British Literature

1800 to the Present

VOLUME II

Third Edition

HAZELTON SPENCER
WALTER E. HOUGHTON
HERBERT BARROWS
DAVID FERRY

D. C. HEATH AND COMPANY
Lexington, Massachusetts Toronto London

British Literature

Edited by

HAZELTON SPENCER
Late of The Johns Hopkins University

WALTER E. HOUGHTON
Wellesley College

HERBERT BARROWS
University of Michigan

DAVID FERRY
Wellesley College

BEVERLY J. LAYMAN
Wellesley College

VOLUME I. OLD ENGLISH TO 1800

Old English Literature
Hazelton Spencer
Beverly J. Layman

Middle English Literature
Hazelton Spencer
Beverly J. Layman

The Seventeenth Century
Hazelton Spencer
Beverly J. Layman
David Ferry

The Eighteenth Century
Hazelton Spencer
David Ferry

VOLUME II. 1800 TO THE PRESENT

The Romantic Period
Hazelton Spencer
David Ferry

The Victorian Period
Walter E. Houghton

The Modern Period
Herbert Barrows

The 1950s and After
Herbert Barrows

Published simultaneously in Canada.

Printed in the United States of America.

International Standard Book Number: 0-669-84137-4

Library of Congress Catalog Card Number: 73-3961

Preface to the Third Edition

The editors of this book have been mindful that literature has always been addressed to what is today called the "general reader" and his enjoyment. The student's intelligent enjoyment of the literature of the British people has been their first concern, both in selecting the texts and in providing explanatory comment. The introductions and notes are designed to supply information which will most readily remove barriers of space and time and permit the reader to confront without obstacle the permanence of the literature's thought and art. The explanatory material constitutes a large body of scholarship, historical and critical; no pains have been spared to make this a work of sound and accurate learning. But the scholarship has constantly been directed to the primary end of allowing the literature to speak for itself.

The first edition of *British Literature* appeared more than two decades ago. Volume I was entirely the work of Hazelton Spencer, late of The Johns Hopkins University. The second volume was the work of Mr. Spencer, Walter E. Houghton of Wellesley College, and Herbert Barrows of the University of Michigan. Mr. Spencer edited and annotated the texts that appeared in "The Romantic Period" and wrote the biographical introductions in that section. Mr. Houghton, with the invaluable aid of his wife, Esther Rhoads Houghton, contributed "The Victorian Period"; Mr. Barrows, "The Modern Period."

The second edition, in 1963, emphasized the incorporation of references to important works of criticism and scholarship that had appeared in the intervening decade. Revisions in Mr. Spencer's sections of the anthology were the work of Edmund G. Miller of the University of New Hampshire. Mr. Houghton and Mr. Barrows made the changes in their sections of the second volume.

British Literature, third edition, is a major revision. In Volume I, Beverly Layman of Wellesley College is responsible for "Old English," "Middle English," "The Renaissance," and "The Seventeenth Century," through Milton; David Ferry of Wellesley College has edited the Restoration section of "The Seventeenth Century," "The Eighteenth Century," and, in Volume II, "The Romantic Period." Walter Houghton and Herbert Barrows have revised their contributions, "The Victorian Period" and "The Modern Period" respectively; Mr. Barrows has added a new section, "The 1950s and After."

The period and biographical introductions, texts and annotations, references and bibliographies, have been extensively rewritten and augmented throughout both volumes. This current scholarship and critical opinion is also reflected in the choice of selections and of authors; some of the important additions to the third edition are listed below.

OLD ENGLISH "Caedmon's Hymn"; Ezra Pound's translation of "The Seafarer."

MIDDLE ENGLISH *Everyman;* Chaucer, "The Wife of Bath's Tale" and "The Miller's Tale."

THE RENAISSANCE John Skelton; Fulke Greville; Spenser, "The Mutability Cantos."

THE SEVENTEENTH CENTURY Jonson's *Volpone;* Thomas Traherne; more poems of John Donne; more of Milton's *Paradise Lost;* John Bunyan, selections from *Pilgrim's Progress.*

THE EIGHTEENTH CENTURY Anne Finch, Charles Churchill; more Johnson, including an excerpt from *Rasselas* and more selections from *The Lives of the . . . Poets;* George Crabbe.

THE ROMANTIC PERIOD Blake, "The Book of Thel," and "The Marriage of Heaven and Hell"; considerable addition to the Wordsworth selections (including more of *The Prelude* and the story of Margaret from Book First of *The Excursion*); John Clare; Keats, "The Fall of Hyperion"; George Darley.

THE VICTORIAN PERIOD Carlyle, "Natural Supernaturalism"; Arnold, "Empedocles on Etna" and, from *Culture and Anarchy,* "Hebraism and Hellenism"; as well as more poems by Clough, Christina Rossetti, and Hopkins.

THE MODERN PERIOD Wilde, *The Importance of Being Earnest;* more poems of Yeats; T. S. Eliot, "Burnt Norton"; Virginia Woolf, excerpts from *A Writer's Diary;* Edward Thomas; Robert Graves; Edwin Muir.

1950S AND AFTER The entire section is new.

New and more numerous illustrations are now strategically interspersed throughout the text of the various period introductions. Each volume, as previously, concludes with Mr. Karl Shapiro's essay on prosody.

The publishers are grateful for the cooperation of the family of the late Hazelton Spencer, whose scholarship and love of literature have continued to be an inspiration in the preparation of this edition.

Acknowledgments

George Gordon, Lord Byron The extracts from *Letters* are from R. E. Prothero's edition of the letters, with the kind permission of Charles Scribner's Sons, the American publishers of the standard edition of Byron.

John Clare "The Groundlark," "Love of Nature," and "The Winter's Spring" are reprinted with the permission of the publisher from *The Poems of John Clare*, J. W. Tibble, ed., copyright 1935 by J. M. Dent & Sons Ltd., London. "Badger" and "An Invite to Eternity" are reprinted with the permission of Curtis Brown Ltd., London, from *Selected Poems and Prose of John Clare*, copyright 1966. "Gipsies," "The Peasant Poet," and "Farewell" are used by permission of Professor Eric Robinson. "Child Harold" is used by permission of David Higham Associates Ltd., London, from *Poems of John Clare's Madness*, Geoffrey Grigson, ed., copyright 1949.

John Keats The extracts from *Letters* are reprinted by kind permission of Maurice Buxton Forman, editor, the Oxford University Press, and AMS Press, Inc., publishers of the 1972 reprint edition.

Arthur Hugh Clough Selections from *The Poems of Arthur Hugh Clough* by A. H. Clough, edited by H. F. Lowry, H.L.P. Norrington, and F. L. Mulhauser are reprinted by permission of the Oxford University Press, copyright 1951.

Matthew Arnold The footnotes to "Empedocles on Etna" are from *Victorian Poets and Poetics*, edited by W. Houghton and G. Robert Stange, second edition, copyright 1968 by the Houghton-Mifflin Company and used with their permission.

Gerard Manley Hopkins "Henry Purcell," "The Windhover," "Pied Beauty," "Felix Randal," "Spelt from Sybil's Leaves," "(Carrion Comfort)," "No Worst, There Is None," "I Wake and Feel the Fell of Dark," "My Own Heart Let Me More Have Pity On," and "Thou Art Indeed Just, Lord" are reprinted by kind permission of the Oxford University Press.

George Meredith Selections from *Selected Poems* by George Meredith, copyright 1897 by George Meredith, 1925 by William M. Meredith, are used by permission of the publishers, Charles Scribner's Sons.

Rudyard Kipling Selections from *Rudyard Kipling's Verse*, Definitive Edition, are reprinted by permission of Mrs. George Bambridge, Doubleday & Company, Inc., and the Macmillan Company of Canada.

Granville Hicks Quotation on p. 406 from *Figures in Transition*, copyright 1939 by The Macmillan Company, used by permission of the publisher.

W. B. Yeats "The Symbolism of Poetry" from W. B. Yeats, *Essays*, copyright 1924 by The Macmillan Company. "The Falling of the Leaves," "An Irish Airman Foresees His Death," "The Fisherman," "Easter, 1916," "The Second Coming," "Sailing to Byzantium," "Among School Children," "Coole Park and Ballylee, 1931," "At Algeciras —A Meditation upon Death," "Lapis Lazuli," "An Acre of Grass," "John Kinsella's Lament for Mrs. Mary Moore," from *The Collected Poems of W. B. Yeats*, copyright 1950 by The Macmillan Company. "Long-Legged Fly," "The Circus Animals' Desertion," and "The Black Tower," from *The Collected Poems of W. B. Yeats*, copyright 1940 by Georgie Yeats, renewed 1968 by Bertha Georgie Yeats, Michael Butler Yeats and Anne Yeats. "A Dialogue of Self and Soul," "Byzantium," and "Crazy Jane and the Bishop," copyright 1933 by The Macmillan Company, renewed 1961 by Bertha Georgie Yeats; "The Cold Heaven," copyright 1912 by The Macmillan Company, renewed 1940 by Georgie Yeats; "The Man Who Dreamed of Faeryland," "To Ireland in the Coming Times," "He Wishes for the Cloths of Heaven," copyright 1906 by The Macmillan Company, renewed 1934 by William Butler Yeats; "Adam's Curse," copyright 1903 by The Macmillan Company, renewed 1931 by William Butler Yeats; "The Wild Swans at Coole," copyright 1919 by The Macmillan Company, renewed 1947 by Bertha Georgie Yeats. Excerpts on pp. 989–91 from *The Autobiography of W. B. Yeats*, copyright 1916 by The Macmillan Company. All selections are reprinted by permission of M. B. Yeats and The Macmillan Companies of New York and Canada.

Thomas Hardy From *Collected Poems* by Thomas Hardy: "No Buyers," copyright 1925 by The Macmillan Company, renewed 1953 by Lloyds Bank Ltd.; "A Broken Appointment," "The Darkling Thrush," "The Convergence of the Twain," "The Going," "The Voice," "Neutral Tones," "Thoughts of Phena," " 'I Look Into My Glass,' " "Drummer Hodge," "A Church Romance," "The Place on the Map," "After a Journey," "The Blinded Bird," "The Children and Sir Nameless," copyright 1925 by The Macmillan Company and reprinted by permission of the Trustees of the Hardy Estate, Macmillan of New York, Macmillan–London & Basingstoke, and The Macmillan Company of Canada Ltd.

Joseph Conrad *The Secret Sharer* reprinted by kind permission of J. M. Dent and Sons Ltd.

T. S. Eliot "Tradition and the Individual Talent" and "The Metaphysical Poets" from *Selected Essays*, New Edition, by T. S. Eliot, copyright, 1932, 1936, 1950, by Harcourt Brace Jovanovich, Inc.; copyright, 1960, 1964, by T. S. Eliot. "The Frontiers of Criticism" from *On Poetry and Poets* by T. S. Eliot, copyright © 1956 by T. S. Eliot and reprinted with the permission of Farrar, Straus & Giroux, Inc. and Faber and Faber Ltd. of London. From *Collected Poems 1909–1962*: "The Love Song of J. Alfred Prufrock," "Preludes," "A Cooking Egg," "Sweeney Among the Nightingales," "The Waste Land," "Burnt Norton," and "The Hollow Men," copyright 1936, by Harcourt Brace Jovanovich, Inc.; copyright © 1943, 1963, 1964, by T. S. Eliot; reprinted by permission of Harcourt Brace

Contents

The Victorian Period

The Modern Period

The 1950s and After

Maps and Illustrations

The Romantic Period

The Romantic Period

There are so many possible definitions of Romanticism as to defy any attempt at summing them up accurately. One can at best sketch out a few tendencies and describe a few of the pressures that make themselves most importantly felt in the literature of this period. The Revolution in France, for example, is a fact whose presence is felt almost everywhere. The intensification of the development of new methods of production and distribution, along with the political and social implications of this development, is apparent in one form or another in very important ways. A conscious and concerted reaction against prevailing characteristics of eighteenth-century style and thought gives shape and character to much of what we read in the Romantic period. This is, of course, more complicated than it looks. The reaction itself may be understood in many ways as a development of the very things it seems to be reacting against. As soon as one has noted a particular phenomenon and labeled it "Romantic," one also realizes that other things contradict, or at least will not confidently support, one's generalization. This is, of course, true of any identifiable literary movement or period, but it is especially noticeable in an age that is particularly conscious of itself as a time of meaningful change.

One hears, for instance, that the Romantic

The Royal Pavilion at Brighton. An Oriental-style palace at an English seaside resort, the much-admired Pavilion was more theatrical design than serious architecture. *Radio Times Hulton Picture Library.*

period is a period of individualism, a time in which there was a significant turning away from abstract speculation in favor of immediate experience. This is a cliché, but, like most clichés, contains some truth. It rests on a complementary cliché, also with truth in it, that the eighteenth century characteristically regarded the universe as essentially fixed, static, hierarchical in structure, mechanical in form—a universe in which man is to be valued primarily for his capacity to think rationally, to construct systems, to categorize, to classify, and to generalize on the basis of enlightened common sense. Of course, one finds oneself saying at once that the eighteenth century is distinguished by writers who were in their own way just as critical of abstractions, just as skeptical of reason untrammeled by experience, just as critical of mechanistic metaphysics, as were any of the Romantic writers. Dr. Johnson is himself an example. So is Burke. So is Boswell's great celebration, in the *Life,* of Johnson's unregenerate and triumphant individuality. So are *Moll Flanders, Tom Jones,* and the engravings of Hogarth. Yet, when all is said and done, it is still true that in the Romantic period there are significant new manifestations of interest in individual and immediate experience and of interest in the criticism of abstractions.

This interest is expressed in many different ways. Though Addison and Steele, in the eighteenth century, and Lamb and Hazlitt, in the nineteenth, are alike interested in the detail of how men ordinarily lead their lives, there is more emphasis in Addison and Steele on the normative, on reasonable codes of manners, morality, and tastes, on what makes men alike; in Lamb and Hazlitt there is more emphasis on individual personality, on what makes men differ. And though the taste for such figures begins in the eighteenth century, the Byronic hero—defining himself against the common herd on the one hand and the more conventional representatives of his own class on the other—is distinctly a Romantic phenomenon:

> *This man*
> *Is of no common order, as his port*
> *And presence here denote; his sufferings*
> *Have been of an immortal nature . . . ;*
> *. . . his knowledge, and his powers and will,*
> *As far as is compatible with clay,*

> *Which clogs the ethereal essence, have been such*
> *As clay hath seldom borne; his aspirations*
> *Have been beyond the dwellers of the earth.*

There was increasing interest, not new but differently and more emphatically stressed, in the odd, the idiosyncratic, the perverse and bizarre. Though this interest was frequently faddish, it can be understood also as a protest against codes of manners and morals perceived as too conventional and too purely reasonable to reflect the diverse possibilities of human personality.

There was also evident an increasing interest—again not new, but differently and more emphatically stressed—in the value of the individual as such, an impulse tending toward the democratic. There are many aspects to Wordsworth's decision to describe "humble and rustic life," but this impulse was certainly one of them. Shelley was a hero of liberty, the enemy of institutional oppression in every form. Byron's maiden speech in the House of Lords was an eloquent defense of some poor workers sentenced for rioting against the introduction of machinery that seemed to them to mean starvation. The attention that Burns's work attracted had to do not only with its intrinsic power but also with the fact that he had been born to follow "his plough, along the mountainside." Perhaps there was something faddish in the vogue for peasant writers, but there was something genuine and important as well, a sense for the worth of every human being, however mean his social status.

THE FRENCH REVOLUTION

There is an obvious connection with the power that the Revolution in France exerted over the imaginations of the writers of the age. Its effect upon England was so profound that some account of it must be given here.

The extravagance and incompetence of the Bourbon kings (whose power was absolute) and of their favorites, together with the strain of two world wars, had left the French government bankrupt; and in desperation the dull-witted though well-meaning Louis XVI sanctioned in 1789 the calling together of the Estates General for the first time in nearly two hundred years. This medieval institution, made up of the nobility, the clergy, and the Third Estate (which was supposed to represent all the rest of the population), could hardly be expected to solve the problems of a society in which most of the intelligence, energy, and economic initiative belonged to a newly risen middle class, and in which the lower classes, long ruthlessly exploited by a parasitic nobility, were at last developing a determination to have their grievances righted. It was therefore probably inevitable that the Third Estate, supported by a small minority of public-spirited nobility and by many of the lower clergy among the representatives of the Church, should presently take control, and so make possible some of the reforms that were desperately needed and intensely desired. Serfdom was abolished, the special privileges of the nobility and clergy were sharply limited, and civil liberties were guaranteed by a Declaration of the Rights of Man similar to the Bill of Rights embodied in the first ten amendments to the Constitution of the United States.

These reforms were moderate enough. Revolutions, however, generate or let loose unforeseen and uncontrollable forces. The fierce resentment of the nobility, the arrogance of Marie Antoinette, the stubborn stupidity of Louis, the threats and intrigues of uniformly hostile neighboring monarchies, made the halfway measures of the moderate party (the Girondists) seem inadequate; and presently the extreme radicals (the Jacobins) began to gain the whip hand. During this period the spirit of the Revolution underwent a basic change. The sporadic and spontaneous outbursts of violence, like the storming of the notorious prison for political offenders known as the Bastille, on July 14, 1789, and the forcible removal of the king from Versailles by the Paris mob toward the end of the same year, were succeeded by the horrible "September Massacres" of imprisoned nobility in 1792, by the execution of the royal family in 1793 (an act as shocking to all Europe as had been the execution of Charles I by the followers of Cromwell), and by the calculated slaughters of the Reign of Terror under Robespierre, which have been made familiar by Carlyle's *The French Revolution* and Dickens's *A Tale of Two Cities*. But the Reign of Terror also had results unforeseen by those who instituted and directed it; they themselves were swept to destruction, leaving a vacuum into which Napoleon stepped in 1795.

THE ENGLISH REACTION

The effect of these events upon England cannot be overstated. At the beginning the Revolution was widely welcomed by liberal thinkers as a long-overdue correction of flagrant political abuses. Blake and Burns were ardent partisans. Wordsworth and Coleridge were both fired with passionate enthusiasm. Coleridge, still a schoolboy at Christ's Hospital in 1789, wrote an "Ode on the Destruction of the Bastille," which hailed the event as a symbol of man's rebelling against entrenched tyranny and recovering his original freedom. Wordsworth, who was in France during most of 1792, was actively associated with the Girondists. On his return to England, when the Reign of Terror was already under way, he wrote (although he did not publish) a long *Letter to the Bishop of Llandaff* upbraiding the latter for his abandonment of the revolutionary cause and urging eloquently and in detail an extreme republican form of government for England. Looking back a decade later, he described the hopes of men like himself in the outcome of the Revolution:

> *I . . . believed*
> *That a benignant spirit was abroad*
> *Which might not be withstood, that poverty*
> *Abject . . . would in a little time*
> *Be found no more, that we should see the earth*
> *Unthwarted in her wish to recompense*
> *The meek, the lowly, patient child of toil,*
> *All institutes for ever blotted out*
> *That legalised exclusion, empty pomp*
> *Abolished, sensual state and cruel power,*
> *Whether by edict of the one or few;*
> *And finally, as sum and crown of all,*
> *Should see the people having a strong hand*
> *In framing their own laws; whence better days*
> *To all mankind.*

But even at the beginning many of the older generation of Englishmen looked askance at what was happening across the Channel. Most influential among them was Edmund Burke, who, in his *Reflections on the Revolution in France* (1790), accurately predicted the violence which was to ensue and warned England against following the course of France (see Volume I). As the progress of the Revolution made it increasingly clear that one form of tyranny was being replaced by another, disaffection toward the French cause grew among English liberals. Moreover, the Revolution soon ceased to be merely a domestic issue and became an active threat to other countries. The revolutionary "people's army" in France, formed to repel the attempts of neighboring monarchs to restore by force the old regime, became imbued with the desire to spread the benefits of the new order throughout Europe, inviting the masses in other countries to rebel against their rulers. By 1793 England was at war with France.

The Tory government, under the leadership of the able but inflexible William Pitt the Younger, was convinced that it had to combat not only the growing military power of France but also the danger of revolt at home. Fearful lest the scenes of violence in France might be reenacted in England if the discontent of the lower classes were fed by revolutionary agitators, it took strongly repressive measures. Any expression of liberal sympathy was liable to interpretation as treason. Spies were set to watch men regarded as dangerous, and various liberals were brought to trial. Public meetings were strictly regulated; freedom of speech was muzzled; freedom of the press was curtailed. No proposal for

internal reform by parliamentary action, however urgently needed, was listened to. Everywhere in England reaction reigned.

This reaction continued throughout the twenty years of turmoil that Europe suffered as a result of Napoleon's grandiose dream of empire. The Corsican was not a monster of the Hitler type; in his early years, at least, he could with some justice claim to be the heir of the Revolution, the bringer of liberty and justice to peoples still oppressed by feudal institutions. He was also able to appeal to the spirit of nationalism which the Revolution kindled—a spirit which, outside of Britain, had scarcely been known in Europe before the latter part of the eighteenth century. The political power that a progressively greater part of the population was now beginning to demand had to be exercised within definite limits set by geography, language, economic interest, and other ties. The masses of people began to identify themselves with the state, as only their rulers had done before. This new spirit of patriotism Napoleon cultivated in France and elsewhere as an instrument in the destruction of the old monarchies.

What he did not see, because of his growing

The Plumb-Pudding in Danger. A contemporary cartoon by James Gillray (1805) mocks the territorial appetites of Sir William Pitt and Napoleon. *The Granger Collection.*

The Victorious Allies. The meeting of Wellington and Prussian Marshal Blucher after "La Belle Alliance" had brought Napoleon to his knees at Waterloo. *Radio Times Hulton Picture Library.*

megalomania, was that nationalism was a two-edged sword: that men in whose minds personal liberty and national sovereignty had become closely linked would have as little liking for his dictatorship as for that of their former rulers. As France had been made a nation, in the modern sense, by the attacks of her neighbors in the early years of the Revolution, so now French aggression against Prussia, Russia, and Spain provoked a similar response. Britain, too, despite the cross currents of internal politics, was unified in a fight for life. Thus Napoleon was finally destroyed by the power that at first he had exploited so successfully. Defeated at Waterloo (1815), he was exiled to Saint Helena, and the Congress of Vienna reestablished the heirs of "legitimate" rulers on all the thrones of Europe.

THE INDUSTRIAL REVOLUTION

In England, where the Tories remained in power and continued their resistance to change, change was long overdue. Even before the war, the beginnings of the Industrial Revolution had created serious economic and social problems. During the war the government had refused to give them enlightened consideration, and at the war's end they were aggravated by the usual aftermath of war—unemployment resulting from the collapse

of war industry and from the return of many soldiers to civilian life, heavy taxation to meet war debts, soaring prices, and the like.

The impact of the Industrial Revolution—a revolution less sudden and spectacular than the political explosion in France, but even more heavily laden with significance for the future—is considered in detail in the introduction to the Victorian period, since it is in that period rather than in the Romantic period that its effects make themselves most conspicuously felt in literature; but something needs to be said of it here. The event that undoubtedly provided the greatest impetus in this revolution was James Watt's invention, about 1765, following the discovery of how to make use of coal, of a really practical steam engine. The most spectacular use of this new resource began about 1785 in the textile industry, in which the eighteenth century had seen a rapid succession of mechanical improvements, alternately in spinning and weaving, each technological triumph in one branch of the industry demanding a corresponding improvement in the other. The invention of the cotton gin by Whitney in 1782, making possible the rapid separation of fiber from seed, was the last important link in a chain of inventions that brought about the expansion of the industry at a speed hitherto unimagined.

Coalbrookdale by Night. The development of coal smelting furnaces in the late eighteenth century led to an expansion of foundries and mines into the Midlands region of England. To Wordsworth and other Romantic poets it was the first step towards the pollution of the English countryside. *Photo, Science Museum, London.*

These technological advantages of such immense ultimate benefit to man were accompanied by terrible evils. The insatiable demand for cotton gave a new and malignant vitality to what had been the dying system of Negro slavery in America—just at the time when the long-sustained efforts of a little band of unselfish men under the leadership of William Wilberforce (1759–1833), struggling against the inertia of the many and the greed of the few, had at last (1807) succeeded in outlawing the monstrous anachronism of slave-trading by English merchants. And it brought to a vast number of the English people themselves a slavery nearly as abominable.

The need for hands to tend the new machines drew laborers from the rural districts (where the enclosure movement was still going on) to huge new "mill towns" like Manchester, emerging like sores upon the face of England, where human life spawned, festered, and died. For it was not only, or mainly, the hands of *men* that were wanted; hands of women and children would do as well, and could be bought more cheaply. Their spirit could also be more easily broken; and if the flesh of ten-year-old children became weak toward the end of a sixteen-hour working day, there were chains to hold them at their machines, and whips in the hands of overseers to keep them awake.

One might suppose that the fathers would have objected; but the family had to eat—or, all too often, the father had to be able to buy the alcohol that would enable him to forget his humiliating helplessness to support his family. Some millowners, also, depended for labor on orphan or pauper children, whom they bought in London or elsewhere of officials who were commendably concerned to save money for the taxpayers, while at the same time lining their own pockets. Where the children went or what happened to them, it was to nobody's interest to inquire. It was not even to the millowners' interest to keep them in decent health. It was cheaper to work them to death and buy more.

These evils were not universal, but they afflicted a vast number of "freeborn Englishmen." They existed in other industries, such as coal mining, and are documented in grisly detail by report after report of royal commissions, from the pages of which emerges an appalling picture of ill-paid drudgery, slum housing, malnutrition, disease, and a high death rate which is all the uglier by contrast with the luxury and extravagance of aristocratic Regency life.[1] As Shelley in *A Defence of Poetry* (1821) was among the first to point out, "all inventions for abridging and combining labour" had led only "to the exasperation of the inequality of mankind"; "the discoveries which should have lightened, have added a weight to the curse imposed on Adam," and "man, having enslaved the elements, remains himself a slave."

Still, one may ask with sincere astonishment and horror why such injustices were tolerated in a supposedly Christian country. Answers are not difficult to find—aside from the normal capacity of human beings to bear with fortitude the misfortunes of their fellows. The Anglican Church, supported largely by the upper classes and their dependents, strongly favored the status quo. Methodism, influential among the laboring classes, turned their thoughts to compensation in a future life. The great Protestant middle class in England in the nineteenth century inherited the Puritan belief that God helps those who help themselves, and that people are poor only because they are lazy and improvident, and therefore neither deserving nor capable of being helped.

Possibly the most potent obstacle to reform, however, was a philosophical one—the application to economic problems of the concept of natural universal law that had been important in eighteenth-century thought: the notion of a clockwork universe created and set in motion by a divine Watchmaker, whose work it was not only futile but also wrong to try to alter. "Thou shalt not tamper with the law of supply and demand" was a sort of Eleventh Commandment, resting on the authority of England's first great economist, Adam Smith, who had published *The Wealth of Nations* in 1776. By no means all the captains of industry conformed to the Marxian stereotype that later developed; many sincerely deplored the sufferings of the workers in their factories. But most of them believed with equal sincerity that nothing could be done to mitigate the evil.

The workers themselves were helpless. Unions were outlawed in 1800 and did not become legal until 1825. The ballot box was a weapon far beyond their reach—not until toward the end of the nineteenth century were ordinary laborers allowed to vote. Moreover, the great new industrial cities like Manchester were entirely unrepresented in Parliament. No reapportionment of the seats in the House of Commons had been made for generations. Areas once thinly populated might now be metropolises; localities once populous enough to deserve a representative might now be almost uninhabited (the notorious "rotten boroughs") and the seat be openly for sale by the wealthy nobleman (as a rule) who owned the land, part of the price, of course, being the member's willingness to vote as he was told.

The only resort, therefore, seemed to be mass protest, peaceful or violent as circumstances might dictate. Violence drew harsh reprisals from the authorities—for example, the death penalty for smashing machines. Even a peaceful gathering might be treated as if it were an insurrection—as when a cavalry charge on a perfectly orderly mass meeting in St. Peter's Field, near Manchester, in 1819, resulted in the death of nine of the crowd and injuries to hundreds (the "Peterloo Massacre," which inspired the eloquence of Shelley's "The Masque of Anarchy"). A vicious circle was constantly in motion—the callousness of the authorities led to demonstrations of popular discontent, and such demonstrations convinced the authorities that repressive measures must be strengthened in the interests of public safety.

But underneath the iron lid of reaction the pressure of a general desire for change was steadily rising. Even during the most critical periods of the war there had been outspoken critics of the government's policy, who could not be silenced by prosecutions, fines, and imprisonment. After the war the protests became louder, and more widespread. Gradually the extremity of the sufferings of the lower classes stimulated the growth of a social conscience in the middle and upper classes, of the humanitarian principles that had

---

[1] The future George IV (1762–1830) was declared prince regent when his father, George III (1738–1820), went mad in 1811. The term *Regency* is frequently used to refer to the second half of the period we are calling *Romantic*.

brought about the abolition of the slave trade and were working (though the great leader in the work, John Howard, had died in 1790) for the reform of a penal code and of a prison system unsurpassed in senseless barbarity by anything in English history. In the late 1820s the tide began to turn. The Great Reform Bill of 1832, forced through Parliament under threat of a popular revolution, corrected the most glaring inequalities in parliamentary representation and thus laid the groundwork for subsequent reforms. It did little to alleviate directly the sufferings of the populace; even yet the vote was given only to owners of a substantial amount of property. Its greatest significance lay in its acceptance of the principle of change. No longer was it to be assumed that the established way of life, the established political, social, and economic system, accorded with changeless laws that man was not to try to tamper with but only to obey. The world was not static but dynamic, not a mechanism but an evolving organism, the future of which was not yet determined, and in the shaping of which men themselves might play a part.

ASPECTS OF THE NATURE OF ROMANTIC LITERATURE

The literature of the time did indeed respond directly to these political and social conditions. The responses were various and complex. And yet it is important to say that Romantic literature does not, generally speaking, operate within assumptions that so deeply characterize the Victorian period: assumptions that prose literature should center upon contemporary problems and offer answers to them; that poetry should be the vehicle of moral guidance or inspiration; that, consequently, literature which does not justify its existence by serving such useful ends must be escapist, a luxury that has no rightful place in the serious business of life. We shall see later how severely some of the Victorian writers, trapped between the popular demand for didacticism and their own leanings toward a purer aestheticism, suffered from the conflict of divided aims. It is Shelley, the passionate social reformer, who said that the supposition that poetry should combat the evil in the world by trying to reform its external wrongs "rests upon a misconception of the manner in which poetry acts to produce the moral improvement of man." It is not "for want

of admirable doctrines that men hate, and despise, and censure, and deceive, and subjugate one another," and a didactic poetry that simply multiplies such doctrines is therefore useless. What we lack is the imaginative awareness that will stimulate us to put our knowledge into action, and it is this that poetry must create. "A man, to be greatly good, must imagine intensely and comprehensively; he must put himself in the place of another, and of many others; the pains and pleasures of his species must become his own. The great instrument of moral good is the imagination; and poetry administers to the effect by acting upon the cause. . . . Poetry strengthens the faculty which is the organ of the moral nature of man, in the same manner as exercise strengthens a limb." So far as literature serves a moral purpose, then, it should quicken the sentiments that are the springs of moral action, rather than teach explicit moral lessons. More broadly, its purpose is to make available to the reader a broader and richer range of experience than he could otherwise have access to, and hence to heighten and intensify his awareness of life—his awareness both of his own nature and of his relation to what lies outside himself.

"What is a Poet? . . . He is a man speaking to men," says Wordsworth. That is to say, he testifies to what it is to be a man, what the essential situation of man is with respect to himself and to nature. And he carries his testimony to other men, like him in what they are but perhaps unlike him in that he is more aware than they, and more articulate. The poet is a man "pleased with his own passions and volitions, and who rejoices more than other men in the spirit of life that is in him; delighting to contemplate similar volitions and passions as manifested in the goings-on of the Universe, and habitually impelled to create them where he does not find them." This implies several obligations that the poet should fulfill.

One is to speak accurately about the world he sees around him. Wordsworth endeavored "at all times . . . to look steadily at my subject," criticizing his predecessors for what he took to be the blurring effects of their conventional epithets and generalized personifications. Coleridge praised him for "the perfect truth of nature in his images and descriptions as taken immediately from nature, and proving a long and genial intimacy with the very spirit which gives the physiognomic expression to all the works of nature . . . . Genius . . . brings out many a vein and many a tint, which escape the eye of common observation, thus raising to the rank of gems what had often been kicked away by the hurrying foot of the traveller on the dusty high road of custom." Keats most certainly exemplifies, though in a much more detailed and luxuriant way, the qualities that Coleridge is praising here. And it is certainly true that one rather common characteristic of the literature of the period is the variety and detail of its natural imagery.

It is possible to exaggerate about this point, to be sure, positing against it a neoclassicism of empty generalization. To do so is, of course, wrong. It is true that Dr. Johnson said: "The business of a poet is to examine not the individual but the species; to remark general properties and large appearances. He does not number the stripes of the tulip . . . ." But he also said, and in the same context: "To a poet nothing can be useless. Whatever is beautiful, and whatever is dreadful, must be familiar to his imagination: he must be conversant with all that is awfully vast or elegantly little. The plants of the garden, the animals of the wood, the minerals of the earth, and meteors of the sky, must all concur to store his mind with inexhaustible variety . . . ." One honors the Romantic ambition to be concrete in its sense imagery, full of pleasure in the actual things of the world, and accurate in describing them. But it would be hard to argue that this passage from Pope—

> Light quirks of music, broken and uneven,
> Make the soul dance upon a jig to Heaven.
> On painted ceilings you devoutly stare,
> Where sprawl the saints of Verrio, or Laguerre,
> On gilded clouds in fair expansion lie,
> And bring all Paradise before your eye—

is less concrete, or less accurate, or less full of pleasure in the actual things of the world than this passage from Keats—

> Conspiring with him how to load and bless
>   With fruit the vines that round the thatch-
>   eaves run;
> To bend with apples the moss'd cottage-trees,
>   And fill all fruit with ripeness to the core;
>   To swell the gourd, and plump the hazel-
>   shells
> With a sweet kernel . . . .

Just so, it is not very profitable to try to choose in such terms between Johnson's

> Love ends with hope; the sinking statesman's door
> Pours in the morning worshiper no more;
> For growing names the weekly scribbler lies,
> To growing wealth the dedicator flies;
> From ev'ry room descends the painted face
> That hung the bright palladium of the place,
> And, smoked in kitchens, or in auctions sold,
> To better features yields the frame of gold;

and Wordsworth's

> The day is come when I again repose
> Here, under this dark sycamore, and view
> These plots of cottage-ground, these orchard-tufts,
> Which at this season, with their unripe fruits,
> Are clad in one green hue, and lose themselves
> 'Mid groves and copses.

Of course, it *would* be profitable to consider how the meanings of words like *concrete, accurate,* and *full of pleasure* change from poet to poet, from age to age. It would not be fair to say that the difference is that the concrete images accurately rendered in Romantic poetry tend to be drawn from nature, those in the eighteenth century from artifacts. There are probably at least as many eighteenth-century passages describing country scenes as there are Romantic ones. And a painting is not in every sense less natural than an apple tree.

If one obligation of the poet as Wordsworth defines him is to speak accurately about the world around him, the other is to look accurately within. Reality includes, of course, what takes place within the consciousness as well as what lies outside. Romantic literature abounds in mental and spiritual autobiography, both verse and prose, ranging from Wordsworth's full-length study of the "growth of a poet's mind" in *The Prelude* to such brief records of transitory moods as Shelley's "Stanzas Written in Dejection, near Naples." Nor do the writers look only into their own minds; beside the literature of introspection stands the literature, equally rich, of imaginative penetration into other minds, the product of what Keats called the "chameleon poet," who immerses himself in the personality of others and loses his own identity in theirs. These two strands of psychological exploration comprise one of the most permanently valuable parts of Romantic literature.

In their wide range the Romantics enter into areas that many eighteenth-century writers would have ignored as too trivial for serious treatment or deplored as morbid deviations from a rational norm of behavior. Freakish quirks of personality; "unedifying" feelings of inexplicable melancholy; delight in indolence; wounded pride; discontent with the limitations of existence; longing for death; irrational prejudices and paradoxical feelings; the vagaries of reverie; the psychology of dreams and nightmares; abnormal and neurotic states of mind; glimmerings of what a later age was to call the subconscious—all these find a place in the Romantic record of human consciousness because they all find a place in that consciousness itself. At times the Romantic writers seem to be striving to record feelings and impressions so vague and elusive that they defy complete articulation. Coleridge speaks in *Biographia Literaria* of readers who "had been accustomed to watch the flux and reflux of their inmost nature, to venture at times into the twilight realms of consciousness, and to feel a deep interest in modes of inmost being."

But the important obligation for the poet, as defined by Wordsworth, is not simply to observe the world outside himself fully and accurately or to describe as well as he can the varieties of human consciousness; it is also to create his poetry in terms of new definitions of man in relation to his natural environment. The poet, representative of and spokesman for man, is "pleased with his own passions and volitions" and delights "to contemplate similar volitions and

Parham Mill, Gillingham by John Constable. Wordsworth's sense of the integration of the life of man and nature is echoed in the landscapes and scenes of rural life painted by Constable and Turner. *From the Collection of Mr. and Mrs. Paul Mellon.*

passions as manifested in the goings-on of the Universe." The world is not a finished and static machine which *has been* created. It is a process of ever-self-refreshing creation and re-creation, and the mind that contemplates it takes the same kind of pleasure in doing so that it takes in contemplating itself, since both mind and nature participate in this process, are indeed but two alternative aspects of it. When Wordsworth says:

> One impulse from a vernal wood
> May teach you more of man,
> Of moral evil and of good,
> Than all the sages can.

> Sweet is the lore which Nature brings;
> Our meddling intellect
> Mis-shapes the beauteous forms of things:—
> We murder to dissect,

he is not in any simple way being anti-intellectual or in any simple way a hater of science. Taken in context, his argument is that our most meaningful responses are responses of the whole being, of the body, of the emotions, as well as of our powers of intellection. He is arguing that we can take lessons in this respect from the vernal wood, from the creatures around us, the birds, and the trees, all of which lack the power of intellection and which participate spontaneously in the harmonious creativity of things. Wordsworth wishes to restore man to a sense of his relationship with the harmonious in nature, finding its counterparts in his own being; for, in Wordsworth's view (and in varying terms, in that of the other principal Romantics) it is there— "To her fair works did Nature link,/The human soul that through me ran."

Perhaps the central identifying proposition of Romanticism in England, this view has many modes of expression and many consequences. It suggests reasons for what is probably the most characteristic situation in Romantic poems: a man alone, or accompanied by another person so closely related to him, so like him in temperament and doctrine, as to be another self, confronts the landscape.

This landscape is more than just a landscape. It is that which demonstrates to the poet the deepest creative workings of the divine in nature; and when the poet's response is worthy, nature reveals to him what he himself is capable

of, and how he participates in the general creativity of things. The principal Romantic triumph, perhaps, was to find a language to convey the complexity of such experience, which was able to be both faithful to objective nature and attentive to the mind's responses, and to demonstrate how, at propitious moments, the workings of nature and of the mind are one:

> Once again
> Do I behold these steep and lofty cliffs,
> That on a wild secluded scene impress
> Thoughts of more deep seclusion; and connect
> The landscape with the quiet of the sky.

Though the dominant Romantic tone about this creative interworking of mind and nature is celebratory, triumphant, there is also in all these poets a countercurrent of pathos. The resources are there, but the poet is not able to use them. Coleridge says, in "Dejection: An Ode":

> And those thin clouds above, in flakes and bars,
> That give away their motion to the stars;
> Those stars, that glide behind them or between,
> Now sparkling, now bedimmed, but always seen:
> Yon crescent Moon, as fixed as if it grew
> In its own cloudless, starless lake of blue;
> I see them all so excellently fair,
> I see, not feel, how beautiful they are!

The eye can see, the brain can understand, how excellently fair they are; but Coleridge lacks at this moment the capacity to respond with his whole being, to summon up from within himself the resources of spontaneous creative life that are the counterparts of the spontaneous creative life in nature. His predicament is in one way peculiar to himself, having to do with his own life history; but it has parallels in Shelley's ironic "A heavy weight of hours has chained and bowed/One too like thee: tameless, and swift, and proud," and in Keats's saying to the nightingale, "Forlorn! the very word is like a bell/To toll me back from thee to my sole self!" and Wordsworth's

> The days gone by
> Return upon me almost from the dawn
> Of life: the hiding-places of man's power
> Open; I would approach them, but they close.
> I see by glimpses now; when age comes on,
> May scarcely see at all . . . .

The human consciousness is both marvelously matched and tragically mismatched to the spontaneous harmony of nature. At its best it can fully participate in the "goings-on of the Universe," but it is an essential characteristic of man that he is not always at his best; his consciousness is not always fully responsive. The "dull brain perplexes and retards," and man's very self-consciousness—his awareness that he is a special being burdened with the knowledge of his separate identity—is inhibiting.

Thus, if the dominant tone in Romantic formulations of the poet's role is celebratory and triumphant, it is precariously maintained for reasons that go beyond the complexity of human personality. Wordsworth says of the poet:

He is the rock of defence for human nature; an upholder and preserver, carrying everywhere with him relationship and love. In spite of difference of soil and climate, of language and manners, of laws and customs: in spite of things silently gone out of mind, and things violently destroyed; the Poet binds together by passion and knowledge the vast empire of human society, as it is spread over the whole earth, and over all time.

This declaration is part of a complex response to many conditions of the world in which he was writing. The poet is the rock of defense, and defense was necessary. There is behind this a sense of the threats inherent in abstraction and mechanism in philosophy and science, of the lost promises of the Revolution abroad, of the real conditions in which most men lead their lives. One of the most poignant aspects of such declarations is that they must be made. There is a powerful feeling of the impoverishment of most men's lives in such definitions of the poet's special mission. Just so, the very celebrations of the beauties of the landscape so frequently encountered in Romantic literature have behind them an unspoken implication of a threatened landscape.

Finally, one should say something about the Romantic taste for the wild, the exotic, the remote—either in time or place—and the mysterious. When Wordsworth and Coleridge set out upon the *Lyrical Ballads,* Wordsworth's subject was to be "things of every day," Coleridge's to transfer "from our inward nature a human interest and a semblance of truth" to "persons and characters supernatural, or at least romantic."

The character—or for that matter the setting—that is romantic in this sense of the word may be, as in the case of the Ancient Mariner, a way of presenting man as the poet essentially defines him, by abstracting him from the familiar and accidental properties of his world; or, as also in the case of the Ancient Mariner, it may be a way of suggesting that the truth about man is more mysterious than commonsense descriptions of him can possibly know.

Raymond Williams has said: "The tendency of Romanticism is towards a vehement rejection of dogmas of method in art, but it is also, very clearly, towards a claim which all good classical theory would have recognized: the claim that the artist's business is to 'read the open secret of the universe.' . . . The artist perceives and represents Essential Reality, and he does so by virtue of his master faculty Imagination. . . . Both Romanticism and Classicism are in this sense idealist theories of art . . . ." In one direction the Romantics sought to read the secret in the commonest things before them; in another they sought to read it by studying the remote and ideal past, by acknowledging the possibility of its strangeness, its wildness, its stubborn resistance to the merely rational.

THE DRAMA AND THE NOVEL

There are two obvious gaps in the Romantic section of this anthology. There are excerpts neither from the drama nor the novel.

The Romantic period is not one of the great creative periods in the history of English drama. The theater was very much alive, as was the opera; plenty of new works were presented. But there was no commanding dramatic talent during this time. Wordsworth, Coleridge, Byron, Shelley, and Keats all tried their hands at writing plays, but the dramatic is far from the center of achievement of all of them. One might, it is true, cite *Prometheus Unbound,* and Byron's *Manfred* and *Cain,* but these are really "dramatic poems" and belong essentially to another genre. (And some critics would also cite Shelley's pseudo-Shakespearean pastiche, *The Cenci.*)

The novel continued to grow and develop vigorously during this time, and it did so both in the direction of romance and of moral and social realism. We have paid some attention below, in the introduction to selections from Sir Walter Scott's poetry, to the novels by which he has

The·THEATRICAL ATLAS·

The Theatrical Atlas. Cruickshank's 1814 drawing of the great tragedian Edmund Kean as Richard III satirically illustrates the dependence of the Regency theatre on the old dramatic repetoire and the new star system. *British Museum.*

achieved such an immense reputation. For us, of course, the great missing figure in this section of the anthology is Jane Austen (1775–1817). Her six published novels (*Northanger Abbey, Pride and Prejudice, Sense and Sensibility, Mansfield Park, Emma,* and *Persuasion*), are glories of the age and of our literature. The extraordinary subtlety and fineness of her language, the Johnsonian scrupulosity of her moral intellect, her emotional delicacy, and her emotional power combine to make an extraordinary achievement. We have remarked that the age was deficient in creative dramatic power. This is so in the drama *per se.* But one might argue that the life of the drama is preserved and developed in the pages of the social comedies of this great writer.

For detailed discussions of the drama and the novel the reader is referred to works listed under "General References" and to standard references to these genres and to the period.

General References

There are a large number of interesting political and social histories of the period, which give some idea of the presiding social issues of the time and something of its ordinary way of life as well. One can cite only a few of them: G. M. Trevelyan's two books, *British History in the Nineteenth Century* (1922) and *English Social History* (1942), and Elie Halévy's *England in 1815* (1949) and *The Liberal Awakening* (1949), have classical status. One can also cite Gilbert Slater's *The Growth of Modern England* (1932) and Alfred Cobban's extremely interesting *Edmund Burke and the Revolt Against the Eighteenth Century* (1929). Two of the most valuable books of recent years which have to do with the connection between literature and social issues are Raymond Williams's *Culture and Society* 1780–1950 (1958) and E. P. Thompson's *The Making of the English Working Class* (1963).

In recent years there has been increasing interest in the intellectual background of the period, the nature of its dominant ideas, and the relation of those ideas to the characteristics of its literature. The work of A. O. Lovejoy, for example, is seminal, in *Romanticism and the History of Ideas* (1948) and *The Great Chain of Being* (1936). Also of great interest on this general level are Basil Willey's *Nineteenth Century Studies* (1955) and Northrop Frye's *A Study of English Romanticism* (1968). Perhaps the two most important books which have to do specifically with Romantic critical and aesthetic theory are W. J. Bate's *From Classic to Romantic* (1946) and Meyer Abrams's *The Mirror and the Lamp* (1953).

There are several very good collections of critical essays having to do with the period in general. Among them are: Robert F. Gleckner and Gerald Enscoe, eds., *Romanticism: Points of View* (1970); Harold Bloom, ed., *Romanticism and Consciousness* (1970); Northrop Frye, ed., *Romanticism Reconsidered* (1963); and F. W. Hilles, ed., *From Sensibility to Romanticism* (1965).

Finally, reference should be made to works about genres other than poetry and to those not covered in this anthology. The following works are useful: Oliver Elton, *A Survey of English Literature* (2 vols., 1928); Ernest A. Baker, *The History of the English Novel,* vol. 6 (1961); Montague Summers, *The Gothic Quest* (1938); J. M. S.

Tompkins, *The Popular Novel in England, 1770–1800* (1932); Edith Birkhead, *The Tale of Terror* (1921); Allardyce Nicoll, *History of Early Nineteenth Century Drama, 1800–1850* (1955). This is probably the place also to mention the two useful though uneven volumes of the Oxford History of English Literature dealing with the period, W. L. Renwick's *English Literature, 1789–1815* (1963) and Ian Jack's *English Literature, 1815–1832* (1963).

William Blake
1757–1827

One can get into a certain amount of trouble trying to distinguish between Coleridge, say, and Blake, with regard to their accounts of how the mind discovers the holy truth of things. Coleridge says, for example, that the "power delegated to nature is all in every part: and by a symbol I mean, not a metaphor or allegory or any other figure of speech or form of fancy, but an actual and essential part of that, the whole of which it represents." Blake has Isaiah the prophet sounding in some ways like this when his interlocutor (Blake) asks him how he "dared so roundly to assert that God spoke" to him, and Isaiah responds: "I saw no God, nor heard any, in a finite organical perception; but my senses discovered the infinite in everything, and as I was then perswaded, & remain confirm'd, that the voice of honest indignation is the voice of God, I cared not for consequences, but wrote." Both of them (and certainly Wordsworth, in theory and in practice) are in rebellion against reports about nature that regard it as simply a collection or arrangement of limited data; both are against accounts of nature—and of human psychology—that are merely reasonable, merely intellectual, or that reduce the truth to what can be discovered by the instruments of rational analysis. But Coleridge and Wordsworth differ from Blake in style, and to a degree which becomes more than a difference in degree. It becomes a difference in kind. Coleridge says: "I seem to myself to behold in the quiet objects, on which I am gazing, more than an arbitrary illustration, more than a mere *simile,* the work of my own fancy. I feel an awe, as if there were before my eyes the same power as that of the reason—the same power in a lower dignity, and therefore a symbol established in the truth of things." Blake says: "The prophets Isaiah and Ezekiel dined with me, and I asked them . . . ," and he says:

> How do you know but ev'ry Bird that
>   cuts the airy way,
> Is an immense world of delight, clos'd by
>   your senses five?

To call Blake more literally a "mystic" than Coleridge or Wordsworth is to beg the question. His style is different, different enough for him to complain that in Wordsworth the natural man rises up against the spiritual man continually. This is to say that, in Blake's view, Wordsworth is not direct and straightforward enough in his way of getting through to divinity. This is not to say that Blake rejects the senses. When he says, "If the doors of perception were cleansed every thing would appear to man as it is, infinite," he is not rejecting perception itself or its sensory organs, but rather is arguing, or confidently declaring, that it is the dirtiness or cloudiness of our perceiving, and the isolation of the egoistic self, by perverse self-limitation, that prevents us from knowing what the world really is. "For man has closed himself up, till he sees all things thro' narrow chinks of his cavern." What he would see if he saw rightly, heard rightly, tasted rightly, smelled rightly, touched

William Blake (1757–1827). The portrait by Thomas Phillips, 1807. *National Portrait Gallery.*

rightly, is not, to use Coleridge's terms, "a symbol established in the truth of things," but an utterly transformed truth of things. Blake says prophetically that "the cherub with his flaming sword is hereby commanded to leave his guard at tree of life; and when he does, the whole creation will be consumed and appear infinite and holy, whereas it now appears finite and corrupt." It is not a vision of Heaven, of an Elsewhere, with all contrarieties abolished, to which one is taken up like an Elijah, away from this world of created things, in all their complexity, and of the senses, in all *their* complexity. It is a vision of *this* world from which "apparent surfaces" have been melted, as by the etcher's acid, "and displaying the infinite which was hid." Wordsworth says: "To me the meanest flower that blows can give/Thoughts that do often lie too deep for tears," and,

> *The budding twigs spread out their fan,*
> *To catch the breezy air;*
> *And I must think, do all I can,*
> *That there was pleasure there.*

For Wordsworth this is seeing symbolically, recognizing that the "quiet objects" on which he is gazing are more than "a mere illustration" but rather "symbols established in the truth of things." But this would be too conditional for Blake. One must see allegorically (in Blake's special sense of the term) that what really *is* is the true world in which no flower is "meanest" in any sense of the word. Wordsworth and Coleridge tell how the traditional hierarchical world can be reinterpreted by the loving imagination so that the blessedness of even the meanest thing can be understood and responded to, but for Blake there is not any hierarchy, in this sense, at all. For Wordsworth and Coleridge the imagination is the highest

A Blake Engraving for The Book of Job, 1825.
Boston Public Library.

faculty in man, and divinity is implicit in it, as it is in the works of nature. For Blake God simply is "the Poetic Genius" and he "only Acts & Is, in existing beings or Men." When the existing man's doors of perception are cleansed, when he has not closed himself up, when he no longer sees all things through narrow chinks of his cavern, then—God acting and being in him—the revelation, the transformation, is total.

There are many different interpretations of Blake's essential quality; and the intricate myths he devised in his career as painter, etcher, and poet are, like anything intricate, susceptible to disagreement.

What has been said so far lends itself perhaps too easily to a view of Blake as seer, and to prophetic and visionary aspects of his style. An important thing to notice about him is the urbanity with which he avoids the solemnity and humorlessness endemic to seers and prophets: "An Angel came to me and said: 'O pitiable foolish young man! O horrible! O dreadful state! consider the hot burning dungeon thou art preparing for thyself to all eternity, to which thou art going in such career.'" The satirist's ear for the exact accent of what he is satirizing, in this case a combination of genteel prissiness and Bible-thumping "fervor" in the angel, reminds us that he is not only a figure of the Romantic period but an eighteenth-century poet as well. So does the epigrammatic conciseness and wit of "Prudence is a rich, ugly old maid courted by Incapacity." And more generally it should be noticed how frequently the accent is exuberant and gay; how *The Book of Thel* is, among other things, a comedy about maidenly timorousness; and how the "inverted" values of *The Marriage of Heaven and Hell* are both deadly serious and a good joke. Blake is in many respects the heir of positive values of the literature of his own eighteenth-century time, even when he despises many of its assumptions. He is a master polemicist and draws on eighteenth-century strengths to be so, just as Byron does.

And he is not merely a polemicist in the cause of his metaphysical views—if "metaphysical" is the right word to use. Blake brings his capacities for irony, for wit, and for what his Isaiah calls "honest indignation," brilliantly to bear on the social conditions of his own time. The quotation of one famous poem will perhaps suffice for what could be many:

> *I wander thro' each charter'd street,*
>   *Near where the charter'd Thames does flow,*
> *And mark in every face I meet*
>   *Marks of weakness, marks of woe.*
>
> *In every cry of every Man,*
>   *In every Infant's cry of fear,*
> *In every voice, in every ban,*
>   *The mind-forg'd manacles I hear.*

Michael Binding Satan by William Blake (watercolor, *ca.* 1805). "And he laid hold on the dragon, that old serpent, which is the Devil, and Satan, and bound him a thousand years."—*Revelation* 20:2. *Courtesy of the Fogg Art Museum, Harvard University, Gift of W. A. White.*

How the Chimney sweeper's cry
 Every black'ning Church appalls;
And the hapless Soldier's sigh
 Runs in blood down Palace walls.

But most thro' midnight streets I hear
 How the youthful Harlot's curse
Blasts the new-born Infant's tear,
 And blights with plagues the Marriage hearse.

Again, the strength of this is in part identifiably eighteenth-century in its conciseness and, in the best sense of the word, its generality. It becomes under-standable not only in terms of Blake's view of what the unredeemed world must necessarily be like, but also as a record of what his London actually was, without regard to any special "Blake perspective." Resisting topicality and mere contemporaneity, it becomes one of our great statements about urban experience. And, of course, its indignation reminds us of that passion for human justice—that social indignation—which in one way or another, at one time in their lives or other, distinguished his Romantic successors as well.

Blake was a shopkeeper's son, born in London in 1757. He was sent to drawing school at ten, and at fourteen apprenticed to an engraver, where he learned the trade that was to bring him much of his modest livelihood throughout his career. After his apprenticeship he briefly attended the art school of the Royal Academy. He made friends with several well-known artists, but his own productions went without any widespread recognition. Meanwhile he was educating himself by reading many of the standard books, always with his marked independence of judgment. He was twenty-four when he married an illiterate girl of twenty. Though childless and poor, they had a long and happy life together. Between the years 1800 and 1803 Blake lived in the village of Felpham, under the patronage, kindly and unimaginative, of a genteel dabbler in poetry, William Hayley. This was a productive and exasperating time for Blake. He returned to London in 1803 and spent the rest of his life there, working for the most part in obscurity. He did, late in life, gain a certain celebrity among younger artists, including the Romantic visionary Samuel Palmer. But his literary reputation, insofar as he had any, ranged pretty much from that of being regarded as a harmless crank to being regarded as harmlessly mad, though talented.

By 1794, the date of publication of the *Songs of Experience*, Blake had also published *The French Revolution, America*, and *The Visions of the Daughters of Albion*." In the next few years, in rapid succession, he published *The Book of Urizen, The Book of Los, Europe, The Song of Los, The Four Zoas, Milton, Jerusalem*, and others, works which are developments and elaborations of his essential attitudes. There is still considerable critical division about these works and their value by comparison with the earlier, and in some opinions more intensely focused, works such as those presented in our selection.

By about 1820 Blake's career as a literary artist was pretty well over. The chief works of his last years are his illustrations of Dante and for the Book of Job. He died in 1827.

TEXTS: The best edition is edited by David V. Erdman, *The Poetry and Prose of William Blake* (1968), with illuminating commentary by Harold Bloom. A great biography of Blake remains to be written, but Alexander Gilchrist's *Life of William Blake: Pictor Ignotus* (1863) and Mona Wilson, *Life of William Blake* (1948) are useful. Critical studies of Blake cover a more than usually wide range of critical persuasions and ideologies. The range may be suggested, at a strong level of competence, by the following: Hazard Adams, *William Blake: A Reading of the Shorter Poems* (1963); Harold Bloom, *Blake's Apocalypse* (1963); S. Foster Damon, *William Blake, His Philosophy and Symbols* (1924); David V. Erdman, *William Blake: Prophet Against Empire* (1954); Peter

Fisher, *The Valley of Vision* (1961); Northrop Frye, *Fearful Symmetry* (1947); E. D. Hirsch, *Innocence and Experience* (1964); Milton Percival, *William Blake's Circle of Destiny* (1938); Kathleen Raine, *Energy and Imagination* (1970); Mark Schorer, *William Blake: The Politics of Vision* (1946). There are several collections of critical essays about Blake, among them Northrup Frye, ed., *William Blake: A Collection of Critical Essays* (1966) and John E. Grant, ed., *Discussions of William Blake* (1961).

The Book of Thel[1]

This poem, probably written in 1789, is ambiguous and difficult. It may in certain respects be compared to Wordsworth's "Resolution and Independence" or Keats's "Ode to a Nightingale," poems in which the human consciousness feels painfully how it differs from the spontaneous creatures of nature, both because of its self-consciousness and because of its special awareness of death.

In the consideration of this poem and of *The Marriage of Heaven and Hell*, the reader is especially referred to Harold Bloom's commentaries in David V. Erdman and Harold Bloom, eds., *The Poetry and Prose of William Blake* (1968).

> *Thel's Motto*
> *Does the eagle know what is in the pit?*
> *Or wilt thou go ask the Mole?*
> *Can Wisdom be put in a silver rod?*
> *Or Love in a golden bowl?*[2]

I

The Daughters of Mne[3] Seraphim led round their sunny flocks,   5
All but the youngest: she in paleness sought the secret air,
To fade away like morning beauty from her mortal day:
Down by the river of Adona her soft voice is heard,
And thus her gentle lamentation falls like morning dew:

"O life of this our spring! why fades the lotus of the water?   10
Why fade these children of the spring, born but to smile & fall?

---

1 The name comes from the Greek for "desire."
2 Ecclesiastes 12.
3 Misprint for "the"?

Ah! Thel is like a wat'ry bow, and like a parting
    cloud;
Like a reflection in a glass; like shadows in the
    water;
Like dreams of infants, like a smile upon an in-
    fant's face;
Like the dove's voice; like transient day; like   15
    music in the air.
Ah! gentle may I lay me down, and gentle rest my
    head,
And gentle sleep the sleep of death, and gentle
    hear the voice
Of him that walketh in the garden in the evening
    time."

The Lilly of the valley, breathing in the humble
    grass,
Answer'd the lovely maid and said: "I am a wat'ry   20
    weed,
And I am very small and love to dwell in lowly
    vales;
So weak, the gilded butterfly scarce perches on my
    head.
Yet I am visited from heaven, and he that smiles
    on all
Walks in the valley and each morn over me spreads
    his hand,
Saying, 'Rejoice, thou humble grass, thou new-   25
    born lilly flower,
Thou gentle maid of silent valleys and of modest
    brooks;
For thou shalt be clothed in light, and fed with
    morning manna,
Till summer's heat melts thee beside the foun-
    tains and the springs
To flourish in eternal vales.' Then why should
    Thel complain?

Why should the mistress of the vales of Har utter   30
    a sigh?"

She ceas'd, & smil'd in tears, then sat down in her
    silver shrine.

Thel answer'd: "O thou little virgin of the peace-
    ful valley,
Giving to those that cannot crave, the voiceless,
    the o'ertired;
Thy breath doth nourish the innocent lamb, he
    smells thy milky garments,
He crops thy flowers while thou sittest smiling in   35
    his face,

Wiping his mild and meekin[4] mouth from all
    contagious taints.
Thy wine doth purify the golden honey; thy per-
    fume,
Which thou dost scatter on every little blade of
    grass that springs,
Revives the milkèd cow, & tames the fire-breath-
    ing steed.
But Thel is like a faint cloud kindled at the ris-   40
    ing sun:
I vanish from my pearly throne, and who shall
    find my place?"

"Queen of the vales," the Lilly answer'd, "ask the
    tender cloud,
And it shall tell thee why it glitters in the morn-
    ing sky,
And why it scatters its bright beauty thro' the
    humid air.
Descend, O little Cloud, & hover before the eyes   45
    of Thel."

The Cloud descended, and the Lilly bow'd her
    modest head
And went to mind her numerous charge among
    the verdant grass.

II

"O little Cloud," the virgin said, "I charge thee
    tell to me
Why thou complainest not when in one hour
    thou fade away:
Then we shall seek thee, but not find. Ah! Thel   50
    is like to thee:
I pass away: yet I complain, and no one hears my
    voice."

The Cloud then shew'd his golden head & his
    bright form emerg'd,
Hovering and glittering on the air before the face
    of Thel.

"O virgin, know'st thou not our steeds drink of
    the golden springs
Where Luvah[5] doth renew his horses? Look'st   55
    thou on my youth,
And fearest thou, because I vanish and am seen
    no more,

---

4 Tender.
5 From "Lover"? One of Blake's four Zoas, the four elements which compose man.

Nothing remains? O maid, I tell thee, when I
    pass away

It is to tenfold life, to love, to peace and raptures
    holy:

Unseen descending, weigh my light wings upon
    balmy flowers,

And court the fair-eyed dew to take me to her   60
    shining tent:

The weeping virgin, trembling, kneels before the
    risen sun,

Till we arise link'd in a golden band and never
    part,

But walk united, bearing food to all our tender
    flowers."

"Dost thou, O little Cloud? I fear that I am not
    like thee,

For I walk thro' the vales of Har, and smell the   65
    sweetest flowers,

But I feed not the little flowers; I hear the war-
    bling birds,

But I feed not the warbling birds; they fly and
    seek their food:

But Thel delights in these no more, because I
    fade away;

And all shall say, 'Without a use this shining
    woman liv'd,

Or did she only live to be at death the food of   70
    worms?' "

The Cloud reclin'd upon his airy throne and
    answer'd thus:

"Then if thou art the food of worms, O virgin of
    the skies,

How great thy use, how great thy blessing! Every
    thing that lives

Lives not alone nor for itself. Fear not, and I will
    call

The weak worm from its lowly bed, and thou   75
    shalt hear its voice.

Come forth, worm of the silent valley, to thy
    pensive queen."

The helpless worm arose, and sat upon the Lilly's
    leaf,

And the bright Cloud sail'd on, to find his part-
    ner in the vale.

III

Then Thel astonish'd view'd the Worm upon its
    dewy bed.

"Art thou a Worm? Image of weakness, art thou   80
    but a Worm?

I see thee like an infant wrapped in the Lilly's
    leaf.

Ah! weep not, little voice, thou canst not speak,
    but thou canst weep.

Is this a Worm? I see thee lay helpless & naked,
    weeping,

And none to answer, none to cherish thee with
    mother's smiles."

The Clod of Clay heard the Worm's voice & rais'd   85
    her pitying head;

She bow'd over the weeping infant, and her life
    exhal'd

In milky fondness; then on Thel she fix'd her
    humble eyes.

"O beauty of the vales of Har! we live not for
    ourselves.

Thou seest me the meanest thing, and so I am in-
    deed.

My bosom of itself is cold, and of itself is dark;   90

But he, that loves the lowly, pours his oil upon
    my head,

And kisses me, and binds his nuptial bands
    around my breast,

And says: 'Thou mother of my children, I have
    loved thee,

And I have given thee a crown that none can take
    away.'

But how this is, sweet maid, I know not, and I   95
    cannot know;

I ponder, and I cannot ponder; yet I live and
    love."

The daughter of beauty wip'd her pitying tears
    with her white veil,

And said: "Alas! I knew not this, and therefore
    did I weep.

That God would love a Worm I knew, and pun-
    ish the evil foot

That wilful bruis'd its helpless form; but that he   100
    cherish'd it

With milk and oil I never knew, and therefore
    did I weep;

And I complain'd in the mild air, because I fade
    away,

And lay me down in thy cold bed, and leave my
    shining lot."

"Queen of the vales," the matron Clay answer'd,
    "I heard thy sighs,

And all thy moans flew o'er my roof, but I have call'd them down.   105

Wilt thou, O Queen, enter my house? 'Tis given thee to enter

And to return: fear nothing, enter with thy virgin feet."

IV

The eternal gates' terrific porter lifted the northern bar:

Thel enter'd in & saw the secrets of the land unknown.

She saw the couches of the dead, & where the fibrous roots   110

Of every heart on earth infixes deep its restless twists:

A land of sorrows & of tears where never smile was seen.

She wander'd in the land of clouds thro' valleys dark, list'ning

Dolours & lamentations; waiting oft beside a dewy grave

She stood in silence, list'ning to the voices of the ground,   115

Till to her own grave plot she came, & there she sat down,

And heard this voice of sorrow breathed from the hollow pit.

"Why cannot the Ear be closed to its own destruction?

Or the glist'ning Eye to the poison of a smile?

Why are Eyelids stor'd with arrows ready drawn,   120

Where a thousand fighting men in ambush lie?

Or an Eye of gifts & graces show'ring fruits & coinèd gold?

Why a Tongue impress'd with honey from every wind?

Why an Ear, a whirlpool fierce to draw creations in?

Why a Nostril wide inhaling terror, trembling, & affright?   125

Why a tender curb upon the youthful burning boy?

Why a little curtain of flesh on the bed of our desire?"

The Virgin started from her seat, & with a shriek

Fled back unhinder'd till she came into the vales of Har.[6]

---

[6] She flees back to the place of innocence, the vales of Har, whether in the rejection of recognition of what she has

from *Poetical Sketches*

This volume, which appeared in 1783, was privately printed at the expense of friends. The first of the following selections is said to have been written before Blake was fourteen.

Song

How sweet I roam'd from field to field,
    And tasted all the summer's pride,
Till I the prince of love beheld,
    Who in the sunny beams did glide!

He shew'd me lilies for my hair,   5
    And blushing roses for my brow;
He led me through his gardens fair,
    Where all his golden pleasures grow.

With sweet May dews my wings were wet,
    And Phoebus fir'd my vocal rage;[1]   10
He caught me in his silken net,
    And shut me in his golden cage.

He loves to sit and hear me sing,
    Then, laughing, sports and plays with me;
Then stretches out my golden wing,   15
    And mocks my loss of liberty.

Song

My silks and fine array,
    My smiles and languish'd air,
By love are driv'n away;
    And mournful lean Despair
Brings me yew to deck my grave: 5
Such end true lovers have.

His face is fair as heav'n,
    When springing buds unfold;
O why to him was't giv'n
    Whose heart is wintry cold?   10
His breast is love's all worship'd tomb,
Where all love's pilgrims come.

Bring me an ax and spade,
    Bring me a winding sheet;

---

been shown, or because of the fullness of her recognition of it.

[1] Fervor.

When I my grave have made,   15
   Let winds and tempests beat:
Then down I'll lie as cold as clay.
True love doth pass away!

Mad Song

The wild winds weep,
   And the night is a-cold;
Come hither, Sleep,
   And my griefs unfold:
But lo! the morning peeps   5
Over the eastern steeps,
And the rustling beds of dawn
The earth do scorn.

Lo! to the vault
   Of pavèd heaven,   10
With sorrow fraught
   My notes are driven:
They strike the ear of night,
Make weep the eyes of day;
They make mad the roaring winds,   15
And with tempests play.

Like a fiend in a cloud,
   With howling woe
After night I do croud,[1]
   And with night will go;   20
I turn my back to the east,
From whence comforts have increas'd;
For light doth seize my brain
With frantic pain.

To the Muses

Whether on Ida's[1] shady brow,
   Or in the chambers of the East,
The chambers of the sun, that now
   From antient melody have ceas'd;

Whether in Heav'n ye wander fair,   5
   Or the green corners of the earth,
Or the blue regions of the air
   Where the melodious winds have birth;

---

[1] Crowd, press on.

[1] The gods of classical mythology visited Mt. Ida, near Troy; Blake is unwarranted, however, in making it a haunt of the Muses.—The complaint of the final stanza is against the neoclassical poetry of the century.

Whether on chrystal rocks ye rove,
   Beneath the bosom of the sea   10
Wand'ring in many a coral grove,
   Fair Nine, forsaking Poetry!

How have you left the antient love
   That bards of old enjoy'd in you!
The languid strings do scarcely move!   15
   The sound is forc'd, the notes are few!

from *Songs of Innocence*

This was the first important example of Blake's "illuminated printing," as he termed his method. He etched the text and the surrounding designs on thirty-one copper plates, printed from these in monochrome, and then illuminated the pages in water color. *Songs of Innocence* was offered for sale in 1789; *Songs of Experience,* produced in the same way, was ready in 1794. Blake soon added a general title page and issued the two sets together as *Songs of Innocence and Experience: Shewing the Two Contrary States of the Human Soul.*

Introduction

Piping down the valleys wild,
   Piping songs of pleasant glee,
On a cloud I saw a child,
   And he laughing said to me:

"Pipe a song about a Lamb!"   5
   So I piped with merry chear.
"Piper, pipe that song again";
   So I piped: he wept to hear.

"Drop thy pipe, thy happy pipe;
   Sing thy songs of happy chear!"   10
So I sang the same again,
   While he wept with joy to hear.

"Piper, sit thee down and write
   In a book, that all may read."
So he vanish'd from my sight,   15
   And I pluck'd a hollow reed,

And I made a rural pen,
   And I stain'd the water clear,
And I wrote my happy songs
   Every child may joy to hear.   20

The Lamb

Little Lamb, who made thee?
Dost thou know who made thee?
Gave thee life, and bid thee feed,
By the stream and o'er the mead;
Gave thee clothing of delight,   5
Softest clothing, wooly, bright;
Gave thee such a tender voice,
Making all the vales rejoice?
Little Lamb, who made thee?
Dost thou know who made thee?   10

Little Lamb, I'll tell thee,
Little Lamb, I'll tell thee:
He is callèd by thy name,
For he calls himself a Lamb,
He is meek, and he is mild;   15
He became a little child.
I a child, and thou a lamb,
We are callèd by his name.
Little Lamb, God bless thee!
Little Lamb, God bless thee!   20

Infant Joy

"I have no name:
I am but two days old."
What shall I call thee?
"I happy am,
Joy is my name."   5
Sweet joy befall thee!

Pretty joy!
Sweet joy, but two days old.
Sweet joy I call thee:
Thou dost smile,
I sing the while,   10
Sweet joy befall thee!

The Little Black Boy

My mother bore me in the southern wild,
And I am black, but O! my soul is white;
White as an angel is the English child,
But I am black, as if bereav'd of light.

My mother taught me underneath a tree,   5

And sitting down before the heat of day,
She took me on her lap and kissèd me,
And, pointing to the east, began to say:

"Look on the rising sun—there God does live,
And gives his light, and gives his heat away;   10
And flowers and trees and beasts and men receive
Comfort in morning, joy in the noonday.

"And we are put on earth a little space,
That we may learn to bear the beams of love;
And these black bodies and this sunburnt face   15
Is but a cloud, and like a shady grove.

"For when our souls have learn'd the heat to
    bear,
The cloud will vanish; we shall hear his voice,
Saying: 'Come out from the grove, my love and
    care,
And round my golden tent like lambs rejoice.'"   20

Thus did my mother say, and kissèd me;
And thus I say to little English boy.
When I from black and he from white cloud free,
And round the tent of God like lambs we joy,

I'll shade him from the heat, till he can bear   25
To lean in joy upon our father's knee;
And then I'll stand and stroke his silver hair,
And be like him, and he will then love me.

A Cradle Song

Sweet dreams, form a shade
O'er my lovely infant's head;
Sweet dreams of pleasant streams
By happy, silent, moony beams.

Sweet sleep, with soft down   5
Weave thy brows an infant crown.
Sweet sleep, Angel mild,
Hover o'er my happy child.

Sweet smiles, in the night
Hover over my delight;   10
Sweet smiles, Mother's smiles,
All the livelong night beguiles.
Sweet moans, dovelike sighs,
Chase not slumber from thy eyes.

Sweet moans, sweeter smiles,
All the dovelike moans beguiles.

Sleep, sleep, happy child,
All creation slept and smil'd;
Sleep, sleep, happy sleep,
While o'er thee thy mother weep. 20

Sweet babe, in thy face
Holy image I can trace.
Sweet babe, once like thee,
Thy maker lay and wept for me,

Wept for me, for thee, for all, 25
When he was an infant small.
Thou his image ever see,
Heavenly face that smiles on thee,

Smiles on thee, on me, on all;
Who became an infant small. 30
Infant smiles are his own smiles;
Heaven and earth to peace beguiles.

The Chimney Sweeper

When my mother died I was very young,
And my father sold me while yet my tongue
Could scarcely cry "'weep! 'weep! 'weep! 'weep!"
So your chimneys I sweep, and in soot I sleep.

There's little Tom Dacre, who cried when his 5
head,
That curl'd like a lamb's, back, was shav'd: so I
said
"Hush, Tom! never mind it, for when your head's
bare
You know that the soot cannot spoil your white
hair."

And so he was quiet, and that very night,
As Tom was a-sleeping, he had such a sight! 10
That thousands of sweepers, Dick, Joe, Ned, and
Jack,
Were all of them lock'd up in coffins of black.

And by came an Angel who had a bright key,
And he open'd the coffins and set them all free;
Then down a green plain leaping, laughing, they 15
run,
And wash in a river, and shine in the Sun.

Then naked and white, all their bags left behind, 15
They rise upon clouds and sport in the wind;
And the Angel told Tom, if he'd be a good boy,
He'd have God for his father, and never want joy. 20

And so Tom awoke; and we rose in the dark,
And got with our bags and our brushes to work.
Tho' the morning was cold, Tom was happy and
warm:
So if all do their duty they need not fear harm.

Nurse's Song

When the voices of children are heard on the
green,
And laughing is heard on the hill,
My heart is at rest within my breast,
And everything else is still.

"Then come home, my children, the sun is gone 5
down,
And the dews of night arise;
Come, come, leave off play, and let us away
Till the morning appears in the skies."

"No, no, let us play, for it is yet day,
And we cannot go to sleep; 10
Besides, in the sky the little birds fly
And the hills are all cover'd with sheep."

"Well, well, go & play till the light fades away,
And then go home to bed."
The little ones leaped & shouted & laugh'd 15
And all the hills echoed.

Holy Thursday[1]

'Twas on a Holy Thursday, their innocent faces
clean,
The children walking two & two, in red & blue &
green,
Grey-headed beadles[2] walk'd before, with wands
as white as snow,
Till into the high dome of Paul's they like
Thames' waters flow.

---

1 Ascension Day, forty days after Easter.
2 Church officials.

O what a multitude they seem'd, these flowers of
    London town!
Seated in companies they sit with radiance all
    their own.
The hum of multitudes was there, but multitudes
    of lambs,
Thousands of little boys & girls raising their in-
    nocent hands.

Now like a mighty wind they raise to heaven the
    voice of song,
Or like harmonious thunderings the seats of
    Heaven among.   10
Beneath them sit the aged men, wise guardians of
    the poor;
Then cherish pity, lest you drive an angel from
    your door.

from *Songs of Experience*
The Tyger

Tyger! Tyger! burning bright
In the forests of the night,
What immortal hand or eye
Could frame thy fearful symmetry?
In what distant deeps or skies   5
Burnt the fire of thine eyes?
On what wings dare he aspire?
What the hand dare seize the fire?

And what shoulder, and what art,
Could twist the sinews of thy heart?   10
And when thy heart began to beat,
What dread hand? and what dread feet?[1]

What the hammer? what the chain?
In what furnace was thy brain?
What the anvil? what dread grasp   15
Dare its deadly terrors clasp?

When the stars threw down their spears,
And water'd heaven with their tears,
Did he smile his work to see?
Did he who made the Lamb make thee?   20

[1] Blake's manuscript shows that he originally intended the
sentence beginning in lines 11 and 12 to run on into another stanza, opening "Could fetch it from the furnace
deep?" Although he decided to cancel that stanza, he was
unwilling to discard the powerful but now incomplete line
12, the punctuation of which he therefore altered to two
question marks.

Tyger! Tyger! burning bright   5
In the forests of the night,
What immortal hand or eye
Dare frame thy fearful symmetry?

The Clod and the Pebble

"Love seeketh not Itself to please,
    Nor for itself hath any care,
But for another gives its ease,
    And builds a Heaven in Hell's despair."

So sung a little Clod of Clay,   5
    Trodden with the cattle's feet,
But a Pebble of the brook
    Warbled out these metres meet:

"Love seeketh only Self to please,
    To bind another to Its delight,   10
Joys in another's loss of ease,
    And builds a Hell in Heaven's despite."

Nurse's Song

When the voices of children are heard on the
    green,
And whisp'rings are in the dale,
The days of my youth rise fresh in my mind,
My face turns green and pale.

Then come home, my children, the sun is gone   5
    down,
And the dews of night arise;
Your spring & your day are wasted in play,
And your winter and night in disguise.

Holy Thursday

Is this a holy thing to see
In a rich and fruitful land,
Babes reduc'd to misery,
Fed with cold and usurous hand?

Is that trembling cry a song?   5
Can it be a song of joy?
And so many children poor?
It is a land of poverty!

And their sun does never shine,
And their fields are bleak & bare,   10
And their ways are fill'd with thorns:
It is eternal winter there.

For where-e'er the sun does shine,
And where-e'er the rain does fall,
Babe can never hunger there,   15
Nor poverty the mind appall.

A Poison Tree

I was angry with my friend:
I told my wrath, my wrath did end.
I was angry with my foe:
I told it not, my wrath did grow.

And I water'd it in fears,   5
Night and morning with my tears;
And I sunnèd it with smiles,
And with soft deceitful wiles.

And it grew both day and night,
Till it bore an apple bright;   10
And my foe beheld it shine,
And he knew that it was mine,

And into my garden stole
When the night had veil'd the pole:
In the morning glad I see   15
My foe outstretch'd beneath the tree.

Ah, Sun-Flower

Ah, Sun-flower! weary of time,
Who countest the steps of the Sun,
Seeking after that sweet golden clime
Where the traveller's journey is done:
Where the Youth pined away with desire,   5
And the pale Virgin shrouded in snow,
Arise from their graves, and aspire
Where my Sun-flower wishes to go.

The Garden of Love

I went to the Garden of Love,
And saw what I never had seen:

A Chapel was built in the midst,
Where I used to play on the green.

And the gates of this Chapel were shut,   5
And "Thou shalt not" writ over the door;
So I turn'd to the Garden of Love
That so many sweet flowers bore;

And I saw it was fillèd with graves,
And tomb-stones where flowers should be;   10
And Priests in black gowns were walking their
      rounds,
And binding with briars my joys and desires.

The Sick Rose

O Rose, thou art sick!
The invisible worm,
That flies in the night,
In the howling storm,

Has found out thy bed   5
Of crimson joy,
And his dark secret love
Does thy life destroy.

A Little Boy Lost

"Nought loves another as itself,
Nor venerates another so,
Nor is it possible to Thought
A greater than itself to know:

"And Father, how can I love you   5
Or any of my brothers more?
I love you like the little bird
That picks up crumbs around the door."

The Priest sat by and heard the child,
In trembling zeal he seiz'd his hair: 10
He led him by his little coat,
And all admir'd the priestly care.

And standing on the altar high,
"Lo! what a fiend is here," said he,
"One who sets reason up for judge   15
Of our most holy Mystery."

The weeping child could not be heard,
   The weeping parents wept in vain;
They strip'd him to his little shirt,
   And bound him in an iron chain;   20

And burn'd him in a holy place,
   Where many had been burn'd before:
The weeping parents wept in vain.
   Are such things done on Albion's[1] shore?

Infant Sorrow

My mother groan'd! my father wept.
Into the dangerous world I leapt:
Helpless, naked, piping loud:
Like a fiend hid in a cloud.

Struggling in my father's hands,   5
Striving against my swadling bands,
Bound and weary I thought best
To sulk upon my mother's breast.

London

I wander thro' each charter'd street,
   Near where the charter'd Thames does flow,
And mark in every face I meet
   Marks of weakness, marks of woe.

In every cry of every Man,   5
   In every Infant's cry of fear,
In every voice, in every ban,
   The mind-forg'd manacles I hear.

How the Chimney sweeper's cry
   Every black'ning Church appalls;   10
And the hapless Soldier's sigh
   Runs in blood down Palace walls.

But most thro' midnight streets I hear
   How the youthful Harlot's curse
Blasts the new-born Infant's tear,   15
   And blights with plagues the Marriage hearse.

The Chimney Sweeper

A little black thing among the snow,
   Crying "'weep! 'weep!" in notes of woe!

---

[1] England's.

"Where are thy father and mother? say?"
   "They are both gone up to the church to pray.

"Because I was happy upon the heath,   5
   And smil'd among the winter's snow,
They clothèd me in the clothes of death,
   And taught me to sing the notes of woe.

"And because I am happy and dance and sing,
   They think they have done me no injury,   10
And are gone to praise God and his Priest and
   King,
   Who make up a heaven of our misery."

Poems from *Manuscripts*

The Rossetti Manuscript (so called because it belonged for a time to the Victorian poet Dante Gabriel Rossetti) is the commonplace-book in which Blake composed many of his poems. Although an editor should normally accept his author's final wording, "Never Seek to Tell Thy Love" is given as it stood before Blake's alterations. The earlier version is far better, and we have no reason to suppose that Blake's revision was final. "A Cradle Song" was evidently intended for *Songs of Experience,* as a contrast to the poem with the same title in *Songs of Innocence;* but for some reason the poet did not use it.

Never Seek to Tell Thy Love

Never seek to tell thy love,
   Love that never told can be;
For the gentle wind doth move
   Silently, invisibly.

I told my love, I told my love,   5
   I told her all my heart,
Trembling, cold, in ghastly fears,
   Ah! she doth depart.

Soon as she was gone from me,
   A traveller came by,   10
Silently, invisibly:
   He took her with a sigh.

A Cradle Song

Sleep! sleep! beauty bright,
Dreaming o'er the joys of night;

Sleep! sleep! in thy sleep
Little sorrows sit and weep.

Sweet Babe, in thy face 5
Soft desires I can trace,
Secret joys and secret smiles,
Little pretty infant wiles.

As thy softest limbs I feel,
Smiles as of the morning steal 10
O'er thy cheek, and o'er thy breast
Where thy little heart does rest.

O! the cunning wiles that creep
In thy little heart asleep.
When thy little heart does wake 15
Then the dreadful lightnings break,

From thy cheek and from thy eye,
O'er the youthful harvest nigh.
Infant wiles and infant smiles
Heaven and Earth of peace beguiles. 20

Eternity

He who bends to himself a Joy
Does the wingèd life destroy;
But he who kisses the Joy as it flies
Lives in Eternity's sunrise.

Mock on Mock on Voltaire, Rousseau

From the 1800–1803 Notebook

Mock on, Mock on Voltaire, Rousseau:[1]
Mock on, Mock on: 'tis all in vain!
You throw the sand against the wind,
And the wind blows it back again.

And every sand becomes a Gem 5
Reflected in the beams divine;
Blown back they blind the mocking Eye,
But still in Israel's paths they shine.

The Atoms of Democritus
And Newton's Particles of light 10

---

[1] In Blake's view enemies of religion, as is also the science of Democritus and of Newton.

Are sands upon the Red sea shore,
Where Israel's tents do shine so bright.

Auguries of Innocence

This poem was left unfinished and unpublished by Blake. The Pickering Manuscript, in which it appears, gets its name from an owner. These couplets were probably written about 1803. They may have been intended simply as jottings from which several poems might later be drawn.

To see a World in a Grain of Sand
And a Heaven in a Wild Flower,
Hold Infinity in the palm of your hand
And Eternity in an hour.
A Robin Redbreast in a Cage 5
Puts all Heaven in a Rage.
A dove-house fill'd with Doves and Pigeons
Shudders Hell thro' all its regions.
A dog starv'd at his Master's Gate
Predicts the ruin of the State. 10
A Horse misus'd upon the Road
Calls to Heaven for Human blood.
Each outcry of the hunted Hare
A fibre from the Brain does tear.
A Skylark wounded in the wing, 15
A Cherubim does cease to sing;
The Game Cock clip'd and arm'd for fight
Does the Rising Sun affright.
Every Wolf's and Lion's howl
Raises from Hell a Human Soul. 20
The wild Deer, wand'ring here and there,
Keeps the Human Soul from Care.
The Lamb misus'd breeds Public Strife
And yet forgives the Butcher's Knife.
The Bat that flits at close of Eve 25
Has left the Brain that won't Believe.
The Owl that calls upon the Night
Speaks the Unbeliever's fright.
He who shall hurt the little Wren
Shall never be belov'd by Men. 30
He who the Ox[1] to wrath has mov'd
Shall never be by Woman lov'd.
The wanton Boy that kills the Fly
Shall feel the Spider's enmity.

---

[1] A London custom, which persisted as late as the second quarter of the nineteenth century, was to turn an ox loose in the street, torment it into a frenzy, and finally hunt it down and kill it.

He who torments the Chafer's Sprite[2]
Weaves a Bower in endless Night.
The Caterpillar on the Leaf
Repeats to thee thy Mother's grief.
Kill not the Moth nor Butterfly,
For the Last Judgment draweth nigh.
He who shall train the Horse to War
Shall never pass the Polar Bar.
The Beggar's Dog and Widow's Cat,
Feed them and thou wilt grow fat.
The Gnat that sings his Summer's Song   45
Poison gets from Slander's tongue.
The poison of the Snake and Newt
Is the sweat of Envy's Foot.
The poison of the Honey Bee
Is the Artist's Jealousy.   50
The Prince's Robes and Beggar's Rags
Are Toadstools on the Miser's Bags.
A Truth that's told with bad intent
Beats all the Lies you can invent.
It is right it should be so;   55
Man was made for Joy and Woe;
And when this we rightly know,
Thro' the World we safely go.
Joy and Woe are woven fine,
A Clothing for the Soul divine.   60
Under every grief and pine
Runs a joy with silken twine.
The Babe is more than Swadling Bands;
Throughout all these Human Lands
Tools were made, and Born were hands,   65
Every Farmer Understands.
Every Tear from Every Eye.
Becomes a Babe in Eternity;
This is caught by Females bright,
And return'd to its own delight.   70
The Bleat, the Bark, Bellow, and Roar
Are Waves that beat on Heaven's Shore.
The Babe that weeps the Rod beneath
Writes Revenge in realms of Death.
The Beggar's Rags, fluttering in Air,   75
Does to Rags the Heavens tear.
The Soldier, arm'd with Sword and Gun,
Palsied strikes the Summer's Sun.
The poor Man's Farthing is worth more
Than all the Gold on Afric's Shore.   80
One Mite wrung from the Lab'rer's hands
Shall buy and sell the Miser's Lands;
Or, if protected from on high,

Does that whole Nation sell and buy.   35
He who mocks the Infant's Faith   85
Shall be mock'd in Age and Death.
He who shall teach the Child to Doubt
The rotting Grave shall ne'er get out.
He who respects the Infant's faith   40
Triumphs over Hell and Death.   90
The Child's Toys and the Old Man's Reasons
Are the Fruits of the Two Seasons.
The Questioner, who sits so sly,
Shall never know how to Reply.   45
He who replies to words of Doubt   95
Doth put the Light of Knowledge out.
The Strongest Poison ever known
Came from Caesar's Laurel Crown.
Nought can Deform the Human Race   50
Like to the Armour's iron brace.   100
When Gold and Gems adorn the Plow
To peaceful Arts shall Envy bow.
A Riddle or the Cricket's Cry
Is to Doubt a fit Reply.   55
The Emmet's[3] Inch and Eagle's Mile   105
Make Lame Philosophy to smile.
He who Doubts from what he sees
Will ne'er Believe, do what you Please.
If the Sun and Moon should Doubt,   60
They'd immediately Go Out.   110
To be in a Passion you Good may do,
But no Good if a Passion is in you.
The Whore and Gambler, by the State
Licens'd, build that Nation's Fate.   65
The Harlot's cry from Street to Street   115
Shall weave Old England's winding Sheet.
The Winner's shout, the Loser's Curse,
Dance before dead England's Hearse.
Every Night and every Morn   70
Some to Misery are Born.   120
Every Morn and every Night
Some are Born to Sweet Delight.
Some are Born to Sweet Delight,
Some are Born to Endless Night.   75
We are led to Believe a Lie   125
When we see not Thro' the Eye,
Which was Born in a Night to perish in a Night,
When the Soul Slept in Beams of Light.
God appears and God is light   80
To those poor Souls who dwell in Night,   130
But does a Human Form Display
To those who Dwell in Realms of Day.

---

2 Beetle's spirit.

3 Ant's.

The Marriage of Heaven and Hell

This work was written between 1790 and 1793. It is a compendium of Blake's central views about the one-ness of body and soul, the relation between reason and energy, the nature of God and what this implies about the workings of the imagination. Moreover, it is full of his particular views about human behavior. It is both an inspirational and a satirical document, and the target of its satire is not only Emmanuel Swedenborg (see note 3) but the manners of men in Blake's England as well.

THE ARGUMENT

Rintrah[1] roars & shakes his fires in the burden'd
   air;
Hungry clouds swag[2] on the deep.

Once meek, and in a perilous path,
The just man kept his course along
The vale of death.   5
Roses are planted where thorns grow,
And on the barren heath
Sing the honey bees.

Then the perilous path was planted,
And a river and a spring   10
On every cliff and tomb,
And on the bleached bones
Red clay brought forth;

Till the villain left the paths of ease,
To walk in perilous paths, and drive   15
The just man into barren climes.

Now the sneaking serpent walks
In mild humility,
And the just man rages in the wilds
Where lions roam.   20

Rintrah roars & shakes his fires in the burden'd
   air;
Hungry clouds swag on the deep.

    As a new heaven is begun, and it is now thirty-three years since its advent, the Eternal Hell revives. And lo! Swedenborg is the Angel   25 sitting at the tomb: his writings are the linen clothes folded up.[3] Now is the dominion of Edom,[4] & the return of Adam into Paradise. See Isaiah xxxiv & xxxv Chap.

    Without Contraries is no progression. Attraction and Repulsion, Reason and Energy, Love   30 and Hate, are necessary to Human existence.

    From these contraries spring what the religious call Good & Evil. Good is the passive that obeys Reason. Evil is the active springing from Energy.

    Good is Heaven. Evil is Hell.

THE VOICE OF THE DEVIL

All Bibles or sacred codes have been the causes of the following Errors:

    1. That Man has two real existing principles: Viz: a Body & a Soul.   40

    2. That Energy, call'd Evil, is alone from the Body; & that Reason, call'd Good, is alone from the Soul.

    3. That God will torment Man in Eternity for following his Energies.

    But the following Contraries to these are True:

    1. Man has no Body distinct from his Soul; for that call'd Body is a portion of Soul discern'd by the five Senses, the chief inlets of Soul in this   50 age.

    2. Energy is the only life, and is from the Body; and Reason is the bound or outward circumference of Energy.

    3. Energy is Eternal Delight.

    Those who restrain desire, do so because theirs is weak enough to be restrained; and the restrainer or reason usurps its place & governs the unwilling.

    And being restrain'd, it by degrees becomes   60 passive, till it is only the shadow of desire.

---

1 The poet himself, associating himself with Old Testament prophets foretelling both destruction and regeneration.
2 Sway violently.

3 Emmanuel Swedenborg (1688–1772), Swedish theologian who founded the New Jerusalem Church. Blake was influenced for a time by his criticisms of other sects but concluded that he had systematized his own thinking into institutional dogma. He is treating Swedenborg ironically here. Swedenborg had announced the coming of the "New Heaven" in 1757, when Blake was born. This is thirty-three years before "The Marriage of Heaven and Hell" and Christ lived for thirty-three years. As Swedenborg was the prophet of the "New Heaven," Blake is here the prophet of "Eternal Hell."
4 The name of Edom is associated in Genesis with Esau, the brother and rival to Jacob, who had received his father's blessing in Esau's place.

The history of this is written in Paradise Lost, & the Governor or Reason is call'd Messiah.

And the original Archangel, or possessor of the command of the heavenly host, is call'd the Devil or Satan, and his children are call'd Sin & Death.

But in the Book of Job, Milton's Messiah is call'd Satan.

For this history has been adopted by both parties.

It indeed appear'd to Reason as if Desire was cast out; but the Devil's account is, that the Messiah fell, & formed a heaven of what he stole from the Abyss.

This is shewn in the Gospel, where he prays to the Father to send the comforter, or Desire, that Reason may have Ideas to build on; the Jehovah of the Bible being no other than he who dwells in flaming fire.

Know that after Christ's death, he became Jehovah.

But in Milton, the Father is Destiny, the Son a Ratio of the five senses, & the Holy-ghost Vacuum!

Note: The reason Milton wrote in fetters when he wrote of Angels & God, and at liberty when of Devils & Hell, is because he was a true Poet and of the Devil's party without knowing it.

A MEMORABLE FANCY

As I was walking among the fires of hell, delighted with the enjoyments of Genius, which to Angels look like torment and insanity, I collected some of their Proverbs; thinking that as the sayings used in a nation mark its character, so the Proverbs of Hell show the nature of Infernal wisdom better than any description of buildings or garments.

When I came home: on the abyss of the five senses, where a flat sided steep frowns over the present world, I saw a mighty Devil[5] folded in black clouds, hovering on the sides of the rock: with corroding fires he wrote the following sentence now perceived by the minds of men, & read by them on earth:

How do you know but ev'ry Bird that cuts the airy way,

Is an immense world of delight, clos'd by your senses five?

---

[5] Blake is "the mighty Devil" here.

PROVERBS OF HELL

In seed time learn, in harvest teach, in winter enjoy.

Drive your cart and your plow over the bones of the dead.

The road of excess leads to the palace of wisdom.

Prudence is a rich, ugly old maid courted by Incapacity.

He who desires but acts not, breeds pestilence.

The cut worm forgives the plow.

Dip him in the river who loves water.

A fool sees not the same tree that a wise man sees.

He whose face gives no light, shall never become a star.

Eternity is in love with the productions of time.

The busy bee has no time for sorrow.

The hours of folly are measur'd by the clock; but of wisdom, no clock can measure.

All wholesome food is caught without a net or a trap.

Bring out number, weight & measure in a year of dearth.

No bird soars too high, if he soars with his own wings.

A dead body revenges not injuries.

The most sublime act is to set another before you.

If the fool would persist in his folly he would become wise.

Folly is the cloke of knavery.

Shame is Pride's cloke.

Prisons are built with stones of Law, Brothels with bricks of Religion.

The pride of the peacock is the glory of God.

The lust of the goat is the bounty of God.

The wrath of the lion is the wisdom of God.

The nakedness of woman is the work of God.

Excess of sorrow laughs. Excess of joy weeps.

The roaring of lions, the howling of wolves, the raging of the stormy sea, and the destructive sword, are portions of eternity too great for the eye of man.

The fox condemns the trap, not himself.

Joys impregnate. Sorrows bring forth.

Let man wear the fell of the lion, woman the fleece of the sheep.

The bird a nest, the spider a web, man friendship.

The selfish, smiling fool, & the sullen, frowning fool shall be both thought wise, that they may be a rod.

What is now proved was once only imagin'd.

The rat, the mouse, the fox, the rabbet watch the roots; the lion, the tyger, the horse, the elephant watch the fruits.

The cistern contains: the fountain overflows.

One thought fills immensity.

Always be ready to speak your mind, and a base man will avoid you.

Every thing possible to be believ'd is an image of truth.

The eagle never lost so much time as when he submitted to learn of the crow.

The fox provides for himself, but God provides for the lion.

Think in the morning. Act in the noon. Eat in the evening. Sleep in the night.

He who has suffer'd you to impose on him, knows you.

As the plow follows words, so God rewards prayers.

The tygers of wrath are wiser than the horses of instruction.

Expect poison from the standing water.

You never know what is enough unless you know what is more than enough.

Listen to the fool's reproach! it is a kingly title!

The eyes of fire, the nostrils of air, the mouth of water, the beard,of earth.

The weak in courage is strong in cunning.

The apple tree never asks the beech how he shall grow; nor the lion, the horse, how he shall take his prey.

The thankful receiver bears a plentiful harvest.

If others had not been foolish, we should be so.

The soul of sweet delight can never be defil'd.

When thou seest an Eagle, thou seest a portion of Genius; lift up thy head!

As the caterpillar chooses the fairest leaves to lay her eggs on, so the priest lays his curse on the fairest joys.

To create a little flower is the labour of ages.

Damn braces. Bless relaxes.

The best wine is the oldest, the best water the newest.

Prayers plow not! Praises reap not!

Joys laugh not! Sorrows weep not!

The head Sublime, the heart Pathos, the genitals Beauty, the hands & feet Proportion.

As the air to a bird or the sea to a fish, so is contempt to the contemptible.

The crow wish'd every thing was black, the owl that every thing was white.

Exuberance is Beauty.

If the lion was advised by the fox, he would be cunning.

Improvement makes strait roads; but the crooked roads without Improvement are roads of Genius.

Sooner murder an infant in its cradle than nurse unacted desires.

Where man is not, nature is barren.

Truth can never be told so as to be understood, and not be believ'd.

Enough! or Too much.

The ancient Poets animated all sensible objects with Gods or Geniuses, calling them by the names and adorning them with the properties of woods, rivers, mountains, lakes, cities, nations, and whatever their enlarged & numerous senses could perceive.

And particularly they studied the genius of each city & country, placing it under its mental deity;

Till a system was formed, which some took advantage of, & enslav'd the vulgar by attempting to realize or abstract the mental deities from their objects: thus began Priesthood;

Choosing forms of worship from poetic tales.

And at length they pronounc'd that the Gods had order'd such things.

Thus men forgot that All deities reside in the human breast.

A MEMORABLE FANCY

The Prophets Isaiah and Ezekiel dined with me, and I asked them how they dared so roundly to assert that God spoke to them; and whether they did not think at the time that they would be misunderstood, & so be the cause of imposition.

Isaiah answer'd: "I saw no God, nor heard any, in a finite organical perception; but my senses discover'd the infinite in everything, and as I was then perswaded, & remain confirm'd, that the voice of honest indignation is the voice of God, I cared not for consequences, but wrote."

Then I asked: "does a firm perswasion that a thing is so, make it so?"

He replied: "All poets believe that it does, & in ages of imagination this firm perswasion removed mountains; but many are not capable of a firm perswasion of any thing."

Then Ezekiel said: "The philosophy of the east taught the first principles of human perception: some nations held one principle for the origin, and some another: we of Israel taught that the Poetic Genius (as you now call it) was the first principle and all the others merely derivative, which was the cause of our despising the Priests & Philosophers of other countries, and prophecying that all Gods would at last be proved to originate in ours & to be the tributaries of the Poetic Genius; it was this that our great poet, King David, desired so fervently & invokes so pathetic'ly, saying by this he conquers enemies & governs kingdoms; and we so loved our God, that we cursed in his name all the deities of surrounding nations, and asserted that they had rebelled: from these opinions the vulgar came to think that all nations would at last be subject to the jews."

"This," said he, "like all firm perswasions, is come to pass; for all nations believe the jews' code and worship the jews' god, and what greater subjection can be?"

I heard this with some wonder, & must confess my own conviction. After dinner I ask'd Isaiah to favour the world with his lost works; he said none of equal value was lost. Ezekiel said the same of his.

I also asked Isaiah what made him go naked and barefoot three years? he answer'd: "the same that made our friend Diogenes, the Grecian."[6]

I then asked Ezekiel why he eat dung, & lay so long on his right & left side?[7] he answer'd, "the desire of raising other men into a perception of the infinite: this the North American tribes practise, & is he honest who resists his genius or conscience only for the sake of present ease or gratification?"

The ancient tradition that the world will be consumed in fire at the end of six thousand years is true, as I have heard from Hell.

For the cherub with his flaming sword is hereby commanded to leave his guard at tree of life;[8] and when he does, the whole creation will be consumed and appear infinite and holy, whereas it now appears finite & corrupt.

This will come to pass by an improvement of sensual enjoyment.

But first the notion that man has a body distinct from his soul is to be expunged; this I shall do by printing in the infernal method, by corrosives, which in Hell are salutary and medicinal, melting apparent surfaces away, and displaying the infinite which was hid.[9]

If the doors of perception were cleansed every thing would appear to man as it is, infinite.

For man has closed himself up, till he sees all things thro' narrow chinks of his cavern.

A MEMORABLE FANCY

I was in a Printing house in Hell, & saw the method in which knowledge is transmitted from generation to generation.

In the first chamber was a Dragon-Man, clearing away the rubbish from a cave's mouth; within, a number of Dragons were hollowing the cave.

In the second chamber was a Viper folding round the rock & the cave, and others adorning it with gold, silver and precious stones.

In the third chamber was an Eagle with wings and feathers of air: he caused the inside of the cave to be infinite; around were numbers of Eagle-like men who built palaces in the immense cliffs.

In the fourth chamber were Lions of flaming fire, raging around & melting the metals into living fluids.

In the fifth chamber were Unnam'd forms, which cast the metals into the expanse.

There they were receiv'd by Men who occupied the sixth chamber, and took the forms of books & were arranged in libraries.

The Giants who formed this world into its

---

6 Diogenes, the fourth-century philosopher, naked in protest against the nature of his world.

7 See Ezekiel 4:4–8.

8 Genesis 3:24.

9 Blake is referring to his own process of etching. The infinite is hidden in the plate; the acid reveals it and thus obliterates the distinction between body and soul. Etching is therefore an instance of, and a metaphor for, a cleansing of the doors of perception, a revelation that joins together what were falsely thought to be distinct—body and soul.

sensual existence, and now seem to live in it in chains, are in truth the causes of its life & the sources of all activity; but the chains are the cunning of weak and tame minds which have power to resist energy; according to the proverb, the weak in courage is strong in cunning.

Thus one portion of being is the Prolific, the other the Devouring: to the Devourer it seems as if the producer was in his chains; but it is not so, he only takes portions of existence and fancies that the whole.

But the Prolific would cease to be Prolific unless the Devourer, as a sea, received the excess of his delights.

Some will say: "Is not God alone the Prolific?" I answer: "God only Acts & Is, in existing beings or Men."

These two classes of men are always upon earth, & they should be enemies: whoever tries to reconcile them seeks to destroy existence.

Religion is an endeavour to reconcile the two.

Note: Jesus Christ did not wish to unite, but to separate them, as in the Parable of sheep and goats! & he says: "I came not to send Peace, but a Sword."[10]

Messiah or Satan or Tempter was formerly thought to be one of the Antediluvians who are our Energies.

A MEMORABLE FANCY

An Angel came to me and said: "O pitiable foolish young man! O horrible! O dreadful state! consider the hot burning dungeon thou art preparing for thyself to all eternity, to which thou art going in such career."

I said: "Perhaps you will be willing to shew me my eternal lot, & we will contemplate together upon it, and see whether your lot or mine is most desirable."

So he took me thro' a stable & thro' a church & down into the church vault, at the end of which was a mill: thro' the mill we went, and came to a cave: down the winding cavern we groped our tedious way, till a void boundless as a nether sky appear'd beneath us, & we held by the roots of trees and hung over this immensity; but I said: "if you please, we will commit ourselves to this void, and see whether providence is here also: if you will not, I will": but he answer'd: "do not presume, O young man, but as we here remain, behold thy lot which will soon appear when the darkness passes away."

So I remain'd with him, sitting in the twisted root of an oak; he was suspended in a fungus, which hung with the head downward into the deep.

By degrees we beheld the infinite Abyss, fiery as the smoke of a burning city; beneath us, at an immense distance, was the sun, black but shining; round it were fiery tracks on which revolv'd vast spiders, crawling after their prey, which flew, or rather swum, in the infinite deep, in the most terrific shapes of animals sprung from corruption; & the air was full of them, & seem'd composed of them: these are Devils, and are called Powers of the air. I now asked my companion which was my eternal lot? he said: "between the black and white spiders."

But now, from between the black & white spiders, a cloud and fire burst and rolled thro' the deep, black'ning all beneath, so that the nether deep grew black as a sea, & rolled with a terrible noise; beneath us was nothing now to be seen but a black tempest, till looking east between the clouds & the waves, we saw a cataract of blood mixed with fire, and not many stones' throw from us appear'd and sunk again the scaly fold of a monstrous serpent; at last, to the east, distant about three degrees, appear'd a fiery crest above the waves; slowly it reared like a ridge of golden rocks, till we discover'd two globes of crimson fire, from which the sea fled away in clouds of smoke; and now we saw it was the head of Leviathan; his forehead was divided into streaks of green & purple like those on a tyger's forehead: soon we saw his mouth & red gills hang just above the raging foam, tinging the black deep with beams of blood, advancing toward us with all the fury of a spiritual existence.

My friend the Angel climb'd up from his station into the mill: I remain'd alone; & then this appearance was no more, but I found myself sitting on a pleasant bank beside a river by moonlight, hearing a harper, who sung to the harp; & his theme was: "The man who never alters his opinion is like standing water, & breeds reptiles of the mind."

But I arose and sought for the mill, & there

---

[10] Matthew 10:34.

I found my Angel, who, surprised, asked me how I escaped?

I answer'd: "All that we saw was owing to your metaphysics; for when you ran away, I found myself on a bank by moonlight hearing a harper. But now we have seen my eternal lot, shall I shew you yours?" he laugh'd at my proposal; but I by force suddenly caught him in my arms, & flew westerly thro' the night, till we were elevated above the earth's shadow; then I flung myself with him directly into the body of the sun; here I clothed myself in white, & taking in my hand Swedenborg's volumes, sunk from the glorious clime, and passed all the planets till we came to saturn: here I stay'd to rest, & then leap'd into the void between saturn & the fixed stars.

"Here," said I, "is your lot, in this space— if space it may be call'd." Soon we saw the stable and the church, & I took him to the altar and open'd the Bible, and lo! it was a deep pit, into which I descended, driving the Angel before me; soon we saw seven houses of brick; one we enter'd; in it were a number of monkeys, baboons, & all of that species, chain'd by the middle, grinning and snatching at one another, but withheld by the shortness of their chains: however, I saw that they sometimes grew numerous, and then the weak were caught by the strong, and with a grinning aspect, first coupled with, & then devour'd, by plucking off first one limb and then another, till the body was left a helpless trunk; this, after grinning & kissing it with seeming fondness, they devour'd too; and here & there I saw one savourily picking the flesh off his own tail; as the stench terribly annoy'd us both, we went into the mill, & I in my hand brought the skeleton of a body, which in the mill was Aristotle's Analytics.

So the Angel said: "thy phantasy has imposed upon me, & thou oughtest to be ashamed."

I answer'd: "we impose on one another, & it is but lost time to converse with you whose works are only Analytics."

Opposition is true Friendship.

I have always found that Angels have the vanity to speak of themselves as the only wise; this they do with a confident insolence sprouting from systematic reasoning.

Thus Swedenborg boasts that what he writes is new: tho' it is only the Contents or Index of already publish'd books.

A man carried a monkey about for a shew, & because he was a little wiser than the monkey, grew vain, and conceiv'd himself as much wiser than seven men. It is so with Swedenborg: he shews the folly of churches, & exposes hypocrites till he imagines that all are religious, & himself the single one on earth that ever broke a net.

Now hear a plain fact: Swedenborg has not written one new truth. Now hear another: he has written all the old falsehoods.

And now hear the reason. He conversed with Angels who are all religious, & conversed not with Devils who all hate religion, for he was incapable thro' his conceited notions.

Thus Swedenborg's writings are a recapitulation of all superficial opinions, and an analysis of the more sublime—but no further.

Have now another plain fact. Any man of mechanical talents may, from the writings of Paracelsus or Jacob Behmen,[11] produce ten thousand volumes of equal value with Swedenborg's, and from those of Dante or Shakespear an infinite number.

But when he has done this, let him not say that he knows better than his master, for he only holds a candle in sunshine.

A MEMORABLE FANCY

Once I saw a Devil in a flame of fire, who arose before an Angel that sat on a cloud, and the Devil utter'd these words:

"The worship of God is: Honouring his gifts in other men, each according to his genius, and loving the greatest men best: those who envy or calumniate great men hate God; for there is no other God."

The Angel hearing this became almost blue; but mastering himself he grew yellow, & at last white, pink, & smiling, and then replied:

"Thou Idolator! is not God One? & is not he visible in Jesus Christ? and has not Jesus Christ given his sanction to the law of ten com-

11 Paracelsus (1493–1541), a magician, astrologer, and alchemist, said to be the founder of modern chemistry. Behmen, or Boehme (1575–1624), a German mystic, whose theory of good and evil is based on the necessity of oppositions.

mandments? and are not all other men fools, sinners, & nothings?"

The Devil answer'd: "bray a fool in a mortar with wheat, yet shall not his folly be beaten out of him; if Jesus Christ is the greatest man, you ought to love him in the greatest degree; now hear how he has given his sanction to the law of ten commandments: did he not mock at the sabbath and so mock the sabbath's God? murder those who were murder'd because of him? turn away the law from the woman taken in adultery? steal the labor of others to support him? bear false witness when he omitted making a defence before Pilate? covet when he pray'd for his disciples, and when he bid them shake off the dust of their feet against such as refused to lodge them? I tell you, no virtue can exist without breaking these ten commandments. Jesus was all virtue, and acted from impulse, not from rules."

When he had so spoken, I beheld the Angel, who stretched out his arms, embracing the flame of fire, & he was consumed and arose as Elijah.

Note: This Angel, who is now become a Devil, is my particular friend; we often read the Bible together in its infernal or diabolical sense, which the world shall have if they behave well.

I have also The Bible of Hell, which the world shall have whether they will or no.

One Law for the Lion & Ox is Oppression.

from *Milton*

Milton: A Poem in 2 Books: To Justify the Ways of God to Men was "written and etched, 1804–1808." It is one of Blake's "Prophetic Books." The Preface denounces the literature of pagan antiquity: "Rouze up, O Young Men of the New Age! . . . We do not want either Greek or Roman Models if we are but just and true to our own Imaginations, those Worlds of Eternity in which we shall live for ever in JESUS OUR LORD."

And did those feet in ancient time
  Walk upon England's mountains green?
And was the holy Lamb of God
  On England's pleasant pastures seen?

And did the Countenance Divine   5
  Shine forth upon our clouded hills?
And was Jerusalem builded here
  Among these dark Satanic mills?

Bring me my Bow of burning gold!
  Bring me my Arrows of desire!   10
Bring me my Spear! O clouds, unfold!
  Bring me my Chariot of fire!

I will not cease from Mental Fight,
  Nor shall my Sword sleep in my hand,
Till we have built Jerusalem   15
  In England's green and pleasant Land.

Robert Burns
1759–1796

Burns lived only thirty-seven years, but long enough to become Scotland's foremost poet. His life falls entirely within the latter half of the eighteenth century. Yet, despite occasional conformity to neoclassical literary patterns, he usually rejected them; and in his passion for freedom, his respect for the common man, his knowledge of nature and love of natural beauty, his interest in local traditions and folklore, and, above all, his faith in emotion and instinct as higher guides than reason, he is Romantic. Though he was familiar with many of the earlier English writers, especially those of his own century, his art was derived less from them than from Scottish poets whose names are now almost or quite forgotten. Sometimes an old song would strike his fancy, and he would make it his own

through rewriting it. The traditional airs of his country deeply moved him; some of his finest lyrics were inspired by them. Aside from the songs, his best verse sprang as directly as any art can from the soil, straight out of the life he knew in his native Ayrshire.

Like many other Scottish liberals, Burns hated Calvinism, or at any rate the state church that John Knox had established. It was the dominant force in Scotland, and its institutions, beginning with the local minister, were able to exert extraordinary pressure on the individual, in terms of issues of morality and orthodoxy. There was resistance to this, even within the church, and Burns was deeply in sympathy with this resistance. A good deal of his verse will be better understood if viewed in relation to this ecclesiastical background. But however he rebelled against the prevailing orthodoxy, Burns was in part a product of Presbyterianism. His father was religious and brought his children up to be so. For all his satirical freedom with the clergy, the poet was a believer at least to the extent of being a Deist. His satire was aimed at hypocrisy, not finally at religion.

As for his political views, he was obliged for his children's sake to keep quiet in public when, toward the close of his life, an expression of sympathy with France might have cost any government employee his job and even his liberty. But his approval of the French Revolution and consequently his desire for reform at home appear in a private letter as late as 1794. "What is there," he wrote of the execution of Louis XVI and his queen, "in delivering over a perjured blockhead and an unprincipled prostitute to the hands of the hangman, that it should arrest . . . attention?"

The eldest of seven children, he was born in 1759 in southwestern Scotland. His father was a gardener, a man of principle who did his best to see to the schooling of his children, which was nevertheless frequently interrupted by the necessity of their farm labor. His mother was illiterate but deeply versed in the old songs and ballads of Scotland, whose music thus began singing in the poet's head. The faithful toil of the whole family, in conditions of extreme poverty, was unable to prevent bankruptcy shortly before the father's death in 1784, leaving Burns the head of the family.

He made a fresh start at Mossgiel, near Ayr, where he became popular for the interest of his conversation and the grace of his personality. He had several love affairs at this time, the most serious with Jean Armour, the daughter of a local contractor who prevented their marriage, though they were later to marry. In 1786 he published *Poems, Chiefly in the Scottish Dialect*. The volume attracted considerable attention not only among the *literati* of Edinburgh but also in London and eventually in America, and for a time Burns was the object of considerable adulation. He estimated its worth shrewdly, well aware that with a few exceptions his flatterers were principally interested in the novelty of a plowman poet, and that their interest would languish.

During his brief career at Edinburgh he became acquainted with James Johnson, an engraver interested in Scottish folksong. With him Burns helped edit *The Scots Musical Museum;* and for tunes unfurnished with suitable words he composed or adapted a number of lyrics, including some of his best. He also contributed to a similar collection, *A Select Collection of Scottish Airs*.

He moved to a farm near Dumfries, combining for a time the difficult career of farmer with a job in the Excise. The farm failed, but the Excise work went reasonably well; and, though he cannot be said to have prospered, he and his family were able to manage. His career as a poet went well in every sense but financial, since he had foolishly sold the copyright for all future printings for a mere hundred guineas. During his final years at Dumfries he was an honored and respected citizen. But the final years were too few. He died of heart disease in 1796 at the age of thirty-seven.

TEXTS: The standard edition is by W. E. Henley and T. F. Henderson, *Works of Robert Burns* (1896–1897). There are several interesting biographical studies: Catherine Carswell, *The Life of Robert Burns* (1950); DeLancey Ferguson, *Pride and Passion* (1939); Franklin Bliss Snyder, *The Life of Robert Burns* (1932). Two important critical studies are: David Daiches, *Robert Burns* (1950); Thomas Crawford, *Burns: A Study of the Poems and Songs* (1960). A more recent study, *Robert Burns: The Man and the Poet* (1970) is by R. T. Fitzhugh.

Green Grow the Rashes, O

Among the inspirations of this lyric, composed when Burns was about twenty-five, was an old song describing how "green grow the rashes, O" and how superior they are to feather beds.

CHORUS

Green grow the rashes,[1] O;
Green grow the rashes, O;
The sweetest hours that e'er I spend,
Are spent among the lasses, O.

There's nought but care on ev'ry han', 5
In every hour that passes, O:
What signifies the life o' man,
An' 'twere na for the lasses, O.

The war'ly race[2] may riches chase,
An' riches still may fly them, O; 10
An' tho' at last they catch them fast,
Their hearts can ne'er enjoy them, O.

But gie me a cannie[3] hour at e'en,
My arms about my dearie, O,
An' war'ly cares an' war'ly men 15
May a' gae tapsalteerie,[4] O!

---

1 Rushes. 2 Worldly folk. 3 Quiet.
4 Go topsy-turvy.

For you sae douce,[5] ye sneer at this;
  Ye're nought but senseless asses, O;
The wisest man the warl' e'er saw,[6]
  He dearly lov'd the lasses, O.   20

Auld[7] Nature swears, the lovely dears
  Her noblest work she classes, O:
Her prentice han' she try'd on man,
  An' then she made the lasses, O.

Holy Willie's Prayer

The subject of this brilliant satire (unpublished till after Burns's death) is William Fisher (1737–1809), an elder and a meddling member of the Session of the church at Mauchline. Burns explains in a note that in 1785 Gavin Hamilton, whom Fisher and the minister had accused of "habitual neglect of church ordinances," appealed to the Presbytery of Ayr, which proceeded to acquit him. Fisher having lost his case, "the Muse overhead him at his devotions."

O Thou, that in the Heavens does dwell,
Wha, as it pleases best Thysel',
Sends ane[1] to Heaven and ten to Hell,
  A' for Thy glory,
And no for ony guid[2] or ill   5
  They've done before Thee!

I bless and praise Thy matchless might,
When thousands Thou hast left in night,
That I am here before Thy sight,
  For gifts an' grace   10
A burning an' a shining light,
  To a' this place.

What was I, or my generation,
That I should get sic[3] exaltation?
I, wha deserv'd most just damnation   15
  For broken laws
Sax thousand years ere my creation,
  Thro' Adam's cause!

When frae my mither's womb I fell,
Thou might hae plung'd me deep in hell,   20
To gnash my gooms, and weep, and wail
  In burning lakes,
Where damnèd devils roar and yell,
  Chain'd to their stakes.

Yet I am here a chosen sample,   25
To show Thy grace is great and ample:
I'm here a pillar o' Thy temple,
  Strong as a rock,
A guide, a buckler, and example
  To a' Thy flock!   30

O Lord, Thou kens[4] what zeal I bear
When drinkers drink, an' swearers swear,
An' singin' here and dancin' there
  Wi' great an' sma';
For I am keepit by Thy fear[5]   35
  Free frae them a'.

But yet, O Lord! confess I must:
At times I'm fash'd[6] wi' fleshy lust;
An' sometimes, too, in warldly trust,
  Vile self gets in;   40
But Thou remembers we are dust,
  Defiled wi' sin.

O Lord! yestreen, Thou kens, wi' Meg—
Thy pardon I sincerely beg—
O, may 't ne'er be a living plague   45
  To my dishonor!
An' I'll ne'er lift a lawless leg
  Again upon her.

Besides, I farther maun[7] avow—
Wi' Leezzie's lass, three times, I trow—   50
But, Lord, that Friday I was fou,[8]
  When I cam near her,
Or else, Thou kens, Thy servant true
  Wad[9] never steer[10] her.

May be Thou lets this fleshly thorn   55
Buffet Thy servant e'en and morn,
Lest he owre[11] proud and high should turn
  That he's sae gifted:
If sae, Thy han' maun e'en be borne
  Until Thou lift it.   60

Lord, bless Thy chosen in this place,
For here Thou has a chosen race!
But God confound their stubborn face
  An' blast their name,
Wha bring Thy elders to disgrace,   65
  An' open shame!

---

[5] As for you, so serious.   [6] Solomon.   [7] Old.

[1] One.   [2] Any good.   [3] Such.

[4] Knowest.   [5] Kept by fear of Thee.   [6] Troubled.
[7] Must.   [8] Full, drunk.   [9] Would.   [10] Touch.
[11] Over, too.

Lord, mind Gau'n Hamilton's deserts:
He drinks, an' swears, an' plays at cartes,
Yet has sae monie takin[12] arts
      Wi' great and sma',   70
Frae God's ain Priest[13] the people's hearts
      He steals awa'.

And when we chasten'd him therefore,
Thou kens how he bred sic a splore,[14]
And set the warld[15] in a roar   75
      O' laughin at us:
Curse Thou his basket and his store,
      Kail[16] an' potatoes!

Lord, hear my earnest cry and pray'r
Against that Presbyt'ry o' Ayr!
Thy strong right hand, Lord, make it bare   80
      Upo' their heads!
Lord, visit them, an' dinna[17] spare,
      For their misdeeds!

O Lord, my God! that glib-tongu'd Aiken,[18]   85
My vera heart and flesh are quakin,
To think how we stood sweatin, shakin,
      An' pish'd[19] wi' dread,
While he, wi' hingin[20] lip an' snakin,[21]
      Held up his head.   90

Lord, in Thy day o' vengeance try him!
Lord, visit him wha did employ him!
And pass not in Thy mercy by them,
      Nor hear their pray'r,
But for Thy people's sake destroy them,   95
      An' dinna spare!

But, Lord, remember me and mine
Wi' mercies temporal and divine,
That I for grace an' gear[22] may shine
      Excell'd by nane;   100
And a' the glory shall be Thine—
      Amen, Amen!

---

12 So many taking.
13 William Auld, the minister at Mauchline.   14 Row.
15 Pronounce as a disyllable by trilling the *r*.
16 Cabbage.—One of the charges against Hamilton was that he had ordered his servants to dig potatoes on a Sunday.   17 Do not.
18 Robert Aiken, of Ayr, Hamilton's counsel.
19 Subjected to contempt.   20 Hanging.   21 Sneering.
22 Wealth.

To a Mouse

On Turning Her Up in Her Nest with the Plough, November, 1785

Wee, sleekit,[1] cow'rin', tim'rous beastie,
O, what a panic's in thy breastie!
Thou need na start awa sae hasty,
      Wi' bickering brattle![2]
I wad be laith to rin[3] an' chase thee,   5
      Wi' murdering pattle![4]

I'm truly sorry man's dominion
Has broken Nature's social union,
An' justifies that ill opinion
      Which makes thee startle   10
At me, thy poor earth-born companion,
      An' fellow-mortal!

I doubt na, whyles,[5] but thou may thieve;
What then? poor beastie, thou maun live!
A daimen icker[6] in a thrave[7]   15
      'S a sma' request;
I'll get a blessin wi' the lave,[8]
      And never miss 't!

Thy wee-bit housie, too, in ruin!
Its silly wa's the win's are strewin'!   20
An' naething, now, to big[9] a new ane,
      O' foggage[10] green!
An' bleak December's win's ensuin',
      Baith snell[11] an' keen!

Thou saw the fields laid bare an' waste,   25
An' weary winter comin' fast,
An' cozie here, beneath the blast,
      Thou thought to dwell,
Till crash! the cruel coulter past
      Out thro' thy cell.   30

That wee bit heap o' leaves an' stibble[12]
Has cost thee monie a weary nibble!
Now thou's turned out, for a' thy trouble,
      But[13] house or hald,[14]
To thole[15] the winter's sleety dribble,   35
      An' cranreuch[16] cauld!

---

1 Sleek.   2 Hasty scamper.   3 Loath to run.
4 Paddle, a kind of narrow spade for digging weeds, cleaning the plowshare, etc.   5 At times.
6 Occasional ear of grain.   7 Twenty-four sheaves.
8 Remnant.   9 Build.   10 Moss.   11 Both harsh.
12 Stubble.   13 Without.   14 Holding, possession.
15 Endure.   16 Hoarfrost.

But, Mousie, thou art no thy lane,[17]
In proving foresight may be vain:
The best-laid schemes o' mice an' men
   Gang aft agley,[18]   40
An' lea'e us nought but grief an' pain,
   For promis'd joy!

Still thou art blest, compared wi' me!
The present only toucheth thee:
But och! I backward cast my e'e,   45
   On prospects drear!
An' forward, tho' I canna see,
   I guess an' fear!

Address to the Deil

The humor of the familiar tone Burns takes with his decidedly un-Miltonic Satan is heightened by his prefixing to this poem two lines from *Paradise Lost* (I, 128–29):

> *O prince, O chief of many thronèd powers,*
> *That led the embattled seraphim to war.*

O Thou! whatever title suit thee—
Auld Hornie, Satan, Nick, or Clootie[1]—
Wha in yon cavern grim an' sootie,
   Clos'd under hatches,   5
Spairges[2] about the brunstane cootie,[3]
   To scaud[4] poor wretches!

Hear me, auld Hangie,[5] for a wee,[6]
An' let poor damnèd bodies be;
I'm sure sma' pleasure it can gie,
   Ev'n to a deil,   10
To skelp[7] an' scaud poor dogs like me
   An' hear us squeel!

Great is thy pow'r, an' great thy fame;
Far kend an' noted is they name;
An' tho' yon lowin heugh's[8] thy hame,
   Thou travels far;   15
An' faith! thou's neither lag,[9] nor lame,
   Nor blate, nor scaur.[10]

Whyles, ranging like a roarin lion,
For prey, a' holes an' corners trying; 20
Whyles, on the strong-wing'd tempest flyin',
   Tirlin the kirks;[11]
Whyles, in the human bosom pryin,
   Unseen thou lurks.

I've heard my rev'rend graunie say, 25
In lanely glens ye like to stray;
Or, where auld ruin'd castles grey
   Nod to the moon,
Ye fright the nightly wand'rer's way,
   Wi' eldritch[12] croon.   30

When twilight did my graunie summon,
To say her pray'rs, douce,[13] honest woman!
Aft yont the dyke she's heard you bummin,[14]
   Wi' eerie drone;
Or, rustlin, through the boortrees[15] comin, 35
   Wi' heavy groan.

Ae dreary, windy, winter night,
The stars shot down wi' sklentin[16] light,
Wi' you mysel, I gat a fright;
   Ayont the lough,[17]   40
Ye, like a rash-buss,[18] stood in sight,
   Wi' waving sugh.[19]

The cudgel in my nieve[20] did shake,
Each bristl'd hair stood like a stake;
When, wi' an eldritch, stoor[21] "quaick, quaick." 45
   Amang the springs,
Awa ye squatter'd like a drake,
   On whistling wings.

Let warlocks[22] grim, an' wither'd hags,
Tell how wi' you, on ragweed nags,   50
They skim the muirs[23] an' dizzy crags,
   Wi' wicked speed;
And in kirk-yards renew their leagues,
   Owre howkit[24] dead.

Thence countra wives, wi' toil an' pain, 55
May plunge an' plunge the kirn[25] in vain;

---

17 Not alone. 18 Often go astray.

1 Hoofie. 2 Splashes. 3 Brimstone bowl.
4 Scald. 5 Hangman, executioner. 6 Bit, jiffy.
7 Spank. 8 Flaming pit is. 9 Backward.
10 Bashful nor timid ("scared").

11 Stripping (i.e., unroofing) the churches.
12 Unearthly. 13 Grave. 14 Humming.
15 Elderbushes. 16 Slanting.
17 Beyond the lake or pond ("loch").
18 Clump of rushes. 19 Moan. 20 Fist.
21 Harsh. 22 Sorcerers. 23 Moors, wastelands.
24 Over dug-up. 25 Churn.

For O! the yellow treasure's taen
    By witching skill;
An' dawtit, twal-pint hawkie's gane
    As yell 's the bill.[26]   60

Thence mystic knots mak great abuse
On young guidmen,[27] fond, keen, an' croose;[28]
When the best wark-lume[29] i' the house,
    By cantraip[30] wit,
Is instant made no worth a louse,
    Just at the bit.[31]   65

When thowes[32] dissolve the snawy hoord,[33]
An' float the jingling icy boord,[34]
Then water-kelpies[35] haunt the foord,
    By your direction,   70
An' nighted trav'llers are allur'd
    To their destruction.

An' aft your moss-traversing spunkies[36]
Decoy the wight that late an' drunk is:
The bleezin, curst, mischievous monkies   75
    Delude his eyes,
Till in some miry slough he sunk is,
    Ne'er mair to rise.

When masons'[37] mystic word an' grip
In storms an' tempests raise you up,   80
Some cock or cat your rage maun stop,[38]
    Or, strange to tell!
The youngest brother ye wad whip
    Aff straught[39] to hell.

Lang syne in Eden's bonie yard,[40]   85
When youthfu' lovers first were pair'd,
An' all the soul of love they shar'd,
    The raptur'd hour,
Sweet on the fragrant flow'ry swaird,
    In shady bow'r;   90

Then you, ye auld, snick-drawing[41] dog!
Ye cam to Paradise incog,

An' play'd on man a cursèd brogue,[42]
    (Black be your fa'![43])
An' gied[44] the infant warld a shog,[45]   95
    'Maist ruin'd a'.

D'ye mind[46] that day, when in a bizz,[47]
Wi' reekit duds, an' reestit gizz,[48]
Ye did present your smoutie phiz[49]
    'Mang better folk,   100
An' sklented on the man of Uzz[50]
    Your spitefu' joke?

An' how ye gat him i' your thrall,
An' brak him out o' house an' hal',
While scabs an' blotches did him gall,   105
    Wi' bitter claw;
An' lowsed[51] his ill-tongued, wicked scawl[52]—
    Was warst ava?[53]

But a' your doings to rehearse,
Your wily snares an' fechtin[54] fierce,   110
Sin' that day Michael did you pierce,[55]
    Down to this time,
Wad ding a Lallan tongue, or Erse,[56]
    In prose or rhyme.

An' now, auld Cloots, I ken ye're thinkin,   115
A certain Bardie's[57] rantin,[58] drinkin,
Some luckless hour will send him linkin,[59]
    To your black Pit;
But faith! he'll turn a corner jinkin',[60]
    An' cheat you yet.   120

But fare-you-weel, auld Nickie-Ben!
O, wad ye tak a thought an' men'![61]
Ye aiblins[62] might—I dinna ken—
    Still hae a stake:[63]
I'm wae[64] to think upo' yon den,   125
    Ev'n for your sake!

---

[26] And the petted, twelve-pint cow has gone as dry as the bull. (A Scots pint equaled two English quarts.)
[27] Goodmen, husbands.   [28] Cocksure.
[29] Tool ("work loom").   [30] Magic.
[31] Crucial moment (of love-making).   [32] Thaws.
[33] Hoard.   [34] Board, i.e., surface ice.
[35] Water demons.   [36] Bog-crossing will-o'-the-wisps.
[37] Burns was a Freemason, but his reference here is jocose.
[38] Must stop (by being sacrificed to you).
[39] Off straight.   [40] Long since in Eden's pretty garden.
[41] I.e., burglarizing. *Snick* = latch.

[42] Trick.   [43] What falls to you, your lot.
[44] Gave.   [45] Jog, shake.   [46] Remember.
[47] Bustle, hurry.
[48] With smoky clothes and scorched wig.
[49] Smutty face.   [50] Job.   [51] Loosed.   [52] Scold.
[53] Worst of all.   [54] Fighting.
[55] Described by Milton in *Paradise Lost*, VI, 321 ff.
[56] Would be too much for a Lowland tongue, or a Gaelic one.   [57] Bardlet, little poet.
[58] Indulgence in high jinks.   [59] Skipping.
[60] Dodging.   [61] Mend (your ways).   [62] Perhaps.
[63] Gambler's chance.   [64] Woeful.

Address to the Unco Guid,[1]
or the Rigidly Righteous

My Son, these maxims make a rule,
An' lump them ay thegither:
The Rigid Righteous is a fool,
The Rigid Wise anither:
The cleanest corn that e'er was dight,[2]
May hae some pyles o' caff[3] in;
So ne'er a fellow-creature slight
For random fits o' daffin.[4]

SOLOMON (Ecclesiastes 7:16)

O ye, wha are sae guid yoursel,
    Sae pious and sae holy,
Ye've nought to do but mark and tell
    Your neebour's fauts and folly;
Whase life is like a weel-gaun[5] mill,   5
    Supplied wi' store o' water;
The heapet happer's[6] ebbing still,
    An' still the clap[7] plays clatter!

Hear me, ye venerable core,[8]
    As counsel for poor mortals   10
That frequent pass douce Wisdom's door
    For glaikit[9] Folly's portals:
I for their thoughtless, careless sakes,
    Would here propone[10] defences,—
Their donsie[11] tricks, their black mistakes,   15
    Their failings and mischances.

Ye see your state wi' theirs compared,
    And shudder at the niffer;[12]
But cast a moment's fair regard,
    What makes the mighty differ?[13]   20
Discount what scant occasion gave;
    That purity ye pride in;
And (what's aft mair than a' the lave)
    Your better art o' hidin'.

Think, when your castigated[14] pulse   25
    Gies[15] now and then a wallop,
What ragings must his veins convulse,
    That still eternal gallop!

Wi' wind and tide fair i' your tail,
    Right on ye scud your sea-way;   30
But in the teeth o' baith to sail,
    It makes an unco lee-way.

See Social-life and Glee sit down
    All joyous and unthinking,
Till, quite transmugrify'd,[16] they're grown   35
    Debauchery and Drinking;
O, would they stay to calculate
    Th' eternal consequences,
Or—your more dreaded hell to state—
    Damnation of expenses!   40

Ye high, exalted, virtuous dames,
    Tied up in godly laces,
Before ye gie poor Frailty names,
    Suppose a change o' cases:
A dear-lov'd lad, convenience snug,   45
    A treach'rous inclination—
But, let me whisper i' your lug,[17]
    Ye're aiblins[18] nae temptation.

Then gently scan your brother man,
    Still gentler sister woman;   50
Tho' they may gang a kennin[19] wrang,
    To step aside is human:
One point must still be greatly dark,
    The moving *why* they do it;
And just as lamely can ye mark   55
    How far perhaps they rue it.

Who made the heart, 'tis He alone
    Decidedly can try us:
He knows each chord, its various tone,
    Each spring, its various bias: 60
Then at the balance let's be mute,
    We never can adjust it;
What's done we partly may compute,
    But know not what's resisted.

To a Louse

On Seeing One on a Lady's Bonnet at Church

Ha! whare ye gaun, ye crowlin' ferlie?[1]
Your impudence protects you sairly:[2]

---

[1] Extraordinarily good.
[2] Grain that was ever winnowed.   [3] Bits of chaff.
[4] Larking.   [5] Well-going.   [6] Heaped-up hopper.
[7] Clapper; the device which, by shaking the hopper, keeps the grain moving down to the grinding stones.
[8] Corps.   [9] Giddy.   [10] Propound.   [11] Perverse.
[12] Exchange.   [13] Big difference.   [14] I.e., disciplined.
[15] Gives.

[16] Transmogrified, transformed.   [17] Ear.
[18] Perhaps.   [19] A tiny bit, the least perceptible bit.

[1] Where are you going, you crawling marvel?
[2] Grievously.

I canna say but ye strunt rarely,[3]
    Owre gauze and lace;
Tho' faith! I fear ye dine but sparely
    On sic a place.   5

Ye ugly, creepin, blastit wonner,[4]
Detested, shunn'd by saunt an' sinner,
How daur ye set your fit[5] upon her,
    Sae fine a lady?   10
Gae somewhere else, and seek your dinner
    On some poor body.

Swith![6] in some beggar's hauffet squattle;[7]
There ye may creep, and sprawl, and sprattle,[8]
Wi' ither kindred, jumping cattle,   15
    In shoals and nations;
Where horn nor bane[9] ne'er daur unsettle
    Your thick plantations.

Now haud[10] ye there! ye're out o' sight
Below the fatt'rils,[11] snug an' tight;   20
Na, faith ye yet! ye'll no be right,
    Till ye've got on it—
The vera tapmost tow'ring height
    O' Miss's bonnet.

My sooth![12] right bauld[13] ye set your nose out,   25
As plump an' grey as onie grozet:[14]
O for some rank, mercurial rozet,[15]
    Or fell, red smeddum![16]
I'd gie ye sic a hearty dose o't,
    Wad dress your droddum![17]   30

I wad na been surpris'd to spy
You on an auld wife's flainen toy;[18]
Or aiblins some bit duddie[19] boy,
    On's wyliecoat;[20]
But Miss's fine Lunardi![21] fye,   35
    How daur ye do't?

O Jenny, dinna toss your head,
An' set your beauties a' abroad![22]

Ye little ken what cursèd speed
    The blastie's makin![23]   40
Thae[24] winks and finger-ends, I dread,
    Are notice takin!

O wad some Power the giftie[25] gie us
To see oursels as ithers see us!
It wad frae monie a blunder free us,   45
    An' foolish notion:
What airs in dress an' gait wad lea'e us,
    An' ev'n devotion!

O, My Luve Is Like a Red, Red Rose

O, my luve is like a red, red rose,
    That's newly sprung in June.
O, my luve is like the melodie,
    That's sweetly play'd in tune.

As fair art thou, my bonie lass,   5
    So deep in luve am I;
And I will luve thee still, my dear,
    Till a' the seas gang dry.

Till a' the seas gang dry, my dear,
    And the rocks melt wi' the sun!   10
And I will luve thee still, my dear,
    While the sands o' life shall run.

And fare thee weel, my only luve,
    And fare thee weel a while!
And I will come again, my luve,   15
    Tho' it were ten thousand mile!

Auld Lang Syne

Burns produced his lyric, in 1788, for an older tune than the one to which it is now sung. He never claimed authorship of this poem, but repeatedly stated that he wrote it down after hearing an old man sing it. Nevertheless no earlier trace of it has ever been discovered.

Should auld acquaintance be forgot,
    And never brought to mind?

---

[3] Strut in fine style.
[4] Blasted wonder.   [5] Foot.   [6] Instantly; i.e., be off!
[7] Temple settle.   [8] Scramble.
[9] Bone; i.e., no comb, of horn or bone.   [10] Hold.
[11] Ribbon ends.   [12] Faith.   [13] Bold.
[14] Gooseberry.   [15] Rosin.   [16] Deadly red powder.
[17] Beat your buttocks.   [18] Flannel trifle, i.e., headdress.
[19] Little ragged.   [20] Undershirt.
[21] "Balloon" bonnet; from the name of a well-known aeronaut.   [22] Abroad.

[23] The blasted thing is making.   [24] Those.
[25] Small gift.

Should auld acquaintance be forgot,
  And auld lang syne![1]

    Chorus. For auld lang syne, my dear,   5
      For auld lang syne,
    We'll tak a cup o' kindness yet
      For auld lang syne!

And surely ye'll be your pint-stowp,[2]
  And surely I'll be mine,   10
And we'll tak a cup o' kindness yet
  For auld lang syne!

We twa hae run about the braes,[3]
  And pou'd[4] the gowans[5] fine,
But we've wander'd monie a weary fit[6]   15
  Sin' auld lang syne.

We twa hae paidl'd in the burn[7]
  From morning sun till dine;[8]
But seas between us braid[9] hae roar'd
  Sin' auld lang syne.   20

And there's a hand, my trusty fiere,[10]
  And gie's a hand o' thine!
And we'll tak a right guid-willie waught,[11]
  For auld lang syne!

Sweet Afton

Flow gently, sweet Afton, among thy green braes!
Flow gently, I'll sing thee a song in thy praise!
My Mary's asleep by thy murmuring stream—
Flow gently, sweet Afton, disturb not her dream!

Thou stock dove whose echo resounds thro' the   5
  glen,
Ye wild whistling blackbirds in yon thorny den,
Thou green-crested lapwing, thy screaming for-
  bear—
I charge you, disturb not my slumbering fair!

How lofty, sweet Afton, thy neighbouring hills,
Far mark'd with the courses of clear, winding rills!   10

There daily I wander, as noon rises high,
My flocks and my Mary's sweet cot in my eye.

How pleasant thy banks and green vallies below,
Where wild in the woodlands the primroses blow!
There oft, as mild Ev'ning weeps over the lea,   15
The sweet-scented birk shades my Mary and me.

Thy crystal stream, Afton, how lovely it glides,
And winds by the cot where my Mary resides!
How wanton thy waters her snowy feet lave,
As, gathering sweet flowerets, she stems thy clear   20
  wave!

Flow gently, sweet Afton, among thy green braes!
Flow gently, sweet river, the theme of my lays!
My Mary's asleep by thy murmuring stream—
Flow gently, sweet Afton, disturb not her dream!

Tam O' Shanter
A Tale

Burns considered this his most finished poem. It was written at Ellisland in 1790 for a volume on Scottish antiquities by Francis Grose (1731–1791),[1] to whom Burns had suggested the inclusion of a drawing of the old ruined church near his birthplace at Alloway, a few miles south of Ayr. Grose agreed, on condition that Burns provide a witch story to accompany the engraving. Already roofless before Burns was born, the haunted kirk is only a couple of hundred yards from the bank of the little river Doon and the "Auld Brig," then the only way of getting over. Fortunately for Tam, no witch could cross running water.

    Of Brownyis and of Bogillis full is this Buke.

                            GAWIN DOUGLAS[2]

When chapman billies[3] leave the street,
And drouthy[4] neebors neebors meet;
As market-days are wearing late,
An' folk begin to tak the gate;[5]
While we sit bousing at the nappy,[6]   5
An' gettin fou and unco happy,

---

1 Old long ago, old times.
2 I.e., pay for your drink.
3 Hillsides.   4 Pulled.   5 Daisies.   6 Foot.
7 Waded ("paddled") in the brook.
8 Dinner time, noon.   9 Broad.   10 Comrade.
11 Good-will drink. Cf. "cup o' kindness," line 7.

1 Now best known for *A Classical Dictionary of the Vulgar Tongue* (1785). He drew his own illustrations for his antiquarian works.
2 The Scottish poet Gavin Douglas (d. 1522); the line, meaning "Of brownies and bogies full is this book," is from the prologue to his translation of Vergil's *Aeneid*.
3 Peddler fellows.   4 Thirsty.   5 Road.
6 Boozing at the ale.

We think na on the lang Scots miles,[7]
The mosses,[8] waters, slaps, and styles,[9]
That lie between us and our hame,
Whare sits our sulky, sullen dame,   10
Gathering her brows like gathering storm,
Nursing her wrath to keep it warm.

This truth fand[10] honest Tam o' Shanter,[11]
As he frae Ayr ae[12] night did canter:
(Auld Ayr, wham ne'er a town surpasses,   15
For honest men and bonie lasses).

O Tam, had'st thou but been sae wise,
As taen thy ain wife Kate's advice!
She tauld thee weel thou was a skellum,[13]
A blethering,[14] blustering, drunken blellum;[15]   20
That frae November till October,
Ae market-day thou was nae sober;
That ilka melder[16] wi' the miller,
Thou sat as lang as thou had siller;[17]
That ev'ry naig was ca'd a shoe on,[18]   25
The smith and thee gat roaring fou on;
That at the Lord's house, even on Sunday,
Thou drank wi' Kirkton Jean[19] till Monday.
She prophesied, that, late or soon,
Thou would be found deep drown'd in Doon,   30
Or catch'd wi' warlocks in the mirk[20]
By Alloway's auld, haunted kirk.

Ah! gentle dames, it gars me greet,[21]
To think how monie counsels sweet,
How monie lengthen'd, sage advices   35
The husband frae the wife despises!

But to our tale:—Ae market-night,
Tam had got planted unco right,
Fast by an ingle, bleezing[22] finely,
Wi' reaming swats,[23] that drank divinely;   40

And at his elbow, Souter[24] Johnie,
His ancient, trusty, drouthy cronie:
Tam lo'ed him like a very brither;
They had been fou for weeks thegither.
The night drave on wi' sangs and clatter;   45
And ay the ale was growing better:
The landlady and Tam grew gracious
Wi' secret favors, sweet and precious:
The Souter tauld his queerest stories;
The landlord's laugh was ready chorus: 50
The storm without might rair[25] and rustle,
Tam did na mind the storm a whistle.

Care, mad to see a man sae happy,
E'en drown'd himsel amang the nappy.
As bees flee hame wi' lades o' treasure,   55
The minutes wing'd their way wi' pleasure;
Kings may be blest but Tam was glorious,
O'er a' the ills o' life victorious!

But pleasures are like poppies spread:
You seize the flow'r, its bloom is shed;   60
Or like the snow falls[26] in the river,
A moment white—then melts for ever;
Or like the borealis race,[27]
That flit ere you can point their place;
Or like the rainbow's lovely form   65
Evanishing amid the storm.
Nae man can tether time or tide;
The hour approaches Tam maun ride:
That hour, o' night's black arch the key-stane,
That dreary hour Tam mounts his beast in;   70
And sic a night he taks the road in,
As ne'er poor sinner was abroad in.

The wind blew as 't wad[28] blawn its last;
The rattling showers rose on the blast;
The speedy gleams the darkness swallow'd;   75
Loud, deep, and lang the thunder bellow'd;
That night, a child might understand,
The Deil had business on his hand.

Weel mounted on his gray mare Meg,
A better never lifted leg,   80
Tam skelpit[29] on thro' dub[30] and mire,
Despising wind, and rain, and fire;

---

[7] The Scotch mile was longer than the English, sometimes by 216 yards.   [8] Bogs.
[9] Openings in fences, and stiles.   [10] Found.
[11] The name of a farm in southern Ayrshire.—The cap called tam-o'-shanter gets its name from the poem.
[12] One.   [13] A good-for-nothing.   [14] Foolish-talking.
[15] Babbler.
[16] Grinding; i.e., every time you took a quantity of grain to be ground.   [17] Silver, money.
[18] Every nag that was knocked a shoe on; i.e., every time you took a horse to be shod.
[19] At Jean's tavern near the church.
[20] By sorcerers in the dark.   [21] Makes me weep.
[22] A fireplace, blazing.   [23] Foaming new ale.

[24] Cobbler.   [25] Roar.   [26] That falls.
[27] Species, kind (of phenomena).
[28] As if it would have.
[29] Went along at a spanking pace.   [30] Puddle.

Whiles[31] holding fast his guid blue bonnet,
Whiles crooning o'er some auld Scots sonnet,[32]
Whiles glow'ring round wi' prudent cares,   85
Lest bogles[33] catch him unawares:
Kirk-Alloway was drawing nigh,
Whare ghaists and houlets[34] nightly cry.

By this time he was cross the ford,
Whare in the snaw the chapman smoor'd;[35]   90
And past the birks and meikle stane,[36]
Whare drunken Charlie brak's neck-bane;
And thro' the whins,[37] and by the cairn,[38]
Whare hunters fand the murder'd bairn;
And near the thorn, aboon[39] the well,   95
Whare Mungo's mither hang'd hersel.
Before him Doon pours all his floods;
The doubling storm roars thro' the woods;
The lightnings flash from pole to pole;
Near and more near the thunders roll: 100
When, glimmering thro' the groaning trees,
Kirk-Alloway seem'd in a bleeze;
Thro' ilka bore[40] the beams were glancing,
And loud resounded mirth and dancing.

Inspiring bold John Barleycorn!   105
What dangers thou canst make us scorn!
Wi' tippenny,[41] we fear nae evil;
Wi' usquebae,[42] we'll face the Devil!
The swats sae ream'd in Tammie's noddle,
Fair play, he car'd na deils a boddle.[43]   110
But Maggie stood right sair astonish'd,
Till, by the heel and hand admonish'd,
She ventur'd forward on the light;
And, wow! Tam saw an unco[44] sight!

Warlocks and witches in a dance: 115
Nae cótillion brent-new frae[45] France,
But hornpipes, jigs, strathspeys,[46] and reels,
Put life and mettle in their heels.
A winnock-bunker[47] in the east,
There sat Auld Nick, in shape o' beast;   120
A tousie tyke,[48] black, grim, and large,

To gie them music was his charge;
He screw'd the pipes and gart them skirl,[49]
Till roof and rafters a' did dirl.[50]
Coffins stood round like open presses,[51]   125
That shaw'd[52] the dead in their last dresses;
And by some devilish cantraip sleight,[53]
Each in its cauld hand held a light:
By which heroic Tam was able
To note upon the haly[54] table   130
A murderer's banes in gibbet-airns;[55]
Twa span-lang, wee, unchristen'd bairns;
A thief, new-cutted frae a rape[56]—
Wi' his last gasp his gab[57] did gape;
Five tomahawks wi' bluid red-rusted;   135
Five scymitars wi' murder crusted;
A garter which a babe had strangled;
A knife a father's throat had mangled—
Whom his ain son o' life bereft—
The grey-hairs yet stack to the heft;[58]   140
Wi' mair o' horrible and awefu',
Which even to name wad be unlawfu':
Three Lawyers' tongues, turned inside out,
Wi' lies seamed like a beggar's clout;[59]
Three Priests'[60] hearts, rotten black as muck, 145
Lay stinking, vile, in every neuk.[61]

As Tammie glower'd,[62] amaz'd, and curious,
The mirth and fun grew fast and furious:
The piper loud and louder blew,
The dancers quick and quicker flew;   150
They reel'd, they set,[63] they cross'd,[64] they
     cleekit,[65]
Till ilka carlin swat and reekit,[66]
And coost her duddies to the wark[67]
And linket[68] at it in her sark![69]

Now Tam, O Tam! had thae been queans,[70]   155
A' plump and strapping in their teens!

31 Sometimes.   32 Song.   33 Bogies, goblins.
34 Ghosts and owls.   35 Smothered.
36 Birches and big stone.   37 Furze, gorse.
38 Pile of stones.   39 Above.   40 Every chink.
41 Twopenny ale.   42 Whisky.
43 Given fair play, he cared not for devils so much as two-
pence (that is, a Scotch coin worth one-third of an English
penny).   44 Uncommon, wondrous.
45 Brand-new from.   46 A relatively slow kind of reel.
47 Window seat.   48 Shaggy dog.

49 Made them squeal.   50 Ring.   51 Cupboards.
52 Showed.   53 Magic trick.   54 Holy.
55 Gallows-irons. The bodies of malefactors were sometimes hung up in chains till only the bones remained.
56 Newly cut down from a rope.   57 Mouth.
58 Stuck to the handle.
59 Patch.—Burns yielded to the advice of friends and
omitted from his books lines 143–46, though they had appeared in Grose's volume and in periodicals.
60 Ministers'.   61 Nook.   62 Stared.
63 Executed a balancing step facing their partners.
64 Crossed over to exchange places with their partners.
65 Seized; i.e., linked arms.
66 Each hag sweat and steamed.
67 Cast her duds (threw off her clothes) for the work.
68 Skipped.   69 Shirt, shift, chemise.
70 These been lasses.

Their sarks, instead o' creeshie flannen,[71]
Been snaw-white seventeen hunder[72] linen!—
Thir breeks[73] o' mine, my only pair,
That ance were plush, o' guid blue hair,
I wad hae gi'en them off my hurdies,[74]   160
For ae blink o'[75] the bonie burdies![76]

But wither'd beldams, auld and droll,
Rigwoodie[77] hags wad spean[78] a foal,
Louping and flinging on a crummock,[79]   165
I wonder didna turn thy stomach!

But Tam kend what was what fu' brawlie;[80]
There was ae winsome wench and wawlie,[81]
That night enlisted in the core[82]
Lang after kend on Carrick[83] shore   170
(For monie a beast to dead she shot,
An' perish'd monie a bonie boat,
And shook baith meikle corn and bear,[84]
And kept the country-side in fear).
Her cutty[85] sark, o' Paisley harn,[86]   175
That while a lassie she had worn,
In longitude tho' sorely scanty,
It was her best, and she was vauntie.—[87]
Ah! little kend thy reverend grannie,
That sark she coft[88] for her wee Nannie,   180
Wi' twa pund Scots[89] ('twas a' her riches),
Wad ever grac'd a dance of witches!
But here my Muse her wing maun cour;[90]
Sic flights are far beyond her power:
To sing how Nannie lap and flang,[91]   185
(A souple jad[92] she was and strang),
And how Tam stood like ane bewitch'd,
And thought his very een enrich'd;
Even Satan glower'd, and fidged fu' fain,[93]
And hotch'd[94] and blew wi' might and main;   190
Till first ae caper, syne[95] anither,

Tam tint[96] his reason a' thegither,[97]
And roars out: "Weel done, Cutty-sark!"
And in an instant all was dark;
And scarcely had he Maggie rallied,   195
When out the hellish legion sallied.

As bees bizz out wi' angry fyke,[98]
When plundering herds[99] assail their byke;[100]
As open[101] pussie's[102] mortal foes,
When, pop! she starts before their nose;   200
As eager runs the market-crowd,
When "Catch the thief!" resounds aloud:
So Maggie runs, the witches follow,
Wi' monie an eldritch skriech and hollo.

Ah, Tam! Ah, Tam! thou'll get thy fairin![103]   205
In hell they'll roast thee like a herrin!
In vain thy Kate awaits thy comin!
Kate soon will be a woefu' woman!
Now, do thy speedy utmost, Meg,
And win the key-stane of the brig;   210
There, at them thou thy tail may toss,
A running stream they dare na cross!
But ere the key-stane she could make,
The fient[104] a tail she had to shake;
For Nannie, far before the rest,   215
Hard upon noble Maggie prest,
And flew at Tam wi' furious ettle;[105]
But little wist[106] she Maggie's mettle!
Ae spring brought off her master hale,[107]
But left behind her ain grey tail: 220
The carlin claught[108] her by the rump,
And left poor Maggie scarce a stump.

Now, wha this tale o' truth shall read,
Ilk man, and mother's son, take heed:
Whene'er to drink you are inclin'd,   225
Or cutty sarks run in your mind,
Think! ye may buy the joys o'er dear:
Remember Tam o' Shanter's mare.

Ye Flowery Banks

Ye flowery banks o' bonie Doon,
    How can ye blume sae fair?

---

71 Greasy flannels.
72 I.e., finely woven (a 1700-thread) fabric.
73 These breeches.   74 Buttocks.   75 Glance at.
76 Maidens.   77 Ropelike, scrawny.
78 Wean; i.e., a hungry foal would turn away from them
in disgust.   79 Leaping and kicking on a stick.
80 Full finely, very well.   81 Choice.
82 Corps; i.e., she had just become a witch.
83 The southern district of Ayrshire.
84 Both much wheat and barley.   85 Short.
86 A coarse linen woven in the famous shawl-town of
Paisley, near Glasgow.   87 Proud.   88 Bought.
89 A pound Scots equaled 20 *pence;* an English pound 20
shillings.   90 Must cower, i.e., lower.
91 Leaped and kicked.   92 Supple jade.
93 Fidgeted full fondly.
94 Jerked (his arm, in playing the bagpipes).   95 Then.

---

96 Lost.   97 Altogether.   98 Fuss.
99 Herdsmen (or boys).
100 Hive.   101 Begin (barking).   102 The hare's.
103 Present at a fair, i.e., reward.   104 Devil ("fiend").
105 Aim.   106 Knew.   107 Whole.   108 Clutched.

How can ye chant, ye little birds,
  And I sae fu' o' care?

Thou'll break my heart, thou bonie bird, 5
  That sings upon the bough:
Thou minds me o' the happy days
  When my fause Luve was true!

Thou'll break my heart, thou bonie bird,
  That sings beside thy mate: 10
For sae I sat, and sae I sang,
  And wist na o' my fate!

Aft hae I roved by bonie Doon
  To see the woodbine twine,
And ilka[1] bird sang o' its luve, 15
  And sae did I o' mine.

Wi' lightsome heart I pu'd a rose
  Frae aff its thorny tree,
And my fause luver staw[2] my rose, 20
  But left the thorn wi' me.

Ae Fond Kiss

Ae fond kiss, and then we sever!
Ae fareweel, and then for ever!
Deep in heart-wrung tears I'll pledge thee,
Warring sighs and groans I'll wage[1] thee.
Who shall say that Fortune grieves him, 5
While the star of hope she leaves him?
Me, nae cheerfu' twinkle lights me,
Dark despair around benights me.

I'll ne'er blame my partial fancy:
Naething could resist my Nancy! 10
But to see her was to love her,
Love but her, and love for ever.
Had we never lov'd sae kindly,
Had we never lov'd sae blindly,
Never met—or never parted— 15
We had ne'er been broken-hearted.

Fare-thee-weel, thou first and fairest!
Fare-thee-weel, thou best and dearest!
Thine be ilka joy and treasure,

Peace, Enjoyment, Love and Pleasure! 20
Ae fond kiss, and then we sever!
Ae fareweel, alas, for ever!
Deep in heart-wrung tears I'll pledge thee,
Warring signs and groans I'll wage thee.

For A' That

These verses of 1795 mark the rising tide of democracy, the same tide that had swept away the Bourbon monarchy in France and was soon to carry Jefferson into the White House. Burns told a friend, "The piece is not really poetry." This statement was probably meant ironically; if not, he was quite wrong.

Is there for[1] honest poverty
  That hings his head, an' a' that?
That coward slave, we pass him by—
  We dare be poor for a' that!
    For a' that, an' a' that, 5
      Our toils obscure, an' a' that,
      The rank is but the guinea's stamp;
      The man's the gowd[2] for a' that.

What tho' on hamely fare we dine,
  Wear hoddin grey,[3] an' a' that? 10
Gie fools their silks, and knaves their wine—
  A man's a man for a' that.
    For a' that, an' a' that,
      Their tinsel show, an' a' that,
      The honest man, tho' e'er sae poor, 15
      Is king o' men for a' that.

Ye see yon birkie,[4] ca'd[5] "a lord,"
  Wha struts, an' stares, an' a' that?
Tho' hundreds worship at his word,
  He's but a cuif[6] for a' that. 20
    For a' that, an' a' that,
      His ribband, star, an' a' that,
      The man o' independent mind,
      He looks and laughs at a' that.

A prince can mak a belted knight, 25
  A marquis, duke, an' a' that!
But an honest man's aboon his might[7]—
  Guid faith, he mauna fa'[8] that!

---

[1] Is there anyone on account of.   [2] Gold.
[3] Coarse gray cloth.   [4] Forward chap.   [5] Called.
[6] Ninny.
[7] Beyond ("above") his power.
[8] Must not claim.

---

[1] Each.   [2] Stole.

[1] Pledge.

For a' that, an' a' that,
    Their dignities, an' a' that,
The pith o' sense an' pride o' worth
    Are higher rank than a' that.

Then let us pray that come it may,
    (As come it will for a' that)
That Sense and Worth o'er a' the earth   35
    May bear the gree[9] an' a' that!
    For a' that, an' a' that,
      It's comin yet for a' that,
    That man to man, the world o'er,
      Shall brithers be for a' that.   40

O, Wert Thou in the Cauld Blast

This song was written a few weeks before Burns died, in honor of Jessy Lewars (d. 1855). She was the young sister of a friend, one of the Excise officers, and had been a great help in the household during the poet's illness. One day when he asked her to play him her

---

[9] Have first place.

favorite tune, he immediately composed these words to it.

O, wert thou in the cauld blast
    On yonder lea, on yonder lea,
My plaidie[1] to the angry airt,[2]
    I'd shelter thee, I'd shelter thee.
Or did Misfortune's bitter storms   5
    Around thee blaw, around thee blaw,
Thy bield[3] should be my bosom,
    To share it a', to share it a'.

Or were I in the wildest waste,
    Sae black and bare, sae black and bare,   10
The desert were a Paradise,
    If thou wert there, if thou wert there.
Or were I monarch o' the globe,
    Wi' thee to reign, wi' thee to reign,
The brightest jewel in my crown   15
    Wad be my queen, wad be my queen.

---

[1] Plaid; the Scot's substitute for a cloak or overcoat.
[2] Quarter, direction of the wind.   [3] Shelter.

William Wordsworth
1770–1850

The story of Wordsworth's long and rather quiet life is easily told. He was born in the Lake District in 1770, son of a lawyer. His mother died when he was eight; his father when he was thirteen. He had four brothers and a sister, Dorothy. In 1787 Wordsworth entered St. John's College, Cambridge, from which he received his bachelor's degree in 1791. In 1790 he had visited France and Switzerland with a friend; the following year, after his graduation, he went back to France, remaining for more than a year. His strong sympathies with the aims of the French Revolution were intensified by his friendship with the soldier-patriot Michel Beaupuy. During this year he had an affair with Marie Anne (Annette) Vallon, the daughter of a surgeon at Blois. Their daughter Caroline was born before Wordsworth returned to England. He acknowledged the paternity of the child, and there continued for years to be an amicable relationship between Annette and the Wordsworth family.

At this time, and for a few years thereafter, Wordsworth was a radical and republican in politics and probably in a sense an atheist in religion; he was particularly under the influence of the author of

Political Justice, William Godwin, who more permanently influenced Shelley's thinking.

When a bequest from an admirer, Raisley Calvert, permitted Wordsworth to concentrate on his career as a poet, he settled first at Racedown, Dorsetshire with his sister in 1795. In this year they met Coleridge; the remarkable collaboration between them began in earnest two years later, the wonderful year of 1797–98, resulting in the *Lyrical Ballads*. In the *Biographia Literaria* Coleridge spells out his and Wordsworth's respective aims: ". . . my endeavours should be directed to persons and characters supernatural, or at least romantic; yet so as to transfer from our inward nature a human interest and a semblance of truth sufficient to procure for these shadows of imagination that willing suspension of disbelief for the moment, which constitutes poetic faith. Mr. Wordsworth, on the other hand, was to propose to himself as his object, to give the charm of novelty to things of every day, and to excite a feeling analogous to the supernatural, by awakening the mind's attention to the lethargy of custom, and directing it to the loveliness and the wonders of the

William Wordsworth (1770–1850). Engraved from a portrait by B. R. Haydon.

world before us. . . ." The volumes, which were dominated by Wordsworth (except that they included *The Rime of the Ancient Mariner*), were published in 1798. They were received with some praise and a good deal of contempt, since they were a really new thing in the world. Many years had to pass before Wordsworth acquired his deserved reputation.

In the following year the Wordsworths and Coleridge went to Germany. On their return the Wordsworths settled into Dove Cottage, Grasmere, in the Lake District. In 1802 Wordsworth was married to Mary Hutchinson, whom he had known since childhood. In 1805 his favorite brother, John, was drowned at sea. In 1810 came an estrangement with Coleridge, temporary in a sense, but the old intimacy was never reestablished. In 1812 two of Mary and William's five children died within six months of each other. In 1813, when Wordsworth was named revenue-stamp distributor for Westmoreland, the family moved to a larger house, Rydal Mount, where Wordsworth spent the rest of his life. In 1843 he became Poet Laureate, and in 1850 he died, the most famous poet of the time.

During all this long life, the poems—apart from such sorrows as the deaths of his children and the mental confusion of his sister in her later years—were the chief events. Their production was steady and voluminous. There is almost universal agreement that the best work falls in the years between 1798 and 1807, the "marvelous decade"—and it was marvelous indeed. In this time he wrote almost all the short poems for which he is valued, including the best of his many sonnets; all of the first version of the great autobiographical poem, *The Prelude* (published in a revised version after Wordsworth's death, in 1850); many of the most vital passages from *The Excursion,* the long moral-didactic poem published in 1814; and a number of other fascinating passages that were intended for ultimate inclusion in *The Recluse,* the philosophical poem, never finished, of which *The Excursion* was to have been a part. One could argue, however, that the later part of the career produced enough first-rate work so that it would have made Wordsworth's reputation even without the greatness of 1798–1807.

It is possible to say many things about Wordsworth's poetry, but there are a few which are essential.

First of all, Wordsworth's central assumptions imply a rejection of many of the central assumptions of the preceding age, or of what, at any rate, he thought of as the central assumption of that age. In his view, for example,

It is remarkable that, excepting the Nocturnal Reverie of Lady Winchelsea, and a passage or two from the "Windsor Forest" of Pope, the poetry of the period intervening between the publication of the "Paradise Lost" and the "Seasons" does not contain a single new image of external nature; and scarcely presents a familiar one from which it can be inferred that the eye of the Poet had been steadily fixed upon his object, much less that his feelings had urged him to work upon it in the spirit of genuine imagination.

The grounds of his criticism are both simple and complex. He thinks that the poets he is criticizing are inaccurate when they write about external nature. This inaccuracy, he believed, was caused by an inadequate investment of emotional and spiritual commitment in the world around them. Furthermore, the "earliest poets of all nations generally wrote from passion excited by real events; they wrote naturally, and as men: feeling powerfully as they did, their language was daring, and figurative." As Wordsworth saw it, the eighteenth century represents a culmination in a process by which men "ambitious of the fame of poets" wanted to produce the same effects as these "earliest poets" but "without being animated by the same passion." Thus their language became mechanical, artificial, empty in spirit, and "differing materially from the real language of men." Such a language cannot possibly describe accurately the world around us, nor can it possibly express with any genuineness the real feelings within us. Poet and reader are put into a false situation both with respect to each other and to "real events," to the real world. The poet, who should be "a man speaking to men," is artificially exalted into a specialist, a man speaking a language which becomes "daily more and more corrupt, thrusting out of sight the plain humanities of Nature by a motley masquerade of tricks, quaintness, hieroglyphics, and enigmas," and the reader is correspondingly victimized.

It is Wordsworth's purpose to make "the plain humanities of Nature" available again, by purifying his language, by speaking a language "really spoken by men," and by directing his attention to the essential, to the "knowledge which all men carry about with them, and to [the] sympathies in which, without any other discipline than that of our daily life, we are fitted to take delight." This is one reason why, in the *Lyrical Ballads,* he chooses to write about "incidents and situations from common life." The

incidents and situations that, for example, Pope writes about are not, in Wordsworth's sense of the terms, "incidents and situations from common life" but rather instances of what Coleridge calls "that school of French poetry, invigorated by English understanding" whose excellence consisted in just and acute observations on men and manners in an artificial state of society." Wordsworth wished to describe incidents taking place in situations that would show forth "the primary laws of our nature." In the *Lyrical Ballads,* therefore, he generally chose scenes "from humble and rustic" life, because in that life "our elementary feelings co-exist in a state of greater simplicity, and, consequently may be more accurately contemplated, and more forcibly communicated; because the manners of rural life germinate from those elementary feelings, and, from the necessary character of rural occupations, are more easily comprehended, and are more durable; and, lastly, because in that condition the passions of men are incorporated with the beautiful and permanent forms of nature." He does not turn to such situations

Hadleigh Castle by John Constable, ca. 1828. Constable's Wordsworthian landscape combines a brooding sense of the past with a commitment to the serenities of rural life. *From the Collection of Mr. and Mrs. Paul Mellon.*

out of any simple kind of primitivism or pastoral longing (though there are elements of both as components of his poetry) but to situations which, from his perspective, will demonstrate in the purest possible fashion what man essentially is. In these situations, he also asserts, men will speak a purer and "more permanent, and far more philosophical language," because such men "hourly communicate with the best objects from which the best part of language is originally derived," and because their place in society keeps them from social vanity. Thus they will speak a language superior to that of poets who "think they are conferring honour upon themselves and their art, in proportion as they separate themselves from the sympathies of men, and indulge in arbitrary and capricious habits of expression . . . ."

Coleridge was right, of course, to point out that the "language really spoken by men" is not in fact necessarily that of Lake District peasants, and that Wordsworth at his best is never really using their language. But Wordsworth's propositions here are a radical model for a myth of the relation of the human consciousness to nature, a myth in terms of which he wrote his best poetry. What the poet speaks about is essentially "certain inherent and indestructible qualities of the human mind, and likewise of certain powers in the great and permanent objects that act upon it, which are equally inherent and indestructible." These qualities of the mind and these powers in nature are brought together auspiciously when the consciousness has properly conditioned itself to respond, has done so by encouraging in itself a "wise passiveness," an open receptivity that is not merely rational or intellectual, but that is able to perceive and in a measure to participate in the "motion" and "spirit" that impels "All thinking things, all objects of all thought,/And rolls through all things."

There is a sadness here. Though Wordsworth is for the most part celebrating the marriage of creative mind to creative nature, many of his poems know that these marriages are precarious triumphs, that man is a complex and self-contradictory creature who frequently defeats his own ends in this regard by his self-consciousness, his sense of personal death, and, in other ways, by his separateness from the rest of nature. He can, at his best, participate through his imagination in the joyous processes of nature, but he is in constant danger of exclusion or self-exclusion from them:

> I heard the sky-lark warbling in the sky;
> And I bethought me of the playful hare:
> Even such a happy Child of earth am I,
> Even as these blissful creatures do I fare;
> Far from the world I walk, and from all care;

> But there may come another day to me—
> Solitude, pain of heart, distress, and poverty.

And there are times when Wordsworth looks back enviously at his own childhood, or at other children, or at the very old, or at those living on the very fringes of society. He sees them as human beings to whom the oneness of nature comes more easily because it comes from the nature of their being, not from the workings of the poetic imagination.

Nevertheless it should be reiterated that the poems *are* mainly celebrations of man's capacity to fuse his own consciousness with the creative workings, the "goings-on," of the universe.

To do this, and to express how it is done, carries certain implications about his language. His simplification and purification of the language is more than just a reaction against what he considers the "gaudy and inane phraseology" of some of his predecessors. It is, as well, the finding of a language that is purified in two ways: it is able to report accurately on the data of one's experience of the natural world and on the data of one's consciousness; and it can convey the mystery of the transaction between mind and nature. Thus "I Wandered Lonely as a Cloud" is both a poem seeking to describe a highly particular experience that occurred to an individual on a particular day, and a symbol, or a reenactment, of the mysterious process itself by which "certain powers in the great and permanent objects . . . act upon" the mind and are acted upon by it. This is true not only of poems taken as a whole but often of individual images in those poems as well. The daffodils in this poem are an example of what Coleridge calls "a symbol established in the truth of things," an "actual and essential part of that, the whole of which [they] also represent." So Wordsworth in his language stands near the head of a new tradition of realism in poetry, and of symbolism as well. He demonstrates how, at the center of Romanticism, the two cannot be separated.

TEXTS: The great standard edition of the poems, *The Poetical Works* (5 vols., 1940–1950), was edited by Ernest de Selincourt and Helen Darbishire. Selincourt also edited the definitive edition of *The Prelude,* bringing together the 1805 and 1830 versions of the poem. He also edited the *Letters* (6 vols., 1935–1939) and the *Journal of Dorothy Wordsworth* (2 vols., 1941). The best biography is Mary Moorman's *William Wordsworth* (2 vols., 1957–1965). Edith Batho's *The Later Wordsworth* (1933), a defense of Wordsworth's so-called "period of decline," has important literary implications but is biographical in its principal emphasis. H. N. Margoliouth's *Wordsworth and Coleridge, 1795–1834* (1953) gives an important account of the relations between the two poets.

Coleridge's *Biographia Literaria* (1817) is of course the most important of all discussions of Wordsworth. The views of Wordsworth by Matthew Arnold, as set forth in *Essays in Criticism: Second Series* (1888), are of permanent importance. Alfred North Whitehead, in *Science and the Modern World* (1925), Basil Willey, in *The Seventeenth Century Background* (1934), and Newton P. Stallknecht, in *Strange Seas of Thought* (1945), have done significant work in placing Wordsworth in relation to the philosophical and scientific thought of his time. Interesting critical studies include: G. Wilson Knight, *The Starlit Dome* (1941); Lionel Trilling, *The Liberal Imagination* (1950); F. W. Bateson, *Wordsworth: A Reinterpretation* (1954); David Ferry, *The Limits of Mortality* (1959); John Jones, *The Egotistical Sublime* (1954); Geoffrey Hartman, *Wordsworth's Poetry, 1787–1814*; David Perkins, *Wordsworth and the Poetry of Sincerity* (1964); Carl Woodring, *Wordsworth* (1968); Jonathan Wordsworth, *The Music of Humanity* (1969); and Richard Onorato, *The Character of the Poet* (1971). The two best works on *The Prelude* are R. D. Havens, *The Mind of a Poet* (1941) and Herbert Lindenberger, *On Wordsworth's Prelude* (1963). There are several collections of critical essays, including M. H. Abrams, ed., *Wordsworth: A Collection of Critical Essays* (1972), J. M. Davis, ed., *Discussions of William Wordsworth* (1964), and G. T. Dunklin, ed., *Wordsworth Centenary Studies* (1951).

Lines Written in Early Spring

The first four of the following poems were composed in 1798 and published in *Lyrical Ballads*.

I heard a thousand blended notes,
While in a grove I sate reclined,
In that sweet mood when pleasant thoughts
Bring sad thoughts to the mind.

To her fair works did Nature link   5
The human soul that through me ran;
And much it grieved my heart to think
What man has made of man.

Through primrose tufts, in that green bower,
The periwinkle trailed its wreaths;   10
And 'tis my faith that every flower
Enjoys the air its breathes.

The birds around me hopped and played,
Their thoughts I cannot measure:—
But the least motion which they made,   15
It seemed a thrill of pleasure.

The budding twigs spread out their fan,
To catch the breezy air;
And I must think, do all I can,
That there was pleasure there.   20

If this belief from heaven be sent,
If such be Nature's holy plan,
Have I not reason to lament
What man has made of man?

Expostulation and Reply

"Why, William, on that old grey stone,
Thus for the length of half a day,
Why, William, sit you thus alone,
And dream your time away?

"Where are your books?—that light bequeathed   5
To Beings else forlorn and blind!
Up! up! and drink the spirit breathed
From dead men to their kind.

"You look round on your Mother Earth,
As if she for no purpose bore you;   10
As if you were her first-born birth,
And none had lived before you!"

One morning thus, by Esthwaite lake,[1]
When life was sweet, I knew not why,
To me my good friend Matthew[2] spake,   15
And thus I made reply:

"The eye—it cannot choose but see;
We cannot bid the ear be still;
Our bodies feel, where'er they be,
Against or with our will.   20

"Nor less I deem that there are Powers
Which of themselves our minds impress;
That we can feed this mind of ours
In a wise passiveness.

---

[1] Esthwaite Water is a lake near Hawkshead, where Wordsworth went to school.
[2] Wordsworth explains that this poem and the next resulted from conversation with "a friend who was somewhat unreasonably attached to modern books of moral philosophy."

"Think you, 'mid all this mighty sum   25
Of things for ever speaking,
That nothing of itself will come,
But we must still be seeking?

"—Then ask not wherefore, here, alone,
Conversing as I may,   30
I sit upon this old grey stone,
And dream my time away."

The Tables Turned

An Evening Scene on the Same Subject

Up! up! my Friend, and quit your books;
Or surely you'll grow double:
Up! up! my Friend, and clear your looks;
Why all this toil and trouble?

The sun, above the mountain's head,   5
A freshening lustre mellow
Through all the long green fields has spread,
His first sweet evening yellow.

Books! 'tis a dull and endless strife:
Come, hear the woodland linnet,   10
How sweet his music! on my life,
There's more of wisdom in it.

And hark! how blithe the throstle sings!
He, too, is no mean preacher:
Come forth into the light of things,   15
Let Nature be your Teacher.

She has a world of ready wealth,
Our minds and hearts to bless—
Spontaneous wisdom breathed by health,
Truth breathed by cheerfulness.   20

One impulse from a vernal wood
May teach you more of man,
Of moral evil and of good,
Than all the sages can.

Sweet is the lore which Nature brings;   25
Our meddling intellect
Mis-shapes the beauteous forms of things:—
We murder to dissect.

Enough of Science and of Art;
Close up those barren leaves;   30
Come forth, and bring with you a heart
That watches and receives.

Lines

Composed a Few Miles above Tintern Abbey, on Revisiting the Banks of the Wye During a Tour. July 13, 1798

In this great poem Wordsworth elaborates the attitude toward nature that is suggested in the first three
of our selections. The noble ruins of Tintern Abbey
stand in a lovely valley in Monmouthshire.

Five years have past; five summers, with the length
Of five long winters! and again I hear
These waters, rolling from their mountain-springs
With a soft inland murmur.—Once again
Do I behold these steep and lofty cliffs,   5
That on a wild secluded scene impress
Thoughts of more deep seclusion; and connect
The landscape with the quiet of the sky.
The day is come when I again repose
Here, under this dark sycamore, and view   10
These plots of cottage-ground, these orchard-tufts,
Which at this season, with their unripe fruits,
Are clad in one green hue, and lose themselves
'Mid groves and copses. Once again I see
These hedge-rows, hardly hedge-rows, little lines   15
Of sportive wood run wild: these pastoral farms,
Green to the very door; and wreaths of smoke
Sent up, in silence, from among the trees!
With some uncertain notice, as might seem
Of vagrant dwellers in the houseless woods,   20
Or of some Hermit's cave, where by his fire
The Hermit sits alone.
                                These beauteous forms,
Through a long absence, have not been to me
As is a landscape to a blind man's eye:
But oft, in lonely rooms, and 'mid the din   25
Of towns and cities, I have owed to them,
In hours of weariness, sensations sweet,
Felt in the blood, and felt along the heart;
And passing even into my purer mind,
With tranquil restoration:—feelings too   30
Of unremembered pleasure: such, perhaps,
As have no slight or trivial influence
On that best portion of a good man's life,
His little, nameless, unremembered, acts

Of kindness and of love. Nor less, I trust,
To them I may have owed another gift,
Of aspect more sublime; that blessèd mood,
In which the burthen of the mystery,
In which the heavy and the weary weight
Of all this unintelligible world,
Is lightened:—that serene and blessèd mood,
In which the affections gently lead us on,—
Until, the breath of this corporeal frame
And even the motion of our human blood
Almost suspended, we are laid asleep
In body, and become a living soul:
While with an eye made quiet by the power
Of harmony, and the deep power of joy,
We see into the life of things.

                            If this
Be but a vain belief, yet, oh! how oft—
In darkness and amid the many shapes
Of joyless daylight; when the fretful stir
Unprofitable, and the fever of the world,
Have hung upon the beatings of my heart—
How oft, in spirit, have I turned to thee,
O sylvan Wye! thou wanderer thro' the woods,
How often has my spirit turned to thee!

    And now, with gleams of half-extinguished
        thought,
With many recognitions dim and faint,
And somewhat of a sad perplexity,
The picture of the mind revives again:
While here I stand, not only with the sense
Of present pleasure, but with pleasing thoughts
That in this moment there is life and food
For future years. And so I dare to hope,
Though changed, no doubt, from what I was
        when first
I came among these hills; when like a roe
I bounded o'er the mountains, by the sides
Of the deep rivers, and the lonely streams,
Wherever nature led: more like a man
Flying from something that he dreads than one
Who sought the thing he loved. For nature then
(The coarser pleasures of my boyish days,
And their glad animal movements all gone by)
To me was all in all.—I cannot paint
What then I was. The sounding cataract
Haunted me like a passion: the tall rock,
The mountain, and the deep and gloomy wood,
Their colours and their forms, were then to me
An appetite; a feeling and a love,
That had no need of a remoter charm,

By thought supplied, nor any interest
Unborrowed from the eye.—That time is past,
And all its aching joys are now no more,
And all its dizzy raptures. Not for this
Faint I, nor mourn nor murmur; other gifts
Have followed; for such loss, I would believe,
Abundant recompense. For I have learned
To look on nature, not as in the hour
Of thoughtless youth; but hearing oftentimes
The still, sad music of humanity,
Nor harsh nor grating, though of ample power
To chasten and subdue. And I have felt
A presence that disturbs me with the joy
Of elevated thoughts; a sense sublime
Of something far more deeply interfused,
Whose dwelling is the light of setting suns,
And the round ocean and the living air,
And the blue sky, and in the mind of man:
A motion and a spirit, that impels
All thinking things, all objects of all thought,
And rolls through all things. Therefore am I still
A lover of the meadows and the woods,
And mountains; and of all that we behold
From this green earth; of all the mighty world
Of eye, and ear,—both what they half create,
And what perceive; well pleased to recognise
In nature and the language of the sense
The anchor of my purest thoughts, the nurse,
The guide, the guardian of my heart, and soul
Of all my moral being.

                    Nor perchance,
If I were not thus taught, should I the more
Suffer my genial spirits to decay:
For thou[1] art with me here upon the banks
Of this fair river; thou my dearest Friend,
My dear, dear Friend; and in thy voice I catch
The language of my former heart, and read
My former pleasures in the shooting lights
Of thy wild eyes. Oh! yet a little while
May I behold in thee what I was once,
My dear, dear Sister! and this prayer I make,
Knowing that Nature never did betray
The heart that loved her; 'tis her privilege,
Through all the years of this our life, to lead
From joy to joy: for she can so inform
The mind that is within us, so impress
With quietness and beauty, and so feed
With lofty thoughts, that neither evil tongues,
Rash judgments, nor the sneers of selfish men,

---

1 His sister Dorothy.

Nor greetings where no kindness is, nor all   130
The dreary intercourse of daily life,
Shall e'er prevail against us, or disturb
Our cheerful faith, that all which we behold
Is full of blessings. Therefore let the moon
Shine on thee in thy solitary walk;   135
And let the misty mountain-winds be free
To blow against thee: and, in after years,
When these wild ecstasies shall be matured
Into a sober pleasure; when thy mind
Shall be a mansion for all lovely forms,   140
Thy memory be as a dwelling-place
For all sweet sounds and harmonies; oh! then,
If solitude, or fear, or pain, or grief,
Should be thy portion, with what healing thoughts
Of tender joy wilt thou remember me,   145
And these my exhortations! Nor, perchance—
If I should be where I no more can hear
Thy voice, nor catch from thy wild eyes these
    gleams
Of past existence—wilt thou then forget
That on the banks of this delightful stream   150
We stood together; and that I, so long
A worshipper of Nature, hither came
Unwearied in that service: rather say
With warmer love—oh! with far deeper zeal
Of holier love. Nor wilt thou then forget   155
That after many wanderings, many years
Of absence, these steep woods and lofty cliffs,
And this green pastoral landscape, were to me
More dear, both for themselves and for thy sake!

There Was a Boy

This poem was one of the few passages from *The
Prelude* to be published in Wordsworth's own lifetime. It appears in Book Fifth, lines 364–97. The
poem was written in 1798. The next poem, "Nutting,"
also written in 1798, was originally intended for inclusion in *The Prelude* but never appeared there.

There was a Boy; ye knew him well, ye cliffs
And islands of Winander!—many a time,
At evening, when the earliest stars began
To move along the edges of the hills,
Rising or setting, would he stand alone,   5
Beneath the trees, or by the glimmering lake;
And there, with fingers interwoven, both hands
Pressed closely palm to palm and to his mouth
Uplifted, he, as through an instrument,

Blew mimic hootings to the silent owls,   10
That they might answer him.—And they would
    shout
Across the watery vale, and shout again,
Responsive to his call,—with quivering peals,
And long halloos, and screams, and echoes loud
Redoubled and redoubled; concourse wild   15
Of jocund din! And, when there came a pause
Of silence such as baffled his best skill:
Then sometimes, in that silence, while he hung
Listening, a gentle shock of mild surprise
Has carried far into his heart the voice   20
Of mountain-torrents; or the visible scene
Would enter unawares into his mind
With all its solemn imagery, its rocks,
Its woods, and that uncertain heaven received
Into the bosom of the steady lake.   25

This boy was taken from his mates, and died
In childhood, ere he was full twelve years old.
Pre-eminent in beauty is the vale
Where he was born and bred: the churchyard
    hangs
Upon a slope above the village-school;   30
And through that churchyard when my way has
    led
On summer-evenings, I believe that there
A long half-hour together I have stood
Mute—looking at the grave in which he lies!

Nutting

——————————————It seems a day
(I speak of one from many singled out)
One of those heavenly days that cannot die;
When, in the eagerness of boyish hope,
I left our cottage-threshold, sallying forth   5
With a huge wallet o'er my shoulders slung,
A nutting-crook in hand; and turned my steps
Tow'rd some far-distant wood, a Figure quaint,
Tricked out in proud disguise of cast-off weeds
Which for that service had been husbanded,   10
By exhortation of my frugal Dame—
Motley accoutrement, of power to smile
At thorns, and brakes, and brambles,—and, in
    truth,
More ragged than need was! O'er pathless rocks,
Through beds of matted fern, and tangled thick-   15
    ets,

Forcing my way, I came to one dear nook
Unvisited, where not a broken bough
Drooped with its withered leaves, ungracious sign
Of devastation; but the hazels rose
Tall and erect, with tempting clusters hung,   20
A virgin scene!—A little while I stood,
Breathing with such suppression of the heart
As joy delights in; and, with wise restraint
Voluptuous, fearless of a rival, eyed
The banquet;—or beneath the trees I sate   25
Among the flowers, and with the flowers I played;
A temper known to those who, after long
And weary expectation, have been blest
With sudden happiness beyond all hope.
Perhaps it was a bower beneath whose leaves   30
The violets of five seasons re-appear
And fade, unseen by any human eye;
Where fairy water-breaks do murmur on
For ever; and I saw the sparkling foam,
And—with my cheek on one of those green stones   35
That, fleeced with moss, under the shady trees,
Lay round me, scattered like a flock of sheep—
I heard the murmur and the murmuring sound,
In that sweet mood when pleasure loves to pay
Tribute to ease; and, of its joy secure,   40
The heart luxuriates with indifferent things,
Wasting its kindliness on stocks and stones,
And on the vacant air. Then up I rose,
And dragged to earth both branch and bough,
     with crash
And merciless ravage: and the shady nook   45
Of hazels, and the green and mossy bower,
Deformed and sullied, patiently gave up
Their quiet being: and unless I now
Confound my present feelings with the past,
Ere from the mutilated bower I turned   50
Exulting, rich beyond the wealth of kings,
I felt a sense of pain when I beheld
The silent trees, and saw the intruding sky.—
Then, dearest Maiden, move along these shades
In gentleness of heart; with gentle hand   55
Touch—for there is a spirit in the woods.

Strange Fits of Passion
Have I Known

This poem and the four that follow it constitute the
"Lucy poems," written in 1799, while Wordsworth
was in Germany.

Strange fits of passion have I known:
And I will dare to tell,
But in the Lover's ear alone,
What once to me befell.

When she I loved looked every day   5
Fresh as a rose in June,
I to her cottage bent my way,
Beneath an evening-moon.

Upon the moon I fixed my eye,
All over the wide lea;[1]   10
With quickening pace my horse drew nigh
Those paths so dear to me.

And now we reached the orchard-plot;
And, as we climbed the hill,
The sinking moon to Lucy's cot   15
Came near, and nearer still.

In one of those sweet dreams I slept,
Kind Nature's gentlest boon!
And all the while my eyes I kept
On the descending moon.   20

My horse moved on; hoof after hoof
He raised, and never stopped:
When down behind the cottage roof,
At once, the bright moon dropped.

What fond and wayward thoughts will slide   25
Into a Lover's head!
"O mercy!" to myself I cried,
"If Lucy should be dead!"[2]

She Dwelt Among the Untrodden Ways

She dwelt among the untrodden ways
     Beside the springs of Dove,[1]
A Maid whom there were none to praise
     And very few to love:

---

1 Meadow or pastureland.
2 The poem originally ended with a stanza that Wordsworth later canceled (see *The Early Letters,* ed. E. de
Selincourt, pp. 205–6):
          I told her this; her laughter light
          Is ringing in my ears;
          And when I think upon that night
          My eyes are dim with tears.

1 A river between Derbyshire and Staffordshire.

A violet by a mossy stone
   Half hidden from the eye!
—Fair as a star, when only one
   Is shining in the sky.

She lived unknown, and few could know
   When Lucy ceased to be;   10
But she is in her grave, and, oh,
   The difference to me!

I Travelled Among Unknown Men

I travelled among unknown men,
   In lands beyond the sea;
Nor, England! did I know till then
   What love I bore to thee.

'Tis past, that melancholy dream!   5
   Nor will I quit thy shore
A second time; for still I seem
   To love thee more and more.

Among thy mountains did I feel
   The joy of my desire;   10
And she I cherished turned her wheel
   Beside an English fire.

Thy mornings showed, thy nights concealed,
   The bowers where Lucy played;
And thine too is the last green field   15
   That Lucy's eyes surveyed.

Three Years She Grew in Sun and Shower

Three years she grew in sun and shower,
Then Nature said, "A lovelier flower
On earth was never sown;
This Child I to myself will take;
She shall be mine, and I will make   5
A Lady of my own.

"Myself will to my darling be
Both law and impulse: and with me
The Girl, in rock and plain,
In earth and heaven, in glade and bower,   10
Shall feel an overseeing power
To kindle or restrain.

"She shall be sportive as the fawn
That wild with glee across the lawn
Or up the mountain springs;   15
And hers shall be the breathing balm,
And hers the silence and the calm
Of mute insensate things.

"The floating clouds their state shall lend
To her; for her the willow bend;   20
Nor shall she fail to see
Even in the motions of the Storm
Grace that shall mould the Maiden's form
By silent sympathy.

"The stars of midnight shall be dear   25
To her; and she shall lean her ear
In many a secret place
Where rivulets dance their wayward round,
And beauty born of murmuring sound
Shall pass into her face.   30

"And vital feelings of delight
Shall rear her form to stately height,
Her virgin bosom swell;
Such thoughts to Lucy I will give
While she and I together live   35
Here in this happy dell."

Thus Nature spake—The work was done—
How soon my Lucy's race was run!
She died, and left to me
This heath, this calm, and quiet scene;   40
The memory of what has been,
And never more will be.

A Slumber Did My Spirit Seal

A slumber did my spirit seal;
   I had no human fears:
She seemed a thing that could not feel
   The touch of earthly years.

No motion has she now, no force;   5
   She neither hears nor sees;
Rolled round in earth's diurnal course,
   With rocks, and stones, and trees.

Lucy Gray *or* Solitude

This poem was also written in 1799, in Germany. Dorothy had told her brother about a little Yorkshire girl drowned in the lock of a canal during a snowstorm. Wordsworth's aim was to tell this story with the simplicity of the old ballads, and yet (as he says in a note) to treat "common life" imaginatively.

Oft I had heard of Lucy Gray:
And, when I crossed the wild,
I chanced to see at break of day
The solitary child.

No mate, no comrade Lucy knew;   5
She dwelt on a wide moor,
—The sweetest thing that ever grew
Beside a human door!

You yet may spy the fawn at play,
The hare upon the green;   10
But the sweet face of Lucy Gray
Will never more be seen.

"To-night will be a stormy night—
You to the town must go;
And take a lantern, Child, to light   15
Your mother through the snow."

"That, Father! will I gladly do:
'Tis scarcely afternoon—
The minster-clock has just struck two,
And yonder is the moon!"   20

At this the Father raised his hook,
And snapped a faggot-band;
He plied his work;—and Lucy took
The lantern in her hand.

Not blither is the mountain roe: 25
With many a wanton stroke
Her feet disperse the powdery snow,
That rises up like smoke.

The storm came on before its time:
She wandered up and down;   30
And many a hill did Lucy climb:
But never reached the town.

The wretched parents all that night
Went shouting far and wide;
But there was neither sound nor sight   35
To serve them for a guide.

At day-break on a hill they stood
That overlooked the moor;
And thence they saw the bridge of wood,
A furlong from their door.   40

They wept—and, turning homeward, cried,
"In heaven we all shall meet";
—When in the snow the mother spied
The print of Lucy's feet.

Then downwards from the steep hill's edge   45
They tracked the footmarks small;
And through the broken hawthorn hedge,
And by the long stone-wall;

And then an open field they crossed:
The marks were still the same;   50
They tracked them on, nor ever lost;
And to the bridge they came.

They followed from the snowy bank
Those footmarks, one by one,
Into the middle of the plank;   55
And further there were none!

—Yet some maintain that to this day
She is a living child;
That you may see sweet Lucy Gray
Upon the lonesome wild.   60

O'er rough and smooth she trips along,
And never looks behind;
And sings a solitary song
That whistles in the wind.

The Fountain

A Conversation

The character of Matthew (who appears also in two other poems, "Matthew" and "The Two April Mornings") is copied at least in part from that of a master in the Hawkshead grammar school, to which Wordsworth was sent at the age of eight. All three poems were composed in 1799 and published in the second edition of *Lyrical Ballads*.

We talked with open heart, and tongue
Affectionate and true,
A pair of friends, though I was young,
And Matthew seventy-two.

We lay beneath a spreading oak,   5
Beside a mossy seat;
And from the turf a fountain[1] broke,
And gurgled at our feet.

"Now Matthew!" said I, "let us match
This water's pleasant tune   10
With some old border-song, or catch
That suits a summer's noon;

"Or of the church-clock and the chimes
Sing here beneath the shade,
That half-mad thing of witty rhymes   15
Which you last April made!"

In silence Matthew lay, and eyed
The spring beneath the tree;
And thus the dear old Man replied,
The grey-haired man of glee: 20

"No check, no stay, this Streamlet fears;
How merrily it goes!
'T will murmur on a thousand years,
And flow as now it flows.

"And here, on this delightful day,   25
I cannot choose but think
How oft, a vigorous man, I lay
Beside this fountain's brink.

"My eyes are dim with childish tears,
My heart is idly stirred,   30
For the same sound is in my ears
Which in those days I heard.

"Thus fares it still in our decay:
And yet the wiser mind
Mourns less for what age takes away   35
Than what it leaves behind.

"The blackbird amid leafy trees,
The lark above the hill,
Let loose their carols when they please,
Are quiet when they will.   40

"With Nature never do *they* wage
A foolish strife; they see
A happy youth, and their old age
Is beautiful and free:

"But we are pressed by heavy laws;   45
And often, glad no more,
We wear a face of joy, because
We have been glad of yore.

"If there be one who need bemoan
His kindred laid in earth,   50
The household hearts that were his own,
It is the man of mirth.

"My days, my Friend, are almost gone,
My life has been approved,
And many love me; but by none   55
Am I enough beloved."

"Now both himself and me he wrongs,
The man who thus complains!
I live and sing my idle songs
Upon these happy plains;   60

"And, Matthew, for thy children dead
I'll be a son to thee!"
At this he grasped my hand, and said,
"Alas! that cannot be."

We rose up from the fountain-side,   65
And down the smooth descent
Of the green sheep-track did we glide;
And through the wood we went;

And, ere we came to Leonard's rock,
He sang those witty rhymes   70
About the crazy old church-clock,
And the bewildered chimes.

---

1 Spring.

Michael

A Pastoral Poem

In "Michael" Wordsworth has attempted, as he says in a letter, "to give a picture of a man, of strong mind and lively sensibility, agitated by two of the most powerful affections of the human heart: the parental affection and the love of property (*landed* property), including the feelings of inheritance, home, and personal and family independence." His success may be judged by the intensity of the quiet line (466), "And never lifted up a single stone." "Michael" was composed in 1800; Wordsworth was living at Grasmere, in the northern lake country.

If from the public way you turn your steps
Up the tumultuous brook of Greenhead Ghyll,[1]
You will suppose that with an upright path
Your feet must struggle; in such bold ascent
The pastoral mountains front you, face to face. 5
But, courage! for around that boisterous brook
The mountains have all opened out themselves,
And made a hidden valley of their own.
No habitation can be seen; but they
Who journey thither find themselves alone 10
With a few sheep, with rocks and stones, and
    kites[2]
That overhead are sailing in the sky.
It is in truth an utter solitude;
Nor should I have made mention of this Dell
But for one object which you might pass by, 15
Might see and notice not. Beside the brook
Appears a straggling heap of unhewn stones!
And to that simple object appertains
A story—unenriched with strange events,
Yet not unfit, I deem, for the fireside, 20
Or for the summer shade. It was the first
Of those domestic tales that spake to me
Of Shepherds, dwellers in the valleys, men
Whom I already loved;—not verily
For their own sakes, but for the fields and hills 25
Where was their occupation and abode.
And hence this Tale, while I was yet a Boy
Careless of books, yet having felt the power
Of Nature, by the gentle agency
Of natural objects, led me on to feel 30
For passions that were not my own, and think
(At random and imperfectly indeed)
On man, the heart of man, and human life.
Therefore, although it be a history
Homely and rude, I will relate the same 35
For the delight of a few natural hearts;
And, with yet fonder feeling, for the sake
Of youthful Poets, who among these hills
Will be my second self when I am gone.

   Upon the forest-side in Grasmere Vale 40
There dwelt a Shepherd, Michael was his name;
An old man, stout of heart, and strong of limb.
His bodily frame had been from youth to age
Of an unusual strength: his mind was keen,
Intense, and frugal, apt for all affairs, 45
And in his shepherd's calling he was prompt
And watchful more than ordinary men.

Hence had he learned the meaning of all winds,
Of blasts of every tone; and oftentimes,
When others heeded not, he heard the South 50
Make subterraneous music, like the noise
Of bagpipers on distant Highland hills.
The Shepherd, at such warning, of his flock
Bethought him, and he to himself would say,
"The winds are now devising work for me!" 55
And, truly, at all times, the storm, that drives
The traveller to a shelter, summoned him
Up to the mountains: he had been alone
Amid the heart of many thousand mists,
That came to him, and left him, on the heights. 60
So lived he till his eightieth year was past.
And grossly that man errs who should suppose
That the green valleys, and the streams and
    rocks,
Were things indifferent to the Shepherd's
    thoughts.
Fields, where with cheerful spirits he had 65
    breathed
The common air; hills, which with vigorous step
He had so often climbed; which had impressed
So many incidents upon his mind
Of hardship, skill or courage, joy or fear;
Which, like a book, preserved the memory 70
Of the dumb animals, whom he had saved,
Had fed or sheltered, linking to such acts
The certainty of honourable gain;
Those fields, those hills—what could they less?
    had laid
Strong hold on his affections, were to him 75
A pleasurable feeling of blind love,
The pleasure which there is in life itself.

   His days had not been passed in singleness.
His Helpmate was a comely matron, old—
Though younger than himself full twenty years. 80
She was a woman of a stirring life,
Whose heart was in her house: two wheels she
    had
Of antique form; this large, for spinning wool;
That small, for flax; and, if one wheel had rest,
It was because the other was at work. 85
The Pair had but one inmate in their house,
An only Child, who had been born to them
When Michael, telling o'er[3] his years, began
To deem that he was old,—in shepherd's phrase,
With one foot in the grave. This only Son,

---

[1] Gully.　　[2] A kind of hawk.

[3] Counting.

With two brave sheep-dogs tried in many a
    storm,
The one of an inestimable worth,
Made all their household. I may truly say,
That they were as a proverb in the vale
For endless industry. When day was gone,   95
And from their occupations out of doors
The Son and Father were come home, even then,
Their labour did not cease; unless when all
Turned to the cleanly supper-board, and there,
Each with a mess of pottage and skimmed milk,   100
Sat round the basket piled with oaten cakes,
And their plain home-made cheese. Yet when the
    meal
Was ended, Luke (for so the Son was named)
And his old Father both betook themselves
To such convenient work as might employ   105
Their hands by the fire-side; perhaps to card
Wool for the Housewife's spindle, or repair
Some injury done to sickle, flail, or scythe,
Or other implement of house or field.

Down from the ceiling, by the chimney's edge, 110
That in our ancient uncouth country style
With huge and black projection overbrowed
Large space beneath, as duly as the light
Of day grew dim the Housewife hung a lamp;
An aged utensil, which had performed   115
Service beyond all others of its kind.
Early at evening did it burn—and late,
Surviving comrade of uncounted hours,
Which, going by from year to year, had found,
And left, the couple neither gay perhaps   120
Nor cheerful, yet with objects and with hopes,
Living a life of eager industry.
And now, when Luke had reached his eighteenth
    year,
There by the light of this old lamp they sate,
Father and Son, while far into the night   125
The Housewife plied her own peculiar[4] work,
Making the cottage through the silent hours
Murmur as with the sound of summer flies.
This light was famous in its neighbourhood,
And was a public symbol of the life   130
That thrifty Pair had lived. For, as it chanced,
Their cottage on a plot of rising ground
Stood single, with large prospect, north and
    south,
High into Easedale, up to Dunmail-Raise,[5]

And westward to the village near the lake;   135
And from this constant light, so regular,
And so far seen, the House itself, by all
Who dwelt within the limits of the vale,
Both old and young, was named THE EVENING
    STAR.

Thus living on through such a length of years, 140
The Shepherd, if he loved himself, must needs
Have loved his Helpmate; but to Michael's heart
This son of his old age was yet more dear—
Less from instinctive tenderness, the same
Fond spirit that blindly works in the blood of 145
    all—
Than that a child, more than all other gifts
That earth can offer to declining man,
Brings hope with it, and forward-looking
    thoughts,
And stirrings of inquietude, when they
By tendency of nature needs must fail.   150
Exceeding was the love he bare to him,
His heart and his heart's joy! For oftentimes
Old Michael, while he was a babe in arms,
Had done him female service, not alone
For pastime and delight, as is the use   155
Of fathers, but with patient mind enforced
To acts of tenderness; and he had rocked
His cradle, as with a woman's gentle hand.

And in a later time, ere yet the Boy
Had put on boy's attire, did Michael love,   160
Albeit of a stern unbending mind,
To have the Young-one in his sight, when he
Wrought in the field, or on his shepherd's stool
Sate with a fettered sheep before him stretched
Under the large old oak, that near his door 165
Stood single, and, from matchless depth of shade,
Chosen for the Shearer's covert from the sun,
Thence in our rustic dialect was called
The CLIPPING TREE, a name which yet it bears.
There, while they two were sitting in the shade, 170
With others round them, earnest all and blithe,
Would Michael exercise his heart with looks
Of fond correction and reproof bestowed
Upon the Child, if he disturbed the sheep
By catching at their legs, or with his shouts 175
Scared them, while they lay still beneath the
    shears.

---

4 Special.
5 A hill south of Thirlmere, on the road between Keswick and Grasmere. Easedale Tarn (pond) lies among the hills southwest of it.

And when by Heaven's good grace the boy
    grew up
A healthy Lad, and carried in his cheek
Two steady roses that were five years old;
Then Michael from a winter coppice cut   180
With his own hand a sapling, which he hooped
With iron, making it throughout in all
Due requisites a perfect shepherd's staff,
And gave it to the Boy; wherewith equipt
He as a watchman oftentimes was placed   185
At gate or gap, to stem or turn the flock;
And, to his office prematurely called,
There stood the urchin, as you will divine,
Something between a hindrance and a help;
And for this cause not always, I believe,   190
Receiving from his Father hire of praise;
Though nought was left undone which staff, or
    voice,
Or looks, or threatening gestures, could perform.

But soon as Luke, full ten years old, could
    stand
Against the mountain blasts; and to the heights,   195
Not fearing toil, nor length of weary ways,
He and his Father daily went, and they
Were as companions, why should I relate
That objects which the Shepherd loved before
Were dearer now? that from the Boy there came   200
Feelings and emanations—things which were
Light to the sun and music to the wind;
And that the old Man's heart seemed born again?

Thus in his Father's sight the Boy grew up:
And now, when he had reached his eighteenth   205
    year,
He was his comfort and his daily hope.

While in this sort the simple household lived
From day to day, to Michael's ear there came
Distressful tidings. Long before the time
Of which I speak, the Shepherd had been bound   210
In surety for his brother's son, a man
Of an industrious life, and ample means;
But unforeseen misfortunes suddenly
Had prest upon him; and old Michael now
Was summoned to discharge the forfeiture,   215
A grievous penalty, but little less
Than half his substance. This unlooked-for
    claim,
At the first hearing, for a moment took
More hope out of his life than he supposed
That any old man ever could have lost.   220

As soon as he had armed himself with strength
To look his trouble in the face, it seemed
The Shepherd's sole resource to sell at once
A portion of his patrimonial fields.
Such was his first resolve; he thought again,   225
And his heart failed him. "Isabel," said he,
Two evenings after he had heard the news,
"I have been toiling more than seventy years,
And in the open sunshine of God's love
Have we all lived; yet, if these fields of ours   230
Should pass into a stranger's hand, I think
That I could not lie quiet in my grave.
Our lot is a hard lot; the sun himself
Has scarcely been more diligent than I;
And I have lived to be a fool at last   235
To my own family. An evil man
That was, and made an evil choice, if he
Were false to us; and, if he were not false,
There are ten thousand to whom loss like this
Had been no sorrow. I forgive him;—but   240
'Twere better to be dumb than to talk thus.

"When I began, my purpose was to speak
Of remedies and of a cheerful hope.
Our Luke shall leave us, Isabel; the land
Shall not go from us, and it shall be free;   245
He shall possess it, free as is the wind
That passes over it. We have, thou know'st,
Another kinsman—he will be our friend
In this distress. He is a prosperous man,
Thriving in trade—and Luke to him shall go,   250
And with his kinsman's help and his own thrift
He quickly will repair this loss, and then
He may return to us. If here he stay,
What can be done? Where every one is poor,
What can be gained?"   255
              At this the old Man paused,
And Isabel sat silent, for her mind
Was busy, looking back into past times.
There's Richard Bateman, thought she to herself,
He was a parish-boy—at the church-door
They made a gathering for him, shillings, pence,   260
And halfpennies, wherewith the neighbours
    bought
A basket, which they filled with pedlar's wares;
And, with this basket on his arm, the lad
Went up to London, found a master there,
Who, out of many, chose the trusty boy   265
To go and overlook his merchandise
Beyond the seas; where he grew wondrous rich,
And left estates and monies to the poor,
And, at his birth-place, built a chapel floored

With marble, which he sent from foreign lands.   270
These thoughts, and many others of like sort,
Passed quickly through the mind of Isabel,
And her face brightened. The old Man was glad,
And thus resumed:—"Well, Isabel! this scheme
These two days has been meat and drink to me.   275
Far more than we have lost is left us yet.
—We have enough—I wish indeed that I
Were younger;—but this hope is a good hope.
Make ready Luke's best garments, of the best
Buy for him more, and let us send him forth   280
To-morrow, or the next day, or to-night:
—If he *could* go, the Boy should go to-night."

Here Michael ceased, and to the fields went
    forth
With a light heart. The Housewife for five days
Was restless morn and night, and all day long   285
Wrought on with her best fingers to prepare
Things needful for the journey of her son.
But Isabel was glad when Sunday came
To stop her in her work: for, when she lay
By Michael's side, she through the last two nights   290
Heard him, how he was troubled in his sleep:
And when they rose at morning she could see
That all his hopes were gone. That day at noon
She said to Luke, while they two by themselves
Were sitting at the door, "Thou must not go: 295
We have no other Child but thee to lose,
None to remember—do not go away,
For if thou leave thy Father he will die."
The Youth made answer with a jocund voice;
And Isabel, when she had told her fears,   300
Recovered heart. That evening her best fare
Did she bring forth, and all together sat
Like happy people round a Christmas fire.

With daylight Isabel resumed her work;
And all the ensuing week the house appeared   305
As cheerful as a grove in Spring: at length
The expected letter from their Kinsman came,
With kind assurances that he would do
His utmost for the welfare of the Boy;
To which, requests were added, that forthwith   310
He might be sent to him. Ten times or more
The letter was read over; Isabel
Went forth to show it to the neighbours round;
Nor was there at that time on English land
A prouder heart than Luke's. When Isabel   315
Had to her house returned, the old Man said,

"He shall depart to-morrow." To this word
The Housewife answered, talking much of things
Which, if at such short notice he should go,
Would surely be forgotten. But at length   320
She gave consent, and Michael was at ease.

Near the tumultuous brook of Greenhead
    Ghyll,
In that deep valley, Michael had designed
To build a Sheep-fold; and, before he heard
The tidings of his melancholy loss,   325
For this same purpose he had gathered up
A heap of stones, which by the streamlet's edge
Lay thrown together, ready for the work.
With Luke that evening thitherward he walked:
And soon as they had reached the place he   330
    stopped,
And thus the old Man spake to him:—"My Son,
To-morrow thou wilt leave me: with full heart
I look upon thee, for thou art the same
That wert a promise to me ere thy birth,
And all thy life hast been my daily joy.   335
I will relate to thee some little part
Of our two histories; 'twill do thee good
When thou art from me, even if I should touch
On things thou canst not know of.—After thou
First cam'st into the world—as oft befalls   340
To new-born infants—thou didst sleep away
Two days, and blessings from thy Father's
    tongue
Then fell upon thee. Day by day passed on,
And still I loved thee with increasing love.
Never to living ear came sweeter sounds   345
Than when I heard thee by our own fire-side
First uttering, without words, a natural tune;
While thou, a feeding babe, didst in thy joy
Sing at thy Mother's breast. Month followed
    month,
And in the open fields my life was passed   350
And on the mountains; else I think that thou
Hadst been brought up upon thy Father's knees.
But we were playmates, Luke: among these hills,
As well thou knowest, in us the old and young
Have played together, nor with me didst thou   355
Lack any pleasure which a boy can know."
Luke had a manly heart; but at these words
He sobbed aloud. The old Man grasped his
    hand,
And said, "Nay, do not take it so—I see
That these are things of which I need not speak.   360
—Even to the utmost I have been to thee

A kind and a good Father: and herein
I but repay a gift which I myself
Received at others' hands; for, though now old
Beyond the common life of man, I still   365
Remember them who loved me in my youth.
Both of them sleep together: here they lived,
As all their Forefathers had done; and, when
At length their time was come, they were not loth
To give their bodies to the family mould.   370
I wished that thou shouldst live the life they
          lived,
But 'tis a long time to look back, my Son,
And see so little gain from threescore years.
These fields were burthened when they came to
          me;
Till I was forty years of age, not more   375
Than half of my inheritance was mine.
I toiled and toiled; God blessed me in my work,
And till these three weeks past the land was free.
—It looks as if it never could endure
Another Master. Heaven forgive me, Luke,   380
If I judge ill for thee, but it seems good
That thou shouldst go."
                    At this the old Man paused;
Then, pointing to the stones near which they
          stood,
Thus, after a short silence, he resumed:
"This was a work for us; and now, my Son,   385
It is a work for me. But, lay one stone—
Here, lay it for me, Luke, with thine own hands.
Nay, Boy, be of good hope;—we both may live
To see a better day. At eighty-four
I still am strong and hale;—do thou thy part;   390
I will do mine:—I will begin again
With many tasks that were resigned to thee:
Up to the heights, and in among the storms,
Will I without thee go again, and do
All works which I was wont to do alone,   395
Before I knew thy face.—Heaven bless thee, Boy!
Thy heart these two weeks has been beating fast
With many hopes; it should be so—yes—yes—
I knew that thou couldst never have a wish
To leave me, Luke: thou hast been bound to me   400
Only by links of love: when thou art gone,
What will be left to us!—But I forget
My purposes. Lay now the corner-stone,
As I requested; and hereafter, Luke,
When thou art gone away, should evil men   405
Be thy companions, think of me, my Son,
And of this moment; hither turn thy thoughts,
And God will strengthen thee: amid all fear

And all temptation, Luke, I pray that thou
May'st bear in mind the life thy Fathers lived, 410
Who, being innocent, did for that cause
Bestir them in good deeds. Now, fare thee well—
When thou return'st, thou in this place wilt see
A work which is not here: a covenant
'Twill be between us; but, whatever fate   415
Befall thee, I shall love thee to the last,
And bear thy memory with me to the grave."

     The Shepherd ended here; and Luke stooped
          down,
And, as his Father had requested, laid
The first stone of the Sheep-fold. At the sight 420
The old Man's grief broke from him; to his heart
He pressed his Son, he kissèd him and wept;
And to the house together they returned.
—Hushed was that House in peace, or seeming
          peace,
Ere the night fell:—with morrow's dawn the Boy   425
Began his journey, and, when he had reached
The public way, he put on a bold face;
And all the neighbours, as he passed their doors,
Came forth with wishes and with farewell
          prayers,
That followed him till he was out of sight.   430

     A good report did from their Kinsman come,
Of Luke and his well-doing: and the Boy
Wrote loving letters, full of wondrous news,
Which, as the Housewife phrased it, were
          throughout
"The prettiest letters that were ever seen."   435
Both parents read them with rejoicing hearts.
So, many months passed on: and once again
The Shepherd went about his daily work
With confident and cheerful thoughts; and now
Sometimes when he could find a leisure hour   440
He to that valley took his way, and there
Wrought at the Sheep-fold. Meantime Luke
          began
To slacken in his duty; and, at length,
He in the dissolute city gave himself
To evil courses: ignominy and shame   445
Fell on him, so that he was driven at last
To seek a hiding-place beyond the seas.

     There is a comfort in the strength of love;
'Twill make a thing endurable, which else
Would overset the brain, or break the heart: 450

I have conversed with more than one who well
Remember the old Man, and what he was
Years after he had heard this heavy news.
His bodily frame had been from youth to age
Of an unusual strength. Among the rocks   455
He went, and still looked up to sun and cloud,
And listened to the wind; and, as before,
Performed all kinds of labour for his sheep,
And for the land, his small inheritance.
And to that hollow dell from time to time   460
Did he repair, to build the Fold of which
His flock had need. 'Tis not forgotten yet
The pity which was then in every heart
For the old Man—and 'tis believed by all
That many and many a day he thither went,   465
And never lifted up a single stone.

    There, by the Sheep-fold, sometimes was he
       seen
Sitting alone, or with his faithful Dog,
Then old, beside him, lying at his feet.
The length of full seven years, from time to time,   470
He at the building of this Sheep-fold wrought,
And left the work unfinished when he died.
Three years, or little more, did Isabel
Survive her Husband: at her death the estate
Was sold, and went into a stranger's hand.   475
The cottage which was named the EVENING STAR
Is gone—the ploughshare has been through the
      ground
On which it stood: great changes have been
      wrought
In all the neighbourhood:—yet the oak is left
That grew beside their door; and the remains   480
Of the unfinished Sheep-fold may be seen
Beside the boisterous brook of Greenhead Ghyll.

My Heart Leaps Up

My heart leaps up when I behold
    A rainbow in the sky:
So was it when my life began;
So is it now I am a man;
So be it when I shall grow old,   5
    Or let me die!
The Child is father of the Man;
And I could wish my days to be
Bound each to each by natural piety.

Resolution and Independence

Wordsworth wrote this poem and the preceding one
at Grasmere in 1802. "This old Man I met a few
hundred yards from my cottage; and the account of
him is taken from his own mouth. I was in the state
of feeling described in the beginning of the poem."
At first in high spirits, the poet has become depressed
as he thinks of how precarious human happiness is,
especially the happiness of poets. Then he meets the
leech gatherer. "I cannot," he wrote in a letter, "conceive a figure more impressive than that of an old
man like this . . . travelling alone . . . carrying with
him his own fortitude, and the necessities which an
unjust state of society has laid upon him."

There was a roaring in the wind all night;
The rain came heavily and fell in floods;
But now the sun is rising calm and bright;
The birds are singing in the distant woods;
Over his own sweet voice the Stock-dove broods;   5
The Jay makes answer as the Magpie chatters;
And all the air is filled with pleasant noise of
    waters.

All things that love the sun are out of doors;
The sky rejoices in the morning's birth;
The grass is bright with rain-drops;—on the   10
    moors
The hare is running races in her mirth;
And with her feet she from the plashy earth
Raises a mist; that, glittering in the sun,
Runs with her all the way, wherever she doth
    run.

I was a Traveller then upon the moor;   15
I saw the hare that raced about with joy;
I heard the woods and distant waters roar;
Or heard them not, as happy as a boy:
The pleasant season did my heart employ:
My old remembrances went from me wholly;   20
And all the ways of men, so vain and melancholy.

But, as it sometimes chanceth, from the might
Of joy in minds that can no further go,
As high as we have mounted in delight
In our dejection do we sink as low;   25
To me that morning did it happen so;
And fears and fancies thick upon me came;
Dim sadness—and blind thoughts, I knew not,
    nor could name.

I heard the sky-lark warbling in the sky;
And I bethought me of the playful hare: 30
Even such a happy Child of earth am I;
Even as these blissful creatures do I fare;
Far from the world I walk, and from all care;
But there may come another day to me—
Solitude, pain of heart, distress, and poverty.   35

My whole life I have lived in pleasant thought,
As if life's business were a summer mood;
As if all needful things would come unsought
To genial faith, still rich in genial good;
But how can He expect that others should   40
Build for him, sow for him, and at his call
Love him, who for himself will take no heed at
    all?

I thought of Chatterton,[1] the marvellous Boy,
The sleepless Soul that perished in his pride;
Of Him who walked in glory and in joy   45
Following his plough, along the mountain-side:[2]
By our own spirits are we deified:
We Poets in our youth begin in gladness;
But thereof come in the end despondency and
    madness.

Now, whether it were by peculiar grace,   50
A leading from above, a something given,
Yet it befell that, in this lonely place,
When I with these untoward[3] thoughts had
    striven,
Beside a pool bare to the eye of heaven
I saw a Man before me unawares: 55
The oldest man he seemed that ever wore grey
    hairs.

As a huge stone is sometimes seen to lie
Couched on the bald top of an eminence;
Wonder to all who do the same espy,
By what means it could thither come, and   60
    whence;
So that it seems a thing endued with sense:
Like a sea-beast crawled forth, that on a shelf
Of rock or sand reposeth, there to sun itself;

Such seemed this Man, not all alive nor dead,

Nor all asleep—in his extreme old age: 65
His body was bent double, feet and head
Coming together in life's pilgrimage;
As if some dire constraint of pain, or rage
Of sickness felt by him in times long past,
A more than human weight upon his frame had   70
    cast.

Himself he propped, limbs, body, and pale face,
Upon a long grey staff of shaven wood:
And, still as I drew near with gentle pace,
Upon the margin of that moorish flood[4]
Motionless as a cloud the old Man stood,   75
That heareth not the loud winds when they call;
And moveth all together, if it move at all.

At length, himself unsettling, he the pond
Stirred with his staff, and fixedly did look
Upon the muddy water, which he conned,   80
As if he had been reading in a book:
And now a stranger's privilege I took;
And, drawing to his side, to him did say,
"This morning gives us promise of a glorious
    day."

A gentle answer did the old Man make,   85
In courteous speech which forth he slowly drew:
And him with further words I thus bespake,
"What occupation do you there pursue?
This is a lonesome place for one like you."
Ere he replied, a flash of mild surprise   90
Broke from the sable orbs of his yet-vivid eyes.

His words came feebly, from a feeble chest,
But each in solemn order followed each,
With something of a lofty utterance drest—
Choice word and measured phrase, above the   95
    reach
Of ordinary men; a stately speech;
Such as grave Livers do in Scotland use,
Religious men, who give to God and man their
    dues.

He told, that to these waters he had come
To gather leeches,[5] being old and poor: 100
Employment hazardous and wearisome!
And he had many hardships to endure:

---

[1] Thomas Chatterton (1752–1770) was fascinated by medieval poetry. He died at eighteen, having won fame with his imitations of it; for a time he succeeded in tricking readers into accepting them as genuine relics of former times.   [2] Robert Burns.   [3] Perverse, wrong.

---

[4] Stream on the moor.
[5] Physicians used them for bleeding patients.

From pond to pond he roamed, from moor to
  moor;
Housing, with God's good help, by choice or
  chance;
And in this way he gained an honest mainte-   105
  nance.

The old Man still stood talking by my side;
But now his voice to me was like a stream
Scarce heard; nor word from word could I divide;
And the whole body of the Man did seem
Like one whom I had met with in a dream;   110
Or like a man from some far region sent,
To give me human strength, by apt admonish-
  ment.

My former thoughts returned: the fear that kills;
And hope that is unwilling to be fed;
Cold, pain, and labour, and all fleshly ills;   115
And mighty Poets in their misery dead.
—Perplexed, and longing to be comforted,
My question eagerly did I renew,
"How is it that you live, and what is it you do?"

He with a smile did then his words repeat;   120
And said that, gathering leeches, far and wide
He travelled; stirring thus about his feet
The waters of the pools where they abide.
"Once I could meet with them on every side;
But they have dwindled long by slow decay;   125
Yet still I persevere, and find them where I may."

While he was talking thus, the lonely place,
The old Man's shape, and speech—all troubled
  me:
In my mind's eye I seemed to see him pace
About the weary moors continually,   130
Wandering about alone and silently.
While I these thoughts within myself pursued,
He, having made a pause, the same discourse
  renewed.

And soon with this he other matter blended,
Cheerfully uttered, with demeanour kind,   135
But stately in the main; and, when he ended,
I could have laughed myself to scorn to find
In that decrepit Man so firm a mind.
"God," said I, "be my help and stay secure;
I'll think of the Leech-gatherer on the lonely   140
  moor!"

To H. C.[1]

Six Years Old

O thou! whose fancies from afar are brought;
Who of thy words dost make a mock apparel,
And fittest to unutterable thought
The breeze-like motion and the self-born carol;
Thou faery voyager! that dost float
In such clear water, that thy boat
May rather seem
To brood on air than on an earthly stream;
Suspended in a stream as clear as sky,
Where earth and heaven do make one imagery;   10
O blessèd vision! happy child!
Thou art so exquisitely wild,
I think of thee with many fears
For what may be thy lot in future years.

I thought of times when Pain might be thy   15
  guest,
Lord of thy house and hospitality;
And Grief, uneasy lover! never rest
But when she sate within the touch of thee.
O too industrious folly!
O vain and causeless melancholy!   20
Nature will either end thee quite;
Or, lengthening out thy season of delight,
Preserve for thee, by individual right,
A young lamb's heart among the full-grown
  flocks.
What hast thou to do with sorrow,   25
Or the injuries of to-morrow?
Thou art a dew-drop, which the morn brings
  forth,
Ill fitted to sustain unkindly shocks,
Or to be trailed along the soiling earth;
A gem that glitters while it lives,   30
And no forewarning gives;
But, at the touch of wrong, without a strife
Slips in a moment out of life.

To a Butterfly

Written in 1802.

I've watched you now a full half-hour,
Self-poised upon that yellow flower;
And, little Butterfly! indeed
I know not if you sleep or feed.

[1] H. C. was Coleridge's son Hartley.

How motionless!—not frozen seas 5
More motionless! and then
What joy awaits you, when the breeze
Hath found you out among the trees,
And calls you forth again!

This plot of orchard-ground is ours; 10
My trees they are, my Sister's flowers;
Here rest your wings when they are weary;
Here lodge as in a sanctuary!
Come often to us, fear no wrong;
Sit near us on the bough! 15
We'll talk of sunshine and of song,
And summer days, when we were young;
Sweet childish days, that were as long
As twenty days are now.

To the Cuckoo

Written in 1804.

O blithe New-comer! I have heard,
I hear thee and rejoice.
O Cuckoo! shall I call thee Bird,
Or but a wandering Voice?

While I am lying on the grass 5
Thy twofold shout I hear;
From hill to hill it seems to pass
At once far off, and near.

Though babbling only to the Vale,
Of sunshine and of flowers, 10
Thou bringest unto me a tale
Of visionary hours.

Thrice welcome, darling of the Spring!
Even yet thou art to me
No bird, but an invisible thing, 15
A voice, a mystery;

The same whom in my schoolboy days
I listened to; that Cry
Which made me look a thousand ways
In bush, and tree, and sky. 20

To seek thee did I often rove
Through woods and on the green;
And thou wert still a hope, a love;
Still longed for, never seen.

And I can listen to thee yet; 25
Can lie upon the plain
And listen, till I do beget
That golden time again.

O blessèd Bird! the earth we pace
Again appears to be 30
An unsubstantial, faery place,
That is fit home for Thee!

She Was a Phantom of Delight

A tribute to the poet's wife, written in 1804.

She was a Phantom of delight
When first she gleamed upon my sight;
A lovely Apparition, sent
To be a moment's ornament;
Her eyes as stars of Twilight fair; 5
Like Twilight's, too, her dusky hair;
But all things else about her drawn
From May-time and the cheerful Dawn;
A dancing Shape, an Image gay,
To haunt, to startle, and way-lay. 10

I saw her upon nearer view,
A Spirit, yet a Woman too!
Her household motions light and free,
And steps of virgin-liberty;
A countenance in which did meet 15
Sweet records, promises as sweet;
A Creature not too bright or good
For human nature's daily food;
For transient sorrows, simple wiles,
Praise, blame, love, kisses, tears, and smiles. 20

And now I see with eye serene
The very pulse of the machine;[1]
A Being breathing thoughtful breath,
A Traveller between life and death;
The reason firm, the temperate will, 25
Endurance, foresight, strength, and skill;
A perfect Woman, nobly planned,
To warn, to comfort, and command;
And yet a Spirit still, and bright
With something of angelic light. 30

---

1 I.e., the whole intricate organism.

I Wandered Lonely as a Cloud

Written in 1804.

I wandered lonely as a cloud
That floats on high o'er vales and hills,
When all at once I saw a crowd,
A host, of golden daffodils;
Beside the lake, beneath the trees,   5
Fluttering and dancing in the breeze.

Continuous as the stars that shine
And twinkle on the milky way,
They stretched in never-ending line
Along the margin of a bay: 10
Ten thousand saw I at a glance,
Tossing their heads in sprightly dance.

The waves beside them danced; but they
Out-did the sparkling waves in glee:
A poet could not but be gay,   15
In such a jocund company:
I gazed—and gazed—but little thought
What wealth the show to me had brought:

For oft, when on my couch I lie
In vacant or in pensive mood,   20
They flash upon that inward eye
Which is the bliss of solitude;
And then my heart with pleasure fills,
And dances with the daffodils.

The Small Celandine

Written in 1804.

There is a Flower, the lesser Celandine,
That shrinks, like many more, from cold and
   rain;
And, the first moment that the sun may shine,
Bright as the sun himself, 'tis out again!

When hailstones have been falling, swarm on   5
   swarm,
Or blasts the green field and the trees distrest,
Oft have I seen it muffled up from harm,
In close self-shelter, like a Thing at rest.

But lately, one rough day, this Flower I passed
And recognised it, though an altered form,   10
Now standing forth an offering to the blast,
And buffeted at will by rain and storm.

I stopped, and said with inly-muttered voice,
"It doth not love the shower, nor seek the cold:
This neither is its courage nor its choice,   15
But its necessity in being old.

"The sunshine may not cheer it, nor the dew;
It cannot help itself in its decay;
Stiff in its members, withered, changed of hue."
And, in my spleen, I smiled that it was grey.   20

To be a Prodigal's Favourite—then, worse truth,
A Miser's Pensioner—behold our lot!
O Man, that from thy fair and shining youth
Age might but take the things Youth needed not!

Ode

Intimations of Immortality from Recollections of Early Childhood

This poem was begun at Grasmere in 1802. "Two years at least," Wordsworth tells us, "passed between the writing of the four first stanzas and the remaining part." As a child, he explains, he was imbued with "a sense of the indomitableness of the Spirit within me. . . . I was often unable to think of external things as having external existence, and I communed with all that I saw as something not apart from, but inherent in, my own immaterial nature. Many times while going to school have I grasped at a wall or tree to recall myself from this abyss of idealism to the reality." That as they grow older the tendency of most men is to reverse their ideas and to become subjugated by material things, Wordsworth goes on to deplore. He does not, however, wish us to take literally his suggestion that the child's consciousness of the ideal may be evidence for a previous state of existence; it is, he says, "far too shadowy a notion to be recommended to faith, as more than an element in our instincts of immortality." But since the idea of preexistence "has entered into the popular creeds of many nations," he feels authorized "to make for my purpose the best use of it I could as a poet."

> *The Child is father of the Man;*
> *And I could wish my days to be*
> *Bound each to each by natural piety.*[1]

I

There was a time when meadow, grove, and
   stream,

---

[1] The conclusion of "My Heart Leaps Up" (see p. 68).

The earth, and every common sight,
     To me did seem
   Apparelled in celestial light,
The glory and the freshness of a dream. 5
It is not now as it hath been of yore;—
     Turn wheresoe'er I may,
        By night or day,
The things which I have seen I now can see no
   more.

II

     The Rainbow comes and goes, 10
     And lovely is the Rose,
     The Moon doth with delight
Look round her when the heavens are bare;
     Waters on a starry night
     Are beautiful and fair; 15
   The sunshine is a glorious birth;
   But yet I know, where'er I go,
That there hath past away a glory from the
   earth.

III

Now, while the birds thus sing a joyous song,
     And while the young lambs bound 20
        As to the tabor's² sound,
To me alone there came a thought of grief:
A timely utterance gave that thought relief,
     And I again am strong:
The cataracts blow their trumpets from the 25
   steep;
No more shall grief of mine the season wrong;
I hear the Echoes through the mountains throng,
The Winds come to me from the fields of sleep,
     And all the earth is gay;
        Land and sea 30
     Give themselves up to jollity,
     And with the heart of May
   Doth every Beast keep holiday;—
        Thou Child of Joy,
Shout round me, let me hear thy shouts, thou 35
   happy Shepherd-boy!

IV

Ye blessèd Creatures, I have heard the call
   Ye to each other make; I see
The heavens laugh with you in your jubilee;
   My heart is at your festival,
     My head hath its coronal, 40

The fulness of your bliss, I feel—I feel it all.
   Oh evil day! if I were sullen
     While Earth herself is adorning,
        This sweet May-morning,
     And the Children are culling 45
        On every side,
     In a thousand valleys far and wide,
     Fresh flowers; while the sun shines
        warm,
And the Babe leaps up on his Mother's arm:—
     I hear, I hear, with joy I hear! 50
        —But there's a Tree, of many, one,
A single Field which I have looked upon,
Both of them speak of something that is gone:
        The Pansy at my feet
        Doth the same tale repeat: 55
Whither is fled the visionary gleam?
Where is it now, the glory and the dream?

V

Our birth is but a sleep and a forgetting:
The Soul that rises with us, our life's Star,
     Hath had elsewhere its setting, 60
        And cometh from afar:
     Not in entire forgetfulness,
     And not in utter nakedness,
But trailing clouds of glory do we come
     From God, who is our home: 65
Heaven lies about us in our infancy!
Shades of the prison-house begin to close
     Upon the growing Boy,
        But He
Beholds the light, and whence it flows, 70
     He sees it in his joy;
The Youth, who daily farther from the east
     Must travel, still is Nature's Priest,
     And by the vision splendid
     Is on his way attended; 75
At length the Man perceives it die away,
And fade into the light of common day.

VI

Earth fills her lap with pleasures of her own;
Yearnings she hath in her own natural kind,
And, even with something of a Mother's mind, 80
     And no unworthy aim,
        The homely Nurse doth all she can
To make her Foster-child, her Inmate Man,
     Forget the glories he hath known,
And that imperial palace whence he came. 85

---

² Little drum's.

VII

Behold the Child among his new-born blisses,
A six years' Darling of a pigmy size!
See, where 'mid work of his own hand he lies,
Fretted by sallies of his mother's kisses,
With light upon him from his father's eyes!   90
See, at his feet, some little plan or chart,
Some fragment from his dream of human life,
Shaped by himself with newly-learnèd art;
    A wedding or a festival,
    A mourning or a funeral;   95
      And this hath now his heart,
    And unto this he frames his song:
      Then will he fit his tongue
To dialogues of business, love, or strife;
    But it will not be long   100
    Ere this be thrown aside,
    And with new joy and pride
The little Actor cons another part;
Filling from time to time his "humorous stage"[3]
With all the Persons, down to palsied Age,   105
That Life brings with her in her equipage;
    As if his whole vocation
    Were endless imitation.

VIII

Thou, whose exterior semblance doth belie
    Thy Soul's immensity;   110
Thou best Philosopher, who yet dost keep
Thy heritage, thou Eye among the blind,
That, deaf and silent, read'st the eternal deep,
Haunted for ever by the eternal mind,—
    Mighty Prophet! Seer blest!   115
    On whom those truths do rest,
Which we are toiling all our lives to find,
In darkness lost, the darkness of the grave;
Thou, over whom thy Immortality
Broods like the Day, a Master o'er a Slave,   120
A Presence which is not to be put by;
Thou little Child, yet glorious in the might
Of heaven-born freedom on thy being's height,
Why with such earnest pains dost thou provoke
The years to bring the inevitable yoke,   125
Thus blindly with thy blessedness at strife?
Full soon thy Soul shall have her earthly freight,
And custom lie upon thee with a weight,
Heavy as frost, and deep almost as life!

---

[3] I.e., all the world's a stage, filled with "persons" or characters of various "humors" or types.

IX

O joy! that in our embers   130
    Is something that doth live,
That nature yet remembers
What was so fugitive!
The thought of our past years in me doth breed
Perpetual benediction: not indeed   135
For that which is most worthy to be blest;
Delight and liberty, the simple creed
Of Childhood, whether busy or at rest,
With new-fledged hope still fluttering in his
    breast:—
    Not for these I raise   140
    The song of thanks and praise;
    But for those obstinate questionings
    Of sense and outward things,
    Fallings from us, vanishings;
    Blank misgivings of a Creature   145
Moving about in worlds not realised,
High instincts before which our mortal Nature
Did tremble like a guilty Thing surprised:
    But for those first affections,
    Those shadowy recollections,   150
    Which, be they what they may,
Are yet the fountain-light of all our day,
Are yet a master-light of all our seeing;
    Uphold us, cherish, and have power to make
Our noisy years seem moments in the being   155
Of the eternal Silence: truths that wake,
    To perish never:
Which neither listlessness, nor mad endeavour,
    Nor Man nor Boy,
Nor all that is at enmity with joy,   160
Can utterly abolish or destroy!
    Hence in a season of calm weather
    Though inland far we be,
Our Souls have sight of that immortal sea
    Which brought us hither,   165
    Can in a moment travel thither,
And see the Children sport upon the shore,
And hear the mighty waters rolling evermore.

X

Then sing, ye Birds, sing, sing a joyous song!
    And let the young Lambs bound   170
    As to the tabor's sound!
We in thought will join your throng,
    Ye that pipe and ye that play,
    Ye that through your hearts to-day
    Feel the gladness of the May!   175

What though the radiance which was once so
   bright
Be now for ever taken from my sight,
  Though nothing can bring back the hour
Of splendour in the grass, of glory in the flower;
     We will grieve not, rather find   180
     Strength in what remains behind;
     In the primal sympathy
     Which having been must ever be;
     In the soothing thoughts that spring
     Out of human suffering;   185
     In the faith that looks through death,
In years that bring the philosophic mind.

XI

And O, ye Fountains, Meadows, Hills, and
   Groves,
Forebode not any severing of our loves!
Yet in my heart of hearts I feel your might;   190
I only have relinquished one delight
To live beneath your more habitual sway.
I love the Brooks which down their channels fret,
Even more than when I tripped lightly as they;
The innocent brightness of a new-born Day   195
      Is lovely yet;
The Clouds that gather round the setting sun
Do take a sober colouring from an eye
That hath kept watch o'er man's mortality;
Another race hath been, and other palms are   200
   won.
Thanks to the human heart by which we live,
Thanks to its tenderness, its joys, and fears,
To me the meanest flower that blows can give
Thoughts that do often lie too deep for tears.

Ode to Duty

Written in 1804.

Stern Daughter of the Voice of God!
O Duty! if that name thou love
Who art a light to guide, a rod
To check the erring, and reprove;
Thou, who art victory and law   5
When empty terrors overawe;
From vain temptations dost set free;
And calm'st the weary strife of frail humanity!

There are who ask not if thine eye
Be on them; who, in love and truth,   10

Where no misgiving is, rely
Upon the genial sense of youth;
Glad Hearts! without reproach or blot;
Who do thy work, and know it not:
Oh! if through confidence misplaced   15
They fail, thy saving arms, dread Power! around
   them cast.

Serene will be our days and bright,
And happy will our nature be,
When love is an unerring light,
And joy its own security.   20
And they a blissful course may hold
Even now, who, not unwisely bold,
Live in the spirit of this creed;
Yet seek thy firm support, according to their
   need.

I, loving freedom, and untried;   25
No sport of every random gust,
Yet being to myself a guide,
Too blindly have reposed my trust:
And oft, when in my heart was heard
Thy timely mandate, I deferred   30
The task, in smoother walks to stray;
But thee I now would serve more strictly, if I
   may.

Through no disturbance of my soul,
Or strong compunction in me wrought,
I supplicate for thy control;   35
But in the quietness of thought:
Me this unchartered freedom tires;
I feel the weight of chance-desires:
My hopes no more must change their name,
I long for a repose that ever is the same.   40

Stern Lawgiver! yet thou dost wear
The Godhead's most benignant grace;
Nor know we anything so fair
As is the smile upon thy face:
Flowers laugh before thee on their beds   45
And fragrance in thy footing treads;
Thou dost preserve the stars from wrong;
And the most ancient heavens, through Thee,
   are fresh and strong.

To humbler functions, awful Power!   50
I call thee: I myself commend
Unto thy guidance from this hour;
Oh, let my weakness have an end!

Give unto me, made lowly wise,
The spirit of self-sacrifice;
The confidence of reason give;   55
And in the light of truth thy Bondman let me
    live!

The Solitary Reaper

Wordsworth traveled in Scotland in 1803; but this
poem, composed in 1805, "was suggested by a beautiful sentence in a MS *Tour in Scotland* written by a
friend," Thomas Wilkinson: "Passed a female who
was reaping alone; she sung in Erse as she bended
over her sickle; the sweetest human voice I ever
heard: her strains were tenderly melancholy, and felt
delicious long after they were heard no more."

Behold her, single in the field,
Yon solitary Highland Lass!
Reaping and singing by herself;
Stop here, or gently pass!
Alone she cuts and binds the grain,   5
And sings a melancholy strain;
O listen! for the Vale profound
Is overflowing with the sound.

No Nightingale did ever chaunt
More welcome notes to weary bands   10
Of travellers in some shady haunt,
Among Arabian sands:
A voice so thrilling ne'er was heard
In spring-time from the Cuckoo-bird,
Breaking the silence of the seas   15
Among the farthest Hebrides.

Will no one tell me what she sings?—[1]
Perhaps the plaintive numbers flow
For old, unhappy, far-off things,
And battles long ago: 20
Or is it some more humble lay,
Familiar matter of to-day?
Some natural sorrow, loss, or pain,
That has been, and may be again?

Whate'er the theme, the Maiden sang   25
As if her song could have no ending;
I saw her singing at her work,
And o'er the sickle bending;—
I listened, motionless and still;
And, as I mounted up the hill,   30
The music in my heart I bore,
Long after it was heard no more.

---

[1] Her song is in Erse i.e., Gaelic.

Stepping Westward

This poem, inspired by an incident during Words-
worth's visit to Scotland in 1803, was composed in
1805. Wordsworth in a note describes how he and
Dorothy, "walking by the side of Loch Ketterine, one
fine evening after sunset, . . . met, in one of the
loneliest parts of that solitary region, two well-dressed
Women, one of whom said to us, by way of greeting,
'What, you are stepping westward?' "

"*What, you are stepping westward?*"—"*Yea.*"
—'T would be a *wildish* destiny,
If we, who thus together roam
In a strange Land, and far from home,
Were in this place the guests of Chance: 5
Yet who would stop, or fear to advance,
Though home or shelter he had none,
With such a sky to lead him on?

The dewy ground was dark and cold;
Behind, all gloomy to behold;   10
And stepping westward seemed to be
A kind of *heavenly* destiny:
I liked the greeting; 't was a sound
Of something without place or bound;
And seemed to give me spiritual right   15
To travel through that region bright.

The voice was soft, and she who spake
Was walking by her native lake:
The salutation had to me
The very sound of courtesy: 20
Its power was felt; and while my eye
Was fixed upon the glowing Sky,
The echo of the voice enwrought
A human sweetness with the thought
Of travelling through the world that lay   25
Before me in my endless way.

Elegiac Stanzas

Suggested by a Picture of Peele Castle, in a Storm, Painted by Sir George Beaumont

Beaumont (1753–1827), a landscape painter and art
collector, was a friend of Wordsworth and of other
poets. The castle is on Piel Island near Walney
Island, off the coast of northern Lancashire, where
Wordsworth seems to have spent part of a college
vacation. This poem was written in 1805.

I was thy neighbour once, thou rugged Pile!
Four summer weeks I dwelt in sight of thee:

I saw thee every day; and all the while
Thy Form was sleeping on a glassy sea.

So pure the sky, so quiet was the air!
So like, so very like, was day to day!
Whene'er I looked, thy Image still was there;
It trembled, but it never passed away.

How perfect was the calm! it seemed no sleep;
No mood, which season takes away, or brings: 10
I could have fancied that the mighty Deep
Was even the gentlest of all gentle Things.

Ah! THEN, if mine had been the Painter's hand,
To express what then I saw; and add the gleam,
The light that never was, on sea or land, 15
The consecration, and the Poet's dream;

I would have planted thee, thou hoary Pile,
Amid a world how different from this!
Beside a sea that could not cease to smile;
On tranquil land, beneath a sky of bliss. 20

Thou shouldst have seemed a treasure-house
divine
Of peaceful years; a chronicle of heaven;—
Of all the sunbeams that did ever shine
The very sweetest had to thee been given.

A Picture had it been of lasting ease, 25
Elysian[1] quiet, without toil or strife;
No motion but the moving tide, a breeze,
Or merely silent Nature's breathing life.

Such, in the fond illusion of my heart,
Such Picture would I at that time have made: 30
And seen the soul of truth in every part,
A steadfast peace that might not be betrayed.

So once it would have been,—'tis so no more;
I have submitted to a new control:
A power is gone, which nothing can restore; 35
A deep distress[2] hath humanised my Soul.

Not for a moment could I now behold
A smiling sea, and be what I have been:
The feeling of my loss will ne'er be old;
This, which I know, I speak with mind serene. 40

---

[1] Like Elysium, in classical mythology the abode of the happy dead.
[2] Wordsworth's brother John had been lost at sea early in the year in which this poem was composed (1805).

Then, Beaumont, Friend! who would have been
the Friend,
If he had lived, of Him whom I deplore,
This work of thine I blame not, but commend; 5
This sea in anger, and that dismal shore.

O 'tis a passionate Work!—yet wise and well, 45
Well chosen is the spirit that is here;
That Hulk which labours in the deadly swell,
This rueful sky, this pageantry of fear!

And this huge Castle, standing here sublime,
I love to see the look with which it braves, 50
Cased in the unfeeling armour of old time,
The lightning, the fierce wind, and trampling
waves.

Farewell, farewell the heart that lives alone,
Housed in a dream, at distance from the Kind!
Such happiness, wherever it be known, 55
Is to be pitied; for 'tis surely blind.

But welcome fortitude, and patient cheer,
And frequent sights of what is to be borne!
Such sights, or worse, as are before me here.—
Not without hope we suffer and we mourn. 60

Sonnets

Upon Westminster Bridge

This sonnet and the next five are connected with Wordsworth's trip to France in August 1802. Accompanied by his sister Dorothy, he spent four weeks at Calais in order to see Annette Vallon and Caroline, now nine years old. This beautiful poem was written on the roof of the coach by which, over Westminster Bridge, he left London in the early morning of July 31.

Earth has not anything to show more fair:
Dull would he be of soul who could pass by
A sight so touching in its majesty:
This City now doth, like a garment, wear
The beauty of the morning; silent, bare, 5
Ships, towers, domes, theatres, and temples lie
Open unto the fields, and to the sky;
All bright and glittering in the smokeless air.
Never did sun more beautifully steep
In his first splendour, valley, rock, or hill; 10
Ne'er saw I, never felt, a calm so deep!
The river glideth at his own sweet will:

Dear God! the very houses seem asleep;
And all that mighty heart is lying still!

It Is a Beauteous Evening

This sonnet was also written at Calais in August 1802.
The child is Wordsworth's French daughter, Caroline.

It is a beauteous evening, calm and free,
The holy time is quiet as a Nun
Breathless with adoration; the broad sun
Is sinking down in its tranquillity;
The gentleness of heaven broods o'er the Sea: 5
Listen! the mighty Being is awake,
And doth with his eternal motion make
A sound like thunder—everlastingly.
Dear Child! dear Girl! that walkest with me here,
If thou appear untouched by solemn thought,   10
Thy nature is not therefore less divine:
Thou liest in Abraham's bosom[1] all the year;
And worshipp'st at the Temple's inner shrine,
God being with thee when we know it not.

To Toussaint L'Ouverture

This great sonnet protests against French imperialism
and tyranny. Toussaint L'Ouverture (1743–1803—his
real name was Pierre Dominique) was the heroic
black general who liberated the oppressed people of
Haiti. He resisted Napoleon's attempt to reestablish
slavery there but was finally defeated. Shortly before
this poem was written, he arrived as a prisoner in
France, where he died less than a year later.

Toussaint, the most unhappy man of men!
Whether the whistling Rustic tend his plough
Within thy hearing, or thy head be now
Pillowed in some deep dungeon's earless den;—
O miserable Chieftain! where and when   5
Wilt thou find patience! Yet die not; do thou
Wear rather in thy bonds a cheerful brow:
Though fallen thyself, never to rise again,
Live, and take comfort. Thou hast left behind
Powers that will work for thee; air, earth, and   10
    skies;
There's not a breathing of the common wind
That will forget thee; thou hast great allies;
Thy friends are exultations, agonies,
And love, and man's unconquerable mind.

1 I.e., in God's presence, See Luke 16:22.

Near Dover

This sonnet and the next two were composed soon
after Wordsworth returned to England in the autumn
of 1802. All were inspired by his realization that
France was again a menace to Europe and by his
hope that England would guard her heritage of
freedom.

Inland, within a hollow vale, I stood;
And saw, while sea was calm and air was clear,
The coast of France—the coast of France how
    near!
Drawn almost into frightful neighbourhood.
I shrunk; for verily the barrier flood   5
Was like a lake, or river bright and fair,
A span of waters; yet what power is there!
What mightiness for evil and for good!
Even so doth God protect us if we be
Virtuous and wise. Winds blow, and waters roll,   10
Strength to the brave, and Power, and Deity;
Yet in themselves are nothing! One decree
Spake laws to *them,* and said that by the soul
Only, the Nations shall be great and free.

London, 1802

Milton! thou shouldst be living at this hour:
England hath need of thee: she is a fen
Of stagnant waters: altar, sword, and pen,
Fireside, the heroic wealth of hall and bower,
Have forfeited their ancient English dower   5
Of inward happiness. We are selfish men;
Oh! raise us up, return to us again;
And give us manners, virtue, freedom, power.
Thy soul was like a Star, and dwelt apart;
Thou hadst a voice whose sound was like the sea: 10
Pure as the naked heavens, majestic, free,
So didst thou travel on life's common way,
In cheerful godliness; and yet thy heart
The lowliest duties on herself did lay.

It Is Not to Be Thought Of

It is not to be thought of that the Flood
Of British freedom, which, to the open sea
Of the world's praise, from dark antiquity
Hath flowed, "with pomp of waters, unwith-
    stood,"[1]

1 From Samuel Daniel's *The Civil Wars*, Book II, Stanza 7.

Roused though it be full often to a mood
Which spurns the check of salutary bands,[2]
That this most famous Stream in bogs and sands
Should perish; and to evil and to good
Be lost for ever. In our halls is hung
Armoury of the invincible Knights of old:
We must be free or die, who speak the tongue
That Shakespeare spake; the faith and morals
   hold
Which Milton held.—In every thing we are
   sprung
Of Earth's first blood, have titles manifold.

The World Is Too Much with Us

This sonnet dates from 1806.

The world is too much with us; late and soon,
Getting and spending, we lay waste our powers:
Little we see in Nature that is ours;
We have given our hearts away, a sordid boon!
This Sea that bares her bosom to the moon;
The winds that will be howling at all hours,
And are up-gathered now like sleeping flowers;
For this, for everything, we are out of tune;
It moves us not.—Great God! I'd rather be
A Pagan suckled in a creed outworn;
So might I, standing on this pleasant lea,
Have glimpses that would make me less forlorn;
Have sight of Proteus rising from the sea;
Or hear old Triton[1] blow his wreathèd horn.

Composed by the Side of Grasmere Lake

Written in 1807.

Clouds, lingering yet, extend in solid bars
Through the grey west; and lo! these waters,
   steeled
By breezeless air to smoothest polish, yield
A vivid repetition of the stars;
Jove, Venus, and the ruddy crest of Mars
Amid his fellows beauteously revealed

2 Bonds, restraints.

1 Sea gods of classical mythology. Proteus had the faculty
of assuming any shape. Triton, son of Neptune, raised
and calmed the waves by blasts on his conch-shell trumpet. *Wreathèd* = spiral.

5 At happy distance from earth's groaning field,
Where ruthless mortals wage incessant wars.
Is it a mirror?—or the nether Sphere
Opening to vie the abyss in which she feeds
Her own calm fires?—But list! a voice is near;
Great Pan himself low-whispering through the
   reeds,
"Be thankful, thou; for, if unholy deeds
Ravage the world, tranquillity is here!"

Surprised by Joy—
Impatient as the Wind

Surprised by joy—impatient as the Wind
I turned to share the transport—Oh! with whom
But Thee, deep buried in the silent tomb,[1]
That spot which no vicissitude can find?
Love, faithful love, recalled thee to my mind—
But how could I forget thee? Through what
   power,
Even for the least division of an hour,
Have I been so beguiled as to be blind
To my most grievous loss!—That thought's re-
   turn
Was the worst pang that sorrow ever bore,
Save one, one only, when I stood forlorn,
Knowing my heart's best treasure was no more;
That neither present time, or years unborn
Could to my sight that heavenly face restore.

The River Duddon, After-Thought

This poem was the last of a series, *The River Duddon*, published in 1820.

I thought of Thee, my partner and my guide,
As being past away.—Vain sympathies!
For, backward, Duddon! as I cast my eyes,
I see what was, and is, and will abide;
Still glides the Stream, and shall for ever glide;
The Form remains, the Function never dies;
While we, the brave, the mighty, and the wise,
We Men, who in our morn of youth defied
The elements, must vanish;—be it so!

1 Wordsworth's daughter Catharine died in 1812. The
poem was written sometime before 1815.

Enough, if something from our hands have power   10
To live, and act, and serve the future hour;
And if, as toward the silent tomb we go,
Through love, through hope, and faith's tran-
   scendent dower,
We feel that we are greater than we know.

Mutability

Written in 1821, except for the last line, which
Wordsworth wrote at sixteen.

From low to high doth dissolution climb,
And sink from high to low, along a scale
Of awful notes, whose concord shall not fail;
A musical but melancholy chime,
Which they can hear who meddle not with crime,   5
Nor avarice, nor over-anxious care.
Truth fails not; but her outward forms that bear
The longest date do melt like frosty rime,
That in the morning whitened hill and plain
And is no more; drop like the tower sublime   10
Of yesterday, which royally did wear
His crown of weeds, but could not even sustain
Some casual shout that broke the silent air,
Or the unimaginable touch of Time.

To ——, in Her Seventieth Year

Written in 1824.

Such age how beautiful! O Lady bright,
Whose mortal lineaments seem all refined
By favouring Nature and a saintly Mind
To something purer and more exquisite
Than flesh and blood; whene'er thou meet'st my   5
   sight,
When I behold thy blanched unwithered cheek,
Thy temples fringed with locks of gleaming white,
And head that droops because the soul is meek,
Thee with the welcome Snowdrop I compare;
That child of winter, prompting thoughts that   10
   climb
From desolation toward the genial prime;
Or with the Moon conquering earth's misty air,
And filling more and more with crystal light
As pensive Evening deepens into night.

from The Excursion, Book First

This excerpt is taken from the long poem Wordsworth published in 1814. *The Excursion* was to
have been one part of three of the "moral and
philosophical" poem *The Recluse* on "Nature, Man,
and Society," which for many years Wordsworth and
Coleridge each thought of as the chief endeavor in
his poetic career. *The Recluse* was never finished.
All we have are *The Excursion*; a beautiful fragment,
"Home at Grasmere," which would have belonged to
the first part; and *The Prelude,* Wordsworth's account of the growth of his own mind, which was
thought of as a kind of preface to the whole.

    The story that takes up most of Book One has
been variously called "The Ruined Cottage," "The
Pedlar," and "The Story of Margaret." The present
version, which is from the 1814 edition of *The
Excursion,* is the last in a series of drafts that Wordsworth began as early as 1795.

    The Wanderer, who tells the poet the story of
Margaret, is, Wordsworth says, an idea of what his
own character "might have become in his circumstances."

    One can profitably compare this poem with
Wordsworth's own "Michael," and both compare
and contrast it with Goldsmith's "The Deserted Village" (see Volume I).

So was He framed; and such his course of life
Who now, with no appendage but a staff,   435
The prized memorial of relinquished toils,
Upon that cottage-bench reposed his limbs,
Screened from the sun. Supine the Wanderer lay,
His eyes as if in drowsiness half shut,
The shadows of the breezy elms above   440
Dappling his face. He had not heard the sound
Of my approaching steps, and in the shade
Unnoticed did I stand some minutes' space.
At length I hailed him, seeing that his hat
Was moist with water-drops, as if the brim   445
Had newly scooped a running stream. He rose,
And ere our lively greeting into peace
Had settled, " 'Tis," said I, "a burning day:
My lips are parched with thirst, but you, it seems,
Have somewhere found relief." He, at the word,   450
Pointing towards a sweet-briar, bade me climb
The fence where that aspiring shrub looked out
Upon the public way. It was a plot
Of garden ground run wild, its matted weeds
Marked with the steps of those, whom, as they   455
   passed,
The gooseberry trees that shot in long lank slips,
Or currants, hanging from their leafless stems,
In scanty strings, had tempted to o'erleap

The broken wall. I looked around, and there,
Where two tall hedge-rows of thick alder boughs   460
Joined in a cold damp nook, espied a well
Shrouded with willow-flowers and plumy fern.
My thirst I slaked, and, from the cheerless spot
Withdrawing, straightway to the shade returned
Where sate the old Man on the cottage-bench;   465
And, while, beside him, with uncovered head,
I yet was standing, freely to respire,
And cool my temples in the fanning air,
Thus did he speak. "I see around me here
Things which you cannot see: we die, my Friend,   470
Nor we alone, but that which each man loved
And prized in his peculiar nook of earth
Dies with him, or is changed; and very soon
Even of the good is no memorial left.
—The Poets, in their elegies and songs   475
Lamenting the departed, call the groves,
They call upon the hills and streams to mourn,
And senseless rocks; nor idly; for they speak,
In these their invocations, with a voice
Obedient to the strong creative power   480
Of human passion. Sympathies there are
More tranquil, yet perhaps of kindred birth,
That steal upon the meditative mind,
And grow with thought. Beside yon spring I
    stood,
And eyed its waters till we seemed to feel   485
One sadness, they and I. For them a bond
Of brotherhood is broken: time has been
When, every day, the touch of human hand
Dislodged the natural sleep that binds them up
In mortal stillness; and they ministered   490
To human comfort. Stooping down to drink,
Upon the slimy foot-stone I espied
The useless fragment of a wooden bowl,
Green with the moss of years, and subject only
To the soft handling of the elements: 495
There let it lie—how foolish are such thoughts!
Forgive them;—never—never did my steps
Approach this door but she who dwelt within
A daughter's welcome gave me, and I loved her
As my own child. Oh, Sir! the good die first,   500
And they whose hearts are dry as summer dust
Burn to the socket. Many a passenger
Hath blessed poor Margaret for her gentle looks,
When she upheld the cool refreshment drawn
From that forsaken spring; and no one came   505
But he was welcome; no one went away
But that it seemed she loved him. She is dead,
The light extinguished of her lonely hut,

The hut itself abandoned to decay,
And she forgotten in the quiet grave.   510

  "I speak," continued he, "of One whose stock
Of virtues bloomed beneath this lowly roof.
She was a Woman of a steady mind,
Tender and deep in her excess of love;
Not speaking much, pleased rather with the joy   515
Of her own thoughts: by some especial care
Her temper had been framed, as if to make
A Being, who by adding love to peace
Might live on earth a life of happiness.
Her wedded Partner lacked not on his side   520
The humble worth that satisfied her heart:
Frugal, affectionate, sober, and withal
Keenly industrious. She with pride would tell
That he was often seated at his loom,
In summer, ere the mower was abroad   525
Among the dewy grass,—in early spring,
Ere the last star had vanished.—They who passed
At evening, from behind the garden fence
Might hear his busy spade, which he would ply,
After his daily work, until the light   530
Had failed, and every leaf and flower were lost
In the dark hedges. So their days were spent
In peace and comfort; and a pretty boy
Was their best hope, next to the God in heaven.

  "Not twenty years ago, but you I think   535
Can scarcely bear it now in mind, there came
Two blighting seasons, when the fields were left
With half a harvest. It pleased Heaven to add
A worse affliction in the plague of war:
This happy Land was stricken to the heart!   540
A Wanderer then among the cottages,
I, with my freight of winter raiment, saw
The hardships of that season: many rich
Sank down, as in a dream, among the poor;
And of the poor did many cease to be,   545
And their place knew them not. Meanwhile,
    abridged
Of daily comforts, gladly reconciled
To numerous self-denials, Margaret
Went struggling on through those calamitous
    years
With cheerful hope, until the second autumn,   550
When her life's Helpmate on a sick-bed lay,
Smitten with perilous fever. In disease
He lingered long; and, when his strength re-
    turned,
He found the little he had stored, to meet

The hour of accident or crippling age,   555
Was all consumed. A second infant now
Was added to the troubles of a time
Laden, for them and all of their degree,
With care and sorrow: shoals of artisans
From ill-requited labour turned adrift   560
Sought daily bread from public charity,
They, and their wives and children—happier far
Could they have lived as do the little birds
That peck along the hedge-rows, or the kite
That makes her dwelling on the mountain rocks!   565

   "A sad reverse it was for him who long
Had filled with plenty, and possessed in peace,
This lonely Cottage. At the door he stood,
And whistled many a snatch of merry tunes
That had no mirth in them; or with his knife   570
Carved uncouth figures on the heads of sticks—
Then, not less idly, sought, through every nook
In house or garden, any casual work
Of use or ornament; and with a strange,
Amusing, yet uneasy, novelty,   575
He mingled, where he might, the various tasks
Of summer, autumn, winter, and of spring.
But this endured not; his good humour soon
Became a weight in which no pleasure was:
And poverty brought on a petted[1] mood   580
And a sore temper: day by day he drooped,
And he would leave his work—and to the town
Would turn without an errand his slack steps;
Or wander here and there among the fields.
One while he would speak lightly of his babes,   585
And with a cruel tongue: at other times
He tossed them with a false unnatural joy:
And 'twas a rueful thing to see the looks
Of the poor innocent children. 'Every smile,'
Said Margaret to me, here beneath these trees,   590
'Made my heart bleed.' "
                          At this the Wanderer paused;
And, looking up to those enormous elms,
He said, " 'Tis now the hour of deepest noon.
At this still season of repose and peace,
This hour when all things which are not at rest   595
Are cheerful; while this multitude of flies
With tuneful hum is filling all the air;
Why should a tear be on an old Man's cheek?
Why should we thus, with an untoward mind,
And in the weakness of humanity,   600
From natural wisdom turn our hearts away;

─────────────────

[1] Irritable.

To natural comfort shut our eyes and ears;
And, feeding on disquiet, thus disturb
The calm of nature with our restless thoughts?"

He spake with somewhat of a solemn tone: 605
But, when he ended, there was in his face
Such easy cheerfulness, a look so mild,
That for a little time it stole away
All recollection; and that simple tale
Passed from my mind like a forgotten sound.   610
A while on trivial things we held discourse,
To me soon tasteless. In my own despite,
I thought of that poor Woman as of one
Whom I had known and loved. He had rehearsed
Her homely tale with such familiar power,   615
With such an active countenance, an eye
So busy, that the things of which he spake
Seemed present; and, attention now relaxed,
A heart-felt chillness crept along my veins.
I rose; and, having left the breezy shade,   620
Stood drinking comfort from the warmer sun,
That had not cheered me long—ere, looking
      found,
Upon that tranquil Ruin, I returned,
And begged of the old Man that, for my sake,
He would resume his story.

                                      He replied,   625
"It were a wantonness, and would demand
Severe reproof, if we were men whose hearts
Could hold vain dalliance with the misery
Even of the dead; contented thence to draw
A momentary pleasure, never marked   630
By reason, barren of all future good.
But we have known that there is often found
In mournful thoughts, and always might be
      found
A power to virtue friendly; wer't not so,
I am a dreamer among men, indeed   635
An idle dreamer! 'Tis a common tale,
An ordinary sorrow of man's life,
A tale of silent suffering, hardly clothed
In bodily form.—But without further bidding
I will proceed.
                          While thus it fared with them,   640
To whom this cottage, till those hapless years,
Had been a blessèd home, it was my chance
To travel in a country far remote;
And when these lofty elms once more appeared
What pleasant expectations lured me on   645

O'er the flat Common!—With quick step I
    reached
The threshold, lifted with light hand the latch;
But, when I entered, Margaret looked at me
A little while; then turned her head away
Speechless,—and, sitting down upon a chair,   650
Wept bitterly. I wist not what to do,
Nor how to speak to her. Poor Wretch! at last
She rose from off her seat, and then,—O Sir!
I cannot *tell* how she pronounced my name:—
With fervent love, and with a face of grief   655
Unutterably helpless, and a look
That seemed to cling upon me, she enquired
If I had seen her husband. As she spake
A strange surprise and fear came to my heart,
Nor had I power to answer ere she told   660
That he had disappeared—not two months gone.
He left his house: two wretched days had past,
And on the third, as wistfully she raised
Her head from off her pillow, to look forth,
Like one in trouble, for returning light,   665
Within her chamber-casement she espied
A folded paper, lying as if placed
To meet her waking eyes. This tremblingly
She opened—found no writing, but beheld
Pieces of money carefully enclosed,   670
Silver and gold. 'I shuddered at the sight,'
Said Margaret, 'for I knew it was his hand
That must have placed it there; and ere that day
Was ended, that long anxious day, I learned,
From one who by my husband had been sent   675
With the sad news, that he had joined a troop
Of soldiers, going to a distant land.
—He left me thus—he could not gather heart
To take a farewell of me; for he feared
That I should follow with my babes, and sink   680
Beneath the misery of that wandering life.'

"This tale did Margaret tell with many tears:
And, when she ended, I had little power
To give her comfort, and was glad to take
Such words of hope from her own mouth as   685
    served
To cheer us both. But long we had not talked
Ere we built up a pile of better thoughts,
And with a brighter eye she looked around
As if she had been shedding tears of joy.
We parted.—'Twas the time of early spring;   690
I left her busy with her garden tools;
And well remember, o'er that fence she looked,
And, while I paced along the foot-way path,

Called out, and sent a blessing after me,
With tender cheerfulness, and with a voice   695
That seemed the very sound of happy thoughts.

"I roved o'er many a hill and many a dale,
With my accustomed load; in heat and cold,
Through many a wood and many an open ground,
In sunshine and in shade, in wet and fair,   700
Drooping or blithe of heart, as might befal;
My best companions now the driving winds,
And now the 'trotting brooks' and whispering
    trees,
And now the music of my own sad steps,
With many a short-lived thought that passed be-   705
    tween,
And disappeared.
        I journeyed back this way,
When, in the warmth of midsummer, the wheat
Was yellow; and the soft and bladed grass,
Springing afresh, had o'er the hay-field spread
Its tender verdure. At the door arrived,   710
I found that she was absent. In the shade,
Where now we sit, I waited her return.
Her cottage, then a cheerful object, wore
Its customary look,—only, it seemed,
The honeysuckle, crowding round the porch,   715
Hung down in heavier tufts; and that bright
    weed,
The yellow stone-crop, suffered to take root
Along the window's edge, profusely grew
Blinding the lower panes. I turned aside,
And strolled into her garden. It appeared   720
To lag behind the season, and had lost
Its pride of neatness. Daisy-flowers and thrift[2]
Had broken their trim border-lines, and straggled
O'er paths they used to deck: carnations, once
Prized for surpassing beauty, and no less   725
For the peculiar pains they had required,
Declined their languid heads, wanting support.
The cumbrous bind-weed, with its wreaths and
    bells,
Had twined about her two small rows of peas,
And dragged them to the earth.
                 Ere this an hour   730
Was wasted.—Back I turned my restless steps;
A stranger passed; and, guessing whom I sought,
He said that she was used to ramble far.—
The sun was sinking in the west; and now

---

2 A tufted wildflower.

I sate with sad impatience. From within   735
Her solitary infant cried aloud;
Then, like a blast that dies away self-stilled,
The voice was silent. From the bench I rose;
But neither could divert nor soothe my thoughts.
The spot, though fair, was very desolate—   740
The longer I remained, more desolate:
And, looking round me, now I first observed
The corner stones, on either side the porch,
With dull red stains discoloured, and stuck o'er
With tufts and hairs of wool, as if the sheep,   745
That fed upon the Common, thither came
Familiarly, and found a couching-place
Even at her threshold. Deeper shadows fell
From these tall elms; the cottage-clock struck
    eight;—
I turned, and saw her distant a few steps.   750
Her face was pale and thin—her figure, too,
Was changed. As she unlocked the door, she said,
'It grieves me you have waited here so long,
But, in good truth, I've wandered much of late;
And, sometimes—to my shame I speak—have need   755
Of my best prayers to bring me back again.'
While on the board she spread our evening meal,
She told me—interrupting not the work
Which gave employment to her listless hands—
That she had parted with her elder child;   760
To a kind master on a distant farm
Now happily apprenticed.—'I perceive
You look at me, and you have cause; to-day
I have been travelling far; and many days
About the fields I wander, knowing this   765
Only, that what I seek I cannot find;
And so I waste my time: for I am changed;
And to myself,' said she, 'have done much wrong
And to this helpless infant. I have slept
Weeping, and weeping have I waked; my tears   770
Have flowed as if my body were not such
As others are; and I could never die.
But I am now in mind and in my heart
More easy; and I hope,' said she, 'that God
Will give me patience to endure the things   775
Which I behold at home.'
                            It would have grieved
Your very soul to see her. Sir, I feel
The story linger in my heart; I fear
'Tis long and tedious; but my spirit clings
To that poor Woman:—so familiarly   780
Do I perceive her manner, and her look,
And presence; and so deeply do I feel
Her goodness, that, not seldom, in my walks

A momentary trance comes over me;
And to myself I seem to muse on One   785
By sorrow laid asleep; or borne away,
A human being destined to awake
To human life, or something very near
To human life, when he shall come again
For whom she suffered. Yes, it would have grieved   790
Your very soul to see her: evermore
Her eyelids drooped, her eyes downward were
    cast;
And, when she at her table gave me food,
She did not look at me. Her voice was low,
Her body was subdued. In every act   795
Pertaining to her house-affairs, appeared
The careless stillness of a thinking mind
Self-occupied; to which all outward things
Are like an idle matter. Still she sighed,
But yet no motion of the breast was seen,   800
No heaving of the heart. While by the fire
We sate together, sighs came on my ear,
I knew not how, and hardly whence they came.

    "Ere my departure, to her care I gave,
For her son's use, some tokens of regard,   805
Which with a look of welcome she received;
And I exhorted her to place her trust
In God's good love, and seek his help by prayer.
I took my staff, and, when I kissed her babe,
The tears stood in her eyes. I left her then   810
With the best hope and comfort I could give:
She thanked me for my wish;—but for my hope
It seemed she did not thank me.
                            I returned,
And took my rounds along this road again
When on its sunny bank the primrose flower   815
Peeped forth, to give an earnest of the Spring.
I found her sad and drooping: she had learned
No tidings of her husband; if he lived,
She knew not that he lived; if he were dead,
She knew not he was dead. She seemed the same   820
In person and appearance; but her house
Bespake a sleepy hand of negligence;
The floor was neither dry nor neat, the hearth
Was comfortless, and her small lot of books,
Which, in the cottage-window, heretofore   825
Had been piled up against the corner panes
In seemly order, now, with straggling leaves
Lay scattered here and there, open or shut,
As they had chanced to fall. Her infant Babe
Had from its mother caught the trick of grief,   830
And sighed among its playthings. I withdrew,

And once again entering the garden saw,
More plainly still, that poverty and grief
Were now come nearer to her: weeds defaced
The hardened soil, and knots of withered grass: 835
No ridges there appeared of clear black mold,
No winter greenness; of her herbs and flowers,
It seemed the better part were gnawed away
Or trampled into earth; a chain of straw,
Which had been twined about the slender stem   840
Of a young apple-tree, lay at its root;
The bark was nibbled round by truant sheep.
—Margaret stood near, her infant in her arms,
And, noting that my eye was on the tree,
She said, 'I fear it will be dead and gone   845
Ere Robert come again.' When to the House
We had returned together, she enquired
If I had any hope:—but for her babe
And for her little orphan boy, she said,
She had no wish to live, that she must die   850
Of sorrow. Yet I saw the idle loom
Still in its place; his Sunday garments hung
Upon the self-same nail; his very staff
Stood undisturbed behind the door.
                                    And when,
In bleak December, I retraced this way,   855
She told me that her little babe was dead,
And she was left alone. She now, released
From her maternal cares, had taken up
The employment common through these wilds,
       and gained,
By spinning hemp, a pittance for herself;   860
And for this end had hired a neighbour's boy
To give her needful help. That very time
Most willingly she put her work aside,
And walked with me along the miry road,
Heedless how far; and, in such piteous sort   865
That any heart had ached to hear her, begged
That, wheresoe'er I went, I still would ask
For him whom she had lost. We parted then—
Our final parting; for from that time forth
Did many seasons pass ere I returned   870
Into this tract again.
                    Nine tedious years;
From their first separation, nine long years,
She lingered in unquiet widowhood;
A Wife and Widow. Needs must it have been
A sore heart-wasting! I have heard, my Friend,   875
That in yon arbour oftentimes she sate
Alone, through half the vacant sabbath day;
And, if a dog passed by, she still would quit
The shade, and look abroad. On this old bench

For hours she sate; and evermore her eye   880
Was busy in the distance, shaping things
That made her heart beat quick. You see that
       path,
Now faint,—the grass has crept o'er its grey line;
There, to and fro, she paced through many a day
Of the warm summer, from a belt of hemp   885
That girt her waist, spinning the long-drawn
       thread
With backward steps. Yet ever as there passed
A man whose garments showed the soldier's red,
Or crippled mendicant in sailor's garb,
The little child who sate to turn the wheel   890
Ceased from his task; and she with faltering voice
Made many a fond enquiry; and when they,
Whose presence gave no comfort, were gone by,
Her heart was still more sad. And by yon gate,
That bars the traveller's road, she often stood,   895
And when a stranger horseman came, the latch
Would lift, and in his face look wistfully:
Most happy, if, from aught discovered there
Of tender feeling, she might dare repeat
The same sad question. Meanwhile her poor Hut   900
Sank to decay; for he was gone, whose hand,
At the first nipping of October frost,
Closed up each chink, and with fresh bands of
       straw
Chequered the green-grown thatch. And so she
       lived
Through the long winter, reckless and alone;   905
Until her house by frost, and thaw, and rain,
Was sapped; and while she slept, the nightly
       damps
Did chill her breast; and in the stormy day
Her tattered clothes were ruffled by the wind,
Even at the side of her own fire. Yet still   910
She loved this wretched spot, nor would for
       worlds
Have parted hence; and still that length of road,
And this rude bench, one torturing hope en-
       deared,
Fast rooted at her heart: and here, my Friend,—
In sickness she remained; and here she died;   915
Last human tenant of these ruined walls!"

   The old Man ceased: he saw that I was moved;
From that low bench, rising instinctively
I turned aside in weakness, nor had power
To thank him for the tale which he had told.   920
I stood, and leaning o'er the garden wall
Reviewed that Woman's sufferings; and it seemed

To comfort me while with a brother's love
I blessed her in the impotence of grief.
Then towards the cottage I returned; and traced   925
Fondly, though with an interest more mild,
That secret spirit of humanity
Which, 'mid the calm oblivious tendencies
Of nature, 'mid her plants, and weeds, and flowers,
And silent overgrowings, still survived.   930
The old Man, noting this, resumed, and said,
"My Friend! enough to sorrow you have given,
The purposes of wisdom ask no more:
Nor more would she have craved as due to One
Who, in her worst distress, had ofttimes felt   935
The unbounded might of prayer; and learned,
     with soul
Fixed on the Cross, that consolation springs,
From sources deeper far than deepest pain,
For the meek Sufferer. Why then should we read
The forms of things with an unworthy eye?   940
She sleeps in the calm earth, and peace is here.
I well remember that those very plumes,
Those weeds, and the high spear-grass on that
     wall,
By mist and silent rain-drops silvered o'er,
As once I passed, into my heart conveyed   945
So still an image of tranquillity,
So calm and still, and looked so beautiful
Amid the uneasy thoughts which filled my mind,
That what we feel of sorrow and despair
From ruin and from change, and all the grief   950
That passing shows of Being leave behind,
Appeared an idle dream, that could maintain,
Nowhere, dominion o'er the enlightened spirit
Whose meditative sympathies repose
Upon the breast of Faith. I turned away,   955
And walked along my road in happiness."

He ceased. Ere long the sun declining shot
A slant and mellow radiance, which began
To fall upon us, while, beneath the trees,
We sate on that low bench: and now we felt,   960
Admonished thus, the sweet hour coming on.
A linnet warbled from those lofty elms,
A thrush sang loud, and other melodies,
At distance heard, peopled the milder air.
The old Man rose, and, with a sprightly mien   965
Of hopeful preparation, grasped his staff;
Together casting then a farewell look
Upon those silent walls, we left the shade;
And, ere the stars were visible, had reached
A village-inn,—our evening resting-place.   970

To a Skylark

Ethereal minstrel! pilgrim of the sky!
Dost thou despise the earth where cares abound?
Or, while the wings aspire, are heart and eye
Both with thy nest upon the dewy ground?
Thy nest which thou canst drop into at will,   5
Those quivering wings composed, that music still!

Leave to the nightingale her shady wood;
A privacy of glorious light is thine;
Whence thou dost pour upon the world a flood
Of harmony, with instinct more divine;   10
Type of the wise who soar, but never roam;
True to the kindred points of Heaven and Home!

Extempore[1] Effusion upon the Death of James Hogg[2]

When first, descending from the moorlands,
I saw the Stream of Yarrow glide
Along a bare and open valley,
The Ettrick Shepherd was my guide.

When last along its banks I wandered,   5
Through groves that had begun to shed
Their golden leaves upon the pathways,
My steps the Border-minstrel[3] led.

The mightly Minstrel breathes no longer,
'Mid mouldering ruins low he lies;   10
And death upon the braes of Yarrow,
Has closed the Shepherd-poet's eyes:

Nor has the rolling year twice measured,
From sign to sign, its stedfast course,
Since every mortal power of Coleridge   15
Was frozen at its marvellous source;[4]

The rapt One, of the godlike forehead,
The heaven-eyed creature sleeps in earth:
And Lamb, the frolic and the gentle,
Has vanished from his lonely hearth.[5]   20

---

1 "Extempore" because Wordsworth wrote the poem in a half hour.
2 James Hogg, "the Ettrick Shepherd," a Scottish poet and prose writer, born in 1770, died in November 1835. The poem was written a few days later.
3 Sir Walter Scott, who died in 1832.
4 Coleridge died in 1834.
5 Charles Lamb, who died in 1834.

Like clouds that rake the mountain-summits,
Or waves that own no curbing hand,
How fast has brother followed brother,
From sunshine to the sunless land!

Yet I, whose lids from infant slumber   25
Were earlier raised, remain to hear
A timid voice, that asks in whispers,
"Who next will drop and disappear?"

Our haughty life is crowned with darkness,
Like London with its own black wreath,   30
On which with thee, O Crabbe! forth-looking
I gazed from Hampstead's breezy heath.[6]

As if but yesterday departed,
Thou too art gone before; but why,
O'er ripe fruit, seasonally gathered,   35
Should frail survivors heave a sigh?

Mourn rather for that holy Spirit,
Sweet as the spring, as ocean deep;
For Her who, ere her summer faded,
Has sunk into a breathless sleep.[7]   40

No more of old romantic sorrows,
For slaughtered Youth or love-lorn Maid!
With sharper grief is Yarrow smitten,
And Ettrick mourns with her their Poet dead.

from The Prelude
or
Growth of a Poet's Mind
An Autobiographical Poem

Wordsworth's preface to *The Excursion* (1814) states:
"Several years ago, when the Author retired to his
native mountains, with the hope of being able to
construct a literary Work that might live, it was a
reasonable thing that he should take a review of his
own mind, and examine how far Nature and Education had qualified him for such employment. As subsidiary to this preparation, he undertook to record, in
verse, the origin and progress of his own powers, as
far as he was acquainted with them. . . . The result
. . . was a determination to compose a philosophical
poem, containing views of Man, Nature, and Society;
and to be entitled 'The Recluse'; as having for its
principal subject the sensations and opinions of a

poet living in retirement. The preparatory poem [*The
Prelude*] is biographical, and conducts the history of
the Author's mind to the point when he was em-
boldened to hope that his faculties were sufficiently
matured for entering upon the arduous labour which
he had proposed to himself. . . ." *The Recluse* was
never completed; *The Excursion,* a long and unsuccessful poem in nine books, was intended as the
second part of it.

As he states in a letter to a friend, Wordsworth's
motive in writing about himself a poem of such
length as *The Prelude* was "not self-conceit . . . but
real humility; I began the work because I was unprepared to treat any more arduous subject, and
diffident of my own powers. Here, at least, I hoped
that . . . I should be sure of succeeding, as I had
nothing to do but describe what I had felt and
thought; therefore could not easily be bewildered."
Begun in 1798, *The Prelude* was all written by 1805
but not published till 1850, after Wordsworth's death.
Meanwhile, it had undergone many revisions. The
text of the following extracts is from the final version.
The great scholarly text by E. de Selincourt (1926),
comparing the differing versions, was revised by Helen
Darbishire (second ed., 1959).

from Book First

INTRODUCTION—CHILDHOOD AND SCHOOL-TIME

Oh there is blessing in this gentle breeze,
A visitant that while it fans my cheek
Doth seem half-conscious of the joy it brings
From the green fields, and from yon azure sky.
Whate'er its mission, the soft breeze can come   5
To none more grateful than to me; escaped
From the vast city, where I long had pined
A discontented sojourner: now free,
Free as a bird to settle where I will.
What dwelling shall receive me? in what vale   10
Shall be my harbour? underneath what grove
Shall I take up my home? and what clear stream
Shall with its murmur lull me into rest?
The earth is all before me.[1] With a heart
Joyous, nor scared at its own liberty,   15
I look about; and should the chosen guide
Be nothing better than a wandering cloud,
I cannot miss my way. I breathe again!
Trances of thought and mountings of the mind
Come fast upon me: it is shaken off,   20
That burthen of my own unnatural self,
The heavy weight of many a weary day
Not mine, and such as were not made for me.
Long months of peace (if such bold word accord

---

[6] The poet George Crabbe, who died in 1832.
[7] Felicia Hemans, a poet, who died in 1835.

[1] Cf. Milton, *Paradise Lost,* XII, 645-49.

With any promises of human life),   25
Long months of ease and undisturbed delight
Are mine in prospect; whither shall I turn,
By road or pathway, or through trackless field,
Up hill or down, or shall some floating thing
Upon the river point me out my course?   30

. . .

Sometimes it suits me better to invent
A tale from my own heart, more near akin
To my own passions and habitual thoughts;[2]
Some variegated story, in the main
Lofty, but the unsubstantial structure melts   225
Before the very sun that brightens it,
Mist into air dissolving! Then a wish,
My last and favourite aspiration, mounts
With yearning toward some philosophic song
Of Truth that cherishes our daily life;   230
With meditations passionate from deep
Recesses in man's heart, immortal verse
Thoughtfully fitted to the Orphean[3] lyre;
But from this awful burthen I full soon
Take refuge and beguile myself with trust   235
That mellower years will bring a riper mind
And clearer insight. Thus my days are passed
In contradiction; with no skill to part
Vague longing, haply[4] bred by want of power,
From paramount impulse not to be withstood,   240
A timorous capacity from prudence,
From circumspection, infinite delay.
Humility and modest awe themselves
Betray me, serving often for a cloak
To a more subtle selfishness; that now   245
Locks every function up in blank reserve,
Now dupes me, trusting to an anxious eye
That with intrusive restlessness beats off
Simplicity and self-presented truth.
Ah! better far than this, to stray about   250
Voluptuously through fields and rural walks,
And ask no record of the hours, resigned
To vacant musing, unreproved neglect
Of all things, and deliberate holiday.
Far better never to have heard the name   255
Of zeal and just ambition, than to live
Baffled and plagued by a mind that every hour
Turns recreant to her task; takes heart again,
Then feels immediately some hollow thought

Hang like an interdict upon her hopes.   260
This is my lot; for either still I find
Some imperfection in the chosen theme,
Or see of absolute accomplishment
Much wanting, so much wanting, in myself,
That I recoil and droop, and seek repose   265
In listlessness from vain perplexity,
Unprofitably travelling toward the grave,
Like a false steward[5] who hath much received
And renders nothing back.

                    Was it for this
That one, the fairest of all rivers, loved   270
To blend his murmurs with my nurse's song,
And, from his alder shades and rocky falls,
And from his fords and shallows, sent a voice
That flowed along my dreams? For this, didst
    thou,
O Derwent! winding among grassy holms[6]   275
Where I was looking on, a babe in arms,
Make ceaseless music that composed my thoughts
To more than infant softness, giving me
Amid the fretful dwellings of mankind
A foretaste, a dim earnest, of the calm   280
That Nature breathes among the hills and groves.
    When he had left the mountains and received
On his smooth breast the shadow of those towers[7]
That yet survive, a shattered monument
Of feudal sway, the bright blue river passed   285
Along the margin of our terrace walk;
A tempting playmate whom we dearly loved.
Oh, many a time have I, a five years' child,
In a small mill-race severed from his stream,
Made one long bathing of a summer's day;   290
Basked in the sun, and plunged and basked again
Alternate, all a summer's day, or scoured
The sandy fields, leaping through flowery groves
Of yellow ragwort; or when rock and hill,
The woods, and distant Skiddaw's lofty height,[8]   295
Were bronzed with deepest radiance, stood alone
Beneath the sky, as if I had been born
On Indian plains, and from my mother's hut
Had run abroad in wantonness, to sport,
A naked savage, in the thunder shower.   300

Fair seed-time had my soul, and I grew up

---

2 Wordsworth has been reviewing the various subjects he had thought of writing about.
3 Exalted. The phrase is from Milton, *Paradise Lost*, III, 17. In Greek mythology the musician Orpheus, son of Apollo, had extraordinary powers.   4 Perhaps.
5 See the parable of the talents, Matthew 25:14–30.
6 Bottoms, low flatlands.—Wordsworth was born at Cockermouth, Cumberland, where the Cocker flows into the Derwent.
7 Of Cockermouth Castle.
8 The fourth highest (3,054 feet) of the peaks in the Lake District.

Fostered alike by beauty and by fear:
Much favoured in my birthplace, and no less
In that belovèd Vale[9] to which erelong
We were transplanted—there were we let loose   305
For sports of wider range. Ere I had told
Ten birth-days, when among the mountain-slopes
Frost, and the breath of frosty wind, had snapped
The last autumnal crocus, 'twas my joy
With store of springes[10] o'er my shoulder hung   310
To range the open heights where woodcocks run
Among the smooth green turf. Through half the
        night,
Scudding away from snare to snare, I plied
That anxious visitation;—moon and stars
Were shining o'er my head. I was alone,   315
And seemed to be a trouble to the peace
That dwelt among them. Sometimes it befell
In these night wanderings, that a strong desire
O'erpowered my better reason, and the bird
Which was the captive of another's toil   320
Became my prey; and when the deed was done
I heard among the solitary hills
Low breathings coming after me, and sounds
Of undistinguishable motion, steps
Almost as silent as the turf they trod.   325

    Nor less when spring had warmed the cul-
        tured[11] Vale
Moved we as plunderers where the mother-bird
Had in high places built her lodge; though mean
Our object and inglorious, yet the end
Was not ignoble. Oh! when I have hung   330
Above the raven's nest, by knots of grass
And half-inch fissures in the slippery rock
But ill sustained, and almost (so it seemed)
Suspended by the blast that blew amain,
Shouldering the naked crag, oh, at that time   335
While on the perilous ridge I hung alone,
With what strange utterance did the loud dry
        wind
Blow through my ear! the sky seemed not a sky
Of earth—and with what motion moved the
        clouds!

    Dust as we are, the immortal spirit grows   340
Like harmony in music; there is a dark
Inscrutable workmanship that reconciles

Discordant elements, makes them cling together
In one society. How strange that all
The terrors, pains, and early miseries,   345
Regrets, vexations, lassitudes interfused
Within my mind, should e'er have borne a part,
And that a needful part, in making up
The calm existence that is mine when I
Am worthy of myself! Praise to the end!   350
Thanks to the means which Nature deigned to
        employ;
Whether her fearless visitings, or those
That came with soft alarm, like hurtless light
Opening the peaceful clouds; or she may use
Severer interventions, ministry   355
More palpable, as best might suit her aim.

    One summer evening (led by her) I found
A little boat tied to a willow tree
Within a rocky cave, its usual home.
Straight I unloosed her chain, and stepping in   360
Pushed from the shore. It was an act of stealth
And troubled pleasure, nor without the voice
Of mountain-echoes did my boat move on;
Leaving behind her still, on either side,
Small circles glittering idly in the moon,   365
Until they melted all into one track
Of sparkling light. But now, like one who rows,
Proud of his skill, to reach a chosen point
With an unswerving line, I fixed my view
Upon the summit of a craggy ridge,   370
The horizon's utmost boundary; for above
Was nothing but the stars and the grey sky.
She was an elfin pinnace; lustily
I dipped my oars into the silent lake,
And, as I rose upon the stroke, my boat   375
Went heaving through the water like a swan;
When, from behind that craggy steep till then
The horizon's bound, a huge peak, black and
        huge,
As if with voluntary power instinct
Upreared its head. I struck and struck again,   380
And growing still in stature the grim shape
Towered up between me and the stars, and still,
For so it seemed, with purpose of its own
And measured motion like a living thing,
Strode after me. With trembling oars I turned,   385
And through the silent water stole my way
Back to the covert of the willow tree;
There in her mooring-place I left my bark,—
And through the meadows homeward went, in
        grave

---

[9] In northern Lancashire, near Lake Windermere; after
his mother's death Wordsworth was sent to school at the
village of Hawkshead in Esthwaite Vale.
[10] Snares, traps.
[11] Cultivated, farmed. Probably the valley of Yewdale,
near Hawkshead.

And serious mood; but after I had seen   390
That spectacle, for many days, my brain
Worked with a dim and undetermined sense
Of unknown modes of being; o'er my thoughts
There hung a darkness, call it solitude
Or blank desertion. No familiar shapes   395
Remained, no pleasant images of trees,
Of sea or sky, no colours of green fields;
But huge and mighty forms, that do not live
Like living men, moved slowly through the mind
By day, and were a trouble to my dreams.   400

Wisdom and Spirit of the universe!
Thou Soul that art the eternity of thought,
That givest to forms and images a breath
And everlasting motion, not in vain
By day or star-light thus from my first dawn   405
Of childhood didst thou intertwine for me
The passions that build up our human soul;
Not with the mean and vulgar works of man,
But with high objects, with enduring things—
With life and nature—purifying thus   410
The elements of feeling and of thought,
And sanctifying, by such discipline,
Both pain and fear, until we recognise
A grandeur in the beatings of the heart.
Nor was this fellowship vouchsafed to me   415
With stinted kindness. In November days,
When vapours rolling down the valley made
A lonely scene more lonesome, among woods
At noon, and 'mid the calm of summer nights,
When, by the margin of the trembling lake,   420
Beneath the gloomy hills homeward I went
In solitude, such intercourse was mine;
Mine was it in the fields both day and night,
And by the waters, all the summer long.

And in the frosty season, when the sun   425
Was set, and visible for many a mile
The cottage windows blazed through twilight
    gloom,
I heeded not their summons: happy time
It was indeed for all of us—for me
It was a time of rapture! Clear and loud   430
The village clock tolled six,—I wheeled about,
Proud and exulting like an untired horse
That cares not for his home. All shod with steel,
We hissed along the polished ice in games
Confederate, imitative of the chase   435
And woodland pleasures,—the resounding horn,
The pack loud chiming, and the hunted hare.

So through the darkness and the cold we flew,
And not a voice was idle; with the din
Smitten, the precipices rang aloud;   440
The leafless trees and every icy crag
Tinkled like iron; while far distant hills
Into the tumult sent an alien sound
Of melancholy not unnoticed, while the stars
Eastward were sparkling clear, and in the west   445
The orange sky of evening died away.
Not seldom from the uproar I retired
Into a silent bay, or sportively
Glanced sideway, leaving the tumultuous throng,
To cut across the reflex of a star   450
That fled, and, flying still before me, gleamed
Upon the glassy plain; and oftentimes,
When we had given our bodies to the wind,
And all the shadowy banks on either side
Came sweeping through the darkness, spinning   455
    still
The rapid line of motion, then at once
Have I, reclining back upon my heels,
Stopped short; yet still the solitary cliffs
Wheeled by me—even as if the earth had rolled
With visible motion her diurnal round!   460
Behind me did they stretch in solemn train,
Feebler and feebler, and I stood and watched
Till all was tranquil as a dreamless sleep.

Ye Presences of Nature in the sky
And on the earth! Ye Visions of the hills!   465
And Souls of lonely places! can I think
A vulgar hope was yours when ye employed
Such ministry, when ye through many a year
Haunting me thus among my boyish sports,
On caves and trees, upon the woods and hills,   470
Impressed upon all forms the characters
Of danger or desire; and thus did make
The surface of the universal earth
With triumph and delight, with hope and fear,
Work like a sea?   475

. . . .

Yes, I remember when the changeful earth,
And twice five summers on my mind had stamped 560
The faces of the moving year, even then
I held unconscious intercourse with beauty
Old as creation, drinking in a pure
Organic pleasure from the silver wreaths
Of curling mist, or from the level plain   565
Of waters coloured by impending clouds.
The sands of Westmoreland, the creeks and
    bays

Of Cumbria's[12] rocky limits, they can tell
How, when the Sea threw off his evening shade
And to the shepherd's hut on distant hills   570
Sent welcome notice of the rising moon,
How I have stood, to fancies such as these
A stranger, linking with the spectacle
No conscious memory of a kindred sight,
And bringing with me no peculiar sense   575
Of quietness or peace; yet have I stood,
Even while mine eye hath moved o'er many a
        league
Of shining water, gathering as it seemed,
Through every hair-breadth in that field of light,
New pleasure like a bee among the flowers.   580

    Thus oft amid those fits of vulgar joy
Which, through all seasons, on a child's pursuits
Are prompt attendants, 'mid that giddy bliss
Which, like a tempest, works along the blood
And is forgotten; even then I felt   585
Gleams like the flashing of a shield;—the earth
And common face of Nature spake to me
Rememberable things; sometimes, 'tis true,
By chance collisions and quaint accidents
(Like those ill-sorted unions, work supposed   590
Of evil-minded fairies), yet not vain
Nor profitless, if haply they impressed
Collateral objects and appearances,
Albeit lifeless then, and doomed to sleep
Until maturer seasons called them forth   595
To impregnate and to elevate the mind.
—And if the vulgar joy by its own weight
Wearied itself out of the memory,
The scenes which were a witness of that joy
Remained in their substantial lineaments   600
Depicted on the brain, and to the eye
Were visible, a daily sight; and thus
By the impressive discipline of fear,
By pleasure and repeated happiness,
So frequently repeated, and by force   605
Of obscure feelings representative
Of things forgotten, these same scenes so bright,
So beautiful, so majestic in themselves,
Though yet the day was distant, did become
Habitually dear, and all their forms   610
And changeful colours by invisible links
Were fastened to the affections.
                        I began
My story early—not misled, I trust,

By an infirmity of love for days
Disowned by memory—ere the birth of spring   615
Planting my snowdrops[13] among winter snows:[14]
Nor will it seem to thee, O Friend![15] so prompt
In sympathy, that I have lengthened out
With fond[16] and feeble tongue a tedious tale.
Meanwhile, my hope has been, that I might fetch   620
Invigorating thoughts from former years;
Might fix the wavering balance of my mind,
And haply meet reproaches too, whose power
May spur me on, in manhood now mature,
To honourable toil. Yet should these hopes   625
Prove vain, and thus should neither I be taught
To understand myself, nor thou to know
With better knowledge how the heart was framed
Of him thou lovest; need I dread from thee
Harsh judgments, if the song be loth to quit   630
Those recollected hours that have the charm
Of visionary things, those lovely forms
And sweet sensations that throw back our life,
And almost make remotest infancy
A visible scene, on which the sun is shining?   635

    One end at least hath been attained; my mind
Hath been revived, and if this genial mood
Desert me not, forthwith shall be brought down
Through later years the story of my life.
The road lies plain before me;—'tis a theme   640
Single and of determined bounds; and hence
I choose it rather at this time, than work
Of ampler or more varied argument,
Where I might be discomfited and lost:
And certain hopes are with me, that to thee   645
This labour will be welcome, honoured Friend!

from Book Second

SCHOOL-TIME (CONTINUED)

· · ·

We ran a boisterous course; the year span
        round
With giddy motion. But the time approached
That brought with it a regular desire
For calmer pleasures, when the winning forms   50
Of Nature were collaterally attached
To every scheme of holiday delight
And every boyish sport, less grateful else

---

12 Cumberland's.

13 This European flower often blossoms while snow is still
on the ground.
14 I.e., I began this account of my life with my childhood.
15 Coleridge.   16 Foolish.

And languidly pursued.
                    When summer came,
Our pastime was, on bright half-holidays,   55
To sweep along the plain of Windermere
With rival oars; and the selected bourne
Was now an Island musical with birds
That sang and ceased not; now a Sister Isle
Beneath the oaks' umbrageous covert, sown   60
With lilies of the valley like a field;
And now a third small Island,[17] where survived
In solitude the ruins of a shrine
Once to Our Lady dedicate, and served
Daily with chaunted rites. In such a race   65
So ended, disappointment could be none,
Uneasiness, or pain, or jealousy:
We rested in the shade, all pleased alike,
Conquered and conqueror. Thus the pride of
    strength,
And the vain-glory of superior skill,   70
Were tempered; thus was gradually produced
A quiet independence of the heart:
And to my Friend who knows me I may add,
Fearless of blame, that hence for future days
Ensued a diffidence and modesty,   75
And I was taught to feel, perhaps too much,
The self-sufficing power of Solitude.

    Our daily meals were frugal, Sabine fare!
More than we wished we knew the blessing then
Of vigorous hunger—hence corporeal strength   80
Unsapped by delicate viands; for, exclude
A little weekly stipend, and we lived
Through three divisions of the quartered year
In penniless poverty. But now to school
From the half-yearly holidays returned,   85
We came with weightier purses, that sufficed
To furnish treats more costly than the Dame[18]
Of the old grey stone, from her scant board, sup-
    plied.
Hence rustic dinners on the cool green ground,
Or in the woods, or by a river side   90
Or shady fountains, while among the leaves
Soft airs were stirring, and the mid-day sun
Unfelt shone brightly round us in our joy.
Nor is my aim neglected if I tell
How sometimes, in the length of those half-years,   95
We from our funds drew largely;—proud to curb,
And eager to spur on, the galloping steed;
And with the courteous inn-keeper, whose stud

Supplied our want, we haply might employ
Sly subterfuge, if the adventure's bound   100
Were distant: some famed temple where of yore
The Druids worshipped, or the antique walls
Of that large abbey,[19] where within the Vale
Of Nightshade, to St. Mary's honour built,
Stands yet a mouldering pile with fractured arch, 105
Belfry, and images, and living trees;
A holy scene!—Along the smooth green turf
Our horses grazed. To more than inland peace,
Left by the west wind sweeping overhead
From a tumultuous ocean, trees and towers   110
In that sequestered valley may be seen,
Both silent and both motionless alike;
Such the deep shelter that is there, and such
The safeguard for repose and quietness.

    Our steeds remounted and the summons given, 115
With whip and spur we through the chauntry flew
In uncouth race, and left the cross-legged knight,
And the stone-abbot, and that single wren
Which one day sang so sweetly in the nave
Of the old church, that—though from recent 120
    showers
The earth was comfortless, and, touched by faint
Internal breezes, sobbings of the place
And respirations, from the roofless walls
The shuddering ivy dripped large drops—yet still
So sweetly 'mid the gloom the invisible bird   125
Sang to herself, that there I could have made
My dwelling-place, and lived for ever there
To hear such music. Through the walls we flew
And down the valley, and, a circuit made
In wantonness of heart, through rough and smooth 130
We scampered homewards. Oh, ye rocks and
    streams,
And that still spirit shed from evening air!
Even in this joyous time I sometimes felt
Your presence, when with slackened step we
    breathed
Along the sides of the steep hills, or when   135
Lighted by gleams of moonlight from the sea
We beat with thundering hoofs the level sand.
                    · · ·

from Book Fourth

SUMMER VACATION

· · ·

Those walks well worthy to be prized and
    loved—

---

17 Lady Holm, a small island in Lake Windermere, in the
Lake District.
18 The schoolmistress.

19 Furness Abbey.

Regretted!—that word, too, was on my tongue,
But they were richly laden with all good,
And cannot be remembered but with thanks
And gratitude, and perfect joy of heart—   135
Those walks in all their freshness now came back
Like a returning Spring. When first I made
Once more the circuit of our little lake,
If ever happiness hath lodged with man,
That day consummate happiness was mine,   140
Wide-spreading, steady, calm, contemplative.
The sun was set, or setting, when I left
Our cottage door, and evening soon brought on
A sober hour, not winning or serene,
For cold and raw the air was, and untuned;   145
But as a face we love is sweetest then
When sorrow damps it, or, whatever look
It chance to wear, is sweetest if the heart
Have fulness in herself; even so with me
It fared that evening. Gently did my soul   150
Put off her veil, and, self-transmuted, stood
Naked, as in the presence of her God.
While on I walked, a comfort seemed to touch
A heart that had not been disconsolate:
Strength came where weakness was not known to   155
    be,
At least not felt; and restoration came
Like an intruder knocking at the door
Of unacknowledged weariness. I took
The balance, and with firm hand weighed myself.
—Of that external scene which round me lay,   160
Little, in this abstraction, did I see;
Remembered less; but I had inward hopes
And swellings of the spirit, was rapt and soothed,
Conversed with promises, had glimmering views
How life pervades the undecaying mind;   165
How the immortal soul with God-like power
Informs, creates, and thaws the deepest sleep
That time can lay upon her; how on earth
Man, if he do but live within the light
Of high endeavours, daily spreads abroad   170
His being armed with strength that cannot fail.
Nor was there want of milder thoughts, of love,
Of innocence, and holiday repose;
And more than pastoral quiet, 'mid the stir
Of boldest projects, and a peaceful end   175
At last, or glorious, by endurance won.
Thus musing, in a wood I sate me down
Alone, continuing there to muse: the slopes
And heights meanwhile were slowly overspread
With darkness, and before a rippling breeze   180
The long lake lengthened out its hoary line,

And in the sheltered coppice where I sate,
Around me from among the hazel leaves,
Now here, now there, moved by the straggling
    wind,
Came ever and anon a breath-like sound,   185
Quick as the pantings of the faithful dog,
The off and on companion of my walk;
And such, at times, believing them to be,
I turned my head to look if he were there;
Then into solemn thought I passed once more.   190

. . .

        Yes, that heartless chase
Of trivial pleasures[20] was a poor exchange
For books and nature at that early age.
'Tis true, some casual knowledge might be gained   300
Of character or life; but at that time,
Of manners put to school I took small note,
And all my deeper passions lay elsewhere.
Far better had it been to exalt the mind
By solitary study, to uphold   305
Intense desire through meditative peace;
And yet for chastisement of these regrets,
The memory of one particular hour
Doth here rise up against me. 'Mid a throng
Of maids and youths, old men, and matrons staid,   310
A medley of all tempers, I had passed
The night in dancing, gaiety, and mirth,
With din of instruments and shuffling feet,
And glancing forms, and tapers glittering,
And unaimed prattle flying up and down;   315
Spirits upon the stretch, and here and there
Slight shocks of young love-liking interspersed,
Whose transient pleasure mounted to the head,
And tingled through the veins. Ere we retired,
The cock had crowed, and now the eastern sky   320
Was kindling, not unseen, from humble copse
And open field, through which the pathway
    wound,
And homeward led my steps. Magnificent
The morning rose, in memorable pomp,
Glorious as e'er I had beheld—in front,   325
The sea lay laughing at a distance; near,
The solid mountains shone, bright as the clouds,
Grain-tinctured, drenched in empyrean light;
And in the meadows and the lower grounds
Was all the sweetness of a common dawn—   330
Dews, vapours, and the melody of birds,
And labourers going forth to till the fields.

---

[20] The poet has just mentioned the distractions that at
this time often occasioned "an inner falling off" from his
true nature and purposes.

Ah! need I say, dear Friend! that to the brim
My heart was full; I made no vows, but vows
Were then made for me; bond unknown to me   335
Was given, that I should be, else sinning greatly,
A dedicated Spirit. On I walked
In thankful blessedness, which yet survives.

. . .

from Book Fifth

BOOKS

When Contemplation, like the night-calm felt
Through earth and sky, spreads widely, and sends
    deep
Into the soul its tranquillising power,
Even then I sometimes grieve for thee, O Man,
Earth's paramount Creature! not so much for   5
    woes
That thou endurest; heavy though that weight
    be,
Cloud-like it mounts, or touched with light di-
    vine
Doth melt away; but for those palms achieved
Through length of time, by patient exercise
Of study and hard thought; there, there, it is   10
That sadness finds its fuel. Hitherto,
In progress through this Verse, my mind hath
    looked
Upon the speaking face of earth and heaven
As her prime teacher, intercourse with man
Established by the sovereign Intellect,   15
Who through that bodily image hath diffused,
As might appear to the eye of fleeting time,
A deathless spirit. Thou also, man! hast wrought,
For commerce of thy nature with herself,
Things that aspire to unconquerable life;   20
And yet we feel—we cannot choose but feel—
That they must perish. Tremblings of the heart
It gives, to think that our immortal being
No more shall need such garments; and yet man,
As long as he shall be the child of earth,   25
Might almost "weep to have" what he may lose,
Nor be himself extinguished, but survive,
Abject, depressed, forlorn, disconsolate.
A thought is with me sometimes, and I say,—
Should the whole frame of earth by inward   30
    throes
Be wrenched, or fire come down from far to
    scorch
Her pleasant habitations, and dry up

Old Ocean, in his bed left singed and bare,
Yet would the living Presence still subsist
Victorious, and composure would ensue,   35
And kindlings like the morning—presage sure
Of day returning and of life revived.
But all the meditations of mankind,
Yea, all the adamantine holds of truth
By reason built, or passion, which itself   40
Is highest reason in a soul sublime;
The consecrated works of Bard and Sage,
Sensuous or intellectual, wrought by men,
Twin labourers and heirs of the same hopes;
Where would they be? Oh! why hath not the   45
    Mind
Some element to stamp her image on
In nature somewhat nearer to her own?
Why, gifted with such powers to send abroad
Her spirit, must it lodge in shrines so frail?

One day, when from my lips a like complaint   50
Had fallen in presence of a studious friend,
He with a smile made answer, that in truth
'T was going far to seek disquietude;
But on the front of his reproof confessed
That he himself had oftentimes given way   55
To kindred hauntings. Whereupon I told,
That once in the stillness of a summer's noon,
While I was seated in a rocky cave
By the sea-side, perusing, so it chanced,
The famous history of the errant knight[21]   60
Recorded by Cervantes, these same thoughts
Beset me, and to height unusual rose,
While listlessly I sate, and, having closed
The book, had turned my eyes toward the wide
    sea.
On poetry and geometric truth,   65
And their high privilege of lasting life,
From all internal injury exempt,
I mused; upon these chiefly: and at length,
My senses yielding to the sultry air,
Sleep seized me, and I passed into a dream.   70
I saw before me stretched a boundless plain
Of sandy wilderness, all black and void,
And as I looked around, distress and fear
Came creeping over me, when at my side,
Close at my side, an uncouth shape appeared   75
Upon a dromedary, mounted high.
He seemed an Arab of the Bedouin tribes:

---

21 *Don Quixote,* in the novel by Miguel Cervantes (1547–
1616).

A lance he bore, and underneath one arm
A stone, and in the opposite hand a shell
Of a surpassing brightness. At the sight
Much I rejoiced, not doubting but a guide
Was present, one who with unerring skill
Would through the desert lead me; and while yet
I looked and looked, self-questioned what this
    freight
Which the new-comer carried through the waste   85
Could mean, the Arab told me that the stone
(To give it in the language of the dream)
Was "Euclid's Elements," and "This," said he,
"Is something of more worth;" and at the word
Stretched forth the shell, so beautiful in shape,   90
In colour so resplendent, with command
That I should hold it to my ear. I did so,
And heard that instant in an unknown tongue,
Which yet I understood, articulate sounds,
A loud prophetic blast of harmony;   95
An Ode, in passion uttered, which foretold
Destruction to the children of the earth
By deluge, now at hand. No sooner ceased
The song, than the Arab with calm look declared
That all would come to pass of which the voice   100
Had given forewarning, and that he himself
Was going then to bury those two books:
The one that held acquaintance with the stars,
And wedded soul to soul in purest bond
Of reason, undisturbed by space or time;   105
The other that was a god, yea many gods,
Had voices more than all the winds, with power
To exhilarate the spirit, and to soothe,
Through every clime, the heart of human kind.
While this was uttering, strange as it may seem,   110
I wondered not, although I plainly saw
The one to be a stone, the other a shell;
Nor doubted once but that they both were books,
Having a perfect faith in all that passed.
Far stronger, now, grew the desire I felt   115
To cleave unto this man; but when I prayed
To share his enterprise, he hurried on
Reckless of me: I followed, not unseen,
For oftentimes he cast a backward look,
Grasping his twofold treasure.—Lance in rest,   120
He rode, I keeping pace with him; and now
He, to my fancy, had become the knight
Whose tale Cervantes tells; yet not the knight,
But was an Arab of the desert too;
Of these was neither, and was both at once.   125
His countenance, meanwhile, grew more
    disturbed;

And, looking backwards when he looked, mine
    eyes
Saw, over half the wilderness diffused,   80
A bed of glittering light: I asked the cause:
"It is," said he, "the waters of the deep   130
Gathering upon us;" quickening then the pace
Of the unwieldy creature he bestrode,
He left me: I called after him aloud;
He heeded not; but, with his twofold charge
Still in his grasp, before me, full in view,   135
Went hurrying o'er the illimitable waste,
With the fleet waters of a drowning world
In chase of him; whereat I waked in terror,
And saw the sea before me, and the book,
In which I had been reading, at my side.   140

    Full often, taking from the world of sleep
This Arab phantom, which I thus beheld,
This semi-Quixote, I to him have given
A substance, fancied him a living man,
A gentle dweller in the desert, crazed   145
By love and feeling, and internal thought
Protracted among endless solitudes;
Have shaped him wandering upon this quest!
Nor have I pitied him; but rather felt
Reverence was due to a being thus employed;   150
And thought that, in the blind and awful lair
Of such a madness, reason did lie couched.
Enow there are on earth to take in charge
Their wives, their children, and their virgin
    loves,
Or whatsoever else the heart holds dear;   155
Enow to stir for these; yea, will I say,
Contemplating in soberness the approach
Of an event so dire, by signs in earth
Or heaven made manifest, that I could share
That maniac's fond anxiety, and go   160
Upon like errand. Oftentimes at least
Me hath such strong entrancement overcome,
When I have held a volume in my hand,
Poor earthly casket of immortal verse,
Shakespeare, or Milton, labourers divine!   165

· · ·

from Book Sixth
CAMBRIDGE AND THE ALPS

· · ·

When from the Vallais we[22] had turned, and
    clomb

---

22 Wordsworth and his friend Robert Jones, with whom
he visited France and Switzerland in the summer of 1790.

Along the Simplon's steep and rugged road,
Following a band of muleteers, we reached
A halting-place, where all together took   565
Their noon-tide meal. Hastily rose our guide,
Leaving us at the board; awhile we lingered,
Then paced the beaten downward way that led
Right to a rough stream's edge, and there broke
     off;
The only track now visible was one   570
That from the torrent's further brink held forth
Conspicuous invitation to ascend
A lofty mountain. After brief delay
Crossing the unbridged stream, that road we
     took,
And clomb with eagerness, till anxious fears   575
Intruded, for we failed to overtake
Our comrades gone before. By fortunate chance,
While every moment added doubt to doubt,
A peasant met us, from whose mouth we learned
That to the spot which had perplexed us first   580
We must descend, and there should find the road,
Which in the stony channel of the stream
Lay a few steps, and then along its banks;
And, that our future course, all plain to sight,
Was downwards, with the current of that stream.   585
Loth to believe what we so grieved to hear,
For still we had hopes that pointed to the clouds,
We questioned him again, and yet again;
But every word that from the peasant's lips
Came in reply, translated by our feelings,   590
Ended in this,—*that we had crossed the Alps.*

     Imagination—here the Power so called
Through sad incompetence of human speech,
That awful Power rose from the mind's abyss
Like an unfathered vapour that enwraps,   595
At once, some lonely traveller. I was lost;
Halted without an effort to break through;
But to my conscious soul I now can say—
"I recognise thy glory:" in such strength
Of usurpation, when the light of sense   600
Goes out, but with a flash that has revealed
The invisible world, doth greatness make abode,
There harbours; whether we be young or old,
Our destiny, our being's heart and home,
Is with infinitude, and only there;   605
With hope it is, hope that can never die,
Effort, and expectation, and desire,
And something evermore about to be.
Under such banners militant, the soul
Seeks for no trophies, struggles for no spoils   610

That may attest her prowess, blest in thoughts
That are their own perfection and reward,
Strong in herself and in beatitude
That hides her, like the mighty flood of Nile
Poured from his fount of Abyssinian clouds   615
To fertilise the whole Egyptian plain.

     The melancholy slackening that ensued
Upon those tidings by the peasant given
Was soon dislodged. Downwards we hurried fast,
And, with the half-shaped road which we had   620
     missed,
Entered a narrow chasm. The brook and road
Were fellow-travellers in this gloomy strait,
And with them did we journey several hours
At a slow pace. The immeasurable height
Of woods decaying, never to be decayed,   625
The stationary blasts of waterfalls,
And in the narrow rent at every turn
Winds thwarting winds, bewildered and forlorn,
The torrents shooting from the clear blue sky,
The rocks that muttered close upon our ears,   630
Black drizzling crags that spake by the way-side
As if a voice were in them, the sick sight
And giddy prospect of the raving stream,
The unfettered clouds and region of the Heavens,
Tumult and peace, the darkness and the light—   635
Were all like workings of one mind, the features
Of the same face, blossoms upon one tree;
Characters of the great Apocalypse,
The types and symbols of Eternity,
Of first, and last, and midst, and without end.   640

• • •

from Book Seventh

RESIDENCE IN LONDON

• • •

     But foolishness and madness in parade,
Though most at home in this their dear domain,   595
Are scattered everywhere, no rarities,
Even to the rudest novice of the Schools.
Me, rather, it employed, to note, and keep
In memory, those individual sights
Of courage, or integrity, or truth,   600
Or tenderness, which there, set off by foil,
Appeared more touching. One will I select—
A Father—for he bore that sacred name;—
Him saw I, sitting in an open square,
Upon a corner-stone of that low wall,   605
Wherein were fixed the iron pales that fenced
A spacious grass-plot; there, in silence, sate
This One Man, with a sickly babe outstretched

Upon his knee, whom he had thither brought
For sunshine, and to breathe the fresher air.   610
Of those who passed, and me who looked at him,
He took no heed; but in his brawny arms
(The Artificer was to the elbow bare,
And from his work this moment had been stolen)
He held the child, and, bending over it,   615
As if he were afraid both of the sun
And of the air, which he had come to seek,
Eyed the poor babe with love unutterable.

As the black storm upon the mountain top
Sets off the sunbeam in the valley, so   620
That huge fermenting mass of human-kind
Serves as a solemn back-ground, or relief,
To single forms and objects, whence they draw,
For feeling and contemplative regard,
More than inherent liveliness and power.   625
How oft, amid those overflowing streets,
Have I gone forward with the crowd, and said
Unto myself, "The face of every one
That passes by me is a mystery!"
Thus have I looked, nor ceased to look, oppressed   630
By thoughts of what and whither, when and how,
Until the shapes before my eyes became
A second-sight procession, such as glides
Over still mountains, or appears in dreams;
And once, far-travelled in such mood, beyond   635
The reach of common indication, lost
Amid the moving pageant, I was smitten
Abruptly, with the view (a sight not rare)
Of a blind Beggar, who, with upright face,
Stood, propped against a wall, upon his chest   640
Wearing a written paper, to explain
His story, whence he came, and who he was.
Caught by the spectacle my mind turned round
As with the might of waters; an apt type
This label seemed of the utmost we can know,   645
Both of ourselves and of the universe;
And, on the shape of that unmoving man,
His steadfast face and sightless eyes, I gazed,
As if admonished from another world.

Though reared upon the base of outward   650
    things,
Structures like these the excited spirit mainly
Builds for herself; scenes different there are,
Full-formed, that take, with small internal help,
Possession of the faculties,—the peace
That comes with night; the deep solemnity   655
Of nature's intermediate hours of rest,

When the great tide of human life stands still:
The business of the day to come, unborn,   660
Of that gone by, locked up, as in the grave;
The blended calmness of the heavens and earth,   660
Moonlight and stars, and empty streets, and
    sounds
Unfrequent as in deserts; at late hours
Of winter evenings, when unwholesome rains
Are falling hard, with people yet astir,
The feeble salutation from the voice   665
Of some unhappy woman, now and then
Heard as we pass, when no one looks about,
Nothing is listened to. But these, I fear,
Are falsely catalogued; things that are, are not,
As the mind answers to them, or the heart   670
Is prompt, or slow, to feel. What say you, then,
To times, when half the city shall break out
Full of one passion, vengeance, rage, or fear?
To executions, to a street on fire,
Mobs, riots, or rejoicings? From these sights   675
Take one,—that ancient festival, the Fair,
Holden where martyrs suffered in past time,[23]
And named of St. Bartholomew; there, see
A work completed to our hands, that lays,
If any spectacle on earth can do,   680
The whole creative powers of man asleep!—
For once, the Muse's help will we implore,
And she shall lodge us, wafted on her wings,
Above the press and danger of the crowd,
Upon some showman's platform. What a shock   685
For eyes and ears! what anarchy and din,
Barbarian and infernal,—a phantasma,
Monstrous in colour, motion, shape, sight, sound!
Below, the open space, through every nook
Of the wide area, twinkles, is alive   690
With heads; the midway region, and above,
Is thronged with staring pictures and huge scrolls,
Dumb proclamations of the Prodigies;
With chattering monkeys dangling from their
    poles,
And children whirling in their roundabouts;   695
With those that stretch the neck and strain the
    eyes,
And crack the voice in rivalship, the crowd
Inviting; with buffoons against buffoons
Grimacing, writhing, screaming,—him who
    grinds
The hurdy-gurdy, at the fiddle weaves,   700

---

23 The fair commemorates the execution of Protestants in
the reign of Mary I, "Bloody Mary" (1516–1558).

Rattles the salt-box, thumps the kettledrum,
And him who at the trumpet puffs his cheeks,
The silver-collared Negro with his timbrel,
Equestrians, tumblers, women, girls, and boys,
Blue-breeched, pink-vested, with high-towering 705
    plumes.—
All moveables of wonder, from all parts,
Are here—Albinos, painted Indians, Dwarfs,
The Horse of knowledge, and the learned Pig,
The Stone-eater, the man that swallows fire,
Giants, Ventriloquists, the Invisible Girl, 710
The Bust that speaks and moves its goggling eyes,
The Wax-work, Clock-work, all the marvellous
    craft
Of modern Merlins, Wild Beasts, Puppet-shows,
All out-o'-the-way, far-fetched, perverted things,
All freaks of nature, all Promethean thoughts 715
Of man, his dullness, madness, and their feats
All jumbled up together, to compose
A Parliament of Monsters.

.   .   .

from Book Eighth

RETROSPECT—LOVE OF NATURE LEADING TO LOVE OF MAN

What sounds are those, Helvellyn,[24] that are
    heard
Up to thy summit, through the depth of air
Ascending, as if distance had the power
To make the sounds more audible? What crowd
Covers, or sprinkles o'er, yon village green? 5
Crowd seems it, solitary hill! to thee,
Though but a little family of men,
Shepherds and tillers of the ground—betimes
Assembled with their children and their wives,
And here and there a stranger interspersed. 10
They hold a rustic fair—a festival,
Such as, on this side now, and now on that,
Repeated through his tributary vales,
Helvellyn, in the silence of his rest,
Sees annually, if clouds towards either ocean 15
Blown from their favourite resting-place, or mists
Dissolved, have left him an unshrouded head.
Delightful day it is for all who dwell
In this secluded glen, and eagerly
They give it welcome. Long ere heat of noon, 20
From byre or field the kine were brought; the
    sheep

Are penned in cotes; the chaffering is begun.
The heifer lows, uneasy at the voice
Of a new master; bleat the flocks aloud.
Booths are there none; a stall or two is here; 25
A lame man or a blind, the one to beg,
The other to make music; hither, too,
From far, with basket, slung upon her arm,
Of hawker's wares—books, pictures, combs, and
    pins—
Some aged woman finds her way again, 30
Year after year, a punctual visitant!
There also stands a speech-maker by rote,
Pulling the strings of his boxed raree-show;
And in the lapse of many years may come
Prouder itinerant, mountebank, or he 35
Whose wonders in a covered wain lie hid.
But one there is, the loveliest of them all,
Some sweet lass of the valley, looking out
For gains, and who that sees her would not buy?
Fruits of her father's orchard are her wares, 40
And with the ruddy produce she walks round
Among the crowd, half pleased with, half
    ashamed
Of, her new office, blushing restlessly.
The children now are rich, for the old to-day
Are generous as the young; and, if content 45
With looking on, some ancient wedded pair
Sit in the shade together; while they gaze,
"A cheerful smile unbends the wrinkled brow,
The days departed start again to life,
And all the scenes of childhood reappear, 50
Faint, but more tranquil, like the changing sun
To him who slept at noon and wakes at eve."[25]
Thus gaiety and cheerfulness prevail,
Spreading from young to old, from old to young,
And no one seems to want his share.—Immense 55
Is the recess, the circumambient world
Magnificent, by which they are embraced:
They move about upon the soft green turf:
How little they, they and their doings, seem,
And all that they can further or obstruct! 60
Through utter weakness pitiably dear,
As tender infants are: and yet how great!
For all things serve them: them the morning
    light
Loves, as it glistens on the silent rocks;
And them the silent rocks, which now from high 65
Look down upon them; the reposing clouds;
The wild brooks prattling from invisible haunts;

---

24 A mountain in the Lake District.

25 These lines (49–52) are quoted from "Malvern Hills"
by Joseph Cottle (1770–1853).

And old Helvellyn, conscious of the stir
Which animates this day their calm abode.

With deep devotion, Nature, did I feel,   70
In that enormous City's turbulent world
Of men and things, what benefit I owed
To thee, and those domains of rural peace,
Where to the sense of beauty first my heart
Was opened; tract more exquisitely fair[26]   75
Than that famed paradise of ten thousand trees,
Or Gehol's matchless gardens, for delight
Of the Tartarian dynasty composed
(Beyond that mighty wall, not fabulous,
China's stupendous mound) by patient toil   80
Of myriads and boon nature's lavish help;
There, in a clime from widest empire chosen,
Fulfilling (could enchantment have done more?)
A sumptuous dream of flowery lawns, with domes
Of pleasure sprinkled over, shady dells   85
For eastern monasteries, sunny mounts
With temples crested, bridges, gondolas,
Rocks, dens, and groves of foliage taught to melt
Into each other their obsequious hues,
Vanished and vanishing in subtle chase,   90
Too fine to be pursued; or standing forth
In no discordant opposition, strong
And gorgeous as the colours side by side
Bedded among rich plumes of tropic birds;
And mountains over all, embracing all;   95
And all the landscape, endlessly enriched
With waters running, falling, or asleep.

But lovelier far than this, the paradise
Where I was reared; in Nature's primitive gifts
Favoured no less, and more to every sense   100
Delicious, seeing that the sun and sky,
The elements, and seasons as they change,
Do find a worthy fellow-labourer there—
Man free, man working for himself, with choice
Of time, and place, and object; by his wants,   105
His comforts, native occupations, cares,
Cheerfully led to individual ends
Or social, and still followed by a train
Unwooed, unthought-of even—simplicity,
And beauty, and inevitable grace.   110

            . . .

              . . . Yet, hail to you   215
Moors, mountains, headlands, and ye hollow
     vales,

---

[26] Ernest de Selincourt, editor of the definitive edition of
The Prelude, refers one to *Paradise Lost*, especially IV,
208–47.

Ye long deep channels for the Atlantic's voice,
Powers of my native region! Ye that seize
The heart with firmer grasp! Your snows and
     streams
Ungovernable, and your terrifying winds,   220
That howl so dismally for him who treads
Companionless your awful solitudes!
There, 't is the shepherd's task the winter long
To wait upon the storms: of their approach
Sagacious, into sheltering coves he drives   225
His flock, and thither from the homestead bears
A toilsome burden up the craggy ways,
And deals it out, their regular nourishment
Strewn on the frozen snow. And when the spring
Looks out, and all the pastures dance with lambs, 230
And when the flock, with warmer weather, climbs
Higher and higher, him his office leads
To watch their goings, whatsoever track
The wanderers choose. For this he quits his home
At day-spring, and no sooner doth the sun   235
Begin to strike him with a fire-like heat,
Than he lies down upon some shining rock,
And breakfasts with his dog. When they have
     stolen,
As is their wont, a pittance from strict time,
For rest not needed or exchange of love,   240
Then from his couch he starts; and now his feet
Crush out a livelier fragrance from the flowers
Of lowly thyme, by Nature's skill enwrought
In the wild turf: the lingering dews of morn
Smoke round him, as from hill to hill he hies,   245
His staff protending like a hunter's spear,
Or by its aid leaping from crag to crag,
And o'er the brawling beds of unbridged streams.
Philosophy, methinks, at Fancy's call,
Might deign to follow him through what he does   250
Or sees in his day's march; himself he feels,
In those vast regions where his service lies,
A freeman, wedded to his life of hope
And hazard, and hard labour interchanged
With that majestic indolence so dear   255
To native man. A rambling schoolboy, thus,
I felt his presence in his own domain,
As of a lord and master, or a power,
Or genius, under Nature, under God,
Presiding; and severest solitude   260
Had more commanding looks when he was there.
When up the lonely brooks on rainy days
Angling I went, or trod the trackless hills
By mists bewildered, suddenly mine eyes
Have glanced upon him distant a few steps,   265

In size a giant, stalking through thick fog,
His sheep like Greenland bears; or, as he stepped
Beyond the boundary line of some hill-shadow,
His form hath flashed upon me, glorified
By the deep radiance of the setting sun: 270
Or him have I descried in distant sky,
A solitary object and sublime,
Above all height! like an aerial cross
Stationed alone upon a spiry rock
Of the Chartreuse, for worship. Thus was man   275
Ennobled outwardly before my sight,
And thus my heart was early introduced
To an unconscious love and reverence
Of human nature; hence the human form
To me became an index of delight,   280
Of grace and honour, power and worthiness.
Meanwhile this creature—spiritual almost
As those of books, but more exalted far;
Far more of an imaginative form
Than the gay Corin of the groves, who lives   285
For his own fancies, or to dance by the hour,
In coronal, with Phyllis[27] in the midst—
Was, for the purposes of kind, a man
With the most common; huband, father; learned,
Could teach, admonish; suffered with the rest   290
From vice and folly, wretchedness and fear;
Of this I little saw, cared less for it,
But something must have felt.

. . .

from Book Ninth

RESIDENCE IN FRANCE

. . .

                    . . . And when we[28] chanced
One day to meet a hunger-bitten girl,   510
Who crept along fitting her languid gait
Unto a heifer's motion, by a cord
Tied to her arm, and picking thus from the lane
Its sustenance, while the girl with pallid hands
Was busy knitting in a heartless mood   515
Of solitude, and at the sight my friend
In agitation said, "'T is against *that*
That we are fighting," I with him believed
That a benignant spirit was abroad
Which might not be withstood, that poverty   520

---

[27] Corin and Phyllis are conventional pastoral names.
[28] Wordsworth and his friend Michel Beaupuy, a French-man of noble family, sympathetic to the Revolution. Wordsworth had come to France in 1791.

Abject as this would in a little time
Be found no more, that we should see the earth
Unthwarted in her wish to recompense
The meek, the lowly, patient child of toil,
All institutes for ever blotted out   525
That legalised exclusion, empty pomp
Abolished, sensual state and cruel power
Whether by edict of the one or few;
And finally, as sum and crown of all,
Should see the people having a strong hand   530
In framing their own laws; whence better days
To all mankind.

. . .

from Book Tenth

RESIDENCE IN FRANCE (CONTINUED)

It was a beautiful and silent day
That overspread the countenance of earth,
Then fading with unusual quietness,—
A day as beautiful as e'er was given
To soothe regret, though deepening what it   5
      soothed,
When by the gliding Loire I paused, and cast
Upon his rich domains, vineyard and tilth,
Green   meadow-ground,   and   many-coloured
      woods,
Again, and yet again, a farewell look;
Then from the quiet of that scene passed on,   10
Bound to the fierce Metropolis. From his throne
The King had fallen,[29] and that invading host—
Presumptuous cloud, on whose black front was
      written
The tender mercies of the dismal wind
That bore it—on the plains of Liberty   15
Had burst innocuous. Say in bolder words,
They—who had come elate as eastern hunters
Banded beneath the Great Mogul, when he
Erewhile went forth from Agra or Lahore,
Rajahs and Omrahs in his train, intent   20
To drive their prey enclosed within a ring
Wide as a province, but, the signal given,
Before the point of the life-threatening spear
Narrowing itself by moments—they, rash men,
Had seen the anticipated quarry turned   25
Into avengers, from whose wrath they fled
In terror. Disappointment and dismay
Remained for all whose fancies had run wild
With evil expectations; confidence
And perfect triumph for the better cause.   30

---

[29] On August 10, 1792.

The State—as if to stamp the final seal
On her security, and to the world
Show what she was, a high and fearless soul,
Exulting in defiance, or heart-stung
By sharp resentment, or belike to taunt   35
With spiteful gratitude the baffled League,
That had stirred up her slackening faculties
To a new transition—when the King was
    crushed,
Spared not the empty throne, and in proud haste
Assumed the body and venerable name   40
Of a Republic. Lamentable crimes,
'T is true, had gone before this hour, dire work
Of massacre, in which the senseless sword
Was prayed to as a judge; but these were past,
Earth free from them for ever, as was thought,— 45
Ephemeral monsters, to be seen but once!
Things that could only show themselves and die.

Cheered with this hope, to Paris I returned,
And ranged, with ardour heretofore unfelt,
The spacious city, and in progress passed   50
The prison where the unhappy Monarch lay,
Associate with his children and his wife
In bondage; and the palace, lately stormed
With roar of cannon by a furious host.
I crossed the square (an empty area then!)   55
Of the Carrousel,[30] where so late had lain
The dead, upon the dying heaped, and gazed
On this and other spots, as doth a man
Upon a volume whose contents he knows
Are memorable, but from him locked up,   60
Being written in a tongue he cannot read,
So that he questions the mute leaves with pain,
And half upbraids their silence. But that night
I felt most deeply in what world I was,
What ground I trod on, and what air I breathed.   65
High was my room and lonely, near the roof
Of a large mansion or hotel, a lodge
That would have pleased me in more quiet
    times;
Nor was it wholly without pleasure then.
With unextinguished taper I kept watch,   70
Reading at intervals; the fear gone by
Pressed on me almost like a fear to come.
I thought of those September massacres,[31]
Divided from me by one little month,
Saw them and touched: the rest was conjured up   75

From tragic fictions or true history,
Remembrances and dim admonishments.
The horse is taught his manage, and no star
Of wildest course but treads back his own steps;
For the spent hurricane the air provides   80
As fierce a successor; the tide retreats
But to return out of its hiding-place
In the great deep; all things have second birth;
The earthquake is not satisfied at once;
And in this way I wrought upon myself,   85
Until I seemed to hear a voice that cried,
To the whole city, "Sleep no more."[32] The trance
Fled with the voice to which it had given birth;
But vainly comments of a calmer mind
Promised soft peace and sweet forgetfulness.   90
The place, all hushed and silent as it was,
Appeared unfit for the repose of night,
Defenceless as a wood where tigers roam.

. . .

As I advanced, all that I saw or felt
Was gentleness and peace. Upon a small   555
And rocky island near, a fragment stood,
(Itself like a sea rock) the low remains
(With shells encrusted, dark with briny weeds)
Of a dilapidated structure, once
A Romish chapel, where the vested priest   560
Said matins at the hour that suited those
Who crossed the sands with ebb of morning tide.
Not far from that still ruin all the plain
Lay spotted with a variegated crowd
Of vehicles and travellers, horse and foot,   565
Wading beneath the conduct of their guide
In loose procession through the shallow stream
Of inland waters; the great sea meanwhile
Heaved at safe distance, far retired. I paused,
Longing for skill to paint a scene so bright   570
And cheerful, but the foremost of the band
As he approached, no salutation given
In the familiar language of the day,
Cried, "Robespierre is dead![33] nor was a doubt,
After strict question, left within my mind   575
That he and his supporters all were fallen.

Great was my transport, deep my gratitude
To everlasting Justice, by this fiat
Made manifest. "Come now, ye golden times,"
Said I forth-pouring on those open sands   580

---

30 In front of the Tuileries, "the palace, lately stormed."
31 The massacre of three thousand Royalists, September 2,
3, 4, 1792.

32 *Macbeth*, II, ii, 35.
33 Robespierre was executed on July 28, 1794.

A hymn of triumph: "as the morning comes
From out the bosom of the night, come ye:
Thus far our trust is verified; behold!
They who with clumsy desperation brought
A river of Blood, and preached that nothing else   585
Could cleanse the Augean stable,[34] by the might
Of their own helper have been swept away;
Their madness stands declared and visible;
Elsewhere will safety now be sought, and earth
March firmly towards righteousness and peace."—   590
Then schemes I framed more calmly, when and
        how
The madding factions might be tranquillised,
And how through hardships manifold and long
The glorious renovation would proceed.
Thus interrupted by uneasy bursts   595
Of exultation, I pursued my way
Along that very shore which I had skimmed
In former days, when—spurring from the Vale
Of Nightshade, and St. Mary's mouldering fane,
And the stone abbot, after circuit made   600
In wantonness of heart, a joyous band
Of schoolboys hastening to their distant home
Along the margin of the moonlight sea—
We beat with thundering hoofs the level sand.[35]

. . .

from Book Eleventh
FRANCE (CONCLUDED)

. . .

This was the time, when, all things tending
        fast
To depravation, speculative schemes—
That promised to abstract the hopes of Man[36]   225
Out of his feelings, to be fixed thenceforth
For ever in a purer element—
Found ready welcome. Tempting region *that*
For Zeal to enter and refresh herself,
Where passions had the privilege to work,   230
And never hear the sound of their own names.

---

[34] To cleanse the Augean stables was one of the labors of Hercules.
[35] These lines recall Book Second, 128–37.
[36] Wordsworth is referring, among other things, to the philosophy of William Godwin (1756–1836), author of *Enquiry Concerning Political Justice*, a powerful influence on, and father-in-law of, Shelley. Wordsworth is here also reflecting the views of Burke, opposed to abstract concepts of liberty, divorced from concrete circumstances and considerations of history. See the selections from Burke in Volume I.

But, speaking more in charity, the dream
Flattered the young, pleased with extremes, nor
        least
With that which makes our Reason's naked self
The object of its fervour. What delight!   235
How glorious! in self-knowledge and self-rule,
To look through all the frailties of the world,
And, with a resolute mastery shaking off
Infirmities of nature, time, and place,
Build social upon personal Liberty,   240
Which, to the blind restraints of general laws,
Superior, magisterially adopts
One guide, the light of circumstances, flashed
Upon an independent intellect.
Thus expectation rose again; thus hope,   245
From her first ground expelled, grew proud once
        more
Oft, as my thoughts were turned to human kind,
I scorned indifference; but, inflamed with thirst
Of a secure intelligence, and sick
Of other longing, I pursued what seemed   250
A more exalted nature; wished that Man
Should start out of his earthy, worm-like state,
And spread abroad the wings of Liberty,
Lord of himself, in undisturbed delight—
A noble aspiration! *yet* I feel   255
(Sustained by worthier as by wiser thoughts)
The aspiration, nor shall ever cease
To feel it;—but return we to our course.

Enough, 't is true—could such a plea excuse
Those aberrations—had the clamorous friends   260
Of ancient Institutions said and done
To bring disgrace upon their very names;
Disgrace, of which, custom and written law,
And sundry moral sentiments as props
Or emanations of those institutes,   265
Too justly bore a part. A veil had been
Uplifted; why deceive ourselves? in sooth,
'T was even so; and sorrow for the man
Who either had not eyes wherewith to see,
Or, seeing, had forgotten! A strong shock   270
Was given to old opinions; all men's minds
Had felt its power, and mine was both let loose,
Let loose and goaded. After what hath been
Already said of patriotic love,
Suffice it here to add, that, somewhat stern   275
In temperament, withal a happy man,
And therefore bold to look on painful things,
Free likewise of the world, and thence more bold,
I summoned my best skill, and toiled, intent

To anatomise the frame of social life;
Yea, the whole body of society
Searched to its heart. Share with me, Friend![37]
   the wish
That some dramatic tale, endued with shapes
Livelier, and flinging out less guarded words
Than suit the work we fashion, might set forth
What then I learned, or think I learned, of
   truth,
And the errors into which I fell, betrayed
By present objects, and by reasonings false
From their beginnings, inasmuch as drawn
Out of a heart that had been turned aside
From Nature's way by outward accidents,
And which was thus confounded, more and more
Misguided, and misguiding. So I fared,
Dragging all precepts, judgments, maxims, creeds,
Like culprits to the bar; calling the mind,
Suspiciously, to establish in plain day
Her titles and her honours; now believing,
Now disbelieving; endlessly perplexed
With impulse, motive, right and wrong, the
   ground
Of obligation, what the rule and whence
The sanction; till, demanding formal *proof,*
And seeking it in every thing, I lost
All feeling of conviction, and, in fine,
Sick, wearied out with contrarieties,
Yielded up moral questions in despair.

   This was the crisis of that strong disease,
This the soul's last and lowest ebb; I drooped,
Deeming our blessèd reason of least use
Where wanted most: "The lordly attributes
Of will and choice," I bitterly exclaimed,
"What are they but a mockery of a Being
Who hath in no concerns of his a test
Of good and evil; knows not what to fear
Or hope for, what to covet or to shun;
And who, if those could be discerned, would yet
Be little profited, would see, and ask
Where is the obligation to enforce?
And, to acknowledged law rebellious, still,
As selfish passion urged, would act amiss;
The dupe of folly, or the slave of crime."

   Depressed, bewildered thus, I did not walk
With scoffers, seeking light and gay revenge
From indiscriminate laughter, nor sate down

280
285
290
295
300
305
310
315
320

In reconcilement with an utter waste
Of intellect; such sloth I could not brook,
(Too well I loved, in that my spring of life,
Pains-taking thoughts, and truth, their dear
   reward)
But turned to abstract science, and there sought
Work for the reasoning faculty enthroned
Where the disturbances of space and time—
Whether in matters various, properties
Inherent, or from human will and power
Derived—find no admission. Then it was—
Thanks to the bounteous Giver of all good!—
That the belovèd Sister[38] in whose sight
Those days were passed, now speaking in a voice
Of sudden admonition—like a brook
That did but *cross* a lonely road, and now
Is seen, heard, felt, and caught at every turn,
Companion never lost through many a league—
Maintained for me a saving intercourse
With my true self; for, though bedimmed and
   changed
Much, as it seemed, I was no further changed
Than as a clouded and a waning moon:
She whispered still that brightness would return;
She, in the midst of all, preserved me still
A Poet, made me seek beneath that name,
And that alone, my office upon earth;
And, lastly, as hereafter will be shown,
If willing audience fail not, Nature's self,
By all varieties of human love
Assisted, led me back through opening day
To those sweet counsels between head and heart
Whence grew that genuine knowledge, fraught
   with peace,
Which, through the later sinkings of this cause,
Hath still upheld me, and upholds me now
In the catastrophe (for so they dream,
And nothing less), when, finally to close
And seal up all the gains of France, a Pope[39]
Is summoned in, to crown an Emperor—
This last opprobrium, when we see a people
That once looked up in faith, as if to Heaven
For manna, take a lesson from the dog
Returning to his vomit; when the sun
That rose in splendour, was alive, and moved
In exultation with a living pomp
Of clouds—his glory's natural retinue—

325
330
335
340
345
350
355
360
365

---

38 Dorothy.
39 Pope Pius VII. The Emperor, of course, is Napoleon.
The event took place in December 1804.

Hath dropped all functions by the gods
    bestowed,
And, turned into a gewgaw, a machine,
Sets like an Opera phantom. 370

. . .

from Book Twelfth

IMAGINATION AND TASTE, HOW IMPAIRED
AND RESTORED

Long time have human ignorance and guilt
Detained us, on what spectacles of woe
Compelled to look, and inwardly oppressed
With sorrow, disappointment, vexing thoughts,
Confusion of the judgment, zeal decayed, 5
And, lastly, utter loss of hope itself
And things to hope for! Not with these began
Our song, and not with these our song must end.
Ye motions of delight, that haunt the sides
Of the green hills; ye breezes and soft airs, 10
Whose subtle intercourse with breathing flowers,
Feelingly watched, might teach Man's haughty
    race
How without injury to take, to give
Without offence; ye who, as if to show
The wondrous influence of power gently used, 15
Bend the complying heads of lordly pines,
And, with a touch, shift the stupendous clouds
Through the whole compass of the sky; ye
    brooks,
Muttering along the stones, a busy noise
By day, a quiet sound in silent night; 20
Ye waves, that out of the great deep steal forth
In a calm hour to kiss the pebbly shore,
Not mute, and then retire, fearing no storm;
And you, ye groves, whose ministry it is
To interpose the covert of your shades, 25
Even as a sleep, between the heart of man
And outward troubles, between man himself,
Not seldom, and his own uneasy heart:
Oh! that I had a music and a voice
Harmonious as your own, that I might tell 30
What ye have done for me. The morning shines,
Nor heedeth Man's perverseness; Spring
    returns,—
I saw the Spring return, and could rejoice,
In common with the children of her love,
Piping on boughs, or sporting on fresh fields, 35
Or boldly seeking pleasure nearer heaven
On wings that navigate cerulean skies.
So neither were complacency, nor peace,
Nor tender yearnings, wanting for my good

Through these distracted times; in Nature still 40
Glorying, I found a counterpoise in her,
Which, when the spirit of evil reached its height,
Maintained for me a secret happiness.

. . .

O Soul of Nature! excellent and fair!
That didst rejoice with me, with whom I, too,
Rejoiced through early youth, before the winds 95
And roaring waters, and in lights and shades
That marched and countermarched about the
    hills
In glorious apparition, Powers on whom
I daily waited, now all eye and now
All ear; but never long without the heart 100
Employed, and man's unfolding intellect:
O Soul of Nature! that, by laws divine
Sustained and governed, still dost overflow
With an impassioned life, what feeble ones
Walk on this earth! how feeble have I been 105
When thou wert in thy strength! Nor this
    through stroke
Of human suffering, such as justifies
Remissness and inaptitude of mind,
But through presumption; even in pleasure
    pleased
Unworthily, disliking here, and there 110
Liking; by rules of mimic art transferred
To things above all art; but more,—for this,
Although a strong infection of the age,
Was never much my habit—giving way
To a comparison of scene with scene, 115
Bent overmuch on superficial things,
Pampering myself with meagre novelties
Of colour and proportion; to the moods
Of time and season, to the moral power,
The affections and the spirit of the place, 120
Insensible. Nor only did the love
Of sitting thus in judgment interrupt
My deeper feelings, but another cause,
More subtle and less easily explained,
That almost seems inherent in the creature, 125
A twofold frame of body and of mind.
I speak in recollection of a time
When the bodily eye, in every stage of life
The most despotic of our senses, gained
Such strength in *me* as often held my mind 130
In absolute dominion. Gladly here,
Entering upon abstruser argument,
Could I endeavour to unfold the means
Which Nature studiously employs to thwart
This tyranny, summons all the senses each 135

To counteract the other, and themselves,
And makes them all, and the objects with which
    all
Are conversant, subservient in their turn
To the great ends of Liberty and Power.
But leave we this: enough that my delights   140
(Such as they were) were sought insatiably.
Vivid the transport, vivid though not profound;
I roamed from hill to hill, from rock to rock,
Still craving combinations of new forms,
New pleasure, wider empire for the sight,   145
Proud of her own endowments, and rejoiced
To lay the inner faculties asleep.
Amid the turns and counterturns, the strife
And various trials of our complex being,
As we grow up, such thraldom of that sense   150
Seems hard to shun. And yet I knew a maid,[40]
A young enthusiast, who escaped these bonds;
Her eye was not the mistress of her heart;
Far less did rules prescribed by passive taste,
Or barren intermeddling subtleties,   155
Perplex her mind; but, wise as women are
When genial circumstance hath favoured them,
She welcomed what was given, and craved no
    more;
Whate'er the scene presented to her view
That was the best, to that she was attuned   160
By her benign simplicity of life,
And through a perfect happiness of soul,
Whose variegated feelings were in this
Sisters, that they were each some new delight.
Birds in the bower, and lambs in the green field,   165
Could they have known her, would have loved;
    methought
Her very presence such a sweetness breathed,
That flowers, and trees, and even the silent hills,
And everything she looked on, should have had
An intimation how she bore herself   170
Towards them and to all creatures. God delights
In such a being; for, her common thoughts
Are piety, her life is gratitude.

Even like this maid, before I was called forth
From the retirement of my native hills,   175
I loved whate'er I saw: nor lightly loved,
But most intensely; never dreamt of aught
More grand, more fair, more exquisitely framed
Than those few nooks to which my happy feet
Were limited. I had not at that time   180

Lived long enough, nor in the least survived
The first diviner influence of this world,
As it appears to unaccustomed eyes.
Worshipping them among the depth of things,
As piety ordained, could I submit   185
To measured admiration, or to aught
That should preclude humility and love?
I felt, observed, and pondered; did not judge,
Yea, never thought of judging; with the gift
Of all this glory filled and satisfied.   190
And afterwards, when through the gorgeous Alps
Roaming, I carried with me the same heart:
In truth, the degradation—howsoe'er
Induced, effect, in whatsoe'er degree,
Of custom that prepares a partial scale   195
In which the little oft outweighs the great;
Or any other cause that hath been named;
Or lastly, aggravated by the times
And their impassioned sounds, which well might
    make
The milder minstrelsies of rural scenes   200
Inaudible—was transient; I had known
Too forcibly, too early in my life,
Visitings of imaginative power
For this to last: I shook the habit off
Entirely and for ever, and again   205
In Nature's presence stood, as now I stand,
A sensitive being, a *creative* soul.

    There are in our existence spots of time,
That with distinct pre-eminence retain
A renovating virtue, whence—depressed   210
By false opinion and contentious thought,
Or aught of heavier or more deadly weight,
In trivial occupations, and the round
Of ordinary intercourse—our minds
Are nourished and invisibly repaired;   215
A virtue, by which pleasure is enhanced,
That penetrates, enables us to mount,
When high, more high, and lifts us up when
    fallen.
This efficacious spirit chiefly lurks
Among those passages of life that give   220
Profoundest knowledge to what point, and how,
The mind is lord and master—outward sense
The obedient servant of her will. Such moments
Are scattered everywhere, taking their date
From our first childhood. I remember well,   225
That once, while yet my inexperienced hand
Could scarcely hold a bridle, with proud hopes
I mounted, and we journeyed towards the hills:

---

40 Dorothy.

An ancient servant of my father's house
Was with me, my encourager and guide: 230
We had not travelled long, ere some mischance
Disjoined me from my comrade; and, through fear
Dismounting, down the rough and stony moor
I led my horse, and, stumbling on, at length
Came to a bottom, where in former times   235
A murderer had been hung in iron chains.
The gibbet-mast had mouldered down, the bones
And iron case were gone; but on the turf,
Hard by, soon after that fell deed was wrought,
Some unknown hand had carved the murderer's   240
   name.
The monumental letters were inscribed
In times long past; but still, from year to year
By superstition of the neighbourhood,
The grass is cleared away, and to this hour
The characters are fresh and visible: 245
A casual glance had shown them, and I fled,
Faltering and faint, and ignorant of the road:
Then, reascending the bare common, saw
A naked pool that lay beneath the hills,
The beacon on the summit, and, more near,   250
A girl, who bore a pitcher on her head,
And seemed with difficult steps to force her way
Against the blowing wind. It was, in truth,
An ordinary sight; but I should need
Colours and words that are unknown to man,   255
To paint the visionary dreariness
Which, while I looked all round for my lost guide,
Invested moorland waste and naked pool,
The beacon crowning the lone eminence,
The female and her garments vexed and tossed   260
By the strong wind. When, in the blessèd hours
Of early love, the loved one at my side,
I roamed, in daily presence of this scene,
Upon the naked pool and dreary crags,
And on the melancholy beacon, fell   265
A spirit of pleasure and youth's golden gleam;
And think ye not with radiance more sublime
For these remembrances, and for the power
They had left behind? So feeling comes in aid
Of feeling, and diversity of strength   270
Attends us, if but once we have been strong.
Oh! mystery of man, from what a depth
Proceed thy honours. I am lost, but see
In simple childhood something of the base
On which thy greatness stands; but this I feel,   275
That from thyself it comes, that thou must give,
Else never canst receive. The days gone by
Return upon me almost from the dawn

Of life: the hiding-places of man's power
Open; I would approach them, but they close.   280
I see by glimpses now; when age comes on,
May scarcely see at all; and I would give,
While yet we may, as far as words can give,
Substance and life to what I feel, enshrining,
Such is my hope, the spirit of the Past   285
For future restoration.—Yet another
Of these memorials:—

                     One Christmas-time,
On the glad eve of its dear holidays,
Feverish, and tired, and restless, I went forth
Into the fields, impatient for the sight   290
Of those led palfreys that should bear us home;
My brothers and myself. There rose a crag,
That, from the meeting-point of two highways
Ascending, overlooked them both, far stretched;
Thither, uncertain on which road to fix   295
My expectation, thither I repaired,
Scout-like, and gained the summit; 't was a day
Tempestuous, dark, and wild, and on the grass
I sate half-sheltered by a naked wall;
Upon my right hand couched a single sheep,   300
Upon my left a blasted hawthorn stood;
With those companions at my side, I watched,
Straining my eyes intensely, as the mist
Gave intermitting prospect of the copse
And plain beneath. Ere we to school returned,—   305
That dreary time,—ere we had been ten days
Sojourners in my father's house, he died;
And I and my three brothers, orphans then,
Followed his body to the grave. The event,
With all the sorrow that it brought, appeared   310
A chastisement; and when I called to mind
That day so lately past, when from the crag
I looked in such anxiety of hope;
With trite reflections of morality,
Yet in the deepest passion, I bowed low   315
To God, Who thus corrected my desires;
And afterwards, the wind and sleety rain,
And all the business of the elements,
The single sheep, and the one blasted tree,
And the bleak music from that old stone wall,   320
The noise of wood and water, and the mist
That on the line of each of those two roads
Advanced in such indisputable shapes;
All these were kindred spectacles and sounds
To which I oft repaired, and thence would drink,   325
As at a fountain; and on winter nights,
Down to this very time, when storm and rain
Beat on my roof, or, haply, at noon-day,

While in a grove I walk, whose lofty trees,
Laden with summer's thickest foliage, rock 330
In a strong wind, some working of the spirit,
Some inward agitations thence are brought,
Whate'er their office, whether to beguile
Thoughts over busy in the course they took,
Or animate an hour of vacant ease. 335

from Book Fourteenth

CONCLUSION

In one of those excursions (may they ne'er
Fade from remembrance!) through the Northern
    tracts
Of Cambria[41] ranging with a youthful friend,
I left Bethgelert's huts at couching-time,
And westward took my way, to see the sun 5
Rise, from the top of Snowdon. To the door
Of a rude cottage at the mountain's base
We came, and roused the shepherd who attends
The adventurous stranger's steps, a trusty guide;
Then, cheered by short refreshment, sallied forth. 10

It was a close, warm, breezeless summer night,
Wan, dull, and glaring, with a dripping fog
Low-hung and thick that covered all the sky;
But, undiscouraged, we began to climb
The mountain-side. The mist soon girt us round, 15
And, after ordinary travellers' talk
With our conductor, pensively we sank
Each into commerce with his private thoughts:
Thus did we breast the ascent, and by myself
Was nothing either seen or heard that checked 20
Those musings or diverted, save that once
The shepherd's lurcher, who, among the crags,
Had to his joy unearthed a hedgehog, teased
His coiled-up prey with barkings turbulent.
This small adventure, for even such it seemed 25
In that wild place and at the dead of night,
Being over and forgotten, on we wound
In silence as before. With forehead bent
Earthward, as if in opposition set
Against an enemy, I panted up 30
With eager pace, and no less eager thoughts.
Thus might we wear a midnight hour away,

---

[41] Medieval Latin name for Wales. Mt. Snowdon, where
this scene takes place, is the highest mountain in northern
Wales.

Ascending at loose distance each from each,
And I, as chanced, the foremost of the band;
When at my feet the ground appeared to brighten, 35
And with a step or two seemed brighter still;
Nor was time given to ask or learn the cause,
For instantly a light upon the turf
Fell like a flash, and lo! as I looked up
The Moon hung naked in a firmament 40
Of azure without cloud, and at my feet
Rested a silent sea of hoary mist.
A hundred hills their dusky backs upheaved
All over this still ocean; and beyond,
Far, far beyond, the solid vapours stretched, 45
In headlands, tongues, and promontory shapes,
Into the main Atlantic, that appeared
To dwindle, and give up his majesty,
Usurped upon far as the sight could reach.
Not so the ethereal vault; encroachment none 50
Was there, nor loss; only the inferior stars
Had disappeared, or shed a fainter light
In the clear presence of the full-orbed Moon,
Who, from her sovereign elevation, gazed
Upon the billowy ocean, as it lay 55
All meek and silent, save that through a rift—
Not distant from the shore whereon we stood,
A fixed abysmal, gloomy, breathing-place—
Mounted the roar of waters, torrents, streams
Innumerable, roaring with one voice! 60
Heard over earth and sea, and, in that hour,
For so it seemed, felt by the starry heavens.

When into air had partially dissolved
That vision, given to spirits of the night
And three chance human wanderers, in calm 65
    thought
Reflected, it appeared to me the type
Of a majestic intellect, its acts
And its possessions, what it has and craves,
What in itself it is, and would become.
There I beheld the emblem of a mind 70
That feeds upon infinity, that broods
Over the dark abyss, intent to hear
Its voices issuing forth to silent light
In one continuous stream; a mind sustained
By recognitions of transcendent power, 75
In sense conducting to ideal form,
In soul of more than mortal privilege.
One function, above all, of such a mind
Had Nature shadowed there, by putting forth,
'Mid circumstances awful and sublime, 80
That mutual domination which she loves

To exert upon the face of outward things,
So moulded, joined, abstracted, so endowed
With interchangeable supremacy,
That men, least sensitive, see, hear, perceive, 85
And cannot choose but feel. The power, which all
Acknowledge when thus moved, which Nature
  thus
To bodily sense exhibits, is the express
Resemblance of that glorious faculty
That higher minds bear with them as their own. 90
This is the very spirit in which they deal
With the whole compass of the universe:
They from their native selves can send abroad
Kindred mutations; for themselves create
A like existence; and, whene'er it dawns 95
Created for them, catch it, or are caught
By its inevitable mastery,
Like angels stopped upon the wing by sound
Of harmony from Heaven's remotest spheres.
Them the enduring and the transient both 100
Serve to exalt; they build up greatest things
From least suggestions; ever on the watch,
Willing to work and to be wrought upon,
They need not extraordinary calls
To rouse them; in a world of life they live, 105
By sensible impressions not enthralled,
But by their quickening impulse made more
  prompt
To hold fit converse with the spiritual world,
And with the generations of mankind
Spread over time, past, present, and to come, 110
Age after age, till Time shall be no more.
Such minds are truly from the Deity,
For they are Powers; and hence the highest bliss
That flesh can know is theirs—the consciousness
Of Whom they are, habitually infused 115
Through every image and through every thought,
And all affections by communion raised
From earth to heaven, from human to divine;
Hence endless occupation for the Soul,
Whether discursive or intuitive; 120
Hence cheerfulness for acts of daily life,
Emotions which best foresight need not fear,
Most worthy then of trust when most intense.
Hence, amid ills that vex and wrongs that crush
Our hearts—if here the words of Holy Writ 125
May with fit reverence be applied—that peace
Which passeth understanding, that repose
In moral judgments which from this pure source
Must come, or will by man be sought in vain.

. . .

from Preface to the Second Edition of *Lyrical Ballads*

The second edition of *Lyrical Ballads* came out in 1801 (misdated 1800) in the first of two volumes, the second of which added new poems by Wordsworth. The essay was altered and expanded in subsequent editions of his poems; eventually it was printed as an appendix. The present text incorporates changes but not all the added material.

The first Volume of these Poems has already been submitted to general perusal. It was published, as an experiment, which, I hoped, might be of some use to ascertain, how far, by fitting to metrical arrangement a selection of the real language of men in a state of vivid sensation, that sort of pleasure and that quantity of pleasure may be imparted, which a Poet may rationally endeavour to impart.

I had formed no very inaccurate estimate of 10 the probable effect of those Poems: I flattered myself that they who should be pleased with them would read them with more than common pleasure: and, on the other hand, I was well aware, that by those who should dislike them, they would be read with more than common dislike. The result has differed from my expectation in this only, that a greater number have been pleased than I ventured to hope I should please. . . .[1] 20

. . .

The principal object, then, proposed in these Poems was to choose incidents and situations from common life, and to relate or describe them, throughout, as far as was possible in a selection of language really used by men, and, at the same time, to throw over them a certain colouring of imagination, whereby ordinary things should be presented to the mind in an unusual aspect; and, further, and above all, to make these incidents and situations interesting by tracing in 30 them, truly though not ostentatiously, the primary laws of our nature: chiefly, as far as regards the manner in which we associate ideas in a state of excitement. Humble and rustic life was gen-

---

[1] At this point Wordsworth mentions Coleridge's contribution of "The Ancient Mariner" and three other poems, and goes on to declare his own unwillingness to engage in an elaborate defense of the new poetic theory.

erally chosen, because, in that condition, the essential passions of the heart find a better soil in which they can attain their maturity, are less under restraint, and speak a plainer and more emphatic language; because in that condition of life our elementary feelings coexist in a state of greater simplicity, and, consequently, may be more accurately contemplated, and more forcibly communicated; because the manners of rural life germinate from those elementary feelings, and, from the necessary character of rural occupations, are more easily comprehended, and are more durable; and, lastly, because in that condition the passions of men are incorporated with the beautiful and permanent forms of nature. The language, too, of these men has been adopted (purified indeed from what appear to be its real defects, from all lasting and rational causes of dislike or disgust) because such men hourly communicate with the best objects from which the best part of language is originally derived; and because, from their rank in society and the sameness and narrow circle of their intercourse, being less under the influence of social vanity, they convey their feelings and notions in simple and unelaborated expressions. Accordingly, such a language, arising out of repeated experience and regular feelings, is a more permanent, and a far more philosophical language, than that which is frequently substituted for it by Poets, who think that they are conferring honour upon themselves and their art, in proportion as they separate themselves from the sympathies of men, and indulge in arbitrary and capricious habits of expression, in order to furnish food for fickle tastes, and fickle appetites, of their own creation.[2]

I cannot, however, be insensible to the present outcry against the triviality and meanness, both of thought and language, which some of my contemporaries have occasionally introduced into their metrical compositions; and I acknowledge that this defect, where it exists, is more dishonourable to the Writer's own character than false refinement or arbitrary innovation, though I should contend at the same time, that it is far less pernicious in the sum of its consequences. From such verses the Poems in these volumes will be found

distinguished at least by one mark of difference, that each of them has a worthy *purpose*. Not that I always began to write with a distinct purpose formally conceived; but habits of meditation have, I trust, so prompted and regulated my feelings, that my descriptions of such objects as strongly excite those feelings, will be found to carry along with them a *purpose*. If this opinion be erroneous, I can have little right to the name of a Poet. For all good poetry is the spontaneous overflow of powerful feelings: and though this be true, Poems to which any value can be attached were never produced on any variety of subjects but by a man who, being possessed of more than usual organic sensibility, had also thought long and deeply. For our continued influxes of feeling are modified and directed by our thoughts, which are indeed the representatives of all our past feelings; and, as by contemplating the relation of these general representatives to each other, we discover what is really important to men, so by the repetition and continuance of this act, our feelings will be connected with important subjects, till at length, if we be originally possessed of much sensibility, such habits of mind will be produced, that, by obeying blindly and mechanically the impulses of those habits, we shall describe objects, and utter sentiments, of such a nature, and in such connection with each other, that the understanding of the Reader must necessarily be in some degree enlightened, and his affections strengthened and purified.

It has been said that each of these Poems has a purpose. Another circumstance must be mentioned which distinguishes these Poems from the popular Poetry of the day; it is this, that the feeling therein developed gives importance to the action and situation, and not the action and situation to the feeling.

A sense of false modesty shall not prevent me from asserting, that the Reader's attention is pointed to this mark of distinction, far less for the sake of these particular Poems than from the general importance of the subject. The subject is indeed important! For the human mind is capable of being excited without the application of gross and violent stimulants; and he must have a very faint perception of its beauty and dignity who does not know this, and who does not further know, that one being is elevated above another, in proportion as he possesses this capability. It

---

2 Wordsworth's note: "It is worth while here to observe, that the affecting parts of Chaucer are almost always expressed in language pure and universally intelligible even to this day."

has therefore appeared to me, that to endeavour to produce or enlarge this capability is one of the best services in which, at any period, a Writer can be engaged; but this service, excellent at all times, is especially so at the present day. For a multitude of causes, unknown to former times, are now acting with a combined force to blunt the discriminating powers of the mind, and, unfitting it for all voluntary exertion, to reduce it to a state of almost savage torpor. The most effective of these causes are the great national events which are daily taking place,[3] and the increasing accumulation of men in cities, where the uniformity of their occupations produces a craving for extraordinary incident, which the rapid communication of intelligence[4] hourly gratifies. To this tendency of life and manners the literature and theatrical exhibitions of the country have conformed themselves. The invaluable works of our elder writers, I had almost said the works of Shakspeare and Milton, are driven into neglect by frantic novels,[5] sickly and stupid German Tragedies,[6] and deluges of idle and extravagant stories in verse.[7]—When I think upon this degrading thirst after outrageous stimulation, I am almost ashamed to have spoken of the feeble endeavour made in these volumes to counteract it; and, reflecting upon the magnitude of the general evil, I should be oppressed with no dishonourable melancholy, had I not a deep impression of certain inherent and indestructible qualities of the human mind, and likewise of certain powers in the great and permanent objects that act upon it, which are equally inherent and indestructible; and were there not added to this impression a belief, that the time is approaching when the evil will be systematically opposed, by men of greater powers, and with far more distinguished success.

Having dwelt thus long on the subjects and aim of these Poems, I shall request the Reader's permission to apprise him of a few circumstances relating to their *style,* in order, among other reasons, that he may not censure me for not having performed what I never attempted. The Reader will find that personifications of abstract ideas rarely occur in these volumes; and are utterly rejected, as an ordinary device to elevate the style, and raise it above prose. My purpose was to imitate, and, as far as possible, to adopt the very language of men; and assuredly such personifications do not make any natural or regular part of that language. They are, indeed, a figure of speech occasionally prompted by passion, and I have made use of them as such; but have endeavoured utterly to reject them as a mechanical device of style, or as a family language which Writers in metre seem to lay claim to by prescription. I have wished to keep the Reader in the company of flesh and blood, persuaded that by so doing I shall interest him. Others who pursue a different track will interest him likewise; I do not interfere with their claim, but wish to prefer[8] a claim of my own. There will also be found in these volumes little of what is usually poetic diction; as much pains has been taken to avoid it as is ordinarily taken to produce it; this has been done for the reason already alleged, to bring my language near to the language of men; and further, because the pleasure which I have proposed to myself to impart, is of a kind very different from that which is supposed by many persons to be the proper object of poetry. Without being culpably particular, I do not know how to give my Reader a more exact notion of the style in which it was my wish and intention to write, than by informing him that I have at all times endeavoured to look steadily at my subject; consequently, there is I hope in these Poems little falsehood of description, and my ideas are expressed in language fitted to their respective importance. Something must have been gained by this practice, as it is friendly to one property of all good poetry, namely, good sense: but it has necessarily cut me off from a large portion of phrases and figures of speech which from father to son have long been regarded as the common inheritance of Poets. I have also thought it expedient to restrict myself still further, having abstained from the use of many expressions, in themselves proper and beautiful, but which have been foolishly repeated by bad Poets, till such feelings of disgust are connected with them as it

---

[3] The war with France, for example.   [4] News.

[5] I.e., the Gothic novels or romances, such as Ann Radcliffe's *The Mysteries of Udolpho* (1794).

[6] Such as the sentimental plays of August von Kotzebue (1761–1819), which were extremely popular in England.

[7] Perhaps an allusion to the earliest work of Scott, written under the influence of German romanticism, as well as the work of some of his predecessors.

[8] Set forth.

is scarcely possible by any art of association to overpower.

If in a poem there should be found a series of lines, or even a single line, in which the language, though naturally arranged, and according to the strict laws of metre, does not differ from that of prose, there is a numerous class of critics, who, when they stumble upon these prosaisms, as they call them, imagine that they have made a notable discovery, and exult over the Poet as over a man ignorant of his own profession. Now these men would establish a canon of criticism which the Reader will conclude he must utterly reject, if he wishes to be pleased with these volumes. And it would be a most easy task to prove to him, that not only the language of a large portion of every good poem, even of the most elevated character, must necessarily, except with reference to the metre, in no respect differ from that of good prose, but likewise that some of the most interesting parts of the best poems will be found to be strictly the language of prose when prose is well written. The truth of this assertion might be demonstrated by innumerable passages from almost all the poetical writings, even of Milton himself. To illustrate the subject in a general manner, I will here adduce a short composition[9] of Gray, who was at the head of those who, by their reasonings, have attempted to widen the space of separation betwixt Prose and Metrical composition, and was more than any other man curiously elaborate in the structure of his own poetic diction.

In vain to me the smiling mornings shine,
And reddening Phoebus lifts his golden fire:
The birds in vain their amorous descant join,
Or cheerful fields resume their green attire.
These ears, alas! for other notes repine;
A different object do these eyes require;
My lonely anguish melts no heart but mine;
And in my breast the imperfect joys expire;
Yet morning smiles the busy race to cheer,
And new-born pleasure brings to happier men;
The fields to all their wonted tribute bear;
To warm their little loves the birds complain.
I fruitless mourn to him that cannot hear,
And weep the more because I weep in vain.

It will easily be perceived, that the only part of this Sonnet which is of any value is the lines printed in Italics; it is equally obvious, that, except in the rhyme, and in the use of the single word "fruitless" for fruitlessly, which is so far a defect, the language of these lines does in no respect differ from that of prose.

By the foregoing quotation it has been shown that the language of Prose may yet be well adapted to Poetry; and it was previously asserted, that a large portion of the language of every good poem can in no respect differ from that of good Prose. We will go further. It may be safely affirmed, that there neither is, nor can be, any *essential* difference between the language of prose and metrical composition. We are fond of tracing the resemblance between Poetry and Painting, and, accordingly, we call them Sisters: but where shall we find bonds of connection sufficiently strict to typify the affinity betwixt metrical and prose composition? They both speak by and to the same organs; the bodies in which both of them are clothed may be said to be of the same substance, their affections are kindred, and almost identical, not necessarily differing even in degree; Poetry[10] sheds no tears "such as Angels weep," but natural and human tears; she can boast of no celestial ichor[11] that distinguishes her vital juices from those of prose; the same human blood circulates through the veins of them both.

If it be affirmed that rhyme and metrical arrangement of themselves constitute a distinction which overturns what has just been said on strict affinity of metrical language with that of prose, and paves the way for other artificial distinctions which the mind voluntarily admits, I answer that the language of such Poetry as is here recommended is, as far as is possible, a selection of the language really spoken by men; that this selection, wherever it is made with true taste and feeling, will of itself form a distinction far

---

9 Sonnet "On the Death of Richard West." West, who was Gray's best friend at Eton, died young in 1742.

10 Wordsworth's note: "I here use the word 'Poetry' (though against my own judgment) as opposed to the word Prose, and synonymous with metrical composition. But much confusion has been introduced into criticism by this contradistinction of Poetry and Prose, instead of the more philosophical one of Poetry and Matter of Fact, or Science. The only strict antithesis to Prose is Metre; nor is this, in truth, a *strict* antithesis, because lines and passages of metre so naturally occur in writing prose, that it would be scarcely possible to avoid them, even were it desirable."
11 In classical mythology, the fluid that flowed instead of blood in the veins of the gods.

greater than would at first be imagined, and will entirely separate the composition from the vulgarity and meanness of ordinary life; and, if metre be super-added thereto, I believe that a dissimilitude will be produced altogether sufficient for the gratification of a rational mind. What other distinction would we have? Whence is it to come? And where is it to exist? Not, surely, where the Poet speaks through the mouths of his characters: it cannot be necessary here, either for elevation of style, or any of its supposed ornaments: for, if the Poet's subject be judiciously chosen, it will naturally, and upon fit occasion, lead him to passions the language of which, if selected truly and judiciously, must necessarily be dignified and variegated, and alive with metaphors and figures. I forbear to speak of an incongruity which would shock the intelligent Reader, should the Poet interweave any foreign splendour of his own with that which the passion naturally suggests: it is sufficient to say that such addition is unnecessary. And, surely, it is more probable that those passages, which with propriety abound with metaphors and figures, will have their due effect, if, upon other occasions where the passions are of a milder character, the style also be subdued and temperate.

But, as the pleasure which I hope to give by the Poems now presented to the Reader must depend entirely on just notions upon this subject, and, as it is in itself of high importance to our taste and moral feelings, I cannot content myself with these detached remarks. And if, in what I am about to say, it shall appear to some that my labour is unnecessary, and that I am like a man fighting a battle without enemies, such persons may be reminded, that, whatever be the language outwardly holden by men, a practical faith in the opinions which I am wishing to establish is almost unknown. If my conclusions are admitted, and carried as far as they must be carried if admitted at all, our judgments concerning the works of the greatest Poets both ancient and modern will be far different from what they are at present, both when we praise, and when we censure: and our moral feelings influencing and influenced by these judgments will, I believe, be corrected and purified.

Taking up the subject, then, upon general grounds, let me ask, what is meant by the word Poet? What is a Poet? To whom does he address himself? And what language is to be expected from him?—He is a man speaking to men: a man, it is true, endowed with more lively sensibility, more enthusiasm and tenderness, who has a greater knowledge of human nature, and a more comprehensive soul, than are supposed to be common among mankind; a man pleased with his own passions and volitions, and who rejoices more than other men in the spirit of life that is in him; delighting to contemplate similar volitions and passions as manifested in the goings-on of the Universe, and habitually impelled to create them where he does not find them. To these qualities he has added a disposition to be affected more than other men by absent things as if they were present; an ability of conjuring up in himself passions, which are indeed far from being the same as those produced by real events, yet (especially in those parts of the general sympathy which are pleasing and delightful) do more nearly resemble the passions produced by real events, than anything which, from the motions of their own minds merely, other men are accustomed to feel in themselves:—whence, and from practice, he has acquired a greater readiness and power in expressing what he thinks and feels, and especially those thoughts and feelings which, by his own choice, or from the structure of his own mind, arise in him without immediate external excitement.

But whatever portion of this faculty we may suppose even the greatest Poet to possess, there cannot be a doubt that the language which it will suggest to him, must often, in liveliness and truth, fall short of that which is uttered by men in real life, under the actual pressure of those passions, certain shadows of which the Poet thus produces, or feels to be produced, in himself.

However exalted a notion we would wish to cherish of the character of a Poet, it is obvious, that while he describes and imitates passions, his employment is in some degree mechanical, compared with the freedom and power of real and substantial action and suffering. So that it will be the wish of the Poet to bring his feelings near to those of the persons whose feelings he describes, nay, for short spaces of time, perhaps, to let himself slip into an entire delusion, and even confound and identify his own feelings with theirs; modifying only the language which is thus suggested to him by a consideration that he describes for a particular purpose, that of giving pleasure. Here, then, he will apply the principle of selection which has been already insisted upon. He will depend upon this for removing what would otherwise be painful or disgusting in the passion; he will feel that there is no necessity to trick out or to elevate nature: and, the more industriously he applies this principle, the deeper will be his faith that no words, which *his* fancy or imagination can suggest, will be to be compared with those which are the emanations of reality and truth.

But it may be said by those who do not object to the general spirit of these remarks, that, as it is impossible for the Poet to produce upon all occasions language as exquisitely fitted for the passion as that which the real passion itself suggests, it is proper that he should consider himself as in the situation of a translator, who does not scruple to substitute excellencies of another kind for those which are unattainable by him; and endeavours occasionally to surpass his original, in order to make some amends for the general inferiority to which he feels that he must submit. But this would be to encourage idleness and unmanly despair. Further, it is the language of men who speak of what they do not understand; who talk of Poetry as of a matter of amusement and idle pleasure; who will converse with us as gravely about a *taste* for Poetry, as they express it, as if it were a thing as indifferent as a taste for rope-dancing, or Frontiniac[12] or Sherry. Aristotle, I have been told, has said, that Poetry is the most philosophic of all writing:[13] it is so: its object is truth, not individual and local, but general, and operative; not standing upon external testimony, but carried alive into the heart by passion; truth which is its own testimony, which gives competence and confidence to the tribunal to which it appeals, and receives them from the same tribunal. Poetry is the image of man and nature. The obstacles which stand in the way of the fidelity of the Biographer and Historian, and of their consequent utility, are incalculably greater than those which are to be encountered by the Poet who comprehends the dignity of his art. The Poet writes under one restriction only, namely, the necessity of giving immediate pleasure to a human Being possessed of that information which may be expected from him, not as a lawyer, a physician, a mariner, an astronomer, or a natural philosopher,[14] but as a Man. Except this one restriction, there is no object standing between the Poet and the image of things; between this, and the Biographer and Historian, there are a thousand.

Nor let this necessity of producing immediate pleasure be considered as a degradation of the Poet's art. It is far otherwise. It is an acknowledgment of the beauty of the Universe, an acknowledgment the more sincere, because not formal, but indirect; it is a task light and easy to him who looks at the world in the spirit of love: further, it is a homage paid to the native and naked dignity of man, to the grand elementary principle of pleasure, by which he knows, and feels, and lives, and moves. We have no sympathy but what is propagated by pleasure: I would not be misunderstood; but wherever we sympathise with pain, it will be found that the sympathy is produced and carried on by subtle combinations with pleasure. We have no knowledge, that is, no general principles drawn from the contemplation of particular facts, but what has been built up by pleasure, and exists in us by pleasure alone. The Man of science, the Chemist and Mathematician, whatever difficulties and disgusts they may have had to struggle with, know and feel this. However painful may be the objects with which the Anatomist's knowledge is connected, he feels that his knowledge is pleasure; and where he has no pleasure he has no knowledge. What then does the Poet? He considers man and the objects that surround him as acting and re-acting upon each other, so as to produce an infinite complexity of pain and pleasure; he considers man in his own nature and in his ordinary life as contemplating this with a certain quantity of immediate knowledge, with certain convictions, intuitions, and deductions, which from habit acquire the quality of intuitions; he considers him as looking upon this complex scene of ideas and sensations, and finding everywhere objects that immediately excite in him sympathies which, from the necessities of his

---

12 Frontignac, a sweet wine of southern France.
13 Aristotle (*Poetics*, IX) says that the truth of poetry is more serious and philosophical than that of history, since the latter deals with the particular and the former with the universal.

14 Student of the natural sciences.

nature, are accompanied by an overbalance of enjoyment.

To this knowledge which all men carry about with them, and to these sympathies in which, without any other discipline than that of our daily life, we are fitted to take delight, the Poet principally directs his attention. He considers man and nature as essentially adapted to each other, and the mind of man as naturally the mirror of the fairest and most interesting properties of nature. And thus the Poet, prompted by this feeling of pleasure, which accompanies him through the whole course of his studies, converses with general nature, with affections akin to those, which, through labour and length of time, the Man of science has raised up in himself, by conversing with those particular parts of nature which are the objects of his studies. The knowledge both of the Poet and the Man of science is pleasure; but the knowledge of the one cleaves to us as a necessary part of our existence, our natural and unalienable inheritance; the other is a personal and individual acquisition, slow to come to us, and by no habitual and direct sympathy connecting us with our fellow-beings. The Man of science seeks truth as a remote and unknown benefactor; he cherishes and loves it in his solitude: the Poet, singing a song in which all human beings join with him, rejoices in the presence of truth as our visible friend and hourly companion. Poetry is the breath and finer spirit of all knowledge; it is the impassioned expression which is in the countenance of all Science. Emphatically may it be said of the Poet, as Shakspeare hath said of man, "that he looks before and after."[15] He is the rock of defence for human nature; an upholder and preserver, carrying everywhere with him relationship and love. In spite of difference of soil and climate, of language and manners, of laws and customs: in spite of things silently gone out of mind, and things violently destroyed; the Poet binds together by passion and knowledge the vast empire of human society, as it is spread over the whole earth, and over all time. The objects of the Poet's thoughts are everywhere; though the eyes and senses of man are, it is true, his favourite guides, yet he will follow wheresoever he can find an atmosphere of sensation in which to

move his wings. Poetry is the first and last of all knowledge—it is as immortal as the heart of man. If the labours of Men of science should ever create any material revolution, direct or indirect, in our condition, and in the impressions which we habitually receive, the Poet will sleep then no more than at present; he will be ready to follow the steps of the Man of science, not only in those general indirect effects, but he will be at his side, carrying sensation into the midst of the objects of the science itself. The remotest discoveries of the Chemist, the Botanist, or Mineralogist, will be as proper objects of the Poet's art as any upon which it can be employed, if the time should ever come when these things shall be familiar to us, and the relations under which they are contemplated by the followers of these respective sciences shall be manifestly and palpably material to us as enjoying and suffering beings. If the time should ever come when what is now called science, thus familiarised to men, shall be ready to put on, as it were, a form of flesh and blood, the Poet will lend his divine spirit to aid the transfiguration, and will welcome the Being thus produced, as a dear and genuine inmate of the household of man.—It is not, then, to be supposed that any one, who holds that sublime notion of Poetry which I have attempted to convey, will break in upon the sanctity and truth of his pictures by transitory and accidental ornaments, and endeavour to excite admiration of himself by arts, the necessity of which must manifestly depend upon the assumed meanness of his subject.

What has been thus far said applies to Poetry in general; but especially to those parts of composition where the Poet speaks through the mouths of his characters; and upon this point it appears to authorise the conclusion that there are few persons of good sense, who would not allow that the dramatic parts of composition are defective, in proportion as they deviate from the real language of nature, and are coloured by a diction of the Poet's own, either peculiar to him as an individual Poet or belonging simply to Poets in general; to a body of men who, from the circumstance of their compositions being in metre, it is expected will employ a particular language.

It is not, then, in the dramatic parts of composition that we look for this distinction of

15 Cf. *Hamlet*, IV, iv, 37.

language; but still it may be proper and necessary where the Poet speaks to us in his own person and character. To this I answer by referring the Reader to the description before given of a Poet. Among the qualities there enumerated as principally conducing to form a Poet, is implied nothing differing in kind from other men, but only in degree. The sum of what was said is, that the Poet is chiefly distinguished from other men by a greater promptness to think and feel without immediate external excitement, and a greater power in expressing such thoughts and feelings as are produced in him in that manner. But these passions and thoughts and feelings are the general passions and thoughts and feelings of men. And with what are they connected? Undoubtedly with our moral sentiments and animal sensations, and with the causes which excite these; with the operations of the elements, and the appearances of the visible universe; with storm and sunshine, with the revolutions of the seasons, with cold and heat, with loss of friends and kindred, with injuries and resentments, gratitude and hope, with fear and sorrow. These, and the like, are the sensations and objects which the Poet describes, as they are the sensations of other men, and the objects which interest them. The Poet thinks and feels in the spirit of human passions. How, then, can his language differ in any material degree from that of all other men who feel vividly and see clearly? It might be *proved* that it is impossible. But supposing that this were not the case, the Poet might then be allowed to use a peculiar language when expressing his feelings for his own gratification, or that of men like himself. But Poets do not write for Poets alone, but for men. Unless therefore we are advocates for that admiration which subsists upon ignorance, and that pleasure which arises from hearing what we do not understand, the Poet must descend from this supposed height; and, in order to excite rational sympathy, he must express himself as other men express themselves. To this it may be added, that while he is only selecting from the real language of men, or, which amounts to the same thing, composing accurately in the spirit of such selection, he is treading upon safe ground, and we know what we are to expect from him. Our feelings are the same with respect to metre; for, as it may be proper to remind the

Reader, the distinction of metre is regular and uniform, and not, like that which is produced by what is usually called POETIC DICTION, arbitrary, and subject to infinite caprices upon which no calculation whatever can be made. In the one case, the Reader is utterly at the mercy of the Poet, respecting what imagery or diction he may choose to connect with the passion; whereas, in the other, the metre obeys certain laws, to which the Poet and Reader both willingly submit because they are certain, and because no interference is made by them with the passion, but such as the concurring testimony of ages has shown to heighten and improve the pleasure which co-exists with it.

It will now be proper to answer an obvious question, namely, Why, professing these opinions, have I written in verse? To this, in addition to such answer as is included in what has been already said, I reply, in the first place, Because, however I may have restricted myself, there is still left open to me what confessedly constitutes the most valuable object of all writing, whether in prose or verse; the great and universal passions of men, the most general and interesting of their occupations, and the entire world of nature before me—to supply endless combinations of forms and imagery. Now, supposing for a moment that whatever is interesting in these objects may be as vividly described in prose, why should I be condemned for attempting to superadd to such description the charm which, by the consent of all nations, is acknowledged to exist in metrical language? To this, by such as are yet unconvinced, it may be answered that a very small part of the pleasure given by Poetry depends upon the metre, and that it is injudicious to write in metre, unless it be accompanied with the other artificial distinctions of style with which metre is usually accompanied, and that, by such deviation, more will be lost from the shock which will thereby be given to the Reader's associations than will be counterbalanced by any pleasure which he can derive from the general power of numbers.[16] In answer to those who still contend for the necessity of accompanying metre with certain appropriate colours of style in order to the accomplishment of its appropriate end, and who also, in my

16 Meter, versification.

opinion, greatly underrate the power of metre in itself, it might, perhaps, as far as relates to these Volumes, have been almost sufficient to observe, that poems are extant, written upon more humble subjects, and in a still more naked and simple style, which have continued to give pleasure from generation to generation. Now, if nakedness and simplicity be a defect, the fact here mentioned affords a strong presumption that poems somewhat less naked and simple are capable of affording pleasure at the present day; and, what I wished *chiefly* to attempt, at present, was to justify myself for having written under the impression of this belief. . . .[17]

I have said that poetry is the spontaneous overflow of powerful feelings: it takes its origin from emotion recollected in tranquillity: the emotion is contemplated till, by a species of reaction, the tranquillity gradually disappears, and an emotion, kindred to that which was before the subject of contemplation, is gradually produced, and does itself actually exist in the mind. In this mood successful composition generally begins, and in a mood similar to this it is carried on; but the emotion, of whatever kind, and in whatever degree, from various causes, is qualified by various pleasures, so that in describing any passions whatsoever, which are voluntarily described, the mind will, upon the whole, be in a state of enjoyment. If Nature be thus cautious to preserve in a state of enjoyment a being so employed, the Poet ought to profit by the lesson held forth to him, and ought especially to take care, that, whatever passions he communicates to his Reader, those passions, if his Reader's mind be sound and vigorous, should always be accompanied with an overbalance of pleasure. Now the music of harmonious metrical language, the sense of difficulty overcome, and the blind association of pleasure which has been previously received from works of rhyme or metre of the same or similar construction, an indistinct perception perpetually renewed of language closely resembling that of real life, and yet, in the circumstance of metre, differing from it so widely—all these imperceptibly make up a complex feeling of delight, which is of the most important use in tempering the painful feeling always found intermingled with powerful descriptions of the deeper passions. This effect is always produced in pathetic and impassioned poetry; while, in lighter compositions, the ease and gracefulness with which the Poet manages his numbers are themselves confessedly a principal source of the gratification of the Reader. All that it is *necessary* to say, however, upon this subject, may be effected by affirming, what few persons will deny, that, of two descriptions, either of passions, manners, or characters, each of them equally well executed, the one in prose and the other in verse, the verse will be read a hundred times where the prose is read once.

Having thus explained a few of my reasons for writing in verse, and why I have chosen subjects from common life, and endeavoured to bring my language near to the real language of men, if I have been too minute in pleading my own cause, I have at the same time been treating a subject of general interest; and for this reason a few words shall be added with reference solely to these particular poems, and to some defects which will probably be found in them. I am sensible that my associations must have sometimes been particular instead of general, and that, consequently, giving to things a false importance, I may have sometimes written upon unworthy subjects; but I am less apprehensive on this account, than that my language may frequently have suffered from those arbitrary connections of feelings and ideas with particular words and phrases, from which no man can altogether protect himself. Hence I have no doubt, that, in some instances, feelings, even of the ludicrous, may be given to my Readers by expressions which appeared to me tender and pathetic. Such faulty expressions, were I convinced they were faulty at present, and that they must necessarily continue to be so, I would willingly take all reasonable pains to correct. But it is dangerous to make these alterations on the simple authority of a few individuals, or even of certain classes of men; for where the understanding of an Author is not convinced, or his feelings altered, this cannot be done without great injury to himself: for his own feelings are his stay and support; and, if he set them aside in one instance, he may be induced to repeat this act till his mind shall lose all confidence in itself, and become utterly debilitated. To this it may be added, that the critic ought never to forget that he is himself

---

[17] A passage on the importance of meter is here omitted.

exposed to the same errors as the Poet, and, perhaps, in a much greater degree: for there can be no presumption in saying of most readers, that it is not probable they will be so well acquainted with the various stages of meaning through which words have passed, or with the fickleness or stability of the relations of particular ideas to each other; and, above all, since they are so much less interested in the subject, they may decide lightly and carelessly.

Long as the Reader has been detained, I hope he will permit me to caution him against a mode of false criticism which has been applied to Poetry, in which the language closely resembles that of life and nature. Such verses have been triumphed over in parodies, of which Dr. Johnson's stanza is a fair specimen:—

> I put my hat upon my head
> And walked into the Strand,[18]
> And there I met another man
> Whose hat was in his hand.

Immediately under these lines let us place one of the most justly-admired stanzas of the "Babes in the Wood."[19]

> These pretty Babes with hand in hand
> Went wandering up and down;
> But never more they saw the Man
> Approaching from the Town.

In both these stanzas the words, and the order of the words, in no respect differ from the most unimpassioned conversation. There are words in both, for example, "the Strand," and "the Town," connected with none but the most familiar ideas; yet the one stanza we admit as admirable, and the other as a fair example of the superlatively contemptible. Whence arises this difference? Not from the metre, not from the language, not from the order of the words; but the *matter* expressed in Dr. Johnson's stanza is contemptible. The proper method of treating trivial and simple verses, to which Dr. Johnson's stanza would be a fair parallelism, is not to say, this is a bad kind of poetry, or, this is not poetry; but, this wants sense; it is neither interesting in itself, nor can *lead* to anything interesting; the images neither originate in that sane state of feeling which arises out of thought, nor can excite thought or feeling in the Reader. This is the only sensible manner of dealing with such verses. Why trouble yourself about the species till you have previously decided upon the genus? Why take pains to prove that an ape is not a Newton, when it is self-evident that he is not a man?

One request I must make of my Reader, which is, that in judging these Poems he would decide by his own feelings genuinely, and not by reflection upon what will probably be the judgment of others. How common is it to hear a person say, I myself do not object to this style of composition, or this or that expression, but, to such and such classes of people it will appear mean or ludicrous! This mode of criticism, so destructive of all sound unadulterated judgment, is almost universal: let the Reader then abide, independently, by his own feelings, and, if he finds himself affected, let him not suffer such conjectures to interfere with his pleasure.

If an Author, by any single composition, has impressed us with respect for his talents, it is useful to consider this as affording a presumption, that on other occasions where we have been displeased, he, nevertheless, may not have written ill or absurdly; and further, to give him so much credit for this one composition as may induce us to review what has displeased us, with more care than we should otherwise have bestowed upon it. This is not only an act of justice, but, in our decisions upon poetry especially, may conduce, in a high degree, to the improvement of our own taste; for an *accurate* taste in poetry, and in all the other arts, as Sir Joshua Reynolds has observed,[20] is an *acquired* talent, which can only be produced by thought and a long-continued intercourse with the best models of composition. This is mentioned, not with so ridiculous a purpose as to prevent the most inexperienced Reader from judging for himself, (I have already said that I wish him to judge for himself;) but merely to temper the rashness of decision, and to suggest, that, if Poetry be a subject on which much time has not been bestowed, the judgment may be erroneous; and that, in many cases, it necessarily will be so.

Nothing would, I know, have so effectually

---

18 One of London's most famous streets.
19 Reprinted in *The Oxford Book of Ballads*, pp. 854–59.

20 In the seventh of the *Discourses* of this eminent eighteenth-century painter.

contributed to further the end which I have in view, as to have shown of what kind the pleasure is, and how that pleasure is produced, which is confessedly produced by metrical composition essentially different from that which I have here endeavoured to recommend: for the Reader will say that he has been pleased by such composition; and what more can be done for him? The power of any art is limited; and he will suspect, that, if it be proposed to furnish him with new friends, that can be only upon condition of his abandoning his old friends. Besides, as I have said, the Reader is himself conscious of the pleasure which he has received from such composition, composition to which he has peculiarly attached the endearing name of Poetry; and all men feel an habitual gratitude, and something of an honourable bigotry, for the objects which have long continued to please them: we not only wish to be pleased, but to be pleased in that particular way in which we have been accustomed to be pleased. There is in these feelings enough to resist a host of arguments; and I should be the less able to combat them successfully, as I am willing to allow, that, in order entirely to enjoy the Poetry which I am recommending, it would be necessary to give up much of what is ordinarily enjoyed. But, would my limits have permitted me to point out how this pleasure is produced, many obstacles might have been removed, and the Reader assisted in perceiving that the powers of language are not so limited as he may suppose; and that it is possible for poetry to give other enjoyments, of a purer, more lasting, and more exquisite nature. This part of the subject has not been altogether neglected, but it has not been so much my present aim to prove, that the interest excited by some other kinds of poetry is less vivid, and less worthy of the nobler powers of the mind, as to offer reasons for presuming, that if my purpose were fulfilled, a species of poetry would be produced, which is genuine poetry; in its nature well adapted to interest mankind permanently, and likewise important in the multiplicity and quality of its moral relations.

From what has been said, and from a perusal of the Poems, the Reader will be able clearly to perceive the object which I had in view: he will determine how far it has been attained; and, what is a much more important question, whether it be worth attaining: and upon the decision of these two questions will rest my claim to the approbation of the Public.

Sir Walter Scott

1771–1832

Scott is the chief exponent of the antiquarian interest that was an important part of the Romantic Movement. Born in Edinburgh, he spent much of his childhood on his grandfather's farm of Sandyknowe in the valley of the Tweed. In that region of ruined castles and abbeys, where for centuries the Border raiders had harried and the tides of Anglo-Scottish war had ebbed and flowed, he stored his head with local history and legend, learning ballads by heart and devouring romances. Later on, in Edinburgh, he found less exhilaration in his law books than in history, medieval literature, travel books, and Shakespeare's plays. He was particularly in love with the medieval —the "Gothic." He delighted in his "raids," both along the Border and among the Highlands, into districts relatively little touched by modernity. He would talk with the oldest inhabitants, listening avidly to legend, folklore, and tales of Jacobite adventure.

His delight in the popular ballads bore early fruit in the most important collection since Percy's *Reliques* (1765): the three volumes of *Minstrelsy of the Scottish Border* (1802–03). A recitation of Coleridge's *Christabel* that he happened to hear impelled him to try his own hand at a metrical romance. In 1805 appeared *The Lay of the Last Minstrel*, the first of the long narrative poems that for a time gave Scott, of all the living British poets, first place in public esteem. *Marmion* was received with great acclaim in 1808, and two years later came the most popular of them all, *The Lady of the Lake*. With *Rokeby* (1812) sales began falling off, largely because of the sudden popularity of Byron's narrative poems; and several later titles made it clear that public taste for Scott's "stale romance," as the youthful Byron contemptuously termed it, had waned. Scott obediently abandoned the genre and turned to another, the historical novel. In it he more than duplicated his success as a poet.

His first novel, *Waverley*, was published anonymously in 1814. It was the first of a long series known as the Waverley Novels; for years Scott averaged two annually. He did not acknowledge his authorship till 1827; but it was an open secret long before then. Among the best of the earlier novels, in which he is more realistic than later, are *Guy Mannering*, *The Antiquary*, *Old Mortality*, *Rob Roy*, and *The Heart of Midlothian*, all published in 1815–18 and set in Scotland. To name only the best of the later, *Ivanhoe* (1819) hardly rises above the level of a good adventure yarn for young people, but Scott incorporates in it several thrilling scenes of England during the reign of Richard Lion-Heart; and *Kenilworth* (1821) takes us, with many historical inaccuracies, to the days of Queen Elizabeth. The France of Louis XI provides the setting of *Quentin Durward* (1823), while in *Redgauntlet* (1824) Scott returns to his native land.

These and many other books made a great deal of money, of which Scott determined at the outset to obtain a larger share than often falls to the lot of authors. Though he had no aptitude for commerce, he became a secret partner in a printing business, sold his copyrights for large sums, and obliged his publishers to employ his firm as printers. He had established himself on an estate called Abbotsford, on the banks of the Tweed near Melrose, in the Border country of southwestern Scotland. There rose an incredible dwelling, a baronial castle, which embodied the dream of a romantic boy who never entirely grew up. In this absurd structure—as absurd as the Gothic novels by which Scott's work was much influenced—he spent the larger part of the rest of his life, in as medieval an atmosphere as money could provide. There he played, in all sincerity, the hospitable role of the great gentleman. Abbotsford became a sinkhole of his fortune. With reckless folly he anticipated (that is, drew out and spent) the profits of books not yet written; and in 1826 his own firm and both its allied publishing houses failed. Scott's imprudence was not the only cause of the crash, but it was a major factor.

He might have tried for a fresh start by recourse to bankruptcy, but he thought that procedure unworthy of a gentleman. The creditors saw they stood to gain if they let him go on working—for them. Scott assumed his share of the debt, and drove his pen more furiously than ever, at history and biography as well as at more novels. In the next two years he earned $200,000; further profits accruing after his death paid his creditors in full. He managed to keep Abbotsford for his children, but his exertions killed him. Even after his first stroke of paralysis in 1830, he toiled doggedly on for another year. In 1832 he died.

Scott's eminence was, and is, due to a remarkable gift for storytelling; but he was a versatile man of letters as well as a popular purveyor of romantic fiction. In addition to important labors as a ballad collector, he brought out monumental editions of Dryden (18 vols., 1808) and Swift (19 vols., 1814). A staunch, irrational Tory, he helped in 1809 to launch the great *Quarterly Review* in London, to compete with the *Edinburgh Review*. In 1813, declining the poet laureateship, he recommended Southey. In 1820 he was made a baronet.

TEXTS: The novels are in many editions. J. L. Robertson, ed., *Poetical Works* (1904); H. J. C. Grierson, ed., *Letters* (12 vols., 1932–37); J. G. Tait, ed., *Journal* (3 vols., 1939–46). About Scott: John Buchan, *Sir Walter Scott* (1932); David Daiches, *Sir Walter Scott and His World* (1971); Donald Davie, *The Heyday of Sir Walter Scott* (1961); John O. Hayen, *Scott: The Critical Heritage* (1970); H. J. C. Grierson, *Sir Walter Scott, Bart.* (1938); Edgar Johnson, *Sir Walter Scott: The Great Unknown* (1970); J. G. Lockhart, *Memoirs of the Life of Sir Walter Scott* (7 vols., 1837–38).

Harp of the North

These are the opening stanzas (note the Spenserian form) of *The Lady of the Lake;* immediately after them the narrative begins.

Harp of the North! that mouldering long hast
   hung
  On the witch-elm[1] that shades Saint Fillan's
    spring,
And down the fitful breeze thy numbers[2] flung,
  Till envious ivy did around thee cling,
Muffling with verdant ringlet every string,—   5
  O minstrel Harp, still must thine accents
    sleep?
'Mid rustling leaves and fountains murmuring,
  Still must thy sweeter sounds their silence
    keep,
Nor bid a warrior smile, nor teach a maid to
   weep?

---

1 Wych-elm, Scotch elm.   2 Measures, i.e., strains.

Not thus, in ancient days of Caledon,[3]   10
   Was thy voice mute amid the festal crowd,
When lay of hopeless love, or glory won,
   Aroused the fearful, or subdued the proud.
At each according pause, was heard aloud
   Thine ardent symphony sublime and high!   15
Fair dames and crested chiefs attention bow'd;
   For still[4] the burden[5] of thy minstrelsy
Was Knighthood's dauntless deed, and Beauty's
     matchless eye.

O wake once more! how rude soe'er the hand
   That ventures o'er thy magic maze to stray;   20
O wake once more! though scarce my skill
     command
   Some feeble echoing of thine earlier lay:
Though harsh and faint, and soon to die away,
   And all unworthy of thy nobler strain,
Yet, if one heart throb higher at its sway,   25
   The wizard note has not been touch'd in vain.
Then silent be no more! Enchantress, wake
     again!

Coronach

The title means *lamentation*. The stanzas are sung,
in *The Lady of the Lake* (III, xvi), by mourners over
the body of the Highland chieftain Duncan.

He is gone on the mountain,
   He is lost to the forest,
Like a summer-dried fountain,
   When our need was the sorest.
The font,[1] reappearing,   5
   From the rain-drops shall borrow,
But to us comes no cheering,
   To Duncan no morrow!

The hand of the reaper
   Takes the ears that are hoary,   10
But the voice of the weeper
   Wails manhood in glory.

The autumn winds rushing
   Waft the leaves that are searest,
But our flower was in flushing,[2]   15
   When blighting was nearest.

Fleet foot on the correi,[3]
   Sage counsel in cumber,[4]
Red hand in the foray,
   How sound is thy slumber!   20
Like the dew on the mountain,
   Like the foam on the river,
Like the bubble on the fountain
   Thou art gone, and for ever!

Proud Maisie

Sung by mad Madge Wildfire in chapter 40 of *The
Heart of Midlothian,* published in 1818.

Proud Maisie is in the wood,
   Walking so early.
Sweet Robin sits on the bush,
   Singing so rarely.

"Tell me, thou bonny bird,   5
   When shall I marry me?"
"When six braw[1] gentlemen
   Kirkward shall carry ye."

"Who makes the bridal bed,
   Birdie, say truly?"   10
"The grey-headed sexton
   That delves the grave duly.

"The glow-worm o'er grave and stone
   Shall light thee steady.
The owl from the steeple sing,   15
   'Welcome, proud lady.' "

---

[3] Caledonia, Scotland.   [4] Ever.   [5] Theme.

[1] Fountain, spring.

[2] Growth, vigor.
[3] Hillside hollow (where game may hide).
[4] Trouble.

[1] Fine.

Samuel Taylor Coleridge

1772–1834

Coleridge is frequently talked about as a brilliant failure. And it is true that the record of his career can be seen as a record of broken promises, if viewed from the perspective of one's sense of his powers. The talents that produced *The Rime of the Ancient Mariner,* "Kubla Khan," "This Lime-Tree Bower My Prison," and "Frost at Midnight" ought to have produced much more than a few other notable poems, ought to have produced many more. The talents that permanently altered the history of literary criticism in his lectures on poetry, on Shakespeare, and especially in the *Biographia Literaria,* ought in the end to have produced, perhaps, a body of work as coherent and lucid as that of his great predecessor Dr. Johnson. They did not. The religious and philosophical writings have been criticized for being fragmented, and, together with some of the critical writings, for owing too much to continental, especially German, writers, and for acknowledging too little of what was owed. But if the contribution of his poems to the changed nature of English poetry was both qualitatively and quantitatively less than that of Wordsworth, it was as essential. And we are still occupied with questions first raised for us by Coleridge, or raised by him in challenging new formulations: questions having to do with the psychology of art, the definition of imagination, the relation between creativity in art and creativity in nature, and the relation of poetry to religious belief. It is as true of Coleridge as it is of Dr. Johnson that one cannot read a Shakesperean play without contending, in one way or another, with the issues he raises; the same is true of his writing about Wordsworth, and of his criticism of the poetry of the preceding age—the poetry of Pope and of Gray. His speculative and philosophical writings were of sufficient power to make John Stuart Mill say that Coleridge led "the revolt of the human mind against the philosophy of the eighteenth century." (For a discussion of some aspects of this revolt, see the introduction to the Romantic period.)

Coleridge's father was vicar of Ottery St. Mary on the Devon coast; there in 1772 the poet was born, the last of fourteen children. The Reverend Mr. Coleridge was also master of the local grammar school and eked out his income by boarding some of his pupils. He died when Coleridge was nine. One of his former students secured the child's admission to a famous London school, Christ's Hospital. Its headmaster, the Reverend James Boyer, was as noted for the soundness of his instruction as for the severity of his discipline. The homesick Coleridge was not in the best rapport with many of his fellow students, and, perhaps as a result, plunged into reading far beyond his years, especially in idealist philosophy, in Plato, and in some of the neoplatonists. Thus he laid the groundwork for many of his adult interests. Charles Lamb, incidentally, attended the school at the same time. He and Coleridge were later to become very close friends.

He entered Cambridge on a scholarship in 1791. A diligent student, at least for a while, he won a medal for a poem in Greek on the slave trade. He also became interested in political philosophy. Then, depressed over some debts, he withdrew from the university and enlisted in the army under the name Silas Tomkyn Comberbacke. Decidedly unfitted for the role of private soldier, he was soon rescued by his brothers, who arranged for his release from the army and for the payment of his debts. He returned to the university, only to leave it again in 1794, without a degree.

This time the attraction was a vague and high-

Samuel Taylor Coleridge (1772–1834). *Radio Times Hulton Picture Library.*

minded scheme for living in a proposed colony of kindred spirits who would "combine the innocence of the patriarchal age with the knowledge and genuine refinements of European culture." "Pantisocracy" —a term compounded of three Greek roots, and signifying an all-equal rule—was the name of the project. Coleridge was influenced to join it by Robert Southey, whom he had met during a visit to Oxford. The Pantisocratic planners talked of setting up a little utopia on the banks of the Susquehanna in the United States. Economic security was to be obtained through a few hours' daily labor by everyone, leaving plenty of time for the pursuit of wisdom. There were to be twelve male Pantisocrats, and each must have a wife. Accordingly, and partly on the rebound from an unhappy love affair, Coleridge found himself married in 1795 to Sara Fricker, one of Southey's sisters-in-law. Funds for going on with the Pantisocratic scheme were not forthcoming: and Southey, to Coleridge's indignation, withdrew from it. The project collapsed, and several years went by before the brothers-in-law were reconciled. Coleridge's marriage began well enough, but before long it became evident that Sara Coleridge was not equipped to be married successfully to Coleridge and that Coleridge was not suited to be married successfully to anyone.

Coleridge set about to find means to support himself and his family. At first he tried lecturing on political questions, preaching for a Unitarian congregation at Bath, and publishing a magazine called *The Watchman*, most of which he wrote himself. All these endeavors came to nothing, but Coleridge did get some support from an admirer, Thomas Poole, a well-to-do tanner, who arranged with a group of other admirers to stake him to about two hundred dollars a year for seven years. At this time Coleridge moved to Nether Stowey in Somersetshire and, shortly after, met William and Dorothy Wordsworth.

The importance of this friendship is almost incalculable, and in two senses of that word. The significance of their intellectual collaboration, of their mutual support, is too great to evaluate with any precision. Furthermore, it is impossible to calculate whether William Wordsworth's influence on Coleridge was greater than Coleridge's on him. Its first great product was the *Lyrical Ballads* volume of 1798, which included *The Rime of the Ancient Mariner*. (What Coleridge has to say about this momentous volume is reprinted below, chapter XIV of *Biographia Literaria*.)

Early in 1798 Coleridge was pledged an annuity of one hundred and fifty pounds a year from Josiah Wedgwood, the great potter, and his brother Thomas. Coleridge received this until 1812, when the Wedgwoods, encountering hard times, had to withdraw it. Its most immediate benefit was that it permitted

Coleridge to spend a year in Germany, much of it at Gottingen, where he learned a good deal more than he had already known about German philosophy.

After his return Coleridge tried his hand briefly at journalism, then settled in the Lake District a few miles from the Wordsworths. He was increasingly unhappy. His marriage was obviously a failure. He fell hopelessly in love with Sara Hutchinson, the sister of Wordsworth's future wife, both knowing that marriage was impossible. His health grew increasingly poor. His opium habit, which had begun sometime earlier, became increasingly demanding.

In 1804 he went to Malta, hoping that the milder climate would improve his health, and to escape the emotional pressures of his situation. He returned two years later, and after that time was effectually separated from his wife. In 1809–10 he got out a new magazine, *The Friend*. This is a case in point about Coleridge's career. It may be seen as yet another symptom in a career full of aborted enterprises, but it remains a very important political and philosophical work. And through the years that followed, he wrote a number of important works, including *The Statesman's Manual*, with its very significant remarks on the nature of symbolism, the lectures on Shakespeare and Milton, a revised version of the play *Remorse* (produced in 1812), the lecture *On Poesy and Art*, the *Aids to Reflection*, and *On the Constitution of Church and State*. A number of these works were to have very deep influence on English philosophical, political, and ecclesiastical thinking. For the literary historian the central work is *Biographia Literaria*, published in 1817. It includes discussions of the nature of poetic imagery and of the distinction between imagination and fancy; it contains a cogent criticism of Wordsworth's theory of poetic diction and a brilliant discussion of Wordsworth's characteristic virtues and defects as a poet. Together with Wordsworth's "Preface to the Second Edition of the *Lyrical Ballads*" and perhaps some of Keats's letters, it has the greatest claim to being the primary document in English Romantic theory.

Coleridge had quarreled with the Wordsworths in 1810—superficially because of the meddling of an officious friend but more deeply because of the strain that would inevitably come into play between people of such different temperaments. The quarrel was patched up, but the old intimacy was never entirely restored.

In 1816 Coleridge moved into the house of a sympathetic physician, James Gillman. Dr. and Mrs. Gillman were devoted to him. Their care and attentiveness helped to bring his opium habit under control, and they provided an atmosphere in which he could in general find some personal ease. He remained in their home for the rest of his life. The

The Mariner's Ship in the Land of Ice. Engraving by Gustave Doré, 1876.

> The ice was here, the ice was there,
> The ice was all around:
> It cracked and growled, and roared and howled,
> Like noises in a swound.

household became increasingly a center for literary men and intellectuals who came to hear the famous spellbinder talk. The last years were years of growing reputation and honor, and of some happiness. Coleridge died there in 1834, after a brief illness.

TEXTS: A definitive edition of Coleridge's works is now under way, directed by Kathleen Coburn. At the present time the most comprehensive collection is the incomplete *Complete Works* edited by W. G. T. Shedd (7 vols., 1884). E. H. Coleridge has edited the *Complete Poetical Works* (2 vols., 1912). John Shawcross has edited the *Biographia Literaria* (2 vols., 1907), with an important critical introduction. The *Miscellaneous Criticism* (1936) and the *Shakespearean Criticism* (2 vols., 1930) have both been edited by T. M. Raysor. The first four volumes of the *Letters* have been edited by E. L. Griggs (1956–1959) and the first two of the *Notebooks* (1957–1961) by Kathleen Coburn. There is a good account of the early career by L. E. Hanson, *The Early Years of Coleridge* (1939) and a more general *Life of Coleridge* (1938) by E. K. Chambers. W. J. Bate has written an

extremely useful short critical biography, *Coleridge* (1968).

Several critical and scholarly studies of Coleridge have achieved virtually classical status, notably John Livingston Lowes, *The Road to Xanadu* (1930), René Wellek, *Immanuel Kant in England* (1931), I. A. Richards, *Coleridge on Imagination* (1934), and Basil Willey, *Nineteenth Century Studies* (1939). H. N. Margoliouth's *Wordsworth and Coleridge, 1795–1834* is a useful account of the relations between the two poets. Humphrey House's *Coleridge* (1953) has come to be regarded as perhaps the best general account written in the past couple of decades. Interesting more recent works include R. H. Fogle, *The Idea of Coleridge's Criticism* (1962), Meyer Abrams, *The Mirror and the Lamp* (1953), Joseph Appleyard, *Coleridge's Philosophy of Literature* (1965), Richard Haven, *Patterns of Consciousness* (1970), Marshall Suter, *The Dark Night of Samuel Taylor Coleridge* (1960), and William Walsh, *Coleridge: The Work and the Relevance* (1967). Norman Fruman has written, in *Coleridge: The Damaged Archangel* (1971), a negative account with which every partisan of Coleridge will have to contend.

There are several collections of critical essays, including Kathleen Coburn, ed., *Coleridge: A Collection of Critical Essays* (1967) and Geoffrey Hartman, ed., *New Perspectives on Wordsworth and Coleridge* (1972).

The Eolian Harp[1]

Composed at Clevedon, Somersetshire

Written in 1795.

My pensive Sara! thy soft cheek reclined
Thus on mine arm, most soothing sweet it is
To sit beside our Cot, our Cot o'ergrown
With white-flower'd Jasmin, and the broad-leav'd Myrtle,
(Meet emblems they of Innocence and Love!)   5
And watch the clouds, that late were rich with light,
Slow saddening round, and mark the star of eve
Serenely brilliant (such should Wisdom be)
Shine opposite! How exquisite the scents
Snatch'd from yon bean-field! and the world *so*   10
    hush'd!
The stilly murmur of the distant Sea

---

1 A stringed instrument for the wind to blow through, when placed in an open window.

Tells us of silence.
          And that simplest Lute,
Placed length-ways in the clasping casement,
     hark!
How by the desultory breeze caress'd,
Like some coy maid half yielding to her lover,   15
It pours such sweet upbraiding, as must needs
Tempt to repeat the wrong! And now, its strings
Boldlier swept, the long sequacious notes
Over delicious surges sink and rise,
Such a soft floating witchery of sound   20
As twilight Elfins make, when they at eve
Voyage on gentle gales from Fairy-Land,
Where Melodies round honey-dropping flowers,
Footless and wild, like birds of Paradise,
Nor pause, nor perch, hovering on untam'd   25
     wing!
O! the one Life within us and abroad,
Which meets all motion and becomes its soul,
A light in sound, a sound-like power in light,
Rhythm in all thought, and joyance every
     where—
Methinks, it should have been impossible   30
Not to love all things in a world so fill'd;
Where the breeze warbles, and the mute still air
Is Music slumbering on her instrument.[2]

And thus, my Love! as on the midway slope
Of yonder hill I stretch my limbs at noon,   35
Whilst through my half-clos'd eye-lids I behold
The sunbeams dance, like diamonds, on the
     main,
And tranquil muse upon tranquillity;
Full many a thought uncall'd and undetain'd,
And many idle flitting phantasies,   40
Traverse my indolent and passive brain,
As wild and various as the random gales
That swell and flutter on this subject Lute!

And what if all of animated nature
Be but organic Harps diversely fram'd,   45
That tremble into thought, as o'er them sweeps
Plastic and vast, one intellectual breeze,
At once the Soul of each, and God of all?

But thy more serious eye a mild reproof
Darts, O beloved Woman! nor such thoughts   50
Dim and unhallow'd dost thou not reject,
And biddest me walk humbly with my God.

---

[2] Lines 26–33 were added in 1817.

Meek Daughter in the family of Christ!
Well hast thou said and holily disprais'd
These shapings of the unregenerate mind;   55
Bubbles that glitter as they rise and break
On vain Philosophy's aye-babbling spring.
For never guiltless may I speak of him,
The Incomprehensible! save when with awe
I praise him, and with Faith that inly *feels*;   60
Who with his saving mercies heal'd me,
A sinful and most miserable man,
Wilder'd and dark, and gave me to possess
Peace, and this Cot, and thee, heart-honour'd
     Maid!

This Lime-Tree Bower
My Prison

[Addressed to Charles Lamb, of the
India House, London]

In the June of 1797 some long-expected friends paid
a visit to the author's cottage; and on the morning of
their arrival, he met with an accident, which disabled
him from walking during the whole time of their stay.
One evening, when they had left him for a few hours,
he composed the following lines in the garden-bower.
(Coleridge's note.)

Well, they are gone, and here must I remain,
This lime-tree bower my prison! I have lost
Beauties and feelings, such as would have been
Most sweet to my remembrance even when age
Had dimm'd mine eyes to blindness! They,   5
     meanwhile,
Friends, whom I never more may meet again,
On springy heath, along the hill-top edge,
Wander in gladness, and wind down, perchance,
To that still roaring dell, of which I told;
The roaring dell, o'erwooded, narrow, deep,   10
And only speckled by the mid-day sun;
Where its slim trunk the ash from rock to rock
Flings arching like a bridge;—that branchless
     ash,
Unsunn'd and damp, whose few poor yellow
     leaves
Ne'er tremble in the gale, yet tremble still,   15
Fann'd by the water-fall! and there my friends
Behold the dark green file of long lank weeds,
That all at once (a most fantastic sight!)
Still nod and drip beneath the dripping edge

Of the blue clay-stone.

           Now, my friends emerge 20
Beneath the wide wide Heaven—and view again
The many-steepled tract magnificent
Of hilly fields and meadows, and the sea,
With some fair bark, perhaps, whose sails light up
The slip of smooth clear blue betwixt two Isles 25
Of purple shadow! Yes! they wander on
In gladness all; but thou, methinks, most glad,
My gentle-hearted Charles![1] for thou hast pined
And hunger'd after Nature, many a year,
In the great City pent, winning thy way 30
With sad yet patient soul, through evil and pain
And strange calamity! Ah! slowly sink
Behind the western ridge, thou glorious Sun!
Shine in the slant beams of the sinking orb,
Ye purple heath-flowers! richlier burn, ye clouds! 35
Live in the yellow light, ye distant groves!
And kindle, thou blue Ocean! So my friend
Struck with deep joy may stand, as I have stood,
Silent with swimming sense; yea, gazing round
On the wide landscape, gaze till all doth seem 40
Less gross than bodily; and of such hues
As veil the Almighty Spirit, when yet he makes
Spirits perceive his presence.

           A delight
Comes sudden on my heart, and I am glad
As I myself were there! Nor in this bower, 45
This little lime-tree bower, have I not mark'd
Much that has sooth'd me. Pale beneath the
    blaze
Hung the transparent foliage; and I watch'd
Some broad and sunny leaf, and lov'd to see
The shadow of the leaf and stem above 50
Dappling its sunshine! And that walnut-tree
Was richly ting'd, and a deep radiance lay
Full on the ancient ivy, which usurps
Those fronting elms, and now, with blackest mass
Makes their dark branches gleam a lighter hue 55
Through the late twilight: and though now the
    bat
Wheels silent by, and not a swallow twitters,
Yet still the solitary humble-bee
Sings in the bean-flower! Henceforth I shall know
That Nature ne'er deserts the wise and pure; 60
No plot so narrow, be but Nature there,
No waste so vacant, but may well employ
Each faculty of sense, and keep the heart

Awake to Love and Beauty! and sometimes
'Tis well to be bereft of promis'd good, 65
That we may lift the soul, and contemplate
With lively joy the joys we cannot share.
My gentle-hearted Charles! when the last rook
Beat its straight path along the dusky air
Homewards, I blest it! deeming its black wing 70
(Now a dim speck, now vanishing in light)
Had cross'd the mighty Orb's dilated glory,
While thou stood'st gazing; or, when all was still,
Flew creeking o'er thy head, and had a charm
For thee, my gentle-hearted Charles, to whom 75
No sound is dissonant which tells of Life.

Kubla Khan

This poem came into being by no ordinary method of composition. Coleridge dreamed it during a sleep induced by opium, subconsciously fusing a number of details from various books (see J. L. Lowes, *The Road to Xanadu*). A prefatory note by Coleridge explains that "in consequence of a slight indisposition, an anodyne had been prescribed, from the effects of which he fell asleep in his chair" while reading Samuel Purchas (d. 1626), the compiler of travel books. In the *Purchas his Pilgrimage* of that devoted follower of Hakluyt occurs this sentence about the enlightened conqueror Kublai Khan (1216–94), founder of the Mongol dynasty in China; Coleridge's eye was on it when he dozed off: "In Xamdu did Cublai Can build a stately Palace, encompassing sixteene miles of plaine ground with a wall, wherein are fertile Meddowes, pleasant springs, delightful Streames, and all sorts of beasts of chase and game, and in the middest thereof a sumptuous house of pleasure, which may be removed from place to place."

    "The Author," proceeds Coleridge, "continued for about three hours in a profound sleep, at least of the external senses, during which time he has the most vivid confidence, that he could not have composed less than from two to three hundred lines; if that indeed can be called composition in which all the images rose up before him as *things*, with a parallel production of the correspondent expressions, without any sensation or consciousness of effort. On awaking he appeared to himself to have a distinct recollection of the whole, and taking his pen, ink, and paper, instantly and eagerly wrote down the lines that are here preserved. At this moment he was unfortunately called out by a person on business from Porlock,[1] and detained by him above an hour, and on his return to his room, found, to his no small surprise and mortification, that though he still retained some vague and dim recollection of the general purport of the vision,

---

[1] Charles Lamb.

[1] A nearby village.

yet, with the exception of some eight or ten scattered lines and images, all the rest had passed away like the images on the surface of a stream into which a stone has been cast, but, alas! without the after restoration of the latter!"

This extraordinary experience took place probably in the summer of 1797. The poem was published with *Christabel* and another in 1816; the original title was "Kubla Khan: Or, A Vision in a Dream. A Fragment."

In Xanadu did Kubla Khan
A stately pleasure-dome decree:
Where Alph, the sacred river, ran
Through caverns measureless to man
   Down to a sunless sea.   5
So twice five miles of fertile ground
With walls and towers were girdled round:
And there were gardens bright with sinuous rills,
Where blossomed many an incense-bearing tree;
And here were forests ancient as the hills,   10
Enfolding sunny spots of greenery.

But oh! that deep romantic chasm which slanted
Down the green hill athwart a cedarn cover!
A savage place! as holy and enchanted
As e'er beneath a waning moon was haunted   15
By woman wailing for her demon-lover!
And from this chasm, with ceaseless turmoil
   seething,
As if this earth in fast thick pants were breathing,
A mighty fountain momently was forced:
Amid whose swift half-intermitted burst   20
Huge fragments vaulted like rebounding hail,
Or chaffy grain beneath the thresher's flail:
And 'mid these dancing rocks at once and ever
It flung up momently the sacred river.
Five miles meandering with a mazy motion   25
Through wood and dale the sacred river ran,
Then reached the caverns measureless to man,
And sank in tumult to a lifeless ocean:
And 'mid this tumult Kubla heard from far
Ancestral voices prophesying war!   30

   The shadow of the dome of pleasure
   Floated midway on the waves;
   Where was heard the mingled measure
   From the fountain and the caves.

It was a miracle of rare device,   35
A sunny pleasure-dome with caves of ice!

   A damsel with a dulcimer
   In a vision once I saw:

It was an Abyssinian maid,
And on her dulcimer she played,   40
Singing of Mount Abora.[2]
Could I revive within me
Her symphony and song,
To such a deep delight 'twould win me,

That with music loud and long,   45
I would build that dome in air,
That sunny dome! those caves of ice!
And all who heard should see them there,
And all should cry, Beware! Beware!
His flashing eyes, his floating hair!   50
Weave a circle round him thrice,[3]
And close your eyes with holy dread,
For he on honey-dew hath fed,
And drunk the milk of Paradise.

The Rime of the Ancient Mariner
In Seven Parts

This poem, composed in 1797–98, was Coleridge's only important contribution to the *Lyrical Ballads* of 1798. Intended as a ballad and to some extent inspired by the specimens in Percy's *Reliques of Ancient English Poetry,* it is closer to that genre than any of the poems from Wordsworth's pen. The marginal gloss was not printed till 1817. In *The Road to Xanadu* (1927) J. L. Lowes has shown how bits of Coleridge's reading coalesced in his subconscious to produce some of the most striking details of the poem. Our text incorporates the poet's revisions.

Argument

How a Ship, having first sailed to the Equator, was driven by Storms to the cold Country towards the South Pole; how the Ancient Mariner cruelly and in contempt of the laws of hospitality killed a Sea-bird and how he was followed by many and strange Judgements: and in what manner he came back to his own Country.

Part I

It is an ancient Mariner,
And he stoppeth one of three.
'By thy long grey beard and glitter-
   ing eye,
Now wherefore stopp'st thou me?

An ancient Mariner meeteth three Gallants bidden to a wedding-feast, and detaineth one.

---

2 Probably derived from the name of a tributary of the Nile, the river Abola, which Coleridge had met in his reading.
3 As a magic protection against his influence.

The Bridegroom's doors are opened wide,   5
And I am next of kin;
The guests are met, the feast is set:
May'st hear the merry din.'

He holds him with his skinny hand,
'There was a ship,' quoth he.   10
'Hold off! unhand me, grey-beard loon!'
Eftsoons[1] his hand dropt he.

He holds him with his glittering
   eye—   *The Wedding-*
   Guest is spell-
The Wedding-Guest stood still,   *bound by the eye*
   of the old sea-
And listens like a three years' child: *faring man, and*   15
   constrained to
The Mariner hath his will.   *hear his tale.*

The Wedding-Guest sat on a stone:
He cannot choose but hear;
And thus spake on the ancient man,
The bright-eyed Mariner.   20

'The ship was cheered, the harbour cleared,
Merrily did we drop
Below the kirk,[2] below the hill,   *The Mariner*
   tells how the
Below the lighthouse top.   *ship sailed south-*
   ward with a good
   wind and fair
The Sun came up upon the left,   *weather, till it*   25
   reached the
Out of the sea came he!   *Line.[3]*
And he shone bright, and on the right
Went down into the sea.

Higher and higher every day,
Till over the mast at noon—'   30
The Wedding-Guest here beat his breast,
For he heard the loud bassoon.

The bride hath paced into the hall,   *The Wedding-*
   Guest heareth
Red as a rose is she;   *the bridal music;*
   but the Mariner
Nodding their heads before her goes   *continueth his*   35
   tale.
The merry minstrelsy.

The Wedding-Guest he beat his breast,
Yet he cannot choose but hear;
And thus spake on that ancient man,
The bright-eyed Mariner.   40

'And now the STORM-BLAST came,
   and he
Was tyrannous and strong: *The ship driven*
   by a storm
He struck with his o'ertaking wings,   *toward the south*
   pole.
And chased us south along.

With sloping masts and dipping prow,   45
As who pursued with yell and blow
Still treads the shadow of his foe,
And forward bends his head,
The ship drove fast, loud roared the blast,
And southward aye we fled.   50

And now there came both mist and snow,
And it grew wondrous cold:
And ice, mast-high, came floating by,
As green as emerald.

And through the drifts the snowy   *The land of*   55
   ice, and of
   clifts[4]   *fearful sounds*
   where no living
Did send a dismal sheen: *thing was to be*
   seen.
Nor shapes of men nor beasts we
   ken—
The ice was all between.

The ice was here, the ice was there,
The ice was all around: 60
It cracked and growled, and roared and howled,
Like noises in a swound![5]

At length did cross an Albatross,   *Till a great sea-*
   bird called the
Thorough[6] the fog it came;   *Albatross, came*
   through the
As if it had been a Christian soul,   *snow-fog, and*   65
   was received
We hailed it in God's name.   *with great joy*
   and hospitality.

It ate the food it ne'er had eat,[7]
And round and round it flew.
The ice did split with a thunder-fit;
The helmsman steered us through!   70

And a good south wind sprung up   *And lo! the*
   Albatross proveth
   behind;   *a bird of good*
   omen, and fol-
The Albatross did follow,   *loweth the ship*
   as it returned
And every day, for food or play,   *northward*
   through fog and
Came to the mariners' hollo!   *floating ice.*

In mist or cloud, on mast or shroud,[8]   75

---

[1] Soon after. This and other archaisms are intended to suggest the style of the medieval ballads.—Wordsworth tells us that he contributed the next stanza.
[2] Church.   [3] Equator.

[4] Cliffs.   [5] Swoon.
[6] Through.   [7] Eaten; pronounced ĕt.
[8] One of the ropes running from the ship's side up to the mast, to secure it laterally.

It perched for vespers nine;
Whiles all the night, through fog-smoke white,
Glimmered the white Moon-shine.'

'God save thee, ancient Mariner! *The ancient Mar-*
From the fiends, that plague thee *iner inhospita-* 80
　　thus!— *bly killeth the*
Why look'st thou so?'—With my *pious bird of*
　　cross-bow *good omen.*
I shot the ALBATROSS.[9]

Part II

The Sun now rose upon the right:
Out of the sea came he,
Still hid in mist, and on the left 85
Went down into the sea.

And the good south wind still blew behind,
But no sweet bird did follow,
Nor any day for food or play
Came to the mariners' hollo! 90

And I had done a hellish thing, *His shipmates cry*
And it would work 'em woe: *out against the*
For all averred, I had killed the bird *ancient Mariner,*
That made the breeze to blow. *for killing the*
bird of good
Ah wretch! said they, the bird to slay, *luck.* 95
That made the breeze to blow!

Nor dim nor red, like God's own *But when the fog*
　　head, *cleared off, they*
The glorious Sun uprist:[10] *justify the same,*
and thus make
Then all averred, I had killed the *themselves ac-*
　　bird *complices in the*
That brought the fog and mist. *crime.* 100
'Twas right, said they, such birds to slay,
That bring the fog and mist.

The fair breeze blew, the white *The fair breeze*
　　foam flew, *continues; the*
The furrow followed free; *ship enters the*
Pacific Ocean,
We were the first[11] that ever burst *and sails north-* 105
Into that silent sea. *ward, even till it*
reaches the Line.

Down dropt the breeze, the sails dropt down,
'Twas sad as sad could be; *The ship hath*
And we did speak only to break *been suddenly*
The silence of the sea! *becalmed.* 110

All in a hot and copper sky,
The bloody Sun, at noon,
Right up above the mast did stand,
No bigger than the Moon.

Day after day, day after day, 115
We stuck, nor breath nor motion;
As idle as a painted ship
Upon a painted ocean.

Water, water, every where, *And the Alba-*
And all the boards did shrink; *tross begins to* 120
Water, water, every where, *be avenged.*
Nor any drop to drink.

The very deep did rot: O Christ!
That ever this should be!
Yea, slimy things did crawl with legs 125
Upon the slimy sea.

About, about, in reel and rout
The death-fires[12] danced at night;
The water, like a witch's oils,
Burnt green and blue and white. 130

And some in dreams assurèd were *A Spirit had fol-*
Of the Spirit that plagued us so; *lowed them; one*
of the invisible
Nine fathom deep he had followed *inhabitants of*
　　us *this planet,*
neither departed
From the land of mist and snow. *souls nor angels;*
concerning whom
the learned Jew,
Josephus, and
the Platonic
And every tongue, through utter *Constantinopoli-* 135
　　drought, *tan, Michael*
Was withered at the root; *Psellus,[13] may*
be consulted.
We could not speak, no more than if *They are very*
We had been choked with soot. *numerous, and*
there is no cli-
mate or element
without one or
more.

Ah! well a-day! what evil looks *The shipmates,*
Had I from old and young! *in their sore* 140
distress, would
Instead of the cross, the Albatross *fain throw the*
About my neck was hung. *whole guilt*
on the ancient
Mariner: in sign
whereof they
hang the dead
sea-bird round
his neck.

---

[9] From this point the text we follow omits quotation marks for the Mariner's story.
[10] I.e., rose. Actually this word is an old form of the present tense.
[11] Another medieval hint; Magellan did not enter the Pacific till 1520.

---

[12] I.e., phosphorescent lights.
[13] Josephus was a famous first-century historian, Psellus

Part III

There passed a weary time. Each throat
Was parched, and glazed each eye.
A weary time! a weary time!   145
How glazed each weary eye,
When looking westward, I beheld
A something in the sky.

The ancient Mariner beholdeth a sign in the element[14] afar off.

At first it seemed a little speck,
And then it seemed a mist;   150
It moved and moved, and took at last
A certain shape, I wist.[15]

A speck, a mist, a shape, I wist!
And still it neared and neared:
As if it dodged a water-sprite,   155
It plunged and tacked and veered.

With throats unslaked, with black
    lips baked,
We could not laugh nor wail;
Through utter drought all dumb we
    stood!
I bit my arm, I sucked the blood,   160
And cried, A sail, a sail!

At its nearer approach, it seemeth him to be a ship; and at a dear ransom he freeth his speech from the bonds of thirst.

With throats unslaked, with black lips baked,
Agape they heard me call:
Gramercy![16] they for joy did grin,
And all at once their breath drew in,   165
As[17] they were drinking all.

A flash of joy;

See! see! (I cried) she tacks no more!
Hither to work us weal;
Without a breeze, without a tide,
She steadies with upright keel!   170

And horror follows. For can it be a ship that comes onward without wind or tide?

The western wave was all a-flame.
The day was well nigh done!
Almost upon the western wave
Rested the broad bright Sun;
When that strange shape drove suddenly   175
Betwixt us and the Sun.

And straight the Sun was flecked with bars,
(Heaven's Mother send us grace!)
As if through a dungeon-grate he
    peered
With broad and burning face.   180

It seemeth him but the skeleton of a ship.

Alas! (thought I, and my heart beat loud)
How fast she nears and nears!
Are those *her* sails that glance in the Sun,
Like restless gossameres?[18]

Are those *her* ribs through which the Sun   185
Did peer, as through a grate?
And is that Woman all her crew?
Is that a DEATH?[19] and are there
    two?
Is DEATH that woman's mate?

And its ribs are seen as bars on the face of the setting Sun.

The Spectre-Woman and her Death-mate, and no other on board the skeleton ship.

Her lips were red, *her* looks were free,   190
Her locks were yellow as gold:
Her skin was as white as leprosy,
The Night-mare LIFE-IN-DEATH was she,
Who thicks man's blood with cold.

Like vessel, like crew!

The naked hulk alongside came,   195
And the twain were casting dice;
'The game is done! I've won!
    I've won!'
Quoth she, and whistles thrice.

Death and Life-in-Death have diced for the ship's crew, and she (the latter) winneth the ancient Mariner.

The Sun's rim dips; the stars rush
    out:
At one stride comes the dark: 200
With far-heard whisper, o'er the sea,
Off shot the spectre-bark.

No twilight within the courts of the Sun.

We listened and looked sideways
    up!
Fear at my heart, as at a cup,
My life-blood seemed to sip!   205
The stars were dim, and thick the night,
The steersman's face by his lamp gleamed white;
From the sails the dew did drip—
Till clomb above the eastern bar
The hornèd Moon, with one bright star   210
Within the nether tip.[20]

At the rising of the Moon,

One after one, by the star-dogged
    Moon,
Too quick for groan or sigh,
Each turned his face with a ghastly pang,
And cursed me with his eye.   215

One after another,

---

a well-known eleventh-century Byzantine philosopher and
politician.   14 Sky.   15 Knew.
16 An exclamation of surprise or thanks.   17 As if.

18 Filmy cobwebs which float in calm air.   19 Skeleton.
20 In a manuscript note Coleridge refers to a sailors' superstition that it is an omen of evil when a star "dogs the
moon."

Four times fifty living men, *His shipmates*
(And I heard nor sigh nor groan) *drop down dead.*
With heavy thump, a lifeless lump,
They dropped down one by one.

The souls did from their bodies *But Life-in-* 220
　fly,— *Death begins*
They fled to bliss or woe! *her work on the*
And every soul, it passed me by, *ancient Mariner.*
Like the whizz of my cross-bow!

Part IV

'I fear thee, ancient Mariner! *The Wedding-*
I fear thy skinny hand! *Guest feareth*
And thou art long, and lank, and brown, *that a Spirit is* 225
As is the ribbed sea-sand.[21] *talking to him;*

I fear thee and thy glittering eye,
And thy skinny hand, so brown.'—
Fear not, fear not, thou Wedding- *But the ancient* 230
　Guest! *Mariner as-*
This body dropt not down. *sureth him*
of his bodily life,
and proceedeth
to relate his
horrible penance.

Alone, alone, all, all alone,
Alone on a wide wide sea!
And never a saint took pity on
My soul in agony. 235

The many men, so beautiful! *He despiseth the*
And they all dead did lie: *creatures of the*
And a thousand thousand slimy things *calm,*
Lived on; and so did I.

I looked upon the rotting sea, *And envieth* 240
And drew my eyes away; *that they*
I looked upon the rotting deck, *should live,*
And there the dead men lay. *and so many lie*
dead.

I looked to heaven, and tried to pray;
But or ever a prayer had gusht, 245
A wicked whisper came, and made
My heart as dry as dust.

I closed my lids, and kept them close,
And the balls like pulses beat;

For the sky and the sea, and the sea and the sky 250
Lay like a load on my weary eye,
And the dead were at my feet.

The cold sweat melted from their *But the curse*
　limbs, *liveth for him in*
Nor rot nor reek did they: *the eye of the*
The look with which they looked on me *dead men.* 255
Had never passed away.

An orphan's curse would drag to hell
A spirit from on high;
But oh! more horrible than that
Is the curse in a dead man's eye! 260
Seven days, seven nights, I saw that *In his loneliness*
　curse, *and fixedness he*
And yet I could not die. *yearneth towards*
the journeying
Moon, and the
stars that still
The moving Moon went up the sky, *sojourn, yet still*
And no where did abide: *move onward;*
Softly she was going up, *and every where*
And a star or two beside— *the blue sky be-* 265
longs to them,
and is their ap-
pointed rest,
and their
Her beams bemocked the sultry *native country*
　main, *and their own*
Like April hoar-frost spread; *natural homes,*
But where the ship's huge shadow *which they enter*
　lay, *unannounced, as*
The charmèd water burnt alway *lords that are cer-* 270
A still and awful red. *tainly expected*
and yet there is a
silent joy at their
arrival.

Beyond the shadow of the ship, *By the light of*
I watched the water-snakes: *the Moon he*
They moved in tracks of shining *beholdeth God's*
　white, *creatures of the*
And when they reared, the elfish light *great calm.* 275
Fell off in hoary flakes.

Within the shadow of the ship
I watched their rich attire:
Blue, glossy green, and velvet black,
They coiled and swam; and every track 280
Was a flash of golden fire.

O happy living things! no tongue *Their beauty and*
Their beauty might declare: *their happiness.*
A spring of love gushed from my heart,
And I blessed them unaware: *He blesseth* 285
Sure my kind saint took pity on me, *them in his*
And I blessed them unaware. *heart.*

---

21 Note by Coleridge: "For the last two lines of this stanza, I am indebted to Mr. Wordsworth. It was on a delightful walk from Nether Stowey to Dulverton, with him and his sister, in the Autumn of 1797, that this Poem was planned, and in part composed."

The self-same moment I could pray; *The spell begins*
And from my neck so free   *to break.*
The Albatross fell off, and sank   290
Like lead into the sea.

Part V

Oh sleep! it is a gentle thing,
Beloved from pole to pole!
To Mary Queen the praise be given!
She sent the gentle sleep from Heaven,   295
That slid into my soul.

The silly²² buckets on the deck,
That had so long remained,   *By grace of the*
I dreamt that they were filled with *holy Mother, the*
    dew;   *ancient Mariner*
                                  is refreshed with
And when I awoke, it rained.   *rain.*   300

My lips were wet, my throat was cold,
My garments all were dank;
Sure I had drunken in my dreams,
And still my body drank.

I moved, and could not feel my limbs: 305
I was so light—almost
I thought that I had died in sleep,
And was a blessèd ghost.

And soon I heard a roaring wind: *He heareth*
It did not come anear;   *sounds and seeth*
But with its sound it shook the sails, *strange sights* 310
                                  and commo-
                                  tions in the
That were so thin and sere.   *sky and the*
                                  element.

The upper air burst into life!
And a hundred fire-flags sheen,²³
To and fro they were hurried about!   315
And to and fro, and in and out,
The wan stars danced between.

And the coming wind did roar more loud,
And the sails did sigh like sedge;
And the rain poured down from one black cloud;   320
The Moon was at its edge.

The thick black cloud was cleft, and still
The Moon was at its side:
Like waters shot from some high crag,
The lightning fell with never a jag,   325
A river steep and wide.

The loud wind never reached the   *The bodies of*
    ship,   *the ship's crew*
                                  are inspired, and
Yet now the ship moved on!   *the ship moves*
Beneath the lightning and the Moon *on:*
The dead men gave a groan.   330

They groaned, they stirred, they all uprose,
Nor spake, nor moved their eyes;
It had been strange, even in a dream,
To have seen those dead men rise.

The helmsman steered, the ship moved on;   335
Yet never a breeze up-blew;
The mariners all 'gan work the ropes,
Where they were wont to do;
They raised their limbs like lifeless tools—
We were a ghastly crew.   340

The body of my brother's son
Stood by me, knee to knee:
The body and I pulled at one rope,
But he said nought to me.

'I fear thee, ancient Mariner!'   *But not by the*   345
Be calm, thou Wedding-Guest!   *souls of the*
                                  men, nor by
'Twas not those souls that fled in *daemons²⁴ of the*
    pain,   *earth or middle*
                                  air, but by a
Which to their corses²⁵ came again, *blessed troop of*
                                  angelic spirits,
But a troop of spirits blest: *sent down by the*
                                  invocation of the
                                  guardian saint.

For when it dawned—they dropped their arms,   350
And clustered round the mast;
Sweet sounds rose slowly through their mouths,
And from their bodies passed.

Around, around, flew each sweet sound,
Then darted to the Sun;   355
Slowly the sounds came back again,
Now mixed, now one by one.

Sometimes a-dropping from the sky
I heard the sky-lark sing;
Sometimes all little birds that are,   360
How they seemed to fill the sea and air
With their sweet jargoning!

And now 'twas like all instruments,
Now like a lonely flute;
And now it is an angel's song,   365
That makes the heavens be mute.

---

²² Useless, because empty.   ²³ Bright.

²⁴ Not demons, but spirits.   ²⁵ Corpses.

It ceased; yet still the sails made on
A pleasant noise till noon,
A noise like of a hidden brook
In the leafy month of June,   370
That to the sleeping woods all night
Singeth a quiet tune.

Till noon we quietly sailed on,
Yet never a breeze did breathe:
Slowly and smoothly went the ship,   375
Moved onward from beneath.

Under the keel nine fathom deep,
From the land of mist and snow,
The spirit slid: and it was he
That made the ship to go.   380
The sails at noon left off their tune,
And the ship stood still also.

The lonesome Spirit from the south-pole carries on the ship as far as the Line, in obedience to the angelic troop, but still requireth vengeance.

The Sun, right up above the mast,
Had fixed her to the ocean:
But in a minute she 'gan stir,   385
With a short uneasy motion—
Backwards and forwards half her length
With a short uneasy motion.

Then like a pawing horse let go,
She made a sudden bound: 390
It flung the blood into my head,
And I fell down in a swound.

How long in that same fit I lay,
I have not[26] to declare;
But ere my living life returned,   395
I heard and in my soul discerned
Two voices in the air.

The Polar Spirit's fellow-daemons, the invisible inhabitants of the element, take part in his wrong; and two of them relate, one to the other, that penance long and heavy for the ancient Mariner hath been accorded to the Polar Spirit, who returneth southward.

'Is it he?' quoth one, 'Is this the man?
By him who died on cross,
With his cruel bow he laid full low   400
The harmless Albatross.

The spirit who bideth by himself
In the land of mist and snow,
He loved the bird that loved the man
Who shot him with his bow.'   405

The other was a softer voice,
As soft as honey-dew:

26 I.e., no power.

Quoth he, 'The man hath penance done,
And penance more will do.'

Part VI

FIRST VOICE

'But tell me, tell me! speak again,   410
Thy soft response renewing—
What makes that ship drive on so fast?
What is the ocean doing?'

SECOND VOICE

'Still as a slave before his lord,
The ocean hath no blast;   415
His great bright eye most silently
Up to the Moon is cast—

If he may know which way to go;
For she guides him smooth or grim.
See, brother, see! how graciously   420
She looketh down on him.'

FIRST VOICE

'But why drives on that ship so fast,
Without or wave or wind?'

The Mariner hath been cast into a trance; for the angelic power causeth the vessel to drive northward faster than human life could endure.

SECOND VOICE

'The air is cut away before,
And closes from behind.   425

Fly, brother, fly! more high, more high!
Or we shall be belated:
For slow and slow that ship will go,
When the Mariner's trance is abated.'

I woke, and we were sailing on   430
As in a gentle weather:
'Twas night, calm night, the moon
    was high;
The dead men stood together.

The supernatural motion is retarded; the Mariner awakes, and his penance begins anew.

All stood together on the deck,
For a charnel-dungeon[27] fitter: 435
All fixed on me their stony eyes,
That in the Moon did glitter.

27 When the digging of a new grave in the churchyard necessitated removal of old bones, they were deposited in the charnel house, or vault. Bodies were sometimes temporarily laid there when the ground was too deeply frozen for digging.

The pang, the curse, with which they died,
Had never passed away:
I could not draw my eyes from theirs,   440
Nor turn them up to pray.

And now this spell was snapt: once   *The curse is*
    more   *finally expiated.*
I viewed the ocean green,
And looked far forth, yet little saw
Of what had else been seen—   445

Like one, that on a lonesome road
Doth walk in fear and dread,
And having once turned round walks on,
And turns no more his head;
Because he knows, a frightful fiend   450
Doth close behind him tread.

But soon there breathed a wind on me,
Nor sound nor motion made:
Its path was not upon the sea,
In ripple or in shade.   455

It raised my hair, it fanned my cheek
Like a meadow-gale of spring—
It mingled strangely with my fears,
Yet it felt like a welcoming.

Swiftly, swiftly flew the ship,   460
Yet she sailed softly too:
Sweetly, sweetly blew the breeze—
On me alone it blew.

Oh! dream of joy! is this indeed   *And the ancient*
The light-house top I see?   *Mariner be-*
                                     holdeth his   465
Is this the hill? is this the kirk? *native*
Is this mine own countree?   *country.*

We drifted o'er the harbour-bar,
And I with sobs did pray—
O let me be awake, my God!   470
Or let me sleep alway.

The harbour-bay was clear as glass,
So smoothly it was strewn!
And on the bay the moonlight lay,
And the shadow of the Moon.   475

The rock shone bright, the kirk no less,
That stands above the rock:
The moonlight steeped in silentness
The steady weathercock.

And the bay was white with silent light,   480
Till rising from the same,   *The angelic*
Full many shapes, that shadows   *spirits leave the*
    were,   *dead bodies,*
In crimson colours came.

A little distance from the prow   *And appear in*
Those crimson shadows were: *their own forms* 485
I turned my eyes upon the deck—   *of light.*
Oh, Christ! what saw I there!

Each corse lay flat, lifeless and flat,
And, by the holy rood![28]
A man all light, a seraph-man,   490
On every corse there stood.

This seraph-band, each waved his hand:
It was a heavenly sight!
They stood as signals to the land,
Each one a lovely light;   495

This seraph-band, each waved his hand,
No voice did they impart—
No voice; but oh! the silence sank
Like music on my heart.

But soon I heard the dash of oars,   500
I heard the Pilot's cheer;
My head was turned perforce away,
And I saw a boat appear.

The Pilot and the Pilot's boy,
I heard them coming fast: 505
Dear Lord in Heaven! it was a joy
The dead men could not blast.

I saw a third—I heard his voice:
It is the Hermit good!
He singeth loud his godly hymns   510
That he makes in the wood.
He'll shrieve[29] my soul, he'll wash away
The Albatross's blood.

Part VII

This Hermit good lives in that   *The Hermit of*
    wood   *the Wood,*
Which slopes down to the sea.   515
How loudly his sweet voice he rears!
He loves to talk with marineres
That come from a far countree.

---

28 Cross.   29 Hear confession and give absolution to.

He kneels at morn, and noon, and eve—
He hath a cushion plump:
It is the moss that wholly hides
The rotted old oak-stump.   520

The skiff-boat neared: I heard them talk,
'Why, this is strange, I trow!
Where are those lights so many and fair,   525
That signal made but now?'

'Strange, by my faith!' the Hermit   *Approacheth the*
    said—   *ship with*
'And they answered not our cheer!   *wonder.*
The planks look warped! and see those sails,
How thin they are and sere!   530
I never saw aught like to them,
Unless perchance it were

Brown skeletons of leaves that lag
My forest-brook along;
When the ivy-tod[30] is heavy with snow,   535
And the owlet whoops to the wolf below,
That eats the she-wolf's young.'

'Dear Lord! it hath a fiendish look—
(The Pilot made reply)
I am a-feared'—'Push on, push on!'   540
Said the Hermit cheerily.

The boat came closer to the ship,
But I nor spake nor stirred;
The boat came close beneath the ship,
And straight a sound was heard.   545

Under the water it rumbled on,   *The ship sud-*
Still louder and more dread: *denly sinketh.*
It reached the ship, it split the bay;
The ship went down like lead.

Stunned by that loud and dreadful   *The ancient*   550
    sound,   *Mariner is*
Which sky and ocean smote,   *saved in the*
Like one that hath been seven days drowned *Pilot's boat.*
My body lay afloat;
But swift as dreams, myself I found
Within the Pilot's boat.   555

Upon the whirl, where sank the ship,
The boat spun round and round;

And all was still, save that the hill
Was telling of the sound.

I moved my lips—the Pilot shrieked   560
And fell down in a fit;
The holy Hermit raised his eyes,
And prayed where he did sit.

I took the oars: the Pilot's boy,
Who now doth crazy go,   565
Laughed loud and long, and all the while
His eyes went to and fro.
'Ha! ha!' quoth he, 'full plain I see,
The Devil knows how to row.'

And now, all in my own countree,   570
I stood on the firm land!
The Hermit stepped forth from the boat,
And scarcely he could stand.

'O shrieve me, shrieve me, holy   *The ancient Mar-*
    man!'   *iner earnestly*
The Hermit crossed[31] his brow.   *entreateth*
                                     the Hermit
                                     to shrieve   575
'Say quick,' quoth he, 'I bid thee   *him; and the*
    say—   *penance of life*
What manner of man art thou?'   *falls on him.*

Forthwith this frame of mine was wrenched
With a woful agony,
Which forced me to begin my tale;   580
And then it left me free.

Since then, at an uncertain hour,   *And ever and*
That agony returns: *anon throughout*
                                     his future life
And till my ghastly tale is told,   *an agony con-*
This heart within me burns.   *straineth him to*
                                     travel from land   585
                                     to land;

I pass, like night, from land to land;
I have strange power of speech;
That moment that his face I see,
I know the man that must hear me:
To him my tale I teach.   590

What loud uproar bursts from that door!
The wedding-guests are there:
But in the garden-bower the bride
And bride-maids singing are:
And hark the little vesper bell,   595
Which biddeth me to prayer!

---

30 Bush.   31 Made the sign of the cross on.

O Wedding-Guest! this soul hath been
Alone on a wide wide sea:
So lonely 'twas, that God himself 600
Scarce seemèd there to be.

O sweeter than the marriage-feast,
'Tis sweeter far to me,
To walk together to the kirk
With a goodly company!—

To walk together to the kirk, 605
And all together pray,
While each to his great Father bends,
Old men, and babes, and loving friends
And youths and maidens gay!

Farewell, farewell! but this I tell 610
To thee, thou Wedding-Guest!
He prayeth well, who loveth well
Both man and bird and beast.

And to teach, by his own example, love and reverence to all things that God made and loveth.

He prayeth best, who loveth best
All things both great and small; 615
For the dear God who loveth us,
He made and loveth all.—

The Mariner, whose eye is bright,
Whose beard with age is hoar, 620
Is gone: and now the Wedding-Guest
Turned from the bridegroom's door.

He went like one that hath been stunned,
And is of sense forlorn:[32]
A sadder and a wiser man, 625
He rose the morrow morn.

Christabel

This strange fragment is one of the numerous projects Coleridge failed to complete. Part I was written at Nether Stowey in 1797–98, Part II at Keswick in 1800; the poet appears to have planned three more.

    Coleridge was unable to get *Christabel* ready in time for the second edition of *Lyrical Ballads;* it remained in manuscript till 1816, when Byron persuaded his own publisher to bring it out. A preface mentions the date of composition; for, now that Scott and Byron were in full blast, Coleridge was afraid he might be accused of following their lead. He also explains that the meter is less irregular than it looks,

---

[32] Bereft of his senses.

"being founded on a new principle: namely, that of counting in each line the accents, not the syllables. Though the latter may vary from seven to twelve, yet in each line the accents will be found to be only four." The principle was, of course, not new at all; it had been used, as we have seen, by medieval writers of alliterative verse. Nor does Coleridge stick consistently to it.

    The key to understanding the poem is the fact that "Geraldine" is at least in part a vampire, that is, a demon which sucks its victims' blood while they sleep. An account Coleridge was subsequently alleged to have given of his intentions may or may not be accurate; Wordsworth doubted whether a settled plan had ever been framed. It seems probable, however, that the vampire is not the actual Geraldine, daughter of Lord Roland de Vaux, but has taken her form. Christabel is good and entirely innocent; her helplessness arises from the spell cast upon her powers of utterance (lines 267 ff., 473 f., 619 f.). Coleridge may have intended to rescue his heroine through the return of her absent fiancé. An interesting "study of the history, background, and purposes" of the poem is A. H. Nethercot's *The Road to Tryermaine* (1939).

Part I

'Tis the middle of night by the castle clock,
And the owls have awakened the crowing cock,
Tu—whit!——Tu—whoo!
And hark, again! the crowing cock,
How drowsily it crew. 5

Sir Leoline, the Baron rich,
Hath a toothless mastiff bitch.
From her kennel beneath the rock
She maketh answer to the clock,
Four for the quarters, and twelve for the hour; 10
Ever and aye, by shine and shower,
Sixteen short howls, not over loud;
Some say, she sees my lady's shroud.

Is the night chilly and dark?
The night is chilly, but not dark. 15
The thin grey cloud is spread on high,
It covers but not hides the sky.
The moon is behind, and at the full;
And yet she looks both small and dull.
The night is chill, the cloud is grey: 20
'Tis a month before the month of May,
And the Spring comes slowly up this way.

The lovely lady, Christabel,
Whom her father loves so well,
What makes her in the wood so late, 25
A furlong from the castle gate?

She had dreams all yesternight
Of her own betrothèd knight;
And she in the midnight wood will pray
For the weal of her lover that's far away.   30

She stole along, she nothing spoke,
The sighs she heaved were soft and low,
And naught was green upon the oak
But moss and rarest mistletoe:
She kneels beneath the huge oak tree,   35
And in silence prayeth she.

The lady sprang up suddenly,
The lovely lady, Christabel!
It moaned as near, as near can be,
But what it is she cannot tell.—   40
On the other side it seems to be,
Of the huge, broad-breasted, old oak tree.

The night is chill; the forest bare;
Is it the wind that moaneth bleak?
There is not wind enough in the air   45
To move away the ringlet curl
From the lovely lady's cheek—
There is not wind enough to twirl
The one red leaf, the last of its clan,
That dances as often as dance it can,   50
Hanging so light, and hanging so high,
On the topmost twig that looks up at the sky.

Hush, beating heart of Christabel!
Jesu, Maria, shield her well!
She folded her arms beneath her cloak,   55
And stole to the other side of the oak.
        What sees she there?

There she sees a damsel bright,
Drest in a silken robe of white,
That shadowy in the moonlight shone: 60
The neck that made that white robe wan,
Her stately neck, and arms were bare;
Her blue-veined feet unsandal'd were,
And wildly glittered here and there
The gems entangled in her hair.   65
I guess, 'twas frightful there to see
A lady so richly clad as she—
Beautiful exceedingly!

Mary mother, save me now!
(Said Christabel,) And who art thou?   70

The lady strange made answer meet,
And her voice was faint and sweet:—
Have pity on my sore distress,
I scarce can speak for weariness:
Stretch forth thy hand, and have no fear!   75
Said Christabel, How camest thou here?
And the lady, whose voice was faint and sweet,
Did thus pursue her answer meet:—

My sire is of a noble line,
And my name is Geraldine: 80
Five warriors seized me yestermorn,
Me, even me, a maid forlorn:
They choked my cries with force and fright,
And tied me on a palfrey white.
The palfrey was as fleet as wind,   85
And they rode furiously behind.
They spurred amain, their steeds were white:
And once we crossed the shade of night.
As sure as Heaven shall rescue me,
I have no thought what men they be;   90
Nor do I know how long it is
(For I have lain entranced I wis[1])
Since one, the tallest of the five,
Took me from the palfrey's back,
A weary woman, scarce alive.   95
Some muttered words his comrades spoke:
He placed me underneath this oak;
He swore they would return with haste;
Whither they went I cannot tell—
I thought I heard, some minutes past,   100
Sounds as of a castle bell.
Stretch forth thy hand (thus ended she),
And help a wretched maid to flee.

Then Christabel stretched forth her hand,
And comforted fair Geraldine: 105
O well, bright dame! may you command
The service of Sir Leoline;
And gladly our stout chivalry[2]
Will he send forth and friends withal[3]
To guide and guard you safe and free   110
Home to your noble father's hall.

She rose: and forth with steps they passed
That strove to be, and were not, fast.
Her gracious stars the lady blest,
And thus spake on sweet Christabel: 115

---

1 Know.   2 Men-at-arms.   3 With them.

All our household are at rest,
The hall as silent as the cell;
Sir Leoline is weak in health,
And may not well awakened be,
But we will move as if in stealth,   120
And I beseech your courtesy,
This night, to share your couch with me.

They crossed the moat, and Christabel
Took the key that fitted well;
A little door she opened straight,   125
All in the middle of the gate;
The gate that was ironed within and without,
Where an army in battle array had marched out.
The lady sank, belike through pain,
And Christabel with might and main   130
Lifted her up, a weary weight,
Over the threshold of the gate:
Then the lady rose again,
And moved, as she were not in pain.[4]

So free from danger, free from fear,   135
They crossed the court: right glad they were.
And Christabel devoutly cried
To the lady by her side,
Praise we the Virgin all divine
Who hath rescued thee from thy distress!   140
Alas, alas! said Geraldine,
I cannot speak for weariness.
So free from danger, free from fear,
They crossed the court: right glad they were.

Outside her kennel, the mastiff old   145
Lay fast asleep, in moonshine cold.
The mastiff old did not awake,
Yet she an angry moan did make!
And what can ail the mastiff bitch?
Never till now she uttered yell   150
Beneath the eye of Christabel.
Perhaps it is the owlet's scritch:
For what can ail the mastiff bitch?

They passed the hall, that echoes still,
Pass as lightly as you will!   155
The brands were flat, the brands were dying,
Amid their own white ashes lying;
But when the lady passed, there came

A tongue of light, a fit of flame;
And Christabel saw the lady's eye,   160
And nothing else saw she thereby,
Save the boss of the shield of Sir Leoline tall,
Which hung in a murky old niche in the wall.
O softly tread, said Christabel,
My father seldom sleepeth well.   165

Sweet Christabel her feet doth bare,
And jealous of the listening air
They steal their way from stair to stair,
Now in glimmer, and now in gloom,
And now they pass the Baron's room,   170
As still as death, with stifled breath!
And now have reached her chamber door;
And now doth Geraldine press down
The rushes of the chamber floor.

The moon shines dim in the open air,   175
And not a moonbeam enters here.
But they without its light can see
The chamber carved so curiously,[5]
Carved with figures strange and sweet,
All made out of the carver's brain,   180
For a lady's chamber meet:
The lamp with twofold silver chain
Is fastened to an angel's feet.

The silver lamp burns dead and dim;
But Christabel the lamp will trim.   185
She trimmed the lamp, and made it bright,
And left it swinging to and fro,
While Geraldine, in wretched plight,
Sank down upon the floor below.

O weary lady, Geraldine,   190
I pray you, drink this cordial wine!
It is a wine of virtuous[6] powers;
My mother made it of wild flowers.

And will your mother pity me,
Who am a maiden most forlorn?   195
Christabel answered—Woe is me!
She died the hour that I was born.
I have heard the grey-haired friar tell
How on her death-bed she did say,
That she should hear the castle-bell   200
Strike twelve upon my wedding-day.
O mother dear! that thou wert here!
I would, said Geraldine, she were!

---

[4] The point being that she could not of herself cross a threshold which had been blessed to keep out evil spirits. Other hints that "Geraldine" is an evil being come in lines 139–42, 148, and 156–59.

---

[5] Exquisitely.   [6] Potent.

But soon with altered voice, said she—
'Off, wandering mother! Peak and pine![7]   205
I have power to bid thee flee.'
Alas! what ails poor Geraldine?
Why stares she with unsettled eye?
Can she the bodiless dead espy?
And why with hollow voice cries she,   210
'Off, woman, off! this hour is mine—
Though thou her guardian spirit be,
Off, woman, off! 'tis given to me.'

Then Christabel knelt by the lady's side,
And raised to heaven her eyes so blue—   215
Alas! said she, this ghastly ride—
Dear lady! it hath wildered you!
The lady wiped her moist cold brow,
And faintly said, ' 'Tis over now!'

Again the wild-flower wine she drank: 220
Her fair large eyes 'gan glitter bright,
And from the floor whereon she sank,
The lofty lady stood upright:
She was most beautiful to see,
Like a lady of a far countree.   225

And thus the lofty lady spake—
'All they who live in the upper sky,
Do love you, holy Christabel!
And you love them, and for their sake
And for the good which me befel,   230
Even I in my degree will try,
Fair maiden, to requite you well.
But now unrobe yourself; for I
Must pray, ere yet in bed I lie.'

Quoth Christabel, So let it be!   235
And as the lady bade, did she.
Her gentle limbs did she undress,
And lay down in her loveliness.

But through her brain of weal and woe
So many thoughts moved to and fro,   240
That vain it were her lids to close;
So half-way from the bed she rose,
And on her elbow did recline
To look at the lady Geraldine.

Beneath the lamp the lady bowed,   245
And slowly rolled her eyes around;
Then drawing in her breath aloud,
Like one that shuddered, she unbound
The cincture[8] from beneath her breast:
Her silken robe, and inner vest,   250
Dropt to her feet, and full in view,
Behold! her bosom and half her side—
A sight to dream of, not to tell!
O shield her! shield sweet Christabel!

Yet Geraldine nor speaks nor stirs;   255
Ah! what a stricken look was hers!
Deep from within she seems half-way
To lift some weight with sick assay,[9]
And eyes the maid and seeks delay;
Then suddenly, as one defied,   260
Collects herself in scorn and pride,
And lay down by the Maiden's side!—
And in her arms the maid she took,
        Ah wel-a-day!
And with low voice and doleful look   265
These words did say:
'In the touch of this bosom there worketh a spell,
Which is lord of thy utterance, Christabel!
Thou knowest to-night, and wilt know to-morrow,
This mark of my shame, this seal of my sorrow;   270
        But vainly thou warrest,
          For this is alone in
        Thy power to declare,
          That in the dim forest
        Thou heard'st a low moaning,   275
And found'st a bright lady, surpassingly fair;
And didst bring her home with thee in love and
    in charity,
To shield her and shelter her from the damp air.'

The Conclusion to Part I

It was a lovely sight to see
The lady Christabel, when she   280
Was praying at the old oak tree.
        Amid the jaggèd shadows
        Of mossy leafless boughs,
        Kneeling in the moonlight,
        To make her gentle vows;   285
Her slender palms together prest,
Heaving sometimes on her breast;
Her face resigned to bliss or bale—

---

[7] Dwindle away. "Geraldine" is driving off the spirit of Christabel's mother, which desires to aid her daughter.— Note that the text we follow is inconsistent in its use of quotation marks.

[8] Belt.
[9] Essay, attempt.

Her face, oh call it fair not pale,
And both blue eyes more bright than clear,   290
Each about to have a tear.

With open eyes (ah woe is me!)
Asleep, and dreaming fearfully,
Fearfully dreaming, yet, I wis,
Dreaming that alone, which is—   295
O sorrow and shame! Can this be she,
The lady, who knelt at the old oak tree?
And lo! the worker of these harms,
That holds the maiden in her arms,
Seems to slumber still and mild,   300
As a mother with her child.

A star hath set, a star hath risen,
O Geraldine! since arms of thine
Have been the lovely lady's prison.
O Geraldine! one hour was thine—   305
Thou'st had thy will![10] By tairn[11] and rill,
The night-birds all that hour were still.
But now they are jubilant anew,
From cliff and tower, tu—whoo! tu—whoo!
Tu—whoo! tu—whoo! from wood and fell![12]   310

And see! the lady Christabel
Gathers herself from out her trance;
Her limbs relax, her countenance
Grows sad and soft; the smooth thin lids
Close o'er her eyes; and tears she sheds—   315
Large tears that leave the lashes bright!
And oft the while she seems to smile
As infants at a sudden light!

Yea, she doth smile, and she doth weep,
Like a youthful hermitess,   320
Beauteous in a wilderness,
Who, praying always, prays in sleep.
And, if she move unquietly,
Perchance, 'tis but the blood so free
Comes back and tingles in her feet.   325
No doubt, she hath a vision sweet.
What if her guardian spirit 'twere,
What if she knew her mother near?
But this she knows, in joys and woes,
That saints will aid if men will call: 330
For the blue sky bends over all!

---

10 As a vampire, "Geraldine" has been sucking Christabel's blood. Cf. lines 374–80 and 453.
11 Pool.   12 Hill.

Part II

Each matin bell, the Baron saith,
Knells us back to a world of death.
These words Sir Leoline first said,
When he rose and found his lady dead: 335
These words Sir Leoline will say
Many a morn to his dying day!

And hence the custom and law began
That still at dawn the sacristan,
Who duly pulls the heavy bell,   340
Five and forty beads must tell
Between each stroke—a warning knell,
Which not a soul can choose but hear
From Bratha Head[13] to Wyndermere.

Saith Bracy the bard, So let it knell!   345
And let the drowsy sacristan
Still count as slowly as he can!
There is no lack of such, I ween,
As well fill up the space between.
In Langdale Pike[14] and Witch's Lair,   350
And Dungeon-ghyll[15] so foully rent,
With ropes of rock and bells of air
Three sinful sextons' ghosts are pent,
Who all give back, one after t'other,
The death-note to their living brother;   355
And oft too, by the knell offended,
Just as their one! two! three! is ended,
The devil mocks the doleful tale
With a merry peal from Borodale.[16]

The air is still! through mist and cloud   360
That merry peal comes ringing loud;
And Geraldine shakes off her dread,
And rises lightly from the bed;
Puts on her silken vestments white,
And tricks her hair in lovely plight,[17]   365
And nothing doubting of her spell
Awakens the lady Christabel.
'Sleep you, sweet lady Christabel?
I trust that you have rested well.'

---

13 Source. Coleridge was living in the Lake District when he composed Part II. The Brathay River flows into the northern end of Lake Windermere. The other place-names are from the same region.
14 Peak.   15 Gorge.
16 Borrowdale, perhaps the most beautiful valley of the District.   17 Plait.

And Christabel awoke and spied
The same who lay down by her side—
O rather say, the same whom she
Raised up beneath the old oak tree!
Nay, fairer yet! and yet more fair! 375
For she belike hath drunken deep
Of all the blessedness of sleep!
And while she spake, her looks, her air
Such gentle thankfulness declare,
That (so it seemed) her girded vests
Grew tight beneath her heaving breasts. 380
'Sure I have sinn'd!' said Christabel,
'Now heaven be praised if all be well!'
And in low faltering tones, yet sweet,
Did she the lofty lady greet
With such perplexity of mind 385
As dreams too lively leave behind.

So quickly she rose, and quickly arrayed
Her maiden limbs, and having prayed
That He, who on the cross did groan,
Might wash away her sins unknown, 390
She forthwith led fair Geraldine
To meet her sire, Sir Leoline.

The lovely maid and the lady tall
Are pacing both into the hall,
And pacing on through page and groom, 395
Enter the Baron's presence-room.

The Baron rose, and while he prest
His gentle daughter to his breast,
With cheerful wonder in his eyes
The lady Geraldine espies, 400
And gave such welcome to the same,
As might beseem so bright a dame!

But when he heard the lady's tale,
And when she told her father's name,
Why waxed Sir Leoline so pale, 405
Murmuring o'er the name again,
Lord Roland de Vaux of Tryermaine?

Alas! they had been friends in youth;
But whispering tongues can poison truth;
And constancy lives in realms above; 410
And life is thorny; and youth is vain;
And to be wroth with one we love
Doth work like madness in the brain.
And thus it chanced, as I divine,
With Roland and Sir Leoline. 415

Each spake words of high disdain 370
And insult to his heart's best brother:
They parted—ne'er to meet again!
But never either found another
To free the hollow heart from paining— 420
They stood aloof, the scars remaining,
Like cliffs which had been rent asunder;
A dreary sea now flows between;—
But neither heat, nor frost, nor thunder,
Shall wholly do away, I ween, 425
The marks of that which once hath been.

Sir Leoline, a moment's space
Stood gazing on the damsel's face:
And the youthful Lord of Tryermaine
Came back upon his heart again. 430

O then the Baron forgot his age,
His noble heart swelled high with rage;
He swore by the wounds in Jesu's side
He would proclaim it far and wide,
With trump and solemn heraldry, 435
That they, who thus had wronged the dame,
Were base as spotted infamy!
'And if they dare deny the same,
My herald shall appoint a week,
And let the recreant traitors seek 440
My tourney court—that there and then
I may dislodge their reptile souls
From the bodies and forms of men!'
He spake: his eye in lightning rolls!
For the lady was ruthlessly seized; and he kenned 445
In the beautiful lady the child of his friend!

And now the tears were on his face,
And fondly in his arms he took
Fair Geraldine, who met the embrace,
Prolonging it with joyous look. 450
Which when she viewed, a vision fell
Upon the soul of Christabel,
The vision of fear, the touch and pain!
She shrunk and shuddered, and saw again—
(Ah, woe is me! Was it for thee, 455
Thou gentle maid! such sights to see?)

Again she saw that bosom old,
Again she felt that bosom cold,
And drew in her breath with a hissing sound:[18]

---

[18] For besides being a vampire "Geraldine" is also a serpent-woman, and Christabel has been affected by contact with her.

Whereat the Knight turned wildly round,   460
And nothing saw, but his own sweet maid
With eyes upraised, as one that prayed.

The touch, the sight, had passed away,
And in its stead that vision blest,
Which comforted her after-rest   465
While in the lady's arms she lay,
Had put a rapture in her breast,
And on her lips and o'er her eyes
Spread smiles like light!
                              With new surprise,
'What ails then my belovèd child?'   470
The Baron said—His daughter mild
Made answer, 'All will yet be well!'
I ween, she had no power to tell
Aught else: so mighty was the spell.

Yet he, who saw this Geraldine,   475
Had deemed her sure a thing divine:
Such sorrow with such grace she blended,
As if she feared she had offended
Sweet Christabel, that gentle maid!
And with such lowly tones she prayed   480
She might be sent without delay
Home to her father's mansion.
                              'Nay!
Nay, by my soul!' said Leoline.
'Ho! Bracy the bard, the charge be thine!
Go thou, with music sweet and loud,   485
And take two steeds with trappings proud,
And take the youth whom thou lov'st best
To bear thy harp, and learn thy song,
And clothe you both in solemn vest,
And over the mountains haste along,   490
Lest wandering folk, that are abroad,
Detain you on the valley road.

'And when he has crossed the Irthing flood,
My merry bard! he hastes, he hastes
Up Knorren Moor, through Halegarth Wood,   495
And reaches soon that castle good
Which stands and threatens Scotland's wastes.

'Bard Bracy! bard Bracy! your horses are fleet,
Ye must ride up the hall, your music so sweet,
More loud than your horses' echoing feet!   500
And loud and loud to Lord Roland call,
Thy daughter is safe in Langdale hall!
Thy beautiful daughter is safe and free—
Sir Leoline greets thee thus through me!

He bids thee come without delay   505
With all thy numerous array
And take thy lovely daughter home:
And he will meet thee on the way
With all his numerous array
White with their panting palfreys' foam: 510
And, by mine honour! I will say,
That I repent me of the day
When I spake words of fierce disdain
To Roland de Vaux of Tryermaine!—
—For since that evil hour hath flown,   515
Many a summer's sun hath shone;
Yet ne'er found I a friend again
Like Roland de Vaux of Tryermaine.'

The lady fell, and clasped his knees,
Her face upraised, her eyes o'erflowing;   520
And Bracy replied, with faltering voice,
His gracious Hail on all bestowing!—
'Thy words, thou sire of Christabel,
Are sweeter than my harp can tell;
Yet might I gain a boon of thee,   525
This day my journey should not be,
So strange a dream hath come to me,
That I had vowed with music loud
To clear yon wood from thing unblest,
Warned by a vision in my rest!   530
For in my sleep I saw that dove,
That gentle bird, whom thou dost love,
And call'st by thy own daughter's name—
Sir Leoline! I saw the same
Fluttering, and uttering fearful moan,   535
Among the green herbs in the forest alone.
Which when I saw and when I heard,
I wonder'd what might ail the bird;
For nothing near it could I see,
Save the grass and green herbs underneath the old   540
        tree.

'And in my dream methought I went
To search out what might there be found;
And what the sweet bird's trouble meant,
That thus lay fluttering on the ground.
I went and peered, and could descry   545
No cause for her distressful cry;
But yet for her dear lady's sake
I stooped, methought, the dove to take,
When lo! I saw a bright green snake
Coiled around its wings and neck.   550
Green as the herbs on which it couched,
Close by the dove's its head it crouched;

And with the dove it heaves and stirs,
Swelling its neck as she swelled hers!
I woke; it was the midnight hour, 555
The clock was echoing in the tower;
But though my slumber was gone by,
This dream it would not pass away—
It seems to live upon my eye!
And thence I vowed this self-same day 560
With music strong and saintly song
To wander through the forest bare,
Lest aught unholy loiter there.'

Thus Bracy said: the Baron, the while,
Half-listening heard him with a smile; 565
Then turned to Lady Geraldine,
His eyes made up of wonder and love;
And said in courtly accents fine,
'Sweet maid, Lord Roland's beauteous dove,
With arms more strong than harp or song, 570
Thy sire and I will crush the snake!'
He kissed her forehead as he spake,
And Geraldine in maiden wise
Casting down her large bright eyes,
With blushing cheek and courtesy fine 575
She turned her from Sir Leoline;
Softly gathering up her train,
That o'er her right arm fell again;
And folded her arms across her chest,
And couched her head upon her breast,[19] 580
And looked askance at Christabel—
Jesu, Maria, shield her well!

A snake's small eye blinks dull and shy;
And the lady's eyes they shrunk in her head,
Each shrunk up to a serpent's eye, 485
And with somewhat of malice, and more of dread,
At Christabel she looked askance!—
One moment—and the sight was fled!
But Christabel in dizzy trance
Stumbling on the unsteady ground 590
Shuddered aloud, with a hissing sound;
And Geraldine again turned round,
And like a thing, that sought relief,
Full of wonder and full of grief,
She rolled her large bright eyes divine 595
Wildly on Sir Leoline.

The maid, alas! her thoughts are gone,
She nothing sees—no sight but one!

---

[19] Like a snake drawing back its head to strike.

The maid, devoid of guile and sin,
I know not how, in fearful wise, 600
So deeply had she drunken in
That look, those shrunken serpent eyes,
That all her features were resigned
To this sole image in her mind:
And passively did imitate 605
That look of dull and treacherous hate!
And thus she stood, in dizzy trance,
Still picturing that look askance
With forced unconscious sympathy
Full before her father's view— 610
As far as such a look could be
In eyes so innocent and blue!

And when the trance was o'er, the maid
Paused awhile, and inly prayed:
Then falling at the Baron's feet, 615
'By my mother's soul do I entreat
That thou this woman send away!'
She said: and more she could not say:
For what she knew she could not tell,
O'er-mastered by the mighty spell. 620

Why is thy cheek so wan and wild,
Sir Leoline? Thy only child
Lies at thy feet, thy joy, thy pride,
So fair, so innocent, so mild;
The same, for whom thy lady died! 625
O by the pangs of her dear mother
Think thou no evil of thy child!
For her, and thee, and for no other,
She prayed the moment ere she died:
Prayed that the babe for whom she died, 630
Might prove her dear lord's joy and pride!
That prayer her deadly pangs beguiled,
Sir Leoline!
And wouldst thou wrong thy only child,
Her child and thine? 635

Within the Baron's heart and brain
If thoughts, like these, had any share,
They only swelled his rage and pain,
And did but work confusion there.
His heart was cleft with pain and rage, 640
His cheeks they quivered, his eyes were wild,
Dishonoured thus in his old age;
Dishonoured by his only child,
And all his hospitality
To the wronged daughter of his friend 645
By more than woman's jealousy

Brought thus to a disgraceful end—
He rolled his eye with stern regard
Upon the gentle minstrel bard,
And said in tones abrupt, austere—   650
'Why, Bracy! dost thou loiter here?
I bade thee hence!' The bard obeyed;
And turning from his own sweet maid,
The agèd knight, Sir Leoline,
Led forth the lady Geraldine!   655

The Conclusion to Part II[20]

A little child, a limber elf,
Singing, dancing to itself,
A fairy thing with red round cheeks,
That always finds, and never seeks,
Makes such a vision to the sight   660
As fills a father's eyes with light;
And pleasures flow in so thick and fast
Upon his heart, that he at last
Must needs express his love's excess
With words of unmeant bitterness.   665
Perhaps 'tis pretty to force together
Thoughts so all unlike each other;
To mutter and mock a broken charm,
To dally with wrong that does no harm.
Perhaps 'tis tender too and pretty   670
At each wild word to feel within
A sweet recoil of love and pity.
And what, if in a world of sin
(O sorrow and shame should this be true!)
Such giddiness of heart and brain   675
Comes seldom save from rage and pain,
So talks as it's most used to do.

Frost at Midnight

Written in 1798.

The Frost performs its secret ministry,
Unhelped by any wind. The owlet's cry
Came loud—and hark, again! loud as before.
The inmates of my cottage, all at rest,
Have left me to that solitude, which suits   5
Abstruser musings: save that at my side

My cradled infant[1] slumbers peacefully.
'Tis calm indeed! so calm, that it disturbs
And vexes meditation with its strange
And extreme silentness. Sea, hill, and wood,   10
This populous village! Sea, and hill, and wood,
With all the numberless goings-on of life,
Inaudible as dreams! the thin blue flame
Lies on my low-burnt fire, and quivers not;
Only that film,[2] which fluttered on the grate,   15
Still flutters there, the sole unquiet thing.
Methinks, its motion in this hush of nature
Gives it dim sympathies with me who live,
Making it a companionable form,
Whose puny flaps and freaks the idling Spirit   20
By its own moods interprets, every where
Echo or mirror seeking of itself,
And makes a toy of Thought.
                    But O! how oft,
How oft, at school, with most believing mind,
Presageful, have I gazed upon the bars,   25
To watch that fluttering *stranger!* and as oft
With unclosed lids, already had I dreamt
Of my sweet birth-place, and the old church-
    tower,
Whose bells, the poor man's only music, rang
From morn to evening, all the hot Fair-day,   30
So sweetly, that they stirred and haunted me
With a wild pleasure, falling on mine ear
Most like articulate sounds of things to come!
So gazed I, till the soothing things, I dreamt,
Lulled me to sleep, and sleep prolonged my   35
    dreams!
And so I brooded all the following morn,
Awed by the stern preceptor's face, mine eye
Fixed with mock study on my swimming book:
Save if the door half opened, and I snatched
A hasty glance, and still my heart leaped up,   40
For still I hoped to see the *stranger's* face,
Townsman, or aunt, or sister more beloved,
My play-mate when we both were clothed alike!

Dear Babe, that sleepest cradled by my side,
Whose gentle breathings, heard in this deep calm,   45
Fill up the interspersèd vacancies
And momentary pauses of the thought!
My babe so beautiful! it thrills my heart
With tender gladness, thus to look at thee,

---

20 We must suppose that the connection between this "conclusion" and the Baron's impatience with his daughter would have been made plainer if Coleridge had finished the poem.

1 Hartley Coleridge (1796–1849), the poet's eldest son.
2 Coleridge's note: ". . . these films are called *strangers* and supposed to portend the arrival of some absent friend."

And think that thou shalt learn far other lore 50
And in far other scenes! For I was reared
In the great city, pent 'mid cloisters dim,
And saw nought lovely but the sky and stars.
But *thou*, my babe! shalt wander like a breeze
By lakes and sandy shores, beneath the crags 55
Of ancient mountain, and beneath the clouds,
Which image in their bulk both lakes and shores
And mountain crags: so shalt thou see and hear
The lovely shapes and sounds intelligible
Of that eternal language, which thy God 60
Utters, who from eternity doth teach
Himself in all, and all things in himself.
Great universal Teacher! he shall mould
Thy spirit, and by giving make it ask.

Therefore all seasons shall be sweet to thee, 65
Whether the summer clothe the general earth
With greenness, or the redbreast sit and sing
Betwixt the tufts of snow on the bare branch
Of mossy apple-tree, while the nigh thatch
Smokes in the sun-thaw; whether the eave-drops 70
fall
Heard only in the trances of the blast,
Or if the secret ministry of frost
Shall hang them up in silent icicles,
Quietly shining to the quiet Moon.

Dejection: An Ode

This poem went through several stages of revision. It was originally composed at Keswick in the spring of 1802; and there are manuscripts which show that, while it was partially inspired by his love for Sara Hutchinson, the Wordsworths were almost equally in Coleridge's mind. The ode was first printed in the *Morning Post* on October 4, Wordsworth's wedding day, but with the directness of the references to him reduced by changing *William* to *Edmund*. Other allusions to him, to Dorothy, and to Sara Hutchinson were left out entirely. Still later, as a consequence of the estrangement, the references to William and his poetry were reduced still further, and an unnamed lady was substituted as the recipient of the poet's good wishes.

These facts are of minor importance, since the poem is mainly about Coleridge. It is himself he is thinking of, far more than a brother poet or a beloved woman. Behind these lines lurks the terrible conviction that his creative powers are waning.

The poem has the following stanza as epigraph:

Late, late yestreen I saw the new Moon,
With the old Moon in her arms;

And I fear, I fear, my Master dear!
We shall have a deadly storm.

Ballad of Sir Patrick Spence

I

Well! If the Bard was weather-wise, who made
The grand old ballad of Sir Patrick Spence,[1]
This night, so tranquil now, will not go hence
Unroused by winds, that ply a busier trade
Than those which mould yon cloud in lazy flakes, 5
Or the dull sobbing draft, that moans and rakes
Upon the strings of this Aeolian lute,[2]
Which better far were mute,
For lo! the New-moon winter-bright!
And overspread with phantom light, 10
(With swimming phantom light o'erspread
But rimmed and circled by a silver thread)
I see the old Moon in her lap, foretelling
The coming-on of rain and squally blast.
And oh! that even now the gust were swelling, 15
And the slant night-shower driving loud and
fast!
Those sounds which oft have raised me, whilst
they awed,
And sent my soul abroad,
Might now perhaps their wonted impulse give,
Might startle this dull pain, and make it move 20
and live!

II

A grief without a pang, void, dark, and drear,
A stifled, drowsy, unimpassioned grief,
Which finds no natural outlet, no relief,
In word, or sigh, or tear—
O Lady![3] in this wan and heartless mood, 25
To other thoughts by yonder throstle woo'd,
All this long eve, so balmy and serene,
Have I been gazing on the western sky,
And its peculiar tint of yellow green:
And still I gaze—and with how blank an eye! 30
And those thin clouds above, in flakes and bars,
That give away their motion to the stars;
Those stars, that glide behind them or between,
Now sparkling, now bedimmed, but always seen:
Yon crescent Moon, as fixed as if it grew 35

1 Reprinted in Volume I.
2 The aeolian harp, popular in this period. It was a box with strings tuned in unison; when it was placed in the wind, its strings vibrated.
3 Formerly *William*, not *Lady*. So also in lines 47, 67.

In its own cloudless, starless lake of blue;
I see them all so excellently fair,
I see, not feel, how beautiful they are!

III

My genial[4] spirits fail;
  And what can these avail   40
To lift the smothering weight from off my breast?
  It were a vain endeavour,
  Though I should gaze for ever
On that green light that lingers in the west:
I may not hope from outward forms to win   45
The passion and the life, whose fountains are
  within.

IV

O Lady! we receive but what we give,
And in our life alone does Nature live:
Ours is her wedding garment, ours her shroud!
  And would we aught behold, of higher worth,   50
Than that inanimate cold world allowed
To the poor loveless ever-anxious crowd,
  Ah! from the soul itself must issue forth
A light, a glory, a fair luminous cloud
  Enveloping the Earth—   55
And from the soul itself must there be sent
  A sweet and potent voice, of its own birth,
Of all sweet sounds the life and element!

V

O pure of heart! thou need'st not ask of me
What this strong music in the soul may be!   60
What, and wherein it doth exist,
This light, this glory, this fair luminous mist,
This beautiful and beauty-making power.
  Joy, virtuous Lady![5] Joy that ne'er was given,
Save to the pure, and in their purest hour,   65
Life, and Life's effluence,[6] cloud at once and
  shower,
Joy, Lady! is the spirit and the power,
Which wedding Nature to us gives in dower
  A new Earth and new Heaven,
Undreamt of by the sensual and the proud—   70
Joy is the sweet voice, Joy the luminous cloud—
  We in ourselves rejoice!
And thence flows all that charms or ear or sight,

All melodies the echoes of that voice,
All colours a suffusion from that light.[7]   75

VI

There was a time when, though my path was
  rough,
  This joy within me dallied with distress,
And all misfortunes were but as the stuff
  Whence Fancy made me dream of happiness:
For hope grew round me, like the twining vine,   80
And fruits, and foliage, not my own, seemed mine.
But now afflictions bow me down to earth:
Nor care I that they rob me of my mirth;
  But oh! each visitation
Suspends what nature gave me at my birth,   85
  My shaping spirit of Imagination.
For not to think of what I needs must feel,
  But to be still and patient, all I can;
And haply by abstruse research to steal
  From my own nature all the natural man—   90
  This was my sole resource, my only plan:
Till that which suits a part infects the whole,
And now is almost grown the habit of my soul.

VII

Hence, viper thoughts, that coil around my mind,
  Reality's dark dream!   95
I turn from you, and listen to the wind,
  Which long has raved unnoticed. What a
  scream
Of agony by torture lengthened out
That lute sent forth! Thou Wind, that rav'st
  without,
  Bare crag, or mountain-tairn,[8] or blasted tree, 100
Or pine-grove whither woodman never clomb,
Or lonely house, long held the witches' home,
  Methinks were fitter instruments for thee,
Mad Lutanist! who in this month of showers,
Of dark-brown gardens, and of peeping flowers,   105
Mak'st Devils' yule, with worse than wintry song,
The blossoms, buds, and timorous leaves among.
  Thou Actor, perfect in all tragic sounds!

---

4 Creative.
5 Formerly *blameless Poet*.   6 Emanation, outflow.

7 The following passage formerly came after line 75:
  "Calm, steadfast Spirit, guided from above,
  O Wordsworth! friend of my devoutest choice,
  Great son of genius! full of light and love
    Thus, thus dost thou rejoice.
  To thee do all things live from pole to pole,
  Their life the eddying of thy living soul.
  Brother and friend of my devoutest choice
  Thus may'st thou ever, evermore rejoice!"
Compare the closing lines of the present version.
8 Pool.

Thou mighty Poet, e'en to frenzy bold!
    What tell'st thou now about?   110
      'Tis of the rushing of an host in rout,
  With groans, of trampled men, with smarting
      wounds—
At once they groan with pain, and shudder with
    the cold!
But hush! there is a pause of deeper silence!
    And all that noise, as of a rushing crowd,   115
With groans, and tremulous shudderings—all is
    over—
    It tells another tale, with sounds less deep and
      loud!
      A tale of less affright,
      And tempered with delight,
As[9] Otway's self[10] had framed the tender lay,—   120
      'Tis of a little child
      Upon a lonesome wild,
Not far from home, but she hath lost her way:
And now moans low in bitter grief and fear,
And now screams loud, and hopes to make her   125
    mother hear.

VIII

'Tis midnight, but small thoughts have I of sleep:
Full seldom may my friend such vigils keep!
Visit her, gentle Sleep! with wings of healing,
    And may this storm be but a mountain-birth,
May all the stars hang bright above her dwelling,   130
    Silent as though they watched the sleeping
      Earth!
      With light heart may she rise,
      Gay fancy, cheerful eyes,
    Joy lift her spirit, joy attune her voice;
To her may all things live, from pole to pole,   135
Their life the eddying of her living soul!
    O simple spirit, guided from above,
Dear Lady! friend devoutest of my choice,
Thus mayest thou ever, evermore rejoice.

Work Without Hope

Lines Composed 21st February 1825

All Nature seems at work. Slugs leave their lair—
The bees are stirring—birds are on the wing—

---

9 As if.

10 Formerly *thou thyself*. The following lines refer to Wordsworth's "Lucy Gray" (p. 61). Thomas Otway wrote two of the best tragedies of the Restoration period.

And Winter slumbering in the open air,
Wears on his smiling face a dream of Spring!
And I the while, the sole unbusy thing,   5
Nor honey make, nor pair, nor build, nor sing.

    Yet well I ken the banks where amaranths blow,
Have traced the fount whence streams of nectar
    flow.
Bloom, O ye amaranths! bloom for whom ye may,
For me ye bloom not! Glide, rich streams, away!   10
With lips unbrightened, wreathless brow, I stroll:
And would you learn the spells that drowse my
    soul?
Work without Hope draws nectar in a sieve,
And Hope without an object cannot live.

from Biographia Literaria

In 1817, soon after its completion, appeared *Biographia Literaria; or Biographical Sketches of My Literary Life and Opinions*. An "immethodical miscellany," as Coleridge acknowledged, it is his literary autobiography, an exposition of his philosophy of poetry, and one of the major documents of Romantic theory. He had formerly accepted as adequately representative of his own views Wordsworth's Preface to *Lyrical Ballads*, with which the following pages should be compared. Since the appearance of the Preface, the but partially healed breach in the poets' friendship had led Coleridge to reexamine points of difference in their theories, especially on the vital question of diction. Of equal interest is his attempt to formulate his conception of what poetry is. *Biographia Literaria* has been edited by J. Shawcross (2 vols., 1907).

from Chapter I

The motives of the present work—Reception of the Author's first publication—The discipline of his taste at school—The effect of contemporary writers on youthful minds—Bowles's sonnets—Comparison between the Poets before and since Mr. Pope.

It has been my lot to have had my name introduced, both in conversation, and in print, more frequently than I find it easy to explain, whether I consider the fewness, unimportance, and limited circulation of my writings, or the retirement and distance in which I have lived, both from the literary and political world. Most often it has been connected with some charge which I could not acknowledge, or some principle which I had never entertained. Nevertheless, had I had no   10 other motive or incitement, the reader would not have been troubled with this exculpation. What my additional purposes were, will be seen in the following pages. It will be found, that the least of what I have written concerns myself personally. I have used the narration chiefly for the purpose of giving a continuity to the work, in part for the sake of the miscellaneous reflections suggested to me by particular events, but still more as introductory to the statement of my principles in Politics, Religion, and Philosophy, and an application of the rules, deduced from philosophical principles, to poetry and criticism. But of the objects which I proposed to myself, it was not the least important to effect, as far as possible, a settlement of the long continued controversy concerning the true nature of poetic diction; and at the same time to define with the utmost impartiality the real *poetic* character of the poet,[1] by whose writings this controversy was first kindled, and has been since fuelled and fanned. . . .

At school I enjoyed the inestimable advantage of a very sensible, though at the same time a very severe master.[2] . . . I learnt from him, that Poetry, even that of the loftiest and, seemingly, that of the wildest odes, had a logic of its own, as severe as that of science; and more difficult, because more subtle, more complex, and dependent on more, and more fugitive causes. In the truly great poets, he would say, there is a reason assignable, not only for every word, but for the position of every word. . . .

In our own English compositions . . . he showed no mercy to phrase, metaphor, or image, unsupported by a sound sense, or where the same sense might have been conveyed with equal force and dignity in plainer words. Lute, harp, and lyre, muse, muses, and inspirations, Pegasus, Parnassus, and Hippocrene were all an abomination to him. In fancy I can almost hear him now, exclaiming *"Harp? Harp? Lyre? Pen and ink, boy, you mean! Muse, boy, Muse? Your Nurse's daughter, you mean! Pierian spring? Oh aye! the cloister-pump, I suppose!"* Nay, certain introductions, similes, and examples were placed by name on a list of interdiction. . . .

I had just entered on my seventeenth year,

when the sonnets of Mr. Bowles,[3] twenty in number, and just then published in a quarto pamphlet, were first made known and presented to me. . . . My earliest acquaintances will not have forgotten the undisciplined eagerness and impetuous zeal, with which I laboured to make proselytes, not only of my companions, but of all with whom I conversed, of whatever rank, and in whatever place. As my school finances did not permit me to purchase copies, I made, within less than a year and a half, more than forty transcriptions, as the best presents I could offer to those, who had in any way won my regard. And with almost equal delight did I receive the three or four following publications of the same author.

Though I have seen and known enough of mankind to be well aware, that I shall perhaps stand alone in my creed, and that it will be well, if I subject myself to no worse charge than that of singularity; I am not therefore deterred from avowing, that I regard, and ever have regarded the obligations of intellect among the most sacred of the claims of gratitude. A valuable thought, or a particular train of thoughts, gives me additional pleasure, when I can safely refer and attribute it to the conversation or correspondence of another. My obligations to Mr. Bowles were indeed important, and for radical good. At a very premature age, even before my fifteenth year, I had bewildered myself in metaphysicks, and in theological controversy. Nothing else pleased me. History, and particular facts, lost all interest in my mind. Poetry (though for a school-boy of that age, I was above par in English versification, and had already produced two or three compositions which, I may venture to say, without reference to my age, were somewhat above mediocrity, and which had gained me more credit than the sound, good sense of my old master was at all pleased with,) poetry itself, yea, novels and romances, became insipid to me. In my friendless wanderings on our *leave-days*,[4] (for I was an orphan and had scarcely any connections in London,) highly was I delighted, if any passenger, especially if he were drest in black,

---

1 Wordsworth.
2 The Rev. James Boyer, long headmaster of Christ's Hospital.

3 The Rev. William Lisle Bowles (1762–1850); the actual merit of his poems scarcely justifies the youthful Coleridge's enthusiasm.
4 Coleridge's note: "The Christ's Hospital phrase, not for holidays altogether, but for those on which the boys are permitted to go beyond the precincts of the school."

would enter into conversation with me. For I soon found the means of directing it to my favorite subjects

> *Of providence, fore-knowledge, will, and fate,*
> *Fixed fate, free will, fore-knowledge absolute,*
> *And found no end, in wandering mazes lost.*[5]

This preposterous pursuit was, beyond doubt, injurious both to my natural powers, and to the progress of my education. It would perhaps have been destructive, had it been continued; but from this I was auspiciously withdrawn, partly indeed by an accidental introduction to an amiable family,[6] chiefly however, by the genial influence of a style of poetry, so tender and yet so manly, so natural and real, and yet so dignified and harmonious, as the sonnets &c. of Mr. Bowles! Well were it for me, perhaps, had I never relapsed into the same mental disease; if I had continued to pluck the flower and reap the harvest from the cultivated surface, instead of delving in the unwholesome quicksilver mines of metaphysic depths. But if in after time I have sought a refuge from bodily pain and mismanaged sensibility in abstruse researches, which exercised the strength and subtlety of the understanding without awakening the feelings of the heart; still there was a long and blessed interval, during which my natural faculties were allowed to expand, and my original tendencies to develop themselves: my fancy, and the love of nature, and the sense of beauty in forms and sounds.

The second advantage, which I owe to my early perusal, and admiration of these poems, . . . bears more immediately on my present subject. Among those with whom I conversed, there were, of course, very many who had formed their taste, and their notions of poetry, from the writings of Mr. Pope and his followers: or to speak more generally, in that school of French poetry, condensed and invigorated by English understanding, which had predominated from the last century. I was not blind to the merits of this school, yet as from inexperience of the world, and consequent want of sympathy with the general subject of these poems, they gave me little pleasure, I doubtless undervalued the *kind,* and

with the presumption of youth withheld from its masters the legitimate names of poets. I saw that the excellence of this kind consisted in just and acute observations on men and manners in an artificial state of society, as its matter and substance: and in the logic of wit, conveyed in smooth and strong epigrammatic couplets, as its *form.* Even when the subject was addressed to the fancy, or the intellect, as in the Rape of the Lock, or the Essay on Man; nay, when it was a consecutive narration, as in that astonishing product of matchless talent and ingenuity, Pope's Translation of the Iliad; still a *point* was looked for at the end of each second line. . . . Meantime the matter and diction seemed to me characterized not so much by poetic thoughts, as by thoughts *translated* into the language of poetry. . . .

The controversies, occasioned by my unfeigned zeal for the honor of a favorite contemporary, then known to me only by his works,[7] were of great advantage in the formation and establishment of my taste and critical opinions. In my defence of the lines running into each other, instead of closing at each couplet, and of natural language, neither bookish, nor vulgar, neither redolent of the lamp, nor of the kennel, such as *I will remember thee;* instead of the same thought tricked up in the rag-fair finery of

> ——*Thy image on her wing*
> *Before my* FANCY'S *eye shall* MEMORY *bring,*

I had continually to adduce the metre and diction of the Greek Poets from Homer to Theocritus inclusive; and still more of our elder English poets from Chaucer to Milton. Nor was this all. But as it was my constant reply to authorities brought against me from later poets of great name, that no authority could avail in opposition to TRUTH, NATURE, LOGIC, and the LAWS of UNIVERSAL GRAMMAR; actuated too by my former passion for metaphysical investigations; I labored at a solid foundation, on which permanently to ground my opinions, in the component faculties of the human mind itself, and their comparative dignity and importance. According to the faculty or source, from which the pleasure given by any poem or passage was de-

---

5 *Paradise Lost,* II, 559–61.
6 Probably the family of Mary Evans, Coleridge's first love.

7 Coleridge did not meet Bowles until 1797.

rived, I estimated the merit of such poem or passage. As the result of all my reading and meditation, I abstracted two critical aphorisms, deeming them to comprise the conditions and criteria of poetic style; first, that not the poem which we have *read,* but that to which we *return,* with the greatest pleasure, possesses the genuine power, and claims the name of *essential poetry.* Second, that whatever lines can be translated into other words of the same language, without diminution of their significance, either in sense, or association, or in any worthy feeling, are so far vicious in their diction. Be it however observed, that I excluded from the list of worthy feelings, the pleasure derived from mere novelty in the reader, and the desire of exciting wonderment at his powers in the author. . . . Our genuine admiration of a great poet is a continuous *under-current* of feeling; it is everywhere present, but seldom anywhere as a separate excitement. I was wont boldly to affirm, that it would be scarcely more difficult to push a stone out from the pyramids with the bare hand, than to alter a word, or the position of a word, in Milton or Shakespeare, (in their most important works at least,) without making the author say something else, or something worse, than he does say. One great distinction, I appeared to myself to see plainly, between, even the characteristic faults of our elder poets, and the false beauty of the moderns. In the former, from DONNE to COWLEY, we find the most fantastic out-of-the-way thoughts, but in the most pure and genuine mother English; in the latter, the most obvious thoughts, in language the most fantastic and arbitrary. Our faulty elder poets sacrificed the passion and passionate flow of poetry, to the subtleties of intellect, and to the starts of wit; the moderns to the glare and glitter of a perpetual, yet broken and heterogeneous imagery, or rather to an amphibious something, made up, half of image, and half of abstract meaning. The one sacrificed the heart to the head; the other both heart and head to point and drapery.

The reader must make himself acquainted with the general style of composition that was at that time deemed poetry, in order to understand and account for the effect produced on me by the SONNETS, the MONODY at MATLOCK, and the HOPE, of Mr. Bowles; for it is peculiar to original genius to become less and less *striking,*

in proportion to its success in improving the taste and judgement of its contemporaries. The poems of WEST,[8] indeed, had the merit of chaste and manly diction, but they were cold, and, if I may so express it, only *dead-coloured;* while in the best of Warton's[9] there is a stiffness, which too often gives them the appearance of imitations from the Greek. Whatever relation therefore of cause or impulse Percy's collection of Ballads[10] may bear to the most *popular* poems of the present day; yet in a more sustained and elevated style, of the then living poets, Bowles and Cowper were, to the best of my knowledge, the first who combined natural thoughts with natural diction; the first who reconciled the heart with the head. . . .

from Chapter IV

The lyrical ballads with the preface—Mr. Wordsworth's earlier poems—On fancy and imagination—The investigation of the distinction important to the fine arts.

. . . It will be sufficient for my purpose, if I have proved, that Mr. Southey's writings no more than my own furnished the original occasion to this fiction of a *new school* of poetry, and to the clamors against its supposed founders and proselytes.[11]

As little do I believe that "Mr. WORDSWORTH'S Lyrical Ballads" were in *themselves* the cause. I speak exclusively of the two volumes[12] so entitled. A careful and repeated examination of these confirms me in the belief, that the omission of less than an hundred lines would have precluded nine-tenths of the criticism on this work. I hazard this declaration, however, on the supposition, that the reader has taken it up, as he would have done any other collection of poems purporting to derive their subjects or interests from the incidents of domestic or ordi-

8 Gilbert West (1703–1756), imitator of Spenser and translator of Pindar and Euripides.
9 Thomas Warton (1728–1790), miscellaneous writer and one of the few eighteenth-century authors of sonnets.
10 Bishop Percy's *Reliques of Ancient English Poetry* (1765).
11 In the preceding chapter Coleridge examines Southey's poetry with this aim in view.
12 The two volumes of the second edition, in which Wordsworth's Preface first appeared. The second volume contained poems by Wordsworth not included in the first edition.

nary life, intermingled with higher strains of meditation which the poet utters in his own person and character; with the proviso, that they were perused without knowledge of, or reference to, the author's peculiar opinions, and that the reader had not had his attention previously directed to those peculiarities. In these, as was actually the case with Mr. Southey's earlier works, the lines and passages which might have offended the general taste, would have been considered as mere inequalities, and attributed to inattention, not to perversity of judgement. The men of business who had passed their lives chiefly in cities, and who might therefore be expected to derive the highest pleasure from acute notices of men and manners conveyed in easy, yet correct and pointed language; and all those who, reading but little poetry, are most stimulated with that species of it, which seems most distant from prose, would probably have passed by the volume altogether. Others more catholic in their taste, and yet habituated to be most pleased when most excited, would have contented themselves with deciding, that the author had been successful in proportion to the elevation of his style and subject. Not a few, perhaps, might by their admiration of "the lines written near Tintern Abbey," those "left upon a Seat under a Yew Tree," the "old Cumberland Beggar," and "Ruth," have been gradually led to peruse with kindred feeling the "Brothers," the "Hart leap well," and whatever other poems in that collection may be described as holding a middle place between those written in the highest and those in the humblest style; as for instance between the "Tintern Abbey," and "the Thorn," or the "Simon Lee." Should their taste submit to no further change, and still remain unreconciled to the colloquial phrases, or the imitations of them, that are, more or less, scattered through the class last mentioned; yet even from the small number of the latter, they would have deemed them but an inconsiderable subtraction from the merit of the whole work; or, what is sometimes not unpleasing in the publication of a new writer, as serving to ascertain the natural tendency, and consequently the proper direction of the author's genius.

In the critical remarks, therefore, prefixed and annexed to the "Lyrical Ballads," I believe that we may safely rest, as the true origin of the unexampled opposition which Mr. Wordsworth's writings have been since doomed to encounter. The humbler passages in the poems themselves were dwelt on and cited to justify the rejection of the theory. What in and for themselves would have been either forgotten or forgiven as imperfections, or at least comparative failures, provoked direct hostility when announced as intentional, as the result of choice after full deliberation. Thus the poems, admitted by *all* as excellent, joined with those which had pleased the far *greater* number, though they formed two-thirds of the whole work, instead of being deemed (as in all right they should have been, even if we take for granted that the reader judged aright) an atonement for the few exceptions, gave wind and fuel to the animosity against both the poems and the poet. . . .

That this conjecture is not wide from the mark, I am induced to believe from the noticeable fact, which I can state on my own knowledge, that the same general censure should have been grounded by almost every different person on some different poem. Among those, whose candour and judgement I estimate highly, I distinctly remember six who expressed their objections to the "Lyrical Ballads" almost in the same words, and altogether to the same purport, at the same time admitting, that several of the poems had given them great pleasure; and, strange as it might seem, the composition which one cited as execrable, another quoted as his favorite. . . . A friend whose *talents* I hold in the highest respect, but whose *judgement* and strong sound sense I have had almost continued occasion to *revere*, making the usual complaints to me concerning both the style and subjects of Mr. Wordsworth's minor poems; I admitted that there were some few of the tales and incidents, in which I could not myself find a sufficient cause for their having been recorded in metre. I mentioned the "Alice Fell" as an instance; "nay," replied my friend with more than usual quickness of manner, "I cannot agree with you *there!*—that, I own, *does* seem to me a remarkably pleasing poem." In the "Lyrical Ballads" . . . I have heard at different times, and from different individuals every single poem *extolled* and *reprobated*, with the exception of those of loftier kind, which as was before observed, seem to have won universal praise. This fact of itself would have made me diffident in my censures, had not a still stronger ground been furnished by the strange contrast of the heat and long continuance of the opposition, with the nature of the faults stated as justifying it. The seductive faults, the dulcia vitia[13] of Cowley, Marini, or Darwin[14] might reasonably be thought capable of corrupting the public judgement for half a century, and require a twenty years' war, campaign after campaign, in order to dethrone the usurper and re-establish the legitimate taste. But that a downright simpleness, under the affectation of simplicity, prosaic words in feeble metre, silly thoughts in childish phrases, and a preference of mean, degrading, or at best trivial associations and characters, should succeed in forming a school of imitators, a company of almost *religious* admirers, and this too among young men of ardent minds, liberal education, and not

with academic laurels unbestowed;

and that this bare and bald *counterfeit* of poetry, which is characterized as *below* criticism, should for nearly twenty years have well-nigh *engrossed* criticism, as the main, if not the only, *butt* of review, magazine, pamphlet, poem, and paragraph;—this is indeed matter of wonder! Of yet greater is it, that the contest should still continue . . . undecided. . . .

During the last year of my residence at Cambridge, I became acquainted with Mr. Wordsworth's first[15] publication entitled "Descriptive Sketches"; and seldom, if ever, was the emergence of an original poetic genius above the literary horizon more evidently announced. In the form, style, and manner of the whole poem, and in the structure of the particular lines and periods, there is an harshness and acerbity connected and combined with words and images all a-glow, which might recall those products of the vegetable world, where gorgeous blossoms rise out of the hard and thorny rind and shell, within which the rich fruit was elaborating. The language was not only peculiar[16] and strong, but at times knotty and contorted, as by its own impatient strength; while the novelty and struggling crowd of images, acting in conjunction with the difficulties of the style, demanded always a greater closeness of attention, than poetry, (at all events, than descriptive poetry) has a right to claim. It not seldom therefore justified the complaint of obscurity. . . .

The poetic PSYCHE, in its process to full development, undergoes as many changes as its Greek namesake, the butterfly.[17] And it is remarkable how soon genius clears and purifies itself from the faults and errors of its earliest products; faults which, in its earliest compositions, are the more obtrusive and confluent, because as heterogeneous elements, which had only a temporary use, they constitute the very *ferment,* by which themselves are carried off. Or we may compare them to some diseases, which must work on the humours, and be thrown out on the surface, in order to secure the patient from their future recurrence. I was in my twenty-fourth year, when I had the happiness of knowing Mr. Wordsworth personally, and while memory lasts, I shall hardly forget the sudden effect produced on my mind, by his recitation of a manuscript poem, which still remains unpublished, but of which the stanza and tone of style were the same as those of *The Female Vagrant,* as originally printed in the first volume of the "Lyrical Ballads." There was here no mark of strained thought, or forced diction, no crowd or turbulence of imagery; and, as the poet hath himself well described in his lines "on re-visiting the Wye,"[18] manly reflection, and human associations had given both variety, and an additional interest to natural objects, which in the passion and appetite of the first love they had seemed to him neither to need or permit. The occasional obscurities, which had risen from an imperfect control over the resources of his native language, had almost wholly disappeared, together with that worse defect of arbitrary and illogical phrases, at once hackneyed, and fantastic, which

---

13 This phrase repeats the sense of the preceding one.
14 Coleridge intends these poets as examples of artificial language and far-fetched conceits. Giambattista Marini or Marino (1569–1625) was an Italian poet. Erasmus Darwin (1731–1802) is more favorably remembered today for his writings on biology than for his poems *The Loves of the Plants* and *The Botanic Garden.*
15 Actually his second.

16 Distinctive.
17 Coleridge quotes (in a note) from "an unpublished poem" of his own ("The Butterfly"):
   "The butterfly the ancient Grecians made
   The soul's fair emblem, and its only name. . . ."
18 "Tintern Abbey."

hold so distinguished a place in the *technique* of ordinary poetry, and will, more or less, alloy the earlier poems of the truest genius, unless the attention has been specifically directed to their worthlessness and incongruity. I did not perceive anything particular in the mere style of the poem alluded to during its recitation, except indeed such difference as was not separable from the thought and manner; and the Spenserian stanza, which always, more or less, recalls to the reader's mind Spenser's own style, would doubtless have authorized, in my then opinion, a more frequent descent to the phrases of ordinary life, than could without an ill effect have been hazarded in the heroic couplet. It was not however the freedom from false taste, whether as to common defects, or to those more properly his own, which made so unusual an impression on my feelings immediately, and subsequently on my judgement. It was the union of deep feeling with profound thought; the fine balance of truth in observing, with the imaginative faculty in modifying the objects observed; and above all the original gift of spreading the tone, the *atmosphere,* and with it the depth and height of the ideal world around forms, incidents, and situations, of which, for the common view, custom had bedimmed all the lustre, had dried up the sparkle and the dew drops. "To find no contradiction in the union of old and new; to contemplate the ANCIENT of days and all his works with feelings as fresh, as if all had then sprang forth at the first creative fiat; characterizes the mind that feels the riddle of the world, and may help to unravel it. To carry on the feelings of childhood into the powers of manhood; to combine the child's sense of wonder and novelty with the appearances, which every day for perhaps forty years had rendered familiar;

With sun and moon and stars throughout the year,
And man and woman;

this is the character and privilege of genius, and one of the marks which distinguish genius from talents. And therefore is it the prime merit of genius and its most unequivocal mode of manifestation, so to represent familiar objects as to awaken in the minds of others a kindred feeling concerning them and that freshness of sensation which is the constant accompaniment of mental,

no less than of bodily, convalescence. Who has not a thousand times seen snow fall on water? Who has not watched it with a new feeling, from the time that he has read Burns's comparison of sensual pleasure

> *To snow that falls upon a river*
> *A moment white—then gone for ever!*[19]

In poems, equally as in philosophic disquisitions, genius produces the strongest impressions of novelty, while it rescues the most admitted truths from the impotence caused by the very circumstance of their universal admission. Truths of all others the most awful and mysterious, yet being at the same time of universal interest, are too often considered as *so* true, that they lose all the life and efficiency of truth, and lie bed-ridden in the dormitory of the soul, side by side with the most despised and exploded errors."[20] . . .

Chapter XIV

Occasion of the Lyrical Ballads, and the objects originally proposed—Preface to the second edition—The ensuing controversy, its causes and acrimony—Philosophic definitions of a poem and poetry with scholia.

During the first year that Mr. Wordsworth and I were neighbours, our conversations turned frequently on the two cardinal points of poetry, the power of exciting the sympathy of the reader by a faithful adherence to the truth of nature, and the power of giving the interest of novelty by the modifying colors of imagination. The sudden charm, which accidents of light and shade, which moonlight or sun-set diffused over a known and familiar landscape, appeared to represent the practicability of combining both. These are the poetry of nature. The thought suggested itself (to which of us I do not recollect) that a series of poems might be composed of two sorts. In the one, the incidents and agents were to be, in part at least, supernatural; and the excellence aimed at was to consist in the interesting of the affections[21] by the dramatic truth of such emotions, as would naturally accompany such situations, supposing them real.

---

19 Misquoted from "Tam o' Shanter," lines 61 ff.
20 This long quotation is from an earlier work by Coleridge, *The Friend*, no. 5.   21 Emotions.

And real in *this* sense they have been to every human being who, from whatever source of delusion, has at any time believed himself under supernatural agency. For the second class, subjects were to be chosen from ordinary life; the characters and incidents were to be such, as will be found in every village and its vicinity, where there is a meditative and feeling mind to seek after them, or to notice them, when they present themselves.

In this idea originated the plan of the "Lyrical Ballads"; in which it was agreed, that my endeavours should be directed to persons and characters supernatural, or at least romantic; yet so as to transfer from our inward nature a human interest and a semblance of truth sufficient to procure for these shadows of imagination that willing suspension of disbelief for the moment, which constitutes poetic faith. Mr. Wordsworth, on the other hand, was to propose to himself as his object, to give the charm of novelty to things of every day, and to excite a feeling analogous to the supernatural, by awakening the mind's attention to the lethargy of custom, and directing it to the loveliness and the wonders of the world before us; an inexhaustible treasure, but for which, in consequence of the film of familiarity and selfish solicitude, we have eyes, yet see not, ears that hear not, and hearts that neither feel nor understand.

With this view I wrote "The Ancient Mariner," and was preparing among other poems, "The Dark Ladie," and the "Christabel," in which I should have more nearly realized my ideal, than I had done in my first attempt. But Mr. Wordsworth's industry had proved so much more successful, and the number of his poems so much greater,[22] that my compositions, instead of forming a balance, appeared rather an interpolation of heterogeneous matter. Mr. Wordsworth added two or three poems written in his own character, in the impassioned, lofty, and sustained diction, which is characteristic of his genius. In this form the "Lyrical Ballads" were published; and were presented by him, as an *experiment*, whether subjects, which from their nature rejected the usual ornaments and extra-colloquial style of poems in general, might not

be so managed in the language of ordinary life as to produce the pleasurable interest, which it is the peculiar business of poetry to impart. To the second edition he added a preface of considerable length; in which, notwithstanding some passages of apparently a contrary import, he was understood to contend for the extension of this style to poetry of all kinds, and to reject as vicious and indefensible all phrases and forms of style that were not included in what he (unfortunately, I think, adopting an equivocal expression) called the language of *real* life. From this preface, prefixed to poems in which it was impossible to deny the presence of original genius, however mistaken its direction might be deemed, arose the whole long-continued controversy. For from the conjunction of perceived power with supposed heresy I explain the inveteracy and in some instances, I grieve to say, the acrimonious passions, with which the controversy has been conducted by the assailants.

Had Mr. Wordsworth's poems been the silly, the childish things, which they were for a long time described as being: had they been really distinguished from the compositions of other poets merely by meanness of language and inanity of thought; had they indeed contained nothing more than what is found in the parodies and pretended imitations of them; they must have sunk at once, a dead weight, into the slough of oblivion, and have dragged the preface along with them. But year after year increased the number of Mr. Wordsworth's admirers. They were found too not in the lower classes of the reading public, but chiefly among young men of strong sensibility and meditative minds; and their admiration (inflamed perhaps in some degree by opposition) was distinguished by its intensity, I might almost say, by its *religious* fervour. These facts, and the intellectual energy of the author, which was more or less consciously felt, where it was outwardly and even boisterously denied, meeting with sentiments of aversion to his opinions, and of alarm at their consequences, produced an eddy of criticism, which would of itself have borne up the poems by the violence, with which it whirled them round and round. With many parts of this preface, in the sense attributed to them, and which the words undoubtedly seem to authorize, I never concurred; but on the contrary objected

---

22 Only four of the twenty-three poems in the first edition were by Coleridge.

to them as erroneous in principle, and as contradictory (in appearance at least) both to other
parts of the same preface, and to the author's
own practice in the greater number of the poems
themselves. Mr. Wordsworth in his recent collection has, I find, degraded this prefatory disquisition to the end of his second volume, to be read
or not at the reader's choice. But he has not, as
far as I can discover, announced any change in
his poetic creed. At all events, considering it as
the source of a controversy, in which I have
been honoured more than I deserve by the frequent conjunction of my name with his, I think
it expedient to declare once for all, in what
points I coincide with his opinions, and in what
points I altogether differ. But in order to render
myself intelligible I must previously, in as few
words as possible, explain my views, first of a
POEM; and secondly, of POETRY itself, in *kind*,
and in *essence*.

The office of philosophical *disquisition*
consists in just *distinction;* while it is the privilege of the philosopher to preserve himself constantly aware, that distinction is not division.
In order to obtain adequate notions of any
truth, we must intellectually separate its distinguishable parts; and this is the technical *process*
of philosophy. But having so done, we must then
restore them in our conceptions to the unity, in
which they actually co-exist; and this is the *result*
of philosophy. A poem contains the same elements as a prose composition; the difference
therefore must consist in a different combination of them, in consequence of a different object
being proposed. According to the difference of
the object will be the difference of the combination. It is possible, that the object may be merely
to facilitate the recollection of any given facts
or observations by artificial arrangement; and
the composition will be a poem, merely because
it is distinguished from prose by metre, or by
rhyme, or by both conjointly. In this, the lowest
sense, a man might attribute the name of a poem
to the well-known enumeration of the days in
the several months:

> *Thirty days hath September,*
> *April, June, and November, &c.*

and others of the same class and purpose. And
as a particular pleasure is found in anticipating

the recurrence of sounds and quantities, all compositions that have this charm super-added,
whatever be their contents, *may* be entitled
poems.

So much for the superficial *form.* A difference of object and contents supplies an additional ground of distinction. The immediate
purpose may be the communication of truths;
either of truth absolute and demonstrable, as in
works of science; or of facts experienced and
recorded, as in history. Pleasure, and that of the
highest and most permanent kind, may *result*
from the *attainment* of the end; but it is not
itself the immediate end. In other works the
communication of pleasure may be the immediate purpose; and though truth, either moral or
intellectual, ought to be the *ultimate* end, yet
this will distinguish the character of the author,
not the class to which the work belongs. Blest
indeed is that state of society, in which the immediate purpose would be baffled by the perversion of the proper ultimate end; in which no
charm of diction or imagery could exempt the
Bathyllus[23] even of an Anacreon, or the Alexis[24]
of Virgil, from disgust and aversion!

But the communication of pleasure may be
the immediate object of a work not metrically
composed; and that object may have been in a
high degree attained, as in novels and romances.
Would then the mere superaddition of metre,
with or without rhyme, entitle *these* to the name
of poems? The answer is, that nothing can permanently please, which does not contain in itself the reason why it is so, and not otherwise.
If metre be superadded, all other parts must be
made consonant with it. They must be such, as
to justify the perpetual and distinct attention to
each part, which an exact correspondent recurrence of accent and sound are calculated to excite. The final definition then, so deduced, may
be thus worded. A poem is that species of composition, which is opposed to works of science,
by proposing for its *immediate* object pleasure,
not truth; and from all other species (having *this*
object in common with it) it is discriminated by
proposing to itself such delight from the *whole,*

---

23 A youth of Samos loved by the tyrant Polycrates (sixth
century B.C.) and mentioned by the Greek poet Anacreon
(d. 488? B.C.).
24 A youth loved by a shepherd in the Second Eclogue of
Vergil.

as is compatible with a distinct gratification from each component *part*.

Controversy is not seldom excited in consequence of the disputants attaching each a different meaning to the same word; and in few instances has this been more striking, than in disputes concerning the present subject. If a man chooses to call every composition a poem, which is rhyme, or measure, or both, I must leave his opinion uncontroverted. The distinction is at least competent to characterize the writer's intention. If it were subjoined, that the whole is likewise entertaining or affecting, as a tale, or as a series of interesting reflections, I of course admit this as another fit ingredient of a poem, and an additional merit. But if the definition sought for be that of a *legitimate* poem, I answer, it must be one, the parts of which mutually support and explain each other; all in their proportion harmonizing with, and supporting the purpose and known influences of metrical arrangement. The philosophic critics of all ages coincide with the ultimate judgement of all countries, in equally denying the praises of a just poem, on the one hand, to a series of striking lines or distiches,[25] each of which, absorbing the whole attention of the reader to itself, disjoins it from its context, and makes it a separate whole, instead of an harmonizing part; and on the other hand, to an unsustained composition, from which the reader collects rapidly the general result, unattracted by the component parts. The reader should be carried forward, not merely or chiefly by the mechanical impulse of curiosity, or by a restless desire to arrive at the final solution; but by the pleasureable activity of mind excited by the attractions of the journey itself. Like the motion of a serpent, which the Egyptians made the emblem of intellectual power; or like the path of sound through the air; at every step he pauses and half recedes, and from the retrogressive movement collects the force which again carries him onward. "Praecipitandus est *liber spiritus*,"[26] says Petronius Arbiter most happily. The epithet, *liber*, here balances the preceding verb; and it is not easy to conceive more meaning condensed in fewer words.

But if this should be admitted as a satisfactory character of a poem, we have still to seek for a definition of poetry. The writings of PLATO, and Bishop TAYLOR,[27] and the "Theoria Sacra" of BURNET,[28] furnish undeniable proofs that poetry of the highest kind may exist without metre, and even without the contradistinguishing objects of a poem. The first chapter of Isaiah (indeed a very large portion of the whole book) is poetry in the most emphatic sense; yet it would be not less irrational than strange to assert, that pleasure, and not truth, was the immediate object of the prophet. In short, whatever *specific* import we attach to the word, poetry, there will be found involved in it, as a necessary consequence, that a poem of any length neither can be, or ought to be, all poetry. Yet if an harmonious whole is to be produced, the remaining parts must be preserved *in keeping* with the poetry; and this can be no otherwise effected than by such a studied selection and artificial arrangement, as will partake of *one,* though not a *peculiar* property of poetry. And this again can be no other than the property of exciting a more continuous and equal attention than the language of prose aims at, whether colloquial or written.

My own conclusions on the nature of poetry, in the strictest use of the word, have been in part anticipated in the preceding disquisition on the fancy and imagination.[29] What is poetry? is so nearly the same question with, what is a poet? that the answer to the one is involved in the solution of the other. For it is a distinction resulting from the poetic genius itself, which sustains and modifies the images, thoughts, and emotions of the poet's own mind.

The poet, described in *ideal* perfection, brings the whole soul of man into activity, with the subordination of its faculties to each other, according to their relative worth and dignity. He diffuses a tone and spirit of unity, that blends, and (as it were) *fuses,* each into each, by that synthetic and magical power, to which I would exclusively appropriate the name of imagina-

---

25 Two-line units of verse.
26 A free spirit ought to be hurled along; i.e., if a poem is to seem inspired. (Petronius [1st century], *Satyricon,* chap. 118.)

27 Jeremy Taylor (1613–1667), author of *The Liberty of Prophesying, Holy Living, Holy Dying,* etc.
28 The Rev. Thomas Burnet (d. 1715). His *Telluris Theoria Sacra* (in an English as well as a Latin text) propounded a fanciful theory of the origin of the earth.
29 In chapter IV Coleridge considered them "distinct and widely different faculties."

tion. This power, first put in action by the will and understanding, and retained under their irremissive,[30] though gentle and unnoticed, controul (*laxis effertur habenis*),[31] reveals itself in the balance or reconciliation of opposite or discordant qualities: of sameness, with difference; of the general, with the concrete; the idea, with the image; the individual, with the representative; the sense of novelty and freshness, with old and familiar objects; a more than usual state of emotion, with more than usual order; judgement ever awake and steady self-possession, with enthusiasm and feeling profound or vehement; and while it blends and harmonizes the natural and the artificial, still subordinates art to nature; the manner to the matter; and our admiration of the poet to our sympathy with the poetry. Doubtless, as Sir John Davies observes of the soul (and his words[32] may with slight alteration be applied, and even more appropriately, to the poetic IMAGINATION)

> *Doubtless this could not be, but that she turns*
> *Bodies to spirit by sublimation strange,*
> *As fire converts to fire the things it burns,*
> *As we our food into our nature change.*
>
> *From their gross matter she abstracts their forms,*
> *And draws a kind of quintessence from things;*
> *Which to her proper [33] nature she transforms*
> *To bear them light on her celestial wings.*
>
> *Thus does she, when from individual states*
> *She doth abstract the universal kinds;*
> *Which then re-clothed in divers names and fates*
> *Steal access through our senses to our minds.*

Finally, GOOD SENSE is the BODY of poetic genius, FANCY its DRAPERY, MOTION its LIFE, and IMAGINATION the SOUL that is everywhere, and in each; and forms all into one graceful and intelligent whole.

Chapter XV

The specific symptoms of poetic power elucidated in a critical analysis of Shakespeare's Venus and Adonis, and Lucrece.

In the application of these principles to purposes of practical criticism as employed in the appraisement of works more or less imperfect, I have endeavoured to discover what the qualities in a poem are, which may be deemed promises and specific symptoms of poetic power, as distinguished from general talent determined to poetic composition by accidental motives, by an act of the will, rather than by the inspiration of a genial and productive nature. In this investigation I could not, I thought, do better, than keep before me the earliest work of the greatest genius, that perhaps human nature has yet produced, our *myriad-minded* Shakespeare. I mean the "Venus and Adonis," and the "Lucrece";[34] works which give at once strong promises of the strength, and yet obvious proofs of the immaturity, of his genius. From these I abstracted the following marks, as characteristics of original poetic genius in general.

1. In the "Venus and Adonis," the first and most obvious excellence is the perfect sweetness of the versification; its adaptation to the subject; and the power displayed in varying the march of the words without passing into a loftier and more majestic rhythm than was demanded by the thoughts, or permitted by the propriety of preserving a sense of melody predominant. The delight in richness and sweetness of sound, even to a faulty excess, if it be evidently original, and not the result of an easily imitable mechanism, I regard as a highly favourable promise in the compositions of a young man. "The man that hath not music in his soul"[35] can indeed never be a genuine poet. Imagery (even taken from nature, much more when transplanted from books, as travels, voyages, and works of natural history); affecting incidents; just thoughts; interesting personal or domestic feelings; and with these the art of their combination or intertexture in the form of a poem; may all by incessant effort be acquired as a trade, by a man of talents and much reading, who, as I once before observed, has mistaken an intense desire of poetic reputation for a natural poetic genius; the love of the arbitrary end for a possession of the peculiar means. But the sense of musical delight, with the power of producing it, is a gift of imagination; and this together with the power of reducing multitude into unity of

---

30 I.e., unremitting, incessant.
31 Is carried along with loose reins. (Inaccurately quoted from Vergil, *Georgics*, II, 364.)
32 Inaccurately quoted from Davies's "Of the Soul of Man," *Nosce Teipsum* (ed. Grosart, I, 43).
33 Own.

34 These poems were printed in 1593 and 1594.
35 Cf. *The Merchant of Venice*, V, i, 83.

effect, and modifying a series of thoughts by some one predominant thought or feeling, may be cultivated and improved, but can never be learned. It is in these that "poeta nascitur non fit."[36]

2. A second promise of genius is the choice of subjects very remote from the private interests and circumstances of the writer himself. At least I have found, that where the subject is taken immediately from the author's personal sensations and experiences, the excellence of a particular poem is but an equivocal mark, and often a fallacious pledge, of genuine poetic power. We may perhaps remember the tale of the statuary,[37] who had acquired considerable reputation for the legs of his goddesses, though the rest of the statue accorded but indifferently with ideal beauty; till his wife, elated by her husband's praises, modestly acknowledged that she herself had been his constant model. In the "Venus and Adonis" this proof of poetic power exists even to excess. It is throughout as if a superior spirit more intuitive, more intimately conscious, even than the characters themselves, not only of every outward look and act, but of the flux and reflux of the mind in all its subtlest thoughts and feelings, were placing the whole before our view; himself meanwhile unparticipating in the passions, and actuated only by that pleasurable excitement, which had resulted from the energetic fervor of his own spirit in so vividly exhibiting what it had so accurately and profoundly contemplated. I think, I should have conjectured from these poems, that even then the great instinct, which impelled the poet to the drama, was secretly working in him, prompting him by a series and never broken chain of imagery, always vivid and, because unbroken, often minute; by the highest effort of the picturesque in words, of which words are capable, higher perhaps than was ever realized by any other poet, even Dante not excepted; to provide a substitute for that visual language, that constant intervention and running comment by tone, look and gesture, which in his dramatic works he was entitled to expect from the players. His Venus and Adonis seem at once the characters themselves and the whole representation of those characters by the most consummate actors.

You seem to be told nothing, but to see and hear everything. Hence it is, that from the perpetual activity of attention required on the part of the reader; from the rapid flow, the quick change, and the playful nature of the thoughts and images; and above all from the alienation, and, if I may hazard such an expression, the utter *aloofness* of the poet's own feelings, from those of which he is at once the painter and the analyst; that though the very subject cannot but detract from the pleasure of a delicate mind, yet never was poem less dangerous on a moral account. Instead of doing as Ariosto,[38] and as, still more offensively, Wieland[39] has done, instead of degrading and deforming passion into appetite, the trials of love into the struggles of concupiscence; Shakespeare has here represented the animal impulse itself, so as to preclude all sympathy with it, by dissipating the reader's notice among the thousand outward images, and now beautiful, now fanciful circumstances, which form its dresses and its scenery; or by diverting our attention from the main subject by those frequent witty or profound reflections, which the poet's ever active mind has deduced from, or connected with, the imagery and the incidents. The reader is forced into too much action to sympathize with the merely passive of our nature. As little can a mind thus roused and awakened be brooded on by mean and indistinct emotion, as the low, lazy mist can creep upon the surface of a lake, while a strong gale is driving it onward in waves and billows.

3. It has been before observed that images, however beautiful, though faithfully copied from nature, and as accurately represented in words, do not of themselves characterize the poet. They become proofs of original genius only as far as they are modified by a predominant passion; or by associated thoughts or images awakened by that passion; or when they have the effect of reducing multitude to unity, or succession to an instant; or lastly, when a human and intellectual life is transferred to them from the poet's own spirit,

Which shoots its being through earth, sea, and air.[40]

36 A poet is born, not made.   37 Sculptor.

38 The Renaissance Italian writer Ludovico Ariosto (1474–1533), author of the romantic epic *Orlando Furioso*.
39 Christoph Martin Wieland (1733–1813), German novelist and poet.
40 From Coleridge's "France: An Ode," line 103.

In the two following lines for instance, there is nothing objectionable, nothing which would preclude them from forming, in their proper place, part of a descriptive poem:

Behold yon row of pines, that shorn and bow'd
Bend from the sea-blast, seen at twilight eve.

But with a small alteration of rhythm, the same words would be equally in their place in a book of topography, or in a descriptive tour. The same image will rise into semblance of poetry if thus conveyed:

Yon row of bleak and visionary pines,
By twilight glimpse discerned, mark! how they flee
From the fierce sea-blast, all their tresses wild
Streaming before them.

I have given this as an illustration, by no means as an instance, of that particular excellence which I had in view, and in which Shakespeare even in his earliest, as in his latest, works surpasses all other poets. It is by this, that he still gives a dignity and a passion to the objects which he presents. Unaided by any previous excitement, they burst upon us at once in life and in power.

Full many a glorious morning have I seen
Flatter the mountain tops with sovereign eye.
                    Shakespeare, Sonnet 33rd.

Not mine own fears, nor the prophetic soul
Of the wide world dreaming on things to come—
*   *   *   *   *   *   *
*   *   *   *   *   *   *
The mortal moon hath her eclipse endur'd,
And the sad augurs mock their own presage;
Incertainties now crown themselves assur'd,
And peace proclaims olives of endless age.
Now with the drops of this most balmy time
My Love looks fresh, and DEATH *to me subscribes!*
Since spite of him, I'll live in this poor rhyme,
While he insults o'er dull and speechless tribes.
And thou in this shalt find thy monument,
When tyrants' crests, and tombs of brass are spent.
                    Sonnet 107.

As of higher worth, so doubtless still more characteristic of poetic genius does the imagery become, when it moulds and colors itself to the circumstances, passion, or character, present and foremost in the mind. For unrivalled instances of this excellence, the reader's own memory will refer him to the LEAR, OTHELLO, in short to which not of the *"great, ever living, dead man's"* dramatic works? "Inopem me copia fecit."[41] How true it is to nature, he has himself finely expressed in the instance of love in Sonnet 98.

From you have I been absent in the spring,
When proud pied April drest in all its trim
Hath put a spirit of youth in every thing,
That heavy Saturn laugh'd and leap'd with him.
Yet nor the lays of birds, nor the sweet smell
Of different flowers in odour and in hue,
Could make me any summer's story tell,
Or from their proud lap pluck them, where they grew:
Nor did I wonder at the lilies white,
Nor praise the deep vermilion in the rose;
They were, tho' sweet, but figures of delight,
Drawn after you, you pattern of all those.
Yet seem'd it winter still, and, you away,
As with your shadow I with these did play!

Scarcely less sure, or if a less valuable, not less indispensable mark

Γονίμου μεν ποιητοῦ——
——ὅστις ῥῆμα γενναῖον λάχοι.[42]

will the imagery supply, when, with more than the power of the painter, the poet gives us the liveliest image of succession with the feeling of simultaneousness!

With this, he breaketh from the sweet embrace
Of those fair arms, that held him to her heart,
And homeward through the dark lawns runs apace:
Look! how a bright star shooteth from the sky,
So glides he in the night from Venus' eye.[43]

4. The last character I shall mention, which would prove indeed but little, except as taken conjointly with the former; yet without which the former could scarce exist in a high degree, and (even if this were possible) would give promises only of transitory flashes and a meteoric power; is DEPTH, and ENERGY OF THOUGHT. No man was ever yet a great poet,

---

41 I.e., the wealth of examples overwhelms me.
42 Of a real poet, one who uttered a noble expression (adapted from Aristophanes, *The Frogs*, lines 96–97).
43 *Venus and Adonis*, lines 811 ff. Coleridge omits the fourth line of the stanza.

without being at the same time a profound philosopher. For poetry is the blossom and the fragrancy of all human knowledge, human thoughts, human passions, emotions, language. In Shakespeare's *poems* the creative power and the intellectual energy wrestle as in a war embrace. Each in its excess of strength seems to threaten the extinction of the other. At length in the DRAMA they were reconciled, and fought each with its shield before the breast of the other. Or like two rapid streams that, at their first meeting within narrow and rocky banks, mutually strive to repel each other and intermix reluctantly and in tumult; but soon finding a wider channel and more yielding shores blend, and dilate, and flow on in one current and with one voice. The "Venus and Adonis" did not perhaps allow the display of the deeper passions. But the story of Lucretia seems to favor and even demand their intensest workings. And yet we find in *Shakespeare's* management of the tale neither pathos, nor any other *dramatic* quality. There is the same minute and faithful imagery as in the former poem, in the same vivid colors, inspirited by the same impetuous vigor of thought, and diverging and contracting with the same activity of the assimilative and of the modifying faculties; and with a yet larger display, a yet wider range of knowledge and reflection; and lastly, with the same perfect dominion, often *domination,* over the whole world of language. What then shall we say? even this; that Shakespeare, no mere child of nature; no automaton of genius; no passive vehicle of inspiration possessed by the spirit, not possessing it; first studied patiently, meditated deeply, understood minutely, till knowledge, become habitual and intuitive, wedded itself to his habitual feelings, and at length gave birth to that stupendous power, by which he stands alone, with no equal or second in his own class; to that power which seated him on one of the two glory-smitten summits of the poetic mountain, with Milton as his compeer, not rival. While the former darts himself forth, and passes into all the forms of human character and passion, the one Proteus of the fire and flood; the other attracts all forms and things to himself, into the unity of his own IDEAL. All things and modes of action shape themselves anew in the being of MILTON, while SHAKESPEARE becomes all things, yet for ever remaining himself. O what great men hast thou not produced, England! my country! truly indeed—

Must we *be free or die, who speak the tongue,*
Which SHAKESPEARE *spake; the faith and morals hold,*
Which MILTON *held. In every thing we are sprung*
Of earth's first blood, have titles manifold!
—WORDSWORTH[44]

from The Statesman's Manual

This is not primarily about literature, but is rather a political, theological, and metaphysical work. The following passages are, however, extremely revealing about Coleridge's attitude toward metaphor, symbol, and allegory.

Now an allegory is but a translation of abstract notions into a picture-language, which is itself nothing but an abstraction from objects of the senses; the principal being more worthless even than its phantom proxy, both alike unsubstantial, and the former shapeless to boot. On the other hand a symbol (ὁ ἔστι ἀει ταυτηγόρικον) is characterized by a translucence of the special in the individual, or of the general in the special, or of the universal in the general; above all by the translucence of the eternal through and in the temporal. It always partakes of the reality which it renders intelligible; and while it enunciates the whole, abides itself as a living part in that unity of which it is the representative. The others are but empty echoes which the fancy arbitrarily associates with apparitions of matter, less beautiful but not less shadowy than the sloping orchard of hillside pasture-field seen in the transparent lake below. Alas, for the flocks that are to be led forth to such pastures! . . .

If you have accompanied me thus far, thoughtful reader, let it not weary you if I digress for a few moments to another book, likewise a revelation of God—the great book of his servant Nature. That in its obvious sense and literal interpretation it declares the being and attributes of the Almighty Father, none but the fool in heart has ever dared gainsay. But it has been the music of gentle and pious minds in all

---

44 Misquoted from the sonnet "It Is Not To Be Thought of," lines 11–14.

ages, it is the poetry of all human nature, to read it likewise in a figurative sense, and to find therein correspondencies and symbols of the spiritual world.

I have at this moment before me, in the flowery meadow, on which my eye is now reposing, one of its most soothing chapters, in which there is no lamenting word, no one character of guilt or anguish. For never can I look and meditate on the vegetable creation without a feeling similar to that with which we gaze at a beautiful infant that has fed itself asleep at its mother's bosom, and smiles in its strange dream of obscure yet happy sensations. The same tender and genial pleasure takes possession of me, and this pleasure is checked and drawn inward by the like aching melancholy, by the same whispered remonstrance, and made restless by a similar impulse of aspiration. It seems as if the soul said to herself: From this state hast thou fallen! Such shouldst thou still become, thy self all permeable to a holier power! thy self at once hidden and glorified by its own transparency, as the accidental and dividuous in this quiet and harmonious object is subjected to the life and light of nature; to that life and light of nature,

I say, which shines in every plant and flower, even as the transmitted power, love and wisdom of God over all fills, and shines through, nature! But what the plant is by an act not its own and unconsciously—that must thou make thyself to become—must by prayer and by a watchful and unresisting spirit, join at least with the preventive and assisting grace to make thyself, in that light of conscience which inflameth not, and with that knowledge which puffeth not up!

But further, and with particular reference to that undivided reason, neither merely speculative or merely practical, but both in one, which I have in this annotation endeavoured to contradistinguish from the understanding, I seem to myself to behold in the quiet objects, on which I am gazing, more than an arbitrary illustration, more than a mere *simile,* the work of my own fancy. I feel an awe, as if there were before my eyes the same power as that of the reason—the same power in a lower dignity, and therefore a symbol established in the truth of things. I feel it alike, whether I contemplate a single tree or flower, or meditate on vegetation throughout the world, as one of the great organs of the life of nature. . . .

Charles Lamb

1775–1834

The kind of essay that Lamb wrote differs markedly from the kind dominant in the preceding century, though it clearly descends from them. It is more informal in tone, more obviously free and easy with the reader, more obviously individual. Its characteristic vice is whimsy, too much of a certain sort of charm; its characteristic virtues are its irreverence toward conventional and received wisdom and the intelligence and independence of its critical judgments. These virtues are evident—whether one always agrees with the views set forth or not—in the following essays.

Lamb was a Londoner, and to the end of his life London was for him a place of wonders. He was actually born within the precincts of an old London institution, the Inner Temple, where his father was a lawyer's clerk. He was seven when he entered another, the school of Christ's Hospital; Coleridge and Leigh Hunt were among his classmates there. One of his best-known essays is a description of "Christ's Hospital Five and Thirty Years Ago." He was not quite fifteen when he left school, and only seventeen when he began to work for the East India Company, the world's largest commercial enterprise, for which he was a bookkeeper for thirty-three years.

On the whole Lamb's essays appear to reflect a sunny life. Yet it was clouded with tragedy. For a time his mind was deranged, and he spent several weeks in an asylum. His recovery was complete; but about a year later, when he was twenty-two, his sister Mary went insane and in his presence killed their invalid mother. On Mary's release from confinement Lamb abandoned all thought of marriage and assumed the burden of caring for her. Mary had long and entirely lucid intervals, but she was subject to recurrent though brief attacks of madness. The record of their life together was a record of exemplary mutual devotion and sympathy.

Lamb's verse, both the early and the late, is of slender value. In his first important literary venture, a book for children, the popular *Tales from Shakespeare* (1807), Mary collaborated; she did the comedies and Charles the tragedies. The following year he edited *Specimens of English Dramatic Poets Who Lived about the Time of Shakespeare,* a book which became a major influence on the so-called Elizabethan Revival. Most of the old dramatists had been neglected during the eighteenth century. Lamb's anthology of short excerpts, with appreciative comments, brought them again into notice; moreover, it established his reputation as a critic.

He and Mary were now living, despite the shadow which always threatened, an uncommonly full life. They were voracious readers and playgoers and haunters of picture galleries. They were also great walkers, who thought nothing of a stroll of twenty or thirty miles. And they were rich in friends, by whom they were much visited. Coleridge and the Wordsworths headed the list, especially Coleridge, whom Lamb described as an "archangel, a little damaged," but also as the "touchstone of all my cogitations." Probably no other Englishman of the time had for intimates as many remarkable men as Lamb did. His circle also included Hazlitt, De Quincey, Southey, Leigh Hunt, the diarist Henry Crabb Robinson, the poet Tom Hood, the philosopher William Godwin, Thomas Barnes (first great editor of the London *Times*), the dramatist Sheridan Knowles, the lawyer and poet Bryan Waller Procter ("Barry Cornwall"), Vincent Novello (organist, composer, and founder of the great music-publishing house), the historical painter Benjamin Robert Haydon, the lawyer and dramatic poet Thomas Noon Talfourd, and a host of lesser lights.

Actually, his early work was undistinguished. He tried to supplement his income with prose fiction, drama, journalism, and children's books. One of his plays, a farce, was put on at Drury Lane; but it was damned on the opening night, and Lamb joined in the hisses lest he be taken for the author. Though he brought out a two-volume edition of his works in 1818, he did not really find himself as a writer till he was forty-five. It was in the pages of a new periodical, the *London Magazine,* that he made during the years 1820–25 his permanent place in English literature with the essays signed "Elia." In them his whimsical personality, his delight in London and its oddities, his fund of human sympathy, and his quaint humor found a perfect medium of expression.

In 1825 he retired from the East India House on a good pension; and, soon after, he and Mary moved to Enfield, a suburb ten miles to the north. Their household included Emma Isola, an orphan they had adopted; shortly before Lamb's death she married the publisher Edward Moxon. In 1833 the Lambs moved for the last time, to Edmonton, one suburb closer to the city—the busses into London ran oftener, as Charles gleefully explained in a letter. His last years were saddened by the death of many friends and by the increasing frequency of Mary's attacks. He died in 1834, but she lived till 1847, on an annuity from the East India Company.

TEXTS: *The Works of Charles and Mary Lamb* (7 vols., 1903–1905) have been edited by E. V. Lucas, who also edited the *Letters* (3 vols., 1935) and wrote the *Life of Charles Lamb* (2 vols., 1921).

Appreciative views of Lamb have been expressed, notably in Edmund Blunden, *Charles Lamb and His Contemporaries* (1933) and Walter Pater, *Appreciations* (1889); an interesting hostile view by Denys Thompson, entitled "Our Debt to Lamb," is in F. R. Leavis, ed., *Determinations* (1934). A more recent work on Lamb is George L. Barnett, *Charles Lamb: The Evolution of Elia* (1964).

The Old Familiar Faces

This poem was written and published in 1798, but the present text agrees with Lamb's revised version. Originally the poem contained, as lines 2–4, a stanza, subsequently and wisely canceled, referring to Lamb's mother and the "day of horrors" when his sister killed her.

Where are they gone, the old familiar faces?

I have had playmates, I have had companions,
In my days of childhood, in my joyful school-days
All, all are gone, the old familiar faces.

I have been laughing, I have been carousing, 5
Drinking late, sitting late, with my bosom cronies,
All, all are gone, the old familiar faces.

I loved a love[1] once, fairest among women;
Closed are her doors on me, I must not see her,
All, all are gone, the old familiar faces. 10

I have a friend,[2] a kinder friend has no man;
Like an ingrate, I left my friend abruptly;
Left him, to muse on the old familiar faces.

---

1 Her name was Anne Simmons.
2 Perhaps Charles Lloyd, a friend of Coleridge's also.

Ghost-like, I paced round the haunts of my child-
   hood.
Earth seemed a desert I was bound to traverse,   15
Seeking to find the old familiar faces.

Friend of my bosom,[3] thou more than a brother,
Why wert not thou born in my father's dwelling?
So might we talk of the old familiar faces—

For some they have died, and some they have left   20
   me,
And some are taken from me; all are departed;
All, all are gone, the old familiar faces.

On the Tragedies of Shakspeare

Considered with Reference to Their Fitness
for Stage Representation

In this essay Lamb argues that the presentation of a
Shakespearean play is necessarily a reduction and distortion of the total experience that we receive from
reading it. This is mainly due to the fact that Shakespeare's subtle analysis of the inner life, of individual
thought and feeling, cannot be translated to the stage;
in the theater it is sacrificed to a primary emphasis on
action, or blurred by rough and conventional modes
of depicting the passions.

    Historically, the essay shows the influence of
Romanticism in the worship of Shakespeare as the
inspired and original genius, the seizing on the internal workings of the mind as the point of primary
interest (cf. Wordsworth's Preface to *Lyrical Ballads*),
and the admiration of great and heroic natures, even
including criminals (cf. the Byronic hero with what
Lamb says about Richard III).

    Lamb contributed the essay to Leigh Hunt's
Reflector (1811). The following text is based on the
1818 *Works*.

Taking a turn the other day in the Abbey, I was
struck with the affected attitude of a figure,
which I do not remember to have seen before,
and which upon examination proved to be a
whole-length of the celebrated Mr. Garrick.[1]
Though I would not go so far with some good
Catholics abroad as to shut players altogether
out of consecrated ground, yet I own I was not
a little scandalized at the introduction of theatrical airs and gestures into a place set apart to   10

---

3 Probably Coleridge.

1 This great actor died in 1779.

remind us of the saddest realities. Going nearer,
I found inscribed under this harlequin figure
the following lines:—

> To paint fair Nature, by divine command,
> Her magic pencil in his glowing hand,
> A Shakspeare rose; then to expand his fame
> Wide o'er this breathing world, a Garrick came.
> Though sunk in death the forms the Poet drew,
> The Actor's genius bade them breathe anew;
> Though, like the bard himself, in night they lay,   10
> Immortal Garrick call'd them back to day:
> And till ETERNITY with power sublime
> Shall mark the mortal hour of hoary TIME,
> SHAKSPEARE and GARRICK like twin stars shall shine,
> And earth irradiate with a beam divine.

    It would be an insult to my readers' under-
standing to attempt anything like a criticism on
this farrago of false thoughts and nonsense. But
the reflection it led me into was a kind of wonder, how, from the days of the actor here celebrated to our own, it should have been the   20
fashion to compliment every performer in his
turn, that has had the luck to please the town
in any of the great characters of Shakspeare, with
the notion of possessing a *mind congenial with
the poet's:* how people should come thus unac-
countably to confound the power of originating
poetical images and conceptions with the faculty
of being able to read or recite the same when put
into words;[2] or what connection that absolute   30
mastery over the heart and soul of man, which
a great dramatic poet possesses, has with those
low tricks upon the eye and ear, which a player
by observing a few general effects, which some
common passion, as grief, anger, &c. usually has
upon the gestures and exterior, can so easily
compass. To know the internal workings and
movements of a great mind, of an Othello or a
Hamlet for instance, the *when* and the *why* and
the *how far* they should be moved; to what pitch   40
a passion is becoming; to give the reins and to

---

2 Lamb's note: "It is observable that we fall into this confusion only in *dramatic* recitations. We never dream that
the gentleman who reads Lucretius in public with great
applause, is therefore a great poet and philosopher; nor
do we find that Tom Davies, the bookseller, who is recorded to have recited the Paradise Lost better than any
man in England in his day (though I cannot help thinking there must be some mistake in this tradition) was
therefore, by his intimate friends, set upon a level with
Milton."

pull in the curb exactly at the moment when the drawing in or the slackening is most graceful; seems to demand a reach of intellect of a vastly different extent from that which is employed upon the bare imitation of the signs of these passions in the countenance or gesture, which signs are usually observed to be most lively and emphatic in the weaker sort of minds, and which signs can after all but indicate some passion, as I said before, anger, or grief, generally; but of the motives and grounds of the passion, wherein it differs from the same passion in low and vulgar natures, of these the actor can give no more idea by his face or gesture than the eye (without a metaphor) can speak, or the muscles utter intelligible sounds. But such is the instantaneous nature of the impressions which we take in at the eye and ear at a playhouse, compared with the slow apprehension oftentimes of the understanding in reading, that we are apt not only to sink the play-writer in the consideration which we pay to the actor, but even to identify in our minds, in a perverse manner, the actor with the character which he represents. It is difficult for a frequent playgoer to disembarrass the idea of Hamlet from the person and voice of Mr. K.[3] We speak of Lady Macbeth, while we are in reality thinking of Mrs. S. Nor is this confusion incidental alone to unlettered persons, who, not possessing the advantage of reading, are necessarily dependent upon the stage-player for all the pleasure which they can receive from the drama, and to whom the very idea of *what an author is* cannot be made comprehensible without some pain and perplexity of mind: the error is one from which persons otherwise not meanly lettered, find it almost impossible to extricate themselves.

Never let me be so ungrateful as to forget the very high degree of satisfaction which I received some years back from seeing for the first time a tragedy of Shakspeare performed, in which those two great performers sustained the principal parts. It seemed to embody and realize conceptions which had hitherto assumed no distinct shape. But dearly do we pay all our life after for this juvenile pleasure, this sense of distinctness. When the novelty is past, we find to our cost that instead of realizing an idea, we have only materialized and brought down a fine vision to the standard of flesh and blood. We have let go a dream, in quest of an unattainable substance.

How cruelly this operates upon the mind, to have its free conceptions thus crampt and pressed down to the measure of a strait-lacing actuality, may be judged from that delightful sensation of freshness, with which we turn to those plays of Shakspeare which have escaped being performed, and to those passages in the acting plays of the same writer which have happily been left out in performance. How far the very custom of hearing any thing *spouted*, withers and blows upon a fine passage, may be seen in those speeches from Henry the Fifth, etc., which are current in the mouths of school-boys from their being to be found in *Enfield Speakers*,[4] and such kind of books. I confess myself utterly unable to appreciate that celebrated soliloquy in Hamlet, beginning "To be or not to be,"[5] or to tell whether it be good, bad or indifferent, it has been so handled and pawed about by declamatory boys and men, and torn so inhumanly from its living place and principle of continuity in the play, till it is become to me a perfect dead member.

It may seem a paradox, but I cannot help being of opinion that the plays of Shakspeare are less calculated for performance on a stage, than those of almost any other dramatist whatever. Their distinguishing excellence is a reason that they should be so. There is so much in them, which comes not under the province of acting, with which eye, and tone, and gesture, have nothing to do.

The glory of the scenic art is to personate passion, and the turns of passion; and the more coarse and palpable the passion is, the more hold upon the eyes and ears of the spectators the performer obviously possesses. For this reason, scolding scenes, scenes where two persons talk themselves into a fit of fury, and then in a surprising manner talk themselves out of it again, have always been the most popular upon our stage. And the reason is plain, because the spectators are here most palpably appealed to, they

---

[3] John Philip Kemble (1757–1823). Mrs. S. in the next sentence is his sister, Sarah Kemble Siddons (1755–1831).

[4] A popular compilation of pieces for declamation, by the Rev. William Enfield.   [5] *Hamlet*, III, i, 56 ff.

are the proper judges in this war of words, they are the legitimate ring that should be formed round such "intellectual prize-fighters." Talking is the direct object of the imitation here. But in all the best dramas, and in Shakspeare above all, how obvious it is, that the form of *speaking*, whether it be in soliloquy or dialogue, is only a medium, and often a highly artificial one, for putting the reader or spectator into possession of that knowledge of the inner structure and workings of mind in a character, which he could otherwise never have arrived at *in that form of composition* by any gift short of intuition. We do here as we do with novels written in the *epistolary form*. How many improprieties, perfect solecisms in letterwriting, do we put up with in Clarissa[6] and other books, for the sake of the delight which that form upon the whole gives us.

But the practice of stage representation reduces every thing to a controversy of elocution. Every character, from the boisterous blasphemings of Bajazet[7] to the shrinking timidity of womanhood, must play the orator. The love-dialogues of Romeo and Juliet, those silver-sweet sounds of lovers' tongues by night; the more intimate and sacred sweetness of nuptial colloquy between an Othello or a Posthumus[8] with their married wives, all those delicacies which are so delightful in the reading, as when we read of those youthful dalliances in Paradise—

> *As beseem'd*
> *Fair couple link'd in happy nuptial league,*
> *Alone:*[9]

by the inherent fault of stage representation, how are these things sullied and turned from their very nature by being exposed to a large assembly; when such speeches as Imogen addresses to her lord, come drawling out of the mouth of a hired actress, whose courtship, though nominally addressed to the personated Posthumus, is manifestly aimed at the spectators, who are to judge of her endearments and her returns of love.

The character of Hamlet is perhaps that by which, since the days of Betterton,[10] a succession of popular performers have had the greatest ambition to distinguish themselves. The length of the part may be one of their reasons. But for the character itself, we find it in a play, and therefore we judge it a fit subject of dramatic representation. The play itself abounds in maxims and reflections beyond any other, and therefore we consider it as a proper vehicle for conveying moral instruction. But Hamlet himself—what does he suffer meanwhile by being dragged forth as a public schoolmaster, to give lectures to the crowd! Why, nine parts in ten of what Hamlet does, are transactions between himself and his moral sense; they are the effusions of his solitary musings, which he retires to holes and corners and the most sequestered parts of the palace to pour forth; or rather, they are the silent meditations with which his bosom is bursting, reduced to *words* for the sake of the reader, who must else remain ignorant of what is passing there. These profound sorrows, these light-and-noise-abhorring ruminations, which the tongue scarce dares utter to deaf walls and chambers, how can they be represented by a gesticulating actor, who comes and mouths them out before an audience, making four hundred people his confidants at once? I say not that it is the fault of the actor so to do; he must pronounce them *ore rotundo;*[11] he must accompany them with his eye, he must insinuate them into his auditory by some trick of eye, tone, or gesture, or he fails. *He must be thinking all the while of his appearance, because he knows that all the while the spectators are judging of it.* And this is the way to represent the shy, negligent, retiring Hamlet.

It is true that there is no other mode of conveying a vast quantity of thought and feeling to a great portion of the audience, who otherwise would never earn it for themselves by reading, and the intellectual acquisition gained this way may, for aught I know, be inestimable; but I am not arguing that Hamlet should not be acted, but how much Hamlet is made another thing by being acted. I have heard much of the wonders which Garrick performed in this part; but as I never saw him, I must have leave to doubt whether the representation of such a character came within the province of his art. Those

---

6 Samuel Richardson's masterpiece (1747–48).
7 A character in Marlowe's *Tamburlaine*.
8 In Shakespeare's *Cymbeline*.
9 *Paradise Lost*, IV, 338–40.   10 Died 1710.

11 With well-rounded utterance (Horace, *Art of Poetry*, line 323).

who tell me of him, speak of his eye, of the magic of his eye, and of his commanding voice: physical properties, vastly desirable in an actor, and without which he can never insinuate meaning into an auditory,—but what have they to do with Hamlet? what have they to do with intellect? In fact, the things aimed at in theatrical representation, are to arrest the spectator's eye upon the form and the gesture, and so to gain a more favourable hearing to what is spoken: it is not what the character is, but how he looks; not what he says, but how he speaks it. I see no reason to think that if the play of Hamlet were written over again by some such writer as Banks or Lillo,[12] retaining the process of the story, but totally omitting all the poetry of it, all the divine features of Shakspeare, his stupendous intellect; and only taking care to give us enough of passionate dialogue, which Banks or Lillo were never at a loss to furnish; I see not how the effect could be much different upon an audience, nor how the actor has it in his power to represent Shakspeare to us differently from his representation of Banks or Lillo. Hamlet would still be a youthful accomplished prince, and must be gracefully personated; he might be puzzled in his mind, wavering in his conduct, seemingly-cruel to Ophelia; he might see a ghost, and start at it, and address it kindly when he found it to be his father; all this in the poorest and most homely language of the servilest creeper after nature that ever consulted the palate of an audience; without troubling Shakspeare for the matter: and I see not but there would be room for all the power which an actor has, to display itself. All the passions and changes of passion might remain: for those are much less difficult to write or act than is thought, it is a trick easy to be attained, it is but rising or falling a note or two in the voice, a whisper with a significant foreboding look to announce its approach, and so contagious the counterfeit appearance of any emotion is, that let the words be what they will, the look and tone shall carry it off and make it pass for deep skill in the passions.

It is common for people to talk of Shakspeare's plays being *so natural;* that every body can understand him. They are natural indeed, they are grounded deep in nature, so deep that the depth of them lies out of the reach of most of us. You shall hear the same persons say that George Barnwell is very natural, and Othello is very natural, that they are both very deep; and to them they are the same kind of thing. At the one they sit and shed tears, because a good sort of young man is tempted by a naughty woman to commit a *trifling peccadillo,* the murder of an uncle or so,[13] that is all, and so comes to an untimely end, which is *so moving;* and at the other, because a blackamoor in a fit of jealousy kills his innocent white wife: and the odds are that ninety-nine out of a hundred would willingly behold the same catastrophe happen to both the heroes, and have thought the rope more due to Othello than to Barnwell. For of the texture of Othello's mind, the inward construction marvellously laid open with all its strengths and weaknesses, its heroic confidences and its human misgivings, its agonies of hate springing from the depths of love, they see no more than the spectators at a cheaper rate, who pay their pennies a-piece to look through the man's telescope in Leicester-fields, see into the inward plot and topography of the moon. Some dim thing or other they see, they see an actor personating a passion, of grief, or anger, for instance, and they recognize it as a copy of the usual external effects of such passions; or at least as being true to *that symbol of the emotion which passes current at the theatre for it,* for it is often no more than that: but of the grounds of the passion, its correspondence to a great or heroic nature, which is the only worthy object of tragedy,—that common auditors know any thing of this, or can

12 John Banks (1652?–1706) wrote several inferior tragedies. George Lillo (1693–1739) is remembered as the author of a domestic tragedy, *The London Merchant, or The History of George Barnwell* (1731), which Lamb describes below.

13 Lamb's note: "If this note could hope to meet the eye of any of the Managers, I would entreat and beg of them, in the name of both the Galleries, that this insult upon the morality of the common people of London should cease to be eternally repeated in the holiday weeks. Why are the 'Prentices of this famous and well-governed city,' instead of an amusement, to be treated over and over again with the nauseous sermon of George Barnwell? Why *at the end of their vistas* are we to place the *gallows?* Were I an uncle, I should not much like a nephew of mine to have such an example placed before his eyes. It is really making uncle-murder too trivial to exhibit it as done upon such slight motives—it is attributing too much to such characters as Millwood;—it is putting things into the heads of good young men, which they would never otherwise have dreamed of. Uncles that think any thing of their lives, should fairly petition the Chamberlain against it."

have any such notions dinned into them by the mere strength of an actor's lungs,—that apprehensions foreign to them should be thus infused into them by storm, I can neither believe, nor understand how it can be possible.

We talk of Shakspeare's admirable observation of life, when we should feel, that not from a petty inquisition into those cheap and every-day characters which surrounded him, as they surround us, but from his own mind, which was, to borrow a phrase of Ben Jonson's, the very "sphere of humanity," he fetched those images of virtue and of knowledge, of which every one of us recognizing a part, think we comprehend in our natures the whole; and oftentimes mistake the powers which he positively creates in us, for nothing more than indigenous faculties of our own minds, which only waited the application of corresponding virtues in him to return a full and clear echo of the same.

To return to Hamlet.—Among the distinguishing features of that wonderful character, one of the most interesting (yet painful) is that soreness of mind which makes him treat the intrusions of Polonius with harshness, and that asperity which he puts on in his interviews with Ophelia. These tokens of an unhinged mind (if they be not mixed in the latter case with a profound artifice of love, to alienate Ophelia by affected discourtesies, so to prepare her mind for the breaking off of that loving intercourse, which can no longer find a place amidst business so serious as that which he has to do) are parts of his character, which to reconcile with our admiration of Hamlet, the most patient consideration of his situation is no more than necessary; they are what we *forgive afterwards,* and explain by the whole of his character, but *at the time* they are harsh and unpleasant. Yet such is the actor's necessity of giving strong blows to the audience, that I have never seen a player in this character, who did not exaggerate and strain to the utmost these ambiguous features,—these temporary deformities in the character. They make him express a vulgar scorn at Polonius which utterly degrades his gentility, and which no explanation can render palatable; they make him shew contempt, and curl up the nose at Ophelia's father,—contempt in its very grossest and most hateful form; but they get applause by it: it is natural, people say; that is, the words are scorn-

ful, and the actor expresses scorn, and that they can judge of: but why so much scorn, and of that sort, they never think of asking.

So to Ophelia.—All the Hamlets that I have ever seen, rant and rave at her as if she had committed some great crime, and the audience are highly pleased, because the words of the part are satirical, and they are enforced by the strongest expression of satirical indignation of which the face and voice are capable. But then, whether Hamlet is likely to have put on such brutal appearances to a lady whom he loved so dearly, is never thought on. The truth is, that in all such deep affections as had subsisted between Hamlet and Ophelia, there is a stock of *supererogatory love* (if I may venture to use the expression), which in any great grief of heart, especially where that which preys upon the mind cannot be communicated, confers a kind of indulgence upon the grieved party to express itself, even to its heart's dearest object, in the language of a temporary alienation; but it is not alienation, it is a distraction purely, and so it always makes itself to be felt by that object: it is not anger, but grief assuming the appearance of anger,— love awkwardly counterfeiting hate, as sweet countenances when they try to frown: but such sternness and fierce disgust as Hamlet is made to shew, is no counterfeit, but the real face of absolute aversion,—of irreconcileable alienation. It may be said he puts on the madman; but then he should only so far put on this counterfeit lunacy as his own real distraction will give him leave; that is, incompletely, imperfectly; not in that confirmed, practised way, like a master of his art, or, as Dame Quickly would say, "like one of those harlotry players."[14]

I mean no disrespect to any actor, but the sort of pleasure which Shakspeare's plays give in the acting seems to me not at all to differ from that which the audience receive from those of other writers; and, *they being in themselves essentially so different from all others,* I must conclude that there is something in the nature of acting which levels all distinctions. And in fact, who does not speak indifferently[15] of the Gamester[16] and of Macbeth as fine stage performances,

---

14 *I Henry IV,* II, iv, 437.
15 I.e., making no distinction between them.
16 A tragedy (1753) by Edward Moore (1712–1757). Mrs. Beverley is a character in it.

and praise the Mrs. Beverley in the same way as the Lady Macbeth of Mrs. S.? Belvidera, and Calista, and Isabella, and Euphrasia,[17] are they less liked than Imogen, or than Juliet, or than Desdemona? Are they not spoken of and remembered in the same way? Is not the female performer as great (as they call it) in one as in the other? Did not Garrick shine, and was he not ambitious of shining, in every drawling tragedy that his wretched day produced,—the productions of the Hooles and the Murphys and the Browns,[18]—and shall he have that honour to dwell in our minds for ever as an inseparable concomitant with Shakspeare? A kindred mind! O who can read that affecting sonnet of Shakspeare which alludes to his profession as a player:—

> Oh for my sake do you with Fortune chide,
> The guilty goddess of my harmless deeds,
> That did not better for my life provide
> Than public means which public custom breeds—
> Thence comes it that my name receives a brand;
> And almost thence my nature is subdued
> To what it works in, like the dyer's hand.[19]

Or that other confession:—

> Alas! 'tis true, I have gone here and there,
> And made myself a motley to thy view,
> Gored mine own thoughts, sold cheap what
> is most dear—[20]

Who can read these instances of jealous self-watchfulness in our sweet Shakspeare, and dream of any congeniality between him and one that, by every tradition of him, appears to have been as mere a player as ever existed; to have had his mind tainted with the lowest players' vices,—envy and jealousy, and miserable cravings after applause; one who in the exercise of his profession was jealous even of the women-performers that stood in his way; a manager full of managerial tricks and stratagems and finesse: that any resemblance should be dreamed of between him and Shakspeare,—Shakspeare who, in the plenitude and consciousness of his own powers, could with that noble modesty, which we can neither imitate nor appreciate, express himself thus of his own sense of his own defects:—

> Wishing me like to one more rich in hope,
> Featured like him, like him with friends possest;
> Desiring this man's art, and that man's scope.[21]

I am almost disposed to deny to Garrick the merit of being an admirer of Shakspeare. A true lover of his excellencies he certainly was not; for would any true lover of them have admitted into his matchless scenes such ribald trash as Tate and Cibber,[22] and the rest of them, that

> With their darkness durst affront his light,[23]

have foisted into the acting plays of Shakspeare? I believe it impossible that he could have had a proper reverence for Shakspeare, and have condescended to go through that interpolated scene in Richard the Third, in which Richard tries to break his wife's heart by telling her he loves another woman, and says, "if she survives this she is immortal." Yet I doubt not he delivered this vulgar stuff with as much anxiety of emphasis as any of the genuine parts; and for acting, it is as well calculated as any. But we have seen the part of Richard lately produce great fame to an actor by his manner of playing it, and it lets us into the secret of acting, and of popular judgements of Shakspeare derived from acting. Not one of the spectators who have witnessed Mr. C's[24] exertions in that part, but has come away with a proper conviction that Richard is a very wicked man, and kills little children in their beds, with something like the pleasure which the giants and ogres in children's books are represented to have taken in that practice; moreover, that he is very close and shrewd, and devilish cunning, for you could see that by his eye.

But is, in fact, this the impression we have in reading the Richard of Shakspeare? Do we

---

17 Characters in, respectively, Thomas Otway's *Venice Preserved* (1682), Nicholas Rowe's *The Fair Penitent* (1703), Thomas Southerne's *The Fatal Marriage* (1694), and Arthur Murphy's *The Grecian Daughter* (1772).
18 John Hoole and the Rev. John Brown were very minor playwrights of Garrick's period. Arthur Murphy (1727–1805), author of a number of successful comedies and tragedies, also wrote a biography of Garrick (1801).
19 Sonnet 111.   20 Sonnet 110.

21 Sonnet 29.
22 Lamb speaks further (below) of Colley Cibber's "improvement" of *Richard III* and Nahum Tate's of *King Lear.*
23 *Paradise Lost,* I, 391.
24 George Frederick Cooke (died 1811) first acted *Richard III* at Covent Garden on October 31, 1801.

feel any thing like disgust, as we do at that butcher-like representation of him that passes for him on the stage? A horror at his crimes blends with the effect which we feel, but how is it qualified, how is it carried off, by the rich intellect which he displays, his resources, his wit, his buoyant spirits, his vast knowledge and insight into characters, the poetry of his part,—not an atom of all which is made perceivable in Mr. C's way of acting it. Nothing but his crimes, his actions, is visible; they are prominent and staring; the murderer stands out, but where is the lofty genius, the man of vast capacity—the profound, the witty, accomplished Richard?

The truth is, the Characters of Shakspeare are so much the objects of meditation rather than of interest or curiosity as to their actions, that while we are reading any of his great criminal characters,—Macbeth, Richard, even Iago,—we think not so much of the crimes which they commit, as of the ambition, the aspiring spirit, the intellectual activity, which prompts them to overleap those moral fences. Barnwell is a wretched murderer; there is a certain fitness between his neck and the rope; he is the legitimate heir to the gallows; nobody who thinks at all can think of any alleviating circumstances in his case to make him a fit object of mercy. Or to take an instance from the higher tragedy, what else but a mere assassin is Glenalvon![25] Do we think of anything but of the crime which he commits, and the rack which he deserves? That is all which we really think about him. Whereas in corresponding characters in Shakspeare, so little do the actions comparatively affect us, that while the impulses, the inner mind in all its perverted greatness, solely seems real and is exclusively attended to, the crime is comparatively nothing. But when we see these things represented, the acts which they do are comparatively every thing, their impulses nothing. The state of sublime emotion into which we are elevated by those images of night and horror which Macbeth is made to utter, that solemn prelude with which he entertains the time till the bell shall strike which is to call him to murder Duncan,—when we no longer read it in a book, when we have given up that vantage-ground of abstraction which reading possesses over seeing, and come to

see a man in his bodily shape before our eyes actually preparing to commit a murder, if the acting be true and impressive, as I have witnessed it in Mr. K's performance of that part, the painful anxiety about the act, the natural longing to prevent it while it yet seems unperpetrated, the too close pressing semblance of reality, give a pain and an uneasiness which totally destroy all the delight which the words in the book convey, where the deed doing never presses upon us with the painful sense of presence: it rather seems to belong to history,—to something past and inevitable, if it has any thing to do with time at all. The sublime images, the poetry alone, is that which is present to our minds in the reading.

So to see Lear acted,—to see an old man tottering about the stage with a walking-stick, turned out of doors by his daughters in a rainy night, has nothing in it but what is painful and disgusting. We want to take him into shelter and relieve him. That is all the feeling which the acting of Lear ever produced in me. But the Lear of Shakspeare cannot be acted. The contemptible machinery by which they mimic the storm which he goes out in, is not more inadequate to represent the horror of the real elements, than any actor can be to represent Lear: they might more easily propose to personate the Satan of Milton upon a stage, or one of Michael Angelo's terrible figures. The greatness of Lear is not in corporal dimension, but in intellectual: the explosions of his passion are terrible as a volcano: they are storms turning up and disclosing to the bottom that sea, his mind, with all its vast riches. It is his mind which is laid bare. This case of flesh and blood seems too insignificant to be thought on; even as he himself neglects it. On the stage we see nothing but corporal infirmities and weakness, the impotence of rage; while we read it, we see not Lear, but we are Lear,—we are in his mind, we are sustained by a grandeur which baffles the malice of daughters and storms; in the aberrations of his reason, we discover a mighty irregular power of reasoning, immethodized from the ordinary purposes of life, but exerting its powers, as the wind blows where it listeth, at will upon the corruptions and abuses of mankind. What have looks, or tones, to do with that sublime identification of his age with that of the *heavens themselves,* when in his reproaches to

25 In John Home's *Douglas* (1756).

them for conniving at the injustice of his children, he reminds them that "they themselves are old"?[26] What gesture shall we appropriate to this? What has the voice or the eye to do with such things? But the play is beyond all art, as the tamperings with it shew: it is too hard and stony; it must have love-scenes, and a happy ending. It is not enough that Cordelia is a daughter, she must shine as a lover too. Tate has put his hook in the nostrils of this Leviathan, for Garrick and his followers, the showmen of the scene, to draw the mighty beast about more easily. A happy ending!—as if the living martyrdom that Lear had gone through,—the flaying of his feelings alive, did not make a fair dismissal from the stage of life the only decorous thing for him. If he is to live and be happy after, if he could sustain this world's burden after, why all his pudder and preparation,—why torment us with all this unnecessary sympathy? As if the childish pleasure of getting his gilt robes and sceptre again could tempt him to act over again his misused station—as if at his years, and with his experience, any thing was left but to die.

Lear is essentially impossible to be represented on a stage. But how many dramatic personages are there in Shakspeare, which though more tractable and feasible (if I may so speak) than Lear, yet from some circumstance, some adjunct to their character, are improper to be shewn to our bodily eye. Othello for instance. Nothing can be more soothing, more flattering to the nobler parts of our natures, than to read of a young Venetian lady of highest extraction, through the force of love and from a sense of merit in him whom she loved, laying aside every consideration of kindred, and country, and colour, and wedding with a *coal-black Moor*—(for such he is represented, in the imperfect state of knowledge respecting foreign countries in those days, compared with our own, or in compliance with popular notions, though the Moors are now well enough known to be by many shades less unworthy of a white woman's fancy)—it is the perfect triumph of virtue over accidents, of the imagination over the senses. She sees Othello's colour in his mind. But upon the stage, when the imagination is no longer the ruling faculty, but we are left to our poor unassisted senses, I

appeal to every one that has seen Othello played, whether he did not, on the contrary, sink Othello's mind in his colour; whether he did not find something extremely revolting in the courtship and wedded caresses of Othello and Desdemona; and whether the actual sight of the thing did not overweigh all that beautiful compromise which we make in reading;—and the reason it should do so is obvious, because there is just so much reality presented to our senses as to give a perception of disagreement, with not enough of belief in the internal motives,—all that which is unseen,—to overpower and reconcile the first and obvious prejudices.[27] What we see upon a stage is body and bodily action; what we are conscious of in reading is almost exclusively the mind, and its movements: and this I think may sufficiently account for the very different sort of delight with which the same play so often affects us in the reading and the seeing.

It requires little reflection to perceive, that if those characters in Shakspeare which are within the precincts of nature, have yet something in them which appeals too exclusively to the imagination, to admit of their being made objects to the senses without suffering a change and a diminution,—that still stronger the objection must lie against representing another line of characters, which Shakspeare has introduced to give a wildness and a supernatural elevation to his scenes, as if to remove them still farther from that assimilation to common life in which their excellence is vulgarly supposed to consist. When we read the incantations of those terrible beings the Witches in Macbeth, though some of the ingredients of their hellish composition savour of the grotesque, yet is the effect upon us other than the most serious and appalling that can be imagined? Do we not feel spell-bound as Macbeth was? Can any mirth accompany a sense of

---

26 *King Lear*, II, iv. 194.

27 Lamb's note: "The error of supposing that because Othello's colour does not offend us in the reading, it should also not offend us in the seeing, is just such a fallacy as supposing that an Adam and Eve in a picture shall affect us just as they do in the poem. But in the poem we for a while have Paradisaical senses given us, which vanish when we see a man and his wife without clothes in the picture. The painters themselves feel this, as is apparent by the awkward shifts they have recourse to, to make them look not quite naked; by a sort of prophetic anachronism, antedating the invention of fig-leaves. So in the reading of the play, we see with Desdemona's eyes; in the seeing of it, we are forced to look with our own."

their presence? We might as well laugh under a consciousness of the principle of Evil himself being truly and really present with us. But attempt to bring these things on to a stage, and you turn them instantly into so many old women, that men and children are to laugh at. Contrary to the old saying, that "seeing is believing," the sight actually destroys the faith; and the mirth in which we indulge at their expense, when we see these creatures upon a stage, seems to be a sort of indemnification which we make to ourselves for the terror which they put us in when reading made them an object of belief,— when we surrendered up our reason to the poet, as children to their nurses and their elders; and we laugh at our fears as children who thought they saw something in the dark, triumph when the bringing in of a candle discovers the vanity of their fears. For this exposure of supernatural agents upon a stage is truly bringing in a candle to expose their own delusiveness. It is the solitary taper and the book that generates a faith in these terrors: a ghost by chandelier light, and in good company, deceives no spectators,—a ghost that can be measured by the eye, and his human dimensions made out at leisure. The sight of a well-lighted house, and a well-dressed audience, shall arm the most nervous child against any apprehensions: as Tom Brown[28] says of the impenetrable skin of Achilles with his impenetrable armour over it, "Bully Dawson would have fought the devil with such advantages."

Much has been said, and deservedly, in reprobation of the vile mixture which Dryden has thrown into the Tempest:[29] doubtless without some such vicious alloy, the impure ears of that age would never have sate out to hear so much innocence of love as is contained in the sweet courtship of Ferdinand and Miranda. But is the Tempest of Shakspeare at all a subject for stage representation? It is one thing to read of an enchanter, and to believe the wondrous tale while we are reading it; but to have a conjuror brought before us in his conjuring-gown, with his spirits about him, which none but himself and some hundred of favoured spectactors before the curtain are supposed to see,

involves such a quantity of the *hateful incredible,* that all our reverence for the author cannot hinder us from perceiving such gross attempts upon the senses to be in the highest degree childish and inefficient. Spirits and fairies cannot be represented, they cannot even be painted,—they can only be believed. But the elaborate and anxious provision of scenery, which the luxury of the age demands, in these cases works a quite contrary effect to what is intended. That which in comedy, or plays of familiar life, adds so much to the life of the imitation, in plays which appeal to the higher faculties positively destroys the illusion which it is introduced to aid. A parlour or a drawing-room,—a library opening into a garden,—a garden with an alcove in it,—a street, or the piazza of Covent-garden, does well enough in a scene; we are content to give as much credit to it as it demands; or rather, we think little about it,—it is little more than reading at the top of a page, "Scene, a Garden"; we do not imagine ourselves there, but we readily admit the imitation of familiar objects. But to think by the help of painted trees and caverns, which we know to be painted, to transport our minds to Prospero, and his island and his lonely cell;[30] or by the aid of a fiddle dexterously thrown in, in an interval of speaking, to make us believe that we hear those super-natural noises of which the isle was full:—the Orrery Lecturer at the Haymarket[31] might as well hope, by his musical glasses cleverly stationed out of sight behind his apparatus, to make us believe that we do indeed hear the chrystal spheres ring out that chime, which if it were to inwrap our fancy long, Milton thinks,

Time would run back and fetch the age of gold,
And speckled Vanity
Would sicken soon and die,
And leprous Sin would melt from earthly mould;
Yea, Hell itself would pass away,
And leave its dolorous mansions to the peering day.[32]

---

28 A miscellaneous writer (1663–1704), in *Observation on Vergil, Ovid, and Homer.* Bully Dawson was a notorious character of Restoration times.
29 Dryden and D'Avenant's adaptation.

30 Lamb's note: "It will be said these things are done in pictures. But pictures and scenes are very different. Painting is a world of itself, but in scene-painting there is the attempt to deceive: and there is the discordancy, never to be got over, between painted scenes and real people."
31 Astronomical lectures were given at the Theater Royal in the Haymarket.
32 From Milton's ode "On the Morning of Christ's Nativity," lines 135–40.

The garden of Eden, with our first parents in it, is not more impossible to be shown on a stage, than the Enchanted Isle, with its no less interesting and innocent first settlers.

The subject of Scenery is closely connected with that of the Dresses, which are so anxiously attended to on our stage. I remember the last time I saw Macbeth played, the discrepancy I felt at the changes of garment which he varied, —the shiftings and reshiftings, like a Romish priest at mass. The luxury of stage-improvements, and the importunity of the public eye, require this. The coronation robe of the Scottish monarch was fairly a counterpart to that which our King wears when he goes to the Parliament-house,—just so full and cumbersome, and set out with ermine and pearls. And if things must be represented, I see not what to find fault with in this. But in reading, what robe are we conscious of? Some dim images of royalty—a crown and sceptre, may float before our eyes, but who shall describe the fashion of it? Do we see in our mind's eye what Webb[33] or any other robe-maker could pattern? This is the inevitable consequence of imitating every thing, to make all things natural. Whereas the reading of a tragedy is a fine abstraction. It presents to the fancy just so much of external appearances as to make us feel that we are among flesh and blood, while by far the greater and better part of our imagination is employed upon the thoughts and internal machinery of the character. But in acting, scenery, dress, the most contemptible things, call upon us to judge of their naturalness.

Perhaps it would be no bad similitude, to liken the pleasure which we take in seeing one of these fine plays acted, compared with that quiet delight which we find in the reading of it, to the different feelings with which a reviewer, and a man that is not a reviewer, reads a fine poem. The accursed critical habit,—the being called upon to judge and pronounce, must make it quite a different thing to the former. In seeing these plays acted, we are affected just as judges. When Hamlet compares the two pictures of Gertrude's first and second husband, who wants to see the pictures? But in the acting, a miniature must be lugged out; which we know not

to be the picture, but only to shew how finely a miniature may be represented. This showing of every thing levels all things: it makes tricks, bows, and curtesies, of importance. Mrs. S. never got more fame by any thing than by the manner in which she dismisses the guests in the banquet-scene in Macbeth: it is as much remembered as any of her thrilling tones or impressive looks. But does such a trifle as this enter into the imaginations of the readers of that wild and wonderful scene? Does not the mind dismiss the feasters as rapidly as it can? Does it care about the gracefulness of the doing it? But by acting, and judging of acting, all these non-essentials are raised into an importance, injurious to the main interest of the play.

I have confined my observations to the tragic parts of Shakspeare. It would be no very difficult task to extend the enquiry to his comedies; and to shew why Falstaff, Shallow, Sir Hugh Evans,[34] and the rest, are equally incompatible with stage representation. The length to which this Essay has run, will make it, I am afraid, sufficiently distasteful to the Amateurs of the Theatre, without going any deeper into the subject at present.

from *Elia*

In 1823 was published in book form the remarkable series which, beginning in 1820, had appeared from time to time in the *London Magazine* over the signature "Elia." This pseudonym was the actual name of an old Italian clerk at the South Sea House, where Lamb had worked for a few months before he was employed by the East India Company. Only the more discriminating of the reviewers, among them Hazlitt and Leigh Hunt, recognized the humanity and humor in these essays. Though they have been repeatedly reprinted, a second edition was not called for in Lamb's lifetime; and his second collection, *The Last Essays of Elia* (1833), met at first with similar indifference. The first American edition of *Elia,* on the other hand, was an immediate success.

New Year's Eve

Every man hath two birth-days: two days, at least, in every year, which set him upon re-

---

33 A maker of theatrical costumes.

34 All characters in *The Merry Wives of Windsor.*

volving the lapse of time, as it affects his mortal duration. The one is that which in an especial manner he termeth *his*. In the gradual desuetude of old observances, this custom of solemnizing our proper birth-day hath nearly passed away, or is left to children, who reflect nothing at all about the matter, nor understand any thing in it beyond cake and orange. But the birth of a New Year is of an interest too wide to be pretermitted by king or cobbler. No one ever regarded the First of January with indifference. It is that from which all date their time, and count upon what is left. It is the nativity of our common Adam.

Of all sound of all bells—(bells, the music nighest bordering upon heaven)—most solemn and touching is the peal which rings out the Old Year. I never hear it without a gathering-up of my mind to a concentration of all the images that have been diffused over the past twelvemonth; all I have done or suffered, performed or neglected—in that regretted time. I begin to know its worth, as when a person dies. It takes a personal colour; nor was it a poetical flight in a contemporary, when he exclaimed

I saw the skirts of the departing Year.[1]

It is no more than what in sober sadness every one of us seems to be conscious of, in that awful leave-taking. I am sure I felt it, and all felt it with me, last night; though some of my companions affected rather to manifest an exhilaration at the birth of the coming year, than any very tendér regrets for the decease of its predecessor. But I am none of those who—

Welcome the coming, speed the parting guest.[2]

I am naturally, beforehand, shy of novelties; new books, new faces, new years,—from some mental twist which makes it difficult in me to face the prospective. I have almost ceased to hope; and am sanguine only in the prospects of other (former) years. I plunge into foregone visions and conclusions. I encounter pell-mell with past disappointments. I am armour-proof against old discouragements. I forgive, or over-

come in fancy, old adversaries. I play over again *for love,* as the gamesters phrase it, games, for which I once paid so dear. I would scarce now have any of those untoward accidents and events of my life reversed. I would no more alter them than the incidents of some well-contrived novel. Methinks, it is better that I should have pined away seven of my goldenest years, when I was thrall to the fair hair, and fairer eyes, of Alice W———n, than that so passionate a love-adventure should be lost. It was better that our family should have missed that legacy, which old Dorrell cheated us of, than that I should have at this moment two thousand pounds *in banco,* and be without the idea of that specious old rogue.

In a degree beneath manhood, it is my infirmity to look back upon those early days. Do I advance a paradox, when I say, that, skipping over the intervention of forty years, a man may have leave to love *himself,* without the imputation of self-love?

If I know aught of myself, no one whose mind is introspective—and mine is painfully so—can have a less respect for his present identity, than I have for the man Elia. I know him to be light, and vain, and humorsome; a notorious * * *; addicted to * * * *; averse from counsel, neither taking it, nor offering it; * * * besides; a stammering buffoon; what you will; lay it on, and spare not; I subscribe to it all, and much more, than thou canst be willing to lay at his door—but for the child Elia—that "other me," there, in the background—I must take leave to cherish the remembrance of that young master—with as little reference, I protest, to this stupid changeling of five-and-forty, as if it had been a child of some other house, and not of my parents. I can cry over its patient small-pox at five, and rougher medicaments. I can lay its poor fevered head upon the sick pillow at Christ's, and wake with it in surprise at the gentle posture of maternal tenderness hanging over it, that unknown had watched its sleep. I know how it shrank from any the least colour of falsehood.—God help thee, Elia, how art thou changed! Thou art sophisticated.—I know how honest, how courageous (for a weakling) it was—how religious, how imaginative, how hopeful! From what have I not fallen, if the child I remember was indeed myself,—and

---

[1] Cf. Coleridge, *Ode to the Departing Year,* line 8.
[2] Pope, translation of the *Odyssey,* XV, 84; translation of Horace, *Satires,* II, ii, 160.

not some dissembling guardian, presenting a false identity, to give the rule to my unpractised steps, and regulate the tone of my moral being!

That I am fond of indulging, beyond a hope of sympathy, in such retrospection, may be the symptom of some sickly idiosyncrasy. Or is it owing to another cause; simply, that being without wife or family, I have not learned to project myself enough out of myself; and having no offspring of my own to dally with, I turn back upon memory, and adopt my own early idea, as my heir and favourite? If these speculations seem fantastical to thee, reader—(a busy man perchance), if I tread out of the way of thy sympathy, and am singularly-conceited only, I retire, impenetrable to ridicule, under the phantom cloud of Elia.

The elders, with whom I was brought up, were of a character not likely to let slip the sacred observance of any old institution; and the ringing out of the Old Year was kept by them with circumstances of peculiar ceremony. —In those days the sound of those midnight chimes, though it seemed to raise hilarity in all around me, never failed to bring a train of pensive imagery into my fancy. Yet I then scarce conceived what it meant, or thought of it as a reckoning that concerned me. Not childhood alone, but the young man till thirty, never feels practically that he is mortal. He knows it indeed, and, if need were, he could preach a homily on the fragility of life; but he brings it not home to himself, any more than in a hot June we can appropriate to our imagination the freezing days of December. But now, shall I confess a truth?—I feel these audits but too powerfully. I begin to count the probabilities of my duration, and to grudge at the expenditure of moments and shortest periods, like misers' farthings. In proportion as the years both lessen and shorten, I set more count upon their periods, and would fain lay my ineffectual finger upon the spoke of the great wheel. I am not content to pass away "like a weaver's shuttle."[3] Those metaphors solace me not, nor sweeten the unpalatable draught of mortality. I care not to be carried with the tide, that smoothly bears human life to eternity; and reluct at[4] the inevitable course of destiny. I am in love with

this green earth; the face of town and country; the unspeakable rural solitudes, and the sweet security of streets. I would set up my tabernacle here. I am content to stand still at the age to which I am arrived; I, and my friends: to be no younger, no richer, no handsomer. I do not want to be weaned by age; or drop, like mellow fruit, as they say, into the grave.—Any alteration, on this earth of mine, in diet or in lodging, puzzles and discomposes me. My household-gods plant a terrible fixed foot, and are not rooted up without blood. They do not willingly seek Lavinian shores.[5] A new state of being staggers me.

Sun, and sky, and breeze, and solitary walks, and summer holidays, and the greenness of fields, and the delicious juices of meats and fishes, and society, and the cheerful glass, and candle-light, and fire-side conversations, and innocent vanities, and jests, and *irony itself*—do these things go out with life?

Can a ghost laugh, or shake his gaunt sides, when you are pleasant with him?

And you, my midnight darlings, my Folios! must I part with the intense delight of having you (huge armfuls) in my embraces? Must knowledge come to me, if it come at all, by some awkward experiment of intuition, and no longer by this familiar process of reading?

Shall I enjoy friendships there, wanting the smiling indications which point me to them here—the recognisable face—the "sweet assurance of a look"[6]—?

In winter this intolerable disinclination to dying—to give it its mildest name—does more especially haunt and beset me. In a genial August noon, beneath a sweltering sky, death is almost problematic. At those times do such poor snakes as myself enjoy an immortality. Then we expand and burgeon. Then are we as strong again, as valiant again, as wise again, and a great deal taller. The blast that nips and shrinks me, puts me in thoughts of death. All things allied to the insubstantial, wait upon that master feeling; cold, numbness, dreams, perplexity; moonlight itself, with its shadowy and spectral appearances,—that cold ghost of the sun, or

---

3 Job 7:6.   4 Resist, rebel against.

5 An allusion to Aeneas, who after the fall of Troy finally settled in Italy ("Lavinian shores").
6 Misquoted from Matthew Roydon's elegy on Sir Philip Sidney.

Phoebus' sickly sister, like that innutritious one denounced in the Canticles:[7]—I am none of her minions—I hold with the Persian.[8]

Whatsoever thwarts, or puts me out of my way, brings death into my mind. All partial evils, like humours, run into that capital plague-sore.—I have heard some profess an indifference to life. Such hail the end of their existence as a port of refuge; and speak of the grave as of some soft arms, in which they may slumber as on a pillow. Some have wooed death—but out upon thee, I say, thou foul, ugly phantom! I detest, abhor, execrate, and (with Friar John[9]) give thee to six-score thousand devils, as in no instance to be excused or tolerated, but shunned as a universal viper; to be branded, proscribed, and spoken evil of! In no way can I be brought to digest thee, thou thin, melancholy *Privation*, or more frightful and confounding *Positive*!

Those antidotes, prescribed against the fear of thee, are altogether frigid and insulting, like thyself. For what satisfaction hath a man, that he shall "lie down with kings and emperors in death,"[10] who in his life-time never greatly coveted the society of such bed-fellows?—or, forsooth, that "so shall the fairest face appear"?[11]—why, to comfort me, must Alice W——n be a goblin? More than all, I conceive disgust at those impertinent and misbecoming familiarities, inscribed upon your ordinary tombstones. Every dead man must take upon himself to be lecturing me with his odious truism, that "such as he now is, I must shortly be." Not so shortly, friend, perhaps, as thou imaginest. In the meantime I am alive. I move about. I am worth twenty of thee. Know thy betters! Thy New Years' days are past. I survive, a jolly candidate for 1821. Another cup of wine —and while that turn-coat bell, that just now mournfully chanted the obsequies of 1820 departed, with changed notes lustily rings in a successor, let us attune to its peal the song made on a like occasion, by hearty, cheerful Mr. Cotton.—[12]

---

7 See Song of Solomon 8:8.   8 I.e., I worship the sun.
9 A character in Rabelais.
10 Cf. Job 3:13–14 and Sir Thomas Browne, *Hydriotaphia*, chapter V, "What time the persons of these ossuaries," etc.
11 From the eighteenth-century poet David Mallet's imitation ballad, *William and Margaret*.
12 Charles Cotton (1630–1687), the friend of Izaak Walton.

THE NEW YEAR.

Hark, the cock crows, and yon bright *star*
Tells us, the day himself's not far;
And see where, breaking from the night,
He gilds the western hills with light.
With him old Janus doth appear,
Peeping into the future year,
With such a look as seems to say,
The prospect is not good that way.
Thus do we rise ill sights to see,
And 'gainst ourselves to prophesy;
When the prophetic fear of things
A more tormenting mischief brings,
More full of soul-tormenting gall,
Than direst mischiefs can befall.
But stay! but stay! methinks my sight,
Better inform'd by clearer light,
Discerns sereneness in that brow,
That all contracted seem'd but now.
His revers'd face may show distaste,
And frown upon the ills are past;
But that which this way looks is clear,
And smiles upon the New-born Year.
He looks too from a place so high,
The year lies open to his eye;
And all the moments open are
To the exact discoverer.
Yet more and more he smiles upon
The happy revolution.
Why should we then suspect or fear
The influences of a year,
So smiles upon us the first morn,
And speaks us good so soon as born?
Plague on't! the last was ill enough,
This cannot but make better proof;
Or, at the worst, as we brush'd through
The last, why so we may this too;
And then the next in reason shou'd
Be superexcellently good:
For the worst ills (we daily see)
Have no more perpetuity
Than the best fortunes that do fall;
Which also bring us wherewithal
Longer their being to support,
Than those do of the other sort:
And who has one good year in three,
And yet repines a destiny,
Appears ungrateful in the case,
And merits not the good he has.
Then let us welcome the New Guest
With lusty brimmers of the best:
Mirth always should Good Fortune *meet*,
And renders e'en Disaster sweet:
And though the Princess turn her back,
Let us but line ourselves with sack,

We better shall by far hold out,
Till the next Year she face about.

How say you, reader—do not these verses smack of the rough magnanimity of the old English vein? Do they not fortify like a cordial; enlarging the heart, and productive of sweet blood, and generous spirits, in the concoction? Where be those puling fears of death, just now expressed or affected?—Passed like a cloud—absorbed in the purging sunlight of clear poetry—clean washed away by a wave of genuine Helicon,[13] your only Spa for these hypochondries.—And now another cup of the generous! and a merry New Year, and many of them, to you all, my masters!

On the Artificial Comedy
of the Last Century

The artificial Comedy, or Comedy of manners, is quite extinct on your stage. Congreve[1] and Farquhar[2] show their heads once in seven years only; to be exploded and put down instantly. The times cannot bear them. Is it for a few wild speeches, an occasional licence of dialogue? I think not altogether. The business of their dramatic characters will not stand the moral test. We screw everything up to that. Idle gallantry in a fiction, a dream, the passing pageant of an evening, startles us in the same way as the alarming indications of profligacy in a son or ward in real life should startle a parent or guardian. We have no such middle emotions as dramatic interests left. We see a stage libertine playing his loose pranks of two hours' duration, and of no after consequence, with the severe eyes which inspect real vices with their bearings upon two worlds. We are spectators to a plot or intrigue (not reducible in life to the point of strict morality), and take it all for truth. We substitute a real for a dramatic person, and

judge him accordingly. We try him in our courts, from which there is no appeal to the *dramatis personæ,* his peers. We have been spoiled with—not sentimental comedy—but a tyrant far more pernicious to our pleasures which has succeeded to it, the exclusive and all-devouring drama of common life; where the moral point is everything; where, instead of the fictitious half-believed personages of the stage (the phantoms of old comedy), we recognize ourselves, our brothers, aunts, kinsfolk, allies, patrons, enemies,—the same as in life,—with an interest in what is going on so hearty and substantial, that we cannot afford our moral judgment, in its deepest and most vital results, to compromise or slumber for a moment. What is *there* transacting, by no modification is made to affect us in any other manner than the same events or characters would do in our relationships of life. We carry our fire-side concerns to the theatre with us. We do not go thither, like our ancestors, to escape from the pressure of reality, so much as to confirm our experience of it; to make assurance double, and take a bond of fate. We must live our toilsome lives twice over, as it was the mournful privilege of Ulysses to descend twice to the shades. All that neutral ground of character, which stood between vice and virtue; or which in fact was indifferent to neither, where neither properly was called in question; that happy breathing-space from the burthen of a perpetual moral questioning—the sanctuary and quiet Alsatia of hunted casuistry—is broken up and disfranchised, as injurious to the interests of society. The privileges of the place are taken away by law. We dare not dally with images, or names, of wrong. We bark like foolish dogs at shadows. We dread infection from the scenic representation of disorder, and fear a painted pustule. In our anxiety that our morality should not take cold, we wrap it up in a great blanket surtout[3] of precaution against the breeze and sunshine.

I confess for myself that (with no great delinquencies to answer for) I am glad for a season to take an airing beyond the diocese of the strict conscience,—not to live always in the precincts of the law-courts,—but now and then, for a dream-while or so, to imagine a world

---

[13] Helicon was the home of the Muses, its stream the source of poetic inspirations.

[1] William Congreve (1670–1729), greatest of the writers of Restoration comedy, author of *Love for Love* and *The Way of the World. The Way of the World* is in Volume I.
[2] George Farquhar (1687–1707), another distinguished writer of comedy, author of *The Recruiting Officer* and *The Beaux' Stratagem.*

[3] A long overcoat.

with no meddling restrictions—to get into recesses, whither the hunter cannot follow me—

> ————*Secret shades*
> *Of woody Ida's inmost grove,*
> *While yet there was no fear of Jove.*

I come back to my cage and my restraint the
fresher and more healthy for it. I wear my
shackles more contentedly for having respired
the breath of an imaginary freedom. I do not
know how it is with others, but I feel the better
always for the perusal of one of Congreve's—
nay, why should I not add even of Wycherley's[4]
—comedies. I am the gayer at least for it; and
I could never connect those sports of a witty
fancy in any shape with any result to be drawn
from them to imitation in real life. They are a
world of themselves almost as much as fairyland.
Take one of their characters, male or female
(with few exceptions they are alike), and place
it in a modern play, and my virtuous indignation shall rise against the profligate wretch as
warmly as the Catos of the pit could desire;
because in a modern play I am to judge of the
right and the wrong. The standard of *police* is
the measure of *political justice.* The atmosphere
will blight it; it cannot live here. It has got into
a moral world, where it has no business, from
which it must needs fall headlong; as dizzy, and
incapable of making a stand, as a Swedenborgian
bad spirit that has wandered unawares into the
sphere of one of his Good Men, or Angels. But
in its own world do we feel the creature is so
very bad?—The Fainalls and the Mirabels, the
Dorimants and the Lady Touchwoods,[5] in their
own sphere, do not offend my moral sense; in
fact they do not appeal to it at all. They seem
engaged in their proper element. They break
through no laws, or conscientious restraints.
They know of none. They have got out of
Christendom into the land—what shall I call
it?—of cuckoldry—the Utopia of gallantry,
where pleasure is duty, and the manners perfect freedom. It is altogether a speculative scene
of things, which has no reference whatever to
the world that is. No good person can be justly
offended as a spectator, because no good person

suffers on the stage. Judged morally, every character in these plays—the few exceptions only are
mistakes—is alike essentially vain and worthless.
The great art of Congreve is especially shown in
this, that he has entirely excluded from his
scenes—some little generosities in the part of
Angelica perhaps excepted—not only anything
like a faultless character, but any pretensions
to goodness or good feelings whatsoever.
Whether he did this designedly, or instinctively,
the effect is as happy, as the design (if design)
was bold. I used to wonder at the strange power
which his Way of the World in particular possesses of interesting you all along in the pursuits
of characters, for whom you absolutely care
nothing—for you neither hate nor love his personages—and I think it is owing to this very indifference for any, that you endure the whole
He has spread a privation of moral light, I will
call it, rather than by the ugly name of palpable
darkness, over his creations; and his shadows
flit before you without distinction or preference.
Had he introduced a good character, a single
gush of moral feeling, a revulsion of the judgment to actual life and actual duties, the impertinent Goshen would have only lighted to
the discovery of deformities, which now are
none, because we think them none.

Translated into real life, the characters of
his, and his friend Wycherley's dramas, are
profligates and strumpets,—the business of their
brief existence, the undivided pursuit of lawless
gallantry. No other spring of action, or possible
motive of conduct, is recognised; principles
which, universally acted upon, must reduce this
frame of things to a chaos. But we do them
wrong in so translating them. No such effects
are produced, in *their* world. When we are
among them, we are amongst a chaotic people.
We are not to judge them by our usages. No
reverend institutions are insulted by their proceedings—for they have none among them. No
peace of families is violated—for no family ties
exist among them. No purity of the marriage
bed is stained—for none is supposed to have a
being. No deep affections are disquieted, no
holy wedlock bands are snapped asunder—for
affection's depth and wedded faith are not of the
growth of that soil. There is neither right nor
wrong,—gratitude or its opposite,—claim or
duty,—paternity or sonship. Of what conse-

---

[4] William Wycherley (1640–1716), author of *The Country
Wife* and *The Plain Dealer.*
[5] Characters in various Restoration comedies.

quence is it to Virtue, or how is she at all concerned about it, whether Sir Simon, or Dapperwit steal away Miss Martha; or who is the father of Lord Froth's or Sir Paul Pliant's children?

The whole is a passing pageant, where we should sit as unconcerned at the issues, for life or death, as at a battle of the frogs and mice. But, like Don Quixote, we take part against the puppets, and quite as impertinently. We dare not contemplate an Atlantis, a scheme, out of which our coxcombical moral sense is for a little transitory ease excluded. We have not the courage to imagine a state of things for which there is neither reward nor punishment. We cling to the painful necessities of shame and blame. We would indict our very dreams.

Amidst the mortifying circumstances attendant upon growing old, it is something to have seen the School for Scandal in its glory.[6] This comedy grew out of Congreve and Wycherley, but gathered some allays of the sentimental comedy which followed theirs. It is impossible that it should be now *acted,* though it continues, at long intervals, to be announced in the bills. Its hero, when Palmer played it at least, was Joseph Surface. When I remember the gay boldness, the graceful solemn plausibility, the measured step, the insinuating voice—to express it in a word—the downright *acted* villainy of the part, so different from the pressure of conscious actual wickedness,—the hypocritical assumption of hypocrisy,—which made Jack so deservedly a favourite in that character, I must needs conclude the present generation of playgoers more virtuous than myself, or more dense. I freely confess that he divided the palm with me with his better brother; that, in fact, I liked him quite as well. Not but there are passages, —like that, for instance, where Joseph is made to refuse a pittance to a poor relation,—incongruities which Sheridan was forced upon by the attempt to join the artificial with the sentimental comedy, either of which must destroy the other—but over these obstructions Jack's manner floated him so lightly, that a refusal from him no more shocked you, than the easy compliance of Charles gave you in reality any pleasure; you got over the paltry question as

quickly as you could, to get back into the regions of pure comedy, where no cold moral reigns. The highly artificial manner of Palmer in this character counteracted every disagreeable impression which you might have received from the contrast, supposing them real, between the two brothers. You did not believe in Joseph with the same faith with which you believed in Charles. The latter was a pleasant reality, the former a no less pleasant poetical foil to it. The comedy, I have said, is incongruous; a mixture of Congreve with sentimental incompatibilities; the gaiety upon the whole is buoyant; but it required the consummate art of Palmer to reconcile the discordant elements.

A player with Jack's talents, if we had one now, would not dare to do the part in the same manner. He would instinctively avoid every turn which might tend to unrealise, and so to make the character fascinating. He must take his cue from his spectators, who would expect a bad man and a good man as rigidly opposed to each other as the death-beds of those geniuses are contrasted in the prints, which I am sorry to say have disappeared from the windows of my old friend Carrington Bowles, of St. Paul's Churchyard memory—(an exhibition as venerable as the adjacent cathedral, and almost coeval) of the bad and good man at the hour of death; where the ghastly apprehensions of the former, —and truly the grim phantom with his reality of a toasting-fork is not to be despised,—so finely contrast with the meek complacent kissing of the rod,—taking it in like honey and butter, —with which the latter submits to the scythe of the gentle bleeder, Time, who wields his lancet with the apprehensive finger of a popular young ladies' surgeon. What flesh, like loving grass, would not covet to meet half-way the stroke of such a delicate mower?—John Palmer was twice an actor in this exquisite part. He was playing to you all the while that he was playing upon Sir Peter and his lady. You had the first intimation of a sentiment before it was on his lips. His altered voice was meant to you, and you were to suppose that his fictitious co-flutterers on the stage perceived nothing at all of it. What was it to you if that half reality, the husband, was over-reached by the puppetry —or the thin thing (Lady Teazle's reputation) was persuaded it was dying of a plethory? The

[6] The comedy by Richard Brinsley Sheridan (1751–1816). See Volume I.

fortunes of Othello and Desdemona were not concerned in it. Poor Jack has passed from the stage in good time, that he did not live to this our age of seriousness. The pleasant old Teazle *King,* too, is gone in good time. His manner would scarce have passed current in our day. We must love or hate—acquit or condemn—censure or pity—exert our detestable coxcombry of moral judgment upon everything. Joseph Surface, to go down now, must be a downright revolting villain—no compromise—his first appearance must shock and give horror—his specious plausibilities, which the pleasurable faculties of our fathers welcomed with such hearty greetings, knowing that no harm (dramatic harm even) could come, or was meant to come, of them, must inspire a cold and killing aversion. Charles (the real canting person of the scene—for the hypocrisy of Joseph has its ulterior legitimate ends, but his brother's professions of a good heart centre in downright self-satisfaction) must be *loved,* and Joseph *hated.* To balance one disagreeable reality with another, Sir Peter Teazle must be no longer the comic idea of a fretful old bachelor bridegroom, whose teasings (while King acted it) were evidently as much played off at you, as they were meant to concern anybody on the stage,—he must be a real person, capable in law of sustaining an injury—a person towards whom duties are to be acknowledged—the genuine crim. con. antagonist of the villainous seducer Joseph. To realise him more, his sufferings under his unfortunate match must have the downright pungency of life—must (or should) make you not mirthful but uncomfortable, just as the same predicament would move you in a neighbour or old friend. The delicious scenes which give the play its name and zest, must affect you in the same serious manner as if you heard the reputation of a dear female friend attacked in your real presence. Crabtree and Sir Benjamin—those poor snakes that live but in the sunshine of your mirth—must be ripened by this hot-bed process of realisation into asps or amphisbænas; and Mrs. Candour—O! frightful!—become a hooded serpent. O! who that remembers Parsons and Dodd—the wasp and butterfly of the School for Scandal—in those two characters; and charming natural Miss Pope, the perfect gentlewoman as

distinguished from the fine lady of comedy, in this latter part—would forego the true scenic delight—the escape from life—the oblivion of consequences—the holiday barring out of the pedant Reflection—those Saturnalia of two or three brief hours, well won from the world—to sit instead at one of our modern plays—to have his coward conscience (that forsooth must not be left for a moment) stimulated with perpetual appeals—dulled rather, and blunted, as a faculty without repose must be—and his moral vanity pampered with images of notional justice, notional beneficence, lives saved without the spectator's risk, and fortunes given away that cost the author nothing?

No piece was, perhaps, ever so completely cast in all its parts as this *manager's comedy.* Miss Farren had succeeded to Mrs. Abington in Lady Teazle; and Smith, the original Charles, had retired when I first saw it. The rest of the characters, with very slight exceptions, remained. I remember it was then the fashion to cry down John Kemble, who took the part of Charles after Smith; but, I thought, very unjustly. Smith, I fancy was more airy, and took the eye with a certain gaiety of person. He brought with him no sombre recollections of tragedy. He had not to expiate the fault of having pleased beforehand in lofty declamation. He had no sins of Hamlet or of Richard to atone for. His failure in these parts was a passport to success in one of so opposite a tendency. But, as far as I could judge, the weighty sense of Kemble made up for more personal incapacity than he had to answer for. His harshest tones in this part came steeped and dulcified in good-humour. He made his defects a grace. His exact declamatory manner, as he managed it, only served to convey the points of his dialogue with more precision. It seemed to head the shafts to carry them deeper. Not one of his sparkling sentences was lost. I remember minutely how he delivered each in succession, and cannot by any effort imagine how any of them could be altered for the better. No man could deliver brilliant dialogue—the dialogue of Congreve or Wycherley—because none understood it—half so well as John Kemble. His Valentine, in Love for Love, was, to my recollection, faultless. He flagged sometimes in the intervals of tragic passion. He would slumber over the level parts of an heroic character. His Macbeth has been known to nod. But he always seemed to me to be particularly alive to pointed and witty dialogue. The relaxing levities of tragedy have not been touched by any since him —the playful court-bred spirit in which he condescended to the players in Hamlet—the sportive relief which he threw into the darker shades of Richard—disappeared with him. He had his sluggish moods, his torpors—but they were the halting-stones and resting-place of his tragedy— politic savings, and fetches of the breath—husbandry of the lungs, where nature pointed him to be an economist—rather, I think, than errors of the judgment. They were, at worst, less painful than the eternal tormenting unappeasable vigilance,—the "lidless dragon eyes," of present fashionable tragedy.

Letters

I. TO SAMUEL TAYLOR COLERIDGE

27 SEPTEMBER, 1796

London

My dearest friend—
White[1] or some of my friends or the public papers by this time may have informed you of the terrible calamities that have fallen on our family. I will only give you the outlines. My poor dear dearest sister in a fit of insanity has been the death of her own mother. I was at hand only time enough to snatch the knife out of her grasp. She is at present in a mad house, from whence I fear she must be moved to an hospital. God has preserved to me my senses,—I eat and drink and sleep, and have my judgment I believe very sound. My poor father was slightly wounded, and I am left to take care of him and my aunt. Mr. Norris[2] of the Bluecoat school has been very kind to us, and we have no other friend, but thank God I am very calm and composed, and able to do the best that remains to do. Write,—as religious a letter as possible—but no mention of what is

gone and done with—with me the former things are passed away, and I have something more to do than to feel—
God almighty
          have us all in
          his keeping.—

                    C. Lamb

Mention nothing of poetry. I have destroyed every vestige of past vanities of that kind. Do as you please, but if you publish, publish mine (I give free leave) without name or initial, and never send me a book, I charge you, your own judgment will convince you not to take notice of this yet to your dear wife.[3]—You look after your family,—I have my reason and strength left to take care of mine. I charge you don't think of coming to see me. Write. I will not see you if you come. God almighty love you and all of us—

II. TO WILLIAM WORDSWORTH

[JANUARY 30, 1801]

Thanks for your Letter and Present.[4] I had already borrowed your second volume. What most please me are, the Song of Lucy . . . .[5] *Simon's sickly daughter*[6] in the Sexton made me *cry.* Next to these are the description of the continuous Echoes in the story of Joanna's laugh,[7] where the mountains and all the scenery absolutely seem alive—and that fine Shaksperian character of the Happy Man, in the Brothers,

> *—that creeps about the fields,*
> *Following his fancies by the hour, to bring*
> *Tears down his cheek, or solitary smiles*
> *Into his face,* until the Setting Sun
> Write Fool upon his forehead.[8]

I will mention one more: the delicate and curious feeling in the wish for the Cumberland

---

1 James White, a friend since their school days at Christ's Hospital.
2 Richard Norris of Christ's Hospital. The Norrises were friends of the family.

3 Who was recovering from childbirth.
4 A copy of the second volume, just published, of *Lyrical Ballads.*—Lamb's letter is not dated, but the postmark is as above.
5 It is evident from the next letter, to Manning, that Lamb refers to "She Dwelt Among the Untrodden Ways." The four dots are in the original letter (now in the library of the University of Texas).
6 "To a Sexton," line 14.
7 In "Poems on the Naming of Places," no. II, "To Joanna."
8 "The Brothers," lines 108–12.

Beggar, that he may have about him the melody of Birds, altho' he hear them not.[9] Here the mind knowingly passes a fiction upon herself, first substituting her own feelings for the Beggar's, and, in the same breath detecting the fallacy, will not part with the wish.—The Poet's Epitaph is disfigured, to my taste by the vulgar satire upon parsons and lawyers in the beginning, and the coarse epithet of pin point[10] in the 6th stanza. All the rest is eminently good, and your own. I will just add that it appears to me a fault in the Beggar, that the instructions conveyed in it are too direct and like a lecture: they don't slide into the mind of the reader, while he is imagining no such matter. An intelligent reader finds a sort of insult in being told, I will teach you how to think upon this subject. This fault, if I am right, is in a ten-thousandth worse degree to be found in Sterne[11] and many many novelists & modern poets, who continually put a sign post up to shew where you are to feel. They set out with assuming their readers to be stupid. Very different from Robinson Crusoe, the Vicar of Wakefield, Roderick Random, and other beautiful bare narratives. There is implied an unwritten compact between Author and reader; I will tell you a story, and I suppose you will understand it. Modern novels "St. Leons"[12] and the like, are full of such flowers as these "Let not my reader suppose," "Imagine, *if you can*"—modest!—&c.—I will here have done with praise and blame. I have written so much, only that you may not think I have passed over your book without observation.—I am sorry that Coleridge has christened his Ancient Marinere[13] "a poet's Reverie"—it is as bad as Bottom the Weaver's declaration[14] that he is not a Lion but only the scenical representation of a Lion. What new idea is gained by this Title, but one subversive of all credit,

which the tale should force upon us, of its truth? For me, I was never so affected with any human tale. After first reading it, I was totally possessed with it for many days—I dislike all the miraculous part of it, but the feelings of the man under the operation of such scenery dragged me along like Tom Piper's magic whistle. I totally differ from your idea that the Marinere should have had a character and profession. This is a beauty in Gulliver's Travels, where the mind is kept in a placid state of little wonderments; but the Ancient Marinere undergoes such trials, as overwhelm and bury all individuality or memory of what he was, like the state of a man in a Bad dream, one terrible peculiarity of which is: that all consciousness of personality is gone. Your other observation is I think as well a little unfounded: the Marinere from being conversant in supernatural events *has* acquired a supernatural and strange cast of *phrase*, eye, appearance, &c. which frighten the wedding guest. You will excuse my remarks, because I am hurt and vexed that you should think it necessary, with a prose apology, to open the eyes of dead men that cannot see. To sum up a general opinion of the second vol.—I do not feel any one poem in it so forcibly as the Ancient Marinere, the Mad Mother,[15] and the Lines at Tintern Abbey in the first.—I could, too, have wished the Critical preface had appeared in a separate treatise. All its dogmas are true and just, and most of them new, *as* criticism. But they associate a *diminishing* idea with the Poems which follow, as having been written for *Experiment* on the public taste, more than having sprung (as they must have done) from living and daily circumstances.—I am prolix, because I am gratified in the opportunity of writing to you, and I don't well know when to leave off. I ought before this to have reply'd to your very kind invitation into Cumberland. With you and your sister I could gang[16] anywhere. But I am afraid whether I shall ever be able to afford so desperate a Journey. Separate from the pleasure of your company, I don't much care if I never see a mountain in my life. I have passed all my days in London, until I have formed as many and intense local attach-

---

9 "The Old Cumberland Beggar," lines 184–85.
10 Wordsworth afterwards removed this expression from "A Poet's Epitaph."
11 The novelist Laurence Sterne (1713–1768), author of *Tristram Shandy* and *A Sentimental Journey*.
12 William Godwin's *St. Leon* (1799).
13 Spellings were more archaic in the first version of this poem.
14 It is actually made by Snug, who plays the role (*A Midsummer Night's Dream*, V, i, 222–30); but the idea of reassuring the ladies originates with Snout, and Bottom elaborates it (III, i, 37 ff.).

---

15 The poem beginning "Her eyes are wild."
16 Go.

ments, as any of you mountaineers can have done with dead nature. The Lighted shops of the Strand and Fleet Street, the innumerable trades, tradesmen and customers, coaches, waggons, playhouses, all the bustle and wickedness round about Covent Garden, the very women of the town,[17] the Watchmen, drunken scenes, rattles,[18] —life awake, if you awake, at all hours of the night, the impossibility of being dull in Fleet Street, the crowds, the very dirt & mud, the Sun shining upon houses and pavements, the print shops, the old book stalls, parsons cheap'ning[19] books, coffee houses, steams of soups from kitchens, the pantomimes, London itself a pantomime and a masquerade,—all these things work themselves into my mind and feed me, without a power of satiating me. The wonder of these sights impells me into night-walks about her crowded streets, and I often shed tears in the motley Strand from fulness of joy at so much Life.—All these emotions must be strange to you. So are your rural emotions to me. But consider, what must I have been doing all my life, not to have lent great portions of my heart with usury to such scenes?—

My attachments are all local, purely local. I have no passion (or have had none since I was in love, and then it was the spurious engendering of poetry & books) to groves and vallies. The rooms where I was born, the furniture which has been before my eyes all my life, a book case which has followed me about (like a faithful dog, only exceeding him in knowledge) wherever I have moved—old chairs, old tables, streets, squares, where I have sunned myself, my old school,—these are my mistresses. Have I not enough, without your mountains? I do not envy you. I should pity you, did I not know, that the Mind will make friends of any thing. Your sun & moon and skys and hills & lakes affect me no more, or scarcely come to me in more venerable characters, than as a gilded room with tapestry and tapers, where I might live with handsome visible objects. I consider the clouds above me but as a roof, beautifully painted but unable to satisfy the mind, and at last, like the pictures of the apartment of a connoisseur, unable to afford him any longer a pleasure. So fading upon

me, from disuse, have been the Beauties of Nature, as they have been confinedly called; so ever fresh & green and warm are all the inventions of men and assemblies of men in this great city. I should certainly have laughed with dear Joanna.[20]

Give my kindest love, *and my sister's*, to D.[21] and yourself and a kiss from me to little Barbara Lewthwaite.[22]

C. Lamb

Thanks for liking my Play!![23]

III. TO THOMAS MANNING [24]

FEB. 15, 1801

I had need be cautious henceforward what opinion I give of the *Lyrical Ballads*. All the North of England are in a turmoil. Cumberland and Westmoreland have already declared a state of war. I lately received from Wordsworth a copy of the second volume, accompanied by an acknowledgment of having received from me many months since a copy of a certain Tragedy,[25] with excuses for not having made any acknowledgment sooner, it being owing to an "almost insurmountable aversion from Letter-writing." This letter I answered in due form and time, and enumerated several of the passages which had most affected me, adding, unfortunately, that no single piece had moved me so forcibly as the Ancient Mariner, The Mad Mother, or the Lines at Tintern Abbey. The Post did not sleep a moment. I received almost instantaneously a long letter of four sweating pages from my Reluctant Letter-Writer, the purport of which was, that he was sorry his 2d vol. had not given me more pleasure (Devil a hint did I give that it had *not pleased me*), and "was compelled to wish that my range of sensibility was more extended, being obliged to believe that I should receive large influxes of happiness and happy thoughts" (I suppose from the *L.B.*) —With a deal of stuff about a certain Union of

---

17 Prostitutes, streetwalkers.
18 Rackets, uproar. 19 Cheapening, bargaining for.

20 See note 7 and the text to which it applies.
21 Dorothy Wordsworth.
22 Who appears in Wordsworth's poem "The Pet-Lamb."
23 *John Woodvil*, a manuscript of which Lamb had sent Wordsworth.
24 One of Lamb's closest friends (1772–1840), mathematician, traveler, and English pioneer in Chinese studies.
25 See note 23.

Tenderness and Imagination, which in the sense he used Imagination was not the characteristic of Shakspeare, but which Milton possessed in a degree far exceeding other Poets: which Union, as the highest species of Poetry, and chiefly deserving that name, "He was most proud to aspire to"; then illustrating the said Union by two quotations from his own 2d vol. (which I had been so unfortunate as to miss). 1st Specimen.—a father addresses his son:

> When thou
> First camest into the World, as it befalls
> To new-born Infants, thou didst sleep away
> Two days: and Blessings from Thy father's Tongue
> Then fell upon thee.[26]

The lines were thus undermarked, and then followed "This Passage, as combining in an extraordinary degree that Union of Imagination and Tenderness which I am speaking of, I consider as one of the Best I ever wrote!"

Second Specimen.—A youth, after years of absence, revisits his native place, and thinks (as most people do) that there has been strange alteration in his absence:—

> And that the rocks
> And everlasting Hills themselves were changed.[27]

You see both these are good Poetry: but after one has been reading Shakspeare twenty of the best years of one's life, to have a fellow start up, and prate about some unknown quality, which Shakspeare possessed in a degree inferior to Milton and *somebody else!!* This was not to be *all* my castigation. Coleridge, who had not written to me some months before, starts up from his bed of sickness to reprove me for my hardy presumption: four long pages, equally sweaty and more tedious, came from him; assuring me that, when the works of a man of true genius such as W. undoubtedly was, do not please me at first sight, I should suspect the fault to lie "in me and not in them," etc., etc., etc., etc., etc. What am I to do with such people? I certainly shall write them a very merry Letter.[28] Writing

to *you,* I may say that the 2d. vol. had no such pieces as the three I enumerated. It is full of original thinking and an observing mind, but it does not often make you laugh or cry.—It too artfully aims at simplicity of expression. And you sometimes doubt if Simplicity be not a cover for Poverty. The best Piece in it I will send you, being *short.* I have grievously offended my friends in the North by declaring my undue preference; but I need not fear you:—

> She dwelt among the untrodden ways
>   Beside the Springs of Dove,
> A maid whom there were few to praise
>   And very few to love.
>
> A violet, by a mossy stone,
>   Half hidden from the eye.
> Fair as a star when only one
>   Is shining in the sky.
>
> She lived unknown; and few could know,
>   When Lucy ceased to be.
> But she is in the grave, and oh!
>   The difference to me.[29]

This is choice and genuine, and so are many, many more. But one does not like to have 'em rammed down one's throat. "Pray, take it—it's very good—let me help you—eat faster."

At length George Dyer's[30] first volume is come to a birth. One volume of three—subscribers being allowed by the prospectus to pay for all at once (tho' it's very doubtful if the rest ever come to anything, this having been already some years getting out). I paid two guineas for you and myself, which entitle us to the whole. I will send you your copy, if you are in a *great hurry.* Meantime you owe me a guinea.

George skipped about like a scorched pea at the receipt of so much cash. To give you a specimen of the beautiful absurdity of the notes, which defy imitation, take one: "Discrimination is not the *aim* of the present volume. It will be more strictly attended to in the next." One of the sonnets purports to have been written in Bedlam![31] This for a man to own![32]

---

26 "Michael," lines 339–43, slightly misquoted.
27 "The Brothers," lines 98–99.
28 If he did, it has apparently not survived.

---

29 Lamb misquotes slightly. For the true text, see p. 59.
30 Unitarian minister (1755–1841), minor poet, essayist, hack writer, eccentric, and friend of Lamb.
31 The insane asylum.   32 Admit.

The rest are addressed to Science, Genius, Melancholy—&c. &c.—two, to the river Cam[33] —an Ode to the Nightingale. Another to Howard,[34] beginning: "Spirit of meek Philanthropy!" One is entitled *The Madman*—"being collected by the author from several Madhouses." It begins: "Yes, yes,—'tis He!" A long poetical satire is addressed to "John Disney, D.D.[35]—his wife and daughter!!!"

Now to my own affairs. I have not taken that thing[36] to Colman, but I have proceeded one step in the business. I have enquired his address, and am promised it in a few days: Meantime three acts and a half are finished galopping, of a Play on a Persian story which I must father in April. But far, very far, from *Antonio*[37] in composition. O Jephtha, Judge of Israel,[38] what a fool I was!

C. Lamb

IV. TO THOMAS MANNING

24TH SEPT., 1802

London

My dear Manning,
Since the date of my last letter I have been a traveller. A strong desire seized me of visiting remote regions. My first impulse was to go and see Paris.[39] It was a trivial objection to my aspiring mind, that I did not understand a word of the language, since I certainly intend some time in my life to see Paris, and equally certainly never intend to learn the language; therefore that could be no objection. However, I am very glad I did not go, because you had left Paris (I see) before I could have set out. I believe, Stoddart[40] promising to go with me another year prevented that plan. My next scheme, (for to my restless, ambitious mind London was become a bed of thorns) was to visit the far-famed Peak in Derbyshire,[41] where the Devil

sits, they say, without breeches. *This* my purer mind rejected as indelicate. And my final resolve was, a tour to the Lakes. I set out with Mary to Keswick, without giving Coleridge any notice; for my time being precious did not admit of it. He received us with all the hospitality in the world, and gave up his time to show us all the wonders of the country. He dwells upon a small hill by the side of Keswick, in a comfortable house, quite enveloped on all sides by a net of mountains: great floundering bears and monsters they seemed, all couchant[42] and asleep. We got in in the evening, travelling in a post-chaise from Penrith,[43] in the midst of a gorgeous sunshine, which transmuted all the mountains into colours, purple, &c., &c. We thought we had got into Fairly Land. But that went off (as it never came again—while we stayed we had no more fine sunsets); and we entered Coleridge's comfortable study just in the dusk, when the mountains were all dark with clouds upon their heads. Such an impression I never received from objects of sight before, nor do I suppose I can ever again. Glorious creatures, fine old fellows, Skiddaw,[44] &c., I never shall forget ye, how ye lay about that night, like an intrenchment; gone to bed, as it seemed for the night, but promising that ye were to be seen in the morning. Coleridge had got a blazing fire in his study; which is a large, antique, ill-shaped room, with an old-fashioned organ, never played upon, big enough for a church, shelves of scattered folios, an Aeolian harp,[45] and an old sofa, half-bed, &c. And all looking out upon the last fading view of Skiddaw and his broad-breasted brethren: what a night! Here we stayed three full weeks, in which time I visited Wordsworth's cottage,[46] where we stayed a day or two with the Clarksons[47] (good people and most hospitable, at whose house we tarried one day and night,) and saw Lloyd.[48] The Wordsworths[49] were gone

---

[33] At Cambridge.
[34] John Howard (d. 1790), the prison reformer. Dyer's "Ode XVIII," in four quatrains, begins "Hard is the lot of meek philanthropy."
[35] A Unitarian clergyman and writer (1746–1816).
[36] Presumably his tragedy (note 23). George Colman the Younger was manager of the Haymarket Theater.
[37] A tragedy by William Godwin; it had recently failed.
[38] Cf. *Hamlet*, II, ii, 422.   [39] He did, in 1822.
[40] John Stoddart, a lawyer and friend, later knighted. His sister married William Hazlitt.   [41] A hill district.

[42] Lying down.
[43] In the northeastern part of the Lake District.
[44] A 3000-foot mountain near Keswick.
[45] A box with strings tuned in unison, to be played on by the wind.   [46] At Grasmere.
[47] Thomas Clarkson (1760–1846) led the crusade against the African slave trade.
[48] Charles Lloyd, minor man of letters, and friend of Coleridge, Lamb, and Manning.
[49] William and Dorothy.

to Calais. They have since been in London and past much time with us: he is now gone into Yorkshire to be married to a girl of small fortune, but he is in expectation of augmenting his own in consequence of the death of Lord Lonsdale,[50] who kept him out of his own in conformity with a plan my lord had taken up in early life of making everybody unhappy. So we have seen Keswick, Grasmere, Ambleside,[51] Ulswater (where the Clarksons live), and a place at the other end of Ulswater—I forget the name —to which we travelled on a very sultry day, over the middle of Helvellyn.[52] We have clambered up to the top of Skiddaw, and I have waded up the bed of Lodore.[53] In fine, I have satisfied myself, that there is such a thing as that which tourists call *romantic*, which I very much suspected before: they make such a spluttering about it, and toss their splendid epithets around them, till they give as dim a light as at four o'clock next morning the lamps do after an illumination. Mary was excessively tired, when she got about half-way up Skiddaw, but we came to a cold rill (than which nothing can be imagined more cold, running over cold stones), and with the reinforcement of a draught of cold water, she surmounted it most manfully. Oh, its fine black head, and the bleak air atop of it, with a prospect of mountains all about, and about, making you giddy; and then Scotland afar off, and the border countries so famous in song and ballad! It was a day that will stand out, like a mountain, I am sure, in my life. But I am returned (I have now been come home near three weeks—I was a month out), and you cannot conceive the degradation I felt at first, from being accustomed to wander free as air among mountains, and bathe in rivers without being controlled by any one, to come home and *work*. I felt very *little*. I had been dreaming I was a very great man. But that is going off, and I find I shall conform in time to that state of life to which it has pleased God to call me. Besides, after all, Fleet-street and the Strand are better places to live in for good and all than

among Skiddaw. Still, I turn back to those great places where I wandered about, participating in their greatness, After all, I could not *live* in Skiddaw. I could spend a year—two, three years —among them, but I must have a prospect of seeing Fleet-street at the end of that time, or I should mope and pine away, I know. Still, Skiddaw is a fine creature. My habits are changing, I think: *i.e.*, from drunk to sober. Whether I shall be happier or not remains to be proved. I shall certainly be more happy in a morning; but whether I shall not sacrifice the fat, and the marrow, and the kidneys, *i.e.*, the night, glorious care-drowning night, that heals all our wrongs, pours wine into our mortifications, changes the scene from indifferent and flat to bright and brilliant!—O Manning, if I should have formed a diabolical resolution, by the time you come to England, of not admitting any spirituous liquors into my house, will you be my guest on such shameworthy terms? Is life, with such limitations, worth trying? The truth is, that my liquors bring a nest of friendly harpies about my house, who consume me. This is a pitiful tale to be read at St. Gothard;[54] but it is just now nearest my heart. Fenwick[55] is a ruined man. He is hiding himself from his creditors, and has sent his wife and children into the country. Fell,[56] my other drunken companion (that has been: nam hic caestus artemque repono[57]), is turned editor of a "Naval Chronicle." Godwin (with a pitiful artificial wife) continues a steady friend, though the same facility does not remain of visiting him often. That Bitch[58] has detached Marshall[59] from his house, Mar-

---

50 Whose estate Wordsworth's father had managed; the heir paid a debt long owed to the Wordsworths.

51 A town near Lake Windermere.

52 Third highest mountain of the Lake District.

53 A brook famous for its fine waterfalls and cascades.

54 The well-known pass over the Alps.

55 John Fenwick, a friend. He was from time to time a journalist, and seems to have ordered his life on the principle that "money kept longer than three days stinks."

56 R. Fell (his given name is unknown). Lamb met Fenwick and Fell through the philosopher and radical William Godwin.

57 For here I lay aside the cestus and the profession (cf. Vergil, *Aeneid*, V, 484). The cestus was the Roman equivalent of a boxing glove, but it was loaded with iron or lead.

58 Godwin's second wife; not Mary Wollstonecraft Godwin (d. 1797), mother of Shelley's second wife, Mary; but the former Mrs. Clairmont, mother of Claire Clairmont (Claire became Byron's mistress and mother of his daughter Allegra). Mrs. Godwin returned Lamb's dislike, but he wrote a number of children's books for her publishing business.

59 Known only as a friend of "the Professor," i.e., Godwin.

shall the man who went to sleep when the "Ancient Mariner" was reading: the old, steady, unalterable friend of the Professor. Holcroft[60] is not yet come to town. I expect to see him, and will deliver your message. How I hate *this part* of a letter. Things come crowding in to say, and no room for 'em. Some things are too little to

be told, *i.e.* to have a preference; some are too big and circumstantial. Thanks for yours, which was most delicious. Would I had been with you, benighted, &c. I fear my head is turned with wandering. I shall never be the same acquiescent being. Farewell: write again quickly, for I shall not like to hazard a letter, not knowing where the fates have carried you. Farewell, my dear fellow.

C. Lamb

---

[60] Thomas Holcroft (1749–1845), playwright, miscellaneous writer, and radical.

Walter Savage Landor

1775–1864

Landor is chiefly famous now for the short lyrics, often founded on classical conventions, that he wrote throughout his long career. Their disciplined elegance is undeniable.

Born into a rich family, he was educated at Rugby and at Oxford. He published his first notable work, the epic *Gebir*, in 1798, fought in Spain against Napoleon, and came into his fortune in 1805. He lived for many years in Italy, at Florence, and returned to England only after separating from his wife. Twenty-odd years later he went back to Italy, where he died in his ninetieth year.

From the beginning Landor was known for his radical republican views and for a temper that got him into trouble with school authorities and with his friends, that brought him into court a number of times, and that helped to end his marriage and estrange him from his children. He never relinquished either his irascibility or his politics.

Besides his lyrics and *Gebir*, he wrote a number of dramas, tragic and historical; several verse narratives; and in prose the *Imaginary Conversations*, the first of which appeared in 1824. These are fictional colloquies between famous persons on diverse subjects of literary, historical, and philosophical interest.

TEXTS: Landor's *Prose* has been edited by C. G. Crump (2 vols., 1891–1893) and his *Poems* by Stephen Wheeler (3 vols., 1937). His biography has been written by R. H. Super, *Landor: A Biography* (1954). Critical writings about him include Malcolm Elwin, *Landor: A Raplevin* (1958) and Robert Pinsky's *Landor's Poetry* (1968). There is also an article by Donald Davie, "The Shorter Poems of Walter Savage Landor," in F. W. Bateson, ed., *Essays in Criticism* (1951).

Mother, I Cannot

An adaptation and expansion of a fragment by Sappho (c. 600 B.C.). This lyric and the next were published in 1806, in Landor's *Simonidea*. The title of this volume is from the name of Simonides of Ceos, another great Greek lyrist of about a century later than Sappho.

Mother, I cannot mind my wheel;
　My fingers ache, my lips are dry:
Oh! if you felt the pain I feel!
　But oh, who ever felt as I?

No longer could I doubt him true;　　　5
　All other men may use deceit:
He always said my eyes were blue,
　And often swore my lips were sweet.

Ah What Avails

Rose Aylmer (1779–1800) was the only daughter of the fourth Baron Aylmer. Landor met her at Swansea, Wales, when she was about seventeen. Not long afterward she accompanied her aunt to Calcutta, where she died suddenly. In later reprints of the poem Landor made a few changes; the following text is that of 1846.

Ah what avails the sceptred race,
　Ah what the form divine!
What every virtue, every grace!
　Rose Aylmer, all were thine.

Rose Aylmer, whom these wakeful eyes 5
   May weep, but never see,
A night of memories and of sighs
   I consecrate to thee.

Dirce

This poem and the next three were published in
Landor's volume of 1831.

Stand close around, ye Stygian set,
   With Dirce in one boat conveyed!
Or Charon,[1] seeing, may forget
   That he is old and she a shade.

Away, My Verse

This lyric and the next are from a section headed
"Ianthe" in the 1831 volume. Others with that name
were printed before and afterwards. Not all are
necessarily to the same lady; but many of the "Ianthe"
poems were addressed to an Irish girl, Sophia Jane
Swift, who became Mrs. Godwin Swifte and subsequently the Countess de Molandé. Landor probably
met her shortly before her first marriage, in 1803. As
far as anyone was the love of his life, she was. That
she became his mistress seems clear. He wanted her
to leave her husband; but she evidently preferred a
conventional Regency liaison to the scandal of a
divorce and remarriage. Swifte died in 1814; meanwhile Landor had married. In 1816 she married her
second husband, who died about 1827. When some
two years later she visited Florence, a sentimental
friendship with Landor sprang from the ashes of their
old love and continued until her death in 1851.

Away, my verse; and never fear,
   As men before such beauty do;
On you she will not look severe,
   She will not turn her eyes from you.

Some happier graces could I lend 5
   That in her memory you should live,
Some little blemishes might blend . . .
   For it would please her to forgive.

---

1 In classical mythology old Charon ferried souls across the
River Styx to Hades.—Landor takes his name for a lovely
lady from a classical fable in which Dirce was the leading
figure.

Past Ruin'd Ilion

Past ruin'd Ilion[1] Helen lives,
   Alcestis[2] rises from the shades;
Verse calls them forth; 'tis verse that gives
   Immortal youth to mortal maids.

Soon shall Oblivion's deepening veil 5
   Hide all the peopled hills you see,
The gay, the proud, while lovers hail
   These many summers you and me.

The tear for fading beauty check,
   For passing glory cease to sigh; 10
One form shall rise above the wreck,
   One name, Ianthe, shall not die.

Twenty Years Hence

Another of the "Ianthe" lyrics, published in 1846.

Twenty years hence my eyes may grow
If not quite dim, yet rather so,
Still yours from others they shall know
    Twenty years hence.

Twenty years hence tho' it may hap 5
That I be call'd to take a nap
In a cool cell where thunder-clap
    Was never heard,

There breathe but o'er my arch of grass
A not too sadly sigh'd *Alas*, 10
And I shall catch, ere you can pass,
    That wingèd word.

Dying Speech of an Old Philosopher

This quatrain appeared in 1849 in the *Examiner*.
Landor wrote it on his seventy-fourth birthday.

I strove with none, for none was worth my strife:
   Nature I loved, and, next to Nature, Art:
I warm'd both hands before the fire of Life;
   It sinks; and I am ready to depart.

---

1 Ilium, Troy.
2 As famous in Greek legend for devotion to her husband
as Helen was for the opposite reason.

To Age

Originally printed in *The Examiner* for June 5, 1852.

Welcome, old friend! These many years
    Have we lived door by door:
The Fates have laid aside their shears[1]
    Perhaps for some few more.

I was indocile at an age   5
    When better boys were taught,
But thou at length hast made me sage,
    If I am sage in aught.

Little I know from other men,
    Too little they from me,   10
But thou has pointed well the pen
    That writes these lines to thee.

Thanks for expelling Fear and Hope,
    One vile, the other vain;
One's scourge, the other's telescope,   15
    I shall not see again:

---

[1] With which Atropos, one of the Fates of Greek myth, cuts the thread of life.

Rather what lies before my feet
    My notice shall engage . . .
He who hath brav'd Youth's dizzy heat
    Dreads not the frost of Age.   20

To My Ninth Decad

Our last two selections were published in 1863. Both are "Ianthe" poems.

To my ninth decad I have tottered on,
    And no soft arm bends now my steps to steady;
She, who once led me where she would, is gone,
    So when he calls me, Death shall find me ready.

Well I Remember

Well I remember how you smiled
    To see me write your name upon
The soft sea-sand . . . *"O! what a child!*
    You think you're writing upon stone!"
I have since written what no tide   5
    Shall ever wash away, what men
Unborn shall read o'er ocean wide
    And find Ianthe's name again.

William Hazlitt

1778–1830

Hazlitt was born in the county of Kent, where his father, a native of Ireland and a graduate of Glasgow, was a Unitarian minister. The Reverend William Hazlitt was a republican and a friend of Benjamin Franklin, as well as the preacher of a liberal doctrine. In 1780 he went back to Ireland to take charge of a small congregation near Cork. His persistent intervention against brutal treatment of American prisoners resulted in a court of inquiry; but it made him so unpopular that, when young William was five, the family left Ireland and began a four-year sojourn in America. A sympathizer with our Revolution, the elder Hazlitt landed on our shores just after its close. He preached, as opportunity offered, from Maryland to Maine; but hostility to Unitarianism was then widespread. On his return to England he was offered a pulpit at Wem, a little Shropshire town near Shrewsbury. His youngest son was educated in a Unitarian seminary in London. He was twenty when he had the

stimulating experience of a meeting with Coleridge, and not long afterward Coleridge introduced him to Wordsworth, by whom he was deeply impressed. He describes these meetings in his famous essay on "My First Acquaintance with Poets," most of which is reprinted below.

Hazlitt did not, however, become a poet, nor for some time a writer of any kind. He was principally attracted to philosophy and painting. For a while he worked under his brother, a pupil of Reynolds and a successful miniaturist. His own portrait of his father was accepted for the Exhibition of 1802. That fall he took advantage of the temporary peace with France to hurry over to Paris and study the pictures in the Louvre. For the French Revolution, and for Napoleon as its heir, Hazlitt conceived a lasting admiration. By the news of Bonaparte's ruin at Waterloo in 1815, says the painter Haydon, Hazlitt seemed for weeks "prostrated in mind and body, he walked about unwashed, unshaved, hardly sober by day, and always intoxicated by night . . . until at length, wakening up as it were from his stupor, he at once left off all stimulating liquors, and never touched them after." The account is overdramatic; at any rate it was not till 1817 that Hazlitt gave up drinking. But that he thought Waterloo a tragedy is true enough. He had called the Emperor's earlier withdrawal to Elba "the abdication of the human race in favour of the hereditary proprietors of the species."

To return to Hazlitt's early career. He did not long remain a painter. Though for several years he kept on with the brush, the conviction grew on him that he would never make a great painter. He began turning to his pen; his first subjects were philosophy, ethics, economics, and politics. In 1808 he married Sarah Stoddart, sister of a well-known lawyer and a friend of the Lambs. She was then thirty-three; Hazlitt was thirty. Miss Stoddart had, besides a small income, a house near Salisbury; for several years it was their home.

1812 was a decisive year, for Hazlitt came before the public with a course of lectures on philosophy and speedily won distinction as a lecturer and as a journalist. He was soon Parliamentary reporter, and afterward dramatic critic, of the *Morning Chronicle*. Later he worked for other papers and contributed many essays and articles to Leigh Hunt's *Examiner*, the *Edinburgh Review*, and other periodicals; some were later published in book form. In the literary and political controversies of his time—they were conducted with a brutality which paralleled the barefisted matches of the prize fighters—Hazlitt battled with appropriate ferocity. His interests—this is one of the most attractive things about him—were uncommonly wide. He knew nearly all the leading writers, and, as some of the following pages demonstrate, had strong reactions concerning their merits and shortcomings.

As a more than merely journalistic critic, Hazlitt won his place in 1817 with a book on *Characters of Shakespeare's Plays;* he confirmed it by a rapid succession of lecture courses on *The English Poets* (delivered in 1818), *The English Comic Writers* (1818–19), and *The Dramatic Literature of the Age of Elizabeth* (1819). All were published soon after he gave them. *The Spirit of the Age* (1825) is a series of sketches of Hazlitt's contemporaries. A hard worker, he kept at his writing to the end. His last book, *Life of Napoleon*, was completed and published only shortly before his death in 1830.

Some aspects of his personal life are not admirable. He was quarrelsome, and sooner or later became estranged from nearly all his friends; Keats,

the Lambs, and the dramatist Sheridan Knowles were exceptions. If he seems to brood over a persecution complex, complaining that "every man's hand is against me," he had some warrant. Particularly in the *Quarterly Review* and *Blackwood's,* he was subjected by the Tories to venomous, blackguardly attacks on his works, his person, and his character. He had a theory to explain this hostility: "I am not, in the ordinary acceptation of the word, a good-natured man—that is, many things annoy me besides what interferes with my own ease and interest. I hate a lie. A piece of injustice wounds me to the quick, though nothing but the report of it reach me. Therefore I have many enemies and few friends." Tarnished as he was in spots, he had heroic traits. Lamb, who did not share his political views, knew he had, and called him "in his natural and healthy state one of the wisest and finest spirits breathing. . . . I think I shall go to my grave without finding, or expecting to find, such another companion."

His relations with women failed to bring happiness. Having separated from his wife several years earlier, he became at the age of forty-four infatuated with the young daughter of a London tailor in whose house he had lodgings. He prevailed on his wife to divorce him, but was unable to induce the girl to marry him. His sensitiveness to the requirements, if not of propriety at any rate of common sense, was at the moment insufficient to keep him from publishing anonymously a transparent account of his unhappy passion in a little book purporting to be fiction called *Liber Amoris* (1823). Naturally, he cuts an absurd figure in it. The following year saw him married again, to a handsome widow with a comfortable income; she is said to have fallen in love with him for his writings. Much of the remainder of his life was spent abroad, in France and Italy. Several years after their marriage the second Mrs. Hazlitt left him; apparently his much-loved son by his first wife came between them. Yet although Hazlitt was afflicted by melancholy, he retained his zest to the end. According to his son his last words were, "I have had a happy life."

Hazlitt is essentially a superb journalist, the greatest of his time. This is true of him even when he is not, strictly speaking, writing as such. His interests were remarkably broad; the energy of his engagement in them was striking; the ease, immediacy, and vivacity of the way he expressed them were extraordinary. He has been called the second best literary critic of his time, next to Coleridge, and this is so in a sense—in the sense that one might consider Wordsworth's and Keats's criticism as not having been intended precisely (or professionally) as such. His criticism differs from that of Coleridge in that one does not ransack it to discover its systematic principles. It is a reflection of the energies and alertness of the man; and the man, like a good journalist, resisted systematization.

TEXTS: P. P. Howe has edited *The Complete Works of William Hazlitt* (21 vols., 1930–1934). There are good selections of the *Essays* edited by Geoffrey Keynes (1930) and Jacob Zeitlin (1926). There is a good biography by Catherine Maclean, *Born Under Saturn* (1944), and an excellent critical biography by Herschel Baker, *William Hazlitt* (1962).

There are interesting discussions of Hazlitt as a critic in W. J. Bate, *Criticism: The Major Texts* (1952), René Wellek, *History of Modern Criticism* (1955), H. W. Garrod, *The Profession of Poetry* (1929), and Elizabeth Schneider, *The Aesthetics of William Hazlitt* (1952). A more recent study is Roy Park, *Hazlitt and the Spirit of the Age* (1971).

from Lectures on the English Poets

Hazlitt delivered this series of eight lectures early in 1818 at the Surrey Institution, a foundation in London for the diffusion of knowledge to the general public. Among his auditors was John Keats. The course proved so successful that it was repeated in the spring. Beginning with a general lecture on poetry, Hazlitt dealt, mostly two at a time, with the leading poets from Chaucer and Spenser on. With respect to his comments on Byron, in the following excerpt, the reader should remember that the first two cantos of Byron's masterpiece, *Don Juan,* were not published until the year after his lecture was delivered. It is greatly to Hazlitt's credit that he was one of the few in England who at once perceived Wordsworth's greatness.

Inexpensive reprints of the *Lectures on the English Poets* are available in Everyman's Library and The World's Classics. In the following notes, "cf." before a reference gives warning that Hazlitt's quotation in the text is not exact.

from Lecture VIII

ON THE LIVING POETS

. . . If Mr. Moore[1] has not suffered enough personally, Lord Byron (judging from the tone of his writings) might be thought to have suffered too much to be a truly great poet. If Mr. Moore

lays himself too open to all the various impulses of things, the outward shews of earth and sky, to every breath that blows, to every stray sentiment that crosses his fancy; Lord Byron shuts himself up too much in the impenetrable gloom of his own thoughts, and buries the natural light of things in "nook monastic."[2] The Giaour, the Corsair, Childe Harold,[3] are all the same person, and they are apparently all himself. The everlasting repetition of one subject, the same dark ground of fiction, with the darker colours of the poet's mind spread over it, the unceasing accumulation of horrors on horror's head,[4] steels the mind against the sense of pain, as inevitably as the unwearied Siren sounds and luxurious monotony of Mr. Moore's poetry make it inaccessible to pleasure. Lord Byron's poetry is as morbid as Mr. Moore's is careless and dissipated. He has more depth of passion, more force and impetuosity, but the passion is always of the same unaccountable character, at once violent and sullen, fierce and gloomy. It is not the passion of a mind struggling with misfortune, or the hopelessness of its desires, but of a mind preying upon itself, and disgusted with, or indifferent to all other things. There is nothing less poetical than this sort of unaccommodating selfishness. There is nothing more repulsive than this sort of ideal absorption of all the interests of others, of the good and ills of life, in the ruling passion and moody abstraction of a single mind, as if it would make itself the centre of the universe, and there was nothing worth cherishing but its intellectual diseases. It is like a cancer, eating into the heart of poetry. But still there is power; and power rivets attention and forces admiration. "He hath a demon":[5] and that is the next thing to being full of the God. His brow collects the scattered gloom: his eye flashes livid fire that withers and consumes. But still we watch the progress of the scathing bolt with interest, and mark the ruin it leaves behind with awe. Within the contracted range of his imagination, he has great unity and truth of keeping. He chooses elements and agents congenial to his mind, the dark and glittering ocean, the frail bark hurry-

---

[1] Hazlitt's criticism of Thomas Moore immediately precedes our excerpt.

[2] *As You Like It,* III, ii, 442.
[3] The heroes (and titles) of three narrative poems by Byron.   [4] *Othello,* III, iii, 370.   [5] Cf. John 10:20.

ing before the storm, pirates and men that "house on the wild sea with wild usages."[6] He gives the tumultuous eagerness of action, and the fixed despair of thought. In vigour of style and force of conception, he in one sense surpasses every writer of the present day. His indignant apothegms are like oracles of misanthropy. He who wishes for "a curse to kill with,"[7] may find it in Lord Byron's writings. Yet he has beauty lurking underneath his strength, tenderness sometimes joined with the frenzy of despair. A flash of golden light sometimes follows from a stroke of his pencil, like a falling meteor. The flowers that adorn his poetry bloom over charnel-houses and the grave! . . .

Walter Scott is the most popular of all the poets of the present day, and deservedly so. He describes that which is most easily and generally understood with more vivacity and effect than any body else. He has no excellences, either of a lofty or recondite kind, which lie beyond the reach of the most ordinary capacity to find out; but he has all the good qualities which all the world agree to understand. His style is clear, flowing, and transparent: his sentiments, of which his style is an easy and natural medium, are common to him with his readers. He has none of Mr. Wordsworth's *idiosyncrasy*. He differs from his readers only in a greater range of knowledge and facility of expression. His poetry belongs to the class of *improvisatori*[8] poetry. It has neither depth, height, nor breadth in it; neither uncommon strength, nor uncommon refinement of thought, sentiment, or language. It has no originality. But if this author has no research, no moving power in his own breast, he relies with the greater safety and success on the force of his subject. He selects a story such as is sure to please, full of incidents, characters, peculiar manners, costume, and scenery; and he tells it in a way that can offend no one. He never wearies or disappoints you. He is communicative and garrulous; but he is not his own hero. He never obtrudes himself on your notice to prevent your seeing the subject. What passes in the poem, passes much as it would have done in reality. The author has little or nothing to do

with it. Mr. Scott has great intuitive power of fancy, great vividness of pencil in placing external objects and events before the eye. The force of his mind is picturesque, rather than *moral*. He gives more of the features of nature than the soul of passion. He conveys the distinct outlines and visible changes in outward objects, rather than "their mortal consequences."[9] He is very inferior to Lord Byron in intense passion, to Moore in delightful fancy, to Mr. Wordsworth in profound sentiment: but he has more picturesque power than any of them; that is, he places the objects themselves, about which *they* might feel and think, in a much more striking point of view, with greater variety of dress and attitude, and with more local truth of colouring. His imagery is Gothic[10] and grotesque. The manners and actions have the interest and curiosity belonging to a wild country and a distant period of time. Few descriptions have a more complete reality, a more striking appearance of life and motion, than that of the warriors in the Lady of the Lake, who start up at the command of Rhoderic Dhu, from their concealment under the fern, and disappear again in an instant.[11] The Lay of the Last Minstrel and Marmion are the first, and perhaps the best of his works. . . . The truth is, there is a modern air in the midst of the antiquarian research of Mr. Scott's poetry. It is history or tradition in masquerade. Not only the crust of old words and images is worn off with time,—the substance is grown comparatively light and worthless. The forms are old and uncouth; but the spirit is effeminate and frivolous. This is a deduction from the praise I have given to his pencil for extreme fidelity, though it has been no obstacle to its drawing-room success. He has just hit the town between the romantic and the fashionable; and between the two, secured all classes of readers on his side. In a word, I conceive that he is to the great poet, what an excellent mimic is to a great actor. There is no determinate impression left on the mind by reading his poetry. It has no results. The reader rises up from the perusal with new images and associations, but he remains the same man that he was before. A great mind is one that moulds the minds of others. Mr. Scott has put the Border

---

6 From a play by Coleridge, *The Piccolomini*, I, iv, 117.
7 Thomas Otway, *Venice Preserved*, II, ii, 57–58.
8 I.e., composed or recited extemporaneously.

9 *Macbeth*, V, iii, 5.   10 Medieval and romantic.
11 Canto V, stanza ix.

Minstrelsy and scattered traditions of the country into easy, animated verse. But the Notes to his poems are just as entertaining as the poems themselves, and his poems are only entertaining.

Mr. Wordsworth is the most original poet now living. He is the reverse of Walter Scott in his defects and excellences. He has nearly all that the other wants, and wants all that the other possesses. His poetry is not external, but internal; it does not depend upon tradition, or story, or old song; he furnishes it from his own mind, and is his own subject. He is the poet of mere sentiment.[12] Of many of the Lyrical Ballads, it is not possible to speak in terms of too high praise, such as Hart-leap Well, the Banks of the Wye,[13] Poor Susan, parts of the Leech-gatherer, the lines to a Cuckoo, to a Daisy, the Complaint, several of the Sonnets, and a hundred others of inconceivable beauty, of perfect originality and pathos. They open a finer and deeper vein of thought and feeling than any poet in modern times has done, or attempted. He has produced a deeper impression, and on a smaller circle, than any other of his contemporaries. His powers have been mistaken by the age, nor does he exactly understand them himself. He cannot form a whole. He has not the constructive faculty. He can give only the fine tones of thought, drawn from his mind by accident or nature, like the sounds drawn from the Aeolian harp by the wandering gale.—He is totally deficient in all the machinery of poetry. His *Excursion,* taken as a whole, notwithstanding the noble materials thrown away in it, is a proof of this. The line labours, the sentiment moves slow, but the poem stands stock-still. The reader makes no way from the first line to the last. It is more than any thing in the world like Robinson Crusoe's boat, which would have been an excellent good boat, and would have carried him to the other side of the globe, but that he could not get it out of the sand where it stuck fast. I did what little I could to help to launch it at the time, but it would not do. I am not, however, one of those who laugh at the attempts or failures of men of genius. It is not my way to cry "Long life to the Conqueror." Success and desert are not with me

synonymous terms; and the less Mr. Wordsworth's general merits have been understood, the more necessary is it to insist upon them. . . .

Mr. Wordsworth is at the head of that which has been denominated the Lake school of poetry; a school which, with all my respect for it, I do not think sacred from criticism or exempt from faults, of some of which faults I shall speak with becoming frankness; for I do not see that the liberty of the press ought to be shackled, or freedom of speech curtailed, to screen either its revolutionary or renegado extravagances. This school of poetry had its origin in the French revolution, or rather in those sentiments and opinions which produced that revolution; and which sentiments and opinions were indirectly imported into this country in translations from the German about that period. Our poetical literature had, towards the close of the last century, degenerated into the most trite, insipid, and mechanical of all things, in the hands of the followers of Pope and the old French school[14] of poetry. It wanted something to stir it up, and it found that something in the principles and events of the French revolution. From the impulse it thus received, it rose at once from the most servile imitation and tamest common-place, to the utmost pitch of singularity and paradox. The change in the belles-lettres was as complete, and to many persons as startling, as the change in politics, with which it went hand in hand. There was a mighty ferment in the heads of statesmen and poets, kings and people. According to the prevailing notions, all was to be natural and new. Nothing that was established was to be tolerated. All the commonplace figures of poetry, tropes,[15] allegories, personifications, with the whole heathen mythology, were instantly discarded; a classical allusion was considered as a piece of antiquated foppery; capital letters were no more allowed in print, than letters-patent of nobility were permitted in real life; kings and queens were dethroned from their rank and station in legitimate tragedy or epic poetry, as they were decapitated elsewhere; rhyme was looked upon as a relic of the feudal system, and regular metre was abolished along with regular govern-

---

12 Sheer feeling.
13 "Tintern Abbey." "The Leech-gatherer," mentioned just beyond, is "Resolution and Independence."

14 Which in Hazlitt's view conformed too closely to the "Rules," formulated by the French neoclassical critics of the seventeenth and eighteenth centuries.
15 Figures of speech.

ment. Authority and fashion, elegance or arrangement, were hooted out of countenance, as pedantry and prejudice. Every one did that which was good in his own eyes. The object was to reduce all things to an absolute level; and a singularly affected and outrageous simplicity prevailed in dress and manners, in style and sentiment. A striking effect produced where it was least expected, something new and original, no matter whether good, bad, or indifferent, whether mean or lofty, extravagant or childish, was all that was aimed at, or considered as compatible with sound philosophy and an age of reason. The licentiousness grew extreme: Coryate's Crudities[16] were nothing to it. The world was to be turned topsy-turvy; and poetry, by the good will of our Adam-wits,[17] was to share its fate and begin *de novo*.[18] It was a time of promise, a renewal of the world and of letters; and the Deucalions,[19] who were to perform this feat of regeneration, were the present poet-laureat[20] and the two authors of the Lyrical Ballads. The Germans, who made heroes of robbers,[21] and honest women of cast-off mistresses, had already exhausted the extravagant and marvellous in sentiment and situation: our native writers adopted a wonderful simplicity of style and matter. The paradox they set out with was, that all things are by nature equally fit subjects for poetry; or that if there is any preference to be given, those that are the meanest and most unpromising are the best, as they leave the greatest scope for the unbounded stores of thought and fancy in the writer's own mind. Poetry had with them "neither buttress nor coigne of vantage to make its pendant bed and procreant cradle."[22] It was not "born so high: its aiery buildeth in the cedar's top, and dallies with the wind, and scorns the sun."[23] It grew like a mushroom out of the ground; or was hidden in it like a truffle, which it required a particular sagacity and industry to find out and dig up. They founded the new school on a principle of sheer humanity, on pure nature void of art. It could not be said of these sweeping reformers and dictators in the republic of letters, that "in their train walked crowns and crownets; that realms and islands, like plates, dropt from their pockets":[24] but they were surrounded, in company with the Muses, by a mixed rabble of idle apprentices and Botany Bay[25] convicts, female vagrants, gipsies, meek daughters in the family of Christ,[26] of ideot boys[27] and mad mothers, and after them "owls and night-ravens flew."[28] They scorned "degrees, priority, and place, insisture, course, proportion, season, form, office, and custom in all line of order":[29]—the distinctions of birth, the vicissitudes of fortune, did not enter into their abstracted, lofty, and levelling calculation of human nature. He who was more than man, with them was none. They claimed kindred only with the commonest of the people: peasants, pedlars, and village-barbers were their oracles and bosom friends. Their poetry, in the extreme to which it professedly tended, and was in effect carried, levels all distinctions of nature and society; has "no figures nor no fantasies,"[30] which the prejudices of superstition or the customs of the world draw in the brains of men; "no trivial fond records"[31] of all that has existed in the history of past ages; it has no adventitious pride, pomp, or circumstance, to set it off; "the marshal's truncheon, nor the judge's robe";[32] neither traditions, reverence, nor ceremony, "that to great ones 'longs":[33] it breaks in pieces the golden images of poetry, and defaces its armorial bearings, to melt them down in the mould of common humanity or of its own upstart self-sufficiency. They took the same method in their new-fangled "metre bal-

---

16 *Coryate's Crudities Hastily Gobbled Up* (1611) by the English traveler Thomas Coryate.
17 Original thinkers and writers.   18 Afresh.
19 In Greek mythology Deucalion and his wife were the only survivors of the Flood.   20 Southey.
21 A reference to Schiller's *Die Räuber* (*The Robbers*, 1781) and possibly to Goethe's *Götz von Berlichingen* (1773).—The next phrase doubtless refers to Lady Milford in Schiller's *Kabale und Liebe* (*Intrigue and Love*, 1784).
22 Cf. *Macbeth*, I, vi, 7–8.
23 Cf. *Richard III*, I, iii, 263–65.

24 Cf. *Antony and Cleopatra*, V, ii, 90–92.
25 The British convict settlement in Australia; Southey wrote several "Botany-Bay Eclogues."—"The Female Vagrant" was the original title of a portion of Wordsworth's poem later called "Guilt and Sorrow," and "Gipsies" is another of his poems.
26 A slight misquotation of line 53, addressed to Coleridge's wife, in his "The Eolian Harp."
27 "The Idiot Boy" is one of Wordsworth's poems. "The Mad Mother" was an early title of another, now called "Her eyes are wild."   28 Unidentified.
29 Cf. Shakespeare's *Troilus and Cressida*, I, iii, 86–88. *Insisture* = steady motion onward.
30 *Julius Caesar*, II, i, 231.
31 *Hamlet*, I, v, 99. *Fond* = foolish, unimportant.
32 *Measure for Measure*, II, ii, 61.   33 Ibid., line 59.

lad-mongering"[34] scheme, which Rousseau did in his prose paradoxes—of exciting attention by reversing the established standards of opinion and estimation in the world. They were for bringing poetry back to its primitive simplicity and state of nature, as he was for bringing society back to the savage state: so that the only thing remarkable left in the world by this change, would be the persons who had produced it. A thorough adept[35] in this school of poetry and philanthropy is jealous of all excellence but his own. He does not even like to share his reputation with his subject; for he would have it all proceed from his own power and originality of mind. Such a one is slow to admire any thing that is admirable; feels no interest in what is most interesting to others, no grandeur in any thing grand, no beauty in any thing beautiful. He tolerates only what he himself creates; he sympathizes only with what can enter into no competition with him, with "the bare trees and mountains bare, and grass in the green field."[36] He sees nothing but himself and the universe. He hates all greatness and all pretensions to it, whether well or ill-founded. His egotism is in some respects a madness; for he scorns even the admiration of himself, thinking it a presumption in any one to suppose that he has taste or sense enough to understand him. He hates all science and all art; he hates chemistry, he hates conchology;[37] he hates Voltaire; he hates Sir Isaac Newton; he hates wisdom; he hates wit; he hates metaphysics, which he says are unintelligible, and yet he would be thought to understand them; he hates prose; he hates all poetry but his own; he hates the dialogues in Shakespeare; he hates music, dancing, and painting; he hates Rubens, he hates Rembrandt; he hates Raphael, he hates Titian; he hates Vandyke; he hates the antique; he hates the Apollo Belvidere;[38] he hates the Venus of Medicis. This is

the reason that so few people take an interest in his writings, because he takes an interest in nothing that others do! . . .

It remains that I should say a few words of Mr. Coleridge; and there is no one who has a better right to say what he thinks of him than I have. "Is there here any dear friend of Caesar? To him I say, that Brutus's love to Caesar was no less than his."[39] But no matter.—His Ancient Mariner is his most remarkable performance, and the only one that I could point out to any one as giving an adequate idea of his great natural powers. It is high German, however, and in it he seems to "conceive of poetry but as a drunken dream, reckless, careless, and heedless, of past, present, and to come."[40] His tragedies (for he has written two) are not answerable[41] to it; they are, except a few poetical passages, drawling sentiment and metaphysical jargon. He has no genuine dramatic talent. There is one fine passage in his Christabel, that which contains the description of the quarrel between Sir Leoline and Sir Roland de Vaux of Tryermaine, who had been friends in youth. . . .[42] But I may say of him here, that he is the only person I ever knew who answered to the idea of a man of genius. He is the only person from whom I ever learnt any thing. There is only one thing he could learn from me in return, but *that* he has not. He was the first poet I ever knew. His genius at that time had angelic wings, and fed on manna. He talked on for ever; and you wished him to talk on for ever. His thoughts did not seem to come with labour and effort; but as if borne on the gusts of genius, and as if the wings of his imagination lifted him from off his feet. His voice rolled on the ear like the pealing organ, and its sound alone was the music of thought. His mind was clothed with wings; and raised on them, he lifted philosophy to heaven. In his descriptions, you then saw the progress of human happiness and liberty in bright and never-ending succession, like the

---

34 Cf. *I Henry IV*, III, i, 130.

35 In the following passage Hazlitt is using journalistic materials he had published about a year before, with reference to Wordsworth. He afterwards repented, alleging that he wrote in fun, and maintaining (not very plausibly) that there was as little of malice as of truth in his statements.

36 Wordsworth, "To My Sister," lines 7–8.

37 That branch of zoology which deals with shells or mollusks.

38 This statue of Apollo derived its second name from its

gallery in the Vatican, as the one of Venus mentioned did from its once having stood in the Medici palace in Rome. —The passage omitted after the next sentence is a short paragraph on Southey.

39 *Julius Caesar*, III, ii, 18–21 (slightly misquoted).

40 Cf. *Measure for Measure*, IV, ii, 149–52.

41 Commensurable, of corresponding value.

42 Here Hazlitt quotes lines 408–30 (see p. 140). Doubtless he mentally applied them to Coleridge and himself.

steps of Jacob's ladder,[43] with airy shapes ascending and descending, and with the voice of God at the top of the ladder. And shall I, who heard him then, listen to him now? Not I! . . . .[44] That spell is broke; that time is gone for ever; that voice is heard no more: but still the recollection comes rushing by with thoughts of long-past years, and rings in my ears with never-dying sound. . . .

On Reason and Imagination

I hate people who have no notion of anything but generalities, and forms, and creeds, and naked propositions, even worse than I dislike those who cannot for the soul of them arrive at the comprehension of an abstract idea. There are those (even among philosophers) who, deeming that all truth is contained within certain outlines and common topics, if you proceed to add colour or relief from individuality, protest against the use of rhetoric as an illogical thing; and if you drop a hint of pleasure or pain as ever entering into "this breathing world,"[1] raise a prodigious outcry against all appeals to the passions.

It is, I confess, strange to me that men who pretend to more than usual accuracy in distinguishing and analysing, should insist that in treating of human nature, of moral good and evil, the nominal differences are alone of any value, or that in describing the feelings and motives of men, any thing that conveys the smallest idea of what those feelings are in any given circumstances, or can by parity of reason ever be in any others, is a deliberate attempt at artifice and delusion—as if a knowledge or representation of things as they really exist (rules and definitions apart) was a proportionable departure from the truth. They stick to the table of contents, and never open the volume of the mind. They are for having maps, not pictures of the world we live in: as much as to say that a bird's-eye view of things contains the truth, the whole truth, and nothing but the truth. If you want to look for the situation of a particular spot, they turn to a pasteboard globe, on which they fix their wandering gaze; and because you cannot find the object of your search in their bald "abridgements," tell you there is no such place, or that it is not worth inquiring after. They had better confine their studies to the celestial sphere and the signs of the zodiac; for there they will meet with no petty details to boggle at, or contradict their vague conclusions. Such persons would make excellent theologians, but are very indifferent philosophers.—To pursue this geographical reasoning a little farther. They may say that the map of a county or shire, for instance, is too large, and conveys a disproportionate idea of its relation to the whole. And we say that their map of the globe is too small, and conveys no idea of it at all.

> —In the world's volume
> Our Britain shows as of it, but not in it;
> In a great pool a swan's nest:[2]

but is it really so? What! the country is bigger than the map at any rate: the representation falls short of the reality, by a million degrees, and you would omit it altogether in order to arrive at a balance of power in the non-entities of the understanding, and call this keeping within the bounds of sense and reason? and whatever does not come within those self-made limits is to be set aside as frivolous or monstrous. But "there are more things between heaven and earth than were ever dreamt of in this philosophy."[3] They cannot get them all in, *of the size of life,* and therefore they reduce them on a graduated scale, till they think they can. So be it, for certain necessary and general purposes, and in compliance with the infirmity of human intellect: but at other times, let us enlarge our conceptions to the dimensions of the original objects; nor let it be pretended that we have outraged truth and nature, because we have encroached on your diminutive mechanical standard. There is no language, no description that can strictly come up to the truth and force of reality: all we have to do is to guide our descriptions and conclusions by the reality. A certain proportion must be kept: we must not

---

43 Genesis 28:12–15.   44 Hazlitt's dots.

1 Shakespeare, *Richard III*, I, i, 21.

2 Cf. Shakespeare, *Cymbeline*, III, iv, 140–42.

3 Cf. Shakespeare, *Hamlet*, I, v, 166–67.

invert the rules of moral perspective. Logic should enrich and invigorate its decisions by the use of imagination; as rhetoric should be governed in its application, and guarded from abuse by the checks of the understanding. Neither, I apprehend, is sufficient alone. The mind can conceive only one or a few things in their integrity: if it proceeds to more, it must have recourse to artificial substitutes, and judge by comparison merely. In the former case, it may select the least worthy, and so distort the truth of things, by giving a hasty preference: in the latter, the danger is that it may refine and abstract so much as to attach no idea at all to them, corresponding with their practical value, or their influence on the minds of those concerned with them. Men act from individual impressions; and to know mankind, we should be acquainted with nature. Men act from passion; and we can only judge of passion by sympathy. Persons of the dry and husky class above spoken of, often seem to think even nature itself an interloper on their flimsy theories. They prefer the shadows in Plato's cave[4] to the actual objects without it. They consider men "as mice in an air-pump,"[5] fit only for their experiments; and do not consider the rest of the universe, or "all the mighty world of eye and ear,"[6] as worth any notice at all. This is making short, but not sure work. Truth does not lie *in vacuo*, any more than in a well. We must improve our concrete experience of persons and things into the contemplation of general rules and principles; but without being grounded in individual facts and feelings, we shall end as we began, in ignorance.

It is mentioned in a short account of the Last Moments of Mr. Fox,[7] that the conversation at the house of Lord Holland (where he died) turning upon Mr. Burke's style, that Noble Person objected to it as too gaudy and meretricious, and said that it was more profuse of flowers than fruit. On which Mr. Fox observed, that though this was a common objection, it appeared to him altogether an unfounded one; that on the contrary, the flowers often concealed the fruit beneath them, and the ornaments of style were rather an hindrance than

an advantage to the sentiments they were meant to set off. In confirmation of this remark, he offered to take down the book, and translate a page any where into his own plain, natural style; and by his doing so, Lord Holland was convinced that he had often missed the thought from having his attention drawn off to the dazzling imagery. Thus people continually find fault with the colours of style as incompatible with the truth of the reasoning, but without any foundation whatever. If it were a question about the figure of two triangles, and any person were to object that one triangle was green and the other yellow, and bring this to bear upon the acuteness or obtuseness of the angles, it would be obvious to remark that the colour had nothing to do with the question. But in a dispute whether two objects are coloured alike, the discovery, that one is green and the other yellow, is fatal. So with respect to moral truth (as distinct from mathematical), whether a thing is good or evil, depends on the quantity of passion, of feeling, of pleasure and pain connected with it, and with which we must be made acquainted in order to come to a sound conclusion, and not on the inquiry, whether it is round or square. Passion, in short, is the essence, the chief ingredient in moral truth; and the warmth of passion is sure to kindle the light of imagination on the objects around it. The "words that glow" are almost inseparable from the "thoughts that burn."[8] Hence logical reason and practical truth are *disparates*. It is easy to raise an outcry against violent invectives, to talk loud against extravagance and enthusiasm, to pick a quarrel with every thing but the most calm, candid, and qualified statement of facts: but there are enormities to which no words can do adequate justice. Are we then, in order to form a complete idea of them, to omit every circumstance of aggravation, or to suppress every feeling of impatience that arises out of the details, lest we should be accused of giving way to the influence of prejudice and passion? This would be to falsify the impression altogether, to misconstrue reason, and fly in the face of nature. Suppose, for instance, that in the discussions on the Slave-Trade, a description to the life was given of the

---

4 *Republic*, Book VII.
5 Edmund Burke, "A Letter to a Noble Lord."
6 Wordsworth, "Tintern Abbey," lines 105–06.
7 The statesman Charles James Fox (1749–1806).

8 Cf. Thomas Gray, "The Progress of Poesy," line 110: "Thoughts that breathe, and words that burn."

horrors of the *Middle Passage*[9] (as it was termed), that you saw the manner in which thousands of wretches, year after year, were stowed together in the hold of a slave-ship, without air, without light, without food, without hope, so that what they suffered in reality was brought home to you in imagination, till you felt in sickness of heart as one of them, could it be said that this was a prejudging of the case, that your knowing the extent of the evil disqualified you from pronouncing sentence upon it, and that your disgust and abhorrence were the effects of a heated imagination? No. Those evils that inflame the imagination and make the heart sick, ought not to leave the head cool. This is the very test and measure of the degree of the enormity, that it involuntarily staggers and appals the mind. If it were a common iniquity, if it were slight and partial, or necessary, it would not have this effect; but it very properly carries away the feelings, and (if you will) overpowers the judgment, because it is a mass of evil so monstrous and unwarranted as not to be endured, even in thought. A man on the rack does not suffer the less, because the extremity of anguish takes away his command of feeling and attention to appearances. A pang inflicted on humanity is not the less real, because it stirs up sympathy in the breast of humanity. Would you tame down the glowing language of justifiable passion into that of cold indifference, of self-complacent, sceptical reasoning, and thus take out the sting of indignation from the mind of the spectator? Not, surely, till you have removed the nuisance by the levers that strong feeling alone can set at work, and have thus taken away the pang of suffering that caused it! Or say that the question were proposed to you, whether, on some occasion, you should thrust your hand into the flames, and were coolly told that you were not at all to consider the pain and anguish it might give you, nor suffer yourself to be led away by any such idle appeals to natural sensibility, but to refer the decision to some abstract, technical ground of propriety, would you not laugh in your adviser's face? Oh! no; where our own interests are concerned, or where we are sincere in our professions of regard, the pretended distinction between sound judgment and

lively imagination is quickly done away with. But I would not wish a better or more philosophical standard of morality, than that we should think and feel towards others as we should, if it were our own case. If we look for a higher standard than this, we shall not find it; but shall lose the substance for the shadow! . . .

With respect to the atrocities committed in the Slave-Trade, it could not be set up as a doubtful plea in their favour, that the actual and intolerable sufferings inflicted on the individuals were compensated by certain advantages in a commercial and political point of view—in a moral sense they *cannot* be compensated. They hurt the public mind: they harden and sear the natural feelings. The evil is monstrous and palpable; the pretended good is remote and contingent. In morals, as in philosophy, *De non apparentibus et non existentibus eadem est ratio.* What does not touch the heart, or come home to the feelings, goes comparatively for little or nothing. A benefit that exists merely in possibility, and is judged of only by the forced dictates of the understanding, is not a set-off against an evil (say of equal magnitude in itself) that strikes upon the senses, that haunts the imagination, and lacerates the human heart. A spectacle of deliberate cruelty, that shocks every one that sees and hears of it, is not to be justified by any calculations of cold-blooded self-interest—is not to be permitted in any case. It is prejudged and self-condemned. Necessity has been therefore justly called "the tyrant's plea."[10] It is no better with the mere doctrine of utility, which is the sophist's plea. Thus, for example, an infinite number of lumps of sugar put into Mr. Bentham's[11] artificial ethical scales would never weigh against the pounds of human flesh, or drops of human blood, that are sacrificed to produce them. The taste of the former on the palate is evanescent; but the others sit heavy on the soul. The one are an object to the imagination: the others only to the understanding. But man is an animal compounded both of imagination and understanding; and, in treating of what is good for man's nature, it is necessary to consider both. A calculation of the mere ultimate advantages, without regard to natural

---

9 The Atlantic voyage from Africa to the West Indies.

10 *Paradise Lost,* IV, 393–94.
11 On Jeremy Bentham see pp. 404–06.

feelings and affections, may improve the external face and physical comforts of society, but will leave it heartless and worthless in itself. In a word, the sympathy of the individual with the consequences of his own act is to be attended to (no less than the consequences themselves) in every sound system of morality; and this must be determined by certain natural laws of the human mind, and not by rules of logic or arithmetic.

The aspect of a moral question is to be judged of very much like the face of a country, by the projecting points, by what is striking and memorable, by that which leaves traces of itself behind, or "casts its shadow before."[12] Millions of acres do not make a picture; nor the calculation of all the consequences in the world a sentiment. We must have some outstanding object for the mind, as well as the eye, to dwell on and recur to—something marked and decisive to give a tone and texture to the moral feelings. Not only is the attention thus roused and kept alive; but what is most important as to the principles of action, the desire of good or hatred of evil is powerfully excited. But all individual facts and history come under the head of what these people call *Imagination*. All full, true, and particular accounts they consider as romantic, ridiculous, vague, inflammatory. As a case in point, one of this school of thinkers[13] declares that he was qualified to write a better History of India from having never been there than if he had, as the last might lead to local distinctions or party-prejudices; that is to say, that he could describe a country better at second-hand than from original observation, or that from having seen no one object, place, or person, he could do ampler justice to the whole. It might be maintained, much on the same principle, that an artist would paint a better likeness of a person after he was dead, from description or different sketches of the face, than from having seen the individual living man. On the contrary, I humbly conceive that the seeing half a dozen wandering Lascars in the streets of London gives one a better idea of the soul of India, that cradle of the world, and (as it were) garden of the sun,

than all the charts, records, and statistical reports that can be sent over, even under the classical administration of Mr. Canning. *Ex uno omnes*.[14] One Hindoo differs more from a citizen of London than he does from all other Hindoos; and by seeing the two first, man to man, you know comparatively and essentially what they are, nation to nation. By a very few specimens you fix the great leading differences, which are nearly the same throughout. Any one thing is a better representative of its kind, than all the words and definitions in the world can be. The sum total is indeed different from the particulars; but it is not easy to guess at any general result, without some previous induction of particulars and appeal to experience.

What can we reason, but from what we know?[15]

Again, it is quite wrong, instead of the most striking illustrations of human nature, to single out the stalest and tritest, as if they were most authentic and infallible; not considering that from the extremes you may infer the means, but you cannot from the means infer the extremes in any case. It may be said that the extreme and individual cases may be retorted upon us:—I deny it, unless it be with truth. The imagination is an *associating* principle; and has an instinctive perception when a thing belongs to a system, or is only an exception to it. For instance, the excesses committed by the victorious besiegers of a town do not attach to the nation committing them, but to the nature of that sort of warfare, and are common to both sides. They may be struck off the score of national prejudices. The cruelties exercised upon slaves, on the other hand, grow out of the relation between master and slave; and the mind intuitively revolts at them as such. The cant about the horrors of the French Revolution is mere cant—every body knows it to be so: each party would have retaliated upon the other: it was a civil war, like that for a disputed succession: the general principle of the right or wrong of the change remains untouched. Neither would these horrors have taken place, except from Prussian manifestos, and treachery within: there were none in the American, and have been

---

12 Cf. Thomas Campbell, "Lochiel's Warning," line 56.
13 The economist and philosopher James Mill (1773–1836), father of John Stuart Mill (see pp. 561–62). He wrote a *History of British India* (1817–18).

14 From one, all (adapted from Vergil's *Aeneid*, II, 65–66).
15 Pope, *An Essay on Man*, I, 18.

none in the Spanish Revolution. The massacre of St. Bartholomew arose out of the principles of that religion which exterminates with fire and sword, and keeps no faith with heretics.—If it be said that nicknames, party watch-words, bugbears, the cry of "No Popery," &c., are continually played off upon the imagination with the most mischievous effect, I answer that most of these bugbears and terms of vulgar abuse have arisen out of abstruse speculation or barbarous prejudice, and have seldom had their root in real facts or natural feelings. Besides, are not general topics, rules, exceptions, endlessly bandied to and fro, and balanced one against the other by the most learned disputants? Have not three-fourths of all the wars, schisms, heart-burnings in the world begun on mere points of controversy?—There are two classes whom I have found given to this kind of reasoning against the use of our senses and feelings in what concerns human nature, *viz.* knaves and fools. The last do it, because they think their own shallow dogmas settle all questions best without any farther appeal; and the first do it, because they know that the refinements of the head are more easily got rid of than the suggestions of the heart, and that a strong sense of injustice, excited by a particular case in all its aggravations, tells more against them than all the distinctions of the jurists. Facts, concrete existences, are stubborn things, and are not so soon tampered with or turned about to any point we please, as mere names and abstractions. Of these last it may be said,

A breath can mar *them, as a breath has made:*[16]

and they are liable to be puffed away by every wind of doctrine, or baffled by every plea of convenience. I wonder that Rousseau gave in to this cant about the want of soundness in rhetorical and imaginative reasoning; and was so fond of this subject, as to make an abridgment of Plato's rhapsodies upon it, by which he was led to expel poets from his commonwealth. Thus two of the most flowery writers are those who have exacted the greatest severity of style from others. Rousseau was too ambitious of an exceedingly technical and scientific mode of reasoning, scarcely

attainable in the mixed questions of human life, (as may be seen in his SOCIAL CONTRACT—a work of great ability, but extreme formality of structure) and it is probable he was led into this error in seeking to overcome his too great warmth of natural temperament and a tendency to indulge merely the impulses of passion. Burke, who was a man of fine imagination, had the good sense (without any of this false modesty) to defend the moral use of the imagination, and is himself one of the grossest instances of its abuse.

It is not merely the fashion among philosophers—the poets also have got into a way of scouting individuality as beneath the sublimity of their pretensions, and the universality of their genius. The philosophers have become mere logicians, and their rivals mere rhetoricians; for as these last must float on the surface, and are not allowed to be harsh and crabbed and recondite like the others, by leaving out the individual, they become common-place. They cannot reason, and they must declaim. Modern tragedy, in particular, is no longer like a vessel making the voyage of life, and tossed about by the winds and waves of passion, but is converted into a handsomely-constructed steamboat, that is moved by the sole expansive power of words. Lord Byron has launched several of these ventures lately (if ventures they may be called) and may continue in the same strain as long as he pleases. We have not now a number of *dramatis personae* affected by particular incidents and speaking according to their feelings, or as the occasion suggests, but each mounting the rostrum, and delivering his opinion on fate, fortune, and the entire consummation of things. The individual is not of sufficient importance to occupy his own thoughts or the thoughts of others. The poet fills his page with *grandes pensées.* He covers the face of nature with the beauty of his sentiments and the brilliancy of his paradoxes. We have the subtleties of the head, instead of the workings of the heart, and possible justifications instead of the actual motives of conduct. This all seems to proceed on a false estimate of individual nature and the value of human life. We have been so used to count by millions of late, that we think the units that compose them nothing, and are so prone to trace remote principles, that we neglect the im-

---

[16] Cf. Goldsmith, *The Deserted Village*, line 54.

mediate results. As an instance of the opposite style of dramatic dialogue, in which the persons speak for themselves, and to one another, I will give, by way of illustration, a passage from an old tragedy, in which a brother has just caused his sister to be put to a violent death.

    Bosola. *Fix your eye here.*
    Ferdinand. *Constantly.*
    Bosola. *Do you not weep?*
Other sins only speak; murther shrieks out:
The element of water moistens the earth;
But blood flies upwards, and bedews the heavens.
    Ferdinand. *Cover her face: mine eyes dazzle; she*
        died young.
    Bosola. *I think not so: her infelicity*
Seem'd to have years too many.
    Ferdinand. *She and I were twins:*
And should I die this instant, I had lived
Her time to a minute.
               Duchess of Malfy, Act iv. Scene 2.

How fine is the constancy with which he first fixes his eye on the dead body, with a forced courage, and then, as his resolution wavers, how natural is his turning his face away, and the reflection that strikes him on her youth and beauty and untimely death, and the thought that they were twins, and his measuring his life by hers up to the present period, as if all that was to come of it were nothing! Now, I would fain ask whether there is not in this contemplation of the interval that separates the beginning from the end of life, of a life too so varied from good to ill, and of the pitiable termination of which the person speaking has been the wilful and guilty cause, enough to "give the mind pause"?[17] Is not that revelation as it were of the whole extent of our being which is made by the flashes of passion and stroke of calamity, a subject sufficiently staggering to have place in legitimate tragedy? Are not the struggles of the will with untoward events and the adverse passions of others as interesting and instructive in the representation as reflections on the mutability of fortune or inevitableness of destiny, or on the passions of men in general? The tragic Muse does not merely utter muffled sounds: but we see the paleness on the cheek, and the life-blood gushing from the heart! The interest we take in

our own lives, in our successes or disappointments, and the *home* feelings that arise out of these, when well described, are the clearest and truest mirror in which we can see the image of human nature. For in this sense each man is a microcosm. What he is, the rest are—whatever his joys and sorrows are composed of, theirs are the same—no more, no less.

One touch of nature makes the whole world kin.[18]

But it must be the genuine touch of nature, not the outward flourishes and varnish of art. The spouting, oracular, didactic figure of the poet no more answers to the living man, than the lay-figure of the painter does. We may well say to such a one,

Thou hast no speculation in those eyes
That thou dost glare with: thy bones are marrowless,
Thy blood is cold![19]

Man is (so to speak) an endless and infinitely varied repetition: and if we know what one man feels, we so far know what a thousand feel in the sanctuary of their being. Our feeling of general humanity is at once an aggregate of a thousand different truths, and it is also the same truth a thousand times told. As is our perception of this original truth, the root of our imagination, so will the force and richness of the general impression proceeding from it be. The boundary of our sympathy is a circle which enlarges itself according to its propulsion from the centre—the heart. If we are imbued with a deep sense of individual weal or woe, we shall be awe-struck at the idea of humanity in general. If we know little of it but its abstract and common properties, without their particular application, their force or degrees, we shall care just as little as we know either about the whole or the individuals. If we understand the texture and vital feeling, we then can fill up the outline, but we cannot supply the former from having the latter given. Moral and poetical truth is like expression in a picture—the one is not to be attained by smearing over a large canvas, nor the other by bestriding a vague topic. In such matters, the

---

[17] Cf. *Hamlet*, III, i, 68.

[18] Shakespeare, *Troilus and Cressida*, III, iii, 175.
[19] Cf. *Macbeth*, III, iv, 94–96.

most pompous sciolists are accordingly found to be the greatest contemners of human life. But I defy any great tragic writer to despise that nature which he understands, or that heart which he has probed, with all its rich bleeding materials of joy and sorrow. The subject may not be a source of much triumph to him, from its alternate light and shade, but it can never become one of supercilious indifference. He must feel a strong reflex interest in it, corresponding to that which he has depicted in the characters of others. Indeed, the object and end of playing, "both at the first and now, is to hold the mirror up to nature,"[20] to enable us to feel for others as for ourselves, or to embody a distinct interest out of ourselves by the force of imagination and passion. This is summed up in the wish of the poet—

To feel what others are, and know myself a man.[21]

If it does not do this, it loses both its dignity and its proper use.

from The Fight

"The Fight" was first published in the *New Monthly Magazine* for February 1822. The contest took place on December 11, 1821, at Hungerford, Berkshire, between Tom Hickman, the Gas-Light Man (1785–1822), and Bill Neate, a butcher from Bristol, mother of champions. This is a classic essay on prize fighting.

——*The* fight, *the* fight's *the thing,*
Wherein I'll catch the conscience of the king.[1]

Where there's a will, there's a way.—I said so to myself, as I walked down Chancery-lane,[2] about half-past six o'clock on Monday the 10th of December, to inquire at Jack Randall's where the fight the next day was to be;[3] and I found

"the proverb" nothing "musty"[4] in the present instance. I was determined to see this fight, come what would, and see it I did, in great style. It was my *first fight,* yet it more than answered my expectations. Ladies! it is to you I dedicate this description; nor let it seem out of character for the fair to notice the exploits of the brave. Courage and modesty are the old English virtues; and may they never look cold and askance on one another! Think, ye fairest of the fair, loveliest of the lovely kind, ye practisers of soft enchantment, how many more ye kill with poisoned baits than ever fell in the ring; and listen with subdued air and without shuddering, to a tale tragic only in appearance, and sacred to the FANCY![5]

I was going down Chancery-lane, thinking to ask at Jack Randall's where the fight was to be, when looking through the glass-door of the *Hole in the Wall,* I heard a gentleman asking the same question *at* Mrs. Randall, as the author of *Waverley* would express it.[6] Now Mrs. Randall stood answering the gentleman's question, with the authenticity of the lady of the Champion of the Light Weights. Thinks I, I'll wait till this person comes out, and learn from him how it is. For to say a truth, I was not fond of going into this house of call for heroes and philosophers, ever since the owner of it (for Jack is no gentleman) threatened once upon a time to kick me out of doors for wanting a mutton-chop at his hospitable board, when the conqueror in thirteen battles was more full of *blue ruin*[7] than of good manners. . . .[8] I . . . was accommodated with a great coat, put up my umbrella to keep off a drizzling mist, and we began to cut through the air like an arrow. The mile-stones disappeared one after another, the rain kept off; Tom Turtle,[9] the trainer, sat before me on the coach-box, with whom I ex-

---

[20] Cf. *Hamlet,* III, ii, 23–25.
[21] Cf. Thomas Gray, "Hymn to Adversity," line 48.

[1] Cf. *Hamlet,* II, ii, 633–34: "the play's the thing," etc.
[2] A London street running between High Holborn and the Strand. The prize fighter Jack Randall kept "The Hole in the Wall" there. It was not unusual for a successful pugilist to keep a "pub," that is, a tavern or saloon.
[3] In those days the location of matches was sometimes kept quiet till the last moment, to avoid interference. They were bloody affairs, fought without gloves, and with no limitation on the number of rounds.

[4] The discontented Hamlet (III, ii, 358–59) alludes to a "musty" proverb about how while the grass grows the steed starves.
[5] The fans and their heroes. All who are interested in a special sport, art, or pursuit.
[6] I.e., as a Scotsman would say.
[7] Cheap gin.
[8] Part of a long paragraph is here omitted. Hazlitt obtains his information, and after some difficulty secures a place on the top of a coach.
[9] According to Hazlitt's son this was John Thurtell (1794–1824), a well-known sporting man.

changed civilities as a gentleman going to the fight; the passion that had transported me an hour before was subdued to pensive regret and conjectural musing on the next day's battle; I was promised a place inside at Reading, and upon the whole, I thought myself a lucky fellow. Such is the force of imagination! On the outside of any other coach on the 10th of December, with a Scotch mist drizzling through the cloudy moonlight air, I should have been cold, comfortless, impatient, and, no doubt, wet through; but seated on the Royal mail, I felt warm and comfortable, the air did me good, the ride did me good, I was pleased with the progress we had made, and confident that all would go well through the journey. When I got inside at Reading, I found Turtle and a stout valetudinarian, whose costume bespoke him one of the FANCY, and who had risen from a three months' sick bed to get into the mail to see the fight. They were intimate, and we fell into a lively discourse. My friend the trainer was confined in his topics to fighting dogs and men, to bears and badgers; beyond this he was "quite chap-fallen,"[10] had not a word to throw at a dog, or indeed very wisely fell asleep, when any other game was started. The whole art of training (I, however, learnt from him) consists in two things, exercise and abstinence, abstinence and exercise, repeated alternately and without end. A yolk of an egg with a spoonful of rum in it is the first thing in a morning, and then a walk of six miles till breakfast. This meal consists of a plentiful supply of tea and toast and beefsteaks. Then another six or seven miles till dinner-time, and another supply of solid beef or mutton with a pint of porter, and perhaps, at the utmost, a couple of glasses of sherry. Martin[11] trains on water, but this increases his infirmity on another very dangerous side. The Gas-man takes now and then a chirping[12] glass (under the rose[13]) to console him, during a six weeks' probation, for the absence of Mrs. Hickman—an agreeable woman, with (I understand) a pretty fortune of two hundred pounds. How matter presses on me! What stubborn things are facts! How in-

exhaustible is nature and art! "It is well," as I once heard Mr. Richmond[14] observe, "to see a variety." He was speaking of cock-fighting as an edifying spectacle. I cannot deny but that one learns more of what *is* (I do not say of what *ought to be*) in this desultory mode of practical study, than from reading the same book twice over, even though it should be a moral treatise. Where was I? I was sitting at dinner with the candidate for the honours of the ring, "where good digestion waits on appetite, and health on both."[15] Then follows an hour of social chat and native glee;[16] and afterwards, to another breathing over heathy hill or dale. Back to supper, and then to bed, and up by six again— Our hero

Follows so the ever-running sun
With profitable ardour—[17]

to the day that brings him victory or defeat in the green fairy circle.[18] Is not this life more sweet than mine?[19] I was going to say; but I will not libel any life by comparing it to mine, which is (at the date of these presents) bitter as coloquintida[20] and the dregs of aconitum! . . .[21]

Our present business was to get beds and a supper at an inn; but this was no easy task. The public-houses were full, and where you saw a light at a private house, and people poking their heads out of the casement to see what was going on, they instantly put them in and shut the window, the moment you seemed advancing with a suspicious overture for accommodation. Our guard and coachman thundered away at the outer gate of the Crown for some time without effect—such was the greater noise within; —and when the doors were unbarred, and we got admittance, we found a party assembled in

---

10 Chopfallen, with jaw hanging. Hazlitt's quotation marks indicate that *Hamlet,* V, i, 212, is in his mind.
11 Jack Martin, the Baker. He had several epic fights with Jack Randall, who was known as the Prime Irish Lad.
12 Cheering.   13 *Sub rosa,* on the sly.

14 Bill Richmond, a black boxer and instructor.
15 Cf. *Macbeth,* III, iv, 38–39.
16 Cf. Burns, "Address to the Unco Guid," line 33 (p. 44).
17 Cf. *Henry V,* IV, i, 293–94.
18 Circles of luxuriant grass used to be called fairy rings. Hazlitt is jocosely confusing them with the prize ring. Matches used to be fought out of doors, on the turf.
19 Cf. *As You Like It,* II, i, 2.
20 *Othello,* I, iii, 355–56. *Coloquintida* = the vine and fruit colocynth; *aconitum* is a poisonous herb.
21 A paragraph is here omitted, describing the rest of the journey, and Hazlitt's reunion with his friend "Joe Toms" (actually Joseph Parkes, a young lawyer), from whom he had become separated on the way.

the kitchen round a good hospitable fire, some sleeping, others drinking, others talking on politics and on the fight. A tall English yeoman (something like Matthews[22] in the face, and quite as great a wag)—

A lusty man to ben an abbot able,—[23]

was making such a prodigious noise about rent and taxes, and the price of corn now and formerly, that he had prevented us from being heard at the gate. The first thing I heard him say was to a shuffling fellow who wanted to be off a bet for a shilling glass of brandy and water —"Confound it, man, don't be *insipid!*" Thinks I, that is a good phrase. It was a good omen. He kept it up so all night, nor flinched with the approach of morning. He was a fine fellow, with sense, wit, and spirit, a hearty body and a joyous mind, free-spoken, frank, convivial—one of that true English breed that went with Harry the Fifth to the siege of Harfleur—"standing like greyhounds in the slips,"[24] &c. We ordered tea and eggs (beds were soon found to be out of the question) and this fellow's conversation was *sauce piquante*. It did one's heart good to see him brandish his oaken towel[25] and to hear him talk. He made mince-meat of a drunken, stupid, red-face, quarrelsome, *frowsy* farmer, whose nose "he moralised into a thousand similes,"[26] making it out a firebrand like Bardolph's.[27] "I'll tell you what, my friend," says he, "the landlady has only to keep you here to save fire and candle. If one was to touch your nose, it would go off like a piece of charcoal." At this the other only grinned like an idiot, the sole variety in his purple face being his little peering grey eyes and yellow teeth; called for another glass, swore he would not stand it; and after many attempts to provoke his humorous antagonist to single combat, which the other turned off (after working him up to a ludicrous pitch of choler) with great adroitness, he fell quietly asleep with a glass of liquor in his hand, which he could not lift to his head. His laugh-

ing persecutor made a speech over him, and turning to the opposite side of the room, where they were all sleeping in the midst of this "loud and furious fun,"[28] said, "There's a scene, by G—d, for Hogarth[29] to paint. I think he and Shakespear were our two best men at copying life." This confirmed me in my good opinion of him. Hogarth, Shakespear, and Nature, were just enough for him (indeed for any man) to know. I said, "You read Cobbett, don't you? At least," says I, "you talk just as well as he writes." He seemed to doubt this. But I said, "We have an hour to spare: if you'll get pen, ink, and paper, and keep on talking, I'll write down what you say; and if it doesn't make a capital Political Register,[30] I'll forfeit my head. You have kept me alive to-night, however. I don't know what I should have done without you." He did not dislike this view of the thing, nor my asking if he was not about the size of Jem Belcher; and told me soon afterwards, in the confidence of friendship, that "the circumstance which had given him nearly the greatest concern in his life, was Cribb's beating Jem[31] after he had lost his eye by racket-playing."—The morning dawns; that dim but yet clear light appears, which weighs like solid bars of metal on the sleepless eyelids; the guests drop down from their chambers one by one—but it was too late to think of going to bed now (the clock was on the stroke of seven), we had nothing for it but to find a barber's (the pole that glittered in the morning sun lighted us to his shop), and then a nine miles' march to Hungerford. The day was fine, the sky was blue, the mists were retiring from the marshy ground, the path was tolerably dry, the sitting-up all night had not done us much harm—at least the cause was good; we talked of this and that with amicable difference, roving and sipping of many subjects, but still invariably we returned to the fight. At length, a mile to the left of Hungerford, on a gentle eminence, we saw the ring surrounded by covered carts, gigs, and carriages, of which hundreds had passed us on the road; Toms[32] gave a youthful

---

22 Charles Matthews (1776–1835), a leading London comedian.
23 Cf. Chaucer, *The Canterbury Tales,* General Prologue, line 167.   24 Cf. *Henry V,* III, i, 31.   25 Staff.
26 Cf. *As You Like It,* II, i, 44–45.
27 Whose red face in *1* and *2 Henry IV, Henry V,* and *The Merry Wives of Windsor* is a stock theme for jesting.

28 Perhaps reminiscent of Burns's "Tam o' Shanter," line 148 (p. 48).   29 The eighteenth-century realist.
30 Cobbett's weekly paper.
31 In 1807 and 1809 the great champion Tom Cribb (1781–1848) beat James Belcher (1781–1811), whose career had been successful till he lost an eye in 1803.
32 See note 21.

shout, and we hastened down a narrow lane to the scene of action.

Reader, have you ever seen a fight? If not, you have a pleasure to come, at least if it is a fight like that between the Gas-man and Bill Neate. The crowd was very great when we arrived on the spot; open carriages were coming up, with streamers flying and music playing, and the country-people were pouring in over hedge and ditch in all directions, to see their hero beat or be beaten. The odds were still on Gas, but only about five to four. Gully[33] had been down to try Neate, and had backed him considerably, which was a damper to the sanguine confidence of the adverse party. About two hundred thousand pounds were pending. The Gas says, he has lost 3000*l.* which were promised him by different gentlemen if he had won. He had presumed too much on himself, which had made others presume on him. This spirited and formidable young fellow seems to have taken for his motto the old maxim, that "there are three things necessary to success in life—*Impudence! Impudence! Impudence!*" It is so in matters of opinion, but not in the FANCY, which is the most practical of all things, though even here confidence is half the battle, but only half. Our friend had vapoured[34] and swaggered too much, as if he wanted to grin and bully his adversary out of the fight. "Alas! the Bristol man was not so tamed!"[35]—"This is *the grave-digger*" (would Tom Hickman exclaim in the moments of intoxication from gin and success, shewing his tremendous right hand), "this will send many of them to their long homes; I haven't done with them yet!" Why should he—though he had licked four of the best men within the hour, yet why should he threaten to inflict dishonorable chastisement on my old master Richmond,[36] a veteran going off the stage, and who has borne his sable honors meekly? Magnanimity, my dear Tom, and bravery, should be inseparable. Or why should he go up to his antagonist, the first time he ever saw him at the Fives[37] Court, and measuring him from head to foot with a glance of contempt, as Achilles surveyed Hector,[38] say to him, "What, are you Bill Neate? I'll knock more blood out of that great carcase of thine, this day fortnight, than you ever knock'd out of a bullock's!" It was not manly, 'twas not fighter-like. If he was sure of victory (as he was not), the less said about it the better. Modesty should accompany the FANCY as its shadow. The best men were always the best behaved. Jem Belcher, the Game Chicken[39] (before whom the Gas-man could not have lived) were civil, silent men. So is Cribb, so is Tom Belcher,[40] the most elegant of sparrers, and not a man for every one to take by the nose. I enlarged on this topic in the mail (while Turtle was asleep), and said very wisely (as I thought) that impertinence was a part of no profession. A boxer was bound to beat his man, but not to thrust his fist, either actually or by implication, in every one's face. Even a highwayman, in the way of trade, may blow out your brains, but if he uses foul language at the same time, I should say he was no gentleman. A boxer, I would infer, need not be a blackguard or a coxcomb, more than another. Perhaps I press this point too much on a fallen man—Mr. Thomas Hickman has by this time learnt that first of all lessons, "That man was made to mourn."[41] He has lost nothing by the late fight but his presumption; and that every man may do as well without! By an over-display of this quality, however, the public had been prejudiced against him, and the *knowing-ones* were taken in. Few but those who had bet on him wished Gas to win. With my own prepossessions on the subject, the result of the 11th of December appeared to me as fine a piece of poetical justice as I had ever witnessed. The difference of weight between the two combatants (14 stone[42] to 12) was nothing to the sporting men. Great, heavy, clumsy, long-armed Bill Neate kicked the beam in the scale of the Gas-man's vanity. The amateurs were frightened at his big

33 John Gully (1783–1863), a retired prize fighter of great fame. 34 Bragged. 35 Cf. Cowper, *The Task*, II, 322. 36 See note 14. Apparently Hazlitt had taken boxing lessons from him. 37 A game similar to handball. The Fives Court was a building near Leicester Square devoted to sports, including boxing. Hazlitt used to play rackets there for hours on end. 38 Cf. *Iliad*, XXII, 260 ff. 39 Henry Pearce (1777–1809), a great fighter. He was a pupil of Jem Belcher, who came out of retirement for a match with him and was beaten. 40 A brother of Jem Belcher and, though not his equal as a slugger, an accomplished boxer. 41 The title of a poem by Burns. 42 An English weight equal to fourteen pounds.

words, and thought that they would make up for the difference of six feet and five feet nine. Truly, the FANCY are not men of imagination. They judge of what has been, and cannot conceive of any thing that is to be. The Gas-man had won hitherto; therefore he must beat a man half as big again as himself—and that to a certainty. Besides, there are as many feuds, factions, prejudices, pedantic notions in the FANCY as in the state or in the schools. Mr. Gully is almost the only cool, sensible man among them, who exercises an unbiassed discretion, and is not a slave to his passions in these matters. But enough of reflections, and to our tale. The day, as I have said, was fine for a December morning. The grass was wet, and the ground miry, and ploughed up with multitudinous feet, except that, within the ring itself, there was a spot of virgin-green closed in and unprofaned by vulgar tread, that shone with dazzling brightness in the mid-day sun. For it was now noon, and we had an hour to wait. This is the trying time. It is then the heart sickens, as you think what the two champions are about, and how short a time will determine their fate. After the first blow is struck, there is no opportunity for nervous apprehensions; you are swallowed up in the immediate interest of the scene—but

> Between the acting of a dreadful thing
> And the first motion, all the interim is
> Like a phantasma, or a hideous dream.[43]

I found it so as I felt the sun's rays clinging to my back, and saw the white wintry clouds sink below the verge of the horizon. "So," I thought, "my fairest hopes have faded from my sight!—so will the Gas-man's glory, or that of his adversary, vanish in an hour." The *swells* were parading in their white box-coats, the outer ring was cleared with some bruises on the heads and shins of the rustic assembly (for the *cockneys*[44] had been distanced by the sixty-six miles); the time drew near, I had got a good stand; a bustle, a buzz, ran through the crowd, and from the opposite side entered Neate, between his second and bottle-holder. He rolled along, swathed in his loose great coat, his knock-knees bending under his huge bulk; and, with a modest cheer-

ful air, threw his hat into the ring. He then just looked round, and began quietly to undress; when from the other side there was a similar rush and an opening made, and the Gas-man came forward with a conscious air of anticipated triumph, too much like the cock-of-the-walk. He strutted about more than became a hero, sucked oranges with a supercilious air, and threw away the skin with a toss of his head, and went up and looked at Neate, which was an act of supererogation.[45] The only sensible thing he did was, as he strode away from the modern Ajax, to fling out his arms, as if he wanted to try whether they would do their work that day. By this time they had stripped, and presented a strong contrast in appearance. If Neate was like Ajax, "with Atlantean[46] shoulders, fit to bear" the pugilistic reputation of all Bristol, Hickman might be compared to Diomed,[47] light, vigorous, elastic, and his back glistened in the sun, as he moved about, like a panther's hide. There was now a dead pause—attention was awe-struck. Who at that moment, big with a great event, did not draw his breath short—did not feel his heart throb? All was ready. They tossed up for the sun, and the Gas-man won. They were led up to the *scratch*—shook hands, and went at it.

In the first round every one thought it was all over. After making play a short time, the Gas-man flew at his adversary like a tiger, struck five blows in as many seconds, three first, and then following him as he staggered back, two more, right and left, and down he fell, a mighty ruin. There was a shout, and I said, "There is no standing this." Neate seemed like a lifeless lump of flesh and bone, round which the Gas-man's blows played with the rapidity of electricity or lightning, and you imagined he would only be lifted up to be knocked down again. It was as if Hickman held a sword or a fire in that right hand of his, and directed it against an unarmed body. They met again, and Neate seemed, not cowed, but particularly cautious. I saw his teeth clenched together and his brows knit close against the sun. He held out both his arms at full length straight before him, like two sledge-hammers, and raised his left an inch or two higher. The

---

43 *Julius Caesar*, II, i, 63–65.
44 Londoners. The rustics, who lived nearer, got there first.

45 An unnecessary action.
46 Strong; resembling Atlas, the Titan who held up the heavens. Hazlitt is quoting *Paradise Lost*, II, 306.
47 One of the Greek heroes in the *Iliad*.

Gas-man could not get over this guard—they struck mutually and fell, but without advantage on either side. It was the same in the next round; but the balance of power was thus restored—the fate of the battle was suspended. No one could tell how it would end. This was the only moment in which opinion was divided; for, in the next, the Gas-man aiming a mortal blow at his adversary's neck, with his right hand, and failing from the length he had to reach, the other returned it with his left at full swing, planted a tremendous blow on his cheek-bone and eyebrow, and made a red ruin of that side of his face. The Gas-man went down, and there was another shout—a roar of triumph as the waves of fortune rolled tumultuously from side to side. This was a settler. Hickman got up, and "grinned horrible a ghastly smile,"[48] yet he was evidently dashed in his opinion of himself; it was the first time he had ever been so punished; all one side of his face was perfect scarlet, and his right eye was closed in dingy blackness, as he advanced to the fight, less confident, but still determined. After one or two rounds, not receiving another such remembrancer, he rallied and went at it with his former impetuosity. But in vain. His strength had been weakened,—his blows could not tell at such a distance,—he was obliged to fling himself at his adversary, and could not strike from his feet; and almost as regularly as he flew at him with his right hand, Neate warded the blow, or drew back out of its reach, and felled him with the return of his left. There was little cautious sparring—no half-hits—no tapping and trifling, none of the *petitmaîtreship*[49] of the art—they were almost all knock-down blows:—the fight was a good stand up fight. The wonder was the half-minute time. If there had been a minute or more allowed between each round, it would have been intelligible how they should by degrees recover strength and resolution; but to see two men smashed to the ground, smeared with gore, stunned, senseless, the breath beaten out of their bodies; and then, before you recover from the shock, to see them rise up with new strength and courage, stand steady to inflict or receive mortal offence, and rush upon each other "like two clouds over the Caspian"[50]—this

is the most astonishing thing of all:—this is the high and heroic state of man! From this time forward the event became more certain every round; and about the twelfth it seemed as if it must have been over. Hickman generally stood with his back to me; but in the scuffle, he had changed positions, and Neate just then made a tremendous lunge at him, and hit him full in the face. It was doubtful whether he would fall backwards or forwards; he hung suspended for a second or two, and then fell back, throwing his hands in the air, and with his face lifted up to the sky. I never saw any thing more terrific than his aspect just before he fell. All traces of life, of natural expression, were gone from him. His face was like a human skull, a death's head, spouting blood. The eyes were filled with blood, the nose streamed with blood, the mouth gaped blood. He was not like an actual man, but like a preternatural, spectral appearance, or like one of the figures in Dante's *Inferno*. Yet he fought on after this for several rounds, still striking the first desperate blow, and Neate standing on the defensive, and using the same cautious guard to the last, as if he had still all his work to do; and it was not till the Gas-man was so stunned in the seventeenth or eighteenth round, that his senses forsook him, and he could not come to time, that the battle was declared over.[51] Ye who despise the FANCY, do something to shew as much *pluck*, or as much self-possession as this, before you assume a superiority which you have never given a single proof of by any one action in the whole course of your lives!—When the Gas-man came to himself, the first words he uttered were, "Where am I? What is the matter?" "Nothing is the matter, Tom—you have lost the battle, but you are the bravest man alive." And Jackson[52] whispered to him, "I am collecting a

---

48 Cf. *Paradise Lost*, II, 846.
49 Little-mastership, dandified mastery.
50 Cf. *Paradise Lost*, II, 714–16.

51 Footnote by Hazlitt: "Scroggins said of the Gas-man, that he thought he was a man of that courage, that if his hands were cut off, he would still fight on with the stumps—like that of Widrington,—

'—In doleful dumps,
Who, when his legs were smitten off,
Still fought upon his stumps.'"

For the gallant squire Witherington, see the ballad "Chevy Chase," lines 93–104, 197–200. Jack Scroggins the Sailor (his real name was John Palmer) was another well-known prize fighter.
52 Presumably the retired prize fighter John ("Gentleman") Jackson (1769–1845), long the sporting world's leading figure. Byron took lessons from him.

purse for you, Tom."—Vain sounds, and unheard at that moment! Neate instantly went up and shook him cordially by the hand, and seeing some old acquaintance, began to flourish with his fists, calling out, "Ah, you always said I couldn't fight—What do you think now?" But all in good humour, and without any appearance of arrogance; only it was evident Bill Neate was pleased that he had won the fight. When it was over, I asked Cribb if he did not think it was a good one? He said, *"Pretty well!"* The carrier-pigeons now mounted into the air, and one of them flew with the news of her husband's victory to the bosom of Mrs. Neate. Alas, for Mrs. Hickman! . . .[53]

from My First Acquaintance with Poets

This essay appeared in the *Liberal* for April, 1823.

My father was a Dissenting Minister at W—m[1] in Shropshire; and in the year 1798 (the figures that compose that date are to me like the "dreaded name of Demogorgon"[2]) Mr. Coleridge came to Shrewsbury, to succeed Mr. Rowe in the spiritual charge of a Unitarian congregation there. He did not come till late on the Saturday afternoon before he was to preach; and Mr. Rowe, who himself went down to the coach in a state of anxiety and expectation, to look for the arrival of his successor, could find no one at all answering the description but a round-faced man in a short black coat (like a shooting jacket) which hardly seemed to have been made for him, but who seemed to be talking at a great rate to his fellow-passengers. Mr. Rowe had scarce returned to give an account of his disappointment, when the round-faced man in black entered, and dissipated all doubts on the subject, by beginning to talk. He did not cease while he staid; nor has he since, that I know of. He held the good town of Shrewsbury in delightful suspense for three weeks that he re-

mained there, "fluttering the *proud Salopians*[3] like an eagle in dove-cote";[4] and the Welsh mountains that skirt the horizon with their tempestuous confusion, agree to have heard no such mystic sounds since the days of

High-born Hoel's harp or soft Llewellyn's lay![5]

As we passed along between W—m and Shrewsbury, and I eyed their blue tops seen through the wintry branches, or the red rustling leaves of the sturdy oak-trees by the road-side, a sound was in my ears as of a Siren's song;[6] I was stunned, startled with it, as from deep sleep; but I had no notion then that I should ever be able to express my admiration to others in motley imagery or quaint allusion, till the light of his genius shone into my soul, like the sun's rays glittering in the puddles of the road. I was at that time dumb, inarticulate, helpless, like a worm by the way-side, crushed, bleeding, lifeless; but now, bursting from the deadly bands that bound them,

With Styx nine times round them,[7]

my ideas float on winged words, and as they expand their plumes, catch the golden light of other years. My soul has indeed remained in its original bondage, dark, obscure, with longings infinite and unsatisfied;[8] my heart, shut up in the prison-house of this rude clay, has never found, nor will it ever find, a heart to speak to; but that my understanding also did not remain dumb and brutish, or at length found a language to express itself, I owe to Coleridge. But this is not to my purpose.

My father lived ten miles from Shrewsbury, and was in the habit of exchanging visits with Mr. Rowe, and with Mr. Jenkins of Whitchurch (nine miles farther on) according to the custom of Dissenting Ministers in each other's neighbourhood. A line of communication is thus established, by which the flame of civil and religious

---

[53] The remainder of the essay tells of the journey back to London.

[1] Wem, a village about ten miles north of Shrewsbury.
[2] *Paradise Lost*, II, 964–65. Demogorgon, a mysterious demon, was formerly credited with "a primordial creative power."

[3] *Salop* is another name for Shropshire.
[4] Cf. Shakespeare's *Coriolanus*, V, vi, 115–16.
[5] Gray, "The Bard," line 28.
[6] In the *Odyssey*, Book XII, the sea nymphs known as the Sirens attempt by their singing to lure the sailors to destruction.
[7] Cf. Pope, "Ode on St. Cecilia's Day," lines 90–91.
[8] Cf. Wordsworth, "The Affliction of Margaret," line 63.

liberty is kept alive, and nourishes its smouldering fire unquenchable, like the fires in the Agamemnon[9] of Aeschylus, placed at different stations, that waited for ten long years to announce with their blazing pyramids the destruction of Troy. Coleridge had agreed to come over to see my father, according to the courtesy of the country, as Mr. Rowe's probable successor; but in the meantime I had gone to hear him preach the Sunday after his arrival. A poet and a philosopher getting up into a Unitarian pulpit to preach the Gospel, was a romance in these degenerate days, a sort of revival of the primitive spirit of Christianity, which was not to be resisted.

It was in January, 1798, that I rose one morning before daylight, to walk ten miles in the mud, and went to hear this celebrated person preach. Never, the longest day I have to live, shall I have such another walk as this cold, raw, comfortless one, in the winter of the year 1798. *Il y a des impressions que ni le tems ni les circonstances peuvent effacer. Dusse-je vivre des siècles entiers, le doux tems de ma jeunesse ne peut renaître pour moi, ni s'effacer jamais dans ma mémoire.*[10] When I got there, the organ was playing the 100th psalm, and, when it was done, Mr. Coleridge rose and gave out his text, "And he went up into the mountain to pray, HIMSELF, ALONE."[11] As he gave out his text, his voice "rose like a steam of rich distilled perfumes,"[12] and when he came to the two last words, which he pronounced loud, deep, and distinct, it seemed to me, who was then young, as if the sounds had echoed from the bottom of the human heart, and as if that prayer might have floated in solemn silence through the universe. The idea of St. John came into mind, "of one crying in the wilderness, who had his loins girt about, and whose food was locusts and wild honey."[13] The preacher then launched into his subject, like an eagle dallying with the wind. The sermon was

upon peace and war; upon church and state—not their alliance, but their separation—on the spirit of the world and the spirit of Christianity, not as the same, but as opposed to one another. He talked of those who had "inscribed the cross of Christ on banners dripping with human gore." He made a poetical and pastoral excursion,—and to shew the fatal effects of war, drew a striking contrast between the simple shepherd boy, driving his team afield, or sitting under the hawthorn, piping to his flock, "as though he should never be old,"[14] and the same poor country-lad, crimped,[15] kidnapped, brought into town, made drunk at an ale-house, turned into a wretched drummer-boy, with his hair sticking on end with powder and pomatum,[16] a long cue at his back, and tricked out in the loathsome finery of the profession of blood.

Such were the notes our once-lov'd poet sung.[17]

And for myself, I could not have been more delighted if I had heard the music of the spheres.[18] Poetry and Philosophy had met together. Truth and Genius had embraced,[19] under the eye and with the sanction of Religion. This was even beyond my hopes. I returned home well satisfied. The sun that was still labouring pale and wan through the sky, obscured by thick mists, seemed an emblem of the *good cause;*[20] and the cold dank drops of dew that hung half melted on the beard of the thistle, had something genial and refreshing in them; for there was a spirit of hope and youth in all nature, that turned every thing into good. The face of nature had not then the brand of JUS DIVINUM[21] on it:

Like to that sanguine flower inscrib'd with woe.[22]

On the Tuesday following, the half-inspired[23] speaker came. I was called down into

9 One of the greatest of the Greek tragedies (fifth century B.C.).

10 There are some impressions which neither time nor circumstances can efface. If I should live for whole centuries, the sweet time of my youth cannot be reborn for me nor ever efface itself in my memory. (Misquoted from Rousseau's epistolary romance *Julie, ou La Nouvelle Héloïse* [1761], Part VI, letter 7.)

11 Cf. John 6:15.   12 Milton, *Comus,* line 556.

13 Cf. Matthew 3:3, 4.

14 From Sir Philip Sidney's *Arcadia,* Book I, chap. 2.

15 Trapped or lured into enlisting.

16 Pomade, hair grease.

17 Cf. Pope, "Epistle to Robert, Earl of Oxford," line 1.

18 The celestial spheres, which according to the Ptolemaic astronomy moved round the earth.   19 Cf. Psalms 85:10.

20 Of liberty and revolution.   21 Divine Right (of kings).

22 Milton, "Lycidas," line 106. The flower is the hyacinth, whose petals were supposed to be marked with the Greek exclamation of lament, *ai, ai.*

23 I.e., in part supernaturally motivated.

the room where he was, and went half-hoping, half-afraid. He received me very graciously, and I listened for a long time without uttering a word. I did not suffer in his opinion by my silence. "For those two hours," he afterwards was pleased to say, "he was conversing with W.H.'s forehead!" His appearance was different from what I had anticipated from seeing him before. At a distance, and in the dim light of the chapel, there was to me a strange wildness in his aspect, a dusky obscurity, and I thought him pitted with the small-pox. His complexion was at that time clear, and even bright—

As are the children of yon azure sheen.[24]

His forehead was broad and high, light as if built of ivory, with large projecting eyebrows, and his eyes rolling beneath them like a sea with darkened lustre. "A certain tender bloom his face o'erspread,"[25] a purple tinge as we see it in the pale thoughtful complexions of the Spanish portrait-painters,[26] Murillo and Velasquez. His mouth was gross, voluptuous, open, eloquent; his chin good-humoured and round; but his nose, the rudder of the face, the index of the will, was small, feeble, nothing—like what he has done. It might seem that the genius of his face as from a height surveyed and projected him (with sufficient capacity and huge aspiration) into the world unknown of thought and imagination, with nothing to support or guide his veering purpose, as if Columbus had launched his adventurous course for the New World in a scallop,[27] without oars or compass. So at least I comment on it after the event. Coleridge in his person was rather above the common size, inclining to the corpulent, or like Lord Hamlet, "somewhat fat and pursy."[28] His hair (now, alas! grey) was then black and glossy as the raven's, and fell in smooth masses over his forehead. This long pendulous hair is peculiar to enthusiasts, to those whose minds tend heavenward; and is traditionally inseparable (though of a different colour) from the pictures of Christ. It ought to belong, as a character, to all who preach *Christ*

crucified, and Coleridge was at that time one of those!

It was curious to observe the contrast between him and my father, who was a veteran in the cause, and then declining into the vale of years.[29] He had been a poor Irish lad, carefully brought up by his parents, and sent to the University of Glasgow (where he studied under Adam Smith[30]) to prepare him for his future destination. It was his mother's proudest wish to see her son a Dissenting Minister. So if we look back to past generations (as far as eye can reach) we see the same hopes, fears, wishes, followed by the same disappointments, throbbing in the human heart; and so we may see them (if we look forward) rising up for ever, and disappearing, like vapourish bubbles, in the human breast! After being tossed about from congregation to congregation in the heats of the Unitarian controversy, and squabbles about the American war, he had been relegated to an obscure village, where he was to spend the last thirty years of his life, far from the only converse that he loved, the talk about disputed texts of Scripture and the cause of civil and religious liberty. Here he passed his days, repining but resigned, in the study of the Bible, and the perusal of the Commentators,—huge folios, not easily got through, one of which would outlast a winter! Why did he pore on these from morn to night (with the exception of a walk in the fields or a turn in the garden to gather broccoli-plants or kidney-beans of his own rearing, with no small degree of pride and pleasure)? Here were "no figures nor no fantasies"[31]—neither poetry nor philosophy—nothing to dazzle, nothing to excite modern curiosity; but to his lack-lustre eyes there appeared, within the pages of the ponderous, unwieldly, neglected tomes, the sacred name of JEHOVAH in Hebrew capitals: pressed down by the weight of the style, worn to the last fading thinness of the understanding, there were glimpses, glimmering notions of the patriarchal wanderings, with palm-trees hovering in the horizon, and processions of camels at the distance of three thousand years; there was Moses with the Burning Bush,[32] the number of the Twelve Tribes, types, shadows, glosses on

---

[24] Cf. James Thomson, *The Castle of Indolence,* II, xxxiii, 7.   [25] Cf. ibid., I, lvii, 3.   [26] Of the seventeenth century.
[27] *Shallop,* a kind of light, open boat.
[28] Short-winded. Misquoted from *Hamlet,* V, ii, 298.

[29] Cf. *Othello,* III, iii, 265–66.
[30] The economist and philosopher (1723–1790).
[31] *Julius Caesar,* II, i, 231.   [32] Exodus 3:1–6.

the law and the prophets; there were discussions (dull enough) on the age of Methuselah,[33] a mighty speculation! there were outlines, rude guesses at the shape of Noah's Ark and of the riches of Solomon's Temple; questions as to the date of the creation, predictions of the end of all things; the great lapses of time, the strange mutations of the globe were unfolded with the voluminous leaf, as it turned over; and though the soul might slumber with an hieroglyphic veil of inscrutable mysteries drawn over it, yet it was in a slumber ill-exchanged for all the sharpened realities of sense, wit, fancy, or reason. My father's life was comparatively a dream; but it was a dream of infinity and eternity, of death, the resurrection, and a judgment to come!

No two individuals were ever more unlike than were the host and his guest. A poet was to my father a sort of nondescript: yet whatever added grace to the Unitarian cause was to him welcome. He could hardly have been more surprised or pleased, if our visitor had worn wings. Indeed, his thoughts had wings; and as the silken sounds rustled round our little wainscoted parlour, my father threw back his spectacles over his forehead, his white hairs mixing with its sanguine hue; and a smile of delight beamed across his rugged cordial face, to think that Truth had found a new ally in Fancy.[34] Besides, Coleridge seemed to take considerable notice of me, and that of itself was enough. He talked very familiarly, but agreeably, and glanced over a variety of subjects. At dinner-time he grew more animated, and dilated in a very edifying manner on Mary Wolstonecraft[35] and Mackintosh.[36] The last, he said, he considered (on my father's speaking of his *Vindiciae Gallicae* as a capital performance) as a clever scholastic man—a master of the topics,—or as the ready warehouse-man of letters, who knew exactly where to lay his hand

on what he wanted, though the goods were not his own. He thought him no match for Burke, either in style or matter. Burke was a metaphysician, Mackintosh a mere logician. Burke was an orator (almost a poet) who reasoned in figures, because he had an eye for nature: Mackintosh, on the other hand, was a rhetorician, who had only an eye to common-places. On this I ventured to say that I had always entertained a great opinion of Burke, and that (as far as I could find) the speaking of him with contempt might be made the test of a vulgar democratical mind. This was the first observation I ever made to Coleridge, and he said it was a very just and striking one. I remember the leg of Welsh mutton and the turnips on the table that day had the finest flavour imaginable. Coleridge added that Mackintosh and Tom Wedgwood[37] (of whom, however, he spoke highly) had expressed a very indifferent opinion of his friend Mr. Wordsworth, on which he remarked to them—"He strides on so far before you, that he dwindles in the distance!" Godwin had once boasted to him of having carried on an argument with Mackintosh for three hours with dubious success; Coleridge told him—"If there had been a man of genius in the room, he would have settled the question in five minutes." He asked me if I had ever seen Mary Wolstonecraft, and I said, I had once for a few moments, and that she seemed to me to turn off Godwin's objections to something she advanced with quite a playful, easy air. He replied, that "this was only one instance of the ascendancy which people of imagination exercised over those of mere intellect." He did not rate Godwin very high[38] (this was caprice or prejudice, real or affected) but he had a great idea of Mrs. Wolstonecraft's powers of conversation, none at all of her talent for book-making. We talked a little about Holcroft.[39] He had been asked if he was not much struck *with* him,

---

[33] According to Genesis 5:27, he lived 969 years.

[34] Hazlitt's note: "My father was one of those who mistook his talent after all. He used to be very much dissatisfied that I preferred his Letters to his Sermons. The last were forced and dry; the first came naturally from him. For ease, half-plays on words, and a supine, monkish, indolent pleasantry, I have never seen them equalled."

[35] A well-known writer (1759–1797), wife of William Godwin and mother of Shelley's second wife. The usual spelling is Wollstonecraft.

[36] Sir James Mackintosh (1765–1832), the Scottish philosopher. He wrote in opposition to Burke, on behalf of the French Revolution.

[37] Brother of the head of the great pottery firm. Their benefaction to Coleridge is described by Hazlitt a little farther on in this essay.

[38] William Godwin (1756–1836), radical philosopher and novelist. Hazlitt's note: "He complained in particular of the presumption of attempting to establish the future immortality of man 'without' (as he said) 'knowing what Death was or what Life was'—and the tone in which he pronounced these two words seemed to convey a complete image of both."

[39] Thomas Holcroft (1745–1809), radical dramatist.

and he said, he thought himself in more danger of being struck *by* him. I complained that he would not let me get on at all, for he required a definition of every the commonest word, explaining, "What do you mean by a *sensation,* Sir? What do you mean by an *idea?*" This, Coleridge said, was barricadoing the road to truth:—it was setting up a turnpike-gate at every step we took. I forget a great number of things, many more than I remember; but the day passed off pleasantly, and the next morning Mr. Coleridge was to return to Shrewsbury. When I came down to breakfast, I found that he had just received a letter from his friend T. Wedgwood, making him an offer of 150*l.* a-year if he chose to wave[40] his present pursuit, and devote himself entirely to the study of poetry and philosophy. Coleridge seemed to make up his mind to close with this proposal in the act of tying on one of his shoes. It threw an additional damp on his departure. It took the wayward enthusiast quite from us to cast him into Deva's winding vales,[41] or by the shores of old romance.[42] Instead of living at ten miles distance, of being the pastor of a Dissenting congregation at Shrewsbury, he was henceforth to inhabit the Hill of Parnassus,[43] to be a shepherd on the Delectable Mountains.[44] Alas! I knew not the way thither, and felt very little gratitude for Mr. Wedgwood's bounty. I was presently relieved from this dilemma; for Mr. Coleridge, asking for a pen and ink, and going to a table to write something on a bit of card, advanced towards me with undulating step, and giving me the precious document, said that that was his address, *Mr. Coleridge, Nether-Stowey, Somersetshire;* and that he should be glad to see me there in a few week's time, and, if I chose, would come half-way to meet me. I was not less surprised than the shepherd-boy (this simile is to be found in Cassandra[45]) when he sees a thunder-bolt fall close at his feet. I stammered out my acknowledgments and acceptance of this offer (I thought Mr. Wedgwood's annuity a trifle to it) as well as I could;

and this mighty business being settled, the poet-preacher took leave, and I accompanied him six miles on the road. It was a fine morning in the middle of winter, and he talked the whole way. The scholar in Chaucer is described as going

—Sounding on his way.[46]

So Coleridge went on his. In digressing, in dilating, in passing from subject to subject, he appeared to me to float in air, to slide on ice. He told me in confidence (going along) that he should have preached two sermons before he accepted the situation at Shrewsbury, one on Infant Baptism, the other on the Lord's Supper, shewing that he could not administer either, which would have effectually disqualified him for the object in view. I observed that he continually crossed me on the way by shifting from one side of the footpath to the other. This struck me as an odd movement; but I did not at that time connect it with any instability of purpose or involuntary change of principle, as I have done since. He seemed unable to keep on in a straight line. He spoke slightingly of Hume[47] (whose essay on Miracles he said was stolen from an objection started in one of South's[48] sermons— *Credat Judaeus Apella!*[49]) I was not very much pleased at this account of Hume, for I had just been reading, with infinite relish, that completest of all metaphysical *choke-pears,*[50] his *Treatise on Human Nature,* to which the *Essays,* in point of scholastic subtlety and close reasoning, are mere elegant trifling, light summer-reading. Coleridge even denied the excellence of Hume's general style, which I think betrayed a want of taste or candour. He however made me amends by the manner in which he spoke of Berkeley.[51] He dwelt particularly on his *Essay on Vision* as a masterpiece of analytical reasoning. So it undoubtedly is. He was exceedingly angry with Dr.

---

40 Waive.

41 *Deva* = the river Dee, in Wales and Cheshire. Cf. Milton, "Lycidas," line 55: "Nor yet where Deva spreads her wizard stream." Hazlitt means that Coleridge decided to dedicate himself to poetry.

42 Wordsworth, "Poems on the Naming of Places," IV, 38.

43 I.e., devote himself to poetry.

44 In John Bunyan's *Pilgrim's Progress.*

45 In the romance *Cassandre* (1642–60) of the French

novelist La Calprenède (Part II, Book 5).

46 Cf. Chaucer, *The Canterbury Tales,* General Prologue, line 307.

47 David Hume (1711–1776), the historian and skeptical philosopher.

48 Robert South (1634–1716), a famous Anglican preacher.

49 Let the Jew Apella believe it—i.e., I shan't. (Horace, *Satires,* I, v, 100.)

50 The sourness of which constricts the throat.

51 For Bishop George Berkeley, the idealistic philosopher (1685–1753), and his verses on America, see Volume I.

Johnson for striking the stone with his foot, in allusion to this author's Theory of Matter and Spirit, and saying, "Thus I confute him, Sir."[52] Coleridge drew a parallel (I don't know how he brought about the connection) between Bishop Berkeley and Tom Paine.[53] He said the one was an instance of a subtle, the other of an acute mind, than which no two things could be more distinct. The one was a shop-boy's quality, the other the characteristic of a philosopher. He considered Bishop Butler[54] as a true philosopher, a profound and conscientious thinker, a genuine reader of nature and of his own mind. He did not speak of his *Analogy*, but of his *Sermons at the Rolls' Chapel*, of which I had never heard. Coleridge somehow always contrived to prefer the *unknown* to the *known*. In this instance he was right. The *Analogy* is a tissue of sophistry, of wire-drawn, theological special-pleading; the *Sermons* (with the Preface to them) are in a fine vein of deep, matured reflection, a candid appeal to our observation of human nature, without pedantry and without bias. I told Coleridge I had written a few remarks, and was sometimes foolish enough to believe that I had made a discovery on the same subject (the *Natural Disinterestedness of the Human Mind*)—and I tried to explain my view of it to Coleridge, who listened with great willingness, but I did not succeed in making myself understood. I sat down to the task shortly afterwards for the twentieth time, got new pens and paper, determined to make clear work of it, wrote a few meagre sentences in the skeleton-style of a mathematical demonstration, stopped half-way down the second page; and, after trying in vain to pump up any words, images, notions, apprehensions, facts, or observations, from that gulph of abstraction in which I had plunged myself for four or five years preceding, gave up the attempt as labour in vain, and shed tears of helpless despondency on the blank unfinished paper. I can write fast enough now. Am I better than I was then? Oh no! One truth discovered, one pang of regret at not being able to express it, is better than all the fluency and flippancy in the world. Would that I could go back to what I then was! Why can we

not revive past times as we can revisit old places? If I had the quaint Muse of Sir Philip Sidney to assist me, I would write a *Sonnet to the Road between W—m and Shrewsbury,* and immortalise every step of it by some fond enigmatical conceit. I would swear that the very milestones had ears, and that Harmer-hill stooped with all its pines, to listen to a poet, as he passed! I remember but one other topic of discourse in this walk. He mentioned Paley,[55] praised the naturalness and clearness of his style, but condemned his sentiments, thought him a mere time-serving casuist, and said that "the fact of his work on Moral and Political Philosophy being made a text-book in our Universities was a disgrace to the national character." We parted at the six-mile stone; and I returned homeward pensive but much pleased. I had met with unexpected notice from a person, whom I believed to have been prejudiced against me. "Kind and affable to me had been his condescension, and should be honoured ever with suitable regard."[56] He was the first poet I had known, and he certainly answered to that inspired name. I had heard a great deal of his powers of conversation, and was not disappointed. In fact, I never met with any thing at all like them, either before or since. I could easily credit the accounts which were circulated of his holding forth to a large party of ladies and gentlemen, an evening or two before, on the Berkeleian Theory, when he made the whole material universe look like a transparency of fine words; and another story (which I believe he has somewhere told himself[57]) of his being asked to a party at Birmingham, of his smoking tobacco and going to sleep after dinner on a sofa, where the company found him to their no small surprise, which was increased to wonder when he started up of a sudden, and rubbing his eyes, looked about him, and launched into a three-hours' description of the third heaven, of which he had had a dream, very different from Mr. Southey's Vision of Judgment, and also from that other Vision of Judgment, which Mr. Murray, the Secretary of the Bridge-street Junto, has taken into his especial keeping![58]

---

52 Cf. Boswell's *Johnson,* ed. Hill, I, 471.
53 The revolutionist and Deist (1737–1809).
54 Joseph Butler (1692–1752), an Anglican theologian.

55 William Paley, author of the long-popular *Evidences of Christianity* (1794).   56 Cf. *Paradise Lost*, VIII, 648–50.
57 Part of this story appears in *Biographia Literaria*, chap. X.
58 Southey's poem describes the entrance of George III

On my way back, I had a sound in my ears, it was the voice of Fancy: I had a light before me, it was the face of Poetry. The one still lingers there, the other has not quitted my side! Coleridge in truth met me half-way on the ground of philosophy, or I should not have been won over to his imaginative creed. I had an uneasy, pleasurable sensation all the time, till I was to visit him. During those months the chill breath of winter gave me a welcoming; the vernal air was balm and inspiration to me. The golden sunsets, the silver star of evening, lighted me on my way to new hopes and prospects. *I was to visit Coleridge in the spring.* This circumstance was never absent from my thoughts, and mingled with all my feelings. I wrote to him at the time proposed, and received an answer postponing my intended visit for a week or two, but very cordially urging me to complete my promise then. This delay did not damp, but rather increased my ardour. In the meantime I went to Llangollen Vale, by way of initiating myself in the mysteries of natural scenery; and I must say I was enchanted with it. I had been reading Coleridge's description of England, in his fine *Ode on the Departing Year,* and I applied it, *con amore,*[59] to the objects before me. That valley was to me (in a manner) the cradle of a new existence: in the river that winds through it, my spirit was baptised in the waters of Helicon![60]

I returned home, and soon after set out on my journey with unworn heart and untired feet. . . .[61]

The next day Wordsworth arrived from Bristol at Coleridge's cottage. I think I see him now. He answered in some degree to his friend's description of him, but was more gaunt and Don Quixote-like. He was quaintly dressed (according to the *costume* of that unconstrained period) in a brown fustian[62] jacket and striped pantaloons. There was something of a roll, a lounge in his gait, not unlike his own Peter Bell.[63] There was a severe, worn pressure of thought about his temples, a fire in his eye (as if he saw something in objects more than the outward appearance), an intense high narrow forehead, a Roman nose, cheeks furrowed by strong purpose and feeling, and a convulsive inclination to laughter about the mouth, a good deal at variance with the solemn, stately expression of the rest of his face. Chantry's[64] bust wants the marking traits; but he was teazed into making it regular and heavy: Haydon's[65] head of him, introduced into the *Entrance of Christ into Jerusalem,* is the most like his drooping weight of thought and expression. He sat down and talked very naturally and freely, with a mixture of clear gushing accents in his voice, a deep guttural intonation, and a strong tincture of the northern *burr,* like the crust on wine. He instantly began to make havoc of the half of a Cheshire cheese on the table, and said triumphantly that "his marriage with experience had not been so unproductive as Mr. Southey's in teaching him a knowledge of the good things of this life." He had been to see the *Castle Spectre,* by Monk Lewis,[66] while at Bristol, and described it very well. He said "it fitted the taste of the audience like a glove." This *ad captandum*[67] merit was however by no means a recommendation of it, according to the severe principles of the new school, which reject rather than court popular effect. Wordsworth, looking out of the low, latticed window, said, "How beautifully the sun sets on that yellow bank!" I thought within myself, "With what eyes these poets see nature!" and ever after, when I saw the sun-set stream upon the objects facing it, conceived I had made a discovery, or thanked Mr. Wordsworth for having made one for me! We went over to All-Foxden[68] again the day following, and Wordsworth read us the story of Peter

into heaven. Byron had written a satire on it. Charles Murray, a lawyer, was secretary of the Constitutional Association for Opposing Disloyal and Seditious Principles; its office was on New Bridge Street, in the Blackfriars district of London.

[59] With love, zestfully.

[60] The Greek mountain in Boeotia where Apollo and the Muses dwelt; to them its springs were sacred.

[61] In a passage here omitted, Hazlitt describes his walk to Nether Stowey and his reception by Coleridge.

[62] A heavy cotton material similar to corduroy.

[63] In the poem thus entitled.

[64] Sir Francis L. Chantrey (d. 1841), a sculptor and painter.

[65] Benjamin Robert Haydon (1786–1846), a historical painter. He also introduced a portrait of Keats into this picture.

[66] Matthew Gregory Lewis (1775–1818), known as "Monk" from the title of one of his romances, wrote "Gothic" novels, plays, and poems; *The Castle Spectre* was a musical play.

[67] *Ad captandum* [*vulgus*], for the sake of pleasing the crowd.

[68] Coleridge had already taken Hazlitt to Alfoxden, but Wordsworth was away.

Bell in the open air; and the comment made upon it by his face and voice was very different from that of some later critics! Whatever might be thought of the poem, "his face was a book where men might read strange matters,"[69] and he announced the fate of his hero in prophetic tones. There is a *chaunt* in the recitation both of Coleridge and Wordsworth, which acts as a spell upon the hearer, and disarms the judgment. Perhaps they have deceived themselves by making habitual use of this ambiguous accompaniment. Coleridge's manner is more full, animated, and varied; Wordsworth's more equable, sustained, and internal. The one might be termed more *dramatic,* the other more *lyrical.* Coleridge has told me that he himself liked to compose in walking over uneven ground, or breaking through the straggling branches of a copse-wood; whereas Wordsworth always wrote (if he could) walking up and down a straight gravel-walk, or in some spot where the continuity of his verse met with no collateral interruption. Returning that same evening, I got into a metaphysical argument with Wordsworth, while Coleridge was explaining the different notes of the nightingale to his sister, in which we neither of us succeeded in making ourselves perfectly clear and intelligible. Thus I passed three weeks at Nether Stowey and in the neighbourhood, generally devoting the afternoons to a delightful chat in an arbour made of bark by the poet's friend Tom Poole, sitting under two fine elm-trees, and listening to the bees humming round us, while we quaffed our *flip*. . . .[70]

---

[69] Cf. *Macbeth,* I, v, 63–64.

[70] Spiced ale.—Most of the remainder of the essay describes "a jaunt down the Bristol Channel, as far as Lynton," made by Coleridge, Hazlitt, and a certain John Chester before Hazlitt's return home.

Thomas Moore
1779–1852

Moore was born in Ireland, the son of a grocer. He was educated at Trinity College, Dublin, then went to London to study law. He brought out some Anacreontic verse which attracted general attention, got an appointment in Bermuda, traveled in the United States, and on the publication (after his return to England) of his *Irish Melodies,* poems with music supplied by others, found himself both a literary and social success. His own singing of his lyrics, along with his easy charm, made him popular at social gatherings; he made a happy marriage with a young actress in 1811. Life seemed to be going more than usually well. But he encountered severe financial troubles and for several years had to seek refuge on the Continent. His five children died, three of them in childhood, two in early adulthood. In politics Moore was a Whig and an advocate of reform. He was, through temperamental, literary, and political congeniality, a friend of Byron, whose biography he wrote in 1830. Other than for his songs Moore was celebrated for the Oriental romance *Lallah Rookh.* His reputation in his own time was far greater than it is today, but some of the songs remain.

TEXTS: A. D. Godley, ed., *Poetical Works* (1910); Sean O'Faolain, ed., *Lyrics and Satires* (1929); J. B. Priestley, ed., *Tom Moore's Diary* (1925). About Moore: S. L. Gwynn, *Thomas Moore* (1924); Howard Mumford Jones, *The Harp That Once* (1937).

The Harp That Once Through Tara's Halls

Both selections are from *Irish Melodies* and were published in 1808.

The harp that once through Tara's[1] halls
    The soul of music shed,
Now hangs as mute on Tara's walls
    As if that soul were fled.—
So sleeps the pride of former days,   5
    So glory's thrill is o'er,
And hearts, that once beat high for praise,
    Now feel that pulse no more.

No more to chiefs and ladies bright
    The harp of Tara swells;   10

---

[1] In a hall on the hill of Tara the Irish kings, bards, and clergy used to deliberate on national affairs.

The chord alone, that breaks at night,
　　Its tale of ruin tells.
Thus Freedom now so seldom wakes,
　　The only throb she gives,
Is when some heart indignant breaks,　　15
　　To show that still she lives.

Believe Me, If All Those Endearing Young Charms

Believe me, if all those endearing young charms,
　　Which I gaze on so fondly to-day,
Were to change by to-morrow, and fleet in my
　　arms,

Like fairy-gifts fading away,
Thou wouldst still be ador'd, as this moment　　5
　　thou art,
　　Let thy loveliness fade as it will,
And around the dear ruin each wish of my heart
　　Would entwine itself verdantly still.

It is not while beauty and youth are thine own,
　　And thy cheeks unprofan'd by a tear,　　10
That the fervour and faith of a soul can be
　　known,
　　To which time will but make thee more dear;
No, the heart that has truly lov'd never forgets,
　　But as truly loves on to the close,
As the sun-flower turns on her god, when he sets,　　15
　　The same look which she turn'd when he rose.

Leigh Hunt
1784–1859

James Henry Leigh Hunt was a friend of many of the greatest literary men of his time—including Keats, some of whose early poems were influenced by Hunt—and as a liberal journalist he fought a good fight, which got him two years in jail. It is for his life more than for his works that he is now respected, though he wrote copiously in verse and prose. He was born at Southgate near London, and educated at Christ's Hospital. In 1808 he and his brother John started a liberal weekly, the *Examiner,* which ran fourteen years. He drew his jail sentence for calling the Prince Regent "a fat Adonis of fifty." He was permitted to have his family with him, and to receive his friends; Byron gave a dinner party in his honor at the jail. In 1822 Shelley and Byron brought Hunt and his family to Italy to found a new magazine. Shelley was drowned a few days later, and the project collapsed. Hunt had a large family; and though he was aided by friends and eventually, after the tide had turned to reform, by the government, he was often in financial straits. On his return to London he tried various journalistic ventures, wrote somewhat acidly of Byron, edited several authors, composed an autobiography, and went on with his verse and essays.

TEXTS: Leigh Hunt's *Poetical Works* have been edited by H. S. Milford (1923) and his *Literary Criticism* by Carolyn W. and Lawrence H. Houtchens (1956). The Houtchens' have also edited his *Dramatic Criticism* (1949) and his *Political* and *Occasional Es-*

says (1962). There is a biography by Edmund Blunden, *Leigh Hunt and His Circle* (1930), and another by Louis Landre, *Leigh Hunt* (1935–1936). The best account of his life, in many ways, is Hunt's own *Autobiography,* edited by J. E. Morpurgo (1948).

The Fish, the Man, and the Spirit

This poem was published in 1836.

TO A FISH

You strange, astonished-looking, angle-faced,
　　Dreary-mouthed, gaping wretches of the sea,
　　Gulping salt-water everlastingly,
Cold-blooded, though with red your blood be
　　graced,
And mute, though dwellers in the roaring waste;　　5
　　And you, all shapes beside, that fishy be,—
　　Some round, some flat, some long, all devilry,
Legless, unloving, infamously chaste:—

O scaly, slippery, wet, swift, staring wights,
　　What is't ye do? What life lead? eh, dull　　10
　　goggles?

How do ye vary your vile days and nights?
    How pass your Sundays? Are ye still but
        joggles
In ceaseless wash? Still nought but gapes and
        bites,
    And drinks, and stares, diversified with
        boggles?[1]

A FISH ANSWERS

Amazing monster! that, for aught I know,   15
    With the first sight of thee didst make our race
    For ever stare! O flat and shocking face,
Grimly divided from the breast below!
Thou that on dry land horribly dost go
    With a split body and most ridiculous pace,   20
    Prong after prong, disgracer of all grace,
Long-useless-finned, haired, upright, unwet, slow!

O breather of the unbreathable, sword-sharp air,
    How canst exist? How bear thyself, thou dry
And dreary sloth? What particle canst share   25
    Of the only blessèd life, the watery?

---

[1] Taking fright and shying away.

I sometimes see of ye an actual *pair*
    Go by! linked fin by fin! most odiously.

THE FISH TURNS INTO A MAN, AND THEN INTO A SPIRIT, AND AGAIN SPEAKS

Indulge thy smiling scorn, if smiling still,
    O man! and loathe, but with a sort of love;   30
    For difference must its use by difference prove,
And, in sweet clang, the spheres with music fill.
One of the spirits am I, that at his will
    Live in what'er has life—fish, eagle, dove—
    No hate, no pride, beneath nought, nor above,   35
A visitor of the rounds of God's sweet skill.

Man's life is warm, glad, sad, 'twixt loves and
        graves,
    Boundless in hope, honoured with pangs
        austere,
Heaven-gazing; and his angel-wings he craves:—
    The fish is swift, small-needing, vague yet   40
        clear,
A cold, sweet, silver life, wrapped in round waves,
    Quickened with touches of transporting fear.

Thomas De Quincey
1785–1859

The second son of a well-to-do dry-goods merchant, De Quincey was born in Manchester in 1785. He was only seven when his father, whom tuberculosis had driven from the damp climate of England, came home to die. Though he was one of eight children, his temperament inclined him to solitude. At a tender age he took to books as to his native element; he was always reader and dreamer. He attended several undistinguished schools, the last at Manchester; from it, as he tells us in the *Confessions,* he ran away. He had inherited money from his father but could not get on with the five guardians who managed it. One of these was his mother, and he went to see her in the course of his flight. After much debate he was allowed to go his way, with a weekly allowance of one guinea, that is, five dollars, then worth in purchasing power a very great deal more than it is today. That summer of 1802 he devoted to a walking trip in Wales, sleeping usually out of doors in a tiny tent of his own manufacture. Next, breaking communications with his family and abandoning the weekly guinea, he

struck out for London, hoping he might talk some moneylender into an advance on his prospects as an heir. He found the moneylenders more cautious than helpful, and spent the winter in dire poverty. He was then seventeen years old. A partial reconciliation with his guardians rescued him from life as a young derelict; they agreed to allow him £100 a year if he would enter Oxford.

This he did in 1803. He made no friends there: to him the interests of the average undergraduate seemed juvenile; and instead of exerting himself to seek out young men of comparable tastes and intelligence, he wrapped himself in a cloak of intellectual pride. His studies were unusual and self-planned. He hired a German to teach him the elements of that language. Then he plunged, quite on his own, into the new German philosophy, against which in later years he turned because it conflicted with orthodox religion. De Quincey was a conservative in such matters, and in politics a lifelong Tory. His second main interest as a student was English literature, a subject then not seriously regarded at Oxford. He was among the warmest admirers of *Lyrical Ballads,* and succeeded in drawing Wordsworth into a corrspondence.

On a visit to London in 1804 he made his first purchase of opium, to relieve neuralgic pains in his face; but he went on using the drug, which he took in the liquid form of laudanum, partly because he was frequently subject to depression. In 1808 he left Oxford, in the midst of his final examinations for the B.A. He had begun them well; but he seems to have worried over them too much, and he was irritated by the authorities' decision that replies during an oral examination in Greek should be made, not in Greek, which he spoke fluently, but in English. At that point De Quincey simply lost interest.

In the meantime his enthusiasms had centered in the North. He had recognized the genius of Wordsworth as soon as he read him. In 1807 he had made the acquaintance of Coleridge; and being now of age and in possession of his share of his father's estate, he had anonymously aided the great man with a present of £300. Later in the same year he had escorted Mrs. Coleridge and the children from Bristol to Keswick. On the way through Grasmere he met the Wordsworths, and stayed on to visit them. For years, till his marriage led to their estrangement, he was among their closest friends, as well as intimate with Coleridge; and when in 1809 the Wordsworths vacated Dove Cottage, De Quincey moved in. He was now in the midst of the Lake School, yet not of it. Opium and procrastination held him back from serious work. In 1817 he was married—beneath him, the Wordsworths thought—to Margaret Simpson, a farmer's daughter of the vicinity. She could neither read nor write; yet the marriage turned out well.

For several years De Quincey had been taking opium daily in appalling quantities; he was broken in health, depressed in mind, paralyzed in will. After he met Margaret Simpson, things improved somewhat, but he never acquired more than intermittent control over the habit. For a considerable period after the respite of 1816–17 he was in the dreadful state described below in "The Pains of Opium." His money had all been spent; and at last, desperate for means, he turned to his pen. In 1821, in two numbers of the *London Magazine,* appeared his *Confessions of an English Opium-Eater.* Still the most famous of his writings, it was an instantaneous success. For several years he was often in London, where Lamb, Hazlitt, and Thomas Hood became his friends. In 1830 he moved with his family—he had eight children —to Edinburgh, in or near which he made his home for the rest of his life. *Blackwood's Magazine,* to which he frequently contributed, was published there; and already he had a number of friends in the city, among them Thomas Carlyle and his wife.

Though there was a steady demand for his work, he was in financial difficulties most of the time —embroiled with (and frequently sued by) the tradesmen he patronized, the owners of the houses he rented, and the publishers with whom he dealt. Sometimes he lived with his family; but often when things got too thick for his tormented psyche, when the children were too noisy, or a process for debt was about to trap him, he would disappear to some secret lodging. From one to another he would dodge like a hunted creature of the woods. His agility in evading the creditors who repeatedly tried to send him to prison was astounding. Once, indeed, he was actually arrested; but the publisher of the *Encyclopaedia Britannica* happened to meet the melancholy procession jailward bound and, in return for the promise of a brace of articles on Shakespeare and Pope, paid the debt and set him free. His last few years, partly through his own earnings, partly from increased income after his mother's death, and partly because his daughters proved capable managers, were less harassed.

The important thing is that this man who coped with life so ineffectively and behaved so differently from the generality of sober citizens wrote a hundred and fifty magazine articles and in the process made a place for himself in the history of English literature. Besides the autobiographical and critical work and the purely imaginative poems in prose from which our selections have been chosen, De Quincey wrote many sketches of poets past and present, and formal articles on history, philosophy, and economics. He spent his last decade chiefly in preparing, with much revision and often expansion, the collected edition of his works brought out at Boston in twenty-two volumes between 1851 and 1859. Among the most remarkable of the creative writings not represented below are *On Murder Considered as One of the Fine Arts* and *The English Mail-Coach.*

TEXTS: The most comprehensive, though not complete, edition of De Quincey's works is *The Collected Writings* (14 vols., 1889–1890), by David Masson. There is a good modern edition of the *Confessions of an English Opium-Eater* by Malcolm Elwin (1956), and an extremely useful selection by Helen Darbishire, *De Quincey's Literary Criticism* (1909). There is also a biography by Elwin, *Thomas De Quincey* (1935), another by Horace A. Eaton, *Thomas De Quincey* (1936), still another by H. S. Davies, *Thomas De Quincey* (1964).

Recent studies of De Quincey's place in literary history include S. K. Proctor, *De Quincey's Theory of Literature* (1943), John E. Jordan, *Thomas De Quincey, Literary Critic* (1952), J. Hillis Miller, *The Disappearance of God* (1963).

from Confessions of an English Opium-Eater

The original version of this curious work—autobiographical, yet essay-like—appeared in the *London Magazine* for September and October, 1821, and was separately reprinted in the year following. Few have been able to resist the fascination of its style and the intimacy of the confession. As for its truth, the narrative is certainly based on fact; but the author did not scruple to heighten his effects: thirty-five years later, in rewriting and greatly enlarging the piece for his collected works, he toned down some of the episodes. He felt, however, that while "as a book of amusement" the revised form was an improvement, something had been lost of the original's "fugitive inspiration" and "extemporaneous excitement." Most critics have preferred the earlier and less discursive version, from which (with the omission of a few of De Quincey's footnotes) our selections are taken. It has been inadequately edited by R. Garnett (1885). The later version is given in Masson's edition of the *Works* (Vol. III).

THE PAINS OF OPIUM

. . . I now pass[1] to what is the main subject of these latter confessions, to the history and journal of what took place in my dreams; for these were the immediate and proximate cause of my acutest suffering.

The first notice I had of any important change going on in this part of my physical economy was from the re-awakening of a state of eye generally incident to childhood, or exalted states of irritability. I know not whether my reader is aware that many children, perhaps most, have a power of painting, as it were, upon the darkness, all sorts of phantoms; in some, that power is simply a mechanic affection of the eye; others have a voluntary, or a semi-voluntary power to dismiss or to summon them; or, as a child once said to me when I questioned him on this matter, "I can tell them to go, and they go; but sometimes they come, when I don't tell them to come." Whereupon I told him that he had almost as unlimited command over apparitions as a Roman centurion[2] over his soldiers.—In the middle of 1817, I think it was, that this faculty became positively distressing to me: at night, when I lay awake in bed, vast processions passed along in mournful pomp; friezes of never-ending stories, that to my feelings were as sad and solemn as if they were stories drawn from times before Oedipus or Priam[3]—before Tyre—before Memphis.[4] And, at the same time, a corresponding change took place in my dreams; a theatre seemed suddenly opened and lighted up within my brain, which presented nightly spectacles of more than earthly splendour. And the four following facts may be mentioned, as noticeable at this time:

1. That, as the creative state of the eye increased, a sympathy seemed to arise between the waking and the dreaming states of the brain in one point—that whatsoever I happened to call up and to trace by a voluntary act upon the darkness was very apt to transfer itself to my dreams; so that I feared to exercise this faculty; for, as Midas turned all things to gold, that yet baffled his hopes and defrauded his human desires,[5] so whatsoever things capable of being visually represented I did but think of in the darkness, immediately shaped themselves into phantoms of the eye; and, by a process apparently no less inevitable, when thus once traced in faint and visionary colours, like writings in sympathetic ink,[6] they were drawn out by the fierce chemistry of my dreams, into insufferable splendour that fretted my heart.

2. For this, and all other changes in my dreams, were accompanied by deep-seated anxiety and gloomy melancholy, such as are wholly incommunicable by words. I seemed every night to descend, not metaphorically, but literally to descend, into chasms and sunless abysses, depths below depths, from which it seemed hopeless that I could ever reascend. Nor did I, by waking, feel that I *had* reascended. This I do not dwell upon; because the state of gloom which attended these gorgeous spectacles, amounting at least to utter darkness, as of some suicidal despondency, cannot be approached by words.

---

[1] After recounting how he suffered in his attempts to break the habit and how an "intellectual torpor" lasted four years.

[2] Captain; he commanded a "century," i.e., one hundred men.

[3] Figures in Greek legend and literature: Oedipus as king of Thebes, Priam as king of Troy.

[4] Tyre, in Lebanon, was in ancient times a Phoenician port; Memphis, now a village near Cairo, was the ancient capital of Egypt.

[5] In Greek mythology this king of Phrygia was granted the faculty of turning everything he touched to gold. He soon asked the god to revoke the gift; for one thing, when he tried to eat, his food turned to gold.

[6] Which is invisible till heat is applied.

3. The sense of space, and in the end, the sense of time, were both powerfully affected. Buildings, landscapes, etc., were exhibited in proportions so vast as the bodily eye is not fitted to receive. Space swelled, and was amplified to an extent of unutterable infinity. This, however, did not disturb me so much as the vast expansion of time; I sometimes seemed to have lived for 70 or 100 years in one night; nay, sometimes had feelings representative of a millennium, passed in that time, or, however, of a duration far beyond the limits of any human experience.

4. The minutest incidents of childhood, or forgotten scenes of later years, were often revived: I could not be said to recollect them; for if I had been told of them when waking, I should not have been able to acknowledge them as parts of my past experience. But placed as they were before me, in dreams like intuitions, and clothed in all their evanescent circumstances and accompanying feelings, I *recognised* them instantaneously. I was once told by a near relative of mine,[7] that having in her childhood fallen into a river, and being on the very verge of death but for the critical assistance which reached her, she saw in a moment her whole life, in its minutest incidents, arrayed before her simultaneously as in a mirror; and she had a faculty developed as suddenly for comprehending the whole and every part. This, from some opium experiences of mine, I can believe; I have, indeed, seen the same thing asserted twice in modern books, and accompanied by a remark which I am convinced is true; viz. that the dread book of account which the Scriptures speak of[8] is, in fact, the mind itself of each individual. Of this, at least, I feel assured, that there is no such thing as *forgetting* possible to the mind; a thousand accidents may and will interpose a veil between our present consciousness and the secret inscriptions on the mind; accidents of the same sort will also rend away this veil; but alike, whether veiled or unveiled, the inscription remains for ever; just as the stars seem to withdraw before the common light of day, whereas, in fact, we all know that it is the light which is drawn over them as a veil— and that they are waiting to be revealed, when the obscuring daylight shall have withdrawn.

Having noticed these four facts as memo-

rably distinguishing my dreams from those of health, I shall now cite a case illustrative of the first fact; and shall then cite any others that I remember, either in their chronological order, or any other that may give them more effect as pictures to the reader.

I had been in youth, and even since, for occasional amusement, a great reader of Livy,[9] whom, I confess, that I prefer, both for style and matter, to any other of the Roman historians; and I had often felt as most solemn and appalling sounds, and most emphatically representative of the majesty of the Roman people, the two words so often occurring in Livy—*Consul Romanus;* especially when the consul is introduced in his military character. I mean to say, that the words king—sultan—regent, &c. or any other titles of those who embody in their own persons the collective majesty of a great people, had less power over my reverential feelings. I had also, though no great reader of history, made myself minutely and critically familiar with one period of English history, namely, the period of the Parliamentary War,[10] having been attracted by the moral grandeur of some who figured in that day, and by the many interesting memoirs which survive those unquiet times. Both these parts of my lighter reading, having furnished me often with matter of reflection, now furnished me with matter for my dreams. Often I used to see, after painting upon the blank darkness a sort of rehearsal whilst waking, a crowd of ladies, and perhaps a festival, and dances. And I heard it said, or I said to myself, "These are English ladies from the unhappy times of Charles I. These are the wives and the daughters of those who met in peace, and sat at the same tables, and were allied by marriage or by blood; and yet, after a certain day in August, 1642, never smiled upon each other again, nor met but in the field of battle; and at Marston Moor, at Newbury, or at Naseby, cut asunder all ties of love by the cruel sabre, and washed away in blood the memory of ancient friendship."—The ladies danced, and looked as lovely as the court of George IV. Yet I knew, even in my dreams, that they had been in the grave for nearly two centuries.—This

---

[7] His mother.   [8] Revelation 20:12.

[9] Author (59 B.C.–17 A.D.) of The *Annals of the Roman People*.
[10] The civil wars of the mid-seventeenth century.

pageant would suddenly dissolve: and, at a clapping of hands, would be heard the heart-quaking sound of *Consul Romanus:* and immediately came "sweeping by,"[11] in gorgeous paludaments,[12] Paulus or Marius,[13] girt round by a company of centurions, with the crimson tunic hoisted on a spear,[14] and followed by the *alalagmos*[15] of the Roman legions.

Many years ago, when I was looking over Piranesi's[16] Antiquities of Rome, Mr. Coleridge, who was standing by, described to me a set of plates by that artist, called his *Dreams,* and which record the scenery of his own visions during the delirium of a fever: some of them (I describe only from memory of Mr. Coleridge's account) representing vast Gothic halls: on the floor of which stood all sorts of engines and machinery, wheels, cables, pulleys, levers, catapults, etc. etc., expressive of enormous power put forth, and resistance overcome. Creeping along the sides of the walls, you perceived a staircase; and upon it, groping his way upwards, was Piranesi himself: follow the stairs a little further, and you perceive it to come to a sudden, abrupt termination, without any balustrade, and allowing no step onwards to him who had reached the extremity, except into the depths below. Whatever is to become of poor Piranesi, you suppose, at least, that his labours must in some way terminate here. But raise your eyes, and behold a second flight of stairs still higher: on which again Piranesi is perceived, but this time standing on the very brink of the abyss. Again elevate your eye, and a still more aerial flight of stairs is beheld; and again is poor Piranesi busy on his aspiring labors: and so on, until the unfinished stairs and Piranesi both are lost in the upper gloom of the hall.—With the same power of endless growth and self-reproduction did my architecture proceed in dreams. In the early stage of my malady, the splendours of my dreams were indeed chiefly architectural: and I beheld such pomp of cities and palaces as was never yet beheld by the waking eye, unless in the clouds. . . . We hear it reported of Dryden, and of Fuseli[17] in modern times, that they thought proper to eat raw meat for the sake of obtaining splendid dreams: how much better, for such a purpose, to have eaten opium, which yet I do not remember that any poet is recorded to have done, except the dramatist Shadwell:[18] and in ancient days, Homer is, I think, rightly reputed to have known the virtues of opium.

To my architecture succeeded dreams of lakes and silvery expanses of water:—these haunted me so much, that I feared (though possibly it will appear ludicrous to a medical man) that some dropsical state or tendency of the brain might thus be making itself (to use a metaphysical word) *objective* and the sentient organ *project* itself as its own object.—For two months I suffered greatly in my head—a part of my bodily structure which had hitherto been so clear from all touch or taint of weakness (physically, I mean) that I used to say of it, as the last Lord Orford[19] said of his stomach, that it seemed likely to survive the rest of my person.—Till now I had never felt a headache even, or any the slightest pain, except rheumatic pains caused by my own folly. However, I got over this attack, though it must have been verging on something very dangerous.

The waters now changed their character,—from translucent lakes, shining like mirrors, they now became seas and oceans. And now came a tremendous change, which, unfolding itself slowly like a scroll, through many months, promised an abiding torment; and, in fact, it never left me until the winding up of my case. Hitherto the human face had mixed often in my dreams, but not despotically, nor with any special power of tormenting. But now that which I have called the tyranny of the human face began to unfold

11 Milton, "Il Penseroso," line 98.
12 Latin *paludamenta,* military cloaks.
13 There were two Roman generals named Paulus. The first was killed fighting the Carthaginians at Cannae (216 B.C.); his son (d. 160 B.C.) defeated the last king of Macedonia. Marius (d. 86 B.C.) was the famous general and politician, victor against foreign foes and opponent of Sulla in the civil war of 88 B.C.
14 De Quincey's note: "The signal which announced a day of battle."
15 De Quincey's note: "A [Greek] word expressing collectively the gathering of the Roman war-cries—*Alála, Alála!*"
16 Giambattista Piranesi (1720–1778), architect, painter, and engraver. His engravings influenced French and English architecture, in the latter case especially the style of Adam. There is no work by Piranesi entitled *Dreams,* but some of his architectural conceptions were not intended realistically.

17 Henry Fuseli (1741–1825), a Swiss painter who had his career in England.
18 Thomas Shadwell (d. 1692), the comic dramatist.
19 Horace Walpole (1717–1797), the connoisseur and letter writer.—*Last* = late.

itself. Perhaps some part of my London life might be answerable for this. Be that as it may, now it was that upon the rocking waters of the ocean the human face began to appear: the sea appeared paved with innumerable faces, up-turned to the heavens: faces imploring, wrathful, despairing, surged upwards by thousands, by myriads, by generations, by centuries:—my agitation was infinite,—my mind tossed—and surged with the ocean.

Literature of Knowledge and Literature of Power

In "Letters to a Young Man Whose Education Has Been Neglected" (*London Magazine,* 1823) De Quincey first expounded the central idea of the following selection, which for the sake of convenience editors have entitled "Literature of Knowledge and Literature of Power." A full comprehension of this distinction and its importance is significant for placing De Quincey in relation to other Romantics. De Quincey acknowledges that it was enforced on him by his long association with Wordsworth. The passage constitutes less than one-seventh of a review of a new edition of Pope, in the *North British Review* for August 1848. De Quincey reprinted the review as an essay in his collected works under the title "Alexander Pope." With one exception, his footnotes have been omitted from the present text.

. . . What is it that we mean by *literature?* Popularly, and amongst the thoughtless, it is held to include everything that is printed in a book. Little logic is required to disturb *that* definition. The most thoughtless person is easily made aware that in the idea of *literature* one essential element is some relation to a general and common interest of man,—so that what applies only to a local, or professional, or merely personal interest, even though presenting itself in the shape of a book, will not belong to Literature. So far the definition is easily narrowed; and it is as easily expanded. For not only is much that takes a station in books not literature; but inversely, much that really *is* literature never reaches a station in books. The weekly sermons of Christendom, that vast pulpit literature which acts so extensively upon the popular mind—to warn, to uphold, to renew, to comfort, to alarm—does not attain the sanctuary of libraries in the ten-thousandth part of its extent. The Drama again,—as,

for instance, the finest part of Shakspere's plays in England, and all leading Athenian plays in the noontide of the Attic[1] stage,—operated as a literature on the public mind, and were (according to the strictest letter of that term) *published* through the audiences that witnessed their representation some time before they were published as things to be read; and they were published in this scenical mode of publication with much more effect than they could have had as books during ages of costly copying or of costly printing.

Books, therefore, do not suggest an idea coextensive and interchangeable with the idea of Literature; since much literature, scenic, forensic,[2] or didactic (as from lecturers and public orators), may never come into books, and much that *does* come into books may connect itself with no literary interest. But a far more important correction, applicable to the common vague idea of literature, is to be sought not so much in a better definition of literature as in a sharper distinction of the two functions which it fulfils. In that great social organ which, collectively, we call literature, there may be distinguished two separate offices that may blend and often *do* so, but capable, severally, of a severe insulation, and naturally fitted for reciprocal repulsion. There is, first, the literature of *knowledge;* and, secondly, the literature of *power.* The function of the first is—to *teach;* the function of the second is—to *move:* the first is a rudder; the second, an oar or a sail. The first speaks to the *mere* discursive understanding; the second speaks ultimately, it may happen, to the higher understanding or reason, but always *through* affections[3] of pleasure and sympathy. Remotely, it may travel towards an object seated in what Lord Bacon calls *dry* light;[4] but, proximately, it does and must operate,—else it ceases to be a literature of *power,*—on and through that *humid* light which clothes itself in the mists and glittering *iris*[5] of human passions, desires, and genial emotions.

Men have so little reflected on the higher

---

[1] I.e., Athenian.   [2] Argumentative.
[3] Feelings.
[4] "The light that a man receiveth by counsel from another is drier and purer than that which cometh from his own understanding and judgment; which is ever infused and drenched in his affections and customs" (Bacon's essay "Of Friendship").   [5] Rainbow.

functions of literature as to find it a paradox if one should describe it as a mean or subordinate purpose of books to give information. But this is a paradox only in the sense which makes it honourable to be paradoxical. Whenever we talk in ordinary language of seeking information or gaining knowledge, we understand the words as connected with something of absolute novelty. But it is the grandeur of all truth which *can* occupy a very high place in human interests that it is never absolutely novel to the meanest of minds: it exists eternally by way of germ or latent principle in the lowest as in the highest, needing to be developed, but never to be planted. To be capable of transplantation is the immediate criterion of a truth that ranges on a lower scale. Besides which, there is a rarer thing than truth, —namely, *power,* or deep sympathy with truth. What is the effect, for instance, upon society, of children? By the pity, by the tenderness, and by the peculiar modes of admiration, which connect themselves with the helplessness, with the innocence, and with the simplicity of children, not only are the primal affections strengthened and continually renewed, but the qualities which are dearest in the sight of heaven,—the frailty, for instance, which appeals to forbearance, the innocence which symbolises the heavenly, and the simplicity which is most alien from the worldly, —are kept up in perpetual remembrance, and their ideals are continually refreshed. A purpose of the same nature is answered by the higher literature, viz. the literature of power. What do you learn from "Paradise Lost"? Nothing at all. What do you learn from a cookery-book? Something new, something that you did not know before, in every paragraph. But would you therefore put the wretched cookery-book on a higher level of estimation than the divine poem? What you owe to Milton is not any knowledge, of which a million separate items are still but a million of advancing steps on the same earthly level; what you owe is *power,*—that is, exercise and expansion to your own latent capacity of sympathy with the infinite, where every pulse and each separate influx is a step upwards, a step ascending as upon a Jacob's ladder[6] from earth to mysterious altitudes above the earth. *All* the

steps of knowledge, from first to last, carry you further on the same plane, but could never raise you one foot above your ancient level of earth: whereas the very *first* step in power is a flight— is an ascending movement into another element where earth is forgotten.

Were it not that human sensibilities are ventilated and continually called out into exercise by the great phenomena of infancy, or of real life as it moves through chance and change, or of literature as it recombines these elements in the mimicries of poetry, romance, &c., it is certain that, like any animal power or muscular energy falling into disuse, all such sensibilities would gradually droop and dwindle. It is in relation to these great *moral* capacities of man that the literature of power, as contradistinguished from that of knowledge, lives and has its field of action. It is concerned with what is highest in man; for the Scriptures themselves never condescended to deal by suggestion or co-operation with the mere discursive understanding: when speaking of man in his intellectual capacity, the Scriptures speak not of the understanding, but of *"the understanding heart,"*[7]—making the heart, i.e. the great *intuitive* (or non-discursive) organ, to be the interchangeable formula for man in his highest state of capacity for the infinite. Tragedy, romance, fairy tale, or epopee,[8] all alike restore to man's mind the ideals of justice, of hope, of truth, of mercy, of retribution, which else (left to the support of daily life in its realities) would languish for want of sufficient illustration.

What is meant, for instance, by *poetic justice*?—It does not mean a justice that differs by its object from the ordinary justice of human jurisprudence; for then it must be confessedly a very bad kind of justice; but it means a justice that differs from common forensic justice by the degree in which it *attains* its object, a justice that is more omnipotent over its own ends, as dealing—not with the refractory elements of earthly life, but with the elements of its own creation, and with materials flexible to its own purest preconceptions. It is certain that, were it not for the Literature of Power, these ideals would often remain amongst us as mere arid notional forms; whereas, by the creative forces

---

[6] In a dream Jacob saw a ladder connecting earth and heaven (Genesis 28:12 ff.).

[7] 1 Kings, 3:9, 12.   [8] Epic poem.

of man put forth in literature, they gain a vernal life of restoration, and germinate into vital activities. The commonest novel, by moving in alliance with human fears and hopes, with human instincts of wrong and right, sustains .and quickens those affections. Calling them into action, it rescues them from torpor. And hence the pre-eminency over all authors that merely *teach* of the meanest that *moves,* or that teaches, if at all, indirectly *by* moving. The very highest work that has ever existed in the Literature of Knowledge is but a *provisional* work: a book upon trial and sufferance, and *quamdiu bene se gesserit.*[9] Let its teaching be even partially revised, let it be but expanded,—nay, even let its teaching be but placed in a better order,—and instantly it is superseded. Whereas the feeblest works in the Literature of Power, surviving at all, survive as finished and unalterable amongst men. For instance, the *Principia* of Sir Isaac Newton[10] was a book *militant* on earth from the first. In all stages of its progress it would have to fight for its existence: 1st, as regards absolute truth; 2dly, when that combat was over, as regards its form or mode of presenting the truth. And as soon as a La Place,[11] or anybody else, builds higher upon the foundations laid by this book, effectually he throws it out of the sunshine into decay and darkness; by weapons won from this book he superannuates and destroys this book, so that soon the name of Newton remains as a mere *nominis umbra,*[12] but his book, as a living power, has transmigrated into other forms. Now, on the contrary, the Iliad, the Prometheus[13] of Aeschylus, the Othello or King Lear, the Hamlet or Macbeth, and the Paradise Lost, are not militant but triumphant[14] for ever, as long as the languages exist in which they speak or can be taught to speak. They never *can* transmigrate into new incarnations. To reproduce *these* in new forms, or variations, even if in some things they should be improved, would be to plagiarise. A good steam-engine is properly superseded by a better.

But one lovely pastoral valley is not superseded by another, nor a statue of Praxiteles by a statue of Michael Angelo. These things are separated not by imparity but by disparity.[15] They are not thought of as unequal under the same standard, but as different in *kind,* and, if otherwise equal, as equal under a different standard. Human works of immortal beauty and works of nature in one respect stand on the same footing: they never absolutely repeat each other, never approach so near as not to differ; and they differ not as better and worse, or simply by more and less: they differ by undecipherable and incommunicable differences, that cannot be caught by mimicries, that cannot be reflected in the mirror of copies, that cannot become ponderable in the scales of vulgar comparison. . . .

At this hour, five hundred years since their creation, the tales of Chaucer, never equalled on this earth for their tenderness, and for life of picturesqueness, are read familiarly by many in the charming language of their natal day, and by others in the modernisations of Dryden, of Pope, and Wordsworth. At this hour, one thousand eight hundred years since their creation, the Pagan tales of Ovid, never equalled on this earth for the gaiety of their movement and the capricious graces of their narrative, are read by all Christendom. This man's people and their monuments are dust; but *he* is alive: he has survived them, as he told us that he had it in his commission to do, by a thousand years; "and *shall* a thousand more."

All the literature of knowledge builds only ground-nests, that are swept away by floods, or confounded by the plough; but the literature of power builds nests in aerial altitudes of temples sacred from violation, or of forests inaccessible to fraud. *This* is a great prerogative of the *power* literature; and it is a greater which lies in the mode of its influence. The *knowledge* literature, like the fashion of this world, passeth away. An Encyclopaedia is its abstract; and, in this respect, it may be taken for its speaking symbol—that before one generation has passed an Encyclopaedia is superannuated; for it speaks through the dead memory and unimpassioned

---

9 As long as it behaves itself.
10 In which (1687) he expounded his theory of gravitation.
11 The Marquis Pierre Simon de Laplace (1749–1827), French astronomer and mathematician.
12 Shadow of a name.
13 One of the great Greek tragedies of the fifth century B.C.
14 Cf. the "Church militant" and "Church triumphant"; i.e., on earth, and eternal.

15 Not by being unequal but by being different.—Praxiteles (fourth century B.C.) and Michelangelo Buonarroti (d. 1564) were among the greatest of sculptors.

GEORGE GORDON, LORD BYRON   223

understanding, which have not the repose of higher faculties, but are continually enlarging and varying their phylacteries.[16] But all literature properly so called—literature κατ᾽ ἐξοχήν,[17]—for the very reason that it is so much more durable than the literature of knowledge, is (and by the very same proportion it is) more intense and electrically searching in its impressions. The directions in which the tragedy of this planet has trained our human feelings to play, and the combinations into which the poetry of this planet has thrown our human passions of love and hatred, of admiration and contempt, exercise a power for bad or good over human life that cannot be contemplated, when stretching through many generations, without a sentiment allied to

awe.[18] And of this let every one be assured—that he owes to the impassioned books which he has read many a thousand more of emotions than he can consciously trace back to them. Dim by their origination, these emotions yet arise in him, and mould him through life, like forgotten incidents of his childhood. . . .

---

10   [16] Small boxes containing certain passages from the Scriptures, worn by the Jews on the head and left arm during prayer.   [17] Par excellence, i.e., preeminently such.

[18] De Quincey's note: "The reason why the broad distinctions between the two literatures of power and knowledge so little fix the attention lies in the fact that a vast proportion of books,—history, biography, travels, miscellaneous essays, &c.,—lying in a middle zone, confound these distinctions, by interblending them. All that we call 'amusement' or 'entertainment' is a diluted form of the power belonging to passion, and also a mixed form; and, where threads of direct *instruction* intermingle in the texture with these threads of *power,* this absorption of the duality into one representative *nuance* neutralises the separate perception of either. Fused into a *tertium quid,* or neutral state, they disappear to the popular eye as the repelling forces which, in fact, they are."

George Gordon, Lord Byron

1788–1824

T. S. Eliot has said: "Of Byron one can say, as of no other English poet of his eminence, that he added nothing to the language, that he discovered nothing in the sounds, and developed nothing in the meaning, of individual words. I cannot think of any other poet of his distinction who might so easily have been an accomplished foreigner writing English." One can accept this generalization. When one compares him to other poets of his own general period, one sees at once that he has had nothing like the creative effect on the language Wordsworth, Keats, or Shelley had, each of whom, in different ways, made profound discoveries in the sounds and meanings of the words they used. Eliot is right in saying that Byron's effects are remarkably diffuse by comparison with other writers of his eminence. And this may yield an explanation of his remarkable popularity, his diffuseness contributing to his availability. His popularity was due, of course, to other things as well. The figure he creates, in *Childe Harold's Pilgrimage,* in *The Corsair,* in *The Giaour,* in *Manfred,* and elsewhere, has in general the qualities associated with popular literature of a certain sort. Indeed, this figure derives directly from the Gothic novel, which had been becoming popular since the middle of the preceding century. A figure glamourously attractive, connected, often in murky and unexplained ways, with sinister

events and personal crimes, bruised by experience, dissipated by it, yet at the same time superior to it, surviving with a spirit damaged yet paradoxically untouched. It is a figure sometimes explicitly related, especially since Milton, with Satan, and not in entirely disapproving ways. Pride and guilt are involved with this figure, and a sense of great powers now exhausted, or for some reason unable to be expended, or willingly withheld. It would in one sense be pretentious to take this figure too seriously. His depths seem deep only because the glamourous shadow cast over them is so self-consciously dark. And yet there is some need that is obviously being filled by his existence.

One can only hazard a few guesses. First, it may be reasonable to suggest a connection between this figure and that of Napoleon, lonely, self-assertive, full of high ambition for the society that he both served and corrupted, unmatchably brave and dangerous, proud, ultimately weak through his own gifts, his own overreaching, and the coalition of "the world" against him. (Obviously here one is trying to reconstruct not necessarily the historical figure but a popular image of him.) The Byronic hero may have been, in a way, a means for both Byron and his public to handle their feelings about Napoleon. Second, it is reasonable to think of the Gothic literature

Lord Byron (1788–1824). The steel engraving, 1862, is from a painting by Chappel. *The Granger Collection.*

from which the Byronic hero derives as itself a Romantic phenomenon, if one can think of it as a sort of protest against the Enlightenment, against the alleged reasonableness of the age in which it began to be written. The very namelessness of the sins, and uncertainties of the virtues, the mysteries of his allegiances, are a form of protest against what is *established,* politically, socially, ethically, and perhaps rationally. It is clear, at any rate, that Byron helped to define an attitude that has by now become traditional for the modern writer. He stands outside the society that he criticizes, doing so by his personal singularity, which seems to constitute a special sort of integrity; yet, at the same time, he is more than usually knowing about that society. He is often cynical and disillusioned both about himself and about the world he criticizes, but is visited at times by moments of high and idealistic aspiration. The sense of the artist as at once sharing the ills of his society and standing far enough from it to criticize it adequately, as being himself not blameless, but nevertheless superior to those around him by virtue of his sensibility, his lack of hypocrisy, and above all his personal style, is an important feature of later English, American,

and continental literature; and Byron is one of its creators. His contribution is not profound and is frequently both theatrical and vulgar, but that is also sometimes part of the style.

Byron was born in London in 1788. His father, who deserted his mother once he had spent her fortune, was a captain in a Guards regiment. His mother, who alternately caressed and abused Byron, pitying him for his lameness, taunting him for it, drank too much and was quarrelsome by temperament. Their relationship was not easy as they lived together in shabby gentility in Aberdeen. When Byron was ten, the death of a great-uncle made him sixth Baron Byron. He attended Harrow and Cambridge, and while still an undergraduate produced his first volume, *Hours of Idleness,* a not very distinguished work harshly criticized by the *Edinburgh Review.* Byron was deeply offended and energetically retaliated a couple of years later with *English Bards, and Scotch Reviewers.*

In the same year he went abroad with a college friend for two years of travel. The war with Napoleon barred the customary Grand Tour, so they went to the Near East, by way of Portugal, Spain, Sardinia, and Malta. Byron visited a Turkish pasha in Albania, stayed in Athens, swam the Dardanelles, and came home in 1811 already Byronic.

The publication in 1812 of the first two cantos of *Childe Harold's Pilgrimage* made Byron immediately famous. In three days the edition was sold out. He followed up his initial hit with some superficial Oriental tales that further developed, or more vividly established, the Byronic hero figure in the consciousness of his readers. *The Giaour, The Bride of Abydos, The Corsair,* and *Lara* were published in rapid succession in 1813–14. *Hebrew Melodies,* containing some of his most celebrated lyrics, appeared in 1815. Meanwhile the rumors of his love affairs enhanced his special sort of reputation. One of these rumors, not confirmed until after his death, had to do with his half-sister, Augusta Leigh.

In 1815 Byron married Anne Isabella Milbanke. This was an error for both, since they could not have been more unsuited; and their relationship was complicated, to say the least, by Lady Byron's knowledge of the affair with Augusta Leigh. The marriage broke up in 1816. Byron departed for the Continent, where he became friends with Shelley and his wife (whose father's stepdaughter was already his mistress). At this time he wrote the third canto of *Childe Harold.* From Switzerland he went to Italy. Before the end of 1817 he had finished the fourth canto of *Childe Harold* and the drama *Manfred;* and in the satirical *Beppo* he had begun to explore new possibilities, writing with a new ease and a new kind of sophistication.

Childe Harold's Pilgrimage: Italy by J.M.W. Turner. "Thy haunts are ever where the dead walls rear/ Their ivy mantles." (Canto IV, ll. 1238–39). *The Tate Gallery.*

The years from 1818 through 1823 were occupied with his prolonged, and in many ways happy, affair with the Countess Teresa Guiccioli, and with the composition of *Don Juan,* the drama *Cain,* and the satire, or polemic, *The Vision of Judgment* (both *Cain* and *The Vision* were written in 1822).

In 1823 Byron volunteered to serve as field agent for a committee that had been formed to aid the Greeks in their rebellion against their Turkish masters. He sailed to Greece and took virtual command of an artillery brigade, under conditions that were extremely difficult because of external political and military circumstances and because of his own health. He died of fever and exhaustion at Missolonghi, in Greece, in April, 1824.

Among the last works, *The Vision of Judgment* and *Don Juan* represent a development of what *Beppo* had promised, a new kind of easiness, an absence of attitudinizing, and the use of verse forms perfectly suited to their purposes, and capable of being handled by him without falsity. These poems have qualities in common with the letters, and the letters suggest an interesting thing about Byron: that he was capable of being something quite different from, and more interesting than, the "Byronic hero" of his own earlier creation. Like the letters the last poems are acute, funny, generous, self-amused, remarkably knowledgable about the world in which

Byron lived, and entirely without illusions about it. If they lack the moral intensity and focus of the best satirical writing, they have these virtues of their own.

TEXTS: E. H. Coleridge and R. E. Prothero have edited Byron's *Works* (13 vols., 1898–1904), which include the poems, letters, and journals. The diaries have been edited by Peter Quennell in *Byron: A Self-Portrait* (2 vols., 1950). The best biography is Leslie A. Marchand's *Byron* (3 vols., 1957). Peter Quennell has contributed several valuable biographical works: *Byron* (1934); *Byron in Italy* (1941); *Byron: The Years of Fame* (1967). One may also mention, among studies of this extraordinary life, C. L. Cline, *Byron, Shelley, and Their Pisan Circle* (1952), Harold Nicolson, *Byron: The Last Journey* (1924), and Iris Origo, *Byron: The Last Attachment* (1949). Two fascinating books by G. Wilson Knight occupy a middle ground between biography and criticism, *Lord Byron: Christian Virtues* (1953) and *Lord Byron's Marriage* (1957).

Among critical works may be listed Michael G. Cooke, *The Blind Man Traces the Circle* (1969); E. J. Lovell, *Byron: The Record of a Quest* (1949); William Marshall, *The Structure of Byron's Major Poems* (1965); J. J. McGann, *Fiery Quest* (1968); Andrew Rutherford, *Byron: A Critical Study* (1961); and Paul West, *Byron and the Spoiler's Art* (1960).

Paul West has edited a collection of critical essays, *Byron* (1963) and Andrew Rutherford another, *Byron: The Critical Heritage* (1970).

Two valuable studies of *Don Juan* are E. F. Boyd, *Byron's Don Juan* (1945) and George M. Ridenour, *The Style of Don Juan* (1960).

from English Bards, and Scotch Reviewers

Byron was only nineteen when, in 1807, he was at work on a satire he intended to call *British Bards;* it was to be an attack on some contemporary poets. In January, 1808, the *Edinburgh Review* came out with a castigation of Byron's *Hours of Idleness* so severe that, as he afterwards acknowledged, it "knocked me down, but," he added, "I got up again." His method of regaining his feet and striking back was to make a careful revision and expansion of his satirical poem. It was published anonymously (though everyone knew it was Byron's) in March 1809, and was an immediate success. Byron kept on adding and repolishing; an enlarged second edition appeared under his name in October. By 1812 a fifth was ready, extending to 1070 lines. Meanwhile Byron had returned from his adventures in the Levant, and was on friendly terms with the Whig leaders Lord and Lady Holland, who are roughly handled in the poem as instigators of the *Edinburgh's* partisan reviewing. Byron suddenly ordered the whole fifth edition burned. Fortunately a few copies escaped, to form the basis of the standard text.

In time Byron repented a number of other rash judgments and expressions; but although the poem is uneven and he was to go far beyond it, a good deal of the poem is still valuable.

Still must I hear?—shall hoarse Fitzgerald[1] bawl
His creaking couplets in a tavern hall,
And I not sing, lest, haply, Scotch Reviews
Should dub me scribbler, and denounce my Muse?
Prepare for rhyme—I'll publish, right or wrong: 5
Fools are my theme; let Satire be my song.

· · ·

I, too, can scrawl, and once upon a time
I poured along the town a flood of rhyme,
A schoolboy freak unworthy praise or blame;
I printed—older children do the same. 50
'Tis pleasant, sure, to see one's name in print;
A Book's a Book, altho' there's nothing in't.

· · ·

A man must serve his time to every trade
Save Censure[2]—Critics all are ready made.

[1] William Thomas Fitzgerald (c. 1759–1829), a poetaster who went about reciting his verses. [2] Criticism.

Take hackneyed jokes from Miller,[3] got by rote, 65
With just enough of learning to misquote;
A mind well skilled to find, or forge, a fault;
A turn for punning—call it Attic salt;[4]
To Jeffrey[5] go, be silent and discreet,
His pay is just ten sterling pounds per sheet:[6] 70
Fear not to lie, 'twill seem a *sharper* hit;
Shrink not from blasphemy, 'twill pass for wit;
Care not for feeling—pass your proper jest,
And stand a Critic, hated yet caressed.

· · ·

Behold! in various throngs the scribbling crew,
For notice eager, pass in long review:
Each spurs his jaded Pegasus[7] apace, 145
And Rhyme and Blank maintain an equal race;
Sonnets on sonnets crowd, and ode on ode;
And Tales of Terror[8] jostle on the road;
Immeasurable measures[9] move along;
For simpering Folly loves a varied song, 150
To strange, mysterious Dulness still the friend,
Admires the strain she cannot comprehend.
Thus Lays of Minstrels[10]—may they be the last!—
On half-strung harps whine mournful to the blast.
While mountain spirits prate to river sprites, 155
That dames may listen to the sound at nights;
And goblin brats, of Gilpin Horner's[11] brood,
Decoy young Border-nobles through the wood,
And skip at every step, Lord knows how high,
And frighten foolish babes, the Lord knows why; 160
While high-born ladies in their magic cell,
Forbidding Knights to read who cannot spell,
Despatch a courier to a wizard's grave,
And fight with honest men to shield a knave.

[3] The name of Joe Miller (1684–1738), a low-comedian at Drury Lane, was without warrant attached to a collection of jokes compiled by John Mottley (1739). It had a long life. [4] Pungent wit.
[5] Francis Jeffrey (1773–1850), founder and editor (1803–29) of the *Edinburgh Review;* subsequently a judge of Scotland's supreme court. He was hostile to the new poetry, and began his famous review of Wordsworth's *Excursion,* "This will never do."
[6] Not of manuscript; the single piece of paper on which a number of pages are printed. In an octavo book there are sixteen pages to the sheet, eight on each side.
[7] The winged horse, symbol of poetic inspiration.
[8] The Gothic novelist, Matthew Gregory ("Monk") Lewis, brought out a collection thus entitled in 1799.
[9] A hit at the varied meters used by the new poets.
[10] Scott's first metrical romance, *The Lay of the Last Minstrel.*
[11] Who figures in a border legend Scott had thought of using for a ballad before he decided to write another full-length romance.

Next view in state, proud prancing on his roan,   165
The golden-crested haughty Marmion,[12]
Now forging scrolls, now foremost in the fight,
Not quite a Felon, yet but half a Knight,
The gibbet or the field prepare to grace—
A mighty mixture of the great and base.   170
And think'st thou, Scott! by vain conceit per-
  chance,
On public taste to foist thy stale romance,
Though Murray with his Miller[13] may combine
To yield thy muse just half-a-crown per line?
No! when the sons of song descend to trade,   175
Their bays[14] are sear, their former laurels fade.
Let such forgo the poet's sacred name,
Who rack their brains for lucre, not for fame:
Still for stern Mammon[15] may they toil in vain!
And sadly gaze on gold they cannot gain!   180
Such be their meed, such still the just reward
Of prostituted Muse and hireling bard!
For this we spurn Apollo's[16] venal son,
And bid a long "good night to Marmion."[17]

These are the themes that claim our plaudits now;   185
These are the Bards to whom the Muse must bow;
While Milton, Dryden, Pope, alike forgot,
Resign their hallowed Bays to Walter Scott.[18]

The time has been, when yet the Muse was young,
When Homer swept the lyre, and Maro[19] sung,   190
An Epic scarce ten centuries could claim,[20]
While awe-struck nations hailed the magic name:
The work of each immortal Bard appears
The single wonder of a thousand years.

Empires have mouldered from the face of earth,   195
Tongues have expired with those who gave them
  birth,
Without the glory such a strain can give,
As even in ruin bids the language live.
Not so with us, though minor Bards content,
On one great work a life of labour spent: 200
With eagle pinion soaring to the skies,
Behold the Ballad-monger Southey[21] rise!
To him let Camoëns, Milton, Tasso[22] yield,
Whose annual strains, like armies, take the field.
First in the ranks see Joan of Arc advance,   205
The scourge of England and the boast of France!
Though burnt by wicked Bedford[23] for a witch,
Behold her statue placed in Glory's niche;
Her fetters burst, and just released from prison,
A virgin Phoenix[24] from her ashes risen.   210
Next see tremendous Thalaba[25] come on,
Arabia's monstrous, wild, and wond'rous son;
Domdaniel's[26] dread destroyer, who o'erthrew
More mad magicians than the world e'er knew.
Immortal Hero! all thy foes o'ercome,   215
For ever reign—the rival of Tom Thumb![27]
Since startled Metre fled before thy face,
Well wert thou doomed the last of all thy race!
Well might triumphant Genii bear thee hence,
Illustrious conqueror of common sense!   220
Now, last and greatest, Madoc spreads his sails,
Cacique[28] in Mexico, and Prince in Wales;
Tells us strange tales, as other travellers do,
More old than Mandeville's,[29] and not so true.
Oh, Southey! Southey! cease thy varied song!   225
A bard may chaunt too often and too long:
As thou art strong in verse, in mercy spare!
A fourth, alas! were more than we could bear.

---

[12] Hero of Scott's historical poem of that name (1808).
[13] The Edinburgh publisher Constable paid Scott a thousand guineas for *Marmion*. Two London publishers, John Murray II and William Miller, bought quarter-shares from Constable.
[14] Leaves of a kind of laurel, and hence a symbol of poetic distinction.
[15] In the New Testament the demon of lust for riches.
[16] God of poetry.   [17] Canto VI, stanza xxviii, line 26.
[18] A dozen years later Byron wrote in his journal (Jan. 12, 1821): "Scott is certainly the most wonderful writer of the day. His novels are a new literature in themselves, and his poetry as good as any—if not better (only on an erroneous system). . . . I like him, too, for his manliness of character, for the extreme pleasantness of his conversation, and his good-nature to myself, personally. . . . I know no reading to which I fall with such alacrity as a work of W. Scott's."
[19] Vergil (Publius Vergilius Maro).
[20] Vergil (70–19 B.C.) lived at least nine centuries after Homer.

---

[21] For Robert Southey (1774–1843), not yet poet laureate, see p. 293. Southey wrote numerous ballads and epics.
[22] All justly famous epic poets. They lived, respectively, in sixteenth-century Portugal, seventeenth-century England, and sixteenth-century Italy.
[23] John of Lancaster (1389–1435), Duke of Bedford. He was an English general, uncle of Henry VI and regent; he delivered Joan to her executioners. Southey wrote an epic on her.
[24] The fabulous bird of Egyptian mythology.
[25] *Thalaba the Destroyer* and *Madoc* (line 221) were other epics by Southey.
[26] In Oriental story a magical meeting place for wizards.
[27] Hero of Henry Fielding's famous burlesque, *The Tragedy of Tragedies, or The Life and Death of Tom Thumb the Great* (1730).
[28] Chief.
[29] Sir John Mandeville was the assumed name of an unknown compiler of a fourteenth-century book of travels.

But if, in spite of all the world can say,
Thou still wilt verseward plod thy weary way;[30]   230
If still in Berkeley-Ballads most uncivil,
Thou wilt devote old women to the devil,[31]
The babe unborn thy dread intent may rue:
"God help thee,"[32] Southey, and thy readers too.

Next comes the dull disciple of thy school,   235
That mild apostate from poetic rule,
The simple Wordsworth, framer of a lay
As soft as evening in his favourite May,
Who warns his friend "to shake off toil and
      trouble,
And quit his books, for fear of growing double";[33] 240
Who, both by precept and example, shows
That prose is verse, and verse is merely prose;
Convincing all, by demonstration plain,
Poetic souls delight in prose insane;
And Christmas stories tortured into rhyme[34]   245
Contain the essence of the true sublime.
Thus, when he tells the tale of Betty Foy,
The idiot mother of "an idiot Boy";
A moon-struck, silly lad, who lost his way,
And, like his bard, confounded night with day;   250
So close on each pathetic part he dwells,
And each adventure so sublimely tells,
That all who view the "idiot in his glory"[35]
Conceive the Bard the hero of the story.

Shall gentle Coleridge pass unnoticed here,   255
To turgid ode and tumid stanza dear?
Though themes of innocence amuse him best,
Yet still Obscurity's a welcome guest.
If Inspiration should her aid refuse
To him who takes a Pixy for a muse,[36]   260
Yet none in lofty numbers can surpass
The bard who soars to elegize an ass:[37]
So well the subject suits his noble mind,
He brays, the Laureate of the long-eared kind.

. . .

---

[30] Cf. Gray's "Elegy," line 3, "The plowman homeward
plods his weary way."
[31] In one of Southey's ballads, "The Old Woman of
Berkeley," the Devil carries off the heroine.
[32] Southey, "The Soldier's Wife," line 3.
[33] Cf. the first stanza of "The Tables Turned," p. 56.—In
his own copy of a later edition of his satire, Byron wrote
"Unjust" in the margin of his lines on Wordsworth and
Coleridge.   [34] See Wordsworth's "The Thorn."
[35] Cf. Wordsworth, "The Idiot Boy," line 452: "Thus
answered Johnny in his glory."
[36] Coleridge entitled an early ode "Songs of the Pixies."
[37] An early poem by Coleridge is "To a Young Ass, Its
Mother Being Tethered Near It."

from The Corsair

The Corsair is the third of Byron's Oriental romances
which in 1813–14 took London by storm. A large part
of their fascination for the reading public sprang from
the identification of the hero—who appears with only
slightly varying lineaments in all—with Byron himself. The Byronic hero, whose preliminary portrait
had been sketched in the first two cantos of *Childe
Harold,* has literary antecedents, especially in the
Gothic novels, but it was Byron who developed the
figure in full detail, and it proved highly influential
on innumerable heroes of poems, novels, and plays,
not to mention young men, European and American,
of taste and sensibility. The following excerpt from
The Corsair is the description of the hero Conrad.
For Byron's most mature handling of the type, the
reader is advised to turn to two of his dramas, *Manfred* (1817) and *Cain* (1822), which are unfortunately
too long to be reprinted here.

. . .

That man of loneliness and mystery,
Scarce seen to smile and seldom heard to sigh;
Whose name appals the fiercest of his crew,   175
And tints each swarthy cheek with sallower hue;
Still sways their souls with that commanding art
That dazzles, leads, yet chills the vulgar heart.
What is that spell, that thus his lawless train
Confess and envy, yet oppose in vain?   180
What should it be that thus their faith can bind?
The power of Thought—the magic of the Mind!
Link'd with success, assumed and kept with skill,
That moulds another's weakness to its will;
Wields with their hands, but, still to these un- 185
      known,
Makes even their mightiest deeds appear his own.
Such hath it been—shall be—beneath the sun
The many still must labour for the one!
'Tis Nature's doom—but let the wretch who toils
Accuse not, hate not *him* who wears the spoils. 190
Oh! if he knew the weight of splendid chains,
How light the balance of his humbler pains!

Unlike the heroes of each ancient race,
Demons in act but Gods at least in face,
In Conrad's form seems little to admire,   195
Though his dark eyebrow shades a glance of fire;
Robust but not Herculean—to the sight
No giant frame sets forth his common height;
Yet, in the whole, who paused to look again,
Saw more than marks the crowd of vulgar men; 200
They gaze and marvel how—and still confess
That thus it is, but why they cannot guess.

Sunburnt his cheek, his forehead high and pale
The sable curls in wild profusion veil;
And oft perforce his rising lip reveals   205
The haughtier thought it curbs, but scarce con-
  ceals.
Though smooth his voice and calm his general
  mien,
Still seems there something he would not have
  seen:
His features' deepening lines and varying hue
At times attracted, yet perplex'd the view,   210
As if within that murkiness of mind
Work'd feelings fearful and yet undefined;
Such might it be—that none could truly tell—
Too close enquiry his stern glance would quell.
There breathe but few whose aspect might defy   215
The full encounter of his searching eye:
He had the skill, when Cunning's gaze would seek
To probe his heart and watch his changing cheek,
At once the observer's purpose to espy,
And on himself roll back his scrutiny,   220
Lest he to Conrad rather should betray
Some secret thought, than drag that chief's to day.
There was a laughing Devil in his sneer,
That raised emotions both of rage and fear;
And where his frown of hatred darkly fell,   225
Hope withering fled—and Mercy sigh'd farewell!

Slight are the outward signs of evil thought,
Within—within—'twas there the spirit wrought!
Love shows all changes—Hate, Ambition, Guile,
Betray no further than the bitter smile;   230
The lip's least curl, the lightest paleness thrown
Along the govern'd aspect, speak alone
Of deeper passions; and to judge their mien,
He, who would see, must be himself unseen.
Then—with the hurried tread, the upward eye,   235
The clenchèd hand, the pause of agony,
That listens, starting, lest the step too near
Approach intrusive on that mood of fear:
Then—with each feature working from the heart,
With feelings loosed to strengthen—not depart,   240
That rise—convulse—contend—that freeze or
  glow,
Flush in the cheek, or damp upon the brow;
Then—Stranger! if thou canst and tremblest not,
Behold his soul—the rest that soothes his lot!
Mark—how that lone and blighted bosom sears   245
The scathing thought of execrated years!
Behold—but who hath seen, or e'er shall see,
Man as himself—the secret spirit free?

Yet was not Conrad thus by Nature sent
To lead the guilty—guilt's worst instrument;   250
His soul was changed, before his deeds had driven
Him forth to war with man and forfeit heaven.
Warp'd by the world in Disappointment's school,
In words too wise, in conduct *there* a fool;
Too firm to yield, and far too proud to stoop,   255
Doom'd by his very virtues for a dupe,
He cursed those virtues as the cause of ill,
And not the traitors who betray'd him still;
Nor deem'd that gifts bestow'd on better men
Had left him joy, and means to give again.   260
Fear'd—shunn'd—belied—ere youth had lost her
  force,
He hated man too much to feel remorse
And thought the voice of wrath a sacred call,
To pay the injuries of some on all.
He knew himself a villain—but he deem'd   265
The rest no better than the thing he seem'd;
And scorn'd the best as hypocrites who hid
Those deeds the bolder spirit plainly did.
He knew himself detested, but he knew
The hearts that loathed him, crouch'd and   270
  dreaded too.
Lone, wild, and strange, he stood alike exempt
From all affection and from all contempt:
His name could sadden and his acts surprise,
But they that fear'd him dared not to despise.
Man spurns the worm, but pauses ere he wake   275
The slumbering venom of the folded snake:
The first may turn—but not avenge the blow;
The last expires—but leaves no living foe;
Fast to the doom'd offender's form it clings,
And he may crush—not conquer—still it stings!   280

None are all evil—quickening round his heart,
One softer feeling would not yet depart:
Oft could he sneer at others as beguiled
By passions worthy of a fool or child;
Yet 'gainst that passion vainly still he strove, 285
And even in him it asks the name of Love!
Yes, it was love—unchangeable—unchanged,
Felt but for one from whom he never ranged;
Though fairest captives daily met his eye,
He shunn'd, nor sought, but coldly pass'd them   290
  by;
Though many a beauty droop'd in prison'd
  bower,
None ever soothed his most unguarded hour.
Yes—it was love; if thoughts of tenderness,
Tried in temptation, strengthen'd by distress,

Unmoved by absence, firm in every clime, 295
And yet—Oh more than all!—untired by time;
Which nor defeated hope, nor baffled wile,
Could render sullen were she near to smile,
Nor rage could fire, nor sickness fret to vent
On her one murmur of his discontent; 300
Which still would meet with joy, with calmness
    part,
Lest that his look of grief should reach her heart:
Which nought removed, nor menaced to re-
    move;—
If there be love in mortals—this was love!
He was a villain—ay—reproaches shower 305
On him—but not the passion, nor its power,
Which only proved, all other virtues gone,
Not guilt itself could quench this loveliest
    one!

. . .

She Walks in Beauty

This lyric belongs to a group called *Hebrew Melodies,*
a title without any special application to some of the
poems. Byron generously gave a number of his newest
lyrics to a young composer, Isaac Nathan (1793–1864),
who published them with settings adapted from old
Jewish airs.

She walks in beauty, like the night
    Of cloudless climes and starry skies;
And all that's best of dark and bright
    Meet in her aspect and her eyes:
Thus mellowed to that tender light 5
    Which heaven to gaudy day denies.

One shade the more, one ray the less,
    Had half impaired the nameless grace
Which waves in every raven tress,
    Or softly lightens o'er her face; 10
Where thoughts serenely sweet express,
    How pure, how dear their dwelling-place.

And on that cheek, and o'er that brow,
    So soft, so calm, yet eloquent,
The smiles that win, the tints that glow, 15
    But tell of days in goodness spent,
A mind at peace with all below,
    A heart whose love is innocent!

When We Two Parted

Neither the date nor the occasion of this fine lyric is
certain. It was first published in 1816.

When we two parted
    In silence and tears,
Half broken-hearted
    To sever for years,
Pale grew thy cheek and cold, 5
    Colder thy kiss;
Truly that hour foretold
    Sorrow to this.

The dew of the morning
    Sunk chill on my brow— 10
It felt like the warning
    Of what I feel now.
Thy vows are all broken,
    And light is thy fame:
I hear thy name spoken, 15
    And share in its shame.

They name thee before me,
    A knell to mine ear;
A shudder comes o'er me—
    Why wert thou so dear? 20
They know not I knew thee,
    Who knew thee too well:—
Long, long shall I rue thee,
    Too deeply to tell.

In secret we met— 25
    In silence I grieve,
That thy heart could forget,
    Thy spirit deceive.
If I should meet thee
    After long years, 30
How should I greet thee?—
    With silence and tears.

Stanzas for Music

This poem, which Byron composed in 1815, came
out of a mood of melancholy inspired by his reflecting
on how much less he was affected emotionally than
would once have been the case by the death of a college friend, the Duke of Dorset, who was killed by a
fall from his horse while hunting.

There's not a joy the world can give like that it
  takes away,
When the glow of early thought declines in Feeling's dull decay;
'Tis not on Youth's smooth cheek the blush alone,
  which fades so fast,
But the tender bloom of heart is gone, ere Youth
  itself be past.

Then the few whose spirits float above the wreck   5
  of happiness
Are driven o'er the shoals of guilt or ocean of excess:
The magnet of their course is gone, or only points
  in vain
The shore to which their shivered sail shall never
  stretch again.
Then the mortal coldness of the soul like death
  itself comes down;
It cannot feel for others' woes, it dare not dream   10
  its own;
That heavy chill has frozen o'er the fountain of
  our tears,
And though the eye may sparkle still, 'tis where
  the ice appears.

Though wit may flash from fluent lips, and mirth
  distract the breast,
Through midnight hours that yield no more their
  former hope of rest;
'Tis but as ivy-leaves around the ruined turret   15
  wreath,
All green and wildly fresh without, but worn and
  gray beneath.

Oh, could I feel as I have felt,—or be what I
  have been,
Or weep as I could once have wept, o'er many a
  vanished scene;
As springs, in deserts found, seem sweet, all brackish though they be,
So, midst the withered waste of life, those tears   20
  would flow to me.

Fare Thee Well

The occasion of these lines was the signing, in March
1816, of the deed of separation by the poet and Lady
Byron. At the head of the poem, which was published
in the same year, stood as a motto lines 408–13 and

419–26 of Coleridge's *Christabel* (p. 140): "Alas! they
had been friends in youth," etc.

Fare thee well! and if for ever,
  Still for ever, fare *thee well*:
Even though unforgiving, never
  'Gainst thee shall my heart rebel.
Would that breast were bared before thee   5
  Where thy head so oft hath lain,
While that placid sleep came o'er thee
  Which thou ne'er canst know again:
Would that breast, by thee glanced over,
  Every inmost thought could show!   10
Then thou would'st at last discover
  'Twas not well to spurn it so.
Though the world for this commend thee—
  Though it smile upon the blow,
Even its praises must offend thee,   15
  Founded on another's woe:
Though my many faults defaced me,
  Could no other arm be found,
Than the one which once embraced me,
  To inflict a cureless wound?   20
Yet, oh yet, thyself deceive not—
  Love may sink by slow decay,
But by sudden wrench, believe not
  Hearts can thus be torn away:
Still thine own its life retaineth—   25
  Still must mine, though bleeding, beat;
And the undying thought which paineth
  Is—that we no more may meet.
These are words of deeper sorrow
  Than the wail above the dead;   30
Both shall live—but every morrow
  Wake us from a widowed bed.
And when thou would'st solace gather—
  When our child's[1] first accents flow—
Wilt thou teach her to say "Father!"   35
  Though his care she must forgo?
When her little hands shall press thee—
  When her lip to thine is pressed—
Think of him whose prayer shall bless thee—
  Think of him thy love *had* blessed!   40
Should her lineaments resemble
  Those thou never more may'st see,

[1] Ada (1815–1852), born shortly before her parents separated. Byron never saw her again. She was married in
1835; three years later her husband was created Earl of
Lovelace. One of her three children married the poet,
anti-imperialist, and Arabian-horse breeder Wilfrid Scawen
Blunt.

Then thy heart will softly tremble
  With a pulse yet true to me.
All my faults perchance thou knowest—   45
  All my madness—none can know;
All my hopes—where'er thou goest—
  Wither—yet with *thee* they go.
Every feeling hath been shaken;
  Pride—which not a world could bow—   50
Bows to thee—by thee forsaken,
  Even my soul forsakes me now:
But 'tis done—all words are idle—
  Words from me are vainer still;
But the thoughts we cannot bridle   55
  Force their way without the will.
Fare thee well! thus disunited—
  Torn from every nearer tie—
Seared in heart—and lone—and blighted—
  More than this I scarce can die.   60

from Childe Harold's Pilgrimage

Byron began this poem in the fall of 1809, in Albania.
The first canto was finished in Greece at the end of
the year; the second in Turkey in March 1810. On
May 3 the poet swam the Dardanelles; midsummer
found him back in Athens. His preface to Cantos I
and II, published in 1812, alludes to their composition in the midst of the scenes described. " A fictitious
character," he continues, "is introduced for the sake
of giving some connection to the piece. . . . Harold is
the child of imagination." Actually, of course, Harold
is modeled on the poet himself—not the whole man,
but Byron as he saw or tried to see himself in certain
moods—despite his declaration in a letter that "I
would not be such a fellow as I have made my hero
for all the world." As for the *Childe* of the title, we
have already met this term in the medieval ballads;
it signifies a youth of noble birth.

  Canto III, reprinted in full below, was written
in less than two months, soon after Byron signed the
separation agreement and left England. He finished
it in June 1816, in Switzerland, after his journey
through Belgium and along the Rhine. Eagerly
awaited by the public, it was brought out in London
that fall. The fourth canto was composed in Italy in
the summer and autumn of 1817, and published the
following spring. "Harold," not greatly in evidence
in Canto III, is in this final canto frankly dropped in
favor of the first personal pronoun. Several passages,
including the closing lines, are given below.

  Childe Harold is not a great poem, but it is an
extraordinary accomplishment. Technical mastery is
displayed in the handling of the Spenserian stanza,
the poem is sprinkled with striking passages, and
considering its length it is well sustained. Byron's

eloquent assertion of his capacity for feeling provided
a precedent and a widely adopted model, both in
the writings and in the actual lives of many of his
contemporaries.

CANTO III

Is thy face like thy mother's, my fair child!
Ada![1] sole daughter of my house and heart?
When last I saw thy young blue eyes they smiled,   50
And then we parted,—not as now we part,
But with a hope.[2]—
                    Awaking with a start,   5
The waters heave around me; and on high
The winds lift up their voices: I depart,
Whither I know not; but the hour's gone by,
When Albion's[3] lessening shores could grieve or
    glad mine eye.

Once more upon the waters! yet once more!   10
And the waves bound beneath me as a steed
That knows his rider. Welcome to their roar!
Swift be their guidance, wheresoe'er it lead!
Though the strained mast should quiver as a
    reed,
And the rent canvas fluttering strew the gale,   15
Still must I on; for I am as a weed,
Flung from the rock, on Ocean's foam to sail
Where'er the surge may sweep, the tempest's
    breath prevail.

In my youth's summer[4] I did sing of One,
The wandering outlaw of his own dark mind;   20
Again I seize the theme, then but begun,
And bear it with me, as the rushing wind
Bears the cloud onwards: in that Tale I find
The furrows of long thought, and dried-up tears,
Which, ebbing, leave a sterile track behind,   25
O'er which all heavily the journeying years
Plod the last sands of life,—where not a flower
    appears.

Since my young days of passion—joy or pain—
Perchance my heart and harp have lost a string—
And both may jar: it may be that in vain   30
I would essay, as I have sung, to sing:
Yet, though a dreary strain, to this I cling;

---

1 See note 1 of preceding poem.
2 That he might see her again; it was slowly and reluctantly that he abandoned hope of a reconciliation with
Lady Byron.   3 England's.
4 Byron was only twenty-one when he wrote Canto I of
this poem.

So that[5] it wean me from the weary dream
Of selfish grief or gladness—so it fling
Forgetfulness around me—it shall seem   35
To me, though to none else, a not ungrateful
    theme.

He, who grown agèd in this world of woe,
In deeds, not years, piercing the depths of life,
So that no wonder waits him—nor below
Can Love or Sorrow, Fame, Ambition, Strife,   40
Cut to his heart again with the keen knife
Of silent, sharp endurance—he can tell
Why Thought seeks refuge in lone caves, yet rife
With airy images, and shapes which dwell
Still unimpaired, though old, in the Soul's   45
    haunted cell.

'Tis to create, and in creating live
A being more intense, that we endow
With form our fancy, gaining as we give
The life we image, even as I do now—
What am I? Nothing: but not so art thou,   50
Soul of my thought! with whom I traverse earth,
Invisible but gazing, as I glow
Mixed with thy spirit, blended with thy birth,
And feeling still with thee in my crushed feelings'
    dearth.

Yet must I think less wildly:—I *have* thought   55
Too long and darkly, till my brain became
In its own eddy boiling and o'erwrought,
A whirling gulf of phantasy and flame;
And thus, untaught in youth my heart to tame,
My springs of life were poisoned. 'Tis too late!   60
Yet am I changed; though still enough the same
In strength to bear what Time can not abate,
And feed on bitter fruits without accusing Fate.

Something too much of this:[6]—but now 'tis past,
And the spell closes with its silent seal.[7]   65
Long absent Harold re-appears at last—
He of the breast which fain no more would feel,
Wrung with the wounds which kill not, but ne'er
    heal;
Yet Time, who changes all, had altered him
In soul and aspect as in age: years steal   70
Fire from the mind as vigour from the limb;

And Life's enchanted cup but sparkles near the
    brim.

His had been quaffed too quickly, and he found
The dregs were wormwood; but he filled again,
And from a purer fount, on holier ground,   75
And deemed its spring perpetual—but in vain!
Still round him clung invisibly a chain
Which galled forever, fettering though unseen,
And heavy though it clanked not; worn with
    pain,
Which pined although it spoke not, and grew   80
    keen,
Entering with every step he took through many
    a scene.

Secure in guarded coldness he had mixed
Again in fancied safety with his kind,
And deemed his spirit now so firmly fixed
And sheathed with an invulnerable mind,   85
That, if no joy, no sorrow lurked behind;
And he, as one, might 'midst the many stand
Unheeded, searching through the crowd to find
Fit speculation—such as in strange land
He found in wonder-works of God and Nature's   90
    hand.

But who can view the ripened rose, nor seek
To wear it? who can curiously behold
The smoothness and the sheen of Beauty's cheek,
Nor feel the heart can never all grow old?
Who can contémplate Fame through clouds un-   95
    fold
The star which rises o'er her steep, nor climb?[8]
Harold, once more within the vortex, rolled
On with the giddy circle, chasing Time,
Yet with a nobler aim than in his Youth's fond
    prime.[9]

But soon he knew himself the most unfit   100
Of men to herd with Man, with whom he held
Little in common; untaught to submit
His thoughts to others, though his soul was
    quelled
In youth by his own thoughts: still uncompelled,
He would not yield dominion of his mind   105
To Spirits against whom his own rebelled,

---

[5] Provided that, if.   [6] *Hamlet*, III, ii, 79.
[7] I.e., on the story ("spell") of my personal affairs is set the seal of silence. He will proceed with *Harold's* story.

[8] I.e., without attempting to climb to the mountain peak where Fame resides.   [9] Foolish spring.

Proud though in desolation—which could find
A life within itself, to breathe without mankind.

Where rose the mountains, there to him were
    friends;
Where rolled the Ocean, thereon was his home;   110
Where a blue sky, and glowing clime, extends,
He had the passion and the power to roam;
The desert, forest, cavern, breaker's foam,
Were unto him companionship; they spake
A mutual language, clearer than the tome   115
Of his land's tongue, which he would oft forsake
For Nature's pages glassed[10] by sunbeams on the
    lake.

Like the Chaldean[11] he could watch the stars,
Till he had peopled them with beings bright
As their own beams; and earth, and earthborn   120
    jars,
And human frailties, were forgotten quite:
Could he have kept his spirit to that flight
He had been happy; but this clay will sink
Its spark immortal, envying it the light
To which it mounts, as if to break the link   125
That keeps us from yon heaven which woos us to
    its brink.

But in Man's dwellings he became a thing
Restless and worn, and stern and wearisome,
Drooped as a wild-born falcon with clipt wing,
To whom the boundless air alone were home: 130
Then came his fit again,[12] which to o'ercome,
As eagerly the barred-up bird will beat
His breast and beak against his wiry dome
Till the blood tinge his plumage—so the heat
Of his impeded Soul would through his bosom   135
    eat.

Self-exiled Harold wanders forth again,
With nought of Hope left—but with less of
    gloom;
The very knowledge that he lived in vain,
That all was over on this side the tomb,
Had made Despair a smilingness assume,   140
Which, though 'twere wild,—as on the plundered
    wreck
When mariners would madly meet their doom

With draughts intemperate on the sinking deck,—
Did yet inspire a cheer, which he forbore to check.

Stop!—for thy tread is on an Empire's dust!   145
An Earthquake's spoil is sepulchered below!
Is the spot marked with no colossal bust?
Nor column trophied for triumphal show?
None;[13] but the *moral's truth*[14] tells simpler so.
As the ground was before, thus let it be;—   150
How that red rain hath made the harvest grow!
And is this all the world has gained by thee,
Thou first and last of Fields! king-making[15] vic-
    tory?

And Harold stands upon this place of skulls,
The grave of France, the deadly Waterloo!   155
How in an hour the Power which gave annuls
Its gifts, transferring fame as fleeting too!—
In "pride of place"[16] here last the Eagle[17] flew,
Then tore with bloody talon the rent plain,
Pierced by the shaft of banded nations through;   160
Ambition's life and labours all were vain—
He wears[18] the shattered links of the World's
    broken chain.

Fit retribution! Gaul[19] may champ the bit
And foam in fetters;—but is earth more free?
Did nations combat to make *One* submit?   165
Or league to teach all Kings true Sovereignty?
What! shall reviving Thraldom again be
The patched-up Idol[20] of enlightened days?
Shall we, who struck the Lion[21] down, shall we
Pay the Wolf[22] homage? proffering lowly gaze   170
And servile knees to Thrones? No; *prove*[23] before
    ye praise!

---

[13] Napoleon was finally defeated at Waterloo, near Brussels, on June 18, 1815, less than a year before Byron visited the field, over which he rode twice.
[14] I.e., that the world reaped no advantage. Byron considered the battle a victory for the forces of reaction.
[15] For the emperor, whom some still considered the heir of the French Revolution, was beaten; the Bourbon, Louis XVIII, was king of France; and the other European monarchs could now feel secure on their thrones.
[16] The height of a bird's, especially a falcon's, flight. Quoted from *Macbeth*, II, iv, 12.   [17] Napoleon.
[18] Under guard, on his way to St. Helena.   [19] France.
[20] The so-called Holy Alliance made by the European monarchs. It became in the minds of liberals a symbol of the prevailing reaction.   [21] Napoleon.
[22] A dangerous but far from royal beast. The application is made in the clause which follows.
[23] Test the quality (of Europe's monarchs).

---

[10] Mirrored.
[11] The Chaldeans of ancient Babylonia were famous astronomers and named a good many stars.
[12] Cf. *Macbeth*, III, iv, 21.

If not, o'er one fallen Despot boast no more!
In vain fair cheeks were furrowed with hot tears
For Europe's flowers long rooted up before
The trampler of her vineyards; in vain, years   175
Of death, depopulation, bondage, fears,
Have all been borne, and broken by the accord
Of roused-up millions: all that most endears
Glory, is when the myrtle wreathes a Sword
Such as Harmodius[24] drew on Athens' tyrant lord.   180

There was a sound of revelry by night,[25]
And Belgium's Capital had gathered then
Her Beauty and her Chivalry—and bright
The lamps shone o'er fair women and brave men;
A thousand hearts beat happily; and when   185
Music arose with its voluptuous swell,
Soft eyes looked love to eyes which spake again,
And all went merry as a marriage bell;
But hush! hark! a deep sound strikes like a rising
    knell!

Did ye not hear it?—No—'twas but the Wind,   190
Or the car rattling o'er the stony street;
On with the dance! let joy be unconfined;
No sleep till morn when Youth and Pleasure meet
To chase the glowing Hours with flying feet—
But hark!——that heavy sound breaks in once   195
    more.
As if the clouds its echo would repeat;
And nearer—clearer—deadlier than before!
Arm! Arm! it is—it is—the cannon's opening
    roar!

Within a windowed niche of that high hall
Sate Brunswick's fated Chieftain;[26] he did hear   200
That sound the first amidst the festival,
And caught its tone with Death's prophetic ear;
And when they smiled because he deemed it near,
His heart more truly knew that peal too well

Which stretched his father on a bloody bier,   205
And roused the vengeance blood alone could
    quell;
He rushed into the field, and, foremost fighting,
    fell.

Ah! then and there was hurrying to and fro—
And gathering tears, and tremblings of distress,
And cheeks all pale, which but an hour ago
Blushed at the praise of their own loveliness;   210
And there were sudden partings, such as press
The life from out young hearts, and choking
    sighs
Which ne'er might be repeated; who could guess
If ever more should meet those mutual eyes,   215
Since upon night so sweet such awful morn could
    rise!

And there was mounting in hot haste—the steed,
The mustering squadron, and the clattering car,
Went pouring forward with impetuous speed,
And swiftly forming in the ranks of war—   220
And the deep thunder peal on peal afar;
And near, the beat of the alarming drum
Roused up the soldier ere the Morning Star;
While thronged the citizens with terror dumb,
Or whispering, with white lips—"The foe! They   225
    come! They come!"

And wild and high the "Cameron's Gathering"[27]
    rose!
The war-note of Lochiel, which Albyn's[28] hills
Have heard, and heard, too, have her Saxon[29]
    foes:
How in the noon of night that pibroch[30] thrills,
Savage and shrill! But with the breath which fills   230
Their mountain-pipe, so fill the mountaineers
With the fierce native daring which instils
The stirring memory of a thousand years,
And Evan's—Donald's,[31] fame rings in each clans-
    man's ears!

---

24 In 514 B.C. the Athenian youths Harmodius and Aris-
togiton, concealing their weapons in myrtle branches,
assassinated the tyrant Hipparchus.
25 This famous passage refers to the ball (also described
by Thackeray in *Vanity Fair*, chaps. 29–32) given by the
Duchess of Richmond in Brussels the evening (June 15)
before the Waterloo campaign opened with the Battle of
Quatre Bras.
26 Friedrich Wilhelm, Duke of Brunswick (1771–1815),
nephew of George III, fell at Quatre Bras. His father,
Duke Karl Wilhelm, was mortally wounded in 1806 at the
Battle of Auerstedt, when the Prussian army under his
command was defeated by Davout, one of Napoleon's
marshals.

27 The tune to which the Camerons gathered for war,
played here as an assembly for the 92nd Highlanders. The
chief of clan Cameron was called Lochiel, from his estate.
28 An old name of northern Scotland.
29 English and Lowland Scotch.
30 Martial music for the bagpipes.
31 Sir Evan Cameron of Lochiel (1629–1719) fought for
the Stuarts in 1652, and raised his clan for them at
Killiecrankie (1689) and again in the uprising of 1715.
His grandson, Sir Donald, fought for Prince Charlie in
1745–46 and, escaping with a wound at Culloden, fled
with him to France. Sir Evan's great-great-grandson, John
Cameron, commanding the 92nd, was mortally wounded
at Quatre Bras on June 16, 1815.

And Ardennes[32] waves above them her green   235
   leaves,
Dewy with Nature's tear-drops, as they pass—
Grieving, if aught inanimate e'er grieves,
Over the unreturning brave,—alas!
Ere evening to be trodden like the grass
Which *now* beneath them, but *above* shall grow   240
In its next verdure, when this fiery mass
Of living Valour, rolling on the foe
And burning with high Hope shall moulder cold
   and low.

Last noon beheld them full of lusty life;—
Last eve in Beauty's circle proudly gay;   245
The Midnight brought the signal-sound of strife,
The morn the marshalling in arms,—the Day
Battle's magnificently-stern array!
The thunder-clouds close o'er it, which when rent
The earth is covered thick with other clay   250
Which her own clay shall cover, heaped and
   pent,[33]
Rider and horse,—friend,—foe—in one red burial
   blent!

Their praise is hymned by loftier harps than
   mine;
Yet one I would select from that proud throng,
Partly because they blend me with his line,   255
And partly that I did his Sire[34] some wrong,
And partly that bright names will hallow song;
And his was of the bravest, and when showered
The death-bolts deadliest the thinned files along,
Even where the thickest of War's tempest   260
   lowered,
They reached no nobler breast than thine, young,
   gallant Howard![35]

There have been tears and breaking hearts for
   thee,
And mine were nothing, had I such to give;

But when I stood beneath the fresh green tree,
Which living waves where thou didst cease to   265
   live,
And saw around me the wide field revive
With fruits and fertile promise, and the Spring
Come forth her work of gladness to contrive,
With all her reckless birds upon the wing,
I turned from all she brought to those she could   270
   not bring.

I turned to thee, to thousands, of whom each
And one as all a ghastly gap did make
In his own kind and kindred, whom to teach
Forgetfulness were mercy for their sake;
The Archangel's trump, not Glory's, must awake   275
Those whom they thirst for; though the sound of
   Fame
May for a moment soothe, it cannot slake
The fever of vain longing, and the name
So honoured but assumes a stronger, bitterer
   claim.

They mourn, but smile at length—and, smiling,   280
   mourn:
The tree will wither long before it fall;
The hull drives on, though mast and sail be torn;
The roof-tree sinks, but moulders on the hall
In massy hoariness; the ruined wall
Stands when its wind-worn battlements are gone;   285
The bars survive the captive they enthral;
The day drags through, though storms keep out
   the sun;
And thus the heart will break, yet brokenly live
   on:

Even as a broken Mirror, which the glass
In every fragment multiplies—and makes   290
A thousand images of one that was
The same—and still the more, the more it breaks;
And thus the heart will do which not forsakes,
Living in shattered guise; and still, and cold,
And bloodless, with its sleepless sorrow aches,   295
Yet withers on till all without is old,
Showing no visible sign, for such things are un-
   told.

There is a very life in our despair,
Vitality of poison,—a quick root
Which feeds these deadly branches; for it were   300
As nothing did we die; but Life will suit
Itself to Sorrow's most detested fruit,

---

32 The forest in Belgium and northeastern France where the United States Army has also made history.
33 Confined.
34 Frederick Howard (1748–1825), fifth Earl of Carlisle, Byron's childhood guardian and his second cousin, whose writings he had insultingly characterized in *English Bards, and Scotch Reviewers,* line 726.
35 Frederick Howard (1785–1815), the Earl's third son, fell at Waterloo late in the evening of the 18th, in the last cavalry charge against the left square of the French Guard. He was temporarily buried on the field, under three trees.

Like to the apples[36] on the Dead Sea's shore,
All ashes to the taste: Did man compute
Existence by enjoyment, and count o'er   305
Such hours 'gainst years of life,—say, would he
    name threescore?

The Psalmist numbered out the years of man:
They are enough; and if thy tale be *true,*
Thou, who didst grudge him even that fleeting
    span,
More than enough, thou fatal Waterloo![37]   310
Millions of tongues record thee, and anew
Their children's lips shall echo them, and say—
"Here, where the sword united nations drew,
Our countrymen were warring on that day!"
And this is much—and all—which will not pass 315
    away.

There sunk the greatest nor the worst of men,[38]
Whose Spirit, antithetically mixed,
One moment of the mightiest, and again
On little objects with like firmness fixed;
Extreme in all things! hadst thou been betwixt, 320
Thy throne had still been thine, or never been;
For daring made thy rise as fall: thou seek'st
Even now to re-assume the imperial mien,[39]
And shake again the world, the Thunderer of the
    scene!

Conqueror and Captive of the Earth art thou!   325
She trembles at thee still, and thy wild name
Was ne'er more bruited in men's minds than now
That thou art nothing, save the jest of Fame,
Who wooed thee once, thy Vassal, and became
The flatterer of thy fierceness—till thou wert 330
A God unto thyself; nor less the same
To the astounded kingdoms all inert,
Who deemed thee for a time whate'er thou didst
    assert.

Oh, more or less than man—in high or low—
Battling with nations, flying from the field;   335
Now making monarchs' necks thy footstool, now
More than thy meanest soldier taught to yield;

An Empire thou could'st crush, command, re-
    build,
But govern not thy pettiest passion, nor,
However deeply in men's spirits skilled,   340
Look through thine own, nor curb the lust of
    War,
Nor learn that tempted Fate will leave the loftiest
    Star.

Yet well thy soul hath brooked the turning tide
With that untaught innate philosophy,
Which, be it Wisdom, Coldness, or deep Pride,   345
Is gall and wormwood to an enemy.
When the whole host of hatred stood hard by,
To watch and mock thee shrinking, thou hast
    smiled
With a sedate and all-enduring eye;—
When Fortune fled her spoiled and favourite   350
    child,
He stood unbowed beneath the ills upon him
    piled.

Sager than in thy fortunes; for in them
Ambition steeled thee on too far to show
That just habitual scorn, which could contemn
Men and their thoughts; 'twas wise to feel, not so 355
To wear it ever on thy lip and brow,
And spurn the instruments thou wert to use
Till they were turned unto thine overthrow:
'Tis but a worthless world to win or lose;
So hath it proved to thee, and all such lot who 360
    choose.

If, like a tower upon a headlong rock,
Thou hadst been made to stand or fall alone,
Such scorn of man had helped to brave the shock;
But men's thoughts were the steps which paved
    thy throne,
Their admiration thy best weapon shone;
The part of Philip's son[40] was thine—not then 365
(Unless aside thy Purple[41] had been thrown)
Like stern Diogenes[42] to mock at men:
For sceptered cynics earth were far too wide a
    den.

But Quiet to quick bosoms is a Hell,
And *there* hath been thy bane; there is a fire   370

---

36 According to travelers, a fruit externally promising but
worthless within.
37 Since the men who fell there were young, whereas in
Psalms 90:10 from seventy to eighty years are specified.
38 Napoleon—neither the greatest nor the worst.
39 He complained that, although his French suite continued to give him an emperor's honors, his British cap-
tors did not.

---

40 Alexander the Great, son of Philip II of Macedon.
41 Symbol of royalty.
42 The Greek cynic philosopher (d. 332 B.C.), a contemporary of Alexander.

And motion of the Soul which will not dwell
In its own narrow being, but aspire
Beyond the fitting medium of desire;
And, but once kindled, quenchless evermore,   375
Preys upon high adventure, nor can tire
Of aught but rest; a fever at the core,
Fatal to him who bears, to all who ever bore.

This makes the madmen who have made men mad
By their contagion; Conquerors and Kings,   380
Founders of sects and systems, to whom add
Sophists, Bards, Statesmen, all unquiet things
Which stir too strongly the soul's secret springs,
And are themselves the fools to those they fool;
Envied, yet how unenviable! what stings   385
Are theirs! One breast laid open were a school
Which would unteach Mankind the lust to shine
      or rule:

Their breath is agitation, and their life
A storm whereon they ride, to sink at last,
And yet so nursed and bigoted to strife,   390
That should their days, surviving perils past,
Melt to calm twilight, they feel overcast
With sorrow and supineness, and so die;
Even as a flame unfed, which runs to waste
With its own flickering, or a sword laid by,   395
Which eats into itself, and rusts ingloriously.

He who ascends to mountain tops shall find
The loftiest peaks most wrapt in clouds and
      snow;
He who surpasses or subdues mankind,
Must look down on the hate of those below.   400
Though high *above* the Sun of Glory glow,
And far *beneath* the Earth and Ocean spread,
Round him are icy rocks, and loudly blow
Contending tempests on his naked head,
And thus reward the toils which to those summits   405
      led.

Away with these! true Wisdom's world will be
Within its own creation, or in thine,
Maternal Nature! for who teems[43] like thee,
Thus on the banks of thy majestic Rhine?
There Harold gazes on a work divine,   410
A blending of all beauties; streams and dells,
Fruit, foliage, crag, wood, cornfield,[44] mountain,
      vine,

And chiefless castles breathing stern farewells
From gray but leafy walls, where Ruin greenly
      dwells.

And there they stand, as stands a lofty mind,   415
Worn, but unstooping to the baser crowd,
All tenantless, save to the crannying Wind,
Or holding dark communion with the Cloud.
There was a day when they were young and proud;
Banners on high, and battles[45] passed below;   420
But they who fought are in a bloody shroud,
And those which waved are shredless dust ere
      now,
And the bleak battlements shall bear no future
      blow.

Beneath these battlements, within those walls,
Power dwelt amidst her passions; in proud state   425
Each robber chief upheld his armèd halls,
Doing his evil will, nor less elate
Than mightier heroes of a longer date.
What want these outlaws[46] conquerors should
      have,
But History's purchased page to call them great?   430
A wider space—an ornamented grave?
Their hopes were not less warm, their souls were
      full as brave.

In their baronial feuds and single fields,
What deeds of prowess unrecorded died!
And Love, which lent a blazon[47] to their shields,   435
With emblems well devised by amorous pride,
Through all the mail of iron hearts would glide;
But still their flame was fierceness, and drew on
Keen contest and destruction near allied,
And many a tower for some fair mischief won,   440
Saw the discoloured Rhine beneath its ruin run.

But Thou, exulting and abounding river!
Making thy waves a blessing as they flow
Through banks whose beauty would endure for-
      ever
Could man but leave thy bright creation so,   445
Nor its fair promise from the surface mow
With the sharp scythe of conflict,—then to see
Thy valley of sweet waters, were to know
Earth paved like Heaven—and to seem such to
      me,

---

[43] Breeds; is productive.—We have left Belgium, and are
southward bound up the Rhine.   [44] Grain field.

[45] Battalions, forces.
[46] What do these outlaws, i.e., the old German robber-
barons, lack which. . . .   [47] A colorful heraldic device.

Even now what wants thy stream?—that it should 450
    Lethe[48] be.

A thousand battles have assailed thy banks,
But these and half their fame have passed away,
And Slaughter heaped on high his weltering
    ranks:
Their very graves are gone, and what are they?
Thy tide washed down the blood of yesterday, 455
And all was stainless, and on thy clear stream
Glassed, with its dancing light, the sunny ray;
But o'er the blackened Memory's blighting dream
Thy waves would vainly roll, all sweeping as they
    seem.

Thus Harold inly said, and passed along, 460
Yet not insensible to all which here
Awoke the jocund birds to early song
In glens which might have made even exile dear:
Though on his brow were graven lines austere,
And tranquil sternness, which had ta'en the place 465
Of feelings fierier far but less severe—
Joy was not always absent from his face,
But o'er it in such scenes would steal with tran-
    sient trace.

Nor was all love shut from him, though his days
Of Passion had consumed themselves to dust. 470
It is in vain that we would coldly gaze
On such as smile upon us; the heart must
Leap kindly back to kindness, though Disgust
Hath weaned it from all worldlings: thus he felt,
For there was soft Remembrance, and sweet Trust 475
In one fond breast,[49] to which his own would
    melt,
And in its tenderer hour on that his bosom dwelt.

And he had learned to love,—I know not why,
For this in such as him seems strange of mood,—
The helpless looks of blooming Infancy, 480
Even in its earliest nurture; what subdued,
To change like this, a mind so far imbued
With scorn of man, it little boots to know;
But thus it was; and though in solitude
Small power the nipped affections have to grow, 485
In him this glowed when all beside had ceased to
    glow.

And there was one soft breast, as hath been said,

Which unto his was bound by stronger ties
Than the church links withal;[50] and,—though
    unwed,
That love was pure—and, far above disguise, 490
Had stood the test of mortal enmities,
Still undivided, and cemented more
By peril, dreaded most in female eyes;
But this was firm, and from a foreign shore
Well to that heart might his these absent greet- 495
    ings pour!

1

The castled Crag of Drachenfels[51]
Frowns o'er the wide and winding Rhine,
Whose breast of waters broadly swells
Between the banks which bear the vine;
And hills all rich with blossomed trees, 500
And fields which promise corn and wine,
And scattered cities crowning these,
Whose far white walls along them shine.
Have strewed a scene, which I should see
With double joy wert *thou* with me. 505

2

And peasant girls, with deep blue eyes,
And hands which offer early flowers,
Walk smiling o'er this Paradise;
Above, the frequent feudal towers
Through green leaves lift their walls of gray; 510
And many a rock which steeply lowers,
And noble arch in proud decay,
Look o'er this vale of vintage-bowers;
But one thing want these banks of Rhine,—
Thy gentle hand to clasp in mine! 515

3

I send the lilies given to me—
Though long before thy hand they touch,
I know that they must withered be,
But yet reject them not as such;
For I have cherished them as dear, 520
Because they yet may meet thine eye,
And guide thy soul to mine even here,—
When thou behold'st them drooping nigh,
And know'st them gathered by the Rhine,
And offered from my heart to thine! 525

---

[48] The river of forgetfulness.
[49] Of his half-sister, Augusta Leigh.
[50] With.
[51] The Dragon's Rock, on the Rhine near Bonn.

4

The river nobly foams and flows—
The charm of this enchanted ground,
And all its thousand turns disclose
Some fresher beauty varying round:
The haughtiest breast its wish might bound   530
Through life to dwell delighted here;
Nor could on earth a spot be found
To Nature and to me so dear—
Could thy dear eyes in following mine
Still sweeten more these banks of Rhine!   535

By Coblentz, on a rise of gentle ground,
There is a small and simple Pyramid
Crowning the summit of the verdant mound;
Beneath its base are Heroes' ashes hid—
Our enemy's—but let not that forbid   540
Honor to Marceau![52] o'er whose early tomb
Tears, big tears, gushed from the rough soldier's
     lid,
Lamenting and yet envying such a doom,
Falling for France, whose rights he battled to re-
     sume.

Brief, brave, and glorious was his young career,—   545
His mourners were two hosts, his friends and foes;
And fitly may the stranger lingering here
Pray for his gallant Spirit's bright repose;—
For he was Freedom's Champion, one of those
The few in number, who had not o'erstept   550
The charter to chastise which she bestows
On such as wield her weapons; he had kept
The whiteness of his soul, and thus men o'er him
     wept.

Here Ehrenbreitstein,[53] with her shattered wall
Black with the miner's blast, upon her height   555
Yet shows of what she was, when shell and ball
Rebounding idly on her strength did light:—
A tower of Victory! from whence the flight
Of baffled foes was watched along the plain:
But Peace destroyed what War could never blight,   560
And laid those proud roofs bare to Summer's
     rain—
On which the iron shower for years had poured
     in vain.

Adieu to thee, fair Rhine! How long delighted
The stranger fain would linger on his way!
Thine is a scene alike where souls united   565
Or lonely Contemplation thus might stray;
And could the ceaseless vultures cease to prey
On self-condemning bosoms, it were here,
Where Nature, nor too somber nor too gay,
Wild but not rude, awful yet not austere,   570
Is to the mellow Earth as Autumn to the year.

Adieu to thee again! a vain adieu!
There can be no farewell to scene like thine;
The mind is coloured by thy every hue;
And if reluctantly the eyes resign   575
Their cherished gaze upon thee, lovely Rhine!
'Tis with the thankful glance of parting praise;
More mighty spots may rise—more glaring shine,
But none unite in one attaching maze,
The brilliant, fair, and soft,—the glories of old   580
     days,

The negligently grand, the fruitful bloom
Of coming ripeness, the white city's sheen,
The rolling stream, the precipice's gloom,
The forest's growth, and Gothic walls between,—
The wild rocks shaped, as they had turrets been,   585
In mockery of man's art; and these withal[54]
A race of faces happy as the scene,
Whose fertile bounties here extend to all,
Still springing o'er thy banks, though Empires
     near them fall.

But these recede. Above me are the Alps,   590
The Palaces of Nature, whose vast walls
Have pinnacled in clouds their snowy scalps,
And throned Eternity in icy halls
Of cold Sublimity, where forms and falls
The Avalanche—the thunderbolt of snow!   595
All that expands the spirit, yet appals,
Gather around these summits, as to show
How Earth may pierce to Heaven, yet leave vain
     man below.

But ere these matchless heights I dare to scan,
There is a spot should not be passed in vain,—   600
Morat![55] the proud, the patriot field! where man

---

[52] François Séverin Marceau (1769–1796), killed at Alten-kirchen. As the inscription relates, he was a soldier at sixteen and a general at twenty-two.
[53] A famous fortress, opposite Coblentz; after a long siege, it was surrendered to the French in 1799, and soon after dismantled.

[54] Along with these.
[55] Between Fribourg and Neuchâtel in Switzerland. At Morat in 1476 the Swiss defeated Charles the Bold, Duke of Burgundy. The bones of the Burgundians were not permanently entombed till 1822.

May gaze on ghastly trophies of the slain,
Nor blush for those who conquered on that plain;
Here Burgundy bequeathed his tombless host,
A bony heap, through ages to remain,   605
Themselves their monument; the Stygian coast[56]
Unsepulchered they roamed, and shrieked each
    wandering ghost.

While Waterloo with Cannae's[57] carnage vies,
Morat and Marathon[58] twin names shall stand;
They were true Glory's stainless victories,   610
Won by the unambitious heart and hand
Of a proud, brotherly, and civic band,
All unbought champions in no princely cause
Of vice-entailed Corruption; they no land
Doomed to bewail the blasphemy of laws   615
Making Kings' rights divine, by some Draconic[59]
    clause.

By a lone wall a lonelier column rears
A gray and grief-worn aspect of old days;
'Tis the last remnant of the wreck of years,
And looks as with the wild-bewildered gaze   620
Of one to stone converted by amaze,
Yet still with consciousness; and there it stands
Making a marvel that it not decays,
When the coeval[60] pride of human hands,
Leveled Aventicum,[61] hath strewed her subject   625
    lands.

And there—oh! sweet and sacred be the name!
Julia[62]—the daughter—the devoted—gave
Her youth to Heaven; her heart, beneath a claim
Nearest to Heaven's, broke o'er a father's grave.
Justice is sworn 'gainst tears, and hers would   630
    crave
The life she lived in—but the Judge was just—
And then she died on him she could not save.
Their tomb was simple, and without a bust,

---

[56] The bank of the mythological River Styx, on the border of Hades.
[57] In southeastern Italy. There in 216 B.C. Hannibal, in one of the most brilliant battles of history, defeated the Romans with great slaughter.
[58] The plain on the coast north of Athens, where in 490 B.C. the Persian invaders were crushed by the Greeks.
[59] Harsh. The Athenian legal code drawn up c. 621 B.C. by Draco was regarded as extremely severe.
[60] Contemporary.
[61] The Roman capital of Helvetia (Switzerland), near Morat. The column was all that remained.
[62] Julius Alpinus was executed by the Romans in 69 A.D. for rebellion. An account of how his daughter, a young priestess, died after an attempt to save him seems to be a Renaissance forgery.

And held within their urn one mind—one heart
    —one dust.

But these are deeds which should not pass away,   635
And names that must not wither, though the
    Earth
Forgets her empires with a just decay,
The enslavers and the enslaved—their death and
    birth;
The high, the mountain-majesty of Worth
Should be—and shall, survivor of its woe,   640
And from its immortality, look forth
In the Sun's face, like yonder Alpine snow,[63]
Imperishably pure beyond all things below.

Lake Leman[64] woos me with its crystal face,
The mirror where the stars and mountains view   645
The stillness of their aspect in each trace
Its clear depth yields of their far height and hue:
There is too much of Man here, to look through
With a fit mind the might which I behold;
But soon in me shall Loneliness renew   650
Thoughts hid, but not less cherished than of old,
Ere mingling with the herd had penned me in
    their fold.

To fly from, need not be to hate, mankind:
All are not fit with them to stir and toil,
Nor is it discontent to keep the mind   655
Deep in its fountain, lest it overboil
In the hot throng, where we become the spoil
Of our infection, till, too late and long,
We may deplore and struggle with the coil,[65]
In wretched interchange of wrong for wrong   660
Midst a contentious world, striving where none
    are strong.

There, in a moment, we may plunge our years
In fatal penitence, and in the blight
Of our own Soul turn all our blood to tears,
And colour things to come with hues of Night;   665
The race of life becomes a hopeless flight
To those that walk in darkness: on the sea
The boldest steer but where their ports invite—
But there are wanderers o'er eternity,

---

[63] Mont Blanc.
[64] Lake Geneva. On the southern shore, near the Shelleys, Byron had taken the Villa Diodati. "Too much of Man," etc. (lines 648 ff.), doubtless refers to his anxiety to secure privacy from tourists who were attracted by his notoriety.
[65] Tumult, trouble.

Whose bark drives on and on, and anchored ne'er 670
    shall be.

Is it not better, then, to be alone,
And love Earth only for its earthly sake?
By the blue rushing of the arrowy Rhone,
Or the pure bosom of its nursing Lake,
Which feeds it as a mother who doth make 675
A fair but froward[66] infant her own care,
Kissing its cries away as these awake;—
Is it not better thus our lives to wear,
Than join the crushing crowd, doomed to inflict
    or bear?

I live not in myself, but I become 680
Portion of that around me; and to me
High mountains are a feeling, but the hum
Of human cities torture: I can see
Nothing to loathe in Nature, save to be
A link reluctant in a fleshly chain, 685
Classed among creatures, when the soul can flee,
And with the sky—the peak—the heaving plain
Of ocean, or the stars, mingle—and not in vain.

And thus I am absorbed, and this is life:—
I look upon the peopled desert past, 690
As on a place of agony and strife,
Where, for some sin, to Sorrow I was cast,
To act and suffer, but remount at last
With a fresh pinion; which I feel to spring,
Though young, yet waxing vigorous as the Blast 695
Which it would cope with, on delighted wing,
Spurning the clay-cold bonds which round our
    being cling.

And when, at length, the mind shall be all free
From what it hates in this degraded form,
Reft of its carnal life, save what shall be 700
Existent happier in the fly and worm,—
When Elements to Elements conform,
And dust is as it should be, shall I not
Feel all I see, less dazzling, but more warm?
The bodiless thought? the Spirit of each spot? 705
Of which, even now, I share at times the im-
    mortal lot?

Are not the mountains, waves, and skies, a part
Of me and of my Soul, as I of them?
Is not the love of these deep in my heart

With a pure passion? should I not contemn 710
All objects, if compared with these? and stem
A tide of suffering, rather than forgo
Such feelings for the hard and worldly phlegm
Of those whose eyes are only turned below,
Gazing upon the ground, with thoughts which 715
    dare not glow?

But this is not my theme; and I return
To that which is immediate, and require
Those who find contemplation in the urn,
To look on One, whose dust was once all fire,—
A native of the land where I respire 720
The clear air for a while—a passing guest,
Where he became a being,—whose desire
Was to be glorious; 'twas a foolish quest,
The which to gain and keep, he sacrificed all rest.

Here the self-torturing sophist, wild Rousseau, 725
The apostle of Affliction, he who threw
Enchantment over Passion, and from Woe
Wrung overwhelming eloquence, first drew
The breath which made him wretched; yet he
    knew
How to make Madness beautiful, and cast 730
O'er erring deeds and thoughts a heavenly hue
Of words, like sunbeams, dazzling as they past
The eyes, which o'er them shed tears feelingly and
    fast.

His love was Passion's essence—as a tree
On fire by lightning; with ethereal flame 735
Kindled he was, and blasted; for to be
Thus and enamoured, were in him the same.
But his was not the love of living dame,
Nor of the dead who rise upon our dreams,
But of ideal Beauty, which became 740
In him existence, and o'erflowing teems
Along his burning page, distempered though it
    seems.

This breathed itself to life in Julie,[67] *this*
Invested her with all that's wild and sweet;
This hallowed, too, the memorable kiss 745
Which every morn his fevered lip would greet,
From hers, who but with friendship his would
    meet;[68]

---

66 Willful.

67 Heroine of *Julie, ou La Nouvelle Héloïse,* a romance
by Jean Jacques Rousseau (1712–1778).
68 In his *Confessions* (II, 9) Rousseau describes the intensity
(much admired by Byron) of his feelings when at the end

But to that gentle touch, through brain and breast
Flashed the thrilled Spirit's love-devouring heat;
In that absorbing sigh perchance more blest   750
Than vulgar minds may be with all they seek
    possest.

His life was one long war with self-sought foes,
Or friends by him self-banished; for his mind
Had grown Suspicion's sanctuary, and chose,
For its own cruel sacrifice, the kind,   755
'Gainst whom he raged with fury strange and
    blind.
But he was phrensied,—wherefore, who may
    know?
Since cause might be which Skill could never
    find;
But he was phrensied by disease or woe,
To that worst pitch of all, which wears a reason-   760
    ing show.

For then he was inspired, and from him came,
As from the Pythian's mystic cave[69] of yore,
Those oracles which set the world in flame,[70]
Nor ceased to burn till kingdoms were no more:
Did he not this for France? which lay, before,   765
Bowed to the inborn tyranny of years?
Broken and trembling to the yoke she bore,
Till by the voice of him and his compeers
Roused up to too much wrath, which follows
    o'ergrown fears?

They made themselves a fearful monument!   770
The wreck of old opinions—things which grew,
Breathed from the birth of Time: the veil they
    rent,
And what behind it lay, all earth shall view;
But good with ill they also overthrew,
Leaving but ruins, wherewith to rebuild   775
Upon the same foundation, and renew
Dungeons and thrones, which the same hour re-
    filled,
As heretofore, because Ambition was self-willed.

But this will not endure, nor be endured!

---

of each morning's walk he exchanged the conventional
kiss of greeting with the Comtesse d'Houdetot, who was
another man's mistress.
[69] The site of Apollo's oracle at Delphi. His priestess, who
uttered the prophecies in a state or appearance of frenzy,
was known as the pythoness.
[70] I.e., he paved the way for the French Revolution.

Mankind have felt their strength, and made it   780
    felt.
They might have used it better, but, allured
By their new vigour, sternly have they dealt
On one another; Pity ceased to melt
With her once natural charities. But they,
Who in Oppression's darkness caved had dwelt,   785
They were not eagles, nourished with the day;
What marvel then, at times, if they mistook their
    prey?

What deep wounds ever closed without a scar?
The heart's bleed longest, and but heal to wear
That which disfigures it; and they who war   790
With their own hopes, and have been vanquished,
    bear
Silence, but not submission: in his lair
Fixed Passion holds his breath, until the hour
Which shall atone for years; none need despair:
It came—it cometh—and will come,—the power   795
To punish or forgive—in *one* we shall be slower.

Clear, placid Leman! thy contrasted lake,
With the wild world I dwelt in, is a thing
Which warns me, with its stillness, to forsake
Earth's troubled waters for a purer spring.   800
This quiet sail is as a noiseless wing
To waft me from distraction; once I loved
Torn Ocean's roar, but thy soft murmuring
Sounds sweet as if a Sister's voice reproved,
That I with stern delights should e'er have been   805
    so moved.

It is the hush of night, and all between
Thy margin and the mountains, dusk, yet clear,
Mellowed and mingling, yet distinctly seen,
Save darkened Jura,[71] whose capt heights appear
Precipitously steep; and drawing near,   810
There breathes a living fragrance from the shore,
Of flowers yet fresh with childhood; on the ear
Drops the light drip of the suspended oar,
Or chirps the grasshopper one good-night carol
    more.

He is an evening reveller who makes   815
His life an infancy, and sings his fill;
At intervals, some bird from out the brakes[72]
Starts into voice a moment, then is still.

---

[71] A mountain range between Switzerland and France.
[72] Thickets.

There seems a floating whisper on the hill,
But that is fancy—for the Starlight dews   820
All silently their tears of Love instill,
Weeping themselves away, till they infuse
Deep into Nature's breast the spirit of her hues.

Ye Stars, which are the poetry of Heaven!
If in your bright leaves we would read the fate   825
Of men and empires,—'tis to be forgiven
That in our aspirations to be great,
Our destinies o'erleap their mortal state,
And claim a kindred with you; for ye are
A Beauty and a Mystery, and create   830
In us such love and reverence from afar,
That Fortune,—Fame,—Power,—Life, have
      named themselves a Star.

All Heaven and Earth are still though not in
      sleep,
But breathless, as we grow when feeling most;
And silent, as we stand in thoughts too deep:—   835
All Heaven and Earth are still. From the high
      host
Of stars to the lulled lake and mountain-coast,
All is concentered in a life intense,
Where not a beam, nor air, nor leaf is lost,
But hath a part of Being, and a sense   840
Of that which is of all Creator and Defence.

Then stirs the feeling infinite, so felt
In solitude, where we are *least* alone;
A truth, which through our being then doth melt,
And purifies from self; it is a tone,   845
The soul and source of Music, which makes
      known
Eternal harmony, and sheds a charm
Like to the fabled Cytherea's zone,[73]
Binding all things with beauty;—'twould disarm
The spectre Death, had he substantial power to   850
      harm.

Not vainly did the early Persian make
His altar the high places, and the peak
Of earth-o'ergazing mountains, and thus take
A fit and unwalled temple, there to seek
The Spirit, in whose honour shrines are weak,   855
Upreared of human hands. Come and compare
Columns and idol-dwellings—Goth or Greek—

With Nature's realms of worship, earth and air—
Nor fix on fond abodes to circumscribe thy
      prayer!

The sky is changed!—and such a change! Oh   860
      Night,
And Storm and Darkness, ye are wondrous strong,
Yet lovely in your strength, as is the light
Of a dark eye in Woman! Far along,
From peak to peak, the rattling crags among
Leaps the live thunder! Not from one lone cloud,   865
But every mountain now hath found a tongue,
And Jura answers, through her misty shroud,
Back to the joyous Alps, who call to her aloud!

And this is in the Night:—most glorious Night!
Thou were not sent for slumber! let me be   870
A sharer in thy fierce and far delight,—
A portion of the tempest and of thee!
How the lit lake shines, a phosphoric sea,
And the big rain comes dancing to the earth!
And now again 'tis black, and now, the glee   875
Of the loud hills shakes with its mountain-mirth,
As if they did rejoice o'er a young Earthquake's
      birth.

Now, where the swift Rhone cleaves his way be-
      tween
Heights which appear as lovers who have parted
In hate, whose mining depths so intervene,   880
That they can meet no more, though broken-
      hearted:
Though in their souls, which thus each other
      thwarted,
Love was the very root of the fond rage
Which blighted their life's bloom, and then de-
      parted:—
Itself expired, but leaving them an age   885
Of years all winters,—war within themselves to
      wage:

Now, where the quick Rhone thus hath cleft his
      way,
The mightiest of the storms hath ta'en his stand:
For here, not one, but many, make their play
And fling their thunder-bolts from hand to hand,   890
Flashing and cast around: of all the band,
The brightest through these parted hills hath
      forked
His lightnings,—as if he did understand,
That in such gaps as Desolation worked,

---

[73] The belt or sash of Venus; worn by a mortal it attracted love.

There the hot shaft should blast whatever therein 895
   lurked.

Sky—Mountains—River—Winds—Lake—
   Lightnings! ye!
With night, and clouds, and thunder—and a
   Soul
To make these felt and feeling, well may be
Things that have made me watchful; the far roll
Of your departing voices, is the knoll[74]   900
Of what in me is sleepless,—if I rest.
But where of ye, O Tempests! is the goal?
Are ye like those within the human breast?
Or do ye find, at length, like eagles, some high
   nest?

Could I embody and unbosom now   905
That which is most within me,—could I wreak
My thoughts upon expression, and thus throw
Soul—heart—mind—passions—feelings—
   strong or weak—
All that I would have sought, and all I seek,
Bear, know, feel—and yet breathe—into *one* 910
   word,
And that one word were Lightning, I would
   speak;
But as it is, I live and die unheard,
With a most voiceless thought, sheathing it as a
   sword.

The Morn is up again, the dewy Morn,
With breath all incense, and with cheek all   915
   bloom—
Laughing the clouds away with playful scorn,
And living as if earth contained no tomb,—
And glowing into day: we may resume
The march of our existence: and thus I,
Still on thy shores, fair Leman! may find room 920
And food for meditation, nor pass by
Much, that may give us pause, if pondered fit-
   tingly.

Clarens![75] sweet Clarens, birthplace of deep Love!
Thine air is the young breath of passionate
   Thought;
Thy trees take root in Love; the snows above,   925
The very Glaciers have his colours caught,

And sun-set into rose-hues sees them wrought
By rays which sleep there lovingly: the rocks,
The permanent crags, tell here of Love, who
   sought
In them a refuge from the worldly shocks,   930
Which stir and sting the Soul with Hope that
   woos, then mocks.

Clarens! by heavenly feet thy paths are trod,—
Undying Love's, who here ascends a throne
To which the steps are mountains; where the God
Is a pervading Life and Light,—so shown   935
Not on those summits solely, nor alone
In the still cave and forest; o'er the flower
His eye is sparkling, and his breath hath blown,
His soft and summer breath, whose tender power
Passes the strength of storms in their most deso- 940
   late hour.

All things are here of *Him;* from the black pines,
Which are his shade on high, and the loud roar
Of torrents, where he listeneth, to the vines
Which slope his green path downward to the
   shore,
Where the bowed Waters meet him, and adore,   945
Kissing his feet with murmurs; and the Wood,
The covert of old trees, with trunks all hoar,
But light leaves, young as joy, stands where it
   stood,
Offering to him, and his, a populous solitude.

A populous solitude of bees and birds,   950
And fairy-formed and many-coloured things,
Who worship him with notes more sweet than
   words,
And innocently open their glad wings,
Fearless and full of life: the gush of springs,
And fall of lofty fountains, and the bend   955
Of stirring branches, and the bud which brings
The swiftest thought of Beauty, here extend
Mingling—and made by Love—unto one mighty
   end.

He who hath loved not, here would learn that
   lore,
And make his heart a spirit; he who knows   960
That tender mystery, will love the more;
For this is Love's recess, where vain men's woes,
And the world's waste, have driven him far from
   those,
For 'tis his nature to advance or die;

---

74 Knell.
75 A village near Vevey on Lake Geneva. The reference
is to the lovers in Rousseau's *La Nouvelle Héloïse.*

He stands not still, but or decays, or grows   965
Into a boundless blessing, which may vie
With the immortal lights, in its eternity!

'Twas not for fiction chose Rousseau this spot,
Peopling it with affections; but he found
It was the scene which Passion must allot   970
To the Mind's purified beings; 'twas the ground
Where early Love his Psyche's zone unbound,[76]
And hallowed it with loveliness: 'tis lone,
And wonderful, and deep, and hath a sound,
And sense, and sight of sweetness; here the Rhone   975
Hath spread himself a couch, the Alps have reared
  a throne.

Lausanne! and Ferney![77] ye have been the abodes
Of Names which unto you bequeathed a name;
Mortals, who sought and found, by dangerous
  roads,
A path to perpetuity of Fame: 980
They were gigantic minds, and their steep aim
Was, Titan-like, on daring doubts to pile
Thoughts which should call down thunder, and
  the flame
Of Heaven again assailed[78]—if Heaven, the while,
On man and man's research could deign do more   985
  than smile.

The one was fire and fickleness, a child
Most mutable in wishes, but in mind
A wit as various,—gay, grave, sage, or wild,—
Historian, bard, philosopher, combined;
He multiplied himself among mankind,   990
The Proteus[79] of their talents: But his own
Breathed most in ridicule,—which, as the wind,
Blew where it listed, laying all things prone,—
Now to o'erthrow a fool, and now to shake a
  throne.

The other, deep and slow, exhausting thought,   995
And hiving wisdom with each studious year,

---

76 For Rousseau's growth in experience there, see his *Confessions*, I, 4.
77 At Ferney or Fernex (near Geneva) lived François Marie Arouet, called Voltaire (1694–1778), and at Lausanne (on the north shore of the Lake) the most famous of English historians, Edward Gibbon (1737–1794).
78 As, in Greek mythology, the Titans attacked and were defeated by the Olympian gods.
79 A sea god who could assume varied forms.—The subject of this stanza is Voltaire; of the next, Gibbon, author of *The Decline and Fall of the Roman Empire*.

In meditation dwelt—with learning wrought,
And shaped his weapon with an edge severe,
Sapping a solemn creed with solemn sneer;[80]
The lord of irony,—that master spell,   1000
Which stung his foes to wrath, which grew from
  fear,
And doomed him to the zealot's ready Hell,
Which answers to all doubts so eloquently well.

Yet, peace be with their ashes,—for by them,
If merited, the penalty is paid;   1005
It is not ours to judge,—far less condemn;
The hour must come when such things shall be
  made
Known unto all,—or hope and dread allayed
By slumber, on one pillow, in the dust,
Which, thus much we are sure, must lie decayed;   1010
And when it shall revive, as is our trust,
'Twill be to be forgiven—or suffer what is just.

But let me quit Man's works, again to read
His Maker's, spread around me, and suspend
This page, which from my reveries I feed,   1015
Until it seems prolonging without end.
The clouds above me to the white Alps tend,
And I must pierce them, and survey whate'er
May be permitted, as my steps I bend
To their most great and growing region, where   1020
The earth to her embrace compels the powers of
  air.

Italia, too! Italia! looking on thee,
Full flashes on the Soul the light of ages,
Since the fierce Carthaginian[81] almost won thee,
To the last halo of the Chiefs and Sages   1025
Who glorify thy consecrated pages;
Thou wert the throne and grave of empires—still,
The fount at which the panting Mind assuages
Her thirst of knowledge, quaffing there her fill,
Flows from the eternal source of Rome's imperial   1030
  hill.

Thus far have I proceeded in a theme
Renewed with no kind auspices:—to feel
We are not what we have been, and to deem
We are not what we should be,—and to steel
The heart against itself; and to conceal,   1035

---

80 Gibbon is sometimes satirical at the expense of Christianity.
81 Hannibal (247–183 B.C.), who invaded Italy.

With a proud caution, love, or hate, or aught,—
Passion or feeling, purpose, grief, or zeal,
Which is the tyrant Spirit of our thought,—
Is a stern task of soul:—No matter,—it is taught.

And for these words, thus woven into song, 1040
It may be that they are a harmless wile,—
The colouring of the scenes which fleet along,
Which I would seize, in passing, to beguile
My breast, or that of others, for a while.
Fame is the thirst of youth,—but I am not 1045
So young as to regard men's frown or smile,
As loss or guerdon of a glorious lot;—
I stood and stand alone,—remembered or forgot.

I have not loved the World, nor the World me;
I have not flattered its rank breath, nor bowed 1050
To its idolatries a patient knee,
Nor coined my cheek to smiles,—nor cried aloud
In worship of an echo: in the crowd
They could not deem me one of such—I stood
Among them, but not of them—in a shroud 1055
Of thoughts which were not their thoughts, and
    still could,
Had I not filed[82] my mind, which thus itself sub-
    dued.

I have not loved the World, nor the World me,—
But let us part fair foes; I do believe,
Though I have found them not, that there may 1060
    be
Words which are things,—hopes which will not
    deceive,
And Virtues which are merciful, nor weave
Snares for the failing: I would also deem
O'er others' griefs that some sincerely grieve—
That two, or one, are almost what they seem,— 1065
That Goodness is no name—and Happiness no
    dream.

My daughter! with thy name this song begun!
My daughter! with thy name thus much shall
    end!—
I see thee not—I hear thee not—but none
Can be so wrapt in thee; Thou art the Friend 1070
To whom the shadows of far years extend:
Albeit my brow thou never should'st behold,
My voice shall with thy future visions blend,

And reach into thy heart,—when mine is cold,
A token and a tone, even from thy father's mould. 1075

To aid thy mind's development,—to watch
Thy dawn of little joys,—to sit and see
Almost thy very growth,—to view thee catch
Knowledge of objects, wonders yet to thee!
To hold thee lightly on a gentle knee, 1080
And print on thy soft cheek a parent's kiss,—
This, it should seem, was not reserved for me—
Yet this was in my nature:—as it is,
I know not what is there, yet something like to
    this.

Yet, though dull Hate as duty should be taught,[83] 1085
I know that thou wilt love me,—though my name
Should be shut from thee, as a spell still fraught
With desolation, and a broken claim:
Though the grave closed between us,—'twere the
    same—
I know that thou wilt love me—though to drain 1090
My blood from out thy being were an aim,
And an attainment,—all would be in vain,—
Still thou would'st love me, still that more than
    life retain.

The child of Love, though born in bitterness,
And nurtured in Convulsion! Of thy sire 1095
These were the elements,—and thine no less.
As yet such are around thee,—but thy fire
Shall be more tempered, and thy hope far higher.
Sweet be thy cradled slumbers! O'er the sea
And from the mountains where I now respire, 1100
Fain would I waft such blessing upon thee,
As—with a sigh—I deem thou might'st have been
    to me!

from CANTO IV

I stood in Venice, on the "Bridge of Sighs";[1]
A Palace and a prison on each hand:
I saw from out the wave her structures rise
As from the stroke of the Enchanter's wand:
A thousand Years their cloudy wings expand 5
Around me, and a dying Glory smiles
O'er the far times, when many a subject land
Look'd to the wingèd Lion's[2] marble piles,

---

82 Defiled (by admitting "their thoughts"). For *filed*, see
Macbeth III, i, 65.

83 By Lady Byron.

1 A covered bridge connecting the ducal palace with the
prison.
2 Symbol of Venice.

Where Venice sate in state, throned on her hundred isles!

She looks a sea Cybele,[3] fresh from Ocean,   10
Rising with her tiara of proud towers
At airy distance, with majestic motion,
A Ruler of the waters and their powers:
And such she was;—her daughters had their dowers
From spoils of nations, and the exhaustless East   15
Poured in her lap all gems in sparkling showers.
In purple was she robed, and of her feast
Monarchs partook, and deemed their dignity increased.

In Venice Tasso's echoes are no more,
And silent rows the songless gondolier;[4]   20
Her palaces are crumbling to the shore,
And Music meets not always now the ear:
Those days are gone—but Beauty still is here.
States fall, arts fade—but Nature doth not die,
Nor yet forget how Venice once was dear,   25
The pleasant place of all festivity,
The Revel of the earth, the Masque of Italy!

But unto us she hath a spell beyond
Her name in story, and her long array
Of mighty shadows, whose dim forms despond   30
Above the Dogeless city's vanished sway;
Ours is a trophy which will not decay
With the Rialto;[5] Shylock and the Moor,[6]
And Pierre,[7] can not be swept or worn away—
The keystones of the Arch! though all were o'er,   35
For us repeopled were[8] the solitary shore.

The Beings of the Mind are not of clay:
Essentially immortal, they create
And multiply in us a brighter ray
And more beloved existence: that which Fate   40
Prohibits to dull life in this our state
Of mortal bondage, by these Spirits supplied,
First exiles, then replaces what we hate;
Watering the heart whose early flowers have died.
And with a fresher growth replenishing the void.   45

. . .

Oh Rome! my Country! City of the Soul!
The orphans of the heart must turn to thee,   695
Lone Mother of dead Empires! and control
In their shut breasts their petty misery.
What are our woes and sufferance? Come and see
The cypress—hear the owl—and plod your way
O'er steps of broken thrones and temples—Ye!   700
Whose agonies are evils of a day—
A world is at our feet as fragile as our clay.

The Niobe[9] of nations! there she stands,
Childless and crownless, in her voiceless woe;
An empty urn within her wither'd hands,   705
Whose holy dust was scatter'd long ago;
The Scipios'[10] tomb contains no ashes now;
The very sepulchres lie tenantless
Of their heroic dwellers: dost thou flow,
Old Tiber![11] through a marble wilderness?   710
Rise, with thy yellow waves, and mantle her distress.

The Goth,[12] the Christian—Time—War—Flood, and Fire,
Have dealt upon the seven-hill'd City's pride;
She saw her glories star by star expire,
And up the steep barbarian Monarchs ride,   715
Where the car[13] climbed the Capitol;[14] far and wide
Temple and tower went down, nor left a site:
Chaos of ruins! who shall trace the void,
O'er the dim fragments cast a lunar light,
And say, "here was, or is," where all is doubly   720
night?

. . .

Can tyrants[15] but by tyrants[16] conquered be,
And Freedom find no Champion and no Child

---

3 I.e., a sea goddess corresponding to the great earth goddess; the latter was depicted wearing a turreted crown.
4 The gondoliers used to sing stanzas from the epic *Jerusalem Delivered* of Torquato Tasso (1554–1595).
5 The business district.
6 In *The Merchant of Venice* and *Othello*.
7 In the fine tragedy *Venice Preserved* (1682) by Thomas Otway.   8 Would be.

9 Her children were slain by the gods of classical mythology; and she, though turned by Zeus into stone, continued weeping for them.
10 The most famous members of this Roman family were: Scipio the Elder, who invaded Africa, thus forcing the Carthaginians to recall from Italy Hannibal, whom he crushed at Zama in 202 B.C.; and Scipio the Younger, who captured Carthage in 146 B.C.
11 The river which flows through Rome. It used periodically to flood parts of the city.
12 Rome was first sacked by the Goths in 410 A.D.
13 Chariot.
14 I.e., to the temple of Jupiter. It was on the Capitoline Hill.
15 I.e., the European monarchs.
16 Such as Napoleon.

Such as Columbia saw arise when she
Sprung forth a Pallas,[17] armed and undefiled?
Or must such minds be nourished in the wild,   860
Deep in the unpruned forest, 'midst the roar
Of cataracts, where nursing Nature smiled
On infant Washington? Has Earth no more
Such seeds within her breast, or Europe no such
    shore?

. . .

Arches on arches! as it were that Rome,
Collecting the chief trophies of her line,   1145
Would build up all her triumphs in one dome,
Her Coliseum[18] stands; the moonbeams shine
As 'twere its natural torches—for divine
Should be the light which streams here,—to il-
    lume
This long-explored but still exhaustless mine   1150
Of Contemplation; and the azure gloom
Of an Italian night, where the deep skies assume

Hues which have words, and speak to ye of
    Heaven,
Floats o'er this vast and wondrous monument,
And shadows forth its glory. There is given   1155
Unto the things of earth, which Time hath bent,
A Spirit's feeling, and where he hath leant
His Hand, but broke his scythe, there is a power
And magic in the ruined battlement,
For which the Palace of the present hour   1160
Must yield its pomp, and wait till Ages are its
    dower.

Oh Time! the Beautifier of the dead,
Adorner of the ruin—Comforter
And only Healer when the heart hath bled;
Time! the Corrector where our judgments err,   1165
The test of Truth, Love—sole philosopher,
For all beside are sophists—from thy thrift,
Which never loses though it doth defer—
Time, the Avenger! unto thee I lift
My hands, and eyes, and heart, and crave of thee   1170
    a gift:

Amidst this wreck, where thou hast made a shrine
And temple more divinely desolate—
Among thy mightier offerings here are mine,
Ruins of years—though few, yet full of fate:—
If thou hast ever seen me too elate,   1175

Hear me not; but if calmly I have borne
Good, and reserved my pride against the hate
Which shall not whelm me, let me not have worn
This iron in my soul in vain—shall *they* not
    mourn?

And Thou, who never yet of human wrong   1180
Left the unbalanced scale, great Nemesis![19]
Here, where the ancient paid thee homage long—
Thou who didst call the Furies[20] from the abyss,
And round Orestes[21] bade them howl and hiss
For that unnatural retribution—just,   1185
Had it but been from hands less near—in this
Thy former realm, I call thee from the dust!
Dost thou not hear my heart?—Awake! thou
    shalt, and must.

It is not that I may not have incurred,
For my ancestral faults or mine, the wound   1190
I bleed withal; and, had it been conferred
With a just weapon, it had flowed unbound;
But now my blood shall not sink in the ground—
To thee I do devote it—*Thou* shalt take
The vengeance, which shall yet be sought and   1195
    found—
Which if *I* have not taken for the sake—
But let that pass—I sleep—but Thou shalt yet
    awake.

And if my voice break forth, 'tis not that now
I shrink from what is suffered: let him speak
Who hath beheld decline upon my brow,   1200
Or seen my mind's convulsion leave it weak;
But in this page a record will I seek.
Not in the air shall these my words disperse,
Though I be ashes; a far hour shall wreak
The deep prophetic fulness of this verse,   1205
And pile on human heads the mountain of my
    curse!

That curse shall be Forgiveness.—Have I not—
Hear me, my mother Earth! behold it, Heaven!—
Have I not had to wrestle with my lot?
Have I not suffered things to be forgiven?   1210
Have I not had my brain seared, my heart riven,

---

17 Pallas Athena or Minerva, goddess of wisdom, who
sprang full-armed from the head of Zeus or Jove.
18 The famous Colosseum, an amphitheater built c. 80 A.D.

19 The classical goddess of just retribution or vengeance.
20 In Greek mythology three snake-haired spirits of
vengeance.
21 The son of Agamemnon; in Greek tragedy he avenges
his father's murder by killing his mother and her lover.

Hopes sapped, name blighted, Life's life lied
  away?
And only not to desperation driven,
Because not altogether of such clay
As rots into the souls of those whom I survey. 1215

From mighty wrongs to petty perfidy
Have I not seen what human things could do?
From the loud roar of foaming calumny
To the small whisper of the as paltry few—
And subtler venom of the reptile crew, 1220
The Janus[22] glance of whose significant eye,
Learning to lie with silence, would *seem* true,
And without utterance, save the shrug or sigh,
Deal round to happy fools its speechless obloquy.

But I have lived, and have not lived in vain: 1225
My mind may lose its force, my blood its fire,
And my frame perish even in conquering pain;
But there is that within me which shall tire
Torture and Time, and breathe when I expire;
Something unearthly, which they deem not of, 1230
Like the remembered tone of a mute lyre,
Shall on their softened spirits sink, and move
In hearts all rocky now the late remorse of Love.

The seal is set.—Now welcome, thou dread
  Power!
Nameless, yet thus omnipotent, which here 1235
Walk'st in the shadow of the midnight hour
With a deep awe, yet all distinct from fear;
Thy haunts are ever where the dead walls rear
Their ivy mantles, and the solemn scene
Derives from thee a sense so deep and clear 1240
That we become a part of what has been,
And grow upon the spot—all-seeing but unseen.

And here the buzz of eager nations ran,
In murmured pity, or loud-roared applause,
As man was slaughtered by his fellow man. 1245
And wherefore slaughtered? wherefore, but be-
  cause
Such were the bloody Circus'[23] genial laws,
And the imperial pleasure.—Wherefore not?
What matters where we fall to fill the maws
Of worms—on battle-plains or listed spot?[24] 1250
Both are but theaters—where the chief actors rot.

I see before me the Gladiator[25] lie:
He leans upon his hand—his manly brow
Consents to death, but conquers agony,
And his drooped head sinks gradually low— 1255
And through his side the last drops, ebbing slow
From the red gash, fall heavy, one by one,
Like the first of a thunder-shower; and now
The arena swims around him—he is gone,
Ere ceased the inhuman shout which hailed the 1260
  wretch who won.

He heard it, but he heeded not—his eyes
Were with his heart—and that was far away;
He recked not of the life he lost nor prize,
But where his rude hut by the Danube lay,
There were his young barbarians all at play, 1265
There was their Dacian[26] mother—he, their sire,
Butchered to make a Roman holiday—
All this rushed with his blood—Shall he expire
And unavenged? Arise! ye Goths, and glut your
  ire!

But here, where Murder breathed her bloody 1270
  steam;—
And here, where buzzing nations choked the ways,
And roared or murmured like a mountain stream
Dashing or winding as its torrent strays;
Here, where the Roman million's blame or praise
Was death or life—the playthings of a crowd— 1275
My voice sounds much—and fall the stars' faint
  rays
On the arena void—seats crushed—walls bowed—
And galleries, where my steps seem echoes
  strangely loud.

A Ruin—yet what Ruin! from its mass
Walls—palaces—half-cities, have been reared; 1280
Yet oft the enormous skeleton ye pass,
And marvel where the spoil could have appeared.
Hath it indeed been plundered, or but cleared?
Alas! developed, opens the decay,
When the colossal fabric's form is neared: 1285
It will not bear the brightness of the day,
Which streams too much on all—years—man—
  have reft away.

---

22 The Roman god of doors and beginnings, depicted with two faces looking opposite ways.
23 A large amphitheater, on whose arena the Romans' "games" were held—especially the Circus Maximus.
24 The area with its "list" or boundary.

25 A famous statue, once thought to represent a dying gladiator.
26 Dacia was a Roman province, conquered in 101–06 by the emperor Trajan. It included parts of modern Hungary, Romania, and Bessarabia.

But when the rising moon begins to climb
Its topmost arch, and gently pauses there—
When the stars twinkle through the loops[27] of
Time,
And the low night-breeze waves along the air
The garland-forest, which the gray walls wear,
Like laurels on the bald first Caesar's head—
When the light shines serene but doth not glare—
Then in this magic circle raise the dead;[28]—   1295
Heroes have trod this spot—'tis on their dust ye
tread.

"While stands the Coliseum, Rome shall stand:
When falls the Coliseum, Rome shall fall;
And when Rome falls—the World." From our
own land
Thus spake the pilgrims o'er this mighty wall   1300
In Saxon times, which we are wont to call
Ancient; and these three mortal things are still
On their foundations, and unaltered all—
Rome and her Ruin past Redemption's skill,
The World—the same wide den—of thieves, or   1305
what ye will.

. . .

Oh! that the Desert were my dwelling-place,   1585
With one fair Spirit for my minister,
That I might all forget the human race,
And, hating no one, love but only her!
Ye elements!—in whose ennobling stir
I feel myself exalted—Can ye not   1590
Accord me such a Being? Do I err
In deeming such inhabit many a spot?
Though with them to converse can rarely be our
lot.

There is a pleasure in the pathless woods,
There is a rapture on the lonely shore,   1595
There is society, where none intrudes,
By the deep Sea, and Music in its roar:
I love not Man the less, but Nature more,
From these our interviews, in which I steal
From all I may be, or have been before,   1600
To mingle with the Universe, and feel
What I can ne'er express—yet cannot all conceal.

Roll on, thou deep and dark blue Ocean—roll!

Ten thousand fleets sweep over thee in vain;
Man marks the earth with ruin—his control   1605
Stops with the shore;—upon the watery plain
The wrecks are all thy deed, nor doth remain
A shadow of man's ravage, save his own,
When, for a moment, like a drop of rain,
He sinks into thy depths with bubbling groan—   1610
Without a grave—unknelled, uncoffined, and un-
known.

His steps are not upon thy path,—thy fields
Are not a spoil for him,—thou dost arise
And shake him from thee; the vile strength he
wields
For Earth's destruction thou dost all despise,   1615
Spurning him from thy bosom to the skies—
And send'st him, shivering in thy playful spray
And howling, to his Gods, where haply lies
His petty hope in some near port or bay,
And dashest him again to Earth:—there let him   1620
lay.[29]

The armaments which thunderstrike the walls
Of rock-built cities, bidding nations quake,
And Monarchs tremble in their Capitals,
The oak Leviathans, whose huge ribs make
Their clay creator the vain title take   1625
Of Lord of thee, and Arbiter of War—
These are thy toys, and, as the snowy flake,
They melt into thy yeast of waves, which mar
Alike the Armada's pride or spoils of Trafalgar.[30]

Thy shores are empires, changed in all save thee—   1630
Assyria—Greece—Rome—Carthage—what   are
they?
Thy waters washed them power while they were
free,
And many a tyrant since; their shores obey
The stranger, slave, or savage; their decay
Has dried up realms to deserts:—not so thou,   1635
Unchangeable, save to thy wild waves' play,
Time writes no wrinkle on thine azure brow—
Such as Creation's dawn beheld, thou rollest now.

---

27 Loopholes, windows.
28 I.e., conjure them up, as the magicians did—within a
charmed circle.—Lines 1297–99 are from the Latin of the
English historian the Venerable Bede (d. 735); quoted by
Gibbon in *The Decline and Fall*, where Byron found the
saying. Gibbon thinks that Bede derived it from English
pilgrims.

29 Lie. In the standard edition this grammatical lapse is
explained on the ground that the author was a lord, and
wrote as well as spoke with an appropriate "careless and
negligent ease"!
30 After its defeat by the English, many ships of the
Spanish Armada of 1588 were wrecked on the homeward
voyage around Scotland and Ireland; and in 1805 the
British lost in a storm a number of the prizes captured
in Nelson's victory at Trafalgar over the French and
Spanish fleets.

Thou glorious mirror, where the Almighty's form
Glasses itself in tempests; in all time,   1640
Calm or convulsed—in breeze, or gale, or storm—
Icing the Pole, or in the torrid clime
Dark-heaving—boundless, endless, and sublime—
The image of Eternity—the throne
Of the Invisible; even from out thy slime   1645
The monsters of the deep are made—each Zone
Obeys thee—thou goest forth, dread, fathomless,
    alone.

And I have loved thee, Ocean! and my joy
Of youthful sports was on thy breast to be
Borne, like thy bubbles, onward: from a boy   1650
I wantoned with thy breakers—they to me
Were a delight; and if the freshening sea
Made them a terror—'twas a pleasing fear,
For I was as it were a Child of thee,
And trusted to thy billows far and near,   1655
And laid my hand upon thy mane—as I do here.

My task is done—my song hath ceased—my
    theme
Has died into an echo; it is fit
The spell should break of this protracted dream.
The torch shall be extinguished which hath lit   1660
My midnight lamp—and what is writ, is writ,—
Would it were worthier! but I am not now
That which I have been—and my visions flit
Less palpably before me—and the glow
Which in my Spirit dwelt is fluttering, faint, and 1665
    low.

Farewell! a word that must be, and hath been—
A sound which makes us linger;—yet—farewell!
Ye! who have traced the Pilgrim to the scene
Which is his last—if in your memories dwell
A thought which once was his—if on ye swell   1670
A single recollection—not in vain
He wore his sandal-shoon and scallop-shell;[31]
Farewell! with *him* alone may rest the pain,
If such there were—with *you*, the Moral of his
    Strain.

So We'll Go No More A-Roving

This lyric originally formed, as did the verses "To
Thomas Moore," parts of letters written in 1817 to

his old companion and brother poet. Byron sent
these letters from Italy on February 28 and July 10,
adding in the latter that the first stanza of "To
Thomas Moore" had been written fifteen years earlier,
when he was leaving England. "So we'll go no more
a-roving" was composed in Lent, during the carnival
at Venice.

So we'll go no more a-roving
    So late into the night,
Though the heart be still as loving,
    And the moon be still as bright.

For the sword outwears its sheath,   5
    And the soul wears out the breast,
And the heart must pause to breathe,
    And Love itself have rest.

Though the night was made for loving,
    And the day returns too soon,   10
Yet we'll go no more a-roving
    By the light of the moon.

To Thomas Moore

My boat is on the shore,
    And my bark is on the sea;
But, before I go, Tom Moore,
    Here's a double health to thee!

Here's a sigh to those who love me,   5
    And a smile to those who hate;
And, whatever sky's above me,
    Here's a heart for every fate.

Though the Ocean roar around me,
    Yet it still shall bear me on;   10
Though a desert shall surround me,
    It hath springs that may be won.

Were't the last drop in the well,
    As I gasped upon the brink,
Ere my fainting spirit fell,   15
    'Tis to thee that I would drink.

With that water, as this wine,
    The libation I would pour
Should be—peace with thine and mine,
    And a health to thee, Tom Moore.   20

---

[31] Worn on the hat by true pilgrims (from the Holy
Land) as a sign, like their sandals, of pilgrimage.

from Don Juan

Byron began the poem in the summer of 1818; the first two cantos were published the following summer. He wrote Cantos III and IV in the winter of 1819–20, and with Canto V they were brought out in August 1821. He set to work on Canto VI in June 1822; by the next March he had finished Canto XVI. Before he left for Greece in 1823, he had begun a seventeenth. The productive energy involved is astonishing, especially if one considers that during the same period he wrote several other long poems and all his plays except *Manfred*.

    Both in the scope he allowed himself and in its verse form (borrowed from a poem by a friend, John Hookham Frere, and through that from Pulci and Ariosto), he found the perfect means for his talents, and his letters give evidence that he knew it.

    The name of Byron's hero should be pronounced in English—*Don Joó-un*.

from CANTO THE FIRST

I want a hero: an uncommon want,
  When every year and month sends forth a new one,
Till, after cloying the gazettes with cant,
  The age discovers he is not the true one;
Of such as these I should not care to vaunt,   5
  I'll therefore take our ancient friend Don Juan—
We all have seen him, in the pantomime,[1]
Sent to the devil somewhat ere his time.

. . .

Brave men were living before Agamemnon[2]
  And since, exceeding valorous and sage,
A good deal like him too, though quite the same   35
  none;
  But then they shone not on the poet's page,
And so have been forgotten;—I condemn none,
  But can't find any in the present age
Fit for my poem (that is, for my new one);
So, as I said, I'll take my friend Don Juan.   40

Most epic poets plunge *"in medias res"*[3]
  (Horace makes this the heroic turnpike road),[4]
And then your hero tells, whene'er you please,
  What went before—by way of episode,

While seated after dinner at his ease,   45
  Beside his mistress in some soft abode,
Palace, or garden, paradise, or cavern,
Which serves the happy couple for a tavern.

That is the usual method, but not mine—
  My way is to begin with the beginning;   50
The regularity of my design
  Forbids all wandering as the worst of sinning,
And therefore I shall open with a line
  (Although it cost me half an hour in spinning)
Narrating somewhat of Don Juan's father,   55
And also of his mother, if you'd rather.

In Seville was he born, a pleasant city,
  Famous for oranges and women,—he
Who has not seen it will be much to pity,
  So says the proverb—and I quite agree;   60
Of all the Spanish towns is none more pretty,
  Cadiz, perhaps—but that you soon may see;—
Don Juan's parents lived beside the river,
A noble stream, and called the Guadalquivir.

His father's name was Jóse—*Don*, of course,—   65
  A true Hidalgo,[5] free from every stain
Of Moor or Hebrew blood, he traced his source
  Through the most Gothic gentlemen of Spain;
A better cavalier ne'er mounted horse,
  Or, being mounted, e'er got down again,   70
Than Jóse, who begot our hero, who
Begot—but that's to come—Well, to renew:

His mother[6] was a learnèd lady, famed
  For every branch of every science known—
In every Christian language ever named,   75
  With virtues equalled by her wit alone:
She made the cleverest people quite ashamed,
  And even the good with inward envy groan,
Finding themselves so very much exceeded,
In their own way, by all the things that she did.   80

. . .

Perfect she was, but as perfection is
  Insipid in this naughty world of ours,
Where our first parents never learned to kiss
  Till they were exiled from their earlier bowers,
Where all was peace, and innocence, and bliss,   140
  (I wonder how they got through the twelve hours),

---

[1] An adaptation of Thomas Shadwell's *The Libertine* (1675).
[2] The king who in Homer commands the Greek army against Troy. For the saying, see Horace, *Odes*, IV, ix, 25.
[3] Into the middle of things. Horace, *Ars Poetica*, line 148.
[4] I.e., Horace says that this is the best route to follow in writing a heroic poem.

[5] Nobleman (of the lower rank).
[6] This portrait, not fully reprinted here, is a caricature of Lady Byron.

Don Jóse, like a lineal son of Eve,
Went plucking various fruit without her leave.

He was a mortal of the careless kind,   145
    With no great love for learning, or the learned,
Who chose to go where'er he had a mind,
    And never dreamed his lady was concerned;
The world, as usual, wickedly inclined
    To see a kingdom or a house o'erturned,   150
Whispered he had a mistress, some said *two*.
But for domestic quarrels *one* will do.

Now Donna Inez had, with all her merit,
    A great opinion of her own good qualities;
Neglect, indeed, requires a saint to bear it,   155
    And such, indeed, she was in her moralities;
But then she had a devil of a spirit,
    And sometimes mixed up fancies with realities,
And let few opportunities escape
Of getting her liege lord into a scrape.   160

This was an easy matter with a man
    Oft in the wrong, and never on his guard;
And even the wisest, do the best they can,
    Have moments, hours, and days, so unprepared,
That you might "brain them with their lady's   165
        fan";[7]
    And sometimes ladies hit exceeding hard,
And fans turn into falchions[8] in fair hands,
And why and wherefore no one understands.

'Tis pity learnèd virgins ever wed
    With persons of no sort of education,   170
Or gentlemen, who, though well born and bred,
    Grow tired of scientific conversation:
I don't choose to say much upon this head,
    I'm a plain man, and in a single station,
But—Oh! ye lords of ladies intellectual,   175
Inform us truly, have they not hen-pecked you all?

Don Jóse and his lady quarrelled—*why*,
    Not any of the many could divine,
Though several thousand people chose to try,
    'Twas surely no concern of theirs nor mine;   180
I loathe that low vice—curiosity;
    But if there's anything in which I shine,
'Tis in arranging all my friends' affairs,
Not having, of my own, domestic cares.

And so I interfered, and with the best   185

Intentions, but their treatment was not kind;
I think the foolish people were possessed,
    For neither of them could I ever find,
Although their porter afterwards confessed—
    But that's no matter, and the worst's behind,   190
For little Juan o'er me threw, down stairs,
A pail of housemaid's water unawares.

A little curly-headed, good-for-nothing,
    And mischief-making monkey from his birth;
His parents ne'er agreed except in doting   195
    Upon the most unquiet imp on earth;
Instead of quarrelling, had they been but both in
    Their senses, they'd have sent young master
        forth
To school, or had him soundly whipped at home,
To teach him manners for the time to come.   200

Don Jóse and the Donna Inez led
    For some time an unhappy sort of life,
Wishing each other, not divorced, but dead;
    They lived respectably as man and wife,   205
Their conduct was exceedingly well-bred,
    And gave no outward signs of inward strife,
Until at length the smothered fire broke out,
And put the business past all kind of doubt.

For Inez called some druggists and physicians,
    And tried to prove her loving lord was *mad*,[9] 210
But as he had some lucid intermissions,
    She next decided he was only *bad;*
Yet when they asked her for her depositions,
    No sort of explanation could be had,
Save that her duty both to man and God   215
Required this conduct—which seemed very odd.

She kept a journal, where his faults were noted,
    And opened certain trunks of books and letters,
All which might, if occasion served, be quoted;
    And then she had all Seville for abettors,   220
Besides her good old grandmother (who doted);
    The hearers of her case became repeaters,
Then advocates, inquisitors, and judges,
Some for amusement, others for old grudges.

And then this best and meekest woman bore   225
    With such serenity her husband's woes,
Just as the Spartan ladies did of yore,
    Who saw their spouses killed, and nobly chose

---

[7] Cf. *I Henry IV*, II, iii, 27.   [8] Swords.

[9] Lady Byron sought medical opinion on her husband's
sanity.

Never to say a word about them more—
   Calmly she heard each calumny that rose,   230
And saw *his* agonies with such sublimity,
That all the world exclaimed, "What magnanim-
   ity!"

No doubt this patience, when the world is damn-
   ing us,
   Is philosophic in our former friends;
'Tis also pleasant to be deem'd magnanimous,   235
   The more so in obtaining our own ends;
And what the lawyers call a *"malus animus"*[10]
   Conduct like this by no means comprehends:
Revenge in person's certainly no virtue,
But then 'tis not *my* fault, if *others* hurt you.   240

And if our quarrels should rip up old stories,
   And help them with a lie or two additional,
I'm not to blame, as you well know—no more is
   Any one else—they were become traditional;
Besides, their resurrection aids our glories   245
   By contrast, which is what we just were wish-
   ing all:
And Science profits by this resurrection—
Dead scandals form good subjects for dissection.

Their friends had tried at reconciliation,
   Then their relations, who made matters worse.   250
('Twere hard to tell upon a like occasion
   To whom it may be best to have recourse—
I can't say much for friend or yet relation):
   The lawyers did their utmost for divorce,
But scarce a fee was paid on either side   255
Before, unluckily, Don José died.
     . . .

Dying intestate, Juan was sole heir
   To a chancery[11] suit, and messuages,[12] and   290
   lands,
Which, with a long minority and care,
   Promised to turn out well in proper hands:
Inez became sole guardian, which was fair,
   And answered but to Nature's just demands;
An only son left with an only mother   295
Is brought up much more wisely than another.

Sagest of women, even of widows, she
   Resolved that Juan should be quite a paragon,
And worthy of the noblest pedigree:

(His Sire was of Castile, his Dam from Ara-   300
   gon):
Then, for accomplishments of chivalry,
   In case our Lord the King should go to war
   again,
He learned the arts of riding, fencing, gunnery,
And how to scale a fortress—or a nunnery.

But that which Donna Inez most desired,   305
   And saw into herself each day before all
The learnèd tutors whom for him she hired,
   Was, that his breeding should be strictly moral:
Much into all his studies she inquired,
   And so they were submitted first to her, all,   310
Arts, sciences, no branch was made a mystery
To Juan's eyes, excepting natural history.[13]

The languages, especially the dead,
   The sciences, and most of all the abstruse,
The arts, at least all such as could be said   315
   To be the most remote from common use,
In all these he was much and deeply read:
   But not a page of anything that's loose,
Or hints continuation of the species,
Was ever suffered, lest he should grow vicious.   320
     . . .

Young Juan waxed in goodliness and grace;   385
   At six a charming child, and at eleven
With all the promise of as fine a face
   As e'er to Man's maturer growth was given:
He studied steadily, and grew apace,
   And seemed, at least, in the right road to   390
   Heaven,
For half his days were passed at church, the other
Between his tutors, confessor, and mother.

At six, I said, he was a charming child,
   At twelve he was a fine, but quiet boy;
Although in infancy a little wild,   395
   They tamed him down amongst them: to de-
   stroy
His natural spirit not in vain they toiled,
   At least it seemed so; and his mother's joy
Was to declare how sage, and still, and steady,
Her young philosopher was grown already.   400

I had my doubts, perhaps I have them still,
   But what I say is neither here nor there:

---

10 Injurious spirit.
11 Formerly the highest English court, and notorious for its delays.
12 Dwellings and lands.

13 I.e., biology.

I knew his father well, and have some skill
    In character—but it would not be fair
From sire to son to augur good or ill: 405
    He and his wife were an ill sorted pair—
But scandal's my aversion—I protest
Against all evil speaking, even in jest.

For my part I say nothing—nothing—but
    This I will say—my reasons are my own—   410
That if I had an only son to put
    To school (as God be praised that I have none),
'Tis not with Donna Inez I would shut
    Him up to learn his catechism alone,
No—no—I'd send him out betimes to college,   415
For there it was I picked up my own knowledge.

For there one learns—'tis not for me to boast,
    Though I acquired—but I pass over *that,*
As well as all the Greek I since have lost:
    I say that there's the place—but *"Verbum* 420
        sat,"[14]
I think I picked up too, as well as most,
    Knowledge of matters—but no matter *what*—
I never married—but, I think, I know
That sons should not be educated so.

Young Juan now was sixteen years of age,   425
    Tall, handsome, slender, but well knit: he
        seemed
Active, though not so sprightly, as a page;
    And everybody but his mother deemed
Him almost man; but she flew in a rage
    And bit her lips (for else she might have 430
        screamed)
If any said so—for to be precocious
Was in her eyes a thing the most atrocious.

Amongst her numerous acquaintance, all
    Selected for discretion and devotion,
There was the Donna Julia, whom to call   435
    Pretty were but to give a feeble notion
Of many charms in her as natural
    As sweetness to the flower, or salt to Ocean,
Her zone[15] to Venus, or his bow to Cupid,
(But this last simile is trite and stupid).   440

The darkness of her Oriental eye
    Accorded with her Moorish origin;

(Her blood was not all Spanish; by the by,
    In Spain, you know, this is a sort of sin;)
When proud Granada fell, and, forced to fly, 445
    Boabdil[16] wept: of Donna Julia's kin
Some went to Africa, some stayed in Spain—
Her great great grandmamma chose to remain.

. . .

However this might be, the race went on   465
    Improving still through every generation,
Until it centred in an only son,
    Who left an only daughter; my narration
May have suggested that this single one
    Could be but Julia (whom on this occasion 470
I shall have much to speak about), and she
Was married, charming, chaste, and twenty-three.

Her eye (I'm very fond of handsome eyes)
    Was large and dark, suppressing half its fire
Until she spoke, then through its soft disguise 475
    Flashed an expression more of pride than ire,
And love than either; and there would arise
    A something in them which was not desire,
But would have been, perhaps, but for the soul
Which struggled through and chastened down the 480
    whole.

Her glossy hair was clustered o'er a brow
    Bright with intelligence, and fair, and smooth;
Her eyebrow's shape was like the aërial bow,
    Her cheek all purple with the beam of youth,
Mounting, at times, to a transparent glow, 485
    As if her veins ran lightning; she, in sooth,
Possessed an air and grace by no means common:
Her stature tall—I hate a dumpy woman.

Wedded she was some years, and to a man
    Of fifty, and such husbands are in plenty; 490
And yet, I think, instead of such a ONE
    'Twere better to have TWO of five-and-twenty,
Especially in countries near the sun:
    And now I think on 't, *"mi vien in mente,"*[17]
Ladies even of the most uneasy virtue
Prefer a spouse whose age is short of thirty. 495

'Tis a sad thing, I cannot choose but say,
    And all the fault of that indecent sun,
Who cannot leave alone our helpless clay,
    But will keep baking, broiling, burning on, 500

---

[14] I.e., *verbum sat sapienti est,* a word to the wise is sufficient.
[15] Belt or sash.

[16] Its last Moorish king, expelled in 1492 by Ferdinand and Isabella.
[17] It comes into my mind.

That howsoever people fast and pray,
  The flesh is frail, and so the soul undone:
What men call gallantry, and gods adultery,
Is much more common where the climate's sultry.

. . .

Alfonso was the name of Julia's lord,
  A man well looking for his years, and who
Was neither much beloved nor yet abhorred: 515
  They lived together as most people do,
Suffering each other's foibles by accord,
  And not exactly either *one* or *two;*
Yet he was jealous, though he did not show it,
For Jealousy dislikes the world to know it.   520

. . .

Juan she saw, and, as a pretty child,   545
  Caressed him often—such a thing might be
Quite innocently done, and harmless styled,
  When she had twenty years, and thirteen he;
But I am not so sure I should have smiled
  When he was sixteen, Julia twenty-three;   550
These few short years make wondrous alterations,
Particularly amongst sun-burnt nations.

Whate'er the cause might be, they had become
  Changed; for the dame grew distant, the youth
    shy,
Their looks cast down, their greetings almost   555
    dumb,
  And much embarrassment in either eye;
There surely will be little doubt with some
  That Donna Julia knew the reason why,
But as for Juan, he had no more notion
Than he who never saw the sea of Ocean.   560

Yet Julia's very coldness still was kind,
  And tremulously gentle her small hand
Withdrew itself from his, but left behind
  A little pressure, thrilling, and so bland
And slight, so very slight, that to the mind   565
  'Twas but a doubt; but ne'er magician's wand
Wrought change with all Armida's[18] fairy art
Like what this light touch left on Juan's heart.

And if she met him, though she smiled no more,
  She looked a sadness sweeter than her smile,   570
As if her heart had deeper thoughts in store
  She must not own, but cherished more the while

For that compression in its burning core;
  Even Innocence itself has many a wile,
And will not dare to trust itself with truth,   575
And Love is taught hypocrisy from youth.

. . .

Then there were sighs, the deeper for suppression,   585
  And stolen glances, sweeter for the theft,
And burning blushes, though for no transgression,
  Tremblings when met, and restlessness when
    left;
All these are little preludes to possession,
  Of which young Passion cannot be bereft,   590
And merely tend to show how greatly Love is
Embarrassed at first starting with a novice.

. . .

She now determined that a virtuous woman
  Should rather face and overcome temptation,   610
That flight was base and dastardly, and no man
  Should ever give her heart the least sensation,
That is to say, a thought beyond the common
  Preference, that we must feel, upon occasion,
For people who are pleasanter than others,   615
But then they only seem so many brothers.

And even if by chance—and who can tell?
  The Devil's so very sly—she should discover
That all within was not so very well,
  And, if still free, that such or such a lover   620
Might please perhaps, a virtuous wife can quell
  Such thoughts, and be the better when they're
    over;
And if the man should ask, 'tis but denial:
I recommend young ladies to make trial.

And, then, there are such things as Love divine,   625
  Bright and immaculate, unmixed and pure,
Such as the angels think so very fine,
  And matrons, who would be no less secure,
Platonic, perfect, "just such love as mine";
  Thus Julia said—and thought so, to be sure;   630
And so I'd have her think, were *I* the man
On whom her reveries celestial ran.

Such love is innocent, and may exist
  Between young persons without any danger.
A hand may first, and then a lip be kissed;   635
  For my part, to such doings I'm a stranger,
But *hear* these freedoms form the utmost list
  Of all o'er which such love may be a ranger:

---

18 A beautiful sorceress in the epic *Jerusalem Delivered* by Tasso. She seduces the crusader Rinaldo.

If people go beyond, 'tis quite a crime,
But not my fault—I tell them all in time. 640

Love, then, but Love within its proper limits,
    Was Julia's innocent determination
In young Don Juan's favour, and to him its
    Exertion might be useful on occasion;
And, lighted at too pure a shrine to dim its 645
    Ethereal lustre, with what sweet persuasion
He might be taught, by Love and her together—
I really don't know what, nor Julia either.

. . .

So much for Julia! Now we'll turn to Juan.
    Poor little fellow! he had no idea
Of his own case, and never hit the true one;
    In feelings quick as Ovid's Miss Medea,[19]
He puzzled over what he found a new one, 685
    But not as yet imagined it could be a
Thing quite in course, and not at all alarming,
Which, with a little patience, might grow charm-
    ing.

Silent and pensive, idle, restless, slow,
    His home deserted for the lonely wood,
Tormented with a wound he could not know,
    His, like all deep grief, plunged in solitude: 690
I'm fond myself of solitude or so,
    But then, I beg it may be understood,
By solitude I mean a Sultan's (not 695
A Hermit's) with a haram[20] for a grot.

. . .

Young Juan wandered by the glassy brooks,
    Thinking unutterable things; he threw
Himself at length within the leafy nooks 715
    Where the wild branch of the cork forest grew;
There poets find materials for their books,
    And every now and then we read them through,
So that their plan and prosody[21] are eligible,
Unless, like Wordsworth, they prove unintelligi- 720
    ble.

He, Juan (and not Wordsworth), so pursued
    His self-communion with his own high soul,
Until his mighty heart, in its great mood,
    Had mitigated part, though not the whole

Of its disease; he did the best he could 725
    With things not very subject to control,
And turned, without perceiving his condition,
Like Coleridge, into a metaphysician.

He thought about himself, and the whole earth,
    Of man the wonderful, and of the stars, 730
And how the deuce they ever could have birth;
    And then he thought of earthquakes, and of
        wars,
How many miles the moon might have in girth,
    Of air-balloons, and of the many bars
To perfect knowledge of the boundless skies;— 735
And then he thought of Donna Julia's eyes.

In thoughts like these true Wisdom may discern
    Longings sublime, and aspirations high,
Which some are born with, but the most part learn
    To plague themselves withal, they know not 740
        why:
'Twas strange that one so young should thus con-
    cern
    His brain about the action of the sky;
If *you* think 'twas Philosophy that this did,
I can't help thinking puberty assisted.

He pored upon the leaves, and on the flowers, 745
    And heard a voice in all the winds; and then
He thought of wood-nymphs and immortal
    bowers,
    And how the goddesses came down to men:
He missed the pathway, he forgot the hours,
    And when he looked upon his watch again, 750
He found how much old Time had been a
    winner—
He also found that he had lost his dinner.

. . .

It was upon a day, a summer's day;—
    Summer's indeed a very dangerous season, 810
And so is spring about the end of May;
    The sun, no doubt, is the prevailing reason;
But whatsoe'er the cause is, one may say,
    And stand convicted of more truth than trea-
        son,
That there are months which nature grows more 815
    merry in,—
March has its hares, and May must have its
    heroine.

'Twas on a summer's day—the sixth of June:
    I like to be particular in dates,

---

[19] The famous sorceress of classical legend who married
Jason. She is the heroine of the tragedy *Medea* by Euripides, but for the present allusion see Ovid, *Metamorphoses*,
VII, 9 ff.
[20] Harem, women's quarters.—*Grot* = cave.
[21] System of versification.

Not only of the age, and year, but moon;
    They are a sort of post-house, where the Fates   820
Change horses, making History change its tune,
    Then spur away o'er empires and o'er states,
Leaving at last not much besides chronology,
Expecting the post-obits[22] of theology.

'Twas on the sixth of June, about the hour   825
    Of half-past six—perhaps still nearer seven—
When Julia sate within as pretty a bower
    As e'er held houri[23] in that heathenish heaven
Described by Mahomet, and Anacreon Moore,[24]
    To whom the lyre and laurels have been given   830
With all the trophies of triumphant song—
He won them well, and may he wear them long!

She sate, but not alone; I know not well
    How this same interview had taken place,
And even if I knew, I should not tell—   835
    People should hold their tongues in any case;
No matter how or why the thing befell,
    But there were she and Juan, face to face—
When two such faces are so, 'twould be wise,
But very difficult, to shut their eyes.   840

How beautiful she looked! her conscious heart
    Glowed in her cheek, and yet she felt no wrong:
Oh Love! how perfect is thy mystic art,
    Strengthening the weak, and trampling on the
        strong!
How self-deceitful is the sagest part   845
    Of mortals whom thy lure hath led along!—
The precipice she stood on was immense,
So was her creed[25] in her own innocence.

She thought of her own strength, and Juan's
    youth,
    And of the folly of all prudish fears,   850
Victorious Virtue, and domestic Truth,
    And then of Don Alfonso's fifty years:
I wish these last had not occurred, in sooth,
    Because that number rarely much endears,

And through all climes, the snowy and the sunny,   855
Sounds ill in love, whate'er it may in money.

. . .

Julia had honour, virtue, truth, and love   865
    For Don Alfonso; and she inly swore,
By all the vows below to Powers above,
    She never would disgrace the ring she wore,
Nor leave a wish which wisdom might reprove;
    And while she pondered this, besides much   870
      more,
One hand on Juan's carelessly was thrown,
Quite by mistake—she thought it was her own;

Unconsciously she leaned upon the other,
    Which played within the tangles of her hair;
And to contend with thoughts she could not   875
      smother
    She seemed, by the distraction of her air.
'Twas surely very wrong in Juan's mother
    To leave together this imprudent pair,
She who for many years had watched her son so—
I'm very certain *mine* would not have done so.   880

The hand which still held Juan's, by degrees
    Gently, but palpably confirmed its grasp,
As if it said, "Detain me, if you please";
    Yet there's no doubt she only meant to clasp
His fingers with a pure Platonic squeeze;   885
    She would have shrunk as from a toad, or asp,
Had she imagined such a thing could rouse
A feeling dangerous to a prudent spouse.

I cannot know what Juan thought of this,
    But what he did, is much what you would do;   890
His young lip thanked it with a grateful kiss,
    And then, abashed at its own joy, withdrew
In deep despair, lest he had done amiss,—
    Love is so very timid when 'tis new:
She blushed, and frowned not, but she strove to   895
    speak,
And held her tongue, her voice was grown so weak.

The sun set, and up rose the yellow moon:
    The Devil's in the moon for mischief; they
Who call'd her CHASTE, methinks, began too soon
    Their nomenclature; there is not a day,   900
The longest, not the twenty-first of June,
    Sees half the business in a wicked way,
On which three single hours of moonshine smile—
And then she looks so modest all the while!

---

22 I.e., post-obit bonds, payable after death. Cf. line 1000.
23 Nymph of the Mohammedan paradise.
24 The poet Thomas Moore (p. 213), translator of *Odes of Anacreon* (1800). Anacreon (died 488? B.C.) survives in a handful of graceful lyrics, but his name became attached to a body of "Anacreontic" verse, much of it amorous. Moore is mentioned here on account of his Oriental poem *Lalla Rookh* (1817).
25 Belief.

There is a dangerous silence in that hour, 905
    A stillness, which leaves room for the full soul
To open all itself, without the power
    Of calling wholly back its self-control;
The silver light which, hallowing tree and tower,
    Sheds beauty and deep softness o'er the whole, 910
Breathes also to the heart, and o'er it throws
A loving languor, which is not repose.

And Julia sate with Juan, half embraced
    And half retiring from the glowing arm,
Which trembled like the bosom where 'twas 915
      placed;
    Yet still she must have thought there was no
      harm,
Or else 'twere easy to withdraw her waist;
    But then the situation had its charm,
And then—God knows what next—I can't go on;
I'm almost sorry that I e'er begun. 920

Oh Plato! Plato! you have paved the way,
    With your confounded fantasies, to more
Immoral conduct by the fancied sway
    Your system feigns o'er the controlless core
Of human hearts, than all the long array 925
    Of poets and romancers:—You're a bore,
A charlatan, a coxcomb—and have been,
At best, no better than a go-between.

And Julia's voice was lost, except in sighs,
    Until too late for useful conversation; 930
The tears were gushing from her gentle eyes,
    I wish, indeed, they had not had occasion;
But who, alas! can love, and then be wise?
    Not that Remorse did not oppose Temptation;
A little still she strove, and much repented, 935
And whispering "I will ne'er consent"—consented.

      . . .

Here my chaste Muse a liberty must take—
    Start not! still chaster reader—she'll be nice
      hence-
Forward, and there is no great cause to quake; 955
    This liberty is a poetic licence,
Which some irregularity may make
    In the design, and as I have a high sense
Of Aristotle and the Rules, 'tis fit
To beg his pardon when I err a bit. 960

This licence is to hope the reader will
    Suppose from June the sixth (the fatal day,

Without whose epoch my poetic skill
    For want of facts would all be thrown away),
But keeping Julia and Don Juan still 965
    In sight, that several months have passed; we'll
      say
'Twas in November, but I'm not so sure
About the day—the era's more obscure.

We'll talk of that anon.—'Tis sweet to hear
    At midnight on the blue and moonlit deep 970
The song and oar of Adria's[26] gondolier,
    By distance mellowed, o'er the waters sweep;
'Tis sweet to see the evening star appear;
    'Tis sweet to listen as the night-winds creep
From leaf to leaf; 'tis sweet to view on high 975
The rainbow, based on ocean, span the sky.

'Tis sweet to hear the watch-dog's honest bark
    Bay deep-mouthed welcome as we draw near
      home;
'Tis sweet to know there is an eye will mark
    Our coming, and look brighter when we come; 980
'Tis sweet to be awakened by the lark,
    Or lulled by falling waters; sweet the hum
Of bees, the voice of girls, the song of birds,
The lisp of children, and their earliest words.

Sweet is the vintage, when the showering grapes 985
    In Bacchanal profusion reel to earth,
Purple and gushing: sweet are our escapes
    From civic revelry to rural mirth;
Sweet to the miser are his glittering heaps,
    Sweet to the father is his first-born's birth, 990
Sweet is revenge—especially to women—
Pillage to soldiers, prize-money to seamen.

Sweet is a legacy, and passing sweet
    The unexpected death of some old lady,
Or gentleman of seventy years complete, 995
    Who've made "us youth"[27] wait too—too long
      already,
For an estate, or cash, or country seat,
    Still breaking, but with stamina so steady
That all the Israelites[28] are fit to mob its
Next owner for their double-damned post-obits. 1000

'Tis sweet to win, no matter how, one's laurels,
    By blood or ink; 'tis sweet to put an end

---

26 The Adriatic's; i.e., in Venice.
27 As the elderly Falstaff describes himself and his associates in *I Henry IV*, II, ii, 89.
28 I.e., Jewish moneylenders.

To strife; 'tis sometimes sweet to have our quar-
    rels,
    Particularly with a tiresome friend:
Sweet is old wine in bottles, ale in barrels;   1005
    Dear is the helpless creature we defend
Against the world; and dear the schoolboy spot
We ne'er forget, though there we are forgot.

But sweeter still than this, than these, than all,
    Is first and passionate Love—it stands alone,   1010
Like Adam's recollection of his fall;
    The Tree of Knowledge has been plucked—
        all's known—
And Life yields nothing further to recall
    Worthy of this ambrosial sin, so shown,
No doubt in fable, as the unforgiven   1015
Fire which Prometheus[29] filched for us from
    Heaven.

      · · ·

'Twas, as the watchmen say, a cloudy night;
    No moon, no stars, the wind was low or loud
By gusts, and many a sparkling hearth was bright   1075
    With the piled wood, round which the family
      crowd;
There's something cheerful in that sort of light,
    Even as a summer sky's without a cloud:
I'm fond of fire, and crickets, and all that,
A lobster salad, and champagne, and chat.   1080

'Twas midnight—Donna Julia was in bed,
    Sleeping, most probably,—when at her door
Arose a clatter might awake the dead,
    If they had never been awoke before,
And that they have been so we all have read,   1085
    And are to be so, at the least, once more;—
The door was fastened, but with voice and fist
First knocks were heard, then "Madam—Madam
    —hist!

"For God's sake, Madam—Madam—here's my
    master,
    With more than half the city at his back—   1090
Was ever heard of such a curst disaster!
    'Tis not my fault—I kept good watch—Alack!
Do pray undo the bolt a little faster—
    They're on the stair just now, and in a crack
Will all be here; perhaps he yet may fly—   1095
Surely the window's not so *very* high!"

By this time Don Alfonso was arrived,
    With torches, friends, and servants in great
      number;
The major part of them had long been wived,
    And therefore paused not to disturb the slum- 1100
      ber
Of any wicked woman, who contrived
    By stealth her husband's temples to encum-
      ber:[30]
Examples of this kind are so contagious,
Were *one* not punished, *all* would be outrageous.

I can't tell how, or why, or what suspicion   1105
    Could enter into Don Alfonso's head;
But for a cavalier of his condition[31]
    It surely was exceedingly ill-bred,
Without a word of previous admonition,
    To hold a levee round his lady's bed,   1110
And summon lackeys, armed with fire and sword,
To prove himself the thing he most abhorred.

Poor Donna Julia! starting as from sleep,
    (Mind—that I do not say—she had not slept),
Began at once to scream, and yawn, and weep;   1115
    Her maid, Antonia, who was an adept,
Contrived to fling the bed-clothes in a heap,
    As if she had just now from out them crept:
I can't tell why she should take all this trouble
To prove her mistress had been sleeping double.   1120

But Julia mistress, and Antonia maid,
    Appeared like two poor harmless women, who
Of goblins, but still more of men afraid,
    Had thought one man might be deterred by
      two,
And therefore side by side were gently laid,   1125
    Until the hours of absence should run
      through,
And truant husband should return, and say,
"My dear,—I was the first who came away."

Now Julia found at length a voice, and cried,
    "In heaven's name, Don Alfonso, what d'ye 1130
      mean?
Has madness seized you? would that I had died
    Ere such a monster's victim I had been!

---

[29] In Greek myth the Titan who was punished by Zeus for stealing fire and giving it to men.

[30] I.e., to make him by her infidelity a cuckold, in whose forehead horns were supposed to grow, the badge of his dishonor.
[31] Rank.

What may this midnight violence betide,
  A sudden fit of drunkenness or spleen?
Dare you suspect me, whom the thought would ¹¹³⁵
    kill?
Search, then, the room!"—Alfonso said, "I will."

He searched, *they* searched, and rummaged
    everywhere,
  Closet and clothes-press, chest and window-
    seat,
And found much linen, lace, and several pair
  Of stockings, slippers, brushes, combs, com- ¹¹⁴⁰
    plete,
With other articles of ladies fair,
  To keep them beautiful, or leave them neat:
Arras they pricked and curtains with their swords,
And wounded several shutters, and some boards.

Under the bed they searched, and there they ¹¹⁴⁵
    found—
  No matter what—it was not that they sought;
They opened windows, gazing if the ground
  Had signs or footmarks, but the earth said
    nought;
And then they stared each other's faces round:
  'Tis odd, not one of all these seekers thought, ¹¹⁵⁰
And seems to me almost a sort of blunder,
Of looking *in* the bed as well as under.

During this inquisition Julia's tongue
  Was not asleep—"Yes, search and search," she
    cried,
"Insult on insult heap, and wrong on wrong! ¹¹⁵⁵
  It was for this that I became a bride!
For this in silence I have suffered long
  A husband like Alfonso at my side;
But now I'll bear no more, nor here remain,
If there be law or lawyers in all Spain. ¹¹⁶⁰

"Yes, Don Alfonso! husband now no more,
  If ever you indeed deserved the name,
Is't worthy of your years?—you have three-score—
  Fifty, or sixty, it is all the same—
Is't wise or fitting, causeless to explore ¹¹⁶⁵
  For facts against a virtuous woman's fame?
Ungrateful, perjured, barbarous Don Alfonso,
How dare you think your lady would go on so?

         ·   ·   ·

"Did not the Italian *Musico* Cazzani ¹¹⁸⁵
  Sing at my heart six months at least in vain?

Did not his countryman, Count Corniani,³²
  Call me the only virtuous wife in Spain?
Were there not also Russians, English, many?
  The Count Strongstroganoff I put in pain, ¹¹⁹⁰
And Lord Mount Coffeehouse, the Irish peer,
Who killed himself for love (with wine) last year.

         ·   ·   ·

"Was it for this you took your sudden journey,
  Under pretence of business indispensable
With that sublime of rascals your attorney,
  Whom I see standing there, and looking
    sensible
Of having played the fool? though both I spurn, ¹²⁰⁵
    he
  Deserves the worst, his conduct's less defen-
    sible,
Because, no doubt, 'twas for his dirty fee,
And not from any love to you nor me.

         ·   ·   ·

"And now, Hidalgo! now that you have thrown ¹²²⁵
  Doubt upon me, confusion over all,
Pray have the courtesy to make it known
  Who is the man you search for? how d'ye call
Him? what's his lineage? let him but be shown—
  I hope he's young and handsome—is he tall? ¹²³⁰
Tell me—and be assured, that since you stain
Mine honour thus, it shall not be in vain.

"At least, perhaps, he has not sixty years,
  At that age he would be too old for slaughter,
Or for so young a husband's jealous fears— ¹²³⁵
  (Antonia! let me have a glass of water.)
I am ashamed of having shed these tears,
  They are unworthy of my father's daughter;
My mother dreamed not in my natal hour,
That I should fall into a monster's power. ¹²⁴⁰

"Perhaps 'tis of Antonia you are jealous,
  You saw that she was sleeping by my side,
When you broke in upon us with your fellows:
  Look where you please—we've nothing, sir, to
    hide;
Only another time, I trust, you'll tell us, ¹²⁴⁵
  Or for the sake of decency abide
A moment at the door, that we may be
Dressed to receive so much good company."

         ·   ·   ·

But Don Alfonso stood with downcast looks,
  And, truth to say, he made a foolish figure;

---

³² The names of both Julia's Italian admirers are based
by Byron on vulgar words.

When, after searching in five hundred nooks,
    And treating a young wife with so much
        rigour,
He gained no point, except some self-rebukes,   1285
    Added to those his lady with such vigour
Had poured upon him for the last half-hour,
Quick, thick, and heavy—as a thunder-shower.

    · · ·

With him retired his *"posse comitatus,"*[33]   1305
    The attorney last, who lingered near the door
Reluctantly, still tarrying there as late as
    Antonia let him—not a little sore
At this most strange and unexplain'd *"hiatus"*
    In Don Alfonso's facts, which just now wore   1310
An awkward look; as he revolved the case,
The door was fastened in his legal face.

No sooner was it bolted, than—Oh Shame!
    Oh Sin! Oh Sorrow! and Oh Womankind!
How can you do such things and keep your fame,   1315
    Unless this world, and t'other too, be blind?
Nothing so dear as an unfilched good name![34]
    But to proceed—for there is more behind:
With much heartfelt reluctance be it said,
Young Juan slipped, half-smothered, from the   1320
    bed.

He had been hid—I don't pretend to say
    How, nor can I indeed describe the where—
Young, slender, and packed easily, he lay,
    No doubt, in little compass, round or square;
But pity him I neither must nor may   1325
    His suffocation by that pretty pair;
'Twere better, sure, to die so, than be shut
With maudlin Clarence in his Malmsey[35] butt.

    · · ·

What's to be done? Alfonso will be back   1345
    The moment he has sent his fools away.
Antonia's skill was put upon the rack,
    But no device could be brought into play—
And how to parry the renewed attack?
    Besides, it wanted but few hours of day: 1350
Antonia puzzled; Julia did not speak,
But pressed her bloodless lip to Juan's cheek.

---

[33] Properly, an armed force summoned by a sheriff to help preserve order.
[34] Cf. *Othello*, III, iii, 159.
[35] A kind of sweet wine. The execution in 1478 of the Duke of Clarence, brother of Edward IV and Richard III, was said to have been finished off by his being drowned in a cask of it.

He turned his lip to hers, and with his hand
    Call'd back the tangles of her wandering hair;
Even then their love they could not all command,   1355
    And half forgot their danger and despair:
Antonia's patience now was at a stand—
    "Come, come, 'tis no time now for fooling
        there,"
She whispered, in great wrath—"I must deposit
This pretty gentleman within the closet."   1360

    · · ·

Now, Don Alfonso entering, but alone,
    Closed the oration of the trusty maid:
She loitered, and he told her to be gone,
    An order somewhat sullenly obeyed;   1380
However, present remedy was none,
    And no great good seemed answered if she
        staid:
Regarding both with slow and sidelong view,
She snuffed the candle, curtsied, and withdrew.

    · · ·

Alfonso closed his speech, and begged her
    pardon,
    Which Julia half withheld, and then half
        granted,
And laid conditions he thought very hard on,   1435
    Denying several little things he wanted:
He stood like Adam lingering near his garden,
    With useless penitence perplexed and haunted,
Beseeching she no further would refuse,
When, lo! he stumbled o'er a pair of shoes.   1440

A pair of shoes!—what then? not much, if they
    Are such as fit with ladies' feet, but these
(No one can tell how much I grieve to say)
    Were masculine; to see them, and to seize,
Was but a moment's act.—Ah! well-a-day!   1445
    My teeth begin to chatter, my veins freeze!
Alfonso first examined well their fashion,
And then flew out into another passion.

He left the room for his relinquished sword,
    And Julia instant to the closet flew.   1450
"Fly, Juan, fly! for Heaven's sake—not a word—
    The door is open—you may yet slip through
The passage you so often have explored—
    Here is the garden-key—Fly—fly—Adieu!
Haste—haste! I hear Alfonso's hurrying feet—   1455
Day has not broke—there's no one in the street."

None can say that this was not good advice,
    The only mischief was, it came too late;

Of all experience 'tis the usual price,
　　A sort of income-tax laid on by fate:　　　1460
Juan had reached the room-door in a trice,
　　And might have done so by the garden-gate,
But met Alfonso in his dressing-gown,
Who threatened death—so Juan knocked him
　　down.

Dire was the scuffle, and out went the light;　1465
　　Antonia cried out "Rape!" and Julia "Fire!"
But not a servant stirred to aid the fight.
　　Alfonso, pommelled to his heart's desire,
Swore lustily he'd be revenged this night;
　　And Juan, too, blasphemed an octave higher;　1470
His blood was up: though young, he was a
　　Tartar,
And not at all disposed to prove a martyr.

Alfonso's sword had dropped ere he could draw it,
　　And they continued battling hand to hand,
For Juan very luckily ne'er saw it;　　　　　1475
　　His temper not being under great command,
If at that moment he had chanced to claw it,
　　Alfonso's days had not been in the land
Much longer.—Think of husbands', lovers' lives!
And how ye may be doubly widows—wives!　1480

Alfonso grappled to detain the foe,
　　And Juan throttled him to get away,
And blood ('twas from the nose) began to flow;
　　At last, as they more faintly wrestling lay,
Juan contrived to give an awkward blow,　　1485
　　And then his only garment quite gave way;
He fled, like Joseph,[36] leaving it; but there,
I doubt,[37] all likeness ends between the pair.

Lights came at length, and men, and maids, who
　　found
　　An awkward spectacle their eyes before；　　1490
Antonia in hysterics, Julia swooned,
　　Alfonso leaning, breathless, by the door;
Some half-torn drapery scattered on the ground,
　　Some blood, and several footsteps, but no
　　more:
Juan the gate gained, turned the key about,　1495
And liking not the inside, locked the out.

Here ends this canto.—Need I sing, or say,
　　How Juan, naked, favoured by the night,

Who favours what she should not, found his way,
　　And reached his home in an unseemly plight?　1500
The pleasant scandal which arose next day,
　　The nine days' wonder which was brought to
　　light,
And how Alfonso sued for a divorce,
Were in the English newspapers, of course.

　　　　　　　. . .

But Donna Inez, to divert the train
　　Of one of the most circulating scandals
That had for centuries been known in Spain,　1515
　　At least since the retirement of the Vandals,[38]
First vowed (and never had she vowed in vain)
　　To Virgin Mary several pounds of candles;
And then, by the advice of some old ladies,
She sent her son to be shipped off from Cadiz.　1520

She had resolved that he should travel through
　　All European climes, by land or sea,
To mend his former morals, and get new,
　　Especially in France and Italy—
(At least this is the thing most people do).　1525
　　Julia was sent into a convent—she
Grieved—but, perhaps, her feelings may be better
Shown in the following copy of her Letter:—

"They tell me 'tis decided you depart:
　　'Tis wise—'tis well, but not the less a pain;　1530
I have no further claim on your young heart,
　　Mine is the victim, and would be again:
To love too much has been the only art
　　I used;—I write in haste, and if a stain
Be on this sheet, 'tis not what it appears;　　1535
My eyeballs burn and throb, but have no tears.

　　　　　　　. . .

"Man's love is of Man's life a thing apart,　　1545
　　'Tis a Woman's whole existence; Man may
　　range
The Court, Camp, Church, the Vessel, and the
　　Mart;
　　Sword, Gown, Gain, Glory, offer in exchange
Pride, Fame, Ambition, to fill up his heart,
　　And few there are whom these cannot es-　1550
　　trange；
Men have all these resources, We but one,
To love again, and be again undone."

　　　　　　　. . .

---

[36] See Genesis 39, especially verse 12.　　[37] Suspect, fear.

[38] Who overran Gaul, Spain, North Africa, and Italy in the fourth and fifth centuries. They migrated from Spain to Africa c. 428.

This was Don Juan's earliest scrape; but whether   1585
   I shall proceed with his adventures is
Dependent on the public altogether;
   We'll see, however, what they say to this:
Their favour in an author's cap's a feather,
   And no great mischief's done by their caprice;   1590
And if their approbation we experience,
Perhaps they'll have some more about a year
   hence.

My poem's epic, and is meant to be
   Divided in twelve books; each book contain-
   ing,
With Love, and War, a heavy gale at sea,   1595
   A list of ships, and captains, and kings reign-
   ing,
New characters; the episodes are three:
   A panoramic view of Hell's in training,
After the style of Virgil and of Homer,
So that my name of Epic's no misnomer.   1600

All these things will be specified in time,
   With strict regard to Aristotle's rules,
The *Vade Mecum*[39] of the true sublime,
   Which makes so many poets, and some fools:
Prose poets like blank-verse, I'm fond of rhyme,   1605
   Good workmen never quarrel with their tools;
I've got new mythological machinery,
And very handsome supernatural scenery.

There's only one slight difference between
Me and my epic brethren gone before,   1610
And here the advantage is my own, I ween
   (Not that I have not several merits more,
But this will more peculiarly be seen);
   They so embellish, that 'tis quite a bore
Their labyrinth of fables to thread through,   1615
Whereas this story's actually true.

If any person doubt it, I appeal
   To History, Tradition, and to Facts,
To newspapers, whose truth all know and feel,
   To plays in five, and operas in three acts;   1620
All these confirm my statement a good deal,
   But that which more completely faith exacts
Is, that myself, and several now in Seville,
Saw Juan's last elopement with the Devil.

If ever I should condescend to prose,   1625
   I'll write poetical commandments, which

Shall supersede beyond all doubt all those
   That went before; in these I shall enrich
My text with many things that no one knows,
   And carry precept to the highest pitch: 1630
I'll call the work "Longinus o'er a Bottle,
Or, Every Poet his *own* Aristotle."

Thou shalt believe in Milton, Dryden, Pope;
   Thou shalt not set up Wordsworth, Coleridge,
   Southey;
Because the first is crazed beyond all hope,   1635
   The second drunk, the third so quaint and
   mouthy:
With Crabbe[40] it may be difficult to cope,
   And Campbell's Hippocrene[41] is somewhat
   drouthy:
Thou shalt not steal from Samuel Rogers,[42] nor
Commit—flirtation with the muse of Moore.[43]   1640

Thou shalt not covet Mr. Sotheby's[44] Muse,
   His Pegasus,[45] nor anything that's his;
Thou shalt not bear false witness like "the
   Blues"[46]—
   (There's *one*, at least, is very fond of this);
Thou shalt not write, in short, but what I   1645
   choose:
   This is true criticism, and you may kiss—
Exactly as you please, or not,—the rod;
But if you don't, I'll lay it on, by G—d!

If any person should presume to assert
   This story is not moral, first, I pray,   1650
That they will not cry out before they're hurt,
   Then that they'll read it o'er again, and say
(But, doubtless, nobody will be so pert),
   That this is not a moral tale, though gay;
Besides, in Canto Twelfth, I mean to show   1655
The very place where wicked people go.

· · ·

---

40 George Crabbe (1754–1832), author of *The Village, The
Parish Register, The Borough,* and other realistic poems.
(See Vol. I.)
41 Waters of a fountain on Mt. Helicon in Greece; i.e.,
poetic inspiration. Thomas Campbell (1777–1844) was extremely popular in his own time for such poems as *The
Pleasures of Hope* and *Gertrude of Wyoming.*
42 Samuel Rogers (1763–1855) enjoyed a reputation far
beyond his merit. He was offered the poet laureateship
when Wordsworth died.   43 See note 24.
44 The poet and translator William Sotheby (1757–1833).
45 The winged horse of classical mythology; i.e., poetic
inspiration.
46 Bluestockings, literary ladies.

---

39 Manual.

But now at thirty years my hair is grey—
   (I wonder what it will be like at forty?
I thought of a peruke the other day—)
   My heart is not much greener; and, in short, I   1700
Have squandered my whole summer while 'twas
   May,
   And feel no more the spirit to retort; I
Have spent my life, both interest and principal,
And deem not, what I deemed—my soul in-
   vincible.

No more—no more—Oh! never more on me   1705
   The freshness of the heart can fall like dew,
Which out of all the lovely things we see
   Extracts emotions beautiful and new,
Hived in our bosoms like the bag o' the bee.
   Think'st thou the honey with those objects 1710
   grew?
Alas! 'twas not in them, but in thy power
To double even the sweetness of a flower.

No more—no more—Oh! never more, my heart,
   Canst thou be my sole world, my universe!
Once all in all, but now a thing apart,   1715
   Thou canst not be my blessing or my curse:
The illusion's gone for ever, and thou art
   Insensible, I trust, but none the worse,
And in thy stead I've got a deal of judgment,
Though Heaven knows how it ever found a 1720
   lodgment.

My days of love are over; me no more
   The charms of maid, wife, and still less of
   widow,
Can make the fool of which they made before,—
   In short, I must not lead the life I did do;
The credulous hope of mutual minds is o'er,   1725
   The copious use of claret is forbid too,
So for a good old-gentlemanly vice,
I think I must take up with avarice.

     . . .

But for the present, gentle reader! and
   Still gentler purchaser! the Bard—that's I—
Must, with permission, shake you by the hand,
   And so—"your humble servant, and Good-
   bye!"
We meet again, if we should understand   1765
Each other; and if not, I shall not try
Your patience further than by this short sample—
'Twere well if others followed my example.

"Go, little Book, from this my solitude!
   I cast thee on the waters—go thy ways!   1770
And if, as I believe, thy vein be good,
   The World will find thee after many days."[47]
When Southey's read, and Wordsworth under-
   stood,
   I can't help putting in my claim to praise—
The four first rhymes are Southey's every line: 1775
For God's sake, reader! take them not for mine.

from CANTO THE SECOND

Oh ye! who teach the ingenuous youth of nations,
   Holland, France, England, Germany, or Spain,
I pray ye flog them upon all occasions,
   It mends their morals, never mind the pain:
The best of mothers and of educations   5
   In Juan's case were but employed in vain,
Since, in a way that's rather of the oddest, he
Became divested of his native modesty.

Had he but been placed at a public school,[1]
   In the third form, or even in the fourth,   10
His daily task had kept his fancy cool,
   At least, had he been nurtured in the North.
Spain may prove an exception to the rule,
   But then exceptions always prove its worth—
A lad of sixteen causing a divorce   15
Puzzled his tutors very much, of course.

     . . .

Well—well; the World must turn upon its axis,   25
   And all Mankind turn with it, heads or tails,
And live and die, make love and pay our taxes,
   And as the veering wind shifts, shift our sails;
The King commands us, and the Doctor quacks
   us.
   The Priest instructs, and so our life exhales,   30
A little breath, love, wine, ambition, fame,
Fighting, devotion, dust,—perhaps a name.

     . . .

But to our tale: the Donna Inez sent
   Her son to Cadiz only to embark;
To stay there had not answered her intent,
   But why?—we leave the reader in the dark—   60
'Twas for a voyage the young man was meant,
   As if a Spanish ship were Noah's ark,
To wean him from the wickedness of earth,
And send him like a Dove of Promise forth.

---

47 From the last stanza of the epilogue to Southey's "The Lay of the Laureate."

1 I.e., a private school, like Eton, Harrow, etc.

Don Juan bade his valet pack his things 65
    According to direction, then received
A lecture and some money: for four springs
    He was to travel; and though Inez grieved
(As every kind of parting has its stings),
    She hoped he would improve—perhaps be- 70
        lieved:
A letter, too, she gave (he never read it)
Of good advice—and two or three of credit.

                    . . .

Juan embarked—the ship got under way,
    The wind was fair, the water passing rough;
A devil of a sea rolls in that bay,
    As I, who've crossed it oft, know well enough;
And, standing upon deck, the dashing spray 85
    Flies in one's face, and makes it weather-tough:
And there he stood to take, and take again,
His first—perhaps his last—farewell of Spain.

I can't but say it is an awkward sight
    To see one's native land receding through 90
The growing waters; it unmans one quite,
    Especially when life is rather new:
I recollect Great Britain's coast looks white,
    But almost every other country's blue,
When gazing on them, mystified by distance, 95
We enter on our nautical existence.

So Juan stood, bewildered on the deck:
    The wind sung, cordage strain'd, and sailors
        swore,
And the ship creaked, the town became a speck,
    From which away so fair and fast they bore. 100
The best of remedies is a beef-steak
    Against sea-sickness: try it, Sir, before
You sneer, and I assure you this is true,
For I have found it answer—so may you.

                    . . .

And Juan wept, and much he sighed and
        thought,
    While his salt tears dropped into the salt sea, 130
"Sweets to the sweet"; (I like so much to quote;
    You must excuse this extract,—'tis where she,
The Queen of Denmark, for Ophelia brought
    Flowers to the grave;[2]) and sobbing often, he
Reflected on his present situation, 135
And seriously resolved on reformation.

"Farewell, my Spain! a long farewell!" he cried,
    "Perhaps I may revisit thee no more,

But die, as many an exiled heart hath died,
    Of its own thirst to see again thy shore: 140
Farewell, where Guadalquivir's waters glide!
    Farewell, my mother! and, since all is o'er,
Farewell, too, dearest Julia!—(here he drew
Her letter out again, and read it through.)

"And oh! if e'er I should forget, I swear— 145
    But that's impossible, and cannot be—
Sooner shall this blue Ocean melt to air,
    Sooner shall Earth resolve itself to sea,
Than I resign thine image, oh, my fair!
    Or think of anything, excepting thee; 150
A mind diseased no remedy can physic—
(Here the ship gave a lurch, and he grew sea-
        sick.)

"Sooner shall Heaven kiss earth—(here he fell
        sicker)
    Oh, Julia! what is every other woe?—
(For God's sake let me have a glass of liquor; 155
    Pedro, Battista, help me down below.)
Julia, my love—(you rascal, Pedro, quicker)—
    Oh, Julia!—(this curst vessel pitches so)—
Belovèd Julia, hear me still beseeching!"
(Here he grew inarticulate with retching.) 160

He felt that chilling heaviness of heart,
    Or rather stomach, which, alas! attends,
Beyond the best apothecary's art,
    The loss of Love, the treachery of friends,
Or death of those we dote on, when a part 165
    Of us dies with them as each fond hope ends:
No doubt he would have been much more pa-
        thetic,
But the sea acted as a strong emetic.

                    . . .

His suite consisted of three servants and
    A tutor, the licentiate[3] Pedrillo,
Who several languages did understand, 195
    But now lay sick and speechless on his pillow
And, rocking in his hammock, longed for land,
    His headache being increased by every billow;
And the waves oozing through the port-hole made
His berth a little damp, and him afraid. 200

'Twas not without some reason, for the wind
    Increased at night, until it blew a gale;
And though 'twas not much to a naval mind,

---

2 *Hamlet*, V, i, 266.

3 Holder of a degree between bachelor and doctor.

Some landsmen would have looked a little
   pale,
For sailors are, in fact, a different kind: 205
   At sunset they began to take in sail,
For the sky showed it would come on to blow,
And carry away, perhaps, a mast or so.

At one o'clock the wind with sudden shift
   Threw the ship right into the trough of the 210
     sea,
Which struck her aft, and made an awkward rift,
   Started the stern-post, also shattered the
Whole of her stern-frame, and, ere she could lift
   Herself from out her present jeopardy,
The rudder tore away: 'twas time to sound   215
The pumps, and there were four feet water found.

      . . .

There she lay, motionless, and seem'd upset;
   The water left the hold, and washed the decks,
And made a scene men do not soon forget;
   For they remember battles, fires, and wrecks,
Or any other thing that brings regret,   245
   Or breaks their hopes, or hearts, or heads, or
     necks:
Thus drownings are much talked of by the divers,
And swimmers, who may chance to be survivors.

Immediately the masts were cut away,
   Both main and mizen; first the mizen went, 250
The main-mast followed: but the ship still lay
   Like a mere log, and baffled our intent.
Foremast and bowsprit were cut down, and they
   Eased her at last (although we never meant
To part with all till every hope was blighted), 255
And then with violence the old ship righted.

It may be easily supposed, while this
   Was going on, some people were unquiet,
That passengers would find it much amiss
   To lose their lives, as well as spoil their diet; 260
That even the able seaman, deeming his
   Days nearly o'er, might be disposed to riot,
As upon such occasions tars will ask
For grog, and sometimes drink rum from the
   cask.

There's nought, no doubt, so much the spirit 265
   calms
   As rum and true religion: thus it was,
Some plundered, some drank spirits, some sung
   psalms,

The high wind made the treble, and as bass
The hoarse harsh waves kept time; fright cured
   the qualms
   Of all the luckless landsmen's sea-sick maws: 270
Strange sounds of wailing, blasphemy, devotion,
Clamoured in chorus to the roaring Ocean.

Perhaps more mischief had been done, but for
   Our Juan, who, with sense beyond his years,
Got to the spirit-room, and stood before   275
   It with a pair of pistols; and their fears,
As if Death were more dreadful by his door
   Of fire than water, spite of oaths and tears,
Kept still aloof the crew, who, ere they sunk,
Thought it would be becoming to die drunk. 280

"Give us more grog," they cried, "for it will be
   All one an hour hence." Juan answer'd, "No!
'Tis true that Death awaits both you and me,
   But let us die like men, not sink below
Like brutes":—and thus his dangerous post kept 285
   he,
   And none liked to anticipate the blow;
And even Pedrillo, his most reverend tutor,
Was for some rum a disappointed suitor.

      . . .

The ship was evidently settling now   345
   Fast by the head; and, all distinction gone,
Some went to prayers again, and made a vow
   Of candles to their saints—but there were none
To pay them with; and some looked o'er the bow;
   Some hoisted out the boats; and there was one 350
That begged Pedrillo for an absolution,
Who told him to be damned—in his confusion.

Some lashed them in their hammocks; some put
   on
   Their best clothes, as if going to a fair;
Some cursed the day on which they saw the Sun, 355
   And gnashed their teeth, and howling, tore
     their hair;
And others went on as they had begun,
   Getting the boats out, being well aware
That a tight boat will live in a rough sea,
Unless with breakers close beneath her lee. 360

The worst of all was, that in their condition,
   Having been several days in great distress,
'Twas difficult to get out such provision
   As now might render their long suffering less:

Men, even when dying, dislike inanition;[4]   365
   Their stock was damaged by the weather's
     stress:
Two casks of biscuit, and a keg of butter,
Were all that could be thrown into the cutter.

But in the long-boat they contrived to stow
   Some pounds of bread, though injured by the   370
     wet;
Water, a twenty-gallon cask or so;
   Six flasks of wine; and they contrived to get
A portion of their beef up from below,
   And with a piece of pork, moreover, met,
But scarce enough to serve them for a luncheon—   375
Then there was rum, eight gallons in a puncheon.

The other boats, the yawl and pinnace, had
   Been stove in the beginning of the gale;
And the long-boat's condition was but bad,
   As there were but two blankets for a sail,   380
And one oar for a mast, which a young lad
   Threw in by good luck over the ship's rail;
And two boats could not hold, far less be stored,
To save one half the people then on board.

'Twas twilight, and the sunless day went down   385
   Over the waste of waters; like a veil,
Which, if withdrawn, would but disclose the
     frown
   Of one whose hate is masked but to assail.
Thus to their hopeless eyes the night was shown,
   And grimly darkled o'er the faces pale,   390
And the dim desolate deep: twelve days had Fear
Been their familiar, and now Death was here.

Some trial had been making at a raft,
   With little hope in such a rolling sea,
A sort of thing at which one would have laughed,   395
   If any laughter at such times could be,
Unless with people who too much have quaffed,
   And have a kind of wild and horrid glee,
Half epileptical, and half hysterical:—
Their preservation would have been a miracle.   400

At half-past eight o'clock, booms, hencoops, spars,
   And all things, for a chance, had been cast
     loose,
That still could keep afloat the struggling tars,
   For yet they strove, although of no great use:

There was no light in heaven but a few stars,   405
   The boats put off o'ercrowded with their
     crews;
She gave a heel, and then a lurch to port,
And, going down head foremost—sunk, in short.

Then rose from sea to sky the wild farewell—
   Then shrieked the timid, and stood still the   410
     brave—
Then some leaped overboard with dreadful yell,
   As[5] eager to anticipate their grave;
And the sea yawned around her like a hell,
   And down she sucked with her the whirling
     wave,
Like one who grapples with his enemy,   415
And strives to strangle him before he die.

And first one universal shriek there rushed,
   Louder than the loud Ocean, like a crash
Of echoing thunder; and then all was hushed,
   Save the wild wind and the remorseless dash   420
Of billows; but at intervals there gushed,
   Accompanied with a convulsive splash,
A solitary shriek, the bubbling cry
Of some strong swimmer in his agony.

The boats, as stated, had got off before,   425
   And in them crowded several of the crew;
And yet their present hope was hardly more
   Than what it had been, for so strong it blew
There was slight chance of reaching any shore;
   And then they were too many, though so few—   430
Nine in the cutter, thirty in the boat,
Were counted in them when they got afloat.

      . . .

Juan got into the long-boat, and there
   Contrived to help Pedrillo to a place;
It seemed as if they had exchanged their care,
   For Juan wore the magisterial face
Which courage gives, while poor Pedrillo's pair   445
   Of eyes were crying for their owner's case:
Battista, though, (a name called shortly Tita),
Was lost by getting at some aqua-vita.[6]

Pedro, his valet, too, he tried to save,
   But the same cause, conducive to his loss,   450
Left him so drunk, he jumped into the wave,
   As o'er the cutter's edge he tried to cross,

---

4 Emptiness.

5 As if.
6 Aqua vitae; brandy, etc.

And so he found a wine-and-watery grave;
    They could not rescue him although so close,
Because the sea ran higher every minute,   455
And for the boat—the crew kept crowding in it.

A small old spaniel,—which had been Don Jóse's,
    His father's, whom he loved, as ye may think,
For on such things the memory reposes
    With tenderness—stood howling on the brink,   460
Knowing, (dogs have such intellectual noses!)
    No doubt, the vessel was about to sink;
And Juan caught him up, and ere he stepped
Off threw him in, then after him he leaped.

He also stuffed his money where he could   465
    About his person, and Pedrillo's too,
Who let him do, in fact, whate'er he would,
    Not knowing what himself to say, or do,
As every rising wave his dread renewed;
    But Juan, trusting they might still get through,   470
And deeming there were remedies for any ill,
Thus re-embarked his tutor and his spaniel.

'Twas a rough night, and blew so stiffly yet,
    That the sail was becalmed between the seas,
Though on the wave's high top too much to set,   475
    They dared not take it in for all the breeze:
Each sea curled o'er the stern, and kept them wet,
    And made them bale without a moment's ease,
So that themselves as well as hopes were damped,
And the poor little cutter quickly swamped.   480

Nine souls more went in her: the long-boat still
    Kept above water, with an oar for mast,
Two blankets stitched together, answering ill
    Instead of sail, were to the oar made fast;
Though every wave rolled menacing to fill,   485
    And present peril all before surpassed,
They grieved for those who perished with the
      cutter,
And also for the biscuit-casks and butter.

· · ·

But man is a carnivorous production,
    And must have meals, at least one meal a day;   530
He cannot live, like woodcocks,[7] upon suction,
    But, like the shark and tiger, must have prey;
Although his anatomical construction
    Bears vegetables, in a grumbling way,

---

[7] This bird feeds chiefly at night. Like the duck it may appear to live by "suction"; actually it depends on solid food.

Your labouring people think beyond all question   535
Beef, veal, and mutton, better for digestion.

And thus it was with this our hapless crew;
    For on the third day there came on a calm,
And though at first their strength it might renew,
    And lying on their weariness like balm,   540
Lulled them like turtles sleeping on the blue
    Of Ocean, when they woke they felt a qualm,
And fell all ravenously on their provision,
Instead of hoarding it with due precision.

The consequence was easily foreseen—   545
    They ate up all they had, and drank their
      wine,
In spite of all remonstrances, and then
    On what, in fact, next day were they to dine?
They hoped the wind would rise, these foolish
      men!
    And carry them to shore; these hopes were fine,   550
But as they had but one oar, and that brittle,
It would have been more wise to save their vic-
    tual.

The fourth day came, but not a breath of air,
    And Ocean slumbered like an unweaned child:
The fifth day, and their boat lay floating there,   555
    The sea and sky were blue, and clear, and
      mild—
With their one oar (I wish they had had a pair)
    What could they do? and Hunger's rage grew
      wild:
So Juan's spaniel, spite of his entreating,
Was killed, and portion'd out for present eating.   560

On the sixth day they fed upon his hide,
    And Juan, who had still refused, because
The creature was his father's dog that died,
    Now feeling all the vulture in his jaws,
With some remorse received (though first denied)   565
    As a great favour one of the fore-paws,
Which he divided with Pedrillo, who
Devoured it, longing for the other too.

The seventh day, and no wind—the burning sun
    Blistered and scorched, and stagnant on the   570
      sea,
They lay like carcasses; and hope was none,
    Save in the breeze that came not: savagely
They glared upon each other—all was done,

Water, and wine, and food,—and you might
    see
The longings of the cannibal arise   575
(Although they spoke not) in their wolfish eyes.

At length one whispered his companion, who
    Whispered another, and thus it went round,
And then into a hoarser murmur grew,
    An ominous, and wild, and desperate sound;   580
And when his comrade's thought each sufferer
    knew,
    'Twas but his own, suppressed till now, he
    found:
And out they spoke of lots for flesh and blood,
And who should die to be his fellow's food.

But ere they came to this, they that day shared   585
    Some leathern caps, and what remained of
    shoes;
And then they looked around them, and de-
    spaired,
    And none to be the sacrifice would choose;
At length the lots were torn up, and prepared,
    But of materials that must shock the Muse—   590
Having no paper, for the want of better,
They took by force from Juan Julia's letter.

Then lots were made, and marked, and mixed,
    and handed
    In silent horror, and their distribution
Lulled even the savage hunger which demanded,   595
    Like the Promethean vulture,[8] this pollution;
None in particular had sought or planned it,
    'Twas Nature gnawed them to the resolution,
By which none were permitted to be neuter—
And the lot fell on Juan's luckless tutor.   600

He but requested to be bled to death:
    The surgeon had his instruments, and bled
Pedrillo, and so gently ebbed his breath,
    You hardly could perceive when he was dead.
He died as born, a Catholic in faith,   605
    Like most in the belief in which they're bred,
And first a little crucifix he kissed,
And then held out his jugular and wrist.

The surgeon, as there was no other fee,
    Had his first choice of morsels for his pains;   610

But being thirstiest at the moment, he
    Preferred a draught from the fast-flowing veins:
Part was divided, part thrown in the sea,
    And such things as the entrails and the brains
Regaled two sharks, who followed o'er the bil-   615
    low—
The sailors ate the rest of poor Pedrillo.

The sailors ate him, all save three or four,
    Who were not quite so fond of animal food;
To these was added Juan, who, before
    Refusing his own spaniel, hardly could   620
Feel now his appetite increased much more;
    'Twas not to be expected that he should,
Even in extremity of their disaster,
Dine with them on his pastor and his master.[9]

'Twas better that he did not; for, in fact,   625
    The consequence was awful in the extreme;
For they, who were most ravenous in the act,
    Went raging mad—Lord! how they did blas-
    pheme!
And foam, and roll, with strange convulsions
    racked,
    Drinking salt-water like a mountain-stream;   630
Tearing, and grinning, howling, screeching,
    swearing,
And, with hyaena-laughter, died despairing.

        . . .

And the same night there fell a shower of rain,   665
    For which their mouths gaped, like the cracks
    of earth
When dried to summer dust; till taught by pain,
    Men really know not what good water's worth;
If you had been in Turkey or in Spain,
    Or with a famished boat's-crew had your berth,   670
Or in the desert heard the camel's bell,
You'd wish yourself where Truth is—in a well.

It poured down torrents, but they were no richer
    Until they found a ragged piece of sheet,
Which served them as a sort of spongy pitcher,   675
    And when they deemed its moisture was com-
    plete,
They wrung it out, and though a thirsty ditcher[10]
    Might not have thought the scanty draught so
    sweet
As a full pot of porter, to their thinking
They ne'er till now had known the joys of drink-   680
    ing.

---

[8] One of the punishments devised by Zeus for the Titan Prometheus, who gave men the gift of fire by stealing it from heaven, was that a bird of prey should tear daily at his liver, which grew whole again by night.

---

[9] I.e., his chaplain and his teacher.   [10] Ditch digger.

And their baked lips, with many a bloody crack,
    Sucked in the moisture, which like nectar
       streamed;
Their throats were ovens, their swoln tongues
    were black,
    As the rich man's[11] in Hell, who vainly
       screamed
To beg the beggar, who could not rain back   685
    A drop of dew, when every drop had seemed
To taste of Heaven—If this be true, indeed,
Some Christians have a comfortable creed.

        . . .

As morning broke, the light wind died away,
    When he who had the watch sung out and 770
       swore,
If 'twas not land that rose with the Sun's ray,
    He wished that land he never might see more;
And the rest rubbed their eyes and saw a bay,
    Or thought they saw, and shaped their course
       for shore;
For shore it was, and gradually grew   775
Distinct, and high, and palpable to view.

And then of these some part burst into tears,
    And others, looking with a stupid stare,
Could not yet separate their hopes from fears,
    And seemed as if they had no further care; 780
While a few prayed—(the first time for some
    years)—
    And at the bottom of the boat three were
Asleep: they shook them by the hand and head,
And tried to awaken them, but found them dead.

        . . .

Meantime the current, with a rising gale,
    Still set them onwards to the welcome shore,
Like Charon's[12] bark of spectres, dull and pale:
    Their living freight was now reduced to four,
And three dead, whom their strength could not 805
    avail
    To heave into the deep with those before,
Though the two sharks still followed them, and
    dashed
The spray into their faces as they splashed.

Famine, despair, cold, thirst and heat, had done
    Their work on them by turns, and thinned 810
       them to

Such things a mother had not known her son
    Amidst the skeletons of that gaunt crew;
By night chilled, by day scorched, thus one by one
    They perished, until withered to these few,
But chiefly by a species of self-slaughter,   815
In washing down Pedrillo with salt water.

As they drew nigh the land, which now was seen
    Unequal in its aspect here and there,
They felt the freshness of its growing green,
    That waved in forest-tops, and smoothed the 820
       air,
And fell upon their glazed eyes like a screen
    From glistening waves, and skies so hot and
       bare—
Lovely seemed any object that should sweep
Away the vast—salt—dread—eternal Deep.

The shore looked wild, without a trace of man,   825
    And girt by formidable waves; but they
Were mad for land, and thus their course they
    ran,
    Though right ahead the roaring breakers lay:
A reef between them also now began
    To show its boiling surf and bounding spray, 830
But finding no place for their landing better,
They ran the boat for shore,—and overset her.

But in his native stream, the Guadalquivir,
    Juan to lave his youthful limbs was wont;
And having learnt to swim in that sweet river, 835
    Had often turned the art to some account:
A better swimmer you could scarce see ever,
    He could, perhaps, have pass'd the Hellespont,
As once (a feat on which ourselves we prided)
Leander, Mr. Ekenhead, and I did.[13]   840

So here, though faint, emaciated, and stark,
    He buoyed his boyish limbs, and strove to ply
With the quick wave, and gain, ere it was dark,
    The beach which lay before him, high and
       dry:
The greatest danger here was from a shark,   845
    That carried off his neighbour by the thigh;
As for the other two, they could not swim,
So nobody arrived on shore but him.

Nor yet had he arrived but for the oar,
    Which, providentially for him, was washed 850

---

[11] For the story of the rich man Dives and the beggar Lazarus, see Luke 16:19ff.
[12] In classical mythology, the ferryman who carries souls over the River Styx.

[13] Byron swam the Hellespont, or Dardanelles, on May 3, 1810. Ekenhead was the naval lieutenant who made the swim with him.

Just as his feeble arms could strike no more,
    And the hard wave o'erwhelm'd him as 'twas
        dashed
Within his grasp; he clung to it, and sore
    The waters beat while he thereto was lashed;
At last, with swimming, wading, scrambling, he   855
Rolled on the beach, half senseless, from the sea:

There, breathless, with his digging nails he clung
    Fast to the sand, lest the returning wave,
From whose reluctant roar his life he wrung,
    Should suck him back to her insatiate grave: 860
And there he lay, full length, where he was flung,
    Before the entrance of a cliff-worn cave,
With just enough of life to feel its pain,
And deem that it was saved, perhaps in vain.

        . . .

How long in his damp trance young Juan lay
    He knew not, for the earth was gone for him,
And Time had nothing of night nor day
    For his congealing blood, and senses dim;
And how this heavy faintness passed away   885
    He knew not, till each painful pulse and limb,
And tingling vein, seemed throbbing back to life,
For Death, though vanquished, still retired with
        strife.

His eyes he opened, shut, again unclosed,
    For all was doubt and dizziness; he thought   890
He still was in the boat, and had but dozed,
    And felt again with his despair o'erwrought,
And wished it death in which he had reposed,
    And then once more his feelings back were
        brought,
And slowly by his swimming eyes was seen   895
A lovely female face of seventeen.

'Twas bending close o'er his, and the small mouth
    Seemed almost prying into his for breath;
And chafing him, the soft warm hand of youth
    Recalled his answering spirits back from   900
        Death;
And, bathing his chill temples, tried to soothe
    Each pulse to animation, till beneath
Its gentle touch and trembling care, a sigh
To these kind efforts made a low reply.

Then was the cordial poured, and mantle flung   905
    Around his scarce-clad limbs; and the fair arm
Raised higher the faint head which o'er it hung;
    And her transparent cheek, all pure and warm,

Pillowed his death-like forehead; then she wrung
    His dewy curls, long drenched by every storm;   910
And watched with eagerness each throb that drew
A sigh from his heaved bosom—and hers, too.

And lifting him with care into the cave,
    The gentle girl, and her attendant,—one
Young, yet her elder, and of brow less grave,   915
    And more robust of figure,—then begun
To kindle fire, and as the new flames gave
    Light to the rocks that roofed them, which the
        sun
Had never seen, the maid, or whatsoe'er
She was, appeared distinct, and tall, and fair.   920

        . . .

And these two tended him, and cheered him both
    With food and raiment, and those soft atten-
        tions,
Which are—as I must own—of female growth,
    And have ten thousand delicate inventions: 980
They made a most superior mess of broth,
    A thing which poesy but seldom mentions,
But the best dish that e'er was cooked since
    Homer's
Achilles order'd dinner for new comers.[14]

I'll tell you who they were, this female pair,   985
    Lest they should seem Princesses[15] in disguise;
Besides, I hate all mystery, and that air
    Of clap-trap, which your recent poets prize;
And so, in short, the girls they really were
    They shall appear before your curious eyes,   990
Mistress and maid; the first was only daughter
Of an old man, who lived upon the water.

A fisherman he had been in his youth,
    And still a sort of fisherman was he;
But other speculations were, in sooth,   995
    Added to his connection with the sea,
Perhaps not so respectable, in truth:
    A little smuggling, and some piracy,
Left him, at last, the sole of many masters
Of an ill-gotten million of piastres.[16]   1000

A fisher, therefore, was he,—though of men,[17]
    Like Peter the Apostle, and he fished

---

14 *Iliad*, IX, 193 ff.
15 Accented in England on the second syllable.
16 Coin of various Eastern countries, including Turkey.
17 Cf. Matthew 4:19.

For wandering merchant-vessels, now and then,
  And sometimes caught as many as he wished;
The cargoes he confiscated,[18] and gain   1005
  He sought in the slave-market too, and dished
Full many a morsel for that Turkish trade,
By which, no doubt, a good deal may be made.

He was a Greek, and on his isle had built
  (One of the wild and smaller Cyclades[19])   1010
A very handsome house from out his guilt,
  And there he lived exceedingly at ease;
Heaven knows what cash he got, or blood he spilt,
  A sad[20] old fellow was he, if you please;
But this I know, it was a spacious building,   1015
Full of barbaric carving, paint, and gilding.

He had an only daughter, called Haidée,
  The greatest heiress of the Eastern Isles;
Besides, so very beautiful was she,
  Her dowry was as nothing to her smiles: 1020
Still in her teens, and like a lovely tree
  She grew to womanhood, and between whiles
Rejected several suitors, just to learn
How to accept a better in his turn.

And walking out upon the beach, below   1025
  The cliff, towards sunset, on that day she
    found,
Insensible,—not dead, but nearly so,—
  Don Juan, almost famished, and half drowned;
But being naked, she was shocked, you know,
  Yet deemed herself in common pity bound,   1030
As far as in her lay, "to take him in,
A stranger"[21] dying—with so white a skin.

But taking him into her father's house
  Was not exactly the best way to save,
But like conveying to the cat the mouse,   1035
  Or people in a trance into their grave;
Because the good old man had so much "νους,"[22]
  Unlike the honest Arab thieves so brave,
He would have hospitably cured the stranger,
And sold him instantly when out of danger.   1040

And therefore, with her maid, she thought it best
  (A virgin always on her maid relies)
To place him in the cave for present rest:
  And when, at last, he opened his black eyes,

Their charity increased about their guest;   1045
  And their compassion grew to such a size,
It opened half the turnpike-gates to Heaven—
  (St. Paul says,[23] 'tis the toll which must be given).

They made a fire,—but such a fire as they
  Upon the moment could contrive with such   1050
Materials as were cast up round the bay,—
  Some broken planks, and oars, that to the touch
Were nearly tinder, since so long they lay,
  A mast was almost crumbled to a crutch;
But, by God's grace, here wrecks were in such   1055
    plenty,
That there was fuel to have furnished twenty.

He had a bed of furs, and a pelisse,[24]
  For Haidée stripped her sables off to make
His couch; and, that he might be more at ease,
  And warm, in case by chance he should awake,   1060
They also gave a petticoat apiece,
  She and her maid,—and promised by daybreak
To pay him a fresh visit, with a dish
For breakfast, of eggs, coffee, bread, and fish.

And thus they left him to his lone repose: 1065
  Juan slept like a top, or like the dead,
Who sleep at last, perhaps (God only knows),
  Just for the present; and in his lullèd head
Not even a vision of his former woes
  Throbbed in accursèd dreams, which some-   1070
    times spread
Unwelcome visions of our former years,
Till the eye, cheated, opens thick with tears.

        .   .   .

And every day by daybreak—rather early
  For Juan, who was somewhat fond of rest—
She came into the cave, but it was merely
  To see her bird reposing in his nest;   1340
And she would softly stir his locks so curly,
  Without disturbing her yet slumbering guest,
Breathing all gently o'er his cheek and mouth,
As o'er a bed of roses the sweet South.[25]

        .   .   .

When Juan woke he found some good things
    ready,
  A bath, a breakfast, and the finest eyes

---

18 Here accented (permissibly) on the second syllable.
19 In the Aegean Sea.   20 Shocking.
21 Cf. Matthew 25:35–36.   22 Mind, good sense.

23 See I Corinthians 13.   24 Fur cloak.
25 South wind. Cf. Shakespeare, *Twelfth Night*, I, i, 5–6,
as emended by Pope and other editors (*south* for *sound*).

That ever made a youthful heart less steady,
　　Besides her maid's, as pretty for their size;
But I have spoken of all this already—　　　　　1365
　　And repetition's tiresome and unwise,—
Well—Juan, after bathing in the sea,
Came always back to coffee and Haidée.

Both were so young, and one so innocent,
　　That bathing passed for nothing; Juan seemed　1370
To her, as 'twere, the kind of being sent,
　　Of whom these two years she had nightly
　　　　dreamed,
A something to be loved, a creature meant
　　To be her happiness, and whom she deemed
To render happy: all who joy would win　　　　1375
Must share it,—Happiness was born a Twin.

It was such pleasure to behold him, such
　　Enlargement of existence to partake
Nature with him, to thrill beneath his touch,
　　To watch him slumbering, and to see him　1380
　　　　wake:
To live with him for ever were too much;
　　But then the thought of parting made her
　　　　quake;
He was her own, her ocean-treasure, cast
Like a rich wreck—her first love, and her last.

And thus a moon rolled on, and fair Haidée　　1385
　　Paid daily visits to her boy, and took
Such plentiful precautions, that still he
　　Remained unknown within his craggy nook;
At last her father's prows put out to sea,
　　For certain merchantmen upon the look,　　1390
Not as of yore to carry off an Io,[26]
But three Ragusan vessels bound for Scio.[27]

Then came her freedom, for she had no mother,
　　So that, her father being at sea, she was
Free as a married woman, or such other　　　　1395
　　Female, as where she likes may freely pass,
Without even the encumbrance of a brother,
　　The freest she that ever gazed on glass:
I speak of Christian lands in this comparison,
Where wives, at least, are seldom kept in gar-　1400
　　rison.

---

[26] A mortal maid, beloved by Zeus and persecuted by his wife. She wandered far, and among her adventures (as rationalized by Herodotus) was abduction by some Phoenician merchants.
[27] Another name for the Aegean island of Chios. Ragusa or Dubrovnik is a port on the eastern side of the Adriatic.

Now she prolonged her visits and her talk
　　(For they must talk), and he had learnt to say
So much as to propose to take a walk,—
　　For little had he wandered since the day
On which, like a young flower snapped from the　1405
　　stalk,
　　Drooping and dewy on the beach he lay,—
And thus they walked out in the afternoon,
And saw the sun set opposite the moon.

It was a wild and breaker-beaten coast,
　　With cliffs above, and a broad sandy shore,　　1410
Guarded by shoals and rocks as by an host,
　　With here and there a creek, whose aspect wore
A better welcome to the tempest-tost;
　　And rarely ceased the haughty billow's roar,
Save on the dead long summer days, which make　1415
The outstretched Ocean glitter like a lake.

．　．　．

The coast—I think it was the coast that I
　　Was just describing—Yes, it *was* the coast—
Lay at this period quiet as the sky,
　　The sands untumbled, the blue waves un-
　　　　tossed,
And all was stillness, save the sea-bird's cry,　　1445
　　And dolphin's leap, and little billow crossed
By some low rock or shelve, that made it fret
Against the boundary it scarcely wet.

And forth they wandered, her sire being gone,
　　As I have said, upon an expedition;　　　　1450
And mother, brother, guardian, she had none,
　　Save Zoe, who, although with due precision
She waited on her lady with the Sun,
　　Thought daily service was her only mission,
Bringing warm water, wreathing her long tresses,　1455
And asking now and then for cast-off dresses.

It was the cooling hour, just when the rounded
　　Red sun sinks down behind the azure hill,
Which then seems as if the whole earth it
　　bounded,
　　Circling all Nature, hushed, and dim, and　1460
　　　　still,
With the far mountain-crescent half surrounded
　　On one side, and the deep sea calm and chill
Upon the other, and the rosy sky
With one star sparkling through it like an eye.

And thus they wandered forth, and hand in hand,　1465
　　Over the shining pebbles and the shells,

Glided along the smooth and hardened sand,
  And in the worn and wild receptacles
Worked by the storms, yet worked as it were
    plann'd
  In hollow halls, with sparry roofs and cells,   1470
They turned to rest; and, each clasped by an arm,
Yielded to the deep Twilight's purple charm.

They looked up to the sky, whose floating glow
  Spread like a rosy Ocean, vast and bright;
They gazed upon the glittering sea below,   1475
  Whence the broad Moon rose circling into
    sight;
They heard the waves splash, and the wind so
    low,
  And saw each other's dark eyes darting light
Into each other—and, beholding this,
Their lips drew near, and clung into a kiss;   1480

A long, long kiss, a kiss of Youth, and Love,
  And Beauty, all concéntrating like rays
Into one focus, kindled from above;
  Such kisses as belong to early days,
Where Heart, and Soul, and Sense, in concert   1485
    move,
  And the blood's lava, and the pulse a blaze,
Each kiss a heart-quake,—for a kiss's strength,
I think, it must be reckoned by its length.

By length I mean duration; theirs endured
  Heaven knows how long—no doubt they never   1490
    reckoned;
And if they had, they could not have secured
  The sum of their sensations to a second:
They had not spoken, but they felt allured,
  As if their souls and lips each other beckoned,
Which, being joined, like swarming bees they   1495
    clung—
Their hearts the flowers from whence the honey
    sprung.

They were alone, but not alone as they
  Who shut in chambers think it loneliness;
The silent Ocean, and the starlight bay,
  The twilight glow, which momently grew less,   1500
The voiceless sands, and dropping caves, that lay
  Around them, made them to each other press,
As if there were no life beneath the sky
Save theirs, and that their life could never die.

They feared no eyes nor ears on that lone beach;   1505
  They felt no terrors from the night; they were

All in all to each other: though their speech
  Was broken words, they *thought* a language
    there,—
And all the burning tongues the Passions teach
  Found in one sigh the best interpreter   1510
Of Nature's oracle—first love,—that all
Which Eve has left her daughters since her fall.

Haidée spoke not of scruples, asked no vows,
  Nor offered any; she had never heard
Of plight and promises to be a spouse,   1515
  Or perils by a loving maid incurred;
She was all which pure Ignorance allows,
  And flew to her young mate like a young bird;
And, never having dreamt of falsehood, she
Had not one word to say of constancy.   1520

She loved, and was belovèd—she adored,
  And she was worshipped after Nature's
    fashion—
Their intense souls, into each other poured,
  If souls could die, had perished in that pas-
    sion,—
But by degrees their senses were restored,   1525
  Again to be o'ercome, again to dash on;
And, beating 'gainst *his* bosom, Haidée's heart
Felt as if never more to beat apart.

Alas! they were so young, so beautiful,
  So lonely, loving, helpless, and the hour   1530
Was that in which the Heart is always full,
  And, having o'er itself no further power,
Prompts deeds Eternity can not annul,
  But pays off moments in an endless shower
Of hell-fire—all prepared for people giving   1535
Pleasure or pain to one another living.

Alas! for Juan and Haidée! they were
  So loving and so lovely—till then never,
Excepting our first parents, such a pair
  Had run the risk of being damned for ever;   1540
And Haidée, being devout as well as fair,
  Had, doubtless, heard about the Stygian river,
And Hell and Purgatory—but forgot
Just in the very crisis she should not.

They look upon each other, and their eyes   1545
  Gleam in the moonlight; and her white arm
    clasps
Round Juan's head, and his around her lies
  Half buried in the tresses which it grasps;

She sits upon his knee, and drinks his sighs,
   He hers, until they end in broken gasps;   1550
And thus they form a group that's quite antique,
Half naked, loving, natural, and Greek.

And when those deep and burning moments
    passed,
   And Juan sunk to sleep within her arms,
She slept not, but all tenderly, though fast,   1555
   Sustained his head upon her bosom's charms;
And now and then her eye to Heaven is cast,
   And then on the pale cheek her breast now
    warms,
Pillowed on her o'erflowing heart, which pants
With all it granted, and with all it grants.   1560

An infant when it gazes on a light,
   A child the moment when it drains the breast,
A devotee when soars the Host[28] in sight,
   An Arab with a stranger for a guest,
A sailor when the prize has struck[29] in fight,   1565
   A miser filling his most hoarded chest,
Feel rapture; but not such true joy are reaping
As they who watch o'er what they love while
   sleeping.

For there it lies so tranquil, so beloved,
   All that it hath of Life with us is living;   1570
So gentle, stirless, helpless, and unmoved,
   And all unconscious of the joy 'tis giving;
All it hath felt, inflicted, passed, and proved,
   Hushed into depths beyond the watcher's div-
    ing;
There lies the thing we love with all its errors   1575
And all its charms, like Death without its terrors.

The lady watched her lover—and that hour
   Of Love's, and Night's, and Ocean's solitude,
O'erflowed her soul with their united power;
   Amidst the barren sand and rocks so rude   1580
She and her wave-worn love had made their
    bower,
   Where nought upon their passion could in-
    trude,
And all the stars that crowded the blue space
Saw nothing happier than her glowing face.

Alas! the love of Women! it is known   1585
   To be a lovely and a fearful thing;

For all of theirs upon that die is thrown,
   And if 'tis lost, Life hath no more to bring
To them but mockeries of the past alone,
   And their revenge is as the tiger's spring,   1590
Deadly, and quick, and crushing; yet, as real
Torture is theirs—what they inflict they feel.

They are right; for Man, to man so oft unjust,
   Is always so to Women: one sole bond
Awaits them—treachery is all their trust;   1595
   Taught to conceal their bursting hearts de-
    spond
Over their idol, till some wealthier lust
   Buys them in marriage—and what rests be-
    yond?
A thankless husband—next a faithless lover—
Then dressing, nursing, praying—and all's over.   1600

Some take a lover, some take drams or prayers,
   Some mind their household, others dissipation,
Some run away, and but exchange their cares,
   Losing the advantage of a virtuous station;
Few changes e'er can better their affairs,   1605
   Theirs being an unnatural situation,
From the dull palace to the dirty hovel:
Some play the devil, and then write a novel.[30]

Haidée was Nature's bride, and knew not this;
   Haidée was Passion's child, born where the   1610
    Sun
Showers triple light, and scorches even the kiss
   Of his gazelle-eyed daughters; she was one
Made but to love, to feel that she was his
   Who was her chosen: what was said or done
Elsewhere was nothing. She had nought to fear,   1615
Hope, care, nor love beyond,—her heart beat
   here.

     . . . .

from CANTO THE THIRD

Hail, Muse! *et cetera.*—We left Juan sleeping,
   Pillowed upon a fair and happy breast,
And watched by eyes that never yet knew weeping,
   And loved by a young heart, too deeply blest
To feel the poison through her spirit creeping,   5
   Or know who rested there, a foe to rest,

---

28 The Eucharistic wafer or bread.
29 The captured ship has hauled down its flag.

30 The eccentric Lady Caroline Lamb, having been (chiefly on her own insistence) one of his mistresses during the Byron craze in London, wrote *Glenarvon* (1816) after their affair was over; she incorporated in it his farewell letter rejecting her.

Had soiled the current of her sinless years,
And turned her pure heart's purest blood to tears!

Oh, Love! what is it in this world of ours
    Which makes it fatal to be loved? Ah, why   10
With cypress branches[1] hast thou wreathed thy
    bowers,
    And made thy best interpreter a sigh?
As those who dote on odours pluck the flowers,
    And place them on their breast—but place
    to die—
Thus the frail beings we would fondly cherish   15
Are laid within our bosoms but to perish.

In her first passion Woman loves her lover,
    In all the others all she loves is Love,
Which grows a habit she can ne'er get over,
    And fits her loosely—like an easy glove,   20
As you may find, whene'er you like to prove[2] her:
    One man alone at first her heart can move;
She then prefers him in the plural number,
Not finding that the additions much encumber.

. . .

Haidée and Juan were not married, but
    The fault was theirs, not mine: it is not fair,   90
Chaste reader, then, in any way to put
    The blame on me, unless you wish they were;
Then if you'd have them wedded, please to shut
    The book which treats of this erroneous pair,
Before the consequences grow too awful;   95
'Tis dangerous to read of loves unlawful.

Yet they were happy,—happy in the illicit
    Indulgence of their innocent desires;
But more imprudent grown with every visit,
    Haidée forgot the island was her Sire's;   100
When we have what we like 'tis hard to miss it,
    At least in the beginning, ere one tires;
Thus she came often, not a moment losing,
Whilst her piratical papa was cruising.

Let not his mode of raising cash seem strange,   105
    Although he fleeced the flags of every nation,
For into a Prime Minister but change
    His title, and 'tis nothing but taxation;
But he, more modest, took an humbler range
    Of Life, and in an honester vocation   110
Pursued o'er the high seas his watery journey,
And merely practised as a sea-attorney.

The good old gentleman had been detained
    By winds and waves, and some important cap-
    tures;
And, in the hope of more, at sea remained,   115
    Although a squall or two had damped his
    raptures,
By swamping one of the prizes; he had chained
    His prisoners, dividing them like chapters
In numbered lots; they all had cuffs and collars,
And averaged each from ten to a hundred dollars.   120

. . .

Then, having settled his marine affairs,   145
    Despatching single cruisers here and there,
His vessel having need of some repairs,
    He shaped his course to where his daughter
    fair
Continued still her hospitable cares;
    But that part of the coast being shoal and bare,   150
And rough with reefs which ran out many a mile,
His port lay on the other side o' the isle.

. . .

Lambro, our sea-solicitor,[3] who had
    Much less experience of dry land than Ocean,
On seeing his own chimney-smoke, felt glad;
    But not knowing metaphysics, had no notion
Of the true reason of his not being sad,   205
    Or that of any other strong emotion;
He loved his child, and would have wept the loss
    of her,
But knew the cause no more than a philosopher.

He saw his white walls shining in the sun,
    His garden trees all shadowy and green;   210
He heard his rivulet's light bubbling run,
    The distant dog-bark; and perceived between
The umbrage of the wood, so cool and dun,
    The moving figures, and the sparkling sheen
Of arms (in the East all arm)—and various dyes   215
Of coloured garbs, as bright as butterflies.

And as the spot where they appear he nears,
    Surprised at these unwonted signs of idling,
He hears—alas! no music of the spheres,
    But an unhallowed, earthly sound of fiddling!   220
A melody which made him doubt his ears,
    The cause being past his guessing or unrid-
    dling;
A pipe, too, and a drum, and shortly after—
A most unoriental roar of laughter.

---

[1] Emblem of sadness.   [2] Test.

[3] Sea lawyer; here = pirate (cf. line 112).

And still more nearly to the place advancing,   225
   Descending rather quickly the declivity,
Through the waved branches o'er the greensward
    glancing,
   'Midst other indications of festivity,
Seeing a troop of his domestics dancing
   Like Dervises,[4] who turn as on a pivot, he   230
Perceived it was the Pyrrhic dance[5] so martial,
To which the Levantines[6] are very partial.

And further on a troop of Grecian girls,
   The first and tallest her white kerchief waving,
Were strung together like a row of pearls,   235
   Linked hand in hand, and dancing; each too
    having
Down her white neck long floating auburn
    curls—
   (The least of which would set ten poets rav-
    ing);
Their leader sang—and bounded to her song
With choral step and voice the virgin throng.   240

And here, assembled cross-legged round their
    trays,
   Small social parties just begun to dine;
Pilaus[7] and meats of all sorts met the gaze,
   And flasks of Samian and Chian wine,[8]
And sherbet cooling in the porous vase;   245
   Above them their dessert grew on its vine;—
The orange and pomegranate nodding o'er,
Dropped in their laps, scarce plucked, their mel-
    low store.

      . . .

Perhaps you think, in stumbling on this feast,
   He flew into a passion, and in fact
There was no mighty reason to be pleased;   315
   Perhaps you prophesy some sudden act,
The whip, the rack, or dungeon at the least,
   To teach his people to be more exact,
And that, proceeding at a very high rate,
He showed the royal *penchants* of a pirate.   320

You're wrong.—He was the mildest mannered
    man

---

[4] Dervishes, members of certain Mohammedan orders, famous for frenzied dances.
[5] An ancient Greek martial dance.
[6] Dwellers in the Levant or eastern Mediterranean countries.
[7] Oriental dishes of rice with meat, chicken, or fish, and spices.   [8] From the Aegean islands of Samos and Chios.

That ever scuttled ship or cut a throat;
   With such true breeding of a gentleman,
    You never could divine his real thought;
No courtier could, and scarcely woman can   325
   Gird more deceit within a petticoat;
Pity he loved adventurous life's variety,
He was so great a loss to good society.

      . . .

Old Lambro passed unseen a private gate,
   And stood within his hall at eventide;
Meantime the lady and her lover sate
   At wassail in their beauty and their pride:
An ivory inlaid table spread with state   485
   Before them, and fair slaves on every side;
Gems, gold, and silver, formed the service mostly,
Mother of pearl and coral the less costly.

The dinner made about a hundred dishes;
   Lamb and pistachio nuts—in short, all meats,   490
And saffron soups, and sweetbreads; and the
    fishes
   Were of the finest that e'er flounced in nets,
Drest to a Sybarite's[9] most pampered wishes;
   The beverage was various sherbets
Of raisin, orange, and pomegranate juice,   495
Squeezed through the rind, which makes it best
    for use.

These were ranged round, each in its crystal ewer,
   And fruits, and date-bread loaves closed the
    repast,
And Mocha's berry, from Arabia pure,
   In small fine China cups, came in at last;   500
Gold cups of filigree, made to secure
   The hand from burning, underneath them
    placed;
Cloves, cinnamon, and saffron too were boiled
Up with the coffee, which (I think) they spoiled.

The hangings of the room were tapestry, made   505
   Of velvet panels, each of different hue,
And thick with damask flowers of silk inlaid;
   And round them ran a yellow border too;
The upper border, richly wrought, displayed,
   Embroidered delicately o'er with blue,   510
Soft Persian sentences, in lilac letters,
From poets, or the moralists their betters.

      . . .

---

[9] The people of the ancient Greek city of Sybaris in southern Italy were notorious for their luxury.

Haidée and Juan carpeted their feet
   On crimson satin, bordered with pale blue;   530
Their sofa occupied three parts complete
   Of the apartment—and appeared quite new;
The velvet cushions (for a throne more meet)
   Were scarlet, from whose glowing center grew
A sun embossed in gold, whose rays of tissue,   535
Meridian-like, were seen all light to issue.

Crystal and marble, plate and porcelain,
   Had done their work of splendour; Indian mats
And Persian carpets, which the heart bled to stain,
   Over the floors were spread; gazelles and cats,   540
And dwarfs and blacks, and such like things, that gain
   Their bread as ministers and favourites (that's
To say, by degradation) mingled there
As plentiful as in a court, or fair.

There was no want of lofty mirrors, and   545
   The tables, most of ebony inlaid
With mother of pearl or ivory, stood at hand,
   Or were of tortoise-shell or rare woods made,
Fretted with gold or silver:—by command
   The greater part of these were ready spread   550
With viands and sherbets in ice—and wine—
Kept for all comers at all hours to dine.

Of all the dresses I select Haidée's:
   She wore two jelicks[10]—one was of pale yellow;
Of azure, pink, and white was her chemise—   555
   'Neath which her breast heaved like a little billow:
With buttons formed of pearls as large as peas,
   All gold and crimson shone her jelick's fellow,
And the striped white gauze baracan[11] that bound her,
Like fleecy clouds about the moon, flowed round her.   560

One large gold bracelet clasped each lovely arm,
   Lockless—so pliable from the pure gold
That the hand stretched and shut it without harm,
   The limb which it adorned its only mold;
So beautiful—its very shape would charm,   565
   And clinging, as if loath to lose its hold,

The purest ore enclosed the whitest skin
That e'er by precious metal was held in.[12]

Around, as Princess of her father's land,
   A like gold bar above her instep rolled   570
Announced her rank;[13] twelve rings were on her hand;
   Her hair was starred with gems; her veil's fine fold
Below her breast was fastened with a band
   Of lavish pearls, whose worth could scarce be told;
Her orange silk full Turkish trousers furled   575
About the prettiest ankle in the world.

Her hair's long auburn waves down to her heel
   Flowed like an Alpine torrent which the sun
Dyes with his morning light,—and would conceal
   Her person if allowed at large to run,   580
And still they seemed resentfully to feel
   The silken fillet's curb, and sought to shun
Their bonds whene'er some Zephyr caught began
To offer his young pinion as her fan.

Round her she made an atmosphere of life,   585
   The very air seemed lighter from her eyes,
They were so soft and beautiful, and rife
   With all we can imagine of the skies,
And pure as Psyche ere she grew a wife—
   Too pure even for the purest human ties;   590
Her overpowering presence made you feel
It would not be idolatry to kneel.

Her eyelashes, though dark as night, were tinged
   (It is the country's custom, but in vain),
For those large black eyes were so blackly fringed,   595
   The glossy rebels mocked the jetty stain,
And in their native beauty stood avenged:
   Her nails were touched with henna; but, again
The power of Art was turned to nothing, for
They could not look more rosy than before.   600

The henna should be deeply dyed to make
   The skin relieved appear more fairly fair;
She had no need of this, day ne'er will break
   On mountain tops more heavenly white than her:

---

10 Vests or bodices.
11 Barracan, a loose outer garment.

12 Byron's note: "This dress is Moorish. . . . As the mother of Haidée was of Fez, her daughter wore the garb of the country."
13 Byron's note: "A mark of sovereign rank in the women of the families of the Deys."

The eye might doubt if it were well awake, 605
    She was so like a vision; I might err,
But Shakespeare also says, 'tis very silly
    "To gild refinèd gold, or paint the lily."[14]

Juan had on a shawl of black and gold,
    But a white baracan, and so transparent 610
The sparkling gems beneath you might behold,
    Like small stars through the milky way ap-
        parent;
His turban, furled in many a graceful fold,
    An emerald aigrette,[15] with Haidée's hair in 't,
Surmounted as its clasp—a glowing crescent, 615
Whose rays shone ever trembling, but incessant.

And now they were diverted by their suite,
    Dwarfs, dancing girls, black eunuchs, and a
        poet,
Which made their new establishment complete;
    The last was of great fame, and liked to show it; 620
His verses rarely wanted their due feet—
    And for his theme—he seldom sung below it,
He being paid to satirise or flatter,
As the Psalm says, "inditing a good matter."[16]

       . . .

He had travelled 'mongst the Arabs, Turks, and 665
    Franks,
    And knew the self-loves of the different na-
        tions;
And having lived with people of all ranks,
    Had something ready upon most occasions—
Which got him a few presents and some thanks.
    He varied with some skill his adulations; 670
To "do at Rome as Romans do," a piece
Of conduct was which *he* observed in Greece.

Thus, usually, when *he* was asked to sing,
    He gave the different nations something na-
        tional;
'Twas all the same to him—"God save the King," 675
    Or "Ça ira,"[17] according to the fashion all:
His Muse made increment of anything,
    From the high lyric down to the low ra-
        tional:[18]

If Pindar sang horse-races,[19] what should hinder
Himself from being as pliable as Pindar? 680

In France, for instance, he would write a chanson;
    In England a six canto quarto tale,
In Spain he'd make a ballad or romance on
    The last war—much the same in Portugal;
In Germany, the Pegasus he'd prance on 685
    Would be old Goethe's—(see what says De
        Staël);[20]
In Italy he'd ape the "Trecentisti";[21]
In Greece, he'd sing some sort of hymn like this
    t' ye:

        1

The Isles of Greece, the Isles of Greece!
    Where burning Sappho[22] loved and sung, 690
Where grew the arts of War and Peace,
    Where Delos rose, and Phoebus sprung![23]
Eternal summer gilds them yet,
But all, except their Sun, is set.

        2

The Scian and the Teian Muse,[24] 695
    The Hero's harp, the Lover's lute,
Have found the fame your shores refuse:
    Their place of birth alone is mute
To sounds which echo further west
Than your Sires' "Islands of the Blest."[25] 700

        3

The mountains look on Marathon[26]—
    And Marathon looks on the sea;

---

14 Cf. Shakespeare, *King John*, IV, ii, 11.
15 Plume.   16 Psalms 45:1.
17 A popular song of the French Revolution: "It will go on."
18 Doubtless Byron is jeering at Southey, praised by Coleridge in *Biographia Literaria*, chap. III, for having achieved success in nearly every form of verse.

19 I.e., in odes celebrating the Olympic victors. The games included chariot races.
20 Mme. de Staël in *De l'Allemagne* (1810) praises Goethe extravagantly.
21 Writers (or artists) of the fourteenth century; among them were Dante, Petrarch, and Boccaccio.
22 The great woman poet who flourished about 600 B.C. on the Aegean island of Lesbos.
23 Phoebus Apollo, god of poetry, music, etc., was born on the island of Delos, which rose from below the Aegean for the express convenience of his mother.
24 Homer, greatest of epic poets (hence, "the Hero's harp"), was according to one account a native of the island of Scio (Chios). Anacreon, who wrote love lyrics, was born (572? B.C.) at the coastal city of Teos in Asia Minor.
25 Which some of the ancients supposed to be in the Atlantic.
26 Where in 490 B.C., on the coastal plain north of Athens, a small army of Greeks defeated an invading horde of Persians.

And musing there an hour alone,
    I dreamed that Greece might still be free;
For standing on the Persians' grave,   705
I could not deem myself a slave.

4

A King sate on the rocky brow
    Which looks o'er sea-born Salamis;[27]
And ships, by thousands, lay below,
    And men in nations;—all were his!   710
He counted them at break of day—
And, when the Sun set, where were they?

5

And where are they? and where art thou,
    My Country? On thy voiceless shore
The heroic lay is tuneless now—   715
    The heroic bosom beats no more!
And must thy Lyre, so long divine,
Degenerate into hands like mine?

6

'Tis something, in the dearth of Fame,
    Though linked among a fettered race,   720
To feel at least a patriot's shame,
    Even as I sing, suffuse my face;
For what is left the poet here?
For Greeks a blush—for Greece a tear.

7

Must *we* but weep o'er days more blest?   725
    Must *we* but blush?—Our fathers bled.
Earth! render back from out thy breast
    A remnant of our Spartan dead!
Of the three hundred grant but three,
To make a new Thermopylae![28]   730

8

What, silent still? and silent all?
    Ah! no;—the voices of the dead

Sound like a distant torrent's fall,
    And answer, "Let one living head,
But one arise,—we come, we come!"   735
'Tis but the living who are dumb.

9

In vain—in vain: strike other chords;
    Fill high the cup with Samian wine!
Leave battles to the Turkish hordes,
    And shed the blood of Scio's vine!   740
Hark! rising to the ignoble call—
How answers each bold Bacchanal!

10

You have the Pyrrhic dance as yet,
    Where is the Pyrrhic phalanx[29] gone?
Of two such lessons, why forget   745
    The nobler and the manlier one?
You have the letters Cadmus[30] gave—
Think ye he meant them for a slave?

11

Fill high the bowl with Samian wine!
    We will not think of themes like these!   750
It made Anacreon's song divine:
    He served—but served Polycrates[31]—
A Tyrant; but our masters then
Were still, at least, our countrymen.

12

The Tyrant of the Chersonese[32]   755
    Was Freedom's best and bravest friend;
That tyrant was Miltiades![33]
    Oh! that the present hour would lend
Another despot of the kind!
Such chains as his were sure to bind.   760

---

27 An island in the Gulf of Aegina, where in 480 B.C., while the Persian King Xerxes looked on from shore, the Athenian fleet won a decisive victory.

28 This pass in central Greece was held for three days in 480 B.C. by Leonidas I of Sparta, with only three hundred men, against the huge army of Xerxes. Though the Spartans learned that the Persians had found another route and would soon be in their rear, they all remained at their posts and died fighting.

29 A formation of heavily armed infantry in close order, used effectively against the Romans by King Pyrrhus (d. 272 B.C.) of Epirus in northwestern Greece.

30 Legendary founder of Thebes, in central Greece, and reputed introducer of the alphabet from Phoenicia.

31 A tyrant of Samos in the sixth century B.C. Anacreon was one of his courtiers.

32 The ancient name of Gallipoli Peninsula, on the north side of the Dardanelles.

33 Who commanded the Athenian army at Marathon. He had formerly ruled the Chersonesus, whence he withdrew on account of Persian hostility.

13

Fill high the bowl with Samian wine!
　　On Suli's rock,[34] and Parga's shore,[35]
Exists the remnant of a line
　　Such as the Doric[36] mothers bore;
And there, perhaps, some seed is sown,　　765
The Heracleidan[37] blood might own.

14

Trust not for freedom to the Franks[38]—
　　They have a king who buys and sells;
In native swords, and native ranks,
　　The only hope of courage dwells;　　770
But Turkish force, and Latin fraud,
Would break your shield, however broad.

15

Fill high the bowl with Samian wine!
　　Our virgins dance beneath the shade—
I see their glorious black eyes shine;　　775
　　But gazing on each glowing maid,
My own the burning tear-drop laves,
To think such breasts must suckle slaves.

16

Place me on Sunium's marbled steep,[39]
　　Where nothing, save the waves and I,　　780
May hear our mutual murmurs sweep;
　　There, swan-like, let me sing and die:
A land of slaves shall ne'er be mine—
Dash down yon cup of Samian wine!

Thus sung, or would, or could, or should have　　785
　　sung,
　　The modern Greek, in tolerable verse;
If not like Orpheus[40] quite, when Greece was
　　young,

Yet in these times he might have done much
　　worse:
His strain displayed some feeling—right or
　　wrong;
　　And feeling, in a poet, is the source　　790
Of others' feeling; but they are such liars,
And take all colours—like the hands of dyers.

But words are things, and a small drop of ink,
　　Falling like dew, upon a thought, produces
That which makes thousands, perhaps millions, 795
　　think;
　　'Tis strange, the shortest letter which man uses
Instead of speech, may form a lasting link
　　Of ages; to what straits old Time reduces
Frail man, when paper—even a rag like this,
Survives himself, his tomb, and all that's his!　　800

And when his bones are dust, his grave a blank,
　　His station, generation, even his nation,
Become a thing, or nothing, save to rank
　　In chronological commemoration,
Some dull MS.[41] oblivion long has sank,　　805
　　Or graven stone found in a barrack's station
In digging the foundation of a closet,[42]
May turn his name up, as a rare deposit.

And Glory long has made the sages smile;
　　'Tis something, nothing, words, illusion, 810
　　wind—
Depending more upon the historian's style
　　Than on the name a person leaves behind:
Troy owes to Homer what whist owes to Hoyle:[43]
　　The present century was growing blind
To the great Marlborough's skill in giving knocks, 815
Until his late Life by Archdeacon Coxe.[44]

Milton's the Prince of poets—so we say;
　　A little heavy, but no less divine:
An independent being in his day—
　　Learned, pious, temperate in love and wine;　　820
But, his life falling into Johnson's way,[45]
　　We're told this great High Priest of all the
　　Nine[46]

---

34 A mountainous region in Epirus (southern Albania). The Suliotes fought heroically against the Turks for Greek independence.　　35 A town near Suli.
36 I.e., Spartan. The Dorians were one of the races that settled in Greece.
37 The Heraclidae, or descendants of Hercules, were the legendary conquerors of the Peloponnesus, the southern part of Greece.
38 I.e. (according to usage in the Levant), Europeans (but not including inhabitants of the Balkan countries).
39 Now Cape Colonni, the southern tip of Attica, southeast of Athens. On it stood a temple to Athena.
40 The Thracian poet and musician of Greek mythology.

41 Pronounce, here, em ess.
42 Water-closet.
43 Edmond Hoyle (1672–1769), the writer on card games, especially whist.
44 William Coxe, an English historian and clergyman; his book on the first Duke of Marlborough (1650–1722), greatest of English soldiers, had appeared in 1818–19.
45 It appears in Dr. Johnson's Lives of the Poets.
46 Nine Muses.

Was whipped at college—a harsh sire—odd
　　spouse,
For the first Mrs. Milton left his house.

All these are, *certes,* entertaining facts,　　　825
　　Like Shakespeare's stealing deer, Lord Bacon's
　　　bribes;[47]
Like Titus' youth, and Ceasar's earliest acts;[48]
　　Like Burns (whom Doctor Currie[49] well de-
　　　scribes);
Like Cromwell's pranks;[50]—but although Truth
　　exacts
　　These amiable descriptions from the scribes,　　830
As most essential to their Hero's story,
They do not much contribute to his glory.

All are not moralists, like Southey, when
　　He prated to the world of "Pantisocracy";
Or Wordsworth unexcised,[51] unhired, who then　　835
　　Seasoned his pedlar[52] poems with democracy;
Or Coleridge, long before his flighty pen
　　Let[53] to the *Morning Post* its aristocracy;[54]
When he and Southey, following the same path,
Espoused two partners (milliners of Bath).[55]　　840

Such names at present cut a convict figure,
　　The very Botany Bay[56] in moral geography;

Their loyal treason, renegado rigour,
　　Are good manure for their more bare biog-
　　　raphy;
Wordsworth's last quarto, by the way, is bigger　845
　　Than any since the birthday of typography;
A drowsy, frowzy poem, called the "Excursion,"[57]
Writ in a manner which is my aversion.

He there builds up a formidable dyke
　　Between his own and others' intellect;　　　850
But Wordsworth's poem, and his followers, like
　　Joanna Southcote's[58] Shiloh and her sect,
Are things which in this century don't strike
　　The public mind,—so few are the elect;
And the new births of both their stale Virginities　855
Have proved but Dropsies, taken for Divinities.

But let me to my story: I must own,
　　If I have any fault, it is digression,
Leaving my people to proceed alone,
　　While I soliloquize beyond expression:　　　860
But these are my addresses from the throne,[59]
　　Which put off business to the ensuing session:
Forgetting each omission is a loss to
The world, not quite so great as Ariosto.[60]

I know that what our neighbours call *"lon-*　865
　　gueurs,"[61]
　　(We've not so good a *word,* but have the *thing,*
In that complete perfection which insures
　　An epic from Bob Southey every spring—)
Form not the true temptation which allures
　　The reader; but 'twould not be hard to bring　870
Some fine examples of the *Epopée,*[62]
To prove its grand ingredient is *Ennui.*

We learn from Horace, "Homer sometimes
　　sleeps";[63]
　　We feel without him,—Wordsworth sometimes
　　wakes,—

---

47 The tradition about Shakespeare has very slight foundations. The accusation that Bacon accepted bribes brought about his fall from political power.
48 Both Julius Ceasar (100–44 B.C.) and the emperor Titus (40?–81 A.D.) are accused of youthful wickedness by the second-century historian Suetonius.
49 The general misunderstanding of Burns's character sprang from the misrepresentations of James Currie, a Scotch physician practicing in Liverpool, who in 1800 brought out a four-volume edition of Burns's poetry with a life of the poet.
50 After the Restoration, attempts were made to blacken Cromwell's character. He was charged, among other offenses, with having been a notorious robber of orchards in his childhood and a roisterer while a student at Cambridge.
51 I.e., before he got his appointment as revenue-stamp distributor (p. 52).
52 Doubtless a reference to Wordsworth's "Peter Bell." Moreover, the central figure of *The Excursion* is "the Wanderer," a philosophical peddler.　　53 Hired out.
54 Byron means this ironically, of course. Coleridge had been a radical, and then recanted. The *Morning Post* was a conservative newspaper to which Coleridge contributed and which also published a number of Wordsworth's poems.
55 This sneer is both snobbish and inaccurate. The older of the Fricker sisters—they were daughters of a bankrupt businessman—became seamstresses. Their home was in Bristol.　　56 The penal colony in Australia.

57 Published in 1814.
58 Joanna Southcott (1750–1814), a notorious religious fanatic, had a following of perhaps 100,000. She announced that she would give birth to Shiloh, a second Messiah, and even named the day. She died two months after the failure of her prophecy.
59 The British king opens every new session of Parliament with a speech "from the throne."
60 The Italian poet and dramatist (1474–1533). Though he left a comedy unfinished, the reference is doubtless to his eminence as an epic poet.
61 Literally, *lengths;* i.e. (here), tedious matters.
62 Epic.　　63 *Ars Poetica,* line 359.

To show with what complacency he creeps,
    With his dear *"Waggoners,"*[64] around his lakes.
He wishes for "a boat" to sail the deeps—
    Of Ocean?—No, of air; and then he makes
Another outcry for "a little boat."[65]   880
And drivels seas to set it well afloat.

If he must fain sweep o'er the ethereal plain,
    And Pegasus runs restive in his "Waggon,"
Could he not beg the loan of Charles's Wain?[66]
    Or pray Medea[67] for a single dragon?
Or if, too classic for his vulgar brain,   885
    He feared his neck to venture such a nag on,
And he must needs mount nearer to the moon,
Could not the blockhead ask for a balloon?

"Pedlars," and "Boats," and "Waggons"! Oh! ye
    shades
    Of Pope and Dryden, are we come to this?   890
That trash of such sort not alone evades
    Contempt, but from the bathos' vast abyss
Floats scumlike uppermost, and these Jack
    Cades[68]
    Of sense and song above your graves may hiss—
The "little boatman" and his *Peter Bell*   895
Can sneer at him who drew "Achitophel"![69]

T' our tale.—The feast was over, the slaves gone,
    The dwarfs and dancing girls had all retired;
The Arab lore and Poet's song were done,
    And every sound of revelry expired;   900
The lady and her lover, left alone,
    The rosy flood of Twilight's sky admired;—
Ave Maria! o'er the earth and sea,
That heavenliest hour of Heaven is worthiest
    thee![70]

Ave Maria! blessèd be the hour!   905
    The time, the clime, the spot, where I so oft
Have felt that moment in its fullest power
    Sink o'er the earth—so beautiful and soft—

While swung the deep bell in the distant tower,
    Or the faint dying day-hymn stole aloft,   910
And not a breath crept through the rosy air,
And yet the forest leaves seemed stirred with
    prayer.

Ave Maria! 'tis the hour of prayer!
    Ave Maria! 'tis the hour of Love!
Ave Maria! may our spirits dare   915
    Look up to thine and to thy Son's above!
Ave Maria! oh that face so fair!
    Those downcast eyes beneath the Almighty
    Dove—
What though 'tis but a pictured image?—strike—
That painting is no idol,—'tis too like.   920

Some kinder casuists are pleased to say,
    In nameless print—that I have no devotion;
But set those persons down with me to pray,
    And you shall see who has the properest notion
Of getting into Heaven the shortest way;   925
    My altars are the mountains and the Ocean,
Earth—air—stars,—all that springs from the
    great Whole,
Who hath produced, and will receive the Soul.

Sweet Hour of Twilight!—in the solitude
    Of the pine forest, and the silent shore   930
Which bounds Ravenna's immemorial wood,
    Rooted where once the Adrian[71] wave flowed
    o'er,
To where the last Caesarean fortress stood,
    Evergreen forest! which Boccaccio's lore
And Dryden's lay[72] made haunted ground to me,   935
How have I loved the twilight hour and thee!

The shrill cicalas,[73] people of the pine,
    Making their summer lives one ceaseless song,
Were the sole echoes, save my steed's and mine,
    And vesper bell's that rose the boughs along;   940
The spectre huntsman of Onesti's line,[74]

---

64 "The Waggoner" (1819).   65 See "Peter Bell" (1798).
66 Charles's Wagon or Wain, the constellation better known to us as the Big Dipper.
67 The sorceress wife of Jason, in classical myth, had a chariot drawn by dragons.
68 John Cade (d. 1450) led a popular uprising and held London for several days before being killed.
69 In a supplementary preface to the 1815 edition of his own poems, Wordsworth includes, besides an implied compliment, two or three strictures on Dryden.
70 The Blessed Virgin. *Ave Maria* = Hail, Mary!

71 Adriatic. Ravenna, on its Italian coast, was once a seaport; under the Byzantine Empire it became the capital of Italy, and "a lovely grove of pines covered the ground where the Roman fleet once rode at anchor" (Gibbon, *Decline and Fall*).
72 In the *Decameron* (V, 8) Boccaccio tells a romantic tale of the extraordinary manner in which a young man of Ravenna persuaded a disdainful young woman to marry him. Dryden retells the story in his *Fables* under the title "Theodore and Honoria."
73 Cicadas, often called locusts.
74 The huntsman of Boccaccio's tale (note 72) was a ghost,

His hell-dogs, and their chase, and the fair
    throng
Which learned from this example not to fly
From a true lover,—shadowed my mind's eye.

Oh, Hesperus![75] thou bringest all good things—   945
    Home to the weary, to the hungry cheer,
To the young bird the parent's brooding wings,
    The welcome stall to the o'erlaboured steer;
Whate'er of peace about our hearthstone clings,
    Whate'er our household gods protect of dear,   950
Are gathered round us by thy look of rest;
Thou bring'st the child, too, to the mother's
    breast.

Soft hour! which wakes the wish and melts the
    heart
Of those who sail the seas, on the first day
When they from their sweet friends are torn   955
    apart;
Or fills with love the pilgrim on his way
As the far bell of Vesper makes him start,
    Seeming to weep the dying day's decay;[76]
Is this a fancy which our reason scorns?
Ah! surely Nothing dies but Something mourns!   960

· · ·

from CANTO THE FOURTH

Nothing so difficult as a beginning
    In poesy, unless perhaps the end;
For oftentimes when Pegasus seems winning
    The race, he sprains a wing, and down we
    tend,
Like Lucifer when hurled from Heaven for sin-   5
    ing;
    Our sin the same, and hard as his to mend,
Being Pride, which leads the mind to soar too far,
Till our own weakness shows us what we are.

But Time, which brings all beings to their level,
    And sharp Adversity, will teach at last   10
Man,—and, as we would hope,—perhaps the
    Devil,

That neither of their intellects are vast:
While Youth's hot wishes in our red veins revel,
    We know not this—the blood flows on too fast;
But as the torrent widens towards the Ocean,   15
We ponder deeply on each past emotion.

As boy, I thought myself a clever fellow,
    And wished that others held the same opinion;
They took it up when my days grew more
    mellow,
    And other minds acknowledged my dominion: 20
Now my sere Fancy "falls into the yellow
    Leaf,"[1] and Imagination droops her pinion,
And the sad truth which hovers o'er my desk
Turns what was once romantic to burlesque.

And if I laugh at any mortal thing,   25
    'Tis that I may not weep; and if I weep,
'Tis that our nature cannot always bring
    Itself to apathy, for we must steep
Our hearts first in the depths of Lethe's[2] spring,
    Ere what we least wish to behold will sleep: 30
Thetis baptized her mortal son in Styx;[3]
A mortal mother would on Lethe fix.

· · ·

Young Juan and his lady-love were left
    To their own hearts' most sweet society;
Even Time the pitiless in sorrow cleft
    With his rude scythe such gentle bosoms; he   60
Sighed to behold them of their hours bereft,
    Though foe to Love; and yet they could not be
Meant to grow old, but die in happy Spring,
Before one charm or hope had taken wing.

Their faces were not made for wrinkles, their   65
    Pure blood to stagnate, their great hearts to
    fail;
The blank grey was not made to blast their hair,
    But like the climes that know nor snow nor
    hail,
They were all summer; lightning might assail
    And shiver them to ashes, but to trail   70
A long and snake-like life of dull decay
Was not for them—they had too little clay.

They were alone once more; for them to be
    Thus was another Eden; they were never

---

pursuing and killing (repeatedly) his cold mistress. The
sight proved an object lesson to the mistress of the suitor,
who was a member of the Onesti family.
[75] The evening star. The first and last lines of this stanza
are adapted from the surviving fragment of an exquisite
lyric by Sappho.
[76] A note by Byron credits the origin of the stanza, thus
far, to Dante, _Purgatory_, VIII, 1–6.

[1] Cf. _Macbeth_, V, iii, 23.
[2] The river of oblivion in Hades.
[3] Another river of Hades. In it the nymph Thetis dipped
her infant son Achilles to make him invulnerable.

Weary, unless when separate: the tree   75
   Cut from its forest root of years—the river
Dammed from its fountain—the child from the
   knee
   And breast maternal weaned at once for
   ever,—
Would wither less than these two torn apart;
Alas! there is no instinct like the Heart—   80

The heart—which may be broken: happy they!
   Thrice fortunate! who of that fragile mould,
The precious porcelain of human clay,
   Break with the first fall: they can ne'er behold
The long year linked with heavy day on day,   85
   And all which must be borne, and never told;
While Life's strange principle will often lie
Deepest in those who long the most to die.

"Whom the gods love die young," was said of
   yore,
   And many deaths do they escape by this: 90
The death of friends, and that which slays even
   more—
   The death of Friendship, Love, Youth, all
   that is,
Except mere breath; and since the silent shore
   Awaits at last even those who longest miss
The old Archer's shafts, perhaps the early grave   95
Which men weep over may be meant to save.

Haidée and Juan thought not of the dead—
   The Heavens, and Earth, and Air, seemed
   made for them:
They found no fault with Time, save that he
   fled;
   They saw not in themselves aught to con-   100
   demn:
Each was the other's mirror, and but read
   Joy sparkling in their dark eyes like a gem,
And knew such brightness was but the reflection
Of their exchanging glances of affection.

The gentle pressure, and the thrilling touch,   105
   The least glance better understood than words,
Which still said all, and ne'er could say too
   much;
   A language, too, but like to that of birds,
Known but to them, at least appearing such
   As but to lovers a true sense affords;   110
Sweet playful phrases, which would seem absurd

To those who have ceased to hear such, or ne'er
   heard—

All these were theirs, for they were children still,
   And children still they should have ever been;
They were not made in the real world to fill   115
   A busy character in the dull scene,
But like two beings born from out a rill,
   A Nymph and her belovèd, all unseen
To pass their lives in fountains and on flowers,
And never know the weight of human hours.   120

Moons changing had rolled on, and changeless
   found
   Those their bright rise had lighted to such joys
As rarely they beheld throughout their round;
   And these were not of the vain kind which cloys,
For theirs were buoyant spirits, never bound   125
   By the mere senses; and that which destroys
Most love—possession—unto them appeared
A thing which each endearment more endeared.

Oh beautiful! and rare as beautiful!
   But theirs was Love in which the Mind de-   130
   lights
To lose itself when the old world grows dull,
   And we are sick of its hack sounds and sights,
Intrigues, adventures of the common school,
   Its petty passions, marriages, and flights,
Where Hymen's torch[4] but brands one strumpet   135
   more,
Whose husband only knows her not a whore.

Hard words—harsh truth! a truth which many
   know.
   Enough.—The faithful and the fairy pair,
Who never found a single hour too slow,
   What was it made them thus exempt from   140
   care?
Young innate feelings all have felt below,
   Which perish in the rest, but in them were
Inherent—what we mortals call romantic,
And always envy, though we deem it frantic.

This is in others a factitious[5] state,   145
   An opium dream of too much youth and read-
   ing,
But was in them their nature or their fate:

---

[4] Symbol of marriage, Hymen being the classical god of
marriage.   [5] Artificial, sham.

No novels e'er had set their young hearts
   bleeding,
For Haidée's knowledge was by no means great,
   And Juan was a boy of saintly breeding;   150
So that there was no reason for their loves
More than for those of nightingales or doves.

They gazed upon the sunset; 'tis an hour
   Dear unto all, but dearest to *their* eyes,
For it had made them what they were: the power   155
   Of Love had first o'erwhelmed them from such
     skies,
When Happiness had been their only dower,
   And Twilight saw them linked in Passion's
     ties;
Charmed with each other, all things charmed
   that brought
The past still welcome as the present thought.   160

I know not why, but in that hour to-night,
   Even as they gazed, a sudden tremor came,
And swept, as 'twere, across their hearts' delight,
   Like the wind o'er a harp-string, or a flame,
When one is shook in sound, and one in sight;   165
   And thus some boding flashed through either
     frame,
And called from Juan's breast a faint low sigh,
While one new tear arose in Haidée's eye.

That large black prophet eye seemed to dilate
   And follow far the disappearing sun,   170
As if their last day of a happy date
   With his broad, bright, and dropping orb were
     gone;
Juan gazed on her as to ask his fate—
   He felt a grief, but knowing cause for none,
His glance inquired of hers for some excuse   175
For feelings causeless, or at least abstruse.

She turned to him, and smiled, but in that sort
   Which makes not others smile; then turned
     aside:
Whatever feeling shook her, it seemed short,
   And mastered by her wisdom or her pride;   180
When Juan spoke, too—it might be in sport—
   Of this their mutual feeling, she replied—
"If it should be so,—but—it cannot be—
Or I at least shall not survive to see."

Juan would question further, but she pressed   185
   His lip to hers, and silenced him with this,

And then dismissed the omen from her breast,
   Defying augury with that fond kiss;
And no doubt of all methods 'tis the best:
   Some people prefer wine—'tis not amiss;   190
I have tried both—so those who would a part take
May choose between the headache and the heart-
   ache.

One of the two, according to your choice,
   Woman or wine, you'll have to undergo;
Both maladies are taxes on our joys: 195
   But which to choose, I really hardly know;
And if I had to give a casting voice,[6]
   For both sides I could many reasons show,
And then decide, without great wrong to either,
It were much better to have both than neither.   200

Juan and Haidée gazed upon each other
   With swimming looks of speechless tenderness,
Which mixed all feelings—friend, child, lover,
     brother—
   All that the best can mingle and express
When two pure hearts are poured in one another,   205
   And love too much, and yet can not love less;
But almost sanctify the sweet excess
By the immortal wish and power to bless.

Mixed in each other's arms, and heart in heart,
   Why did they not then die?—they had lived   210
     too long
Should an hour come to bid them breathe apart;
   Years could but bring them cruel things or
     wrong;
The World was not for them—nor the World's
   art
   For beings passionate as Sappho's song;
Love was born *with* them, *in* them, so intense,   215
It was their very Spirit—not a sense.

They should have lived together deep in woods,
   Unseen as sings the nightingale; they were
Unfit to mix in these thick solitudes
   Called social, haunts of Hate, and Vice, and   220
     Care:
How lonely every freeborn creature broods!
   The sweetest song-birds nestle in a pair;
The eagle soars alone; the gull and crow
Flock o'er their carrion, just like men below.

---

6 Deciding vote.

Now pillowed cheek to cheek, in loving sleep,   225
   Haidée and Juan their siesta took,
A gentle slumber, but it was not deep,
   For ever and anon a something shook
Juan, and shuddering o'er his frame would creep;
   And Haidée's sweet lips murmured like a   230
      brook
A wordless music, and her face so fair
Stirred with her dream, as rose-leaves with the air.

Or as the stirring of a deep clear stream
   Within an Alpine hollow, when the wind
Walks o'er it, was she shaken by the dream,   235
   The mystical Usurper of the mind—
O'erpowering us to be whate'er may seem
   Good to the soul which we no more can bind;
Strange state of being! (for 'tis still to be)
Senseless to feel, and with sealed eyes to see.   240

She dreamed of being alone on the sea-shore,
   Chained to a rock; she knew not how, but stir
She could not from the spot, and the loud roar
   Grew, and each wave rose roughly, threatening
      her;
And o'er her upper lip they seemed to pour,   245
   Until she sobbed for breath, and soon they
      were
Foaming o'er her lone head, so fierce and high—
Each broke to drown her, yet she could not die.

Anon—she was released, and then she strayed
   O'er the sharp shingles[7] with her bleeding feet,   250
And stumbled almost every step she made:
   And something rolled before her in a sheet,
Which she must still pursue howe'er afraid:
   'Twas white and indistinct, nor stopped to
      meet
Her glance nor grasp, for still she gazed and   255
      grasped,
And ran, but it escaped her as she clasped.

The dream changed:—in a cave she stood, its
      walls
   Were hung with marble icicles, the work
Of ages on its water-fretted halls,
   Where waves might wash, and seals might   260
      breed and lurk;
Her hair was dripping, and the very balls
   Of her black eyes seemed turned to tears, and
      mirk[8]

The sharp rocks looked below each drop they
      caught,
Which froze to marble as it fell,—she thought.

And wet, and cold, and lifeless at her feet,   265
   Pale as the foam that frothed on his dead brow,
Which she essayed in vain to clear, (how sweet
   Were once her cares, how idle seemed they
      now!)
Lay Juan, nor could aught renew the beat
   Of his quenched heart: and the sea dirges low   270
Rang in her sad ears like a Mermaid's song,
And that brief dream appeared a life too long.

And gazing on the dead, she thought his face
   Faded, or altered into something new—
Like to her Father's features, till each trace   275
   More like and like to Lambro's aspect grew—
With all his keen worn look and Grecian grace;
   And starting, she awoke, and what to view?
Oh! Powers of Heaven! what dark eye meets she
      there?
'Tis—'tis her father's—fixed upon the pair!   280

Then shrieking, she arose, and shrieking fell,
   With joy and sorrow, hope and fear, to see
Him whom she deemed a habitant where dwell
   The ocean-buried, risen from death, to be
Perchance the death of one she loved too well: 285
   Dear as her father had been to Haidée,
It was a moment of that awful kind—
I have seen such—but must not call to mind.

Up Juan sprang to Haidée's bitter shriek,
   And caught her falling, and from off the wall   290
Snatched down his sabre, in hot haste to wreak
   Vengeance on him who was the cause of all:
Then Lambro, who till now forbore to speak,
   Smiled scornfully, and said, "Within my call,
A thousand scimitars await the word;   295
Put up, young man, put up your silly sword."

And Haidée clung around him; "Juan, 'tis—
   'Tis Lambro—'tis my father! Kneel with me—
He will forgive us—yes—it must be—yes.
   Oh! dearest father, in this agony   300
Of pleasure and of pain—even while I kiss
   Thy garment's hem with transport, can it be
That doubt should mingle with my filial joy?
Deal with me as thou wilt, but spare this boy."

---

7 Pebbles on a stony beach.   8 Murk, dark.

High and inscrutable the old man stood,   305
    Calm in his voice, and calm within his eye—
Not always signs with him of calmest mood:
    He looked upon her, but gave no reply;
Then turned to Juan, in whose cheek the blood
    Oft came and went, as there resolved to die;   310
In arms, at least, he stood, in act to spring
On the first foe whom Lambro's call might bring.

"Young man, your sword"; so Lambro once more
    said:
    Juan replied, "Not while this arm is free."
The old man's cheek grew pale, but not with   315
    dread,
    And drawing from his belt a pistol he
Replied, "Your blood be then on your own head."
    Then looked close at the flint, as if to see
'Twas fresh—for he had lately used the lock—
And next proceeded quietly to cock.   320

It has a strange quick jar upon the ear,
    That cocking of a pistol, when you know
A moment more will bring the sight to bear
    Upon your person, twelve yards off, or so;
A gentlemanly distance, not too near,   325
    If you have got a former friend for foe;
But after being fired at once or twice,
The ear becomes more Irish, and less nice.[9]

Lambro presented,[10] and one instant more
    Had stopped this Canto, and Don Juan's   330
    breath,
When Haidée threw herself her boy before;
    Stern as her sire: "On me," she cried, "let
    Death
Descend—the fault is mine; this fatal shore
    He found—but sought not. I have pledged my
    faith;
I love him—I will die with him: I knew   335
    Your nature's firmness—know your daughter's
    too."

A minute past, and she had been all tears,
    And tenderness, and infancy; but now
She stood as one who championed human fears—
    Pale, statue-like, and stern, she wooed the   340
    blow;

And tall beyond her sex, and their compeers,
    She drew up to her height, as if to show
A fairer mark; and with a fixed eye scanned
Her Father's face—but never stopped his hand.

He gazed on her, and she on him; 'twas strange   345
    How like they looked! the expression was the
    same;
Serenely savage, with a little change
    In the large dark eye's mutual-darted flame;
For she, too, was as one who could avenge,
    If cause should be—a Lioness, though tame.   350
Her Father's blood before her Father's face
Boiled up, and proved her truly of his race.

I said they were alike, their features and
    Their stature, differing but in sex and years;
Even to the delicacy of their hand   355
    There was resemblance, such as true blood
    wears;
And now to see them, thus divided, stand
    In fixed ferocity, when joyous tears
And sweet sensations should have welcomed
    both,
Shows what the passions are in their full growth. 360

The father paused a moment, then withdrew
    His weapon, and replaced it; but stood still,
And looking on her, as to look her through,
    "Not *I*," he said, "have sought this stranger's
    ill;
Not *I* have made this desolation: few   365
    Would bear such outrage, and forbear to kill;
But I must do my duty—how thou hast
Done thine, the present vouches for the past.

"Let him disarm; or, by my father's head,
    His own shall roll before you like a ball!"   370
He raised his whistle, as the word he said,
    And blew; another answered to the call,
And rushing in disorderly, though led,
    And armed from boot to turban, one and all,
Some twenty of his train came, rank on rank;   375
He gave the word,—"Arrest or slay the Frank."

Then, with a sudden movement, he withdrew
    His daughter; while compressed within his
    clasp,
'Twixt her and Juan interposed the crew;
    In vain she struggled in her father's grasp—   380

---

[9] Delicate, finicky. Byron professes to think that constant listening to their own speech must accustom Irish ears to harshness.   [10] Aimed.

His arms were like a serpent's coil: then flew
   Upon their prey, as darts an angry asp,
The file of pirates—save the foremost, who
Had fallen, with his right shoulder half cut
   through.

The second had his cheek laid open; but   385
   The third, a wary, cool old sworder, took
The blows upon his cutlass, and then put
   His own well in; so well, ere you could look,
His man was floored, and helpless at his foot,
   With the blood running like a little brook   390
From two smart sabre gashes, deep and red—
One on the arm, the other on the head.

And then they bound him where he fell, and bore
   Juan from the apartment: with a sign
Old Lambro bade them take him to the shore,   395
   Where lay some ships which were to sail at
   nine.
They laid him in a boat, and plied the oar
   Until they reached some galliots,[11] placed in
   line;
On board of one of these, and under hatches,
They stowed him, with strict orders to the   400
   watches.

The world is full of strange vicissitudes,
   And here was one exceedingly unpleasant:
A gentleman so rich in the world's goods,
   Handsome and young, enjoying all the present,
Just at the very time when he least broods   405
   On such a thing, is suddenly to sea sent,
Wounded and chained so that he cannot move,
And all because a lady fell in love.

     . . . .

The last sight which she saw was Juan's gore,
   And he himself o'ermastered and cut down;
His blood was running on the very floor
   Where late he trod, her beautiful, her own;   460
Thus much she viewed an instant and no more,—
   Her struggles ceased with one convulsive
   groan;
On her Sire's arm, which until now scarce held
Her writhing, fell she like a cedar felled.

A vein had burst, and her sweet lips' pure dyes   465
   Were dabbled with the deep blood which ran
   o'er;

And her head drooped, as when the lily lies
   O'ercharged with rain: her summoned hand-
   maids bore
Their lady to her couch with gushing eyes;
   Of herbs and cordials they produced their   470
   store,
But she defied all means they could employ,
Like one Life could not hold, nor Death destroy.

Days lay she in that state unchanged, though
   chill—
   With nothing livid, still her lips were red;
She had no pulse, but Death seemed absent still; 475
   No hideous sign proclaimed her surely dead;
Corruption came not in each mind to kill
   All hope; to look upon her sweet face bred
New thoughts of Life, for it seemed full of soul—
She had so much, Earth could not claim the   480
   whole.

The ruling passion, such as marble shows
   When exquisitely chiselled, still lay there,
But fixed as marble's unchanged aspect throws
   O'er the fair Venus,[12] but for ever fair;
O'er the Laocoön's all eternal throes,[13]   485
   And ever-dying Gladiator's[14] air,
Their energy like life forms all their fame,
Yet looks not life, for they are still the same.—

She woke at length, but not as sleepers wake,
   Rather the dead, for Life seemed something   490
   new,
A strange sensation which she must partake
   Perforce, since whatsoever met her view
Struck not on memory, though a heavy ache
   Lay at her heart, whose earliest beat still true
Brought back the sense of pain without the cause, 495
For, for a while, the Furies made a pause.

She looked on many a face with vacant eye,
   On many a token without knowing what:
She saw them watch her without asking why,
   And recked not who around her pillow sat;   500

---

11 Small, swift galleys, propelled by oars and sails.

12 From references elsewhere it is clear that Byron means the Venus de' Medici at Florence.

13 Another piece of classical sculpture, representing the legendary Trojan priest and his two sons being crushed by huge serpents sent by the goddess Athena to punish Laocoön for his skepticism over the wooden horse by means of which the Greeks got into the city.

14 A famous statue once thought to represent a dying gladiator; cf. *Childe Harold*, IV, 1252 ff. (p. 250).

Not speechless, though she spoke not—not a sigh
  Relieved her thoughts—dull silence and quick
     chat
Were tried in vain by those who served; she gave
No sign, save breath, of having left the grave.

Her handmaids tended, but she heeded not;   505
  Her Father watched, she turned her eyes away;
She recognized no being, and no spot,
  However dear or cherished in their day;
They changed from room to room—but all for-
     got—
  Gentle, but without memory she lay;   510
At length those eyes, which they would fain be
     weaning
Back to old thoughts, waxed full of fearful mean-
     ing.

And then a slave bethought her of a harp;
  The harper came, and tuned his instrument;
At the first notes, irregular and sharp,   515
  On him her flashing eyes a moment bent,
Then to the wall she turned as if to warp
  Her thoughts from sorrow through her heart
     re-sent;
And he began a long low island-song
Of ancient days, ere Tyranny grew strong.   520

Anon her thin wan fingers beat the wall
  In time to his old tune; he changed the theme,
And sung of Love; the fierce name struck through
     all
  Her recollection; on her flashed the dream
Of what she was, and is, if ye could call   525
  To be so being; in a gushing stream
The tears rushed forth from her o'erclouded
     brain,
Like mountain mists at length dissolved in rain.

Short solace, vain relief!—Thought came too
     quick,
  And whirled her brain to madness; she arose   530
As one who ne'er had dwelt among the sick,
  And flew at all she met, as on her foes;
But no one ever heard her speak or shriek,
  Although her paroxysm drew towards its
     close;—
Hers was a frenzy which disdained to rave,   535
Even when they smote her, in the hope to save.

Yet she betrayed at times a gleam of sense;

Nothing could make her meet her Father's
     face,
Though on all other things with looks intense
  She gazed, but none she ever could retrace;   540
Food she refused, and raiment; no pretence
  Availed for either; neither change of place,
Nor time, nor skill, nor remedy, could give her
Senses to sleep—the power seemed gone for ever.

Twelve days and nights she withered thus; at last,   545
  Without a groan, or sigh, or glance, to show
A parting pang, the spirit from her passed:
  And they who watched her nearest could not
     know
The very instant, till the change that cast
  Her sweet face into shadow, dull and slow,   550
Glazed o'er her eyes—the beautiful, the black—
Oh! to possess such lustre—and then lack!

She died, but not alone; she held, within,
  A second principle of Life, which might
Have dawned a fair and sinless child of sin;   555
  But closed its little being without light,
And went down to the grave unborn, wherein
  Blossom and bough lie withered with one
     blight;
In vain the dews of Heaven descend above
The bleeding flower and blasted fruit of Love.   560

Thus lived—thus died she; never more on her
  Shall Sorrow light, or Shame. She was not
     made
Through years or moons the inner weight to bear,
  Which colder hearts endure till they are laid
By age in earth: her days and pleasures were   565
  Brief, but delightful—such as had not staid
Long with her destiny; but she sleeps well
By the sea-shore, whereon she loved to dwell.

That isle is now all desolate and bare,
  Its dwellings down, its tenants passed away;   570
None but her own and Father's grave is there,
  And nothing outward tells of human clay;
Ye could not know where lies a thing so fair,
  No stone is there to show, no tongue to say,
What was; no dirge, except the hollow sea's,   575
Mourns o'er the beauty of the Cyclades.[15]

But many a Greek maid in a loving song
  Sighs o'er her name; and many an islander

---

[15] The islands off southeastern Greece.

With her Sire's story makes the night less long;
   Valour was his, and Beauty dwelt with her: 580
If she loved rashly, her life paid for wrong—
   A heavy price must all pay who thus err,
In some shape; let none think to fly the danger,
For soon or late Love is his own avenger. . . .

Stanzas Written on the Road Between Florence and Pisa

Oh, talk not to me of a name great in story—
The days of our Youth are the days of our glory;
And the myrtle and ivy[1] of sweet two-and-twenty
Are worth all your laurels,[2] though ever so plenty.

What are garlands and crowns to the brow that is   5
   wrinkled?
'Tis but as a dead flower with May-dew be-
   sprinkled:
Then away with all such from the head that is
   hoary,
What care I for the wreaths that can *only* give
   glory?

Oh Fame!—if I e'er took delight in thy praises,
'Twas less for the sake of thy high-sounding   10
   phrases,
Than to see the bright eyes of the dear One dis-
   cover,
She thought that I was not unworthy to love her.

There chiefly I sought thee, *there* only I found
   thee;
Her Glance was the best of the rays that surround
   thee;
When it sparkled o'er aught that was bright in   15
   my story,
I knew it was Love, and I felt it was Glory.

The Vision of Judgment

Written in 1821. Robert Southey (1774–1843), Coleridge's brother-in-law, and friend of Wordsworth, was
a poet, historian, and political writer. A radical in
youth, he was conservative later on. He was made
Poet Laureate in 1813 and was widely regarded by
liberals as a turncoat. Certainly *his* poem "A Vision
of Judgment" was sycophantic. Byron's poem, written
a few months after Southey's, parodies its structure
while it ridicules its content.

I

Saint Peter sat by the celestial gate:
   His keys were rusty, and the lock was dull,
So little trouble had been given of late;
   Not that the place by any means was full,
But since the Gallic era "eighty-eight"[1]   5
   The devils had ta'en a longer, stronger pull,
And "a pull altogether," as they say
At sea—which drew most souls another way.

II

The angels all were singing out of tune,
   And hoarse with having little else to do,   10
Excepting to wind up the sun and moon,
   Or curb a runaway young star or two,
Or wild colt of a comet, which too soon
   Broke out of bounds o'er th' ethereal blue,
Splitting some planet with its playful tail,   15
As boats are sometimes by a wanton whale.

III

The guardian seraphs had retired on high,
   Finding their charges past all care below;
Terrestrial business fill'd nought in the sky
   Save the recording angel's black bureau;   20
Who found, indeed, the facts to multiply
   With such rapidity of vice and woe,
That he had stripp'd off both his wings in quills,
And yet was in arrear of human ills.

IV

His business so augmented of late years,   25
   That he was forced, against his will no doubt,
(Just like those cherubs, earthly ministers,)
   For some resource to turn himself about,
And claim the help of his celestial peers,
   To aid him ere he should be quite worn out   30
By the increased demand for his remarks;
Six angels and twelve saints were named his clerks.

V

This was a handsome board—at least for heaven;
   And yet they had even then enough to do,

---

[1] Symbols of love and wine.—This lyric was written in 1821.   [2] All the laurels (i.e., fame and prizes) there are.

[1] The beginning of the French Revolution.

So many conquerors' cars were daily driven,   35
  So many kingdoms fitted up anew;
Each day too slew its thousands six or seven,
  Till at the crowning carnage, Waterloo,
They threw their pens down in divine disgust—
The page was so besmear'd with blood and dust.   40

VI

This by the way; 'tis not mine to record
  What angels shrink from: even the very devil
On this occasion his own work abhorr'd,
  So surfeited with the infernal revel:
Though he himself had sharpen'd every sword,   45
  It almost quench'd his innate thirst of evil.
(Here Satan's sole good work deserves insertion—
'Tis, that he has both generals in reversion.)

VII

Let's skip a few short years of hollow peace,
  Which peopled earth no better, hell as wont,   50
And heaven none—they form the tyrant's lease,
  With nothing but new names subscribed
    upon 't;
'Twill one day finish: meantime they increase,
  "With seven heads and ten horns," and all in
    front,[2]
Like Saint John's foretold beast; but ours are   55
  born
Less formidable in the head than horn.

VIII

In the first year of freedom's second dawn
  Died George the Third; although no tyrant,
    one
Who shielded tyrants, till each sense withdrawn
  Left him nor mental nor external sun: 60
A better farmer ne'er brush'd dew from lawn,
  A worse king never left a realm undone!
He died—but left his subjects still behind,
One half as mad—and t'other no less blind.

IX

He died! his death made no great stir on earth;   65
  His burial made some pomp; there was profu-
    sion
Of velvet, gilding, brass, and no great dearth
  Of aught but tears—save those shed by collu-
    sion.

---

2 See Revelation 13.

For these things may be bought at their true
  worth;
  Of elegy there was the due infusion—   70
Bought also; and the torches, cloaks, and banners,
Heralds, and relics of old Gothic manners,

X

Form'd a sepulchral melodrame. Of all
  The fools who flock'd to swell or see the show,
Who cared about the corpse? The funeral   75
  Made the attraction, and the black the woe.
There throbb'd not there a thought which pierced
  the pall;
  And when the gorgeous coffin was laid low,
It seem'd the mockery of hell to fold
The rottenness of eighty years in gold.   80

XI

So mix his body with the dust! It might
  Return to what it *must* far sooner, were
The natural compound left alone to fight
  Its way back into earth, and fire, and air;
But the unnatural balsams merely blight   85
  What nature made him at his birth, as bare
As the mere million's base unmummied clay—
Yet all his spices but prolong decay.

XII

He's dead—and upper earth with him has done;
  He's buried; save the undertaker's bill,   90
Or lapidary scrawl, the world is gone
  For him, unless he left a German will;
But where's the proctor who will ask his son?
  In whom his qualities are reigning still,
Except that household virtue, most uncommon,   95
Of constancy to a bad, ugly woman.

XIII

"God save the king!" It is a large economy
  In God to save the like; but if he will
Be saving, all the better; for not one am I
  Of those who think damnation better still: 100
I hardly know too if not quite alone am I
  In this small hope of bettering future ill
By circumscribing, with some slight restriction,
The eternity of hell's hot jurisdiction.

XIV

I know this is unpopular; I know   105
  'Tis blasphemous; I know one may be damn'd

For hoping no one else may e'er be so;
 I know my catechism; I know we're cramm'd
With the best doctrines till we quite o'erflow;
 I know that all save England's church have 110
  shamm'd,
And that the other twice two hundred churches
And synagogues have made a *damn'd* bad pur-
 chase.

XV

God help us all! God help me too! I am,
 God knows, as helpless as the devil can wish,
And not a whit more difficult to damn, 115
 Than is to bring to land a late-hook'd fish,
Or to the butcher to purvey the lamb;
 Not that I'm fit for such a noble dish,
As one day will be that immortal fry
Of almost everybody born to die. 120

XVI

Saint Peter sat by the celestial gate,
 And nodded o'er his keys; when, lo! there came
A wondrous noise he had not heard of late—
 A rushing sound of wind, and stream, and
  flame;
In short, a roar of things extremely great, 125
 Which would have made aught save a saint
  exclaim;
But he, with first a start and then a wink,
Said, "There's another star gone out, I think!"

XVII

But ere he could return to his repose,
 A cherub flapp'd his right wing o'er his eyes— 130
At which St. Peter yawn'd, and rubb'd his nose:
 "Saint porter," said the angel, "prithee rise!"
Waving a goodly wing, which glow'd, as glows
 An earthly peacock's tail, with heavenly dyes:
To which the saint replied, "Well, what's the 135
  matter?
 Is Lucifer come back with all this clatter?"

XVIII

"No," quoth the cherub; "George the Third is
 dead."
 "And who *is* George the Third?" replied the
  apostle:
"*What George? what Third?*" "The king of England," said

The angel. "Well! he won't find kings to jostle 140
Him on his way; but does he wear his head;
 Because the last we saw here had a tustle,
And ne'er would have got into heaven's good
  graces,
Had he not flung his head in all our faces.[3]

XIX

"He was, if I remember, king of France; 145
 That head of his, which could not keep a
  crown
On earth, yet ventured in my face to advance
 A claim to those of martyrs—like my own:
If I had had my sword, as I had once
 When I cut ears off, I had cut him down; 150
But having but my *keys,* and not my brand,
I only knock'd his head from out his hand.

XX

"And then he set up such a headless howl,
 That all the saints came out and took him in;
And there he sits by St. Paul, cheek by jowl; 155
 That fellow Paul—the parvenù! The skin
Of St. Bartholomew, which makes his cowl
 In heaven, and upon earth redeem'd his sin
So as to make a martyr, never sped
Better than did this weak and wooden head. 160

XXI

"But had it come up here upon its shoulders,
 There would have been a different tale to tell:
The fellow-feeling in the saint's beholders
 Seems to have acted on them like a spell;
And so this very foolish head heaven solders 165
 Back on its trunk: it may be very well,
And seems the custom here to overthrow
Whatever has been wisely done below."

XXII

The angel answer'd, "Peter! do not pout:
 The king who comes has head and all entire, 170
And never knew much what it was about—
 He did as doth the puppet—by its wire,
And will be judged like all the rest, no doubt:
 My business and your own is not to inquire
Into such matters, but to mind our cue—
Which is to act as we are bid to do." 175

---

[3] Louis XVI, guillotined in 1793.

XXIII

While thus they spake, the angelic caravan,
    Arriving like a rush of mighty wind,
Cleaving the fields of space, as doth the swan
    Some silver stream (say Ganges, Nile, or Inde,   180
Or Thames, or Tweed), and 'midst them an old
    man
    With an old soul, and both extremely blind,
Halted before the gate, and in his shroud
Seated their fellow-traveller on a cloud.

XXIV

But bringing up the rear of this bright host   185
    A Spirit of a different aspect waved
His wings, like thunder-clouds above some coast
    Whose barren beach with frequent wrecks is
    paved;
His brow was like the deep when tempest-toss'd;
    Fierce and unfathomable thoughts engraved   190
Eternal wrath on his immortal face,
And *where* he gazed a gloom pervaded space.

XXV

As he drew near, he gazed upon the gate
    Ne'er to be enter'd more by him or Sin,
With such a glance of supernatural hate,   195
    As made Saint Peter wish himself within;
He patter'd with his keys at a great rate,
    And sweated through his apostolic skin:
Of course his perspiration was but ichor,[4]
Or some such other spiritual liquor.   200

XXVI

The very cherubs huddled all together,
    Like birds when soars the falcon; and they felt
A tingling to the tip of every feather,
    And form'd a circle like Orion's belt
Around their poor old charge; who scarce knew   205
    whither
    His guards had led him, though they gently
    dealt
With royal manes (for by many stories,
And true, we learn the angels all are Tories).

XXVII

As things were in this posture, the gate flew
    Asunder, and the flashing of its hinges   210

Flung over space an universal hue
    Of many-colour'd flame, until its tinges
Reach'd even our speck of earth, and made a new
    Aurora borealis spread its fringes
O'er the North Pole; the same seen, when ice-   215
    bound,
By Captain Parry's crew, in "Melville's Sound."[5]

XXVIII

And from the gate thrown open issued beaming
    A beautiful and mighty Thing of Light,
Radiant with glory, like a banner streaming
    Victorious from some world-o'erthrowing fight: 220
My poor comparisons must needs be teeming
    With earthly likenesses, for here the night
Of clay obscures our best conceptions, saving
Johanna Southcote,[6] or Bob Southey raving.

XXIX

'Twas the archangel Michael: all men know   225
    The make of angels and archangels, since
There's scarce a scribbler has not one to show,
    From the fiends' leader to the angels' prince.
There also are some altar-pieces, though
    I really can't say that they much evince   230
One's inner notions of immortal spirits;
But let the connoisseurs explain *their* merits.

XXX

Michael flew forth in glory and in good;
    A goodly work of him from whom all glory
And good arise; the portal past—he stood;   235
    Before him the young cherubs and saints
    hoary—
(I say *young*, begging to be understood
    By looks, not years; and should be very sorry
To state, they were not older than St. Peter,
But merely that they seem'd a little sweeter).   240

XXXI

The cherubs and the saints bow'd down before
    That arch-angelic hierarch, the first
Of essences angelical, who wore
    The aspect of a god; but this ne'er nursed

---

4 The blood of the gods.

5 Edward Parry had led an expedition to find the North-
west Passage.
6 Joanna Southcott or Southcote, a raving prophetess and
fanatic, who attracted a huge following before her death
in 1814.

Pride in his heavenly bosom, in whose core   245
   No thought, save for his Master's service, durst
Intrude, however glorified and high;
   He knew him but the viceroy of the sky.

XXXII

He and the sombre silent Spirit met—
   They knew each other both for good and ill;   250
Such was their power, that neither could forget
   His former friend and future foe; but still
There was a high, immortal, proud regret
   In either's eye, as if 'twere less their will
Than destiny to make the eternal years   255
Their date of war, and their "champ clos" the
     spheres.[7]

XXXIII

But here they were in neutral space: we know
   From Job, that Satan hath the power to pay
A heavenly visit thrice a year or so;
   And that the "sons of God," like those of clay,   260
Must keep him company; and we might show
   From the same book, in how polite a way
The dialogue is held between the Powers
Of Good and Evil—but 'twould take up hours.

XXXIV

And this is not a theologic tract,   265
   To prove with Hebrew and with Arabic
If Job be allegory or a fact,
   But a true narrative; and thus I pick
From out the whole but such and such an act
   As sets aside the slightest thought of trick.   270
'Tis every tittle true, beyond suspicion,
And accurate as any other vision.

XXXV

The spirits were in neutral space, before
   The gate of heaven; like eastern thresholds is
The place where Death's grand cause is argued   275
     o'er,
   And souls despatch'd to that world or to this;
And therefore Michael and the other wore
   A civil aspect: though they did not kiss,
Yet still between his Darkness and his Brightness
There pass'd a mutual glance of great politeness.   280

---

7 *Champ clos*, an enclosed field, is a jousting term.

XXXVI

The Archangel bow'd, not like a modern beau,
   But with a graceful oriental bend,
Pressing one radiant arm just where below
   The heart in good men is supposed to tend.
He turn'd as to an equal, not too low,   285
   But kindly; Satan met his ancient friend
With more hauteur, as might an old Castilian
Poor noble meet a mushroom rich civilian.

XXXVII

He merely bent his diabolic brow
   An instant; and then raising it, he stood   290
In act to assert his right or wrong, and show
   Cause why King George by no means could or
     should
Make out a case to be exempt from woe
   Eternal, more than other kings, endued
With better sense and hearts, whom history men-   295
     tions,
Who long have "paved hell with their good in-
     tentions."

XXXVIII

Michael began: "What wouldst thou with this
     man,
   Now dead, and brought before the Lord? What
     ill
Hath he wrought since his mortal race began,
   That thou canst claim him? Speak! and do thy   300
     will,
If it be just: if in this earthly span
   He hath been greatly failing to fulfil
His duties as a king and mortal, say,
And he is thine; if not, let him have way."

XXXIX

"Michael!" replied the Prince of Air, "even here,   305
   Before the Gate of him thou servest, must
I claim my subject: and will make appear
   That as he was my worshipper in dust,
So shall he be in spirit, although dear
   To thee and thine, because nor wine nor lust   310
Were of his weaknesses; yet on the throne
He reign'd o'er millions to serve me alone.

XL

"Look to *our* earth, or rather *mine*; it was,
Once, more thy master's: but I triumph not

In this poor planet's conquest; nor, alas!   315
    Need he thou servest envy me my lot:
With all the myriads of bright worlds which pass
    In worship round him, he may have forgot
Yon weak creation of such paltry things:
I think few worth damnation save their kings,—   320

XLI

"And these but as a kind of quit-rent, to
    Assert my right as lord: and even had
I such an inclination, 'twere (as you
    Well know) superfluous; they are grown so bad,
That hell has nothing better left to do   325
    Than leave them to themselves: so much more
      mad
And evil by their own internal curse,
Heaven cannot make them better, nor I worse.

XLII

"Look to the earth, I said, and say again:
    When this old, blind, mad, helpless, weak,   330
      poor worm[8]
Began in youth's first bloom and flush to reign,
    The world and he both wore a different form,
And much of earth and all the watery plain
    Of ocean call'd him king: through many a
      storm
His isles had floated on the abyss of time;   335
For the rough virtues chose them for their clime.

XLIII

"He came to his sceptre young; he leaves it old:
    Look to the state in which he found his realm,
And left it; and his annals too behold,
    How to a minion first he gave the helm;[9]   340
How grew upon his heart a thirst for gold,
    The beggar's vice, which can but overwhelm
The meanest hearts; and for the rest, but glance
Thine eye along America and France.

XLIV

" 'Tis true, he was a tool from first to last   345
(I have the workmen safe); but as a tool
So let him be consumed. From out the past
    Of ages, since mankind have known the rule
Of monarchs—from the bloody rolls amass'd

Of sin and slaughter—from the Cæsar's   350
    school,
Take the worst pupil; and produce a reign
More drench'd with gore, more cumber'd with the
    slain.

XLV

"He ever warr'd with freedom and the free:
    Nations as men, home subjects, foreign foes,
So that they utter'd the word 'Liberty!'   355
    Found George the Third their first opponent.
      Whose
History was ever stain'd as his will be
    With national and individual woes?
I grant his household abstinence; I grant
His neutral virtues, which most monarchs want;   360

XLVI

"I know he was a constant consort; own
    He was a decent sire, and middling lord.
All this is much, and most upon a throne;
    As temperance, if at Apicius' board,[10]
Is more than at an anchorite's supper shown.[11]   365
    I grant him all the kindest can accord;
And this was well for him, but not for those
Millions who found him what oppression chose.

XLVII

"The New World shook him off; the Old yet
    groans
    Beneath what he and his prepared, if not   370
Completed: he leaves heirs on many thrones
    To all his vices, without what begot
Compassion for him—his tame virtues; drones
    Who sleep, or despots who have now forgot
A lesson which shall be re-taught them, wake   375
Upon the thrones of earth; but let them quake!

XLVIII

"Five millions of the primitive, who hold
    The faith which makes ye great on earth, im-
    plored
A *part* of that vast *all* they held of old,—
    Freedom to worship—not alone your Lord,   380
Michael, but you, and you, Saint Peter! Cold
    Must be your souls, if you have not abhorr'd

---

8 Byron is echoing Shelley's "England in 1819." See p. 329.
9 Lord Bute, George's prime minister early in his reign.

10 Apicius, a famous food-lover in Tiberius's time, said to have written a cookbook.
11 An anchorite is a religious hermit.

The foe to Catholic participation
In all the license of a Christian nation.

XLIX

"True! he allow'd them to pray God; but as   385
   A consequence of prayer, refused the law
Which would have placed them upon the same
      base
   With those who did not hold the saints in
      awe."[12]
But here Saint Peter started from his place,
   And cried, "You may the prisoner withdraw: 390
Ere heaven shall ope her portals to this Guelph,[13]
While I am guard, may I be damn'd myself!

L

"Sooner will I with Cerberus exchange[14]
   My office (and *his* is no sinecure)
Than see this royal Bedlam bigot range   395
   The azure fields of heaven, of that be sure!"
"Saint!" replied Satan, "you do well to avenge
   The wrongs he made your satellites endure;
And if to this exchange you should be given,
I'll try to coax *our* Cerberus up to heaven."   400

LI

Here Michael interposed: "Good saint! and devil!
   Pray, not so fast; you both outrun discretion.
Saint Peter! you were wont to be more civil!
   Satan! excuse this warmth of his expression,
And condescension to the vulgar's level: 405
   Even saints sometimes forget themselves in ses-
      sion.
Have you got more to say?"—"No."—"If you
      please,
I'll trouble you to call your witnesses."

LII

Then Satan turn'd and waved his swarthy hand,
   Which stirr'd with its electric qualities   410
Clouds farther off than we can understand,
   Although we find him sometimes in our skies;
Infernal thunder shook both sea and land

In all the planets, and hell's batteries
Let off the artillery, which Milton mentions   415
As one of Satan's most sublime inventions.[15]

LIII

This was a signal unto such damn'd souls
   As have the privilege of their damnation
Extended far beyond the mere controls
   Of worlds past, present, or to come; no station 420
Is theirs particularly in the rolls
   Of hell assign'd; but where their inclination
Or business carries them in search of game,
They may range freely—being damn'd the same.

LIV

They're proud of this—as very well they may,   425
   It being a sort of knighthood, or gilt key
Struck in their loins; or like to an "entré"
   Up the back stairs, or such free-masonry.
I borrow my comparisons from clay,
   Being clay myself. Let not those spirits be   430
Offended with such base low likenesses;
We know their posts are nobler far than these.

LV

When the great signal ran from heaven to hell—
   About ten million times the distance reckon'd
From our sun to its earth, as we can tell   435
   How much time it takes up, even to a second,
For every ray that travels to dispel
   The fogs of London, through which, dimly
      beacon'd,
The weathercocks are gilt some thrice a year,
If that the *summer* is not too severe:—   440

LVI

I say that I can tell—'twas half a minute:
   I know the solar beams take up more time
Ere, packed up for their journey, they begin it;
   But then their telegraph is less sublime,
And if they ran a race, they would not win it   445
   'Gainst Satan's couriers bound for their own
      clime.
The sun takes up some years for every ray
To reach its goal—the devil not half a day.

LVII

Upon the verge of space, about the size
   Of half-a-crown, a little speck appear'd   450

---

12 Byron is referring to George III's implacable hostility to assuring Catholics of equal political rights. The "five million" are the Irish.
13 The family name of the royal house George belonged to, the Hanoverians.
14 The monstrous dog that guards Hades.

15 *Paradise Lost*, VI, 484–85.

(I've seen a something like it in the skies
   In the Ægean, ere a squall); it near'd,
And, growing bigger, took another guise;
   Like an aërial ship it tack'd, and steer'd,
Or *was* steer'd (I am doubtful of the grammar   455
Of the last phrase, which makes the stanza stam-
    mer;—

LVIII

But take your choice); and then it grew a cloud;[16]
   And so it was—a cloud of witnesses.
But such a cloud! No land e'er saw a crowd
   Of locusts numerous as the heavens saw these;   460
They shadow'd with their myriads space; their
    loud
And varied cries were like those of wild geese
(If nations may be liken'd to a goose),
And realised the phrase of "hell broke loose."

LIX

Here crash'd a sturdy oath of stout John Bull,   465
   Who damn'd away his eyes as heretofore:
There Paddy brogued "By Jasus!"—"What's your
    wull?"
   The temperate Scot exclaim'd: the French
    ghost swore
In certain terms I shan't translate in full,
   As the first coachman will; and 'midst the war,   470
The voice of Jonathan was heard to express,[17]
"*Our* president is going to war, I guess."

LX

Besides there were the Spaniard, Dutch, and
    Dane;
   In short, an universal shoal of shades,
From Otaheite's isle to Salisbury Plain,[18]   475
   Of all climes and professions, years and trades,
Ready to swear against the good king's reign,
   Bitter as clubs in cards are against spades:
All summon'd by this grand "subpœna," to
Try if kings mayn't be damn'd like me or you.   480

LXI

When Michael saw this host, he first grew pale,
   As angels can; next, like Italian twilight,

He turn'd all colours—as a peacock's tail,
   Or sunset streaming through a Gothic skylight
In some old abbey, or a trout not stale,   485
   Or distant lightning on the horizon *by* night,
Or a fresh rainbow, or a grand review
Of thirty regiments in red, green, and blue.

LXII

Then he address'd himself to Satan: "Why—
   My good old friend, for such I deem you, 490
    though
Our different parties make us fight so shy,
   I ne'er mistake you for a *personal* foe;
Our difference is *political,* and I
   Trust that, whatever may occur below,
You know my great respect for you: and this   495
Makes me regret whate'er you do amiss—

LXIII

"Why, my dear Lucifer, would you abuse
   My call for witnesses? I did not mean
That you should half of earth and hell produce;
   'Tis even superfluous, since two honest, clean, 500
True testimonies are enough: we lose
   Our time, nay, our eternity, between
The accusation and defence: if we
Hear both, 'twill stretch our immortality."

LXIV

Satan replied, "To me the matter is   505
   Indifferent, in a personal point of view:
I can have fifty better souls than this
   With far less trouble than we have gone
    through
Already; and I merely argued his
   Late majesty of Britain's case with you   510
Upon a point of form: you may dispose
Of him; I've kings enough below, God knows!"

LXV

Thus spoke the Demon (late call'd "multifaced"
   By multo-scribbling Southey). "Then we'll call
One or two persons of the myriads placed   515
   Around our congress, and dispense with all
The rest," quoth Michael: "Who may be so
    graced
   As to speak first? there's choice enough—who
    shall

---

[16] Byron is probably recalling *Paradise Lost,* II, 636–43, and also *The Rime of the Ancient Mariner,* III, 149–56.
[17] I.e., a Yankee voice.
[18] Otaheite is Tahiti.

It be?" Then Satan answer'ed, "There are many;
But you may choose Jack Wilkes as well as any."[19]   520

LXVI

A merry cock-eyed, curious-looking sprite
 Upon the instant started from the throng,
Dress'd in a fashion now forgotten quite;
 For all the fashions of the flesh stick long
By the people in the next world; where unite   525
 All the costumes since Adam's, right or wrong,
From Eve's fig-leaf down to the petticoat,
Almost as scanty, of days less remote.

LXVII

The spirit look'd around upon the crowds
 Assembled, and exclaim'd, "My friends of all   530
The spheres, we shall catch cold amongst these
  clouds;
 So let's to business: why this general call?
If those are freeholders I see in shrouds,
 And 'tis for an election that they bawl,
Behold a candidate with unturn'd coat!   535
 Saint Peter, may I count upon your vote?"

LXVIII

"Sir," replied Michael, "you mistake; these things
 Are of a former life, and what we do
Above is more august; to judge of kings
 Is the tribunal met: so now you know."   540
"Then I presume those gentlemen with wings,"
 Said Wilkes, "are cherubs; and that soul below
Looks much like George the Third, but to my
  mind
A good deal older—Bless me! is he blind?"

LXIX

"He is what you behold him, and his doom   545
 Depends upon his deeds," the Angel said.
"If you have aught to arraign in him, the tomb
 Gives license to the humblest beggar's head
To lift itself against the loftiest."—"Some,"
 Said Wilkes, "don't wait to see them laid in   550
  lead,

---

[19] John Wilkes, who died in 1797 after a career of opposition to the government. He was a member of Parliament for Middlesex, and also was elected lord mayor of London. His famous meeting with Dr. Johnson, who disapproved of his politics and his morals, but was charmed by him, is recounted in our excerpts from Boswell's *Life*, in Volume I.

For such a liberty—and I, for one,
Have told them what I thought beneath the sun."

LXX

"*Above* the sun repeat, then, what thou hast
 To urge against him," said the Archangel.
  "Why,"
Replied the spirit, "since old scores are past,   555
 Must I turn evidence? In faith, not I.
Besides, I beat him hollow at the last,
 With all his Lords and Commons: in the sky
I don't like ripping up old stories, since
His conduct was but natural in a prince.   560

LXXI

"Foolish, no doubt, and wicked, to oppress
 A poor unlucky devil without a shilling;
But then I blame the man himself much less
 Than Bute and Grafton,[20] and shall be un-
  willing
To see him punish'd here for their excess,   565
 Since they were both damn'd long ago, and
  still in
Their place below: for me, I have forgiven,
And vote his 'habeas corpus' into heaven."

LXXII

"'Wilkes," said the Devil, "I understand all this;
 You turn'd to half a courtier ere you died,   570
And seem to think it would not be amiss
 To grow a whole one on the other side
Of Charon's ferry; you forget that *his*
 Reign is concluded; whatsoe'er betide,
He won't be sovereign more: you've lost your   575
  labour
For at the best he will but be your neighbour.

LXXIII

"However, I knew what to think of it,
 When I beheld you in your jesting way
Flitting and whispering round about the spit
 Where Belial, upon duty for the day,   580
With Fox's lard was basting William Pitt,[21]
 His pupil; I knew what to think, I say:

---

[20] Grafton, one of George's ministers.
[21] Charles James Fox, the great rival of William Pitt, and opponent of the war against the French which Pitt, as prime minister, conducted. Fox was very fat.

That fellow even in hell breeds farther ills;
I'll have him *gagg'd*—'twas one of his own bills.

LXXIV

"Call Junius!" From the crowd a shadow stalk'd,[22]   585
    And at the name there was a general squeeze,
So that the very ghosts no longer walk'd
    In comfort, at their own aërial ease,
But were all ramm'd, and jamm'd (but to be
    balk'd,
    As we shall see), and jostled hands and knees,   590
Like wind compress'd and pent within a bladder
Or like a human colic, which is sadder.

LXXV

The shadow came—a tall, thin, grey-hair'd figure,
    That look'd as it had been a shade on earth;
Quick in its motions, with an air of vigour,   595
    But nought to mark its breeding or its birth:
Now it wax'd little, then again grew bigger,
    With now an air of gloom, or savage mirth;
But as you gazed upon its features, they
Changed every instant—to *what,* none could say.   600

LXXVI

The more intently the ghosts gazed, the less
    Could they distinguish whose the features
    were;
The Devil himself seem'd puzzled even to guess;
    They varied like a dream—now here, now
    there;
And several people swore from out the press,   605
    They knew him perfectly; and one could swear
He was his father: upon which another
Was sure he was his mother's cousin's brother:

LXXVII

Another, that he was a duke, or knight,
    An orator, lawyer, or a priest,   610
A nabob, a man-midwife; but the wight
    Mysterious changed his countenance at least
As oft as they their minds: though in full sight
    He stood, the puzzle only was increased;
The man was a phantasmagoria in   615
Himself—he was so volatile and thin.

22 "Junius" wrote against George III's government in the late 1760s and early 70s. He was probably Sir Philip Francis.

LXXVIII

The moment that you had pronounced him *one,*
    Presto! his face changed, and he was another;
And when that change was hardly well put on,
    It varied, till I don't think his own mother   620
(If that he had a mother) would her son
    Have known, he shifted so from one to t'other;
Till guessing from a pleasure grew a task,
At this epistolary "Iron Mask."

LXXIX

For sometimes he like Cerberus would seem—   625
    "Three gentlemen at once" (as sagely says
Good Mrs. Malaprop); then you might deem
    That he was not even *one;* now many rays
Were flashing round him; and now a thick steam
    Hid him from sight—like fogs on London   630
    days:
Now Burke, now Tooke, he grew to people's
    fancies,
And certes often like Sir Philip Francis.

LXXX

I've an hypothesis—'tis quite my own;
    I never let it out till now, for fear
Of doing people harm about the throne,   635
    And injuring some minister or peer,
On whom the stigma might perhaps be blown;
    It is—my gentle public, lend thine ear!
'Tis, that what Junius we are wont to call
Was *really, truly,* nobody at all.   640

LXXXI

I don't see wherefore letters should not be
    Written without hands, since we daily view
Them written without heads; and books, we see,
    Are fill'd as well without the latter too:
And really till we fix on somebody   645
    For certain sure to claim them as his due,
Their author, like the Niger's mouth, will bother
The world to say if *there* be mouth or author.

LXXXII

"And who and what art thou?" the Archangel
    said.
    "For *that* you may consult my title-page,"   650
Replied this mighty shadow of a shade:
    "If I have kept my secret half an age,

I scarce shall tell it now."—"Canst thou upbraid,"
   Continued Michael, "George Rex, or allege
Aught further?" Junius answer'd, "You had better   655
First ask him for *his* answer to my letter:

LXXXIII

"My charges upon record will outlast
   The brass of both his epitaph and tomb."
"Repent'st thou not," said Michael, "of some past
   Exaggeration? something which may doom   660
Thyself if false, as him if true? Thou wast
   Too bitter—is it not so?—in thy gloom
Of passion?"—"Passion!" cried the phantom dim,
"I loved my country, and I hated him.

LXXXIV

"What I have written, I have written: let   665
   The rest be on his head or mine!" So spoke
Old "Nominis Umbra;" and while speaking yet,[23]
   Away he melted in celestial smoke.
Then Satan said to Michael, "Don't forget
   To call George Washington, and John Horne   670
     Tooke,[24]
And Franklin;"—but at this time there was heard
A cry for room, though not a phantom stirr'd.

LXXXV

At length with jostling, elbowing, and the aid
   Of cherubim appointed to that post,
The devil Asmodeus to the circle made[25]   675
   His way, and look'd as if his journey cost
Some trouble. When his burden down he laid,[26]
   "What's this?" cried Michael; "why, 'tis not a
     ghost?"
"I know it," quoth the incubus; "but he
Shall be one, if you leave the affair to me.   680

LXXXVI

"Confound the renegado! I have sprain'd
   My left wing, he's so heavy; one would think
Some of his works about his neck were chain'd.
   But to the point; while hovering o'er the brink

Of Skiddaw (where as usual it still rain'd),[27]   685
   I saw a taper, far below me, wink,
And stooping, caught this fellow at a libel—
No less on history than the Holy Bible.

LXXXVII

"The former is the devil's scripture, and
   The latter yours, good Michael: so the affair   690
Belongs to all of us, you understand.
   I snatch'd him up just as you see him there,
And brought him off for sentence out of hand:
   I've scarcely been ten minutes in the air—
At least a quarter it can hardly be: 695
I dare say that his wife is still at tea."

LXXXVIII

Here Satan said, "I know this man of old,
   And have expected him for some time here;
A sillier fellow you will scarce behold,
   Or more conceited in his petty sphere: 700
But surely it was not worth while to fold
   Such trash below your wing, Asmodeus dear:
We had the poor wretch safe (without being
     bored
With carriage) coming of his own accord.

LXXXIX

"But since he's here, let's see what he has done."   705
   "Done!" cried Asmodeus, "he anticipates
The very business you are now upon,
   And scribbles as if head clerk to the Fates.
Who knows to what his ribaldry may run,
   When such an ass as this, like Balaam's,   710
     prates?"[28]
"Let's hear," quoth Michael, "what he has to say:
You know we're bound to that in every way."

XC

Now the bard, glad to get an audience, which
   By no means often was his case below,
Began to cough, and hawk, and hem, and pitch   715
   His voice into that awful note of woe
To all unhappy hearers within reach
   Of poets when the tide of rhyme's in flow;
But stuck fast with his first hexameter,
Not one of all whose gouty feet would stir.   720

---

23 *Stat Nominis Umbra,* "a shadow stands in place of the name," the motto for the collection of his polemical letters.
24 Tooke was another opponent of government policy, and identified with liberal causes.
25 Asmodeus, the Jewish "king of the demons," sometimes associated with Beelzebub or Apollyon.
26 His burden is Southey.

---

27 Skiddaw, a Lake District mountain. Southey lived in the Lake District.
28 See Numbers 22:28.

XCI

But ere the spavin'd dactyls could be spurr'd
    Into recitative, in great dismay
Both cherubim and seraphim were heard
    To murmur loudly through their long array;
And Michael rose ere he could get a word   725
    Of all his founder'd verses under way,
And cried, "For God's sake stop, my friend! 'twere
        best—
Non Di, non homines—you know the rest."[29]

XCII

A general bustle spread throughout the throng,
    Which seem'd to hold all verse in detestation;   730
The angels had of course enough of song
    When upon service; and the generation
Of ghosts had heard too much in life, not long
    Before, to profit by a new occasion:
The monarch, mute till then, exclaim'd, "What!   735
        what!
Pye come again? No more—no more of that!"[30]

XCIII

The tumult grew; an universal cough
    Convulsed the skies, as during a debate,
When Castlereagh has been up long enough[31]
    (Before he was first minister of state,   740
I mean—the *slaves hear now*); some cried "Off,
        off!"
    As at a farce; till, grown quite desperate,
The bard Saint Peter pray'd to interpose
(Himself an author) only for his prose.

XCIV

The varlet was not an ill-favour'd knave;   745
    A good deal like a vulture in the face,
With a hook nose and a hawk's eye, which gave
    A smart and sharper-looking sort of grace
To his whole aspect, which, though rather grave,
    Was by no means so ugly as his case;   750
But that, indeed, was hopeless as can be,
Quite a poetic felony *"de se."*[32]

---

[29] "Neither gods nor men can put up with a bad poet."—
Horace, *The Art of Poetry.*
[30] Henry James Pye, Southey's predecessor as laureate.
[31] Viscount Castlereagh was foreign secretary from 1812
to 1822. He represented Britain at the Congress of Vienna
and was identified with repression and reaction, in Byron's
view.   [32] Suicide.

XCV

Then Michael blew his trump, and still'd the
        noise
    With one still greater, as is yet the mode
On earth besides; except some grumbling voice,   755
    Which now and then will make a slight inroad
Upon decorous silence, few will twice
    Lift up their lungs when fairly overcrow'd;
And now the bard could plead his own bad cause,
With all the attitudes of self-applause.   760

XCVI

He said—(I only give the heads)—he said,
    He meant no harm in scribbling; 'twas his way
Upon all topics; 'twas, besides, his bread,
    Of which he butter'd both sides; 'twould
        delay
Too long the assembly (he was pleased to dread), 765
    And take up rather more time than a day,
To name his works—he would but cite a few—
"Wat Tyler"—"Rhymes on Blenheim"—"Water-
        loo."

XCVII

He had written praises of a regicide;
    He had written praises of all kings what ever;   770
He had written for republics far and wide,
    And then against them bitterer than ever:
For pantisocracy he once had cried[33]
    Aloud, a scheme less moral than 'twas clever;
Then grew a hearty anti-jacobin—   775
Had turn'd his coat—and would have turn'd his
        skin.

XCVIII

He had sung against all battles, and again
    In their high praise and glory; he had call'd
Reviewing "the ungentle craft," and then
    Become as base a critic as e'er crawl'd—   780
Fed, paid, and pamper'd by the very men
    By whom his muse and morals had been
        maul'd:
He had written much blank verse, and blanker
        prose
And more of both than anybody knows.

---

[33] Pantisocracy: Southey's abortive scheme, as a young
man, to establish an ideal colony in the United States
with Coleridge and others.

XCIX

He had written Wesley's life:—here turning 785
    round
  To Satan, "Sir, I'm ready to write yours,
In two octavo volumes, nicely bound,
  With notes and preface, all that most allures
The pious purchaser; and there's no ground
For fear, for I can choose my own reviewers: 790
So let me have the proper documents,
That I may add you to my other saints."

C

Satan bow'd, and was silent. "Well, if you,
  With amiable modesty, decline
My offer, what says Michael? There are few 795
  Whose memoirs could be render'd more divine.
Mine is a pen of all work; not so new
  As it was once, but I would make you shine
Like your own trumpet. By the way, my own
Has more of brass in it, and is as well blown. 800

CI

"But talking about trumpets, here's my Vision!
  Now you shall judge, all people; yes, you shall
Judge with my judgment, and by my decision
  Be guided who shall enter heaven or fall.
I settle all these things by intuition, 805
  Times present, past, to come, heaven, hell, and
    all,
Like King Alfonso. When I thus see double,
I save the Deity some worlds of trouble."[34]

CII

He ceased, and drew forth an MS.; and no
  Persuasion on the part of devils, saints, 810
Or angels, now could stop the torrent; so
  He read the first three lines of the contents;
But at the fourth, the whole spiritual show
  Had vanish'd, with variety of scents,
Ambrosial and sulphureous, as they sprang, 815
Like lightning, off from his "melodious twang."[35]

CIII

Those grand heroics acted as a spell:
  The angels stopp'd their ears and plied their
    pinions;
The devils ran howling, deafen'd, down to hell;
  The ghosts fled, gibbering, for their own do- 820
    minions—
(For 'tis not yet decided where they dwell,
  And I leave every man to his opinions);
Michael took refuge in his trump—but, lo!
His teeth were set on edge, he could not blow!

CIV

Saint Peter, who has hitherto been known 825
  For an impetuous saint, upraised his keys,
And at the fifth line knock'd the poet down;
  Who fell like Phaëton, but more at ease,[36]
Into his lake, for there he did not drown;
  A different web being by the Destinies 830
Woven for the Laureate's final wreath, whene'er
Reform shall happen either here or there.

CV

He first sank to the bottom—like his works,
  But soon rose to the surface—like himself;
For all corrupted things are buoy'd like corks, 835
  By their own rottenness, light as an elf,
Or wisp that flits o'er a morass: he lurks,
  It may be, still, like dull books on a shelf,
In his own den, to scrawl some "Life" or "Vi-
    sion,"
As Welborn says—"the devil turn'd precisian."[37] 840

CVI

As for the rest, to come to the conclusion
  Of this true dream, the telescope is gone
Which kept my optics free from all delusion,
  And show'd me what I in my turn have shown;
All I saw farther, in the last confusion, 845
  Was, that King George slipp'd into heaven
    for one;
And when the tumult dwindled to a calm,
I left him practising the hundredth psalm.

---

34 Byron's note: "King Alfonso of Castile, speaking of the Ptolemaic system, said that 'had he been consulted at the creation of the world, he would have spared the Maker some absurdities.'"
35 Byron is referring to an anecdote in the works of the seventeenth-century writer John Aubrey, in which a ghost made such a noise as it disappeared.

36 Apollo's son.
37 A character from a play by Philip Massinger, a seventeenth-century playwright. A "precisian" is a Puritan.

On This Day I Complete My Thirty-Sixth Year

'Tis time this heart should be unmoved,
    Since others it hath ceased to move:
Yet, though I cannot be beloved,
    Still let me love!

My days are in the yellow leaf;[1]   5
    The flowers and fruits of Love are gone;
The worm, the canker, and the grief
    Are mine alone!

The fire that on my bosom preys
    Is lone as some Volcanic isle;   10
No torch is kindled at its blaze—
    A funeral pile.

The hope, the fear, the jealous care,
    The exalted portion of the pain
And power of love, I cannot share,   15
    But wear the chain.

But 'tis not *thus*—and 'tis not *here*—
    Such thoughts should shake my soul, nor *now*,
Where Glory decks the hero's bier,
    Or binds his brow.   20

The Sword, the Banner, and the Field,
    Glory and Greece, around me see!
The Spartan, borne upon his shield,[2]
    Was not more free.

Awake! (not Greece—she *is* awake!)   25
    Awake, my spirit! Think through *whom*
Thy life-blood tracks its parent lake,
    And then strike home!

Tread those reviving passions down,
    Unworthy manhood!—unto thee   30
Indifferent should the smile or frown
    Of Beauty be.

If thou regret'st thy youth, *why live?*
    The land of honourable death
Is here:—up to the Field, and give   35
    Away thy breath!

Seek out—less often sought than found—
    A soldier's grave, for thee the best;
Then look around, and choose thy ground,
    And take thy Rest.   40

---

1 Cf. *Macbeth*, V, iii, 23.—Byron wrote this poem at Missolonghi on Jan. 22, 1824, less than three months before he died.
2 I.e., killed doing his duty, and carried home on his shield.

Letters

I. TO FRANCIS HODGSON[1]

JULY 16, 1809

Lisbon

Thus far have we pursued our route, and seen all sorts of marvellous sights, palaces, convents, etc.;—which, being to be heard in my friend Hobhouse's[2] forthcoming Book of Travels, I shall not anticipate by smuggling any account whatsoever to you in a private and clandestine manner. I must just observe that the village of Cintra in Estremadura[3] is the most beautiful, perhaps, in the world.

I am very happy here, because I loves oranges, and talks bad Latin to the monks, who understand it, as it is like their own,—and I goes into society (with my pocket-pistols), and I swims in the Tagus all across at once, and I rides on an ass or a mule, and swears Portuguese, and have got a diarrhoea and bites from the mosquitoes. But what of that? Comfort must not be expected by folks that go a pleasuring. . . .

Hodgson! send me the news, and the deaths and defeats and capital crimes and the misfortunes of one's friends; and let us hear of literary matters, and the controversies and the criticisms. All this will be pleasant—*Suave mari magno*,[4] etc. Talking of that, I have been sea-sick, and sick of the sea. Adieu.

Yours faithfully, etc.

---

1 Hodgson (1781–1852), a son-in-law of Byron's headmaster at Harrow, was a minor but prolific man of letters and one of the poet's best friends. In 1813 Byron enabled him to marry by presenting him with £1000. He was afterwards a country parson and eventually Provost of Eton.
2 John Cam Hobhouse (1786–1869), Byron's traveling companion, lifelong friend, and executor. He afterward held important ministerial posts in the British government.
3 The Portuguese, not the Spanish, province.
4 The opening words of Lucretius, *De Rerum Natura*, Book II: "It is sweet when on the great sea [the winds trouble the waters, to behold from the land the great hardship of someone else; not because there is pleasure to be had from anyone's being afflicted, but because it is sweet to see from what evils one is free]."

II. TO HIS MOTHER

NOVEMBER 12, 1809

Prevesa[5]

My dear Mother,—

I have now been some time in Turkey: this place is on the coast, but I have traversed the interior of the province of Albania on a visit to the Pacha. I left Malta in the *Spider,* a brig of war, on the 21st of September, and arrived in eight days at Prevesa. I thence have been about 50 miles, as far as Tepaleen, his Highness's country palace, where I stayed three days. The name of the Pacha is *Ali,*[6] and he is considered a man of the first abilities: he governs the whole of Albania (the ancient Illyricum), Epirus, and part of Macedonia. His son, Vely Pacha, to whom he has given me letters, governs the Morea,[7] and has great influence in Egypt; in short, he is one of the most powerful men in the Ottoman empire. When I reached Yanina,[8] the capital, after a journey of three days over the mountains, through a country of the most picturesque beauty, I found that Ali Pacha was with his army in Illyricum, besieging Ibrahim Pacha in the castle of Berat.[9] He had heard that an Englishman of rank was in his dominions, and had left orders in Yanina with the commandant to provide a house, and supply me with every kind of necessary *gratis;* and, though I have been allowed to make presents to the slaves, etc., I have not been permitted to pay for a single article of household consumption.

I rode out on the vizier's[10] horses, and saw the palaces of himself and grandsons: they are splendid, but too much ornamented with silk and gold. I then went over the mountains through Zitza, a village with a Greek monastery (where I slept on my return), in the most beautiful situation (always excepting Cintra, in Portugal) I ever beheld. In nine days I reached Tepaleen.[11] Our journey was much prolonged by the torrents that had fallen from the moun-tains, and intersected the roads. I shall never forget the singular scene on entering Tepaleen at five in the afternoon, as the sun was going down. It brought to my mind (with some change of *dress,* however) Scott's description of Branksome Castle in his *Lay,*[12] and the feudal system. The Albanians, in their dresses (the most magnificent in the world, consisting of a long *white kilt,* gold-worked cloak, crimson velvet gold-laced jacket and waistcoat, silver-mounted pistols and daggers), the Tartars with their high caps, the Turks in the vast pelisses[13] and turbans, the soldiers and black slaves with the horses, the former in groups in an immense large open gallery in front of the palace, the latter placed in a kind of cloister below it, two hundred steeds ready caparisoned to move in a moment, couriers entering or passing out with the despatches, the kettle-drums beating, boys calling the hour from the minaret of the mosque, altogether, with the singular appearance of the building itself, formed a new and delightful spectacle to a stranger. I was conducted to a very handsome apartment, and my health inquired after by the vizier's secretary, *à-la-mode Turque!*[14]

The next day I was introduced to Ali Pacha. I was dressed in a full suit of staff uniform, with a very magnificent sabre, etc. The vizier received me in a large room paved with marble; a fountain was playing in the centre; the apartment was surrounded by scarlet ottomans.[15] He received me standing, a wonderful compliment from a Mussulman, and made me sit down on his right hand. I have a Greek interpreter for general use, but a physician of Ali's named Femlario, who understands Latin, acted for me on this occasion. His first question was, why, at so early an age, I left my country?—(the Turks have no idea of travelling for amusement). He then said, the English minister,[16] Captain Leake, had told him I was of a great family, and desired his respects to my mother; which I now, in the name of Ali Pacha, present to you. He said he was certain I was a man of birth, because I had small ears, curling hair, and little white hands, and expressed himself pleased with my

---

[5] In northwestern Greece, then a part of the Turkish Empire.
[6] Known as the Rob Roy of Albania, the tyrant Ali (1741–1822) was a brilliant soldier and administrator.
[7] Southern Greece, the peninsula of Peloponnesus.
[8] Ioannina, at the foot of the Pindus Mountains in northwestern Greece (Epirus). [9] In central Albania.
[10] Ali was nominally the Turkish governor.
[11] Tepelini, in southern Albania, on the way to Berat.

[12] *The Lay of the Last Minstrel,* Canto I.
[13] Furred cloaks.
[14] In Turkish style. [15] Backless couches.
[16] An emissary of the British government, which aided Ali with munitions.

appearance and garb. He told me to consider him as a father whilst I was in Turkey, and said he looked on me as his son. Indeed, he treated me like a child, sending me almonds and sugared sherbet, fruit and sweetmeats, twenty times a day. He begged me to visit him often, and at night, when he was at leisure. I then, after coffee and pipes, retired for the first time. I saw him thrice afterwards. It is singular that the Turks, who have no hereditary dignities, and few great families, except the Sultans, pay so much respect to birth; for I found my pedigree more regarded than my title.

To-day I saw the remains of the town of Actium,[17] near which Antony lost the world, in a small bay, where two frigates could hardly manoeuvre: a broken wall is the sole remnant. On another part of the gulf stand the ruins of Nicopolis, built by Augustus in honour of his victory. Last night I was at a Greek marriage; but this and a thousand things more I have neither time nor *space* to describe. . . .

I am going to-morrow, with a guard of fifty men, to Patras[18] in the Morea, and thence to Athens, where I shall winter. Two days ago I was nearly lost in a Turkish ship of war, owing to the ignorance of the captain and crew, though the storm was not violent. Fletcher[19] yelled after his wife, the Greeks called on all the saints, the Mussulmans on Alla; the captain burst into tears and ran below deck, telling us to call on God; the sails were split, the main-yard shivered, the wind blowing fresh, the night setting in, and all our chance was to make Corfu, which is in possession of the French, or (as Fletcher pathetically termed it) "a watery grave." I did what I could to console Fletcher, but finding him incorrigible, wrapped myself up in my Albanian capote (an immense cloak), and lay down on deck to wait the worst. I have learnt to philosophise in my travels; and if I had not, complaint was useless. Luckily the wind abated, and only drove us on the coast of Suli, on the main land, where we landed, and proceeded, by the help of the natives, to Prevesa again; but I shall not trust Turkish sailors in future, though the Pacha had ordered one of his own galliots[20] to take me to Patras. I am therefore going as far as Missolonghi by land, and there have only to cross a small gulf to get to Patras.

Fletcher's next epistle will be full of marvels. We were one night lost for nine hours in the mountains in a thunder-storm, and since nearly wrecked. In both cases Fletcher was sorely bewildered, from apprehensions of famine and banditti in the first, and drowning in the second instance. His eyes were a little hurt by the lightning, or crying (I don't know which), but are now recovered. When you write, address to me at Mr. Strané's, English consul, Patras, Morea.

I could tell you I know not how many incidents that I think would amuse you, but they crowd on my mind as much as they would swell my paper, and I can neither arrange them in the one, nor put them down on the other, except in the greatest confusion. I like the Albanians much; they are not all Turks; some tribes are Christians. But their religion makes little difference in their manner or conduct. They are esteemed the best troops in the Turkish service. I lived on my route, two days at once, and three days again, in a barrack at Salora, and never found soldiers so tolerable, though I have been in the garrisons of Gibraltar and Malta, and seen Spanish, French, Sicilian, and British troops in abundance. I have had nothing stolen, and was always welcome to their provision and milk. Not a week ago an Albanian chief, (every village has its chief, who is called Primate), after helping us out of the Turkish galley in her distress, feeding us, and lodging my suite, consisting of Fletcher, a Greek, two Athenians, a Greek priest, and my companion, Mr. Hobhouse, refused any compensation but a written paper stating that I was well received; and when I pressed him to accept a few sequins,[21] "No," he replied; "I wish you to love me, not to pay me." These are his words. . . .

I am going to Athens, to study modern Greek, which differs much from the ancient, though radically similar. I have no desire to return to England, nor shall I, unless compelled by absolute want, and Hanson's[22] neglect; but I

---

[17] Off which, in the famous battle of 31 B.C., Antony and Cleopatra were defeated by the fleet of Octavius, the future emperor Augustus.
[18] Near the entrance to the Gulf of Corinth.
[19] William Fletcher, Byron's valet; he was with Byron till the end came at Missolonghi.

[20] Small, swift galleys, using both sails and oars.
[21] A gold coin worth about $2.25.
[22] John Hanson, Byron's solicitor.

shall not enter into Asia for a year or two, as I have much to see in Greece, and I may perhaps cross into Africa, at least the Egyptian part. Fletcher, like all Englishmen, is very much dissatisfied, though a little reconciled to the Turks by a present of eighty piastres from the vizier, which, if you consider every thing, and the value of specie here, is nearly worth ten guineas English. He has suffered nothing but from cold, heat, and vermin, which those who lie in cottages and cross mountains in a cold country must undergo, and of which I have equally partaken with himself; but he is not valiant, and is afraid of robbers and tempests. I have no one to be remembered to in Enland, and wish to hear nothing from it, but that you are well, and a letter or two on business from Hanson, whom you may tell to write. I will write when I can, and beg you to believe me,

Your affectionate son,
Byron

III. TO THOMAS MOORE

SEPT. 20, 1814

Newstead Abbey

Here's to her who long
  Hath waked the poet's sigh!
The girl who gave to song
  What gold could never buy.

My dear Moore,—I am going to be married—that is, I am accepted, and one usually hopes the rest will follow. My mother of the Gracchi[23] (that *are* to be) *you* think too strait-laced for me, although the paragon of only children, and invested with "golden opinions of all sorts of men,"[24] and full of "most blest conditions"[25] as Desdemona herself. Miss Milbanke is the lady, and I have her father's invitation to proceed there[26] in my elect capacity,—which, however, I cannot do till I have settled some business in London, and got a blue coat.

She is said to be an heiress, but of that I know nothing certainly, and shall not enquire. But I do know, that she has talents and excellent qualities; and you will not deny her judgment, after having refused six suitors and taken me.

Now, if you have any thing to say against this, pray do; my mind's made up, positively fixed, determined, and therefore I will listen to reason, because now it can do no harm. Things may occur to break it off, but I will hope not. In the mean time, I tell you (a *secret,* by the by, —at least, till I know she wishes it to be public) that I have proposed and am accepted. You need not be in a hurry to wish me joy, for one mayn't be married for months. I am going to town tomorrow: but expect to be here, on my way there, within a fortnight.

If this had not happened, I should have gone to Italy. In my way down,[27] perhaps, you will meet me at Nottingham, and come over with me here. I need not say that nothing will give me greater pleasure. I must, of course, reform thoroughly; and, seriously, if I can contribute to her happiness, I shall secure my own. She is so good a person, that—that—in short, I wish I was a better.

Ever, etc.

IV. TO THOMAS MOORE

JANUARY 28, 1817

Venice

Your letter of the 8th is before me. The remedy for your plethora is simple—abstinence. I was obliged to have recourse to the like some years ago, I mean in point of *diet,* and, with the exception of some convivial weeks and days, (it might be months, now and then), have kept to Pythagoras[28] ever since. For all this, let me hear that you are better. You must not *indulge* in "filthy beer," nor in porter, nor eat *suppers*— the last are the devil to those who swallow dinner. . . .

I am truly sorry to hear of your father's misfortune—cruel at any time, but doubly cruel in advanced life.[29] However, you will, at least,

---

23 "Cornelia, the Mother of the Gracchi" was the simple inscription on a statue to the memory of this Roman matron of the second century B.C., famous for her remark to a visiting lady who asked to see her jewels, "These are my jewels," as she presented her children. Her sons, Tiberius and Gaius Gracchus, lost their lives through political activities as democratic leaders.
24 Cf. *Macbeth,* I, vii, 33.   25 Cf. *Othello,* II, i, 255.
26 To the Milbankes' house in the county of Durham. The proposal and acceptance were by letter.

---

27 From London, i.e. (here), northward.
28 To this Greek philosopher and mathematician of the sixth century B.C. was ascribed the doctrine that the end of earthly existence is purification of the soul.
29 The elder Moore, formerly a grocer and wine dealer,

have the satisfaction of doing your part by him, and, depend upon it, it will not be in vain. Fortune, to be sure, is a female, but not such a b—[30] as the rest (always excepting your wife and my sister from such sweeping terms); for she generally has some justice in the long run. I have no spite against her, though, between her and Nemesis, I have had some sore gauntlets to run —but then I have done my best to deserve no better. But to *you,* she is a good deal in arrear, and she will come round—mind if she don't: you have the vigour of life, of independence, of talent, spirit, and character all with you. What you can do for yourself, you have done and will do; and surely there are some others in the world who would not be sorry to be of use, if you would allow them to be useful, or at least attempt it.

I think of being in England in the spring. If there is a row, by the sceptre of King Ludd,[31] but I'll be one;[32] and if there is none, and only a continuance of "this meek,[33] piping time of peace," I will take a cottage a hundred yards to the south of your abode, and become your neighbour; and we will compose such canticles, and hold such dialogues, as shall be the terror of the *Times* (including the newspaper of that name), and the wonder, and honour, and praise of the *Morning Chronicle*[34] and posterity.

I rejoice to hear of your forthcoming[35] in February—though I tremble for the "magnificence," which you attribute to the new *Childe Harold.* I am glad you like it; it is a fine indistinct piece of poetical desolation, and my favourite. I was half mad during the time of its composition, between metaphysics, mountains, lakes, love unextinguishable, thoughts unutterable, and the nightmare of my own delinquencies. I should, many a good day, have blown my brains out, but for the recollection that it would

have given pleasure to my mother-in-law; and, even *then,* if I could have been certain to haunt her—but I won't dwell upon these trifling family matters.

Venice is in the *estro*[36] of her carnival, and I have been up these last two nights at the ridotto[37] and the opera, and all that kind of thing. Now for an adventure. A few days ago a gondolier brought me a billet without a subscription,[38] intimating a wish on the part of the writer to meet me either in gondola, or at the island of San Lazaro, or at a third rendezvous, indicated in the note. "I know the country's disposition well"—in Venice "they do let Heaven see those tricks they dare not show,"[39] etc., etc.; so, for all response, I said that neither of the three places suited me; but that I would either be at home at ten at night *alone,* or be at the ridotto at midnight, where the writer might meet me masked. At ten o'clock I was at home and alone (Marianna[40] was gone with her husband to a conversazione[41]), when the door of my apartment opened, and in walked a well-looking and (for an Italian) *bionda*[42] girl of about nineteen, who informed me that she was married to the brother of my *amorosa,* and wished to have some conversation with me. I made a decent reply, and we had some talk in Italian and Romaic[43] (her mother being a Greek of Corfu), when, lo! in a very few minutes, in marches, to my very great astonishment, Marianna Segati, *in propria persona,*[44] and, after making a most polite courtesy to her sister-in-law and to me, without a single word seizes her said sister-in-law by the hair, and bestows upon her some sixteen slaps, which would have made your ear ache only to hear their echo. I need not describe the screaming which ensued. The luckless visitor took flight. I seized Marianna, who, after several vain efforts to get away in pursuit of the enemy, fairly went into fits in my arms; and, in spite of reasoning, eau de Cologne, vinegar, half a pint of water, and God knows what other waters beside, continued so till past midnight.

After damning my servants for letting peo-

had been dismissed from his post as barrack-master at Dublin.

[30] Thus the Prothero edition, without indicating whether the abbreviation is Byron's or an editor's.
[31] A legendary king of ancient Britain.
[32] Take part in it. The allusion is doubtless to the possibility that the widespread radical agitation might lead to violence.
[33] Shakespeare wrote "weak" (*Richard III,* I, i, 24).
[34] The *Times* was Tory, the *Chronicle* Whig.
[35] The long-delayed publication of Moore's Oriental poem *Lalla Rookh,* though it was not for several months after this letter.

[36] Ardor.   [37] Masked ball.
[38] Note without a signature.   [39] *Othello, III,* iii, 201–03.
[40] Marianna Segati, one of Byron's current mistresses. She was the vicious and avaricious wife of the tradesman in whose house he lodged.   [41] I.e., social gathering.
[42] Blond.   [43] Modern Greek.   [44] In very person.

ple in without apprizing me, I found that Marianna in the morning had seen her sister-in-law's gondolier on the stairs, and, suspecting that his apparition boded her no good, had either returned of her own accord, or been followed by her maids or some other spy of her people to the conversazione, from whence she returned to perpetrate this piece of pugilism. I had seen fits before, and also some small scenery of the same genus in and out of our island: but this was not all. After about an hour, in comes—who? why, Signor Segati, her lord and husband, and finds me with his wife fainting upon a sofa, and all the apparatus of confusion, dishevelled hair, hats, handkerchiefs, salts, smelling bottles—and the lady as pale as ashes, without sense or motion. His first question was, "What is all this?" The lady could not reply—so I did. I told him the explanation was the easiest thing in the world; but, in the mean time, it would be as well to recover his wife—at least, her senses. This came about in due time of suspiration and respiration.

You need not be alarmed—jealousy is not the order of the day in Venice, and daggers are out of fashion; while duels, on love matters, are unknown—at least, with the husbands. But, for all this, it was an awkward affair; and though he must have known that I made love to Marianna, yet I believe he was not, till that evening, aware of the extent to which it had gone. It is very well known that almost all the married women have a lover; but it is usual to keep up the forms, as in other nations. I did not, therefore, know what the devil to say. I could not out with the truth, out of regard to her, and I did not choose to lie for my sake;—besides, the thing told itself. I thought the best way would be to let her explain it as she chose (a woman being never at a loss—the devil always sticks by them)—only determining to protect and carry her off, in case of any ferocity on the part of the Signor. I saw that he was quite calm. She went to bed, and next day —how they settled it, I know not, but settle it they did. Well—then I had to explain to Marianna about this never-to-be-sufficiently-confounded sister-in-law; which I did by swearing innocence, eternal constancy, etc., etc. . . .[45] But the sister-in-law, very much discomposed with being treated in such wise, has (not having her own shame before her eyes) told the affair to half Venice, and the servants (who were summoned by the fight and the fainting) to the other half. But, here, nobody minds such trifles, except to be amused by them. I don't know whether you will be so, but I have scrawled a long letter out of these follies.

Believe me ever, etc.

V. TO JOHN MURRAY

APRIL 6, 1819

Venice

Dear Sir,—The Second Canto of *Don Juan* was sent, on Saturday last, by post, in 4 packets, two of 4, and two of three sheets each, containing in all two hundred and seventeen stanzas, octave measure. But I will permit no curtailments, except those mentioned about Castlereagh and the two *Bobs*[46] in the Introduction. You sha'n't make *Canticles* of my Cantos. The poem will please, if it is lively; if it is stupid, it will fail: but I will have none of your damned cutting and slashing. If you please, you may publish *anonymously;* it will perhaps be better; but I will battle my way against them all, like a Porcupine.

So you and Mr. Foscolo,[47] etc., want me to undertake what you call a "great work"? an Epic Poem, I suppose, or some such pyramid. I'll try no such thing; I hate tasks. And then "seven or eight years"! God send us all well this day three months, let alone years. If one's years can't be better employed than in sweating poesy, a man had better be a ditcher. And works, too! —is *Childe Harold* nothing? You have so many "*divine*" poems, is it nothing to have written a *Human* one? without any of your worn-out machinery. Why, man, I could have spun the

---

45 See note 30.

46 Robert Southey, the poet laureate, and Robert Stewart, better known as Viscount Castlereagh than by his subsequent title of Marquis of Londonderry. It was Castlereagh who sent Napoleon to St. Helena; he was foreign secretary and leader of the House of Commons from 1812 till his suicide in 1822.

47 This letter was in answer to one from Murray, Byron's publisher, on March 19. Ugo Foscolo (1778–1827), Italian writer, patriot, soldier in the Napoleonic armies, and professor at Padua, was now a refugee in England. Murray had written: "Here is Foscolo at my side, deploring that a man of your genius will not occupy some six or eight years in the composition of a work and subject worthy of you."

thoughts of the four cantos of that poem into twenty, had I wanted to book-make, and its passion into as many modern tragedies. Since you want *length,* you shall have enough of *Juan,* for I'll make 50 cantos.

And Foscolo, too! Why does *he* not do something more than the *Letters of Ortis,*[48] and a tragedy, and pamphlets? He has good fifteen years more at his command than I have: what has he done all that time?—proved his Genius, doubtless, but not fixed its fame, nor done his utmost.

Besides, I mean to write my best work in *Italian,* and it will take me nine years more thoroughly to master the language; and then if my fancy exists, and I exist too, I will try what I *can* do *really.* As to the Estimation of the English which you talk of,[49] let them calculate what it is worth, before they insult me with their insolent condescension.

I have not written for their pleasure. If they are pleased, it is that they chose to be so; I have never flattered their opinions, nor their pride; nor will I. Neither will I make "Ladies' books" *al dilettar le femine e la plebe.*[50] I have written from the fullness of my mind, from passion, from impulse, from many motives, but not for their "sweet voices."

I know the precise worth of popular applause, for few Scribblers have had more of it; and if I chose to swerve into their paths, I could retain it, or resume it, or increase it. But I neither love ye, nor fear ye; and though I buy with ye and sell with ye, and talk with ye, I will neither eat with ye, drink with ye, nor pray with ye.[51] They made me, without my search, a species of popular Idol; they, without reason or judgment, beyond the caprice of their good pleasure, threw down the Image from its pedestal; it was not broken with the fall, and they would, it seems, again replace it—but they shall not.

You ask about my health: about the beginning of the year I was in a state of great exhaustion, attended by such debility of Stomach that nothing remained upon it; and I was obliged to reform my "way of life," which was conducting me from the "yellow leaf"[52] to the Ground, with all deliberate speed. I am better in health and morals, and very much yours ever,

B[n.]

VI.   TO THE COUNTESS GUICCIOLI

AUGUST 25, 1819

Bologna

My dear Teresa,—

I have read this book[53] in your garden;—my love, you were absent, or else I could not have read it. It is a favourite book of yours, and the writer was a friend of mine. You will not understand these English words, and *others* will not understand them—which is the reason I have not scrawled them in Italian. But you will recognize the hand-writing of him who passionately loved you, and you will divine that, over a book which was yours, he could only think of love. In that word, beautiful in all languages, but most so in yours—*Amor mio*[54]—is comprised my existence here and hereafter. I feel I exist here, and I fear that I shall exist hereafter,—to *what* purpose you will decide; my destiny rests with you, and you are a woman, seventeen years of age, and two out of a convent. I wish that you had stayed there, with all my heart,—or, at least, that I had never met you in your married state.

But all this is too late. I love you, and you love me,—at least, you *say so,* and *act* as if you *did* so, which last is a great consolation in all events. But *I* more than love you, and cannot cease to love you.

Think of me, sometimes, when the Alps and the ocean divide us,—but they never will, unless you *wish* it.

Byron

VII.   TO PERCY BYSSHE SHELLEY

APRIL 26, 1821

Ravenna

The child[55] continues doing well, and the ac-

---

[48] In which, in 1798, he expressed his disapproval of Napoleon's handing Venice over to Austria.
[49] Murray had written that he wished Byron would allow himself "to be fully aware" of the "high estimation" in which he was held by his countrymen.
[50] To delight the women and the mob.
[51] Cf. *The Merchant of Venice,* I, iii, 36–39.

[52] Cf. *Macbeth,* V, iii, 22–23.
[53] This letter was written on the last page of Teresa's copy of *Corinne,* a novel (1807) by Mme. de Staël, whom Byron had met and liked in London and Switzerland.
[54] My love.
[55] Byron's daughter by Claire Clairmont. Allegra was now four, and Byron had placed her in a convent.

counts are regular and favourable. It is gratifying to me that you and Mrs. Shelley do not disapprove of the step which I have taken, which is merely temporary.

I am very sorry to hear what you say of Keats—is it *actually* true? I did not think criticism had been so killing.[56] Though I differ from you essentially in your estimate of his performances, I so much abhor all unnecessary pain, that I would rather he had been seated on the highest peak of Parnassus than have perished in such a manner. Poor fellow! though with such inordinate self-love he would probably have not been very happy. I read the review of *Endymion* in the *Quarterly*. It was severe,—but surely not so severe as many reviews in that and other journals upon others.

I recollect the effect on me of the *Edinburgh* on my first poem; it was rage, and resistance, and redress—but not despondency nor despair. I grant that those are not amiable feelings; but, in this world of bustle and broil, and especially in the career of writing, a man should calculate upon his powers of *resistance* before he goes into the arena.

Expect not life from pain nor danger free,
Nor deem the doom of man reversed for thee.[57]

You know my opinion of *that second-hand* school of poetry. You also know my high opinion of your own poetry,—because it is of *no* school. I read *Cenci*[58]—but, besides that I think the *subject* essentially *undramatic*, I am not an admirer of our old dramatists *as models*. I deny that the English have hitherto had a drama at all. Your *Cenci*, however, was a work of power, and poetry. As to *my* drama,[59] pray revenge yourself upon it, by being as free as I have been with yours.

I have not yet got your *Prometheus*,[60] which I long to see. I have heard nothing of mine, and do not know that it is yet published. I have

published a pamphlet[61] on the Pope controversy, which you will not like. Had I known that Keats was dead—or that he was alive and so sensitive—I should have omitted some remarks[62] upon his poetry, to which I was provoked by his *attack* upon *Pope*,[63] and my disapprobation of *his own* style of writing.

You want me to undertake a great poem—I have not the inclination nor the power. As I grow older, the indifference—*not* to life, for we love it by instinct—but to the stimuli of life, increases. Besides, this late failure of the Italians[64] has latterly disappointed me for many reasons,—some public, some personal. My respects to Mrs. S.

Yours ever,
B

P.S. Could not you and I contrive to meet this summer? Could not you take a run here *alone?*

VIII. TO JOHN MURRAY

SEPTEMBER 24th 1821

Ravenna

Dear Murray—

I have been thinking over our late correspondence, and wish to propose to you the following articles for our future:—

1stly That you shall write to me of yourself, of the health, wealth, and welfare of all friends; but of *me* (*quoad*[65] *me*) little or nothing.

2dly That you shall send me Soda powders, tooth-powder, tooth-brushes, or any such antiodontalgic[66] or chemical articles, as heretofore, *ad libitum*,[67] upon being re-imbursed for the same.

3dly That you shall *not* send me any modern, or (as they are called) *new*, publications in *English whatsoever*, save and excepting any writing, prose or verse, of (or reasonably presumed to

56 Keats had died at Rome in February 1821. Already the legend was circulating that a severe review in the *Quarterly* in 1818 had caused his fatal illness.
57 Cf. Dr. Johnson, *The Vanity of Human Wishes*, lines 155–56.   58 Shelley's tragedy *The Cenci* (1819).
59 Byron's historical tragedy *Marino Faliero, Doge of Venice;* it had in fact been published five days before, though Byron did not yet know that.
60 Shelley's "lyrical drama," *Prometheus Unbound* (1820).

61 *Letter . . . on the Rev. W. L. Bowles's Strictures on the Life and Writings of Pope* (March 1821).
62 In *Observations upon "Observations." A Second Letter to John Murray* (written in March 1821 but not published till 1835).
63 In Keats's "Sleep and Poetry," lines 193–206.
64 Risings by the Neapolitans and the Piedmontese had recently been crushed by the Austrians.
65 As far as.   66 Anti-toothache.   67 As you please.

be of) Walter Scott, Crabbe,[68] Moore, Campbell,[69] Rogers,[70] Gifford,[71] Joanna Baillie,[72] Irving[73] (the American), Hogg,[74] Wilson (*Isle of Palms* man),[75] or *any* especial *single* work of fancy which is thought to be of considerable merit; *Voyages* and *travels,* provided that they are *neither in Greece, Spain, Asia Minor, Albania, nor Italy,* will be welcome. Having travelled the countries mentioned, I know that what is said of them can convey nothing farther which I desire to know about them. No other English works whatsoever.

4[thly] That you send me *no periodical works* whatsoever—*no Edinburgh, Quarterly, Monthly,* nor any Review, Magazine, or Newspapers, English or foreign, of any description.

5[thly] That you send me *no opinions* whatsoever, either *good, bad,* or *indifferent,* of yourself, or your friends, or others, concerning any work, or works, of mine, past, present, or to come.

6[thly] That all negotiations in matters of business between you and me pass through the medium of the Hon[ble] Douglas Kinnaird,[76] my friend and trustee, or Mr. Hobhouse,[77] as *Alter Ego,*[78] and tantamount to myself during my absence, or presence.

Some of these propositions may at first seem strange, but they are founded. The quantity of trash I have received as books is incalculable, and neither amused nor instructed. Reviews and Magazines are at the best but ephemeral and superficial reading: *who thinks* of the *grand article* of *last year* in any *given review?* In the next place, if they regard *myself,* they tend to increase *Egotism;* if favourable, I do not deny that the

praise *elates,* and if unfavourable, that the abuse *irritates*—the latter may conduct me to inflict a species of Satire, which would neither do good to you nor to your friends: *they* may smile *now,* and so may *you;* but if I took you all in hand, it would not be difficult to cut you up like gourds. I did as much by as powerful people at nineteen years old, and I know little as yet in three-and-thirty, which should prevent me from making all your ribs Gridirons for your hearts, if such were my propensity. But it is *not.* Therefore let me hear none of your provocations. If any thing occurs so very *gross* as to require my notice, I shall hear of it from my personal friends. For the rest, I merely request to be left in ignorance.

The same applies to opinions, *good, bad,* or *indifferent,* of persons in conversation or correspondence: these do not *interrupt,* but they *soil* the *current* of my *Mind.* I am sensitive enough, but *not* till I am *touched;* and *here* I am beyond the touch of the short arms of literary England, except the few feelers of the Polypus that crawl over the Channel in the way of Extract.

All these precautions *in* England would be useless: the libeller or the flatterer would there reach me in spite of all; but in Italy we know little of literary England, and think less, except what reaches us through some garbled and brief extract in some miserable Gazette. For *two years* (excepting two or three articles cut out and sent to *you,* by the post) I never read a newspaper which was not forced upon me by some accident, and know, upon the whole, as little of England as you all do of Italy, and God knows *that* is little enough, with all your travels, etc., etc., etc. The English travellers *know Italy* as *you* know Guernsey: how much is *that?*

If any thing occurs so violently gross or personal as requires notice, Mr. D[s] Kinnaird will let me *know;* but of *praise* I desire to hear *nothing.*

You will say, "to what tends all this?" I will answer THAT;—to keep my mind *free and unbiassed* by all paltry and personal irritabilities of praise or censure;—to let my Genius take its natural direction, while my feelings are like the dead, who know nothing and feel nothing of all or aught that is said or done in their regard.

If you can observe these conditions, you

---

[68] The realistic poet George Crabbe (1754–1832), author of *The Village,* etc. (See Volume I.)

[69] The popular poet (1777–1844). See page 265, footnote 41.

[70] The poet Samuel Rogers (1763–1855), author of *The Pleasures of Memory.*

[71] The critic and poet William Gifford (1756–1826), first editor (1809–24) of the *Quarterly Review.*

[72] Scottish playwright and poet (1762–1851).

[73] Washington Irving (1783–1859), whose romantic *The Sketch Book* had appeared in 1820.

[74] James Hogg, the Scottish poet and miscellaneous writer (1770–1835), called "the Ettrick Shepherd."

[75] The miscellaneous writer John Wilson, "Christopher North" (1785–1854); *The Isle of Palms* was his first volume of poetry.

[76] A banker, member of the Drury Lane committee, and trustee for Lady Byron's marriage settlement.

[77] See note 2 of this series.   [78] Other self.

will spare yourself and others some pain: let me not be worked upon to rise up; for if I do, it will not be for a little. If you can *not* observe these conditions, we shall cease to be correspondents, but *not friends;* for I shall always be

Yours ever and truly,
Byron

P.S.—I have taken these resolutions not from any irritation against *you* or *yours,* but simply upon reflection that all reading, either praise or censure, of myself has done me harm. When I was in Switzerland and Greece, I was out of the way of hearing either, and *how I wrote there!* In Italy I am out of the way of it too; but latterly, partly through my fault, and partly through your kindness in wishing to send me the *newest* and most periodical publications, I have had a crowd of reviews, etc., thrust upon me, which have bored me with their jargon, of one kind or another, and taken off my attention from greater objects. You have also sent me a parcel of trash of poetry, for no reason that I can conceive, unless to provoke me to write a new *English Bards.* Now *this* I wish to avoid; for if ever I *do,* it will be a strong production; and I desire peace, as long as the fools will keep their nonsense out of my way.

IX. TO JOHN MURRAY
AUGUST 3ᵈ 1822

Pisa

Dear Sir,—

. . . I presume you have heard that Mr. Shelley and Capt. Williams[79] were lost on the 7ᵗʰ Ultᵒ [80] in their passage from Leghorn to Spezia in their own open boat. You may imagine the state of their families: I never saw such a scene, nor wish to see such another.

You were all brutally mistaken about Shelley, who was, without exception, the *best* and least selfish man I ever knew. I never knew one who was not a beast in comparison.

Yours ever,
N. B.[81]

---

79 Edward Williams, a friend of Byron and Shelley, was lost on the final voyage of the latter's yacht.
80 Ultimo, last; i.e., of last month.
81 Lady Byron's uncle, Lord Wentworth, died in 1815, leaving a life interest in his property to her mother, Lady Milbanke, who then took the name Lady Noel. When his mother-in-law died early in 1822, Byron was a substantial beneficiary, since according to the terms of the separation his wife and he shared equally in the income from the property. He promptly added the surname Noel to his own.

Percy Bysshe Shelley
1792–1822

George Santayana says of Shelley that he was

one of these spokesmen of the a priori, *one of these nurslings of the womb, like a bee or a butterfly; a dogmatic, inspired, perfect, and incorrigible creature. He was innocent and cruel, swift and wayward, illuminated and blind. Being a finished child of nature, not a joint product, like most of us, of nature, history, and society, he abounded miraculously in his own clear sense, but was obtuse to the droll, miscellaneous lessons of fortune. The cannonade of hard, inexplicable facts that knocks into most of us what little wisdom we have left Shelley dazed and sore, perhaps, but uninstructed. When the storm was over, he began chirping again his own natural note. If the world continued to confine and beset him, he hated the world and gasped for freedom.*

What is primary in Shelley's poetry is the unremitting intensity of his idealism. This is primary in his life as well. His delight was to embody his sense of the ideal in absolute images of that ideal. The other side of the coin of his delight is the purity of his outrage against those institutions that, in his view, combined throughout history to prevent men from realizing the ideal in their actual experience. Between his delight and his outrage, to be sure, there are not many gradations of tone, which is to say that Shelley is not much interested in the ordinary condition of men, in the sense that the ordinary condition may be defined as a mixture of good and evil, pleasure and suffering. One of the things we probably mean when we say that we possess a humane literature is that most of our writers do in some sense accept, and even value, the mixed character of our actual experience in this world. It is what identifies us as being men. But Shelley is angelic in his radical vision, usually beautifully so, in the purity of his outrage and his delight:

> A heavy weight of hours has chained and
>   bowed
> One too like thee: tameless, and swift
>   and proud

Or:

IONE Sister, it is not earthly . . . How it glides
> Under the leaves! how on its head there
>   burns
> A light, like a green star, whose emerald
>   beams
> Are twined with its fair hair! how, as it
>   moves,
> The splendour drops in flakes upon the
>   grass!
> Know'st thou it?

PANTHEA It is the delicate spirit
> That guides the earth through Heaven.
>   From afar
> The populous constellations call that light
> The loveliest of the planets . . . .

Or:

SPIRIT OF THE HOUR
> My vision then grew clear, and I could see
> Into the mysteries of the universe.
> Dizzy as with delight I floated down,
> Winnowing the lightsome air with lan-
>   guid plumes,
> My coursers sought their birthplace in
>   the sun,
> Where they will live henceforth exempt
>   from toil,
> Pasturing flowers of vegetable fire . . . .

Such passages as these do "abound miraculously" in Shelley's "own clear sense," but one must say that their intensity, and the amazing delicacy achieved within that intensity, would not have been possible if he were not both "illuminated" and "blind," "obtuse to the droll, miscellaneous lessons of fortune."

But this is not the whole story. To say that Shelley is visionary—and being visionary in his way has its consequences—is not to deny the powerful and learned intelligence behind everything he wrote. Sometimes it even takes worldly and witty form, as in *Peter Bell the Third* or some passages of *The Masque of Anarchy*. Some of the lyrics conform to our formulation about the "angelic" character of Shelley's imagination, but not all of them, and these include some of the best. Santayana's formulations

Percy Bysshe Shelley (1792–1822). Engraved from an original portrait painted by Amelia Curran in 1819. *The Granger Collection.*

perhaps do not exclude, but they do not acknowledge those qualities in Shelley's poetry and prose which led George Bernard Shaw to think of him as a political and social hero, and to call him a significant influence on the labor movement in England. (And it has been argued—perhaps incorrectly—that *The Cenci*, Shelley's Shakespearean drama, demonstrates genuine dramatic powers.) Nevertheless, one should mainly emphasize Shelley's intensity, and his extraordinary power to turn that intensity into music; one should emphasize the uncompromising character of his imagination; and one should emphasize the cost of this, since his poetry seems to live mainly at its own extremes.

Shelley in his life is all of a piece with Shelley in his poetry. The unremitting intensity with which he sought to realize the ideal in the actual is what encouraged behavior of such sweetness and generosity as to lead Byron to say after his death: "You were all brutally mistaken about Shelley, who was, without exception, the *best* and least selfish man I ever knew. I never knew one who was not a beast in comparison." It also encouraged such behavior as the astonishingly blind and insensitive communications with his first wife after his desertion of her—or, in other cases, especially with women, the rapidity with which his idealization of them could alter to outrage and scorn.

Shelley was born in Sussex, the eldest child of a country squire, and the eldest grandson of a wealthy baronet. His father was a conventional and conservative man; true to his type, he was alarmed when it began to appear that his son was brilliant, fearless, and contemptuous of accepted religious, political, and ethical codes. Shelley began his preparation at an academy near London, where he acquired a permanent taste for the physical sciences, especially chemistry and electricity. Then he spent six years at Eton, spectacularly ill-adjusted to that atmosphere. At Oxford he was a puzzle to his fellow students and to the faculty, almost solitary, buried in reading of his own choice, always ready to raise his voice in vehement argument against all ideas and institutions that he considered inimical to freedom. He was only eighteen when his privately printed essay, *The Necessity of Atheism,* had the result of getting him and his friend Thomas Jefferson Hogg expelled from the university.

Shelley went up to London, where he became interested in Harriet Westbrook, a friend of his sisters' whom he thought a convert to his social views. Though he was opposed in principle to the institution of marriage, they eloped and were married. The marriage, which caused consternation and rage in both families, went badly almost from the start.

It was during this period that Shelley wrote *Queen Mab,* a long, bad, extremely interesting philosophical poem, which set forth in detail ethical and political ideas that Shelley maintained all his life. His ideas owe much to a number of different writers but were most directly indebted to the radical thinker William Godwin, whose book *Political Justice* held that the ills of modern society derive from the imperfections of institutions and not from man himself, who is inherently good. With all its faults, *Queen Mab* became an influential document in the history of English political and social thought.

In the spring of 1814 Shelley fell in love with Godwin's daughter Mary, the daughter also of Mary Wollstonecraft. Godwin was infuriated, though his fury did not prevent him from sponging on Shelley for nearly the rest of Shelley's life. Shelley and Mary were not married until the end of 1816, after the squalid and pitiable suicide of Shelley's first wife. Though the relationship between Shelley and Harriet had been complicated on both sides from the beginning, it is impossible not to assign some blame to Shelley, both for Harriet's fate and for his own response to it.

Shelley tried to regain custody of his two children by his first wife, but was prevented by court action. In the meantime he wrote the long poem *Alastor,* incoherently beautiful, and the longest step forward so far in the development of his characteristic style. In the summer of 1816 he and Mary spent time in Switzerland, where they became friends with Byron. They were accompanied on this journey by Claire Clairmont, Godwin's stepdaughter. She was Byron's mistress at the time and bore him a daughter. During this summer abroad Shelley wrote "Hymn to Intellectual Beauty" and "Mont Blanc." In 1817, living in England again, he wrote the long political allegory, *The Revolt of Islam,* which is like *Queen Mab* in being poetically unsuccessful and in being extremely interesting as an exposition of Shelley's characteristic views.

In 1818 the Shelleys returned to Italy, partly in rage at the court that had deprived him of his children, partly out of fear that his children by Mary would also be taken from him, and partly for reasons of Shelley's health. They never returned to England. The years that remained were both tragic and extraordinarily productive. Two of their children died, and their deaths caused considerable strain and even partial estrangement between Shelley and Mary. There were also difficulties because of the personality of Claire Clairmont, who still accompanied them, and attendant difficulties in dealing with Byron. But in 1818–19 Shelley wrote the great *Prometheus Unbound,* and in 1819 the "Ode to the West Wind," the drama *The Cenci,* the polemical *The Masque of Anarchy,* and other political poems occasioned by repressive measures of the English government during this year. In 1820 he wrote *The Witch of Atlas;* in 1821 *Epipsychidion,* "Adonais" (the elegy for Keats), and *Hellas,* a visionary drama written to honor the Greek struggle for independence from Turkey. In 1822 he was engaged in writing *The Triumph of Life.* And throughout this time he produced most of the famous lyrics.

But in July of 1822 Shelley, who had been living at Pisa, near Byron, set out from Leghorn in his sailboat, accompanied by his friend Edward Williams and a young sailor. The boat was lost in a storm. Several days later Shelley's body washed ashore. In one of his pockets was a volume of Sophocles; in the other a volume of Keats. The body was cremated on the shore, in Byron's presence, and Shelley's ashes buried in the Protestant Cemetery at Rome, not far from the graves of his children and that of Keats.

TEXTS: The standard texts are as follows: R. Ingpen and W. E. Peck, eds., *Complete Works* (10 vols., 1926–1930); Thomas Hutchinson, ed., *Complete*

The Peterloo Massacre. A contemporary drawing of the incident in 1819 which fired Shelley's anger in "The Masque of Anarchy" and other poems. *Radio Times Hulton Picture Library.*

Poetical Works (1933); David Lee Clarke, ed., *Shelley's Prose* (1954); F. L. Jones, ed., *Letters* (2 vols., 1964). *The Life of Percy Bysshe Shelley* (1858), by Shelley's friend T. J. Hogg, is an important document. Edmund Blunden's biography, *Shelley: A Life Story* (1946), is good, and Newman Ivey White's *Shelley* (2 vols., 1940), the most authoritative account, is indispensable.

Three essays by celebrated literary figures have been extremely influential in the criticism of Shelley: Matthew Arnold's in *Essays in Criticism: Second Series* (1888); William Butler Yeats's in *Essays* (1924); and George Santayana's in *Winds of Doctrine* (1913).

A number of works have explored Shelley's ideas in their relation to philosophical and scientific traditions, among them: Carl Grabo, *A Newton Among Poets* (1930); Kenneth Neill Cameron, *The Young Shelley* (1950); J. N. Notopolous, *The Platonism of Shelley;* and C. E. Pulos, *The Deep Truth: A Study of Shelley's Scepticism* (1954).

Critical works include: Carlos Baker, *Shelley's Major Poetry* (1948); Harold Bloom, *Shelley's Myth-*making (1959); David Perkins, *The Quest for Permanence* (1959); Earl Wasserman, *The Subtler Language* (1959); Earl Wasserman, *Shelley* (1971); and G. M. Mathews, *Shelley* (1970). George M. Ridenour has edited a collection of critical essays, *Shelley* (1965).

Hymn to Intellectual Beauty

According to his wife, the idea for this poem came to Shelley when he was circumnavigating Lake Geneva with Byron in the summer of 1816.

The awful shadow of some unseen Power
  Floats though unseen among us,—visiting
  This various world with as inconstant wing
As summer winds that creep from flower to
    flower,—
Like moonbeams that behind some piny moun- 5
    tain shower,

It visits with inconstant glance
  Each human heart and countenance;
Like hues and harmonies of evening,—
  Like clouds in starlight widely spread,—
  Like memory of music fled,—   10
  Like aught that for its grace may be
Dear, and yet dearer for its mystery.

Spirit of BEAUTY, that dost consecrate
  With thine own hues all thou dost shine upon
  Of human thought or form,—where art thou 15
    gone?
Why dost thou pass away and leave our state,
This dim vast vale of tears, vacant and desolate?
  Ask why the sunlight not for ever
  Weaves rainbows o'er yon mountain-river,
Why aught should fail and fade that once is 20
  shown,
  Why fear and dream and death and birth
  Cast on the daylight of this earth
  Such gloom,—why man has such a scope
For love and hate, despondency and hope?

No voice from some sublimer world hath ever 25
  To sage or poet these responses[1] given—
  Therefore the names of Demon,[2] Ghost, and
    Heaven,
Remain the records of their vain endeavour,
Frail spells—whose uttered charm might not avail
  to sever,
  From all we hear and all we see,   30
  Doubt, chance, and mutability.
Thy light alone—like mist o'er mountains driven,
  Or music by the night-wind sent
  Through strings of some still instrument,
  Or moonlight on a midnight stream,   35
Gives grace and truth to life's unquiet dream.

Love, Hope, and Self-esteem, like clouds depart
  And come, for some uncertain moments lent.
  Man were immortal, and omnipotent,
Didst thou, unknown and awful as thou art, 40
Keep with thy glorious train firm state within his
  heart.

Thou messenger of sympathies,
  That wax and wane in lovers' eyes—
Thou—that to human thought art nourishment,
  Like darkness to a dying flame!   45
  Depart not as thy shadow came,
  Depart not—lest the grave should be,
Like life and fear, a dark reality.

While yet a boy I sought for ghosts, and sped
  Through many a listening chamber, cave and 50
  ruin,
  And starlight wood, with fearful steps pursuing
Hopes of high talk with the departed dead.
I called on poisonous names with which our
  youth is fed;
  I was not heard—I saw them not—
  When musing deeply on the lot   55
Of life, at that sweet time when winds are wooing
  All vital things that wake to bring
  News of birds and blossoming,—
  Sudden, thy shadow fell on me;
I shrieked, and clasped my hands in ecstasy! 60

I vowed that I would dedicate my powers
  To thee and thine—have I not kept the vow?
  With beating heart and streaming eyes, even
    now
I call the phantoms of a thousand hours
Each from his voiceless grave: they have in vi- 65
  sioned bowers
  Of studious zeal or love's delight
  Outwatched with me the envious night—
They know that never joy illumed my brow
  Unlinked with hope that thou wouldst free
  This world from its dark slavery,   70
  That thou—O awful LOVELINESS,
Wouldst give whate'er these words cannot express.

The day becomes more solemn and serene
  When noon is past—there is a harmony
  In autumn, and a lustre in its sky,   75
Which through the summer is not heard or seen,
As if it could not be, as if it had not been!
  Thus let thy power, which like the truth
  Of nature on my passive youth
Descended, to my onward life supply   80
  Its calm—to one who worships thee,
  And every form containing thee,
  Whom, SPIRIT fair, thy spells did bind
To fear himself, and love all human kind.

Ozymandias[1]

I met a traveller from an antique land
Who said: Two vast and trunkless legs of stone
Stand in the desert. . . Near them, on the sand,
Half sunk, a shattered visage lies, whose frown,
And wrinkled lip, and sneer of cold command,   5
Tell that its sculptor well those passions read
Which yet survive, stamped on these lifeless
    things,
The hand that mocked them, and the heart that
    fed:[2]
And on the pedestal these words appear:
"My name is Ozymandias, king of kings: 10
Look on my works, ye Mighty, and despair!"
Nothing beside remains. Round the decay
Of that colossal wreck, boundless and bare
The lone and level sands stretch far away.

Stanzas

Written in Dejection, near Naples

The mood of desolation in this poem, composed late
in 1818, was chiefly due to Shelley's ill health and to
a temporary estrangement from his wife following
the death of their baby daughter Clara.

The sun is warm, the sky is clear,
    The waves are dancing fast and bright;
Blue isles and snowy mountains wear
    The purple noon's transparent might;
    The breath of the moist earth is light,   5
Around its unexpanded buds;
    Like many a voice of one delight,
The winds, the birds, the ocean-floods,
The City's voice itself is soft, like Solitude's.

I see the Deep's untrampled floor   10
    With green and purple sea-weeds strown;
I see the waves upon the shore,
    Like light dissolved in star-showers, thrown:
    I sit upon the sands alone;
The lightning of the noontide ocean   15
    Is flashing round me, and a tone
Arises from its measured motion,

How sweet! did any heart now share in my emo-
    tion.

Alas! I have nor hope nor health,
    Nor peace within nor calm around,   20
Nor that content surpassing wealth
    The sage in meditation found,
    And walked with inward glory crowned;
Nor fame, nor power, nor love, nor leisure.
    Others I see whom these surround;   25
Smiling they live, and call life pleasure;—
To me that cup has been dealt in another measure.

Yet now despair itself is mild,
    Even as the winds and waters are;
I could lie down like a tired child,   30
    And weep away the life of care
    Which I have borne and yet must bear,
Till death like sleep might steal on me,
    And I might feel in the warm air
My cheek grow cold, and hear the sea   35
Breathe o'er my dying brain its last monotony.

Some might lament that I were cold,
    As I, when this sweet day is gone,
Which my lost heart, too soon grown old,
    Insults with this untimely moan;   40
    They might lament—for I am one
Whom men love not,—and yet regret;
    Unlike this day, which, when the sun
Shall on its stainless glory set,
Will linger, though enjoyed, like joy in memory   45
    yet.

from **Prometheus Unbound**

This great lyrical drama was written in 1818 and
1819. Its subject was suggested by Aeschylus' tragedy
Prometheus Bound. That play tells how the heroic
Titan who stole fire from heaven and gave it to mankind was condemned by Zeus to be chained to Mt.
Caucasus and tortured daily by a vulture preying on
his liver, which constantly renewed itself. In the
Greek myth, Zeus and Prometheus are eventually
reconciled. In Shelley's conception the hero, Prometheus, who represents all man's potentialities for
good, is the bringer of civilization and, though Christlike in forgiving his enemy, nevertheless remains
implacably defiant. The overthrow of Jupiter, who
stands for all the tyrannies of institutions and of
custom, is inevitable, since it is Shelley's view that
there is a principle in history making for the triumph

---

1 Ozymandias is the Greek name for the great Egyptian
King Ramses II (1295–25 B.C.).
2 The *hand* is the sculptor's, who imitated or represented
("mocked") the monarch's passions; the *heart* is the king's
—it nourished those passions.

of the good. The play is great not because it is greatly dramatic but because it provided Shelley with his most expansive occasion for the writing of celebratory verse, and he brought his most extraordinary powers to this occasion.

Both our excerpts (aside from the two songs that follow) are from Act III, just after the fall of Jupiter.

ACT III, SCENE II

The Mouth of a great River in the Island Atlantis. OCEAN *is discovered reclining near the Shore;* APOLLO *stands beside him.*

OCEAN. He[1] fell, thou sayest, beneath his conqueror's frown?

APOLLO. Ay, when the strife was ended which made dim
The orb I rule, and shook the solid stars,
The terrors of his eye illumined heaven
With sanguine light, through the thick ragged skirts   5
Of the victorious darkness, as he fell:
Like the last glare of day's red agony,
Which, from a rent among the fiery clouds,
Burns far along the tempest-wrinkled deep.

OCEAN. He sunk to the abyss? To the dark void?   10

APOLLO. An eagle so caught in some bursting cloud
On Caucasus, his thunder-baffled wings
Entangled in the whirlwind, and his eyes
Which gazed on the undazzling sun, now blinded
By the white lightning, while the ponderous hail   15
Beats on his struggling form, which sinks at length
Prone, and the aërial ice clings over it.

OCEAN. Henceforth the fields of Heaven-reflecting sea
Which are my realm, will heave, unstained with blood,
Beneath the uplifting winds, like plains of corn   20
Swayed by the summer air; my streams will flow
Round many-peopled continents, and round
Fortunate isles; and from their glassy thrones
Blue Proteus[2] and his humid nymphs shall mark
The shadow of fair ships, as mortals see   25
The floating bark of the light-laden moon
With that white star, its sightless pilot's crest,
Borne down the rapid sunset's ebbing sea;

Tracking their path no more by blood and groans,
And desolation, and the mingled voice   30
Of slavery and command; but by the light
Of wave-reflected flowers, and floating odours,
And music soft, and mild, free, gentle voices,
That sweetest music, such as spirits love.

APOLLO. And I shall gaze not on the deeds   35
which make
My mind obscure with sorrow, as eclipse
Darkens the sphere I guide; but list, I hear
The small, clear, silver lute of the young Spirit
That sits i' the morning star.

OCEAN.   Thou must away;
Thy steeds will pause at even, till when farewell: 40
The loud deep calls me home even now to feed it
With azure calm out of the emerald urns
Which stand for ever full beside my throne.
Behold the Nereids[3] under the green sea,
Their wavering limbs borne on the wind-like stream,   45
Their white arms lifted o'er their streaming hair
With garlands pied and starry sea-flower crowns,
Hastening to grace their mighty sister's joy.
                    (*A sound of waves is heard.*)
It is the unpastured sea hungering for calm.
Peace, Monster; I come now. Farewell.

APOLLO.   Farewell.   50

ACT III, SCENE III

Caucasus. PROMETHEUS, HERCULES, IONE, *the* EARTH, SPIRITS, ASIA, *and* PANTHEA, *borne in the Car with the* SPIRIT OF THE HOUR. HERCULES *unbinds* PROMETHEUS, *who descends.*

HERCULES. Most glorious among Spirits, thus doth strength
To wisdom, courage, and long-suffering love,
And thee, who art the form they animate,
Minister like a slave.

PROMETHEUS.   Thy gentle words
Are sweeter even than freedom long desired   5
And long delayed.
                    Asia, thou light of life,
Shadow of beauty unbeheld: and ye,
Fair sister nymphs,[4] who made long years of pain
Sweet to remember, through your love and care:
Henceforth we will not part. There is a cave,   10
All overgrown with trailing odorous plants,

---

[1] Jupiter.   [2] A sea-god, Poseidon's shepherd.

[3] Daughters of a sea-god, Nereus.
[4] Ione and Panthea, Asia's sisters.

Which curtain out the day with leaves and
    flowers,
And paved with veinèd emerald, and a fountain
Leaps in the midst with an awakening sound.
From its curved roof the mountain's frozen tears   15
Like snow, or silver, or long diamond spires,
Hang downward, raining forth a doubtful light:
And there is heard the ever-moving air,
Whispering without from tree to tree, and birds,
And bees; and all around are mossy seats,   20
And the rough walls are clothed with long soft
    grass;
A simple dwelling, which shall be our own:
Where we will sit and talk of time and change,
As the world ebbs and flows, ourselves unchanged.
What can hide man from mutability?   25
And if ye sigh, then I will smile; and thou,
Ione, shalt chant fragments of sea-music,
Until I weep, when ye shall smile away
The tears she brought, which yet were sweet to
    shed.
We will entangle buds and flowers and beams   30
Which twinkle on the fountain's brim, and make
Strange combinations out of common things,
Like human babes in their brief innocence;
And we will search, with looks and words of love,
For hidden thoughts, each lovelier than the last,   35
Our unexhausted spirits; and like lutes
Touched by the skill of the enamoured wind,
Weave harmonies divine, yet ever new,
From difference sweet where discord cannot be;
And hither come, sped on the charmèd winds,   40
Which meet from all the points of heaven, as bees
From every flower aëreal Enna feeds,[5]
At their known island-homes in Himera,[6]
The echoes of the human world, which tell
Of the low voice of love, almost unheard,   45
And dove-eyed pity's murmured pain, and music,
Itself the echo of the heart, and all
That tempers or improves man's life, now free;
And lovely apparitions,—dim at first,
Then radiant, as the mind, arising bright   50
From the embrace of beauty (whence the forms
Of which these are the phantoms) casts on them
The gathered rays which are reality—
Shall visit us, the progeny immortal
Of Painting, Sculpture, and rapt Poesy,   55

And arts, though unimagined, yet to be.
The wandering voices and the shadows these
Of all that man becomes, the mediators
Of that best worship love, by him and us
Given and returned; swift shapes and sounds,   60
    which grow
More fair and soft as man grows wise and kind,
And, veil by veil, evil and error fall:
Such virtue has the cave and place around.
         (*Turning to the* SPIRIT OF THE HOUR.)
For thee, fair Spirit, one toil remains. Ione,
Give her that curvèd shell, which Proteus old   65
Made Asia's nuptial boon, breathing within it
A voice to be accomplished, and which thou
Didst hide in grass under the hollow rock.
    IONE. Thou most desired Hour, more loved
    and lovely
Than all thy sisters, this is the mystic shell;   70
See the pale azure fading into silver
Lining it with a soft yet glowing light:
Looks it not like lullèd music sleeping there?
    SPIRIT. It seems in truth the fairest shell of
    Ocean:
Its sound must be at once both sweet and strange.   75
    PROMETHEUS. Go, borne over the cities of man-
    kind
Outspeed the sun around the orbèd world;
And as thy chariot cleaves the kindling air,
Thou breathe into the many-folded shell,
Loosening its mighty music; it shall be   80
As thunder mingled with clear echoes: then
Return; and thou shalt dwell beside our cave.

Two Songs *from* Prometheus Unbound

The first of the following lyrics is sung to close
Act II by Asia, Prometheus' love, who generally
represents nature. The second is the concluding passage in the play, celebrating the fall of Jupiter and
the freeing of Prometheus, and prophesying the
future happiness of the world.

MY SOUL IS AN ENCHANTED BOAT

My soul is an enchanted boat,
    Which, like a sleeping swan, doth float
Upon the silver waves of thy sweet singing;
    And thine doth like an Angel sit
    Beside the helm conducting it,   5
Whilst all the winds with melody are ringing.
    It seems to float ever, for ever,

---

[5] Enna was the place where Proserpina was gathering
flowers when she was ravished away to Hades by Pluto.
[6] A town in Sicily, named for Himeros, the brother of
Eros, the god of love.

Upon that many-winding river,
Between mountains, woods, abysses,
A Paradise of wildernesses!   10
Till, like one in slumber bound,
Borne to the ocean, I float, down, around,
Into a sea profound, of ever-spreading sound:

Meanwhile thy Spirit lifts its pinions
In Music's most serene dominions;   15
Catching the winds that fan that happy Heaven.
And we sail on, away, afar,
Without a course, without a star,
But by the instinct of sweet music driven;
Till through Elysian garden islets   20
By thee, most beautiful of pilots,
Where never mortal pinnace glided,
The boat of my desire is guided:
Realms where the air we breathe is Love,
Which in the winds and on the waves doth move, 25
Harmonizing this Earth with what we feel above.

We have passed Age's icy caves,
And Manhood's dark and tossing waves,
And Youth's smooth ocean, smiling to betray:
Beyond the glassy gulphs we flee   30
Of shadow-peopled Infancy,
Through Death and Birth, to a diviner day;
A Paradise of vaulted bowers
Lit by downward-gazing flowers,
And watery paths that wind between   35
Wildernesses calm and green,
Peopled by shapes too bright to see,
And rest, having beheld; somewhat like thee;
Which walk upon the sea, and chant melodiously!

THIS IS THE DAY

This is the Day, which down the void Abysm
At the Earth-born's spell yawns for Heaven's
    despotism,
    And Conquest is dragged captive through the
        deep;
Love, from its awful throne of patient power
In the wise heart, from the last giddy hour   5
    Of dread endurance, from the slippery, steep,
And narrow verge of crag-like agony, springs
And folds over the world its healing wings.

Gentleness, Virtue, Wisdom, and Endurance,—
These are the seals of that most firm assurance 10
    Which bars the pit over Destruction's strength;
And if, with infirm hand, Eternity,

Mother of many acts and hours, should free
    The serpent that would clasp her with his
        length,
These are the spells by which to re-assume   15
An empire o'er the disentangled Doom.

To suffer woes which Hope thinks infinite;
To forgive wrongs darker than death or night;
    To defy Power, which seems omnipotent;
To love, and bear; to hope till Hope creates   20
From its own wreck the thing it contemplates:
    Neither to change, nor falter, nor repent;
This, like thy glory, Titan, is to be
Good, great and joyous, beautiful and free;
This is alone Life, Joy, Empire, and Victory.   25

The Masque of Anarchy
Written on the Occasion of the
Massacre at Manchester

On a day in the summer of 1819 thousands of citizens assembled at St. Peter's Field in Manchester in a mass meeting called by the advocates of reform. The militia, ordered to arrest the speaker, lost their heads and sabered the workers. Several persons were killed and many wounded. The national administration upheld the local authorities. News of Peterloo, as the bloody affair was called in derisive contrast with the Army's victory at Waterloo, roused Shelley to a white heat of indignation, out of which was written the following powerful poem. Shelley sent it to Leigh Hunt for publication in the *Examiner;* but Hunt withheld it till 1832, the year of the Reform Bill, when it was brought out in separate form.

As I lay asleep in Italy
There came a voice from over the Sea,
And with great power it forth led me
To walk in the visions of Poesy.

I met Murder on the way—   5
He had a mask like Castlereagh;[1]
Very smooth he looked, yet grim;
Seven bloodhounds followed him.

All were fat, and well they might
Be in admirable plight,   10

---

[1] Robert Stewart (1769–1822), second Marquis of Londonderry, better known by his earlier title of Viscount Castlereagh, foreign secretary and leader of the House of Commons (1812–22). Three years after Shelley wrote his poem, Castlereagh gratified the liberals by cutting his own throat.

For one by one, and two by two,
He tossed them human hearts to chew,
Which from his wide cloak he drew.

Next came Fraud, and he had on,
Like Eldon,[2] an ermined gown;[3]   15
His big tears, for he wept well,
Turned to millstones as they fell,

And the little children, who
Round his feet played to and fro,
Thinking every tear a gem,   20
Had their brains knocked out by them.

Clothed with the Bible, as with light,
And the shadows of the night,
Like Sidmouth,[4] next, Hypocrisy
On a crocodile rode by.   25

And many more Destructions played
In this ghastly masquerade,
All disguised, even to the eyes,
Like Bishops, lawyers, peers, and spies.

Last came Anarchy: he rode   30
On a white Horse splashed with blood;
He was pale even to the lips,
Like Death in the Apocalypse.[5]

And he wore a kingly crown;
In his hand a sceptre shone;   35
On his brow this mark I saw—
"I AM GOD, AND KING, AND LAW!"

With a pace stately and fast,
Over English land he past,
Trampling to a mire of blood   40
The adoring multitude.

And a mighty troop around
With their trampling shook the ground,
Waving each a bloody sword
For the service of their Lord.   45

And, with glorious triumph, they
Rode through England, proud and gay,
Drunk as with intoxication
Of the wine of desolation.

O'er fields and towns, from sea to sea,   50
Past the pageant swift and free,
Tearing up, and trampling down,—
Till they came to London town.

And each dweller, panic-stricken,
Felt his heart with terror sicken   55
Hearing the tempestuous cry
Of the triumph of Anarchy.

For with pomp to meet him came,
Clothed in arms like blood and flame,
The hired Murderers, who did sing   60
"Thou art God, and Law, and King.

"We have waited, weak and lone,
For thy coming, Mighty One!
Our purses are empty, our swords are cold;
Give us glory, and blood, and gold."   65

Lawyers and priests, a motley crowd,
To the earth their pale brows bowed;
Like a bad prayer not over-loud,
Whispering—"Thou art Law and God."

Then all cried with one accord,   70
"Thou art King, and God, and Lord;
Anarchy, to thee we bow,—
Be thy name made holy now!"

And Anarchy, the Skeleton,
Bowed and grinned to every one,   75
As well as if his education
Had cost ten millions to the Nation.

For he knew the Palaces
Of our Kings were rightly his;
His the sceptre, crown, and globe,   80
And the gold-inwoven robe.

So he sent his slaves before
To seize upon the Bank and Tower,[6]
And was proceeding with intent
To meet his pensioned parliament,   85

2 John Scott (1751–1838), first Earl of Eldon, almost continuously lord chancellor from 1801 to 1827, and center of the government's resistance to reform. In his judicial capacity he had pronounced Shelley unfit to be the guardian of his children by his first wife, Harriet.
3 Worn by judges.
4 Henry Addington (1757–1844), first Viscount Sidmouth, was home secretary from 1812 to 1821. His policy of repression led directly to the outrage at Manchester.
5 Revelation 6:8.

6 The Bank of England and the Tower of London.

When one fled past, a Maniac maid,
And her name was Hope, she said:
But she looked more like Despair,
And she cried out in the air:

"My father Time is weak and grey   90
With waiting for a better day;
See how idiot-like he stands,
Fumbling with his palsied hands!

"He has had child after child,
And the dust of death is piled   95
Over every one but me—
Misery, oh, Misery!"

Then she lay down in the street,
Right before the horses' feet,
Expecting,[7] with a patient eye,   100
Murder, Fraud, and Anarchy;

When between her and her foes
A mist, a light, an image rose,—
Small at first, and weak, and frail
Like the vapour of a vale: 105

Till as clouds grow on the blast,
Like tower-crowned giants, striding fast,
And glare with lightnings as they fly,
And speak in thunder to the sky,

It grew—a Shape[8] arrayed in mail   110
Brighter than the viper's scale,
And upborne on wings whose grain[9]
Was as the light of sunny rain.

On its helm, seen far away,
A planet, like the Morning's, lay;   115
And those plumes its light rained through
Like a shower of crimson dew.

With step as soft as wind it past
O'er the heads of men—so fast
That they knew the presence there,   120
And looked,—and all was empty air.

As flowers beneath May's footstep waken,
As stars from Night's loose hair are shaken,
As waves arise when loud winds call,
Thoughts sprung where'er that step did fall.   125

And the prostrate multitude
Looked—and ankle-deep in blood,
Hope, that maiden most serene,
Was walking with a quiet mien:

And Anarchy, the ghastly birth,   130
Lay dead earth upon the earth;
The Horse of Death, tameless as wind,
Fled, and with his hoofs did grind
To dust the murderers thronged behind.

A rushing light of clouds and splendour,   135
A sense, awakening and yet tender,
Was heard and felt—and at its close
These words of joy and fear arose:

As if their own indignant Earth,
Which gave the Sons of England birth,   140
Had felt their blood upon her brow,
And shuddering with a mother's throe

Had turnèd every drop of blood
By which her face had been bedewed
To an accent unwithstood,—   145
As if her heart had cried aloud:

"Men of England, Heirs of Glory,
Heroes of unwritten story,
Nurslings of one mighty Mother,
Hopes of her, and one another;   150

"Rise like Lions after slumber,
In unvanquishable number;
Shake your chains to earth like dew
Which in sleep had fallen on you:—
Ye are many—they are few.   155

"What is Freedom?—ye can tell
That which slavery is, too well—
For its very name has grown
To an echo of your own.

" 'Tis to work, and have such pay   160
As just keeps life from day to day
In your limbs,—as in a cell,
For the tyrants' use to dwell:

"So that ye for them are made
Loom, and plough, and sword, and spade,—   165
With or without your own will, bent
To their defence and nourishment.

---

[7] Awaiting.
[8] According to Hunt, Public Enlightenment. See line 125.
[9] Color.

" 'Tis to see your children weak
With their mothers pine and peak,
When the winter winds are bleak:—   170
They are dying whilst I speak.

" 'Tis to hunger for such diet
As the rich man in his riot[10]
Casts to the fat dogs that lie
Surfeiting beneath his eye.   175

" 'Tis to let the Ghost of Gold[11]
Take from Toil a thousandfold
More than e'er its substance could
In the tyrannies of old:

"Paper coin—that forgery   180
Of the title-deeds which ye
Hold to something of the worth
Of the inheritance of Earth.

" 'Tis to be a slave in soul
And to hold no strong controul   185
Over your own wills, but be
All that others make of ye.

"And at length when ye complain
With a murmur weak and vain,
'Tis to see the Tyrant's crew   190
Ride over your wives and you—
Blood is on the grass like dew!

"Then it is to feel revenge,
Fiercely thirsting to exchange
Blood for blood—and wrong for wrong:—   195
Do not thus when ye are strong!

"Birds find rest in narrow nest
When weary of their wingèd quest;
Beasts find fare in woody lair
When storm and snow are in the air.   200

"Horses, oxen, have a home,
When from daily toil they come;
Household dogs, when the wind roars,
Find a home within warm doors.

"Asses, swine, have litter spread   205
And with fitting food are fed;
All things have a home but one—
Thou, O Englishman, hast none!

"This is Slavery: savage men,
Or wild beasts within a den,   210
Would endure not as ye do:—
But such ills they never knew.

"What art thou, Freedom? Oh, could slaves
Answer from their living graves
This demand—tyrants would flee   215
Like a dream's dim imagery:

"Thou art not, as impostors say,
A shadow soon to pass away,
A superstition, and a name
Echoing from the cave of Fame.   220

"For the labourer thou art bread,
And a comely table spread,
From his daily labour come
In a neat and happy home.

"Thou art clothes, and fire, and food   225
For the trampled multitude:—
No—in countries that are free
Such starvation cannot be
As in England now we see.

"To the rich thou art a check;   230
When his foot is on the neck
Of his victim, thou dost make
That he treads upon a snake.

"Thou art Justice—ne'er for gold
May thy righteous laws be sold   235
As laws are in England: thou
Shield'st alike the high and low.

"Thou art Wisdom—freemen never
Dream that God will damn forever
All who think those things untrue   240
Of which Priests make such ado.

"Thou art Peace—never by thee
Would blood and treasure wasted be
As tyrants wasted them, when all
Leagued to quench thy flame in Gaul.[12]   245

"What if English toil and blood
Was poured forth, even as a flood?
It availed, O Liberty!
To dim, but not extinguish thee.

---

10 Revelry.   11 I.e., paper, securities.

12 I.e., to suppress the French Revolution and Napoleon.

"Thou art Love—the rich have kist
Thy feet, and like him following[13] Christ,
Give their substance to the free
And through the rough world follow thee:

"Or turn their wealth to arms, and make
War for thy belovèd sake   255
On wealth, and war, and fraud—whence they
Drew the power which is their prey.

"Science. Poetry and Thought
Are thy lamps; they make the lot
Of the dwellers in a cot   260
So serene, they curse it not.

"Spirit, patience, gentleness,
All that can adorn and bless,
Art thou. . . let deeds, not words, express
Thine exceeding loveliness.   265

"Let a great Assembly be
Of the fearless and the free,
On some spot of English ground
Where the plains stretch wide around.

"Let the blue sky overhead,   270
The green earth on which ye tread,
All that must eternal be,
Witness the solemnity.

"From the corners uttermost
Of the bounds of English coast;   275
From every hut, village and town
Where those who live and suffer, moan
For others' misery or their own;

"From the workhouse and the prison
Where, pale as corpses newly risen,   280
Woman, children, young and old,
Groan for pain, and weep for cold;

"From the haunts of daily life
Where is waged the daily strife
With common wants and common cares,   285
Which sows the human heart with tares,

"Lastly, from the palaces,
Where the murmur of distress
Echoes, like the distant sound
Of a wind alive around   290

250 "Those prison-halls of wealth and fashion,
Where some few feel such compassion,
For those who groan, and toil, and wail,
As must make their brethren pale;—

"Ye who suffer woes untold,   295
Or to feel or to behold
Your lost country bought and sold
With a price of blood and gold;—

"Let a vast Assembly be;
And with great solemnity   300
Declare with measured words that ye
Are, as God has made ye, free.

"Be your strong and simple words
Keen to wound as sharpened swords,
And wide as targes[14] let them be,   305
With their shade to cover ye.

"Let the tyrants pour around
With a quick and startling sound,
Like the loosening of a sea,
Troops of armed emblazonry.   310

"Let the charged artillery drive
Till the dead air seems alive
With the clash of clanging wheels,
And the tramp of horses' heels.

"Let the fixèd bayonet   315
Gleam with sharp desire to wet
Its bright point in English blood,
Looking keen, as one for food.

"Let the horsemen's scimitars
Wheel and flash, like sphereless[15] stars   320
Thirsting to eclipse their burning
In a sea of death and mourning.

"Stand ye calm and resolute,
Like a forest, close and mute,
With folded arms, and looks which are   325
Weapons of unvanquished war;

"And let Panic, who outspeeds
The career of armèd steeds,
Pass, a disregarded shade,
Through your phalanx[16] undismayed.   330

---

13 Him who follows.

14 Shields.
15 I.e., escaped from their fixed spheres or orbits.
16 Close-packed formation.

"Let the Laws of your own land,
Good or ill, between ye stand,
Hand to hand, and foot to foot,
Arbiters of the dispute:—

"The old laws of England—they   335
Whose reverend heads with age are grey,
Children of a wiser day;
And whose solemn voice must be
Thine own echo—Liberty!

"On those who first should violate   340
Such sacred heralds in their state
Rest the blood that must ensue. . .
And it will not rest on you.

"And if then the tyrants dare,
Let them ride among you there,   345
Slash, and stab, and maim, and hew,—
What they like, that let them do.

"With folded arms and steady eyes,
And little fear, and less surprise,
Look upon them as they slay,   350
Till their rage has died away.

"Then they will return with shame
To the place from which they came,
And the blood thus shed will speak
In hot blushes on their cheek.   355

"Every woman in the land
Will point at them as they stand. . .
They will hardly dare to greet
Their acquaintance in the street,

"And the bold, true warriors   360
Who have hugged Danger in the wars,
Will turn to those who would be free,
Ashamed of such base company.

"And that slaughter to the Nation
Shall steam up like inspiration,   365
Eloquent, oracular;
A volcano heard afar.

"And these words shall then become
Like Oppression's thundered doom
Ringing through each heart and brain,   370
Heard again—again—again:—

" 'Rise like Lions after slumber,
In unvanquishable number;
Shake your chains to earth, like dew
Which in sleep had fallen on you:—   375
Ye are many—they are few.' "

Song to the Men of England

Composed in the fall of 1819.

Men of England, wherefore plough
For the lords who lay ye low?
Wherefore weave with toil and care
The rich robes your tyrants wear?

Wherefore feed, and clothe, and save,   5
From the cradle to the grave,
Those ungrateful drones who would
Drain your sweat—nay, drink your blood?

Wherefore, Bees of England, forge
Many a weapon, chain, and scourge,   10
That these stingless drones may spoil
The forced produce of your toil?

Have ye leisure, comfort, calm,
Shelter, food, love's gentle balm?
Or what is it ye buy so dear   15
With your pain and with your fear?

The seed ye sow, another reaps;
The wealth ye find, another keeps;
The robes ye weave, another wears;
The arms ye forge, another bears.   20

Sow seed,—but let no tyrant reap;
Find wealth,—let no impostor heap;
Weave robes,—let not the idle wear;
Forge arms,—in your defence to bear.

Shrink to your cellars, holes, and cells;   25
In halls ye deck another dwells.
Why shake the chains ye wrought? Ye see
The steel ye tempered glance on ye.

With plough and spade, and hoe and loom,
Trace your grave, and build your tomb,   30
And weave your winding-sheet, till fair
England be your sepulchre.

England in 1819

An old, mad, blind, despised, and dying king,[1]—
Princes, the dregs of their dull race, who flow
Through public scorn—mud from a muddy
    spring;
Rulers, who neither see, nor feel, nor know,
But leech-like to their fainting country cling,   5
Till they drop, blind in blood, without a blow;
A people starved and stabbed in the untilled
    field,—
An army, which liberticide and prey
Makes as a two-edged sword to all who wield;
Golden and sanguine[2] laws which tempt and slay;   10
Religion Christless, Godless—a book sealed;
A Senate,—Time's worst statute[3] unrepealed,—
Are graves, from which a glorious Phantom may
Burst, to illumine our tempestuous day.

Ode to the West Wind

The basic meter of the "Ode," written in 1819, is
an Italian one called *terza rima:* each tercet or set of
three lines is laced to the next by rime, line 2 of
each tercet riming with lines 1 and 3 of the following
tercet (*aba bcb cdc,* etc.). Shelley makes a brilliant
variation in this pattern by writing strophes of fourteen lines, each composed of four tercets plus a
couplet which rimes with line 2 of the preceding
tercet (*aba bcb cdc ded ee*).

1

O wild West Wind, thou breath of Autumn's
    being,
Thou, from whose unseen presence the leaves
    dead
Are driven, like ghosts from an enchanter fleeing,

Yellow, and black, and pale, and hectic red,
Pestilence-stricken multitudes: O thou,   5
Who chariotest to their dark wintry bed

The wingèd seeds, where they lie cold and low,
Each like a corpse within its grave, until
Thine azure sister[1] of the Spring shall blow

Her clarion o'er the dreaming earth, and fill   10
(Driving sweet buds like flocks to feed in air)
With living hues and odours plain and hill.

Wild Spirit, which art moving everywhere;
Destroyer and preserver; hear, oh, hear!

2

Thou on whose stream, 'mid the steep sky's com-   15
    motion,
Loose clouds like Earth's decaying leaves are
    shed,
Shook from the tangled boughs of Heaven and
    Ocean,

Angels of rain and lightning: there are spread
On the blue surface of thine airy surge,
Like the bright hair uplifted from the head   20

Of some fierce Maenad,[2] even from the dim verge
Of the horizon to the zenith's height,
The locks of the approaching storm. Thou dirge

Of the dying Year, to which this closing[3] night
Will be the dome of a vast sepulchre,   25
Vaulted with all thy congregated might

Of vapours, from whose solid atmosphere
Black rain, and fire, and hail will burst: oh, hear!

3

Thou who didst waken from his summer dreams
The blue Mediterranean, where he lay,   30
Lulled by the coil of his crystalline streams,

Beside a pumice[4] isle in Baiae's[5] bay,
And saw in sleep old palaces and towers
Quivering within the wave's intenser day,

All overgrown with azure moss and flowers   35
So sweet, the sense faints picturing them! Thou
For whose path the Atlantic's level powers

Cleave themselves into chasms, while far below
The sea-blooms and the oozy woods which wear
The sapless foliage of the ocean know   40

---

[1] George III (d. 1820).
[2] Laws founded on gold and blood.
[3] Imposing penalties on Catholics.

[1] The south wind.

---

[2] Nymph attending Bacchus.
[3] I.e., closing down on the world.   [4] I.e., volcanic.
[5] Ruins of a Roman town near Naples, partially under-
water.

Thy voice, and suddenly grow grey with fear,
And tremble and despoil themselves: oh, hear!

4

If I were a dead leaf thou mightest bear;
If I were a swift cloud to fly with thee;
A wave to pant beneath thy power, and share   45

The impulse of thy strength, only less free
Than thou, O uncontrollable! If even
I were as in my boyhood, and could be

The comrade of thy wanderings over Heaven,
As then, when to outstrip thy skiey speed   50
Scarce seemed a vision; I would ne'er have striven

As thus with thee in prayer in my sore need.
Oh! lift me as a wave, a leaf, a cloud!
I fall upon the thorns of life! I bleed!

A heavy weight of hours has chained and bowed   55
One too like thee: tameless, and swift, and proud.

5

Make me thy lyre, even as the forest is:
What if my leaves are falling like its own!
The tumult of thy mighty harmonies

Will take from both a deep, autumnal tone,   60
Sweet though in sadness. Be thou, Spirit fierce,
My spirit! Be thou me, impetuous one!

Drive my dead thoughts over the universe
Like withered leaves to quicken a new birth!
And, by the incantation of this verse,   65

Scatter, as from an unextinguished hearth
Ashes and sparks, my words among mankind!
Be through my lips to unawakened Earth

The trumpet of a prophecy! O Wind,
If Winter comes, can Spring be far behind?   70

The Indian Serenade

This lyric and the one following were written in 1819.

I arise from dreams of thee
   In the first sweet sleep of night,
When the winds are breathing low,
   And the stars are shining bright:

I arise from dreams of thee,   5
   And a spirit in my feet
Hath led me—who knows how?
   To thy chamber window, sweet!

The wandering airs they faint
   On the dark, the silent stream;   10
The Champak[1] odours fail
   Like sweet thoughts in a dream;
The nightingale's complaint,
   It dies upon her heart,
As I must die on thine,   15
   O belovèd as thou art!

Oh lift me from the grass!
   I die! I faint! I fail!
Let thy love in kisses rain
   On my lips and eyelids pale.   20
My cheek is cold and white, alas!
   My heart beats loud and fast,—
Oh! press it close to thine again,
   Where it will break at last.

Love's Philosophy

The fountains mingle with the river,
   And the rivers with the ocean;
The winds of Heaven mix for ever
   With a sweet emotion;
Nothing in the world is single;   5
   All things by a law divine
In one another's being mingle;—
   Why not I with thine?

See the mountains kiss high Heaven,
   And the waves clasp one another;   10
No sister flower would be forgiven
   If it disdained its brother;
And the sunlight clasps the earth,
   And the moonbeams kiss the sea:
What is all this sweet work worth,   15
   If thou kiss not me?

The Cloud

The date of this poem is uncertain; it was probably
finished in Italy in 1820, the year of its publication.

I bring fresh showers for the thirsting flowers,
   From the seas and the streams;

---

1 Or champac, an East Indian tree of the magnolia family.

I bear light shade for the leaves when laid
In their noonday dreams.
From my wings are shaken the dews that waken   5
The sweet buds every one,
When rocked to rest on their mother's breast,
As she dances about the sun.
I wield the flail of the lashing hail,
And whiten the green plains under,   10
And then again I dissolve it in rain,
And laugh as I pass in thunder.

I sift the snow on the mountains below,
And their great pines groan aghast;
And all the night 'tis my pillow white,   15
While I sleep in the arms of the blast.
Sublime on the towers of my skiey bowers,
Lightning my pilot sits;
In a cavern under is fettered the thunder,—
It struggles and howls at fits;   20
Over earth and ocean, with gentle motion,
This pilot[1] is guiding me,
Lured by the love of the genii that move
In the depths of the purple sea;
Over the rills, and the crags, and the hills,   25
Over the lakes and the plains,
Wherever he dream under mountain or stream
The Spirit he loves remains;
And I all the while bask in Heaven's blue smile,
Whilst he is dissolving in rains.   30

The sanguine sunrise, with his meteor eyes,
And his burning plumes outspread,
Leaps on the back of my sailing rack,[2]
When the morning star shines dead:
As on the jag of a mountain crag,   35
Which an earthquake rocks and swings,
An eagle alit one moment may sit
In the light of its golden wings.
And when sunset may breathe, from the lit sea
beneath,
Its ardours of rest and of love,   40
And the crimson pall of eve may fall
From the depth of Heaven above,
With wings folded I rest, on mine airy nest,
As still as a brooding dove.

That orbèd maiden with white fire laden,   45
Whom mortals call the moon,
Glides glimmering o'er my fleece-like floor,
By the midnight breezes strewn;
And wherever the beat of her unseen feet,
Which only the angels hear,   50

May have broken the woof of my tent's thin roof,
The stars peep behind her and peer;
And I laugh to see them whirl and flee,
Like a swarm of golden bees,
When I widen the rent in my wind-built tent,   55
Till the calm rivers, lakes, and seas,
Like strips of the sky fallen through me on high,
Are each paved with the moon and these.

I bind the sun's throne with a burning zone,[3]
And the moon's with a girdle of pearl;   60
The volcanos are dim, and the stars reel and
swim,
When the whirlwinds my banner unfurl.
From cape to cape, with a bridge-like shape,
Over a torrent sea,
Sunbeam-proof, I hang like a roof,—   65
The mountains its columns be.
The triumphal arch through which I march
With hurricane, fire, and snow,
When the Powers of the air are chained to my
chair,
Is the millioncoloured bow;   70
The sphere-fire above its soft colours wove,
While the moist Earth was laughing below.

I am the daughter of earth and water,
And the nursling of the sky;
I pass through the pores of the ocean and shores;   75
I change, but I cannot die.
For after the rain, when with never a stain
The pavilion of Heaven is bare,
And the winds and sunbeams with their convex
gleams,
Build up the blue dome of air,   80
I silently laugh at my own cenotaph,[4]
And out of the caverns of rain,
Like a child from the womb, like a ghost from
the tomb,
I arise and unbuild it again.

To a Skylark

This poem was written at Leghorn in the early summer of 1820.

Hail to thee, blithe Spirit!—
Bird thou never wert!—

---

[1] Electricity.   [2] Mass of high, scudding cloud.

[3] Belt.
[4] An empty tomb built as a monument; i.e., the "blue dome" of the sky.

That from Heaven, or near it,
　　Pourest thy full heart
In profuse strains of unpremeditated art.   5

　　Higher still and higher
　　　From the earth thou springest
　　Like a cloud of fire;
　　　The blue deep thou wingest,
And singing still dost soar, and soaring ever sing-   10
est.

　　In the golden lightning
　　　Of the sunken sun,
　　O'er which clouds are bright'ning,
　　　Thou dost float and run;
Like an unbodied joy whose race is just begun.   15

　　The pale purple even
　　　Melts around thy flight;
　　Like a star of Heaven,
　　　In the broad daylight
Thou art unseen,—but yet I hear thy shrill de-   20
light,

　　Keen as are the arrows
　　　Of that silver sphere,
　　Whose intense lamp narrows
　　　In the white dawn clear
Until we hardly see—we feel that it is there: 25

　　All the earth and air
　　　With thy voice is loud,
　　As, when Night is bare,
　　　From one lonely cloud
The moon rains out her beams, and Heaven is   30
overflowed.

　　What thou art we know not;
　　　What is most like thee?
　　From rainbow-clouds there flow not
　　　Drops so bright to see
As from thy presence showers a rain of melody.   35

　　Like a Poet hidden
　　　In the light of thought,
　　Singing hymns unbidden
　　　Till the world is wrought
To sympathy with hopes and fears it heeded not: 40

　　Like a high-born maiden
　　　In a palace-tower,

　　Soothing her love-laden
　　　Soul in secret hour
With music sweet as love, which overflows her   45
bower:

　　Like a glow-worm golden
　　　In a dell of dew,
　　Scattering unbeholden[1]
　　　Its aërial hue
Among the flowers and grass which screen it from   50
the view:

　　Like a rose embowered
　　　In its own green leaves,
　　By warm winds deflowered,
　　　Till the scent it gives
Makes faint with too much sweet those heavy   55
wingèd thieves.

　　Sound of vernal showers
　　　On the twinkling grass;
　　Rain-awakened flowers,
　　　All that ever was
Joyous and clear and fresh, thy music doth sur-   60
pass.

　　Teach us, Sprite[2] or Bird,
　　　What sweet thoughts are thine;
　　I have never heard
　　　Praise of love or wine
That panted forth a flood of rapture so divine: 65

　　Chorus hymeneal,[3]
　　　Or triumphal chaunt,
　　Matched with thine, would be all
　　　But an empty vaunt,
A thing wherein we feel there is some hidden   70
want.

　　What objects are the fountains
　　　Of thy happy strain?
　　What fields or waves or mountains?
　　　What shapes of sky or plain?
What love of thine own kind? what ignorance of   75
pain?

　　With thy clear keen joyance
　　　Langour cannot be:
　　Shadow of annoyance
　　　Never came near thee:
Thou lovest—but ne'er knew love's sad satiety.   80

---

1 Unseen.　　2 Spirit.　　3 Marriage song.

Waking or asleep
   Thou of death must deem
Things more true and deep
   Than we mortals dream,
Or how could thy notes flow in such a crystal   85
stream?

   We look before and after,
     And pine for what is not:
   Our sincerest laughter
     With some pain is fraught;
Our sweetest songs are those that tell of saddest   90
thought.

   Yet if we could scorn
     Hate and pride and fear;
   If we were things born
     Not to shed a tear,
I know not how thy joy we ever should come   95
near.

   Better than all measures
     Of delightful sound—
   Better than all treasures
     That in books are found,
Thy skill to poet were,[4] thou scorner of the   100
ground!

   Teach[5] me half the gladness
     That thy brain must know,
   Such harmonious madness[6]
     From my lips would flow
The world should listen then—as I am listening   105
now.

Hymn of Pan

I

From the forests and highlands
   We come, we come;
From the river-girt islands,
   Where loud waves are dumb
     Listening to my sweet pipings.   5
The wind in the reeds and the rushes,
   The bees on the bells of thyme,
The birds on the myrtle bushes,
   The cicale above in the lime,

And the lizards below in the grass,
Were as silent as ever old Tmolus[1] was,   10
     Listening to my sweet pipings.

II

Liquid Peneus[2] was flowing,
   And all dark Tempe lay
In Pelion's shadow, outgrowing   15
   The light of the dying day,
     Speeded by my sweet pipings.
The Sileni, and Sylvans, and Fauns,
   And the Nymphs of the woods and the waves,
To the edge of the moist river-lawns,   20
   And the brink of the dewy caves,
And all that did then attend and follow,
Were silent with love, as you now, Apollo,
     With envy of my sweet pipings.

III

I sang of the dancing stars,   25
   I sang of the daedal Earth,
And of Heaven—and the giant wars,
   And Love, and Death, and Birth,—
     And then I changed my pipings,—
Singing how down the vale of Maenalus   30
   I pursued a maiden and clasped a reed.
Gods and men, we are all deluded thus!
   It breaks in our bosom and then we bleed:
All wept, as I think both ye now would,
If envy or age had not frozen your blood,   35
     At the sorrow of my sweet pipings.

Hymn of Apollo

I

The sleepless Hours who watch me as I lie,
   Curtained with star-inwoven tapestries
From the broad moonlight of the sky,
   Fanning the busy dreams from my dim eyes,—
Waken me when their Mother, the gray Dawn,   5
Tells them that dreams and that the moon is
   gone.

II

Then I arise, and climbing Heaven's blue dome,
   I walk over the mountains and the waves,

---

[4] Would be.   [5] If thou wouldst teach.
[6] Inspired poetry.

[1] Tmolus and Pelion are mountains in Greece.
[2] A river in the Vale of Tempe.

Leaving my robe upon the ocean foam;
　　My footsteps pave the clouds with fire; the　10
　　　　caves
Are filled with my bright presence, and the air
Leaves the green Earth to my embraces bare.

III

The sunbeams are my shafts, with which I kill
　　Deceit, that loves the night and fears the day;
All men who do or even imagine ill　15
　　Fly me, and from the glory of my ray
Good minds and open actions take new might,
Until diminished by the reign of Night.

IV

I feed the clouds, the rainbows and the flowers
　　With their aethereal colours; the moon's globe　20
And the pure stars in their eternal bowers
　　Are cinctured with my power as with a robe;
Whatever lamps on Earth or Heaven may shine
Are portions of one power, which is mine.

V

I stand at noon upon the peak of Heaven,　25
　　Then with unwilling steps I wander down
Into the clouds of the Atlantic even;
　　For grief that I depart they weep and frown:
What look is more delightful than the smile
With which I soothe them from the western isle?　30

VI

I am the eye with which the Universe
　　Beholds itself and knows itself divine;
All harmony of instrument or verse,
　　All prophecy, all medicine is mine,
All light of art or nature;—to my song　35
Victory and praise in its own right belong.

Adonais

An Elegy on the Death of John Keats, Author of Endymion, Hyperion, Etc.

This famous poem in Spenserian stanzas, written at
Pisa in the late spring of 1821, laments the death of
Keats at Rome several months earlier. The poets were
not well acquainted; it was some time after Keats's
death that the sad news reached Shelley. Had he
known Keats better, he could never have supposed

that, as he states in a preface here omitted, a savage
review had killed him.

"Adonais," like "Lycidas," follows the ancient
tradition of pastoral elegy; hence the name, another
form of *Adonis*, the unfortunate youth beloved by
Venus and celebrated by numerous poets and painters.
No more than Milton's "Lycidas" does Shelley's poem
spring from an outburst of sorrow for a personal
loss. The subject is the lot of the genius in general,
and especially his liability to misunderstanding and
even persecution by the dull and ignorant. Typically
Shelleyan is the poetic statement of Platonic faith
in the Ideal and in the individual spirit's capacity
for reunion with it. The epigraph is Shelley's translation of an epigram which may be by Plato:

Thou wert the morning star among the living,
　　Ere thy fair light had fled—
Now, having died, thou art as Hesperus, giving
　　New splendour to the dead.

I weep for Adonais—he is dead!
Oh, weep for Adonais! though our tears
Thaw not the frost which binds so dear a head!
And thou, sad Hour, selected from all years
To mourn our loss, rouse thy obscure com-　5
　　peers,[1]
And teach them thine own sorrow; say, With
　　me
Died Adonais; till the Future dares
Forget the Past, his fate and fame shall be
An echo and a light unto eternity!

Where wert thou, mighty Mother,[2] when he　10
　　lay,
When thy Son lay, pierced by the shaft which
　　flies
In darkness?[3] where was lorn Urania
When Adonais died? With veilèd eyes,
'Mid listening Echoes, in her Paradise
She sate, while one,[4] with soft enamoured　15
　　breath,
Rekindled all the fading melodies,
With which, like flowers that mock the corse
　　beneath,
He had adorned and hid the coming bulk of
　　Death.

---

1 Companions, hours still hidden ("obscure") because in
the future.
2 The Heavenly One (because she is the Muse of astronomy); but *Urania* is also one of the epithets for Aphrodite:
the Uranian Venus was goddess of heavenly love and thus
of the Ideal or, in Shelley's phrase, "Intellectual Beauty."
3 I.e., the arrow shot by an anonymous reviewer.
4 Of the Echoes.

Oh, weep for Adonais—he is dead!
Wake, melancholy Mother, wake and weep!   20
Yet wherefore? Quench within their burning
    bed
Thy fiery tears, and let thy loud heart keep,
Like his, a mute and uncomplaining sleep;
For he is gone, where all things wise and fair
Descend;—oh, dream not that the amorous   25
    Deep
Will yet restore him to the vital air;
Death feeds on his mute voice, and laughs at our
    despair.

Most musical of mourners, weep again!
Lament anew, Urania!—He[5] died,
Who was the Sire of an immortal strain,   30
Blind, old, and lonely,—when his country's
    pride
The priest, the slave, and the liberticide
Trampled and mocked with many a loathèd
    rite
Of lust and blood; he went, unterrified,
Into the gulph of death; but his clear Sprite   35
Yet reigns o'er earth, the third[6] among the sons
    of light.

Most musical of mourners, weep anew!
Not all to that bright station dared to climb;
And happier they their happiness who knew,
Whose tapers yet burn through that night of   40
    time
In which suns perished; others more sublime,
Struck by the envious wrath of man or God,
Have sunk, extinct in their refulgent prime;
And some yet live, treading the thorny road,
Which leads, through toil and hate, to Fame's   45
    serene abode.

But now, thy youngest, dearest one has per-
    ished,
The nursling of thy widowhood, who grew,
Like a pale flower by some sad maiden cher-
    ished,
And fed with true-love tears, instead of dew,[7]
Most musical of mourners, weep anew!   50
Thy extreme hope, the loveliest and the last,

The bloom, whose petals, nipt before they
    blew,
Died on the promise of the fruit, is waste;
The broken lily lies—the storm is overpast.

To that high Capital,[8] where kingly Death   55
Keeps his pale court in beauty and decay,
He came; and bought, with price of purest
    breath,
A grave among the eternal.—Come away!
Haste, while the vault of blue Italian day
Is yet his fitting charnel-roof! while still   60
He lies, as if in dewy sleep he lay;
Awake him not! surely he takes his fill
Of deep and liquid rest, forgetful of all ill.

He will awake no more, oh, never more!—
Within the twilight chamber spreads apace   65
The shadow of white Death, and at the door
Invisible Corruption waits to trace
His extreme[9] way to her dim dwelling-place;
The eternal Hunger[10] sits, but pity and awe
Soothe her pale rage, nor dares she to deface   70
So fair a prey, till darkness, and the law
Of change, shall o'er his sleep the mortal curtain
    draw.

Oh, weep for Adonais!—The quick Dreams,[11]
The passion-wingèd Ministers of thought,
Who were his flocks, whom near the living   75
    streams
Of his young spirit he fed, and whom he taught
The love which was its music, wander not.—
Wander no more, from kindling brain to brain,
But droop there, whence they sprung; and
    mourn their lot
Round the cold heart, where, after their sweet   80
    pain,[12]
They ne'er will gather strength, or find a home
    again.

And one with trembling hands clasps his cold
    head,
And fans him with her moonlight wings, and
    cries,
"Our love, our hope, our sorrow, is not dead;

---

5 Milton.
6 It is evident from *A Defence of Poetry* that Shelley considered Homer and Dante Milton's two great predecessors
as epic poets.
7 An allusion to Keats's "Isabella."

8 Rome.   9 Adonais' last.
10 Corruption, which consumes the body in the grave.
11 Poems, poetic ideas.
12 The pangs of the poet in giving them birth.

See, on the silken fringe of his faint eyes,   85
Like dew upon a sleeping flower, there lies
A tear some Dream has loosened from his
    brain."
Lost Angel of a ruined Paradise![13]
She knew not 'twas her own,—as with no stain
She faded, like a cloud which had outwept its   90
    rain.

One from a lucid urn of starry dew
Washed his light limbs, as if embalming them;
Another clipt her profuse locks, and threw
The wreath upon him, like an anadem,[14]
Which frozen tears instead of pearls begem;   95
Another in her wilful grief would break
Her bow and wingèd reeds[15]—as if to stem
A greater loss with one which was more weak—
And dull the barbèd fire against his frozen cheek.

Another Splendour[16] on his mouth alit,   100
That mouth whence it was wont to draw the
    breath
Which gave it strength to pierce the guarded
    wit,[17]
And pass into the panting heart beneath
With lightning and with music: the damp
    death
Quenched its caress upon his icy lips;   105
And, as a dying meteor stains a wreath
Of moonlight vapour, which the cold night
    clips,[18]
It flushed through his pale limbs, and passed to
    its eclipse.

And others came . . . Desires and Adorations,
Wingèd Persuasions and veiled Destinies,   110
Splendours, and Glooms, and glimmering In-
    carnations
Of hopes and fears, and twilight Phantasies;
And Sorrow, with her family of Sighs,
And Pleasure, blind with tears, led by the
    gleam
Of her own dying smile instead of eyes,   115
Came in slow pomp;—the moving pomp might
    seem
Like pageantry of mist on an autumnal stream.

All he had loved, and moulded into thought,
From shape, and hue, and odour, and sweet
    sound,
Lamented Adonais. Morning sought   120
Her eastern watch-tower, and her hair un-
    bound,
Wet with the tears which should adorn the
    ground,
Dimmed the aërial eyes that kindle day;
Afar the melancholy thunder moaned,
Pale Ocean in unquiet slumber lay,   125
And the wild winds flew round, sobbing in their
    dismay.

Lost Echo sits amid the voiceless mountains,
And feeds her grief with his remembered lay,
And will no more reply to winds or fountains,
Or amorous birds perched on the young green   130
    spray,
Or herdsman's horn, or bell at closing day;
Since she can mimic not his lips, more dear
Than those[19] for whose disdain she pined
    away
Into a shadow of all sounds:—a drear
Murmur, between their songs, is all the woodmen   135
    hear.

Grief made the young Spring wild, and she
    threw down
Her kindling buds, as if she Autumn were,
Or they dead leaves; since her delight is flown,
For whom should she have waked the sullen
    Year?
To Phoebus was not Hyacinth[20] so dear,   140
Nor to himself Narcissus, as to both
Thou, Adonais; wan they stand and sere
Amid the faint companions of their youth,
With dew all turned to tears; odour, to sighing
    ruth.

Thy spirit's sister, the lorn nightingale,   145
Mourns not her mate with such melodious
    pain;
Not so the eagle, who like thee could scale
Heaven, and could nourish in the sun's do-
    main

---

13 Adonais' mind.   14 Chaplet, garland.
15 Arrows by which the thoughts of Keats's poems were
shot into the "guarded wit" (see line 102).
16 I.e., "dream," poetic conception.
17 I.e., unresponsive minds.   18 Embraces.

19 Of Narcissus, the youth (enamored of himself) for
whom, in the myth, the nymph Echo pined away till she
was only a voice.
20 The youth Hyacinthus, loved by Phoebus Apollo, who
accidentally killed him. From his blood sprang the flower.

Her mighty youth with morning, doth com-
  plain,
Soaring and screaming round her empty nest, 150
As Albion[21] wails for thee: the curse of Cain
Light on his head[22] who pierced thy innocent
  breast,
And scared the angel soul that was its earthly
  guest!

Ah woe is me! Winter is come and gone,
But grief returns with the revolving year; 155
The airs and streams renew their joyous tone;
The ants, the bees, the swallows reappear;
Fresh leaves and flowers deck the dead Seasons'
  bier;
The amorous birds now pair in every brake,
And build their mossy homes in field and 160
  brere;[23]
And the green lizard, and the golden snake,
Like unimprisoned flames, out of their trance
  awake.

Through wood and stream and field and hill
  and Ocean
A quickening life from the Earth's heart has
  burst,
As it has ever done, with change and motion, 165
From the great morning of the world when
  first
God dawned on Chaos; in its stream immersed
The lamps of Heaven flash with a softer light;
All baser things pant with life's sacred thirst;
Diffuse themselves; and spend in love's delight, 170
The beauty and the joy of their renewèd might.

The leprous corpse touched by this spirit
  tender
Exhales itself in flowers of gentle breath;
Like incarnations of the stars, when splendour
Is changed to fragrance, they illumine death 175
And mock the merry worm that wakes be-
  neath;
Nought we know, dies. Shall that alone which
  knows
Be as a sword consumed before the sheath
By sightless[24] lightning?—Th' intense atom
  glows

A moment, then is quenched in a most cold re- 180
  pose.

Alas! that all we loved of him should be,
But for our grief, as if it had not been,
And grief itself be mortal! Woe is me!
Whence are we, and why are we? of what scene
The actors or spectators? Great and mean 185
Meet massed in death, who lends what life
  must borrow.[25]
As long as skies are blue, and fields are green,
Evening must usher night, night urge the mor-
  row,
Month follow month with woe, and year wake
  year to sorrow.

He will awake no more, oh, never more! 190
"Wake thou," cried Misery, "childless Mother!
  rise
Out of thy sleep, and slake in thy heart's core
A wound more fierce than his with tears and
  sighs."
And all the Dreams that watched Urania's
  eyes,
And all the Echoes whom their sister's song 195
Had held in holy silence, cried, "Arise!"
Swift as a Thought by the snake Memory
  stung,
From her ambrosial rest the fading Splendour
  sprung.

She rose like an autumnal Night, that springs
Out of the East, and follows wild and drear 200
The golden Day, which, on eternal wings,
Even as a ghost abandoning a bier,
Had left the Earth a corpse. Sorrow and fear
So struck, so roused, so rapt Urania;
So saddened round her like an atmosphere 205
Of stormy mist; so swept her on her way
Even to the mournful place where Adonais lay.

Out of her secret Paradise she sped,
Through camps and cities rough with stone,
  and steel,
And human hearts, which to her aery tread 210

---

21 England.   22 The reviewer in the *Quarterly*.
23 Briar.
24 Invisible. Everything of which we can have actual

knowledge, i.e., all matter, is imperishable (line 177).
How strange that the part of us which is conscious should
perish, as if (lines 178–79) a bolt of lightning should
destroy the sword (the mind) without destroying the sheath
(the body).
25 I.e., the great reality is not life but death.

Yielding not, wounded the invisible
Palms of her tender feet where'er they fell:
And barbèd tongues, and thoughts more sharp
    than they,
Rent the soft Form they never could repel,
Whose sacred blood, like the young tears of 215
    May,
Paved with eternal flowers that undeserving way.

In the death-chamber for a moment Death,
Shamed by the presence of that living Might,
Blushed to annihilation, and the breath
Revisited those lips, and life's pale light 220
Flashed through those limbs, so late her dear
    delight.
"Leave me not wild and drear and comfortless,
As silent lightning leaves the starless night!
Leave me not!" cried Urania: her distress
Roused Death: Death rose and smiled, and met 225
    her vain caress.

"Stay yet awhile! speak to me once again;
Kiss me, so long but as a kiss may live;
And in my heartless[26] breast and burning
    brain
That word, that kiss, shall all thoughts else
    survive,
With food of saddest memory kept alive, 230
Now thou art dead, as if it were a part
Of thee, my Adonais! I would give
All that I am to be as thou now art,
But I am chained to Time, and cannot thence de-
    part!

"O gentle child, beautiful as thou wert, 235
Why didst thou leave the trodden paths of
    men
Too soon, and with weak hands though mighty
    heart
Dare the unpastured dragon[27] in his den?
Defenceless as thou wert, oh! where was then
Wisdom the mirrored shield,[28] or scorn the 240
    spear?
Or hadst thou waited the full cycle, when
Thy spirit should have filled its crescent sphere,

The monsters of life's waste had fled from thee
    like deer.

"The herded[29] wolves, bold only to pursue;
The obscene ravens, clamorous o'er the dead; 245
The vultures to the conqueror's banner true
Who feed where Desolation first has fed,
And whose wings rain contagion;—how they
    fled,
When, like Apollo, from his golden bow,
The Pythian[30] of the age one arrow sped 250
And smiled!—The spoilers tempt no second
    blow,—
They fawn on the proud feet that spurn them
    lying low.

"The sun comes forth, and many reptiles
    spawn;
He sets, and each ephemeral insect then
Is gathered into death without a dawn, 255
And the immortal stars awake again;
So it is in the world of living men:
A godlike mind soars forth, in its delight
Making earth bare and veiling Heaven,[31] and
    when
It sinks, the swarms that dimmed or shared its 260
    light
Leave to its kindred lamps[32] the spirit's awful
    night."

Thus ceased she: and the mountain shepherds
    came,
Their garlands sere, their magic mantles rent;
The Pilgrim of Eternity,[33] whose fame
Over his living head like Heaven is bent, 265
An early but enduring monument,
Came, veiling all the lightnings of his song
In sorrow; from her wilds Ierne sent
The sweetest lyrist of her saddest wrong,[34]
And love taught grief to fall like music from his 270
    tongue.

---

26 Because her heart was with Adonais.
27 I.e., boldly seek out and expose yourself to the world's harshness, as Perseus in the Greek myth confronted Medusa, the snaky-haired Gorgon.
28 The Gorgon's gaze could turn anyone to stone. Perseus looked at her reflection in his shield.

29 Running in pack; i.e., the critics.
30 Apollo was given this epithet for slaying the huge serpent known as the Python. The allusion is to Byron and his *English Bards, and Scotch Reviewers.*
31 Like the sun making the earth bright and unclouded, and the other heavenly bodies invisible.
32 The other heavenly bodies; i.e., other poets.
33 Byron, the Pilgrim of *Childe Harold.*
34 Ireland sent Tom Moore. Actually, however, he did not contribute a lamentation for Keats.

Midst others of less note, came one frail
    Form,[35]
A phantom among men; companionless
As the last cloud of an expiring storm
Whose thunder is its knell; he, as I guess,
Had gazed on Nature's naked loveliness,   275
Actaeon-like,[36] and now he fled astray
With feeble steps o'er the world's wilderness,
And his own thoughts, along that rugged way,
Pursued, like raging hounds, their father and
    their prey.

A pardlike[37] Spirit beautiful and swift—   280
A Love in desolation masked;—a Power
Girt round with weakness;—it can scarce up-
    lift
The weight of the superincumbent hour;
It is a dying lamp, a falling shower,
A breaking billow;—even whilst we speak   285
Is it not broken? On the withering flower
The killing sun smiles brightly: on a cheek
The life can burn in blood, even while the heart
    may break.

His head was bound with pansies[38] over-blown,
And faded violets, white, and pied, and blue;   290
And a light spear topped with a cypress cone,
Round whose rude shaft dark ivy-tresses grew
Yet dripping with the forest's noonday dew,
Vibrated, as the ever-beating heart
Shook the weak hand that grasped it; of that   295
    crew
He came the last, neglected and apart;
A herd-abandoned deer struck by the hunter's
    dart.

All stood aloof, and at his partial[39] moan
Smiled through their tears; well knew that
    gentle band
Who in another's fate now wept his own;   300
As in the accents of an unknown[40] land
He sung new sorrow; sad Urania scanned
The Stranger's mien, and murmured, "Who
    art thou?"

He answered not, but with a sudden hand
Made bare his branded and ensanguined brow,   305
Which was like Cain's or Christ's—oh! that it
    should be so!

What softer voice is hushed over the dead?
Athwart what brow is that dark mantle
    thrown?
What form leans sadly o'er the white death-
    bed,
In mockery of monumental stone,—   310
The heavy heart heaving without a moan?
If it be He,[41] who, gentlest of the wise,
Taught, soothed, loved, honoured the departed
    one,
Let me not vex, with inharmonious sighs,
The silence of that heart's accepted sacrifice.   315

Our Adonais has drunk poison—oh,
What deaf and viperous murderer could crown
Life's early cup with such a draught of woe?
The nameless worm[42] would now itself dis-
    own:
It felt, yet could escape the magic tone   320
Whose prelude held all envy, hate, and wrong,
But what was howling in one breast alone,
Silent with expectation of the song,
Whose master's hand is cold, whose silver lyre
    unstrung.

Live thou, whose infamy is not thy fame!   325
Live! fear no heavier chastisement from me,
Thou noteless blot on a remembered name!
But be thyself, and know thyself to be!
And ever at thy season be thou free
To spill the venom when thy fangs o'erflow: 330
Remorse and Self-contempt shall cling to thee;
Hot Shame shall burn upon thy secret brow,
And like a beaten hound tremble thou shalt—as
    now.

Nor let us weep that our delight is fled[43]
Far from these carrion kites that scream below;   335
He wakes or sleeps with the enduring dead;

---

35 Shelley.
36 Actaeon, in Greek myth, saw Diana bathing. He was
punished by being changed into a stag and hunted to his
death by his own hounds.
37 Leopard-like.
38 Symbol of thought, as the violet is of modesty, the
cypress of mourning, and the ivy of poets.
39 Sympathetic.   40 I.e., to Urania.

41 Leigh Hunt, one of Shelley's best friends. See p. 214.
42 Serpent; i.e., the anonymous reviewer in the *Quarterly*
for April 1818 (published in September). It was the Tory
critic John Wilson Croker (1780–1857), though Keats's
friends suspected another.
43 With this stanza comes the "turn" of the poem; Shelley
begins soaring to a higher elevation.

Thou canst not soar where he is sitting now.—
Dust to the dust! but the pure spirit shall flow
Back to the burning fountain whence it came,
A portion of the Eternal, which must glow   340
Through time and change, unquenchably the
    same,
Whilst thy cold embers[44] choke the sordid hearth
    of shame.

Peace, peace! he is not dead, he doth not
    sleep—
He hath awakened from the dream of life:
'Tis we, who, lost in stormy visions, keep   345
With phantoms an unprofitable strife,
And, in mad trance, strike with our spirit's
    knife
Invulnerable nothings.—*We* decay
Like corpses in a charnel;[45] fear and grief
Convulse us and consume us day by day,   350
And cold hopes swarm like worms within our liv-
    ing clay.

He has outsoared the shadow of our night;
Envy and calumny and hate and pain,
And that unrest which men miscall delight,
Can touch him not and torture not again;   355
From the contagion of the world's slow stain
He is secure, and now can never mourn
A heart grown cold, a head grown grey in
    vain;
Nor, when the spirit's self has ceased to burn,
With sparkless ashes load an unlamented urn.   360

He lives, he wakes—'tis Death is dead, not he;
Mourn not for Adonais.—Thou young Dawn,
Turn all thy dew to splendour, for from thee
The spirit thou lamentest is not gone;
Ye caverns and ye forests, cease to moan!   365
Cease, ye faint flowers and fountains, and thou
    Air,
Which like a mourning veil thy scarf hadst
    thrown
O'er the abandoned Earth, now leave it bare
Even to the joyous stars which smile on its des-
    pair!

He is made one with Nature: there is heard   370
His voice in all her music, from the moan
Of thunder to the song of night's sweet bird;

He is a presence to be felt and known
In darkness and in light, from[46] herb and
    stone,—
Spreading itself where'er that Power[47] may   375
    move
Which has withdrawn his being to its own;
Which wields the world with never-wearied
    love,
Sustains it from beneath, and kindles it above.

He is a portion of the loveliness
Which once he made more lovely: he doth   380
    bear
His part, while the one Spirit's plastic[48] stress
Sweeps through the dull dense world, com-
    pelling there
All new successions to the forms they wear;
Torturing th' unwilling dross that checks its
    flight
To its own likeness, as[49] each mass may bear.   385
And bursting in its beauty and its might
From trees and beasts and men into the Heaven's
    light.

The splendours of the firmament of time
May be eclipsed, but are extinguished not:
Like stars to their appointed height they   390
    climb,
And death is a low mist which cannot blot
The brightness it may veil. When lofty
    thought
Lifts a young heart above its mortal lair,
And love and life contend in it for what
Shall be its earthly doom, the dead live there[50]   395
And move like winds of light on dark and stormy
    air.

The inheritors of unfulfilled renown
Rose from their thrones, built beyond mortal
    thought,
Far in the Unapparent. Chatterton[51]
Rose pale,—his solemn agony had not   400
Yet faded from him; Sidney,[52] as he fought
And as he fell and as he lived and loved,

---

44 The reviewer's ashes.   45 Charnel house, sepulchre.

46 Emanating from.
47 The Eternal, the burning fountain (line 339), the creative source of all.   48 Molding, creating.
49 According as, to such extent as.
50 In the young heart.
51 In 1770, at the age of eighteen, this young poet killed
himself.
52 Sir Philip Sidney (1554–1586).

Sublimely mild, a Spirit without spot,
Arose; and Lucan,[53] by his death approved:
Oblivion as they rose shrank like a thing re- 405
   proved.

And many more, whose names on Earth are
   dark,
But whose transmitted effluence cannot die
So long as fire outlives the parent spark,
Rose, robed in dazzling immortality.
"Thou art become as one of us," they cry; 410
"It was for thee yon kingless sphere has long
Swung blind[54] in unascended majesty,
Silent alone amid an Heaven of song.
Assume thy wingèd throne, thou Vesper[55] of our
   throng!"

Who mourns for Adonais? Oh come forth, 415
Fond wretch![56] and know thyself and him
   aright.
Clasp with thy panting soul the pendulous
   Earth;
As from a centre, dart thy spirit's light
Beyond all worlds, until its spacious might
Satiate the void circumference: then shrink 420
Even to a point within our day and night;
And keep thy heart light lest it make thee sink
When hope has kindled hope, and lured thee to
   the brink.[57]

Or go to Rome, which is the sepulchre,
Oh, not of him, but of our joy: 'tis nought 425
That ages, empires, and religions there
Lie buried in the ravage they have wrought;
For such as he can lend,—they borrow not
Glory[58] from those who made the world their
   prey;
And he is gathered to the kings of thought 430
Who waged contention with their time's de-
   cay,
And of the past are all that cannot pass away.

Go thou to Rome,—at once the Paradise,
The grave, the city, and the wilderness;

And where its wrecks like shattered mountains 435
   rise,
And flowering weeds, and fragrant copses dress
The bones of Desolation's nakedness,
Pass, till the Spirit of the spot shall lead
Thy footsteps to a slope of green access,[59]
Where, like an infant's smile, over the dead 440
A light of laughing flowers along the grass is
   spread;

And grey walls moulder round, on which dull
   Time
Feeds, like slow fire upon a hoary brand;
And one keen pyramid[60] with wedge sublime,
Pavilioning the dust of him who planned 445
This refuge for his memory, doth stand
Like flame transformed to marble; and be-
   neath,
A field is spread, on which a newer band
Have pitched in Heaven's smile their camp of
   death,
Welcoming him we lose with scarce-extinguished 450
   breath.

Here pause: these graves are all too young as
   yet
To have outgrown the sorrow which consigned
Its charge to each; and if the seal is set,
Here, on one fountain of a mourning mind,[61]
Break it not thou! too surely shalt thou find 455
Thine own well full, if thou returnest home,
Of tears and gall. From the world's bitter wind
Seek shelter in the shadow of the tomb.
What Adonais is, why fear we to become?

The One[62] remains, the many change and pass; 460
Heaven's light forever shines, Earth's shadows
   fly;
Life, like a dome of many-coloured glass,
Stains[63] the white radiance of Eternity,
Until Death tramples it to fragments.—Die,

---

[53] The Roman poet Lucan (39–65), author of the epic *Pharsalia*, killed himself after Nero had condemned him to death. [54] Without light.
[55] Or Hesper, the evening star.
[56] Presumably Shelley. [57] Of death.
[58] I.e., by being buried there Keats confers distinction on Rome.

[59] The Protestant cemetery. Shelley's ashes were soon buried there, too.
[60] The tomb of Gaius Cestius, a Roman praetor and tribune.
[61] Shelley's son William had been buried there in 1819. The graves are all "young" because the cemetery was new.
[62] The Platonic Idea, the eternal and ultimate reality, as contrasted with "Earth's shadows," the impermanent and merely individual phenomena of life.
[63] I.e., breaks up into individual and fragmentary colors.

If thou wouldst be with that which thou dost 465
seek![64]
Follow where all is fled!—Rome's azure sky,
Flowers, ruins, statues, music, words, are weak
The glory they transfuse with fitting truth to
speak.

Why linger, why turn back, why shrink, my
Heart?
Thy hopes are gone before: from all things 470
here
They have departed; thou shouldst now de-
part!
A light is past from the revolving year,
And man, and woman; and what still is dear
Attracts to crush, repels to make thee wither.
The soft sky smiles,—the low wind whispers 475
near:
'Tis Adonais calls! oh, hasten thither,—
No more let Life divide what Death can join to-
gether.

That Light whose smile kindles the Universe,
That Beauty in which all things work and
move,
That Benediction which the eclipsing Curse 480
Of birth can quench not, that sustaining Love
Which, through the web of being, blindly
wove
By man and beast and earth and air and sea,
Burns bright or dim, as each are mirrors of
The fire for which all thirst,—now beams on 485
me,
Consuming the last clouds of cold mortality.

The breath[65] whose might I have invoked in
song
Descends on me; my spirit's bark is driven,
Far from the shore, far from the trembling
throng
Whose sails were never to the tempest given; 490
The massy earth and spherèd skies are riven!
I am borne darkly, fearfully, afar;
Whilst, burning through the inmost veil of
Heaven,
The soul of Adonais, like a star,
Beacons from the abode where the Eternal are. 495

---

64 The One (line 460).
65 Of the spirit of the universe.

Choruses *from* Hellas

Hellas, written at Pisa in the fall of 1821, is another
of Shelley's "lyrical dramas." He calls it "a series of
lyric pictures," but his aim was to help identify the
Greek war of independence with "the cause of civilisation and social improvement. . . . We are all,"
he continues in his preface, "Greeks. Our laws, our
literature, our religion, our arts, have their roots in
Greece." This British government was still pro-Turk;
but Shelley, rejoicing in the success of a Spanish
revolution, predicts that the peoples of Greece, Italy,
and Germany will yet rise triumphant against the
tyrants and their "bloody sceptres." It is, he holds,
Platonic idealism and the great thought of the past
that will eventually bring about a liberated world.

WORLDS ON WORLDS

Worlds on worlds are rolling ever
  From creation to decay,
Like the bubbles on a river,
  Sparkling, bursting, borne away.
    But they are still immortal   5
    Who, through birth's orient portal
And death's dark chasm hurrying to and fro,
    Clothe their unceasing flight
    In the brief dust and light
Gathered around their chariots as they go;   10
    New shapes they still may weave,
    New gods, new laws receive;
Bright or dim are they, as the robes they last
    On Death's bare ribs had cast.

A power[1] from the unknown God,   15
    A Promethean[2] conqueror came;
Like a triumphal path he trod
    The thorns of death and shame.
    A mortal shape to him
    Was like the vapour dim   20
Which the orient planet animates with light;
    Hell, Sin, and Slavery came,
    Like bloodhounds mild and tame,
Nor preyed, until their Lord had taken flight;
    The moon of Mahomet   25
    Arose, and it shall set:
While blazoned as on Heaven's immortal noon
    The cross leads generations on.

Swift as the radiant shapes of sleep
    From one whose dreams are Paradise   30

---

1 Jesus.
2 I.e., like the civilizing Titan, Prometheus, who gave man
fire.

Fly, when the fond wretch wakes to weep,
  And Day peers forth with her blank eyes;
    So fleet, so faint, so fair,
    The Powers of earth and air
Fled from the folding-star[3] of Bethlehem: 35
  Apollo, Pan, and Love,
  And even Olympian Jove,[4]
Grew weak, for killing Truth had glared on them;
  Our hills and seas and streams,
  Dispeopled of their dreams, 40
Their waters turned to blood, their dew to tears,
  Wailed for the golden years.[5]

THE WORLD'S GREAT AGE

The world's great age[6] begins anew,
  The golden years return,
The earth doth like a snake renew
  Her winter weeds[7] outworn:
Heaven smiles, and faiths and empires gleam 5
Like wrecks of a dissolving dream.

A brighter Hellas rears its mountains
  From waves serener far;
A new Peneus[8] rolls his fountains
  Against the morning-star. 10
Where fairer Tempes bloom, there sleep
Young Cyclads[9] on a sunnier deep.

A loftier Argo[10] cleaves the main,
  Fraught with a later prize;
Another Orpheus[11] sings again, 15
  And loves, and weeps, and dies.
A new Ulysses leaves once more
Calypso[12] for his native shore.

Oh, write no more the tale of Troy,
  If earth Death's scroll must be! 20
Nor mix with Laian[13] rage the joy
  Which dawns upon the free:
Although a subtler Sphinx renew
Riddles of death Thebes never knew.

Another Athens shall arise, 25
  And to remoter time
Bequeath, like sunset to the skies,
  The splendour of its prime;
And leave, if nought so bright may live,
All earth can take or Heaven can give. 30

Saturn and Love their long repose[14]
  Shall burst, more bright and good
Than all who fell, than One who rose,
  Than many unsubdued:
Not gold, not blood, their altar dowers, 35
But votive tears and symbol flowers.

Oh, cease! must hate and death return?
  Cease! must men kill and die?
Cease! drain not to its dregs the urn
  Of bitter prophecy. 40
The world is weary of the past,—
Oh, might it die or rest at last!

Time

During 1821 Shelley composed besides longer poems—among them "Adonais" and *Hellas*—a number of his finest short lyrics.

Unfathomable Sea, whose waves are years;
  Ocean of Time, whose waters of deep woe

---

[3] The evening star, at whose appearance the sheep are gathered into the fold.

[4] I.e., the pagan gods of Greece and Rome: Apollo, of the sun, poetry, and music; Pan, of flocks and herds, of woods and wild life; Venus, of love and beauty; Jove or Zeus, dweller on Mt. Olympus, home of the classical deities.

[5] In classical fable the age of primeval simplicity, before Jove drove Saturn from the throne of heaven.

[6] See note 5.—This is the final chorus of the poem. Shelley remarks in a note that it "is indistinct and obscure, as the event of the living drama whose arrival it foretells."

[7] I.e., the garments or trappings of the long ages of evil.

[8] Or Salambria, a river in Thessaly, Greece. It flows through the beautiful valley of Tempe.

[9] The Cyclades, islands in the southwestern Aegean.

[10] The ship in which Jason sailed to win the Golden Fleece.

[11] The fabled Thracian poet and musician who journeyed to Hades and nearly succeeded in bringing back his wife Eurydice.

[12] The nymph who tried to induce the Greek hero, home-ward bound from the Trojan War, to remain on her island.

[13] King Laius of Thebes was the father of Oedipus. The misfortunes of this family are prominent among the subjects of Greek poetry and tragedy. It was Oedipus who solved the riddle of the Sphinx.

[14] From Shelley's note: "Saturn and Love were among the deities of a real or imaginary state of innocence and happiness. *All* those *who fell*, or the Gods of Greece, Asia, and Egypt; the *One who rose*, or Jesus Christ, at whose appearance the idols of the Pagan World were amerced [punished by being deprived] of their worship; and *the many unsubdued*, or the monstrous objects of the idolatry of China, India, the Antarctic islands, and the native tribes of America, certainly have reigned over the under-standings of men in conjunction or in succession, during periods in which all we know of evil has been in a state of portentous, and, until the revival of learning [the Renaissance], perpetually increasing, activity."

Are brackish with the salt of human tears!
　Thou shoreless flood, which in thy ebb and
　　flow
Claspest the limits of mortality!　　　　　　5
And sick of prey, yet howling on for more,
Vomitest thy wrecks on its inhospitable shore;
　Treacherous in calm, and terrible in storm,
　　Who shall put forth on thee,
　　Unfathomable Sea?　　　　　　　　　　10

To Night

Swiftly walk o'er the western wave,
　　Spirit of Night!
Out of the misty eastern cave,
Where, all the long and lone daylight,
Thou wovest dreams of joy and fear,　　　　5
Which make thee terrible and dear,—
　　Swift be thy flight!

Wrap thy form in a mantle grey,
　　Star-inwrought!
Blind with thine hair the eyes of Day,　　　10
Kiss her until she be wearied out;
Then wander o'er city, and sea, and land,
Touching all with thine opiate wand—
　　Come, long sought!

When I arose and saw the dawn,　　　　　15
　　I sighed for thee;
When light rode high, and the dew was gone,
And noon lay heavy on flower and tree,
And the weary Day turned to his rest,
Lingering like an unloved guest,　　　　　20
　　I sighed for thee.

Thy brother Death came, and cried,
　　"Wouldst thou me?"
Thy sweet child Sleep, the filmy-eyed,
Murmured like a noontide bee,　　　　　25
"Shall I nestle near thy side?
Wouldst thou me?"—And I replied,
　　"No, not thee!"

Death will come when thou art dead,
　　Soon, too soon:　　　　　　　　　　30
Sleep will come when thou art fled;
Of neither would I ask the boon
I ask of thee, belovèd Night,—
Swift be thine approaching flight,
　　Come soon, soon!　　　　　　　　　35

Mutability

In company with a longer poem, *Epipsychidion,* this lyric and probably several of those that follow it appear to be inspired by Shelley's regret over the marriage of convenience in the fall of 1821 of Emilia Viviani, a beautiful Italian girl with whom he and his wife had become acquainted somewhat less than a year before. Emilia and the poet had not fallen in love, but were aware of an unusual spiritual sympathy for each other which Shelley, who was deeply moved, realized was unlikely to continue after her wedding.

The flower that smiles to-day
　　To-morrow dies;
All that we wish to stay,
　　Tempts and then flies;
What is this world's delight?　　　　　　5
Lightning that mocks the night,
　　Brief even as bright.

Virtue, how frail it is!
　　Friendship how rare!
Love, how it sells poor bliss　　　　　　10
　　For proud despair!
But we, though soon they fall,
Survive their joy, and all
　　Which ours we call.

Whilst skies are blue and bright,　　　　15
　　Whilst flowers are gay,
Whilst eyes that change ere night
　　Make glad the day;
Whilst yet the calm hours creep,
Dream thou—and from thy sleep　　　　20
　　Then wake to weep.

A Lament

O world! O life! O time!
On whose last steps I climb
　Trembling at that where I had stood before;
When will return the glory of your prime?
　　No more—oh, never more!　　　　　5

Out of the day and night
A joy has taken flight;
　Fresh Spring, and Summer, and Winter hoar,
Move my faint heart with grief,—but with delight
　　No more—oh, never more!　　　　　10

To ——

Music, when soft voices die,
Vibrates in the memory;
Odours, when sweet violets sicken,
Live within the sense they quicken.
Rose-leaves, when the rose is dead,   5
Are heaped for the belovèd's bed;
And so thy thoughts, when thou art gone,
Love itself shall slumber on.

A Dirge

The remaining lyrics were written in 1822.

Rough wind, that moanest loud
  Grief too sad for song;
Wild wind, when sullen cloud
  Knells all the night long;
Sad storm, whose tears are vain,   5
Bare woods, whose branches strain,
Deep caves and dreary main,
  Wail, for the world's wrong!

Lines: When the Lamp Is Shattered

When the lamp is shattered,
The light in the dust lies dead;
  When the cloud is scattered,
The rainbow's glory is shed.
  When the lute is broken,   5
Sweet tones are remembered not;
  When the lips have spoken,
Loved accents are soon forgot.

  As music and splendour
Survive not the lamp and the lute,   10
  The heart's echoes render
No song when the spirit is mute:—
  No song but sad dirges,
Like the wind in a ruined cell,
  Or the mournful surges   15
That ring the dead seaman's knell.

  When hearts have once mingled,
Love first leaves the well-built nest;
  The weak one is singled

To endure what it once possest.   20
  O Love! who bewailest
The frailty of all things here,
  Why chose you the frailest
For your cradle, your home, and your bier?

  Its passions will rock thee,   25
As the storms rock the ravens on high:
  Bright reason will mock thee,
Like the sun from a wintry sky.
  From thy nest every rafter
Will rot, and thine eagle home   30
  Leave thee naked to laughter,
When leaves fall and cold winds come.

To Jane: "The Keen Stars Were Twinkling"

I

The keen stars were twinkling,
And the fair moon was rising among them,
    Dear Jane!
  The guitar was tinkling,
But the notes were not sweet till you sung them   5
    Again.

II

  As the moon's soft splendour
O'er the faint cold starlight of Heaven
    Is thrown,
  So your voice most tender
To the strings without soul had then given   10
    Its own.

III

  The stars will awaken,
Though the moon sleep a full hour later,
    To-night;
  No leaf will be shaken
Whilst the dews of your melody scatter   15
    Delight.

IV

  Though the sound overpowers,
Sing again, with your dear voice revealing
    A tone
  Of some world far from ours,
Where music and moonlight and feeling   20
    Are one.

from A Defence of Poetry

This manifesto is one of the major expositions of the reasons why thoughtful men, whether artists or scientists, consider poetry and its functions of first-rate importance. Shelley intended to carry on the discussion in a second and a third Part; but he completed only Part I, about two-thirds of which is here reprinted. The occasion of the treatise was a whimsical attack on Romantic poetry by a gifted friend of Shelley's, Thomas Love Peacock (1785–1866), a minor poet, scholar, and miscellaneous writer, chiefly celebrated for his satirical novels. Peacock's *The Four Ages of Poetry* appeared in 1820. Shelley wrote his rejoinder in 1821; but on account of his death and the subsequent troubles of the Hunts, who were to publish it, the *Defence* remained in manuscript till 1840. The principal literary influences on its conceptions are Plato and Sir Philip Sidney's *The Defense of Poesy* (see Volume I).

The version printed in 1840, which is followed in our selections, was edited by Leigh Hunt's brother John and by Mary Shelley; they wisely removed a number of counterblasts to Peacock's remarks, in order to emphasize the essay's general application. The changes are discussed in a useful edition: *Peacock's Four Ages of Poetry, Shelley's Defence of Poetry, Browning's Essay on Shelley,* edited by H. F. B. Brett-Smith (1921). Another good edition, confined to Shelley's essay, is A. S. Cook's (1891).

According to one mode of regarding those two classes of mental action, which are called reason and imagination, the former may be considered as mind contemplating the relations borne by one thought to another, however produced; and the latter, as mind acting upon those thoughts so as to colour them with its own light, and composing from them, as from elements, other thoughts, each containing within itself the principle of its own integrity. The one is the τὸ ποιεῖν,[1] or the principle of synthesis, and has for its objects those forms which are common to universal nature and existence itself; the other is the τὸ λογίζειν,[2] or principle of analysis, and its action regards the relations of things, simply as relations; considering thoughts, not in their integral unity, but as the algebraical representations which conduct to certain general results. Reason is the enumeration of quantities already known; imagination is the perception of the value of those quantities, both separately and as a whole. Reason respects the differences, and

imagination the similitudes of things. Reason is to imagination as the instrument to the agent, as the body to the spirit, as the shadow to the substance.

Poetry, in a general sense, may be defined to be "the expression of the imagination"; and poetry is connate with the origin of man. Man is an instrument over which a series of external and internal impressions are driven, like the alternations of an ever-changing wind over an Aeolian lyre, which move it by their motion to ever-changing melody. But there is a principle within the human being, and perhaps within all sentient beings, which acts otherwise than in the lyre, and produces not melody alone, but harmony, by an internal adjustment of the sounds or motions thus excited to the impressions which excite them. It is as if the lyre could accommodate its chords to the motions of that which strikes them, in a determined proportion of sound; even as the musician can accommodate his voice to the sound of the lyre. A child at play by itself will express its delight by its voice and motions; and every inflexion of tone and every gesture will bear exact relation to a corresponding antitype in the pleasurable impressions which awakened it; it will be the reflected image of that impression; and as the lyre trembles and sounds after the wind has died away, so the child seeks, by prolonging in its voice and motions the duration of the effect, to prolong also a consciousness of the cause. In relation to the objects which delight a child, these expressions are what poetry is to higher objects. The savage (for the savage is to ages what the child is to years) expresses the emotions produced in him by surrounding objects in a similar manner; and language and gesture, together with plastic or pictorial imitation, become the image of the combined effect of those objects and his apprehension of them. Man in society, with all his passions and his pleasures, next becomes the object of the passions and pleasures of man; an additional class of emotions produces an augmented treasure of expression; and language, gesture, and the imitative arts, become at once the representation and the medium, the pencil and the picture, the chisel and the statue, the chord and the harmony. The social sympathies, or those laws from which as from its elements society results, begin to develop themselves from the moment that two human

---

1 Making.
2 Reasoning.

beings coexist; the future is contained within the present as the plant within the seed; and equality, diversity, unity, contrast, mutual dependence, become the principles alone capable of affording the motives according to which the will of a social being is determined to action, inasmuch as he is social; and constitute pleasure in sensation, virtue in sentiment, beauty in art, truth in reasoning, and love in the intercourse of kind. Hence men, even in the infancy of society, observe a certain order in their words and actions, distinct from that of the objects and the impressions represented by them, all expression being subject to the laws of that from which it proceeds. But let us dismiss those more general considerations which might involve an inquiry into the principles of society itself, and restrict our view to the manner in which the imagination is expressed upon its forms.

In the youth of the world, men dance and sing and imitate natural objects, observing in these actions, as in all others, a certain rhythm or order. And, although all men observe a similar, they observe not the same order, in the motions of the dance, in the melody of the song, in the combinations of language, in the series of their imitations of natural objects. For there is a certain order or rhythm belonging to each of these classes of mimetic representation, from which the hearer and the spectator receive an intenser and purer pleasure than from any other: the sense of an approximation to this order has been called taste by modern writers. Every man, in the infancy of art, observes an order which approximates more or less closely to that from which this highest delight results: but the diversity is not sufficiently marked, as that its gradations should be sensible, except in those instances where the predominance of this faculty of approximation to the beautiful (for so we may be permitted to name the relation between this highest pleasure and its cause) is very great. Those in whom it exists to excess are poets, in the most universal sense of the word; and the pleasure resulting from the manner in which they express the influence of society or nature upon their own minds, communicates itself to others, and gathers a sort of reduplication from the community. Their language is vitally metaphorical; that is, it marks the before unapprehended relations of things and perpetuates their

apprehension, until words, which represent them, become, through time, signs for portions or classes of thought, instead of pictures of integral thoughts; and then, if no new poets should arise to create afresh the associations which have been thus disorganised, language will be dead to all the nobler purposes of human intercourse. These similitudes or relations are finely said by Lord Bacon to be "the same footsteps of nature impressed upon the various subjects of the world"[3] —and he considers the faculty which perceives them as the storehouse of axioms common to all knowledge. In the infancy of society every author is necessarily a poet, because language itself is poetry; and to be a poet is to apprehend the true and the beautiful, in a word, the good which exists in the relation subsisting, first between existence and perception, and secondly between perception and expression. Every original language near to its source is in itself the chaos of a cyclic poem; the copiousness of lexicography and the distinctions of grammar are the works of a later age, and are merely the catalogue and the forms of the creations of poetry.

But poets, or those who imagine and express this indestructible order, are not only the authors of language and of music, of the dance, and architecture, and statuary, and painting; they are the institutors of laws and the founders of civil society, and the inventors of the arts of life, and the teachers, who draw into a certain propinquity with the beautiful and the true that partial apprehension of the agencies of the invisible world which is called religion. Hence all original religions are allegorical, or susceptible of allegory, and, like Janus,[4] have a double face of false and true. Poets, according to the circumstances of the age and nation in which they appeared, were called, in the earlier epochs of the world, legislators or prophets: a poet essentially comprises and unites both these characters. For he not only beholds intensely the present as it is, and discovers those laws according to which present things ought to be ordered, but he beholds the future in the present, and his thoughts are the germs of the flower and the fruit of latest time. Not that I assert poets to be prophets in

---

3 Cf. *The Advancement of Learning*, II, v, 3.
4 The Roman god of doors, depicted with two faces looking in opposite directions.

the gross sense of the word, or that they can fore-tell the form as surely as they foreknow the spirit of events: such is the pretence of superstition, which would make poetry an attribute of proph-ecy, rather than prophecy an attribute of poetry. A poet participates in the eternal, the infinite, and the one; as far as relates to his conceptions, time and place and number are not. The gram-matical forms which express the moods of time, and the difference of persons, and the distinction of place, are convertible with respect to the high-est poetry without injuring it as poetry; and the choruses of Aeschylus, and the book of Job, and Dante's Paradise, would afford, more than any other writings, examples of this fact, if the limits of this essay did not forbid citation. The crea-tions of sculpture, painting, and music, are il-lustrations still more decisive.

Language, colour, form, and religious and civil habits of action, are all the instruments and materials of poetry; they may be called poetry by that figure of speech which considers the effect as a synonyme of the cause. But poetry in a more restricted sense expresses those arrangements of language, and especially metrical language, which are created by that imperial faculty, whose throne is curtained within the invisible nature of man. And this springs from the nature itself of lan-guage, which is a more direct representation of the actions and passions of our internal being, and is susceptible of more various and delicate combinations, than colour, form, or motion, and is more plastic and obedient to the control of that faculty of which it is the creation. For language is arbitrarily produced by the imagination, and has relation to thoughts alone; but all other mate-rials, instruments, and conditions of art, have relations among each other, which limit and in-terpose between conception and expression. The former is as a mirror which reflects, the latter as a cloud which enfeebles, the light of which both are mediums of communication. Hence the fame of sculptors, painters, and musicians, although the intrinsic powers of the great masters of these arts may yield in no degree to that of those who have employed language as the hieroglyphic of their thoughts, has never equalled that of poets in the restricted sense of the term; as two per-formers of equal skill will produce unequal effects from a guitar and a harp. The fame of legislators and founders of religions, so long as

their institutions last, alone seems to exceed that of poets in the restricted sense; but it can scarcely be a question, whether, if we deduct the celebrity which their flattery of the gross opinions of the vulgar usually conciliates, together with that which belonged to them in their higher character of poets, any excess will remain.

We have thus circumscribed the word poetry within the limits of that art which is the most familiar and the most perfect expression of the faculty itself. It is necessary, however, to make the circle still narrower, and to determine the distinction between measured and unmeasured language; for the popular division into prose and verse is inadmissible in accurate philosophy.

Sounds as well as thoughts have relation both between each other and towards that which they represent, and a perception of the order of those relations has always been found connected with a perception of the order of the relations of thoughts. Hence the language of poets has ever affected a certain uniform and harmonious re-currence of sound, without which it were not poetry, and which is scarcely less indispensable to the communication of its actions, than the words themselves, without reference to that pe-culiar order. Hence the vanity of translation; it were as wise to cast a violet into a crucible that you might discover the formal principle of its colour and odour, as seek to transfuse from one language into another the creations of a poet. The plant must spring again from its seed, or it will bear no flower—and this is the burden of the curse of Babel.

An observation of the regular mode of the recurrence of harmony in the language of poet-ical minds, together with its relation to music, produced metre, or a certain system of traditional forms of harmony and language. Yet it is by no means essential that a poet should accommodate his language to this traditional form, so that the harmony, which is its spirit, be observed. The practice is indeed convenient and popular, and to be preferred, especially in such composition as includes much action; but every great poet must inevitably innovate upon the example of his predecessors in the exact structure of his peculiar versification. The distinction between poets and prose writers is a vulgar error. The distinction between philosophers and poets has been anticipated. Plato was essentially a poet—

the truth and splendour of his imagery, and the melody of his language, are the most intense that it is possible to conceive. He rejected the measure of the epic, dramatic, and lyrical forms, because he sought to kindle a harmony in thoughts divested of shape and action, and he forbore to invent any regular plan of rhythm which would include, under determinate forms, the varied pauses of his style. Cicero sought to imitate the cadence of his periods, but with little success. Lord Bacon was a poet. His language has a sweet and majestic rhythm, which satisfies the sense, no less than the almost superhuman wisdom of his philosophy satisfies the intellect; it is a strain which distends, and then bursts the circumference of the reader's mind, and pours itself forth together with it into the universal element with which it has perpetual sympathy. All the authors of revolutions in opinion are not only necessarily poets as they are inventors, nor even as their words unveil the permanent analogy of things by images which participate in the life of truth; but as their periods are harmonious and rhythmical, and contain in themselves the elements of verse; being the echo of the eternal music. Nor are those supreme poets, who have employed traditional forms of rhythm on account of the form and action of their subjects, less capable of perceiving and teaching the truth of things, than those who have omitted that form. Shakespeare, Dante, and Milton (to confine ourselves to modern writers) are philosophers of the very loftiest power.

A poem is the very image of life expressed in its eternal truth. There is this difference between a story and a poem,[5] that a story is a catalogue of detached facts, which have no other connexion than time, place, circumstance, cause, and effect; the other is the creation of actions according to the unchangeable forms of human nature, as existing in the mind of the Creator, which is itself the image of all other minds. The one is partial, and applies only to a definite period of time, and a certain combination of events which can never again recur; the other is universal, and contains within itself the germ of a relation to whatever motives or actions have place in the possible varieties of human nature. Time, which destroys the beauty and the use of the story of particular facts, stripped of the poetry which should invest them, augments that of poetry, and for ever develops new and wonderful applications of the eternal truth which it contains. Hence epitomes have been called[6] the moths of just history; they eat out the poetry of it. A story of particular facts is as a mirror which obscures and distorts that which should be beautiful: poetry is a mirror which makes beautiful that which is distorted.

The parts of a composition may be poetical, without the composition as a whole being a poem. A single sentence may be considered as a whole, though it may be found in the midst of a series of unassimilated portions; a single word even may be a spark of inextinguishable thought. And thus all the great historians, Herodotus, Plutarch, Livy, were poets; and although the plan of these writers, especially that of Livy, restrained them from developing this faculty in its highest degree, they made copious and ample amends for their subjection, by filling all the interstices of their subjects with living images.

Having determined what is poetry, and who are poets, let us proceed to estimate its effects upon society.

Poetry is ever accompanied with pleasure: all spirits upon which it falls open themselves to receive the wisdom which is mingled with its delight. In the infancy of the world, neither poets themselves nor their auditors are fully aware of the excellence of poetry: for it acts in a divine and unapprehended manner, beyond and above consciousness; and it is reserved for future generations to contemplate and measure the mighty cause and effect in all the strength and splendour of their union. Even in modern times, no living poet ever arrived at the fullness of his fame; the jury which sits in judgement upon a poet, belonging as he does to all time, must be composed of his peers: it must be empanelled by time from the selectest of the wise of many generations. A poet is a nightingale, who sits in darkness and sings to cheer its own solitude with sweet sounds; his auditors are as men entranced by the melody of an unseen musician, who feel that they are

---

[5] This distinction rests on Aristotle's assertion (*Poetics*, IX, 1–4) that poetry is more philosophical and serious than history, since the former deals with the general and the latter with the particular.

[6] By Bacon, *The Advancement of Learning*, II, ii, 4. *Epitomes* = abstracts, compendiums.

moved and softened, yet know not whence or why. The poems of Homer and his contemporaries were the delight of infant Greece; they were the elements of that social system which is the column upon which all succeeding civilisation has reposed. Homer embodied the ideal perfection of his age in human character; nor can we doubt that those who read his verses were awakened to an ambition of becoming like to Achilles, Hector, and Ulysses: the truth and beauty of friendship, patriotism, and persevering devotion to an object, were unveiled to their depths in these immortal creations: the sentiments of the auditors must have been refined and enlarged by a sympathy with such great and lovely impersonations, until from admiring they imitated, and from imitation they identified themselves with the objects of their admiration. Nor let it be objected, that these characters are remote from moral perfection, and that they are by no means to be considered as edifying patterns for general imitation. Every epoch, under names more or less specious, has deified its peculiar errors; Revenge is the naked idol of the worship of a semi-barbarous age; and Self-deceit is the veiled image of unknown evil, before which luxury and satiety lie prostrate. But a poet considers the vices of his contemporaries as a temporary dress in which his creations must be arrayed, and which cover without concealing the eternal proportions of their beauty. An epic or dramatic personage is understood to wear them around his soul, as he may the ancient armour or the modern uniform around his body; whilst it is easy to conceive a dress more graceful than either. The beauty of the internal nature cannot be so far concealed by its accidental vesture, but that the spirit of its form shall communicate itself to the very disguise, and indicate the shape it hides from the manner in which it is worn. A majestic form and graceful motions will express themselves through the most barbarous and tasteless costume. Few poets of the highest class have chosen to exhibit the beauty of their conceptions in its naked truth and splendour; and it is doubtful whether the alloy of costume, habit, &c., be not necessary to temper this planetary music for mortal ears.[7]

7 A figurative allusion to the old belief that the "spheres," revolving around the earth, made music unheard by human beings.

The whole objection, however, of the immorality of poetry rests upon a misconception of the manner in which poetry acts to produce the moral improvement of man. Ethical science arranges the elements which poetry has created, and propounds schemes and proposes examples of civil and domestic life: nor is it for want of admirable doctrines that men hate, and despise, and censure, and deceive, and subjugate one another. But poetry acts in another and diviner manner. It awakens and enlarges the mind itself by rendering it the receptacle of a thousand unapprehended combinations of thought. Poetry lifts the veil from the hidden beauty of the world, and makes familiar objects be as if they were not familiar; it reproduces all that it represents, and the impersonations clothed in its Elysian[8] light stand thenceforward in the minds of those who have once contemplated them, as memorials of that gentle and exalted content which extends itself over all thoughts and actions with which it coexists. The great secret of morals is love; or a going out of our own nature, and an identification of ourselves with the beautiful which exists in thought, action, or person, not our own. A man, to be greatly good, must imagine intensely and comprehensively; he must put himself in the place of another and of many others; the pains and pleasures of his species must become his own. The great instrument of moral good is the imagination; and poetry administers to the effect by acting upon the cause. Poetry enlarges the circumference of the imagination by replenishing it with thoughts of ever new delight, which have the power of attracting and assimilating to their own nature all other thoughts, and which form new intervals and interstices whose void for ever craves fresh food. Poetry strengthens the faculty which is the organ of the moral nature of man, in the same manner as exercise strengthens a limb. A poet therefore would do ill to embody his own conceptions of right and wrong, which are usually those of his place and time, in his poetical creations, which participate in neither. By this assumption of the inferior office of interpreting the effect, in which perhaps after all he might acquit himself but imperfectly, he would resign a glory in the participation in the cause. There was little danger

8 Blissful.

that Homer, or any of the eternal poets, should have so far misunderstood themselves as to have abdicated this throne of their widest dominion. Those in whom the poetical faculty, though great, is less intense, as Euripides, Lucan,[9] Tasso, Spenser, have frequently affected[10] a moral aim, and the effect of their poetry is diminished in exact proportion to the degree in which they compel us to advert to this purpose. . . .[11]

But let us not be betrayed from a defence into a critical history of poetry and its influence on society. Be it enough to have pointed out the effects of poets, in the large and true sense of the word, upon their own and all succeeding times.

But poets have been challenged[12] to resign the civic crown to reasoners and mechanists, on another plea. It is admitted that the exercise of the imagination is most delightful, but it is alleged that that of reason is more useful. Let us examine, as the grounds of this distinction, what is here meant by utility. Pleasure or good, in a general sense, is that which the consciousness of a sensitive and intelligent being seeks, and in which, when found, it acquiesces. There are two kinds of pleasure, one durable, universal and permanent; the other transitory and particular. Utility may either express the means of producing the former or the latter. In the former sense, whatever strengthens and purifies the affections, enlarges the imagination, and adds spirit to sense, is useful. But a narrower meaning may be assigned to the word utility, confining it to express that which banishes the importunity of the wants of our animal nature, the surrounding men with security of life, the dispersing the grosser delusions of superstition, and the conciliating such a degree of mutual forbearance among men as may consist with the motives of personal advantage.

Undoubtedly the promoters of utility, in this limited sense, have their appointed office in society. They follow the footsteps of poets, and copy the sketches of their creations into the book of common life. They make space, and give time. Their exertions are of the highest value, so long as they confine their administration of the concerns of the inferior powers of our nature within the limits due to the superior ones. But whilst the sceptic destroys gross superstitions, let him spare to deface, as some of the French writers have defaced, the eternal truths charactered upon the imaginations of men. Whilst the mechanist abridges, and the political economist combines, labour, let them beware that their speculations, for want of correspondence with those first principles which belong to the imagination, do not tend, as they have in modern England, to exasperate at once the extremes of luxury and want. They have exemplified the saying, "To him that hath, more shall be given; and from him that hath not, the little that he hath shall be taken away."[13] The rich have become richer, and the poor have become poorer; and the vessel of the state is driven between the Scylla and Charybdis[14] of anarchy and despotism. Such are the effects which must ever flow from an unmitigated exercise of the calculating faculty.

It is difficult to define pleasure in its highest sense; the definition involving a number of apparent paradoxes. For, from an inexplicable defect of harmony in the constitution of human nature, the pain of the inferior is frequently connected with the pleasures of the superior portions of our being. Sorrow, terror, anguish, despair itself, are often the chosen expressions of an approximation to the highest good. Our sympathy in tragic fiction depends on this principle; tragedy delights by affording a shadow of the pleasure which exists in pain. This is the source also of the melancholy which is inseparable from the sweetest melody. The pleasure that is in sorrow is sweeter than the pleasure of pleasure itself. And hence the saying, "It is better to go to the house of mourning than to the house of mirth."[15] Not that this highest species of pleasure is necessarily linked with pain. The delight of love and friendship, the ecstasy of the admiration of nature, the joy of the perception and still

9 For this Roman epic poet (d. 65 A.D.) Shelley had an exaggerated liking; hence his inappropriate mention here in company with the great author of Greek tragedy, the famous epic poet of the Italian Renaissance, and Spenser.
10 Cultivated.
11 The foregoing paragraphs constitute slightly less than the first third of the treatise. Shelley proceeds with a discussion of poetic drama and an historical survey of poetry and its bearing on civilization. The rest of our selection amounts to nearly the last third of the *Defence*.
12 By Peacock, in the last four paragraphs of his attack.

13 Cf. Mark 4:25.
14 The famous rock and whirlpool which menaced navigation between Sicily and Italy.
15 Cf. Ecclesiastes 7:2.

more of the creation of poetry, is often wholly unalloyed.

The production and assurance of pleasure in this highest sense is true utility. Those who produce and preserve this pleasure are poets or poetical philosophers.

The exertions of Locke, Hume, Gibbon, Voltaire, Rousseau,[16] and their disciples, in favour of oppressed and deluded humanity, are entitled to the gratitude of mankind. Yet it is easy to calculate the degree of moral and intellectual improvement which the world would have exhibited, had they never lived. A little more nonsense would have been talked for a century or two; and perhaps a few more men, women, and children burnt as heretics. We might not at this moment have been congratulating each other on the abolition[17] of the Inquisition in Spain. But it exceeds all imagination to conceive what would have been the moral condition of the world if neither Dante, Petrarch, Boccaccio, Chaucer, Shakespeare, Calderon,[18] Lord Bacon, nor Milton, had ever existed; if Raphael and Michael Angelo had never been born; if the Hebrew poetry had never been translated; if a revival of the study of Greek literature had never taken place; if no monuments of ancient sculpture had been handed down to us; and if the poetry of the religion of the ancient world had been extinguished together with its belief. The human mind could never, except by the intervention of these excitements, have been awakened to the invention of the grosser sciences, and that application of analytical reasoning to the aberrations of society, which it is now attempted to exalt over the direct expression of the inventive and creative faculty itself.

We have more moral, political, and historical wisdom, than we know how to reduce into practice; we have more scientific and economical knowledge than can be accommodated to the just distribution of the produce which it multiplies. The poetry, in these systems of thought, is concealed by the accumulation of facts and calculating processes. There is no want of knowledge respecting what is wisest and best in morals,

government, and political economy, or at least what is wiser and better than what men now practise and endure. But we let "*I dare not* wait upon *I would,* like the poor cat in the adage."[19] We want the creative faculty to imagine that which we know; we want the generous impulse to act that which we imagine; we want the poetry of life: our calculations have outrun conception; we have eaten more than we can digest. The cultivation of those sciences which have enlarged the limits of the empire of man over the external world, has, for want of the poetical faculty, proportionally circumscribed those of the internal world; and man, having enslaved the elements, remains himself a slave. To what but a cultivation of the mechanical arts in a degree disproportioned to the presence of the creative faculty, which is the basis of all knowledge, is to be attributed the abuse of all invention for abridging and combining labour, to the exasperation[20] of the inequality of mankind? From what other cause has it arisen that the discoveries which should have lightened, have added a weight to the curse imposed on Adam? Poetry, and the principle of Self, of which money is the visible incarnation, are the God and Mammon of the world.

The functions of the poetical faculty are twofold: by one it creates new materials of knowledge, and power, and pleasure; by the other it engenders in the mind a desire to reproduce and arrange them according to a certain rhythm and order, which may be called the beautiful and the good. The cultivation of poetry is never more to be desired than at periods when, from an excess of the selfish and calculating principle, the accumulation of the materials of external life exceed the quantity of the power of assimilating them to the internal laws of human nature. The body has then become too unwieldy for that which animates it.

Poetry is indeed something divine. It is at once the centre and circumference of knowledge; it is that which comprehends all science, and that to which all science must be referred. It is at the same time the root and blossom of all other systems of thought; it is that from which all spring, and that which adorns all; and that which, if blighted, denies the fruit and the seed,

---

[16] Shelley's note: "Although Rousseau has been thus classed, he was essentially a poet. The others, even Voltaire, were mere reasoners."   [17] In the preceding year.
[18] The Spanish dramatist and poet Pedro Calderón de la Barca (1600–1681).

[19] *Macbeth,* I, vii, 44–45.   [20] Intensification.

and withholds from the barren world the nourishment and the succession of the scions of the tree of life. It is the perfect and consummate surface and bloom of all things; it is as the odour and the colour of the rose to the texture of the elements which compose it, as the form and splendour of unfaded beauty to the secrets of anatomy and corruption. What were virtue, love, patriotism, friendship,—what were the scenery of this beautiful universe which we inhabit; what were our consolations on this side of the grave— and what were our aspirations beyond it, if poetry did not ascend to bring light and fire from those eternal regions where the owl-winged faculty of calculation dare not ever soar? Poetry is not like reasoning, a power to be exerted according to the determination of the will. A man cannot say, "I will compose poetry." The greatest poet even cannot say it; for the mind in creation is as a fading coal, which some invisible influence, like an inconstant wind, awakens to transitory brightness; this power arises from within, like the colour of a flower which fades and changes as it is developed, and the conscious portions of our nature are unprophetic either of its approach or its departure. Could this influence be durable in its original purity and force, it is impossible to predict the greatness of the results; but when composition begins, inspiration is already on the decline, and the most glorious poetry that has ever been communicated to the world is probably a feeble shadow of the original conceptions of the poet. I appeal to the greatest poets of the present day, whether it is not an error to assert that the finest passages of poetry are produced by labour and study. The toil and the delay recommended by critics can be justly interpreted to mean no more than a careful observation of the inspired moments, and an artificial connection of the spaces between their suggestions, by the intertexture of conventional expressions; a necessity only imposed by the limitedness of the poetical faculty itself: for Milton conceived the Paradise Lost as a whole before he executed it in portions. We have his own authority also for the Muse having "dictated" to him the "unpremeditated song."[21] And let this be an answer to those who would allege the fifty-six various readings of the first line of the Orlando Furioso.[22] Compositions so produced are to poetry what mosaic is to painting. This instinct and intuition of the poetical faculty is still more observable in the plastic and pictorial arts; a great statue or picture grows under the power of the artist as a child in the mother's womb; and the very mind which directs the hands in formation, is incapable of accounting to itself for the origin, the gradations, or the media of the process.

Poetry is the record of the best and happiest moments of the happiest and best minds. We are aware of evanescent visitations of thought and feeling, sometimes associated with place or person, sometimes regarding our own mind alone, and always arising unforeseen and departing unbidden, but elevating and delightful beyond all expression: so that even in the desire and the regret they leave, there cannot but be pleasure, participating as it does in the nature of its object. It is as it were the interpenetration of a diviner nature through our own; but its footsteps are like those of a wind over the sea, which the coming calm erases, and whose traces remain only, as on the wrinkled sand which paves it. These and corresponding conditions of being are experienced principally by those of the most delicate sensibility and the most enlarged imagination; and the state of mind produced by them is at war with every base desire. The enthusiasm of virtue, love, patriotism, and friendship, is essentially linked with such emotions; and whilst they last, self appears as what it is, an atom to a Universe. Poets are not only subject to these experiences as spirits of the most refined organisation, but they can colour all that they combine with the evanescent hues of this ethereal world; a word, a trait in the representation of a scene or a passion, will touch the enchanted chord, and reanimate, in those who have ever experienced these emotions, the sleeping, the cold, the buried image of the past. Poetry thus makes immortal all that is best and most beautiful in the world; it arrests the vanishing apparitions which haunt the interlunations[23] of life, and veiling them, or[24] in language or in form, sends them forth among mankind, bearing sweet news of kindred joy to those with whom their sisters abide—

21 Cf. *Paradise Lost*, IX, 20–24.

22 The epic masterpiece of Lodovico Ariosto (1474–1533).
23 I.e., dark intervals.　24 Either.

abide, because there is no portal of expression from the caverns of the spirit which they inhabit into the universe of things. Poetry redeems from decay the visitations of the divinity in man.

Poetry turns all things to loveliness; it exalts the beauty of that which is most beautiful, and it adds beauty to that which is most deformed; it marries exultation and horror, grief and pleasure, eternity and change; it subdues to union, under its light yoke, all irreconcilable things. It transmutes all that it touches, and every form moving within the radiance of its presence is changed by wondrous sympathy to an incarnation of the spirit which it breathes: its secret alchemy turns to potable gold the poisonous waters which flow from death through life; it strips the veil of familiarity from the world, and lays bare the naked and sleeping beauty, which is the spirit of its forms.

All things exist as they are perceived; at least in relation to the percipient. "The mind is its own place, and of itself can make a heaven of hell, a hell of heaven."[25] But poetry defeats the curse which binds us to be subjected to the accident of surrounding impressions. And whether it spreads its own figured curtain, or withdraws life's dark veil from before the scene of things, it equally creates for us a being within our being. It makes us the inhabitant of a world to which the familiar world is a chaos. It reproduces the common universe of which we are portions and percipients, and it purges from our inward sight the film of familiarity which obscures from us the wonder of our being. It compels us to feel that which we perceive, and to imagine that which we know. It creates anew the universe, after it has been annihilated in our minds by the recurrence of impressions blunted by reiteration. It justifies the bold and true word of Tasso: *Non merita nome di creatore, se non Iddio ed il Poeta.*[26]

A poet, as he is the author to others of the highest wisdom, pleasure, virtue and glory, so he ought personally to be the happiest, the best, the wisest, and the most illustrious of men. As to his glory, let time be challenged to declare whether the fame of any other institutor of human life be comparable to that of a poet. That he is the wisest, the happiest, and the best, inasmuch as he is a poet, is equally incontrovertible: the greatest poets have been men of the most spotless virtue, of the most consummate prudence, and, if we could look into the interior of their lives, the most fortunate of men: and the exceptions, as they regard those who possessed the poetic faculty in a high yet inferior degree, will be found on consideration to confine rather than destroy the rule. Let us for a moment stoop to the arbitration of popular breath, and usurping and uniting in our own persons the incompatible characters of accuser, witness, judge and executioner, let us decide without trial, testimony, or form, that certain motives of those who are "there sitting where we dare not soar,"[27] are reprehensible. Let us assume that Homer was a drunkard, that Virgil was a flatterer, that Horace was a coward, that Tasso was a madman, that Lord Bacon was a peculator, that Raphael was a libertine, that Spenser was a poet laureate. It is inconsistent with this division of our subject to cite living poets, but posterity has done ample justice to the great names now referred to. Their errors have been weighed and found to have been dust in the balance;[28] if their sins "were as scarlet, they are now white as snow":[29] they have been washed in the blood of the mediator and the redeemer,[30] time. Observe in what a ludicrous chaos the imputations of real or fictitious crime have been confused in the contemporary calumnies against poetry and poets; consider how little is, as it appears—or appears, as it is; look to your own motives, and judge not, lest ye be judged.[31]

Poetry, as has been said, differs in this respect from logic, that it is not subject to the control of the active powers of the mind, and that its birth and recurrence have no necessary connexion with the consciousness or will. It is presumptuous to determine that these are the necessary conditions of all mental causation, when mental effects are experienced insusceptible of being referred to them. The frequent recurrence of the poetical power, it is obvious to suppose, may produce in the mind a habit of

---

[25] *Paradise Lost,* I, 254–55.
[26] None deserves the name of creator save God and the poet.

[27] Cf. *Paradise Lost,* IV, 829.
[28] Cf. Daniel 5:27 and Isaiah 40:15.   [29] Cf. Isaiah 1:18.
[30] Cf. Revelation 7:14 and Hebrews 9:14–15, 12:24.
[31] Matthew 7:1.

order and harmony correlative with its own nature and with its effects upon other minds. But in the intervals of inspiration, and they may be frequent without being durable, a poet becomes a man, and is abandoned to the sudden reflux of the influences under which others habitually live. But as he is more delicately organized than other men, and sensible to pain and pleasure, both his own and that of others, in a degree unknown to them, he will avoid the one and pursue the other with an ardour proportioned to this difference. And he renders himself obnoxious to calumny, when he neglects to observe the circumstances under which these objects of universal pursuit and flight have disguised themselves in one another's garments.

But there is nothing necessarily evil in this error, and thus cruelty, envy, revenge, avarice, and the passions purely evil, have never formed any portion of the popular imputations on the lives of poets.

I have thought it most favourable to the cause of truth to set down these remarks according to the order in which they were suggested to my mind, by a consideration of the subject itself, instead of observing the formality of a polemical reply;[32] but if the view which they contain be just, they will be found to involve a refutation of the arguers against poetry, so far at least as regards the first division of the subject. I can readily conjecture what should have moved the gall of some learned and intelligent writers who quarrel with certain versifiers; I, like them, confess myself unwilling to be stunned by the Theseids of the hoarse Codri of the day. Bavius and Maevius[33] undoubtedly are, as they ever were, insufferable persons. But it belongs to a philosophical critic to distinguish rather than confound.

The first part of these remarks has related to poetry in its elements and principles; and it has been shewn, as well as the narrow limits assigned them would permit, that what is called poetry, in a restricted sense, has a common source with all other forms of order and of beauty, according to which the materials of human life are susceptible of being arranged, and which is poetry in an universal sense.

The second part will have for its object an application of these principles to the present state of the cultivation of poetry, and a defence of the attempt to idealise the modern forms of manners and opinions, and compel them into a subordination to the imaginative and creative faculty. For the literature of England, an energetic development of which has ever preceded or accompanied a great and free development of the national will, has arisen as it were from a new birth. In spite of the low-thoughted envy which would undervalue contemporary merit, our own will be a memorable age in intellectual achievements, and we live among such philosophers and poets as surpass beyond comparison any who have appeared since the last national struggle for civil and religious liberty.[34] The most unfailing herald, companion, and follower of the awakening of a great people to work a beneficial change in opinion or institution, is poetry. At such periods there is an accumulation of the power of communicating and receiving intense and impassioned conceptions respecting man and nature. The persons in whom this power resides, may often as far as regards many portions of their nature, have little apparent correspondence with that spirit of good of which they are the ministers. But even whilst they deny and abjure, they are yet compelled to serve, the power which is seated on the throne of their own soul. It is impossible to read the compositions of the most celebrated writers of the present day without being startled with the electric life which burns within their words. They measure the circumference and sound the depths of human nature with a comprehensive and all-penetrating spirit, and they are themselves perhaps the most sincerely astonished at its manifestations; for it is less their spirit than the spirit of the age. Poets are the hierophants[35] of an unapprehended inspiration; the mirrors of the gigantic shadows which futurity casts upon the present; the words which express what they understand not; the trumpets which sing to battle and feel not what they inspire; the influence which is moved not, but moves. Poets are the unacknowledged legislators of the world.

---

32 To Peacock's treatise.
33 A *Theseid* would be a poem on the subject of Theseus, the legendary ruler of Athens. Juvenal (*Satires*, I, 1–2) alludes to a bad one by "Codrus," possibly a fictitious name. Bavius and Maevius are mentioned as jealous poetasters by Vergil (*Eclogues*, III, 90) and Horace (*Epodes*, X).

34 In the seventeenth century.
35 Priests, explainers of mysteries.

John Clare

1793–1864

Clare was born in Northamptonshire of very humble stock, his parents being nearly illiterate, their circumstances remarkably poor. Clare made himself a reader and, inspired by what he read, wrote a great deal. One of his poems was noticed by a local bookseller, who called his work to the attention of Taylor and Hessey, the publishers of Keats. They published his first volume, *Poems Descriptive of Rural Life and Scenery* (1820). It had a strong success and for a time Clare was lionized. No doubt its success was in part a result of Clare's origins and reflected the current fashion for peasant poets. This was really more than a fashion, since it also reflected directions in attitude about the sources of poetic inspiration and original genius. There are connections here not only with the significance of the Robert Burns phenomenon but also with Wordsworth's declaration in the Preface to *Lyrical Ballads* that the language of peasants, of men "who hourly communicate with the best objects from which the best part of language is originally derived," is "a more permanent, and a far more philosophical language than that which is frequently substituted for it by Poets."

Clare's success was not repeated, however, and there followed years of privation and struggle. In 1837 he had a mental breakdown and spent most of the rest of his life in an insane asylum.

The poems betray the not always assimilated influence of other poets, especially Shakespeare, Wordsworth, Coleridge, Byron, and the standard later eighteenth-century writers; but they nevertheless manage a remarkable freshness, exactness of observation, and range of feeling. And they are sometimes terrifying in the directness with which his distress is communicated.

TEXTS: The *Poems* have been edited by J. W. Tibble (2 vols., 1935). Geoffrey Grigson has edited *Poems of John Clare's Madness* (1949). E. Robinson and G. Summerfield have edited *The Later Poems of John Clare* (1964). Anne and J. W. Tibble have written a biography, *Clare: His Life and Poetry* (1956).

Critical studies are as yet not numerous. John Middleton Murry, *John Clare and Other Studies* (1950) may be mentioned, as well as John Heath-Stubbs, *The Darkling Plain* (1950), and Robert Pinsky, " 'That Sweet Man, John Clare,' " in *The Rarer Action*, Alan Cheuse and Richard Koffler, eds. (1970).

The texts of "The Badger," "Gipsies," "Invite to Eternity," "Peasant Poet," and "Farewell" are from *Selected Poems and Prose of John Clare*, Eric Robinson and Geoffrey Summerfield, eds. (1966). The others are from Tibble's edition, which supplies capitalization and punctuation.

The Badger[1]

The badger grunting on his woodland track
With shaggy hide and sharp nose scrowed[2] with black
Roots in the bushes and the woods and makes
A great hugh[3] burrow in the ferns and brakes

With nose on ground he runs a awkard pace   5
And anything will beat him in the race
The shepherds dog will run him to his den
Followed and hooted by the dogs and men
The woodman when the hunting comes about
Go round at night to stop the foxes out   10
And hurrying through the bushes ferns and brakes
Nor sees the many holes the badger makes
And often through the bushes to the chin
Breaks the old holes and tumbles headlong in

When midnight comes a host of dogs and men   15
Go out and track the badger to his den
And put a sack within the hole and lye
Till the old grunting badger passes bye
He comes and hears they let the strongest loose
The old fox hears the noise and drops the goose   20
The poacher shoots and hurrys from the cry
And the old hare half wounded buzzes bye
They get a forked stick to bear him down
And clapt the dogs and bore him to the town
And bait him all the day with many dogs   25
And laugh and shout and fright the scampering hogs
He runs along and bites at all he meets
They shout and hollo down the noisey streets

He turns about to face the loud uproar
And drives the rebels to their very doors   30
The frequent stone is hurled where ere they go
When badgers fight and every ones a foe

---

[1] This poem and the following two were written between 1835 and 1837.   [2] Marked.   [3] Huge.

The dogs are clapt and urged to join the fray
The badger turns and drives them all away
Though scarcly half as big dimute and small   35
He fights with dogs for hours and beats them all
The heavy mastiff savage in the fray
Lies down and licks his feet and turns away
The bull dog knows his match and waxes cold
The badger grins and never leaves his hold   40
He drives the crowd and follows at their heels
And bites them through the drunkard swears and
   reels

The frighted women takes the boys away
The blackguard laughs and hurrys on the fray
He tries to reach the woods a awkard race   45
But sticks and cudgels quickly stop the chace
He turns agen and drives the noisey crowd
And beats the many dogs in noises loud
He drives away and beats them every one
And then they loose them all and set them on   50
He falls as dead and kicked by boys and men
Then starts and grins and drives the crowd agen
Till kicked and torn and beaten out he lies
And leaves his hold and cackles groans and dies

Some keep a baited badger tame as hog   55
And tame him till he follows like the dog
They urge him on like dogs and show fair play
He beats and scarcely wounded goes away
Lapt up as if asleep he scorns to fly
And seizes any dog that ventures nigh   60
Clapt like a dog he never bites the men
But worrys dogs and hurrys to his den
They let him out and turn a harrow down
And there he fights the host of all the town
He licks the patting hand and trys to play   65
And never trys to bite or run away
And runs away from noise in hollow trees
Burnt by the boys to get a swarm of bees

The Groundlark

Close where the milking maidens pass,
   In roots and twitches[1] drest
Within a little bunch of grass
   A groundlark made her nest.

The maiden touched her with her gown   5
   And often frit[2] her out,

----

[1] Spear-grasses.   [2] Frightened.

And looked and set her bucket down
   But never found it out.

The eggs were large and spotted round
And dark as is the fallow ground;   10
The schoolboy kicked the grass in play
   But danger never guessed;
And when they came to mow the hay
   They found an empty nest.

Gipsies

The gipsies seeking sheltering woods again
With droves of horses flock to marston lane
And trample on dead leaves and hear the sound
And look and see the black clouds gather round
And set their camps and free from muck and   5
   mire
And gather stolen sticks to make the fire
The roasted hedgehog bitter though as gall
Is eaten up and relished by them all
They know the woods and every foxes den
And get their livings far away from men   10
The shooters ask them where to find the game
The rabbits know them and are almost tame
The aged woman tawney with the smoke
Go with the winds and crack the rotten oak

from Child Harold[1]

Written in 1841.

For in that hamlet lives my rising sun,
Whose beams hath cheered me all my lorn life
   long.
My heart to nature there was early won,
For she was nature's self—and still my song
Is her through sun and shade, through right and   5
   wrong.
On her my memory for ever dwells,
The flowers of Eden, evergreen of song.
Truth in my heart the same love story tells—
I love the music of those village bells.

----

[1] Clare is imitating Byron's Spenserian stanzas in his
Childe Harold's Pilgrimage, though not always with the
hexameter final line.

The blackbird startles from the homestead hedge, 10
Raindrops and leaves fall yellow as he springs.
Such images are nature's sweetest pledge,
For me there's music in his rustling wings,
'Prink prink' he cries and loud the robin sings.
The small hawk like a shot drops from the sky 15
Close to my feet for mice and creeping things,
Then swift as thought again he suthers[2] by,
And hides among the clouds from the pursuing
eye.

The lightning's vivid flashes rend the cloud
That rides like castled crags along the sky, 20
And splinters them to fragments—while aloud
The thunders, heaven's artillery, vollies bye:
Trees crash, earth trembles, beasts prepare to fly.
Almighty, what a crash—yet man is free
And walks unhurt while danger seems so nigh. 25
Heaven's archway now the rainbow seems to be
That spans the eternal round of earth and sky
and sea.

A shock, a moment, in the wrath of God
Is long as hell's eternity to all.
His thunderbolts leave life but as the clod, 30
Cold and inanimate; their temples fall
Beneath his frown to ashes, the eternal pall
Of wrath sleeps o'er the ruins where they fell,
And nought of memory may their creeds recall
The sin of Sodom was a moment's yell. 35
Fire's deathbed theirs, their first grave the last
hell.

The towering willow with its pliant boughs
Sweeps its grey foliage to the autumn wind.
The level grounds where oft a group of cows
Huddled together close—or propped behind 40
An hedge or hovel ruminate and find
The peace—as walks and health and I pursue;
For nature's every place is still resigned
To happiness—new life's in every view,
And here I comfort seek and early joys renew. 45

The lake that held a mirror to the sun
Now curves with wrinkles in the stillest place.
The autumn wind sounds hollow as a gun,
And water stands in every swampy place.

---

2 Flies past, his wings making a sighing sound.

Yet in these fens peace, harmony, and grace, 50
The attributes of nature, are allied.
The barge with naked mast, in sheltered place
Beside the brig, close to the bank is tied,
While small waves plashes by its bulky side.

Absence in love is worse than any fate: 55
Summer is winter's desert, and the spring
Is like a ruined city desolate.
Joy dies, and hope retires on feeble wing,
Nature sinks heedless—birds unheeded sing.
'Tis solitude in cities, crowds all move 60
Like living death, though all to life still cling.
The strongest, bitterest thing that life can prove
Is woman's undisguise of hate and love.

An Invite to Eternity

Wilt thou go with me sweet maid
Say maiden wilt thou go with me
Through the valley depths of shade
Of night and dark obscurity
Where the path hath lost its way 5
Where the sun forgets the day
Where there's nor life nor light to see
Sweet maiden wilt thou go with me

Where stones will turn to flooding streams
Where plains will rise like ocean waves 10
Where life will fade like visioned dreams
And mountains darken into caves
Say maiden wilt thou go with me
Through this sad non-identity
Where parents live and are forgot 15
And sisters live and know us not

Say maiden wilt thou go with me
In this strange death of life to be
To live in death and be the same
Without this life or home or name 20
At once to be and not to be
That was and is not—yet to see
Things pass like shadows—and the sky
Above, below, around us lie.

The land of shadows wilt thou trace 25
And look nor know each others face
The present mixed with reasons gone
And past and present all as one

Say maiden can thy life be led
To join the living with the dead   30
Then trace thy footsteps on with me
We're wed to one eternity

Love of Nature

I love thee, nature, with a boundless love,
    The calm of earth, the storm of roaring woods;
The winds breathe happiness where'er I rove,
    There's life's own music in the swelling floods.
My heart is in the thunder-melting clouds,   5
    The snow-capt mountain, and the rolling sea;
And hear ye not the voice where darkness shrouds
    The heavens? There lives happiness for me.

Death breathes its pleasures when it speaks of
    him;
    My pulse beats calmer while his lightnings   10
    play.
My eye, with earth's delusions waxing dim,
    Clears with the brightness of eternal day.
The elements crash round me: it is he!
    Calmly I hear his voice and never start.
From Eve's posterity I stand quite free,   15
    Nor feel her curses rankle round my heart.

Love is not here. Hope is, and at his voice—
    The rolling thunder and the roaring sea—
My pulses leap, and with the hills rejoice;
    Then strife and turmoil are at end for me,   20
No matter where life's ocean leads me on;
    For nature is my mother, and I rest,
When tempests trouble and the sun is gone,
    Like to a weary child upon her breast.

The Winter's Spring

The winter comes; I walk alone,
    I want no birds to sing;
To those who keep their hearts their own,
    The winter is the spring.
No flowers to please—no bees to hum—   5
The coming spring's already come.

I never want the Christmas rose
    To come before its time;
The seasons, each as God bestows,
    Are simple and sublime.   10

I love to see the snowstorm hing:[1]
'Tis but the winter garb of spring.

I never want the grass to bloom:
    The snowstorm's best in white.
I love to see the tempest come   15
    And love its piercing light.
The dazzled eyes that love to cling
O'er snow-white meadows see the spring.

The Peasant Poet

He loved the brook's soft sound
    The swallow swimming by
He loved the daisy covered ground
    The cloud bedappled sky
To him the dismal storm appeared   5
    The very voice of God
And where the Evening rock was reared
    Stood Moses with his rod
And every thing his eyes surveyed
    The insects i' the brake   10
Where[1] creatures God almighty made
    He loved them for his sake
A silent man in lifes affairs
    A thinker from a Boy
A Peasant in his daily cares—   15
    The Poet in his joy

To John Clare

Well, honest John, how fare you now at home?
The spring is come, and birds are building nests;
The old cock-robin to the sty is come,
With olive feathers and its ruddy breast;
And the old cock, with wattles and red comb,   5
Struts with the hens, and seems to like some best,
Then crows, and looks about for little crumbs,
Swept out by little folks an hour ago;
The pigs sleep in the sty; the bookman comes—
The little boy lets home-close nesting go,   10
And pockets tops and taws, where daisies blow,
To look at the new number just laid down,
With lots of pictures, and good stories too,
And Jack the Giant-killer's high renown.

---

1 Hang.

1 Clare usually writes "where" for "were."

Farewell

Farewell to the bushy clump
Closte[1] to the river
And the flags where the butter bump[2]
Hides in for ever
Farewell to the weedy nook   5
Hemmed in by waters
Farewell to the millers brook
And his three bonny daughters
Farewell to them all
While in prison I lye   10
In the prison o thrall
Seems nought but the sky

Shut out are the green fields
And birds i' the bushes

I' the prison yard nothing builds   15
Black birds or thrushes
Farewell to the old Mill
And dash o the waters
To the Miller and dearer still
To his three bonny daughters   20

I' the neak[3] the large burdock
Grows near the green willow
I' the flood round the moorcock
Dashes under the billow
To the old Mill farewell   25
To the lock pens and waters
To the Miller himself
And his three bonny daughters

---

[1] Close.
[2] Bittern.

[3] Nook. Clare often used Scots words, imagining sometimes that he *was* Robert Burns.

John Keats

1795–1821

Keats was born in London, where his father kept a livery stable. His first schooling was at the suburban private establishment of John Clarke, whose son Charles Cowden Clarke encouraged an early interest in literature. When Keats was eight, his father died in an accident. A year later his mother remarried, but a year after that left her husband, taking her four children to live with their grandmother. The grandmother made a will, leaving eight thousand pounds to be shared by the children on their coming of age. Keats's mother died in 1809 and his grandmother in 1814. Her estate was tied up in litigation, and Keats was never to come into effective possession of his share. The estate and, to some degree, the lives of all four children were for the rest of their childhoods mostly under the control of one of their two guardians, Richard Abbey, not a very sympathetic figure.

Keats had been apprenticed since 1811 to a surgeon apothecary at Edmonton. Four years later he withdrew to commence medical studies at Guy's and St. Thomas's Hospitals in London. It was at this point that his literary life really began. By, or soon after, the summer of 1816, when he passed his examinations and received his certificate for practice as an apothecary, he had met Leigh Hunt (who printed a sonnet of his in the *Examiner*), and through him William Hazlitt, Charles Lamb, Shelley, and the painter B. R. Haydon. Before 1816 was over, Keats had decided that his vocation was poetry rather than medicine. And in October of 1816 he wrote his first great sonnet, "On First Looking into Chapman's Homer," an extraordinarily impressive poem in the subtlety of its organization.

In 1817 he published a small book of poems and worked on the ambitious long poem *Endymion*, which was published the following spring. In 1817 and 1818 *Blackwood's Magazine* ran a series of articles on "The Cockney School of Poetry," the fourth of which contained an attack on Keats, one explainable not only in literary terms but also because Keats was an associate of the radical Hunt. In September there was an article in the *Quarterly*, the source of the baseless notion—

> *Who killed John Keats?*
> *"I," says the Quarterly,*
> *So savage and Tartarly;*
> *"'Twas one of my feats."*[1]

---

[1] Byron.

John Keats, 1795–1821. Painting by William Hilton after a portrait by Keats's friend Joseph Severn. *The Granger Collection.*

—that a hostile review had broken the poet's spirit and was the cause of his early death.

Keats had spent the summer of 1818 on a walking tour of the North. Illness, a cough, and sore throat forced him to abandon it. He returned to London, where he spent the fall and part of the winter nursing his brother Tom, who was dying, and working on his second long poem, *Hyperion.* It remained unfinished, but the fragment shows remarkable advances over *Endymion.* The earlier poem is full of both felicities and excesses. *Hyperion* is an experiment in much greater austerity and authoritative weight. Its Miltonism shows, but it shows brilliantly.

On December 1 Tom died of the tuberculosis that had killed their mother and was to kill Keats himself.

The fall of 1818 was significant also because of the meeting of Keats and Fanny Brawne. Keats's relationship with her was never entirely untroubled, but the once widely held notion that she was a trivial-minded and cold-hearted person who would have been entirely unworthy of Keats has by now been pretty well dispelled. They became engaged in the winter of 1819.

With the beginning of 1819 also begins an astonishing period in the history of poetry. In January and February Keats wrote the superbly assured

"medieval" erotic masterpiece, "The Eve of St. Agnes." In April he wrote "La Belle Dame Sans Merci," "On the Sonnet," and the "Ode to Psyche"; in May the "Ode to a Nightingale," the "Ode on Melancholy," and the "Ode on a Grecian Urn." The summer was spent working on the narrative poem *Lamia* and also on his revision of *Hyperion,* the dream-vision *The Fall of Hyperion.* On September 19, 1819, he wrote the last of his great poems, "To Autumn."

In February of 1820 he experienced a serious hemorrhaging of the lungs. He recognized its significance at once. By the time the great 1820 volume of his poems was published in the summer, the disease had become acute. In September he left England, on doctors' advice going to Italy to get away from the English climate. He was accompanied by his friend Joseph Severn, the painter. Shortly after they settled in Rome, Keats suffered a severe relapse and, after weeks of terrible suffering, died in February of 1821. He was buried in the Protestant Cemetery at Rome, in a grave part of whose epitaph was written by Keats himself: "Here lies one whose name was writ in water." But he had also said, in a letter the previous October: "I shall be among the English poets after my death."

It is customary to speak of the richness, abundance, and sensuousness of Keats's poetry—and with good reason. It used to be among the possible implications of such terms, as critics used them, that his work was all sense and feeling, to the exclusion

Keats on His Deathbed, 1821. Severn sketched this touching portrait while sitting up with poet during his final illness. *Radio Times Hulton Picture Library.*

or suppression of thought. This is rightly no longer the case. The poetry—and the great letters—give evidence of a wonderfully thoughtful and attentive intellect, playful, speculative, serious, wide-ranging in its considerations. It is an intellect that had not come to define a fully coherent ideological point of view, in the sense that this is true of Wordsworth, say, or of Shelley. Perhaps it never would have. Perhaps it is of its essential nature that it should look first this way, then that. To say this is not to say that his mind is a chaos or inchoate, or that it has no central assumptions. Keats's mind, his consciousness, is an *embodied* consciousness, which is to say that his thinking is always deeply implicated in the context of his sense experience and of his emotions. He is always aware that this is so and, furthermore, is always aware that this is no simple matter. When Keats says, "The Imagination may be compared to Adam's dream—he awoke and found it truth," he has in mind no facile mindless triumph of comforting illusion over mundane reality. When he says, "O for a Life of Sensations rather than of Thoughts," he says it with a conscious and self-amused oversimplicity, in the light of his admiration for "a complex Mind—one that is imaginative, and at the same time careful of its fruits—who would exist partly on Sensation partly on thought—to whom it is necessary that years should bring the philosophic Mind." When he praises Shakespeare for being capable of "remaining in uncertainties, mysteries, doubts, without any irritable reaching after fact and reason," and complains of Coleridge that he "would let go by a fine isolated verisimilitude caught from the Penetralium of mystery, from being incapable of remaining content with half-knowledge," he is not being anti-intellectual. He is rejecting the dominance of that aspect of the intellect which analyzes, categorizes, abstracts, and so seeks to press home and resolve all doubts, disengaging intellect from its proper sensuous and emotional context. The result is the abolition—or the appearance of the abolition—of the ultimate complex mystery of things. Another way to state this is to say that Keats is rejecting, or resisting, the impulse to seek out what might lie beyond what the embodied consciousness can experience. The ultimate complex mystery of things makes itself available, though not solvable, to a full and integrated response of mind, body, and emotions, taken together. When Keats says, in the "Ode to a Nightingale,"

> Away! away! for I will fly to thee,
>   Not charioted by Bacchus and his pards,
> But on the viewless wings of Poesy,
>   Though the dull brain perplexes and retards,

it is the "dull brain" that is the unembodied consciousness, that is mere rational intellection; the movement is "away" into a more full emotional, sensuous, intellectual experience. It is characteristic of Keats, though, that he recognizes the paradoxes here. He realizes that in a sense the movement is also "away" as if into another world, and that the full exercise of the embodied consciousness has aspects which are like a loss of consciousness, which are like a kind of death; the fullest and most generous embrace of experience by the personality may be a kind of surrender of the personality. And beyond even this, he recognizes that this surrender can never be as complete as that of the nightingale, singing "of summer in full-throated ease," effortlessly at one with the landscape. Even the embodied consciousness, even the richest and most fully integrated response of body, mind, feelings, being human, is self-conscious. Feeling itself distinct from the landscape to which it responds, it must be tolled back from the nightingale to its sole self. The point is not that the poem arrives at any answers to the questions it asks. The poem itself is content to remain "in uncertainties, mysteries, doubts"; in this it is characteristic of Keats at his best.

One should say further about the richness, abundance, and sensuousness of his poetry that there is another way in which it is the manifestation in actual poetic practice of his conviction that the whole being should be brought to one's experience of the world. Terms like "rich," "abundant," and "sensuous," mean something quite different when applied to *Endymion* than they do when applied to *Hyperion;* something else again when applied to "The Eve of St. Agnes"; yet again to the "Ode on Melancholy"; and again to "To Autumn." Nor is this entirely (though it is partly) a matter of the history of his stylistic development. It is further evidence of the variety of response he was willing to bring to experience, and this too has to do with his resistance to the systematic and categorical. Finally, it should be pointed out that the use of such terms need not forbid the use of terms like "austere" and "disciplined." It is remarkable that a poet as young as Keats was producing such an abundance of rich new imagery and rich new cadences, and organizing and orchestrating them so subtly and definitively.

TEXTS: The standard texts are Ernest de Selincourt, ed., *Poems* (1926); H. W. Garrod, ed., *Poetical Works* (1958); Hyder E. Rollins, ed., *Letters, 1814–1821* (2 vols., 1958). Rollins also edited an invaluable collection of correspondence and memorabilia of those around Keats, *The Keats Circle* (2 vols., 1948).

There are four impressive modern biographies: W. J. Bate, *John Keats* (1963); Douglas Bush, *John Keats* (1966); Robert Gittings, *John Keats* (1968);

and Aileen Ward, *John Keats* (1963). Everything considered, Bate's is probably the best. But all of them are valuable.

There is a high tide of Keats criticism. One can only indicate a certain range by citing a few titles: W. J. Bate, *The Stylistic Development of John Keats* (1945); A. C. Bradley, *Oxford Lectures on Poetry* (1909); J. R. Caldwell, *John Keats's Fancy* (1945); C. L. Finney, *The Evolution of Keats's Poetry* (1936); George H. Ford, *Keats and the Victorians* (1944); John Jones, *John Keats's Dream of Truth* (1969); John Middleton Murry, *Keats* (1955); David Perkins, *The Quest for Permanence* (1959); Clarence D. Thorpe, *The Mind of John Keats* (1926); Earl R. Wasserman, *The Finer Tone* (1953).

W. J. Bate has edited a good collection of critical essays, *Keats* (1964).

On First Looking into Chapman's Homer

Keats wrote the following lines in the fall of 1816 after sitting up all night with Cowden Clarke, enchanted by his admission to the heroic world of Homer. George Chapman (1559?–1634), one of Shakespeare's leading contemporaries in tragedy and comedy, translated both the *Iliad* and the *Odyssey*.

Much have I travell'd in the realms of gold,
  And many goodly states and kingdoms seen;
  Round many western islands have I been
Which bards in fealty to Apollo[1] hold.
Oft of one wide expanse had I been told   5
  That deep-brow'd Homer ruled as his demesne;
  Yet did I never breathe its pure serene
Till I heard Chapman speak out loud and bold:
Then felt I like some watcher of the skies
  When a new planet swims into his ken;   10
Or like stout Cortez[2] when with eagle eyes
  He star'd at the Pacific—and all his men
Look'd at each other with a wild surmise—
  Silent, upon a peak in Darien.[3]

On Seeing the Elgin Marbles

At the British Museum may still be seen the collection of Greek sculptures, especially from the Parthenon, brought back to London by the seventh Earl of Elgin and sold by him in 1816 to the British government.

My spirit is too weak—mortality
  Weighs heavily on me like unwilling sleep,
  And each imagin'd pinnacle and steep
Of godlike hardship tells me I must die
Like a sick Eagle looking at the sky.   5
  Yet 'tis a gentle luxury to weep
  That I have not the cloudy winds to keep
Fresh for the opening of the morning's eye.
Such dim-conceivèd glories of the brain
  Bring round the heart an undescribable feud;   10
So do these wonders a most dizzy pain,
  That mingles Grecian grandeur with the rude
Wasting of old Time—with a billowy main—
  A sun—a shadow of a magnitude.

To My Brothers

Written in 1816.

Small, busy flames play through the fresh laid coals,
  And their fresh cracklings o'er our silence creep
  Like whispers of the household gods that keep
A gentle empire o'er fraternal souls.
And while, for rhymes, I search around the poles,   5
  Your eyes are fix'd, as in poetic sleep,
  Upon the lore so voluble and deep,
That aye at fall of night our care condoles.
This is your birth-day Tom, and I rejoice
  That thus it passes smoothly, quietly.   10
Many such eves of gently whisp'ring noise
  May we together pass, and calmly try
What are this world's true joys,—ere the great voice,
  From its fair face, shall bid our spirits fly.

On the Sea

It keeps eternal whisperings around
  Desolate shores, and with its mighty swell
  Gluts twice ten thousand caverns, till the spell
Of Hecate[1] leaves them their old shadowy sound.

---

[1] The god of poetry.
[2] It was actually Balboa who made the discovery.
[3] The Isthmus of Panama.

---

[1] Goddess of magic, associated with the moon and tides.

Often 'tis in such gentle temper found,   5
  That scarcely will the very smallest shell
    Be moved for days from whence it sometime
      fell,
When last the winds of heaven were unbound.
Oh ye! who have your eye-balls vexed and tired,
  Feast them upon the wideness of the Sea;   10
    Oh ye! whose ears are dinn'd with uproar
      rude,
    Or fed too much with cloying melody,—
      Sit ye near some old cavern's mouth, and
        brood
Until ye start, as if the sea-nymphs quired![2]

from Endymion

Keats's first long poem, *Endymion: A Poetic Romance,*
written in 1817, retells the old myth of the mortal
youth with whom the moon goddess fell in love.
These lines are from Book I.

A thing of beauty is a joy for ever:
Its loveliness increases; it will never
Pass into nothingness; but still will keep
A bower quiet for us, and a sleep
Full of sweet dreams, and health, and quiet   5
  breathing.
Therefore, on every morrow, are we wreathing
A flowery band to bind us to the earth,
Spite of despondence, of the inhuman dearth
Of noble natures, of the gloomy days,
Of all the unhealthy and o'er-darkened ways   10
Made for our searching: yet, in spite of all,
Some shape of beauty moves away the pall
From our dark spirits. Such the sun, the moon,
Trees old, and young sprouting a shady boon
For simple sheep; and such are daffodils   15
With the green world they live in; and clear rills
That for themselves a cooling covert make
'Gainst the hot season; the mid forest brake,
Rich with a sprinkling of fair musk-rose blooms:
And such too is the grandeur of the dooms   20
We have imagined for the mighty dead;
All lovely tales that we have heard or read:
An endless fountain of immortal drink,
Pouring unto us from the heaven's brink.

     . . .

  Full in the middle of this pleasantness
There stood a marble altar, with a tress   90

Of flowers budded newly; and the dew
Had taken fairy phantasies to strew
Daisies upon the sacred sward last eve,
And so the dawnèd light in pomp receive.
For 'twas the morn: Apollo's upward fire   95
Made every eastern cloud a silvery pyre
Of brightness so unsullied, that therein
A melancholy spirit well might win
Oblivion, and melt out his essence fine
Into the winds: rain-scented eglantine   100
Gave temperate sweets to that well-wooing sun;
The lark was lost in him; cold springs had run
To warm their chilliest bubbles in the grass;
Man's voice was on the mountains; and the mass
Of nature's lives and wonders puls'd tenfold   105
To feel this sun-rise and its glories old.

  Now while the silent workings of the dawn
Were busiest, into that self-same lawn
All suddenly, with joyful cries, there sped
A troop of little children garlanded;   110
Who gathering round the altar, seem'd to pry
Earnestly round as wishing to espy
Some folk of holiday: nor had they waited
For many moments, ere their ears were sated
With a faint breath of music, which ev'n then   115
Fill'd out its voice, and died away again.
Within a little space again it gave
Its airy swellings, with a gentle wave,
To light-hung leaves, in smoothest echoes break-
    ing
Through copse-clad vallies,—ere their death, o'er- 120
    taking
The surgy murmurs of the lonely sea.

  And now, as deep into the wood as we
Might mark a lynx's eye, there glimmered light
Fair faces and a rush of garments white,
Plainer and plainer showing, till at last   125
Into the widest alley they all past,
Making directly for the woodland altar.
O kindly muse! let not my weak tongue falter
In telling of this goodly company,
Of their old piety, and of their glee: 130
But let a portion of ethereal dew
Fall on my head, and presently unmew
My soul; that I may dare, in wayfaring,
To stammer where old Chaucer us'd to sing.

  Leading the way, young damsels danced along, 135
Bearing the burden of a shepherd song;

---

2 Choired.

Each having a white wicker over brimm'd
With April's tender younglings: next, well
    trimm'd,
A crowd of shepherds with as sunburnt looks
As may be read of in Arcadian books;   140
Such as sat listening round Apollo's pipe,
When the great deity, for earth too ripe,
Let his divinity o'erflowing die
In music, through the vales of Thessaly:
Some idly trail'd their sheep-hooks on the ground, 145
And some kept up a shrilly mellow sound
With ebon-tipped flutes: close after these,
Now coming from beneath the forest trees,
A venerable priest full soberly,
Begirt with ministring looks: always his eye   150
Stedfast upon the matted turf he kept,
And after him his sacred vestments swept.
From his right hand there swung a vase, milk-
    white,
Of mingled wine, out-sparkling generous light;
And in his left he held a basket full   155
Of all sweet herbs that searching eye could cull:
Wild thyme, and valley-lillies whiter still
Than Leda's[1] love, and cresses from the rill.
His agèd head, crowned with beechen wreath,
Seem'd like a poll of ivy in the teeth   160
Of winter hoar. Then came another crowd
Of shepherds, lifting in due time aloud
Their share of the ditty. After them appear'd,
Up-followed by a multitude that rear'd
Their voices to the clouds, a fair wrought car, 165
Easily rolling so as scarce to mar
The freedom of three steeds of dapple brown:
Who stood therein did seem of great renown
Among the throng. His youth was fully blown,
Showing like Ganymede[2] to manhood grown; 170
And, for those simple times, his garments were
A chieftain king's: beneath his breast, half bare,
Was hung a silver bugle, and between
His nervy knees there lay a boar-spear keen.
A smile was on his countenance; he seem'd, 175
To common lookers on, like one who dream'd
Of idleness in groves Elysian:
But there were some who feelingly could scan
A lurking trouble in his nether lip,
And see that oftentimes the reins would slip 180
Through his forgotten hands: then would they
    sigh,

And think of yellow leaves, of owlets' cry,
Of logs piled solemnly.—Ah, well-a-day,
Why should our young Endymion pine away!

Soon the assembly, in a circle rang'd,   185
Stood silent round the shrine: each look was
    chang'd
To sudden veneration: women meek
Beckon'd their sons to silence; while each cheek
Of virgin bloom paled gently for slight fear.
Endymion too, without a forest peer,   190
Stood, wan, and pale, and with an awèd face,
Among his brothers of the mountain chace.
In midst of all, the venerable priest
Eyed them with joy from greatest to the least,
And, after lifting up his agèd hands,   195
Thus spake he: "Men of Latmos! shepherd
    bands!
Whose care it is to guard a thousand flocks:
Whether descended from beneath the rocks
That overtop your mountains; whether come
From vallies where the pipe is never dumb; 200
Or from your swelling downs, where sweet air
    stirs
Blue hare-bells lightly, and where prickly furze
Buds lavish gold; or ye, whose precious charge
Nibble their fill at ocean's very marge,
Whose mellow reeds are touch'd with sounds 205
    forlorn
By the dim echoes of old Triton's horn:[3]
Mothers and wives! who day by day prepare
The scrip, with needments, for the mountain air;
And all ye gentle girls who foster up
Udderless lambs, and in a little cup   210
Will put choice honey for a favoured youth:
Yea, every one attend! for in good truth
Our vows are wanting to our great god Pan.[4]
Are not our lowing heifers sleeker than
Night-swollen mushrooms? Are not our wide 215
    plains
Speckled with countless fleeces? Have not rains
Green'd over April's lap? No howling sad
Sickens our fearful ewes; and we have had
Great bounty from Endymion our lord.
The earth is glad: the merry lark has pour'd 220
His early song against yon breezy sky,
That spreads so clear o'er our solemnity."

Thus ending, on the shrine he heap'd a spire

---

[1] Leda was Helen of Troy's mother, seduced by Zeus in the form of a swan.
[2] Ganymede was the gods' cupbearer.

---

[3] Triton was a sea-god.
[4] God of nature.

Of teeming sweets, enkindling sacred fire;
Anon he stain'd the thick and spongy sod   225
With wine, in honour of the shepherd-god.
Now while the earth was drinking it, and while
Bay leaves were crackling in the fragrant pile,
And gummy frankincense was sparkling bright
'Neath smothering parsley, and a hazy light   230
Spread greyly eastward, thus a chorus sang:

"O thou, whose mighty palace roof doth hang
From jagged trunks, and overshadoweth
Eternal whispers, glooms, the birth, life, death
Of unseen flowers in heavy peacefulness;   235
Who lov'st to see the hamadryads dress
Their ruffled locks where meeting hazels darken;
And through whole solemn hours dost sit, and
          hearken
The dreary melody of bedded reeds—
In desolate places, where dank moisture breeds   240
The pipy hemlock to strange overgrowth;
Bethinking thee, how melancholy loth
Thou wast to lose fair Syrinx[5]—do thou now,
By thy love's milky brow!
By all the trembling mazes that she ran,   245
Hear us, great Pan!

"O thou, for whose soul-soothing quiet, turtles
Passion their voices cooingly 'mong myrtles,
What time thou wanderest at eventide
Through sunny meadows, that outskirt the side   250
Of thine enmossèd realms: O thou, to whom
Broad leavèd fig trees even now foredoom
Their ripen'd fruitage; yellow girted bees
Their golden honeycombs; our village leas
Their fairest blossom'd beans and poppied corn;   255
The chuckling linnet its five young unborn,
To sing for thee; low creeping strawberries
Their summer coolness; pent up butterflies
Their freckled wings; yea, the fresh budding year
All its completions—be quickly near,   260
By every wind that nods the mountain pine,
O forester divine!

"Thou, to whom every faun and satyr flies
For willing service; whether to surprise
The squatted hare while in half sleeping fit;   265
Or upward ragged precipices flit
To save poor lambkins from the eagle's maw;
Or by mysterious enticement draw

Bewildered shepherds to their path again;
Or to tread breathless round the frothy main,   270
And gather up all fancifullest shells
For thee to tumble into Naiads' cells,[6]
And, being hidden, laugh at their out-peeping;
Or to delight thee with fantastic leaping,
The while they pelt each other on the crown   275
With silvery oak apples, and fir cones brown—
By all the echoes that about thee ring,
Hear us, O satyr king!

"O Hearkener to the loud clapping shears
While ever and anon to his shorn peers   280
A ram goes bleating: Winder of the horn,
When snouted wild-boars routing tender corn
Anger our hunstmen: Breather round our farms,
To keep off mildews, and all weather harms:
Strange ministrant of undescribèd sounds,   285
That come a swooning over hollow grounds,
And wither drearily on barren moors:
Dread opener of the mysterious doors
Leading to universal knowledge—see,
Great son of Dryope,[7]   290
The many that are come to pay their vows
With leaves about their brows!

"Be still the unimaginable lodge
For solitary thinkings; such as dodge
Conception to the very bourne of heaven,   295
Then leave the naked brain: be still the leaven,
That spreading in this dull and clodded earth
Gives it a touch ethereal—a new birth:
Be still a symbol of immensity;
A firmament reflected in a sea;   300
An element filling the space between;
An unknown—but no more: we humbly screen
With uplift hands our foreheads, lowly bending,
And giving out a shout most heaven rending,
Conjure thee to receive our humble Pæan,   305
Upon thy Mount Lycean!"[8] . . .

On Sitting Down to Read *King Lear* Again

This poem and the three that follow were written
in 1818.

---

[5] Syrinx was turned into a reed, escaping from Pan. Pan's
pipes, with which he played his natural music, was made
from the reed.

[6] Naiads are water nymphs.
[7] Mother of Pan. Hermes was his father, according to
some legends.
[8] A sacred mountain in Asia Minor.

O golden tongued Romance, with serene lute!
    Fair-plumèd Syren, Queen of far-away!
    Leave melodizing on this wintry day,
Shut up thine olden pages, and be mute:
Adieu! for, once again, the fierce dispute   5
    Betwixt damnation and impassion'd clay
    Must I burn through; once more humbly assay
The bitter-sweet of this Shakespearian fruit:
Chief Poet! and ye clouds of Albion,
    Begetters of our deep eternal theme!   10
When through the old oak Forest I am gone,
    Let me not wander in a barren dream,
But, when I am consumèd in the fire,
Give me new Phoenix wings to fly at my desire.

When I Have Fears

When I have fears that I may cease to be
    Before my pen has glean'd my teeming brain,
Before high-pilèd books, in charact'ry,[1]
    Hold like rich garners the full-ripen'd grain;
When I behold, upon the night's starr'd face,   5
    Huge cloudy symbols of a high romance,
And think that I may never live to trace
    Their shadows, with the magic hand of
        chance;
And when I feel, fair creature of an hour,
    That I shall never look upon thee more,   10
Never have relish in the faery power
    Of unreflecting love!—then on the shore
Of the wide world I stand alone, and think
Till love and fame to nothingness do sink.

The Eve of St. Agnes

All through the year 1819 Keats kept polishing and
repolishing these Spenserian stanzas. The result is a
work of astounding craftsmanship, wrought with care
for every glowing piece in the mosaic of minute
pictorial detail. It falls within that department of
the era's poetry which includes the narrative verse
of Scott and Coleridge's *Christabel,* the department
of imitative medieval romance.

St. Agnes' Eve[1]—Ah, bitter chill it was!
    The owl, for all his feathers, was a-cold;

The hare limp'd trembling through the frozen
        grass,
    And silent was the flock in woolly fold:
Numb were the Beadsman's fingers, while he   5
        told[2]
    His rosary, and while his frosted breath,
    Like pious incense from a censer old,
    Seem'd taking flight for heaven, without a
        death,
Past the sweet Virgin's picture, while his prayer
    he saith.

His prayer he saith, this patient, holy man;   10
    Then takes his lamp, and riseth from his knees,
And back returneth, meagre, barefoot, wan,
    Along the chapel aisle by slow degrees:
    The sculptur'd dead, on each side, seem to
        freeze,
    Emprison'd in black, purgatorial rails:[3]   15
    Knights, ladies, praying in dumb orat'ries,[4]
    He passeth by; and his weak spirit fails
To think how they may ache in icy hoods and
    mails.

Northward he turneth through a little door,
    And scarce three steps, ere Music's golden   20
        tongue
Flatter'd to tears this agèd man and poor;
    But no—already had his deathbell rung;
    The joys of all his life were said and sung:
    His was harsh penance on St. Agnes' Eve:
    Another way he went, and soon among   25
    Rough ashes sat he for his soul's reprieve,
And all night kept awake, for sinners' sake to
    grieve.

That ancient Beadsman heard the prelude soft;
    And so it chanc'd, for many a door was wide,
From hurry to and fro. Soon, up aloft,   30
    The silver, snarling trumpets 'gan to chide:
    The level chambers, ready with their pride,
    Were glowing to receive a thousand guests:
    The carvèd angels, ever eager-eyed,
    Star'd, where upon their heads the cornice   35
        rests,

---

[1] Characters, letters, writing.

[1] The night of January 20, supposed to be the year's coldest.

[2] I.e., counted the beads as he repeated his Ave Marias. A beadsman is an inmate of an almshouse, required to pray for the soul of its founder.
[3] I.e., sculptured in garments ("rails") appropriate to purgatory.
[4] Oratories, small chapels, "dumb" because tenanted by statues.

With hair blown back, and wings put cross-wise
    on their breasts.

At length burst in the argent[5] revelry,
With plume, tiara, and all rich array,
Numerous as shadows haunting fairily
The brain, new stuff'd, in youth, with tri-   40
    umphs gay
Of old romance. These let us wish away,
And turn, sole-thoughted, to one Lady there,
Whose heart had brooded, all that wintry day,
On love, and wing'd St. Agnes' saintly care,
As she had heard old dames full many times   45
    declare.

They told her how, upon St. Agnes' Eve,
Young virgins might have visions of delight,[6]
And soft adorings from their loves receive
Upon the honey'd middle of the night,
If ceremonies due they did aright;   50
As, supperless to bed they must retire,
And couch supine their beauties, lily white;
Nor look behind, nor sideways, but require[7]
Of Heaven with upward eyes for all that they
    desire.

Full of this whim was thoughtful Madeline: 55
The music, yearning like a God in pain,
She scarcely heard: her maiden eyes divine,
Fix'd on the floor, saw many a sweeping train[8]
Pass by—she heeded not at all: in vain
Came many a tiptoe, amorous cavalier,   60
And back retir'd; not cool'd by high disdain,
But she saw not: her heart was otherwhere:
She sigh'd for Agnes' dreams, the sweetest of the
    year.

She danc'd along with vague, regardless eyes,
Anxious her lips, her breathing quick and   65
    short:
The hallow'd hour was near at hand: she sighs
Amid the timbrels,[9] and the throng'd resort
Of whisperers in anger, or in sport;
'Mid looks of love, defiance, hate, and scorn,
Hoodwink'd[10] with faery fancy; all amort,[11]   70

Save to St. Agnes and her lambs[12] unshorn,
And all the bliss to be before to-morrow morn.

So, purposing each moment to retire,
She linger'd still. Meantime, across the moors,
Had come young Porphyro, with heart on fire   75
For Madeline. Beside the portal doors,
Buttress'd from moonlight, stands he, and im-
    plores
All saints to give him sight of Madeline,
But for one moment in the tedious hours,
That he might gaze and worship all unseen;   80
Perchance speak, kneel, touch, kiss—in sooth
    such things have been.

He ventures in: let no buzz'd whisper tell:
All eyes be muffled, or a hundred swords
Will storm his heart, Love's fev'rous citadel:
For him, those chambers held barbarian   85
    hordes,
Hyena foemen, and hot-blooded lords,
Whose very dogs would execrations howl
Against his lineage: not one breast affords
Him any mercy, in that mansion foul,
Save one old beldame, weak in body and in soul.   90

Ah, happy chance! the agèd creature came,
Shuffling along with ivory-headed wand,
To where he stood, hid from the torch's flame,
Behind a broad hall-pillar, far beyond
The sound of merriment and chorus bland: 95
He startled her; but soon she knew his face,
And grasp'd his fingers in her palsied hand,
Saying, "Mercy, Porphyro! hie thee from this
    place;
They are all here to-night, the whole blood-
    thirsty race!

"Get hence! get hence! there's dwarfish Hilde-   100
    brand;
He had a fever late, and in the fit
He cursèd thee and thine, both house and
    land:
Then there's that old Lord Maurice, not a whit
More tame for his gray hairs—Alas me! flit!
Flit like a ghost away."—"Ah, Gossip[13] dear,   105
We're safe enough; here in this arm-chair sit,

---

5 Silver, shining.
6 I.e., a revelation of their future husbands, who will
appear and feast with them.   7 Ask.
8 Not, says Keats in a letter, "for 'concourse of passers by,'
but for 'skirts' sweeping along the floor."
9 Tambourines.   10 Blinded.
11 Lifeless, i.e., oblivious.

---

12 St. Agnes is regularly depicted with lambs. It was an
annual custom to bless two lambs and shear them; nuns
then spun the wool.
13 Godmother; here, elderly friend.

And tell me how"—"Good Saints! not here,
    not here;
Follow me, child, or else these stones will be thy
    bier."

He followed through a lowly archèd way,
Brushing the cobwebs with his lofty plume,   110
And as she muttered "Well-a—well-a-day!"
He found him in a little moonlight room,
Pale, lattic'd, chill, and silent as a tomb.
"Now tell me where is Madeline," said he,
"O tell me, Angela, by the holy loom   115
Which none but secret sisterhood may see,
When they St. Agnes' wool are weaving piously."

"St. Agnes! Ah! it is St. Agnes' Eve—
Yet men will murder upon holy days:
Thou must hold water in a witch's sieve,   120
And be liege-lord of all the Elves and Fays,
To venture so: it fills me with amaze
To see thee, Porphyro!—St. Agnes' Eve!
God's help! my lady fair the conjuror plays
This very night: good angels her deceive!   125
But let me laugh awhile, I've mickle[14] time to
    grieve."

Feebly she laugheth in the languid moon,
While Porphyro upon her face doth look,
Like puzzled urchin on an agèd crone
Who keepeth clos'd a wond'rous riddle-book,   130
As spectacled she sits in chimney nook.
But soon his eyes grew brilliant, when she told
His lady's purpose; and he scarce could
    brook[15]
Tears, at the thought of those enchantments
    cold
And Madeline asleep in lap of legends old.   135

Sudden a thought came like a full-blown rose,
Flushing his brow, and in his painèd heart
Made purple riot: then doth he propose
A stratagem, that makes the beldame start:
"A cruel man and impious thou art: 140
Sweet lady, let her pray, and sleep, and dream
Alone with her good angels, far apart
From wicked men like thee. Go, go! I deem
Thou canst not surely be the same that thou
    didst seem."

"I will not harm her, by all saints I swear,"   145
Quoth Porphyro: "O may I ne'er find grace
When my weak voice shall whisper its last
    prayer,
If one of her soft ringlets I displace,
Or look with ruffian passion in her face:
Good Angela, believe me by these tears;   150
Or I will, even in a moment's space,
Awake, with horrid shout, my foemen's ears,
And beard them, though they be more fang'd
    than wolves and bears."

"Ah! why wilt thou affright a feeble soul?
A poor, weak, palsy-stricken, churchyard thing,   155
Whose passing-bell may ere the midnight toll;
Whose prayers for thee, each morn and eve-
    ning,
Were never miss'd."—Thus plaining, doth she
    bring
A gentler speech from burning Porphyro;
So woful, and of such deep sorrowing,   160
That Angela gives promise she will do
Whatever he shall wish, betide her weal or woe.

Which was, to lead him, in close secrecy,
Even to Madeline's chamber, and there hide
Him in a closet, of such privacy   165
That he might see her beauty unespied,
And win perhaps that night a peerless bride,
While legion'd faeries pac'd the coverlet,
And pale enchantment held her sleepy-eyed.
Never on such a night have lovers met,   170
Since Merlin paid his Demon all the monstrous
    debt.[16]

"It shall be as thou wishest," said the Dame:
"All cates[17] and dainties shall be storèd there
Quickly on this feast-night: by the tambour
    frame[18]
Her own lute thou wilt see: no time to spare,   175
For I am slow and feeble, and scarce dare
On such a catering trust my dizzy head.
Wait here, my child, with patience; kneel in
    prayer
The while: Ah! thou must needs the lady wed,
Or may I never leave my grave among the dead."   180

---

14 Much.
15 Restrain (a meaning not recognized by the dictionary).
16 King Arthur's wizard, Merlin, was said to be a demon's son. He fell in love with Vivien, and with the black magic she learned from him she destroyed him.
17 Delicacies, provisions.
18 The double hoop on which material is stretched tight for embroidering.

So saying, she hobbled off with busy fear.
The lover's endless minutes slowly pass'd;
The dame return'd, and whisper'd in his ear
To follow her; with agèd eyes aghast
From fright of dim espial. Safe at last, 185
Through many a dusky gallery, they gain
The maiden's chamber, silken, hush'd, and
    chaste;
Where Porphyro took covert, pleased amain.[19]
His poor guide hurried back with agues in her
    brain.

Her falt'ring hand upon the balustrade, 190
Old Angela was feeling for the stair,
When Madeline, St. Agnes' charmèd maid,
Rose, like a missioned spirit, unaware:
With silver taper's light, and pious care,
She turn'd, and down the agèd gossip led 195
To a safe level matting. Now prepare,
Young Porphyro, for gazing on that bed;
She comes, she comes again, like ring-dove fray'd[20]
    and fled.

Out went the taper as she hurried in;
Its little smoke, in pallid moonshine, died: 200
She clos'd the door, she panted, all akin
To spirits of the air, and visions wide:
No uttered syllable, or, woe betide!
But to her heart, her heart was voluble,
Paining with eloquence her balmy side; 205
As though a tongueless nightingale should
    swell
Her throat in vain, and die, heart-stifled, in her
    dell.

A casement high and triple-arch'd there was,
All garlanded with carven imag'ries
Of fruits, and flowers, and bunches of knot- 210
    grass,
And diamonded with panes of quaint device,
Innumerable of stains and splendid dyes,
As are the tiger-moth's deep-damask'd[21] wings;
And in the midst, 'mong thousand heraldries,
And twilight saints, and dim emblazonings, 215
A shielded scutcheon blush'd with blood of
    queens and kings.

Full on this casement shone the wintry moon,

And threw warm gules[22] on Madeline's fair
    breast,
As down she knelt for heaven's grace and
    boon;
Rose-bloom fell on her hands, together prest, 220
And on her silver cross soft amethyst,
And on her hair a glory, like a saint:
She seem'd a splendid angel, newly drest,
Save wings, for heaven:—Porphyro grew faint:
She knelt, so pure a thing, so free from mortal 225
    taint.

Anon his heart revives: her vespers done,
Of all its wreathèd pearls her hair she frees;
Unclasps her warmèd jewels one by one;
Loosens her fragrant boddice; by degrees
Her rich attire creeps rustling to her knees: 230
Half-hidden, like a mermaid in sea-weed,
Pensive awhile she dreams awake, and sees,
In fancy, fair St. Agnes in her bed,
But dares not look behind, or all the charm is
    fled.

Soon, trembling in her soft and chilly nest, 235
In sort of wakeful swoon, perplex'd she lay,
Until the poppied[23] warmth of sleep oppress'd
Her soothèd limbs, and soul fatigued away;
Flown, like a thought, until the morrow-day;
Blissfully haven'd both from joy and pain; 240
Clasp'd like a missal where swart Paynims
    pray;[24]
Blinded alike from sunshine and from rain,
As though a rose should shut, and be a bud again.

Stol'n to this paradise, and so entranced,
Porphyro gazed upon her empty dress, 245
And listened to her breathing, if it chanced
To wake into a slumberous tenderness;
Which when he heard, that minute did he
    bless,
And breath'd himself: then from the closet
    crept,
Noiseless as fear in a wide wilderness, 250
And over the hush'd carpet, silent, stept,
And 'tween the curtains peep'd, where, lo!—how
    fast she slept.

---

19 Greatly.   20 Frightened.
21 I.e., colored.

22 Heraldic term for reds.
23 Since opium is a derivative of the poppy.
24 Fastened shut with clasps, as a missal (the book containing the words of the Mass) might be in a country
peopled by dark-skinned pagans, who would have no use
for it in their prayers.

Then by the bed-side, where the faded moon
Made a dim, silver twilight, soft he set
A table, and, half anguish'd, threw thereon   255
A cloth of woven crimson, gold, and jet:—
O for some drowsy Morphean amulet![25]
The boisterous, midnight, festive clarion,
The kettle-drum, and far-heard clarionet,
Affray his ears, though but in dying tone:—   260
The hall door shuts again, and all the noise is
     gone.

And still she slept an azure-lidded sleep,
In blanchèd linen, smooth, and lavender'd,
While he from forth the closet brought a heap
Of candied apple, quince, and plum, and   265
     gourd;
With jellies soother[26] than the creamy curd,
And lucent syrops, tinct with cinnamon;
Manna and dates, in argosy[27] transferr'd
From Fez; and spicèd dainties, every one,
From silken Samarcand to cedar'd Lebanon.   270

These delicates he heap'd with glowing hand
On golden dishes and in baskets bright
Of wreathèd silver: sumptuous they stand
In the retired quiet of the night,
Filling the chilly room with perfume light.—   275
"And now, my love, my seraph fair, awake!
Thou art my heaven, and I thine eremite:[28]
Open thine eyes, for meek St. Agnes' sake,
Or I shall drowse beside thee, so my soul doth
     ache."

Thus whispering, his warm, unnervèd arm   280
Sank in her pillow. Shaded was her dream
By the dusk curtains:—'twas a midnight charm
Impossible to melt as icèd stream:
The lustrous salvers in the moonlight gleam;
Broad golden fringe upon the carpet lies: 285
It seem'd he never, never could redeem
From such a stedfast spell his lady's eyes;
So mus'd awhile, entoil'd in woofèd phantasies.[29]

Awakening up, he took her hollow lute,—
Tumultuous,—and, in chords that tenderest   290
     be,

He played an ancient ditty, long since mute,
In Provence called "La belle dame sans
     mercy":[30]
Close to her ear touching the melody;—
Wherewith disturb'd, she utter'd a soft moan:
He ceased—she panted quick—and suddenly   295
Her blue affrayèd eyes wide open shone:
Upon his knees he sank, pale as smooth-sculp-
     tured stone.

Her eyes were open, but she still beheld,
Now wide awake, the vision of her sleep:
There was a painful change, that nigh expell'd   300
The blisses of her dream so pure and deep
At which fair Madeline began to weep,
And moan forth witless[31] words with many a
     sigh;
While still her gaze on Porphyro would keep;
Who knelt, with joinèd hands and piteous eye,   305
Fearing to move or speak, she look'd so dream-
     ingly.

"Ah, Porphyro!" said she, "but even now
Thy voice was at sweet tremble in mine ear,
Made tuneable with every sweetest vow;
And those sad eyes were spiritual and clear: 310
How changed thou art! how pallid, chill, and
     drear!
Give me that voice again, my Porphyro,
Those looks immortal, those complainings
     dear!
Oh leave me not in this eternal woe,
For if thou diest, my Love, I know not where   315
     to go."

Beyond a mortal man impassion'd far
At these voluptuous accents, he arose,
Ethereal, flush'd, and like a throbbing star
Seen mid the sapphire heaven's deep repose;
Into her dream he melted, as the rose   320
Blendeth its odour with the violet,—
Solution sweet: meantime the frost-wind blows
Like Love's alarum pattering the sharp sleet
Against the window-panes; St. Agnes' moon
     hath set.

'Tis dark: quick pattereth the flaw-blown[32]   325
     sleet:

[25] Charm. Morpheus was god of sleep.
[26] Smoother. On the feast, see note 6.
[27] Large merchant ship.
[28] Hermit, i.e., devotee.
[29] Interwoven fantasies.

[30] The beautiful lady without pity.
[31] Meaningless.   [32] Gust-blown.

"This is no dream, my bride, my Madeline!"
'Tis dark: the icèd gusts still rave and beat:
"No dream, alas! alas! and woe is mine!
Porphyro will leave me here to fade and
          pine.—
Cruel! what traitor could thee hither bring? 330
I curse not, for my heart is lost in thine,
Though thou forsakest a deceivèd thing;—
A dove forlorn and lost with sick unprunèd
     wing."

"My Madeline! sweet dreamer! lovely bride!
Say, may I be for aye thy vassal blest?   335
Thy beauty's shield, heart-shap'd and vermeil[33]
     dyed?
Ah, silver shrine, here will I take my rest
After so many hours of toil and quest,
A famish'd pilgrim,—saved by miracle.
Though I have found, I will not rob thy nest 340
Saving of thy sweet self; if thou think'st well
To trust, fair Madeline, to no rude infidel.

"Hark! 'tis an elfin storm from faery land,
Of haggard seeming,[34] but a boon indeed:
Arise—arise! the morning is at hand;—   345
The bloated wassaillers will never heed:—
Let us away, my love, with happy speed;
There are no ears to hear, or eyes to see,—
Drowned all in Rhenish[35] and the sleepy
     mead:[36]
Awake! arise! my love, and fearless be,   350
For o'er the southern moors I have a home for
     thee."

She hurried at his words, beset with fears,
For there were sleeping dragons all around,
At glaring watch, perhaps, with ready spears—
Down the wide stairs a darkling way they 355
     found.—
In all the house was heard no human sound.
A chain-drooped lamp was flickering by each
     door;
The arras, rich with horseman, hawk, and
     hound,
Flutter'd in the besieging wind's uproar;
And the long carpets rose along the gusty floor. 360

They glide, like phantoms, into the wide hall;

Like phantoms, to the iron porch they glide,
Where lay the Porter, in uneasy sprawl,
With a huge empty flaggon by his side:
The wakeful bloodhound rose, and shook his 365
     hide,
But his sagacious eye an inmate owns:[37]
By one, and one, the bolts full easy slide:—
The chains lie silent on the footworn stones;—
The key turns, and the door upon its hinges
     groans.

And they are gone: ay, ages long ago   370
These lovers fled away into the storm.
That night the Baron dreamt of many a woe,
And all his warrior-guests, with shade and form
Of witch, and demon, and large coffin-worm,
Were long be-nightmar'd. Angela the old   375
Died palsy-twitch'd, with meagre face de-
     form;[38]
The Beadsman, after thousand aves told,
For aye unsought-for slept among his ashes cold.

La Belle Dame Sans Merci

A Ballad

The theme of the fairy lover is from folklore; it
appears in a number of the old ballads. Keats probably got his title (The Beautiful Lady without Pity)
from a poem, once attributed to Chaucer, by the
early fifteenth-century Frenchman Alain Chartier; if
so, that was the sum of his indebtedness, except for
his reading in medieval ballads and romances in
general. Keats's laborious revisions usually improved
his lines, but not here. The following is the earlier of
two versions. It was written in the spring of 1819.

O what can ail thee, knight-at-arms,
     Alone and palely loitering?
The sedge has wither'd from the lake
     And no birds sing!

O what can ail thee, knight-at-arms,   5
     So haggard and so woe-begone?
The squirrel's granary is full,
     And the harvest's done.

I see a lilly on thy brow,
     With anguish moist and fever dew,   10

---

[33] Vermilion.
[34] Wild appearance.   [35] Rhine wine.
[36] A medieval drink of fermented honey and water.

[37] Acknowledges.   [38] Deformed.

And on thy cheeks a fading rose
   Fast withereth too.

I met a lady in the meads
   Full beautiful, a faery's child;
Her hair was long, her foot was light   15
   And her eyes were wild.

I made a garland for her head,
   And bracelets too, and fragrant zone;[1]
She looked at me as she did love,
   And made sweet moan.   20

I set her on my pacing steed,
   And nothing else saw all day long,
For sidelong would she bend, and sing
   A faery's song.

She found me roots of relish sweet,   25
   And honey wild, and manna dew,
And sure in language strange she said—
   "I love thee true."

She took me to her elfin grot,
   And there she wept, and sigh'd full sore,   30
And there I shut her wild wild eyes
   With kisses four.

And there she lullèd me asleep,
   And there I dream'd—Ah! woe betide!
The latest dream I ever dream'd   35
   On the cold hill side.

I saw pale kings and princes too,
   Pale warriors, death-pale were they all;
They cried—"La Belle Dame sans Merci
   Thee hath in thrall!"   40

I saw their starved lips in the gloam,
   With horrid warning gapèd wide;
And I awoke, and found me here,
   On the cold hill's side.

And this is why I sojourn here,   45
   Alone and palely loitering,
Though the sedge has wither'd from the lake,
   And no birds sing.

---

1 Girdle, sash.

On the Sonnet

If by dull rhymes our English must be chain'd,
And, like Andromeda,[1] the Sonnet sweet
Fetter'd, in spite of painèd loveliness,
Let us find out, if we must be constrain'd,
Sandals more interwoven and complete   5
To fit the naked foot of Poesy:
Let us inspect the Lyre, and weigh the stress
Of every chord, and see what may be gain'd
By ear industrious, and attention meet;
Misers of sound and syllable, no less   10
Than Midas[2] of his coinage, let us be
Jealous of dead leaves in the bay wreath crown;
So, if we may not let the Muse be free,
She will be bound with garlands of her own.

To Sleep

Written in the spring of 1819.

O soft embalmer of the still midnight,
   Shutting, with careful fingers and benign,
Our gloom-pleas'd eyes, embower'd from the
     light,
   Enshaded in forgetfulness divine:
O soothest Sleep! if so it please thee, close   5
   In midst of this thine hymn my willing eyes,
Or wait the "Amen," ere thy poppy throws
   Around my bed its lulling charities.
Then save me, or the passèd day will shine
Upon my pillow, breeding many woes,—   10
   Save me from curious Conscience, that still
     lords
Its strength for darkness, burrowing like a mole;
   Turn the key deftly in the oilèd wards,
And seal the hushèd casket of my soul.

Bright Star

Originally composed in the spring of 1819, this sonnet was once thought to be Keats's last, because on

---

1 Andromeda was chained to a rock in the sea and her
life threatened by a sea monster sent by Poseidon. Perseus
rescued her.
2 Midas was the Phyrgian king who could, disastrously
for himself, turn anything to gold.

September 28, 1820, on his way out to Italy, he copied it on a blank page in a volume of Shakespeare.

Bright star! would I were steadfast as thou art—
    Not in lone splendour hung aloft the night
And watching, with eternal lids apart,
    Like nature's patient, sleepless Eremite,[1]
The moving waters at their priestlike task   5
    Of pure ablution round earth's human shores,
Or gazing on the new soft fallen mask
    Of snow upon the mountains and the moors—
No—yet still steadfast, still unchangeable,
    Pillow'd upon my fair love's ripening breast,   10
To feel for ever its soft fall and swell,
    Awake for ever in a sweet unrest,
Still, still to hear her tender-taken breath,
And so live ever—or else swoon to death.

Ode to Psyche

This is the first of the great odes written in the spring of 1819. The story of Cupid and Psyche appears in Apuleius' *The Golden Ass,* a work of the second century A.D. Psyche was punished, by his deserting her, for looking at her theretofore invisible lover Cupid. She was made immortal by Jupiter after having wandered the earth looking for Cupid, while being persecuted by Venus.

O Goddess! hear these tuneless numbers, wrung
    By sweet enforcement and remembrance dear,
And pardon that thy secrets should be sung
    Even into thine own soft-conchèd ear:
Surely I dreamt to-day, or did I see   5
    The wingèd Psyche with awaken'd eyes?
I wander'd in a forest thoughtlessly,
    And, on the sudden, fainting with surprise,
Saw two fair creatures, couchèd side by side
    In deepest grass, beneath the whisp'ring roof   10
    Of leaves and trembled blossoms, where there
        ran
        A brooklet, scarce espied:

'Mid hush'd, cool-rooted flowers, fragrant-eyed,
    Blue, silver-white, and budded Tyrian,
They lay calm-breathing on the bedded grass;   15
    Their arms embracèd, and their pinions too;
    Their lips touch'd not, but had not bade adieu,

[1] Hermit.

As if disjoinèd by soft-handled slumber,
And ready still past kisses to outnumber
    At tender eye-dawn of aurorean love: 20
        The wingèd boy I knew;
    But who wast thou, O happy, happy dove?
        His Psyche true!

O latest born and loveliest vision far
    Of all Olympus' faded hierarchy!   25
Fairer than Phœbe's sapphire-region'd star,[1]
    Or Vesper, amorous glow-worm of the sky;[2]
Fairer than these, though temple thou hast none,
        Nor altar heap'd with flowers;
Nor virgin-choir to make delicious moan   30
        Upon the midnight hours;
No voice, no lute, no pipe, no incense sweet
    From chain-swung censer teeming;
No shrine, no grove, no oracle, no heat
    Of pale-mouth'd prophet dreaming.   35

O brightest! though too late for antique vows,
    Too, too late for the fond believing lyre,
When holy were the haunted forest boughs,
    Holy the air, the water, and the fire;
Yet even in these days so far retir'd   40
    From happy pieties, thy lucent fans,
    Fluttering among the faint Olympians,
I see, and sing, by my own eyes inspired.
So let me be thy choir, and make a moan
        Upon the midnight hours;   45
Thy voice, thy lute, thy pipe, thy incense sweet
    From swingèd censer teeming;
Thy shrine, thy grove, thy oracle, thy heat
    Of pale-mouth'd prophet dreaming.

Yes, I will be thy priest, and build a fane   50
    In some untrodden region of my mind,
Where branchèd thoughts, new grown with pleas-
        ant pain,
    Instead of pines shall murmur in the wind:
Far, far around shall those dark-cluster'd trees
    Fledge the wild-ridgèd mountains steep by   55
        steep;
And there by zephyrs, streams, and birds, and
        bees,
    The moss-lain Dryads[3] shall be lull'd to sleep;
And in the midst of this wide quietness

[1] Phoebe's star is the moon.
[2] Vesper, the evening star.
[3] Dryads are wood-nymphs.

A rosy sanctuary will I dress
With the wreath'd trellis of a working brain,   60
　With buds, and bells, and stars without a
　　name,
With all the gardener Fancy e'er could feign,
　Who breeding flowers, will never breed the
　　same:
And there shall be for thee all soft delight
　That shadowy thought can win,   65
A bright torch, and a casement ope at night,
　To let the warm Love in!

Ode to a Nightingale

The poem was written substantially in one sitting, on
a morning probably very early in May of 1819.

I

My heart aches, and a drowsy numbness pains
　My sense, as though of hemlock I had drunk,
Or emptied some dull opiate to the drains
　One minute past, and Lethe-wards had sunk:[1]
'Tis not through envy of thy happy lot,   5
　But being too happy in thine happiness,—
　　That thou, light-wingèd Dryad of the trees,[2]
　　　In some melodious plot
　Of beechen green, and shadows numberless,
　　Singest of summer in full-throated ease.   10

II

O, for a draught of vintage! that hath been
　Cool'd a long age in the deep-delvèd earth,
Tasting of Flora[3] and the country green,
　Dance, and Provençal song, and sunburnt
　　mirth!
O for a beaker full of the warm South,   15
　Full of the true, the blushful Hippocrene,[4]
　　With beaded bubbles winking at the brim,
　　　And purple-stainèd mouth;
That I might drink, and leave the world unseen,
　And with thee fade away into the forest dim: 20

III

Fade far away, dissolve, and quite forget
　What thou among the leaves hast never known,

The weariness, the fever, and the fret
　Here, where men sit and hear each other
　　groan;
Where palsy shakes a few, sad, last gray hairs,   25
　Where youth grows pale, and spectre-thin, and
　　dies;
Where but to think is to be full of sorrow
　And leaden-eyed despairs,
Where Beauty cannot keep her lustrous eyes,
　Or new Love pine at them beyond to-morrow.   30

IV

Away! away! for I will fly to thee,
　Not charioted by Bacchus and his pards,[5]
But on the viewless wings of Poesy,
　Though the dull brain perplexes and retards:
Already with thee! tender is the night,   35
　And haply the Queen-Moon is on her throne,
　　Cluster'd around by all her starry Fays;
　　　But here there is no light,
Save what from heaven is with the breezes
　　blown
　　Through verdurous glooms and winding   40
　　mossy ways.

V

I cannot see what flowers are at my feet,
　Nor what soft incense hangs upon the boughs,
But, in embalmèd darkness, guess each sweet
　Wherewith the seasonable month endows
The grass, the thicket, and the fruit-tree wild;   45
　White hawthorn, and the pastoral eglantine;
　　Fast fading violets cover'd up in leaves;
　　　And mid-May's eldest child,
　The coming musk-rose, full of dewy wine,
　　The murmurous haunt of flies on summer   50
　　eves.

VI

Darkling I listen; and, for many a time
　I have been half in love with easeful Death,
Call'd him soft names in many a mused rhyme,
　To take into the air my quiet breath;
Now more than ever seems it rich to die,   55
　To cease upon the midnight with no pain,
　　While thou art pouring forth thy soul
　　abroad
　　　In such an ecstasy!

---

[1] Lethe was the river of forgetfulness in the underworld.
[2] A Dryad is a wood-nymph.
[3] Flora was Roman goddess of spring and of flowers.
[4] The Muses' fountain on Mt. Helicon.

[5] Bacchus was god of wine; "pards" are leopards.

Still wouldst thou sing, and I have ears in
    vain—
  To thy high requiem become a sod.   60

VII

Thou wast not born for death, immortal Bird!
  No hungry generations tread thee down;
The voice I hear this passing night was heard
  In ancient days by emperor and clown:
Perhaps the self-same song that found a path   65
    Through the sad heart of Ruth, when, sick
      for home,
      She stood in tears amid the alien corn;[6]
        The same that oft-times hath
  Charm'd magic casements, opening on the
    foam
  Of perilous seas, in faery lands forlorn.   70

VIII

Forlorn! the very word is like a bell
  To toll me back from thee to my sole self!
Adieu! the fancy cannot cheat so well
  As she is fam'd to do, deceiving elf.
Adieu! adieu! thy plaintive anthem fades   75
    Past the near meadows, over the still stream,
      Up the hill-side; and now 'tis buried deep
        In the next valley-glades:
  Was it a vision, or a waking dream?
      Fled is that music:—Do I wake or sleep?   80

Ode on a Grecian Urn

Apparently written shortly after the preceding poem.

I

Thou still unravish'd bride of quietness,
  Thou foster-child of silence and slow time,
Sylvan historian, who canst thus express
  A flowery tale more sweetly than our rhyme:
What leaf-fring'd legend haunts about thy shape   5
  Of deities or mortals, or of both,
    In Tempe or the dales of Arcady?[1]

---

[6] See the Book of Ruth, 2.

[1] Tempe, a valley in Thessaly, and Arcady, Arcadia, the domain of Pan, both regions associated in pastoral literature with loveliness and fruitfulness.

What men or gods are these? What maidens
    loth?
What mad pursuit? What struggle to escape?   60
    What pipes and timbrels? What wild ec- 10
    stasy?

II

Heard melodies are sweet, but those unheard
  Are sweeter; therefore, ye soft pipes, play on;
Not to the sensual ear, but, more endear'd,
  Pipe to the spirit ditties of no tone:
Fair youth, beneath the trees, thou canst not 15
    leave
  Thy song, nor ever can those trees be bare;
    Bold Lover, never, never canst thou kiss,
Though winning near the goal—yet, do not
    grieve;
  She cannot fade, though thou hast not thy
    bliss,
    For ever wilt thou love, and she be fair!   20

III

Ah, happy, happy boughs! that cannot shed
  Your leaves, nor ever bid the Spring adieu;
And, happy melodist, unwearièd,
  For ever piping songs for ever new;
More happy love! more happy, happy love!   25
  For ever warm and still to be enjoy'd,
    For ever panting, and for ever young;
All breathing human passion far above,
  That leaves a heart high-sorrowful and cloy'd,
    A burning forehead, and a parching tongue.   30

IV

Who are these coming to the sacrifice?
  To what green altar, O mysterious priest,
Lead'st thou that heifer lowing at the skies,
  And all her silken flanks with garlands drest?
What little town by river or sea shore,   35
  Or mountain-built with peaceful citadel,
    Is emptied of this folk, this pious morn?
And, little town, thy streets for evermore
  Will silent be; and not a soul to tell
    Why thou art desolate, can e'er return.   40

V

O Attic shape! Fair attitude! with brede[2]
  Of marble men and maidens overwrought,

---

[2] "Attic" is Greek; "brede" is a piece of braiding or embroidery.

With forest branches and the trodden weed;
   Thou, silent form, dost tease us out of thought
As doth eternity: Cold Pastoral!   45
   When old age shall this generation waste,
      Thou shalt remain, in midst of other woe
Than ours, a friend to man, to whom thou say'st,
   "Beauty is truth, truth beauty,—that is all
      Ye know on earth, and all ye need to know."   50

Ode on Melancholy

No, no, go not to Lethe, neither twist
   Wolf's-bane, tight-rooted, for its poisonous
      wine;
Nor suffer thy pale forehead to be kiss'd
   By nightshade, ruby grape of Proserpine;[1]
Make not your rosary of yew-berries,   5
   Nor let the beetle, nor the death-moth be
      Your mournful Psyche,[2] nor the downy owl
A partner in your sorrow's mysteries;
   For shade to shade will come too drowsily,
      And drown the wakeful anguish of the soul.   10

But when the melancholy fit shall fall
   Sudden from heaven like a weeping cloud,
That fosters the droop-headed flowers all,
   And hides the green hill in an April shroud;
Then glut thy sorrow on a morning rose,   15
   Or on the rainbow of the salt sand-wave,
   Or on the wealth of globèd peonies;
Or if thy mistress some rich anger shows,
   Emprison her soft hand, and let her rave,
      And feed deep, deep upon her peerless eyes.   20

She[3] dwells with Beauty—Beauty that must die;
   And Joy, whose hand is ever at his lips
Bidding adieu; and aching Pleasure nigh,
   Turning to poison while the bee-mouth sips:
Ay, in the very temple of Delight   25
   Veil'd Melancholy has her sovran shrine,
      Though seen of none save him whose
         strenuous tongue
   Can burst Joy's grape against his palate fine;
His soul shall taste the sadness of her might,
      And be among her cloudy trophies hung.   30

---

[1] Queen of the underworld.
[2] Butterfly, symbol of the soul.
[3] Melancholy.

The Fall of Hyperion

A Dream

Written mostly in the summer and early fall of
1819, this is an extremely uneven fragment, much
more so than the earlier fragment, *Hyperion*. But
it is in some ways more impressive. *Hyperion* leans
very heavily indeed on the example of Milton, and
does so with extraordinarily impressive skill. In *The
Fall of Hyperion*, Keats is clearly attempting to work
out a style for a long poem that would be as decidedly his own as the style, or styles, he had so
triumphantly achieved for shorter forms. He is not
as yet successful, and was never to be, since death
intervened; but the attempt is admirable. In content
the poem raises (in the first half) some questions
about poetry and the poet that were clearly of the
first importance to Keats. The relation of the poet
on the one hand to the dreamer, on the other to
the responsible man of action, sheds light, though
uncertain and flickering light, on Keats's attitudes
toward his own work at this stage of his career, his
pride in it, and his uncertainties as well. With regard
to such subjects the poem is a document in the history of nineteenth-century attitudes toward the poet
and his function as special and as different in kind
from that of other men. The poem leaves it unclear
where Keats stands.

CANTO I

Fanatics have their dreams, wherewith they weave
A paradise for a sect; the savage too
From forth the loftiest fashion of his sleep
Guesses at Heaven; pity these have not
Trac'd upon vellum or wild Indian leaf   5
The shadows of melodious utterance.
But bare of laurel they live, dream, and die;
For Poesy alone can tell her dreams,
With the fine spell of words alone can save
Imagination from the sable charm   10
And dumb enchantment. Who alive can say,
"Thou art no Poet—may'st not tell thy dreams?"
Since every man whose soul is not a clod
Hath visions, and would speak, if he had loved,
And been well nurtured in his mother tongue.   15
Whether the dream now purpos'd to rehearse
Be poet's or fanatic's will be known
When this warm scribe my hand is in the grave.

   Methought I stood where trees of every clime,
Palm, myrtle, oak, and sycamore, and beech,   20
With plantain, and spice-blossoms, made a
   screen;

In neighbourhood of fountains (by the noise
Soft-showering in my ears), and, (by the touch
Of scent,) not far from roses. Turning round
I saw an arbour with a drooping roof   25
Of trellis vines, and bells, and larger blooms,
Like floral censers, swinging light in air;
Before its wreathèd doorway, on a mound
Of moss, was spread a feast of summer fruits,
Which, nearer seen, seem'd refuse of a meal   30
By angel tasted or our Mother Eve;
For empty shells were scattered on the grass,
And grape-stalks but half bare, and remnants
     more,
Sweet-smelling, whose pure kinds I could not
     know.
Still was more plenty than the fabled horn[1]   35
Thrice emptied could pour forth, at banqueting
For Proserpine return'd to her own fields,[2]
Where the white heifers low. And appetite
More yearning than on Earth I ever felt
Growing within, I ate deliciously;   40
And, after not long, thirsted, for thereby
Stood a cool vessel of transparent juice
Sipp'd by the wander'd bee, the which I took,
And, pledging all the mortals of the world,
And all the dead whose names are in our lips,   45
Drank. That full draught is parent of my theme.
No Asian poppy nor elixir fine
Of the soon-fading jealous Caliphat;[3]
No poison gender'd in close monkish cell,
To thin the scarlet conclave of old men,[4]   50
Could so have rapt unwilling life away.
Among the fragrant husks and berries crush'd,
Upon the grass I struggled hard against
The domineering potion; but in vain:
The cloudy swoon came on, and down I sank,   55
Like a Silenus[5] on an antique vase.
How long I slumber'd 'tis a chance to guess.
When sense of life return'd, I started up
As if with wings; but the fair trees were gone,
The mossy mound and arbour were no more: 60
I look'd around upon the carvèd sides

Of an old sanctuary with roof august,
Builded so high, it seem'd that filmed clouds
Might spread beneath, as o'er the stars of heaven;
So old the place was, I remember'd none   65
The like upon the Earth: what I had seen
Of grey cathedrals, buttress'd walls, rent towers,
The superannuations of sunk realms,
Or Nature's rocks toil'd hard in waves and winds,
Seem'd but the faulture of decrepit things   70
To that eternal domèd Monument.—
Upon the marble at my feet there lay
Store of strange vessels and large draperies,
Which needs had been of dyed asbestos wove,
Or in that place the moth could not corrupt,   75
So white the linen, so, in some, distinct
Ran imageries from a sombre loom.
All in a mingled heap confus'd there lay
Robes, golden tongs, censer and chafing-dish,
Girdles, and chains, and holy jewelries.   80

  Turning from these with awe, once more I
     rais'd
My eyes to fathom the space every way;
The embossed roof, the silent massy range
Of columns north and south, ending in mist
Of nothing, then to eastward, where black gates   85
Were shut against the sunrise evermore.—
Then to the west I look'd, and saw far off
An image, huge of feature as a cloud,
At level of whose feet an altar slept,
To be approach'd on either side by steps,   90
And marble balustrade, and patient travail
To count with toil the innumerable degrees.
Towards the altar sober-paced I went,
Repressing haste, as too unholy there;
And, coming nearer, saw beside the shrine   95
One minist'ring;[6] and there arose a flame.—
When in mid-May the sickening East wind
Shifts sudden to the south, the small warm rain
Melts out the frozen incense from all flowers,
And fills the air with so much pleasant health   100
That even the dying man forgets his shroud;—
Even so that lofty sacrificial fire,
Sending forth Maian[7] incense, spread around
Forgetfulness of everything but bliss,
And clouded all the altar with soft smoke;   105
From whose white fragrant curtains thus I heard
Language pronounc'd: "If thou canst not ascend

---

1 The horn of plenty.
2 Proserpine, or Persephone, daughter of Zeus and Demeter, carried off to the underworld by Pluto, and finally permitted by Zeus to spend half the year in the living world, half in the underworld. Her return is with the growing of crops in the spring.
3 Mohammedan rulers.
4 The College of Cardinals.
5 Silenus was the drunken foster-father and attendant of Dionysus.

6 Moneta, admonisher, who had been Mnemosyne, memory, in the first *Hyperion.*
7 Maia was one of the Pleiades.

These steps, die on that marble where thou art.
Thy flesh, near cousin to the common dust,
Will parch for lack of nutriment—thy bones 110
Will wither in few years, and vanish so
That not the quickest eye could find a grain
Of what thou now art on that pavement cold.
The sands of thy short life are spent this hour,
And no hand in the universe can turn 115
Thy hourglass, if these gummèd leaves be burnt
Ere thou canst mount up these immortal steps."
I heard, I look'd: two senses both at once,
So fine, so subtle, felt the tyranny
Of that fierce threat and the hard task proposed. 120
Prodigious seem'd the toil; the leaves were yet
Burning—when suddenly a palsied chill
Struck from the pavèd level up my limbs,
And was ascending quick to put cold grasp
Upon those streams that pulse beside the throat: 125
I shriek'd, and the sharp anguish of my shriek
Stung my own ears—I strove hard to escape
The numbness; strove to gain the lowest step.
Slow, heavy, deadly was my pace: the cold
Grew stifling, suffocating, at the heart; 130
And when I clasp'd my hands I felt them not.
One minute before death, my iced foot touch'd
The lowest stair; and as it touch'd, life seem'd
To pour in at the toes: I mounted up,
As once fair angels on a ladder flew[8] 135
From the green turf to Heaven—"Holy Power,"
Cried I, approaching near the hornèd shrine,
"What am I that should so be saved from death?
What am I that another death come not
To choke my utterance, sacrilegious, here?" 140
Then said the veiled shadow—"Thou has felt
What 'tis to die and live again before
Thy fated hour, that thou hadst power to do so
Is thy own safety; thou hast dated on
Thy doom."—"High Prophetess," said I, "purge 145
    off,
Benign, if so it please thee, my mind's film."—[9]
"None can usurp this height," return'd that
    shade,
"But those to whom the miseries of the world
Are misery, and will not let them rest.
All else who find a haven in the world, 150
Where they may thoughtless sleep away their
    days,

If by a chance into this fane they come,
Rot on the pavement where thou rottedst half."—
"Are there not thousands in the world," said I,
Encourag'd by the sooth voice of the shade, 155
"Who love their fellows even to the death,
Who feel the giant agony of the world,
And more, like slaves to poor humanity,
Labour for mortal good? I sure should see
Other men here; but I am here alone." 160
"Those whom thou spak'st of are no vision'ries,"
Rejoin'd that voice—"They are no dreamers
    weak,
They seek no wonder but the human face;
No music but a happy-noted voice—
They come not here, they have no thought to 165
    come—
And thou art here, for thou art less than they—
What benefit canst thou do, or all thy tribe,
To the great world? Thou art a dreaming thing,
A fever of thyself—think of the Earth;
What bliss even in hope is there for thee? 170
What haven? every creature hath its home;
Every sole man hath days of joy and pain,
Whether his labours be sublime or low—
The pain alone; the joy alone; distinct:
Only the dreamer venoms all his days, 175
Bearing more woe than all his sins deserve.
Therefore, that happiness be somewhat shar'd,
Such things as thou art are admitted oft
Into like gardens thou didst pass erewhile,
And suffer'd in these temples: for that cause 180
Thou standest safe beneath this statue's knees."
"That I am favour'd for unworthiness,
By such propitious parley medicin'd
In sickness not ignoble, I rejoice,
Aye, and could weep for love of such award." 185
So answer'd I, continuing, "If it please,
Majestic shadow, tell me: sure not all
Those melodies sung into the World's ear
Are useless: sure a poet is a sage;
A humanist, physician to all men. 190
That I am none I feel, as vultures feel
They are no birds when eagles are abroad.
What am I then: Thou spakest of my tribe:
What tribe?" The tall shade veil'd in drooping
    white
Then spake, so much more earnest, that the 195
    breath
Moved the thin linen folds that drooping hung
About a golden censer from the hand
Pendent—"Art thou not of the dreamer tribe?

---

[8] Jacob's ladder; see Genesis 28, and *Paradise Lost*, III,
510–16.
[9] A curious echo here of the sonnet "To Sleep." See
page 373.

The poet and the dreamer are distinct,
Diverse, sheer opposite, antipodes.   200
The one pours out a balm upon the World,
The other vexes it." Then shouted I
Spite of myself, and with a Pythia's spleen,[10]
"Apollo! faded! O far flown Apollo!
Where is thy misty pestilence to creep   205
Into the dwellings, through the door crannies
Of all mock lyrists, large self worshipers
And careless Hectorers in proud bad verse.
Though I breathe death with them it will be life
To see them sprawl before me into graves.   210
Majestic shadow, tell me where I am,
Whose altar this: for whom this incense curls;
What image this whose face I cannot see,
For the broad marble knees; and who thou art,
Of accent feminine so courteous?"   215

    Then the tall shade, in drooping linens veil'd,[11]
Spoke out, so much more earnest, that her breath
Stirr'd the thin folds of gauze that drooping hung
About a golden censer from her hand
Pendent; and by her voice I knew she shed   220
Long-treasured tears. "This temple, sad and lone,
Is all spar'd from the thunder of a war
Foughten long since by giant hierarchy
Against rebellion: this old image here,
Whose carvèd features wrinkled as he fell,[12]   225
Is Saturn's; I Moneta, left supreme
Sole Priestess of this desolation,"—
I had no words to answer, for my tongue,
Useless, could find about its roofèd home
No syllable of a fit majesty   230
To make rejoinder to Moneta's mourn.
There was a silence, while the altar's blaze
Was fainting for sweet food: I look'd thereon,
And on the pavèd floor, where nigh were piled
Faggots of cinnamon, and many heaps   235
Of other crispèd spice-wood—then again
I look'd upon the altar, and its horns
Whiten'd with ashes, and its lang'rous flame,
And then upon the offerings again;
And so by turns—till sad Moneta cried,   240
"The sacrifice is done, but not the less
Will I be kind to thee for thy good will.
My power, which to me is still a curse,
Shall be to thee a wonder; for the scenes

Still swooning vivid through my globèd brain,   245
With an electral changing misery,
Thou shalt with those dull mortal eyes behold,
Free from all pain, if wonder pain thee not."
As near as an immortal's spherèd words
Could to a mother's soften, were these last: 250
And yet I had a terror of her robes,
And chiefly of the veils, that from her brow
Hung pale, and curtain'd her in mysteries,
That made my heart too small to hold its blood.
This saw that Goddess, and with sacred hand   255
Parted the veils. Then saw I a wan face,
Not pin'd by human sorrows, but bright-blanch'd
By an immortal sickness which kills not;
It works a constant change, which happy death
Can put no end to; deathwards progressing   260
To no death was that visage; it had past
The lilly and the snow; and beyond these
I must not think now, though I saw that face—
But for her eyes I should have fled away.
They held me back, with a benignant light,   265
Soft mitigated by divinest lids
Half-closed, and visionless entire they seem'd
Of all external things;—they saw me not,
But in blank splendor, beam'd like the mild
    moon,
Who comforts those she sees not, who knows not 270
What eyes are upward cast. As I had found
A grain of gold upon a mountain side,
And twing'd with avarice strain'd out my eyes
To search its sullen entrails rich with ore,
So at the view of sad Moneta's brow,   275
I ach'd to see what things the hollow brain
Behind enwombèd: what high tragedy
In the dark secret chambers of her skull
Was acting, that could give so dread a stress
To her cold lips, and fill with such a light   280
Her planetary eyes; and touch her voice
With such a sorrow—"Shade of Memory!"—
Cried I, with act adorant at her feet,
"By all the gloom hung round thy fallen house,
By this last temple, by the golden age,   285
By great Apollo, thy dear Foster Child,
And by thyself, forlorn divinity,
The pale Omega[13] of a withered race,
Let me behold, according as thou saidst,
What in thy brain so ferments to and fro!"   290
No sooner had this conjuration pass'd

---

10 Pythia was a priestess of Apollo.
11 Compare the next few lines with lines 194–98. Keats
was apparently going to drop the earlier passage.
12 Saturn, father of Zeus and deposed by him.

---

13 Omega, the last letter in the Greek alphabet signifies
the end.

My devout lips, than side by side we stood
(Like a stunt bramble by a solemn pine)
Deep in the shady sadness of a vale,[14]
Far sunken from the healthy breath of morn,   295
Far from the fiery noon and eve's one star.
Onward I look'd beneath the gloomy boughs,
And saw, what first I thought an image huge,
Like to the image pedestal'd so high
In Saturn's temple. Then Moneta's voice   300
Came brief upon mine ear—"So Saturn sat
When he had lost his Realms—" whereon there
    grew
A power within me of enormous ken
To see as a god sees, and take the depth
Of things as nimbly as the outward eye   305
Can size and shape pervade. The lofty theme
At those few words hung vast before my mind,
With half-unravel'd web. I set myself
Upon an eagle's watch, that I might see,
And seeing ne'er forget. No stir of life   310
Was in this shrouded vale, not so much air
As in the zoning of a summer's day
Robs not one light seed from the feather'd grass,
But where the dead leaf fell there did it rest:
A stream went voiceless by, still deaden'd more   315
By reason of the fallen divinity
Spreading more shade; the Naiad 'mid her reeds
Prest her cold finger closer to her lips.

Along the margin-sand large footmarks went
No farther than to where old Saturn's feet   320
Had rested, and there slept, how long a sleep!
Degraded, cold, upon the sodden ground
His old right hand lay nerveless, listless, dead,
Unsceptred; and his realmless eyes were clos'd,
While his bow'd head seem'd listening to the   325
    Earth,
His ancient mother, for some comfort yet.

It seem'd no force could wake him from his
    place;
But there came one who, with a kindred hand
Touch'd his wide shoulders after bending low
With reverence, though to one who knew it not.   330
Then came the griev'd voice of Mnemosyne,[15]
And griev'd I hearken'd. "That divinity
Whom thou saw'st step from yon forlornest wood,
And with slow pace approach our fallen King,

Is Thea, softest-natur'd of our Brood."[16]   335
I mark'd the Goddess in fair statuary
Surpassing wan Moneta by the head,
And in her sorrow nearer woman's tears.
There was a listening fear in her regard,
As if calamity had but begun;   340
As if the vanward clouds of evil days
Had spent their malice, and the sullen rear
Was with its storèd thunder labouring up.
One hand she press'd upon that aching spot
Where beats the human heart, as if just there,   345
Though an immortal, she felt cruel pain;
The other upon Saturn's bended neck
She laid, and to the level of his hollow ear
Leaning with parted lips, some words she spake
In solemn tenor and deep organ tune;   350
Some mourning words, which in our feeble
    tongue
Would come in this-like accenting; how frail
To that large utterance of the early Gods!

"Saturn! look up—and for what, poor lost
    King?
I have no comfort for thee; no not one;   355
I cannot cry, wherefore thus sleepest thou?
For Heaven is parted from thee, and the Earth
Knows thee not, so afflicted, for a God;
And Ocean too, with all its solemn noise,
Has from thy sceptre pass'd, and all the air   360
Is emptied of thine hoary majesty:
Thy thunder, captious at the new command,
Rumbles reluctant o'er our fallen house;
And thy sharp lightning, in unpracticed hands,
Scorches and burns our once serene domain.   365
With such remorseless speed still come new woes,
That unbelief has not a space to breathe.
Saturn! sleep on:—Me thoughtless, why should I
Thus violate thy slumbrous solitude?
Why should I ope thy melancholy eyes?   370
Saturn, sleep on, while at thy feet I weep."

As when upon a trancèd summer-night
Forests, branch-charmèd by the earnest stars,
Dream, and so dream all night without a noise,
Save from one gradual solitary gust,   375
Swelling upon the silence; dying off;
As if the ebbing air had but one wave;
So came these words, and went; the while in tears
She prest her fair large forehead to the earth,

[14] From this point on, Keats returns, with some alterations, to the original *Hyperion*.
[15] Apparent slip for Moneta.

[16] Hyperion's wife and sister.

Just where her fallen hair might spread in curls, 380
A soft and silken mat for Saturn's feet.
Long, long those two were postured motionless,
Like sculpture builded-up upon the grave
Of their own power. A long awful time
I look'd upon them: still they were the same; 385
The frozen God still bending to the earth,
And the sad Goddess weeping at his feet,
Moneta silent. Without stay or prop,
But my own weak mortality, I bore
The load of this eternal quietude, 390
The unchanging gloom, and the three fixèd
    shapes
Ponderous upon my senses, a whole moon.
For by my burning brain I measured sure
Her silver seasons shedded on the night,
And ever day by day methought I grew 395
More gaunt and ghostly.—Oftentimes I pray'd
Intense, that Death would take me from the Vale
And all its burthens—gasping with despair
Of change, hour after hour I curs'd myself;
Until old Saturn rais'd his faded eyes, 400
And look'd around and saw his kingdom gone,
And all the gloom and sorrow of the place,
And that fair kneeling Goddess at his feet.
As the moist scent of flowers, and grass, and
    leaves,
Fills forest dells with a pervading air, 405
Known to the woodland nostril, so the words
Of Saturn fill'd the mossy glooms around,
Even to the hollows of time-eaten oaks,
And to the windings of the foxes' hole,
With sad low tones, while thus he spake, and 410
    sent
Strange musings to the solitary Pan.
"Moan, brethren, moan; for we are swallow'd up
And buried from all Godlike exercise
Of influence benign on planets pale,
And peaceful sway above man's harvesting, 415
And all those acts which Deity supreme
Doth ease its heart of love in. Moan and wail,
Moan, brethren, moan; for lo, the rebel spheres
Spin round, the stars their ancient courses keep,
Clouds still with shadowy moisture haunt the 420
    earth,
Still suck their fill of light from sun and moon;
Still buds the tree, and still the sea-shores mur-
    mur;
There is no death in all the Universe,
No smell of death—there shall be death—Moan,
    moan,

Moan, Cybele,[17] moan; for thy pernicious Babes 425
Have changed a god into a shaking Palsy.
Moan, brethren, moan, for I have no strength left,
Weak as the reed—weak—feeble as my voice—
O, O, the pain, the pain of feebleness.
Moan, moan, for still I thaw—or give me help; 430
Throw down those imps, and give me victory.
Let me hear other groans, and trumpets blown
Of triumph calm, and hymns of festival,
From the gold peaks of Heaven's high-pilèd
    clouds;
Voices of soft proclaim, and silver stir 435
Of strings in hollow shells; and let there be
Beautiful things made new for the surprise
Of the sky-children." So he feebly ceas'd,
With such a poor and sickly sounding pause,
Methought I heard some old man of the earth 440
Bewailing earthly loss; nor could my eyes
And ears act with that pleasant unison of sense
Which marries sweet sound with the grace of
    form,
And dolorous accent from a tragic harp
With large-limb'd visions.—More I scrutinized: 445
Still fix'd he sat beneath the sable trees,
Whose arms spread straggling in wild serpent
    forms,
With leaves all hush'd; his awful presence there
(Now all was silent) gave a deadly lie
To what I erewhile heard—only his lips 450
Trembled amid the white curls of his beard.
They told the truth, though, round, the snowy
    locks
Hung nobly, as upon the face of heaven
A mid-day fleece of clouds. Thea arose,
And stretched her white arm through the hollow 455
    dark,
Pointing some whither: whereat he too rose
Like a vast giant, seen by men at sea
To grow pale from the waves at dull midnight.
They melted from my sight into the woods;
Ere I could turn, Moneta cried, "These twain 460
Are speeding to the families of grief,
Where roof'd in by black rocks they waste, in pain
And darkness, for no hope."—And she spake on,
As ye may read who can unwearied pass
Onward from the Antichamber of this dream, 465
Where even at the open doors awhile
I must delay, and glean my memory
Of her high phrase:—perhaps no further dare.

---

17 Cybele was Saturn's wife.

CANTO II

"Mortal, that thou may'st understand aright,
I humanize my sayings to thine ear,
Making comparisons of earthly things;
Or thou might'st better listen to the wind,
Whose language is to thee a barren noise, 5
Though it blows legend-laden thro' the trees.—
In melancholy realms big tears are shed,
More sorrow like to this, and such like woe,
Too huge for mortal tongue, or pen of scribe.
The Titans fierce,[18] self hid or prison bound, 10
Groan for the old allegiance once more,
Listening in their doom for Saturn's voice.
But one of our whole eagle-brood still keeps
His sov'reignty, and rule, and majesty;
Blazing Hyperion[19] on his orbèd fire 15
Still sits, still snuffs the incense teeming up
From Man to the Sun's God: yet unsecure.
For as upon the earth dire prodigies
Fright and perplex, so also shudders he:
Nor at dog's howl or gloom-bird's Even screech, 20
Or the familiar visitings of one
Upon the first toll of his passing bell:
But horrors, portioned to a giant nerve,
Make great Hyperion ache. His palace bright,
Bastion'd with pyramids of glowing gold, 25
And touch'd with shade of bronzèd obelisks,
Glares a blood-red thro' all the thousand courts,
Arches, and domes, and fiery galleries:
And all its curtains of Aurorian clouds
Flush angerly; when he would taste the wreaths 30
Of incense breathed aloft from sacred hills,
Instead of sweets, his ample palate takes
Savour of poisonous brass and metals sick.
Wherefore when harbour'd in the sleepy West,
After the full completion of fair day, 35
For rest divine upon exalted couch
And slumber in the arms of melody,
He paces through the pleasant hours of ease
With strides colossal, on from hall to hall;
While far within each aisle and deep recess 40
His wingèd minions in close clusters stand
Amaz'd, and full of fear; like anxious men,
Who on a wide plain gather in sad troops,
When earthquakes jar their battlements and
    towers.
Even now, while Saturn, roused from icy trance, 45
Goes, step for step, with Thea from yon woods,

Hyperion, leaving twilight in the rear,
Is sloping to the threshold of the West.—
Thither we tend."—Now in clear light I stood,
Reliev'd from the dusk vale. Mnemosyne 50
Was sitting on a square-edg'd polish'd stone,
That in its lucid depth reflected pure
Her priestess-garments.—My quick eyes ran on
From stately nave to nave, from vault to vault,
Through bow'rs of fragrant and enwreathèd light 55
And diamond-pavèd lustrous long arcades.
Anon rush'd by the bright Hyperion;
His flaming robes stream'd out beyond his heels,
And gave a roar, as if of earthly fire,
That scared away the meek ethereal hours, 60
And made their dove-wings tremble. On he flared.

To Autumn

Season of mists and mellow fruitfulness,
    Close bosom-friend of the maturing sun;
Conspiring with him how to load and bless
    With fruit the vines that round the thatch-
        eaves run;
To bend with apples the moss'd cottage-trees, 5
    And fill all fruit with ripeness to the core;
        To swell the gourd, and plump the hazel
            shells
    With a sweet kernel; to set budding more,
And still more, later flowers for the bees,
Until they think warm days will never cease, 10
        For Summer has o'er-brimm'd their clammy
            cells.

Who hath not seen thee oft amid thy store?
    Sometimes whoever seeks abroad may find
Thee sitting careless on a granary floor,
    Thy hair soft-lifted by the winnowing wind; 15
Or on a half-reap'd furrow sound asleep,
    Drows'd with the fume of poppies, while thy
        hook
        Spares the next swath and all its twinèd
            flowers:
And sometimes like a gleaner thou dost keep
    Steady thy laden head across a brook; 20
    Or by a cyder-press, with patient look,
        Thou watchest the last oozings hours by
            hours.

Where are the songs of Spring? Ay, where are
    they?

---

[18] The Titans had been overthrown with Saturn.
[19] Hyperion, god of the sun before Apollo.

Think not of them, thou hast thy music too,—
While barrèd clouds bloom the soft-dying day, 25
   And touch the stubble-plains with rosy hue;
Then in a wailful choir the small gnats mourn
   Among the river sallows,[1] borne aloft
     Or sinking as the light wind lives or dies;
And full-grown lambs loud bleat from hilly 30
     bourn,[2]
Hedge-crickets sing; and now with treble soft
   The redbreast whistles from a garden-croft;[3]
     And gathering swallows twitter in the skies.

Letters

I. TO BENJAMIN BAILEY[1]

[NOVEMBER 22, 1817]

My dear Bailey,

   . . . O I wish I was as certain of the end of all your troubles as that of your momentary start about the authenticity of the Imagination. I am certain of nothing but of the holiness of the Heart's affections and the truth of Imagination —What the imagination seizes as Beauty must be truth—whether it existed before or not—for I have the same Idea of all our Passions as of Love: they are all, in their sublime, creative of essential 10 Beauty. In a Word, you may know my favorite Speculation by my first Book and the little song I sent in my last[2]—which is a representation from the fancy of the probable mode of operating in these Matters. The Imagination may be compared to Adam's dream[3]—he awoke and found it truth. I am the more zealous in this affair, because I have never yet been able to perceive how any thing can be known for truth by consecutive reasoning—and yet it must be. Can it be that 20 even the greatest Philosopher ever arrived at his goal without putting aside numerous objections? However it may be, O for a Life of Sensations[4]

---

[1] Willows.   [2] Region.   [3] Enclosure.

[1] This friend (1791–1853) was a student at Oxford; Keats wrote Book III of *Endymion* while staying with him there in the summer of 1817. Bailey became a clergyman.—A very few spellings in these letters have been altered, and some points of punctuation changed or introduced, in the interest of clearness, but most of Keats's idiosyncrasies of spelling, punctuation, and capitalization have been retained.

[2] The song "O Sorrow," in Keats's letter of Nov. 3.

[3] Of the creation of Eve (*Paradise Lost*, VIII, 460–90; cf. lines 292–311).

[4] I.e., intuitions.—The quotation that follows is unidentified.

rather than of Thoughts! It is "a Vision in the form of Youth," a Shadow of reality to come— and this consideration has further convinced me, for it has come as auxiliary to another favourite Speculation of mine, that we shall enjoy ourselves hereafter by having what we called happiness on Earth repeated in a finer tone and so repeated. And yet such a fate can only befall those who delight in Sensation rather than hunger as you do after Truth. Adam's dream will do here and 10 seems to be a conviction that Imagination and its empyreal reflection is the same as human Life and its Spiritual repetition. But, as I was saying—the simple imaginative Mind may have its rewards in the repetition of its own silent Working coming continually on the Spirit with a fine Suddenness—to compare great things with small—have you never by being Surprised with an old Melody—in a delicious place—by a delicious voice, felt over again your very Specula- 20 tions and Surmises at the time it first operated on your Soul—do you not remember forming to yourself the Singer's face more beautiful than it was possible and yet with the elevation of the Moment you did not think so? Even then you were mounted on the Wings of Imagination so high—that the Prototype must be hereafter—that delicious face you will see. What a time! I am continually running away from the subject— sure this cannot be exactly the case with a com- 30 plex Mind—one that is imaginative, and at the same time careful of its fruits—who would exist partly on Sensation partly on thought—to whom it is necessary that years should bring the philosophic Mind[5]—such a one I consider yours and therefore it is necessary to your eternal Happiness that you not only drink this old Wine of Heaven, which I shall call the redigestion of our most ethereal Musings on Earth; but also increase in knowledge and know all things. I am glad to 40 hear you are in a fair way for Easter—you will soon get through your unpleasant reading, and then!—but the world is full of troubles and I have not much reason to think myself pesterd with many. . . .

   You perhaps at one time thought there was such a thing as Worldly Happiness to be arrived at, at certain periods of time marked out—you have of necessity from your disposition been thus

---

[5] Quoted from Wordsworth, "Ode: Intimations of Immortality," line 190.

led away—I scarcely remember counting upon any Happiness—I look not for it if it be not in the present hour—nothing startles me beyond the Moment. The setting Sun will always set me to rights, or if a Sparrow come before my Window I take part in its existence and pick about the Gravel. The first thing that strikes me on hearing a Misfortune having befalled another is this. "Well it cannot be helped—he will have the pleasure of trying the resources of his spirit"—and I beg now my dear Bailey that hereafter should you observe any thing cold in me not to put it to the account of heartlessness but abstraction—for I assure you I sometimes feel not the influence of a Passion or affection during a whole week—and so long this sometimes continues I begin to suspect myself, and the genuineness of my feelings at other times—thinking them a few barren Tragedy-tears. My brother Tom is much improved—he is going to Devonshire—whither I shall follow him—at present I am just arrived at Dorking to change the Scene—change the Air and give me a spur to wind up my Poem,[6] of which there are wanting 500 Lines. . . .

Your affectionate friend
John Keats—

II. TO GEORGE AND THOMAS KEATS

[DECEMBER 21, 1817]

My dear Brothers,

. . . I spent Friday evening with Wells, and went next morning to see Death on the Pale Horse. It is a wonderful picture, when West's age is considered; But there is nothing to be intense upon; no woman one feels mad to kiss, no face swelling into reality—The excellence of every art is its intensity, capable of making all disagreeables evaporate, from their being in close relationship with Beauty and Truth. Examine "King Lear," and you will find this exemplified throughout; but in this picture we have unpleasantness without any momentous depth of speculation excited, in which to bury its repulsiveness—The picture is larger than "Christ rejected."

I dined with Haydon the Sunday after you left, and had a very pleasant day, I dined too (for I have been out too much lately) with Horace Smith, and met his two Brothers, with Hill and Kingston, and one Du Bois. They only served to convince me, how superior humour is to wit in respect to enjoyment—These men say things which make one start, without making one feel; they are all alike; their manners are alike; they all know fashionables; they have a mannerism in their eating and drinking, in their mere handling a Decanter—They talked of Kean and his low company—Would I were with that Company instead of yours, said I to myself! I know such like acquaintance will never do for me, and yet I am going to Reynolds on Wednesday. Brown and Dilke walked with me and back from the Christmas pantomine. I had not a dispute but a disquisition, with Dilke on various subjects; several things dove-tailed in my mind, and at once it struck me what quality went to form a Man of Achievement, especially in Literature, and which Shakespeare possessed so enormously—I mean *Negative Capability,* that is, when a man is capable of being in uncertainties, mysteries, doubts, without any irritable reaching after fact and reason—Coleridge, for instance, would let go by a fine isolated verisimilitude caught from the Penetralium of mystery, from being incapable of remaining content with half-knowledge. This pursued through volumes would perhaps take us no further than this, that with a great poet the sense of Beauty overcomes every other consideration, or rather obliterates all consideration.

Shelley's poem [*The Revolt of Islam*] is out, and there are words about its being objected to as much as "Queen Mab" was. Poor Shelley, I think he has his Quota of good qualities, in sooth la!! Write soon to your most sincere friend and affectionate Brother

John

III. TO JOHN HAMILTON REYNOLDS[7]

[FEBRUARY 3, 1818]

Hampstead, TUESDAY

My dear Reynolds,

I thank you for your dish of Filberts[8]—Would I could get a basket of them by way of dessert every day for the sum of two-pence—Would we were a sort of ethereal Pigs, and turn'd loose to feed upon spiritual Mast and Acorns—which would be merely being a squirrel and feed

---

6 *Endymion.*

7 One of Keats's best friends (1794–1852), a minor poet, humorist, and writer of farces.

8 He means two sonnets Reynolds had sent for criticism, by the twopenny post. They were afterwards printed, but are in fact pretty poor.

upon filberts, for what is a squirrel but an airy pig, or a filbert but a sort of archangelical acorn? About the nuts being worth cracking, all I can say is that where there are a throng of delightful Images ready drawn, simplicity is the only thing. The first is the best on account of the first line, and the "arrow—foil'd of its antler'd food," and moreover (and this is the only word or two I find fault with, the more because I have had so much reason to shun it as a quicksand) the last has "tender and true." We must cut this, and not be rattlesnaked into any more of the like—It may be said that we ought to read our Contemporaries, that Wordsworth &c. should have their due from us. But, for the sake of a few fine imaginative or domestic passages, are we to be bullied into a certain Philosophy engendered in the whims of an Egotist? Every man has his speculations, but every man does not brood and peacock over them till he makes a false coinage and deceives himself. Many a man can travel to the very bourne of Heaven, and yet want confidence to put down his half-seeing. Sancho[9] will invent a Journey heavenward as well as any body. We hate poetry that has a palpable design upon us—and if we do not agree, seems to put its hand in its breeches pocket. Poetry should be great and unobtrusive, a thing which enters into one's soul, and does not startle it or amaze it with itself, but with its subject.—How beautiful are the retired flowers! how would they lose their beauty were they to throng into the highway crying out, "admire me, I am a violet!—dote upon me, I am a primrose!" Modern poets differ from the Elizabethans in this. Each of the moderns like an Elector of Hanover governs his petty state, and knows how many straws are swept daily from the Causeways in all his dominions and has a continual itching that all the Housewives should have their coppers well scoured: the antients were Emperors of vast Provinces, they had only heard of the remote ones and scarcely cared to visit them.—I will cut all this—I will have no more of Wordsworth or Hunt[10] in particular—Why should we be of the tribe of Manasseh, when we can wander with Esau?[11]

why should we kick against the Pricks,[12] when we can walk on Roses? Why should we be owls, when we can be Eagles? Why be teased with "nice Eyed wagtails,"[13] when we have in sight "the Cherub Contemplation"?[14]—Why with Wordsworth's "Matthew with a bough of wilding in his hand"[15] when we can have Jacques "under an oak[16] &c."?—The secret of the Bough of Wilding will run through your head faster than I can write it—Old Matthew spoke to him some years ago on some nothing, and because he happens in an Evening Walk to imagine the figure of the Old Man—he must stamp it down in black and white, and it is henceforth sacred—I don't mean to deny Wordsworth's grandeur and Hunt's merit, but I mean to say we need not be teazed with grandeur and merit when we can have them uncontaminated and unobtrusive. Let us have the old Poets, and Robin Hood. Your letter and its sonnets gave me more pleasure than will the 4th Book of Childe Harold and the whole of anybody's life and opinions. In return for your Dish of filberts, I have gathered a few Catkins, I hope they'll look pretty. . . .[17]

In the hope that these Scribblings will be some amusement for you this evening—I remain copying on the Hill

Yr sincere friend and Co-scribbler,
John Keats.

IV. TO JOHN TAYLOR[18]

27 FEBY—[1818]

Hampstead

My dear Taylor,

Your alteration strikes me as being a great improvement—the page looks much better. And

---

9 Sancho Panza, the clownish and unquixotic retainer of Don Quixote; he is unable to follow his master's soaring ideas.
10 On Leigh Hunt, see p. 214.
11 Esau, who sold his birthright for a mess of pottage

(Genesis 25:29–34), was the eldest son of the patriarch Isaac, whose son Jacob did his brother out of his father's blessing (Genesis 27); hence Esau became a wanderer wild and free. Manasseh was the eldest son of Jacob's favorite son Joseph, and received that name in honor of Joseph's getting rich in Egypt (Genesis 41:51). It means *forgetting*; "God," said Joseph, "hath made me forget all my toil."
12 Goads. Quoted from Acts 9:5.
13 Leigh Hunt, "The Nymphs," II, 170.
14 Milton, "Il Penseroso," line 54.
15 Wordsworth, "The Two April Mornings," lines 59–60. *Wilding* = an uncultivated plant, especially the wild apple.   16 Cf. *As You Like It*, II, i, 30–31.
17 Here Keats inserts his own poems "Robin Hood" and "Lines on the Mermaid Tavern."
18 The publisher (1781–1864) of Keats's second and third volumes.

now I will attend to the Punctuations you speak of—the comma should be at *soberly,*[19] and in the other passage the comma should follow *quiet.*[20] I am extremely indebted to you for this attention and also for your after admonitions—It is a sorry thing for me that any one should have to overcome Prejudices in reading my Verses—that affects me more than any hyper-criticism on any particular Passage. In *Endymion* I have most likely but moved into the Go-cart from the leading strings. In Poetry I have a few Axioms, and you will see how far I am from their Centre. 1st. I think Poetry should surprise by a fine excess and not by Singularity—it should strike the Reader as a wording of his own highest thoughts, and appear almost a Remembrance—2nd. Its touches of Beauty should never be half way thereby making the reader breathless instead of content: the rise, the progress, the setting of imagery should like the Sun come natural to him—shine over him and set soberly although in magnificence leaving him in the Luxury of twilight—but it is easier to think what Poetry should be than to write it—and this leads me on to another axiom. That if Poetry comes not as naturally as the Leaves to a tree it had better not come at all. However it may be with me I cannot help looking into new countries with "O for a Muse of Fire to ascend!"[21] If Endymion serves me as a Pioneer perhaps I ought to be content. I have great reason to be content, for thank God I can read and perhaps understand Shakspeare to his depths, and I have I am sure many friends, who, if I fail, will attribute any change in my Life and Temper to Humbleness rather than to Pride—to a cowering under the Wings of great Poets rather than to a Bitterness that I am not appreciated. I am anxious to get *Endymion* printed that I may forget it and proceed. I have coppied the 3rd Book and have begun the 4th. On running my Eye over the Proofs—I saw one Mistake—I will notice it presently and also any others if there be any. There should be no comma in "the raft branch down sweeping from a tall ash top."[22] I have besides made one or two alterations and also altered the 13 Line Page 32 to make sense of it as you will see. I will take care the Printer shall not trip up my Heels. There should be no dash after Dryope in this Line "Dryope's lone lulling of her child."[23] . . .

> Your sincere and obligd friend
> *John Keats*—

P.S. You shall have a short *Preface* in good time—

V. TO BENJAMIN ROBERT HAYDON[24]

MARCH 14, 1818

Teignmouth SATURD. MORN

My dear Haydon—
. . . Here's some doggrel for you. . . .

Where be ye going, you Devon Maid,
　　And what have you there i' the Basket?
Ye tight little fairy—just fresh from the dairy,
　　Will ye give me some cream if I ask it?

I love your Meads and I love your flowers　　5
　　And I love your junkets mainly;[25]
But 'hind the door, I love kissing more,
　　O look not so disdainly!

I love your Hills and I love your dales
　　And I love your flocks a-bleating—　　10
But O on the heather to lie together
　　With both our hearts a-beating.

I'll put your Basket all safe in a nook
　　And your shawl I hang up on this willow,
And we will sigh in the daisy's eye　　15
　　And Kiss on a grass green pillow.

I know not if this rhyming fit has done anything—it will be safe with you if worthy to put among my Lyrics. . . . I think of seeing the Dart[26] and Plymouth—but I don't know. It has as yet been a Mystery to me how and when Wordsworth went. I can't help thinking he has returned to his Shell—with his beautiful Wife and his enchanting Sister. It is a great Pity that People should by associating themselves with the finest things, spoil them. Hunt has damned Hampstead[27] and Masks and Sonnets and Italian tales—Wordsworth has damned the lakes—Milman

19 *Endymion*, I, 149.　　20 Ibid., I, 247.
21 Cf. the first line of Shakespeare's *Henry V.*
22 *Endymion*, I, 334-35.

23 Ibid., I, 495.
24 A historical painter (1786-1846).　　25 Extremely.
26 A river in Devonshire.
27 The London suburb where Keats lived.

has damned the old drama[28]—West[29] has damned —wholesale—Peacock[30] has damned satire, Ollier[31] has damn'd Music—Hazlitt has damned the bigotted and the blue-stockined; how durst the Man?! he is your only good damner and if ever I am damn'd—damn me if I shouldn't like him to damn me. It will not be long ere I see you, but I thought I would just give you a line out of Devon—

Yours affectionately
John Keats

Remember me to all we know

VI. TO JOHN HAMILTON REYNOLDS

MAY 3rd [1818]

Teignmouth

My dear Reynolds.

. . . Were I to study physic or rather Medecine again, I feel it would not make the least difference in my Poetry; when the Mind is in its infancy a Bias is in reality a Bias, but when we have acquired more strength, a Bias becomes no Bias. Every department of Knowledge we see excellent and calculated towards a great whole. I am so convinced of this, that I am glad at not having given away my medical Books, which I shall again look over to keep alive the little I know thitherwards. . . . An extensive knowledge is needful to thinking people—it takes away the heat and fever; and helps, by widening speculation, to ease the Burden of the Mystery:[32] a thing I begin to understand a little, and which weighed upon you in the most gloomy and true sentence in your Letter. The difference of high Sensations with and without knowledge appears to me this—in the latter case we are falling continually ten thousand fathoms deep and being blown up again without wings and with all [the] horror of a bare shoulderd creature—in the former case, our shoulders are fledge, and we go thro' the same air and space without fear. . . .

You may be anxious to know for fact to what sentence in your Letter I allude. You say, "I fear there is little chance of any thing else in this life." You seem by that to have been going through with a more painful and acute zest the same labyrinth that I have—I have come to the same conclusion thus far. My Branchings out therefrom have been numerous: one of them is the consideration of Wordsworth's genius and as a help, in the manner of gold being the meridian Line of worldly wealth,—how he differs from Milton.—And here I have nothing but surmises, from an uncertainty whether Milton's apparently less anxiety for Humanity proceeds from his seeing further or no than Wordsworth: And whether Wordsworth has in truth epic passion, and martyrs himself to the human heart, the main region of his song. In regard to his genius alone—we find what he says true as we have experienced, and we can judge no further but by larger experience—for axioms in philosophy are not axioms until they are proved upon our pulses: We read fine things but never feel them to the full until we have gone the same steps as the Author.—I know this is not plain; you will know exactly my meaning when I say that now I shall relish Hamlet more than I ever have done—Or, better—You are sensible no Man can set down Venery as a bestial or joyless thing until he is sick of it and therefore all philosophizing on it would be mere wording. Until we are sick, we understand not;—in fine, as Byron says, "Knowledge is Sorrow";[33] and I go on to say that "Sorrow is Wisdom"—and further for aught we can know for certainty "Wisdom is folly"!—So you see how I have run away from Wordsworth, and Milton, and shall still run away from what was in my head, to observe, that some kind of letters are good squares, others handsome ovals, and other some orbicular, others spheroid—and why should not there be another species with two rough edges like a Rat-trap? I hope you will find all my long letters of that species, and all will be well; for by merely touching the spring delicately and ethereally, the rough edged will fly immediately into a proper compactness; and thus you may make a

---

28 The poet and historian Henry Hart Milman (1791–1868). His verse drama *Fazio* had been produced in London on February 5.
29 The American painter Benjamin West (1738–1820), established in London, had succeeded Reynolds as president of the Royal Academy.
30 Thomas Love Peacock (1785–1866), Shelley's friend, author of miscellaneous works, especially novels.
31 Charles Ollier (1788–1859), an amateur of the flute, was a member of the firm that had published Keats's first volume.
32 Wordsworth, "Tintern Abbey," line 38.

---

33 Cf. *Manfred,* I, i, 10.

good wholesome loaf, with your own leven in it, of my fragments—If you cannot find this said Rat-trap sufficiently tractable—alas for me, it being an impossibility in grain for my ink to stain otherwise: If I scribble long letters I must play my vagaries. I must be too heavy, or too light, for whole pages—I must be quaint and free of Tropes[34] and figures—I must play my draughts[35] as I please, and for my advantage and your erudition, crown a white with a black, or a black with a white, and move into black or white, far and near as I please—I must go from Hazlitt to Patmore,[36] and make Wordsworth and Coleman[37] play at leap-frog—or keep one of them down a whole half-holiday at fly the garter[38]— "from Gray to Gay, from Little to Shakespeare"[39] —Also, as a long cause requires two or more sittings of the Court, so a long letter will require two or more sittings of the Breech—wherefore I shall resume after dinner.—

Have you not seen a Gull, an orc,[40] a Sea Mew, or any thing to bring this Line to a proper length, and also fill up this clear part; that like the Gull I may *dip*[41]—I hope, not out of sight— and also, like a Gull, I hope to be lucky in a good sized fish—This crossing a letter is not without its association—for chequer work leads us naturally to a Milkmaid, a Milkmaid to Hogarth, Hogarth to Shakespeare, Shakespeare to Hazlitt, Hazlitt to Shakespeare—and thus by merely pulling an apron string we set a pretty peal of Chimes at work—Let them chime on while, with your patience, I will return to Wordsworth— whether or no he has an extended vision or a circumscribed grandeur—whether he is an eagle in his nest, or on the wing—And to be more explicit and to show you how tall I stand by the giant, I will put down a simile of human life as far as I now perceive it; that is, to the point to which I say we both have arrived at—Well—I compare human life to a large Mansion of Many Apartments, two of which I can only describe, the doors of the rest being as yet shut upon me. The first we step into we call the infant or thoughtless Chamber, in which we remain as long as we do not think—We remain there a long while, and notwithstanding the doors of the second Chamber remain wide open, showing a bright appearance, we care not to hasten to it; but are at length imperceptibly impelled by the awakening of this thinking principle within us —we no sooner get into the second Chamber, which I shall call the Chamber of Maiden-Thought, than we become intoxicated with the light and the atmosphere, we see nothing but pleasant wonders, and think of delaying there for ever in delight: However among the effects this breathing is father of is that tremendous one of sharpening one's vision into the heart and nature of Man—of convincing one's nerves that the world is full of Misery and Heartbreak, Pain, Sickness, and oppression—whereby this Chamber of Maiden-Thought becomes gradually darken'd and at the same time on all sides of it many doors are set open—but all dark—all leading to dark passages—We see not the ballance of good and evil. We are in a Mist. *We* are now in that state —We feel the "burden of the Mystery." To this Point was Wordsworth come, as far as I can conceive, when he wrote "Tintern Abbey," and it seems to me that his Genius is explorative of those dark Passages. Now if we live, and go on thinking, we too shall explore them—he is a Genius and superior [to] us, in so far as he can, more than we, make discoveries, and shed a light in them—Here I must think Wordsworth is deeper than Milton—though I think it has depended more upon the general and gregarious advance of intellect, than individual greatness of Mind. . . . The Reformation produced such immediate and great benefits, that Protestantism was considered under the immediate eye of heaven, and its own remaining Dogmas and superstitions, then, as it were, regenerated, constituted those resting places and seeming sure points of Reasoning—from that I have mentioned, Milton, whatever he may have thought in the sequel, appears to have been content with these by his writings—He did not think into the human heart, as Wordsworth has done—Yet Milton as a Philosopher, had sure as great powers as Wordsworth—What is then to be inferr'd? O

---

[34] Figures of speech.   [35] Checkers.
[36] Peter George Patmore (1786–1855), a voluminous writer and father of the Victorian poet Coventry Patmore.
[37] George Colman the Younger (1762–1836), a leading playwright.
[38] A variety of the game of leapfrog.
[39] Cf. Pope. *Essay on Man*, IV, 380: "From grave to gay, from lively to severe." "Little" was one of Tom Moore's pseudonyms.   [40] Grampus.
[41] Part of this letter was "crossed," i.e., written with lines running both horizontally and vertically. "Dip" was the first word to be obscured by this crisscross method.

many things—It proves there is really a grand march of intellect—It proves that a mighty providence subdues the mightiest Minds to the service of the time being, whether it be in human Knowledge or Religion—I have often pitied a Tutor who has to hear "Nom:[42] Musa" so often dinn'd into his ears—I hope you may not have the same pain in this scribbling—I may have read these things before, but I never had even a thus dim perception of them; and moreover I like to say my lesson to one who will endure my tediousness for my own sake—After all there is certainly something real in the World—Moore's present to Hazlitt[43] is real—I like that Moore, and am glad I saw him at the Theatre just before I left Town. Tom[44] has spit a leetle blood this afternoon, and that is rather a damper—but I know —the truth is there is something real in the World. Your third Chamber of Life shall be a lucky and a gentle one—stored with the wine of love—and the Bread of Friendship. When you see George[45] if he should not have received a letter from me tell him he will find one at home most likely—tell Bailey[46] I hope soon to see him —Remember me to all. The leaves have been out here, for mony a day—I have written to George for the first stanzas of my Isabel[47]—I shall have them soon and will copy the whole out for you.

Your affectionate friend
John Keats.

VII. TO FANNY KEATS

JULY 2nd [1818]

Dumfries

My dear Fanny,

I intended to have written to you from Kirkudbright[48] the town I shall be in to-morrow—but I will write now because my Knapsack has worn my coat in the Seams, my coat has gone to the Taylors and I have but one Coat to my back in these parts. I must tell you how I went to Liverpool with George and our new Sister and the Gentleman my fellow traveller through the Summer and Autumn—We had a tolerable journey to Liverpool—which I left the next morning before George was up for Lancaster—Then we set off from Lancaster on foot with our Knapsacks on, and have walked a Little zig zag through the mountains and Lakes of Cumberland and Westmoreland—We came from Carlisle yesterday to this place—We are employed in going up Mountains, looking at strange towns, prying into old ruins, and eating very hearty breakfasts. Here we are full in the Midst of broad Scotch "How is it a' wi' yoursel"—the Girls are walking about bare footed and in the worst cottages the Smoke finds its way out of the door. I shall come home full of news for you and for fear I should choak you by too great a dose at once I must make you used to it by a letter or two. We have been taken for travelling Jewellers, Razor sellers and Spectacle venders because friend Brown wears a pair—The first place we stopped at with our Knapsacks contained one Richard Bradshaw, a notorious tippler—He stood in the shape of a ʒ and ballanced himself as well as he could saying with his nose right in Mr Brown's face "Do—yo—u sell Spect—ta—cles?" Mr Abbey[49] says we are Don Quixotes—tell him we are more generally taken for Pedlars. All I hope is that we may not be taken for excisemen in this whiskey country— We are generally up about 5 walking before breakfast and we complete our 20 Miles before dinner—Yesterday we visited Burns's Tomb and this morning the fine Ruins of Lincluden[50]—I had done thus far when my coat came back fortified at all points—so as we lose no time we set forth again through Galloway—all very pleasant and pretty with no fatigue when one is used to it —We are in the midst of Meg Merrilies' country of whom I suppose you have heard. . . .[51]

My dear Fanny I am ashamed of writing you such stuff, nor would I if it were not for being tired after my day's walking, and ready to tumble

---

42 Nominative; i.e., has to hear students decline nouns, etc.
43 Perhaps a presentation copy of Moore's *The Fudge Family in Paris,* which he had given Hazlitt in April.
44 Keats's sick brother, who died toward the end of 1818.
45 Keats's other brother.
46 See note 1.   47 "Isabella, or the Pot of Basil."
48 Kirkcudbright (pronounced *Kirkoóbry*), in southwestern Scotland. Fanny Keats was John's sister. Their brother George with his bride was emigrating to the United States. Keats had said good-by at Liverpool and then set off on a northern tour with his friend Charles Armitage Brown (1786–1842), a writer for periodicals.

49 Richard Abbey, who had been Keats's guardian. Fanny lived with the Abbeys.
50 A Benedictine abbey founded in the twelfth century near Dumfries.
51 Here Keats inserts a ballad on the gypsy and also some nonsense verses about his tour. He resumes his letter at Newton Steward on July 4.

into bed so fatigued that when I am asleep you might sew my nose to my great toe and trundle me round the town like a Hoop, without waking me—Then I get so hungry—a Ham goes but a very little way and fowls are like Larks to me—A Batch of Bread I make no more ado with than a sheet of parliament;[52] and I can eat a Bull's head as easily as I used to do Bull's eyes[53]—I take a whole string of Pork Sausages down as easily as a Pen'orth of Lady's fingers—Oh dear I must soon be contented with an acre or two of oaten cake, a hogshead of Milk and a Cloaths basket of Eggs morning noon and night when I get among the Highlanders—Before we see them we shall pass into Ireland and have a chat with the Paddies, and look at the Giant's Cause-way which you must have heard of—I have not time to tell you particularly for I have to send a Journal to Tom of whom you shall hear all particulars or from me when I return. Since I began this we have walked sixty miles to Newton Stewart at which place I put in this Letter—to-night we sleep at Glenluce—tomorrow at Portpatrick and the next day we shall cross in the passage boat to Ireland—I hope Miss Abbey has quite recovered—Present my Respects to her and to M^r and Mrs Abbey—God bless you—

Your affectionate Brother
John

Do write me a Letter directed to *Inverness,* Scotland—

VIII. TO JAMES AUGUSTUS HESSEY[54]

[OCTOBER 9, 1818]

My dear Hessey,

You are very good in sending me the letters[55] from the Chronicle—and I am very bad in not acknowledging such a kindness sooner—pray forgive me.—It has so chanced that I have had that paper every day—I have seen to-day's. I cannot but feel indebted to those Gentlemen who have taken my part—As for the rest, I begin to get a little acquainted with my own strength and weakness.—Praise or blame has but a momentary effect on the man whose love of beauty in the abstract makes him a severe critic on his own Works. My own domestic criticism has given me pain without comparison beyond what Blackwood or the Quarterly could possibly inflict, and also when I feel I am right, no external praise can give me such a glow as my own solitary re-perception & ratification of what is fine. J. S.[56] is perfectly right in regard to the slip-shod Endymion. That it is so is no fault of mine.—No! —though it may sound a little paradoxical. It is as good as I had power to make it—by myself. Had I been nervous about its being a perfect piece, & with that view asked advice, & trembled over every page, it would not have been written; for it is not in my nature to fumble—I will write independently.—I have written independently *without Judgment.*—I may write independently, & *with Judgment* hereafter. The Genius of Poetry must work out its own salvation in a man: It cannot be matured by law and precept, but by sensation & watchfulness in itself. That which is creative must create itself—In Endymion, I leaped headlong into the Sea, and thereby have become better acquainted with the Soundings, the quicksands, & the rocks, than if I had stayed upon the green shore, and piped a silly pipe, and took tea & comfortable advice.—I was never afaid of failure; for I would sooner fail than not be among the greatest. But I am nigh getting into a rant. So, with remembrances to Taylor and Woodhouse[57] &c I am

Y^rs very sincerely
John Keats

IX. TO RICHARD WOODHOUSE[58]

TUESDAY 27 OCT. 1818

My dear Woodhouse,

Your Letter gave me a great satisfaction; more on account of it friendliness, than any relish of that matter in it which is accounted so acceptable in the "genus irritabile." The best answer

---

52 Parliament-cake, gingerbread.
53 A kind of hard, round candy.
54 Taylor's junior partner in the publishing firm. See note 18.
55 On Oct. 3 and 8 two letters to the editor had appeared in the *Morning Chronicle* protesting against the *Quarterly's* attack on Keats.

56 The signature of the earlier of the letters.
57 Richard Woodhouse (1788–1834), a young lawyer, literary adviser to Taylor and Hessey, and an admirer of Keats.
58 See note 57.

I can give you is in a clerk-like manner to make some observations on two principle points, which seem to point like indices into the midst of the whole pro and con, about genius, and views and atchievements and ambition and cœtera. 1st. As to the poetical. Character itself (I mean that sort of which, if I am any thing, I am a Member; that sort distinguished from the wordsworthian or egotistical sublime; which is a thing per se and stands alone) it is not itself—it has no self —it is every thing and nothing—It has no character—it enjoys light and shade; it lives in gusto, be it foul or fair, high or low, rich or poor, mean or elevated—It has as much delight in conceiving an Iago as an Imogen. What shocks the virtuous philosopher, delights the camelion Poet. It does no harm from its relish of the dark side of things any more than from its taste for the bright one; because they both end in speculation. A Poet is the most unpoetical of any thing in existence; because he has no Identity—he is continually in for—and filling some other Body—The Sun, the Moon, the Sea and Men and Women who are creatures of impulse are poetical and have about them an unchangeable attribute—the poet has none; no identity—he is certainly the most unpoetical of all God's Creatures. If then he has no self, and if I am a Poet, where is the Wonder that I should say I would write no more? Might I not at that very instant have been cogitating on the Characters of Saturn and Ops?[59] It is a wretched thing to confess; but is a very fact that not one word I ever utter can be taken for granted as an opinion growing out of my identical nature—how can it, when I have no nature? When I am in a room with People if I ever am free from speculating on creations of my own brain, then not myself goes home to myself: but the identity of every one in the room begins to press upon me that I am in a very little time an[ni]hilated—not only among Men; it would be the same in a Nursery of children: I know not whether I make myself wholly understood: I hope enough so to let you see that no dependence is to be placed on what I said that day.

In the second place I will speak of my views, and of the life I purpose to myself. I am ambitious of doing the world some good: if I should be spared that may be the work of maturer years

—in the interval I will assay to reach to as high a summit in Poetry as the nerve bestowed upon me will suffer. The faint conceptions I have of Poems to come brings the blood frequently into my forehead. All I hope is that I may not lose all interest in human affairs—that the solitary indifference I feel for applause even from the finest Spirits, will not blunt any acuteness of vision I may have. I do not think it will—I feel assured I should write from the mere yearning and fondness I have for the Beautiful even if my night's labours should be burnt every morning, and no eye ever shine upon them. But even now I am perhaps not speaking from myself: but from some character in whose soul I now live. I am sure however that this next sentence is from myself. I feel your anxiety, good opinion and friendliness in the highest degree, and am

Your's most sincerely
John Keats

X. TO FANNY BRAWNE
JULY 8th [1819]

My sweet Girl,

Your Letter gave me more delight than any thing in the world but yourself could do; indeed I am almost astonished that any absent one should have that luxurious power over my senses which I feel. Even when I am not thinking of you I receive your influence and a tenderer nature steeling upon me. All my thoughts, my unhappiest days and nights, have I find not at all cured me of my love of Beauty, but made it so intense that I am miserable that you are not with me: or rather breathe in that dull sort of patience that cannot be called Life. I never knew before, what such a love as you have made me feel, was; I did not believe in it; my Fancy was afraid of it, lest it should burn me up. But if you will fully love me, though there may be some fire, 'twill not be more than we can bear when moistened and bedewed with Pleasures. You mention "horrid people" and ask me whether it depend upon them, whether I see you again. Do understand me, my love, in this. I have so much of you in my heart that I must turn Mentor when I see a chance of harm beffaling you. I would never see any thing but Pleasure in your eyes, love on your lips, and Happiness in your steps. I would wish to see you among those amusements suitable to your inclinations and spirits; so that

---

[59] Wife of Saturn, mother of Jupiter.

our loves might be a delight in the midst of Pleasures agreeable enough, rather than a resource from vexations and cares. But I doubt much, in case of the worst, whether I shall be philosopher enough to follow my own Lessons: if I saw my resolution give you a pain I could not. Why may I not speak of your Beauty, since without that I could never have lov'd you? I cannot conceive any beginning of such love as I have for you but Beauty. There may be a sort of love for which, without the least sneer at it, I have the highest respect and can admire it in others: but it has not the richness, the bloom, the full form, the enchantment of love after my own heart. So let me speak of your Beauty, though to my own endangering; if you could be so cruel to me as to try elsewhere its Power. You say you are affraid I shall think you do not love me—in saying this you make me ache the more to be near you. I am at the diligent use of my faculties here,[60] I do not pass a day without sprawling some blank verse or tagging some rhymes; and here I must confess, that (since I am on that subject) I love you the more in that I believe you have liked me for my own sake and for nothing else. I have met with women whom I really think would like to be married to a Poem and to be given away by a Novel. I have seen your Comet,[61] and only wish it was a sign that poor Rice[62] would get well whose illness makes him rather a melancholy companion: and the more so as to conquer his feelings and hide them from me, with a forc'd Pun. I kiss'd your writing over in the hope you had indulg'd me by leaving a trace of honey—What was your dream? Tell it me and I will tell you the interpretation thereof.

Ever yours, my love!

John Keats

Do not accuse me of delay—we have not here an opportunity of sending letters every day. Write speedily.

XI. TO FANNY BRAWNE

[FEBRUARY 1820?]

My dear Fanny,

Do not let your mother suppose that you hurt me by writing at night. For some reason or other your last night's note was not so treasureable as former ones. I would fain that you call me *Love* still. To see you happy and in high spirits is a great consolation to me—still let me believe that you are not half so happy as my restoration would make you. I am nervous, I own, and may think myself worse than I really am; if so you must indulge me, and pamper with that sort of tenderness you have manifested towards me in different Letters. My sweet creature when I look back upon the pains and torments I have suffer'd for you from the day I left you to go to the isle of Wight; the extasies in which I have pass'd some days and the miseries in their turn, I wonder the more at the Beauty which has kept up the spell so fervently. When I send this round I shall be in the front parlour watching to see you show yourself for a minute in the garden. How illness stands as a barrier betwixt me and you! Even if I was well—I must make myself as good a Philosopher as possible. Now I have had opportunities of passing nights anxious and awake I have found other thoughts intrude upon me. "If I should die," said I to myself, "I have left no immortal work behind me—nothing to make my friends proud of my memory—but I have lov'd the principle of beauty in all things, and if I had had time I would have made myself remember'd." Thoughts like these came very feebly whilst I was in health and every pulse beat for you—now you divide with this (may *I* say it?) "Last infirmity of noble minds"[63] all my reflection.

God bless you, Love.

J. Keats

XII. TO CHARLES ARMITAGE BROWN[64]

1 NOVEMBER [1820]

Naples

My dear Brown,

Yesterday we were let out of Quarantine, during which my health suffered more from bad air and the stifled cabin than it had done the whole voyage. The fresh air revived me a little, and I hope I am well enough this morning to write to you a short calm letter;—if that can be called one, in which I am afraid to speak of what I would fainest dwell upon. As I have gone thus far into it, I must go on a little:—perhaps it may

---

60 Keats is writing from Newport, Isle of Wight.

61 One was visible early that July.

62 Keats's friend James Rice, of whom not much is known.

63 Cf. Milton, "Lycidas," line 71.   64 See note 48.

relieve the load of WRETCHEDNESS which presses upon me. The persuasion that I shall see her[65] no more will kill me. I cannot q— My dear Brown, I should have had her when I was in health, and I should have remained well. I can bear to die—I cannot bear to leave her. O, God! God! God! Everything I have in my trunks that reminds me of her goes through me like a spear. The silk lining she put in my travelling cap scalds my head. My imagination is horribly vivid about her—I see her—I hear her. There is nothing in the world of sufficient interest to divert me from her a moment. This was the case when I was in England; I cannot recollect, without shuddering, the time that I was a prisoner at Hunt's, and used to keep my eyes fixed on Hampstead all day. Then there was a good hope of seeing her again—Now!—O that I could be buried near where she lives! I am afraid to write to her—to receive a letter from her—to see her handwriting would break my heart—even to hear of her anyhow, to see her name written, would be more than I can bear. My dear Brown, what am I to do? Where can I look for consolation or ease? If I had any chance of recovery, this passion would kill me. Indeed, through the whole of my illness, both at your house and at Kentish Town,[66] this fever has never ceased wearing me out. When you write to me, which you will do immediately, write to Rome (*poste restante*)[67]— if she is well and happy, put a mark thus +; if——

Remember me to all. I will endeavour to bear my miseries patiently. A person in my state of health should not have such miseries to bear. Write a short note to my sister, saying you have heard from me. Severn[68] is very well. If I were in better health I would urge your coming to Rome. I fear there is no one can give me any comfort. Is there any news of George? O, that something fortunate had ever happened to me or my brothers!—then I might hope,—but despair is forced upon me as a habit. My dear Brown, for my sake, be her advocate for ever. I cannot say a word about Naples; I do not feel at all concerned in the thousand novelties around me. I

am afraid to write to her—I should like her to know that I do not forget her. Oh, Brown, I have coals of fire in my breast. It surprises me that the human heart is capable of containing and bearing so much misery. Was I born for this end? God bless her, and her mother, and my sister, and George, and his wife, and you, and all!

Your ever affectionate friend,
John Keats

Thursday.—I was a day too early for the Courier. He sets out now. I have been more calm to-day, though in a half dread of not continuing so. . . . I must leave off. You bring my thoughts too near to Fanny. God bless you!

XIII. TO CHARLES ARMITAGE BROWN
30 NOVEMBER 1820

Rome

My dear Brown,

'Tis the most difficult thing in the world to me to write a letter. My stomach continues so bad, that I feel it worse on opening any book, —yet I am much better than I was in quarantine. Then I am afraid to encounter the pro-ing and con-ing of anything interesting to me in England. I have an habitual feeling of my real life having passed, and that I am leading a posthumous existence. God knows how it would have been—but it appears to me—however, I will not speak of that subject. I must have been at Bedhampton nearly at the time you were writing to me from Chichester—how unfortunate—and to pass on the river too! There was my star predominant! I cannot answer anything in your letter, which followed me from Naples to Rome, because I am afraid to look it over again. I am so weak (in mind) that I cannot bear the sight of any handwriting of a friend I love so much as I do you. Yet I ride the little horse, and, at my worst, even in a quarantine, summoned up more puns, in a sort of desperation, in one week than in any year of my life. There is one thought enough to kill me; I have been well, healthy, alert, &c., walking with her, and now—the knowledge of contrast, feeling for light and shade, all that information (primitive sense) necessary for a poem, are great enemies to the recovery of the stomach. There, you rogue, I put you to the

---

[65] Fanny Brawne.
[66] Then, like Hampstead, a northern suburb of London.
[67] I.e., to be held till called for.
[68] Joseph Severn (1793–1879), a painter and friend of Keats, whom he had accompanied to Italy.

torture; but you must bring your philosophy to bear, as I do mine, really, or how should I be able to live? Dr. Clark is very attentive to me; he says, there is very little the matter with my lungs, but my stomach, he says, is very bad. I am well disappointed in hearing good news from George, for it runs in my head we shall all die young.[69] I have not written to Reynolds yet, which he must think very neglectful; being anxious to send him a good account of my health, I have delayed it from week to week. If I recover, I will do all in my power to correct the mistakes made during sickness; and if I should not, all my faults will be forgiven. Severn is very well, though he leads so dull a life with me. Remember me to all friends, and tell Haslam[70] I should not have left London without taking leave of him, but from being so low in body and mind. Write to George as soon as you receive this, and tell him how I am, as far as you can guess; and also a note to my sister—who walks about my imagination like a ghost—she is so like Tom. I can scarcely bid you good-bye, even in a letter. I always made an awkward bow.

God bless you!
John Keats

[69] George had settled in Louisville, Kentucky; he died there in 1841. Fanny Keats died in 1889, aged eighty-six.

[70] William Haslam (1795–1851), a businessman and Keats's devoted friend.

George Darley

1795–1846

Darley was born in Ireland and educated at Trinity College. Like Thomas Lovell Beddoes, he represents some results of the interest at this time in Elizabethan and Jacobean lyrics and drama. His most famous work is the long poem *Nepenthe,* but he wrote a great deal in other forms as well, including prose.

TEXTS: Ramsay Colles, ed., *Complete Poetical Works* (1908). See also C. C. Abbott, *The Life and Letters* (1928); and John Heath-Stubbs, *The Darkling Plain* (1950).

from Nepenthe

O blest unfabled Incense Tree,[1]
That burns in glorious Araby,
With red scent chalicing the air,
Till earth-life grow Elysian there!

Half buried to her flaming breast
In this bright tree, she makes her nest,
Hundred-sunned Phœnix! when she must
Crumble at length to hoary dust!

Her gorgeous death-bed! her rich pyre
Burnt up with aromatic fire!
Her urn, sight high from spoiler men!
Her birthplace when self-born again!

The mountainless green wilds among,
Here ends she her unechoing song!
With amber tears and odorous sighs
Mourned by the desert where she dies!

The Luring-On[1]

When westering winds the ocean soothe,
    Till calm as Heaven's blue waste it be,
How sweet to glide from smooth to smooth,
    Like halcyons of the under sea!

How brave to tread the glistening sands
    That lie in amber wreaths below:
The twisted toil of faery hands
    Condemned to swing them to and fro!

My bright harp with its golden tongue,
    Speaks sweetly thro' the lucid wave,
And says its chords need scarce be rung,
    While floods so soft its bosom lave.

[1] The "source" for this poem is Shakespeare's "The Phoenix and the Turtle."

[1] This poem and the next are from "Siren Songs."

Broad-handed Neptune aye will beat
  In milder mood this harp of mine;
So think not, if the song be sweet,   15
  Think not the melody is mine!

The Mermaidens' Vesper-Hymn

Troop home to silent grots and caves!
  Troop home! and mimic as you go
The mournful winding of the waves
  Which to their dark abysses flow.

At this sweet hour, all things beside   5
  In amorous pairs to covert creep;
The swans that brush the evening tide
  Homeward in snowy couples keep.

In his green den the murmuring seal
  Close by his sleek companion lies;   10
While singly we to bedward steal,
  And close in fruitless sleep our eyes.

In bowers of love men take their rest,
  In loveless bowers we sigh alone,
With bosom-friends are others blest,—   15
  But we have none! but we have none!

Thomas Lovell Beddoes
1803–1849

The renewed interest in Elizabethan and Jacobean literature that characterizes this period manifests itself in poems like these of Beddoes.

    The son of a well-known doctor, he was educated at the Charterhouse and Oxford, and then went to Germany to study anatomy at Göttingen. He was still an undergraduate when his poetic drama *The Bride's Tragedy* was published and enthusiastically reviewed. Most of his adult life was spent in Germany and Switzerland; not much is known about its details. He wrote a great deal, but only a little was published in his own lifetime. His most famous work, *Death's Jest-Book,* a play imitative of Jacobean effects, was published after his death, which was by suicide.

    The *Works* have been edited by H. W. Donner (1935), and the life, *Thomas Lovell Beddoes: The Making of a Poet,* is also by Donner (1935).

The Phantom-Wooer[1]

I

A ghost, that loved a lady fair,
Ever in the starry air
  Of midnight at her pillow stood;
And, with a sweetness skies above
The luring words of human love,   5
  Her soul the phantom wooed.

Sweet and sweet is their poisoned note.
The little snakes of silver throat,
In mossy skulls that nest and lie,
Ever singing 'die, oh! die.'   10

II

Young soul put off your flesh, and come
With me into the quiet tomb,
  Our bed is lovely, dark, and sweet;
The earth will swing us, as she goes,
Beneath our coverlid of snows,   15
  And the warm leaden sheet.
Dear and dear is their poisoned note,
The little snakes of silver throat,
In mossy skulls that nest and lie,
Ever singing 'die, oh! die.'   20

Threnody[1]

    Far away,
      As we hear
The song of wild swans winging
    Through the day,
The thought of him, who is no more, comes   5
  ringing

---

[1] Written before 1848.

[1] Written before 1848.

On my ear.
Gentle fear
On the breast
Of my memory comes breaking,
Near and near,
As night winds' murmurous music waking
Seas at rest.

As the blest
Tearful eye
Sees the sun behind the ocean   15
Red i' th' west,
10 Grow pale, and in changing hues and fading
motion
Wane and die:

So do I
Wake or dream   20

The Victorian Period

From a painting by Sir Edwin Landseer.

The Victorian Period

THE CHARACTER OF THE AGE

When a writer in the *Edinburgh Review* for July 1858 asked himself how best to describe "the remarkable period in which our own lot is cast," he did not call it the age of democracy or industry or science; still less, the age of moral earnestness and complacency. He seized on one characteristic which affirmed "a fact equally obvious and certain, . . . that we are living in *an age of transition;*—a period when changes, deeply and permanently affecting the whole condition of mankind, are occurring more rapidly, as well as [more] extensively, than at any prior time in human history." Other ages, of course, notably the Renaissance and the seventeenth century, have been periods of unusually rapid change and transition. What distinguishes the nineteenth century is the widespread consciousness of what

H.R.H. Queen Victoria Opening the Crystal Palace in 1851. The brainchild of the Prince Consort, the Great Exposition was accomplished in the face of considerable opposition and was a resounding commercial success. The Palace itself, enclosing over 700,000 square feet in a frail-seeming filigree of iron and glass, was constructed in only nine months. It seemed a marvel to the Victorians and exemplified the era's fascination with technology and applied science. *Engraving by Cruickshank from Radio Times Hulton Picture Library.*

was taking place. As Mill pointed out in his important essays of 1831 on *The Spirit of the Age* (the first of which, printed below, is a fine introduction to the period), "The idea of comparing one's own age with former ages . . . had occurred to philosophers; but it never before was itself the dominant idea of any age." Never before had men been so acutely aware that their own times were "distinguished in a very remarkable manner from the times which preceded them." What did the Victorians mean by the times which preceded them? What did they think, by contrast, distinguished their own age?

In their minds the past was not the Romantic period and not even the eighteenth century. It was the Middle Ages. From their perspective it was the medieval tradition from which they had irrevocably broken—Christian orthodoxy under the rule of the Church, and civil government under the rule of king and nobility; the social structure of fixed classes, each with its recognized rights and duties; and the economic organization of village agriculture and town guilds. The breakup of this whole pattern of life and thought began with the Renaissance and Reformation, continued, quietly but steadily, through the next two centuries of philosophical rationalism and expanding business, and finally reached a point of conscious recognition when it "invaded outward objects." The French Revolution (1789), with its democratic appeal to the Rights of Man and its atheistical worship of the Goddess of Reason, was the first overt manifestation, in Mill's opinion, that Europe had entered into a state of transition. But in England the signs were not clearly recognized until the 1820s, at the threshold of the Victorian period.

Then it was that the rising agitation for an extension of the suffrage showed "that those were indeed new men, who insisted upon being governed in a new way." The new men were the captains of industry; and the new form of government which they demanded—and attained in 1832 with the passage of the Reform Bill—was a middle-class democracy. But the bloodless revolution that brought them to political power was simply the result of the more fundamental industrial and agrarian revolutions which gave them financial power. The crucial inventions—the steam engine, the spinning jenny, the water frame, the power loom, smelting by pit coal,

and the application of the steam engine to blast furnaces—all date from the second half of the eighteenth century. In the following decades, the great improvement in the means of communication achieved by more canals, macadam roads, railways, and steamboats hastened the growth of large-scale manufacturing by making possible a vast expansion of commerce. And just when the factories needed workmen in large numbers, the enclosure acts, as well as a sizable increase of population, provided the manpower.

This industrial expansion radically altered the character of economic life:

In the towns the old theory of a "limited" and "well-regulated" trade, based on the local monopoly of a chartered few, subjecting themselves to a common set of rules about trade and apprenticeship, was . . . abandoned for the new principle of open world-competition wherein all traders who could muster the capital and enterprise were invited to buy in the cheapest market and sell in the dearest, and to hire their labour wherever they liked and on what conditions each could secure. The change, in town as well as country, caused a wide cleavage of sympathy and of interest between classes which had previously shared, each in its degree, the common advantages of a fixed system of life and work; now that everyone scrambled for himself, the rich became richer and the poor poorer. (G. M. Trevelyan)

Small wonder that in 1833 Bulwer-Lytton made the point that although "every age may be called an age of transition, . . . in our age the transition is *visible*." The first great change which sets off the Victorian era from the past was the arrival of big business and middle-class government.

The second is of a wholly different nature, though no less impressive and radical. It is the emergence, on a wide scale, of religious doubt, meaning either outright skepticism and the adoption of some purely secular and agnostic philosophy, or, more commonly, a state of hesitation and uncertainty, often half conscious, not merely between belief and unbelief in a supernatural reality, but also between conflicting forms of faith. If there is a supernatural reality, is its character revealed in Protestantism? (and if so, in which form of Protestantism?) or in Roman Catholicism? or simply in Theism? It is quite true that infidelity had been common among the eighteenth-century intellectuals, but it was not until the 1820s that the religious tradition began to lose its unquestioned authority in society as a whole, and that the doubt which once had hung, as Carlyle says, "in the background of our world," spread outward to the middle ground, and later to the foreground. By 1870, after the theory of evolution and Biblical criticism had added their dissolving influences, John Morley might well say that the age was "characteristically and cardinally an epoch of transition in the very foundations of belief and conduct."

The Victorian period was therefore conditioned, in its thinking, in its psychological atmosphere, in its moral and intellectual temper, by the two overwhelming facts that mark the difference between the nineteenth century and any previous period of modern history: bourgeois industrial society and the disintegration of Christian thought. Those crucial factors, which are everywhere reflected, directly or indirectly, in Victorian literature, are summed up in two pertinent descriptions of the time, the first by Herbert Spencer, the second by John Ruskin:

Throughout the civilized world, especially in England, and above all in America, social activity is almost wholly expended in material development. To subjugate Nature, and bring the powers of production and distribution to their highest perfection, is the task of our age. . . . When the chief desideratum is industrial growth, honour is most conspicuously given to that which generally indicates the aiding of industrial growth. The English nation at present displays what we may call the commercial diathesis.

There never yet was a generation of men (savage or civilized) who, taken as a body, so wofully fulfilled the words "having no hope, and without God in the world," as the present civilized European race. . . . Nearly all our powerful men in this age of the world are unbelievers; the best of them in doubt and misery; the worst in reckless defiance; the plurality, in plodding hesitation, doing, as well as they can, what practical work lies ready to their hands. . . . Our earnest poets and deepest thinkers are doubtful and indignant (Tennyson, Carlyle).

Could not both quotations apply as well, almost, to our own period? We have a tendency to adopt a scornful or amused attitude toward the Victorians, as though we were quite different— and much superior. But the fact is that our social and religious situation is fundamentally the same; the age of transition still continues, and no social institutions nor any philosophy of life remotely so stable and widely accepted as those of the Middle Ages have yet emerged. That is why Victorian literature, especially its prose, is so alive today. It explores the very problems raised by the industrial and intellectual revolutions that are our problems too. Its analysis and criticism, both pro and con, of democracy and dictatorship, of free enterprise and socialism, and its various efforts to resolve the conflict of religion and science, speak to us directly. 1850 simply marks an earlier stage of the ideological conflicts of the 1970s. Their original shape and the various solutions that were proposed, first in the social area and then in the religious, are outlined in the sections that follow.

SOCIETY: THE PHILOSOPHY OF THE MIDDLE CLASS

On the strength of the Industrial Revolution, the new capitalists became the most powerful class in English society—potentially, but not yet actually. For they were excluded from the political life of the nation. The world of the 1820s was still the world of the old aristocracy in which a whole series of laws restrained the liberty of everyone who was not an aristocrat. Consider the humiliating position in the year 1825 of a successful Manchester businessman who happened to be a Presbyterian or a Congregationalist, a Baptist, a Quaker, or a Methodist, maybe a Jew or a Roman Catholic, in short anything except an Anglican (a member of the Church of England). And he probably wasn't an Anglican, because the middle class since the seventeenth century had been very largely Puritan; it was the aristocracy that was solidly Anglican. This admirable citizen could not hold any office under the Crown, in the army, navy, or civil service; he could not sit on the Town Corporation, the governing board of his city; he could not graduate from either Oxford or Cambridge (the only universities in England at the time); he could not run his business efficiently because he was hampered by innumerable and now antiquated restrictions, especially a long series of Navigation Acts. Above all, he had no voice in the national government: he had no vote and, still worse, no representation in Parliament because the electoral districts had been drawn up centuries before, when Manchester and other industrial cities did not exist, and had never been revised. These are the circumstances in which Victorian liberalism was born. The middle class demanded freedom from the old aristocratic-Anglican restrictions. They wanted an extension of the franchise and the repeal of class legislation. This meant, theoretically, a democratic, or at any rate a partly democratic, form of government to replace the old constitution in which England had been ruled by the king and an oligarchy of landed nobility; and it meant, so far as power was concerned, that the government should be severely limited to the function of keeping public order, and should no longer interfere with the equal liberties of all citizens, regardless of creed or wealth. This is the liberal program that was carried to success between 1825 and 1835. The passage of the Reform Bill in 1832, which enfranchised half the middle class (the upper capitalist group), signalized its victory.

The political philosophy that expressed and formulated the concrete demands of the bourgeoisie had been worked out through the eighteenth century, notably by Locke and Rousseau, and had been given embodiment in the French Rights of Man and in our own Declaration of Independence. For the Victorians, however, it was Jeremy Bentham and his disciples, known as the Utilitarians, who provided the middle class with their political theory. Bentham's starting point was the assumption that, whatever their pretensions, men are motivated, at bottom, by self-interest—that is to say, their real aim in life is to have as much pleasure and suffer as little pain as possible. It followed, therefore, that the purpose of government should be to promote "the greatest happiness of the greatest number." Whatever made for general happiness he called a useful law or a useful act of government. Whatever made for general unhappiness was a useless law or a useless act of government; hence the term Utilitarianism in its political application. On this premise Bentham based his argument for democracy. Would a monarchy promote the greatest good of the greatest number? By no means; it would promote the greatest good of the monarch. Would an oligarchy do it? Again no; it would promote its own good. Would a democracy do it? Yes, obviously, because then the government would be in the hands of the

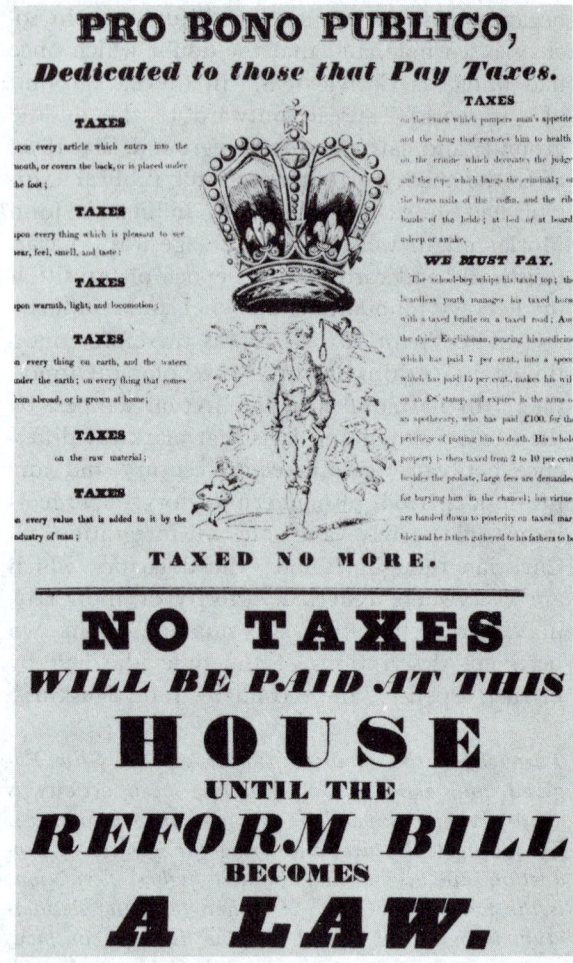

A Middle-Class Revolution. A handbill urging passage of the Reform Bill of 1832. *The Granger Collection.*

people, and the people would inevitably act for the greatest good of the people. Later in the century, John Stuart Mill put the liberal argument for democracy on firmer and wider grounds (see p. 564).

Finally, on the extent of state control, it is quite true that Bentham's first principle could have justified almost any amount of interference. If the purpose of government is to promote the general happiness, then it *may* do anything, and *should* do anything, that will achieve that end —even, in theory, the abolition of private property. And as a matter of fact, Benthamism had its influence, ironically enough, on the growth of English Socialism. Ironically, because no one would have been more horrified at such a result than the Benthamites. After all, their sympathies, conscious or otherwise, were strongly middle-class; and they staunchly believed in the utility of private property and the maximum amount of personal and business freedom. From their point of view, government would promote the general happiness by interfering just as little as possible. It *could* do anything, but it *would* do very little. And for two reasons, as stated by Bentham:

The motto, or watchword of government, . . . ought to be—Be quiet. For this quietism there are two main reasons:—1. Generally speaking, any interference . . . on the part of government is needless. . . . There is no one who knows what is for your interest, so well as yourself—no one who is disposed with so much ardor and constancy to pursue it. 2. Generally speaking, it is moreover likely to be pernicious . . . by the restraint or constraint imposed on the free agency of the individual. Pain is the general concomitant of the sense of such restraint, wherever it is experienced. . . . With few exceptions, and those not very considerable ones, the attainment of the maximum enjoyment will be most effectually secured by leaving each individual to pursue his own maximum of enjoyment.

Then Bentham adds a statement that at once reveals the connection of his theory with the economic desires of the middle class: *"Security* and *freedom* are all that industry requires. The request which agriculture, manufacturers, and commerce present to governments, is modest and reasonable as that which Diogenes made to Alexander: 'Stand out of my sunshine.' " In a word, the policy of the government should be *laissez faire*—hands off.

Especially with regard to business. The middle-class theory of political economy, which Bentham and the Utilitarians adopted, had been first formulated by Adam Smith in his famous and influential book on *The Wealth of Nations* (1776). He had argued that if the real value of the annual produce of a nation's land and labor was to be increased (as, of course, it should be), the government must limit itself to three duties: protecting the country from foreign invasion, protecting every citizen from the oppression of any other citizen, and erecting certain public institutions like law courts, post offices, and schools. Moreover, business was to be free not only from government interference but also from the whole system of local and guild regulation which, as we saw earlier, was breaking down in fact. If only all forms of preference and restraint were removed, and every man, worker or capitalist, "as long as he does not violate the laws of justice, is left perfectly free to pursue his own interest his own way, and to bring both his industry and capital into competition with those of any other man, or order of men," then the economic machine would function "naturally" and most efficiently—for the greatest good of the greatest number. Nothing is more characteristic

"Hurrying" Coal. Before the passage of the Mines Act of 1842, drawing coal wagons as heavy as 400 pounds was a job for children, especially girls under 14 years old who could fit through the narrow passages. *Radio Times Hulton Picture Library.*

of the liberal mind than this confidence in "free enterprise," this faith that unrestricted competition is at once the ideal means to develop the individual (the strongest survive, the weakest go down) and to give society the best products at the lowest prices.

The blessings of this liberal economy were not particularly apparent, however, to the millions of men, women, and children who, in the absence of any protection from either the state or effective trade unions, were exploited with a ruthlessness that has perhaps never been paralleled.

Official reports describe children of from six to eight working ten or twelve hours a day as stocking weavers, often fainting at their work, and slowly losing their eyesight. They describe needle-women who received 1½ pence for a shirt, and others who were paid 4½ pence a week for working sixteen hours a day on neckties. They speak of child labor in the mines, arsenic poisoning in the potteries, men fined for talking at their work, women in the last stages of pregnancy fined for sitting down. They record that one-fifth of the population of Liverpool lived in cellars, that 12,000 persons lived in 1400 houses in a London block four hundred yards square, that twenty persons could be found lying huddled on the floor of a single Glasgow room. This was the fruit of the industrial revolution.[1]

Efforts to relieve this situation by government action were few and feeble until late in the century, for the theory of *laissez faire,* which Adam Smith had applied to commerce, had been extended to industry by T. R. Malthus and David Ricardo. They were the creators of what Carlyle later called "the dismal science." "Dismal" is a masterly understatement for their theoretical argument against any alleviation of these appalling conditions, whether by government action or by private charity. The supposed "iron laws" of supply and demand made all interference useless. If wages were raised, population would increase, and the larger supply of labor would simply bring wages back to where they had been. Charity, public or private, not only encouraged idleness but tended to increase population and therefore to lower wages and intensify the struggle for survival. "To prevent the

recurrence of misery, is, alas! beyond the power of man." The only possible alleviation was for the workers to limit the number of their children, and thus, by decreasing the supply of labor, to increase their wages.

Finally, implicit in the whole theory of liberalism, political and economic, is a new theory of society. It is no longer thought of in feudal terms as an organism or a partnership like a family, whose various members, each holding a fixed status in the hierarchy, were united by mutual obligations and loyalties. It is now considered a collection of individuals, each motivated by self-interest, each free to sell or purchase his labor in free competition at the best possible price. The bond between man and man is solely contractual, or, in Carlyle's famous phrase, "cash-nexus." But this is all to the good, because to do the best for yourself is to do the best for society. That is the very core of the liberal faith.

So much for the abstractions of philosophy. What is the concrete outlook of the middle class? Or to put it another way, what did it feel like to belong to a society dedicated to commercial expansion? Under what conditions would you have lived? By what characteristic goals, personal and national? By what moral ideals and intellectual standards of value? When those questions are explored, we can then answer for ourselves the more important question of whether or not the temper of society today is very different.

In such a competitive system, business success, or even survival, demanded an economic struggle far beyond anything known before. And since new and ever more distant sources of supply were being opened up by the railroad and the steamship, there was the additional battle for new markets. Moreover, as the standard of living went up, the measure of sufficiency went up too; and the son fought for comforts that his father had had no incentive to strive for. Under these conditions the pressure of work was immensely increased. England became in literal fact the workshop of the world; and Englishmen, Emerson estimated, worked three times as hard as other Europeans. In the professions, too, the immense competition for preferment made work and hard work "the only way now-a-days to rise."

---

[1] Granville Hicks, *Figures in Transition*, p. 6.

W. R. Greg's picture of English life in 1851 is hardly exaggerated:

The excessive toil required in nearly every occupation —the severity of the struggle for existence—the strain upon the powers of every man who runs the race of life in this land and age of high excitement, . . . is by no means confined to the lower orders. Throughout the whole community we are all called to labour too early and compelled to labour too severely and too long. We live sadly too fast. Our existence, in nearly all ranks, is a crush, a struggle, and a strife.

As Greg notices, the competition was not only stiff but fast. The tempo of business life had increased with its size:

Compare the magnitude and complexity of your business transactions, the rapidity, decision, and energy with which they have to be conducted, the incessant strain of thought and care which they involve, with the easy, methodical round of commerce in the days when the goods train, the ocean steamship, and the electric telegraph were unknown. (J. B. Brown in 1871)

These inventions, incidentally, stepped up the speed of life throughout the society; and though faster machines have been invented in our own times, the feeling of being rushed was every bit as great then as now. "That constant sense of being driven—not precisely like 'dumb' cattle, but cattle who must read, write, and talk more in twenty-four hours than twenty-four hours will permit, can never have been known to them." That sounds exactly like someone today talking of the Victorians. Actually it is Frances Cobbe in 1864 talking of the *pre*-Victorians.

The high pressure of business life was further intensified by the characteristic goals of a bourgeois society. When Herbert Spencer referred to England as being in the "commercial diathesis," he at once added, "and the undue admiration for wealth appears to be its concomitant—a relation still more conspicuous in the worship of 'the almighty dollar' by the Americans." But it was not so much wealth itself that motivated the economic struggle and won prestige as it was the social position that wealth could buy. The passion for money was complemented by the passion for social advancement. By 1840 Mill found the latter a major characteristic of English life:

In England, as well as in America, it appears to foreigners, and even to Englishmen recently returned from a foreign country, as if everybody had but one wish—to improve his condition, never to enjoy it; as if no Englishman cared to cultivate either the pleasures or the virtues corresponding to his station in society, but solely to get out of it as quickly as possible; or if that cannot be done, and until it is done, to seem to have got out of it.

It was the breakdown of class barriers, consequent upon the increasing wealth of the bourgeoisie and the declining wealth of the aristocracy, which made this ambition practical. "Now that a man may make money," said Ruskin, "and rise in the world, and associate himself, unreproached, with people once far above him, . . . it becomes a veritable shame to him to remain in the state he was born in, and everybody thinks it is his *duty* to try to be a 'gentleman.'" We must recognize the precision and importance, here, of the word "duty." The ambition to better one's position was rationalized by the liberal theory, mentioned above, that to do the best for yourself was to do the best for society. Beatrice Webb has described the creed of self-advancement as she knew it in her own middle-class home:

It was the bounden duty of every citizen to better his social status; to ignore those beneath him, and to aim steadily at the top rung of the social ladder. Only by this persistent pursuit by each individual of his own and his family's interest would the highest general level of civilisation be attained. . . . No one of the present generation realises with what sincerity and fervour these doctrines were held by the representative men and women of the mid-Victorian middle class.

However hard their conditions of life, their mood—and therefore the mood of the age—was highly optimistic. Individual success was part cause, part result of national success. England, too, was making money and advancing up the national ladder. Before Germany and the United States began to catch up late in the century, she had no rivals in industrial power, and from 1850 to 1914 was top nation of the world. Englishmen had good reason to view their achievement with pride and satisfaction, and natural, if not good, reason to view it, by moments, with a complacent

Victorian Contrasts. Between the rising middle classes and the life of the poor the gap was ever-widening. An affection for decoration and a passion for possession produced the style typified by this cluttered drawing room. *Radio Times Hulton Picture Library.*

and bumptious air of self-congratulation. Macaulay talked of his countrymen as "the greatest and most highly civilised people that ever the world saw," and boasted of their carrying "the means of locomotion and correspondence, every mechanical art, every manufacture, everything that promotes the convenience of life, to a perfection which our ancestors would have thought magical." (See also the salute to English science and commerce by Carlyle in the selection from *Past and Present,* Book III, Chap. 5.)

We notice here the identification of civilization with material power; and it is true that Victorian pride was often founded on a childish admiration for mere size and quantity: longer lines of railroads, more tons of coal, greater national income. (See Arnold's criticism, p. 859.) But not entirely. The worship of science and industry often sprang from a spontaneous admiration of the power of man to conquer nature, to discover her secrets, and to transform her material resources into productive usefulness.

Why is Manchester at 5:30 A.M., with all the factory whistles blowing, a thrilling sight even to a man like Carlyle, so indignant at the condition of the workers and the Mammonism of the capitalists? Because it symbolizes "the triumph of man over matter" and bears victorious witness to his "manufacturing, commercial, economic *skill.*" It is the new sense of enormous technological and executive power, "the mastery, the achieve of the thing," quite as much as its actual "fruits," that won the glowing admiration of the Victorians and provoked much of their patriotic pride.

If they viewed the present with satisfaction, they looked to the future with unbounded hope. It was an age of great expectations. With so much already accomplished, and in so short a time, what wonders lie ahead! Macaulay's glamorous prophecy of the world of 1930—the population quadrupled, national income enormously expanded, "machines constructed on principles yet undiscovered" in every house, etc. (in the

Dog Leap Stairs, Newcastle, about 1880. Life in the streets was marked by drab scarcity and unrelieved plainness. *Radio Times Hulton Picture Library.*

concluding paragraphs of the selection from "Southey's Colloquies.")—is a perfect index not only to the confident faith in progress but to its scientific basis and its predominantly material character. The law of Baconian philosophy, Macaulay said, is that "a point which yesterday was invisible is its goal today, and will be its starting-post tomorrow"; its end and aim, to increase the comforts and mitigate the pains of human life. After a hundred years of such progress, we are no longer so certain that it is the *summum bonum,* or that Baconian science is the only philosophy we need. It is fair to add, however, that Macaulay and the middle class believed that scientific progress would mean moral progress as well. And to some extent they were right. Better health and better morals go together, as Kingsley and Dickens never tired of pointing out. Better conditions of living, consequent upon the cheaper cost of clothing and household supplies, make for a happier and more law-abiding population. But this line of thought

was pushed to fantastic extremes. It was supposed (by Macaulay) that "every improvement of the means of locomotion . . . tends to remove national and provincial antipathies, and to bind together all the branches of the great human family," until—war would be a thing of the past! Nothing Victorian is more curious, and ironic, than the confident association of world peace with scientific progress, on the ground that international communication would replace the prejudice of insularity by friendly understanding and provide each nation with a ready market for its goods. Indeed, Herbert Spencer thought that the new industrial age *must* put an end to war by diffusing economic opportunities and benefits over the whole world, and making peace a requirement of prosperity. As capital became international and a thousand investments crossed every frontier, international peace would become a necessity. Great expectations indeed! And in Tennyson's "Locksley Hall" they even include "the Parliament of man, the Federation of the world." As a matter of fact, our own desire for world federation has its source in scientific progress, but of a kind the Victorians never conceived of. The age of optimism is long past.

Consonant with their conception of progress is the middle-class attitude toward intellectual culture. In lives so immersed in business, the test of value is utility conceived in terms of tangible and practical results. Thought is only useful, therefore, if it issues in better machinery, political, social, or mechanical. The investigation of truth as truth, the free play of the mind on subjects of "no practical account," is viewed with indifference and sometimes scorn. The man of action is exalted at the expense of the thinker and the artist; and the humanities, art, philosophy, literature, even history, are condemned as useless or patronized for "cultural"—that is, social—reasons. With heavy sarcasm, a writer in the Utilitarian *Westminster Review* asked to be informed how the "pursuit of literature and poetry . . . is to conduce towards cotton-spinning." The Society for the Diffusion of Useful Knowledge was founded in 1827, and the liberal reviews carried on a campaign to transform the old classical education into the study, primarily, of the natural and social sciences. Even a man like Charles Kingsley could tell the students of Wellington College that "only the knowledge which you get by observation" is power, and that the shrewd fellow who has an eye for facts and can turn them "to some particular use" will leave the man of book learning far behind in the race of life. The notion that books may so broaden and deepen one's knowledge of life, and so sharpen one's perceptions, that he can judge more intelligently and live more wisely, has dropped out of Kingsley's mind, and, to a large extent, out of the Victorian—in fact, the modern —mind. In bourgeois society the conception of utility became too narrow to include the great but intangible utility of the humanities, or to recognize the importance of what Arnold called "the whole life of the intelligence." This is not to imply that the age of Mill and Darwin did not make significant contributions to thought, or that there were not many Victorians who valued intellectual culture in theory and demonstrated it in practice—to the point in some cases, notably those of Newman and Arnold, of attacking the contemporary "preference of doing to thinking." But when we realize that "intellectuals" like Carlyle and J. A. Froude, Kingsley and Macaulay, were so infected by the bias of commercial life that they could support that preference (though for other reasons too, as we shall see), we have a measure of how deeply antiintellectualism had permeated Victorian society.

But whatever its blindness to intellectual values, the middle class was keenly alive to moral values; and these are ultimately the more important. As W. E. H. Lecky pointed out, the Victorians owed their commercial success, personal and national, less to their intellect than to their character, specifically to their possession of what he significantly calls the "industrial virtues." "Temperance, industry, integrity, frugality, self-reliance, and self-restraint are the means by which the great masses of men rise from penury to comfort, and it is the nations in which these qualities are most diffused that in the long run are the most prosperous." These virtues had the further sanction of Puritanism, which had always been strong, and still was, among the middle class. The greatest, that is, the most compulsive, of them all was the second which Lecky mentions: industry. The duty to work (and conversely the sinfulness of not working) was at once a Puritan dogma and an economic necessity for social and financial success. Under that double

A Ward for the "Casual Poor" at Marylebone Workhouse. Established by the Poor Law of 1834, workhouses were a more efficient and impersonal method of dealing with the problem of poverty than the parish dole they replaced. Carlyle characterized them as "Poor-Law Bastilles." *The Granger Collection.*

pressure it was built into the Victorian temper so firmly that we still feel its urgency today. The younger Thomas Arnold wrote of his father: "For all his children, the precept flowed steadily from his life, still more from his lips, '*Work.*' Not, work at this or that—but, work." The Victorians could not understand what the Romantics meant by "wise passiveness." It was a contradiction in terms, and morally suspect. The only excuse for idleness was illness, even among the gentry. Sir Michael, in Miss Braddon's novel, *Lady Audley's Secret*, went "to his dressing-room to prepare for dinner after a day of lazy enjoyment, that is only legitimate for an invalid."

It is quite true, of course, that the ethical code was not always obeyed. There is plenty of evidence of immorality among the moral Victorians. Their ideal was too high for human nature: hence the discrepancy between their professions and their practice, which we now call their hypocrisy. But on the whole, public and private life reached a higher level of moral probity than ever before or since. Certainly the Victorians would have been shocked by our moral skepticism, our bland uncertainty of what, if any, moral principles we should live by.

THE REACTION AGAINST POLITICAL LIBERALISM AND INDUSTRIAL SOCIETY

Although the middle-class philosophy of life we have been examining dominated the age, it did not go unchallenged. It was supported by Macaulay, Herbert Spencer, and Huxley (for the most part), but it was severely attacked by most of the Victorian "prophets." Dickens and Mrs. Gaskell, Kingsley and Disraeli in the novel, Tennyson and Mrs. Browning in verse, and in expository prose Carlyle and Ruskin, Newman and Mill, Arnold and William Morris subjected its political liberalism, its worldly ambitions, its conception of man and society to searching criticism. Only Newman and Morris, however, ended with complete rejection. The others— and this is characteristic of the time—arrived at some compromise. At one point or another, they were in sympathy with the middle-class creed. Their aim was not to destroy it, but to check its inhuman tendencies and reintroduce the intellectual and spiritual ideals which it was forfeiting.

The attack on political-economic liberalism came from two directions, from the right and the left. In both cases it was fired by what Carlyle called "the Condition-of-England Question," the existence side by side of tremendous wealth and abject poverty. The suffering of the masses called for action; but so entrenched was the theory of *laissez faire* that the government would not act. Under these conditions it was inevitable that two opposing theories should have arisen: Tory Paternalism on the right and Socialism on the left.

The former, which first appears in the later work of Coleridge and Robert Southey (for the latter, see p. 492), was the creed of Carlyle, Ruskin, and Disraeli. It emphasized the old feudal theory of a governing aristocracy that was responsible for the welfare of the whole nation. Democracy was a snare and a delusion. To entrust the country to the ignorant masses, without education or political experience, was not only absurd, it was dangerous as well. The majority might well vote the confiscation of private property: had they not done so once in France? The fear of democracy, which was felt even by lib-

erals like Macaulay (see his "Letter on Democracy") and by democrats like Mill, was natural enough at the time. No, the government should remain in the hands of an aristocracy, which usually meant the landed nobility, though Carlyle in middle life advocated the dictatorship of a Hero or else a new aristocracy of talent composed of the Captains of Industry. But in whatever form, this autocratic government was to carry out a program of labor legislation that would put an end at once to the appalling conditions of proletarian life. Factory acts and mine acts to limit the hours of work and make the conditions of work safer and more sanitary; free emigration to the colonies and a public works program to solve overpopulation and unemployment; a national system of free public schools; the establishment of semipermanent contracts so that laborers could not suddenly be thrown out of work—these are some of the remedies that were suggested (see, for example, chap. 3 from Book IV of *Past and Present,* below). Though they stop short of public ownership of industry, they point directly toward the collectivistic theory of the state which had grown up in England by the eighties and nineties, and which arrived in America with the Roosevelt New Deal. But the New Dealers were called "liberals." The change in the meaning of the term is significant. In the nineteenth century the liberals, as we have seen, were the businessmen who wished to free society from special aristocratic privileges and to establish equal social and economic freedom for all. We need not disparage their achievement if we recognize the truth of Carlyle's charge that this freedom meant, in fact, freedom for the "haves" and slavery for the "have-nots." The worker was free to refuse the job at the local factory at the local wage—but if he did, he starved. He was legally free but actually in chains. This explains why, in our sense of the term—freeing the underprivileged from injustice through government action—the Tory paternalists of Victorian times were more liberal than the Liberals.

By the same token so were the Socialists. Socialism may be viewed as a parallel movement "from below," by the workers themselves, to gain the help of the state. It differs from Tory Paternalism by being democratic and by pushing beyond collectivism toward state ownership of utilities, land, and the major industries. In the Victorian period it first appeared in Robert Owen's scheme for cooperative communities; emerged as the radical wing of Chartism (the working-class movement of the thirties and forties for universal manhood suffrage); won the guarded support of John Stuart Mill (who decided that even Communism was superior to the system of unreformed, *laissez-faire* capitalism, and advocated the nationalization of land); and finally arrived in the 1880s when the influence of Marx at last began to count and the Fabian Society (out of which the Labor Party grew) was founded. On the whole, however, Socialism was more of a threat than a living movement in the period. It added fear to the moral and humanitarian appeal of the Tory Paternalists and thus contributed, indirectly, to the series of factory acts and mine acts that Tory pressure put through Parliament.

Consistently with their conception of government, the Paternalists denounced the Liberal theory of an atomic society in which each individual pursued his own interest, within the law, and the sole bond between man and man was "cash-nexus." Society, they asserted, was an organic whole like a family, and its guiding principle should be "one for all and all for one." The relationship of capital and labor, therefore, should be that of partners in a joint enterprise, animated by a spirit on the one side of humane consideration, and on the other of trust and obedience. Such a "philosophy" implies a much higher conception of human nature than that of the Utilitarians. Man is not a selfish animal motivated exclusively by self-interest. He is a child of God, blessed with a divine conscience and an innate capacity for human loyalty and pity. Not pleasure, therefore, but duty is the guide of life, and a man's true goal is not personal success, but the unselfish service of society as an end in itself. By this gospel Carlyle, the spokesman for Paternalism, hoped to preach the Captains of Industry out of their Mammonism and to turn the warfare of capital and labor into the peaceful cooperation of humane executives and loyal, obedient workers.

Though they might reject one or another part of this program, all of the great Victorian critics shared its central idealism. All of them felt, as Mill did, that an England whose celebrity had come to rest "upon her docks, her canals, her railroads" was "void of lofty aspirations." All of them agreed with Tennyson that "the inspiration of ideals" was badly needed to "combat the cynical indifference, the intellectual selfishness, the sloth of will, the utilitarian materialism of a transition age"; and with Arnold that people needed a higher conception of progress and a sounder basis for national pride than bigger and faster machines and greater and greater wealth. Even at their best the qualities developed by commercial life seemed to the Victorian critics "not precisely those by which mankind raise themselves to the perfection of their nature," either moral or intellectual.

Bourgeois society was not, of course, lacking in moral emphasis, as we have seen; but its morality was both too narrowly identified with strict adherence to the letter of the law and too rigidly restricted to the efficient training of character for successful action (the industrial virtues like honesty, thrift, strenuous work are self-centered). Lecky found public opinion very severe in judging crimes of passion and drink, and very lenient in judging those "of ambition, cupidity, envy, malevolence, and callous selfishness," which lie beyond the reach of law. Mill noticed more than once the contrast between the greater technical virtue of the English and the higher ideals of the Continental nations, especially the French. The following passage is at once a brilliant analysis of "middle-class morality" and a plea for something higher:

One of the commonest types of character among us is that of a man all whose ambition is self-regarding; who has no higher purpose in life than to enrich or raise in the world himself and his family; who never dreams of making the good of his fellow-creatures or of his country an habitual object, further than giving away, annually or from time to time, certain sums in charity; but who has a conscience sincerely alive to whatever is generally considered wrong, and would scruple to use any very illegitimate means for attaining his self-interested objects. While it will often happen in other countries that men whose feelings and whose active energies point strongly in an unselfish direction, who have the love of their country, of human improvement, of human freedom, even of virtue, in great strength, and of whose thoughts and activity a large share is devoted to disinterested objects, will yet, in the pursuit of these or of any other objects that they strongly desire, permit themselves to do wrong things which the other man, though intrinsically, and taking the whole of his character, farther removed from what a human being ought to be, could not bring himself to commit. It is of no use to debate which of these two states of mind is the best, or rather the least bad. It is quite possible to cultivate the conscience and the sentiments too. Nothing hinders us from so training a man that he will not, even for a disinterested purpose, violate the moral law, and also feeding and encouraging those high feelings, on which we mainly rely for lifting men above low and sordid objects, and giving them a higher conception of what constitutes success in life.

How was this to be done? Partly by preaching a higher morality on the lines laid down by Carlyle, mentioned a moment ago, and adapted to Utilitarianism by Mill himself (see Mill's *Autobiography*, p. 573). Partly by the contemplation of "great characters in history, or even in fiction." Because the heroic image was the direct counterpoise to the "economic man," in theory and practice, it became the principal means by which the Victorian idealists tried to instill a nobler spirit into a commercial society.

The modern world says—"Mind your own business, and leave others to take care of theirs"; and whoever among us aspires to more than the negative abstaining from wrong, is left to his own guidance. There is no help for him, no instruction, no modern ideal which shall be to him what the heroes were to the young Greek or Roman, or the martyrs to the Middle-Age Christian. (J. A. Froude)

Further, the elevating effect on character so much needed might be achieved, as Mill also suggested, by the contemplation of beauty, both in nature and in art. Though it has no direct application to conduct, it lifts us out of our selfish concerns and helps to create a broad, sympathetic frame of mind. This third suggestion is best illustrated by Ruskin. His lifelong effort to quicken the appreciation of beauty in nature as well as in painting and architecture—and in both areas for its moral no less than its aesthetic values—was a one-man crusade to counteract the growing ugliness of urban and suburban England and the impoverishment of life when measured solely by utilitarian standards.

Finally, Newman and Arnold, as well as Mill, attacked the antiintellectualism that is indigenous to the business mind. In Newman's *Idea of a University* and in Arnold's essays on "The Function of Criticism" and "Hellenism and Hebraism" the limitation of thought to practical ends and the Philistine notion that the liberal arts are useless are attacked with brilliant argument and satire. But the counter-ideal was not the "pure" intellectual or the academic scholar. What they wanted was the full development of all sides of human nature until modern man, whose mind and emotions are now divorced and whose faculties are narrowed to the demands of practical existence, shall again become an integrated human being.

THE RELIGIOUS SITUATION

As we can see from Carlyle's *Sartor Resartus* (completed in 1831), the second great factor that conditioned the thought and temper of the Victorians—the decline of religious faith—had already reached a crucial stage by 1830. The rise of the critical spirit at the Renaissance, reinforced by the new science of the seventeenth century, made it impossible for Christianity to stand any longer on ecclesiastical and traditional authority. It had either to be defended by reason, or abandoned for a rational religion of nature (Deism). In both cases the philosophers argued the existence of God from the need of a first cause or creator of the world, and from the belief that a universe which everywhere seemed so beautifully designed (from the stars in their courses to the intricate functioning of bodily organs) must have had an intelligent and beneficent architect. It was therefore reasonable to suppose that he intended a moral order based on moral laws as simple and clear as the physical laws of the natural order. And finally, since on earth the good were seldom rewarded and the evil often unpunished, it seemed equally reasonable to suppose a heaven and a hell where a just God would right the balance. To stop at this point was to be a Deist. The defenders of Christianity merely went on to argue that a wise and benevolent God would certainly have made a definite revelation through Jesus Christ of the great truths which all men needed to know for salvation; and they cited for proof the fact that such a revelation was foretold in the Old

Testament by prophecies and confirmed in the New by miracles. This line of defense was developed in a long series of books called "Evidences of Christianity."

But by the nineteenth century it was sterile. The "Evidences" were useless, and even Deism was insecure. For this, David Hume is largely responsible. In his *Dialogues concerning Natural Religion* (1779) he turned the weapon of reason against reason itself. As to the argument from a first cause, how do we know, he asked, that the earth *was* created at a moment in time? Isn't it just as reasonable—or unreasonable—to assume that the universe was eternal and existed from the beginning as to assume a creator who is eternal and existed from the beginning? In like manner, how do we know that there ever was a chaos for a god to shape into order and design? Maybe design and order were the original form of nature. Because justice does not exist on earth, can we be sure it exists after death—if there *is* any "after death"? In short, by submitting religion to the strict test of fact and reason, Hume decided that skepticism, in the sense of agnosticism (the belief that we cannot prove or disprove supernatural truths), was the only reasonable position. Such a conclusion, which was implicit in Gibbon's well-known account of Christianity in the *Decline and Fall of the Roman Empire* (chaps. 15, 16), made religious faith impossible. Impossible, that is, so long as one relied upon reason. But by demonstrating the dead end of the rational approach, Hume opened up, in effect, the possibility of a fresh approach through the imagination and the feelings. This important development and the various forms of religion it fathered will be discussed below.

While eighteenth-century religious thought was growing colder and weaker, the contemporary course of philosophy, under the same influence of scientific rationalism, was taking a more and more naturalistic, and even materialistic, direction. Starting from Bacon and Descartes, and developed by Locke and Hartley, Hume and Bentham, a series of axioms, in direct or indirect conflict with the religious tradition, had been built up. Nothing happens in nature except by physical causes: There is no supernatural interference, divine or demonic; and miracles, including the Incarnation, never

occurred. All knowledge comes originally from experience—sensations are impressed upon a passive mind, likened to soft wax—and is then developed automatically by association (the fire-burn-pain association, for example, teaches the child that stoves are hot and dangerous). Consequently, men are the products of their environment in mind and character. What they do—or what they desire to do—is conditioned by the basic impulse of human nature, the avoidance of pain and the appetite for pleasure. They are therefore motivated by self-interest, and they act virtuously, so far as they do, out of fear of the law and public opinion.

This, of course, is no adequate summary of eighteenth-century philosophy. It simply isolates those ideas which, when combined with Hume's religious skepticism, undermined the entire Christian scheme of things, metaphysical and ethical—indeed, any religious view of life. The result was what Carlyle called "The Everlasting No," the denial of all the spiritual and moral beliefs of the past, until what was left was a universe "all void of Life, of Purpose, of Volition, even of Hostility: it was one huge, dead, immeasurable steam-engine, rolling on, in its dead indifference, to grind me limb from limb." That chapter is eloquent testimony to the destructive impact of eighteenth-century rationalism in the opening decades of the nineteenth century. The Utilitarians, the economists, the fashionable world had no religious faith and no morality of any breadth and power.

But at this point the progress of disbelief was checked by a countermovement of religious faith, in one form or another, which held back the tide through the thirties and forties, until a fresh wave of skepticism, resulting from Biblical criticism and the scientific theory of evolution, swept over England in the fifties and sixties and made doubt a characteristic of the whole society. Though the religious revival took various forms, its approach to the problem of faith was the same in all cases. Belief had to be based not on reason (Hume had disposed of that) but on "experience": on the intuitive apprehension of God in nature or in the conscience or in moments of high and noble feeling (which seem God-inspired); or on a "conversion" in which one feels the immediate presence of God; or on proving the truth of Christianity by actual trial, finding that it works. This approach is clearly indebted to the Romantic insistence on living experience in place of abstract speculation, and the complementary reliance on the inner authority of intuition or the "feelings of the heart" as guides to truth and conduct in place of reason.

It was altogether natural, therefore, that the religious revival among the Romantics took the form of belief in divine immanence, sometimes called Pantheism. In Wordsworth, Coleridge, and Shelley, in Goethe and Novalis in Germany (writers who influencd Carlyle), the aesthetic exaltation in the presence of natural beauty, especially in its more sublime forms (the starlit sky, the ocean, mountain peaks) became a religious exaltation in which they felt the presence of a supernatural spirit. If to this awareness we add the emotions of wonder, awe, and reverence that go with it, and the moral effect of feeling purified of all that is selfish and evil, we have the Religion of Nature, which became for Carlyle and Ruskin and thousands of Victorians a faith they could turn to, either in place of Christianity or as a reassuring support to Christian beliefs they could no longer accept on ecclesiastical or Biblical authority alone. (For Carlyle, see p. 440; for Ruskin, p. 629–30.)

This double function was also served by another form of natural (as opposed to revealed) religion that starts from personal experience. This is Theism. Here one finds God in the phenomenon of conscience. The inner voice, demanding moral action, insisting on the priority of duty over pleasure, is either interpreted directly as that of an all-powerful Judge and Governor (Newman), or is made the basis from which one deduces the existence of God and a moral universe (Kant, Fichte, and, under their influence, Carlyle). This "argument" could be used, as it was by Newman, to support Christianity. But many Victorians who could not accept the Christian revelation, especially those shaped by the Puritan tradition, found in Theism, with its strong moral urgency (ethically much stronger than Pantheism), an answer to their need. In fact, as the Romantic spirit waned, and the Puritan revival gained in force, the Religion of Nature was more and more displaced by this Religion of Conscience. It is characteristic of

the time that the former is chiefly emphasized in *Sartor Resartus* (1833), while in *Past and Present* (1843) the latter stands almost alone—and Carlyle has emerged as perhaps the major Victorian prophet of Theism.

Meanwhile the subversive influence of eighteenth-century rationalism had been met by a powerful revival of Christianity that had taken three forms: Protestant, Liberal, and Anglo-Catholic. The Protestant revival, which is the earliest, had been initiated as far back as 1738 by John and Charles Wesley, the founders of the new Protestant sect of Methodism. In reaction against the optimistic and rational form of contemporary religion, the Wesleyans returned to the Puritan insistence on original sin and salvation by faith. By his own efforts man could not hope to live a virtuous life or to go to heaven. His whole nature had to be miraculously transformed by the grace of God. He had to be born again of the Spirit. But how? Certainly not by any external sacramental system administered by a church. Solely by the experience of "conversion." This was the tremendous moment when the sinner, in an access of repentance, cried out to Christ for mercy, and suddenly felt the inrush of divine grace. From that day forth he was a regenerate man, his heart filled with the love of God, his life a constant and spontaneous exercise of virtue, his soul saved. And his mind never in the slightest doubt. For his belief in God did not rest on any dubious argument, but on the very experience of the Divine Presence in the act of conversion.

This revival of Puritanism was not limited to the Methodists. It permeated the Church of England, where the disciples of Wesley who remained behind became the Low Church party, known as the "Evangelicals." They were famous for their ethical piety, their founding of foreign missions and Bible societies, and their philanthropic activities. William Wilberforce and Zachary Macaulay, father of Thomas Babington, played important roles in the antislavery movement. But it was their moral fervor—one might say their Puritan conscience—that left the deepest mark on their age. The moral strictness, which in any case would have characterized a new industrial society, was strongly colored and intensified by Evangelicalism. It is the primary source of the Victorian sense of sin, which prohibited dancing, cardplaying, and the theater as things of the devil, made prudery and the maiden blush conventions of decency, forbade the reading of any literature which dealt with evil (even Charlotte Brontë thought one had better omit the comedies of Shakespeare), and turned Sunday into a day of gloom on which church services could be supplemented only by *Paradise Lost, Pilgrim's Progress,* or perhaps some pious story of Mrs. Sherwood's about "wicked girls who had gone to balls, dying immediately after of fever."

Although Evangelicalism penetrated into aristocratic and university circles, it was too fervid and emotional to capture the more highly educated or socially conservative classes. In these areas the Christian revival took other directions. Under the leadership of Thomas Arnold, the famous headmaster of Rugby and the father of Matthew, there grew up in the 1820s a school of Liberal Protestantism that later included F. D. Maurice and Charles Kingsley, Benjamin Jowett (the translator of Plato), Tennyson and Matthew Arnold. Thomas Arnold saw that the new spirit of the country, as represented by the Utilitarians, was at once secular and commercial. The crucial need of the time, therefore, was a strong state church "to Christianize the nation, and introduce the principles of Christianity into men's social and civil relations." But much of the nation belonged, not to the established Church of England, but to one or another of the Protestant sects. Hence Arnold's program to turn the Church of England into a truly national Protestant Church, a Broad Church. Why not? With the exception of Catholics and Unitarians, did not all Christians, he asked, "have a common ground in all that is essential in Christianity"? And this common ground was the worship of Jesus Christ, the Son of God, and the desire to live in holy and virtuous imitation of His life. True, this would mean that each sect would have to give up some of its special dogmas and the Church of England abandon its Thirty-nine Articles. But what matter? "Christian unity and the perfection of Christ's Church are independent of theological Articles of opinion; consisting in a certain moral state and moral and religious affections, which have existed in good Christians of all ages and all communions." This divorce of religion from theology, in which the

former becomes a matter of feeling and conduct, and the latter a matter of opinion (to be believed or not, as the individual pleases), is highly characteristic of Victorian life. And even more so, perhaps, of Protestantism today. The fact is, of course, that theological dogmas—the Trinity, the Incarnation, the Atonement, the Redemption, to name only the most important—are miraculous. If they are subjected to the strict test of scientific fact and law, they are destroyed. And they had been destroyed, or had survived in name only, under the eighteenth-century examination of reason, to the point where Christianity, as we have seen, was in serious danger. But suppose the ground were shifted and the whole movement of theology, starting in St. John and St. Paul, continuing through the medieval schoolmen and the Protestant reformers, were seen as a huge monument to the subtlety and sophistication of the human intellect. Then one would turn back to the first three Gospels to find the true and simple "Religion of Christ"—namely, there is a God whose divine nature was revealed in Jesus Christ our Saviour, in the love and worship of whom is our moral strength and the promise of heavenly immortality. If you doubt it, try it; the practical results will prove the assumptions true. By this liberal faith Christianity might be saved in the modern world, and given so broad a basis that the union of all Protestants would be possible. Through one great national church, exerting its wide influence throughout society, the twin evils of the age, doubt and greed, might be destroyed.

But a group of men at Oxford, led by Newman, John Keble, and E. B. Pusey, did not believe it. On the contrary they were convinced that Liberalism would "make shipwreck of Christian faith" and was, in fact, the "halfway house" to atheism. For where was the process of casting out dogma and miracle to stop? In an age of doubt another generation might find even Arnold's belief in the Incarnation incredible, and Christianity might disintegrate into Theism, which in turn might easily dissolve into some nonreligious form of ethical culture and humanitarian service. And these fears were not idle: the prophecy largely came to pass. The Oxford Movement, which Newman and Keble initiated in 1833 with a series of *Tracts for the Times,* was an attempt to save Christianity from its Liberal friends as well as its Utilitarian enemies, by insisting on its dogmatic and miraculous character. The great dogmas, they said, form a body of divinely revealed truth that would be sacrilege—and religious suicide—to submit to rational examination and human judgment. They are simply *given* on the supreme authority of God. The first principle of the Oxford Movement, as Newman said, was "the principle of dogma: my battle was with liberalism; by liberalism I meant the anti-dogmatic principle and its developments." (See Newman's "Note on Liberalism," especially the definition on p. 535 and the eighteen propositions at the end.)

The second principle was Catholicism, Anglo-Catholicism. When the Church of England cut its ties with Rome in the sixteenth century, it had attempted to steer a middle course, to retain *some* Catholic and adopt *some* Protestant doctrines and ceremonies. Although this rather ambiguous compromise satisfied the majority, it did not satisfy either the Puritans on the left, who wished to purify the Church from all Catholicism and make it entirely Protestant, or the Anglo-Catholics on the right, who felt that Protestantism had already gone too far and that the Catholic elements of the liturgy should be emphasized. In the minds of the latter, the English Church was not a new church set up at the Reformation, but a branch of the original Apostolic Church founded by Christ to be the guardian of dogma and the ark of salvation (by means of the sacraments administered by a priesthood possessing supernatural power). In course of time this Church of God had been corrupted by certain Roman Catholic errors like the doctrines of purgatory and transubstantiation. These had now been rightly rejected, along with the headship of the Pope. But unfortunately the Reformation had introduced new Protestant errors: salvation by faith alone; the denial that the sacraments were channels of grace, which had led in turn to denying the supernatural power of the priesthood; and worst of all, the shifting of supreme authority from the Church to the Bible, so that the individual reader became, in effect, the ultimate judge and interpreter of divine truth. Anglo-Catholicism was the attempt in the seventeenth century under Archbishop Laud to make the Church of England adopt a Catholic, though not quite a Roman Catholic,

interpretation of Christianity. It had not succeeded, but its principles had been kept alive through the eighteenth century in various country parsonages, in one of which John Keble had been brought up.

The Oxford Movement was a revival of this Anglican tradition, a new attempt to make the Church of England Anglo-Catholic:

We were upholding that primitive Christianity which was delivered for all time by the early teachers of the Church, and which was registered and attested in the Anglican formularies and by the Anglican divines. That ancient religion had well nigh faded away out of the land, through the political changes of the last 150 years, and it must be restored. It would be in fact a second Reformation:—a better reformation, for it would be a return not to the sixteenth century, but to the seventeenth. (Newman)

If it succeeded, the miraculous and dogmatic character of Christianity could be preserved and protected by the reestablishment of ecclesiastical authority; and Christianity could be saved not only from the misguided efforts of the Liberal Protestants but from the greater destructive force of modern skepticism.

For a while the movement won wide support, both among the clergy and also among many Victorians who found a welcome refuge from religious doubts and perplexities in Catholic authority. But the opposing forces were too strong. The Low Church party of the Evangelicals and the Broad Church party of the Liberals could unite with fighting conviction against such a High and Catholic conception of the Church. And both could appeal to the latent fear of Rome that is deeply ingrained in the English temper. When the showdown came, the English bishops reaffirmed the traditional Protestant interpretation of the liturgy and the Articles—and Newman turned to the only living Catholic church. His conversion to Rome in 1845 was a further blow to the movement he had led. But it remained alive; and the Anglo-Catholics today form a strong minority in the Church of England and the Episcopal Church of America.

The religious revival, in both the non-Christian and Christian forms we have examined, was sufficiently strong to check the influence of eighteenth-century rationalism and to make it possible for most Victorians of the first generation (1830–1860) to maintain a supernatural faith. But not easily or firmly. The very existence of competing solutions, the clash of Theists and Christians, of Evangelicals and Liberals and Anglo-Catholics, and the inevitable raising of difficulties which otherwise would never have arisen, created an atmosphere which tended, ironically, to turn the very effort to dispel doubt into a fresh cause of doubt. ("Doubt" means primarily lack of firm convictions, beliefs only half believed, though the situation pushed some of the half-believers into becoming non-believers.) Another intangible but important source of doubt was the secular and naturalistic direction of contemporary life and thought. Where so much energy was being devoted, and so successfully, to the expansion of business and the increase of physical comfort, where the popular mind was fascinated by science, by its extraordinary inventions and its new knowledge of the universe no less than by its glamorous promises of far greater conquests to come, the religious point of view was difficult to maintain. "I am sometimes startled," said one Victorian, "to find to what a halt my old theological trains of thought and sentiment have come; I have never deliberately discarded them, but the scientific atmosphere seems to paralyse them." This must have been so in thousands of cases. Indeed, if Victorian science dealt religion a blow from which it has never recovered (and it is impossible to see how, even granting the vigorous life of many churches, one can call modern society religious), it was not so much by its shocking discoveries in evolution as by its silent attraction of the human mind away from a supernatural orientation.

But the discoveries carried weight. Through the eighteenth century and well into the nineteenth, the universe was still thought of as static. God had created the solar system at one moment in time, complete and perfect just as it was today and would always be till the end of the world. And everyone knew when this great event had occurred: it was in 4004 B.C.—according to one scholar, on October 23, at 9 A.M. The first dent in this static universe was made by a Frenchman named Laplace in 1799, when he advanced the nebular hypothesis.

It taught that the solar system existed originally as a great gaseous nebula with a central kernel; as the mass cooled, the center condensed into the revolving sun, and the outer parts became revolving rings, which in turn condensed into the planets circling round the sun. With this hypothesis the idea of evolution was born. The next step was to explain the development of the earth from an incandescent state to its present condition. In the important work of James Hutton and especially Charles Lyell (*Principles of Geology*, 1830) the older theory of catastrophic changes by violent earthquakes or volcanic eruptions was replaced by the modern theory of uniformitarianism: all geological changes have occurred by the uniform operation of physical causes now in daily operation. Just as the surface of the globe is being changed today by the action of rain, rivers, the sea, and chemical decomposition, so it has always been changed. This meant that the date of the creation had to be radically revised, because only in terms of a tremendous period of time could one account by natural causes for the formation of so many layers of strata. Not 4004 B.C. but something closer to 1,000,000,000 B.C. was the truth.

The existence of strata from epochs separated by immense periods of time made the literal interpretation of Genesis no longer possible. All forms of animal life were plainly *not* created on the fifth and sixth days, but at widely separated periods. When the fossil remains of fish were found in the lower strata, reptiles in higher, birds and then mammals, including finally man, in the highest, the idea of *biological* evolution was inescapable. But it may be noticed that the first conception, which was widely established by 1850, was not what we would mean today by the term, and not what Darwin meant. The later meaning is that of an evolution of species, one from another, by natural means. The earlier concept still retained the notion of special creation, only not at one time. At widely separated intervals God created new species on what seemed to be an ascending scale, ending with the creation of man in His own image. This is all that most Victorians (and very likely Tennyson in *In Memoriam*) meant by evolution before Darwin. But once the principle of development by natural causes had been accepted in geology, it was very difficult to reject it in biology. The problem was to extend the principle of uniformitarianism to biological evolution.

Though Darwin was not the first to do this (the Frenchman Lamarck had put forward a tentative theory in 1815), his *Origin of Species* (1859) was the epoch-making statement of evolution by natural causes. Taking over a suggestion by Thomas Malthus in his *Theory of Population* (1798)—that since population increases at a much higher rate than the supply of food, the poorest classes constantly live on the edge of starvation and only the strongest individuals survive in the struggle for existence—Darwin argued that in the jungle the same situation would produce a natural process of selection. Only those varieties best fitted to cope with their environment would survive to form new species, while those unequal to the struggle would die out. (For a detailed explanation of Darwin's theory, see Huxley's review of *The Origin of Species,* printed below.) In itself this explanation did not go unchallenged, and there is a school of Neo-Lamarckians today. But the mass of evidence which Darwin brought forward was so impressive that the fact of a natural evolution, in one way or another, of all forms of life "from some one primordial form or sperm" gained wide and permanent acceptance.

One can vaguely imagine the explosion which this theory set off. In one terrible blow it seemed to destroy the traditional conceptions of man, of nature, and of the origin of religion and morality; and to substitute for each an interpretation that was deeply distressing. Man was reduced to an animal, the descendant of apes. Nature, which had been the witness of a divine and beneficent God and a source of moral elevation, became a battlefield in which individuals and species alike fought for their lives, and the victor was the best, not morally but physically, the toughest and the roughest and the quickest on the kill. If *this* nature was the creation of God, then God, as Tennyson put it, "is disease, murder and rapine." Or if not, then either there is no God and no immortality but only Nature, indifferent to all moral values, impelling all things to a life of instinctive cruelty ending in death; or else God and Nature are locked in an incredible and inexplicable strife. These terrible alternatives are all present, directly or by implication, in the famous passage of *In Memoriam* (see poems 54–56) where Tennyson expresses the profound doubts that the evolutionary view of nature had raised in the Victorian mind.

They were further increased when Darwin's principle of the struggle for survival was applied to the evolution of human society, and the origin of morals and religion was explained in purely naturalistic terms (see concluding passage of selection from Huxley's *Essays on Some Controverted Questions*). The "tiger" instincts were first checked when animals combined, in the family or the pack, to fight together for better survival, and therefore tacitly agreed not to fight one another for the time being. Human society then made the important advance on wolf society of agreeing to use the force of the whole body against individuals who violated the truce and in favor of those who observed it. In this way moral laws naturally developed; a conscience which demands their fulfillment was built into man through ages of tribal punishment and reward; and ideals of social service and self-sacrifice were created through ages of tribal praise, all in the cause of better personal survival by means of multiple and combined strength. Apparently it was not God who placed a conscience in man, and apparently virtuous conduct had nothing to do with His supposed will, or with an individual's supposed survival after death, but only with the will of the tribe, and the survival of the tribe (and the individual) here and now. As for high ideals, they were nothing at bottom but a disguised form of selfishness.

In this context it is easy to explain the origin and function of religion. It begins when primitive men imagine gods in the sun or the rain; and then, in the cause of survival from storms and droughts, the tribe institutes sacrifices and prayers to placate the gods and win their aid. Presently religion takes over the already existing moral code. Since no natural explanation of moral laws is known, a supernatural one is assumed, and the laws of the tribe are called the laws of its tribal gods. This in turn gives those laws a more powerful sanction, since to violate them is now to evoke the wrath of the gods. Thus religion, because it helps greatly to curb the centrifugal force of animal instincts and to increase the cohesive power of morality, makes its natural contribution to tribal, and therefore individual, survival. In short, religion is not in the least an objective, supernatural reality that has been revealed by God to man, in the first century, by His only-begotten Son. It is a psychological superstition of such value in the struggle for existence that it has become a basic element of social life.

It was still possible, however, to be a Darwinian and at the same time to retain a belief in God as the creator of life. In claiming that "all living things . . . which have ever lived on this earth have descended from some one primordial form," Darwin had gone on at once to add, "into which life was first breathed by the Creator." And breathed, one could suppose, with full and purposive knowledge of the great process of development which He initiated, a development not only from lower to higher forms of life, but from the violence of tribal society up to the law-abiding civilization of nineteenth-century Europe. If evolution was the principle of the universe, it was a divine principle. Progress was God's providence. And if progress *on* earth, why not also, on the same terms of moral growth, progress *from* earth to heaven? This desperate attempt to seize the weapons of the enemy and use them in self-defense may be seen, along with the contrary implications of science, in Tennyson's *In Memoriam* (see poems 82, 118, and the end of the "Epilogue"). But aside from the fact that this religious reading of evolution was difficult to reconcile with "Nature red in tooth and claw," it was directly impugned by a fresh attack on human nature. The reduction of man to an animal was followed by his reduction to a machine.

Darwin might talk of God breathing life into the first sperm, but Huxley and other scientists would not believe that in the vast evolution of all things from some purely material beginning, like a spiral nebula, there was any moment of supernatural intervention. Why was not life itself a natural result of certain chemical elements uniting under exactly the right, fortuitous conditions? In his sensational essay "On the Physical Basis of Life" (1868), Huxley argued that the property of "life" or "vitality" was as much a product of the combination of oxygen, hydrogen, nitrogen, and carbon forming the protoplasm that is common to all living beings, as the property of "aquosity" is the result of the combination of oxygen and hydrogen forming water. If so, man has no spirit or soul independent of the body, but only a brain in which molecular changes, determined by external stimuli, give automatic rise to all our thoughts and all our actions. For Huxley, as for many physiologists and biologists today, man is simply a human automaton, a "physico-chemical organism, the lineal descendant of some bit of primordial slime; all his hopes and aspirations, . . . all his self-sacrifice and knowledge, are the result of the peculiar laws governing the chemical reactions that ultimately go to produce his behavior" (J. H. Randall). This extension of the realm of matter and law to a point where it includes human life itself is the Victorian nightmare:

Science frees us in many ways . . . from the bodily terror which the savage feels. But she replaces that, in the minds of many, by a moral terror which is far more overwhelming. Am I—a man is driven to ask— am I, and all I love, the victims of an organized tyranny, from which there can be no escape—for there is not even a tyrant from whom I may perhaps beg mercy? Are we only helpless particles, at best separate parts of the wheels of a vast machine, which will use us till it has worn us away, and ground us to powder? Are our bodies—and if so, why not our souls?—the puppets, yea, the creatures of necessary circumstances, and all our strivings and sorrows only vain beatings against the wires of our cage? . . . Tell us not that the world is governed by universal law; the news is not comfortable, but simply horrible. . . . (Charles Kingsley)

What made the anti-Christian conclusions of modern science doubly disturbing was their direct conflict with the Bible. From the beginning Protestantism had substituted the Scriptures for the Church as the supreme source of authority. They were the Word of God, inspired by Him, and therefore worthy of unquestioning belief. The early Puritans and their Methodist-Evangelical descendants in the Victorian period preached, as Huxley says (p. 683), "the necessity, on pain of reprobation in this world and damnation in the next, of accepting, in the strict and literal sense, every statement contained in the Protestant Bible." Even Christians who did not go so far, and were ready to admit the propriety of mystical or allegorical interpretations, thought of the Bible as unlike any other book, a direct revelation of God's truth. That is why the anti-Biblical conclusions of modern science were far more shocking to the Victorians than they were, say, to Roman Catholics on the Continent. Science was not merely advancing antireligious theories; the theories threatened the sacred foundation of Christian faith. If a chapter here and a passage there were shown to be erroneous, where was the process going to stop? As Huxley put the ominous possibility, "if Scripture has been discovered 'not to be worthy of unquestioning belief,' faith 'in the supernatural itself' is, so far, undermined."

The destructive analysis of the Bible was not, however, the actual work of the scientists, nor were the new discoveries in science the only source of doubt about its reliability. In the late eighteenth century the so-called Higher Criticism had been inaugurated in Germany by literary and historical scholars. What they did was simply to treat the Bible like any other ancient book, and to extend the methods of scholarship from classical to Biblical studies. In doing so they followed three lines of criticism (as Huxley points out in the "Prologue" to *Some Controverted Questions*): scientific historical criticism, centering on the separation of historical fact from fable and legend, and using comparative mythology to show that many supposed facts in the Bible, like Noah's flood, were common products of the mythopoetic faculty in all primitive peoples; scientific literary criticism, meaning the study of Biblical languages and literary forms, which showed that the Scriptures were written by many authors at widely different times and that certain dogmas had resulted from a literal reading of what was a conventional metaphor; and finally, scientific physical criticism, the testing of the Bible against modern scientific knowledge, with serious consequences not only for Genesis but also for the miracles of the New Testament.

For a while the Higher Criticism reached only a few English thinkers—notably Thomas Arnold, who was its first, cautious exponent in England, and George Eliot, who was converted by it from Evangelical Christianity to agnosticism. But on the publication of *Essays and Reviews* in 1860 (written by seven English scholars and theologians), it broke over the public mind —and exactly one year after the explosive publication of *The Origin of Species*. Evolution and

Biblical criticism converged in the 1860s until, as Matthew Arnold reported, there was "not a creed which is not shaken, not an accredited dogma which is not shown to be questionable, not a received tradition which does not threaten to dissolve." The doubt which through the early decades of the century had been checked or half buried now became a conscious and recognized fact of English life. By the 1880s most educated Englishmen were either "deniers or doubters"; and our modern inheritance was complete. We were to live in a secular no less than an industrial society.

How did it feel to exist in this Victorian world of religious tension between the forces of renewed affirmation and of fresh denial? What effects did the total situation have on the temper of the time? What habits of thought, what moral attitudes should we attribute either to the revival of faith or to its radical decline?

As we have noticed in tracing the impact of evolution and Biblical criticism, the Victorians found religious doubt painful and disturbing to a degree that we can now hardly understand. If it is true, as Clifford Bax has claimed, that most people today do not bother their heads with "thoughts of 'God' or 'the soul'" and that "they behave, indeed, as though neither existed," nothing could be less Victorian. A hundred years ago men filled their books and magazines with endless discussions of God and the soul—indeed, you might say that *they* behaved as though *terrified* that neither existed. For we have Carlyle's word for it that the age was "at once destitute of faith and terrified at scepticism." Why the terror? Why could the Victorians not accept doubt or unbelief as indifferently as we do, or pretend to do?

Partly because it was new. Christian faith had for centuries been an assumption of European thought; and now suddenly in the nineteenth century, in the early manhood of men like Carlyle and Kingsley, Ruskin and Matthew Arnold, the foundation of the universe began to tremble. "Those who dwell in the tower of ancient faiths look about them," wrote John Morley, "in constant apprehension, misgiving, and wonder, with the hurried uneasy mien of people living amid earthquakes. The air seems full of missiles and all is doubt, hesitation, and shivering expectancy." We who have never been disinherited because we have never known religious certainty can only imagine the distress of the first sudden catastrophe. But the loss, or the threatened loss, of century-old beliefs was disturbing not only in itself but in its ominous implications as well. The Victorians imagined, or foresaw, that the decline of religion would have moral and social consequences of the direst kind. If men ceased to believe in God and a future life, the great sanctions of moral action would be gone; and once they were gone, the selfish passions of individuals and nations would be unleashed, and society would disintegrate into violence and war. Finally, and perhaps most immediately painful, was the sense of frustration that the loss of faith imposed on many sensitive minds. Men had so long lived and acted within a framework of Christian thought, giving their lives purpose and meaning, that its collapse could leave them at loose ends, their active energies "paralysed . . . by enfeebling doubts." The closing stanzas of Arnold's "Scholar-Gipsy" are an eloquent expression of "the sick fatigue" and the baffled wills of those "half-believers of our casual creeds" who "hesitate and falter life away." Under all their fine optimism, the Victorians at heart were filled with anxiety. So are we, but ours is political, while theirs was mainly religious.

Anxiety demands, and if possible compels, resolution. Because they found doubt so painful, the Victorians demanded something to believe in, or to think they believed in. The age, as Lord Acton acutely noted, was distracted between the difficulty of belief and the intense need of believing. Hence the paradoxical psychology of the period. On the one hand, the disintegration of traditional authority and the spread of the scientific attitude, emphasizing detached examination and empirical evidence, encouraged a spirit of critical inquiry. On the other, the pain of doubt dictated an almost frantic desire to welcome any new authority, any new philosophy of life, religous or naturalistic, with uncritical promptness.

It was not the acceptance of any single body of doctrine that distinguished the Victorian, but his insistent attitude of acceptance, his persistent belief in (but only rare examination of) the credentials of Authority, his innate desire to affirm and conform rather than to reject or to question. (A. C. Ward)

The crucial bearing of this psychology on Victorian literature, for writers and readers alike, will be considered below.

Finally, we may notice how various intellectual and moral attitudes already attributed to the influence of middle-class industrialism were equally indebted to the religious situation. The antiintellectualism of business was reinforced by the fear of speculation. At a time when modern thought was undermining belief and men were terrified of skepticism, surely it was best to leave well enough alone and go about one's job. This was the conclusion not only of individuals like Carlyle and Kingsley but also of public opinion. Religious thought that issued in any but orthodox conclusions was treated with the same weapons of social stigma and professional obstruction used today against similar freedom of political thought. (Mill's analysis of the situation and his fine defense of the free pursuit of truth are on pp. 593–96.) Furthermore, if the policy of "Don't think, work hard" was a protection against doubt, it was also a cure for those who caught the disease. "Let him who gropes painfully in darkness or uncertain light," says Carlyle, remember that " 'Doubt of any sort cannot be removed except by Action.' " And he therefore closes his "Everlasting Yea" with a fervid injunction to "Produce! Produce! Were it but the pitifullest infinitesimal fraction of a Product, produce it, in God's name! . . . Work while it is called Today; for the Night cometh, wherein no man can work." Out of its context would anyone imagine that this was not the daily chant of the Captains of Industry? The Intellectual and Industrial Revolutions met together in the gospel of work, with the powerful encouragement of Puritan ethics. The child of business and doubt was an antiintellectual.

He was also a man of the highest moral rectitude, at least in theory. If the revival of Puritanism strengthened the concern with morality natural in a bourgeois society, so did the decline of belief. When the old religious sanctions were losing their force, all the more need to stress the social obligations of virtuous conduct, and for agnostics to prove, by word and example, that moral living was not dependent on supernatural beliefs. On a famous occasion when George Eliot mentioned the three words which had so long been "inspiring trumpet-calls of men, —the words *God, Immortality, Duty,—*" she

"Work" by Ford Madox Brown. The approving observers of the labor are, at right, Carlyle (in hat) and the Reverend F. D. Maurice, founder of a college for working men. *City Art Gallery, Manchester.*

"pronounced, with terrible earnestness, how inconceivable was the *first,* how unbelievable was the *second,* and yet how peremptory and absolute the *third.*" It is because the first two words have lost their meaning that the third is given such passionate affirmation. In George Eliot's novels, as in the essays of other leading agnostics like Mill and Huxley, a Religion of Humanity is made a new basis for morals. The service of man displaces the service of God; a heaven on earth, not after death, becomes the goal of life; and the inspiration to share in the building of a finer humanity is made the sufficient source of ethical control and altruistic action. Closely related to this secular religion is another that centers on an ideal image, in this case not that of Man but of Men, the Religion of Hero-Worship. The preoccupation of Victorian literature with legendary heroes—Greek, medieval, and Teutonic—was partly motivated, as we have seen, by the need

to supplant the commercial spirit by a heroic spirit; but partly also by the need to find a substitute for the old supernatural faith. In Carlyle's *Heroes and Hero-Worship* the heroic image has taken the place of the divine image; and the germ of Christianity, its living core in contrast to its dead theological forms, is said to be "hero-worship, heartfelt prostrate admiration, submission, burning, boundless, for a noblest godlike Form of Man." The same need to endow a natural object with spiritual values lies behind the complementary idealization of woman, with its romantic-chivalric view of love (see the Brownings especially) and its sentimentalizing of the home and family life.

LITERATURE

IF we compare the literature of the Victorian age with the literature that preceded it or followed it, in the Romantic or the Modern period, we are struck by its public character and its public importance. Of the great Romantic writers, only Byron and Scott were widely read, and essentially for entertainment. Wordsworth, Shelley, Keats, Hazlitt, and Lamb had each a following of devotees, but it was small. Moreover, although Romantic art sometimes dealt with contemporary political, economic, and religious problems, it did not center upon them nor did it handle them in a form likely to attract the general reader. If we add to these facts the antiartistic bias of both Utilitarianism and Evangelicalism, we can readily understand why the prestige of literature in 1830 had sunk to a low ebb. "A poet in our times," as Peacock ironically noticed,

is a semi-barbarian in a civilized community. He lives in the days that are past. His ideas, thoughts, feelings, associations, are all with barbarous manners, obsolete customs, and exploded superstitions. The march of his intellect is like that of a crab, backward. . . . In whatever degree poetry is cultivated, it must necessarily be to the neglect of some branch of useful study; and it is a lamentable spectacle to see minds capable of better things running to seed in the specious indolence of these empty, aimless mockeries of intellectual exertion.

On the whole, the situation today is very similar. Modern literature is a "thing apart"—too esoteric in content, too subtle and difficult in form, to reach any but a small audience of "intellectuals." The modern writer has no status. It is not to him but to specialists, or journalists, that people turn for answers to the pressing problems of our time. Only the novel on the level of entertainment commands a reading public of any size.

But between these two periods, for the fifty years from 1830 to 1880, literature was a living medium of culture. Because at its best it was in close touch with the general life of the time and spoke in a language that was simple without being flat or conventional, it commanded a wide audience. And the prestige of the writer was little short of amazing. If Carlyle's high claim (p. 450) that the Man of Letters was "our most important modern person," possessed of intuitive insight into "the True, Divine and Eternal," and therefore "the light of the world, . . . guiding it, like a sacred Pillar of Fire, in its dark pilgrimage" (a theory derived from the Romantic conception of

the natural genius), if this was, at bottom, a counterdefiance hurled at Philistine indifference and a kind of self-sustaining boast, it came, nonetheless, to be widely acknowledged not only by writers but by readers as well. According to Mill, Carlyle "made Artist the term for expressing the highest order of moral and intellectual greatness."

Mill's choice of adjectives is significant. The public nature and the public importance of Victorian literature rested precisely there, on its moral and intellectual character, and not on its imaginative re-creation of life. The task of the writer, as Arnold put it, was "not to exhibit all the kingdoms of human life and the glory of them like Shakspeare, but to interpret human life afresh." It was his natural task in an age of radical transition, when the Church and the aristocracy had lost their traditional authority, when the most fundamental questions in politics and religion cried out for new answers, and men were in need of guidance and inspiration. Under such conditions his inevitable role, as we see plainly in Carlyle's Lecture V ("The Hero as Man of Letters"), was that of a prophet. It was a platitude of Victorian criticism that authors were a modern priesthood whose duty was to "enlighten and encourage and purify public opinion." The essential style of this prose was described by Walter Bagehot in a revealing article called "The First Edinburgh Reviewers." The difference, he said, between ancient and modern writing of a philosophical kind was due to the fact that "we must instruct so many persons." So long as he wrote for a small group of educated men, the writer could be "systematic, suggesting all arguments, analyzing all difficulties, discussing all doubts"; but now that he must write for the multitude, "impatient of system, desirous of brevity, puzzled by formality," he had to give his ideas a simpler and shorter expression:

In this transition from ancient writing to modern, the review-like essay and the essay-like review fill a large space. Their small bulk, their slight pretension to systematic completeness,—their avowal, it might be said, of necessary incompleteness—the facility of changing the subject, of selecting points to attack, of exposing only the best corner for defense, are great temptations. . . . Unquestionably the Spectator *and* Tatler, *and such like writings, had opened a similar vein; but their size was too small: they could only deal with small fragments or the extreme essence of a subject; they could not give a view of what was complicated, or analyze what was involved. The modern man must be told what to think; shortly, no doubt, but he* must *be told it. The essay-like criticism of modern times is about the length which he likes. The* Edinburgh Review, *which began the system, may be said to be, in this country, the commencement on large topics of suitable views for sensible persons.*

The *Edinburgh Review* (Whig) was followed by the *Quarterly* (Tory), the *Westminster* (Utilitarian), and scores of others. The Victorian period is the golden age of the periodical at its highest level, where it is a vehicle for the best intelligence of the time. As that would suggest, much of the work of Macaulay and Arnold, Carlyle and Mill and Huxley, first appeared in the reviews. Some of their most famous books—Arnold's *Culture and Anarchy,* for example, and Huxley's *Science and the Christian Tradition*—were collections of essays reprinted from periodicals. Even whole books (*Past and Present* is a clear case) explore a range of loosely connected ideas in a series of essay-like chapters.

But the intellectual character of the age was as important as its democratic audience in making the essay a "natural" for the time. When there was no longer any accepted body of beliefs, and men were wrestling with a multitude of new facts and tentative theories, they saw truth in fragments—and wrote it in essays. Furthermore, the very limitation of length, which allowed the writer, as Bagehot says, to avoid "analyzing all difficulties, discussing all doubts," was entirely welcome to a public which wanted solutions and not deeper—and more confusing—analysis.

This last point bears directly on style. At a time when doubt was painful and the will to believe intense, what people craved above all was to be told—and in no uncertain terms. They did not want balanced arguments in a cool and measured style. They wanted positive doctrine expressed with eloquent and dogmatic conviction. When Carlyle taught Froude a creed which saved him from atheism, "the lesson came from one who seemed 'to speak with authority and not as the Scribes,' as if what he said was absolute certainty beyond question or cavil." Had it not been so, Froude might not have been saved. One critic excused Ruskin's "arrogance and dogma-

tism" on the extraordinary ground that "even error, eloquently advocated with the honest conviction that it is truth, is better than truth coldly believed and languidly proclaimed"—extraordinary only if we forget that it was an age "at once destitute of faith and terrified at scepticism." For their part the prophets were not only willing to meet the public demand; they had their own good reasons for adopting the tone of authority. When each school of political or religious thought (often with its own periodical) was fighting its rivals, the sectarian spirit encouraged dogmatism. When the prestige of intuition that marked the Romantic reaction against eighteenth-century rationalism was at its height, and the artist was endowed with an almost mystical power of insight, the writer might well substitute authoritative statement for logical argument. What Spencer said of Carlyle could be applied to many, though not all, of the prose prophets: he "never set out from premises and reasoned his way to conclusions, but habitually dealt in intuitions and dogmatic assertions."

To speak more precisely, the prophets were men of letters writing prophetic literature. Their prose has usually been thought of as ideas treated with rhetorical skill. But within the last fifteen years or so, teachers and scholars have come to feel that the achievement of Carlyle, Newman, Arnold, and Ruskin—to mention only the greatest names—was the kind of thing they were accustomed to think of "as the peculiar activity of poets and novelists."[2] In a novel we expect a series of incidents—linked by a plot—a cast of characters, dialogue or monologue (speaking voices), ideas and value judgments—explicit and implicit—pictures of places and scenery, and imagery—descriptive and figurative. When all the elements are fused, the result is a personal vision or reading of life which can only be described in shorthand. Compare a book like *Past and Present*: it has not only the life of the monastery with its sharply drawn monks, but also telling incidents, each centering on a character (Columbus on the voyage to America, rugged Brindly, John Bull, the poor Irish widow with

[2] A good statement of this theory, to which the editors of this book are indebted, is the Introduction to *The Art of Victorian Prose,* ed. George Levine and William Madden, 1968. Also see the critical essays that follow.

typhus); there is not only dialogue but monologue as well, often in close conjunction with statements of political ideas and moral judgments; perhaps above all, there is vivid imagery.

Our life is not a mutual helpfulness; but rather, cloaked under due laws-of-war, named "fair competition" and so forth, it is a mutual hostility. We have profoundly forgotten everywhere that Cash-payment *is not the sole relation of human beings; we think, nothing doubting, that it absolves and liquidates all engagements of man. "My starving workers?" answers the rich Millowner: "Did not I hire them fairly in the market? Did I not pay them, to the last sixpence, the sum covenanted for? What have I to do with them more?"—Verily Mammon-Worship is a melancholy creed.*

Surely this is the work of an artist; and taken as a symbol of the whole, it illustrates the literary forms of self-expression which create a Carlylean vision of England in 1843.

Between the prophetic literature of prose and that of poetry and fiction, one may make a rough distinction on the lines laid down by Carlyle. The former is intended to persuade, to affect public opinion; the latter to inspire, to affect the character. In the one case, doctrine is central; in the other, "noble sentiments," in the form of either moral reflections or ideal images —usually both at once. George Eliot felt that the function of the novelist was "that of the *aesthetic,* not the doctrinal teacher,—the rousing of the nobler emotions, which make mankind desire the social right, not the prescribing of special measures." For Arnold, the function of poetry in an age when traditional religion was dying was "to interpret life for us, to console us, to sustain us."

This moral pressure on the artist was apparent in the 1830s, when a reaction against the verbal beauties of Shelley and Keats and the wild, passionate heroes of Byron called for a literature of "noble images and thoughts." Tennyson was forced to abandon his early romantic poetry of mood and impression to supply the age with moral reflections or heroic characters. Browning, whose natural gift was for detached observation, was induced by Elizabeth Barrett and the gospel of Carlyle to make some of his studies of men and women illustrations of moral aspiration. Though Arnold complained in 1849

that under the influence of Wordsworth verse had become "a channel for thinking aloud, instead of making anything," much of his own poetry is filled with moral reflection; or, when that is not the case, offers "some noble action of a heroic time" to inspire and sustain an anxious generation. And there is no doubt that the prophetic purpose was welcomed. In at least one Victorian home where the parents had been "emancipated" by reading Darwin and Huxley, and where no one mentioned the Bible or went to church, the children were brought up on the Greek pantheon and the Arthurian Round Table. In the living room hung a picture of Sir Galahad by Frederick Watts, with the quotation from Tennyson:

> *My strength is as the strength of ten,*
> *Because my heart is pure.*

On the library table was a finely bound copy of *The Poetical Works of Robert Browning* containing his modern version of chivalric love and his high doctrine of aspiration toward impossible goals:

> *'Tis not what man Does which exalts him, but what man Would do!*

In literal fact the Victorian poets became, as Carlyle predicted, a modern priesthood.

It must not be supposed that in itself a didactic intention is fatal to a work of art; still less that poetry of noble images or moral reflection is bad poetry. Shakespeare and Milton may be cited at once to the contrary. The critical estimate depends on the treatment. The noble image must not be too noble; the hero must be a human being and not an idealized abstraction or a self-conscious preacher of his own virtues (like Galahad in the quotation from Tennyson just given). Moral reflections must be translated into music and image, not simply stated (as they might be in a treatise or a sermon, as they *are* in the line by Browning quoted above). They must be "experienced" by the sensibility of the artist, not merely "thought" by the mind. Or they must arise implicitly from the concrete presentation of character and action, instead of being explicitly injected. The Victorian record, in these respects, is varied. All one can say is that the strong demand of the age for high ideals and moral guidance made artistic success more difficult to achieve, though by no means impossible.

Furthermore, these pressures were not always operative; and a considerable body of Victorian poetry is innocent of prophetic intention. By moments the poets turned away from the needs and problems of the time, and away from its "unpoetic" environment of dirt and smoke and cutthroat competition, to seek relief in some image of ideal beauty, of woods and flowers, of faraway places and olden times—ancient Greece or medieval England, the Orient or a land of lotos-eating. Side by side with the motive to instruct and inspire was the motive to escape. It is because the heroic image could satisfy both motives at once—and meet both desires in their readers—that the Victorian writers turned so often to the mythology of Greece and Scandinavia and the legends of a time when knighthood was in flower. It is highly significant that when Arnold told the poet to abandon thinking and writing about the problems of the age, he suggested that instead he ought "to delight himself with the contemplation of some noble action of a heroic time, and to enable others, through his representation of it, to delight in it also." You have your cake and eat it too—escape to the glamour of heroic adventure and feel the moral inspiration of a noble action. This double effect is produced by Arnold's "Sohrab and Rustum," Tennyson's *Idylls of the King*, Morris's *Earthly Paradise*—and in prose by Kingsley's *Heroes, or Greek Fairy Tales*.

But for all these distractions, a considerable body of Victorian verse is simply a record of living experience. In his "Essay on Shelley" Browning described not only the subjective poet who searches his soul for divine wisdom, but also the objective poet who chooses to deal with "the noisy, complex, yet imperfect exhibitions of human nature in the manifold experience of man around him." Certainly many of Browning's men and women are sketched with psychological penetration. We may also remember that however inconsistent with other statements of his (the inconsistency is inevitable in a period of intellectual uncertainty), Arnold could also insist on a poetry that should "appeal to the great primary human affections: to those elementary feelings which subsist permanently in the race. . . ." Perhaps chief among these feelings at the time were those of dejection and despair, rising from the breakdown of traditional ideas and modes of life, and often accompanied by the sense of isolation, loneliness, and nostalgia. The more sensitive Victorians felt like displaced persons, cut off from a divine relationship, divided from families and friends by religious differences, and unwilling to enter the amoral world of industrial struggle. This is the creative background that lies behind the early poems of Tennyson and some of the finest lyrics of *In Memoriam;* Arnold's "Dover Beach," "The Scholar-Gipsy," "Stanzas from the Grande Chartreuse," and the second "Isolation: To Marguerite"; most of the poetry of Clough; and nearly all of that of Hardy. Because we ourselves are also caught in the same world, or a worse one, we find that these expressions of anxiety and loneliness speak to us with immediacy.

Starting in the 1850s the Pre-Raphaelites (the Rossettis, Morris, and Swinburne were the chief poets) inaugurated a movement that later evolved into the Aesthetes and Decadents of the nineties (Oscar Wilde and the early Yeats), with Walter Pater as chief philosopher-critic. Among these men there was considerable diversity of opinion and practice, but they all agreed on one thing, that it was *not* the business of art to instruct or inspire, nor the function of an artist to be a prophet. Art, as the battle cry put it, was for art's sake, and an artist—was an artist. But what did this mean, in theory and in fact? The various answers are implicit in Morris's lecture on Pre-Raphaelitism (see below).

The Aesthetic Movement began in 1848 when a new and radical group of painters, who called themselves Pre-Raphaelites, first exhibited their pictures. What was radical was their insistence that an artist should paint what he saw regardless of the traditional "rules" of painting. In technical terms they were Naturalists: they were imitating nature as they experienced it directly instead of nature as it had been portrayed by earlier painters; and they were painting "naturally," in forms and colors faithful to their experience, not in those which had come down in the art schools of Europe since the Renaissance as the "right" techniques. A passage from Ruskin describes the situation against which they were revolting, and incidentally explains the term "Pre-Raphaelitism":

It being required to produce a poet on canvas, what is our way of setting to work? We begin, in all probability, by telling the youth of fifteen or sixteen, that Nature is full of faults, and that he is to improve her; but that Raphael is perfection, and that the more he copies Raphael the better; that after much copying of Raphael, . . . he is to try to do something very clever, all out of his own head, but yet this clever something is to be properly subjected to Raphaelesque rules, is to have a principal light occupying one-seventh of its space, and a principal shadow occupying one-third of the same; that no two people's heads in the picture are to be turned the same way, and that all the personages represented are to possess ideal beauty of the highest order, which ideal beauty consists partly in a Greek outline of nose, partly in proportions expressible in decimal fractions between the lips and chin. . . . This I say is the kind of teaching which . . . we give to our young men. And we wonder we have no painters!

In short, Pre-Raphaelitism was a return, not to the form and style of early Italian painting, but to its freedom from the requirement of painting ideal figures according to the rules that Raphael had laid down. As Morris points out (p. 900), the same revolt had occurred fifty years earlier in literature when Wordsworth and Coleridge had led the reaction against neoclassical conventions in poetry and had set up the contrary aim of keeping the eye on the object, that is, imitating nature as they saw it—which explains why Ruskin can say that "the Pre-Raphaelite school was headed, in literary power, by Wordsworth." In origin, therefore, the Aesthetic Movement was not antididactic: it was antiacademic. But the primary insistence on fidelity to experience was, in effect, a rejection of the prophetic principle, and an extension to painting of the Romantic principle of Naturalism.

The Pre-Raphaelites, however, were neo-Romantic in a further sense, which explains why, for all their talk about Naturalism, their art was realistic only in its sharply realized detail and not in the least as an account of contemporary life. On the contrary, they deliberately turned away from the ugly, noisy world of industrial England, from the problems and doubts of an age of transition, to a far more beautiful and heroic past, ancient or medieval, secular or Christian. We may say "deliberately" because, though this tendency had appeared, as we have noticed, in Tennyson and Arnold, it was in direct contradiction to their prophetic creed and their normal practice. But the Pre-Raphaelites openly called themselves tellers of tales and "dreamers of dreams," whose only purpose was to provide the pleasure of escaping into a romantic world of the past. Indeed, in the "Apology" prefixed to *The Earthly Paradise* (see p. 890) Morris explicitly denied that he had any power to ease "the heavy trouble, the bewildering care that weighs us down" or any intention of setting "the crooked straight." He aimed only "to build a shadowy isle of bliss midmost the beating of the steely [Victorian] sea." In short, he was not a prophet but "the idle singer of an empty day."

In poetry this romantic withdrawal from contemporary life took two forms, both suggested in Morris's lecture. The first was narrative or dramatic verse, where the primary focus is on characters seen at a moment of emotional crisis (for example, Rossetti's "Troy-Town" or Morris's "Defence of Guenevere"). The indebtedness here to Browning is obvious, and was frankly acknowledged; but, as we should expect, Rossetti and Morris adopted only his dramatic technique and not his moralism, and they injected it into a form closer to the ballad than to the dramatic monologue.

The second kind of aesthetic poetry, which eventually displaced the first in importance, is indicated by Morris's reference to the ornamental and decorative side of the movement. It is a poetry of color and sound where imagery and rhythm are used, not to describe living characters or express human emotions, but to invoke a vague and intangible mood of beauty (see Morris's "Blue Closet" on the pictorial side, and Swinburne's "Garden of Proserpine" on the musical side). In terms of *literary* history, this decorative poetry abstracted the form of Romantic verse from its content, combining the imagery of Keats with the lyrical rhythm of Shelley; and in doing so, it rejected all ideas, whether abstract or psychological. In fact, at its furthest development, in some of Swinburne, in the early Yeats, even concretely defined objects have disappeared and what is left is an

Pre-Raphaelite Painting. The preoccupation of the Victorian mind and the Pre-Raphaelite sensibilities with medieval themes is exemplified by a painting of the marriage of Saint George and Princess Sabra by Rossetti. *The Tate Gallery.*

"almost bodiless emotion." In terms of *intellectual* history, it marks the extreme withdrawal of the artist from the contemporary world into the Ivory Tower of the aesthetic imagination. There, and there only, could Yeats find a room where "tapestry, full of the blue and bronze of peacocks, fell over the doors, and shut out all history and activity untouched with beauty and peace." That room is symbol at once for the poetry and the poetic mind of the later Aesthetic Movement.

This was the dead end. In Hopkins and Hardy we see the start of that reaction against sensuous beauties of style and thinness, or pre-

ciousness, of experience which prepared the way for modern poetry. "My generation," said Yeats, in later life when he had outgrown his early theory and practice, threw over "poetical diction" and began the search "for hard positive subject-matter"—but in the spirit of art, not prophecy. Modern poetry may be viewed as a profounder development, under the influence of the French Symbolists, of the principle of Art for Art's Sake.

General References

For the political history of the period see G. M. Trevelyan, *British History in the Nineteenth*

Queen Victoria in 1897. A sensible and somewhat stubborn woman, Victoria was early influenced by the ideas of her cousin-husband, Prince Albert of Saxe-Coburg. Her devotion to the Prince Consort caused her to withdraw from her intense involvement with political affairs after his death in 1861. A picture of Albert is on her bracelet. *Gernsheim Collection, University of Texas at Austin.*

Century (1938); or, more briefly, J. A. Williamson, *The Evolution of England* (1931), chaps. 8–10.

For social and intellectual history the reader may consult J. H. Randall, Jr., *The Making of the Modern Mind* (1940 ed.), chaps. 11–15, on the important background of eighteenth-century thought, and chaps. 16-22 on the nineteenth century; G. M. Young, *Victorian England: Portrait of an Age* (1936); Walter E. Houghton, *The Victorian Frame of Mind, 1830–1870* (1957); Raymond Williams, *Culture and Society, 1780–1950* (1958); W. L. Burn, *The Age of Equipoise: A Study of the Mid-Victorian Generation* (1964); G. M. Trevelyan, *English Social History* (illustrated ed. in 4 vols., 1949), Vol. IV; Raymond Chapman, *The Victorian Debate: English Literature and Society, 1832–1901* (1968).

But the best social and intellectual history of the period is to be found in contemporary biography. Among the most revealing and representative are: A. P. Stanley, *The Life and Correspondence of Dr. Thomas Arnold* (1844); Edmund Gosse, *Father and Son* (1907); *Letters and Memorials of Charles Kingsley,* edited by his wife (abridged ed., 2 vols., 1877); John Stuart Mill, *Autobiography* (1873); John Morley, *Recollections* (2 vols., 1917), I, 3–144; and H. F. Brown, *John Addington Symonds, A Biography* (1894).

In addition, many Victorian novels throw significant light on the age. Dickens's *Hard Times* (1854); Disraeli's *Coningsby* (1844) and *Sybil: or The Two Nations* (1845); Mrs. Elizabeth Gaskell's *Mary Barton* (1848) and *North and South* (1855); and Kingsley's *Alton Locke* (1850) deal with political and economic problems. Religious and moral questions are central in Samuel Butler's *Way of All Flesh* (1903, but written about 1880); Kingsley's *Yeast* (1851); Trollope's *Barchester Towers* (1857); and Mrs. Humphry Ward's *Robert Elsmere* (1888).

There is no adequate account of Victorian literature as a whole. Oliver Elton, *A Survey of English Literature, 1780–1880* (4 vols., 1920), Vols. III and IV, is the best general guide that exists. *From Dickens to Hardy,* ed. Boris Ford (1958), is the best recent survey. Some special studies in literature are Jerome Buckley's *The Victorian Temper* (1951), largely on the rise and fall of the "moral aesthetic"; Graham Hough, *The Last Romantics* (1949); A. H. Warren, *English Poetic Theory, 1825–1865* (1950); Basil Willey's two books: *Nineteenth Century Studies: Coleridge to Matthew Arnold* (1949) and *More Nineteenth Century Studies: A Group of Honest Doubters* (1955); John Holloway, *The Victorian Sage* (1953); Frank Kermode, *Romantic Image* (1957); J. Hillis Miller, *The Disappearance of God* (1963), and George L. Levine, *The Boundaries of Fiction* (1968). Isobel Armstrong, *Victorian Scrutinies: Reviews of Poetry, 1830–1870* (1972) centers attention on Tennyson and Arnold and has a long and illuminating essay on poetic theory. The best account of the literary scene in the last decade of the century is in W. B. Yeats's *Autobiography.*

Thomas Carlyle

1795–1881

The thought and temper of the age is nowhere more fully revealed than in the work of Thomas Carlyle. Like so many Victorians, he started with traditional Christianity, passed through a period of doubt amounting for a while to outright disbelief in any supernatural order, and ended by the recovery of his faith in a new form, or new forms, of religion that seemed credible, as Christianity did not, in the light of modern thought. In politics his opposition to Benthamite liberalism and *laissez faire* and his plea for a strong government to support labor legislation are characteristic not only of conservatives like Disraeli and Ruskin, but also of the "new" liberals in the sixties and seventies, Mill, Huxley, and Chamberlain. When we add to this pattern of thought his insistence upon the value of work and the importance of duty, his worship of heroes, and his ambivalent attitude toward commercial society (scorn for its low ideals but enthusiasm for its industrial achievements), we see that he reflects the full range of the Victorian temper.

Thomas Carlyle (1795–1881). One of the most influential writers of the Victorian period, Carlyle was a prose writer whose sources of inspiration were intuitive and poetic. His prophetic writing style resonated with biblical echoes and the influence of the German transcendentalism of Kant, Fichte, and Goethe. *The Granger Collection.*

Carlyle was born in Scotland in 1795, the son of humble parents who brought him up in the ethic and theology of Puritanism. In 1809 he entered Edinburgh University to prepare himself for the ministry, but his scientific and philosophical studies undermined his religious faith. After a period of schoolteaching he returned to Edinburgh in 1818 to study law, but soon abandoned it for literature. The new religious philosophy that he had found in the contemporary German poets and philosophers he first discussed in a series of articles for the *Edinburgh Review* and presently embodied in the semiautobiographical *Sartor Resartus* (the tailor with a new suit of clothes), published in 1833. Meanwhile he had married Jane Welsh in 1826; and after visiting London in 1831, where they met the leading writers of the day, especially John Stuart Mill, they settled there permanently in 1835. With suggestions and helpful materials from Mill, Carlyle now wrote his famous *History of the French Revolution* (1837). Henceforth history and biography were his major fields of work: his *Heroes and Hero-Worship* (1841) is a collection of biographies from Odin and Mohammed to Napoleon; *Past and Present* (1843) combines the history of a medieval monastery with essays on contemporary politics; in the *Letters and Speeches of Cromwell* (1845) and *The History of Frederick the Great* (1858–65) he fused history, biography, and political theory in the autocratic image of the hero. When he died in 1881, he seemed to most Victorians the great prophet of the age.

When Carlyle arrived at Edinburgh in 1809, he was shocked to find that most of his professors and fellow students treated Christianity, and to some extent even Deism, with cool acquiescence or outright ridicule. This was the fruit of eighteenth-century rationalism, stemming from Bacon and Descartes, Locke and Newton in the previous century, and developed by Hartley, Hume, and Bentham. (See the outline on pp. 413–414 of the introduction to the Victorian period, which gives this essential background for understanding Carlyle.) In the work of these philosophers he found that all he had been taught to believe was denied, at least implicitly: there was no God immediately active in human life, or no God at all; man was not endowed with free will or with a God-given conscience, nor motivated by any unselfish sense of duty to God and society; and obviously, there was no original sin, no Incarnation or Atonement, and no Biblical miracles. This is the world into which Carlyle sank down from 1809 to 1818, and which he describes in the chapter from *Sartor Resartus* appropriately called "The Everlasting No." That chapter ends, however, with the start of his journey back to faith, the moment of sudden defiance, in August 1822, when once and for all he repudiated the whole conception of a "dead, steam-engine" universe without purpose or volition. *That* he would *not* believe in. But what *was* he to believe in? He found an answer in German Transcendentalism, notably in Kant, Fichte, and Goethe, where he met a view of man and nature at all points opposite to that of eighteenth-century rationalism. In this view the mind, far from being passive, is itself an active agent of knowledge (what we "know" is the product of both mind and experience, the former interpreting the latter); in addition to reason, there is a higher faculty of knowledge, an intuitive power of insight into the nonphysical truths of religion, morality, and politics; matter is not the ultimate reality, but only an appearance in consciousness (the way the world appears to an organism that possesses a human mind and human senses); man is born with a moral will or conscience, able and free to choose between right and wrong; the highest goal of life is not pleasure but duty (meaning both the passive duty of accepting pain and suffering—what Carlyle calls "the worship of sorrow"—and the active duty of work); and finally, above all, there is a God immediately present in the universe: Nature is a symbol, manifestation, or "garment" of the divine spirit in the same way that a man's gestures or facial expressions may be said to manifest his personality. So fortified, Carlyle could again believe, not in Christianity, but in a religion that was part pantheism, part theism; and could thus answer "The Everlasting No" with "The Everlasting Yea."

But in the last analysis he did not rest his faith on the mystical-metaphysical idea of the universe as a symbolic manifestation of God. What he felt in nature, as we see in the chapter "Natural Supernaturalism," was not so much the presence of a divine spirit as a sense of mystery, the profound mystery of human existence and the equally profound mystery beneath the facts of physical science. All our science is merely descriptive. It tells us that this object has these properties, that this law acts in that way, but *why* the properties or *why* the action is unknown. And since science permeated the Victorian mind, Carlyle's argument from mystery to God was bound to speak more persuasively than the mystical-metaphysical argument of German philosophy. What is mysterious, he said, is inexplicable (without natural explanation), and therefore supernatural, and therefore indirectly a witness to, or revelation of, a divine power:

Science has done much for us; but it is a poor science that would hide from us the great deep sacred infinitude of Nescience, whither we can never penetrate, on which all science swims as a mere superficial film. This world, after all our science and sciences, is still a miracle; wonderful, inscrutable, magical [i.e., supernatural] and more [i.e., divine], to whosoever will think of it.

It is not an accident that this passage appears in the opening paragraphs of *Heroes and Hero-Worship,* for the hero, as Carlyle conceived of him, was not only the man who found God behind the mystery of the universe, but was himself another finite revelation of the Infinite. He was literally inspired, a Seer or Prophet able to perceive intuitively what God wills or what he plans for mankind. "Really his utterances, are they not a kind of 'revelation'? . . . We must listen before all to him," as we no longer can listen to the Church or the Bible. Christ himself is reduced by Carlyle to "the greatest of all Heroes," and the germ of Christianity is said to be "hero-worship, heartfelt prostrate admiration, submission, burning, boundless, for a noblest godlike Form of Man." From there it is only a step to the secular cult of the hero and the Victorian effort to find in heroic legends or heroic lives the moral inspiration no longer supplied by religion.

That means, in effect, the substitution of the writer for the priest; and this too is explicit in Carlyle's book. His hero is not simply a political or military leader; he is also an intellectual leader. In "The Hero as Man of Letters," we see the Victorian conception of the writer as prophet, taking the place of the old Christian priesthood, providing a new religion, or at least the moral guidance and inspiration that men were ceasing to find in the Church.

This conception provides the best perspective for understanding Carlyle's peculiar—and at first baffling—style. Its essential character is prophetic. Like that of the Old Testament prophets, his method is not analysis, explanation, logical argument. It is passionate exhortation, confident statements on matters highly debatable, frequent imperatives ("Know it of a truth that . . ."), direct addresses to the reader in a charged and idiomatic speech (the prophet speaking to *you*), and a "shock" technique that startles one into attention by sudden, rapid shifts of form or by strange and often grotesque metaphors and illustrations. All this, with a minimum of logical argument, was exactly the right style for both the Victorian prophet and his disciples. However irritating it may be today, it was enormously popular with a generation longing to be told what to believe, and in no uncertain or debatable terms. And quite apart from this public demand, Carlyle's whole conception of the writer pointed in the same direction. If intuition rather than reason is his great faculty, then positive statement and not rational argument will be his natural technique.

The figure of the hero is closely linked with Carlyle's theory of history and his practice in historical writing. In theory he conceived of history, too, as a revelation of God: in the success and fate of nations we can see the hand of Providence rewarding virtue and punishing evil. But since history is made by great men and not by impersonal economic forces, great men are "the inspired (speaking and acting) Texts of that divine Book of Revelation"—the texts on which the historian preaches. *The History of the French Revolution* (1837), which centers on Mirabeau and Danton, was written to show the manifest judgment of God upon the dissolute, luxury-loving court of Versailles. But it was also written simply to bring the men and the events vividly to life. For Carlyle often forgot his didactic theory, and under the influence of Scott made history a vivid re-creation of the

past. In this respect he belongs with Macaulay; though where Macaulay's art is narrative, Carlyle's is dramatic. He sees the past in a series of scenes, complete with dialogue and stage setting (see the selections from Book II of *Past and Present*). In one respect, however, these two historians are radically different. Because Carlyle saw the institutions of the past as so many efforts—successful then though now worn out—to embody the *permanent* spiritual goals of man (for religious faith, for political order, and so on), he could look at earlier times with a sympathy impossible for any liberal like Macaulay, who viewed his superstitious and autocratic ancestors with superior disdain. This explains why Carlyle inserted a sketch of medieval life, feudal and monastic, into a book on modern politics. *Past and Present* says, in effect, let us remember the living ideals of the past and give them new forms for the present: the ideal of religion in a new non-Catholic, non-Christian form; of work and service in a new secular, nonascetic form; of feudal authority in a new social organization where a natural aristocracy

Capital and Labor (from *Punch*, 1847). "Life was never a May-game for men: in all times the lot of the dumb millions born to toil was defaced with manifold sufferings, injustices, heavy burdens, avoidable and unavoidable; not play at all, but hard work that made the sinews sore and the heart sore." (*Past and Present*). *Radio Times Hulton Picture Library*.

of talent shall take the place of the old landed aristocracy and again govern the country with a strong and paternal hand.

As this last "ideal" implies, *Past and Present* is a bitter arraignment of the Victorian liberal-business world. Carlyle cut under the worship of material success, the hurrahs for liberty and the blessings of competition, to expose the ugliness, physical and spiritual, of modern industrial society. Not that he was hostile to business as such. He was as ready as Macaulay to celebrate its industrial achievements; and under their spell as ready to turn antiintellectual and to exalt practical action at the expense of theoretical speculation (see Book III, chap. 5, "The English")—even readier, because for Carlyle work was not only an economic requirement, not only a Puritan command; it was also a protection against the dangerous atheistical tendency of modern thought and a cure for modern doubt (see page 444). What Carlyle attacked was not business but the worldly and selfish spirit of the new industrialists, concerned only with their personal success, financial and social. And he attacked their political creed. He saw that their boasted policy of freedom (no government interference) meant, in fact, freedom for the capitalist but hardly for the laborer who had to take the job in the local factory at the local wage or go unemployed—and be free to starve. He saw that the liberal theory of society as a collection of free individuals, bound together only by a "cash-nexus," free from any personal obligations or responsibilities like those of feudal or family society, competing freely in an open market, might produce better goods at lower prices, but might also produce much worse human beings, devoid of charity, permeated by bitter and open hostility, especially between capital and labor.

The fundamental solution was a spiritual rebirth. No amount of tinkering with the machinery of government would produce a good society. That could only be done by producing good men through a powerful religious revival. If the Captains of Industry would recognize the reality of God and hear His voice in their conscience, commanding a life of duty and brotherly love—that is to say, if they would become heroic—they would cast out their Mammonism and treat their workers with justice and humanity; while the workers for their part would give their leaders the loyalty and devotion due to genuine heroes. But in the meanwhile, pending this utopia, something might be done to improve the appalling "condition-of-England" by a strong, paternalistic state that would carry through a program of labor legislation (see Book IV, chap. 3, "The One Institution"); and by giving this political power not to the people (democracy seemed madness to Carlyle) but to a hero-dictator if possible, otherwise to a talented aristocracy

—not the old, idle, pigeon-shooting, landed aristocracy, but a new aristocracy of brains and energy to be recruited from the Captains of Industry purged of their Mammonism and converted to Carlyle's religious and moral idealism.

TEXTS: The standard edition is *The Works of Thomas Carlyle,* ed. H. D. Traill (Centenary Edition, 30 vols., 1896–99). The best life is by J. A. Froude (4 vols., 1882–84); though not always reliable, this is a brilliantly written biography, full of illuminating letters and journals. For critical interpretation, one may consult the essays in Basil Willey's *Nineteenth Century Studies* (1949); John Holloway, *The Victorian Sage* (1953); and George Levine, *The Boundaries of Fiction* (1968). Also see Albert J. LaValley's *Carlyle and the Idea of the Modern: Studies in Carlyle's Prophetic Literature and Its Relation to Blake, Nietzsche, Marx, and Others* (1968).

from Sartor Resartus

Book II, Chapter 7

THE EVERLASTING NO[1]

Under the strange nebulous envelopment, wherein our Professor[2] has now shrouded himself, no doubt but his spiritual nature is nevertheless progressive, and growing: for how can the "Son of Time,"[3] in any case, stand still? We behold him, through those dim years, in a state of crisis, of transition: his mad Pilgrimings, and general solution into aimless Discontinuity, what is all this but a mad Fermentation; wherefrom, the fiercer it is, the clearer product will one day 10 evolve itself?

Such transitions are ever full of pain: thus the Eagle when he molts is sickly; and, to attain his new beak, must harshly dash-off the old one upon rocks. What Stoicism soever our Wanderer, in his individual acts and motions, may affect, it is clear that there is a hot fever of anarchy and

---

[1] The title means the spirit of negation, denying any possible moral or spiritual values, positing instead a wholly materialistic universe, "all void of Life, of Purpose, of Volition, even of Hostility . . . one huge, dead, immeasurable Steam-engine, rolling on, in its dead indifference."
[2] Diogenes Teufelsdröckh, the hero of *Sartor Resartus* and the mouthpiece for Carlyle's ideas. The book purports to be his autobiography edited by Carlyle, who refers to himself as "the Editor." [3] Man.

misery raging within; coruscations of which flash out: as, indeed, how could there be other? Have we not seen him disappointed, bemocked of Destiny, through long years? All that the young heart might desire and pray for has been denied; nay, as in the last worst instance,[4] offered and then snatched away. Ever an "excellent Passivity";[5] but of useful, reasonable Activity, essential to the former as Food to Hunger, nothing granted: till at length, in this wild Pilgrimage, he must forcibly seize for himself an Activity, though useless, unreasonable. Alas, his cup of bitterness, which had been filling drop by drop, ever since that first "ruddy morning" in the Hinterschlag Gymnasium,[6] was at the very lip; and then with that poison-drop, of the Towgood-and-Blumine business, it runs over, and even hisses over in a deluge of foam.

He himself says once, with more justice than originality: "Man is, properly speaking, based upon Hope; he has no other possession but Hope; this world of his is emphatically the 'Place of Hope.' " What, then, was our Professor's possession? We see him, for the present, quite shut-out from Hope; looking not into the golden orient, but vaguely all round into a dim copper firmament, pregnant with earthquake and tornado.

Alas, shut-out from Hope, in a deeper sense than we yet dream of! For, as he wanders wearisomely through this world, he has now lost all tidings of another and higher. Full of religion, or at least of religiosity, as our Friend has since exhibited himself, he hides not that, in those days, he was wholly irreligious: "Doubt had darkened into Unbelief," says he; "shade after shade goes grimly over your soul, till you have the fixed, starless, Tartarean[7] black." To such readers as have reflected, what can be called reflecting, on man's life, and happily discovered, in contradiction to much Profit-and-Loss Philosophy,[8] speculative and practical, that Soul is *not* synonymous with Stomach; who understand, therefore, in our Friend's words, "that, for man's well-being, Faith is properly the one thing needful; how, with it, Martyrs, otherwise weak, can cheerfully endure the shame and the cross; and without it, Worldlings puke-up their sick existence, by suicide, in the midst of luxury": to such, it will be clear that, for a pure moral nature, the loss of his religious Belief was the loss of everything. Unhappy young man! All wounds, the crush of long-continued Destitution, the stab of false Friendship, and of false Love, all wounds in thy so genial heart, would have healed again, had not its life-warmth been withdrawn. Well might he exclaim, in his wild way: "Is there no God, then; but at best an absentee God, sitting idle, ever since the first Sabbath, at the outside of his Universe, and *seeing* it go?[9] Has the word Duty no meaning; is what we call Duty no divine Messenger and Guide, but a false earthly Fantasm, made-up of Desire and Fear, of emanations from the Gallows and from Doctor Graham's Celestial Bed?[10] Happiness of an approving Conscience! Did not Paul of Tarsus, whom admiring men have since named Saint, feel that *he* was 'the chief of sinners,' and Nero of Rome, jocund in spirit (*wohlgemuth*), spend much of his time in fiddling?[11] Foolish Wordmonger, and Motive-grinder, who in thy Logic-mill[12] hast an earthly mechanism for the Godlike itself, and wouldst fain grind me out Virtue from the husks of Pleasure,[13]—I tell thee, Nay! To the unregener-

---

4 The loss of his beloved Blumine to his friend Towgood, described in the previous chapter.

5 Teufelsdröckh tells us he had early learned to "bear and forbear," and as a child had been held down by "a strait bond of Obedience." The resultant passivity, a combination of acceptance and renunciation, was excellent so far as it went, but it was negative inasmuch as it was not the product of active choice.

6 It was a "red sunny Whitsuntide morning" when Teufelsdröckh went to school for the first time to the Strike-behind Academy.

7 Tartarus was the lowest and darkest region of hell.

8 The reference is to Utilitarianism with its doctrine that a good or virtuous action is one that produces a total balance of pleasure over pain; a bad or vicious action, one producing more pain than pleasure. One must, so to speak, calculate the Profit (pleasure) against the Loss (pain). To Carlyle this seemed an utterly sensual (stomach) philosophy. He opposes to it, in the next sentences, a "higher" one of service to God and man, regardless of pain. Not pleasure but duty is man's true goal.

9 The eighteenth-century Deistic position, in which God was viewed as a mechanic or celestial clockmaker, who having created the world and set it going was then content to let it function without his participation or even his presence.

10 Graham, an eighteenth-century quack, invented a bed said to cure impotence, an example of the Desire just mentioned.

11 By tradition Nero is supposed to have fiddled while Rome burned.

12 A pun on the name of James Mill, one of the most ardent Utilitarians.

13 Benthamite education aimed at making virtuous acts

ate Prometheus Vinctus[14] of a man, it is ever the bitterest aggravation of his wretchedness that he is conscious of Virtue, that he feels himself the victim not of suffering only, but of injustice. What then? Is the heroic inspiration we name Virtue but some Passion; some bubble of the blood, bubbling in the direction others *profit* by? I know not: only this I know, If what thou namest Happiness be our true aim, then are we all astray. With Stupidity and sound digestion man may front much. But what, in these dull unimaginative days, are the terrors of Conscience to the diseases of the Liver! Not on Morality, but on Cookery, let us build our stronghold: there brandishing our frying-pan, as censer, let us offer sweet incense to the Devil, and live at ease on the fat things *he* has provided for his Elect!"

Thus has the bewildered Wanderer to stand, as so many have done, shouting question after question into the Sibyl-cave[15] of Destiny, and receive no Answer but an Echo. It is all a grim Desert, this once-fair world of his; wherein is heard only the howling of wild-beasts, or the shrieks of despairing, hate-filled men; and no Pillar of Cloud by day, and no Pillar of Fire by night, any longer guides the Pilgrim.[16] To such length has the spirit of Inquiry carried him. "But what boots it (*was thut's*)?" cries he; "it is but the common lot in this era. Not having come to spiritual majority prior to the *Siècle de Louis Quinze*,[17] and not being born purely a Loghead (*Dummkopf*), thou hadst no other outlook. The whole world is, like thee, sold to Unbelief; their old Temples of the Godhead, which for long have not been rainproof, crumble down; and men ask now: Where is the Godhead; our eyes never saw him?"

Pitiful enough were it, for all these wild utterances, to call our Diogenes wicked. Unprofitable servants as we all are,[18] perhaps at no era of his life was he more decisively the Servant of Goodness, the Servant of God, than even now when doubting God's existence. "One circumstance I note," says he: "after all the nameless woe that Inquiry, which for me, what it is not always, was genuine Love of Truth, had wrought me, I nevertheless still loved Truth, and would bate no jot[19] of my allegiance to her. 'Truth!' I cried, 'though the Heavens crush me for following her: no Falsehood! though a whole celestial Lubberland[20] were the price of Apostasy.' In conduct it was the same. Had a divine Messenger from the clouds, or miraculous Handwriting on the wall, convincingly proclaimed to me *This thou shalt do,* with what passionate readiness, as I often thought, would I have done it, had it been leaping into the infernal Fire. Thus, in spite of all Motive-grinders, and Mechanical Profit-and-Loss Philosophies, with the sick ophthalmia and hallucination they had brought on, was the Infinite nature of Duty still dimly present to me: living without God in the world,[21] of God's light I was not utterly bereft; if my as yet sealed eyes, with their unspeakable longing, could nowhere see Him, nevertheless in my heart He was present, and His heaven-written Law still stood legible and sacred there."

Meanwhile, under all these tribulations, and temporal and spiritual destitutions, what must the Wanderer, in his silent soul, have endured! "The painfullest feeling," writes he, "is that of your own Feebleness (*Unkraft*); ever, as the English Milton says, to be weak is the true misery.[22] And yet of your Strength there is and can be no clear feeling, save by what you have prospered in, by what you have done. Between vague wavering Capability and fixed indubitable Performance, what a difference! A certain inarticulate Self-consciousness dwells dimly in us; which only our Works can render articulate and decisively discernible. Our Works are the mirror wherein the spirit first sees its natural lineaments. Hence, too, the folly of that impossible Precept, *Know thyself;* till it be translated into this partially possible one, *Know what thou canst work at.*

"But for me, so strangely unprosperous had

---

pleasant (by praise, rewards, etc.) and vicious acts painful (by blame, punishment, etc.).

[14] Prometheus Bound represents a man of genius suffering under, but defying, an unjust fate.

[15] The Sibyl was reputed to know the innermost secrets of the universe.

[16] As happened to the Israelites in their flight from Egypt (Exodus 13:21–22).

[17] The century of Louis XV; i.e., the eighteenth century, known as one of rationalism and skepticism. See "The Hero as Man of Letters," below.

[18] Luke 17:10.

[19] Abate not the smallest part.

[20] Land of luxurious ease.   [21] Ephesians 2:12.

[22] *Paradise Lost,* I, 157.

I been, the net-result of my Workings amounted as yet simply to—Nothing. How then could I believe in my Strength, when there was as yet no mirror to see it in? Ever did this agitating, yet, as I now perceive, quite frivolous question, remain to me insoluble: Hast thou a certain Faculty, a certain Worth, such even as the most have not; or art thou the completest Dullard of these modern times? Alas! the fearful Unbelief is unbelief in yourself; and how could I believe? Had not my first, last Faith in myself, when even to me the Heavens seemed laid open, and I dared to love, been all-too cruelly belied? The speculative Mystery of Life grew ever more mysterious to me; neither in the practical Mystery[23] had I made the slightest progress, but been everywhere buffeted, foiled, and contemptuously cast out. A feeble unit in the middle of a threatening Infinitude, I seemed to have nothing given me but eyes, whereby to discern my own wretchedness. Invisible yet impenetrable walls, as of Enchantment, divided me from all living: was there, in the wide world, any true bosom I could press trustfully to mine? O Heaven, No, there was none! I kept a lock upon my lips: why should I speak much with that shifting variety of so-called Friends, in whose withered, vain and too-hungry souls, Friendship was but an incredible tradition? In such cases, your resource is to talk little, and that little mostly from the Newspapers. Now when I look back, it was a strange isolation I then lived in. The men and women around me, even speaking with me, were but Figures: I had, practically, forgotten that they were alive, that they were not merely automatic. In the midst of their crowded streets, and assemblages, I walked solitary; and (except as it was my own heart, not another's, that I kept devouring) savage also, as the tiger in his jungle. Some comfort it would have been, could I, like a Faust,[24] have fancied myself tempted and tormented of the Devil; for a Hell, as I imagine, without Life, though only diabolic Life, were more frightful: but in our age of Down-pulling and Disbelief, the very Devil has been pulled down, you cannot so much as believe in a Devil.

To me the Universe was all void of Life, of Purpose, of Volition, even of Hostility: it was one huge, dead, immeasurable Steam-engine, rolling on, in its dead indifference, to grind me limb from limb. O, the vast gloomy, solitary Golgotha,[25] and Mill of Death! Why was the Living banished thither companionless, conscious? Why, if there is no Devil; nay, unless the Devil is your God?"

A prey incessantly to such corrosions, might not, moreover, as the worst aggravation to them, the iron constitution even of a Teufelsdröckh threaten to fail? We conjecture that he has known sickness; and, in spite of his locomotive habits, perhaps sickness of the chronic sort. Hear this, for example: "How beautiful to die of broken-heart, on Paper! Quite another thing in practice; every window of your Feeling, even of your Intellect, as it were, begrimed and mud-bespattered, so that no pure ray can enter; a whole Drugshop in your inwards; the foredone soul drowning slowly in quagmires of Disgust!"

Putting all which external and internal miseries together, may we not find in the following sentences, quite in our Professor's still vein, significance enough? "From Suicide a certain aftershine (*Nachschein*) of Christianity withheld me: perhaps also a certain indolence of character; for, was not that a remedy I had at any time within reach? Often, however, was there a question present to me: Should some one now, at the turning of that corner, blow thee suddenly out of Space, into the other World, or other No-world, by pistol-shot,—how were it? On which ground, too, I have often, in sea-storms and sieged cities and other death-scenes, exhibited an imperturbability, which passed, falsely enough, for courage.

"So had it lasted," concludes the Wanderer, "so had it lasted, as in bitter protracted Death-agony, through long years. The heart within me, unvisited by any heavenly dewdrop, was smouldering in sulphurous, slow-consuming fire. Almost since earliest memory I had shed no tear; or once only when I, murmuring half-audibly, recited Faust's Deathsong, that wild *Selig der den er im Siegesglanze findet* (Happy whom he[26]

---

23 Occupation, profession.
24 A medieval German scholar who sold his soul to the Devil in return for a life of hedonistic pleasure. Carlyle quotes below from Goethe's poem on the subject.

25 The scene of Jesus's crucifixion; literally, place of skulls.
26 Death.

finds in Battle's splendour), and thought that of this last Friend even I was not forsaken, that Destiny itself could not doom me not to die. Having no hope, neither had I any definite fear, were it of Man or of Devil: nay, I often felt as if it might be solacing, could the Arch-Devil himself, though in Tartarean terrors, but rise to me, that I might tell him a little of my mind. And yet, strangely enough, I lived in a continual, indefinite, pining fear; tremulous, pusillanimous, apprehensive of I knew not what: it seemed as if all things in the Heavens above and the Earth beneath would hurt me; as if the Heavens and the Earth were but boundless jaws of a devouring monster, wherein I, palpitating, waited to be devoured.

"Full of such humour, and perhaps the miserablest man in the whole French Capital or Suburbs, was I, one sultry Dog-day, after much perambulation, toiling along the dirty little *Rue Saint-Thomas de l'Enfer*,[27] among civic rubbish enough, in a close atmosphere, and over pavements hot as Nebuchadnezzar's Furnace;[28] whereby doubtless my spirits were little cheered; when, all at once, there rose a Thought in me, and I asked myself: 'What *art* thou afraid of? Wherefore, like a coward, dost thou forever pip and whimper, and go cowering and trembling? Despicable biped! what is the sum-total of the worst that lies before thee? Death? Well, Death; and say the pangs of Tophet[29] too, and all that the Devil and Man may, will, or can do against thee! Hast thou not a heart; canst thou not suffer whatsoever it be; and, as a Child of Freedom, though outcast, trample Tophet itself under thy feet, while it consumes thee? Let it come, then; I will meet it and defy it!' And as I so thought, there rushed like a stream of fire over my whole soul; and I shook base Fear away from me forever. I was strong, of unknown strength; a spirit, almost a god. Ever from that time, the temper of my misery was changed: not Fear or whining Sorrow was it, but Indignation and grim fire-eyed Defiance.

"Thus had the EVERLASTING No (*das ewige Nein*) pealed authoritatively through all the recesses of my Being, of my ME; and then was it that my whole ME stood up, in native God-created majesty, and with emphasis recorded its Protest. Such a Protest, the most important transaction in Life, may that same Indignation and Defiance, in a psychological point of view, be fitly called. The Everlasting No had said: 'Behold, thou art fatherless, outcast, and the Universe is mine (the Devil's)'; to which my whole ME now made answer: '*I* am not thine, but Free, and forever hate thee!'[30]

"It is from this hour that I incline to date my Spiritual New-birth, or Baphometic[31] Fire-baptism; perhaps I directly thereupon began to be a Man."

Book II, Chapter 9

THE EVERLASTING YEA

"Temptations in the Wilderness!"[32] exclaims Teufelsdröckh: "Have we not all to be tried with such? Not so easily can the old Adam,[33] lodged in us by birth, be dispossessed. Our Life is compassed round with Necessity; yet is the meaning of Life itself no other than Freedom, than Voluntary Force;[34] thus have we a warfare; in the beginning, especially, a hard-fought battle. For the God-given mandate, *Work thou in Well-doing*, lies mysteriously written, in Promethean[35] Prophetic Characters, in our hearts; and leaves us no rest, night or day, till it be deciphered and obeyed; till it burn forth, in our conduct, a

---

27 As the scene of Teufelsdröckh's experience Carlyle chose Paris because it typified all that was most skeptical and materialistic in French thought, and this particular street because of its infernal name.

28 The furnace prepared by the king of Babylon for the cremation of three Jews who would not worship a golden image (Daniel 3).

29 Hell.

30 See note 1. The importance of this experience lies in Teufelsdröckh's realization that he can protest against a wholly materialistic conception of the universe. His very "Indignation and grim fire-eyed Defiance" proved to him that there was something in his "whole Me," as distinct from the "mere Me" (the bodily part, belonging solely to the natural order), something which seemed not earth-created but God-created or of the spirit.

31 Baphomet was an idol whose rites included baptism by fire.

32 A reference to Christ's forty days in the wilderness. This section has repeated images from the gospel account (Matthew 4:1–11).

33 Original sin.

34 Life, he admits, is determined in some ways (we have to eat, sleep, and die, or be burned if we touch a hot stove), but still its meaning, its central characteristic, is voluntary force, i.e., moral freedom or free-will; hence the warfare and battle he goes on to mention between choosing the good or choosing the old Adam.

35 Fiery, from Prometheus' gift of fire to man. Characters = letters.

visible, acted Gospel of Freedom. And as the clay-given mandate, *Eat thou and be filled*,[36] at the same time persuasively proclaims itself through every nerve,—must there not be a confusion, a contest, before the better Influence can become the upper?

"To me nothing seems more natural than that the Son of Man, when such God-given mandate first prophetically stirs within him, and the Clay must now be vanquished or vanquish,—should be carried of the spirit into grim Solitudes, and there fronting the Tempter do grimmest battle with him; defiantly setting him at naught, till he yield and fly. Name it as we choose: with or without visible Devil, whether in the natural Desert of rocks and sands, or in the populous moral Desert of selfishness and baseness,—to such Temptation are we all called. Unhappy if we are not! Unhappy if we are but Half-men, in whom that divine handwriting has never blazed forth, all-subduing, in true sun-splendour; but quivers dubiously amid meaner lights: or smoulders, in dull pain, in darkness, under earthly vapours!—Our Wilderness is the wide World in an Atheistic Century; our Forty Days are long years of suffering and fasting: nevertheless, to these also comes an end. Yes, to me also was given, if not Victory, yet the consciousness of Battle, and the resolve to persevere therein while life or faculty is left. To me also, entangled in the enchanted forests, demon-peopled, doleful of sight and of sound, it was given, after weariest wanderings, to work out my way into the higher sunlit slopes—of that Mountain[37] which has no summit, or whose summit is in Heaven only!"

He says elsewhere, under a less ambitious figure; as figures are, once for all, natural to him: "Has not thy Life been that of most sufficient men (*tüchtigen Männer*) thou hast known in this generation? An outflush of foolish young Enthusiasm, like the first fallow-crop,[38] wherein are as many weeds as valuable herbs: this all parched away, under the Droughts of practical and spiritual Unbelief, as Disappointment, in thought and act, often-repeated gave rise to Doubt, and Doubt gradually settled into Denial! If I have had a second-crop, and now see the perennial greensward, and sit under umbrageous cedars, which defy all Drought (and Doubt); herein too, be the Heavens praised, I am not without examples, and even exemplars."

So that, for Teufelsdröckh also, there has been a "glorious revolution":[39] these mad shadow-hunting and shadow-hunted Pilgrimings of his were but some purifying "Temptation in the Wilderness," before his apostolic work (such as it was) could begin; which Temptation is now happily over, and the Devil once more worsted! Was "that high moment in the *Rue de l'Enfer*," then, properly the turning-point of the battle; when the Fiend said, *Worship me, or be torn in shreds;* and was answered valiantly with an *Apage Satana?*[40]—Singular Teufelsdröckh, would thou hadst told thy singular story in plain words! But it is fruitless to look there, in those Paper-bags,[41] for such. Nothing but innuendoes, figurative crotchets: a typical Shadow, fitfully wavering, prophetico-satiric; no clear logical Picture. "How paint to the sensual eye," asks he once, "what passes in the Holy-of-Holies of Man's Soul; in what words, known to these profane times, speak even afar-off of the unspeakable?" We ask in turn: Why perplex these times, profane as they are, with needless obscurity, by omission and by commission? Not mystical only is our Professor, but whimsical; and involves himself, now more than ever, in eye-bewildering *chiaroscuro*.[42] Successive glimpses, here faithfully imparted, our more gifted readers must endeavour to combine for their own behoof.

He says: "The hot Harmattan[43] wind had raged itself out; its howl went silent within me; and the long-deafened soul could now hear. I paused in my wild wanderings; and sat me down to wait, and consider; for it was as if the hour of change drew nigh. I seemed to surrender, to renounce utterly, and say: "Fly, then, false shadows of Hope; I will chase you no more, I will believe

---

36 The Devil's suggestion to Christ in the wilderness to follow his selfish desires for the pleasures of life—money, fame, sex, worldly success, etc.
37 Of insight or revelation.
38 The first crop after a field has lain fallow.

39 A purely verbal reference to the Revolution of 1688, which was known as "glorious" because it saved England both from absolutism and from Roman Catholicism.
40 "Get thee hence, Satan."
41 The manuscript of Teufelsdröckh's autobiography was found crammed into six paper bags.
42 A pictorial term used here to mean alternations of clarity and obscurity.   43 From the Sahara Desert.

you no more. And ye too, haggard spectres of Fear, I care not for you; ye too are all shadows and a lie. Let me rest here: for I am way-weary and life-weary; I will rest here, were it but to die: to die or to live is alike to me; alike insignificant."—And again: "Here, then, as I lay in that CENTRE OF INDIFFERENCE;[44] cast, doubtless by benignant upper Influence, into a healing sleep, the heavy dreams rolled gradually away, and I awoke to a new Heaven and a new Earth. The first preliminary moral Act, Annihilation of Self (*Selbsttödtung*), had been happily accomplished;[45] and my mind's eyes were now unsealed, and its hands ungyved."[46]

Might we not also conjecture that the following passage refers to his Locality, during this same "healing sleep"; that his Pilgrim-staff lies cast aside here, on "the high table-land"; and indeed that the repose is already taking wholesome effect on him? If it were not that the tone, in some parts, has more of riancy,[47] even of levity, than we could have expected! However, in Teufelsdröckh, there is always the strangest Dualism: light dancing, with guitar-music, will be going on in the forecourt, while by fits from within comes the faint whimpering of woe and wail. We transcribe the piece entire:

"Beautiful it was to sit there, as in my skyey Tent, musing and meditating; on the high table-land, in front of the Mountains; over me, as roof, the azure Dome, and around me, for walls, four azure-flowing curtains,—namely, of the Four azure Winds, on whose bottom-fringes also I have seen gilding. And then to fancy the fair Castles, that stood sheltered in these Mountain hollows; with their green flower-lawns, and white dames and damosels, lovely enough: or better still, the straw-roofed Cottages, wherein stood many a Mother baking bread, with her children round her:—all hidden and protect-

ingly folded-up in the valley-folds; yet there and alive, as sure as if I beheld them. Or to see, as well as fancy, the nine Towns and Villages, that lay round my mountain-seat, which, in still weather, were wont to speak to me (by their steeple-bells) with metal tongue; and, in almost all weather, proclaimed their vitality by repeated Smoke-clouds; whereon, as on a culinary horologue, I might read the hour of the day. For it was the smoke of cookery, as kind housewives at morning, midday, eventide, were boiling their husbands' kettles; and ever a blue pillar rose up into the air, successively or simultaneously, from each of the nine, saying, as plainly as smoke could say: Such and such a meal is getting ready here. Not uninteresting! For you have the whole Borough, with all its love-makings and scandal-mongeries, contentions and contentments, as in miniature, and could cover it all with your hat.—If, in my wide Wayfarings, I had learned to look into the business of the World in its details, here perhaps was the place for combining it into general propositions, and deducing inferences therefrom.

"Often also could I see the black Tempest marching in anger through the distance: round some Schreckhorn,[48] as yet grim-blue, would the eddying vapour gather, and there tumultuously eddy, and flow down like a mad witch's hair; till, after a space, it vanished, and, in the clear sunbeam, your Schreckhorn stood smiling grim-white, for the vapour had held snow. How thou fermentest and elaboratest in thy great fermenting-vat and laboratory of an Atmosphere, of a World, O Nature!—Or what is Nature? Ha! why do I not name thee GOD? Art thou not the 'Living Garment of God'? O Heavens, is it, in very deed, HE, then, that ever speaks through thee; that lives and loves in thee, that lives and loves in me?[49]

"Fore-shadows, call them rather fore-splendours, of that Truth, and Beginning of Truths, fell mysteriously over my soul. Sweeter than Day-

---

[44] This is the title and the theme of the chapter between "The Everlasting No" and "The Everlasting Yea." After Teufelsdröckh had found himself able to defy the materialistic conception of the universe, he remained for a period in a state of indifference. Released from his previous "continual, indefinite, pining fear," he sought for the time being only rest and inactivity.

[45] This is the first, preliminary moral act because the rejection of Self has not yet burned forth in his conduct (cf. the first paragraph of this chapter); he has not yet begun to work in welldoing.

[46] Unshackled.   [47] Gaiety.

[48] An Alpine peak.

[49] This leap from Nature to pantheism (the immanence of God in Nature and Man) has its psychological source in the shift of scenery from a black, angry tempest to clear sunbeams on a snowy summit, suggesting the change from the darkness of doubt to the sunlit splendors of faith (cf. the second paragraph). For the "Garment of God," see p. 432 of the introduction to Carlyle.

spring to the Shipwrecked in Nova Zembla;[50] ah, like the mother's voice to her little child that strays bewildered, weeping, in unknown tumults; like soft streamings of celestial music to my too-exasperated heart, came that Evangel. The Universe is not dead and demoniacal, a charnel-house with spectres; but godlike, and my Father's!

"With other eyes, too, could I now look upon my fellow man: with an infinite Love, an infinite Pity. Poor, wandering, wayward man! Art thou not tried, and beaten with stripes, even as I am? Ever, whether thou bear the royal mantle or the beggar's gabardine, art thou not so weary, so heavy-laden; and thy Bed of Rest is but a Grave. O my Brother, my Brother, why cannot I shelter thee in my bosom, and wipe away all tears from thy eyes!—Truly, the din of many-voiced Life, which, in this solitude, with the mind's organ, I could hear, was no longer a maddening discord, but a melting one; like inarticulate cries, and sobbings of a dumb creature, which in the ear of Heaven are prayers. The poor Earth, with her poor joys, was now my needy Mother, not my cruel Stepdame; Man, with his so mad Wants and so mean Endeavors, had become the dearer to me; and even for his sufferings and his sins, I now first named him Brother. Thus was I standing in the porch of that 'Sanctuary of Sorrow';[51] by strange, steep ways, had I too been guided thither; and ere long its sacred gates would open, and the 'Divine Depth of Sorrow'[52] lie disclosed to me."

The Professor says, he here first got eye on the Knot that had been strangling him, and straightway could unfasten it, and was free. "A vain interminable controversy," writes he, "touching what is at present called Origin of Evil, or some such thing, arises in every soul, since the beginning of the world; and in every soul, that would pass from idle Suffering into actual Endeavouring, must first be put an end to. The most, in our time, have to go content with a simple, incomplete enough Suppression of this controversy; to a few, some Solution of it is indispensable. In every new era, too, such Solution comes-out in different terms; and ever the Solution of the last era has become obsolete, and is found unserviceable. For it is man's nature to change his Dialect from century to century; he cannot help it though he would. The authentic *Church-Catechism* of our present century has not yet fallen into my hands: meanwhile, for my own private behoof, I attempt to elucidate the matter so. Man's Unhappiness, as I construe, comes of his Greatness; it is because there is an Infinite in him, which with all his cunning he cannot quite bury under the Finite. Will the whole Finance Ministers and Upholsterers and Confectioners of modern Europe undertake, in joint-stock company, to make one Shoeblack HAPPY? They cannot accomplish it, above an hour or two: for the Shoeblack also has a Soul quite other than his Stomach; and would require, if you consider it, for his permanent satisfaction and saturation, simply this allotment, no more, and no less: *God's infinite Universe altogether to himself*, therein to enjoy infinitely, and fill every wish as fast as it rose. Oceans of Hochheimer,[53] a Throat like that of Ophiuchus:[54] speak not of them; to the infinite Shoeblack they are as nothing. No sooner is your ocean filled, than he grumbles that it might have been of better vintage. Try him with half of a Universe, of an Omnipotence, he sets to quarrelling with the proprietor of the other half, and declares himself the most maltreated of men.— Always there is a black spot in our sunshine: it is even, as I said, the *Shadow of Ourselves*.[55]

"But the whim we have of Happiness is somewhat thus. By certain valuations, and averages, of our own striking, we come upon some sort of average terrestrial lot; this we fancy belongs to us by nature, and of indefeasible right. It is simple payment of our wages, of our deserts;

---

50 Scene of a Dutch shipwreck in 1596.
51 The Sanctuary of Sorrow (of pain, suffering, etc.) was the name of a hall where Wilhelm Meister, in Goethe's novel, is taken to view some murals representing the life of Christ. Christian love and pity, with the resulting sense of brotherhood, are in marked contrast to the self-centered misery, hostility, and isolation that Teufelsdröckh had felt in "The Everlasting No." But they have brought him only to the porch; he has still to enter and discover the central message of Christianity.
52 See below, where it is called the "Worship of Sorrow." The next paragraphs attack the worship of Happiness, not because it is evil, but because it is insatiable and irrational.

53 A choice Rhenish wine.
54 A mythological giant, after whom the constellation was probably named.
55 Man's sense of the infinite which will not allow him a definitive limit to his desires.

requires neither thanks nor complaint; only such *overplus* as there may be do we account Happiness; any *deficit* again is Misery. Now consider that we have the valuation of our own deserts ourselves, and what a fund of Self-conceit there is in each of us,—do you wonder that the balance should so often dip the wrong way, and many a Blockhead cry: See there, what a payment; was ever worthy gentleman so used!—I tell thee, Blockhead, it all comes of thy Vanity; of what thou *fanciest* those same deserts of thine to be. Fancy that thou deservest to be hanged (as is most likely), thou wilt feel it happiness to be only shot: fancy that thou deservest to be hanged in a hair-halter, it will be a luxury to die in hemp.[56]

"So true it is, what I then said, that *the Fraction of Life can be increased in value not so much by increasing your Numerator as by lessening your Denominator.* Nay, unless my Algebra deceive me, *Unity* itself divided by *Zero* will give *Infinity.* Make thy claim of wages a zero, then; thou hast the world under thy feet. Well did the Wisest of our time[57] write: 'It is only with Renunciation (*Entsagen*) that Life, properly speaking, can be said to begin.'

"I asked myself: What is this that, ever since earliest years, thou hast been fretting and fuming, and lamenting and self-tormenting, on account of? Say it in a word: is it not because thou art not HAPPY? Because the THOU (sweet gentleman) is not sufficiently honoured, nourished, soft-bedded, and lovingly cared-for? Foolish soul! What Act of Legislature was there that *thou* shouldst be Happy? A little while ago thou hadst no right to *be* at all. What if thou wert born and predestined not to be Happy, but to be Unhappy! Art thou nothing other than a Vulture, then, that fliest through the Universe seeking after somewhat to *eat;* and shrieking dolefully because carrion enough is not given thee? Close thy *Byron;* open thy *Goethe.*"[58]

"*Es leuchtet mir ein,* I see a glimpse of it!" cries he elsewhere: "there is in man a HIGHER than Love of Happiness: he can do without Happiness, and instead thereof find Blessedness! Was it not to preach-forth this same HIGHER that sages and martyrs, the Poet and the Priest, in all times, have spoken and suffered; bearing testimony, through life and through death, of the Godlike that is in Man, and how in the Godlike only has he Strength and Freedom? Which God-inspired Doctrine art thou also honoured to be taught; O Heavens! and broken with manifold merciful Afflictions, even till thou become contrite, and learn it! O, thank thy Destiny for these; thankfully bear what yet remain: thou hadst need of them; the Self in thee needed to be annihilated. By benignant fever-paroxysms is Life rooting out the deep-seated chronic Disease, and triumphs over Death. On the roaring billows of Time, thou art not engulfed, but borne aloft into the azure of Eternity. Love not Pleasure; love God. This is the EVERLASTING YEA, wherein all contradiction is solved: wherein whoso walks and works, it is well with him."

And again: "Small is it that thou canst trample the Earth with its injuries under thy feet, as old Greek Zeno[59] trained thee: thou canst love the Earth while it injures thee, and even because it injures thee; for this a Greater than Zeno was needed, and he too was sent. Knowest thou that '*Worship of Sorrow*'?[60] The Temple thereof, founded some eighteen centuries ago, now lies in ruins, overgrown with jungle, the habitation of doleful creatures: nevertheless, venture forward; in a low crypt, arched out of falling fragments, thou findest the Altar still there, and its sacred Lamp perennially burning."[61]

Without pretending to comment on which strange utterances, the Editor will only remark, that there lies beside them much of a still more questionable character; unsuited to the general

---

[56] It was more painful to be hanged with a rope made of hair than with a hempen rope.

[57] Goethe, the German author, who wrote *Wilhelm Meister,* which Carlyle had translated.

[58] Close thy Byron pouring out his woes and despairs because his search for Happiness is thwarted, and open thy Goethe with his gospel of self-renunciation.

[59] Stoic philosopher (flourished c. 300 B.C.) who taught men to despise the pleasures and injuries of life as of no consequence compared with the pursuit of virtue.

[60] Christ was greater than Zeno in that he taught men to love those who injured them, and even to recognize the positive value of the suffering involved, of all suffering—that it helps to annihilate the Self (see middle of previous paragraph, and remember "Be ye made perfect through suffering"). The "Worship of Sorrow" is the acceptance of suffering as good.

[61] I.e., in spite of the skepticism and materialism of the eighteenth century, the soul of Christianity is still burningly alive.

apprehension; nay, wherein he himself does not see his way. Nebulous disquisitions on Religion, yet not without bursts of splendour; on the "perennial continuance of Inspiration"; on Prophecy; that there are "true Priests, as well as Baal-Priests,[62] in our own day": with more of the like sort. We select some fractions, by way of finish to this farrago.

"Cease, my much-respected Herr von Voltaire,"[63] thus apostrophises the Professor: "shut thy sweet voice; for the task appointed thee seems finished. Sufficiently hast thou demonstrated this proposition, considerable or otherwise: That the Mythus of the Christian Religion looks not in the eighteenth century as it did in the eighth. Alas, were thy six-and-thirty quartos, and the six-and-thirty thousand other quartos and folios, and flying sheets or reams, printed before and since on the same subject, all needed to convince us of so little! But what next? Wilt thou help us to embody the divine Spirit of that Religion in a new Mythus, in a new vehicle and vesture, that our Souls, otherwise too like perishing, may live? What! thou hast no faculty in that kind? Only a torch for burning, no hammer for building? Take our thanks, then, and—thyself away.

"Meanwhile what are antiquated Mythuses to me? Or is the God present, felt in my own heart, a thing which Herr von Voltaire will dispute out of me; or dispute into me? To the 'Worship of Sorrow' ascribe what origin and genesis thou pleasest, *has* not that Worship originated, and been generated; is it not *here*? Feel it in thy heart, and then say whether it is of God! This is Belief; all else is Opinion,—for which latter whoso will, let him worry and be worried."

"Neither," observes he elsewhere, "shall ye tear-out one another's eyes, struggling over 'Plenary Inspiration,'[64] and such-like: try rather to get a little even Partial Inspiration, each of you for yourself. One BIBLE I know,[65] of whose Plenary Inspiration doubt is not so much as possible; nay with my own eyes I saw the God's-Hand writing it: thereof all other Bibles are but Leaves,—say, in Picture-Writing to assist the weaker faculty."

Or to give the wearied reader relief, and, bring it to an end, let him take the following perhaps more intelligible passage:

"To me, in this our life," says the Professor, "which is an internecine warfare with the Time-spirit,[66] other warfare seems questionable. Hast thou in any way a Contention with thy brother, I advise thee, think well what the meaning thereof is. If thou gauge it to the bottom, it is simply this: 'Fellow, see! thou art taking more than thy share of Happiness in the world, something from *my* share: which, by the Heavens, thou shalt not; nay, I will fight thee rather.'—Alas, and the whole lot to be divided is such a beggarly matter, truly a 'feast of shells,' for the substance has been spilled out: not enough to quench one Appetite; and the collective human species clutching at them!—Can we not, in all such cases, rather say: 'Take it, thou too-ravenous individual; take that pitiful additional fraction of a share, which I reckoned mine, but which thou so wantest; take it with a blessing: would to Heaven I had enough for thee!'—Fichte's *Wissenschaftslehre*[67] be, 'to a certain extent, Applied Christianity,' surely to a still greater extent, so is this. We have here not a Whole Duty of Man, yet a Half Duty, namely, the Passive half,[68] could we but do it, as we can demonstrate it!

"But indeed Conviction, were it never so excellent, is worthless till it convert itself into Conduct. Nay, properly Conviction is not possible till then; inasmuch as all Speculation is by nature endless, formless, a vortex amid vortices:

---

62 Priests who served the pagan divinity Baal; i.e., priests of a false religion.

63 Voltaire for Teufelsdröckh was the great antagonist of all positive, creative religious belief. He was purely destructive.

64 The doctrine that every word of the Bible was inspired by God.

65 Man's heart. The "Worship of Sorrow" is so exalted and extraordinary a feeling that it must be God-inspired. Elsewhere Carlyle says that "Christianity, the worship of Sorrow," has its verification "in mysterious, ineffaceable characters . . . written in the purest nature of man."

66 The constant struggle of man to survive despite the passing of time, which will in the end destroy him.

67 The German philosopher Johann Gottlieb Fichte (1762–1814) taught that the highest wisdom lay in pursuing one's duty rather than one's happiness. This involves a renunciation which is akin to Christian teaching.

68 That is, the necessity for renunciation, for loving God and our brother humans, and for realizing the value of suffering. Work, as he goes on to say, is the Active half of one's duty.

only by a felt indubitable certainty of Experience does it find any centre to revolve round, and so fashion itself into a system. Most true is it, as a wise man teaches us,[69] that 'Doubt of any sort cannot be removed except by Action.' On which ground, too, let him who gropes painfully in darkness or uncertain light, and prays vehemently that the dawn may ripen into day, lay this other precept well to heart, which to me was of invaluable service: *'Do the Duty which lies nearest thee,'* which thou knowest to be a Duty! Thy second Duty will already have become clearer.[70]

"May we not say, however, that the hour of Spiritual Enfranchisement is even this: When your Ideal World, wherein the whole man has been dimly struggling and inexpressibly languishing to work, becomes revealed and thrown open; and you discover, with amazement enough, like the Lothario in *Wilhelm Meister,* that your 'America'[71] is here or nowhere'? The Situation that has not its Duty, its Ideal, was never yet occupied by man. Yes here, in this poor, miserable, hampered, despicable Actual, wherein thou even now standest, here or nowhere is thy Ideal: work it out therefrom; and working, believe, live, be free. Fool! the Ideal is in thyself, the impediment too is in thyself: thy Condition is but the stuff thou art to shape that same Ideal out of: what matters whether such stuff be of this sort or that, so the Form thou give it be heroic, be poetic? O thou that pinest in the imprisonment of the Actual, and criest bitterly to the gods for a kingdom wherein to rule and create, know this of a truth: the thing thou seekest is already with thee, 'here or nowhere,' couldst thou only see!

"But it is with man's Soul as it was with Nature: the beginning of Creation is—Light. Till the eye have vision, the whole members are in bonds. Divine moment, when over the tempest-tost Soul, as once over the wild-weltering Chaos, it is spoken: Let there be light! Ever to

the greatest that has felt such moment, is it not miraculous and God-announcing,[72] even as, under simpler figures, to the simplest and least. The mad primeval Discord is hushed; the rudely-jumbled conflicting elements bind themselves into separate Firmaments: deep silent rock-foundations are built beneath; and the skyey vault with its everlasting Luminaries above: instead of a dark wasteful Chaos, we have a blooming, fertile, Heaven-encompassed World.

"I too could now say to myself: Be no longer a Chaos, but a World, or even Worldkin. Produce! Produce! Were it but the pitifullest infinitesimal fraction of a Product, produce it, in God's name! 'Tis the utmost thou hast in thee: out with it, then. Up, up! Whatsoever thy hand findeth to do, do it with thy whole might. Work while it is called Today; for the Night cometh, wherein no man can work."[73]

Book III, Chapter 8

NATURAL SUPERNATURALISM[1]

It is in his stupendous Section, headed *Natural Supernaturalism,* that the Professor first becomes a Seer; and, after long effort, such as we have witnessed, finally subdues under his feet this refractory Clothes-Philosophy,[2] and takes victorious possession thereof. Phantasms enough he has had to struggle with; "Cloth-webs and Cob-webs," of Imperial Mantles, Superannuated Symbols, and what not: yet still did he courageously pierce through. Nay, worst of all, two quite mysterious, world-embracing Phantasms, TIME and SPACE, have ever hovered round him,

---

[69] Goethe in *Wilhelm Meister.*

[70] So Teufelsdröckh's doubt is not removed by the preceding arguments, but only by doing the nearest duty and then feeling the "indubitable certainty" of having followed a "God-given mandate, *'Work thou in Welldoing'.*" Thus the Passive half of Duty becomes "Conviction" only when the Active half is being done. As he goes on to say, by "Working, believe, live, be free."

[71] Land of opportunity or ideal world.

[72] Again, the moment when one discovers his Ideal, the work he is best fitted to do, is so exalting it seems "miraculous and God-announcing." Cf. lines 14–21.

[73] The last lines are echoes of Ecclesiastes 9:10 and John 9:4.

[1] In 1832, as he was finishing *Sartor,* Carlyle wrote in his diary: "A strange feeling of the mystery and wonderfulness of life, of the super-natural, haunts and grows upon me." This chapter is an attempt to explain and illustrate this feeling that the natural world and every natural object and event is *miraculous* (i.e., in some respects inexplicable by logic or scientific law); and therefore *super-natural;* and therefore *divine.* Cf. the introduction to Carlyle, paragraph 4, which is a good headnote to this chapter.

[2] Carlyle's term for the philosophy of the book: see the last sentence of this paragraph.

perplexing and bewildering: but with these also he now resolutely grapples, these also he victoriously rends asunder. In a word, he has looked fixedly on Existence, till, one after the other, its earthly hulls and garnitures have all melted away; and now, to his rapt vision, the interior celestial Holy of Holies lies disclosed.

Here, therefore, properly it is that the Philosophy of Clothes attains to Transcendentalism;[3] this last leap, can we but clear it, takes us safe into the promised land, where *Palingenesia*,[4] in all senses, may be considered as beginning. "Courage, then!" may our Diogenes exclaim, with better right than Diogenes the First once did.[5] This stupendous Section we, after long painful meditation, have found not to be unintelligible; but, on the contrary, to grow clear, nay radiant, and all-illuminating. Let the reader, turning on it what utmost force of speculative intellect is in him, do his part; as we, by judicious selection and adjustment, shall study to do ours:

"Deep has been, and is, the significance of Miracles," thus quietly begins the Professor; "far deeper perhaps than we imagine. Meanwhile, the question of questions were: What specially is a Miracle? To that Dutch King of Siam, an icicle had been a miracle; whoso had carried with him an air-pump, and vial of vitriolic ether, might have worked a miracle. To my Horse, again, who unhappily is still more unscientific, do not I work a miracle, and magical '*Open sesame!*' every time I please to pay twopence, and open for him an impassable *Schlagbaum*, or shut Turnpike?

" 'But is not a real Miracle simply a violation of the Laws of Nature?' ask several. Whom I answer by this new question: Where are the Laws of Nature? To me perhaps the rising of one from the dead were no violation of these Laws, but a confirmation; were some far deeper Law, now first penetrated into, and by Spiritual Force, even as the rest have all been, brought to bear on us with its Material Force.

"Here too may some inquire, not without astonishment: On what ground shall one, that can make Iron swim, come and declare that therefore he can teach Religion? To us, truly, of the Nineteenth Century, such declaration were inept enough; which nevertheless to our fathers, of the First Century, was full of meaning.[6]

" 'But is it not the deepest Law of Nature that she be constant?' cries an illuminated class: 'Is not the Machine of the Universe fixed to move by unalterable rules?' Probable enough, good friends: nay I, too, must believe that the God, whom ancient inspired men assert to be 'without variableness or shadow of turning,' does indeed never change; that Nature, that the Universe, which no one whom it so pleases can be prevented from calling a Machine, does move by the most unalterable rules. And now of you, too, I make the old inquiry: What those same unalterable rules, forming the complete Statute-Book of Nature, may possibly be?

"They stand written in our Works of Science, say you; in the accumulated records of Man's Experience?—Was Man with his Experience present at the Creation, then, to see how it all went on? Have any deepest scientific individuals yet dived down to the foundations of the Universe, and gauged everything there? Did the Maker take them into His counsel; that they read His groundplan of the incomprehensible All; and can say, This stands marked therein, and no more than this? Alas, not in anywise! These scientific individuals have been nowhere but where we also are; have seen some handbreadths deeper than we see into the Deep that is infinite, without bottom as without shore.

"Laplace's Book on the Stars, wherein he exhibits that certain Planets, with their Satellites, gyrate round our worthy Sun, at a rate and in a course, which, by greatest good fortune, he and the like of him have succeeded in detecting,—is to me as precious as to another. But is this what thou namest 'Mechanism of the Heavens,' and 'System of the World'; this, wherein Sirius and the Pleiades, and all Herschel's Fifteen-thousand Suns per minute,[7] being left out, some paltry

---

3 I.e., truths that transcend sensory experience.
4 Rebirth.
5 Near the end of a long lecture, Diogenes cried, "Courage, friends! I see land!"

6 What was a miracle in the first century, entitling its performer to teach religion—viz., a floating piece of iron (2 Kings 6:5–7)—was no miracle in the nineteenth century and the builder of iron ships no prophet.
7 Sir William Herschel was an English astronomer who discovered a vast number of new stars per astronomical minute, the sixtieth part of a degree.

handful of Moons, and inert Balls, had been—looked at, nicknamed, and marked in the Zodiacal Way-bill; so that we can now prate of their Whereabout; their How, their Why, their What, being hid from us, as in the signless Inane?[8]

"System of Nature! To the wisest man, wide as is his vision, Nature remains of quite *infinite* depth, of quite infinite expansion; and all Experience thereof limits itself to some few computed centuries and measured square-miles. The course of Nature's phases, on this our little fraction of a Planet, is partially known to us: but who knows what deeper courses these depend on; what infinitely larger Cycle (of causes) our little Epicycle revolves on? To the Minnow every cranny and pebble, and quality and accident, of its little native Creek may have become familiar: but does the Minnow understand the Ocean Tides and periodic Currents, the Tradewinds, and Monsoons, and Moon's Eclipses; by all which the condition of its little Creek is regulated, and may, from time to time (*un*miraculously enough), be quite overset and reversed? Such a minnow is Man; his Creek this Planet Earth; his Ocean the immeasurable All; his Monsoons and periodic Currents the mysterious Course of Providence through Æons of Æons.

"We speak of the Volume of Nature: and truly a Volume it is,—whose Author and Writer is God. To read it! Dost thou, does man, so much as well know the Alphabet thereof? With its Words, Sentences, and grand descriptive Pages, poetical and philosophical, spread out through Solar Systems, and Thousands of Years, we shall not try thee. It is a Volume written

in celestial hieroglyphs, in the true Sacred-writing; of which even Prophets are happy that they can read here a line and there a line. As for your Institutes, and Academies of Science, they strive bravely; and, from amid the thick-crowded, inextricably intertwisted hieroglyphic writing, pick out, by dextrous combination, some Letters in the vulgar Character, and therefrom put together this and the other economic[9] Recipe, of high avail in Practice. That Nature is more than some boundless Volume of such Recipes, or huge, well-nigh inexhaustible Domestic-Cookery Book, of which the whole secret will in this manner one day evolve itself, the fewest dream.[10]

"Custom," continues the Professor, "doth make dotards of us all. Consider well, thou wilt find that Custom is the greatest of Weavers; and weaves air-raiment for all the Spirits of the Universe; whereby indeed these dwell with us visibly, as ministering servants, in our houses and workshops; but their spiritual nature becomes, to the most, forever hidden. Philosophy complains that Custom has hoodwinked us, from the first; that we do everything by Custom, even Believe by it; that our very Axioms, let us boast of Freethinking as we may, are oftenest simply such Beliefs as we have never heard questioned. Nay, what is Philosophy throughout but a continual battle against Custom; an ever-renewed effort to *transcend* the sphere of blind Custom, and so become Transcendental?

"Innumerable are the illusions and legerdemain-tricks of Custom: but of all these, perhaps the cleverest is her knack of persuading us that the Miraculous, by simple repetition, ceases to be Miraculous. True, it is by this means we live; for man must work as well as wonder: and herein is Custom so far a kind nurse, guiding him to his true benefit. But she is a fond foolish nurse, or rather we are false foolish nurselings, when, in our resting and reflecting hours, we prolong the same deception. Am I to view the Stupendous with stupid indifference, because I have seen it twice, or two-hundred, or two-million times? There is no reason in Nature

---

8 Works of science like Laplace's *Mecanique Céleste* are studies of second causes—the physical causes of certain physical results—which are normally stated in mathematical formulae. But there are three other types of causation in "the *complete* Statute-Book of Nature," which Laplace and his fellow scientists are ignorant of—the How, the Why, and the What. The How is the first cause: how was the universe originally created? The Why is the final cause: why was the universe created and each thing in it?—to what end or purpose? The What is the efficient cause: what makes things act as they do? The cause that makes water boil at sea-level at 100 degrees centigrade is the efficient cause, but we do not know *what* it is. The boiling point of water is simply a *mysterious fact*. These three mysterious causes seem to be mentioned in the previous paragraph: the first cause, certainly, in lines 22–29; the efficient causes are included in the next question, and the final causes in the "groundplan of the . . . All."

9 Of or pertaining to man's needs and therefore "of high avail in Practice."

10 Few dream that the study of nature is far more than the study of these second causes that produce the practical results we desire.

or in Art why I should: unless, indeed, I am a mere Work-Machine, for whom the divine gift of Thought were no other than the terrestrial gift of Steam is to the Steam-engine; a power whereby cotton might be spun, and money and money's worth realised.

"Notable enough too, here as elsewhere, wilt thou find the potency of Names; which indeed are but one kind of such custom-woven, wonder-hiding Garments. Witchcraft, and all manner of Spectre-work, and Demonology, we have now named Madness and Diseases of the Nerves. Seldom reflecting that still the new question comes upon us: What is Madness, what are Nerves? Ever, as before, does Madness remain a mysterious-terrific, altogether *infernal* boiling-up of the Nether Chaotic Deep, through this fair-painted Vision of Creation, which swims thereon, which we name the Real. Was Luther's Picture of the Devil less a Reality, whether it were formed within the bodily eye, or without it?[11] In every the wisest Soul lies a whole world of internal Madness, an authentic Demon-Empire; out of which, indeed, his world of Wisdom has been creatively built together, and now rests there, as on its dark foundations does a habitable flowery Earth-rind.[12]

"But deepest of all illusory Appearances, for hiding Wonder, as for many other ends, are your two grand fundamental world-enveloping Appearances, SPACE and TIME.[13] These, as spun and woven for us from before Birth itself, to clothe our celestial ME for dwelling here, and yet to blind it,—lie all-embracing, as the universal canvas, or warp and woof, whereby all minor Illusions, in this Phantasm Existence, weave and paint themselves. In vain, while here on Earth, shall you endeavour to strip them off; you can, at best, but rend them asunder for moments, and look through.

"Fortunatus had a wishing Hat, which when he put on, and wished himself Anywhere, behold he was There. By this means had Fortunatus triumphed over Space, he had annihilated Space; for him there was no Where, but all was Here. Were a Hatter to establish himself, in the Wahngasse of Weissnichtwo,[14] and make felts of this sort for all mankind, what a world we should have of it! Still stranger, should, on the opposite side of the street, another Hatter establish himself; and, as his fellow-craftsman made Space-annihilating Hats, make Time-annihilating! Of both would I purchase, were it with my last groschen; but chiefly of this latter. To clap-on your felt, and, simply by wishing that you were Any*where,* straightway to be *There!* Next to clap-on your other felt, and, simply by wishing that you were Any*when,* straightway to be *Then!* This were indeed the grander: shooting at will from the Fire-Creation of the World to its Fire-Consummation; here historically present in the First Century, conversing face to face with Paul and Seneca; there prophetically in the Thirty-first, conversing also face to face with other Pauls and Senecas, who as yet stand hidden in the depth of that late Time!

"Or thinkest thou it were impossible, unimaginable? Is the Past annihilated, then, or only past; is the Future nonexistent, or only future? Those mystic faculties of thine, Memory and Hope, already answer: already through those mystic avenues, thou the Earth-blinded summonest both Past and Future, and communest with them, though as yet darkly, and with mute beckonings. The curtains of Yesterday drop down, the curtains of Tomorrow roll up; but Yesterday and Tomorrow both *are.* Pierce through the Time-element, glance into the Eternal. Believe what thou findest written in the sanctuaries of Man's Soul, even as all Thinkers, in all ages, have devoutly read it there: that Time and Space are not God, but creations of God; that with God as it is a universal HERE, so is it an everlasting Now.

"And seest thou therein any glimpse of IMMORTALITY?—O Heaven! Is the white Tomb

---

11 The Devil who appeared to Luther was real enough whether seen by his eye or by his deranged imagination.
12 The wisest soul has creatively put together his world of wisdom out of a world of internal madness. Cf. making Order out of Chaos.
13 In the Kantian philosophy, here adopted by Carlyle, Space and Time are "forms of thought," ways in which we see one object or event in relation to another, either spatially or temporally. They are therefore not external realities but appearances; they are how two or more things appear after they pass through the mind—spread-out and strung-along, or in the past, present, or future.

14 Illusion-street of Knows-not-where, the town in which *Sartor Resartus* is supposed to have been published; see Book I, chap. 1.

of our Loved One, who died from our arms, and had to be left behind us there, which rises in the distance, like a pale, mournfully receding Milestone, to tell how many toilsome uncheered miles we have journeyed on alone,—but a pale spectral Illusion! Is the lost Friend still mysteriously Here, even as we are Here mysteriously, with God!—Know of a truth that only the Time-shadows have perished, or are perishable; that the real Being of whatever was, and whatever is, and whatever will be, *is* even now and forever. This, should it unhappily seem new, thou mayest ponder at thy leisure; for the next twenty years, or the next twenty centuries: believe it thou must; understand it thou canst not.

"That the Thought-forms, Space and Time, wherein, once for all, we are sent into this Earth to live, should condition and determine our whole Practical reasonings, conceptions, and imagings or imaginings, seems altogether fit, just, and unavoidable. But that they should, furthermore, usurþ such sway over pure spiritual Meditation, and blind us to the wonder everywhere lying close on us, seems nowise so. Admit Space and Time to their due rank as Forms of Thought; nay even, if thou wilt, to their quite undue rank of Realities: and consider, then, with thyself how their thin disguises hide from us the brightest God–effulgences! Thus, were it not miraculous, could I stretch forth my hand and clutch the Sun? Yet thou seest me daily stretch forth my hand and therewith clutch many a thing, and swing it hither and thither. Art thou a grown baby, then, to fancy that the Miracle lies in miles of distance, or in pounds avoirdupois of weight; and not to see that the true inexplicable God-revealing Miracle lies in this, that I can stretch forth my hand at all; that I have free Force to clutch aught therewith? Innumerable other of this sort are the deceptions, and wonder-hiding stupefactions, which Space practises on us.

"Still worse is it with regard to Time. Your grand anti-magician, and universal wonder-hider, is this same lying Time. Had we but the Time-annihilating Hat, to put on for once only, we should see ourselves in a World of Miracles, wherein all fabled or authentic Thaumaturgy, and feats of Magic, were outdone. But unhappily we have not such a Hat; and man, poor fool that he is, can seldom and scantily help himself without one.

"Were it not wonderful, for instance, had Orpheus, or Amphion, built the walls of Thebes by the mere sound of his Lyre? Yet tell me, Who built these walls of Weissnichtwo; summoning out all the sandstone rocks, to dance along from the *Steinbruch*[15] (now a huge Troglodyte[16] Chasm, with frightful green-mantled pools); and shape themselves into Doric and Ionic pillars, squared ashlar[17] houses and noble streets? Was it not the still higher Orpheus, or Orpheuses, who, in past centuries, by the divine Music of Wisdom, succeeded in civilising Man? Our highest Orpheus walked in Judea, eighteen-hundred years ago: his sphere-melody, flowing in wild native tones, took captive the ravished souls of men; and, being of a true sphere-melody still flows and sounds, though now with thousandfold accompaniments, and rich symphonies, through all our hearts; and modulates, and divinely leads them. Is that a wonder, which happens in two hours; and does it cease to be wonderful if happening in two million? Not only was Thebes built by the music of an Orpheus; but without the music of some inspired Orpheus was no city ever built, no work that man glories in ever done.

"Sweep away the Illusion of Time; glance, if thou have eyes, from the near moving-cause to its far-distant Mover: The stroke that came transmitted through a whole galaxy of elastic balls, was it less a stroke than if the last ball only had been struck, and sent flying? O, could I (with the Time-annihilating Hat) transport thee direct from the Beginnings to the Endings, how were thy eyesight unsealed, and thy heart set flaming in the Light-sea of celestial wonder! Then sawest thou that this fair Universe, were it in the meanest province thereof, is in very deed the star-domed City of God; that through every star, through every grass-blade, and most through every Living Soul, the glory of a present God still beams.[18] But Nature, which is the Time-vesture of God, and reveals Him to the wise, hides Him from the foolish.

---

15 Quarry.

16 Primitive cave-dweller.

17 Hewn stone.

18 If one could see at a glance the whole evolution of the universe from beginning to end, and the integral place of everything in it (know the How and the Why and the What), he would recognize everywhere the miraculous work of God. The last clause probably is not a statement of divine immanence, as it could be, quoted out of context; for here one *sees* the "City of God," the thing He created.

"Again, could anything be more miraculous than an actual authentic Ghost? The English Johnson longed, all his life, to see one; but could not, though he went to Cock Lane, and thence to the church-vaults, and tapped on coffins. Foolish Doctor! Did he never, with the mind's eye as well as with the body's, look round him into that full tide of human Life he so loved; did he never so much as look into Himself? The good Doctor was a Ghost,[19] as actual and authentic as heart could wish; well-nigh a million of Ghosts were travelling the streets by his side. Once more I say, sweep away the illusion of Time; compress the threescore years into three minutes: what else was he, what else are we? Are we not Spirits, that are shaped into a body, into an Appearance; and that fade away again into air and Invisibility? This is no metaphor, it is a simple scientific *fact;* we start out of Nothingness, take figure, and are Apparitions; round us, as round the veriest spectre, is Eternity; and to Eternity minutes are as years and æons. Come there not tones of Love and Faith, as from celestial harp-strings, like the Song of beatified Souls? And again, do not we squeak and jibber (in our discordant, screech-owlish debatings and recriminatings); and glide bodeful, and feeble, and fearful; or uproar (*poltern*), and revel in our mad Dance of the Dead,—till the scent of the morning air summons us to our still Home; and dreamy Night becomes awake and Day? Where now is Alexander of Macedon: does the steel Host, that yelled in fierce battle-shouts at Issus and Arbela,[20] remain behind him; or have they all vanished utterly, even as perturbed Goblins must? Napoleon too, and his Moscow Retreats and Austerlitz Campaigns! Was it all other than the veriest Spectre-hunt; which has now, with its howling tumult that made Night hideous, flitted away? —Ghosts! There are nigh a thousand-million walking the Earth openly at noontide; some half-hundred have vanished from it, some half-hundred have arisen in it, ere thy watch ticks once.

"O Heaven, it is mysterious, it is awful to consider that we not only carry each a future Ghost within Him; but are, in very deed, Ghosts! These Limbs, whence had we them; this stormy Force; this life-blood with its burning Passion? They are dust and shadow; a Shadow-system gathered round our ME; wherein, through some moments or years, the Divine Essence is to be revealed in the Flesh. That warrior on his strong war-horse, fire flashes through his eyes; force dwells in his arm and heart: but warrior and war-horse are a vision; a revealed Force, nothing more. Stately they tread the Earth, as if it were a firm substance: fool! the Earth is but a film; it cracks in twain, and warrior and war-horse sink beyond plummet's sounding. Plummet's? Fantasy herself will not follow them. A little while ago, they were not; a little while, and they are not, their very ashes are not.

"So has it been from the beginning, so will it be to the end. Generation after generation takes to itself the Form of a Body; and forth-issuing from Cimmerian Night, on Heaven's mission APPEARS. What Force and Fire is in each he expends: one grinding in the mill of Industry; one hunter-like climbing the giddy Alpine heights of Science; one madly dashed in pieces on the rocks of Strife, in war with his fellow:—and then the Heaven-sent is recalled; his earthly Vesture falls away, and soon even to sense becomes a vanished Shadow. Thus, like some wild-flaming, wild-thundering train of Heaven's Artillery, does this mysterious MANKIND thunder and flame, in long-drawn, quick-succeeding grandeur, through the unknown Deep. Thus, like a God-created, fire-breathing Spirit-host, we emerge from the Inane; haste stormfully across the astonished Earth; then plunge again into the Inane. Earth's mountains are levelled, and her seas filled up, in our passage: can the Earth, which is but dead and a vision, resist Spirits which have reality and are alive? On the hardest adamant some footprint of us is stamped-in; the last Rear of the host will read traces of the earliest Van. But whence?—O Heaven, whither? Sense knows not; Faith knows not; only that it is through Mystery to Mystery, from God and to God.

'*We* are such stuff
As dreams are made of, and our little Life
Is rounded with a sleep!' "[21]

---

19 The soul or spirit of a person that appears to the living in bodily form. If we appeared for only three minutes instead of threescore years, we should all be recognized as ghosts.
20 Two towns where Alexander defeated the Persians.

21 From Shakespeare's *Tempest*, IV, i, 156–58.

from On Heroes, Hero-Worship and the Heroic in History[1]

from Lecture V

THE HERO AS MAN OF LETTERS

Johnson, Rousseau, Burns

Hero-gods, Prophets, Poets, Priests are forms of Heroism that belong to the old ages, make their appearance in the remotest times; some of them have ceased to be possible long since, and cannot any more show themselves in this world. The Hero as *Man of Letters,* again, of which class we are to speak today, is altogether a product of these new ages; and so long as the wondrous art of *Writing,* or of Ready-writing which we call *Printing,* subsists, he may be expected to continue, as one of the main forms of Heroism for all future ages. He is, in various respects, a very singular phenomenon.

He is new, I say; he has hardly lasted above a century in the world yet. Never, till about a hundred years ago, was there seen any figure of a Great Soul living apart in that anomalous manner; endeavouring to speak-forth the inspiration that was in him by Printed Books, and find place and subsistence by what the world would please to give him for doing that. Much had been sold and bought, and left to make its own bargain in the marketplace; but the inspired wisdom of a Heroic Soul never till then, in that naked manner. He, with his copyrights and copy-wrongs,[2] in his squalid garret, in his rusty coat; ruling (for this is what he does), from his grave, after death, whole nations and generations who would, or would not, give him bread while living,—is a rather curious spectacle! Few shapes of Heroism can be more unexpected.

Alas, the Hero from of old has had to cramp himself into strange shapes: the world knows not well at any time what to do with him, so foreign is his aspect in the world! It seemed absurd to us, that men, in their rude admiration, should take some wise great Odin for a god, and worship him as such; some wise great Mahomet for one god-inspired, and religiously follow his Law for twelve centuries: but that a wise great Johnson, a Burns, a Rousseau, should be taken for some idle nondescript, extant in the world to amuse idleness, and have a few coins and applauses thrown him, that he might live thereby; *this* perhaps, as before hinted, will one day seem a still absurder phasis of things!—Meanwhile, since it is the spiritual always that determines the material, this same Man-of-Letters Hero must be regarded as our most important modern person.[3] He, such as he may be, is the soul of all. What he teaches, the whole world will do and make. The world's manner of dealing with him is the most significant feature of the world's general position. Looking well at his life, we may get a glance, as deep as is readily possible for us, into the life of those singular centuries which have produced him, in which we ourselves live and work.

There are genuine Men of Letters, and not genuine; as in every kind there is a genuine and a spurious. If *Hero* be taken to mean genuine, then I say the Hero as Man of Letters will be found discharging a function for us which is ever honourable, ever the highest; and was once well known to be the highest. He is uttering-forth, in such way as he has, the inspired soul of him; all that a man, in any case, can do. I say *inspired;* for what we call "originality," "sincerity," "genius," the heroic quality we have no good name for, signifies that. The Hero is he who lives in the inward sphere of things, in the True, Divine and Eternal, which exists always, unseen to most, under the Temporary, Trivial: his being is in that; he declares that abroad, by act or speech as it may be, in declaring himself abroad. His life, as we said before, is a piece of the everlasting heart of Nature herself: all men's life is,—but the weak many know not the fact, and are untrue to it, in most times; the strong few are strong, heroic, perennial, because it cannot be hidden from them. The Man of Letters, like every Hero, is there to proclaim this in such sort as he can. Intrinsically it is the same function which the old generations named a man

---

[1] This is the title of the published lectures, originally delivered at London, May 1840, on the hero as divinity, as prophet, as poet, as priest, as man of letters, and as king.
[2] Reference to the widespread piracy of books whereby the author lost all return for his work.

[3] This high estimate of the role of the man of letters was by no means peculiar to Carlyle. It was prevalent both in England and on the Continent, and the man of letters was often regarded in the light of a prophet. See the next paragraphs.

Prophet, Priest, Divinity for doing; which all manner of Heroes, by speech or by act, are sent into the world to do.

Fichte the German Philosopher delivered, some forty years ago at Erlangen, a highly remarkable Course of Lectures on this subject: *"Ueber das Wesen des Gelehrten,* On the Nature of the Literary Man." Fichte, in conformity with the Transcendental Philosophy, of which he was a distinguished teacher, declares first: That all things which we see or work with in this Earth, especially we ourselves and all persons, are as a kind of vesture or sensuous Appearance: that under all there lies, as the essence of them, what he calls the "Divine Idea of the World"; this is the Reality which "lies at the bottom of all Appearance." To the mass of men no such Divine Idea is recognisable in the world; they live merely, says Fichte, among the superficialities, practicalities and shows of the world, not dreaming that there is anything divine under them. But the Man of Letters is sent hither specially that he may discern for himself, and make manifest to us, this same Divine Idea; in every new generation it will manifest itself in a new dialect; and he is there for the purpose of doing that. Such is Fichte's phraseology; with which we need not quarrel. It is his way of naming what I here, by other words, am striving imperfectly to name; what there is at present no name for: The unspeakable Divine Significance, full of splendour, of wonder and terror, that lies in the being of every man, of every thing,—the Presence of the God who made every man and thing. Mahomet taught this in his dialect; Odin in his: it is the thing which all thinking hearts, in one dialect or another, are here to teach.

Fichte calls the Man of Letters, therefore, a Prophet, or as he prefers to phrase it, a Priest, continually unfolding the Godlike to men: Men of Letters are a perpetual Priesthood, from age to age, teaching all men that a God is still present in their life; that all "Appearance," whatsoever we see in the world, is but as a vesture for the "Divine Idea of the World," for "that which lies at the bottom of Appearance." In the true Literary Man there is thus ever, acknowledged or not by the world, a sacredness: he is the light of the world; the world's Priest;—guiding it, like a sacred Pillar of Fire, in its dark pilgrimage through the waste of Time. Fichte discriminates with sharp zeal the *true* Literary Man, what we here call the *Hero* as Man of Letters, from multitudes of false unheroic. Whoever lives not wholly in this Divine Idea, or living partially in it, struggles not, as for the one good, to live wholly in it, —he is, let him live where else he like, in what pomps and prosperities he like, no Literary Man; he is, says Fichte, a "Bungler, *Stümper."* Or at best, if he belong to the prosaic provinces, he may be a "Hodman";[4] Fichte even calls him elsewhere a "Nonentity," and has in short no mercy for him, no wish that *he* should continue happy among us! This is Fichte's notion of the Man of Letters. It means, in its own form, precisely what we here mean.

In this point of view, I consider that, for the last hundred years, by far the notablest of all Literary Men is Fichte's countryman, Goethe. To that man too, in a strange way, there was given what we may call a life in the Divine Idea of the World; vision of the inward divine mystery: and strangely, out of his Books, the world rises imaged once more as godlike, the workmanship and temple of a God. Illuminated all, not in fierce impure fire-splendour as of Mahomet,[5] but in mild celestial radiance;—really a Prophecy in these most unprophetic times; to my mind, by far the greatest, though one of the quietest, among all the great things that have come to pass in them. Our chosen specimen of the Hero as Literary Man would be this Goethe. And it were a very pleasant plan for me here to discourse of his heroism: for I consider him to be a true Hero; heroic in what he said and did, and perhaps still more in what he did not say and did not do; to me a noble spectacle: a great heroic ancient man, speaking and keeping silence as an ancient Hero, in the guise of a most modern, high-bred, high-cultivated Man of Letters! We have had no such spectacle; no man capable of affording such, for the last hundred-and-fifty years.

But at present, such is the general state of knowledge about Goethe, it were worse than useless to attempt speaking of him in this case. Speak as I might, Goethe, to the great majority of you, would remain problematic, vague; no

4 Here used to mean one who is capable only of unthinking manual labor.
5 In "The Hero as Prophet," Carlyle speaks of Mahomet as "a fiery mass of Life . . . to *kindle* the world."

impression but a false one could be realised. Him we must leave to future times. Johnson, Burns, Rousseau, three great figures from a prior time, from a far inferior state of circumstances, will suit us better here. Three men of the Eighteenth Century; the conditions of their life far more resemble what those of ours still are in England, than what Goethe's in Germany were. Alas, these men did not conquer like him; they fought bravely, and fell. They were not heroic bringers of the light, but heroic seekers of it. They lived under galling conditions; struggling as under mountains of impediment, and could not unfold themselves into clearness, or victorious interpretation of that "Divine Idea." It is rather the *Tombs* of three Literary Heroes that I have to show you. There are the monumental heaps, under which three spiritual giants lie buried. Very mournful, but also great and full of interest for us. We will linger by them for a while.

Complaint is often made, in these times, of what we call the disorganised condition of society: how ill many arranged forces of society fulfil their work; how many powerful forces are seen working in a wasteful, chaotic, altogether unarranged manner. It is too just a complaint, as we all know. But perhaps if we look at this of Books and the Writers of Books, we shall find here, as it were, the summary of all other disorganisation;—a sort of *heart*, from which, and to which, all other confusion circulates in the world! Considering what Book-writers do in the world, and what the world does with Bookwriters, I should say, It is the most anomalous thing the world at present has to show.—We should get into a sea far beyond sounding, did we attempt to give account of this: but we must glance at it for the sake of our subject. The worst element in the life of these three Literary Heroes was, that they found their business and position such a chaos. On the beaten road there is tolerable travelling; but it is sore work, and many have to perish, fashioning a path through the impassable!

Our pious Fathers, feeling well what importance lay in the speaking of man to men, founded churches, made endowments, regulations; everywhere in the civilised world there is a Pulpit, environed with all manner of complex dignified appurtenances and furtherances, that

therefrom a man with the tongue may, to best advantage, address his fellow-men. They felt that this was the most important thing; that without this there was no good thing. It is a right pious work, that of theirs; beautiful to behold! But now with the art of Writing, with the art of Printing, a total change has come over that business. The Writer of a Book, is not he a Preacher preaching not to this parish or that, on this day or that, but to all men in all times and places? Surely it is of the last importance that *he* do his work right, whoever do it wrong;—that the *eye* report not falsely, for then all the other members are astray! Well; how he may do his work, whether he do it right or wrong, or do it at all, is a point which no man in the world has taken the pains to think of. To a certain shopkeeper, trying to get some money for his books, if lucky, he is of some importance; to no other man of any. Whence he came, whither he is bound, by what ways he arrived, by what he might be furthered on his course, no one asks. He is an accident in society. He wanders like a wild Ishmaelite,[6] in a world of which he is as the spiritual light, either the guidance or the misguidance!

Certainly the Art of Writing is the most miraculous of all things man has devised. Odin's *Runes* were the first form of the work of a Hero;[7] *Books,* written words, are still miraculous *Runes,* the latest form! In Books lies the *soul* of the whole Past Time; the articulate audible voice of the Past, when the body and material substance of it has altogether vanished like a dream. Mighty fleets and armies, harbours and arsenals, vast cities, high-domed, many-engined,—they are precious, great: but what do they become? Agamemnon, the many Agamemnons, Pericleses, and their Greece;[8] all is gone now to some ruined fragments, dumb mournful wrecks and blocks: but the Books of Greece! There Greece, to every thinker, still very literally lives; can be called-up

---

6 The Biblical image of the lonely Ishmael in the desert was a favorite with Carlyle.

7 In "The Hero as Divinity" Carlyle suggests that Odin was "the inventor of Letters" and defines runes as "the Scandinavian Alphabet."

8 Agamemnon was the legendary leader of the Greeks in the war against Troy, and Pericles was a great statesman and orator in Athens (fifth century B.C.). As men of action rather than men of letters, they left behind them, according to Carlyle, nothing but ruined fragments.

again into life. No magic *Rune* is stranger than a Book. All that Mankind has done, thought, gained or been: it is lying as in magic preservation in the pages of Books. They are the chosen possession of men.

Do not Books still accomplish *miracles,* as *Runes* were fabled to do? They persuade men. Not the wretchedest circulating-library novel, which foolish girls thumb and con in remote villages, but will help to regulate the actual practical weddings and households of those foolish girls. So "Celia" felt, so "Clifford"[9] acted: the foolish Theorem of Life, stamped into those young brains, comes out as a solid Practice one day. Consider whether any *Rune* in the wildest imagination of Mythologist ever did such wonders as, on the actual firm Earth, some Books have done! What built St. Paul's Cathedral? Look at the heart of the matter, it was that divine Hebrew Book,—the word partly of the man Moses, an outlaw tending his Midianitish herds, four-thousand years ago, in the wilderness of Sinai![10] It is the strangest of things, yet nothing is truer. With the art of Writing, of which Printing is a simple, an inevitable and comparatively insignificant corollary, the true reign of miracles for mankind commenced. It related, with a wondrous new contiguity and perpetual closeness, the Past and Distant with the Present in time and place; all times and all places with this our actual Here and Now. All things were altered for men; all modes of important work of men: teaching, preaching, governing, and all else.

To look at Teaching, for instance. Universities are a notable, respectable product of the modern ages. Their existence too is modified, to the very basis of it, by the existence of Books. Universities arose while there were yet no Books procurable; while a man, for a single Book, had to give an estate of land. That, in those circumstances, when a man had some knowledge to communicate, he should do it by gathering the learners round him, face to face, was a necessity for him. If you wanted to know what Abelard knew, you must go and listen to Abelard.[11]

Thousands, as many as thirty-thousand, went to hear Abelard and that metaphysical theology of his. And now for any other teacher who had also something of his own to teach, there was a great convenience opened: so many thousands eager to learn were already assembled yonder; of all places the best place for him was that. For any third teacher it was better still; and grew ever the better, the more teachers there came. It only needed now that the King took notice of this new phenomenon; combined or agglomerated the various schools into one school; gave it edifices, privileges, encouragements, and named it *Universitas,* or School of all Sciences: the University of Paris, in its essential characters, was there. The model of all subsequent Universities; which down even to these days, for six centuries now, have gone on to found themselves. Such, I conceive, was the origin of Universities.

It is clear, however, that with this simple circumstance, facility of getting Books, the whole conditions of the business from top to bottom were changed. Once invent Printing, you metamorphosed all Universities, or superseded them! The Teacher needed not now to gather men personally round him, that he might *speak* to them what he knew: print it in a Book, and all learners far and wide, for a trifle, had it each at his own fireside, much more effectually to learn it!—Doubtless there is still peculiar virtue in Speech; even writers of Books may still, in some circumstances, find it convenient to speak also,— witness our present meeting here! There is, one would say, and must ever remain while man has a tongue, a distinct province for Speech as well as for Writing and Printing. In regard to all things this must remain: to Universities among others. But the limits of the two have nowhere yet been pointed out, ascertained; much less put in practice: the University which would completely take-in that great new fact, of the existence of Printed Books, and stand on a clear footing for the Nineteenth Century as the Paris one did for the Thirteenth, has not yet come into existence. If we think of it, all that a University, or final highest School can do for us, is still but what the first School began doing,—teach us to *read.* We learn to *read,* in various languages, in various sciences; we learn the alphabet and letters of all manner of Books. But the place where we are to get knowledge, even theoretic

---

9 Stock figures of the sentimental novel.
10 The word of Moses embodied in the Old Testament is part of the Christian religion, of which St. Paul's is a temple.
11 Peter Abelard (1079–1142), famous philosopher and teacher at the University of Paris.

knowledge, is the Books themselves! It depends on what we read, after all manner of Professors have done their best for us. The true University of these days is a Collection of Books.

But to the Church itself, as I hinted already, all is changed, in its preaching, in its working, by the introduction of Books. The Church is the working recognised Union of our Priests or Prophets, of those who by wise teaching guide the souls of men. While there was no Writing, even while there was no Easy-writing or *Printing,* the preaching of the voice was the natural sole method of performing this. But now with Books!—He that can write a true Book, to persuade England, is not he the Bishop and Archbishop, the Primate of England and of All England? I many a time say, the writers of Newspapers, Pamphlets, Poems, Books, those *are* the real working effective Church of a modern country. Nay not only our preaching, but even our worship, is not it too accomplished by means of Printed Books? The noble sentiment which a gifted soul has clothed for us in melodious words, which brings melody into our hearts,—is not this essentially, if we will understand it, of the nature of worship? There are many, in all countries, who, in this confused time, have no other method of worship. He who, in any way, shows us better than we knew before that a lily of the fields is beautiful, does he not show it us as an effluence of the Fountain of all Beauty; as the *handwriting,* made visible there, of the great Maker of the Universe? He has sung for us, made us sing with him, a little verse of a sacred Psalm. Essentially so. How much more he who sings, who says, or in any way brings home to our heart the noble doings, feelings, darings and endurances of a brother man! He has verily touched our hearts as with a live coal *from the altar.* Perhaps there is no worship more authentic.

Literature, so far as it is Literature, is an "apocalypse of Nature," a revealing of the "open secret." It may well enough be named, in Fichte's style, a "continuous revelation" of the Godlike in the Terrestrial and Common. The Godlike does ever, in very truth, endure there; is brought out, now in this dialect, now in that, with various degrees of clearness: all true gifted Singers and Speakers are, consciously or unconsciously, doing so. The dark stormful indigna-

tion of a Byron, so wayward and perverse, may have touches of it; nay the withered mockery of a French sceptic,[12]—his mockery of the False, a love and worship of the True. How much more the sphere-harmony of a Shakspeare, of a Goethe; the cathedral-music of a Milton! They are something too, those humble genuine lark-notes of a Burns,—skylark, starting from the humble furrow,[13] far overhead into the blue depths, and singing to us so genuinely there! For all true singing is of the nature of worship; as indeed all true *working* may be said to be,[14]—whereof such *singing* is but the record, and fit melodious representation, to us. Fragments of a real "Church Liturgy" and "Body of Homilies," strangely disguised from the common eye, are to be found weltering in that huge froth-ocean of Printed Speech we loosely call Literature! Books are our Church too.

Or turning now to the Government of men. Witenagemote,[15] old Parliament, was a great thing. The affairs of the nation were there deliberated and decided; what we were to *do* as a nation. But does not, though the name Parliament subsists, the parliamentary debate go on now, everywhere and at all times, in a far more comprehensive way, *out* of Parliament altogether? Burke said there were Three Estates in Parliament; but, in the Reporters' Gallery yonder, there sat a *Fourth Estate* more important far than they all.[16] It is not a figure of speech, or a witty saying; it is a literal fact,—very momentous to us in these times. Literature is our Parliament too. Printing, which comes necessarily out of Writing, I say often, is equivalent to Democracy: invent Writing, Democracy is inevitable. Writing brings Printing; brings universal everyday extempore Printing, as we see at present. Whoever can speak, speaking now to the whole nation, becomes a power, a branch of government, with inalienable weight in law-making, in all acts of authority. It matters not what rank he has, what revenues or garnitures: the requisite

---

12 A characteristic reference to Voltaire.

13 The image echoes that in Burns's poem "To a Mountain Daisy," lines 7–12.

14 Compare Carlyle's glorification of work at the close of "The Everlasting Yea."

15 The Anglo-Saxon Parliament.

16 The three estates were by tradition the nobility, the clergy, and the people. At the time of the French Revolution the press came to be known as "The Fourth Estate."

thing is, that he have a tongue which others will listen to; this and nothing more is requisite. The nation is governed by all that has tongue in the nation: Democracy is virtually *there*. Add only, that whatsoever power exists will have itself, by and by, organised; working secretly under bandages, obscurations, obstructions, it will never rest till it get to work free, unencumbered, visible to all. Democracy virtually extant will insist on becoming palpably extant.—

On all sides, are we not driven to the conclusion that, of the things which man can do or make here below, by far the most momentous, wonderful and worthy are the things we call Books! Those poor bits of rag-paper with black ink on them;—from the Daily Newspaper to the sacred Hebrew Book, what have they not done, what are they not doing!—For indeed, whatever be the outward form of the thing (bits of paper, as we say, and black ink), is it not verily, at bottom, the highest act of man's faculty that produces a Book? It is the *Thought* of man; the true thaumaturgic virtue; by which man works all things whatsoever. All that he does, and brings to pass, is the vesture of a Thought. This London City, with all its houses, palaces, steam-engines, cathedrals, and huge immeasurable traffic and tumult, what is it but a Thought, but millions of Thoughts made into One;—a huge immeasurable Spirit of a Thought, embodied in brick, in iron, smoke, dust, Palaces, Parliaments, Hackney Coaches, Katherine Docks, and the rest of it! Not a brick was made but some man had to *think* of the making of that brick.—The thing we called "bits of paper with traces of black ink," is the *purest* embodiment a Thought of man can have. No wonder it is, in all ways, the activest and noblest.

All this, of the importance and supreme importance of the Man of Letters in modern Society, and how the Press is to such a degree superseding the Pulpit, the Senate, the *Senatus Academicus*[17] and much else, has been admitted for a good while; and recognised often enough, in late times, with a sort of sentimental triumph and wonderment. It seems to me, the Sentimental by and by will have to give place to the Practical. If Men of Letters *are* so incalculably influential, actually performing such work for us

from age to age, and even from day to day, then I think we may conclude that Men of Letters will not always wander like unrecognised unregulated Ishmaelites among us! Whatsoever thing, as I said above, has virtual unnoticed power will cast-off its wrappages, bandages, and step-forth one day with palpably articulated, universally visible power. That one man wear the clothes, and take the wages, of a function which is done by quite another:[18] there can be no profit in this; this is not right, it is wrong. And yet, alas, the *making* of it right,—what a business, for long times to come! Sure enough, this that we call Organisation of the Literary Guild is still a great way off, encumbered with all manner of complexities. If you asked me what were the best possible organisation for the Men of Letters in modern society; the arrangement of furtherance and regulation, grounded the most accurately on the actual facts of their position and of the world's position,—I should beg to say that the problem far exceeded my faculty! It is not one man's faculty; it is that of many successive men turned earnestly upon it, that will bring-out even an approximate solution. What the best arrangement were, none of us could say. But if you ask, Which is the worst? I answer: This which we now have, that Chaos should sit umpire in it;[19] this is the worst. To the best, or any good one, there is yet a long way.

One remark I must not omit, That royal or parliamentary grants of money are by no means the chief thing wanted! To give our Men of Letters stipends, endowments and all furtherance of cash, will do little towards the business. On the whole, one is weary of hearing about the omnipotence of money. I will say rather that, for a genuine man, it is no evil to be poor; that there ought to be Literary Men poor,—to show whether they are genuine or not! Mendicant Orders, bodies of good men doomed to *beg*, were instituted in the Christian Church; a most natural and even necessary development of the spirit of Christianity. It was itself founded on

---

17 The governing body of a university.

18 A restatement of the earlier proposition that writers are now doing work for which the clergy, the politicians, and the professors are receiving the credit and the remuneration.

19 Cf. Milton's *Paradise Lost*, II, 907–8:

"Chaos umpire sits
And by decision more embroils the fray."

Poverty, on Sorrow, Contradiction, Crucifixion, every species of worldly Distress and Degradation. We may say, that he who has not known those things, and learned from them the priceless lessons they have to teach, has missed a good opportunity of schooling. To beg, and go barefoot, in coarse woollen cloak with a rope round your loins, and be despised of all the world, was no beautiful business;—nor an honourable one in any eye, till the nobleness of those who did so had made it honoured of some!

Begging is not in our course at the present time: but for the rest of it, who will say that a Johnson is not perhaps the better for being poor? It is needful for him, at all rates, to know that outward profit, that success of any kind is *not* the goal he has to aim at. Pride, vanity, ill-conditioned egoism of all sorts, are bred in his heart, as in every heart; need, above all, to be cast-out of his heart,—to be, with whatever pangs, torn-out of it, cast-forth from it, as a thing worthless. Byron, born rich and noble, made-out even less than Burns, poor and plebeian. Who knows but, in that same "best possible organisation" as yet far off, Poverty may still enter as an important element? What if our Men of Letters, men setting-up to be Spiritual Heroes, were still *then*, as they now are, a kind of "involuntary monastic order"; bound still to this same ugly Poverty,—till they had tried what was in it too, till they had learned to make it too do for them! Money, in truth, can do much, but it cannot do all. We must know the province of it, and confine it there; and even spurn it back, when it wishes to get farther.

Besides, were the money-furtherances, the proper season for them, the fit assigner of them, all settled,—how is the Burns to be recognized that merits these? He must pass through the ordeal, and prove himself. *This* ordeal; this wild welter of a chaos which is called Literary Life: this too is a kind of ordeal! There is clear truth in the idea that a struggle from the lower classes of society, towards the upper regions and rewards of society, must ever continue. Strong men are born there, who ought to stand elsewhere than there. The manifold, inextricably complex, universal struggle of these constitutes, and must constitute, what is called the progress of society. For Men of Letters, as for all other sorts of men. How to regulate that struggle?

There is the whole question. To leave it as it is, at the mercy of blind Chance; a whirl of distracted atoms, one cancelling the other; one of the thousand arriving saved, nine-hundred-and-ninety-nine lost by the way; your royal Johnson languishing inactive in garrets, or harnessed to the yoke of Printer Cave;[20] your Burns dying broken-hearted as a Gauger;[21] your Rousseau driven into mad exasperation, kindling French Revolutions by his paradoxes:[22] this, as we said, is clearly enough the *worst* regulation. The *best*, alas, is far from us!

And yet there can be no doubt but it is coming; advancing on us, as yet hidden in the bosom of centuries: this is a prophecy one can risk. For so soon as men get to discern the importance of a thing, they do infallibly set about arranging it, facilitating, forwarding it; and rest not till, in some approximate degree, they have accomplished that. I say, of all Priesthoods, Aristocracies, Governing Classes at present extant in the world, there is no class comparable for importance to that Priesthood of the Writers of Books. This is a fact which he who runs may read,—and draw inferences from. "Literature will take care of itself," answered Mr. Pitt,[23] when applied-to for some help for Burns. "Yes," adds Mr. Southey, "it will take care of itself; *and of you too,* if you do not look to it!"

The result to individual Men of Letters is not the momentous one; they are but individuals, an infinitesimal fraction of the great body; they can struggle on, and live or else die, as they have been wont. But it deeply concerns the whole society, whether it will set its *light* on high places, to walk thereby; or trample it under foot, and scatter it in all ways of wild waste (not without conflagration), as heretofore! Light is the one thing wanted for the world. Put wisdom in the head of the world, the world will fight its battle victoriously, and be the best world man can make it. I call this anomaly of a disorganic Literary Class the heart of all other anomalies, at once product and parent; some good

---

20 Cave was the editor and owner of the *Gentleman's Magazine,* to which Johnson was a contributor during his early impoverished years in London.
21 Excise officer.
22 The reference is probably to his *Social Contract* (1762), a plea for democracy.
23 The younger William Pitt, Prime Minister of England from 1783 to 1801 and from 1804 to 1806.

arrangement for that would be as the *punctum saliens*[24] of a new vitality and just arrangement for all. Already, in some European countries, in France, in Prussia, one traces some beginnings of an arrangement for the Literary Class; indicating the gradual possiblity of such. I believe that it is possible; that it will have to be possible.

By far the most interesting fact I hear about the Chinese is one on which we cannot arrive at clearness, but which excites endless curiosity even in the dim state: this namely, that they do attempt to make their Men of Letters their Governors! It would be rash to say, one understood how this was done, or with what degree of success it was done. All such things must be very *unsuccessful;* yet a small degree of success is precious; the very attempt how precious! There does seem to be, all over China, a more or less active search everywhere to discover the men of talent that grow up in the young generation. Schools there are for every one: a foolish sort of training, yet still a sort. The youths who distinguish themselves in the lower school are promoted into favourable stations in the higher, that they may still more distinguish themselves,—forward and forward: it appears to be out of these that the Official Persons, and incipient Governors, are taken. These are they whom they *try* first, whether they can govern or not. And surely with the best hope: for they are the men that have already shown intellect. Try them: they have not governed or administered as yet; perhaps they cannot; but there is no doubt they *have* some Understanding,—without which no man can! Neither is Understanding a *tool,* as we are too apt to figure; "it is a *hand* which can handle any tool." Try these men: they are of all others the best worth trying.—Surely there is no kind of government, constitution, revolution, social apparatus or arrangement, that I know of in this world, so promising to one's scientific curiosity as this. The man of intellect at the top of affairs: this is the aim of all constitutions and revolutions, if they have any aim. For the man of true intellect, as I assert and believe always, is the noble-hearted man withal, the true, just, humane and valiant man. Get *him* for governor, all is got; fail to get him, though you had Con-

stitutions plentiful as blackberries, and a Parliament in every village, there is nothing yet got!—

These things look strange, truly; and are not such as we commonly speculate upon. But we are fallen into strange times; these things will require to be speculated upon; to be rendered practicable, to be in some way put in practice. These, and many others. On all hands of us, there is the announcement, audible enough, that the old Empire of Routine has ended; that to say a thing has long been, is no reason for its continuing to be. The things which have been are fallen into decay, are fallen into incompetence; large masses of mankind, in every society of our Europe, are no longer capable of living at all by the things which have been. When millions of men can no longer by their utmost exertion gain food for themselves, and "the third man for thirty-six weeks each year is short of third-rate potatoes,"[25] the things which have been must decidedly prepare to alter themselves!—I will now quit this of the organisation of Men of Letters.

Alas, the evil that pressed heaviest on those Literary Heroes of ours[26] was not the want of organisation for Men of Letters, but a far deeper one; out of which, indeed, this and so many other evils for the Literary Man, and for all men, had, as from their fountain, taken rise. That our Hero as Man of Letters had to travel without highway, companionless, through an inorganic chaos,—and to leave his own life and faculty lying there, as a partial contribution towards *pushing* some highway through it: this, had not his faculty itself been so perverted and paralysed, he might have put-up with, might have considered to be but the common lot of Heroes. His fatal misery was the *spiritual paralysis,* so we may name it, of the Age in which his life lay; whereby his life too, do what he might, was half-paralysed! The Eighteenth was a *Scepti-*

---

24 A point from which to spring into action.

25 Carlyle is quoting from memory his own essay on "Chartism," chap. 4: "Ireland has near seven millions of working people, the third unit of whom . . . has not for thirty weeks each year as many third-rate potatoes as will suffice him."

26 Carlyle switches here from consideration of men of letters in general to specific observations about the three writers he has chosen to discuss and the age in which they lived. The following paragraphs provide a summary of Carlyle's scornful reaction to the eighteenth century.

cal Century; in which little word there is a whole Pandora's Box[27] of miseries. Scepticism means not intellectual Doubt alone, but moral Doubt; all sorts of *in*fidelity, insincerity, spiritual paralysis. Perhaps, in few centuries that one could specify since the world began, was a life of Heroism more difficult for a man. That was not an age of Faith,—an age of Heroes! The very possibility of Heroism had been, as it were, formally abnegated in the minds of all. Heroism was gone forever; Triviality, Formulism and Common-place were come forever. The "age of miracles" had been, or perhaps had not been; but it was not any longer. An effete world; wherein Wonder, Greatness, Godhood could not now dwell;—in one word, a godless world!

How mean, dwarfish are their ways of thinking, in this time,—compared not with the Christian Shakspeares and Miltons, but with the old Pagan Skalds,[28] with any species of believing men! The living TREE Igdrasil,[29] with the melodious prophetic waving of its world-wide boughs, deep-rooted as Hela, has died-out into the clanking of a World-MACHINE. "Tree" and "Machine": contrast these two things. I, for my share, declare the world to be no machine! I say that it does *not* go by wheel-and-pinion "motives," self-interests, checks, balances; that there is something far other in it than the clank of spinning-jennies, and parliamentary majorities; and, on the whole, that it is not a machine at all!—The old Norse Heathen had a truer notion of God's-world than these poor Machine-Sceptics: the old Heathen Norse were *sincere*[30] men. But for these poor Sceptics there was no sincerity, no truth. Half-truth and hearsay was called truth. Truth, for most men, meant plausibility; to be measured by the number of votes you could get. They had lost any notion that sincerity was possible, or of what sincerity was. How many Plausibilities asking, with unaffected surprise and the air of offended virtue, What! am not I sincere? Spiritual Paralysis, I say, nothing left but a Mechanical

life, was the characteristic of that century. For the common man, unless happily he stood *below* his century and belonged to another prior one, it was impossible to be a Believer, a Hero; he lay buried, unconscious, under these baleful influences. To the strongest man, only with infinite struggle and confusion was it possible to work himself half-loose; and lead as it were, in an enchanted, most tragical way, a spiritual death-in-life, and be a Half-Hero!

Scepticism is the name we give to all this; as the chief symptom, as the chief origin of all this. Concerning which so much were to be said! It would take many Discourses, not a small fraction of one Discourse, to state what one feels about that Eighteenth Century and its ways. As indeed this, and the like of this, which we now call Scepticism, is precisely the black malady and life-foe, against which all teaching and discoursing since man's life began has directed itself: the battle of Belief against Unbelief is the never-ending battle! Neither is it in the way of crimination that one would wish to speak. Scepticism, for that century, we must consider as the decay of old ways of believing, the preparation afar off for new better and wider ways,—an inevitable thing. We will not blame men for it; we will lament their hard fate. We will understand that destruction of old *forms* is not destruction of everlasting *substances;* that Scepticism, as sorrowful and hateful as we see it, is not an end but a beginning.

The other day speaking, without prior purpose that way, of Bentham's theory of man and man's life,[31] I chanced to call it a more beggarly one than Mahomet's. I am bound to say, now when it is once uttered, that such is my deliberate opinion. Not that one would mean offence against the man Jeremy Bentham, or those who respect and believe him. Bentham himself, and even the creed of Bentham, seems to me com-

---

27 A casket in Greek mythology, which when opened by Pandora released upon the world innumerable mental and physical ills.

28 Ancient Scandinavian poets.

29 The skalds sang of "the Ash-tree of Existence [which] has its roots deep-down in the kingdoms of Hela or Death; its trunk reaches up heaven-high, spreads its boughs over the whole Universe." ("The Hero as Divinity")

30 Carlyle's use of this word tends to be personal. In general, he equates sincerity with belief and insincerity with skepticism. Cf. "A world all sincere, a believing world." ("The Hero as Priest")

31 In his lecture on "The Hero as Prophet," where he delivered the following blast: "Benthamee Utility, virtue by Profit and Loss; reducing this God's-world to a dead brute Steam-engine, the infinite celestial Soul of Man to a kind of Hay-balance for weighing hay and thistles on, pleasures and pains on. . . ." Cf. note 8 to Book II, chap. 7 of *Sartor Resartus.*

paratively worthy of praise. It is a determinate *being* what all the world, in a cowardly half-and-half manner, was tending to be. Let us have the crisis; we shall either have death or the cure. I call this gross, steam-engine Utilitarianism an approach towards new Faith. It was a laying-down of cant; a saying to oneself: "Well then, this world is a dead iron machine, the god of it Gravitation and selfish Hunger; let us see what, by checking and balancing, and good adjustment of tooth and pinion, can be made of it!" Benthamism has something complete, manful, in such fearless committal of itself to what it finds true; you may call it Heroic, though a Heroism with its *eyes* put out! It is the culminating point, and fearless ultimatum, of what lay in the half-and-half state, pervading man's whole existence in that Eighteenth Century. It seems to me, all deniers of Godhood, and all lip-believers of it, are bound to be Benthamites, if they have courage and honesty. Benthamism is an *eyeless* Heroism: the Human Species, like a hapless blinded Samson grinding in the Philistine Mill, clasps convulsively the pillars of its Mill; brings huge ruin down, but ultimately deliverance withal.[32] Of Bentham I meant to say no harm.

But this I do say, and would wish all men to know and lay to heart, that he who discerns nothing but Mechanism in the Universe has in the fatalest way missed the secret of the Universe altogether. That all Godhood should vanish out of men's conception of this Universe seems to me precisely the most brutal error,—I will not disparage Heathenism by calling it a Heathen error,—that men could fall into. It is not true; it is false at the very heart of it. A man who thinks so will think *wrong* about all things in the world; this original sin will vitiate all other conclusions he can form. One might call it the most lamentable of Delusions,—not forgetting Witchcraft itself! Witchcraft worshipped at least a living Devil; but this worships a dead iron Devil; no God, not even a Devil!—Whatsoever is noble, divine, inspired, drops thereby out of life. There remains everywhere in life a despicable *caput-mortuum;*[33] the mechanical hull, all

soul fled out of it. How can a man act heroically? The "Doctrine of Motives" will teach him that it is, under more or less disguise, nothing but a wretched love of Pleasure, fear of Pain; that Hunger, of applause, of cash, of whatsoever victual it may be, is the ultimate fact of man's life. Atheism, in brief;—which does indeed frightfully punish itself. The man, I say, is become spiritually a paralytic man; this godlike Universe a dead mechanical steam-engine, all working by motives, checks, balances, and I know not what; wherein, as in the detestable belly of some Phalaris'-Bull[34] of his own contriving, he the poor Phalaris sits miserably dying!

Belief I define to be the healthy act of a man's mind. It is a mysterious indescribable process, that of getting to believe;—indescribable, as all vital acts are. We have our mind given us, not that it may cavil and argue, but that it may see into something, give us clear belief and understanding about something, whereon we are then to proceed to act. Doubt, truly, is not itself a crime. Certainly we do not rush out, clutch-up the first thing we find, and straightway believe that! All manner of doubt, inquiry, σκέψις as it is named, about all manner of objects, dwells in every reasonable mind. It is the mystic working of the mind, on the object it is *getting* to know and believe. Belief comes out of all this, above ground, like the tree from its hidden *roots.* But now if, even on common things, we require that a man keep his doubts *silent,* and not babble of them till they in some measure become affirmations or denials; how much more in regard to the highest things, impossible to speak-of in words at all! That a man parade his doubt, and get to imagine that debating and logic (which means at best only the manner of *telling* us your thought, your belief or disbelief, about a thing) is the triumph and true work of what intellect he has: alas, this is as if you should *overturn* the tree, and instead of green boughs, leaves and fruits, show us ugly taloned roots turned-up into the air,—and no growth, only death and misery going-on![35]

---

32 Samson, blinded by the Philistines and set to grinding corn, seized the pillars of the temple and brought the building crashing to earth (Judges 16).—There is again a play upon the name of the Utilitarian thinker, James Mill.   33 Skull.

34 A brazen bull made for the Sicilian tyrant Phalaris (sixth century B.C.), in which he roasted his victims.
35 Carlyle believed, with Coleridge and the German transcendentalists, that the triumph and true work of the intellect was not logic but intuition or "pure reason."

For the Scepticism, as I said, is not intellectual only; it is moral also; a chronic atrophy and disease of the whole soul. A man lives by believing something; not by debating and arguing about many things. A sad case for him when all that he can manage to believe is something he can button in his pocket, and with one or the other organ eat and digest! Lower than that he will not get. We call those ages in which he gets so low the mournfulest, sickest and meanest of all ages. The world's heart is palsied, sick: how can any limb of it be whole? Genuine Acting ceases in all departments of the world's work; dextrous Similitude of Acting begins. The world's wages are pocketed, the world's work is not done. Heroes have gone-out; Quacks have come-in. Accordingly, what Century, since the end of the Roman world, which also was a time of scepticism, simulacra and universal decadence, so abounds with Quacks as that Eighteenth? Consider them, with their tumid sentimental vapouring about virtue, benevolence,—the wretched Quack-squadron, Cagliostro[36] at the head of them! Few men were without quackery; they had got to consider it a necessary ingredient and amalgam for truth. Chatham,[37] our brave Chatham himself, comes down to the House, all wrapt and bandaged; he "has crawled out in great bodily suffering," and so on;—*forgets,* says Walpole, that he is acting the sick man; in the fire of debate, snatches his arm from the sling, and oratorically swings and brandishes it! Chatham himself lives the strangest mimetic life, half-hero, half-quack, all along. For indeed the world is full of dupes; and you have to gain the *world's* suffrage! How the duties of the world will be done in that case, what quantities of error, which means failure, which means sorrow and misery, to some and to many, will gradually accumulate in all provinces of the world's business, we need not compute.

It seems to me, you lay your finger here on the heart of the world's maladies, when you call it a Sceptical World. An insincere world; a godless untruth of a world! It is out of this, as I consider, that the whole tribe of social pestilences, French Revolutions, Chartisms,[38] and what not, have derived their being,—their chief necessity to be. This must alter. Till this alter, nothing can beneficially alter. My one hope of the world, my inexpugnable consolation in looking at the miseries of the world, is that this is altering. Here and there one does now find a man who knows, as of old, that this world is a Truth, and no Plausibility and Falsity; that he himself is alive, not dead or paralytic; and that the world is alive, instinct with Godhood, beautiful and awful, even as in the beginning of days! One man once knowing this, many men, all men, must by and by come to know it. It lies there clear, for whosoever will take the *spectacles* off his eyes and honestly look, to know! For such a man the Unbelieving Century, with its unblessed Products, is already past: a new century is already come. The old unblessed Products and Performances, as solid as they look, are Phantasms, preparing speedily to vanish. To this and the other noisy, very great-looking Simulacrum with the whole world huzzahing at its heels, he can say, composedly stepping aside: Thou art not *true;* thou art not extant, only semblant; go thy way!—Yes, hollow Formulism, gross Benthamism, and other unheroic atheistic Insincerity is visibly and even rapidly declining. An unbelieving Eighteenth Century is but an exception, —such as now and then occurs. I prophesy that the world will once more become *sincere;* a believing world; with *many* Heroes in it, a heroic world! It will then be a victorious world; never till then.

Or indeed what of the world and its victories? Men speak too much about the world. Each one of us here, let the world go how it will, and be victorious or not victorious, has he not a Life of his own to lead? One Life; a little gleam of Time between two Eternities; no second chance to us for evermore! It were well for *us* to live not as fools and simulacra, but as wise and realities. The world's being saved will not save us; nor the world's being lost destroy us.

---

[36] Count Cagliostro Palermo (1743–1795), a notorious charlatan who pretended to sell eternal youth.
[37] William Pitt the Elder (1708–1778). The incident is related by Horace Walpole (1717–1797) in his *Memoirs of the Reign of George the Third.*

[38] A movement which took its name from a charter drawn up by leaders of the workingmen embodying certain relatively moderate demands for popular rights. Carlyle discussed the movement at length in his tract "Chartism" in 1839. The agitation came to a climax in 1848, when the workers marched toward London to present a petition to Parliament but were repulsed by government troops and the leaders imprisoned or killed.

We should look to ourselves: there is great merit here in the "duty of staying at home"! And, on the whole, to say truth, I never heard of "worlds" being "saved" in any other way. That mania of saving worlds is itself a piece of the Eighteenth Century with its windy sentimentalism. Let us not follow it too far. For the saving of the *world* I will trust confidently to the Maker of the world; and look a little to my own saving, which I am more competent to!— In brief, for the world's sake, and for our own, we will rejoice greatly that Scepticism, Insincerity, Mechanical Atheism, with all their poison-dews, are going, and as good as gone.—

Now it was under such conditions, in those times of Johnson, that our Men of Letters had to live. Times in which there was properly no truth in life. Old truths had fallen nigh dumb; the new lay yet hidden, not trying to speak. That Man's Life here below was a Sincerity and Fact, and would for ever continue such, no new intimation, in that dusk of the world, had yet dawned. No intimation; not even any French Revolution,—which we define to be a Truth once more, though a Truth clad in hellfire! How different was the Luther's pilgrimage, with its assured goal,[39] from the Johnson's, girt with mere traditions, suppositions, grown now incredible, unintelligible! Mahomet's Formulas[40] were of "wood waxed and oiled," and could be *burnt* out of one's way: poor Johnson's were far more difficult to burn.—The strong man will ever find *work,* which means difficulty, pain, to the full measure of his strength. But to make-out a victory, in those circumstances of our poor Hero as Man of Letters, was perhaps more difficult than in any. Not obstruction, disorganisation, Bookseller Osborne and Fourpence-halfpenny a day;[41] not this alone; but the light of his own soul was taken from him. No landmark on the Earth; and, alas, what is that to having no loadstar in the Heaven! We need not wonder

that none of those Three men rose to victory.[42] That they fought truly is the highest praise. With a mournful sympathy we will contemplate, if not three living victorious Heroes, as I said, the Tombs of three fallen Heroes! They fell for us too; making a way for us. There are the mountains which they hurled abroad in their confused War of the Giants; under which, their strength and life spent, they now lie buried. . . .

from Past and Present

Book II, Chapter 2

ST. EDMUNDSBURY[1]

The *Burg*, Bury, or "Berry" as they call it, of St. Edmund is still a prosperous brisk Town; beautifully diversifying, with its clear brick houses, ancient clean streets, and twenty or fifteen thousand busy souls, the general grassy face of Suffolk; looking out right pleasantly, from its hill-slope, towards the rising Sun: and on the eastern edge of it, still runs, long, black and massive, a range of monastic ruins; into the wide internal spaces of which the stranger is admitted on payment of one shilling. Internal spaces laid out, at present, as a botanic garden. Here stranger or townsman, sauntering at his leisure amid these vast grim venerable ruins, may persuade himself that an Abbey of St. Edmundsbury did once exist; nay there is no doubt of it: see here the ancient massive Gateway, of architecture interesting to the eye of Dilettantism;[2] and farther on, that other ancient Gateway, now about to tumble, unless Dilettantism, in these very months, can subscribe money to cramp it and prop it!

Here, sure enough, is an Abbey; beautiful in the eye of Dilettantism. Giant Pedantry also will step in, with its huge *Dugdale* and other enormous *Monasticons*[3] under its arm, and cheer-

---

[39] Of the Reformation.

[40] The Formulas attacked by Mahomet were the contemporary idolatries. They could be *"burnt* out of one's way" because the originally sincere faith (now nothing but empty formulism) had been symbolized in wooden idols, rubbed with oil and wax.

[41] Dr. Johnson's restricted finances are constantly stressed by Boswell in his *Life,* where also is related Johnson's quarrel with Thomas Osborne, for whom he had prepared a *Catalogue of the Library of the Earl of Oxford.*

[42] Johnson, Rousseau, and Burns, whom Carlyle goes on to discuss after this preliminary essay.

[1] *Past and Present* was published in 1843. The whole of Book II, entitled "The Ancient Monk," is devoted to an account of life in the monastery of St. Edmundsbury. For its significance, see the introduction to Carlyle.

[2] One of the objects of Carlyle's attack in *Past and Present* is the lack of seriousness and responsibility on the part of the governing classes. "We must," he says "exchange our dilettantisms for sincerities."

[3] Sir William Dugdale, seventeenth-century English anti-

fully apprise you, That this was a very great Abbey, owner and indeed creator of St. Edmund's Town itself, owner of wide lands and revenues; nay that its lands were once a county of themselves; that indeed King Canute or Knut was very kind to it, and gave St. Edmund[4] his own gold crown off his head, on one occasion: for the rest, that the Monks were of such and such a genus, such and such a number; that they had so many carucates[5] of land in this hundred, and so many in that; and then farther that the large Tower or Belfry was built by such a one, and the smaller Belfry was built by &c., &c.—Till human nature can stand no more of it; till human nature desperately take refuge in forgetfulness, almost in flat disbelief of the whole business, Monks, Monastery, Belfries, Carucates and all! Alas, what mountains of dead ashes, wreck and burnt bones, does assiduous Pedantry dig up from the Past Time, and name it History, and Philosophy of History; till, as we say, the human soul sinks wearied and bewildered; till the Past Time seems all one infinite incredible grey void, without sun, stars, hearth-fires, or candlelight; dim offensive dust-whirlwinds filling universal Nature; and over your Historical Library, it is as if all the Titans had written for themselves: DRY RUBBISH SHOT[6] HERE!

And yet these grim old walls are not a dilettantism and dubiety; they are an earnest fact. It was a most real and serious purpose they were built for! Yes, another world it was, when these black ruins, white in their new mortar and fresh chiselling, first saw the sun as walls, long ago. Gauge not, with thy dilettante compasses, with that placid dilettante simper, the Heaven's-Watchtower of our Fathers, the fallen God's-Houses, the Golgotha[7] of true Souls departed!

Their architecture, belfries, land-carucates?

Yes,—and that is but a small item of the matter. Does it never give thee pause, this other strange item of it, that men then had a *soul*,—not by hearsay alone, and as a figure of speech; but as a truth that they *knew*, and practically went upon! Verily it was another world then. Their Missals[8] have become incredible, a sheer platitude, sayest thou? Yes, a most poor platitude; and even, if thou wilt, an idolatry and blasphemy, should anyone persuade *thee* to believe them, to pretend praying by them. But yet it is pity we had lost tidings of our souls:—actually we shall have to go in quest of them again, or worse in all ways will befall! A certain degree of soul, as Ben Jonson reminds us, is indispensable to keep the very body from destruction of the frightfullest sort; to "save us," says he, "the expense of *salt*."[9] Ben has known men who had soul enough to keep their body and five senses from becoming carrion, and save salt:—men, and also Nations. You may look in Manchester[10] Hunger-mobs and Corn-law Commons Houses, and various other quarters, and say whether either soul or else salt is not somewhat wanted at present!—

Another world, truly: and this present poor distressed world might get some profit by looking wisely into it, instead of foolishly. But at lowest, O dilettante friend, let us know always that it *was* a world, and not a void infinite of grey haze with phantasms swimming in it. These old St. Edmundsbury walls, I say, were not peopled with phantasms; but with men of flesh and blood, made altogether as we are. Had thou and I then been, who knows but we ourselves had taken refuge from an evil Time, and fled to dwell here, and meditate on an Eternity, in such fashion as we could? Alas, how like an old osseous fragment, a broken blackened shinbone of the old dead Ages, this black ruin looks out, not yet covered by the soil; still indicating what a once gigantic Life lies buried there! It is dead now, and dumb; but was alive once, and spake. For twenty generations, here was the earthly arena where painful[11] living men worked out their

---

quarian, author of a history of British monasteries, *Monasticon Anglicanum*. Carlyle takes many a sly dig at antiquarian pedantry in these chapters.
[4] Edmund, king of East Anglia from 855 to 870, was the owner of the land on which the monastery was built in his memory. He was killed by invading Danes. Because he had been a just man and a good landlord he became venerated as a saint, according to Carlyle. He was far from being a contemporary of Canute, who ruled England from 1017 to 1035.
[5] Measure of land signifying as much as could be tilled by an eight-ox plow in a year.
[6] Deposited.
[7] Cemetery.

---

[8] The books containing the prayers and ritual of the Mass.
[9] If we are without souls, we are no better than dead carrion and, therefore, will need salt to keep us from rotting.
[10] Manchester was the scene of particular hardship and unrest among the workers.
[11] Painstaking; i.e., serious, as opposed to dilettante.

life-wrestle,—looked at by Earth, by Heaven and Hell. Bells tolled to prayers; and men, of many humours, various thoughts, chanted vespers, matins;—and round the little islet of their life rolled forever (as round ours still rolls, though we are blind and deaf) the illimitable Ocean, tinting all things with *its* eternal hues and reflexes; making strange prophetic music! How silent now; all departed, clean gone. The World-Dramaturgist has written: *Exeunt.*[12] The devouring Time-Demons have made away with it all: and in its stead, there is either nothing; or what is worse, offensive universal dust-clouds, and grey eclipse of Earth and Heaven, from "dry rubbish shot here!"—

Truly it is no easy matter to get across the chasm of Seven Centuries, filled with such material. But here, of all helps, is not a Boswell the welcomest; even a small Boswell?[13] Veracity, true simplicity of heart, how valuable are these always! He that speaks what *is* really in him, will find men to listen, though under never such impediments. Even gossip, springing free and cheery from a human heart, this too is a kind of veracity and *speech;*—much preferable to pedantry and inane grey haze! Jocelin is weak and garrulous, but he is human. Through the thin watery gossip of our Jocelin, we do get some glimpses of that deep-buried Time; discern veritably, though in a fitful intermittent manner, these antique figures and their life-method, face to face! Beautifully, in our earnest loving glance, the old centuries melt from opaque to partially translucent, transparent here and there; and the void black Night, one finds, is but the summing-up of innumerable peopled luminous *Days.* Not parchment Chartularies,[14] Doctrines of the Constitution, O Dryasdust; not altogether, my erudite friend!—

Readers who please to go along with us into this poor *Jocelini Chronica* shall wander inconveniently enough, as in wintry twilight, through some poor stripped hazel-grove, rustling with foolish noises, and perpetually hindering

the eyesight; but across which, here and there, some real human figure is seen moving: very strange; whom we could hail if he would answer;[15]—and we look into a pair of eyes deep as our own, *imaging* our own, but all unconscious of us; to whom we for the time are become as spirits and invisibles!

Book II, Chapter 4

ABBOT HUGO

It is true, all things have two faces, a light one and a dark. It is true, in three centuries much imperfection accumulates; many an Ideal, monastic or other, shooting forth into practice as it can, grows to a strange enough Reality; and we have to ask with amazement, Is this your Ideal? For, alas, the Ideal always has to grow in the Real, and to seek out its bed and board there, often in a very sorry way. No beautifullest Poet is a Bird-of-Paradise, living on perfumes; sleeping in the ether with outspread wings. The Heroic, *independent* of bed and board, is found in Drury-Lane Theatre[16] only; to avoid disappointments, let us bear this in mind.

By the law of Nature, too, all manner of Ideals have their fatal limits and lot; their appointed periods, of youth, of maturity or perfection, of decline, degradation, and final death and disappearance. There is nothing born but has to die. Ideal monasteries, once grown real, do seek bed and board in this world; do find it more and more successfully; do get at length too intent on finding it, exclusively intent on that. They are then like diseased corpulent bodies fallen idiotic, which merely eat and sleep; *ready* for "dissolution,"[17] by a Henry the Eighth or some other. Jocelin's St. Edmundsbury is still far from this last dreadful state: but here too the reader will prepare himself to see an Ideal not sleeping in the ether like a bird-of-paradise, but roosting as the common wood-fowl do, in an imperfect, un-

---

12 Stage direction: "They go out."

13 I.e., a chatty day-by-day account, like Boswell's in his *Life of Johnson.* Just such an account of life in St. Edmundsbury was the source of Carlyle's information about the monastery, "the 'Chronicle,' or private Boswellean Notebook, of Jocelin, a certain old St. Edmundsbury Monk." The *Chronicle* covers the years 1173–1202.

14 Registers of charters.

15 This reflects the central nature of Carlyle's historiography—the imaginative realization of the past so that characters and events are vividly brought to life.

16 I.e., is a fiction, not a reality.

17 Carlyle is playing upon the word, using it in its primary meaning in connection with his image as well as in its political meaning with reference to the drastic action of Henry VIII in the mid-sixteenth century in suppressing the monasteries.

comfortable, more or less contemptible manner!—

Abbot Hugo, as Jocelin, breaking at once into the heart of the business, apprises us, had in those days grown old, grown rather blind, and his eyes were somewhat darkened, *aliquantulum caligaverunt oculi ejus.* He dwelt apart very much, in his *Talamus* or peculiar Chamber; got into the hands of flatterers, a set of mealy-mouthed persons who strove to make the passing hour easy for him,—for him easy, and for themselves profitable; accumulating in the distance mere mountains of confusion. Old Dominus Hugo sat inaccessible in this way, far in the interior, wrapped in his warm flannels and delusions; inaccessible to all voice of Fact; and bad grew ever worse with us. Not that our worthy old *Dominus Abbas* was inattentive to the divine offices, or to the maintenance of a devout spirit in us or in himself; but the Account-Books of the Convent fell into the frightfullest state, and Hugo's annual Budget grew yearly emptier, or filled with futile expectations, fatal deficit, wind and debts!

His one worldly care was to raise ready money; sufficient for the day is the evil thereof. And how he raised it: From usurious insatiable Jews; every fresh Jew sticking on him like a fresh horseleech, sucking his and our life out; crying continually, Give, give! Take one example instead of scores. Our *Camera*[18] having fallen into ruin, William the Sacristan received charge to repair it; strict charge, but no money; Abbot Hugo would, and indeed could, give him no fraction of money. The *Camera* in ruins and Hugo penniless and inaccessible, Willelmus Sacrista borrowed Forty Marcs (some Seven-and-twenty Pounds) of Benedict the Jew, and patched up our Camera again. But the means of repaying him? There were no means. Hardly could *Sacrista, Cellerarius,*[19] or any public officer, get ends to meet, on the indispensablest scale, with their shrunk allowances: ready money had vanished.

Benedict's Twenty-seven pounds grew rapidly at compound-interest; and at length, when it had amounted to a Hundred pounds, he, on a day of settlement, presents the account to Hugo himself. Hugo already owed him another Hundred of his own; and so here it has become Two Hundred! Hugo, in a fine frenzy, threatens to depose the Sacristan, to do this and do that; but, in the meanwhile, How to quiet your insatiable Jew? Hugo, for this couple of hundreds, grants the Jew his bond for Four hundred payable at the end of four years. At the end of four years there is, of course, still no money; and the Jew now gets a bond for Eight hundred and eighty pounds, to be paid by instalments, Four-score pounds every year. Here was a way of doing business!

Neither yet is this insatiable Jew satisfied or settled with: he had papers against us of "small debts fourteen years old"; his modest claim amounts finally to "Twelve hundred pounds besides interest";—and one hopes he never got satisfied in this world; one almost hopes he was one of those beleaguered Jews who hanged themselves in York Castle shortly afterwards, and had his usances and quittances and horseleech papers[20] summarily set fire to! For approximate justice will strive to accomplish itself; if not in one way, then in another. Jews, and also Christians and Heathens, who accumulate in this manner, though furnished with never so many parchments, do, at times, "get their grinder-teeth successively pulled out of their head, each day a new grinder," till they consent to disgorge again. A sad fact,—worth reflecting on.

Jocelin, we see, is not without secularity: Our *Dominus Abbas* was intent enough on the divine offices; but then his Account-Books—?— One of the things that strike us most, throughout, in Jocelin's *Chronicle,* and indeed in Eadmer's[21] *Anselm,* and other old monastic Books, written evidently by pious men, is this, That there is almost no mention whatever of "personal religion" in them; that the whole gist of their thinking and speculation seems to be the

---

18 Council chamber.
19 The monks in charge, respectively, of the room where the sacred utensils, vestments, etc. were kept, and of the wine cellar and other provisions.

20 Usances, literally, are periods of time allowed for the payment of foreign bills of exchange—here used for the documents involved; quittances are receipts; a horseleech is a rapacious person, here turned into an adjective modifying "papers" (cf. Proverbs 30:14–15).
21 Monk of Canterbury, intimate friend and biographer of Anselm, who was Archbishop of Canterbury from 1093 to 1109.

"privileges of our order," "strict exaction of our dues," "God's honour" (meaning the honour of our Saint), and so forth. Is not this singular? A body of men, set apart for perfecting and purifying their own souls, do not seem disturbed about that in any measure: the "Ideal" says nothing about its idea; says much about finding bed and board for itself! How is this?

Why, for one thing, bed and board are a matter very apt to come to speech: it is much easier to *speak* of them than of ideas; and they are sometimes much more pressing with some! Nay, for another thing, may not this religious reticence, in these devout good souls, be perhaps a merit, and sign of health in them? Jocelin, Eadmer, and such religious men, have as yet nothing of "Methodism";[22] no Doubt or even root of Doubt. Religion is not a diseased self-introspection, an agonizing inquiry: their duties are clear to them, the way of supreme good plain, indisputable, and they are travelling on it. Religion lies over them like an all-embracing heavenly canopy, like an atmosphere and life-element, which is not spoken of, which in all things is presupposed without speech. Is not serene or complete Religion the highest aspect of human nature; as serene Cant, or complete No-religion, is the lowest and miserablest? Between which two, all manner of earnest Methodisms, introspections, agonizing inquiries, never so morbid, shall play their respective parts, not without approbation.

But let any reader fancy himself one of the Brethren in St. Edmundsbury Monastery under such circumstances! How can a Lord Abbot, all stuck over with horseleeches of this nature, front the world? He is fast losing his life-blood, and the Convent will be as one of Pharaoh's lean kine.[23] Old monks of experience draw their hoods deeper down; careful what they say: the monk's first duty is obedience. Our Lord the King, hearing of such work, sends down his Almoner to make investigations: but what boots it? Abbot Hugo assembles us in Chapter; asks,

"If there is any complaint?" Not a soul of us dare answer, "Yes, thousands!" but we all stand silent, and the Prior even says that things are in a very comfortable condition. Whereupon old Abbot Hugo, turning to the royal messenger, says, "You see!"—and the business terminates in that way. I, as a brisk-eyed, noticing youth and novice, could not help asking of the elders, asking of Magister Samson in particular: Why he, well-instructed and a knowing man, had not spoken out, and brought matters to a bearing?[24] Magister Samson was Teacher of the Novices, appointed to breed us up to the rules, and I loved him well. "*Fili mi,*" answered Samson, "the burnt child shuns the fire. Dost thou not know, our Lord the Abbot sent me once to Acre in Norfolk, to solitary confinement and bread and water, already? The Hinghams, Hugo and Robert, have just got home from banishment for speaking. This is the hour of darkness: the hour when flatterers rule and are believed. *Videat Dominus,* let the Lord see, and judge."

In very truth, what could poor old Abbot Hugo do? A frail old man; and the Philistines were upon him,—that is to say, the Hebrews. He had nothing for it but to shrink away from them; get back into his warm flannels, into his warm delusions again. Happily, before it was quite too late, he bethought him of pilgriming to St. Thomas of Canterbury. He set out, with a fit train, in the autumn days of the year 1180; near Rochester City, his mule threw him, dislocated his poor kneepan, raised incurable inflammatory fever; and the poor old man got his dismissal from the whole coil at once. St. Thomas à Becket, though in a circuitous way, had *brought* deliverance! Neither Jew usurers, nor grumbling monks, nor other importunate despicability of men or mud-elements afflicted Abbot Hugo any more; but he dropped his rosaries, closed his account-books, closed his old eyes, and lay down into the long sleep. Heavy-laden hoary old Dominus Hugo, fare thee well!

One thing we cannot mention without a due thrill of horror: namely, that, in the empty exchequer of Dominus Hugo, there was not found one penny to distribute to the Poor that they might pray for his soul! By a kind of godsend, Fifty shillings did, in the very nick of time,

---

[22] Carlyle distrusted Methodism as a morbid kind of egoism, "with its eye forever turned on its own navel; asking itself with torturing anxiety of Hope and Fear, 'Am I right? am I wrong? Shall I be saved? shall I not be damned?'"

[23] The lean cattle seen by the king of Egypt in a dream, signifying seven years of poor harvests (Genesis 41:27–30).

[24] I.e., into the open.

fall due, or seem to fall due, from one of his Farmers (the *Firmarius de Palegrava*), and he paid it, and the Poor had it; though, alas, this too only *seemed* to fall due, and we had it to pay again afterwards. Dominus Hugo's apartments were plundered by his servants, to the last portable stool, in a few minutes after the breath was out of his body. Forlorn old Hugo, fare thee well forever.

Book II, Chapter 8

THE ELECTION

Accordingly[25] our Prior assembles us in Chapter; and, we adjuring him before God to do justly, nominates, not by our selection, yet with our assent, Twelve Monks, moderately satisfactory. Of whom are Hugo Third-Prior, Brother Dennis a venerable man, Walter the *Medicus*, Samson *Subsacrista,* and other esteemed characters,— though Willelmus *Sacrista*, of the red nose,[26] too is one. These shall proceed straightway to Waltham;[27] and there elect the Abbot as they may and can. Monks are sworn to obedience; must not speak too loud, under penalty of foot-gyves, limbo, and bread and water: yet monks too would know what it is they are obeying. The St. Edmundsbury Community has no hustings,[28] ballot-box, indeed no open voting: yet by various vague manipulations, pulse-feelings, we struggle to ascertain what its virtual aim is, and succeed better or worse.

This question, however, rises; alas, a quite preliminary question: Will the *Dominus Rex* allow us to choose freely? It is to be hoped! Well, if so, we agree to choose one of our own Convent. If not, if the *Dominus Rex* will force a stranger on us, we decide on demurring, the Prior and his Twelve shall demur: we can appeal, plead, remonstrate; appeal even to the Pope, but trust it will not be necessary. Then there is this other question, raised by Brother Samson: What if the Thirteen should not themselves be able to agree? Brother Samson *Subsacrista,* one remarks, is ready oftenest with some question, some suggestion, that has wisdom in it. Though a servant of servants, and saying little, his words all tell, having sense in them; it seems by his light mainly that we steer ourselves in this great dimness.

What if the Thirteen should not themselves be able to agree? Speak, Samson, and advise.— Could not, hints Samson, Six of our venerablest elders be chosen by us, a kind of electoral committee, here and now: of these, "with their hand on the Gospels, with their eye on the *Sacrosancta*," we take oath that they will do faithfully; let these, in secret and as before God, agree on Three whom they reckon fittest; write their names in a Paper, and deliver the same sealed, forthwith, to the Thirteen: one of those Three the Thirteen shall fix on, if permitted. If not permitted, that is to say, if the *Dominus Rex* force us to demur,—the Paper shall be brought back unopened, and publicly burned, that no man's secret bring him into trouble.

So Samson advises, so we act; wisely, in this and in other crises of the business. Our electoral committee, its eye on the *Sacrosancta*, is soon named, soon sworn; and we striking up the Fifth Psalm, *"Verba mea,*

> *Give ear unto my words, O Lord,*
> *My meditation weigh,"*

march out chanting, and leave the Six to their work in the Chapter here. Their work, before long, they announce as finished: they, with their eye on the Sacrosancta, imprecating the Lord to weigh and witness their meditation, have fixed on Three Names, and written them in this Sealed Paper. Let Samson Subsacrista, general servant of the party, take charge of it. On the morrow morning, our Prior and his Twelve will be ready to get under way.

This then is the ballot-box and electoral winnowing-machine they have at St. Edmundsbury: a mind fixed on the Thrice Holy, an appeal to God on high to witness their meditation: by far the best, and indeed the only good electoral winnowing-machine,—if men have souls in them. Totally worthless, it is true, and even hideous

---

[25] Electoral procedure, as indicated at the close of the preceding chapter, required an embassy of the prior and twelve other monks to the king, under whose supervision the election was to be made.

[26] Jocelin has previously complained of Willelmus's drinking.

[27] Waltham was the site of a famous abbey about twelve miles northeast of London. At this moment of crisis, King Henry II, who had the final say in the choice of a new abbot, was resident there.

[28] Temporary platform for political speakers.

and poisonous, if men have no souls. But without soul, alas what winnowing-machine in human elections can be of avail? We cannot get along without soul; we stick fast, the mournfullest spectacle; and salt itself will not save us![29]

On the morrow morning, accordingly, our Thirteen set forth; or rather our Prior and Eleven; for Samson, as general servant of the party, has to linger, settling many things. At length he too gets upon the road; and, "carrying the sealed Paper in a leather pouch hung round his neck; and *froccum bajulans in ulnis*" (thanks to thee Bozzy Jocelin), "his frock-skirts looped over his elbow," showing substantial stern-works, tramps stoutly along. Away across the Heath, not yet of Newmarket[30] and horse-jockeying; across your Fleam-dike and Devil's-dike,[31] no longer useful as a Mercian East-Anglian boundary or bulwark: continually towards Waltham, and the Bishop of Winchester's House there, for his Majesty is in that. Brother Samson, as purse-bearer, has the reckoning always, when there is one, to pay; "delays are numerous," progress none of the swiftest.

But, in the solitude of the Convent, Destiny thus big and in her birthtime, what gossiping, what babbling, what dreaming of dreams! The secret of the Three our electoral elders alone know: some Abbot we shall have to govern us; but which Abbot, O which! One Monk discerns in a vision of the night-watches, that we shall get an Abbot of our own body, without needing to demur: a prophet appeared to him clad all in white, and said, "Ye shall have one of yours, and he will rage among you like a wolf, *saeviet ut lupus.*" Verily!—then which of ours? Another Monk now dreams: he has seen clearly which; a certain Figure taller by head and shoulders than the other two, dressed in alb and *pallium*,[32] and with the attitude of one about to fight;—which tall Figure a wise Editor would rather not name at this stage of the business! Enough that the vision is true: that Saint Edmund himself, pale and awful, seemed to rise from his Shrine, with naked feet, and say audibly, "He, *ille*, shall veil my feet"; which part of the vision also proves true. Such guessing, visioning, dim perscrutation of the momentous future: the very cloth-makers, old women, all townsfolk speak of it, "and more than once it is reported in St. Edmundsbury, This one is elected; and then, This one and That other." Who knows?

But now, sure enough, at Waltham "on the Second Sunday of Quadragesima," which Dryasdust declares to mean the 22nd day of February, year 1182, Thirteen St. Edmundsbury Monks are, at last, seen processioning towards the Winchester Manorhouse; and in some high Presence-chamber, and Hall of State, get access to Henry II in all his glory. What a Hall,—not imaginary in the least, but entirely real and indisputable, though so extremely dim to us; sunk in the deep distances of Night! The Winchester Manorhouse has fled bodily, like a Dream of the old Night; not Dryasdust himself can show a wreck of it. House and people, royal and episcopal, lords and varlets, where are they? Why *there*, I say, Seven Centuries off; sunk *so* far in the Night, there they *are*; peep through the blankets of the old Night, and thou wilt see! King Henry himself is visibly there, a vivid, noble-looking man, with grizzled beard, in glittering uncertain costume; with earls round him, and bishops and dignitaries, in the like. The Hall is large, and has for one thing an altar near it,—chapel and altar adjoining it; but what gilt seats, carved tables, carpeting of rush-cloth, what arras-hangings,[33] and huge fire of logs:—alas, it has Human Life in it; and is not that the grand miracle, in what hangings or costume soever?—

The *Dominus Rex*, benignantly receiving our Thirteen with their obeisance, and graciously declaring that he will strive to act for God's honour, and the Church's good, commands, "by the Bishop of Winchester and Geoffrey the Chancellor,"—*Galfridus Cancellarius*, Henry's and the Fair Rosamond's authentic Son[34] present here!—commands, "That they, the said Thirteen, do now withdraw, and fix upon Three from their own Monastery." A work soon done; the Three hanging ready round Samson's neck, in that leather pouch of his. Breaking the seal, we find the names,—what think *ye* of it, ye higher dignitaries, thou indolent Prior, thou Willelmus

[29] See note 9.
[30] Scene later of a celebrated race track.
[31] Channels of water, originally fortified boundaries between the low-lying lands of East Anglia and her neighbor to the west, Mercia.   [32] Ecclesiastical vestments.
[33] Tapestries.   [34] Henry's natural son.

Sacrista with the red bottle-nose?—the names, in this order: of Samson *Subsacrista,* of Roger the distressed Cellarer,[35] of Hugo *Tertius-Prior.*

The higher dignitaries, all omitted here, "flush suddenly red in the face"; but have nothing to say. One curious fact and question certainly is, How Hugo Third-Prior, who was of the electoral committee, came to nominate *himself* as one of the Three? A curious fact, which Hugo Third-Prior has never yet entirely explained, that I know of!—However, we return, and report to the King our Three names; merely altering the order; putting Samson last, as lowest of all. The King, at recitation of our Three, asks us: "Who are they? Were they born in my domain? Totally unknown to me! You must nominate three others." Whereupon Willelmus Sacrista says, "Our Prior must be named, *quia caput nostrum est,* being already our head." And the Prior responds, "Willelmus Sacrista is a fit man, *bonus vir est,*"—for all his red nose. Tickle me, Toby, and I'll tickle thee![36] Venerable Dennis too is named; none in his conscience can say nay. There are now Six on our List. "Well," said the King, "they have done it swiftly, they! *Deus est cum eis.*"[37] The Monks withdraw again; and Majesty revolves, for a little, with his *Pares* and *Episcopi,*[38] Lords or "*Law-wards*"[39] and Soul-Overseers, the thoughts of the royal breast. The Monks wait silent in an outer room.

In short while, they are next ordered, To add yet another three; but not from their own Convent; from other Convents, "for the honour of my kingdom." Here,—what is to be done here? We will demur, if need be! We do name three, however, for the nonce: the Prior of St. Faith's, a good Monk of St. Neot's, a good Monk of St. Alban's; good men all; all made abbots and dignitaries since, at this hour. There are now Nine upon our List. What the thoughts of the Dominus Rex may be farther? The Dominus Rex, thanking graciously, sends out word that we shall now strike off three. The three strangers are instantly struck off. Willelmus Sacrista adds,

that he will of his own accord decline,—a touch of grace and respect for the *Sacrosancta,* even in Willelmus! The King then orders us to strike off a couple more; then yet one more: Hugo Third-Prior goes, and Roger *Cellerarius,* and venerable Monk Dennis;—and now there remain on our List two only, Samson Subsacrista and the Prior.

Which of these two? It were hard to say,—by Monks who may get themselves foot-gyved and thrown into limbo for speaking! We humbly request that the Bishop of Winchester and Geoffrey the Chancellor may again enter, and help us to decide. "Which do you want?" asks the Bishop. Venerable Dennis made a speech, "commending the persons of the Prior and Samson; but always in the corner of his discourse, *in angulo sui sermonis,* brought Samson in." "I see!" said the Bishop: "We are to understand that your Prior is somewhat remiss; that you want to have him you call Samson for Abbot." "Either of them is good," said venerable Dennis, almost trembling; "but we would have the better, if it pleased God." "Which of the two *do* you want?" inquires the Bishop pointedly. "Samson!" answered Dennis; "Samson!" echoed all of the rest that durst speak or echo anything: and Samson is reported to the King accordingly. His Majesty, advising of it for a moment, orders that Samson be brought in with the other Twelve.

The King's Majesty, looking at us somewhat sternly, then says: "You present to me Samson; I do not know him: had it been your Prior, whom I do know, I should have accepted him: however, I will now do as you wish. But have a care of yourselves. By the true eyes of God, *per veros oculos Dei,* if you manage badly, I will be upon you!" Samson, therefore, steps forward, kisses the King's feet; but swiftly rises erect again, swiftly turns towards the altar, uplifting with the other Twelve, in clear tenor-note, the Fifty-first Psalm, "*Miserere mei Deus,*

> *After thy loving-kindness, Lord,*
> *Have mercy upon* me";

with firm voice, firm step and head, no change in his countenance whatever. "By God's eyes," said the King, "that one, I think, will govern the Abbey well." By the same oath (charged to your Majesty's account), I too am precisely of that

---

35 Distressed by his financial difficulties in providing for the monastery.
36 Proverbial: say a good word for me, and I'll say one for you.
37 God is with them.   38 Peers and bishops.
39 The etymology "guardians of the law" is strictly Carlyle's own.

opinion! It is some while since I fell in with a likelier man anywhere than this new Abbot Samson. Long life to him, and may the Lord *have* mercy on him as Abbot!

Thus, then, have the St. Edmundsbury Monks, without express ballot-box or other good winnowing-machine, contrived to accomplish the most important social feat a body of men can do, to winnow out the man that is to govern them: and truly one sees not that, by any winnowing-machine whatever, they could have done it better. O ye kind Heavens, there is in every Nation and Community *a fittest,* a wisest, bravest, best; whom could we find and make King over us, all were in very truth well;—the best that God and Nature had permitted *us* to make it![40] By what art discover him? Will the Heavens in their pity teach us no art; for our need of him is great!

Ballot-boxes, Reform Bills, winnowing-machines: all these are good, or are not so good;—alas, brethren, how *can* these, I say, be other than inadequate, be other than failures, melancholy to behold? Dim all souls of men to the divine, the high and awful meaning of Human Worth and Truth, we shall never, by all the machinery in Birmingham, discover the True and Worthy. It is written, "if we are ourselves valets, there shall exist no hero for us; we shall not know the hero when we see him";—we shall take the quack for a hero; and cry, audibly through all ballot-boxes and machinery whatsoever, Thou art he; be thou King over us!

What boots it? Seek only deceitful Speciosity, money with gilt carriages, "fame" with newspaper-paragraphs, whatever name it bear, you will find only deceitful Speciosity; godlike Reality will be forever far from you. The Quack shall be legitimate inevitable King of you; no earthly machinery able to exclude the Quack. Ye shall be born thralls of the Quack, and suffer

under him, till your hearts are near broken, and no French Revolution or Manchester Insurrection, or partial or universal volcanic combustions and explosions, never so many, can do more than "change the *figure* of your Quack"; the essence of him remaining, for a time and times.—"How long, O Prophet?" say some, with a rather melancholy sneer. Alas, ye *un*prophetic, ever till this come about: Till deep misery, if nothing softer will, have driven you out of your Speciosities *into* your Sincerities; and you find that there either is a Godlike in the world, or else ye are an unintelligible madness; that there is a God, as well as a Mammon and a Devil, and a Genius of Luxuries and canting Dilettantisms and Vain Shows! How long that will be, compute for yourselves. My unhappy brothers!—

Book III,[41] Chapter 2

GOSPEL OF MAMMONISM

Reader, even Christian Reader as thy title goes, hast thou any notion of Heaven and Hell? I rather apprehend, not. Often as the words are on our tongue, they have got a fabulous or semi-fabulous character for most of us, and pass on like a kind of transient similitude, like a sound signifying little.

Yet it is well worth while for us to know, once and always, that they are not a similitude, nor a fable nor semi-fable; that they are an everlasting highest fact! "No Lake of Sicilian or other sulphur burns now anywhere in these ages," sayest thou? Well, and if there did not! Believe that there does not; believe it if thou wilt, nay hold by it as a real increase, a rise to higher stages, to wider horizons and empires. All this has vanished, or has not vanished; believe as thou wilt as to all this. But that an Infinite of Practical Importance,[42] speaking with strict arithmetical exactness, an *Infinite,* has vanished or can vanish from the Life of any Man: this thou shalt not believe! O brother, the Infinite of Terror, of Hope, of Pity, did it not at any moment disclose itself to thee, indubitable, unnameable? Came it never, like the gleam of *pre*ternatural eternal Oceans, like the voice of old Eternities, far-sounding through thy heart of

---

40 Carlyle's ideal: the rule of the wise hero as king. This cannot be achieved, however, until men become serious rather than dilettante and believe again in the underlying spiritual reality of the universe. For the present "we have quietly closed our eyes to the eternal Substance of things, and opened them only to the Shows and Shams of things," and are therefore unable to recognize the true hero. The implication is that the monks of St. Edmundsbury were able to recognize the fittest, wisest, bravest, best among themselves, because in spite of their human weaknesses they were at heart believing men.

---

41 Book III is entitled "The Modern Worker."
42 That has practical effect upon our lives.

hearts? Never? Alas, it was not thy Liberalism, then; it was thy Animalism! The Infinite is more sure than any other fact. But only men can discern it; mere building beavers, spinning arachnes, much more the predatory vulturous and vulpine species, do not discern it well!—

"The word Hell," says Sauerteig,[43] "is still frequently in use among the English People: but I could not without difficulty ascertain what they meant by it. Hell generally signifies the Infinite Terror, the thing a man *is* infinitely afraid of, and shudders and shrinks from, struggling with his whole soul to escape from it. There is a Hell therefore, if you will consider, which accompanies man, in all stages of his history, and religious or other development: but the Hells of men and Peoples differ notably. With Christians it is the infinite terror of being found guilty before the Just Judge. With old Romans, I conjecture, it was the terror not of Pluto,[44] for whom probably they cared little, but of doing unworthily, doing unvirtuously, which was their word for un*man*fully. And now what is it, if you pierce through his Cants, his oft-repeated Hearsays, what he calls his Worships and so forth,—what is it that the modern English soul does, in very truth, dread infinitely, and contemplate with entire despair? What *is* his Hell, after all these reputable, oft-repeated Hearsays, what is it? With hesitation, with astonishment, I pronounce it to be: The terror of 'Not succeeding'; of not making money, fame, or some other figure in the world,—chiefly of not making money! Is not that a somewhat singular Hell?"

Yes, O Sauerteig, it is very singular. If we do not "succeed," where is the use of us? We had better never have been born. "Tremble intensely," as our friend the Emperor of China says: *there* is the black Bottomless of Terror; what Sauerteig calls the "Hell of the English!"— But indeed this Hell belongs naturally to the Gospel of Mammonism, which also has its corresponding Heaven. For there *is* one Reality among so many Phantasms; about one thing we are entirely in earnest: The making of money. Working Mammonism does divide the world with idle game-preserving Dilettantism:—thank Heaven that there is even a Mammonism, *anything* we are in earnest about! Idleness is worst, Idleness alone is without hope: work earnestly at anything, you will by degrees learn to work at almost all things. There is endless hope in work, were it even work at making money.

True, it must be owned, we for the present, with our Mammon-Gospel, have come to strange conclusions. We call it a Society; and go about professing openly the totallest separation, isolation. Our life is not a mutual helpfulness; but rather, cloaked under due laws-of-war, named "fair competition" and so forth, it is a mutual hostility. We have profoundly forgotten everywhere that *Cash-payment* is not the sole relation of human beings; we think, nothing doubting, that *it* absolves and liquidates all engagements of man. "My starving workers?" answers the rich Millowner: "Did not I hire them fairly in the market? Did I not pay them, to the last sixpence, the sum covenanted for? What have I to do with them more?"—Verily Mammon-worship is a melancholy creed. When Cain, for his own behoof, had killed Abel, and was questioned, "Where is thy brother?" he too made answer, "Am I my brother's keeper?" Did I not pay my brother *his* wages, the thing he had merited from me?

O sumptuous Merchant-Prince, illustrious game-preserving Duke, is there no way of "killing" thy brother but Cain's rude way! "A good man by the very look of him, by his very presence with us as a fellow wayfarer in this Life-pilgrimage, *promises* so much": woe to him if he forget all such promises, if he never know that they were given! To a deadened soul, seared with the brute Idolatry of Sense, to whom going to Hell is equivalent to not making money, all "promises," and moral duties, that cannot be pleaded for in Courts of Request,[45] address themselves in vain. Money he can be ordered to pay, but nothing more. I have not heard in all Past History, and expect not to hear in all Future History, of any Society anywhere under God's Heaven supporting itself on such Philosophy. The Universe is not made so; it is made otherwise than so. The man or nation of men that thinks it is made so, marches forward nothing doubting, step after step, but marches—whither we know! In these last two

---

43 A mouthpiece for some of Carlyle's comments on the English. He is presented as a "picturesque tourist" observing the English scene.   44 Judge of the Underworld.

45 Courts in which money disputes were heard.

centuries of Atheistic Government (near two centuries now, since the blessed restoration of his Sacred Majesty, and Defender of the Faith, Charles Second), I reckon that we have pretty well exhausted what of "firm earth" there was for us to march on;—and are now, very ominously, shuddering, reeling, and let us hope trying to recoil, on the cliff's edge!—

For out of this that we call Atheism come so many other *isms* and falsities, each falsity with its misery at its heels!—A SOUL is not like wind (*spiritus,* or breath) contained within a capsule; the ALMIGHTY MAKER is not like a Clockmaker that once, in old immemorial ages, having *made* his Horologe of a Universe, sits ever since and sees it go![46] Not at all. Hence comes Atheism; come, as we say, many other *isms;* and as the sum of all, comes Valetism, the *reverse* of Heroism; sad root of all woes whatsoever. For indeed, as no man ever saw the above-said wind-element enclosed within its capsule, and finds it at bottom more deniable than conceivable; so too he finds, in spite of Bridgewater Bequests,[47] your Clockmaker Almighty an entirely questionable affair, a deniable affair;—and accordingly denies it, and along with it so much else. Alas, one knows not what and how much else! For the faith in an Invisible, Unnameable, Godlike, present everywhere in all that we see and work and suffer, is the essence of all faith whatsoever; and that once denied, or still worse, asserted with lips only, and out of bound prayerbooks only, what other thing remains believable? That Cant well-ordered is marketable Cant; that Heroism means gas-lighted Histrionism;[48] that seen with "clear eyes" (as they call Valet-eyes), no man is a Hero, or ever was a Hero, but all men are Valets and Varlets. The accursed practical quintessence of all sorts of Unbelief! For if there be now no Hero, and the Histrio himself begin to be seen into, what hope is there for the seed of Adam here below? We are the doomed everlasting prey of the Quack; who, now in this guise, now in that, is to filch us, to pluck and eat us, by such modes as are convenient for him. For the modes and guises I care little. The Quack once in-

evitable, let him come swiftly, let him pluck and eat me;—swiftly, that I may at least have done with him; for in his Quack-world I can have no wish to linger. Though he slay me, yet will I *not* trust in him. Though he conquer nations, and have all the Flunkeys of the Universe shouting at his heels, yet will I know well that *he* is an Inanity; that for him and his there is no continuance appointed, save only in Gehenna and the Pool.[49] Alas, the Atheist world, from its utmost summits of Heaven and Westminster Hall,[50] downwards through poor seven-feet Hats[51] and "Unveracities fallen hungry," down to the lowest cellars and neglected hunger-dens of it, is very wretched.

One of Dr. Alison's Scotch facts struck us much.[52] A poor Irish Widow, her husband having died in one of the Lanes of Edinburgh, went forth with her three children, bare of all resource, to solicit help from the Charitable Establishments of that City. At this Charitable Establishment and then at that she was refused; referred from one to the other, helped by none; —till she had exhausted them all; till her strength and heart failed her: she sank down in typhus-fever; died, and infected her Lane with fever, so that "seventeen other persons" died of fever there in consequence. The humane Physician asks thereupon, as with a heart too full for speaking, Would it not have been *economy* to help this poor Widow? She took typhus-fever, and killed seventeen of you!—Very curious. The forlorn Irish Widow applies to her fellow-creatures, as if saying, "Behold I am sinking, bare of help: ye must help me! I am your sister, bone of your bone; one God made us: ye must help me!" They answer, "No, impossible; thou art no sister of ours." But she proves her sisterhood; her typhus-fever kills *them:* they actually were her brothers, though denying it! Had human creature ever to go lower for a proof?

For, as indeed was very natural in such case, all government of the Poor by the Rich has long ago been given over to Supply-and-de-

[46] See note 9 to *Sartor Resartus,* Book II, chap. 7.
[47] A sum of £8,000 left by the Earl of Bridgewater for the best treatise on God as the mechanistic creator of the universe.
[48] Play acting, i.e., sham.
[49] Hell.
[50] A seat in Parliament is the heaven of an atheist world.
[51] An advertising scheme described in Book II, chap. 1, as a contemptible example of sham and dupery.
[52] Carlyle himself gives the reference to *Observations on the Management of the Poor in Scotland,* by William Pulteney Alison, M.D. (Edinburgh, 1840).

mand, Laissez-faire[53] and such like, and universally declared to be "impossible." "You are no sister of ours; what shadow of proof is there? Here are our parchments, our padlocks, proving indisputably our money-safes to be *ours,* and you to have no business with them. Depart! It is impossible!"—Nay, what wouldst thou thyself have us do? cry indignant readers. Nothing, my friends,—till you have got a soul for yourselves again. Till then all things are "impossible." Till then I cannot even bid you buy, as the old Spartans would have done, two-pence worth of powder and lead, and compendiously shoot to death this poor Irish Widow:[54] even that is "impossible" for you. Nothing is left but that she prove her sisterhood by dying, and infecting you with typhus. Seventeen of you lying dead will not deny such proof that she *was* flesh of your flesh; and perhaps some of the living may lay it to heart.

"Impossible": of a certain two-legged animal with feathers it is said, if you draw a distinct chalk-circle round him, he sits imprisoned, as if girt with the iron ring of Fate; and will die there, though within sight of victuals,—or sit in sick misery there, and be fatted to death. The name of this poor two-legged animal is—Goose;[55] and they make of him, when well fattened, *Pâté de foie gras,*[56] much prized by some!

Book III, Chapter 5

THE ENGLISH

And yet, with all thy theoretic platitudes, what a depth of practical sense in thee, great England! A depth of sense, of justice, and courage; in which, under all emergencies and world-bewilderments, and under this most complex of emergencies we now live in, there is still hope, there is still assurance!

The English are a dumb people. They can do great acts, but not describe them. Like the old Romans, and some few others, *their* Epic Poem is written on the Earth's surface: England her Mark! It is complained that they have no artists: one Shakespeare indeed; but for Raphael only a Reynolds; for Mozart nothing but a Mr. Bishop:[57] not a picture, not a song. And yet they did produce one Shakespeare: consider how the element of Shakespearean melody does lie imprisoned in their nature; reduced to unfold itself in mere Cottonmills, Constitutional Governments, and such like;—all the more interesting when it does become visible, as even in such unexpected shapes it succeeds in doing! Goethe spoke of the Horse, how impressive, almost affecting it was that an animal of such qualities should stand obstructed so; its speech nothing but an inarticulate neighing, its handiness mere *hoof*iness, the fingers all constricted, tied together, the finger-nails coagulated into a mere hoof, shod with iron. The more significant, thinks he, are those eye-flashings of the generous noble quadruped; those prancings, curvings of the neck clothed with thunder.

A Dog of Knowledge has free utterance; but the Warhorse is almost mute, very far from free! It is even so. Truly, your freest utterances are not by any means always the best: they are the worst rather; the feeblest, trivialest; their meaning prompt, but small, ephemeral. Commend me to the silent English, to the silent Romans. Nay, the silent Russians too I believe to be worth something: are they not even now drilling, under much obloquy, an immense semi-barbarous half-world from Finland to Kamtschatka[58] into rule, subordination, civilization, —really in an old Roman fashion; speaking no word about it; quietly hearing all manner of vituperative Able Editors speak! While your ever-talking, ever-gesticulating French, for example, what are they at this moment drilling?— Nay, of all animals, the freest of utterance, I should judge, is the genus *Simia:* go into the Indian woods, say all Travellers, and look what a brisk, adroit, unresting Ape-population it is!

The spoken Word, the written Poem, is said to be an epitome of the man; how much more the done Work. Whatsoever of morality

---

53 See the introduction to Carlyle.
54 The Spartans killed off their helots or slaves when they became too numerous.
55 In claiming that it is impossible to do anything about the deplorable condition of the poor, Englishmen are acting like geese.
56 A rich paste made of fatted goose livers.
57 Raphael (1483–1520), an Italian and one of the world's greatest painters, in comparison with whom the English portrait painter Sir Joshua Reynolds (1723–1792) holds an inferior rank. The comparison in the realm of music is even more destructive of the prestige of England. The great Austrian composer Mozart (1756–1791) is contrasted with a minor contemporary figure, Sir Henry Bishop (1786–1855).
58 A peninsula in northeastern Siberia.

and of intelligence; what of patience, perseverance, faithfulness, of method, insight, ingenuity, energy; in a word, whatsoever of Strength the man had in him will lie written in the Work he does. To work: why, it is to try himself against Nature, and her everlasting unerring Laws; these will tell a true verdict as to the man. So much of virtue and of faculty did *we* find in him; so much and no more! He had such capacity of harmonizing himself with *me* and my unalterable ever-veracious Laws; of co-operating and working as *I* bade him;—and has prospered, and has not prospered, as you see!—Working as great Nature bade him: does not that mean virtue of a kind; nay, of all kinds? Cotton can be spun and sold, Lancashire operatives can be got to spin it, and at length one has the woven webs and sells them, by following Nature's regulations in that matter: by not following Nature's regulations, you have them not. You have them not; —there is no Cotton-web to sell: Nature finds a bill against you; your "Strength" is not Strength, but Futility! Let faculty be honoured, so far as it is faculty. A man that can succeed in working is to me always a man.

How one loves to see the burly figure of him, this thick-skinned, seemingly opaque, perhaps sulky, almost stupid Man of Practice, pitted against some light adroit Man of Theory, all equipped with clear logic, and able anywhere to give you Why for Wherefore! The adroit Man of Theory, so light of movement, clear of utterance, with his bow full-bent and quiver full of arrow-arguments,—surely he will strike down the game, transfix everywhere the heart of the matter; triumph everywhere, as he proves that he shall and must do? To your astonishment, it turns out oftenest No. The cloudy-browed, thick-soled, opaque Practicality, with no logic utterance, in silence mainly, with here and there a low grunt or growl, has in him what transcends all logic-utterance: a Congruity with the Unuttered. The Speakable, which lies atop, as a superficial film, or outer skin, is his or is not his: but the Doable, which reaches down to the World's centre, you find him there!

The rugged Brindly[59] has little to say for himself; the rugged Brindley, when difficulties accumulate on him, retires silent, "generally to his bed"; retires "sometimes for three days together to his bed, that he may be in perfect privacy there," and ascertain in his rough head how the difficulties can be overcome. The ineloquent Brindley, behold he *has* chained seas together; his ships do visibly float over valleys, invisibly through the hearts of mountains; the Mersey and the Thames, the Humber and the Severn have shaken hands: Nature most audibly answers, Yea! The man of Theory twangs his full-bent bow: Nature's Fact ought to fall stricken, but does not: his logic-arrow glances from it as from a scaly dragon, and the obstinate Fact keeps walking its way. How singular! At bottom, you will have to grapple closer with the dragon; take it home to you, by real faculty, not by seeming faculty; try whether you are stronger or it is stronger. Close with it, wrestle it: sheer obstinate toughness of muscle; but much more, what we call toughness of heart, which will mean persistence hopeful and even desperate, unsubduable patience, composed candid openness, clearness of mind: all this shall be "strength" in wrestling your dragon; the whole man's real strength is in this work, we shall get the measure of him here.

Of all the Nations in the world at present the English are the stupidest in speech, the wisest in action. As good as a "dumb" Nation, I say, who cannot speak, and have never yet spoken, —spite of the Shakespeares and Miltons who show us what possibilities there are!—O Mr. Bull, I look in that surly face of thine with a mixture of pity and laughter, yet also with wonder and veneration. Thou complainest not, my illustrious friend; and yet I believe the heart of thee is full of sorrow, of unspoken sadness, seriousness,—profound melancholy (as some have said) the basis of thy being. Unconsciously, for thou speakest of nothing, this great Universe is great to thee. Not by levity of floating, but by stubborn force of swimming, shalt thou make thy way. The Fates sing of thee that thou shalt many times be thought an ass and a dull ox, and shalt with a godlike indifference believe it. My friend,—and it is all untrue, nothing ever falser in point of fact! Thou art of those great ones whose greatness the small passer-by does not discern. Thy very stupidity is wiser than their wisdom. A grand *vis inertiae*[60] is in thee;

---

[59] James Brindley (1716-1772), an engineer who constructed many aqueducts and canals.

[60] Inert strength.

how many grand qualities unknown to small men! Nature alone knows thee, acknowledges the bulk and strength of thee: thy Epic, unsung in words, is written in huge characters on the face of this Planet,—sea-moles, cotton-trades, railways, fleets and cities, Indian Empires, Americas, New-Hollands; legible throughout the Solar System!

But the dumb Russians too, as I said, they, drilling all wild Asia and wild Europe into military rank and file, a terrible yet hitherto a prospering enterprise, are still dumber. The old Romans also could not *speak,* for many centuries:—not till the world was theirs, and so many speaking Greekdoms, their logic-arrows all spent, had been absorbed and abolished. The logic-arrows, how they glanced futile from obdurate thick-skinned Facts; Facts to be wrestled down only by the real vigour of Roman thews! —As for me, I honour, in these loud-babbling days, all the Silent rather. A grand Silence that of Romans;—nay the grandest of all, is it not that of the gods! Even Triviality, Imbecility, that can sit silent, how respectable is it in comparison! The "talent of silence" is our fundamental one. Great honour to him whose Epic is a melodious hexameter Iliad; not a jingling Sham-Iliad, nothing true in it but the hexameters and forms merely. But still greater honour, if his Epic be a mighty Empire slowly built together, a mighty Series of Heroic Deeds,—a mighty Conquest over Chaos; *which* Epic the "Eternal Melodies" have, and must have, informed and dwelt in, as *it* sung itself! There is no mistaking that latter Epic. Deeds are greater than Words. Deeds have such a life, mute but undeniable, and grow as living trees and fruit-trees do; they people the vacuity of Time, and make it green and worthy. Why should the oak prove logically that it ought to grow, and will grow? Plant it, try it; what gifts of diligent judicious assimilation and secretion it has, of progress and resistance, of *force* to grow, will then declare themselves. My much-honoured, illustrious, extremely inarticulate Mr. Bull!—

Ask Bull his spoken opinion of any matter, —oftentimes the force of dullness can no farther go. You stand silent, incredulous, as over a platitude that borders on the Infinite. The man's Churchisms, Dissenterisms, Puseyisms, Benthamisms, College Philosophies, Fashionable Litera-

tures, are unexampled in this world.[61] Fate's prophecy is fulfilled; you call the man an ox and an ass. But set him once to work,—respectable man! His spoken sense is next to nothing, nine-tenths of it palpable *non*sense: but his unspoken sense, his inner silent feeling of what is true, what does agree with fact, what is doable and what is not doable,—this seeks its fellow in the world. A terrible worker; irresistible against marshes, mountains, impediments, disorder, incivilization; everywhere vanquishing disorder, leaving it behind him as method and order. He "retires to his bed three days," and considers!

Nay withal, stupid as he is, our dear John, —ever, after infinite tumblings, and spoken platitudes innumerable from barrel-heads and parliament-benches, he does settle down somewhere about the just conclusion; you are certain that his jumblings and tumblings will end, after years or centuries, in the stable equilibrium. Stable equilibrium, I say; centre-of-gravity lowest; —not the unstable, with centre-of-gravity highest, as I have known it done by quicker people! For indeed, do but jumble and tumble sufficiently, you avoid that worse fault, of settling with your centre-of-gravity highest; your centre-of-gravity is certain to come lowest, and to stay there. If slowness, what we in our impatience call "stupidity," be the price of stable equilibrium over unstable, shall we grudge a little slowness? Not the least admirable quality of Bull is, after all, that of remaining insensible to logic; holding out for considerable periods, ten years or more, as in this of the Corn-Laws,[62] after all arguments and shadow of arguments have faded away from him, till the very urchins on the street titter at the arguments he brings. Logic,—Λογική, the "Art of Speech,"—does indeed speak so and so; clear enough: nevertheless Bull still shakes his head; will see whether nothing else *illogical,* not yet "spoken," not yet able to be "spoken," do not lie in the business, as there so often does!—My firm

---

61 The English mind is muddled by all the contemporary controversies. Puseyism was the High Church movement.
62 The very high tariffs imposed on imported grain, in the interest of the land-owning aristocracy. The workers were severely hurt by the resulting high price of bread. In 1841–42, R. D. Altick calculates that they had to pay a shilling a loaf when their average wage was 15 shillings a week (i.e., earning $100 a week and having to pay $6.67 for each loaf of bread).

belief is, that, finding himself now enchanted, hand-shackled, foot-shackled, in Poor-Law Bastilles[63] and elsewhere, he will retire three days to his bed, and *arrive* at a conclusion or two! His three-years "total stagnation of trade,"[64] alas, is not that a painful enough "lying in bed to consider himself"? Poor Bull!

Bull is a born Conservative; for this too I inexpressibly honour him. All great Peoples are conservative; slow to believe in novelties; patient of much error in actualities; deeply and for ever certain of the greatness that is in Law, in Custom once solemnly established, and now long recognized as just and final.—True, O Radical Reformer, there is no Custom that can, properly speaking, be final; none. And yet thou seest *Customs* which, in all civilized countries, are accounted final; nay, under the Old-Roman name of *Mores*, are accounted *Morality*, Virtue, Laws of God Himself. Such, I assure thee, not a few of them are; such almost all of them once were. And greatly do I respect the solid character,— a blockhead, thou wilt say; yes, but a well-conditioned blockhead, and the best-conditioned,— who esteems all "Customs once solemnly acknowledged" to be ultimate, divine, and the rule for a man to walk by, nothing doubting, not inquiring farther. What a time of it had we, were all men's life and trade still, in all parts of it, a problem, a hypothetic seeking, to be settled by painful Logics and Baconian Inductions! The Clerk in Eastcheap[65] cannot spend the day in verifying his Ready-Reckoner; he must take it as verified, true and indisputable; or his Bookkeeping by Double Entry will stand still. "Where is your Posted Ledger?" asks the Master at night. —"Sir," answers the other, "I was verifying my Ready-Reckoner, and find some errors. The Ledger is—!"—Fancy such a thing!

True, all turns on your Ready-Reckoner being moderately correct,—being *not* insupportably incorrect! A Ready-Reckoner which has led to distinct entries in your Ledger such as these: "*Creditor* an English People by fifteen hundred years of good Labour; and *Debtor* to lodging in enchanted Poor-Law Bastilles: *Creditor* by conquering the largest Empire the Sun ever saw; and *Debtor* to Donothingism and 'Impossible' written on all departments of the government thereof: *Creditor* by mountains of gold ingots earned; and *Debtor* to No Bread purchasable by them":—*such* Ready-Reckoner, methinks, is beginning to be suspect; nay is ceasing, and has ceased, to be suspect! Such Ready-Reckoner is a Solecism in Eastcheap; and must, whatever be the press of business, and will and shall be rectified a little. Business can go on no longer with *it*. The most Conservative English People, thickest-skinned, most patient of Peoples, is driven alike by its Logic and its Unlogic, by things "spoken," and by things not yet spoken or very speakable, but only felt and very unendurable, to be wholly a Reforming People. Their Life as it is has ceased to be longer possible for them.

Urge not this noble silent People: rouse not the Berserkir-rage[66] that lies in them! Do you know their Cromwells, Hampdens, their Pyms and Bradshaws?[67] Men very peaceable, but men that can be made very terrible! Men who, like their old Teutsch Fathers in Agrippa's days,[68] "have a soul that despises death"; to whom "death," compared with falsehoods and injustices, is light;—"in whom there is a rage unconquerable by the immortal gods!" Before this, the English People have taken very preternatural-looking Spectres by the beard; saying virtually: "And if thou *wert* 'preternatural'? Thou with thy 'divine-rights' grown diabolic wrongs? Thou, —not even 'natural'; decapitable; totally extinguishable!"—Yes, just so godlike as this People's patience was, even so godlike will and must its impatience be. Away, ye scandalous Practical Solecisms, children actually of the Prince of Darkness; ye have near broken our hearts; we can and will endure you no longer. Begone, we say; depart, while the play is good! By the Most High God, whose sons and born missionaries true men are, ye shall not continue here! You and

---

[63] Workhouses. These were established by the Poor Law of 1834; and, though they made for more efficient care of the poor, they were less "personal" than the earlier parish dole and seemed like prisons. Carlyle attacked them for dealing with people as so many objects rather than as individual human beings.

[64] See note 85.

[65] Financial district of London.

[66] The berserk was in Norse folklore a warrior subject to fits of frenzy in battle.

[67] Men who were roused by the evils of their time to become leaders of the Puritan Revolution in the middle of the seventeenth century.

[68] Germanic tribes living in the time of Agrippa (63–12 B.C.).

we have become incompatible; can inhabit one house no longer. Either you must go, or we. Are ye ambitious to try *which* it shall be?

O my Conservative friends, who still specially name and struggle to approve yourselves "Conservative," would to Heaven I could persuade you of this world-old fact, than which Fate is not surer, That Truth and Justice alone are *capable* of being "conserved" and preserved! The thing which is unjust, which is *not* according to God's Law, will you, in a God's Universe, try to conserve that? It is so old, say you? Yes, and the hotter haste ought *you*, of all others, to be in to let it grow no older! If but the faintest whisper in your hearts intimate to you that it is not fair, —hasten, for the sake of Conservatism itself, to probe it rigorously, to cast it forth at once and for ever if guilty. How will or can you preserve *it*, the thing that is not fair? "Impossibility" a thousandfold is marked on that. And ye call yourselves Conservatives, Aristocracies:—ought not honour and nobleness of mind, if they had departed from all the Earth elsewhere, to find their last refuge with you? Ye unfortunate!

The bough that is dead shall be cut away, for the sake of the tree itself. Old? Yes, it is too old. Many a weary winter has it swung and creaked there, and gnawed and fretted, with its dead wood, the organic substance and still living fibre of this good tree; many a long summer has its ugly naked brown defaced the fair green umbrage; every day it has done mischief, and that only: off with it, for the tree's sake, if for nothing more; let the Conservatism that would preserve cut *it* away. Did no wood-forester apprise you that a dead bough with its dead root left sticking there is extraneous, poisonous; is as a dead iron spike, some horrid rusty ploughshare driven into the living substance;—nay is far worse; for in every windstorm ("commercial crisis" or the like), it frets and creaks, jolts itself to and fro, and cannot lie quiet as your dead iron spike would.

If I were the Conservative Party of England (which is another bold figure of speech), I would not for a hundred thousand pounds an hour allow those Corn-Laws to continue! Potosi and Golconda[69] put together would not purchase my assent to them. Do you count what treasuries of bitter indignation they are laying up for you in every just English heart? Do you know what questions, not as to Corn-prices and Sliding-scales alone,[70] they are *forcing* every reflective Englishman to ask himself? Questions insoluble, or hitherto unsolved; deeper than any of our Logic-plummets hitherto will sound: questions deep enough,—which it were better that we did not name even in thought! You are forcing us to think of them, to begin uttering them. The utterance of them is begun; and where will it be ended, think you? When two millions of one's brother-men sit in Workhouses, and five millions, as is insolently said, "rejoice in potatoes," there are various things that must be begun, let them end where they can.

Book III, Chapter 11

LABOUR

For there is a perennial nobleness, and even sacredness, in Work. Were he never so benighted, forgetful of his high calling, there is always hope in a man that actually and earnestly works: in Idleness alone is there perpetual despair. Work, never so Mammonish, mean, *is* in communication with Nature; the real desire to get Work done will itself lead one more and more to truth, to Nature's appointments and regulations, which are truth.

The latest Gospel in this world is, Know thy work and do it. "Know thyself": long enough has that poor "self" of thine tormented thee; thou wilt never get to "know" it, I believe! Think it not thy business, this of knowing thyself; thou art an unknowable individual: know what thou canst work at; and work at it, like a Hercules! That will be thy better plan.

It has been written, "an endless significance lies in Work"; a man perfects himself by working. Foul jungles are cleared away, fair seed-fields rise instead, and stately cities; and withal the man himself first ceases to be a jungle and foul unwholesome desert thereby. Consider how, even in the meanest sorts of Labour, the whole soul of a man is composed into a kind of real harmony, the instant he sets himself to work!

---

69 Sites of fabulous treasure.

70 In 1828 Wellington introduced a sliding-scale for import duties on corn (i.e.,. wheat): the duties rose as the price in the English market rose, so that the latter was always protected.

Doubt, Desire, Sorrow, Remorse, Indignation, Despair itself, all these like helldogs lie beleaguering the soul of the poor dayworker, as of every man: but he bends himself with free valour against his task, and all these are stilled, all these shrink murmuring far off into their caves. The man is now a man. The blessed glow of Labour in him, is it not as purifying fire, wherein all poison is burnt up, and of sour smoke itself there is made bright blessed flame!

Destiny, on the whole, has no other way of cultivating us. A formless Chaos, once set it *revolving*, grows round and ever rounder; ranges itself, by mere force of gravity, into strata, spherical courses; is no longer a Chaos, but a round compacted World. What would become of the Earth, did she cease to revolve? In the poor old Earth, so long as she revolves, all inequalities, irregularities disperse themselves; all irregularities are incessantly becoming regular. Hast thou looked on the Potter's wheel,—one of the venerablest objects; old as the Prophet Ezekiel and far older? Rude lumps of clay, how they spin themselves up, by mere quick whirling, into beautiful circular dishes. And fancy the most assiduous Potter, but without his wheel; reduced to make dishes, or rather amorphous botches, by mere kneading and baking! Even such a Potter were Destiny, with a human soul that would rest and lie at ease, that would not work and spin! Of an idle unrevolving man the kindest Destiny, like the most assiduous Potter without wheel, can bake and knead nothing other than a botch; let her spend on him what expensive colouring, what gilding and enamelling she will, he is but a botch. Not a dish; no, a bulging, kneaded, crooked, shambling, squint-cornered, amorphous botch,—a mere enamelled vessel of dishonour! Let the idle think of this.

Blessed is he who has found his work; let him ask no other blessedness. He has a work, a life-purpose; he has found it, and will follow it! How, as a free-flowing channel, dug and torn by noble force through the sour mud-swamp of one's existence, like an ever-deepening river there, it runs and flows;—draining off the sour festering water, gradually from the root of the remotest grass-blade; making, instead of pestilential swamp, a green fruitful meadow with its clear-flowing stream. How blessed for the meadow itself, let the stream and *its* value be great

or small! Labour is Life: from the inmost heart of the Worker rises his god-given Force, the sacred celestial Life-essence breathed into him by Almighty God; from his inmost heart awakens him to all nobleness,—to all knowledge, "self-knowledge" and much else, so soon as Work fitly begins. Knowledge? The knowledge that will hold good in working, cleave thou to that; for Nature herself accredits that, says Yea to that. Properly thou hast no other knowledge but what thou hast got by working: the rest is yet all a hypothesis of knowledge; a thing to be argued of in schools, a thing floating in the clouds, in endless logic-vortices, till we try it and fix it. "Doubt, of whatever kind, can be ended by Action alone."

And again, hast thou valued Patience, Courage, Perseverance, Openness to light; readiness to own thyself mistaken, to do better next time? All these, all virtues, in wrestling with the dim brute Powers of Fact, in ordering of thy fellows in such wrestle, there and elsewhere not at all, thou wilt continually learn. Set down a brave Sir Christopher[71] in the middle of black ruined Stone-heaps, of foolish unarchitectural Bishops, redtape Officials, idle Nell-Gwyn Defenders of the Faith;[72] and see whether he will ever raise a Paul's Cathedral out of all that, yea or no! Rough, rude, contradictory are all things and persons, from the mutinous masons and Irish hodmen, up to the idle Nell-Gwyn Defenders, to blustering redtape Officials, foolish unarchitectural Bishops. All these things and persons are there not for Christopher's sake and his Cathedral's; they are there for their own sake mainly! Christopher will have to conquer and constrain all these,—if he be able. All these are against him. Equitable Nature herself, who carries her mathematics and architectonics not on the face of her, but deep in the hidden heart of her,—Nature herself is but partially for him; will be wholly against him, if he constrain her not! His very money, where is it to come from? The pious munificence of England lies far-scat-

71 Sir Christopher Wren (1632–1723), the architect of St. Paul's Cathedral, responsible for rebuilding large sections of London after the Great Fire (1666).
72 Kings like Charles II. Part of his royal title was Defender of the Faith. Nell Gwyn, the actress, was his avowed mistress.

tered, distant, unable to speak, and say, "I am here";—must be spoken to before it can speak. Pious munificence, and all help, is so silent, invisible like the gods; impediment, contradictions manifold are so loud and near! O brave Sir Christopher, trust thou in those, notwithstanding, and front all these;[73] understand all these; by valiant patience, noble effort, insight, by man's-strength, vanquish and compel all these,—and, on the whole, strike down victoriously the last topstone of that Paul's Edifice; thy monument for certain centuries, the stamp "Great Man" impressed very legibly on Portland stone there!—

Yes, all manner of help, and pious response from Men or Nature, is always what we call silent; cannot speak or come to light, till it be seen, till it be spoken to. Every noble work is at first "impossible." In very truth, for every noble work the possibilities will lie diffused through Immensity; inarticulate, undiscoverable except to faith. Like Gideon thou shalt spread out thy fleece at the door of thy tent; see whether under the wide arch of Heaven there be any bounteous moisture, or none. Thy heart and life-purpose shall be as a miraculous Gideon's fleece, spread out in silent appeal to Heaven, and from the kind Immensities, what from the poor unkind Localities and town and country Parishes there never could, blessed dew-moisture to suffice thee shall have fallen![74]

Work is of a religious nature:—work is of a *brave* nature; which it is the aim of all religion to be. All work of man is as the swimmer's: a waste ocean threatens to devour him; if he front it not bravely, it will keep its word. By incessant wise defiance of it, lusty rebuke and buffet of it, behold how it loyally supports him, bears him as its conqueror along. "It is so," says Goethe, "with all things that man undertakes in this world."

Brave Sea-captain, Norse Sea-king,—Columbus, my hero, royallest Sea-king of all! it is no friendly environment this of thine, in the waste deep waters; around thee mutinous discouraged souls, behind thee disgrace and ruin, before thee the unpenetrated veil of Night. Brother, these wild water-mountains, bounding from their deep bases (ten miles deep, I am told), are not entirely there on thy behalf! Meseems *they* have other work than floating thee forward:—and the huge Winds, that sweep from Ursa Major[75] to the Tropics and Equators, dancing their giant-waltz through the kingdoms of Chaos and Immensity, they care little about filling rightly or filling wrongly the small shoulder-of-mutton sails in this cockle-skiff of thine! Thou art not among articulate-speaking friends, my brother; thou art among immeasurable dumb monsters, tumbling, howling wide as the world here. Secret, far off, invisible to all hearts but thine, there lies a help in them: see how thou wilt get at that. Patiently thou wilt wait till the mad Southwester spend itself, saving thyself by dexterous science of defence, the while: valiantly, with swift decision, wilt thou strike in, when the favouring East, the Possible, springs up. Mutiny of men thou wilt sternly repress; weakness, despondency, thou wilt cheerily encourage: thou wilt swallow down complaint, unreason, weariness, weakness of others and thyself;—how much wilt thou swallow down! There shall be a depth of Silence in thee, deeper than this Sea, which is but ten miles deep: a Silence unsoundable; known to God only. Thou shalt be a Great Man. Yes, my World-Soldier, thou of the World Marine-service,—thou wilt have to be *greater* than this tumultuous unmeasured World here round thee is: thou, in thy strong soul, as with wrestler's arms, shalt embrace it, harness it down; and make it bear thee on,—to new Americas, or whither God wills!

Book III, Chapter 13

DEMOCRACY

If the Serene Highnesses and Majesties do not take note of that,[76] then, as I perceive, *that* will take note of itself! The time for levity, insincerity, and idle babble and play-acting, in all kinds, is gone by; it is a serious, grave time. Old long-vexed questions, not yet solved in logical words or parliamentary laws, are fast solving

---

73 The antecedent of "those" is "pious munificence, and all help"; of "these," "impediment, contradictions manifold."

74 Gideon's fleece was found to be wet with dew while the ground around was dry (Judges 6:36–38).

75 The Great Bear or Big Dipper, a constellation in the northern sky.

76 The antecedent of "that" is in the closing paragraph of the preceding chapter: "The proper Epic of this world . . . is now 'Tools and the Man.' " Carlyle means that the major problem of his time is industry and the worker.

themselves in facts, somewhat unblessed to behold! This largest of questions, this question of Work and Wages, which ought, had we heeded Heaven's voice, to have begun two generations ago or more, cannot be delayed longer without hearing Earth's voice. "Labour" will verily need to be somewhat "organized," as they say,—God knows with what difficulty. Man will actually need to have his debts and earnings a little better paid by man; which, let Parliaments speak of them, or be silent of them, are eternally his due from man, and cannot, without penalty and at length not without death-penalty, be withheld. How much ought to cease among us straightway; how much ought to begin straightway, while the hours yet are!

Truly they are strange results to which this of leaving all to "Cash";[77] of quietly shutting up the God's Temple, and gradually opening wide-open the Mammon's Temple, with "Laissez-faire, and Every man for himself,"—have led us in these days! We have Upper, speaking Classes, who indeed do "speak" as never man spake before; the withered flimsiness, godless baseness and barrenness of whose Speech might of itself indicate what kind of Doing and practical Governing went on under it! For Speech is the gaseous element out of which most kinds of Practice and Performance, especially all kinds of moral Performance, condense themselves, and take shape; as the one is, so will the other be. Descending, accordingly, into the Dumb Class in its Stockport[78] Cellars and Poor-Law Bastilles, have we not to announce that they also are hitherto unexampled in the History of Adam's Posterity?

Life was never a May-game for men: in all times the lot of the dumb millions born to toil was defaced with manifold sufferings, injustices, heavy burdens, avoidable and unavoidable; not play at all, but hard work that made the sinews sore and the heart sore. As bond-slaves, *villani, bordarii, sochemanni,* nay indeed as dukes, earls and kings, men were oftentimes made weary of their life; and had to say, in the sweat of their brow and of their soul, Behold, it is not sport, it is grim earnest, and our back can bear no more! Who knows not what massacrings and harryings there have been; grinding, long-continuing, unbearable injustices,—till the heart had to rise in madness, and some *"Eu Sachsen, nimith euer sachses,* You Saxons, out with your gully-knives, then!" You Saxons, some "arrestment," partial "arrestment of the Knaves and Dastards" has become indispensable!—The page of Dryasdust is heavy with such details.

And yet I will venture to believe that in no time, since the beginnings of Society, was the lot of those same dumb millions of toilers so entirely unbearable as it is even in the days now passing over us. It is not to die, or even to die of hunger, that makes a man wretched; many men have died; all men must die,—the last exit of us all is in a Fire-Chariot of Pain. But it is to live miserable we know not why; to work sore and yet gain nothing; to be heart-worn, weary, yet isolated, unrelated, girt-in with a cold universal Laissez-faire: it is to die slowly all our life long, imprisoned in a deaf, dead, Infinite Injustice, as in the accursed iron belly of a Phalaris' Bull![79] This is and remains forever intolerable to all men whom God has made. Do we wonder at French Revolutions, Chartisms, Revolts of Three Days? The times, if we will consider them, are really unexampled.

Never before did I hear of an Irish Widow reduced to "prove her sisterhood by dying of typhus-fever and infecting seventeen persons,"— saying in such undeniable way, "You *see* I was your sister!" Sisterhood, brotherhood, was often forgotten; but not till the rise of these ultimate Mammon and Shotbelt Gospels did I ever see it so expressly denied. If no pious Lord or *Lawward* would remember it, always some pious Lady ("*Hlaf dig,*" Benefactress, "*Loaf-giveress,*" they say she is,—blessings on her beautiful heart!) was there, with mild mother-voice and hand, to remember it; some pious thoughtful *Elder,* what we now call "Prester," *Presbyter* or "Priest," was there to put all men in mind of it, in the name of the God who had made all.

Not even in Black Dahomey[80] was it ever,

---

77 I.e., the theory that the only responsibility of the employer to his employee was that of wages.
78 Used here as a symbol of the degraded living conditions of the workers. It was the site of a singularly grim crime committed because of poverty and starvation, which Carlyle related in Book I, chap. 1. For Poor-Law Bastilles see note 63.

79 See p. 459, n. 34.
80 On the west coast of Africa, where the explorer Mungo Park (1771–1806) was once taken ill.

I think, forgotten to the typhus-fever length.
Mungo Park, resourceless, had sunk down to die
under the Negro Village-Tree, a horrible White
object in the eyes of all. But in the poor Black
Woman, and her daughter who stood aghast at
him, whose earthly wealth and funded capital
consisted of one small calabash of rice, there
lived a heart richer than "*Laissez-faire*": they,
with a royal munificence, boiled their rice for
him; they sang all night to him, spinning assiduous on their cotton distaffs, as he lay to sleep:
"Let us pity the poor white man; no mother has
he to fetch him milk, no sister to grind him
corn!" Thou poor black Noble One,—thou *Lady*
too: did not a God make thee too; was there not
in thee too something of a God!—

Gurth, born thrall of Cedric the Saxon,
has been greatly pitied by Dryasdust and others.
Gurth, with the brass collar round his neck,
tending Cedric's pigs in the glades of the wood,
is not what I call an exemplar of human felicity:
but Gurth, with the sky above him, with the free
air and tinted boscage and umbrage round him,
and in him at least the certainty of supper and
social lodging when he came home; Gurth to me
seems happy, in comparison with many a Lancashire and Buckinghamshire man of these days,
not born thrall of anybody! Gurth's brass collar
did not gall him: Cedric *deserved* to be his
Master. The pigs were Cedric's, but Gurth too
would get his parings of them. Gurth had the
inexpressible satisfaction of feeling himself related indissolubly, though in a rude brass-collar
way, to his fellow-mortals in this Earth. He had
superiors, inferiors, equals.—Gurth is now
"emancipated" long since; has what we call
"Liberty." Liberty, I am told, is a Divine thing.
Liberty when it becomes the "Liberty to die by
starvation" is not so divine!

Liberty? The true liberty of a man, you
would say, consisted in his finding out, or being
forced to find out, the right path, and to walk
thereon. To learn, or to be taught, what work
he actually was able for; and then by permission,
persuasion, and even compulsion, to set about
doing of the same! That is his true blessedness,
honour, "liberty" and maximum of wellbeing:
if liberty be not that, I for one have small care
about liberty.[81] You do not allow a palpable

madman to leap over precipices; you violate his
liberty, you that are wise; and keep him, were it
in strait-waistcoats, away from the precipices!
Every stupid, every cowardly and foolish man is
but a less palpable madman: his true liberty
were that a wiser man, that any and every wiser
man, could, by brass collars, or in whatever
milder or sharper way, lay hold of him when he
was going wrong, and order and compel him to
go a little righter. O, if thou really art my *Senior,*
Seigneur, my *Elder,* Presbyter or Priest,—if thou
art in very deed my *Wiser,* may a beneficent
instinct lead and impel thee to "conquer" me, to
command me! If thou do know better than I
what is good and right, I conjure thee in the
name of God, force me to do it; were it by never
such brass collars, whips and handcuffs, leave
me not to walk over precipices! That I have been
called, by all the Newspapers, a "free man" will
avail me little, if my pilgrimage have ended in
death and wreck. O that the Newspapers had
called me slave, coward, fool, or what it pleased
their sweet voices to name me, and I had attained
not death, but life!—Liberty requires new definitions.

A conscious abhorrence and intolerance of
Folly, of Baseness, Stupidity, Poltroonery and all
that brood of things, dwells deep in some men:
still deeper in others an *unconscious* abhorrence
and intolerance, clothed moreover by the beneficent Supreme Powers in what stout appetites,
energies, egoisms so-called, are suitable to it;—
these latter are your Conquerors, Romans, Nor-
mans, Russians, Indo-English; Founders of what
we call Aristocracies. Which indeed have they
not the most "divine right" to found;—being
themselves very truly Ἄριστοι, BRAVEST, BEST;
and conquering generally a confused rabble of
WORST, or at lowest, clearly enough, of WORSE?
I think their divine right, tried, with affirmatory
verdict, in the greatest Law-Court known to me,
was good! A class of men who are dreadfully exclaimed against by Dryasdust; of whom nevertheless beneficent Nature has oftentimes had
need; and may, alas, again have need.

When, across the hundredfold poor scepti-
cisms, trivialisms, and constitutional cobwebberies of Dryasdust, you catch any glimpse of a

---

81 Carlyle uses the term to mean freedom from passions that blind one to knowing his true work and that prevent
him from doing it.

William the Conqueror, a Tancred of Haute-ville[82] or such like,—do you not discern veritably some rude outline of a true God-made King; whom not the Champion of England cased in tin,[83] but all Nature and the Universe were calling to the throne? It is absolutely necessary that he get thither. Nature does not mean her poor Saxon children to perish, of obesity, stupor or other malady, as yet: a stern Ruler and Line of Rulers therefore is called in,—a stern but most beneficent *perpetual House-Surgeon* is by Nature herself called in, and even the appropriate *fees* are provided for him! Dryasdust talks lamentably about Hereward and the Fen Counties; fate of Earl Waltheof;[84] Yorkshire and the North reduced to ashes; all of which is undoubtedly lamentable. But even Dryasdust apprises me of one fact: "A child, in this William's reign, might have carried a purse of gold from end to end of England." My erudite friend, it is a fact which outweighs a thousand! Sweep away thy constitutional, sentimental, and other cobwebberies; look eye to eye, if thou still have any eye, in the face of this big burly William Bastard: thou wilt see a fellow of most flashing discernment, of most strong lion-heart;—in whom, as it were, within a frame of oak and iron, the gods have planted the soul of "a man of genius"! Dost thou call that nothing? I call it an immense thing!—Rage enough was in this Willelmus Conquaestor, rage enough for his occasions;—and yet the essential element of him, as of all such men, is not scorching *fire*, but shining illuminative *light*. Fire and light are strangely interchangeable; nay, at bottom, I have found them different forms of the same most godlike "elementary substance" in our world: a thing worth stating in these days. The essential element of this Conquaestor is, first of all, the most sun-eyed perception of what *is* really what on this God's-Earth;—which, thou wilt find, does mean at bottom "Justice," and "Virtues" not a few: *Conformity* to what the Maker has seen good to make; that, I suppose, will mean Justice and a Virtue or two?—

Dost thou think Willelmus Conquaestor would have tolerated ten years' jargon, one hour's jargon, on the propriety of killing Cotton-manufactures by partridge Corn-Laws?[85] I fancy, this was not the man to knock out of his night's-rest with nothing but a noisy bedlamism in your mouth! "Assist us still better to bush the partridges; strangle Plugson who spins the shirts?" —"*Par la Splendeur de Dieu!*"—Dost thou think Willelmus Conquaestor, in this new time, with Steam-engine Captains of Industry on one hand of him, and Joe-Manton Captains of Idleness on the other, would have doubted which *was* really the Best; which did deserve strangling, and which not?

I have a certain indestructible regard for Willelmus Conquaestor. A resident House-Surgeon, provided by Nature for her beloved English People, and even furnished with the requisite fees, as I said; for he by no means felt himself doing Nature's work, this Willelmus, but his own work exclusively! And his own work withal it was; informed "*par la Splendeur de Dieu.*"—I say, it is necessary to get the work out of such a man, however harsh that be! When a world, not yet doomed for death, is rushing down to ever-deeper Baseness and Confusion, it is a dire necessity of Nature's to bring in her ARISTOCRACIES, her BEST, even by forcible methods. When their descendants or representatives cease entirely to *be* the Best, Nature's poor world will very soon rush down again to Baseness; and it becomes a dire necessity of Nature's to cast them out. Hence French Revolutions, Five-point Charters,[86] Democracies, and a mournful list of *Etceteras*, in these our afflicted times.

To what extent Democracy has now reached, how it advances irresistible with ominous, ever-increasing speed, he that will open

---

82 A Norman leader in the First Crusade.
83 A traditional impersonation of St. George, who appears in armor at the coronation ceremonies to guarantee the king's right to the throne.
84 Two Anglo-Saxon heroes, famous for their resistance to William.

85 Note that besides the workers (see note 62), the industrialists suffered from the Corn Laws. For one thing, countries that were potential buyers of British manufactured goods needed to sell their grain to pay for them, but this kind of foreign exchange was shut off by the Corn Laws. Furthermore, grain-producing countries, in reprisal, set up high tariffs of their own on goods the British wanted to sell them. Hence England suffered from overproduction: its manufactured products found no buyers at home or abroad. On p. 475, col. 1, lines 3–7, Carlyle speaks of John Bull's "three-years 'total stagnation of trade.'" Just below, Plugson is his symbolic figure of the manufacturer; Joe Manton was the fashionable gunsmith of the dilettante and idle aristocrats. "Par la Splendeur de Dieu!" was a favorite oath of William the Conqueror.
86 See "Heroes and Hero Worship," note 38.

his eyes on any province of human affairs may discern. Democracy is everywhere the inexorable demand of these ages, swiftly fulfilling itself. From the thunder of Napoleon battles, to the jabbering of Open-vestry in St. Mary Axe,[87] all things announce Democracy. A distinguished man, whom some of my readers will hear again with pleasure, thus writes to me what in these days he notes from the Wahngasse of Weissnicht-wo, where our London fashions seem to be in full vogue. Let us hear the Herr Teufelsdröckh[88] again, were it but the smallest word!

"Democracy, which means despair of finding any Heroes to govern you, and contented putting up with the want of them,—alas, thou too, *mein Lieber*, seest well how close it is of kin to *Atheism*, and other sad *Isms*: he who discovers no God whatever, how shall he discover Heroes, the visible Temples of God?—Strange enough meanwhile it is, to observe with what thoughtlessness, here in our rigidly Conservative Country, men rush into Democracy with full cry. Beyond doubt, his Excellenz the Titular-Herr Ritter Kauderwälsch von Pferdefuss-Quacksalber, he our distinguished Conservative Premier himself,[89] and all but the thicker-headed of his Party, discern Democracy to be inevitable as death, and are even desperate of delaying it much!

"You cannot walk the streets without beholding Democracy announce itself: the very Tailor has become, if not properly Sansculottic, which to him would be ruinous,[90] yet a Tailor unconsciously symbolizing, and prophesying with his scissors, the reign of Equality. What now is our fashionable coat? A thing of superfinest texture, of deeply meditated cut; with Malines-lace cuffs; quilted with gold; so that a man can carry, without difficulty, an estate of land on his back? *Keineswegs*, By no manner of means! The Sumptuary Laws[91] have fallen into such a state of desuetude as was never before seen. Our fashionable coat is an amphibium between barn-sack and drayman's doublet. The cloth of it is studiously coarse; the colour a speckled soot-black or rust-brown grey;—the nearest approach to a Peasant's. And for shape,—thou shouldst see it! The last consummation of the year now passing over us is definable as Three Bags; a big bag for the body, two small bags for the arms, and by way of collar a hem! The first Antique Cheruscan[92] who, of felt-cloth or bear's-hide, with bone or metal needle, set about making himself a coat, before Tailors had yet awakened out of Nothing,—did not he make it even so? A loose wide poke for body, with two holes to let out the arms; this was his original coat: to which holes it was soon visible that two small loose pokes, or sleeves, easily appended, would be an improvement.

"Thus has the Tailor-art, so to speak, overset itself, like most other things; changed its centre-of-gravity; whirled suddenly over from zenith to nadir. Your Stulz,[93] with huge somerset, vaults from his high shopboard down to the depths of primal savagery,—carrying much along with him! For I will invite thee to reflect that the Tailor, as topmost ultimate froth of Human Society, is indeed swift-passing, evanescent, slippery to decipher; yet significant of much, nay of all. Topmost evanescent froth, he is churned up from the very lees, and from all intermediate regions of the liquor. The general outcome he, visible to the eye, of what men aimed to do, and were obliged and enabled to do, in this one public department of symbolizing themselves to each other by covering of their skins. A smack of all Human Life lies in the Tailor: its wild struggles towards beauty, dignity, freedom, victory; and how, hemmed in by Sedan and Huddersfield,[94] by Nescience, Dullness, Prurience, and other sad necessities and laws of Nature, it has attained just to this: Grey savagery of Three Sacks with a hem!

"When the very Tailor verges towards

---

[87] An attempt to allow expression of the will of all tax-paying parishioners, considered a democratic innovation.

[88] Teufelsdröckh, the hero of *Sartor Resartus*, is a professor at the University of Weissnichtwo (I-know-not-where). *Wahngasse* = Delusion Alley.

[89] This is a characteristically vituperative set of names for Sir Robert Peel, who was prime minister when *Past and Present* was being written. The general meaning is "one who talks nonsense."

[90] The Sansculottes were a group of poor and extreme radicals active in the French Revolution. Inasmuch as such men could not afford culottes or knee breeches, it would be ruinous for the tailoring trade if they came to dominate the political scene.

[91] Restrictions on expenditure for dress, furniture, etc.

[92] Member of an early German tribe.

[93] A fashionable London tailor.

[94] Two cloth-manufacturing centers, one in France, the other in Yorkshire.

Sansculottism, is it not ominous? The last Divinity of poor mankind dethroning himself; sinking *his* taper too, flame downmost, like the Genius of Sleep or of Death; admonitory that Tailor-time shall be no more!—For, little as one could advise Sumptuary Laws at the present epoch, yet nothing is clearer than that where ranks do actually exist, strict division of costumes will also be enforced; that if we ever have a new[95] Hierarchy and Aristocracy, acknowledged veritably as such, for which I daily pray Heaven, the Tailor will re-awaken; and be, by volunteering and appointment, consciously and unconsciously, a safeguard of that same."—Certain farther observations, from the same invaluable pen, on our never-ending changes of mode, our "perpetual nomadic and even ape-like appetite for change and mere change" in all the equipments of our existence, and the "fatal revolutionary character" thereby manifested, we suppress for the present. It may be admitted that Democracy, in all meanings of the word, is in full career; irresistible by any Ritter Kauderwälsch or other Son of Adam, as times go. "Liberty" is a thing men are determined to have.

But truly, as I had to remark in the meanwhile, "the liberty of not being oppressed by your fellow man" is an indispensable, yet one of the most insignificant fractional parts of Human Liberty. No man oppresses thee, can bid thee fetch or carry, come or go, without reason shown. True; from all men thou art emancipated: but from Thyself and from the Devil—? No man, wiser, unwiser, can make thee come or go: but thy own futilities, bewilderments, thy false appetites for Money, Windsor Georges[96] and such like? No man oppresses thee, O free and independent Franchiser: but does not this stupid Porter-pot oppress thee? No Son of Adam can bid thee come or go; but this absurd Pot of Heavy-wet,[97] this can and does! Thou art the thrall not of Cedric the Saxon, but of thy own brutal appetites, and this scoured dish of liquor.

And thou pratest of thy "liberty"? Thou entire blockhead!

Heavy-wet and gin: alas, these are not the only kinds of thraldom. Thou who walkest in a vain show, looking out with ornamental dilettante sniff, and serene supremacy, at all Life and all Death; and amblest jauntily; perking up thy poor talk into crotchets, thy poor conduct into fatuous somnambulisms;—and *art* as an "enchanted Ape"[98] under God's sky, where thou mightest have been a man, had proper Schoolmasters and Conquerors, and Constables with cat-o'-nine tails, been vouchsafed thee: dost thou call that "liberty"? Or your unreposing Mammon-worshipper, again, driven, as if by Galvanisms, by Devils and Fixed-Ideas, who rises early and sits late, chasing the impossible; straining every faculty to "fill himself with the east wind,"—how merciful were it, could you, by mild persuasion or by the severest tyranny so-called, check him in his mad path, and turn him into a wiser one! All painful tyranny, in that case again, were but mild "surgery"; the pain of it cheap, as health and life, instead of galvanism and fixed-idea, are cheap at any price.

Sure enough, of all paths a man could strike into, there *is*, at any given moment, a *best path* for every man; a thing which, here and now, it were of all things *wisest* for him to do;—which could he be but led or driven to do, he were then doing "like a man," as we phrase it; all men and gods agreeing with him, the whole Universe virtually exclaiming Well-done to him! His success, in such case, were complete; his felicity a maximum. This path, to find this path and walk in it, is the one thing needful for him. Whatsoever forwards him in that, let it come to him even in the shape of blows and spurnings, is liberty: whatsoever hinders him, were it wardmotes, open-vestries, poll-booths, tremendous cheers, rivers of heavy-wet, is slavery.

The notion that a man's liberty consists in giving his vote at election-hustings, and saying, "Behold now I too have my twenty-thousandth part of a Talker in our National Palaver;[99]

[95] The word "new" is of vital importance; Carlyle is disgusted with the idle aristocracy of birth and inherited possessions, and looks for a *new* aristocracy, comprised of active, working Captains of Industry, freed of their Mammonism.
[96] Orders of St. George were decorations bestowed by the king at Windsor. They symbolize here the urge for social climbing.
[97] Strong malt beverage.
[98] In Book III, chap 3, Carlyle has described a race of men living by the Dead Sea who were changed by enchantment into chattering apes because they had made no use of their souls.
[99] Parliament.

will not all the gods be good to me?"—is one of the pleasantest! Nature nevertheless is kind at present; and puts it into the heads of many, almost of all. The liberty especially which has to purchase itself by social isolation, and each man standing separate from the other, having "no business with him" but a cash-account: this is such a liberty as the Earth seldom saw;—as the Earth will not long put up with, recommend it how you may. This liberty turns out, before it have long continued in action, with all men flinging up their caps round it, to be, for the Working Millions, a liberty to die by want of food; for the Idle Thousands and Units, alas, a still more fatal liberty to live in want of work; to have no earnest duty to do in this God's-World any more. What becomes of a man in such predicament? Earth's Laws are silent; and Heaven's speak in a voice which is not heard. No work, and the ineradicable need of work, give rise to new very wondrous life-philosophies, new very wondrous life-practices! Dilettantism, Pococurantism,[100] Beau-Brummelism,[101] with perhaps an occasional, half-mad, protesting burst of Byronism, establish themselves: at the end of a certain period,—if you go back to "the Dead Sea," there is, say our Moslem friends, a very strange "Sabbath-day" transacting itself there![102] —Brethren, we know but imperfectly yet, after ages of Constitutional Government, what Liberty and Slavery are.

Democracy, the chase of Liberty in that direction, shall go its full course; unrestrainable by him of Pferdefuss-Quacksalber, or any of *his* household. The Toiling Millions of Mankind, in most vital need and passionate instinctive desire of Guidance, shall cast away False-Guidance; and hope, for an hour, that No-Guidance will suffice them: but it can be for an hour only. The smallest item of human Slavery is the oppression of man by his Mock-Superiors; the palpablest, but I say at bottom the smallest. Let him shake off such oppression, trample it indignantly under his feet; I blame him not, I pity and commend him. But oppression by your Mock-Su-

periors well shaken off, the grand problem yet remains to solve: That of finding government by your Real-Superiors! Alas, how shall we ever learn the solution of that, benighted, bewildered, sniffing, sneering, god-forgetting unfortunates as we are? It is a work for centuries; to be taught us by tribulations, confusions, insurrections, obstructions; who knows if not by conflagration and despair! It is a lesson inclusive of all other lessons; the hardest of all lessons to learn.

One thing I do know: Those Apes, chattering on the branches by the Dead Sea, never got it learned; but chatter there to this day. To them no Moses need come a second time;[103] a thousand Moseses would be but so many painted Phantasms, interesting Fellow-Apes of new strange aspect,—whom they would "invite to dinner," be glad to meet with in lion-soirées. To them the voice of Prophecy, of heavenly monition, is quite ended. They chatter there, all Heaven shut to them, to the end of the world. The unfortunates! Oh, what is dying of hunger, with honest tools in your hand, with a manful purpose in your heart, and much real labour lying round you done, in comparison? You honestly quit your tools; quit a most muddy confused coil of sore work, short rations, of sorrows, dispiritments and contradictions, having now honestly done with it all;—and await, not entirely in a distracted manner, what the Supreme Powers, and the Silences and the Eternities may have to say to you.

A second thing I know: This lesson will have to be learned,—under penalties! England will either learn it, or England also will cease to exist among Nations. England will either learn to reverence its Heroes, and discriminate them from its Sham-Heroes and Valets and gaslighted Histrios; and to prize them as the audible God's-voice, amid all inane jargons and temporary market-cries, and say to them with heart-loyalty, "Be ye King and Priest, and Gospel and Guidance for us": or else England will continue to worship new and ever-new forms of Quackhood,—and so, with what resiliences and reboundings matters little, go down to the

---

100 Indifferentism.
101 Dandyism. Beau Brummell was the outstanding fop of the early nineteenth century.
102 See note 98 on the enchanted apes. "Their worship on the Sabbath now is to roost there, with unmusical screeches, and half-remember that they had souls."

103 The Dwellers by the Dead Sea might have escaped their fate if they had listened to Moses, who was sent to warn them, but they did not recognize the hero in him: rather they found him a humbug and a bore. See Book III, chap. 3.

Father of Quacks! Can I dread such things of England? Wretched, thick-eyed, gross-hearted mortals, why will ye worship lies, and "Stuffed Clothes-suits, created by the ninth-parts of men!"[104] It is not your purses that suffer; your farm-rents, your commerces, your mill-revenues, loud as ye lament over these; no, it is not these alone, but a far deeper than these: it is your souls that lie dead, crushed down under despicable Nightmares, Atheisms, Brain-fumes; and are not souls at all, but mere succedanea[105] for *salt* to keep your bodies and their appetites from putrefying! Your cotton-spinning and thrice-miraculous mechanism, what is this too, by itself, but a larger kind of Animalism? Spiders can spin, Beavers can build and show contrivance: the Ant lays up accumulation of capital, and has, for aught I know, a Bank of Antland. If there is no soul in man higher than all that, did it reach to sailing on the cloud-rack and spinning sea-sand; then I say, man is but an animal, a more cunning kind of brute: he has no soul, but only a succedaneum for salt. Whereupon, seeing himself to be truly of the beasts that perish, he ought to admit it, I think;—and also straightway universally to kill himself; and so, in a manlike manner, at least, *end,* and wave these brute-worlds *his* dignified farewell!—

Book IV, Chapter 3

THE ONE INSTITUTION[106]

What our Government can do in this grand Problem of the Working Classes of England? Yes, supposing the insane Corn-Laws totally abolished, all speech of them ended, and "from ten to twenty years of new possibility to live and find wages" conceded us in consequence: What the English Government might be expected to accomplish or attempt towards rendering the existence of our Labouring Millions somewhat less anomalous, somewhat less impossible, in the years that are to follow those "ten or twenty," if either "ten" or "twenty" there be? . . .

Of Time-Bill, Factory-Bill and other such Bills the present Editor has no authority to speak. He knows not, it is for others than he to know, in what specific ways it may be feasible to interfere, with Legislation, between the Workers and the Master-Workers;—knows only and sees, what all men are beginning to see, that Legislative interference, and interferences not a few are indispensable; that as a lawless anarchy of supply-and-demand, on market-wages alone, this province of things cannot longer be left. Nay interference has begun: there are already Factory Inspectors,—who seem to have no *lack* of work. Perhaps there might be Mine-Inspectors too:—might there not be Furrowfield Inspectors[107] withal, and ascertain for us how on seven-and-sixpence a week a human family does live! Interference has begun; it must continue, must extensively enlarge itself, deepen and sharpen itself. Such things cannot longer be idly lapped in darkness, and suffered to go on unseen: the Heavens do see them; the curse, not the blessing of the Heavens is on an Earth that refuses to see them.

Again, are not Sanitary Regulations possible for a Legislature? The old Romans had their Aediles;[108] who would, I think, in direct contravention to supply-and-demand, have rigorously seen rammed up into total abolition many a foul cellar in our Southwarks, Saint-Gileses, and dark poison-lanes; saying sternly, "Shall a Roman man dwell there?" The Legislature, at whatever cost of consequences, would have had to answer, "God forbid!"—The Legislature, even as it now is, could order all dingy Manufacturing Towns to cease from their soot and darkness; to let-in the blessed sunlight, the blue of Heaven, and become clear and clean; to burn their coal-smoke, namely, and make flame of it. Baths, free air, a wholesome temperature, ceilings twenty feet high, might be ordained, by Act of Parliament, in all establishments licensed as Mills. There are such Mills already extant; —honour to the builders of them![109] The Legislature can say to others: Go ye and do likewise; better if you can.

Every toiling Manchester, its smoke and soot all burnt, ought it not, among so many world-wide conquests, to have a hundred acres

---

104 Old proverb: "Nine tailors make a man." The contemporary leaders of England seem to Carlyle to be tailors' dummies or quacks.

105 Substitutes.

106 The one orderly arrangement; here, of society.

107 Agricultural inspectors.

108 Building inspectors.

109 Robert Owen and a few of his enlightened contemporaries.

or so of free green-field, with trees on it, conquered, for its little children to disport in; for its all-conquering workers to take a breath of twilight air in? You would say so! A willing Legislature could say so with effect. A willing Legislature could say very many things! And to whatsoever "vested interest," or suchlike, stood up, gainsaying merely, "I shall lose profits,"—the willing Legislature would answer, "Yes, but my sons and daughters will gain health, and life, and a soul."—"What is to become of our Cotton-trade?" cried certain Spinners, when the Factory Bill[110] was proposed; "What is to become of our invaluable Cotton-trade?" The Humanity of England answered steadfastly: "Deliver me these rickety perishing souls of infants, and let your Cotton-trade take its chance. God Himself commands the one thing; not God especially the other. We cannot have prosperous Cotton-trades at the expense of keeping the Devil a partner in them!"—

Bills enough, were the Corn-Law Abrogation Bill once passed, and a Legislature willing! Nay this one Bill, which lies yet unenacted, a right Education Bill, is not this of itself the sure parent of innumerable wise Bills,—wise regulations, practical methods and proposals, gradually ripening towards the state of Bills? To irradiate with intelligence, that is to say, with order, arrangement and all blessedness, the Chaotic, Unintelligent: how, except by educating, *can* you accomplish this? That thought, reflection, articulate utterance and understanding be awakened in these individual million heads, which are the atoms of your Chaos: there is no other way of illuminating any Chaos! The sum-total of intelligence that is found in it, determines the extent of order that is possible for your Chaos,—the feasibility and rationality of what your Chaos will dimly demand from you, and will gladly obey when proposed by you! It is an exact equation; the one accurately measures the other.—If the whole English People, during these "twenty years of respite," be not educated, with at least schoolmaster's educating, a tremendous responsibility, before God and men, will rest somewhere! How dare any man, especially a man calling himself minister of God, stand up in any Parliament or place, under any

pretext or delusion, and for a day or an hour forbid God's Light to come into the world, and bid the Devil's Darkness continue in it one hour more! For all light and science, under all shapes, in all degrees of perfection, is of God; all darkness, nescience, is of the Enemy of God. "The schoolmaster's creed is somewhat awry?" Yes, I have found few creeds entirely correct; few light-beams shining *white,* pure of admixture: but of all creeds and religions now or ever before known, was not that of thoughtless thriftless Animalism, of Distilled Gin, and Stupor and Despair, unspeakably the least orthodox? We will exchange *it* even with Paganism, with Fetishism; and, on the whole, must exchange it with something.

An effective "Teaching Service" I do consider that there must be; some Education Secretary, Captain-General of Teachers, who will actually contrive to get us *taught.* Then again, why should there not be an "Emigration Service," and Secretary, with adjuncts, with funds, forces, idle Navy-ships, and ever-increasing apparatus; in fine an *effective system* of Emigration; so that, at length, before our twenty years of respite ended, every honest willing Workman who found England too strait, and the "Organization of Labour" not yet sufficiently advanced, might find likewise a bridge built to carry him into new Western Lands, there to "organize" with more elbow-room some labour for himself? There to be a real blessing, raising new corn for us, purchasing new webs and hatchets from us; leaving us at least in peace;—instead of staying here to be a Physical-Force Chartist,[111] unblessed and no blessing! Is it not scandalous to consider that a Prime Minister could raise within the year, as I have seen it done, a Hundred and Twenty Millions Sterling to shoot the French;[112] and we are stopped short for want of the hundredth part of that to keep the English living? The bodies of the English living, and the souls of the English living:—these two "Services," an Education Service and an Emigration Service, these with others will actually have to be organized!

A free bridge for Emigrants: why, we should then be on a par with America itself, the

---

110 The Factory Act of 1833, by which the working hours of women and children were restricted.

111 Chartists were divided into two categories according to the methods they advocated for obtaining the Charter: Moral Force Chartists and Physical Force Chartists.
112 To defeat Napoleon.

most favoured of all lands that have no government; and we should have, besides, so many traditions and mementoes of priceless things which America has cast away. We could proceed deliberately to "organize Labour," not doomed to perish unless we effected it within year and day;—every willing Worker that proved superfluous, finding a bridge ready for him. This verily will have to be done; the Time is big with this. Our little Isle is grown too narrow for us; but the world is wide enough yet for another Six Thousand Years. England's sure markets will be among new Colonies of Englishmen in all quarters of the Globe. All men trade with all men, when mutually convenient; and are even bound to do it by the Maker of men. Our friends of China, who guiltily refused to trade, in these circumstances,—had we not to argue with them, in cannon-shot at last, and convince them that they ought to trade![113] "Hostile Tariffs" will arise, to shut us out; and then again will fall, to let us in: but the Sons of England, speakers of the English language were it nothing more, will in all times have the ineradicable predisposition to trade with England. Mycale was the *Pan-Ionion*,[114] rendezvous of all the Tribes of Ion, for old Greece: why should not London long continue the *All-Saxon-home,* rendezvous of all the "Children of the Harz-Rock,"[115] arriving, in select samples, from the Antipodes and elsewhere, by steam and otherwise, to the "season" here!—What a Future; wide as the world, if we have the heart and heroism for it,—which, by Heaven's blessing, we shall:

> *Keep not standing fixed and rooted,*
> *Briskly venture, briskly roam;*
> *Head and hand, where'er thou foot it,*
> *And stout heart are still at home.*
>
> *In what land the sun does visit,*
> *Brisk are we, whate'er betide:*
> *To give space for wandering is it*
> *That the world was made so wide.*[116]

Fourteen hundred years ago, it was by a consider-

able "Emigration Service," never doubt it, by much enlistment, discussion and apparatus, that we ourselves arrived in this remarkable Island,—and got into our present difficulties among others!

It is true the English Legislature, like the English People, is of slow temper; essentially conservative. In our wildest periods of reform, in the Long Parliament itself, you notice always the invincible instinct to hold fast by the Old; to admit the *minimum* of New; to expand, if it be possible, some old habit or method, already found fruitful, into new growth for the new need. It is an instinct worthy of all honour; akin to all strength and all wisdom. The Future hereby is not dissevered from the Past, but based continuously on it; grows with all the vitalities of the Past, and is rooted down deep into the beginnings of us. The English Legislature is entirely repugnant to believe in "new epochs." The English Legislature does not occupy itself with epochs; has, indeed, other business to do than looking at the Time-Horologe and hearing it tick! Nevertheless new epochs do actually come; and with them new imperious peremptory necessities; so that even an English Legislature has to look up, and admit, though with reluctance, that the hour has struck. The hour having struck, let us not say "impossible":—it will have to be possible! "Contrary to the habits of Parliament, the habits of Government"? Yes: but did any Parliament or Government ever sit in a Year Forty-three before? One of the most original, unexampled years and epochs; in several important respects totally unlike any other! For Time, all-edacious and all-feracious,[117] does run on: and the Seven Sleepers,[118] awakening hungry after a hundred years, find that it is not their old nurses who can now give them suck!

For the rest, let not any Parliament, Aristocracy, Millocracy, or Member of the Governing Class, condemn with much triumph this small specimen of "remedial measures"; or ask again, with the least anger, of this Editor, What is to be done, How that alarming problem of the Work-

---

113 The First Opium War, 1839–42, brought about by the desire of English traders to import opium from China.
114 A shrine on the slope of Mt. Mycale in Asia Minor, the scene of a festival in which the twelve cities of the Ionian league periodically participated.
115 A reference probably to the Germanic origin of the Saxons, the Harz Mountains being a range in Germany.
116 Translated from Goethe's *Wilhelm Meister*.

117 All-devouring and all-fruitful.
118 Seven Christian youths who, according to legend, concealed themselves in a cave near Ephesus in the third century in order to escape pagan persecution and did not waken for two or three hundred years, by which time they found Christianity established.

ing Classes is to be managed? Editors are not here, foremost of all, to say How. A certain Editor thanks the gods that nobody pays him three hundred thousand pounds a year, two hundred thousand, twenty thousand, or any similar sum of cash for saying How;—that his wages are very different, his work somewhat fitter for him. An Editor's stipulated work is to apprise *thee* that it must be done. The "way to do it,"— is to try it, knowing that thou shalt die if it be not done. There is the bare back, there is the web of cloth; thou shalt cut me a coat to cover the bare back, thou whose trade it is. "Impossible"? Hapless Fraction,[119] dost thou discern Fate there, half unveiling herself in the gloom of the future, with her gibbet-cords, her steel-whips, and very authentic Tailor's Hell; waiting to see whether it is "possible"? Out with thy scissors, and cut that cloth or thy own windpipe!

Book IV, Chapter 4

CAPTAINS OF INDUSTRY

If I believed that Mammonism with its adjuncts was to continue henceforth the one serious principle of our existence, I should reckon it idle to solicit remedial measures from any Government, the disease being insusceptible of remedy. Government can do much, but it can in no wise do all. Government, as the most conspicuous object in Society, is called upon to give signal of what shall be done; and, in many ways, to preside over, further, and command the doing of it. But the Government cannot do, by all its signalling and commanding, what the Society is radically indisposed to do. In the long-run every Government is the exact symbol of its People, with their wisdom and unwisdom; we have to say, Like People like Government.—The main substance of this immense Problem of Organizing Labour, and first of all of Managing the Working Classes, will, it is very clear, have to be solved by those who stand practically in the middle of it; by those who themselves work and preside over work. Of all that can be enacted by any Parliament in regard to it, the germs must already lie potentially extant in those two Classes, who are to obey such enactment. A Human Chaos *in*

which there is no light, you vainly attempt to irradiate by light shed *on* it: order never can arise there.

But it is my firm conviction that the "Hell of England" will *cease* to be that of "not making money"; that we shall get a nobler Hell and a nobler Heaven! I anticipate light *in* the Human Chaos, glimmering, shining more and more; under manifold true signals from without That light shall shine. Our deity no longer being Mammon,—O Heavens, each man will then say to himself: "Why such deadly haste to make money? I shall not go to Hell, even if I do not make money! There is another Hell, I am told!" Competition, at railway-speed, in all branches of commerce and work will then abate:—good felt-hats for the head, in every sense, instead of seven-feet lath-and-plaster hats on wheels,[120] will then be discoverable! Bubble-periods, with their panics and commercial crises, will again become infrequent; steady modest industry will take the place of gambling speculation. To be a noble Master, among noble Workers, will again be the first ambition with some few; to be a rich Master only the second. How the Inventive Genius of England, with the whirr of its bobbins and billy-rollers shoved somewhat into the backgrounds of the brain, will contrive and devise, not cheaper produce exclusively, but fairer distribution of the produce at its present cheapness! By degrees, we shall again have a Society with something of Heroism in it, something of Heaven's Blessing on it; we shall again have, as my German friend asserts, "instead of Mammon-Feudalism with unsold cotton-shirts and Preservation of the Game, noble just Industrialism and Government by the Wisest!"

It is with the hope of awakening here and there a British man to know himself for a man and divine soul, that a few words of parting admonition, to all persons to whom the Heavenly Powers have lent power of any kind in this land, may now be addressed. And first to those same Master-Workers, Leaders of Industry; who stand nearest, and in fact powerfullest, though not most prominent, being as yet in too many senses a Virtuality[121] rather than an Actuality.

The Leaders of Industry, if Industry is

---

119 Again a reference to the old proverb, "Nine tailors make a man."

120 See Book III, chap. 2, note 51.
121 I.e., a potentiality.

ever to be led, are virtually the Captains of the World(!) if there be no nobleness in them, there will never be an Aristocracy more. But let the Captains of Industry consider: once again, are they born of other clay than the old Captains of Slaughter; doomed for ever to be no Chivalry, but a mere gold-plated *Doggery,*—what the French well name *Canaille,* "Doggery" with more or less gold carrion at its disposal? Captains of Industry are the true Fighters, henceforth recognizable as the only true ones: Fighters against Chaos, Necessity and the Devils and Jötuns;[122] and lead on Mankind in that great, and alone true, and universal warfare; the stars in their courses fighting for them, and all Heaven and all Earth saying audibly, Well done! Let the Captains of Industry retire into their own hearts, and ask solemnly, If there is nothing but vulturous hunger for fine wines, valet reputation and gilt carriages, discoverable there? Of hearts made by the Almighty God I will not believe such a thing. Deep-hidden under wretchedest god-forgetting Cants, Epicurisms, Dead-Sea Apisms; forgotten as under foulest fat Lethe mud and weeds, there is yet, in all hearts born into this God's-World, a spark of the Godlike slumbering. Awake, O nightmare sleepers; awake, arise, or be for ever fallen! This is not playhouse poetry; it is sober fact. Our England, our world cannot live as it is. It will connect itself with a God again, or go down with nameless throes and fire-consummation to the Devils. Thou who feelest aught of such a Godlike stirring in thee, any faintest intimation of it as through heavy-laden dreams, follow *it,* I conjure thee. Arise, save thyself, be one of those that save thy country.

Bucaniers, Chactaw Indians, whose supreme aim in fighting is that they may get the scalps, the money, that they may amass scalps and money; out of such came no Chivalry, and never will! Out of such came only gore and wreck, infernal rage and misery; desperation quenched in annihilation. Behold it, I bid thee, behold there, and consider! What is it that thou have a hundred thousand-pound bills laid up in thy strong-room, a hundred scalps hung up in thy wigwam? I value not them or thee. Thy scalps and thy thousand-pound bills are as yet nothing, if no nobleness from within irradiate them; if no

Chivalry, in action, or in embryo ever struggling towards birth and action, be there.

Love of men cannot be bought by cash-payment; and without love, men cannot endure to be together. You cannot lead a Fighting World without having it regimented, chivalried: the thing, in a day, becomes impossible; all men in it, the highest at first, the very lowest at last, discern consciously, or by a noble instinct, this necessity. And can you any more continue to lead a Working World unregimented, anarchic? I answer, and the Heavens and Earth are now answering, No! The thing becomes not "in a day" impossible; but in some two generations it does. Yes, when fathers and mothers, in Stockport hunger-cellars, begin to eat their children, and Irish widows have to prove their relationship by dying of typhus-fever; and amid Governing "Corporations of the Best and Bravest," busy to preserve their game by "bushing," dark millions of God's human creatures start up in mad Chartisms, impracticable Sacred-Months,[123] and Manchester Insurrections;—and there is a virtual Industrial Aristocracy as yet only half-alive, spell-bound amid money-bags and ledgers; and an actual Idle Aristocracy seemingly near dead in somnolent delusions, in trespasses and double-barrels; "sliding," as on inclined-planes, which every new year they *soap* with new Hansard's-jargon[124] under God's sky, and so are "sliding" ever faster, towards a "scale"[125] and balance-scale whereon is written *Thou art found Wanting:*—in such days, after a generation or two, I say, it does become, even to the low and simple, very palpably impossible! No Working World, any more than a Fighting World, can be led on without a noble Chivalry of Work, and laws and fixed rules which follow out of that,—far nobler than any Chivalry of Fighting was. As an anarchic multitude on mere Supply-and-demand, it is becoming inevitable that we dwindle in horrid suicidal convulsion, and self-abrasion, frightful to the imagination, into *Chactaw* Workers. With wigwams and scalps,—with palaces and thousand-pound bills; with savagery, depopulation,

---

122 Giants of Norse mythology.

123 An allusion to the revolutionary calendar adopted in France in 1793; here, a symbol of the French Revolution itself.
124 Discussion in Parliament. Journals of the debates were published by Hansard.
125 Cf. note 70, on the sliding-scale of duties on corn.

chaotic desolation! Good Heavens, will not one French Revolution and Reign of Terror suffice us, but must there be two? There will be two if needed; there will be twenty if needed; there will be precisely as many as are needed. The Laws of Nature will have themselves fulfilled. That is a thing certain to me.

Your gallant battle-hosts and work-hosts, as the others did, will need to be made loyally yours; they must and will be regulated, methodically secured in their just share of conquest under you;—joined with you in veritable brotherhood, sonhood, by quite other and deeper ties than those of temporary day's wages! How would mere redcoated regiments, to say nothing of chivalries, fight for you, if you could discharge them on the evening of the battle, on payment of the stipulated shillings,—and they discharge you on the morning of it! Chelsea Hospitals,[126] pensions, promotions, rigorous lasting covenant on the one side and on the other, are indispensable even for a hired fighter. The Feudal Baron, much more,—how could he subsist with mere temporary mercenaries round him, at sixpence a day; ready to go over to the other side, if sevenpence were offered? He could not have subsisted;—and his noble instinct saved him from the necessity of even trying! The Feudal Baron had a Man's Soul in him; to which anarchy, mutiny, and the other fruits of temporary mercenaries, were intolerable: he had never been a Baron otherwise, but had continued a Chactaw and Bucanier. He felt it precious, and at last it became habitual, and his fruitful enlarged existence included it as a necessity, to have men round him who in heart loved him; whose life he watched over with rigour yet with love; who were prepared to give their life for him, if need came. It was beautiful; it was human! Man lives not otherwise, nor can live contented, anywhere or anywhen. Isolation is the sum-total of wretchedness to man. To be cut off, to be left solitary: to have a world alien, not your world; all a hostile camp for you; not a home at all, of hearts and faces who are yours, whose you are! It is the frightfullest enchantment; too truly a work of the Evil One. To have neither superior, nor inferior, nor equal, united manlike to you. Without father, without child, without brother. Man knows no sadder destiny.

"How is each of us," exclaims Jean Paul,[127] "so lonely in the wide bosom of the All!" Encased each as in his transparent "ice-palace"; our brother visible in his, making signals and gesticulations to us;—visible, but for ever unattainable: on his bosom we shall never rest, nor he on ours. It was not a God that did this; no!

Awake, ye noble Workers, warriors in the one true war: all this must be remedied. It is you who are already half-alive, whom I will welcome into life; whom I will conjure in God's name to shake off your enchanted sleep, and live wholly! Cease to count scalps, gold-purses; not in these lies your or our salvation. Even these, if you count only these, will not be left. Let bucaniering be put far from you; alter, speedily abrogate all laws of the bucaniers, if you would gain any victory that shall endure. Let God's justice, let pity, nobleness and manly valour, with more gold-purses or with fewer, testify themselves in this your brief Life-transit to all the Eternities, the Gods and Silences. It is to you I call; for ye are not dead, ye are already half-alive: there is in you a sleepless dauntless energy, the prime-matter of all nobleness in man. Honour to you in your kind. It is to you I call: ye know at least this, That the mandate of God to His creature man is: Work! The future Epic of the World rests not with those that are near dead, but with those that are alive, and those that are coming into life.

Look around you. Your world-hosts are all in mutiny, in confusion, destitution; on the eve of fiery wreck and madness! They will not march farther for you, on the sixpence a day and supply-and-demand principle: they will not; nor ought they, nor can they. Ye shall reduce them to order, begin reducing them. To order, to just subordination; noble loyalty in return for noble guidance. Their souls are driven nigh mad; let yours be sane and ever saner. Not as a bewildered bewildering mob; but as a firm regimented mass, with real captains over them, will these men march any more. All human interests, combined human endeavours, and social growths in this world, have, at a certain stage of their development, required organising: and Work, the grandest of human interests, does now require it.

God knows, the task will be hard: but no

---

[126] For disabled soldiers.

[127] Johann Paul Richter (1763–1825), German author.

noble task was ever easy. This task will wear away your lives, and the lives of your sons and grandsons: but for what purpose, if not for tasks like this, were lives given to men? Ye shall cease to count your thousand-pound scalps, the noble of you shall cease! Nay, the very scalps, as I say, will not long be left if you count on these. Ye shall cease wholly to be barbarous vulturous Chactaws, and become noble European Nineteenth-Century Men. Ye shall know that Mammon, in never such gigs and flunkey "respectabilities," is not the alone God; that of himself he is but a Devil, and even a Brute-god.

Difficult? Yes, it will be difficult. The short-fibre cotton; that too was difficult. The waste cotton-shrub, long useless, disobedient, as the thistle by the wayside,—have ye not conquered it; made it into beautiful bandana webs; white woven shirts for men; bright-tinted air-garments wherein flit goddesses? Ye have shivered mountains asunder, made the hard iron pliant to you

as soft putty: the Forest-giants, Marsh-jötuns bear sheaves of golden grain; Aegir the Sea-demon himself stretches his back for a sleek highway to you, and on Firehorses and Windhorses ye career. Ye are most strong. Thor red-bearded, with his blue sun-eyes, with his cheery heart and strong thunder-hammer, he and you have prevailed. Ye are most strong, ye Sons of the icy North, of the far East,—far marching from your rugged Eastern Wildernesses, hitherward from the grey Dawn of Time! Ye are Sons of the *Jötun*-land; the land of Difficulties Conquered. Difficult? You must try this thing. Once try it with the understanding that it will and shall have to be done. Try it as ye try the paltrier thing, making of money! I will bet on you once more, against all Jötuns, Tailor-gods, Double-barrelled Law-wards,[128] and Denizens of Chaos whatsoever!

---

[128] The idle aristocracy (lords) shooting partridges with double-barreled guns.

Thomas Babington Macaulay
1800–1859

We noticed in the introduction to the Victorian period that the Victorians thought of themselves as living in a changed world, a new outer world of big business and middle-class government, and a new inner world of religious doubt. Macaulay is a perfect index to the first of these two changes. He is the great spokesman of the middle class, or, more exactly, of the upper-middle class of businessmen who rose to power with the Industrial Revolution and who dominated the political and social order of the Victorian age. He gives us their philosophy of life in the broad sense that includes their ideals and attitudes as well as their specific beliefs.

Both by inheritance and by training Macaulay was well equipped to speak for the Captains of Industry. He was born in 1800, and thus reached maturity at exactly the time when the manufacturing system and the political agitation for extending the suffrage were first attracting wide attention. His father, Zachary Macaulay, was a wealthy London businessman, a leading Evangelical in religion, and a Tory in politics. The son was a precocious boy who formed the habit early in life of constant reading in both history and literature, and of writing, too. Be-

fore he was eight he had written a compendium of universal history and started two heroic poems in the manner of Scott. In 1818 he went to Cambridge, where he came under an influence exactly opposite to the Tory-Evangelical atmosphere of his home. This was Benthamism, which a brilliant group of young liberals was ardently preaching. They were crying out for a democratic form of government and the disestablishment of the Church of England. The crucial result of this influence on Macaulay was his adoption of a middle position. In religion he became a Broad Churchman, supporting the state church but eager to see it "liberalized" in doctrine, with major stress placed on Christian ethics. In politics he discarded his Toryism but refused to go to any democratic extremes. In short, he became a Whig Liberal, willing to reform the Church and eager to extend the suffrage to the middle class but no further.

When he left college in 1824, he had two great ambitions, to succeed in literature and in politics. He fulfilled both. In 1825 his essay on Milton, crammed with liberal doctrines, made him famous almost overnight; it was published, quite rightly, in the great Whig periodical, the *Edinburgh Review*. In the next

Thomas Babington Macaulay (1800–1859). As an M.P., administrative adviser to India, and author of the famous *History*, Macaulay was dedicated to laissez-faire and the ideal of material progress. However, being a liberal, he also spoke out for the political emancipation of Catholics and Jews. *The Granger Collection.*

five years he wrote a series of brilliant essays for the same magazine, striking at the Tories to the right and the Benthamites to the left, and urging a compromise that would "amend, conciliate, and preserve," precisely the position of the liberal Whigs of the 1820s. In 1830 he won a seat in the House of Commons, where his speeches in support of the 1832 Reform Bill marked the alliance of the Whigs with the middle-class industrialists.

In the years that followed, Macaulay was sent to India, to draw up the Indian penal code and reorganize Indian education on Western lines; continued, on his return, to follow his double career of literature and politics; and on his defeat for reelection in 1847, retired from public life to write his famous, and enormously popular, *History of England.* In 1857 he was raised to the peerage and became a Whig lord. In 1859, when he died, he was buried in Westminster Abbey, easily the most outstanding writer of the age in fame and popularity.

Such an amazing record of success must not blind us to his limitations. His mind was vigorous and sturdy, able to grasp broad principles and broad emotions, but insensitive to subtleties of thought and nuances of feeling. His command of ideas was infe-

rior to his command of words: he was an orator rather than a thinker, and more of a debater than a seeker for truth. Above all, he had no capacity for growth. What he believed when he left Cambridge he always believed. He never reexamined his premises. This gave him a narrow strength. He knew where he stood and he stood there rigidly. And what he stood on was the Whig-Liberal creed, in politics and religion, which fitted the needs and desires of the middle-class capitalists.

In 1829 Robert Southey, the friend of Wordsworth and Coleridge, published a book called *Sir Thomas More: or, Colloquies on the Progress and Prospects of Society.* Almost every page of it stated some opinion which outraged Macaulay's stolid convictions, so that his fighting review of it defines his political-economic position in black and white. Southey had once been a radical supporter of democracy and the French Revolution, but frightened by the Reign of Terror, the confiscation of property, and the attack on Switzerland in 1798, he swung violently in the other direction and became an extreme reactionary, opposed to all liberal reforms and advocating a strong autocratic government in the hands of the aristocracy and the Anglican Church. Against such blind reaction Macaulay's attack is welcome.

But there was another side of Southey's book much less ugly, and another side of Macaulay's review much less attractive. Southey was one of the first to recognize the terrible cost in human suffering of the factory system—the long hours and low wages, child labor, the slum conditions in the new industrial cities, the displacement of the old personal and human relationship of employer and employee in small factories and shops by the strictly business one of "cash-nexus," and above all the slavery of the worker in a system where, without the help of a union, he had to accept what he was offered or go unemployed. To this indictment Macaulay replies that there is less unemployment in the towns than in the country and that men now live longer in Manchester and Leeds than they used to! After which evasion, he pounces with devastating but empty rhetoric on the passage (pp. 495–96) where Southey seems to attack the factories on aesthetic grounds but primarily is using architecture as a symbol of moral conditions. (The force of "Mammon's temples" and "helotry" should be noted; and to make his real meaning clear to everyone except Macaulay, Southey ends by saying that these edifices are "as offensive to the eye *as to the mind.*") It is true that at one point Macaulay admits that the laboring classes in England suffer severe hardships, but he adds at once that they are no worse off than the same classes on the Continent. To which Southey might have replied, "Two wrongs do not make a right." In the first years of industrial achievement, it was hard to see the cost of the system, nor were the new capitalists eager to look the ugly facts in the face. Rhetorical sophistry was an easier way out.

Given their contrasting views of the factory system, their opposite political theories logically follow. Southey wants a strong aristocratic government which will enact a program of labor legislation—factory acts, an emigration service to the colonies to solve overpopulation, a great national works program to solve unemployment. If the state can vote millions for war, why not for war on poverty and destitution? But for the liberal Macaulay the duties of government are strictly limited to protecting the persons and property of the people from attack. A strong state not only will crush individual freedom and initiative, but may well be a blundering, fumbling bureaucracy. Therefore, *laissez faire, laissez faire!* To which Southey answers, yes, government interference is bad, but to do nothing and let these appalling conditions continue is worse. Finally, in Macaulay's last paragraph we see the economic foundation of his political theory. If capital is "to find its most lucrative course," the government must keep hands off—and balance the budget.

On one thing, however, Southey and Macaulay saw eye to eye. They both hated democracy, Southey any democracy, Macaulay anything more than a middle-class democracy. The famous letter to Commodore Randall of the New York Yacht Club advances a prophetic and challenging thesis: that full democracy will lead either directly to communism and the end of civilization (the end, that is, of private property), or indirectly to dictatorship and the end of liberty—indirectly, because to ward off communism the middle class will be forced to back a dictatorship of the right. Many would agree with this analysis, though they might not welcome one or the other alternative. Others will feel that the real danger of communism lies, not in democracy as such, but in the very system Macaulay is defending, a completely laissez-faire policy which does nothing to solve the explosive miseries and injustices of trade cycles, unemployment, large disparity of income. Certainly, Macaulay's letter is fair warning to any democracy which does not meet the economic problems of a capitalist economy.

The essay on Bacon is an exact complement to the essay on Southey. Both start from the same middle-class ideal of material progress; the difference is that in the Southey essay Macaulay has advocated the best *political* means of attaining that goal, and in the Bacon essay he advocates the best *intellectual* means or method of attaining it, namely, the application of science to industry and medicine. The important thing, however, in the "Bacon" is its revelation of the standard of values which the worship of science and industry produced. Macaulay assumes that in order to be valuable any action or study must be useful (it must issue in practical and tangible results) and it must be progressive (it must change and improve). The two are closely connected, since progress tends to be measured in terms of improved efficiency. These initial assumptions, especially utility, lead to the antiintellectualism and the antiidealism for which the essay is notorious. If practical results are exalted, theory and speculation, philosophy and art, as well as high ideals that cannot be achieved, will be considered useless; and the thinker (philosopher, theologian, artist) will seem of little account compared with the man of action, the scientist or businessman, who gets things done. Macaulay is so dominated by these attitudes that he can dismiss all the work of sixty generations of thinkers before Bacon as words, words, words; and can imagine that because the moral ideal of Stoicism was never achieved, it bore no "fruit" (as though no one had ever been better or happier for having tried, however unsuccessfully, to live like a Stoic). In the final paragraph we notice the emphasis on psychiatry, in which Macaulay recognizes scientific method applied to problems of conduct, and the divorce of religion from theology (religion is useful because it provides ethical restraints and the consoling promise of immortality; theology is not only useless but purely fanciful, since its "truths" cannot be scientifically demonstrated). In all these respects the essay is of central importance for revealing the effect on values, modern as well as Victorian, of a scientific, industrial society, and for showing us the resulting loss as well as the gain.

Macaulay's greatest work is his *History of England.* Although it covers only the reigns of James II and William and Mary, the plan was to deal with all the transactions, social life as well as political events, "which took place between the Revolution which brought the Crown into harmony with the Parliament [the Whig revolution of 1688], and the Revolution which brought the Parliament into harmony with the nation [the middle-class revolution of 1832]." Macaulay had two intentions. The first was to show the progress of liberty, as his plan suggests, and the progress of material wealth and power (so that the *History* complements the essays on Southey and Bacon); the second was to adapt the method of Scott to the writing of history and give "to truth those attractions which have been usurped by fiction":

To make the past present, to bring the distant near, to place us in the society of a great man or on the eminence which overlooks the field of a mighty battle, to invest with the reality of human flesh and blood beings whom we are too much inclined to consider as personified qualities in an allegory, to

call up our ancestors before us with all their pe-
culiarities of language, manners, and garb, to show
us over their houses, to seat us at their tables, to
rummage their old-fashioned wardrobes, to explain
the uses of their ponderous furniture, these parts of
the duty which properly belongs to the historian
have been appropriated by the historical novelist.

Macaulay succeeded brilliantly in both intentions.
His Whig view of history is still dominant, and his
imaginative re-creation of the past has never, except
perhaps by Carlyle, been equaled.

TEXTS: The best edition of the *History of
England* is that edited by C. H. Firth (6 vols., 1913–
15). The standard biography is *The Life and Letters
of Lord Macaulay* by G. O. Trevelyan (2 vols., 1876).
John Clive's fine *Macaulay: The Shaping of the Historian* (New York, 1973) covers the early life, 1800–
1837. Arthur Bryant's *Macaulay* (1932) is a competent
study, which includes a bibliography. Mark Pattison's
article in the eleventh edition of the *Encyclopaedia
Britannica* and Leslie Stephen's essay in *Hours in a
Library* (1874–79), Vol. II, are valuable Victorian es-
timates. For the study of Macaulay as a historian, his
aims and methods, his virtues and limitations, C. H.
Firth's *Commentary on Macaulay's History of England* (1938) is almost indispensable. The two essays
reprinted here are from Macaulay's *Critical and Historical Essays,* ed. F. C. Montague (3 vols., 1903).

from Southey's Colloquies[1]

. . . We now come to the conversations which
pass between Mr. Southey and Sir Thomas More,[2]
or rather between two Southeys, equally eloquent, equally angry, equally unreasonable, and
equally given to talking about what they do not
understand. Perhaps we could not select a better
instance of the spirit which pervades the whole
book than the passages in which Mr. Southey
gives his opinion of the manufacturing system.
There is nothing which he hates so bitterly. It is,
according to him, a system more tyrannical than

that of the feudal ages, a system of actual servi-
tude, a system which destroys the bodies and
degrades the minds of those who are engaged in
it. He expresses a hope that the competition of
other nations may drive us out of the field; that
our foreign trade may decline; and that we may
thus enjoy a restoration of national sanity and
strength. But he seems to think that the extermination of the whole manufacturing population
would be a blessing, if the evil could be removed
in no other way.

Mr. Southey does not bring forward a
single fact in support of these views; and, as it
seems to us, there are facts which lead to a very
different conclusion. In the first place, the poor-
rate is very decidedly lower in the manufacturing
than in the agricultural districts. If Mr. Southey
will look over the Parliamentary returns on this
subject, he will find that the amount of parochial
relief required by the labourers in the different
counties of England is almost exactly in inverse
proportion to the degree in which the manufacturing system has been introduced into those
counties. The returns for the years ending in
March 1825, and in March 1828, are now before
us. In the former year we find the poor-rate
highest in Sussex, about twenty shillings to every
inhabitant. Then come Buckinghamshire, Essex,
Suffolk, Bedfordshire, Huntingdonshire, Kent,
and Norfolk. In all these the rate is above fifteen
shillings a head. We will not go through the
whole. Even in Westmoreland and the North
Riding of Yorkshire, the rate is at more than
eight shillings. In Cumberland and Monmouthshire, the most fortunate of all the agricultural
districts, it is at six shillings. But in the West
Riding of Yorkshire, it is as low as five shillings:
and when we come to Lancashire, we find it at
four shillings, one-fifth of what it is in Sussex.
The returns of the year ending in March 1828
are a little, and but a little, more unfavourable
to the manufacturing districts. Lancashire, even
in that season of distress, required a smaller
poor-rate than any other district, and little more
than one-fourth of the poor-rate raised in Sussex.
Cumberland alone, of the agricultural districts,
was as well off as the West Riding of Yorkshire.
These facts seem to indicate that the manufacturer is both in a more comfortable and in a
less dependent situation than the agricultural
labourer.

---

[1] This selection is from Macaulay's review of *Sir Thomas
More: or, Colloquies on the Progress and Prospects of
Society,* by Robert Southey, London, 1829. See the intro-
duction to Macaulay.

[2] Southey cast his book into the form of discussions between himself and the ghost of Sir Thomas More, the
great humanist and statesman who was executed by order
of Henry VIII because he would not disavow the supremacy of the Pope.

As to the effect of the manufacturing system on the bodily health, we must beg leave to estimate it by a standard far too low and vulgar for a mind so imaginative as that of Mr. Southey, the proportion of births and deaths. We know that, during the growth of this atrocious system, this new misery, to use the phrases of Mr. Southey, this new enormity, this birth of a portentous age, this pest which no man can approve whose heart is not seared or whose understanding has not been darkened, there has been a great diminution of mortality, and that this diminution has been greater in the manufacturing towns than anywhere else. The mortality still is, as it always was, greater in towns than in the country. But the difference has diminished in an extraordinary degree. There is the best reason to believe that the annual mortality of Manchester, about the middle of the last century, was one in twenty-eight. It is now reckoned at one in forty-five. In Glasgow and Leeds a similar improvement has taken place. Nay, the rate of mortality in those three great capitals of the manufacturing districts is now considerably less than it was, fifty years ago, over England and Wales, taken together, open country and all. We might with some plausibility maintain that the people live longer because they are better fed, better lodged, better clothed, and better attended in sickness, and that these improvements are owing to that increase of national wealth which the manufacturing system has produced.

Much more might be said on this subject. But to what end? It is not from bills of mortality and statistical tables that Mr. Southey has learned his political creed. He cannot stoop to study the history of the system which he abuses, to strike the balance between the good and evil which it has produced, to compare district with district, or generation with generation. We will give his own reason for his opinion, the only reason which he gives for it, in his own words:—

We remained a while in silence looking upon the assemblage of dwellings below. Here, and in the adjoining hamlet of Millbeck, the effects of manufactures and of agriculture may be seen and compared. The old cottages are such as the poet and the painter equally delight in beholding. Substantially built of the native stone without mortar, dirtied with no white lime, and their long low roofs covered with slate, if they had been raised by the magic of some indigenous Amphion's music,[3] the materials could not have adjusted themselves more beautifully in accord with the surrounding scene; and time has still further harmonized them with weather stains, lichens, and moss, short grasses, and short fern, and stone-plants of various kinds. The ornamented chimneys, round or square, less adorned than those which, like little turrets, crest the houses of the Portuguese peasantry; and yet not less happily suited to their place; the hedge of clipt box beneath the windows, the rose-bushes beside the door, the little patch of flower-ground, with its tall hollyhocks in front; the garden beside, the bee-hives, and the orchard with its bank of daffodils and snow-drops, the earliest and the profusest in these parts, indicate in the owners some portion of ease and leisure, some regard to neatness and comfort, some sense of natural, and innocent, and healthful enjoyment. The new cottages of the manufacturers are upon the manufacturing pattern— naked, and in a row.

"How is it," said I, "that everything which is connected with manufactures presents such features of unqualified deformity? From the largest of Mammon's temples[4] down to the poorest hovel in which his helotry are stalled, these edifices have all one character. Time will not mellow them; nature will neither clothe nor conceal them; and they will remain always as offensive to the eye as to the mind."

Here is wisdom. Here are the principles on which nations are to be governed. Rose-bushes and poor-rates, rather than steam-engines and independence. Mortality and cottages with weather-stains, rather than health and long life with edifices which time cannot mellow. We are told, that our age has invented atrocities beyond the imagination of our fathers; that society has been brought into a state compared with which extermination would be a blessing; and all because the dwellings of cotton-spinners are naked and rectangular. Mr. Southey has found out a way, he tells us, in which the effects of manufactures and agriculture may be compared. And what is this way? To stand on a hill, to look at a cottage and a factory, and to see which is the prettier. Does Mr. Southey think that the body of the English peasantry live, or ever lived, in substantial or ornamented cottages, with box-hedges, flower-gardens, bee-hives, and orchards? If not, what is his parallel worth? We despise those

---

3 An allusion to the legend that the walls of Thebes built themselves to the sound of Amphion's lyre.

4 The temples of Mammon, god of greed, are the factories.

mock philosophers, who think that they serve the cause of science by depreciating literature and the fine arts.[5] But if anything could excuse their narrowness of mind, it would be such a book as this. It is not strange that, when one enthusiast makes the picturesque the test of political good, another should feel inclined to proscribe altogether the pleasures of taste and imagination.

Thus it is that Mr. Southey reasons about matters with which he thinks himself perfectly conversant. We cannot, therefore, be surprised to find that he commits extraordinary blunders when he writes on points of which he acknowledges himself to be ignorant. He confesses that he is not versed in political economy, and that he has neither liking nor aptitude for it; and he then proceeds to read the public a lecture concerning it which fully bears out his confession.

"All wealth," says Sir Thomas More, "in former times was tangible. It consisted in land, money, or chattels, which were either of real or conventional value."

Montesinos,[6] as Mr. Southey somewhat affectedly calls himself, answers thus:—

"Jewels, for example, and pictures, as in Holland, where indeed at one time tulip bulbs answered the same purpose."

"That bubble," says Sir Thomas, "was one of those contagious insanities to which communities are subject. All wealth was real, till the extent of commerce rendered a paper currency necessary; which differed from precious stones and pictures in this important point, that there was no limit to its production."

"We regard it," says Montesinos, "as the representative of real wealth; and, therefore, limited always to the amount of what it represents."

"Pursue that notion," answers the ghost, "and you will be in the dark presently. Your provincial banknotes, which constitute almost wholly the circulating medium of certain districts, pass current to-day. To-morrow tidings may come that the house which issued them has stopt payment, and what do they represent then? You will find them the shadow of a shade."

We scarcely know at which end to begin to disentangle this knot of absurdities. We might ask, why it should be a greater proof of insanity in men to set a high value on rare tulips than on rare stones, which are neither more useful nor more beautiful? We might ask how it can be said that there is no limit to the production of paper money, when a man is hanged if he issues any in the name of another, and is forced to cash what he issues in his own? But Mr. Southey's error lies deeper still. "All wealth," says he, "was tangible and real till paper currency was introduced." Now, was there ever, since men emerged from a state of utter barbarism, an age in which there were no debts? Is not a debt, while the solvency of the debtor is undoubted, always reckoned as part of the wealth of the creditor? Yet is it tangible and real wealth? Does it cease to be wealth, because there is the security of a written acknowledgment for it? And what else is paper currency? Did Mr. Southey ever read a banknote? If he did, he would see that it is a written acknowledgment of a debt, and a promise to pay that debt. The promise may be violated: the debt may remain unpaid: those to whom it was due may suffer: but this is a risk not confined to cases of paper currency: it is a risk inseparable from the relation of debtor and creditor. Every man who sells goods for anything but ready money runs the risk of finding that what he considered as part of his wealth one day is nothing at all the next day. Mr. Southey refers to the picture-galleries of Holland. The pictures were undoubtedly real and tangible possessions. But surely it might happen that a burgomaster might owe a picture-dealer a thousand guilders for a Teniers.[7] What in this case corresponds to our paper money is not the picture, which is tangible, but the claim of the picture-dealer on his customer for the price of the picture; and this claim is not tangible. Now, would not the picture-dealer consider this claim as part of his wealth? Would not a tradesman who knew of the claim give credit to the picture-dealer the more readily on account of the claim? The burgomaster might be ruined. If so, would not those consequences follow which, as Mr. Southey tells us, were never heard of till paper

5 The Benthamite Utilitarians.
6 The name of a chivalric hero in Spanish legend. Southey used it to point up his romantic Toryism.

7 A painting by an artist named David Teniers, either the father (1582–1649) or the son (1610–1690), both of whom had the same Christian name.

money came into use? Yesterday this claim was worth a thousand guilders. To-day what is it? The shadow of a shade.

It is true that, the more readily claims of this sort are transferred from hand to hand, the more extensive will be the injury produced by a single failure. The laws of all nations sanction, in certain cases, the transfer of rights not yet reduced into possession. Mr. Southey would scarcely wish, we should think, that all indorsements of bills and notes should be declared invalid. Yet even if this were done, the transfer of claims would imperceptibly take place, to a very great extent. When the baker trusts the butcher, for example, he is in fact, though not in form, trusting the butcher's customers. A man who owes large bills to tradesmen, and fails to pay them, almost always produces distress through a very wide circle of people with whom he never dealt.

In short, what Mr. Southey takes for a difference in kind is only a difference of form and degree. In every society men have claims on the property of others. In every society there is a possibility that some debtors may not be able to fulfil their obligations. In every society, therefore, there is wealth which is not tangible, and which may become the shadow of a shade.

Mr. Southey then proceeds to a dissertation on the national debt, which he considers in a new and most consolatory light, as a clear addition to the income of the country.

"You can understand," says Sir Thomas, "that it constitutes a great part of the national wealth."

"So large a part," answers Montesinos, "that the interest amounted, during the prosperous times of agriculture, to as much as the rental of all the land in Great Britain; and at present to the rental of all lands, all houses, and all other fixed property put together."

The Ghost and Laureate agree that it is very desirable that there should be so secure and advantageous a deposit for wealth as the funds afford. Sir Thomas then proceeds:—

"Another and far more momentous benefit must not be overlooked; the expenditure of an annual interest, equalling, as you have stated, the present rental of all fixed property."

"That expenditure," quoth Montesinos, "gives employment to half the industry in the kingdom, and feeds half the mouths. Take, indeed, the weight of the national debt from this great and complicated social machine, and the wheels must stop."

From this passage we should have been inclined to think that Mr. Southey supposes the dividends to be a free gift periodically sent down from heaven to the fundholders, as quails and manna were sent to the Israelites,[8] were it not that he has vouchsafed, in the following question and answer, to give the public some information which, we believe, was very little needed.

"Whence comes the interest?" says Sir Thomas.

"It is raised," answers Montesinos, "by taxation."

Now, has Mr. Southey ever considered what would be done with this sum if it were not paid as interest to the national creditor? If he would think over this matter for a short time, we suspect that the "momentous benefit" of which he talks would appear to him to shrink strangely in amount. A fundholder, we will suppose, spends dividends amounting to five hundred pounds a year; and his ten nearest neighbours pay fifty pounds each to the tax-gatherer, for the purpose of discharging the interest of the national debt. If the debt were wiped out, a measure, be it understood, which we by no means recommend, the fundholder would cease to spend his five hundred pounds a year. He would no longer give employment to industry, or put food into the mouths of labourers. This Mr. Southey thinks a fearful evil. But is there no mitigating circumstance? Each of the ten neighbours of our fundholder has fifty pounds a year more than formerly. Each of them will, as it seems to our feeble understandings, employ more industry and feed more mouths than formerly. The sum is exactly the same. It is in different hands. But on what grounds does Mr. Southey call upon us to believe that it is in the hands of men who will spend it less liberally or less judiciously? He seems to think that nobody but a fundholder can employ the poor; that, if a tax is remitted, those who formerly used to pay it proceed immediately to dig holes in the earth, and to bury the sum which the Government had been accustomed to take; that no

8 As they were fleeing from Egypt.

money can set industry in motion till such money has been taken by the tax-gatherer out of one man's pocket and put into another man's pocket. We really wish that Mr. Southey would try to prove this principle, which is indeed the foundation of his whole theory of finance: for we think it right to hint to him that our hardhearted and unimaginative generation will expect some more satisfactory reason than the only one with which he has yet favoured it, namely, a similitude touching evaporation and dew.

Both the theory and the illustration, indeed, are old friends of ours. In every season of distress which we can remember, Mr. Southey has been proclaiming that it is not from economy, but from increased taxation, that the country must expect relief; and he still, we find, places the undoubting faith of a political Diafoirus, in his

Resaignare, repurgare, et reclysterizare.[9]

"A people," he tells us, "may be too rich, but a government cannot be so."

"A state," says he, "cannot have more wealth at its command than may be employed for the general good, a liberal expenditure in national works being one of the surest means of promoting national prosperity; and the benefit being still more obvious, of an expenditure directed to the purposes of national improvement. But a people may be too rich."

We fully admit that a state cannot have at its command more wealth than may be employed for the general good. But neither can individuals, or bodies of individuals, have at their command more wealth than may be employed for the general good. If there be no limit to the sum which may be usefully laid out in public works and national improvement, then wealth, whether in the hands of private men or of the Government, may always, if the possessors choose to spend it usefully, be usefully spent. The only ground, therefore, on which Mr. Southey can possibly maintain that a govern-

ment cannot be too rich, but that a people may be too rich, must be this, that governments are more likely to spend their money on good objects than private individuals.

But what is useful expenditure? "A liberal expenditure in national works," says Mr. Southey, "is one of the surest means for promoting national prosperity." What does he mean by national prosperity? Does he mean the wealth of the State? If so, his reasoning runs thus: The more wealth a state has the better; for the more wealth a state has the more wealth it will have. This is surely something like that fallacy, which is ungallantly termed a lady's reason. If by national prosperity he means the wealth of the people, of how gross a contradiction is Mr. Southey guilty. A people, he tells us, may be too rich: a government cannot: for a government can employ its riches in making the people richer. The wealth of the people is to be taken from them, because they have too much, and laid out in works, which will yield them more.

We are really at a loss to determine whether Mr. Southey's reason for recommending large taxation is that it will make the people rich, or that it will make them poor. But we are sure that, if his object is to make them rich, he takes the wrong course. There are two or three principles respecting public works, which, as an experience of vast extent proves, may be trusted in almost every case.

It scarcely ever happens that any private man or body of men will invest property in a canal, a tunnel, or a bridge, but from an expectation that the outlay will be profitable to them. No work of this sort can be profitable to private speculators, unless the public be willing to pay for the use of it. The public will not pay of their own accord for what yields no profit or convenience to them. There is thus a direct and obvious connection between the motive which induces individuals to undertake such a work, and the utility of the work.

Can we find any such connection in the case of a public work executed by a government? If it is useful, are the individuals who rule the country richer? If it is useless, are they poorer? A public man may be solicitous for his credit. But is not he likely to gain more credit by an useless display of ostentatious architecture in a great town than by the best road or the best

---

9 Diafoirus is an ignorant quack in Molière's *Le Malade Imaginaire.* He tries to sound impressive by Latinizing the only remedies he has heard of: bleeding, purgation, and enema. By the remedy of taxation, according to Macaulay, Southey would cure the people of having too much money.

THOMAS BABINGTON MACAULAY 499

canal in some remote province? The fame of public works is a much less certain test of their utility than the amount of toll collected at them. In a corrupt age, there will be direct embezzlement. In the purest age, there will be abundance of jobbing. Never were the statesmen of any country more sensitive to public opinion, and more spotless in pecuniary transactions, than those who have of late governed England. Yet we have only to look at the buildings recently erected in London for a proof of our rule. In a bad age, the fate of the public is to be robbed outright. In a good age, it is merely to have the dearest and the worst of everything.

Buildings for State purposes the State must erect. And here we think that, in general, the State ought to stop. We firmly believe that five hundred thousand pounds subscribed by individuals for rail-roads or canals would produce more advantage to the public than five millions voted by Parliament for the same purpose. There are certain old saws about the master's eye and about everybody's business, in which we place very great faith.

There is, we have said, no consistency in Mr. Southey's political system. But if there be in his political system any leading principle, any one error which diverges more widely and variously than any other, it is that of which his theory about national works is a ramification. He conceives that the business of the magistrate is, not merely to see that the persons and property of the people are secure from attack, but that he ought to be a jack-of-all-trades, architect, engineer, schoolmaster, merchant, theologian, a Lady Bountiful in every parish, a Paul Pry in every house, spying, eaves-dropping, relieving, admonishing, spending our money for us, and choosing our opinions for us. His principle is, if we understand it rightly, that no man can do anything so well for himself as his rulers, be they who they may, can do it for him, and that a government approaches nearer and nearer to perfection, in proportion as it interferes more and more with the habits and notions of individuals.

He seems to be fully convinced that it is in the power of government to relieve all the distresses under which the lower orders labour. Nay, he considers doubt on this subject as impious. We cannot refrain from quoting his argument on this subject. It is a perfect jewel of logic:—

"Many thousands in your metropolis," says Sir Thomas More, "rise every morning without knowing how they are to subsist during the day; as many of them, where they are to lay their heads at night. All men, even the vicious themselves, know that wickedness leads to misery: but many, even among the good and the wise, have yet to learn that misery is almost as often the cause of wickedness."

"There are many," says Montesinos, "who know this, but believe that it is not in the power of human institutions to prevent this misery. They see the effect, but regard the causes as inseparable from the condition of human nature."

"As surely as God is good," replies Sir Thomas, "so surely there is no such thing as necessary evil. For, by the religious mind, sickness, and pain, and death, are not to be accounted evils."

Now if sickness, pain, and death, are not evils, we cannot understand why it should be an evil that thousands should rise without knowing how they are to subsist. The only evil of hunger is that it produces first pain, then sickness, and finally death. If it did not produce these, it would be no calamity. If these are not evils, it is no calamity. We will propose a very plain dilemma: either physical pain is an evil, or it is not an evil. If it is an evil, then there is necessary evil in the universe: if it is not, why should the poor be delivered from it?

Mr. Southey entertains as exaggerated a notion of the wisdom of governments as of their power. He speaks with the greatest disgust of the respect now paid to public opinion. That opinion is, according to him, to be distrusted and dreaded; its usurpation ought to be vigorously resisted; and the practice of yielding to it is likely to ruin the country. To maintain police is, according to him, only one of the ends of government. The duties of a ruler are patriarchal and paternal. He ought to consider the moral discipline of the people as his first object, to establish a religion, to train the whole community in that religion, and to consider all dissenters as his own enemies.

"Nothing," says Sir Thomas, "is more certain, than that religion is the basis upon which civil government rests; that from religion power derives its authority, laws their efficacy, and both their zeal and sanction; and it is necessary that this religion be established as for the security of the state, and for the welfare of the people, who would otherwise be moved to and fro with every wind of doctrine. A state is secure in proportion as the people are attached to its institutions; it is, therefore, the first and plainest rule of sound policy, that the people be trained up in the way they should go. The state that neglects this prepares its own destruction; and they who train them in any other way are undermining it. Nothing in abstract science can be more certain than these positions are."

"All of which," answers Montesinos, "are nevertheless denied by our professors of the arts Babblative and Scribblative: some in the audacity of evil designs, and others in the glorious assurance of impenetrable ignorance."

The greater part of the two volumes before us is merely an amplification of these paragraphs. What does Mr. Southey mean by saying that religion is demonstrably the basis of civil government? He cannot surely mean that men have no motives except those derived from religion for establishing and supporting civil government, that no temporal advantage is derived from civil government, that men would experience no temporal inconvenience from living in a state of anarchy? If he allows, as we think he must allow, that it is for the good of mankind in this world to have civil government, and that the great majority of mankind have always thought it for their good in this world to have civil government, we theh have a basis for government quite distinct from religion. It is true that the Christian religion sanctions government, as it sanctions everything which promotes the happiness and virtue of our species. But we are at a loss to conceive in what sense religion can be said to be the basis of government, in which religion is not also the basis of the practices of eating, drinking, and lighting fires in cold weather. Nothing in history is more certain than that government has existed, has received some obedience, and has given some protection, in times in which it derived no support from religion, in times in which there was no religion that influenced the hearts and lives of men. It was not from dread of Tartarus, or from belief

in the Elysian fields,[10] that an Athenian wished to have some institutions which might keep Orestes from filching his cloak, or Midias from breaking his head.[11] "It is from religion," says Mr. Southey, "that power derives its authority, and laws their efficacy." From what religion does our power over the Hindoos derive its authority, or the law in virtue of which we hang Brahmins[12] its efficacy? For thousands of years civil government has existed in almost every corner of the world, in ages of priestcraft, in ages of fanaticism, in ages of Epicurean indifference, in ages of enlightened piety. However pure or impure the faith of the people might be, whether they adored a beneficent or a malignant power, whether they thought the soul mortal or immortal, they have, as soon as they ceased to be absolute savages, found out their need of civil government, and instituted it accordingly. It is as universal as the practice of cookery. Yet, it is as certain, says Mr. Southey, as anything in abstract science, that government is founded on religion. We should like to know what notion Mr. Southey has of the demonstrations of abstract science. A very vague one, we suspect.

The proof proceeds. As religion is the basis of government, and as the State is secure in proportion as the people are attached to public institutions, it is therefore, says Mr. Southey, the first rule of policy, that the government should train the people in the way in which they should go; and it is plain that those who train them in any other way are undermining the State.

Now it does not appear to us to be the first object that people should always believe in the established religion and be attached to the established government. A religion may be false. A government may be oppressive. And whatever support government gives to false religions, or religion to oppressive governments, we consider as a clear evil.

The maxim, that governments ought to train the people in the way in which they should go, sounds well. But is there any reason for believing that a government is more likely to lead

---

10 Tartarus and the Elysian fields are respectively Hades and the land of the happy dead in Greek mythology.
11 Orestes and Midias seem to be used merely as representative Greek names.
12 The Hindus are a religious group in India, of which the Brahmins are a caste.

the people in the right way than the people to fall into the right way of themselves? Have there not been governments which were blind leaders of the blind? Are there not still such governments? Can it be laid down as a general rule that the movement of political and religious truth is rather downwards from the government to the people than upwards from the people to the government? These are questions which it is of importance to have clearly resolved. Mr. Southey declaims against public opinion, which is now, he tells us, usurping supreme power. Formerly, according to him, the laws governed; now public opinion governs. What are laws but expressions of the opinion of some class which has power over the rest of the community? By what was the world ever governed but by the opinion of some person or persons? By what else can it ever be governed? What are all systems, religious, political, or scientific, but opinions resting on evidence more or less satisfactory? The question is not between human opinion and some higher and more certain mode of arriving at truth, but between opinion and opinion, between the opinions of one man and another, or of one class and another, or of one generation and another. Public opinion is not infallible; but can Mr. Southey construct any institutions which shall secure to us the guidance of an infallible opinion? Can Mr Southey select any family, any profession, any class, in short, distinguished by any plain badge from the rest of the community, whose opinion is more likely to be just than this much abused public opinion? Would he choose the peers, for example? Or the two hundred tallest men in the country? Or the poor Knights of Windsor?[13] Or children who are born with cauls? Or the seventh sons of seventh sons? We cannot suppose that he would recommend popular election; for that is merely an appeal to public opinion. And to say that society ought to be governed by the opinion of the wisest and best, though true, is useless. Whose opinion is to decide who are the wisest and best?

Mr. Southey and many other respectable people seem to think that, when they have once proved the moral and religious training of the people to be a most important object, it follows, of course, that it is an object which the government ought to pursue. They forget that we have to consider, not merely the goodness of the end, but also the fitness of the means. Neither in the natural nor in the political body have all members the same office. There is surely no contradiction in saying that a certain section of the community may be quite competent to protect the persons and property of the rest, yet quite unfit to direct our opinions, or to superintend our private habits.

So strong is the interest of a ruler to protect his subjects against all depredations and outrages except his own, so clear and simple are the means by which this end is to be effected, that men are probably better off under the worst governments in the world than they would be in a state of anarchy. Even when the appointment of magistrates has been left to chance, as in the Italian Republics, things have gone on far better than if there had been no magistrates at all, and if every man had done what seemed right in his own eyes. But we see no reason for thinking that the opinions of the magistrate on speculative questions are more likely to be right than those of any other man. None of the modes by which a magistrate is appointed, popular election, the accident of the lot, or the accident of birth, affords, as far as we can perceive, much security for his being wiser than any of his neighbours. The chance of his being wiser than all his neighbours together is still smaller. Now we cannot understand how it can be laid down that it is the duty and the right of one class to direct the opinions of another, unless it can be proved that the former class is more likely to form just opinions than the latter.

The duties of government would be, as Mr. Southey says that they are, paternal, if a government were necessarily as much superior in wisdom to a people as the most foolish father, for a time, is to the most intelligent child, and if a government loved a people as fathers generally love their children. But there is no reason to believe that a government will have either the paternal warmth of affection or the paternal superiority of intellect. Mr. Southey might as well say that the duties of the shoemaker are paternal, and that it is an usurpation in any man not of the craft to say that his shoes are bad and to

---

[13] An order of retired soldiers, with headquarters at Windsor.

insist on having better. The division of labour would be no blessing, if those by whom a thing is done were to pay no attention to the opinion of those for whom it is done. The shoemaker, in the *Relapse,*[14] tells Lord Foppington that his Lordship is mistaken in supposing that his shoe pinches. "It does not pinch; it cannot pinch; I know my business; and I never made a better shoe." This is the way in which Mr. Southey would have a government treat a people who usurp the privilege of thinking. Nay, the shoemaker of Vanbrugh has the advantage in the comparison. He contented himself with regulating his customer's shoes, about which he had peculiar means of information, and did not presume to dictate about the coat and hat. But Mr. Southey would have the rulers of a country prescribe opinions to the people, not only about politics, but about matters concerning which a government has no peculiar sources of information, and concerning which any man in the streets may know as much and think as justly as the King, namely religion and morals.

Men are never so likely to settle a question rightly as when they discuss it freely. A government can interfere in discussion only by making it less free than it would otherwise be. Men are most likely to form just opinions when they have no other wish than to know the truth, and are exempt from all influence, either of hope or fear. Government, as government, can bring nothing but the influence of hopes and fears to support its doctrines. It carries on controversy, not with reasons, but with threats and bribes. If it employs reasons, it does so, not in virtue of any powers which belong to it as a government. Thus, instead of a contest between argument and argument, we have a contest between argument and force. Instead of a contest in which truth, from the natural constitution of the human mind, has a decided advantage over falsehood, we have a contest in which truth can be victorious only by accident.

And what, after all, is the security which this training gives to governments? Mr. Southey would scarcely propose that discussion should be more effectually shackled, that public opinion should be more strictly disciplined into con-

formity with established institutions, than in Spain and Italy. Yet we know that the restraints which exist in Spain and Italy have not prevented atheism from spreading among the educated classes, and especially among those whose office it is to minister at the altars of God. All our readers know how, at the time of the French Revolution, priest after priest came forward to declare that his doctrine, his ministry, his whole life, had been a lie, a mummery during which he could scarcely compose his countenance sufficiently to carry on the imposture. This was the case of a false, or at least of a grossly corrupted religion. Let us take then the case of all others most favourable to Mr. Southey's argument. Let us take that form of religion which he holds to be the purest, the system of the Arminian[15] part of the Church of England. Let us take the form of government which he most admires and regrets, the government of England in the time of Charles the First. Would he wish to see a closer connection between Church and State than then existed? Would he wish for more powerful ecclesiastical tribunals? for a more zealous king? for a more active primate? Would he wish to see a more complete monopoly of public instruction given to the Established Church? Could any government do more to train the people in the way in which he would have them go? And in what did all this training end? The Report of the state of the Province of Canterbury, delivered by Laud[16] to his master at the close of 1639, represents the Church of England as in the highest and most palmy state. So effectually had the Government pursued that policy which Mr. Southey wishes to see revived that there was scarcely the least appearance of dissent. Most of the bishops stated that all was well among their flocks. Seven or eight persons in the diocese of Peterborough had seemed refractory to the Church, but had made ample submission. In Norfolk and Suffolk all whom there had been reason to suspect had made profession of conformity, and appeared to

---

[14] A comedy by the Restoration dramatist Sir John Vanbrugh (1666–1726).

[15] The High Church party under Charles I, upholders of the divine right of kings and of strong ecclesiastical authority.
[16] William Laud (1573–1645) as Archbishop of Canterbury was one of Charles's outstanding supporters in attempting to defend the Church of England against Puritanism and the royal prerogative against the Commons. He was impeached by the Long Parliament and beheaded.

observe it strictly. It is confessed that there was a little difficulty in bringing some of the vulgar in Suffolk to take the sacrament at the rails in the chancel. This was the only open instance of nonconformity which the vigilant eye of Laud could detect in all the dioceses of his twenty-one suffragans, on the very eve of a revolution in which primate, and Church, and monarch, and monarchy were to perish together.

At which time would Mr. Southey pronounce the constitution more secure: in 1639, when Laud presented this Report to Charles; or now, when thousands of meetings openly collect millions of dissenters, when designs against the tithes[17] are openly avowed, when books attacking not only the Establishment, but the first principles of Christianity, are openly sold in the streets? The signs of discontent, he tells us, are stronger in England now than in France when the States-General[18] met: and hence he would have us infer that a revolution like that of France may be at hand. Does he not know that the danger of states is to be estimated, not by what breaks out of the public mind, but by what stays in it? Can he conceive anything more terrible than the situation of a government which rules without apprehension over a people of hypocrites, which is flattered by the press and cursed in the inner chambers, which exults in the attachment and obedience of its subjects, and knows not that those subjects are leagued against it in a freemasonry of hatred, the sign of which is every day conveyed in the glance of ten thousand eyes, the pressure of ten thousand hands, and the tone of ten thousand voices? Profound and ingenious policy! Instead of curing the disease, to remove those symptoms by which alone its nature can be known! To leave the serpent his deadly sting, and deprive him only of his warning rattle!

When the people whom Charles had so assiduously trained in the good way had rewarded his paternal care by cutting off his head, a new kind of training came into fashion. Another government arose[19] which, like the former, considered religion as its surest basis, and the religious discipline of the people as its first duty. Sanguinary laws were enacted against libertinism; profane pictures were burned; drapery was put on indecorous statues; the theatres were shut up; fast-days were numerous; and the Parliament resolved that no person should be admitted into any public employment, unless the House should be first satisfied of his vital godliness. We know what was the end of this training. We know that it ended in impiety, in filthy and heartless sensuality, in the dissolution of all ties of honour and morality. We know that at this very day scriptural phrases, scriptural names, perhaps some scriptural doctrines excite disgust and ridicule, solely because they are associated with the austerity of that period.

Thus has the experiment of training the people in established forms of religion been twice tried in England on a large scale, once by Charles and Laud, and once by the Puritans. The High Tories of our time still entertain many of the feelings and opinions of Charles and Laud, though in a mitigated form; nor is it difficult to see that the heirs of the Puritans are still amongst us. It would be desirable that each of these parties should remember how little advantage or honour it formerly derived from the closest alliance with power, that it fell by the support of rulers and rose by their opposition, that of the two systems that in which the people were at any time drilled was always at that time the unpopular system, that the training of the High Church ended in the reign of the Puritans, and that the training of the Puritans ended in the reign of the harlots.[20]

This was quite natural. Nothing is so galling to a people not broken in from the birth as a paternal, or, in other words, a meddling government, a government which tells them what to read, and say, and eat, and drink, and wear. Our fathers could not bear it two hundred years ago; and we are not more patient than they. Mr. Southey thinks that the yoke of the Church is dropping off because it is loose. We feel convinced that it is borne only because it is easy, and that, in the instant in which an attempt is made to tighten it, it will be flung away. It will be

---

17 Taxes established by the government for the support of the state Church, or Establishment.
18 An assembly that met in Paris just before the outbreak of the French Revolution, so named from its being composed of members of the three estates, clergy, nobility, and people.
19 The Commonwealth, 1649–60.

20 After the restoration of the monarchy in 1660 there was a period of marked licentiousness, doubtless a reaction against the repressions of the Puritan period.

neither the first nor the strongest yoke that has been broken asunder and trampled under foot in the day of the vengeance of England.

How far Mr. Southey would have the Government carry its measures for training the people in the doctrines of the Church, we are unable to discover. In one passage Sir Thomas More asks with great vehemence,

"Is it possible that your laws should suffer the unbelievers to exist as a party? Vetitum est adeo sceleris nihil?"[21]

Montesinos answers: "They avow themselves in defiance of the laws. The fashionable doctrine which the press at this time maintains is, that this is a matter in which the laws ought not to interfere, every man having a right, both to form what opinion he pleases upon religious subjects, and to promulgate that opinion."

It is clear, therefore, that Mr. Southey would not give full and perfect toleration to infidelity. In another passage, however, he observes with some truth, though too sweepingly, that "any degree of intolerance short of that full extent which the Papal Church exercises where it has the power, acts upon the opinions which it is intended to suppress, like pruning upon vigorous plants; they grow the stronger for it." These two passages, put together, would lead us to the conclusion that, in Mr. Southey's opinion, the utmost severity ever employed by the Roman Catholic Church in the days of its greatest power ought to be employed against unbelievers in England; in plain words, that Carlile and his shopmen ought to be burned in Smithfield,[22] and that every person who, when called upon, should decline to make a solemn profession of Christianity ought to suffer the same fate. We do not, however, believe that Mr. Southey would recommend such a course, though his language would, according to all the rules of logic, justify us in supposing this to be his meaning. His opinions form no system at all. He never sees, at one glance, more of a question than will furnish matter for one flowing and well-turned sentence; so that it would be the height of unfairness to charge him personally with holding a doctrine merely because that doctrine is deducible,

though by the closest and most accurate reasoning, from the premises which he has laid down. We are, therefore, left completely in the dark as to Mr. Southey's opinions about toleration. Immediately after censuring the Government for not punishing infidels, he proceeds to discuss the question of the Catholic disabilities, now, thank God, removed, and defends them on the ground that the Catholic doctrines tend to persecution, and that the Catholics persecuted when they had power.

"They must persecute," says he, "if they believe their own creed, for conscience-sake; and if they do not believe it, they must persecute for policy; because it is only by intolerance that so corrupt and injurious a system can be upheld."

That unbelievers should not be persecuted is an instance of national depravity at which the glorified spirits stand aghast. Yet a sect of Christians is to be excluded from power, because those who formerly held the same opinions were guilty of persecution. We have said that we do not very well know what Mr. Southey's opinion about toleration is. But, on the whole, we take it to be this, that everybody is to tolerate him, and that he is to tolerate nobody.

We will not be deterred by any fear of misrepresentation from expressing our hearty approbation of the mild, wise, and eminently Christian manner in which the Church and the Government have lately acted with respect to blasphemous publications. We praise them for not having thought it necessary to encircle a religion pure, merciful, and philosophical, a religion to the evidence of which the highest intellects have yielded, with the defences of a false and bloody superstition. The ark of God was never taken till it was surrounded by the arms of earthly defenders.[23] In captivity, its sanctity was sufficient to vindicate it from insult, and to lay the hostile fiend prostrate on the threshold of his own temple. The real security of Christianity is to be found in its benevolent morality, in its exquisite adaptation to the human heart, in the facility with which its scheme accommodates itself to the capacity of every human intellect, in the consolation which it bears to the house of mourning, in the light with which it brightens

---

21 "Is nothing now forbidden to the wicked?"
22 Scene of a cattle market in London where heretics were burned at the stake under Mary Tudor.

23 Actually until the Israelites carried it into battle, hoping it would bring divine aid in defeating the Philistines.

the great mystery of the grave. To such a system it can bring no addition of dignity or of strength, that it is part and parcel of the common law. It is not now for the first time left to rely on the force of its own evidences and the attractions of its own beauty. Its sublime theology confounded the Grecian schools in the fair conflict of reason with reason. The bravest and wisest of the Caesars found their arms and their policy unavailing, when opposed to the weapons that were not carnal and the kingdom that was not of this world. The victory which Porphyry and Diocletian failed to gain[24] is not, to all appearance, reserved for any of those who have, in this age, directed their attacks against the last restraint of the powerful and the last hope of the wretched. The whole history of Christianity shows, that she is in far greater danger of being corrupted by the alliance of power, than of being crushed by its opposition. Those who thrust temporal sovereignty upon her treat her as their prototypes treated her author. They bow the knee, and spit upon her; they cry "Hail!" and smite her on the cheek; they put a sceptre in her hand, but it is a fragile reed; they crown her, but it is with thorns; they cover with purple the wounds which their own hands have inflicted on her; and inscribe magnificent titles over the cross on which they have fixed her to perish in ignominy and pain.

The general view which Mr. Southey takes of the prospects of society is very gloomy; but we comfort ourselves with the consideration that Mr. Southey is no prophet. He foretold, we remember, on the very eve of the abolition of the Test and Corporation Acts,[25] that these hateful laws were immortal, and that pious minds would long be gratified by seeing the most solemn religious rite of the Church profaned for the purpose of upholding her political supremacy. In the book before us, he says that Catholics cannot possibly be admitted into Parliament until those whom Johnson called "the bottomless Whigs"[26] come into power. While the book was in the press, the prophecy was falsified; and a Tory of the Tories,[27] Mr. Southey's own favourite hero, won and wore that noblest wreath, "Ob cives servatos."[28]

The signs of the times, Mr. Southey tells us, are very threatening. His fears for the country would decidedly preponderate over his hopes, but for his firm reliance on the mercy of God. Now, as we know that God has once suffered the civilised world to be overrun by savages, and the Christian religion to be corrupted by doctrines which made it, for some ages, almost as bad as Paganism, we cannot think it inconsistent with his attributes that similar calamities should again befall mankind.

We look, however, on the state of the world, and of this kingdom in particular, with much greater satisfaction and with better hopes. Mr. Southey speaks with contempt of those who think the savage state happier than the social. On this subject, he says, Rousseau[29] never imposed on him even in his youth. But he conceives that a community which has advanced a little way in civilisation is happier than one which has made greater progress. The Britons in the time of Caesar were happier, he suspects, than the English of the nineteenth century. On the whole, he selects the generation which preceded the Reformation as that in which the people of this country were better off than at any time before or since.

This opinion rests on nothing, as far as we can see, except his own individual associations. He is a man of letters; and a life destitute of literary pleasures seems insipid to him. He abhors the spirit of the present generation, the severity of its studies, the boldness of its inquiries, and the disdain with which it regards some old prejudices by which his own mind is held in bondage. He dislikes an utterly unenlightened

24 Porphyry, a Greek philosopher of the third century, attacked Christianity by argument; the Emperor Diocletian (245–313), by physical persecution.
25 Both the Corporation Act (1661) and the Test Act (1673) forbade the holding of public office by anyone who would not receive communion according to the rites of the Church of England once a year. They were repealed in 1828.
26 Dr. Johnson, Boswell relates, said of a friend, "Sir, he is a cursed Whig, a *bottomless* Whig, as they all are now." He meant that the Whigs lacked a core or bottom of sound principles.
27 Catholic Emancipation was granted under the ministry of the Duke of Wellington, the last of the old Tories, in 1829, probably only to avert civil war, a concession that evidently took Southey by surprise.
28 "On behalf of the delivered citizens."
29 Jean Jacques Rousseau (1712–1778), French philosopher who won wide acclaim by his attack on civilization and concomitant praise of a state of nature.

age; he dislikes an investigating and reforming age. The first twenty years of the sixteenth century would have exactly suited him. They furnished just the quantity of intellectual excitement which he requires. The learned few read and wrote largely. A scholar was held in high estimation. But the rabble did not presume to think; and even the most inquiring and independent of the educated classes paid more reverence to authority, and less to reason, than is usual in our time. This is a state of things in which Mr. Southey would have found himself quite comfortable; and, accordingly, he pronounces it the happiest state of things ever known in the world.

The savages were wretched, says Mr. Southey; but the people in the time of Sir Thomas More were happier than either they or we. Now we think it quite certain that we have the advantage over the contemporaries of Sir Thomas More, in every point in which they had any advantage over savages.

Mr. Southey does not even pretend to maintain that the people in the sixteenth century were better lodged or clothed than at present. He seems to admit that in these respects there has been some little improvement. It is indeed a matter about which scarcely any doubt can exist in the most perverse mind that the improvements of machinery have lowered the price of manufactured articles, and have brought within the reach of the poorest some conveniences which Sir Thomas More or his master could not have obtained at any price.

The labouring classes, however, were, according to Mr. Southey, better fed three hundred years ago than at present. We believe that he is completely in error on this point. The condition of servants in noble and wealthy families, and of scholars at the Universities, must surely have been better in those times than that of day-labourers; and we are sure that it was not better than that of our workhouse paupers. From the household book of the Northumberland family, we find that in one of the greatest establishments of the kingdom the servants lived very much as common sailors live now. In the reign of Edward the Sixth the state of the students at Cambridge is described to us, on the very best authority, as most wretched. Many of them dined on pottage made of a farthing's worth of beef with a little salt and oatmeal, and literally nothing else. This

account we have from a contemporary master of St. John's. Our parish poor now eat wheaten bread. In the sixteenth century the labourer was glad to get barley, and was often forced to content himself with poorer fare. In Harrison's introduction to Holinshed[30] we have an account of the state of our working population in the "golden days," as Mr. Southey calls them, "of good Queen Bess." "The gentilitie," says he, "commonly provide themselves sufficiently of wheat for their own tables, whylest their household and poore neighbours in some shires are inforced to content themselves with rye or barleie; yea, and in time of dearth, many with bread made eyther of beanes, peason, or otes, or of altogether, and some acornes among. I will not say that this extremity is oft so well to be seen in time of plentie as of dearth; but if I should I could easily bring my trial: for albeit there be much more grounde eared nowe almost in everye place then hathe beene of late yeares, yet such a price of corne continueth in each towne and markete, without any just cause, that the artificer and poore labouring man is not able to reach unto it, but is driven to content himself with horse-corne." We should like to see what the effect would be of putting any parish in England now on allowance of "horse-corne." The helotry of Mammon[31] are not, in our day, so easily enforced to content themselves as the peasantry of that happy period, as Mr. Southey considers it, which elapsed between the fall of the feudal and the rise of the commercial tyranny.

"The people," says Mr. Southey, "are worse fed than when they were fishers." And yet in another place he complains that they will not eat fish. "They have contracted," says he, "I know not how, some obstinate prejudice against a kind of food at once wholesome and delicate, and everywhere to be obtained cheaply and in abundance, were the demand for it as general as it ought to be." It is true that the lower orders have an obstinate prejudice against fish. But hunger has no such obstinate prejudices. If what was formerly a common diet is now eaten only in times of severe pressure, the inference is plain. The people must be fed with what they at

---

30 William Harrison (1534–1593) wrote a "Description of England" that was published with Holinshed's *Chronicles* in 1577.
31 The laborers.

least think better food than that of their ancestors.

The advice and medicine which the poorest labourer can now obtain, in disease, or after an accident, is far superior to what Henry the Eighth could have commanded. Scarcely any part of the country is out of the reach of practitioners who are probably not so far inferior to Sir Henry Halford as they are superior to Dr. Butts.[32] That there has been a great improvement in this respect, Mr. Southey allows. Indeed he could not well have denied it. "But," says he, "the evils for which these sciences are the palliative, have increased since the time of the Druids, in a proportion that heavily overweighs the benefit of improved therapeutics." We know nothing either of the diseases or the remedies of the Druids. But we are quite sure that the improvement of medicine has far more than kept pace with the increase of disease during the last three centuries. This is proved by the best possible evidence. The term of human life is decidedly longer in England than in any former age, respecting which we possess any information on which we can rely. All the rants in the world about picturesque cottages and temples of Mammon will not shake this argument. No test of the physical well-being of society can be named so decisive as that which is furnished by bills of mortality. That the lives of the people of this country have been gradually lengthening during the course of several generations, is as certain as any fact in statistics; and that the lives of men should become longer and longer, while their bodily condition during life is becoming worse and worse, is utterly incredible.

Let our readers think over these circumstances. Let them take into the account the sweating sickness and the plague. Let them take into the account that fearful disease which first made its appearance in the generation to which Mr. Southey assigns the palm of felicity, and raged through Europe with a fury at which the physician stood aghast, and before which the people were swept away by myriads. Let them consider the state of the northern counties, constantly the scene of robberies, rapes, massacres, and conflagrations. Let them add to all this the fact that seventy-two thousand persons suffered death by the hands of the executioner during the reign of Henry the Eighth, and judge between the nineteenth and the sixteenth century.

We do not say that the lower orders in England do not suffer severe hardships. But, in spite of Mr. Southey's assertions, and in spite of the assertions of a class of politicians, who, differing from Mr. Southey in every other point, agree with him in this, we are inclined to doubt whether the labouring classes here really suffer greater physical distress than the labouring classes of the most flourishing countries of the Continent.

It will scarcely be maintained that the lazzaroni[33] who sleep under the porticoes of Naples, or the beggars who besiege the convents of Spain, are in a happier situation than the English commonalty. The distress which has lately been experienced in the northern part of Germany, one of the best governed and most prosperous regions of Europe, surpasses, if we have been correctly informed, anything which has of late years been known among us. In Norway and Sweden the peasantry are constantly compelled to mix bark with their bread; and even this expedient has not always preserved whole families and neighbourhoods from perishing together of famine. An experiment has lately been tried in the kingdom of the Netherlands, which has been cited to prove the possibility of establishing agricultural colonies on the waste lands of England, but which proves to our minds nothing so clearly as this, that the rate of subsistence to which the labouring classes are reduced in the Netherlands is miserably low, and very far inferior to that of the English paupers. No distress which the people here have endured for centuries approaches to that which has been felt by the French in our own time. The beginning of the year 1817 was a time of great distress in this island. But the state of the lowest classes here was luxury compared with that of the people of France. We find in Magendie's[34] *Journal de Physiologie Expérimentale* a paper on a point of physiology connected with the distress of that season. It appears that the inhabitants of six departments, Aix, Jura, Doubs,

---

32 The former was physician to George IV, William IV, and Victoria; the latter to Henry VIII.

33 Beggars.
34 François Magendie (1783–1855), French physiologist.

Haute Saone, Vosges, and Saone-et-Loire, were reduced first to oatmeal and potatoes, and at last to nettles, beanstalks, and other kinds of herbage fit only for cattle; that when the next harvest enabled them to eat barley-bread, many of them died from intemperate indulgence in what they thought an exquisite repast; and that a dropsy of a peculiar description was produced by the hard fare of the year. Dead bodies were found on the roads and in the fields. A single surgeon dissected six of these, and found the stomach shrunk, and filled with the unwholesome aliments which hunger had driven men to share with beasts. Such extremity of distress as this is never heard of in England, or even in Ireland. We are, on the whole, inclined to think, though we would speak with diffidence on a point on which it would be rash to pronounce a positive judgment without a much longer and closer investigation than we have bestowed upon it, that the labouring classes of this island, though they have their grievances and distresses, some produced by their own improvidence, some by the errors of their rulers, are on the whole better off as to physical comforts than the inhabitants of any equally extensive district of the old world. For this very reason, suffering is more acutely felt and more loudly bewailed here than elsewhere. We must take into the account the liberty of discussion, and the strong interest which the opponents of a ministry always have to exaggerate the extent of the public disasters. There are countries in which the people quietly endure distress that here would shake the foundations of the State, countries in which the inhabitants of a whole province turn out to eat grass with less clamour than one Spitalfields[35] weaver would make here, if the overseers were to put him on barley-bread. In those new commonwealths in which a civilised population has at its command a boundless extent of the richest soil, the condition of the labourer is probably happier than in any society which has lasted for many centuries. But in the old world we must confess ourselves unable to find any satisfactory record of any great nation, past or present, in which the working classes have been in a more comfortable situation than in England during the last thirty years. When this island was thinly peopled, it was barbarous: there was little capital; and that little was insecure. It is now the richest and most highly civilised spot in the world; but the population is dense. Thus we have never known that golden age which the lower orders in the United States are now enjoying. We have never known an age of liberty, of order, and of education, an age in which the mechanical sciences were carried to a great height, yet in which the people were not sufficiently numerous to cultivate even the most fertile valleys. But, when we compare our own condition with that of our ancestors, we think it clear that the advantages arising from the progress of civilisation have far more than counterbalanced the disadvantages arising from the progress of population. While our numbers have increased tenfold, our wealth has increased a hundredfold. Though there are so many more people to share the wealth now existing in the country than there were in the sixteenth century, it seems certain that a greater share falls to almost every individual than fell to the share of any of the corresponding class in the sixteenth century. The King keeps a more spendid court. The establishments of the nobles are more magnificent. The esquires are richer; the merchants are richer; the shopkeepers are richer. The serving-man, the artisan, and the husbandman, have a more copious and palatable supply of food, better clothing, and better furniture. This is no reason for tolerating abuses, or for neglecting any means of ameliorating the condition of our poorer countrymen. But it is a reason against telling them, as some of our philosophers are constantly telling them, that they are the most wretched people who ever existed on the face of the earth.

We have already adverted to Mr. Southey's amusing doctrine about national wealth. A state, says he, cannot be too rich; but a people may be too rich. His reason for thinking this is extremely curious.

A people may be too rich, because it is the tendency of the commercial, and more especially of the manufacturing system, to collect wealth rather than to diffuse it. Where wealth is necessarily employed in any of the speculations of trade, its increase is in proportion to its amount. Great capitalists become like pikes in a fish-pond who devour the weaker fish; and it is but too certain, that the poverty of one

---

[35] A district in London largely given over to the weaving of silk.

part of the people seems to increase in the same ratio as the riches of another. There are examples of this in history. In Portugal, when the high tide of wealth flowed in from the conquests in Africa and the East, the effect of that great influx was not more visible in the augmented splendour of the court, and the luxury of the higher ranks, than in the distress of the people.

Mr. Southey's instance is not a very fortunate one. The wealth which did so little for the Portuguese was not the fruit either of manufactures or of commerce carried on by private individuals. It was the wealth, not of the people, but of the Government and its creatures, of those who, as Mr. Southey thinks, can never be too rich. The fact is, that Mr. Southey's proposition is opposed to all history, and to the phaenomena which surround us on every side. England is the richest country in Europe, the most commercial country, and the country in which manufactures flourish most. Russia and Poland are the poorest countries in Europe. They have scarcely any trade, and none but the rudest manufactures. Is wealth more diffused in Russia and Poland than in England? There are individuals in Russia and Poland whose incomes are probably equal to those of our richest countrymen. It may be doubted whether there are not, in those countries, as many fortunes of eighty thousand a year as here. But are there as many fortunes of two thousand a year, or of one thousand a year? There are parishes in England which contain more people of between three hundred and three thousand pounds a year than could be found in all the dominions of the Emperor Nicholas. The neat and commodious houses which have been built in London and its vicinity, for people of this class, within the last thirty years, would of themselves form a city larger than the capitals of some European kingdoms. And this is the state of society in which the great proprietors have devoured a smaller!

The cure which Mr. Southey thinks that he has discovered is worthy of the sagacity which he has shown in detecting the evil. The calamities arising from the collection of wealth in the hands of a few capitalists are to be remedied by collecting it in the hands of one great capitalist, who has no conceivable motive to use it better than other capitalists, the all-devouring State.

It is not strange that, differing so widely from Mr. Southey as to the past progress of society, we should differ from him also as to its probable destiny. He thinks, that to all outward appearance, the country is hastening to destruction; but he relies firmly on the goodness of God. We do not see either the piety or the rationality of thus confidently expecting that the Supreme Being will interfere to disturb the common succession of causes and effects. We, too, rely on his goodness, on his goodness as manifested, not in extraordinary interpositions, but in those general laws which it has pleased him to establish in the physical and in the moral world. We rely on the natural tendency of the human intellect to truth, and on the natural tendency of society to improvement. We know no well-authenticated instance of a people which has decidedly retrograded in civilisation and prosperity, except from the influence of violent and terrible calamities, such as those which laid the Roman Empire in ruins, or those which, about the beginning of the sixteenth century, desolated Italy. We know of no country which, at the end of fifty years of peace and tolerably good government, has been less prosperous than at the beginning of that period. The political importance of a state may decline, as the balance of power is disturbed by the introduction of new forces. Thus the influence of Holland and of Spain is much diminished. But are Holland and Spain poorer than formerly? We doubt it. Other countries have outrun them. But we suspect that they have been positively, though not relatively, advancing. We suspect that Holland is richer than when she sent her navies up the Thames,[36] that Spain is richer than when a French king was brought captive to the footstool of Charles the Fifth.[37]

History is full of the signs of this natural progress of society. We see in almost every part of the annals of mankind how the industry of individuals, struggling up against wars, taxes, famines, conflagrations, mischievous prohibitions, and more mischievous protections, creates faster than governments can squander, and repairs whatever invaders can destroy. We see the wealth of nations increasing, and all the arts of life approaching nearer and nearer to perfection,

---

[36] Climax of the First Dutch War, 1665–67.
[37] Francis I of France became a prisoner of Charles I of Spain (who as Holy Roman Emperor was Charles V) at the Battle of Pavia, 1525.

in spite of the grossest corruption and the wildest profusion on the part of rulers.

The present moment is one of great distress.[38] But how small will that distress appear when we think over the history of the last forty years;[39] a war, compared with which all other wars sink into insignificance; taxation, such as the most heavily taxed people of former times could not have conceived; a debt larger than all the public debts that ever existed in the world added together; the food of the people studiously rendered dear; the currency imprudently debased, and imprudently restored. Yet is the country poorer than in 1790? We firmly believe that, in spite of all the misgovernment of her rulers, she has been almost constantly becoming richer and richer. Now and then there has been a stoppage, now and then a short retrogression; but as to the general tendency there can be no doubt. A single breaker may recede; but the tide is evidently coming in.

If we were to prophesy that in the year 1930 a population of fifty millions, better fed, clad, and lodged than the English of our time, will cover these islands, that Sussex and Huntingdonshire will be wealthier than the wealthiest parts of the West Riding of Yorkshire now are, that cultivation, rich as that of a flower-garden, will be carried up to the very tops of Ben Nevis and Helvellyn,[40] that machines constructed on principles yet undiscovered will be in every house, that there will be no highways but railroads, no travelling but by steam, that our debt, vast as it seems to us, will appear to our great-grandchildren a trifling encumbrance, which might easily be paid off in a year or two, many people would think us insane. We prophesy nothing; but this we say: If any person had told the Parliament which met in perplexity and terror after the crash in 1720 that in 1830 the wealth of England would surpass all their wildest dreams, that the annual revenue would equal the principal of that debt which they considered as an intolerable burden, that for one man of ten thousand pounds then living there would be five men of fifty thousand pounds, that London would be twice as large and twice as populous, and that nevertheless the rate of mortality would have diminished to one half of what it then was, that the post-office would bring more into the exchequer than the excise and customs had brought in together under Charles the Second, that stage-coaches would run from London to York in twenty-four hours, that men would be in the habit of sailing without wind, and would be beginning to ride without horses, our ancestors would have given as much credit to the prediction as they gave to *Gulliver's Travels*. Yet the prediction would have been true; and they would have perceived that it was not altogether absurd, if they had considered that the country was then raising every year a sum which would have purchased the fee-simple of the revenue of the Plantagenets,[41] ten times what supported the Government of Elizabeth, three times what, in the time of Cromwell, had been thought intolerably oppressive. To almost all men the state of things under which they have been used to live seems to be the necessary state of things. We have heard it said that five per cent. is the natural interest of money, that twelve is the natural number of a jury, that forty shillings is the natural qualification of a county voter. Hence it is that, though in every age everybody knows that up to his own time progressive improvement has been taking place, nobody seems to reckon on any improvement during the next generation. We cannot absolutely prove that those are in error who tell us that society has reached a turning point, that we have seen our best days. But so said all who came before us, and with just as much apparent reason. "A million a year will beggar us," said the patriots of 1640. "Two millions a year will grind the country to powder," was the cry in 1660. "Six millions a year, and a debt of fifty millions!" exclaimed Swift, "the high allies have been the ruin of us."[42] "A

---

[38] 1830 was a year of agitation in England, leading up to the fall of Wellington and the installation of the Whig reformers under Lord Grey.

[39] The last forty years had witnessed the French Revolution and the Napoleonic Wars, both of which had repercussions in England; and England had participated in the defeat of Bonaparte. Moreover, during those forty years the reactionary Tories had been, in Macaulay's opinion, "misgoverning."

[40] Mountains in Scotland and the English Lake District, respectively, both in isolated and rugged terrain.

[41] Would have been sufficient to purchase absolute possession of the land which yielded the revenues of the Plantagenet family, England's rulers from 1154 to 1485.

[42] In the War of the Spanish Succession, 1701–12, when Holland and Austria fought as allies of England.

hundred and forty millions of debt!" said Junius;[43] "well may we say that we owe Lord Chatham more than we shall ever pay, if we owe him such a load as this." "Two hundred and forty millions of debt!" cried all the statesmen of 1783 in chorus; "what abilities, or what economy on the part of a minister, can save a country so burdened?" We know that if, since 1783, no fresh debt had been incurred, the increased resources of the country would have enabled us to defray that debt at which Pitt, Fox, and Burke stood aghast, nay, to defray it over and over again, and that with much lighter taxation than what we have actually borne. On what principle is it that, when we see nothing but improvement behind us, we are to expect nothing but deterioration before us?

It is not by the intermeddling of Mr. Southey's idol, the omniscient and omnipotent State, but by the prudence and energy of the people, that England has hitherto been carried forward in civilisation; and it is to the same prudence and the same energy that we now look with comfort and good hope. Our rulers will best promote the improvement of the nation by strictly confining themselves to their own legitimate duties, by leaving capital to find its most lucrative course, commodities their fair price, industry and intelligence their natural reward, idleness and folly their natural punishment, by maintaining peace, by defending property, by diminishing the price of law, and by observing strict economy in every department of the State. Let the Government do this: the People will assuredly do the rest.

from Francis Bacon[1]

. . . The chief peculiarity of Bacon's philosophy seems to us to have been this, that it aimed at things altogether different from those which his predecessors had proposed to themselves. This was his own opinion. "Finis scientiarum," says he, "a nemine adhuc bene positus est."[2] And again, "Omnium gravissimus error in deviatione ab ultimo doctrinarum fine consistit."[3] "Nec ipsa meta," says he elsewhere, "adhuc ulli, quod sciam, mortalium posita est et defixa."[4] The more carefully his works are examined, the more clearly, we think, it will appear that this is the real clue to his whole system, and that he used means different from those used by other philosophers, because he wished to arrive at an end altogether different from theirs.

What then was the end which Bacon proposed to himself? It was, to use his own emphatic expression, "fruit." It was the multiplying of human enjoyments and the mitigating of human sufferings. It was "the relief of man's estate." It was "commodis humanis inservire."[5] It was "efficaciter operari ad sublevanda vitae humanae incommoda."[6] It was "dotare vitam humanam novis inventis et copiis."[7] It was "genus humanum novis operibus et potestatibus continuo dotare."[8] This was the object of all his speculations in every department of science, in natural philosophy, in legislation, in politics, in morals.

Two words form the key of the Baconian doctrine, Utility and Progress. The ancient philosophy disdained to be useful, and was content to be stationary. It dealt largely in theories of moral perfection, which were so sublime that they never could be more than theories; in attempts to solve insoluble enigmas; in exhortations to the attainment of unattainable frames of mind. It could not condescend to the humble office of ministering to the comfort of human beings. All the schools contemned that office as degrading; some censured it as immoral. Once indeed Posidonius, a distinguished writer of the age of Cicero and Caesar, so far forgot himself as

---

43 Pseudonym of a Whig political writer, author of a series of letters, 1769–71, attacking Lord North, Chancellor of the Exchequer, and George III.
1 From a review by Macaulay in the *Edinburgh Review* for July, 1837, of *The Works of Francis Bacon, Lord Chancellor of England*, edited by Basil Montagu, London, 1825–34.

2 "The goal of the sciences has not as yet been well defined by anyone." (*Novum Organum*, Lib. 1, aph. 81.) The title references in parentheses in this selection are Macaulay's.
3 "The most serious error of all consists in deviation from the ultimate end of learning." (*De Augmentis*, Lib. 1.)
4 "Nor has the limit itself been set and established up to now by any man, so far as I know." (*Cogitata et Visa*.)
5 "To advance human comforts." (*De Augmentis*, Lib. 7, cap. 1.)
6 "To work effectually to remove the discomforts of human life." (*De Augmentis*, Lib. 2, cap. 2.)
7 "To endow human life with new discoveries and powers." (*Novum Organum*, Lib. 1, aph. 81.)
8 "Ever anew to endow mankind with new achievements and powers." (*Cogitata et Visa*.)

to enumerate, among the humbler blessings which mankind owed to philosophy, the discovery of the principle of the arch, and the introduction of the use of metals. This eulogy was considered as an affront, and was taken up with proper spirit. Seneca[9] vehemently disclaims these insulting compliments. Philosophy, according to him, has nothing to do with teaching men to rear arched roofs over their heads. The true philosopher does not care whether he has an arched roof or any roof. Philosophy has nothing to do with teaching men the uses of metals. She teaches us to be independent of all material substances, of all mechanical contrivances. The wise man lives according to nature. Instead of attempting to add to the physical comforts of his species, he regrets that his lot was not cast in that golden age when the human race had no protection against the cold but the skins of wild beasts, no screen from the sun but a cavern. To impute to such a man any share in the invention or improvement of a plough, a ship, or a mill is an insult. "In my own time," says Seneca, "there have been inventions of this sort, transparent windows, tubes for diffusing warmth equally through all parts of a building, shorthand, which has been carried to such a perfection that a writer can keep pace with the most rapid speaker. But the inventing of such things is drudgery for the lowest slaves; philosophy lies deeper. It is not her office to teach men how to use their hands. The object of her lessons is to form the soul. *Non est, inquam, instrumentorum ad usus necessarios opifex.*"[10] If the *non* were left out, this last sentence would be no bad description of the Baconian philosophy, and would, indeed, very much resemble several expressions in the *Novum Organum*.[11] "We shall next be told," exclaims Seneca, "that the first shoemaker was a philosopher." For our own part, if we are forced to make our choice between the first shoemaker and the author of the three books On Anger,[12] we pronounce for the shoemaker. It may be worse to be angry than to be wet. But shoes have kept millions from being wet; and we

doubt whether Seneca ever kept anybody from being angry.

It is very reluctantly that Seneca can be brought to confess that any philosopher had ever paid the smallest attention to anything that could possibly promote what vulgar people would consider as the well-being of mankind. He labours to clear Democritus[13] from the disgraceful imputation of having made the first arch, and Anacharsis[14] from the charge of having contrived the potter's wheel. He is forced to own that such a thing might happen; and it may also happen, he tells us, that a philosopher may be swift of foot. But it is not in his character of philosopher that he either wins a race or invents a machine. No, to be sure. The business of a philosopher was to declaim in praise of poverty with two millions sterling out at usury, to meditate epigrammatic conceits about the evils of luxury, in gardens which moved the envy of sovereigns, to rant about liberty, while fawning on the insolent and pampered freedmen of a tyrant, to celebrate the divine beauty of virtue with the same pen which had just before written a defence of the murder of a mother by a son.[15]

From the cant of this philosophy, a philosophy meanly proud of its own unprofitableness, it is delightful to turn to the lessons of the great English teacher. We can almost forgive all the faults of Bacon's life when we read that singularly graceful and dignified passage: "Ego certe, ut de me ipso, quod res est, loquar, et in iis quae nunc edo, et in iis quae in posterum meditor, dignitatem ingenii et nominis mei, si qua sit, saepius sciens et volens projicio, dum commodis humanis inserviam; quique architectus fortasse in philosophia et scientiis esse debeam, etiam operarius, et bajulus, et quidvis demum fio, cum haud pauca quae omnino fieri necesse sit, alii autem ob innatum superbiam subterfugiant, ipsi sustineam et exsequar."[16]

---

9 Seneca (*c.* 4 B.C.–65 A.D.), Roman Stoic philosopher, who was the tutor of the Emperor Nero.
10 "She is not, I say, the maker of instruments for necessary purposes."
11 One of Bacon's most important works.
12 Seneca was the author of *De Ira*.

13 Greek philosopher (born *c.* 460 B.C.) whose learning and interests embraced other fields than pure philosophy, among which was mechanics.
14 Anacharsis came to Athens from Scythia in the sixth century B.C. to study philosophy.
15 This is evidently intended in part as a portrait of Seneca.
16 "But I, certainly, to say how the matter stands with myself alone, both in respect to what I am now producing and in what I intend hereafter, often advisedly and deliberately throw aside the dignity of my name and wit, if such exist, in my endeavor to advance human comforts;

This *philanthropia,* which, as he said in one of the most remarkable of his early letters, "was so fixed in his mind, as it could not be removed," this majestic humility, this persuasion that nothing can be too insignificant for the attention of the wisest, which is not too insignificant to give pleasure or pain to the meanest, is the great characteristic distinction, the essential spirit of the Baconian philosophy. We trace it in all that Bacon has written on Physics, on Laws, on Morals. And we conceive that from this peculiarity all the other peculiarities of his system directly and almost necessarily sprang.

The spirit which appears in the passage of Seneca to which we have referred tainted the whole body of the ancient philosophy from the time of Socrates[17] downwards, and took possession of intellects with which that of Seneca cannot for a moment be compared. It pervades the dialogues of Plato. It may be distinctly traced in many parts of the works of Aristotle. Bacon has dropped hints from which it may be inferred that, in his opinion, the prevalence of this feeling was in a great measure to be attributed to the influence of Socrates. Our great countryman evidently did not consider the revolution which Socrates effected in philosophy as a happy event, and constantly maintained that the earlier Greek speculators, Democritus in particular, were, on the whole, superior to their more celebrated successors.

Assuredly if the tree which Socrates planted and Plato watered is to be judged of by its flowers and leaves, it is the noblest of trees. But if we take the homely test of Bacon, if we judge of the tree by its fruits, our opinion of it may perhaps be less favourable. When we sum up all the useful truths which we owe to that philosophy, to what do they amount? We find, indeed, abundant proofs that some of those who cultivated it were men of the first order of intel-

lect. We find among their writings incomparable specimens both of dialectical and rhetorical art. We have no doubt that the ancient controversies were of use, in so far as they served to exercise the faculties of the disputants; for there is no controversy so idle that it may not be of use in this way. But, when we look for something more, for something which adds to the comforts or alleviates the calamities of the human race, we are forced to own ourselves disappointed. We are forced to say with Bacon that this celebrated philosophy ended in nothing but disputation, that it was neither a vineyard nor an olive-ground, but an intricate wood of briars and thistles, from which those who lost themselves in it brought back many scratches and no food. . . .[18]

Words, and more words, and nothing but words, had been all the fruit of all the toil of all the most renowned sages of sixty generations. But the days of this sterile exuberance were numbered. . . .[19]

At this time Bacon appeared . . . . The philosophy which he taught was essentially new. It differed from that of the celebrated ancient teachers, not merely in method, but also in object. Its object was the good of mankind, in the sense in which the mass of mankind always have understood and always will understand the word good. "Meditor," said Bacon, "instaurationem philosophiae ejusmodi quae nihil inanis aut abstracti habeat, quaeque vitae humanae conditiones in melius provehat."[20]

The difference between the philosophy of Bacon and that of his predecessors cannot, we think, be better illustrated than by comparing his views on some important subjects with those of Plato. We select Plato, because we conceive that he did more than any other person towards giving to the minds of speculative men that bent which they retained till they received from

---

and being one who should properly, perhaps, be an architect in philosophy and the sciences, I turn common laborer, hodman, anything that is wanted; taking upon myself the burden and execution of many things that must needs be done, and that others, through an inborn pride, shrink from and decline." (*De Augmentis,* Lib. 7, cap. 1).
17 Macaulay notes that prior to Socrates (420–399 B.C.) philosophers had been mainly occupied with the observation and explanation of physical phenomena, whereas after his time philosophy concerned itself with increasingly abstract questions.

18 In a passage here omitted, Macaulay gives further particulars as to the nature of the ancient philosophy and its continuing influence down to Bacon's day.
19 In another omitted passage, Macaulay mentions the causes that "predisposed the public mind to a change"—principally the Reformation.
20 "I contemplate a reorganization of philosophy which shall be neither empty nor abstract and which shall improve the conditions of human existence." (*Redargutio Philosophiarum.*)

Bacon a new impulse in a diametrically opposite direction.

It is curious to observe how differently these great men estimated the value of every kind of knowledge. Take Arithmetic for example. Plato, after speaking slightly of the convenience of being able to reckon and compute in the ordinary transactions of life, passes to what he considers as a far more important advantage. The study of the properties of numbers, he tells us, habituates the mind to the contemplation of pure truth, and raises us above the material universe. He would have his disciples apply themselves to this study, not that they may be able to buy or sell, not that they may qualify themselves to be shopkeepers or travelling merchants, but that they may learn to withdraw their minds from the ever-shifting spectacle of this visible and tangible world, and to fix them on the immutable essences of things.

Bacon, on the other hand, valued this branch of knowledge, only on account of its uses with reference to that visible and tangible world which Plato so much despised. He speaks with scorn of the mystical arithmetic of the later Platonists, and laments the propensity of mankind to employ, on mere matters of curiosity, powers the whole exertion of which is required for purposes of solid advantage. He advises arithmeticians to leave these trifles, and to employ themselves in framing convenient expressions, which may be of use in physical researches.

The same reasons which led Plato to recommend the study of arithmetic led him to recommend also the study of mathematics. The vulgar crowd of geometricians, he says, will not understand him. They have practice always in view. They do not know that the real use of the science is to lead men to the knowledge of abstract, essential, eternal truth. Indeed, if we are to believe Plutarch, Plato carried this feeling so far that he considered geometry as degraded by being applied to any purpose of vulgar utility. Archytas, it seems, had framed machines of extraordinary power on mathematical principles. Plato remonstrated with his friend, and declared that this was to degrade a noble intellectual exercise into a low craft, fit only for carpenters and wheelwrights. The office of geometry, he said, was to discipline the mind, not to minister to the base wants of the body. His interference

was successful; and from that time, according to Plutarch, the science of mechanics was considered as unworthy of the attention of a philosopher.[21]

Archimedes[22] in a later age imitated and surpassed Archytas. But even Archimedes was not free from the prevailing notion that geometry was degraded by being employed to produce anything useful. It was with difficulty that he was induced to stoop from speculation to practice. He was half ashamed of those inventions which were the wonder of hostile nations, and always spoke of them slightingly as mere amusements, as trifles in which a mathematician might be suffered to relax his mind after intense application to the higher parts of his science.

The opinion of Bacon on this subject was diametrically opposed to that of the ancient philosophers. He valued geometry chiefly, if not solely, on account of those uses, which to Plato appeared so base. And it is remarkable that the longer Bacon lived the stronger this feeling became. When in 1605 he wrote the two books on the *Advancement of Learning*, he dwelt on the advantages which mankind derived from mixed mathematics; but he at the same time admitted that the beneficial effect produced by mathematical study on the intellect, though a collateral advantage, was "no less worthy than that which was principal and intended." But it is evident that his views underwent a change. When, near twenty years later, he published the *De Augmentis*, which is the *Treatise on the Advancement of Learning*, greatly expanded and carefully corrected, he made important alterations in the part which related to mathematics. He condemned with severity the high pretensions of the mathematicians, "delicias et fastum mathematicorum."[23] Assuming the well-being of the human race to be the end of knowledge, he pronounced that mathematical science could claim no higher rank than that of an appendage or auxiliary to other sciences. Mathe-

---

21 Plutarch was a famous Greek historian (46?–120?) best known as the author of the *Parallel Lives*. According to Macaulay's own note, the incident related about Archytas, philosopher, mathematician, and statesman of the fifth century B.C., is taken from Plutarch's *Symposiaca*, viii, and *Life of Marcellus*.
22 Mathematician who lived at Syracuse in the third century B.C.
23 "The daintiness and pride of mathematicians."

matical science, he says, is the handmaid of natural philosophy; she ought to demean herself as such; and he declares that he cannot conceive by what ill chance it has happened that she presumes to claim precedence over her mistress. He predicts—a prediction which would have made Plato shudder—that as more and more discoveries are made in physics, there will be more and more branches of mixed mathematics. Of that collateral advantage the value of which, twenty years before, he rated so highly, he says not one word. This omission cannot have been the effect of mere inadvertence. His own treatise was before him. From that treatise he deliberately expunged whatever was favourable to the study of pure mathematics, and inserted several keen reflections on the ardent votaries of that study. This fact, in our opinion, admits of only one explanation. Bacon's love of those pursuits which directly tend to improve the condition of mankind, and his jealousy of all pursuits merely curious, had grown upon him, and had, it may be, become immoderate. He was afraid of using any expression which might have the effect of inducing any man of talents to employ in speculations, useful only to the mind of the speculator, a single hour which might be employed in extending the empire of man over matter. If Bacon erred here, we must acknowledge that we greatly prefer his error to the opposite error of Plato. We have no patience with a philosophy which, like those Roman matrons who swallowed abortives in order to preserve their shapes, takes pains to be barren for fear of being homely.

Let us pass to astronomy. This was one of the sciences which Plato exhorted his disciples to learn, but for reasons far removed from common habits of thinking. "Shall we set down astronomy," says Socrates,[24] "among the subjects of study?" "I think so," answers his young friend Glaucon: "to know something about the seasons, the months, and the years is of use for military purposes, as well as for agriculture and navigation." "It amuses me," says Socrates, "to see how afraid you are, lest the common herd of people should accuse you of recommending useless studies." He then proceeds, in that pure and magnificent diction which, as Cicero said, Jupi-

ter would use if Jupiter spoke Greek, to explain, that the use of astronomy is not to add to the vulgar comforts of life, but to assist in raising the mind to the contemplation of things which are to be perceived by the pure intellect alone. The knowledge of the actual motions of the heavenly bodies Socrates considers as of little value. The appearances which make the sky beautiful at night are, he tells us, like the figures which a geometrician draws on the sand, mere examples, mere helps to feeble minds. We must get beyond them; we must attain to an astronomy which is as independent of the actual stars as geometrical truth is independent of the lines of an ill-drawn diagram. This is, we imagine, very nearly, if not exactly, the astronomy which Bacon compared to the ox of Prometheus, a sleek, well-shaped hide, stuffed with rubbish, goodly to look at, but containing nothing to eat. He complained that astronomy had, to its great injury, been separated from natural philosophy, of which it was one of the noblest provinces, and annexed to the domain of mathematics. The world stood in need, he said, of a very different astronomy, of a living astronomy, of an astronomy which should set forth the nature, the motion, and the influences of the heavenly bodies, as they really are.

On the greatest and most useful of all human inventions, the invention of alphabetical writing, Plato did not look with much complacency. He seems to have thought that the use of letters had operated on the human mind as the use of the go-cart in learning to walk, or of corks in learning to swim, is said to operate on the human body. It was a support which, in his opinion, soon became indispensable to those who used it, which made vigorous exertion first unnecessary and then impossible. The powers of the intellect would, he conceived, have been more fully developed without this delusive aid. Men would have been compelled to exercise the understanding and the memory, and, by deep and assiduous meditation, to make truth thoroughly their own. Now, on the contrary, much knowledge is traced on paper, but little is engraved in the soul. A man is certain that he can find information at a moment's notice when he wants it. He therefore suffers it to fade from his mind. Such a man cannot in strictness be said to know anything. He has the show without

---

24 In Plato's *Republic*, Book VII.

the reality of wisdom. These opinions Plato has put into the mouth of an ancient king of Egypt.[25] But it is evident from the context that they were his own; and so they were understood to be by Quinctilian.[26] Indeed they are in perfect accordance with the whole Platonic system.

Bacon's views, as may easily be supposed, were widely different. The powers of the memory, he observes, without the help of writing, can do little towards the advancement of any useful science. He acknowledges that the memory may be disciplined to such a point as to be able to perform very extraordinary feats. But on such feats he sets little value. The habits of his mind, he tells us, are such that he is not disposed to rate highly any accomplishment, however rare, which is of no practical use to mankind. As to these prodigious achievements of the memory, he ranks them with the exhibitions of rope-dancers and tumblers. "These two performances," he says, "are much of the same sort. The one is an abuse of the powers of the body; the other is an abuse of the powers of the mind. Both may perhaps excite our wonder; but neither is entitled to our respect."

To Plato, the science of medicine appeared to be of very disputable advantages. He did not indeed object to quick cures for acute disorders, or for injuries produced by accidents. But the art which resists the slow sap of a chronic disease, which repairs frames enervated by lust, swollen by gluttony, or inflamed by wine, which encourages sensuality by mitigating the natural punishment of the sensualist, and prolongs existence when the intellect has ceased to retain its entire energy, had no share of his esteem. A life protracted by medical skill he pronounced to be a long death. The exercise of the art of medicine ought, he said, to be tolerated, so far as that art may serve to cure the occasional distempers of men whose constitutions are good. As to those who have bad constitutions, let them die; and the sooner the better. Such men are unfit for war, for magistracy, for the management of their domestic affairs, for severe study and speculation. If they engage in any vigorous mental exercise, they are troubled with giddiness and fulness of the head, all which they lay to the

account of philosophy. The best thing that can happen to such wretches is to have done with life at once. He quotes mythical authority in support of this doctrine; and reminds his disciples that the practice of the sons of Aesculapius,[27] as described by Homer, extended only to the cure of external injuries.

Far different was the philosophy of Bacon. Of all the sciences, that which he seems to have regarded with the greatest interest was the science which, in Plato's opinion, would not be tolerated in a well-regulated community. To make men perfect was no part of Bacon's plan. His humble aim was to make imperfect men comfortable. The beneficence of his philosophy resembled the beneficence of the common Father, whose sun rises on the evil and the good, whose rain descends for the just and the unjust. In Plato's opinion man was made for philosophy; in Bacon's opinion philosophy was made for man; it was a means to an end; and that end was to increase the pleasures and to mitigate the pains of millions who are not and cannot be philosophers. That a valetudinarian who took great pleasure in being wheeled along his terrace, who relished his boiled chicken and his weak wine and water, and who enjoyed a hearty laugh over the Queen of Navarre's tales,[28] should be treated as a *caput lupinum*[29] because he could not read the *Timaeus*[30] without a headache, was a notion which the humane spirit of the English school of wisdom altogether rejected. Bacon would not have thought it beneath the dignity of a philosopher to contrive an improved garden chair for such a valetudinarian, to devise some way of rendering his medicines more palatable, to invent repasts which he might enjoy, and pillows on which he might sleep soundly; and this though there might not be the smallest hope that the mind of the poor invalid would ever rise to the contemplation of the ideal beautiful and the ideal good. As Plato had cited the religious legends of Greece to justify his contempt for the more recondite parts of the art of

---

25 In his *Phaedrus*, 274-75.
26 Or Quintilian, famous Roman rhetorician (35?-100?).
27 Aesculapius, as portrayed by Homer in the *Iliad,* was the founder of medical art, and his sons were the doctors who accompanied the Greek army to Troy.
28 A collection of love stories, the *Heptameron*, made by Marguerite, Queen of Navarre (1492-1549).
29 An outlaw.
30 One of Plato's more difficult dialogues.

healing, Bacon vindicated the dignity of that art by appealing to the example of Christ, and reminded men that the great Physician of the soul did not disdain to be also the physician of the body.

When we pass from the science of medicine to that of legislation, we find the same difference between the systems of these two great men. Plato, at the commencement of the *Dialogue on Laws,* lays it down as a fundamental principle that the end of legislation is to make men virtuous. It is unnecessary to point out the extravagant conclusions to which such a proposition leads. Bacon well knew to how great an extent the happiness of every society must depend on the virtue of its members; and he also knew what legislators can and what they cannot do for the purpose of promoting virtue. The view which he has given of the end of legislation, and of the principal means for the attainment of that end, has always seemed to us eminently happy, even among the many happy passages of the same kind with which his works abound. "Finis et scopus quem leges intueri atque ad quem jussiones et sanctiones suas dirigere debent, non alius est quam ut cives feliciter degant. Id fiet si pietate et religione recte instituti, moribus honesti, armis adversus hostes externos tuti, legum auxilio adversus seditiones et privatas injurias muniti, imperio et magistratibus obsequentes, copiis et opibus locupletes et florentes fuerint."[31] The end is the well-being of the people. The means are the imparting of moral and religious education; the providing of everything necessary for defence against foreign enemies; the maintaining of internal order; the establishing of a judicial, financial, and commercial system, under which wealth may be rapidly accumulated and securely enjoyed.

Even with respect to the form in which laws ought to be drawn, there is a remarkable difference of opinion between the Greek and the Englishman. Plato thought a preamble essential; Bacon thought it mischievous. Each was consistent with himself. Plato, considering the moral improvement of the people as the end of legislation, justly inferred that a law which commanded and threatened, but which neither convinced the reason, nor touched the heart, must be a most imperfect law. He was not content with deterring from theft a man who still continued to be a thief at heart, with restraining a son who hated his mother from beating his mother. The only obedience on which he set much value was the obedience which an enlightened understanding yields to reason, and which a virtuous disposition yields to precepts of virtue. He really seems to have believed that, by prefixing to every law an eloquent and pathetic exhortation, he should, to a great extent, render penal enactments superfluous. Bacon entertained no such romantic hopes; and he well knew the practical inconveniences of the course which Plato recommended. "Neque nobis," says he, "prologi legum qui inepti olim habiti sunt, et leges introducunt disputantes non jubentes, utique placerent, si priscos mores ferre possemus. . . . Quantum fieri potest prologi evitentur, et lex incipiat a jussione."[32]

Each of the great men whom we have compared intended to illustrate his system by a philosophical romance; and each left his romance imperfect. Had Plato lived to finish the *Critias,* a comparison between that noble fiction and the new *Atlantis*[33] would probably have furnished us with still more striking instances than any which we have given. It is amusing to think with what horror he would have seen such an institution as Solomon's House[34] rising in his republic: with what vehemence he would have ordered the brew-houses, the perfume-houses, and the dispensatories to be pulled down; and with what inexorable rigour he

---

31 "The end and scope which laws should have in view, and to which they should direct their decrees and sanctions, is no other than the happiness of the citizens. And this will be effected if the citizens be rightly trained in piety and religion, sound in morality, protected by arms against foreign enemies, guarded by the shield of the laws against civil discords and private injuries, obedient to the government and the magistrates, and rich and flourishing in forces and wealth." (*De Augmentis,* Lib. 8, cap. 3, aph. 5.)

32 "Nor do I approve the preambles to laws, which were formerly considered impertinent, and which present the laws as disputations rather than as commands so that they may be acceptable, if we could endure the ancient customs. As much as possible preambles should be avoided and the law should begin with its enactment." (*De Augmentis,* Lib. 8, cap. 3, aph. 69.)

33 The *New Atlantis* by Bacon.

34 The ideal college described in the *New Atlantis,* "dedicated to the study of the works and creatures of God," all with a strictly practical bias.

would have driven beyond the frontier all the Fellows of the College, Merchants of Light and Deprecators, Lamps and Pioneers.

To sum up the whole, we should say that the aim of the Platonic philosophy was to exalt man into a god. The aim of the Baconian philosophy was to provide man with what he requires while he continues to be man. The aim of the Platonic philosophy was to raise us far above vulgar wants. The aim of the Baconian philosophy was to supply our vulgar wants. The former aim was noble; but the latter was attainable. Plato drew a good bow; but, like Acestes in Virgil, he aimed at the stars; and therefore, though there was no want of strength or skill, the shot was thrown away. His arrow was indeed followed by a track of dazzling radiance, but it struck nothing.

Volans liquidis in nubibus arsit arundo
Signavitque viam flammis, tenuisque recessit
Consumpta in ventos.[35]

Bacon fixed his eye on a mark which was placed on the earth, and within bow-shot, and hit it in the white. The philosophy of Plato began in words and ended in words, noble words indeed, words such as were to be expected from the finest of human intellects exercising boundless dominion over the finest of human languages. The philosophy of Bacon began in observations and ended in arts.

The boast of the ancient philosophers was that their doctrine formed the minds of men to a high degree of wisdom and virtue. This was indeed the only practical good which the most celebrated of those teachers even pretended to effect; and undoubtedly, if they had effected this, they would have deserved far higher praise than if they had discovered the most salutary medicines or constructed the most powerful machines. But the truth is that, in those very matters in which alone they professed to do any good to mankind, in those very matters for the sake of which they neglected all the vulgar interests of mankind, they did nothing, or worse than nothing. They promised what was impracticable; they despised what was practicable; they filled the world with long words and long beards; and they left it as wicked and as ignorant as they found it.

An acre in Middlesex is better than a principality in Utopia. The smallest actual good is better than the most magnificent promises of impossibilities. The wise man of the Stoics would, no doubt, be a grander object than a steam-engine. But there are steam-engines. And the wise man of the Stoics is yet to be born. A philosophy which should enable a man to feel perfectly happy while in agonies of pain would be better than a philosophy which assuages pain. But we know that there are remedies which will assuage pain; and we know that the ancient sages liked the toothache just as little as their neighbours. A philosophy which should extinguish cupidity would be better than a philosophy which should devise laws for the security of property. But it is possible to make laws which shall, to a very great extent, secure property. And we do not understand how any motives which the ancient philosophy furnished could extinguish cupidity. We know indeed that the philosophers were no better than other men. From the testimony of friends as well as of foes, from the confessions of Epictetus[36] and Seneca, as well as from the sneers of Lucian[37] and the fierce invectives of Juvenal,[38] it is plain that these teachers of virtue had all the vices of their neighbours, with the additional vice of hypocrisy. Some people may think the object of the Baconian philosophy a low object, but they cannot deny that, high or low, it has been attained. They cannot deny that every year makes an addition to what Bacon called "fruit." They cannot deny that mankind have made, and are making, great and constant progress in the road which he pointed out to them. Was there any such progressive movement among the ancient philosophers? After they had been declaiming eight hundred years, had they made the world better than when they began? Our belief is that, among the philosophers themselves, instead of a progressive improvement there was a progressive degeneracy. An abject

---

35 "For, as through cloud and rain the arrow was flying, it kindled, Marking its track with fire; then vanished from sight in the heavens, Wholly consumed." (*Aeneid*, V, 525–27. Connington's translation.)

36 Outstanding Stoic philosopher of the first century A.D.
37 Greek satirist (c. 120–180), who made mock of philosophers in general.
38 Roman poet and satirist (60?–140), who also disparaged philosophers.

superstition which Democritus or Anaxagoras[39] would have rejected with scorn, added the last disgrace to the long dotage of the Stoic and Platonic schools. Those unsuccessful attempts to articulate which are so delightful and interesting in a child shock and disgust in an aged paralytic; and in the same way, those wild and mythological fictions which charm us, when we hear them lisped by Greek poetry in its infancy, excite a mixed sensation of pity and loathing, when mumbled by Greek philosophy in its old age. We know that guns, cutlery, spy-glasses, clocks, are better in our time than they were in the time of our fathers, and were better in the time of our fathers than they were in the time of our grandfathers. We might, therefore, be inclined to think that, when a philosophy which boasted that its object was the elevation and purification of the mind, and which for this object neglected the sordid office of ministering to the comforts of the body, had flourished in the highest honour during many hundreds of years, a vast moral amelioration must have taken place. Was it so? Look at the schools of this wisdom four centuries before the Christian era and four centuries after that era. Compare the men whom those schools formed at those two periods. Compare Plato and Libanius.[40] Compare Pericles and Julian.[41] This philosophy confessed, nay boasted, that for every end but one it was useless. Had it attained that one end?

Suppose that Justinian, when he closed the schools of Athens,[42] had called on the last few sages who still haunted the Portico, and lingered round the ancient plane-trees, to show their title to public veneration: suppose that he had said: "A thousand years have elapsed since, in this famous city, Socrates posed Protagoras and Hippias;[43] during those thousand years a large proportion of the ablest men of every generation has been employed in constant efforts to bring to perfection the philosophy which you teach; that philosophy has been munificently patronised by the powerful; its professors have been held in the highest esteem by the public; it has drawn to itself almost all the sap and vigour of the human intellect: and what has it effected? What profitable truth has it taught us which we should not equally have known without it? What has it enabled us to do which we should not have been equally able to do without it?" Such questions, we suspect, would have puzzled Simplicius and Isidore.[44] Ask a follower of Bacon what the new philosophy, as it was called in the time of Charles the Second, has effected for mankind, and his answer is ready: "It has lengthened life; it has mitigated pain; it has extinguished diseases; it has increased the fertility of the soil; it has given new securities to the mariner; it has furnished new arms to the warrior; it has spanned great rivers and estuaries with bridges of form unknown to our fathers; it has guided the thunderbolt innocuously from heaven to earth; it has lighted up the night with the splendour of day; it has extended the range of the human vision; it has multiplied the power of the human muscles; it has accelerated motion; it has annihilated distance; it has facilitated intercourse, correspondence, all friendly offices, all despatch of business; it has enabled man to descend to the depths of the sea, to soar into the air, to penetrate securely into the noxious recesses of the earth, to traverse the land in cars which whirl along without horses, and the ocean in ships which run ten knots an hour against the wind. These are but a part of its fruits, and of its first fruits. For it is a philosophy which never rests, which has never attained, which is never perfect. Its law is progress. A point which yesterday was invisible is its goal to-day, and will be its starting-post to-morrow."

Great and various as the powers of Bacon were, he owes his wide and durable fame chiefly to this, that all those powers received their direction from common sense. His love of the vulgar useful, his strong sympathy with the popular

---

[39] Two early Greek philosophers, the first of whom propounded an atomic theory of the universe, while the latter believed in reason as a metaphysical principle. It is uncertain at just what specific "superstition" Macaulay is aiming, but he mentions almost immediately below some of the "late" philosophers, who are known to have dabbled in magic, divination, etc.

[40] Greek sophist and commentator (314–393), who was specifically charged with studying magic.

[41] Pericles was a leading Athenian statesman (fifth century B.C.) in the time of Greece's greatest intellectual vigor. Julian (331–363) was emperor of Rome in the days of its decadence; his devotion to classical philosophy was undercut by his belief in such superstitions as divination and sacrificial offerings.

[42] By an imperial edict in 529.

[43] Interlocutors in Plato's *Protagoras*.

[44] Among the last of the Neo-Platonists. Simplicius was actually teaching at the Academy when Justinian closed it.

notions of good and evil, and the openness with which he avowed that sympathy, are the secret of his influence. There was in his system no cant, no illusion. He had no anointing for broken bones, no fine theories *de finibus*,[45] no arguments to persuade men out of their senses. He knew that men, and philosophers as well as other men, do actually love life, health, comfort, honour, security, the society of friends, and do actually dislike death, sickness, pain, poverty, disgrace, danger, separation from those to whom they are attached. He knew that religion, though it often regulates and moderates these feelings, seldom eradicates them; nor did he think it desirable for mankind that they should be eradicated. The plan of eradicating them by conceits like those of Seneca, or syllogisms like those of Chrysippus,[46] was too preposterous to be for a moment entertained by a mind like his. He did not understand what wisdom there could be in changing names where it was impossible to change things; in denying that blindness, hunger, the gout, the rack, were evils, and calling them ἀποπροήγμενα;[47] in refusing to acknowledge that health, safety, plenty, were good things, and dubbing them by the name of ἀδιάφορα.[48] In his opinions on all these subjects, he was not a Stoic, nor an Epicurean, nor an Academic, but what would have been called by Stoics, Epicureans, and Academics a mere ἰδιώτης, a mere common man. And it was precisely because he was so that his name makes so great an era in the history of the world. It was because he dug deep that he was able to pile high. It was because, in order to lay his foundations, he went down into those parts of human nature which lie low, but which are not liable to change, that the fabric which he reared has risen to so stately an elevation, and stands with such immovable strength.

We have sometimes thought that an amusing fiction might be written, in which a disciple of Epictetus and a disciple of Bacon should be introduced as fellow-travellers. They come to a village where the small-pox has just begun to rage, and find houses shut up, intercourse suspended, the sick abandoned, mothers weeping in terror over their children. The Stoic assures the dismayed population that there is nothing bad in the small-pox, and that to a wise man disease, deformity, death, the loss of friends, are not evils. The Baconian takes out a lancet and begins to vaccinate. They find a body of miners in great dismay. An explosion of noisome vapours has just killed many of those who were at work; and the survivors are afraid to venture into the cavern. The Stoic assures them that such an accident is nothing but a mere ἀποπροήγμενον.[49] The Baconian, who has no such fine word at his command, contents himself with devising a safety-lamp. They find a shipwrecked merchant wringing his hands on the shore. His vessel with an inestimable cargo has just gone down, and he is reduced in a moment from opulence to beggary. The Stoic exhorts him not to seek happiness in things which lie without himself, and repeats the whole chapter of Epictetus πρὸς τοὺς τήν ἀπορίαν δεδοικότας[50] The Baconian constructs a diving-bell, goes down in it, and returns with the most precious effects from the wreck. It would be easy to multiply illustrations of the difference between the philosophy of thorns and the philosophy of fruit, the philosophy of words and the philosophy of works.

Bacon has been accused of overrating the importance of those sciences which minister to the physical well-being of man, and of underrating the importance of moral philosophy; and it cannot be denied that persons who read the *Novum Organum* and the *De Augmentis,* without adverting to the circumstances under which those works were written, will find much that may seem to countenance the accusation. It is certain, however, that, though in practice he often went very wrong, and though, as his historical work and his essays prove, he did not hold, even in theory, very strict opinions on points of political morality, he was far too wise a man not to know how much our well-being depends on the regulation of our minds. The world for which he wished was not, as some people seem to imagine, a world of water-wheels, power-looms, steam-carriages, sensualists, and knaves. He would have been as ready as Zeno himself[51] to maintain that no bodily comforts which could

---

45 Concerning final ends or purposes.
46 A leader of the Stoic school at Athens. He stated many of the Stoic ideas in the form of syllogisms.
47 "Things relatively evil."   48 "Things indifferent."

49 "Relative evil."   50 "To those who fear poverty."
51 The founder of the Stoic school of philosophy. His teachings were roughly those outlined here by Macaulay.

be devised by the skill and labour of a hundred generations would give happiness to a man whose mind was under the tyranny of licentious appetite, of envy, of hatred, or of fear. If he sometimes appeared to ascribe importance too exclusively to the arts which increase the outward comforts of our species, the reason is plain. Those arts had been most unduly depreciated. They had been represented as unworthy of the attention of a man of liberal education . . . had undoubtedly caused many arts which were of the greatest utility, and which were susceptible of the greatest improvements, to be neglected by speculators, and abandoned to joiners, masons, smiths, weavers, apothecaries. It was necessary to assert the dignity of those arts, to bring them prominently forward, to proclaim that, as they have a most serious effect on human happiness, they are not unworthy of the attention of the highest human intellects. Again, it was by illustrations drawn from these arts that Bacon could most easily illustrate his principles. It was by improvements effected in these arts that the soundness of his principles could be most speedily and decisively brought to the test, and made manifest to common understandings. He acted like a wise commander who thins every other part of his line to strengthen a point where the enemy is attacking with peculiar fury, and on the fate of which the event of the battle seems likely to depend. In the *Novum Organum,* however, he distinctly and most truly declares that his philosophy is no less a Moral than a Natural Philosophy, that, though his illustrations are drawn from physical science, the principles which those illustrations are intended to explain are just as applicable to ethical and political inquiries as to inquiries into the nature of heat and vegetation. . . . .

from The History of England from the Accession of James the Second

from Chapter I

I purpose to write the history of England from the accession of King James the Second[1] down to a time which is within the memory of men still living. I shall recount the errors which, in a few months, alienated a loyal gentry and priesthood from the House of Stuart. I shall trace the course of that revolution which terminated the long struggle between our sovereigns and their parliaments, and bound up together the rights of the people and the title of the reigning dynasty. I shall relate how the new settlement was, during many troubled years, successfully defended against foreign and domestic enemies; how, under that settlement, the authority of law and the security of property were found to be compatible with a liberty of discussion and of individual action never before known; how, from the auspicious union of order and freedom, sprang a prosperity of which the annals of human affairs had furnished no example; how our country, from a state of ignominious vassalage, rapidly rose to the place of umpire among European powers; how her opulence and her martial glory grew together; how, by wise and resolute good faith, was gradually established a public credit fruitful of marvels which, to the statesmen of any former age, would have seemed incredible; how a gigantic commerce gave birth to a maritime power, compared with which every other maritime power, ancient or modern, sinks into insignificance; how Scotland, after ages of enmity, was at length united to England, not merely by legal bonds,[2] but by indissoluble ties of interest and affection; how, in America, the British colonies rapidly became far mightier and wealthier than the realms which Cortes and Pizarro[3] had added to the dominions of Charles the Fifth; how, in Asia, British adventurers founded an empire[4] not less splendid, and more durable, than that of Alexander.[5]

Nor will it be less my duty faithfully to record disasters mingled with triumphs, and great national crimes and follies far more humiliating than any disaster. It will be seen that

[1] 1685.—The selections from the *History* are so full of allusive material that it has seemed wise to provide annotation only where a clear reading of the meaning depends upon it. The text used is from *The Complete Writings of Lord Macaulay,* edited by Lady Trevelyan, 20 vols. in 10 (New York, 1898).
[2] The union took place in 1707.
[3] Soldiers and explorers of the first half of the sixteenth century, subjects of Charles V of Spain. The former conquered Mexico; the latter, Peru.
[4] India.
[5] Alexander the Great in the fourth century B.C. conquered Greece, Asia Minor, Egypt, and Persia.

even what we justly account our chief blessings were not without alloy. It will be seen that the system which effectually secured our liberties against the encroachments of kingly power gave birth to a new class of abuses, from which absolute monarchies are exempt. It will be seen that, in consequence partly of unwise interference, and partly of unwise neglect, the increase of wealth and the extension of trade produced, together with immense good, some evils from which poor and rude societies are free. It will be seen how, in two important dependencies of the crown, wrong was followed by just retribution; how imprudence and obstinacy broke the ties which bound the North American colonies to the parent state; how Ireland, cursed by the domination of race over race, and of religion over religion, remained indeed a member of the empire, but a withered and distorted member, adding no strength to the body politic, and reproachfully pointed at by all who feared or envied the greatness of England.

Yet, unless I greatly deceive myself, the general effect of this chequered narrative will be to excite thankfulness in all religious minds, and hope in the breasts of all patriots. For the history of our country during the last hundred and sixty years is eminently the history of physical, of moral, and of intellectual improvement. Those who compare the age on which their lot has fallen with a golden age which exists only in their imagination, may talk of degeneracy and decay; but no man who is correctly informed as to the past will be disposed to take a morose or desponding view of the present.

I should very imperfectly execute the task which I have undertaken, if I were merely to treat of battles and sieges, of the rise and fall of administrations, of intrigues in the palace, and of debates in the Parliament. It will be my endeavour to relate the history of the people as well as the history of the government; to trace the progress of useful and ornamental arts; to describe the rise of religious sects and the changes of literary taste; to portray the manners of successive generations; and not to pass by with neglect even the revolutions which have taken place in dress, furniture, repasts, and public amusements. I shall cheerfully bear the reproach of having descended below the dignity of history, if I can succeed in placing before the English of the nineteenth century a true picture of the life of their ancestors. . . .

from Chapter 9

. . . Meanwhile the fleet of William[6] was on the German Ocean. It was on the evening of Thursday the first of November[7] that he put to sea the second time. The wind blew fresh from the east. The armament, during twelve hours, held a course toward the north-west. The light vessels sent out by the English Admiral for the purpose of obtaining intelligence brought back news which confirmed the prevailing opinion that the enemy would try to land in Yorkshire. All at once, on a signal from the Prince's ship, the whole fleet tacked, and made sail for the British Channel. The same breeze which favored the voyage of the invaders prevented Dartmouth[8] from coming out of the Thames. His ships were forced to strike yards and topmasts; and two of his frigates, which had gained the open sea, were shattered by the violence of the weather and driven back into the river.

The Dutch fleet ran fast before the gale, and reached the Straits[9] at about ten in the morning of Saturday, the third of November. William himself, in the Brill, led the way. More than six hundred vessels, with canvas spread to a favorable wind, followed in his train. The transports were in the centre. The men-of-war, more than fifty in number, formed an outer rampart. Herbert, with the title of Lieutenant Admiral General, commanded the whole fleet. His post was in the rear, and many English sailors, inflamed against Popery, and attracted by high pay, served under him. It was not without great difficulty that the Prince had prevailed on some Dutch officers of high reputation to submit to the authority of a stranger. But the arrangement

6 William III (1650–1702), originally William of Orange, son of the eldest daughter of Charles I, and husband of his cousin, Princess Mary, elder daughter of James II. William and Mary ruled together from 1689 to 1694; after her death William reigned alone from 1694 to 1702. When James II, who was a Roman Catholic, tried to rule as an absolute monarch, 1685–88, seven representative leaders of both the Tories and the Whigs invited William, then Prince of Orange in Holland, to invade England and become the king. His first effort failed; this is the account of his second and successful attack.
7 1688.
8 The British naval commander.
9 Between Dover and Calais.

was eminently judicious. There was in the King's fleet much discontent, and an ardent zeal for the Protestant faith. But within the memory of old mariners the Dutch and English navies had thrice, with heroic spirit and various fortune, contended for the empire of the sea. Our sailors had not forgotten the broom with which Tromp had threatened to sweep the Channel, or the fire which De Ruyter had lighted in the dockyards of the Medway.[10] Had the rival nations been once more brought face to face on the element of which both claimed the sovereignty, all other thoughts might have given place to mutual animosity. A bloody and obstinate battle might have been fought. Defeat would have been fatal to William's enterprise. Even victory would have deranged all his deeply meditated schemes of policy. He therefore wisely determined that the pursuers, if they overtook him, should be hailed in their own mother-tongue, and adjured, by an admiral under whom they had served, and whom they esteemed,[11] not to fight against old messmates for Popish tyranny. Such an appeal might possibly avert a conflict. If a conflict took place, one English commander would be opposed to another; nor would the pride of the islanders be wounded by learning that Dartmouth had been compelled to strike to Herbert.

Happily William's precautions were not necessary. Soon after mid-day he passed the Straits. His fleet spread to within a league of Dover on the north, and of Calais on the south. The men-of-war on the extreme right and left saluted both fortresses at once. The troops appeared under arms on the decks. The flourish of trumpets, the clash of cymbals, and the rolling of drums were distinctly heard at once on the English and French shores. An innumerable company of gazers blackened the white beach of Kent. Another mighty multitude covered the coast of Picardy. Rapin de Thoyras, who, driven by persecution from his country, had taken service in the Dutch army, and now went with the Prince to England, described the spectacle, many years later, as the most magnificent and affecting that

was ever seen by human eyes. At sunset the armament was off Beachy Head. Then the lights were kindled. The sea was in a blaze for many miles. But the eyes of all the steersmen were directed throughout the night to three huge lanterns which flamed on the stern of the Brill.

Meanwhile a courier had been riding post from Dover Castle to Whitehall with news that the Dutch had passed the Straits and were steering westward. It was necessary to make an immediate change in all the military arrangements. Messengers were despatched in every direction. Officers were roused from their beds at dead of night. At three on the Sunday morning there was a great muster by torch-light in Hyde Park. The King had sent several regiments northward in the expectation that William would land in Yorkshire. Expresses were despatched to recall them. All the forces except those which were necessary to keep the peace of the capital were ordered to move to the West. Salisbury was appointed as the place of rendezvous; but, as it was thought possible that Portsmouth might be the first point of attack, three battalions of Guards and a strong body of cavalry set out for that fortress. In a few hours it was known that Portsmouth was safe; and these troops then received orders to change their route and hasten to Salisbury.

When Sunday the fourth of November dawned, the cliffs of the Isle of Wight were full in view of the Dutch armament. That day was the anniversary both of William's birth and of his marriage. Sail was slackened during part of the morning; and divine service was performed on board of the ships. In the afternoon and through the night the fleet held on its course. Torbay was the place where the Prince intended to land. But the morning of Monday the fifth of November was hazy. The pilot of the Brill could not discern the sea marks, and carried the fleet too far to the west. The danger was great. To return in the face of the wind was impossible. Plymouth was the next port. But at Plymouth a garrison had been posted under the command of the Earl of Bath. The landing might be opposed; and a check might produce serious consequences. There could be little doubt, moreover, that by this time the royal fleet had got out of the Thames and was hastening full sail down the Channel. Russell saw the whole extent of the peril, and exclaimed to Burnet, "You may go to

---

10 Dutch commanders in the war with England, 1652–67. The first had defeated Admiral Blake in 1652, and then sailed up the Channel with a broom at his masthead to denote that he had swept the enemy from the seas; the Medway is a river in Kent which flows into the estuary of the Thames.

11 Lord Herbert, mentioned just above.

prayers, Doctor. All is over." At that moment the wind changed: a soft breeze sprang up from the south: the mist dispersed: the sun shone forth; and, under the mild light of an autumnal noon, the fleet turned back, passed round the lofty cape of Berry Head, and rode safe in the harbor of Torbay.

Since William looked on that harbor its aspect has greatly changed. The amphitheatre which surrounds the spacious basin now exhibits everywhere signs of prosperity and civilization. At the north-eastern extremity has sprung up a great watering-place, to which strangers are attracted from the most remote parts of our island by the Italian softness of the air: for in that climate the myrtle flourishes unsheltered; and even the winter is milder than the Northumbrian April. The inhabitants are about ten thousand in number. The newly built churches and chapels, the baths and libraries, the hotels and public gardens, the infirmary and the museum, the white streets, rising terrace above terrace, the gay villas peeping from the midst of shrubberies and flower-beds, present a spectacle widely differing from any that in the seventeenth century England could show. At the opposite end of the bay lies, sheltered by Berry Head, the stirring market-town of Brixham, the wealthiest seat of our fishing trade. A pier and a haven were formed there at the beginning of the present century, but have been found insufficient for the increasing traffic. The population is about six thousand souls. The shipping amounts to more than two hundred sail. The tonnage exceeds many times the tonnage of the port of Liverpool under the kings of the House of Stuart. But Torbay, when the Dutch fleet cast anchor there, was known only as a haven where ships sometimes took refuge from the tempests of the Atlantic. Its quiet shores were undisturbed by the bustle either of commerce or of pleasure; and the huts of ploughmen and fishermen were thinly scattered over what is now the site of crowded marts and of luxurious pavilions.[12]

The peasantry of the coast of Devonshire remembered the name of Monmouth with affection, and held Popery in detestation.[13] They therefore crowded down to the sea-side with provisions and offers of service. The disembarkation instantly commenced. Sixty boats conveyed the troops to the coast. Mackay was sent on shore first with the British regiments. The Prince soon followed. He landed where the quay of Brixham now stands. The whole aspect of the place has been altered. Where we now see a port crowded with shipping, and a market-place swarming with buyers and sellers, the waves then broke on a desolate beach; but a fragment of the rock on which the deliverer stepped from his boat has been carefully preserved, and is set up as an object of public veneration in the centre of that busy wharf.

As soon as the Prince had planted his foot on dry ground he called for horses. Two beasts, such as the small yeoman of that time were in the habit of riding, were procured from the neighboring village. William and Schomberg mounted and proceeded to examine the country.

As soon as Burnet[14] was on shore he hastened to the Prince. An amusing dialogue took place between them. Burnet poured forth his congratulations with genuine delight, and then eagerly asked what were His Highness's plans. Military men are seldom disposed to take counsel with gownsmen on military matters; and William regarded the interference of unprofessional advisers, in questions relating to war, with even more than the disgust ordinarily felt by soldiers on such occasions. But he was at that moment in an excellent humor, and, instead of signifying his displeasure by a short and cutting reprimand, graciously extended his hand, and answered his chaplain's question by another question: "Well, Doctor, what do you think of predestination now?" The reproof was so delicate that Burnet, whose perceptions were not very fine, did not perceive it. He answered with great fervor that he should never forget the signal manner in which Providence had favored their undertaking.[15]

During the first day the troops who had gone on shore had many discomforts to endure. The earth was soaked with rain. The baggage was still on board of the ships. Officers of high rank were compelled to sleep in wet clothes on the

---

12 Passages like this on English progress often appear in the *History:* cf. end of next paragraph.
13 The Duke of Monmouth (1649–1685) who, in his unsuccessful rebellion against James II, had landed on the coast of Devonshire.

14 Bishop Gilbert Burnet (1643–1715), a liberal churchman now serving as William's chaplain.
15 Burnet, apparently, had questioned predestination.

wet ground: the Prince himself had no better quarters than a hut afforded. His banner was displayed on the thatched roof; and some bedding brought from the Brill was spread for him on the floor. There was some difficulty about landing the horses; and it seemed probable that this operation would occupy several days. But on the following morning the prospect cleared. The wind was gentle. The water in the bay was as even as glass. Some fishermen pointed out a place where the ships could be brought within sixty feet of the beach. This was done; and in three hours many hundreds of horses swam safely to shore.

The disembarkation had hardly been effected when the wind rose again, and swelled into a fierce gale from the west. The enemy coming in pursuit down the Channel had been stopped by the same change of weather which enabled William to land. During two days the King's fleet lay on an unruffled sea in sight of Beachy Head. At length Dartmouth was able to proceed. He passed the Isle of Wight, and one of his ships came in sight of the Dutch top-masts in Torbay. Just at this moment he was encountered by the tempest, and compelled to take shelter in the harbor of Portsmouth. At that time James, who was not incompetent to form a judgment on a question of seamanship, declared himself perfectly satisfied that his admiral had done all that man could do, and had yielded only to irresistible hostility of the winds and waves. At a later period the unfortunate prince began, with little reason, to suspect Dartmouth of treachery, or at least of slackness.

The weather had indeed served the Protestant cause so well that some men of more piety than judgment fully believed the ordinary laws of nature to have been suspended for the preservation of the liberty and religion of England. Exactly a hundred years before, they said, the Armada,[16] invincible by man, had been scattered by the wrath of God. Civil freedom and divine truth were again in jeopardy; and again the obedient elements had fought for the good cause. The wind had blown strong from the east while the Prince wished to sail down the Channel, had turned to the south when he wished to enter Torbay, had sunk to a calm during the disembarkation, and, as soon as the disembarkation was completed, had risen to a storm, and had met the pursuers in the face. Nor did men omit to remark that, by an extraordinary coincidence, the Prince had reached our shores on a day on which the Church of England commemorated, by prayer and thanksgiving, the wonderful escape of the royal House and of the three Estates from the blackest plot ever devised by Papists. Carstairs, whose suggestions were sure to meet with attention from the Prince, recommended that, as soon as the landing had been effected, public thanks should be offered to God for the protection so conspicuously accorded to the great enterprise. This advice was taken, and with excellent effect. The troops, taught to regard themselves as favorites of heaven, were inspired with new courage; and the English people formed the most favorable opinion of a general and an army so attentive to the duties of religion. . . .

On the morning of Saturday, the eighth of December, the King's Commissioners reached Hungerford. The Prince's body-guard was drawn up to receive them with military respect. Bentinck welcomed them and proposed to conduct them immediately to his master. They expressed a hope that the Prince would favor them with a private audience; but they were informed that he had resolved to hear them and answer them in public. They were ushered into his bed-chamber, where they found him surrounded by a crowd of noblemen and gentlemen. Halifax,[17] whose rank, age, and abilities entitled him to precedence, was spokesman. The proposition which the Commssioners had been instructed to make was that the points in dispute should be referred to the Parliament, for which the writs were already sealing, and that in the meantime the Prince's army would not come within thirty or forty miles of London. Halifax, having explained that this was the basis on which he and his colleagues were prepared to treat, put into William's hand a letter from the King and retired. William opened the letter, and seemed unusually moved. It was the first letter which he had received from his father-in-law since they had become avowed enemies. Once they had been on good terms and had written to each

---

[16] The Spanish Armada, which planned an invasion of England in 1588, was defeated by bad weather and by Sir Francis Drake.

[17] Charles Montagne, Earl of Halifax (1661–1715).

other familiarly; nor had they, even when they began to regard each other with suspicion and aversion, banished from their correspondence those forms of kindness which persons nearly related by blood and marriage commonly use. The letter which the Commissioners had brought was drawn up by a secretary in diplomatic form and in the French language. I have had many letters from the King," said William, "but they were all in English, and in his own hand." He spoke with a sensibility which he was little in the habit of displaying. Perhaps he thought at that moment how much reproach his enterprise, just, beneficent, and necessary as it was, must bring on him and on his wife who was devoted to him. Perhaps he repined at the hard fate which had placed him in such a situation that he could fulfil his public duties only by breaking through domestic ties, and envied the happier condition of those who are not responsible for the welfare of nations and Churches. But such thoughts, if they rose in his mind, were firmly suppressed. He requested the Lords and gentlemen whom he had convoked on this occasion to consult together, unrestrained by his presence, as to the answer which ought to be returned. To himself, however, he reserved the power of deciding in the last resort, after hearing their opinion. He then left them, and retired to Littlecote Hall, a manor-house situated about two miles off, and renowned down to our own times, not more on account of its venerable architecture and furniture than on account of a horrible and mysterious crime which was perpetrated there in the days of the Tudors.

Before he left Hungerford, he was told that Halifax had expressed a great desire to see Burnet. In this desire there was nothing strange; for Halifax and Burnet had long been on terms of friendship. No two men, indeed, could resemble each other less. Burnet was utterly destitute of delicacy and tact. Halifax's taste was fastidious, and his sense of the ludicrous morbidly quick. Burnet viewed every act and every character through a medium distorted and colored by party spirit. The tendency of Halifax's mind was always to see the faults of his allies more strongly than the faults of his opponents. Burnet was, with all his infirmities, and through all the vicissitudes of a life passed in circumstances not very favorable to piety a sincerely pious man.

The sceptical and sarcastic Halifax lay under the imputation of infidelity. Halifax, therefore, often incurred Burnet's indignant censure; and Burnet was often the butt of Halifax's keen and polished pleasantry. Yet they were drawn to each other by a mutual attraction, liked each other's conversation, appreciated each other's abilities, interchanged opinions freely, and interchanged also good offices in perilous times. It was not, however, merely from personal regard that Halifax now wished to see his old acquaintance. The Commissioners must have been anxious to know what was the Prince's real aim. He had refused to see them in private; and little could be learned from what he might say in a formal and public interview. Almost all those who were admitted to his confidence were men taciturn and impenetrable as himself. Burnet was the only exception. He was notoriously garrulous and indiscreet. Yet circumstances had made it necessary to trust him; and he would doubtless, under the dexterous management of Halifax, have poured out secrets as fast as words. William knew this well, and, when he was informed that Halifax was asking for the Doctor, could not refrain from exclaiming, "If they get together there will be fine tattling." Burnet was forbidden to see the Commissioners in private: but he was assured in very courteous terms that his fidelity was regarded by the Prince as above all suspicion; and, that there might be no ground for complaint, the prohibition was made general.

That afternoon the noblemen and gentlemen whose advice William had asked met in the great room of the principal inn at Hungerford. Oxford[18] was placed in the chair; and the King's overtures were taken into consideration. It soon appeared that the assembly was divided into two parties, a party anxious to come to terms with the King, and a party bent on his destruction. The latter party had the numerical superiority: but it was observed that Shrewsbury, who of all the English nobles was supposed to enjoy the largest share of William's confidence, though a Whig, sided on this occasion with the Tories.[19] After much altercation the question was put. The majority was for rejecting the

---

18 Robert Harley, Earl of Oxford and Mortimer (1661–1724).
19 The two English political parties: in general, the Whigs were left of center and the Tories right.

proposition which the royal Commissioners had been instructed to make. The resolution of the assembly was reported to the Prince at Littlecote. On no occasion during the whole course of his eventful life did he show more prudence and self-command. He could not wish the negotiation to succeed. But he was far too wise a man not to know that, if unreasonable demands made by him should cause it to fail, public feeling would no longer be on his side. He therefore overruled the opinion of his too eager followers, and declared his determination to treat on the basis proposed by the King. Many of the Lords and gentlemen assembled at Hungerford remonstrated: a whole day was spent in bickering: but William's purpose was immovable. He declared himself willing to refer all the questions in dispute to the Parliament which had just been summoned, and not to advance within forty miles of London. On his side he made some demands which even those who were least disposed to commend him allowed to be moderate. He insisted that the existing statutes should be obeyed till they should be altered by competent authority, and that all persons who held offices without a legal qualification should be forthwith dismissed. The deliberations of the Parliament, he justly conceived, could not be free if it was to sit surrounded by Irish regiments while he and his army lay at a distance of several marches. He therefore thought it reasonable that, since his troops were not to advance within forty miles of London on the west, the King's troops should fall back as far to the east. There would thus be, round the spot where the Houses were to meet, a wide circle of neutral ground. Within that circle, indeed, there were two fastnesses of great importance to the people of the capital— the Tower, which commanded their dwellings, and Tilbury Fort, which commanded their maritime trade. It was impossible to leave their places ungarrisoned. William, therefore, proposed that they should be temporarily intrusted to the care of the City of London. It might possibly be convenient that, when the Parliament assembled, the King should repair to Westminster with a body-guard. The Prince announced that, in that case, he should claim the right of repairing thither with an equal number of soldiers. It seemed to him just that, while military operations were suspended, both the armies should be considered as alike engaged in the service of the English nation, and should be alike maintained out of the English revenue. Lastly, he required some guarantee that the King would not take advantage of the armistice for the purpose of introducing a French force into England. The point where there was most danger was Portsmouth. The Prince did not insist that this important fortress should be delivered up to him, but proposed that it should, during the truce, be under the government of an officer in whom both himself and James could confide.

The propositions of William were framed with a punctilious fairness, such as might have been expected rather from a disinterested umpire pronouncing an award than from a victorious prince dictating to a helpless enemy. No fault could be found with them from the partisans of the King. But among the Whigs there was much murmuring. They wanted no reconciliation with their old master. They thought themselves absolved from all allegiance to him. They were not disposed to recognize the authority of a Parliament convoked by his writ. They were averse to an armistice; and they could not conceive why, if there was to be an armistice, it should be an armistice on equal terms. By all the laws of war the stronger party had a right to take advantage of his strength; and what was there in the character of James to justify any extraordinary indulgence? Those who reasoned thus little knew from how elevated a point of view, and with how discerning an eye, the leader whom they censured contemplated the whole situation of England and Europe. They were eager to ruin James, and would therefore either have refused to treat with him on any conditions, or have imposed on him conditions insupportably hard. To the success of William's vast and profound scheme of policy it was necessary that James should ruin himself by rejecting conditions ostentatiously liberal. The event proved the wisdom of the course which the majority of the Englishmen at Hungerford were inclined to condemn.

On Sunday, the ninth of December, the Prince's demands were put in writing, and delivered to Halifax. The Commissioners dined at Littlecote. A splendid assemblage had been invited to meet them. The old hall, hung with coats of mail which had seen the wars of the Roses, and with portraits of gallants who had adorned the court of Philip and Mary,[20] was now crowded with peers and generals. In such a throng a short question and answer might be exchanged without attracting notice. Halifax seized this opportunity, the first which had presented itself, of extracting all that Burnet knew or thought. "What is it that you want?" said the dexterous diplomatist: "do you wish to get the King into your power?" "Not at all," said Burnet: "we would not do the least harm to his person." "And if he were to go away?" said Halifax. "There is nothing," said Burnet, "so much to be wished." There can be no doubt that Burnet expressed the general sentiment of the Whigs in the Prince's camp. They were all desirous that James should fly from the country: but only a few of the wisest among them understood how important it was that his flight should be ascribed by the nation to his own folly and perverseness, and not to harsh usage and well-grounded apprehension. It seemed probable that, even in the extremity to which he was now reduced, all his enemies united would have been unable to effect his complete overthrow had he not been his own worst enemy: but while his Commissioners were laboring to save him, he was laboring as earnestly to make all their efforts useless. . . .

On the morning of Monday, the tenth of December, the King learned that his wife and son had begun their voyage with a fair prospect of reaching their destination.[21] About the same time a courier arrived with despatches from Hungerford. Had James been a little more discerning, or a little less obstinate, those despatches would have induced him to reconsider all his plans. The Commissioners wrote hopefully. The conditions proposed by the conqueror were strangely liberal. The King himself could not refrain from exclaiming that they were more favorable than he could have expected. He might indeed not unreasonably suspect that they had been framed with no friendly design: but this mattered nothing; for, whether they were offered in the hope that, by closing with them, he would lay the ground for a happy reconciliation, or, as is more likely, in the hope that, by rejecting them, he would exhibit himself to the whole nation as utterly unreasonable and incorrigible, his course was equally clear. In either case his policy was to accept them promptly and to observe them faithfully.

But it soon appeared that William had perfectly understood the character with which he had to deal, and, in offering those terms which the Whigs at Hungerford had censured as too indulgent, had risked nothing. The solemn farce by which the public had been amused since the retreat of the royal army from Salisbury was prolonged during a few hours. All the Lords who were still in the capital were invited to the palace that they might be informed of the progress of the negotiation which had been opened by their advice. Another meeting of Peers was appointed for the following day. The Lord Mayor and the Sheriffs of London were summoned to attend the King. He exhorted them to perform their duties vigorously, and owned that he had thought it expedient to send his wife and child out of the country, but assured them that he would himself remain at his post. While he uttered this unkingly and unmanly falsehood, his fixed purpose was to depart before daybreak. Already he had intrusted his most valuable movables to the care of several foreign ambassadors. His most important papers had been deposited with the Tuscan minister. But before the flight there was still something to be done. The tyrant pleased himself with the thought that he might avenge himself on a people who had been impatient of his despotism by inflicting on them, at parting, all the evils of anarchy. He ordered the Great Seal and the writs for the new Parliament to be brought to his apartment. The writs he threw into the fire. Some which had been already sent out he annulled by an instrument drawn up in legal form. To Feversham he wrote a letter which could be understood only as a command to disband the army. Still, however, he concealed, even from his chief ministers, his intention of absconding. Just before he retired he directed Jeffreys to be in the closet early on the morrow, and, while stepping into bed, whispered to Mulgrave that the news from Hungerford was highly satisfactory. Everybody withdrew except the Duke of Northumberland. This young man, a natural

---

[20] Probably the court of Philip II of Spain (1527–1598), whose second wife was Mary Tudor of England.
[21] France and the court of Louis XIV.

son of Charles the Second by the Duchess of Cleveland, commanded a troop of Life Guards, and was a Lord of the Bedchamber. It seems to have been then the custom of the court that, in the Queen's absence, a Lord of the Bedchamber should sleep on a pallet in the King's room; and it was Northumberland's turn to perform this duty.

At three in the morning of Tuesday, the eleventh of December, James rose, took the Great Seal in his hand, laid his commands on Northumberland not to open the door of the bedchamber till the usual hour, and disappeared through a secret passage, the same passage probably through which Huddleston had been brought to the bedside of the late King.[22] Sir Edward Hales was in attendance with a hackney-coach. James was conveyed to Millbank, where he crossed the Thames in a small wherry. As he passed Lambeth, he flung the Great Seal into the midst of the stream, where, after many months, it was accidently caught by a fishing-net and dragged up.

At Vauxhall he landed. A carriage and horses had been stationed there for him; and he immediately took the road toward Sheerness, where a boy belonging to the Custom-house had been ordered to await his arrival.

Letter on Democracy[1]

May 23, 1857

Holly Lodge, Kensington, London

Dear Sir:

You are surprised to learn that I have not a high opinion of Mr. Jefferson,[2] and I am surprised at your surprise. I am certain that I never wrote a line, and that I never in Parliament—a place where it is the fashion to court the populace—uttered a word, indicating an opinion that

the Supreme authority in a State ought to be trusted to the majority of citizens told by the head;[3] in other words to the poorest and most ignorant part of society. I have long been convinced that institutions purely democratic must, sooner or later destroy liberty or civilization, or both. In Europe, where the population is dense, the effect of such institutions would be instantaneous.

What happened lately in France is an example. In 1848 a pure democracy was established there.[4] During a short time there was reason to expect a general spoliation, a national bankruptcy, a new partition of the soil, a maximum of prices, a ruinous load of taxation laid on the rich for the purpose of supporting the poor in idleness. Such a system would, in twenty years, have made France as poor and barbarous as the France of the Carlovingians. Happily, the danger was averted; and now there is a despotism, a silent tribune, an enslaved press. Liberty is gone but civilization has been saved.

I have not the smallest doubt that, if we had a purely democratic Government here, the effect would be the same. Either the poor would plunder the rich and civilization would perish, or order and prosperity would be saved by a strong military government, and liberty would perish.

You may think that your country enjoys an exemption from these evils; I will frankly own to you that I am of a very different opinion. Your fate I believe to be certain, though it is deferred by a physical cause. As long as you have a boundless extent of fertile and unoccupied land, your laboring population will be far more at ease than the laboring population of the old world; and while that is the case the Jefferson politics may continue to exist without causing any fatal calamity. But the time will come when New England will be as thickly settled as Old England. Wages will be as low, and will fluctuate as much with you as with us. You will have your Manchesters and Birminghams. And in those Manchesters and Birminghams hundreds

---

22 Charles II, who reigned from 1660 to 1685.

1 Addressed to Commodore H. S. Randall of the New York Yacht Club, and reprinted from the *Review of Reviews and World's Work*, XC (July, 1934), 38–39.
2 Thomas Jefferson (1743–1826), drafter of the American Declaration of Independence and third president of the United States.

3 Counted by individuals, i.e., universal manhood suffrage.
4 The Second French Republic, set up on February 24, 1848, provided for universal suffrage and instituted various socialistic measures but, lacking strong and experienced leadership, it quickly succumbed to the political intrigues of Louis-Napoleon, first as president and then as emperor.

and thousands of artisans will sometimes be out of work. Then your institutions will be fairly brought to the test. Distress everywhere makes the labourer mutinous and discontented, and inclines him to listen with eagerness to agitators, who tell him that it is a monstrous iniquity that one man should have a million while another cannot get a full meal.

In bad years there is plenty of grumbling here, and sometimes a little rioting; but it matters little, for here the sufferers are not the rulers. The supreme power is in the hands of a class numerous indeed, but select—of an educated class—of a class which is and knows itself to be, deeply interested in the security of property and the maintenance of order. Accordingly, the malcontents are gently but firmly restrained. The bad time is got over without robbing the wealthy to relieve the indigent. The springs of national prosperity soon begin to flow again; work is plentiful, wages rise and all is tranquillity and cheerfulness. I have seen England pass, three or four times, through such critical seasons as I have described.

Through such seasons the United States will have to pass in the course of the next century, if not of this. How will you pass through them? I heartily wish you good deliverance. But my reason is quite plain that your Government will never be able to restrain a distressed and discontented majority. For, with you the majority is the government, and has the rich, who are always the minority, absolutely at its mercy. The day will come when in the State of New York, a multitude of people, none of whom has had more than half a breakfast, or expects to have more than half a dinner, will choose a Legislature. Is it possible to doubt what sort of Legislature will be chosen? On one side is a statesman preaching patience, respect for vested rights, strict observance of public faith; on the other is a demagogue, ranting about the tyranny of the capitalists and usurers, and asking why anybody should be permitted to drink champagne and to ride in a carriage while thousands of honest folks are in want of necessaries. Which of the two candidates is likely to be preferred by a workman who hears his children cry for bread?

I seriously apprehend you will, in some season of adversity as I have described, do things that will prevent prosperity from returning; that you will act like people who should, in a season of scarcity, partake of absolute famine. There will be, I fear, spoliation. The spoliation will increase the distress. The distress will produce fresh spoliation. There is nothing to stop you. Your Constitution is all sail and no anchor.

As I said before, when a society has entered on its downward progress either civilization or liberty must perish. Either some Caesar or Napoleon will seize the rein of Government with a strong hand or your republic will be as fearfully plundered and laid waste by barbarians in the Twentieth Century as the Roman Empire was in the Fifth—with this difference that the Huns and Vandals who ravaged the Roman Empire came from without, and that your Huns and Vandals have been engendered within your country by your own institutions.

Thinking this, of course, I cannot reckon Jefferson among the benefactors of mankind.

Yours respectfully,
Thomas Babington Macaulay

John Henry Newman
1801–1890

John Henry Newman was the most highly gifted of all the Victorians. He possessed both a subtle mind and a sensitive imagination. He was at once a thinker and an artist. He could use language to record the most inward "modes of being," whether his own or other men's, and he could use it with superb rhetorical force to move and persuade. He was a great man and a great writer.

Newman was born at London in 1801, the son of a rather worldly banker and a rather pious mother. In early life he had various mystical or quasi-mystical experiences. He sometimes "thought life might be a dream, or I an Angel, and all this world a deception, my fellow-angels by a playful device . . . deceiving me with the semblance of a material world." In the beauty of nature he found a reflection or symbol of divine beauty. In the voice of conscience he felt the presence "of a Supreme Governor, a Judge, holy, just, powerful, all-seeing, retributive." But though his mother had taught him his catechism and taken him to the Church of England on Sundays, this religious awareness was unconnected with any definite creed; and indeed it did not hold a central place in his mind or heart. Then in 1816 occurred the major event of his life, an event which changed him so radically that he found it difficult, he said, to recognize the identity of the boy before it and after it. Under the influence of the Reverend Walter Mayers, a devout Evangelical who was one of his teachers at the boarding school to which he had been sent in 1808, Newman experienced an "inward conversion" which brought him two new and everlasting convictions: the absolute certainty of two "supreme and luminously self-evident beings, myself [i.e., his immortal soul] and my Creator," and the truth of the central dogmas of Christianity, revealed by God through Christ—Original Sin, the Trinity, the Incarnation, the Atonement, Redemption, and the Resurrection. From this time to his death seventy-four years later, Newman believed unwaveringly in the reality of God and personal immortality, and in

John Henry Newman (1801–1890). Newman represented one of the two major reactions to the breakdown of religious certainty that assailed the Victorian mind. The Oxford Movement was a reaffirmation of the Catholic elements in the dogmas and liturgy of the Church of England. The engraving is after the painting by Sir W. C. Ross, 1847. *British Museum.*

the miraculous and dogmatic character of Christianity. His later changes, from Evangelicalism to Anglo-Catholicism to Roman Catholicism, resulted from changing conceptions of the importance and meaning of various dogmas and subsidiary doctrines, especially the doctrine of the Church.

In 1817 he went to Oxford, where he became a brilliant student, and though he blew up in the final examinations and failed to receive high honors, he was elected in 1822 a fellow of Oriel College, at that time the outstanding college in the university. So opened a new chapter in his life, for not one of his new companions was an Evangelical. John Keble was an Anglo-Catholic; the rest were liberal Protestants.

At first Newman was drawn toward the liberals, but when he recognized the antidogmatic tendency of their thinking, he not only turned *away* from religious liberalism, he turned *against* it, convinced that if Christianity were to survive in the modern world, liberalism would have to be crushed. Years later, in a speech at Rome when he was made a cardinal (1879), he said, "For thirty, forty, fifty years [i.e., since 1829] I have resisted to the best of my powers the spirit of Liberalism in religion. Never did Holy Church need champions against it more sorely than now, when, alas! it is an error overspreading, as a snare, the whole earth." This is the central clue, not only to Newman's life, but to the Oxford Movement which he and his friends initiated. Its first principle was "the principle of dogma: my battle was with liberalism; by liberalism I meant the anti-dogmatic principle and its developments." Its second principle was Catholicism, Anglo-Catholicism. The connection is of the highest importance. Newman became a Catholic partly because Catholicism offered him a position from which, better than any other in his time, he could fight liberalism.

But what exactly did he mean by liberalism in religion? and why did he think it would make shipwreck of Christianity? He wrote the famous "Note on Liberalism" in answer to those questions. Liberalism meant, in the first place, the refusal to accept anything on authority, whether of the Bible or the creeds or the church. Belief was a matter of private judgment. One had to decide for himself what was true; he had to satisfy his own reason (see Propositions 1 and 9 at the end of the "Note"). This meant, in effect, the denial of any definite body of revealed truth to be accepted on faith. But to Newman the great dogmas of Christianity were a revelation of God, given on His supreme authority, and embodied at scattered places in the New Testament and in summary form in the three creeds. If they were subjected to reason and private judgment, one person accepting some, another accepting others, the whole dogmatic structure would disintegrate. Religion would no longer rest on any objective body of truth. Dogmas would be simply matters of opinion which this person or that church happened to believe (see Proposition 3). And Christianity would become a mixture of pious feeling and Christian ethics. Newman was right. The simple "Religion of Christ" (defined in the introduction to the Victorian period, p. 416) has become the religion of most Protestants today.

What is "wrong" with it? It is unstable. It tends to disintegrate, actually if not consciously, into ethical culture and moral humanitarianism. All religious people have periods of spiritual dryness when they lose the immediate sense of God. When that happens to a liberal, he has nothing to fall back upon, no structure of belief, no ecclesiastical life, to which his religious emotions have become attached, and which can sustain him and hold him until—partly through these very objects—he can recover the central experience of divine reality. And if at the same time he is living in a world where atheism and agnosticism are all around him, where the secular and scientific atmosphere is thick, the chances are a hundred to one that he will lose the supernatural life of his religion altogether and drift downward into a naturalistic religion of humanity and social service. That is why Newman called liberalism the halfway house to atheism. That is why he hated it, not merely because he was a Catholic, not merely because he believed in dogmatic Christianity, but because he was fighting to save religion in the modern world. It is a measure of his extraordinary insight that he saw, far more clearly than they did, where the Oriel liberals were going, and saw the necessity of defending revelation from the destructive force of reason if religion were to survive.

No wonder, at this crucial moment, that John Keble and his younger friend, Hurrell Froude, both Anglo-Catholics, came to exert a determining influence on Newman's personal life and public career. Anglo-Catholicism offered him the idea of a visible church founded by Christ to be the ark of salvation, through the power of the sacraments, and the guardian of dogma. This idea had been embodied in the theology, the polity, and the ritual of the Church of the fourth and fifth centuries. That original Catholic and Apostolic Church was therefore the right and true model of what the Church of England ought to be, but unfortunately was not, because it had been corrupted at the Reformation by various Protestant errors, like belief in salvation by faith alone, assertion of the supreme authority of the Bible, and denial of the supernatural power of the priesthood. The Oxford Movement was the attempt to reform the Church of England on Catholic lines, Catholic but not Roman Catholic, since the Anglo-Catholics deny the head-

Dr. Thomas Arnold (1795–1842). Arnold, Newman's ideological adversary, was head of the Broad Church movement which sought to liberalize the doctrinal base of the Anglican Church so as to encompass all Protestant groups, especially Evangelicals. *The Granger Collection.*

ship of the Pope and various Roman dogmas relating to the sacraments, purgatory, the Virgin, etc., which they consider medieval corruptions of primitive doctrine. (Cf. a somewhat different account of Anglo-Catholicism in the introduction to the Victorian period, p. 417, which brings out its seventeenth-century antecedents.)

Beginning in 1833 Newman and his friends published a series of *Tracts for the Times,* pleading for a Catholic interpretation of the Church. The movement won wide support among the clergy; but when it failed to win the official approval of the bishops, who insisted on the traditional Protestant interpretation, Newman had no recourse, he felt, but to secede and join the Roman Church. His "shocking" conversion, which he later explained in his superb autobiography, *Apologia pro Vita Sua* (1864), occurred in 1845.

Newman's life and thought were informed by two great objects: religion and education, Christianity and the Liberal Arts. In the Oxford years the former had dominated his mind; when he became a Roman Catholic and was asked to be the rector of a Catholic university to be founded at Dublin, he turned much of his attention to the latter. In 1852 he delivered the famous lectures on *The Scope and Nature of University Education,* to which he later added ten more essays on *University Subjects;* the two series were published together in 1873 as *The Idea of a University.* This book is Newman's apologia for a liberal education, complementing the *Apologia* for his Catholic Christianity.

In the 1852 lectures Newman had to defend his position against two quite different enemies: on the one hand, against the utilitarians, who could see no "use" in such an impractical education; and on the other, against the Catholics in Ireland, and elsewhere, who could only view with alarm the study of modern subjects like natural science and philosophy as a dangerous threat to Catholic orthodoxy. It is because both enemies, especially the first, are still with us that Newman's fine defense of a liberal education is as relevant today as it was a century ago.

What is the function of a liberal arts college? Should it try to prepare men and women for professional and business careers? Certainly not. That is the job of vocational schools of law and medicine, business and engineering. Should it aim to train character, to quicken the moral and religious side of human nature? Again no. That is the function of the family and the church. The right and sole end of higher education is the cultivation of the intellect. "It contemplates neither moral impression nor mechanical production; it professes to exercise the mind neither in art [professional skills] nor in duty; its function is intellectual culture." Why?

First, because knowledge is capable of being its own end, though it may and does have further ends. Human beings seek perfection. They admire and enjoy the beauty of trees irrespective of any fruit they bear, the beauty of moral character irrespective of particular action. "In like manner there is a beauty, there is a perfection, of the intellect" irrespective of anything it may accomplish. But in what does it consist? What *is* a perfectly cultivated mind? Certainly it is not a mind that is merely stored with knowledge; and the educated man is not the student who has taken courses in a wide range of subjects and who can "talk about" Egyptian art and feudalism and Wordsworth's theory of poetry and family life in American society. This is mere knowledge, cultural veneer. The mind is stocked but unchanged. Education means the enlightenment or enlargement of the mind.

The enlargement consists, not merely in the passive reception into the mind of a number of ideas hitherto unknown to it, but in the mind's energetic and simultaneous action upon and towards and among those new ideas, which are rushing in upon it. . . . It is a making the objects of our knowledge subjectively our own, or, to use a familiar word, it is a digestion of what we receive, into the substance of our

previous state of thought; and without this no enlargement is said to follow. There is no enlargement, unless there be a comparison of ideas one with another, as they come before the mind, and a systematizing of them. We feel our minds to be growing and expanding then, when we not only learn, but refer what we learn to what we know already.

That is the very heart of the matter—and the very thing most often neglected. The tragedy of education is that most students, and many teachers, spend hundreds of hours in learning new ideas without stopping to bring them into contact with their old assumptions, or ever asking what their value and meaning is *now to them.* Most B.A.'s are therefore "only possessed by their knowledge, not possessed of it."

But even when it "works," is a liberal education really valuable? The perfection of the intellect may be a legitimate end in its own right, but if it has no other, is it worth the time and expense of four years in college? Perhaps we should do better to study practical subjects which would prepare us for practical life. This vocational pressure began in the nineteenth century. It reflects both the democratic extension of education, once confined to men of leisure, to the middle and lower classes, and the modern commercial environment that grew up after the Industrial Revolution. But at bottom it rests on ignorance of the larger and intangible utility of a liberal education. Newman calls attention to the value of the latter in training men to think and reason, to compare and discriminate and analyze. The educated man is likely to be a better lawyer or doctor or broker. This at least is recognized in theory. What is almost totally overlooked is that the educated man is likely to be a better *man,* not morally but intellectually, a more intelligent human being; and therefore able, a little more wisely, to make the judgments and decisions everyone is called on constantly to make. The process of assimilating knowledge, of comparing what we learn with what we know, issues in "an acquired faculty of judgment, of clear-sightedness, of sagacity, of wisdom, of philosophical reach of mind, and of intellectual self-possession and repose." Is anything short of moral and spiritual power *more* useful?

TEXTS: The standard biography is by Wilfred Ward (2 vols., 1912), but it deals almost entirely with the Roman Catholic half of Newman's life. For the early years, see Maisie Ward, *Young Mr. Newman* (1948). R. H. Hutton, *Cardinal Newman* (1905) is a good short biography. C. F. Harrold, *John Henry Newman: An Expository and Critical Study of His Mind, Thought, and Art* (1945) is the best work of criticism in English. George Levine has a good essay in *The Boundaries of Fiction* (1968). The most scholarly edition of the *Apologia pro Vita Sua* is that edited, with introduction and notes, by Martin J. Svaglic (1967); the best edition for the student is a paperback edited by Dwight Culler (1956). Dwight Culler's *The Imperial Intellect* (1955) is an excellent study of *The Idea of a University*.

from Apologia pro Vita Sua

Note A

LIBERALISM

I have been asked to explain more fully what it is I mean by "Liberalism," because merely to call it the Anti-dogmatic Principle is to tell very little about it. An explanation is the more necessary, because such good Catholics and distinguished writers as Count Montalembert[1] and Father Lacordaire[2] use the word in a favourable sense, and claim to be Liberals themselves. "The only singularity," says the former of the two in describing his friend, "was his Liberalism. By a phenomenon, at that time unheard of, this convert, this seminarist, this confessor of nuns, was just as stubborn a liberal, as in the days when he was a student and a barrister."—Life (transl.), p. 19.

I do not believe that it is possible for me to differ in any important matter from two men whom I so highly admire. In their general line of thought and conduct I enthusiastically concur, and consider them to be before their age. And it would be strange indeed if I did not read with a special interest, in M. de Montalembert's beautiful volume, of the unselfish aims, the thwarted projects, the unrequited toils, the grand and tender resignation of Lacordaire. If I hesitate to adopt their language about Liberalism, I impute the necessity of such hesitation to some

differences between us in the use of words or in the circumstances of country; and thus I reconcile myself to remaining faithful to my own conception of it, though I cannot have their voices to give force to mine. Speaking then in my own way, I proceed to explain what I meant as a Protestant by Liberalism, and to do so in connexion with the circumstances under which that system of opinion came before me at Oxford.

If I might presume to contrast Lacordaire and myself, I should say, that we had been both of us inconsistent;—he, a Catholic, in calling himself a Liberal; I, a Protestant, in being an Anti-liberal; and moreover, that the cause of this inconsistency had been in both cases one and the same. That is, we were both of us such good conservatives, as to take up with what we happened to find established in our respective countries, at the time when we came into active life. Toryism was the creed of Oxford; he inherited, and made the best of, the French Revolution.

When, in the beginning of the present century, not very long before my own time, after many years of moral and intellectual declension, the University of Oxford woke up to a sense of its duties, and began to reform itself,[3] the first instruments of this change, to whose zeal and courage we all owe so much, were naturally thrown together for mutual support, against the numerous obstacles which lay in their path, and stood out in relief from the body of residents, who, though many of them men of talent themselves, cared little for the object which the others had at heart. These Reformers, as they may be called, were for some years members of scarcely more than three or four Colleges; and their own Colleges, as being under their direct influence, of course had the benefit of those stricter views of discipline and teaching, which they themselves were urging on the University. They had, in no long time, enough of real progress in their several spheres of exertion, and enough of reputation out of doors, to warrant them in considering themselves the *élite* of the place; and it is not wonderful if they were in consequence led to look down upon the majority of Colleges, which had not kept pace with the reform, or which had been

---

1 Comte Charles René de Montalembert (1810–1870) was a Roman Catholic politician and historian whose liberal ideas with regard to education, ecclesiastical jurisdiction, etc., irritated the more conservative elements in his church; but he raised no questions of dogma.

2 Père Lacordaire (1802–1861) was a more pronounced radical, advocating separation of church and state, the freeing of education from both state and church domination, popular sovereignty in civil affairs, etc. He too was a liberal in ecclesiastical politics but not in theology.

---

3 It was awakened by a series of articles in the *Edinburgh Review*, 1808–10, pointing out its wealth and privilege and its antiquated and perfunctory educational system.

hostile to it. And, when those rivalries of one man with another arose, whether personal or collegiate, which befall literary and scientific societies, such disturbances did but tend to raise in their eyes the value which they had already set upon academical distinction, and increase their zeal in pursuing it. Thus was formed an intellectual circle or class in the University,—men, who felt they had a career before them, as soon as the pupils, whom they were forming, came into public life; men, whom non-residents, whether country parsons or preachers of the Low Church, on coming up from time to time to the old place, would look at, partly with admiration, partly with suspicion, as being an honour indeed to Oxford, but withal exposed to the temptation of ambitious views, and to the spiritual evils signified in what is called the "pride of reason."

Nor was this imputation altogether unjust; for, as they were following out the proper idea of a University, of course they suffered more or less from the moral malady incident to such a pursuit. The very object of such great institutions lies in the cultivation of the mind and the spread of knowledge; if this object, as all human objects, has its dangers at all times, much more would these exist in the case of men, who were engaged in a work of reformation, and had the opportunity of measuring themselves, not only with those who were their equals in intellect, but with the many, who were below them. In this select circle or class of men, in various Colleges, the direct instruments and the choice fruit of real University Reform, we see the rudiments of the Liberal party.

Whenever men are able to act at all, there is the chance of extreme and intemperate action; and therefore, when there is exercise of mind, there is the chance of wayward or mistaken exercise. Liberty of thought is in itself a good; but it gives an opening to false liberty. Now by Liberalism I mean false liberty of thought, or the exercise of thought upon matters, in which, from the constitution of the human mind, thought cannot be brought to any successful issue, and therefore is out of place. Among such matters are first principles of whatever kind; and of these the most sacred and momentous are especially to be reckoned the truths of Revelation. Liberalism then is the mistake of subjecting to human judgment those revealed doctrines which are in

their nature beyond and independent of it, and of claiming to determine on intrinsic grounds the truth and value of propositions which rest for their reception simply on the external authority of the Divine Word.

Now certainly the party of whom I have been speaking, taken as a whole, were of a character of mind out of which Liberalism might easily grow up, as in fact it did; certainly they breathed around an influence which made men of religious seriousness shrink into themselves. But, while I say as much as this, I have no intention whatever of implying that the talent of the University, in the years before and after 1820, was liberal in its theology, in the sense in which the bulk of the educated classes through the country are liberal now. I would not for the world be supposed to detract from the Christian earnestness, and the activity in religious works, above the average of men, of many of the persons in question. They would have protested against their being supposed to place reason before faith, or knowledge before devotion; yet I do consider that they unconsciously encouraged and successfully introduced into Oxford a licence of opinion which went far beyond them. In their day they did little more than take credit to themselves for enlightened views, largeness of mind, liberality of sentiment, without drawing the line between what was just and what was inadmissible in speculation,[4] and without seeing the tendency of their own principles; and engrossing, as they did, the mental energy of the University, they met for a time with no effectual hindrance to the spread of their influence, except (what indeed at the moment was most effectual, but not of an intellectual character) the thoroughgoing Toryism and traditionary Church-of-Englandism of the great body of the Colleges and Convocation.[5]

Now and then a man of note appeared in the Pulpit or Lecture Rooms of the University, who was a worthy representative of the more religious and devout Anglicans. These belonged chiefly to the High-Church party; for the party

[4] Cf. the definition of Liberalism in the preceding paragraph. Their two other characteristics are mentioned just above—placing reason above faith and knowledge before devotion.

[5] The assembly of all the masters of art and doctors of the higher faculties which has final control of university affairs.

called Evangelical[6] never has been able to breathe freely in the atmosphere of Oxford, and at no time has been conspicuous, as a party, for talent or learning. But of the old High Churchmen several exerted some sort of Anti-liberal influence in the place, at least from time to time, and that influence of an intellectual nature. Among these especially may be mentioned Mr. John Miller, of Worcester College, who preached the Bampton Lecture in the year 1817. But, as far as I know, he who turned the tide, and brought the talent of the University round to the side of the old theology, and against what was familiarly called "march-of-mind," was Mr. Keble.[7] In and from Keble the mental activity of Oxford took that contrary direction which issued in what was called Tractarianism.[8]

Keble was young in years, when he became a University celebrity, and younger in mind. He had the purity and simplicity of a child. He had few sympathies with the intellectual party, who sincerely welcomed him as a brilliant specimen of young Oxford. He instinctively shut up before literary display, and pomp and donnishness of manner, faults which always will beset academical notabilities. He did not respond to their advances. His collision with them (if it may be so called) was thus described by Hurrell Froude[9] in his own way. "Poor Keble!" he used gravely to say, "he was asked to join the aristocracy of talent, but he soon found his level." He went into the country, but his instance serves to prove that men need not, in the event, lose that influence which is rightly theirs, because they happen to be thwarted in the use of the channels natural and proper to its exercise. He did not lose his place in the minds of men because he was out of their sight.

Keble was a man who guided himself and formed his judgments, not by processes of reason, by inquiry or by argument, but, to use the word in a broad sense, by authority. Conscience is an authority; the Bible is an authority; such is the Church; such is Antiquity; such are the

words of the wise; such are hereditary lessons; such are ethical truths; such are historical memories, such are legal saws and state maxims; such are proverbs; such are sentiments, presages, and prepossessions. It seemed to me as if he ever felt happier, when he could speak or act under some such primary or external sanction; and could use argument mainly as a means of recommending or explaining what had claims on his reception prior to proof. He even felt a tenderness, I think, in spite of Bacon, for the Idols of the Tribe and the Den, of the Market and the Theatre.[10] What he hated instinctively was heresy, insubordination, resistance to things established, claims of independence, disloyalty, innovation, a critical, censorious spirit. And such was the main principle of the school which in the course of years was formed around him; nor is it easy to set limits to its influence in its day; for multitudes of men, who did not profess its teaching, or accept its peculiar doctrines, were willing nevertheless, or found it to their purpose, to act in company with it.

Indeed for a time it was practically the champion and advocate of the political doctrines of the great clerical interest through the country,[11] who found in Mr. Keble and his friends an intellectual, as well as moral support to their cause, which they looked for in vain elsewhere. His weak point, in their eyes, was his consistency; for he carried his love of authority and old times so far, as to be more than gentle towards the Catholic Religion, with which the Toryism of Oxford and of the Church of England had no sympathy. Accordingly, if my memory be correct, he never could get himself to throw his heart into the opposition made to Catholic Emancipation,[12] strongly as he revolted from the politics and the instruments by means of which that Emancipation was won. I fancy he would have

---

6 See Introduction, p. 415.
7 John Keble (1792–1866), by whom Newman was profoundly influenced. Together with Newman and Hurrell Froude, he originated the Oxford Movement.
8 I.e., the Oxford Movement. The term was derived from *Tracts for the Times;* see p. 532.
9 A fellow of Oriel and an intimate friend of Newman, deeply Anglo-Catholic in his thought.

10 As defined by Sir Francis Bacon, these are false notions which arise from the limitations of human nature, from the constitution of the individual, from the association of men, and from unfounded philosophical systems, respectively.
11 These political doctrines were just the opposite of Liberal propositions 12, 14, and 15 printed below, and were now emphasized the more because the Liberal government was threatening to disestablish the state Church of England (which meant withdrawing its financial support) and to alter its liturgy.
12 The bill to admit Catholics to Parliament was passed in 1829 against loud Tory opposition.

had no difficulty in accepting Dr. Johnson's saying about "the first Whig";[13] and it grieved and offended him that the "Via prima salutis"[14] should be opened to the Catholic body from the Whig quarter. In spite of his reverence for the Old Religion, I conceive that on the whole he would rather have kept its professors beyond the pale of the Constitution with the Tories, than admit them on the principles of the Whigs. Moreover, if the Revolution of 1688[15] was too lax in principle for him and his friends, much less, as is very plain, could they endure to subscribe to the revolutionary doctrines of 1776 and 1789,[16] which they felt to be absolutely and entirely out of keeping with theological truth.

The Old Tory or Conservative party in Oxford had in it no principle or power of development, and that from its very nature and constitution: it was otherwise with the Liberals. They represented a new idea, which was but gradually learning to recognise itself, to ascertain its characteristics and external relations, and to exert an influence upon the University. The party grew, all the time that I was in Oxford, even in numbers, certainly in breadth and definiteness of doctrine, and in power. And, what was a far higher consideration, by the accession of Dr. Arnold's pupils,[17] it was invested with an elevation of character which claimed the respect even of its opponents. On the other hand, in proportion as it became more earnest and less self-applauding, it became more free-spoken; and members of it might be found who, from the mere circumstance of remaining firm to their original professions, would in the judgment of the world, as to their public acts, seem to have left it for the Conservative camp. Thus, neither in its component parts nor in its policy, was it the same in 1832, 1836, and 1841, as it was in 1845.

These last remarks will serve to throw light upon a matter personal to myself, which I have introduced into my Narrative, and to which my attention has been pointedly called, now that my Volume is coming to a second edition.

It has been strongly urged upon me to reconsider the following passages which occur in it: "The men who had driven me from Oxford were distinctly the Liberals, it was they who had opened the attack upon Tract 90," p. 197, and "I found no fault with the Liberals; they had beaten me in a fair field," p. 205.

I am very unwilling to seem ungracious, or to cause pain in any quarter; still I am sorry to say I cannot modify these statements. It is surely a matter of historical fact that I left Oxford upon the University proceedings of 1841;[18] and in those proceedings, whether we look to the Heads of Houses or the resident Masters, the leaders, if intellect and influence make men such, were members of the Liberal party. Those who did not lead, concurred or acquiesced in them,— I may say, felt a satisfaction. I do not recollect any Liberal who was on my side on that occasion. Excepting the Liberal, no other party as a party, acted against me. I am not complaining of them; I deserved nothing else at their hands. They could not undo in 1845,[19] even had they wished it (and there is no proof they did), what they had done in 1841. In 1845, when I had already given up the contest for four years, and my part in it had passed into the hands of others, then some of those who were prominent against me in 1841, feeling (what they had not felt in 1841) the danger of driving a number of my followers to Rome, and joined by younger friends who had come into University importance since 1841 and felt kindly towards me, adopted a course more consistent with their principles, and proceeded to shield from the zeal of the Hebdomadal Board,[20] not me, but professedly, all parties through the country,—Tractarians, Evangelicals, Liberals in general,—who had to subscribe to the Anglican formularies,[21] on the ground that

---

13 Boswell reports in his *Life of Dr. Johnson* that Johnson claimed the first Whig was the Devil.
14 The first way or step of [political] salvation.
15 The Whig Revolution, which forced James II off the throne and transferred power from the king to Parliament.
16 The American Declaration of Independence and the French Rights of Man. Cf. Proposition 17 below.
17 From Rugby, where Thomas Arnold, the father of Matthew, was headmaster. His liberal views on theology and church reform were deeply impressed upon his students.

18 The bitter attack by the Heads of the Oxford Colleges upon Newman's interpretation, in Tract 90, of the Thirty-nine Articles, which define the basic beliefs of the Church of England. He had attempted to show that they did not preclude the doctrines of Anglo-Catholicism.
19 The year in which Newman became a Roman Catholic.
20 A board of seven set up to initiate and canvass matters that were to be submitted to Convocation.
21 The Thirty-nine Articles.

those formularies, rigidly taken, were, on some point or other, a difficulty to all parties alike. . . .

I conclude this notice of Liberalism in Oxford, and the party which was antagonistic to it, with some propositions in detail, which, as a member of the latter, and together with the High Church, I earnestly denounced and abjured.

1. No religious tenet is important, unless reason shows it to be so.

Therefore, *e.g.*[22] the doctrine of the Athanasian Creed is not to be insisted on, unless it tends to convert the soul; and the doctrine of the Atonement is to be insisted on, if it does convert the soul.

2. No one can believe what he does not understand. Therefore, *e.g.* there are no mysteries in true religion.

3. No theological doctrine is any thing more than an opinion which happens to be held by bodies of men.

Therefore, *e.g.* no creed, as such, is necessary for salvation.

4. It is dishonest in a man to make an act of faith in what he has not had brought home to him by actual proof.

Therefore, *e.g.* the mass of men ought not absolutely to believe in the divine authority of the Bible.

5. It is immoral in a man to believe more than he can spontaneously receive as being congenial to his moral and mental nature.

Therefore, *e.g.* a given individual is not bound to believe in eternal punishment.

6. No revealed doctrines or precepts may reasonably stand in the way of scientific conclusions.

Therefore, *e.g.* Political Economy may reverse our Lord's declarations about poverty and riches, or a system of Ethics may teach that the highest condition of body is ordinarily essential to the highest state of mind.

7. Christianity is necessarily modified by the growth of civilization, and the exigencies of times.

Therefore, *e.g.* the Catholic priesthood, though necessary in the Middle Ages, may be superseded now.

8. There is a system of religion more simply true than Christianity as it has ever been received.

Therefore, *e.g.* we may advance that Christianity is the "corn of wheat" which has been dead for 1800 years, but at length will bear fruit; and that Mahometanism is the manly religion, and existing Christianity the womanish.

9. There is a right of Private Judgment: that is, there is no existing authority on earth competent to interfere with the liberty of individuals in reasoning and judging for themselves about the Bible and its contents, as they severally please.

Therefore, *e.g.* religious establishments requiring subscription are Anti-christian.

10. There are rights of conscience such, that every one may lawfully advance a claim to profess and teach what is false and wrong in matters, religious, social, and moral, provided that to his private conscience it seems absolutely true and right.

Therefore, *e.g.* individuals have a right to preach and practise fornication and polygamy.

11. There is no such thing as a national or state conscience.

Therefore, *e.g.* no judgments can fall upon a sinful or infidel nation.

12. The civil power has no positive duty, in a normal state of things, to maintain religious truth.

Therefore, *e.g.* blasphemy and sabbath-breaking are not rightly punishable by law.

13. Utility and expedience are the measure of political duty.

Therefore, *e.g.* no punishment may be enacted, on the ground that God commands it: *e.g.* on the text, "Whoso sheddeth man's blood, by man shall his blood be shed."

14. The Civil Power may dispose of Church property without sacrilege.

Therefore, *e.g.* Henry VIII. committed no sin in his spoliations.[23]

15. The Civil Power has the right of ecclesiastical jurisdiction and administration.

Therefore, *e.g.* Parliament may impose articles of faith on the Church or suppress Dioceses.

---

[22] Each Liberal proposition is followed by a deduction that is intended to be a *reductio ad absurdum*.

[23] His dissolution of the monasteries and appropriation of their property.

16. It is lawful to rise in arms against legitimate princes.

Therefore, *e.g.* the Puritans in the seventeenth century, and the French in the eighteenth, were justified in their Rebellion and Revolution respectively.

17. The people are the legitimate source of power.

Therefore, *e.g.* Universal Suffrage is among the natural rights of man.

18. Virtue is the child of knowledge, and vice of ignorance.

Therefore, *e.g.* education, periodical literature, railroad travelling, ventilation, drainage, and the arts of life, when fully carried out, serve to make a population moral and happy.

All of these propositions, and many others too, were familiar to me thirty years ago,[24] as in the number of the tenets of Liberalism, and, while I gave in to none of them except No. 12, and perhaps No. 11, and partly No. 1, before I began to publish, so afterwards I wrote against most of them in some part or other of my Anglican works. . . .

I need hardly say that the above Note is mainly historical. How far the Liberal party of 1830–40 really held the above eighteen Theses, which I attributed to them, and how far and in what sense I should oppose those Theses now, could scarcely be explained without a separate Dissertation.

from The Idea of a University

from Discourse V

KNOWLEDGE ITS OWN END

A University may be considered with reference either to its Students or to its Studies; and the principle, that all Knowledge is a whole and the separate Sciences[1] parts of one, which I have hitherto been using in behalf of its studies, is equally important when we direct our attention to its students. Now then I turn to the students, and shall consider the education which,

by virtue of this principle, a University will give them; and thus I shall be introduced, Gentlemen, to the second question, which I proposed to discuss, viz. whether and in what sense its teaching, viewed relatively to the taught, carries the attribute of Utility[2] along with it.

1

I have said that all branches of knowledge are connected together, because the subject-matter of knowledge is intimately united in itself, as being the acts and the work of the Creator. Hence it is that the Sciences, into which our knowledge may be said to be cast, have multiplied bearings one on another, and an internal sympathy, and admit, or rather demand, comparison and adjustment. They complete, correct, balance each other. This consideration, if well-founded, must be taken into account, not only as regards the attainment of truth, which is their common end, but as regards the influence which they exercise upon those whose education consists in the study of them. I have said already, that to give undue prominence to one is to be unjust to another; to neglect or supersede these is to divert those from their proper object. It is to unsettle the boundary lines between science and science, to disturb their action, to destroy the harmony which binds them together. Such a proceeding will have a corresponding effect when introduced into a place of education. There is no science but tells a different tale, when viewed as a portion of a whole, from what it is likely to suggest when taken by itself, without the safeguard, as I may call it, of others.

Let me make use of an illustration. In the combination of colours, very different effects are produced by a difference in their selection and juxtaposition; red, green, and white change their shades, according to the contrast to which they are submitted. And, in like manner, the drift and meaning of a branch of knowledge

---

24 He is writing in 1864.

1 I.e., the separate branches or fields of knowledge.

2 This discourse is a reply to those who charged liberal or humane studies with "remoteness from the occupations and duties of life, to which they are the formal introduction." It should be compared with Macaulay's description and advocacy of Baconian philosophy, whose aim "was to supply our vulgar wants." Newman had Bacon and Macaulay's essay on him specifically in view, as well as a series of articles in the *Edinburgh Review* 1808–10, attacking classical education at Oxford.

varies with the company in which it is introduced to the student. If his reading is confined simply to one subject, however such division of labour may favour the advancement of a particular pursuit, a point into which I do not here enter, certainly it has a tendency to contract his mind. If it is incorporated with others, it depends on those others as to the kind of influence which it exerts upon him. Thus the Classics, which in England are the means of refining the taste, have in France subserved the spread of revolutionary and deistical doctrines. In Metaphysics, again, Butler's[3] *Analogy of Religion,* which has had so much to do with the conversion to the Catholic faith of members of the University of Oxford, appeared to Pitt and others, who had received a different training, to operate only in the direction of infidelity. And so again, Watson, Bishop of Llandaff, as I think he tells us in the narrative of his life, felt the science of Mathematics to indispose the mind to religious belief, while others see in its investigations the best parallel, and thereby defence, of the Christian Mysteries. In like manner, I suppose, Arcesilaus would not have handled logic as Aristotle, nor Aristotle have criticized poets as Plato; yet reasoning and poetry are subject to scientific rules.

It is a great point then to enlarge the range of studies which a University professes, even for the sake of the students; and, though they cannot pursue every subject which is open to them, they will be the gainers by living among those and under those who represent the whole circle. This I conceive to be the advantage of a seat of universal learning, considered as a place of education. An assemblage of learned men, zealous for their own sciences, and rivals of each other, are brought, by familiar intercourse and for the sake of intellectual peace, to adjust together the claims and relations of their respective subjects of investigation. They learn to respect, to consult, to aid each other. Thus is created a pure and clear atmosphere of thought, which the student also breathes, though in his own case he only pursues a few sciences out of the multitude. He profits by an intellectual tradition, which is independent of particular teachers, which guides him in his choice of subjects, and duly interprets for him those which he chooses. He apprehends the great outlines of knowledge, the principles on which it rests, the scale of its parts, its lights and its shades, its great points and its little, as he otherwise cannot apprehend them. Hence it is that his education is called "Liberal."[4] A habit of mind is formed which lasts through life, of which the attributes are, freedom, equitableness, calmness, moderation, and wisdom; or what in a former Discourse I have ventured to call a philosophical habit. This then I would assign as the special fruit of the education furnished at a University, as contrasted with other places of teaching or modes of teaching. This is the main purpose of a University in its treatment of its students.

And now the question is asked me, What is the *use* of it? and my answer will constitute the main subject of the Discourses which are to follow.

2

Cautious and practical thinkers, I say, will ask of me, what, after all, is the gain of this Philosophy, of which I make such account, and from which I promise so much. Even supposing it to enable us to exercise the degree of trust exactly due to every science respectively, and to estimate precisely the value of every truth which is anywhere to be found, how are we better for this master view of things, which I have been extolling? Does it not reverse the principle of the division of labour? will practical objects be obtained better or worse by its cultivation? to what then does it lead? where does it end? what does it do? how does it profit? what does it promise? Particular sciences are respectively the basis of definite arts, which carry on to results tangible and beneficial the truths which are the subjects of the knowledge attained; what is the Art of this science of sciences? what is the fruit of such a Philosophy? what are we proposing to effect, what inducements do we hold out to the Catholic community, when we set about the enterprise of founding a University?

---

[3] Joseph Butler (1692–1752). The *Analogy,* as Newman tells us in the *Apologia,* had a profound effect upon his thinking, but it was probably only through his admiration and interpretation that it had anything like the influence attributed to it here.

[4] As distinguished from a professional or vocational education.

I am asked what is the end of University Education, and of the Liberal or Philosophical Knowledge which I conceive it to impart: I answer, that what I have already said has been sufficient to show that it has a very tangible, real, and sufficient end, though the end cannot be divided from that knowledge itself. Knowledge is capable of being its own end. Such is the constitution of the human mind, that any kind of knowledge, if it be really such, is its own reward. And if this is true of all knowledge, it is true also of that special Philosophy, which I have made to consist in a comprehensive view of truth in all its branches, of the relations of science to science, of their mutual bearings, and their respective values. What the worth of such an acquirement is, compared with other objects which we seek,—wealth or power or honour or the conveniences and comforts of life, I do not profess here to discuss; but I would maintain, and mean to show, that it is an object, in its own nature so really and undeniably good, as to be the compensation of a great deal of thought in the compassing, and a great deal of trouble in the attaining.

Now, when I say that Knowledge is, not merely a means to something beyond it, or the preliminary of certain arts into which it naturally resolves, but an end sufficient to rest in and to pursue for its own sake, surely I am uttering no paradox, for I am stating what is both intelligible in itself, and has ever been the common judgment of philosophers and the ordinary feeling of mankind. I am saying what at least the public opinion of this day ought to be slow to deny, considering how much we have heard of late years, in opposition to Religion, of entertaining, curious, and various knowledge. I am but saying what whole volumes have been written to illustrate, viz. by a "selection from the records of Philosophy, Literature, and Art, in all ages and countries, of a body of examples, to show how the most unpropitious circumstances have been unable to conquer an ardent desire for the acquisition of knowledge."[5] That further advantages accrue to us and redound to others by its possession, over and above what it is in itself, I am very far indeed from denying; but,

independent of these, we are satisfying a direct need of our nature in its very acquisition; and, whereas our nature, unlike that of the inferior creation, does not at once reach its perfection, but depends, in order to it, on a number of external aids and appliances, Knowledge, as one of the principal of these, is valuable for what its very presence in us does for us after the manner of a habit, even though it be turned to no further account, nor subserve any direct end.

3

Hence it is that Cicero, in enumerating the various heads of mental excellence, lays down the pursuit of Knowledge for its own sake, as the first of them. "This pertains most of all to human nature," he says, "for we are all of us drawn to the pursuit of Knowledge; in which to excel we consider excellent, whereas to mistake, to err, to be ignorant, to be deceived, is both an evil and a disgrace."[6] And he considers Knowledge the very first object to which we are attracted, after the supply of our physical wants. After the calls and duties of our animal existence, as they may be termed, as regards ourselves, our family, and our neighbours, follows, he tells us, "the search after truth. Accordingly, as soon as we escape from the pressure of necessary cares, forthwith we desire to see, to hear, and to learn; and consider the knowledge of what is hidden or is wonderful a condition of our happiness."

This passage, though it is but one of many similar passages in a multitude of authors, I take for the very reason that it is so familiarly known to us; and I wish you to observe, Gentlemen, how distinctly it separates the pursuit of Knowledge from those ulterior objects to which certainly it can be made to conduce, and which are, I suppose, solely contemplated by the persons who would ask of me the use of a University or Liberal Education. So far from dreaming of the cultivation of Knowledge directly and mainly in order to our physical comfort and enjoyment, for the sake of life and person, of health, of the conjugal and family union, of the social tie and civil security, the great Orator implies, that it is only after our physical and

---

[5] The quotation is from the Introduction to *Pursuit of Knowledge under Difficulties* by George Craik.

[6] At the beginning of his *De Officiis*.

political needs are supplied, and when we are "free from necessary duties and cares," that we are in a condition for "desiring to see, to hear, and to learn." Nor does he contemplate in the least degree the reflex or subsequent action of Knowledge, when acquired, upon those material goods which we set out by securing before we seek it; on the contrary, he expressly denies its bearing upon social life altogether, strange as such a procedure is to those who live after the rise of the Baconian philosophy,[7] and he cautions us against such a cultivation of it as will interfere with our duties to our fellow-creatures. "All these methods," he says, "are engaged in the investigation of truth; by the pursuit of which to be carried off from public occupations is a transgression of duty. For the praise of virtue lies altogether in action; yet intermissions often occur, and then we recur to such pursuits; not to say that the incessant activity of the mind is vigorous enough to carry us on in the pursuit of knowledge, even without any exertion of our own." The idea of benefiting society by means of "the pursuit of science and knowledge," did not enter at all into the motives which he would assign for their cultivation.

This was the ground of the opposition which the elder Cato made to the introduction of Greek Philosophy among his countrymen, when Carneades[8] and his companions, on occasion of their embassy, were charming the Roman youth with their eloquent expositions of it. The fit representative of a practical people, Cato estimated everything by what it produced; whereas the Pursuit of Knowledge promised nothing beyond Knowledge itself. He despised that refinement or enlargement of mind of which he had no experience.

4

Things, which can bear to be cut off from everything else and yet persist in living, must have life in themselves; pursuits, which issue in nothing, and still maintain their ground for ages, which are regarded as admirable, though they have not as yet proved themselves to be useful, must have their sufficient end in themselves, whatever it turn out to be. And we are brought to the same conclusion by considering the force of the epithet, by which the knowledge under consideration is popularly designated. It is common to speak of "*liberal* knowledge," of the "*liberal* arts and studies," and of a "*liberal* education," as the especial characteristic or property of a University and of a gentleman; what is really meant by the word? Now, first, in its grammatical sense it is opposed to *servile;* and by "servile work" is understood, as our catechisms inform us, bodily labour, mechanical employment, and the like, in which the mind has little or no part. Parallel to such servile works are those arts, if they deserve the name, of which the poet speaks,[9] which owe their origin and their method to hazard, not to skill; as, for instance, the practice and operations of an empiric. As far as this contrast may be considered as a guide into the meaning of the word, liberal education and liberal pursuits are exercises of mind, of reason, of reflection.

But we want something more for its explanation, for there are bodily exercises which are liberal, and mental exercises which are not so. For instance, in ancient times the practitioners in medicine were commonly slaves; yet it was an art as intellectual in its nature, in spite of the pretence, fraud, and quackery with which it might then, as now, be debased, as it was heavenly in its aim. And so in like manner, we contrast a liberal education with a commercial education or a professional; yet no one can deny that commerce and the professions afford scope for the highest and most diversified powers of mind. There is then a great variety of intellectual exercises, which are not technically called "liberal"; on the other hand, I say, there are exercises of the body which do receive that appellation. Such, for instance, was the palaestra,[10] in ancient times; such the Olympic games, in which strength and dexterity of body as well as of mind gained the prize. In Xenophon[11] we read of the young Persian nobility being taught

---

7 To Bacon practical usefulness was the justification of knowledge. See Macaulay's essay on Bacon, above.
8 A Greek skeptic philosopher who so alarmed the Roman statesman Cato (234–149 B.C.) by the charm which his eloquent sophistries were exerting in Rome that he was sent back to Athens.

9 Agathon (fifth century B.C.) as quoted by Aristotle in the *Nicomachean Ethics,* VI, according to Newman's own note.
10 Wrestling.
11 Greek historian of the fifth century B.C.

to ride on horseback and to speak the truth; both being among the accomplishments of a gentleman. War, too, however rough a profession, has ever been accounted liberal, unless in cases when it becomes heroic, which would introduce us to another subject.

Now comparing these instances together, we shall have no difficulty in determining the principle of this apparent variation in the application of the term which I am examining. Manly games, or games of skill, or military prowess, though bodily, are, it seems, accounted liberal; on the other hand, what is merely professional, though highly intellectual, nay, though liberal in comparison of trade and manual labour, is not simply called liberal, and mercantile occupations are not liberal at all. Why this distinction? because that alone is liberal knowledge, which stands on its own pretensions, which is independent of sequel, expects no complement, refuses to be *informed* (as it is called) by any end, or absorbed into any art, in order duly to present itself to our contemplation. The most ordinary pursuits have this specific character, if they are self-sufficient and complete; the highest lose it, when they minister to something beyond them. It is absurd to balance, in point of worth and importance, a treatise on reducing fractures with a game of cricket or a fox-chase; yet of the two the bodily exercise has that quality which we call "liberal," and the intellectual has not. And so of the learned professions altogether, considered merely as professions; although one of them be the most popularly beneficial, and another the most politically important, and the third the most intimately divine of all human pursuits, yet the very greatness of their end, the health of the body, or of the commonwealth, or of the soul, diminishes, not increases, their claim to the appellation "liberal," and that still more, if they are cut down to the strict exigencies of that end. If, for instance, Theology instead of being cultivated as a contemplation, be limited to the purposes of the pulpit or be represented by the catechism, it loses—not its usefulness, not its divine character, not its meritoriousness, (rather it gains a claim upon these titles by such charitable condescension),—but it does lose the particular attribute which I am illustrating; just as a face worn by tears and fasting loses its beauty, or a labourer's hand loses

its delicateness;—for Theology thus exercised is not simple knowledge, but rather is an art or a business making use of Theology. And thus it appears that even what is supernatural need not be liberal, nor need a hero be a gentleman, for the plain reason that one idea is not another idea. And in like manner the Baconian Philosophy, by using its physical sciences in the service of man, does thereby transfer them from the order of Liberal Pursuits to, I do not say the inferior, but the distinct class of the Useful. And, to take a different instance, hence again, as is evident, whenever personal gain is the motive, still more distinctive an effect has it upon the character of a given pursuit; thus racing, which was a liberal exercise in Greece, forfeits its rank in times like these, so far as it is made the occasion of gambling.

All that I have been now saying is summed up in a few characteristic words of the great Philosopher.[12] "Of possessions," he says, "those rather are useful, which bear fruit; those *liberal, which tend to enjoyment*. By fruitful, I mean, which yield revenue; by enjoyable, where *nothing accrues of consequence beyond the using*." . . .

6

Now bear with me, Gentlemen, if what I am about to say, has at first sight a fanciful appearance. Philosophy, then, or Science, is related to Knowledge in this way:—Knowledge is called by the name of Science or Philosophy, when it is acted upon, informed, or if I may use a strong figure, impregnated by Reason. Reason is the principle of that intrinsic fecundity of Knowledge, which, to those who possess it, is its especial value, and which dispenses with the necessity of their looking abroad for any end to rest upon external to itself. Knowledge, indeed, when thus exalted into a scientific form, is also power; not only is it excellent in itself, but whatever such excellence may be, it is something more, it has a result beyond itself. Doubtless; but that is a further consideration, with which I am not concerned. I only say that, prior to its being a power, it is a good; that it is, not only an instrument, but an end. I know well it may resolve

---

12 Aristotle. The quotation, according to Newman, is taken from the *Rhetoric*, I, 5.

itself into an art, and terminate in a mechanical process, and in tangible fruit; but it also may fall back upon that Reason which informs it, and resolve itself into Philosophy. In one case it is called Useful Knowledge, in the other Liberal. The same person may cultivate it in both ways at once; but this again is a matter foreign to my subject; here I do but say that there are two ways of using Knowledge, and in matter of fact those who use it in one way are not likely to use it in the other, or at least in a very limited measure. You see, then, here are two methods of Education; the end of the one is to be philosophical, of the other to be mechanical; the one rises towards general ideas, the other is exhausted upon what is particular and external. Let me not be thought to deny the necessity, or to decry the benefit, of such attention to what is particular and practical, as belongs to the useful or mechanical arts; life could not go on without them; we owe our daily welfare to them; their exercise is the duty of the many, and we owe to the many a debt of gratitude for fulfilling that duty. I only say that Knowledge, in proportion as it tends more and more to be particular, ceases to be Knowledge. It is a question whether Knowledge can in any proper sense be predicated of the brute creation; without pretending to metaphysical exactness of phraseology, which would be unsuitable to an occasion like this, I say, it seems to me improper to call that passive sensation, or perception of things, which brutes seem to possess, by the name of Knowledge. When I speak of Knowledge, I mean something intellectual, something which grasps what it perceives through the senses; something which takes a view of things; which sees more than the senses convey; which reasons upon what it sees, and while it sees; which invests it with an idea. It expresses itself, not in a mere enunciation, but by an enthymeme:[13] it is of the nature of science from the first, and in this consists its dignity. The principle of real dignity in Knowledge, its worth, its desirableness, considered irrespectively of its results, is this germ within it of a scientific or a philosophical process. This is how it comes to be an end in itself; this is why it admits of being called Liberal. Not to

know the relative disposition of things is the state of slaves or children; to have mapped out the Universe is the boast, or at least the ambition, of Philosophy.

Moreover, such knowledge is not a mere extrinsic or accidental advantage, which is ours to-day and another's to-morrow, which may be got up from a book, and easily forgotten again, which we can command or communicate at our pleasure, which we can borrow for the occasion, carry about in our hand, and take into the market; it is an acquired illumination, it is a habit, a personal possession, and an inward endowment. And this is the reason, why it is more correct, as well as more usual, to speak of a University as a place of education, than of instruction, though, when knowledge is concerned, instruction would at first sight have seemed the more appropriate word. We are instructed, for instance, in manual exercises, in the fine and useful arts, in trades, and in ways of business; for these are methods, which have little or no effect upon the mind itself, are contained in rules committed to memory, to tradition, or to use, and bear upon an end external to themselves. But education is a higher word; it implies an action upon our mental nature, and the formation of a character; it is something individual and permanent, and is commonly spoken of in connexion with religion and virtue. When, then, we speak of the communication of Knowledge as being Education, we thereby really imply that that Knowledge is a state or condition of mind; and since cultivation of mind is surely worth seeking for its own sake, we are thus brought once more to the conclusion, which the word "Liberal" and the word "Philosophy" have already suggested, that there is a Knowledge, which is desirable, though nothing come of it, as being of itself a treasure, and a sufficient remuneration of years of labour.

7

This, then, is the answer which I am prepared to give to the question with which I opened this Discourse. Before going on to speak of the object of the Church in taking up Philosophy, and the uses to which she puts it, I am prepared to maintain that Philosophy is its own end, and, as I conceive, I have now begun the proof of

---

[13] A form of reasoning in which one premise is understood but not expressed.

it. I am prepared to maintain that there is a knowledge worth possessing for what it is, and not merely for what it does; and what minutes remain to me today I shall devote to the removal of some portion of the indistinctness and confusion with which the subject may in some minds be surrounded.

It may be objected then, that, when we profess to seek Knowledge for some end or other beyond itself, whatever it be, we speak intelligibly; but that, whatever men may have said, however obstinately the idea may have kept its ground from age to age, still it is simply unmeaning to say that we seek Knowledge for its own sake, and for nothing else; for that it ever leads to something beyond itself, which therefore is its end, and the cause why it is desirable;— moreover, that this end is twofold, either of this world or of the next; that all knowledge is cultivated either for secular objects or for eternal; that if it is directed to secular objects, it is called Useful Knowledge, if to eternal, Religious or Christian Knowledge;—in consequence, that if, as I have allowed, this Liberal Knowledge does not benefit the body or estate, it ought to benefit the soul; but if the fact be really so, that it is neither a physical or a secular good on the one hand, nor a moral good on the other, it cannot be a good at all, and is not worth the trouble which is necessary for its acquisition.

And then I may be reminded that the professors of this Liberal or Philosophical Knowledge have themselves, in every age, recognized this exposition of the matter, and have submitted to the issue in which it terminates; for they have ever been attempting to make men virtuous; or, if not, at least have assumed that refinement of mind was virtue, and that they themselves were the virtuous portion of mankind. This they have professed on the one hand; and on the other, they have utterly failed in their professions, so as ever to make themselves a proverb among men, and a laughing-stock both to the grave and the dissipated portion of mankind, in consequence of them. Thus they have furnished against themselves both the ground and the means of their own exposure, without any trouble at all to anyone else. In a word, from the time that Athens was the University of the world, what has Philosophy taught men, but to promise without practising, and to aspire

without attaining? What has the deep and lofty thought of its disciples ended in but eloquent words?[14] Nay, what has its teaching ever meditated, when it was boldest in its remedies for human ill, beyond charming us to sleep by its lessons, that we might feel nothing at all? like some melodious air, or rather like those strong and transporting perfumes, which at first spread their sweetness over everything they touch, but in a little while do but offend in proportion as they once pleased us. Did Philosophy support Cicero under the disfavour of the fickle populace,[15] or nerve Seneca to oppose an imperial tyrant?[16] It abandoned Brutus,[17] as he sorrowfully confessed, in his greatest need, and it forced Cato, as his panegyrist strangely boasts, into the false position of defying heaven.[18] How few can be counted among its professors, who, like Polemon,[19] were thereby converted from a profligate course, or like Anaxagoras,[20] thought the world well lost in exchange for its possession? The philosopher in *Rasselas*[21] taught a superhuman doctrine, and then succumbed without an effort to a trial of human affection.

"He discoursed," we are told, "with great energy on the government of the passions. His look was venerable, his action graceful, his pronunciation clear, and his diction elegant. He showed, with great strength of sentiment and variety of illustration, that human nature is

---

14 Compare Bacon's view as set forth in Macaulay's essay, even to the verbal echo: "The philosophy of Plato began in words and ended in words" (p. 518).

15 Plutarch describes in detail how low-spirited Cicero became in exile, so dejected "as none could have expected in a man who had devoted so much of his life to study and learning."

16 Instead of opposing Nero, for whom he had been both tutor and virtual regent, Seneca tried to retire from public affairs.

17 On the eve of their final battle with Antony, Brutus, according to Plutarch, confessed to Cassius that his philosophy was insufficient to enable him to accept the fate of defeat, and that if the issue were against them he would kill himself, which he did.

18 Cato the Younger, in Plutarch's account, defied heaven by declaring that he was master of his own life or death and committing suicide.

19 A profligate Athenian youth who accidentally heard a philosopher discourse on temperance and was induced thereby to become abstemious. He later became head of the Platonic school in Athens.

20 A Greek philosopher of the fifth century B.C. who sold all his worldly goods in order to devote himself to philosophy.

21 A novel by Samuel Johnson.

degraded and debased, when the lower faculties predominate over the higher. He communicated the various precepts given, from time to time, for the conquest of passion, and displayed the happiness of those who had obtained the important victory, after which man is no longer the slave of fear, nor the fool of hope. . . . He enumerated many examples of heroes immovable by pain or pleasure, who looked with indifference on those modes or accidents to which the vulgar give the names of good and evil."

Rasselas in a few days found the philosopher in a room half darkened, with his eyes misty, and his face pale. "Sir," said he, "you have come at a time when all human friendship is useless; what I suffer cannot be remedied, what I have lost cannot be supplied. My daughter, my only daughter, from whose tenderness I expected all the comforts of my age, died last night of a fever." "Sir," said the prince, "mortality is an event by which a wise man can never be surprised; we know that death is always near, and it should therefore always be expected." "Young man," answered the philosopher, "you speak like one who has never felt the pangs of separation." "Have you, then, forgot the precept," said Rasselas, "which you so powerfully enforced? . . . consider that external things are naturally variable, but truth and reason are always the same." "What comfort," said the mourner, "can truth and reason afford me? Of what effect are they now, but to tell me that my daughter will not be restored?"

8

Better, far better, to make no professions, you will say, than to cheat others with what we are not, and to scandalize them with what we are. The sensualist, or the man of the world, at any rate, is not the victim of fine words, but pursues a reality and gains it. The Philosophy of Utility, you will say, Gentlemen, has at least done its work; and I grant it,—it aimed low, but it has fulfilled its aim.[22] If that man of great intellect who has been its Prophet in the conduct of life played false to his own professions,[23] he was not bound by his philosophy to be true to his friend or faithful in his trust. Moral virtue was not the line in which he undertook to instruct men; and though, as the poet calls him, he were the "meanest" of mankind,[24] he was so in what may be called his private capacity and without any prejudice to the theory of induction. He had a right to be so, if he chose, for anything that the Idols of the den or the theatre[25] had to say to the contrary. His mission was the increase of physical enjoyment and social comfort;[26] and most wonderfully, most awfully has he fulfilled his conception and his design. Almost day by day have we fresh and fresh shoots, and buds, and blossoms, which are to ripen into fruit, on that magical tree of Knowledge which he planted, and to which none of us perhaps, except the very poor, but owes, if not his present life, at least his daily food, his health, and general well-being. He was the divinely provided minister of temporal benefits to all of us so great, that, whatever I am forced to think of him as a man, I have not the heart, from mere gratitude, to speak of him severely. And, in spite of the tendencies of his philosophy, which are, as we see at this day, to depreciate, or to trample on Theology, he has himself, in his writings, gone out of his way, as if with a prophetic misgiving of those tendencies, to insist on it as the instrument of that beneficent Father, who, when He came on earth in visible form, took on Him first and most prominently the office of assuaging the bodily wounds of human nature.[27] And truly, like the old mediciner in the tale, "he sat diligently at his work, and hummed, with cheerful countenance, a pious song"; and then in turn "went out singing into the meadows so gaily, that those who had seen him from afar might well have thought it was a youth gathering flowers for his beloved, instead of an old physician gathering healing herbs in the morning dew."[28]

Alas, that men, in the action of life or in their heart of hearts, are not what they seem to

---

[22] Direct allusion to Macaulay's essay: "Some people may think the object of the Baconian philosophy a low object, but they cannot deny that, high or low, it has been attained." See p. 518.

[23] Bacon as Lord Chancellor was charged with bribery, and, indeed, admitted corruption and neglect.

[24] Pope in his *Essay on Man* termed Bacon "the wisest, brightest, meanest of mankind."

[25] See note 10 to *Apologia pro Vita Sua* above.

[26] "It will be seen that on the whole I agree with Lord Macaulay in his Essay on Bacon's Philosophy. I do not know whether he would agree with me." (Newman)

[27] "*De Augment.* IV, 2, vid. Macaulay's Essay." (Newman) See pp. 516-17.

[28] "Fouqué's *Unknown Patient*." (Newman) The parallel is between the "old mediciner" and Bacon.

be in their moments of excitement, or in their trances or intoxications of genius,—so good, so noble, so serene! Alas, that Bacon too in his own way should after all be but the fellow of those heathen philosophers who in their disadvantages had some excuse for their inconsistency, and who surprise us rather in what they did say than in what they did not do! Alas, that he too, like Socrates or Seneca, must be stripped of his holyday coat, which looks so fair, and should be but a mockery amid his most majestic gravity of phrase; and, for all his vast abilities, should, in the littleness of his own moral being, but typify the intellectual narrowness of his school! However, granting all this, heroism after all was not his philosophy:—I cannot deny he has abundantly achieved what he proposed. His is simply a Method whereby bodily discomforts and temporal wants are to be most effectually removed from the greatest number; and already, before it has shown any signs of exhaustion, the gifts of nature, in their most artificial shapes and luxurious profusion and diversity, from all quarters of the earth, are, it is undeniable, by its means brought even to our doors, and we rejoice in them.

9

Useful Knowledge then, I grant, has done its work; and Liberal Knowledge as certainly has not done its work,—that is, supposing, as the objectors assume, its direct end, like Religious Knowledge, is to make men better; but this, I will not for an instant allow, and, unless I allow it, those objectors have said nothing to the purpose. I admit, rather I maintain, what they have been urging, for I consider Knowledge to have its end in itself. For all its friends, or its enemies, may say, I insist upon it, that it is as real a mistake to burden it with virtue or religion as with the mechanical arts. Its direct business is not to steel the soul against temptation or to console it in affliction, any more than to set the loom in motion, or to direct the steam carriage; be it ever so much the means or the condition of both material and moral advancement, still, taken by and in itself, it as little mends our hearts as it improves our temporal circumstances. And if its eulogists claim for it such a power, they commit the very same kind of encroachment on a province not their own as

the political economist who should maintain that his science educated him for casuistry or diplomacy. Knowledge is one thing, virtue is another; good sense is not conscience, refinement is not humility, nor is largeness and justness of view faith. Philosophy, however enlightened, however profound, gives no command over the passions, no influential motives, no vivifying principles. Liberal Education makes not the Christian, not the Catholic, but the gentleman. It is well to be a gentleman, it is well to have a cultivated intellect, a delicate taste, a candid, equitable, dispassionate mind, a noble and courteous bearing in the conduct of life;—these are the connatural qualities of a large knowledge; they are the objects of a University; I am advocating, I shall illustrate and insist upon them; but still, I repeat, they are no guarantee for sanctity or even for conscientiousness, they may attach to the man of the world, to the profligate, to the heartless,—pleasant, alas, and attractive as he shows when decked out in them. Taken by themselves, they do but seem to be what they are not; they look like virtue at a distance, but they are detected by close observers, and on the long run; and hence it is that they are popularly accused of pretence and hypocrisy, not, I repeat, from their own fault, but because their professors and their admirers persist in taking them for what they are not, and are officious in arrogating for them a praise to which they have no claim. Quarry the granite rock with razors, or moor the vessel with a thread of silk; then may you hope with such keen and delicate instruments as human knowledge and human reason to contend against those giants, the passion and the pride of man.

Surely we are not driven to theories of this kind, in order to vindicate the value and dignity of Liberal Knowledge. Surely the real grounds on which its pretensions rest are not so very subtle or abstruse, so very strange or improbable. Surely it is very intelligible to say, and that is what I say here, that Liberal Education, viewed in itself, is simply the cultivation of the intellect, as such, and its object is nothing more or less than intellectual excellence. Everything has its own perfection, be it higher or lower in the scale of things; and the perfection of one is not the perfection of another. Things animate, inanimate, visible, invisible, all are good in their kind, and have a *best* of themselves, which is an object of pursuit. Why do you take such pains with your garden or your park? You see to your walks and turf and shrubberies; to your trees and drives; not as if you meant to make an orchard of the one, or corn or pasture land of the other, but because there is a special beauty in all that is goodly in wood, water, plain, and slope, brought all together by art into one shape, and grouped into one whole. Your cities are beautiful, your palaces, your public buildings, your territorial mansions, your churches; and their beauty leads to nothing beyond itself. There is a physical beauty and a moral; there is a beauty of person, there is a beauty of our moral being, which is natural virtue; and in like manner there is a beauty, there is a perfection, of the intellect. There is an ideal perfection in these various subject-matters, towards which individual instances are seen to rise, and which are the standards for all instances whatever. The Greek divinities and demigods, as the statuary has moulded them, with their symmetry of figure and their high forehead and their regular features, are the perfection of physical beauty. The heroes, of whom history tells, Alexander, or Caesar, or Scipio, or Saladin, are the representatives of that magnanimity or self-mastery which is the greatness of human nature. Christianity too has its heroes, and in the supernatural order, and we call them Saints. The artist puts before him beauty of feature and form; the poet, beauty of mind; the preacher, the beauty of grace: then intellect too, I repeat, has its beauty, and it has those who aim at it. To open the mind, to correct it, to refine it, to enable it to know, and to digest, master, rule, and use its knowledge, to give it power over its own faculties, application, flexibility, method, critical exactness, sagacity, resource, address, eloquent expression, is an object as intelligible (for here we are inquiring, not what the object of a Liberal Education is worth, nor what use the Church makes of it, but what it is in itself), I say, an object as intelligible as the cultivation of virtue, while, at the same time, it is absolutely distinct from it.

10

This indeed is but a temporal object, and a transitory possession: but so are other things in themselves which we make much of and pursue.

The moralist will tell us that man, in all his functions, is but a flower which blossoms and fades, except so far as a higher principle breathes upon him, and makes him and what he is immortal. Body and mind are carried on into an eternal state of being by the gifts of Divine Munificence; but at first they do but fail in a failing world; and if the powers of intellect decay, the powers of the body have decayed before them, and, as an Hospital or an Almshouse, though its end be ephemeral, may be sanctified to the service of religion, so surely may a University, even were it nothing more than I have as yet described it. We attain to heaven by using this world well, though it is to pass away; we perfect our nature, not by undoing it, but by adding to it what it more than nature, and directing it towards aims higher than its own.

from Discourse VI

KNOWLEDGE VIEWED IN RELATION TO LEARNING

1

It were well if the English, like the Greek language, possessed some definite word to express, simply and generally, intellectual proficiency or perfection, such as "health," as used with reference to the animal frame, and "virtue," with reference to our moral nature. . . .

In default of a recognized term, I have called the perfection or virtue of the intellect by the name of philosophy, philosophical knowledge, enlargement of mind, or illumination; terms which are not uncommonly given to it by writers of this day; but, whatever name we bestow on it, it is, I believe, as a matter of history, the business of a University to make this intellectual culture its direct scope, or to employ itself in the education of the intellect,—just as the work of a Hospital lies in healing the sick or wounded, of a Riding or Fencing School, or of a Gymnasium, in exercising the limbs, of an Almshouse, in aiding and solacing the old, of an Orphanage, in protecting innocence, of a Penitentiary, in restoring the guilty. I say, a University, taken in its bare idea, and before we view it as an instrument of the Church, has this object and this mission; it contemplates neither moral impression nor mechanical production; it professes to exercise the mind neither in art[29] nor in duty; its function is intellectual culture; here it may leave its scholars, and it has done its work when it has done as much as this. It educates the intellect to reason well in all matters, to reach out towards truth, and to grasp it.

2

. . . I have then to investigate, in the Discourses which follow, those qualities and characteristics of the intellect in which its cultivation issues or rather consists; and, with a view of assisting myself in this undertaking, I shall recur to certain questions which have already been touched upon. These questions are three: viz. the relation of intellectual culture, first, to *mere* knowledge; secondly, to *professional* knowledge; and thirdly, to *religious* knowledge. In other words, are *acquirements* and *attainments* the scope of a University Education? or *expertness in particular arts and pursuits?* or *moral and religious proficiency?* or something besides these three? These questions I shall examine in succession, with the purpose I have mentioned; and I hope to be excused, if, in this anxious undertaking, I am led to repeat what, either in these Discourses or elsewhere, I have already put upon paper. And first, of *Mere Knowledge,* or Learning, and its connexion with intellectual illumination or Philosophy.

3

I suppose the *primâ-facie* view which the public at large would take of a University, considering it as a place of Education, is nothing more or less than a place for acquiring a great deal of knowledge on a great many subjects. Memory is one of the first developed of the mental faculties; a boy's business when he goes to school is to learn, that is, to store up things in his memory. For some years his intellect is little more than an instrument for taking in facts, or a receptacle for storing them; he welcomes them as fast as they come to him; he lives on what is without; he has his eyes ever about him; he has a lively susceptibility of impressions; he imbibes information of every kind; and little does he make his own in a true sense of the word, living rather upon his neighbours all around him. He has opinions, religious, political, and literary, and, for a boy, is very positive in them and sure about them; but he gets them from his schoolfellows, or his masters, or his parents, as the case may be. Such as he is in his other relations, such also is he in his school exercises; his mind is observant, sharp, ready, retentive; he is almost passive in the acquisition of knowledge. I say this in no disparagement of the idea of a clever boy. Geography, chronology, history, language, natural history, he heaps up the matter of these studies as treasures for a future day. It is the seven years of plenty with him: he gathers in by handfuls, like the Egyptians, without counting;[30] and though, as time goes on, there is exercise for his argumentative powers in the Elements of Mathematics, and for his taste in the Poets and Orators, still, while at school, or at least, till quite the last years of his time, he acquires, and little more; and when he is leaving for the University, he is mainly the creature of foreign influences and circumstances, and made up of accidents, homogeneous or not, as the case may be. Moreover, the moral habits, which are a boy's praise, encourage and assist this result; that is, diligence, assiduity, regularity, despatch, persevering application; for these are the direct conditions of acquisition, and naturally lead to it. Acquirements, again, are emphatically producible, and at a moment; they are a something to show, both for master and scholar; an audience, even though ignorant themselves of the subjects of an examination, can comprehend when questions are answered and when they are not. Here again is a reason why mental culture is in the minds of men identified with the acquisition of knowledge.

The same notion possesses the public mind, when it passes on from the thought of a school to that of a University: and with the best of reasons so far as this, that there is no true culture without acquirements, and that philosophy presupposes knowledge. It requires a great deal of reading, or a wide range of information, to warrant us in putting forth our opinions on any serious subject; and without such learning the most original mind may be able indeed to dazzle, to

---

[29] Used here in the sense of a mechanical or vocational skill.

[30] Under the direction of Joseph in the seven years of plenty as provision against the seven years of famine that were to follow (Genesis 41:49).

amuse, to refute, to perplex, but not to come to any useful result or any trustworthy conclusion. There are indeed persons who profess a different view of the matter, and even act upon it. Every now and then you will find a person of vigorous or fertile mind, who relies upon his own resources, despises all former authors, and gives the world, with the utmost fearlessness, his views upon religion, or history, or any other popular subject. And his works may sell for a while; he may get a name in his day; but this will be all. His readers are sure to find in the long run that his doctrines are mere theories, and not the expression of facts, that they are chaff instead of bread, and then his popularity drops as suddenly as it rose.

Knowledge, then, is the indispensable condition of expansion of mind, and the instrument of attaining to it; this cannot be denied, it is ever to be insisted on; I begin with it as a first principle; however, the very truth of it carries men too far, and confirms to them the notion that it is the whole of the matter. A narrow mind is thought to be that which contains little knowledge; and an enlarged mind, that which holds a great deal; and what seems to put the matter beyond dispute is, the fact of the great number of studies which are pursued in a University, by its very profession. Lectures are given on every kind of subject; examinations are held; prizes awarded. There are moral, metaphysical, physical Professors; Professors of languages, of history, of mathematics, of experimental science. Lists of questions are published, wonderful for their range and depth, variety and difficulty; treatises are written, which carry upon their very face the evidence of extensive reading or multifarious information; what then is wanting for mental culture to a person of large reading and scientific attainments? what is grasp of mind but acquirement? where shall philosophical repose be found, but in the consciousness and enjoyment of large intellectual possessions?

And yet this notion is, I conceive, a mistake, and my present business is to show that it is one, and that the end of a Liberal Education is not mere knowledge, or knowledge considered in its *matter;* and I shall best attain my object, by actually setting down some cases, which will be generally granted to be instances of the process of enlightenment or enlargement of mind, and others which are not, and thus, by the comparison, you will be able to judge for yourselves, Gentlemen, whether Knowledge, that is, acquirement, is after all the real principle of the enlargement, or whether that principle is not rather something beyond it.

4

For instance,[31] let a person, whose experience has hitherto been confined to the more calm and unpretending scenery of these islands, whether here or in England, go for the first time into parts where physical nature puts on her wilder and more awful forms, whether at home or abroad, as into mountainous districts; or let one, who has ever lived in a quiet village, go for the first time to a great metropolis,—then I suppose he will have a sensation which perhaps he never had before. He has a feeling not in addition or increase of former feelings, but of something different in its nature. He will perhaps be borne forward, and find for a time that he has lost his bearings. He has made a certain progress, and he has a consciousness of mental enlargement; he does not stand where he did, he has a new centre, and a range of thoughts to which he was before a stranger.

Again, the view of the heavens which the telescope opens upon us, if allowed to fill and possess the mind, may almost whirl it round and make it dizzy. It brings in a flood of ideas, and is rightly called an intellectual enlargement, whatever is meant by the term.

And so again, the sight of beasts of prey and other foreign animals, their strangeness, the originality (if I may use the term) of their forms and gestures and habits and their variety and independence of each other, throw us out of ourselves into another creation, and as if under another Creator, if I may so express the temptation which may come on the mind. We seem to have new faculties, or a new exercise for our faculties, by this addition to our knowledge; like a prisoner, who, having been accustomed to wear manacles or fetters, suddenly finds his arms and legs free.

31 "The pages which follow are taken almost *verbatim* from the author's 14th (Oxford) University Sermon, which, at the time of writing this Discourse, he did not expect ever to reprint." (Newman)

Hence Physical Science generally, in all its departments, as bringing before us the exuberant riches and resources, yet the orderly course, of the Universe, elevates and excites the student, and at first, I may say, almost takes away his breath, while in time it exercises a tranquilizing influence upon him.

Again, the study of history is said to enlarge and enlighten the mind, and why? because, as I conceive, it gives it a power of judging of passing events, and of all events, and a conscious superiority over them, which before it did not possess.

And in like manner, what is called seeing the world, entering into active life, going into society, travelling, gaining acquaintance with the various classes of the community, coming into contact with the principles and modes of thought of various parties, interests, and races, their views, aims, habits and manners, their religious creeds and forms of worship,—gaining experience how various yet how alike men are, how low-minded, how bad, how opposed, yet how confident in their opinions; all this exerts a perceptible influence upon the mind, which it is impossible to mistake, be it good or be it bad, and is popularly called its enlargement.

And then again, the first time the mind comes across the arguments and speculations of unbelievers, and feels what a novel light they cast upon what he has hitherto accounted sacred; and still more, if it gives in to them and embraces them, and throws off as so much prejudice what it has hitherto held, and, as if waking from a dream, begins to realize to its imagination that there is now no such thing as law and the transgression of law, that sin is a phantom, and punishment a bugbear, that it is free to sin, free to enjoy the world and the flesh; and still further, when it does enjoy them, and reflects that it may think and hold just what it will, that "the world is all before it where to choose," and what system to build up as its own private persuasion; when this torrent of wilful thoughts rushes over and inundates it, who will deny that the fruit of the tree of knowledge, or what the mind takes for knowledge, has made it one of the gods, with a sense of expansion and elevation, —an intoxication in reality, still, so far as the subjective state of the mind goes, an illumination? Hence the fanaticism of individuals or nations, who suddenly cast off their Maker. Their eyes are opened; and, like the judgment-stricken king in the Tragedy,[32] they see two suns, and a magic universe, out of which they look back upon their former state of faith and innocence with a sort of contempt and indignation, as if they were then but fools, and the dupes of imposture.

On the other hand, Religion has its own enlargement, and an enlargement, not of tumult, but of peace. It is often remarked of uneducated persons, who have hitherto thought little of the unseen world, that, on their turning to God, looking into themselves, regulating their hearts, reforming their conduct, and meditating on death and judgment, heaven and hell, they seem to become, in point of intellect, different beings from what they were. Before, they took things as they came, and thought no more of one thing than another. But now every event has a meaning; they have their own estimate of whatever happens to them; they are mindful of times and seasons, and compare the present with the past; and the world, no longer dull, monotonous, unprofitable, and hopeless, is a various and complicated drama, with parts and an object, and an awful moral.

5

Now from these instances, to which many more might be added, it is plain, first, that the communication of knowledge certainly is either a condition or the means of that sense of enlargement or enlightenment, of which at this day we hear so much in certain quarters: this cannot be denied; but next, it is equally plain, that such communication is not the whole of the process. The enlargement consists, not merely in the passive reception into the mind of a number of ideas hitherto unknown to it, but in the mind's energetic and simultaneous action upon and towards and among those new ideas, which are rushing in upon it. It is the action of a formative power, reducing to order and meaning the matter of our acquirements; it is a making the objects of our knowledge subjectively our own, or, to use a familiar word, it is a digestion of what we receive, into the substance of our previous state of thought; and without this no enlargement is

---

32 The king of Thebes in the *Bacchae* of Euripides.

said to follow. There is no enlargement, unless there be a comparison of ideas one with another, as they come before the mind, and a systematizing of them. We feel our minds to be growing and expanding *then,* when we not only learn, but refer what we learn to what we know already. It is not the mere addition to our knowledge that is the illumination; but the locomotion, the movement onwards, of that mental centre, to which both what we know, and what we are learning, the accumulating mass of our acquirements, gravitates. And therefore a truly great intellect, and recognized to be such by the common opinion of mankind, such as the intellect of Aristotle, or of St. Thomas, or of Newton, or of Goethe, (I purposely take instances within and without the Catholic pale, when I would speak of the intellect as such,) is one which takes a connected view of old and new, past and present, far and near, and which has an insight into the influence of all these one on another; without which there is no whole, and no centre. It possesses the knowledge, not only of things, but also of their mutual and true relations; knowledge, not merely considered as acquirement, but as philosophy.

Accordingly, when this analytical, distributive, harmonizing process is away, the mind experiences no enlargement, and is not reckoned as enlightened or comprehensive, whatever it may add to its knowledge. For instance, a great memory, as I have already said, does not make a philosopher, any more than a dictionary can be called a grammar. There are men who embrace in their minds a vast multitude of ideas, but with little sensibility about their real relations towards each other. These may be antiquarians, annalists, naturalists; they may be learned in the law; they may be versed in statistics; they are most useful in their own place; I should shrink from speaking disrespectfully of them; still, there is nothing in such attainments to guarantee the absence of narrowness of mind. If they are nothing more than well-read men, or men of information, they have not what specially deserves the name of culture of mind, or fulfils the type of Liberal Education.

In like manner, we sometimes fall in with persons who have seen much of the world, and of the men who, in their day, have played a conspicuous part in it, but who generalize nothing, and have no observation, in the true sense of the word. They abound in information in detail, curious and entertaining, about men and things; and, having lived under the influence of no very clear or settled principles, religious or political, they speak of every one and every thing, only as so many phenomena, which are complete in themselves, and lead to nothing, not discussing them, or teaching any truth, or instructing the hearer, but simply talking. No one would say that these persons, well informed as they are, had attained to any great culture of intellect or to philosophy.

The case is the same still more strikingly where the persons in question are beyond dispute men of inferior powers and deficient education. Perhaps they have been much in foreign countries, and they receive, in a passive, otiose, unfruitful way, the various facts which are forced upon them there. Seafaring men, for example, range from one end of the earth to the other; but the multiplicity of external objects, which they have encountered, forms no symmetrical and consistent picture upon their imagination; they see the tapestry of human life, as it were, on the wrong side, and it tells no story. They sleep, and they rise up, and they find themselves, now in Europe, now in Asia; they see visions of great cities and wild regions; they are in the marts of commerce, or amid the islands of the South; they gaze on Pompey's Pillar,[33] or on the Andes; and nothing which meets them carries them forward or backward, to any idea beyond itself. Nothing has a drift or relation; nothing has a history or a promise. Every thing stands by itself, and comes and goes in its turn, like the shifting scenes of a show, which leave the spectator where he was. Perhaps you are near such a man on a particular occasion, and expect him to be shocked or perplexed at something which occurs; but one thing is much the same to him as another, or, if he is perplexed, it is as not knowing what to say, whether it is right to admire, or to ridicule, or to disapprove, while conscious that some expression of opinion is expected from him; for in fact he has no standard of judgment at all, and no landmarks to guide him to a conclusion. Such is mere acquisition, and, I repeat, no one would dream of calling it philosophy.

---

33 At Alexandria.

6

Instances, such as these, confirm, by the contrast, the conclusion I have already drawn from those which preceded them. That only is true enlargement of mind which is the power of viewing many things at once as one whole, of referring them severally to their true place in the universal system, of understanding their respective values, and determining their mutual dependence. Thus is that form of Universal Knowledge, of which I have on a former occasion spoken, set up in the individual intellect, and constitutes its perfection. Possessed of this real illumination, the mind never views any part of the extended subject-matter of Knowledge without recollecting that it is but a part, or without the associations which spring from this recollection. It makes every thing in some sort lead to every thing else; it would communicate the image of the whole to every separate portion, till that whole becomes in imagination like a spirit, every where pervading and penetrating its component parts, and giving them one definite meaning. Just as our bodily organs, when mentioned, recall their function in the body, as the word "creation" suggests the Creator, and "subjects" a sovereign, so, in the mind of the Philosopher, as we are abstractedly conceiving of him, the elements of the physical and moral world, sciences, arts, pursuits, ranks, offices, events, opinions, individualities, are all viewed as one, with correlative functions and as gradually by successive combinations converging, one and all, to the true centre.

To have even a portion of this illuminative reason and true philosophy is the highest state to which nature can aspire, in the way of intellect; it puts the mind above the influences of chance and necessity, above anxiety, suspense, unsettlement, and superstition, which is the lot of the many. Men, whose minds are possessed with some one object, take exaggerated views of its importance, are feverish in the pursuit of it, make it the measure of things which are utterly foreign to it, and are startled and despond if it happens to fail them. They are ever in alarm or in transport. Those, on the other hand, who have no object or principle whatever to hold by, lose their way, every step they take. They are thrown out, and do not know what to think or say, at every fresh juncture; they have no view

of persons, or occurrences, or facts, which come suddenly upon them, and they hang upon the opinion of others, for want of internal resources. But the intellect, which has been disciplined to the perfection of its powers, which knows, and thinks while it knows, which has learned to leaven the dense mass of facts and events with the elastic force of reason, such an intellect cannot be partial, cannot be exclusive, cannot be impetuous, cannot be at a loss, cannot but be patient, collected, and majestically calm, because it discerns the end in every beginning, the origin in every end, the law in every interruption, the limit in each delay; because it ever knows where it stands, and how its path lies from one point to another. It is the τετράγωνος[34] of the Peripatetic,[35] and has the "nil admirari" of the Stoic,[36]—

Felix qui potuit rerum cognoscere causas,
Atque metus omnes, inexorabile fatum
Subjecit pedibus, strepitumque Acherontis avari.[37]

There are men who, when in difficulties, originate at the moment vast ideas or dazzling projects; who, under the influence of excitement, are able to cast a light, almost as if from inspiration, on a subject or course of action which comes before them; who have a sudden presence of mind equal to any emergency, rising with the occasion, and an undaunted magnanimous bearing, and an energy and keenness which is but made intense by opposition. This is genius, this is heroism; it is the exhibition of a natural gift, which no culture can teach, at which no Institution can aim; here, on the contrary, we are concerned, not with mere nature, but with training and teaching. That perfection of the Intellect, which is the result of Education, and its *beau idéal*, to be imparted to individuals in their respective measures, is the clear, calm, accurate vision and comprehension of all things, as far as the finite mind can embrace them, each in its

---

34 Square or symbol of perfect development.
35 The disciples of Aristotle were called Peripatetics because of the master's habit of walking about as he taught them.
36 The phrase, meaning "be moved by nothing," is often cited as the keystone of the Stoic philosophy, which taught indifference to both pleasure and pain.
37 From Vergil's *Georgics*, II, 490–93: "Happy is he who could know the causes of things and put under his feet all fears and inexorable fate and the roar of greedy Acheron."

place, and with its own characteristics upon it. It is almost prophetic from its knowledge of history; it is almost heart-searching from its knowledge of human nature; it has almost supernatural charity from its freedom from littleness and prejudice; it has almost the repose of faith, because nothing can startle it; it has almost the beauty and harmony of heavenly contemplation, so intimate is it with the eternal order of things and the music of the spheres.

7

And now, if I may take for granted that the true and adequate end of intellectual training and of a University is not Learning or Acquirement, but rather, is Thought or Reason exercised upon Knowledge, or what may be called Philosophy, I shall be in a position to explain the various mistakes which at the present day beset the subject of University Education.

I say then, if we would improve the intellect, first of all, we must ascend; we cannot gain real knowledge on a level; we must generalize, we must reduce to method, we must have a grasp of principles, and group and shape our acquisitions by means of them. It matters not whether our field of operation be wide or limited; in every case, to command it, is to mount above it. Who has not felt the irritation of mind and impatience created by a deep, rich country, visited for the first time, with winding lanes, and high hedges, and green steeps, and tangled woods, and every thing smiling indeed, but in a maze? The same feeling comes upon us in a strange city, when we have no map of its streets. Hence you hear of practised travellers, when they first come into a place, mounting some high hill or church tower, by way of reconnoitring its neighbourhood. In like manner, you must be above your knowledge, not under it, or it will oppress you; and the more you have of it, the greater will be the load. The learning of a Salmasius[38] or a Burman,[39] unless you are its master, will be your tyrant. "Imperat aut servit";[40] if you can wield it with a strong arm, it is a great weapon; otherwise,

Vis consili expers
Mole ruit suâ.[41]

You will be overwhelmed, like Tarpeia,[42] by the heavy wealth which you have exacted from tributary generations. . . .

8

. . . I will tell you, Gentlemen, what has been the practical error of the last twenty years—not to load the memory of the student with a mass of undigested knowledge, but to force upon him so much that he has rejected all. It has been the error of distracting and enfeebling the mind by an unmeaning profusion of subjects; of implying that a smattering in a dozen branches of study is not shallowness, which it really is, but enlargement, which it is not; of considering an acquaintance with the learned names of things and persons, and the possession of clever duodecimos, and attendance on eloquent lecturers, and membership with scientific institutions, and the sight of the experiments of a platform and the specimens of a museum, that all this was not dissipation of mind, but progress. All things now are to be learned at once, not first one thing, then another, not one well, but many badly. Learning is to be without exertion, without attention, without toil; without grounding, without advance, without finishing. There is to be nothing individual in it; and this, forsooth, is the wonder of the age. What the steam engine does with matter, the printing press is to do with mind; it is to act mechanically, and the population is to be passively, almost unconsciously enlightened, by the mere multiplication and dissemination of volumes. Whether it be the school boy, or the school girl, or the youth at college, or the mechanic in the town, or the politician in the senate, all have been the victims in one way or other of this most preposterous and pernicious of delusions. Wise men have lifted up their voices in vain; and at length, lest their own institutions should be outshone and should disappear in the folly of the hour, they have been obliged, as far as they could with a good conscience, to humour a spirit which they could not withstand, and

---

38 Very learned French scholar of the first half of the seventeenth century.
39 Either one of two eminent Dutch classical scholars having identical names in the seventeenth and eighteenth centuries.
40 "It rules or it serves."

41 "Strength deprived of wisdom is destroyed by its own weight" (Horace, *Odes,* III, iv, 65).
42 A Roman maiden who betrayed her city to the Sabines and was then crushed by the invaders under their shields.

make temporizing concessions at which they could not but inwardly smile.

It must not be supposed that, because I so speak, therefore I have some sort of fear of the education of the people: on the contrary, the more education they have, the better, so that it is really education. Nor am I an enemy to the cheap publication of scientific and literary works, which is now in vogue: on the contrary, I consider it a great advantage, convenience, and gain; that is, to those to whom education has given a capacity for using them. Further, I consider such innocent recreations as science and literature are able to furnish will be a very fit occupation of the thoughts and the leisure of young persons, and may be made the means of keeping them from bad employments and bad companions. Moreover, as to that superficial acquaintance with chemistry, and geology, and astronomy, and political economy, and modern history, and biography, and other branches of knowledge, which periodical literature and occasional lectures and scientific institutions diffuse through the community, I think it a graceful accomplishment, and a suitable, nay, in this day a necessary accomplishment, in the case of educated men. Nor, lastly, am I disparaging or discouraging the thorough acquisition of any one of these studies, or denying that, as far as it goes, such thorough acquisition is a real education of the mind. All I say is, call things by their right names, and do not confuse together ideas which are essentially different. A thorough knowledge of one science and a superficial acquaintance with many, are not the same thing; a smattering of a hundred things or a memory for detail, is not a philosophical or comprehensive view. Recreations are not education; accomplishments are not education. Do not say, the people must be educated, when, after all, you only mean, amused, refreshed, soothed, put into good spirits and good humour, or kept from vicious excesses. I do not say that such amusements, such occupations of mind, are not a great gain; but they are not education. You may as well call drawing and fencing education, as a general knowledge of botany or conchology. Stuffing birds or playing stringed instruments is an elegant pastime, and a resource to the idle, but it is not education; it does not form or cultivate the intellect. Education is a high word: it is the preparation for knowledge, and it is the imparting of knowledge in propor-

tion to that preparation. We require intellectual eyes to know withal, as bodily eyes for sight. We need both objects and organs intellectual; we cannot gain them without setting about it; we cannot gain them in our sleep, or by hap-hazard. The best telescope does not dispense with eyes; the printing press or the lecture room will assist us greatly, but we must be true to ourselves, we must be parties in the work. A University is, according to the usual designation, an Alma Mater, knowing her children one by one, not a foundry, or a mint, or a treadmill.

9

I protest to you, Gentlemen, that if I had to choose between a so-called University, which dispensed with residence and tutorial superintendence, and gave its degrees to any person who passed an examination in a wide range of subjects, and a University which had no professors or examinations at all, but merely brought a number of young men together for three or four years, and then sent them away as the University of Oxford is said to have done some sixty years since, if I were asked which of these two methods was the better discipline of the intellect,—mind, I do not say which is *morally* the better, for it is plain that compulsory study must be a good and idleness an intolerable mischief,—but if I must determine which of the two courses was the more successful in training, moulding, enlarging the mind, which sent out men the more fitted for their secular duties, which produced better public men, men of the world, men whose names would descend to posterity, I have no hesitation in giving the preference to that University which did nothing, over that which exacted of its members an acquaintance with every science under the sun. And, paradox as this may seem, still if results be the test of systems, the influence of the public schools and colleges of England, in the course of the last century, at least will bear out one side of the contrast as I have drawn it. What would come, on the other hand, of the ideal systems of education which have fascinated the imagination of this age, could they ever take effect, and whether they would not produce a generation frivolous, narrow-minded, and resourceless, intellectually considered, is a fair subject for debate; but so far is certain, that the Universities and scholastic establishments, to which I refer, and which did little more than bring together first boys and then youths in large numbers, these institutions, with miserable deformities on the side of morals, with a hollow profession of Christianity, and a heathen code of ethics,—I say, at least they can boast of a succession of heroes and statesmen, of literary men and philosophers, of men conspicuous for great natural virtues, for habits of business, for knowledge of life, for practical judgment, for cultivated tastes, for accomplishments, who have made England what it is,—able to subdue the earth, able to domineer over Catholics.

How is this to be explained? I suppose as follows: When a multitude of young men, keen, open-hearted, sympathetic, and observant, as young men are, come together and freely mix with each other, they are sure to learn one from another, even if there be no one to teach them; the conversation of all is a series of lectures to each, and they gain for themselves new ideas and views, fresh matter of thought, and distinct principles for judging and acting, day by day. An infant has to learn the meaning of the information which its senses convey to it, and this seems to be its employment. It fancies all that the eye presents to it to be close to it, till it actually learns the contrary, and thus by practice does it ascertain the relations and uses of those first elements of knowledge which are necessary for its animal existence. A parallel teaching is necessary for our social being, and it is secured by a large school or a college; and this effect may be fairly called in its own department an enlargement of mind. It is seeing the world on a small field with little trouble; for the pupils or students come from very different places, and with widely different notions, and there is much to generalize, much to adjust, much to eliminate, there are inter-relations to be defined, and conventional rules to be established, in the process, by which the whole assemblage is moulded together, and gains one tone and one character.

Let it be clearly understood, I repeat it, that I am not taking into account moral or religious considerations; I am but saying that that youthful community will constitute a whole, it will embody a specific idea, it will represent a doctrine, it will administer a code of conduct, and it will furnish principles of thought and action. It

will give birth to a living teaching, which in course of time will take the shape of a self-perpetuating tradition, or a *genius loci*,[43] as it is sometimes called; which haunts the home where it has been born, and which imbues and forms, more or less, and one by one, every individual who is successively brought under its shadow. Thus it is that, independent of direct instruction on the part of Superiors, there is a sort of self-education in the academic institutions of Protestant England; a characteristic tone of thought, a recognized standard of judgment is found in them, which, as developed in the individual who is submitted to it, becomes a twofold source of strength to him, both from the distinct stamp it impresses on his mind, and from the bond of union which it creates between him and others,—effects which are shared by the authorities of the place, for they themselves have been educated in it, and at all times are exposed to the influence of its ethical atmosphere. Here then is a real teaching, whatever be its standards and principles, true or false; and it at least tends towards cultivation of the intellect; it at least recognizes that knowledge is something more than a sort of passive reception of scraps and details; it is a something, and it does a something, which never will issue from the most strenuous efforts of a set of teachers, with no mutual sympathies and no inter-communion, of a set of examiners with no opinions which they dare profess, and with no common principles, who are teaching or questioning a set of youths who do not know them, and do not know each other, on a large number of subjects, different in kind, and connected by no wide philosophy, three times a week, or three times a year, or once in three years, in chill lecture-rooms or on a pompous anniversary.

10

Nay, self-education in any shape, in the most restricted sense, is preferable to a system of teaching which, professing so much, really does so little for the mind. Shut your College gates against the votary of knowledge, throw him back upon the searchings and the efforts of his own mind; he will gain by being spared an entrance into your Babel. Few, indeed, there are who can

---

43 Spirit or atmosphere of the place.

dispense with the stimulus and support of instructors, or will do any thing at all, if left to themselves. And fewer still (though such great minds are to be found), who will not, from such unassisted attempts, contract a self-reliance and a self-esteem, which are not only moral evils, but serious hindrances to the attainment of truth. And next to none, perhaps, or none, who will not be reminded from time to time of the disadvantage under which they lie, by their imperfect grounding, by the breaks, deficiencies, and irregularities of their knowledge, by the eccentricity of opinion and the confusion of principle which they exhibit. They will be too often ignorant of what every one knows and takes for granted, of that multitude of small truths which fall upon the mind like dust, impalpable and ever accumulating; they may be unable to converse, they may argue perversely, they may pride themselves on their worst paradoxes or their grossest truisms, they may be full of their own mode of viewing things, unwilling to be put out of their way, slow to enter into the minds of others;—but, with these and whatever other liabilities upon their heads, they are likely to have more thought, more mind, more philosophy, more true enlargement, than those earnest but ill-used persons, who are forced to load their minds with a score of subjects against an examination, who have too much on their hands to indulge themselves in thinking or investigation, who devour premise and conclusion together with indiscriminate greediness, who hold whole sciences on faith, and commit demonstrations to memory, and who too often, as might be expected, when their period of education is passed, throw up all they have learned in disgust, having gained nothing really by their anxious labours, except perhaps the habit of application.

Yet such is the better specimen of the fruit of that ambitious system which has of late years been making way among us: for its result on ordinary minds, and on the common run of students, is less satisfactory still; they leave their place of education simply dissipated and relaxed by the multiplicity of subjects, which they have never really mastered, and so shallow as not even to know their shallowness. How much better, I say, is it for the active and thoughtful intellect, where such is to be found, to eschew the College and the University altogether, than to submit to drudgery so ignoble, a mockery so contumelious! How much more profitable for the independent mind, after the mere rudiments of education, to range through a library at random, taking down books as they meet him, and pursuing the trains of thought which his mother wit suggests! How much healthier to wander into the fields, and there with the exiled Prince to find "tongues in the trees, books in the running brooks"![44] How much more genuine an education is that of the poor boy in the Poem[45]—a Poem, whether in conception or in execution, one of the most touching in our language—who, not in the wide world, but ranging day by day around his widowed mother's home, "a dexterous gleaner" in a narrow field, and with only such slender outfit

> *as the village school and books a few Supplied,*

contrived from the beach, and the quay, and the fisher's boat, and the inn's fireside, and the tradesman's shop, and the shepherd's walk, and the smuggler's hut, and the mossy moor, and the screaming gulls, and the restless waves, to fashion for himself a philosophy and a poetry of his own!

But in a large subject, I am exceeding my necessary limits. Gentlemen, I must conclude abruptly; and postpone any summing up of my argument, should that be necessary, to another day.

from Discourse VII

KNOWLEDGE VIEWED IN RELATION TO PROFESSIONAL SKILL

1

I have been insisting, in my two preceding Discourses, first, on the cultivation of the intellect, as an end which may reasonably be pursued for

---

44 Shakespeare's *As You Like It,* II, 1, 16.
45 "Crabbe's *Tales of the Hall.* This Poem, let me say, I read on its first publication, above thirty years ago, with extreme delight, and have never lost my love of it; and on taking it up lately, found I was even more touched by it than heretofore. A work which can please in youth and age, seems to fulfil (in logical language) the *accidental definition* of a Classic. [A further course of twenty years has past, and I bear the same witness in favour of this Poem.]" (Newman)

its own sake; and next, on the nature of that cultivation, or what that cultivation consists in. Truth of whatever kind is the proper object of the intellect; its cultivation then lies in fitting it to apprehend and contemplate truth. Now the intellect in its present state, with exceptions which need not here be specified, does not discern truth intuitively, or as a whole. We know, not by a direct and simple vision, not at a glance, but, as it were, by piecemeal and accumulation, by a mental process, by going round an object, by the comparison, the combination, the mutual correction, the continual adaptation, of many partial notions, by the employment, concentration, and joint action of many faculties and exercises of mind. Such a union and concert of the intellectual powers, such an enlargement and development, such a comprehensiveness, is necessarily a matter of training. And again, such a training is a matter of rule; it is not mere application, however exemplary, which introduces the mind to truth, nor the reading many books, nor the getting up many subjects, nor the witnessing many experiments, nor the attending many lectures. All this is short of enough; a man may have done it all, yet be lingering in the vestibule of knowledge:—he may not realize what his mouth utters; he may not see with his mental eye what confronts him; he may have no grasp of things as they are; or at least he may have no power at all of advancing one step forward of himself, in consequence of what he has already acquired, no power of discriminating between truth and falsehood, of sifting out the grains of truth from the mass, of arranging things according to their real value, and, if I may use the phrase, of building up ideas. Such a power is the result of a scientific formation of mind; it is an acquired faculty of judgment, of clear-sightedness, of sagacity, of wisdom, of philosophical reach of mind, and of intellectual self-possession and repose,—qualities which do not come of mere acquirement. The bodily eye, the organ for apprehending material objects, is provided by nature; the eye of the mind, of which the object is truth, is the work of discipline and habit.

This process of training, by which the intellect, instead of being formed or sacrificed to some particular or accidental purpose, some specific trade or profession, or study or science, is disciplined for its own sake, for the perception of its own proper object, and for its own highest culture, is called Liberal Education; and though there is no one in whom it is carried as far as is conceivable, or whose intellect would be a pattern of what intellects should be made, yet there is scarcely any one but may gain an idea of what real training is, and at least look towards it, and make its true scope and result, not something else, his standard of excellence; and numbers there are who may submit themselves to it, and secure it to themselves in good measure. And to set forth the right standard, and to train according to it, and to help forward all students towards it according to their various capacities, this I conceive to be the business of a University.

2

Now this is what some great men are very slow to allow; they insist that Education should be confined to some particular and narrow end, and should issue in some definite work, which can be weighed and measured. They argue as if everything, as well as every person, had its price; and that where there has been a great outlay, they have a right to expect a return in kind. This they call making Education and Instruction "useful," and "Utility" becomes their watchword. With a fundamental principle of this nature, they very naturally go on to ask, what there is to show for the expense of a University; what is the real worth in the market of the article called "a Liberal Education," on the supposition that it does not teach us definitely how to advance our manufactures, or to improve our lands, or to better our civil economy; or again, if it does not at once make this man a lawyer, that an engineer, and that a surgeon; or at least if it does not lead to discoveries in chemistry, astronomy, geology, magnetism, and science of every kind.

This question, as might have been expected, has been keenly debated in the present age, and formed one main subject of the controversy, to which I referred in the Introduction to the present Discourses, as having been sustained in the first decade of this century by a celebrated Northern Review on the one hand, and defenders of the University of Oxford on the other.[46]

---

[46] The impractical nature of Oxford education was attacked in the *Edinburgh Review*, 1808–10. The University was defended in the first instance by its Professor of

Hardly had the authorities of that ancient seat of learning, waking from their long neglect, set on foot a plan for the education of the youth committed to them, than the representatives of science and literature in the city, which has sometimes been called the Northern Athens,[47] remonstrated, with their gravest arguments and their most brilliant satire, against the direction and shape which the reform was taking. Nothing would content them, but that the University should be set to rights on the basis of the philosophy of Utility; a philosophy, as they seem to have thought, which needed but to be proclaimed in order to be embraced. In truth, they were little aware of the depth and force of the principles on which the academical authorities were proceeding, and, this being so, it was not to be expected that they would be allowed to walk at leisure over the field of controversy which they had selected. Accordingly they were encountered in behalf of the University by two men of great name and influence in their day,[48] of very different minds, but united, as by Collegiate ties, so in the clear-sighted and large view which they took of the whole subject of Liberal Education; and the defence thus provided for the Oxford studies has kept its ground to this day. . . .

5

. . . Let us take "useful," as Locke[49] takes it, in its proper and popular sense, and then we enter upon a large field of thought, to which I cannot do justice in one Discourse, though to-day's is all the space that I can give to it. I say, let us take "useful" to mean, not what is simply good, but what *tends* to good, or is the *instrument* of good; and in this sense also, Gentlemen, I will show

you how a liberal education is truly and fully a useful, though it be not a professional, education. "Good" indeed means one thing, and "useful" means another; but I lay it down as a principle, which will save us a great deal of anxiety, that, though the useful is not always good, the good is always useful. Good is not only good, but reproductive of good; this is one of its attributes; nothing is excellent, beautiful, perfect, desirable for its own sake, but it overflows, and spreads the likeness of itself all around it. Good is prolific; it is not only good to the eye, but to the taste; it not only attracts us, but it communicates itself; it excites first our admiration and love, then our desire and our gratitude, and that, in proportion to its intenseness and fulness in particular instances. A great good will impart great good. If then the intellect is so excellent a portion of us, and its cultivation so excellent, it is not only beautiful, perfect, admirable, and noble in itself, but in a true and high sense it must be useful to the possessor and to all around him; not useful in any low, mechanical, mercantile sense, but as diffusing good, or as a blessing, or a gift, or power, or a treasure, first to the owner, then through him to the world. I say then, if a liberal education be good, it must necessarily be useful too.

6

You will see what I mean by the parallel of bodily health. Health is a good in itself, though nothing came of it, and is especially worth seeking and cherishing; yet, after all, the blessings which attend its presence are so great, while they are so close to it and so redound back upon it and encircle it, that we never think of it except as useful as well as good, and praise and prize it for what it does, as well as for what it is, though at the same time we cannot point out any definite and distinct work or production which it can be said to effect. And so as regards intellectual culture, I am far from denying utility in this large sense as the end of Education, when I lay it down, that the culture of the intellect is a good in itself and its own end: I do not exclude from the idea of intellectual culture what it cannot but be, from the very nature of things; I only deny that we must be able to point out, before we have any right to call it useful, some art, or business, or profession, or trade, or work, as resulting from

Poetry, Edward Copleston, followed by John Davison, Fellow of Oriel College. That the attack did, however, pave the way for certain needed reforms is pointed out by Newman in his "Note on Liberalism."

47 Edinburgh.   48 Copleston and Davison.

49 In the passage that has been omitted at the beginning of this section, Newman cites the celebrated seventeenth-century philosopher John Locke and his nineteenth-century disciples as "condemning the ordinary subjects in which boys are instructed at school, on the ground that they are not needed by them in after life." The authors of the articles in the *Edinburgh Review* (see note 46) are identified with Locke in asking the question which Newman here proposes to answer: "What other measure of dignity in intellectual labour is there but usefulness?"

it, and as its real and complete end. The parallel is exact:—As the body may be sacrificed to some manual or other toil, whether moderate or oppressive, so may the intellect be devoted to some specific profession; and I do not call *this* the culture of the intellect. Again, as some member or organ of the body may be inordinately used and developed, so may memory, or imagination, or the reasoning faculty; and *this* again is not intellectual culture. On the other hand, as the body may be tended, cherished, and exercised with a simple view to its general health, so may the intellect also be generally exercised in order to its perfect state; and this *is* its cultivation.

Again, as health ought to precede labour of the body, and as a man in health can do what an unhealthy man cannot do, and as of this health the properties are strength, energy, agility, graceful carriage and action, manual dexterity, and endurance of fatigue, so in like manner general culture of mind is the best aid to professional and scientific study, and educated men can do what illiterate cannot; and the man who has learned to think and to reason and to compare and to discriminate and to analyse, who has refined his taste, and formed his judgment, and sharpened his mental vision, will not indeed at once be a lawyer, or a pleader, or an orator, or a statesman, or a physician, or a good landlord, or a man of business, or a soldier, or an engineer, or a chemist, or a geologist, or an antiquarian, but he will be placed in that state of intellect in which he can take up any one of the sciences or callings I have referred to, or any other for which he has a taste or special talent, with an ease, a grace, a versatility, and a success, to which another is a stranger. In this sense then, and as yet I have said but a very few words on a large subject, mental culture is emphatically *useful*.

If then I am arguing, and shall argue, against Professional or Scientific knowledge as the sufficient end of a University Education, let me not be supposed, Gentlemen, to be disrespectful towards particular studies, or arts, or vocations, and those who are engaged in them. In saying that Law or Medicine is not the end of a University course, I do not mean to imply that the University does not teach Law or Medicine. What indeed can it teach at all, if it does not teach something particular? It teaches *all* knowledge by teaching all *branches* of knowledge, and in no other way. I do but say that there will be this distinction as regards a Professor of Law, or of Medicine, or of Geology, or of Political Economy, in a University and out of it, that out of a University he is in danger of being absorbed and narrowed by his pursuit, and of giving Lectures which are the Lectures of nothing more than a lawyer, physician, geologist, or political economist; whereas in a University he will just know where he and his science stand, he has come to it, as it were, from a height, he has taken a survey of all knowledge, he is kept from extravagance by the very rivalry of other studies, he has gained from them a special illumination and largeness of mind and freedom and self-possession, and he treats his own in consequence with a philosophy and a resource, which belongs not to the study itself, but to his liberal education.

This then is how I should solve the fallacy, for so I must call it, by which Locke and his disciples would frighten us from cultivating the intellect, under the notion that no education is useful which does not teach us some temporal calling, or some mechanical art, or some physical secret. I say that a cultivated intellect, because it is a good in itself, brings with it a power and a grace to every work and occupation which it undertakes, and enables us to be more useful, and to a greater number. There is a duty we owe to human society as such, to the state to which we belong, to the sphere in which we move, to the individuals towards whom we are variously related, and whom we successively encounter in life; and that philosophical or liberal education, as I have called it, which is the proper function of a University, if it refuses the foremost place to professional interests, does but postpone them to the formation of the citizen, and, while it subserves the larger interests of philanthropy, prepares also for the successful prosecution of those merely personal objects, which at first sight it seems to disparage. . . .

10

. . . Today I have confined myself to saying that that training of the intellect, which is best for the individual himself, best enables him to discharge his duties to society. The Philosopher, indeed, and the man of the world differ in their very notion, but the methods, by which they are respectively formed, are pretty much the same. The Philosopher has the same command of matters of thought, which the true citizen and gentleman has of matters of business and conduct. If then a practical end must be assigned to a University course, I say it is that of training good members of society. Its art is the art of social life, and its end is fitness for the world. It neither confines its views to particular professions on the one hand, nor creates heroes or inspires genius on the other. Works indeed of genius fall under no art; heroic minds come under no rule; a University is not a birthplace of poets or of immortal authors, of founders of schools, leaders of colonies, or conquerors of nations. It does not promise a generation of Aristotles or Newtons, of Napoleons or Washingtons, of Raphaels or Shakespeares, though such miracles of nature it has before now contained within its precincts. Nor is it content on the other hand with forming the critic or the experimentalist, the economist or the engineer, though such too it includes within its scope. But a University training is the great ordinary means to a great but ordinary end; it aims at raising the intellectual tone of society, at cultivating the public mind, at purifying the national taste, at supplying true principles to popular enthusiasm and fixed aims to popular aspiration, at giving enlargement and sobriety to the ideas of the age, at facilitating the exercise of political power, and refining the intercourse of private life. It is the education which gives a man a clear conscious view of his own opinions and judgments, a truth in developing them, an eloquence in expressing them, and a force in urging them. It teaches him to see things as they are, to go right to the point, to disentangle a skein of thought, to detect what is sophistical, and to discard what is irrelevant. It prepares him to fill any post with credit, and to master any subject with facility. It shows him how to accommodate himself to others, how to throw himself into their state of mind, how to bring before them his own, how to influence them, how to come to an understanding with them, how to bear with them. He is at home in any society, he has common ground with every class; he knows when to speak and when to be silent; he is able to converse, he is able to listen; he can ask a question pertinently, and gain a lesson seasonably, when he has nothing to impart himself; he is ever ready, yet never in the way; he is a pleasant companion, and a comrade you can depend upon; he knows when to be serious and when to trifle, and he has a sure tact which enables him to trifle with gracefulness and to be serious with effect. He has the repose of a mind which lives in itself, while it lives in the world, and which has resources for its happiness at home when it cannot go abroad. He has a gift which serves him in public, and supports him in retirement, without which good fortune is but vulgar, and with which failure and disappointment have a charm. The art which tends to make a man all this, is in the object which it pursues as useful as the art of wealth or the art of health, though it is less susceptible of method, and less tangible, less certain, less complete in its result.

John Stuart Mill

1806–1873

John Stuart Mill was born in 1806, the eldest son of James Mill, the ardent disciple and personal friend of Bentham. From his birth, therefore, Mill was dedicated to the cause of Utilitarianism. To that end he was subjected to a rigorous and thorough education, with his father as teacher. He began the study of Greek at the age of three and Latin at eight, covered much of ancient and modern history and philosophy before he was thirteen, did considerable work in physical science and mathematics, and then completed his education at sixteen with a close study of Bentham and the political economists whom Bentham admired, Adam Smith, Ricardo, and Malthus, all of whom advocated a policy of laissez faire. In method this education was almost entirely intellectual. Mill's mind was so well trained in logical analysis and his sensibility so well starved (literature and art were of small account in Utilitarian theory) that he became, as he confesses, a reasoning machine. As for religious and moral training, the former did not exist (James

Mill was an agnostic, and his son, therefore, was "one of the very few examples, in this country, of one who has, not thrown off religious belief, but never had it"); while the latter was Utilitarian in principle and method. Starting from the assumption that men are motivated almost entirely by the desire for pleasure. Bentham's plan was to make the social—that is, the moral—action pleasurable and the antisocial, antimoral action painful. This was already being done, to some extent, by law and public opinion, but far better results might be achieved by a rigorous discipline in early life. Whenever a child did a social act or adopted a social attitude, he was to be praised or given a tangible reward; whenever the reverse, he was to be blamed or punished. In this way unbreakable associations would supposedly be built up between social good and personal pleasure, between social harm and personal pain, until ultimately the grown man would "instinctively" do the unselfish thing, though his motivation, of course, would be selfish. This was the system tried out on young Mill; but with the additional twist of teaching him to associate his own greatest happiness with a life of positive service to society. By day he was to earn his living at the East India Company (where he started as a clerk in 1823 and rose to the second highest office before the company was taken over by the state in 1858 and Mill retired from business). But by night, and on weekends and vacations, he was to reform society on Utilitarian lines. He was to persuade people of the value of democracy, of an enlightened self-interest, of

John Stuart Mill (1806–1873). Mill began as a disciple of his father and Jeremy Bentham, but moved from strict Utilitarianism to a new, more idealistic political and economic liberalism. *The Granger Collection.*

an education wider than the classics which would include modern science and political economy, and all other projects which Bentham and James Mill were advocating (see selection from chapter 5 of the *Autobiography* for a summary). The main vehicle for this propaganda was the *Westminster Review,* founded in 1824 as an organ of Utilitarianism to rival the Tory *Quarterly Review* and the Whig *Edinburgh Review.*

Then in 1826, when Mill was twenty, occurred the event which changed his life and widened his thinking far beyond the bounds of Benthamism. This was a severe nervous breakdown which brought him to the edge of suicide. As A. W. Levi has suggested,[1] its real cause, unknown to Mill, probably lay in a repressed desire for the death of his father (which is the explanation for the sense of guilt Mill recognized but could not explain: see p. 570). This was the result partly of long years of fear and hatred, bred by James Mill's irritable temper and his severe discipline, unmitigated by any tenderness of feeling; and partly of the frustrated wish to escape from a parental domination so strong that the boy could not call his soul his own or stand on his own feet. No wonder, therefore, that his reading of Marmontel's passage relating the death of a father and the delighted assumption of his place by the son, started the process of recovery (Mill being able in this substituted form to rejoice in what he secretly and guiltily desired for himself, and thus to rid himself partially of his repressed emotions). But in that pre-Freudian age, he had no conscious inkling of the real facts. He, therefore, explained his breakdown in another way, of no significance as explanation, but of great significance for the development of his thought.

In the early weeks of depression, he had asked himself how he would feel if all his dreams for social improvement were fulfilled. The answer should have been "Superlatively happy," since he had been taught to identify his own happiness with that of society; but the answer was "Miserable." Plainly, something was wrong with his Benthamite education. In a highly important but difficult passage of chapter 5, he concludes that the theory of association was sound enough, but that the linkage between personal happiness and social good must have been too weak and too much exposed to dissolution. In all such associations there must be "something artificial and casual." Why *should* my own pleasure be tied up with social good rather than with personal achievement or anything else? The linkage is arbitrarily made by the parent; and in Mill's case had been made entirely by the instruments of "praise and blame, reward and punishment." But logical analysis, in which he had been almost exclusively trained, is exactly the faculty

---

[1] *Psycho-Analytical Review,* XXXII (1945), 88–101.

best calculated to "separate ideas which have only casually clung together." This, clearly, was what had happened. How could it have been prevented, and be prevented in the future? First, through making the associations stronger and more intense by presenting social action as something thrilling and exciting on its own account, a heroic crusade for humanity, and not merely something which can win the reformer praise and reward. Then his personal feelings would be far more intimately attached to humanitarian goals, and would less readily yield to analysis. And perhaps they would not yield at all if, second, analytical training were supplemented, and its dominance checked, by a training of the feelings and the imagination.

This rationale of his breakdown led Mills to two radical changes in his intellectual outlook. He decided that although happiness was the aim of life, it was only to be attained, as a by-product, from the pursuit of some other object, the happiness of others or the improvement of mankind, "followed not as a means, but as itself an ideal end." The other crucial change lay in the method by which he thought a good society might be attained. The great need, he decided, was not for better public opinion and better institutions, political and educational; it was for better men. Social progress depended at bottom on "the internal culture of the individual," of the whole individual, of his feelings no less than his intellect. And by the cultivation of the feelings, Mill meant the development of the moral as well as the aesthetic sensibility. What he wanted, therefore, and what almost all of his work was intended to forward, directly or indirectly, was self-development, sometimes meaning the development of one's individual personality (following one's own genius), sometimes meaning the development of all one's potentialities of mind and character and imagination.

It is obvious that these two changes in the foundations of Mill's philosophy, presently confirmed by his reading of Wordsworth, carried him at once outside Benthamism. Indeed, they were cardinal doctrines of the anti-Benthamite school of Wordsworth, Coleridge, and Carlyle, and of the German philosophers and poets they admired. Mill himself noticed the parallel of the first with Carlyle's "anti-self-consciousness theory" (see "The Everlasting Yea") and remarked of the second that the Germano-Coleridgean philosophers looked on "the culture of the inward man as the problem of problems" (cf. Carlyle's focus on individual regeneration, and his reference to external social reforms as Morison's pills). In short, Mill's breakdown proved a blessing in disguise. It widened his personal friendships to include not only Carlyle, with whom he was on intimate terms for many years, but also the Coleridgeans F. D. Maurice and John Sterling. It widened his reading to include

Kant, Fichte, Goethe, along with the French romantic historians Guizot and Michelet and the French philosophers Saint-Simon and Comte, who were challenging laissez-faire capitalism and propounding a theory of history in which organic periods of belief like the Middle Ages were succeeded by critical periods of doubt and transition like the present (see p. 577f. and the chapter from Mill's *Spirit of the Age*). It led to his conviction that no creed ever contained more than half of the truth and that the whole truth lay in a synthesis of opposing views (of which his own later work was to be an example). It inspired that fine, and very un-Victorian, plea "to consider one's opponents as one's allies, as people climbing the hill on the other side."

So long as Mill was a Benthamite, he had thought of liberty as something essentially negative. It meant freedom *from* interference; and the function of government was solely to maintain law and order. This was the cornerstone of early Victorian liberalism; it is perfectly exemplified in Macaulay's essay on Southey. But Mill now came to think of liberty as something positive. It meant freedom *to* develop and grow to one's full capacity. As a result, his evaluation of democracy changed and deepened (see his *Representative Government*, 1861). Once, under the influence of Bentham and James Mill, he had advocated democracy because only when govern-

Jeremy Bentham (1748–1832). Bentham's Utilitarian philosophy seemed to Mill wholly negative and left out the essential elements of freedom and individuality. *The Granger Collection.*

ment was in the hands of the people would it act for the greatest good of the people—and not for the greatest good of a monarch or an oligarchy. Now he saw that it was also valuable because, if the people had to manage their own government, national and local, they would gain in self-reliance and self-dependence: their active faculties would be developed and their social feelings stimulated. In theory the Benthamites would have accepted a dictator provided he governed for the greatest good of society. But not Mill, because from his point of view dictatorship, however benevolent, promotes dependence and passive obedience. It curbs the very development of individuality which democracy encourages. In one other particular Mill extended democratic theory. The Benthamites never went beyond manhood suffrage. Mill argued for universal suffrage on the grounds that women too must be represented if *their* greatest good was not to be overlooked, and that they too needed the stimulus of self-development that democracy provides.

If a free society is one in which all individuals have the maximum opportunity to grow to their full capacity, moral and intellectual, is this best attained under laissez-faire capitalism? Mill had thought so once, but when he saw the suffering of the laboring classes in the 1840s and read *Past and Present,* he became convinced that a majority of the nation had no such opportunity under the existing system. "The generality of labourers in this and most other countries," he wrote in his *Principles of Political Economy* (1848), "have as little choice of occupation or freedom of locomotion, are practically as dependent on fixed rules and on the will of others, as they could be on any system short of actual slavery." And then he spoke those astonishing words, at once the measure of his own capacity for growth and of his remarkable open-mindedness, "The restraints of Communism would be freedom in comparison with the present condition of the majority of the human race." So it was that Mill, the liberal, in the cause of gaining greater freedom for the have-nots, came to advocate a greater and greater extension of government action—high inheritance taxes, state control of public utilities, the nationalization of land—until finally he called himself a socialist and talked of a time when all men would be required to work and the division of labor would be made on an acknowledged principle of justice. But he saw the dilemma. If the creation of a society where all should have an equal freedom to grow meant the erection of an all-powerful state, the very freedom he was seeking would be destroyed, and individual liberty would be crushed beneath an omnipotent regimentation. How, he asked, can we unite "the greatest individual liberty of action, with a common ownership in the raw material of the globe, and an equal participation of all

in the benefits of combined labour"? That was "the social problem of the future"—and it still is.

This gives us the right perspective on the famous essay *On Liberty* (1859), which has been called the finest expression of Victorian, and modern, liberalism. If a large measure of social control was necessary to insure equal freedom for all, a set limit to political and social power was also necessary if individuality was to be preserved. That limit was self-protection. "The only purpose for which power can be rightfully exercised over any member of a civilised community, against his will, is to prevent harm to others. . . . Over himself, over his own body and mind, the individual is sovereign" (p. 588).

The danger at the time was not the tyranny of the state but that of public opinion—the tendency of Victorian society, as of all societies, "to fetter the development, and, if possible, prevent the formation, of any individuality not in harmony with its ways," by using the weapons of social stigma and ostracism. In chapter 2 Mill attacks the effort to curb freedom of thought and speech; in chapter 3 the effort to curb freedom of action and character. The former is a fine exposure of the Victorian attempt to suppress speculation for fear it might undermine religious belief and consequently moral order. As Mill points out, in an age terrified of skepticism it was wholly natural to defend traditional doctrines because they were useful, and to stigmatize anyone who questioned them in the name of truth. In such an atmosphere not only was speculation *dis*couraged, but hypocrisy was *en*couraged, outward conformity to the accepted beliefs but inward dissent. That important connection between Victorian antiintellectualism and Victorian hypocrisy is brought out in the last paragraphs of the selection. "The ban placed on all inquiry which does not end in the orthodox conclusions" thwarted the development of great minds either by turning them away from the pursuit of truth altogether, or by forcing them into timid and sophistical efforts to fit "their own conclusions to premises which they have internally renounced."

In chapter 3 it is the development of character, meaning both a person's individual bent and all his capacities, which Mill finds jeopardized, unconsciously by modern democratic civilization, and consciously by public opinion. He recognized—what is even truer today—that people were living more and more in the same world—hearing the same things, going to the same places, sharing the same ambitions—as class lines were breaking down and science was providing better and faster means of communication. As a result, one of the two prerequisites for promoting individuality, variety of situations, was steadily disappearing. This lay beyond control, but the other prerequisite, freedom from social pressure, might and should be demanded in opposition to democratic and

Puritan public opinion. In any democracy the "average" or "typical" citizen may readily be made the standard to which all must conform on pain of being criticized as "different"; and if that society is also strongly Puritan, the slightest deviation from a rigid and severe moral code will be sufficient to incite public ostracism. Moreover, since Puritanism exalted the Christian doctrine of self-denial, and viewed the passions and the intellect as dangerous faculties to be kept severely in check, it was naturally a force in Victorian society running counter to Mill's deepest convictions. " 'Pagan self-assertion,' " he insists, "is one of the elements of human worth, as well as 'Christian self-denial.' There is a Greek ideal of self-development, which the Platonic and Christian ideal of self-government blends with, but does not supersede." This is the core of Matthew Arnold's famous essay on "Hebraism and Hellenism"; for Arnold, with his plea for the intellectual life and the rounded development of human nature, is the follower of Mill.

TEXTS: The *Collected Works of John Stuart Mill,* ed. F. E. L. Priestley and John M. Robson (Toronto, 1963–), is in progress. The definitive edition of the *Autobiography,* with a preface by John Jacob Coss, was published in New York (1924), and can now be bought in paperback; the first edition (1873), which differs very slightly, was edited by Harold Laski for The World's Classics (1924). *Utilitarianism, On Liberty,* and *Representative Government* share a volume in the Everyman's Library. Mill's major essays have been collected as *Dissertations and Discussions* (4 or 5 volumes depending on the edition): see especially "Civilization," "Bentham," and "Coleridge." *The Spirit of the Age* has been edited by F. von Hayek (1942). The best biography is by St. John Packe (1954); and the best study, I think, is by John M. Robson, *The Improvement of Mankind: The Social and Political Thought of John Stuart Mill.* For his literary criticism see Mill's *Literary Essays,* ed. Edward Alexander (1967) and Robson's "Mill's Theory of Poetry," *University of Toronto Quarterly,* XXIX (July 1960), 420–38.

from Autobiography

from Chapter 4

YOUTHFUL PROPAGANDISM. THE WESTMINSTER REVIEW

. . . At this period,[1] when Liberalism seemed to be becoming the tone of the time, when improve-

ment of institutions was preached from the highest places, and a complete change of the constitution of Parliament was loudly demanded in the lowest, it is not strange that attention should have been roused by the regular appearance in controversy of what seemed a new school of writers, claiming to be the legislators and theorists of this new tendency. The air of strong conviction with which they wrote, when scarcely any one else seemed to have an equally strong faith in as definite a creed; the boldness with which they tilted against the very front of both the existing political parties; their uncompromising profession of opposition to many of the generally received opinions, and the suspicion they lay under of holding others still more heterodox than they professed; the talent and verve of at least my father's articles, and the appearance of a corps behind him sufficient to carry on a Review;[2] and finally, the fact that the Review was bought and read, made the so-called Bentham school in philosophy and politics fill a greater place in the public mind than it had held before, or has ever again held since other equally earnest schools of thought have arisen in England. As I was in the headquarters of it, knew of what it was composed, and as one of the most active of its very small number, might say without undue assumption, *quorum pars magna fui,*[3] it belongs to me more than to most others, to give some account of it.

This supposed school, then, had no other existence than what was constituted by the fact, that my father's writings and conversation drew round him a certain number of young men who had already imbibed, or who imbibed from him, a greater or smaller portion of his very decided political and philosophical opinions. The notion that Bentham was surrounded by a band of disciples who received their opinions from his lips, is a fable to which my father did justice in his "Fragment on Mackintosh,"[4] and which, to all who knew Mr. Bentham's habits of life and manner of conversation, is simply ridiculous. The influence which Bentham exercised was by his writings. Through them he has produced, and is producing, effects on the condition of man-

---

[1] The 1820s.—The *Autobiography,* on which Mill worked at intervals during the last twenty years of his life, was published in 1873, shortly after his death.

[2] The *Westminster Review,* the organ of the Utilitarians or Benthamites, founded in 1824.

[3] I was a great part of it.

[4] Sir James Mackintosh (1765–1832) was a Scottish philosopher.

kind, wider and deeper, no doubt, than any which can be attributed to my father. He is a much greater name in history. But my father exercised a far greater personal ascendancy. He *was* sought for the vigour and instructiveness of his conversation, and did use it largely as an instrument for the diffusion of his opinions. I have never known any man who could do such ample justice to his best thoughts in colloquial discussion. His perfect command over his great mental resources, the terseness and expressiveness of his language and the moral earnestness as well as intellectual force of his delivery, made him one of the most striking of all argumentative conversers: and he was full of anecdote, a hearty laugher, and, when with people whom he liked, a most lively and amusing companion. It was not solely, or even chiefly, in diffusing his merely intellectual convictions that his power showed itself: it was still more through the influence of a quality, of which I have only since learnt to appreciate the extreme rarity: that exalted public spirit, and regard above all things to the good of the whole, which warmed into life and activity every germ of similar virtue that existed in the minds he came in contact with: the desire he made them feel for his approbation, the shame at his disapproval; the moral support which his conversation and his very existence gave to those who were aiming at the same objects, and the encouragement he afforded to the faint-hearted or desponding among them, by the firm confidence which (though the reverse of sanguine as to the results to be expected in any one particular case) he always felt in the power of reason, the general progress of improvement, and the good which individuals could do by judicious effort.

It was my father's opinions which gave the distinguishing character to the Benthamic or utilitarian propagandism of that time. They fell singly, scattered from him, in many directions, but they flowed from him in a continued stream principally in three channels. One was through me, the only mind directly formed by his instructions, and through whom considerable influence was exercised over various young men, who became in their turn, propagandists. A second was through some of the Cambridge contemporaries of Charles Austin,[5] who, either initiated by him or under the general mental impulse which he gave, had adopted many opinions allied to those of my father, and some of the more considerable of whom afterwards sought my father's acquaintance and frequented his house. Among these may be mentioned Strutt, afterwards Lord Belper, and the present Lord Romilly, with whose eminent father, Sir Samuel, my father had of old been on terms of friendship. The third channel was that of a younger generation of Cambridge undergraduates, contemporary, not with Austin, but with Eyton Tooke,[6] who were drawn to that estimable person by affinity of opinions, and introduced by him to my father: the most notable of these was Charles Buller.[7] Various other persons individually received and transmitted a considerable amount of my father's influence: for example, Black[8] (as before mentioned) and Fonblanque:[9] most of these, however, we accounted only partial allies; Fonblanque, for instance, was always divergent from us on many important points. But indeed there was by no means complete unanimity among any portion of us, nor had any of us adopted implicitly all my father's opinions. For example, although his Essay on Government was regarded probably by all of us as a masterpiece of political wisdom, our adhesion by no means extended to the paragraph of it, in which he maintains that women may consistently with good government, be excluded from the suffrage, because their interest is the same with that of men. From this doctrine, I, and all those who formed my chosen

5 A slightly older contemporary of Mill, who had been much influenced by James Mill. Earlier in the *Auto-*

biography Mill says: "It is my belief that much of the notion popularly entertained of the tenets and sentiments of what are called Benthamites or Utilitarians had its origin in paradoxes thrown out by Charles Austin."

6 A member of the early Utilitarian Society, a group planned by Mill, as he tells us earlier, in the winter of 1822–23, "to be composed of young men agreeing in fundamental principles—acknowledging Utility as their standard in ethics and politics. . . . The number never, I think, reached ten, and the society was broken up in 1826." He mentions Tooke as one of the members who became his intimate companions.

7 English statesman (1806–1848), who had a considerable share, aided by Mill himself, in drawing up the famous Durham report on North America, which first laid down the general principles of the British Commonwealth of Nations.

8 John Black (1783–1855), the editor of the *Morning Chronicle*, under whose aegis the paper "became to a considerable extent a vehicle of the opinions of the Utilitarian Radicals." (Mill)

9 Albany Fonblanque (1793–1872), one of the principal contributors to the *Morning Chronicle*.

associates, most positively dissented. It is due to my father to say that he denied having intended to affirm that women *should* be excluded, any more than men under the age of forty, concerning whom he maintained, in the very next paragraph, an exactly similar thesis. He was, as he truly said, not discussing whether the suffrage had better be restricted, but only (assuming that it is to be restricted) what is the utmost limit of restriction, which does not necessarily involve a sacrifice of the securities for good government. But I thought then, as I have always thought since, that the opinion which he acknowledged, no less than that which he disclaimed, is as great an error as any of those against which the Essay was directed; that the interest of women is included in that of men exactly as much and no more, as the interest of subjects is included in that of kings; and that every reason which exists for giving the suffrage to anybody, demands that it should not be withheld from women. This was also the general opinion of the younger proselytes; and it is pleasant to be able to say that Mr. Bentham, on this important point, was wholly on our side.

But though none of us, probably, agreed in every respect with my father, his opinions, as I said before, were the principal element which gave its colour and character to the little group of young men who were the first propagators of what was afterwards called "Philosophic Radicalism." Their mode of thinking was not characterized by Benthamism in any sense which has relation to Bentham as a chief or guide, but rather by a combination of Bentham's point of view with that of the modern political economy, and with the Hartleian[10] metaphysics. Malthus's population principle[11] was quite as much a banner, and point of union among us, as any opinion specially belonging to Bentham. This great doctrine, originally brought forward as an argument against the indefinite improvability of human affairs, we took up with ardent zeal in the contrary sense, as indicating the sole means of realizing that improvability by securing full employment at high wages to the whole labouring population through a voluntary restriction of the increase of their numbers. The other leading characteristics of the creed, which we held in common with my father, may be stated as follows:

In politics, an almost unbounded confidence in the efficacy of two things: representative government, and complete freedom of discussion. So complete was my father's reliance on the influence of reason over the minds of mankind, whenever it is allowed to reach them, that he felt as if all would be gained if the whole population were taught to read, if all sorts of opinions were allowed to be addressed to them by word and in writing, and if by means of the suffrage they could nominate a legislature to give effect to the opinions they adopted. He thought that when the legislature no longer represented a class interest, it would aim at the general interest, honestly and with adequate wisdom; since the people would be sufficiently under the guidance of educated intelligence, to make in general a good choice of persons to represent them, and having done so, to leave to those whom they had chosen a liberal discretion. Accordingly aristocratic rule, the government of the Few in any of its shapes, being in his eyes the only thing which stood between mankind and an administration of their affairs by the best wisdom to be found among them, was the object of his sternest disapprobation, and a democratic suffrage the principal article of his political creed, not on the ground of liberty, Rights of Man, or any of the phrases, more or less significant, by which, up to that time, democracy had usually been defended, but as the most essential of "securities for good government." In this, too, he held fast only to what he deemed essentials; he was comparatively indifferent to monarchical or republican forms—far more so than Bentham, to whom a king, in the character of "corrupter-general," appeared necessarily very noxious. Next to aristocracy, an established church, or corporation of priests, as being by position the great depravers of religion, and interested in opposing the progress of the human mind, was the object of his greatest detestation; though he disliked no clergyman personally who did not deserve it, and was on terms of sincere friendship with several. In ethics, his moral feelings were ener-

---

[10] Of David Hartley (c. 1705–1757), materialist philosopher and founder of English associational psychology.
[11] That since population increases in a geometrical and means of subsistence only in an arithmetical ratio, mankind was constantly and inevitably subject to crime, disease, and war.

getic and rigid on all points which he deemed important to human well being, while he was supremely indifferent in opinion (though his indifference did not show itself in personal conduct) to all those doctrines of the common morality, which he thought had no foundation but in asceticism and priestcraft. He looked forward, for example, to a considerable increase of freedom in the relations between the sexes, though without pretending to define exactly what would be, or ought to be, the precise conditions of that freedom. This opinion was connected in him with no sensuality either of a theoretical or of a practical kind. He anticipated, on the contrary, as one of the beneficial effects of increased freedom, that the imagination would no longer dwell upon the physical relation and its adjuncts, and swell this into one of the principal objects of life; a perversion of the imagination and feelings, which he regarded as one of the deepest seated and most pervading evils in the human mind. In psychology, his fundamental doctrine was the formation of all human character by circumstances, through the universal Principle of Association, and the consequent unlimited possibility of improving the moral and intellectual condition of mankind by education. Of all his doctrines none was more important than this, or needs more to be insisted on: unfortunately there is none which is more contradictory to the prevailing tendencies of speculation, both in his time and since.

These various opinions were seized on with youthful fanaticism by the little knot of young men of whom I was one: and we put into them a sectarian spirit, from which, in intention at least, my father was wholly free. What we (or rather a phantom substituted in the place of us) were sometimes, by a ridiculous exaggeration, called by others, namely a "school," some of us for a time really hoped and aspired to be. The French *philosophes*[12] of the eighteenth century were the example we sought to imitate, and we hoped to accomplish no less results. No one of the set went to so great excesses in this boyish ambition as I did; which might be shown by many particulars, were it not an useless waste of space and time.

All this, however, is properly only the outside of our existence; or, at least, the intellectual part alone, and no more than one side of that. In attempting to penetrate inward, and give any indication of what we were as human beings, I must be understood as speaking only of myself, of whom alone I can speak from sufficient knowledge; and I do not believe that the picture would suit any of my companions without many and great modifications.

I conceive that the description so often given of a Benthamite, as a mere reasoning machine, though extremely inapplicable to most of those who have been designated by that title, was during two or three years of my life not altogether untrue of me. It was perhaps as applicable to me as it can well be to any one just entering into life, to whom the common objects of desire must in general have at least the attraction of novelty. There is nothing very extraordinary in this fact: no youth of the age I then was, can be expected to be more than one thing, and this was the thing I happened to be. Ambition and desire of distinction, I had in abundance; and zeal for what I thought the good of mankind was my strongest sentiment, mixing with and colouring all others. But my zeal was as yet little else, at that period of my life, than zeal for speculative opinions. It had not its root in genuine benevolence, or sympathy with mankind; though these qualities held their due place in my ethical standard. Nor was it connected with any high enthusiasm for ideal nobleness. Yet of this feeling I was imaginatively very susceptible; but there was at that time an intermission of its natural aliment, poetical culture, while there was a superabundance of the discipline antagonistic to it, that of mere logic and analysis. Add to this that, as already mentioned, my father's teachings tended to the undervaluing of feeling. It was not that he was himself coldhearted or insensible; I believe it was rather from the contrary quality; he thought that feeling could take care of itself; that there was sure to be enough of it if actions were properly cared about. Offended by the frequency with which, in ethical and philosophical controversy, feeling is made the ultimate reason and justification of conduct, instead of being itself called on

12 A name given to a group of writers, most of whom were French, who were skeptics in religion, materialists in philosophy, and hedonists in ethics. Principal representatives included Diderot, D'Alembert, Helvetius, and Condorcet.

for a justification, while, in practice, actions the effect of which on human happiness is mischievous, are defended as being required by feeling, and the character of a person of feeling obtains a credit for desert, which he thought only due to actions, he had a real impatience of attributing praise to feeling, or of any but the most sparing reference to it, either in the estimation of persons or in the discussion of things. In addition to the influence which this characteristic in him, had on me and others, we found all the opinions to which we attached most importance, constantly attacked on the ground of feeling. Utility was denounced as cold calculation; political economy as hard-hearted; anti-population doctrines as repulsive to the natural feelings of mankind. We retorted by the word "sentimentality," which, along with "declamation" and "vague generalities," served us as common terms of opprobrium. Although we were generally in the right, as against those who were opposed to us, the effect was that the cultivation of feeling (except the feelings of public and private duty), was not in much esteem among us, and had very little place in the thoughts of most of us, myself in particular. What we principally thought of, was to alter people's opinions; to make them believe according to evidence, and know what was their real interest, which when they once knew, they would, we thought, by the instrument of opinion, enforce a regard to it upon one another. While fully recognising the superior excellence of unselfish benevolence and love of justice, we did not expect the regeneration of mankind from any direct action on those sentiments, but from the effect of educated intellect, enlightening the selfish feelings. Although this last is prodigiously important as a means of improvement in the hands of those who are themselves impelled by nobler principles of action, I do not believe that any one of the survivors of the Benthamites or Utilitarians of that day, now relies mainly upon it for the general amendment of human conduct.

From this neglect both in theory and in practice of the cultivation of feeling, naturally resulted, among other things, an undervaluing of poetry, and of Imagination generally, as an element of human nature. It is, or was, part of the popular notion of Benthamites, that they are enemies of poetry: this was partly true of

Bentham himself; he used to say that "all poetry is misrepresentation": but in the sense in which he said it, the same might have been said of all impressive speech; of all representation or inculcation more oratorical in its character than a sum in arithmetic. An article of Bingham's[13] in the first number of the Westminster Review, in which he offered as an explanation of something which he disliked in Moore,[14] that "Mr. Moore *is* a poet, and therefore is *not* a reasoner," did a good deal to attach the notion of hating poetry to the writers in the Review. But the truth was that many of us were great readers of poetry; Bingham himself had been a writer of it, while as regards me (and the same thing might be said of my father), the correct statement would be, not that I disliked poetry, but that I was theoretically indifferent to it. I disliked any sentiments in poetry which I should have disliked in prose; and that included a great deal. And I was wholly blind to its place in human culture, as a means of educating the feelings. But I was always personally very susceptible to some kinds of it. In the most sectarian period of my Benthamism, I happened to look into Pope's Essay on Man, and though every opinion in it was contrary to mine, I well remember how powerfully it acted on my imagination. Perhaps at that time poetical composition of any higher type than eloquent discussion in verse, might not have produced a similar effect on me: at all events I seldom gave it an opportunity. This, however, was a mere passive state. Long before I had enlarged in any considerable degree, the basis of my intellectual creed, I had obtained in the natural course of my mental progress, poetic culture of the most valuable kind, by means of reverential admiration for the lives and characters of heroic persons; especially the heroes of philosophy.[15] The same inspiring effect which so many of the benefactors of mankind have left on record that they had experienced from Plutarch's Lives,[16] was produced on

13 Peregrine Bingham (1788–1864), a frequent contributor in the early days of the *Westminster Review*. "The literary and artistic department [of the first number] had rested chiefly on Mr. Bingham." (Mill)
14 Thomas Moore (1779–1852), Irish poet; see p. 213.
15 For Mill's identification of "poetic culture" with the cultivation of the moral sensibility, see p. 574.
16 Plutarch wrote the *Lives* to provide inspiring examples of wise and heroic conduct.

me by Plato's pictures of Socrates,[17] and by some modern biographies, above all by Condorcet's Life of Turgot;[18] a book well calculated to rouse the best sort of enthusiasm, since it contains one of the wisest and noblest of lives, delineated by one of the wisest and noblest of men. The heroic virtue of these glorious representatives of the opinions with which I sympathized, deeply affected me, and I perpetually recurred to them as others do to a favourite poet, when needing to be carried up into the more elevated regions of feeling and thought. I may observe by the way that this book cured me of my sectarian follies. The two or three pages beginning "Il regardait toute secte comme nuisible,"[19] and explaining why Turgot always kept himself perfectly distinct from the Encyclopedists,[20] sank deeply into my mind. I left off designating myself and others as Utilitarians, and by the pronoun "we" or any other collective designation, I ceased to *afficher*[21] sectarianism. My real inward sectarianism I did not get rid of till later, and much more gradually. . . .

from Chapter 5

A CRISIS IN MY MENTAL HISTORY. ONE STAGE ONWARD

For some years after this time[22] I wrote very little, and nothing regularly, for publication: and great were the advantages which I derived from the intermission. It was of no common importance to me, at this period, to be able to digest and mature my thoughts for my own mind only, without any immediate call for giving them out in print. Had I gone on writing, it would have much disturbed the important transformation in my opinions and character, which took place during those years. The origin of this transformation, or at least the process by which I was prepared for it, can only be explained by turning some distance back.

17 In *The Republic.*
18 Turgot was an eighteenth-century French statesman who endeavored to effect liberal reforms until his dismissal by Louis XVI. Such a figure naturally appealed to Mill, as it had to the liberal *philosophe* Condorcet.
19 He considered all sects or schools as harmful.
20 Another name for the French *philosophes,* applied because they published their "subversive" ideas in the form of a harmless-looking encyclopedia.
21 Literally, to advertise by placards; here, to proclaim publicly.
22 1828.

From the winter of 1821, when I first read Bentham, and especially from the commencement of the Westminster Review, I had what might truly be called an object in life; to be a reformer of the world. My conception of my own happiness was entirely identified with this object. The personal sympathies I wished for were those of fellow labourers in this enterprise. I endeavoured to pick up as many flowers as I could by the way; but as a serious and permanent personal satisfaction to rest upon, my whole reliance was placed on this; and I was accustomed to felicitate myself on the certainty of a happy life which I enjoyed, through placing my happiness in something durable and distant, in which some progress might be always making, while it could never be exhausted by complete attainment. This did very well for several years, during which the general improvement going on in the world and the idea of myself as engaged with others in struggling to promote it, seemed enough to fill up an interesting and animated existence. But the time came when I awakened from this as from a dream. It was in the autumn of 1826. I was in a dull state of nerves, such as everybody is occasionally liable to; unsusceptible to enjoyment or pleasurable excitement; one of those moods when what is pleasure at other times, becomes insipid or indifferent; the state, I should think, in which converts to Methodism usually are, when smitten by their first "conviction of sin." In this frame of mind it occurred to me to put the question directly to myself: "Suppose that all your objects in life were realized; that all the changes in institutions and opinions which you are looking forward to, could be completely effected at this very instant: would this be a great joy and happiness to you?" And an irrepressible self-consciousness distinctly answered, "No!" At this my heart sank within me: the whole foundation on which my life was constructed fell down. All my happiness was to have been found in the continual pursuit of this end. The end had ceased to charm, and how could there ever again be any interest in the means? I seemed to have nothing left to live for.

At first I hoped that the cloud would pass away of itself; but it did not. A night's sleep, the sovereign remedy for the smaller vexations of life, had no effect on it. I awoke to a renewed consciousness of the woful fact. I carried it with me into all companies, into all occupations. Hardly anything had power to cause me even a few minutes' oblivion of it. For some months the cloud seemed to grow thicker and thicker. The lines in Coleridge's "Dejection"—I was not then acquainted with them—exactly describe my case:

A grief without a pang, void, dark and drear,
A drowsy, stifled, unimpassioned grief,
Which finds no natural outlet or relief
In word, or sigh, or tear.

In vain I sought relief from my favourite books; those memorials of past nobleness and greatness from which I had always hitherto drawn strength and animation. I read them now without feeling, or with the accustomed feeling *minus* all its charm; and I became persuaded, that my love of mankind, and of excellence for its own sake, had worn itself out. I sought no comfort by speaking to others of what I felt. If I had loved any one sufficiently to make confiding my griefs a necessity, I should not have been in the condition I was. I felt, too, that mine was not an interesting, or in any way respectable distress. There was nothing in it to attract sympathy. Advice, if I had known where to seek it, would have been most precious. The words of Macbeth to the physician[23] often occurred to my thoughts. But there was no one on whom I could build the faintest hope of such assistance. My father, to whom it would have been natural to me to have recourse in any practical difficulties, was the last person to whom, in such a case as this, I looked for help. Everything convinced me that he had no knowledge of any such mental state as I was suffering from, and that even if he could be made to understand it, he was not the physician who could heal it. My education, which was wholly his work, had been conducted without any regard to the possibility of its ending in this result; and I saw no use in giving him the pain of thinking that his plans had failed, when the failure was probably irremediable, and, at all events, beyond the power of

his remedies. Of other friends, I had at that time none to whom I had any hope of making my condition intelligible. It was however abundantly intelligible to myself; and the more I dwelt upon it, the more hopeless it appeared.

My course of study had led me to believe, that all mental and moral feelings and qualities, whether of a good or of a bad kind, were the results of association; that we love one thing, and hate another, take pleasure in one sort of action or contemplation, and pain in another sort, through the clinging of pleasurable or painful ideas to those things, from the effect of education or of experience. As a corollary from this, I had always heard it maintained by my father, and was myself convinced, that the object of education should be to form the strongest possible associations of the salutary class; associations of pleasure with all things beneficial to the great whole, and of pain with all things hurtful to it. This doctrine appeared inexpugnable; but it now seemed to me, on retrospect, that my teachers had occupied themselves but superficially with the means of forming and keeping up these salutary associations. They seemed to have trusted altogether to the old familiar instruments, praise and blame, reward and punishment. Now, I did not doubt that by these means, begun early, and applied unremittingly, intense associations of pain and pleasure, especially of pain, might be created, and might produce desires and aversions capable of lasting undiminished to the end of life. But there must always be something artificial and casual in associations thus produced. The pains and pleasures thus forcibly associated with things, are not connected with them by any natural tie; and it is therefore, I thought, essential to the durability of these associations, that they should have become so intense and inveterate as to be practically indissoluble, before the habitual exercise of the power of analysis had commenced. For I now saw, or thought I saw, what I had always before received with incredulity—that the habit of analysis has a tendency to wear away the feelings: as indeed it has, when no other mental habit is cultivated, and the analysing spirit remains without its natural complements and correctives. The very excellence of analysis (I argued) is that it tends to weaken and undermine whatever is the result of

---

23 "Canst thou not minister to a mind diseas'd,
  Pluck from the memory a rooted sorrow,
  Raze out the written troubles of the brain,
  And with some sweet oblivious antidote
  Cleanse the stuff'd bosom of that perilous stuff
  Which weighs upon the heart?" (*Macbeth*, V, iii, 40–45)

prejudice; that it enables us mentally to separate ideas which have only casually clung together: and no associations whatever could ultimately resist this dissolving force, were it not that we owe to analysis our clearest knowledge of the permanent sequences in nature; the real connexions between Things, not dependent on our will and feelings; natural laws, by virtue of which, in many cases, one thing is inseparable from another in fact; which laws, in proportion as they are clearly perceived and imaginatively realized, cause our ideas of things which are always joined together in Nature, to cohere more and more closely in our thoughts. Analytic habits may thus even strengthen the associations between causes and effects, means and ends, but tend altogether to weaken those which are, to speak familiarly, a *mere* matter of feeling. They are therefore (I thought) favourable to prudence and clear-sightedness, but a perpetual worm at the root both of the passions and of the virtues; and, above all, fearfully undermine all desires, and all pleasures, which are the effects of association, that is, according to the theory I held, all except the purely physical and organic; of the entire insufficiency of which to make life desirable, no one had a stronger conviction than I had. These were the laws of human nature, by which, as it seemed to me, I had been brought to my present state. All those to whom I looked up, were of opinion that the pleasure of sympathy with human beings, and the feelings which made the good of others, and especially of mankind on a large scale, the object of existence, were the greatest and surest sources of happiness. Of the truth of this I was convinced, but to know that a feeling would make me happy if I had it, did not give me the feeling. My education, I thought, had failed to create these feelings in sufficient strength to resist the dissolving influence of analysis, while the whole course of my intellectual cultivation had made precocious and premature analysis the inveterate habit of my mind. I was thus, as I said to myself, left stranded at the commencement of my voyage, with a well-equipped ship and a rudder, but no sail; without any real desire for the ends which I had been so carefully fitted out to work for: no delight in virtue, or the general good, but also just as little in anything else. The fountains of vanity and ambition seemed to have

dried up within me, as completely as those of benevolence. I had had (as I reflected) some gratification of vanity at too early an age: I had obtained some distinction, and felt myself of some importance, before the desire of distinction and of importance had grown into a passion: and little as it was which I had attained, yet having been attained too early, like all pleasures enjoyed too soon, it had made me *blasé* and indifferent to the pursuit. Thus neither selfish nor unselfish pleasures were pleasures to me. And there seemed no power in nature sufficient to begin the formation of my character anew, and create in a mind now irretrievably analytic, fresh associations of pleasure with any of the objects of human desire.

These were the thoughts which mingled with the dry heavy dejection of the melancholy winter of 1826–7. During this time I was not incapable of my usual occupations. I went on with them mechanically, by the mere force of habit. I had been so drilled in a certain sort of mental exercise, that I could still carry it on when all the spirit had gone out of it. I even composed and spoke several speeches at the debating society, how, or with what degree of success, I know not. Of four years continual speaking at that society, this is the only year of which I remember next to nothing. Two lines of Coleridge, in whom alone of all writers I have found a true description of what I felt, were often in my thoughts, not at this time (for I had never read them), but in a later period of the same mental malady:

Work without hope draws nectar in a sieve,
And hope without an object cannot live.[24]

In all probability my case was by no means so peculiar as I fancied it, and I doubt not that many others have passed through a similar state; but the idiosyncrasies of my education had given to the general phenomenon a special character, which made it seem the natural effect of causes that it was hardly possible for time to remove. I frequently asked myself, if I could, or if I was bound to go on living, when life must be passed in this manner. I generally answered to myself, that I did not think I could possibly bear it beyond a year. When, however, not more than

---

24 The last lines of "Work Without Hope."

half that duration of time had elapsed, a small ray of light broke in upon my gloom. I was reading, accidentally, Marmontel's "Memoires,"[25] and came to the passage which relates his father's death, the distressed position of the family, and the sudden inspiration by which he, then a mere boy, felt and made them feel that he would be everything to them—would supply the place of all that they had lost. A vivid conception of the scene and its feelings came over me, and I was moved to tears. From this moment my burden grew lighter. The oppression of the thought that all feeling was dead within me, was gone. I was no longer hopeless: I was not a stock or a stone. I had still, it seemed, some of the material out of which all worth of character, and all capacity for happiness, are made. Relieved from my ever present sense of irremediable wretchedness, I gradually found that the ordinary incidents of life could again give me some pleasure; that I could again find enjoyment, not intense, but sufficient for cheerfulness, in sunshine and sky, in books, in conversation, in public affairs; and that there was, once more, excitement, though of a moderate kind, in exerting myself for my opinions, and for the public good. Thus the cloud gradually drew off, and I again enjoyed life: and though I had several relapses, some of which lasted many months, I never again was as miserable as I had been.

The experiences of this period had two very marked effects on my opinions and character. In the first place, they led me to adopt a theory of life, very unlike that on which I had before acted, and having much in common with what at that time I certainly had never heard of, the anti-self-consciousness theory of Carlyle.[26] I never, indeed, wavered in the conviction that happiness is the test of all rules of conduct, and the end of life. But I now thought that this end was only to be attained by not making it the direct end. Those only are happy (I thought) who have their minds fixed on some object other than their own happiness; on the happiness of others, on the improvement of mankind, even on some art or pursuit, followed not as a means, but as itself an ideal end. Aiming thus at some-

thing else, they find happiness by the way. The enjoyments of life (such was now my theory) are sufficient to make it a pleasant thing, when they are taken *en passant,* without being made a principal object. Once make them so, and they are immediately felt to be insufficient. They will not bear a scrutinizing examination. Ask yourself whether you are happy, and you cease to be so. The only chance is to treat, not happiness, but some end external to it, as the purpose of life. Let your self-consciousness, your scrutiny, your self-interrogation, exhaust themselves on that; and if otherwise fortunately circumstanced you will inhale happiness with the air you breathe, without dwelling on it or thinking about it, without either forestalling it in imagination, or putting it to flight by fatal questioning. This theory now became the basis of my philosophy of life. And I still hold to it as the best theory for all those who have but a moderate degree of sensibility and of capacity for enjoyment, that is, for the great majority of mankind.

The other important change which my opinions at this time underwent, was that I, for the first time, gave its proper place, among the prime necessities of human well-being, to the internal culture of the individual. I ceased to attach almost exclusive importance to the ordering of outward circumstances, and the training of the human being for speculation and for action.

I had now learnt by experience that the passive susceptibilities needed to be cultivated as well as the active capacities, and required to be nourished and enriched as well as guided. I did not, for an instant, lose sight of, or undervalue, that part of the truth which I had seen before; I never turned recreant to intellectual culture, or ceased to consider the power and practice of analysis as an essential condition both of individual and of social improvement. But I thought that it had consequences which required to be corrected, by joining other kinds of cultivation with it. The maintenance of a due balance among the faculties, now seemed to me of primary importance. The cultivation of the feelings became one of the cardinal points in my ethical and philosophical creed.[27] And my thoughts and

---

25 *Mémoires d'un père* (1804) by Jean François Marmontel.
26 The theory that to seek consciously for happiness is to miss it, a conclusion which Mill now draws for himself. For Carlyle, see p. 442.

---

27 It should be noticed that Mill means to include, and with primary emphasis, the *moral* feelings. Cf. the next paragraph.

inclinations turned in an increasing degree towards whatever seemed capable of being instrumental to that object.

I now began to find meaning in the things which I had read or heard about the importance of poetry and art as instruments of human culture. But it was some time longer before I began to know this by personal experience. The only one of the imaginative arts in which I had from childhood taken great pleasure, was music; the best effect of which (and in this it surpasses perhaps every other art) consists in exciting enthusiasm; in winding up to a high pitch those feelings of an elevated kind which are already in the character, but to which this excitement gives a glow and a fervour, which, though transitory at its utmost height, is precious for sustaining them at other times. This effect of music I had often experienced; but like all my pleasurable susceptibilities it was suspended during the gloomy period. I had sought relief again and again from this quarter, but found none. After the tide had turned, and I was in process of recovery, I had been helped forward by music, but in a much less elevated manner. I at this time first became acquainted with Weber's Oberon,[28] and the extreme pleasure which I drew from its delicious melodies did me good, by showing me a source of pleasure to which I was as susceptible as ever. The good, however, was much impaired by the thought, that the pleasure of music (as is quite true of such pleasure as this was, that of mere tune) fades with familiarity, and requires either to be revived by intermittence, or fed by continual novelty. And it is very characteristic both of my then state, and of the general tone of my mind at this period of my life, that I was seriously tormented by the thought of the exhaustibility of musical combinations. The octave consists only of five tones and two semitones, which can be put together in only a limited number of ways, of which but a small proportion are beautiful: most of these, it seemed to me, must have been already discovered, and there could not be room for a long succession of Mozarts and Webers, to strike out, as these had done, entirely new and surpassingly rich veins of musical beauty. This source of anxiety may, perhaps, be thought to resemble that of the philosophers of Laputa,[29] who feared lest the sun should be burnt out. It was, however, connected with the best feature in my character, and the only good point to be found in my very unromantic and in no way honourable distress. For though my dejection, honestly looked at, could not be called other than egotistical, produced by the ruin, as I thought, of my fabric of happiness, yet the destiny of mankind in general was ever in my thoughts, and could not be separated from my own. I felt that the flaw in my life, must be a flaw in life itself; that the question was, whether, if the reformers of society and government could succeed in their objects, and every person in the community were free and in a state of physical comfort, the pleasures of life, being no longer kept up by struggle and privation, would cease to be pleasures. And I felt that unless I could see my way to some better hope than this for human happiness in general, my dejection must continue; but that if I could see such an outlet, I should then look on the world with pleasure; content as far as I was myself concerned, with any fair share of the general lot.

This state of my thoughts and feelings made the fact of my reading Wordsworth for the first time (in the autumn of 1828), an important event in my life. I took up the collection of his poems from curiosity, with no expectation of mental relief from it, though I had before resorted to poetry with that hope. In the worst period of my depression, I had read through the whole of Byron (then new to me), to try whether a poet, whose peculiar department was supposed to be that of the intenser feelings, could rouse any feeling in me. As might be expected, I got no good from this reading, but the reverse. The poet's state of mind was too like my own. His was the lament of a man who had worn out all pleasures, and who seemed to think that life, to all who possess the good things of it, must necessarily be the vapid, uninteresting thing which I found it. His Harold and Manfred had the same burden on them which I had; and I was not in a frame of mind to desire any comfort from the vehement sensual passion of his Giaours, or the sullenness of his Laras. But while Byron was

---

28 An English romantic opera by Carl Maria von Weber, first produced in London in 1826.

29 In *Gulliver's Travels*, Part III, which satirizes the absurdities and impracticalities into which abstract philosophers, mathematicians, etc., may fall.

exactly what did not suit my condition, Wordsworth was exactly what did. I had looked into the Excursion two or three years before, and found little in it; and I should probably have found as little, had I read it at this time. But the miscellaneous poems, in the two-volume edition of 1815 (to which little of value was added in the latter part of the author's life), proved to be the precise thing for my mental wants at that particular juncture.

In the first place, these poems addressed themselves powerfully to one of the strongest of my pleasurable susceptibilities, the love of rural objects and natural scenery; to which I had been indebted not only for much of the pleasure of my life, but quite recently for relief from one of my longest relapses into depression. In this power of rural beauty over me, there was a foundation laid for taking pleasure in Wordsworth's poetry; the more so, as his scenery lies mostly among mountains, which, owing to my early Pyrenean excursion,[30] were my ideal of natural beauty. But Wordsworth would never have had any great effect on me, if he had merely placed before me beautiful pictures of natural scenery. Scott does this still better than Wordsworth, and a very second-rate landscape does it more effectually than any poet. What made Wordsworth's poems a medicine for my state of mind, was that they expressed, not mere outward beauty, but states of feeling, and of thought coloured by feeling, under the excitement of beauty. The seemed to be the very culture of the feelings, which I was in quest of. In them I seemed to draw from a source of inward joy, of sympathetic and imaginative pleasure, which could be shared in by all human beings; which had no connexion with struggle or imperfection, but would be made richer by every improvement in the physical or social condition of mankind. From them I seemed to learn what would be the perennial sources of happiness, when all the greater evils of life shall have been removed. And I felt myself at once better and happier as I came under their influence. There have certainly been, even in our own age, greater poets than Wordsworth; but poetry of deeper and loftier feeling could not have done for me at that time what his did. I needed to be made to feel that

there was real, permanent happiness in tranquil contemplation. Wordsworth taught me this, not only without turning away from, but with a greatly increased interest in the common feelings and common destiny of human beings. And the delight which these poems gave me, proved that with culture of this sort, there was nothing to dread from the most confirmed habit of analysis. At the conclusion of the Poems came the famous Ode, falsely called Platonic,[31] "Intimations of Immortality": in which, along with more than his usual sweetness of melody and rhythm, and along with the two passages of grand imagery but bad philosophy so often quoted, I found that he too had had similar experience to mine; that he also had felt that the first freshness of youthful enjoyment of life was not lasting; but that he had sought for compensation, and found it, in the way in which he was now teaching me to find it. The result was that I gradually, but completely, emerged from my habitual depression and was never again subject to it. I long continued to value Wordsworth less according to his intrinsic merits, than by the measure of what he had done for me. Compared with the greatest poets, he may be said to be the poet of unpoetical natures, possessed of quiet and contemplative tastes. But unpoetical natures are precisely those which require poetic cultivation. This cultivation Wordsworth is much more fitted to give, than poets who are intrinsically far more poets than he.

It so fell out that the merits of Wordsworth were the occasion of my first public declaration of my new way of thinking, and separation from those of my habitual companions who had not undergone a similar change. The person with whom at that time I was most in the habit of comparing notes on such subjects was Roebuck,[32] and I induced him to read Wordsworth, in whom he also at first seemed to find much to admire: but I, like most Wordsworthians, threw myself into strong antagonism to Byron, both as a poet and as to his influence on the character. Roebuck, all whose instincts were those of action and struggle, had, on the con-

---

[30] Made with family friends in 1820.

[31] Wordsworth himself protested that the ode was not an expression of Platonic philosophy.
[32] John Arthur Roebuck (1801–1879), a member of Mill's early Utilitarian Society, 1823–26, who later became a politician and reformer.

trary, a strong relish and great admiration of Byron, whose writings he regarded as the poetry of human life, while Wordsworth's, according to him, was that of flowers and butterflies. We agreed to have the fight out at our Debating Society,[33] where we accordingly discussed for two evenings the comparative merits of Byron and Wordsworth, propounding and illustrating by long recitations our respective theories of poetry: Sterling[34] also, in a brilliant speech, putting forward his particular theory. This was the first debate on any weighty subject in which Roebuck and I had been on opposite sides. The schism between us widened from this time more and more, though we continued for some years longer to be companions. In the beginning, our chief divergence related to the cultivation of the feelings. Roebuck was in many respects very different from the vulgar notion of a Benthamite or Utilitarian. He was a lover of poetry and of most of the fine arts. He took great pleasure in music, in dramatic performances, especially in painting, and himself drew and designed landscapes with great facility and beauty. But he never could be made to see that these things have any value as aids in the formation of character. Personally, instead of being, as Benthamites are supposed to be, void of feeling, he had very quick and strong sensibilities. But, like most Englishmen who have feelings, he found his feelings stand very much in his way. He was much more susceptible to the painful sympathies than to the pleasurable, and looking for his happiness elsewhere, he wished that his feelings should be deadened rather than quickened. And, in truth, the English character, and English social circumstances, make it so seldom possible to derive happiness from the exercise of the sympathies, that it is not wonderful if they count for little in an Englishman's scheme of life. In most other countries the paramount importance of the sympathies as a constituent of individual happiness is an axiom, taken for granted rather than needing any formal statement; but most English thinkers almost seem to regard them as necessary evils, required for keeping men's actions benevolent and compassionate. Roebuck was, or appeared to be, this kind of Englishman. He saw little good in any cultivation of the feelings, and none at all in cultivating them through the imagination, which he thought was only cultivating illusions. It was in vain I urged on him that the imaginative emotion which an idea, when vividly conceived, excites in us, is not an illusion but a fact, as real as any of the other qualities of objects; and far from implying anything erroneous and delusive in our mental apprehension of the object, is quite consistent with the most accurate knowledge and most perfect practical recognition of all its physical and intellectual laws and relations. The intensest feeling of the beauty of a cloud lighted by the setting sun, is no hindrance to my knowing that the cloud is vapour of water, subject to all the laws of vapours in a state of suspension; and I am just as likely to allow for, and act on, these physical laws whenever there is occasion to do so, as if I had been incapable of perceiving any distinction between beauty and ugliness.

While my intimacy with Roebuck diminished, I fell more and more into friendly intercourse with our Coleridgian adversaries in the Society, Frederick Maurice[35] and John Sterling, both subsequently so well known, the former by his writings, the latter through the biographies by Hare[36] and Carlyle. Of these two friends, Maurice was the thinker, Sterling the orator, and impassioned expositor of thoughts which, at this period, were almost entirely formed for him by Maurice.

With Maurice I had for some time been acquainted through Eyton Tooke, who had known him at Cambridge, and although my discussions with him were almost always disputes, I had carried away from them much that helped to build up my new fabric of thought, in the same way as I was deriving much from Coleridge, and from the writings of Goethe and other German authors which I read during these years. . . . I found the fabric of my old and taught opinions giving way in many fresh places, and I never allowed it to fall to pieces, but was

---

[33] The London Debating Society, organized (1825) and originally supported mainly by Mill and Roebuck.
[34] John Sterling (1806–1844), man of letters, friend of Coleridge, Wordsworth, and Carlyle, the last of whom wrote his biography.
[35] Frederick Denison Maurice (1805–1872), clergyman, leader of the Broad Church and the Christian Socialist movements.
[36] Julius Hare (1795–1855), editor of Sterling's *Essays and Tales* and author of a life of Sterling.

incessantly occupied in weaving it anew. I never, in the course of my transition, was content to remain, for ever so short a time, confused and unsettled. When I had taken in any new idea, I could not rest till I had adjusted its relation to my old opinions, and ascertained exactly how far its effect ought to extend in modifying or superseding them. . . .

If I am asked, what system of political philosophy I substituted for that which, as a philosophy, I had abandoned, I answer, No system; only a conviction that the true system was something much more complex and many-sided than I had previously had any idea of, and that its office was to supply, not a set of model institutions, but principles from which the institutions suitable to any given circumstances might be deduced. The influences of European, that is to say, Continental, thought, and especially those of the reaction of the nineteenth century against the eighteenth, were now streaming in upon me. They came from various quarters: from the writings of Coleridge, which I had begun to read with interest even before the change in my opinions; from the Coleridgians with whom I was in personal intercourse; from what I had read of Goethe; from Carlyle's early articles in the Edinburgh and Foreign Reviews, though for a long time I saw nothing in these (as my father saw nothing in them to the last) but insane rhapsody. From these sources, and from the acquaintance I kept up with the French literature of the time, I derived, among other ideas which the general turning upside down of the opinions of European thinkers had brought uppermost, these in particular: That the human mind has a certain order of possible progress, in which some things must precede others, an order which governments and public instructors can modify to some, but not to an unlimited extent: that all questions of political institutions are relative, not absolute, and that different stages of human progress not only *will* have, but *ought* to have, different institutions: that government is always either in the hands, or passing into the hands, of whatever is the strongest power in society, and that what this power is, does not depend on institutions, but institutions on it: that any general theory or philosophy of politics supposes a previous theory of human progress, and that this is the same thing with a philosophy of his-

tory. These opinions, true in the main, were held in an exaggerated and violent manner by the thinkers with whom I was now most accustomed to compare notes, and who, as usual with a reaction, ignored that half of the truth which the thinkers of the eighteenth century saw. But though, at one period of my progress, I for some time undervalued that great century, I never joined in the reaction against it, but kept as firm hold of one side of the truth as I took of the other. The fight between the nineteenth century and the eighteenth always reminded me of the battle about the shield, one side of which was white and the other black. I marvelled at the blind rage with which the combatants rushed against one another. I applied to them, and to Coleridge himself, many of Coleridge's sayings about half truths;[37] and Goethe's device, "many-sidedness,"[38] was one which I would most willingly, at this period, have taken for mine.

The writers by whom, more than by any others, a new mode of political thinking was brought home to me, were those of the St. Simonian school[39] in France. In 1829 and 1830 I became acquainted with some of their writings. They were then only in the earlier stages of their speculations. They had not yet dressed out their philosophy as a religion, nor had they organized their scheme of Socialism. They were just beginning to question the principle of hereditary property. I was by no means prepared to go with them even this length; but I was greatly struck with the connected view which they for the first time presented to me, of the natural order of human progress; and especially with their division of all history into organic periods and critical periods. During the organic periods (they said) mankind accept with firm conviction some positive creed, claiming jurisdiction over all their actions, and containing more or less of truth and adaptation to the needs of humanity.

---

37 In Mill's essay on Coleridge, quoting from the latter's *Literary Remains,* iii, 145, he says: "Almost all errors he holds to be 'truths misunderstood,' 'half-truths taken as the whole,' though not the less, but the more dangerous on that account."

38 One of Goethe's maxims (no. 1337): "Let us then be many-sided."

39 So called after Claude Henri Saint-Simon (1760–1825) and considered the founders of French Socialism, in which the state would own all property and the worker would be rewarded according to the quality and quantity of his work.

Under its influence they make all the progress compatible with the creed, and finally outgrow it; when a period follows of criticism and negation, in which mankind lose their old convictions without acquiring any new ones, of a general or authoritative character, except the conviction that the old are false. The period of Greek and Roman polytheism, so long as really believed in by instructed Greeks and Romans, was an organic period, succeeded by the critical or sceptical period of the Greek philosophers. Another organic period came in with Christianity. The corresponding critical period began with the Reformation, has lasted ever since, still lasts, and cannot altogether cease until a new organic period has been inaugurated by the triumph of a yet more advanced creed. These ideas, I knew, were not peculiar to the St. Simonians; on the contrary, they were the general property of Europe, or at least of Germany and France, but they had never, to my knowledge, been so completely systematized as by these writers, nor the distinguishing characteristics of a critical period so powerfully set forth; for I was not then acquainted with Fichte's Lectures on "The Characteristics of the Present Age."[40] In Carlyle, indeed, I found bitter denunciations of an "age of unbelief," and of the present age as such, which I, like most people at that time, supposed to be passionate protests in favour of the old modes of belief. But all that was true in these denunciations, I thought that I found more calmly and philosophically stated by the St. Simonians. Among their publications, too, there was one which seemed to me far superior to the rest; in which the general idea was matured into something much more definite and instructive. This was an early work of Auguste Comte,[41] who then called himself, and even announced himself in the title-page as, a pupil of Saint Simon. In this tract M. Comte first put forth the doctrine, which he afterwards so copiously illustrated, of the natural succession of three stages in every department of human knowledge: first, the theological, next the metaphysical, and lastly, the positive stage; and contended, that social science must be subject to the same law; that the feudal and Catholic system was the concluding phasis of the theological state of the social science, Protestantism the commencement, and the doctrines of the French Revolution the consummation, of the metaphysical; and that its positive state was yet to come. This doctrine harmonized well with my existing notions, to which it seemed to give a scientific shape. I already regarded the methods of physical science as the proper models for political. But the chief benefit which I derived at this time from the trains of thought suggested by the St. Simonians and by Comte, was, that I obtained a clearer conception than ever before of the peculiarities of an era of transition in opinion, and ceased to mistake the moral and intellectual characteristics of such an era, for the normal attributes of humanity. I looked forward, through the present age of loud disputes but generally weak convictions, to a future which shall unite the best qualities of the critical with the best qualities of the organic periods; unchecked liberty of thought, unbounded freedom of individual action in all modes not hurtful to others; but also, convictions as to what is right and wrong, useful and pernicious, deeply engraven on the feelings by early education and general unanimity of sentiment, and so firmly grounded in reason and in the true exigencies of life, that they shall not, like all former and present creeds, religious, ethical, and political, require to be periodically thrown off and replaced by others.

M. Comte soon left the St. Simonians, and I lost sight of him and his writings for a number of years. But the St. Simonians I continued to cultivate. I was kept *au courant* of[42] their progress by one of their most enthusiastic disciples, M. Gustave d'Eichthal, who about that time passed a considerable interval in England. I was introduced to their chiefs, Bazard and Enfantin, in 1830; and as long as their public teachings and proselytism continued, I read nearly everything they wrote. Their criticisms on the common doctrines of Liberalism seemed to me full of

---

40 In these lectures the German philosopher Johann Gottlieb Fichte (1762–1814) brilliantly arraigned the eighteenth century as an age of skepticism.
41 Auguste Comte (1798–1857), founder of the positivist philosophy, in which only positive facts and observable phenomena, with the objective relations of these and the laws which determine them, are recognized, all inquiry into theology and metaphysics being abandoned. Furthermore, it postulates a "positive stage" of human development in which the laws of science become the proper models for the structure of society.

42 In touch with.

important truth; and it was partly by their writings that my eyes were opened to the very limited and temporary value of the old political economy, which assumes private property and inheritance as indefeasible facts, and freedom of production and exchange as the *dernier mot*[43] of social improvement. The scheme gradually unfolded by the St. Simonians, under which the labour and capital of society would be managed for the general account of the community, every individual being required to take a share of labour, either as thinker, teacher, artist, or producer, all being classed according to their capacity, and remunerated according to their work, appeared to me a far superior description of Socialism to Owen's.[44] Their aim seemed to me desirable and rational, however their means might be inefficacious; and though I neither believed in the practicability, nor in the beneficial operation of their social machinery, I felt that the proclamation of such an ideal of human society could not but tend to give a beneficial direction to the efforts of others to bring society, as at present constituted, nearer to some ideal standard. I honoured them most of all for what they have been most cried down for—the boldness and freedom from prejudice with which they treated the subject of family, the most important of any, and needing more fundamental alterations than remain to be made in any other great social institution, but on which scarcely any reformer has the courage to touch. In proclaiming the perfect equality of men and women, and an entirely new order of things in regard to their relations with one another, the St. Simonians, in common with Owen and Fourier,[45] have entitled themselves to the grateful remembrance of future generations.

In giving an account of this period of my life, I have only specified such of my new impressions as appeared to me, both at the time and since, to be a kind of turning points, marking a definite progress in my mode of thought.

But these few selected points give a very insufficient idea of the quantity of thinking which I carried on respecting a host of subjects during these years of transition. Much of this, it is true, consisted in rediscovering things known to all the world, which I had previously disbelieved, or disregarded. But the rediscovery was to me a discovery, giving me plenary possession of the truths, not as traditional platitudes, but fresh from their source: and it seldom failed to place them in some new light, by which they were reconciled with, and seemed to confirm while they modified, the truths less generally known which lay in my early opinions, and in no essential part of which I at any time wavered. All my new thinking only laid the foundation of these more deeply and strongly, while it often removed misapprehension and confusion of ideas which had perverted their effect. For example, during the later returns of my dejection, the doctrine of what is called Philosophical Necessity weighed on my existence like an incubus. I felt as if I was scientifically proved to be the helpless slave of antecedent circumstances; as if my character and that of all others had been formed for us by agencies beyond our control, and was wholly out of our own power. I often said to myself, what a relief it would be if I could disbelieve the doctrine of the formation of character by circumstances; and remembering the wish of Fox[46] respecting the doctrine of resistance to governments, that it might never be forgotten by kings, nor remembered by subjects, I said that it would be a blessing if the doctrine of necessity could be believed by all *quoad*[47] the characters of others, and disbelieved in regard to their own. I pondered painfully on the subject, till gradually I saw light through it. I perceived, that the word Necessity, as a name for the doctrine of Cause and Effect applied to human action, carried with it a misleading association; and that this association was the operative force in the depressing and paralysing influence which I had experienced: I saw that though our character is formed by circumstances, our own desires can do much to shape those circumstances; and that what is really inspiriting

---

[43] Last word.
[44] Because in the theory of Robert Owen (1771–1858), wealthy mill-owner and founder of several socialist communities, there was to be no distinction in remuneration according to the work done. All men were to receive "from the general store of the community" what they required.
[45] Charles Fourier (1772–1837) was one of the earliest French communists.
[46] Charles James Fox (1749–1806), liberal and humanitarian statesman, distinguished by his opposition to George III and the ultraconservative Tories in the government.
[47] As to, in regard to.

and ennobling in the doctrine of freewill, is the conviction that we have real power over the formation of our own character; that our will, by influencing some of our circumstances, can modify our future habits or capabilities of willing. All this was entirely consistent with the doctrine of circumstances, or rather, was that doctrine itself, properly understood. From that time I drew in my own mind, a clear distinction between the doctrine of circumstances, and Fatalism; discarding altogether the misleading word Necessity. The theory, which I now for the first time rightly apprehended, ceased altogether to be discouraging, and besides the relief to my spirits, I no longer suffered under the burden, so heavy to one who aims at being a reformer in opinions, of thinking one doctrine true, and the contrary doctrine morally beneficial. The train of thought which had extricated me from this dilemma, seemed to me, in after years, fitted to render a similar service to others; and it now forms the chapter on Liberty and Necessity in the concluding Book of my system of Logic.

Again, in politics, though I no longer accepted the doctrine of the Essay on Government[48] as a scientific theory; though I ceased to consider representative domocracy as an absolute principle, and regarded it as a question of time, place, and circumstance; though I now looked upon the choice of political institutions as a moral and educational question more than one of material interests, thinking that it ought to be decided mainly by the consideration, what great improvement in life and culture stands next in order for the people concerned, as the condition of their further progress, and what institutions are most likely to promote that; nevertheless, this change in the premises of my political philosophy did not alter my practical political creed as to the requirements of my own time and country. I was as much as ever a Radical and Democrat for Europe, and especially for England. I thought the predominance of the aristocratic classes, the noble and the rich, in the English constitution, an evil worth any struggle to get rid of; not on account of taxes, or any such comparatively small inconvenience, but as the great demoralizing agency in the country. Demoralizing, first, because it made the conduct of the Government an example of gross public immorality, through the predominance of private over public interests in the State, and the abuse of the powers of legislation for the advantage of classes. Secondly, and in a still greater degree, because the respect of the multitude always attaching itself principally to that which, in the existing state of society, is the chief passport to power; and under English institutions, riches, hereditary or acquired, being the almost exclusive source of political importance; riches, and the signs of riches, were almost the only things really respected, and the life of the people was mainly devoted to the pursuit of them. I thought, that while the higher and richer classes held the power of government, the instruction and improvement of the mass of the people were contrary to the self-interest of those classes, because tending to render the people more powerful for throwing off the yoke: but if the democracy obtained a large, and perhaps the principal share, in the governing power, it would become the interest of the opulent classes to promote their education, in order to ward off really mischievous errors, and especially those which would lead to unjust violations of property. On these grounds I was not only as ardent as ever for democratic institutions, but earnestly hoped that Owenite, St. Simonian, and all other anti-property doctrines might spread widely among the poorer classes; not that I thought those doctrines true, or desired that they should be acted on, but in order that the higher classes might be made to see that they had more to fear from the poor when uneducated, than when educated. . . .

I have already mentioned Carlyle's earlier writings as one of the channels through which I received the influences which enlarged my early narrow creed; but I do not think that those writings, by themselves, would ever have had any effect on my opinions. What truths they contained, though of the very kind which I was already receiving from other quarters, were presented in a form and vesture less suited than any other to give them access to a mind trained as mine had been. They seemed a haze of poetry and German metaphysics, in which almost the only clear thing was a strong animosity to most of the opinions which were the basis of my mode of thought; religious scepticism, utilitarianism, the doctrine of circumstances, and the

---

48 By his father, James Mill.

attaching any importance to democracy, logic, or political economy. Instead of my having been taught anything, in the first instance, by Carlyle, it was only in proportion as I came to see the same truths through media more suited to my mental constitution, that I recognized them in his writings. Then, indeed, the wonderful power with which he put them forth made a deep impression upon me, and I was during a long period one of his most fervent admirers; but the good his writings did me, was not as philosophy to instruct, but as poetry to animate. Even at the time when our acquaintance commenced, I was not sufficiently advanced in my new modes of thought, to appreciate him fully; a proof of which is, that on his showing me the manuscript of Sartor Resartus, his best and greatest work, which he had just then finished, I made little of it; though when it came out about two years afterwards in Fraser's Magazine I read it with enthusiastic admiration and the keenest delight. I did not seek and cultivate Carlyle less on account of the fundamental differences in our philosophy. He soon found out that I was not "another mystic," and when for the sake of my own integrity I wrote to him a distinct profession of all those of my opinions which I knew he most disliked, he replied that the chief difference between us was that I "was as yet consciously nothing of a mystic." I do not know at what period he gave up the expectation that I was destined to become one; but though both his and my opinions underwent in subsequent years considerable changes, we never approached much nearer to each other's modes of thought than we were in the first years of our acquaintance. I did not, however, deem myself a competent judge of Carlyle. I felt that he was a poet, and that I was not; that he was a man of intuition, which I was not; and that as such, he not only saw many things long before me, which I could only when they were pointed out to me, hobble after and prove, but that it was highly probable he could see many things which were not visible to me even after they were pointed out. I knew that I could not see round him, and could never be certain that I saw over him; and I never presumed to judge him with any definiteness, until he was interpreted to me by one greatly the superior of us both—who was more a poet than he, and more a thinker than I—whose own

mind and nature included his, and infinitely more.[49] . . .

from The Spirit of the Age,[1] No. 1

The "spirit of the age" is in some measure a novel expression. I do not believe that it is to be met with in any work exceeding fifty years in antiquity. The idea of comparing one's own age with former ages, or with our notion of those which are yet to come, had occurred to philosophers; but it never before was itself the dominant idea of any age.

It is an idea essentially belonging to an age of change. Before men begin to think much and long on the peculiarities of their own times, they must have begun to think that those times are, or are destined to be, distinguished in a very remarkable manner from the times which preceded them. Mankind are then divided, into those who are still what they were, and those who have changed: into the men of the present age, and the men of the past. To the former, the spirit of the age is a subject of exultation; to the latter, of terror; to both, of eager and anxious interest. The wisdom of ancestors, and the march of intellect, are bandied from mouth to mouth; each phrase originally an expression of respect and homage, each ultimately usurped by the partisans of the opposite catch-word, and in the bitterness of their spirit, turned into the sarcastic jibe of hatred and insult.

The present times possess this character. A change has taken place in the human mind; a change which, being effected by insensible gradations, and without noise, had already proceeded far before it was generally perceived. When the fact disclosed itself, thousands awoke

---

[49] The subject of this extraordinary eulogy is Mrs. Harriet Taylor, with whom Mill fell violently in love, and whom he subsequently married.

[1] "I attempted," says Mill, "in the beginning of 1831, to embody in a series of articles, headed 'The Spirit of the Age,' some of my new opinions, and especially to point out in the character of the present age, the anomalies and evils characteristic of the transition from a system of opinions which had worn out, to another only in process of being formed." The articles appeared in the *Examiner,* a radical weekly, from January through May, and were signed merely "A. B." Most of the first article is reprinted here.

as from a dream. They knew not what processes had been going on in the minds of others, or even in their own, until the change began to invade outward objects; and it became clear that those were indeed new men, who insisted upon being governed in a new way.

But mankind are now conscious of their new position. The conviction is already not far from being universal, that the times are pregnant with change; and that the nineteenth century will be known to posterity as the era of one of the greatest revolutions of which history has preserved the remembrance, in the human mind, and in the whole constitution of human society. Even the religious world teems with new interpretations of the Prophecies, foreboding mighty changes near at hand. It is felt that men are henceforth to be held together by new ties, and separated by new barriers; for the ancient bonds will now no longer unite, nor the ancient boundaries confine. Those men who carry their eyes in the back of their heads and can see no other portion of the destined track of humanity than that which it has already travelled, imagine that because the old ties are severed mankind henceforth are not to be connected by any ties at all; and hence their affliction, and their awful warnings. For proof of this assertion, I may refer to the gloomiest book ever written by a cheerful man—Southey's "Colloquies on the Progress and Prospects of Society";[2] a very curious and not uninstructive exhibition of one of the points of view from which the spirit of the age may be contemplated. They who prefer the ravings of a party politician to the musings of a recluse, may consult a late article in Blackwood's Magazine,[3] under the same title which I have prefixed to this paper. For the reverse of the picture, we have only to look into any popular newspaper or review.

Amidst all this indiscriminate eulogy and abuse, these undistinguishing hopes and fears, it seems to be a very fit subject for philosophical inquiry, what the spirit of the age really is; and how or wherein it differs from the spirit of any other age. The subject is deeply impor-

tant: for, whatever we may think or affect to think of the present age, we cannot get out of it; we must suffer with its sufferings, and enjoy with its enjoyments; we must share in its lot, and, to be either useful or at ease, we must even partake its character. No man whose good qualities were mainly those of another age, ever had much influence on his own. And since every age contains in itself the germ of all future ages as surely as the acorn contains the future forest, a knowledge of our own age is the fountain of prophecy—the only key to the history of posterity. It is only in the present that we can know the future; it is only through the present that it is in our power to influence that which is to come.

Yet, because our own age is *familiar* to us, we are presumed, if I may judge from appearances, to know it by nature. A statesman, for example, if it be required of him to have studied any thing at all (which, however, is more than I would venture to affirm) is supposed to have studied history—which is at best the spirit of ages long past, and more often the mere inanimate carcass without the spirit: but is it ever asked (or to whom does the question ever occur?) whether he understands his own age? Yet that also is history, and the most important part of history, and the only part which a man may know and understand, with absolute certainty, by using the proper means. He may learn in a morning's walk through London more of the history of England during the nineteenth century, than all the professed English histories in existence will tell him concerning the other eighteen: for, the obvious and universal facts, which every one sees and no one is astonished at, it seldom occurs to any one to place upon record; and posterity, if it learn the rule, learns it, generally, from the notice bestowed by contemporaries on some accidental exception. Yet are politicians and philosophers perpetually exhorted to judge of the present by the past, when the present alone affords a fund of materials for judging, richer than the whole stores of the past, and far more accessible.

But it is unadvisable to dwell longer on this topic, lest we should be deemed studiously to exaggerate that want, which we desire that the reader should think ourselves qualified to supply. It were better, without further preamble,

---

[2] See Macaulay's essay on "Southey's Colloquies," reprinted above.
[3] In the issue of December 1830 by David Robinson, London journalist (*Wellesley Index to Victorian Periodicals*, Vol. I).

to enter upon the subject, and be tried by our ideas themselves, rather than by the need of them.

The first of the leading peculiarities of the present age is, that it is an age of transition. Mankind have outgrown old institutions and old doctrines, and have not yet acquired new ones. When we say outgrown, we intend to prejudge nothing. A man may not be either better or happier at six-and-twenty, that he was at six years of age: but the same jacket which fitted him then, will not fit him now.

The prominent trait just indicated in the character of the present age, was obvious a few years ago only to the more discerning: at present it forces itself upon the most inobservant. Much might be said, and shall be said on a fitting occasion, of the mode in which the old order of things has become unsuited to the state of society and of the human mind. But when almost every nation on the continent of Europe has achieved, or is in the course of rapidly achieving, a change in its form of government; when our own country, at all former times the most attached in Europe to its old institutions, proclaims almost with one voice that they are vicious both in the outline and in the details, and that they *shall* be renovated, and purified, and made fit for civilized man, we may assume that a part of the effects of the cause just now pointed out, speak sufficiently loudly for themselves. To him who can reflect, even these are but indications which tell of a more vital and radical change. Not only, in the conviction of almost all men, things as they are, are wrong— but, according to that same conviction, it is not by remaining in the old ways that they can be set right. Society demands, and anticipates, not merely a new machine, but a machine constructed in another manner. Mankind will not be led by their old maxims, nor by their old guides; and they will not choose either their opinions or their guides as they have done heretofore. The ancient constitutional texts were formerly spells which would call forth or allay the spirit of the English people at pleasure: what has become of the charm? Who can hope to sway the minds of the public by the old maxims of law, or commerce, or foreign policy, or ecclesiastical policy? Whose feelings are now roused by the mottoes and watch-words of Whig

and Tory? And what Whig or Tory could command ten followers in the warfare of politics by the weight of his own personal authority? Nay, what landlord could call forth his tenants, or what manufacturer his men? Do the poor respect the rich, or adopt their sentiments? Do the young respect the old, or adopt their sentiments? Of the feelings of our ancestors it may almost be said that we retain only such as are the natural and necessary growth of a state of human society, however constituted; and I only adopt the energetic expression of a member of the House of Commons, less than two years ago, in saying of the young men, even of that rank in society, that they are ready to advertise for opinions.

Since the facts are so manifest, there is the more chance that a few reflections on their causes, and on their probable consequences, will receive whatever portion of the reader's attention they may happen to deserve.

With respect, then, to the discredit into which old institutions and old doctrines have fallen, I may premise, that this discredit is, in my opinion, perfectly deserved. Having said this, I may perhaps hope, that no perverse interpretation will be put upon the remainder of my observations, in case some of them should not be quite so conformable to the sentiments of the day as my commencement might give reason to expect. The best guide is not he who, when people are in the right path, merely praises it, but he who shows them the pitfalls and the precipices by which it is endangered; and of which, as long as they were in the wrong road, it was not so necessary that they should be warned.

There is one very easy, and very pleasant way of accounting for this general departure from the modes of thinking of our ancestors: so easy, indeed, and so pleasant, especially to the hearer, as to be very convenient to such writers for hire or for applause, as address themselves not to the men of the age that is gone by, but to the men of the age which has commenced. This explanation is that which ascribes the altered state of opinion and feeling to the growth of the human understanding. According to this doctrine, we reject the sophisms and prejudices which misled the uncultivated minds of our ancestors, because we have learnt too much, and have become too wise, to be imposed upon by such sophisms and such prejudices. It is our knowledge and our sagacity which keep us free from these gross errors. We have now risen to the capacity of perceiving our true interests; and it is no longer in the power of impostors and charlatans to deceive us.

I am unable to adopt this theory. Though a firm believer in the improvement of the age, I do not believe that its improvement has been of this kind. The grand achievement of the present age is the *diffusion* of *superficial* knowledge; and that surely is no trifle, to have been accomplished by a single generation. The persons who are in possession of knowledge adequate to the formation of sound opinions by their own lights, form also a constantly increasing number, but hitherto at all times a small one. It would be carrying the notion of the march of intellect too far, to suppose that an average man of the present day is superior to the greatest men of the beginning of the eighteenth century; yet they *held* many opinions which we are fast renouncing. The intellect of the age, therefore, is not the cause which we are in search of. I do not perceive that, in the mental training which has been received by the immense majority of the reading and thinking part of my countrymen, or in the kind of knowledge and other intellectual aliment which has been supplied to them, there is any thing likely to render them much less accessible to the influence of imposture and charlatanerie than there ever was. . . . Neither do I see, in such observations as I am able to make upon my cotemporaries, evidence that they have any principle within them which renders them much less liable now than at any former period to be misled by sophisms and prejudices. All I see is, that the opinions which have been transmitted to them from their ancestors, are not the kind of sophisms and prejudices which are fitted to possess any considerable ascendancy in their altered frame of mind. And I am rather inclined to account for this fact in a manner not reflecting such extraordinarily great honour upon the times we live in, as would result from the theory by which all is ascribed to the superior expansion of our understandings.

The intellectual tendencies of the age, considered both on the favourable and on the unfavourable side, it will be necessary, in the prosecution of the present design, to review and analyse in some detail. For the present it may be enough to remark, that it is seldom safe to ground a positive estimate of a character upon mere negatives: and that the faults or the prejudices, which a person, or an age, or a nation *has not,* go but a very little way with a wise man towards forming a high opinion of them. A person may be without a single prejudice, and yet utterly unfit for every purpose in nature. To have erroneous convictions is one evil; but to have no strong or deep-rooted convictions at all, is an enormous one. Before I compliment either a man or a generation upon having got rid of their prejudices, I require to know what they have substituted in lieu of them.

Now, it is self-evident that no fixed opinions have yet generally established themselves in the place of those which we have abandoned; that no new doctrines, philosophical or social, as yet command, or appear likely soon to command, an assent at all comparable in unanimity to that which the ancient doctrines could boast of while they continued in vogue. So long as this intellectual anarchy shall endure, we may be warranted in believing that we are in a fair way to become wiser than our forefathers; but it would be premature to affirm that we are already wiser. We have not yet advanced beyond the unsettled state, in which the mind is, when it has recently found itself out in a grievous error, and has not yet satisfied itself of the truth. The men of the present day rather incline to an opinion than embrace it; few, except the very penetrating, or the very presumptuous, have full confidence in their own convictions. This is not a state of health, but, at the best, of convalescence. It is a necessary stage in the progress of civilization, but it is attended with numerous evils; as one part of a road may be rougher or more dangerous than another, although every step brings the traveller nearer to his desired end.

Not increase of wisdom, but a cause of the reality of which we are better assured, may serve to account for the decay of prejudices; and this is, increase of discussion. Men may not reason better, concerning the great questions in which human nature is interested, but they reason more. Large subjects are discussed more, and longer, and by more minds. Discussion has penetrated deeper into society; and if no greater numbers than before have attained the higher degrees of intelligence, fewer grovel in that state of abject stupidity, which can only co-exist with utter apathy and sluggishness.

The progress which we have made, is precisely that sort of progress which increase of discussion suffices to produce, whether it be attended with increase of wisdom or no. To discuss, and to question established opinions, are merely two phrases for the same thing. When all opinions are questioned, it is in time found out what are those which will not bear a close examination. Ancient doctrines are then put upon their proofs; and those which were originally errors, or have become so by change of circumstances, are thrown aside. Discussion does this. It is by discussion, also, that true opinions are discovered and diffused. But this is not so certain a consequence of it as the weakening of error. To be rationally assured that a given doctrine is *true,* it is often necessary to examine and weigh an immense variety of facts. One single well-established fact, clearly irreconcilable with a doctrine, is sufficient to prove that it is *false.* Nay, opinions often upset themselves by their own incoherence; and the impossibility of their being well-founded may admit of being brought home to a mind not possessed of so much as one positive truth. All the inconsistencies of an opinion with itself, with obvious facts, or even with other prejudices, discussion evolves and makes manifest: and indeed this mode of refutation, requiring less study and less real knowledge than any other, is better suited to the inclination of most disputants. But the moment, and the mood of mind, in which men break loose from an error, is not, except in natures very happily constituted, the most favourable to those mental processes which are necessary to the investigation of truth. What led them wrong at first, was generally nothing else but the incapacity of seeing more than one thing at a time; and that incapacity is apt to stick to them when they have turned their eyes in an altered direction. They usually resolve that the new light which has broken in upon them shall be the sole light; and they wilfully and passionately blew out the ancient lamp, which, though it did not show them what they now see, served very well to enlighten the objects in its immediate neighbourhood. Whether men adhere to old opinions or adopt new ones, they have in general an invincible propensity to split the truth, and take half, or less than half of it; and a habit of erecting their quills and bristling up like a porcupine against any one who brings them the other half, as if he were attempting to deprive them of the portion which they have.

I am far from denying, that, besides getting rid of error, we are also continually enlarging the stock of positive truth. In physical science and art, this is too manifest to be called in question; and in the moral and social sciences, I believe it to be as undeniably true. The wisest men in every age generally surpass in wisdom the wisest of any preceding age, because the wisest men possess and profit by the constantly increasing accumulation of the ideas of all ages: but the multitude (by which I mean the majority of all ranks) have the ideas of their own age, and no others: and if the multitude of one age are nearer to the truth than the multitude of another, it is only in so far as they are guided and influenced by the authority of the wisest among them. . . .

from On Liberty

from Chapter 1

INTRODUCTORY

The subject of this Essay is not the so-called Liberty of the Will, so unfortunately opposed to the misnamed doctrine of Philosophical Necessity;[1] but Civil, or Social Liberty: the nature and limits of the power which can be legitimately exercised by society over the individual. A question seldom stated, and hardly ever discussed, in general terms, but which profoundly influences the practical controversies of the age by its latent presence, and is likely soon to make itself recognized as the vital question of the future. It is so far from being new, that, in a certain sense, it has divided mankind, almost from the remotest ages; but in the stage of prog-

---

[1] The reference is to the issue between the belief that man is free to choose what he will do and the opposed doctrine that his every action is determined ultimately by external factors.

ress into which the more civilized portions of the species have now entered, it presents itself under new conditions, and requires a different and more fundamental treatment.

The struggle between Liberty and Authority is the most conspicuous feature in the portions of history with which we are earliest familiar, particularly in that of Greece, Rome, and England. But in old times this contest was between subjects, or some classes of subjects, and the Government. By liberty, was meant protection against the tyranny of the political rulers. The rulers were conceived (except in some of the popular governments of Greece) as in a necessarily antagonistic position to the people whom they ruled. They consisted of a governing One, or a governing tribe or caste, who derived their authority from inheritance or conquest, who, at all events, did not hold it at the pleasure of the governed, and whose supremacy men did not venture, perhaps did not desire, to contest, whatever precautions might be taken against its oppressive exercise. Their power was regarded as necessary, but also as highly dangerous; as a weapon which they would attempt to use against their subjects, no less than against external enemies. To prevent the weaker members of the community from being preyed upon by innumerable vultures, it was needful that there should be an animal of prey stronger than the rest, commissioned to keep them down. But as the king of the vultures would be no less bent upon preying on the flock than any of the minor harpies, it was indispensable to be in a perpetual attitude of defence against his beak and claws. The aim, therefore, of patriots was to set limits to the power which the ruler should be suffered to exercise over the community; and this limitation was what they meant by liberty. It was attempted in two ways. First, by obtaining a recognition of certain immunities, called political liberties or rights, which it was to be regarded as a breach of duty in the ruler to infringe, and which, if he did infringe, specific resistance, or general rebellion, was held to be justifiable. A second, and generally a later expedient, was the establishment of constitutional checks, by which the consent of the community, or of a body of some sort, supposed to represent its interests, was made a necessary condition to some of the more important acts of the governing power. To the first of these modes of limitation, the ruling power, in most European countries, was compelled, more or less, to submit. It was not so with the second; and, to attain this, or when already in some degree possessed, to attain it more completely, became everywhere the principal object of the lovers of liberty. And so long as mankind were content to combat one enemy by another, and to be ruled by a master, on condition of being guaranteed more or less efficaciously against his tyranny, they did not carry their aspirations beyond this point.

A time, however, came, in the progress of human affairs, when men ceased to think it a necessity of nature that their governors should be an independent power, opposed in interest to themselves. It appeared to them much better that the various magistrates of the State should be their tenants or delegates, revocable at their pleasure. In that way alone, it seemed, could they have complete security that the powers of government would never be abused to their disadvantage. By degrees this new demand for elective and temporary rulers became the prominent object of the exertions of the popular party, wherever any such party existed; and superseded, to a considerable extent, the previous efforts to limit the power of rulers. As the struggle proceeded for making the ruling power emanate from the periodical choice of the ruled, some persons began to think that too much importance had been attached to the limitation of the power itself. *That* (it might seem) was a resource against rulers whose interests were habitually opposed to those of the people. What was now wanted was, that the rulers should be identified with the people; that their interest and will should be the interest and will of the nation. The nation did not need to be protected against its own will. There was no fear of its tyrannizing over itself. Let the rulers be effectually responsible to it, promptly removable by it, and it could afford to trust them with power of which it could itself dictate the use to be made. Their power was but the nation's own power, concentrated, and in a form convenient for exercise. This mode of thought, or rather perhaps of feeling, was common among the last generation of European liberalism, in the Continental section of which it still apparently predominates. Those who admit any limit to what a government may do, except in the case of such governments as they think ought not to exist, stand out as brilliant exceptions among the political thinkers of the Continent. A similar tone of sentiment might by this time have been prevalent in our own country, if the circumstances which for a time encouraged it, had continued unaltered.

But, in political and philosophical theories, as well as in persons, success discloses faults and infirmities which failure might have concealed from observation. The notion, that the people have no need to limit their power over themselves, might seem axiomatic, when popular government was a thing only dreamed about, or read of as having existed at some distant period of the past. Neither was that notion necessarily disturbed by such temporary aberrations as those of the French Revolution, the worst of which were the work of an usurping few, and which, in any case, belonged, not to the permanent working of popular institutions, but to a sudden and convulsive outbreak against monarchical and aristocratic despotism. In time, however, a democratic republic came to occupy a large portion of the earth's surface, and made itself felt as one of the most powerful members of the community of nations; and elective and responsible government became subject to the observations and criticisms which wait upon a great existing fact. It was now perceived that such phrases as "self-government," and "the power of the people over themselves," do not express the true state of the case. The "people" who exercise the power are not always the same people with those over whom it is exercised; and the "self-government" spoken of is not the government of each by himself, but of each by all the rest. The will of the people, moreover, practically means the will of the most numerous or the most active *part* of the people; the majority, or those who succeed in making themselves accepted as the majority; the people, consequently, *may* desire to oppress a part of their number; and precautions are as much needed against this as against any other abuse of power. The limitation, therefore, of the power of government over individuals loses none of its importance when the holders of power are regularly accountable to the community, that is, to the strongest party therein. This view of things, recommending it-self equally to the intelligence of thinkers and to the inclination of those important classes in European society to whose real or supposed interests democracy is adverse, has had no difficulty in establishing itself; and in political speculations "the tyranny of the majority" is now generally included among the evils against which society requires to be on its guard.

Like other tyrannies, the tyranny of the majority was at first, and is still vulgarly, held in dread, chiefly as operating through the acts of the public authorities. But reflecting persons perceived that when society is itself the tyrant —society collectively, over the separate individuals who compose it—its means of tyrannizing are not restricted to the acts which it may do by the hands of its political functionaries. Society can and does execute its own mandates: and if it issues wrong mandates instead of right, or any mandates at all in things with which it ought not to meddle, it practises a social tyranny more formidable than many kinds of political oppression, since, though not usually upheld by such extreme penalties, it leaves fewer means of escape, penetrating much more deeply into the details of life, and enslaving the soul itself. Protection, therefore, against the tyranny of the magistrate is not enough: there needs protection also against the tyranny of the prevailing opinion and feeling; against the tendency of society to impose, by other means than civil penalties, its own ideas and practices as rules of conduct on those who dissent from them; to fetter the development, and, if possible, prevent the formation, of any individuality not in harmony with its ways, and compel all characters to fashion themselves upon the model of its own. There is a limit to the legitimate interference of collective opinion with individual independence: and to find that limit, and maintain it against encroachment, is as indispensable to a good condition of human affairs, as protection against political despotism. . . .

The object of this Essay is to assert one very simple principle, as entitled to govern absolutely the dealings of society with the individual in the way of compulsion and control, whether the means used be physical force in the form of legal penalties, or the moral coercion of public opinion. That principle is, that the sole end for which mankind are warranted, individually or collectively, in interfering with the liberty of action of any of their number, is self-protection. That the only purpose for which power can be rightfully exercised over any member of a civilised community, against his will, is to prevent harm to others. His own good, either physical or moral, is not a sufficient warrant. He cannot rightfully be compelled to do or forbear because it will be better for him to do so, because it will make him happier, because, in the opinions of others, to do so would be wise, or even right. These are good reasons for remonstrating with him, or reasoning with him, or persuading him, or entreating him, but not for compelling him, or visting him with any evil in case he do otherwise. To justify that, the conduct from which it is desired to deter him, must be calculated to produce evil to some one else. The only part of the conduct of any one, for which he is amenable to society, is that which concerns others. In the part which merely concerns himself, his independence is, of right, absolute. Over himself, over his own body and mind, the individual is sovereign.

It is, perhaps, hardly necessary to say that this doctrine is meant to apply only to human beings in the maturity of their faculties. We are not speaking of children, or of young persons below the age which the law may fix as that of manhood or womanhood. Those who are still in a state to require being taken care of by others, must be protected against their own actions as well as against external injury. For the same reason, we may leave out of consideration those backward states of society in which the race itself may be considered as in its nonage. The early difficulties in the way of spontaneous progress are so great, that there is seldom any choice of means for overcoming them; and a ruler full of the spirit of improvement is warranted in the use of any expedients that will attain an end, perhaps otherwise unattainable. Despotism is a legitimate mode of government in dealing with barbarians, provided the end be their improvement, and the means justified by actually effecting that end. Liberty, as a principle, has no application to any state of things anterior to the time when mankind have become capable of being improved by free and equal discussion. Until then, there is nothing for them but implicit obedience to an Akbar or a Charlemagne,[2] if they are so fortunate as to find one.

But as soon as mankind have attained the capacity of being guided to their own improvement by conviction or persuasion (a period long since reached in all nations with whom we need here concern ourselves), compulsion, either in the direct form or in that of pains and penalties for non-compliance, is no longer admissible as a means to their own good, and justifiable only for the security of others.

It is proper to state that I forgo any advantage which could be derived to my argument from the idea of abstract right, as a thing independent of utility. I regard utility as the ultimate appeal on all ethical questions; but it must be utility in the largest sense, grounded on the permanent interests of man as a progressive being. Those interests, I contend, authorize the subjection of individual spontaneity to external control, only in respect to those actions of each, which concern the interest of other people. If any one does an act hurtful to others, there is a prima facie case for punishing him, by law, or, where legal penalties are not safely applicable, by general disapprobation. There are also many positive acts for the benefit of others, which he may rightfully be compelled to perform; such as, to give evidence in a court of justice; to bear his fair share in the common defence, or in any other joint work necessary to the interest of the society of which he enjoys the protection; and to perform certain acts of individual beneficence, such as saving a fellow creature's life, or interposing to protect the defenceless against ill-usage, things which whenever it is obviously a man's duty to do, he may rightfully be made responsible to society for not doing. A person may cause evil to others not only by his actions but by his inaction, and in either case he is justly accountable to them for the injury. The latter case, it is true, requires a much more cautious exercise of compulsion than the former. To make any one answerable for doing evil to others, is the rule; to make him answerable for not preventing evil, is, comparatively speaking, the exception. Yet there are many cases clear enough and grave enough to justify that exception. In all things which regard the external relations of the individual, he is *de jure*[3] amenable to those whose

---

2 Akbar Khan (1566–1605), Mogul emperor of Hindustan. Charlemagne (742–815), king of the Franks and later emperor of the West.
3 By law.

interests are concerned, and if need be, to society as their protector. There are often good reasons for not holding him to the responsibility; but these reasons must arise from the special expediencies of the case: either because it is a kind of case in which he is on the whole likely to act better, when left to his own discretion, than when controlled in any way in which society have it in their power to control him; or because the attempt to exercise control would produce other evils, greater than those which it would prevent. When such reasons as these preclude the enforcement of responsibility, the conscience of the agent himself should step into the vacant judgement-seat, and protect those interests of others which have no external protection; judging himself all the more rigidly, because the case does not admit of his being made accountable to the judgement of his fellow creatures.

But there is a sphere of action in which society, as distinguished from the individual, has, if any, only an indirect interest; comprehending all that portion of a person's life and conduct which affects only himself, or if it also affects others, only with their free, voluntary, and undeceived consent and participation. When I say only himself, I mean directly, and in the first instance: for whatever affects himself, may affect others through himself; and the objection which may be grounded on this contingency will receive consideration in the sequel. This, then, is the appropriate region of human liberty. It comprises, first, the inward domain of consciousness; demanding liberty of conscience, in the most comprehensive sense; liberty of thought and feeling; absolute freedom of opinion and sentiment on all subjects, practical or speculative, scientific, moral, or theological. The liberty of expressing and publishing opinions may seem to fall under a different principle, since it belongs to that part of the conduct of an individual which concerns other people; but, being almost of as much importance as the liberty of thought itself, and resting in great part on the same reasons, is practically inseparable from it. Secondly, the principle requires liberty of tastes and pursuits; of framing the plan of our life to suit our own character; of doing as we like, subject to such consequences as may follow: without impediment from our fellow creatures, so long as what we do does not harm them, even though they should think our conduct foolish, perverse,

or wrong. Thirdly, from this liberty of each individual, follows the liberty, within the same limits, of combination among individuals; freedom to unite, for any purpose not involving harm to others: the persons combining being supposed to be of full age, and not forced or deceived.

No society in which these liberties are not, on the whole, respected, is free, whatever may be its form of government; and none is completely free in which they do not exist absolute and unqualified. The only freedom which deserves the name, is that of pursuing our own good in our own way, so long as we do not attempt to deprive others of theirs, or impede their efforts to obtain it. Each is the proper guardian of his own health, whether bodily, or mental and spiritual. Mankind are greater gainers by suffering each other to live as seems good to themselves, than by compelling each to live as seems good to the rest.

Though this doctrine is anything but new, and, to some persons, may have the air of a truism, there is no doctrine which stands more directly opposed to the general tendency of existing opinion and practice. Society has expended fully as much effort in the attempt (according to its lights) to compel people to conform to its notions of personal, as of social excellence. The ancient commonwealths thought themselves entitled to practise, and the ancient philosophers countenanced, the regulation of every part of private conduct by public authority, on the ground that the State had a deep interest in the whole bodily and mental discipline of every one of its citizens; a mode of thinking which may have been admissible in small republics surrounded by powerful enemies, in constant peril of being subverted by foreign attack or internal commotion, and to which even a short interval of relaxed energy and self-command might so easily be fatal, that they could not afford to wait for the salutary permanent effects of freedom. In the modern world, the greater size of political communities, and, above all, the separation between spiritual and temporal authority (which placed the direction of men's consciences in other hands than those which controlled their worldly affairs), prevented so great an interference by law in the details of private life; but the engines of moral repression have been wielded more strenuously against divergence from the reigning opinion in self-regarding, than even in social matters; religion, the most powerful of the elements which have entered into the formation of moral feeling, having almost always been governed either by the ambition of a hierarchy, seeking control over every department of human conduct, or by the spirit of Puritanism. And some of those modern reformers who have placed themselves in strongest opposition to the religions of the past, have been no way behind either churches or sects in their assertion of the right of spiritual domination: M. Comte, in particular, whose social system, as unfolded in his *Système de Politique Positive,* aims at establishing (though by moral more than by legal appliances) a despotism of society over the individual, surpassing anything contemplated in the political ideal of the most rigid disciplinarian among the ancient philosophers.[4]

Apart from the peculiar tenets of individual thinkers, there is also in the world at large an increasing inclination to stretch unduly the powers of society over the individual, both by the force of opinion and even by that of legislation: and as the tendency of all the changes taking place in the world is to strengthen society, and diminish the power of the individual, this encroachment is not one of the evils which tend spontaneously to disappear, but, on the contrary, to grow more and more formidable. The disposition of mankind, whether as rulers or as fellow citizens to impose their own opinions and inclinations as a rule of conduct on others, is so energetically supported by some of the best and by some of the worst feelings incident to human nature, that it is hardly ever kept under restraint by anything but want of power; and as the power is not declining, but growing, unless a strong barrier of moral conviction can be raised against the mischief, we must expect, in the present circumstances of the world, to see it increase.

from Chapter 2

OF THE LIBERTY OF THOUGHT AND DISCUSSION

. . . In the present age—which has been described as "destitute of faith, but terrified at scepticism"[5] —in which people feel sure, not so much that their opinions are true, as that they should not know what to do without them—the claims of an opinion to be protected from public attack are rested not so much on its truth, as on its importance to society. There are, it is alleged, certain beliefs, so useful, not to say indispensable to well-being, that it is as much the duty of governments to uphold those beliefs, as to protect any other of the interests of society. In a case of such necessity, and so directly in the line of their duty, something less than infallibility may, it is maintained, warrant, and even bind, governments, to act on their own opinion, confirmed by the general opinion of mankind. It is also often argued, and still oftener thought, that none but bad men would desire to weaken these salutary beliefs; and there can be nothing wrong, it is thought, in restraining bad men, and prohibiting what only such men would wish to practise. This mode of thinking makes the justification of restraints on discussion not a question of the truth of doctrines, but of their usefulness; and flatters itself by that means to escape the responsibility of claiming to be an infallible judge of opinions. But those who thus satisfy themselves, do not perceive that the assumption of infallibility is merely shifted from one point to another. The usefulness of an opinion is itself matter of opinion: as disputable, as open to discussion, and requiring discussion as much, as the opinion itself. There is the same need of an infallible judge of opinions to decide an opinion to be noxious, as to decide it to be false, unless the opinion condemned has full opportunity of defending itself. And it will not do to say that the heretic may be allowed to maintain the utility or harmlessness of his opinion, though forbidden to maintain its truth. The truth of an opinion is part of its utility. If we would know whether or not it is desirable that a proposition should be believed, is it possible to exclude the consideration of whether or not it is true? In the opinion, not of bad men, but of the best men, no belief which is contrary to truth can be really useful: and can you prevent such men from urging that plea, when they are charged with culpability for denying some doctrine which they are told is useful, but which they believe to be false? Those who are on the side of received opinions, never fail to take all possible advantage of this plea; you do not find *them* handling the question of utility as if it could be completely abstracted

---

4 See chap. 5 of Mill's *Autobiography,* note 41. Comte in sketching the ideal positivist society finally denied to the individual every right save that of doing his duty.
5 By Carlyle in his essay on Sir Walter Scott (1838).

from that of truth: on the contrary, it is, above all, because their doctrine is the "truth," that the knowledge or the belief of it is held to be so indispensable. There can be no fair discussion of the question of usefulness, when an argument so vital may be employed on one side, but not on the other. And in point of fact, when law or public feeling do not permit the truth of an opinion to be disputed, they are just as little tolerant of a denial of its usefulness. The utmost they allow is an extenuation of its absolute necessity, or of the positive guilt of rejecting it.

In order more fully to illustrate the mischief of denying a hearing to opinions because we, in our own judgement, have condemned them, it will be desirable to fix down the discussion to a concrete case; and I choose, by preference, the cases which are least favourable to me— in which the argument against freedom of opinion, both on the score of truth and on that of utility, is considered the strongest. Let the opinions impugned be the belief in a God and in a future state, or any of the commonly received doctrines of morality. To fight the battle on such ground, gives a great advantage to an unfair antagonist; since he will be sure to say (and many who have no desire to be unfair will say it internally), Are these the doctrines which you do not deem sufficiently certain to be taken under the protection of law? Is the belief in a God one of the opinions, to feel sure of which, you hold to be assuming infallibility? But I must be permitted to observe, that it is not the feeling sure of a doctrine (be it what it may) which I call an assumption of infallibility. It is the undertaking to decide that question *for others,* without allowing them to hear what can be said on the contrary side. And I denounce and reprobate this pretension not the less, if put forth on the side of my most solemn convictions. However positive any one's persuasion may be, not only of the falsity but of the pernicious consequences—not only of the pernicious consequences, but (to adopt expressions which I altogether condemn) the immorality and impiety of an opinion; yet if, in pursuance of that private judgement, though backed by the public judgement of his country or his cotemporaries, he prevents the opinion from being heard in its defence, he assumes infallibility. And so far from the assumption being less objectionable or less dangerous because the opinion is called immoral or impious, this is the case of all others in which it is most fatal. These are exactly the occasions on which the men of one generation commit those dreadful mistakes, which excite the astonishment and horror of posterity. It is among such that we find the instances memorable in history, when the arm of the law has been employed to root out the best men and the noblest doctrines; with deplorable success as to the men, though some of the doctrines have survived to be (as if in mockery) invoked, in defence of similar conduct towards those who dissent from *them,* or from their received interpretation.

Mankind can hardly be too often reminded, that there was once a man named Socrates, between whom and the legal authorities and public opinion of his time, there took place a memorable collision. Born in an age and country abounding in individual greatness, this man has been handed down to us by those who best knew both him and the age, as the most virtuous man in it; while *we* know him as the head and prototype of all subsequent teachers of virtue, the source equally of the lofty inspiration of Plato and the judicious utilitarianism of Aristotle, *"i maëstri di color che sanno,"*[6] the two headsprings of ethical as of all other philosophy. This acknowledged master of all the eminent thinkers who have since lived—whose fame, still growing after more than two thousand years, all but outweighs the whole remainder of the names which make his native city illustrious —was put to death by his countrymen, after a judicial conviction, for impiety and immorality. Impiety, in denying the gods recognized by the State; indeed his accuser asserted (see the *Apologia*) that he believed in no gods at all. Immorality, in being, by his doctrines and instructions, a "corruptor of youth." Of these charges the tribunal, there is every ground for believing, honestly found him guilty, and condemned the man who probably of all then born had deserved best of mankind, to be put to death as a criminal.

To pass from this to the only other instance of judicial iniquity, the mention of which, after the condemnation of Socrates, would not be an anticlimax: the event which took place on Cal-

---

[6] Mill has put into the plural the description which Dante gave of Aristotle in *The Divine Comedy:* "The master of those who know."

vary rather more than eighteen hundred years ago. The man who left on the memory of those who witnessed his life and conversation, such an impression of his moral grandeur, that eighteen subsequent centuries have done homage to him as the Almighty in person, was ignominiously put to death, as what? As a blasphemer. Men did not merely mistake their benefactor; they mistook him for the exact contrary of what he was, and treated him as that prodigy of impiety, which they themselves are now held to be, for their treatment of him. The feelings with which mankind now regard these lamentable transactions, especially the later of the two, render them extremely unjust in their judgement of the unhappy actors. These were, to all appearance, not bad men—not worse than men commonly are, but rather the contrary; men who possessed in a full, or somewhat more than a full measure, the religious, moral, and patriotic feelings of their time and people: the very kind of men who, in all times, our own included, have every chance of passing through life blameless and respected. The high-priest who rent his garments when the words were pronounced, which, according to all the ideas of his country, constituted the blackest guilt, was in all probability quite as sincere in his horror and indignation, as the generality of respectable and pious men now are in the religious and moral sentiments they profess; and most of those who now shudder at his conduct, if they had lived in his time, and been born Jews, would have acted precisely as he did. Orthodox Christians who are tempted to think that those who stoned to death the first martyrs must have been worse men than they themselves are, ought to remember that one of those persecutors was Saint Paul.

Let us add one more example, the most striking of all, if the impressiveness of an error is measured by the wisdom and virtue of him who falls into it. If ever any one, possessed of power, had grounds for thinking himself the best and most enlightened among his cotemporaries, it was the Emperor Marcus Aurelius.[7] Absolute monarch of the whole civilized world, he preserved through life not only the most unblemished justice, but what was less to be expected

from his Stoical breeding, the tenderest heart. The few failings which are attributed to him, were all on the side of indulgence: while his writings, the highest ethical product of the ancient mind, differ scarcely perceptibly, if they differ at all, from the most characteristic teachings of Christ. This man, a better Christian in all but the dogmatic sense of the word, than almost any of the ostensibly Christian sovereigns who have since reigned, persecuted Christianity. Placed at the summit of all the previous attainments of humanity, with an open, unfettered intellect, and a character which led him of himself to embody in his moral writings the Christian ideal, he yet failed to see that Christianity was to be a good and not an evil to the world, with his duties to which he was so deeply penetrated. Existing society he knew to be in a deplorable state. But such as it was, he saw, or thought he saw, that it was held together, and prevented from being worse, by belief and reverence of the received divinities. As a ruler of mankind, he deemed it his duty not to suffer society to fall in pieces; and saw not how, if its existing ties were removed, any others could be formed which could again knit it together. The new religion openly aimed at dissolving these ties: unless, therefore, it was his duty to adopt that religion, it seemed to be his duty to put it down. Inasmuch then as the theology of Christianity did not appear to him true or of divine origin; inasmuch as this strange history of a crucified God was not credible to him, and a system which purported to rest entirely upon a foundation to him so wholly unbelievable, could not be foreseen by him to be that renovating agency which, after all abatements, it has in fact proved to be; the gentlest and most amiable of philosophers and rulers, under a solemn sense of duty, authorized the persecution of Christianity. To my mind this is one of the most tragical facts in all history. It is a bitter thought, how different a thing the Christianity of the world might have been, if the Christian faith had been adopted as the religion of the empire under the auspices of Marcus Aurelius instead of those of Constantine.[8] But it would be equally unjust to him and false to truth, to deny, that no one plea which can be urged for

---

[7] Roman emperor from 161 to 180.

[8] Roman emperor from 306 to 337.

punishing anti-Christian teaching, was wanting to Marcus Aurelius for punishing, as he did, the propagation of Christianity. No Christian more firmly believes that Atheism is false, and tends to the dissolution of society, than Marcus Aurelius believed the same things of Christianity; he who, of all men then living, might have been thought the most capable of appreciating it. Unless any one who approves of punishment for the promulgation of opinions, flatters himself that he is a wiser and better man than Marcus Aurelius—more deeply versed in the wisdom of his time, more elevated in his intellect above it—more earnest in his search for truth, or more single-minded in his devotion to it when found; —let him abstain from that assumption of the joint infallibility of himself and the multitude, which the great Antoninus[9] made with so unfortunate a result.

Aware of the impossibility of defending the use of punishment for restraining irreligious opinions, by any argument which will not justify Marcus Antoninus, the enemies of religious freedom, when hard pressed, occasionally accept this consequence, and say, with Dr. Johnson, that the persecutors of Christianity were in the right; that persecution is an ordeal through which truth ought to pass, and always passes successfully, legal penalties being, in the end, powerless against truth, though sometimes beneficially effective against mischievous errors. This is a form of the argument for religious intolerance, sufficiently remarkable not to be passed without notice.

A theory which maintains that truth may justifiably be persecuted because persecution cannot possibly do it any harm, cannot be charged with being intentionally hostile to the reception of new truths; but we cannot commend the generosity of its dealing with the persons to whom mankind are indebted for them. To discover to the world something which deeply concerns it, and of which it was previously ignorant; to prove to it that it had been mistaken on some vital point of temporal or spiritual interest, is as important a service as a human being can render to his fellow creatures, and in certain cases, as in those of the early Christians and of the Re-

formers, those who think with Dr. Johnson believe it to have been the most precious gift which could be bestowed on mankind. That the authors of such splendid benefits should be requited by martyrdom; that their reward should be to be dealt with as the vilest of criminals, is not, upon this theory, a deplorable error and misfortune, for which humanity should mourn in sackcloth and ashes, but the normal and justifiable state of things. The propounder of a new truth, according to this doctrine, should stand, as stood, in the legislation of the Locrians,[10] the proposer of a new law, with a halter round his neck, to be instantly tightened if the public assembly did not, on hearing his reasons, then and there adopt his proposition. People who defend this mode of treating benefactors, cannot be supposed to set much value on the benefit; and I believe this view of the subject is mostly confined to the sort of persons who think that new truths may have been desirable once, but that we have had enough of them now.

But, indeed, the dictum that truth always triumphs over persecution, is one of those pleasant falsehoods which men repeat after one another till they pass into commonplaces, but which all experience refutes. History teems with instances of truth put down by persecution. If not suppressed for ever, it may be thrown back for centuries. . . . Persecution has always succeeded, save where the heretics were too strong a party to be effectually persecuted. No reasonable person can doubt that Christianity might have been extirpated in the Roman Empire. It spread, and became predominant, because the persecutions were only occasional, lasting but a short time, and separated by long intervals of almost undisturbed propagandism. It is a piece of idle sentimentality that truth, merely as truth, has any inherent power denied to error, of prevailing against the dungeon and the stake. Men are not more zealous for truth than they often are for error, and a sufficient application of legal or even of social penalties will generally succeed in stopping the propagation of either. The real advantage which truth has, consists in this, that when an opinion is true, it may be extinguished once, twice, or many times, but in the course of ages there will generally be found persons to

---

[9] The emperor's full name was Marcus Aurelius Antoninus.

[10] Ancient inhabitants of a division of middle Greece.

rediscover it, until some one of its reappearances falls on a time when from favourable circumstances it escapes persecution until it has made such head as to withstand all subsequent attempts to suppress it.

It will be said, that we do not now put to death the introducers of new opinions: we are not like our fathers who slew the prophets, we even build sepulchres to them. It is true we no longer put heretics to death; and the amount of penal infliction which modern feeling would probably tolerate, even against the most obnoxious opinions, is not sufficient to extirpate them. But let us not flatter ourselves that we are yet free from the stain even of legal persecution. Penalties for opinion, or at least for its expression, still exist by law; and their enforcement is not, even in these times, so unexampled as to make it at all incredible that they may some day be revived in full force. In the year 1857, at the summer assizes of the county of Cornwall, an unfortunate man, said to be of unexceptionable conduct in all relations of life, was sentenced to twenty-one months' imprisonment, for uttering, and writing on a gate, some offensive words concerning Christianity. Within a month of the same time, at the Old Bailey, two persons, on two separate occasions, were rejected as jurymen, and one of them grossly insulted by the judge and by one of the counsel, because they honestly declared that they had no theological belief; and a third, a foreigner, for the same reason, was denied justice against a thief. This refusal of redress took place in virtue of the legal doctrine, that no person can be allowed to give evidence in a court of justice, who does not profess belief in a God (any god is sufficient) and in a future state; which is equivalent to declaring such persons to be outlaws, excluded from the protection of the tribunals; who may not only be robbed or assaulted with impunity, if no one but themselves, or persons of similar opinions, be present, but any one else may be robbed or assaulted with impunity, if the proof of the fact depends on their evidence. The assumption on which this is grounded is that the oath is worthless, of a person who does not believe in a future state; a proposition which betokens much ignorance of history in those who assent to it (since it is historically true that a large proportion of infidels in all ages have been persons of distinguished integrity and honour); and would be maintained by no one who had the smallest conception how many of the persons in greatest repute with the world, both for virtues and for attainments, are well known, at least to their intimates, to be unbelievers. The rule, besides, is suicidal, and cuts away its own foundation. Under pretence that atheists must be liars, it admits the testimony of all atheists who are willing to lie, and rejects only those who brave the obloquy of publicly confessing a detested creed rather than affirm a falsehood. A rule thus self-convicted of absurdity so far as regards its professed purpose, can be kept in force only as a badge of hatred, a relic of persecution; a persecution, too, having the peculiarity, that the qualification for undergoing it, is the being clearly proved not to deserve it. The rule, and the theory it implies, are hardly less insulting to believers than to infidels. For if he who does not believe in a future state, necessarily lies, it follows that they who do believe are only prevented from lying, if prevented they are, by the fear of hell. We will not do the authors and abettors of the rule the injury of supposing, that the conception which they have formed of Christian virtue is drawn from their own consciousness.

These, indeed, are but rags and remnants of persecution, and may be thought to be not so much an indication of the wish to persecute, as an example of that very frequent infirmity of English minds, which makes them take a preposterous pleasure in the assertion of a bad principle, when they are no longer bad enough to desire to carry it really into practice. But unhappily there is no security in the state of the public mind, that the suspension of worse forms of legal persecution, which has lasted for about the space of a generation, will continue. In this age the quiet surface of routine is as often ruffled by attempts to resuscitate past evils, as to introduce new benefits. What is boasted of at the present time as the revival of religion, is always, in narrow and uncultivated minds, at least as much the revival of bigotry; and where there is the strong permanent leaven of intolerance in the feelings of a people, which at all times abides in the middle classes of this country, it needs but little to provoke them into actively persecuting those whom they have never ceased to think proper objects of persecution.[11] For it is this—it is the opinions men entertain, and the feelings they cherish, respecting those who disown the beliefs they deem important, which makes this country not a place of mental freedom. For a long time past, the chief mischief of the legal penalties is that they strengthen the social stigma. It is that stigma which is really effective, and so effective is it, that the profession of opinions which are under the ban of society is much less common in England, than is, in many other countries, the avowal of those which incur risk of judicial punishment. In respect to all persons but those whose pecuniary circumstances make them independent of the goodwill of other people, opinion, on this subject, is as efficacious as law; men might as well be imprisoned, as excluded from the means of earning their bread. Those whose bread is already secured, and who desire no favours from men in power, or from bodies of men, or from the public, have nothing to fear from the open avowal of any opinions, but to be ill-thought of and ill-spoken of, and this it ought not to require a very heroic mould to enable them to bear. There is no room for any appeal *ad misericordiam*[12] in behalf of such persons. But though we do not now inflict so much evil on those who think differently from us, as it was formerly our custom to do, it may be that we do ourselves as much evil as ever by our treatment of them. Socrates was put to death, but the Socratic philosophy rose like the sun in heaven, and spread its illumination over the whole intellectual firmament. Christians were cast to the lions, but the Christian church grew up a stately and spreading tree, overtopping the older and less vigorous growths, and stifling them by its shade. Our merely social intolerance kills no one, roots out no opinions, but induces men to disguise them, or to abstain from any active effort for their diffusion. With us, heretical opinions do not perceptibly gain, or even lose, ground in each decade or generation; they never blaze out far and wide, but continue to smoulder in the narrow circles of thinking and studious persons among whom they originate, without ever lighting up the general affairs of mankind with either a true or a deceptive light. And thus is kept up a state of things very satisfactory to some minds, because, without the unpleasant process of fining or imprisoning anybody, it maintains all prevailing opinions outwardly undisturbed, while it does not absolutely interdict the exercise of reason by dissentients afflicted with the malady of thought. A convenient plan for having peace in the intellectual world, and keeping all things going on therein very much as they do already. But the price paid for this sort of intellectual pacification, is the sacrifice of the entire moral courage of the human mind. A state of things in which a large portion of the most active and inquiring intellects find it advisable to keep the general principles and grounds of their convictions within their own breasts, and attempt, in what they address to the public, to fit as much as they can of their own conclusions to premises which they have internally renounced, cannot send forth the open, fearless characters, and logical, consistent intellects who once adorned the thinking world. The sort of men who can be looked for under it, are either mere conformers to commonplace, or time-servers for truth, whose arguments on all great subjects are meant for their hearers, and are not those which have convinced themselves. Those who avoid this alternative, do so by narrowing their thoughts and interest to things which can be

---

11 "Ample warning may be drawn from the large infusion of the passions of a persecutor, which mingled with the general display of the worst parts of our national character on the occasion of the Sepoy insurrection. The ravings of fanatics or charlatans from the pulpit may be unworthy of notice; but the heads of the Evangelical party have announced as their principle for the government of Hindoos and Mohammedans, that no schools be supported by public money in which the Bible is not taught, and by necessary consequence that no public employment be given to any but real or pretended Christians. An under-Secretary of State, in a speech delivered to his constituents on November 12, 1857, is reported to have said: 'Toleration of their faith' (the faith of a hundred millions of British subjects), 'the superstition which they called religion, by the British Government, had had the effect of retarding the ascendancy of the British name, and preventing the salutary growth of Christianity. . . . Toleration was the great corner-stone of the religious liberties of this country; but do not let them abuse that precious word toleration. As he understood it, it meant the complete liberty to all, freedom of worship, *among Christians, who worshipped upon the same foundation.* It meant toleration of all sects and denominations of *Christians who believed in the one mediation.*' I desire to call attention to the fact, that a man who has been deemed fit to fill a high office in the government of this country, under a liberal Ministry, maintains the doctrine that all who do not believe in the divinity of Christ are beyond the pale of toleration. Who, after this imbecile display, can indulge the illusion that religious persecution has passed away, never to return?" (Mill)

12 To mercy or pity.

spoken of without venturing within the region of principles, that is, to small practical matters, which would come right of themselves, if but the minds of mankind were strengthened and enlarged, and which will never be made effectually right until then: while that which would strengthen and enlarge men's minds, free and daring speculation on the highest subjects, is abandoned.

Those in whose eyes this reticence on the part of heretics is no evil, should consider in the first place, that in consequence of it there is never any fair and thorough discussion of heretical opinions; and that such of them as could not stand such a discussion, though they may be prevented from spreading, do not disappear. But it is not the minds of heretics that are deteriorated most, by the ban placed on all inquiry which does not end in the orthodox conclusions. The greatest harm done is to those who are not heretics, and whose whole mental development is cramped, and their reason cowed, by the fear of heresy. Who can compute what the world loses in the multitude of promising intellects combined with timid characters, who dare not follow out any bold, vigorous, independent train of thought, lest it should land them in something which would admit of being considered irreligious or immoral? Among them we may occasionally see some man of deep conscientiousness, and subtle and refined understanding, who spends a life in sophisticating with an intellect which he cannot silence, and exhausts the resources of ingenuity in attempting to reconcile the promptings of his conscience and reason with orthodoxy, which yet he does not, perhaps, to the end succeed in doing. No one can be a great thinker who does not recognise, that as a thinker it is his first duty to follow his intellect to whatever conclusions it may lead. Truth gains more even by the errors of one who, with due study and preparation, thinks for himself, than by the true opinions of those who only hold them because they do not suffer themselves to think. Not that it is solely, or chiefly, to form great thinkers, that freedom of thinking is required. On the contrary, it is as much and even more indispensable, to enable average human beings to attain the mental stature which they are capable of. There have been, and may again be, great individual thinkers, in a general atmosphere of mental slavery. But there never has been, nor ever will be, in that atmosphere, an intellectually active people. When any people has made a temporary approach to such a character, it has been because the dread of heterodox speculation was for a time suspended. Where there is a tacit convention that principles are not to be disputed; where the discussion of the greatest questions which can occupy humanity is considered to be closed, we cannot hope to find that generally high scale of mental activity which has made some periods of history so remarkable. Never when controversy avoided the subjects which are large and important enough to kindle enthusiasm, was the mind of a people stirred up from its foundations, and the impulse given which raised even persons of the most ordinary intellect to something of the dignity of thinking beings. Of such we have had an example in the condition of Europe during the times immediately following the Reformation; another, though limited to the Continent and to a more cultivated class, in the speculative movement of the latter half of the eighteenth century; and a third, of still briefer duration, in the intellectual fermentation of Germany during the Goethian and Fichtean period. These periods differed widely in the particular opinions which they developed; but were alike in this, that during all three the yoke of authority was broken. In each, an old mental despotism had been thrown off, and no new one had yet taken its place. The impulse given at these three periods has made Europe what it now is. Every single improvement which has taken place either in the human mind or in institutions, may be traced distinctly to one or other of them. Appearances have for some time indicated that all three impulses are wellnigh spent; and we can expect no fresh start, until we again assert our mental freedom. . . .

Chapter 3

OF INDIVIDUALITY, AS ONE OF THE ELEMENTS OF WELL-BEING

Such being the reasons which make it imperative that human beings should be free to form opinions, and to express their opinions without reserve; and such the baneful consequences to the intellectual, and through that to the moral nature of man, unless this liberty is either conceded, or asserted in spite of prohibition; let us next examine whether the same reasons do not require that men should be free to act upon their opinions—to carry these out in their lives, without hindrance, either physical or moral, from their fellow men, so long as it is at their own risk and peril. This last proviso is of course indispensable. No one pretends that actions should be as free as opinions. On the contrary, even opinions lose their immunity, when the circumstances in which they are expressed are such as to constitute their expression a positive instigation to some mischievous act. An opinion that corn-dealers are starvers of the poor, or that private property is robbery, ought to be unmolested when simply circulated through the press, but may justly incur punishment when delivered orally to an excited mob assembled before the house of a corn-dealer, or when handed about among the same mob in the form of a placard. Acts, of whatever kind, which, without justifiable cause, do harm to others, may be, and in the more important cases absolutely require to be, controlled by the unfavourable sentiments, and, when needful, by the active interference of mankind. The liberty of the individual must be thus far limited; he must not make himself a nuisance to other people. But if he refrains from molesting others in what concerns them, and merely acts according to his own inclination and judgement in things which concern himself, the same reasons which show that opinion should be free, prove also that he should be allowed, without molestation, to carry his opinions into practice at his own cost. That mankind are not infallible; that their truths, for the most part, are only half-truths; that unity of opinion, less resulting from the fullest and freest comparison of opposite opinions, is not desirable, and diversity not an evil, but a good, until mankind are much more capable than at present of recognizing all sides of the truth, are principles applicable to men's modes of action, not less than to their opinions. As it is useful that while mankind are imperfect there should be different opinions, so is it that there should be different experiments of living; that free scope should be given to varieties of character, short of injury to others; and that the worth of different modes of life should be proved practically, when any one thinks fit to try them.

It is desirable, in short, that in things which do not primarily concern others, individuality should assert itself. Where, not the person's own character, but the traditions or customs of other people are the rule of conduct, there is wanting one of the principal ingredients of human happiness, and quite the chief ingredient of individual and social progress.

In maintaining this principle, the greatest difficulty to be encountered does not lie in the appreciation of means towards an acknowledged end, but in the indifference of persons in general to the end itself. If it were felt that the free development of individuality is one of the leading essentials of well-being; that it is not only a co-ordinate element with all that is designated by the terms civilization, instruction, education, culture, but is itself a necessary part and condition of all those things; there would be no danger that liberty should be undervalued, and the adjustment of the boundaries between it and social control would present no extraordinary difficulty. But the evil is, that individual spontaneity is hardly recognized by the common modes of thinking, as having any intrinsic worth, or deserving any regard on its own account. The majority, being satisfied with the ways of mankind as they now are (for it is they who make them what they are), cannot comprehend why those ways should not be good enough for everybody; and what is more, spontaneity forms no part of the ideal of the majority of moral and social reformers, but is rather looked on with jealousy, as a troublesome and perhaps rebellious obstruction to the general acceptance of what these reformers, in their own judgement, think would be best for mankind. Few persons, out of Germany, even comprehend the meaning of the doctrine which Wilhelm von Humboldt, so eminent both as a savant and as a politician, made the text of a treatise—that "the end of man, or that which is prescribed by the eternal or immutable dictates of reason, and not suggested by vague and transient desires, is the highest and most harmonious development of his powers to a complete and consistent whole"; that, therefore, the object "towards which every human being must ceaselessly direct his efforts, and on which especially those who design to influence their fellow men must ever keep their eyes, is the individuality of power and development";

that for this there are two requisites, "freedom, and variety of situations"; and that from the union of these arise "individual vigour and manifold diversity," which combine themselves in "originality."[13]

Little, however, as people are accustomed to a doctrine like that of Von Humboldt, and surprising as it may be to them to find so high a value attached to individuality, the question, one must nevertheless think, can only be one of degree. No one's idea of excellence in conduct is that people should do absolutely nothing but copy one another. No one would assert that people ought not to put into their mode of life, and into the conduct of their concerns, any impress whatever of their own judgement, or of their own individual character. On the other hand, it would be absurd to pretend that people ought to live as if nothing whatever had been known in the world before they came into it; as if experience had as yet done nothing towards showing that one mode of existence, or of conduct, is preferable to another. Nobody denies that people should be so taught and trained in youth, as to know and benefit by the ascertained results of human experience. But it is the privilege and proper condition of a human being, arrived at the maturity of his faculties, to use and interpret experience in his own way. It is for him to find out what part of recorded experience is properly applicable to his own circumstances and character. The traditions and customs of other people are, to a certain extent, evidence of what their experience has taught *them*; presumptive evidence, and as such, have a claim to his deference: but, in the first place, their experience may be too narrow; or they may not have interpreted it rightly. Secondly, their interpretation of experience may be correct, but unsuitable to him. Customs are made for customary circumstances, and customary characters; and his circumstances or his character may be uncustomary. Thirdly, though the customs be both good as customs, and suitable to him, yet to conform to custom, merely *as* custom, does not educate or develop in him any of the qualities which are the distinctive endowment of a human being. The human faculties of per-

ception, judgement, discriminative feeling, mental activity, and even moral preference, are exercised only in making a choice. He who does anything because it is the custom, makes no choice. He gains no practice either in discerning or in desiring what is best. The mental and moral, like the muscular powers, are improved only by being used. The faculties are called into no exercise by doing a thing merely because others do it, no more than by believing a thing only because others believe it. If the grounds of an opinion are not conclusive to the person's own reason, his reason cannot be strengthened, but is likely to be weakened, by his adopting it: and if the inducements to an act are not such as are consentaneous to his own feelings and character (where affection, or the rights of others, are not concerned) it is so much done towards rendering his feelings and character inert and torpid, instead of active and energetic.

He who lets the world, or his own portion of it, choose his plan of life for him, has no need of any other faculty than the ape-like one of imitation. He who chooses his plan for himself, employs all his faculties. He must use observation to see, reasoning and judgement to foresee, activity to gather materials for decision, discrimination to decide, and when he has decided, firmness and self-control to hold to his deliberate decision. And these qualities he requires and exercises exactly in proportion as the part of his conduct which he determines according to his own judgement and feelings is a large one. It is possible that he might be guided in some good path, and kept out of harm's way, without any of these things. But what will be his comparative worth as a human being? It really is of importance, not only what men do, but also what manner of men they are that do it. Among the works of man, which human life is rightly employed in perfecting and beautifying, the first in importance surely is man himself. Supposing it were possible to get houses built, corn grown, battles fought, causes tried, and even churches erected and prayers said, by machinery—by automatons in human form—it would be a considerable loss to exchange for these automatons even the men and women who at present inhabit the more civilized parts of the world, and who assuredly are but starved specimens of what nature can and will

[13] *The Sphere and Duties of Government,* from the German of Baron Wilhelm von Humboldt, pp. 11–13. (Mill)

produce. Human nature is not a machine to be built after a model, and set to do exactly the work prescribed for it, but a tree, which requires to grow and develop itself on all sides, according to the tendency of the inward forces which make it a living thing.

It will probably be conceded that it is desirable people should exercise their understandings, and that an intelligent following of custom, or even occasionally an intelligent deviation from custom, is better than a blind and simply mechanical adhesion to it. To a certain extent it is admitted, that our understanding should be our own: but there is not the same willingness to admit that our desires and impulses should be our own likewise; or that to possess impulses of our own, and of any strength, is anything but a peril and a snare. Yet desires and impulses are as much a part of a perfect human being, as beliefs and restraints: and strong impulses are only perilous when not properly balanced; when one set of aims and inclinations is developed into strength, while others, which ought to co-exist with them, remain weak and inactive. It is not because men's desires are strong that they act ill; it is because their consciences are weak. There is no natural connexion between strong impulses and a weak conscience. The natural connexion is the other way. To say that one person's desires and feelings are stronger and more various than those of another, is merely to say that he has more of the raw material of human nature, and is therefore capable, perhaps of more evil, but certainly of more good. Strong impulses are but another name for energy. Energy may be turned to bad uses; but more good may always be made of an energetic nature, than of an indolent and impassive one. Those who have most natural feeling, are always those whose cultivated feelings may be made the strongest. The same strong susceptibilities which make the personal impulses vivid and powerful, are also the source from whence are generated the most passionate love of virtue, and the sternest self-control. It is through the cultivation of these, that society both does its duty and protects its interests: not by rejecting the stuff of which heroes are made, because it knows not how to make them. A person whose desires and impulses are his own—are the expression of his own nature, as it has been developed and modified by his own culture—is said to have a character. One whose desires and impulses are not his own, has no character, no more than a steam-engine has a character. If, in addition to being his own, his impulses are strong, and are under the government of a strong will, he has an energetic character. Whoever thinks that individuality of desires and impulses should not be encouraged to unfold itself, must maintain that society has no need of strong natures—is not the better for containing many persons who have much character—and that a high general average of energy is not desirable.

In some early states of society, these forces might be, and were, too much ahead of the power which society then possessed of disciplining and controlling them. There has been a time when the element of spontaneity and individuality was in excess, and the social principle had a hard struggle with it. The difficulty then was, to induce men of strong bodies or minds to pay obedience to any rules which required them to control their impulses. To overcome this difficulty, law and discipline, like the Popes struggling against the Emperors, asserted a power over the whole man, claiming to control all his life in order to control his character—which society had not found any other sufficient means of binding. But society has now fairly got the better of individuality; and the danger which threatens human nature is not the excess, but the deficiency, of personal impulses and preferences. Things are vastly changed, since the passions of those who were strong by station or by personal endowment were in a state of habitual rebellion against laws and ordinances, and required to be rigorously chained up to enable the persons within their reach to enjoy any particle of security. In our times, from the highest class of society down to the lowest, every one lives as under the eye of a hostile and dreaded censorship. Not only in what concerns others, but in what concerns only themselves, the individual or the family do not ask themselves—what do I prefer? or, what would suit my character and disposition? or, what would allow the best and highest in me to have fair play, and enable it to grow and thrive? They ask themselves, what is suitable to my position? what is usually done by persons of my station and pecuniary circumstances? or (worse still) what is usually done by persons of a station and circumstances superior to mine? I do not mean that they choose what is customary, in preference to what suits their own inclination. It does not occur to them to have any inclination, except for what is customary. Thus the mind itself is bowed to the yoke: even in what people do for pleasure, conformity is the first thing thought of; they like in crowds; they exercise choice only among things commonly done: peculiarity of taste, eccentricity of conduct, are shunned equally with crimes: until by dint of not following their own nature, they have no nature to follow: their human capacities are withered and starved: they become incapable of any strong wishes or native pleasures, and are generally without either opinions or feelings of home growth, or properly their own. Now is this, or is it not, the desirable condition of human nature?

It is so, on the Calvinistic theory. According to that, the one great offence of man is self-will. All the good of which humanity is capable, is comprised in obedience. You have no choice; thus you must do, and no otherwise: "whatever is not a duty, is a sin." Human nature being radically corrupt, there is no redemption for any one until human nature is killed within him. To one holding this theory of life, crushing out any of the human faculties, capacities, and susceptibilities, is no evil: man needs no capacity, but that of surrendering himself to the will of God: and if he uses any of his faculties for any other purpose but to do that supposed will more effectually, he is better without them. This is the theory of Calvinism; and it is held, in a mitigated form, by many who do not consider themselves Calvinists; the mitigation consisting in giving a less ascetic interpretation to the alleged will of God; asserting it to be his will that mankind should gratify some of their inclinations; of course not in the manner they themselves prefer, but in the way of obedience, that is, in a way prescribed to them by authority; and, therefore, by the necessary conditions of the case, the same for all.

In some such insidious form there is at present a strong tendency to this narrow theory of life, and to the pinched and hidebound type of human character which it patronizes. Many persons, no doubt, sincerely think that human beings thus cramped and dwarfed, are as their Maker designed them to be; just as many have thought that trees are a much finer thing when clipped into pollards, or cut out into figures of animals, than as nature made them. But if it be any part of religion to believe that man was made by a good Being, it is more consistent with that faith to believe, that this Being gave all human faculties that they might be cultivated and unfolded, not rooted out and consumed, and that he takes delight in every nearer approach made by his creatures to the ideal conception embodied in them, every increase in any of their capabilities of comprehension, of action, or of enjoyment. There is a different type of human excellence from the Calvinistic; a conception of humanity as having its nature bestowed on it for other purposes than merely to be abnegated. "Pagan self-assertion" is one of the elements of human worth, as well as "Christian self-denial."[14] There is a Greek ideal of self-development, which the Platonic and Christian ideal of self-government blends with, but does not supersede. It may be better to be a John Knox than an Alcibiades, but it is better to be a Pericles than either;[15] nor would a Pericles, if we had one in these days, be without anything good which belonged to John Knox.

It is not by wearing down into uniformity all that is individual in themselves, but by cultivating it and calling it forth, within the limits imposed by the rights and interests of others, that human beings become a noble and beautiful object of contemplation; and as the works partake the character of those who do them, by the same process human life also becomes rich, diversified, and animating, furnishing more abundant aliment to high thoughts and elevating feelings, and strengthening the tie which binds every individual to the race, by making the race infinitely better worth belonging to. In proportion to the development of his individuality, each person becomes more valuable to himself, and is therefore capable of being more valuable to others. There is a greater fullness of life about

14 Sterling's *Essays*. (Mill)

15 John Knox was a sixteenth-century Scotch reformer and statesman, and a leading Calvinist. Though Alcibiades, Athenian politician and general of the fifth century B.C., was a person of greater charm and wider interests, his moral weakness places him below Knox. Better than either to Mill is the fully rounded character of another fifth-century Athenian, the statesman Pericles.

his own existence, and when there is more life in the units there is more in the mass which is composed of them. As much compression as is necessary to prevent the stronger specimens of human nature from encroaching on the rights of others, cannot be dispensed with; but for this there is ample compensation even in the point of view of human development. The means of development which the individual loses by being prevented from gratifying his inclinations to the injury of others, are chiefly obtained at the expense of the development of other people. And even to himself there is a full equivalent in the better development of the social part of his nature, rendered possible by the restraint put upon the selfish part. To be held to rigid rules of justice for the sake of others, develops the feelings and capacities which have the good of others for their object. But to be restrained in things not affecting their good, by their mere displeasure, develops nothing valuable, except such force of character as may unfold itself in resisting the restraint. If acquiesced in, it dulls and blunts the whole nature. To give any fair play to the nature of each, it is essential that different persons should be allowed to lead different lives. In proportion as this latitude has been exercised in any age, has that age been noteworthy to posterity. Even despotism does not produce its worst effects, so long as individuality exists under it; and whatever crushes individuality is despotism, by whatever name it may be called, and whether it professes to be enforcing the will of God or the injunctions of men.

Having said that Individuality is the same thing with development, and that it is only the cultivation of individuality which produces, or can produce, well-developed human beings, I might here close the argument: for what more or better can be said of any condition of human affairs, than that it brings human beings themselves nearer to the best thing they can be? or what worse can be said of any obstruction to good, than that it prevents this? Doubtless, however, these considerations will not suffice to convince those who most need convincing; and it is necessary further to show, that these developed human beings are of some use to the undeveloped—to point out to those who do not desire liberty, and would not avail themselves of it, that they may be in some intelligible

manner rewarded for allowing other people to make use of it without hindrance.

In the first place, then, I would suggest that they might possibly learn something from them. It will not be denied by anybody, that originality is a valuable element in human affairs. There is always need of persons not only to discover new truths, and point out when what were once truths are no longer, but also to commence new practices, and set the example of more enlightened conduct, and better taste and sense in human life. This cannot well be gainsaid by anybody who does not believe that the world has already attained perfection in all its ways and practices. It is true that this benefit is not capable of being rendered by everybody alike: there are but few persons, in comparison with the whole of mankind, whose experiments, if adopted by others, would be likely to be any improvement on established practice. But these few are the salt of the earth; without them, human life would become a stagnant pool. Not only is it they who introduce good things which did not before exist; it is they who keep the life in those which already existed. If there were nothing new to be done, would human intellect cease to be necessary? Would it be a reason why those who do the old things should forget why they are done, and do them like cattle, not like human beings? There is only too great a tendency in the best beliefs and practices to degenerate into the mechanical; and unless there were a succession of persons whose ever-recurring originality prevents the grounds of those beliefs and practices from becoming merely traditional, such dead matter would not resist the smallest shock from anything really alive, and there would be no reason why civilization should not die out, as in the Byzantine Empire. Persons of genius, it is true, are, and are always likely to be, a small minority; but in order to have them, it is necessary to preserve the soil in which they grow. Genius can only breathe freely in an *atmosphere* of freedom. Persons of genius are, *ex vi termini*,[16] *more* individual than any other people—less capable, consequently, of fitting themselves, without hurtful compression, into any of the small number of moulds which society provides in order to save its members the trouble of forming their own character. If from

---

16 By definition.

timidity they consent to be forced into one of these moulds, and to let all that part of themselves which cannot expand under the pressure remain unexpanded, society will be little the better for their genius. If they are of a strong character, and break their fetters, they become a mark for the society which has not succeeded in reducing them to commonplace, to point at with solemn warning as "wild," "erratic," and the like; much as if one should complain of the Niagara river for not flowing smoothly between its banks like a Dutch canal.

I insist thus emphatically on the importance of genius, and the necessity of allowing it to unfold itself freely both in thought and in practice, being well aware that no one will deny the position in theory, but knowing also that almost every one, in reality, is totally indifferent to it. People think genius a fine thing if it enables a man to write an exciting poem, or paint a picture. But in its true sense, that of originality in thought and action, though no one says that it is not a thing to be admired, nearly all, at heart, think that they can do very well without it. Unhappily this is too natural to be wondered at. Originality is the one thing which unoriginal minds cannot feel the use of. They cannot see what it is to do for them: how should they? If they could see what it would do for them, it would not be originality. The first service which originality has to render them, is that of opening their eyes: which being once fully done, they would have a chance of being themselves original. Meanwhile, recollecting that nothing was ever yet done which some one was not the first to do, and that all good things which exist are the fruits of originality, let them be modest enough to believe that there is something still left for it to accomplish, and assure themselves that they are more in need of originality, the less they are conscious of the want.

In sober truth, whatever homage may be professed, or even paid, to real or supposed mental superiority, the general tendency of things throughout the world is to render mediocrity the ascendant power among mankind. In ancient history, in the middle ages, and in a diminishing degree through the long transition from feudality to the present time, the individual was a power in himself; and if he had either great talents or a high social position, he was a considerable power.

At present individuals are lost in the crowd. In politics it is almost a triviality to say that public opinion now rules the world. The only power deserving the name is that of masses, and of governments while they make themselves the organ of the tendencies and instincts of masses. This is as true in the moral and social relations of private life as in public transactions. Those whose opinions go by the name of public opinion, are not always the same sort of public: in America they are the whole white population; in England, chiefly the middle class. But they are always a mass, that is to say, collective mediocrity. And what is a still greater novelty, the mass do not now take their opinions from dignitaries in Church or State, from ostensible leaders, or from books. Their thinking is done for them by men much like themselves, addressing them or speaking in their name, on the spur of the moment, through the newspapers. I am not complaining of all this. I do not assert that any thing better is compatible, as a general rule, with the present low state of the human mind. But that does not hinder the government of mediocrity from being mediocre government. No government by a democracy or a numerous aristocracy, either in its political acts or in the opinions, qualities, and tone of mind which it fosters, ever did or could rise above mediocrity, except in so far as the sovereign Many have let themselves be guided (which in their best times they always have done) by the counsels and influence of a more highly gifted and instructed One or Few. The initiation of all wise or noble things, comes and must come from individuals; generally at first from some one individual. The honour and glory of the average man is that he is capable of following that initiative; that he can respond internally to wise and noble things, and be led to them with his eyes open. I am not countenancing the sort of "hero-worship" which applauds the strong man of genius for forcibly seizing on the government of the world and making it do his bidding in spite of itself. All he can claim is, freedom to point out the way. The power of compelling others into it, is not only inconsistent with the freedom and development of all the rest, but corrupting to the strong man himself. It does seem, however, that when the opinions of masses of merely average men are everywhere become or becoming the dominant power, the counterpoise and corrective to that tendency would be, the more and more pronounced individuality of those who stand on the higher eminences of thought. It is in these circumstances most especially, that exceptional individuals, instead of being deterred, should be encouraged in acting differently from the mass. In other times there was no advantage in their doing so, unless they acted not only differently, but better. In this age, the mere example of nonconformity, the mere refusal to bend the knee to custom, is itself a service. Precisely because the tyranny of opinion is such as to make eccentricity a reproach, it is desirable, in order to break through that tyranny, that people should be eccentric. Eccentricity has always abounded when and where strength of character has abounded; and the amount of eccentricity in a society has generally been proportional to the amount of genius, mental vigour, and moral courage which it contained. That so few now dare to be eccentric, marks the chief danger of the time.

I have said that it is important to give the freest scope possible to uncustomary things, in order that it may in time appear which of these are fit to be converted into customs. But independence of action, and disregard of custom, are not solely deserving of encouragement for the chance they afford that better modes of action, and customs more worthy of general adoption, may be struck out; nor is it only persons of decided mental superiority who have a just claim to carry on their lives in their own way. There is no reason that all human existence should be constructed on some one or some small number of patterns. If a person possesses any tolerable amount of common sense and experience, his own mode of laying out his existence is the best, not because it is the best in itself, but because it is his own mode. Human beings are not like sheep; and even sheep are not undistinguishably alike. A man cannot get a coat or a pair of boots to fit him, unless they are either made to his measure, or he has a whole warehouseful to choose from: and is it easier to fit him with a life than with a coat, or are human beings more like one another in their whole physical and spiritual conformation than in the shape of their feet? If it were only that people have diversities of taste, that is reason enough for not attempting to shape them all after one model. But different persons also require different conditions for their spiritual development; and can no more exist healthily in the same moral, than all the variety of plants can in the same physical, atmosphere and climate. The same things which are helps to one person towards the cultivation of his higher nature, are hindrances to another. The same mode of life is a healthy excitement to one, keeping all his faculties of action and enjoyment in their best order, while to another it is a distracting burthen, which suspends or crushes all internal life. Such are the differences among human beings in their sources of pleasure, their susceptibilities of pain, and the operation on them of different physical and moral agencies, that unless there is a corresponding diversity in their modes of life, they neither obtain their fair share of happiness, nor grow up to the mental, moral, and aesthetic stature of which their nature is capable. Why then should tolerance, as far as the public sentiment is concerned, extend only to tastes and modes of life which extort acquiesence by the multitude of their adherents? Nowhere (except in some monastic institutions) is diversity of taste entirely unrecognized; a person may, without blame, either like or dislike rowing, or smoking, or music, or athletic exercises, or chess, or cards, or study, because both those who like each of these things, and those who dislike them, are too numerous to be put down. But the man, and still more the woman, who can be accused either of doing "what nobody does," or of not doing "what everybody does," is the subject of as much depreciatory remark as if he or she had committed some grave moral delinquency. Persons require to possess a title, or some other badge of rank, or of the consideration of people of rank, to be able to indulge somewhat in the luxury of doing as they like without detriment to their estimation. To indulge somewhat, I repeat: for whoever allow themselves much of that indulgence, incur the risk of something worse than disparaging speeches—they are in peril of a commission *de lunatico*,[17] and of having their property taken from them and given to their relations.[18]

---

17 Commission of lunacy to decide on the sanity of an individual.

18 "There is something both contemptible and frightful in the sort of evidence on which, of late years, any person can be judicially declared unfit for the management of his affairs; and after his death, his disposal of his property

There is one characteristic of the present direction of public opinion, peculiarly calculated to make it intolerant of any marked demonstration of individuality. The general average of mankind are not only moderate in intellect, but also moderate in inclinations: they have no tastes or wishes strong enough to incline them to do anything unusual, and they consequently do not understand those who have, and class all such with the wild and intemperate whom they are accustomed to look down upon. Now, in addition to this fact which is general, we have only to suppose that a strong movement has set in towards the improvement of morals, and it is evident what we have to expect. In these days such a movement has set in; much has actually been effected in the way of increased regularity of conduct, and discouragement of excesses; and there is a philanthropic spirit abroad, for the exercise of which there is no more inviting field than the moral and prudential improvement of our fellow creatures. These tendencies of the times cause the public to be more disposed than at most former periods to prescribe general rules of conduct, and endeavour to make every one conform to the approved standard. And that standard, express or tacit, is to desire nothing strongly. Its ideal of character is to be without any marked character; to maim by compression, like a Chinese lady's foot, every part of human

nature which stands out prominently, and tends to make the person markedly dissimilar in outline to commonplace humanity.

As is usually the case with ideals which exclude one-half of what is desirable, the present standard of approbation produces only an inferior imitation of the other half. Instead of great energies guided by vigorous reason, and strong feelings strongly controlled by a conscientious will, its result is weak feelings and weak energies, which therefore can be kept in outward conformity to rule without any strength either of will or of reason. Already energetic characters on any large scale are becoming merely traditional. There is now scarcely any outlet for energy in this country except business. The energy expended in this may still be regarded as considerable. What little is left from that employment, is expended on some hobby; which may be a useful, even a philanthropic hobby, but is always some one thing, and generally a thing of small dimensions. The greatness of England is now all collective: individually small, we only appear capable of anything great by our habit of combining; and with this our moral and religious philanthropists are perfectly contented. But it was men of another stamp than this that made England what it has been; and men of another stamp will be needed to prevent its decline.

The despotism of custom is everywhere the standing hindrance to human advancement, being in unceasing antagonism to that disposition to aim at something better than customary, which is called, according to circumstances, the spirit of liberty, or that of progress or improvement. The spirit of improvement is not always a spirit of liberty, for it may aim at forcing improvements on an unwilling people; and the spirit of liberty, in so far as it resists such attempts, may ally itself locally and temporarily with the opponents of improvement; but the only unfailing and permanent source of improvement is liberty, since by it there are as many possible independent centres of improvement as there are individuals. The progressive principle, however, in either shape, whether as the love of liberty or of improvement, is antagonistic to the sway of Custom, involving at least emancipation from that yoke; and the contest between the two constitutes the chief interest of the history of mankind. The greater part of the world has,

can be set aside, if there is enough of it to pay the expenses of litigation—which are charged on the property itself. All the minute details of his daily life are pried into, and whatever is found which, seen through the medium of the perceiving and describing faculties of the lowest of the low, bears an appearance unlike absolute commonplace, is laid before the jury as evidence of insanity, and often with success; the jurors being little, if at all, less vulgar and ignorant than the witnesses; while the judges, with that extraordinary want of knowledge of human nature and life which continually astonishes us in English lawyers, often help to mislead them. These trials speak volumes as to the state of feeling and opinion among the vulgar with regard to human liberty. So far from setting any value on individuality—so far from respecting the right of each individual to act, in things indifferent, as seems good to his own judgement and inclinations, judges and juries cannot even conceive that a person in a state of sanity can desire such freedom. In former days, when it was proposed to burn atheists, charitable people used to suggest putting them in a mad-house instead: it would be nothing surprising nowadays were we to see this done, and the doers applauding themselves, because, instead of persecuting for religion, they had adopted so humane and Christian a mode of treating these unfortunates, not without a silent satisfaction at their having thereby obtained their deserts." (Mill) properly speaking, no history, because the despotism of Custom is complete. This is the case over the whole East. Custom is there, in all things, the final appeal; justice and right mean conformity to custom; the argument of custom no one, unless some tyrant intoxicated with power, thinks of resisting. And we see the result. Those nations must once have had originality; they did not start out of the ground populous, lettered, and versed in many of the arts of life; they made themselves all this, and were then the greatest and most powerful nations of the world. What are they now? The subjects or dependents of tribes whose forefathers wandered in the forests when theirs had magnificent palaces and gorgeous temples, but over whom custom exercised only a divided rule with liberty and progress. A people, it appears, may be progressive for a certain length of time, and then stop: when does it stop? When it ceases to possess individuality. If a similar change should befall the nations of Europe, it will not be in exactly the same shape: the despotism of custom with which these nations are threatened is not precisely stationariness. It proscribes singularity, but it does not preclude change, provided all change together. We have discarded the fixed costumes of our forefathers; every one must still dress like other people, but the fashion may change once or twice a year. We thus take care that when there is change it shall be for change's sake, and not from any idea of beauty or convenience; for the same idea of beauty or convenience would not strike all the world at the same moment, and be simultaneously thrown aside by all at another moment. But we are progressive as well as changeable: we continually make new inventions in mechanical things, and keep them until they are again superseded by better; we are eager for improvement in politics, in education, even in morals, though in this last our idea of improvement chiefly consists in persuading or forcing other people to be as good as ourselves. It is not progress that we object to; on the contrary, we flatter ourselves that we are the most progressive people who ever lived. It is individuality that we war against: we should think we had done wonders if we had made ourselves all alike; forgetting that the unlikeness of one person to another is generally the first thing which draws the attention of either to the imperfection of his own type, and the superiority

of another, or the possibility, by combining the advantages of both, of producing something better than either. We have a warning example in China—a nation of much talent, and, in some respects, even wisdom, owing to the rare good fortune of having been provided at an early period with a particularly good set of customs, the work, in some measure, of men to whom even the most enlightened European must accord, under certain limitations, the title of sages and philosophers. They are remarkable, too, in the excellence of their apparatus for impressing, as far as possible, the best wisdom they possess upon every mind in the community, and securing that those who have appropriated most of it shall occupy the posts of honour and power. Surely the people who did this have discovered the secret of human progressiveness, and must have kept themselves steadily at the head of the movement of the world. On the contrary, they have become stationary—have remained so for thousands of years; and if they are ever to be farther improved, it must be by foreigners. They have succeeded beyond all hope in what English philanthropists are so industriously working at—in making a people all alike, all governing their thoughts and conduct by the same maxims and rules; and these are the fruits. The modern *régime* of public opinion is, in an unorganized form, what the Chinese educational and political systems are in an organized; and unless individuality shall be able successfully to assert itself against this yoke, Europe, notwithstanding its noble antecedents and its professed Christianity, will tend to become another China.

What is it that has hitherto preserved Europe from this lot? What has made the European family of nations an improving, instead of a stationary portion of mankind? Not any superior excellence in them, which, when it exists, exists as the effect, not as the cause; but their remarkable diversity of character and culture. Individuals, classes, nations, have been extremely unlike one another: they have struck out a great variety of paths, each leading to something valuable; and although at every period those who travelled in different paths have been intolerant of one another, and each would have thought it an excellent thing if all the rest could have been compelled to travel his road, their attempts to thwart each other's development have rarely had any permanent success, and each has in time endured to receive the good which the others have offered. Europe is, in my judgement, wholly indebted to this plurality of paths for its progressive and many-sided development. But it already begins to possess this benefit in a considerably less degree. It is decidedly advancing towards the Chinese ideal of making all people alike. M. de Tocqueville,[19] in his last important work, remarks how much more the Frenchmen of the present day resemble one another, than did those even of the last generation. The same remark might be made of Englishmen in a far greater degree. In a passage already quoted from Wilhelm von Humboldt, he points out two things as necessary conditions of human development, because necessary to render people unlike one another; namely, freedom, and variety of situations. The second of these two conditions is in this country every day diminishing. The circumstances which surround different classes and individuals, and shape their characters, are daily becoming more assimilated. Formerly, different ranks, different neighbourhoods, different trades and professions, lived in what might be called different worlds; at present, to a great degree in the same. Comparatively speaking, they now read the same things, listen to the same things, see the same things, go to the same places, have their hopes and fears directed to the same objects, have the same rights and liberties, and the same means of asserting them. Great as are the differences of position which remain, they are nothing to those which have ceased. And the assimilation is still proceeding. All the political changes of the age promote it, since they all tend to raise the low and to lower the high. Every extension of education promotes it, because education brings people under common influences, and gives them access to the general stock of facts and sentiments. Improvements in the means of communication promote it, by bringing the in-

habitants of distant places into personal contact, and keeping up a rapid flow of changes of residence between one place and another. The increase of commerce and manufactures promotes it, by diffusing more widely the advantages of easy circumstances, and opening all objects of ambition, even the highest, to general competition, whereby the desire of rising becomes no longer the character of a particular class, but of all classes. A more powerful agency than even all these, in bringing about a general similarity among mankind, is the complete establishment, in this and other free countries, of the ascendancy of public opinion in the State. As the various social eminences which enabled persons entrenched on them to disregard the opinion of the multitude, gradually become levelled; as the very idea of resisting the will of the public, when it is positively known that they have a will, disappears more and more from the minds of practical politicians; there ceases to be any social support for nonconformity—any substantive power in society, which, itself opposed to the ascendancy of numbers, is interested in taking under its protection opinions and tendencies at variance with those of the public.

The combination of all these causes forms so great a mass of influences hostile to Individuality, that it is not easy to see how it can stand its ground. It will do so with increasing difficulty, unless the intelligent part of the public can be made to feel its value—to see that it is good there should be differences, even though not for the better, even though, as it may appear to them, some should be for the worse. If the claims of Individuality are ever to be asserted, the time is now, while much is still wanting to complete the enforced assimilation. It is only in the earlier stages that any stand can be successfully made against the encroachment. The demand that all other people shall resemble ourselves, grows by what it feeds on. If resistance waits till life is reduced *nearly* to one uniform type, all deviations from that type will come to be considered impious, immoral, even monstrous and contrary to nature. Mankind speedily become unable to conceive diversity, when they have been for some time unaccustomed to see it.

---

[19] Alexis Charles de Tocqueville (1805–1859), French statesman and writer on political theory, author of a famous study of American democracy. Like Mill, who admired him greatly, he was troubled by the idea that democracy and universal state education would make for a uniformly dull level of intelligence and for conformity of opinion.

John Ruskin

1819–1900

Ruskin was born at London in 1819, the only child of a wealthy merchant with artistic and literary interests, and a mother who was a devout Evangelical. This double influence, aesthetic and moral, colored the whole of Ruskin's life and work. Most of his formal education before he went to Oxford in 1837 consisted of a rigid course in the Bible, given by his mother in the mornings, and another, less rigid, in English literature, which his father read aloud in the evenings or the boy pursued in the family library during the afternoons. But observation was as important as books, ultimately more so, in the development of his taste and sensibility. Since he was not allowed to play with toys or with boys (his mother was afraid he might get hurt, physically or morally), he was forced to spend long hours "tracing the squares and comparing the colors of my carpet, . . . or counting the bricks in the opposite houses," with the important result that his eye was trained to sharp and accurate perception. After carpets and bricks, he began to observe nature, first in his garden at

Herne Hill, and then with increasing delight on summer travels with his parents, when he discovered the English landscape, the ocean at Dover, the lakes and mountains of Westmorland, and finally the splendors of the Alps. But his response to nature was scientific as well as aesthetic. He looked at the strata of the Alps as well as at their beauty; and brought home from his summer trips specimens of rocks and flowers which he examined closely and described in detail for the catalogue he wrote of his own museum. As a matter of fact, his first published work appeared in a magazine of natural history, and his scientific studies had an important influence later on his theory of art.

But the romantic interest in nature predominated. It led him presently to sketching trees and mountains, and to spending hours in art shops and museums looking at landscapes. Then in 1833 the discovery of Turner's engravings of the Italian lakes "determined," he says, "the main tenor of my life," that is, made him a critic of art. For when his hero was viciously attacked in the reviews, Ruskin leapt to his defense (and that of other modern painters of landscape) and published, at the age of twenty-four, a remarkable book called *Modern Painters* (1843). To some extent it advanced a theory of aesthetics, which we shall consider in a moment, but for the most part it was filled with striking descriptions of nature drawn from his own experience, and set down to prove that Turner's landscapes, contrary to the charge that they were fantastic, were true to life. As he says himself, in a revealing passage, it was not his knowledge or his love of art (both of which were relatively slight in 1843) but of mountains and the sea which made him feel he could judge more justly of Turner than others could.

The aesthetic development here outlined did not take place, however, without the counterinfluence of Ruskin's Evangelical training. Because the Puritan tradition had always been suspicious of sensuous pleasures, like those of natural beauty and the arts in general, it was impossible for the boy to enjoy either nature or painting "straight" without a feeling of guilt. His first ecstatic glimpse of mountain scenery was dashed by an "alarmed sense of the sin of being so happy among the hills," so that he felt a profane and rebellious character, compared to his mother.[1] No wonder he spoke later of nature as coming to him "often in the form of a temptation."

John Ruskin (1819–1900). As a follower of Carlyle and a socialist, Ruskin hoped to "spread the love and knowledge of art among all classes." This portrait was painted by Edward Millais, one of the original members of the Pre-Raphaelite Brotherhood. *Radio Times Hulton Picture Library.*

---

[1] To be sure, this reaction occurred on a Sunday, but it would have been only less in degree, not different in kind, on a weekday.

But also, by great good luck, it came to him in another form, as a "safeguard," he calls it (the choice of the word is revealing). "It was . . . inconsistent with every evil feeling, with spite, anger, covetousness, discontent, and every other hateful passion"; and though it did not strengthen his character, it had much power in molding it. Furthermore, he felt a "Sanctity in the whole of nature," and interpreted the joy he experienced as the satisfaction "of a sort of heart-hunger" by "the presence of a Great and Holy Spirit." These experiences, recounted in the important chapter on "The Moral of Landscape" (printed below), remind us at once of Wordsworth and Carlyle, to whom, Ruskin later said, he owed much; and certainly the religio-moral view of nature, which conditioned his earliest reactions, was an inheritance from the Romantics. It thus provided the saving reconciliation of aesthetics and ethics, of father and mother, which he so badly needed. For if the sky was "fitted in all its functions for the perpetual comfort and exalting of the heart, for soothing it and purifying it from its dross and dust," why not also a painting of the sky? And if so, the art of landscape—maybe all great art rightly looked at—was not a sinful or an idle form of amusement. It was something of the greatest importance to society. In 1844 Ruskin wrote his *apologia* in a letter which might have been addressed to his mother—or to his own conscience:

Now observe—I am not engaged in selfish cultivation of critical acumen, but in ardent endeavour to spread the love and knowledge of art among all classes, . . . and [in] directing the public to expect and the artist to intend—an earnest and elevating moral influence in all that they admire and achieve.

The theory of art which Ruskin developed in the successive volumes of *Modern Painters* (from Volume I in 1843 to Volume V in 1860) was founded squarely on his personal experience. He read the standard works on aesthetics (by Burke, Reynolds, Coleridge, and Hazlitt), but it was his own reactions to nature, romantic, scientific, and Evangelical, which determined his critical principles.

The first of these may be called Naturalism. This was the doctrine, first asserted for literature by the Romantics and for painting by Ruskin (though there are anticipations in Hazlitt), that the artist should describe nature as he saw it, and not, as the neoclassicists had maintained, "nature to advantage dressed"; and that he should do so in whatever form naturally fitted his materials regardless of the "rules" or conventions of art laid down in neoclassical criticism. (See the introduction to the Victorian period, pp. 427–28, and the important quotation there

from Ruskin.) Furthermore, "nature as he saw it" meant the concrete object in all of its detailed particularity, and not the general type which had been the focus of eighteenth-century art. But between the Naturalism of the Romantics and that of Ruskin there is an important difference. Ruskin took the element of realism in Romantic poetry (which he noticed in the imagery of Wordsworth, Byron, and Keats) and made it central. His dictum that art must produce on the beholder's mind "precisely the impression which the reality would have produced" has no parallel in Romantic criticism. It came from the influence of his scientific studies (he pointed out that natural science had rendered our knowledge of nature "fruitful in accumulation and exquisite in accuracy"), and from his desire that a landscape should give him as nearly as possible the same experience he loved at first-hand and took in through a pair of very sharp eyes. The boy who stared at the pattern of carpets and studied the formation of strata became the critic who said, "He who is closest to Nature is best. . . . The more facts you give, the greater you are."

Not that Ruskin thought art should be merely photographic. He made room for an element of selection and arrangement even in what he called "imitative realism" (in the engraving of famous churches and lakes, or the painting of the Dutch School). And still further, he always maintained that the highest form of art was "imaginative realism." (See p. 626 where the two forms are contrasted, and there called Historical and Poetical painting.) The great artist does not give the facts as such, but the impression they made on his mind, the essential character or quality of his experience. Indeed, Ruskin's insistence that "the virtue of the Imagination is its reaching, by intuition and intensity of gaze (not by reasoning, but by its authoritative opening and revealing power), a more essential truth than is seen at the surface of things" was a valuable protest (and still is today) against the mistaken notion, engendered by science, that reason alone is a valid instrument of truth and that the poetic imagination dreams up charming and quite unreal pictures of life. Ruskin saw that the "truth of impression" grasped by the imagination of a great artist deepens and sharpens our perceptions of human experience. But this "impression" was to be painted realistically, in clear outline and finished detail. Ruskin hated Impressionism because his own impressions were always realistic. His theory of Naturalism, therefore, applies to the painting of the Pre-Raphaelites (whom he both influenced and defended), and to the literature of realism, in the poetry of Browning and the novels of the mid-Victorians, but not to the later work of the Symbolists and Impressionists.

Furthermore, we have to recognize that Ruskin hated or disparaged even realism in certain forms. He looks at a realistic picture by Teniers, the Flemish painter, of sots quarreling over their dice and calls it "an entirely base and evil picture. It is an expression of delight in . . . a vile thing." He looks at a Dutch painting of taverns and interiors with its clarity and detail and finds it trivial because the subjects are trivial. In both cases the two things that are lacking—and his insistence on which qualifies his realistic naturalism and completes his theory of art—are beauty and nobility. Great art must be beautiful, though not at the expense of truth. The beauty must not be achieved by removing everything ugly, nor by making the object an idealization of life. "Great art accepts Nature as she is"; it admits, in subordinate place, what is ugly or evil, and it then "directs the eyes and thoughts to what is most perfect in her," that is, to a beauty of face or form, mountain or tree, which *does* exist, however rare and uncommon it may be. Finally, in the doctrine of nobility we hear the voice of the Victorian prophet, brought up an Evangelical and molded by the moral idealism of the age, defining poetry, whether in verse or paint, as "the suggestion, by the imagination, of noble grounds for the noble emotions," and setting up as the greatest subject of art the heroic image, "the acts or meditations of great men." Ruskin's theory of art, taken as a whole, owed its enormous vogue to its combination of the realistic-scientific taste that was new to the age with the reassertion of those aesthetic and moral values of the past which modern civilization threatened to destroy.

Broadly speaking, a work of art may be looked at in two ways, directly as the expression of experience, or indirectly as a revelation of the artist and his time. The first approach is critical, the second biographical and historical. In Ruskin's earliest work (Volumes I and II of *Modern Painters*) the first point of view is predominant; but when he turned from painting to architecture (where the relationship between art and society is always conspicuous) and wrote *The Seven Lamps of Architecture* (1849) and *The Stones of Venice* (1851 and 1853), he became more and more preoccupied with the character of the age which built the buildings or painted the pictures under examination, whether ancient or modern. But his point of view was not what we would call "scientific" or "scholarly." It was not open or detached. Though he ceased to be an Evangelical under the skeptical influences of the time, he never ceased to be a moralist. We have just seen how this affected his critical theory, and we could predict that it would make his historical search for the character of the artist or the society behind the art a search for its *moral* character.

But moral in a wide sense of the term that includes political and economic life. Under the influence of *Past and Present,* Ruskin became increasingly concerned with the evils of industrialism—the greed and selfishness of the new capitalists, the suffering of the workers under laissez-faire liberalism, and in particular the reduction of men to machines by the assembly-line methods of the modern factory. "For my own part," he cries out, "I will put up with this state of things, passively, not an hour longer. . . . I simply cannot paint, nor read, nor look at minerals, nor do anything else that I like, and the very light of the morning sky, when there is any—which is seldom, nowadays, near London [or Bradford, where he gave the lecture on "Traffic"]—has become hateful to me, because of the misery that I know of, and see signs of, where I know it not, which no imagination can interpret too bitterly. Therefore, . . . I will endure it no longer quietly; but henceforward, with any few or many who will help, do my poor best to abate this misery." This was the state of mind which filled his architectural works with bitter arraignments of industrial civilization as he saw it reflected directly in modern, or indirectly, by contrast, in Greek or Gothic, building (see "The Nature of Gothic," printed below); and which eventually led him to abandon art criticism altogether, in later life, and to write a series of political and economic tracts for the times, most notably *Unto This Last* (1862), *The Crown of Wild Olive* (1866), in which the brilliant lecture on "Traffic" appeared, and the letters addressed to workingmen called *Fors Clavigera* (1871–84).

On the positive side, what did Ruskin have to propose? First, that so far as possible men should abandon the machines which were degrading workers into human automatons and robbing work of any incentive but money, and return, for the most part, to the old system of handicrafts where a man might use his creative imagination and find pride and pleasure in making a table or a pair of shoes. No doubt this proposal (though Morris took it quite seriously) was a futile effort to sweep back the tide with a broom. But what Ruskin says, in "The Nature of Gothic," about the destructive effect of machines on human nature is profoundly true. He may even be right about the source of the angry discontent of the proletariat that is promoting the rise of communism, namely, not low wages or envy of the rich, but bitter revulsion, however unconscious, against the degradation of life which their mechanical work is forcing upon them. But needless to say, Ruskin had little hope of setting back the clock. His more practical suggestions follow, in general, the Tory Paternalism he learned from Scott and his early travels (see p. 611), and from Carlyle. This meant, on the political side, the rejection of democracy in favor of a strong central government which would carry interference even farther than Carlyle had thought of, to the point of establishing old-age pensions, providing work for the unemployed, and regulating wages and prices—in short, a highly controlled capitalist economy. It is not surprising that Ruskin has been called one of the fathers of English Socialism. But political reformation would not be enough —indeed, it would only touch the surface. At bottom, the great need was for moral regeneration. Though the lecture on "Traffic" is mainly a superb attack on the worldliness and irresponsibility of the big businessmen who sat listening, it included Ruskin's plea for a heroism of trade. Why should not a merchant conceive of his function as a soldier does of his, as that of serving his country rather than serving himself? of being a captain with men to lead and be responsible for? of being capable, if necessary, of the courage and self-sacrifice of a hero? In short, the heroic manufacturer would produce the best quality of goods at a small profit, constantly consider the welfare of his workmen, and stand ready to accept the fortunes of war, however destructive of his own prosperity. But the achievement of such an ideal was not very likely in a society where both the Christian and the feudal traditions were dying or dead. The trouble with Victorian idealism is not that it was too idealistic (so is Christian morality, and its influence has been tremendous) but that it had nothing to build on, no philosophy of life widely and firmly established which could support and sustain it. The Bradford millionaires who heard "Traffic" could not have shrugged it off, as they undoubtedly did, had they had any real belief in the Gospels, or any living sense of a society where classes were bound together by mutual responsibilities. And Ruskin is really aware of this. He knows what goddess they adore, and how empty of heroism her followers must be. His phrasing admits it. "If one could contrive to attach the notion of conquest to them [feeding and clothing a population] anyhow!" No wonder his plea for idealism is so wistful beside the anger of his incisive attack on the worship of "Getting-on."

TEXTS: The standard edition, filled with reproductions of Ruskin's own drawings to illustrate the text, is that edited by E. T. Cook and A. Wedderburn (39 vols., 1903–12). The best biography is Ruskin's own autobiography called *Praeterita*. Two good studies that combine biography with critical interpretation are *John Ruskin*, by R. H. Wilenski (1933), and *The Darkening Glass: A Portrait of Ruskin's Genius*, by J. D. Rosenberg (1961). There are useful essays in *The Victorian Temper* (1951) by Jerome Buckley and *The Last Romantics* (1949) by Graham Hough.

from Praeterita[1]

from Chapter 1

THE SPRINGS OF WANDEL[2]

I am, and my father was before me, a violent Tory of the old school;—Walter Scott's school, that is to say, and Homer's.[3] I name these two out of the numberless great Tory writers, because they were my own two masters. I had Walter Scott's novels, and the *Iliad* (Pope's translation), for constant reading when I was a child, on weekdays: on Sundays their effect was tempered by *Robinson Crusoe* and the *Pilgrim's Progress;* my mother having it deeply in her heart to make an evangelical clergyman of me. Fortunately, I had an aunt more evangelical than my mother; and my aunt gave me cold mutton for Sunday's dinner,[4] which—as I much preferred it hot— greatly diminished the influence of the *Pilgrim's Progress;* and the end of the matter was, that I got all the noble imaginative teaching of Defoe and Bunyan, and yet—am not an evangelical clergyman.

I had, however, still better teaching than theirs, and that compulsorily, and every day of the week.

Walter Scott and Pope's Homer were reading of my own election, and my mother forced me, by steady daily toil, to learn long chapters of the Bible by heart; as well as to read it every syllable through, aloud, hard names and all, from Genesis to the Apocalypse, about once a year: and to that discipline—patient, accurate, and resolute—I owe, not only a knowledge of the book, which I find occasionally serviceable, but much of my general power of taking pains, and the best part of my taste in literature. From Walter Scott's novels I might easily, as I grew older, have fallen to other people's novels; and Pope might, perhaps, have led me to take Johnson's English, or Gibbon's, as types of lan-

1 This is the title, meaning "Things Past," that Ruskin gave to his autobiography, written between 1885 and 1889.
2 The sources of a small stream near which Ruskin played as a child.
3 A little below, Ruskin defines the Toryism of Scott and Homer as "a most sincere love of kings, and dislike of everybody who attempted to disobey them."
4 The Evangelicals were strict observers of the Sabbath, and Ruskin's aunt would not allow a hot meal to be prepared on Sunday.

guage;[5] but, once knowing the 32d of Deuteronomy, the 119th Psalm, the 15th of 1st Corinthians, the Sermon on the Mount, and most of
the Apocalypse, every syllable by heart, and
having always a way of thinking with myself what
words meant, it was not possible for me, even in
the foolishest times of youth, to write entirely
superficial or formal English; and the affectation
of trying to write like Hooker and George
Herbert[6] was the most innocent I could have
fallen into.

From my own chosen masters, then, Scott
and Homer, I learned the Toryism which my
best afterthought has only served to confirm.

That is to say, a most sincere love of kings,
and dislike of everybody who attempted to disobey them. Only, both by Homer and Scott, I
was taught strange ideas about kings, which I
find for the present much obsolete; for, I perceived that both the author of the *Iliad* and the
author of *Waverley* made their kings, or king-
loving persons, do harder work than anybody
else. Tydides or Idomeneus always killed twenty
Trojans to other people's one, and Redgauntlet
speared more salmon than any of the Solway
fishermen; and—which was particularly a subject of admiration to me—I observed that they
not only did more, but in proportion to their
doings *got* less than other people—nay, that the
best of them were even ready to govern for
nothing! and let their followers divide any
quantity of spoil or profit. Of late it has seemed
to me that the idea of a king has become exactly
the contrary of this, and that it has been supposed the duty of superior persons generally to
govern less, and get more, than anybody else. So
that it was, perhaps, quite as well that in those
early days my contemplation of existent kingship
was a very distant one.[7]

The aunt who gave me cold mutton on
Sundays was my father's sister: she lived at
Bridge-end, in the town of Perth, and had a
garden full of gooseberry-bushes, sloping down
to the Tay, with a door opening to the water,
which ran past it, clear-brown over the pebbles
three or four feet deep; swift-eddying,—an infinite thing for a child to look down into.

My father began business as a wine-mer-
chant, with no capital, and a considerable
amount of debts bequeathed him by my grandfather. He accepted the bequest, and paid them
all before he began to lay by anything for himself,—for which his best friends called him a
fool, and I, without expressing any opinion as
to his wisdom, which I knew in such matters to
be at least equal to mine, have written on the
granite slab over his grave that he was "an entirely honest merchant." As days went on he
was able to take a house in Hunter Street,
Brunswick Square, No. 54, (the windows of it,
fortunately for me, commanded a view of a
marvellous iron post, out of which the water-
carts were filled through beautiful little trap-
doors, by pipes like boa-constrictors; and I was
never weary of contemplating that mystery, and
the delicious dripping consequent); and as years
went on, and I came to be four or five years old,
he could command a postchaise and pair for
two months in the summer, by help of which,
with my mother and me, he went the round
of his country customers (who liked to see the
principal of the house his own traveller); so
that, at a jog-trot pace, and through the panoramic opening of the four windows of a post-
chaise, made more panoramic still to me because
my seat was a little bracket in front, (for we
used to hire the chaise regularly for the two
months out of Long Acre, and so could have
it bracketed and pocketed as we liked,) I saw all
the high-roads, and most of the cross ones, of
England and Wales; and great part of lowland
Scotland, as far as Perth, where every other year
we spent the whole summer; and I used to read
the *Abbot* at Kinross, and the *Monastery* in
Glen Farg, which I confused with "Glendearg,"
and thought that the White Lady had as certainly lived by the streamlet in that glen of the
Ochils, as the Queen of Scots in the island of
Loch Leven.[8]

To my farther great benefit, as I grew
older, I thus saw nearly all the noblemen's houses
in England; in reverent and healthy delight of

---

[5] Ruskin has in mind the rather formalized styles of Dr.
Johnson and of the historian Edward Gibbon.
[6] Richard Hooker and George Herbert were also formal
stylists, of the seventeenth century, but their language
was closer to that of the King James version of the Bible.
[7] Ruskin is referring to the unedifying manners and
morals at the English court under George IV (1820–30).

[8] *The Abbot* and *The Monastery* are both novels by Scott.
Mary Queen of Scots appears in the former and the White
Lady in the latter.

uncovetous admiration,—perceiving, as soon as I could perceive any political truth at all, that it was probably much happier to live in a small house, and have Warwick Castle to be astonished at, than to live in Warwick Castle and have nothing to be astonished at; but that, at all events, it would not make Brunswick Square in the least more pleasantly habitable, to pull Warwick Castle down. And at this day, though I have kind invitations enough to visit America, I could not, even for a couple of months, live in a country so miserable as to possess no castles.

Nevertheless, having formed my notion of kinghood chiefly from the FitzJames of the *Lady of the Lake,* and of noblesse from the Douglas there, and the Douglas in *Marmion,*[9] a painful wonder soon arose in my child-mind, why the castles should now be always empty. Tantallon was there; but no Archibald of Angus: —Stirling, but no Knight of Snowdoun. The galleries and gardens of England were beautiful to see—but his Lordship and her Ladyship were always in town, said the housekeepers and gardeners. Deep yearning took hold of me for a kind of "Restoration," which I began slowly to feel that Charles the Second had not altogether effected, though I always wore a gilded oak-apple very piously in my button-hole on the 29th of May.[10] It seemed to me that Charles the Second's Restoration had been, as compared with the Restoration I wanted, much as that gilded oak-apple to a real apple. And as I grew wiser, the desire for sweet pippins instead of bitter ones, and Living Kings instead of dead ones, appeared to me rational as well as romantic; and gradually it has become the main purpose of my life to grow pippins, and its chief hope, to see Kings.[11] . . .

Nor did I painfully wish, what I was never permitted for an instant to hope, or even imagine, the possession of such things as one saw in toy-shops. I had a bunch of keys to play with, as long as I was capable only of pleasure in what glittered and jingled; as I grew older, I had a cart, and a ball; and when I was five or six years old, two boxes of well-cut wooden bricks. With these modest, but, I still think, entirely sufficient possessions, and being always summarily whipped if I cried, did not do as I was bid, or tumbled on the stairs, I soon attained serene and secure methods of life and motion; and could pass my days contentedly in tracing the squares and comparing the colours of my carpet;—examining the knots in the wood of the floor, or counting the bricks in the opposite houses; with rapturous intervals of excitement during the filling of the water-cart, through its leathern pipe, from the dripping iron post at the pavement edge; or the still more admirable proceedings of the turncock, when he turned and turned till a fountain sprang up in the middle of the street. But the carpet, and what patterns I could find in bed-covers, dresses, or wall-papers to be examined, were my chief resources, and my attention to the particulars in these was soon so accurate, that when at three and a half I was taken to have my portrait painted by Mr. Northcote,[12] I had not been ten minutes alone with him before I asked him why there were holes in his carpet. The portrait in question represents a very pretty child with yellow hair, dressed in a white frock like a girl, with a broad light-blue sash and blue shoes to match; the feet of the child wholesomely large in proportion to its body; and the shoes still more wholesomely large in proportion to the feet. . . .

My mother had, as she afterward told me, solemnly "devoted me to God" before I was born; in imitation of Hannah.[13]

Very good women are remarkably apt to make away with their children prematurely, in this manner: the real meaning of the pious act being, that, as the sons of Zebedee are not (or at least they hope not), to sit on the right and left of Christ, in His kingdom, their own sons may perhaps, they think, in time be advanced to that respectable position in eternal life; especially if they ask Christ very humbly for it every day: and they always forget in the most naïve way that the position is not His to give![14]

---

9 That is, from Scott, who was the author of these two narrative poems.

10 Anniversary of the restoration of Charles II in 1660.

11 "The St. George's Company was founded [by Ruskin] for the promotion of agricultural instead of town life: and my only hope of prosperity for England, or any other country, in whatever life they lead, is in their discovering and obeying men capable of Kinghood." (Ruskin)

12 James Northcote, a disciple of Sir Joshua Reynolds, and a distinguished portrait and historical painter.

13 The mother of Samuel, who dedicated him to the service of the Lord (I Samuel 1).

14 The wife of Zebedee asked that her sons James and John might sit in these positions, and Jesus replied that not he but God would make the decision (Matthew 20:20–23).

"Devoting me to God," meant, as far as my mother knew herself what she meant, that she would try to send me to college, and make a clergyman of me: and I was accordingly bred for "the Church." My father, who—rest be to his soul—had the exceedingly bad habit of yielding to my mother in large things and taking his own way in little ones, allowed me, without saying a word, to be thus withdrawn from the sherry trade as an unclean thing; not without some pardonable participation in my mother's ultimate views for me. For, many and many a year afterward, I remember, while he was speaking to one of our artist friends, who admired Raphael, and greatly regretted my endeavors to interfere with that popular taste,[15]—while my father and he were condoling with each other on my having been impudent enough to think I could tell the public about Turner[16] and Raphael,—instead of contenting myself, as I ought, with explaining the way of their souls' salvation to them—and what an amiable clergyman was lost in me,—"Yes," said my father, with tears in his eyes—(true and tender tears, as ever father shed,) "he would have been a Bishop."

Luckily for me, my mother, under these distinct impressions of her own duty, and with such latent hopes of my future eminence, took me very early to church;—where, in spite of my quiet habits, and my mother's golden vinaigrette, always indulged to me there, and there only, with its lid unclasped that I might see the wreathed open pattern above the sponge, I found the bottom of the pew so extremely dull a place to keep quiet in, (my best story-books being also taken away from me in the morning,) that, as I have somewhere said before, the horror of Sunday used even to cast its prescient gloom as far back in the week as Friday—and all the glory of Monday, with church seven days removed again, was no equivalent for it.

Notwithstanding, I arrived at some abstract in my own mind of the Rev. Mr. Howell's sermons; and occasionally, in imitation of him, preached a sermon at home over the red sofa cushions;—this performance being always called for by my mother's dearest friends, as the great accomplishment of my childhood. The sermon was, I believe, some eleven words long;—very exemplary, it seems to me, in that respect—and I still think must have been the purest gospel, for I know it began with, "People, be good.". . .

from Chapter 2

HERNE-HILL ALMOND BLOSSOMS

When I was about four years old my father found himself able to buy the lease of a house on Herne Hill, a rustic eminence four miles south of the "Standard in Cornhill";[17] of which the leafy seclusion remains, in all essential points of character, unchanged to this day: certain Gothic splendors, lately indulged in by our wealthier neighbors, being the only serious innovations; and these are so graciously concealed by the fine trees of their grounds, that the passing viator remains unappalled by them; and I can still walk up and down the piece of road between the Fox tavern and the Herne Hill station, imagining myself four years old.

Our house was the northernmost of a group which stand accurately on the top or dome of the hill, where the ground is for a small space level, as the snows are, (I understand,) on the dome of Mont Blanc; presently falling, however, in what may be, in the London clay formation, considered a precipitous slope, to our valley of Chamouni (or of Dulwich) on the east; and with a softer descent into Cold Harbour-lane on the west: on the south, no less beautifully declining to the dale of the Effra, (doubtless shortened from Effrena, signifying the "Unbridled" river; recently, I regret to say, bricked over for the convenience of Mr. Biffin, chemist, and others); while on the north, prolonged indeed with slight depression some half mile or so, and receiving, in the parish of Lambeth, the chivalric title of "Champion Hill," it plunges down at last to efface itself in the plains of Peckham, and the rural barbarism of Goose Green.

The group, of which our house was the quarter, consisted of two precisely similar part-

[15] Ruskin had originally greatly admired Raphael, but on a visit to Rome in 1840 he began to have reservations; he continued to admire the earlier work of the artist but felt that his later work embodied false ideals and conventions which finally made him "the ruin of art." Ruskin's reaction is, of course, closely akin to that of the Pre-Raphaelites. See last six paragraphs of the introduction to the Victorian period.

[16] J. M. W. Turner (1775-1851), English landscape painter and principal subject of Ruskin's *Modern Painters*, Vol. I (1843).

[17] A water tower in the central part of London, from which outlying distances were commonly measured.

ner-couples of houses, gardens and all to match;
still the two highest blocks of buildings seen
from Norwood on the crest of the ridge; so that
the house itself, three-storied, with garrets above,
commanded, in those comparatively smokeless
days, a very notable view from its garret windows, of the Norwood hills on one side, and the
winter sunrise over them; and of the valley of
the Thames on the other, with Windsor tele-
scopically clear in the distance, and Harrow,
conspicuous always in fine weather to open
vision against the summer sunset. It had front
and back garden in sufficient proportion to its
size; the front, richly set with old evergreens,
and well-grown lilac and laburnum; the back,
seventy yards long by twenty wide, renowned
over all the hill for its pears and apples, which
had been chosen with extreme care by our predecessor, (shame on me to forget the name of a
man to whom I owe so much!)—and possessing
also a strong old mulberry tree, a tall white-
heart cherry tree, a black Kentish one, and an
almost unbroken hedge, all round, of alternate
gooseberry and currant bush; decked, in due season, (for the ground was wholly beneficent,) with
magical splendor of abundant fruit: fresh green,
soft amber, and rough-bristled crimson bending
the spinous branches; clustered pearl and pendant ruby joyfully discoverable under the large
leaves that looked like vine.

The differences of primal importance
which I observed between the nature of this
garden, and that of Eden, as I had imagined it,
were, that, in this one, *all* the fruit was forbidden; and there were no companionable beasts:
in other respects the little domain answered
every purpose of Paradise to me; and the climate,
in that cycle of our years, allowed me to pass
most of my life in it. My mother never gave me
more to learn than she knew I could easily get
learnt, if I set myself honestly to work, by twelve
o'clock. She never allowed anything to disturb
me when my task was set; if it was not said
rightly by twelve oclock, I was kept in till I knew
it, and in general, even when Latin Grammar
came to supplement the Psalms, I was my own
master for at least an hour before half-past one
dinner, and for the rest of the afternoon.

My mother, herself finding her chief personal pleasure in her flowers, was often planting
or pruning beside me, at least if I chose to stay
beside *her*. I never thought of doing anything

behind her back which I would not have done
before her face; and her presence was therefore
no restraint to me; but, also, no particular pleasure, for, from having always been left so much
alone, I had generally my own little affairs to
see after; and, on the whole, by the time I
was seven years old, was already getting too
independent, mentally, even of my father and
mother; and, having nobody else to be dependent upon, began to lead a very small, perky,
contented, conceited, Cock-Robinson-Crusoe sort
of life, in the central point which it appeared to
me, (as it must naturally appear to geometrical
animals,) that I occupied in the universe.

This was partly the fault of my father's
modesty; and partly of his pride. He had so
much more confidence in my mother's judgment
as to such matters than in his own, that he never
ventured even to help, much less to cross her,
in the conduct of my education; on the other
hand, in the fixed purpose of making an ecclesiastical gentleman of me, with the superfinest of manners, and access to the highest circles
of fleshly and spiritual society, the visits to
Croydon, where I entirely loved my aunt, and
young baker-cousins, became rarer and more
rare: the society of our neighbors on the hill
could not be had without breaking up our regular and sweetly selfish manner of living; and on
the whole, I had nothing animate to care for,
in a childish way, but myself, some nests of
ants, which the gardener would never leave
undisturbed for me, and a sociable bird or two;
though I never had the sense or perseverance
to make one really tame. But that was partly
because, if ever I managed to bring one to be the
least trustful of me, the cats got it.

Under these circumstances, what powers of
imagination I possessed, either fastened themselves on inanimate things—the sky, the leaves,
and pebbles, observable within the walls of
Eden,—or caught at any opportunity of flight
into regions of romance, compatible with the
objective realities of existence in the nineteenth
century, within a mile and a quarter of Camberwell Green.

Herein my father, happily, though with
no definite intention other than of pleasing me,
when he found he could do so without infringing
any of my mother's rules, became my guide. I
was particularly fond of watching him shave;
and was always allowed to come into his room

in the morning (under the one in which I am now writing), to be the motionless witness of that operation. Over his dressing-table hung one of his own water-colour drawings, made under the teaching of the elder Nasmyth;[18] I believe, at the High School of Edinburgh. It was done in the early manner of tinting, which, just about the time when my father was at the High School, Dr. Monro[19] was teaching Turner; namely, in grey under-tints of Prussian blue and British ink, washed with warm colour afterward on the lights. It represented Conway Castle, with its Frith,[20] and, in the foreground, a cottage, a fisherman, and a boat at the water's edge.

When my father had finished shaving, he always told me a story about this picture. The custom began without any initial purpose of his, in consequence of my troublesome curiosity whether the fisherman lived in the cottage, and where he was going to in the boat. It being settled, for peace' sake, that he *did* live in the cottage, and was going in the boat to fish near the castle, the plot of the drama afterward gradually thickened; and became, I believe, involved with that of the tragedy of *Douglas,* and of the *Castle Spectre,*[21] in both of which pieces my father had performed in private theatricals, before my mother, and a select Edinburgh audience, when he was a boy of sixteen, and she, at grave twenty, a model housekeeper, and very scornful and religiously suspicious of theatricals. But she was never weary of telling me, in later years, how beautiful my father looked in his Highland dress, with the high black feathers.

In the afternoons, when my father returned (always punctually) from his business, he dined, at half-past four, in the front parlor, my mother sitting beside him to hear the events of the day, and give counsel and encouragement with respect to the same;—chiefly the last, for my father was apt to be vexed if orders for sherry fell the least short of their due standard, even for a day or two. I was never present at this time, however, and only avouch what I relate by hearsay and probable conjecture; for between four and six

it would have been a grave misdemeanor in me if I so much as approached the parlor door. After that, in summer time, we were all in the garden as long as the day lasted; tea under the white-heart cherry tree; or in winter and rough weather, at six o'clock in the drawing-room,—I having my cup of milk, and slice of bread-and-butter, in a little recess, with a table in front of it, wholly sacred to me; and in which I remained in the evenings as an Idol in a niche, while my mother knitted, and my father read to her,—and to me, so far as I chose to listen.

The series of the Waverley novels, then drawing toward its close, was still the chief source of delight in all households caring for literature; and I can no more recollect the time when I did not know them than when I did not know the Bible; but I have still a vivid remembrance of my father's intense expression of sorrow mixed with scorn, as he threw down *Count Robert of Paris,*[22] after reading three or four pages; and knew that the life of Scott was ended: the scorn being a very complex and bitter feeling in him,—partly, indeed, of the book itself, but chiefly of the wretches who were tormenting and selling the wrecked intellect, and not a little, deep down, of the subtle dishonesty which had essentially caused the ruin. My father never could forgive Scott his concealment of the Ballantyne partnership.

Such being the salutary pleasures of Herne Hill, I have next with deeper gratitude to chronicle what I owe to my mother for the resolutely consistent lessons which so exercised me in the Scriptures as to make every word of them familiar to my ear in habitual music,—yet in that familiarity reverenced, as transcending all thought, and ordaining all conduct.

This she effected, not by her own sayings or personal authority; but simply by compelling me to read the book thoroughly, for myself. As soon as I was able to read with fluency, she began a course of Bible work with me, which never ceased till I went to Oxford. She read alternate verses with me, watching, at first, every intonation of my voice, and correcting the false

18 Scottish portrait and landscape painter.
19 Physician and art patron, from whom, according to Ruskin, Turner got "some practical teaching."
20 Either a wooded park or an estuary.
21 Two late eighteenth-century dramas, the first by John Home, the second by M. G. Lewis.

22 Scott was a very ill man when he wrote this, his next to last novel. He was actually writing himself to death in an endeavor to pay off his share of the debt incurred by the failure of his publisher, with whom he had been a business partner. Although the parnership was concealed, there does not seem to have been any dishonest intention.

ones, till she made me understand the verse, if within my reach, rightly, and energetically. It might be beyond me altogether; that she did not care about; but she made sure that as soon as I got hold of it at all, I should get hold of it by the right end.

In this way she began with the first verse of Genesis, and went straight through, to the last verse of the Apocalypse; hard names, numbers, Levitical law, and all; and began again at Genesis the next day. If a name was hard, the better the exercise in pronunciation,—if a chapter was tiresome, the better lesson in patience,—if loathsome, the better lesson in faith that there was some use in its being so outspoken. After our chapters, (from two to three a day, according to their length, the first thing after breakfast, and no interruption from servants allowed,— none from vistors, who either joined in the reading or had to stay upstairs,—and none from any visitings or excursions, except real travelling,) I had to learn a few verses by heart, or repeat, to make sure I had not lost, something of what was already known; and, with the chapters thus gradually possessed from the first word to the last, I had to learn the whole body of the fine old Scottish paraphrases,[23] which are good, melodious, and forceful verse; and to which, together with the Bible itself, I owe the first cultivation of my ear in sound.

It is strange that of all the pieces of the Bible which my mother thus taught me, that which cost me most to learn, and which was, to my child's mind, chiefly repulsive—the 119th Psalm—has now become of all the most precious to me, in its overflowing and glorious passion of love for the Law of God, in opposition to the abuse of it by modern preachers of what they imagine to be His gospel.

But it is only by deliberate effort that I recall the long morning hours of toil, as regular as sunrise,—toil on both sides equal—by which, year after year, my mother forced me to learn these paraphrases, and chapters, (the eighth of 1st Kings being one—try it, good reader, in a leisure hour!) allowing not so much as a syllable to be missed or misplaced; while every sentence was required to be said over and over again till she was satisfied with the accent of it. I recollect a struggle between us of about three weeks, concerning the accent of the "of" in the lines

"Shall any following spring revive
The ashes of the urn?"—

I insisting, partly in childish obstinacy, and partly in true instinct for rhythm, (being wholly careless on the subject both of urns and their contents,) on reciting it with an accented *of*. It was not, I say, till after three weeks' labor, that my mother got the accent lightened on the "of" and laid on the ashes, to her mind. But had it taken three years she would have done it, having once undertaken to do it. And, assuredly, had she not done it,—well, there's no knowing what would have happened; but I am very thankful she *did*.

I have just opened my oldest (in use) Bible, —a small, closely, and very neatly printed volume it is, printed in Edinburgh by Sir D. Hunter Blair and J. Bruce, Printers to the King's Most Excellent Majesty, in 1816. Yellow, now, with age; and flexible, but not unclean, with much use; except that the lower corners of the pages at 8th of 1st Kings, and 32d Deuteronomy, are worn somewhat thin and dark, the learning of these two chapters having cost me much pains. My mother's list of the chapters with which, thus learned, she established my soul in life,[24] has just fallen out of it. I will take what indulgence the incurious reader can give me, for printing the list thus accidentally occurrent:

Exodus	chapters	15th and 20th.
2 Samuel	"	1st, from 17th verse to the end.
1 Kings	"	8th.
Psalms	"	23rd, 32nd, 90th, 91st, 103rd, 112th, 119th, 139th.
Proverbs	"	2nd, 3rd, 8th, 12th.
Isaiah	"	58th.
Matthew	"	5th, 6th, 7th.
Acts	"	26th.
1 Corinthians	"	13th, 15th.
James	"	4th.
Revelation	"	5th, 6th.

---

23 *Translations and Paraphrases in Verse collected and prepared by . . . the Church of Scotland, in order to be sung in Churches.* The quotation below is from this collection.

24 "This expression . . . has naturally been supposed by some readers to mean that my mother at this time made me vitally and evangelically religious. The fact was far otherwise. I meant only that she gave me secure *ground* for all future life, practical or spiritual. See the paragraph next following." (Ruskin)

And truly, though I have picked up the elements of a little further knowledge—in mathematics, meteorology, and the like, in after life,—and owe not a little to the teaching of many people, this maternal installation of my mind in that property of chapters, I count very confidently the most precious, and, on the whole, the one *essential* part of all my education.

And it is perhaps already time to mark what advantage and mischief, by the chances of life up to seven years old, had been irrevocably determined for me.

I will first count my blessings (as a not unwise friend once recommended me to do, continually; whereas I have a bad trick of always numbering the thorns in my fingers and not the bones in them).

And for best and truest beginning of all blessings, I had been taught the perfect meaning of Peace, in thought, act, and word.

I never had heard my father's or mother's voice once raised in any question with each other; nor seen an angry, or even slightly hurt or offended, glance in the eyes of either. I had never heard a servant scolded; nor even suddenly, passionately, or in any severe manner, blamed. I had never seen a moment's trouble or disorder in any household matter; nor anything whatever either done in a hurry, or undone in due time. I had no conception of such a feeling as anxiety; my father's occasional vexation in the afternoons, when he had only got an order for twelve butts after expecting one for fifteen, as I have just stated, was never manifested to *me;* and itself related only to the question whether his name would be a step higher or lower in the year's list of sherry exporters; for he never spent more than half his income, and therefore found himself little incommoded by occasional variations in the total of it. I had never done any wrong that I knew of—beyond occasionally delaying the commitment to heart of some improving sentence, that I might watch a wasp on the window-pane, or a bird in the cherry tree; and I had never seen any grief.

Next to this quite priceless gift of Peace, I had received the perfect understanding of the natures of Obedience and Faith. I obeyed word, or lifted finger, of father or mother, simply as a ship her helm; not only without idea of resistance, but receiving the direction as a part of my own life and force, and helpful law, as necessary to me in every moral action as the law of gravity in leaping. And my practice in Faith was soon complete: nothing was ever promised me that was not given; nothing ever threatened me that was not inflicted, and nothing ever told me that was not true.

Peace, obedience, faith; these three for chief good; next to these, the habit of fixed attention with both eyes and mind—on which I will not further enlarge at this moment, this being the main practical faculty of my life, causing Mazzini[25] to say of me, in conversation authentically reported, a year or two before his death, that I had "the most analytic mind in Europe." An opinion in which, so far as I am acquainted with Europe, I am myself entirely disposed to concur.

Lastly, an extreme perfection in palate and all other bodily senses, given by the utter prohibition of cake, wine, comfits, or, except in carefullest restriction, fruit; and by fine preparation of what food was given me. Such I esteem the main blessings of my childhood;—next, let me count the equally dominant calamities.

First, that I had nothing to love.

My parents were—in a sort—visible powers of nature to me, no more loved than the sun and the moon: only I should have been annoyed and puzzled if either of them had gone out; (how much, now, when both are darkened!)—still less did I love God; not that I had any quarrel with Him, or fear of Him; but simply found what people told me was His service, disagreeable; and what people told me was His book, not entertaining. I had no companions to quarrel with, neither; nobody to assist, and nobody to thank. Not a servant was ever allowed to do anything for me, but what it was their duty to do; and why should I have been grateful to the cook for cooking, or the gardener for gardening,—when the one dared not give me a baked potato without asking leave, and the other would not let my ants' nest alone, because they made the walks untidy? The evil consequence of all this was not, however, what might perhaps have been expected, that I grew up selfish or unaffectionate; but that, when affection did come, it came with violence utterly rampant and unmanageable, at least by me, who never before had anything to manage.

---

25 The famous Italian patriot, for whom Ruskin had great admiration.

For (second of chief calamities) I had nothing to endure. Danger or pain of any kind I knew not: my strength was never exercised, my patience never tried, and my courage never fortified. Not that I was ever afraid of anything, —either ghosts, thunder, or beasts; and one of the nearest approaches to insubordination which I was ever tempted into as a child, was in passionate effort to get leave to play with the lion's cubs in Wombwell's menagerie.

Thirdly. I was taught no precision nor etiquette of manners; it was enough if, in the little society we saw, I remained unobtrusive, and replied to a question without shyness: but the shyness came later, and increased as I grew conscious of the rudeness arising from the want of social discipline, and found it impossible to acquire, in advanced life, dexterity in any bodily exercise, skill in any pleasing accomplishment, or ease and tact in ordinary behavior.

Lastly, and chief of evils. My judgment of right and wrong, and powers of independent action, were left entirely undeveloped; because the bridle and blinkers were never taken off me. Children should have their times of being off duty, like soldiers; and when once the obedience, if required, is certain, the little creature should be very early put for periods of practice in complete command of itself; set on the bare-backed horse of its own will, and left to break it by its own strength. But the ceaseless authority exercised over my youth left me, when cast out at last into the world, unable for some time to do more than drift with its vortices.

My present verdict, therefore, on the general tenor of my education at that time, must be, that it was at once too formal and too luxurious; leaving my character, at the most important moment for its construction, cramped indeed, but not disciplined; and only by protection innocent, instead of by practice virtuous.

from Modern Painters, Volume III

from Chapter 1

OF THE RECEIVED OPINIONS TOUCHING THE "GRAND STYLE"[1]

... It seems to me, and may seem to the reader, strange that we should need to ask the question,

"What is poetry?" Here is a word we have been using all our lives, and, I suppose, with a very distinct idea attached to it; and when I am now called upon to give a definition of this idea, I find myself at a pause. What is more singular, I do not at present recollect hearing the question often asked, though surely it is a very natural one; and I never recollect hearing it answered, or even attempted to be answered. In general, people shelter themselves under metaphors, and while we hear poetry described as an utterance of the soul, an effusion of Divinity, or voice of nature, or in other terms equally elevated and obscure, we never attain anything like a definite explanation of the character which actually distinguishes it from prose.

I come, after some embarrassment, to the conclusion, that poetry "is the suggestion, by the imagination, of noble grounds for the noble emotions." I mean, by the noble emotions, those four principal sacred passions—Love, Veneration, Admiration, and Joy (this latter especially, if unselfish); and their opposites—Hatred, Indignation (or Scorn), Horror, and Grief,—this last, when unselfish, becoming Compassion. These passions in their various combinations constitute what is called "poetical feeling," when they are felt on noble grounds, that is, on great and true grounds. Indignation, for instance, is a poetical feeling, if excited by serious injury; but it is not a poetical feeling if entertained on being cheated out of a small sum of money. It is very possible the manner of the cheat may have been such as to justify considerable indigation; but the feeling is nevertheless not poetical unless the grounds of it be large as well as just. In like manner, energetic admiration may be excited in certain minds by a display of fireworks, or a street of handsome shops; but the feeling is not poetical, because the grounds of it are false, and therefore ignoble. There is in reality nothing to deserve admiration either in the firing of packets of gunpowder, or in the display of the stocks of warehouses. But admiration excited by the budding of a flower is a poetical feeling, because it is impossible that this manifestation of spiritual

---

[1] The word "style" is used in a wide sense, which covers content as well as form. The "Grand Style" may be paraphrased as "Great Art." In this chapter Ruskin begins his discussion of what determines greatness in art by examining some of Sir Joshua Reynolds' theories, in the course of which he is led to the definition of poetry which follows. Note that he uses "poetry" to mean the artistic use of either colors or language, so that the definition amounts to a definition of art.

power and vital beauty can ever be enough admired.

Farther, it is necessary to the existence of poetry that the grounds of these feelings should be *furnished by the imagination*. Poetical feeling, that is to say, mere noble emotion, is not poetry. It is happily inherent in all human nature deserving the name, and is found often to be purest in the least sophisticated. But the power of assembling, by *the help of the imagination*, such images as will excite these feelings, is the power of the poet or literally of the "Maker."

Now this power of exciting the emotions depends of course on the richness of the imagination, and on its choice of those images which, in combination, will be most effective, or, for the particular work to be done, most fit. And it is altogether impossible for a writer not endowed with invention to conceive what tools a true poet will make use of, or in what way he will apply them, or what unexpected results he will bring out by them; so that it is vain to say that the details of poetry ought to possess, or ever do possess, any *definite* character. Generally speaking, poetry runs into finer and more delicate details than prose; but the details are not poetical because they are more delicate, but because they are employed so as to bring out an affecting result. For instance, no one but a true poet would have thought of exciting our pity for a bereaved father by describing his way of locking the door of his house:

Perhaps to himself at that moment he said,
"The key I must take, for my Ellen is dead."
But of this in my ears not a word did he speak;
And he went to the chase with a tear on his
    cheek.[2]

In like manner, in painting, it is altogether impossible to say beforehand what details a great painter may make poetical by his use of them to excite noble emotions: and we shall, therefore, find presently that a painting is to be classed in the great or inferior schools, not according to the kind of details which it represents, but according to the uses for which it employs them.

It is only farther to be noticed, that infinite confusion has been introduced into this subject by the careless and illogical custom of opposing

painting to poetry, instead of regarding poetry as consisting in a noble use, whether of colours or words. Painting is properly to be opposed to *speaking* or *writing*, but not to *poetry*. Both painting and speaking are methods of expression. Poetry is the employment of either for the noblest purposes. . . .

from Chapter 3

OF THE REAL NATURE OF GREATNESS OF STYLE

. . . The best way will be, therefore, I think, to sketch out at once in this chapter, the different characters which really constitute "greatness" of style,[3] and to indicate the principal directions of the outbranching misapprehensions of them; then, in the succeeding chapters, to take up in succession those which need more talk about them, and follow out at leisure whatever inquiries they may suggest.

I. CHOICE OF NOBLE SUBJECT.—Greatness of style consists, then: first, in the habitual choice of subjects of thought which involve wide interests and profound passions, as opposed to those which involve narrow interests and slight passions. The style is greater or less in exact proportion to the nobleness of the interests and passions involved in the subject. The habitual choice of sacred subjects, such as the Nativity, Transfiguration, Crucifixion (if the choice be sincere), implies that the painter has a natural disposition to dwell on the highest thoughts of which humanity is capable; it constitutes him so far forth a painter of the highest order, as, for instance, Leonardo,[4] in his painting of the Last Supper: he who delights in representing the acts or meditations of great men, as, for instance, Raphael painting the School of Athens, is, so far forth, a painter of the second order: he who represents the passions and events of ordinary life, of the third. And in this ordinary life, he who represents deep thoughts and sorrows, as, for instance, Hunt,[5] in his Claudio and Isabella, and

---

[2] The last stanza of "The Childless Father" by Wordsworth.

[3] In the passage omitted at the beginning of this chapter Ruskin points out that "we have at all times some instinctive sense that the function of one painter is greater than that of another" and that our problem is to determine a true measure of this greatness.

[4] Leonardo da Vinci (1452–1519).

[5] Holman Hunt (1827–1910) was a leader in the Pre-Raphaelite movement. His "Claudio and Isabella," exhibited at the Royal Academy in 1853, was much admired by Ruskin.

such other works, is of the highest rank in his sphere: and he who represents the slight malignities and passions of the drawing-room, as, for instance, Leslie,[6] of the second rank; he who represents the sports of boys, or simplicities of clowns, as Webster[7] or Teniers,[8] of the third rank; and he who represents brutalities and vices (for delight in them, and not for rebuke of them), of no rank at all, or rather of a negative rank, holding a certain order in the abyss.

The reader will, I hope, understand how much importance is to be attached to the sentence in the first parenthesis, "if the choice be sincere"; for choice of subjects is, of course, only available as a criterion of the rank of the painter, when it is made from the heart. Indeed, in the lower orders of painting, the choice is always made from such heart as the painter has; for his selection of the brawls of peasants or sports of children can, of course, proceed only from the fact that he has more sympathy with such brawls or pastimes than with nobler subjects. But the choice of the higher kind of subjects is often insincere; and may, therefore, afford no real criterion of the painter's rank. The greater number of men who have lately painted religious or heroic subjects have done so in mere ambition, because they had been taught that it was a good thing to be a "high-art"[9] painter; and the fact is that, in nine cases out of ten, the so-called historical or "high-art" painter is a person infinitely inferior to the painter of flowers or still life. He is, in modern times, nearly always a man who has great vanity without pictorial capacity, and differs from the landscape or fruit painter merely in misunderstanding and overestimating his own powers. He mistakes his vanity for inspiration, his ambition for greatness of soul, and takes pleasure in what he calls "the ideal," merely because

he has neither humility nor capacity enough to comprehend the real.

But also observe, it is not enough even that the choice be sincere. It must also be wise. It happens very often that a man of weak intellect, sincerely desiring to do what is good and useful, will devote himself to high art subjects because he thinks them the only ones on which time and toil can be usefully spent, or, sometimes, because they are really the only ones he has pleasure in contemplating. But not having intellect enough to enter into the minds of truly great men, or to imagine great events as they really happened, he cannot become a great painter; he degrades the subjects he intended to honour, and his work is more utterly thrown away, and his rank as an artist in reality lower, than if he had devoted himself to the imitation of the simplest objects of natural history. The works of Overbeck[10] are a most notable instance of this form of error.

It must also be remembered, that in nearly all the great periods of art the choice of subject has not been left to the painter. His employer,—abbot, baron, or monarch,—determined for him whether he should earn his bread by making cloisters bright with choirs of saints, painting coats of arms on leaves of romances, or decorating presence-chambers with complimentary mythology; and his own personal feelings are ascertainable only by watching, in the themes assigned to him, what are the points in which he seems to take most pleasure. Thus, in the prolonged ranges of varied subjects with which Benozzo Gozzoli decorated the cloisters of Pisa, it is easy to see that love of simple domestic incident, sweet landscape, and glittering ornament, prevails slightly over the solemn elements of religious feeling, which, nevertheless, the spirit of the age instilled into him in such measure as to form a very lovely and noble mind, though still one of the second order. In the work of Orcagna, an intense solemnity and energy in the sublimest groups of his figures, fading away as he touches inferior subjects, indicates that his home was among the archangels, and his rank among the first of the sons of men: while Correggio,[11] in

6 Charles Robert Leslie (1794–1859), American-born English painter of fashionable life.

7 Thomas Webster, minor painter of the nineteenth century whose interests lay in school and village scenes.

8 There were two Dutch painters of this name, in the sixteenth and seventeenth centuries respectively, both of them of the realistic school.

9 In chapter 1 of this volume Ruskin says that for the last hundred and fifty years critics have used the terms " 'High Art,' 'Great or Ideal style,' and other such, as descriptive of a certain noble manner of painting," and have characterized "as 'vulgar,' or 'low,' or 'realist,' another manner of painting and conceiving." The distinction includes, of course, the subject matter.

10 Nineteenth-century German painter who, upon his conversion to Roman Catholicism, devoted himself entirely to sacred subjects. His pictures were full of devout feeling but hard in color and outline.

11 All three of the painters here described belonged to the Italian Renaissance.

the sidelong grace, artificial smiles, and purple languors of his saints, indicates the inferior instinct which would have guided his choice in quite other directions, had it not been for the fashion of the age, and the need of the day.

It will follow, of course, from the above considerations, that the choice which characterizes the school of high art is seen as much in the treatment of a subject as in its selection, and that the expression of the thoughts of the persons represented will always be the first thing considered by the painter who worthily enters that highest school. For the artist who sincerely chooses the noblest subject will also choose chiefly to represent what makes that subject noble, namely, the various heroism or other noble emotions of the persons represented. If, instead of this, the artist seeks only to make his picture agreeable by the composition of its masses and colours, or by any other merely pictorial merit, as fine drawing of limbs, it is evident, not only that any other subject would have answered his purpose as well, but that he is unfit to approach the subject he has chosen, because he cannot enter into its deepest meaning, and therefore cannot in reality have chosen it for that meaning. Nevertheless, while the expression is always to be the first thing considered, all other merits must be added to the utmost of the painter's power; for until he can both colour and draw beautifully he has no business to consider himself a painter at all,[12] far less to attempt the noblest subjects of painting; and, when he has once possessed himself of these powers, he will naturally and fitly employ them to deepen and perfect the impression made by the sentiment of his subject.

The perfect unison of expression, as the painter's main purpose, with the full and natural exertion of his pictorial power in the details of the work, is found only in the old Pre-Raphaelite periods, and in the modern Pre-Raphaelite school.[13] In the works of Giotto, Angelico, Orcagna, John Bellini, and one or two more,

these two conditions of high art are entirely fulfilled, so far as the knowledge of those days enable them to be fulfilled; and in the modern Pre-Raphaelite school they are fulfilled nearly to the uttermost. Hunt's Light of the World is, I believe, the most perfect instance of expressional purpose with technical power, which the world has yet produced.

Now in the Post-Raphaelite period of ancient art, and in the spurious high art of modern times, two broad forms of error divide the schools; the one consisting in (A) the superseding of expression by technical excellence, and the other in (B) the superseding of technical excellence by expression.

(A). Superseding expression by technical excellence.—This takes place most frankly, and therefore most innocently, in the work of the Venetians.[14] They very nearly ignore expression altogether, directing their aim exclusively to the rendering of external truths of colour and form. Paul Veronese will make the Magdalene wash the feet of Christ with a countenance as absolutely unmoved as that of any ordinary servant bringing a ewer to her master, and will introduce the supper at Emmaus[15] as a background to the portraits of two children playing with a dog. Of the wrongness or rightness of such a proceeding we shall reason in another place; at present we have to note it merely as displacing the Venetian work from the highest or expressional rank of art. But the error is generally made in a more subtle and dangerous way. The artist deceives himself into the idea that he is doing all he can do to elevate his subject by treating it under rules of art, introducing into it accurate science, and collecting for it the beauties of (so-called) ideal form; whereas he may, in reality, be all the while sacrificing his subject to his own vanity or pleasure, and losing truth, nobleness, and impressiveness for the sake of delightful lines or creditable pedantries.

(B). Superseding technical excellence by expression.—This is usually done under the influence of another kind of vanity. The artist desires that men should think he has an elevated soul,

12 The stress which Ruskin laid upon subject matter or content sometimes tends to obscure his insistence upon, and assumption of, technical skill as an indispensable prerequisite to any artistic excellence.
13 The old periods, of course, were those before the time of Raphael (1483–1520). The modern school, of which Ruskin was an ardent champion, is described in the last six paragraphs of the introduction to the Victorian period.

14 Chief among the great Venetian painters were Titian, Giorgione, Tintoretto, and Veronese.
15 The meal that Jesus ate with two of his disciples at a village outside Jerusalem after his resurrection (Luke 24:13–35).

affects to despise the ordinary excellence of art, contemplates with separated egotism[16] the course of his own imaginations or sensations, and refuses to look at the real facts round about him, in order that he may adore at leisure the shadow of himself. He lives in an element of what he calls tender emotions and lofty aspirations; which are, in fact, nothing more than very ordinary weaknesses or instincts, contemplated through a mist of pride. A large range of modern German art comes under this head.

A more interesting and respectable form of this error is fallen into by some truly earnest men, who, finding their powers not adequate to the attainment of great artistical excellence, but adequate to rendering, up to a certain point, the expression of the human countenance, devote themselves to that object alone, abandoning effort in other directions, and executing the accessories of their pictures feebly or carelessly. With these are associated another group of philosophical painters, who suppose the artistical merits of other parts *adverse* to the expression, as drawing the spectator's attention away from it, and who paint in grey colour, and imperfect light and shade, by way of enforcing the purity of their conceptions. Both these classes of conscientious but narrow-minded artists labour under the same grievous mistake of imagining that wilful fallacy can ever be either pardonable or helpful. They forget that colour, if used at all, must be either true or false, and that what *they* call chastity, dignity, and reserve, is to the eye of any person accustomed to nature, pure, bold, and impertinent falsehood. It does not, in the eyes of any soundly minded man, exalt the expression of a female face that the cheeks should be painted of the colour of clay, nor does it in the least enhance his reverence for a saint to find the scenery around him deprived, by his presence, of sunshine.[17] It is an important consolation, however, to reflect that no artist ever fell into any of these last three errors (under head B.) who had really the capacity of becoming a great painter. No man ever despised colour who could produce

it; and the error of these sentimentalists and philosophers is not so much in the choice of their manner of painting, as in supposing themselves capable of painting at all. Some of them might have made efficient sculptors, but the greater number had their mission in some other sphere than that of art, and would have found, in works of practical charity, better employment for their gentleness and sentimentalism, than in denying to human beauty its colour, and to natural scenery its light; in depriving heaven of its blue, and earth of its bloom, valour of its glow, and modesty of its blush.

II. LOVE OF BEAUTY.—The second characteristic of the great school of art is, that it introduces in the conception of its subject as much beauty as is possible, consistently with truth.[18]

---

[16] An egotism that has separated him from the ordinary artist.

[17] Ruskin has mainly in view here the academic painting of the period, against which the Pre-Raphaelites rebelled. That he was also thinking of Rembrandt is clear from section III.

[18] "As here, for the first time, I am obliged to use the terms Truth and Beauty in a kind of opposition, I must therefore stop for a moment to state clearly the relation of these two qualities of art; and to protest against the vulgar and foolish habit of confusing truth and beauty with each other. People with shallow powers of thought, desiring to flatter themselves with the sensation of having attained profundity, are continually doing the most serious mischief by introducing confusion into plain matters, and then valuing themselves on being confounded. Nothing is more common than to hear people who desire to be thought philosophical, declare that 'beauty is truth,' and 'truth is beauty.' I would most earnestly beg every sensible person who hears such an assertion made to nip the germinating philosopher in his ambiguous bud; and beg him, if he really believes his own assertion, never thenceforward to use two words for the same thing. The fact is, truth and beauty are entirely distinct, though often related, things. One is a property of statements, the other of objects. The statement that 'two and two make four' is true, but it is neither beautiful nor ugly, for it is invisible; a rose is lovely, but it is neither true nor false, for it is silent. That which shows nothing cannot be fair, and that which asserts nothing cannot be false. Even the ordinary use of the words false and true as applied to artificial and real things, is inaccurate. An artificial rose is not a 'false' rose, it is not a rose at all. The falseness is in the person who states, or induces the belief, that it *is* a rose.

"Now, therefore, in things concerning art, the words true and false are only to be rightly used while the picture is considered as a statement of facts. The painter asserts that this which he has painted is the form of a dog, a man, or a tree. If it be *not* the form of a dog, a man, or a tree, the painter's statement is false; and therefore we justly speak of a false line, or false colour; not that any line or colour can in themselves be false, but they become so when they convey a statement that they resemble something which they do *not* resemble. But the beauty of the lines or colours is wholly independent of any such statement. They may be beautiful lines, though quite inaccurate, and ugly lines, though quite faithful. A picture may be frightfully ugly, which represents with fidelity some base circumstance of daily life; and a painted win-

For instance, in any subject consisting of a number of figures, it will make as many of those figures beautiful as the faithful representation of humanity will admit. It will not deny the facts of ugliness or decrepitude, or relative inferiority and superiority of feature as necessarily manifested in a crowd, but it will, so far as it is in its power, seek for and dwell upon the fairest forms, and in all things insist on the beauty that is in them, not on the ugliness. In this respect, schools of art become higher in exact proportion to the degree in which they apprehend and love the beautiful. Thus, Angelico, intensely loving all spiritual beauty, will be of the highest rank; and Paul Veronese and Correggio, intensely loving physical and corporeal beauty, of the second rank; and Albert Dürer, Rubens, and in general the Northern artists, apparently insensible to beauty, and caring only for truth, whether shapely or not, of the third rank; and Teniers and Salvator, Caravaggio, and other such worshippers of the depraved, of no rank, or, as we said before, of a certain order in the abyss.

The corruption of the schools of high art, so far as this particular quality is concerned, consists in the sacrifice of truth to beauty. Great art dwells on all that is beautiful; but false art omits or changes all that is ugly. Great art accepts Nature as she is, but directs the eyes and thoughts to what is most perfect in her; false art saves itself the trouble of direction by removing or altering whatever it thinks objectionable. The evil results of which proceeding are twofold.

First.[19] That beauty deprived of its proper foils and adjuncts ceases to be enjoyed as beauty, just as light deprived of all shadow ceases to be enjoyed as light. A white canvas cannot produce an effect of sunshine; the painter must darken it in some places before he can make it look luminous in others; nor can an uninterrupted succession of beauty produce the true effect of beauty; it must be foiled by inferiority before its own power can be developed. Nature has for the most part mingled her inferior and nobler elements as she mingles sunshine with shade, giving due use and influence to both, and the painter who chooses to remove the shadow, perishes in the burning desert he has created. The truly high and beautiful art of Angelico is continually refreshed and strengthened by his frank portraiture of the most ordinary features of his brother monks, and of the recorded peculiarities of ungainly sanctity; but the modern German and Raphaelesque schools lose all honour and nobleness in barber-like admiration of handsome faces, and have, in fact, no real faith except in straight noses and curled hair. Paul Veronese opposes the dwarf to the soldier, and the negress to the queen;[20] Shakspeare places Caliban beside Miranda, and Autolycus beside Perdita;[21] but the vulgar idealist withdraws his beauty to the safety of the saloon,[22] and his innocence to the seclusion of the cloister; he pretends that he does this in delicacy of choice and purity of sentiment, while in truth he has neither courage to front the monster, nor wit enough to furnish the knave.

It[23] is only by the habit of representing faithfully all things, that we can truly learn what is beautiful, and what is not. The ugliest objects contain some element of beauty; and in all, it is an element peculiar to themselves, which cannot be separated from their ugliness, but must either be enjoyed together with it, or not at all. The more a painter accepts nature as he finds it, the more unexpected beauty he discovers in what he at first despised; but once let him arrogate the right of rejection, and he will gradually contract

dow may be exquisitely beautiful, which represents men with eagles' faces, and dogs with blue heads and crimson tails (though, by the way, this is not in the strict sense *false* art, as we shall see hereafter, inasmuch as it means no assertion that men ever *had* eagles' faces). If this were not so, it would be impossible to sacrifice truth to beauty; for to attain the one would always be to attain the other. But, unfortunately, this sacrifice is exceedingly possible, and it is chiefly this which characterises the false schools of high art, so far as high art consists in the pursuit of beauty. For although truth and beauty are independent of each other, it does not follow that we are at liberty to pursue whichever we please. They are indeed separable, but it is wrong to separate them; they are to be sought together in the order of their worthiness; that is to say, truth first, and beauty afterwards. High art differs from low art in possessing an excess of beauty in addition to its truth, not in possessing an excess of beauty inconsistent with truth." (Ruskin)
19 "Evil first, that we lose the true *force* of beauty." (Ruskin, marginal summary)

20 In his pictures "Alexander and the Family of Darius" and "The Queen of Sheba," respectively.
21 In *The Tempest* and *The Winter's Tale*, respectively.
22 The English equivalent of the French salon, meaning a large room for social purposes or for the exhibition of works of art.
23 "Evil second,—we lose the true *quantity* of beauty." (Ruskin, marginal summary)

his circle of enjoyment, until what he supposed to be nobleness of selection ends in narrowness of perception. Dwelling perpetually upon one class of ideas, his art becomes at once monstrous and morbid; until at last he cannot faithfully represent even what he chooses to retain; his discrimination contracts into darkness, and his fastidiousness fades into fatuity.

High art, therefore, consists neither in altering, nor in improving nature; but in seeking throughout nature for "whatsoever things are lovely, and whatsoever things are pure";[24] in loving these, in displaying to the utmost of the painter's power such loveliness as is in them, and directing the thoughts of others to them by winning art, or gentle emphasis. Of the degree in which this can be done, and in which it may be permitted to gather together, without falsifying, the finest forms or thoughts, so as to create a sort of perfect vision, we shall have to speak hereafter: at present, it is enough to remember that art (*caeteris paribus*)[25] is great in exact proportion to the love of beauty shown by the painter, provided that love of beauty forfeit no atom of truth.

III. SINCERITY.—The next[26] characteristic of great art is that it includes the largest possible quantity of Truth in the most perfect possible harmony. If it were possible for art to give all the truths of nature, it ought to do it. But this is not possible. Choice must always be made of some facts which *can* be represented, from among others which must be passed by in silence, or even, in some respects, misrepresented. The inferior artist chooses unimportant and scattered truths; the great artist chooses the most necessary first, and afterwards the most consistent with these, so as to obtain the greatest possible and most harmonious *sum*. For instance, Rembrandt always chooses to represent the exact force with which the light on the most illumined part of an object is opposed to its obscurer portions. In order to obtain this, in most cases, not very important truth, he sacrifices the light and colour of five sixths of his picture; and the expression of every character of objects which depends on tenderness of shape or tint. But he obtains his single truth, and what picturesque and forcible

expression is dependent upon it, with magnificent skill and subtlety. Veronese, on the contrary, chooses to represent the great relations of visible things to each other, to the heaven above, and to the earth beneath them. He holds it more important to show how a figure stands relieved from delicate air, or marble wall; how as a red, or purple, or white figure, it separates itself, in clear discernibility, from things not red, nor purple, nor white; how infinite daylight shines round it; how innumerable veils of faint shadow invest it; how its blackness and darkness are, in the excess of their nature, just as limited and local as its intensity of light: all this, I say, he feels to be more important than showing merely the exact *measure* of the spark of sunshine that gleams on a dagger-hilt, or glows on a jewel. All this, moreover, he feels to be harmonious,—capable of being joined in one great system of spacious truth. And with inevitable watchfulness, inestimable subtlety, he unites all this in tenderest balance, noting in each hair's-breadth of colour, not merely what its rightness or wrongness is in itself, but what its relation is to every other on his canvas; restraining, for truth's sake, his exhaustless energy; reining back, for truth's sake, his fiery strength; veiling, before truth, the vanity of brightness; penetrating, for truth, the discouragement of gloom; ruling his restless invention with a rod of iron; pardoning no error, no thoughtlessness, no forgetfulness; and subduing all his powers, impulses, and imaginations, to the arbitrament of a merciless justice, and the obedience of an incorruptible verity.

I give this instance with respect to colour and shade; but, in the whole field of art, the difference between the great and inferior artists is of the same kind, and may be determined at once by the question, which of them conveys the largest sum of truth?

It follows from this principle,[27] that in general all *great* drawing is *distinct* drawing; for truths which are rendered indistinctly might, for the most part, as well not be rendered at all. There are, indeed, certain facts of mystery, and facts of indistinctness, in all objects, which must have their proper place in the general harmony, and the reader will presently find me, when we

---

24 Philippians 4:8.
25 Other things being equal.
26 "I name them in order of *increasing*, not decreasing importance." (Ruskin)

27 "Corollary 1st: Great art is generally distinct." (Ruskin, marginal summary)

come to that part of our investigation, telling him that all good drawing must in some sort be *in*distinct. We may, however, understand this apparent contradiction, by reflecting that the highest knowledge always involves a more advanced perception of the fields of the unknown; and, therefore, it may most truly be said, that to know anything well involves a profound sensation of ignorance, while yet it is equally true that good and noble knowledge is distinguished from vain and useless knowledge chiefly by its clearness and distinctness, and by the vigorous consciousness of what is known and what is not.

So in art. The best drawing involves a wonderful perception and expression of indistinctness; and yet all noble drawing is separated from the ignoble by its distinctness, by its fine expression and firm assertion of *Something*; whereas the bad drawing, without either firmness or fineness, expresses and asserts *Nothing*. The first thing, therefore, to be looked for as a sign of noble art, is a clear consciousness of what is drawn and what is not; the bold statement, and frank confession—"*This* I know," "*that* I know not"; and, generally speaking, all haste, slurring, obscurity, indecision, are signs of low art, and all calmness, distinctness, luminousness, and positiveness, of high art.

It follows, secondly, from this principle,[28] that as the great painter is always attending to the sum and harmony of his truths rather than to one or the other of any group, a quality of Grasp is visible in his work, like the power of a great reasoner over his subject, or a great poet over his conception, manifesting itself very often in missing out certain details or less truths (which, though good in themselves, he finds are in the way of others), and in a sweeping manner of getting the beginnings and ends of things shown at once, and the squares and depths rather than the surfaces: hence, on the whole, a habit of looking at large masses rather than small ones; and even a physical largeness of handling, and love of working, if possible, on a large scale; and various other qualities, more or less imperfectly expressed by such technical terms as breadth, massing, unity, boldness, &c., all of which are, indeed, great qualities when they mean breadth of truth, weight of truth, unity of

truth, and courageous assertion of truth; but which have all their correlative errors and mockeries, almost universally mistaken for them,—the breadth which has no contents, the weight which has no value, the unity which plots deception, and the boldness which faces out fallacy.

And it is to be noted especially respecting largeness of scale, that though for the most part it is characteristic of the more powerful masters, they having both more invention wherewith to fill space (as Ghirlandajo wished that he might paint all the walls of Florence),[29] and, often, an impetuosity of mind which makes them like free play for hand and arm (besides that they usually desire to paint everything in the foreground of their picture of the natural size), yet, as this largeness of scale involves the placing of the picture at a considerable distance from the eye, and this distance involves the loss of many delicate details, and especially of the subtle lines of expression in features, it follows that the masters of refined detail and human expression are apt to prefer a small scale to work upon; so that the chief masterpieces of expression which the world possesses are small pictures by Angelico, in which the figures are rarely more than six or seven inches high; in the best works of Raphael and Leonardo the figures are almost always less than life; and the best works of Turner do not exceed the size of 18 inches by 12.

As its greatness depends on the sum of truth, and this sum of truth can always be increased by delicacy of handling, it follows that all great art must have this delicacy to the utmost possible degree.[30] This rule is infallible and inflexible. All coarse work is the sign of low art. Only, it is to be remembered, that coarseness must be estimated by the distance from the eye; it being necessary to consult this distance, when great, by laying on touches which appear coarse when seen near; but which, so far from being coarse, are, in reality, more delicate in a master's work than the finest close handling, for they involve a calculation of result, and are laid on with a subtlety of sense precisely correspondent to that

---

28 "Corollory 2nd: Great art is generally large in masses and in scale." (Ruskin, marginal summary)

29 This great fifteenth-century master of fresco is reported by Vasari to have complained, "Now that I have begun to get into the spirit and comprehend the method of this art, I grudge that they do not commission me to paint the whole circuit of the walls of Florence with stories."

30 "Corollary 3rd: Great art is always delicate." (Ruskin, marginal summary)

with which a good archer draws his bow; the spectator seeing in the action nothing but the strain of the strong arm, while there is, in reality, in the finger and eye, an ineffably delicate estimate of distance, and touch on the arrow plume. And, indeed, this delicacy is generally quite perceptible to those who know what the truth is, for strokes by Tintoret or Paul Veronese, which were done in an instant, and look to an ignorant spectator merely like a violent dash of loaded colour (and are, as such, imitated by blundering artists), are, in fact, modulated by the brush and finger to that degree of delicacy that no single grain of the colour could be taken from the touch without injury; and little golden particles of it, not the size of a gnat's head, have important share and function in the balances of light in a picture perhaps fifty feet long. Nearly *every* other rule applicable to art has some exception but this. This has absolutely none. All great art is delicate art, and all coarse art is bad art. Nay, even to a certain extent, all *bold* art is bad art; for boldness is not the proper word to apply to the courage and swiftness of a great master, based on knowledge, and coupled with fear and love. There is as much difference between the boldness of the true and the false masters, as there is between the courage of a pure woman and the shamelessness of a lost one.

IV. INVENTION.—The last characteristic of great art is that it must be inventive, that is, be produced by the imagination. In this respect, it must precisely fulfil the definition already given of poetry; and not only present grounds for noble emotion, but furnish these grounds by *imaginative power*. Hence there is at once a great bar fixed between the two schools of Lower and Higher Art. The lower merely copies what is set before it, whether in portrait, landscape, or still-life; the higher either entirely imagines its subject, or arranges the materials presented to it, so as to manifest the imaginative power in all the three phases which have been already explained in the second volume.

And this was the truth which was confusedly present in Reynolds's mind when he spoke, as above quoted, of the difference between Historical and Poetical painting.[31] *Every relation of the plain facts which the painter saw* is proper *historical* painting. If those facts are unimportant (as that he saw a gambler quarrel with another gambler, or a sot enjoying himself with another sot), then the history is trivial; if the facts are important (as that he saw such and such a great man look thus, or act thus, at such a time), then the history is noble: in each case perfect truth of narrative being supposed, otherwise the whole thing is worthless, being neither history nor poetry, but plain falsehood. And farther, as greater or less elegance and precision are manifested in the relation or painting of the incidents, the merit of the work varies; so that, what with difference of subject, and what with difference of treatment, historical painting falls or rises in changeful eminence, from Dutch trivialities[32] to a Velasquez[33] portrait, just as historical talking or writing varies in eminence, from an old woman's story-telling up to Herodotus.[34] Besides which, certain operations of the imagination come into play inevitably, here and there, so as to touch the history with some light of poetry, that is, with some light shot forth of the narrator's mind, or brought out by the way he has put the accidents together: and wherever the imagination has thus had anything to do with the matter at all (and it must be somewhat cold work where it has not), then, the confines of the lower and higher schools touching each other, the work is coloured by both; but there is no reason why, therefore, we should in the least confuse the historical and poetical characters, any more than that we should confuse blue with crimson, because they may overlap each other, and produce purple.

Now, historical or simply narrative art is very precious in its proper place and way, but it is never *great* art until the poetical or imaginative power touches it; and in proportion to the stronger manifestation of this power, it becomes greater and greater, while the highest art is purely imaginative, all its materials being wrought into their form by invention. . . .

31 Ruskin in chapter 1 sums up Reynolds's distinction: painting is historical when it attends "to literal truth and 'minute exactness in the details of nature modified by accident'" and poetical when it attends only "to the invariable."

32 Ruskin is thinking of the domestic and familiar scenes favored by the Dutch painters.

33 Perhaps the greatest of Spanish painters, noted particularly for his portraits.

34 Greek historian of the fifth century B.C., known as "the father of history."

Farther, imaginative art always *includes* historical art; so that, strictly speaking, according to the analogy above used, we meet with the pure blue, and with the crimson ruling the blue and changing it into kingly purple, but not with the pure crimson: for all imagination must deal with the knowledge it has before accumulated; it never produces anything but by combination or contemplation. Creation, in the full sense, is impossible to it. And the mode in which the historical faculties are included by it is often quite simple, and easily seen. Thus, in Hunt's great poetical picture of the Light of the World, the whole thought and arrangement of the picture being imaginative, the several details of it are wrought out with simple portraiture; the ivy, the jewels, the creeping plants, and the moonlight being calmly studied or remembered from the things themselves. But of all these special ways in which the invention works with plain facts, we shall have to treat farther afterwards.

And now, finally, since this poetical power includes the historical, if we glance back to the other qualities required in great art, and put all together, we find that the sum of them is simply the sum of all the powers of man. For as (1) the choice of the high subject involves all conditions of right moral choice, and as (2) the love of beauty involves all conditions of right admiration, and as (3) the grasp of truth involves all strength of sense, evenness of judgment, and honesty of purpose, and as (4) the poetical power involves all swiftness of invention, and accuracy of historical memory, the sum of all these powers is the sum of the human soul. Hence we see why the word "Great" is used of this art. It is literally great. It compasses and calls forth the entire human spirit, whereas any other kind of art, being more or less small or narrow, compasses and calls forth only *part* of the human spirit. Hence the idea of its magnitude is a literal and just one, the art being simply less or greater in proportion to the number of faculties it exercises and addresses. And this is the ultimate meaning of the definition I gave of it long ago,[35] as containing the "greatest number of the greatest ideas."

Such, then, being the characters required in order to constitute high art, if the reader will think over them a little, and over the various ways in which they may be falsely assumed, he will easily perceive how spacious and dangerous a field of discussion they open to the ambitious critic, and of error to the ambitious artist; he will see how difficult it must be, either to distinguish what is truly great art from the mockeries of it, or to rank the real artists in anything like a progressive system of greater and less. For it will have been observed that the various qualities which form greatness are partly inconsistent with each other (as some virtues are, docility and firmness for instance), and partly independent of each other; and the fact is, that artists differ not more by mere capacity, than by the component *elements* of their capacity, each possessing in very different proportions the several attributes of greatness; so that, classed by one kind of merit, as, for instance, purity of expression, Angelico will stand highest; classed by another, sincerity of manner, Veronese will stand highest, classed by another, love of beauty, Leonardo will stand highest, and so on: hence arise continual disputes and misunderstandings among those who think that high art must always be one and the same, and that great artists ought to unite all great attributes in an equal degree.

In one of the exquisitely finished tales of Marmontel, a company of critics are received at dinner by the hero of the story, an old gentleman, somewhat vain of his *acquired* taste, and his niece, by whose incorrigible *natural* taste he is seriously disturbed and tormented. During the entertainment, "On parcourut tous les genres de littérature, et pour donner plus d'essor à l'érudition et à la critique, on mit sur le tapis cette question toute neuve, sçavoir, lequel méritoit la préférence de Corneille ou de Racine. L'on disoit même là-dessus les plus belles choses du monde, lorsque la petite nièce, qui n'avoit pas dit un mot, s'avisa de demander naïvement lequel des deux fruits, de l'orange ou de la pêche, avoit le goût le plus exquis et méritoit le plus d'éloges. Son oncle rougit de sa simplicité, et les convives baissèrent tous les yeux sans daigner répondre à cette bêtise. Ma nièce, dit Fintac, à votre âge, il faut sçavoir écouter, et se taire."[36]

35 In the first volume of *Modern Painters*, 1843.

36 "Le Connoisseur" in his *Contes moraux*. The quoted passage may be translated: "They discussed all kinds of literature and, to allow greater flights of erudition and

I cannot close this chapter with shorter or better advice to the reader, than merely, whenever he hears discussions about the relative merits of great masters, to remember the young lady's question. It is, indeed, true that there *is* a relative merit, that a peach is nobler than a hawthorn berry, and still more a hawthorn berry than a bead of the nightshade; but in each rank of fruits, as in each rank of masters, one is endowed with one virtue, and another with another; their glory is their dissimilarity, and they who propose to themselves in the training of an artist that he should unite the colouring of Tintoret, the finish of Albert Dürer, and the tenderness of Correggio, are no wiser than a horticulturist would be, who made it the object of his labour to produce a fruit which should unite in itself the lusciousness of the grape, the crispness of the nut, and the fragrance of the pine.

And from these considerations one most important practical corollary is to be deduced, with the good help of Mademoiselle Agathe's[37] simile, namely, that the greatness or smallness of a man is, in the most conclusive sense, determined for him at his birth, as strictly as it is determined for a fruit whether it is to be a currant or an apricot. Education, favourable circumstances, resolution, and industry can do much; in a certain sense they do *everything;* that is to say, they determine whether the poor apricot shall fall in the form of a green bead, blighted by the east wind, and be trodden under foot, or whether it shall expand into tender pride, and sweet brightness of golden velvet. But apricot out of currant,—great man out of small,—did never yet art or effort make; and, in a general way, men have their excellence nearly fixed for them when they are born; a little cramped and frost-bitten on one side, a little sun-burnt and fortune-spotted on the other, they reach, between good and evil chances, such size and taste as

generally belong to the men of their calibre, and, the small in their serviceable bunches, the great in their golden isolation, have, these no cause for regret, nor those for distain.

Therefore it is, that every system of teaching is false which holds forth "great art" as in any wise to be taught to students, or even to be aimed at by them. Great art is precisely that which never was, nor will be taught, it is pre-eminently and finally the expression of the spirits of great men; so that the only wholesome teaching is that which simply endeavours to fix those characters of nobleness in the pupil's mind, of which it seems easily susceptible; and without holding out to him, as a possible or even probable result, that he should ever paint like Titian, or carve like Michael Angelo, enforces upon him the manifest possibility, and assured duty, of endeavouring to draw in a manner at least honest and intelligible; and cultivates in him those general charities of heart, sincerities of thought, and graces of habit which are likely to lead him, throughout life, to prefer openness to affectation, realities to shadows, and beauty to corruption.

from Chapter 17

THE MORAL OF LANDSCAPE[38]

. . . The first thing which I remember, as an event in life,[39] was being taken by my nurse to the brow of Friar's Crag on Derwentwater; the intense joy, mingled with awe, that I had in looking through the hollows in the mossy roots, over the crag, into the dark lake, has associated itself more or less with all twining roots of trees ever since. Two other things I remember, as, in a sort, beginnings of life;— crossing Shapfells (being let out of the chaise to run up the hills), and going through Glenfarg, near Kinross, in a winter's morning, when the rocks were hung with icicles; these being culminating points in an early life of more trav-

---

criticism, they proposed this entirely original question, namely, which was to be preferred, Corneille or Racine. They were just saying the finest things in the world, when the little niece, who had not said a word, took it into her head to ask naïvely which of the two fruits, oranges or pears, had the more delicious taste and deserved the greatest praise. Her uncle blushed for her simplicity and the guests lowered their eyes without condescending to reply to this stupidity. 'My niece,' said Fintac, 'at your age you should know how to listen and keep quiet.' "

37 The niece in Marmontel's tale.

38 Ruskin proposes to discuss in this chapter what are the probable or usual effects of taking pleasure in nature or landscape. Are they good or bad? And he feels that in the case of no one else can he judge these effects so well as in his own, particularly in earliest youth.

39 I.e., the first event in the history of his pleasure in nature.

elling than is usually indulged to a child.[40] In such journeyings, whenever they brought me near hills, and in all mountain ground and scenery, I had a pleasure, as early as I can remember, and continuing till I was eighteen or twenty, infinitely greater than any which has been since possible to me in anything; comparable for intensity only to the joy of a lover in being near a noble and kind mistress, but no more explicable or definable than that feeling of love itself. Only thus much I can remember, respecting it, which is important to our present subject.

First: it was never independent of associated thought. Almost as soon as I could see or hear, I had got reading enough to give me associations with all kinds of scenery; and mountains, in particular, were always partly confused with those of my favourite book, Scott's *Monastery;* so that Glenfarg and all other glens were more or less enchanted to me, filled with forms of hesitating creed about Christie of the Clint Hill, and the monk Eustace; and with a general presence of White Lady[41] everywhere. I also generally knew, or was told by my father and mother, such simple facts of history as were necessary to give more definite and justifiable association to other scenes which chiefly interested me, such as the ruins of Lochleven and Kenilworth; and thus my pleasure in mountains or ruins was never, even in earliest childhood, free from a certain awe and melancholy, and general sense of the meaning of death, though, in its principal influence, entirely exhilarating and gladdening.

Secondly: it was partly dependent on contrast with a very simple and unamused mode of general life: I was born in London, and accustomed, for two or three years, to no other prospect than that of the brick walls over the way; had no brothers nor sisters, nor companions; and though I could always make myself happy in a quiet way, the beauty of the mountains had an additional charm of change and adventure which a country-bred child would not have felt.

Thirdly: there was no definite religious feeling mingled with it. I partly believed in ghosts and fairies; but supposed that angels belonged entirely to the Mosaic dispensation, and cannot remember any single thought or feeling connected with them. I believed that God was in heaven, and could hear me and see me; but this gave me neither pleasure nor pain, and I seldom thought of it at all. I never thought of nature as God's work, but as a separate fact or existence.

Fourthly: it was entirely unaccompanied by powers of reflection or invention. Every fancy that I had about nature was put into my head by some book; and I never reflected about anything till I grew older; and then, the more I reflected, the less nature was precious to me: I could then make myself happy, by thinking, in the dark, or in the dullest scenery; and the beautiful scenery became less essential to my pleasure.

Fifthly: it was, according to its strength, inconsistent with every evil feeling, with spite, anger, covetousness, discontent, and every other hateful passion; but would associate itself deeply with every just and noble sorrow, joy, or affection. It had not, however, always the power to repress what was inconsistent with it; and, though only after stout contention, might at last be crushed by what it had partly repressed. And as it only acted by setting one impulse against another, though it had much power in moulding the character, it had hardly any in strengthening it; it formed temperament, but never instilled principle; it kept me generally good-humoured and kindly, but could not teach me perseverance or self-denial: what firmness or principle I had was quite independent of it; and it came itself nearly as often in the form of a temptation as of a safeguard, leading me to ramble over hills when I should have been learning lessons, and lose days in reveries which I might have spent in doing kindnesses.

Lastly: although there was no definite religious sentiment mingled with it, there was a continual perception of Sanctity in the whole of nature, from the slightest thing to the vastest; —an instinctive awe, mixed with delight; an indefinable thrill, such as we sometimes imagine to indicate the presence of a disembodied spirit. I could only feel this perfectly when I was alone; and then it would often make me shiver from head to foot with the joy and fear of it, when

---

[40] For Ruskin's description of his early travels with his parents, see chap. 1 from *Praeterita,* above.
[41] All these characters are to be found in *The Monastery.*

after being some time away from hills, I first got to the shore of a mountain river, where the brown water circled among the pebbles, or when I saw the first swell of distant land against the sunset, or the first low broken wall, covered with mountain moss. I cannot in the least *describe* the feeling; but I do not think this is my fault, nor that of the English language, for, I am afraid, no feeling *is* describable. If we had to explain even the sense of bodily hunger to a person who had never felt it, we should be hard put to it for words; and this joy in nature seemed to me to come of a sort of heart-hunger, satisfied with the presence of a Great and Holy spirit. These feelings remained in their full intensity till I was eighteen or twenty, and then, as the reflective and practical power increased, and the "cares of this world" gained upon me, faded gradually away, in the manner described by Wordsworth in his *Intimations of Immortality*.

I cannot, of course, tell how far I am justified in supposing that these sensations may be reasoned upon as common to children in general. In the same degree they are not of course common, otherwise children would be, most of them, very different from what they are in their choice of pleasures. But, as far as such feelings exist, I apprehend they are more or less similar in their nature and influence; only producing different characters according to the elements with which they are mingled. Thus, a very religious child may give up many pleasures to which its instincts lead it, for the sake of irksome duties; and an inventive child would mingle its love of nature with watchfulness of human sayings and doings: but I believe the feelings I have endeavoured to describe are the pure landscape-instinct; and the likelihoods of good or evil resulting from them may be reasoned upon as generally indicating the usefulness or danger of the modern love and study of landscape. . . .

from The Stones of Venice, Volume II

from Chapter 6

THE NATURE OF GOTHIC[1]

. . . . I shall endeavour . . . to give the reader in this chapter an idea, at once broad and defi-

nite, of the true nature of *Gothic* architecture, properly so called. . . .

. . . We shall find that Gothic architecture has external forms and internal elements. Its elements are certain mental tendencies of the builders, legibly expressed in it; as fancifulness, love of variety, love of richness, and such others. Its external forms are pointed arches, vaulted roofs, etc. And unless both the elements and the forms are there, we have no right to call the style Gothic. It is not enough that it has the Form, if it have not also the power and life. It is not enough that it has the Power, if it have not the form. We must therefore inquire into each of these characters successively; and determine first, what is the Mental Expression, and secondly, what the Material Form of Gothic architecture, properly so called.

Mental Power or Expression. What characters, we have to discover, did the Gothic builders love, or instinctively express in their work, as distinguished from all other builders?

. . . I believe . . . that the characteristic or moral elements of Gothic are the following, placed in the order of their importance:

1. Savageness.
2. Changefulness.
3. Naturalism.
4. Grotesqueness.
5. Rigidity.
6. Redundance.

These characters are here expressed as belonging to the building; as belonging to the builder, they would be expressed thus:—1. Savageness or Rudeness. 2. Love of Change. 3. Love of Nature. 4. Disturbed Imagination. 5. Obstinacy. 6. Generosity. . . . I shall proceed to examine them in their order.

1. SAVAGENESS.—I am not sure when the word "Gothic" was first generically applied to the architecture of the North; but I presume that, whatever the date of its original usage, it was intended to imply reproach, and express the barbaric character of the nations among whom that architecture arose. It never implied that they were literally of Gothic lineage, far less that their architecture had been originally invented by the Goths themselves; but it did imply that they and their buildings together

---

[1] The rough, general definition of Gothic is that style of architecture prevalent in Western Europe from the twelfth to the fifteenth century, of which the chief characteristic is the pointed arch.

exhibited a degree of sternness and rudeness, which in contradistinction to the character of Southern and Eastern nations, appeared like a perpetual reflection of the contrast between the Goth and the Roman in their first encounter. And when that fallen Roman, in the utmost impotence of his luxury, and insolence of his guilt, became the model for the imitation of civilized Europe, at the close of the so-called Dark ages,[2] the word Gothic became a term of unmitigated contempt, not unmixed with aversion. From that contempt, by the exertion of the antiquaries and architects of this century, Gothic architecture has been sufficiently vindicated; and perhaps some among us, in our admiration of the magnificent science of its structure, and sacredness of its expression, might desire that the term of ancient reproach should be withdrawn, and some other, of more apparent honourableness, adopted in its place. There is no chance, as there is no need, of such a substitution. As far as the epithet was used scornfully, it was used falsely; but there is no reproach in the word, rightly understood; on the contrary, there is a profound truth, which the instinct of mankind almost unconsciously recognizes. It is true, greatly and deeply true, that the architecture of the North is rude and wild; but it is not true, that, for this reason, we are to condemn it, or despise. Far otherwise: I believe it is in this very character that it deserves our profoundest reverence.

The charts of the world which have been drawn up by modern science have thrown into a narrow space the expression of a vast amount of knowledge, but I have never yet seen any one pictorial enough to enable the spectator to imagine the kind of contrast in physical character which exists between Northern and Southern countries. We know the differences in detail, but we have not that broad glance and grasp which would enable us to feel them in their fulness. We know that gentians grow on the Alps, and olives on the Apennines; but we do not enough conceive for ourselves that variegated mosaic of the world's surface which a bird sees in its migration, that difference between the district of the gentian and of the olive which the stork and the swallow see far off, as they lean upon the sirocco[3] wind. Let us, for a moment, try to raise ourselves even above the level of their flight, and imagine the Mediterranean lying beneath us like an irregular lake, and all its ancient promontories sleeping in the sun: here and there an angry spot of thunder, a gray stain of storm, moving upon the burning field; and here and there a fixed wreath of white volcano smoke, surrounded by its circle of ashes; but for the most part a great peacefulness of light, Syria and Greece, Italy and Spain, laid like pieces of a golden pavement into the seablue, chased, as we stoop nearer to them, with bossy beaten work of mountain chains, and glowing softly with terraced gardens, and flowers heavy with frankincense, mixed among masses of laurel, and orange, and plumy palm, that abate with their gray-green shadows the burning of the marble rocks, and of the ledges of porphyry sloping under lucent sand. Then let us pass farther toward the north, until we see the orient colors change gradually into a vast belt of rainy green, where the pastures of Switzerland, and poplar valleys of France, and dark forests of the Danube and Carpathians stretch from the mouths of the Loire to those of the Volga, seen through clefts in gray swirls of rain-cloud and flaky veils of the mist of the brooks, spreading low along the pasture lands: and then, farther north still, to see the earth heave into mighty masses of leaden rock and heathy moor, bordering with a broad waste of gloomy purple that belt of field and wood, and splintering into irregular and grisly islands amidst the northern seas, beaten by storm, and chilled by ice-drift, and tormented by furious pulses of contending tide, until the roots of the last forests fail from among the hill ravines, and the hunger of the north wind bites their peaks into barrenness; and, at last, the wall of ice, durable like iron, sets, deathlike, its white teeth against us out of the polar twilight. And, having once traversed in thought this gradation of the zoned iris[4] of the earth in all its material vastness, let us go

---

[2] Roughly the period from 400 to 1400. The Middle or Dark Ages came to a close with the beginnings of the Italian Renaissance, at which time the example of all excellence was deemed to be in Greek and Roman antiquity.

[3] A hot wind blowing northward from Africa across the southern Mediterranean countries.

[4] Ruskin imagines the different zones on the curving surface of the earth to appear like the bands of color in a rainbow when viewed from the great height he has stipulated. Iris, in Greek myth, was the personification of the rainbow.

down nearer to it, and watch the parallel change in the belt of animal life; the multitudes of swift and brilliant creatures that glance in the air and sea, or tread the sands of the southern zone; striped zebras and spotted leopards, glistening serpents, and birds arrayed in purple and scarlet. Let us contrast their delicacy and brilliancy of color, and swiftness of motion, with the frost-cramped strength, and shaggy covering, and dusky plumage of the northern tribes; contrast the Arabian horse with the Shetland, the tiger and leopard with the wolf and bear, the antelope with the elk, the bird of paradise with the osprey; and then, submissively acknowledging the great laws by which the earth and all that it bears are ruled throughout their being, let us not condemn, but rejoice in the expression by man of his own rest in the statutes of the lands that gave him birth.[5] Let us watch him with reverence as he sets side by side the burning gems, and smooths with soft sculpture the jasper pillars, that are to reflect a ceaseless sunshine, and rise into a cloudless sky: but not with less reverence let us stand by him, when, with rough strength and hurried stroke, he smites an uncouth animation out of the rocks which he has torn from among the moss of the moorland, and heaves into the darkened air the pile of iron buttress and rugged wall, instinct with work of an imagination as wild and wayward as the northern sea; creatures of ungainly shape and rigid limb, but full of wolfish life; fierce as the winds that beat, and changeful as the clouds that shade them.

There is, I repeat, no degradation, no reproach in this, but all dignity and honourableness: and we should err grievously in refusing either to recognize as an essential character of the existing architecture of the North, or to admit as a desirable character in that which it yet may be, this wildness of thought, and roughness of work; this look of mountain brotherhood between the cathedral and the Alp; this magnificence of sturdy power, put forth only the more energetically because the fine finger-touch was chilled away by the frosty wind, and the eye dimmed by the moor-mist, or blinded by the hail; this outspeaking of the strong spirit of men who may not gather redundant fruitage from the earth, nor bask in dreamy benignity of sunshine, but must break the rock for bread, and cleave the forest for fire, and show, even in what they did for their delight, some of the hard habits of the arm and heart that grew on them as they swung the ax or pressed the plough.

If, however, the savageness of Gothic architecture, merely as an expression of its origin among Northern nations, may be considered, in some sort, a noble character, it possesses a higher nobility still, when considered as an index, not of climate, but of religious principle.

In the 13th and 14th paragraphs of Chapter XXI of the first volume of this work, it was noticed that the systems of architectural ornament, properly so called, might be divided into three:—1. Servile ornament, in which the execution or power of the inferior workman is entirely subjected to the intellect of the higher;—2. Constitutional ornament, in which the executive inferior power is, to a certain point, emancipated and independent, having a will of its own, yet confessing its inferiority and rendering obedience to higher powers;—and 3. Revolutionary ornament, in which no executive inferiority is admitted at all. I must here explain the nature of these divisions at somewhat greater length.

Of Servile ornament, the principal schools are the Greek, Ninevite, and Egyptian; but their servility is of different kinds. The Greek masterworkman was far advanced in knowledge and power above the Assyrian or Egyptian. Neither he nor those for whom he worked could endure the appearance of imperfection in anything; and therefore, what ornament he appointed to be done by those beneath him was composed of mere geometrical forms,—balls, ridges, and perfectly symmetrical foliage,—which could be executed with absolute precision by line and rule, and were as perfect in their way, when completed, as his own figure sculpture. The Assyrian and Egyptian, on the contrary, less cognizant of accurate form in anything, were content to allow their figure sculpture to be executed by inferior workmen, but lowered the method of its treatment to a standard which every workman could reach, and then trained him by discipline so rigid, that there was no chance of his falling beneath the standard appointed. The Greek gave to the lower workman no subject which he could

---

[5] Let us admire man's acceptance of the geographical conditions under which he must live and the fact that his artistic efforts or expressions are suited to these conditions.

not perfectly execute. The Assyrian gave him subjects which he could only execute imperfectly, but fixed a legal standard for his imperfection. The workman was, in both systems, a slave.

But in the mediaeval, or especially Christian, system of ornament, this slavery is done away with altogether; Christianity having recognized, in small things as well as great, the individual value of every soul. But it not only recognizes its value; it confesses its imperfection, in only bestowing dignity upon the acknowledgment of unworthiness. That admission of lost power and fallen nature, which the Greek or Ninevite felt to be intensely painful, and, as far as might be, altogether refused, the Christian makes daily and hourly, contemplating the fact of it without fear, as tending, in the end, to God's greater glory. Therefore, to every spirit which Christianity summons to her service, her exhortation is: Do what you can, and confess frankly what you are unable to do; neither let your effort be shortened for fear of failure, nor your confession silenced for fear of shame. And it is, perhaps, the principal admirableness of the Gothic schools of architecture, that they thus receive the results of the labor of inferior minds; and out of fragments full of imperfection, and betraying that imperfection in every touch, indulgently raise up a stately and unaccusable whole.

But the modern English mind has this much in common with that of the Greek, that it intensely desires, in all things, the utmost completion or perfection compatible with their nature. This is a noble character in the abstract, but becomes ignoble when it causes us to forget the relative dignities of that nature itself, and to prefer the perfectness of the lower nature to the imperfection of the higher; not considering that as, judged by such a rule, all the brute animals would be preferable to man, because more perfect in their functions and kind, and yet are always held inferior to him, so also in the works of man, those which are more perfect in their kind are always inferior to those which are, in their nature, liable to more faults and shortcomings. For the finer the nature, the more flaws it will show through the clearness of it; and it is a law of this universe, that the best things shall be seldomest seen in their best form. The wild grass grows well and strongly, one year with another;

but the wheat is, according to the greater nobleness of its nature, liable to the bitterer blight. And therefore, while in all things that we see or do, we are to desire perfection, and strive for it, we are nevertheless not to set the meaner thing, in its narrow accomplishment, above the nobler thing, in its mighty progress; not to esteem smooth minuteness above shattered majesty; not to prefer mean victory to honorable defeat; not to lower the level of our aim, that we may the more surely enjoy the complacency of success. But, above all, in our dealings with the souls of other men, we are to take care how we check, by severe requirement or narrow caution, efforts which might otherwise lead to a noble issue; and, still more, how we withhold our admiration from great excellencies, because they are mingled with rough faults. Now, in the make and nature of every man, however rude or simple, whom we employ in manual labor, there are some powers for better things; some tardy imagination, torpid capacity of emotion, tottering steps of thought, there are, even at the worst; and in most cases it is all our own fault that they *are* tardy or torpid. But they cannot be strengthened, unless we are content to take them in their feebleness, and unless we prize and honor them in their imperfection above the best and most perfect manual skill. And this is what we have to do with all our labourers; to look for the *thoughtful* part of them, and get that out of them, whatever we lose for it, whatever faults and errors we are obliged to take with it. For the best that is in them cannot manifest itself, but in company with much error. Understand this clearly: You can teach a man to draw a straight line, and to cut one; to strike a curved line, and to carve it; and to copy and carve any number of given lines or forms, with admirable speed and perfect precision; and you find his work perfect of its kind: but if you ask him to think about any of those forms, to consider if he cannot find any better in his own head, he stops; his execution becomes hesitating; he thinks, and ten to one he thinks wrong; ten to one he makes a mistake in the first touch he gives to his work as a thinking being. But you have made a man of him for all that. He was only a machine before, an animated tool.

And observe, you are put to stern choice in this matter. You must either make a tool of the creature, or a man of him. You cannot make both. Men were not intended to work with the accuracy of tools, to be precise and perfect in all their actions. If you will have that precision out of them, and make their fingers measure degrees like cogwheels, and their arms strike curves like compasses, you must unhumanize them. All the energy of their spirits must be given to make cogs and compasses of themselves. All their attention and strength must go to the accomplishment of the mean act. The eye of the soul must be bent upon the finger-point, and the soul's force must fill all the invisible nerves that guide it, ten hours a day, that it may not err from its steely precision, and so soul and sight be worn away, and the whole human being be lost at last—a heap of sawdust, so far as its intellectual work in this world is concerned: saved only by its Heart, which cannot go into the form of cogs and compasses, but expands, after the ten hours are over, into fireside humanity. On the other hand, if you will make a man of the working creature, you cannot make a tool. Let him but begin to imagine, to think, to try to do anything worth doing; and the engine-turned precision is lost at once. Out come all his roughness, all his dulness, all his incapability; shame upon shame, failure upon failure, pause after pause: but out comes the whole majesty of him also; and we know the height of it only when we see the clouds settling upon him. And, whether the clouds be bright or dark, there will be transfiguration behind and within them.

And now, reader, look round this English room of yours, about which you have been proud so often, because the work of it was so good and strong, and the ornaments of it so finished. Examine again all those accurate mouldings, and perfect polishings, and unerring adjustments of the seasoned wood and tempered steel. Many a time you have exulted over them, and thought how great England was, because her slightest work was done so thoroughly. Alas! if read rightly, these perfectnesses are signs of a slavery in our England a thousand times more bitter and more degrading than that of the scourged African, or helot Greek. Men may be beaten, chained, tormented, yoked like cattle, slaughtered like summer flies, and yet remain in one sense, and the best sense, free. But to smother their souls with them, to blight and hew into rotting pollards the suckling branches of their human intelligence, to make the flesh and skin which, after the worm's work on it, is to see God, into leathern thongs to yoke machinery with,—this it is to be slave-masters indeed; and there might be more freedom in England, though her feudal lords' lightest words were worth men's lives, and though the blood of the vexed husbandman dropped in the furrows of her fields, than there is while the animation of her multitudes is sent like fuel to feed the factory smoke, and the strength of them is given daily to be wasted into the fineness of a web, or racked into the exactness of a line.

And, on the other hand, go forth again to gaze upon the old cathedral front, where you have smiled so often at the fantastic ignorance of the old sculptors: examine once more those ugly goblins, and formless monsters, and stern statues, anatomiless and rigid; but do not mock at them, for they are signs of the life and liberty of every workman who struck the stone; a freedom of thought, and rank in scale of being, such as no laws, no charters, no charities can secure; but which it must be the first aim of all Europe at this day to regain for her children.

Let me not be thought to speak wildly or extravagantly. It is verily this degradation of the operative into a machine, which, more than any other evil of the times, is leading the mass of the nations everywhere into vain, incoherent, destructive struggling for a freedom of which they cannot explain the nature to themselves. Their universal outcry against wealth, and against nobility, is not forced from them either by the pressure of famine, or the sting of mortified pride. These do much, and have done much in all ages; but the foundations of society were never yet shaken as they are at this day. It is not that men are ill fed, but that they have no pleasure in the work by which they make their bread, and therefore look to wealth as the only means of pleasure. It is not that men are pained by the scorn of the upper classes, but they cannot endure their own; for they feel that the kind of labor to which they are condemned is verily a degrading one, and makes them less than men. Never had the upper classes so much sympathy with the lower, or charity for them, as they have at this day, and yet never were they so much hated by them: for, of old, the separation between the noble and the poor was merely a wall built by law; now it is a veritable difference in level of standing, a precipice between upper and lower grounds in the field of humanity, and there is pestilential air at the bottom of it. I know not if a day is ever to come when the nature of right freedom will be understood, and when men will see that to obey another man, to labor for him, yield reverence to him or to his place, is not slavery. It is often the best kind of liberty,— liberty from care. The man who says to one, Go, and he goeth, and to another, Come, and he cometh, has, in most cases, more sense of restraint and difficulty than the man who obeys him. The movements of the one are hindered by the burden on his shoulder; of the other, by the bridle on his lips: there is no way by which the burden may be lightened; but we need not suffer from the bridle if we do not champ at it. To yield reverence to another, to hold ourselves and our lives at his disposal, is not slavery; often it is the noblest state in which a man can live in this world. There is, indeed, a reverence which is servile, that is to say, irrational or selfish: but there is also noble reverence, that is to say, reasonable and loving; and a man is never so noble as when he is reverent in this kind; nay, even if the feeling pass the bounds of mere reason, so that it be loving, a man is raised by it. Which had, in reality, most of the serf nature in him,—the Irish peasant who was lying in wait yesterday for his landlord, with his musket muzzle thrust through the ragged hedge;[6] or that old mountain servant, who 200 years ago, at Inverkeithing, gave up his own life and the lives of his seven sons for his chief?— as each fell, calling forth his brother to the death, "Another for Hector!"[7] And therefore, in all ages and all countries, reverence has been paid and sacrifice made by men to each other, not only without complaint, but rejoicingly; and famine, and peril, and sword, and all evil, and all shame, have been borne willingly in the causes of masters and kings; for all these gifts of the heart ennobled the men who gave, not less than the men who received them, and nature prompted, and God rewarded the sacrifice. But to feel their souls withering within them, unthanked, to find their whole being sunk into an unrecognized abyss, to be counted off into a heap of mechanism, numbered with its wheels, and weighed with its hammer strokes,—this, nature bade not,—this, God blesses not,—this, humanity for no long time is able to endure.

We have much studied and much perfected, of late, the great civilized invention of the division of labor; only we give it a false name. It is not, truly speaking, the labor that is divided; but the men:— Divided into mere segments of men—broken into small fragments and crumbs of life; so that all the little piece of intelligence that is left in a man is not enough to make a pin, or a nail, but exhausts itself in making the point of a pin or the head of a nail. Now it is a good and desirable thing, truly, to make many pins in a day; but if we could only see with what crystal sand their points were polished,—sand of human soul, much to be magnified before it can be discerned for what it is—we should think there might be some loss in it also. And the great cry that rises from all our manufacturing cities, louder than their furnace blast, is all in very deed for this,—that we manufacture everything there except men; we blanch cotton, and strengthen steel, and refine sugar, and shape pottery; but to brighten, to strengthen, to refine, or to form a single living spirit, never enters into our estimate of advantages. And all the evil to which that cry is urging our myriads can be met only in one way: not by teaching nor preaching, for to teach them is but to show them their misery, and to preach to them, if we do nothing more than preach, is to mock at it. It can be met only by a right understanding, on the part of all classes, of what kinds of labour are good for men, raising them, and making them happy; by a determined sacrifice of such convenience, or beauty, or cheapness as is to be got only by the degradation of the workman; and by equally determined demand for the products and results of healthy and ennobling labor.

And how, it will be asked, are these products to be recognized, and this demand to be regulated? Easily: by the observance of three broad and simple rules:

---

[6] At the time Ruskin was writing, agrarian discontent was running high in Ireland; several landlords had been murdered by discontented tenants.
[7] The incident is recounted in the preface to Scott's *The Fair Maid of Perth,* according to Ruskin.

1. Never encourage the manufacture of any article not absolutely necessary, in the production of which *Invention* has no share.

2. Never demand an exact finish for its own sake, but only for some practical or noble end.

3. Never encourage imitation or copying of any kind, except for the sake of preserving record of great works.

The second of these principles is the only one which directly rises out of the consideration of our immediate subject; but I shall briefly explain the meaning and extent of the first also, reserving the enforcement of the third for another place.

1. Never encourage the manufacture of anything not necessary, in the production of which invention has no share.

For instance. Glass beads are utterly unnecessary, and there is no design or thought employed in their manufacture. They are formed by first drawing out the glass into rods; these rods are chopped up into fragments of the size of beads by the human hand, and the fragments are then rounded in the furnace. The men who chop up the rods sit at their work all day, their hands vibrating with a perpetual and exquisitely timed palsy, and the beads dropping beneath their vibration like hail. Neither they, nor the men who draw out the rods or fuse the fragments, have the smallest occasion for the use of any single human faculty; and every young lady, therefore, who buys glass beads is engaged in the slave-trade and in a much more cruel one than that which we have so long been endeavouring to put down.[8]

But glass cups and vessels may become the subjects of exquisite invention; and if in buying these we pay for the invention, that is to say, for the beautiful form, or color, or engraving, and not for mere finish of execution, we are doing good to humanity.

So, again, the cutting of precious stones, in all ordinary cases, requires little exertion of any mental faculty; some tact and judgment in avoiding flaws, and so on, but nothing to bring out the whole mind. Every person who wears cut jewels merely for the sake of their value is, therefore, a slave-driver.

But the working of the goldsmith, and the various designing of grouped jewellery and enamel-work, may become the subject of the most noble human intelligence. Therefore, money spent in the purchase of well-designed plate, of precious engraved vases, cameos, or enamels, does good to humanity; and, in work of this kind, jewels may be employed to heighten its splendor; and their cutting is then a price paid for the attainment of a noble end, and thus perfectly allowable.

I shall perhaps press this law farther elsewhere, but our immediate concern is chiefly with the second, namely, never to demand an exact finish, when it does not lead to a noble end. For observe, I have only dwelt upon the rudeness of Gothic, or any other kind of imperfectness, as admirable, where it was impossible to get design or thought without it. If you are to have the thought of a rough and untaught man, you must have it in a rough and untaught way; but from an educated man, who can without effort express his thoughts in an educated way, take the graceful expression, and be thankful. Only *get* the thought, and do not silence the peasant because he cannot speak good grammar, or until you have taught him his grammar. Grammar and refinement are good things, both, only be sure of the better thing first. And thus in art, delicate finish is desirable from the greatest masters, and is always given by them. In some places Michael Angelo, Leonardo, Phidias, Perugino, Turner, all finished with the most exquisite care; and the finish they give always leads to the fuller accomplishment of their noble purposes. But lower men than these cannot finish, for it requires consummate knowledge to finish consummately, and then we must take their thoughts as they are able to give them. So the rule is simple: Always look for invention first, and after that, for such execution as will help the invention, and as the inventor is capable of without painful effort, and *no more.* Above all, demand no refinement of execution where there is no thought, for that is slaves' work, unredeemed. Rather choose rough work than smooth work, so only that the practical purpose be answered, and never imagine there is reason to be proud of anything that may be accomplished by patience and sand-paper.

I shall only give one example, which however will show the reader what I mean, from

---

[8] Slavery had been abolished in British colonies in 1833; the effort at the time Ruskin was writing was to suppress it throughout the world, particularly in America.

the manufacture already alluded to, that of glass. Our modern glass is exquisitely clear in its substance, true in its form, accurate in its cutting. We are proud of this. We ought to be ashamed of it. The old Venice glass was muddy, inaccurate in all its forms, and clumsily cut, if at all. And the old Venetian was justly proud of it. For there is this difference between the English and Venetian workman, that the former thinks only of accurately matching his patterns, and getting his curves perfectly true and his edges perfectly sharp, and becomes a mere machine for rounding curves and sharpening edges; while the old Venetian cared not a whit whether his edges were sharp or not, but he invented a new design for every glass that he made, and never moulded a handle or a lip without a new fancy in it. And therefore, though some Venetian glass is ugly and clumsy enough when made by clumsy and uninventive workmen, other Venetian glass is so lovely in its forms that no price is too great for it; and we never see the same form in it twice. Now you cannot have the finish and the varied form too. If the workman is thinking about his edges, he cannot be thinking of his design; if of his design, he cannot think of his edges. Choose whether you will pay for the lovely form or the perfect finish, and choose at the same moment whether you will make the worker a man or a grindstone.

Nay, but the reader interrupts me,—"If the workman can design beautifully, I would not have him kept at the furnace. Let him be taken away and made a gentleman, and have a studio, and design his glass there, and I will have it blown and cut for him by common workmen, and so I will have my design and my finish too."

All ideas of this kind are founded upon two mistaken suppositions: the first, that one man's thoughts can be, or ought to be, executed by another man's hands; the second, that manual labour is a degradation, when it is governed by intellect.

On a large scale, and in work determinable by line and rule, it is indeed both possible and necessary that the thoughts of one man should be carried out by the labour of others; in this sense I have already defined the best architecture to be the expression of the mind of manhood by the hands of childhood. But on a smaller scale, and in a design which cannot be mathematically defined, one man's thoughts can never

be expressed by another: and the difference between the spirit of touch of the man who is inventing, and of the man who is obeying directions, is often all the difference between a great and a common work of art. How wide the separation is between original and second-hand execution, I shall endeavour to show elsewhere; it is not so much to our purpose here as to mark the other and more fatal error of despising manual labor when governed by intellect; for it is no less fatal an error to despise it when thus regulated by intellect, than to value it for its own sake. We are always in these days endeavouring to separate the two; we want one man to be always thinking, and another to be always working, and we call one a gentleman, and the other an operative; whereas the workman ought often to be thinking, and the thinker often to be working, and both should be gentleman, in the best sense. As it is, we make both ungentle, the one envying, the other despising, his brother; and the mass of society is made up of morbid thinkers, and miserable workers. Now it is only by labour that thought can be made healthy, and only by thought that labour can be made happy, and the two cannot be separated with impunity. It would be well if all of us were good handicraftsmen in some kind, and the dishonor of manual labour done away with altogether; so that though there should still be a trenchant distinction of race between nobles and commoners, there should not, among the latter, be a trenchant distinction of employment, as between idle and working men, or between men of liberal and illiberal professions. All professions should be liberal, and there should be less pride felt in peculiarity of employment, and more in excellence of achievement. And yet more, in each several profession, no master should be too proud to do its hardest work. The painter should grind his own colors; the architect work in the mason's yard with his men; the master-manufacturer be himself a more skilful operative than any man in his mills; and the distinction between one man and another be only in experience and skill, and the authority and wealth which these must naturally and justly obtain.

I should be led far from the matter in hand, if I were to pursue this interesting subject. Enough, I trust, has been said to show the reader that the rudeness or imperfection which at first rendered the term "Gothic" one of reproach is indeed, when rightly understood, one of the most noble characters of Christian architecture, and not only a noble but an *essential* one. It seems a fantastic paradox, but it is nevertheless a most important truth, that no architecture can be truly noble which is *not* imperfect. And this is easily demonstrable. For since the architect, whom we will suppose capable of doing all in perfection, cannot execute the whole with his own hands, he must either make slaves of his workmen in the old Greek, and present English fashion, and level his work to a slave's capacities, which is to degrade it; or else he must take his workmen as he finds them, and let them show their weaknesses together with their strength, which will involve the Gothic imperfection, but render the whole work as noble as the intellect of the age can make it.

But the principle may be stated more broadly still. I have confined the illustration of it to architecture, but I must not leave it as if true of architecture only. Hitherto I have used the words imperfect and perfect merely to distinguish between work grossly unskilful, and work executed with average precision and science; and I have been pleading that any degree of unskilfulness should be admitted, so only that the labourer's mind had room for expression. But, accurately speaking, no good work whatever can be perfect, and *the demand for perfection is always a sign of a misunderstanding of the ends of art.*

This for two reasons, both based on everlasting laws. The first, that no great man ever stops working till he has reached his point of failure: that is to say, his mind is always far in advance of his powers of execution, and the latter will now and then give way in trying to follow it; besides that he will aways give to the inferior portions of his work only such inferior attention as they require; and according to his greatness he becomes so accustomed to the feeling of dissatisfaction with the best he can do, that in moments of lassitude or anger with himself he will not care though the beholder be dissatisfied also. I believe there has only been one man who would not acknowledge this necessity, and strove always to reach perfection, Leonardo; the end of his vain effort being merely that he would take ten years to a picture and

leave it unfinished. And therefore, if we are to have great men working at all, or less men doing their best, the work will be imperfect, however beautiful. Of human work none but what is bad can be perfect, in its own bad way.[9]

The second reason is, that imperfection is in some sort essential to all that we know of life. It is the sign of life in a mortal body, that is to say, of a state of progress and change. Nothing that lives is, or can be, rigidly perfect; part of it is decaying, part nascent. The foxglove blossom,—a third part bud, a third part past, a third part in full bloom,—is a type of the life of this world. And in all things that live there are certain irregularities and deficiencies which are not only signs of life, but sources of beauty. No human face is exactly the same in its lines on each side, no leaf perfect in its lobes, no branch in its symmetry. All admit irregularity as they imply change; and to banish imperfection is to destroy expression, to check exertion, to paralyze vitality. All things are literally better, lovelier, and more beloved for the imperfections which have been divinely appointed, that the law of human life may be Effort, and the law of human judgment, Mercy.

Accept this then for a universal law, that neither architecture nor any other noble work of man can be good unless it be imperfect; and let us be prepared for the otherwise strange fact, which we shall discern clearly as we approach the period of the Renaissance, that the first cause of the fall of the arts of Europe was a relentless requirement of perfection, incapable alike either of being silenced by veneration for greatness, or softened into forgiveness of simplicity.

Thus far then of the Rudeness or Savageness, which is the first mental element of Gothic architecture. It is an element in many other healthy architectures also, as in Byzantine and Romanesque;[10] but true Gothic cannot exist without it. . . .

---

[9] "The Elgin marbles are supposed by many persons to be 'perfect.' In the most important portions they indeed approach perfection, but only there. The draperies are unfinished, the hair and wool of the animals are unfinished, and the entire bas-reliefs of the frieze are roughly cut." (Ruskin)

[10] The former flourished in the Byzantine Empire in the fifth and sixth centuries; the latter in the countries of southern Europe that had come under Roman domination, roughly from the fifth to the twelfth century.

from The Crown of Wild Olive[1]

Lecture II

TRAFFIC[2]

My good Yorkshire friends, you asked me down here among your hills that I might talk to you about this Exchange you are going to build; but, earnestly and seriously asking you to pardon me, I am going to do nothing of the kind. I cannot talk, or at least can say very little, about this same Exchange. I must talk of quite other things, though not willingly;—I could not deserve your pardon, if, when you invited me to speak on one subject, I *wilfully* spoke on another. But I cannot speak, to purpose, of anything about which I do not care; and most simply and sorrowfully I have to tell you, in the outset, that I do *not* care about this Exchange of yours.

If, however, when you sent me your invitation, I had answered, "I won't come, I don't care about the Exchange of Bradford," you would have been justly offended with me, not knowing the reason of so blunt a carelessness. So I have come down, hoping that you will patiently let me tell you why, on this, and many other such occasions, I now remain silent, when formerly I should have caught at the opportunity of speaking to a gracious audience.

In a word, then, I do not care about this Exchange—because *you* don't; and because you know perfectly well I cannot make you. Look at the essential conditions of the case, which you, as businessmen, know perfectly well, though perhaps you think I forget them. You are going to spend £30,000, which to you, collectively, is nothing; the buying a new coat is, as to the cost of it, a much more important matter of consideration to me, than building a new Exchange is to you. But you think you may as well have the right thing for your money. You know there are a great many odd styles of architecture about; you don't want to do anything ridiculous; you hear of me, among others, as a respectable architectural man-milliner; and you send for me, that

I may tell you the leading fashion; and what is, in our shops, for the moment, the newest and sweetest thing in pinnacles.

Now, pardon me for telling you frankly, you cannot have good architecture merely by asking people's advice on occasion. All good architecture is the expression of national life and character, and it is produced by a prevalent and eager national taste, or desire for beauty. And I want you to think a little of the deep significance of this word "taste"; for no statement of mine has been more earnestly or oftener controverted than that good taste is essentially a moral quality. "No," say many of my antagonists, "taste is one thing, morality is another. Tell us what is pretty: we shall be glad to know that; but we need no sermons—even were you able to preach them, which may be doubted."

Permit me, therefore, to fortify this old dogma of mine somewhat. Taste is not only a part and an index of morality;—it is the ONLY morality. The first, and last, and closest trial question to any living creature is, "What do you like?" Tell me what you like, and I'll tell you what you are. Go out into the street, and ask the first man or woman you meet, what their "taste" is; and if they answer candidly, you know them, body and soul. "You, my friend in the rags, with the unsteady gait, what do *you* like?" "A pipe and a quartern of gin." I know you. "You, good woman, with the quick step and tidy bonnet, what do you like?" "A swept hearth, and a clean tea-table; and my husband opposite me, and a baby at my breast." Good, I know you also. "You, little girl with the golden hair and the soft eyes, what do you like?" "My canary, and a run among the wood hyacinths." "You, little boy with the dirty hands, and the low forehead, what do you like?" "A shy at the sparrows, and a game at pitch farthing." Good; we know them all now. What more need we ask?

"Nay," perhaps you answer; "we need rather to ask what these people and children do, than what they like. If they *do* right, it is no matter that they like what is wrong; and if they *do* wrong, it is no matter that they like what is right. Doing is the great thing; and it does not matter that the man likes drinking, so that he does not drink; nor that the little girl likes to be kind to her canary, if she will not learn her lessons; nor that the little boy likes throwing stones at the

---

1 The victor at the ancient Olympic Games was rewarded simply with a wreath made of the leaves of the wild olive. Ruskin's title is intended to suggest that honor alone, rather than riches, should be our goal.

2 Delivered at the Town Hall, Bradford, April 21, 1864. *Traffic* means trade

sparrows, if he goes to the Sunday school." Indeed, for a short time, and in a provisional sense, this is true. For if, resolutely, people do what is right, in time to come they like doing it. But they only are in a right moral state when they *have* come to like doing it; and as long as they don't like it, they are still in a vicious state. The man is not in health of body who is always thinking of the bottle in the cupboard, though he bravely bears his thirst; but the man who heartily enjoys water in the morning, and wine in the evening, each in its proper quantity and time. And the entire object of true education is to make people not merely *do* the right things, but *enjoy* the right things:—not merely industrious, but to love industry—not merely learned, but to love knowledge—not merely pure, but to love purity—not merely just, but to hunger and thirst after justice.

But you may answer or think, "Is the liking for outside ornaments,—for pictures, or statutes, or furniture, or architecture, a moral quality?" Yes, most surely, if a rightly set liking. Taste for *any* pictures or statues is not a moral quality, but taste for good ones is. Only here again we have to define the word "good." I don't mean by "good," clever—or learned—or difficult in the doing. Take a picture by Teniers, of sots quarrelling over their dice;[3] it is an entirely clever picture; so clever that nothing in its kind has ever been done equal to it; but it is also an entirely base and evil picture. It is an expression of delight in the prolonged contemplation of a vile thing, and delight in that is an "unmannered," or "immoral" quality. It is "bad taste" in the profoundest sense—it is the taste of the devils. On the other hand, a picture of Titian's, or a Greek statue, or a Greek coin, or a Turner landscape, expresses delight in the perpetual contemplation of a good and perfect thing. That is an entirely moral quality—it is the taste of the angels. And all delight in fine art, and all love of it, resolve themselves into simple love of that which deserves love. That deserving is the quality which we call "loveliness"—(we ought to have an opposite word, hateliness, to be said of the things which deserve to be hated); and it is not an indifferent nor optional thing whether we

love this or that; but it is just the vital function of all our being. What we *like* determines what we *are,* and is the sign of what we are; and to teach taste is inevitably to form character.

As I was thinking over this, in walking up Fleet Street the other day, my eye caught the title of a book standing open in a bookseller's window. It was—"On the necessity of the diffusion of taste among all classes." "Ah," I thought to myself, "my classifying friend, when you have diffused your taste, where will your classes be? The man who likes what you like, belongs to the same class with you, I think. Inevitably so. You may put him to other work if you choose; but, by the condition you have brought him into, he will dislike the work as much as you would yourself. You get hold of a scavenger or a costermonger, who enjoyed the Newgate Calendar[4] for literature, and 'Pop goes the Weasel' for music. You think you can make him like Dante and Beethoven? I wish you joy of your lessons; but if you do, you have made a gentleman of him:—he won't like to go back to his costermongering."

And so completely and unexceptionally is this so, that, if I had time tonight, I could show you that a nation cannot be affected by any vice, or weakness, without expressing it, legibly, and for ever, either in bad art, or by want of art; and that there is no national virtue, small or great, which is not manifestly expressed in all the art which circumstances enable the people possessing that virtue to produce. Take, for instance, your great English virtue of enduring and patient courage. You have at present in England only one art of any consequence—that is, iron-working. You know thoroughly well how to cast and hammer iron. Now, do you think, in those masses of lava which you build volcanic cones to melt, and which you forge at the mouths of the Infernos you have created; do you think on those iron plates, your courage and endurance are not written for ever,—not merely with an iron pen, but on iron parchment? And take also your great English vice—European vice—vice of all the world—vice of all other worlds that roll or shine in heaven, bearing with them yet the atmosphere of hell—the vice of jealousy, which brings competition into your commerce, treachery into your

---

[3] Probably the picture "Flemish Tap-Room" by the younger Teniers (1610–1690).

[4] An account of the crimes committed by the inmates of Newgate Prison which used to be published at regular intervals.

councils, and dishonour into your wars—that vice which has rendered for you, and for your next neighbouring nation, the daily occupations of existence no longer possible, but with the mail upon your breasts and the sword loose in its sheath;[5] so that at last, you have realised for all the multitudes of the two great peoples who lead the so-called civilisation of the earth,—you have realised for them all, I say, in person and in policy, what was once true only of the rough Border riders of your Cheviot hills—

> *They carved at the meal*
> *With gloves of steel,*
> *And they drank the red wine through the*
> *helmet barr'd;*[6]—

do you think that this national shame and dastardliness of heart are not written as legibly on every rivet of your iron armour as the strength of the right hands that forged it?

Friends, I know not whether this thing be the more ludicrous or the more melancholy. It is quite unspeakably both. Suppose, instead of being now sent for by you, I had been sent for by some private gentleman, living in a suburban house, with his garden separated only by a fruit wall from his next door neighbour's; and he had called me to consult with him on the furnishing of his drawing-room. I begin looking about me, and find the walls rather bare; I think such and such a paper might be desirable—perhaps a little fresco here and there on the ceiling—a damask curtain or so at the windows. "Ah," says my employer, "damask curtains, indeed! That's all very fine, but you know I can't afford that kind of thing just now!" "Yet the world credits you with a splendid income!" "Ah, yes," says my friend, "but do you know, at present I am obliged to spend it nearly all in steel-traps?" "Steel-traps! for whom?" "Why, for that fellow on the other side the wall, you know; we're very good friends, capital friends; but we are obliged to keep our traps set on both sides of the wall; we could not possibly keep on friendly terms without them,

and our spring guns. The worst of it is, we are both clever fellows enough; and there's never a day passes that we don't find out a new trap, or a new gun-barrel, or something; we spend about fifteen millions a year each in our traps, take it altogether; and I don't see how we're to do with less." A highly comic state of life for two private gentlemen! but for two nations, it seems to me, not wholly comic. Bedlam would be comic, perhaps, if there were only one madman in it; and your Christmas pantomime is comic, when there is only one clown in it; but when the whole world turns clown, and paints itself red with its own heart's blood instead of vermilion, it is something else than comic, I think.

Mind, I know a great deal of this is play, and willingly allow for that. You don't know what to do with yourselves for a sensation: fox-hunting and cricketing will not carry you through the whole of this unendurably long mortal life: you liked popguns when you were schoolboys, and rifles and Armstrongs are only the same things better made: but then the worst of it is, that what was play to you when boys, was not play to the sparrows; and what is play to you now, is not play to the small birds of State neither; and for the black eagles, you are somewhat shy of taking shots at them, if I mistake not.[7]

I must get back to the matter in hand, however. Believe me, without farther instance, I could show you, in all time, that every nation's vice, or virtue, was written in its art: the soldiership of early Greece; the sensuality of late Italy; the visionary religion of Tuscany; the splendid human energy of Venice. I have no time to do this tonight (I have done it elsewhere before now); but I proceed to apply the principle to ourselves in a more searching manner.

I notice that among all the new buildings which cover your once wild hills, churches and schools are mixed in due, that is to say, in large proportion, with your mills and mansions; and I notice also that the churches and schools are almost always Gothic, and the mansions and

---

5 Ruskin is here inveighing against the foreign policy of England, particularly during the second term of Palmerston as prime minister, and deploring the mutually suspicious attitudes of France and England. The English were frightened at the renewed threat of invasion by France under Louis Napoleon.

6 Scott's *Lay of the Last Minstrel*, Canto I, stanza 4.

7 The small birds of state were Poland and Denmark. The former made a bid for freedom from Russia, which Palmerston's cabinet would not support; and the latter was attacked by Prussia and Austria, again without intervention from England. The black eagle was the Austrian insignia, and the Order of the Black Eagle was a Prussian military decoration.

mills are never Gothic. May I ask the meaning of this? for, remember, it is peculiarly a modern phenomenon. When Gothic was invented, houses were Gothic as well as churches; and when the Italian style superseded the Gothic, churches were Italian as well as houses. If there is a Gothic spire to the Cathedral of Antwerp, there is a Gothic belfry to the Hôtel de Ville at Brussels; if Inigo Jones builds an Italian Whitehall, Sir Christopher Wren[8] builds an Italian St. Paul's. But now you live under one school of architecture, and worship under another. What do you mean by doing this? Am I to understand that you are thinking of changing your architecture back to Gothic; and that you treat your churches experimentally, because it does not matter what mistakes you make in a church? Or am I to understand that you consider Gothic a preeminently sacred and beautiful mode of building, which you think, like the fine frankincense, should be mixed for the tabernacle only, and reserved for your religious services? For if this be the feeling, though it may seem at first as if it were graceful and reverent, at the root of the matter, it signifies neither more nor less than that you have separated your religion from your life.

For consider what a wide significance this fact has: and remember that it is not you only, but all the people of England, who are behaving thus, just now.

You have all got into the habit of calling the church "the house of God." I have seen, over the doors of many churches, the legend actually carved, "*This* is the house of God and this is the gate of heaven." Now, note where that legend comes from, and of what place it was first spoken.[9] A boy leaves his father's house to go on a long journey on foot, to visit his uncle: he has to cross a wild hill-desert; just as if one of your own boys had to cross the wolds to visit an uncle at Carlisle. The second or third day your boy finds himself somewhere between Hawes and Brough, in the midst of the moors, at sunset. It is stony ground, and boggy; he cannot go one foot farther that night. Down he lies, to sleep, on Wharnside, where best he may, gathering a few of the stones together to put under his head;—so wild the place is, he cannot get anything but stones. And there, lying under the broad night, he has a dream; and he sees a ladder set up on the earth, and the top of it reaches to heaven, and the angels of God are seen ascending and descending upon it. And when he wakes out of his sleep, he says, "How dreadful is this place; surely this is none other than the house of God, and this is the gate of heaven." This PLACE, observe; not this church; not this city; not this stone, even, which he puts up for a memorial—the piece of flint on which his head was lain. But this *place*; this windy slope of Wharnside; this moorland hollow, torrent-bitten, snow-blighted; this *any* place where God lets down the ladder. And how are you to know where that will be? or how are you to determine where it may be, but by being ready for it always? Do you know where the lightning is to fall next? You *do* know that, partly; you can guide the lightning; but you cannot guide the going forth of the Spirit, which is as that lightning when it shines from the east to the west.

But the perpetual and insolent warping of that strong verse to serve a merely ecclesiastical purpose,[10] is only one of the thousand instances in which we sink back into gross Judaism. We call our churches "temples." Now, you know perfectly well they are *not* temples. They have never had, never can have, anything whatever to do with temples. They are "synagogues"—"gathering places"—where you gather yourselves together as an assembly; and by not calling them so, you again miss the force of another mighty text—"Thou, when thou prayest, shalt not be as the hypocrites are; for they love to pray standing in the *churches*" [we should translate it], "that they may be seen of men. But thou, when thou prayest, enter into thy closet, and when thou hast shut thy door, pray to thy Father,"—which is, not in chancel nor in aisle, but "in secret."[11]

Now, you feel, as I say this to you—I know you feel—as if I were trying to take away the

---

[8] Two seventeenth-century English architects, exponents of the classic style. The former designed the banqueting hall for the new palace of Whitehall.

[9] See Genesis 28 for the story of Jacob's journey and his dream of the ladder let down from heaven.

[10] As a Protestant and an Evangelical, Ruskin attacks in these two paragraphs the stress laid by Roman and Anglo Catholics upon church and temple as the house of God and gate to heaven. To him worship and salvation were respectively the function and the reward of the heart alone, independent of any ecclesiastical building or priesthood. It was precisely this emphasis upon the external forms of worship that led Thomas Arnold, as well as Ruskin, to say that the spirit behind the Oxford Movement was Judaism.   [11] Cf. Matthew 6:5-6.

honour of your churches. Not so; I am trying to prove to you the honour of your houses and your hills; not that the Church is not sacred—but that the whole Earth is. I would have you feel what careless, what constant, what infectious sin there is in all modes of thought, whereby, in calling your churches only "holy," you call your hearths and homes "profane"; and have separated yourselves from the heathen by casting all your household gods to the ground, instead of recognising, in the places of their many and feeble Lares,[12] the presence of your One and Mighty Lord and Lar.

"But what has all this to do with our Exchange?" you ask me, impatiently. My dear friends, it has just everything to do with it; on these inner and great questions depend all the outer and little ones; and if you have asked me down here to speak to you, because you had before been interested in anything I have written, you must know that all I have yet said about architecture was to show this. The book I called *The Seven Lamps* was to show that certain right states of temper and moral feeling were the magic powers by which all good architecture, without exception, had been produced. *The Stones of Venice* had, from beginning to end, no other aim than to show that the Gothic architecture of Venice had risen out of, and indicated in all its features, a state of pure national faith, and of domestic virtue; and that its Renaissance architecture had arisen out of, and in all its features indicated, a state of concealed national infidelity, and of domestic corruption. And now, you ask me what style is best to build in, and how can I answer, knowing the meaning of the two styles, but by another question—do you mean to build as Christians or as Infidels? And still more—do you mean to build as honest Christians or as honest Infidels? as thoroughly and confessedly either one or the other? You don't like to be asked such rude questions. I cannot help it; they are of much more importance than this Exchange business; and if they can be at once answered, the Exchange business settles itself in a moment. But before I press them farther, I must ask leave to explain one point clearly.

In all my past work, my endeavour has been to show that good architecture is essentially religious—the production of a faithful and virtuous, not of an infidel and corrupted people. But in the course of doing this, I have had also to show that good architecture is not *ecclesiastical*. People are so apt to look upon religion as the business of the clergy, not their own, that the moment they hear of anything depending on "religion," they think it must also have depended on the priesthood; and I have had to take what place was to be occupied between these two errors, and fight both, often with seeming contradiction. Good architecture is the work of good and believing men; therefore, you say, at least some people say, "Good architecture must essentially have been the work of the clergy, not of the laity." No—a thousand times no; good architecture[13] has always been the work of the commonalty, *not* of the clergy. "What," you say, "those glorious cathedrals—the pride of Europe—did their builders not form Gothic architecture?" No; they corrupted Gothic architecture. Gothic was formed in the baron's castle, and the burgher's street. It was formed by the thoughts, and hands, and powers of labouring citizens and warrior kings. By the monk it was used as an instrument for the aid of his superstition; when that superstition became a beautiful madness, and the best hearts of Europe vainly dreamed and pined in the cloister, and vainly raged and perished in the crusade,—through that fury of perverted faith and wasted war, the Gothic rose also to its loveliest, most fantastic, and, finally, most foolish dreams; and in those dreams was lost.

I hope, now, that there is no risk of your misunderstanding me when I come to the gist of what I want to say tonight;—when I repeat, that every great national architecture has been the result and exponent of a great national religion. You can't have bits of it here, bits there—you must have it everywhere or nowhere. It is not the monopoly of a clerical company—it is not the exponent of a theological dogma—it is not the hieroglyphic writing of an initiated priesthood; it is the manly language of a people inspired by resolute and common purpose, and rendering resolute and common fidelity to the legible laws of an undoubted God.

---

12 The Roman divinities of the household.

13 "And all other arts, for the most part; even of incredulous and secularly-minded commonalties." (Ruskin, 1873)

Now there have as yet been three distinct schools of European architecture. I say, European, because Asiatic and African architectures belong so entirely to other races and climates, that there is no question of them here; only, in passing, I will simply assure you that whatever is good or great in Egypt, and Syria, and India, is just as good or great for the same reasons as the buildings on our side of the Bosphorus. We Europeans, then, have had three great religions: the Greek, which was the worship of the God of Wisdom and Power; the Mediaeval, which was the worship of the God of Judgment and Consolation; the Renaissance, which was the worship of the God of Pride and Beauty; these three we have had—they are past,—and now, at last, we English have got a fourth religion, and a God of our own, about which I want to ask you. But I must explain these three old ones first.

I repeat, first, the Greeks essentially worshipped the God of Wisdom; so that whatever contended against their religion,—to the Jews a stumbling-block,—was, to the Greeks—*Foolishness*.[14]

The first Greek idea of deity was that expressed in the word, of which we keep the remnant in our words "*Di*-urnal" and "*Di*-vine"— the god of *Day*, Jupiter the revealer. Athena is his daughter, but especially daughter of the Intellect, springing armed from the head. We are only with the help of recent investigation beginning to penetrate the depth of meaning couched under the Athenaic symbols: but I may note rapidly, that her aegis, the mantle with the serpent fringes, in which she often, in the best statues, is represented as folding up her left hand, for better guard; and the Gorgon,[15] on her shield, are both representative mainly of the chilling horror and sadness (turning men to stone, as it were) of the outmost and superficial spheres of knowledge—that knowledge which separates, in bitterness, hardness, and sorrow, the heart of the full-grown man from the heart of the child. For out of imperfect knowledge spring terror, dis-

sension, danger, and disdain; but from perfect knowledge, given by the full-revealed Athena, strength and peace, in sign of which she is crowned with the olive spray, and bears the resistless spear.

This, then, was the Greek conception of purest Deity; and every habit of life, and every form of his art developed themselves from the seeking this bright, serene, resistless wisdom; and setting himself, as a man, to do things evermore rightly and strongly;[16] not with any ardent affection or ultimate hope; but with a resolute and continent energy of will, as knowing that for failure there was no consolation, and for sin there was no remission. And the Greek architecture rose unerring, bright, clearly defined, and self-contained.

Next followed in Europe the great Christian faith, which was essentially the religion of Comfort. Its great doctrine is the remission of sins; for which cause, it happens, too often, in certain phases of Christianity, that sin and sickness themselves are partly glorified, as if, the more you had to be healed of, the more divine was the healing. The practical result of this doctrine, in art, is a continual contemplation of sin and disease, and of imaginary states of purification from them; thus we have an architecture conceived in a mingled sentiment of melancholy and aspiration, partly severe, partly luxuriant, which will bend itself to every one of our needs, and every one of our fancies, and be strong or weak with us, as we are strong or weak ourselves. It is, of all architecture, the basest, when base people build it—of all, the noblest, when built by the noble.

And now note that both these religions— Greek and Mediaeval—perished by falsehood in their own main purpose. The Greek religion of Wisdom perished in a false philosophy—"Op-

---

14 The reference is to I Corinthians 1:23: "But we preach Christ crucified, unto the Jews a stumblingblock, and unto the Greeks foolishness."
15 In Greek mythology Athena lent her shield to Perseus for the slaying of the Gorgon Medusa, one glance at whose face would have turned him into stone. In gratitude he placed the Gorgon's head, with its fatal power still inherent, upon the shield before returning it to the goddess.
16 "It is an error to suppose that the Greek worship, or seeking, was chiefly of Beauty. It was essentially of rightness and strength, founded on Forethought; the principal character of Greek art is not beauty, but design: and the Dorian Apollo-worship and Athenian Virgin-worship are both expressions of adoration of divine wisdom and purity. Next to these great deities, rank, in power over the national mind, Dionysus and Ceres, the givers of human strength and life; then, for heroic example, Hercules. There is no Venus-worship among the Greeks in the great times: and the Muses are essentially teachers of Truth, and of its harmonies." (Ruskin)

positions of science, falsely so called."[17] The Mediaeval religion of Consolation perished in false comfort; in remission of sins given lyingly. It was the selling of absolution that ended the Mediaeval faith;[18] and I can tell you more, it is the selling of absolution which, to the end of time, will mark false Christianity. Pure Christianity gives her remission of sins only by *ending* them; but false Christianity gets her remission of sins by *compounding for* them. And there are many ways of compounding for them. We English have beautiful little quiet ways of buying absolution, whether in low Church or high, far more cunning than any of Tetzel's trading.[19]

Then, thirdly, there followed the religion of Pleasure, in which all Europe gave itself to luxury, ending in death. First, *bals masqués* in every saloon,[20] and then guillotines in every square. And all these three worships issue in vast temple building. Your Greek worshipped Wisdom, and built you the Parthenon[21]—the Virgin's temple. The Mediaeval worshipped Consolation, and built you Virgin temples also—but to our Lady of Salvation. Then the Revivalist[22] worshipped beauty, of a sort, and built you Versailles and the Vatican.[23] Now, lastly, will you tell me what *we* worship, and what *we* build?

You know we are speaking always of the real, active, continual, national worship; that by which men act, while they live; not that which they talk of, when they die. Now, we have, indeed, a nominal religion, to which we pay tithes of property and sevenths of time;[24] but we have also a practical and earnest religion, to which we devote nine-tenths of our property and six-sevenths of our time. And we dispute a great deal about the nominal religion: but we are all unanimous about this practical one; of which I think you will admit that the ruling goddess may be best generally described as the "Goddess of Getting-on," or "Britannia of the Market." The Athenians had an "Athena Agoraia," or Athena of the Market; but she was a subordinate type of their goddess, while our Britannia Agoraia is the principal type of ours. And all your architectural works are, of course, built to her. It is long since you built a great cathedral; and how you would laugh at me if I proposed building a cathedral on the top of one of these hills of yours, to make it an Acropolis! But your railroad mounds, vaster than the walls of Babylon; your railroad stations, vaster than the temple of Ephesus, and innumerable; your chimneys, how much more mighty and costly than cathedral spires! your harbour-piers; your warehouses; your exchanges!—all these are built to your great Goddess of "Getting-on"; and she has formed, and will continue to form, your architecture, as long as you worship her; and it is quite vain to ask me to tell you how to build to *her;* you know far better than I.

There might, indeed, on some theories, be a conceivably good architecture for Exchanges—that is to say, if there were any heroism in the fact or deed of exchange which might be typically carved on the outside of your building. For, you know, all beautiful architecture must be adorned with sculpture or painting; and for sculpture or painting, you must have a subject. And hitherto it has been a received opinion among the nations of the world that the only right subjects for either, were *heroisms* of some sort. Even on his pots and his flagons, the Greek put a Hercules slaying lions, or an Apollo slaying serpents, or Bacchus slaying melancholy giants, and earthborn despondencies. On his temples, the Greek put contests of great warriors in founding states, or of gods with evil spirits. On his houses and temples alike, the Christian put carvings of angels conquering devils; or of hero-martyrs exchanging this world for another; subject inap-

---

17 This is probably a reference to the destructive effect of the questionings of the Sophists, who undermined faith in the early Olympian deities and the moral and intellectual ideals associated with them. It was a later manifestation of the same skeptical tendency that Paul warned Timothy against: "O Timothy, keep that which is committed to thy trust, avoiding profane and vain babblings, and oppositions of science falsely so called" (I Timothy 6:20).

18 It was one of the abuses attacked by Luther in his demands for a reformation within the Catholic church, demands which produced in the end the establishment of the various Reformed or Protestant churches of central and northwestern Europe.

19 Tetzel was the papal agent by whose sale of indulgences or absolution Luther's remonstrances were specifically evoked.

20 Masked balls in every drawing room.

21 Temple of Athena built on an eminence overlooking Athens, the Acropolis.

22 Those who wished to revive classical antiquity.

23 The palaces of the French kings and of the Pope, respectively.

24 One-tenth of our income and one day of our week.

propriate, I think, to our direction of exchange here. And the Master of Christians not only left His followers without any orders as to the sculpture of affairs of exchange on the outside of buildings, but gave some strong evidence of His dislike of affairs of exchange within them.[25] And yet there might surely be a heroism in such affairs; and all commerce become a kind of selling of doves, not impious. The wonder has always been great to me, that heroism has never been supposed to be in any wise consistent with the practice of supplying people with food, or clothes; but rather with that of quartering one's self upon them for food, and stripping them of their clothes. Spoiling of armour is an heroic deed in all ages; but the selling of clothes, old or new, has never taken any colour of magnanimity. Yet one does not see why feeding the hungry and clothing the naked should ever become base businesses, even when engaged in on a large scale. If one could contrive to attach the notion of conquest to them anyhow! so that, supposing there were anywhere an obstinate race, who refused to be comforted, one might take some pride in giving them compulsory comfort![26] and, as it were, "*occupying* a country" with one's gifts, instead of one's armies? If one could only consider it as much a victory to get a barren field sown, as to get an eared field stripped; and contend who should build villages, instead of who should "carry" them! Are not all forms of heroism conceivable in doing these serviceable deeds? You doubt who is strongest? It might be ascertained by push of spade, as well as push of sword. Who is wisest? There are witty things to be thought of in planning other business than campaigns. Who is bravest? There are always the elements to fight with, stronger than men; and nearly as merciless.

The only absolutely and unapproachably heroic element in the soldier's work seems to be —that he is paid little for it—and regularly: while you traffickers, and exchangers, and others occupied in presumably benevolent business, like to be paid much for it—and by chance. I never can make out how it is that a *knight*-errant does not expect to be paid for his trouble, but a *pedlar*-errant always does;—that people are willing to take hard knocks for nothing, but never to sell ribands cheap; that they are ready to go on fervent crusades, to recover the tomb of a buried God, but never on any travels to fulfil the orders of a living one;—that they will go anywhere barefoot to preach their faith, but must be well bribed to practise it, and are perfectly ready to give the Gospel gratis, but never the loaves and fishes.[27]

If you chose to take the matter up on any such soldierly principle; to do your commerce, and your feeding of nations, for fixed salaries; and to be as particular about giving people the best food, and the best cloth, as soldiers are about giving them the best gunpower, I could carve something for you on your exchange worth looking at. But I can only at present suggest decorating its frieze with pendant purses; and making its pillars broad at the base, for the sticking of bills. And in the innermost chambers of it there might be a statue of Britannia of the Market, who may have, perhaps advisably, a partridge for her crest, typical at once of her courage in fighting for noble ideas, and of her interest in game; and round its neck, the inscription in golden letters, "Perdix fovit quae non peperit."[28] Then, for her spear, she might have a weaver's beam; and on her shield, instead of St. George's Cross, the Milanese boar, semi-fleeced, with the town of Gennesaret proper, in the field;[29] and the legend, "In the best market,"[30] and her corslet, of leather, folded over her

---

[25] When he drove the money-changers from the temple.
[26] "Quite serious, all this, though it reads like jest." (Ruskin, 1873)

[27] "Please think over this paragraph, too briefly and antithetically put, but one of those which I am happiest in having written." (Ruskin, 1873) The loaves and fishes, of course, are an allusion to Christ's feeding of the multitude.
[28] "*Jeremiah*, XVII, 11 (best in Septuagint and Vulgate). 'As the partridge, fostering what she brought not forth, so he that getteth riches, not by right, shall leave them in the midst of his days, and at his end shall be a fool.'" (Ruskin)
[29] The substitution of the Milanese boar for the Cross of St. George which was usually portrayed on Britannia's shield is intended to symbolize England's turning away from the ideals of chivalry exemplified by St. George, her patron saint, to greed and reliance on guns and armor plate (which Ruskin has stigmatized above), since the Milanese had been particularly noted as armorers. By association Ruskin apparently moved from the boar (wild swine) to the Biblical story of the Gadarene swine who became possessed of demons. On two other occasions when he referred to this miracle (in *Fors Clavigera*, letter 61), Ruskin also located the scene at Gennesaret instead of Gadara.
[30] Allusion to the slogan of laissez-faire capitalism, "Buy

heart in the shape of a purse, with thirty slits in it, for a piece of money to go in at, on each day of the month. And I doubt not but that people would come to see your exchange, and its goddess, with applause.

Nevertheless, I want to point out to you certain strange characters in this goddess of yours. She differs from the great Greek and Mediaeval deities essentially in two things—first, as to the continuance of her presumed power; secondly, as to the extent of it.

First, as to the Continuance.

The Greek Goddess of Wisdom gave continual increase of wisdom, as the Christian Spirit of Comfort (or Comforter) continual increase of comfort. There was no question, with these, of any limit or cessation of function. But with your Agora Goddess, that is just the most important question. Getting on—but where to? Gathering together—but how much? Do you mean to gather always—never to spend? If so, I wish you joy of your goddess, for I am just as well off as you, without the trouble of worshipping her at all. But if you do not spend, somebody else will— somebody else must. And it is because of this (among many other such errors) that I have fearlessly declared your so-called science of Political Economy to be no science; because, namely, it has omitted the study of exactly the most important branch of the business—the study of *spending*. For spend you must, and as much as you make, ultimately. You gather corn:—will you bury England under a heap of grain; or will you, when you have gathered, finally eat? You gather gold:—will you make your house-roofs of it, or pave your streets with it? That is still one way of spending it. But if you keep it, that you may get more, I'll give you more; I'll give you all the gold you want—all you can imagine—if you can tell me what you'll do with it. You shall have thousands of gold pieces;—thousands of thousands—millions—mountains, of gold: where will you keep them? Will you put an Olympus of silver upon a golden Pelion—make Ossa like a wart?[31] Do you think the rain and dew would

then come down to you, in the streams from such mountains, more blessedly than they will down the mountains which God has made for you, of moss and whinstone? But it is not gold that you want to gather! What is it? greenbacks? No; not those neither. What is it then—is it ciphers after a captial I? Cannot you practise writing ciphers, and write as many as you want! Write ciphers for an hour every morning, in a big book, and say every evening, I am worth all those naughts more than I was yesterday. Won't that do? Well, what in the name of Plutus[32] is it you want? Not gold, not greenbacks, not ciphers after a capital I? You will have to answer, after all, "No; we want, somehow or other, money's *worth*." Well, what is that? Let your Goddess of Getting-on discover it, and let her learn to stay therein.

Second. But there is yet another question to be asked respecting this Goddess of Getting-on. The first was of the continuance of her power; the second is of its extent.

Pallas[33] and the Madonna were supposed to be all the world's Pallas, and all the world's Madonna. They could teach all men, and they could comfort all men. But, look strictly into the nature of the power of your Goddess of Getting-on; and you will find she is the Goddess —not of everybody's getting on—but only of somebody's getting on. This is a vital, or rather deathful, distinction. Examine it in your own ideal of the state of national life which this Goddess is to evoke and maintain. I asked you what it was, when I was last here;[34]—you have never told me. Now, shall I try to tell you?

Your ideal of human life then is, I think, that it should be passed in a pleasant undulating world, with iron and coal everywhere underneath it. On each pleasant bank of this world is to be a beautiful mansion, with two wings; and stables, and coach-houses; a moderately-sized park; a large garden and hothouses; and pleasant carriage drives through the shrubberies. In this mansion are to live the favoured votaries of the Goddess; the English gentleman, with his gracious wife, and his beautiful family; always able to have the boudoir and the jewels for the

---

in the cheapest and sell in the dearest market." Ruskin in 1873 made the following annotation: "Meaning, fully, 'We have brought our pigs to it.'"
31 In Greek mythology, the giants in attempting to reach Mount Olympus (or heaven) piled the mountains Pelion and Ossa one upon the other.

32 God of riches.
33 Pallas Athena, goddess of wisdom.
34 Ruskin had delivered a previous lecture at Bradford in 1859 at the inauguration of the Bradford School of Design.

wife, and the beautiful ball dresses for the daughters, and hunters for the sons, and a shooting in the Highlands for himself. At the bottom of the bank, is to be the mill; not less than a quarter of a mile long, with one steam engine at each end, and two in the middle, and a chimney three hundred feet high. In this mill are to be in constant employment from eight hundred to a thousand workers, who never drink, never strike, always go to church on Sunday, and always express themselves in respectful language.

Is not that, broadly, and in the main features, the kind of thing you propose to yourselves? It is very pretty indeed, seen from above; not at all so pretty, seen from below. For, observe, while to one family this deity is indeed the Goddess of Getting-on, to a thousand families she is the Goddess of *not* Getting-on. "Nay," you say, "they have all their chance." Yes, so has every one in a lottery, but there must always be the same number of blanks. "Ah! but in a lottery it is not skill and intelligence which take the lead, but blind chance." What then! do you think the old practice, that "they should take who have the power, and they should keep who can," is less iniquitous, when the power has become power of brains instead of fist? and that, though we may not take advantage of a child's or a woman's weakness, we may of a man's foolishness? "Nay, but finally, work must be done, and some one must be at the top, some one at the bottom." Granted, my friends. Work must always be, and captains of work must always be; and if you in the least remember the tone of any of my writings, you must know that they are thought unfit for this age, because they are always insisting on need of government, and speaking with scorn of liberty. But I beg you to observe that there is a wide difference between being captains or governors of work, and taking the profits of it. It does not follow, because you are general of an army, that you are to take all the treasure, or land, it wins (if it fight for treasure or land); neither, because you are king of a nation, that you are to consume all the profits of the nation's work. Real kings, on the contrary, are known invariably by their doing quite the reverse of this—by their taking the least possible quantity of the nation's work for themselves. There is no test of real kinghood so infallible

as that. Does the crowned creature live simply, bravely, unostentatiously? probably he *is* a King. Does he cover his body with jewels, and his table with delicates? in all probability he is *not* a King. It is possible he may be, as Solomon was; but that is when the nation shares his splendour with him. Solomon made gold, not only to be in his own palace as stones, but to be in Jerusalem as stones. But, even so, for the most part, these splendid kinghoods expire in ruin, and only the true kinghoods live, which are of royal labourers governing loyal labourers; who, both leading rough lives, establish the true dynasties. Conclusively you will find that because you are king of a nation, it does not follow that you are to gather for yourself all the wealth of that nation; neither, because you are king of a small part of the nation, and lord over the means of its maintenance—over field, or mill, or mine, —are you to take all the produce of that piece of the foundation of national existence for yourself.

You will tell me I need not preach against these things, for I cannot mend them. No, good friends, I cannot; but you can, and you will; or something else can and will. Even good things have no abiding power—and shall these evil things persist in victorious evil? All history shows, on the contrary, that to be the exact thing they never can do. Change *must* come; but it is ours to determine whether change of growth, or change of death. Shall the Parthenon be in ruins on its rock, and Bolton priory[35] in its meadow, but these mills of yours be the consummation of the buildings of the earth, and their wheels be as the wheels of eternity? Think you that "men may come, and men may go," but—mills—go on for ever?[36] Not so; out of these, better or worse shall come; and it is for you to choose which.

I know that none of this wrong is done with deliberate purpose. I know, on the contrary, that you wish your workmen well; that you do much for them, and that you desire to do more for them, if you saw your way to such benevolence safely. I know that even all this wrong and misery are brought about by a warped sense of duty, each of you striving to do his best; but,

---

35 Ruins of a beautiful abbey in Yorkshire.
36 Cf. Tennyson's "The Brook": "Men may come, and men may go, but I go on for ever."

unhappily, not knowing for whom this best should be done. And all our hearts have been betrayed by the plausible impiety of the modern economist,[37] telling us that, "To do the best for ourselves, is finally to do the best for others." Friends, our great Master said not so; and most absolutely we shall find this world is not made so. Indeed, to do the best for others, is finally to do the best for ourselves; but it will not do to have our eyes fixed on that issue. The Pagans had got beyond that. Hear what a Pagan says of this matter; hear what were, perhaps, the last written words of Plato,—if not the last actually written (for this we cannot know), yet assuredly in fact and power his parting words—in which, endeavouring to give full crowning and harmonious close to all his thoughts, and to speak the sum of them by imagined sentence of the Great Spirit, his strength and his heart fail him, and the words cease, broken off for ever.

They are at the close of the dialogue called *Critias,* in which he describes, partly from real tradition, partly in ideal dream, the early state of Athens; and the genesis, and order, and religion, of the fabled isle of Atlantis; in which genesis he conceives the same first perfection and final degeneracy of man, which in our own Scriptural tradition is expressed by saying that the Sons of God inter-married with the daughters of men, for he supposes the earliest race to have been indeed the children of God; and to have corrupted themselves, until "their spot was not the spot of his children." And this, he says, was the end; that indeed "through many generations, so long as the God's nature in them yet was full, they were submissive to the sacred laws, and carried themselves lovingly to all that had kindred with them in divineness; for their uttermost spirit was faithful and true, and in every wise great; so that, in *all meekness of wisdom, they dealt with each other,* and took all the chances of life; and despising all things except virtue, they cared little what happened day by day, and *bore lightly the burden* of gold and of possessions; for they saw that, if *only their common love and virtue increased, all these things would be increased together with them;* but to set their esteem and ardent pursuit upon material possession would be to lose that first, and their virtue and affection together with it. And by such reasoning, and what of the divine nature remained in them, they gained all this greatness of which we have already told; but when the God's part of them faded and became extinct, being mixed again and again, and effaced by the prevalent mortality; and the human nature at last exceeded, they then became unable to endure the courses of fortune; and fell into shapelessness of life, and baseness in the sight of him who could see, having lost everything that was fairest of their honour; while to the blind hearts which could not discern the true life, tending to happiness, it seemed that they were then chiefly noble and happy, being filled with all iniquity of inordinate possession and power. Whereupon, the God of Gods, whose Kinghood is in laws, beholding a once just nation thus cast into misery, and desiring to lay such punishment upon them as might make them repent into restraining, gathered together all the gods into his dwelling place, which from heaven's centre overlooks whatever has part in creation; and having assembled them, he said"—

The rest is silence.[38] Last words of the chief wisdom of the heathen, spoken of this idol of riches; this idol of yours; this golden image, high by measureless cubits, set up where your green fields of England are furnace-burnt into the likeness of the plain of Dura:[39] this idol, forbidden to us, first of all idols, by our own Master and faith; forbidden to us also by every human lip that has ever, in any age or people, been accounted of as able to speak according to the purposes of God. Continue to make that forbidden deity your principal one, and soon no more art, no more science, no more pleasure will be possible. Catastrophe will come; or, worse than catastrophe, slow mouldering and withering into Hades. But if you can fix some conception of a true human state of life to be striven for—life, good for all men, as for yourselves; if you can determine some honest and simple order of exis-

---

[37] The liberals. See introduction to the Victorian period, p. 407.

[38] Hamlet's last words. Ruskin means that the *Critias* was broken off at this point.

[39] Plain in the province of Babylon where Nebuchadnezzar set up the golden idol. "Furnace-burnt" may be intended to recall the fiery furnace into which Shadrach, Meshach, and Abednego were cast for refusing to worship the idol (Daniel 3).

tence; following those trodden ways of wisdom which are pleasantness, and seeking her quiet and withdrawn paths, which are peace;—then, and so sanctifying wealth into "common-wealth," all your art, your literature, your daily labours, your domestic affection, and citizen's duty, will join and increase into one magnificent harmony. You will know then how to build, well enough; you will build with stone well, but with flesh better; temples not made with hands, but riveted of hearts; and that kind of marble, crimson-veined, is indeed eternal.

Thomas Henry Huxley
1825–1895

In his *Notebooks* Samuel Butler has an entry headed "Personified Science":

Science is being daily more and more personified and anthropomorphised into a god. By and by they will say that science took our nature upon him, and sent down his only begotten son, Charles Darwin, or Huxley, into the world so that those who believe in him, etc.

This indicates the real significance of Huxley (far more than of Darwin) in the history of Victorian thought.[1] He was *the* prophet of science. What was he sent down to reveal? First, the revolutionary discoveries of the age in geology and biology. With wonderful clarity and illustrative power, in a long series of popular lectures and articles, he explained to the Victorians the theories of evolution which had been put forward in technical language by men like Lyell and Darwin. But he was more than a brilliant popularizer. He was a philosopher who thought science the key to all truth and who wanted to extend the application of scientific theory and method to all fields of knowledge. This meant testing the validity of traditional beliefs, especially religious beliefs as expressed in the Bible, by a scientific standard of proof. It meant asking, What does science tell us about the universe in which we live? the origin and nature of man? the source and sanction of morality? the beginnings of religion? the forces of cohesion and disruption in society? In short, Huxley aimed at nothing less than a complete reconstruction of thought in the light of science. The range of his writing, therefore, goes far beyond science itself to include philosophy, ethics, religion, political theory, and education. "To promote the increase of natural knowledge and to forward the application of scien-

tific methods of investigation to all the problems of life" were the two great objects he had in view.

But the pursuit of these goals involved him in two other causes, both of which are reflected, and their importance emphasized, by the fact that Huxley's enthusiastic reception in America in 1876 was given not so much to "the preacher of new doctrines" as to the champion "of *freedom* and *sincerity*." These additional roles were forced upon him by the religious situation. Alarmed by the skeptical implications of science, the churches appealed to the authority of the

Thomas Henry Huxley (1825–1895). Differing with the advocates of the classical literary education, Huxley emphasized the primacy of science in producing an educated man and alleviating the sufferings of humanity. In the battle over evolution, he called himself "Darwin's bull-dog." *National Portrait Gallery.*

---

[1] For the factual details of Huxley's life, see his own "Autobiography," printed below.

Bible, every statement of which was still widely considered to be the word of God and therefore to be accepted without question. If science came to different conclusions, it was wrong; if scientists, relying on "carnal reason," denied any of its truths, they were morally reprehensible (see p. 682). No wonder Huxley waved the liberal banner and demanded the right of free thought and free speech even when they were anti-Christian or antireligious, and the right to follow reason even when it ran counter to religious authority. How important this role was, in his own mind, can be seen at the end of his "Autobiography," where he thinks his worldly honors of small account compared with his contribution to "the new Reformation" (see p. 658 and the note).

Finally, Huxley became something like an apostle of veracity to a generation which found itself caught between belief and unbelief, and often forced, by social pressures or psychological fears, into professing to believe what in fact it only half-believed or gravely doubted. Against such insincerities and evasions, however natural at the time, he struck with telling force, and his demand that men "rest in no lie" gave many later Victorians the courage to express their doubts or their outright disbelief.

The essay on "Science and Culture" is a plea for the study of science against the opposition of both the businessmen, who were slow to perceive its practical possibilities, and the scholars and schoolmasters, who clung to the old classical education. The argument, therefore, stresses the contribution of scientific education to industrial progress, on the one hand; and on the other, to culture—that is, to our understanding of human life. The battle to get science into the curriculum has long since been won, but its vocational value has almost submerged its cultural value, until today it is rarely taught as a liberal subject. Huxley would hardly approve of a science curriculum exclusively devoted to training chemists and engineers. He would insist that it contain historical courses which would explore the successive impacts of scientific discoveries upon man's moral, religious, and philosophical outlook.

On the other hand, the essay also reveals how seriously the cult of science could undermine the cultural values of the humanities. Though Huxley professes to recognize that unless the study of science is combined with the study of literature (in the wide sense that includes philosophy and history) the result will be a lopsided man, in point of fact he exalts science at the expense of literature. He is willing to say that men preparing for a career in medicine, business, or science need not bother with a literary education. He is willing to accept Sir Josiah Mason's College as providing "a fairly complete culture" be-

cause instruction in the English, French, and German *languages* is to be offered. He calls "literary or artistic culture a never-failing source of pleasures" that are morally wholesome, without pointing out that their real value lies in their power to extend our knowledge and quicken our perceptions of life. He can even claim that "the free employment of reason, in accordance with scientific method, is the sole method of reaching truth," which is at once to question the validity of much of our intellectual inheritance; for it is not to logic but to intuition that we owe the most important insights men have had into moral and religious life. In short, Huxley is right in insisting on the values of science, but his overinsistence upon them, with the consequent disparagement of the humanities, reveals the destructive influence of the scientific mind upon our cultural tradition.

Even more serious has been its similar effect on the religious tradition. The antireligious implications of nineteenth-century science (described at length in the introduction to the Victorian period) may be summarized here in a series of propositions, all of which Huxley maintained. The universe, to all intents and purposes, is infinite in space and infinite in time. It is not static but dynamic, in a continuous process of evolution which started from some "primordial molecular arrangement" and has been going on ever since by scientific laws. Organic life began when hydrogen, oxygen, nitrogen, and carbon came together in a complex relationship under just the right climatic conditions. Its origin, therefore, was completely material. From this original sperm all later life has naturally descended: man is an animal, and animals are merely physical automata. All of man's actions and thoughts are determined by molecular changes in the brain, which are determined by external stimuli, which in turn are simply parts of the great mechanism of cause and effect that "composes the sum of existence." Consequently, man has no immaterial soul or spirit, and no moral will that is free to control his thinking or his conduct. He is simply a human automaton. This is the scientific picture of the universe which had emerged by 1870, and which Huxley did so much to publicize. And yet, in the very teeth of these propositions, he could turn around and say that in a world so full of misery and ignorance, it is "the plain duty of each and all of us to try to make the little corner he can influence somewhat less miserable and somewhat less ignorant than it was before he entered it." The automaton can choose to make the world a better place! The fact is that Huxley was not only a scientist, but he was also a humanist and a humanitarian; and the first self was always arriving at conclusions which the second could not endure. He therefore tried, with dubious success, to sit on two stools at once. So did

Tennyson and many other Victorians unable to deny either the logic of mechanistic science or the inner assurance of free will. The situation still exists, as Whitehead has pointed out:

> A scientific realism, based on mechanism, is conjoined with an unwavering belief in the world of men and of the higher animals as being composed of self-determining organisms. This radical inconsistency at the basis of modern thought accounts for much that is half-hearted and wavering in our civilisation.

The same tension can be seen in Huxley's ethics. On the one hand, he derived the moral will and moral laws from the automatic working of Darwin's principle of natural selection. In the cause of better survival, men banded together into tribes, which meant that they had to establish certain moral laws so that they could work together. These were enforced by tribal punishments on all who disobeyed them, with the result that out of fear (but ultimately for the sake of personal survival) a conscience was gradually instilled into primitive man. At the same time, social ideals were set up exalting duty and self-sacrifice because they could add further weight to the force of conscience in giving the tribe greater cohesive strength—and the individual a greater chance of survival. Altruism, therefore, was simply a disguised form of selfishness.

These are the beliefs of Huxley the scientist (see pp. 689–90). But Huxley the humanist can talk of an "innate sense of moral beauty and ugliness," which is possessed by a few "men of moral genius, to whom we owe ideals of duty and visions of moral perfection" unattainable by ordinary persons, and from whom the latter derive an inspiration to spend their lives trying to embody these ideals in the actual world. One of the essays ends with an appeal to all of us to strive upward "towards those high peaks, where, resting in eternal calm, reason [ethical reason or moral intuition] discerns the undefined but bright ideal of the highest Good." This is the language of moral idealism. It is the language of Plato. And it never appeared in any natural history of morality. The logic of science was always leading Huxley to a position that his humanism repudiated. But he could not let go his hold of either.

Both sides of his mind can be seen again in the two volumes that he devoted directly to the subject of religion (Science and Hebrew Tradition and Science and Christian Tradition, to both of which the "Prologue," printed below, was a general preface). On the one hand, he applied the new scientific criticism (historical, literary, and physical) to the Bible, with the intention of disproving or rationalizing the entire body of supernatural dogma and miracle. When he finished, the Bible had been reduced to a typical primitive document full of superstition and myth. But his liberal opponents insisted that no amount of Biblical criticism could disprove the core of religion, the belief in God and immortality. Huxley, forced reluctantly to agree, added a corollary. He said, "Right, there is no disproof of those beliefs, but don't forget, there is no proof of them either"; and by proof he meant objective evidence capable of public verification. This is the agnostic position, standing between faith and atheism; not denial of belief but denial that we have sufficient reason to believe. Huxley himself coined the term agnosticism (literally, "no knowledge") in 1869 to describe, with proper caution, the conclusions of the scientific mind. But we must remember that there is the genuine agnostic, honestly in doubt, earnestly trying to discover whether or not there is a supernatural order; and there is the polemical agnostic, at heart an atheist, but too smart to claim that there is no supernatural order, though ready enough to propagate his conviction by insinuation and aspersion. Huxley was a polemical agnostic (see his real belief in note 15 of the "Prologue" to Essays on Some Controverted Questions, but his official agnosticism in the text above; and notice the brilliant antireligious rhetoric on p. 681, where he stacks all the cards on the side of naturalism). Nevertheless, Huxley the humanist was only too eager to "save" both the Bible and the Church. Both had to be purged of their supernatural and theological elements, but when that was done, the residue would be sound morality. The function of both, he thought, ought to be "the setting before men's minds of an ideal of true, just, and pure living." This Victorian reduction of religion and the Sunday service to moral and humanitarian inspiration has largely captured the Protestant churches. But one may wonder if the inspiration can have much compulsion when it is divorced from the faith which once gave it meaning and power.

TEXTS: The standard biography is the Life and Letters of Thomas Henry Huxley, by his son, Leonard Huxley (2 vols., London, 1900; New York, 1901). The best general study is by Cyril Bibby, Thomas Henry Huxley: Scientist, Humanist, and Educator (1959); but also see William Irvine's Apes, Angels, and Victorians: The Study of Darwin, Huxley, and Evolution (1955). On his style, see Aldous Huxley, "T. H. Huxley as a Man of Letters" in Huxley Memorial Lectures at the Imperial College of Science and Technology (London, 1932), and Walter E. Houghton, "The Rhetoric of T. H. Huxley," University of Toronto Quarterly, XVIII (1948–49), 159–75.

Autobiography

*And when I consider, in one view, the many things
. . . which I have upon my hands, I feel the burlesque
of being employed in this manner at my time of
life. But, in another view, and taking in all circumstances, these things, as trifling as they may appear,
no less than things of greater importance, seem to be
put upon me to do. . . .*

—BISHOP BUTLER[1] to the DUCHESS OF SOMERSET

The "many things" to which the Duchess's correspondent here refers are the repairs and improvements of the episcopal seat at Auckland. I doubt
if the great apologist, greater in nothing than
in the simple dignity of his character, would
have considered the writing an account of himself as a thing which could be put upon him to
do, whatever circumstances might be taken in.
But the good bishop lived in an age when a
man might write books and yet be permitted to
keep his private existence to himself; in the pre-
Boswellian epoch, when the germ of the photog-
rapher lay in the womb of the distant future,
and the interviewer who pervades our age was
an unforeseen, indeed unimaginable, birth of
time.

At present, the most convinced believer in
the aphorism *"Bene qui latuit, bene vixit,"*[2] is
not always able to act up to it. An importunate
person informs him that his portrait is about
to be published and will be accompanied by a
biography which the importunate person proposes to write. The sufferer knows what that
means; either he undertakes to revise the "biography" or he does not. In the former case, he
makes himself responsible; in the latter, he
allows the publication of a mass of more or less
fulsome inaccuracies for which he will be held
responsible by those who are familiar with the
prevalent art of self-advertisement. On the whole,
it may be better to get over the "burlesque of
being employed in this manner" and do the
thing himself.

It was by reflections of this kind that, some
years ago, I was led to write and permit the
publication of the subjoined sketch.

[1] Bishop Joseph Butler (1692–1752), author of the widely
read *Analogy of Religion*.
[2] "He who has lived inconspicuously has lived well."
(Ovid, *Tristia*, III, iv, 25).

I was born about eight o'clock in the morning on the 4th of May, 1825, at Ealing, which
was, at that time, as quiet a little country village
as could be found within half-a-dozen miles of
Hyde Park Corner. Now it is a suburb of London with, I believe, 30,000 inhabitants. My father
was one of the masters in a large semipublic
school which at one time had a high reputation.
I am not aware that any portents preceded
my arrival in this world, but, in my childhood,
I remember hearing a traditional account of
the manner in which I lost the chance of an
endowment of great practical value. The windows of my mother's room were open, in consequence of the unusual warmth of the weather.
For the same reason, probably, a neighboring
beehive had swarmed, and the new colony, pitch-
ing on the window-sill, was making its way into
the room when the horrified nurse shut down the
sash. If that well-meaning woman had only abstained from her ill-timed interference, the
swarm might have settled on my lips, and I
should have been endowed with that mellifluous
eloquence which, in this country, leads far more
surely than worth, capacity, or honest work, to
the highest places in Church and State. But the
opportunity was lost, and I have been obliged
to content myself through life with saying what
I mean in the plainest of plain language, than
which, I suppose, there is no habit more ruinous
to a man's prospects of advancement.

Why I was christened Thomas Henry I do
not know; but it is a curious chance that my
parents should have fixed for my usual denomination upon the name of that particular Apostle
with whom I have always felt most sympathy.
Physically and mentally I am the son of my
mother so completely—even down to peculiar
movements of the hands, which made their appearance in me as I reached the age she had
when I noticed them—that I can hardly find
any trace of my father in myself, except an inborn faculty for drawing, which unfortunately,
in my case, has never been cultivated, a hot
temper, and that amount of tenacity of purpose
which unfriendly observers sometimes call obstinacy.

My mother was a slender brunette, of an
emotional and energetic temperament, and possessed of the most piercing black eyes I ever saw
in a woman's head. With no more education

than other women of the middle classes in her day, she had an excellent mental capacity. Her most distinguishing characteristic, however, was rapidity of thought. If one ventured to suggest she had not taken much time to arrive at any conclusion, she would say, "I cannot help it, things flash across me." That peculiarity has been passed on to me in full strength; it has often stood me in good stead; it has sometimes played me sad tricks, and it has always been a danger. But, after all, if my time were to come over again, there is nothing I would less willingly part with than my inheritance of mother wit.

I have next to nothing to say about my childhood. In later years my mother, looking at me almost reproachfully, would sometimes say, "Ah! you were such a pretty boy!" whence I had no difficulty in concluding that I had not ful-filled my early promise in the matter of looks. In fact, I have a distinct recollection of certain curls of which I was vain, and of a conviction that I closely resembled that handsome, courtly gentleman, Sir Herbert Oakley, who was vicar of our parish, and who was as a god to us coun-try folk, because he was occasionally visited by the then Prince George of Cambridge. I remem-ber turning my pinafore wrong side forwards in order to represent a surplice, and preaching to my mother's maids in the kitchen as nearly as possible in Sir Herbert's manner one Sunday morning when the rest of the family were at church. That is the earliest indication I can call to mind of the strong clerical affinities which my friend Mr. Herbert Spencer has always ascribed to me, though I fancy they have for the most part remained in a latent state.

My regular school training was of the brief-est, perhaps fortunately, for though my way of life has made me acquainted with all sorts and conditions of men, from the highest to the lowest, I deliberately affirm that the society I fell into at school was the worst I have ever known. We boys were average lads, with much the same inherent capacity for good and evil as any others; but the people who were set over us cared about as much for our intellectual and moral welfare as if they were baby-farmers. We were left to the operation of the struggle for existence among ourselves, and bullying was the least of the ill practices current among us. Almost the only cheerful reminiscence in connection with the place which

arises in my mind is that of a battle I had with one of my classmates, who had bullied me until I could stand it no longer. I was a very slight lad, but there was a wildcat element in me which, when roused, made up for lack of weight, and I licked my adversary effectually. However, one of my first experiences of the extremely rough-and-ready nature of justice, as exhibited by the course of things in general, arose out of the fact that I—the victor—had a black eye, while he—the van-quished—had none, so that I got into disgrace and he did not. We made it up, and thereafter I was unmolested. One of the greatest shocks I ever received in my life was to be told a dozen years afterwards by the groom who brought me my horse in a stable-yard in Sydney that he was my quondam antagonist. He had a long story of family misfortune to account for his position, but at that time it was necessary to deal very cau-tiously with mysterious strangers in New South Wales, and on inquiry I found that the unfor-tunate young man had not only been "sent out," but had undergone more than one colonial con-viction.

As I grew older, my great desire was to be a mechanical engineer, but the fates were against this and, while very young, I commenced the study of medicine under a medical brother-in-law. But, though the Institute of Mechanical Engineers would certainly not own me, I am not sure that I have not all along been a sort of mechanical engineer *in partibus infidelium*.[3] I am now occasionally horrified to think how very little I ever knew or cared about medicine as the art of healing. The only part of my professional course which really and deeply interested me way physiology, which is the mechanical engi-neering of living machines; and, notwithstanding that natural science has been my proper business, I am afraid there is very little of the genuine naturalist in me. I never collected anything, and species work was always a burden to me; what I cared for was the architectural and engi-neering part of the business, the working out the wonderful unity of plan in the thousands and thousands of diverse living constructions, and the modifications of similar apparatuses to serve di-verse ends. The extraordinary attraction I felt

---

[3] "In heathen or foreign parts." Huxley is here thinking of himself as a mechanical engineer in the "foreign" field of physiology.

towards the study of the intricacies of living structure nearly proved fatal to me at the outset. I was a mere boy—I think between thirteen and fourteen years of age—when I was taken by some older student friends of mine to the first post-mortem examination I ever attended. All my life I have been most unfortunately sensitive to the disagreeables which attend anatomical pursuits, but on this occasion my curiosity overpowered all other feelings, and I spent two or three hours in gratifying it. I did not cut myself, and none of the ordinary symptoms of dissection-poison supervened, but poisoned I was somehow, and I remember sinking into a strange state of apathy. By way of a last chance, I was sent to the care of some good, kind people, friends of my father's, who lived in a farmhouse in the heart of Warwickshire. I remember staggering from my bed to the window on the bright spring morning after my arrival, and throwing open the casement. Life seemed to come back on the wings of the breeze, and to this day the faint odor of wood-smoke, like that which floated across the farmyard in the early morning, is as good to me as the "sweet south upon a bed of violets." I soon recovered, but for years I suffered from occasional paroxysms of internal pain, and from that time my constant friend, hypochondriacal dyspepsia, commenced his half century of cotenancy of my fleshly tabernacle.

Looking back on my *Lehrjahre*,[4] I am sorry to say that I do not think that any account of my doings as a student would tend to edification. In fact, I should distinctly warn ingenuous youth to avoid imitating my example. I worked extremely hard when it pleased me, and when it did not—which was a very frequent case—I was extremely idle (unless making caricatures of one's pastors and masters is to be called a branch of industry), or else wasted my energies in wrong directions. I read everything I could lay hands upon, including novels, and took up all sorts of pursuits to drop them again quite as speedily. No doubt it was very largely my own fault, but the only instruction from which I ever obtained the proper effect of education was that which I received from Mr. Wharton Jones, who was the lecturer on physiology at the Charing Cross School of Medicine. The extent and precision of his knowledge impressed me greatly, and the severe exactness of his method of lecturing was quite to my taste. I do not know that I have ever felt so much respect for anybody as a teacher before or since. I worked hard to obtain his approbation, and he was extremely kind and helpful to the youngster who, I am afraid, took up more of his time than he had any right to do. It was he who suggested the publication of my first scientific paper—a very little one—in the *Medical Gazette* of 1845, and most kindly corrected the literary faults which abounded in it, short as it was; for at that time, and for many years afterwards, I detested the trouble of writing, and would take no pains over it.

It was in the early spring of 1846, that, having finished my obligatory medical studies and passed the first M.B. examination at the London University—though I was still too young to qualify at the College of Surgeons—I was talking to a fellow student (the present eminent physician, Sir Joseph Fayrer), and wondering what I should do to meet the imperative necessity for earning my own bread, when my friend suggested that I should write to Sir William Burnett, at that time Director-General for the Medical Service of the Navy, for an appointment. I thought this rather a strong thing to do, as Sir William was personally unknown to me, but my cheery friend would not listen to my scruples, so I went to my lodgings and wrote the best letter I could devise. A few days afterwards I received the usual official circular of acknowledgement, but at the bottom there was written an instruction to call at Somerset House on such a day. I thought that looked like business, so at the appointed time I called and sent in my card, while I waited in Sir William's anteroom. He was a tall, shrewd-looking old gentleman, with a broad Scotch accent—and I think I see him now as he entered with my card in his hand. The first thing he did was to return it, with the frugal reminder that I should probably find it useful on some other occasion. The second was to ask whether I was an Irishman. I suppose the air of modesty about my appeal must have struck him. I satisfied the Director-General that I was English to the backbone, and he made some inquiries as to my student career, finally desiring me to hold myself ready for examination. Having passed this, I was in Her Majesty's Service, and entered on the

[4] Student years.

books of Nelson's old ship, the *Victory,* for duty at Haslar Hospital, about a couple of months after I made my application.

My official chief at Haslar was a very remarkable person, the late Sir John Richardson, an excellent naturalist, and far-famed as an indomitable Arctic traveler. He was a silent, reserved man, outside the circle of his family and intimates; and, having a full share of youthful vanity, I was extremely disgusted to find that "Old John," as we irreverent youngsters called him, took not the slightest notice of my worshipful self either the first time I attended him, as it was my duty to do, or for some weeks afterwards. I am afraid to think of the lengths to which my tongue may have run on the subject of the churlishness of the chief, who was, in truth, one of the kindest-hearted and most considerate of men. But one day, as I was crossing the hospital square, Sir John stopped me, and heaped coals of fire on my head by telling me that he had tried to get me one of the resident appointments, much coveted by the assistant surgeons, but that the Admiralty had put in another man. "However," said he, "I mean to keep you here till I can get you something you will like," and turned upon his heel without waiting for the thanks I stammered out. That explained how it was I had not been packed off to the West Coast of Africa like some of my juniors, and why, eventually, I remained altogether seven months at Haslar.

After a long interval, during which "Old John" ignored my existence almost as completely as before, he stopped me again as we met in a casual way, and describing the service on which the *Rattlesnake* was likely to be employed, said that Captain Owen Stanley, who was to command the ship, had asked him to recommend an assistant surgeon who knew something of science; would I like that? Of course I jumped at the offer. "Very well, I give you leave; go to London at once and see Captain Stanley." I went, saw my future commander, who was very civil to me, and promised to ask that I should be appointed to his ship, as in due time I was. It is a singular thing that, during the few months of my stay at Haslar, I had among my messmates two future Directors-General of the Medical Service of the Navy (Sir Alexander Armstrong and Sir John Watt-Reid), with the present President of the College of Physicians and my kindest of doctors, Sir Andrew Clark.

Life on board Her Majesty's ships in those days was a very different affair from what it is now, and ours was exceptionally rough, as we were often many months without receiving letters or seeing any civilized people but ourselves. In exchange, we had the interest of being about the last voyagers, I suppose, to whom it could be possible to meet with people who knew nothing of firearms—as we did on the south coast of New Guinea—and of making acquaintance with a variety of interesting savage and semicivilized people. But, apart from experience of this kind and the opportunities offered for scientific work, to me, personally, the cruise was extremely valuable. It was good for me to live under sharp discipline; to be down on the realities of existence by living on bare necessaries; to find out how extremely well worth living life seemed to be when one woke up from a night's rest on a soft plank, with the sky for canopy and cocoa and weevily biscuit the sole prospect for breakfast; and, more especially, to learn to work for the sake of what I got for myself out of it, even if it all went to the bottom and I along with it. My brother officers were as good fellows as sailors ought to be and generally are, but, naturally, they neither knew nor cared anything about my pursuits, nor understood why I should be so zealous in pursuit of the objects which my friends, the middies, christened "Buffons," after the title conspicuous on a volume of the *Suites à Buffon,*[5] which stood on my shelf in the chart room.

During the four years of our absence, I sent home communication after communication to the "Linnean Society,"[6] with the same result as that obtained by Noah when he sent the raven out of his ark. Tired at last of hearing nothing about them, I determined to do or die, and in 1849 I drew up a more elaborate paper and forwarded it to the Royal Society.[7] This was my dove, if I had only known it. But owing to the movements of the ship, I heard nothing of that either until my return to England in the latter end of the year 1850, when I found that it was printed and published, and that a huge packet

---

[5] Supplements to the *Histoire Naturelle,* written by the great French naturalist Georges Buffon (1707–1788).

[6] Founded in 1788 for the promotion of zoology and botany and named for the Swedish botanist Carl von Linné.

[7] The Royal Society was the oldest scientific society in England, founded in 1662.

of separate copies awaited me. When I hear some of my young friends complain of want of sympathy and encouragement, I am inclined to think that my naval life was not the least valuable part of my education.

Three years after my return were occupied by a battle between my scientific friends on the one hand and the Admiralty on the other, as to whether the latter ought, or ought not, to act up to the spirit of a pledge they had given to encourage officers who had done scientific work by contributing to the expense of publishing mine. At last the Admiralty, getting tired, I suppose, cut short the discussion by ordering me to join a ship, which thing I declined to do, and as Rastignac, in the *Père Goriot,* says to Paris, I said to London, *"à nous deux."*[8] I desired to obtain a Professorship of either Physiology or Comparative Anatomy, and as vacancies occurred I applied, but in vain. My friend, Professor Tyndall, and I were candidates at the same time, he for the Chair of Physics and I for that of Natural History in the University of Toronto, which, fortunately, as it turned out, would not look at either of us. I say fortunately, not from any lack of respect for Toronto, but because I soon made up my mind that London was the place for me, and hence I have steadily declined the inducements to leave it, which have at various times been offered. At last, in 1854, on the translation of my warm friend Edward Forbes, to Edinburgh, Sir Henry De la Beche, the Director-General of the Geological Survey, offered me the post Forbes vacated of Paleontologist and Lecturer on Natural History. I refused the former point-blank, and accepted the latter only provisionally, telling Sir Henry that I did not care for fossils, and that I should give up Natural History as soon as I could get a physiological post. But I held the office for thirty-one years, and a large part of my work has been paleontological.

At that time I disliked public speaking, and had a firm conviction that I should break down every time I opened my mouth. I believe I had every fault a speaker could have (except talking at random or indulging in rhetoric), when I spoke to the first important audience I ever addressed, on a Friday evening at the Royal Institution,[9] in 1852. Yet, I must confess to having been guilty, *malgré moi,*[10] of as much public speaking as most of my contemporaries, and for the last ten years it ceased to be so much of a bugbear to me. I used to pity myself for having to go through this training, but I am now more disposed to compassionate the unfortunate audiences, especially my ever-friendly hearers at the Royal Institution, who were the subjects of my oratorical experiments.

The last thing that it would be proper for me to do would be to speak of the work of my life, or to say at the end of the day whether I think I have earned my wages or not. Men are said to be partial judges of themselves. Young men may be—I doubt if old men are. Life seems terribly foreshortened as they look back, and the mountain they set themselves to climb in youth turns out to be a mere spur of immeasurably higher ranges when, with failing breath, they reached the top. But if I may speak of the objects I have had more or less definitely in view since I began the ascent of my hillock, they are briefly these: To promote the increase of natural knowledge and to forward the application of scientific methods of investigation to all the problems of life to the best of my ability, in the conviction, which has grown with my growth and strengthened with my strength, that there is no alleviation for the sufferings of mankind except veracity of thought and of action, and the resolute facing of the world as it is when the garment of make-believe by which pious hands have hidden its uglier features is stripped off.

It is with this intent that I have subordinated any reasonable, or unreasonable, ambition for scientific fame which I may have permitted myself to entertain to other ends: to the popularization of science; to the development and organization of scientific education; to the endless series of battles and skirmishes over evolution; and to untiring opposition to that ecclesiastical spirit, that clericalism, which in England, as everywhere else, and to whatever denomination it may belong, is the deadly enemy of science.

In striving for the attainment of these objects, I have been but one among many, and I shall be well content to be remembered, or even not remembered, as such. Circumstances, among which I am proud to reckon the devoted kindness

---

8 *Le Père Goriot* is a novel by Honoré de Balzac (1799-1850). The French phrase means, "Now the issue is squarely between the two of us."

9 A scientific society. 10 In spite of myself.

of many friends, have led to my occupation of various prominent positions, among which the Presidency of the Royal Society is the highest. It would be mock modesty on my part, with these and other scientific honors which have been bestowed upon me, to pretend that I have not succeeded in the career which I have followed, rather because I was driven into it than of my own free will; but I am afraid I should not count even these things as marks of success if I could not hope that I had somewhat helped that movement of opinion which has been called the New Reformation.[11]

Science and Culture[1]

Six years ago, as some of my present hearers may remember, I had the privilege of addressing a large assemblage of the inhabitants of this city, who had gathered together to do honor to the memory of their famous townsman, Joseph Priestley;[2] and, if any satisfaction attaches to posthumous glory, we may hope that the *manes*[3] of the burnt-out philosopher were then finally appeased.

No man, however, who is endowed with a fair share of common sense, and not more than a fair share of vanity, will identify either contemporary or posthumous fame with the highest good; and Priestley's life leaves no doubt that he, at any rate, set a much higher value upon the advancement of knowledge, and the promotion of that freedom of thought which is at once the cause and the consequence of intellectual progress.

Hence I am disposed to think that, if Priestley could be amongst us today, the occasion of our meeting would afford him even greater pleasure than the proceedings which celebrated the centenary of his chief discovery.[4] The kindly heart would be moved, the high sense of social duty would be satisfied, by the spectacle of well-earned wealth neither squandered in tawdry luxury and vainglorious show, nor scattered with the careless charity which blesses neither him that gives nor him that takes, but expended in the execution of a well-considered plan for the aid of present and future generations of those who are willing to help themselves.

We shall all be of one mind thus far. But it is needful to share Priestley's keen interest in physical science; and to have learned, as he had learned, the value of scientific training in fields of inquiry apparently far remote from physical science; in order to appreciate, as he would have appreciated, the value of the noble gift which Sir Josiah Mason has bestowed upon the inhabitants of the Midland district.

For us children of the nineteenth century, however, the establishment of a college under the conditions of Sir Josiah Mason's Trust, has a significance apart from any which it could have possessed a hundred years ago. It appears to be an indication that we are reaching the crisis of the battle, or rather of the long series of battles, which have been fought over education in a campaign which began long before Priestley's time, and will probably not be finished just yet.

In the last century, the combatants were the champions of ancient literature on the one side, and those of modern literature on the other; but, some thirty years ago, the contest became complicated by the appearance of a third army, ranged round the banner of physical science.

I am not aware that anyone has authority to speak in the name of this new host. For it must be admitted to be somewhat of a guerilla force, composed largely of irregulars, each of whom fights pretty much for his own hand. But the impressions of a full private, who has seen a good deal of service in the ranks, respecting the present position of affairs and the conditions of a permanent peace, may not be devoid of interest; and I do not know that I could make a better

11 Cf. Huxley's letter to his wife in 1873: "The part I have to play is not to found a new school of thought or to reconcile the antagonisms of the old schools. We are in the midst of a gigantic movement greater than that which preceded and produced the Reformation, and really only the continuation of that movement. But there is nothing new in the ideas which lie at the bottom of the movement, nor is any reconcilement possible between free thought and traditional authority."

1 This essay was originally delivered on October 1, 1880, as a lecture at the opening of the new Science College founded by Sir Josiah Mason at Birmingham.

2 A distinguished scientist and political economist as well as a Unitarian clergyman (1733–1804). Because of his liberal sympathies and the panic engendered by the French Revolution, his house was attacked and burned by a mob in 1791. Both his scientific instruments and his manuscripts were destroyed.

3 Ancestral spirits.

4 That of oxygen.

use of the present opportunity than by laying them before you.

From the time that the first suggestion to introduce physical science into ordinary education was timidly whispered, until now, the advocates of scientific education have met with opposition of two kinds. On the one hand, they have been pooh-poohed by the men of business who pride themselves on being the representatives of practicality; while, on the other hand, they have been excommunicated by the classical scholars, in their capacity of Levites in charge of the ark of culture and monopolists of liberal education.[5]

The practical men believed that the idol whom they worship—rule of thumb—has been the source of the past prosperity, and will suffice for the future welfare of the arts and manufactures. They were of opinion that science is speculative rubbish; that theory and practice have nothing to do with one another; and that the scientific habit of mind is an impediment, rather than aid, in the conduct of ordinary affairs.

I have used the past tense in speaking of the practical men—for although they were very formidable thirty years ago, I am not sure that the pure species has not been extirpated. In fact, so far as mere argument goes, they have been subjected to such a *feu d'enfer*[6] that it is a miracle if any have escaped. But I have remarked that your typical practical man has an unexpected resemblance to one of Milton's angels. His spiritual wounds, such as are inflicted by logical weapons, may be as deep as a well and as wide as a church door, but beyond shedding a few drops of ichor, celestial or otherwise, he is no whit the worse. So, if any of these opponents be left, I will not waste time in vain repetition of the demonstrative evidence of the practical value of science; but knowing that a parable will sometimes penetrate where syllogisms fail to effect an entrance, I will offer a story for their consideration.

Once upon a time, a boy,[7] with nothing to depend upon but his own vigorous nature, was thrown into the thick of the struggle for existence in the midst of a great manufacturing population. He seems to have had a hard fight, inasmuch as, by the time he was thirty years of age, his total disposable funds amounted to twenty pounds. Nevertheless, middle life found him giving proof of his comprehension of the practical problems he had been roughly called upon to solve, by a career of remarkable prosperity.

Finally, having reached old age with its well-earned surroundings of "honor, troops of friends," the hero of my story bethought himself of those who were making a like start in life, and how he could stretch out a helping hand to them.

After long and anxious reflection this successful practical man of business could devise nothing better than to provide them with the means of obtaining "sound, extensive, and practical scientific knowledge." And he devoted a large part of his wealth and five years of incessant work to this end.

I need not point the moral of a tale which, as the solid and spacious fabric of the Scientific College assures us, is no fable, nor can anything which I could say intensify the force of this practical answer to practical objections.

We may take it for granted then, that, in the opinion of those best qualified to judge, the diffusion of thorough scientific education is an absolutely essential condition of industrial progress; and that the college which has been opened today will confer an inestimable boon upon those whose livelihood is to be gained by the practice of the arts and manufactures of the district.

The only question worth discussion is, whether the conditions, under which the work of the college is to be carried out, are such as to give it the best possible chance of achieving permanent success.

Sir Josiah Mason, without doubt most wisely, has left very large freedom of action to the trustees, to whom he proposes ultimately to commit the administration of the college, so that they may be able to adjust its arrangements in accordance with the changing conditions of the future. But, with respect to three points, he has laid most explicit injunctions upon both administrators and teachers.

Party politics are forbidden to enter into the minds of either, so far as the work of the college is concerned; theology is as sternly ban-

[5] Using the Biblical designation of those appointed to guard the Ark of the Lord, Huxley implies that the classical scholars, i.e., the universities, are endowing their particular culture with an aura of sanctity that may well be founded on mere tradition.
[6] Barrage (literally, hell-fire).
[7] Sir Josiah Mason.

ished from its precincts; and finally, it is especially declared that the college shall make no provision for "mere literary instruction and education."

It does not concern me at present to dwell upon the first two injunctions any longer than may be needful to express my full conviction of their wisdom. But the third prohibition brings us face to face with those other opponents of scientific education, who are by no means in the moribund condition of the practical man, but alive, alert, and formidable.

It is not impossible that we shall hear this express exclusion of "literary instruction and education" from a college which, nevertheless, professes to give a high and efficient education, sharply criticized. Certainly the time was that the Levites of culture would have sounded their trumpets against its walls as against an educational Jericho.[8]

How often have we not been told that the study of physical science is incompetent to confer culture; that it touches none of the higher problems of life; and, what is worse, that the continual devotion to scientific studies tends to generate a narrow and bigoted belief in the applicability of scientific methods to the search after truth of all kinds? How frequently one has reason to observe that no reply to a troublesome argument tells so well as calling its author a "mere scientific specialist." And, as I am afraid it is not permissible to speak of this form of opposition to scientific education in the past tense, may we not expect to be told that this, not only omission, but prohibition, of "mere literary instruction and education" is a patent example of scientific narrow-mindedness?

I am not acquainted with Sir Josiah Mason's reasons for the action which he has taken; but if, as I apprehend is the case, he refers to the ordinary classical course of our schools and universities by the name of "mere literary instruction and education," I venture to offer sundry reasons of my own in support of that action.

For I hold very strongly by two convictions. The first is that neither the discipline nor the subject-matter of classical education is of such direct value to the student of physical science as to justify the expenditure of valuable time upon either; and the second is, that for the purpose of attaining real culture, an exclusively scientific education is at least as effectual as an exclusively literary education.

I need hardly point out to you that these opinions, especially the latter, are diametrically opposed to those of the great majority of educated Englishmen, influenced as they are by school and university traditions. In their belief, culture is obtainable only by a liberal education; and a liberal education is synonymous, not merely with education and instruction in literature, but in one particular form of literature, namely, that of Greek and Roman antiquity. They hold that the man who has learned Latin and Greek, however little, is educated; while he who is versed in other branches of knowledge, however deeply, is a more or less respectable specialist, not admissible into the cultured caste. The stamp of the educated man, the university degree, is not for him.

I am too well acquainted with the generous catholicity of spirit, the true sympathy with scientific thought, which pervades the writings of our chief apostle of culture[9] to identify him with these opinions; and yet one may cull from one and another of those epistles to the Philistines, which so much delight all who do not answer to that name, sentences which lend them some support.

Mr. Arnold tells us that the meaning of culture is "to know the best that has been thought and said in the world."[10] It is the criticism of life contained in literature. That criticism regards "Europe as being, for intellectual and spiritual purposes, one great confederation, bound to a joint action and working to a common result; and whose members have, for their common outfit, a knowledge of Greek, Roman, and Eastern antiquity, and of one another. Special, local, and temporary advantages being put out of account, that modern nation will in the intellectual

---

[8] As the walls of Jericho in the Bible story were destroyed by the blowing of the Levites' trumpets (Joshua 6), so the proponents of classical culture would once have tried to destroy the College by a loud noise of protest.

[9] The reference is to Matthew Arnold. Huxley refers to Arnold's essays as "epistles to the Philistines" because Arnold, using the parallel of the Biblical account of the struggle of the Hebrews with their enemies, had termed the enemies of culture—and in this category he included the whole English middle class—"Philistines."

[10] The two quotations from Arnold in this paragraph are from his essay "The Function of Criticism at the Present Time" reprinted below.

and spiritual sphere make most progress, which most thoroughly carries out this program. And what is that but saying that we too, all of us, as individuals, the more thoroughly we carry it out, shall make the more progress?"

We have here to deal wth two distinct propositions. The first, that a criticism of life is the essence of culture; the second, that literature contains the materials which suffice for the construction of such criticism.

I think that we must all assent to the first proposition. For culture certainly means something quite different from learning or technical skill. It implies the possession of an ideal, and the habit of critically estimating the value of things by comparison with a theoretic standard.[11] Perfect culture should supply a complete theory of life, based upon a clear knowledge alike of its possibilities and of its limitations.

But we may agree to all this, and yet strongly dissent from the assumption that literature alone is competent to supply this knowledge. After having learned all that Greek, Roman, and Eastern antiquity have thought and said, and all that modern literatures have to tell us, it is not self-evident that we have laid a sufficiently broad and deep foundation for that criticism of life which constitutes culture.

Indeed, to anyone acquainted with the scope of physical science, it is not at all evident. Considering progress only in the "intellectual and spiritual sphere," I find myself wholly unable to admit that either nations or individuals will really advance, if their common outfit draws nothing from the stores of physical science. I should say that an army, without weapons of precision and with no particular base of operations, might more hopefully enter upon a campaign on the Rhine, than a man, devoid of a knowledge of what physical science has done in the last century, upon a criticism of life.

When a biologist meets with an anomaly, he instinctively turns to the study of development to clear it up. The rationale of contradictory opinions may with equal confidence be sought in history.

It is, happily, no new thing that Englishmen should employ their wealth in building and endowing institutions for educational purposes. But, five or six hundred years ago, deeds of foundation expressed or implied conditions as nearly as possible contrary to those which have been thought expedient by Sir Josiah Mason. That is to say, physical science was practically ignored, while a certain literary training was enjoined as a means to the acquirement of knowledge which was essentially theological.

The reason of this singular contradiction between the actions of men alike animated by a strong and disinterested desire to promote the welfare of their fellows, is easily discovered.

At that time, in fact, if anyone desired knowledge beyond such as could be obtained by his own observation, or by common conversation, his first necessity was to learn the Latin language, inasmuch as all the higher knowledge of the western world was contained in works written in that language. Hence, Latin grammar, with logic and rhetoric, studied through Latin, were the fundamentals of education. With respect to the substance of the knowledge imparted through this channel, the Jewish and Christian Scriptures, as interpreted and supplemented by the Romish Church, were held to contain a complete and infallibly true body of information.

Theological dicta were, to the thinkers of those days, that which the axioms and definitions of Euclid are to the geometers of these. The business of the philosophers of the Middle Ages was to deduce from the data furnished by the theologians, conclusions in accordance with ecclesiastical decrees. They were allowed the high privilege of showing, by logical process, how and why that which the Church said was true, must be true. And if their demonstrations fell short of or exceeded this limit, the Church was maternally ready to check their aberrations; if need were by the help of the secular arm.

Between the two, our ancestors were furnished with a compact and complete criticism of life. They were told how the world began and how it would end; they learned that all material existence was but a base and insignificant blot upon the fair face of the spiritual world, and that nature was, to all intents and purposes, the playground of the devil; they learned that the earth is the center of the visible universe, and that man is the cynosure of things terrestrial; and more

---

11 This, and not Arnold's definition above, is correct. To possess an ideal, one must "know the best that has been thought and said in the world," but culture has then to form the habit of comparison.

especially was it inculcated that the course of nature had no fixed order, but that it could be, and constantly was, altered by the agency of innumerable spiritual beings, good and bad, according as they were moved by the deeds and prayers of men. The sum and substance of the whole doctrine was to produce the conviction that the only thing really worth knowing in this world was how to secure that place in a better which, under certain conditions, the Church promised.

Our ancestors had a living belief in this theory of life, and acted upon it in their dealings with education, as in all other matters. Culture meant saintliness—after the fashion of the saints of those days; the education that led to it was, of necessity, theological; and the way to theology lay through Latin.

That the study of nature—further than was requisite for the satisfaction of everyday wants—should have any bearing on human life was far from the thoughts of men thus trained. Indeed, as nature had been cursed for man's sake, it was an obvious conclusion that those who meddled with nature were likely to come into pretty close contact with Satan. And, if any born scientific investigator followed his instincts, he might safely reckon upon earning the reputation, and probably upon suffering the fate, of a sorcerer.

Had the western world been left to itself in Chinese isolation, there is no saying how long this state of things might have endured. But, happily, it was not left to itself. Even earlier than the thirteenth century, the development of Moorish civilization in Spain and the great movement of the Crusades had introduced the leaven which, from that day to this, has never ceased to work. At first, through the intermediation of Arabic translations, afterwards by the study of the originals, the western nations of Europe became acquainted with the writings of the ancient philosophers and poets, and, in time, with the whole of the vast literature of antiquity.

Whatever there was of high intellectual aspiration or dominant capacity in Italy, France, Germany, and England, spent itself for centuries in taking possession of the rich inheritance left by the dead civilizations of Greece and Rome. Marvelously aided by the invention of printing, classical learning spread and flourished. Those who possessed it prided themselves on having attained the highest culture then within the reach of mankind.

And justly. For, saving Dante on his solitary pinnacle, there was no figure in modern literature at the time of the Renascence to compare with the men of antiquity; there was no art to compete with their sculpture; there was no physical science but that which Greece had created. Above all, there was no other example of perfect intellectual freedom—of the unhesitating acceptance of reason as the sole guide to truth and the supreme arbiter of conduct.

The new learning necessarily soon exerted a profound influence upon education. The language of the monks and schoolmen seemed little better than gibberish to scholars fresh from Virgil and Cicero, and the study of Latin was placed upon a new foundation. Moreover, Latin itself ceased to afford the sole key to knowledge. The student who sought the highest thought of antiquity, found only a second-hand reflection of it in Roman literature, and turned his face to the full light of the Greeks. And after a battle, not altogether dissimilar to that which is at present being fought over the teaching of physical science, the study of Greek was recognized as an essential element of all higher education.

Thus the Humanists, as they were called, won the day; and the great reform which they effected was of incalculable service to mankind. But the Nemesis of all reformers is finality; and the reformers of education, like those of religion, fell into the profound, however common, error of mistaking the beginning for the end of the work of reformation.

The representatives of the Humanists, in the nineteenth century, take their stand upon classical education as the sole avenue to culture, as firmly as if we were still in the age of Renascence. Yet, surely, the present intellectual relations of the modern and the ancient worlds are profoundly different from those which obtained three centuries ago. Leaving aside the existence of a great and characteristically modern literature, of modern painting, and, especially, of modern music, there is one feature of the present state of the civilized world which separates it more widely from the Renascence than the Renascence was separated from the Middle Ages.

This distinctive character of our own times lies in the vast and constantly increasing part which is played by natural knowledge. Not only is our daily life shaped by it, not only does the prosperity of millions of men depend upon it, but our whole theory of life has long been influenced, consciously or unconsciously, by the general conceptions of the universe which have been forced upon us by physical science.

In fact, the most elementary acquaintance with the results of scientific investigation shows us that they offer a broad and striking contradiction to the opinion so implicitly credited and taught in the Middle Ages.

The notions of the beginning and the end of the world entertained by our forefathers are no longer credible. It is very certain that the earth is not the chief body in the material universe, and that the world is not subordinated to man's use. It is even more certain that nature is the expression of a definite order with which nothing interferes, and that the chief business of mankind is to learn that order and govern themselves accordingly. Moreover this scientific "criticism of life" presents itself to us with different credentials from any other. It appeals not to authority, nor to what anybody may have thought or said, but to nature. It admits that all our interpretations of natural fact are more or less imperfect and symbolic, and bids the learner seek for truth not among words but among things. It warns us that the assertion which outstrips evidence is not only a blunder but a crime.

The purely classical education advocated by the representatives of the Humanists in our day, gives no inkling of all this. A man may be a better scholar than Erasmus,[12] and know no more of the chief causes of the present intellectual fermentation than Erasmus did. Scholarly and pious persons, worthy of all respect, favor us with allocutions upon the sadness of the antagonism of science to their medieval way of thinking, which betray an ignorance of the first principles of scientific investigation, an incapacity for understanding what a man of science means by veracity, and an unconsciousness of the weight of established scientific truths, which is almost comical.

There is no great force in the *tu quoque*[13] argument, or else the advocates of scientific edu-

cation might fairly enough retort upon the modern Humanists that they may be learned specialists, but that they possess no such sound foundation for a criticism of life as deserves the name of culture. And, indeed, if we were disposed to be cruel, we might urge that the Humanists have brought this reproach upon themselves, not because they are too full of the spirit of the ancient Greek, but because they lack it.

The period of the Renascence is commonly called that of the "Revival of Letters," as if the influences then brought to bear upon the mind of Western Europe have been wholly exhausted in the field of literature. I think it is very commonly forgotten that the revival of science, effected by the same agency, although less conspicuous, was not less momentous.

In fact, the few and scattered students of nature of that day picked up the clue to her secrets exactly as it fell from the hands of the Greeks a thousand years before. The foundations of mathematics were so well laid by them, that our children learn their geometry from a book written for the schools of Alexandria two thousand years ago.[14] Modern astronomy is the natural continuation and development of the work of Hipparchus and of Ptolemy; modern physics of that of Democritus and of Archimedes; it was long before modern biological science outgrew the knowledge bequeathed to us by Aristotle, by Theophrastus, and by Galen.

We cannot know all the best thoughts and sayings of the Greeks unless we know what they thought about natural phenomena. We cannot fully apprehend their criticism of life unless we understand the extent to which that criticism was affected by scientific conceptions. We falsely pretend to be the inheritors of their culture, unless we are penetrated, as the best minds among them were, with an unhesitating faith that the free employment of reason, in accordance with scientific method, is the sole method of reaching truth.

Thus I venture to think that the pretensions of our modern Humanists to the possession of the monopoly of culture and to the exclusive inheritance of the spirit of antiquity must be abated, if not abandoned. But I should be very sorry that anything I have said should be taken

---

12 The Dutch classical scholar (1466–1536) was reputed to be the most learned man of his time.
13 "You, too." If it's true of me, it's just as true of you.

14 By Euclid.

to imply a desire on my part to depreciate the value of classical education, as it might be and as it sometimes is. The native capacities of mankind vary no less than their opportunities; and while culture is one, the road by which one man may best reach it is widely different from that which is most advantageous to another. Again, while scientific education is yet inchoate and tentative, classical education is thoroughly well organized upon the practical experience of generations of teachers. So that, given ample time for learning and estimation for ordinary life, or for a literary career, I do not think that a young Englishman in search of culture can do better than follow the course usually marked out for him, supplementing its deficiencies by his own efforts.

But for those who mean to make science their serious occupation; or who intend to follow the profession of medicine; or who have to enter early upon the business of life; for all these, in my opinion, classical education is a mistake; and it is for this reason that I am glad to see "mere literary education and instruction" shut out from the curriculum of Sir Josiah Mason's College, seeing that its inclusion would probably lead to the introduction of the ordinary smattering of Latin and Greek.

Nevertheless, I am the last person to question the importance of genuine literary education, or to suppose that intellectual culture can be complete without it. An exclusively scientific training will bring about a mental twist as surely as an exclusively literary training. The value of the cargo does not compensate for a ship's being out of trim; and I should be very sorry to think that the Scientific College would turn out none but lopsided men.

There is no need, however, that such a catastrophe should happen. Instruction in English, French, and German is provided, and thus the three greatest literatures of the modern world are made accessible to the student.

English and German, and especially the latter language, are absolutely indispensable to those who desire full knowledge in any department of science. But even supposing that the knowledge of these languages acquired is not more than sufficient for purely scientific purposes, every Englishman has, in his native tongue, an almost perfect instrument of literary expression; and, in his own literature, models of every kind

of literary excellence. If an Englishman cannot get literary culture out of his Bible, his Shakespeare, his Milton, neither, in my belief, will the profoundest study of Homer and Sophocles, Virgil and Horace, give it to him.

Thus, since the constitution of the college makes sufficient provision for literary as well as for scientific education, and since artistic instruction is also contemplated, it seems to me that a fairly complete culture is offered to all who are willing to take advantage of it.

But I am not sure that at this point the "practical" man, scotched[15] but not slain, may ask what all this talk about culture has to do with an institution, the object of which is defined to be "to promote the prosperity of the manufactures and the industry of the country." He may suggest that what is wanted for this end is not culture, nor even a purely scientific discipline, but simply a knowledge of applied science.

I often wish that this phrase, "applied science," had never been invented. For it suggests that there is a sort of scientific knowledge of direct practical use, which can be studied apart from another sort of scientific knowledge, which is of no practical utility, and which is termed "pure science." But there is no more complete fallacy than this. What people call applied science is nothing but the application of pure science to particular classes of problems. It consists of deductions from those general principles, established by reasoning and observation, which constitute pure science. No one can safely make these deductions until he has a firm grasp of the principles; and he can obtain that grasp only by personal experience of the operations of observation and of reasoning on which they are founded.

Almost all the processes employed in the arts and manufactures fall within the range either of physics or of chemistry. In order to improve them, one must thoroughly understand them; and no one has a chance of really understanding them, unless he has obtained that mastery of principles and that habit of dealing with facts, which is given by long-continued and well-directed purely scientific training in the physical and the chemical laboratory. So that there really is no question as to the necessity of purely scientific discipline, even if the work of

15 Gashed. Cf. *Macbeth,* III, ii. 13.

the college were limited by the narrowest interpretation of its stated aims.

And, as to the desirableness of a wider culture than that yielded by science alone, it is to be recollected that the improvement of manufacturing processes is only one of the conditions which contribute to the prosperity of industry. Industry is a means and not an end; and mankind work only to get something which they want. What that something is depends partly on their innate, and partly on their acquired, desires.

If the wealth resulting from prosperous industry is to be spent upon the gratification of unworthy desires, if the increasing perfection of manufacturing processes is to be accompanied by an increasing debasement of those who carry them on, I do not see the good of industry and prosperity.

Now it is perfectly true that men's views of what is desirable depend upon their characters; and that the innate proclivities to which we give that name are not touched by any amount of instruction. But it does not follow that even mere intellectual education may not, to an indefinite extent, modify the practical manifestation of the characters of men in their actions, by supplying them with motives unknown to the ignorant. A pleasure-loving character will have pleasure of some sort; but, if you give him the choice, he may prefer pleasures which do not degrade him to those which do. And this choice is offered to every man, who possesses in literary or artistic culture a never-failing source of pleasures, which are neither withered by age, nor staled by custom, nor embittered in the recollection by the pangs of self-reproach.

If the institution opened today fulfills the intention of its founder, the picked intelligences among all classes of the population of this district will pass through it. No child born in Birmingham, henceforward, if he have the capacity to profit by the opportunities offered to him, first in the primary and other schools, and afterwards in the Scientific College, need fail to obtain, not merely the instruction, but the culture most appropriate to the conditions of his life.

Within these walls, the future employer and the future artisan may sojourn together for a while, and carry, through all their lives, the stamp of the influences then brought to bear upon them. Hence, it is not beside the mark to remind you, that the prosperity of industry depends not merely upon the improvement of manufacturing processes, not merely upon the ennobling of the individual character, but upon a third condition, namely, a clear understanding of the conditions of social life, on the part of both the capitalist and the operative, and their agreement upon common principles of social action. They must learn that social phenomena are as much the expression of natural laws as any others; that no social arrangements can be permanent unless they harmonize with the requirements of social statics and dynamics;[16] and that, in the nature of things, there is an arbiter whose decisions execute themselves.

But this knowledge is only to be obtained by the application of the methods of investigation adopted in physical researches to the investigation of the phenomena of society. Hence, I confess, I should like to see one addition made to the excellent scheme of education propounded for the college, in the shape of provision for the teaching of sociology. For though we are all agreed that party politics are to have no place in the instruction of the college; yet in this country, practically governed as it is now by universal suffrage, every man who does his duty must exercise political functions. And, if the evils which are inseparable from the good of political liberty are to be checked, if the perpetual oscillation of nations between anarchy and despotism is to be replaced by the steady march of self-restraining freedom; it will be because men will gradually bring themselves to deal with political, as they now deal with scientific questions; to be as ashamed of undue haste and partisan prejudice in the one case as in the other; and to believe that the machinery of society is at least as delicate as that of a spinning-jenny, and as little likely to be improved by the meddling of those who have not taken the trouble to master the principles of its action.

In conclusion, I am sure that I make myself the mouthpiece of all present in offering to the venerable founder of the institution, which now commences its beneficent career, our congratula-

[16] The laws of society, as they affect either its successive states or its development from one state to the next.

tions on the completion of his work; and in expressing the conviction, that the remotest posterity will point to it as a crucial instance of the wisdom which natural piety leads all men to ascribe to their ancestors.

from Darwiniana[1]

from THE ORIGIN OF SPECIES

Mr. Darwin's long-standing and well-earned scientific eminence probably renders him indifferent to that social notoriety which passes by the name of success; but if the calm spirit of the philosopher have not yet wholly superseded the ambition and the vanity of the carnal man within him, he must be well satisfied with the results of his venture in publishing the "Origin of Species." Overflowing the narrow bounds of purely scientific circles, the "species question" divides with Italy and the Volunteers the attention of general society.[2] Everybody has read Mr. Darwin's book, or, at least, has given an opinion upon its merits or demerits; pietists, whether lay or ecclesiastic, decry it with the mild railing which sounds so charitable; bigots denounce it with ignorant invective; old ladies of both sexes consider it a decidedly dangerous book; and even savants, who have no better mud to throw, quote antiquated writers to show that its author is no better than an ape himself; while every philosophical thinker hails it as a veritable Whitworth gun[3] in the armoury of liberalism; and all competent naturalists and physiologists, whatever their opinions as to the ultimate fate of the doctrines put forth, acknowledge that the work in which they are embodied is a solid contribution to knowledge and inaugurates a new epoch in natural history.

Nor has the discussion of the subject been restrained within the limits of conversation.

When the public is eager and interested, reviewers must minister to its wants; and the genuine *littérateur*[4] is too much in the habit of acquiring his knowledge from the book he judges —as the Abyssinian is said to provide himself with steaks from the ox which carries him—to be withheld from criticism of a profound scientific work by the mere want of the requisite preliminary scientific acquirement; while, on the other hand, the men of science who wish well to the new views, no less than those who dispute their validity, have naturally sought opportunities of expressing their opinions. Hence it is not surprising that almost all the critical journals have noticed Mr. Darwin's work at greater or less length; and so many disquisitions, of every degree of excellence, from the poor product of ignorance, too often stimulated by prejudice, to the fair and thoughtful essay of the candid student of Nature, have appeared, that it seems an almost hopeless task to attempt to say anything new upon the question.

But it may be doubted if the knowledge and acumen of prejudged scientific opponents, and the subtlety of orthodox special pleaders, have yet exerted their full force in mystifying the real issues of the great controversy which has been set afoot, and whose end is hardly likely to be seen by this generation; so that, at this eleventh hour, and even failing anything new, it may be useful to state afresh that which is true, and to put the fundamental positions advocated by Mr. Darwin in such a form that they may be grasped by those whose special studies lie in other directions. And the adoption of this course may be the more advisable, because, notwithstanding its great deserts, and indeed partly on account of them, the "Origin of Species" is by no means an easy book to read—if by reading is implied the full comprehension of an author's meaning. . . .

Thus while it may be doubted if, for some years, any one is likely to be competent to pronounce judgment on all the issues raised by Mr. Darwin, there is assuredly abundant room for him, who, assuming the humbler, though perhaps as useful, office of an interpreter between the "Origin of Species" and the public, contents himself with endeavouring to point out the nature of the problems which it discusses; to dis-

---

[1] In *Darwiniana* (1893) Huxley collected his most important essays and lectures on evolution. The present essay was a review (1860) of Darwin's *The Origin of Species by Means of Natural Selection, or The Preservation of Favored Races in the Struggle for Life* (1859).
[2] 1859–61 were the years of Garibaldi's attempt to drive the Austrians out of Italy. The events were followed with great interest in England. In 1859, fear of the ambitions of Napoleon III resulted in the formation of a Volunteer Corps.
[3] A gun with the latest improvements.

[4] Professional man of letters.

tinguish between the ascertained facts and the theoretical views which it contains; and finally, to show the extent to which the explanation it offers satisfies the requirements of scientific logic. At any rate, it is this office which we purpose to undertake in the following pages.

It may be safely assumed that our readers have a general conception of the nature of the objects to which the word "species" is applied; but it has, perhaps, occurred to a few, even to those who are naturalists *ex professo*,[5] to reflect, that, as commonly employed, the term has a double sense and denotes two very different orders of relations. When we call a group of animals, or of plants, a species, we may imply thereby, either that all these animals or plants have some common peculiarity of form or structure; or, we may mean that they possess some common functional character. That part of biological science which deals with form and structure is called Morphology—that which concerns itself with function, Physiology—so that we may conveniently speak of these two senses, or aspects, of "species"—the one as morphological, the other as physiological. Regarded from the former point of view, a species is nothing more than a kind of animal or plant, which is distinctly definable from all others, by certain constant, and not merely sexual, morphological peculiarities. Thus horses form a species, because the group of animals to which that name is applied is distinguished from all others in the world by the following constantly associated characters. They have—1, A vertebral column; 2, Mammae; 3, A placental embryo; 4, Four legs; 5, A single well-developed toe in each foot provided with a hoof; 6, A bushy tail; and 7, Callosities on the inner sides of both the fore and the hind legs. The asses, again, form a distinct species, because, with the same characters, as far as the fifth in the above list, all asses have tufted tails, and have callosities only on the inner side of the forelegs. If animals were discovered having the general characters of the horse, but sometimes with callosities only on the fore-legs, and more or less tufted tails; or animals having the general characters of the ass, but with more or less bushy tails, and sometimes with callosities on both pairs of legs, besides being intermediate in other re-

spects—the two species would have to be merged into one. They could no longer be regarded as morphologically distinct species, for they would not be distinctly definable one from the other. . . .

The student of Nature wonders the more and is astonished the less, the more conversant he becomes with her operations; but of all the perennial miracles she offers to his inspection, perhaps the most worthy of admiration is the development of a plant or of an animal from its embryo. Examine the recently laid egg of some common animal, such as a salamander or newt. It is a minute spheroid in which the best microscope will reveal nothing but a structureless sac, enclosing a glairy[6] fluid, holding granules in suspension. But strange possibilities lie dormant in that semi-fluid globule. Let a moderate supply of warmth reach its watery cradle, and the plastic matter undergoes changes so rapid, yet so steady and purposelike in their succession, that one can only compare them to those operated by a skilled modeller upon a formless lump of clay. As with an invisible trowel, the mass is divided and subdivided into smaller and smaller portions, until it is reduced to an aggregation of granules not too large to build withal the finest fabrics of the nascent organism. And, then, it is as if a delicate finger traced out the line to be occupied by the spinal column, and moulded the contour of the body; pinching up the head at one end, the tail at the other, and fashioning flank and limb into due salamandrine proportions, in so artistic a way, that, after watching the process hour by hour, one is almost involuntarily possessed by the notion, that some more subtle aid to vision than an achromatic,[7] would show the hidden artist, with his plan before him, striving with skilful manipulation to perfect his work.

As life advances, and the young amphibian ranges the waters, the terror of his insect contemporaries, not only are the nutritious particles supplied by its prey, by the addition of which to its frame, growth takes place, laid down, each in its proper spot, and in such due proportion to the rest, as to reproduce the form, the colour, and the size, characteristic of the parental stock; but even the wonderful powers of reproducing lost

---

[5] By profession.

[6] Resembling white of egg.

[7] Special type of microscope.

parts possessed by these animals are controlled by the same governing tendency. Cut off the legs, the tail, the jaws, separately or all together, and, as Spallanzani showed long ago, these parts not only grow again, but the redintegrated limb is formed on the same type as those which were lost. The new jaw, or leg, is a newt's, and never by any accident more like that of a frog. What is true of the newt is true of every animal and of every plant; the acorn tends to build itself up again into a woodland giant such as that from whose twig it fell; the spore of the humblest lichen reproduces the green or brown incrustation which gave it birth; and at the other end of the scale of life, the child that resembled neither the paternal nor the maternal side of the house would be regarded as a kind of monster.

So that the one end to which, in all living beings, the formative impulse is tending—the one scheme which the Archaeus[8] of the old speculators strives to carry out, seems to be to mould the offspring into the likeness of the parent. It is the first great law of reproduction, that the offspring tends to resemble its parent or parents, more closely than anything else.

Science will some day show us how this law is a necessary consequence of the more general laws which govern matter; but, for the present, more can hardly be said than that it appears to be in harmony with them. We know that the phaenomena of vitality are not something apart from other physical phaenomena, but one with them; and matter and force are the two names of the one artist who fashions the living as well as the lifeless. Hence living bodies should obey the same great laws as other matter —nor, throughout Nature, is there a law of wider application than this, that a body impelled by two forces takes the direction of their resultant. But living bodies may be regarded as nothing but extremely complex bundles of forces held in a mass of matter, as the complex forces of a magnet are held in the steel by its coercive force; and, since the differences of sex are comparatively slight, or, in other words, the sum of the forces in each has a very similar tendency, their resultant, the offspring, may reasonably be expected to deviate but little from a course parallel to either, or to both.

Represent the reason of the law to ourselves by what physical metaphor or analogy we will, however, the great matter is to apprehend its existence and the importance of the consequences deducible from it. For things which are like to the same are like to one another; and if, in a great series of generations, every offspring is like its parent, it follows that all the offspring and all the parents must be like one another; and that, given an original parental stock, with the opportunity of undisturbed multiplication, the law in question necessitates the production, in course of time, of an indefinitely large group, the whole of the members of which are at once very similar and are blood relations, having descended from the same parent, or pair of parents. The proof that all the members of any given group of animals, or plants, had thus descended, would be ordinarily considered sufficient to entitle them to the rank of physiological species, for most physiologists consider species to be definable as "the offspring of a single primitive stock."

But though it is quite true that all those groups we call species *may*, according to the known laws of reproduction, have descended from a single stock, and though it is very likely they really have done so, yet this conclusion rests on deduction and can hardly hope to establish itself upon a basis of observation. And the primitiveness of the supposed single stock, which, after all, is the essential part of the matter, is not only a hypothesis, but one which has not a shadow of foundation, if by "primitive" be meant "independent of any other living being." A scientific definition, of which an unwarrantable hypothesis forms an essential part, carries its condemnation within itself; but, even supposing such a definition were, in form, tenable, the physiologist who should attempt to apply it in Nature would soon find himself involved in great, if not inextricable, difficulties. As we have said, it is indubitable that offspring *tend* to resemble the parental organism, but it is equally true that the similarity attained never amounts to identity either in form or in structure. There is always a certain amount of deviation, not only from the precise characters of a single parent, but when, as in most animals and many plants, the sexes are lodged in distinct individuals, from an exact mean between the two parents. And indeed, on general principles, this slight deviation seems as intelligible as the general similarity, if we reflect how complex the

---

[8] A kind of indwelling spirit posited by early medical research.

co-operating "bundles of forces" are, and how improbable it is that, in any case, their true resultant shall coincide with any mean between the more obvious characters of the two parents. Whatever be its cause, however, the co-existence of this tendency to minor variation with the tendency to general similarity, is of vast importance in its bearing on the question of the origin of species.

As a general rule, the extent to which an offspring differs from its parent is slight enough; but, occasionally, the amount of difference is much more strongly marked, and then the divergent offspring receives the name of a Variety. Multitudes, of what there is every reason to believe are such varieties, are known, but the origin of very few has been accurately recorded, and of these we will select two as more especially illustrative of the main features of variation. The first of them is that of the "Ancon" or "Otter" sheep, of which a careful account is given by Colonel David Humphreys, F.R.S., in a letter to Sir Joseph Banks, published in the "Philosophical Transactions" for 1813. It appears that one Seth Wright, the proprietor of a farm on the banks of the Charles River, in Massachusetts, possessed a flock of fifteen ewes and a ram of the ordinary kind. In the year 1791, one of the ewes presented her owner with a male lamb, differing, for no assignable reason, from its parents by a proportionally long body and short bandy legs, whence it was unable to emulate its relatives in those sportive leaps over the neighbours' fences, in which they were in the habit of indulging, much to the good farmer's vexation.

The second case is that detailed by a no less unexceptionable authority than Réaumur, in his "Art de faire éclore les Poulets."[9] A Maltese couple, named Kelleia, whose hands and feet were constructed upon the ordinary human model, had born to them a son, Gratio, who possessed six perfectly movable fingers on each hand, and six toes, not quite so well formed, on each foot. No cause could be assigned for the appearance of this unusual variety of the human species.

Two circumstances are well worthy of remark in both these cases. In each, the variety appears to have arisen in full force, and, as it

were, per saltum;[10] a wide and definite difference appearing, at once, between the Ancon ram and the ordinary sheep; between the six-fingered and six-toed Gratio Kelleia and ordinary men. In neither case is it possible to point out any obvious reason for the appearance of the variety. Doubtless there were determining causes for these as for all other phaenomena; but they do not appear, and we can be tolerably certain that what are ordinarily understood as changes in physical conditions, as in climate, in food, or the like, did not take place and had nothing to do with the matter. It was no case of what is commonly called adaptation to circumstances; but, to use a conveniently erroneous phrase, the variations arose spontaneously. The fruitless search after final causes leads their pursuers a long way; but even those hardy teleologists, who are ready to break through all the laws of physics in chase of their favourite will-o'-the-wisp, may be puzzled to discover what purpose could be attained by the stunted legs of Seth Wright's ram or the hexadactyle members of Gratio Kelleia.

Varieties then arise we know not why; and it is more than probable that the majority of varieties have arisen in this "spontaneous" manner, though we are, of course, far from denying that they may be traced, in some cases, to distinct external influences; which are assuredly competent to alter the character of the tegumentary covering, to change colour, to increase or diminish the size of muscles, to modify constitution, and, among plants, to give rise to the metamorphosis of stamens into petals, and so forth. But however they may have arisen, what especially interests us at present is, to remark that, once in existence, many varieties obey the fundamental law of reproduction that like tends to produce like; and their offspring exemplify it by tending to exhibit the same deviation from the parental stock as themselves. Indeed, there seems to be, in many instances, a prepotent influence about a newly-arisen variety which gives it what one may call an unfair advantage over the normal descendants from the same stock. This is strikingly exemplified by the case of Gratio Kelleia, who married a woman with the ordinary pentadactyle extremities, and had by her four children, Salvator, George, André, and Marie. Of these children Salvator, the eldest boy, had six fingers

9 "How to Hatch Chickens." Réaumur (1683–1757) was a French scientist and inventor.

10 Literally, at a leap; all at once.

and six toes, like his father; the second and third, also boys, had five fingers and five toes, like their mother, though the hands and feet of George were slightly deformed. The last, a girl, had five fingers and five toes, but the thumbs were slightly deformed. The variety thus reproduced itself purely in the eldest, while the normal type reproduced itself purely in the third, and almost purely in the second and last: so that it would seem, at first, as if the normal type were more powerful than the variety. But all these children grew up and intermarried with normal wives and husband, and then, note what took place: Salvator had four children, three of whom exhibited the hexadactyle members of their grandfather and father, while the youngest had the pentadactyle limbs of the mother and grandmother; so that here, notwithstanding a double pentadactyle dilution of the blood, the hexadactyle variety had the best of it. The same prepotency of the variety was still more markedly exemplified in the progeny of two of the other children, Marie and George. Marie (whose thumbs only were deformed) gave birth to a boy with six toes, and three other normally formed children; but George, who was not quite so pure a pentadactyle, begot, first, two girls, each of whom had six fingers and toes; then a girl with six fingers on each hand and six toes on the right foot, but only five toes on the left; and lastly, a boy with only five fingers and toes. In these instances, therefore, the variety, as it were, leaped over one generation to reproduce itself in full force in the next. Finally, the purely pentadactyle André was the father of many children, not one of whom departed from the normal parental type.

If a variation which approaches the nature of a monstrosity can strive thus forcibly to reproduce itself, it is not wonderful that less aberrant modifications should tend to be preserved even more strongly; and the history of the Ancon sheep is, in this respect, particularly instructive. With the "'cuteness" characteristic of their nation, the neighbours of the Massachusetts farmer imagined it would be an excellent thing if all his sheep were imbued with the stay-at-home tendencies enforced by Nature upon the newly-arrived ram; and they advised Wright to kill the old patriarch of his fold, and install the Ancon ram in his place. The result justified their

sagacious anticipations, and coincided very nearly with what occurred to the progeny of Gratio Kelleia. The young lambs were almost always either pure Ancons, or pure ordinary sheep. But when sufficient Ancon sheep were obtained to interbreed with one another, it was found that the offspring was always pure Ancon. Colonel Humphreys, in fact, states that he was acquainted with only "one questionable case of a contrary nature." Here, then, is a remarkable and well-established instance, not only of a very distinct race being established *per saltum,* but of that race breeding "true" at once, and showing no mixed forms, even when crossed with another breed.

By taking care to select Ancons of both sexes, for breeding from, it thus became easy to establish an extremely well-marked race; so peculiar that, even when herded with other sheep, it was noted that the Ancons kept together. And there is every reason to believe that the existence of this breed might have been indefinitely protracted; but the introduction of the Merino sheep, which were not only very superior to the Ancons in wool and meat, but quite as quiet and orderly, led to the complete neglect of the new breed, so that, in 1813, Colonel Humphreys found it difficult to obtain the specimen, the skeleton of which was presented to Sir Joseph Banks. We believe that, for many years, no remnant of it has existed in the United States.

Gratio Kelleia was not the progenitor of a race of six-fingered men, as Seth Wright's ram became a nation of Ancon sheep, though the tendency of the variety to perpetuate itself appears to have been fully as strong in the one case as in the other. And the reason of the difference is not far to seek. Seth Wright took care not to weaken the Ancon blood by matching his Ancon ewes with any but males of the same variety, while Gratio Kelleia's sons were too far removed from the patriarchal times to intermarry with their sisters; and his grand-children seem not to have been attracted by their six-fingered cousins. In other words, in the one example a race was produced, because, for several generations, care was taken to *select* both parents of the breeding stock from animals exhibiting a tendency to vary in the same direction; while, in the other, no race was evolved, because no such selection was exercised. A race is a propagated variety; and as, by the laws of reproduction, offspring tend to assume the parental forms, they will be more likely to propagate a variation exhibited by both parents than that possessed by only one.

There is no organ of the body of an animal which may not, and does not, occasionally, vary more or less from the normal type; and there is no variation which may not be transmitted and which, if selectively transmitted, may not become the foundation of a race. This great truth, sometimes forgotten by philosophers, has long been familiar to practical agriculturists and breeders; and upon it rest all the methods of improving the breeds of domestic animals, which, for the last century, have been followed with so much success in England. Colour, form, size, texture of hair or wool, proportions of various parts, strength or weakness of constitution, tendency to fatten or to remain lean, to give much or little milk, speed, strength, temper, intelligence, special instincts; there is not one of these characters the transmission of which is not an every-day occurrence within the experience of cattle-breeders, stock-farmers, horse-dealers, and dog and poultry fanciers. Nay, it is only the other day that an eminent physiologist, Dr. Brown-Séquard, communicated to the Royal Society his discovery that epilepsy, artificially produced in guinea-pigs, by a means which he has discovered, is transmitted to their offspring.

But a race, once produced, is no more a fixed and immutable entity than the stock whence it sprang; variations arise among its members, and as these variations are transmitted like any others, new races may be developed out of the pre-existing one *ad infinitum,* or, at least, within any limit at present determined. Given sufficient time and sufficiently careful selection, and the multitude of races which may arise from a common stock is as astonishing as are the extreme structural differences which they may present. A remarkable example of this is to be found in the rock-pigeon, which Mr. Darwin has, in our opinion, satisfactorily demonstrated to be the progenitor of all our domestic pigeons, of which there are certainly more than a hundred well-marked races. The most noteworthy of these races are, the four great stocks known to the "fancy" as tumblers, pouters, carriers, and fantails; birds which not only differ most singularly in size, colour, and habits, but in the form of the beak and of the skull; in the proportions of the beak to the skull; in the number of tail-feathers; in the absolute and relative size of the feet; in the presence or absence of the uropygial gland; in the number of vertebrae in the back; in short, in precisely those characters in which the genera and species of birds differ from one another.

And it is most remarkable and instructive to observe, that none of these races can be shown to have been originated by the action of changes in what are commonly called external circumstances, upon the wild rock-pigeon. On the contrary, from time immemorial pigeon-fanciers have had essentially similar methods of treating their pets, which have been housed, fed, protected and cared for in much the same way in all pigeonries. In fact, there is no case better adapted than that of the pigeons to refute the doctrine which one sees put forth on high authority, that "no other characters than those founded on the development of bone for the attachment of muscles" are capable of variation. In precise contradition of this hasty assertion, Mr. Darwin's researches prove that the skeleton of the wings in domestic pigeons has hardly varied at all from that of the wild type; while, on the other hand, it is in exactly those respects, such as the relative length of the beak and skull, the number of the vertebrae, and the number of the tail-feathers, in which muscular exertion can have no important influence, that the utmost amount of variation has taken place.

We have said that the following out of the properties exhibited by physiological species would lead us into difficulties, and at this point they begin to be obvious; for if, as the result of spontaneous variation and of selective breeding, the progeny of a common stock may become separated into groups distinguished from one another by constant, not sexual, morphological characters, it is clear that the physiological definition of species is likely to clash with the morphological definition. No one would hesitate to describe the pouter and the tumbler as distinct species, if they were found fossil, or if their skins and skeletons were imported, as those of exotic wild birds commonly are—and without doubt, if considered alone, they are good and distinct morphological species. On the other hand, they are not physiological species, for they are descended from a common stock, the rock-pigeon.

Under these circumstances, as it is admitted on all sides that races occur in Nature, how are we to know whether any apparently distinct animals are really of different physiological species, or not, seeing that the amount of morphological difference is no safe guide? Is there any test of a physiological species? The usual answer of physiologists is in the affirmative. It is said that such a test is to be found in the phaenomena of hybridisation—in the results of crossing races, as compared with the results of crossing species.

So far as the evidence goes at present, individuals, of what are certainly known to be mere races produced by selection, however distinct they may appear to be, not only breed freely together, but the offspring of such crossed races are perfectly fertile with one another. Thus, the spaniel and the greyhound, the dray-horse and the Arab, the pouter and the tumbler, breed together with perfect freedom, and their mongrels, if matched with other mongrels of the same kind, are equally fertile.

On the other hand, there can be no doubt that the individuals of many natural species are either absolutely infertile if crossed with individuals of other species, or, if they give rise to hybrid offspring, the hybrids so produced are infertile when paired together. The horse and the ass, for instance, if so crossed, give rise to the mule, and there is no certain evidence of offspring ever having been produced by a male and female mule. The unions of the rock-pigeon and the ring-pigeon appears to be equally barren of result. Here, then, says the physiologist, we have a means of distinguishing any two true species from any two varieties. If a male and a female, selected from each group, produce offspring, and that offspring is fertile with others produced in the same way, the groups are races and not species. If, on the other hand, no result ensues, or if the offspring are infertile with others produced in the same way, they are true physiological species. The test would be an admirable one, if, in the first place, it were always practicable to apply it, and if, in the second, it always yielded results susceptible of a definite interpretation. . . .

Up to this point, we have been dealing with matters of fact, and the statements which we have laid before the reader would, to the best of our knowledge, be admitted to contain a fair exposition of what is at present known respecting the essential properties of species, by all who have studied the question. And whatever may be his theoretical views, no naturalist will probably be disposed to demur to the following summary of that exposition:—

Living beings, whether animals or plants, are divisible into multitudes of distinctly definable kinds, which are morphological species. They are also divisible into groups of individuals, which breed freely together, tending to reproduce their like, and are physiological species. Normally resembling their parents, the offspring of members of these species are still liable to vary; and the variation may be perpetuated by selection, as a race, which race, in many cases, presents all the characteristics of a morphological species. But it is not as yet proved that a race ever exhibits, when crossed with another race of the same species, those phaenomena of hybridisation which are exhibited by many species when crossed with other species. On the other hand, not only is it not proved that all species give rise to hybrids infertile *inter se,* but there is much reason to believe that, in crossing, species exhibit every gradation from perfect sterility to perfect fertility.

Such are the most essential characteristics of species. Even were man not one of them—a member of the same system and subject to the same laws—the question of their origin, their causal connexion, that is, with the other phaenomena of the universe, must have attracted his attention, as soon as his intelligence had raised itself above the level of his daily wants.

Indeed history relates that such was the case, and has embalmed for us the speculations upon the origin of living beings, which were among the earliest products of the dawning intellectual activity of man. In those early days positive knowledge was not to be had, but the craving after it needed, at all hazards, to be satisfied, and according to the country, or the turn of thought, of the speculator, the suggestion that all living things arose from the mud of the Nile, from a primeval egg, or from some more anthropomorphic agency, afforded a sufficient resting-place for his curiosity. The myths of Paganism are as dead as Osiris or Zeus, and the man who should revive them, in opposition to the knowledge of our time, would be justly laughed to scorn; but the coeval imaginations current among the rude inhabitants of Palestine, recorded by writers whose very name and age are admitted by every scholar to be unknown, have unfortunately not yet shared their fate, but, even at this day, are regarded by nine-tenths of the civilised world as the authoritative standard of fact and the criterion of the justice of scientific conclusions, in all that relates to the origin of things, and, among them, of species. In this nineteenth century, as at the dawn of modern physical science, the cosmogony of the semi-barbarous Hebrew is the incubus of the philosopher and the opprobrium of the orthodox. Who shall number the patient and earnest seekers after truth, from the days of Galileo until now, whose lives have been embittered and their good name blasted by the mistaken zeal of Bibliolaters? Who shall count the host of weaker men whose sense of truth has been destroyed in the effort to harmonise impossibilities—whose life has been wasted in the attempt to force the generous new wine of Science into the old bottles of Judaism, compelled by the outcry of the same strong party?

It is true that if philosophers have suffered, their cause has been amply avenged. Extinguished theologians lie about the cradle of every science as the strangled snakes beside that of Hercules; and history records that whenever science and orthodoxy have been fairly opposed, the latter has been forced to retire from the lists, bleeding and crushed if not annihilated; scotched, if not slain. But orthodoxy is the Bourbon[11] of the world of thought. It learns not, neither can it forget; and though, at present, bewildered and afraid to move, it is as willing as ever to insist that the first chapter of Genesis contains the beginning and the end of sound science; and to visit, with such petty thunderbolts as its half-paralysed hands can hurl, those who refuse to degrade Nature to the level of primitive Judaism.

Philosophers, on the other hand, have no such aggressive tendencies. With eyes fixed on the noble goal to which "per aspera et ardua"[12]

they tend, they may, now and then, be stirred to momentary wrath by the unnecessary obstacles with which the ignorant, or the malicious, encumber, if they cannot bar, the difficult path; but why should their souls be deeply vexed? The majesty of Fact is on their side, and the elemental forces of Nature are working for them. Not a star comes to the meridian at its calculated time but testifies to the justice of their methods—their beliefs are "one with the falling rain and with the growing corn." By doubt[13] they are established, and open inquiry is their bosom friend. Such men have no fear of traditions however venerable, and no respect for them when they become mischievous and obstructive; but they have better than mere antiquarian business in hand, and if dogmas, which ought to be fossil but are not, are not forced upon their notice, they are too happy to treat them as non-existent.

The hypotheses respecting the origin of species which profess to stand upon a scientific basis, and, as such, alone demand serious attention, are of two kinds. The one, the "special creation" hypothesis, presumes every species to have originated from one or more stocks, these not being the result of the modification of any other form of living matter—or arising by natural agencies—but being produced, as such, by a supernatural creative act.

The other, the so-called "transmutation" hypothesis, considers that all existing species are the result of the modification of pre-existing species, and those of their predecessors, by agencies similar to those which at the present day produce varieties and races, and therefore in an altogether natural way; and it is a probable, though not a necessary consequence of this hypothesis, that all living beings have arisen from a single stock. With respect to the origin of this primitive stock, or stocks, the doctrine of the origin of species is obviously not necessarily concerned. The transmutation hypothesis, for example, is perfectly consistent either with the conception of a special creation of the primitive germ, or with the supposition of its having arisen, as a modification of inorganic matter, by natural causes.

The doctrine of special creation owes its

---

11 The Bourbons were the ruling family of France, whose inability to change with the times eventually cost them the throne.
12 Through bitterness and difficulty.

13 I.e., their role is to question.

existence very largely to the supposed necessity of making science accord with the Hebrew cosmogony; but it is curious to observe that, as the doctrine is at present maintained by men of science, it is as hopelessly inconsistent with the Hebrew view as any other hypothesis.

If there be any result which has come more clearly out of geological investigation than another, it is, that the vast series of extinct animals and plants is not divisible, as it was once supposed to be, into distinct groups, separated by sharply-marked boundaries. There are not great gulfs between epochs and formations—no successive periods marked by the appearance of plants, of water animals, and of land animals, *en masse*. Every year adds to the list of links between what the older geologists supposed to be widely separated epochs: witness the crags linking the drift with older tertiaries; the Maestricht beds linking the tertiaries with the chalk; the St. Cassian beds exhibiting an abundant fauna of mixed mesozoic and palaeozoic types, in rocks of an epoch once supposed to be eminently poor in life; witness, lastly, the incessant disputes as to whether a given stratum shall be reckoned devonian or carboniferous, silurian or devonian, cambrian or silurian.

This truth is further illustrated in a most interesting manner by the impartial and highly competent testimony of M. Pictet, from whose calculations of what percentage of the genera of animals, existing in any formation, lived during the preceding formation, it results that in no case is the proportion less than *one-third,* or 33 per cent. It is the triassic formation, or the commencement of the mesozoic epoch, which has received the smallest inheritance from preceding ages. The other formations not uncommonly exhibit 60, 80, or even 94 per cent. of genera in common with those whose remains are imbedded in their predecessor. Not only is this true, but the subdivisions of each formation exhibit new species characteristic of, and found only in, them; and, in many cases, as in the lias for example, the separate beds of these subdivisions are distinguished by well-marked and peculiar forms of life. A section, a hundred feet thick, will exhibit, at different heights, a dozen species of ammonite, none of which passes beyond its particular zone of limestone, or clay, into the zone below it or into that above it; so that those who adopt the

doctrine of special creation must be prepared to admit, that at intervals of time, corresponding with the thickness of these beds, the Creator thought fit to interfere with the natural course of events for the purpose of making a new ammonite. It is not easy to transplant oneself into the frame of mind of those who can accept such a conclusion as this, on any evidence short of absolute demonstration; and it is difficult to see what is to be gained by so doing, since, as we have said, it is obvious that such a view of the origin of living beings is utterly opposed to the Hebrew cosmogony. Deserving no aid from the powerful arm of Bibliolatry, then, does the received form of the hypothesis of special creation derive any support from science or sound logic? Assuredly not much. The arguments brought forward in its favour all take one form: If species were not supernaturally created, we cannot understand the facts x, or y, or z; we cannot understand the structure of animals or plants, unless we suppose they were contrived for special ends; we cannot understand the structure of the eye, except by supposing it to have been made to see with; we cannot understand instincts, unless we suppose animals to have been miraculously endowed with them.

As a question of dialectics, it must be admitted that this sort of reasoning is not very formidable to those who are not to be frightened by consequences. It is an *argumentum ad ignorantiam*—take this explanation or be ignorant. But suppose we prefer to admit our ignorance rather than adopt a hypothesis at variance with all the teachings of Nature? Or, suppose for a moment we admit the explanation, and then seriously ask ourselves how much the wiser are we; what does the explanation explain? Is it any more than a grandiloquent way of announcing the fact, that we really know nothing about the matter? A phaenomenon is explained when it is shown to be a case of some general law of Nature; but the supernatural interposition of the Creator can, by the nature of the case, exemplify no law, and if species have really arisen in this way, it is absurd to attempt to discuss their origin.

Or, lastly, let us ask ourselves whether any amount of evidence which the nature of our faculties permits us to attain, can justify us in asserting that any phaenomenon is out of the reach of natural causation. To this end it is obviously necessary that we should know all the consequences to which all possible combinations, continued through unlimited time, can give rise. If we knew these, and found none competent to originate species, we should have good ground for denying their origin by natural causation. Till we know them, any hypothesis is better than one which involves us in such miserable presumption.

But the hypothesis of special creation is not only a mere specious mask for our ignorance; its existence in Biology marks the youth and imperfection of the science. For what is the history of every science but the history of the elimination of the notion of creative, or other interferences, with the natural order of the phaenomena which are the subject-matter of that science? When Astronomy was young "the morning stars sang together for joy," and the planets were guided in their courses by celestial hands. Now, the harmony of the stars has resolved itself into gravitation according to the inverse squares of the distances, and the orbits of the planets are deducible from the laws of the forces which allow a schoolboy's stone to break a window. The lightning was the angel of the Lord; but it has pleased Providence, in these modern times, that science should make it the humble messenger of man, and we know that every flash that shimmers about the horizon on a summer's evening is determined by ascertainable conditions, and that its direction and brightness might, if our knowledge of these were great enough, have been calculated.

The solvency of great mercantile companies rests on the validity of the laws which have been ascertained to govern the seeming irregularity of that human life which the moralist bewails as the most uncertain of things; plague, pestilence, and famine are admitted, by all but fools, to be the natural result of causes for the most part fully within human control, and not the unavoidable tortures inflicted by wrathful Omnipotence upon His helpless handiwork.

Harmonious order governing eternally continuous progress—the web and woof of matter and force interweaving by slow degrees, without a broken thread, that veil which lies between us and the Infinite—that universe which alone we know or can know; such is the picture which science draws of the world, and in proportion as any part of that picture is in unison with the rest, so may we feel sure that it is rightly painted. Shall Biology alone remain out of harmony with her sister sciences?

Such arguments against the hypothesis of the direct creation of species as these are plainly enough deducible from general considerations; but there are, in addition, phaenomena exhibited by species themselves, and yet not so much a part of their very essence as to have required earlier mention, which are in the highest degree perplexing, if we adopt the popularly accepted hypothesis. Such are the facts of distribution in space and in time; the singular phaenomena brought to light by the study of development; the structural relations of species upon which our systems of classification are founded; the great doctrines of philosophical anatomy, such as that of homology, or of the community of structural plan exhibited by large groups of species differing very widely in their habits and functions.

The species of animals which inhabit the sea on opposite sides of the isthmus of Panama are wholly distinct;[14] the animals and plants which inhabit islands are commonly distinct from those of the neighbouring mainlands, and yet have a similarity of aspect. The mammals of the latest tertiary epoch in the Old and New Worlds belong to the same genera, or family groups, as those which now inhabit the same great geographical area. The crocodilian reptiles which existed in the earliest secondary epoch were similar in general structure to those now living, but exhibit slight differences in their vertebrae, nasal passages, and one or two other points. The guinea-pig has teeth which are shed before it is born, and hence can never subserve the masticatory purpose for which they seem contrived, and, in like manner, the female dugong has tusks which never cut the gum. All the members of the same great group run through similar conditions in their development, and all their parts, in the adult state, are arranged according to the same plan. Man is more like a gorilla than a gorilla is like a lemur. Such are a few, taken at random, among the multitudes of similar facts which modern research has established; but when the student seeks for an explanation of them from the supporters of the received hypothesis of the

14 "Recent investigations tend to show that this statement is not strictly accurate." (Huxley, 1870)

origin of species, the reply he receives is, in substance, of Oriental simplicity and brevity—"Mashallah! it so pleases God!" There are different species on opposite sides of the isthmus of Panama, because they were created different on the two sides. The pliocene mammals are like the existing ones, because such was the plan of creation; and we find rudimental organs and similarity of plan, because it has pleased the Creator to set before Himself a "divine exemplar or archetype," and to copy it in His works; and somewhat ill, those who hold this view imply, in some of them. That such verbal hocus-pocus should be received as science will one day be regarded as evidence of the low state of intelligence in the nineteenth century, just as we amuse ourselves with the phraseology about Nature's abhorrence of a vacuum; wherewith Torricelli's[15] compatriots were satisfied to explain the rise of water in a pump. And be it recollected that this sort of satisfaction works not only negative but positive ill, by discouraging inquiry, and so depriving man of the usufruct of one of the most fertile fields of his great patrimony, Nature.

The objections to the doctrine of the origin of species by special creation which have been detailed, must have occurred, with more or less force, to the mind of every one who has seriously and independently considered the subject. It is therefore no wonder that, from time to time, this hypothesis should have been met by counter hypotheses, all as well, and some better founded than itself; and it is curious to remark that the inventors of the opposing views seem to have been led into them as much by their knowledge of geology, as by their acquaintance with biology. In fact, when the mind has once admitted the conception of the gradual production of the present physical state of our globe, by natural causes operating through long ages of time, it will be little disposed to allow that living beings have made their appearance in another way....

Impelled towards the hypothesis of the transmutation of species, partly by his general cosmological and geological views; partly by the conception of a graduated, though irregularly branching, scale of being, which had arisen out of his profound study of plants and of the lower forms of animal life, Lamarck,[16] whose general line of thought often closely resembles that of De Maillet,[17] made a great advance upon the crude and merely speculative manner in which that writer deals with the question of the origin of living beings, by endeavouring to find physical causes competent to effect that change of one species into another, which De Maillet had only supposed to occur. And Lamarck conceived that he had found in Nature such causes, amply sufficient for the purpose in view. It is a physiological fact, he says, that organs are increased in size by action, atrophied by inaction; it is another physiological fact that modifications produced are transmissible to offspring. Change the actions of an animal, therefore, and you will change its structure, by increasing the development of the parts newly brought into use and by the diminution of those less used; but by altering the circumstances which surround it you will alter its actions, and hence, in the long run, change of circumstance must produce change of organisation. All the species of animals, therefore, are, in Lamarck's view, the result of the indirect action of changes of circumstance, upon those primitive germs which he considered to have originally arisen, by spontaneous generation, within the waters of the globe. It is curious, however, that Lamarck should insist so strongly as he has done, that circumstances never in any degree directly modify the form or the organisation of animals, but only operate by changing their wants and consequently their actions; for he thereby brings upon himself the obvious question, How, then, do plants, which cannot be said to have wants or actions, become modified? To this he replies, that they are modified by the changes in their nutritive processes, which are effected by changing circumstances; and it does not seem to have occurred to him that such changes might be as well supposed to take place among animals.

When we have said that Lamarck felt that mere speculation was not the way to arrive at the origin of species, but that it was necessary, in order to the establishment of any sound theory

15 Italian physicist (1608–1647) who discovered the principle of the barometer.

16 Jean Baptiste Lamarck (1774–1829), celebrated French naturalist, one of the founders of the doctrine of biological evolution.

17 Benoît de Maillet, French consul-general in Egypt, whose speculations on the origin of the earth and its inhabitants were published anonymously in 1748.

on the subject, to discover by observation or otherwise, some *vera causa*,[18] competent to give rise to them; that he affirmed the true order of classification to coincide with the order of their development one from another; that he insisted on the necessity of allowing sufficient time, very strongly; and that all the varieties of instinct and reason were traced back by him to the same cause as that which has given rise to species, we have enumerated his chief contributions to the advance of the question. On the other hand, from his ignorance of any power in Nature competent to modify the structure of animals, except the development of parts, or atrophy of them, in consequence of a change of needs, Lamarck was led to attach infinitely greater weight than it deserves to this agency, and the absurdities into which he was led have met with deserved condemnation. Of the struggle for existence, on which, as we shall see, Mr. Darwin lays such great stress, he had no conception; indeed, he doubts whether there really are such things as extinct species, unless they be such large animals as may have met their death at the hands of man; and so little does he dream of there being any other destructive causes at work, that, in discussing the possible existence of fossil shells, he asks, "Pourquoi d'ailleurs seroient-ils perdues dès que l'homme n'a pu opérer leur destruction?"[19] ("Phil. Zool.," vol. i. p. 77.) Of the influence of selection Lamarck has as little notion, and he makes no use of the wonderful phaenomena which are exhibited by domesticated animals, and illustrate its powers. The vast influence of Cuvier[20] was employed against the Lamarckian views, and, as the untenability of some of his conclusions was easily shown, his doctrines sank under the opprobrium of scientific, as well as of theological, heterodoxy. Nor have the efforts made of late years to revive them tended to re-establish their credit in the minds of sound thinkers acquainted with the facts of the case; indeed it may be doubted whether Lamarck has not suffered more from his friends than from his foes.

Two years ago, in fact, though we venture to question if even the strongest supporters of the special creation hypothesis had not, now and then, an uneasy consciousness that all was not right, their position seemed more impregnable than ever, if not by its own inherent strength, at any rate by the obvious failure of all the attempts which had been made to carry it. On the other hand, however much the few, who thought deeply on the question of species, might be repelled by the generally received dogmas, they saw no way of escaping from them save by the adoption of suppositions so little justified by experiment or by observation as to be at least equally distasteful.

The choice lay between two absurdities and a middle condition of uneasy scepticism; which last, however unpleasant and unsatisfactory, was obviously the only justifiable state of mind under the circumstances.

Such being the general ferment in the minds of naturalists, it is no wonder that they mustered strong in the rooms of the Linnaean Society,[21] on the 1st of July of the year 1858, to hear two papers by authors living on opposite sides of the globe, working out their results independently, and yet professing to have discovered one and the same solution of all the problems connected with species. The one of these authors was an able naturalist, Mr. Wallace,[22] who had been employed for some years in studying the productions of the islands of the Indian Archipelago, and who had forwarded a memoir embodying his views to Mr. Darwin, for communication to the Linnaean Society. On perusing the essay, Mr. Darwin was not a little surprised to find that it embodied some of the leading ideas of a great work which he had been preparing for twenty years, and parts of which, containing a development of the very same views, had been perused by his private friends fifteen or sixteen years before. Perplexed in what manner to do full justice both to his friend and to himself, Mr. Darwin placed the matter in the hands of Dr. Hooker and Sir Charles Lyell, by whose advice he communicated a brief abstract of his own views to the Linnaean Society, at the same time that Mr. Wallace's paper was read. Of that abstract, the work on the "Origin of Species" is an enlargement; but a complete statement of Mr. Darwin's

---

[18] True cause.
[19] "Besides, why should they have been lost since man could not have brought about their destruction?"
[20] Georges Cuvier (1769–1832), French naturalist, founder of the science of comparative anatomy.

[21] Society for the promotion of zoology and botany.
[22] Alfred Russell Wallace (1823–1913).

doctrine is looked for in the large and well-illustrated work which he is said to be preparing for publication.

The Darwinian hypothesis has the merit of being eminently simple and comprehensible in principle, and its essential positions may be stated in a very few words: all species have been produced by the development of varieties from common stocks; by the conversion of these, first into permanent races and then into new species, by the process of *natural selection,* which process is essentially identical with that artificial selection by which man has originated the races of domestic animals—the *struggle for existence* taking the place of man, and exerting, in the case of natural selection, that selective action which he performs in artificial selection.

The evidence brought forward by Mr. Darwin in support of his hypothesis is of three kinds. First, he endeavours to prove that species may be originated by selection; secondly, he attempts to show that natural causes are competent to exert selection; and thirdly, he tries to prove that the most remarkable and apparently anomalous phaenomena exhibited by the distribution, development, and mutual relations of species, can be shown to be deducible from the general doctrine of their origin, which he propounds, combined with the known facts of geological change; and that, even if all these phaenomena are not at present explicable by it, none are necessarily inconsistent with it.

There cannot be a doubt that the method of inquiry which Mr. Darwin has adopted is not only rigorously in accordance with the canons of scientific logic, but that it is the only adequate method. Critics exclusively trained in classics or in mathematics, who have never determined a scientific fact in their lives by induction from experiment or observation, prate learnedly about Mr. Darwin's method, which is not inductive enough, not Baconian enough, forsooth, for them. But even if practical acquaintance with the process of scientific investigation is denied them, they may learn, by the perusal of Mr. Mill's admirable chapter "On the Deductive Method,"[23] that there are multitudes of scientific inquiries in which the method of pure induction helps the investigator but a very little way.

"The mode of investigation," says Mr. Mill, "which, from the proved inapplicability of direct methods of observation and experiment, remains to us as the main source of the knowledge we possess, or can acquire, respecting the conditions and laws of recurrence of the more complex phaenomena, is called, in its most general expression, the deductive method, and consists of three operations: the first, one of direct induction; the second, of ratiocination; and the third, of verification."

Now, the conditions which have determined the existence of species are not only exceedingly complex, but, so far as the great majority of them are concerned, are necessarily beyond our cognisance. But what Mr. Darwin has attempted to do is in exact accordance with the rule laid down by Mr. Mill; he has endeavoured to determine certain great facts inductively, by observation and experiment; he has then reasoned from the data thus furnished; and lastly, he has tested the validity of his ratiocination by comparing his deductions with the observed facts of Nature. Inductively, Mr. Darwin endeavours to prove that species arise in a given way. Deductively, he desires to show that, if they arise in that way, the facts of distribution, development, classification, &c., may be accounted for, *i.e.* may be deduced from their mode of origin, combined with admitted changes in physical geography and climate, during an indefinite period. And this explanation, or coincidence of observed with deduced facts, is, so far as it extends, a verification of the Darwinian view.

There is no fault to be found with Mr. Darwin's method, then; but it is another question whether he has fulfilled all the conditions imposed by that method. Is it satisfactorily proved, in fact, that species may be originated by selection? that there is such a thing as natural selection? that none of the phaenomena exhibited by species are inconsistent with the origin of species in this way? If these questions can be answered in the affirmative, Mr. Darwin's view steps out of the rank of hypotheses into those of proved theories; but, so long as the evidence at present adduced falls short of enforcing that affirmation, so long, to our minds, must the new doctrine be content to remain among the former—an extremely valuable, and in the highest degree probable, doctrine, indeed the only extant hypothesis which is worth anything in a scientific

23 In John Stuart Mill's *System of Logic* (1843).

point of view; but still a hypothesis, and not yet the theory of species.

After much consideration, and with assuredly no bias against Mr. Darwin's views, it is our clear conviction that, as the evidence stands, it is not absolutely proven that a group of animals, having all the characters exhibited by species in Nature, has ever been originated by selection, whether artificial or natural. Groups having the morphological character of species—distinct and permanent races in fact—have been so produced over and over again; but there is no positive evidence, at present, that any group of animals has, by variation and selective breeding, given rise to another group which was, even in the least degree, infertile with the first. Mr. Darwin is perfectly aware of this weak point, and brings forward a multitude of ingenious and important arguments to diminish the force of the objection. We admit the value of these arguments to their fullest extent; nay, we will go so far as to express our belief that experiments, conducted by a skilful physiologist, would very probably obtain the desired production of mutually more or less infertile breeds from a common stock, in a comparatively few years; but still, as the case stands at present, this "little rift within the lute"[24] is not to be disguised nor overlooked.

In the remainder of Mr. Darwin's argument our own private ingenuity has not hitherto enabled us to pick holes of any great importance; and judging by what we hear and read, other adventurers in the same field do not seem to have been much more fortunate. It has been urged, for instance, that in his chapters on the struggle for existence and on natural selection, Mr. Darwin does not so much prove that natural selection does occur, as that it must occur; but, in fact, no other sort of demonstration is attainable. A race does not attract our attention in Nature until it has, in all probability, existed for a considerable time, and then it is too late to inquire into the conditions of its origin. Again, it is said that there is no real analogy between the selection which takes place under domestication, by human influence, and any operation which can be effected by Nature, for man interferes intelligently. Reduced to its elements, this argument implies that an effect produced with trouble by an intelligent agent must, *a fortiori*,[25] be more

troublesome, if not impossible, to an unintelligent agent. Even putting aside the question whether Nature, acting as she does according to definite and invariable laws, can be rightly called an unintelligent agent, such a position as this is wholly untenable. Mix salt and sand, and it shall puzzle the wisest of men, with his mere natural appliances, to separate all the grains of sand from all the grains of salt; but a shower of rain will effect the same object in ten minutes. And so, while man may find it tax all his intelligence to separate any variety which arises, and to breed selectively from it, the destructive agencies incessantly at work in Nature, if they find one variety to be more soluble in circumstances than the other, will inevitably, in the long run, eliminate it.

A frequent and a just objection to the Lamarckian hypothesis of the transmutation of species is based upon the absence of transitional forms between many species. But against the Darwinian hypothesis this argument has no force. Indeed, one of the most valuable and suggestive parts of Mr. Darwin's work is that in which he proves, that the frequent absence of transitions is a necessary consequence of his doctrine, and that the stock whence two or more species have sprung, need in no respect be intermediate between these species. If any two species have arisen from a common stock in the same way as the carrier and the pouter, say, have arisen from the rock-pigeon, then the common stock of these two species need be no more intermediate between the two than the rock-pigeon is between the carrier and pouter. Clearly appreciate the force of this analogy, and all the arguments against the origin of species by selection, based on the absence of transitional forms, fall to the ground. And Mr. Darwin's position might, we think, have been even stronger than it is if he had not embarrassed himself with the aphorism, *"Natura non facit saltum,"*[26] which turns up so often in his pages. We believe, as we have said above, that Nature does make jumps now and then, and a recognition of the fact is of no small importance in disposing of many minor objections to the doctrine of transmutation.

But we must pause. The discussion of Mr. Darwin's arguments in detail would lead us far beyond the limits within which we proposed, at

---

24 I.e., flaw in the argument.
25 With stronger reason.

26 Nature does not make jumps. See p. 669.

starting, to confine this article. Our object has been attained if we have given an intelligible, however brief, account of the established facts connected with species, and of the relation of the explanation of those facts offered by Mr. Darwin to the theoretical views held by his predecessors and his contemporaries, and, above all, to the requirements of scientific logic. We have ventured to point out that it does not, as yet, satisfy all those requirements; but we do not hesitate to assert that it is as superior to any preceding or contemporary hypothesis, in the extent of observational and experimental basis on which it rests, in its rigorously scientific method, and in its power of explaining biological phaenomena, as was the hypothesis of Copernicus to the speculations of Ptolemy.[27] But the planetary orbits turned out to be not quite circular after all, and, grand as was the service Copernicus rendered to science, Kepler and Newton had to come after him. What if the orbit of Darwinism should be a little too circular? What if species should offer residual phaenomena, here and there, not explicable by natural selection? Twenty years hence naturalists may be in a position to say whether this is, or is not, the case; but in either event they will owe the author of "The Origin of Species" an immense debt of gratitude. We should leave a very wrong impression on the reader's mind if we permitted him to suppose that the value of that work depends wholly on the ultimate justification of the theoretical views which it contains. On the contrary, if they were disproved tomorrow, the book would still be the best of its kind—the most compendious statement of well-sifted facts bearing on the doctrine of species that has ever appeared. The chapters on Variation, on the Struggle for Existence, on Instinct, on Hybridism, on the Imperfection of the Geological Record, on Geographical Distribution, have not only no equals, but, so far as our knowledge goes, no competitors, within the range of biological literature. And viewed as a whole, we do not believe that, since the publication of Von Baer's[28] "Researches on Development," thirty years ago, any work has appeared calculated to exert so large an influence, not only on the future of Biology, but in extending the domination of Science over regions of thought into which she has, as yet, hardly penetrated.

from Essays upon Some Controverted Questions[1]

PROLOGUE

Le plus grand service qu'on puisse rendre à la science est d'y faire place nette avant d'y rien construire.
—CUVIER.[2]

Most of the Essays comprised in the present volume have been written during the last six or seven years, without premeditated purpose or intentional connection, in reply to attacks upon doctrines which I hold to be well founded; or in refutation of allegations respecting matters lying within the province of natural knowledge, which I believe to be erroneous; and they bear the mark of their origin in the controversial tone which pervades them.

Of polemical writing, as of other kinds of warfare, I think it may be said, that it is often useful, sometimes necessary, and always more or less of an evil. It is useful, when it attracts attention to topics which might otherwise be neglected; and when, as does sometimes happen, those who come to see a contest remain to think. It is necessary, when the interests of truth and of justice are at stake. It is an evil, in so far as controversy always tends to degenerate into quarrelling, to swerve from the great issue of what is right and what is wrong to the very small question of who is right and who is wrong. I venture to hope that the useful and the necessary were more conspicuous than the evil attributes of literary militancy, when these papers were first published; but I have had some hesitation about reprinting them. If I may judge by my own taste, few literary dishes are less appetising than cold controversy; moreover, there is an air of unfairness about the

---

[27] A tremendous step forward was taken when Copernicus proved (1543) that Ptolemy was mistaken in thinking that the earth was the center of the universe.

[28] Karl Ernst von Baer (1792–1876), Estonian-born German naturalist and pioneer embryologist.

---

[1] This volume (1892) was later expanded into two books, *Science and Hebrew Tradition* and *Science and Christian Tradition*. The "Prologue" was then reprinted in the latter.

[2] "The greatest service one can render to knowledge is to clear the ground before starting to build anything." On Cuvier see note 20 of the preceding selection.

presentation of only one side of a discussion, and a flavour of unkindness in the reproduction of "winged words," which, however appropriate at the time of their utterance, would find a still more appropriate place in oblivion. Yet, since I could hardly ask those who have honoured me by their polemical attentions to confer lustre on this collection, by permitting me to present their lucubrations along with my own; and since it would be a manifest wrong to them to deprive their, by no means rare, vivacities of language of such justification as they may derive from similar freedoms on my part; I came to the conclusion that my best course was to leave the essays just as they were written; assuring my honourable adversaries that any heat of which signs may remain was generated, in accordance with the law of the conservation of energy, by the force of their own blows, and has long since been dissipated into space.

But, however the polemical concomitants of these discussions may be regarded—or better, disregarded—there is no doubt either about the importance of the topics of which they treat, or as to the public interest in the "Controverted Questions" with which they deal. Or rather, the Controverted Question; for disconnected as these pieces may, perhaps, appear to be, they are, in fact, concerned only with different aspects of a single problem, with which thinking men have been occupied, ever since they began seriously to consider the wonderful frame of things in which their lives are set, and to seek for trustworthy guidance among its intricacies.

Experience speedily taught them that the shifting scenes of the world's stage have a permanent background; that there is order amidst the seeming confusion, and that many events take place according to unchanging rules. To this region of familiar steadiness and customary regularity they gave the name of Nature. But, at the same time, their infantile and untutored reason, little more, as yet, than the playfellow of the imagination, led them to believe that this tangible, commonplace, orderly world of Nature was surrounded and interpenetrated by another intangible and mysterious world, no more bound by fixed rules than, as they fancied, were the thoughts and passions which coursed through their minds and seemed to exercise an intermittent and capricious rule over their bodies. They

attributed to the entities, with which they peopled this dim and dreadful region, an unlimited amount of that power of modifying the course of events of which they themselves possessed a small share, and thus came to regard them as not merely beyond, but above, Nature.

Hence arose the conception of a "Supernature" antithetic to "Nature"—the primitive dualism of a natural world "fixed in fate" and a supernatural, left to the free play of volition—which has pervaded all later speculation and, for thousands of years, has exercised a profound influence on practice. For it is obvious that, on this theory of the Universe, the successful conduct of life must demand careful attention to both worlds; and, if either is to be neglected, it may be safer that it should be Nature. In any given contingency, it must doubtless be desirable to know what may be expected to happen in the ordinary course of things; but it must be quite as necessary to have some inkling of the line likely to be taken by supernatural agencies able, and possibly willing, to suspend or reverse that course. Indeed, logically developed, the dualistic theory must needs end in almost exclusive attention to Supernature, and in trust that its overruling strength will be exerted in favour of those who stand well with its denizens. On the other hand, the lessons of the great schoolmaster, experience, have hardly seemed to accord with this conclusion. They have taught, with considerable emphasis, that it does not answer to neglect Nature; and that, on the whole, the more attention paid to her dictates the better men fare.

Thus the theoretical antithesis brought about a practical antagonism. From the earliest times of which we have any knowledge, Naturalism and Supernaturalism have consciously, or unconsciously, competed and struggled with one another; and the varying fortunes of the contest are written in the records of the course of civilisation, from those of Egypt and Babylonia, six thousand years ago, down to those of our own time and people.

These records inform us that, so far as men have paid attention to Nature, they have been rewarded for their pains. They have developed the Arts which have furnished the conditions of civilised existence; and the Sciences, which have been a progressive revelation of reality and have afforded the best discipline of the mind in the methods of discovering truth. They have accumulated a vast body of universally accepted knowledge; and the conceptions of man and of society, of morals and of law, based upon that knowledge, are every day more and more, either openly or tacitly, acknowledged to be the foundations of right action.

History also tells us that the field of the supernatural has rewarded its cultivators with a harvest, perhaps not less luxuriant, but of a different character. It has produced an almost infinite diversity of Religions. These, if we set aside the ethical concomitants upon which natural knowledge also has a claim, are composed of information about Supernature; they tell us of the attributes of supernatural beings, of their relations with Nature, and of the operations by which their interference with the ordinary course of events can be secured or averted. It does not appear, however, that supernaturalists have attained to any agreement about these matters, or that history indicates a widening of the influence of supernaturalism on practice, with the onward flow of time. On the contrary, the various religions are, to a great extent, mutually exclusive; and their adherents delight in charging each other, not merely with error, but with criminality, deserving and ensuing[3] punishment of infinite severity. In singular contrast with natural knowledge, again, the acquaintance of mankind with the supernatural appears the more extensive and the more exact, and the influence of supernatural doctrines upon conduct the greater, the further back we go in time and the lower the stage of civilisation submitted to investigation. Historically, indeed, there would seem to be an inverse relation between supernatural and natural knowledge. As the latter has widened, gained in precision and in trustworthiness, so has the former shrunk, grown vague and questionable; as the one has more and more filled the sphere of action, so has the other retreated into the region of meditation, or vanished behind the screen of mere verbal recognition.

Whether this difference of the fortunes of Naturalism and of Supernaturalism is an indication of the progress, or of the regress, of humanity; of a fall from, or an advance towards, the higher life; is a matter of opinion. The point to which I wish to direct attention is that the difference exists and is making itself felt. Men are growing to be seriously alive to the fact that the historical evolution of humanity, which is generally, and I venture to think not unreasonably, regarded as progress, has been, and is being, accompanied by a co-ordinate elimination of the supernatural from its originally large occupation of men's thoughts. The question—How far is this process to go?—is, in my apprehension, the Controverted Question of our time. . . .[4]

My memory, unfortunately, carries me back to the fourth decade of the nineteenth century, when the evangelical flood had a little abated and the tops of certain mountains were soon to appear, chiefly in the neighbourhood of Oxford; but when nevertheless, bibliolatry was rampant; when church and chapel alike proclaimed, as the oracles of God, the crude assumptions of the worst informed and, in natural sequence, the most presumptuously bigoted, of all theological schools.

In accordance with promises made on my behalf, but certainly without my authorisation, I was very early taken to hear "sermons in the vulgar tongue." And vulgar enough often was the tongue in which some preacher, ignorant alike of literature, of history, of science, and even of theology, outside that patronised by his own narrow school, poured forth, from the safe entrenchment of the pulpit, invectives against those who deviated from his notion of orthodoxy. From dark allusions to "sceptics" and "infidels," I became aware of the existence of people who trusted in carnal reason; who audaciously doubted that the world was made in six natural days, or that the deluge was universal; perhaps even went so far as to question the literal accuracy of the story of Eve's temptation, or of Balaam's ass; and from the horror of the tones in which they were mentioned, I should have been justified in drawing the conclusion that these rash men belonged to the criminal classes. At the same time, those who were more directly responsible for providing me with the knowledge

---

[3] Bringing about as a consequence.

[4] The passage which has been omitted here gives a summary historical account of the various manifestations of belief in the supernatural, culminating in the Methodist and Evangelical movements of the late eighteenth century.

essential to the right guidance of life (and who sincerely desired to do so), imagined they were discharging that most sacred duty by impressing upon my childish mind the necessity, on pain of reprobation in this world and damnation in the next, of accepting, in the strict and literal sense, every statement contained in the Protestant Bible. I was told to believe, and I did believe, that doubt about any of them was a sin, not less reprehensible than a moral delict. I suppose that, out of a thousand of my contemporaries, nine hundred, at least, had their minds systematically warped and poisoned, in the name of the God of truth, by like discipline. I am sure that, even a score of years later, those who ventured to question the exact historical accuracy of any part of the Old Testament and *a fortiori*[5] of the Gospels, had to expect a pitiless shower of verbal missiles, to say nothing of the other disagreeable consequences which visit those who, in any way, run counter to that chaos of prejudices called public opinion. . . .

Among the watchers of the course of the world of thought, some view with delight and some with horror, the recrudescence of Supernaturalism which manifests itself among us, in shapes ranged along the whole flight of steps, which, in this case, separates the sublime from the ridiculous—from Neo-Catholicism and Innerlight mysticism,[6] at the top, to unclean things, not worthy of mention in the same breath, at the bottom. In my poor opinion, the importance of these manifestations is often greatly over-estimated. The extant forms of Supernaturalism have deep roots in human nature, and will undoubtedly die hard; but, in these latter days, they have to cope with an enemy whose full strength is only just beginning to be put out, and whose forces, gathering strength year by year, are hemming them round on every side. This enemy is Science, in the acceptation of systematised natural knowledge, which, during the last two centuries, has extended those methods of investigation, the worth of which is confirmed by daily appeal to Nature, to every region in which the Supernatural has hitherto been recognised.

When scientific historical criticism reduced the annals of heroic Greece and of regal Rome to the level of fables; when the unity of authorship of the *Iliad* was successfully assailed by scientific literary criticism; when scientific physical criticism, after exploding the geocentric theory of the universe and reducing the solar system itself to one of millions of groups of like cosmic specks, circling, at unimaginable distances from one another through infinite space, showed the supernaturalistic theories of the duration of the earth and of life upon it, to be as inadequate as those of its relative dimensions and importance had been; it needed no prophetic gift to see that, sooner or later, the Jewish and the early Christian records would be treated in the same manner; that the authorship of the Hexateuch[7] and of the Gospels would be as severely tested; and that the evidence in favour of the veracity of many of the statements found in the Scriptures would have to be strong indeed, if they were to be opposed to the conclusions of physical science. In point of fact, so far as I can discover, no one competent to judge of the evidential strength of these conclusions, ventures now to say that the biblical accounts of the creation and of the deluge are true in the natural sense of the words of the narratives. The most modern Reconcilers venture upon is to affirm, that some quite different sense may be put upon the words; and that this non-natural sense may, with a little trouble, be manipulated into some sort of non-contradiction of scientific truth.

My purpose, in the essay (XVI.) which treats of the narrative of the Deluge, was to prove, by physical criticism, that no such event as that described ever took place; to exhibit the untrustworthy character of the narrative demonstrated by literary criticism; and, finally, to account for its origin, by producing a form of those ancient legends of pagan Chaldaea, from which the biblical compilation is manifestly derived. I have yet to learn that the main propositions of this essay can be seriously challenged.

---

5 Even more so.

6 Neo-Catholicism was the movement inaugurated by Newman repudiating the Protestant Reformation and stressing instead the affinity of the English Church with that of Rome. Huxley discusses the movement in the passage that has been omitted just above. Inner-light mysticism was the position of such extreme Protestant sects as the Quakers, who rejected the authority of both the Bible and the Church in favor of guidance by divine inspiration.

---

7 The first six books of the Bible.

In the essays (II., III.) on the narrative of the Creation, I have endeavoured to controvert the assertion that modern science supports, either the interpretation put upon it by Mr. Gladstone,[8] or any interpretation which is compatible with the general sense of the narrative, quite apart from particular details. The first chapter of Genesis teaches the supernatural creation of the present forms of life; modern science teaches that they have come about by evolution. The first chapter of Genesis teaches the successive origin—firstly, of all the plants, secondly, of all the aquatic and aerial animals, thirdly, of all the terrestrial animals, which now exist—during distinct intervals of time; modern science teaches that, throughout all the duration of an immensely long past, so far as we have any adequate knowledge of it (that is as far back as the Silurian epoch), plants, aquatic, aerial, and terrestrial animals have co-existed; that the earliest known are unlike those which at present exist; and that the modern species have come into existence as the last terms of a series, the members of which have appeared one after another. Thus, far from confirming the account in Genesis, the results of modern science, so far as they go, are in principle, as in detail, hopelessly discordant with it.

Yet, if the pretensions to infallibility set up, not by the ancient Hebrew writings themselves, but by the ecclesiastical champions and friends from whom they may well pray to be delivered, thus shatter themselves against the rock of natural knowledge, in respect of the two most important of all events, the origin of things and the palingenesis[9] of terrestrial life, what historical credit dare any serious thinker attach to the narratives of the fabrication of Eve, of the Fall, of the commerce between the *Bene Elohim*[10] and the daughters of men, which lie between the creational and the diluvial legends? And, if these are to lose all historical worth, what becomes of the infallibility of those who, according to the later scriptures, have accepted them, argued from them, and staked far-reaching dogmatic conclusions upon their historical accuracy?

It is the merest ostrich policy for contemporary ecclesiasticism to try to hide its Hexateuchal head—in the hope that the inseparable connection of its body with pre-Abrahamic legends may be overlooked. The question will still be asked, if the first nine chapters of the Pentateuch[11] are unhistorical, how is the historical accuracy of the remainder to be guaranteed? What more intrinsic claim has the story of the Exodus than that of the Deluge, to belief? If God did not walk in the Garden of Eden, how can we be assured that he spoke from Sinai?

In some other of the following essays (IX., X., XI., XII., XIV., XV.) I have endeavoured to show that sober and well-founded physical and literary criticism plays no less havoc with the doctrine that the canonical scriptures of the New Testament "declare incontrovertibly the actual historical truth in all records." We are told that the Gospels contain a true revelation of the spiritual world—a proposition which, in one sense of the word "spiritual," I should not think it necessary to dispute. But, when it is taken to signify that everything we are told about the world of spirits in these books is infallibly true; that we are bound to accept the demonology which constitutes an inseparable part of their teaching; and to profess belief in a Supernaturalism as gross as that of any primitive people—it is at any rate permissible to ask why? Science may be unable to define the limits of possibility, but it cannot escape from the moral obligation to weigh the evidence in favour of any alleged wonderful occurrence; and I have endeavoured to show that the evidence for the Gadarene miracle[12] is altogether worthless. We have simply three, partially discrepant, versions of a story, about the primitive form, the origin, and the authority for which we know absolutely nothing. But the evidence in favour of the Gadarene miracle is as good as that for any other.

Elsewhere, I have pointed out that it is utterly beside the mark to declaim against these conclusions on the ground of their asserted tendency to deprive mankind of the consolations of the Christian faith, and to destroy the founda-

---

8 The great political leader of the liberal party in Victorian England. In 1885 he attempted to prove that the order of creation given in Genesis is supported by the evidence of science.
9 Birth.
10 Sons of God (see Genesis 6:2).

11 The first five books of the Bible.
12 By which Jesus cast out the devils from a madman into a herd of swine (Mark 5:1–20; cf. Matthew 8:28–34, Luke 8:26–40).

tions of morality; still less to brand them with the question-begging vituperative appellation of "infidelity." The point is not whether they are wicked; but, whether, from the point of view of scientific method, they are irrefragably true. If they are, they will be accepted in time, whether they are wicked, or not wicked. Nature, so far as we have been able to attain to any insight into her ways, recks little about consolation and makes for righteousness by very round-about paths. And, at any rate, whatever may be possible for other people, it is becoming less and less possible for the man who puts his faith in scientific methods of ascertaining truth, and is accustomed to have that faith justified by daily experience, to be consciously false to his principle in any matter. But the number of such men, driven into the use of scientific methods of inquiry and taught to trust them, by their education, their daily professional and business needs, is increasing and will continually increase. The phraseology of Supernaturalism may remain on men's lips, but in practice they are Naturalists. The magistrate who listens with devout attention to the precept "Thou shalt not suffer a witch to live" on Sunday, on Monday dismisses, as intrinsically absurd, a charge of bewitching a cow brought against some old woman; the superintendent of a lunatic asylum who substituted exorcism for rational modes of treatment would have but a short tenure of office; even parish clerks doubt the utility of prayers for rain, so long as the wind is in the east; and an outbreak of pestilence sends men, not to the churches, but to the drains. In spite of prayers for the success of our arms and *Te Deums* for victory, our real faith is in big battalions and keeping our powder dry; in knowledge of the science of warfare; in energy, courage, and discipline. In these, as in all other practical affairs, we act on the aphorism *"Laborare est orare"*;[13] we admit that intelligent work is the only acceptable worship; and that, whether there be a Supernature or not, our business is with Nature.

It is important to note that the principle of the scientific Naturalism of the latter half of the nineteenth century, in which the intellectual movement of the Renascence has culminated, and which was first clearly formulated by Descartes,[14] leads not to the denial of the existence of any Supernature;[15] but simply to the denial of the validity of the evidence adduced in favour of this, or of that, extant form of Supernaturalism.

Looking at the matter from the most rigidly scientific point of view, the assumption that, amidst the myriads of worlds scattered through endless space, there can be no intelligence, as much greater than man's as his is greater than a blackbeetle's; no being endowed with powers of influencing the course of nature as much greater than his, as his is greater than a snail's, seems to me not merely baseless, but impertinent. Without stepping beyond the analogy of that which is known, it is easy to people the cosmos with entities, in ascending scale, until we reach something practically indistinguishable from omnipotence, omnipresence, and omniscience. If our intelligence can, in some matters, surely reproduce the past of thousands of years ago and anticipate the future, thousands of years hence, it is clearly within the limits of possibility that some greater intellect, even of the same order, may be able to mirror the whole past and the whole future; if the universe is penetrated by a medium of such a nature that a magnetic needle on the earth answers to a commotion in the sun, an omnipresent agent is also conceivable; if our insignificant knowledge gives us some influence over events, practical omniscience may confer indefinably greater power. Finally, if evidence that a thing may be, were equivalent to proof that it is, analogy might justify the construction of a naturalistic theology and demonology not less wonderful than the current supernatural; just as it might justify the peopling of Mars, or of Jupiter, with living forms to which terrestrial biology offers no parallel. Until human life is longer and the duties of the present press less heavily, I do not think that wise men will occupy themselves with Jovian, or Martian, natural

---

13 "To work is to pray."

14 René Descartes (1596–1650) rejected traditional authority of every sort, founding his philosophy on "clear and distinct ideas."

15 "I employ the words 'Supernature' and 'Supernatural' in their popular senses. For myself, I am bound to say that the term 'Nature' covers the totality of that which is. The world of psychical phenomena appears to me to be as much part of 'Nature' as the world of physical phenomena; and I am unable to perceive any justification for cutting the Universe into two halves, one natural and one supernatural." (Huxley)

history; and they will probably agree to a verdict of "not proven" in respect of naturalistic theology, taking refuge in that agnostic confession, which appears to me to be the only position for people who object to say that they know what they are quite aware they do not know. As to the interests of morality, I am disposed to think that if mankind could be got to act up to this last principle in every relation of life, a reformation would be effected such as the world has not yet seen; an approximation to the millennium, such as no supernaturalistic religion has ever yet succeeded, or seems likely ever to succeed, in effecting.

I have hitherto dwelt upon scientific Naturalism chiefly in its critical and destructive aspect. But the present incarnation of the spirit of the Renascence differs from its predecessor in the eighteenth century, in that it builds up, as well as pulls down.

That of which it has laid the foundation, of which it is already raising the superstructure, is the doctrine of evolution. But so many strange misconceptions are current about this doctrine—it is attacked on such false grounds by its enemies, and made to cover so much that is disputable by some of its friends, that I think it well to define as clearly as I can, what I do not and what I do understand by the doctrine.

I have nothing to say to any "Philosophy of Evolution." Attempts to construct such a philosophy may be as useful, nay, even as admirable, as was the attempt of Descartes to get at a theory of the universe by the same *a priori* road;[16] but, in my judgment, they are as premature. Nor, for this purpose, have I to do with any theory of the "Origin of Species," much as I value that which is known as the Darwinian theory. That the doctrine of natural selection presupposes evolution is quite true; but it is not true that evolution necessarily implies natural selection. In fact, evolution might conceivably have taken place without the development of groups possessing the characters of species.

For me, the doctrine of evolution is no speculation, but a generalisation of certain facts, which may be observed by any one who will take the necessary trouble. These facts are those which are classed by biologists under the heads of Embryology and of Palaeontology. Embryology

proves that every higher form of individual life becomes what it is by a process of gradual differentiation from an extremely low form; palaeontology proves, in some cases, and renders probable in all, that the oldest types of a group are the lowest; and that they have been followed by a gradual succession of more and more differentiated forms. It is simply a fact, that evolution of the individual animal and plant is taking place, as a natural process, in millions and millions of cases every day; it is a fact, that the species which have succeeded one another in the past, do, in many cases, present just those morphological relations, which they must possess, if they had proceeded, one from the other, by an analogous process of evolution.

The alternative presented, therefore, is: either the forms of one and the same type—say, *e.g.,* that of the Horse tribe—arose successively but independently of one another, at intervals, during myriads of years; or, the later forms are modified descendants of the earlier. And the latter supposition is so vastly more probable than the former, that rational men will adopt it, unless satisfactory evidence to the contrary can be produced. The objection sometimes put forward, that no one yet professes to have seen one species pass into another, comes oddly from those who believe that mankind are all descended from Adam. Has any one then yet seen the production of negroes from a white stock, or *vice versâ?* Moreover, is it absolutely necessary to have watched every step of the progress of a planet, to be justified in concluding that it really does go round the sun? If so, astronomy is in a bad way.

I do not, for a moment, presume to suggest that some one, far better acquainted than I am with astronomy and physics; or that a master of the new chemistry, with its extraordinary revelations; or that a student of the development of human society, of language, and of religions, may not find a sufficient foundation for the doctrine of evolution in these several regions. On the contrary, I rejoice to see that scientific investigation, in all directions, is tending to the same result. And it may well be, that it is only my long occupation with biological matters that leads me to feel safer among them than anywhere else. Be that as it may, I take my stand on the facts of embryology and of paleontology; and I hold that our present knowledge of these facts is sufficiently thorough and extensive to justify

---

[16] By deductive logic, without reference to observed facts.

the facts of embryology and of palaeontology; and theological speculations will have to accommodate themselves to some such common body of established truths as the following:—

1. Plants and animals have existed on our planet for many hundred thousand, probably millions, of years. During this time, their forms, or species, have undergone a succession of changes, which eventually gave rise to the species which constitute the present living population of the earth. There is no evidence, nor any reason to suspect, that this secular process of evolution is other than a part of the ordinary course of nature; there is no more ground for imagining the occurrence of supernatural intervention, at any moment in the development of species in the past, than there is for supposing such intervention to take place, at any moment in the development of an individual animal or plant, at the present day.

2. At present, every individual animal or plant commences its existence as an organism of extremely simple anatomical structure; and it acquires all the complexity it ultimately possesses by gradual differentiation into parts of various structure and function. When a series of specific forms of the same type, extending over a long period of past time, is examined, the relation between the earlier and the later forms is analogous to that between earlier and later stages of individual development. Therefore, it is a probable conclusion that, if we could follow living beings back to their earlier states, we should find them to present forms similar to those of the individual germ, or, what comes to the same thing, of those lowest known organisms which stand upon the boundary line between plants and animals. At present, our knowledge of the ancient living world stops very far short of this point.

3. It is generally agreed, and there is certainly no evidence to the contrary, that all plants are devoid of consciousness; that they neither feel, desire, nor think. It is conceivable that the evolution of the primordial living substance should have taken place only along the plant line. In that case, the result might have been a wealth of vegetable life, as great, perhaps as varied, as at present, though certainly widely different from the present flora, in the evolution of which animals have played so great a part. But the living world thus constituted would be simply an admirable piece of unconscious machinery, the working out of which lay potentially in its primitive composition; pleasure and pain would have no place in it; it would be a veritable Garden of Eden without any tree of the knowledge of good and evil. The question of the moral government of such a world could no more be asked, than we could reasonably seek for a moral purpose in a kaleidoscope.

4. How far down the scale of animal life the phenomena of consciousness are manifested, it is impossible to say. No one doubts their presence in his fellow-men; and, unless any strict Cartesians are left, no one doubts that mammals and birds are to be reckoned creatures that have feelings analogous to our smell, taste, sight, hearing, touch, pleasure, and pain. For my own part, I should be disposed to extend this analogical judgment a good deal further. On the other hand, if the lowest forms of plants are to be denied consciousness, I do not see on what ground it is to be ascribed to the lowest animals. I find it hard to believe that an infusory animalcule, foraminifer, or a fresh-water polype is capable of feeling; and, in spite of Shakspere, I have doubts about the great sensitiveness of the "poor beetle that we tread upon." The question is equally perplexing when we turn to the stages of development of the individual. Granted a fowl feels; that the chick just hatched feels; that the chick when it chirps within the egg may possibly feel; what is to be said of it on the fifth day, when the bird is there, but with all its tissues nascent? Still more, on the first day, when it is nothing but a flat cellular disk? I certainly cannot bring myself to believe that this disk feels. Yet if it does not, there must be some time in the three weeks, between the first day and the day of hatching, when, as a concomitant, or a consequence, of the attainment by the brain of the chick of a certain stage of structural evolution, consciousness makes its appearance. I have frequently expressed my incapacity to understand the nature of the relation between consciousness and a certain anatomical tissue, which is thus established by observation. But the fact remains that, so far as observation and experiment go, they teach us that the psychical phenomena are dependent on the physical.

In like manner, if fishes, insects, scorpions, and such animals as the pearly nautilus, possess feeling, then undoubtedly consciousness was present in the world as far back as the Silurian epoch. But, if the earliest animals were similar to our rhizopods and monads, there must have been some time, between the much earlier epoch in which they constituted the whole animal population and the Silurian, in which feeling dawned, in consequence of the organism having reached the stage of evolution on which it depends.

5. Consciousness has various forms, which may be manifested independently of one another. The feelings of light and colour, of sound, of touch, though so often associated with those of pleasure and pain, are, by nature, as entirely independent of them as is thinking. An animal devoid of the feelings of pleasure and of pain, may nevertheless exhibit all the effects of sensation and purposive action. Therefore, it would be a justifiable hypothesis that, long after organic evolution had attained to consciousness, pleasure and pain were still absent. Such a world would be without either happiness or misery; no act could be punished and none could be rewarded; and it could have no moral purpose.

6. Suppose, for argument's sake, that all mammals and birds are subjects of pleasure and pain. Then we may be certain that these forms of consciousness were in existence at the beginning of the Mesozoic epoch. From that time forth, pleasure has been distributed without reference to merit, and pain inflicted without reference to demerit, throughout all but a mere fraction of the higher animals. Moreover, the amount and the severity of the pain, no less than the variety and acuteness of the pleasure, have increased with every advance in the scale of evolution. As suffering came into the world, not in consequence of a fall, but of a rise, in the scale of being, so every further rise has brought more suffering. As the evidence stands, it would appear that the sort of brain which characterises the highest mammals and which, so far as we know, is the indispensable condition of the highest sensibility, did not come into existence before the Tertiary epoch. The primordial anthropoid was probably, in this respect, on much the same footing as his pithecoid kin.[17] Like them he stood upon his "natural rights," gratified all his desires to the best of his ability, and was as in-

capable of either right or wrong doing as they. It would be as absurd as in their case, to regard his pleasures, any more than theirs, as moral rewards, and his pains, any more than theirs, as moral punishments.

7. From the remotest ages of which we have any cognizance, death has been the natural and, apparently, the necessary concomitant of life. In our hypothetical world (3),[18] inhabited by nothing but plants, death must have very early resulted from the struggle for existence: many of the crowd must have jostled one another out of the conditions on which life depends. The occurrence of death, as far back as we have any fossil record of life, however, needs not to be proved by such arguments; for, if there had been no death there would have been no fossil remains, such as the great majority of those we met with. Not only was there death in the world, as far as the record of life takes us; but, ever since mammals and birds have been preyed upon by carnivorous animals, there has been painful death, inflicted by mechanisms specially adapted for inflicting it.

8. Those who are acquainted with the closeness of the structural relations between the human organisation and that of the mammals which come nearest to him, on the one hand; and with the palaeontological history of such animals as horses and dogs, on the other; will not be disposed to question the origin of man from forms which stand in the same sort of relation to *Homo sapiens,* as *Hipparion* does to *Equus.* I think it a conclusion, fully justified by analogy, that, sooner or later, we shall discover the remains of our less specialised primatic ancestors in the strata which have yielded the less specialised equine and canine quadrupeds. At present, fossil remains of men do not take us back further than the later part of the Quarternary epoch; and, as was to be expected, they do not differ more from existing men, than Quaternary horses differ from existing horses. Still earlier we find traces of man, in implements such as are used by the ruder savages at the present day. Later, the remains of the palaeolithic and neolithic[19] conditions take us gradually from the savage state to the civilisations of Egypt and of Mycenae;

---

17 The manlike ape was on much the same footing as the apelike man.

18 As described in the paragraph above numbered 3.
19 Of the early and later stone ages, respectively.

though the true chronological order of the remains actually discovered may be uncertain.

9. Much has yet to be learned, but, at present, natural knowledge affords no support to the notion that men have fallen from a higher to a lower state. On the contrary, everything points to a slow natural evolution; which, favoured by the surrounding conditions in such localities as the valleys of the Yangtse-kang, the Euphrates, and the Nile, reached a relatively high pitch, five or six thousand years ago; while, in many other regions, the savage condition has persisted down to our day. In all this vast lapse of time there is not a trace of the occurrence of any general destruction of the human race; not the smallest indication that man has been treated on any other principles than the rest of the animal world.

10. The results of the process of evolution in the case of man, and in that of his more nearly allied contemporaries, have been marvellously different. Yet it is easy to see that small primitive differences of a certain order, must, in the long run, bring about a wide divergence of the human stock from the others. It is a reasonable supposition that, in the earliest human organisms, an improved brain, a voice more capable of modulation and articulation, limbs which lent themselves better to gesture, a more perfect hand, capable among other things of imitating form in plastic or other material, were combined with the curiosity, the mimetic tendency, the strong family affection of the next lower group; and that they were accompanied by exceptional length of life and a prolonged minority. The last two peculiarities are obviously calculated to strengthen the family organisation, and to give great weight to its educative influences. The potentiality of language, as the vocal symbol of thought, lay in the faculty of modulating and articulating the voice. The potentiality of writing, as the visual symbol of thought, lay in the hand that could draw; and in the mimetic tendency, which, as we know, was gratified by drawing, as far back as the days of Quaternary man. With speech as the record, in tradition, of the experience of more than one generation; with writing as the record of that of any number of generations; the experience of the race, tested and corrected generation after generation, could be stored up and made the starting point for fresh progress. Having these perfectly natural factors of the evolutionary process in man before us, it seems unnecessary to go further a-field in search of others.

11. That the doctrine of evolution implies a former state of innocence of mankind is quite true; but, as I have remarked, it is the innocence of the ape and of the tiger, whose acts, however they may run counter to the principles of morality, it would be absurd to blame. The lust of the one and the ferocity of the other are as much provided for in their organisation, are as clear evidences of design, as any other features that can be named.

Observation and experiment upon the phenomena of society soon taught men that, in order to obtain the advantages of social existence, certain rules must be observed. Morality commenced with society. Society is possible only upon the condition that the members of it shall surrender more or less of their individual freedom of action. In primitive societies, individual selfishness is a centrifugal force of such intensity that it is constantly bringing the social organisation to the verge of destruction. Hence the prominence of the positive rules of obedience to the elders; of standing by the family or the tribe in all emergencies; of fulfilling the religious rites, nonobservance of which is conceived to damage it with the supernatural powers, belief in whose existence is one of the earliest products of human thought; and of the negative rules, which restrain each from meddling with the life or property of another.

12. The highest conceivable form of human society is that in which the desire to do what is best for the whole, dominates and limits the action of every member of that society. The more complex the social organisation the greater the number of acts from which each man must abstain, if he desires to do that which is best for all. Thus the progressive evolution of society means increasing restriction of individual freedom in certain directions.

With the advance of civilisation, and the growth of cities and of nations by the coalescence of families and of tribes, the rules which constitute the common foundation of morality and of law became more numerous and complicated, and the temptations to break or evade many of them stronger. In the absence of a clear apprehension of the natural sanctions of these rules, a supernatural sanction was assumed; and imagination supplied the motives which reason was supposed to be incompetent to furnish. Religion, at first independent of morality, gradually took morality under its protection; and the supernaturalists have ever since tried to persuade mankind that the existence of ethics is bound up with that of supernaturalism.

I am not of that opinion. But, whether it is correct or otherwise, it is very clear to me that, as Beelzebub is not to be cast out by the aid of Beelzebub, so morality is not to be established by immorality. It is, we are told, the special peculiarity of the devil that he was a liar from the beginning. If we set out in life with pretending to know that which we do not know; with professing to accept for proof evidence which we are well aware is inadequate; with wilfully shutting our eyes and our ears to facts which militate against this or that comfortable hypothesis; we are assuredly doing our best to deserve the same character.

I have not the presumption to imagine that, in spite of all my efforts, errors may not have crept into these propositions. But I am tolerably confident that time will prove them to be substantially correct. And if they are so, I confess I do not see how any extant supernaturalistic system can also claim exactness. That they are irreconcilable with the biblical cosmogony, anthropology, and theodicy is obvious; but they are no less inconsistent with the sentimental Deism of the "Vicaire Savoyard"[20] and his numerous modern progeny. It is as impossible, to my mind, to suppose that the evolutionary process was set going with full foreknowledge of the result and yet with what we should understand by a purely benevolent intention, as it is to imagine that the intention was purely malevolent. And the prevalence of dualistic theories from the earliest times to the present day—whether in the shape of the doctrine of the inherently evil nature of matter; of an Ahriman;[21] of a hard and cruel Demiurge;[22] of a diabolical "prince of this world," show how widely this difficulty has been felt.

Many seem to think that, when it is admitted that the ancient literature, contained in our Bibles, has no more claim to infallibility than any other ancient literature; when it is proved that the Israelites and their Christian successors accepted a great many supernaturalistic theories and legends which have no better foundation than those of heathenism, nothing remains to be done but to throw the Bible aside as so much waste paper.

I have always opposed this opinion. It appears to me that if there is anybody more objectionable than the orthodox Bibliolater it is the heterodox Philistine, who can discover in a literature which, in some respects, has no superior, nothing but a subject for scoffing and an occasion for the display of his conceited ignorance of the debt he owes to former generations.

Twenty-two years ago I pleaded for the use of the Bible as an instrument of popular education, and I venture to repeat what I then said:

"Consider the great historical fact that, for three centuries, this book has been woven into the life of all that is best and noblest in English history; that it has become the national Epic of Britain and is as familiar to gentle and simple,[23] from John o' Groat's House to Land's End,[24] as Dante and Tasso once were to the Italians; that it is written in the noblest and purest English and abounds in exquisite beauties of mere literary form; and, finally, that it forbids the veriest hind, who never left his village, to be ignorant of the existence of other countries and other civilisations and of a great past, stretching back to the furthest limits of the oldest nations in the world. By the study of what other book could children be so much humanised and made to feel that each figure in that vast historical procession fills, like themselves, but a momentary space in the interval between the Eternities; and earns the blessings or the curses of all time, according to its effort to do good and hate evil, even as they also are earning their payment for their work?"

At the same time, I laid stress upon the necessity of placing such instruction in lay hands; in the hope and belief, that it would thus gradually accommodate itself to the coming changes of opinion; that the theology and the legend

---

[20] A mouthpiece for Jean Jacques Rousseau in *Emile*.
[21] The principle of evil in the Zoroastrian system.
[22] Creator of the world in the Platonic philosophy.

[23] To gentleman and simple peasant.
[24] The extreme northern and extreme southern points of England, respectively.

would drop more and more out of sight, while the perennially interesting historical, literary, and ethical contents would come more and more into view.

I may add yet another claim of the Bible to the respect and the attention of a democratic age. Throughout the history of the western world, the Scriptures, Jewish and Christian, have been the great instigators of revolt against the worst forms of clerical and political despotism. The Bible has been the *Magna Charta* of the poor and of the oppressed; down to modern times, no State has had a constitution in which the interests of the people are so largely taken into account, in which the duties, so much more than the privileges, of rulers are insisted upon, as that drawn up for Israel in Deuteronomy and in Leviticus; nowhere is the fundamental truth that the welfare of the State, in the long run, depends on the uprightness of the citizen so strongly laid down. Assuredly, the Bible talks no trash about the rights of man; but it insists on the equality of duties, on the liberty to bring about that righteousness which is somewhat different from struggling for "rights"; on the fraternity of taking thought for one's neighbour as for one's self.

So far as such equality, liberty, and fraternity are included under the democratic principles which assume the same names, the Bible is the most democratic book in the world. As such it began, through the heretical sects, to undermine the clerico-political despotism of the middle ages, almost as soon as it was formed, in the eleventh century; Pope and King had as much as they could do to put down the Albigenses and the Waldenses in the twelfth and thirteenth centuries; the Lollards and the Hussites gave them still more trouble in the fourteenth and fifteenth; from the sixteenth century onward, the Protestant sects have favoured political freedom in proportion to the degree in which they have refused to acknowledge any ultimate authority save that of the Bible.

But the enormous influence which has thus been exerted by the Jewish and Christian Scriptures has had no necessary connection with cosmogonies, demonologies, and miraculous interferences. Their strength lies in their appeals, not to the reason, but to the ethical sense. I do not say that even the highest biblical ideal is exclusive of others or needs no supplement. But I do believe that the human race is not yet, possibly may never be, in a position to dispense with it.

Alfred, Lord Tennyson
1809–1892

Tennyson's appointment as poet laureate in 1850 was altogether fitting, for more than anyone else he expressed in verse the dominant ideas and attitudes of the period: the passionate belief in progress, the conservative pride in English freedom, the religious doubts but the triumph of faith (and a broad, liberal faith outside creeds and ecclesiastical forms), and, above all, the moral earnestness and the moral idealism which exalted Duty, Love, and the Home. Today, much of this poetry is dated, but Tennyson still commands a living interest for three reasons. His lyrics are among the finest in the language. His development from a late Romantic into a Victorian poet has great historical significance. And, thirdly, his poetry contains a strain of anti-Victorianism, unnoticed or explained away by the Victorians, which demands a fresh critical and psychological approach.

Tennyson was born in 1809 at Somersby in Lincolnshire, not far from the North Sea. His father was the rector of the parish church, a man of literary and artistic tastes, and of bitter and irritable temper. In this environment Alfred started early to write verse, and to develop the somber and melancholy spirit that colors much of his work. Hallam Tennyson reported that "More than once Alfred, scared by his father's fits of despondency, went out through the black night, and threw himself on a grave in the churchyard, praying to be beneath the sod himself." No doubt there is an element here of youthful romantic posturing, but it is probably true, as W. H. Auden has claimed, that Tennyson's most genuine and personal feelings were almost entirely those of loneliness, depression, and the desire for death. Certainly those are the dominant notes in the poems which he contributed to a joint volume, with his brothers Charles and Frederick, in 1827, and they inform the "Song,"

Alfred, Lord Tennyson (1809–1892). Perhaps the first man of letters to become a national celebrity during his lifetime, the poet laureate moved twice to escape admirers and sycophants. Lakes, mountains, and roses were named after him, and every detail of his lifestyle and clothing was reported in the popular press. *The Granger Collection.*

"Mariana," and "Tithonus," the first selections below.

After being educated largely at home by his father, Tennyson entered Cambridge in 1828, where he came under a new and important influence. This was a group of young intellectuals called the Apostles, one of whom, Arthur Henry Hallam, became his closest friend. The Apostles were great admirers, not only of Wordsworth, but of two obscure modern poets named Shelley and Keats; indeed, in 1829 they published the first English edition of Shelley's *Adonais,* his elegy on the death of Keats. The double effect of these new literary idols is apparent in Tennyson's second volume, *Poems, Chiefly Lyrical* (1830). They suggested, on the one hand, the possibility of combining the pictorial imagery of Keats with the musical rhythms of Shelley and thus creating an aesthetic poetry of mood and atmosphere; and on the other, they suggested (Shelley in particular) a poetry almost the reverse of this, of philosophical and political ideas.

The first genre, which was to reappear later in the work of the Pre-Raphaelites and the young Yeats, is to be clearly distinguished from Romantic poetry,

however much it may be derived from it. If we compare Keats's "To Autumn" (p. 383) with Tennyson's "Song" on the same subject (p. 694), we see at once that where Keats describes an object, Tennyson invokes a mood. In the one case, the reader "sees" autumn; in the other, he doesn't "see" anything; he simply feels a mixture of emotions (depression, dejection, weariness, fatigue, the sense of decay and death) that combine to create an intangible but none the less vivid impression. In short, Tennyson's poem is not about autumn at all; autumn simply provided the set of images which he needed to communicate a particular mood. In the same way, "Mariana" is not about a woman who has lost her lover: the woman and the refrain are merely the principal images which combine with those of lonely remoteness and dilapidation to evoke a similar mood of melancholia. ("Tithonus," by contrast, *does* center on a human situation, which in this case, as in Romantic poetry in general as distinct from aesthetic poetry, is the source of the emotions of fatigue and weariness.) In "The Sea-Fairies" rhythm replaces imagery as the dominant technique for evoking an impression of bright and rapid motion. It is perhaps the finest piece of music in English verse before Swinburne.

If this was Tennyson's starting point, why did he shift, or try to shift, his theory and practice of poetry from Romantic aestheticism to Victorian didacticism, in the large sense that covers lofty sentiments and ideals? The first and immediate answer is the Apostles. They *were* apostles because they felt commissioned to "preach to the sons of men dwelling in outer darkness new truths in regard to literature and religion, the cultivation of a loftier philosophy, a purer poetry, higher ideals in life and letters." Judged by this aim, they could only feel that Tennyson was misdirecting his poetic gift. R. C. Trench took him aside and said, "Tennyson, we cannot live in art." His friend George Venables told him his verse was too largely imbued with magic to appeal to popular taste, and urged him to base his poetry more on the "broad and common interests of the time," of which he ought to be the artistic exponent and unifier. Tennyson "pondered all that had been said," and presently began to write "with a deeper and a fuller insight into the requirements of the age." Of the age, because the program of the Apostles simply reflected the need of the period, not only for new truths—new liberal truths—in religion and politics, but also loftier ideals in life, philosophy, and poetry to counteract the "low" view of man and society for which the three B's were responsible—Byron, Business, and Benthamism. (See the introduction to the Victorian period, pp. 407–08, 412–13.)

This new conception of his role, which had behind it the further authority of both Wordsworth and Shelley, is announced by Tennyson in "The Poet" (where the influence of the "Ode to the West Wind" is apparent), and reflected in the two poems that follow, "You Ask Me, Why" and "Sir Galahad." But Tennyson's conversion was far from wholehearted. "Alas for me!" he wrote to Hallam, "I have more of the beautiful than the good!" This explains the conflict of intentions which spoils both "The Palace of Art" and "Oenone." Although the former was written to support the warning of his fellow apostle, R. C. Trench, that "we cannot live in art," and to preach the moral lessons announced in the introductory poem "To ____" (probably Trench), the fact is that Tennyson is so concerned with his lengthy description of the palace and its paintings, and so vague about the soul's pilgrimage at the end, that the poem falls between two stools. In "Oenone," heartbroken grief, pictorial beauties (which Oenone stops at every moment to phrase with conscious artistry), and a Victorian sermon from Athene compete together for the distracted reader's attention.

The second aspect of Tennyson's development from 1830 to 1842, in addition to the shift in his theory of poetry, was the increase of his early melancholia and a growing distaste for Victorian society. The 1832 volume was severely criticized in contemporary reviews by Lockhart and Croker; in 1833 Arthur Hallam suddenly died, leaving Tennyson not only stricken with grief but filled with profoundly distressing doubts about the beneficence of a God who could sanction the death of so remarkable a man as Hallam on the very threshold of a great career; in 1836 he fell in love with Emily Sellwood, but their engagement was broken off a few years later, and a long period of trying and uncertain relationship followed before they were eventually married in 1850; Finally, Tennyson was beset with financial difficulties: when his father died in 1831, he left his son a small patrimony which the poet later invested in Dr. Allen's wood-carving machine, only to lose every penny, and to fall into "so severe a hypochondria . . . that his friends despaired of his life." But in 1842 the tide began to turn. His new volume of poems, published in that year, was well received. In 1845 he was given a government pension. *The Princess* (1847), on the emancipation of women, was followed in 1850 by the famous *In Memoriam* and the poet-laureateship; and though *Maud* (1855) was not a popular success, the first four *Idylls of the King* (1859) established him firmly as the great poet of the age and the major exponent of Victorian ideals. When he died in 1892, he was buried, of course, in Westminster Abbey.

Five years later the official biography by his son Hallam was the life of Tennyson the Victorian prophet—and yet, here and there, like curious excres-

cences, the text was punctuated by some very un-Victorian, even sometimes anti-Victorian, remarks. The poet laureate had once laughed at a tremendous "duty-woman," had claimed it was right to enjoy leisure, had thought a glacier covered with debris looked "as if a thousand London seasons had passed over it," had spoken of "a mighty wave of evil passing over the world," and had called the Victorian period "an age of lies, and also an age of stinks."

This bitter note of criticism, reinforced by his own misfortunes, brought into his poetry a deeper level of feeling and perception, and an unexpected strain of ambivalence. In "Ulysses" the unheroic desire to abandon the responsibilities of daily life and set sail on a romantic voyage of endless adventure (drinking life to the lees) is followed by the heroic appeal to strive, to conquer, and not to yield. To Victorian critics the moral of "The Lotos-Eaters" seemed to be "that the law of life is labour, and to reject it is to lose all that makes life worth living" (A. C. Bradley), but the modern reader will recognize the *qualified* attraction of sunbathing ease on far-away islands, and bring the poem into touch with "The Sea-Fairies." Only the final stanza, inserted into the revised version published in 1842, introduces a moral condemnation that is unprepared for and jarring. The jilted lover of "Locksley Hall" is at once critical of the age (and ready to retreat to an oriental Eden far from railroads and "march of mind") and at the same time enthusiastic about its magnificent progress, western style, especially in science. In "The Vision of Sin" the fruits of evil are patent, but the protagonist is not a debauched sinner but a bitter satirist of moral hypocrisy, political passions, and the hollowness of human endeavor. He is closer to Juvenal or Swift than to a Victorian parson.

In their final form the *Idylls of the King* were intended to show the disastrous consequences that followed from the initial sin of Lancelot and Guinevere: the spread of evil through the community, which breeds loss of pure faith in God and the Moral Law, which then turns religion from "practical goodness and holiness to superstition," that is, to selfish searching for visions of the Holy Grail (the reference is to the ascetic and ecclesiastical emphasis of the Oxford Movement). This "moral" was then supplemented by heroic or ideal images of courage and love. But no one can read the *Idylls* without feeling Tennyson's delight in the beauty and glamour of days when knighthood and not Victorianism was in flower. In descriptions of armor and Gothic towers, in tales of magic and adventure, the aesthetic-escapist sensibility found renewed expression. But here and there, most noticeably in the earlier *Idylls*, Tennyson's insight into the darker sides of human experience is released. If "Lancelot and Elaine" contains an ideal picture of pure and innocent love, it also contains, and centrally, a picture of burnt-out and disillusioned love, where a man and woman are held together out of habit and waning sexual attraction in a relationship they have not power to break. This is Tennyson's finest study in human psychology. It is, like "The Vision of Sin," a moral but not a moralistic poem.

The death of his close friend Arthur Hallam in 1833 inspired the series of lyric poems which Tennyson eventually published in 1850 as *In Memoriam*. In some of them he gives poignant expression to his grief (see for example Nos. 7 and 11), while in others he explores the religious problem—doubt vs. faith—which the event inevitably raised, especially in the mind of a Victorian. Under the liberal influence of the Apostles, Tennyson had already sloughed off much of Christian theology until his religion was reduced, as it was for many Victorians, to a simple faith in God, in a divine moral law speaking through conscience, and in the immortality of the soul. But the new science of evolution threatened to destroy all religious belief whatever. What Tennyson did, and what made the poem so significant at the time, was to recognize the arguments of "atheistical science" (see the introduction to the Victorian period, pp. 418-20, which has several references to *In Memoriam*), and then, in one way or another, to question them or to reject them. He did this first by simply repudiating the notion that man was merely a product of nature dying a natural death in a universe of mechanical force. To believe it would be to deny everything that makes life worth living, to deny our inmost feelings of freedom and dignity. I will *not* believe it! Then, once a godless universe is defied, the way back to faith is opened up (cf. the end of Carlyle's "Everlasting No"). Tennyson based his belief in God and immortality on "what is highest within us," meaning either moments of exalted, unselfish love, which seemed to attest a moral nature made in God's image, or moments of outright mystical experience in which he felt the presence of Arthur Hallam in heaven, or of the divine spirit itself. Finally, attempting to turn the flank of the enemy, he argued (less persuasively from the modern viewpoint) that evolution might be given a moral and religious interpretation. Yet the founding of faith on inner feeling and mystical insight, if more difficult to achieve in our increasingly skeptical and scientific environment, is nevertheless as valid as ever.

As a matter of fact, Tennyson himself never attained a firm belief. "An Omnipotent Creator Who would make such a painful world," he once admitted, "is to me *sometimes* as hard to believe in as to believe in blind matter behind everything." Hence the quality of Tennyson's faith—not really faith at all, but simply a hope, a guess, a trust that the religious

reading of life was true. It is no accident that those words, especially "trust," echo through the poem. *In Memoriam* is not a record of faith nor of doubt. It is an expression of trust.

That, indeed, is the conclusion we would come to from balancing the brighter lyrics against the darker ones (No. 106 against No. 56), and especially from noticing the ambivalence present in so many of the poems (like No. 54 and No. 123). Perhaps more than anything else, it is Tennyson's fidelity to his real feelings that makes *In Memoriam* impressive today. The refusal to pretend to feel more than he does, the recognition of emotions that contradict what he asserts, and the artistic ability to find the words of qualified affirmation that express precisely the necessary degree of ambivalence—this is an achievement we can recognize and appreciate in the 1970s.

TEXTS: Tennyson's *Works,* with his own notes, have been edited by Hallam Tennyson in nine volumes (1908) and in one volume (1913). The most scholarly edition of the poetry is *The Complete Poems,* ed. Christopher Ricks (1969). Charles Tennyson's *Alfred Tennyson* (1949) has not displaced Hallam Tennyson's *Alfred Lord Tennyson: A Memoir* (2 vols., 1897) as the standard biography. This is indispensable for the letters and conversations and the large amount of contemporary comment by men like Jowett, Sidgwick, and Spedding that it reprints. *Critical Essays on the Poetry of Tennyson,* ed. John Killam, reprints the most important articles of recent years; and, together with W. H. Auden's introduction to *A Selection from the Poems of Alfred Lord Tennyson* (1944) and the essay in Basil Willey's *More Nineteenth Century Studies: a Group of Honest Doubters* (1956), it shows how much of his poetry is still alive and significant.

Note: Throughout the poetry, spelling has been modernized, but original punctuation has been kept. A colon is used sometimes to mean "as follows" but primarily indicates a longer pause than a semicolon and a shorter one than a period.

Song

I

A spirit haunts the year's last hours
Dwelling amid these yellowing bowers:
   To himself he talks;
For at eventide, listening earnestly,
At his work you may hear him sob and sigh
   In the walks;
   Earthward he boweth the heavy stalks

5

Of the mouldering flowers.
　　Heavily hangs the broad sunflower
　　　　Over its grave i' the earth so chilly;   10
　　Heavily hangs the hollyhock,
　　　　Heavily hangs the tiger-lily.

II

The air is damp, and hushed, and close,
As a sick man's room when he taketh repose
　　An hour before death;   15
My very heart faints and my whole soul grieves
At the moist rich smell of the rotting leaves,
　　And the breath
　　Of the fading edges of box beneath,
And the year's last rose.   20
　　Heavily hangs the broad sunflower
　　　　Over its grave i' the earth so chilly;
　　Heavily hangs the hollyhock,
　　　　Heavily hangs the tiger-lily.

Mariana

"Mariana in the moated grange."
Measure for Measure

With blackest moss the flower-plots
　　Were thickly crusted, one and all:
The rusted nails fell from the knots
　　That held the pear to the gable-wall.
The broken sheds looked sad and strange: 5
　　Unlifted was the clinking latch;
　　Weeded and worn the ancient thatch
Upon the lonely moated grange,
　　She only said, "My life is dreary,
　　　　He cometh not," she said;   10
　　She said, "I am aweary, aweary,
　　　　I would that I were dead!"

Her tears fell with the dews at even;
　　Her tears fell ere the dews were dried;
She could not look on the sweet heaven,   15
　　Either at morn or eventide.
After the flitting of the bats,
　　When thickest dark did trance the sky,
　　She drew her casement-curtain by,
And glanced athwart the glooming flats.   20
　　She only said, "The night is dreary,
　　　　He cometh not," she said;
　　She said, "I am aweary, aweary,
　　　　I would that I were dead!"

Upon the middle of the night,   25
　　Waking she heard the night-fowl crow:
The cock sung out an hour ere light:
　　From the dark fen the oxen's low
Came to her; without hope of change,
　　In sleep she seemed to walk forlorn,   30
　　Till cold winds woke the gray-eyed morn
About the lonely moated grange.
　　She only said, "The day is dreary,
　　　　He cometh not," she said;
　　She said, "I am aweary, aweary,   35
　　　　I would that I were dead!"

About a stone-cast from the wall
　　A sluice with blackened waters slept,
And o'er it many, round and small,
　　The clustered marish-mosses crept.   40
Hard by a poplar shook alway,
　　All silver-green with gnarlèd bark:
　　For leagues no other tree did mark
The level waste, the rounding gray.
　　She only said, "My life is dreary,   45
　　　　He cometh not," she said;
　　She said, "I am aweary, aweary,
　　　　I would that I were dead!"

And ever when the moon was low,
　　And the shrill winds were up and away,   50
In the white curtain, to and fro,
　　She saw the gusty shadow sway.
But when the moon was very low,
　　And wild winds bound within their cell,
　　The shadow of the poplar fell   55
Upon her bed, across her brow.
　　She only said, "The night is dreary,
　　　　He cometh not," she said;
　　She said, "I am aweary, aweary,
　　　　I would that I were dead!"   60

All day within the dreamy house,
　　The doors upon their hinges creaked;
The blue fly sung in the pane; the mouse
　　Behind the mouldering wainscot shrieked,
Or from the crevice peered about,   65
　　Old faces glimmered through the doors,
　　Old footsteps trod the upper floors,
Old voices called her from without.
　　She only said, "My life is dreary,
　　　　He cometh not," she said;   70
　　She said, "I am aweary, aweary,
　　　　I would that I were dead!"

The sparrow's chirrup on the roof,
   The slow clock ticking, and the sound
Which to the wooing wind aloof   75
   The poplar made, did all confound
Her sense; but most she loathed the hour
   When the thick-moted sunbeam lay
Athwart the chambers, and the day
Was sloping toward his western bower.   80
     Then said she, "I am very dreary,
       He will not come," she said;
     She wept, "I am aweary, aweary,
       O God, that I were dead!"

Tithonus[1]

The woods decay, the woods decay and fall,
The vapors weep their burthen to the ground,
Man comes and tills the field and lies beneath,
And after many a summer dies the swan.
Me only cruel immortality   5
Consumes: I wither slowly in thine arms,
Here at the quiet limit of the world,
A white-haired shadow roaming like a dream
The ever-silent spaces of the East,
Far-folded mists, and gleaming halls of morn.   10

   Alas! for this gray shadow, once a man—
So glorious in his beauty and thy choice,
Who madest him thy chosen, that he seemed
To his great heart none other than a God!
I asked thee, "Give me immortality."   15
Then didst thou grant mine asking with a smile,
Like wealthy men who care not how they give.
But thy strong Hours indignant worked their
   wills,
And beat me down and marred and wasted me,
And though they could not end me, left me   20
   maimed

To dwell in presence of immortal youth,
Immortal age beside immortal youth,
And all I was, in ashes. Can thy love,
Thy beauty, make amends, though even now,
Close over us, the silver star,[2] thy guide,   25
Shines in those tremulous eyes that fill with tears
To hear me? Let me go: take back thy gift:
Why should a man desire in any way
To vary from the kindly race of men,
Or pass beyond the goal of ordinance   30
Where all should pause, as is most meet for all?

   A soft air fans the cloud apart; there comes
A glimpse of that dark world where I was born.
Once more the old mysterious glimmer steals
From thy pure brows, and from thy shoulders   35
   pure,
And bosom beating with a heart renewed.
Thy cheek begins to redden through the gloom,
Thy sweet eyes brighten slowly close to mine,
Ere yet they blind the stars, and the wild team[3]
Which love thee, yearning for thy yoke, arise,   40
And shake the darkness from their loosened
   manes,
And beat the twilight into flakes of fire.

   Lo! ever thus thou growest beautiful
In silence, then before thine answer given
Departest, and thy tears are on my cheek.   45

   Why wilt thou ever scare me with thy tears,
And make me tremble lest a saying learnt,
In days far-off, on that dark earth, be true?
"The Gods themselves cannot recall their gifts."

   Ay me! ay me! with what another heart   50
In days far-off, and with what other eyes
I used to watch—if I be he that watched—
The lucid outline forming round thee; saw
The dim curls kindle into sunny rings;
Changed with thy mystic change, and felt my   55
   blood
Glow with the glow that slowly crimsoned all
Thy presence and thy portals, while I lay,
Mouth, forehead, eyelids, growing dewy-warm
With kisses balmier than half-opening buds
Of April, and could hear the lips that kissed   60
Whispering I knew not what of wild and sweet,

---

[1] Aurora (or Eos), goddess of the dawn, loved Tithonus and secured for him from Zeus eternal life; but, since she had failed to ask for immortal youth, he gradually grew older and feebler until at last he begged to be allowed to die. According to the myth, he was finally changed into a grasshopper.
"The basic conflicts of the poem are those between light and dark, warmth and cold, beauty and ugliness, youth and age. But the ultimate mood and attitude of the poem go beyond its dramatic situation, the problem of love between Tithonus and Eos, . . . to express a more profound contrast, a revulsion from the terms of all life and health and a yearning for death." (Mary Donahue Ellmann)

[2] The morning star.
[3] The horses which drew the chariot of dawn.

Like that strange song I heard Apollo sing,
While Ilion like a mist rose into towers.[4]

    Yet hold me not for ever in thine East:
How can my nature longer mix with thine?   65
Coldly thy rosy shadows bathe me, cold
Are all thy lights, and cold my wrinkled feet
Upon thy glimmering thresholds, when the steam
Floats up from those dim fields about the homes
Of happy men that have the power to die,   70
And grassy barrows of the happier dead.
Release me, and restore me to the ground;
Thou seëst all things, thou wilt see my grave:
Thou wilt renew thy beauty morn by morn;
I earth in earth forget these empty courts,   75
And thee returning on thy silver wheels.

The Sea-Fairies[1]

Slow sailed the weary mariners and saw,
Betwixt the green brink and the running foam,
Sweet faces, rounded arms, and bosoms pressed
To little harps of gold; and while they mused
Whispering to each other half in fear,   5
Shrill music reached them on the middle sea.

Whither away, whither away, whither away? fly
    no more.
Whither away from the high green field, and the
    happy blossoming shore?
Day and night to the billow the fountain calls:
Down shower the gambolling waterfalls   10
From wandering over the lea:
Out of the live-green heart of the dells
They freshen the silvery-crimson shells,
And thick with white bells the clover-hill swells
High over the full-toned sea: 15
O, hither, come hither and furl your sails,
Come hither to me and to me:
Hither, come hither and frolic and play;
Here it is only the mew that wails;
We will sing to you all the day: 20
Mariner, mariner, furl your sails,
For here are the blissful downs and dales,
And merrily, merrily carol the gales,

And the spangle dances in bight and bay,
And the rainbow forms and flies on the land   25
Over the islands free;
And the rainbow lives in the curve of the sand;
Hither, come hither and see;
And the rainbow hangs on the poising wave,
And sweet is the color of cove and cave,   30
And sweet shall your welcome be:
O, hither, come hither, and be our lords,
For merry brides are we:
We will kiss sweet kisses, and speak sweet words:
O, listen, listen, your eyes shall glisten   35
With pleasure and love and jubilee:
O, listen, listen, your eyes shall glisten
When the sharp clear twang of the golden chords
Runs up the ridgèd sea.
Who can light on as happy a shore   40
All the world o'er, all the world o'er?
Whither away? listen and stay: mariner, mariner,
    fly no more.

The Lady of Shalott

Part 1

On either side the river lie
Long fields of barley and of rye,
That clothe the wold and meet the sky;
And through the field the road runs by
    To many-towered Camelot;[1]   5
And up and down the people go,
Gazing where the lilies blow
Round an island there below,
    The island of Shalott.

Willows whiten,[2] aspens quiver,   10
Little breezes dusk and shiver
Through the wave that runs for ever
By the island in the river
    Flowing down to Camelot.
Four gray walls, and four gray towers,   15
Overlook a space of flowers,
And the silent isle imbowers
    The Lady of Shalott.

By the margin, willow-veiled,
Slide the heavy barges trailed   20

---

4 The walls of Troy were said to have risen to the music
of Apollo.

1 The sirens who tempted Odysseus and his mariners on
their way home from Troy.

---

1 The seat of King Arthur's court.
2 The wind turns up the white underside of the leaves.

By slow horses; and unhailed
The shallop flitteth silken-sailed
    Skimming down to Camelot:
But who hath seen her wave her hand?
Or at the casement seen her stand? 25
Or is she known in all the land,
    The Lady of Shalott?

Only reapers, reaping early
In among the bearded barley,
Hear a song that echoes cheerly 30
From the river winding clearly,
    Down to towered Camelot:
And by the moon the reaper weary,
Piling sheaves in uplands airy,
Listening, whispers " 'Tis the fairy 35
    Lady of Shalott."

Part 2

There she weaves by night and day
A magic web with colors gay.
She has heard a whisper say,
A curse is on her if she stay 40
    To look down to Camelot.
She knows not what the curse may be,
And so she weaveth steadily,
And little other care hath she,
    The Lady of Shalott. 45

And moving through a mirror clear
That hangs before her all the year,
Shadows of the world appear.
There she sees the highway near
    Winding down to Camelot: 50
There the river eddy whirls,
And there the surly village-churls,
And the red cloaks of market girls,
    Pass onward from Shalott.

Sometimes a troop of damsels glad, 55
An Abbot on an ambling pad,[3]
Sometimes a curly shepherd-lad,
Or long-haired page in crimson clad,
    Goes by to towered Camelot;
And sometimes through the mirror blue 60
The knights come riding two and two:
She hath no loyal knight and true,
    The Lady of Shalott.

But in her web she still delights
To weave the mirror's magic sights, 65
For often through the silent nights
A funeral, with plumes and lights
    And music, went to Camelot:
Or when the moon was overhead,
Came two young lovers lately wed; 70
"I am half sick of shadows," said
    The Lady of Shalott.

Part 3

A bow-shot from her bower-eaves,
He rode between the barley-sheaves,
The sun came dazzling through the leaves, 75
And flamed upon the brazen greaves
    Of bold Sir Lancelot.
A red-cross knight forever kneeled
To a lady in his shield,
That sparkled on the yellow field, 80
    Beside remote Shalott.

The gemmy bridle glittered free,
Like to some branch of stars we see
Hung in the golden Galaxy.[4]
The bridle bells rang merrily 85
    As he rode down to Camelot:
And from his blazoned baldric slung
A mighty silver bugle hung,
And as he rode his armor rung,
    Beside remote Shalott. 90

All in the blue unclouded weather
Thick-jeweled shone the saddle-leather,
The helmet and the helmet-feather
Burned like one burning flame together,
    As he rode down to Camelot. 95
As often through the purple night,
Below the starry clusters bright,
Some bearded meteor, trailing light,
    Moves over still Shalott.

His broad clear brow in sunlight glowed; 100
On burnished hooves his war-horse trode;
From underneath his helmet flowed
His coal-black curls as on he rode,
    As he rode down to Camelot.
From the bank and from the river 105
He flashed into the crystal mirror,
"Tirra lirra," by the river
    Sang Sir Lancelot.

---

3 An easy-gaited horse.

4 The Milky Way.

She left the web, she left the loom,
She made three paces through the room,　　　110
She saw the water-lily bloom,
She saw the helmet and the plume,
　　　She looked down to Camelot.
Out flew the web and floated wide;
The mirror cracked from side to side;　　　115
"The curse is come upon me," cried
　　　The Lady of Shalott.

Part 4

In the stormy east-wind straining,
The pale yellow woods were waning,
The broad stream in his banks complaining,　　　120
Heavily the low sky raining
　　　Over towered Camelot;
Down she came and found a boat
Beneath a willow left afloat,
And round about the prow she wrote　　　125
　　　The Lady of Shalott.

And down the river's dim expanse
Like some bold seër in a trance,
Seeing all his own mischance—
With a glassy countenance　　　130
　　　Did she look to Camelot.
And at the closing of the day
She loosed the chain, and down she lay;
The broad stream bore her far away,
　　　The Lady of Shalott.　　　135

Lying, robed in snowy white
That loosely flew to left and right—
The leaves upon her falling light—
Through the noises of the night
　　　She floated down to Camelot:　　　140
And as the boat-head wound along
The willowy hills and fields among,
They heard her singing her last song,
　　　The Lady of Shalott.

Heard a carol, mournful, holy,　　　145
Chanted loudly, chanted lowly,
Till her blood was frozen slowly,
And her eyes were darkened wholly,
　　　Turned to towered Camelot.
For ere she reached upon the tide　　　150
The first house by the water-side,
Singing in her song she died,
　　　The Lady of Shalott.

Under tower and balcony,
By garden-wall and gallery,　　　155
A gleaming shape she floated by,
Dead-pale between the houses high,
　　　Silent into Camelot.
Out upon the wharfs they came,
Knight and burgher, lord and dame,　　　160
And round the prow they read her name,
　　　The Lady of Shalott.

Who is this? And what is here?
And in the lighted palace near
Died the sound of royal cheer;　　　165
And they crossed themselves for fear,
　　　All the knights at Camelot:
But Lancelot mused a little space;
He said, "She has a lovely face;
God in his mercy lend her grace,　　　170
　　　The Lady of Shalott."[5]

The Poet

The poet in a golden clime was born,
　　　With golden stars above;
Dowered with the hate of hate, the scorn of scorn,
　　　The love of love.

He saw through life and death, through good and　　　5
　　　ill,
　　　He saw through his own soul,
The marvel of the everlasting will,
　　　An open scroll,

Before him lay: with echoing feet he threaded
　　　The secretest walks of fame:　　　10
The viewless arrows of his thoughts were headed
　　　And winged with flame,

Like Indian reeds[1] blown from his silver tongue,
　　　And of so fierce a flight,

---

5 "Like many of Tennyson's poems, 'The Lady of Shalott'
assumes the quality of parable rather than of strict allegory. The tower, the loom, the mirror, the maiden
herself, have no consistent figurative meaning, but the
reader is tempted to consider the Lady in her tower as
representing the poet, the loom as art, and the mirror as
poetic imagination. If the images have these meanings,
. . . the poem suggests that the artist must remain in aloof
detachment, observing life only in the mirror of the
imagination, not mixing in it directly. Once the artist attempts to live the life of ordinary men his poetic gift,
it would seem, dies." (G. Robert Stange)

1 Arrows blown from a blowpipe.

From Calpe unto Caucasus[2] they sung,
    Filling with light

And vagrant melodies the winds which bore
    Them earthward till they lit;
Then, like the arrow-seeds of the field flower,[3]
    The fruitful wit   20

Cleaving, took root, and springing forth anew
    Where'er they fell, behold,
Like to the mother plant in semblance, grew
    A flower all gold,

And bravely furnished all abroad to fling   25
    The wingèd shafts of truth,
To throng with stately blooms the breathing
    spring
        Of Hope and Youth.

So[4] many minds did gird their orbs with beams,
    Though one did fling the fire.   30
Heaven flowed upon the soul in many dreams
    Of high desire.

Thus truth was multiplied on truth, the world
    Like one great garden showed,
And through the wreaths of floating dark up-   35
    curled,
        Rare sunrise flowed.

And Freedom reared in that august sunrise
    Her beautiful bold brow,
When rites and forms[5] before his burning eyes
    Melted like snow.   40

There was no blood upon her maiden robes
    Sunned by those orient skies;
But round about the circles of the globes
    Of her keen eyes[6]

And in her raiment's hem was traced in flame   45
    WISDOM, a name to shake
All evil dreams of power—a sacred name.
        And when she spake,

Her words did gather thunder as they ran,
    And as the lightning to the thunder   50

---

[2] From Gibraltar to the Caucasus Mountains, that is, through Europe from its western to its eastern limits.
[3] The dandelion.
[4] Thus.
[5] The old tyrannical forms of monarchy and the church.
[6] The word "wisdom" (see the next lines) is reflected in her eyes.

Which follows it, riving the spirit of man,   15
    Making earth wonder,

So was their meaning to her words. No sword
    Of wrath her right arm whirled,
But one poor poet's scroll, and with *his* word   55
    She shook the world.

You Ask Me, Why, Though Ill at Ease

You ask me, why, though ill at ease,
    Within this region I subsist,
    Whose spirits falter in the mist,
And languish for the purple seas.

It is the land that freemen till,   5
    That sober-suited Freedom chose,
    The land, where girt with friends or foes
A man may speak the thing he will;

A land of settled government,
    A land of just and old renown,   10
    Where Freedom slowly broadens down
From precedent to precedent:

Where faction seldom gathers head,
    But by degrees to fullness wrought,
    The strength of some diffusive thought   15
Hath time and space to work and spread.

Should banded unions persecute
    Opinion, and induce a time
    When single thought is civil crime,
And individual freedom mute;   20

Though Power should make from land to land
    The name of Britain trebly great—
    Though every channel of the State
Should fill and choke with golden sand—

Yet waft me from the harbor-mouth,   25
    Wild wind! I seek a warmer sky,
    And I will see before I die
The palms and temples of the South.

Sir Galahad

My good blade carves the casques[1] of men,
    My tough lance thrusteth sure,
My strength is as the strength of ten,
    Because my heart is pure.

---

[1] Helmets.

The shattering trumpet shrilleth high,
  The hard brands shiver on the steel,
The splintered spear-shafts crack and fly,
  The horse and rider reel:
They reel, they roll in clanging lists,   10
  And when the tide of combat stands,
Perfume and flowers fall in showers,
  That lightly rain from ladies' hands.

How sweet are looks that ladies bend
  On whom their favors fall!
For them I battle till the end,   15
  To save from shame and thrall:
But all my heart is drawn above,
  My knees are bowed in crypt and shrine:
I never felt the kiss of love,
  Nor maiden's hand in mine.   20
More bounteous aspects on me beam,
  Me mightier transports move and thrill;
So keep I fair through faith and prayer
  A virgin heart in work and will.

When down the stormy crescent[2] goes,   25
  A light before me swims,
Between dark stems the forest glows,
  I hear a noise of hymns.
Then by some secret shrine I ride;
  I hear a voice but none are there;   30
The stalls are void, the doors are wide,
  The tapers burning fair.
Fair gleams the snowy altar-cloth,
  The silver vessels sparkle clean,
The shrill bell rings, the censer swings,   35
  And solemn chaunts resound between.

Sometimes on lonely mountain-meres
  I find a magic bark;
I leap on board: no helmsman steers:
  I float till all is dark.   40
A gentle sound, an awful light!
  Three angels bear the holy Grail:[3]
With folded feet, in stoles of white,
  On sleeping wings they sail.
Ah, blessed vision! blood of God!   45
  My spirit beats her mortal bars,
As down dark tides the glory slides,
  And star-like mingles with the stars.

When on my goodly charger borne   5
  Through dreaming towns I go,   50
The cock crows ere the Christmas morn,
  The streets are dumb with snow.
The tempest crackles on the leads,[4]
  And, ringing, springs from brand and mail;
But o'er the dark a glory spreads,   55
  And gilds the driving hail.
I leave the plain, I climb the height;
  No branchy thicket shelter yields;
But blessèd forms in whistling storms
  Fly o'er waste fens and windy fields.   60

A maiden knight—to me is given
  Such hope, I know not fear;
I yearn to breathe the airs of heaven
  That often meet me here.
I muse on joy that will not cease,   65
  Pure spaces clothed in living beams,
Pure lilies of eternal peace,
  Whose odors haunt my dreams;
And, stricken by an angel's hand,
  This mortal armor that I wear,   70
This weight and size, this heart and eyes,
  Are touched, are turned to finest air.

The clouds are broken in the sky,
  And through the mountain-walls
A rolling organ-harmony   75
  Swells up, and shakes and falls.
Then move the trees, the copses nod,
  Wings flutter, voices hover clear:
"O just and faithful knight of God!
  Ride on! the prize is near."   80
So pass I hostel, hall, and grange;
  By bridge and ford, by park and pale,
All-armed I ride, whate'er betide,
  Until I find the holy Grail.

To ———.

With the Following Poem[1]

I send you here a sort of allegory,
(For you will understand it) of a soul,

---

[2] The new moon.

[3] The cup in which Joseph of Arimathea was said to have caught the drops of blood that fell from Christ on the cross, and which supposedly he had brought to England.

[4] Leaded roofs.

[1] The dedication is probably to R. C. Trench, one of the Cambridge Apostles, who took Tennyson aside and warned him that "we cannot live in art." That remark, according to Tennyson, was the "inspiration" for "The Palace of Art," which follows.

A sinful soul possessed of many gifts,
A spacious garden full of flowering weeds,
A glorious Devil, large in heart and brain,　　　5
That did love Beauty only (Beauty seen
In all varieties of mould and mind),
And Knowledge for its beauty; or if Good,
Good only for its beauty, seeing not
That Beauty, Good, and Knowledge, are three　10
　　sisters
That dote upon each other, friends to man,
Living together under the same roof,
And never can be sundered without tears.
And he that shuts Love out, in turn shall be
Shut out from Love, and on her threshold lie　15
Howling in outer darkness. Not for this
Was common clay ta'en from the common earth
Moulded by God, and tempered with the tears
Of angels to the perfect shape of man.

The Palace of Art

I built my soul a lordly pleasure-house,
　　Wherein at ease for aye to dwell.
I said, "O Soul, make merry and carouse,
　　Dear soul, for all is well."

A huge crag-platform, smooth as burnished brass,　5
　　I chose. The rangèd ramparts bright
From level meadow-bases of deep grass
　　Suddenly scaled the light.

Thereon I built it firm. Of ledge or shelf
　　The rock rose clear, or winding stair.　　10
My soul would live alone unto herself
　　In her high palace there.

And "while the world runs round and round," I
　　said,
　　"Reign thou apart, a quiet king,
Still as, while Saturn whirls, his steadfast shade　15
　　Sleeps on his luminous ring."[1]

To which my soul made answer readily:
　　"Trust me, in bliss I shall abide
In this great mansion, that is built for me,
　　So royal-rich and wide."　　20

---

[1] The shadow of whirling Saturn cast on the luminous ring that surrounds the planet appears to be motionless.

*　*　*　*　*

Four courts I made, East, West, and South and
　　North,
　　In each a squarèd lawn, wherefrom
The golden gorge of dragons spouted forth
　　A flood of fountain-foam.

And round the cool green courts there ran a row　25
　　Of cloisters, branched like mighty woods,
Echoing all night to that sonorous flow
　　Of spouted fountain-floods.

And round the roofs a gilded gallery
　　That lent broad verge to distant lands,　　30
Far as the wild swan wings, to where the sky
　　Dipped down to sea and sands.

From those four jets four currents in one swell
　　Across the mountain streamed below
In misty folds, that floating as they fell　　35
　　Lit up a torrent-bow.

And high on every peak a statue seemed
　　To hang on tiptoe, tossing up
A cloud of incense of all odor steamed
　　From out a golden cup.　　40

So that she thought, "And who shall gaze upon
　　My palace with unblinded eyes,
While this great bow will waver in the sun,
　　And that sweet incense rise?"

For that sweet incense rose and never failed,　45
　　And, while day sank or mounted higher,
The light aërial gallery, golden-railed,
　　Burnt like a fringe of fire.

Likewise the deep-set windows, stained and
　　traced,
　　Would seem slow-flaming crimson fires　　50
From shadowed grots of arches interlaced,
　　And tipped with frost-like spires.

*　*　*　*　*

Full of long-sounding corridors it was,
　　That over-vaulted grateful gloom,
Through which the livelong day my soul did pass,　55
　　Well-pleased, from room to room.

Full of great rooms and small the palace stood,
　　All various, each a perfect whole

From living Nature, fit for every mood
    And change of my still soul.

For some were hung with arras green and blue,
    Showing a gaudy summer-morn,
Where with puffed cheek the belted hunter blew
    His wreathèd bugle-horn.

One seemed all dark and red—a tract of sand,
    And some one pacing there alone,
Who paced for ever in a glimmering land,
    Lit with a low large moon.

One showed an iron coast and angry waves.
    You seemed to hear them climb and fall
And roar rock-thwarted under bellowing caves
    Beneath the windy wall.

And one, a full-fed river winding slow
    By herds upon an endless plain,
The ragged rims of thunder brooding low,
    With shadow-streaks of rain.

And one, the reapers at their sultry toil.
    In front they bound the sheaves. Behind
Were realms of upland, prodigal in oil,
    And hoary to the wind.[2]

And one a foreground black with stones and slags,
    Beyond, a line of heights, and higher
All barred with long white cloud the scornful crags,
    And highest, snow and fire.

And one, an English home—gray twilight poured
    On dewy pastures, dewy trees,
Softer than sleep—all things in order stored,
    A haunt of ancient Peace.

Nor these alone, but every landscape fair,
    As fit for every mood of mind,
Or gay, or grave, or sweet, or stern, was there
    Not less than truth designed.

        *   *   *   *   *

Or the maid-mother by a crucifix,
    In tracts of pasture sunny-warm,
Beneath branch-work of costly sardonyx
    Sat smiling, babe in arm.

Or in a clear-walled city on the sea,
    Near gilded organ-pipes, her hair
Wound with white roses, slept Saint Cecily;[3]
    An angel looked at her.

Or thronging all one porch of Paradise
    A group of Houris[4] bowed to see
The dying Islamite,[5] with hands and eyes
    That said, We wait for thee.

Or mythic Uther's deeply-wounded son[6]
    In some fair space of sloping greens
Lay, dozing in the vale of Avalon,[7]
    And watched by weeping queens.

Or hollowing one hand against his ear,
    To list a foot-fall, ere he saw
The wood-nymph, stayed the Ausonian king to hear
    Of wisdom and of law.[8]

Or over hills with peaky tops engrailed,[9]
    And many a tract of palm and rice,
The throne of Indian Cama[10] slowly sailed
    A summer fanned with spice.

Or sweet Europa's mantle blew unclasped,
    From off her shoulder backward borne:
From one hand drooped a crocus: one hand grasped
    The mild bull's golden horn.[11]

Or else flushed Ganymede,[12] his rosy thigh
    Half-buried in the Eagle's down,
Sole as a flying star shot through the sky
    Above the pillared town.

Nor these alone: but every legend fair
    Which the supreme Caucasian mind[13]

---

2 Cf. note 2 to "The Lady of Shalott."

3 Patron saint of music.
4 Maidens who lived in the Mohammedan paradise.
5 Mohammedan.
6 King Arthur.
7 Earthly paradise to which Arthur was borne by the queens referred to in the next line.
8 Numa, early Roman king (*Ausonian* = Italian), was counseled by the nymph Egeria.   9 Indented.
10 God of love in Hindu mythology.
11 Europa, princess of Phoenicia, was courted by Zeus in the disguise of a white bull.
12 Trojan boy whom Zeus, in the form of an eagle, carried off to Olympus and made the cupbearer of the gods.
13 Race.

Carved out of Nature for itself, was there,
    Not less than life, designed.

       *   *   *   *   *

Then in the towers I placed great bells that
    swung,
    Moved of themselves, with silver sound;   130
And with choice paintings of wise men I hung
    The royal dais round.

For there was Milton like a seraph strong,
    Beside him Shakespeare bland and mild;
And there the world-worn Dante grasped his 135
    song,
    And somewhat grimly smiled.

And there the Ionian father of the rest;[14]
    A million wrinkles carved his skin;
A hundred winters snowed upon his breast,
    From cheek and throat and chin.   140

Above, the fair hall-ceiling stately-set
    Many an arch high up did lift,
And angels rising and descending met
    With interchange of gift.

Below was all mosaic choicely planned   145
    With cycles of the human tale
Of this wide world, the times of every land
    So wrought, they will not fail.

The people here, a beast of burden slow,
    Toiled onward, pricked with goads and stings; 150
Here played a tiger, rolling to and fro
    The heads and crowns of kings;

Here rose an athlete, strong to break or bind
    All force in bonds that might endure,
And here once more like some sick man declined, 155
    And trusted any cure.

But over these she trod: and those great bells
    Began to chime. She took her throne:
She sat betwixt the shining Oriels,
    To sing her songs alone.   160

And through the topmost Oriels' colored flame
    Two god-like faces gazed below;
Plato the wise, and large-browed Verulam,[15]
    The first of those who know.

And all those names, that in their motion were 165
    Full-welling fountain-heads of change,
Betwixt the slender shafts were blazoned fair
    In diverse raiment strange:

Through which the lights, rose, amber, emerald,
    blue,
    Flushed in her temples and her eyes,   170
And from her lips, as morn from Memnon,[16] drew
    Rivers of melodies.

No nightingale delighteth to prolong
    Her low preamble all alone,
More than my soul to hear her echoed song 175
    Throb through the ribbèd stone;

Singing and murmuring in her feastful mirth,
    Joying to feel herself alive,
Lord over Nature, lord of the visible earth,
    Lord of the senses five;   180

Communing with herself: "All these are mine,
    And let the world have peace or wars,
'Tis one to me." She—when young night divine
    Crowned dying day with stars,

Making sweet close of his delicious toils— 185
    Lit light in wreaths and anadems,[17]
And pure quintessences of precious oils
    In hollowed moons of gems,

To mimic heaven; and clapped her hands and
    cried,
    "I marvel if my still delight   190
In this great house so royal-rich, and wide,
    Be flattered to the height.

"O all things fair to sate my various eyes!
    O shapes and hues that please me well!
O silent faces of the Great and Wise, 195
    My Gods, with whom I dwell!

"O god-like isolation which art mine,
    I can but count thee perfect gain,
What time I watch the darkening droves of swine
    That range on yonder plain.   200

"In filthy sloughs they roll a prurient skin,
    They graze and wallow, breed and sleep;

---

[14] Homer.
[15] Francis Bacon.

[16] A statue near Thebes in Egypt supposed to respond with music to the first rays of the sun.   [17] Garlands.

And oft some brainless devil enters in,
    And drives them to the deep."

Then of the moral instinct would she prate   205
    And of the rising from the dead,
As hers by right of full-accomplished Fate;
    And at the last she said:

"I take possession of man's mind and deed.
    I care not what the sects may brawl.   210
I sit as God holding no form of creed,
    But contemplating all."

      *   *   *   *   *

Full oft the riddle of the painful earth
    Flashed through her as she sat alone,
Yet not the less held she her solemn mirth,   215
    And intellectual throne.

And so she throve and prospered: so three years
    She prospered: on the fourth she fell,
Like Herod, when the shout was in his ears,[18]
    Struck through with pangs of hell.   220

Lest she should fail and perish utterly,
    God, before whom ever lie bare
The abysmal deeps of Personality,
    Plagued her with sore despair.

When she would think, where'er she turned her   225
    sight
    The airy hand confusion wrought,
Wrote, "Mene, mene,"[19] and divided quite
    The kingdom of her thought.

Deep dread and loathing of her solitude
    Fell on her, from which mood was born   230
Scorn of herself, again, from out that mood
    Laughter at her self-scorn.

"What! is not this my place of strength," she said,
    "My spacious mansion built for me,
Whereof the strong foundation-stones were laid   235
    Since my first memory?"

---

18 As the people shouted their praise of him as a god,
Herod was struck down by the angel of the Lord "because
he gave not God the glory." (Acts 12:21–23)
19 One of the words of warning written on the wall of
Belshazzar's palace which David interpreted as meaning,
"God hath numbered thy kingdom, and finished it" (Daniel 5:17–31).

But in dark corners of her palace stood
    Uncertain shapes; and unawares
On white-eyed phantasms weeping tears of blood,
    And horrible nightmares,   240

And hollow shades enclosing hearts of flame,
    And, with dim fretted foreheads all,
On corpses three-months-old at noon she came,
    That stood against the wall.

A spot of dull stagnation, without light   245
    Or power of movement, seemed my soul,
'Mid onward-sloping motions infinite
    Making for one sure goal.

A still salt pool, locked in with bars of sand,
    Left on the shore; that hears all night   250
The plunging seas draw backward from the land
    Their moon-led waters white.

A star that with the choral starry dance
    Joined not, but stood, and standing saw
The hollow orb of moving Circumstance   255
    Rolled round by one fixed law.

Back on herself her serpent pride had curled.
    "No voice," she shrieked in that lone hall,
"No voice breaks through the stillness of this
    world:
        One deep, deep silence all!"   260

She, moldering with the dull earth's moldering
    sod,
    Inwrapt tenfold in slothful shame,
Lay there exilèd from eternal God,
    Lost to her place and name;

And death and life she hated equally,   265
    And nothing saw, for her despair,
But dreadful time, dreadful eternity,
    No comfort anywhere;

Remaining utterly confused with fears,
    And ever worse with growing time,   270
And ever unrelieved by dismal tears,
    And all alone in crime:

Shut up as in a crumbling tomb, girt round
    With blackness as a solid wall,
Far off she seemed to hear the dully sound   275
    Of human footsteps fall:

As in strange lands a traveler walking slow,
    In doubt and great perplexity,
A little before moon-rise hears the low
    Moan of an unknown sea;   280

And knows not if it be thunder, or a sound
    Of rocks thrown down, or one deep cry
Of great wild beasts; then thinketh, "I have
        found
    A new land, but I die."

She howled aloud, "I am on fire within.   285
    There comes no murmur of reply.
What is it that will take away my sin,
    And save me lest I die?"

So when four years were wholly finishèd,
    She threw her royal robes away.   290
"Make me a cottage in the vale," she said,
    "Where I may mourn and pray.

"Yet pull not down my palace towers, that are
    So lightly, beautifully built:
Perchance I may return with others there   295
    When I have purged my guilt."

Oenone[1]

There lies a vale in Ida, lovelier
Than all the valleys of Ionian hills.
The swimming vapor slopes athwart the glen,
Puts forth an arm, and creeps from pine to pine,
And loiters, slowly drawn. On either hand   5
The lawns and meadow-ledges midway down
Hang rich in flowers, and far below them roars
The long brook falling through the cloven ravine
In cataract after cataract to the sea.
Behind the valley topmost Gargarus[2]   10
Stands up and takes the morning: but in front
The gorges, opening wide apart, reveal
Troas and Ilion's columned citadel,[3]
The crown of Troas.
                    Hither came at noon
Mournful Oenone, wandering forlorn   15

Of Paris, once her playmate on the hills.
Her cheek had lost the rose, and round her neck
Floated her hair or seemed to float in rest.
She, leaning on a fragment twined with vine,
Sang to the stillness, till the mountain-shade   20
Sloped downward to her seat from the upper cliff.

    "O mother Ida, many-fountained Ida,
Dear mother Ida, harken ere I die.
For now the noonday quiet holds the hill:
The grasshopper is silent in the grass: 25
The lizard, with his shadow on the stone,
Rests like a shadow, and the winds are dead.
The purple flower droops: the golden bee
Is lily-cradled: I alone awake.
My eyes are full of tears, my heart of love,   30
My heart is breaking, and my eyes are dim,
And I am all aweary of my life.

    "O mother Ida, many-fountained Ida,
Dear mother Ida, harken ere I die.
Hear me, O Earth, hear me, O Hills, O Caves   35
That house the cold crowned snake! O mountain
        brooks,
I am the daughter of a River-God,
Hear me, for I will speak, and build up all
My sorrow with my song, as yonder walls
Rose slowly to a music slowly breathed,[4]   40
A cloud that gathered shape: for it may be
That, while I speak of it, a little while
My heart may wander from its deeper woe.

    "O mother Ida, many-fountained Ida,
Dear mother Ida, harken ere I die.   45
I waited underneath the dawning hills,
Aloft the mountain lawn was dewy-dark,
And dewy-dark aloft the mountain pine:
Beautiful Paris, evil-hearted Paris,
Leading a jet-black goat white-horned, white-   50
        hooved,
Came up from reedy Simois all alone.

    "O mother Ida, harken ere I die.
Far-off the torrent called me from the cleft;
Far up the solitary morning smote
The streaks of virgin snow. With down-dropt eyes   55
I sat alone: white-breasted like a star
Fronting the dawn he moved; a leopard skin
Drooped from his shoulder, but his sunny hair

---

[1] A nymph, daughter of Mt. Ida and the river Simois,
both near Troy. She was beloved by Paris until the fatal
day when he awarded the apple engraved "for the fairest"
to Aphrodite. Aphrodite gave him Helen of Troy in return—and Oenone was deserted.
[2] Highest peak of Mt. Ida.
[3] The region surrounding Troy, and Troy itself.

[4] See "Tithonus," note 4.

Clustered about his temples like a God's:
And his cheek brightened as the foam-bow brightens
When the wind blows the foam, and all my heart
Went forth to embrace him coming ere he came.

"Dear mother Ida, harken ere I die.
He smiled, and opening out his milk-white palm
Disclosed a fruit of pure Hesperian gold,   65
That smelt ambrosially,[5] and while I looked
And listened, the full-flowing river of speech
Came down upon my heart.
                    "'My own Oenone,
Beautiful-browed Oenone, my own soul,
Behold this fruit, whose gleaming rind ingraven   70
"For the most fair," would seem to award it thine,
As lovelier than whatever Oread haunt
The knolls of Ida, loveliest in all grace
Of movement, and the charm of married brows.'

"Dear mother Ida, harken ere I die.   75
He prest the blossom of his lips to mine,
And added, 'This was cast upon the board,
When all the full-faced presence of the Gods
Ranged in the halls of Peleus;[6] whereupon
Rose feud, with question unto whom 'twere due: 80
But light-foot Iris[7] brought it yester-eve,
Delivering, that to me, by common voice
Elected umpire, Herè comes to-day,
Pallas and Aphroditè, claiming each
This meed of fairest.[8] Thou, within the cave   85
Behind yon whispering tuft of oldest pine,
Mayst well behold them unbeheld, unheard
Hear all, and see thy Paris judge of Gods.'

"Dear mother Ida, harken ere I die.
It was the deep midnoon: one silvery cloud   90
Had lost his way between the piney sides
Of this long glen. Then to the bower they came,
Naked they came to that smooth-swarded bower,
And at their feet the crocus brake like fire,
Violet, amaracus, and asphodel,   95
Lotos and lilies: and a wind arose,
And overhead the wandering ivy and vine,
This way and that, in many a wild festoon

Ran riot, garlanding the gnarlèd boughs
With bunch and berry and flower through and through.   100

"O mother Ida, harken ere I die.
On the tree-tops, a crested peacock lit,[9]
And o'er him flowed a golden cloud, and leaned
Upon him, slowly dropping fragrant dew.
Then first I heard the voice of her, to whom   105
Coming through Heaven, like a light that grows
Larger and clearer, with one mind the Gods
Rise up for reverence. She to Paris made
Proffer of royal power, ample rule
Unquestioned, overflowing revenue   110
Wherewith to embellish state, 'from many a vale
And river-sundered champaign clothed with corn,
Or labored mines undrainable of ore.
Honor,' she said, 'and homage, tax and toll,
From many an inland town and haven large,   115
Mast-thronged beneath her shadowing citadel
In glassy bays among her tallest towers.'

"O mother Ida, harken ere I die.
Still she spake on and still she spake of power,
'Which in all action is the end of all;   120
Power fitted to the season; wisdom-bred
And throned of wisdom — from all neighbor crowns
Alliance and allegiance, till thy hand
Fail from the sceptre-staff. Such boon from me,
From me, Heaven's Queen, Paris, to thee king-   125
born,
A shepherd all thy life but yet king-born,
Should come most welcome, seeing men, in power
Only, are likest gods, who have attained
Rest in a happy place and quiet seats
Above the thunder, with undying bliss   130
In knowledge of their own supremacy.'

"Dear mother Ida, harken ere I die.
She ceased, and Paris held the costly fruit
Out at arm's-length, so much the thought of power
Flattered his spirit; but Pallas where she stood   135
Somewhat apart, her clean and barèd limbs
O'erthwarted with the brazen-headed spear
Upon her pearly shoulder leaning cold,
The while, above, her full and earnest eye
Over her snow-cold breast and angry cheek   140
Kept watch, waiting decision, made reply.

---

[5] A fruit like the golden apples guarded by the Hesperides which smells like ambrosia, the food of the gods.
[6] At the wedding feast of Thetis and Peleus.
[7] Messenger of the gods.
[8] Herè is Juno, the wife of Jupiter; Pallas Athena, or Minerva, is the goddess of wisdom; Aphroditè is Venus, goddess of love and beauty.

[9] Bird sacred to Here.

" 'Self-reverence, self-knowledge, self-control,
These three alone lead life to sovereign power.
Yet not for power (power of herself
Would come uncalled for) but to live by law,   145
Acting the law we live by without fear;
And, because right is right, to follow right
Were wisdom in the scorn of consequence.'

"Dear mother Ida, harken ere I die.
Again she said: 'I woo thee not with gifts.   150
Sequel of guerdon[10] could not alter me
To fairer. Judge thou me by what I am,
So shalt thou find me fairest.
                          Yet, indeed,
If gazing on divinity disrobed
Thy mortal eyes are frail to judge of fair,   155
Unbiassed by self-profit, oh! rest thee sure
That I shall love thee well and cleave to thee,
So that my vigor, wedded to thy blood,
Shall strike within thy pulses, like a God's,
To push thee forward through a life of shocks,   160
Dangers, and deeds, until endurance grow
Sinewed with action, and the full-grown will,
Circled through all experiences, pure law,
Commeasure perfect freedom.'[11]
                          "Here she ceased,
And Paris pondered, and I cried, 'O Paris,   165
Give it to Pallas!' but he heard me not,
Or hearing would not hear me, woe is me!

"O mother Ida, many-fountained Ida,
Dear mother Ida, harken ere I die.
Idalian Aphroditè beautiful,   170
Fresh as the foam, new-bathed in Paphian wells,[12]
With rosy slender fingers backward drew
From her warm brows and bosom her deep hair
Ambrosial, golden round her lucid throat
And shoulder: from the violets her light foot   175
Shone rosy-white, and o'er her rounded form
Between the shadows of the vine-bunches
Floated the glowing sunlights, as she moved.

"Dear mother Ida, harken ere I die.
She with a subtle smile in her mild eyes,   180

The herald of her triumph, drawing nigh
Half-whispered in his ear, 'I promise thee
The fairest and most loving wife in Greece,'
She spoke and laughed: I shut my sight for fear:
But when I looked, Paris had raised his arm,   185
And I beheld great Herè's angry eyes,
As she withdrew into the golden cloud,
And I was left alone within the bower;
And from that time to this I am alone,
And I shall be alone until I die.   190

"Yet, mother Ida, harken ere I die.
Fairest—why fairest wife? am I not fair?
My love hath told me so a thousand times.
Methinks I must be fair, for yesterday,
When I past by, a wild and wanton pard,[13]   195
Eyed like the evening star, with playful tail
Crouched fawning in the weed. Most loving is
    she?
Ah me, my mountain shepherd, that my arms
Were wound about thee, and my hot lips prest
Close, close to thine in that quick-falling dew   200
Of fruitful kisses, thick as Autumn rains
Flash in the pools of whirling Simois.

"O mother, hear me yet before I die.
They came, they cut away my tallest pines,[14]
My dark tall pines, that plumed the craggy ledge   205
High over the blue gorge, and all between
The snowy peak and snow-white cataract
Fostered the callow eaglet—from beneath
Whose thick mysterious boughs in the dark morn
The panther's roar came muffled, while I sat   210
Low in the valley. Never, never more
Shall lone Oenone see the morning mist
Sweep through them; never see them overlaid
With narrow moon-lit slips of silver cloud,
Between the loud stream and the trembling stars.   215

"O mother, hear me yet before I die.
I wish that somewhere in the ruined folds,
Among the fragments tumbled from the glens,
Of the dry thickets, I could meet with her
The Abominable,[15] that uninvited came   220
Into the fair Peleïan banquet-hall,
And cast the golden fruit upon the board,

---

10 Reward.
11 The moral will, having gone through the circle of experience, will become pure law to the individual, which is a thing commensurate with perfect freedom from all evil.
12 Idalium and Paphos were towns where Aphroditè was worshiped. She was said to have landed at Paphos after her birth in the sea.

13 Leopard.
14 To build ships with which to sail across the Aegean Sea to Greece, where Helen was living.
15 Eris, goddess of discord.

And bred this change; that I might speak my
   mind,
And tell her to her face how much I hate
Her presence, hated both of Gods and men.   225

   "O mother, hear me yet before I die.
Hath he not sworn his love a thousand times,
In this green valley, under this green hill,
Ev'n on this hand, and sitting on this stone?
Sealed it with kisses? watered it with tears?   230
O happy tears, and how unlike to these!
O happy Heaven, how canst thou see my face?
O happy earth, how canst thou bear my weight?
O death, death, death, thou ever-floating cloud,
There are enough unhappy on this earth,   235
Pass by the happy souls, that love to live:
I pray thee, pass before my light of life,
And shadow all my soul, that I may die.
Thou weighest heavy on the heart within,
Weigh heavy on my eyelids: let me die.   240

   "O mother, hear me yet before I die.
I will not die alone, for fiery thoughts
Do shape themselves within me, more and more,
Whereof I catch the issue, as I hear
Dead sounds at night come from the inmost hills,   245
Like footsteps upon wool. I dimly see
My far-off doubtful purpose,[16] as a mother
Conjectures of the features of her child
Ere it is born: her child!—a shudder comes
Across me: never child be born of me,   250
Unblest, to vex me with his father's eyes!

   "O mother, hear me yet before I die.
Hear me, O earth. I will not die alone,
Lest their shrill happy laughter come to me
Walking the cold and starless road of Death   255
Uncomforted, leaving my ancient love
With the Greek woman. I will rise and go
Down into Troy, and ere the stars come forth
Talk with the wild Cassandra,[17] for she says
A fire dances before her, and a sound   260
Rings ever in her ears of armèd men.
What this may be I know not, but I know
That, wheresoe'er I am by night and day,
All earth and air seem only burning fire."

---

[16] To refuse Paris's request that she heal the wound which she foresees he will receive in the Trojan War, and thus to gain her revenge. This explains her statement (lines 242 and 253) that she will not die alone.
[17] Daughter of Priam, gifted with the power of prophecy. She foretold the Trojan War.

Ulysses

It little profits that an idle king,
By this still hearth, among these barren crags,[1]
Matched with an agèd wife, I mete and dole
Unequal laws unto a savage race,
That hoard, and sleep, and feed, and know not   5
   me.

I cannot rest from travel: I will drink
Life to the lees: all times I have enjoyed
Greatly, have suffered greatly, both with those
That loved me, and alone; on shore, and when
Through scudding drifts the rainy Hyades[2]   10
Vexed the dim sea: I am become a name;
For always roaming with a hungry heart
Much have I seen and known: cities of men
And manners, climates, councils, governments,
Myself not least, but honored of them all;   15
And drunk delight of battle with my peers,
Far on the ringing plains of windy Troy.
I am a part of all that I have met;
Yet all experience is an arch wherethrough
Gleams that untraveled world, whose margin   20
   fades
For ever and for ever when I move.
How dull it is to pause, to make an end,
To rust unburnished, not to shine in use!
As though to breathe were life. Life piled on life
Were all too little, and of one to me   25
Little remains; but every hour is saved
From that eternal silence, something more,[3]
A bringer of new things; and vile it were
For some three suns to store and hoard myself,
And this gray spirit yearning in desire   30
To follow knowledge like a sinking star,
Beyond the utmost bound of human thought.

   This is my son, mine own Telemachus,
To whom I leave the scepter and the isle—
Well-loved of me, discerning to fulfil   35
This labor, by slow prudence to make mild
A rugged people, and through soft degrees
Subdue them to the useful and the good.
Most blameless is he, centered in the sphere
Of common duties, decent not to fail   40

---

[1] Of the island of Ithaca, off the west coast of Greece, the home of Ulysses, to which he had returned, after ten years of wandering, from Troy.
[2] A group of stars associated with the rainy season.
[3] I.e., may be something more than just another hour.

In offices of tenderness, and pay
Meet adoration to my household gods,
When I am gone. He works his work, I mine.

There lies the port; the vessel puffs her sail:
There gloom the dark broad seas. My mariners,   45
Souls that have toiled, and wrought, and thought
    with me—
That ever with a frolic welcome took
The thunder and the sunshine, and opposed
Free hearts, free foreheads—you and I are old;
Old age hath yet his honor and his toil;   50
Death closes all: but something ere the end,
Some work of noble note, may yet be done,
Not unbecoming men that strove with Gods.
The lights begin to twinkle from the rocks:
The long day wanes: the slow moon climbs: the   55
    deep
Moans round with many voices. Come, my friends,
'Tis not too late to seek a newer world.
Push off, and sitting well in order smite
The sounding furrows; for my purpose holds
To sail beyond the sunset, and the baths   60
Of all the western stars, until I die.
It may be that the gulfs will wash us down:
It may be we shall touch the Happy Isles,[4]
And see the great Achilles, whom we knew.
Though much is taken, much abides; and though   65
We are not now that strength which in old days
Moved earth and heaven, that which we are, we
    are;
One equal temper of heroic hearts,
Made weak by time and fate, but strong in will
To strive, to seek, to find, and not to yield.[5]   70

The Lotos-Eaters

"Courage!" he said,[1] and pointed toward the
    land,
"This mounting wave will roll us shoreward
    soon."

---

4 The abode of the Greek heroes after death.
5 Tennyson told his son that the poem was written shortly
after Arthur Hallam's death, "and gave my feeling about
the need of going forward, and braving the struggle of
life." But it also gives his feeling of escaping the struggle
of life by the distraction of endless experience for its
own sake.

1 Ulysses speaking to his men on their way back from Troy
to Ithaca.

In the afternoon they came unto a land
In which it seemèd always afternoon.
All round the coast the languid air did swoon,   5
Breathing like one that hath a weary dream.
Full-faced above the valley stood the moon;
And like a downward smoke, the slender stream
Along the cliff to fall and pause and fall did seem.

A land of streams! some, like a downward smoke,   10
Slow-dropping veils of thinnest lawn, did go;
And some through wavering lights and shadows
    broke,
Rolling a slumbrous sheet of foam below.
They saw the gleaming river seaward flow
From the inner land: far off, three mountain-   15
    tops,
Three silent pinnacles of agèd snow,
Stood sunset-flushed; and, dewed with showery
    drops,
Up-clomb the shadowy pine above the woven
    copse.

The charmèd sunset lingered low adown
In the red West; through mountain clefts the dale   20
Was seen far inland, and the yellow down
Bordered with palm, and many a winding vale
And meadow, set with slender galingale;[2]
A land where all things always seemed the same!
And round about the keel with faces pale,   25
Dark faces pale against that rosy flame,
The mild-eyed melancholy Lotos-eaters came.

Branches they bore of that enchanted stem,
Laden with flower and fruit, whereof they gave
To each, but whoso did receive of them,   30
And taste, to him the gushing of the wave
Far far away did seem to mourn and rave
On alien shores; and if his fellow spake,
His voice was thin, as voices from the grave;
And deep-asleep he seemed, yet all awake,   35
And music in his ears his beating heart did make.

They sat them down upon the yellow sand,
Between the sun and moon upon the shore;
And sweet it was to dream of Fatherland,
Of child, and wife, and slave; but evermore   40
Most weary seemed the sea, weary the oar,
Weary the wandering fields of barren foam.
Then some one said, "We will return no more";

---

2 A kind of grass.

And all at once they sang, "Our island home
Is far beyond the wave; we will no longer roam." 45

CHORIC SONG

I

There is sweet music here that softer falls
Than petals from blown roses on the grass,
Or night-dews on still waters between walls
Of shadowy granite, in a gleaming pass;
Music that gentlier on the spirit lies, 50
Than tired eyelids upon tired eyes;
Music that brings sweet sleep down from the
    blissful skies.
Here are cool mosses deep,
And through the moss the ivies creep,
And in the stream the long-leaved flowers weep, 55
And from the craggy ledge the poppy hangs in
    sleep.

II

Why are we weighed upon with heaviness,
And utterly consumed with sharp distress,
While all things else have rest from weariness?
All things have rest: why should we toil alone, 60
We only toil, who are the first things,
And make perpetual moan,
Still from one sorrow to another thrown;
Nor ever fold our wings,
And cease from wanderings, 65
Nor steep our brows in slumber's holy balm;
Nor harken what the inner spirit sings,
"There is no joy but calm!"
Why should we only toil, the roof and crown of
    things?

III

Lo! in the middle of the wood, 70
The folded leaf is wooed from out the bud
With winds upon the branch, and there
Grows green and broad, and takes no care,
Sun-steeped at noon, and in the moon
Nightly dew-fed; and turning yellow 75
Falls, and floats adown the air.
Lo! sweetened with the summer light,
The full-juiced apple, waxing over-mellow,
Drops in a silent autumn night.
All its allotted length of days, 80
The flower ripens in its place,
Ripens and fades, and falls, and hath no toil,
Fast-rooted in the fruitful soil.

IV

Hateful is the dark-blue sky,
Vaulted o'er the dark-blue sea. 85
Death is the end of life; ah, why
Should life all labor be?
Let us alone. Time driveth onward fast,
And in a little while our lips are dumb.
Let us alone. What is it that will last? 90
All things are taken from us, and become
Portions and parcels of the dreadful Past.
Let us alone. What pleasure can we have
To war with evil? Is there any peace
In ever climbing up the climbing wave? 95
All things have rest, and ripen toward the grave
In silence; ripen, fall and cease:
Give us long rest or death, dark death, or dream-
    ful ease.

V

How sweet it were, hearing the downward stream,
With half-shut eyes ever to seem 100
Falling asleep in a half-dream!
To dream and dream, like yonder amber light,
Which will not leave the myrrh-bush on the
    height;
To hear each other's whispered speech;
Eating the Lotos day by day, 105
To watch the crisping ripples on the beach,
And tender curving lines of creamy spray;
To lend our hearts and spirits wholly
To the influence of mild-minded melancholy;
To muse and brood and live again in memory, 110
With those old faces of our infancy
Heaped over with a mound of grass,
Two handfuls of white dust, shut in an urn of
    brass!

VI

Dear is the memory of our wedded lives,
And dear the last embraces of our wives 115
And their warm tears: but all hath suffered
    change:
For surely now our household hearths are cold:
Our sons inherit us: our looks are strange:
And we should come like ghosts to trouble joy.
Or else the island princes over-bold 120
Have eat our substance, and the minstrel sings
Before them of the ten years' war in Troy,
And our great deeds, as half-forgotten things.
Is there confusion in the little isle?

Let what is broken so remain.
The gods are hard to reconcile:
'Tis hard to settle order once again.
There *is* confusion worse than death,
Trouble on trouble, pain on pain,
Long labor unto agèd breath,   130
Sore task to hearts worn out by many wars
And eyes grown dim with gazing on the pilot-
    stars.

VII

But, propped on beds of amaranth[3] and moly,[4]
How sweet (while warm airs lull us, blowing
    lowly)
With half-dropped eyelid still,   135
Beneath a heaven dark and holy,
To watch the long bright river drawing slowly
His waters from the purple hill—
To hear the dewy echoes calling
From cave to cave through the thick-twinèd vine—   140
To watch the emerald-colored water falling
Through many a wov'n acanthus-wreath divine![5]
Only to hear and see the far-off sparkling brine,
Only to hear were sweet, stretched out beneath
    the pine.

VIII

The Lotos blooms below the barren peak: 145
The Lotos blows by every winding creek:
All day the wind breathes low with mellower
    tone:
Through every hollow cave and alley lone
Round and round the spicy downs the yellow
    Lotos-dust is blown.
We have had enough of action, and of motion   150
    we,
Rolled to starboard, rolled to larboard, when the
    surge was seething free,
Where the wallowing monster spouted his foam-
    fountains in the sea.
Let us swear an oath, and keep it with an equal
    mind,
In the hollow Lotos-land to live and lie reclined
On the hills like Gods together, careless of man-   155
    kind.
For they lie beside their nectar, and the bolts are
    hurled

Far below them in the valleys, and the clouds are   125
    lightly curled
Round their golden houses, girdled with the
    gleaming world:
Where they smile in secret, looking over wasted
    lands,
Blight and famine, plague and earthquake, roar-   160
    ing deeps and fiery sands,
Clanging fights, and flaming towns, and sinking
    ships, and praying hands.
But they smile, they find a music centered in a
    doleful song
Steaming up, a lamentation and an ancient tale
    of wrong,
Like a tale of little meaning though the words are
    strong;
Chanted from an ill-used race of men that cleave   165
    the soil,
Sow the seed, and reap the harvest with enduring
    toil,
Storing yearly little dues of wheat, and wine and
    oil;
Till they perish and they suffer—some, 'tis whis-
    pered—down in hell
Suffer endless anguish, others in Elysian valleys
    dwell,[6]
Resting weary limbs at last on beds of asphodel.   170
Surely, surely, slumber is more sweet than toil,
    the shore
Than labor in the deep mid-ocean, wind and
    wave and oar;
O rest ye, brother mariners, we will not wander
    more.[7]

Locksley Hall

Comrades, leave me here a little, while as yet 'tis
    early morn:
Leave me here, and when you want me, sound
    upon the bugle-horn.

---

3 A flower that could not fade.
4 An herb of magical power.
5 Acanthus was a plant sacred to the gods.

6 The Elysian fields were the paradise of the Greeks.
7 "By introducing into the second version of the poem
this comparison of the lotos-eaters to the Lucretian gods,
aloof 'from all human interests and elevated action,' living in 'an Epicurean and therefore hard-hearted repose,
sweetened not troubled by the endless wail from the
earth' (*Memoir*, I, 504), Tennyson injected a moral-religious judgment into an amoral poem, and suddenly asked
the reader to condemn what had earlier been presented
as largely attractive and desirable. Did he try to "save"
a poem of escape by tacking on a moral?" (R. C. Haynes)

'Tis the place, and all around it, as of old, the
    curlews[1] call,
Dreary gleams about the moorland flying over
    Locksley Hall;[2]

Locksley Hall, that in the distance overlooks the
    sandy tracts,
And the hollow ocean-ridges roaring into cata-
    racts.

Many a night from yonder ivied casement, ere I
    went to rest,
Did I look on great Orion sloping slowly to the
    West.

Many a night I saw the Pleiads, rising through
    the mellow shade,
Glitter like a swarm of fire-flies tangled in a silver   10
    braid.

Here about the beach I wandered, nourishing a
    youth sublime
With the fairy tales of science, and the long result
    of Time;

When the centuries behind me like a fruitful
    land reposed;
When I clung to all the present for the promise
    that it closed:

When I dipped into the future far as human eye   15
    could see;
Saw the Vision of the world, and all the wonder
    that would be.—

In the spring a fuller crimson comes upon the
    robin's breast;
In the spring the wanton lapwing gets himself
    another crest;

In the spring a livelier iris changes on the burn-
    ished dove;[3]
In the spring a young man's fancy lightly turns   20
    to thoughts of love.

Then her cheek was pale and thinner than should
    be for one so young,

And her eyes on all my motions with a mute
    observance hung.

And I said, "My cousin Amy, speak and speak the
    truth to me,
Trust me, cousin, all the current of my being sets   5
    to thee."

On her pallid cheek and forehead came a color   25
    and a light,
As I have seen the rosy red flushing in the
    northern night.

And she turned—her bosom shaken with a sud-
    den storm of sighs—
All the spirit deeply dawning in the dark of
    hazel eyes—

Saying, "I have hid my feelings, fearing they
    should do me wrong";
Saying, "Dost thou love me, cousin?" weeping, "I   30
    have loved thee long."

Love took up the glass of Time, and turned it in
    his glowing hands;
Every moment, lightly shaken, ran itself in golden
    sands.

Love took up the harp of Life, and smote on all
    the chords with might;
Smote the chord of Self, that, trembling, passed
    in music out of sight.

Many a morning on the moorland did we hear   35
    the copses ring,
And her whisper thronged my pulses with the
    fulness of the Spring.

Many an evening by the waters did we watch the
    stately ships,
And our spirits rushed together at the touching
    of the lips.

O my cousin, shallow-hearted! O my Amy, mine
    no more!
O the dreary, dreary moorland! O the barren,   40
    barren shore!

Falser than all fancy fathoms, falser than all songs
    have sung,

---

1 Long-billed shore birds.
2 Tennyson said he meant "to express the flying gleams of
light across a dreary moorland."
3 The rainbow colors on the dove's neck become brighter
during the mating season.

Puppet to a father's threat, and servile to a
    shrewish tongue![4]

Is it well to wish thee happy?—having known
    me—to decline
On a range of lower feelings and a narrower heart
    than mine!

Yet it shall be; thou shalt lower to his level day   45
    by day,
What is fine within thee growing coarse to sym-
    pathize with clay.

As the husband is, the wife is: thou are mated
    with a clown,
And the grossness of his nature will have weight
    to drag thee down.

He will hold thee, when his passion shall have
    spent its novel force,
Something better than his dog, a little dearer   50
    than his horse.

What is this? his eyes are heavy: think not they
    are glazed with wine.
Go to him: it is thy duty: kiss him; take his hand
    in thine.

It may be my lord is weary, that his brain is over-
    wrought:
Soothe him with thy finer fancies, touch him with
    thy lighter thought.

He will answer to the purpose, easy things to   55
    understand—
Better thou wert dead before me, though I slew
    thee with my hand!

Better thou and I were lying, hidden from the
    heart's disgrace,
Rolled in one another's arms, and silent in a last
    embrace.

Cursèd be the social wants that sin against the
    strength of youth!
Cursèd be the social lies that warp us from the   60
    living truth!

Cursèd be the sickly forms that err from honest
    Nature's rule!
Cursèd be the gold that gilds the straitened fore-
    head of the fool!

Well—'tis well that I should bluster!—Hadst
    thou less unworthy proved—
Would to God—for I had loved thee more than
    ever wife was loved.

Am I mad, that I should cherish that which bears   65
    but bitter fruit?
I will pluck it from my bosom, though my heart
    be at the root.

Never, though my mortal summers to such length
    of years should come
As the many-wintered crow that leads the clang-
    ing rookery home.

Where is comfort? in division of the records of
    the mind?
Can I part her from herself, and love her, as I   70
    knew her, kind?

I remember one that perished: sweetly did she
    speak and move:
Such a one do I remember, whom to look at was
    to love.

Can I think of her as dead, and love her for the
    love she bore?
No—she never loved me truly: love is love for
    evermore.

Comfort? comfort scorned of devils! this is truth   75
    the poet sings,[5]
That a sorrow's crown of sorrow is remembering
    happier things.

Drug thy memories, lest thou learn it, lest thy
    heart be put to proof,
In the dead unhappy night, and when the rain is
    on the roof.

Like a dog, he[6] hunts in dreams, and thou art
    staring at the wall,
Where the dying night-lamp flickers, and the   80
    shadows rise and fall.

---

[4] I.e., she weakly yielded to her parents' desire that she
marry another man, of more wealth and social position.

[5] Dante in the *Inferno*, V, 121.   [6] Amy's husband.

Then a hand shall pass before thee, pointing to
    his drunken sleep,
To thy widowed marriage-pillows, to the tears
    that thou wilt weep.

Thou shalt hear the "Never, never," whispered
    by the phantom years,
And a song from out the distance in the ringing
    of thine ears;

And an eye shall vex thee, looking ancient kind-   85
    ness on thy pain.
Turn thee, turn thee on thy pillow; get thee to
    thy rest again.

Nay, but Nature brings thee solace; for a tender
    voice will cry.
'Tis a purer life than thine; a lip to drain thy
    trouble dry.

Baby lips will laugh me down: my latest rival
    brings thee rest.
Baby fingers, waxen touches, press me from the   90
    mother's breast.

Oh, the child too clothes the father with a dear-
    ness not his due.
Half is thine and half is his: it will be worthy of
    the two.

Oh, I see thee old and formal, fitted to thy petty
    part,
With a little hoard of maxims preaching down a
    daughter's heart.

"They were dangerous guides, the feelings—she   95
    herself was not exempt—
Truly, she herself had suffered"—Perish in thy
    self-contempt!

Overlive it—lower yet—be happy! wherefore
    should I care?
I myself must mix with action, lest I wither by
    despair.

What is that which I should turn to, lighting
    upon days like these?
Every door is barred with gold, and opens but to   100
    golden keys.

Every gate is thronged with suitors, all the
    markets overflow.

I have but an angry fancy; what is that which I
    should do?

I had been content to perish, falling on the
    foeman's ground,
When the ranks are rolled in vapor, and the
    winds are laid with sound.

But the jingling of the guinea helps the hurt that   105
    Honor feels,
And the nations do but murmur, snarling at each
    other's heels.

Can I but relive in sadness? I will turn that earlier
    page.
Hide me from my deep emotion, O thou won-
    drous Mother-Age!

Make me feel the wild pulsation that I felt before
    the strife,
When I heard my days before me, and the tumult   110
    of my life;

Yearning for the large excitement that the coming
    years would yield,
Eager-hearted as a boy when first he leaves his
    father's field,

And at night along the dusky highway near and
    nearer drawn,
Sees in heaven the light of London flaring like a
    dreary dawn;

And his spirit leaps within him to be gone before   115
    him then,
Underneath the light he looks at, in among the
    throngs of men:

Men, my brothers, men the workers, ever reaping
    something new:
That which they have done but earnest of the
    things that they shall do:

For I dipped into the future, far as human eye
    could see,
Saw the Vision of the world, and all the wonder   120
    that would be;

Saw the heavens fill with commerce, argosies of
    magic sails,
Pilots of the purple twilight, dropping down
    with costly bales;

Heard the heavens fill with shouting, and there
rained a ghastly dew

From the nations' airy navies grappling in the
central blue;

Far along the world-wide whisper of the south-   125
wind rushing warm,

With the standards of the peoples plunging
through the thunder-storm;

Till the war-drum throbbed no longer, and the
battle-flags were furled

In the Parliament of man, the Federation of the
world.

There the common sense of most shall hold a
fretful realm in awe,

And the kindly earth shall slumber, lapped in   130
universal law.

So I triumphed ere my passion sweeping through
me left me dry,

Left me with the palsied heart, and left me with
the jaundiced eye;

Eye, to which all order festers, all things here are
out of joint:

Science moves, but slowly slowly, creeping on
from point to point:

Slowly comes a hungry people, as a lion creeping   135
nigher,

Glares at one that nods and winks behind a
slowly dying fire.

Yet I doubt not through the ages one increasing
purpose runs,

And the thoughts of men are widened with the
process of the suns.[7]

What is that to him that reaps not harvest of his
youthful joys,

Though the deep heart of existence beat forever   140
like a boy's?

Knowledge comes, but wisdom lingers, and I
linger on the shore,

And the individual withers, and the world is
more and more.[8]

Knowledge comes, but wisdom lingers, and he
bears a laden breast,

Full of sad experience, moving toward the stillness of his rest.

Hark, my merry comrades call me, sounding on   145
the bugle-horn,

They to whom my foolish passion were a target
for their scorn:

Shall it not be scorn to me to harp on such a
moldered string?

I am shamed through all my nature to have loved
so slight a thing.

Weakness to be wroth with weakness! woman's
pleasure, woman's pain—

Nature made them blinder motions bounded in a   150
shallower brain:

Woman is the lesser man, and all thy passions,
matched with mine,

Are as moonlight unto sunlight, and as water
unto wine—

Here at least, where nature sickens, nothing. Ah,
for some retreat

Deep in yonder shining Orient, where my life
began to beat;

Where in wild Mahratta-battle[9] fell my father   155
evil-starred;—

I was left a trampled orphan, and a selfish uncle's
ward.

Or to burst all links of habit—there to wander
far away,

On from island unto island at the gateways of the
day.

Larger constellations burning, mellow moons and
happy skies,

Breadths of tropic shade and palms in cluster,   160
knots of Paradise.

---

7 The passage of the years.

8 Many Victorians, notably Mill and Arnold, felt that the
advance of democracy was forcing people to become more
and more alike, that is, more and more like "the average
man."

9 In a battle in India against the tribe of the Mahrattas.

Never comes the trader, never floats an European
    flag,
Slides the bird o'er lustrous woodland, swings the
    trailer[10] from the crag;

Droops the heavy-blossomed bower, hangs the
    heavy-fruited tree—
Summer isles of Eden lying in dark-purple
    spheres of sea.

There methinks would be enjoyment more than   165
    in this march of mind,
In the steamship, in the railway, in the thoughts
    that shake mankind.

There the passions cramped no longer shall have
    scope and breathing space;
I will take some savage woman, she shall rear my
    dusky race.

Iron jointed, supple-sinewed, they shall dive, and
    they shall run,
Catch the wild goat by the hair, and hurl their   170
    lances in the sun;

Whistle back the parrot's call, and leap the rain-
    bows of the brooks,
Not with blinded eyesight poring over miserable
    books—

Fool, again the dream, the fancy! but I *know* my
    words are wild,
But I count the gray barbarian lower than the
    Christian child.

I, to herd with narrow foreheads, vacant of our   175
    glorious gains,
Like a beast with lower pleasures, like a beast
    with lower pains!

Mated with a squalid savage—what to me were
    sun or clime?
I the heir of all the ages, in the foremost files of
    time—

I that rather held it better men should perish
    one by one,
Than that earth should stand at gaze like   180
    Joshua's moon in Ajalon![11]

---

10 A trailing vine.
11 Joshua commanded the moon to stand still in the
valley of Ajalon (Joshua 10:12-13).

Not in vain the distance beacons. Forward, for-
    ward let us range,
Let the great world spin for ever down the ring-
    ing grooves of change.

Through the shadow of the globe we sweep into
    the younger day:
Better fifty years of Europe than a cycle of Cathay.

Mother-Age (for mine I knew not) help me as   185
    when life begun:
Rift the hills, and roll the waters, flash the light-
    nings, weigh the Sun.

Oh, I see the crescent promise of my spirit hath
    not set.
Ancient founts of inspiration well through all my
    fancy yet.

Howsoever these things be, a long farewell to
    Locksley Hall!
Now for me the woods may wither, now for me   190
    the roof-tree fall.

Comes a vapor from the margin, blackening over
    heath and holt,[12]
Cramming all the blast before it, in its breast a
    thunderbolt.

Let it fall on Locksley Hall, with rain or hail, or
    fire or snow;
For the mighty wind arises, roaring seaward, and
    I go.

The Vision of Sin

I

I had a vision when the night was late:
A youth came riding toward a palace-gate.
He rode a horse with wings, that would have
    flown,
But that his heavy rider kept him down.[1]

---

12 Wood or copse.

1 Tennyson is drawing an analogy between this youth and
Bellerophon, who tried to fly to heaven on the winged
horse Pegasus, but fell. For the full meaning cf. Tennyson's remark (*Memoir*, II, 337), "The higher moral imagination enslaved to sense is like an eagle caught by the feet
in a snare, baited with carrion, so that it cannot use its
wings to soar."

And from the palace came a child of sin,
And took him by the curls, and led him in,
Where sat a company with heated eyes,
Expecting when a fountain should arise:
A sleepy light upon their brows and lips— 10
As when the sun, a crescent of eclipse,
Dreams over lake and lawn, and isles and capes—
Suffused them, sitting, lying, languid shapes,
By heaps of gourds, and skins of wine, and piles
    of grapes.

II

Then methought I heard a mellow sound,
Gathering up from all the lower ground; 15
Narrowing in to where they sat assembled
Low voluptuous music winding trembled,
Woven in circles: they that heard it sighed,
Panted hand-in-hand with faces pale,
Swung themselves, and in low tones replied; 20
Till the fountain spouted, showering wide
Sleet of diamond-drift and pearly hail;
Then the music touched the gates and died;
Rose again from where it seemed to fail,
Stormed in orbs of song, a growing gale; 25
Till thronging in and in, to where they waited,
As 't were a hundred-throated nightingale,
The strong tempestuous treble throbbed and
    palpitated;
Ran into its giddiest whirl of sound,
Caught the sparkles, and in circles, 30
Purple gauzes, golden hazes, liquid mazes,
Flung the torrent rainbow round:[2]
Then they started from their places,
Moved with violence, changed in hue,
Caught each other with wild grimaces, 35
Half-invisible to the view,
Wheeling with precipitate paces
To the melody, till they flew,
Hair, and eyes, and limbs, and faces,
Twisted hard in fierce embraces, 40
Like to Furies, like to Graces,
Dashed together in blinding dew:[3]
Till, killed with some luxurious agony,

The nerve-dissolving melody 5
Fluttered headlong from the sky. 45

III

And then I looked up toward a mountain-tract,
That girt the region with high cliff and lawn:
I saw that every morning, far withdrawn
Beyond the darkness and the cataract,
God made Himself an awful rose of dawn, 50
Unheeded: and detaching, fold by fold,
From those still heights, and, slowly drawing
    near,
A vapor heavy, hueless, formless, cold,
Came floating on for many a month and year,
Unheeded:[4] and I thought I would have spoken, 55
And warned that madman ere it grew too late:
But, as in dreams, I could not. Mine was broken,
When that cold vapor touched the palace gate,
And linked again.[5] I saw within my head
A gray and gap-toothed man as lean as death, 60
Who slowly rode across a withered heath,
And lighted at a ruined inn, and said:

IV

"Wrinkled ostler, grim and thin!
    Here is custom come your way;
Take my brute, and lead him in, 65
    Stuff his ribs with mouldy hay.

"Bitter barmaid, waning fast!
    See that sheets are on my bed;[6]
What! the flower of life is past:
    It is long before you wed. 70

"Slipshod waiter, lank and sour,
    At the Dragon[7] on the heath!
Let us have a quiet hour,
    Let us hob-and-nob with Death.

---

2 The fountain rising from below (doubtless Tennyson means to suggest from hell) is probably a fountain of music, and the succeeding images of water and wind represent the "river" and "storm" of Bacchanalian song. The impressionistic technique is striking.
3 Another fine piece of impressionism. *Dew* means *mist*. The Graces and the Furies suggest the combination of sensuous beauty and sadistic passion.

4 According to Tennyson, the "mists of satiety," which come down from the heights because they are the threatened punishment of God upon a life of sensuality. But both God and the approaching punishment are unheeded by the youth. The metaphor of a stream of vapor with its epithets (heavy, hueless, formless, cold) is chosen for contrast with the music imagery above, to underscore the difference between satiety and the first excited indulgence.
5 My dream was broken, and then linked up again with a new image of the madman years later.
6 An invitation, which the barmaid refuses (see the next two lines).
7 The name of the inn.

"I am old, but let me drink; 75
  Bring me spices, bring me wine;
I remember, when I think,
  That my youth was half divine.[8]

"Wine is good for shriveled lips,
  When a blanket wraps the day, 80
When the rotten woodland drips,
  And the leaf is stamped in clay.

"Sit thee down, and have no shame,
  Cheek by jowl, and knee by knee:
What care I for any name? 85
  What for order or degree?

"Let me screw thee up a peg:[9]
  Let me loose thy tongue with wine:
Callest thou that thing a leg?
  Which is thinnest? Thine or mine? 90

"Thou shalt not be saved by works;
  Thou hast been a sinner too:
Ruined trunks on withered forks,
  Empty scarecrows, I and you!

"Fill the cup and fill the can: 95
  Have a rouse[10] before the morn:
Every moment dies a man,
  Every moment one is born.[11]

"We are men of ruined blood;
  Therefore comes it we are wise. 100
Fish are we that love the mud,
  Rising to no fancy-flies.[12]

"Name and fame! to fly sublime
  Through the courts, the camps, the schools,

Is to be the ball of Time, 105
  Bandied by the hands of fools.

"Friendship!—to be two in one—
  Let the canting liar pack!
Well I know, when I am gone,
  How she mouths behind my back. 110

"Virtue!—to be good and just—
  Every heart, when sifted well,
Is a clot of warmer dust,
  Mixed with cunning sparks of hell.

"O, we two as well can look 115
  Whited thought and cleanly life
As the priest, above his book
  Leering at his neighbor's wife.

"Fill the cup and fill the can:
  Have a rouse before the morn: 120
Every moment dies a man,
  Every moment one is born.

"Drink, and let the parties[13] rave:
  They are filled with idle spleen;
Rising, falling, like a wave, 125
  For they know not what they mean.

"He that roars for liberty
  Faster binds a tyrant's power;[14]
And the tyrant's cruel glee
  Forces on the freer hour. 130

"Fill the can, and fill the cup:
  All the windy ways of men
Are but dust that rises up,
  And is lightly laid again.

"Greet her with applausive breath, 135
  Freedom, gaily doth she tread;
In her right a civic wreath,
  In her left a human head.

"No, I love not what is new;
  She is of an ancient house: 140

---

8 Cf. line 3.
9 A notch or degree (cf. previous line). Let me raise you up with a drink so that you'll feel my equal (which he is in the sense brought out in the next stanza).
10 Carouse.
11 Human life is just an endless round of birth and death, death and birth; hence the emotional attitude of weary futility that the lines express.
12 This is the key stanza. The "hero" is by no means merely a debauched sinner, and the poem is not a moralistic sermon on the results of sin. From living in the mud, the sinner has become wise to the illusions of life. He has learned, for one thing, to penetrate below fair exteriors to the ugliness that often lies beneath. Lines 103–18 give three examples of "fancy-flies": name and fame, friendship, and virtue.

13 The political parties. Lines 123–50 describe the futile course of politics, action and reaction. Cf. Tennyson (Memoir, II, 339): "Action and Reaction is the miserable see-saw of our child-world."
14 Cf. Tennyson (Memoir, II, 338): "Violent, selfish, unreasoning democracy would bring . . . the iron rule of a Cromwell"—as it had brought the iron rule of Napoleon.

And I think we know the hue
    Of that cap upon her brows.[15]

"Let her go! her thirst she slakes
    Where the bloody conduit runs,
Then her sweetest meal she makes   145
    On the first-born of her sons.

"Drink to lofty hopes that cool—
    Visions of a perfect State:
Drink we, last, the public fool,
    Frantic love and frantic hate.   150

"Chant me now some wicked stave,[16]
    Till thy drooping courage rise,
And the glow-worm of the grave
    Glimmer in thy rheumy eyes.

"Fear not thou to loose thy tongue;   155
    Set thy hoary fancies free;
What is loathsome to the young
    Savors well to thee and me.

"Change, reverting to the years,[17]
    When thy nerves could understand   160
What there is in loving tears,
    And the warmth of hand in hand.

"Tell me tales of thy first love—
    April hopes, the fools of chance;
Till the graves begin to move,   165
    And the dead begin to dance.[18]

"Fill the can, and fill the cup:
    All the windy ways of men
Are but dust that rises up,
    And is lightly laid again.   170

"Trooping from their mouldy dens
    The chap-fallen[19] circle spreads:
Welcome, fellow-citizens,
    Hollow hearts and empty heads![20]

"You are bones, and what of that?   175
    Every face, however full,
Padded round with flesh and fat,
    Is but modeled on a skull.

"Death is king, and Vivat Rex[21]
    Tread a measure on the stones,   180
Madam—if I know your sex,
    From the fashion of your bones.

"No, I cannot praise the fire
    In your eye—nor yet your lip;
All the more do I admire   185
    Joints of cunning workmanship.

"Lo! God's likeness—the ground-plan—
    Neither modeled, glazed, nor framed:
Buss[22] me, thou rough sketch of man,
    Far too naked to be shamed!   190

"Drink to Fortune, drink to Chance,
    While we keep a little breath!
Drink to heavy Ignorance![23]
    Hob-and-nob with brother Death!

"Thou art mazed,[24] the night is long,   195
    And the longer night is near:
What! I am not all as wrong
    As a bitter jest is dear.[25]

"Youthful hopes, by scores, to all,
    When the locks are crisp and curled;   200
Unto me my maudlin gall
    And my mockeries of the world.

"Fill the cup, and fill the can:
    Mingle madness, mingle scorn!
Dregs of life, and lees of man: 205
    Yet we will not die forlorn."[26]

V

The voice grew faint: there came a further
    change:

---

[15] The red cap of the French revolutionists.
[16] Song.
[17] No, change that and sing instead of the years of youth.
[18] The ghosts of those you loved.
[19] Jaw-fallen. The image is that of a gaping skeleton.
[20] Cf. line 94. Here and in the next stanzas the process of stripping off the illusions of life is extended from the moral and political orders to man himself. Under life, so to speak, is death.

[21] Long live the king.   [22] Kiss.
[23] Of both the past (cf. lines 75–78, 163–64) and the future (the actual fact of death).   [24] Drunk.
[25] What! You question my interpretation of life? I am not as far from being wrong as a bitter jest, like my interpretation, is from being dear (appreciated). Or, in looser paraphrase, my bitter jests are more true than welcome.
[26] Hopeless and abandoned. The prophecy is fulfilled in the next stanza.

Once more uprose the mystic mountain-range:
Below were men and horses pierced with worms,
And slowly quickening into lower forms;   210
By shards[27] and scurf[28] of salt, and scum of dross,
Old plash[29] of rains, and refuse patched with
    moss.
Then some one spake: "Behold! it was a crime
Of sense avenged by sense that wore with time."
Another said: "The crime of sense became   215
The crime of malice,[30] and is equal blame."
And one: "He had not wholly quenched his
    power;
A little grain of conscience made him sour."[31]
At last I heard a voice upon the slope
Cry to the summit, "Is there any hope?"   220
To which an answer pealed from that high land,
But in a tongue no man could understand;
And on the glimmering limit far withdrawn
God made Himself an awful rose of dawn.

Break, Break, Break

Break, break, break,
  On thy cold gray stones, O Sea!
And I would that my tongue could utter
  The thoughts that arise in me.

O well for the fisherman's boy,   5
  That he shouts with his sister at play!
O well for the sailor lad,
  That he sings in his boat on the bay!

And the stately ships go on
  To their haven under the hill;   10
But O for the touch of a vanished hand,
  And the sound of a voice that is still!

Break, break, break
  At the foot of thy crags, O Sea!
But the tender grace of a day that is dead   15
  Will never come back to me.

---

27 Broken chinaware.   28 Scaly incrustation.
29 Puddles.
30 "The sensualist becomes worn out by his senses" (Tennyson's note), as predicted in lines 51–55.
31 The first two judgments are not wrong, but they leave out the all-important fact, demonstrated in section IV, that the man still had power (the power of insight) and a conscience which made him sour. As a result (see the last lines), God holds out the bright promise of salvation.

Sweet and Low[1]

Sweet and low, sweet and low,
  Wind of the western sea,
Low, low, breathe and blow,
  Wind of the western sea!
Over the rolling waters go,   5
Come from the dying moon, and blow,
  Blow him again to me;
While my little one, while my pretty one, sleeps.

Sleep and rest, sleep and rest,
  Father will come to thee soon;   10
Rest, rest, on mother's breast,
  Father will come to thee soon;
Father will come to his babe in the nest,
Silver sails all out of the west
  Under the silver moon: 15
Sleep, my little one, sleep, my pretty one, sleep.

The Splendor Falls
on Castle Walls

The splendor falls on castle walls
  And snowy summits old in story:
The long light shakes across the lakes,
  And the wild cataract leaps in glory.
Blow, bugle, blow, set the wild echoes flying,   5
Blow, bugle; answer, echoes, dying, dying, dying.

  O hark, O hear! how thin and clear,
    And thinner, clearer, farther going!
  O sweet and far from cliff and scar
    The horns of Elfland faintly blowing!   10
Blow, let us hear the purple glens replying:
Blow, bugle; answer, echoes, dying, dying, dying.

  O love, they die in yon rich sky,
    They faint on hill or field or river;
  Our echoes roll from soul to soul,   15
    And grow for ever and for ever.
Blow, bugle, blow, set the wild echoes flying,
And answer, echoes, answer, dying, dying, dying.

Tears, Idle Tears

Tears, idle tears, I know not what they mean,
Tears from the depth of some divine despair

---

1 This lyric and the next six are from *The Princess* (1847; 2nd ed., 1850).

Rise in the heart, and gather to the eyes,
In looking on the happy Autumn-fields,
And thinking of the days that are no more.   5

Fresh as the first beam glittering on a sail,
That brings our friends up from the underworld,
Sad as the last which reddens over one
That sinks with all we love below the verge;
So sad, so fresh, the days that are no more.   10

Ah, sad and strange as in dark summer dawns
The earliest pipe of half-awakened birds
To dying ears, when unto dying eyes
The casement slowly grows a glimmering square;
So sad, so strange, the days that are no more.   15

Dear as remembered kisses after death,
And sweet as those by hopeless fancy feigned
On lips that are for others; deep as love,
Deep as first love, and wild with all regret;
O Death in Life, the days that are no more.   20

Home They Brought
Her Warrior Dead

Home they brought her warrior dead:
  She nor swooned nor uttered cry:
All her maidens, watching, said,
  "She must weep or she will die."

Then they praised him, soft and low,   5
  Called him worthy to be loved,
Truest friend and noblest foe;
  Yet she neither spoke nor moved.

Stole a maiden from her place,
  Lightly to the warrior stepped,   10
Took the face-cloth from the face;
  Yet she neither moved nor wept.

Rose a nurse of ninety years,
  Set his child upon her knee—
Like summer tempest came her tears—   15
  "Sweet my child, I live for thee."

Ask Me No More

Ask me no more: the moon may draw the sea;
  The cloud may stoop from heaven and take
    the shape
  With fold to fold, of mountain or of cape;

But O too fond, when have I answered thee?
    Ask me no more.   5

Ask me no more: what answer should I give?
  I love not hollow cheek or faded eye:
    Yet, O my friend, I will not have thee die!
Ask me no more, lest I should bid thee live;
    Ask me no more.   10

Ask me no more: thy fate and mine are sealed:
  I strove against the stream and all in vain:
    Let the great river take me to the main:
No more, dear love, for at a touch I yield;
    Ask me no more.   15

Now Sleeps the Crimson Petal

Now sleeps the crimson petal, now the white;
Nor waves the cypress in the palace walk;
Nor winks the gold fin in the porphyry font:
The fire-fly wakens: waken thou with me.

Now droops the milkwhite peacock like a   5
    ghost,
And like a ghost she glimmers on to me.

Now lies the Earth all Danaë[1] to the stars,
And all thy heart lies open unto me.

Now slides the silent meteor on, and leaves
A shining furrow, as thy thoughts in me.   10

Now folds the lily all her sweetness up,
And slips into the bosom of the lake:
So fold thyself, my dearest, thou, and slip
Into my bosom and be lost in me.

Come Down, O Maid

Come down, O maid, from yonder mountain
    height:
What pleasure lives in height (the shepherd sang)
In height and cold, the splendor of the hills?
But cease to move so near the Heavens, and cease
To glide a sunbeam by the blasted Pine,   5
To sit a star upon the sparkling spire;
And come, for Love is of the valley, come,
For Love is of the valley, come thou down

---

[1] Princess to whom Zeus descended in the form of a golden shower.

And find him; by the happy threshold, he,
Or hand in hand with Plenty in the maize,   10
Or red with spirted purple of the vats,
Or foxlike in the vine;[1] nor cares to walk
With Death and Morning on the silver horns,[2]
Nor wilt thou snare him in the white ravine,
Nor find him dropped upon the firths of ice,[3]   15
That huddling slant in furrow-cloven falls
To roll the torrent out of dusky doors:
But follow; let the torrent dance thee down
To find him in the valley; let the wild
Lean-headed Eagles yelp alone, and leave   20
The monstrous ledges there to slope, and spill
Their thousand wreaths of dangling water-smoke,
That like a broken purpose waste in air:
So waste not thou; but come; for all the vales
Await thee; azure pillars of the hearth[4]   25
Arise to thee; the children call, and I
Thy shepherd pipe, and sweet is every sound,
Sweeter thy voice, but every sound is sweet;
Myriads of rivulets hurrying through the lawn,
The moan of doves in immemorial elms,   30
And murmuring of innumerable bees.

The Eagle

Fragment

He clasps the crag with crooked hands;
Close to the sun in lonely lands,
Ringed with the azure world, he stands.

The wrinkled sea beneath him crawls;
He watches from his mountain walls,   5
And like a thunderbolt he falls.

from In Memoriam A. H. H.[1]

Obiit 1833

PROLOGUE

Strong Son of God, Immortal Love,
Whom we, that have not seen thy face,
By faith, and faith alone, embrace,
Believing where we cannot prove;

Thine are these orbs of light and shade;[2]   5
Thou madest Life in man and brute;
Thou madest Death; and lo, thy foot
Is on the skull which thou hast made.

Thou wilt not leave us in the dust:
Thou madest man, he knows not why,   10
He thinks he was not made to die;
And thou hast made him: thou art just.

Thou seemest human and divine,
The highest, holiest manhood, thou:
Our wills are ours, we know not how,   15
Our wills are ours, to make them thine.

Our little systems[3] have their day;
They have their day and cease to be:
They are but broken lights of thee,
And thou, O Lord, art more than they.   20

We have but faith: we cannot know;
For knowledge is of things we see;
And yet we trust it comes from thee,
A beam in darkness: let it grow.

Let knowledge grow from more to more,   25
But more of reverence in us dwell;
That mind and soul, according well,
May make one music as before,[4]

But vaster. We are fools and slight;
We mock thee when we do not fear: 30
But help thy foolish ones to bear;
Help thy vain worlds to bear thy light.

Forgive what seemed my sin in me;
What seemed my worth since I began;
For merit lives from man to man,   35
And not from man, O Lord, to thee.

Forgive my grief for one removed,
Thy creature, whom I found so fair.
I trust he lives in thee, and there
I find him worthier to be loved.   40

---

[1] Like the foxes who lurked in the vines of tender grapes (Song of Solomon 2:15).
[2] Peaks in the alps.   [3] Glaciers.
[4] Columns of smoke.

[1] Tennyson's close friend, Arthur Henry Hallam, whom he met at Cambridge, and who died in Vienna at the age of twenty-two.

---

[2] Literally, the planets, partly in the light of the sun, partly in the shade; but Tennyson means to suggest the light of life and the shadow of death.
[3] Of theology and philosophy.
[4] Before the separation effected by modern science, which has driven the mind to deny what the soul feels or longs for.

Forgive these wild and wandering cries,[5]
    Confusions of a wasted youth;
    Forgive them where they fail in truth,
And in thy wisdom make me wise.

2

Old Yew, which graspest at the stones
    That name the underlying dead,
    Thy fibres net the dreamless head,
Thy roots are rapt about the bones.

The seasons bring the flower again,   5
    And bring the firstling to the flock;
    And in the dusk of thee, the clock
Beats out the little lives of men.

O not for thee the glow, the bloom,
    Who changest not in any gale,   10
    Nor branding summer suns avail
To touch thy thousand years of gloom:

And gazing on thee, sullen tree,
    Sick for thy stubborn hardihood,
    I seem to fail from out my blood   15
And grow incorporate into thee.

3

O Sorrow, cruel fellowship,
    O Priestess in the vaults of Death,
    O sweet and bitter in a breath,
What whispers from thy lying lip?

"The stars," she whispers, "blindly run;   5
    A web is woven across the sky;
    From out waste places comes a cry,
And murmurs from the dying sun:[6]

"And all the phantom, Nature, stands—
    With all her music in her tone,   10
    A hollow echo of my own,[7]—
A hollow form with empty hands."

And shall I take a thing so blind,[8]
    Embrace her as my natural good;
    Or crush her, like a vice of blood,   15
Upon the threshold of the mind?

5

I sometimes hold it half a sin
    To put in words the grief I feel;
    For words, like Nature, half reveal
And half conceal the Soul within.

But, for the unquiet heart and brain,   5
    A use in measured language lies;
    The sad mechanic exercise,
Like dull narcotics, numbing pain.

In words, like weeds,[9] I'll wrap me o'er,
    Like coarsest clothes against the cold: 10
    But that large grief which these enfold
Is given in outline and no more.

6

One writes, that "Other friends remain,"
    That "Loss is common to the race"—
    And common is the commonplace,
And vacant chaff well meant for grain.

That loss is common would not make   5
    My own less bitter, rather more:
    Too common! Never morning wore
To evening, but some heart did break.

O father, wheresoe'er thou be,
    Who pledgest now thy gallant son;   10
    A shot, ere half thy draught be done,
Hath stilled the life that beat from thee.

O mother, praying God will save
    Thy sailor,—while thy head is bowed,
    His heavy-shotted hammock-shroud   15
Drops in his vast and wandering grave.

Ye know no more than I who wrought
    At that last hour to please him well;
    Who mused on all I had to tell,
And something written, something thought;   20

Expecting still his advent home;
    And ever met him on his way
    With wishes, thinking, "here to-day,"
Or, "here to-morrow will he come."

O somewhere, meek, unconscious dove,   25
    That sittest ranging[10] golden hair;
    And glad to find thyself so fair,
Poor child, that waitest for thy love!

---

5 The 131 short lyrics, written at various times between 1833 and 1850, which comprise the poem.
6 Because his sorrow lacks the resolution of firm faith, it calls up the vision of a mechanical universe which answers to no divine purpose. The sun is dying because it will some day lose its heat.
7 That is, of Sorrow's own despairing tone.
8 As this sorrow and its reading of the universe.

9 Garments of mourning.
10 Arranging.

For now her father's chimney glows
    In expectation of a guest;   30
    And thinking "this will please him best,"
She takes a riband or a rose;

For he will see them on to-night;
    And with the thought her color burns;
    And, having left the glass, she turns   35
Once more to set a ringlet right;

And, even when she turned, the curse
    Had fallen, and her future Lord
    Was drowned in passing thro' the ford,
Or killed in falling from his horse.   40

O what to her shall be the end?
    And what to me remains of good?
    To her, perpetual maidenhood,
And unto me no second friend.

7

Dark house,[11] by which once more I stand
    Here in the long unlovely street,
    Doors, where my heart was used to beat
So quickly, waiting for a hand,

A hand that can be clasped no more—   5
    Behold me, for I cannot sleep,
    And like a guilty thing I creep
At earliest morning to the door.

He is not here; but far away
    The noise of life begins again,
    And ghastly through the drizzling rain   10
On the bald street breaks the blank day.

11

Calm is the morn without a sound,
    Calm as to suit a calmer grief,
    And only through the faded leaf
The chestnut pattering to the ground:

Calm and deep peace on this high wold,   5
    And on these dews that drench the furze,
    And all the silvery gossamers
That twinkle into green and gold:

Calm and still light on yon great plain
    That sweeps with all its autumn bowers,   10
    And crowded farms and lessening towers,
To mingle with the bounding main:

Calm and deep peace in this wide air,
    These leaves that redden to the fall;
    And in my heart, if calm at all,   15
If any calm, a calm despair:

Calm on the seas, and silver sleep,
    And waves that sway themselves in rest,
    And dead calm in that noble breast
Which heaves but with the heaving deep.[12]   20

27

I envy not in any moods
    The captive void of noble rage,
    The linnet born within the cage,
That never knew the summer woods:

I envy not the beast that takes   5
    His license in the field of time,
    Unfettered by the sense of crime,
To whom a conscience never wakes;

Nor, what may count itself as blest,
    The heart that never plighted troth   10
    But stagnates in the weeds of sloth;
Nor any want-begotten rest.[13]

I hold it true, whate'er befall;
    I feel it, when I sorrow most;
    'Tis better to have loved and lost   15
Than never to have loved at all.

28

The time draws near the birth of Christ:[14]
    The moon is hid; the night is still;
    The Christmas bells from hill to hill
Answer each other in the mist.

Four voices of four hamlets round,   5
    From far and near, on mead and moor,
    Swell out and fail, as if a door
Were shut between me and the sound:

Each voice four changes[15] on the wind,
    That now dilate, and now decrease,   10
    Peace and goodwill, goodwill and peace,
Peace and goodwill, to all mankind.

---

11 Where Hallam had lived.

12 The body of Hallam is being brought home by ship to England.
13 Nor any peace of mind purchased by the lack of some valuable quality or experience.
14 Christmas of 1833, the year of Hallam's death.
15 Sequences in which a peal of bells is rung.

This year I slept and woke with pain,
    I almost wished no more to wake,
    And that my hold on life would break   15
Before I heard those bells again:

But they my troubled spirit rule,
    For they controlled me when a boy;
    They bring me sorrow touched with joy,
The merry merry bells of Yule.   20

30

With trembling fingers did we weave
    The holly round the Christmas hearth;
    A rainy cloud possessed the earth,
And sadly fell our Christmas-eve.

At our old pastimes in the hall   5
    We gamboled, making vain pretense
    Of gladness, with an awful sense
Of one mute Shadow watching all.

We paused: the winds were in the beech:
    We heard them sweep the winter land;   10
    And in a circle hand-in-hand
Sat silent, looking each at each.

Then echo-like our voices rang;
    We sung, though every eye was dim,
    A merry song we sang with him   15
Last year: impetuously we sang:

We ceased: a gentler feeling crept
    Upon us: surely rest is meet:
    "They rest," we said, "their sleep is sweet,"
And silence followed, and we wept.   20

Our voices took a higher range;
    Once more we sang: "They do not die
    Nor lose their mortal sympathy,
Nor change to us, although they change;

"Rapt from the fickle and the frail   25
    With gathered power, yet the same,
    Pierces the keen seraphic flame
From orb to orb, from veil to veil."[16]

Rise, happy morn, rise, holy morn,
    Draw forth the cheerful day from night: 30
    O Father, touch the east, and light
The light that shone when Hope was born.[17]

50

Be near me when my light is low,
    When the blood creeps, and the nerves prick
    And tingle; and the heart is sick,
And all the wheels of Being slow.

Be near me when the sensuous frame   5
    Is racked with pangs that conquer trust;
    And Time, a maniac scattering dust,
And Life, a Fury slinging flame.

Be near me when my faith is dry,
    And men[18] the flies of latter spring,   10
    That lay their eggs, and sting and sing
And weave their petty cells and die.

Be near me when I fade away,
    To point the term of human strife,[19]
    And on the low dark verge of life   15
The twilight of eternal day.

54

O yet we trust that somehow good
    Will be the final goal of ill,
    To pangs of nature, sins of will,
Defects of doubt, and taints of blood;

That nothing walks with aimless feet;   5
    That not one life shall be destroyed,
    Or cast as rubbish to the void,
When God hath made the pile complete;

That not a worm is cloven in vain;
    That not a moth with vain desire   10
    Is shriveled in a fruitless fire,
Or but subserves another's gain.[20]

Behold, we know not anything;
    I can but trust that good shall fall
    At last—far off—at last, to all,   15
And every winter change to spring.

---

16 The soul, freed from the flesh but its essence unchanged, passes from world to world in successively higher embodiments.

17 With Christ, who brought the hope of immortality.
18 And men seem.
19 To point to the end of human life.
20 In the struggle for survival.

So runs my dream: but what am I?
    An infant crying in the night:
    An infant crying for the light:
And with no language but a cry.   20

55

The wish, that of the living whole
    No life may fail beyond the grave,
    Derives it not from what we have
The likest God within the soul?[21]

Are God and Nature then at strife,   5
    That Nature lends such evil dreams?
    So fareful of the type[22] she seems,
So careless of the single life;

That I, considering everywhere
    Her secret meaning in her deeds,
    And finding that of fifty seeds   10
She often brings but one to bear,

I falter where I firmly trod,
    And falling with my weight of cares
    Upon the great world's altar-stairs
That slope through darkness up to God,   15

I stretch lame hands of faith, and grope,
    And gather dust and chaff, and call
    To what I feel is Lord of all,
And faintly trust the larger hope.[23]   20

56

"So careful of the type?" but no.
    From scarpèd cliff and quarried stone
    She cries, "A thousand types are gone:
I care for nothing, all shall go.[24]

"Thou makest thine appeal to me: 5
    I bring to life, I bring to death:
    The spirit does but mean the breath:
I know no more." And he, shall he,

Man, her last work, who seemed so fair,
    Such splendid purpose in his eyes,   10
    Who rolled the psalm to wintry skies,
Who built him fanes of fruitless prayer,

Who trusted God was love indeed
    And love Creation's final law—
    Though Nature, red in tooth and claw   15
With ravine, shrieked against his creed—

Who loved, who suffered countless ills,
    Who battled for the True, the Just,
    Be blown about the desert dust,
Or sealed within the iron hills?   20

No more? A monster then, a dream,
    A discord.[25] Dragons of the prime,
    That tare each other in their slime,
Were mellow music matched with him.[26]

O life as futile, then, as frail!   25
    O for thy voice[27] to soothe and bless!
    What hope of answer, or redress?
Behind the veil, behind the veil.

78

Again at Christmas did we weave
    The holly round the Christmas hearth;
    The silent snow possessed the earth,
And calmly fell our Christmas-eve:

The yule-clog[28] sparkled keen with frost,   5
    No wing of wind the region swept,
    But over all things brooding slept
The quiet sense of something lost.

As in the winters left behind,
    Again our ancient games had place,   10
    The mimic picture's breathing grace,[29]
And dance and song and hoodman-blind.

---

21 That is, from Love, which makes us long for the survival of every life after death.
22 The species.
23 Expressed in lines 1–2.
24 Nature is as careless of the species as of the individual, as we can see from the fossil remains of dead species discovered in quarried stone and scarped cliff (a cliff cut away perpendicularly, so that the strata in which fossils are embedded are exposed).

25 Is that the whole story? Then man is a monster (a beast in human shape), a dream that vanishes (since he has no immortal soul), a discord (when his hopes and traditions clash so violently with what appear to be the facts: cf. Prologue, lines 27–28, and note 4).
26 Because they at least had no delusions of spiritual life and survival, and were therefore more harmoniously adjusted to existence than man.   27 Hallam's.
28 Log.—This is the second Christmas after Hallam's death.
29 Tableaux of famous paintings.

Who showed a token of distress?
    No single tear, no mark of pain:
    O sorrow, then can sorrow wane?   15
O grief, can grief be changed to less?

O last regret, regret can die!
    No—mixed with all this mystic frame,
    Her deep relations are the same,
But with long use her tears are dry.   20

82

I wage not any feud with Death
    For changes wrought on form and face;
    No lower life that earth's embrace
May breed with him, can fright my faith.

Eternal process moving on,   5
    From state to state the spirit walks;[30]
    And these are but the shattered stalks,
Or ruined chrysalis of one.[31]

Nor blame I Death, because he bare[32]
    The use of virtue[33] out of earth: 10
    I know transplanted human worth
Will bloom to profit, otherwhere.

For this alone on Death I wreak
    The wrath that garners in my heart;
    He put our lives so far apart   15
We cannot hear each other speak.

96

You[34] say, but with no touch of scorn,
    Sweet-hearted, you, whose light-blue eyes
    Are tender over drowning flies,
You tell me, doubt is Devil-born.

I know not: one[35] indeed I knew   5
    In many a subtle question versed,
    Who touched a jarring lyre at first,
But ever strove to make it true:

Perplexed in faith, but pure in deeds,
    At last he beat his music out.   10
    There lives more faith in honest doubt,
Believe me, than in half the creeds.[36]

He fought his doubts and gathered strength,
    He would not make his judgment blind,
    He faced the specters of the mind   15
And laid them: thus he came at length

To find a stronger faith his own;
    And Power was with him in the night,
    Which makes the darkness and the light,
And dwells not in the light alone,   20

But in the darkness and the cloud,
    As over Sinaï's peaks of old,
    While Israel made their gods of gold,[37]
Although the trumpet blew so loud.

104

The time draws near the birth of Christ;[38]
    The moon is hid, the night is still;
    A single church below the hill
Is pealing, folded in the mist.

A single peal of bells below,   5
    That wakens at this hour of rest
    A single murmur in the breast,
That these are not the bells I know.

Like strangers' voices here they sound
    In lands where not a memory strays,   10
    Nor landmark breathes of other days,
But all is new unhallowed ground.

---

30 As the body passes into lower forms of life, the spirit moves upward into higher states (cf. No. 30).
31 "These" seems to refer to line 2. The general meaning is that the dead body is but the shattered support or ruined chrysalis of one state of the spirit.   32 Bore.
33 The practice of virtue by Hallam, or in other words, the virtuous Hallam.
34 Some woman of simple faith.   35 Hallam.

36 These lines must be read with what follows. In doubt that is honestly, i.e., openly and squarely, faced and fought, there lies potentially a much stronger, because firmer, faith than that of half the people who claim to be orthodox believers (and often scorn the doubters as sinners: cf. line 4) but whose faith is really weak because they have purchased it dishonestly by refusing to face any arguments to the contrary (by making their judgment blind).
37 God dwells in the darkness of doubt just as he dwelt in the darkness over Mt. Sinai when he was hidden in a storm cloud. Below, the Israelites were worshipping the golden calf (which may be an allusion to the Victorians whose doors are barred with gold, and open but to golden keys: see "Locksley Hall," line 100).
38 The Christmas of 1837. The family had moved from Somersby to Epping Forest.

105

Tonight ungathered let us leave
　　This laurel, let this holly stand:
　　We live within the stranger's land,
And strangely falls our Christmas-eve.

Our father's dust is left alone　　　　　　　5
　　And silent under other snows:
　　There in due time the woodbine blows,
The violet comes, but we are gone.

No more shall wayward grief abuse
　　The genial hour with mask and mime;　　10
　　For change of place, like growth of time,
Has broke the bond of dying use.

Let cares that petty shadows cast,
　　By which our lives are chiefly proved,
　　A little spare the night I loved,　　　　　15
And hold it solemn to the past.

But let no footstep beat the floor,
　　Nor bowl of wassail mantle[39] warm;
　　For who would keep an ancient form
Through which the spirit breathes no more?　20

Be neither song, nor game, nor feast;
　　Nor harp be touched, nor flute be blown;
　　No dance, no motion, save alone
What lightens in the lucid east

Of rising worlds[40] by yonder wood.　　　　25
　　Long sleeps the summer in the seed;
　　Run out your measured arcs, and lead
The closing cycle rich in good.[41]

106

Ring out, wild bells, to the wild sky,
　　The flying cloud, the frosty light:
　　The year is dying in the night;
Ring out, wild bells, and let him die.

Ring out the old, ring in the new,　　　　　5
　　Ring, happy bells, across the snow:
　　The year is going, let him go;
Ring out the false, ring in the true.

Ring out the grief that saps the mind,
　　For those that here we see no more;　　　10
　　Ring out the feud of rich and poor,
Ring in redress to all mankind.

Ring out a slowly dying cause,
　　And ancient forms of party strife;
　　Ring in the nobler modes of life,　　　　15
With sweeter manners, purer laws.

Ring out the want, the care, the sin,
　　The faithless coldness of the times;
　　Ring out, ring out my mournful rhymes,
But ring the fuller minstrel in.　　　　　　20

Ring out false pride in place and blood,
　　The civic slander and the spite;
　　Ring in the love of truth and right,
Ring in the common love of good.

Ring out old shapes of foul disease;　　　　25
　　Ring out the narrowing lust of gold;
　　Ring out the thousand wars of old,
Ring in the thousand years of peace.

Ring in the valiant man and free,
　　The larger heart, the kindlier hand;　　　30
　　Ring out the darkness of the land,
Ring in the Christ that is to be.[42]

116

Is it, then, regret for buried time
　　That keenlier in sweet April wakes,
　　And meets the year, and gives and takes
The colors of the crescent prime?

Not all: the songs, the stirring air,　　　　5
　　The life re-orient out of dust,
　　Cry through the sense to hearten trust
In that which made the world so fair.

Not all regret: the face will shine
　　Upon me, while I must alone;　　　　　　10
　　And that dear voice, I once have known,
Still speak to me of me and mine:

---

39 Wine with a cover of froth.　　40 Stars.
41 The final period of perfection: cf. the next poem and
the very last stanza of *In Memoriam*.

42 According to his son (*Memoir*, I, 326), Tennyson
thought "that the forms of Christian religion would alter;
but that the spirit of Christ would still grow from more
to more"; and he looked forward to a time "when the
controversies of creeds shall have vanished."

Yet less of sorrow lives in me
    For days of happy commune dead;
    Less yearning for the friendship fled,   15
Than some strong bond which is to be.

118

Contemplate all this work of Time,
    The giant laboring in his youth;
    Nor dream of human love and truth,
As dying Nature's earth and lime;[43]

But trust that those we call the dead   5
    Are breathers of an ampler day
    For[44] ever nobler ends. They[45] say,
The solid earth whereon we tread

In tracts of fluent heat began,[46]
    And grew to seeming-random forms,   10
    The seeming prey of cyclic storms,[47]
Till at the last arose the man;[48]

Who throve and branched from clime to clime,
    The herald of a higher race,[49]
    And of himself in higher place,[50]   15
If so he type this work of time

Within himself, from more to more;[51]
    Or,[52] crowned with attributes of woe
    Like glories, move his course, and show
That life is not as idle ore,   20

But iron dug from central gloom,
    And heated hot with burning fears,
    And dipped in baths of hissing tears,
And battered with the shocks of doom

---

43 Do not dream that the human spirit dies with the natural body made of earth and lime.
44 For the purpose of.
45 The astronomers and the geologists.
46 A reference to the nebular hypothesis. See the introduction to the Victorian period, p. 418.
47 Periodic cataclysms. The line refers to the older theory of geological change which Lyell attacked. See the introduction, p. 418.
48 From lower forms of life? By special creation of God? Either may be the reading, and Tennyson may have intended the ambiguity.   49 Of men on earth.
50 Than on the earth.
51 Provided he imitate the progressive work of time in his own moral life (cf. the last stanza).
52 Or (see the next lines) provided he make pain and suffering the instruments of moral growth.

To shape and use. Arise and fly   25
    The reeling Faun, the sensual feast;
    Move upward, working out the beast,
And let the ape and tiger die.

120

I trust I have not wasted breath:[53]
    I think we are not wholly brain,
    Magnetic mockeries;[54] not in vain,
Like Paul with beasts, I fought with Death;[55]

Not only[56] cunning casts in clay: 5
    Let Science prove we are, and then
    What matters Science unto men,
At least to me? I would not stay.

Let him, the wiser man[57] who springs
    Hereafter, up from childhood shape   10
    His action like the greater ape,
But I was *born* to other things.

123

There rolls the deep where grew the tree.
    O earth, what changes hast thou seen!
    There where the long street roars, hath been
The stillness of the central sea.

The hills are shadows, and they flow   5
    From form to form, and nothing stands;
    They melt like mist, the solid lands,
Like clouds they shape themselves and go.

But in my spirit will I dwell,[58]
    And dream my dream, and hold it true;   10
    For though my lips may breathe adieu,
I cannot think the thing farewell.

---

53 Breath that wastes away till it ceases at death. I trust I am not merely mortal.
54 Human automatons controlled by magnetic force: cf. the introduction, p. 420.
55 I fought against the view of human life as ending in death, as Paul did also, who likened the fight to a battle with beasts (I Corinthians 15:32).
56 We are not merely.
57 Made wiser by science. The tone is ironic.
58 Not in my senses, which would lead me to think that nothing whatever was permanent or lasting (not even a soul), and that everything is part of a meaningless process of change.

124

That which we dare invoke to bless;
 Our dearest faith; our ghastliest doubt;[59]
 He, They, One, All;[60] within, without;
The Power in darkness whom we guess;

I found Him not in world or sun,   5
 Or eagle's wing, or insect's eye;
 Nor through the questions men may try,
The petty cobwebs we have spun:[61]

If e'er when faith had fallen asleep,
 I heard a voice "believe no more"   10
 And heard an ever-breaking shore
That tumbled in the Godless deep;[62]

A warmth within the breast would melt
 The freezing reason's colder part,
 And like a man in wrath the heart   15
Stood up and answered "I have felt."[63]

No, like a child in doubt and fear:
 But that blind clamor made me wise;
 Then was I as a child that cries,
But, crying, knows his father near;[64]   20

And what I am[65] beheld again
 What is,[66] and no man understands;
 And out of darkness came the hands
That reach through nature, molding men.[67]

130

Thy voice is on the rolling air;
 I hear thee where the waters run;
 Thou standest in the rising sun,
And in the setting thou art fair.

What art thou then? I cannot guess;   5
 But though I seem in star and flower
 To feel thee some diffusive power,
I do not therefore love thee less:

My love involves the love before;
 My love is vaster passion now;   10
 Though mixed with God and Nature thou,
I seem to love thee more and more.

Far off thou art, but ever nigh;
 I have thee still, and I rejoice;
 I prosper, circled with thy voice;   15
I shall not lose thee though I die.

131

O living will[68] that shalt endure
 When all that seems[69] shall suffer shock,
 Rise in the spiritual rock,
Flow through our deeds and make them pure,[70]

That we may lift from out of dust   5
 A voice as unto him that hears,
 A cry above the conquered years
To one that with us works, and trust,

With faith that comes of self-control,
 The truths that never can be proved   10
 Until we close with all we loved,
And all we flow from, soul in soul.

from EPILOGUE

. . . A soul shall draw from out the vast[71]
And strike his being into bounds,[72]

And, moved through life of lower phase,[73]   125
 Result in man, be born and think,
 And act and love, a closer link
Betwixt us and the crowning race

---

[59] The subject or object of both faith and doubt.
[60] However we may think of this object, as God or the gods, or as an impersonal "unity in all things or all things together" (Bradley).
[61] He did not deduce the existence of God in eighteenth-century fashion by claiming that design in nature pointed to a designer, nor from any rational arguments.
[62] That is, felt the atheistical implications of No. 123, lines 1–8.
[63] Known spiritual reality from experience. But that is a boast. Tennyson at once corrects himself and gives the real facts in the next stanza.
[64] When he cried out like a child in doubt and fear, that blind clamor brought him wisdom because he felt the immediate sense of a father (i.e., a divine Father) close by. The lines describe a religious-mystical experience by analogy with a psychological experience in childhood.
[65] My spirit or soul.   [66] Spiritual reality.
[67] Contrast this high moment of faith with the end of No. 55.

[68] According to Tennyson, he meant the moral will in man.
[69] All that seems so lasting.
[70] In I Corinthians 10:4, Christ is called a spiritual rock. May the moral will of man, inspired by the love or example of Christ, flow through our deeds.
[71] The child of Edmund Lushington and Tennyson's sister Cecilia, whose marriage is celebrated in the "Epilogue."
[72] The womb.
[73] The embryonic development roughly parallels the successive stages of animal evolution.

Of those that, eye to eye, shall look
　　On knowledge; under whose command　　130
　　Is Earth and Earth's, and in their hand
Is Nature like an open book;

No longer half-akin to brute,
　　For all we thought and loved and did,
　　And hoped, and suffered, is but seed　　135
Of what in them is flower and fruit;

Whereof the man, that with me trod
　　This planet, was a noble type
　　Appearing ere the times were ripe,
That friend of mine who lives in God,　　140

That God, which ever lives and loves,
　　One God, one law, one element,
　　And one far-off divine event,
To which the whole creation moves.

from Idylls of the King

Dedication

These to His Memory[1]—since he held them dear,
Perchance as finding there unconsciously
Some image of himself—I dedicate,
I dedicate, I consecrate with tears—
These Idylls.
　　　　　　And indeed He seems to me　　5
Scarce other than my king's ideal knight,
"Who reverenced his conscience as his king;
Whose glory was, redressing human wrong;
Who spake no slander, no, nor listened to it;
Who loved one only and who clave to her—"[2]　　10
Her—over all whose realms to their last isle,
Commingled with the gloom of imminent war,
The shadow of His loss drew like eclipse,
Darkening the world. We have lost him: he is
　　gone:
We know him now: all narrow jealousies　　15
Are silent; and we see him as he moved,
How modest, kindly, all-accomplished, wise,
With what sublime repression of himself,
And in what limits, and how tenderly;

Not swaying to this faction or to that;　　20
Not making his high place the lawless perch
Of winged ambitions, nor a vantage-ground
For pleasure; but through all this tract of years
Wearing the white flower of a blameless life,
Before a thousand peering littlenesses,　　25
In that fierce light which beats upon a throne,
And blackens every blot: for where is he,
Who dares foreshadow for an only son
A lovelier life, a more unstained, than his?
Or how should England dreaming of *his* sons　　30
Hope more for these than some inheritance
Of such a life, a heart, a mind as thine,
Thou noble Father of her Kings to be,
Laborious for her people and her poor—
Voice in the rich dawn of an ampler day—　　35
Far-sighted summoner of War and Waste
To fruitful strifes and rivalries of peace—
Sweet nature gilded by the gracious gleam
Of letters, dear to Science, dear to Art,
Dear to thy land[3] and ours, a Prince indeed,　　40
Beyond all titles, and a household name,
Hereafter, through all times, Albert the Good.
　　　Break not, O woman's-heart, but still en-
　　　　dure;
Break not, for thou art Royal, but endure,
Remembering all the beauty of that star　　45
Which shone so close beside Thee that ye made
One light together, but has passed and leaves
The Crown a lonely splendor.
　　　　　　　　　　　May all love,
His love, unseen but felt, o'ershadow Thee,
The love of all Thy sons encompass Thee,　　50
The love of all Thy daughters cherish Thee,
The love of all Thy people comfort Thee,
Till God's love set Thee at his side again!

LANCELOT AND ELAINE

Elaine the fair, Elaine the lovable,
Elaine, the lily maid of Astolat,
High in her chamber up a tower to the east
Guarded the sacred shield of Lancelot;
Which first she placed where morning's earliest　　5
　　ray
Might strike it, and awake her with the gleam;
Then fearing rust or soilure fashioned for it
A case of silk, and braided thereupon
All the devices blazoned on the shield
In their own tint, and added, of her wit,　　10

---

[1] Prince Albert, consort of Queen Victoria. He died in 1861.
[2] A paraphrase of King Arthur's speech in "Guinevere," one of the *Idylls*, where he summarizes the code of the Round Table.

[3] Saxe-Coburg-Gotha in Germany, the Prince's native land.

A border fantasy of branch and flower,
And yellow-throated nestling in the nest.
Nor rested thus content, but day by day,
Leaving her household and good father, climbed
That eastern tower, and entering barred her door,   15
Stripped off the case, and read the naked shield,
Now guessed a hidden meaning in his arms,
Now made a pretty history to herself
Of every dint a sword had beaten in it,
And every scratch a lance had made upon it,   20
Conjecturing when and where: this cut is fresh;
That ten years back; this dealt him at Caerlyle;
That at Caerleon; this at Camelot:
And ah God's mercy, what a stroke was there!
And here a thrust that might have killed, but   25
    God
Broke the strong lance, and rolled his enemy
    down,
And saved him: so she lived in fantasy.

How came the lily maid by that good shield
Of Lancelot, she that knew not ev'n his name?
He left it with her, when he rode to tilt   30
For the great diamond in the diamond jousts,
Which Arthur had ordained, and by that name
Had named them, since a diamond was the prize.

For Arthur, long before they crowned him
    King,
Roving the trackless realms of Lyonnesse,   35
Had found a glen, gray boulder and black tarn.[4]
A horror lived about the tarn, and clave
Like its own mists to all the mountain side:
For here two brothers, one a king, had met
And fought together; but their names were lost;   40
And each had slain his brother at a blow;
And down they fell and made the glen abhorred:
And there they lay till all their bones were
    bleached,
And lichened into color with the crags:
And he, that once was king, had on a crown   45
Of diamonds, one in front, and four aside.
And Arthur came, and laboring up the pass,
All in a misty moonshine, unawares
Had trodden that crowned skeleton, and the
    skull
Brake from the nape, and from the skull the   50
    crown
Rolled into light, and turning on its rims

Fled like a glittering rivulet to the tarn:
And down the shingly scaur[5] he plunged, and
    caught,
And set it on his head, and in his heart
Heard murmurs, "Lo, thou likewise shalt be   55
    King."

Thereafter, when a King, he had the gems
Plucked from the crown, and showed them to his
    knights,
Saying, "These jewels, whereupon I chanced
Divinely,[6] are the kingdom's, not the King's—
For public use: henceforward let there be,   60
Once every year, a joust for one of these:
For so by nine years' proof we needs must learn
Which is our mightiest, and ourselves shall grow
In use of arms and manhood, till we drive
The heathen,[7] who, some say, shall rule the land   65
Hereafter, which God hinder." Thus he spoke:
And eight years past, eight jousts had been, and
    still
Had Lancelot won the diamond of the year,
With purpose to present them to the Queen,
When all were won; but meaning all at once   70
To snare her royal fancy with a boon
Worth half her realm, had never spoken word.

Now for the central diamond and the last
And largest, Arthur, holding then his court
Hard on the river nigh the place which now   75
Is this world's hugest,[8] let proclaim a joust
At Camelot, and when the time drew nigh
Spake (for she had been sick) to Guinevere,
"Are you so sick, my Queen, you cannot move
To these fair jousts?" "Yea, lord," she said, "ye   80
    know it."
"Then will ye miss," he answered, "the great
    deeds
Of Lancelot, and his prowess in the lists,
A sight ye love to look on." And the Queen
Lifted her eyes, and they dwelt languidly
On Lancelot, where he stood beside the King.   85
He, thinking that he read her meaning there,
"Stay with me, I am sick; my love is more
Than many diamonds," yielded; and a heart
Love-loyal to the least wish of the Queen
(However much he yearned to make complete   90

---

4 Mountain lake.
5 Steep bank covered with loose gravel.
6 By divine guidance.
7 The Angles, Saxons, and Jutes.
8 London.

The tale of diamonds for his destined boon)
Urged him to speak against the truth, and say,
"Sir King, mine ancient wound is hardly whole,
And lets me from the saddle"; and the King
Glanced first at him, then her, and went his way. 95
No sooner gone than suddenly she began:

   "To blame, my lord Sir Lancelot, much to
     blame!
Why go ye not to these fair jousts? the knights
Are half of them our enemies, and the crowd
Will murmur, 'Lo the shameless ones, who take 100
Their pastime now the trustful King is gone!'"
Then Lancelot vexed at having lied in vain:
"Are ye so wise? ye were not once so wise,
My Queen, that summer, when ye loved me first.
Then of the crowd ye took no more account 105
Than of the myriad cricket of the mead,
When its own voice clings to each blade of grass,
And every voice is nothing. As to knights,
Them surely can I silence with all ease.
But now my loyal worship is allowed 110
Of all men: many a bard, without offence,
Has linked our names together in his lay,
Lancelot, the flower of bravery, Guinevere,
The pearl of beauty: and our knights at feast
Have pledged us in this union, while the King 115
Would listen smiling. How then? is there more?
Has Arthur spoken aught? or would yourself,
Now weary of my service and devoir,
Henceforth be truer to your faultless lord?"[9]

   She broke into a little scornful laugh: 120
"Arthur, my lord, Arthur, the faultless King,
That passionate perfection, my good lord—
But who can gaze upon the Sun in heaven?
He never spake word of reproach to me,
He never had a glimpse of mine untruth, 125
He cares not for me: only here to-day
There gleamed a vague suspicion in his eyes:
Some meddling rogue has tampered with him—
     else
Rapt in this fancy of his Table Round,
And swearing men to vows impossible, 130
To make them like himself: but, friend, to me
He is all fault who hath no fault at all:
For who loves me must have a touch of earth;

The low sun makes the color:[10] I am yours,
Not Arthur's, as ye know, save by the bond.[11] 135
And therefore hear my words: go to the jousts:
The tiny-trumpeting gnat can break our dream
When sweetest; and the vermin voices here
May buzz so loud—we scorn them, but they
     sting."

   Then answered Lancelot, the chief of knights: 140
"And with what face, after my pretext made,
Shall I appear, O Queen, at Camelot, I
Before a King who honors his own word,
As if it were his God's?"
          "Yea," said the Queen,
"A moral child without the craft to rule, 145
Else had he not lost me: but listen to me,
If I must find you wit: we hear it said
That men go down before your spear at a touch,
But knowing you are Lancelot; your great name,
This conquers: hide it therefore; go unknown: 150
Win! by this kiss you will:[12] and our true King
Will then allow your pretext, O my knight,
As all for glory; for to speak him true,
Ye know right well, how meek soe'er he seem,
No keener hunter after glory breathes. 155
He loves it in his knights more than himself:
They prove to him his work: win and return."

   Then got Sir Lancelot suddenly to horse,
Wroth at himself. Not willing to be known,
He left the barren-beaten thoroughfare, 160
Chose the green path that showed the rarer foot,
And there among the solitary downs,
Full often lost in fancy, lost his way;
Till as he traced in faintly-shadowed track,
That all in loops and links among the dales 165
Ran to the Castle of Astolat, he saw
Fired from the west, far on a hill, the towers.
Thither he made, and blew the gateway horn.
Then came an old, dumb, myriad-wrinkled man,
Who let him into lodging and disarmed. 170
And Lancelot marvelled at the wordless man;
And issuing found the Lord of Astolat
With two strong sons, Sir Torre and Sir Lavaine,
Moving to meet him in the castle court;
And close behind them stepped the lily maid 175

---

[9] The captious and weary tone of this speech, so lacking in any feeling of love, indicates at once the burnt-out character of the love affair.

[10] Contrast line 123. The clouds are bright with attractive color only when the sun is low, near the earth, at rising or setting.
[11] The matter-of-fact tone reinforces the implications mentioned in note 9. [12] A very casual kiss.

Elaine, his daughter: mother of the house
There was not: some light jest among them rose
With laughter dying down as the great knight
Approached them: then the Lord of Astolat:
"Whence comest thou, my guest, and by what   180
    name
Livest between the lips? for by thy state
And presence I might guess thee chief of those,
After the King, who eat in Arthur's halls.
Him have I seen: the rest, his Table Round,
Known as they are, to me they are unknown."   185

Then answered Lancelot, the chief of knights:
"Known am I, and of Arthur's hall, and known,
What I by mere mischance have brought, my
    shield.
But since I go to joust as one unknown
At Camelot for the diamond, ask me not,   190
Hereafter ye shall know me—and the shield—
I pray you lend me one, if such you have,
Blank, or at least with some device not mine."

Then said the Lord of Astolat, "Here is
    Torre's:
Hurt in his first tilt was my son, Sir Torre.   195
And so, God wot, his shield is blank enough.
His ye can have." Then added plain Sir Torre,
"Yea, since I cannot use it, ye may have it."
Here laughed the father saying, "Fie, Sir Churl,
Is that an answer for a noble knight?   200
Allow him![13] but Lavaine, my younger here,
He is so full of lustihood, he will ride,
Joust for it, and win, and bring it in an hour,
And set it in this damsel's golden hair,
To make her thrice as wilful as before."   205

"Nay, father, nay good father, shame me not
Before this noble knight," said young Lavaine,
"For nothing. Surely I but played on Torre:
He seemed so sullen, vexed he could not go:
A jest, no more! for, knight, the maiden dreamt   210
That some one put this diamond in her hand,
And that it was too slippery to be held,
And slipped and fell into some pool or stream,
The castle-well, belike; and then I said
That *if* I went and *if* I fought and won it   215
(But all was jest and joke among ourselves)
Then must she keep it safelier. All was jest.[14]

But, father, give me leave, an if he will,
To ride to Camelot with this noble knight:
Win shall I not, but do my best to win: 220
Young as I am, yet would I do my best."

"So ye will grace me," answered Lancelot,
Smiling a moment, "with your fellowship
O'er these waste downs whereon I lost myself,
Then were I glad of you as guide and friend: 225
And you shall win this diamond,—as I hear
It is a fair large diamond,—if ye may,
And yield it to this maiden, if ye will."
"A fair large diamond," added plain Sir Torre,
"Such be for queens, and not for simple maids."   230
Then she, who held her eyes upon the ground,
Elaine, and heard her name so tossed about,
Flushed slightly at the slight disparagement
Before the stranger knight, who, looking at her,
Full courtly, yet not falsely, thus returned: 235
"If what is fair be but for what is fair,
And only queens are to be counted so,
Rash were my judgment then, who deem this
    maid
Might wear as fair a jewel as is on earth,
Not violating the bond of like to like."   240

He spoke and ceased: the lily maid Elaine,
Won by the mellow voice before she looked,
Lifted her eyes, and read his lineaments.
The great and guilty love he bare the Queen,
In battle with the love he bare his lord,   245
Had marred his face, and marked it ere his time.
Another sinning on such heights with one,
The flower of all the west and all the world,
Had been the sleeker for it: but in him
His mood was often like a fiend, and rose   250
And drove him into wastes and solitudes
For agony, who was yet a living soul.[15]
Marred as he was, he seemed the goodliest man
That ever among ladies ate in hall,
And noblest, when she lifted up her eyes.   255
However marred, of more than twice her years,
Seamed with an ancient swordcut on the cheek,
And bruised and bronzed, she lifted up her eyes

---

[13] Forgive him.
[14] But not entirely, one suspects. The truth lies somewhere between the father's account of the incident, which
puts the worst interpretation upon it (the Lord of Astolat manages to take a crack at all three of his children),
and Lavaine's, which puts it in the best light.
[15] Whose soul was still alive, not deadened by sin. But
the poem suggests that Lancelot's "agony" was as much
disgust at himself and the whole weary "situation" which
he cannot break with as it was a sense of guilt. See lines
1230–31 and his final speech at the end.

And loved him, with that love which was her
    doom.

Then the great knight, the darling of the 260
    court,
Loved of the loveliest, into that rude hall
Stepped with all grace, and not with half disdain
Hid under grace, as in a smaller time,[16]
But kindly man moving among his kind:
Whom they with meats and vintage of their best 265
And talk and minstrel melody entertained.
And much they asked of court and Table Round,
And ever well and readily answered he:
But Lancelot, when they glanced at Guinevere,
Suddenly speaking of the wordless man, 270
Heard from the Baron that, ten years before,
The heathen caught and reft him of his tongue.
"He learnt and warned me of their fierce design
Against my house, and him they caught and
    maimed;
But I, my sons, and little daughter fled 275
From bonds or death, and dwelt among the woods
By the great river in a boatman's hut.
Dull days were those, till our good Arthur broke
The Pagan yet once more on Badon hill."

"O there, great lord, doubtless," Lavaine said, 280
    rapt
By all the sweet and sudden passion of youth
Toward greatness in its elder, "you have fought.
O tell us—for we live apart—you know
Of Arthur's glorious wars." And Lancelot spoke
And answered him at full, as having been 285
With Arthur in the fight which all day long
Rang by the white mouth of the violent Glem;
And in the four loud battles by the shore
Of Duglas; that on Bassa; then the war
That thundered in and out the gloomy skirts 290
Of Celidon the forest; and again
By castle Gurnion, where the glorious King
Had on his cuirass worn our Lady's Head,
Carved of one emerald centered in a sun
Of silver rays, that lightened as he breathed; 295
And at Caerleon had he helped his lord,
When the strong neighings of the wild white
    Horse
Set every gilded parapet shuddering;
And up in Agned-Cathregonion too,
And down the waste sand-shores of Trath Treroit, 300

Where many a heathen fell; "and on the mount
Of Badon I myself beheld the King
Charge at the head of all his Table Round,
And all his legions crying Christ and him,
And break them; and I saw him, after, stand 305
High on a heap of slain, from spur to plume
Red as the rising sun with heathen blood,
And seeing me, with a great voice he cried,
'They are broken, they are broken!' for the King,
However mild he seems at home, nor cares 310
For triumph in our mimic wars, the jousts—
For if his own knight cast him down, he laughs
Saying, his knights are better men than he—
Yet in this heathen war the fire of God
Fills him: I never saw his like: there lives 315
No greater leader."
           While he uttered this,
Low to her own heart said the lily maid,
"Save your great self, fair lord"; and when he
    fell
From talk of war to traits of pleasantry—
Being mirthful he, but in a stately kind— 320
She still took note that when the living smile
Died from his lips, across him came a cloud
Of melancholy severe, from which again,
Whenever in her hovering to and fro
The lily maid had striven to make him cheer, 325
There brake a sudden-beaming tenderness
Of manners and of nature; and she thought
That all was nature,[17] all, perchance, for her.
And all night long his face before her lived,
As when a painter, poring on a face, 330
Divinely through all hindrance finds the man
Behind it, and so paints him that his face,
The shape and color of a mind and life,
Lives for his children, ever at its best
And fullest; so the face before her lived, 335
Dark-splendid, speaking in the silence, full
Of noble things, and held her from her sleep.
Till rathe[18] she rose, half-cheated in the thought
She needs must bid farewell to sweet Lavaine.
First as in fear, step after step, she stole 340
Down the long tower-stairs, hesitating:
Anon, she heard Sir Lancelot cry in the court,
"This shield, my friend, where is it?" and Lavaine
Passed inward, as she came from out the tower.
There to his proud horse Lancelot turned, and 345
    smoothed
The glossy shoulder, humming to himself.

---

[16] A lesser age.

[17] Natural, spontaneous.   [18] Early.

Half-envious of the flattering hand, she drew
Nearer and stood. He looked, and more amazed
Than if seven men had set upon him, saw
The maiden standing in the dewy light.   350
He had not dreamed she was so beautiful.
Then came on him a sort of sacred fear,
For silent, though he greeted her, she stood
Rapt on his face as if it were a God's.
Suddenly flashed on her a wild desire,   355
That he should wear her favor at the tilt.
She braved a riotous heart in asking for it.
"Fair lord, whose name I know not—noble it is,
I well believe, the noblest—will you wear
My favor at this tourney?" "Nay," said he,   360
"Fair lady, since I never yet have worn
Favor of any lady in the lists.
Such is my wont, as those, who know me, know."
"Yea, so," she answered; "then in wearing mine
Needs must be lesser likelihood, noble lord,   365
That those who know should know you." And he
   turned
Her counsel up and down within his mind,
And found it true, and answered, "True, my
   child.
Well, I will wear it:[19] fetch it out to me:
What is it?" and she told him "A red sleeve   370
Broidered with pearls," and brought it: then he
   bound
Her token on his helmet, with a smile
Saying, "I never yet have done so much
For any maiden living," and the blood
Sprang to her face and filled her with delight;   375
But left her all the paler, when Lavaine
Returning brought the yet-unblazoned shield,
His brother's; which he gave to Lancelot,
Who parted with his own to fair Elaine:
"Do me this grace, my child, to have my shield   380
In keeping till I come." "A grace to me,"
She answered, "twice to-day. I am your squire!"
Whereat Lavaine said, laughing, "Lily maid,
For fear our people call you lily maid
In earnest, let me bring your color back;   385
Once, twice, and thrice: now get you hence to
   bed":
So kissed her, and Sir Lancelot his own hand,[20]
And thus they moved away: she stayed a minute,
Then made a sudden step to the gate, and there—
Her bright hair blown about the serious face   390

Yet rosy-kindled with her brother's kiss—
Paused by the gateway, standing near the shield
In silence, while she watched their arms far-off
Sparkle, until they dipped below the downs.
Then to her tower she climbed, and took the   395
   shield,
There kept it, and so lived in fantasy.

     Meanwhile the new companions passed away
Far o'er the long backs of the bushless downs,
To where Sir Lancelot knew there lived a knight
Not far from Camelot, now for forty years   400
A hermit, who had prayed, labored and prayed,
And ever laboring had scooped himself
In the white rock a chapel and a hall
Of massive columns, like a shorecliff cave,
And cells and chambers: all were fair and dry;   405
The green light from the meadows underneath
Struck up and lived along the milky roofs;
And in the meadows tremulous aspen-trees
And poplars made a noise of falling showers.
And thither wending there that night they bode.   410

     But when the next day broke from under-
   ground,
And shot red fire and shadows through the cave,
They rose, heard mass, broke fast, and rode away:
Then Lancelot saying, "Hear, but hold my name
Hidden, you ride with Lancelot of the Lake,"   415
Abashed Lavaine, whose instant reverence,
Dearer to true young hearts than their own
   praise,
But left him leave to stammer, "Is it indeed?"
And after muttering "The great Lancelot,"
At last he got his breath and answered, "One,   420
One have I seen—that other, our liege lord,
The dread Pendragon, Britain's King of kings,
Of whom the people talk mysteriously,
He will be there—then were I stricken blind
That minute, I might say that I had seen."   425

     So spake Lavaine, and when they reached the
   lists
By Camelot in the meadow, let his eyes
Run through the peopled gallery which half
   round
Lay like a rainbow fall'n upon the grass,
Until they found the clear-faced King, who sat   430
Robed in red samite, easily to be known,
Since to his crown the golden dragon clung,
And down his robe the dragon writhed in gold,

---

[19] Because of her argument? her beauty? her flattery?
[20] Kissed his hand to her.

And from the carven-work behind him crept
Two dragons gilded, sloping down to make   435
Arms for his chair, while all the rest of them
Through knots and loops and folds innumerable
Fled ever through the woodwork, till they found
The new design wherein they lost themselves,
Yet with all ease, so tender was the work: 440
And, in the costly canopy o'er him set,
Blazed the last diamond of the nameless king.

    Then Lancelot answered young Lavaine and
       said,
"Me you call great: mine is the firmer seat,
The truer lance: but there is many a youth   445
Now crescent,[21] who will come to all I am
And overcome it; and in me there dwells
No greatness, save it be some far-off touch
Of greatness to know well I am not great:
There is the man." And Lavaine gaped upon him   450
As on a thing miraculous, and anon
The trumpets blew; and then did either side,
They that assailed, and they that held the lists,
Set lance in rest, strike spur, suddenly move,
Meet in the midst, and there so furiously   455
Shock, that a man far-off might well perceive,
If any man that day were left afield,
The hard earth shake, and a low thunder of arms.
And Lancelot bode a little, till he saw
Which were the weaker; then he hurled into it   460
Against the stronger: little need to speak
Of Lancelot in his glory! King, duke, earl,
Count, baron—whom he smote, he overthrew.

    But in the field were Lancelot's kith and kin,
Ranged with the Table Round that held the lists,   465
Strong men, and wrathful that a stranger knight
Should do and almost overdo the deeds
Of Lancelot; and one said to the other, "Lo!
What is he? I do not mean the force alone—
The grace and versatility of the man!   470
Is it not Lancelot?" "When has Lancelot worn
Favor of any lady in the lists?
Not such his wont, as we, that know him, know."
"How then? who then?" a fury seized them all,
A fiery family passion for the name   475
Of Lancelot, and a glory one with theirs.
They couched their spears and pricked their
    steeds, and thus,

---

[21] Growing up.

Their plumes driv'n backward by the wind they
    made
In moving, all together down upon him
Bare, as a wild wave in the wide North-sea,   480
Green-glimmering toward the summit, bears, with
    all
Its stormy crests that smoke against the skies,
Down on a bark, and overbears the bark,
And him that helms it, so they overbore
Sir Lancelot and his charger, and a spear   485
Down-glancing lamed the charger, and a spear
Pricked sharply his own cuirass, and the head
Pierced through his side, and there snapped, and
    remained.

    Then Sir Lavaine did well and worshipfully;
He bore a knight of old repute to the earth,   490
And brought his horse to Lancelot where he lay.
He up the side, sweating with agony, got,
But thought to do while he might yet endure,
And being lustily holpen by the rest,
His party,—though it seemed half-miracle   495
To those he fought with,—drave his kith and
    kin,
And all the Table Round that held the lists,
Back to the barrier; then the trumpets blew
Proclaiming his the prize, who wore the sleeve
Of scarlet, and the pearls; and all the knights,   500
His party, cried "Advance and take thy prize
The diamond"; but he answered, "Diamond me
No diamonds! for God's love, a little air!
Prize me no prizes, for my prize is death!
Hence will I, and I charge you, follow me not."   505

    He spoke, and vanished suddenly from the field
With young Lavaine into the poplar grove.
There from his charger down he slid, and sat,
Gasping to Sir Lavaine, "Draw the lance-head":
"Ah my sweet lord Sir Lancelot," said Lavaine,   510
"I dread me, if I draw it, you will die."
But he, "I die already with it: draw—
Draw,"—and Lavaine drew, and Sir Lancelot
    gave
A marvellous great shriek and ghastly groan,
And half his blood burst forth, and down he sank   515
For the pure pain, and wholly swooned away.
Then came the hermit out and bare him in,
There stanched his wound; and there, in daily
    doubt
Whether to live or die, for many a week
Hid from the wild world's rumor by the grove   520

Of poplars with their noise of falling showers,
And ever-tremulous aspen-trees, he lay.

But on that day when Lancelot fled the lists,
His party, knights of utmost North and West,
Lords of waste marches, kings of desolate isles,   525
Came round their great Pendragon, saying to
    him,
"Lo, Sire, our knight, through whom we won the
    day,
Hath gone sore wounded, and hath left his prize
Untaken, crying that his prize is death."
"Heaven hinder," said the King, "that such an   530
    one,
So great a knight as we have seen to-day—
He seemed to me another Lancelot—
Yea, twenty times I thought him Lancelot—
He must not pass uncared for. Wherefore, rise,
O Gawain, and ride forth and find the knight.   535
Wounded and wearied needs must he be near.
I charge you that you get at once to horse.
And, knights and kings, there breathes not one of
    you
Will deem this prize of ours is rashly given:
His prowess was too wondrous. We will do him   540
No customary honor: since the knight
Came not to us, of us to claim the prize,
Ourselves will send it after. Rise and take
This diamond, and deliver it, and return,
And bring us where he is, and how he fares,   545
And cease not from your quest until ye find."

So saying, from the carven flower above,
To which it made a restless heart, he took,
And gave, the diamond: then from where he sat
At Arthur's right, with smiling face arose,   550
With smiling face and frowning heart, a Prince
In the mid might and flourish of his May,
Gawain, surnamed The Courteous, fair and
    strong,
And after Lancelot, Tristram, and Geraint
And Gareth, a good knight, but therewithal   555
Sir Modred's brother, and the child of Lot,[22]
Nor often loyal to his word, and now
Wroth that the King's command to sally forth
In quest of whom he knew not, made him leave
The banquet, and concourse of knights and kings.   560

So all in wrath he got to horse and went;
While Arthur to the banquet, dark in mood,

Passed, thinking "Is it Lancelot who hath come
Despite the wound he spake of, all for gain
Of glory, and hath added wound to wound,   565
And ridd'n away to die?" So feared the King,
And, after two days' tarriance there, returned.
Then when he saw the Queen, embracing asked,
"Love, are you yet so sick?" "Nay, lord," she said.
"And where is Lancelot?" Then the Queen   570
    amazed,
"Was he not with you? won he not your prize?"
"Nay, but one like him." "Why that like was he."
And when the King demanded how she knew,
Said, "Lord, no sooner had ye parted from us,
Than Lancelot told me of a common talk   575
That men went down before his spear at a touch,
But knowing he was Lancelot; his great name
Conquered; and therefore would he hide his
    name
From all men, ev'n the King, and to this end
Had made the pretext of a hindering wound,   580
That he might joust unknown of all, and learn
If his old prowess were in aught decayed;
And added, 'Our true Arthur, when he learns,
Will well allow my pretext, as for gain
Of purer glory.' "

            Then replied the King: 585
"Far lovelier in our Lancelot had it been,
In lieu of idly dallying with the truth,
To have trusted me as he hath trusted thee.
Surely his King and most familiar friend
Might well have kept his secret. True, indeed,   590
Albeit I know my knights fantastical,
So fine a fear in our large Lancelot
Must needs have moved my laughter: now re-
    mains
But little cause for laughter: his own kin—
Ill news, my Queen, for all who love him, this!—   595
His kith and kin, not knowing, set upon him;
So that he went sore wounded from the field:
Yet good news too: for goodly hopes are mine
That Lancelot is no more a lonely heart.[23]
He wore, against his wont, upon his helm   600
A sleeve of scarlet, broidered with great pearls,
Some gentle maiden's gift."

               "Yea, lord," she said,
"Thy hopes are mine," and saying that, she
    choked,
And sharply turned about to hide her face,

---

22 Brother of a traitor and child of another.

23 Are the final words ironic? If so, line 595, just above,
is pointed.

Passed to her chamber, and there flung herself 605
Down on the great King's couch, and writhed
    upon it,
And clenched her fingers till they bit the palm,
And shrieked out "Traitor" to the unhearing
    wall,
Then flashed into wild tears, and rose again,
And moved about her palace, proud and pale. 610

    Gawain the while through all the region round
Rode with his diamond, wearied of the quest,
Touched at all points, except the poplar grove,
And came at last, though late, to Astolat:
Whom glittering in enamelled arms the maid 615
Glanced at, and cried, "What news from Camelot,
    lord?
What of the knight with the red sleeve?" "He
    won."
"I knew it," she cried. "But parted from the
    jousts
Hurt in the side," whereat she caught her breath;
Through her own side she felt the sharp lance go; 620
Thereon she smote her hand: wellnigh she
    swooned:
And, while he gazed wonderingly at her, came
The Lord of Astolat out, to whom the Prince
Reported who he was, and on what quest
Sent, that he bore the prize and could not find 625
The victor, but had ridd'n a random round
To seek him, and had wearied of the search.
To whom the Lord of Astolat, "Bide with us,
And ride no more at random, noble Prince!
Here was the knight, and here he left a shield; 630
This will he send or come for: furthermore
Our son is with him; we shall hear anon,
Needs must we hear." To this the courteous
    Prince
Accorded with his wonted courtesy,
Courtesy with a touch of traitor in it, 635
And stayed; and cast his eyes on fair Elaine:
Where could be found face daintier? then her
    shape
From forehead down to foot, perfect—again
From foot to forehead exquisitely turned:[24]
"Well—If I bide, lo! this wild flower for me!" 640
And oft they met among the garden yews,
And there he set himself to play upon her
With sallying wit, free flashes from a height

Above her, graces of the court, and songs,
Sighs, and slow smiles, and golden eloquence 645
And amorous adulation, till the maid
Rebelled against it, saying to him, "Prince,
O loyal nephew of our noble King,
Why ask you not to see the shield he left,
Whence you might learn his name? Why slight 650
    your King,
And lose the quest he sent you on, and prove
No surer than our falcon yesterday,
Who lost the hern we slipped her at, and went
To all the winds?" "Nay, by mine head," said he,
"I lose it, as we lose the lark in heaven, 655
O damsel, in the light of your blue eyes;
But an ye will it let me see the shield."
And when the shield was brought, and Gawain
    saw
Sir Lancelot's azure lions, crowned with gold,
Ramp in the field, he smote his thigh, and 660
    mocked:
"Right was the King! our Lancelot! that true
    man!"
"And right was I," she answered merrily, "I,
Who dreamed my knight the greatest knight of
    all."
"And if I dreamed," said Gawain, "that you love
This greatest knight, your pardon! lo, ye know 665
    it![25]
Speak therefore: shall I waste myself in vain?"
Full simple was her answer, "What know I?
My brethren have been all my fellowship;
And I, when often they have talked of love,
Wished it had been my mother, for they talked, 670
Meseemed, of what they knew not; so myself—
I know not if I know what true love is,
But if I know, then, if I love not him,
I know there is none other I can love."
"Yea, by God's death," said he, "ye love him well, 675
But would not, knew ye what all others know,
And whom he loves." "So be it," cried Elaine,
And lifted her fair face and moved away:
But he pursued her, calling, "Stay a little!
One golden minute's grace! he wore your sleeve: 680
Would he break faith with one I may not name?
Must our true man change like a leaf at last?
Nay—like enow: why then, far be it from me
To cross our mighty Lancelot in his loves!

---

[24] What Gawain saw when he looked at Elaine, or more exactly, the way he looked at Elaine, is intended to contrast with Lancelot's view of her at lines 348–51.

[25] The elliptical phrasing seems to mean, "If I've made love to you when you love another, I shall ask your pardon, as you know I would."

And, damsel, for I deem you know full well
Where your great knight is hidden, let me leave
My quest with you; the diamond also: here!
For if you love, it will be sweet to give it;
And if he love, it will be sweet to have it
From your own hand; and whether he love or 690
    not,
A diamond is a diamond.[26] Fare you well
A thousand times!—a thousand times farewell!
Yet, if he love, and his love hold, we two
May meet at court hereafter: there, I think,
So ye will learn the courtesies of the court, 695
We two shall know each other."

                                Then he gave,
And slightly kissed the hand to which he gave,
The diamond, and all wearied of the quest
Leapt on his horse, and carolling as he went
A true-love ballad, lightly rode away. 700

    Thence to the court he passed; there told the
        King
What the King knew, "Sir Lancelot is the knight."
And added, "Sire, my liege, so much I learnt;
But failed to find him, though I rode all round
The region: but I lighted on the maid 705
Whose sleeve he wore; she loves him; and to her,
Deeming our courtesy is the truest law,
I gave the diamond: she will render it;
For by mine head she knows his hiding-place."

    The seldom-frowning King frowned, and re- 710
        plied,
"Too courteous truly! ye shall go no more
On quest of mine, seeing that ye forget
Obedience is the courtesy due to kings."

    He spake and parted. Wroth, but all in awe,
For twenty strokes of the blood, without a word, 715
Lingered that other, staring after him;
Then shook his hair, strode off, and buzzed
    abroad
About the maid of Astolat, and her love.
All ears were pricked at once, all tongues were
    loosed:
"The maid of Astolat loves Sir Lancelot, 720
Sir Lancelot loves the maid of Astolat."
Some read the King's face, some the Queen's, and
    all

Had marvel what the maid might be, but most 685
Predoomed her as unworthy. One old dame
Came suddenly on the Queen with the sharp 725
    news.
She, that had heard the noise of it before,
But sorrowing Lancelot should have stooped so
    low,[27]
Marred her friend's aim with pale tranquillity.
So ran the tale like fire about the court,
Fire in dry stubble a nine-days' wonder flared: 730
Till even the knights at banquet twice or thrice
Forgot to drink to Lancelot and the Queen,
And pledging Lancelot and the lily maid
Smiled at each other, while the Queen, who sat
With lips severely placid, felt the knot 735
Climb in her throat, and with her feet unseen
Crushed the wild passion out against the floor
Beneath the banquet, where the meats became
As wormwood, and she hated all who pledged.

    But far away the maid in Astolat, 740
Her guiltless rival, she that ever kept
The one-day-seen Sir Lancelot in her heart,
Crept to her father, while he mused alone,
Sat on his knee, stroked his gray face and said,
"Father, you call me wilful, and the fault 745
Is yours who let me have my will, and now,
Sweet father, will you let me lose my wits?"
"Nay," said he, "surely." "Wherefore, let me
    hence,"
She answered, "and find out our dear Lavaine."
"Ye will not lose your wits for dear Lavaine: 750
Bide," answered he: "we needs must hear anon
Of him, and of that other." "Ay," she said,
"And of that other, for I needs must hence
And find that other, wheresoe'er he be,
And with mine own hand give his diamond to 755
    him,
Lest I be found as faithless in the quest
As yon proud Prince who left the quest to me.
Sweet father, I behold him in my dreams
Gaunt as it were the skeleton of himself,
Death-pale, for lack of gentle maiden's aid. 760
The gentler-born the maiden, the more bound,
My father, to be sweet and serviceable
To noble knights in sickness, as ye know
When these have worn their tokens: let me hence
I pray you." Then her father nodding said, 765

---

26 A fine summary of Gawain's philosophy.

27 The lines are her reply to the old dame, in indirect
discourse.

"Ay, ay, the diamond: wit ye well, my child,
Right fain were I to learn this knight were whole,
Being our greatest: yea, and you must give it—
And sure I think this fruit is hung too high
For any mouth to gape for save a queen's—   770
Nay, I mean nothing: so then, get you gone,
Being so very wilful you must go."

Lightly, her suit allowed, she slipped away,
And while she made her ready for her ride,
Her father's latest word hummed in her ear,   775
"Being so very wilful you must go,"
And changed itself and echoed in her heart,
"Being so very wilful you must die."
But she was happy enough and shook it off,
As we shake off the bee that buzzes at us;   780
And in her heart she answered it and said,
"What matter, so I help him back to life?"
Then far away with good Sir Torre for guide
Rode o'er the long backs of the bushless downs
To Camelot, and before the city-gates   785
Came on her brother with a happy face
Making a roan horse caper and curvet
For pleasure all about a field of flowers:
Whom when she saw, "Lavaine," she cried,
    "Lavaine,
How fares my lord Sir Lancelot?" He amazed,   790
"Torre and Elaine! why here? Sir Lancelot!
How know ye my lord's name is Lancelot?"
But when the maid had told him all her tale,
Then turned Sir Torre, and being in his moods
Left them, and under the strange-statued gate,   795
Where Arthur's wars were rendered mystically,
Passed up the still rich city to his kin,
His own far blood, which dwelt at Camelot;
And her, Lavaine across the poplar grove
Led to the caves: there first she saw the casque   800
Of Lancelot on the wall: her scarlet sleeve,
Though carved and cut, and half the pearls away,
Streamed from it still; and in her heart she
    laughed,
Because he had not loosed it from his helm,
But meant once more perchance to tourney in it.   805
And when they gained the cell wherein he slept,
His battle-writhen arms and mighty hands
Lay naked on the wolfskin, and a dream
Of dragging down his enemy made them move.
Then she that saw him lying unsleek, unshorn,   810
Gaunt as it were the skeleton of himself,
Uttered a little tender dolorous cry.
The sound not wonted in a place so still

Woke the sick knight, and while he rolled his
    eyes
Yet blank from sleep, she started to him, saying,   815
"Your prize the diamond sent you by the King":
His eyes glistened: she fancied "Is it for me?"
And when the maid had told him all the tale
Of King and Prince, the diamond sent, the quest
Assigned to her not worthy of it, she knelt   820
Full lowly by the corners of his bed,
And laid the diamond in his open hand.
Her face was near, and as we kiss the child
That does the task assigned, he kissed her face.
At once she slipped like water to the floor.   825
"Alas," he said, "your ride hath wearied you.
Rest must you have." "No rest for me," she said;
"Nay, for near you, fair lord, I am at rest."
What might she mean by that? his large black
    eyes,
Yet larger through his leanness, dwelt upon her,   830
Till all her heart's sad secret blazed itself
In the heart's colors on her simple face;
And Lancelot looked and was perplexed in mind,
And being weak in body said no more;
But did not love the color; woman's love,   835
Save one, he not regarded, and so turned
Sighing, and feigned a sleep until he slept.

Then rose Elaine and glided through the
    fields,
And passed beneath the weirdly-sculptured gates
Far up the dim rich city to her kin;   840
There bode the night: but woke with dawn, and
    passed
Down through the dim rich city to the fields,
Thence to the cave: so day by day she passed
In either twilight ghost-like to and fro
Gliding, and every day she tended him,   845
And likewise many a night: and Lancelot
Would, though he called his wound a little hurt
Whereof he should be quickly whole, at times
Brain-feverous in his heat and agony, seem
Uncourteous, even he: but the meek maid   850
Sweetly forbore him ever, being to him
Meeker than any child to a rough nurse,
Milder than any mother to a sick child,
And never woman yet, since man's first fall,
Did kindlier unto man, but her deep love   855
Upbore her; till the hermit, skilled in all
The simples and the science of that time,
Told him that her fine care had saved his life.
And the sick man forgot her simple blush,

Would call her friend and sister, sweet Elaine,
Would listen for her coming and regret
Her parting step, and held her tenderly,
And loved her with all love except the love
Of man and woman when they love their best,
Closest and sweetest, and had died the death   865
In any knightly fashion for her sake.
And peradventure had he seen her first
She might have made this and that other world
Another world for the sick man; but now
The shackles of an old love straitened him,   870
His honor rooted in dishonor stood,
And faith unfaithful kept him falsely true.[28]

Yet the great knight in his mid-sickness made
Full many a holy vow and pure resolve.
These, as but born of sickness, could not live: 875
For when the blood ran lustier in him again,
Full often the bright image of one face,
Making a treacherous quiet in his heart,
Dispersed his resolution like a cloud.
Then if the maiden, while that ghostly grace[29]   880
Beamed on his fancy, spoke, he answered not,
Or short and coldly, and she knew right well
What the rough sickness meant, but what this
    meant
She knew not, and the sorrow dimmed her sight,
And drave her ere her time across the fields   885
Far into the rich city, where alone
She murmured, "Vain, in vain: it cannot be.
He will not love me: how then? must I die?"
Then as a little helpless innocent bird,
That has but one plain passage of few notes,   890
Will sing the simple passage o'er and o'er
For all an April morning, till the ear
Wearies to hear it, so the simple maid
Went half the night repeating, "Must I die?"
And now to right she turned, and now to left,   895
And found no ease in turning or in rest;
And "Him or death," she muttered, "death or
    him,"
Again and like a burthen,[30] "Him or death."

But when Sir Lancelot's deadly hurt was
    whole,
To Astolat returning rode the three.   900

There morn by morn, arraying her sweet self   860
In that wherein she deemed she looked her best,
She came before Sir Lancelot, for she thought,
"If I be loved, these are my festal robes,
If not, the victim's flowers before he fall."[31]   905
And Lancelot ever pressed upon the maid
That she should ask some goodly gift of him
For her own self or hers; "and do not shun
To speak the wish most near to your true heart;
Such service have ye done me, that I make   910
My will of yours, and Prince and Lord am I
In mine own land, and what I will I can."
Then like a ghost she lifted up her face,
But like a ghost without the power to speak.
And Lancelot saw that she withheld her wish,   915
And bode among them yet a little space
Till he should learn it; and one morn it chanced
He found her in among the garden yews,
And said, "Delay no longer, speak your wish,
Seeing I go to-day": then out she brake: 920
"Going? and we shall never see you more.
And I must die for want of one bold word."
"Speak: that I live to hear," he said, "is yours."
Then suddenly and passionately she spoke:
"I have gone mad. I love you: let me die."   925
"Ah, sister," answered Lancelot, "what is this?"
And innocently extending her white arms,
"Your love," she said, "your love—to be your
    wife."
And Lancelot answered, "Had I chosen to wed,
I had been wedded earlier, sweet Elaine: 930
But now there never will be wife of mine."
"No, no," she cried, "I care not to be wife,
But to be with you still, to see your face,
To serve you, and to follow you through the
    world."
And Lancelot answered, "Nay, the world, the   935
    world,
All ear and eye, with such a stupid heart
To interpret ear and eye, and such a tongue
To blare its own interpretation—nay,
Full ill then should I quit your brother's love,
And your good father's kindness." And she said,   940
"Not to be with you, not to see your face—
Alas for me then, my good days are done."
"Nay, noble maid," he answered, "ten times nay!
This is not love: but love's first flash in youth,
Most common: yea, I know it of mine own self: 945
And you yourself will smile at your own self

---

[28] His faith to Guinevere, which was unfaithfulness to
her husband and his king, Arthur, and kept him true to
her and false to him.
[29] The image of Guinevere.
[30] Refrain.

---

[31] Sacrificial animals were decorated with flowers.

Hereafter, when you yield your flower of life
To one more fitly yours, not thrice your age:[32]
And then will I, for true you are and sweet
Beyond mine old belief in womanhood,   950
More specially should your good knight be poor,
Endow you with broad land and territory
Even to the half my realm beyond the seas,[33]
So that would make you happy: furthermore,
Ev'n to the death, as though ye were my blood,   955
In all your quarrels will I be your knight.
This will I do, dear damsel, for your sake,
And more than this I cannot."
                                 While he spoke
She neither blushed nor shook, but deathly-pale
Stood grasping what was nearest, then replied: 960
"Of all this will I nothing"; and so fell,
And thus they bore her swooning to her tower.

    Then spake, to whom through those black
        walls of yew
Their talk had pierced, her father: "Ay, a flash,
I fear me, that will strike my blossom dead.   965
Too courteous are ye, fair Lord Lancelot.
I pray you, use some rough discourtesy
To blunt or break her passion."
                                 Lancelot said,
"That were against me: what I can I will";
And there that day remained, and toward even   970
Sent for his shield: full meekly rose the maid,
Stripped off the case, and gave the naked shield;
Then, when she heard his horse upon the stones,
Unclasping flung the casement back, and looked
Down on his helm, from which her sleeve had   975
    gone.
And Lancelot knew the little clinking sound;
And she by tact of love was well aware
That Lancelot knew that she was looking at him.
And yet he glanced not up, nor waved his hand,
Nor bade farewell, but sadly rode away.   980
This was the one discourtesy that he used.

    So in her tower alone the maiden sat.
His very shield was gone; only the case,
Her own poor work, her empty labor, left.
But still she heard him, still his picture formed   985
And grew between her and the pictured wall.
Then came her father, saying in low tones,
"Have comfort," whom she greeted quietly.

32 The exaggeration is deliberate. He is only a little more
than twice her age (see line 256).
33 His ancestral estates were in Brittany.

Then came her brethren saying, "Peace to thee,
Sweet sister," whom she answered with all calm.   990
But when they left her to herself again,
Death, like a friend's voice from a distant field
Approaching through the darkness, called; the
    owls
Wailing had power upon her, and she mixed
Her fancies with the sallow-rifted glooms   995
Of evening, and the moanings of the wind.

    And in those days she made a little song,
And called her song "The Song of Love and
    Death,"
And sang it: sweetly could she make and sing.

    "Sweet is true love though given in vain, in   1000
        vain;
And sweet is death who puts an end to pain:
I know not which is sweeter, no, not I.

    "Love, art thou sweet? then bitter death must
        be:
Love, thou art bitter; sweet is death to me.
O Love, if death be sweeter, let me die.   1005

    "Sweet love, that seems not made to fade away,
Sweet death, that seems to make us loveless clay,
I know not which is sweeter, no, not I.

    "I fain would follow love, if that could be;
I needs must follow death, who calls for me;   1010
Call and I follow, I follow! let me die."

    High with the last line scaled her voice, and
        this,
All in a fiery dawning wild with wind
That shook her tower, the brothers heard, and
        thought
With shuddering, "Hark the Phantom of the   1015
        house
That ever shrieks before a death," and called
The father, and all three in hurry and fear
Ran to her, and lo! the blood-red light of dawn
Flared on her face, she shrilling, "Let me die!"

    As when we dwell upon a word we know,   1020
Repeating, till the word we know so well
Becomes a wonder, and we know not why,
So dwelt the father on her face, and thought
"Is this Elaine?" till back the maiden fell,
Then gave a languid hand to each, and lay,   1025
Speaking a still good-morrow with her eyes.

At last she said, "Sweet brothers, yesternight
I seemed a curious little maid again,
As happy as when we dwelt among the woods,
And when ye used to take me with the flood   1030
Up the great river in the boatman's boat.
Only ye would not pass the cape
That has the poplar on it: there ye fixed
Your limit, oft returning with the tide.
And yet I cried because ye would not pass   1035
Beyond it, and far up the shining flood
Until we found the palace of the King.
And yet ye would not; but this night I dreamed
That I was all alone upon the flood,
And then I said, 'Now shall I have my will':   1040
And there I woke, but still the wish remained.
So let me hence that I may pass at last
Beyond the poplar and far up the flood,
Until I find the palace of the King.
There will I enter in among them all,   1045
And no man there will dare to mock at me;
But there the fine Gawain will wonder at me,
And there the great Sir Lancelot muse at me;
Gawain, who bade a thousand farewells to me,
Lancelot, who coldly went, nor bade me one: 1050
And there the King will know me and my love,
And there the Queen herself will pity me,
And all the gentle court will welcome me,
And after my long voyage I shall rest!"

"Peace," said her father, "O my child, ye seem   1055
Light-headed, for what force is yours to go
So far, being sick? and wherefore would ye look
On this proud fellow again, who scorns us all?"

Then the rough Torre began to heave and
    move,
And bluster into stormy sobs and say,   1060
"I never loved him: an I meet with him,
I care not howsoever great he be,
Then will I strike at him and strike him down,
Give me good fortune, I will strike him dead,
For this discomfort he hath done the house."   1065

To whom the gentle sister made reply,
"Fret not yourself, dear brother, nor be wroth,
Seeing it is no more Sir Lancelot's fault
Not to love me, than it is mine to love
Him of all men who seems to me the highest."   1070

"Highest?" the father answered, echoing
    "highest?"

(He meant to break the passion in her) "nay,
Daughter, I know not what you call the highest;
But this I know, for all the people know it,
He loves the Queen, and in an open shame: 1075
And she returns his love in open shame;
If this be high, what is it to be low?"

Then spake the lily maid of Astolat:
"Sweet father, all too faint and sick am I
For anger: these are slanders: never yet   1080
Was noble man but made ignoble talk.
He makes no friend who never made a foe.
But now it is my glory to have loved
One peerless, without stain: so let me pass,
My father, howsoe'er I seem to you,   1085
Not all unhappy, having loved God's best
And greatest, though my love had no return:
Yet, seeing you desire your child to live,
Thanks, but you work against your own desire;
For if I could believe the things you say   1090
I should but die the sooner; wherefore cease,
Sweet father, and bid call the ghostly man
Hither, and let me shrive me clean,[34] and die."

So when the ghostly man had come and gone,
She with a face, bright as for sin forgiven,   1095
Besought Lavaine to write as she devised
A letter, word for word; and when he asked
"Is it for Lancelot, is it for my dear lord?
Then will I bear it gladly"; she replied,
"For Lancelot and the Queen and all the world,   1100
But I myself must bear it." Then he wrote
The letter she devised; which being writ
And folded, "O sweet father, tender and true,
Deny me not," she said—"ye never yet
Denied my fancies—this, however strange,   1105
My latest: lay the letter in my hand
A little ere I die, and close the hand
Upon it; I shall guard it even in death.
And when the heat is gone from out my heart,
Then take the little bed on which I died   1110
For Lancelot's love, and deck it like the Queen's
For richness, and me also like the Queen
In all I have of rich, and lay me on it.
And let there be prepared a chariot-bier
To take me to the river, and a barge   1115
Be ready on the river, clothed in black.
I go in state to court, to meet the Queen.

---

[34] Call the priest to give me absolution, so that I may be
cleansed of sin.

There surely I shall speak for mine own self,
And none of you can speak for me so well.
And therefore let our dumb old man alone 1120
Go with me, he can steer and row, and he
Will guide me to that palace, to the doors."

She ceased: her father promised; whereupon
She grew so cheerful that they deemed her death
Was rather in the fantasy than the blood. 1125
But ten slow mornings passed, and on the eleventh
Her father laid the letter in her hand,
And closed the hand upon it, and she died.
So that day there was dole in Astolat.

But when the next sun brake from under- 1130
    ground,
Then, those two brethren slowly with bent brows
Accompanying, the sad chariot-bier
Passed like a shadow through the field, that shone
Full-summer, to that stream whereon the barge,
Palled all its length in blackest samite, lay. 1135
There sat the lifelong creature of the house,
Loyal, the dumb old servitor, on deck,
Winking his eyes, and twisted all his face.
So those two brethren from the chariot took
And on the black decks laid her in her bed, 1140
Set in her hand a lily, o'er her hung
The silken case with braided blazonings,
And kissed her quiet brows, and saying to her
"Sister, farewell for ever," and again
"Farewell, sweet sister," parted all in tears. 1145
Then rose the dumb old servitor, and the dead,
Oared by the dumb, went upward with the
    flood—
In her right hand the lily, in her left
The letter—all her bright hair streaming down—
And all the coverlid was cloth of gold 1150
Drawn to her waist, and she herself in white
All but her face, and that clear-featured face
Was lovely, for she did not seem as dead,
But fast asleep, and lay as though she smiled.

That day Sir Lancelot at the palace craved 1155
Audience of Guinevere, to give at last
The price of half a realm, his costly gift,
Hard-won and hardly won with bruise and blow,
With deaths of others, and almost his own,
The nine-years-fought-for diamonds: for he saw 1160
One of her house, and sent him to the Queen
Bearing his wish, whereto the Queen agreed
With such and so unmoved a majesty

She might have seemed her statue, but that he,
Low-drooping till he wellnigh kissed her feet 1165
For loyal awe, saw with a sidelong eye
The shadow of some piece of pointed lace,
In the Queen's shadow, vibrate on the walls,[35]
And parted, laughing in his courtly heart.

All in an oriel on the summer side, 1170
Vine-clad, of Arthur's palace toward the stream,
They met, and Lancelot kneeling uttered,
    "Queen,
Lady, my liege, in whom I have my joy,
Take, what I had not won except for you,
These jewels, and make me happy, making them 1175
An armlet for the roundest arm on earth,
Or necklace for a neck to which the swan's
Is tawnier than her cygnet's:[36] these are words:
Your beauty is your beauty, and I sin
In speaking, yet O grant my worship of it 1180
Words, as we grant grief tears. Such sin in words
Perchance, we both can pardon:[37] but, my Queen,
I hear of rumors flying through your court.
Our bond, as not the bond of man and wife,
Should have in it an absoluter trust 1185
To make up that defect: let rumors be:
When did not rumors fly? these, as I trust
That you trust me in your own nobleness,
I may not well believe that you believe."

While thus he spoke, half turned away, the 1190
    Queen
Brake from the vast oriel-embowering vine
Leaf after leaf, and tore, and cast them off,
Till all the place whereon she stood was green;
Then, when he ceased, in one cold passive hand
Received at once and laid aside the gems 1195
There on a table near her, and replied:

"It may be, I am quicker of belief
Than you believe me, Lancelot of the Lake.
Our bond is not the bond of man and wife.
This good is in it, whatsoe'er of ill, 1200
It be broken easier. I for you
This many a year have done despite and wrong
To one whom ever in my heart of hearts

---

35 That is, saw that she was trembling (with jealous anger).
36 The neck of the young swan, or cygnet, is tawny or yellowish. Compared with yours even the swan's white neck is tawnier than a cygnet's.
37 To this point the speech is completely formal and courtly.

I did acknowledge nobler. What are these?
Diamonds for me! they had been thrice their 1205
    worth
Being your gift, had you not lost your own.
To loyal hearts the value of all gifts
Must vary as the giver's. Not for me!
For her! for your new fancy. Only this
Grant me, I pray you: have your joys apart. 1210
I doubt not that however changed, you keep
So much of what is graceful: and myself
Would shun to break those bounds of courtesy
In which as Arthur's Queen I move and rule:
So cannot speak my mind. An end to this! 1215
A strange one! yet I take it with Amen.
So pray you, add my diamonds to her pearls;
Deck her with these; tell her, she shines me down:
An armlet for an arm to which the Queen's
Is haggard, or a necklace for a neck 1220
O as much fairer—as a faith once fair
Was richer than these diamonds—hers not
    mine—
Nay, by the mother of our Lord himself,
Or hers or mine, mine now to work my will—
She shall not have them."
                Saying which she seized, 1225
And, through the casement standing wide for
    heat,
Flung them, and down they flashed, and smote
    the stream.
Then from the smitten surface flashed, as it were,
Diamonds to meet them, and they passed away.
Then while Sir Lancelot leaned, in half disdain 1230
At love, life, all things, on the window ledge,
Close underneath his eyes, and right across
Where these had fallen, slowly, slowly passed the
    barge
Whereon the lily maid of Astolat
Lay smiling, like a star in blackest night. 1235

But the wild Queen, who saw not, burst away
To weep and wail in secret; and the barge,
On to the palace-doorway sliding, paused.
There two stood armed, and kept the door; to
    whom,
All up the marble stair, tier over tier, 1240
Were added mouths that gaped, and eyes that
    asked
"What is it?" but that oarsman's haggard face,
As hard and still as is the face that men
Shape to their fancy's eye from broken rocks
On some cliff-side, appalled them, and they said, 1245

"He is enchanted, cannot speak—and she,
Look how she sleeps—the Fairy Queen, so fair!
Yea, but how pale! what are they? flesh and
    blood?
Or come to take the King to Fairyland?
For some do hold our Arthur cannot die, 1250
But that he passes into Fairyland."

While thus they babbled of the King, the King
Came girt with knights: then turned the tongue-
    less man
From the half-face to the full eye, and rose
And pointed to the damsel, and the doors. 1255
So Arthur bade the meek Sir Percivale
And pure Sir Galahad to uplift the maid;
And reverently they bore her into hall.
Then came the fine Gawain and wondered at her,
And Lancelot later came and mused at her, 1260
And last the Queen herself, and pitied her:
But Arthur spied the letter in her hand,
Stooped, took, brake seal, and read it; this was
    all:

"Most noble lord, Sir Lancelot of the Lake,
I, sometime called the maid of Astolat, 1265
Come, for you left me taking no farewell,
Hither, to take my last farewell of you.
I loved you, and my love had no return,
And therefore my true love has been my death.
And therefore to our Lady Guinevere, 1270
And to all other ladies, I make moan:
Pray for my soul, and yield me burial.
Pray for my soul thou too, Sir Lancelot,
As thou art a knight peerless."
                Thus he read;
And ever in the reading, lords and dames 1275
Wept, looking often from his face who read
To hers which lay so silent, and at times,
So touched were they, half-thinking that her lips,
Who had devised the letter, moved again.

Then freely spoke Sir Lancelot to them all: 1280
"My lord liege Arthur, and all ye that hear,
Know that for this most gentle maiden's death
Right heavy am I; for good she was and true,
But loved me with a love beyond all love
In women, whomsoever I have known. 1285
Yet to be loved makes not to love again;
Not at my years, however it hold in youth.
I swear by truth and knighthood that I gave
No cause, not willingly, for such a love:

To this I call my friends in testimony,   1290
Her brethren, and her father, who himself
Besought me to be plain and blunt, and use,
To break her passion, some discourtesy
Against my nature: what I could, I did.
I left her and I bade her no farewell;   1295
Though, had I dreamt the damsel would have
    died,
I might have put my wits to some rough use,
And helped her from herself."
                  Then said the Queen
(Sea was her wrath, yet working after storm)
"Ye might at least have done her so much grace, 1300
Fair lord, as would have helped her from her
    death."[38]
He raised his head, their eyes met and hers fell,
He adding:
           "Queen, she would not be content
Save that I wedded her, which could not be.
Then might she follow me through the world, 1305
    she asked;
It could not be. I told her that her love
Was but the flash of youth, would darken down
To rise hereafter in a stiller flame
Toward one more worthy of her—then would I,
More specially were he, she wedded, poor,   1310
Estate them with large land and territory
In mine own realm beyond the narrow seas,
To keep them in all joyance: more than this
I could not; this she would not, and she died."

He pausing, Arthur answered, "O my knight,   1315
It will be to thy worship,[39] as my knight,
And mine, as head of all our Table Round,
To see that she be buried worshipfully."[40]

So toward that shrine which then in all the
    realm
Was richest, Arthur leading, slowly went   1320
The marshalled Order of their Table Round,
And Lancelot sad beyond his wont, to see
The maiden buried, not as one unknown,
Nor meanly, but with gorgeous obsequies,
And mass, and rolling music, like a queen.   1325
And when the knights had laid her comely head
Low in the dust of half-forgotten kings,
Then Arthur spake among them, "Let her tomb
Be costly, and her image thereupon,

And let the shield of Lancelot at her feet   1330
Be carven, and her lily in her hand.
And let the story of her dolorous voyage
For all true hearts be blazoned on her tomb
In letters gold and azure!" which was wrought
Thereafter; but when now the lords and dames 1335
And people, from the high door streaming, brake
Disorderly, as homeward each, the Queen,
Who marked Sir Lancelot where he moved apart,
Drew near, and sighed in passing, "Lancelot,
Forgive me; mine was jealousy in love."   1340
He answered with his eyes upon the ground,
"That is love's curse; pass on, my Queen, for-
    given."
But Arthur, who beheld his cloudy brows,
Approached him, and with full affection said,

"Lancelot, my Lancelot, thou in whom I have 1345
Most joy and most affiance,[41] for I know
What thou hast been in battle by my side,
And many a time have watched thee at the tilt
Strike down the lusty and long practised knight,
And let the younger and unskilled go by   1350
To win his honor and to make his name,
And loved thy courtesies and thee, a man
Made to be loved; but now I would to God,
Seeing the homeless trouble in thine eyes,
Thou couldst have loved this maiden, shaped, it 1355
    seems,
By God for thee alone, and from her face,
If one may judge the living by the dead,
Delicately pure and marvellously fair,
Who might have brought thee, now a lonely man
Wifeless and heirless, noble issue, sons   1360
Born to the glory of thy name and fame,
My knight, the great Sir Lancelot of the Lake."

Then answered Lancelot: "Fair she was, my
    King,
Pure, as you ever wish your knights to be.
To doubt her fairness were to want an eye,   1365
To doubt her pureness were to want a heart—
Yea, to be loved, if what is worthy love
Could bind him, but free love will not be bound."

"Free love, so bound, were freëst," said the
    King.
"Let love be free; free love is for the best: 1370
And, after heaven, on our dull side of death,

---

[38] Have prevented her death.   [39] Honor.
[40] Honorably.

[41] Reliance.

What should be best, if not so pure a love
Clothed in so pure a loveliness? yet thee
She failed to bind, though being, as I think,
Unbound as yet, and gentle, as I know." 1375

And Lancelot answered nothing, but he went,
And at the inrunning of a little brook
Sat by the river in a cove, and watched
The high reed wave, and lifted up his eyes
And saw the barge that brought her moving 1380
    down,
Far-off, a blot upon the stream, and said
Low in himself, "Ah simple heart and sweet,
Ye loved me, damsel, surely with a love
Far tenderer than my Queen's. Pray for thy soul?
Ay, that will I. Farewell too—now at last— 1385
Farewell, fair lily. 'Jealousy in love?'
Not rather[42] dead love's harsh heir, jealous pride?
Queen, if I grant the jealousy as of love,
May not your crescent[43] fear for name and fame
Speak, as it waxes, of a love that wanes? 1390
Why did the King dwell on my name to me?
Mine own name shames me, seeming a reproach,
Lancelot, whom the Lady of the Lake
Caught from his mother's arms—the wondrous
    one
Who passes through the vision of the night— 1395
She chanted snatches of mysterious hymns
Heard on the winding waters, eve and morn
She kissed me saying, 'Thou art fair, my child,
As a king's son,' and often in her arms
She bare me, pacing on the dusky mere. 1400
Would she had drowned me in it, where'er it be!
For what am I? what profits me my name
Of greatest knight? I fought for it, and have it:
Pleasure to have it, none; to lose it, pain;
Now grown a part of me: but what use in it? 1405
To make men worse by making my sin known?

Or sin seem less, the sinner seeming great?
Alas for Arthur's greatest knight, a man
Not after Arthur's heart! I needs must break
These bonds that so defame me: not without 1410
She wills it: would I, if she willed it? nay,
Who knows? but if I would not, then may God,
I pray him, send a sudden Angel down
To seize me by the hair and bear me far,
And fling me deep in that forgotten mere, 1415
Among the tumbled fragments of the hills."

So groaned Sir Lancelot in remorseful pain,
Not knowing he should die a holy man.

Crossing the Bar

Sunset and evening star,
    And one clear call for me!
And may there be no moaning of the bar,
    When I put out to sea,

But such a tide as moving seems asleep, 5
    Too full for sound and foam,
When that which drew from out the boundless
    deep
    Turns again home.

Twilight and evening bell,
    And after that the dark! 10
And may there be no sadness of farewell,
    When I embark;

For though from out our bourne of Time and
    Place
    The flood may bear me far,
I hope to see my Pilot face to face 15
    When I have crossed the bar.

Robert Browning
1812–1889

Browning was born in 1812 at Camberwell, a suburb of London. His father, who held a post in the Bank of England, had well-developed tastes for history, art, and music; his mother, like Ruskin's, was a devout Puritan, though with a sunnier disposition, which the boy inherited. And like Ruskin again, he was largely educated at home, where he read widely in his father's library, finding most delight in history and in modern poetry (Scott, Byron, and especially Shelley, his great idol). So nourished, he assimilated much of the Romantic temper, the thirst for knowledge and experience, an ardent longing for the Ideal,

---

[42] Was it not rather.   [43] Growing.

and a marked self-consciousness. All these characteristics are reflected in his first long poem, *Pauline* (1833), which Browning later described in two passages that throw important light on his development as a poet:

The following Poem was written in pursuance of a foolish plan which occupied me mightily for a time, and which had for its object the enabling me to assume & realize I know not how many different characters;—meanwhile the world was never to guess that "Brown, Smith, Jones & Robinson" (as the spelling books have it) the respective authors of this poem, the other novel, such an opera, such a speech, etc. etc. were no other than one and the same individual. The present abortion was the first work of the Poet *of the batch, who would have been more legitimately* myself *than most of the others; but I surrounded him with all manner of (to my then notion) poetical accessories, and had planned quite a delightful life for him. (1837)*

The thing was my earliest attempt at "poetry always dramatic in principle, and so many utterances of so many imaginary persons, not mine," which I have since written according to a scheme less extravagant and scale less impracticable than were ventured upon in this crude preliminary sketch. (1867)

The words in quotation marks in the second statement (Browning is quoting himself) define the central principle of his aesthetics, on which he wrote the long series of dramatic monologues which began to appear in the 1840s and comprise his two main volumes, appropriately called *Men and Women* (1855) and *Dramatis Personae* (1864). But in 1832, as the first statement reveals, Browning's temperament was entirely too subjective to make the plan anything other than a slightly disguised series of personal confessions in the Romantic tradition. Or to put the same thing differently, he was too much under the influence of Byron (all of whose heroes are Byron) and of Shelley (whose record of his own poetic sensibility in *Alastor* was the immediate model for *Pauline*) to write dramatic poetry. Consequently, in despite of his plan, his first poem was really an account of his own youthful soul, which he imagined he had concealed under a dramatic framework.

But he was quickly disabused. In a review written by John Stuart Mill, the author was credited with "considerable poetic powers" but with "a more intense and morbid self-consciousness" than Mill had ever known in any sane human being. The world *had* guessed—and easily—that the protagonist was the poet. Browning was humiliated—and *Pauline* was promptly called an "abortion." His next poems, *Paracelsus* (1835) and *Sordello* (1840), were more explicitly dramatic, but the protagonists of both were still romantic characters in search of a philosophy, and still very like Robert Browning. Years later he is reported to have said that "his early poems were so transparent in their [personal] meaning as to draw down upon him the ridicule of the critics, and that, boy as he was, this ridicule and censure stung him into quite another style of writing"—that is to say, into a style that was in fact, and not in pretense, "dramatic in principle."

But no amount of criticism would have produced this transformation if Browning had been merely a Victorian Shelley. The truth was, however, that in addition to ardent idealism, he possessed a sharp eye for psychological realities and a considerable gift for detached observation of human nature. This side of his temperament was exercised and developed by ten years of playwriting (1837–47), during which Shakespeare took the place of Shelley as his poetic model. His plays were not successful. The action was constantly impeded by long speeches in which the characters analyzed their emotions or justified their conduct. But what was a liability on the stage might be a virtue in poetry if the method of self-analysis were transferred to short character sketches in the form of dramatic speeches.

Robert Browning (1812–1889). The ten years Browning spent writing unsuccessful plays helped him to develop his bent for the dramatic monologue. This poetic form enabled him to speak through his characters while remaining detached and critical. *National Portrait Gallery.*

Exactly when and how Browning made that all-important discovery and thus found his true bent is unknown, but it was certainly affected by three things. One was Shakespeare's soliloquies. The second was the poetry of John Donne, so frequently quoted in the letters to Elizabeth Barrett (1845–46). In Donne's "Elegies" he found realistic studies of men and women, and in the "Songs and Sonnets" a series of dramatic monologues, idiomatic in diction and rhythm, psychological in focus, and emotionally intense (the poem often beginning with a passionate outburst at a moment of crisis). Finally, the old plan of a group of long biographical poems like *Pauline,* written in a romantic style, in which he would assume "many different characters," lay in the back of his mind, ready to be transformed, under the combined influences of the theater, Shakespeare, and Donne, into a series of short, dramatic monologues in which the several protagonists would reveal their own characters through the medium of natural speech.

The affinity with Donne not only suggests that in many ways Browning is the most modern of the Victorian poets, with the exception perhaps of Hopkins; it also gives the right clue to his contemporary reputation. For Donne made the same appeal to the younger generation of Jacobeans that Browning did to the younger generation of Rossetti and Morris, John Morley and Pater. To any Jacobean tired of the "literary" verse of Spenser and Sidney, of pastorals and allegories and Petrarchan conceits, Donne offered a poetry at once more passionately alive and more psychologically profound. In the same way the younger Victorians were delighted to find in Browning a range and intensity of experience quite lacking in contemporary verse. Morley's reaction in 1869 is revealing:

The truth is, we have for long been so debilitated by pastorals, by graceful presentation of the Arthurian legend for drawing-rooms, by idylls, . . . by verse directly didactic, that a rude blast of air from the outside welter of human realities is apt to give a shock, that might well show in what simpleton's paradise we have been living. The ethics of the rectory parlour set to sweet music, the respectable aspirations of the sentimental curate married to exquisite verse, the everlasting glorification of domestic sentiment, . . . all this might seem to be making valetudinarians of us all. . . .

[From Browning] there comes out a long procession of human figures, infinitely various in form and thought, in character and act; a group of men and women, eager, passionate, indifferent; tender and ravenous, mean and noble, humorous and profound. . . . And they all come out with a certain Shakespearian fulness, vividness, directness. Above all, they are
every one of them men and women, with free play of human life in limb and feature, as in an antique sculpture. So much of modern art, in poetry as in painting, runs to mere drapery.

That might have been said by a Jacobean in the early 1600s with Spenser and Donne in his mind. In the same vein Walter Pater not only praised Browning for renouncing the "selfish serenities of wild-wood and dream-palace" to observe the acts of living men, but also found that his concern with psychological analysis made him "the most modern, to modern people the most important, of poets." It is because the point of view reflected in these passages, both negatively in the reaction against didactic and aesthetic verse, and positively in the taste for psychological realism, became widespread by 1920 that Browning probably has a wider appeal today than either Tennyson or Arnold.

Even his obscurity is modern: the touch-and-go allusions that demand extensive knowledge on the reader's part; the plunging *in medias res* without explanation of who is speaking or where and when; above all, the elliptical syntax and the sudden jump from thought to thought without benefit of connecting links. With reference to the last, Julia Wedgwood once protested to Browning, in terms often echoed later by readers of Eliot and Auden, against his use of "hieroglyphics." "You must treat us respectfully," she said, "and not fling us torn scraps of meaning, leaving us to supply the gaps." And the explanation, in both cases, is the same. "I have observed," wrote Elizabeth Barrett, ". . . that a good deal of what is called obscurity in you, arises from a habit of very subtle association; so subtle, that you are probably unconscious of it, . . . the effect of which is to throw together on the same level and in the same light, things of likeness and unlikeness—till the reader grows confused as I did." But Browning was no more unconscious of this than Eliot. When Ruskin complained of his obscurity, he answered, "You ought, I think, to keep pace with the thought tripping from ledge to ledge of my 'glaciers,' as you call them; not stand poking your alpenstock into the holes, and demonstrating that no foot could have stood there;— suppose it sprang over there?" And a moment later, apropos of a particular jump, he adds the revealing remark, "The whole is all but a simultaneous feeling with me." In modern verse the same effort to reflect the very movement of the mind, and therefore to discard the logical and grammatical connections which falsify the immediacy of experience, is carried much further. No reader of Eliot will find Browning's obscurity difficult, or fail to understand its main function. And, in any event, it is only a matter of the line. His poems as a whole are far longer, far more discursive, than modern work. But to the Victorians, as Elizabeth Barrett says, his condensed phrasing was all very new and confusing.

So was another characteristic of his poetry which is modern. This is his willingness to present "bad" characters without the moral condemnation his mid-Victorian readers expected. At times he could adopt an almost clinical view of a criminal (the lover of Porphyria or the woman in "The Laboratory"), or still worse, he could treat with sympathy what obviously called for instant reproof (the life of Lippo Lippi and the lovers in "Respectability"). On one occasion Browning criticized his wife for being without a "scientific interest in evil"; and on another claimed that "all morbidness of the soul is worth the soul's study." Related to this suspension of judgment is his habit of implying opposite judgments, so that the reader must balance the good with the evil and arrive at his own conclusion, somewhere between the warm approval or the righteous condemnation which Victorian morality demanded. As one critic has recently said, "The Duke of Ferrara may not be all bad even though he seems to have had his last wife murdered; and his Duchess may not be all saint, even though she smiled sweetly at everyone." The Bishop who orders his tomb "alternately shocks and delights, in a poem which is neither an indictment of the Italian Renaissance nor a panegyric." I suspect, however, that the earnest Victorians failed to realize that Browning's own attitude was ambivalent. They condemned Duke and Bishop outright. And unfortunately this one-sided reading has been carried down into modern textbooks and anthologies, where we may be told, for example, that the Friar in the Spanish Cloister is filled with the passion of hate, or that Andrea del Sarto is "the kind of man Browning considers most contemptible (worse than an energetic criminal)."

But even so, even though the Victorians *could* find a "moral" in Browning's neutral or balanced studies of dubious characters, the lesson was obviously blurred and weakened by his dramatic detachment. As one critic pointed out to him in 1846, it was not "by the dramatic medium that poets teach most impressively. . . . It is too difficult for the common reader to analyse, and to discern between the vivid and the earnest." Consequently, as that implies, the critic begged him "to speak yourself out of that personality which God made, and with the voice which He tuned"; and, because he had thought so deeply on life and its ends, to teach others what he had learned "in the directest and most impressive way, the mask thrown off."

What made this comment so important for Browning's development was that the critic was Elizabeth Barrett. The famous love affair is too well known to need retelling. They were married in 1846 and lived in Italy until Mrs. Browning's death in 1861. After that Browning returned to London to become a popular guest at dinner parties, and to write, for the most part, a series of long poems, most notably *The Ring and the Book* (1869).

In the meanwhile, though his form continued to be dramatic, his intention, under his wife's influence and the pressure of the time, became more and more prophetic. The purpose of the artist defined in "Fra Lippo Lippi" (at lines 282ff.), to paint the shapes of things just as they are so that men may become more aware of the world, is crossed and to some extent displaced by the purpose "to rule—by thought insight to deed." It is this didactic strain, and still more the particular nature of the thought that Browning came to teach, which make him a Victorian poet in the sense of being foreign to contemporary taste. But we must remember that the modern characteristics isolated above, especially the dramatic monologue, had direct influence on the work of Ezra Pound and T. S. Eliot, and that Eliot did much to promote the Donne revival.

In itself Browning's ethical philosophy, partly Puritan, partly Romantic, in which life is conceived of as a moral testing ground—those who strive for high goals are spiritually successful, while those who succeed in attaining low aims really fail—can still carry weight. But it is harder to accept his glorification of the moral struggle as a heroic battle in which "good" is certain of victory, and the gallant warrior certain of a heaven where his goal will be reached. Browning's poetry, though filled with tragedy, is never tragic. The relative ease of his own life and the complacent optimism in his environment blinded him, for all his psychological insight, to the deepest levels of experience. The objection may be put in another form. He was so ready to exalt the life of aspiration—what matter the failure, fight on, strive ever, there as here—that he could be horribly oblivious to the pain involved. Is there any other body of poetry so filled with defeat and frustration and so lacking in suffering? That is why a poem like "The Last Ride Together" seems shallow: it is romantic in the derogatory sense. And the criticism bites hard in a period like ours, so acutely aware of suffering and so suspicious of romantic idealizations.

Browning's philosophy of love is equally vulnerable today. The theory of "elective affinities," of two people and two only made for each other; the idea of the "critical moment" when the great lover goes forward regardless of obstacles and continues to love regardless of the outcome, while the little lover draws back out of selfish or worldly considerations; and above all, as these doctrines imply, the idealization of romantic love into what he calls the "summum bonum," the highest of all goals of aspiration—these attitudes, for better or worse, are now more likely to stir ridicule than inspiration.

But in the 1880s, when the Browning Societies were being founded all over England and America, his philosophy of life and love was not only alive, it was the conservative leaven which gave his poetry a range of appeal that no other poet of the time could command. For here was psychological realism and full-blooded life combined with all the moral idealism one could ask for, not just in an ethic of aspiration, but best of all in a conception of love that recognized human passion and yet made it a spiritual inspiration. Here, indeed, was the perfect poet-prophet for the later Victorians who wanted to open the door wide enough to let in a good blast of fresh air, but who did not want to leave the Victorian home. In the next generation the exodus made Browning's philosophy a liability. Fortunately it does not appear in many of his best poems and where it does, it is sometimes conceived dramatically (as in "Andrea del Sarto"), so that whatever may be our personal disagreement, we recognize its psychological rightness in the mouth of the speaker.

TEXTS: The best text is *The Works of Robert Browning* (Centenary Edition), edited by F. G. Kenyon (10 vols., 1912). A good selection with useful introduction and notes is *Browning: Pippa Passes and Shorter Poems,* edited by J. E. Baker (1947). The standard biography is by H. W. Griffin and H. C. Minchin (3rd ed. revised, 1938). W. C. De Vane's *Browning Handbook* (1955 ed.) gives dates of writing, publication, sources, etc. Betty Miller's *Robert Browning. A Portrait* (1952) is a lively study that uses some concepts of modern psychology. A useful book is Park Honan's *Browning's Characters: A Study in Poetic Techniques* (1961). Robert Langbaum's *The Poetry of Experience* (1963) is largely devoted to Browning. Two collections of essays by various modern critics have been edited by Philip Drew (1966) and by Boyd Litzinger and K. L. Knickerbocker (1965).

My Last Duchess

Ferrara[1]

That's my last Duchess painted on the wall,
Looking as if she were alive. I call
That piece a wonder, now: Frà Pandolf's[2] hands
Worked busily a day, and there she stands.
Will 't please you sit and and look at her? I said   5
"Frà Pandolf" by design, for never read
Strangers like you that pictured countenance,
The depth and passion of its earnest glance,
But to myself they turned (since none puts by
The curtain I have drawn for you, but I)   10
And seemed as they would ask me, if they durst,
How such a glance came there; so, not the first
Are you to turn and ask thus. Sir, 't was not
Her husband's presence only, called that spot
Of joy into the Duchess' cheek: perhaps   15
Frà Pandolf chanced to say "Her mantle laps
Over my lady's wrist too much," or "Paint
Must never hope to reproduce the faint
Half-flush that dies along her throat": such stuff
Was courtesy, she thought, and cause enough   20
For calling up that spot of joy. She had
A heart—how shall I say?—too soon made glad,
Too easily impressed; she liked whate'er
She looked on, and her looks went everywhere.
Sir, 't was all one! My favor at her breast,   25
The dropping of the daylight in the West,
The bough of cherries some officious fool
Broke in the orchard for her, the white mule
She rode with round the terrace—all and each
Would draw from her alike the approving speech,   30
Or blush, at least. She thanked men,—good! but
    thanked
Somehow—I know not how—as if she ranked
My gift of a nine-hundred-years-old name
With anybody's gift. Who'd stoop to blame
This sort of trifling? Even had you skill   35
In speech—(which I have not)—to make your
    will
Quite clear to such an one, and say, "Just this
Or that in you disgusts me; here you miss,
Or there exceed the mark"—and if she let
Herself be lessoned so, nor plainly set   40
Her wits to yours, forsooth, and made excuse,
—E'en then would be some stooping; and I choose
Never to stoop. Oh sir, she smiled, no doubt,
Whene'er I passed her; but who passed without
Much the same smile? This grew; I gave com-   45
    mands;
Then all smiles stopped together.[3] There she
    stands
As if alive. Will 't please you rise? We'll meet

---

[1] Place, the Italian town of Ferrara; time, the Rennaissance. The Duke of Ferrara speaks to the Count's envoy.
[2] Brother Pandolf, an imaginary painter.

[3] Browning explained that "the commands were that she should be put to death, or he might have had her shut up in a convent."

The company below, then. I repeat,
The Count your master's known munificence
Is ample warrant that no just pretence   50
Of mine for dowry will be disallowed;
Though his fair daughter's self, as I avowed
At starting, is my object. Nay, we'll go
Together down, sir! Notice Neptune, though,
Taming a sea-horse, thought a rarity,   55
Which Claus of Innsbruck[4] cast in bronze for me!

Count Gismond

Aix in Provence[1]

I

Christ God who savest man, save most
    Of men Count Gismond who saved me!
Count Gauthier, when he chose his post,
    Chose time and place and company
To suit it; when he struck at length   5
My honor, 'twas with all his strength.

II

And doubtlessly ere he could draw
    All points to one, he must have schemed!
That miserable morning saw
    Few half so happy as I seemed,   10
While being dressed in queen's array
To give our tourney prize away.

III

I thought they loved me, did me grace
    To please themselves; 'twas all their deed;
God makes, or fair or foul, our face;   15
    If showing mine so caused to bleed
My cousins' hearts, they should have dropped
A word, and straight the play had stopped.

IV

They, too, so beauteous! Each a queen
    By virtue of her brow and breast;   20

Not needing to be crowned, I mean,
    As I do. E'en when I was dressed,
Had either of them spoke, instead
Of glancing sideways with still head!

V

But no: they let me laugh, and sing   25
    My birthday song quite through, adjust
The last rose in my garland, fling
    A last look on the mirror, trust
My arms to each an arm of theirs,
And so descend the castle-stairs—   30

VI

And come out on the morning-troop
    Of merry friends who kissed my cheek,
And called me queen, and made me stoop
    Under the canopy—(a streak
That pierced it, of the outside sun,   35
Powdered with gold its gloom's soft dun)—

VII

And they could let me take my state
    And foolish throne amid applause
Of all come there to celebrate
    My queen's-day—Oh I think the cause   40
Of much was, they forgot no crowd
Makes up for parents in their shroud!

VIII

However that be, all eyes were bent
    Upon me, when my cousins cast
Theirs down; 'twas time I should present   45
    The victor's crown, but . . . there, 'twill last
No long time . . . the old mist again
Blinds me as then it did.[2] How vain!

IX

See! Gismond's at the gate, in talk
    With his two boys: I can proceed.   50
Well, at that moment, who should stalk
    Forth boldly—to my face, indeed—
But Gauthier, and he thundered "Stay!"
And all stayed. "Bring no crowns, I say!

---

4 An imaginary sculptor.

1 Place, the town of Aix in Provence, a section of southern France; time, the Middle Ages. The wife of Count Gismond speaks to a friend of hers named Adela. The poem was originally grouped with "My Last Duchess," and the two together were called *Italy and France*.

2 At the memory of that moment, everything goes blank again, as it did originally.

X

"Bring torches! Wind the penance-sheet   55
　　About her! Let her shun the chaste,
Or lay herself before their feet!
　　Shall she whose body I embraced
A night long, queen it in the day?
For honor's sake no crowns, I say!"   60

XI

I? What I answered? As I live,
　　I never fancied such a thing
As answer possible to give.
　　What says the body when they spring
Some monstrous torture-engine's whole   65
Strength on it? No more says the soul.

XII

Till out strode Gismond; then I knew
　　That I was saved. I never met
His face before, but, at first view,
　　I felt quite sure that God had set   70
Himself to Satan; who would spend
A minute's mistrust on the end?

XIII

He strode to Gauthier, in his throat
　　Gave him the lie, then struck his mouth
With one back-handed blow that wrote   75
　　In blood men's verdict there. North, South,
East, West, I looked. The lie was dead,
And damned, and truth stood up instead.

XIV

This glads me most, that I enjoyed
　　The heart of the joy, with my content   80
In watching Gismond unalloyed
　　By any doubt of the event:
God took that on him—I was bid
Watch Gismond for my part: I did.

XV

Did I not watch him while he let   85
　　His armorer just brace his greaves,
Rivet his hauberk, on the fret
　　The while! His foot . . . my memory leaves
No least stamp out, nor how anon
He pulled his ringing gauntlets on.   90

XVI

And e'en before the trumpet's sound
　　Was finished, prone lay the false knight,
Prone as his lie, upon the ground:
　　Gismond flew at him, used no sleight
O' the sword, but open-breasted drove,   95
Cleaving till out the truth he clove.

XVII

Which done, he dragged him to my feet
　　And said, "Here die, but end thy breath
In full confession, lest thou fleet
　　From my first, to God's second death![3]   100
Say, hast thou lied?" And, "I have lied
To God and her," he said, and died.[4]

XVIII

Then Gismond, kneeling to me, asked
　　—What safe my heart holds, though no word
Could I repeat now, if I tasked   105
　　My powers for ever, to a third
Dear even as you are. Pass the rest
Until I sank upon his breast.

XIX

Over my head his arm he flung
　　Against the world; and scarce I felt   110
His sword (that dripped by me and swung)
　　A little shifted in its belt:
For he began to say the while
How South our home lay many a mile.

XX

So 'mid the shouting multitude   115
　　We two walked forth to never more
Return. My cousins have pursued
　　Their life, untroubled as before
I vexed them. Gauthier's dwelling-place
God lighten! May his soul find grace!   120

---

[3] Damnation.

[4] The temptation to suspect that Gauthier was a rejected lover who knew whereof he spoke has to be put aside because the poem upholds the medieval confidence in the ordeal by duel (see again lines 70–72, 79–83). Was he the instrument of a plot devised by the envious cousins to ruin the speaker's character?

XXI

Our elder boy has got the clear
  Great brow;[5] though when his brother's black
Full eye shows scorn, it[6] . . . Gismond here?
  And have you brought my tercel[7] back?
I just was telling Adela   125
How many birds it struck since May.

Soliloquy of the Spanish Cloister

I

Gr-r-r—there go, my heart's abhorrence!
  Water your damned flower-pots, do!
If hate killed men, Brother Lawrence,
  God's blood, would not mine kill you!
What? your myrtle-bush wants trimming?   5
  Oh, that rose has prior claims—
Needs its leaden vase filled brimming?
  Hell dry you up with its flames!

II

At the meal we sit together:
  Salve tibi![1] I must hear   10
Wise talk of the kind of weather,
  Sort of season, time of year:
Not a plenteous cork-crop: scarcely
  Dare we hope oak-galls,[2] *I doubt:*
What's the Latin name for "parsley"?   15
  What's the Greek name for Swine's Snout?

III

Whew! We'll have our platter burnished,
  Laid with care on our own shelf!
With a fire-new spoon we're furnished,
  And a goblet for ourself,   20
Rinsed like something sacrificial
  Ere 'tis fit to touch our chaps—
Marked with L for our initial!
  (He-he! There his lily snaps!)

IV

Saint, forsooth! While brown Dolores   25
  Squats outside the Convent bank

With Sanchicha, telling stories,
  Steeping tresses in the tank,
Blue-black, lustrous, thick like horsehairs,
  —Can't I see his dead eye glow,   30
Bright as 'twere a Barbary corsair's?[3]
  (That is, if he'd let it show!)

V

When he finishes refection,[4]
  Knife and fork he never lays
Cross-wise, to my recollection,   35
  As do I, in Jesu's praise.
I the Trinity illustrate,
  Drinking watered orange-pulp—
In three sips the Arian[5] frustrate;
  While he drains his at one gulp.   40

VI

Oh, those melons! If he's able
  We're to have a feast! so nice!
One goes to the Abbot's table,
  All of us get each a slice.
How go on your flowers? None double?   45
  Not one fruit-sort can you spy?
Strange!—And I, too, at such trouble
  Keep them close-nipped on the sly!

VII

There's a great text in Galatians,[6]
  Once you trip on it, entails   50
Twenty-nine distinct damnations,
  One sure, if another fails:
If I trip him just a-dying,
  Sure of heaven as sure can be,
Spin him round and send him flying   55
  Off to hell, a Manichee?[7]

VIII

Or, my scrofulous French novel
  On gray paper with blunt type!

---

[5] Of his father.   [6] It too resembles his father's eye.
[7] Male falcon used in hunting.

[1] "Hail to thee." The italics here and in lines 13–15 are used to indicate remarks of Brother Lawrence's which the friar is quoting.
[2] Oak apples produced on the leaves of the oak, valuable for their tannic acid.

[3] Pirate from the coast of north Africa.
[4] Dinner.
[5] Follower of Arius, the fourth-century heretic who denied the dogma of the Trinity.   [6] Galatians 3:10.
[7] If I can trip him into some Manichean heresy (into saying, for example, that both Good and Evil are in eternal opposition, when the orthodox Christian view is that God, the Good, is alone eternal), I can send him to hell.

Simply glance at it, you grovel
    Hand and foot in Belial's gripe: 60
If I double down its pages
    At the woeful sixteenth print,
When he gathers his greengages,
    Ope a sieve and slip it in't?

IX

Or, there's Satan!—one might venture   65
    Pledge one's soul to him, yet leave
Such a flaw in the indenture
    As he'd miss till, past retrieve,
Blasted lay that rose-acacia
    We're so proud of![8] Hy, Zy, Hine[9] . . .   70
'St, there's Vespers! *Plena gratiâ,*
    Ave, Virgo![10] Gr-r-r—you swine![11]

Porphyria's Lover[1]

The rain set early in to-night,
    The sullen wind was soon awake,
It tore the elm-tops down for spite,
    And did its worst to vex the lake:[2]
    I listened with heart fit to break.   5
When glided in Porphyria; straight
    She shut the cold out and the storm,
And kneeled and made the cheerless grate
    Blaze up, and all the cottage warm;
Which done, she rose, and from her form   10
Withdrew the dripping cloak and shawl,
    And laid her soiled gloves by, untied
Her hat and let the damp hair fall,
    And, last, she sat down by my side
    And called me. When no voice replied,   15

She put my arm about her waist,
    And made her smooth white shoulder bare,
And all her yellow hair displaced,
    And, stooping, made my cheek lie there,
    And spread, o'er all, her yellow hair,   20
Murmuring how she loved me—she
    Too weak, for all her heart's endeavor,
To set its struggling passion free
    From pride, and vainer ties dissever,
    And give herself to me forever.   25
But passion sometimes would prevail,
    Nor could to-night's gay feast restrain
A sudden thought of one so pale
    For love of her, and all in vain:
    So, she was come through wind and rain.   30
Be sure I looked up at her eyes
    Happy and proud; at last I knew
Porphyria worshipped me;[3] surprise
    Made my heart swell, and still it grew
    While I debated what to do.   35
That moment she was mine, mine, fair,
    Perfectly pure and good: I found
A thing to do, and all her hair
    In one long yellow string I wound
    Three times her little throat around,   40
And strangled her. No pain felt she;
    I am quite sure she felt no pain.
As a shut bud that holds a bee,
    I warily oped her lids: again
    Laughed the blue eyes without a stain.   45
And I untightened next the tress
    About her neck; her cheek once more
Blushed bright beneath my burning kiss:
    I propped her head up as before,
    Only, this time my shoulder bore   50
Her head, which droops upon it still:
    The smiling rosy little head,
So glad it has its utmost will,
    That all it scorned at once is fled,
    And I, its love, am gained instead!   55
Porphyria's love: she guessed not how
    Her darling one wish would be heard.[4]
And thus we sit together now,
    And all night long we have not stirred,
    And yet God has not said a word!   60

[8] Or I might make a bargain with Satan to give him my soul if he guaranteed to take Brother Lawrence's to hell, but with a flaw in the contract which would allow me to escape.
[9] Possibly an incantation used in black magic.
[10] "Hail, Virgin, full of grace."
[11] It is customary to assume that the poem is "a brilliant analysis of the passion of hate," but is "hate" the right word for the petty spite of lines 45–48 and the ingenious, half-amused play of fancy in lines 49–70? The speaker is mean and malicious, certainly, but Brother Lawrence was a great big bore.

[1] Printed originally with another study in abnormal psychology ("Johannes Agricola"), under the overall title *Madhouse Cells.*
[2] The scenery is partly symbolic.

[3] It is at this point that the speaker ceases to be rational.
[4] The problem of the poem is the tone of lines 36–57. Is it the quiet, businesslike voice of a man believing what he says, or that of a psychopathic murderer getting his revenge and defending himself with a wild rationalization?

"How They Brought the Good News from Ghent to Aix"[1]

[16—]

I

I sprang to the stirrup, and Joris, and he;
I galloped, Dirck galloped, we galloped all three;
"Good speed!" cried the watch, as the gate-bolts
    undrew;
"Speed!" echoed the wall to us galloping through;
Behind shut the postern,[2] the lights sank to rest,   5
And into the midnight we galloped abreast.

II

Not a word to each other; we kept the great pace
Neck by neck, stride by stride, never changing our
    place;
I turned in my saddle and made its girths tight,
Then shortened each stirrup, and set the pique[3]   10
    right,
Rebuckled the cheek-strap, chained slacker the
    bit,
Nor galloped less steadily Roland a whit.

III

'Twas moonset at starting; but while we drew
    near
Lokeren, the cocks crew and twilight dawned
    clear;
At Boom, a great yellow star came out to see;   15
At Duffeld, 'twas morning as plain as could be;
And from Mecheln church-steeple we heard the
    half-chime,
So Joris broke silence with, "Yet there is time!"

IV

At Aershot, up leaped of a sudden the sun,
And against him the cattle stood black every one,   20
To stare through the mist at us galloping past,
And I saw my stout galloper Roland at last,
With resolute shoulders, each butting away
The haze, as some bluff river headland its spray:

V

And his low head and crest, just one sharp ear   25
    bent back
For my voice, and the other pricked out on his
    track;
And one eye's black intelligence,—ever that
    glance
O'er its white edge at me, his own master,
    askance!
And the thick heavy spume-flakes which aye and
    anon
His fierce lips shook upwards in galloping on.   30

VI

By Hasselt, Dirck groaned; and cried Joris, "Stay
    spur!
Your Roos galloped bravely, the fault's not in
    her,
We'll remember at Aix"—for one heard the quick
    wheeze
Of her chest, saw the stretched neck and stagger-
    ing knees,
And sunk tail, and horrible heave of the flank,   35
As down on her haunches she shuddered and
    sank.

VII

So, we were left galloping, Joris and I,
Past Looz and past Tongres, no cloud in the sky;
The broad sun above laughed a pitiless laugh,
'Neath our feet broke the brittle bright stubble   40
    like chaff;
Till over by Dalhem a dome-spire sprang white,
And "Gallop," gasped Joris, "for Aix is in sight!"

VIII

"How they'll greet us!"—and all in a moment his
    roan
Rolled neck and croup over, lay dead as a stone;
And there was my Roland to bear the whole   45
    weight
Of the news which alone could save Aix from her
    fate,
With his nostrils like pits full of blood to the
    brim,
And with circles of red for his eye-sockets' rim.

IX

Then I cast loose my buffcoat, each holster let
    fall,

---

1 From Ghent in Belgium to Aix-la-Chapelle in West
Prussia, a hundred miles away. The towns mentioned lie
on the road between the two. Browning said that the
incident was imaginary.
2 The gate of the walled city of Ghent.
3 Pommel of the saddle.

Shook off both my jack-boots, let go belt and all,   50
Stood up in the stirrup, leaned, patted his ear,
Called my Roland his pet-name, my horse with-
    out peer;
Clapped my hands, laughed and sang, any noise,
    bad or good,
Till at length into Aix Roland galloped and
    stood.

X

And all I remember is—friends flocking round   55
As I sat with his head 'twixt my knees on the
    ground;
And no voice but was praising this Roland of
    mine,
As I poured down his throat our last measure of
    wine,
Which (the burgesses voted by common consent)
Was no more than his due who brought good   60
    news from Ghent.

Home-Thoughts, from Abroad

I

Oh, to be in England
Now that April's there,
And whoever wakes in England
Sees, some morning, unaware,
That the lowest boughs and the brushwood sheaf   5
Round the elm-tree bole are in tiny leaf,
While the chaffinch sings on the orchard bough
In England—now!

II

And after April, when May follows,
And the whitethroat builds, and all the swallows!   10
Hark, where my blossomed pear-tree in the hedge
Leans to the field and scatters on the clover
Blossoms and dewdrops—at the bent spray's
    edge—
That's the wise thrush; he sings each song twice
    over,
Lest you should think he never could recapture   15
The first fine careless rapture!
And though the fields look rough with hoary dew,
All will be gay when noontide wakes anew
The buttercups, the little children's dower
—Far brighter than this gaudy melon-flower!   20

Home-Thoughts, from the Sea

Nobly, nobly Cape Saint Vincent[1] to the North-
    west died away;
Sunset ran, one glorious blood-red, reeking into
    Cadiz Bay;
Bluish 'mid the burning water, full in face
    Trafalgar[2] lay;
In the dimmest North-east distance dawned
    Gibraltar grand and gray;
"Here and here did England help me; how can I   5
    help England?"—say,
Whoso turns as I, this evening, turn to God to
    praise and pray,
While Jove's planet rises yonder, silent over
    Africa.

The Bishop Orders His Tomb at Saint Praxed's Church[1]

Rome, 15—

Vanity, saith the preacher, vanity![2]
Draw round my bed: is Anselm keeping back?
Nephews[3]—sons mine . . . ah God, I know not![4]
    Well—
She, men would have to be your mother once,
Old Gandolf[5] envied me, so fair she was!   5
What's done is done, and she is dead beside,

---

1 At the southwestern tip of Portugal, where Nelson defeated the Spanish fleet in 1797.
2 The cape, east of Cadiz Bay on the southern coast of
Spain, where Nelson won his famous victory (1805) over
the French and Spanish.

1 Ruskin said he knew "of no other piece of modern
English, prose or poetry, in which there is so much told,
as in these lines, of the Renaissance spirit,—its worldliness, inconsistency, pride, hypocrisy, ignorance of itself,
love of art, of luxury, and of good Latin." This may be
true, but the poem is not about a period but a man, a
human being first, and second, a bishop who lived in the
Renaissance.
2 Cf. Ecclesiastes 1:2. Does the Bishop speak this line per-
functorily? Or genuinely, as a comment on human life and
his own in particular? Cf. similar remarks throughout
the poem.
3 A euphemism for illegitimate sons.
4 The repetition of this phrase at line 39 shows that it
does not here express doubt as to whether or not the
sons are his. It seems to mean, I know not whether I am
damned or saved; or (cf. line 10), I know not how or
what life is; or (cf. lines 13 and 113), "Do I live, am I
dead?" Probably all these alternatives are vaguely present
in his mind at once.   5 His predecessor.

Dead long ago, and I am Bishop since,
And as she died so must we die ourselves,
And thence ye may perceive the world's a dream.
Life, how and what is it? As here I lie 10
In this state-chamber, dying by degrees,
Hours and long hours in the dead night, I ask
"Do I live, am I dead?" Peace, peace seems all.
Saint Praxed's ever was the church for peace;
And so, about this tomb of mine. I fought 15
With tooth and nail to save my niche, ye know:
—Old Gandolf cozened me, despite my care;
Shrewd was that snatch from out the corner South
He graced his carrion with, God curse the same!
Yet still my niche is not so cramped but thence 20
One sees the pulpit o' the epistle-side,[6]
And somewhat of the choir, those silent seats,
And up into the aery dome where live
The angels, and a sunbeam 's sure to lurk:
And I shall fill my slab of basalt there, 25
And 'neath my tabernacle[7] take my rest,
With those nine columns round me, two and two,
The odd one at my feet where Anselm stands:
Peach-blossom marble all, the rare, the ripe
As fresh-poured red wine of a mighty pulse. 30
—Old Gandolf with his paltry onion-stone,[8]
Put me where I may look at him! True peach,
Rosy and flawless: how I earned the prize!
Draw close: that conflagration of my church
—What then? So much was saved if aught were missed![9] 35
My sons, ye would not be my death? Go dig
The white-grape vineyard where the oil-press stood,
Drop water gently till the surface sink,
And if ye find . . . Ah, God I know not, I! . . .
Bedded in store of rotten figleaves soft, 40
And corded up in a tight olive-frail,[10]
Some lump, ah God, of *lapis lazuli*,
Big as a Jew's head cut off at the nape,
Blue as a vein o'er the Madonna's breast . . .
Sons, all have I bequeathed you, villas, all, 45
That brave Frascati villa with its bath,

So, let the blue lump poise between my knees,
Like God the Father's globe on both his hands
Ye worship in the Jesu Church[11] so gay,
For Gandolf shall not choose but see and burst! 50
Swift as a weaver's shuttle fleet our years:[12]
Man goeth to the grave, and where is he?
Did I say basalt for my slab, sons? Black—
'T was ever antique-black[13] I meant! How else
Shall ye contrast my frieze to come beneath? 55
The bas-relief in bronze ye promised me,
Those Pans and Nymphs ye wot of, and perchance
Some tripod, thyrsus,[14] with a vase or so,
The Saviour at his sermon on the mount,
Saint Praxed in a glory,[15] and one Pan 60
Ready to twitch the Nymph's last garment off,
And Moses with the tables . . . but I know
Ye mark me not! What do they whisper thee,
Child of my bowels, Anselm? Ah, ye hope
To revel down my villas while I gasp 65
Bricked o'er with beggar's mouldy travertine[16]
Which Gandolf from his tomb-top[17] chuckles at!
Nay, boys, ye love me—all of jasper, then!
'T is jasper ye stand pledged to, lest I grieve.
My bath must needs be left behind, alas! 70
One block, pure green as a pistachio-nut,
There's plenty jasper somewhere in the world—
And have I not Saint Praxed's ear to pray
Horses for ye, and brown Greek manuscripts,
And mistresses with great smooth marbly limbs? 75
—That's if ye carve my epitaph aright,
Choice Latin, picked phrase, Tully's every word,
No gaudy ware like Gandolf's second line—
Tully, my masters? Ulpian serves his need![18]
And then how I shall lie through centuries, 80
And hear the blessed mutter of the mass,
And see God made and eaten all day long,[19]
And feel the steady candle-flame, and taste
Good strong thick stupefying incense-smoke!

---

6 The right-hand side as one faces the altar.
7 The canopy.
8 Inferior grade of marble that peels off in layers.
9 If the lapis lazuli had been missed after the fire, he would have said he saved it. But fortunately it was not, and he buried it for later—and personal—use. This is a nice observation of where a conscience may draw the line.
10 Olive basket.
11 Church of Il Jesu in Rome.
12 Cf. Job 7:6: "My days are swifter than a weaver's shuttle. . . ."
13 A black marble, more beautiful than basalt.
14 Designs for the frieze: a stool like that on which the priestess of Apollo sat when she spoke oracular prophecies at Delphi, or the staff carried by the followers of Bacchus, the god of wine.
15 With a halo.   16 Cheap limestone.
17 The effigy of Gandolf sculptured on top of his tomb.
18 The decadent Latin of Domitius Ulpianus, a Roman jurist of the third century, far inferior to that of Cicero.
19 A reference to the doctrine of transubstantiation.

For as I lie here, hours of the dead night, 85
Dying in state and by such slow degrees,
I fold my arms as if they clasped a crook,
And stretch my feet forth straight as stone can
    point,
And let the bedclothes, for a mortcloth,[20] drop
Into great laps and folds of sculptor's-work: 90
And as yon tapers dwindle, and strange thoughts
Grow, with a certain humming in my ears,
About the life before I lived this life,
And this life too, popes, cardinals and priests,
Saint Praxed at his sermon on the mount,[21] 95
Your tall pale mother with her talking eyes,
And new-found agate urns as fresh as day,
And marble's language, Latin pure, discreet,
—Aha, ELUCESCEBAT[22] quoth our friend?
No Tully, said I, Ulpian at the best! 100
Evil and brief hath been my pilgrimage.
All *lapis*, all, sons! Else I give the Pope
My villas! Will ye ever eat my heart?
Ever your eyes were as a lizard's quick,
They glitter like your mother's for my soul, 105
Or ye would heighten my impoverished frieze,
Piece out its starved design, and fill my vase
With grapes, and add a vizor and a Term,[23]
And to the tripod ye would tie a lynx
That in his struggle throws the thyrsus down, 110
To comfort me on my entablature
Whereon I am to lie till I must ask
"Do I live, am I dead?" There, leave me, there!
For ye have stabbed me with ingratitude
To death—ye wish it—God, ye wish it! Stone— 115
Gritstone,[24] a-crumble! Clammy squares which
    sweat
As if the corpse they keep were oozing through—
And no more *lapis* to delight the world!
Well, go! I bless ye. Fewer tapers there,
But in a row: and, going, turn your backs 120
—Ay, like departing altar-ministrants,
And leave me in my church, the church for peace,
That I may watch at leisure if he leers—
Old Gandolf—at me, from his onion-stone,
As still he envied me, so fair she was! 125

---

[20] Funeral pall.
[21] The confusion of St. Praxed (a woman) with Christ shows that his mind is wandering. Cf. their juxtaposition in lines 59–60.
[22] "He was famous," a word in the inscription on Gandolf's tomb. This at best is Ulpian Latin. The pure, Ciceronian form would have been *elucebat*.
[23] A mask and a bust on a pedestal.
[24] Coarse sandstone.

The Laboratory

Ancien Régime[1]

I

Now that I, tying thy glass mask[2] tightly,
May gaze through these faint smokes curling
    whitely,
As thou pliest thy trade in this devil's-smithy—
Which is the poison to poison her, prithee?

II

He is with her, and they know that I know 5
Where they are, what they do: they believe my
    tears flow
While they laugh, laugh at me, at me fled to the
    drear
Empty church, to pray God in, for them!—I am
    here.

III

Grind away, moisten and mash up thy paste,
Pound at thy powder,—I am not in haste! 10
Better sit thus, and observe thy strange things,
Than go where men wait me and dance at the
    King's.

IV

That in the mortar—you call it a gum?
Ah, the brave tree whence such gold oozings
    come!
And yonder soft phial, the exquisite blue, 15
Sure to taste sweetly,—is that poison too?

V

Had I but all of them, thee and thy treasures,
What a wild crowd of invisible pleasures!
To carry pure death in an ear-ring, a casket,
A signet, a fan-mount, a filigree basket! 20

VI

Soon, at the King's, a mere lozenge to give,
And Pauline should have just thirty minutes to
    live!

---

[1] The "Old Order" of aristocratic life in France before the Revolution. Lines 19–20 suggest that the time is the Renaissance.
[2] A mask worn to protect the face against radiant heat, originally in glassworks.

But to light a pastile,[3] and Elise, with her head
And her breast and her arms and her hands,
    should drop dead![4]

VII

Quick—is it finished? The colour's too grim!   25
Why not soft like the phial's, enticing and dim?
Let it brighten her drink, let her turn it and stir,
And try it and taste, ere she fix and prefer![5]

VIII

What a drop! She's not little, no minion[6] like me!
That's why she ensnared him: this never will free   30
The soul from those masculine eyes,—say "no!"
To that pulse's magnificent come-and-go.

IX

For only last night, as they whispered, I brought
My own eyes to bear on her so, that I thought
Could I keep them one half minute fixed, she   35
    would fall
Shrivelled; she fell not; yet this does it all!

X

Not that I bid you spare her the pain;
Let death be felt and the proof remain:
Brand, burn up, bite into its grace—
He is sure to remember her dying face!   40

XI

Is it done? Take my mask off! Nay, be not morose;
It kills her, and this prevents seeing it close:
The delicate droplet, my whole fortune's fee!
If it hurts her, beside, can it ever hurt me?

XII

Now, take all my jewels, gorge gold to your fill,   45
You may kiss me, old man, on my mouth if you
    will!
But brush this dust off me, lest horror it brings
Ere I know it—next moment I dance at the
    King's!

---

[3] A cone of paste burned as a perfume, in this case poisonous perfume.
[4] Pauline and Elise are two other women she would be happy to see poisoned.
[5] Ere she decides exactly how she prefers it.
[6] A small, delicate person.

Meeting at Night

I

The gray sea and the long black land;
And the yellow half-moon large and low;
And the startled little waves that leap
In fiery ringlets from their sleep,
As I gain the cove with pushing prow,   5
And quench its speed i' the slushy sand.

II

Then a mile of warm sea-scented beach;
Three fields to cross till a farm appears;
A tap at the pane, the quick sharp scratch
And blue spurt of a lighted match,   10
And a voice less loud, through its joys and fears,
Than the two hearts beating each to each!

Parting at Morning

Round the cape of a sudden came the sea,
And the sun looked over the mountain's rim:
And straight was a path of gold for him,[1]
And the need of a world of men for me.[2]

Love Among the Ruins

I

Where the quiet-colored end of evening smiles
    Miles and miles
On the solitary pastures where our sheep
    Half-asleep
Tinkle homeward through the twilight, stray or   5
    stop
    As they crop—
Was the site once of a city great and gay,
    (So they say)
Of our country's very capital, its prince
    Ages since   10
Held his court in, gathered councils, wielding far
    Peace or war.

---

[1] For the sun.
[2] Browning said of the two poems taken together, "It is *his* confession of how fleeting is the belief (implied in the first part) that such raptures are self-sufficient and enduring—as for a time they appear."

II

Now,—the country does not even boast a tree,
    As you see,
To distinguish slopes of verdure, certain rills   15
    From the hills
Intersect and give a name to, (else they run
    Into one)
Where the domed and daring palace shot its
    spires
    Up like fires   20
O'er the hundred-gated circuit of a wall
    Bounding all,
Made of marble, men might march on nor be
    pressed,
    Twelve abreast.

III

And such plenty and perfection, see, of grass   25
    Never was!
Such a carpet as, this summer-time, o'er-spreads
    And embeds
Every vestige of the city, guessed alone,
    Stock or stone—   30
Where a multitude of men breathed joy and woe
    Long ago;
Lust of glory pricked their hearts up, dread of
    shame
    Struck them tame;
And that glory and that shame alike, the gold   35
    Bought and sold.

IV

Now,—the single little turret that remains
    On the plains,
By the caper[1] overrooted, by the gourd
    Overscored,   40
While the patching houseleek's[2] head of blossom
    winks
    Through the chinks—
Marks the basement whence a tower in ancient
    time
    Sprang sublime,
And a burning ring, all round, the chariots traced   45
    As they raced,
And the monarch and his minions and his dames
    Viewed the games.

V

And I know, while thus the quiet-colored eve
    Smiles to leave   50
To their folding, all our many-tinkling fleece
    In such peace,
And the slopes and rills in undistinguished gray
    Melt away—
That a girl with eager eyes and yellow hair   55
    Waits me there
In the turret whence the charioteers caught soul
    For the goal,
When the king looked, where she looks now,
    breathless, dumb
    Till I come.   60

VI

But he looked upon the city, every side,
    Far and wide,
All the mountains topped with temples, all the
    glades'
    Colonnades,
All the causeys,[3] bridges, aqueducts,—and then,   65
    All the men!
When I do come, she will speak not, she will
    stand,
    Either hand
On my shoulder, give her eyes the first embrace
    Of my face,   70
Ere we rush, ere we extinguish sight and speech
    Each on each.

VII

In one year they sent a million fighters forth
    South and North,
And they built their gods a brazen pillar high   75
    As the sky,
Yet reserved a thousand chariots in full force—
    Gold, of course.
Oh heart! oh blood that freezes, blood that burns!
    Earth's returns   80
For whole centuries of folly, noise and sin!
    Shut them in,
With their triumphs and their glories and the
    rest!
    Love is best.

---

[1] A brambly bush.
[2] Small plant with clustered petals.

[3] Causeways, i.e., raised roads across low ground.

"Childe Roland to the Dark Tower Came"

(See Edgar's song in "Lear")

The title is derived from Edgar's mad song in *King Lear*, III, iv, 171–73:

> Child Rowland to the dark tower came,
> His word was still—Fie, foh, and fum,
> I smell the blood of a British man.

Browning's contemporaries felt that his poems must contain some ethical statement, and tried to interpret "Childe Roland" as a moral allegory. However, Browning himself refuted this approach by saying: ". . . I was conscious of no allegorical intention in writing it. . . . Childe Roland came upon me as a kind of dream. I had to write it, then and there, and I finished it the same day, I believe. But it was simply that I had to do it. I did not know then what I meant beyond that, and I'm sure I don't know now. But I am very fond of it." (Lillian Whiting, *The Brownings,* Boston, 1917, p. 261)

If, instead of searching for allegory, one allows the sensuous suggestions of the poem to work on him, he will find that diction, imagery, and situation fuse to create a complex symbol. The situation is immediately suggested by the title. A "childe" is a young knight who has not yet proved himself. "Roland" reminds one of the *Chanson de Roland* and the knights of Charlemagne. And the chivalric romances, which often center on an heroic quest, are full of towers where people are imprisoned and from which they are sometimes rescued. But here the tower is a dark tower and later turns out to be a "round squat turret, blind as the fool's heart." This strikes the ironic and unromantic note which gives the poem its unexpected tone. The hero is endowed with traditional courage and determination, but strangely enough—to the Victorians if not to us— has lost all dedication to a great goal, and now longs only to be done with his quest. The journey that tests his character is not a series of actions, defeating dragons, magicians, and evil knights, but a series of objects or images which are sinister, horrible, and frightening. And when he reaches his goal he sacrifices his life in heroic style—for what?

I

My first thought was, he lied in every word,
  That hoary cripple, with malicious eye
  Askance to watch the working of his lie
On mine, and mouth scarce able to afford
Suppression of the glee, that pursed and scored   5
  Its edge, at one more victim gained thereby.

II

What else should he be set for, with his staff?
  What, save to waylay with his lies, ensnare
  All travellers who might find him posted there,
And ask the road? I guessed what skull-like laugh   10
Would break, what crutch 'gin write my epitaph
  For pastime in the dusty thoroughfare,

III

If at his counsel I should turn aside
  Into that ominous tract which, all agree,
  Hides the Dark Tower. Yet acquiescingly   15
I did turn as he pointed: neither pride
Nor hope rekindling at the end descried,
  So much as gladness that some end might be.[1]

IV

For, what with my whole world-wide wandering,
  What with my search drawn out through   20
    years, my hope
  Dwindled into a ghost not fit to cope
With that obstreperous joy success would bring,—
I hardly tried now to rebuke the spring
  My heart made, finding failure in its scope.[2]

V

As when a sick man very near to death   25
  Seems dead indeed, and feels begin and end
  The tears and takes the farewell of each friend,
And hears one bid the other go, draw breath
Freelier outside, ("since all is o'er," he saith,
  "And the blow fallen no grieving can amend;")   30

VI

While some discuss if near the other graves
  Be room enough for this, and when a day
  Suits best for carrying the corpse away,
With care about the banners, scarves and staves:
And still the man hears all, and only craves   35
  He may not shame such tender love and stay.

---

[1] The hoary cripple misdirects travelers from the highroad to the ominous tract which hides the Dark Tower, knowing that there they will meet certain death. Childe Roland at once sees through his lies and recognizes the road to his goal. But the mood with which he approaches the end of his quest is one of gladness only because the long effort will be finished.

[2] These lines are clarified by stanza vii.

VII

Thus, I had so long suffered in this quest,
  Heard failure prophesied so oft, been writ
  So many times among "The Band"—to wit,
The knights who to the Dark Tower's search   40
  addressed
Their steps—that just to fail as they, seemed best,
  And all the doubt was now—should I be fit?

VIII

So, quiet as despair, I turned from him,
  That hateful cripple, out of his highway
  Into the path he pointed. All the day   45
Had been a dreary one at best, and dim
Was settling to its close, yet shot one grim
  Red leer to see the plain catch its estray.[3]

IX

For mark! no sooner was I fairly found
  Pledged to the plain, after a pace or two,   50
  Than, pausing to throw backward a last view
O'er the safe road, 'twas gone; gray plain all
  round:
Nothing but plain to the horizon's bound.
  I might go on; naught else remained to do.

X

So, on I went. I think I never saw   55
  Such starved ignoble nature; nothing throve:
  For flowers—as well expect a cedar grove!
But cockle, spurge, according to their law
Might propagate their kind, with none to awe,[4]
  You'd think; a burr had been a treasure-trove.   60

XI

No! penury, inertness and grimace,
  In some strange sort, were the land's portion. "See
  Or shut your eyes," said Nature peevishly,
"It nothing skills: I cannot help my case:
'Tis the Last Judgment's fire must cure this place,   65
  Calcine[5] its clods and set my prisoners free."

---

[3] Someone who has strayed from the highroad.
[4] That is, with no flowers or no gardener to overawe and
restrain their growth.
[5] Pulverize by heat.

XII

If there pushed any ragged thistle-stalk
  Above its mates, the head was chopped; the
    bents[6]
  Were jealous else. What made those holes and
    rents
In the dock's harsh swarth leaves, bruised as to   70
  balk
All hope of greenness? 'tis a brute must walk
  Pashing their life out, with a brute's intents.

XIII

As for the grass, it grew as scant as hair
  In leprosy; thin dry blades pricked the mud
  Which underneath looked kneaded up with   75
    blood.
One stiff blind horse, his every bone a-stare,
Stood stupefied, however he came there:
  Thrust out past service from the devil's stud!

XIV

Alive? he might be dead for aught I know,
  With that red gaunt and colloped[7] neck   80
    a-strain,
  And shut eyes underneath the rusty mane;
Seldom went such grotesqueness with such woe;
I never saw a brute I hated so;
  He must be wicked to deserve such pain.

XV

I shut my eyes and turned them on my heart.   85
  As a man calls for wine before he fights,
  I asked one draught of earlier, happier sights,
Ere fitly I could hope to play my part.
Think first, fight afterwards—the soldier's art:
  One taste of the old time sets all to rights.   90

XVI

Not it! I fancied Cuthbert's reddening face
  Beneath its garniture of curly gold,
  Dear fellow, till I almost felt him fold
An arm in mine to fix me to the place,
That way he used. Alas, one night's disgrace!   95
  Out went my heart's new fire and left it cold.

---

[6] Coarse grasses.
[7] Ridged in folds.

XVII

Giles then, the soul of honour—there he stands
   Frank as ten years ago when knighted first.
   What honest man should dare (he said) he
     durst.
Good—but the scene shifts—faugh! what hang- 100
   man hands
Pin to his breast a parchment? His own bands
   Read it. Poor traitor, spit upon and curst!

XVIII

Better this present than a past like that;
   Back therefore to my darkening path again!
   No sound, no sight as far as eye could strain. 105
Will the night send a howlet or a bat?
I asked: when something on the dismal flat
   Came to arrest my thoughts and change their
     train.

XIX

A sudden little river crossed my path
   As unexpected as a serpent comes. 110
   No sluggish tide congenial to the glooms;
This, as it frothed by, might have been a bath
For the fiend's glowing hoof—to see the wrath
   Of its black eddy bespate[8] with flakes and
     spumes.

XX

So petty yet so spiteful! All along, 115
   Low scrubby alders kneeled down over it;
   Drenched willows flung them headlong in a fit
Of mute despair, a suicidal throng:
The river which had done them all the wrong,
   Whate'er that was, rolled by, deterred no whit. 120

XXI

Which, while I forded,—good saints, how I feared
   To set my foot upon a dead man's cheek,
   Each step, or feel the spear I thrust to seek
For hollows, tangled in his hair or beard!
—It may have been a water-rat I speared, 125
   But, ugh! it sounded like a baby's shriek.

XXII

Glad was I when I reached the other bank.
   Now for a better country. Vain presage!

---

8 Spattered.

Who were the strugglers, what war did they
    wage,
Whose savage trample thus could pad the dank 130
Soil to a plash?[9] Toads in a poisoned tank,
   Or wild cats in a red-hot iron cage—

XXIII

The fight must so have seemed in that fell cirque.
   What penned them there, with all the plain
    to choose?
   No foot-print leading to that horrid mews,[10] 135
None out of it. Mad brewage set to work
Their brains, no doubt, like galley-slaves the
   Turk
   Pits for his pastime, Christians against Jews.

XXIV

And more than that—a furlong on—why, there!
   What bad use was that engine for, that wheel, 140
   Or brake, not wheel—that harrow fit to reel
Men's bodies out like silk? with all the air
Of Tophet's tool, on earth left unaware,
   Or brought to sharpen its rusty teeth of steel.[11]

XXV

Then came a bit of stubbed ground, once a wood, 145
   Next a marsh, it would seem, and now mere
    earth
   Desperate and done with; (so a fool finds
    mirth,
Makes a thing and then mars it, till his mood
Changes and off he goes!) within a rood—
   Bog, clay and rubble, sand and stark black 150
    dearth.

XXVI

Now blotches rankling, colored gay and grim,
   Now patches where some leanness of the soil's
   Broke into moss or substances like boils;
Then came some palsied oak, a cleft in him
Like a distorted mouth that splits its rim 155
   Gaping at death, and dies while it recoils.

---

9 A puddle.
10 Pen or coop.
11 The "engine" probably meant an instrument of torture.
A "brake" is a harrow, a large tool set with metal teeth
or disks that is dragged over plowed land to break the
clods. "Tophet" is hell.

XXVII

And just as far as ever from the end!
    Naught in the distance but the evening, naught
    To point my footstep further! At the thought,
A great black bird, Apollyon's bosom-friend,[12]   160
Sailed past, nor beat his wide wing dragon-penned[13]
    That brushed my cap—perchance the guide I sought.

XXVIII

For, looking up, aware I somehow grew,
    'Spite of the dusk, the plain had given place
    All round to mountains—with such name to 165
grace
Mere ugly heights and heaps now stolen in view.
How thus they had surprised me,—solve it, you!
    How to get from them was no clearer case.

XXIX

Yet half I seemed to recognize some trick
    Of mischief happened to me, God knows 170
when—
    In a bad dream perhaps. Here ended, then,
Progress this way. When, in the very nick
Of giving up, one time more, came a click
    As when a trap shuts—you're inside the den!

XXX

Burningly it came on me all at once,   175
    This was the place! those two hills on the right,
    Crouched like two bulls locked horn in horn in fight;
While to the left, a tall scalped mountain . . . Dunce,
Dotard, a-dozing at the very nonce,
    After a life spent training for the sight!   180

XXXI

What in the midst lay but the Tower itself?
    The round squat turret, blind[14] as the fool's heart,
    Built of brown stone, without a counterpart

In the whole world. The tempest's mocking elf
Points to the shipman thus the unseen shelf   185
He strikes on, only when the timbers start.

XXXII

Not see? because of night perhaps?—why, day
    Came back again for that! before it left,
    The dying sunset kindled through a cleft:
The hills, like giants at a hunting, lay,   190
Chin upon hand, to see the game at bay,—
    "Now stab and end the creature—to the heft!"[15]

XXXIII

Not hear? when noise was everywhere! it tolled
    Increasing like a bell. Names in my ears
    Of all the lost adventurers my peers,—   195
How such a one was strong, and such was bold,
And such was fortunate, yet each of old
    Lost, lost![16] one moment knelled the woe of years.

XXXIV

There they stood, ranged along the hill-sides, met
    To view the last of me, a living frame   200
    For one more picture! in a sheet of flame
I saw them and I knew them all. And yet
Dauntless the slug-horn[17] to my lips I set,
    And blew. *Childe Roland to the Dark Tower came.*"[18]

Fra Lippo Lippi[1]

I am poor brother Lippo, by your leave!
You need not clap your torches to my face.

---

12 The devil's friend: see Revelation 9:11.
13 Pinioned.
14 Windowless.

15 Heft is a variant spelling of *haft*, the handle of a cutting tool or weapon. The meaning here is to stab deeply, up to the handle of Roland's sword.
16 Members of "The Band" (see stanza vii), heroes who have found the Dark Tower and lost their lives.
17 Trumpet.
18 His triumph is simply that he "came" to the Dark Tower and dauntlessly blew his horn. A moment later the "creature" (line 192) killed him (so that the story-teller is a ghost, like each of his comrades. Think of the modern unheroic, existential hero who has no faith in any action or any cause, but finds the value of life simply in the courage to be.

1 Filippo Lippi, a Carmelite friar and painter, who lived at Florence in the fifteenth century.

Zooks,[2] what's to blame? you think you see a
    monk!
What, 'tis past midnight, and you go the rounds,
And here you catch me at an alley's end   5
Where sportive ladies leave their doors ajar?
The Carmine's my cloister: hunt it up,
Do,—harry out, if you must show your zeal,
Whatever rat, there, haps on his wrong hole,
And nip each softling of a wee white mouse,   10
Weke, weke, that's crept to keep him company!
Aha, you know your betters! Then, you'll take
Your hand away that's fiddling on my throat,
And please to know me likewise. Who am I?
Why, one, sir, who is lodging with a friend   15
Three streets off—he's a certain . . . how d'ye call?
Master—a . . . Cosimo of the Medici,[3]
I' the house that caps the corner. Boh! you were
    best![4]
Remember and tell me, the day you're hanged,
How you affected such a gullet's-gripe!   20
But you, sir, it concerns you that your knaves
Pick up a manner nor discredit you:
Zooks, are we pilchards,[5] that they sweep the
    streets
And count fair prize what comes into their net?
He's Judas to a tittle, that man is![6]   25
Just such a face! Why, sir, you make amends.
Lord, I'm not angry! Bid your hangdogs go
Drink out this quarter-florin to the health
Of the munificent House that harbors me
(And many more beside, lads! more beside!)   30
And all's come square again. I'd like his face—
His, elbowing on his comrade in the door
With the pike and lantern,—for the slave[7] that
    holds
John Baptist's head a-dangle by the hair
With one hand ("Look you, now," as who should   35
    say)
And his weapon in the other, yet unwiped!
It's not your chance to have a bit of chalk,
A wood-coal or the like? or you should see!

Yes, I'm the painter, since you style me so.
What, brother Lippo's doings, up and down,   40
You know them and they take you? like enough!
I saw the proper twinkle in your eye—
'Tell you, I liked your looks at very first.
Let's sit and set things straight now, hip to
    haunch.
Here's spring come, and the nights one makes up   45
    bands
To roam the town and sing out carnival,
And I've been three weeks shut within my mew,[8]
A-painting for the great man, saints and saints
And saints again. I could not paint all night—
Ouf! I leaned out of window for fresh air.   50
There came a hurry of feet and little feet,
A sweep of lute-strings, laughs, and whiffs of
    song,—
Flower o' the broom,
Take away love, and our earth is a tomb!
Flower o' the quince,   55
I let Lisa go, and what good in life since?
Flower o' the thyme—and so on. Round they
    went.
Scarce had they turned the corner when a titter
Like the skipping of rabbits by moonlight,—
    three slim shapes,
And a face that looked up . . . zooks, sir, flesh and   60
    blood,
That's all I'm made of! Into shreds it went,
Curtain and counterpane and coverlet,
All the bed-furniture—a dozen knots,
There was a ladder! Down I let myself,
Hands and feet, scrambling somehow, and so   65
    dropped,
And after them. I came up with the fun
Hard by Saint Laurence,[9] hail fellow, well met,—
Flower o' the rose,
If I've been merry, what matter who knows?
And so as I was stealing back again   70
To get to bed and have a bit of sleep
Ere I rise up to-morrow and go work
On Jerome knocking at his poor old breast
With his great round stone to subdue the flesh,[10]
You snap me of the sudden. Ah, I see!   75
Though your eye twinkles still, you shake your
    head—

---

2 Gadzooks (an oath).
3 Banker and patron of the arts (1389–1464), the real ruler
of Florence.
4 "You do well to take your hand off my throat," which
the guard does instantly on hearing the name of Cosimo.
The "you" in line 21 is the captain of the group.
5 A kind of cheap fish.
6 One of the guard whom Lippo, with the sharp eye of a
painter, has just noticed.
7 That is, as a model for the slave in the picture he goes
on to describe. On John the Baptist's death see Mark
6:17-28.

8 Coop or pen.
9 The church of San Lorenzo.
10 Picture of St. Jerome (340–420) on which Lippo is
working. According to Vasari, he painted it for Cosimo di
Medici.

Mine's shaved—a monk, you say—the sting's in
    that!
If Master Cosimo announced himself,
Mum's the word naturally; but a monk!
Come, what am I a beast for? tell us, now!   80
I was a baby when my mother died
And father died and left me in the street.
I starved there, God knows how, a year or two
On fig-skins, melon-parings, rinds and shucks,
Refuse and rubbish. One fine frosty day,   85
My stomach being empty as your hat,
The wind doubled me up and down I went.
Old Aunt Lapaccia trussed me[11] with one hand,
(Its fellow was a stinger as I knew)
And so along the wall, over the bridge,   90
By the straight cut to the convent. Six words there,
While I stood munching my first bread that
    month:
"So boy, you're minded," quoth the good fat
    father
Wiping his own mouth, 'twas refection-time,—
"To quit this very miserable world?   95
Will you renounce" . . . "the mouthful of bread?"
    thought I;
By no means! Brief, they made a monk of me;
I did renounce the world, its pride and greed,
Palace, farm, villa, shop, and banking-house,
Trash, such as these poor devils of Medici   100
Have given their hearts to—all at eight years old.
Well, sir, I found in time, you may be sure,
'Twas not for nothing—the good bellyful,
The warm serge and the rope that goes all round,
And day-long blessed idleness beside!   105
"Let's see what the urchin's fit for"—that came
    next.
Not overmuch their way, I must confess.
Such a to-do! They tried me with their books:
Lord, they'd have taught me Latin in pure waste!
Flower o' the clove,   110
All the Latin I construe is, "amo" I love!
But, mind you, when a boy starves in the streets
Eight years together, as my fortune was,
Watching folk's faces to know who will fling
The bit of half-stripped grape-bunch he desires,   115
And who will curse or kick him for his pains,—
Which gentleman processional[12] and fine,
Holding a candle to the Sacrament,
Will wink and let him lift a plate and catch

The droppings of the wax to sell again,   120
Or holla for the Eight[13] and have him whipped,—
How say I?—nay, which dog bites, which lets drop
His bone from the heap of offal in the street,—
Why, soul and sense of him grow sharp alike,
He learns the look of things, and none the less   125
For admonition from the hunger-pinch.
I had a store of such remarks, be sure,
Which, after I found leisure, turned to use.
I drew men's faces on my copy-books,
Scrawled them within the antiphonary's[14] marge,   130
Joined legs and arms to the long music-notes,
Found eyes and nose and chin for A's and B's,
And made a string of pictures of the world
Betwixt the ins and outs of verb and noun,
On the wall, the bench, the door. The monks   135
    looked black.
"Nay," quoth the Prior, "turn him out, d'ye say?
In no wise. Lose a crow and catch a lark.
What if at last we get our man of parts,
We Carmelites, like those Camaldolese
And Preaching Friars,[15] to do our church up fine   140
And put the front on it that ought to be!"
And hereupon he bade me daub away.
Thank you! my head being crammed, the walls
    a blank,
Never was such prompt disemburdening.
First, every sort of monk, the black and white,   145
I drew them, fat and lean: then, folk at church,
From good old gossips waiting to confess
Their cribs[16] of barrel-droppings, candle-ends,—
To the breathless fellow at the altar-foot,
Fresh from his murder, safe[17] and sitting there   150
With the little children round him in a row
Of admiration, half for his beard and half
For that white anger of his victim's son
Shaking a fist at him with one fierce arm,
Signing himself with the other because of Christ   155
(Whose sad face on the cross sees only this
After the passion of a thousand years)
Till some poor girl, her apron o'er her head,
(Which the intense eyes looked through) came at
    eve
On tiptoe, said a word, dropped in a loaf,   160
Her pair of earrings and a bunch of flowers
(The brute took growling), prayed, and so was
    gone.

---

11 Held me up firmly.
12 Gentleman walking in a religious procession.

13 The magistrates of Florence.   14 Choir-book's.
15 Two rival religious orders.
16 Thefts.
17 Because he cannot be arrested in the church.

I painted all, then cried " 'Tis ask and have;
Choose, for more's ready!"—laid the ladder flat,
And showed my covered bit of cloister-wall.   165
The monks closed in a circle and praised loud
Till checked, taught what to see and not to see,
Being simple bodies,—"That's the very man!
Look at the boy who stoops to pat the dog!
That woman's like the Prior's niece who comes   170
To care about his asthma: it's the life!"
But there my triumph's straw-fire flared and
    funked;
Their betters took their turn to see and say:
The Prior and the learned pulled a face
And stopped all that in no time. "How? what's   175
    here?
Quite from the mark of painting, bless us all!
Faces, arms, legs, and bodies like the true
As much as pea and pea! it's devil's-game!
Your business is not to catch men with show,
With homage to the perishable clay,   180
But lift them over it, ignore it all,
Make them forget there's such a thing as flesh.
Your business is to paint the souls of men—
Man's soul, and it's a fire, smoke . . . no, it's
    not . . .
It's vapor done up like a new-born babe—   185
(In that shape when you die it leaves your mouth)
It's . . . well, what matters talking, it's the soul!
Give us no more of body than shows soul!
Here's Giotto, with his Saint a-praising God,
That sets us praising,—why not stop with him?[18]   190
Why put all thoughts of praise out of our head
With wonder at lines, colors, and what not?
Paint the soul, never mind the legs and arms!
Rub all out, try at it a second time.
Oh, that white smallish female with the breasts,   195
She's just my niece . . . Herodias, I would say,—
Who went and danced and got men's heads cut
    off![19]
Have it all out!" Now, is this sense, I ask?
A fine way to paint soul, by painting body
So ill, the eye can't stop there, must go further   200
And can't fare worse! Thus, yellow does for white
When what you put for yellow's simply black,

And any sort of meaning looks intense
When all beside itself means and looks naught.
Why can't a painter lift each foot in turn,   205
Left foot and right foot, go a double step,
Make his flesh liker and his soul more like,
Both in their order? Take the prettiest face,
The Prior's niece . . . patron-saint—is it so pretty
You can't discover if it means hope, fear,   210
Sorrow or joy? won't beauty go with these?
Suppose I've made her eyes all right and blue,
Can't I take breath and try to add life's flash,
And then add soul and heighten them three-fold?
Or say there's beauty with no soul at all—   215
(I never saw it—put the case the same—)
If you get simple beauty and naught else,
You get about the best thing God invents:
That's somewhat: and you'll find the soul you
    have missed,
Within yourself, when you return him thanks.   220
"Rub all out!" Well, well, there's my life, in
    short,
And so the thing has gone on ever since.
I'm grown a man no doubt, I've broken bounds:
You should not take a fellow eight years old
And make him swear to never kiss the girls.   225
I'm my own master, paint now as I please—
Having a friend, you see, in the Corner-house!
Lord, it's fast holding by the rings in front[20]—
Those great rings serve more purposes than just
To plant a flag in, or tie up a horse!   230
And yet the old schooling sticks, the old grave
    eyes
Are peeping o'er my shoulder as I work,
The heads shake still—"It's art's decline, my son!
You're not of the true painters, great and old;
Brother Angelico's the man, you'll find: 235
Brother Lorenzo stands his single peer:[21]
Fag on at flesh, you'll never make the third!"
Flower o' the pine,
You keep your mistr . . . manners, and I'll stick
    to mine!
I'm not the third, then: bless us, they must know!   240
Don't you think they're the likeliest to know,
They with their Latin? So, I swallow my rage,
Clench my teeth, suck my lips in tight, and paint

---

18 That is, why not continue to follow the medieval conception of painting exemplified by Giotto (1276–1337)? Lippo and Masaccio (line 276) led the reaction that introduced realism.
19 It was not Herodias but her daughter Salome who at Herodias' instigation asked Herod to reward her dancing by giving her John the Baptist's head on a platter (cf. lines 33–34 and note 7).

20 The iron rings on the front of the palace give Lippo something to hold fast by, which makes them symbols for the protection and patronage of Cosimo.
21 Fra Angelico and Lorenzo Monaco were painters who worked in the medieval tradition against which Lippo was revolting.

To please them—sometimes do and sometimes
    don't;
For, doing most, there's pretty sure to come   245
A turn, some warm eve finds me at my saints—
A laugh, a cry, the business of the world—
(*Flower o' the peach,*
Death for us all, and his own life for each!)
And my whole soul revolves, the cup runs over,   250
The world and life's too big to pass for a dream,
And I do these wild things in sheer despite,
And play the fooleries you catch me at,
In pure rage! The old mill-horse, out at grass
After hard years, throws up his stiff heels so,   255
Although the miller does not preach to him
The only good of grass is to make chaff.
What would men have? Do they like grass or no—
May they or mayn't they? all I want's the thing
Settled for ever one way. As it is,   260
You tell too many lies and hurt yourself:
You don't like what you only like too much,
You do like what, if given you at your word,
You find abundantly detestable.
For me, I think I speak as I was taught;   265
I always see the garden and God there
A-making man's wife: and, my lesson learned,
The value and significance of flesh,
I can't unlearn ten minutes afterwards.

    You understand me: I'm a beast, I know.   270
But see, now—why, I see as certainly
As that the morning-star's about to shine,
What will hap some day. We've a youngster here
Comes to our convent, studies what I do,
Slouches and stares and lets no atom drop: 275
His name is Guidi—he'll not mind the monks—
They call him Hulking Tom, he lets them talk—
He picks my practice up[22]—he'll paint apace,
I hope so—though I never live so long,
I know what's sure to follow. You be judge!   280
You speak no Latin more than I, belike;
However, you're my man, you've seen the world
—The beauty and the wonder and the power,
The shapes of things, their colors, lights and
    shades,
Changes, surprises,—and God made it all!   285
—For what? Do you feel thankful, ay or no,
For this fair town's face, yonder river's line,
The mountain round it and the sky above,

Much more the figures of man, woman, child,
These are the frame to? What's it all about?   290
To be passed over, despised? or dwelt upon,
Wondered at? oh, this last of course!—you say.
But why not do as well as say,—paint these
Just as they are, careless what comes of it?
God's works—paint any one, and count it crime   295
To let a truth slip. Don't object, "His works
Are here already; nature is complete:
Suppose you reproduce her—(which you can't)
There's no advantage! you must beat her, then."
For, don't you mark? we're made so that we love   300
First when we see them painted, things we have
    passed
Perhaps a hundred times nor cared to see;
And so they are better, painted—better to us,
Which is the same thing. Art was given for that;
God uses us to help each other so,   305
Lending our minds out. Have you noticed, now,
Your cullion's[23] hanging face? A bit of chalk,
And trust me but you should, though! How much
    more,
If I drew higher things with the same truth!
That were to take the Prior's pulpit-place,   310
Interpret God to all of you! Oh, oh,
It makes me mad to see what men shall do
And we in our graves! This world's no blot for us,
Nor blank; it means intensely, and means good:
To find its meaning is my meat and drink.   315
"Ay, but you don't so instigate to prayer!"
Strikes in the Prior: "when your meaning's plain
It does not say to folk—remember matins,
Or, mind you fast next Friday!" Why, for this
What need of art at all? A skull and bones,   320
Two bits of stick nailed crosswise, or, what's best,
A bell to chime the hour with, does as well.
I painted a Saint Laurence six months since
At Prato, splashed the fresco in fine style:
"How looks my painting, now the scaffold's   325
    down?"
I ask a brother: "Hugely," he returns—
"Already not one phiz of your three slaves
Who turn the Deacon off his toasted side,
But's scratched and prodded to our heart's con-
    tent,
The pious people have so eased their own   330
With coming to say prayers there in a rage:
We get on fast to see the bricks beneath.[24]

---

22 Tommaso Guidi, more commonly known as Masaccio, was more probably Lippo's master than his pupil, but both shared the same theory.

23 Rascal's.
24 Lippo's mural of St. Lawrence, showing him being turned over on the gridiron so that his other side may be

Expect another job this time next year,
For pity and religion grow i' the crowd—
Your painting serves its purpose!" Hang the 335
   fools![25]
   —That is—you'll not mistake an idle word
Spoke in a huff by a poor monk, God wot,
Tasting the air this spicy night which turns
The unaccustomed head like Chianti wine!
Oh, the church knows! don't misreport me, now! 340
It's natural a poor monk out of bounds
Should have his apt word to excuse himself:
And hearken how I plot to make amends.
I have bethought me: I shall paint a piece
. . . There's for you! Give me six months, then 345
   go, see
Something in Sant' Ambrogio's![26] Bless the nuns!
They want a cast o' my office.[27] I shall paint
God in the midst, Madonna and her babe,
Ringed by a bowery flowery angel-brood,
Lilies and vestments and white faces, sweet 350
As puff on puff of grated orris-root
When ladies crowd to Church at midsummer.
And then i' the front, of course a saint or two—
Saint John, because he saves the Florentines,[28]
Saint Ambrose, who puts down in black and 355
   white
The convent's friends and gives them a long day,
And Job, I must have him there past mistake,
The man of Uz (and Us without the z,
Painters who need his patience). Well, all these
Secured at their devotion, up shall come 360
Out of a corner[29] when you least expect,
As one by a dark stair into a great light,
Music and talking, who but Lippo! I!—
Mazed, motionless, and moonstruck—I'm the
   man!
Back I shrink—what is this I see and hear? 365
I, caught up with my monk's-things by mistake,
My old serge gown and rope that goes all round,
I, in this presence, this pure company!
Where's a hole, where's a corner for escape?

Then steps a sweet angelic slip of a thing 370
Forward, puts out a soft palm—"Not so fast!"
—Addresses the celestial presence, "nay—
He made you and devised you, after all,
Though he's none of you! Could Saint John
   there draw—
His camel-hair make up a painting-brush? 375
We come to brother Lippo for all that,
Iste perfecit opus!"[30] So, all smile—
I shuffle sideways with my blushing face
Under the cover of a hundred wings
Thrown like a spread of kirtles when you're gay 380
And play hot cockles,[31] all the doors being shut,
Till, wholly unexpected, in there pops
The hothead husband! Thus I scuttle off
To some safe bench behind, not letting go
The palm of her, the little lily thing 385
That spoke the good word for me in the nick,
Like the Prior's niece . . . Saint Lucy, I would
   say.[32]
And so all's saved for me, and for the church
A pretty picture gained. Go, six months hence!
Your hand, sir, and good-by: no lights, no lights! 390
The street's hushed, and I know my own way
   back,
Don't fear me! There's the grey beginning.
   Zooks!

A Toccata of Galuppi's[1]

I

O Galuppi, Baldassaro, this is very sad to find!
I can hardly misconceive you; it would prove me
   deaf and blind;
But although I take your meaning, 'tis with such
   a heavy mind!

---

broiled, was so realistic that people have scratched at the three torturers until the paint has almost been worn off, exposing the bricks beneath. Prato is a town near Florence.
25 Since it was hardly Lippo's purpose to promote religion in this way.
26 In the convent in Florence, whose patron saint is St. Ambrose; there Lippo painted "The Coronation of the Virgin," which he goes on to describe.
27 An example of my art.
28 John the Baptist, patron saint of Florence.
29 Of the picture.

---

30 "This man made the work," words which appear in the painting near Lippo, who is in the lower right-hand corner.
31 A game.
32 The "sweet angelic slip of a thing" who steps forward to defend him in the picture is St. Lucy, for whom the Prior's niece has again served as model (cf. lines 170, 195–96, 208–09).

1 Baldassare Galuppi was a Venetian composer of the eighteenth century, "good alike at grave and gay" music (see line 26). In the poem the speaker is playing one of his toccatas, a casual piece, light in tone and free in movement. But the poem is not about Galuppi nor about music, nor even, strictly speaking, about the Venetians whom Galuppi and the toccata call up in the speaker's mind as he listens. It is about the speaker himself.

II

Here you come with your old music, and here's
    all the good it brings.[2]
What, they lived once thus at Venice where the   5
    merchants were the kings,
Where St. Mark's is, where the Doges used to wed
    the sea with rings?[3]

III

Aye, because the sea's the street there; and 'tis
    arched by . . . what you call . . .
Shylock's bridge with houses on it,[4] where they
    kept the carnival:
I was never out of England—it's as if I saw it all.

IV

Did young people take their pleasure when the   10
    sea was warm in May?
Balls and masks begun at midnight, burning ever
    to mid-day,
When they made up fresh adventures for the
    morrow, do you say?

V

Was a lady such a lady, cheeks so round and lips
    so red,—
On her neck the small face buoyant, like a bell-
    flower on its bed,
O'er the breast's superb abundance where a man   15
    might base his head?

VI

Well, and it was graceful of them—they'd break
    talk off and afford—
She, to bite her mask's black velvet—he, to finger
    on his sword,
While you sat and played Toccatas, stately at the
    clavichord?

VII

What? Those lesser thirds so plaintive, sixths
    diminished, sigh on sigh,
Told them something? Those suspensions, those   20
    solutions—"Must we die?"[5]
Those commiserating sevenths—"Life might last!
    we can but try!"[6]

VIII

"Were you happy?"—"Yes."—"And are you still
    as happy?"—"Yes. And you?"
—"Then, more kisses!"—"Did *I* stop them, when
    a million seemed so few?"
Hark, the dominant's persistence till it must be
    answered to!

IX

So, an octave struck the answer.[7] Oh, they praised   25
    you, I dare say!
"Brave Galuppi! that was music! good alike at
    grave and gay!
I can always leave off talking when I hear a
    master play!"

X

Then they left you for their pleasure: till in due
    time, one by one,
Some with lives that came to nothing, some with
    deeds as well undone,
Death stepped tacitly and took them where they   30
    never see the sun.[8]

XI

But when I sit down to reason, think to take my
    stand nor swerve,
While I triumph o'er a secret wrung from nature's
    close reserve,

---

[2] These first four lines must be reread at the end of the poem. They are the speaker's final comment on the second strand of thought which the music suggests, in lines 31–45.
[3] The Doge, who was the chief magistrate of Venice, threw a ring into the Adriatic once a year to symbolize the "marriage" of Venice, a great commercial power, with the sea.
[4] The Rialto, a bridge over the Grand Canal.

[5] The musical terms refer to dissonant effects that suggest the idea of death to the listening dancers.
[6] The "sevenths" give a more pleasing effect, awakening a more hopeful idea.
[7] The dominant is answered in the tonic, an octave above the first presentation of the theme. Although with the "commiserating sevenths" life seemed possible, in a kind of pleasing melancholy, the inevitable solution reinforces the idea of death. (This note is adapted from one by Prof. J. E. Baker.)
[8] Into their graves. Only the virtuous gain the reward of immortality (cf. lines 38–43).

In you come with your cold music till I creep
through every nerve.[9]

XII

Yes, you, like a ghostly cricket, creaking where a
house was burned:
"Dust and ashes, dead and done with, Venice   35
spent what Venice earned.
The soul, doubtless, is immortal—where a soul
can be discerned.

XIII

"Yours for instance: you know physics, something
of geology,
Mathematics are your pastime; souls shall rise in
their degree;
Butterflies may dread extinction—you'll not die,
it cannot be!

XIV

"As for Venice and her people, merely born to   40
bloom and drop,
Here on earth they bore their fruitage, mirth and
folly were the crop:
What of soul was left, I wonder, when the kissing
had to stop?

XV

"Dust and ashes!" So you creak it, and I want
the heart to scold.[10]
Dear dead women, with such hair, too,—what's
become of all the gold
Used to hang and brush their bosoms? I feel   45
chilly and grown old.[11]

---

[9] Suddenly the taunting tone of the music, which has
been reflecting the speaker's moral judgment on the
pleasure-loving Venetians, seems to be turned upon his
own complacent superiority—explicitly on his belief in
immortality, which he thought he had triumphantly
maintained in the face of his scientific investigations. The
irony in lines 36–39 is emphatic.
[10] Not Galuppi, but the Venetians he has been rapping
for their "mirth and folly," but no longer has the heart to
scold now that his capacity to feel different and superior
has been undermined (by recognizing that he too may be
as mortal as they).
[11] This second reversal of attitude follows from the first.
Once his moral-religious complacency is gone, he can see
the charm and beauty of Venetian life—and now, by contrast, no longer feel self-righteous, but "chilly and grown
old." The poem is a remarkable study of a moment of
self-criticism, in which one's egotistic pretensions are
suddenly pricked.

My Star

All that I know
    Of a certain star
Is, it can throw
    (Like the angled spar[1])
Now a dart of red,
    Now a dart of blue;
Till my friends have said
    They would fain see, too,
My star that dartles the red and the blue!
Then it stops like a bird; like a flower, hangs   10
    furled:
    They must solace themselves with the Saturn
    above it.
What matter to me if their star is a world?
    Mine has opened its soul to me; therefore I
    love it.

Respectability

I

Dear, had the world in its caprice
    Deigned to proclaim "I know you both,
    Have recognized your plighted troth,
Am sponsor for you: live in peace!"[1]—
How many precious months and years   5
    Of youth had passed, that speed so fast,
    Before we found it out at last,
The world, and what it fears?[2]

II

How much of priceless life were spent[3]
    With men that every virtue decks,   10
    And women models of their sex,
Society's true ornament,—
Ere we dared wander, nights like this,
    Through wind and rain,[4] and watch the Seine,
    And feel the Boulevard break again   15
To warmth and light and bliss?

---

[1] Iceland spar which acts like a prism, breaking the light
into different colors.

[1] That is, "You may live together as lovers."
[2] Before we discovered that what the world fears and condemns is any violation of its respectable conventions.
[3] How much of priceless freedom to live our own lives
would have been spent. . . .
[4] Symbolic of freedom to do the unconventional.

III

I know! the world proscribes not love;
    Allows my finger to caress
    Your lips' contour and downiness,
Provided it supply a glove.[5]
The world's good word!—the Institute![6]   20
    Guizot receives Montalembert![7]
    Eh? Down the court three lampions[8] flare:
Put forward your best foot![9]

The Last Ride Together

I

I said—Then, dearest, since 'tis so,
Since now at length my fate I know,
Since nothing all my love avails,
Since all, my life seemed meant for, fails,
    Since this was written and needs must be—   5
My whole heart rises up to bless
Your name in pride and thankfulness!
Take back the hope you gave,—I claim
Only a memory of the same,
—And this beside, if you will not blame,   10
    Your leave for one more last ride with me.

II

My mistress bent that brow of hers;
Those deep dark eyes where pride demurs
When pity would be softening through,
Fixed me a breathing-while or two   15
    With life or death in the balance: right!
The blood replenished me again;
My last thought was at least not vain:
I and my mistress, side by side,
Shall be together, breathe and ride,   20
So, one day more am I deified.
    Who knows but the world may end tonight?

III

Hush! if you saw some western cloud
All billowy-bosomed, over-bowed
By many benedictions—sun's   25
And moon's and evening-star's at once—
    And so, you, looking and loving best,
Conscious grew, your passion drew
Cloud, sunset, moonrise, star-shine too,
Down on you, near and yet more near,   30
Till flesh must fade for heaven was here!—
Thus leant she and lingered—joy and fear!
    Thus lay she a moment on my breast.

IV

Then we began to ride. My soul
Smoothed itself out, a long-cramped scroll   35
Freshening and fluttering in the wind.
Past hopes already lay behind.
    What need to strive with a life awry?
Had I said that, had I done this,
So might I gain, so might I miss.   40
Might she have loved me? just as well
She might have hated, who can tell!
Where had I been now if the worst befell?
    And here we are riding, she and I.

V

Fail I alone, in words and deeds?   45
Why, all men strive and who succeeds?
We rode; it seemed my spirit flew,
Saw other regions, cities new,
    As the world rushed by on either side.
I thought,—All labor, yet no less   50
Bear up beneath their unsuccess.
Look at the end of work, contrast
The petty done, the undone vast,
This present of theirs with the hopeful past!
    I hoped she would love me; here we ride.   55

VI

What hand and brain went ever paired?
What heart alike conceived and dared?
What act proved all its thought had been?
What will but felt the fleshly screen?
    We ride and I see her bosom heave.
There's many a crown for who can reach.[1]   60

---

[5] Provided we wear the gloves of respectability it supplies to cover the naked fact of love—i.e., provided we get married.

[6] The Institute of France on the left bank of the Seine, which they are just passing.

[7] Guizot, the constitutional royalist, welcomes the liberal Montalembert, whom he really hated as a political enemy, into the French Academy (which met in the Institute). The world's good word countenances even hypocrisy in the cause of propriety.

[8] Elaborate lamps in the courtyard of the Institute.

[9] Be respectable now for ten yards!

---

[1] Many a crown for those who aim only at objects they can reach.

Ten lines, a statesman's life in each!²
The flag struck on a heap of bones,
A soldier's doing! what atones?
They scratch his name on the Abbey stones.³   65
    My riding is better, by their leave.

VII

What does it all mean, poet? Well,
Your brains beat into rhythm, you tell
What we felt only; you expressed
You hold things beautiful the best,   70
    And pace them in rhyme so, side by side.
'Tis something, nay 'tis much: but then,
Have you yourself what's best for men?
Are you—poor, sick, old ere your time—
Nearer one whit your own sublime   75
Than we who never have turned a rhyme?
    Sing, riding's a joy! For me, I ride.

VIII

And you, great sculptor—so, you gave
A score of years to Art, her slave,
And that's your Venus, whence we turn   80
To yonder girl that fords the burn!⁴
    You acquiesce, and shall I repine?
What, man of music, you grown gray
With notes and nothing else to say,
Is this your sole praise from a friend,   85
"Greatly his opera's strains intend,
But in music we know how fashions end!"
    I gave my youth; but we ride, in fine.

IX

Who knows what's fit for us? Had fate
Proposed bliss here should sublimate⁵   90
My being—had I signed the bond—
Still one must lead some life beyond,
    Have a bliss to die with, dim-descried.
This foot once planted on the goal,
This glory-garland round my soul,   95
Could I descry such? Try and test!
I sink back shuddering from the quest.
Earth being so good, would heaven seem best?
    Now, heaven and she are beyond this ride.

X

And yet—she has not spoke so long!   100
What if heaven be that, fair and strong
At life's best, with our eyes upturned
Whither life's flower is first discerned,
    We, fixed so, ever should so abide?
What if we still ride on, we two   105
With life forever old yet new,
Changed not in kind but in degree,
The instant made eternity,—
And heaven just prove that I and she
    Ride, ride together, for ever ride?   110

Andrea del Sarto

(Called "The Faultless Painter"¹)

But do not let us quarrel any more,
No, my Lucrezia; bear with me for once:
Sit down and all shall happen as you wish.
You turn your face, but does it bring your heart?
I'll work then for your friend's friend, never fear,   5
Treat his own subject after his own way,
Fix his own time, accept too his own price,
And shut the money into this small hand
When next it takes mine. Will it? tenderly?
Oh, I'll content him,—but to-morrow, Love!   10
I often am much wearier than you think,
This evening more than usual, and it seems
As if—forgive now—should you let me sit
Here by the window with your hand in mine
And look a half-hour forth on Fiesole,²   15
Both of one mind, as married people use,³
Quietly, quietly the evening through,
I might get up to-morrow to my work
Cheerful and fresh as ever. Let us try.

---

² Ten lines of eulogy in the history books.
³ On his tombstone in Westminster Abbey.
⁴ Brook.
⁵ Exalt to its highest pitch.

---

¹ Florentine painter (1486–1531), famous for his technical skill but also for his lack of "grandeur, richness, and force," and therefore a perfect example of Browning's philosophy of "failure in success," complementing the "success in failure" of the lover in "The Last Ride Together." But the poem is not the exemplum for a moral; it is a study in character. In Vasari's account of Andrea (see note 9), which is the main source of the poem, Browning's imagination seized primarily, not on the "faultless" idea, but on the statement that "there was a certain timidity of mind, a sort of diffidence and want of force in his nature." Consequently, he wrote an analysis of the kind of person we call pathetically weak. All of Andrea's various attitudes may be traced to this central characteristic.
² Suburb of Florence.   ³ Are accustomed to do.

To-morrow, how you shall be glad for this!
Your soft hand is a woman of itself,
And mine the man's bared breast she curls inside.
Don't count the time lost, neither; you must serve
For each of the five pictures we require:
It saves a model. So! keep looking so— 25
My serpentining beauty, rounds on rounds!
—How could you ever prick those perfect ears,
Even to put the pearl there! oh, so sweet—
My face, my moon, my everybody's moon,
Which everybody looks on and calls his, 30
And, I suppose, is looked on by in turn,
While she looks—no one's: very dear, no less.
You smile? why, there's my picture ready made,
There's what we painters call our harmony!
A common greyness silvers everything,— 35
All in a twilight, you and I alike
—You, at the point of your first pride in me
(That's gone you know),—but I, at every point;
My youth, my hope, my art, being all toned down
To yonder sober pleasant Fiesole. 40
There's the bell clinking from the chapel-top;
That length of convent-wall across the way
Holds the trees safer, huddled more inside;
The last monk leaves the garden; days decrease,
And autumn grows, autumn in everything. 45
Eh? the whole seems to fall into a shape
As if I saw alike my work and self
And all that I was born to be and do,
A twilight-piece. Love, we are in God's hand.
How strange now, looks the life he makes us lead; 50
So free we seem, so fettered fast we are!
I feel He laid the fetter: let it lie!
This chamber for example—turn your head—
All that's behind us! you don't understand
Nor care to understand about my art, 55
But you can hear at least when people speak:
And that cartoon,[4] the second from the door
—It is the thing, Love! so such things should be—
Behold Madonna!—I am bold to say.
I can do with my pencil what I know, 60
What I see, what at bottom of my heart
I wish for, if I ever wish so deep—
Do easily, too—when I say, perfectly,
I do not boast, perhaps: yourself are judge,
Who listened to the Legate's[5] talk last week, 65
And just as much they used to say in France.
At any rate 'tis easy, all of it!

No sketches first, no studies, that's long past: 20
I do what many dream of, all their lives,
—Dream? strive to do, and agonize to do, 70
And fail in doing. I could count twenty such
On twice your fingers, and not leave this town,
Who strive—you don't know how the others strive
To paint a little thing like that you smeared
Carelessly passing with your robes afloat,— 75
Yet do much less, so much less, Someone says,[6]
(I know his name, no matter)—so much less!
Well, less is more, Lucrezia: I am judged.
There burns a truer light of God in them,
In their vexed beating stuffed and stopped-up brain, 80
Heart, or whate'er else, than goes on to prompt
This low-pulsed forthright craftsman's hand of mine.
Their works drop groundward, but themselves, I know,
Reach many a time a heaven that's shut to me,
Enter and take their place there sure enough, 85
Though they come back and cannot tell the world.
My works are nearer heaven, but I sit here.
The sudden blood of these men! at a word—
Praise them, it boils, or blame them, it boils too.
I, painting from myself and to myself, 90
Know what I do, am unmoved by men's blame
Or their praise either. Somebody remarks
Morello's[7] outline there is wrongly traced,
His hue mistaken; what of that? or else,
Rightly traced and well ordered; what of that? 95
Speak as they please, what does the mountain care?
Ah, but a man's reach should exceed his grasp,
Or what's a heaven for? all is silver-grey
Placid and perfect with my art: the worse!
I know both what I want and what might gain, 100
And yet how profitless to know, to sigh
"Had I been two, another and myself,
Our head would have o'erlooked the world!" No doubt.
Yonder's a work now, of that famous youth
The Urbinate[8] who died five years ago. 105
('Tis copied, George Vasari[9] sent it me.)

4 Preliminary drawing for a painting.
5 The Pope's envoy.

6 Michelangelo (see lines 184 and 199).
7 Mountain north of Florence.
8 Raphael (1483–1520), who was born at Urbino.
9 The pupil of Andrea and the author of *The Lives of the Most Eminent Painters, Sculptors, and Architects.*

Well, I can fancy how he did it all,
Pouring his soul, with kings and popes to see,
Reaching, that heaven might so replenish him,
Above and through his art—for it gives way;   110
That arm is wrongly put—and there again—
A fault to pardon in the drawing's lines,
Its body, so to speak: its soul is right,
He means right—that, a child may understand.
Still, what an arm! and I could alter it: 115
But all the play, the insight and the stretch—
Out of me, out of me! And wherefore out?
Had you enjoined them on me, given me soul,
We might have risen to Rafael, I and you!
Nay, Love, you did give all I asked, I think—   120
More than I merit, yes, by many times.
But had you—oh, with the same perfect brow,
And perfect eyes, and more than perfect mouth,
And the low voice my soul hears, as a bird
The fowler's pipe, and follows to the snare—   125
Had you, with these the same, but brought a
     mind!
Some women do so. Had the mouth there urged
"God and the glory! never care for gain.
The present by the future, what is that?
Live for fame, side by side with Agnolo![10]   130
Rafael is waiting: up to God, all three!"
I might have done it for you. So it seems:
Perhaps not. All is as God over-rules.
Beside, incentives come from the soul's self;
The rest avail not. Why do I need you?   135
What wife had Rafael, or has Agnolo?
In this world, who can do a thing, will not;
And who would do it, cannot, I perceive:
Yet the will's somewhat—somewhat, too, the
     power—
And thus we half-men struggle. At the end,   140
God, I conclude, compensates, punishes.
'Tis safer for me, if the award be strict,
That I am something underrated here,
Poor this long while, despised, to speak the truth.
I dared not, do you know, leave home all day,   145
For fear of chancing on the Paris lords.
The best is when they pass and look aside;
But they speak sometimes; I must bear it all.
Well may they speak! That Francis, that first
     time,
And that long festal year at Fontainebleau![11]   150

I surely then could sometimes leave the ground,
Put on the glory, Rafael's daily wear,
In that humane great monarch's golden look,—
One finger in his beard or twisted curl
Over his mouth's good mark that made the smile,   155
One arm about my shoulder, round my neck,
The jingle of his gold chain in my ear,
I painting proudly with his breath on me,
All his court round him, seeing with his eyes,
Such frank French eyes, and such a fire of souls   160
Profuse, my hand kept plying by those hearts,—
And, best of all, this, this, this face beyond,
This in the background, waiting on my work,
To crown the issue with a last reward!
A good time, was it not, my kingly days?   165
And had you not grown restless . . . but I know—
'Tis done and past; 'twas right, my instinct said;
Too live the life grew, golden and not grey,
And I'm the weak-eyed bat no sun should tempt
Out of the grange whose four walls make his   170
     world.
How could it end in any other way?
You called me, and I came home to your heart.
The triumph was—to reach and stay there; since
I reached it ere the triumph, what is lost?
Let my hands frame your face in your hair's gold,   175
You beautiful Lucrezia that are mine!
"Rafael did this, Andrea painted that;
The Roman's[12] is the better when you pray,
But still the other's Virgin was his wife—"
Men will excuse me. I am glad to judge   180
Both pictures in your presence; clearer grows
My better fortune, I resolve to think.
For, do you know, Lucrezia, as God lives,
Said one day Agnolo, his very self,
To Rafael . . . I have known it all these years . . . 185
(When the young man was flaming out his
     thoughts
Upon a palace-wall for Rome to see,
Too lifted up in heart because of it)
"Friend, there's a certain sorry little scrub
Goes up and down our Florence, none cares how,   190
Who, were he set to plan and execute
As you are, pricked on by your popes and kings,
Would bring the sweat into that brow of yours!"
To Rafael's!—And indeed the arm is wrong.
I hardly dare . . . yet, only you to see,   195

---

10 Michelangelo.
11 In 1518 Andrea was invited by King Francis I of France
to decorate his palace at Fontainebleau. When he was
sent back to Florence to buy paintings for the King, he

---

used the money to build a house for himself and Lucrezia (which explains his fear of meeting any Paris lords
who might recognize him).
12 Raphael's.

Give the chalk here—quick, thus the line should
    go!
Ay, but the soul! he's Rafael! rub it out!
Still, all I care for, if he spoke the truth
(What he? why, who but Michel Agnolo?
Do you forget already words like those?) 200
If really there was such a chance, so lost,—
Is, whether you're—not grateful—but more
    pleased.
Well, let me think so. And you smile indeed!
This hour has been an hour! Another smile?
If you would sit thus by me every night 205
I should work better, do you comprehend?
I mean that I should earn more, give you more.
See, it is settled dusk now; there's a star;
Morello's gone, the watch-lights show the wall,
The cue-owls speak the name we call them by. 210
Come from the window, love,—come in, at last,
Inside the melancholy little house
We built to be so gay with. God is just.
King Francis may forgive me; oft at nights
When I look up from painting, eyes tired out, 215
The walls become illumined, brick from brick
Distinct, instead of mortar, fierce bright gold,
That gold of his I did cement them with!
Let us but love each other. Must you go?
That Cousin[13] here again? he waits outside? 220
Must see you—you, and not with me? Those
    loans?
More gaming debts to pay? you smiled for that?
Well, let smiles buy me! have you more to spend?
While hand and eye and something of a heart
Are left me, work's my ware, and what's it worth? 225
I'll pay my fancy. Only let me sit
The grey remainder of the evening out,
Idle, you call it, and muse perfectly
How I could paint, were I but back in France,
One picture, just one more—the Virgin's face, 230
Not yours this time! I want you at my side
To hear them—that is, Michel Agnolo—
Judge all I do and tell you of its worth.
Will you? To-morrow, satisfy your friend.
I take the subjects for his corridor, 235
Finish the portrait out of hand—there, there,
And throw him in another thing or two
If he demurs; the whole should prove enough
To pay for this same Cousin's freak. Beside,
What's better and what's all I care about, 240
Get you the thirteen scudi[14] for the ruff!

Love, does that please you? Ah, but what does he,
The Cousin! what does he to please you more?

    I am grown peaceful as old age to-night.
I regret little, I would change still less. 245
Since there my past life lies, why alter it?
The very wrong to Francis!—it is true
I took his coin, was tempted and complied,
And built this house and sinned, and all is said.
My father and my mother died of want. 250
Well, had I riches of my own? you see
How one gets rich! Let each one bear his lot.
They were born poor, lived poor, and poor they
    died:
And I have labored somewhat in my time
And not been paid profusely. Some good son 255
Paint my two hundred pictures—let him try!
No doubt, there's something strikes a balance.
    Yes,
You loved me quite enough, it seems tonight.
This must suffice me here. What would one have?
In heaven, perhaps, new chances, one more 260
    chance—
Four great walls in the New Jerusalem,[15]
Meted on each side by the angel's reed,
For Leonard,[16] Rafael, Agnolo and me
To cover—the three first without a wife,
While I have mine! So—still they overcome 265
Because there's still Lucrezia,—as I choose.

    Again the Cousin's whistle! Go, my Love.

Memorabilia

I

Ah, did you once see Shelley plain,
    And did he stop and speak to you
And did you speak to him again?
    How strange it seems and new!

II

But you were living before that, 5
    And also you are living after;
And the memory I started at—
    My starting moves your laughter.

---

13 Euphemism for lover.   14 Italian coins.

15 Heaven (see Revelation 21:10–21).
16 Leonardo da Vinci.

III

I crossed a moor, with a name of its own
   And a certain use in the world no doubt,   10
Yet a hand's-breadth of it shines alone
   'Mid the blank miles round about:

IV

For there I picked up on the heather
   And there I put inside my breast
A molted feather, an eagle feather!   15
   Well, I forget the rest.

Two in the Campagna[1]

I

I wonder do you feel to-day
   As I have felt since, hand in hand,
We sat down on the grass, to stray
   In spirit better through the land,
This morn of Rome and May?   5

II

For me, I touched a thought, I know,
   Has tantalized me many times,
(Like turns of thread the spiders throw
   Mocking across our path) for rhymes
To catch at and let go.[2]   10

III

Help me to hold it! First it left
   The yellowing fennel, run to seed
There, branching from the brickwork's cleft,
   Some old tomb's ruin: yonder weed
Took up the floating weft,[3]   15

IV

Where one small orange cup amassed
   Five beetles,—blind and green they grope

---

[1] The Campagna, a large open plain outside Rome, is dotted with ancient ruins (hence the metaphor of "Rome's ghost" in line 25).
[2] The thread of thought that he has never been able to express in rimes is like the thread that a spider throws across a path, attaching it to a branch, letting go, then swinging down to attach it to a stone (these objects being similes for the rimes).
[3] Cross-thread (a weaving term) of my thought.

Among the honey-meal: and last,
   Everywhere on the grassy slope
I traced it. Hold it fast!   20

V

The champaign[4] with its endless fleece
   Of feathery grasses everywhere!
Silence and passion, joy and peace,
   An everlasting wash of air—
Rome's ghost since her decease.   25

VI

Such life here, through such lengths of hours,
   Such miracles performed in play,
Such primal naked forms of flowers,
   Such letting nature have her way
While heaven looks from its towers!   30

VII

How say you? Let us, O my dove,
   Let us be unashamed of soul,
As earth lies bare to heaven above!
   How is it under our control
To love or not to love?   35

VIII

I would that you were all to me,
   You that are just so much, no more.[5]
Nor yours nor mine, nor slave nor free!
   Where does the fault lie? What the core
O' the wound, since wound must be?   40

IX

I would I could adopt your will,
   See with your eyes, and set my heart
Beating by yours, and drink my fill
   At your soul's springs,—your part my part
In life, for good and ill.   45

X

No. I yearn upward, touch you close,
   Then stand away. I kiss your cheek,

---

[4] The Campagna.
[5] The obvious meaning (that I am only half in love with you) is rendered very doubtful by the next three stanzas.

Catch your soul's warmth,—I pluck the rose
    And love it more than tongue can speak—
Then the good minute goes.[6]   50

XI

Already how am I so far
    Out of that minute? Must I go
Still like the thistle-ball, no bar,
    Onward, whenever light winds blow,
Fixed by no friendly star?[7]   55

XII

Just when I seemed about to learn![8]
    Where is the thread now? Off again!
The old trick! Only I discern—
    Infinite passion, and the pain
Of finite hearts that yearn.[9]   60

A Grammarian's Funeral

Shortly After the Revival of Learning in Europe

Let us begin and carry up this corpse,
    Singing together.
Leave we the common crofts, the vulgar thorpes[1]
    Each in its tether
Sleeping safe on the bosom of the plain,   5
    Cared-for till cock-crow:
Look out if yonder be not day again
    Rimming the rock-row![2]

---

[6] Since this stanza implies that they share the fullness of love, what they lack is simply the complete sense of oneness and identity of will described in lines 41–45. The correct reading of lines 34–38 is thus made clear. The lovers have this oneness only by moments, after which they again feel their individual identities and know the sense of separation.

[7] Must I always lack the steady and overpowering influence of one star? Cf. lines 41–45.

[8] To learn the answers to the questions in lines 39–40, and follow the thread of his thought to a satisfactory conclusion.

[9] Though why this should be so, what is the core of the wound, I cannot discern. If lines 11–30 are now reread, their general purpose becomes clear. In the Campagna Browning feels the joy and peace of complete fulfillment. But that is in nature; human nature is different. There finite hearts feel an infinite passion and know the pain of its frustration.

[1] The enclosed fields and the small villages (in the valley).

[2] The morning sun is just striking the rocky top of the mountain.

That's the appropriate country; there, man's thought,
    Rarer, intenser,   10
Self-gathered for an outbreak, as it ought,
    Chafes in the censer.
Leave we the unlettered plain its herd and crop;
    Seek we sepulture
On a tall mountain, cited to the top,   15
    Crowded with culture!
All the peaks soar, but one the rest excels;
    Clouds overcome it;
No! yonder sparkle is the citadel's
    Circling its summit.   20
Thither our path lies; wind we up the heights;
    Wait ye the warning?
Our low life was the level's and the night's;
    He's for the morning.
Step to a tune, square chests, erect each head,   25
    'Ware the beholders!
This is our master, famous, calm and dead,
    Borne on our shoulders.

Sleep, crop and herd! sleep, darkling thorpe and croft,
    Safe from the weather!   30
He, whom we convoy to his grave aloft,
    Singing together,
He was a man born with thy face and throat,
    Lyric Apollo!
Long he lived nameless: how should spring take note   35
    Winter would follow?
Till lo, the little touch, and youth was gone!
    Cramped and diminished,
Moaned he, "New measures, other feet anon!
    My dance is finished"?   40
No, that's the world's way: (keep the mountain-side,
    Make for the city!)
He knew the signal, and stepped on with pride
    Over men's pity;
Left play for work, and grappled with the world   45
    Bent on escaping:[3]
"What's in the scroll," quoth he, "thou keepest furled?
    Show me their shaping,

---

[3] Grappled with the meaning of life, which seems bent on escaping our understanding.

Theirs who most studied man, the bard and
    sage,[4]—
      Give!"—So, he gowned him,[5]   50
Straight got by heart that book to its last page:
    Learned, we found him.
Yea, but we found him bald too, eyes like lead,
    Accents uncertain:
"Time to taste life," another would have said,   55
    "Up with the curtain!"
This man said rather, "Actual life comes next?
    Patience a moment!
Grant I have mastered learning's crabbed text,
    Still there's the comment.   60
Let me know all! Prate not of most or least,
    Painful or easy!
Even to the crumbs I'd fain eat up the feast,
    Ay, nor feel queasy."
Oh, such a life as he resolved to live,   65
    When he had learned it,
When he had gathered all books had to give!
    Sooner, he spurned it.
Image the whole, then execute the parts—
    Fancy the fabric   70
Quite, ere you build, ere steel strike fire from
    quartz,
    Ere mortar dab brick!

(Here's the town-gate reached: there's the market-
    place
    Gaping before us.)
Yea, this in him was the peculiar grace   75
    (Hearten our chorus!)
That before living he'd learn how to live—
    No end to learning:
Earn the means first—God surely will contrive
    Use for our earning.   80
Others mistrust and say, "But time escapes:
    Live now or never!"
He said, "What's time? Leave Now for dogs and
    apes!
    Man has Forever."
Back to his book then: deeper drooped his head: 85
    Calculus[6] racked him:
Leaden before, his eyes grew dross of lead:
    Tussis[7] attacked him.

"Now, master, take a little rest!"—not he!
    (Caution redoubled,   90
Step two abreast, the way winds narrowly!)
    Not a whit troubled
Back to his studies, fresher than at first,
    Fierce as a dragon
He (soul-hydroptic[8] with a sacred thirst)   95
    Sucked at the flagon.
Oh, if we draw a circle premature,
    Heedless of far gain,
Greedy for quick returns of profit, sure
    Bad is our bargain!   100
Was it not great? did not he throw on God,
    (He loves the burthen)—
God's task to make the heavenly period
    Perfect the earthen?
Did not he magnify the mind, show clear   105
    Just what it all meant?
He would not discount life, as fools do here,
    Paid by instalment.
He ventured neck or nothing—heaven's success
    Found, or earth's failure: 110
"Wilt thou trust death or not?" He answered
    "Yes:
    Hence with life's pale lure!"
That low man seeks a little thing to do,
    Sees it and does it:
This high man, with a great thing to pursue,   115
    Dies ere he knows it.
That low man goes on adding one to one,
    His hundred's soon hit:
This high man, aiming at a million,
    Misses an unit.   120
That, has the world here—should he need the
    next,
    Let the world mind him!
This, throws himself on God, and unperplexed
    Seeking shall find him.
So, with the throttling hands of death at strife,   125
    Ground he at grammar;
Still, through the rattle,[9] parts of speech were
    rife;
    While he could stammer
He settled *Hoti's* business—let it be!—
    Properly based *Oun*—   130
Gave us the doctrine of the enclitic *De*,[10]
    Dead from the waist down.

---

[4] "Their shaping" means either what manner of men they were or what their creative interpretation of life was.
[5] Put on a scholar's gown.
[6] The disease called the stone.
[7] A bronchial cough.

[8] Soul-thirsty.
[9] Death rattle in his throat.
[10] The italicized words are Greek particles which were discussed by the Renaissance philologists.

Well, here's the platform, here's the proper place:
    Hail to your purlieus,
All ye highfliers of the feathered race,   135
    Swallows and curlews!
Here's the top-peak; the multitude below
    Live, for they can, there:
This man decided not to Live but Know—
    Bury this man there?   140
Here—here's his place, where meteors shoot,
    clouds form,
    Lightnings are loosened,
Stars come and go! Let joy break with the storm,
    Peace let the dew send!
Lofty designs must close in like effects: 145
    Loftily lying,
Leave him—still loftier than the world suspects,
    Living and dying.[11]

Prospice[1]

Fear death?—to feel the fog in my throat,
    The mist in my face,
When the snows begin, and the blasts denote
    I am nearing the place,
The power of the night, the press of the storm,   5
    The post of the foe;
Where he stands, the Arch Fear in a visible form,
    Yet the strong man must go:
For the journey is done and the summit attained,
    And the barriers fall,   10
Though a battle's to fight ere the guerdon be
    gained,
    The reward of it all.
I was ever a fighter, so—one fight more,
    The best and the last!
I would hate that death bandaged my eyes, and   15
    forbore,
    And bade me creep past.

No! let me taste the whole of it, fare like my peers
    The heroes of old,
Bear the brunt, in a minute pay glad life's arrears
    Of pain, darkness and cold.   20
For sudden the worst turns the best to the brave,
    The black minute's at end,
And the elements' rage, the fiend-voices that rave,
    Shall dwindle, shall blend,
Shall change, shall become first a peace out of   25
    pain,
    Then a light, then thy breast,
O thou soul of my soul! I shall clasp thee again,
    And with God be the rest!

Adam, Lilith, and Eve

One day it thundered and lightened.
Two women, fairly frightened,
Sank to their knees, transformed, transfixed,
At the feet of the man who sat betwixt;
And "Mercy!" cried each—"if I tell the truth   5
Of a passage in my youth!"

Said This:[1] "Do you mind the morning
I met your love with scorning?
As the worst of the venom left my lips,
I thought, 'If, despite this lie, he strips   10
The mask from my soul with a kiss—I crawl
His slave,—soul, body and all!' "

Said That:[2] "We stood to be married;
The priest, or someone, tarried;
'If Paradise-door prove locked?' smiled you.   15
I thought, as I nodded, smiling too,
'Did one, that's away, arrive—nor late
Nor soon should unlock Hell's gate!' "[3]

It ceased to lighten and thunder.
Up started both in wonder,   20
Looked round and saw that the sky was clear,
Then laughed, "Confess you believed us, Dear!"
"I saw through the joke!" the man replied.[4]
They re-seated themselves beside.[5]

---

11 Browning's attitude toward the grammarian seems to be somewhat ambiguous. The reader senses a note of criticism, perhaps directed at pedantry, perhaps at compulsive work. But primarily Browning seems to be praising a Renaissance humanist for devoting his whole soul to the complete fulfilment of a high purpose, namely, the absolute mastery of ancient literature as a key to wise living (and such a mastery would rightly include the necessity to understand the most subtle points of grammar, indeed, the passion to do so; cf. line 63), and for the faith that what he cannot accomplish here will be achieved in heaven.

1 "Look forward." The poem was probably written soon after Mrs. Browning's death in 1861.

1 Lilith, Adam's mate before he married Eve.
2 Eve.
3 If only the man I really love would arrive, I wouldn't unlock hell's gate by marrying you.
4 The remark is double-edged. To them it means (or rather, they are willing to assume that it means), "Yes, I saw that you were only joking"; but to himself and to the reader it means, "I saw through the whole wretched joke, your false pretensions of a lifetime, and your latest attempt to make me think your true confessions were only a joke."
5 As if nothing had happened. The poem is a wonderfully

Epilogue to *Asolando*[1]

At the midnight in the silence of the sleep-time,
    When you set your fancies free,
Will they pass to where—by death, fools think,
        imprisoned—
Low he lies who once so loved you, whom you
        loved so,
    —Pity me?   5

Oh to love so, be so loved, yet so mistaken!
    What had I on earth to do
With the slothful, with the mawkish, the un-
        manly?
Like the aimless, helpless, hopeless, did I drivel—
        Being—who?   10

One who never turned his back but marched
        breast forward,
    Never doubted clouds would break,
Never dreamed, though right were worsted, wrong
        would triumph,
Held[2] we fall to rise, are baffled to fight better,
    Sleep to wake.   15

No, at noonday in the bustle of man's work-time
    Greet the unseen with a cheer!
Bid him forward, breast and back as either should
        be,
    "Strive and thrive!" cry "Speed,—fight on, fare
        ever
        There as here!"   20

Arthur Hugh Clough

1819–1861

Clough was born at Liverpool in 1819 and educated at Rugby, where he came under the powerful influence of Thomas Arnold and Liberal Protestantism (see introduction, p. 416). But, when he arrived at Oxford in 1837, his faith was disturbed by the rival claim of Newman's Anglo-Catholicism; and presently, as he felt the combined impact of scientific materialism, of Biblical criticism, and of modern writers like George Sand, Goethe, Emerson, and especially Carlyle—none of whom, in the strict sense, was a Christian—he was deeply disturbed. Though at times he achieved some sense of belief in an unnameable and unknowable divine spirit, and a life of duty and work as a realization of divine purpose (see "Qui laborat, orat"), the highly qualified faith of "That There Are Powers Above Us I Admit" is more characteristic: he "will not say they will not give us aid." This is the state of doubt—not denial but profound uncertainty—which runs through much of Clough's poetry, whether religious or secular. Was the scientific or the religious view of man and the universe true? How could either be proved? Were old beliefs entirely wrong? or new ones wholly right? Could anyone say for certain what we are or why we are here?

And yet Clough found his contemporaries rushing to one or another conclusion, and either defending their choice with dogmatic zeal, or ignoring the upsetting facts of science and Biblical criticism, and clinging blindly to tradition (see the sonnet printed below).

Out of this "vortex of philosophism and discussion," as he called the Oxford of the 1840s, Clough developed the special frame of mind that Henry Sidgwick, the professor of philosophy at Cambridge, described in 1869 in a passage on Clough and the modern spirit:

His point of view and habit of mind are less singular in England in the year 1869 than they were in 1859, and much less than they were in 1849. We are growing year by year more introspective and self-conscious: the current philosophy leads us to a close, patient, and impartial observation and analysis of our mental processes. . . . We are growing at the same time more unreserved and unveiled in our expression; in conversations, in journals and books, we more and more say and write what we actually do think and feel, and not what we intend to think or should desire to feel. We are growing also more skeptical in the proper sense of the word: we suspend our judgment much more than our predecessors, and much more contentedly: we see that there are many sides to many questions: the opinions that we do hold we hold if not more loosely, at least more at arm's length: we can imagine how they appear to others, and can conceive ourselves not holding them. We are losing in faith

---

wry comment on the masks (of scorn, of love, of ignorance) that people put on in order to live together with some show of peace and stability, and continue to wear even when they have been seen through. Cf. Guizot's mask in "Respectability," p. 775.

[1] The last poem in Browning's last book, *Asolando*.
[2] Maintained.

and confidence . . . and we are gaining in impartiality and comprehensiveness of sympathy. In each of these respects, Clough, if he were still alive, would find himself gradually more and more at home in the changing world.

When we add to this the intellectual character of his verse, the extensive use of irony (see "The Latest Decalogue," just below), and the plain idiomatic style devoid of sensuous diction and incantatory rhythm, we recognize that in many respects Clough is the most modern of the Victorian poets. He often reminds one of Auden or MacLeish.

Through the 1840s Clough's mind was introspective and self-centered, but the other side of his nature—the flair for social observation in modes of amused comedy or angry satire—was occasionally breaking through in short poems; and the more painful and baffled the introspection became, the more eager he was to turn toward objective poetry. The first necessity was to resign his fellowship at Oriel and to leave Oxford, which he did in 1848. Almost at once he wrote the first of the three long poems on which his claim to high rank as a poet is largely based. *The Bothie of Tober-na-Vuolich* (1848) is a delightful account of a reading party of Oxonians in the Highlands, combining a love story with amusing character sketches, descriptions of scenery, gentle satire, and serious reflections on social and moral questions. A year later he composed *Amours de Voyage* (1849), another love story, laid in Rome at the time of the 1848 revolt, with an intellectual as hero struggling with indecision—to propose or not to propose—a situation which Clough handles with sympathy and irony. Finally in 1850 he wrote *Dipsychus,* meaning double-minded, a poetic drama modeled on Goethe's *Faust,* in which "the conflict of the tender conscience and the world" is presented in a series of dialogues between Dipsychus, the idealist who is aware of earthy instincts and worldly standards in himself, and the Spirit, witty, single-minded, amoral—laughing at idealism and exalting the way of the World. Though the poem continues the serio-comic mode of *Amours de Voyage* and explores the problem of to act or not to act with greater subtlety, it represents a return to the "impartial observation and analysis of our mental processes" which was predominant in his earlier work.

It is these three poems, all too long unfortunately to reprint here in full, along with a score of shorter poems like those which follow, that make Clough one of the major Victorian poets. In an essay written in 1882, R. H. Hutton placed him with his peers:

For my own part, though I should not assert that Clough is the great poet of our age, I should agree heartily with Mr. Lowell that he will in future generations rank among the highest of our time, and that especially he will be ranked with Matthew Arnold, as having found a voice for this self-questioning age— a voice of greater range and richness even, and of a deeper pathos.

TEXTS: The definitive text, here used by kind permission of the Oxford Press, is *The Poems of Arthur Hugh Clough,* edited by H. F. Lowry, A. L. P. Norrington, and F. L. Mulhauser (1951). Mulhauser has also edited a two-volume selection from Clough's letters (1957). The fullest edition of his prose essays was published by Buckner Trawick (1964). The best biography is that by Lady Katharine Chorley (1962). The fullest study of Clough's work, set against the background of his age, is *Arthur Hugh Clough, 1819–1861,* written in French by Paul Veyriras (1964). *The Poetry of Clough,* by Walter E. Houghton (1963), is a useful introduction. The Victorian essays by Walter Bagehot in *Literary Studies,* (1879), by R. H. Hutton in *Literary Essays* (1871), and by Henry Sidgwick in *Miscellaneous Essays and Addresses* (1904) are still valuable.

The Latest Decalogue

Thou shalt have one God only; who
Would be at the expense of two?
No graven images may be
Worshiped, except the currency:
Swear not at all; for for thy curse   5
Thine enemy is none the worse:
At church on Sunday to attend
Will serve to keep the world thy friend:
Honour thy parents; that is, all
From whom advancement may befall: 10
Thou shalt not kill; but need'st not strive
Officiously to keep alive:
Do not adultery commit;
Advantage rarely comes of it:
Thou shalt not steal; an empty feat,   15
When it's so lucrative to cheat:
Bear not false witness; let the lie
Have time on its own wings to fly:
Thou shalt not covet; but tradition
Approves all forms of competition.   20

The sum of all is, thou shalt love,
If any body, God above:
At any rate shall never labour
More than thyself to love thy neighbour.

Is It True, Ye Gods

Is it true, ye gods, who treat us
As the gambling fool is treated,
O ye, who ever cheat us,
And let us feel we're cheated!
Is it true that poetical power,   5
The gift of heaven, the dower
Of Apollo and the Nine,
The inborn sense, "the vision and the faculty
        divine,"[1]
All we glorify and bless
In our rapturous exaltation,   10
All invention, and creation,
Exuberance of fancy, and sublime imagination,
All a poet's fame is built on,
The fame of Shakespeare, Milton,
Of Wordsworth, Byron, Shelley,   15
Is in reason's grave precision,
Nothing more, nothing less,
Than a peculiar conformation,
Constitution, and condition
Of the brain and of the belly?[2]   20
Is it true, ye gods who cheat us?
And that's the way ye treat us?

Oh say it, all who think it,
Look straight, and never blink it!
If it is so, let it be so,   25
And we will all agree so;
But the plot has counterplot,
It may be, and yet be not.[3]

"Old Things Need Not
Be Therefore True"

"Old things need not be therefore true,"
O brother men, nor yet the new;

---

[1] Wordsworth's description of the poetic imagination (*The Excursion*, I, 79).
[2] See the introduction, p. 420.
[3] If "and" is emphasized, the line may be an antinomy, in which case both statements may be true. In an antinomy different inferences may be correctly drawn from different principles. The fact that the plot has a counterplot supports this reading. "In reason's grave precision" (Kant's *Verstand*), a poet is a physical machine; but by pure reason (Kant's *Vernunft*), he is a being with free will and sublime imagination. Cf. Carlyle, *Sartor Resartus*, Book I, chap. 10, entitled "Pure Reason": "To the vulgar eye of Logic . . . What is man? An omnivorous Biped that wears Breeches. To the eye of Pure Reason what is he? A Soul, a Spirit, a divine Apparition."

Ah! still awhile the old thought retain,
And yet consider it again!

The souls of now two thousand years   5
Have laid up here their toils and tears,
And all the earnings of their pain,—
Ah, yet consider that again!

We! what do *we* see? each a space
Of some few yards before his face;   10
Does that the whole wide plan explain?
Ah, yet consider it again!

Alas! the great World goes its way,
And takes its truth from each new day;
They do not quit, nor can retain,   15
Far less consider it again!

To Spend Uncounted Years of Pain

To spend uncounted years of pain,
Again, again, and yet again,
In working out in heart and brain
    The problem of our being here;
To gather facts from far and near,   5
Upon the mind to hold them clear,
And, knowing more may yet appear,
Unto one's latest breath to fear
The premature result to draw—
Is this the object, end and law,   10
    And purpose of our being here?

Qui Laborat, Orat[1]

O only Source of all our light and life,
    Whom as our truth, our strength, we see and
        feel,
But whom the hours of mortal moral strife
    Alone aright reveal!

Mine inmost soul, before Thee inly brought,   5
    Thy presence owns ineffable, divine;
Chastised each rebel self-encentered thought,
    My will adoreth Thine.

With eye down-dropt, if then this earthly mind
    Speechless remain, or speechless e'en depart;   10

---

[1] Literally, "He who works, prays."

Nor seek to see—for what of earthly kind
   Can see Thee as Thou art?—

If well-assured 'tis but profanely bold
   In thought's abstractest forms to seem to see,
It dare not dare the dread communion hold   15
   In ways unworthy Thee,

O not unowned, Thou shalt unnamed forgive,
   In worldly walks the prayerless heart prepare;
And if in work its life it seem to live,
   Shalt make that work be prayer.[2]   20

Nor times shall lack, when while the work it
    plies,
   Unsummoned powers the blinding film shall
    part,
And scarce by happy tears made dim, the eyes
   In recognition start.

But, as thou willest, give or e'en forbear   25
   The beatific supersensual sight,
So, with Thy blessing blest, that humbler prayer
   Approach Thee morn and night.

That There Are Powers Above Us I Admit

That there are powers above us I admit;
It may be true too
That while we walk the troublous tossing sea,
That when we see the o'ertopping waves advance,
And when [we] feel our feet beneath us sink,   5
There are who walk beside us; and the cry
That rises so spontaneous to the lips,
The "Help us or we perish," is not nought,[1]
An evanescent spectrum of disease.
It may be that in deed and not in fancy,   10
A hand that is not ours upstays our steps,
A voice that is not ours commands the waves,
Commands the waves, and whispers in our ear,

O thou of little faith, why didst thou doubt?
At any rate—   15
That there are beings above us, I believe,
And when we lift up holy hands of prayer,
I will not say they will not give us aid.

from Seven Sonnets

4

But whether in the uncoloured light of truth
This inward strong assurance be, indeed,[1]
More than the self-willed arbitrary creed,
Manhood's inheritor to the dream of youth;
Whether to shut out fact because forsooth   5
To live were insupportable unfreed,[2]
Be not or be the service of untruth;
Whether this vital confidence be more
Than his, who upon death's immediate brink
Knowing, perforce determines to ignore;   10
Or than the bird's, that when the hunter's near,
Burying her eyesight, can forget her fear;
Who about this shall tell us what to think?

Say Not the Struggle Nought Availeth

Say not the struggle nought availeth,
   The labour and the wounds are vain,
The enemy faints not, nor faileth,
   And as things have been, they remain.

If hopes were dupes, fears may be liars;   5
   It may be, in yon smoke concealed,
Your comrades chase e'en now the fliers,
   And, but for you, possess the field.

For while the tired waves, vainly breaking,
   Seem here no painful inch to gain,   10
Far back through creeks and inlets making
   Came, silent, flooding in, the main.

And not by eastern windows only,
   When daylight comes, comes in the light,

---

[2] Clough suggests that since vocal prayers may be too "profanely bold" in their attempt to address the Unnameable or describe the Unknowable, a life of earnest work in the service of man may be a better expression of praise and devotion, or (lines 27–28, below) a better approach to God.

[1] The reference is to the two scenes in Matthew (8:23–26 and 14:24–32) involving Christ and the terrified disciples during a storm at sea.

---

[1] The reference is to the immortality of the soul.
[2] Chained or tied down to fact. After this line the MS leaves a blank for the seventh line of the sonnet, which would have rimed -eed.

In front, the sun climbs slow, how slowly,
  But westward, look, the land is bright.   15

O Let Me Love My Love
unto Myself Alone[1]

O let me love my love unto myself alone,
And know my knowledge to the world unknown;
No witness to the vision call,
Beholding, unbeheld of all;
And worship thee, with thee withdrawn, apart,   5
Whoe'er, whate'er thou art,
Within the closest veil of mine own inmost heart.

Better it were, thou sayest,[2] to consent,
Feast while we may, and live ere life be spent;
Close up clear eyes, and call the unstable sure,   10
The unlovely lovely, and the filthy pure;
In self-belyings, self-deceivings roll,
And lose in Action, Passion, Talk, the soul.

Nay, better far to mark off thus much air
And call it heaven, place bliss and glory there;   15
Fix perfect homes in the unsubstantial sky,
And say, what is not, will be by-and-by;
What here exists not, must exist elsewhere.
But play no tricks upon thy soul, O man;
Let fact be fact, and life the thing it can.   20

"There Is No God," the Wicked Saith[1]

"There is no God," the wicked saith,
  "And truly it's a blessing,
For what he might have done with us
  It's better only guessing."

"There is no God," a youngster thinks,   5
  "Or really, if there may be,
He surely didn't mean a man
  Always to be a baby."

"There is no God, or if there is,"
  The tradesman thinks," 'twere funny   10
If he should take it ill in me
  To make a little money."

"Whether there be," the rich man says,
  "It matters very little,
For I and mine, thank somebody,   15
  Are not in want of victual."

Some others, also, to themselves
  Who scarce so much as doubt it,
Think there is none, when they are well,
  And do not think about it.   20

But country folks who live beneath
  The shadow of the steeple;
The parson and the parson's wife,
  And mostly married people;

Youths green and happy in first love,   25
  So thankful for illusion;
And men caught out in what the world
  Calls guilt, in first confusion;

And almost every one when age,
  Disease, or sorrows strike him,   30
Inclines to think there is a God,
  Or something very like Him.

Jacob[1]

My sons, and ye the children of my sons,
Jacob your father goes upon his way,
His pilgrimage is being accomplished.
Come near, and hear him ere his words are o'er.
Not as my father's or his father's days,   5
As Isaac's days or Abraham's, have been mine;
Not as the days of those that in the field
Walked at the eventide to meditate,
And haply to the tent returning found

---

[1] From *Dipsychus*, Scene IV, lines 82–101. The notes for this poem and the next two are reprinted from *Victorian Poetry and Poetics*, ed. W. E. Houghton and G. R. Stange, by kind permission of the Houghton Mifflin Company.
[2] The Spirit who is talking with Dipsychus and whose worldly philosophy Dipsuchus sums up sardonically in the next lines.

[1] From *Dipsychus*, Scene V, lines 154–85. Spoken by the Spirit in the sharp and perhaps cynical tones of the man of the world.

---

[1] The occasion of this dramatic monologue is the dying speech of Jacob to his sons, but unlike the account in Genesis 49, where Jacob discusses what will happen to the sons in the future, Clough has him dwell, with sorrow and remorse, on his own life of hard and sometimes treacherous struggle, so different, he feels, from the "antique pure simplicity" and the close communion with God which characterized the days of his grandfather Abraham and his father Isaac. The background of the poem is in Genesis 25, 27–35, 37–38, 47–49.

ARTHUR HUGH CLOUGH 789

Angels at nightfall waiting at their door.
They communed, Israel wrestled with the Lord.[2]
No, not as Abraham's or as Isaac's days,
My sons, have been Jacob your father's days,
Evil and few, attaining not to theirs
In number, and in worth inferior much.[3]
As a man with his friend, walked they with God,
In his abiding presence they abode,
And all their acts were open to his face.
But I have had to force mine eyes away,
To lose, almost to shun, the thoughts I loved,
To bend down to the work, to bare the breast,
And struggle, feet and hands, with enemies;
To buffet and to battle with hard men,
With men of selfishness and violence;
To watch by day and calculate by night,
To plot and think of plots, and through a land
Ambushed with guile, and with strong foes beset,
To win with art safe wisdom's peaceful way.
Alas! I know, and from the outset knew,
The first-born faith, the singleness of soul,
The antique pure simplicity with which
God and good angels communed undispleased,
Is not; it shall not any more be said
That of a blameless and a holy kind
The chosen race, the seed of promise, comes.
The royal high prerogatives, the dower
Of innocence and perfectness of life,
Pass not unto my children from their sire
As unto me they came of mine; they fit
Neither to Jacob nor to Jacob's race.
Think ye, my sons, in this extreme old age
And in this failing breath, that I forget
How on the day when from my father's door,
In bitterness and ruefulness of heart,
I from my parents set my face and felt
I never more again should look on theirs,—
How on that day I seemed unto myself
Another Adam from his home cast out,
And driven abroad into a barren land,
Cursed for his sake, and mocking still with thorns
And briars that labour and that sweat of brow
He still must spend to live? Sick of my days,
I wished not life, but cried out, Let me die;[4]

But at Luz God came to me; in my heart
He put a better mind, and showed me how,
While we discern it not and least believe,
On stairs invisible betwixt his heaven
And our unholy, sinful, toilsome earth
Celestial messengers of loftiest good
Upward and downward pass continually.[5]
Many, since Jacob on the field of Luz
Set up the stone he slept on, unto God,
Many have been the troubles of my life;
Sins in the field and sorrows in the tent,
In mine own household anguish and despair,
And gall and wormwood mingled with my love.
The time would fail me should I seek to tell
Of a child wronged and cruelly revenged
(Accursed was that anger, it was fierce,
That wrath, for it was cruel),[6] or of strife
And jealousy and cowardice, with lies
Mocking a father's misery;[7] deeds of blood,
Pollutions, sicknesses, and sudden deaths,
These many things against me many times.
The ploughers have ploughed deep upon my back,
And made deep furrows; blessed be his name
Who hath delivered Jacob out of all,
And left within his spirit hope of good.
Come near to me, my sons: your father goes,
The hour of his departure draweth nigh.
Ah me! this eager rivalry of life,
This cruel conflict for pre-eminence,
This keen supplanting of the dearest kin,[8]
Quick seizure and fast unrelaxing hold
Of vantage-place; the stony-hard resolve,
The chase, the competition, and the craft
Which seems to be the poison of our life

upon him the birthright that belonged to his brother
Esau (Genesis 27), he was forced to flee into Mesopotamia
to escape his brother's revenge.
[5] At Luz, Jacob dreamed (Genesis 28:12), "and behold a
ladder set up on earth, and the top of it reached to
heaven: and behold the angels of God ascending and descending on it."
[6] The child is Dinah, violated by Schechem, and revenged
by her brothers Levi and Simeon when they slew not only
Schechem and his father but all the males of their tribe.
See Genesis 34. In his dying speech Jacob says (49:7),
"Cursed be their anger, for it was fierce; and their wrath,
for it was cruel."
[7] The reference is mainly to the jealousy his sons felt for
their brother Joseph, who was Jacob's favorite, and to the
lie they told their father, that Joseph had been killed by
a wild beast. See Genesis 37.
[8] The word "Jacob" meant "the supplanter," in reference
to his stealing the birthright from Esau.

[2] They communed with God, but I only wrestled with
Him. Israel was the name given to Jacob by God when
he wrestled with Him. (Genesis 32:24–32)
[3] Cf. Genesis 47:9: "And Jacob said unto Pharaoh, . . .
few and evil have the days of the years of my life been,
and have not attained unto the days of the years of the
life of my fathers in the days of their pilgrimage."
[4] After Jacob had tricked his aged father into bestowing

And yet is the condition of our life!
To have done things on which the eye with
    shame
Looks back, the closed hand clutching still the   90
    prize![9]
Alas! what of all these things shall I say?
Take me away unto thy sleep, O God!
I thank thee it is over, yet I think
It was a work appointed me of thee.

How is it? I have striven all my days   95
To do my duty to my house and hearth,
And to the purpose of my father's race,
Yet is my heart therewith not satisfied.[10]

---

[9] As the word "competition" rightly suggests, Clough intends Jacob's life to suggest, but not explicitly to symbolize, the commercial life of the Victorian world. In comparison with the usual portrait of the hard, calculating businessman, the analysis here is more subtle and probably closer to reality. On this level we may perhaps consider the earlier period of "antique pure simplicity" as a somewhat idealized view (natural enough in a man who came later) of the age before the Industrial Revolution and the tense struggle for survival which it initiated.

But That from Slow Dissolving Pomps of Dawn

But that from slow dissolving pomps of dawn
No verity of slowly strengthening light
Early or late hath issued; that the day
Scarce-shown, relapses rather, self-withdrawn,
Back to the glooms of ante-natal night,   5
For this, O human beings, mourn we may.

---

[10] If you did not know the author of "Jacob," you might well guess it was by Browning. Why would you be wrong?

Matthew Arnold
1822–1888

Matthew Arnold (1822–1888). Of all Victorian men of letters, Arnold had perhaps the most thorough and direct experience of life as it was lived among all classes. *Radio Times Hulton Picture Library.*

Arnold was the famous son of a famous father. Thomas Arnold was the headmaster of Rugby, a leader of the Broad Church school of Liberal Protestantism (see the introduction to the Victorian period, p. 416), and a very earnest Victorian who summoned his boys to a life of moral warfare and strenuous work. The son was something of a black sheep. Partly in reaction against his father, he cultivated the elegant airs of a dandy. At Oxford, where he matriculated in 1841 after a school education at Winchester and Rugby, he went fishing when he should have been studying, wore wondrous waistcoats in the latest French fashion, and entertained his friends with practical jokes and "a genial amount of ribaldry." But there was nothing light or gay about the poems that he published in 1849. Even his sister, to say nothing of his Oxford associates, found the volume "almost like a new Introduction to him. . . . I felt there was so much more of . . . practical questioning in Matt's book than I was at all prepared for; in fact that it showed a knowledge of life and conflict which was strangely like experience if it was not the thing itself; and this . . . I should not have looked for."

The key words here are "questioning" and "conflict." The fact is that Arnold's dandyism was largely a mask, either adopted deliberately to hide an inner distress of mind he did not want to discuss, or assumed instinctively as a kind of laughing that he might not weep. For he was suffering from the disease of the nineteenth century, the collapse of traditional beliefs, especially in religion, as the waves of modern thought—science and Utilitarianism and Biblical criticism—broke over his head at Oxford, to leave him, as they left his friend Clough, without compass or stars, in a painful darkness of indecision and doubt (see the description of the Victorians in "The Scholar-Gipsy," lines 161–230). He felt himself "wandering between two worlds, one dead, the other powerless to be born, with nowhere yet to rest my head" (lines 85–87).

As this statement implies, Arnold's melancholy is shot through with a sense of loneliness. The old relationship between man and God, and between man and nature (cf. Wordsworth), is broken, leaving man alone in an indifferent universe of mechanical law. The decay of the old social structure, under industrial and democratic pressure, and the rise of the large impersonal city have put an end to the binding associations of fixed classes and small communities. The individual is thus thrown back upon himself in painful isolation, both cosmic and social. (See especially the two poems to Marguerite.) In the last analysis it is this poetry of "depression and ennui," combined as it usually is with nostalgia for an earlier world of youth and joy, that carries the accent of passionate and genuine experience.

But the Victorian son of Thomas Arnold could hardly approve of it. He resolved "to make a habitual war on depression and low spirits," and to remember that "nothing can absolve us from the duty of doing all we can to keep alive our courage and activity." But how? What philosophy could take the place of his lost Christianity and give him, and his age, renewed strength and inspiration? The question led Arnold to different answers, with the result, as he said himself, that his poems cannot be made to square in all their parts. They are fragments, because "I am fragments." And no one should plague himself "to find a consistent meaning."

One answer was the Stoicism of Epictetus and Marcus Aurelius, with its doctrines of self-reliance and the imitation of nature. So long as men depend on external things for their happiness, on the attainment of wealth or fame or love, they are doomed to disappointment and frustration. Only by achieving *self*-dependence through mastering their possessive passions and adopting an attitude of Stoic detachment can they gain inner calm and peace of mind. This did not mean, however, that man was to turn away from active life in the world. Since his goal was to "live according to nature," and all things had a "natural" function to pursue—the vine to bear grapes, the sun to shine—man was to serve society in whatever role "naturally" fitted his temper and abilities. This is what Arnold means by "quiet work," in the world but not of it, as contrasted with the battling, noisy work that is motivated by personal and worldly ambitions. In one respect, however, Arnold found Stoicism unsatisfactory. "The burden [it] laid upon man is well-nigh greater than he can bear." It said, Renounce your natural desires and you will be serene. But most men, Arnold felt, including himself, needed something more hopeful and inspiring "to make moral action perfect."

This something was religion, whose paramount virtue is that "it has *lighted up* morality; that it has supplied the emotion and inspiration needful for carrying the sage along the narrow way perfectly, for carrying the ordinary man along it at all"; and more than any other religion Christianity has manifested this virtue "with unexampled splendour." What he had in mind was partly the figure of Christ and partly the Christian ethic, in particular the Puritan-Christian ethic which lays major emphasis on moral struggle and aspiration rather than on forgiveness and humility—on warring against evil, within and without, and on living a strenuous life of hard labor in the service of God by serving society. There is much that harmonizes here with the ethic of Stoicism, but there is a clear distinction between "quiet work" and "strenuous work," between emphasizing detachment and emphasizing active effort. (Cf. "Quiet Work" and "Self-Dependence" with "The Better Part" and "Morality.")

Finally, the search for a constructive philosophy led Arnold to a third answer, one which is indebted both to his sympathy with aristocracy and his admiration for dynamic personality—that is, for the decisive force he so badly lacked himself and which he recognized in his father. This is the hero worship that is seen in "Sohrab and Rustum," the inspiring image of a great man, great in courage and energy, still greater in moral character; and if not noble by birth, always noble in spirit. "I am glad you like the Gipsy Scholar," he wrote to his friend Clough, "but what does it *do* for you? Homer *animates*—Shakespeare *animates*—in its poor way I think Sohrab and Rustum *animates*—the Gipsy Scholar at best awakens a pleasing melancholy. But this is not what we want. 'The complaining millions of men darken in labour and pain'—what they want is something to *animate* and *ennoble* them."

This, he goes on to say, is "the basis of . . . my poetics." It is true that the principles laid down in the preface to the 1853 *Poems* are classical: the insistence on organic structure and the subordination of the parts to the whole, the rejection of subjective analysis for an objective story, and the choice of ancient rather than of modern subjects. But to think of the essay as a classical protest against Romanticism is to pick it up by the wrong handle. Its basic motivation was the desire to provide an age of "spiritual discomfort" with a poetry that would "inspirit and rejoice"; and to *that* end modern subjects and introspective analyses, both of which could only increase one's depression, are rejected. The right focus of poetry is said to be "some noble action of a heroic time" in which no incidental beauties of imagery will distract the reader's attention and so "impair the grandiose effect of the whole." This is the theory on which "Sohrab and Rustum" was conceived and written. But most of Arnold's poems are more representative of his later poetics, which found that poetry interpreted life in two ways—"by expressing with magical felicity the physiognomy and movement of the outward world [of nature], and . . . by expressing, with inspired conviction, the ideas and laws of the inward world of man's moral and spiritual nature." In both ways, he says, "it *reconciles* him [man] with himself and the universe." In the former it does so through the calming effect of natural beauty (cf. "The Scholar-Gipsy"); in the latter by the inspiration not only of heroic action but also of moral statement or injunction (cf. such poems as "Quiet Work" and "Self-Dependence").

After publishing three volumes of verse between 1849 and 1853, Arnold ceased to write poetry, except occasionally; and in 1857, when he was elected Professor of Poetry at Oxford, he began his career as a Victorian critic, not only of literature (in two volumes of *Essays in Criticism*, 1865 and 1888) but also of society and politics (in *Culture and Anarchy*, 1869) and of religion (in *Literature and Dogma*, 1873). But the dividing lines are loose and the divisions somewhat arbitrary, because almost everywhere Arnold's attention is centered on the contemporary situation. What is wrong with Victorian life?—and what can be done about it?

Perhaps his basic answer to these questions appears in the brilliant essay, "The Function of Criticism at the Present Time," which introduced the *Essays in Criticism* of 1865. What, he asks, is "at present the bane of criticism in this country? It is that practical considerations cling to it and stifle it. . . . Our organs of criticism [the reviews] are organs of men and parties having practical ends to serve, and with them those practical ends are the first thing and the play of mind second." The *Edinburgh Review* serves the Whigs, the *Quarterly* the Tories, etc. This is because the Englishman sets such high value on what is political and practical, so much indeed that he comes to dislike and neglect even "ideas as such, and . . . the whole life of intelligence; practice is everything, a free play of the mind is nothing." Thus, Arnold's attack is extended from the bane of

criticism to antiintellectualism in general.[1] What is needed is the disinterested love of speculation on all subjects, for its own sake. Criticism, real criticism, is essentially an exercise of this faculty, but to a particular end: "Its business is . . . simply to know the best that is known and thought in the world, and by in its turn making this known, to create a current of true and fresh ideas."

To approach such an achievement, the critic must possess a wide range of knowledge—theology, philosophy, history, art, scholarship—drawn from "Greek, Roman, and Eastern antiquity" and from at least one great literature, in the broad sense, besides his own. He must know, as we should say today, the "great books" from the Greeks to the present; and he must be alive to the world around him. From this background he can endeavor "to see the object as in itself it really is," or, as Arnold also says, "to see things as they really are"—that is in their ultimate nature and truth—and thus "to establish a new order of ideas, if not absolutely true, yet true by comparison with that which it displaces; to make the best ideas prevail." The value of such a criticism goes beyond the judgment of books as such. "By making the mind dwell upon what is excellent in itself," it keeps men from self-satisfaction and leads them toward perfection.

The culture of *Culture and Anarchy* (1869) evolved from Arnold's conception of criticism. Observing in the preface to the first edition that "a notion of something bookish, pedantic, and futile has got itself more or less connected with the word culture," Arnold gives his own, very different conception:

The whole scope of the essay is to recommend culture as the great help out of our present difficulties; culture being a pursuit of our total perfection by means of getting to know, on all the matters which most concern us, the best which has been thought and said in the world; and through this knowledge, turning a stream of fresh and free thought upon our stock notions and habits, which we now follow staunchly but mechanically. . . .

A moment later he emphasizes the fact that "this inward operation is the very life and essence of culture," so that the character of perfection as culture sees it is "not a having and a resting, but a growing and a becoming."

The term "total perfection," however, refers to more than that; it includes all that culture con-

---

1 Antiintellectualism is discussed at length in chapter 5 of Walter E. Houghton's *Victorian Frame of Mind*.

ceives to be the perfection of man and society. Later in the Preface, Arnold explains:

Culture, which is the study of perfection, leads us, as we in the following pages have shown, to conceive of true human perfection as a harmonious perfection, developing all sides of our humanity, and as a general perfection, developing all parts of our society. . . . All which, in what follows, is said about Hebraism and Hellenism, has for its main result to show how our Puritans, ancient and modern . . . have developed one side of their humanity at the expense of all others, and have become incomplete and mutilated men in consequence.

They have developed the moral side of human nature, "the obligation of duty, self-control, and work," but only at the expense of a rounded development. In this way Arnold's book becomes an analysis of what is wrong with the Victorian character and what may be done about it—here its one-sided moralism to be mended by the cultivation of a full humanity through the addition of "beauty and intelligence," or, in a phrase of Swift's, "sweetness and light." Indeed sweetness and light are so important, and the lack of them so damaging, that their pursuit is often called the pursuit of perfection, when strictly speaking the latter is the pursuit of the complete man, including the moral will. They are so important that they became the title of chapter I, which is concerned with culture and its implications. In a similar way, the harmonious development of character may be called culture when, in fact, it is an ideal *conceived* by culture.

The opening pages of the book, reminiscent of "The Function of Criticism," are difficult and misleading. Instead of defining culture, Arnold emphasizes two grounds or desires or origins of it. Starting from curiosity, he finds it can be "a desire after the things of the mind simply for their own sakes and for the pleasure of seeing things as they are" [seeing them in their ultimate nature and truth through the study of the best that has been known and said] and so becoming a more intelligent being.

But this view is essentially self-centered, as paragraph 6 makes clear. There is another view "in which all the love of our neighbors, the impulses toward action, help, and beneficence, the desire for removing human error, clearing human confusion, and diminishing human misery, the noble aspiration to leave the world better and happier than we found it," in which all of these things come in as "the main and pre-eminent" grounds of culture. "Culture is then properly described, not as having its origin in curiosity, but as having its origin in the love of [moral and social] perfection; it is *a study of perfection*."

It moves not only by the passion for knowledge, but primarily by the passion for doing good. And "this culture is more interesting and more far-reaching than the other."

But in the summary statement that follows, there is only one culture with two aims or endeavors: "to see things as they are, to draw towards a knowledge of the universal order which seems intended and aimed at in the world . . ." and "to make it [the first endeavor] *prevail*." Plainly the purpose of culture, as of criticism, is the pursuit of intelligence and the desire to get *its* wisdom adopted.

If there is any doubt of this, one should remember that everywhere else Arnold speaks, not of this or that culture, but of culture, "with its disinterested pursuit of perfection, culture, simply trying to see things as they are, in order to seize on the best and to make it prevail"; that nothing more is ever said about alleviating human misery or leaving the world a better place (indeed, the ignoring of suffering has been a common criticism of the book); and that the chapter ends by saying that culture seeks "to make the best that has been thought and known in the world current everywhere; to make all men live in an atmosphere of sweetness and light, where they may use ideas, as it uses them itself freely—nourished, and not bound by them." This is the *social idea;* and the men of culture are the true apostles—of charity? of loving one's neighbor? of the religion of humanity?—no, "of equality." For they possess not only the "best knowledge, the best ideas of the time" but also "a passion for diffusing, for making them prevail," everywhere and in all classes.

If one now rereads the opening paragraph of "Sweetness and Light" and realizes the attacks that were being made on culture as motivated by "mere exclusiveness and vanity," mere personal pride, he can understand why Arnold replied with a misleading emphasis on moral objectives: it was inspired more by polemics than clarity.

The inevitable tension between culture and religion over the clashing ideals of human nature perfect on all sides and human nature perfect on the moral side emerges in chapter I and is then expanded and developed in chapter IV, "Hebraism and Hellenism."

TEXTS: C. B. Tinker and H. F. Lowry have edited the definitive text of the *Poetical Works* (1950), but reference should be made to *The Poems of Matthew Arnold,* ed. Kenneth Allott (1965). The *Complete Prose Works,* ed. H. R. Super, began to appear in 1960 and will soon be completed. An expurgated selection of the *Letters* was brought out by G.W.E. Russell (2 vols., 1895; 2nd ed., 1901); but more important for the poetry is *The Letters of Matthew Arnold to Arthur Hugh Clough*, ed. H. F. Lowry (1932). The best general study of Arnold's life and thought is by Lionel Trilling (1939). *The Poetry of Matthew Arnold: A Commentary*, by C. B. Tinker and H. F. Lowry (1940), is a handbook that provides valuable information on sources and compositional history. Kenneth Allott's *Matthew Arnold* (1955) is a useful essay with a bibliography. On Arnold's prose style, see the chapter in John Holloway's *The Victorian Sage* (1953). Recent critical studies of the poetry and poetics are A. Dwight Culler's *Imaginative Reason: The Poetry of Matthew Arnold* (1966); and G. Robert Stange's *Matthew Arnold: The Poet as Humanist* (1967).

Quiet Work

One lesson, Nature, let me learn of thee,
One lesson which in every wind is blown,
One lesson of two duties kept at one
Though the loud world proclaim their enmity—

Of toil unsevered from tranquillity!   5
Of labor, that in lasting fruit outgrows
Far noisier schemes, accomplished in repose,
Too great for haste, too high for rivalry!

Yes, while on earth a thousand discords ring,
Man's fitful uproar mingling with his toil,   10
Still do thy sleepless ministers move on,

Their glorious tasks in silence perfecting;
Still working, blaming still our vain turmoil,
Laborers that shall not fail, when man is gone.

To a Friend[1]

Who prop, thou ask'st, in these bad days, my
      mind?—
He much, the old man,[2] who, clearest-souled of
      men,
Saw The Wide Prospect,[3] and the Asian Fen,[4]
And Tmolus hill, and Smyrna bay,[5] though blind.

---

1 Probably Clough.
2 Homer.
3 Arnold explains that this phrase is a literal translation of the Greek word Europe, and suggests that it described the appearance of the European coast as seen by the Greeks from Asia Minor.
4 "The name Asia, again, comes, it has been thought, from the muddy fens of the rivers of Asia Minor." (Arnold)
5 A mountain and a seaport in Asia Minor.

Much he,[6] whose friendship I not long since won,   5
That halting slave, who in Nicopolis
Taught Arrian, when Vespasian's brutal son
Cleared Rome of what most shamed him.[7] But be
      his[8]

My special thanks, whose even-balanced soul,
From first youth tested up to extreme old age,   10
Business could not make dull, nor passion wild;

Who saw life steadily, and saw it whole;[9]
The mellow glory of the Attic stage,
Singer of sweet Colonus,[10] and its child.[11]

Shakespeare

Others abide our question. Thou art free.
We ask and ask—Thou smilest and art still,
Out-topping knowledge. For the loftiest hill,
Who to the stars uncrowns his majesty,

Planting his steadfast footsteps in the sea,   5
Making the heaven of heavens his dwelling-place,
Spares but the cloudy border of his base
To the foiled searching of mortality;

And thou, who didst the stars and sunbeams
      know,
Self-schooled, self-scanned, self-honored, self-   10
      secure,
Didst tread on earth unguessed at.—Better so!

All pains the immortal spirit must endure,
All weakness which impairs, all griefs which bow,
Find their sole speech in that victorious brow.

In Harmony with Nature

To a Preacher

"In harmony with Nature?" Restless fool,
Who with such heat dost preach what were to
      thee,

---

6 Epictetus, the Stoic philosopher (60?–140?).
7 Who taught Arrian, the Greek historian, in Nicopolis in Greece after the Emperor Domitian, shamed by philosophy, drove Epictetus out of Rome.   8 Sophocles.
9 As a whole, coherently, not in fragments.
10 In his *Oedipus at Colonus*.
11 He was born at Colonus near Athens.

When true, the last impossibility—
To be like Nature strong, like Nature cool!

Know, man hath all which Nature hath, but 5
    more,
And in that *more* lie all his hopes of good.
Nature is cruel, man is sick of blood;
Nature is stubborn, man would fain adore;

Nature is fickle, man hath need of rest;
Nature forgives no debt, and fears no grave; 10
Man would be mild, and with safe conscience
    blest.

Man must begin, know this, where Nature ends;
Nature and man can never be fast friends.
Fool, if thou canst not pass her, rest her slave!

The Forsaken Merman

Come, dear children, let us away;
Down and away below!
Now my brothers call from the bay,
Now the great winds shoreward blow,
Now the salt tides seaward flow; 5
Now the wild white horses play,
Champ and chafe and toss in the spray.
Children dear, let us away!
This way, this way!

Call her once before you go— 10
Call once yet!
In a voice that she will know:
"Margaret! Margaret!"
Children's voices should be dear
(Call once more) to a mother's ear; 15
Children's voices, wild with pain—
Surely she will come again!
Call her once and come away;
This way, this way!
"Mother dear, we cannot stay! 20
The wild white horses foam and fret."
Margaret! Margaret!

Come, dear children, come away down;
Call no more!
One last look at the white-walled town, 25
And the little gray church on the windy shore,
Then come down!
She will not come though you call all day;
Come away, come away!

Children dear, was it yesterday 30
We heard the sweet bells over the bay?
In the caverns where we lay,
Through the surf and through the swell,
The far-off sound of a silver bell?
Sand-strewn caverns, cool and deep, 35
Where the winds are all asleep;
Where the spent lights quiver and gleam,
Where the salt weed sways in the stream,
Where the sea-beasts, ranged all round,
Feed in the ooze of their pasture-ground; 40
Where the sea-snakes coil and twine,
Dry their mail and bask in the brine;
Where great whales come sailing by,
Sail and sail, with unshut eye,
Round the world for ever and aye? 45
When did music come this way?
Children dear, was it yesterday?

Children dear, was it yesterday
(Call yet once) that she went away?
Once she sate with you and me, 50
On a red gold throne in the heart of the sea,
And the youngest sate on her knee.
She combed its bright hair, and she tended it
    well,
When down swung the sound of a far-off bell.
She sighed, she looked up through the clear green 55
    sea;
She said: "I must go, for my kinsfolk pray
In the little gray church on the shore to-day.
'Twill be Easter-time in the world—ah me!
And I lose my poor soul, Merman! here with
    thee."
I said: "Go up, dear heart, through the waves; 60
Say thy prayer, and come back to the kind sea-
    caves."
She smiled, she went up through the surf in the
    bay.
Children dear, was it yesterday?

    Children dear, were we long alone?
"The sea grows stormy, the little ones moan; 65
Long prayers," I said, "in the world they say;
Come!" I said; and we rose through the surf in
    the bay.
We went up the beach, by the sandy down
Where the sea-stocks bloom, to the white-walled
    town;
Through the narrow paved streets, where all was 70
    still,
To the little gray church on the windy hill.

From the church came a murmur of folk at their
    prayers,
But we stood without in the cold blowing airs.
We climbed on the graves, on the stones worn
    with rains,
And we gazed up the aisle through the small   75
    leaded panes.
She sate by the pillar; we saw her clear:
"Margaret, hist! come quick, we are here!
Dear heart," I said, "we are long alone;
The sea grows stormy, the little ones moan."
But, ah, she gave me never a look,   80
For her eyes were sealed to the holy book!
Loud prays the priest; shut stands the door.
Come away, children, call no more!
Come away, come down, call no more!

    Down, down, down!   85
Down to the depths of the sea!
She sits at her wheel in the humming town,
Singing most joyfully.
Hark what she sings: "O joy, O joy,
For the humming street, and the child with its   90
    toy!
For the priest, and the bell,[1] and the holy well;[2]
For the wheel where I spun,
And the blessed light of the sun!"
And so she sings her fill,
Singing most joyfully,   95
Till the spindle drops from her hand,
And the whizzing wheel stands still.
She steals to the window, and looks at the sand,
And over the sand at the sea;
And her eyes are set in a stare;   100
And anon there breaks a sigh,
And anon there drops a tear,
From a sorrow-clouded eye,
And a heart sorrow-laden,
A long, long sigh;   105
For the cold strange eyes of a little Mermaiden
And the gleam of her golden hair.

    Come away, away children;
Come children, come down!
The hoarse wind blows coldly;
Lights shine in the town.   110
She will start from her slumber
When gusts shake the door;
She will hear the winds howling,
Will hear the waves roar.   115
We shall see, while above us
The waves roar and whirl,
A ceiling of amber,
A pavement of pearl.
Singing: "Here came a mortal,   120
But faithless was she!
And alone dwell for ever
The kings of the sea."

But, children, at midnight,
When soft the winds blow,   125
When clear falls the moonlight,
When spring-tides are low;
When sweet airs come seaward
From heaths starred with broom,
And high rocks throw mildly   130
On the blanched sands a gloom;
Up the still, glistening beaches,
Up the creeks we will hie,
Over banks of bright seaweed
The ebb-tide leaves dry.   135
We will gaze, from the sand-hills,
At the white, sleeping town;
At the church on the hill-side—
And then come back down.
Singing: "There dwells a loved one,   140
But cruel is she!
She left lonely for ever
The kings of the sea."[3]

Memorial Verses

April, 1850

Goethe in Weimar sleeps, and Greece,
Long since, saw Byron's struggle cease.[1]
But one such death remained to come;

---

[1] The bell that is rung at the consecration of the bread
and the wine in the Mass.
[2] The font where holy water is kept.

[3] Is this poem an allegory of Protestantism and the disciplined life of work (in plain whites and grays) vs.
paganism and the sensuous life of nature (in reds and
golds)? If it is, it is also a supernatural poem on Coleridge's formula (see his *Biographia Literaria*), where just
enough reality is injected into a world of faery fantasy to
procure our "willing suspension of disbelief." For the
reality, cf. the two poems to Marguerite.

[1] Goethe died at Weimar in 1832; Byron in Greece in
1824.

The last poetic voice is dumb—
We stand today by Wordsworth's tomb.   5

When Byron's eyes were shut in death,
We bowed our head and held our breath.
He taught us little; but our soul
Had *felt* him like the thunder's roll.
With shivering heart the strife we saw   10
Of passion with eternal law;
And yet with reverential awe
We watched the fount of fiery life
Which served for that Titanic strife.

   When Goethe's death was told, we said: 15
Sunk, then, is Europe's sagest head.
Physician of the iron age,[2]
Goethe has done his pilgrimage.
He took the suffering human race,
He read each wound, each weakness clear;   20
And struck his fingers on the place,
And said: *Thou ailest here, and here!*
He looked on Europe's dying hour
Of fitful dream and feverish power;
His eye plunged down the weltering strife,   25
The turmoil of expiring life—
He said: *The end is everywhere,*
Art still has truth, take refuge there!
And he was happy, if to know
Causes of things, and far below   30
His feet to see the lurid flow
Of terror, and insane distress,
And headlong fate, be happiness.[3]

And Wordsworth!—Ah, pale ghosts, rejoice!
For never has such soothing voice   35
Been to your shadowy world conveyed,
Since erst, at morn, some wandering shade
Heard the clear song of Orpheus come

Through Hades, and the mournful gloom.[4]
Wordsworth has gone from us—and ye,   40
Ah, may ye feel his voice as we!
He too upon a wintry clime
Had fallen—on this iron time
Of doubts, disputes, distractions, fears.
He found us when the age had bound   45
Our souls in its benumbing round;
He spoke, and loosed our heart in tears.
He laid us as we lay at birth
On the cool flowery lap of earth,
Smiles broke from us and we had ease;   50
The hills were round us, and the breeze
Went o'er the sun-lit fields again;
Our foreheads felt the wind and rain.
Our youth returned; for there was shed
On spirits that had long been dead,   55
Spirits dried up and closely furled,
The freshness of the early world.[5]

Ah! since dark days still bring to light
Man's prudence and man's fiery might,
Time may restore us in his course   60
Goethe's sage mind and Byron's force;
But where will Europe's latter hour
Again find Wordsworth's healing power?
Others will teach us how to dare,
And against fear our breast to steel;   65
Others will strengthen us to bear—
But who, ah! who, will make us feel?
The cloud of mortal destiny,
Others will front it fearlessly—
But who, like him, will put it by?   70

Keep fresh the grass upon his grave
O Rotha,[6] with thy living wave!
Sing him thy best! for few or none
Hears thy voice right, now he is gone.

Self-Dependence

Weary of myself, and sick of asking
What I am, and what I ought to be,

---

[2] The age of war and revolution, political and intellectual (1789–1832). Cf. the further definition of iron time in lines 43–44. Both Arnold and Carlyle viewed Goethe as the perfect type of the artist as prophet (hence, "physician").

[3] These lines are a paraphrase of Vergil (*Georgics*, II, 490 ff.). Arnold expects the reader not only to recognize them as such but to remember the context, where the poet "who hath availed to know the causes of things, and hath laid all fears and immitigable Fate and the roar of hungry Acheron under his feet" is contrasted with the poet who turns away from the problems and discords of society to live content by "stream and woodland" (Mackail's translation). Since the latter is clearly the poet (Wordsworth) of the next verse paragraph, the lines carry an extra suggestion which makes them transitional.

[4] On the occasion when Orpheus sang for Pluto, god of the underworld, in return for which Pluto agreed to give him back his wife, Eurydice.

[5] Cf. "The Scholar-Gipsy," where the "iron time" is described in detail (including its benumbing effect, line 146), and where the beauty of the Oxford countryside is presented as a refuge and a source of refreshment.

[6] Stream near Grasmere, where Wordsworth was buried.

At this vessel's prow I stand, which bears me
Forwards, forwards, o'er the starlit sea.

And a look of passionate desire 5
O'er the sea and to the stars I send:
"Ye who from my childhood up have calmed me,
Calm me, ah, compose me to the end!

"Ah, once more," I cried, "ye stars, ye waters,
On my heart your mighty charm renew; 10
Still, still let me, as I gaze upon you,
Feel my soul becoming vast like you!"

From the intense, clear, star-sown vault of heaven,
Over the lit sea's unquiet way,
In the rustling night-air came the answer: 15
"Wouldst thou *be* as these are? *Live* as they.[1]

"Unaffrighted by the silence round them,
Undistracted by the sights they see,
These demand not that the things without them
Yield them love, amusement, sympathy. 20

"And with joy the stars perform their shining,
And the sea its long moon-silvered roll;
For self-poised they live, nor pine with noting
All the fever of some differing soul.

"Bounded by themselves, and unregardful 25
In what state God's other works may be,
In their own tasks all their powers pouring,
These attain the mighty life you see."

O air-born voice! long since, severely clear,
A cry like thine in mine own heart I hear: 30
"Resolve to be thyself; and know that he,
Who finds himself, loses his misery!"[2]

A Summer Night

In the deserted, moon-blanched street,
How lonely rings the echo of my feet!
Those windows, which I gaze at, frown,
Silent and white, unopening down,

Repellent as the world;—but see, 5
A break between the housetops shows
The moon! and, lost behind her, fading dim
Into the dewy dark obscurity
Down at the far horizon's rim,
Doth a whole tract of heaven disclose! 10

And to my mind the thought
Is on a sudden brought
Of a past night, and a far different scene.
Headlands stood out into the moon-lit deep
As clearly as at noon; 15

The spring-tide's brimming flow
Heaved dazzlingly between;
Houses, with long white sweep,
Girdled the glistening bay;
Behind, through the soft air, 20
The blue haze-cradled mountains spread away,
That night was far more fair—
But the same restless pacings to and fro,
And the same vainly throbbing heart was there,
And the same bright, calm moon. 25

And the calm moonlight seems to say:
Hast thou then still the old unquiet breast,
That neither deadens into rest,
Nor ever feels the fiery glow
That whirls the spirit from itself away, 30
But fluctuates to and fro,
Never by passion quite possessed
And never quite benumbed by the world's sway?—
And I, know not if to pray
Still to be what I am, or yield and be 35
Like all the other men I see.

For most men in a brazen prison live,
Where, in the sun's hot eye,
With heads bent o'er their toil, they languidly
Their lives to some unmeaning taskwork give, 40
Dreaming of nought beyond their prison-wall.
And as, year after year,
Fresh products of their barren labor fall
From their tired hands, and rest
Never yet comes more near, 45
Gloom settles slowly down over their breast;
And while they try to stem
The waves of mournful thought by which they
    are prest,
Death in their prison reaches them,
Unfreed, having seen nothing, still unblest. 50

---

[1] This line is a criticism of Arnold's previous attitude (in lines 9–12), where his appreciation of the stars was merely aesthetic, for their sublime beauty alone, without regard to their moral lesson of how to live.
[2] By "finding himself" Arnold means not only finding one's true nature, but also (cf. the stars) living a life which that nature is fitted for—in Stoic terms, "living according to nature."

And the rest, a few,
Escape their prison and depart
On the wide ocean of life anew.
There the freed prisoner, where'er his heart
Listeth, will sail; 55
Nor does he know how there prevail,
Despotic on that sea,
Trade-winds which cross it from eternity.[1]
Awhile he holds some false way, undebarred
By thwarting signs, and braves 60
The freshening wind and blackening waves.
And then the tempest strikes him; and between
The lightning-bursts is seen
Only a driving wreck,
And the pale master on his spar-strewn deck 65
With anguished face and flying hair
Grasping the rudder hard,
Still bent to make some port he knows not where,
Still standing for some false, impossible shore.
And sterner comes the roar 70
Of sea and wind, and through the deepening
  gloom
Fainter and fainter wreck and helmsman loom,
And he too disappears, and comes no more.

Is there no life, but these alone?
Madman or slave, must man be one?[2] 75

Plainness and clearness without shadow of stain!
Clearness divine!
Ye heavens, whose pure dark regions have no sign
Of languor, though so calm, and, though so great,
Are yet untroubled and unpassionate; 80
Who, though so noble, share in the world's toil,
And, though so tasked, keep free from dust and
  soil![3]
I will not say that your mild deeps retain
A tinge, it may be, of their silent pain
Who have longed deeply once, and longed in 85
  vain[4]—
But I will rather say that you remain
A world above man's head, to let him see
How boundless might his soul's horizons be,
How vast, yet of what clear transparency!
How it were good to abide there, and breathe 90
  free;

---

[1] Moral laws which he ignores at his peril.
[2] The slave of lines 37–50 or the madman of lines 51–73.
[3] Cf. "Quiet Work."
[4] This is an aside. What Arnold wants to say follows in lines 86–92. But he feels, from his own experience, that the stoical attitude of the stars is partly a refuge from disappointed hopes.

How fair a lot to fill
Is left to each man still!

The Buried Life

Light flows our war of mocking words, and yet,
Behold, with tears mine eyes are wet!
I feel a nameless sadness o'er me roll.
Yes, yes, we know that we can jest,
We know, we know that we can smile! 5
But there's a something in this breast,
To which thy light words bring no rest,
And thy gay smiles no anodyne.
Give me thy hand, and hush awhile,
And turn those limpid eyes on mine, 10
And let me read there, love! thy inmost soul.

Alas! is even love too weak
To unlock the heart, and let it speak?
Are even lovers powerless to reveal
To one another what indeed they feel? 15
I knew the mass of men concealed
Their thoughts, for fear that if revealed
They would by other men be met
With blank indifference, or with blame reproved;
I knew they lived and moved 20
Tricked in disguises, alien to the rest
Of men, and alien to themselves—and yet
The same heart beats in every human breast!

But we, my love!—doth a like spell benumb
Our hearts, our voices?—must we too be dumb? 25

Ah! well for us, if even we,
Even for a moment, can get free
Our heart, and have our lips unchained;
For that which seals them hath been deep-
  ordained!

Fate, which foresaw 30
How frivolous a baby man would be—
By what distractions he would be possessed,
How he would pour himself in every strife,
And well-nigh change his own identity—
That it might keep from his capricious play 35
His genuine self, and force him to obey
Even in his own despite his being's law,
Bade through the deep recesses of our breast
The unregarded river of our life
Pursue with indiscernible flow its way; 40

And that we should not see
The buried stream, and seem to be
Eddying at large in blind uncertainty,
Though driving on with it eternally.

But often, in the world's most crowded streets,   45
But often, in the din of strife,
There rises an unspeakable desire
After the knowledge of our buried life;
A thirst to spend our fire and restless force
In tracking out our true, original course;   50
A longing to inquire
Into the mystery of this heart which beats
So wild, so deep in us—to know
Whence our lives come and where they go.
And many a man in his own breast then delves,   55
But deep enough, alas! none ever mines.
And we have been on many thousand lines,
And we have shown, on each, spirit and power;
But hardly have we, for one little hour,
Been on our own line, have we been ourselves[1]—   60
Hardly had skill to utter one of all
The nameless feelings that course through our
     breast,
But they course on for ever unexpressed.
And long we try in vain to speak and act
Our hidden self, and what we say and do   65
Is eloquent, is well—but 'tis not true![2]
And then we will no more be racked
With inward striving, and demand
Of all the thousand nothings of the hour
Their stupefying power;[3]   70
Ah yes, and they benumb us at our call!
Yet still, from time to time, vague and forlorn,
From the soul's subterranean depth upborne
As from an infinitely distant land,
Come airs, and floating echoes, and convey   75
A melancholy into all our day.

Only—but this is rare—
When a belovèd hand is laid in ours,
When, jaded with the rush and glare
Of the interminable hours,   80
Our eyes can in another's eyes read clear,
When our world-deafened ear

Is by the tones of a loved voice caressed—
A bolt is shot back somewhere in our breast,
And a lost pulse of feeling stirs again.   85
The eye sinks inward, and the heart lies plain,
And what we mean, we say, and what we would,
     we know.
A man becomes aware of his life's flow,
And hears its winding murmur; and he sees
The meadows where it glides, the sun, the breeze.   90

And there arrives a lull in the hot race
Wherein he doth for ever chase
That flying and elusive shadow, rest.
An air of coolness plays upon his face,
And an unwonted calm pervades his breast.   95
And then he thinks he knows
The hills where his life rose,
And the sea where it goes.

Morality

We cannot kindle when we will
The fire which in the heart resides;
The spirit bloweth and is still,
In mystery our soul abides.
     But tasks in hours of insight willed,   5
     Can be through hours of gloom fulfilled.

With aching hands and bleeding feet
We dig and heap, lay stone on stone;
We bear the burden and the heat
Of the long day, and wish 'twere done.   10
     Not till the hours of light return,
     All we have built do we discern.

Then, when the clouds are off the soul,
When thou dost bask in Nature's eye,
Ask, how she viewed thy self-control,   15
Thy struggling, tasked morality—
     Nature, whose free, light, cheerful air,
     Oft made thee, in thy gloom, despair.

And she, whose censure thou dost dread,
Whose eyes thou wast afraid to seek,   20
See, on her face a glow is spread,
A strong emotion on her cheek!
     "Ah, child," she cries, "that strife divine,
     Whence was it, for it is not mine?

---

[1] Cf. the last lines of "Self-Dependence."
[2] The implication seems to be that if we could know and follow the hidden self, we could live more fully because then the subconscious drive referred to in lines 30–44 and the conscious will would be synchronized and the personality integrated.
[3] Their power to deaden or numb the pain of "inward striving."

"There is no effort on *my* brow—
I do not strive, I do not weep;
I rush with the swift spheres and glow
In joy, and when I will, I sleep.[1]
    Yet that severe, that earnest air,
    I saw, I felt it once—but where?

"I knew not yet the gauge of time,
Nor wore the manacles of space;
I felt it in some other clime,
I saw it in some other place.
    'Twas when the heavenly house I trod,
    And lay upon the breast of God."[2]

Sohrab and Rustum

An Episode

And the first gray of morning filled the east,
And the fog rose out of the Oxus stream.[1]
But all the Tartar camp along the stream
Was hushed, and still the men were plunged in
    sleep;
Sohrab alone, he slept not;[2] all night long   5
He had lain wakeful, tossing on his bed;
But when the gray dawn stole into his tent,
He rose, and clad himself, and girt his sword,
And took his horseman's cloak, and left his tent,
And went abroad into the cold wet fog,   10
Through the dim camp to Peran-Wisa's[3] tent.
    Through the black Tartar tents he passed,
      which stood
Clustering like bee-hives on the low flat strand
Of Oxus, where the summer-floods o'erflow
When the sun melts the snows in high Pamere;[4]   15
Through the black tents he passed, o'er that low
    strand,

And to a hillock came, a little back   25
From the stream's brink—the spot where first a
    boat,
Crossing the stream in summer, scrapes the land.
The men of former times had crowned the top   20
With a clay fort; but that was fall'n, and now
The Tartars built there Peran-Wisa's tent,
A dome of laths, and o'er it felts were spread.
And Sohrab came there, and went in, and stood
Upon the thick piled[5] carpets in the tent,   25
And found the old man sleeping on his bed
Of rugs and felts, and near him lay his arms.
And Peran-Wisa heard him, though the step
Was dulled; for he slept light, an old man's sleep;
And he rose quickly on one arm, and said:—   30
    "Who art thou? for it is not yet clear dawn.
Speak! is there news, or any night alarm?"
    But Sohrab came to the bedside, and said:—
"Thou know'st me, Peran-Wisa! it is I.
The sun is not yet risen, and the foe   35
Sleep; but I sleep not; all night long I lie
Tossing and wakeful, and I come to thee.
For so did King Afrasiab bid me seek
Thy counsel, and to heed thee as thy son,
In Samarcand, before the army marched;   40
And I will tell thee what my heart desires.
Thou know'st if, since from Ader-baijan[6] first
I came among the Tartars and bore arms,
I have still served Afrasiab well, and shown,
At my boy's years, the courage of a man.   45
This too thou know'st, that while I still bear on
The conquering Tartar ensigns through the
    world,
And beat the Persians back on very field,
I seek one man, one man, and one alone—
Rustum, my father; who I hoped should greet,   50
Should one day greet, upon some well-fought
    field,
His not unworthy, not inglorious son.
So I long hoped, but him I never find.
Come then, hear now, and grant me what I ask.
Let the two armies rest to-day; but I   55
Will challenge forth the bravest Persian lords
To meet me, man to man; if I prevail,
Rustum will surely hear it; if I fall—
Old man, the dead need no one, claim no kin.
Dim is the rumor of a common fight,   60

---

[1] Nature symbolizes a nonmoral life of rich and varied experience, free from the struggle to discipline the moral will to a life of concentrated work. (Cf. the life of the poet which Arnold once set out to live and his life as an inspector of schools, fulfilled in many hours of gloom, though the latter came later, after the poem was written.)
[2] Before the creation (hence lines 31-32). Nature as well as Morality is divine in origin, but the moral life is the higher, closer to God. The poem brings out the cost involved (both the joy lost, and the pain endured) of choosing the latter.

[1] A great river in central Asia.
[2] Although a Persian by birth, Sohrab has taken service under Afrasiab, king of the Tartars.
[3] The general of the Tartar army.
[4] Plateau in central Asia.

---

[5] Heavy-napped.
[6] Province in northwestern Persia where Sohrab's mother lived (cf. line 590).

Where host meets host, and many names are
    sunk;
But of a single combat fame speaks clear."
    He spoke; and Peran-Wisa took the hand
Of the young man in his, and sighed, and said:—
    "O Sohrab, an unquiet heart is thine!   65
Canst thou not rest among the Tartar chiefs,
And share the battle's common chance with us
Who love thee, but must press for ever first,
In single fight incurring single risk,
To find a father thou hast never seen?   70
That were far best, my son, to stay with us
Unmurmuring; in our tents, while it is war,
And when 'tis truce, then in Afrasiab's towns.
But, if this one desire indeed rules all,
To seek out Rustum—seek him not through   75
    fight!
Seek him in peace, and carry to his arms,
O Sohrab, carry an unwounded son!
But far hence seek him, for he is not here.
For now it is not as when I was young,
When Rustum was in front of every fray;   80
But now he keeps apart, and sits at home,
In Seistan,[7] with Zal, his father old.
Whether that his own mighty strength at last
Feels the abhorred approaches of old age,
Or in some quarrel with the Persian King.   85
There go!—Thou wilt not? Yet my heart fore-
    bodes
Danger or death awaits thee on this field.
Fain would I know thee safe and well, though
    lost
To us; fain therefore send thee hence, in peace
To seek thy father, not seek single fights   90
In vain:—but who can keep the lion's cub
From ravening, and who govern Rustum's son?
Go, I will grant thee what thy heart desires."
    So said he, and dropped Sohrab's hand, and
    left
His bed, and the warm rugs whereon he lay;   95
And o'er his chilly limbs his woollen coat
He passed, and tied his sandals on his feet,
And threw a white cloak round him, and he took
In his right hand a ruler's staff, no sword;
And on his head he set his sheep-skin cap,   100
Black, glossy, curled, the fleece of Kara-Kul;[8]
And raised the curtain of his tent, and called
His herald to his side, and went abroad.
    The sun by this had risen, and cleared the fog

From the broad Oxus and the glittering sands.   105
And from their tents the Tartar horsemen filed
Into the open plain; so Haman bade—
Haman, who next to Peran-Wisa ruled
The host, and still was in his lusty prime.
From their black tents, long files of horse, they   110
    streamed;
As when some gray November morn the files,
In marching order spread, of long-necked cranes
Stream over Casbin and the southern slopes
Of Elburz, from the Aralian estuaries,
Or some frore[9] Caspian reed-bed, southward   115
    bound
For the warm Persian sea-board—so they
    streamed.
The Tartars of the Oxus, the King's guard,
First, with black sheep-skin caps and with long
    spears;
Large men, large steeds; who from Bokhara come
And Khiva, and ferment the milk of mares.   120
Next, the more temperate Toorkmuns of the
    south,
The Tukas, and the lances of Salore,
And those from Attruck and the Caspian sands;
Light men and on light steeds, who only drink
The acrid milk of camels, and their wells.   125
And then a swarm of wandering horse, who came
From far, and a more doubtful service owned;
The Tartars of Ferghana, from the banks
Of the Jaxartes, men with scanty beards
And close-set skull caps; and those wilder hordes   130
Who roam o'er Kipchak and the northern waste,
Kalmucks and unkempt Kuzzaks, tribes who stray
Nearest the Pole, and wandering Kirghizzes,
Who come on shaggy ponies from Pamere;
These all filed out from camp into the plain.   135
And on the other side the Persians formed;—
First a light cloud of horse, Tartars they seemed,
The Ilyats of Khorassan; and behind,
The royal troops of Persia, horse and foot,
Marshalled battalions bright in burnished steel.   140
But Peran-Wisa with his herald came,
Threading the Tartar squadrons to the front,
And with his staff kept back the foremost ranks.
And when Ferood, who led the Persians, saw
That Peran-Wisa kept the Tartars back,   145
He took his spear, and to the front he came,
And checked his ranks, and fixed them where
    they stood.

---

7 Region bordering on eastern Persia.
8 Of karakul sheep, from the province of Bokhara.

9 Frozen.

And the old Tartar came upon the sand
Betwixt the silent hosts, and spake, and said:—
  "Ferood, and ye, Persians and Tartars, hear!   150
Let there be truce between the hosts to-day.
But choose a champion from the Persian lords
To fight our champion Sohrab, man to man."
    As, in the country, on a morn in June,
When the dew glistens on the pearlèd ears,   155
A shiver runs through the deep corn for joy—
So, when they heard what Peran-Wisa said,
A thrill through all the Tartar squadrons ran
Of pride and hope for Sohrab, whom they loved.
    But as a troop of pedlars, from Cabool,   160
Cross underneath the Indian Caucasus,
That vast sky-neighboring mountain of milk
      snow;
Crossing so high, that, as they mount, they pass
Long flocks of travelling birds dead on the snow,
Choked by the air, and scarce can they themselves   165
Slake their parched throats with sugared mul-
      berries—
In single file they move, and stop their breath,
For fear they should dislodge the o'erhanging
      snows—
So the pale Persians held their breath with fear.
    And to Ferood his brother chiefs came up   170
To counsel; Gudurz and Zoarrah came,
And Feraburz, who ruled the Persian host
Second, and was the uncle of the King;
These came and counselled, and then Gudurz
      said:—
    "Ferood, shame bids us take their challenge   175
      up,
Yet champion have we none to match this youth.
He has the wild stag's foot, the lion's heart.
But Rustum came last night; aloof he sits
And sullen, and has pitched his tents apart.
Him will I seek, and carry to his ear   180
The Tartar challenge, and this young man's
      name.
Haply he will forget his wrath, and fight.
Stand forth the while, and take their challenge
      up."
    So spake he; and Ferood stood forth and
      cried:—
"Old man, be it agreed as thou hast said!   185
Let Sohrab arm, and we will find a man."
    He spake: and Peran-Wisa turned, and strode
Back through the opening squadrons to his tent.
But through the anxious Persians Gudurz ran,
And crossed the camp which lay behind, and   190
    reached,
Out on the sands beyond it, Rustum's tents.
Of scarlet cloth they were, and glittering gay,
Just pitched; the high pavilion in the midst
Was Rustum's, and his men lay camped around.
And Gudurz entered Rustum's tent, and found   195
Rustum; his morning meal was done, but still
The table stood before him, charged with food—
A side of roasted sheep, and cakes of bread,
And dark green melons; and there Rustum sate
Listless, and held a falcon on his wrist,   200
And played with it; but Gudurz came and stood
Before him; and he looked, and saw him stand,
And with a cry sprang up and dropped the bird,
And greeted Gudurz with both hands, and said:—
    "Welcome! these eyes could see no better sight.   205
What news? but sit down first, and eat and drink."
    But Gudurz stood in the tent-door, and said:—
"Not now! a time will come to eat and drink,
But not to-day; to-day has other needs.
The armies are drawn out, and stand at gaze;   210
For from the Tartars is a challenge brought
To pick a champion from the Persian lords
To fight their champion—and thou know'st his
      name—
Sohrab men call him, but his birth is hid.
O Rustum, like thy might is this young man's!   215
He has the wild stag's foot, the lion's heart;
And he is young, and Iran's[10] chiefs are old,
Or else too weak; and all eyes turn to thee.
Come down and help us, Rustum, or we lose!"
    He spoke; but Rustum answered with a   220
      smile:—
"Go to! if Iran's chiefs are old, then I
Am older; if the young are weak, the King
Errs strangely; for the King, for Kai Khosroo,
Himself is young, and honors younger men,
And lets the agèd molder to their graves.   225
Rustum he loves no more, but loves the young—
The young may rise at Sohrab's vaunts, not I.
For what care I, though all speak Sohrab's fame?
For would that I myself had such a son,
And not that one slight helpless girl I have—   230
A son so famed, so brave, to send to war,
And I to tarry with the snow-haired Zal,
My father, whom the robber Afghans vex,
And clip his borders short, and drive his herds,
And he has none to guard his weak old age.   235
There would I go, and hang my armor up,

10 Persia's.

And with my great name fence that weak old
    man,
And spend the goodly treasures I have got,
And rest my age, and hear of Sohrab's fame,
And leave to death the hosts of thankless kings,   240
And with these slaughterous hands draw sword
    no more."
    He spoke, and smiled; and Gudurz made
    reply:—
"What then, O Rustum, will men say to this,
When Sohrab dares our bravest forth, and seeks
Thee most of all, and thou, whom most he seeks,   245
Hidest thy face? Take heed lest men should say:
Like some old miser, Rustum hoards his fame,
And shuns to peril it with younger men."
    And, greatly moved, then Rustum made
    reply:—
"O Gudurz, wherefore dost thou say such words?   250
Thou knowest better words than this to say.
What is one more, one less, obscure or famed,
Valiant or craven, young or old, to me?
Are not they mortal, am not I myself?
But who for men of nought would do great deeds?   255
Come, thou shall see how Rustum hoards his
    fame!
But I will fight unknown, and in plain arms;[11]
Let not men say of Rustum, he was matched
In single fight with any mortal man."
    He spoke, and frowned; and Gudurz turned,   260
    and ran
Back quickly through the camp in fear and joy—
Fear at his wrath, but joy that Rustum came.
But Rustum strode to his tent-door, and called
His followers in, and bade them bring his arms,
And clad himself in steel; the arms he chose   265
Were plain, and on his shield was no device,
Only his helm was rich, inlaid with gold,
And, from the fluted spine atop, a plume
Of horsehair waved, a scarlet horsehair plume.
So armed, he issued forth; and Ruksh, his horse,   270
Followed him like a faithful hound at heel—
Ruksh, whose renown was noised through all the
    earth,
The horse, whom Rustum on a foray once
Did in Bokhara by the river find
A colt beneath its dam, and drove him home,   275
And reared him; a bright bay, with lofty crest,
Dight[12] with a saddle-cloth of broidered green

Crusted with gold, and on the ground were
    worked
All beasts of chase, all beasts which hunters know.
So followed, Rustum left his tents, and crossed   280
The camp, and to the Persian host appeared.
And all the Persians knew him, and with shouts
Hailed; but the Tartars knew not who he was.
And dear as the wet diver to the eyes
Of his pale wife who waits and weeps on shore,   285
By sandy Bahrein, in the Persian Gulf,
Plunging all day in the blue waves, at night,
Having made up his tale of precious pearls,
Rejoins her in their hut upon the sands—
So dear to the pale Persians Rustum came.   290
    And Rustum to the Persian front advanced,
And Sohrab armed in Haman's tent, and came.
And as afield the reapers cut a swath
Down through the middle of a rich man's corn,
And on each side are squares of standing corn,   295
And in the midst a stubble, short and bare—
So on each side were squares of men, with spears
Bristling, and in the midst, the open sand.
And Rustum came upon the sand, and cast
His eyes toward the Tartar tents, and saw   300
Sohrab come forth, and eyed him as he came.
    As some rich woman, on a winter's morn,
Eyes through her silken curtains the poor drudge
Who with numb blackened fingers makes her
    fire—
At cock-crow, on a starlit winter's morn,   305
When the frost flowers the whitened window-
    panes—
And wonders how she lives, and what the
    thoughts
Of that poor drudge may be; so Rustum eyed
The unknown adventurous youth, who from afar
Came seeking Rustum, and defying forth   310
All the most valiant chiefs; long he perused
His spirited air, and wondered who he was.
For very young he seemed, tenderly reared;
Like some young cypress, tall, and dark, and
    straight,
Which in a queen's secluded garden throws   315
Its slight dark shadow on the moonlit turf,
By midnight, to a bubbling fountain's sound—
So slender Sohrab seemed, so softly reared.
And a deep pity entered Rustum's soul
As he beheld him coming; and he stood,   320
And beckoned to him with his hand, and said:—
    "O thou young man, the air of Heaven is soft,
And warm, and pleasant; but the grave is cold!

---

11 Without the markings which would reveal his identity.
12 Caparisoned.

Heaven's air is better than the cold dead grave.
Behold me! I am vast, and clad in iron, 325
And tried; and I have stood on many a field
Of blood, and I have fought with many a foe—
Never was that field lost, or that foe saved.
O Sohrab, wherefore wilt thou rush on death?
Be governed! quit the Tartar host, and come 330
To Iran, and be as my son to me,
And fight beneath my banner till I die!
There are no youths in Iran brave as thou."

    So he spake, mildly; Sohrab heard his voice,
The mighty voice of Rustum, and he saw 335
His giant figure planted on the sand,
Sole, like some single tower, which a chief
Has builded on the waste in former years
Against the robbers; and he saw that head,
Streaked with its first gray hairs;—hope filled his 340
    soul,
And he ran forward and embraced his knees,
And clasped his hand within his own, and said:—

    "O, by thy father's head! by thine own soul!
Art thou not Rustum? speak! art thou not he?"

    But Rustum eyed askance the kneeling youth, 345
And turned away, and spake to his own soul:—
    "Ah me, I muse what this young fox may
    mean!
False, wily, boastful, are these Tartar boys.
For if I now confess this thing he asks,
And hide it not, but say: *Rustum is here!* 350
He will not yield indeed, nor quit our foes,
But he will find some pretext not to fight,
And praise my fame, and proffer courteous gifts,
A belt or sword perhaps, and go his way.
And on a feast-tide, in Afrasiab's hall, 355
In Samarcand, he will arise and cry:
'I challenged once, when the two armies camped
Beside the Oxus, all the Persian lords
To cope with me in single fight; but they
Shrank, only Rustum dared; then he and I 360
Changed gifts, and went on equal terms away.'
So will he speak, perhaps, while men applaud;
Then were the chiefs of Iran shamed through
    me."

    And then he turned, and sternly spake
    aloud:—
"Rise! wherefore dost thou vainly question thus 365
Of Rustum? I am here, whom thou hast called
By challenge forth; make good thy vaunt, or
    yield!
Is it with Rustum only thou wouldst fight?
Rash boy, men look on Rustum's face and flee!

For well I know, that did great Rustum stand 370
Before thy face this day, and were revealed,
There would be then no talk of fighting more.
But being what I am, I tell thee this—
Do thou record it in thine inmost soul:
Either thou shalt renounce thy vaunt and yield, 375
Or else thy bones shall strew this sand, till winds
Bleach them, or Oxus with his summer-floods,
Oxus in summer wash them all away."

    He spoke; and Sohrab answered, on his feet:—
"Art thou so fierce? Thou wilt not fright me so! 380
I am no girl, to be made pale by words.
Yet this thou hast said well, did Rustum stand
Here on this field, there were no fighting then.
But Rustum is far hence, and we stand here.
Begin! thou art more vast, more dread than I, 385
And thou art proved, I know, and I am young—
But yet success sways with the breath of Heaven.
And though thou thinkest that thou knowest sure
Thy victory, yet thou canst not surely know.
For we are all, like swimmers in the sea, 390
Poised on the top of a huge wave of fate,
Which hangs uncertain to which side to fall.
And whether it will heave us up to land,
Or whether it will roll us out to sea,
Back out to sea, to the deep waves of death, 395
We know not, and no search will make us know;
Only the event will teach us in its hour."

    He spoke, and Rustum answered not, but
    hurled
His spear; down from the shoulder, down it came,
As on some partridge in the corn a hawk, 400
That long has towered in the airy clouds,
Drops like a plummet; Sohrab saw it come,
And sprang aside, quick as a flash; the spear
Hissed, and went quivering down into the sand,
Which it sent flying wide;—then Sohrab threw 405
In turn, and full struck Rustum's shield; sharp
    rang,
The iron plates rang sharp, but turned the spear.
And Rustum seized his club, which none but he
Could wield; an unlopped trunk it was, and
    huge,
Still rough—like those which men in treeless 410
    plains
To build them boats fish from the flooded rivers,
Hyphasis or Hydaspes, when, high up
By their dark springs, the wind in winter-time
Has made in Himalayan forests wrack,
And strewn the channels with torn boughs—so 415
    huge

The club which Rustum lifted now, and struck
One stroke; but again Sohrab sprang aside,
Lithe as the glancing snake, and the club came
Thundering to earth, and leaped from Rustum's
    hand.
And Rustum followed his own blow, and fell   420
To his knees, and with his fingers clutched the
    sand;
And now might Sohrab have unsheathed his
    sword,
And pierced the mighty Rustum while he lay
Dizzy, and on his knees, and choked with sand;
But he looked on, and smiled, nor bared his   425
    sword,
But courteously drew back, and spoke, and
    said:—
    "Thou strik'st too hard! that club of thine will
      float
Upon the summer-floods, and not my bones.
But rise, and be not wroth! not wroth am I;
No, when I see thee, wrath forsakes my soul.   430
Thou say'st, thou art not Rustum; be it so!
Who art thou then, that canst so touch my soul?
Boy as I am, I have seen battles too—
Have waded foremost in their bloody waves,
And heard their hollow roar of dying men;   435
But never was my heart thus touched before.
Are they from Heaven, these softenings of the
    heart?
O thou old warrior, let us yield to Heaven!
Come, plant we here in earth our angry spears,
And make a truce, and sit upon this sand,   440
And pledge each other in red wine, like friends,
And thou shalt talk to me of Rustum's deeds.
There are enough foes in the Persian host,
Whom I may meet, and strike, and feel no pang;
Champions enough Afrasiab has, whom thou   445
Mayst fight; fight *them,* when they confront thy
    spear!
But oh, let there be peace 'twixt thee and me!"
    He ceased, but while he spake, Rustum had
      risen,
And stood erect, trembling with rage; his club
He left to lie, but had regained his spear,   450
Whose fiery point now in his mailed right-hand
Blazed bright and baleful, like that autumn-star,[13]
The baleful sign of fevers; dust had soiled
His stately crest, and dimmed his glittering arms.
His breast heaved, his lips foamed, and twice his   455
    voice

---

[13] Sirius, the Dog Star.

Was choked with rage; at last these words broke
    way:—
    "Girl! nimble with thy feet, not with thy
      hands!
Curled minion, dancer, coiner of sweet words!
Fight, let me hear thy hateful voice no more!
Thou art not in Afrasiab's gardens now   460
With Tartar girls, with whom thou art wont to
    dance;
But on the Oxus-sands, and in the dance
Of battle, and with me, who make no play
Of war; I fight it out, and hand to hand.
Speak not to me of truce, and pledge, and wine!   465
Remember all thy valor; try thy feints
And cunning! all the pity I had is gone;
Because thou hast shamed me before both the
    hosts
With thy light skipping tricks, and thy girl's
    wiles."
    He spoke, and Sohrab kindled at his taunts,   470
And he too drew his sword; at once they rushed
Together, as two eagles on one prey
Come rushing down together from the clouds,
One from the east, one from the west; their
    shields
Dashed with a clang together, and a din   475
Rose, such as that the sinewy woodcutters
Make often in the forest's heart at morn,
Of hewing axes, crashing trees—such blows
Rustum and Sohrab on each other hailed.
And you would say that sun and stars took part   480
In that unnatural conflict; for a cloud
Grew suddenly in Heaven, and darkened the sun
Over the fighters' heads; and a wind rose
Under their feet, and moaning swept the plain,
And in a sandy whirlwind wrapped the pair.   485
In gloom they twain were wrapped, and they
    alone;
For both the on-looking hosts on either hand
Stood in broad daylight, and the sky was pure,
And the sun sparkled on the Oxus stream.
But in the gloom they fought, with bloodshot   490
    eyes
And laboring breath; first Rustum struck the
    shield
Which Sohrab held stiff out; the steel-spiked
    spear
Rent the tough plates, but failed to reach the
    skin,
And Rustum plucked it back with angry groan.
Then Sohrab with his sword smote Rustum's   495
    helm,

Nor clove its steel quite through; but all the crest
He shore away, and that proud horsehair plume,
Never till now defiled, sank to the dust;
And Rustum bowed his head; but then the gloom
Grew blacker, thunder rumbled in the air,　500
And lightnings rent the cloud; and Ruksh, the
　　horse,
Who stood at hand, uttered a dreadful cry;—
No horse's cry was that, most like the roar
Of some pained desert-lion, who all day
Hath trailed the hunter's javelin in his side,　505
And comes at night to die upon the sand.
The two hosts heard that cry, and quaked for
　　fear,
And Oxus curdled as it crossed his stream.
But Sohrab heard, and quailed not, but rushed
　　on,
And struck again; and again Rustum bowed　510
His head; but this time all the blade, like glass,
Sprang in a thousand shivers on the helm,
And in his hand the hilt remained alone.
Then Rustum raised his head; his dreadful eyes
Glared, and he shook on high his menacing spear,　515
And shouted: *Rustum!*—Sohrab heard that
　　shout,
And shrank amazed; back he recoiled one step,
And scanned with blinking eyes the advancing
　　form;
And then he stood bewildered; and he dropped
His covering shield, and the spear pierced his side.　520
He reeled, and staggering back, sank to the
　　ground;
And then the gloom dispersed, and the wind fell,
And the bright sun broke forth, and melted all
The cloud; and the two armies saw the pair—
Saw Rustum standing, safe upon his feet,　525
And Sohrab, wounded, on the bloody sand.
　　Then, with a bitter smile, Rustum began:—
"Sohrab, thou thoughtest in thy mind to kill
A Persian lord this day, and strip his corpse,
And bear thy trophies to Afrasiab's tent.　530
Or else that the great Rustum would come down
Himself to fight, and that thy wiles would move
His heart to take a gift, and let thee go.
And then that all the Tartar host would praise
Thy courage or thy craft, and spread thy fame,　535
To glad thy father in his weak old age.
Fool, thou art slain, and by an unknown man!
Dearer to the red jackals shalt thou be
Than to thy friends, and to thy father old."
　　And, with a fearless mien, Sohrab replied:—　540
"Unknown thou art; yet thy fierce vaunt is vain.

Thou dost not slay me, proud and boastful man!
No! Rustum slays me, and this filial heart.
For were I matched with ten such men as thee,
And I were that which till to-day I was,　545
They should be lying here, I standing there.
But that belovèd name unnerved my arm—
That name, and something, I confess, in thee,
Which troubles all my heart, and made my shield
Fall; and thy spear transfixed an unarmed foe.　550
And now thou boastest, and insult'st my fate.
But hear thou this, fierce man, tremble to hear:
The mighty Rustum shall avenge my death!
My father, whom I seek through all the world,
He shall avenge my death, and punish thee!"　555
　　As when some hunter in the spring hath found
A breeding eagle sitting on her nest,
Upon the craggy isle of a hill-lake,
And pierced her with an arrow as she rose,
And followed her to find her where she fell　560
Far off;—anon her mate comes winging back
From hunting, and a great way off descries
His huddling young left sole; at that, he checks
His pinion, and with short uneasy sweeps
Circles above his eyry, with loud screams　565
Chiding his mate back to her nest; but she
Lies dying, with the arrow in her side,
In some far stony gorge out of his ken,
A heap of fluttering feathers—never more
Shall the lake glass her, flying over it;　570
Never the black and dripping precipices
Echo her stormy scream as she sails by—
As that poor bird flies home, nor knows his loss,
So Rustum knew not his own loss, but stood
Over his dying son, and knew him not.　575
　　But, with a cold incredulous voice, he said:—
"What prate is this of fathers and revenge?
The mighty Rustum never had a son."
　　And, with a failing voice, Sohrab replied:—
"Ah! yes, he had! and that lost son am I.　580
Surely the news will one day reach his ear,
Reach Rustum, where he sits, and tarries long,
Somewhere, I know not where, but far from here;
And pierce him like a stab, and make him leap
To arms, and cry for vengeance upon thee.　585
Fierce man, bethink thee, for an only son!
What will that grief, what will that vengeance
　　be?
Oh, could I live, till I that grief had seen!
Yet him I pity not so much, but her,
My mother, who in Ader-baijan dwells　590
With that old king, her father, who grows gray
With age, and rules over the valiant Koords.

Her most I pity, who no more will see
Sohrab returning from the Tartar camp,
With spoils and honor, when the war is done.   595
But a dark rumor will be bruited up,
From tribe to tribe, until it reach her ear;
And then will that defenceless woman learn
That Sohrab will rejoice her sight no more,
But that in battle with a nameless foe,   600
By the far-distant Oxus, he is slain."

    He spoke; and as he ceased, he wept aloud,
Thinking of her he left, and his own death.
He spoke; but Rustum listened, plunged in
    thought.
Nor did he yet believe it was his son   605
Who spoke, although he called back names he
    knew;
For he had had sure tidings that the babe,
Which was in Ader-baijan born to him,
Had been a puny girl, no boy at all—
So that sad mother sent him word, for fear   610
Rustum should take the boy, to train in arms.
And so he deemed that either Sohrab took,
By a false boast, the style of Rustum's son;
Or that men gave it him, to swell his fame.
So deemed he; yet he listened, plunged in thought   615
And his soul set to grief, as the vast tide
Of the bright rocking Ocean sets to shore
At the full moon; tears gathered in his eyes;
For he remembered his own early youth,
And all its bounding rapture; as, at dawn,   620
The shepherd from his mountain-lodge descries
A far, bright city, smitten by the sun,
Through many rolling clouds—so Rustum saw
His youth; saw Sohrab's mother, in her bloom;
And that old king, her father, who loved well   625
His wandering guest, and gave him his fair child
With joy; and all the pleasant life they led,
They three, in that long-distant summer-time—
The castle, and the dewy woods, and hunt
And hound, and morn on those delightful hills   630
In Ader-baijan. And he saw that youth,
Of age and looks to be his own dear son,
Piteous and lovely, lying on the sand,
Like some rich hyacinth which by the scythe
Of an unskilful gardener has been cut,   635
Mowing the garden grass-plots near its bed,
And lies, a fragrant tower of purple bloom,
On the mown, dying grass—so Sohrab lay,
Lovely in death, upon the common sand.
And Rustum gazed on him with grief, and   640
    said:—
    "O Sohrab, thou indeed art such a son

Whom Rustum, wert thou his, might well have
    loved.
Yet here thou errest, Sohrab, or else men
Have told thee false—thou art not Rustum's son.
For Rustum had no son; one child he had—   645
But one—a girl; who with her mother now
Plies some light female task, nor dreams of us—
Of us she dreams not, nor of wounds, nor war."
    But Sohrab answered him in wrath; for now
The anguish of the deep-fixed spear grew fierce,   650
And he desired to draw forth the steel,
And let the blood flow free, and so to die—
But first he would convince his stubborn foe;
And, rising sternly on one arm, he said:—
    "Man, who art thou who dost deny my words?   655
Truth sits upon the lips of dying men,
And falsehood, while I lived, was far from mine.
I tell thee, pricked upon this arm I bear
That seal which Rustum to my mother gave,
That she might prick it on the babe she bore."   660
    He spoke; and all the blood left Rustum's
        cheeks,
And his knees tottered, and he smote his hand
Against his breast, his heavy mailed hand,
That the hard iron corslet clanked aloud;
And to his heart he pressed the other hand,   665
And in a hollow voice he spake, and said:—
    "Sohrab, that were a proof which could not lie!
If thou show this, then art thou Rustum's son."
    Then, with weak hasty fingers, Sohrab loosed
His belt, and near the shoulder bared his arm,   670
And showed a sign in faint vermilion points
Pricked; as a cunning workman, in Pekin,
Pricks with vermilion some clear porcelain vase,
An emperor's gift—at early morn he paints,
And all day long, and, when night comes, the   675
    lamp
Lights up his studious forehead and thin hands—
So delicately pricked the sign appeared
On Sohrab's arm, the sign of Rustum's seal.
It was that griffin, which of old reared Zal,
Rustum's great father, whom they left to die,   680
A helpless babe, among the mountain-rocks;
Him that kind creature found, and reared, and
    loved—
Then Rustum took it for his glorious sign.
And Sohrab bared that image on his arm,
And himself scanned it long with mournful eyes,   685
And then he touched it with his hand and
    said:—
    "How say'st thou? Is that sign the proper sign

Of Rustum's son, or of some other man's?"
　He spoke; but Rustum gazed, and gazed, and stood
Speechless; and then he uttered one sharp cry: 690
O boy—thy father!—and his voice choked there.
And then a dark cloud passed before his eyes,
And his head swam, and he sank down to earth.
But Sohrab crawled to where he lay, and cast
His arms about his neck, and kissed his lips, 695
And with fond faltering fingers stroked his cheeks,
Trying to call him back to life; and life
Came back to Rustum, and he oped his eyes,
And they stood wide with horror; and he seized
In both his hands the dust which lay around, 700
And threw it on his head, and smirched his hair,—
His hair, and face, and beard, and glittering arms;
And strong convulsive groanings shook his breast,
And his sobs choked him; and he clutched his sword,
To draw it, and forever let life out. 705
But Sohrab saw his thought, and held his hands,
And with a soothing voice he spake, and said:—
　"Father, forbear! for I but meet to-day
The doom that at my birth was written down
In Heaven, and thou art Heaven's unconscious 710
　hand.
Surely my heart cried out that it was thou,
When first I saw thee; and thy heart spoke too,
I know it! but fate trod those promptings down
Under its iron heel; fate, fate engaged
The strife, and hurled me on my father's spear. 715
But let us speak no more of this! I find
My father; let me feel that I have found!
Come, sit beside me on this sand, and take
My head betwixt thy hands, and kiss my cheeks,
And wash them with thy tears, and say: My son! 720
Quick! quick! for numbered are my sands of life,
And swift; for like the lightning to this field
I came, and like the wind I go away—
Sudden, and swift, and like a passing wind.
But it was writ in Heaven that this should be." 725
　So said he, and his voice released the heart
Of Rustum, and his tears broke forth; he cast
His arms round his son's neck, and wept aloud,
And kissed him. And awe fell on both the hosts,
When they saw Rustum's grief; and Ruksh, the 730
　horse,
With his head bowing to the ground and mane
Sweeping the dust, came near, and in mute woe

First to the one then to the other moved
His head, as if inquiring what their grief
Might mean; and from his dark, compassionate 735
　eyes,
The big warm tears rolled down, and caked the sand.
But Rustum chid him with stern voice, and said:—
　"Ruksh, now thou grievest; but O Ruksh, thy feet
Should first have rotted on their nimble joints,
Or ere they brought thy master to this field!" 740
　But Sohrab looked upon the horse and said:—
Is this, then, Ruksh? How often, in past days,
My mother told me of thee, thou brave steed,
My terrible father's terrible horse! and said,
That I should one day find thy lord and thee. 745
Come, let me lay my hand upon thy mane!
O Ruksh, thou art more fortunate than I;
For thou hast gone where I shall never go,
And snuffed the breezes of my father's home.
And thou hast trod the sands of Seistan, 750
And seen the River of Helmund, and the Lake
Of Zirrah; and the aged Zal himself
Has often stroked thy neck, and given thee food,
Corn in a golden platter soaked with wine,
And said: O Ruksh! bear Rustum well!—but I 755
Have never known my grandsire's furrowed face,
Nor seen his lofty house in Seistan,
Nor slaked my thirst at the clear Helmund stream;
But lodged among my father's foes, and seen
Afrasiab's cities only, Samarcand, 760
Bokhara, and lone Khiva in the waste,
And the black Toorkmun tents; and only drunk
The desert rivers, Moorghab and Tejend,
Kohik, and where the Kalmuks feed their sheep,
The northern Sir; and this great Oxus stream, 765
The yellow Oxus, by whose brink I die."
　Then, with a heavy groan, Rustum bewailed:—
"Oh, that its waves were flowing over me!
Oh, that I saw its grains of yellow silt
Roll tumbling in the current o'er my head!" 770
　But, with a grave mild voice, Sohrab replied:—
"Desire not that, my father! thou must live.
For some are born to do great deeds, and live,
As some are born to be obscured, and die.
Do thou the deeds I die too young to do, 775
And reap a second glory in thine age;
Thou art my father, and thy gain is mine.
But come! thou seest this great host of men

Which follow me; I pray thee, slay not these!
Let me entreat for them; what have they done? 780
They followed me, my hope, my fame, my star.
Let them all cross the Oxus back in peace.
But me thou must bear hence, not send with
    them,
But carry me with thee to Seistan,
And place me on a bed, and mourn for me, 785
Thou, and the snow-haired Zal, and all thy
    friends.
And thou must lay me in that lovely earth,
And heap a stately mound above my bones,
And plant a far-seen pillar over all.
That so the passing horseman on the waste 790
May see my tomb a great way off, and cry:
Sohrab, the mighty Rustum's son, lies there,
Whom his great father did in ignorance kill!
And I be not forgotten in my grave."
    And, with a mournful voice, Rustum re- 795
    plied:—
"Fear not! as thou hast said, Sohrab, my son,
So shall it be; for I will burn my tents,
And quit the host, and bear thee hence with me,
And carry thee away to Seistan,
And place thee on a bed, and mourn for thee, 800
With the snow-headed Zal, and all my friends.
And I will lay thee in that lovely earth,
And heap a stately mound above thy bones,
And plant a far-seen pillar over all,
And men shall not forget thee in thy grave. 805
And I will spare thy host; yea, let them go!
Let them all cross the Oxus back in peace!
What should I do with slaying any more?
For would that all whom I have ever slain
Might be once more alive; my bitterest foes, 810
And they who were called champions in their
    time,
And through whose death I won that fame I
    have—
And I were nothing but a common man,
A poor, mean soldier, and without renown,
So thou mightest live too, my son, my son! 815
Or rather would that I, even I myself,
Might now be lying on this bloody sand,
Near death, and by an ignorant stroke of thine,
Not thou of mine! and I might die, not thou;
And I, not thou, be borne to Seistan; 820
And Zal might weep above my grave, not thine;
And say: *O son, I weep thee not too sore,*
For willingly, I know, thou met'st thine end!
But now in blood and battles was my youth,

And full of blood and battles is my age, 825
And I shall never end this life of blood."
    Then, at the point of death, Sohrab replied:—
"A life of blood indeed, thou dreadful man!
But thou shalt yet have peace; only not now,
Not yet! but thou shalt have it on that day, 830
When thou shalt sail in a high-masted ship,
Thou and the other peers of Kai Khosroo,
Returning home over the salt blue sea,
From laying thy dear master in his grave."
    And Rustum gazed on Sohrab's face, and 835
    said:—
"Soon be that day, my son, and deep that sea!
Till then, if fate so wills, let me endure."
    He spoke; and Sohrab smiled on him, and took
The spear, and drew it from his side, and eased
His wound's imperious anguish; but the blood 840
Came welling from the open gash, and life
Flowed with the stream;—all down his cold white
    side
The crimson torrent ran, dim now and soiled,
Like the soiled tissue of white violets
Left, freshly gathered, on their native bank, 845
By children whom their nurses call with haste
Indoors from the sun's eye; his head drooped low,
His limbs grew slack; motionless, white, he lay—
White, with eyes closed; only when heavy gasps,
Deep heavy gasps quivering through all his frame, 850
Convulsed him back to life, he opened them,
And fixed them feebly on his father's face;
Till now all strength was ebbed, and from his
    limbs
Unwillingly the spirit fled away,
Regretting the warm mansion which it left, 855
And youth, and bloom, and this delightful world.
    So, on the bloody sand, Sohrab lay dead;
And the great Rustum drew his horseman's cloak
Down o'er his face, and sate by his dead son.
As those black granite pillars, once high-reared 860
By Jemshid in Persepolis,[14] to bear
His house, now 'mid their broken flights of steps
Lie prone, enormous, down the mountain side—
So in the sand lay Rustum by his son.
    And night came down over the solemn waste, 865
And the two gazing hosts, and that sole pair,
And darkened all; and a cold fog, with night,
Crept from the Oxus. Soon a hum arose,
As of a great assembly loosed, and fires

---

[14] Capital city of ancient Persia, of which Jemshid was a
legendary king.

Began to twinkle through the fog; for now
Both armies moved to camp, and took their meal;
The Persians took it on the open sands
Southward, the Tartars by the river marge;
And Rustum and his son were left alone.

But the majestic river floated on, 875
Out of the mist and hum of that low land,
Into the frosty starlight, and there moved,
Rejoicing,   through   the   hushed   Chorasmian
   waste,[15]
Under the solitary moon;—he flowed
Right for the polar star, past Orgunjè,[16] 880
Brimming, and bright, and large; then sands
   begin
To hem his watery march, and dam his streams,
And split his currents; that for many a league
The shorn and parcelled Oxus strains along
Through beds of sand and matted rushy isles— 885
Oxus, forgetting the bright speed he had
In his high mountain-cradle in Pamere,
A foiled circuitous wanderer—till at last
The longed-for dash of waves is heard, and wide
His luminous home of waters opens, bright 890
And tranquil, from whose floor the new-bathed
   stars
Emerge, and shine upon the Aral Sea.[17]

Requiescat[1]

Strew on her roses, roses,
   And never a spray of yew!
In quiet she reposes;
   Ah, would that I did too!

Her mirth the world required; 5
   She bathed it in smiles of glee.
But her heart was tired, tired,
   And now they let her be.

Her life was turning, turning, 870
   In mazes of heat and sound.
But for peace her soul was yearning, 10
   And now peace laps her round.

Her cabined, ample spirit, 875
   It fluttered and failed for breath.
To-night it doth inherit 15
   The vasty hall of death.

The Scholar-Gipsy[1]

Go, for they call you, shepherd, from the hill;
   Go, shepherd, and untie the wattled cotes![2]
      No longer leave thy wistful flock unfed,
   Nor let thy bawling fellows rack their throats,
      Nor the cropped herbage shoot another head. 5
         But when the fields are still,
   And the tired men and dogs all gone to rest,
      And only the white sheep are sometimes seen
      Cross and recross the strips of moon-blanched
         green,
   Come, shepherd, and again begin the quest![3] 10

Here, where the reaper was at work of late—
   In this high field's dark corner, where he leaves
      His coat, his basket, and his earthen cruse,
   And in the sun all morning binds the sheaves,
      Then here, at noon, comes back his stores 15
         to use—
      Here will I sit and wait,

---

15 Khiva in Turkestan.
16 Village on the Oxus.
17 The function of the final paragraph, which is to create a feeling of quiet peace and reassurance after the
tragedy, is achieved partly on the direct level by an image
of natural beauty, partly on a symbolic level by the
suggestion—it is only a suggestion—that the Oxus stands
for the stream of human life, which begins with the
bright strength of youth, has to endure being shorn of its
potentialities and foiled of its hopes, but finally reaches
its "luminous home."

1 "May she rest [in peace]."

1 There was very lately a lad in the University of Oxford,
who was by his poverty forced to leave his studies there;
and at last to join himself to a company of vagabond gipsies. Among these extravagant people, by the insinuating subtilty of his carriage, he quickly got so much of
their love and esteem as that they discovered to him their
mystery. After he had been a pretty while exercised in
the trade, there chanced to ride by a couple of scholars,
who had formerly been of his acquaintance. They quickly
spied out their old friend among the gipsies; and he gave
them an account of the necessity which drove him to that
kind of life, and told them that the people he went with
were not such impostors as they were taken for, but that
they had a traditional kind of learning among them, and
could do wonders by the power of imagination, their
fancy binding that of others: that himself had learned
much of their art, and when he had compassed the whole
secret, he intended, he said, to leave their company, and
give the world an account of what he had learned.—
Glanvil's *Vanity of Dogmatizing*, 1661. (Affixed to the
poem by Arnold himself.)
2 Sheepfolds made of interwoven twigs.
3 The search for the Scholar-Gipsy (see line 63).

While to my ear from uplands far away
 The bleating of the folded flocks is borne,
  With distant cries of reapers in the corn—
All the live murmur of a summer's day. 20

Screened is this nook o'er the high, half-reaped
 field,
 And here till sun-down, shepherd! will I be.
  Through the thick corn the scarlet poppies
   peep,
 And round green roots and yellowing stalks I
  see
  Pale pink convolvulus in tendrils creep; 25
   And air-swept lindens yield
Their scent, and rustle down their perfumed
 showers
 Of bloom on the bent grass where I am laid,
 And bower me from the August sun with
  shade;
 And the eye travels down to Oxford's towers. 30

And near me on the grass lies Glanvil's book—
 Come, let me read the oft-read tale again!
  The story of the Oxford scholar poor,
 Of pregnant parts and quick inventive brain,
  Who, tired of knocking at preferment's 35
   door,
   One summer-morn forsook
His friends, and went to learn the gipsy-lore,
 And roamed the world with that wild
  brotherhood,
 And came, as most men deemed, to little
  good,
 But came to Oxford and his friends no more. 40

But once, years after, in the country-lanes,
 Two scholars, whom at college erst he knew,
  Met him, and of his way of life enquired;
 Whereat he answered, that the gipsy-crew,
  His mates, had arts to rule as they desired 45
   The workings of men's brains,
And they can bind them to what thoughts they
 will.[4]
  "And I," he said, "the secret of their art,
 When fully learned, will to the world
  impart;
 But it needs heaven-sent moments for this 50
  skill."

This said, he left them, and returned no more.—
 But rumors hung about the country-side,
  That the lost Scholar long was seen to stray,
 Seen by rare glimpses, pensive and tongue-tied,
  In hat of antique shape, and cloak of gray, 55
   The same the gipsies wore.
Shepherds had met him on the Hurst[5] in
 spring;
 At some lone alehouse in the Berkshire
  moors,
 On the warm ingle-bench,[6] the smock-
  frocked boors[7]
Had found him seated at their entering, 60

But, 'mid their drink and clatter, he would fly.
 And I myself seem half to know thy looks,
  And put the shepherds, wanderer! on thy
   trace;
 And boys who in lone wheatfields scare the
  rooks
  I ask if thou hast passed their quiet place; 65
   Or in my boat I lie
Moored to the cool bank in the summer-heats,
 'Mid wide grass meadows which the sun-
  shine fills,
 And watch the warm, green-muffled Cumner
  hills,
 And wonder if thou haunt'st their shy retreats. 70

For most, I know, thou lov'st retired ground!
 Thee at the ferry Oxford riders blithe,
  Returning home on summer-nights, have
  met
 Crossing the stripling Thames at Bab-lock-
  hithe,
  Trailing in the cool stream thy fingers wet, 75
   As the punt's rope chops round;[8]
And leaning backward in a pensive dream,
 And fostering in thy lap a heap of flowers
 Plucked in shy fields and distant Wychwood
  bowers,
 And thine eyes resting on the moonlit stream. 80

And then they land, and thou art seen no more!—
 Maidens, who from the distant hamlets come
  To dance around the Fyfield elm in May,

---

[4] Cf. note 1. The arts are those of hypnotism, as the rest
of the passage from Glanvil, not quoted by Arnold, makes
clear.

[5] A hill outside Oxford. All the proper names in the
following stanzas are of places in the environs of Oxford.
[6] Bench in the chimney corner. [7] Peasants.
[8] The rope which pulls the ferryboat across the Thames
is shaken about by the wind.

Oft through the darkening fields have seen thee roam,
  Or cross a stile into the public way.   85
    Oft thou hast given them store
Of flowers—the frail-leafed, white anemony,
  Dark bluebells drenched with dews of summer eves,
  And purple orchises with spotted leaves—
But none hath words she can report of thee.   90

And, above Godstow Bridge, when hay-time's here
  In June, and many a scythe in sunshine flames,
  Men who through those wide fields of breezy grass
  Where black-winged swallows haunt the glittering Thames,
  To bathe in the abandoned lasher pass,[9]   95
    Have often passed thee near
Sitting upon the river bank o'ergrown;
  Marked thine outlandish garb, thy figure spare,
  Thy dark vague eyes, and soft abstracted air—
But, when they came from bathing, thou wast gone!   100

At some lone homestead in the Cumner hills,
  Where at her open door the housewife darns,
  Thou hast been seen, or hanging on a gate
To watch the threshers in the mossy barns.
  Children, who early range these slopes and late   105
    For cresses from the rills,
Have known thee eying, all an April-day,
  The springing pastures and the feeding kine;
  And marked thee, when the stars come out and shine,
Through the long dewy grass move slow away.   110

In autumn, on the skirts of Bagley Wood—
  Where most the gipsies by the turf-edged way
    Pitch their smoked tents, and every bush you see
  With scarlet patches tagged and shreds of gray,
    Above the forest-ground called Thessaly—   115
    The blackbird, picking food,
Sees thee, nor stops his meal, nor fears at all;

So often has he known thee past him stray,
  Rapt, twirling in thy hand a withered spray,
  And waiting for the spark from heaven to fall.   120

And once, in winter, on the causeway chill
  Where home through flooded fields foot-travellers go,
    Have I not passed thee on the wooden bridge,
  Wrapped in thy cloak and battling with the snow,
    Thy face toward Hinksey and its wintry   125
    ridge?
    And thou hast climbed the hill,
  And gained the white brow of the Cumner range;
    Turned once to watch, while thick the snowflakes fall,
    The line of festal light in Christ-Church hall[10]—
Then sought thy straw in some sequestered   130
grange.

But what—I dream! Two hundred years are flown
  Since first thy story ran through Oxford halls,
  And the grave Granvil did the tale inscribe
  That thou wert wandered from the studious walls
    To learn strange arts, and join a gipsy-tribe;   135
    And thou from earth art gone
Long since, and in some quiet churchyard laid—
  Some country-nook, where o'er thy unknown grave
  Tall grasses and white flowering nettles wave,
Under a dark, red-fruited yew-tree's shade.   140

—No, no, thou hast not felt the lapse of hours!
  For what wears out the life of mortal men?
    'Tis that from change to change their being rolls;
  'Tis that repeated shocks, again, again,
    Exhaust the energy of strongest souls   145
    And numb the elastic powers.
  Till having used our nerves with bliss and teen,[11]

---

[9] Pool below a dam.

[10] The dining hall at Christ Church College.
[11] Sorrow.

And tired upon a thousand schemes our wit,
To the just-pausing Genius[12] we remit
Our worn-out life, and are—what we have   150
been.

Thou hast not lived, why shouldst thou perish,
so?
Thou hadst *one* aim, *one* business, *one* desire;
Else wert thou long since numbered with
the dead!
Else hadst thou spent, like other men, thy fire!
The generations of thy peers are fled,   155
And we ourselves shall go;
But thou possessest an immortal lot,
And we imagine thee exempt from age
And living as thou liv'st on Glanvil's page,
Because thou hadst—what we, alas! have not.   160

For early didst thou leave the world, with powers
Fresh, undiverted to the world without,
Firm to their mark, not spent on other
things;
Free from the sick fatigue, the languid doubt,
Which much to have tried, in much been   165
baffled, brings.
O life unlike to ours!
Who fluctuate idly without term or scope,
Of whom each strives, nor knows for what
he strives,
And each half lives a hundred different
lives;
Who wait like thee, but not, like thee, in hope.   170

Thou waitest for the spark from heaven! and we,
Light half-believers of our casual creeds,
Who never deeply felt, nor clearly willed,
Whose insight never has borne fruit in deeds,
Whose vague resolves never have been   175
fulfilled;
For whom each year we see
Breeds new beginnings, disappointments new;
Who hesitate and falter life away,
And lose to-morrow the ground won to-
day—
Ah! do not we, wanderer! await it too?   180

Yes, we await it!—but it still delays,
And then we suffer! and amongst us one,
Who most has suffered, takes dejectedly

His seat upon the intellectual throne;
And all his store of sad experience he   185
Lays bare of wretched days;
Tells us his misery's birth and growth and
signs,
And how the dying spark of hope was fed,
And how the breast was soothed, and how
the head,
And all his hourly varied anodynes.[13]   190

This for our wisest![14] and we others pine,
And wish the long unhappy dream would end,
And waive all claim to bliss, and try to bear;
With close-lipped patience for our only friend,
Sad patience, too near neighbor to de-   195
spair—
But none has hope like thine!
Thou through the fields and through the
woods dost stray,
Roaming the country-side, a truant boy,
Nursing thy project in unclouded joy,
And every doubt long blown by time away.   200

O born in days when wits were fresh and clear,
And life ran gaily as the sparkling Thames;
Before this strange disease of modern life,
With its sick hurry, its divided aims,
Its heads o'ertaxed, its palsied hearts, was   205
rife—
Fly hence, our contact fear!
Still fly, plunge deeper in the bowering wood!
Averse, as Dido did with gesture stern
From her false friend's approach in Hades
turn,[15]
Wave us away, and keep thy solitude!   210

Still nursing the unconquerable hope,[16]
Still clutching the inviolable shade,
With a free, onward impulse brushing
through,
By night, the silvered branches of the glade—
Far on the forest-skirts, where none pursue,   215
On some mild pastoral slope

---

12 The Spirit who gave us life just barely pauses to receive it back again.
13 Palliatives as distinguished from curative drugs.
14 The reference is either to Goethe or to Tennyson. Lines
185–90 fit *In Memoriam* perfectly, and line 184 could refer to the laureateship. It is true that Arnold did not consider Tennyson "our wisest," but the last phrase may simply mean, "the one who is thought or called our wisest"
(since he has been placed on the intellectual throne).
15 Dido, who had killed herself when Aeneas deserted her,
turned away from him scornfully when he visited Hades.
16 Cf. line 120.

Emerge, and resting on the moonlit pales
  Freshen thy flowers as in former years
  With dew, or listen with enchanted ears,
From the dark dingles,[17] to the nightingales! 220

But fly our paths, our feverish contact fly!
  For strong the infection of our mental strife,
  Which, though it gives no bliss, yet spoils
    for rest;
  And we should win thee from thy own fair
    life,
  Like us distracted, and like us unblest. 225
    Soon, soon thy cheer would die,
  Thy hopes grow timorous, and unfixed thy
    powers,
    And thy clear aims be cross and shifting
      made;
    And then thy glad perennial youth would
      fade,
  Fade, and grow old at last, and die like ours. 230

Then fly our greetings, fly our speech and smiles!
  —As some grave Tyrian[18] trader, from the sea,
  Descried at sunrise an emerging prow
  Lifting the cool-haired creepers stealthily,[19]
    The fringes of a southward-facing brow 235
      Among the Aegaean isles;
  And saw the merry Grecian coaster come,
    Freighted with amber grapes, and Chian
      wine,
    Green, bursting figs, and tunnies[20] steeped
      in brine—
  And knew the intruders on his ancient home, 240

The young light-hearted masters of the waves—
  And snatched his rudder, and shook out more
    sail;
  And day and night held on indignantly
  O'er the blue Midland waters with the gale,
    Betwixt the Syrtes[21] and soft Sicily, 245
      To where the Atlantic raves
  Outside the western straits;[22] and unbent sails

There, where down cloudy cliffs, through
    sheets of foam,
  Shy traffickers, the dark Iberians[23] come;
And on the beach undid his corded bales.[24] 250

Stanzas from the Grande Chartreuse[1]

Through Alpine meadows soft-suffused
With rain, where thick the crocus blows,
Past the dark forges long disused,
The mule-track from Saint Laurent[2] goes.
The bridge is crossed, and slow we ride, 5
Through forest, up the mountain-side.

The autumnal evening darkens round,
The wind is up, and drives the rain;
While, hark! far down, with strangled sound
Doth the Dead Guier's[3] stream complain, 10
Where that wet smoke, among the woods,
Over his boiling cauldron broods.

Swift rush the spectral vapors white
Past limestone scars with ragged pines,
Showing—then blotting from our sight!— 15
Halt—through the cloud-drift something shines!
High in the valley, wet and drear,
The huts of Courrerie[4] appear.

Strike leftward! cries our guide; and higher
Mounts up the stony forest-way. 20
At last the encircling trees retire;
Look! through the showery twilight gray
What pointed roofs are these advance?—
A palace of the Kings of France?

---

17 Wooded dells.
18 Tyre, in Asia Minor, was the chief city of the Phoenicians, who controlled the Mediterranean trade until the rise of the Greeks.
19 The foliage overhanging a cliff at the entrance to a harbor.
20 Fish.
21 Gulf of Sidra on the northern coast of Africa.
22 Beyond the straits of Gibraltar.

23 Early inhabitants of the Spanish peninsula.
24 The appropriateness of this famous simile is somewhat dubious. The analogies between the Tyrian trader and the Scholar-Gipsy, and between the Greeks and either the Oxford scholars of Glanvil's time or the modern Victorians who have just been described, are less obvious than their differences. The best that can be said is that the Tyrian trader has "one aim, one business, one desire" which he can achieve if he turns away from "civilization" and flies to the dark Iberians (the gipsies). But his (commercial) aim is definite where the Scholar-Gipsy's aim is indefinite; and the trader shows no interest whatever in the beauties of nature, which, in point of fact, the Scholar-Gipsy flies to.

1 Carthusian monastery in the Alps, visited by Arnold in 1851.
2 Village near the monastery.
3 River near the monastery.
4 Another mountain village.

Approach, for what we seek is here!
Alight, and sparely sup, and wait
For rest in this outbuilding near;
Then cross the sward and reach that gate.
Knock; pass the wicket! Thou art come
To the Carthusians' world-famed home. 30

The silent courts, where night and day
Into their stone-carved basins cold
The splashing icy fountains play—
The humid corridors behold!
Where, ghostlike in the deepening night, 35
Cowled forms brush by in gleaming white.

The chapel, where no organ's peal
Invests the stern and naked prayer—
With penitential cries they kneel
And wrestle; rising then, with bare 40
And white uplifted faces stand,
Passing the Host[5] from hand to hand;

Each takes, and then his visage wan
Is buried in his cowl once more.
The cells!—the suffering Son of Man 45
Upon the wall—the knee-worn floor—
And where they sleep, that wooden bed,
Which shall their coffin be, when dead!

The library, where tract and tome
Not to feed priestly pride are there, 50
To hymn the conquering march of Rome,
Nor yet to amuse, as ours are!
They paint of souls the inner strife,
Their drops of blood, their death in life.

The garden, overgrown—yet mild, 55
See, fragrant herbs are flowering there!
Strong children of the Alpine wild
Whose culture is the brethren's care;
Of human tasks their only one,
And cheerful works beneath the sun. 60

Those halls, too, destined to contain
Each its own pilgrim-host of old,
From England, Germany, or Spain—
All are before me! I behold
The House, the Brotherhood austere! 65
—And what am I, that I am here?

25
For rigorous teachers seized my youth,
And purged its faith, and trimmed its fire,
Showed me the high, white star of Truth,
There bade me gaze, and there aspire.[6] 70
Even now their whispers pierce the gloom:
What dost thou in this living tomb?

Forgive me, masters of the mind!
At whose behest I long ago
So much unlearnt, so much resigned— 75
I come not here to be your foe!
I seek these anchorites, not in ruth,
To curse and to deny your truth;[7]

Not as their friend, or child, I speak!
But as, on some far northern strand, 80
Thinking of his own Gods, a Greek
In pity and mournful awe might stand
Before some fallen Runic stone—
For both were faiths, and both are gone.[8]

Wandering between two worlds, one dead, 85
The other powerless to be born,[9]
With nowhere yet to rest my head,
Like these, on earth I wait forlorn.
Their faith, my tears, the world deride—
I come to shed them at their side. 90

Oh, hide me in your gloom profound,
Ye solemn seats of holy pain!
Take me, cowled forms, and fence me round,
Till I possess my soul again;
Till free my thoughts before me roll, 95
Not chafed by hourly false control!

For the world cries your faith is now
But a dead time's exploded dream;

5 The consecrated bread in the service of the Mass. But since it is never passed from hand to hand, Arnold must have confused the Host with the Pax (a crucifix).

6 The rationalists (Goethe in one way, Mill and the scientists in another) who insisted he follow the truth of fact and reason to the exclusion not only of Catholic Christianity, Roman and Anglican, but even of his father's Liberal Protestantism (cf. lines 74–75).
7 Not in repentance for my faith in reason.
8 A runic stone is a religious tablet written in early Germanic characters. Arnold likens himself to a rational Greek who has lost his faith in the gods (as Arnold has lost his in Liberal Protestantism) and who therefore feels "pity and mournful awe" before another exploded superstition, German paganism (as Arnold does before Roman Catholicism).
9 In the age of transition (cf. introduction to Victorian period, opening section), when the old religious philosophy of life is dead, and no new one has yet been formulated.

My melancholy, sciolists[10] say,
Is a passed mode, an outworn theme— 100
As if the world had ever had
A faith, or sciolists been sad![11]

Ah, if it *be* passed, take away,[12]
At least, the restlessness, the pain;
Be man henceforth no more a prey 105
To these out-dated stings again!
The nobleness of grief is gone—
Ah, leave us not the fret alone!

But—if you cannot give us ease—
Last of the race of them who grieve 110
Here leave us to die out with these
Last of the people who believe!
Silent, while years engrave the brow;
Silent—the best are silent now.

Achilles ponders in his tent,[13] 115
The kings of modern thought are dumb;
Silent they are, though not content,
And wait to see the future come.
They have the grief men had of yore,
But they contend and cry no more. 120

Our fathers watered with their tears[14]
This sea of time whereon we sail,
Their voices were in all men's ears
Who passed within their puissant hail.
Still the same ocean round us raves, 125
But we stand mute, and watch the waves.

For what availed it, all the noise
And outcry of the former men?—
Say, have their sons achieved more joys,
Say, is life lighter now than then? 130
The sufferers died, they left their pain—
The pangs which tortured them remain.

What helps it now, that Byron bore,
With haughty scorn which mocked the smart,

Through Europe to the Aetolian shore[15] 135
The pageant of his bleeding heart?
That thousands counted every groan,
And Europe made his woe her own?

What boots it, Shelley! that the breeze
Carried thy lovely wail away, 140
Musical through Italian trees
Which fringe thy soft blue Spezzian bay?[16]
Inheritors of thy distress
Have restless hearts one throb the less?

Or we are easier, to have read, 145
O Obermann![17] the sad, stern page,
Which tells us how thou hidd'st thy head
From the fierce tempest of thine age
In the lone brakes of Fontainebleau,
Or chalets near the Alpine snow? 150

Ye slumber in your silent grave!—
The world, which for an idle day
Grace to your mood of sadness gave,
Long since hath flung her weeds away.
The eternal trifler breaks your spell; 155
But we—we learnt your lore[18] too well!

Years hence, perhaps, may dawn an age,
More fortunate, alas! than we,
Which without hardness will be sage,
And gay without frivolity. 160
Sons of the world, oh, speed those years;
But, while we wait, allow our tears!

Allow them! We admire with awe
The exulting thunder of your race;
You give the universe your law, 165
You triumph over time and space!
Your pride of life, your tireless powers,
We laud them, but they are not ours.

We are like children reared in shade
Beneath some old-world abbey wall, 170
Forgotten in a forest-glade,
And secret from the eyes of all.

---

[10] Men of superficial knowledge.
[11] The world and the sciolists can talk this way only because the one has never known the real meaning of faith and the other has never known sadness.
[12] In this stanza and the next Arnold is again addressing his "rigorous teachers" of lines 66–78.
[13] Whom Achilles stands for, if anyone in particular, is unknown. He symbolizes the "kings of modern thought" who have withdrawn from the struggle to solve the religious problem.
[14] The melancholy romantics of the previous age.
[15] To the shore of the Greek province where Byron died.
[16] Shelley spent his last days on the shore of the Gulf of Spezia.
[17] Etienne Pivert de Sénancour (1770–1846), author of a philosophic romance called *Obermann*. He died at Fontainebleau near Paris.
[18] Your melancholy grief.

Deep, deep the greenwood round them waves,
Their abbey, and its close of graves!

But, where the road runs near the stream,   175
Oft through the trees they catch a glance
Of passing troops in the sun's beam—
Pennon, and plume, and flashing lance!
Forth to the world those soldiers fare,
To life, to cities, and to war!   180

And through the wood, another way,
Faint bugle-notes from far are borne,
Where hunters gather, staghounds bay,
Round some fair forest-lodge at morn.
Gay dames are there, in sylvan green;   185
Laughter and cries—those notes between!

The banners flashing through the trees
Make their blood dance and chain their eyes;
That bugle-music on the breeze
Arrests them with a charmed surprise.   190
Banner by turns and bugle woo:
Ye shy recluses, follow too!

O children, what do ye reply?—
"Action and pleasure, will ye roam
Through these secluded dells to cry   195
And call us?—but too late ye come!
Too late for us your call ye blow,
Whose bent was taken long ago.

"Long since we pace this shadowed nave;
We watch those yellow tapers shine,   200
Emblems of hope over the grave,
In the high altar's depth divine;
The organ carries to our ear
Its accents of another sphere.

"Fenced early in this cloistral round   205
Of reverie, of shade, of prayer,
How should we grow in other ground?
How can we flower in foreign air?
—Pass, banners, pass, and bugles, cease;
And leave our desert to its peace!"   210

Isolation. To Marguerite[1]

We were apart; yet day by day,
I bade my heart more constant be.

I bade it keep the world away,
And grow a home for only thee;
Nor feared but thy love likewise grew,   5
Like mine, each day, more tried, more true.

The fault was grave! I might have known,
What far too soon, alas! I learned—
The heart can bind itself alone,
And faith may oft be unreturned.   10
Self-swayed our feelings ebb and swell—
Thou lov'st no more;—Farewell! Farewell!

Farewell!—and thou, thou lonely heart,
Which never yet without remorse
Even for a moment didst depart   15
From thy remote and spherèd course
To haunt the place where passions reign—
Back to thy solitude again!

Back! with the conscious thrill of shame
Which Luna felt, that summer-night,   20
Flash through her pure immortal frame,
When she forsook the starry height
To hang over Endymion's sleep
Upon the pine-grown Latmian steep.[2]

Yet she, chaste queen, had never proved   25
How vain a thing is mortal love,
Wandering in Heaven, far removed.
But thou hast long had place to prove
This truth—to prove, and make thine own:
"Thou hast been, shalt be, art, alone."   30

Or, if not quite alone, yet they
Which touch thee are unmating things—
Ocean and clouds and night and day;
Lorn autumns and triumphant springs;
And life, and others' joy and pain,   35
And love, if love, of happier men.

Of happier men—for they, at least,
Have *dreamed* two human hearts might blend
In one, and were through faith released
From isolation without end   40
Prolonged; nor knew, although not less
Alone than thou, their loneliness.

---

1 This poem and the following one are taken from a series
of seven poems published under the heading *Switzerland*.

Who Marguerite was is not known. Arnold pronounced
the name as a disyllable.
2 Diana, goddess of the moon and of chastity, fell in love
with the shepherd Endymion, whom she found sleeping on
Mt. Latmos.

To Marguerite—Continued

Yes! in the sea of life enisled,
With echoing straits between us thrown,
Dotting the shoreless watery wild,
We mortal millions live *alone*.
The islands feel the enclasping flow,   5
And then their endless bounds they know.

But when the moon their hollows lights,
And they are swept by balms of spring,
And in their glens, on starry nights,
The nightingales divinely sing;   10
And lovely notes, from shore to shore,
Across the sounds and channels pour—

Oh! then a longing like despair
Is to their farthest caverns sent;
For surely once, they feel, we were   15
Parts of a single continent!
Now round us spreads the watery plain—
Oh might our marges meet again![1]

Who ordered, that their longing's fire
Should be, as soon as kindled, cooled?   20
Who renders vain their deep desire?—
A God, a God[2] their severance ruled!
And bade betwixt their shores to be
The unplumbed, salt, estranging sea.

The Better Part[1]

Long fed on boundless hopes, O race of man,
How angrily thou spurn'st all simpler fare!
"Christ," some one says, "was human as we are;
No judge eyes us from Heaven, our sin to scan;

"We live no more, when we have done our   5
      span."—
"Well, then, for Christ," thou answerest, "who
      can care?

From sin, which Heaven records not, why
      forbear?
Live we like brutes our life without a plan!"

So answerest thou; but why not rather say:
"Hath man no second life?—*Pitch this one high!*   10
Sits there no judge in Heaven, our sin to see?—

"*More strictly, then, the inward judge obey!*
Was Christ a man like us? *Ah! let us try
If we then, too, can be such men as he!*"

Dover Beach

The sea is calm to-night.
The tide is full, the moon lies fair
Upon the straits;—on the French coast the light
Gleams and is gone; the cliffs of England stand,
Glimmering and vast, out in the tranquil bay.   5
Come to the window, sweet is the night-air!
Only, from the long line of spray
Where the sea meets the moon-blanched land,
Listen! you hear the grating roar
Of pebbles which the waves draw back, and fling,   10
At their return, up the high strand,
Begin, and cease, and then again begin,
With tremulous cadence slow, and bring
The eternal note of sadness in.

Sophocles long ago   15
Heard it on the Aegaean, and it brought
Into his mind the turbid ebb and flow
Of human misery;[1] we
Find also in the sound a thought,
Hearing it by this distant northern sea.   20

The Sea of Faith
Was once, too, at the full, and round earth's
      shore
Lay like the folds of a bright girdle furled.
But now I only hear
Its melancholy, long, withdrawing roar,   25
Retreating, to the breath
Of the night-wind, down the vast edges drear
And naked shingles of the world.[2]

---

[1] Stanzas 2 and 3 suggest that when people feel a sense of romance (spring, moonlight, and nightingales merge into a symbol), they experience a longing for the companionship of human beings, which seems so natural that they feel as though communion were something men must once have had and now have somehow lost.
[2] I.e., a fate or destiny.

[1] Originally called "Anti-Desperation."

---

[1] The reference is to a passage in *Antigone*, lines 583 ff.
[2] Shingles are pebbled beaches. Though what is retreating is mainly religious faith, it is also faith of any kind, any coherent philosophy of the world that can make life meaningful.

Ah, love, let us be true
To one another! for the world, which seems   30
To lie before us like a land of dreams,
So various, so beautiful, so new,
Hath really neither joy, nor love, nor light,
Nor certitude, nor peace, nor help for pain;
And we are here as on a darkling plain   35
Swept with confused alarms of struggle and
     flight,
Where ignorant armies clash by night.[3]

The Last Word

Creep into thy narrow bed,
Creep, and let no more be said!
Vain thy onset! all stands fast.
Thou thyself must break at last.

Let the long contention cease!   5
Geese are swans, and swans are geese.
Let them have it how they will!
Thou art tired; best be still.

They out-talked thee, hissed thee, tore thee?
Better men fared thus before thee;   10
Fired their ringing shot and passed,
Hotly charged—and sank at last.

Charge once more, then, and be dumb!
Let the victors, when they come,
When the forts of folly fall,   15
Find thy body by the wall!

Empedocles on Etna[1]
A Dramatic Poem

This is Arnold's major work and one of the most impressive long poems written in the Victorian period.

[3] Cf. J. A. Symonds in his diary for 1865: "Scepticism is my spirit. In my sorest needs I have had no actual faith, and have said to destruction. 'Thou art my sister.' To the skirts of human love I have clung, and I cling blindly. But all else is chaos—a mountain chasm filled with tumbling mists."
    It should be noticed that the moonlit scene of stanza one takes on symbolic meaning in the final stanza. The world that lies before him from the Dover cliffs is a beautiful world but it is not the real world. It is a world clothed in moonlight, a land of dreams. The real world is a land of darkness where ignorant armies clash by night.

[1] I am grateful to the Houghton Mifflin Co. for permission to reprint the footnotes to "Empedocles on Etna," which

Empedocles was an early Greek philosopher, poet, doctor, and statesman, living in Sicily in the fifth century B.C., who was supposed to have leaped into the crater of Mt. Etna. But the subject of the poem is the historical character *as he might have appeared in the mid-nineteenth century.* He is the brother of Sénancour, of Clough, and of Arnold himself. Act I centers on "modern thought": the scientific picture of the universe emerging at the time, together with a new philosophy, largely Stoic, with which man may face a world devoid of religious or ethical meaning. In Act II, the portrayal of Empedocles' state of mind is a dramatic expression of what Arnold called "modern feeling," namely, "depression and ennui." Arnold's comments on his poem are in the opening paragraphs of the 1853 Preface to *Poems* and the following outline he jotted down on a MS. now in the Yale library:
    "He is a philosopher.
    "He has not the religious consolation of other men, facile because adapted to their weaknesses, or because shared by all around and charging the atmosphere they breathe.
    "He sees things as they are—the world as it is—God as he is: in their stern simplicity.
    "The sight is a severe and mind-tasking one: to know the mysteries which are communicated to others by fragments, in parables.
    "But he started towards it in hope: his first glimpses of it filled him with joy: he had friends who shared his hope & joy & communicated to him theirs: even now he does not deny that the sight is capable of affording rapture & the purest peace.
    "But his friends are dead: the world is all against him, & incredulous of the truth: his mind is overtasked by the effort to hold fast so great & severe a truth in solitude: the atmosphere he breathes not being modified by the presence of human life, is too rare for him. He perceives still the truth of the truth [sic], but cannot be transported and rapturously agitated by its grandeur: his spring and elasticity of mind are gone: he is clouded, oppressed, dispirited, without hope & energy.
    "Before he becomes the victim of depression & overtension of mind, to the utter deadness to joy, grandeur, spirit, and animated life, he desires to die; to be reunited with the universe, before by exaggerating his human side he has become utterly estranged from it."

Persons

EMPEDOCLES.
PAUSANIAS, a *Physician.*
CALLICLES, a *young Harp-player.*
The Scene of the Poem is on Mount Etna; at

I originally wrote for *Victorian Poetry and Poetics,* edited with G. Robert Stange, second edition, Boston, 1968. [W. E. H.]

first in the forest region, afterwards on the summit of the mountain.

ACT I

Scene I

Morning. A Pass in the forest region of Etna.

CALLICLES (*Alone, resting on a rock by the path.*)

The mules, I think, will not be here this hour;
They feel the cool wet turf under their feet
By the stream-side, after the dusty lanes
In which they have toiled all night from Catana,[2]
And scarcely will they budge a yard. O Pan,   5
How gracious is the mountain at this hour!
A thousand times have I been here alone,
Or with the revellers from the mountain-towns,
But never on so fair a morn;—the sun
Is shining on the brilliant mountain-crests,   10
And on the highest pines; but farther down,
Here in the valley, is in shade; the sward
Is dark, and on the stream the mist still hangs;
One sees one's footprints crushed in the wet
    grass,
One's breath curls in the air; and on these pines   15
That climb from the stream's edge, the long gray
    tufts,
Which the goats love, are jewelled thick with
    dew.
Here will I stay till the slow litter comes.
I have my harp too—that is well.—Apollo!
What mortal could be sick or sorry here?   20
I know not in what mind Empedocles,
Whose mules I followed, may be coming up,
But if, as most men say, he is half mad
With exile, and with brooding on his wrongs,
Pausanias, his sage friend, who mounts with him,   25
Could scarce have lighted on a lovelier cure.
The mules must be below, far down. I hear
Their tinkling bells, mixed with the song of
    birds,
Rise faintly to me—now it stops!—Who's here?
Pausanias! and on foot? alone?

PAUSANIAS

                    And thou, then?   30
I left thee supping with Peisianax,[3]
With thy head full of wine, and thy hair
    crowned,

Touching thy harp as the whim came on thee,
And praised and spoiled by master and by guests
Almost as much as the new dancing-girl.   35
Why hast thou followed us?

CALLICLES

                    The night was hot,
And the feast past its prime; so we slipped out,
Some of us, to the portico to breathe;—
Peisianax, thou know'st, drinks late;—and then,
As I was lifting my soiled garland off,   40
I saw the mules and litter in the court,
And in the litter sate Empedocles;
Thou, too, wast with him. Straightaway I sped
    home:
I saddled my white mule, and all night long
Through the cool lovely country followed you,   45
Passed you a little since as morning dawned,
And have this hour sate by the torrent here,
Till the slow mules should climb in sight again.
And now?

PAUSANIAS

                    And now, back to the town with speed!
Crouch in the wood first, till the mules have   50
    passed;
They do but halt, they will be here anon.
Thou must be viewless to Empedocles;
Save mine, he must not meet a human eye.
One of his moods is on him that thou know'st;
I think, thou wouldst not vex him.

CALLICLES

                    No—and yet   55
I would fain stay, and help thee tend him. Once
He knew me well, and would oft notice me;
And still, I know not how, he draws me to him,
And I could watch him with his proud sad
    face,
His flowing locks and gold-encircled brow   60
And kingly gait, for ever; such a spell
In his severe looks, such a majesty
As drew of old the people after him,
In Agrigentum and Olympia,
When his star reigned, before his banishment,[4]   65

---

[2] Town at the foot of Mt. Etna.
[3] See the next note.

[4] The passage is based on the notes Arnold made from various accounts of Empedocles: "He travelled in the East, to Greece & Olympia where he claimed & received great attention. . . . Returning to Sicily, he found the aristocrats uppermost at Agrigentum, the children of his early foes: he was repulsed [by] them & coming to Syracuse, abode in the house of Pisianax, a wealthy man, on the side of the city nearest to Ætna. Pausanias son of Anchities, the famous physician, & his friend, followed him."

Is potent still on me in his decline.
But oh! Pausanias, he is changed of late;
There is a settled trouble in his air
Admits no momentary brightening now,
And when he comes among his friends at feasts,   70
'Tis as an orphan among prosperous boys.
Thou know'st of old he loved this harp of mine,
When first he sojourned with Peisianax;
He is now always moody, and I fear him;
But I would serve him, soothe him, if I could,   75
Dared one but try.

PAUSANIAS

Thou wast a kind child ever!
He loves thee, but he must not see thee now.
Thou hast indeed a rare touch on thy harp,
He loves that in thee, too;—there was a time
(But that is passed), he would have paid[5] thy   80
        strain
With music to have drawn the stars from heaven.
He hath his harp and laurel with him still,
But he has laid the use of music by,
And all which might relax his settled gloom.
Yet thou may'st try thy playing, if thou wilt—   85
But thou must keep unseen; follow us on,
But at a distance! in these solitudes,
In this clear mountain-air, a voice will rise,
Though from afar, distinctly; it may soothe him.
Play when we halt, and, when the evening comes   90
And I must leave him (for his pleasure is
To be left musing these soft nights alone
In the high unfrequented mountain-spots),
Then watch him, for he ranges swift and far,
Sometimes to Etna's top, and to the cone;   95
But hide thee in the rocks a great way down,
And try thy noblest strains, my Callicles,
With the sweet night to help thy harmony!
Thou wilt earn my thanks sure, and perhaps his.

CALLICLES

More than a day and night, Pausanias,   100
Of this fair summer-weather, on these hills,
Would I bestow to help Empedocles.
That needs no thanks; one is far better here
Than in the broiling city in these heats.
But tell me, how hast thou persuaded him   105
In this his present fierce, man-hating mood,
To bring thee out with him alone on Etna?

PAUSANIAS

Thou hast heard all men speaking of Pantheia

The woman who at Agrigentum lay
Thirty long days in a cold trance of death,   110
And whom Empedocles called back to life.
Thou art too young to note it, but his power
Swells with the swelling evil of this time,
And holds men mute to see where it will rise.
He could stay swift diseases in old days,   115
Chain madmen by the music of his lyre,
Cleanse to sweet airs the breath of poisonous
        streams,
And in the mountain-chinks inter the winds.
This he could do of old; but now, since all
Clouds and grows daily worse in Sicily,   120
Since broils tear us in twain, since this new
        swarm
Of sophists has got empire in our schools
Where he was paramount,[6] since he is banished
And lives a lonely man in triple gloom—
He grasps the very reins of life and death.   125
I asked him of Pantheia yesterday,
When we were gathered with Peisianax,
And he made answer, I should come at night
On Etna here, and be alone with him,
And he would tell me, as his old, tried friend,   130
Who still was faithful, what might profit me;
That is, the secret of this miracle.

CALLICLES

Bah! Thou a doctor! Thou art superstitious,
Simple Pausanias, 'twas no miracle!
Pantheia, for I know her kinsmen well,   135
Was subject to these trances from a girl.
Empedocles would say so, did he deign;
But he still lets the people, whom he scorns,
Gape and cry *wizard* at him, if they list.
But thou, thou art no company for him!   140
Thou art as cross, as soured as himself!
Thou hast some wrong from thine own citizens,
And then thy friend is banished, and on that,
Straightway thou fallest to arraign the times,
As if the sky was impious not to fall.   145
The sophists are no enemies of his;
I hear, Gorgias, their chief, speaks nobly of him,
As of his gifted master, and once friend.
He is too scornful, too high-wrought, too bitter.
'Tis not the times, 'tis not the sophists vex him;   150
There is some root of suffering in himself,
Some secret and unfollowed vein of woe,

---

5 Requited.

6 The sophists were professional teachers who tended to debase the serious study of rhetoric and logic by making them instruments of specious ("sophistical") persuasion.

Which makes the time look black and sad to him.
Pester him not in this his sombre mood
With questionings about an idle tale,   155
But lead him through the lovely mountain-paths,
And keep his mind from preying on itself,
And talk to him of things at hand and common,
Not miracles! thou art a learned man,
But credulous of fables as a girl.   160

PAUSANIAS
And thou, a boy whose tongue outruns his knowl-
    edge,
And on whose lightness blame is thrown away.
Enough of this! I see the litter wind
Up by the torrent-side, under the pines.
I must rejoin Empedocles. Do thou   165
Crouch in the brushwood till the mules have
    passed;
Then play thy kind part well. Farewell till night!

Scene II

*Noon. A Glen on the highest skirts of the woody
region of Etna.*

EMPEDOCLES——PAUSANIAS

PAUSANIAS
The noon is hot. When we have crossed the
    stream,
We shall have left the woody tract, and come
Upon the open shoulder of the hill.
See how the giant spires of yellow bloom
Of the sun-loving gentian, in the heat,   5
Are shining on those naked slopes like flame!
Let us rest here; and now, Empedocles,
Pantheia's history!
        A harp-note below is heard.

EMPEDOCLES
         Hark! what sound was that
Rose from below? If it were possible,
And we were not so far from human haunt,   10
I should have said that some one touched a harp.
Hark! there again!

PAUSANIAS
         'Tis the boy Callicles,
The sweetest harp-player in Catana.
He is for ever coming on these hills,
In summer, to all country-festivals,   15
With a gay revelling band; he breaks from them
Sometimes, and wanders far among the glens.
But heed him not, he will not mount to us;

I spoke with him this morning. Once more,
    therefore,
Instruct me of Pantheia's story, Master,   20
As I have prayed thee.

EMPEDOCLES
         That? and to what end?

PAUSANIAS
It is enough that all men speak of it.
But I will also say, that when the Gods
Visit us as they do with sign and plague,
To know those spells of thine which stay their   25
    hand
Were to live free from terror.

EMPEDOCLES
         Spells? Mistrust them!
Mind is the spell which governs earth and
    heaven.
Man has a mind with which to plan his safety;
Know that, and help thyself!

PAUSANIAS
         But thine own words?
"The wit and counsel of man was never clear,   30
Troubles confound the little wit he has."[7]
Mind is a light which the Gods mock us with,
To lead those false who trust it.
        The harp sounds again.

EMPEDOCLES
         Hist! once more!
Listen, Pausanias!—Ay, 'tis Callicles;
I know these notes among a thousand. Hark!   35

CALLICLES
(Sings unseen, from below)
The track winds down to the clear stream,
To cross the sparkling shallows; there
The cattle love to gather, on their way
To the high mountain-pastures, and to stay,
Till the rough cow-herds drive them past,   40
Knee-deep in the cool ford; for 'tis the last
Of all the woody, high, well-watered dells
On Etna; and the beam
Of noon is broken there by chestnut-boughs
Down its steep verdant sides; the air   45
Is freshened by the leaping stream, which throws
Eternal showers of spray on the mossed roots

---

[7] Cf. Empedocles in John Burnet, *Early Greek Philosophy*,
4th ed., Fragment #2, p. 204: "For straitened are the
powers that are spread over their bodily parts [that is,
apparently, their sensory perceptions], and many are the
woes that burst in on them and blunt the edge of their
careful thoughts!"

Of trees, and veins of turf, and long dark shoots
Of ivy-plants, and fragrant hanging bells
Of hyacinths, and on late anemonies,   50
That muffle its wet banks; but glade,
And stream, and sward, and chestnut-trees,
End here; Etna beyond, in the broad glare
Of the hot noon, without a shade,
Slope behind slope, up to the peak, lies bare;   55
The peak, round which the white clouds play.

    In such a glen, on such a day,
    On Pelion, on the grassy ground,
    Chiron, the aged Centaur lay,
    The young Achilles standing by.   60
The Centaur taught him to explore
The mountains; where the glens are dry
And the tired Centaurs come to rest,
And where the soaking springs abound
And the straight ashes grow for spears,   65
And where the hill-goats come to feed,
And the sea-eagles build their nest.
He showed him Phthia far away,
And said: O boy, I taught this lore
To Peleus, in long distant years!   70
He told him of the Gods, the stars,
The tides;—and then of mortal wars,
And of the life which heroes lead
Before they reach the Elysian place
And rest in the immortal mead;   75
And all the wisdom of his race.[8]

The music below ceases and EMPEDOCLES *speaks,*
accompanying himself in a solemn manner on
his harp.

    The out-spread world to span
    A cord the Gods first slung,
    And then the soul of man
    There, like a mirror, hung,   80
And bade the winds through space impel the
    gusty toy.

    Hither and thither spins
    The wind-borne, mirroring soul,

---

[8] On Mt. Pelion, from which his birthplace Phthia can
be seen, Achilles is instructed by Chiron in the same wisdom the Centaur had taught his father Peleus "in long
distant years"—the traditional knowledge of gods and
immortality and how to live like a hero. The comparison
and contrast with the instruction of Pausanias by Empedocles that follows shows why Arnold chose the myth.

    A thousand glimpses wins,
    And never sees a whole;   85
Looks once, and drives elsewhere, and leaves its
    last employ.

    The Gods laugh in their sleeve
    To watch man doubt and fear,
    Who knows not what to believe
    Since he sees nothing clear,   90
And dares stamp nothing false where he finds
    nothing sure.

    Is this, Pausanias, so?
    And can our souls not strive,
    But with the winds must go,
    And hurry where they drive?   95
Is fate indeed so strong, man's strength indeed
    so poor?

    I will not judge. That man,
    Howbeit, I judge as lost,
    Whose mind allows a plan,
    Which would degrade it most;   100
And he treats doubt the best who tries to see
    least ill.

    Be not, then, fear's blind slave!
    Thou art my friend; to thee,
    All knowledge that I have,
    All skill I wield, are free.   105
Ask not the latest news of the last miracle,

    Ask not what days and nights
    In trance Pantheia lay,
    But ask how thou such sights
    May'st see without dismay;   110
Ask what most helps when known, thou son of
    Anchitus!

    What? hate, and awe, and shame
    Fill thee to see our time;
    Thou feelest thy soul's frame
    Shaken and out of chime?   115
What? life and chance go hard with thee too, as
    with us;

    Thy citizens, 'tis said,
    Envy thee and oppress,
    Thy goodness no men aid,
    All strive to make it less;   120
Tyranny, pride, and lust, fill Sicily's abodes;

Heaven is with earth at strife,
Signs make thy soul afraid,
The dead return to life,
Rivers are dried, winds stayed;   125
Scarce can one think in calm, so threatening
    are the Gods;

And we feel, day and night,
The burden of ourselves—
Well, then, the wiser wight
In his own bosom delves,   130
And asks what ails him so, and gets what cure
    he can.

The sophist sneers: Fool, take
Thy pleasure, right or wrong.[9]
The pious wail: Forsake
A world these sophists throng.   135
Be neither saint not sophist-led, but be a man!

These hundred doctors try
To preach thee to their school.
We have the truth! they cry;
And yet their oracle,   140
Trumpet it as they will, is but the same as thine.

Once read thy own breast right,
And thou hast done with fears;
Man gets no other light,
Search he a thousand years.   145
Sink in thyself! there ask what ails thee, at that
    shrine!

What makes thee struggle and rave?
Why are men ill at ease?—
'Tis that the lot they have
Fails their own will to please;   150
For man would make no murmuring, were his
    will obeyed.[10]

And why is it, that still
Man with his lot thus fights?—
'Tis that he makes this *will*
The measure of his *rights,*   155
And believes Nature outraged if his will's gain-
    said.

Couldst thou, Pausanias, learn
How deep a fault is this;

Couldst thou but once discern
Thou has no *right* to bliss,   160
No title from the Gods to welfare and repose;

Then thou wouldst look less mazed
Whene'er of bliss debarred,
Nor think the Gods were crazed
When thy own lot went hard.   165
But we are all the same—the fools of our own
    woes!

For, from the first faint morn
Of life, the thirst for bliss
Deep in man's heart is born;
And, sceptic as he is,   170
He fails not to judge clear if this be quenched or
    no.

Nor is the thirst to blame.
Man errs not that he deems
His welfare his true aim,
He errs because he dreams   175
The world does but exist that welfare to bestow.

We mortals are no kings
For each of whom to sway
A new-made world up-springs,
Meant merely for his play;   180
No, we are strangers here; the world is from
    of old.

In vain our pent wills fret,
And would the world subdue.
Limits we did not set
Condition all we do;   185
Born into life we are, and life must be our mold.

Born into life!—man grows
Forth from his parents' stem,
And blends their bloods, as those
Of theirs are blent in them;   190
So each new man strikes root into a far foretime.

Born into life!—we bring
A bias with us here,
And, when here, each new thing
Affects us we come near;   195
To tunes we did not call our being must keep
    chime.

Born into life!—in vain,
Opinions, those or these,

---

[9] This is an extension of the amoral attitude present in sophistical reasoning: cf. note 5.
[10] Here and in the following lines "will" means "desire."

Unaltered to retain
The obstinate mind decrees;   200
Experience, like a sea, soaks all-effacing in.[11]

Born into life!—who lists
May what is false hold dear,
And for himself make mists
Through which to see less clear;   205
The world is what it is, for all our dust and din.

Born into life!—'tis we,
And not the world, are new;
Our cry for bliss, our plea,
Others have urged it too—   210
Our wants have all been felt, our errors made
before.

No eye could be too sound
To observe a world so vast,
No patience too profound
To sort what's here amassed;   215
How man may here best live no care too great to
explore.

But we—as some rude guest
Would change, where'er he roam,
The manners there professed
To those he brings from home—   220
We mark not the world's course, but would
have *it* take *ours.*

The world's course proves the terms
On which man wins content;
Reason the proof confirms—
We spurn it, and invent   225
A false course for the world, and for ourselves,
false powers.[12]

Riches we wish to get,
Yet remain spendthrifts still;
We would have health, and yet
Still use our bodies ill;   230
Bafflers of our own prayers, from youth to life's
last scenes.

We would have inward peace,
Yet will not look within;
We would have misery cease,
Yet will not cease from sin;   235
We want all pleasant ends, but will use no harsh
means;

We do not what we ought,
What we ought not, we do,
And lean upon the thought
That chance will bring us through;   240
But our own acts, for good or ill, are mightier
powers.

Yet, even when man forsakes
All sin,—is just, is pure,
Abandons all which makes
His welfare insecure,—   245
Other existences there are, that clash with ours.

Like us, the lightning-fires
Love to have scope and play;
The stream, like us, desires
An unimpeded way;   250
Like us, the Libyan wind delights to roam at
large.

Streams will not curb their pride
The just man not to entomb,
Nor lightnings go aside
To give his virtues room;   255
Nor is that wind less rough which blows a good
man's barge.

Nature, with equal mind,
Sees all her sons at play;
Sees man control the wind,
The wind sweep man away;   260
Allows the proudly-riding and the foundering
bark.

And, lastly, though of ours
No weakness spoil our lot,
Though the non-human powers
Of Nature harm us not,   265
The ill deeds of other men make often *our* life
dark.

What were the wise man's plan?—
Through this sharp, toil-set life,
To work as best he can,
And win what's won by strife.—   270

---

[11] But a wise and supple mind, it is implied, would alter his opinions to fit the conditions of human life. As it is, it takes bitter experience to drown the false opinions "the obstinate mind decrees."

[12] Instead of accepting the world as it is and attaining the "content" that is possible, we invent an unreal world whose course is less indifferent to us, and for ourselves powers of achieving happiness we do not possess.

But we an easier way to cheat our pains have
found.[13]

    Scratched by a fall, with moans
    As children of weak age
    Lend life to the dumb stones
    Whereon to vent their rage,   275
And bend their little fists, and rate the senseless
ground;

    So, loath to suffer mute,
    We, peopling the void air,
    Make Gods to whom to impute
    The ills we ought to bear;   280
With God and Fate to rail at, suffering easily.[14]

    Yet grant—as sense long missed
    Things that are now perceived,
    And much may still exist
    Which is not yet believed—   285
Grant that the world were full of Gods we cannot see;

    All things the world which fill
    Of but one stuff are spun,
    That we who rail are still,
    With what we rail at, one;   290
One with the o'erlabored Power that through the
breadth and length

    Of earth, and air, and sea,
    In men, and plants, and stones,
    Hath toil perpetually,
    And travails, pants, and moans;   295
Fain would do all things well, but sometimes fails
in strength.

    And patiently exact
    This universal God
    Alike to any act
    Proceeds at any nod,   300
And quietly declaims the cursings of himself.[15]

    This is not what man hates,

---

[13] This positive philosophy is amplified at lines 397–426,
but first Empedocles deals with an easier way to reckon
with the ills of life.
[14] The main line of thought continues at line 307. Lines
282–306 suggest that the only God that is, is a pantheistic
Power or World-soul, acting both in nature and in man.
[15] Because this universal God has predetermined whatever happens.

    Yet he can curse but this.
    Harsh Gods and hostile Fates
    Are dreams! this only *is*—   305
Is everywhere; sustains the wise, the foolish elf.

    Nor only, in the intent
    To attach blame elsewhere,
    Do we at will invent
    Stern Powers who make their care   310
To embitter human life, malignant Deities;

    But, next, we would reverse
    The scheme ourselves have spun,
    And what we made to curse
    We now would lean upon,   315
And feign kind Gods who perfect what man
vainly tries.

    Look, the world tempts our eye,
    And we would know it all!
    We map the starry sky,
    We mine this earthen ball,   320
We measure the sea-tides, we number the sea-
sands;

    We scrutinise the dates
    Of long-past human things,
    The bounds of effaced states,
    The lines of deceased kings;   325
We search out dead men's words, and works of
dead men's hands;

    We shut our eyes, and muse
    How our own minds are made,
    What springs of thought they use,
    How rightened, how betrayed—   330
And spend our wit to name what most employ
unnamed.

    But still, as we proceed
    The mass swells more and more
    Of volumes yet to read,
    Of secrets yet to explore.   335
Our hair grows gray, our eyes are dimmed, our
heat is tamed;

    We rest our faculties,
    And thus address the Gods:
    "True science if there is,
    It stays in your abodes!   340
Man's measures cannot mete the immeasurable
All.

"You only can take in
The world's immense design.
Our desperate search was sin,
Which henceforth we resign,   345
Sure only that your mind sees all things which
befal."

Fools! That in man's brief term
He cannot all things view,
Affords no ground to affirm
That there are Gods who do;   350
Nor does being weary prove that he has where
to rest.

Again.—Our youthful blood
Claims rapture as its right;
The world, a rolling flood
Of newness and delight,   355
Draws in the enamored gazer to its shining breast;

Pleasure, to our hot grasp,
Gives flowers after flowers;
With passionate warmth we clasp
Hand after hand in ours;   360
Now do we soon perceive how fast our youth is
spent.

At once our eyes grow clear!
We see, in blank dismay,
Year posting after year,
Sense after sense decay;   365
Our shivering heart is mined by secret discontent;

Yet still, in spite of truth,
In spite of hopes entombed,
That longing of our youth
Burns ever unconsumed,   370
Still hungrier for delight as delights grow more
rare.

We pause; we hush our heart,
And thus address the Gods:
"The world hath failed to impart
The joy our youth forebodes,   375
Failed to fill up the void which in our breasts
we bear.

"Changeful till now, we still
Looked on to something new;
Let us, with changeless will,
Henceforth look on to you,   380
To find with you the joy we in vain here require!"

Fools! That so often here
Happiness mocked our prayer,
I think, might make us fear
A like event elsewhere;   385
Make us, not fly to dreams, but moderate desire.

And yet, those who know
Themselves, who wisely take
Their way through life, and bow
To what they cannot break,   390
Why should I say that life need yield but *moderate* bliss?

Shall we, with temper spoiled,
Health sapped by living ill,
And judgment all embroiled
By sadness and self-will,   395
Shall *we* judge what for man is not true bliss or
is?

Is it so small a thing
To have enjoyed the sun,
To have lived light in the spring,
To have loved, to have thought, to have   400
done;
To have advanced true friends, and beat down
baffling foes—

That we must feign a bliss
Of doubtful future date,
And, while we dream on this,
Lose all our present state,   405
And relegate to worlds yet distant our repose?

Not much, I know, you prize
What pleasures may be had,
Who look on life with eyes
Estranged, like mine, and sad;   410
And yet the village-churl feels the truth more
than you,

Who's loath to leave this life
Which to him little yields—
His hard-tasked sunburnt wife,
His often-labored fields,   415
The boors with whom he talked, the country-
spots he knew.

But thou, because thou hear'st
Men scoff at Heaven and Fate,

Because the Gods thou fear'st
Fail to make blest thy state, 420
Tremblest, and wilt not dare to trust the joys
there are!

I say: Fear not! Life still
Leaves human effort scope.
But, since life teems with ill,
Nurse no extravagant hope; 425
Because thou must not dream, thou need'st not
then despair![16]

*A long pause. At the end of it the notes of a
harp below are again heard, and* CALLICLES
sings:—

Far, far from here,
The Adriatic breaks in a warm bay
Among the green Illyrian hills; and there
The sunshine in the happy glens is fair, 430
And by the sea, and in the brakes.
The grass is cool, the sea-side air
Buoyant and fresh, the mountain flowers
More virginal and sweet than ours.
And there, they say, two bright and aged snakes, 435
Who once were Cadmus and Harmonia,[17]
Bask in the glens or on the warm sea-shore,
In breathless quiet, after all their ills;
Nor do they see their country, nor the place
Where the Sphinx lived among the frowning 440
hills,
Nor the unhappy palace of their race,
Nor Thebes, nor the Ismenus, any more.

There those two live, far in the Illyrian
brakes!
They had stayed long enough to see,
In Thebes, the billow of calamity 445
Over their own dear children rolled,

Curse upon curse, pang upon pang,
For years, they sitting helpless in their home,
A gray old man and woman; yet of old
The Gods had to their marriage come, 450
And at the banquet all the Muses sang.

Therefore they did not end their days
In sight of blood; but were rapt, far away,
To where the west-wind plays,
And murmurs of the Adriatic come 455
To those untrodden mountain-lawns; and there
Placed safely in changed forms, the pair
Wholly forget their first sad life, and home,
And all that Theban woe, and stray
For ever through the glens, placid and dumb.[18] 460

EMPEDOCLES
That was my harp-player again!—where is he?
Down by the stream?

PAUSANIAS
                    Yes, Master, in the wood.

EMPEDOCLES
He ever loved the Theban story well!
But the day wears. Go now, Pausanias,
For I must be alone. Leave me one mule; 465
Take down with thee the rest to Catana.
And for young Callicles, thank him from me;
Tell him, I never failed to love his lyre—
But he must follow me no more to-night.

PAUSANIAS
Thou wilt return to-morrow to the city? 470

EMPEDOCLES
Either to-morrow or some other day,
In the sure revolutions of the world,
Good friend, I shall revisit Catana.
I have seen many cities in my time,
Till mine eyes ache with the long spectacle, 475
And I shall doubtless see them all again;
Thou know'st me for a wanderer from of old.
Meanwhile, stay me not now. Farewell, Pausanias!
        He departs on his way up the mountain.

PAUSANIAS (*alone*)
I dare not urge him further—he must go;
But he is strangely wrought!—I will speed back 480

---

16 The core of Empedocles' sermon (lines 397–426) is
Stoic, but with a strain of Epicureanism derived from
Lucretius.

17 Cadmus was the builder and ruler of Thebes. His marriage to Harmonia was attended by all the Olympian
gods. Because he had killed a serpent sacred to Mars, a
heavy fatality hung over his family, which led to the
violent death of some of his children and grandchildren.
In great unhappiness he prayed to be changed into a
creature apparently so much favored by the gods, and was
transformed into a serpent. When Harmonia received the
same response to her prayer, they were "rapt far away"
to the Illyrian hills north of Greece. The Ismenus,
mentioned in line 442, is a river near Thebes.

18 This lovely idyll seems intended by Callicles to relax
Empedocles' "settled gloom" by a vision of quiet happiness
in the midst of nature far from the unhappy life of
Agrigentum: cf. Scene I, lines 76–125. For the effect on
Empedocles, see line 483.

And bring Peisianax to him from the city;
His counsel could once soothe him. But, Apollo!
How his brow lightened as the music rose!
Callicles must wait here, and play to him;
I saw him through the chestnuts far below,   485
Just since, down at the stream.—Ho! Callicles!

He descends, calling.

ACT II

Evening. The Summit of Etna.

EMPEDOCLES

                                        Alone!—
On this charred, blackened, melancholy waste,
Crowned by the awful peak, Etna's great mouth.
Round which the sullen vapor rolls—alone!
Pausanias is far hence, and that is well,   5
For I must henceforth speak no more with man.
He hath his lesson too, and that debt's paid;
And the good, learned, friendly, quiet man
May bravelier front his life, and in himself
Find henceforth energy and heart. But I—   10
The weary man, the banished citizen,
Whose banishment is not his greatest ill,
Whose weariness no energy can reach,
And for whose hurt courage is not the cure—
What should I do with life and living more?   15

    No, thou art come too late, Empedocles!
And the world hath the day, and must break thee,
Not thou the world. With men thou canst not
    live,
Their thoughts, their ways, their wishes, are not
    thine;
And being lonely thou art miserable,   20
For something has impaired thy spirit's strength,
And dried its self-sufficing fount of joy.
Thou canst not live with men nor with thyself—
O sage! O sage!—Take then the one way left;
And turn thee to the elements, thy friends,   25
Thy well-tried friends, thy willing ministers,
And say: Ye helpers, hear Empedocles,
Who asks this final service at your hands!
Before the sophist-brood hath overlaid
The last spark of man's consciousness with   30
    words[1]—
Ere quite the being of man, ere quite the world

Be disarrayed of their divinity—
Before the soul lose all her solemn joys,
And awe be dead, and hope impossible,
And the soul's deep eternal night come on—   35
Receive me, hide me, quench me, take me home!

He advances to the edge of the crater. Smoke and fire break forth with a loud noise, and CALLICLES *is heard below singing:*—

The lyre's voice is lovely everywhere;
In the court of Gods, in the city of men,
And in the lonely rock-strewn mountain-glen,
In the still mountain air.   40

Only to Typho it sounds hatefully;
To Typho only, the rebel o'erthrown,
Through whose heart Etna drives her roots of
    stone
To imbed them in the sea.

Wherefore dost thou groan so loud?   45
Wherefore do thy nostrils flash,
Through the dark night, suddenly,
Typho, such red jets of flame?—
Is thy tortured heart still proud?
Is thy fire-scathed arm still rash?   50
Still alert thy stone-crushed frame?
Does thy fierce soul still deplore
Thine ancient rout by the Cilician hills,
And that curst treachery on the Mount of Gore?[2]
Do thy bloodshot eyes still weep   55
The fight which crowned thine ills,
Thy last mischance on this Sicilian deep?
Hast thou sworn, in thy sad lair,
Where erst the strong sea-currents sucked thee
    down,
Never to cease to writhe, and try to rest,   60
Letting the sea-stream wander through thy hair?
That thy groans, like thunder pressed,
Begin to roll, and almost drown
The sweet notes whose lulling spell
Gods and the race of mortals love so well,   65
When through thy caves thou hearest music
    swell?

---

[1] "Consciousness" seems to be used here in the broad sense of mind. Empedocles is afraid that through long immersion in the verbal sophistries he hears all about him, he may be unable to think clearly and honestly.

[2] "Mount Hæmus, so called, said the legend, from Typho's blood spilt on it in his last battle with Zeus, when the giant's strength failed, owing to the Destinies having a short time before given treacherously to him, for his refreshment, perishable fruits. See Apollodorus, *Bibliotheca*, book i, chap. vi." (Arnold's note) The relevance of this third song of Callicles is pointed out below in lines 89–107.

But an awful pleasure bland
Spreading o'er the Thunderer's face,
When the sound climbs near his seat,
The Olympian council sees;   70
As he lets his lax right hand,
Which the lightnings doth embrace,
Sink upon his mighty knees.
And the eagle, at the beck
Of the appeasing, gracious harmony,   75
Droops all his sheeny, brown, deep-feathered
      neck,
Nestling nearer to Jove's feet;
While o'er his sovereign eye
The curtains of the blue films slowly meet
And the white Olympus-peaks   80
Rosily brighten, and the soothed Gods smile
At one another from their golden chairs,
And no one round the charmed circle speaks.
Only the loved Hebe bears
The cup about, whose draughts beguile   85
Pain and care, with a dark store
Of fresh-pulled violets wreathed and nodding
      o'er;
And her flushed feet glow on the marble floor.

EMPEDOCLES
He fables, yet speaks truth!
The brave, impetuous heart yields everywhere   90
To the subtle, contriving head;
Great qualities are trodden down,
And littleness united
Is become invincible.

These rumblings are not Typho's groans, I   95
      know!
These angry smoke-bursts
Are not the passionate breath
Of the mountain-crushed, tortured, intractable
      Titan king—
But over all the world
What suffering is there not seen   100
Of plainness oppressed by cunning,
As the well-counselled Zeus oppressed
That self-helping son of earth!
What anguish of greatness,
Railed and hunted from the world,   105
Because its simplicity rebukes
This envious, miserable age!

I am weary of it.
—Lie there, ye ensigns
Of my unloved preëminence   110

In an age like this!
Among a people of children,
Who thronged me in their cities,
Who worshipped me in their houses,
And asked, not wisdom,   115
But drugs to charm with,
But spells to mutter—
All the fool's armory of magic!—Lie there,
My golden circlet,
My purple robe!3   120

CALLICLES (*from below*)
As the sky-brightening south-wind clears the day,
And makes the massed clouds roll,
The music of the lyre blows away
The clouds which wrap the soul.
Oh! that Fate had let me see   125
That triumph of the sweet persuasive lyre,
That famous, final victory,
When jealous Pan with Marsyas did conspire;4
When, from far Parnassus' side,
Young Apollo, all the pride   130
Of the Phrygian flutes to tame,
To the Phrygian highlands came;
Where the long green reed-beds sway
In the rippled waters gray
Of that solitary lake   135
Where Mæander's springs are born;
Whence the ridged pine-wooded roots
Of Messogis westward break,
Mounting westward, high and higher.
There was held the famous strife;   140
There the Phrygian brought his flutes,
And Apollo brought his lyre;
And, when now the westering sun
Touched the hills, the strife was done,
And the attentive Muses said: 145
"Marsyas, thou art vanquishèd!"
Then Apollo's minister
Hanged upon a branching fir
Marsyas, that unhappy Faun,
And began to whet his knife.   150
But the Maenads,5 who were there,
Left their friend, and with robes flowing
In the wind, and loose dark hair
O'er their polished bosoms blowing,

---

3 Symbols of civic power.
4 Marsyas, a faun of Phyrgia, urged on by Pan, rashly
challenged Apollo to a musical contest on the understanding that the winner might do what he wished with the
loser. When Apollo won, he decided to flay Marsyas alive.
5 Female followers of Bacchus.

Each her ribboned tambourine
Flinging on the mountain-sod,
With a lovely frightened mien
Came about the youthful God.
But he turned his beauteous face   160
Haughtily another way,
From the grassy sun-warmed place
Where in proud repose he lay,
With one arm over his head,
Watching how the whetting sped.

    But aloof, on the lake-strand,   165
Did the young Olympus stand,
Weeping at his master's end;
For the Faun had been his friend.
For he taught him how to sing,
And he taught him flute-playing.   170
Many a morning had they gone
To the glimmering mountain-lakes,
And had torn up by the roots
The tall crested water-reeds
With long plumes and soft brown seeds,   175
And had carved them into flutes,
Sitting on a tabled stone
Where the shoreward ripple breaks.
And he taught him how to please
The red-snooded Phrygian girls,   180
Whom the summer evening sees
Flashing in the dance's whirls
Underneath the starlit trees
In the mountain-villages.
Therefore now Olympus stands,   185
At his master's piteous cries
Pressing fast with both his hands
His white garment to his eyes,
Not to see Apollo's scorn;—
Ah, poor Faun, poor Faun! ah, poor **Faun!**   190

EMPEDOCLES
And lie thou there,
My laurel bough!
Scornful Apollo's ensign, lie thou there![6]
Though thou hast been my shade in the world's
    heat—
Though I have loved thee, lived in honoring   195
    thee—
Yet lie thou there,
My laurel bough!

I am weary of thee.   155
I am weary of the solitude
Where he who bears thee must abide—   200
Of the rocks of Parnassus,
Of the gorge of Delphi,
Of the moonlit peaks, and the caves.
Thou guardest them, Apollo!
Over the grave of the slain Pytho,[7]   205
Though young, intolerably severe!
Thou keepest aloof the profane,
But the solitude oppresses thy votary!
The jars of men reach him not in thy valley—
But can life reach him?   210
Thou fencest him from the multitude—
Who will fence him from himself?
He hears nothing but the cry of the torrents,
And the beating of his own heart.
The air is thin, the veins swell,   215
The temples tighten and throb there—
Air! air!

Take thy bough, set me free from my solitude;
I have been enough alone!

Where shall thy votary fly then? back to men?—   220
But they will gladly welcome him once more,
And help him to unbend his too tense thought,
And rid him of the presence of himself,
And keep their friendly chatter at his ear,
And haunt him, till the absence from himself,   225
That other torment, grow unbearable;[8]
And he will fly to solitude again,
And he will find its air too keen for him,
And so change back; and many thousand times
Be miserably bandied to and fro   230
Like a sea-wave, betwixt the world and thee,
Thou young, implacable God! and only death
Can cut his oscillations short, and so
Bring him to poise. There is no other way.

And yet what days were those, Parmenides!   235
When we were young, when we could number
    friends
In all the Italian cities like ourselves,
When with elated hearts we joined your train,

---

[6] Complementing the effect of Typho's story, the tale of Apollo's pride and scorn persuades Empedocles to give up the poetic as well as the political life.

[7] Serpent who lived on Mt. Parnassus, slain by Apollo.
[8] At line 212 just above he had wanted to fly from himself. But there is no inconsistency. The self he would be fenced from is "the weary man," deeply despondent; the self he cannot bear to lose, under the pressure of social chatter, is his individuality.

Ye Sun-born Virgins! on the road of truth.[9]
Then we could still enjoy, then neither thought 240
Nor outward things were closed and dead to us;
But we received the shock of mighty thoughts
On simple minds with a pure natural joy;
And if the sacred load oppressed our brain,
We had the power to feel the pressure eased, 245
The brow unbound, the thoughts flow free again,
In the delightful commerce of the world.
We had not lost our balance then, nor grown
Thought's slaves, and dead to every natural joy.[10]
The smallest thing could give us pleasure then— 250
The sports of the country-people,
A flute-note from the woods,
Sunset over the sea;
Seed-time and harvest,
The reapers in the corn, 255
The vinedresser in his vineyard,
The village-girl at her wheel.

Fulness of life and power of feeling, ye
Are for the happy, for the souls at ease,
Who dwell on a firm basis of content! 260
But he, who has outlived his prosperous days—
But he, whose youth fell on a different world
From that on which his exiled age is thrown—
Whose mind was fed on other food, was trained
By other rules than are in vogue to-day— 265
Whose habit of thought is fixed, who will not
    change,
But, in a world he loves not, must subsist
In ceaseless opposition, be the guard
Of his own breast, fettered to what he guards,
That the world win no mastery over him— 270
Who has no friend, no fellow left, not one;
Who has no minute's breathing space allowed
To nurse his dwindling faculty of joy—
Joy and the outward world must die to him,
As they are dead to me. 275

---

9 Arnold's note referred the reader to the Greek lines of
Parmenides, a philosopher and contemporary of Empedocles, which he has here paraphrased. The Virgins were
probably the daughters of Helios, the sun-god to whom
the island of Sicily was sacred.
10 In these important lines, 240–249, Empedocles seems to
be fusing two ideas by saying (1) that once he was flexible
enough to enjoy both the life of thought in solitude and
the life of friendly intercourse in society, and (2) that he
enjoyed them both because then he possessed a unified
sensibility (in which the senses, emotions, imagination,
and reason were all active together), able to digest every
kind of experience, whether that of ideas or of the
natural objects he goes on to mention in the next lines.

A long pause, during which EMPEDOCLES *remains
motionless, plunged in thought. The night
deepens. He moves forward and gazes round him,
and proceeds:—*

And you, ye stars,
Who slowly begin to marshal,
As of old, in the fields of heaven,
Your distant, melancholy lines!
Have you, too, survived yourselves? 280
Are you, too, what I fear to become?
You, too, once lived;
You, too, moved joyfully
Among august companions,
In an older world, peopled by Gods, 285
In a mightier order,
The radiant, rejoicing, intelligent Sons of
    Heaven.
But now, ye kindle
Your lonely, cold-shining lights,
Unwilling lingerers 290
In the heavenly wilderness,
For a younger, ignoble world;
And renew, by necessity,
Night after night your courses,
In echoing, unneared silence, 295
Above a race you know not—
Uncaring and undelighted,
Without friend and without home;
Weary like us, though not
Weary with our weariness. 300

No, no, ye stars! there is no death with you,
No languor, no decay! languor and death,
They are with me, not you! ye are alive—
Ye, and the pure dark ether where ye ride
Brilliant above me! And thou, fiery world, 305
That sapp'st the vitals of this terrible mount
Upon whose charred and quaking crust I stand—
Thou, too, brimmest with life!—the sea of cloud,
That heaves its white and billowy vapors up
To moat this isle of ashes from the world, 310
Lives; and that other fainter sea, far down,
O'er whose lit floor a road of moonbeams leads
To Etna's Liparëan sister-fires
And the long dusky line of Italy—
That mild and luminous floor of waters lives, 315
With held-in joy swelling its heart; I only,
Whose spring of hope is dried, whose spirit has
    failed,
I, who have not, like these, in solitude

Maintained courage and force, and in myself
Nursed an immortal vigor—I alone   320
Am dead to life and joy, therefore I read
In all things my own deadness.

> *A long silence. He continues:*—

Oh, that I could glow like this mountain!
Oh, that my heart bounded with the swell of sea!
Oh, that my soul were full of light as the stars!   325
Oh, that it brooded over the world like the air!

But no, this heart will glow no more; thou art
A living man no more, Empedocles!
Nothing but a devouring flame of thought—
But a naked, eternally restless mind!   330

> *After a pause:*—

To the elements it came from
Everything will return—
Our bodies to earth,
Our blood to water,
Heat to fire,   335
Breath to air.
They were well born, they will be well entombed—
But mind? . . .

And we might gladly share the fruitful stir
Down in our mother earth's miraculous womb;   340
Well would it be
With what rolled of us in the stormy main;
We might have joy, blent with the all-bathing air,
Or with the nimble, radiant life of fire.

But mind, but thought—   345
If these have been the master part of us—
Where will *they* find their parent element?
What will receive *them,* who will call *them* home?[11]
But we shall still be in them, and they in us,
And we shall be the strangers of the world,   350
And they will be our lords, as they are now;
And keep us prisoners of our consciousness,
And never let us clasp and feel the All

But through their forms, and modes, and stifling veils.[12]
And we shall be unsatisfied as now;   355
And we shall feel the agony of thirst,
The ineffable longing for the life of life
Baffled for ever; and still thought and mind
Will hurry us with them on their homeless march,
Over the unallied unopening earth,   360
Over the unrecognising sea; while air
Will blow us fiercely back to sea and earth,
And fire repel us from its living waves.
And then we shall unwillingly return
Back to this meadow of calamity,   365
This uncongenial place, this human life;
And in our individual human state
Go through the sad probation all again,
To see if we will poise our life at last,
To see if we will now at last be true   370
To our own only true, deep-buried selves,
Being one with which we are one with the whole world;
Or whether we will once more fall away
Into some bondage of the flesh or mind,
Some slough of sense, or some fantastic maze   375
Forged by the imperious lonely thinking-power.[13]
And each succeeding age in which we are born
Will have more peril for us than the last;
Will goad our senses with a sharper spur,
Will fret our minds to an intenser play,   380
Will make ourselves harder to be discerned.
And we shall struggle awhile, gasp and rebel—
And we shall fly for refuge to past times,
Their soul of unworn youth, their breath of greatness;
And the reality will pluck us back,   385
Knead us in its hot hand, and change our nature.
And we shall feel our powers of effort flag,
And rally them for one last fight—and fail;
And we shall sink in the impossible strife,
And be astray for ever.

> Slave of sense   390
> I have in no wise been;—but slave of thought? . . .

---

11 The background is the ancient belief that human beings are composed of the four basic elements and return to them at death. But if the mind (the abstract, logical mind divorced from feeling) has been dominant, Arnold suggests, it would have nothing to return to.

12 If men become "thought's slaves," they are prisoners of the mind, never able to know the world directly through experience, but only at one remove, through the forms and modes of logic, which are therefore, in effect, stifling veils.

13 Lonely because to be cut off from concrete experience is to live alone in the ivory tower of the mind. In this context the true, deep-buried self would seem to be the balanced sensibility described in lines 240–49.

And who can say: I have been always free,
Lived ever in the light of my own soul?—
I cannot; I have lived in wrath and gloom,
Fierce, disputatious, ever at war with man,   395
Far from my own soul, far from warmth and
    light.
But I have not grown easy in these bonds—
But I have not denied what bonds these were.
Yea, I take myself to witness,
That I have loved no darkness,   400
Sophisticated no truth,
Nursed no delusion,
Allowed no fear!

    And therefore, O ye elements! I know—
Ye know it too—it hath been granted me   405
Not to die wholly, not to be all enslaved.
I feel it in this hour. The numbing cloud
Mounts off my soul; I feel it, I breathe free.

Is it but for a moment?
    —Ah, boil up, ye vapors!   410

Leap and roar, thou sea of fire!
My soul glows to meet you.
Ere it flag, ere the mists
Of despondency and gloom
Rush over it again,   415
Receive me, save me!14

            He plunges into the crater.

CALLICLES
(*from below*)

Through the black, rushing smoke-bursts,
Thick breaks the red flame;
All Etna heaves fiercely
Her forest-clothed frame.   420

Not here, O Apollo!
Are haunts meet for thee.
But, where Helicon breaks down
In cliff to the sea,

Where the moon-silvered inlets   425
Send far their light voice
Up the still vale of Thisbe,
O speed, and rejoice!15

On the sward at the cliff-top
Lie strewn the white flocks,   430
On the cliff-side the pigeons
Roost deep in the rocks.

In the moonlight the shepherds,
Soft lulled by the rills,
Lie wrapped in their blankets   435
Asleep on the hills.

—What forms are these coming
So white through the gloom?
What garments out-glistening
The gold-flowered broom?   440

What sweet-breathing presence
Out-perfumes the thyme?
What voices enrapture
The night's balmy prime?—

'Tis Apollo comes leading   445
His choir, the Nine.16
—The leader is fairest,
But all are divine.

They are lost in the hollows!
They stream up again!   450
What seeks on this mountain
The glorified train?—

They bathe on this mountain,
In the spring by their road;
Then on to Olympus,   455
Their endless abode.

—Whose praise do they mention?
Of what is it told?—
What will be for ever;
What was from of old.   460

First hymn they the Father
Of all things; and then,
The rest of immortals,17
The action of men.

The day in his hotness,   465
The strife with the palm;

---

14 For the direct motivation of suicide, cf. lines 23–36 of
this act and Arnold's own statement given in the headnote to the poem, last paragraph.
15 Helicon was the mountain of the Muses in Greece near

the "inlets" of the Gulf of Corinth, and Thisbe a village
in the valley below.
16 The Muses.
17 "Rest" here means "repose."

The night in her silence,
The stars in their calm.[18]

Preface to *Poems*, 1853

In two small volumes of Poems, published anonymously, one in 1849, the other in 1852, many of the Poems which compose the present volume have already appeared. The rest are now published for the first time.

I have, in the present collection, omitted the poem from which the volume published in 1852 took its title.[1] I have done so, not because the subject of it was a Sicilian Greek born between two and three thousand years ago, although many persons would think this a sufficient reason. Neither have I done so because I had, in my own opinion, failed in the delineation which I intended to effect. I intended to delineate the feelings of one of the last of the Greek religious philosophers, one of the family of Orpheus and Musaeus,[2] having survived his fellows, living on into a time when the habits of Greek thought and feeling had begun fast to change, character to dwindle, the influence of the Sophists[3] to prevail. Into the feelings of a man so situated there entered much that we are accustomed to consider as exclusively modern; how much, the fragments of Empedocles himself which remain to us are sufficient at least to indicate. What those who are familiar only with the great monuments of early Greek genius suppose to be its exclusive characteristics, have disappeared; the calm, the cheerfulness, the disinterested objectivity have disappeared; the dialogue of the mind with itself has commenced; modern problems have presented themselves; we hear already the doubts, we witness the discouragement, of Hamlet and of Faust.

The representation of such a man's feelings

must be interesting, if consistently drawn. We all naturally take pleasure, says Aristotle,[4] in any imitation or representation whatever: this is the basis of our love of poetry: and we take pleasure in them, he adds, because all knowledge is naturally agreeable to us; not to the philosopher only, but to mankind at large. Every representation therefore which is consistently drawn may be supposed to be interesting, inasmuch as it gratifies this natural interest in knowledge of all kinds. What is *not* interesting, is that which does not add to our knowledge of any kind; that which is vaguely conceived and loosely drawn; a representation which is general, indeterminate, and faint, instead of being particular, precise, and firm.

Any accurate representation may therefore be expected to be interesting; but, if the representation be a poetical one, more than this is demanded. It is demanded, not only that it shall interest, but also that it shall inspirit and rejoice the reader: that it shall convey a charm, and infuse delight. For the Muses, as Hesiod says,[5] were born that they might be "a forgetfulness of evils, and a truce from cares": and it is not enough that the poet should add to the knowledge of men, it is required of him also that he should add to their happiness. "All art," says Schiller, "is dedicated to Joy, and there is no higher and no more serious problem, than how to make men happy. The right art is that alone, which creates the highest enjoyment."

A poetical work, therefore, is not yet justified when it has been shown to be an accurate, and therefore interesting representation; it has to be shown also that it is a representation from which men can derive enjoyment. In presence of the most tragic circumstances represented in a work of art, the feeling of enjoyment, as is well known, may still subsist: the representation of the most utter calamity, of the liveliest anguish, is not sufficient to destroy it: the more tragic the situation, the deeper becomes the enjoyment; and the situation is more tragic in proportion as it becomes more terrible.

What then are the situations, from the representation of which, though accurate, no poetical enjoyment can be derived? They are

---

[18] Callicles the poet sings of the poetic life of contemplation, ranging over the divine and human worlds, in pointed comparison with the life Empedocles had once lived (lines 240–57) and in poignant contrast with the life of abstract thought he had adopted.

[1] "Empedocles on Etna."
[2] Legendary Greek poets and musicians. Orpheus was the father of Musaeus.
[3] Greek teachers of philosophy and rhetoric whose influence led to the placing of greater emphasis on ingenious argument than on the substance of truth.

[4] *Poetics*, IV, 2–5.
[5] Early Greek poet in his *Theogony*.

those in which the suffering finds no vent in action; in which a continuous state of mental distress is prolonged, unrelieved by incident, hope, or resistance; in which there is everything to be endured, nothing to be done. In such situations there is inevitably something morbid, in the description of them something monotonous. When they occur in actual life, they are painful, not tragic; the representation of them in poetry is painful also.

To this class of situations, poetically faulty as it appears to me, that of Empedocles, as I have endeavoured to represent him, belongs; and I have therefore excluded the poem from the present collection.

And why, it may be asked, have I entered into this explanation respecting a matter so unimportant as the admission or exclusion of the poem in question? I have done so, because I was anxious to avow that the sole reason for its exclusion was that which has been stated above; and that it has not been excluded in deference to the opinion which many critics of the present day appear to entertain against subjects chosen from distant times and countries: against the choice, in short, of any subjects but modern ones.

"The poet," it is said,[6] and by an intelligent critic, "the poet who would really fix the public attention must leave the exhausted past, and draw his subjects from matters of present import, and *therefore* both of interest and novelty."

Now this view I believe to be completely false. It is worth examining, inasmuch as it is a fair sample of a class of critical dicta everywhere current at the present day, having a philosophical form and air, but no real basis in fact; and which are calculated to vitiate the judgement of readers of poetry, while they exert, so far as they are adopted, a misleading influence on the practice of those who make it.

What are the eternal objects of poetry, among all nations and at all times? They are actions; human actions; possessing an inherent interest in themselves, and which are to be communicated in an interesting manner by the art of the poet. Vainly will the latter imagine that he has everything in his own power; that he can make an intrinsically inferior action equally

delightful with a more excellent one by his treatment of it: he may indeed compel us to admire his skill, but his work will possess, within itself, an incurable defect.

The poet, then, has in the first place to select an excellent action; and what actions are the most excellent? Those, certainly, which most powerfully appeal to the great primary human affections: to those elementary feelings which subsist permanently in the race, and which are independent of time. These feelings are permanent and the same; that which interests them is permanent and the same also. The modernness or antiquity of an action, therefore, has nothing to do with its fitness for poetical representation; this depends upon its inherent qualities. To the elementary part of our nature, to our passions, that which is great and passionate is eternally interesting; and interesting solely in proportion to its greatness and to its passion. A great human action of a thousand years ago is more interesting to it than a smaller human action of today, even though upon the representation of this last the most consummate skill may have been expended, and though it has the advantage of appealing by its modern language, familiar manners, and contemporary allusions, to all our transient feelings and interests. These, however, have no right to demand of a poetical work that it shall satisfy them; their claims are to be directed elsewhere. Poetical works belong to the domain of our permanent passions: let them interest these, and the voice of all subordinate claims upon them is at once silenced.

Achilles, Prometheus, Clytemnestra, Dido—what modern poem presents personages as interesting, even to us moderns, as these personages of an "exhausted past"? We have the domestic epic dealing with the details of modern life, which pass daily under our eyes; we have poems representing modern personages in contact with the problems of modern life, moral, intellectual, and social; these works have been produced by poets the most distinguished of their nation and time; yet I fearlessly assert that *Hermann and Dorothea, Childe Harold, Jocelyn,* the *Excursion,*[7] leave the reader cold in comparison with the effect produced upon him by the latter books

---

6 "In the *Spectator* of April 2, 1853. The words quoted were not used with reference to poems of mine." (Arnold)

7 Narrative and philosophical poems by Goethe, Byron, Lamartine, and Wordsworth.

of the *Iliad,* by the *Oresteia,* or by the episode of Dido.[8] And why is this? Simply because in the three last-named cases the action is greater, the personages nobler, the situations more intense: and this is the true basis of the interest in a poetical work, and this alone.

It may be urged, however, that past actions may be interesting in themselves, but that they are not to be adopted by the modern poet, because it is impossible for him to have them clearly present to his own mind, and he cannot therefore feel them deeply, nor represent them forcibly. But this is not necessarily the case. The externals of a past action, indeed, he cannot know with the precision of a contemporary; but his business is with its essentials. The outward man of Oedipus[9] or of Macbeth, the houses in which they lived, the ceremonies of their courts, he cannot accurately figure to himself; but neither do they essentially concern him. His business is with their inward man; with their feelings and behaviour in certain tragic situations, which engage their passions as men; these have in them nothing local and casual; they are as accessible to the modern poet as to a contemporary.

The date of an action, then, signifies nothing: the action itself, its selection and construction, this is what is all-important. This the Greeks understood far more clearly than we do. The radical difference between their poetical theory and ours consists, as it appears to me, in this: that, with them, the poetical character of the action in itself, and the conduct of it, was the first consideration; with us, attention is fixed mainly on the value of the separate thoughts and images which occur in the treatment of an action. They regarded the whole; we regard the parts. With them, the action predominated over the expression of it; with us, the expression predominates over the action. Not that they failed in expression, or were inattentive to it; on the contrary, they are the highest models of expression, the unapproached masters of the *grand style:*[10] but their expression is so excellent be-

cause it is so admirably kept in its right degree of prominence; because it is so simple and so well subordinated; because it draws its force directly from the pregnancy of the matter which it conveys. For what reason was the Greek tragic poet confined to so limited a range of subjects? Because there are so few actions which united in themselves, in the highest degree, the conditions of excellence; and it was not thought that on any but an excellent subject could an excellent poem be constructed. A few actions, therefore, eminently adapted for tragedy, maintained almost exclusive possession of the Greek tragic stage. Their significance appeared inexhaustible; they were as permanent problems, perpetually offered to the genius of every fresh poet. This too is the reason of what appears to us moderns a certain baldness of expression in Greek tragedy; of the triviality with which we often reproach the remarks of the chorus, where it takes part in the dialogue: that the action itself, the situation of Orestes, or Merope, or Alcmaeon,[11] was to stand the central point of interest, unforgotten, absorbing, principal; that no accessories were for a moment to distract the spectator's attention from this, that the tone of the parts was to be perpetually kept down, in order not to impair the grandiose effect of the whole. The terrible old mythic story on which the drama was founded stood, before he entered the theatre, traced in its bare outlines upon the spectator's mind; it stood in his memory, as a group of statuary, faintly seen, at the end of a long and dark vista: then came the poet, embodying outlines, developing situations, not a word wasted, not a sentiment capriciously thrown in: stroke upon stroke, the drama proceeded: the light deepened upon the group; more and more it revealed itself to the rivetted gaze of the spectator: until at last, when the final words were spoken, it stood before him in broad sunlight, a model of immortal beauty.

This was what a Greek critic demanded; this was what a Greek poet endeavoured to effect. It signified nothing to what time an action belonged. We do not find that the *Persae* occupied a particularly high rank among the dramas of Aeschylus because it represented a matter of contemporary interest: this was not what a cultivated Athenian required. He required that the perma-

---

8 Cf. the opening sentence of this paragraph. Clytemnestra, the wife of Agamemnon, is in Aeschylus' *Oresteia.*

9 King of Thebes and hero of Sophocles' *Oedipus Tyrannus.*

10 That is, great art. Cf. Arnold's definition in his *On Translating Homer: Last Words:* "The grand style arises in poetry, when a noble nature, poetically gifted, treats with simplicity or with severity a serious subject."

---

11 Three heroic characters in Greek tragedies, each of whom was involved in avenging a family murder.

nent elements of his nature should be moved; and dramas of which the action, though taken from a long-distant mythic time, yet was calculated to accomplish this in a higher degree than that of the *Persae,* stood higher in his estimation accordingly. The Greeks felt, no doubt, with their exquisite sagacity of taste, that an action of present times was too near them, too much mixed up with what was accidental and passing, to form a sufficiently grand, detached, and self-subsistent object for a tragic poem. Such objects belonged to the domain of the comic poet, and of the lighter kinds of poetry. For the more serious kinds, for *pragmatic* poetry, to use an excellent expression of Polybius,[12] they were more difficult and severe in the range of subjects which they permitted. Their theory and practice alike, the admirable treatise of Aristotle, and the unrivalled works of their poets, exclaim with a thousand tongues—"All depends upon the subject; choose a fitting action, penetrate yourself with the feeling of its situations; this done, everything else will follow."

But for all kinds of poetry alike there was one point on which they were rigidly exacting; the adaptability of the subject to the kind of poetry selected, and the careful construction of the poem.

How different a way of thinking from this is ours! We can hardly at the present day understand what Menander meant, when he told a man who inquired as to the progress of his comedy that he had finished it, not having yet written a single line, because he had constructed the action of it in his mind. A modern critic would have assured him that the merit of his piece depended on the brilliant things which arose under his pen as he went along. We have poems which seem to exist merely for the sake of single lines and passages; not for the sake of producing any total impression. We have critics who seem to direct their attention merely to detached expressions, to the language about the action, not to the action itself. I verily think that the majority of them do not in their hearts believe that there is such a thing as a total-impression to be derived from a poem at all, or to be demanded from a poet; they think the term a commonplace of metaphysical criticism. They

will permit the poet to select any action he pleases, and to suffer that action to go as it will, provided he gratifies them with occasional bursts of fine writing, and with a shower of isolated thoughts and images. That is, they permit him to leave their poetical sense ungratified, provided that he gratifies their rhetorical sense and their curiosity. Of his neglecting to gratify these, there is little danger; he needs rather to be warned against the danger of attempting to gratify these alone; he needs rather to be perpetually reminded to prefer his action to everything else; so to treat this, as to permit its inherent excellences to develop themselves, without interruption from the intrusion of his personal peculiarities: most fortunate when he most entirely succeeds in effacing himself, and in enabling a noble action to subsist as it did in nature.

But the modern critic not only permits a false practice: he absolutely prescribes false aims. "A true allegory of the state of one's own mind in a representative history," the poet is told, "is perhaps the highest thing that one can attempt in the way of poetry."[13] And accordingly he attempts it. An allegory of the state of one's own mind, the highest problem of an art which imitates actions! No, assuredly, it is not, it never can be so: no great poetical work has ever been produced with such an aim. *Faust* itelf, in which something of the kind is attempted, wonderful passages as it contains, and in spite of the unsurpassed beauty of the scenes which relate to Margaret, *Faust* itself, judged as a whole, and judged strictly as a poetical work, is defective: its illustrious author, the greatest poet of modern times, the greatest critic of all times, would have been the first to acknowledge it; he only defended his work, indeed, by asserting it to be "something incommensurable."

The confusion of the present times is great, the multitude of voices counselling different things bewildering, the number of existing works capable of attracting a younger writer's attention and of becoming his models, immense: what he wants is a hand to guide him through the confusion, a voice to prescribe to him the aim which he should keep in view, and to explain to him that the value of the literary works which offer themselves to his attention is relative to their

---

12 The Greek historian of the second century B.C. Pragmatic poetry means poetry concerned with the business of life, social and personal.

13 The critic was David Masson, writing in the *North British Review* for August, 1853: see *The Wellesley Index to Victorian Periodicals,* ed. W. E. Houghton, Vol. I.

power of helping him forward on his road towards this aim. Such a guide the English writer at the present day will nowhere find. Failing this, all that can be looked for, all indeed that can be desired, is, that his attention should be fixed on excellent models; that he may reproduce, at any rate, something of their excellence, by penetrating himself with their works and by catching their spirit, if he cannot be taught to produce what is excellent independently.

Foremost among these models for the English writer stands Shakespeare: a name the greatest perhaps of all poetical names; a name never to be mentioned without reverence. I will venture, however, to express a doubt whether the influence of his works, excellent and fruitful for the readers of poetry, for the great majority, has been an unmixed advantage to the writers of it. Shakespeare indeed chose excellent subjects—the world could afford no better than *Macbeth,* or *Romeo and Juliet,* or *Othello:* he had no theory respecting the necessity of choosing subjects of present import, or the paramount interest attaching to allegories of the state of one's own mind; like all great poets, he knew well what constituted a poetical action; like them, wherever he found such an action, he took it; like them, too, he found his best in past times. But to these general characteristics of all great poets he added a special one of his own; a gift, namely, of happy, abundant, and ingenious expression, eminent and unrivalled; so eminent as irresistibly to strike the attention first in him and even to throw into comparative shade his other excellences as a poet. Here has been the mischief. These other excellences were his fundamental excellences *as a poet;* what distinguishes the artist from the mere amateur, says Goethe, is *Architectonicè* in the highest sense; that power of execution which creates, forms, and constitutes: not the profoundness of single thoughts, not the richness of imagery, not the abundance of illustration. But these attractive accessories of a poetical work being more easily seized than the spirit of the whole, and these accessories being possessed by Shakespeare in an unequalled degree, a young writer having recourse to Shakespeare as his model runs great risk of being vanquished and absorbed by them, and, in consequence, of reproducing, according to the measure of his power, these, and these alone. Of this pre-

pondering quality of Shakespeare's genius, accordingly, almost the whole of modern English poetry has, it appears to me, felt the influence. To the exclusive attention on the part of his imitators to this, it is in a great degree owing that of the majority of a modern poetical works the details alone are valuable, the composition worthless. In reading them one is perpetually reminded of that terrible sentence on a modern French poet,—*il dit tout ce qu'il veut, mais malheureusement il n'a rien à dire.*[14]

Let me give an instance of what I mean. I will take it from the works of the very chief among those who seem to have been formed in the school of Shakespeare; of one whose exquisite genius and pathetic death render him forever interesting. I will take the poem of *Isabella, or the Pot of Basil,* by Keats. I choose this rather than the *Endymion,* because the latter work (which a modern critic has classed with the *Faery Queen!*), although undoubtedly there blows through it the breath of genius, is yet as a whole so utterly incoherent, as not strictly to merit the name of a poem at all. The poem of *Isabella,* then, is a perfect treasure-house of graceful and felicitous words and images: almost in every stanza there occurs one of those vivid and picturesque turns of expression, by which the object is made to flash upon the eye of the mind, and which thrill the reader with a sudden delight. This one short poem contains, perhaps, a greater number of happy single expressions which one could quote than all the extant tragedies of Sophocles. But the action, the story? The action in itself is an excellent one; but so feebly is it conceived by the poet, so loosely constructed, that the effect produced by it, in and for itself, is absolutely null. Let the reader, after he has finished the poem of Keats, turn to the same story in the *Decameron:*[15] he will then feel how pregnant and interesting the same action has become in the hands of a great artist, who above all things delineates his object; who subordinates expression to that which it is designed to express.

I have said that the imitators of Shakespeare, fixing their attention on his wonderful

---

14 "He says all he wishes to, but unfortunately he has nothing to say." The poet referred to is Théophile Gautier (1811–1872), the leader of the French school of Art for Art's Sake.

15 By Boccaccio: the fifth novel of the fourth day.

gift of expression, have directed their imitation to this, neglecting his other excellences. These excellences, the fundamental excellences of poetical art, Shakespeare no doubt possessed them— possessed many of them in a splendid degree; but it may perhaps be doubted whether even he himself did not sometimes give scope to his faculty of expression to the prejudice of a higher poetical duty. For we must never forget that Shakespeare is the great poet he is from his skill in discerning and firmly conceiving an excellent action, from his power of intensely feeling a situation, of intimately associating himself with a character; not from his gift of expression, which rather even leads him astray, degenerating sometimes into a fondness for curiosity of expression, into an irritability of fancy, which seems to make it impossible for him to say a thing plainly, even when the press of the action demands the very directest language, or its level character the very simplest. Mr. Hallam,[16] than whom it is impossible to find a saner and more judicious critic, has had the courage (for at the present day it needs courage) to remark, how extremely and faultily difficult Shakespeare's language often is. It is so: you may find main scenes in some of his greatest tragedies, *King Lear,* for instance, where the language is so artificial, so curiously tortured, and so difficult, that every speech has to be read two or three times before its meaning can be comprehended. This over-curiousness of expression is indeed but the excessive employment of a wonderful gift—of the power of saying a thing in a happier way than any other man; nevertheless, it is carried so far that one understands what M. Guizot[17] meant when he said that Shakespeare appears in his language to have tried all styles except that of simplicity. He has not the severe and scrupulous self-restraint of the ancients, partly, no doubt, because he had a far less cultivated and exacting audience. He has indeed a far wider range than they had, a far richer fertility of thought; in this respect he rises above them. In his strong conception of his subject, in the genuine way in which he is penetrated with it, he resembles them, and is unlike the moderns.

But in the accurate limitation of it, the conscientious rejection of superfluities, the simple and rigorous development of it from the first line of his work to the last, he falls below them, and comes nearer to the moderns. In his chief works, besides what he has of his own, he has the elementary soundness of the ancients; he has their important action and their large and broad manner; but he has not their purity of method. He is therefore a less safe model; for what he has of his own is personal, and inseparable from his own rich nature; it may be imitated and exaggerated, it cannot be learned or applied as an art. He is above all suggestive; more valuable, therefore, to young writers as men than as artists. But clearness of arrangement, rigour of development, simplicity of style—these may to a certain extent be learned: and these may, I am convinced, be learned best from the ancients, who, although infinitely less suggestive than Shakespeare, are thus, to the artist, more instructive.

What then, it will be asked, are the ancients to be our sole models? the ancients with their comparatively narrow range of experience, and their widely different circumstances? Not, certainly, that which is narrow in the ancients, nor that in which we can no longer sympathize. An action like the action of the *Antigone* of Sophocles, which turns upon the conflict between the heroine's duty to her brother's corpse and that to the laws of her country, is no longer one in which it is possible that we should feel a deep interest. I am speaking too, it will be remembered, not of the best sources of intellectual stimulus for the general reader, but of the best models of instruction for the individual writer. This last may certainly learn of the ancients, better than anywhere else, three things which it is vitally important for him to know:—the all-importance of the choice of a subject; the necessity of accurate construction; and the subordinate character of expression. He will learn from them how unspeakably superior is the effect of the one moral impression left by a great action treated as a whole, to the effect produced by the most striking single thought or by the happiest image. As he penetrates into the spirit of the great classical works, as he becomes gradually aware of their intense significance, their noble simplicity, and their calm pathos, he will be convinced that it is this effect, unity and profoundness of moral im-

---

[16] Henry Hallam (1777–1859) in his *Introduction to the Literature of Europe in the Fifteenth, Sixteenth, and Seventeenth Centuries,* chap. 23.
[17] The French historian (1787–1874) in his preface to *Shakespeare and His Times.*

pression, at which the ancient poets aimed; that it is this which constitutes the grandeur of their works, and which makes them immortal. He will desire to direct his own efforts towards producing the same effect. Above all, he will deliver himself from the jargon of modern criticism, and escape the danger of producing poetical works conceived in the spirit of the passing time, and which partake of its transitoriness.

The present age makes great claims upon us: we owe it service, it will not be satisfied without our admiration. I know not how it is, but their commerce with the ancients appears to me to produce, in those who constantly practise it, a steadying and composing effect upon their judgement, not of literary works only, but of men and events in general. They are like persons who have had a very weighty and impressive experience; they are more truly than others under the empire of facts, and more independent of the language current among those with whom they live. They wish neither to applaud nor to revile their age: they wish to know what it is, what it can give them, and whether this is what they want. What they want, they know very well; they want to educe and cultivate what is best and noblest in themselves: they know, too, that this is no easy task—χαλεπὸν, as Pittacus said, χαλεπὸν ἐσθλὸν ἔμμεναι[18]—and they ask themselves sincerely whether their age and its literature can assist them in the attempt. If they are endeavouring to practise any art, they remember the plain and simple proceedings of the old artists, who attained their grand results by penetrating themselves with some noble and significant action, not by inflating themselves with a belief in the preeminent importance and greatness of their own times. They do not talk of their mission, nor of interpreting their age, nor of the coming poet; all this, they know, is the mere delirium of vanity; their business is not to praise their age, but to afford to the men who live in it the highest pleasure which they are capable of feeling. If asked to afford this by means of subjects drawn from the age itself, they ask what special fitness the present age has for supplying them. They are told that it is an era of progress, an age commissioned to carry out the great ideas of industrial development and social amelioration. They reply that with all this they can do nothing; that the elements they need for the exercise of their art are great actions, calculated powerfully and delightfully to affect what is permanent in the human soul; that so far as the present age can supply such actions, they will gladly make use of them; but that an age wanting in moral grandeur can with difficulty supply such, and an age of spiritual discomfort with difficulty be powerfully and delightfully affected by them.

A host of voices will indignantly rejoin that the present age is inferior to the past neither in moral grandeur nor in spiritual health. He who possesses the discipline I speak of will content himself with remembering the judgements passed upon the present age, in this respect, by the men of strongest head and widest culture whom it has produced; by Goethe and by Niebuhr.[19] It will be sufficient for him that he knows the opinions held by these two great men respecting the present age and its literature; and that he feels assured in his own mind that their aims and demands upon life were such as he would wish, at any rate, his own to be; and their judgement as to what is impeding and disabling such as he may safely follow. He will not, however, maintain a hostile attitude towards the false pretensions of his age; he will content himself with not being overwhelmed by them. He will esteem himself fortunate if he can succeed in banishing from his mind all feelings of contradiction, and irritation, and impatience; in order to delight himself with the contemplation of some noble action of a heroic time, and to enable others, through his representation of it, to delight in it also.

I am far indeed from making any claim, for myself, that I possess this discipline; or for the following poems, that they breathe its spirit. But I say, that in the sincere endeavour to learn and practise, amid the bewildering confusion of our times, what is sound and true in poetical art, I seemed to myself to find the only sure guidance, the only solid footing, among the ancients. They, at any rate, knew what they wanted in art, and we do not. It is this uncertainty which is disheartening, and not hostile criticism. How often

---

[18] "It is hard to be excellent." Pittacus was one of the Seven Sages of Greece.

[19] A German historian of Rome, contemporary with Goethe.

have I felt this when reading words of disparagement or of cavil: that it is the uncertainty as to what is really to be aimed at which makes our difficulty, not the dissatisfaction of the critic, who himself suffers from the same uncertainty. *Non me tua fervida terrent Dicta; . . . Dii me terrent, et Jupiter hostis.*[20]

Two kinds of *dilettanti,* says Goethe, there are in poetry: he who neglects the indispensable mechanical part, and thinks he has done enough if he shows spirituality and feeling; and he who seeks to arrive at poetry merely by mechanism, in which he can acquire an artisan's readiness, and is without soul and matter. And he adds, that the first does most harm to art, and the last to himself. If we must be *dilettanti:* if it is impossible for us, under the circumstances amidst which we live, to think clearly, to feel nobly, and to delineate firmly: if we cannot attain to the mastery of the great artists—let us, at least, have so much respect for our art as to prefer it to ourselves. Let us not bewilder our successors: let us transmit to them the practice of poetry, with its boundaries and wholesome regulative laws, under which excellent works may again, perhaps, at some future time, be produced, not yet fallen into oblivion through our neglect, not yet condemned and cancelled by the influence of their eternal enemy, caprice.

from Essays in Criticism, First Series

I

from THE FUNCTION OF CRITICISM AT THE PRESENT TIME[1]

Many objections have been made to a proposition which, in some remarks of mine on translating Homer, I ventured to put forth; a proposition about criticism, and its importance at the present day. I said that "of the literature of France and Germany, as of the intellect of Europe in general, the main effort, for now many years, has been a critical effort; the endeavor, in all branches of knowledge, theology, philosophy, history, art, science, to see the object as in itself it really is." I added, that owing to the operation in English literature of certain causes, "almost the last thing for which one would come to English literature is just that very thing which now Europe most desires—criticism"; and that the power and value of English literature was thereby impaired. More than one rejoinder declared that the importance I here assigned to criticism was excessive, and asserted the inherent superiority of the creative effort of the human spirit over its critical effort. And the other day, having been led by a Mr. Shairp's excellent notice of Wordsworth,[2] to turn again to his biography, I found, in the words of this great man, whom I, for one, must always listen to with the profoundest respect, a sentence passed on the critic's business, which seems to justify every possible disparagement of it. Wordsworth says in one of his letters:

"The writers in these publications" (the Reviews), "while they prosecute their inglorious employment, cannot be supposed to be in a state of mind very favorable for being affected by the finer influences of a thing so pure as genuine poetry."

And a trustworthy reporter of his conversation quotes a more elaborate judgment to the same effect:

"Wordsworth holds the critical power very low, infinitely lower than the inventive; and he said to-day that if the quantity of time consumed in writing critiques on the works of others were given to original composition, of whatever kind it might be, it would be much better employed; it would make a man find out sooner his own level, and it would do infinitely less mischief. A false or malicious criticism may do much injury to the minds of others; a stupid invention, either in prose or verse, is quite harmless."

It is almost too much to expect of poor human nature, that a man capable of producing some effect in one line of literature, should, for the greater good of society, voluntarily doom himself to impotence and obscurity in another. Still less is this to be expected from men addicted to the composition of the "false or mali-

---

20 Vergil's *Aeneid,* XII, 894–95: "Your hot words do not frighten me. . . . The gods frighten me, and Jupiter as my enemy."

1 First published in November 1864. For a commentary see the introduction to Arnold.

2 John Campbell Shairp, "Wordsworth: The Man and the Poet," *North British Review,* XLI (1864), 1–54.

cious criticism" of which Wordsworth speaks. However, everybody would admit that a false or malicious criticism had better never have been written. Everybody, too, would be willing to admit, as a general proposition, that the critical faculty is lower than the inventive. But is it true that criticism is really, in itself, a baneful and injurious employment; is it true that all time given to writing critiques on the works of others would be much better employed if it were given to original composition of whatever kind this may be? Is it true that Johnson had better have gone on producing more *Irenes*[3] instead of writing his *Lives of the Poets;* nay, is it certain that Wordsworth himself was better employed in making his Ecclesiastical Sonnets than when he made his celebrated Preface,[4] so full of criticism, and criticism of the works of others? Wordsworth was himself a great critic, and it is to be sincerely regretted that he has not left us more criticism; Goethe was one of the greatest of critics, and we may sincerely congratulate ourselves that he has left us so much criticism. Without wasting time over the exaggeration which Wordsworth's judgment on criticism clearly contains, or over an attempt to trace the causes— not difficult, I think, to be traced—which may have led Wordsworth to this exaggeration, a critic may with advantage seize an occasion for trying his own conscience, and for asking himself of what real service, at any given moment, the practice of criticism either is, or may be made, to his own mind and spirit, and to the minds and spirits of others.

The critical power is of lower rank than the creative. True; but in assenting to this proposition, one or two things are to be kept in mind. It is undeniable that the exercise of a creative power, that a free creative activity, is the true function of man; it is proved to be so by man's finding in it his true happiness. But it is undeniable, also, that men may have the sense of exercising this free creative activity in other ways than in producing great works of literature or art; if it were not so, all but a very few men would be shut out from the true happiness of all men. They may have it in well-doing, they may have it in learning, they may have it even in

criticizing. This is one thing to be kept in mind. Another is, that the exercise of the creative power in the production of great works of literature or art, however high this exercise of it may rank, is not at all epochs and under all conditions possible; and that therefore labor may be vainly spent in attempting it, which might with more fruit be used in preparing for it, in rendering it possible. This creative power works with elements, with materials; what if it has not those materials, those elements, ready for its use? In that case it must surely wait till they are ready. Now, in literature—I will limit myself to literature, for it is about literature that the question arises—the elements with which the creative power works are ideas; the best ideas on every matter which literature touches, current at the time. At any rate we may lay it down as certain that in modern literature no manifestation of the creative power not working with these can be very important or fruitful. And I say *current* at the time, not merely accessible at the time; for creative literary genius does not principally show itself in discovering new ideas, that is rather the business of the philosopher. The grand work of literary genius is a work of synthesis and exposition, not of analysis and discovery; its gift lies in the faculty of being happily inspired by a certain intellectual and spiritual atmosphere, by a certain order of ideas, when it finds itself in them; of dealing divinely with these ideas, presenting them in the most effective and attractive combinations, making beautiful works with them, in short. But it must have the atmosphere, it must find itself amidst the order of ideas, in order to work freely; and these it is not so easy to command. This is why great creative epochs in literature are so rare; this is why there is so much that is unsatisfactory in the productions of many men of real genius; because, for the creation of a master-work of literature two powers must concur, the power of the man and the power of the moment, and the man is not enough without the moment; the creative power has, for its happy exercise, appointed elements, and those elements are not in its own control.

Nay, they are more within the control of the critical power. It is the business of the critical power, as I said in the words already quoted, "in all branches of knowledge, theology, philosophy, history, art, science, to see the object as in itself

---

[3] Dr. Johnson's *Irene* (1749) was an unsuccessful play.
[4] To the second edition of *Lyrical Ballads* (pp. 108–18).

it really is." Thus it tends, at last, to make an intellectual situation of which the creative power can profitably avail itself. It tends to establish an order of ideas, if not absolutely true, yet true by comparison with that which it displaces; to make the best ideas prevail. Presently these new ideas reach society, the touch of truth is the touch of life, and there is a stir and growth everywhere; out of this stir and growth come the creative epochs of literature.

Or, to narrow our range, and quit these considerations of the general march of genius and of society—considerations which are apt to become too abstract and impalpable—every one can see that a poet, for instance, ought to know life and the world before dealing with them in poetry; and life and the world being in modern times very complex things, the creation of a modern poet, to be worth much, implies a great critical effort behind it; else it would be a comparatively poor, barren, and short-lived affair. This is why Byron's poetry had so little endurance in it, and Goethe's so much; both Byron and Goethe had a great productive power, but Goethe's was nourished by a great critical effort providing the true materials for it, and Byron's was not; Goethe knew life and the world, the poet's necessary subjects, much more comprehensively and thoroughly than Byron. He know a great deal more of them, and he knew them much more as they really are.

It has long seemed to me that the burst of creative activity in our literature, through the first quarter of this century, had about it in fact something premature; and that from this cause its productions are doomed, most of them, in spite of the sanguine hopes which accompanied and do still accompany them, to prove hardly more lasting than the productions of far less splendid epochs. And this prematureness comes from its having proceeded without having its proper data, without sufficient materials to work with. In other words, the English poetry of the first quarter of this century, with plenty of energy, plenty of creative force, did not know enough. This makes Byron so empty of matter, Shelley so incoherent, Wordsworth even, profound as he is, yet so wanting in completeness and variety. Wordsworth cared little for books, and disparaged Goethe. I admire Wordsworth, as he is, so much that I cannot wish him different; and it is vain, no doubt, to imagine such a man

different from what he is, to suppose that he could have been different. But surely the one thing wanting to make Wordsworth an even greater poet than he is—his thought richer, and his influence of wider application—was that he should have read more books, among them, no doubt, those of that Goethe whom he disparaged without reading him.

But to speak of books and reading may easily lead to a misunderstanding here. It was not really books and reading that lacked to our poetry at this epoch; Shelley had plenty of reading, Coleridge had immense reading. Pindar and Sophocles—as we all say so glibly, and often with so little discernment of the real import of what we are saying—had not many books; Shakespeare was no deep reader. True; but in the Greece of Pindar and Sophocles, in the England of Shakespeare, the poet lived in a current of ideas in the highest degree animating and nourishing to the creative power; society was, in the fullest measure, permeated by fresh thought, intelligent and alive. And this state of things is the true basis for the creative power's exercise, in this it finds its data, its materials, truly ready for its hand; all the books and reading in the world are only valuable as they are helps to this. Even when this does not actually exist, books and reading may enable a man to construct a kind of semblance of it in his own mind, a world of knowledge and intelligence in which he may live and work. This is by no means an equivalent to the artist for the nationally diffused life and thought of the epochs of Sophocles or Shakespeare; but, besides that it may be a means of preparation for such epochs, it does really constitute, if many share in it, a quickening and sustaining atmosphere of great value. Such an atmosphere the many-sided learning and the long and widely-combined critical effort of Germany formed for Goethe, when he lived and worked. There was no national glow of life and thought there, as in the Athens of Pericles or the England of Elizabeth. That was the poet's weakness. But there was a sort of equivalent for it in the complete culture and unfettered thinking of a large body of Germans. That was his strength. In the England of the first quarter of this century there was neither a national glow of life and thought, such as we had in the age of Elizabeth, nor yet a culture and a force of learning and criticism such as were to be found in Germany. Therefore the creative power of poetry wanted, for success in the highest sense, materials and a basis; a thorough interpretation of the world was necessarily denied to it.

At first sight it seems strange that out of the immense stir of the French Revolution and its age should not have come a crop of works of genius equal to that which came out of the stir of the great productive time of Greece, or out of that of the Renaissance, with its powerful episode the Reformation. But the truth is that the stir of the French Revolution took a character which essentially distinguished it from such movements as these. These were, in the main, disinterestedly intellectual and spiritual movements; movements in which the human spirit looked for its satisfaction in itself and in the increased play of its own activity. The French Revolution took a political, practical character. The movement which went on in France under the old régime, from 1700 to 1789, was far more really akin than that of the Revolution itself to the movement of the Renaissance; the France of Voltaire and Rousseau told far more powerfully upon the mind of Europe than the France of the Revolution. Goethe reproached this last expressly with having "thrown quiet culture back." Nay, and the true key to how much in our Byron, even in our Wordsworth, is this!—that they had their source in a great movement of feeling, not in a great movement of mind. The French Revolution, however, that object of so much blind love and so much blind hatred, found undoubtedly its motive-power in the intelligence of men, and not in their practical sense;—this is what distinguishes it from the English Revolution of Charles the First's time. This is what makes it a more spiritual event than our Revolution, an event of much more powerful and world-wide interest, though practically less successful—it appeals to an order of ideas which are universal, certain, permanent. 1789 asked of a thing, Is it rational? 1642 asked of a thing, Is it legal? or, when it went furthest, Is it according to conscience? This is the English fashion, a fashion to be treated, within its own sphere, with the highest respect; for its success, within its own sphere, has been prodigious. But what is law in one place is not law in another; what is law here to-day is not law even here to-morrow; and as for conscience, what is binding on one man's conscience is not binding

on another's. The old woman who threw her stool at the head of the surpliced minister in the Tron Church at Edinburgh[5] obeyed an impulse to which millions of the human race may be permitted to remain strangers. But the prescriptions of reason are absolute, unchanging, of universal validity; *to count by tens is the easiest way of counting*—that is a proposition of which every one, from here to the Antipodes, feels the force; at least I should say so if we did not live in a country where it is not impossible that any morning we may find a letter in the *Times* declaring that a decimal coinage is an absurdity. That a whole nation should have been penetrated with an enthusiasm for pure reason, and with an ardent zeal for making its prescriptions triumph, is a very remarkable thing, when we consider how little of mind or anything so worthy and quickening as mind, comes into the motives which alone, in general, *impel* great masses of men. In spite of the extravagant direction given to this enthusiasm, in spite of the crimes and follies in which it lost itself, the French Revolution derives from the force, truth, and universality of the ideas which it took for its law, and from the passion with which it could inspire a multitude for these ideas, a unique and still living power; it is—it will probably long remain—the greatest, the most animating event in history. And as no sincere passion for the things of the mind, even though it turn out in many respects an unfortunate passion, is ever quite thrown away and quite barren of good, France has reaped from hers one fruit—the natural and legitimate fruit, though not precisely the grand fruit she expected: she is the country in Europe where *the people* is most alive.

But the mania for giving an immediate political and practical application to all these fine ideas of the reason was fatal. Here an Englishman is in his element: on this theme we can all go for hours. And all we are in the habit of saying on it has undoubtedly a great deal of truth. Ideas cannot be too much prized in and for themselves, cannot be too much lived with; but to transport them abruptly into the world of politics and practice, violently to revolutionize this world to their bidding—that is quite another

---

[5] Janet Geddes thus protested against the imposition of the English liturgy on the Scotch Church by Charles I in 1637.

thing. There is the world of ideas and there is the world of practice; the French are often for suppressing the one and the English the other; but neither is to be suppressed. A member of the House of Commons said to me the other day: "That a thing is an anomaly, I consider to be no objection to it whatever." I venture to think he was wrong; that a thing is an anomaly *is* an objection to it, but absolutely and in the sphere of ideas: it is not necessarily, under such and such circumstances, or at such and such a moment, an objection to it in the sphere of politics and practice. Joubert[6] has said beautifully: "C'est la force et le droit qui règlent toutes choses dans le monde; la force en attendant le droit." Force and right are the governors of this world; force till right is ready. *Force till right is ready;* and till right is ready, force, the existing order of things, is justified, is the legitimate ruler. But right is something moral, and implies inward recognition, free assent of the will; we are not ready for right—*right,* so far as we are concerned, *is not ready*—until we have attained this sense of seeing it and willing it. The way in which for us it may change and transform force, the existing order of things, and become, in its turn, the legitimate ruler of the world, will depend on the way in which, when our time comes, we see it and will it. Therefore for other people enamored of their own newly discerned right, to attempt to impose it upon us as ours, and violently to substitute their right for our force, is an act of tyranny, and to be resisted. It sets at nought the second great half of our maxim, *force till right is ready.* This was the grand error of the French Revolution; and its movement of ideas, by quitting the intellectual sphere and rushing furiously into the political sphere, ran, indeed, a prodigious and memorable course, but produced no such intellectual fruit as the movement of ideas of the Renaissance, and created, in opposition to itself, what I may call an *epoch of concentration.* The great force of that epoch of concentration was England; and the great voice of that epoch of concentration was Burke. It is the fashion to treat Burke's writings on the French Revolution as superannuated and conquered by the event; as the eloquent but unphilosophical tirades of bigotry and prejudice. I will not deny that they

are often disfigured by the violence and passion of the moment, and that in some directions Burke's view was bounded, and his observation therefore at fault. But on the whole, and for those who can make the needful corrections, what distinguishes these writings is their profound, permanent, fruitful, philosophical truth. They contain the true philosophy of an epoch of concentration, dissipate the heavy atmosphere which its own nature is apt to engender round it, and make its resistance rational instead of mechanical.

But Burke is so great because, almost alone in England, he brings thought to bear upon politics, he saturates politics with thought. It is his accident that his ideas were at the service of an epoch of concentration, not of an epoch of expansion; it is his characteristic that he so lived by ideas, and had such a source of them welling up within him, that he could float even an epoch of concentration and English Tory politics with them. It does not hurt him that Dr. Price[7] and the Liberals were displeased with him; it does not even hurt him that George the Third and the Tories were enchanted with him. His greatness is that he lived in a world which neither English Liberalism nor English Toryism is apt to enter; the world of ideas, not the world of catchwords and party habits. So far is it from being really true of him that he "to party gave up what was meant for mankind,"[8] that at the very end of his fierce struggle with the French Revolution, after all his invectives against its false pretensions, hollowness, and madness, with his sincere conviction of its mischievousness, he can close a memorandum on the best means of combating it, some of the last pages he ever wrote—the *Thoughts on French Affairs,* in December 1791—with these striking words:

"The evil is stated, in my opinion, as it exists. The remedy must be where power, wisdom, and information, I hope, are more united with good intentions than they can be with me. I have done with this subject, I believe, for ever. It has given me many anxious moments for the last two years. *If a great change is to be made in*

---

[6] French moralist of the nineteenth century.

[7] The nonconformist Richard Price, who preached a sermon in praise of the French Revolution that Burke singled out for special attack in his famous *Reflections on the French Revolution* (1790).
[8] Goldsmith in his "Retaliation."

human affairs, the minds of men will be fitted to it; the general opinions and feelings will draw that way. Every fear, every hope will forward it; and then they who persist in opposing this mighty current in human affairs, will appear rather to resist the decrees of Providence itself, than the mere designs of men. They will not be resolute and firm, but perverse and obstinate."

That return of Burke upon himself has always seemed to me one of the finest things in English literature, or indeed in any literature. That is what I call living by ideas: when one side of a question has long had your earnest support, when all your feelings are engaged, when you hear all round you no language but one, when your party talks this language like a steam-engine and can imagine no other—still to be able to think, still to be irresistibly carried, if so it be, by the current of thought to the opposite side of the question, and, like Balaam, to be unable to speak anything *but what the Lord has put in your mouth.*[9] I know nothing more striking, and I must add that I know nothing more un-English.

For the Englishman in general is like my friend the Member of Parliament, and believes, point-blank, that for a thing to be an anomaly is absolutely no objection to it whatever. He is like the Lord Auckland of Burke's day, who, in a memorandum on the French Revolution, talks of "certain miscreants, assuming the name of philosophers, who have presumed themselves capable of establishing a new system of society." The Englishman has been called a political animal, and he values what is political and practical so much that ideas easily become objects of dislike in his eyes, and thinkers "miscreants," because ideas and thinkers have rashly meddled with politics and practice. This would be all very well if the dislike and neglect confined themselves to ideas transported out of their own sphere, and meddling rashly with practice; but they are inevitably extended to ideas as such, and to the whole life of intelligence; practice is everything, a free play of the mind is nothing. The notion of the free play of the mind upon all subjects being a pleasure in itself, being an object of desire, being an essential provider of elements without which a nation's spirit, whatever compensations it may have for them, must, in the long run, die of inanition, hardly enters into an Englishman's thoughts. It is noticeable that the word *curiosity*, which in other languages is used in a good sense, to mean, as a high and fine quality of man's nature, just this disinterested love of a free play of the mind on all subjects, for its own sake,—it is noticeable, I say, that this word has in our language no sense of the kind, no sense but a rather bad and disparaging one. But criticism, real criticism, is essentially the exercise of this very quality. It obeys an instinct prompting it to try to know the best that is known and thought in the world, irrespectively of practice, politics, and everything of the kind; and to value knowledge and thought as they approach this best, without the intrusion of any other considerations whatever. This is an instinct for which there is, I think, little original sympathy in the practical English nature, and what there was of it has undergone a long benumbing period of blight and suppression in the epoch of concentration which followed the French Revolution.

But epochs of concentration cannot well endure for ever; epochs of expansion, in the due course of things, follow them. Such an epoch of expansion seems to be opening in this country. In the first place all danger of a hostile forcible pressure of foreign ideas upon our practice has long disappeared; like the traveller in the fable,[10] therefore, we begin to wear our cloak a little more loosely. Then, with a long peace, the ideas of Europe steal gradually and amicably in, and mingle, though in infinitesimally small quantities at a time, with our own notions. Then, too, in spite of all that is said about the absorbing and brutalizing influence of our passionate material progress, it seems to be indisputable that this progress is likely, though not certain, to lead in the end to an apparition of intellectual life; and that man, after he has made himself perfectly comfortable and has now to determine what to do with himself next, may begin to remember that he has a mind, and that the mind may be made the source of great pleasure. I grant it is mainly the privilege of faith, at present, to discern this end to our railways, our business, and our fortune-making; but we shall see if, here as elsewhere, faith is not in the end the true prophet. Our ease, our travelling, and our un-

---

[9] Numbers 22:35, 38.

[10] Of the wind and the sun in Aesop.

bounded liberty to hold just as hard and securely as we please to the practice to which our notions have given birth, all tend to beget an inclination to deal a little more freely with these notions themselves, to canvass them a little, to penetrate a little into their real nature. Flutterings of curiosity, in the foreign sense of the word, appear amongst us, and it is in these that criticism must look to find its account. Criticism first; a time of true creative activity, perhaps—which, as I have said, must inevitably be preceded amongst us by a time of criticism—hereafter, when criticism has done its work.

It is of the last importance that English criticism should clearly discern what rule for its course, in order to avail itself of the field now opening to it, and to produce fruit for the future, it ought to take. The rule may be summed up in one word—disinterestedness. And how is criticism to show disinterestedness? By keeping aloof from what is called "the practical view of things"; by resolutely following the law of its own nature, which is to be a free play of the mind on all subjects which it touches. By steadily refusing to lend itself to any of those ulterior, political, practical considerations about ideas, which plenty of people will be sure to attach to them, which perhaps ought often to be attached to them, which in this country at any rate are certain to be attached to them quite sufficiently, but which criticism has really nothing to do with. Its business is, as I have said, simply to know the best that is known and thought in the world, and by in its turn making this known, to create a current of true and fresh ideas. Its business is to do this with inflexible honesty, with due ability; but its business is to do no more, and to leave alone all questions of practical consequences and applications, questions which will never fail to have due prominence given to them. Else criticism, besides being really false to its own nature, merely continues in the old rut which it has hitherto followed in this country, and will certainly miss the chance now given to it.

For what is at present the bane of criticism in this country? It is that practical considerations cling to it and stifle it. It subserves interests not its own. Our organs of criticism are organs of men and parties having practical ends to serve, and with them those practical ends are the first thing and the play of mind the second; so much play of mind as is compatible with the prosecution of those practical ends is all that is wanted. An organ like the *Revue des Deux Mondes,* having for its main function to understand and utter the best that is known and thought in the world, existing, it may be said, as just an organ for a free play of the mind, we have not. But we have the *Edinburgh Review,* existing as an organ of the old Whigs, and for as much play of the mind as may suit its being that; we have the *Quarterly Review,* existing as an organ of the Tories, and for as much play of mind as may suit its being that; we have the *British Quarterly Review,* existing as an organ of the political Dissenters, and for as much play of mind as may suit its being that; we have the *Times,* existing as an organ of the common, satisfied, well-to-do Englishman, and for as much play of mind as may suit its being that. And so on through all the various fractions, political and religious, of our society; every fraction has, as such, its organ of criticism, but the notion of combining all fractions in the common pleasure of a free disinterested play of mind meets with no favor. Directly this play of mind wants to have more scope, and to forget the pressure of practical considerations a little, it is checked, it is made to feel the chain. We saw this the other day in the extinction, so much to be regretted, of the *Home and Foreign Review.* Perhaps in no organ of criticism in this country was there so much knowledge, so much play of mind; but these could not save it. The *Dublin Review* subordinates play of mind to the practical business of English and Irish Catholicism, and lives. It must needs be that men should act in sects and parties, that each of these sects and parties should have its organ, and should make this organ subserve the interests of its action; but it would be well, too, that there should be a criticism, not the minister of these interests, not their enemy, but absolutely and entirely independent of them. No other criticism will ever attain any real authority or make any real way towards its end,—the creating a current of true and fresh ideas.

It is because criticism has so little kept in the pure intellectual sphere, has so little detached itself from practice, has been so directly polemical and controversial, that it has so ill accomplished, in this country, its best spiritual work; which is to keep man from a self-satisfaction which is retarding and vulgarizing, to lead him towards perfection, by making his mind dwell upon what is excellent in itself, and the absolute beauty and fitness of things. A polemical practical criticism makes men blind even to the ideal imperfection of their practice, makes them willingly assert its ideal perfection, in order the better to secure it against attack; and clearly this is narrowing and baneful for them. If they were reassured on the practical side, speculative considerations of ideal perfection they might be brought to entertain, and their spiritual horizon would thus gradually widen. Sir Charles Adderley[11] says to the Warwickshire farmers:

Talk of the improvement of breed! Why, the race we ourselves represent, the men and women, the old Anglo-Saxon race, are the best breed in the whole world. . . . The absence of a too enervating climate, too unclouded skies, and a too luxurious nature, has produced so vigorous a race of people, and has rendered us so superior to all the world.

Mr. Roebuck[12] says to the Sheffield cutlers:

I look around me and ask what is the state of England? Is not property safe? Is not every man able to say what he likes? Can you not walk from one end of England to the other in perfect security? I ask you whether, the world over or in past history, there is anything like it? Nothing. I pray that our unrivalled happiness may last.

Now obviously there is a peril for poor human nature in words and thoughts of such exuberant self-satisfaction, until we find ourselves safe in the streets of the Celestial City.

*Das wenige verschwindet leicht dem Blicke
Der vorwärts sieht, wie viel noch übrig bleibt—*

says Goethe; "the little that is done seems nothing when we look forward and see how much we have yet to do." Clearly this is a better line of reflection for weak humanity, so long as it remains on this earthly field of labor and trial. But neither Sir Charles Adderley nor Mr. Roebuck is by nature inaccessible to considerations of this sort. They only lose sight of them

owing to the controversial life we all lead, and the practical form which all speculation takes with us. They have in view opponents whose aim is not ideal, but practical; and in their zeal to uphold their own practice against these innovators, they go so far as even to attribute to this practice an ideal perfection. Somebody has been wanting to introduce a six-pound franchise,[13] or to abolish church-rates,[14] or to collect agricultural statistics by force, or to diminish local self-government. How natural, in reply to such proposals, very likely improper or ill-timed, to go a little beyond the mark and to say stoutly, "such a race of people as we stand, so superior to all the world! The old Anglo-Saxon race, the best breed in the whole world! I pray that our unrivalled happiness may last! I ask you whether, the world over or in past history, there is anything like it?" And so long as criticism answers this dithyramb by insisting that the old Anglo-Saxon race would be still more superior to all others if it had no church-rates, or that our unrivalled happiness would last yet longer with a six-pound franchise, so long will the strain, "The best breed in the whole world!" swell louder and louder, everything ideal and refining will be lost out of sight, and both the assailed and their critics will remain in a sphere, to say the truth, perfectly unvital, a sphere in which spiritual progression is impossible. But let criticism leave church-rates and the franchise alone, and in the most candid spirit, without a single lurking thought of practical innovation, confront with our dithyramb this paragraph on which I stumbled in a newspaper immediately after reading Mr. Roebuck:

A shocking child murder has just been committed at Nottingham. A girl named Wragg left the workhouse there on Saturday morning with her young illegitimate child. The child was soon afterwards found dead on Mapperly Hills, having been strangled. Wragg is in custody.

Nothing but that; but, in juxtaposition with the absolute eulogies of Sir Charles Adderley and Mr. Roebuck, how eloquent, how suggestive are those few lines! "Our old Anglo-Saxon breed,

---

11 A Tory politician.
12 John Arthur Roebuck, a prominent radical and Utilitarian.

13 A law allowing all men to vote who own land or buildings whose rental value amounts to at least £6 per annum. The 1832 Reform Bill established the £10 franchise.
14 Taxes legally imposed by the state Church of England.

the best in the whole world!"—how much that is harsh and ill-favored there is in this best! *Wragg!* If we are to talk of ideal perfection, of "the best in the whole world," has any one reflected what a touch of grossness in our race, what an original shortcoming in the more delicate spiritual perceptions, is shown by the natural growth amongst us of such hideous names— Higginbottom, Stiggins, Bugg! In Ionia and Attica they were luckier in this respect than "the best race in the world"; by the Ilissus[15] there was no Wragg, poor thing! And "our unrivalled happiness";—what an element of grimness, bareness, and hideousness mixes with it and blurs it; the workhouse, the dismal Mapperly Hills—how dismal those who have seen them will remember; —the gloom, the smoke, the cold, the strangled illegitimate child! "I ask you whether, the world over or in past history, there is anything like it?" Perhaps not, one is inclined to answer; but at any rate, in that case, the world is very much to be pitied. And the final touch—short, bleak and inhuman: *Wragg is in custody.* The sex lost in the confusion of our unrivalled happiness; or (shall I say?) the superfluous Christian name lopped off by the straightforward vigor of our old Anglo-Saxon breed! There is profit for the spirit in such contrasts as this; criticism serves the cause of perfection by establishing them. By eluding sterile conflict, by refusing to remain in the sphere where alone narrow and relative conceptions have any worth and validity, criticism may diminish its momentary importance, but only in this way has it a chance of gaining admittance for those wider and more perfect conceptions to which all its duty is really owed. Mr. Roebuck will have a poor opinion of an adversary who replies to his defiant songs of triumph only by murmuring under his breath, *Wragg is in custody;* but in no other way will these songs of triumph be induced gradually to moderate themselves, to get rid of what in them is excessive and offensive, and to fall into a softer and truer key.

It will be said that it is a very subtle and indirect action which I am thus prescribing for criticism, and that, by embracing in this manner the Indian virtue of detachment and abandoning the sphere of practical life, it condemns itself to a slow and obscure work. Slow and obscure it may be, but it is the only proper work of criticism. The mass of mankind will never have any ardent zeal for seeing things as they are;[16] very inadequate ideas will always satisfy them. On these inadequate ideas reposes, and must repose, the general practice of the world. That is as much as saying that whoever sets himself to see things as they are will find himself one of a very small circle; but it is only by this small circle resolutely doing its own work that adequate ideas will ever get current at all. The rush and roar of practical life will always have a dizzying and attracting effect upon the most collected spectator, and tend to draw him into its vortex; most of all will this be the case where that life is so powerful as it is in England. But it is only by remaining collected, and refusing to lend himself to the point of view of the practical man, that the critic can do the practical man any service; and it is only by the greatest sincerity in pursuing his own course, and by at last convincing even the practical man of his sincerity, that he can escape misunderstandings which perpetually threaten him.

For the practical man is not apt for fine distinctions, and yet in these distinctions truth and the highest culture greatly find their account. But it is not easy to lead a practical man—unless you reassure him as to your practical intentions, you have no chance of leading him—to see that a thing which he has always been used to look at from one side only, which he greatly values, and which, looked at from that side, quite deserves, perhaps, all the prizing and admiring which he bestows upon it—that this thing, looked at from another side, may appear much less beneficent and beautiful, and yet retain all its claims to our practical allegiance. Where shall we find language innocent enough, how shall we make the spotless purity of our intentions evident enough, to enable us to say to the political Englishman that the British constitution itself, which, seen from the practical side, looks such a magnificent organ of progress and virtue, seen from the speculative side—with its compromises, its love of facts, its horror of theory, its studied

---

15 A famous river near Athens.

16 This important phrase, often used in *Culture and Anarchy,* has the same meaning as "seeing the object as in itself it really is" (opening paragraph of this essay)—that is, seeing them in their ultimate nature and truth. This is mainly achieved by a knowledge of "the best that is known and thought in the world."

avoidance of clear thoughts—that, seen from this side, our august constitution sometimes looks —forgive me, shade of Lord Somers![17]—a colossal machine for the manufacture of Philistines?[18] How is Cobbett[19] to say this and not be misunderstood, blackened as he is with the smoke of a lifelong conflict in the field of political practice? how is Mr. Carlyle to say it and not be misunderstood, after his furious raid into this field with his *Latter-day Pamphlets?* how is Mr. Ruskin, after his pugnacious political economy? I say, the critic must keep out of the region of immediate practice in the political, social, humanitarian sphere, if he wants to make a beginning for that more free speculative treatment of things, which may perhaps one day make its benefits felt even in this sphere, but in a natural and thence irresistible manner.

Do what he will, however, the critic will still remain exposed to frequent misunderstandings, and nowhere so much as in this country. For here people are particularly indisposed even to comprehend that without this free disinterested treatment of things, truth and the highest culture are out of the question. So immersed are they in practical life, so accustomed to take all their notions from this life and its processes, that they are apt to think that truth and culture themselves can be reached by the processes of this life, and that it is an impertinent singularity to think of reaching them in any other. "We are all *terrae filii*,"[20] cries their eloquent advocate; "all Philistines together. Away with the notion of proceeding by any other way than the way dear to the Philistines; let us have a social movement, let us organize and combine a party to pursue truth and new thought, let us call it *the liberal party,* and let us all stick to each other, and back each other up. Let us have no nonsense about independent criticism, and intellectual delicacy, and the few and the many. Don't let us trouble ourselves about foreign thought; we shall invent the whole thing for ourselves as we go along. If one of us speaks well, applaud him; if one of us

speaks ill, applaud him too; we are all in the same movement, we are all liberals, we are all in pursuit of truth." In this way the pursuit of truth becomes really a social, practical, pleasurable affair, almost requiring a chairman, a secretary, and advertisements; with the excitement of a little resistance, an occasional scandal, to give the happy sense of difficulty overcome; but, in general, plenty of bustle and very little thought. To act is so easy, as Goethe says; to think is so hard! It is true that the critic has many temptations to go with the stream, to make one of the party movement, one of these *terrae filii;* it seems ungracious to refuse to be a *terrae filius,* when so many excellent people are; but the critic's duty is to refuse, or, if resistance is vain, at least to cry with Obermann: *Périssons en résistant.*[21] . . .

I lately heard a man of thought and energy contrasting the want of ardor and movement which he now found amongst young men in this country with what he remembered in his own youth, twenty years ago. "What reformers we were then!" he exclaimed; "what a zeal we had! how we canvassed every institution in Church and State, and were prepared to remodel them all on first principles!" He was inclined to regret, as a spiritual flagging, the lull which he saw. I am disposed rather to regard it as a pause in which the turn to a new mode of spiritual progress is being accomplished. Everything was long seen, by the young and ardent amongst us, in inseparable connection with politics and practical life. We have pretty well exhausted the benefits of seeing things in this connection, we have got all that can be got by so seeing them. Let us try a more disinterested mode of seeing them; let us betake ourselves more to the serener life of the mind and spirit. This life, too, may have its excesses and dangers; but they are not for us at present. Let us think of quietly enlarging our stock of true and fresh ideas, and not, as soon as we get an idea or half an idea, be running out with it into the street, and trying to make it rule there. Our ideas will, in the end, shape the world all the better for maturing a little. Perhaps in fifty years' time it will in the English House of Commons be an objection to an institution that it is an anomaly, and my friend the Member of

---

17 The chairman of the committee that drew up the Declaration of Rights in 1689.
18 The enemies of the Israelites in the Old Testament. This is Arnold's famous term for the Victorian middle classes, the enemies of culture, neither possessing nor respecting "sweetness and light."
19 Radical journalist (1762–1835).
20 "Sons of the earth."

21 "Let us die resisting," from *Obermann* (1804), by the French romantic Etienne de Sénancour.

Parliament will shudder in his grave. But let us in the meanwhile rather endeavor that in twenty years' time it may, in English literature, be an objection to a proposition that it is absurd. That will be a change so vast, that the imagination almost fails to grasp it. *Ab integro saeclorum nascitur ordo.*[22]

If I have insisted so much on the course which criticism must take where politics and religion are concerned, it is because, where these burning matters are in question, it is most likely to go astray. I have wished, above all, to insist on the attitude which criticism should adopt towards things in general; on its right tone and temper of mind. But then comes another question as to the subject-matter which literary criticism should seek. Here in general, its course is determined for it by the idea which is the law of its being; the idea of a disinterested endeavor to learn and propagate the best that is known and thought in the world, and thus to establish a current of fresh and true ideas. By the very nature of things, as England is not all the world, much of the best that is known and thought in the world cannot be of English growth, must be foreign; by the nature of things, again, it is just this that we are least likely to know, while English thought is streaming in upon us from all sides, and takes excellent care that we shall not be ignorant of its existence. The English critic, therefore, must dwell much on foreign thought, and with particular heed on any part of it, which, while significant and fruitful in itself, is for any reason specially likely to escape him. Again, judging is often spoken of as the critic's one business, and so in some sense it is; but the judgment which almost insensibly forms itself in a fair and clear mind, along with fresh knowledge, is the valuable one; and thus knowledge, and ever fresh knowledge, must be the critic's great concern for himself. And it is by communicating fresh knowledge, and letting his own judgment pass along with it—but insensibly, and in the second place, not the first, as a sort of companion and clue, not as an abstract lawgiver—that he will generally do most good to his readers. Sometimes, no doubt, for the sake of establishing an author's

place in literature, and his relation to a central standard (and if this is not done, how are we to get at our *best in the world?*) criticism may have to deal with a subject-matter so familiar that fresh knowledge is out of the question, and then it must be all judgment; an enunciation and detailed application of principles. Here the great safeguard is never to let oneself become abstract, always to retain an intimate and lively consciousness of the truth of what one is saying, and, the moment this fails us, to be sure that something is wrong. Still, under all circumstances, this mere judgment and application of principles is, in itself, not the most satisfactory work to the critic; like mathematics, it is tautological, and cannot well give us, like fresh learning, the sense of creative activity.

But stop, someone will say; all this talk is of no practical use to us whatever; this criticism of yours is not what we have in our minds when we speak of criticism; when we speak of critics and criticism, we mean critics and criticism of the current English literature of the day; when you offer to tell criticism of its function, it is to this criticism that we expect you to address yourself. I am sorry for it for I am afraid I must disappoint these expectations. I am bound by my own definition of criticism: *a disinterested endeavor to learn and propagate the best that is known and thought in the world.* How much of current English literature comes into this "best that is known and thought in the world"? Not very much, I fear; certainly less, at this moment, than of the current literature of France or Germany. Well, then, am I to alter my definition of criticism, in order to meet the requirements of a number of practising English critics, who, after all, are free in their choice of a business? that would be making criticism lend itself to one of those alien practical considerations, which, I have said, are so fatal to it. One may say, indeed, to those who have to deal with the mass—so much better disregarded—of current English literature, that they may at all events endeavor, in dealing with this, to try it, so far as they can, by the standard of the best that is known and thought in the world: one may say, that to get anywhere near this standard, every critic should try and possess one great literature, at least, besides his own; and the more unlike his own, the better. But, after all, the criticism I am really

---

22 From Vergil's fourth *Eclogue:* "The cycle of periods is born anew." The Greeks held a theory that after 72,000 years, starting with the Golden Age and declining to the Age of Iron, the whole cycle began again.

concerned with—the criticism which alone can much help us for the future, the criticism which, throughout Europe, is at the present moment meant, when so much stress is laid on the importance of criticism and the critical spirit—is a criticism which regards Europe as being, for intellectual and spiritual purposes, one great confederation, bound to a joint action and working to a common result; and whose members have, for their proper outfit, a knowledge of Greek, Roman, and Eastern antiquity, and of one another. Special, local, and temporary advantages being put out of account, that modern nation will in the intellectual and spiritual sphere make most progress, which most thoroughly carries out this programme. And what is that but saying that we too, all of us, as individuals, the more thoroughly we carry it out, shall make the more progress?

There is so much inviting us!—what are we to take? what will nourish us in growth towards perfection? That is the question which, with the immense field of life and literature lying before him, the critic has to answer: for himself first, afterwards for others. In this idea of the critic's business the essays brought together in the following pages have had their origin; in this idea, widely different as are their subjects, they have, perhaps, their unity.

I conclude with what I said at the beginning: to have the sense of creative activity is the great happiness and the great proof of being alive, and it is not denied to criticism to have it; but then criticism must be sincere, simple, flexible, ardent, ever widening its knowledge. Then it may have, in no contemptible measure, a joyful sense of creative activity; a sense which a man of insight and conscience will prefer to what he might derive from a poor, starved, fragmentary, inadequate creation. And at some epochs no other creation is possible.

Still, in full measure, the sense of creative activity belongs only to genuine creation; in literature we must never forget that. But what true man of letters ever can forget it? It is no such common matter for a gifted nature to come into possession of a current of true and living ideas, and to produce amidst the inspiration of them, that we are likely to underrate it. The epochs of Aeschylus and Shakespeare make us feel their pre-eminence. In an epoch like those is,

no doubt, the true life of literature; there is the promised land, towards which criticism can only beckon. That promised land it will not be ours to enter, and we shall die in the wilderness: but to have desired to enter it, to have saluted it from afar, is already, perhaps, the best distinction among contemporaries; it will certainly be the best title to esteem with posterity.

from Culture and Anarchy[1]

Estote ergo vos perfecti![2]

INTRODUCTION

In one of his speeches a short time ago, that fine speaker and famous Liberal, Mr. Bright, took occasion to have a fling at the friends and preachers of culture. "People who talk about what they call *culture!*" said he, contemptuously; "by which they mean a smattering of the two dead languages of Greek and Latin." And he went on to remark, in a strain with which modern speakers and writers have made us very familiar, how poor a thing this culture is, how little good it can do to the world, and how absurd it is for its possessors to set much store by it. And the other day a younger Liberal than Mr. Bright, one of a school whose mission it is to bring into order and system that body of truth with which the earlier Liberals merely fumbled, a member of the University of Oxford, and a very clever writer, Mr. Frederic Harrison, developed, in the systematic and stringent manner of his school, the thesis which Mr. Bright had propounded in only general terms. "Perhaps the very silliest cant of the day," said Mr. Frederic Harrison, "is the cant about culture. Culture is a desirable quality in a critic of new books, and sits well on a professor of *belles-lettres;* but as applied to politics, it means simply a turn for small fault-finding, love of selfish ease, and indecision in action. The man of culture is in politics one of the poorest mortals alive. For simple pedantry and want of good sense no man is his equal. No assumption is too

---

1 First published in 1869. Chapter titles were added in the second edition of 1875, and many personal names omitted. The third and definitive edition, here followed, came out in 1883.

2 "Be ye therefore perfect"—from Matthew 5:48 in the Vulgate version.

unreal, no end is too unpractical for him. But the active exercise of politics requires common sense, sympathy, trust, resolution, and enthusiasm, qualities which your man of culture has carefully rooted up, lest they damage the delicacy of his critical olfactories. Perhaps they are the only class of responsible beings in the community who cannot with safety be entrusted with power."[3]

Now for my part I do not wish to see men of culture asking to be entrusted with power; and, indeed, I have freely said, that in my opinion the speech most proper, at present, for a man of culture to make to a body of his fellow-countrymen who get him into a committee-room, is Socrates's: *Know thyself!* and this is not a speech to be made by men wanting to be entrusted with power. For this very indifference to direct political action I have been taken to task by the *Daily Telegraph,* coupled, by a strange perversity of fate, with just that very one of the Hebrew prophets whose style I admire the least, and called "an elegant Jeremiah." It is because I say (to use the words which the *Daily Telegraph* puts in my mouth):—"You mustn't make a fuss because you have no vote,—that is vulgarity; you mustn't hold big meetings to agitate for reform bills and to repeal corn laws,—that is the very height of vulgarity,"—it is for this reason that I am called, sometimes an elegant Jeremiah, sometimes a spurious Jeremiah, a Jeremiah about the reality of whose mission the writer in the *Daily Telegraph* has his doubts. It is evident, therefore, that I have so taken my line as not to be exposed to the whole brunt of Mr. Frederic Harrison's censure. Still, I have often spoken in praise of culture, I have striven to make all my works and ways serve the interests of culture. I take culture to be something a great deal more than what Mr. Frederic Harrison and others call it: "a desirable quality in a critic of new books." Nay, even though to a certain extent I am disposed to agree with Mr. Frederic Harrison, that men of culture are just the class of responsible beings in this community of ours who cannot properly, at present, be entrusted with power, I am not sure that I do not think this the fault of our community rather than of the men of culture. In

short, although, like Mr. Bright and Mr. Frederic Harrison, and the editor of the *Daily Telegraph,* and a large body of valued friends of mine, I am a Liberal, yet I am a Liberal tempered by experience, reflection, and renouncement, and I am, above all, a believer in culture. Therefore I propose now to try and inquire, in the simple unsystematic way which best suits both my taste and my powers, what culture really is, what good it can do, what is our own special need of it; and I shall seek to find some plain grounds on which a faith in culture,—both my own faith in it and the faith of others,—may rest securely.

Chapter I

SWEETNESS AND LIGHT[1]

The disparagers of culture make its motive curiosity; sometimes, indeed, they make its motive mere exclusiveness and vanity. The culture which is supposed to plume itself on a smattering of Greek and Latin is a culture which is begotten by nothing so intellectual as curiosity; it is valued either out of sheer vanity and ignorance or else as an engine of social and class distinction, separating its holder, like a badge or title, from other people who have not got it. No serious man would call this *culture,* or attach any value to it, as culture, at all. To find the real ground for the very different estimate which serious people will set upon culture, we must find some motive for culture in the terms of which may lie a real ambiguity; and such a motive the word *curiosity* gives us.

I have before now pointed out[2] that we English do not, like the foreigners, use this word in a good sense as well as in a bad sense. With us the word is always used in a somewhat disapproving sense. A liberal and intelligent eagerness about the things of the mind may be meant by a foreigner when he speaks of curiosity, but with us the word always conveys a certain notion of frivolous and unedifying activity. In the *Quarterly Review,* some little time ago,[3] was an estimate

---

[3] From Harrison's "Our Venetian Constitution," *Fortnightly Review* for March, 1867; later reprinted as "Parliament before Reform," in *Order and Progress,* 1875.

[1] First delivered as Arnold's final lecture as Professor of Poetry at Oxford, June 7, 1867, and published in the July issue of the *Cornhill Magazine.*
[2] In "The Function of Criticism at the Present Time."
[3] In January 1866, written by Frank T. Marzials: see *The Wellesley Index to Victorian Periodicals,* Vol. I.

of the celebrated French critic, M. Sainte-Beuve, and a very inadequate estimate it in my judgment was. And its inadequacy consisted chiefly in this: that in our English way it left out of sight the double sense really involved in the word *curiosity*, thinking enough was said to stamp M. Sainte-Beuve with blame if it was said that he was impelled in his operations as a critic by curiosity, and omitting either to perceive that M. Sainte-Beuve himself, and many other people with him, would consider that this was praiseworthy and not blameworthy, or to point out why it ought really to be accounted worthy of blame and not of praise. For as there is a curiosity about intellectual matters which is futile, and merely a disease, so there is certainly a curiosity,—a desire after the things of the mind simply for their own sakes and for the pleasure of seeing them as they are,[4]—which is, in an intelligent being, natural and laudable. Nay, and the very desire to see things as they are implies a balance and regulation of mind which is not often attained without fruitful effort, and which is the very opposite of the blind and diseased impulse of mind which is what we mean to blame when we blame curiosity. Montesquieu says: "The first motive which ought to impel us to study is the desire to augment the excellence of our nature, and to render an intelligent being yet more intelligent." This is the true ground to assign for the genuine scientific[5] passion, however manifested, and for culture, viewed simply as a fruit of this passion; and it is a worthy ground, even though we let the term *curiosity* stand to describe it.

But there is of culture another view, in which not solely the scientific passion, the sheer desire to see things as they are, natural and proper in an intelligent being, appears as the ground of it. There is a view in which all the love of our neighbour, the impulses towards action, help, and beneficence, the desire for removing human error, clearing human confusion, and diminishing human misery, the noble aspiration to leave the world better and happier than we found it,—motives eminently such as are called social,—come in as part of the grounds of culture, and the main and pre-eminent part. Culture is then properly described not as having

its origin in curiosity, but as having its origin in the love of perfection; it is *a study of perfection*. It moves by the force, not merely or primarily of the scientific passion for pure knowledge, but also of the moral and social passion for doing good. As, in the first view of it, we took for its worthy motto Montesquieu's words: "To render an intelligent being yet more intelligent!" so, in the second view of it, there is no better motto which it can have than these words of Bishop Wilson:[6] "To make reason and the will of God prevail!"[7]

Only, whereas the passion for doing good is apt to be overhasty in determining what reason and the will of God say, because its turn is for acting rather than thinking and it wants to be beginning to act; and whereas it is apt to take its own conceptions, which proceed from its own state of development and share in all the imperfections and immaturities of this, for a basis of action; what distinguishes culture is, that it is possessed by the scientific passion as well as by the passion of doing good; that it demands worthy notions of reason and the will of God, and does not readily suffer its own crude conceptions to substitute themselves for them. And knowing that no action or institution can be salutary and stable which is not based on reason and the will of God, it is not so bent on acting and instituting, even with the great aim of diminishing human error and misery ever before its thoughts, but that it can remember that acting and instituting are of little use, unless we know how and what we ought to act and to institute.

This culture is more interesting and more far-reaching than that other, which is founded solely on the scientific passion for knowing. But it needs times of faith and ardour, times when the intellectual horizon is opening and widening all round us, to flourish in. And is not the close

---

4 See note 16 of the preceding essay.
5 Learned.

6 Thomas Wilson (1663–1755) in his "Sacra Privata," *Works* (1796), II, 303. Also see note 7 and the text it is attached to.
7 The important word is "prevail," in contrast to learning the truth for our own personal pleasure. "Reason" is not logic but the intuitive reason whose aim is to see things as they are in their ultimate truth; and in so doing it would see "the will of God." Thus "reason and the will of God" belong with the first description of culture, "prevail" with the second: see the next paragraph and the summary paragraph beginning, "The moment this view of culture . . ." where the two descriptions are merged into one thing with two aims.

and bounded intellectual horizon within which we have long lived and moved now lifting up, and are not new lights finding free passage to shine in upon us? For a long time there was no passage for them to make their way in upon us, and then it was of no use to think of adapting the world's action to them. Where was the hope of making reason and the will of God prevail among people who had a routine which they had christened reason and the will of God, in which they were inextricably bound, and beyond which they had no power of looking? But now the iron force of adhesion to the old routine,—social, political, religious,—has wonderfully yielded; the iron force of exclusion of all which is new has wonderfully yielded. The danger now is, not that people should obstinately refuse to allow anything but their old routine to pass for reason and the will of God, but either that they should allow some novelty or other to pass for these too easily, or else that they should underrate the importance of them altogether, and think it enough to follow action for its own sake, without troubling themselves to make reason and the will of God prevail therein. Now, then, is the moment for culture to be of service, culture which believes in making reason and the will of God prevail, believes in perfection, is the study and pursuit of perfection, and is no longer debarred, by a rigid invincible exclusion of whatever is new, from getting acceptance for its ideas, simply because they are new.

The moment this view of culture is seized, the moment it is regarded not solely as the endeavour to see things as they are, to draw towards a knowledge of the universal order which seems to be intended and aimed at in the world, and which it is a man's happiness to go along with or his misery to go counter to,—to learn, in short, the will of God,—the moment, I say, culture is considered not merely as the endeavour to *see* and *learn* this, but as the endeavour, also, to make it *prevail,* the moral, social, and beneficent character of culture becomes manifest. The mere endeavour to see and learn the truth for our own personal satisfaction is indeed a commencement for making it prevail, a preparing the way for this, which always serves this, and is wrongly, therefore, stamped with blame absolutely in itself and not only in its caricature and degeneration. But perhaps it has got stamped with blame,

and disparaged with the dubious title of curiosity, because in comparison with this wider endeavour of such great and plain utility it looks selfish, petty, and unprofitable.[8]

And religion, the greatest and most important of the efforts by which the human race has manifested its impulse to perfect itself,—religion, that voice of the deepest human experience,—does not only enjoin and sanction the aim which is the great aim of culture, the aim of setting ourselves to ascertain what perfection is and to make it prevail; but also, in determining generally in what human perfection consists, religion comes to a conclusion identical with that which culture,—culture seeking the determination of this question through *all* the voices of human experience which have been heard upon it, of art, science, poetry, philosophy, history, as well as of religion, in order to give a greater fulness and certainty to its solution,—likewise reaches. Religion says: *The kingdom of God is within you;* and culture, in like manner, places human perfection in an *internal* condition, in the growth and predominance of our humanity proper, as distinguished from our animality. It places it in the ever-increasing efficacy and in the general harmonious expansion of those gifts of thought and feeling, which make the peculiar dignity, wealth, and happiness of human nature. As I have said on a former occasion:[9] "It is in making endless additions to itself, in the endless expansion of its powers, in endless growth in wisdom and beauty, that the spirit of the human race finds its ideal. To reach this ideal, culture is an indispensable aid, and that is the true value of culture." Not a having and a resting, but a growing and a becoming, is the character of perfection as culture conceives it; and here, too, it coincides with religion.

And because men are all members of one great whole, and the sympathy which is in human nature will not allow one member to be indifferent to the rest or to have a perfect welfare independent of the rest, the expansion of our humanity, to suit the idea of perfection which culture forms, must be a *general* expansion. Perfection, as culture conceives it, is not possible while

---

[8] For a comment on these opening paragraphs, see the close of the introduction to Arnold.
[9] In *A French Eton,* in *Works,* ed. Super, II, 318.

the individual remains isolated. The individual is required, under pain of being stunted and enfeebled in his own development if he disobeys, to carry others along with him in his march towards perfection, to be continually doing all he can to enlarge and increase the volume of the human stream sweeping thitherward. And here, once more, culture lays on us the same obligation as religion which says, as Bishop Wilson has admirably put it, that "to promote the kingdom of God is to increase and hasten one's own happiness."

But, finally, perfection,—as culture from a thorough disinterested study of human nature and human experience learns to conceive it,—is a harmonious expansion of *all* the powers which make the beauty and worth of human nature, and is not consistent with the over-development of any one power at the expense of the rest. Here culture goes beyond religion, as religion is generally conceived by us.

If culture, then, is a study of perfection, and of harmonious perfection, general perfection, and perfection which consists in becoming something rather than in having something, in an inward condition of the mind and spirit, not in an outward set of circumstances,—it is clear that culture, instead of being the frivolous and useless thing which Mr. Bright, and Mr. Frederic Harrison, and many other Liberals are apt to call it, has a very important function to fulfil for mankind. And this function is particularly important in our modern world, of which the whole civilisation is, to a much greater degree than the civilisation of Greece and Rome, mechanical and external, and tends constantly to become more so. But above all in our own country has culture a weighty part to perform, because here that mechanical character, which civilisation tends to take everywhere, is shown in the most eminent degree. Indeed nearly all the characters of perfection, as culture teaches us to fix them, meet in this country with some powerful tendency which thwarts them and sets them at defiance. The idea of perfection as an *inward* condition of the mind and spirit is at variance with the mechanical and material civilisation in esteem with us, and nowhere, as I have said, so much in esteem as with us. The idea of perfection as a *general* expansion of the human family is at variance with our strong individualism, our hatred of all

limits to the unrestrained swing of the individual's personality, our maxim of "every man for himself." Above all, the idea of perfection as a *harmonious* expansion of human nature is at variance with our want of flexibility, with our inaptitude for seeing more than one side of a thing, with our intense energetic absorption in the particular pursuit we happen to be following. So culture has a rough task to achieve in this country. Its preachers have, and are likely long to have, a hard time of it, and they will much oftener be regarded, for a great while to come, as elegant or spurious Jeremiahs than as friends and benefactors. That, however, will not prevent their doing in the end good service if they persevere. And, meanwhile, the mode of action they have to pursue, and the sort of habits they must fight against, ought to be made quite clear for every one to see, who may be willing to look at the matter attentively and dispassionately.

Faith in machinery, is, I said, our besetting danger; often in machinery most absurdly disproportioned to the end which this machinery, if it is to do any good at all, is to serve; but always in machinery, as if it had a value in and for itself. What is freedom but machinery? what is population but machinery? what is coal but machinery? what are railroads but machinery? what is wealth but machinery? what are, even, religious organisations but machinery? Now almost every voice in England is accustomed to speak of these things as if they were precious ends in themselves, and therefore had some of the characters of perfection indisputably joined to them. I have before now noticed Mr. Roebuck's stock argument for proving the greatness and happiness of England as she is, and for quite stopping the mouths of all gainsayers. Mr. Roebuck is never weary of reiterating this argument of his, so I do not know why I should be weary of noticing it. "May not every man in England say what he likes?"—Mr. Roebuck perpetually asks; and that, he thinks, is quite sufficient, and when every man may say what he likes, our aspirations ought to be satisfied. But the aspirations of culture, which is the study of perfection, are not satisfied, unless what men say, when they may say what they like, is worth saying,—has good in it, and more good than bad. In the same way the *Times*, replying to some foreign strictures on the dress, looks, and behaviour of the English abroad, urges that the English ideal is that every one should be free to do and to look just as he likes. But culture indefatigably tries, not to make what each raw person may like the rule by which he fashions himself; but to draw ever nearer to a sense of what is indeed beautiful, graceful, and becoming, and to get the raw person to like that.

And in the same way with respect to railroads and coal. Every one must have observed the strange language current during the late discussions as to the possible failures of our supplies of coal. Our coal, thousands of people were saying, is the real basis of our national greatness; if our coal runs short, there is an end of the greatness of England. But what *is* greatness?—culture makes us ask. Greatness is a spiritual condition worthy to excite love, interest, and admiration; and the outward proof of possessing greatness is that we excite love, interest, and admiration. If England were swallowed up by the sea tomorrow, which of the two, a hundred years hence, would most excite the love, interest, and admiration of mankind,—would most, therefore, show the evidences of having possessed greatness,—the England of the last twenty years, or the England of Elizabeth, of a time of splendid spiritual effort, but when our coal, and our industrial operations depending on coal, were very little developed? Well, then, what an unsound habit of mind it must be which makes us talk of things like coal or iron as constituting the greatness of England, and how salutary a friend is culture, bent on seeing things as they are, and thus dissipating delusions of this kind and fixing standards of perfection that are real!

Wealth, again, that end to which our prodigious works for material advantage are directed, —the commonest of commonplaces tells us how men are always apt to regard wealth as a precious end in itself; and certainly they have never been so apt thus to regard it as they are in England at the present time. Never did people believe anything more firmly than nine Englishmen out of ten at the present day believe that our greatness and welfare are proved by our being so very rich. Now, the use of culture is that it helps us, by means of its spiritual standard of perfection, to regard wealth as but machinery, and not only to say as a matter of words that we regard wealth as but machinery, but really to perceive and feel that it is so. If it were not for this purging effect

wrought upon our minds by culture, the whole world, the future as well as the present, would inevitably belong to the Philistines. The people who believe most that our greatness and welfare are proved by our being very rich, and who most give their lives and thoughts to becoming rich, are just the very people whom we call Philistines.[10] Culture says: "Consider these people, then, their way of life, their habits, their manners, the very tones of their voice; look at them attentively; observe the literature they read, the things which give them pleasure, the words which come forth out of their mouths, the thoughts which make the furniture of their minds; would any amount of wealth be worth having with the condition that one was to become just like these people by having it?" And thus culture begets a dissatisfaction which is of the highest possible value in stemming the common tide of men's thoughts in a wealthy and industrial community, and which saves the future, as one may hope, from being vulgarised, even if it cannot save the present.

Population, again, and bodily health and vigour, are things which are nowhere treated in such an unintelligent, misleading, exaggerated way as in England. Both are really machinery; yet how many people all around us do we see rest in them and fail to look beyond them! Why, one has heard people, fresh from reading certain articles of the *Times* on the Registrar-General's returns of marriages and births in this country, who would talk of our large English families in quite a solemn strain, as if they had something in itself beautiful, elevating, and meritorious in them; as if the British Philistine would have only to present himself before the Great Judge with his twelve children, in order to be received among the sheep as a matter of right!

But bodily health and vigour, it may be said, are not to be classed with wealth and population as mere machinery; they have a more real and essential value. True; but only as they are more intimately connected with a perfect spiritual condition than wealth or population are. The moment we disjoin them from the idea of a perfect spiritual condition, and pursue them, as we do pursue them, for their own sake and as ends in themselves, our worship of them

---

10 See p. 852, note 18.

becomes as mere worship of machinery, as our worship of wealth or population, and as unintelligent and vulgarising a worship as that is. Every one with anything like an adequate idea of human perfection has distinctly marked this subordination to higher and spiritual ends of the cultivation of bodily vigour and activity. "Bodily exercise profiteth little; but godliness is profitable unto all things," says the author of the Epistle to Timothy. And the utilitarian Franklin says just as explicitly:—"Eat and drink such an exact quantity as suits the constitution of thy body, *in reference to the services of the mind.*" But the point of view of culture, keeping the mark of human perfection simply and broadly in view, and not assigning to this perfection, as religion or utilitarianism assigns to it, a special and limited character, this point of view, I say, of culture is best given by these words of Epictetus:[11]—"It is a sign of ἀφυΐα," says he,—that is, of a nature not finely tempered,—"to give yourselves up to things which relate to the body; to make, for instance, a great fuss about exercise, a great fuss about eating, a great fuss about drinking, a great fuss about walking, a great fuss about riding. All these things ought to be done merely by the way: the formation of the spirit and character must be our real concern." This is admirable; and, indeed, the Greek word εὐφυΐα, a finely tempered nature, gives exactly the notion of perfection as culture brings us to conceive it: a harmonious perfection, a perfection in which the characters of beauty and intelligence are both present, which unites "the two noblest of things,"—as Swift, who of one of the two, at any rate, had himself all too little, most happily calls them in his *Battle of the Books,*—"the two noblest of things, *sweetness and light.*"[12] The εὐφυής is the man who tends towards sweetness and light; the ἀφυής, on the other hand, is our Philistine. The immense spiritual significance of the Greeks

is due to their having been inspired with this central and happy idea of the essential character of human perfection; and Mr. Bright's misconception of culture, as a smattering of Greek and Latin, comes itself, after all, from this wonderful significance of the Greeks having affected the very machinery of our education, and is in itself a kind of homage to it.

In thus making sweetness and light to be characters of perfection, culture is of like spirit with poetry, follows one law with poetry. Far more than on our freedom, our population, and our industrialism, many amongst us rely upon our religious organisations to save us. I have called religion a yet more important manifestation of human nature than poetry, because it has worked on a broader scale for perfection, and with greater masses of men. But the idea of beauty and of a human nature perfect on all its sides, which is the dominant idea of poetry,[13] is a true and invaluable idea, though it has not yet had the success that the idea of conquering the obvious faults of our animality, and of a human nature perfect on the moral side,—which is the dominant idea of religion,—has been enabled to have; and it is destined, adding to itself the religious idea of a devout energy, to transform and govern the other.

The best art and poetry of the Greeks, in which religion and poetry are one, in which the idea of beauty and of a human nature perfect on all sides adds to itself a religious and devout energy, and works in the strength of that, is on this account of such surpassing interest and instructiveness for us, though it was,—as, having regard to the human race in general, and, indeed, having regard to the Greeks themselves, we must own,—a premature attempt, an attempt which for success needed the moral and religious fibre in humanity to be more braced and developed than it had yet been. But Greece did not err in having the idea of beauty, harmony, and complete human perfection, so present and paramount. It is impossible to have this idea too

11 The Roman Stoic philosopher (60?–120?).

12 "Light" is obviously a metaphor for "intelligence," but though "sweetness" may be one for "beauty," its chief meanings in Arnold are (1) politeness and graciousness of manners, usually associated with the aristocracy (*Works*, ed. Super, V, 124, but qualified on p. 140), and (2) a calm, serenity of temper—"indulgence," in contrast to acrimony and polemical fierceness: see ibid., p. 143, where the "spirit of indulgence" is called "a necessary part of sweetness"; and pp. 111–12, where without sweetness of temper Arnold says there can be no light, and without light no recognition of the value of sweetness.

13 Cf. "On the Modern Element in Literature," (1857), in *Works*, ed. Super, I, 28: "The peculiar characteristic of the highest literature—the poetry—of the fifth century in Greece . . . is its *adequacy* . . . that it represents the highly developed human nature of that age—human nature developed in a number of directions, politically, socially, religiously, morally developed—in its completest and most harmonious development. . . ."

present and paramount; only, the moral fibre must be braced too. And we, because we have braced the moral fibre, are not on that account in the right way, if at the same time the idea of beauty, harmony, and complete human perfection, is wanting or misapprehended amongst us; and evidently it *is* wanting or misapprehended at present. And when we rely as we do on our religious organisations, which in themselves do not and cannot give us this idea, and think we have done enough if we make them spread and prevail, then, I say, we fall into our common fault of overvaluing machinery.

Nothing is more common than for people to confound the inward peace and satisfaction which follows the subduing of the obvious faults of our animality with what I may call absolute inward peace and satisfaction,—the peace and satisfaction which are reached as we draw near to complete spiritual perfection, and not merely to moral perfection, or rather to relative moral perfection. No people in the world have done more and struggled more to attain this relative moral perfection than our English race has. For no people in the world has the command to *resist the devil,* to *overcome the wicked one,* in the nearest and most obvious sense of those words, had such a pressing force and reality. And we have had our reward, not only in the great worldly prosperity which our obedience to this command has brought us, but also, and far more, in great inward peace and satisfaction. But to me few things are more pathetic than to see people, on the strength of the inward peace and satisfaction which their rudimentary efforts towards perfection have brought them, employ, concerning their incomplete perfection and the religious organisations within which they have found it, language which properly applies only to complete perfection, and is a far-off echo of the human soul's prophecy of it. Religion itself, I need hardly say, supplies them in abundance with this grand language. And very freely do they use it; yet it is really the severest possible criticism of such an incomplete perfection as alone we have yet reached through our religious organisations.

The impulse of the English race towards moral development and self-conquest has nowhere so powerfully manifested itself as in Puritanism. Nowhere has Puritanism found so adequate an expression as in the religious organisation of the Independents.[14] The modern Independents have a newspaper, the *Nonconformist,* written with great sincerity and ability. The motto, the standard, the profession of faith which this organ of theirs carries aloft, is: "The Dissidence of Dissent and the Protestantism of the Protestant religion." There is sweetness and light, and an ideal of complete harmonious human perfection! One need not go to culture and poetry to find language to judge it. Religion, with its instinct for perfection, supplies language to judge it, language, too, which is in our mouths every day. "Finally, be of one mind, united in feeling," says St. Peter.[15] There is an ideal which judges the Puritan ideal: "The Dissidence of Dissent and the Protestantism of the Protestant religion!" And religious organisations like this are what people believe in, rest in, would give their lives for! Such, I say, is the wonderful virtue of even the beginnings of perfection, of having conquered even the plain faults of our animality that the religious organisation which has helped us to do it can seem to us something precious, salutary, and to be propagated, even when it wears such a brand of imperfection on its forehead as this. And men have got such a habit of giving to the language of religion a special application, of making it a mere jargon, that for the condemnation which religion itself passes on the shortcomings of their religious organisations they have no ear; they are sure to cheat themselves and to explain this condemnation away. They can only be reached by the criticism which culture, like poetry, speaking a language not to be sophisticated, and resolutely testing these organisations by the ideal of a human perfection complete on all sides, applies to them.

But men of culture and poetry, it will be said, are again and again failing, and failing conspicuously, in the necessary first stage to a harmonious perfection, in the subduing of the great obvious faults of our animality, which it is the glory of these religious organisations to have helped us to subdue. True, they do often so fail. They have often been without the virtues as well as the faults of the Puritan; it has been one of

---

14 The Congregationalists, who believed in the right of each congregation to govern itself independently.
15 I Peter 3:8.

their dangers that they so felt the Puritan's faults that they too much neglected the practice of his virtues. I will not, however, exculpate them at the Puritan's expense. They have often failed in morality, and morality is indispensable. And they have been punished for their failure, as the Puritan has been rewarded for his performance. They have been punished wherein they erred; but their ideal of beauty, of sweetness and light, and a human nature complete on all its sides, remains the true ideal of perfection still; just as the Puritan's ideal of perfection remains narrow and inadequate, although for what he did well he has been richly rewarded. Notwithstanding the mighty results of the Pilgrim Fathers' voyage, they and their standard of perfection are rightly judged when we figure to ourselves Shakspeare or Virgil,—souls in whom sweetness and light, and all that in human nature is most humane, were eminent,—accompanying them on their voyage, and think what intolerable company Shakspeare and Virgil would have found them! In the same way let us judge the religious organisations which we see all around us. Do not let us deny the good and the happiness which they have accomplished; but do not let us fail to see clearly that their idea of human perfection is narrow and inadequate, and that the Dissidence of Dissent and the Protestantism of the Protestant religion will never bring humanity to its true goal. As I said with regard to wealth: Let us look at the life of those who live in and for it,—so I say with regard to the religious organisations. Look at the life imaged in such a newspaper as the *Nonconformist,*—a life of jealousy of the Establishment,[16] disputes, tea-meetings, openings of chapels, sermons; and then think of it as an ideal of a human life completing itself on all sides, and aspiring with all its organs after sweetness, light, and perfection!

Another newspaper, representing, like the *Nonconformist,* one of the religious organisations of this country, was a short time ago giving an account of the crowd at Epsom on the Derby day,[17] and of all the vice and hideousness which was to be seen in that crowd; and then the writer turned suddenly round upon Professor Huxley,[18]

and asked him how he proposed to cure all this vice and hideousness without religion. I confess I felt disposed to ask the asker this question: and how do you propose to cure it with such a religion as yours? How is the ideal of a life so unlovely, so unattractive, so incomplete, so narrow, so far removed from a true and satisfying ideal of human perfection, as is the life of your religious organisation as you yourself reflect it, to conquer and transform all this vice and hideousness? Indeed, the strongest plea for the study of perfection as pursued by culture, the clearest proof of the actual inadequacy of the idea of perfection held by the religious organisations,—expressing, as I have said, the most widespread effort which the human race has yet made after perfection,—is to be found in the state of our life and society with these in possession of it, and having been in possession of it I know not how many hundred years. We are all of us included in some religious organisation or other; we all call ourselves, in the sublime and aspiring language of religion which I have before noticed, *children of God.* Children of God;—it is an immense pretension!—and how are we to justify it? By the works which we do, and the words which we speak. And the work which we collective children of God do, our grand centre of life, our *city* which we have builded for us to dwell in, is London! London, with its unutterable external hideousness, and with its internal canker of *publicè egestas, privatim opulentia,*[19]—to use the words which Sallust puts into Cato's mouth about Rome,—unequalled in the world! The word, again, which we children of God speak, the voice which most hits our collective thought, the newspaper with the largest circulation in England, nay, with the largest circulation in the whole world, is the *Daily Telegraph!*[20] I say that when our religious organizations,— which I admit to express the most considerable effort after perfection that our race has yet made,—land us in no better result than this, it is high time to examine carefully their idea of perfection, to see whether it does not leave out of account sides and forces of human nature which we might turn to great

16 The Church of England.
17 The day of the horse races.
18 The scientist and agnostic.

19 "Publicly, for most people, privation; privately, for a few, great wealth." From the *Catiline* of Sallust, the Roman historian (86–35 B.C.).
20 The first penny newspaper in England, founded in 1855.

use; whether it would not be more operative if it were more complete. And I say that the English reliance on our religious organisations and on their ideas of human perfection just as they stand, is like our reliance on freedom, on muscular Christianity,[21] on population, on coal, on wealth,—mere belief in machinery, and unfruitful; and that it is wholesomely counteracted by culture, bent on seeing things as they are, and on drawing the human race onwards to a more complete, a harmonious perfection.

Culture, however, shows its single-minded love of perfection, its desire simply to make reason and the will of God prevail, its freedom from fanaticism, by its attitude towards all this machinery, even while it insists that it *is* machinery. Fanatics, seeing the mischief men do themselves by their blind belief in some machinery or other, —whether it is wealth and industrialism, or whether it is the cultivation of bodily strength and activity, or whether it is a political organisation,—or whether it is a religious organisation,— oppose with might and main the tendency to this or that political and religious organisation, or to games and athletic exercises, or to wealth and industrialism, and try violently to stop it. But the flexibility which sweetness and light give, and which is one of the rewards of culture pursued in good faith, enables a man to see that a tendency may be necessary, and even, as a preparation for something in the future, salutary, and yet that the generations or individuals who obey this tendency are sacrificed to it, that they fall short of the hope of perfection by following it; and that its mischiefs are to be criticised, lest it should take too firm a hold and last after it has served its purpose.

Mr. Gladstone well pointed out, in a speech at Paris,—and others have pointed out the same thing,—how necessary is the present great movement towards wealth and industrialism, in order to lay broad foundations of material well-being for the society of the future. The worst of these justifications is, that they are generally addressed to the very people engaged, body and soul, in the movement in question; at all events, that they are always seized with the greatest avidity by these people, and taken by them as quite justify-

ing their life; and that thus they tend to harden them in their sins. Now, culture admits the necessity of the movement towards fortune-making and exaggerated industrialism, readily allows that the future may derive benefit from it; but insists, at the same time, that the passing generations of industrialists,—forming, for the most part, the stout main body of Philistinism,—are sacrificed to it. In the same way, the result of all the games and sports which occupy the passing generation of boys and young men may be the establishment of a better and sounder physical type for the future to work with. Culture does not set itself against the games and sports; it congratulates the future, and hopes it will make a good use of its improved physical basis; but it points out that our passing generation of boys and young men is, meantime, sacrificed. Puritanism was perhaps necessary to develop the moral fibre of the English race, Nonconformity[22] to break the yoke of ecclesiastical domination over men's minds and to prepare the way for freedom of thought in the distant future; still, culture points out that the harmonious perfection of generations of Puritans and Nonconformists has been, in consequence, sacrificed. Freedom of speech may be necessary for the society of the future, but the young lions of the *Daily Telegraph* in the meanwhile are sacrificed. A voice for every man in his country's government may be necessary for the society of the future, but meanwhile Mr. Beales and Mr. Bradlaugh are sacrificed.[23]

Oxford, the Oxford of the past, has many faults; and she has heavily paid for them in defeat, in isolation, in want of hold upon the modern world. Yet we in Oxford, brought up amidst the beauty and sweetness of that beautiful place, have not failed to seize one truth,—the truth that beauty and sweetness are essential characters of a complete human perfection. When I insist on this, I am all in the faith and tradition

---

21 A term used of Charles Kingsley and his followers who laid religious emphasis on animal spirits, physical strength, etc.

22 All of the Protestant denominations which were not the episcopal Church of England and who fought that Church because it alone was sustained by the State. Also called Dissent.

23 The young writers of the *Daily Telegraph* were often loud asserters of freedom of speech in the extreme form which rejects all authority and claims that the individual should think and speak whatever he considers true. Like them, Edmond Beales and Charles Bradlaugh were examples of extreme and unbalanced supporters of liberalism, in this case of manhood suffrage in particular.

of Oxford. I say boldly that this our sentiment for beauty and sweetness, our sentiment against hideousness and rawness, has been at the bottom of our attachment to so many beaten causes, of our opposition to so many triumphant movements. And the sentiment is true, and has never been wholly defeated, and has shown its power even in its defeat. We have not won our political battles, we have not carried our main points, we have not stopped our adversaries' advance, we have not marched victoriously with the modern world; but we have told silently upon the mind of the country, we have prepared currents of feeling which sap our adversaries' position when it seems gained, we have kept up our own communications with the future. Look at the course of the great movement which shook Oxford to its centre some thirty years ago! It was directed, as any one who reads Dr. Newman's *Apology* may see, against what in one word may be called "Liberalism."[24] Liberalism prevailed; it was the appointed force to do the work of the hour; it was necessary, it was inevitable that it should prevail. The Oxford movement was broken, it failed; our wrecks are scattered on every shore:—

Quae regio in terris nostri non plena laboris?[25]

But what was it, this liberalism, as Dr. Newman saw it, and as it really broke the Oxford movement? It was the great middle-class liberalism, which had for the cardinal points of its belief the Reform Bill of 1832, and local self-government, in politics; in the social sphere, free-trade, unrestricted competition, and the making of large industrial fortunes; in the religious sphere, the Dissidence of Dissent and the Protestantism of the Protestant religion. I do not say that other and more intelligent forces than this were not opposed to the Oxford movement: but this was the force which really beat it; this was the force which Dr. Newman felt himself fighting with;[26] this was the force which till only the other day seemed to be the paramount force in this country, and to be in possession of the future; this was the

force whose achievements fill Mr. Lowe[27] with such inexpressible admiration, and whose rule he was so horror-struck to see threatened. And where is this great force of Philistinism now? It is thrust into the second rank, it is become a power of yesterday, it has lost the future. A new power has suddenly appeared,[28] a power which it is impossible yet to judge fully, but which is certainly a wholly different force from middle-class liberalism; different in its cardinal points of belief, different in its tendencies in every sphere. It loves and admires neither the legislation of middle-class Parliaments, nor the local self-government of middle-class vestries,[29] nor the unrestricted competition of middle-class industrialists, nor the dissidence of middle-class Dissent and the Protestantism of middle-class Protestant religion. I am not now praising this new force, or saying that its own ideals are better; all I say is, that they are wholly different. And who will estimate how much the currents of feeling created by Dr. Newman's movements, the keen desire for beauty and sweetness which it nourished, the deep aversion it manifested to the hardness and vulgarity of middle-class liberalism, the strong light it turned on the hideous and grotesque illusions of middle-class Protestantism,— who will estimate how much all these contributed to swell the tide of secret dissatisfaction which has mined the ground under self-confident liberalism of the last thirty years, and has prepared the way for its sudden collapse and supersession? It is in this manner that the sentiment of Oxford for beauty and sweetness conquers, and in this manner long may it continue to conquer!

In this manner it works to the same end as culture, and there is plenty of work for it yet to do. I have said that the new and more democratic force which is now superseding our old middle-class liberalism cannot yet be rightly judged. It has its main tendencies still to form. We hear promises of its giving us administrative reform, law reform, reform of education, and I know not what; but those promises come rather

---

24 See Newman's "Note on Liberalism," pp. 534–39.
25 "What country in the world is not full [does not know] of our toil and trouble?" (Vergil's *Aeneid*, I, 460)
26 This seems very unlikely since Newman felt he was beaten by the spread of *religious* liberalism: See source in note 24.

27 Robert Lowe was a middle-class liberal who was horrified by the extension of the suffrage (by the 1867 Reform Bill) to the proletariat in the towns.
28 The town democracy.
29 The vestry in Anglican churches is a group of members who manage its temporal affairs.

from its advocates, wishing to make a good plea for it and to justify it for superseding middle-class liberalism, than from clear tendencies which it has itself yet developed. But meanwhile it has plenty of well-intentioned friends against whom culture may with advantage continue to uphold steadily its ideal of human perfection; that this is *an inward spiritual activity, having for its characters increased sweetness, increased light, in-life, increased sympathy.* Mr. Bright, who has a foot in both worlds, the world of middle-class liberalism and the world of democracy, but who brings most of his ideas from the world of middle-class liberalism in which he was bred, always inclines to inculcate that faith in machinery to which, as we have seen, Englishmen are so prone, and which has been the bane of middle-class liberalism. He complains with a sorrowful indignation of people who "appear to have no proper estimate of the value of the franchise"; he leads his disciples to believe,—what the Englishman is always too ready to believe,—that the having a vote, like the having a large family, or a large business, or large muscles, has in itself some edifying and perfecting effect upon human nature. Or else he cries out to the democracy,— "the men," as he calls them, "upon whose shoulders the greatness of England rests,"—he cries out to them: "See what you have done! I look over this country and see the cities you have built, the railroads you have made, the manufactures you have produced, the cargoes which freight the ships of the greatest mercantile navy the world has ever seen! I see that you have converted by your labours what was once a wilderness, these islands, into a fruitful garden; I know that you have created this wealth, and are a nation whose name is a word of power throughout all the world." Why, this is just the very style of laudation with which Mr. Roebuck or Mr. Lowe debauches the minds of the middle classes, and makes such Philistines of them. It is the same fashion of teaching a man to value himself not on what he *is*, not on his progress in sweetness and light, but on the number of the railroads he has constructed, or the bigness of the tabernacle he has built.[30] Only the middle classes are told they have done it all with their

energy, self-reliance, and capital, and the democracy are told they have done it all with their hands and sinews. But teaching the democracy to put its trust in achievements of this kind is merely training them to be Philistines to take the place of the Philistines whom they are superseding; and they too, like the middle class, will be encouraged to sit down at the banquet of the future without having on a wedding garment, and nothing excellent can then come from them. Those who know their besetting faults, those who have watched them and listened to them, or those who will read the instructive account recently given of them by one of themselves, the *Journeyman Engineer*,[31] will agree that the idea which culture sets before us of perfection,—an increased spiritual activity, having for its characters increased sweetness, increased light, increased life, increased sympathy,—is an idea which the new democracy needs far more than the idea of the blessedness of the franchise, or the wonderfulness of its own industrial performances.

Other well-meaning friends of this new power are for leading it, not in the old ruts of middle-class Philistinism, but in ways which are naturally alluring to the feet of democracy, though in this country they are novel and untried ways. I may call them the ways of Jacobinism.[32] Violent indignation with the past, abstract systems of renovation applied wholesale, a new doctrine drawn up in black and white for elaborating down to the very smallest details a rational society for the future,—these are the ways of Jacobinism. Mr. Frederic Harrison and other disciples of Comte,[33]—one of them, Mr. Congreve, is an old friend of mine, and I am glad to have an opportunity of publicly expressing my respect for his talents and character,—are among the friends of democracy who are for leading it in paths of this kind. Mr. Frederic Harrison is very hostile to culture, and from a natural

---

[30] A reference to the huge metropolitan tabernacle built by Charles Haddon Spurgeon, the most popular Nonconformist preacher of the time.

[31] The pseudonym of Thomas Wright, who wrote a book on *Some Habits and Customs of the Working Classes* (1867).

[32] Of the extreme party in the French Revolution, the Jacobins.

[33] The French philosopher (1798–1857) who also influenced Mill. He advocated a strong centralized government in the hands of industrialists which would organize all phases of economic life, and a Religion of Humanity founded on the worship of great men. Both schemes illustrate Arnold's previous sentence.

enough motive; for culture is the eternal opponent of the two things which are the signal marks of Jacobinism,—its fierceness, and its addiction to an abstract system. Culture is always assigning to system-makers and systems a smaller share in the bent of human destiny than their friends like. A current in people's minds sets towards new ideas; people are dissatisfied with their old narrow stock of Philistine ideas, Anglo-Saxon ideas, or any other; and some man, some Bentham or Comte, who has the real merit of having early and strongly felt and helped the new current, but who brings plenty of narrowness and mistakes of his own into his feeling and help of it, is credited with being the author of the whole current, the fit person to be entrusted with its regulation and to guide the human race.

The excellent German historian of the mythology of Rome, Preller, relating the introduction at Rome under the Tarquins of the worship of Apollo, the god of light, healing, and reconciliation, will have us observe that it was not so much the Tarquins who brought to Rome the new worship of Apollo, as a current in the mind of the Roman people which set powerfully at that time towards a new worship of this kind, and away from the old run of Latin[34] and Sabine religious ideas. In a similar way, culture directs our attention to the natural current there is in human affairs, and to its continual working, and will not let us rivet our faith upon any one man and his doings. It makes us see not only his good side, but also how much in him was of necessity limited and transient; nay, it even feels a pleasure, a sense of an increased freedom and of an ampler future, in so doing.

I remember, when I was under the influence of a mind to which I feel the greatest obligations, the mind of a man who was the very incarnation of sanity and clear sense, a man the most considerable, it seems to me, whom America has yet produced,—Benjamin Franklin,—I remember the relief with which, after long feeling the sway of Franklin's imperturbable common-sense, I came upon a project of his for a new version of the Book of Job, to replace the old version, the style of which, says Franklin, has become obsolete, and thence less agreeable. "I give," he continues, "a few verses, which may serve as a sample of the kind of version I would recommend." We all recollect the famous verse in our translation: "Then Satan answered the Lord and said: 'Doth Job fear God for nought?'" Franklin makes this: "Does your Majesty imagine that Job's good conduct is the effect of mere personal attachment and affection?" I well remember how, when first I read that, I drew a deep breath of relief, and said to myself: "After all, there is a stretch of humanity beyond Franklin's victorious good sense!" So, after hearing Bentham cried loudly up as the renovator of modern society, and Bentham's mind and ideas proposed as the rulers of our future, I open the *Deontology*.[35] There I read: "While Xenophon was writing his history and Euclid teaching geometry, Socrates and Plato were talking nonsense under pretence of talking wisdom and morality. This morality of theirs consisted in words; this wisdom of their was the denial of matters known to every man's experience." From the moment of reading that, I am delivered from the bondage of Bentham! the fanaticism of his adherents can touch me no longer. I feel the inadequacy of his mind and ideas for supplying the rule of human society, for perfection.

Culture tends always thus to deal with the men of a system, of disciples, of a school; with men like Comte, or the late Mr. Buckle, or Mr. Mill.[36] However much it may find to admire in these personages, or in some of them, it nevertheless remembers the text: "Be not ye called Rabbi!"[37] and it soon passes on from any Rabbi. But Jacobinism loves a Rabbi; it does not want to pass on from its Rabbi in pursuit of a future and still unreached perfection; it wants its Rabbi and his ideas to stand for perfection, that they may with the more authority recast the world; and for Jacobinism, therefore, culture,—eternally passing onwards and seeking,—is an impertinence

34 I.e., of Latium, the district of Italy that included Rome. The Sabine district was northeast of Latium.

35 Jeremy Bentham (1748–1832) was the founder of Utilitarianism and the leader of the philosophic radicalism that inspired the Liberalism of the period. His *Deontology, or The Science of Morality,* was published in 1834.

36 John Stuart Mill, the disciple of Bentham who later came strongly under the influence of Carlyle and Coleridge, and in turn influenced Arnold. Thomas Henry Buckle wrote a *History of Civilization in England* (1857, 1861) that attempted to put history on a scientific basis and to explain the social laws that determine the character and progress of institutions and beliefs.

37 Matthew 23:8. *Rabbi* means *Master.*

and an offence. But culture, just because it resists this tendency of Jacobinism to impose on us a man with limitations and errors of his own along with the true ideas of which he is the organ, really does the world and Jacobinism itself a service.

So, too, Jacobinism, in its fierce hatred of the past and of those whom it makes liable for the sins of the past, cannot away with the in-exhaustible indulgence proper to culture, the consideration of circumstances, the severe judg-ment of actions joined to the merciful judgment of persons. "The man of culture is in politics," cries Mr. Frederic Harrison, "one of the poorest mortals alive!" Mr. Frederic Harrison wants to be doing business, and he complains that the man of culture stops him with a "turn for small fault-finding, love of selfish ease, and indecision in action." Of what use is culture, he asks, except for "a critic of new books or a professor of *belles-lettres?*" Why, it is of use because in presence of the fierce exasperation which breathes, or rather, I may say, hisses through the whole production in which Mr. Frederic Harrison asks that ques-tion, it reminds us that the perfection of human nature is sweetness and light. It is of use because, like religion,—that other effort after perfection, —it testifies, that, where bitter envying and strife are, there is confusion and every evil work.

The pursuit of perfection, then, is the pur-suit of sweetness and light. He who works for sweetness and light, works to make reason and the will of God prevail. He who works for machinery, he who works for hatred, works only for confusion. Culture looks beyond machinery, culture hates hatred; culture has one great pas-sion, the passion for sweetness and light. It has one even yet greater!—the passion for making them *prevail*. It is not satisfied till we *all* come to a perfect man; it knows that the sweetness and light of the few must be imperfect until the raw and unkindled masses of humanity are touched with sweetness and light. If I have not shrunk from saying that we must work for sweetness and light, so neither have I shrunk from saying that we must have a broad basis, must have sweetness and light for as many as possible. Again and again I have insisted how those are the happy moments of humanity, how those are the marking epochs of a people's life, how those are the flowering times for literature and art and all the

creative power of genius, when there is a *national* glow of life and thought, when the whole of society is in the fullest measure permeated by thought, sensible to beauty, intelligent and alive. Only it must be *real* thought and *real* beauty; *real* sweet-ness and *real* light. Plenty of people will try to give the masses, as they call them, an intellectual food prepared and adapted in the way they think proper for the actual condition of the masses. The ordinary popular literature is an example of this way of working on the masses. Plenty of people will try to indoctrinate the masses with the set of ideas and judgments constituting the creed of their own profession or party. Our re-ligious and political organisations give an ex-ample of this way of working on the masses. I condemn neither way; but culture works differ-ently. It does not try to teach down to the level of inferior classes; it does not try to win them for this or that sect of its own, with ready-made judgments and watchwords. It seeks to do away with classes; to make the best that has been thought and known in the world current every-where; to make all men live in an atmosphere of sweetness and light, where they may use ideas, as it uses them itself, freely,—nourished, and not bound by them.

This is the *social idea;* and the men of culture are the true apostles of equality. The great men of culture are those who have had a passion for diffusing, for making prevail, for carrying from one end of society to the other, the best knowledge, the best ideas of their time; who have laboured to divest knowledge of all that was harsh, uncouth, difficult, abstract, profes-sional, exclusive; to humanise it, to make it efficient outside the clique of the cultivated and learned, yet still remaining the *best* knowledge and thought of the time, and a true source, therefore, of sweetness and light. Such a man was Abelard[38] in the Middle Ages, in spite of all his imperfections; and thence the boundless emotion and enthusiasm which Abelard excited. Such were Lessing and Herder[39] in Germany, at the end of the last century; and their services to Germany were in this way inestimably precious. Generations will pass, and literary monuments will accumulate, and works far more perfect

---

[38] The great scholastic philosopher who taught at Paris.
[39] German philosophers of the eighteenth century.

than the works of Lessing and Herder will be produced in Germany; and yet the names of these two men will fill a German with a reverence and enthusiasm such as the names of the most gifted masters will hardly awaken. And why? Because they *humanised* knowledge; because they broadened the basis of life and intelligence; because they worked powerfully to diffuse sweetness and light, to make reason and the will of God prevail. With Saint Augustine they said: "Let us not leave thee alone to make in the secret of thy knowledge, as thou didst before the creation of the firmament, the division of light from darkness; let the children of thy spirit, placed in their firmament, make their light shine upon the earth, mark the division of night and day, and announce the revolution of the times; for the old order is passed, and the new arises; the night is spent, the day is come forth; and thou shalt crown the year with thy blessing, when thou shalt send forth labourers into thy harvest sown by other hands than theirs; when thou shalt send forth new labourers to new seedtimes, whereof the harvest shall be not yet."[40]

Chapter IV

HEBRAISM AND HELLENISM

This fundamental ground[1] is our preference of doing to thinking. Now this preference is a main element in our nature, and as we study it we find ourselves opening up a number of large questions on every side.

Let me go back for a moment to Bishop Wilson, who says: "First, never go against the best light you have; secondly, take care that your light be not darkness." We show, as a nation, laudable energy and persistence in walking according to the best light we have, but are not quite careful enough, perhaps, to see that our light be not darkness. This is only another version of the old story that energy is our strong point and favourable characteristic, rather than

intelligence. But we may give to this idea a more general form still, in which it will have a yet larger range of application. We may regard this energy driving at practice, this paramount sense of the obligation of duty, self-control, and work, this earnestness in going manfully with the best light we have, as one force. And we may regard the intelligence driving at those ideas which are, after all, the basis of right practice, the ardent sense for all the new and changing combinations of them which man's development brings with it, the indomitable impulse to know and adjust them perfectly, as another force. And these two forces we may regard as in some sense rivals,— rivals not by the necessity of their own nature, but as exhibited in man and his history,—and rivals dividing the empire of the world between them. And to give these forces names from the two races of men who have supplied the most signal and splendid manifestations of them, we may call them respectively the forces of Hebraism and Hellenism. Hebraism and Hellenism,—between these two points of influence moves our world. At one time it feels more powerfully the attraction of one of them, at another time of the other; and it ought to be, though it never is, evenly and happily balanced between them.

The final aim of both Hellenism and Hebraism, as of all great spiritual disciplines, is no doubt the same: man's perfection or salvation. The very language which they both of them use in schooling us to reach this aim is often identical. Even when their language indicates by variation,—sometimes a broad variation, often a but slight and subtle variation,—the different courses of thought which are uppermost in each discipline, even then the unity of the final end and aim is still apparent. To employ the actual words of that discipline with which we ourselves are all of us most familiar, and the words of which, therefore, come most home to us, that final end and aim is "that we might be partakers of the divine nature."[2] These are the words of a Hebrew apostle, but of Hellenism and Hebraism alike this is, I say, the aim. When the two are confronted, as they very often are confronted, it is nearly always with what I may call a rhetorical purpose; the speaker's whole design is to exalt and enthrone one of the two, and he uses the

---

[40] *Confessions*, xiii, 18.

[1] These words refer to the end of chap. III, where Arnold has announced that he will now seek "for the very ground and cause" of our hostility to some public recognition of what right reason dictates. For "right reason" see note 7 to chap. I, "Sweetness and Light."

---

[2] II Peter 1:4.

other only as a foil and to enable him the better to give effect to his purpose. Obviously, with us, it is usually Hellenism which is thus reduced to minister to the triumph of Hebraism. There is a sermon on Greece and the Greek spirit by a man never to be mentioned without interest and respect, Frederick Robertson,[3] in which this rhetorical use of Greece and the Greek spirit, and the inadequate exhibition of them necessarily consequent upon this, is almost ludicrous, and would be censurable if it were not to be explained by the exigencies of a sermon. On the other hand, Heinrich Heine,[4] and other writers of his sort, give us the spectacle of the tables completely turned, and of Hebraism brought in just as a foil and contrast to Hellenism, and to make the superiority of Hellenism more manifest. In both these cases there is injustice and misrepresentation. The aim and end of both Hebraism and Hellenism is, as I have said, one and the same, and this aim and end is august and admirable.

Still, they pursue this aim by very different courses. The uppermost idea with Hellenism is to see things as they really are;[5] the uppermost idea with Hebraism is conduct and obedience. Nothing can do away with this ineffaceable difference. The Greek quarrel with the body and its desires is, that they hinder right thinking; the Hebrew quarrel with them is, that they hinder right acting. "He that keepeth the law, happy is he;" "Blessed is the man that feareth the Eternal, that delighteth greatly in his commandments;"— that is the Hebrew notion of felicity; and, pursued with passion and tenacity, this notion would not let the Hebrew rest till, as is well known, he had at last got out of the law a network of prescriptions to enwrap his whole life, to govern every moment of it, every impulse, every action. The Greek notion of felicity, on the other hand, is perfectly conveyed in these words of a great French moralist: "C'est le bonheur des hommes," —when? when they abhor that which is evil?— no; when they exercise themselves in the law of the Lord day and night?—no; when they die

daily?—no; when they walk about the New Jerusalem with palms in their hands?—no; but when they think aright, when their thought hits: "quand ils pensent juste."[6] At the bottom of both the Greek and the Hebrew notion is the desire, native in man, for reason and the will of God, the feeling after the universal order,—in a word, the love of God. But, while Hebraism seizes upon certain plain, capital intimations of the universal order, and rivets itself, one may say, with unequalled grandeur of earnestness and intensity on the study and observance of them, the bent of Hellenism is to follow, with flexible activity, the whole play of the universal order, to be apprehensive of missing any part of it, of sacrificing one part to another, to slip away from resting in this or that intimation of it, however capital. An unclouded clearness of mind, an unimpeded play of thought, is what this bent drives at. The governing idea of Hellenism is *spontaneity of consciousness;* that of Hebraism, *strictness of conscience.*

Christianity changed nothing in this essential bent of Hebraism to set doing above knowing. Self-conquest, self-devotion, the following not our own individual will, but the will of God, *obedience,* is the fundamental idea of this form, also, of the discipline to which we have attached the general name of Hebraism. Only, as the old law and the network of prescriptions with which it enveloped human life were evidently a motive-power not driving and searching enough to produce the result aimed at,—patient continuance in well-doing, self-conquest,—Christianity substituted for them boundless devotion to that inspiring and affecting pattern of self-conquest offered by Jesus Christ; and by the new motive-power, of which the essence was this, though the love and admiration of Christian churches have for centuries been employed in varying, amplifying, and adorning the plain description of it, Christianity, as St. Paul truly says, "establishes the law," and in the strength of the ampler power which she has thus supplied to fulfil it, has accomplished the miracles, which we all see, of her history.

So long as we do not forget that both

---

[3] A famous Victorian preacher, very sympathetic with working-class movements.

[4] German poet (1797–1856), a Jew by birth, who worshipped the Greeks. See Arnold's essay in *Essays in Criticism* (1865).

[5] See p. 851, note 16, and p. 870, lines 8–13.

[6] Frederick the Great, quoted by Sainte-Beuve (in *Works*, ed. Super, p. 436, derived from Coulling): "It is the happiness of men when they think rightly."

Hellenism and Hebraism are profound and admirable manifestations of man's life, tendencies, and powers, and that both of them aim at a like final result, we can hardly insist too strongly on the divergence of line and of operation with which they proceed. It is a divergence so great that it most truly, as the prophet Zechariah says, "has raised up thy sons, O Zion, against thy sons, O Greece!"[7] The difference whether it is by doing or by knowing that we set most store, and the practical consequences which follow from this difference, leave their mark on all the history of our race and of its development. Language may be abundantly quoted from both Hellenism and Hebraism to make it seem that one follows the same current as the other towards the same goal. They are, truly, borne towards the same goal; but the currents which bear them are infinitely different. It is true, Solomon will praise knowing: "Understanding is a well-spring of life unto him that hath it."[8] And in the New Testament, again, Jesus Christ is a "light," and "truth makes us free." It is true, Aristotle will undervalue knowing: "In what concerns virtue," says he, "three things are necessary—knowledge, deliberate will, and perseverance; but whereas the two last are all-important, the first is a matter of little importance."[9] It is true that with the same impatience with which St. James enjoins a man to be not a forgetful hearer, but a *doer of the word,* Epictetus exhorts us to *do* what we have demonstrated to ourselves we ought to do; or he taunts us with futility, for being armed at all points to prove that lying is wrong, yet all the time continuing to lie.[10] It is true, Plato, in words which are almost the words of the New Testament or the Imitation, calls life a learning to die.[11] But underneath the superficial agreement the fundamental divergence still subsists. The understanding of Solomon is "the walking in the way of the commandments;" this is "the way of peace," and it is of this that blessedness comes. In the New Testament, the truth which gives us the peace of God and makes us free, is the love of Christ constraining us to crucify, as he did, and with a like purpose of moral regeneration,

the flesh with its affections and lusts, and thus establishing, as we have seen, the law.[12] The moral virtues, on the other hand, are with Aristotle but the porch and access to the intellectual, and with these last is blessedness. That partaking of the divine life, which both Hellenism and Hebraism, as we have said, fix as their crowning aim, Plato expressly denies to the man of practical virtue merely, of self-conquest with any other motive than that of perfect intellectual vision. He reserves it for the lover of pure knowledge, of seeing things as they really are,—the φιλομαθής.[13]

Both Hellenism and Hebraism arise out of the wants of human nature, and address themselves to satisfying those wants. But their methods are so different, they lay stress on such different points, and call into being by their respective disciplines such different activities, that the face which human nature presents when it passes from the hands of one of them to those of the other, is no longer the same. To get rid of one's ignorance, to see things as they are, and by seeing them as they are to see them in their beauty, is the simple and attractive ideal which Hellenism holds out before human nature; and from the simplicity and charm of this ideal, Hellenism, and human life in the hands of Hellenism, is invested with a kind of aërial ease, clearness, and radiancy; they are full of what we call sweetness and light. Difficulties are kept out of view, and the beauty and rationalness of the ideal have all our thoughts. "The best man is he who most tries to perfect himself, and the happiest man is he who most feels that he *is* perfecting himself,"—this account of the matter by Socrates, the true Socrates of the *Memorabilia,*[14] has something so simple, spontaneous, and unsophisticated about it, that it seems to fill us with clearness and hope when we hear it. But there is a saying which I have heard attributed to Mr. Carlyle about Socrates,—a very happy saying, whether it is really Mr. Carlyle's or not,—which excellently marks the essential point in which Hebraism differs from Hellenism. "Socrates," this saying goes, "is terribly *at ease in Zion.*"[15] Hebraism,—

---

7 Zechariah 9:13.
8 Proverbs 16:22.
9 *Nichomachean Ethics,* II, iv, 3.
10 James 1:22; Epictetus, *Encheiridion,* 35, 52.
11 *Phaedo,* 64A.

12 I Kings 3:14; Galatians 5:24.
13 *Nichomachean Ethics,* X, viii; the idea may be found in Plato's *Phaedo,* 82D–83E and the *Republic,* V, 475D–480.
14 Xenophon, *Memorabilia,* IV, viii, 6.
15 In a letter of Carlyle's to J. L. Davies: for details see *Works,* ed. Super, V, 437

and here is the source of its wonderful strength, —has always been severely preoccupied with an awful sense of the impossibility of being at ease in Zion;[16] of the difficulties which oppose themselves to man's pursuit or attainment of that perfection of which Socrates talks so hopefully, and, as from this point of view one might almost say, so glibly. It is all very well to talk of getting rid of one's ignorance, of seeing things in their reality, seeing them in their beauty; but how is this to be done when there is something which thwarts and spoils all our efforts?

This something is *sin;* and the space which sin fills in Hebraism, as compared with Hellenism, is indeed prodigious. This obstacle to perfection fills the whole scene, and perfection appears remote and rising away from earth, in the background. Under the name of sin, the difficulties of knowing oneself and conquering oneself which impede man's passage to perfection, become, for Hebraism, a positive, active entity hostile to man, a mysterious power which I heard Dr. Pusey[17] the other day, in one of his impressive sermons, compare to a hideous hunchback seated on our shoulders, and which it is the main business of our lives to hate and oppose. The discipline of the Old Testament may be summed up as a discipline teaching us to abhor and flee from sin; the discipline of the New Testament, as a discipline teaching us to die to it. As Hellenism speaks of thinking clearly, seeing things in their essence and beauty, as a grand and precious feat for man to achieve, so Hebraism speaks of becoming conscious of sin, of awakening to a sense of sin, as a feat of this kind. It is obvious to what wide divergence these differing tendencies, actively followed, must lead. As one passes and repasses from Hellenism to Hebraism, from Plato to St. Paul, one feels inclined to rub one's eyes and ask oneself whether man is indeed a gentle and simple being, showing the traces of a noble and divine nature; or an unhappy chained captive, labouring with groanings that cannot be uttered to free himself from the body of this death.

Apparently it was the Hellenic conception of human nature which was unsound, for the world could not live by it. Absolutely to call it

unsound, however, is to fall into the common error of its Hebraising enemies; but it was unsound at that particular moment of man's development, it was premature. The indispensable basis of conduct and self-control, the platform upon which alone the perfection aimed at by Greece can come into bloom, was not to be reached by our race so easily; centuries of probation and discipline were needed to bring us to it. Therefore the bright promise of Hellenism faded, and Hebraism ruled the world. Then was seen that astonishing spectacle, so well marked by the often-quoted words of the prophet Zechariah, when men of all languages of the nations took hold of the skirt of him that was a Jew, saying:—"*We will go with you, for we have heard that God is with you.*"[18] And the Hebraism which thus received and ruled a world all gone out of the way and altogether become unprofitable, was, and could not but be, the later, the more spiritual, the more attractive development of Hebraism. It was Christianity; that is to say, Hebraism aiming at self-conquest and rescue from the thrall of vile affections, not by obedience to the letter of a law, but by conformity to the image of a self-sacrificing example. To a world stricken with moral enervation Christianity offered its spectacle of an inspired self-sacrifice; to men who refused themselves nothing, it showed one who refused himself everything;— "*my Saviour banished joy!*" says George Herbert.[19] When the *alma Venus,* the life-giving and joy-giving power of nature, so fondly cherished by the Pagan world, could not save her followers from self-dissatisfaction and ennui, the severe words of the apostle came bracingly and refreshingly: "Let no man deceive you with vain words, for because of these things cometh the wrath of God upon the children of disobedience."[20] Through age after age and generation after generation, our race, or all that part of our race which was most living and progressive, was *baptized into a death;* and endeavoured, by suffering in the flesh, to cease from sin. Of this endeavour, the animating labours and afflictions of early Christianity, the touching asceticism of mediæval Christianity, are the great historical manifestations. Literary monuments of it, each

---

16 Amos 6:1; Zion is Jerusalem and its Hebraism.
17 Dr. E. B. Pusey (1800–1882), Professor of Hebrew at Oxford and one of the leaders of the Oxford Movement.

18 Zechariah 8:23.
19 The seventeenth–century religious poet.
20 Ephesians 5:6.

in its own way incomparable, remain in the Epistles of St. Paul, in St. Augustine's Confessions, and in the two original and simplest books of the Imitation.[21]

Of two disciplines laying their main stress, the one, on clear intelligence, the other, on firm obedience; the one, on comprehensively knowing the grounds of one's duty, the other, on diligently practising it; the one, on taking all possible care (to use Bishop Wilson's words again) that the light we have be not darkness, the other, that according to the best light we have we diligently walk,—the priority naturally belongs to that discipline which braces all man's moral powers, and founds for him an indispensable basis of character. And, therefore, it is justly said of the Jewish people, who were charged with setting powerfully forth that side of the divine order to which the words *conscience* and *self-conquest* point, that they were "entrusted with the oracles of God;"[22] as it is justly said of Christianity, which followed Judaism and which set forth this side with a much deeper effectiveness and a much wider influence, that the wisdom of the old Pagan world was foolishness compared to it. No words of devotion and admiration can be too strong to render thanks to these beneficent forces which have so borne forward humanity in its appointed work of coming to the knowledge and possession of itself; above all, in those great moments when their action was the wholesomest and the most necessary.

But the evolution of these forces, separately and in themselves, is not the whole evolution of humanity,—their single history is not the whole history of man; whereas their admirers are always apt to make it stand for the whole history. Hebraism and Hellenism are, neither of them, the *law* of human development, as their admirers are prone to make them; they are, each of them, *contributions* to human development,—august contributions, invaluable contributions; and each showing itself to us more august, more invaluable, more preponderant over the other, according to the moment in which we take them, and the relation in which we stand to them. The nations of our modern world, children of that immense and salutary movement which broke up

the Pagan world, inevitably stand to Hellenism in a relation which dwarfs it, and to Hebraism in a relation which magnifies it. They are inevitably prone to take Hebraism as the law of human development, and not as simply a contribution to it, however precious. And yet the lesson must perforce be learned, that the human spirit is wider than the most priceless of the forces which bear it onward, and that to the whole development of man Hebraism itself is, like Hellenism, but a contribution.

Perhaps we may help ourselves to see this clearer by an illustration drawn from the treatment of a single great idea which has profoundly engaged the human spirit, and has given it eminent opportunities for showing its nobleness and energy. It surely must be perceived that the idea of immortality, as this idea rises in its generality before the human spirit, is something grander, truer, and more satisfying, than it is in the particular forms by which St. Paul, in the famous fifteenth chapter of the Epistle to the Corinthians, and Plato, in the *Phaedo,* endeavour to develop and establish it. Surely we cannot but feel, that the argumentation with which the Hebrew apostle goes about to expound this great idea is, after all, confused and inconclusive; and that the reasoning, drawn from analogies of likeness and equality, which is employed upon it by the Greek philosopher, is over-subtle and sterile. Above and beyond the inadequate solutions which Hebraism and Hellenism here attempt, extends the immense and august problem itself, and the human spirit which gave birth to it. And this single illustration may suggest to us how the same thing happens in other cases also.

But meanwhile, by alternations of Hebraism and Hellenism, of a man's intellectual and moral impulses, of the effort to see things as they really are, and the effort to win peace by self-conquest, the human spirit proceeds; and each of these two forces has its appointed hours of culmination and seasons of rule. As the great movement of Christianity was a triumph of Hebraism and man's moral impulses, so the great movement which goes by the name of the Renascence was an uprising and re-instatement of man's intellectual impulses and of Hellenism. We in England, the devoted children of Protestantism, chiefly know the Renascence by its subordinate and secondary side of the Reformation.

---

21 The two first books (Arnold).
22 Romans 3:2.

The Reformation has been often called a Hebraising revival, a return to the ardour and sincereness of primitive Christianity. No one, however, can study the development of Protestantism and of Protestant churches without feeling that into the Reformation too,—Hebraising child of the Renascence and offspring of its fervour, rather than its intelligence, as it undoubtedly was,—the subtle Hellenic leaven of the Renascence found its way, and that the exact respective parts, in the Reformation, of Hebraism and of Hellenism, are not easy to separate. But what we may with truth say is, that all which Protestantism was to itself clearly conscious of, all which it succeeded in clearly setting forth in words, had the characters of Hebraism rather than of Hellenism. The Reformation was strong, in that it was an earnest return to the Bible and to doing from the heart the will of God as there written. It was weak, in that it never consciously grasped or applied the central idea of the Renascence,—the Hellenic idea of pursuing, in all lines of activity, the law and science, to use Plato's words, of things as they really are.[23] Whatever direct superiority, therefore, Protestantism had over Catholicism was a moral superiority, a superiority arising out of its greater sincerity and earnestness,—at the moment of its apparition at any rate,—in dealing with the heart and conscience. Its pretensions to an intellectual superiority are in general quite illusory. For Hellenism, for the thinking side in man as distinguished from the acting side, the attitude of mind of Protestantism towards the Bible in no respect differs from the attitude of mind of Catholicism towards the Church. The mental habit of him who imagines that Balaam's ass spoke, in no respect differs from the mental habit of him who imagines that a Madonna of wood or stone winked; and the one, who says that God's Church makes him believe what he believes, and the other, who says that God's Word makes him believe what he believes, are for the philosopher perfectly alike in not really and truly knowing, when they say *God's Church* and *God's Word,* what it is they say, or whereof they affirm.

In the sixteenth century, therefore, Hellenism re-entered the world, and again stood in presence of Hebraism,—a Hebraism renewed and purged. Now, it has not been enough observed, how, in the seventeenth century, a fate befell Hellenism in some respects analogous to that which befell it at the commencement of our era. The Renascence, that great re-awakening of Hellenism, that irresistible return of humanity to nature and to seeing things as they are, which in art, in literature, and in physics, produced such splendid fruits, had, like the anterior Hellenism of the Pagan world, a side of moral weakness and of relaxation or insensibility of the moral fibre, which in Italy showed itself with the most startling plainness, but which in France, England, and other countries was very apparent too. Again this loss of spiritual balance, this exclusive preponderance given to man's perceiving and knowing side, this unnatural defect of his feeling and acting side, provoked a reaction. Let us trace that reaction where it most nearly concerns us.

Science[24] has now made visible to everybody the great and pregnant elements of difference which lie in race, and in how signal a manner they make the genius and history of an Indo-European people vary from those of a Semitic people. Hellenism is of Indo-European growth, Hebraism is of Semitic growth; and we English, a nation of Indo-European stock, seem to belong naturally to the movement of Hellenism. But nothing more strongly marks the essential unity of man, than the affinities we can perceive, in this point or that, between members of one family of peoples and members of another. And no affinity of this kind is more strongly marked than that likeness in the strength and prominence of the moral fibre, which notwithstanding immense elements of difference, knits in some special sort the genius and history of us English, and our American descendants across the Atlantic, to the genius and history of the Hebrew people. Puritanism, which has been so great a power in the English nation, and in the strongest part of the English nation, was originally the reaction in the seventeenth century of the conscience and moral sense of our race, against the moral indifference and lax rule of conduct which in the sixteenth century came in with the Renascence. It was a reaction of Hebraism against Hellenism; and it powerfully manifested itself, as was natural, in

---

23 *Republic,* VII, 532.

24 Ethnology.

a people with much of what we call a Hebraising turn, with a signal affinity for the bent which was the master-bent of Hebrew life. Eminently Indo-European by its *humour*,[25] by the power it shows, through this gift, of imaginatively acknowledging the multiform aspects of the problem of life, and of thus getting itself unfixed from its own over-certainty, of smiling at its own over-tenacity, our race has yet (and a great part of its strength lies here), in matters of practical life and moral conduct, a strong share of the assuredness, the tenacity, the intensity of the Hebrews. This turn manifested itself in Puritanism, and has had a great part in shaping our history for the last two hundred years. Undoubtedly it checked and changed amongst us that movement of the Renascence which we see producing in the reign of Elizabeth such wonderful fruits. Undoubtedly it stopped the prominent rule and direct development of that order of ideas which we call by the name of Hellenism, and gave the first rank to a different order of ideas. Apparently, too, as we said of the former defeat of Hellenism, if Hellenism was defeated, this shows that Hellenism was imperfect, and that its ascendency at that moment would not have been for the world's good.

Yet there is a very important difference between the defeat inflicted on Hellenism by Christianity eighteen hundred years ago, and the check given to the Renascence by Puritanism. The greatness of the difference is well measured by the difference in force, beauty, significance, and usefulness, between primitive Christianity and Protestantism. Eighteen hundred years ago it was altogether the hour of Hebraism. Primitive Christianity was legitimately and truly the ascendant force in the world at that time, and the way of mankind's progress lay through its full development. Another hour in man's development began in the fifteenth century, and the main road of his progress then lay for a time through Hellenism. Puritanism was no longer the central current of the world's progress, it was a side stream crossing the central current and checking it. The cross and the check may have been necessary and salutary, but that does not do away with the essential difference between the main stream of man's advance and a cross or side stream. For more than two hundred years the main stream of man's advance has moved towards knowing himself and the world, seeing things as they are, spontaneity of consciousness; the main impulse of a great part, and that the strongest part, of our nation has been towards strictness of conscience. They have made the secondary the principal at the wrong moment, and the principal they have at the wrong moment treated as secondary. This contravention of the natural order has produced, as such contravention always must produce, a certain confusion and false movement,[26] of which we are now beginning to feel, in almost every direction, the inconvenience. In all directions our habitual courses of action seem to be losing efficaciousness, credit, and control, both with others and even with ourselves. Everywhere we see the beginnings of confusion, and we want a clue to some sound order and authority. This we can only get by going back upon the actual instincts and forces which rule our life, seeing them as they really are, connecting them with other instincts and forces, and enlarging our whole view and rule of life.

---

25 Disposition, state of mind.

26 Cf. the Preface (1883 ed.), p. xlii: "Now, and for us, it is a time to Hellenise, and to praise knowing; for we have Hebraised too much, and have over-valued doing."

Dante Gabriel Rossetti

1828–1882

Dante Gabriel Rossetti was a rarely endowed individual, having to a high degree the gift not only of poetic but also of pictorial expression. Indeed, so evenly balanced were these two sides of his artistic temperament that his pictures sometimes seem the plastic expression of his poetic inspiration, and his poems often create the impression of paintings. Actually he often dealt with the same subject in both media, writing sonnets for his pictures or depicting the subjects of his poems on canvas. A contemporary critic notes that Rossetti, "the poet-painter," was unable to dissever his pictorial from his poetic faculty, and Rossetti himself all but identified the two arts when he declared, "If any man has any poetry in him he should paint it," which is essentially what he strove to do with both color and words.

Born in London in 1828, the son of an exiled Italian patriot, this doubly talented youth grew up in a household where culture and politics, mainly Italian, were the major preoccupations: the simple home welcomed sooner or later almost all the Italians who had fled to England to escape Austrian tyranny, and was at the same time a meeting place for those of literary, musical, and artistic interests. The father, who had both musical and poetic talents, was a devoted student of Dante. As his political hopes grew dim, he gradually gave himself up almost exclusively to the interpretation of the great Florentine, who became, we are told, a kind of familiar spirit in the house, "a sacred and benign, though mysteriously invisible visitor."

Dante's influence upon young Dante Gabriel did not remain completely ethereal, for the son in turn began to pore over the *Divina Commedia* and more especially over the *Vita Nuova*. At first it was no doubt the pictorial qualities that appealed to his sensuous imagination, but there was also a strain of mysticism in him which responded to Dante's conception of the final fulfillment of human love and beauty in the divine. Moreover, he was at the same time discovering with delight the glowing and picturesque character of the Middle Ages as portrayed in Malory, in Scott, and in Keats. Here was a world to which he, like William Morris, instinctively felt he belonged, with all its wealth of color and romance and its chivalric tradition of courtly love. Thus stirred, it is small wonder that when he decided to bend his main efforts to painting, he should find the drab tones and academic conventionalism of contemporary art both lifeless and intolerable, "wishy-

Dante Gabriel Rossetti (1828–1882). Rossetti rejected the strict formalism of academy painting in favor of forms and colors which arise directly from the experience and perceptions of the artist himself. This portrait of him at the age of 25 is by his friend and Pre-Raphaelite brother, Holman Hunt. *Published with the permission of the Birmingham Museum and Art Gallery.*

washy to the last degree." It was primarily "in the Italian painters from Giotto to Leonardo, and in certain early Flemish and German painters," that he recognized some of the qualities which had exerted such a spell over him in poetry, "a manifest emotional sincerity, expressed sometimes in a lofty and solemn way, and sometimes with a candid *naïveté;* . . . strong evidences of grace, decorative charm." To rescue English painting from its worn-out traditions by returning to the spirit of those early painters, he joined in 1848 with Holman Hunt and Edward Millais to form the Pre-Raphaelite Brotherhood (see the introduction to the Victorian period, p. 427). His brother William asserted that the basis of their new start was to be "serious and elevated invention of subject, along with earnest scrutiny of visible facts, and an earnest endeavour to present them veraciously and exactly." This careful observation and reproduction of visible facts was what Morris had in mind years later when he singled out naturalism as the "special and particular doctrine" of the school. (See p. 900.) To spread their ideas the group started in 1850 a short-lived magazine, *The Germ*. Nearly a dozen poems were contributed by Rossetti, chief among which was "The Blessed Damozel," the very epitome of his Pre-Raphaelite ideals. The subject is elevated, but at the same time heaven and its inhabitants are depicted in the most candid and naturalistic terms; the details are earnestly studied and accurately presented, while the color and imagery are full of decorative charm. Whatever the immediate occasion for the poem, it is clearly a reflection of Rossetti's deep and lifelong preoccupation with Dante and with the story of his semimystical devotion to Beatrice, for the blessed damozel is certainly an echo of Dante's portrayal of his lady in Paradise. But the echo, by its very nature, has undergone transformation. The lady who leaned out from the gold bar of heaven has retained far more of her earthly attributes than the Beatrice of the "Paradiso." With all of his appreciation of Dante's transcendentally spiritualized love, Rossetti remained a man whose sensuous perceptions could not be separated from his spiritual ideals, so that the poem conveys an atmosphere of almost opulent beauty that contrasts markedly with Dante's austerity. Indeed, so striking are the plastic elements that the reader may well ask himself whether he has been reading a poem or looking at a picture, an effect which attains to what Rossetti once proclaimed to be the supreme perfection: "the point of meeting where the two [picture and poem] are most identical."

The same plastic effect tends to dominate in other poems where he is depicting more contemporary and more earthly scenes. "My Sister's Sleep" describes one of those incidents that William Morris termed distinctive of the naturalistic painting of the Pre-Raphaelite group (see p. 901), an incident taken from ordinary modern life; but again the poem is a picture, with the same conscientious attention to accurate presentment of physical detail. Rossetti painted another contemporary scene in his dramatic monologue "Jenny," written under the influence of Robert Browning, for whom at one period he experienced an intense admiration. Here again, although the emotional and psychological factors are much more in evidence, it is still the pictorial impression that is dominant.

These, however, are scenes and incidents such as Rossetti usually eschewed; his love of beauty and color and romance, coupled to his fascination with Dante and with the semimystical traditions of chivalry, led him more often to medieval subjects. One of the earliest and best of his poems on such subjects is "Sister Helen." Though the same pictorial imagination is recognizable in this study of the almost demoniacal cruelty engendered by unrequited love and jealousy, there is a comparative lack of either decorative or colorful detail. The power of the narrative is enforced by the austerity of diction and image that perfectly reflect the stark scene and the grim emotions, as well as by the skillful use of the refrain to communicate Helen's inner excitement and final despair.

With his mind thus filled with themes and images of the Middle Ages in general and of Dante in particular, it is hardly surprising that when, in 1850, Rossetti fell in love with Elizabeth Siddal, he should have identified himself and her with Dante and Beatrice, an identity which was emphasized by Lizzie's posing for his pictures of the latter. Nor is it too surprising that during the next ten years Rossetti, although mainly busied with his painting, and distracted by his troubled and prolonged engagement and subsequent marriage (1860) to the beautiful but difficult Miss Siddal—a union which was soon terminated by her death under circumstances that did not preclude the possibility of suicide—should still have found time to translate the *Vita Nuova* and some of Dante's sonnets, as well as poems by various of his predecessors and contemporaries. These he published in 1861 as *The Early Italian Poets,* later revising and rearranging them under the title of *Dante and His Circle* (1874).

He had planned to publish his own poetry separately shortly after the volume of Italian translations, but the project was temporarily halted when, in 1862, in a fit of remorse he put his manuscripts into his wife's coffin. This impulsive and somewhat histrionic gesture was an attempt to atone to Lizzie for the unhappiness he felt he had caused her. In the first flush of his attachment he had viewed her in an aura of Dantesque mysticism, but as the stress of their personalities and circumstances revealed with ever-increasing clarity that he was no Dante and Lizzie no Beatrice, he tasted keen disillusionment and frustration, and, finally, bitter self-reproach. No doubt the galling realization of the gulf between his earlier dream and the actuality is responsible for the tone of desolation and vain regret that sounds in many of the sonnets which he was writing during this period and which eventually formed part of his sequence, *The House of Life*. But Rossetti, whatever his bitterness and disillusionment, could not escape the influence that had been such a dominating force from his earliest years. He was still "half lost in medievalism and Dante," as Ruskin complained to the Brownings in 1859. He still dreamed of love as he had found it in the *Vita Nuova,* "love sublimed to heavenly mood," although time had proved it so foreign to his own experience and nature. The mystical fulfillment that had been so signally wanting in his relations with Lizzie, he now looked for in his love for Jane Morris, the wife of his friend and one-time disciple William Morris. Thus, joined with vain regret for the past, there is in these sonnets an equally vain hope for the future, and that hope, by the very nature of the case, led full circle round to vain regret for what might have been.

Written over a period of more than thirty years, the completed series of a hundred and one sonnets makes no attempt to present a consecutive story or to trace an ordered psychological development; rather, as the poet himself explains, each sonnet is "a moment's monument." For obvious personal reasons both Rossetti and later his brother and editor, William, made every effort to obscure the exact autobiographical bearing of the sonnets; it is nevertheless quite clear that the sonnets do reflect for the most part Rossetti's experiences and moods, and are attempts to translate these into a semi-Platonic and allegorical idiom. While there are lines which do recapture momentarily the naturalistic and pictorial qualities of some of his other poems, specifically descriptions of nature or natural settings, the sonnets are on the whole noticeably abstract and stylized, full of symbolic imagery and elaborate personification. But occasionally, when the intensity of the underlying mood of remorse or longing does break through the conventionalized expression of the medieval tradition, we can recognize and respond to the emotions of a living man.

It was not until 1869, when he feared that his eyesight might be failing, that Rossetti took the necessary steps to have the manuscripts of his poems recovered from Lizzie's grave. After some revision and addition, he published in April, 1870, the first collection of his own work, *Poems.* The publication gave rise in October to a scurrilous denunciation by Robert Buchanan in the *Contemporary Review,* entitled "The Fleshly School of Poetry—Mr. D. G. Rossetti," which lashed out at the sensualism of Rossetti's poems, designating *The House of Life* a very hotbed of offensive ideas and nasty phrases. To a man in a less morbidly sensitive state, the attack might have proved irritating enough; but to Rossetti, whose mind was already showing signs of paranoid delusions of persecution, it seemed "the first symptom in a widespread conspiracy for crushing his fair fame as an artist and a man, and for hounding him out of honest society." He suffered a breakdown the following May, and his brother tells us that henceforth till the close of his life Rossetti was a changed man, although during his

The Blessed Damozel. Completed thirty years after the poem, Rossetti's painting perfectly evokes the lush sentimentality of the verse. *Fogg Art Museum, Harvard University, Grenville L. Winthrop Bequest.*

last ten years he did work actively at his painting and in 1881 published his *Ballads and Sonnets* and a revised edition of his *Poems.*

TEXTS: The standard edition is *Collected Works of Dante Gabriel Rossetti,* edited by his brother William (2 vols., 1886). P. F. Baum published a separate edition of *The House of Life,* with extensive commentary, in 1928. The collected letters are being edited by Oswald Doughty and J. R. Wahl in 4 vols. (1965–67). The most recent and exhaustive biography is *A Victorian Romantic: Dante Gabriel Rossetti,* by Oswald Doughty (1949). There is a good essay by Graham Hough in *The Last Romantics* (1949).

The Blessed Damozel[1]

The blessed damozel leaned out
   From the gold bar of Heaven;
Her eyes were deeper than the depth
   Of waters stilled at even;
She had three lilies in her hand,   5
   And the stars in her hair were seven.

Her robe, ungirt from clasp to hem,
   No wrought flowers did adorn,
But a white rose of Mary's gift,
   For service meetly worn;[2]   10
Her hair that lay along her back
   Was yellow like ripe corn.[3]

Herseemed[4] she scarce had been a day
   One of God's choristers;
The wonder was not yet quite gone   15
   From that still look of hers;
Albeit, to them she left, her day
   Had counted as ten years.

(To one, it is ten years of years.
   . . . Yet now, and in this place,   20
Surely she leaned o'er me—her hair
   Fell all about my face. . . .
Nothing: the autumn-fall of leaves.
   The whole year sets apace.)

It was the rampart of God's house   25
   That she was standing on;
By God built over the sheer depth
   The which is Space begun;
So high, that looking downward thence
   She scarce could see the sun.   30

It lies in Heaven, across the flood
   Of ether, as a bridge.
Beneath, the tides of day and night
   With flame and darkness ridge
The void, as low as where this earth   35
   Spins like a fretful midge.

Around her, lovers, newly met
   'Mid deathless love's acclaims,
Spoke evermore among themselves
   Their heart-remembered names;   40
And the souls mounting up to God
   Went by her like thin flames.

And still she bowed herself and stooped
   Out of the circling charm;
Until her bosom must have made   45
   The bar she leaned on warm,
And the lilies lay as if asleep
   Along her bended arm.

From the fixed place of Heaven she saw
   Time like a pulse shake fierce   50
Through all the worlds. Her gaze still strove
   Within the gulf to pierce
Its path; and now she spoke as when
   The stars sang in their spheres.[5]

The sun was gone now; the curled moon   55
   Was like a little feather
Fluttering far down the gulf; and now
   She spoke through the still weather.
Her voice was like the voice the stars
   Had when they sang together.   60

(Ah, sweet! Even now, in that bird's song,
   Strove not her accents there,
Fain to be harkened? When those bells
   Possessed the midday air,
Strove not her steps to reach my side   65
   Down all the echoing stair?)

"I wish that he were come to me,
   For he will come," she said.
"Have I not prayed in Heaven?—on earth,
   Lord, Lord, has he not prayed?   70
Are not two prayers a perfect strength?
   And shall I feel afraid?

"When round his head the aureole clings,
   And he is clothed in white,
I'll take his hand and go with him   75
   To the deep wells of light;
As unto a stream we will step down,
   And bathe there in God's sight.

---

[1] The word "damozel" is an early form of the French "demoiselle" or English "damsel." Rossetti, many years after writing the poem, attributed its origin to his admiration for Poe's "Raven." "I saw," he is reported to have said, "that Poe had done the utmost it was possible to do with grief of the lover on earth, and I determined to reverse the conditions."

[2] The white rose is a symbol of virginity and therefore a fitting flower to be worn by one in the service of Mary.

[3] In England *corn* is a general term for grain.

[4] It seemed to her.

[5] It was a common belief in ancient times that the stars made a singing noise as they moved in their spheres.

"We two will stand beside that shrine,
    Occult, withheld, untrod,   80
Whose lamps are stirred continually
    With prayer sent up to God;
And see our old prayers, granted, melt
    Each like a little cloud.

"We two will lie i' the shadow of   85
    That living mystic tree[6]
Within whose secret growth the Dove[7]
    Is sometimes felt to be,
While every leaf that His plumes touch
    Saith His Name audibly.   90

"And I myself will teach to him,
    I myself, lying so,
The songs I sing here; which his voice
    Shall pause in, hushed and slow,
And find some knowledge at each pause,   95
    Or some new thing to know."

(Alas! We two, we two, thou say'st!
    Yea, one wast thou with me
That once of old. But shall God lift
    To endless unity   100
The soul whose likeness with thy soul
    Was but its love for thee?)

"We two," she said, "will seek the groves
    Where the lady Mary is,
With her five handmaidens, whose names   105
    Are five sweet symphonies,
Cecily, Gertrude, Magdalen,
    Margaret, and Rosalys.[8]

"Circlewise sit they, with bound locks
    And foreheads garlanded;   110
Into the fine cloth white like flame
    Weaving the golden thread,
To fashion the birth-robes for them
    Who are just born, being dead.

"He shall fear, haply, and be dumb;   115
    Then will I lay my cheek
To his, and tell about our love,
    Not once abashed or weak;
And the dear Mother will approve
    My pride, and let me speak.   120

"Herself shall bring us, hand in hand,
    To Him round whom all souls
Kneel, the clear-ranged unnumbered heads
    Bowed with their aureoles;
And angels meeting us shall sing   125
    To their citherns and citoles.[9]

"There will I ask of Christ the Lord
    Thus much for him and me:—
Only to live as once on earth
    With Love,—only to be,   130
As then awhile, forever now,
    Together, I and he."

She gazed and listened and then said,
    Less sad of speech than mild,—
"All this is when he comes." She ceased.   135
    The light thrilled toward her, filled
With angels in strong level flight.
    Her eyes prayed, and she smiled.

(I saw her smile.) But soon their path
    Was vague in distant spheres: 140
And then she cast her arms along
    The golden barriers,
And laid her face between her hands,
    And wept. (I heard her tears.)

My Sister's Sleep[1]

She fell asleep on Christmas Eve.
    At length the long-ungranted shade
    Of weary eyelids overweighed
The pain naught else might yet relieve.

Our mother, who had leaned all day   5
    Over the bed from chime to chime,
    Then raised herself for the first time,
And as she sat her down, did pray.

Her little work-table was spread
    With work to finish. For the glare   10
    Made by her candle, she had care
To work some distance from the bed.

---

[6] Cf. Revelation 22:2.   [7] The Holy Spirit.
[8] The names of the saints attending Mary are chosen purely for the musical effect.

[9] Medieval musical instruments.

[1] "This little poem, written in 1847, was printed in a periodical [*The Germ*] at the outset of 1850. The metre, which is used by several old English writers, became celebrated a month or two later on the publication of '*In Memoriam*.'" (Rossetti) The poem is not based upon any autobiographical facts.

Without, there was a cold moon up,
　　Of winter radiance sheer and thin;
　　The hollow halo it was in
Was like an icy crystal cup.　　　　　　　　　15

Through the small room, with subtle sound
　　Of flame, by vents the fireshine drove
　　And reddened. In its dim alcove
The mirror shed a clearness round.　　　　　20

I had been sitting up some nights,
　　And my tired mind felt weak and blank;
　　Like a sharp strengthening wine it drank
The stillness and the broken lights.

Twelve struck. That sound, by dwindling years　25
　　Heard in each hour,[2] crept off; and then
　　The ruffled silence spread again,
Like water that a pebble stirs.

Our mother rose from where she sat;
　　Her needles, as she laid them down,　　　30
　　Met lightly, and her silken gown
Settled: no other noise than that.

"Glory unto the Newly Born!"
　　So, as said angels, she did say,
　　Because we were in Christmas Day,　　　35
Though it would still be long till morn.

Just then in the room over us
　　There was a pushing back of chairs,
　　As some who had sat unawares
So late, now heard the hour, and rose.　　　40

With anxious softly-stepping haste
　　Our mother went where Margaret lay,
　　Fearing the sounds o'erhead—should they
Have broken her long watched-for rest!

She stooped an instant, calm, and turned,　45
　　But suddenly turned back again;
　　And all her features seemed in pain
With woe, and her eyes gazed and yearned.

For my part, I but hid my face,
　　And held my breath, and spoke no word:　50
　　There was none spoken; but I heard
The silence for a little space.

Our mother bowed herself and wept;
　　And both my arms fell, and I said,
　　"God knows I knew that she was dead."　55
And there, all white, my sister slept.

Then kneeling, upon Christmas morn
　　A little after twelve o'clock
　　We said, ere the first quarter struck,
"Christ's blessing on the newly born!"　　　60

The Ballad of Dead Ladies[1]
François Villon, 1450

Tell me now in what hidden way is
　　Lady Flora the lovely Roman?
Where's Hipparchia, and where is Thaïs,[2]
　　Neither of them the fairer woman?
　　Where is Echo, beheld of no man,　　　5
Only heard on river and mere,—
　　She whose beauty was more than human? . . .
But where are the snows of yester-year?

Where's Héloïse, the learned nun,
　　For whose sake Abeillard, I ween,　　　10
Lost manhood and put priesthood on?[3]
　　(From Love he won such dule and teen!)
　　And where, I pray you, is the Queen[4]
Who willed that Buridan should steer
　　Sewed in a sack's mouth down the Seine? . . .　15
But where are the snows of yester-year?

---

[1] This is a translation of the "Ballade des Dames du Temps Jadis" by François Villon (b. 1431), whose irregular life and haunting songs captured the imaginations of many later writers. Rossetti was much attracted by medieval literary forms. The *ballade* is a French form composed of three eight-line stanzas and a concluding four-line "envoy," each ending with the same line by way of refrain. Strictly speaking, the same rimes should be employed throughout, in the order *ababbcbc* (*bcbc* for the envoy), but Rossetti introduces fresh *a* and *b* rimes in each stanza.

[2] Flora was a famous courtesan of Rome, Hipparchia a Greek courtesan, and Thaïs an Athenian lady of like profession.

[3] Héloïse was the beautiful niece of a church official, who fell in love with her teacher, the famous philosopher and theologian, Abelard (1079–1142). They eloped, and the uncle was so incensed that he caused Abelard to be set upon and emasculated. As a result Abelard became a monk and Héloïse a nun, and the reward of their love was sorrow and pain.

[4] The Queen was Margaret of Burgundy, who used to have her lovers, among whom was the scholar Buridan, sewn in sacks and thrown into the Seine.

---

[2] Because old people tend to sleep less than others, they hear the striking of all the hours.

White Queen Blanche, like a queen of lilies,[5]
   With a voice like any mermaiden,—
Bertha Broadfoot, Beatrice, Alice,[6]
   And Ermengarde the lady of Maine,[7]—   20
And that good Joan[8] whom Englishmen
At Rouen doomed and burned her there,—
   Mother of God, where are they then? . . .
But where are the snows of yester-year?

Nay, never ask this week, fair lord,   25
   Where they are gone, nor yet this year,
Except with this for an overword,—
   But where are the snows of yester-year?

Sister Helen[1]

"Why did you melt your waxen man,
             Sister Helen?
Today is the third since you began."
"The time was long, yet the time ran,
             Little brother."   5
        (O Mother, Mary Mother,
Three days today, between Hell and Heaven!)

"But if you have done your work aright,
             Sister Helen,
You'll let me play, for you said I might."   10
"Be very still in your play tonight,
             Little brother."
        (O Mother, Mary Mother,
Third night, tonight, between Hell and Heaven!)

"You said it must melt ere vesper-bell,   15
             Sister Helen;
If now it be molten, all is well."
"Even so,—nay, peace! you cannot tell,
             Little brother."
        (O Mother, Mary Mother,   20
Oh, what is this, between Hell and Heaven?)

"Oh, the waxen knave was plump today,
             Sister Helen;

How like dead folk he has dropped away!"
"Nay now, of the dead what can you say,   25
             Little brother?"
        (O Mother, Mary Mother,
What of the dead, between Hell and Heaven?)

"See, see, the sunken pile of wood,
             Sister Helen,   30
Shines through the thinned wax red as blood!"
"Nay now, when looked you yet on blood,
             Little brother?"
        (O Mother, Mary Mother,
How pale she is, between Hell and Heaven!)   35

"Now close your eyes, for they're sick and sore,
             Sister Helen,
And I'll play without the gallery door."
"Aye, let me rest—I'll lie on the floor,
             Little brother."   40
        (O Mother, Mary Mother,
What rest tonight, between Hell and Heaven?)

"Here high up in the balcony,
             Sister Helen,
The moon flies face to face with me."   45
"Aye, look and say whatever you see,
             Little brother."
        (O Mother, Mary Mother,
What sight tonight, between Hell and Heaven?)

"Outside it's merry in the wind's wake,   50
             Sister Helen;
In the shaken trees the chill stars shake."
"Hush, heard you a horse-tread as you spake,
             Little brother?"
        (O Mother, Mary Mother,   55
What sound tonight, between Hell and Heaven?)

"I hear a horse-tread, and I see,
             Sister Helen,
Three horsemen that ride terribly."
"Little brother, whence come the three,   60
             Little brother?"
        (O Mother, Mary Mother,
Whence should they come, between Hell and
    Heaven?)

"They come by the hill-verge from Boyne Bar,[2]
             Sister Helen,   65
And one draws nigh, but two are afar."

---

5 Perhaps Blanche of Castille, or perhaps a figment of Villon's imagination.
6 Bertha Broadfoot, in epic accounts, is the mother of Charlemagne. The identity of Beatrice and Alice is uncertain. The poet may well not have had any specific ladies in mind.
7 A countess of Anjou in France.   8 Joan of Arc.

1 The ballad is based on the superstition that melting the waxen image of a person will bring about his suffering and death.

2 At the mouth of the river of that name in Ireland.

"Look, look, do you know them who they are,
          Little brother?"
          (*O Mother, Mary Mother,*
Who should they be, between Hell and Heaven?)   70

"Oh, it's Keith of Eastholm rides so fast,
          Sister Helen,
For I know the white mane on the blast."
"The hour has come, has come at last,
          Little brother!"   75
          (*O Mother, Mary Mother,*
Her hour at last, between Hell and Heaven!)

"He has made a sign and called Halloo!
          Sister Helen,
And he says that he would speak with you."   80
"Oh, tell him I fear the frozen dew,
          Little brother."
          (*O Mother, Mary Mother,*
Why laughs she thus, between Hell and Heaven?)

"The wind is loud, but I hear him cry,   85
          Sister Helen,
That Keith of Ewern's like to die."
"And he and thou, and thou and I,
          Little brother."
          (*O Mother, Mary Mother,*   90
And they and we, between Hell and Heaven!)

"Three days ago, on his marriage-morn,
          Sister Helen,
He sickened, and lies since then forlorn."
"For bridegroom's side is the bride a thorn,   95
          Little brother?"
          (*O Mother, Mary Mother,*
Cold bridal cheer, between Hell and Heaven!)

"Three days and nights he has lain abed,
          Sister Helen,   100
And he prays in torment to be dead."
"The thing may chance, if he have prayed,
          Little brother!"
          (*O Mother, Mary Mother,*
If he have prayed, between Hell and Heaven!)   105

"But he has not ceased to cry today,
          Sister Helen,
That you should take your curse away."
"*My* prayer was heard,—he need but pray,
          Little brother!"   110
          (*O Mother, Mary Mother,*
Shall God not hear, between Hell and Heaven?)

"But he says, till you take back your ban,
          Sister Helen,
His soul would pass, yet never can."   115
"Nay then, shall I slay a living man,[3]
          Little brother?"
          (*O Mother, Mary Mother,*
A living soul, between Hell and Heaven!)

"But he calls for ever on your name,   120
          Sister Helen,
And says that he melts before a flame."
"My heart for his pleasure fared the same,
          Little brother."
          (*O Mother, Mary Mother,*   125
Fire at the heart, between Hell and Heaven!)

"Here's Keith of Westholm riding fast,
          Sister Helen,
For I know the white plume on the blast."
"The hour, the sweet hour I forecast,   130
          Little brother!"
          (*O Mother, Mary Mother,*
Is the hour sweet, between Hell and Heaven?)

"He stops to speak, and he stills his horse,
          Sister Helen;   135
But his words are drowned in the wind's course."
"Nay hear, nay hear, you must hear perforce,
          Little brother!"
          (*O Mother, Mary Mother,*
What word now heard, between Hell and   140
Heaven?)

"Oh, he says that Keith of Ewern's cry,
          Sister Helen,
Is ever to see you ere he die."
"In all that his soul sees, there am I,
          Little brother!"   145
          (*O Mother, Mary Mother,*
The soul's one sight, between Hell and Heaven!)

"He sends a ring and a broken coin,[4]
          Sister Helen,

---

[3] A piece of sophistry: if Helen would retract her curse, her victim, Keith of Ewern, could die; but this, says Helen, would be to kill a living man. Like her other replies, this is merely to evade the pleas for help.
[4] Helen and Keith had pledged their troth by breaking a coin in two and each one retaining a half.

And bids you mind the banks of Boyne." 150
"What else he broke will he ever join,
         Little brother?"
           (O Mother, Mary Mother,
No, never joined, between Hell and Heaven!)

"He yields you these and craves full fain, 155
         Sister Helen,
You pardon him in his mortal pain."
"What else he took will he give again,
         Little brother?"
           (O Mother, Mary Mother, 160
Not twice to give, between Hell and Heaven!)

"He calls your name in an agony,
         Sister Helen,
That even dead Love must weep to see."
"Hate, born of Love, is blind as he, 165
         Little brother!"
           (O Mother, Mary Mother,
Love turned to hate, between Hell and Heaven!)

"Oh, it's Keith of Keith now that rides fast,
         Sister Helen, 170
For I know the white hair on the blast."
"The short short hour will soon be past,
         Little brother!"
           (O Mother, Mary Mother,
Will soon be past, between Hell and Heaven!) 175

"He looks at me and he tries to speak,
         Sister Helen,
But oh! his voice is sad and weak!"
"What here should the mighty Baron seek,
         Little brother?" 180
           (O Mother, Mary Mother,
Is this the end, between Hell and Heaven?)

"Oh, his son still cries, if you forgive,
         Sister Helen,
The body dies but the soul shall live." 185
"Fire shall forgive me as I forgive,[5]
         Little brother!"
           (O Mother, Mary Mother,
As she forgives, between Hell and Heaven!)

"Oh, he prays you, as his heart would rive,[6] 190
         Sister Helen,
To save his dear son's soul alive."

"Fire cannot slay it; it shall thrive,[7]
         Little brother!"
           (O Mother, Mary Mother, 195
Alas, alas, between Hell and Heaven!)

"He cries to you, kneeling in the road,
         Sister Helen,
To go with him for the love of God!"
"The way is long to his son's abode, 200
         Little brother."
           (O Mother, Mary Mother,
The way is long, between Hell and Heaven!)

"A lady's here, by a dark steed brought,
         Sister Helen, 205
So darkly clad, I saw her not."
"See her now or never see aught,
         Little brother!"
           (O Mother, Mary Mother,
What more to see, between Hell and Heaven?) 210

"Her hood falls back, and the moon shines fair,
         Sister Helen,
On the Lady of Ewern's golden hair."
"Blest hour of my power and her despair,
         Little brother!" 215
           (O Mother, Mary Mother,
Hour blest and banned, between Hell and
    Heaven!)

"Pale, pale her cheeks, that in pride did glow,
         Sister Helen,
'Neath the bridal-wreath three days ago." 220
"One morn for pride and three days for woe,
         Little brother!"
           (O Mother, Mary Mother,
Three days, three nights, between Hell and
    Heaven!)

"Her clasped hands stretch from her bending 225
    head,
         Sister Helen;
With the loud wind's wail her sobs are wed."
"What wedding-strains hath her bridal-bed,
         Little brother?"
           (O Mother, Mary Mother, 230
What strain but death's, between Hell and
    Heaven!)

---

[5] Hell fire will burn me as I burn this image. In neither case will there be forgiveness.

[6] As if his heart would burst with sorrow.

[7] It shall thrive only in the sense that it will never die, for part of the effect of the curse is that it shall never find peace but remain between heaven and hell.

"She may not speak, she sinks in a swoon,
                    Sister Helen,—
She lifts her lips and gasps on the moon."
"Oh! might I but hear her soul's blithe tune,   235
                    Little brother!"
          (O Mother, Mary Mother,
Her woe's dumb cry, between Hell and Heaven!)

"They've caught her to Westholm's saddle-bow,
                    Sister Helen,   240
And her moonlit hair gleams white in its flow."
"Let it turn whiter than winter snow,
                    Little brother!"
          (O Mother, Mary Mother,
Woe-withered gold, between Hell and Heaven!)   245

"O Sister Helen, you heard the bell,
                    Sister Helen!
More loud than the vesper-chime it fell."
"No vesper-chime, but a dying knell,
                    Little brother!"   250
          (O Mother, Mary Mother,
His dying knell, between Hell and Heaven!)

"Alas! but I fear the heavy sound,
                    Sister Helen;
Is it in the sky or in the ground?"   255
"Say, have they turned their horses round,
                    Little brother?"
          (O Mother, Mary Mother,
What would she more, between Hell and
          Heaven?)

"They have raised the old man from his knee,   260
                    Sister Helen,
And they ride in silence hastily."
"More fast the naked soul doth flee,
                    Little brother!"
          (O Mother, Mary Mother,   265
The naked soul, between Hell and Heaven!)

"Flank to flank are the three steeds gone,
                    Sister Helen,
But the lady's dark steed goes alone."
"And lonely her bridegroom's soul hath flown,   270
                    Little brother."
          (O Mother, Mary Mother,
The lonely ghost, between Hell and Heaven!)

"Oh, the wind is sad in the iron chill,
                    Sister Helen,   275
And weary sad they look by the hill."

"But he and I are sadder still,
                    Little brother!"
          (O Mother, Mary Mother,
Most sad of all, between Hell and Heaven!)   280

"See, see, the wax has dropped from its place,
                    Sister Helen,
And the flames are winning up apace!"
"Yet here they burn but for a space,[8]
                    Little brother!"   285
          (O Mother, Mary Mother,
Here for a space, between Hell and Heaven!)

"Ah! what white thing at the door has crossed,
                    Sister Helen?
Ah! what is this that sighs in the frost?"   290
"A soul that's lost as mine is lost,
                    Little brother!"
          (O Mother, Mary Mother,
Lost, lost, all lost, between Hell and Heaven!)

from The House of Life

A Sonnet Sequence[1]

A Sonnet is a moment's monument,—
    Memorial from the Soul's eternity
        To one dead deathless hour. Look that it be,
Whether for lustral[2] rite or dire portent,
Of its own arduous fulness reverent: 5
    Carve it in ivory or in ebony,
        As Day or Night may rule; and let Time see
Its flowering crest impearled and orient.

A Sonnet is a coin: its face reveals
    The soul,—its converse, to what Power 'tis   10
        due:—
Whether for tribute to the august appeals
    Of Life, or dower in Love's high retinue,
It serve; or, 'mid the dark wharf's cavernous
        breath,
In Charon's[3] palm it pay the toll to Death.

---

8 The implication is that in hell they burn eternally.

1 The title is derived from astrology, where the heavens are divided into houses, the chief of which is the House of Life. In other words, the sonnets purport to be a comment upon life. Actually they are primarily reflections on three subjects: life, love, and death.   2 Purifying.
3 Charon was the ferryman who, for a coin, rowed the dead across the Styx to the Underworld.   4 I.e., clouds.

4. LOVESIGHT

When do I see thee most, beloved one?
 When in the light the spirits of mine eyes
 Before thy face, their altar, solemnize
The worship of that Love through thee made
  known?
Or when in the dusk hours (we two alone,)   5
 Close-kissed and eloquent of still replies
 Thy twilight-hidden glimmering visage lies,
And my soul only sees thy soul its own?

O love, my love! if I no more should see
Thyself, nor on the earth the shadow of thee,   10
 Nor image of thine eyes in any spring,—
How then should sound upon Life's darkening
  slope
The ground-whirl of the perished leaves of Hope,
 The wind of Death's imperishable wing?

19. SILENT NOON

Your hands lie open in the long fresh grass,—
 The finger-points look through like rosy
  blooms:
 Your eyes smile peace. The pasture gleams and
  glooms
'Neath billowing skies[4] that scatter and amass.
All round our nest, far as the eye can pass,   5
 Are golden kingcup-fields with silver edge
 Where the cow-parsley skirts the hawthorn-
  hedge.[5]
'Tis visible silence, still as the hour-glass.

Deep in the sun-searched growths the dragon-fly
Hangs like a blue thread loosened from the sky:—   10
 So this winged hour is dropt to us from above.
Oh! clasp we to our hearts, for deathless dower,
This close-companioned inarticulate hour
 When twofold silence was the song of love.

24. PRIDE OF YOUTH

Even as a child, of sorrow that we give
 The dead, but little in his heart can find,
 Since without need of thought to his clear
  mind
Their turn it is to die and his to live:—
Even so the winged New Love smiles to receive   5
 Along his eddying plumes the auroral wind,
 Nor, forward glorying, casts one look behind
Where night-rack shrouds the Old Love fugitive.

There is a change in every hour's recall,
 And the last cowslip in the fields we see   10
 On the same day with the first corn-poppy.
Alas for hourly change! Alas for all
The loves that from his hand proud Youth lets
  fall,
 Even as the beads of a told rosary!

51. WILLOWWOOD, 3[6]

"O ye, all ye that walk in Willowwood,
 That walk with hollow faces burning white;
What fathom-depth of soul-struck widowhood,
 What long, what longer hours, one lifelong
  night,
Ere ye again, who so in vain have wooed   5
 Your last hope lost, who so in vain invite
Your lips to that their unforgotten food,
 Ere ye, ere ye again shall see the light.

Alas! the bitter banks in Willowwood,
 With tear-spurge wan, with blood-wort burn-   10
  ing red:
Alas! if ever such a pillow could
 Steep deep the soul in sleep till she were
  dead,—
Better all life forget her than this thing,
That Willowwood should hold her wandering!"

56. TRUE WOMAN[7]

1. Herself

To be a sweetness more desired than Spring;
 A bodily beauty more acceptable
 Than the wild rose-tree's arch that crowns the
  fell;[8]
To be an essence more environing[9]
Than wine's drained juice; a music ravishing   5
 More than the passionate pulse of Philo-
  mel;[10]—
 To be all this 'neath one soft bosom's swell
That is the flower of life:—how strange a thing!

How strange a thing to be what Man can know
 But as a sacred secret! Heaven's own screen   10
Hides her soul's purest depth and loveliest glow;

---

[4] Fields of buttercups, edged with silvery-leafed cow-parsley.

[6] There is a series of four sonnets under this title. The wood indicated is one of weeping willows, traditionally symbolizing a mourning lover. It is probably the general mood of separation and the anguish of thwarted love that is described rather than a biographical event.
[7] Three sonnets bear this title. The second has the subtitle "Her Love"; the third, "Her Heaven." [8] Cliff.
[9] Permeating. [10] The nightingale.

Closely withheld, as all things most unseen,—
The wave-bowered pearl,—the heart-shaped
    seal of green
That flecks the snowdrop underneath the snow.

69. AUTUMN IDLENESS

This sunlight shames November where he grieves
    In dead red leaves, and will not let him shun
    The day, though bough with bough be over-
      run.
But with a blessing every glade receives
High salutation; while from hillock-eaves   5
    The deer gaze calling, dappled white and dun,
    As if, being foresters of old, the sun
Had marked them with the shade of forest-leaves.

Here dawn today unveiled her magic glass;[11]
    Here noon now gives the thirst and takes the   10
      dew;
Till eve bring rest when other good things pass.
    And here the lost hours the lost hours renew[12]
While I still lead my shadow o'er the grass,
    Nor know, for longing, that which I should do.

77. SOUL'S BEAUTY[13]

Under the arch of Life, where love and death,
    Terror and mystery, guard her shrine, I saw
    Beauty enthroned; and though her gaze struck
      awe,
I drew it in as simply as my breath.   5
Hers are the eyes which, over and beneath,
    The sky and sea bend on thee,—which can
      draw,
    By sea or sky or woman, to one law,
The allotted bondman of her palm and wreath.

This is that Lady Beauty, in whose praise
    Thy voice and hand shake still,—long known   10
    to thee
      By flying hair and fluttering hem,[14]—the
      beat
    Following her daily of thy heart and feet,

---

[11] Dew or frost reflecting the sunlight.

[12] I am now losing time as I live over in memory the past hours which are lost. The second "lost" may mean merely past and gone or may have the added sense of "wasted." The line may be compared with the sonnet "Lost Days," printed below.

[13] This sonnet and the next, according to William Rossetti, were written respectively for Rossetti's pictures entitled Sibylla Palmifera and Lilith.

[14] Heretofore the poet has known beauty only through fleeting glimpses.

How passionately and irretrievably,
In what fond flight, how many ways and days!

78. BODY'S BEAUTY

Of Adam's first wife, Lilith, it is told
    (The witch he loved before the gift of Eve,)
    That, ere the snake's, her sweet tongue could
      deceive,
And her enchanted hair was the first gold.
And still she sits, young while the earth is old,   5
    And, subtly of herself contemplative,
    Draws men to watch the bright web she can
      weave,
Till heart and body and life are in its hold.

The rose and poppy are her flowers; for where
    Is he not found, O Lilith, whom shed scent   10
And soft-shed kisses and soft sleep shall snare?
    Lo! as that youth's eyes burned at thine, so
      went
    Thy spell through him, and left his straight
      neck bent
And round his heart one strangling golden hair.

86. LOST DAYS

The lost days of my life until to-day,
    What were they, could I see them on the street
    Lie as they fell? Would they be ears of wheat
Sown once for food but trodden into clay?
Or golden coins squandered and still to pay?   5
    Or drops of blood dabbling the guilty feet?
    Or such spilt water as in dreams must cheat
The undying throats of Hell, athirst alway?

I do not see them here; but after death
    God knows I know the faces I shall see,   10
Each one a murdered self, with low last breath.
    "I am thyself,—what hast thou done to me?"
    "And I—and I—thyself," (lo! each one saith,)
    "And thou thyself to all eternity!"

97. A SUPERSCRIPTION[15]

Look in my face; my name is Might-have-been;
    I am also called No-more, Too-late, Farewell;
    Unto thine ear I hold the dead-sea shell
Cast up thy Life's foam-fretted feet between;

---

[15] Mr. Doughty suggests that the title refers to the new love for Janey Morris " 'superscribed' as it were, upon his heart as on a palimpsest; written, that is, upon the old love." Certainly the sonnet is charged with a haunting sense of an old love that will not allow itself to be forgotten.

Unto thine eyes the glass where that is seen   5
  Which had Life's form and Love's, but by my
    spell
  Is now a shaken shadow intolerable,
Of ultimate things unuttered the frail screen.

Mark me, how still I am! But should there dart
  One moment through thy soul the soft sur-   10
    prise
  Of that winged Peace which lulls the breath
    of sighs,[16]—
Then shalt thou see me smile, and turn apart
Thy visage to mine ambush at thy heart
  Sleepless with cold commemorative eyes.

101. THE ONE HOPE[17]

When vain desire at last and vain regret
  Go hand in hand to death, and all is vain,
  What shall assuage the unforgotten pain
And teach the unforgetful to forget?
Shall Peace be still a sunk stream long unmet,—   5
  Or may the soul at once in a green plain
  Stoop through the spray of some sweet life-
    fountain
And cull the dew-drenched flowering amulet?

---

[16] I.e., of perfect love fulfilled.
[17] The one hope is that of eternal union in the hereafter with "the woman supremely beloved upon earth."

Ah! when the wan soul in that golden air
  Between the scriptured petals softly blown   10
  Peers breathless for the gift of grace un-
    known,—
Ah! let none other alien spell soe'er
But only the one Hope's one name be there,—
  Not less nor more, but even that word alone.

The Woodspurge

The wind flapped loose, the wind was still,
Shaken out dead from tree and hill:
I had walked on at the wind's will,—
I sat now, for the wind was still.

Between my knees my forehead was,—   5
My lips, drawn in, said not Alas!
My hair was over in the grass,
My naked ears heard the day pass.

My eyes, wide open, had the run
Of some ten weeds to fix upon;   10
Among those few, out of the sun,
The woodspurge flowered, three cups in one.

From perfect grief there need not be
Wisdom or even memory:
One thing then learnt remains to me,—   15
The woodspurge has a cup of three.

William Morris
1834–1896

William Morris was born in 1834 and brought up on his father's country estate at Woodford in Essex. In his early years he developed what was to be a life-long love of the Middle Ages, partly from reading Scott, partly from excursions to old Essex churches and a visit to Canterbury Cathedral at the age of eight which "left on his mind an ineffaceable impression of the glory of Gothic architecture." As a result, he was prepared to respond sympathetically to the High Church influence at Marlborough, where he went to boarding school, and before he entered Oxford in 1853 he had become an Anglo-Catholic. There he read church history, the *Tracts for the Times,* and masses of medieval chronicles; and he presently decided to enter the ministry. But the attraction of Anglo-Catholicism for him lay more in its ritual and its architecture than in its theology—more in its beauty than in its truth. For at bottom Morris's temperament was strongly aesthetic; and it was only a matter of time before art displaced religion as his major interest.

    The change was foreshadowed by his enthusiastic reading of Malory's *Morte Darthur,* of Keats and Shelley, along with Tennyson (especially the early Romantic poems), then Chaucer and Browning; and in prose, Ruskin's *Modern Painters* and *The Stones of Venice* and Carlyle's *Past and Present,* which were taken for "inspired and absolute truth" (though not so much for their social gospel—that influence came later—as for their medievalism, and in the case of Ruskin, for his enthusiastic account of Gothic). The plan to take orders was dropped; "art

William Morris (1834–1896). A founder of the Aesthetic Movement and a gentle socialist, Morris loved the old England, its old inns, old songs, and old leisures. Through the Hammersmith Socialist League he worked for the amelioration of conditions in the new England he found so ugly. *The Granger Collection.*

and literature were no longer thought of as hand-maids to religion, but as ends to be pursued for their own sake" (Art for Art's Sake), and Morris decided to become an architect. Then, at London in 1856 as he was beginning the study of architecture, he met Rossetti and came into direct contact with the Pre-Raphaelite Movement. This crucial influence led him first to painting and then to poetry, with the result that in 1858 he published what is perhaps the finest volume of Pre-Raphaelite verse, *The Defence of Guenevere and Other Poems.*

The chief characteristics of this work are suggested by Morris's lecture on Pre-Raphaelitism (pp. 899–904). Though the Naturalism which he first takes up applies mainly to painting, it is responsible for the sharp, pictorial detail in the poetry of both Rossetti and Morris. The very opening lines of "The Defence of Guenevere,"

But, knowing now that they would have her speak,
She threw her wet hair backward from her brow,
Her hand close to her mouth touching her cheek,

are the lines of a painter trained to realistic observation, especially one who had read Ruskin's *Modern*

Painters, and of a poet schooled in the Romantics, particularly in Keats (Arnold's description of Keats's imagery on p. 840 might apply equally well to Morris's). But as these lines suggest, and as Morris goes on to state in his lecture, Pre-Raphaelite art was primarily centered not on the description of natural facts, but on "telling some kind of a story." Many of the pictures present dramatic incidents taken from the Bible, or from medieval, Shakespearean, or Romantic literature. Half of Morris's volume consists of narrative poems like "The Haystack in the Floods"; or dramatic studies of character in the manner of Browning without his moralistic strain ("The Defence of Guenevere"); or poems where the lyrical and the dramatic are fused into a striking and original form, as in "The Eve of Crécy" with its combination of speaking voice and musical refrain. In this poetry there is nothing dreamy or remote from life. Its violent action and intense emotion brought into Victorian poetry a vitality and range of feeling which had been quite lacking in Tennyson and Arnold, and was just beginning to appear, at a lower emotional level, in Browning. Only in the minor sense that these poems portray medieval and not modern life can they be called escapist.

But side by side with them stood other poems which warrant that epithet. These illustrate the third characteristic of Pre-Raphaelitism which Morris speaks of, its decorative and ornamental art. A poem like "The Blue Closet" is a piece of tapestry. The figures are almost lifeless, the story hardly exists, dramatic speech is gone. What we have is a vague, intangible mood made out of color and sound, perfectly achieved and perfectly empty of human significance. It is simply a charming piece of decoration that draws the mind completely away, not only from the troubled and ugly world of the nineteenth century but also from life itself. As such, it is the forerunner of the "pure" aesthetic verse of Swinburne and the early Yeats.

Morris's interest in decorative art was not limited to poetry. In 1861 he founded Morris and Company, where he and a group of craftsmen made stained-glass windows, tapestries, carpets, furniture (he invented the Morris chair), and wallpapers. The impulse here was by no means merely aesthetic. It was also, if indirectly, social. In both respects its main source was Ruskin's chapter on "The Nature of Gothic" in *The Stones of Venice,* where the mechanical work devoid of pleasure which men had to do in the modern factory was contrasted with the joyous creative activity of the workmen who built the Gothic cathedrals. From this observation Morris, as well as Ruskin, drew two conclusions: that so far as possible handcrafts should be revived, and that the modern system of high-pressure competitive capitalism, which was turning out thousands of things that no one

A scene from *Two Gentlemen of Verona* by Holman Hunt. This sentimental painting illustrates the characteristics of Pre-Raphaelitism praised by Morris: naturalism, decorativeness, and epical quality. *Published with the permission of the Birmingham Museum and Art Gallery.*

really needed at the cost of turning thousands of men into machines, should be replaced by some form of socialism. Both conclusions are found in the essay on "The Art of the People" (1879). A few years later, after reading Karl Marx, Morris became a socialist. But he failed to realize that while the triumph of socialism would transfer control of the machines from the bourgeoisie to the proletariat, it would leave the machines as powerful and as deadly to the human spirit as ever. His mistake came from imagining that everyone shared his own longing for a simple life of creative activity, and consequently that once the people came to power they would abandon the machines, except those necessary to perform disagreeable work. The Revolution, he thought, would usher in a happy society in which creative pleasure would be available to everyone, either directly in handiwork or indirectly as an avocation to fill one's leisure; and art would again "be made by the people and for the people, as a happiness to the maker and the user."

If we may dismiss Morris's socialism as Utopian,

we must recognize the truth—for our time as well as his—of what he says about the state of the arts. Indeed, perhaps the best thing in "The Art of the People" is his acute analysis of a society divided between a public, on the one hand, which thinks "Art is at best trifling" and whose very leaders of thought know nothing and feel nothing about it except a vague sense of repulsion; and on the other hand, as a consequence, a small group of artists who despise the common herd and hold themselves aloof from the major concerns of modern life, to live in a palace of art and write a poetry of faraway times or purely verbal beauty. This, of course, applies to Morris himself and his own poetry in the fifties and sixties (in *Jason* and *The Earthly Paradise* as well as *The Defence of Guenevere*). In those years he had turned away from "politico-social subjects" because "on the whole I see that things are in a muddle, and I have no power or vocation to set them right," and therefore made his work "the embodiment of dreams in one form or another" (cf. "An Apology"). But now

THIS IS THE PICTURE OF THE OLD HOUSE BY THE THAMES TO WHICH THE PEOPLE OF THIS STORY WENT ❧ HEREAFTER FOLLOWS THE BOOK IT. SELF WHICH IS CALLED NEWS FROM NOWHERE OR AN EPOCH OF REST & IS WRITTEN BY WILLIAM MORRIS ❧❧

News from Nowhere. Morris's *News from Nowhere* is a naive and delightful work of socialist propaganda, a utopian novel whose characters have no use for money, machinery, or manufactured goods. The decorative title page is from the edition published by Morris's own Kelmscott Press.

that socialism offered a solution, Morris renounced his renunciation and became, in his later prose work, a late Victorian prophet. From that new perspective he could criticize the divorce between public and artist that grew up in his time and has grown even sharper in our own. Indeed, if we change only one aspect of his analysis, and substitute an esoteric, obscure art for a delicate, aesthetic art, his description of the state of affairs is as valid today as it was in 1879. For "the general tendency of civilisation," which he found responsible for the situation, is still the same, still industrial and scientific, still concerned not with art but with making "machines for carrying on the competition in buying and selling, . . . and machines for the violent destruction of life."

TEXTS: The standard edition of Morris is the *Collected Works,* edited by May Morris (24 vols., 1910–15). The best biography, which also illuminates the Pre-Raphaelite Movement, is by J. W. Mackail (2 vols., 1899). Walter Pater's "Aesthetic Poetry" (1868) is in his *Appreciations* (1889 ed.), and Graham Hough's essay is in *The Last Romantics* (1949). The

best recent books are Edward Palmer Thompson's *William Morris, Romantic to Revolutionary* (1962) and Paul Thompson's *The Work of William Morris* (1967).

An Apology[1]

Of Heaven or Hell I have no power to sing,
I cannot ease the burden of your fears,
Or make quick-coming death a little thing,
Or bring again the pleasure of past years,
Nor for my words shall ye forget your tears,　　5
Or hope again for aught that I can say,
The idle singer of an empty day.

But rather, when aweary of your mirth,
From full hearts still unsatisfied ye sigh,
And, feeling kindly unto all the earth,　　10
Grudge every minute as it passes by,
Made the more mindful that the sweet days die—
Remember me a little then I pray,
The idle singer of an empty day.

The heavy trouble, the bewildering care　　15
That weighs us down who live and earn our
　　bread,
These idle verses have no power to bear;
So let me sing of names rememberèd,
Because they, living not, can ne'er be dead,
Or long time take their memory quite away　　20
From us poor singers of an empty day.

Dreamer of dreams, born out of my due time,
Why should I strive to set the crooked straight?
Let it suffice me that my murmuring rhyme
Beats with light wing against the ivory gate,[2]　　25
Telling a tale not too importunate
To those who in the sleepy region stay,
Lulled by the singer of an empty day.

Folk say, a wizard to a northern king
At Christmas-tide such wondrous things did　　30
　　show,

1 The prefatory poem to *The Earthly Paradise* (1868–70), a collection of stories from Greek and Norse mythology. The four poems that follow it are from *The Defence of Guenevere and Other Poems* (1858).
2 According to Greek legend, the ivory gate was the gate through which false dreams issued. Morris's "rhyme" does not pretend to express truth, but only to create a dream world of shadowy bliss (cf. line 38).

That through one window men beheld the spring,
And through another saw the summer glow,
And through a third the fruited vines a-row,
While still, unheard, but in its wonted way,
Piped the drear wind of that December day.   35

So with this Earthly Paradise it is,
If ye will read aright, and pardon me,
Who strive to build a shadowy isle of bliss
Midmost the beating of the steely sea,
Where tossed about all hearts of men must be;   40
Whose ravening monsters mighty men shall slay,
Not the poor singer of an empty day.

The Haystack in the Floods[1]

Had she come all the way for this,
To part at last without a kiss?
Yea, had she borne the dirt and rain
That her own eyes might see him slain
Beside the haystack in the floods?   5

Along the dripping leafless woods,
The stirrup touching either shoe,
She rode astride as troopers do;
With kirtle kilted[2] to her knee,
To which the mud splashed wretchedly;   10
And the wet dripped from every tree
Upon her head and heavy hair,
And on her eyelids broad and fair;
The tears and rain ran down her face.
By fits and starts they rode apace,   15
And very often was his place
Far off from her; he had to ride
Ahead, to see what might betide
When the roads crossed; and sometimes, when
There rose a murmuring from his men,   20
Had to turn back with promises;
Ah me! she had but little ease;
And often for pure doubt and dread
She sobbed, made giddy in the head
By the swift riding; while, for cold,   25
Her slender fingers scarce could hold
The wet reins; yea, and scarcely, too,
She felt the foot within her shoe
Against the stirrup: all for this,

To part at last without a kiss   30
Beside the haystack in the floods.

For when they neared that old soaked hay,
They saw across the only way
That Judas, Godmar, and the three
Red running lions dismally   35
Grinned from his pennon,[3] under which
In one straight line along the ditch,
They counted thirty heads.
                           So then,
While Robert turned round to his men,
She saw at once the wretched end,   40
And, stooping down, tried hard to rend
Her coif the wrong way from her head,
And hid her eyes;[4] while Robert said:
"Nay, love, 'tis scarcely two to one;
At Poictiers where we made them run   45
So fast—why, sweet my love, good cheer,
The Gascon frontier is so near,
Nought after us."
                 But, "O!" she said,
"My God! my God! I have to tread
The long way back without you; then   50
The court at Paris; those six men;[5]
The gratings of the Chatelet;[6]
The swift Seine on some rainy day
Like this, and people standing by,
And laughing, while my weak hands try   55
To recollect how strong men swim.[7]
All this, or else a life with him,[8]
For which I should be damned at last;
Would God that this next hour were past!"

He answered not, but cried his cry,   60
"St. George[9] for Marny!" cheerily;
And laid his hand upon her rein.
Alas! no man of all his train
Gave back that cheery cry again;
And, while for rage his thumb beat fast   65
Upon his sword-hilt, some one cast
About his neck a kerchief long,
And bound him.
               Then they went along

1 Sir Robert de Marny, an English knight, and his mistress, Jehane, are riding hard for Gascony, which was in British hands. The date is 1356, shortly after the English victory over the French at Poitiers.   2 Tucked up.

3 Godmar's banner bearing his family crest.
4 She tried to turn her cap about so that the longer part (ordinarily at the back) would cover her eyes and prevent her from seeing Robert slain.   5 The judges.
6 The bars of the Châtelet prison in Paris.
7 In the trial by water, she would be judged innocent of being a witch if she sank and drowned; if she swam, guilty, and then burned (cf. line 108).   8 Godmar.
9 Patron saint of England.

To Godmar; who said: "Now, Jehane,
Your lover's life is on the wane   70
So fast, that, if this very hour
You yield not as my paramour,
He will not see the rain leave off—
Nay, keep your tongue from gibe and scoff,
Sir Robert, or I slay you now."   75

She laid her hand upon her brow,
Then gazed upon the palm, as though
She thought her forehead bled, and—"No!"
She said, and turned her head away,
As there were nothing else to say,   80
And everything were settled: red
Grew Godmar's face from chin to head:
"Jehane, on yonder hill there stands
My castle, guarding well my lands:
What hinders me from taking you,   85
And doing that I list to do
To your fair wilful body, while
Your knight lies dead?"
                              A wicked smile
Wrinkled her face, her lips grew thin,
A long way out she thrust her chin: 90
"You know that I should strangle you
While you were sleeping; or bite through
Your throat, by God's help—ah!" she said,
"Lord Jesus, pity your poor maid!
For in such wise they hem me in,   95
I cannot choose but sin and sin,
Whatever happens: yet I think
They could not make me eat or drink,
And so should I just reach my rest."
"Nay, if you do not my behest,   100
O Jehane! though I love you well,"
Said Godmar, "would I fail to tell
All that I know?" "Foul lies," she said.
"Eh? lies, my Jehane? by God's head,
At Paris folks would deem them true!   105
Do you know, Jehane, they cry for you:
'Jehane the brown! Jehane the brown!
Give us Jehane to burn or drown!'—
Eh—gag me Robert!—sweet my friend,
This were indeed a piteous end   110
For those long fingers, and long feet,
And long neck, and smooth shoulders sweet;
An end that few men would forget
That saw it—So, an hour yet:
Consider, Jehane, which to take   115
Of life or death!"
                     So, scarce awake,

Dismounting, did she leave that place,
And totter some yards: with her face
Turned upward to the sky she lay,
Her head on a wet heap of hay,   120
And fell asleep: and while she slept,
And did not dream, the minutes crept
Round to the twelve again; but she,
Being waked at last, sighed quietly,
And strangely childlike came, and said: 125
"I will not." Straightway Godmar's head,
As though it hung on strong wires, turned
Most sharply round, and his face burned.

For Robert—both his eyes were dry,
He could not weep, but gloomily   130
He seemed to watch the rain; yea, too,
His lips were firm; he tried once more
To touch her lips; she reached out, sore
And vain desire so tortured them,
The poor gray lips, and now the hem   135
Of his sleeve brushed them.
                              With a start
Up Godmar rose, thrust them apart;
From Robert's throat he loosed the bands
Of silk and mail; with empty hands
Held out, she stood and gazed, and saw   140
The long bright blade without a flaw
Glide out from Godmar's sheath, his hand
In Robert's hair; she saw him bend
Back Robert's head; she saw him send
The thin steel down; the blow told well,   145
Right backward the knight Robert fell,
And moaned as dogs do, being half dead,
Unwitting, as I deem: so then
Godmar turned grinning to his men,
Who ran, some five or six, and beat   150
His head to pieces at their feet.

Then Godmar turned again and said:
"So, Jehane, the first fitte[10] is read!
Take note, my lady, that your way
Lies backward to the Chatelet!"   155
She shook her head and gazed awhile
At her cold hands with a rueful smile,
As though this thing had made her mad.

This was the parting that they had
Beside the haystack in the floods.   160

---

10 Part of a song or tale.

The Defence of Guenevere[1]

But, knowing now that they would have her
    speak,
She threw her wet hair backward from her brow,
Her hand close to her mouth touching her cheek,

As though she had had there a shameful blow,
And feeling it shameful to feel aught but shame   5
All through her heart, yet felt her cheek burned
    so,

She must a little touch it; like one lame
She walked away from Gauwaine, with her head
Still lifted up; and on her cheek of flame

The tears dried quick; she stopped at last and   10
    said:
"O knights and lords, it seems but little skill[2]
To talk of well-known things past now and dead.

"God wot[3] I ought to say, I have done ill,
And pray you all forgiveness heartily!
Because you must be right, such great lords—still   15

"Listen, suppose your time were come to die,
And you were quite alone and very weak;
Yea, laid a dying while very mightily

"The wind was ruffling up the narrow streak
Of river through your broad lands running well: 20
Suppose a hush should come, then some one
    speak:

" 'One of these cloths is heaven, and one is hell,
Now choose one cloth for ever; which they be,
I will not tell you, you must somehow tell

" 'Of your own strength and mightiness; here,   25
    see!'
Yea, yea, my lord,[4] and you to ope your eyes,
At foot of your familiar bed to see

"A great God's angel standing, with such dyes,
Not known on earth, on his great wings, and
    hands
Held out two ways, light from the inner skies   30

"Showing him well, and making his commands
Seem to be God's commands, moreover, too,
Holding within his hands the cloths on wands;

"And one of these strange choosing cloths was
    blue,
Wavy and long, and one cut short and red;   35
No man could tell the better of the two.

"After a shivering half-hour you said:
'God help! heaven's color, the blue'; and he said,
    'hell.'[5]
Perhaps you then would roll upon your bed,

"And cry to all good men that loved you well,   40
'Ah Christ! if only I had known, known, known';
Launcelot went away, then I could tell,[6]

"Like wisest man how all things would be, moan,
And roll and hurt myself, and long to die,
And yet fear much to die for what was sown.   45

"Nevertheless you, O Sir Gauwaine, lie,

---

[1] Guenevere is speaking in self-defense at her trial for adultery. She and Launcelot had been trapped by Agravaine and Modred, who had persuaded King Arthur on a hunting expedition to send back word to his queen that he could not return that night. Thereupon, as the conspirators hoped, she had arranged a rendezvous with Launcelot and they had been caught together in her room. (Lines 242–81 give her account of the incident.) One of the conspirators and her chief accuser at the trial is Gauwaine, brother of Agravaine, who had just finished his speech as the poem opens. To support his accusation of adultery, he has cited not only the occasion just mentioned but also a former occasion at the castle of Mellyagraunce when some of Guenevere's knights who had been wounded were placed in her chambers, and next morning blood was found on her bed—which had provoked a previous charge of adultery, by Mellyagraunce (rightly enough, in fact, but it was not the blood of a wounded knight, as Mellyagraunce thought, but that of Launcelot, who had cut his arm crawling through the barred window of Guenevere's bedroom). At that time she had been saved by Launcelot from being burnt at the stake, the punishment for adultery (and therefore what she is now threatened with again). He had defended her honor in trial by battle with Mellyagraunce (see lines 167–221).
[2] Use. [3] Knows.
[4] Gauwaine.

[5] Guenevere implies that her original choice of Launcelot instead of Arthur as the object of her admiration and friendship was just about as accidental (things being so evenly divided) and certainly as innocent of evil intentions as the choice of a blue cloth over a red cloth; and yet, through no fault of hers, it turned out to be the wrong (because evil) choice.
[6] Because she then knew, for the first time, that she loved him passionately and not merely as a friend, and had therefore, in fact, though unwittingly, chosen "hell" when she found him more attractive than Arthur.

Whatever may have happened through these
    years,
God knows I speak truth, saying that you lie."[7]

Her voice was low at first, being full of tears,
But as it cleared, it grew full loud and shrill,   50
Growing a windy shriek in all men's ears,

A ringing in their startled brains, until
She said that Gauwaine lied, then her voice sunk,
And her great eyes began again to fill,

Though still she stood right up, and never   55
    shrunk,
But spoke on bravely, glorious lady fair!
Whatever tears her full lips may have drunk,

She stood, and seemed to think, and wrung her
    hair,
Spoke out at last with no more trace of shame,
With passionate twisting of her body there: 60

"It chanced upon a day that Launcelot came
To dwell at Arthur's court: at Christmastime
This happened; when the heralds sung his name,

" 'Son of King Ban of Benwick,' seemed to chime
Along with all the bells that rang that day,   65
O'er the white roofs, with little change of rhyme.

"Christmas and whitened winter passed away,
And over me the April sunshine came,
Made very awful with black hail-clouds, yea

"And in the Summer I grew white with flame,   70
And bowed my head down—Autumn, and the
    sick
Sure knowledge things would never be the same,

"However often Spring might be most thick
Of blossoms and buds, smote on me, and I grew
Careless of most things, let the clock tick, tick,   75

"To my unhappy pulse, that beat right through
My eager body: while I laughed out loud,
And let my lips curl up at false or true,

"Seemed cold and shallow without any cloud.
Behold my judges, then the cloths were brought;   80

While I was dizzied thus, old thoughts would
    crowd,

"Belonging to the time ere I was bought
By Arthur's great name and his little love;
Must I give up for ever then, I thought,

"That which I deemed would ever round me   85
    move
Glorifying all things; for a little word,
Scarce ever meant at all, must I now prove

"Stone-cold for ever?[8] Pray you, does the Lord
Will that all folks should be quite happy and
    good?
I love God now a little; if this cord   90

"Were broken,[9] once for all what striving could
Make me love anything in earth or heaven?
So day by day it grew, as if one should

"Slip slowly down some path worn smooth and
    even,
Down to a cool sea on a summer day;   95
Yet still in slipping was there some small leaven

"Of stretched hands catching small stones by the
    way,
Until one surely reached the sea at last,
And felt strange new joy as the worn head lay

"Back, with the hair like sea-weed; yea all past   100
Sweat of the forehead, dryness of the lips,
Washed utterly out by the dear waves o'ercast,

"In the lone sea, far off from any ships!
Do I not know now of a day in Spring?
No minute of that wild day ever slips   105

"From out my memory; I hear thrushes sing,
And wheresoever I may be, straightway
Thoughts of it all come up with most fresh sting;

"I was half mad with beauty on that day,
And went without my ladies all alone,   110
In a quiet garden walled round every way;

---

[7] Whatever my relations with Launcelot have been, they
have not been adulterous.

[8] Must I give up love for ever because I once said, but
scarcely meant it, that I would "love, honor, and obey"?
[9] If this tie with Launcelot were severed, I could never
love anything again, not even God.

"I was right joyful of that wall of stone,
That shut the flowers and trees up with the sky,
And trebled all the beauty: to the bone,

"Yea right through to my heart, grown very shy 115
With weary thoughts, it pierced, and made me
      glad;
Exceedingly glad, and I knew verily,

"A little thing just then had made me mad;
I dared not think, as I was wont to do,
Sometimes, upon my beauty; if I had 120

"Held out my long hand up against the blue,
And, looking on the tenderly darkened fingers,
Thought that by rights one ought to see quite
      through,

"There, see you, where the soft still light yet
      lingers,
Round by the edges; what should I have done, 125
If this had joined with yellow spotted singers,

"And startling green drawn upward by the sun?[10]
But shouting, loosed out, see now! all my hair,
And trancedly stood watching the west wind run

"With faintest half-heard breathing sound—why 130
      there
I lose my head e'en now in doing this;
But shortly listen—In that garden fair

"Came Launcelot walking; this is true, the kiss
Wherewith we kissed in meeting that spring day,
I scarce dare talk of the remembered bliss, 135

"When both our mouths went wandering in one
      way,
And aching sorely, met among the leaves;
Our hands being left behind strained far away.

"Never within a yard of my bright sleeves
Had Launcelot come before—and now, so nigh! 140
After that day why is it Guenevere grieves?

"Nevertheless you, O Sir Gauwaine, lie,
Whatever happened on through all those years,
God knows I speak truth, saying that you lie.

"Being such a lady could I weep these tears 145
If this were true? A great queen such as I
Having sinned this way, straight her conscience
      sears;

"And afterwards she liveth hatefully,
Slaying and poisoning, certes never weeps,—
Gauwaine, be friends now, speak me lovingly. 150

"Do I not see how God's dear pity creeps
All through your frame, and trembles in your
      mouth?[11]
Remember in what grave your mother sleeps,

"Buried in some place far down in the south,
Men are forgetting as I speak to you; 155
By her head severed in that awful drouth

"Of pity that drew Agravaine's fell blow,
I pray your pity![12] let me not scream out
For ever after, when the shrill winds blow

"Through half your castle-locks! let me not shout 160
For ever after in the winter night
When you ride out alone! in battle-rout

"Let not my rusting tears make your sword
      light![13]
Ah! God of mercy, how he turns away!
So, ever must I dress[14] me to the fight; 165

"So—let God's justice work! Gauwaine, I say,
See me hew down your proofs: yea, all men know
Even as you said how Mellyagraunce one day,

"One bitter day in *la Fausse Garde*,[15] for so
All good knights held it after, saw— 170
Yea, sirs, by cursed unknightly outrage;[16] though

---

10 If the sight of the blue sky seen through or behind her
uplifted hand were joined with the further beauty of
singing thrushes (cf. line 106) and spring-green leaves.

11 I.e., God's pity *should* creep, etc., for the reason which
follows.

12 In the name of another woman, your own mother and
King Arthur's sister, who was accused of infidelity and
violently slain by your brother Agravaine in an "awful
drouth [lack] of pity," I beg of you to act otherwise—to
pity me and spare my life.

13 Be careful lest my tears of injured innocence rust your
sword and make it light (weak)—that is, lest your guilty
conscience paralyze your ability to fight.   14 Address.

15 Literally, the False Prison, which is the name Guenevere
gives Mellyagraunce's castle because he had attacked her
knights when they were unarmed and had carried Guenevere off to his castle as a prisoner.

16 Coming to her bedside before she was up.

"You, Gauwaine, held his word without a flaw,
This Mellyagraunce saw blood upon my bed—
Whose blood then pray you? is there any law

"To make a queen say why some spots of red 175
Lie on her coverlet? or will you say,
'Your hands are white, lady, as when you wed,

" 'Where did you bleed?' and must I stammer
out, 'Nay,
I blush indeed, fair lord, only to rend
My sleeve up to my shoulder, where there lay 180

" 'A knife-point last night': so must I defend
The honor of the lady Guenevere?
Not so, fair lords, even if the world should end

"This very day, and you were judges here
Instead of God. Did you see Mellyagraunce 185
When Launcelot stood by him? what white fear

"Curdled his blood, and how his teeth did dance,
His side sink in? as my knight cried and said:
'Slayer of unarmed men, here is a chance!

" 'Setter of traps,[17] I pray you guard your head, 190
By God I am so glad to fight with you,
Stripper of ladies, that my hand feels lead

" 'For driving weight; hurrah now! draw and do,
For all my wounds are moving in my breast,
And I am getting mad with waiting so.' 195

"He struck his hands together o'er the beast,
Who fell down flat and grovelled at his feet,
And groaned at being slain so young—'at least.'

"My knight said, 'Rise you, sir, who are so fleet
At catching ladies, half-armed will I fight, 200
My left side all uncovered!' then I weet,[18]

"Up sprang Sir Mellyagraunce with great delight
Upon his knave's face; not until just then
Did I quite hate him, as I saw my knight

"Along the lists look to my stake and pen[19] 205

With such a joyous smile, it made me sigh
From agony beneath my waist-chain, when

"The fight began, and to me they drew nigh;
Ever Sir Launcelot kept him on the right,
And traversed warily, and ever high 210

"And fast leapt caitiff's sword, until my knight
Sudden threw up his sword to his left hand,
Caught it, and swung it; that was all the fight,

"Except a spout of blood on the hot land;
For it was hottest summer; and I know 215
I wondered how the fire,[20] while I should stand,

"And burn, against the heat, would quiver so,
Yards above my head; thus these matters went;
Which things were only warnings of the woe

"That fell on me. Yet Mellyagraunce was shent,[21] 220
For Mellyagraunce had fought against the Lord;
Therefore, my lords, take heed lest you be blent

"With all this wickedness;[22] say no rash word
Against me, being so beautiful; my eyes,
Wept all away to gray, may bring some sword 225

"To drown you in your blood; see my breast
rise,
Like waves of purple sea, as here I stand;
And how my arms are moved in wonderful wise,

"Yea also at my full heart's strong command,
See through my long throat how the words go up 230
In ripples to my mouth; how in my hand

"The shadow lies like wine within a cup
Of marvellously colored gold; yea now
This little wind is rising, look you up,

"And wonder how the light is falling so 235
Within my moving tresses: will you dare,
When you have looked a little on my brow,

"To say this thing is vile? or will you care
For any plausible lies of cunning woof,
When you can see my face with no lie there 240

---

17 After Launcelot had undertaken to defend Guenevere's honor in trial by battle, Mellyagraunce had sprung a trap in the floor and pitched him into a dungeon, from which he had escaped just in time to rescue Guenevere.
18 Know.   19 Enclosure for a prisoner.

20 She had been sentenced to be burned for adultery.
21 Disgraced and destroyed.
22 *Blent with* may mean either blended with (i.e., involved in) or blinded by.

"For ever? am I not a gracious proof—
'But in your chamber Launcelot was found'—
Is there a good knight then would stand aloof,

"When a queen says with gentle queenly sound:
'O true as steel, come now and talk with me,   245
I love to see your step upon the ground

"'Unwavering, also well I love to see
That gracious smile light up your face, and hear
Your wonderful words, that all mean verily

"'The thing they seem to mean: good friend, so   250
    dear
To me in everything, come here to-night,
Or else the hours will pass most dull and drear;

"'If you come not, I fear this time I might
Get thinking over much of times gone by,
When I was young, and green hope was in sight;   255

"'For no man cares now to know why I sigh;
And no man comes to sing me pleasant songs,
Nor any brings me the sweet flowers that lie

"'So thick in the gardens; therefore one so longs
To see you, Launcelot; that we may be   260
Like children once again, free from all wrongs

"'Just for one night.' Did he not come to me?
What thing could keep true Launcelot away
If I said 'Come'? There was one less than three

"In my quiet room that night, and we were gay;   265
Till sudden I rose up, weak, pale, and sick,
Because a bawling broke our dream up, yea

"I looked at Launcelot's face and could not
    speak,
For he looked helpless too, for a little while;
Then I remembered how I tried to shriek,   270

"And could not, but fell down; from tile to tile
The stones they threw up rattled o'er my head
And made me dizzier; till within a while

"My maids were all about me, and my head
On Launcelot's breast was being soothed away   275
From its white chattering, until Launcelot said—

"By God! I will not tell you more to-day,

Judge any way you will—what matters it?
You know quite well the story of that fray,

"How Launcelot stilled their bawling, the mad   280
    fit
That caught up Gauwaine[23]—all, all, verily,
But just that which would save me; these things
    flit.

"Nevertheless you, O Sir Gauwaine, lie,
Whatever may have happened these long years,
God knows I speak truth, saying that you lie!   285

"All I have said is truth, by Christ's dear tears."
She would not speak another word, but stood
Turned sideways; listening, like a man who hears

His brother's trumpet sounding through the
    wood
Of his foes' lances. She leaned eagerly,   290
And gave a slight spring sometimes, as she could

At last hear something really; joyfully
Her cheek grew crimson, as the headlong speed
Of the roan charger drew all men to see,
The knight who came was Launcelot at good   295
    need.[24]

The Eve of Crécy[1]

Gold on her head, and gold on her feet,
And gold where the hems of her kirtle meet,
And a golden girdle round my sweet;—
    Ah! qu'elle est belle La Marguerite.[2]

Margaret's maids are fair to see,   5
Freshly dressed and pleasantly;
Margaret's hair falls down to her knee;—
    Ah! qu'elle est belle La Marguerite.

---

[23] The fit of mad suspicion which has made him accuse
her.
[24] Just in the nick of time, to save her again from death
at the stake.

[1] The poem is spoken by Sir Lambert du Bois, a French
knight in impoverished circumstances, who is dreaming
of the glory and the wealth which he imagines he will
gain in the next day's battle of Crécy (1346), and which
will enable him to marry Margaret. The pathos and the
irony of the poem lie in the fact that the French were
to be defeated in the battle.
[2] How beautiful is Marguerite.

If I were rich I would kiss her feet,
I would kiss the place where the gold hems meet, 10
And the golden girdle round my sweet—
    Ah! qu'elle est belle La Marguerite.

Ah me! I have never touched her hand;
When the arriere-ban[3] goes through the land,
Six basnets under my pennon stand;[4]— 15
    Ah! qu'elle est belle La Marguerite.

And many an one grins under his hood:
"Sir Lambert du Bois, with all his men good,
Has neither food nor firewood."—
    Ah! qu'elle est belle La Marguerite. 20

If I were rich I would kiss her feet,
And the golden girdle of my sweet,
And thereabouts where the gold hems meet;
    Ah! qu'elle est belle La Marguerite.

Yet even now it is good to think, 25
While my few poor varlets grumble and drink
In my desolate hall, where the fires sink,—
    Ah! qu'elle est belle La Marguerite.

Of Margaret sitting glorious there,
In glory of gold and glory of hair, 30
And glory of glorious face most fair;—
    Ah! qu'elle est belle La Marguerite.

Likewise to-night I make good cheer,
Because this battle draweth near:
For what have I to lose or fear?— 35
    Ah! qu'elle est belle La Marguerite.

For, look you, my horse is good to prance
A right fair measure in this war-dance,
Before the eyes of Philip of France;[5]—
    Ah! qu'elle est belle La Marguerite. 40

And sometime it may hap, perdie,
While my new towers stand up three and three,
And my hall gets painted fair to see—
    Ah! qu'elle est belle La Marguerite—

That folks may say: "Times change, by the rood, 45

For Lambert, banneret[6] of the wood,[7]
Has heaps of food and firewood;—
    Ah! qu'elle est belle La Marguerite.

"And wonderful eyes, too, under the hood
Of a damsel of right noble blood." 50
St. Ives, for Lambert of the wood!—
    Ah! qu'elle est belle La Marguerite.

The Blue Closet[1]

THE DAMOZELS

Lady Alice, Lady Louise,
Between the wash of the tumbling seas
We are ready to sing, if so ye please;
So lay your long hands on the keys;
      Sing: *"Laudate pueri."*[2] 5

And ever the great bell overhead
Boomed in the wind a knell for the dead,
Though no one tolled it, a knell for the dead.

LADY LOUISE

Sister, let the measure swell
Not too loud; for you sing not well 10
If you drown the faint boom of the bell;
      He is weary, so am I.

And ever the chevron[3] overhead
Flapped on the banner of the dead;
(Was he asleep, or was he dead?) 15

LADY ALICE

Alice the Queen, and Louise the Queen,
Two damozels wearing purple and green,
Four lone ladies dwelling here
From day to day and year to year;
And there is none to let us go; 20

---

3 Proclamation calling men to arms.
4 Only six helmeted men stand under my banner.
5 The king of France, Philip VI.

6 A knight who could lead vassals to battle under his own heraldic banner.
7 This phrase is a translation of his name: cf. line 18.

1 Lady Louise is in love with Arthur, who rode off wearing her scarf and was never heard of again. He returns, apparently, at the end of the poem as a ghost, and leads Lady Louise, her sister, Lady Alice, and their two damozels across the bridge to the land of death. But the situation is very vague and of no importance.
2 "Let the children praise [the Lord]"—the opening words of a medieval hymn.
3 Device of honor on Arthur's banner, which he has left in the Blue Closet.

To break the locks of the doors below,
Or shovel away the heaped-up snow;
And when we die no man will know
That we are dead: but they give us leave,
Once every year on Christmas-eve, 25
To sing in the Closet Blue one song;
And we should be so long, so long,
If we dared, in singing; for dream on dream,
They float on in a happy stream;
Float from the gold strings, float from the keys, 30
Float from the opened lips of Louise;
But, alas! the sea-salt oozes through
The chinks of the tiles of the Closet Blue.
And ever the great bell overhead
Booms in the wind a knell for the dead, 35
The wind plays on it a knell for the dead.

> *They sing all together*

How long ago was it, how long ago,
He came to this tower with hands full of snow?

"Kneel down, O love Louise, kneel down!" he
said,
And sprinkled the dusty snow over my head. 40

He watched the snow melting, it ran through my
hair,
Ran over my shoulders, white shoulders and
bare.

"I cannot weep for thee, poor love Louise,
For my tears are all hidden deep under the seas;

"In a gold and blue casket she keeps all my tears, 45
But my eyes are no longer blue, as in old years;

"Yea, they grow gray with time, grow small and
dry,
I am so feeble now, would I might die."

> *And in truth the great bell overhead*
> *Left off his pealing for the dead,* 50
> *Perchance because the wind was dead.*

Will he come back again, or is he dead?
O! is he sleeping, my scarf round his head?

Or did they strangle him as he lay there,
With the long scarlet scarf I used to wear? 55

Only I pray thee, Lord, let him come here!

Both his soul and his body to me are most dear.

Dear Lord, that loves me, I wait to receive
Either body or spirit this wild Christmas-eve.

> *Through the floor shot up a lily red,* 60
> *With a patch of earth from the land of*
> *the dead,*
> *For he was strong in the land of the*
> *dead.*

What matter that his cheeks were pale,
His kind kissed lips all gray?
"O love Louise, have you waited long?" 65
"O my lord Arthur, yea."

What if his hair that brushed her cheek
Was stiff with frozen rime?
His eyes were grown quite blue again,
As in the happy time. 70

"O, love Louise, this is the key
Of the happy golden land!
O, sisters, cross the bridge with me,
My eyes are full of sand.
What matter that I cannot see, 75
If ye take me by the hand?"

> *And ever the great bell overhead,*
> *And the tumbling seas mourned for the*
> *dead;*
> *For their song ceased, and they were*
> *dead.*

from Address on the Collection of Paintings of the English Pre-Raphaelite School in the City of Birmingham Museum and Art Gallery on Friday, October 24, 1891[1]

Mr. Kenrick has said that I am going to address you on the subject of Art, but it is clear that that subject is a very wide one and that I must limit myself very considerably. Not only so, even if I were to speak about all the pictures exhibited here, the subject would be again such a very

---

[1] Reprinted from *William Morris; Artist, Writer, Socialist,* edited by May Morris (Oxford, 1936), by permission of Basil Blackwell, the publisher.

wide one, that there would be no end of it. So I must limit myself still further. Therefore I propose to speak to you almost entirely, according to the light I have, of that school of painters once called the pre-Raphaelites, and who perhaps should still be called pre-Raphaelites. There is all the more reason for my doing so because, as a matter of fact, their doctrines have been successful; they have impressed themselves upon the present generation, at any rate of the English people, and, I think to a certain extent, have influenced also the artists of France. In fact, they have exercised a very great influence on the works of art that are now current. I mean, even apart from the magnificent works that have been produced by the leaders of that School, the School itself has made its mark upon the age.

Let us consider what these pre-Raphaelites were. They were certainly a very small body of men. The three original leaders, the chief members of the pre-Raphaelite Brotherhood, as you probably know, were Dante Gabriel Rossetti, Everett Millais, and Holman Hunt; but there were others who belonged to the School, though they were not actually enrolled in the Brotherhood. The most noteworthy of these painters, in the early days of the School, were Ford Madox Brown and Arthur Hughes. Later on your fellow-townsman, Burne-Jones, became a friend and fellow-worker of the above named men. There were several others, but those named were not only the greatest, but also the most characteristic.

However, these few young men, wholly unknown till they *forced* the public to recognize them, began what must be called a really audacious attempt; a definite revolt against the Academical Art which brooded over all the Schools of civilized Europe at the time.[2] In point of fact I think, in considering the revolt of the pre-Raphaelites, one must look upon it as a portion of the general revolt against Academicism in Literature as well as in Art. In Literature the revolt had taken place much earlier. There were many reasons for that; but the principal one seems to me to be that the Art of Painting, being so much more technical than Literature, depends much more upon tradition than Literature does, and that tradition, however much it may have

lost its original position, however poor a tradition may be, and however deficient in positive, in creative power, nevertheless retains the negative and conservative power, and keeps people from changing the general tendency of the Art; whereas the sister Art of Literature depends less on traditions, and is more individual than that of Painting, though less than many think, and consequently the necessity for a revolt is sooner felt, and the effect of it is more easily and plainly to be seen.

Before I go further I may as well give something like an approximate date. If I am wrong I see at least one friend in this room who can correct me. It seems to me that somewhere about the year 1848 will cover the date for the first general appearance of the pre-Raphaelites before the public.

Well, let us consider, first of all, what their first and underlying doctrine was. What was the special and particular standpoint they took up? Because in all revolts there is one special and particular principle which, so to speak, swallows up all others, which is so engrossing that those who are carrying on the revolt can scarcely see any other side to what they are doing than that which embodies this particular doctrine. Well, I think that the special and particular doctrine of the pre-Raphaelites is not very far to seek. It is, in one word, Naturalism.

That is to say the pre-Raphaelites started by saying, "You have Nature before you, what you have to do is to copy Nature and you will produce something which at all events is worth people's attention." Now that at first sight seems a self-evident proposition. But you must not forget what I said just now as to that worn-out tradition which was dominating the whole of the artistic schools of Europe at the time. I remember distinctly myself, as a boy, that when I had pictures offered to my notice I could not understand what they were about at all. I said, "Oh, well, that is all right. It has got the sort of thing in it which there ought to be in a picture. There is nothing to be said against it, no doubt. I cannot say I would have it other than that, because it is clearly the proper thing to do." But really I took very little interest in it, and I should think that would be the case with nine hundred and ninety-nine out of every thousand of those people who had not received definite technical instruction in the art, who were not formally artists. I should have said, but just now my friend Mr. Wallis rather corrected me on that point, that even up to the present day the greater part of what I should call the laymen in these matters of the Arts do not feel any very great exultation when they see an Old Master. If they are suddenly introduced to an Old Master I venture to think they are more or less disappointed with the impression that it makes upon them.

Well, what the pre-Raphaelites really practically said was this, "We are going to break with this poor and worn-out tradition which has tyrannized over us so long. We are going in point of fact to present you with something that is natural." And I must say that they certainly did do so. They did paint fully intending to be, and fully succeeding in being naturalistic, and I should have thought most people would have thought that the public would have received this attempt with acclamation, with joy, that they would have said: "Here at last is something we can understand. Here are visible sheep; here are such and such things as we have seen them, as we see them every day, exceedingly like the things in question. There may be short-comings here and there, very probably, but after all we understand what it means. This is addressed to us, the public, and not merely to artists prejudiced in favour of certain traditions."

But strange to say, the public did exactly the reverse of receiving these paintings with acclamation. What they really said was "These things are monsters. They are not like nature." They did not mean that; they meant to say "They are not like pictures." They certainly were not, as pictures then were, but they assuredly were like nature; you could not possibly get out of that. However as I tell you, the public received these attempts as revolutionary attempts of young men always are received, with jeers, because they also were under the influence of the academical tradition.

But there was one man, at all events, who although he had been brought up in a very different school from that of the pre-Raphaelites, in what I should call the old-fashioned Drawing Master School (I do not mean to use the word with any sort of contempt but merely as an explanatory word)—who although he was brought up in that school, and although his master was Mr. J. D. Harding—a name you know very well —really looked at these pre-Raphaelite paintings with open eyes. That man I need scarcely tell you was John Ruskin. He immediately came forward as the champion of those young men before the public. And no doubt they needed such a champion very badly.

However, they made way and they finally won, in the first place great personal reputation, thoroughly well deserved, and they also achieved success as a School; as far as their root doctrine, Naturalism, is concerned they destroyed the old feeble Academical tradition.

But now one has got to say a little more about what one means by the word Naturalism. I can conceive, I fancy most of you can conceive, a certain kind of Naturalism which would not be very interesting. There is a good deal of talk about such Naturalism as that nowadays. It means but very little more than bare statements of fact by means of the Art of painting, and it seems to me that pictures painted with that end in view, unless—as not very seldom happens by the bye—in spite of the theory they have other things to help them, will be scarcely works of Art. They will be rather something on the border-line between works of Art and scientific statements. Now the pre-Raphaelite pictures were not in the least like that, because besides the mere presentment of natural facts, they aimed at another kind of thing which was far more important. The painters aimed, some of them no doubt much more than others, at the conscientious presentment of incident. In other words they certainly had entirely come to the conclusion that not only was it necessary that they should paint well, but that this painting, this good painting, the excellent execution, the keen eyesight, the care, the skill, and so on, should be the instrument for telling some kind of story to the beholder. That you see completes the Naturalism. Granted that you have something to say, and that you say it well by means of the Art of Painting, you are then, and then only, a Naturalistic Painter.

No doubt in the early days of pre-Raphaelitism, in talk at all events, it was rather the fashion to decry the use of any sort of convention in dealing with the works of painting which were produced in the reaction against the aforesaid tyranny of a weak, poor and unworthy convention. But as a matter of fact every work of Art whether it is imitative or whether it is suggestive, must be founded on some convention or other. It seems to me that the real point of the thing—and that I think the pre-Raphaelites understood instinctively—is that that convention shall not be so to say, a conventional convention. It must be a convention that you have found out for yourself in some way or another, whether that has been deduced from history, or whether you yourself have been able to hit upon it by the light of nature. In any case, this you must understand, that it is absolutely impossible to give a really literal transcript of nature. You must have some convention. You know in the old story about Parrhasios and Zeuxis, Parrhasios says, "Zeuxis deceived the birds but I deceived Zeuxis."[3] This story, though instructive in some respects, makes a mistake. Zeuxis would never have deceived the birds: Zeuxis himself was very much easier to deceive than the birds, because Zeuxis was a man, and had an imagination, which was all his life telling him some kind of a story, which story was connected with the actual sights that passed before his eyes. Well the Naturalism of the pre-Raphaelites which did not stop at the simple presentment of scientific fact but went further and conscientiously considered the due and proper incidents that were necessary in order to make a work of Art, was founded on a genuinely *natural* convention.

I have so far spoken of two sides of the qualities that go to make a great work of plastic Art: presentation of nature and the telling of a story. There is also however a third side necessary in a work of Art: and that third side was both less considered by the public, and was much more difficult to put before it: that side was the ornamental function of the Art. No picture it seems to me is complete unless it is something more than a representation of nature and the teller of a tale. It ought also to have a definite, harmonious, conscious beauty. It ought to be ornamental. It ought to be possible for it to be part of a beautiful whole in a room or church or hall. Now of the original pre-Raphaelites, Rossetti was the man who mostly felt that side

of the Art of painting: all his pictures have a decorative quality as an essential, and not as a mere accident of them, and not unnaturally, because of all his fellows he had most sense of the historical connection of the Arts. His mind was formed on that looking into history which is such a marked feature of the general revolt against Academicism: and whoever looks into history will find living Art there always decorative.

But this decorative side of the school needed another man to complete its development, and did not fail to get him—your townsman, Burne-Jones—of whom, indeed, I feel some difficulty in speaking as the truth demands, because he is such a close friend of mine. But I must say that he added the element of *perfect* ornamentation, the completely decorative side of the Art. In fact, when the pre-Raphaelite School was completed by this representative man, it then became apparent that what pre-Raphaelitism was, was sufficiently indicated by its name. That is to say, it was the continuation of the art that had been current throughout Europe before Raphael marked the completion of the period when art became academical, i.e., inorganic; the so-called renaissance.

It has become clear that the "new" school which was received at one time with such volleys of scorn and has since made its way so vigorously, was really nothing more or less than a branch of the great Gothic Art which once pervaded all Europe. I will repeat that the characteristics of that Gothic Art were in the main three. The first was Love of Nature—not, mind you, of the mere dead surface of it—but Love of Nature as the only instrument for telling a tale of some sort or another. Love of nature is the first element in the Gothic Art; next is the epical quality, and joined to those two things is what people very often think perhaps is the only quality it has got, and that is its ornamental quality. These qualities you may say it shares with the ancient organic Schools of Art, the Greek above all, (though it seems to me that it outgoes them in its epical and ornamental developments,) but at least one quality distinguishes it from them, the *romantic* quality, as I must call it for lack of a better word; and this quality is eminently characteristic of both Rossetti and Burne-Jones, but especially of the

---

[3] Greek painters who strove to outdo each other in creating an illusion of actual reality. Zeuxis boasted that birds tried to eat the grapes in one of his pictures.

latter. It is an element of the epical quality (as notably in Homer), though it is not the whole of it; and is necessary to the utmost refinement, abundance and enduring interest of decoration; though I admit that it is rather to be felt than defined.

And I must say, that you will find throughout the whole of the history of the Arts, that when artists are thinking in the main of conscientiously telling a story their works are really much more beautiful, much more fitted for the ornamenting of public buildings than when they are only thinking of producing works of *mere* ornament. How this comes about it would take long to say, but so it is. Perhaps it may seem at first something like a paradox to you. I am afraid however I must add another paradox to it, and say, that when people talk most about Works of Art, generally speaking at that period they do least in art. Well we must take that home to ourselves for after all we are in that position. We must acknowledge that in these times of the world we have got a great deal of backway to make up. We are forced to talk about Art, clearly not because it is in a satisfactory condition, but because it is in a very unsatisfactory condition: or else why should we have to say anything about it?

A word or two of summing up the characteristics of the individual members of the pre-Raphaelite School. I should say that as a representative of its pure naturalism, not thinking so much about tale-telling as about the presentment of natural form, Millais was the leader, and that the three, Dante Gabriel Rossetti, Holman Hunt and Ford Madox Brown were all of them equally concerned with the conscientious presentation of incident. You will find in looking at their pictures that they always want to knock in the nail hard on this point: that there is always something going on, there is something being done in the picture. They say, "Here is an event"; and at their best they are successful in doing what every genuine artist tries to do—in really convincing the beholder that the events they represent could have happened in no other way than the way in which they represent them. That is the end and aim of what, for want of a better word, I will call dramatic Art: perhaps epical Art would be a better word. And Rossetti

and Burne-Jones are those members of the school whose conscientious presentation of events deals with romantic subjects in a romantic way, and *consequently* includes decoration as an essential.

Now I must just say one word about the fact that both Rossetti and Burne-Jones have had very little to do with representing the scenes of ordinary modern life as they go on before your eyes. One has often heard that brought against the "Romantic" artists, as a shortcoming. Now, quite plainly, I must say that I think it *is* a shortcoming. But is the shortcoming due to the individual artist, or is it due to the public at large? for my part I think the latter. When an artist has really a very keen sense of beauty, I venture to think that he can not literally represent an event that takes place in modern life. He must add something or another to qualify or soften the ugliness and sordidness of the surroundings of life in our generation. That is not only the case with pictures, if you please: it is the case also in literature. Two examples occur to my mind at this moment. Let us take the novels of such a man as Hardy, or the others who write more or less in the same way. They are supposed to represent scenes of modern life in their novels. But do they? I say they do not; because they take care to surround these modern scenes with an atmosphere of out-of-the-way country life, which we ourselves never by any chance see. If you go down into the country you won't see Mr. Hardy's heroes and heroines walking about, I assure you. You will see a very different kind of thing from that when you meet the ordinary British farmer or the ordinary British agricultural labourer walking about, and more especially—excuse me—more especially when you see their wives and daughters walking about. I am very sorry, but so it is. Well, I say the difficulty is even greater, perhaps, for the painter. In painting, you cannot get so far away from the facts as you can in literature. Nevertheless I think those of you who have seen Walker's pictures (and if you have seen them you must have admired them, for they are exceedingly beautiful and exceedingly skilful) will have perceived that his countrymen: his haymakers, his carters and all the rest of them: are really not modern English carters and haymakers: they are carters and haymakers that have stepped down from the frieze of the Parthenon.[4] The agricultural Briton is not built like that, or is built like that very rarely. Sometimes you may get people of that kind amongst waifs and strays: amongst, perhaps, the gipsies, but never amongst the ordinary working people of the country. Well, of course Art is free to everybody, and by all means, if anyone is really moved by the spirit to treat modern subjects, let him do so, and do it in the best way he can; but, on the other hand, I don't think he has a right, under the circumstances and considering the evasions he is absolutely bound to make, to lay any blame on his brother artist who turns back again to the life of past times; or who, shall we rather say, since his imagination must have some garb or another, naturally takes the raiment of some period in which the surroundings of life were not ugly but beautiful.

Well, I have tried as well as I could to give you some idea of the general principles of the pre-Raphaelite School. I say that those principles, so far as they inculcated pure naturalism, have more or less succeeded: I mean in producing a continuous School. So far as they inculcated the conscientious representation of incident—their special side—they have not succeeded so well, because, after all, for the production of works of that kind you want either artists of startling and stupendous genius, of whom very few can be born in one epoch, or else a great homogeneous school of tradition, which is able to use up all the various qualities of the lesser men and combine them in a harmonious whole. On the other hand, the ornamental aim of the School has made less impression still upon the age. That cannot be wondered at, because, after all, the ornamental side of the Art is but a part of architecture, and architecture cannot flourish unless it is the spontaneous expression of the pleasure and the will of the whole people. In these days let us admit it at once: and that is one reason why these galleries hung with pictures, each one complete in itself, are interesting to us: whatever you can get out of Art can not be got out of the combined efforts of the people at large, but must be simply the work and the expression of individual genius, individual capac-

ity, working towards a certain end. And I recur to what I was talking about just now, and say that I think one reason why there is much to be said for that Art which deals with the life of the past, or rather with the artist's imagination of it, is because only so can the artist have at his back in the form of history anything like that traditional combined idea of Art which once was common to the whole people. That, I think, is perhaps, after all, the real inner reason why it is so very difficult to represent the life which is round about us at the present day. . . .

from The Art of the People

Delivered before the Birmingham Society of Arts and School of Design, February 19, 1879

"And the men of labour spent their strength in daily struggling for bread to maintain the vital strength they labour with: so living in a daily circulation of sorrow, living but to work, and working but to live, as if daily bread were the only end of a wearisome life, and a wearisome life the only occasion of daily bread."—DANIEL DEFOE

. . . To me, and I hope to you, Art is a very serious thing, and cannot by any means be dissociated from the weighty matters that occupy the thoughts of men; and there are principles underlying the practice of it, on which all serious-minded men may—nay, must—have their own thoughts. It is on some of these that I ask your leave to speak, and to address myself, not only to those who are consciously interested in the arts, but to all those also who have considered what the progress of civilization promises and threatens to those who shall come after us: what there is to hope and fear for the future of the arts, which were born with the birth of civilization and will only die with its death—what on this side of things, the present time of strife and doubt and change is preparing for the better time, when the change shall have come, the strife be lulled, and the doubt cleared: this is a question, I say, which is indeed weighty, and may well interest all thinking men. . . .

The aim of your Society and School of Arts is, as I understand it, to further those arts by education widely spread. A very great object is

---

4 That is, they have the idealized character of Phidias' statues, which adorned the Greek temple of the Parthenon at Athens.

that, and well worthy of the reputation of this great city; but since Birmingham has also, I rejoice to know, a great reputation for not allowing things to go about shamming life when the brains are knocked out of them, I think you should know and see clearly what it is you have undertaken to further by these institutions, and whether you really care about it, or only languidly acquiesce in it—whether, in short, you know it to the heart, and are indeed part and parcel of it, with your own will, or against it; or else have heard say that it is a good thing if anyone care to meddle with it.

If you are surprised at my putting that question for your consideration, I will tell you why I do so. There are some of us who love Art most, and I may say most faithfully, who see for certain that such love is rare nowadays. We cannot help seeing, that besides a vast number of people, who (poor souls!) are sordid and brutal of mind and habits, and have had no chance or choice in the matter, there are many highminded, thoughtful, and cultivated men who inwardly think the arts to be a foolish accident of civilization—nay, worse perhaps, a nuisance, a disease, a hindrance to human progress. Some of these, doubtless, are very busy about other sides of thought. They are, as I should put it, so *artistically* engrossed by the study of science, politics, or what not, that they have necessarily narrowed their minds by their hard and praiseworthy labours. But since such men are few, this does not account for a prevalent habit of thought that looks upon Art as at best trifling.

What is wrong, then, with us or the arts, since what was once accounted so glorious, is now deemed paltry?

The question is no light one; for, to put the matter in its clearest light, I will say that the leaders of modern thought do for the most part sincerely and single-mindedly hate and despise the arts; and you know well that as the leaders are, so must the people be; and that means that we who are met together here for the furthering of Art by wide-spread education are either deceiving ourselves and wasting our time, since we shall one day be of the same opinion as the best men among us, or else we represent a small minority that is right, as minorities sometimes are, while those upright men aforesaid, and the great mass of civilized men, have been blinded by untoward circumstances.

That we are of this mind—the minority that is right—is, I hope, the case. I hope we know assuredly that the arts we have met together to further are necessary to the life of man, if the progress of civilization is not to be as causeless as the turning of a wheel that makes nothing.

How, then, shall we, the minority, carry out the duty which our position thrusts upon us, of striving to grow into a majority?

If we could only explain to those thoughtful men, and the millions of whom they are the flower, what the thing is that we love, which is to us as the bread we eat, and the air we breathe, but about which they know nothing and feel nothing, save a vague instinct of repulsion, then the seed of victory might be sown. This is hard indeed to do; yet if we ponder upon a chapter of ancient or mediaeval history, it seems to me some glimmer of a chance of doing so breaks in upon us. Take for example a century of the Byzantine Empire, weary yourselves with reading the names of the pedants, tyrants, and taxgatherers to whom the terrible chain which long-dead Rome once forged, still gave the power of cheating people into thinking that they were necessary lords of the world. Turn then to the lands they governed, and read and forget a long string of the causeless murders of Northern and Saracen pirates and robbers. That is pretty much the sum of what so-called history has left us of the tale of those days—the stupid languor and the evil deeds of kings and scoundrels. Must we turn away then, and say that all was evil? How then did men live from day to day? How then did Europe grow into intelligence and freedom? It seems there were others than those of whom history (so called) has left us the names and the deeds. These, the raw material for the treasury and the slave-market, we now call "the people," and we know that they were working all that while. Yes, and that their work was not merely slaves' work, the meal-trough before them and the whip behind them; for though history (so called) has forgotten them, yet their work has not been forgotten, but has made another history —the history of Art. There is not an ancient city in the East or the West that does not bear some token of their grief, and joy, and hope. From

Ispahan[1] to Northumberland, there is no building built between the seventh and seventeenth centuries that does not show the influence of the labour of that oppressed and neglected herd of men. No one of them, indeed, rose high above his fellows. There was no Plato, or Shakespeare, or Michael Angelo amongst them. Yet scattered as it was among many men, how strong their thought was, how long it abided, how far it travelled!

And so it was ever through all those days when Art was so vigorous and progressive. Who can say how little we should know of many periods, but for their art? History (so called) has remembered the kings and warriors, because they destroyed; Art has remembered the people, because they created.

I think, then, that this knowledge we have of the life of past times gives us some token of the way we should take in meeting those honest and single-hearted men who above all things desire the world's progress, but whose minds are, as it were, sick on this point of the arts. Surely you may say to them: When all is gained that you (and we) so long for, what shall we do then? That great change which we are working for, each in his own way, will come like other changes, as a thief in the night, and will be with us before we know it; but let us imagine that its consummation has come suddenly and dramatically, acknowledged and hailed by all right-minded people; and what shall we do then, lest we begin once more to heap up fresh corruption for the woeful labour of ages once again? I say, as we turn away from the flagstaff where the new banner has been just run up; as we depart, our ears yet ringing with the blare of the heralds' trumpets that have proclaimed the new order of things, what shall we turn to then, what *must* we turn to then?

To what else, save to our work, our daily labour?

With what, then, shall we adorn it when we have become wholly free and reasonable? It is necessary toil, but shall it be toil only? Shall all we can do with it be to shorten the hours of that toil to the utmost, that the hours of leisure may be long beyond what men used to hope for? and what then shall we do with the leisure,

if we say that all toil is irksome? Shall we sleep it all away?—Yes, and never wake up again, I should hope, in that case.

What shall we do then? what shall our necessary hours of labour bring forth?

That will be a question for all men in that day when many wrongs are righted, and when there will be no classes of degradation on whom the dirty work of the world can be shovelled; and if men's minds are still sick and loathe the arts, they will not be able to answer that question.

Once men sat under grinding tyrannies, amidst violence and fear so great, that nowadays we wonder how they lived through twenty-four hours of it, till we remember that then, as now, their daily labour was the main part of their lives, and that that daily labour was sweetened by the daily creation of Art; and shall we who are delivered from the evils they bore, live drearier days than they did? Shall men, who have come forth from so many tyrannies, bind themselves to yet another one, and become the slaves of nature, piling day upon day of hopeless, useless toil? Must this go on worsening till it comes to this at last—that the world shall have come into its inheritance, and with all foes conquered and nought to bind it, shall choose to sit down and labour for ever amidst grim ugliness? How, then, were all our hopes cheated, what a gulf of despair should we tumble into then!

In truth, it cannot be; yet if that sickness of repulsion to the arts were to go on hopelessly, nought else would be, and the extinction of the love of beauty and imagination would prove to be the extinction of civilization. But that sickness the world will one day throw off, yet will, I believe, pass through many pains in so doing, some of which will look very like the death-throes of Art, and some, perhaps, will be grievous enough to the poor people of the world; since hard necessity, I doubt, works many of the world's changes, rather than the purblind striving to see, which we call the foresight of man.

Meanwhile, remember that I asked just now, what was amiss in Art or in ourselves that this sickness was upon us. Nothing is wrong or can be with Art in the abstract—that must always be good for mankind, or we are all wrong together: but with Art as we of these latter days have known it, there is much wrong; nay, what

---

[1] A city in Iran, once the capital of Persia.

are we here for to-night if that is not so? were not the schools of art founded all over the country some thirty years ago because we had found out that popular art was fading—or perhaps had faded out from amongst us?

As to the progress made since then in this country—and in this country only, if at all—it is hard for me to speak without being either ungracious or insincere, and yet speak I must. I say, then, that an apparent external progress in some ways is obvious, but I do not know how far that is hopeful, for time must try it, and prove whether it be a passing fashion or the first token of a real stir among the great mass of civilized men. To speak quite frankly, and as one friend to another, I must needs say that even as I say those words they seem too good to be true. And yet—who knows?—so wont are we to frame history for the future as well as for the past, so often are our eyes blind both when we look backward and when we look forward, because we have been gazing so intently at our own days, our own lines. May all be better than I think it!

At any rate let us count our gains, and set them against less hopeful signs of the times. In England, then—and as far as I know, in England only—painters of pictures have grown, I believe, more numerous, and certainly more conscientious in their work, and in some cases—and this more especially in England—have developed and expressed a sense of beauty which the world has not seen for the last three hundred years. This is certainly a very great gain, which is not easy to over-estimate, both for those who make the pictures and those who use them.

Furthermore, in England, and in England only, there has been a great improvement in architecture and the arts that attend it—arts which it was the special province of the aforementioned schools to revive and foster. This, also, is a considerable gain to the users of the works so made, but I fear a gain less important to most of those concerned in making them.

Against these gains we must, I am very sorry to say, set the fact not easy to be accounted for, that the rest of the civilized world (so called) seems to have done little more than stand still in these matters; and that among ourselves these improvements have concerned comparatively few people, the mass of our population not being in the least touched by them; so that the great bulk of our architecture—the art which most depends on the taste of the people at large—grows worse and worse every day.

I must speak also of another piece of discouragement before I go further. I daresay many of you will remember how emphatically those who first had to do with the movement of which the foundation of our art-schools was a part, called the attention of our pattern-designers to the beautiful works of the East. This was surely most well judged of them, for they bade us look at an art at once beautiful, orderly, living in our own day, and above all, popular. Now, it is a grievous result of the sickness of civilization that this art is fast disappearing before the advance of western conquest and commerce—fast, and every day faster. While we are met here in Birmingham to further the spread of education in art, Englishmen in India are, in their shortsightedness, actively destroying the very sources of that education—jewellery, metal-work, pottery, calico-printing, brocade-weaving, carpet-making—all the famous and historical arts of the great peninsula have been for long treated as matters of no importance, to be thrust aside for the advantage of any paltry scrap of so-called commerce; and matters are now speedily coming to an end there. . . .

I have just shown you for one thing that lovers of Indian and Eastern Art, including as they do the heads of our institutions for art education, and I am sure many among what are called the governing classes, are utterly powerless to stay its downward course. The general tendency of civilization is against them, and is too strong for them.

Again, though many of us love architecture dearly, and believe that it helps the healthiness both of the body and soul to live among beautiful things, we of the big towns are mostly compelled to live in houses which have become a by-word of contempt for their ugliness and inconvenience. The stream of civilization is against us, and we cannot battle against it.

Once more, those devoted men who have upheld the standard of truth and beauty amongst us, and whose pictures, painted amidst difficulties that none but a painter can know, show great qualities of mind unsurpassed in any age— these great men have but a narrow circle that can understand their works, and are utterly unknown to the great mass of the people: civilization is so much against them, that they cannot move the people.

Therefore, looking at all this, I cannot think that all is well with the root of the tree we are cultivating. Indeed, I believe that if other things were but to stand still in the world, this improvement before mentioned would lead to a kind of art which, in that impossible case, would be in a way stable, would perhaps stand still also. This would be an art cultivated professedly by a few, and for a few, who would consider it necessary—a duty, if they could admit duties—to despise the common herd, to hold themselves aloof from all that the world has been struggling for from the first, to guard carefully every approach to their palace of art. It would be a pity to waste many words on the prospect of such a school of art as this, which does in a way, theoretically at least, exist at present, and has for its watchword a piece of slang that does not mean the harmless thing it seems to mean—art for art's sake. Its foredoomed end must be, that art at last will seem too delicate a thing for even the hands of the initiated to touch; and the initiated must at last sit still and do nothing—to the grief of no one.

Well, certainly, if I thought you were come here to further such an art as this I could not have stood up and called you *friends;* though such a feeble folk as I have told you of one could scarce care to call foes.

Yet, as I say, such men exist, and I have troubled you with speaking of them, because I know that those honest and intelligent people, who are eager for human progress, and yet lack part of the human senses and are anti-artistic, suppose that such men are artists, and that this is what art means, and what it does for people, and that such a narrow, cowardly life is what we, fellow-handicraftsmen, aim at. I see this taken for granted continually, even by many who, to say truth, ought to know better, and I long to put the slur from off us; to make people understand that we, least of all men, wish to widen the gulf between the classes, nay, worse still, to make new classes of elevation, and new classes of degradation—new lords and new slaves; that we, least of all men, want to cultivate the "plant called man" in different ways—here stingily, there wastefully: I wish people to understand that the art we are striving for is a good thing which all can share, which will elevate all; in good sooth, if all people do not soon share it there will soon be none to share; if all are not elevated by it, mankind will lose the elevation it has gained. Nor is such an art as we long for a vain dream; such an art once was in times that were worse than these, when there was less courage, kindness, and truth in the world than there is now; such an art there will be hereafter, when there will be more courage, kindness, and truth than there is now in the world.

Let us look backward in history once more for a short while, and then steadily forward till my words are done: I began by saying that part of the common and necessary advice given to Art students was to study antiquity; and no doubt many of you, like me, have done so; have wandered, for instance, through the galleries of the admirable museum of South Kensington, and, like me, have been filled with wonder and gratitude at the beauty which has been born from the brain of man. Now, consider, I pray you, what these wonderful works are, and how they were made; and indeed, it is neither in extravagance nor without due meaning that I use the word "wonderful" in speaking of them. Well, these things are just the common household goods of those past days, and that is one reason why they are so few and so carefully treasured. They were common things in their own day, used without fear of breaking or spoiling—no rarities then—and yet we have called them "wonderful."

And how were they made? Did a great artist draw the designs for them—a man of cultivation, highly paid, daintily fed, carefully housed, wrapped up in cotton wool, in short, when he was not at work? By no means. Wonderful as these works are, they were made by "common fellows," as the phrase goes, in the common course of their daily labour. Such were the men we honour in honouring those works. And their labour—do you think it was irksome to them? Those of you who are artists know very well that it was not; that it could not be. Many a grin of pleasure I'll be bound—and you will not contradict me—went to the carrying through of those mazes of mysterious beauty, to the invention of those strange beasts and birds and flowers that we ourselves have chuckled over at South Kensington. While they were at work, at least, these men were not unhappy, and I suppose they worked most days, and the most part of the day, as we do.

Or those treasures of architecture that we study so carefully nowadays—what are they? how were they made? There are great minsters among them, indeed, and palaces of kings and lords, but not many; and, noble and awe-inspiring as these may be, they differ only in size from the little grey church that still so often makes the common-place English landscape beautiful, and the little grey house that still, in some parts of the country at least, makes an English village a thing apart, to be seen and pondered on by all who love romance and beauty. These form the mass of our architectural treasures, the houses that everyday people lived in, the unregarded churches in which they worshipped.

And, once more, who was it that designed and ornamented them? The great architect, carefully kept for the purpose, and guarded from the common troubles of common men? By no means. Sometimes, perhaps, it was the monk, the ploughman's brother; oftenest his other brother, the village carpenter, smith, mason, what not— "a common fellow," whose common everyday labour fashioned works that are to-day the wonder and despair of many a hard-working "cultivated" architect. And did he loathe his work? No, it is impossible. I have seen, as we most of us have, work done by such men in some out-of-the-way hamlet—where to-day even few strangers ever come, and whose people seldom go five miles from their own doors; in such places, I say, I have seen work so delicate, so careful, and so inventive, that nothing in its way could go further. And I will assert, without fear of contradiction, that no human ingenuity can produce work such as this without pleasure being a third party to the brain that conceived and the hand that fashioned it. Nor are such works rare. The throne of the great Plantagenet, or the great Valois, was no more daintily carved than the seat of the village mass-john,[2] or the chest of the yeoman's good-wife.

So, you see, there was much going on to

make life endurable in those times. Not every day, you may be sure, was a day of slaughter and tumult, though the histories read almost as if it were so; but every day the hammer chinked on the anvil, and the chisel played about the oak beam, and never without some beauty and invention being born of it, and consequently some human happiness.

That last word brings me to the very kernel and heart of what I have come here to say to you, and I pray you to think of it most seriously —not as to my words, but as to a thought which is stirring in the world, and will one day grow into something.

That thing which I understand by real art is the expression by man of his pleasure in labour. I do not believe he can be happy in his labour without expressing that happiness; and especially is this so when he is at work at anything in which he specially excels. A most kind gift is this of nature, since all men, nay, it seems all things too, must labour; so that not only does the dog take pleasure in hunting, and the horse in running, and the bird in flying, but so natural does the idea seem to us, that we imagine to ourselves that the earth and the very elements rejoice in doing their appointed work; and the poets have told us of the spring meadows smiling, of the exultation of the fire, of the countless laughter of the sea.

Nor until these latter days has man ever rejected this universal gift, but always, when he has not been too much perplexed, too much bound by disease or beaten down by trouble, has striven to make his work at least happy. Pain he has too often found in his pleasure, and weariness in his rest, to trust to these. What matter if his happiness lie with what must be always with him—his work?

And, once more, shall we, who have gained so much, forgo this gain, the earliest, most natural gain of mankind? If we have to a great extent done so, as I verily fear we have, what strange foglights must have misled us; or rather let me say, how hard pressed we must have been in the battle with the evils we have overcome, to have forgotten the greatest of all evils. I cannot call it less than that. If a man has work to do which he despises, which does not satisfy his natural and rightful desire for pleasure, the greater part of his life must pass unhappily and without self-

2 Priest, from Mas or Mass (Master) John, a name once applied contemptuously to a Scotch Presbyterian minister.

respect. Consider, I beg of you, what that means, and what ruin must come of it in the end.

If I could only persuade you of this, that the chief duty of the civilized world to-day is to set about making labour happy for all, to do its utmost to minimize the amount of unhappy labour—nay, if I could only persuade some two or three of you here present—I should have made a good night's work of it.

Do not, at any rate, shelter yourselves from any misgiving you may have behind the fallacy that the art-lacking labour of to-day is happy work: for the most of men it is not so. It would take long, perhaps, to show you, and make you fully understand that the would-be art which it produces is joyless. But there is another token of its being most unhappy work, which you cannot fail to understand at once—a grievous thing that token is—and I beg of you to believe that I feel the full shame of it, as I stand here speaking of it; but if we do not admit that we are sick, how can we be healed? This hapless token is, that the work done by the civilized world is mostly dishonest work. Look now: I admit that civilization does make certain things well, things which it knows, consciously or unconsciously, are necessary to its present unhealthy condition. These things, to speak shortly, are chiefly machines for carrying on the competition in buying and selling called falsely commerce; and machines for the violent destruction of life—that is to say, materials for two kinds of war; of which kinds the last is no doubt the worst, not so much in itself perhaps, but because on this point the conscience of the world is beginning to be somewhat pricked. But, on the other hand, matters for the carrying on of a dignified daily life, that life of mutual trust, forbearance, and help, which is the only real life of thinking men— these things the civilized world makes ill, and even increasingly worse and worse.

If I am wrong in saying this, you know well I am only saying what is widely thought, nay widely said too, for that matter. Let me give an instance, familiar enough, of that widespread opinion. There is a very clever book of pictures now being sold at the railway bookstalls, called *The British Working Man, by one who does not believe in him*—a title and a book which make me both angry and ashamed, because the two express much injustice, and not a little truth in their quaint, and necessarily exaggerated way. It is quite true, and very sad to say, that if any one nowadays wants a piece of ordinary work done by gardener, carpenter, mason, dyer, weaver, smith, what you will, he will be a lucky rarity if he get it well done. He will, on the contrary, meet on every side with evasion of plain duties, and disregard of other men's rights; yet I cannot see how the "British Working Man" is to be made to bear the whole burden of this blame, or indeed the chief part of it. I doubt if it be possible for a whole mass of men to do work to which they are driven, and in which there is no hope and no pleasure, without trying to shirk it—at any rate, shirked it has always been under such circumstances. On the other hand, I know that there are some men so right-minded, that they will, in despite of irksomeness and hopelessness, drive right through their work. Such men are the salt of the earth. But must there not be something wrong with a state of society which drives these into that bitter heroism, and the most part into shirking, into the depths often of half-conscious self-contempt and degradation? Be sure that there is, that the blindness and hurry of civilization as it now is, have to answer a heavy charge as to that enormous amount of pleasureless work —work that tries every muscle of the body and every atom of the brain, and which is done without pleasure and without aim—work which everybody who has to do with tries to shuffle off in the speediest way that dread of starvation or ruin will allow him.

I am as sure of one thing as that I am living and breathing, and it is this: that the dishonesty in the daily arts of life, complaints of which are in all men's mouths, and which I can answer for it does exist, is the natural and inevitable result of the world in the hurry of the war of the counting-house, and the war of the battlefield, having forgotten—of all men, I say, each for the other, having forgotten that pleasure in our daily labour which nature cries out for as its due.

Therefore, I say again, it is necessary to the further progress of civilization that men should turn their thoughts to some means of limiting, and in the end of doing away with, degrading labour.

I do not think my words hitherto spoken

have given you any occasion to think that I mean by this either hard or rough labour; I do not pity men much for their hardships, especially if they be accidental; not necessarily attached to one class or one condition, I mean. Nor do I think (I were crazy or dreaming else) that the work of the world can be carried on without rough labour; but I have seen enough of that to know that it need not be by any means degrading. To plough the earth, to cast the net, to fold the flock—these, and such as these, which are rough occupations enough, and which carry with them many hardships, are good enough for the best of us, certain conditions of leisure, freedom, and due wages being granted. As to the bricklayer, the mason, and the like—these would be artists, and doing not only necessary, but beautiful, and therefore happy work, if art were anything like what it should be. No, it is not such labour as this which we need to do away with, but the toil which makes the thousand and one things which nobody wants, which are used merely as the counters for the competitive buying and selling, falsely called commerce, which I have spoken of before—I know in my heart, and not merely by my reason, that this toil cries out to be done away with. But, besides that, the labour which now makes things good and necessary in themselves, merely as counters for the commercial war aforesaid, needs regulating and reforming. Nor can this reform be brought about save by art; and if we were only come to our right minds, and could see the necessity for making labour sweet to all men, as it is now to very few—the necessity, I repeat; lest discontent, unrest, and despair should at last swallow up all society—If we, then, with our eyes cleared, could but make some sacrifice of things which do us no good, since we unjustly and uneasily possess them, then indeed I believe we should sow the seeds of a happiness which the world has not yet known, of a rest and content which would make it what I cannot help thinking it was meant to be: and with that seed would be sown also the seed of real art, the expression of man's happiness in his labour—an art made by the people, and for the people, as a happiness to the maker and the user.

That is the only real art there is, the only art which will be an instrument to the progress of the world, and not a hindrance. Nor can I seriously doubt that in your hearts you know that it is so, all of you, at any rate, who have in you an instinct for art. I believe that you agree with me in this, though you may differ from much else that I have said. I think assuredly that this is the art whose welfare we have met together to further, and the necessary instruction in which we have undertaken to spread as widely as may be.

Thus I have told you something of what I think is to be hoped and feared for the future of Art; and if you ask me what I expect as a practical outcome of the admission of these opinions, I must say at once that I know, even if we were all of one mind, and that what I think the right mind on this subject, we should still have much work and many hindrances before us; we should still have need of all the prudence, foresight, and industry of the best among us; and, even so, our path would sometimes seem blind enough. And, to-day, when the opinions which we think right, and which one day will be generally thought so, have to struggle sorely to make themselves noticed at all, it is early days for us to try to see our exact and clearly mapped road. I suppose you will think it too commonplace of me to say that the general education that makes men think, will one day make them think rightly upon art. Commonplace as it is, I really believe it, and am indeed encouraged by it, when I remember how obviously this age is one of transition from the old to the new, and what a strange confusion, from out of which we shall one day come, our ignorance and half-ignorance is like to make of the exhausted rubbish of the old and the crude rubbish of the new, both of which lie so ready to our hands.

But, if I must say, furthermore, any words that seem like words of practical advice, I think my task is hard, and I fear I shall offend some of you whatever I say; for this is indeed an affair of morality, rather than of what people call art.

However, I cannot forget that, in my mind, it is not possible to dissociate art from morality, politics, and religion. Truth in these great matters of principle is of one, and it is only in formal treatises that it can be split up diversely. I must also ask you to remember how I have already said, that though my mouth alone speaks, it speaks, however feebly and disjointedly, the thoughts of many men better than myself. And further, though when thing are tending to the best, we shall still, as aforesaid, need our best men to lead us quite right; yet even now surely, when it is far from that, the least of us can do some yeoman's service to the cause, and live and die not without honour.

So I will say that I believe there are two virtues much needed in modern life, if it is ever to become sweet; and I am quite sure that they are absolutely necessary in the sowing the seed of an *art which is to be made by the people and for the people, as a happiness to the maker and the user*. These virtues are honesty, and simplicity of life. To make my meaning clearer I will name the opposing vice of the second of these—luxury to wit. Also I mean by honesty, the careful and eager giving his due to every man, the determination not to gain by any man's loss, which in my experience is not a common virtue.

But note how the practice of either of these virtues will make the other easier to us. For if our wants are few, we shall have but little chance of being driven by our wants into injustice; and if we are fixed in the principle of giving every man his due, how can our self-respect bear that we should give too much to ourselves?

And in art, and in that preparation for it without which no art that is stable or worthy can be, the raising, namely, of those classes which have heretofore been degraded, the practice of these virtues would make a new world of it. For if you are rich, your simplicity of life will both go towards smoothing over the dreadful contrast between waste and want, which is the great horror of civilized countries, and will also give an example and standard of dignified life to those classes which you desire to raise, who, as it is indeed, being like enough to rich people, are given both to envy and to imitate the idleness and waste that the possession of much money produces.

Nay, and apart from the morality of the matter, which I am forced to speak to you of, let me tell you that though simplicity in art may be costly as well as uncostly, at least it is not wasteful, and nothing is more destructive to art than the want of it. I have never been in any rich man's house which would not have looked the better for having a bonfire made outside of it of nine-tenths of all that it held. Indeed, our sacrifice on the side of luxury will, it seems to me, be little or nothing: for, as far as I can make out, what people usually mean by it, is either a gathering of possessions which are sheer vexations to the owner, or a chain of pompous circumstance, which checks and annoys the rich man at every step. Yes, luxury cannot exist without slavery of some kind or other, and its abolition will be blessed, like the abolition of other slaveries, by the freeing both of the slaves and of their masters.

Lastly, if, besides attaining to simplicity of life, we attain also to the love of justice, then will all things be ready for the new springtime of the arts. For those of us that are employers of labour, how can we bear to give any man less money than he can decently live on, less leisure than his education and self-respect demand? or those of us who are workmen, how can we bear to fail in the contract we have undertaken, or to make it necessary for a foreman to go up and down spying out our mean tricks and evasions? or we the shopkeepers—can we endure to lie about our wares, that we may shuffle off our losses on to someone else's shoulders? or we the public—how can we bear to pay a price for a piece of goods which will help to trouble one man, to ruin another, and starve a third? Or, still more, I think, how can we bear to use, how can we enjoy something which has been a pain and a grief for the maker to make?

And now, I think, I have said what I came to say. I confess that there is nothing new in it, but you know the experience of the world is that a thing must be said over and over again before any great number of men can be got to listen to it. Let my words to-night, therefore, pass for one of the necessary times that the thought in them must be spoken out.

For the rest I believe that, however seriously these words may be gainsaid, I have been speaking to an audience in whom any words spoken from a sense of duty and in hearty good-will, as mine have been, will quicken thought and sow some good seed. At any rate, it is good for a man who thinks seriously to face his fellows, and speak out whatever really burns in him, so that men may seem less strange to one another, and misunderstanding, the fruitful cause of aimless strife, may be avoided.

But if to any of you I have seemed to speak hopelessly, my words have been lacking in art; and you must remember that hopelessness would have locked my mouth, not opened it. I am, indeed, hopeful, but can I give a date to the accomplishment of my hope, and say that it will happen in my life or yours?

But I will say at least, Courage! for things wonderful, unhoped-for, glorious, have happened even in this short while I have been alive.

Yes, surely these times are wonderful and fruitful of change, which, as it wears and gathers new life even in its wearing, will one day bring better things for the toiling days of men, who, with freer hearts and clearer eyes, will once more gain the sense of outward beauty, and rejoice in it.

Meanwhile, if these hours be dark, as, indeed, in many ways they are, at least do not let us sit deedless, like fools and fine gentlemen, thinking the common toil not good enough for us, and beaten by the muddle; but rather let us work like good fellows trying by some dim candle-light to set our workshop ready against to-morrow's daylight—that to-morrow, when the civilized world, no longer greedy, strifeful, and destructive, shall have a new art, a glorious art, made by the people and for the people, as a happiness to the maker and the user.

Algernon Charles Swinburne

1837–1909

Swinburne, who was of aristocratic stock, was slight and delicate in build, but was so fired with nervous energy that he was in a constant ferment of physical activity and intellectual excitement. Too restive to accept the usual restraints of university life, he left Oxford without a degree to take up a Bohemian existence in London. In the succeeding twenty years he wrote and published feverishly both poetry and criticism, until by 1879 his erratic and uncontrolled way of living had so burnt up his limited physique that he was on the verge of collapse, and was led to retire into seclusion and almost complete inactivity for the remaining thirty years of his life.

From 1859 to 1879, however, staid but troubled Victorian England had no more outspoken rebel than Swinburne, and his right-minded contemporaries regarded him with a mixture of horror and fear. They remembered Shelley's revolt some two generations before. Only, to make matters worse, this new outbreak was the more extravagant on the one hand because of the somewhat flamboyant temperament of Swinburne, and the more insidious on the other because the lyrical cadences of his verse were so charming that almost in spite of oneself one was attracted to poetry filled with noxious and revolutionary themes. The radical character of his mind was unnoticed at first in his brilliant reproduction of the form of Greek tragedy in *Atalanta in Calydon* (1865), but with the publication of *Poems and Ballads* (1866) it became clear that here was a threat to all that the Victorians were struggling to uphold. The representa-tive "Hymn to Proserpine" not only extolled that goddess but likewise condemned the sway of the pale Galilean as gray, lifeless, sorrowful, and even worse, as transitory:

Yet thy kingdom shall pass, Galilean, thy dead shall go down to thee dead.

Shocking as this scorn of Christianity was in itself, it provoked less of an outcry than the ideal which was exalted in its stead—no mere abstract Platonism, as in the case of Shelley, but an unabashed naturalism, a glorification of man's senses and the free expansion of his whole being, mental and physical. So violent, indeed, was Swinburne's rejection of the stultifying morality of his time that he could not resist the temptation to exaggerate those sensuous elements most likely to offend his readers, in such poems, for instance, as "Laus Veneris" and "Sapphics." It was, says Thomas Hardy, "as though a garland of red roses had fallen about the hood of some smug nun."

In addition to release from the gloom of Christian doctrine and escape from moral prudishness, there was yet a third freedom championed by Swinburne, as it had been by Shelley too, namely, political liberty. Under the influence of Mazzini, Swinburne pleaded for the cause of Italian nationalism; stirred by Victor Hugo, he bitterly denounced Louis Napoleon for betraying the French Republic. These were the preoccupations which later inspired his *Songs Before Sunrise* (1871), although the challenge to the

Algernon Charles Swinburne (1837–1909). A radical such as English poetry had not seen since Shelley, Swinburne trampled with enthusiasm on ideals of Victorian morality and promoted an unashamed sensuousness. *Radio Times Hulton Picture Library.*

hierarchy in both church and state had already been clearly sounded in "A Song in Time of Order, 1852" (*Songs and Ballads*), in which Bonaparte was termed a bastard and the Pope was condemned to the galleys. Similarly, his admiration for freedom and democracy in the New World inspired "To Walt Whitman in America," which gave voice to his disgust with the discords of Europe and begged that the vivifying spirit of American liberty might "rise and remain and take station" in the Old World as well.

Just as he considered America the home of political freedom, so he saw the ancient world as the scene of moral and social freedom. This attitude, together with an unusually fine knowledge of both Greek and Latin literature, accounts for his fascination with classical models and themes. It was, he felt, primarily in pre-Christian times that man had been truly free, free of the bonds of a sorrowing asceticism and a hypocritical prudery. But in the Middle Ages, too, he found, in such subjects as the Tannhäuser Venus and in such poets as Villon, outspoken delight in sensuous enjoyment and defiance of conventional

tabus; and it was only natural that he should have hailed his own contemporary, Charles Baudelaire, for these same qualities.

A corollary to his demand for freedom from the shackles of contemporary standards was his reaction against the current didactic and moralistic tendencies of Victorian poetry; and in his essay on Baudelaire (1862) he flares out, "Critical students . . . seem to have pretty well forgotten that a poet's business is presumably to write good verses, and by no means to redeem the age and remould society." Now this from a poet who in his own way was trying his best to remold society and redeem the age from tyranny as well as from cant and hypocrisy calls for an explanation. Aware of this, Swinburne in an essay on Victor Hugo attempted a reconciliation, defining his position in terms of the contemporary Aesthetic Movement: "The one primary requisite of art is artistic worth; art for art's sake first, and then all things shall be added to her—or if not, it is a matter of quite secondary importance. . . . On the other hand we refuse to admit that art of the highest kind may not ally itself with moral or religious passion, with the ethics or the politics of a nation or an age." This statement of Swinburne's poetic creed was in conformity with both his temperament and his gifts. It allowed him to give free rein to his love of sound and pattern, of metrical brilliance, and of song for singing's sake, and thus to become, on the musical side, the leading poet of the Aesthetic Movement; yet it justified the intense expression of his moral, social, and political convictions.

There was, however, a fundamental flaw in Swinburne which kept him from realizing the ideal he had set up. He was too facile, too undisciplined. He allowed his thought to become blurred in a maze of beautiful sound, and he let himself be floated away on a sea of words—words as such, in which even the image was sometimes lost or distorted. The result was a vagueness and diffusion, which, on occasion, almost nullifies meaning, and which, of course, accounts for the length of many of his poems, where he seems literally unable to set a term. He had a genius for words; but, as Hopkins remarked with Swinburne in mind, "words only are only words."

TEXTS: The standard edition is *The Complete Works* (20 vols., 1925–27) edited by Sir Edmund Gosse and T. J. Wise. Perhaps the best biography is G. Lafourcade's *Swinburne. A Literary Biography* (1932). R. L. Peters's *The Crown of Apollo* (1965) is a valuable study of Swinburne's poetics. The liveliest essays are T. S. Eliot's "Swinburne as Poet" (1920), reprinted in his *Selected Essays* (1932), and J. D. Rosenberg's "Swinburne," *Victorian Studies*, XI (1967),

131–52. E.M.W. Tillyard analyzes "Hertha" in his *Five Poems* (1948).

Choruses *from* Atalanta in Calydon

1

When the hounds of spring are on winter's traces,
  The mother of months[1] in meadow or plain
Fills the shadows and windy places
  With lisp of leaves and ripple of rain;
And the brown bright nightingale amorous   5
Is half assuaged for Itylus,
For the Thracian ships and the foreign faces,
  The tongueless vigil, and all the pain.[2]

Come with bows bent and with emptying of
    quivers,
  Maiden most perfect, lady of light,   10
With a noise of winds and many rivers,
  With a clamor of waters, and with might;
Bind on thy sandals, O thou most fleet,
Over the splendor and speed of thy feet;
For the faint east quickens, the wan west shivers, 15
  Round the feet of the day and the feet of the
    night.

Where shall we find her, how shall we sing to her,
  Fold our hands round her knees, and cling?
O that man's heart were as fire and could spring
    to her,
  Fire, or the strength of the streams that spring! 20
For the stars and the winds are unto her
As raiment, as songs of the harp-player;
For the risen stars and the fallen cling to her,
  And the southwest-wind and the west-wind
    sing.

For winter's rains and ruins are over,   25
  And all the season of snows and sins;
The days dividing lover and lover,
  The light that loses, the night that wins;
And time remembered is grief forgotten,

And frosts are slain and flowers begotten,   30
And in green underwood and cover
  Blossom by blossom the spring begins.

The full streams feed on flower of rushes,
  Ripe grasses trammel a traveling foot,
The faint fresh flame of the young year flushes 35
  From leaf to flower and flower to fruit;
And fruit and leaf are as gold and fire,
And the oat[3] is heard above the lyre,
And the hoofèd heel of a satyr crushes
  The chestnut-husk at the chestnut-root.   40

And Pan by noon and Bacchus by night,
  Fleeter of foot than the fleet-foot kid,
Follows with dancing and fills with delight
  The Maenad and the Bassarid;[4]
And soft as lips that laugh and hide   45
The laughing leaves of the trees divide,
And screen from seeing and leave in sight
  The god pursuing, the maiden hid.

The ivy falls with the Bacchanal's hair
  Over her eyebrows hiding her eyes;   50
The wild vine slipping down leaves bare
  Her bright breast shortening into sighs;
The wild vine slips with the weight of its leaves,
But the berried ivy catches and cleaves
To the limbs that glitter, the feet that scare   55
  The wolf that follows, the fawn that flies.

2

Before the beginning of years
  There came to the making of man
Time, with a gift of tears;
  Grief, with a glass that ran;   60
Pleasure, with pain for leaven;
  Summer, with flowers that fell;
Remembrance fallen from heaven,
  And madness risen from hell;
Strength without hands to smite;   65
  Love that endures for a breath:
Night, the shadow of light,
  And life, the shadow of death.

And the high gods took in hand
  Fire, and the falling of tears,   70
And a measure of sliding sand
  From under the feet of the years;

---

1 Diana or Artemis, mother of months because goddess of the moon.
2 These lines refer to the rape of Philomela by her brother-in-law, Tereus, king of Thrace. To ensure silence about his misdeed, Tereus tore out his victim's tongue, but she still managed to inform her sister Procne. Procne in revenge killed her son Itylus and fed his body to his unsuspecting father. The sisters then fled, Procne in the shape of a swallow, Philomela in that of a nightingale.

3 Musical pipe made of an oat straw, played by shepherds.
4 Followers of Bacchus.

And froth and drift of the sea;
  And dust of the laboring earth;
And bodies of things to be   75
  In the houses of death and of birth;
And wrought with weeping and laughter,
  And fashioned with loathing and love
With life before and after
  And death beneath and above,   80
For a day and a night and a morrow,
  That his strength might endure for a span
With travail and heavy sorrow,
  The holy spirit of man.

From the winds of the north and the south 85
  They gathered as unto strife;
They breathed upon his mouth,
  They filled his body with life;
Eyesight and speech they wrought
  For the veils of the soul therein,   90
A time for labor and thought,
  A time to serve and to sin;
They gave him light in his ways,
  And love, and a space for delight,
And beauty and length of days,   95
  And night, and sleep in the night.
His speech is a burning fire;
  With his lips he travaileth;
In his heart is a blind desire,
  In his eyes foreknowledge of death; 100
He weaves, and is clothed with derision;
  Sows, and he shall not reap;
His life is a watch or a vision
  Between a sleep and a sleep.

Hymn to Proserpine

(After the Proclamation in Rome of the Christian Faith)[1]

Vicisti, Galilæe[2]

I have lived long enough, having seen one thing, that love hath an end;
Goddess and maiden and queen, be near me now and befriend.
Thou art more than the day or the morrow, the seasons that laugh or that weep;

For these give joy and sorrow; but thou, Proserpina, sleep.
Sweet is the treading of wine, and sweet the feet 5
  of the dove;
But a goodlier gift is thine than foam of the grapes or love.
Yea, is not even Apollo, with hair and harpstring of gold,
A bitter God to follow, a beautiful God to behold?
I am sick of singing: the bays[3] burn deep and chafe: I am fain
To rest a little from praise and grievous pleasure 10
  and pain.
For the Gods we know not of, who give us our daily breath,
We know they are cruel as love or life, and lovely as death.
O Gods dethroned and deceased, cast forth, wiped out in a day!
From your wrath is the world released, redeemed from your chains, men say.
New Gods[4] are crowned in the city; their flowers 15
  have broken your rods;
They are merciful, clothed with pity, the young compassionate Gods.
But for me their new device is barren, the days are bare;
Things long past over suffice, and men forgotten that were.
Time and the Gods are at strife; ye dwell in the midst thereof,
Draining a little life from the barren breasts of 20
  love.
I say to you, cease, take rest; yea, I say to you all, be at peace,
Till the bitter milk of her breast and the barren bosom shall cease.
Wilt thou yet take all, Galilean? but these thou shalt not take,
The laurel, the palms and the paean, the breast of the nymphs in the brake;
Breasts more soft than a dove's that tremble with 25
  tenderer breath;
And all the wings of the Loves, and all the joy before death;
All the feet of the hours that sound as a single lyre,

---

1 After Constantine's Edict of Milan (313), which proclaimed official toleration of the Christian religion.
2 "You have conquered, O Galilean"—reported to have been the dying words of the Emperor Julian (d. 363), who in his lifetime had denied Christianity.

3 The bay or laurel leaves forming the poet's crown.
4 The Christian saints.

Dropped and deep in the flowers, with strings
that flicker like fire.

More than these wilt thou give, things fairer
than all these things?

Nay, for a little we live, and life hath mutable   30
wings.

A little while and we die; shall life not thrive
as it may?

For no man under the sky lives twice, outliving
his day.

And grief is a grievous thing, and a man hath
enough of his tears:

Why should he labor, and bring fresh grief to
blacken his years?

Thou hast conquered, O pale Galilean; the world   35
has grown gray from thy breath;

We have drunken of things Lethean,[5] and fed
on the fulness of death.

Laurel is green for a season, and love is sweet
for a day;

But love grows bitter with treason, and laurel
outlives not May.

Sleep, shall we sleep after all? for the world is
not sweet in the end;

For the old faiths loosen and fall, the new years   40
ruin and rend.

Fate is a sea without shore, and the soul is a rock
that abides;

But her ears are vexed with the roar and her face
with the foam of the tides.

O lips that the live blood faints in, the leavings
of racks and rods!

O ghastly glories of saints, dead limbs of gibbeted
Gods!

Though all men abase them before you in spirit,   45
and all knees bend,

I kneel not neither adore you, but standing, look
to the end.

All delicate days and pleasant, all spirits and
sorrows are cast

Far out with the foam of the present that sweeps
to the surf of the past:

Where beyond the extreme sea-wall, and between
the remote sea-gates,

Waste water washes, and tall ships founder, and   50
deep death waits:

Where, mighty with deepening sides, clad about
with the seas as with wings,

And impelled of invisible tides, and fulfilled of
unspeakable things,

White-eyed and poisonous-finned, shark-toothed
and serpentine-curled,

Rolls, under the whitening wind of the future,
the wave of the world.

The depths stand naked in sunder behind it, the   55
storms flee away;

In the hollow before it the thunder is taken and
snared as a prey;

In its sides is the north-wind bound; and its salt
is of all men's tears;

With light of ruin, and sound of changes, and
pulse of years;

With travail of day after day, and with trouble
of hour upon hour;

And bitter as blood is the spray; and the crests   60
are as fangs that devour:

And its vapor and storm of its steam as the sighing of spirits to be;

And its noise as the noise in a dream; and its
depth as the roots of the sea:

And the height of its heads as the height of the
utmost stars of the air:

And the ends of the earth at the might thereof
tremble, and time is made bare.

Will ye bridle the deep sea with reins, will ye   65
chasten the high sea with rods?

Will ye take her to chain her with chains, who
is older than all ye Gods?

All ye as a wind shall go by, as a fire shall ye
pass and be past;

Ye are Gods, and behold, ye shall die, and the
waves be upon you at last.

In the darkness of time, in the deeps of the years,
in the changes of things,

Ye shall sleep as a slain man sleeps, and the   70
world shall forget you for kings.

Though the feet of thine high priests tread where
thy lords and our forefathers trod,

Though these that were Gods are dead, and thou
being dead are a God,

Though before thee the throned Cytherean[6] be
fallen, and hidden her head,

Yet thy kingdom shall pass, Galilean, thy dead
shall go down to thee dead.

Of the maiden thy mother men sing as a goddess   75
with grace clad around;

---

[5] Lethe, the river of forgetfulness, was crossed by the dead
on their way to the Underworld.
[6] Aphrodite, or Venus, reputedly born of the foam near
Cythera.

Thou art throned where another was king; where another was queen she is crowned.

Yea, once we had sight of another: but now she is queen, say these.

Not as thine, not as thine was our mother, a blossom of flowering seas,

Clothed round with the world's desire as with raiment, and fair as the foam,

And fleeter than kindled fire, and a goddess, and mother of Rome.[7]   80

For thine came pale and a maiden, and sister to sorrow; but ours,

Her deep hair heavily laden with odor and color of flowers,

White rose of the rose-white water, a silver splendor, a flame,

Bent down unto us that besought her, and earth grew sweet with her name.

For thine came weeping, a slave among slaves, and rejected; but she   85

Came flushed from the full-flushed wave, and imperial, her foot on the sea.

And the wonderful waters knew her, the winds and the viewless ways,

And the roses grew rosier, and bluer the sea-blue stream of the bays.

Ye are fallen, our lords, by what token? we wist that ye should not fall.

Ye were all so fair that are broken; and one more fair than ye all.   90

But I turn to her still, having seen she shall surely abide in the end;

Goddess and maiden and queen, be near me now and befriend.

O daughter of earth, of my mother, her crown and blossom of birth,

I am also, I also, thy brother; I go as I came unto earth.

In the night where thine eyes are as moons are in heaven, the night where thou art,   95

Where the silence is more than all tunes, where sleep overflows from the heart,

Where the poppies are sweet as the rose in our world, and the red rose is white,

And the wind falls faint as it blows with the fume of the flowers of the night,

And the murmur of spirits that sleep in the shadow of Gods from afar

Grows dim in thine ears and deep as the deep dim soul of a star,   100

In the sweet low light of thy face, under heavens untrod by the sun,

Let my soul with their souls find place, and forget what is done and undone.

Thou art more than the Gods who number the days of our temporal breath;

For these give labor and slumber; but thou, Proserpina, death.

Therefore now at thy feet I abide for a season in silence. I know   105

I shall die as my fathers died, and sleep as they sleep; even so.

For the glass of the years is brittle wherein we gaze for a span;

A little soul for a little bears up this corpse which is man.

So long I endure, no longer; and laugh not again, neither weep.

For there is no God found stronger than death;   110 and death is a sleep.

The Garden of Proserpine[1]

Here, where the world is quiet;
  Here, where all trouble seems
Dead winds' and spent waves' riot
  In doubtful dreams of dreams;
I watch the green field growing   5
For reaping folk and sowing,
For harvest-time and mowing,
  A sleepy world of streams.

I am tired of tears and laughter,
  And men that laugh and weep;   10
Of what may come hereafter
  For men that sow to reap:
I am weary of days and hours,
Blown buds of barren flowers,
Desires and dreams and powers   15
  And everything but sleep.

Here life has death for neighbor,
  And far from eye or ear
Wan waves and wet winds labor,
  Weak ships and spirits steer;   20
They drive adrift, and whither
They wot not who make thither;

---

[7] Aeneas was believed to have been the son of Aphrodite.

[1] The land of the dead, whose queen is Proserpine.

But no such winds blow hither,
　　And no such things grow here.

No growth of moor or coppice,   25
　　No heather-flower or vine,
But bloomless buds of poppies,
　　Green grapes of Proserpine,
Pale beds of blowing rushes
Where no leaf blooms or blushes   30
Save this whereout she crushes
　　For dead men deadly wine.

Pale, without name or number,
　　In fruitless fields of corn,
They bow themselves and slumber   35
　　All night till light is born;
And like a soul belated,
In hell and heaven unmated,
By cloud and mist abated
　　Comes out of darkness morn.   40

Though one were strong as seven,
　　He too with death shall dwell,
Nor wake with wings in heaven,
　　Nor weep for pains in hell;
Though one were fair as roses,   45
His beauty clouds and closes;
And well though love reposes,
　　In the end it is not well.

Pale, beyond porch and portal,
　　Crowned with calm leaves, she stands   50
Who gathers all things mortal
　　With cold immortal hands;
Her languid lips are sweeter
Than love's who fears to greet her,
To men that mix and meet her   55
　　From many times and lands.

She waits for each and other,
　　She waits for all men born;
Forgets the earth her mother,
　　The life of fruits and corn;   60
And spring and seed and swallow
Take wing for her and follow
Where summer song rings hollow
　　And flowers are put to scorn.

There go the loves that wither,   65
　　The old lives with wearier wings;
And all dead years draw thither,
　　And all disastrous things;

Dead dreams of days forsaken,
Blind buds that snows have shaken,   70
Wild leaves that winds have taken,
　　Red strays of ruined springs.

We are not sure of sorrow,
　　And joy was never sure;
To-day will die to-morrow;   75
　　Time stoops to no man's lure;
And love, grown faint and fretful,
With lips but half regretful
Sighs, and with eyes forgetful
　　Weeps that no loves endure.   80

From too much love of living,
　　From hope and fear set free,
We thank with brief thanksgiving
　　Whatever gods may be
That no life lives for ever;   85
That dead men rise up never;
That even the weariest river
　　Winds somewhere safe to sea.

Then star nor sun shall waken,
　　Nor any change of light: 90
Nor sound of waters shaken,
　　Nor any sound or sight:
Nor wintry leaves nor vernal,
Nor days nor things diurnal;
Only the sleep eternal   95
　　In an eternal night.

A Ballad of François Villon[1]

Prince of All Ballad-Makers

Bird of the bitter bright gray golden morn
　　Scarce risen upon the dusk of dolorous years,
First of us all the sweetest singer born,
　　Whose far shrill note the world of new men
　　　hears
　　Cleave the cold shuddering shade as twilight   5
　　　clears;
When song new-born put off the old world's
　　attire[2]

---

[1] Villon, the great fifteenth-century French poet, was also
a thief and a rascal who was more than once in prison
and had a narrow escape from the gallows. Swinburne's
praise of such a social reprobate naturally scandalized
his critics, but the skill with which he imitated Villon's
favorite stanzaic form delighted his admirers.
[2] Swinburne considers Villon the first of the modern, as
distinguished from the medieval, poets.

And felt its tune on her changed lips expire,
  Writ foremost on the roll of them that came
Fresh girt for service of the latter lyre,
  Villon, our sad bad glad mad brother's name!   10

Alas the joy, the sorrow, and the scorn,
  That clothed thy life with hopes and sins and
    fears,
And gave thee stones for bread and tares for corn
  And plume-plucked gaol-birds for thy starve-
    ling peers
  Till death clipped close their flight with   15
    shameful shears;
Till shifts came short[3] and loves were hard to
  hire,
When lilt of song nor twitch of twangling wire
  Could buy thee bread or kisses; when light
    fame
Spurned like a ball and haled through brake
  and briar,
  Villon, our sad bad glad mad brother's name!   20

Poor splendid wings so frayed and soiled and
  torn!
  Poor kind wild eyes so dashed with light quick
    tears!
Poor perfect voice, most blithe when most for-
  lorn,
  That rings athwart the sea whence no man
    steers,
  Like joy-bells crossed with death-bells in our   25
    ears!
What far delight has cooled the fierce desire
That like some ravenous bird was strong to tire
  On that frail flesh and soul consumed with
    flame,
But left more sweet than roses to respire,
  Villon, our sad bad glad mad brother's name?   30

ENVOI

Prince of sweet songs made out of tears and fire,
A harlot was thy nurse, a God thy sire;[4]
  Shame soiled thy song, and song assoiled thy
    shame,
But from thy feet now death has washed the mire,
Love reads out first at head of all our quire,   35
  Villon, our sad bad glad mad brother's name.

---

[3] A shift was a woman's garment. The meaning is, "Till
there was a shortage of women."
[4] Although baseborn, Villon was a son of Apollo, god
of poetry.

Hertha[1]

I am that which began;
  Out of me the years roll;
Out of me God and man;
  I am equal[2] and whole;
God changes, and man, and the form of them   5
  bodily; I am the soul.

Before ever land was,
  Before ever the sea,
Or soft hair of the grass,
  Or fair limbs of the tree,
Or the flesh-colored fruit of my branches, I was,   10
  and thy soul was in me.

First life on my sources
  First drifted and swam;
Out of me are the forces
  That save it or damn;
Out of me man and woman, and wild-beast and   15
  bird; before God was, I am.[3]

Beside or above me
  Nought is there to go;
Love or unlove me,
  Unknow me or know,
I am that which unloves me and loves; I am   20
  stricken, and I am the blow.

I the mark that is missed
  And the arrows that miss,
I the mouth that is kissed
  And the breath in the kiss,
The search, and the sought, and the seeker, the   25
  soul and the body that is.

I am that thing which blesses
  My spirit elate;
That which caresses
  With hands uncreate[4]
My limbs unbegotten that measure the length of   30
  the measure of fate.

---

[1] The speaker in this poem is the Germanic goddess of
earth and growth, whom Swinburne here makes the
original source of all being. He regarded this poem as one
of his best in that it had "lyric force and music" combined with "condensed and clarified thought."
[2] All of one nature.
[3] Cf. the words of Jesus in John 8:58, "Before Abraham
was, I am," echoed here probably with satiric intent.
[4] Not created, but having always existed; cf. "unbegotten"
in the next line.

But what thing dost thou now,
  Looking Godward, to cry
"I am I, thou art thou,
  I am low, thou art high"?
I am thou, whom thou seekest to find him; find   35
  thou but thyself, thou art I.

I the grain and the furrow,
  The plough-cloven clod
And the ploughshare drawn thorough,
  The germ and the sod,
The deed and the doer, the seed and the sower,   40
  the dust which is God.

Hast thou known how I fashioned thee,
  Child, underground?
Fire that impassioned thee,
  Iron that bound,
Dim changes of water, what thing of all these   45
  hast thou known of or found?

Canst thou say in thine heart
  Thou hast seen with thine eyes
With what cunning of art
  Thou wast wrought in what wise,
By what force of what stuff thou wast shapen,   50
  and shown on my breast to the skies?

Who hath given, who hath sold it thee,
  Knowledge of me?
Hath the wilderness told it thee?
    Hast thou learnt of the sea?
Hast thou communed in spirit with night? have   55
  the winds taken counsel with thee?

Have I set such a star
  To show light on thy brow
That thou sawest from afar
  What I show to thee now?
Have ye spoken as brethren together, the sun   60
  and the mountains and thou?

What is here, dost thou know it?
  What was, has thou known?
Prophet nor poet
  Nor tripod[5] nor throne
Nor spirit nor flesh can make answer, but only   65
  thy mother alone.

Mother, not maker,
  Born, and not made;
Though her children forsake her,
  Allured or afraid,
Praying prayers to the God of their fashion, she   70
  stirs not for all that have prayed.

A creed is a rod,
  And a crown is of night;
But this thing is God,
  To be man with thy might,
To grow straight in the strength of thy spirit,   75
  and live out thy life as the light.

I am in thee to save thee,
  As my soul in thee saith;
Give thou, as I gave thee,
  Thy life-blood and breath,
Green leaves of thy labor, white flowers of thy   80
  thought, and red fruit of thy death.

Be the ways of thy giving
  As mine were to thee;
The free life of thy living,
  Be the gift of it free;
Not as servant to lord, nor as master to slave,   85
  shalt thou give thee to me.

O children of banishment,
  Souls overcast,
Were the lights ye see vanish meant
  Always to last,
Ye would know not the sun overshining the shad-   90
  ows and stars overpast.

I that saw where ye trod
  The dim paths of the night
Set the shadow called God
  In your skies to give light;
But the morning of manhood is risen, and the   95
  shadowless soul is in sight.

The tree many-rooted
  That swells to the sky
With frondage red-fruited
  The life-tree am I;[6]
In the buds of your lives is the sap of my leaves: 100
  ye shall live and not die.

---

[5] The priestess at the famous oracular shrine of Apollo at Delphi sat upon a tripod. The reference here is probably to the church or priesthood.

[6] In Germanic mythology, the tree Igdrasil.

But the Gods of your fashion
   That take and that give,
In their pity and passion
   That scourge and forgive,
They are worms that are bred in the bark that 105
   falls off; they shall die and not live.

My own blood is what stanches
   The wounds in my bark;
Stars caught in my branches
   Make day of the dark,
And are worshipped as suns till the sunrise shall 110
   tread out their fires as a spark.

Where dead ages hide under
   The live roots of the tree,
In my darkness the thunder
   Makes utterance of me;
In the clash of my boughs with each other ye 115
   hear the waves sound of the sea.

That noise is of Time,
   As his feathers are spread
And his feet set to climb
   Through the boughs overhead,
And my foliage rings round him and rustles, 120
   and branches are bent with his tread.

The storm-winds of ages
   Blow through me and cease,
The war-wind that rages,
   The spring-wind of peace,
Ere the breath of them roughen my tresses, ere 125
   one of my blossoms increase.

All sounds of all changes,
   All shadows and lights
On the world's mountain-ranges
   And stream-riven heights,
Whose tongue is the wind's tongue and language 130
   of storm-clouds on earth-shaking nights;

All forms of all faces,
   All works of all hands
In unsearchable places
   Of time-stricken lands,
All death and all life, and all reigns and all 135
   ruins, drop through me as sands.

Though sore be my burden
   And more than ye know,

And my growth have no guerdon
   But only to grow,
Yet I fail not of growing for lightnings above 140
   me or deathworms below.

These too have their part in me,
   As I too in these;
Such fire is at heart in me,
   Such sap is this tree's,
Which hath in it all sounds and all secrets of 145
   infinite lands and of seas.

In the spring-colored hours
   When my mind was as May's,
There brake forth of me flowers
   By centuries of days,
Strong blossoms with perfume of manhood, shot 150
   out from my spirit as rays.

And the sound of them springing
   And smell of their shoots
Were as warmth and sweet singing
   And strength to my roots;
And the lives of my children made perfect with 155
   freedom of soul were my fruits.

I bid you but be;
   I have need not of prayer;
I have need of you free
   As your mouths of mine air;
That my heart may be greater within me, behold- 160
   ing the fruits of me fair.

More fair than strange fruit is
   Of faiths ye espouse;
In me only the root is
   That blooms in your boughs;
Behold now your God that ye made you, to feed 165
   him with faith of your vows.

In the darkening and whitening
   Abysses adored,
With dayspring and lightning
   For lamp and for sword,
God thunders in heaven, and his angels are red 170
   with the wrath of the Lord.

O my sons, O too dutiful
   Towards Gods not of me,
Was not I enough beautiful?
   Was it hard to be free?

For behold, I am with you, am in you and of 175
  you; look forth now and see.

Lo, winged with world's wonders,
  With miracles shod,
With the fires of his thunders
  For raiment and rod,
God trembles in heaven, and his angels are white 180
  with the terror of God.

For his twilight[7] is come on him,
  His anguish is here;
And his spirits gaze dumb on him,
  Grown gray from his fear;
And his hour taketh hold on him stricken, the 185
  last of his infinite year.

Thought made him and breaks him,
  Truth slays and forgives;
But to you, as time takes him,
  This new thing it gives,
Even love, the beloved Republic, that feeds upon 190
  freedom and lives.

For truth only is living,
  Truth only is whole,
And the love of his giving
  Man's polestar and pole;
Man, pulse of my center, and fruit of my body, 195
  and seed of my soul.

One birth of my bosom;
  One beam of mine eye;
One topmost blossom
  That scales the sky;
Man, equal and one with me, man that is made 200
  of me, man that is I.

To Walt Whitman in America

Send but a song oversea for us,
  Heart of their hearts who are free,
Heart of their singer, to be for us
  More than our singing can be;
Ours, in the tempest at error, 5

With no light but the twilight of terror;[1]
  Send us a song oversea!

Sweet-smelling of pine-leaves and grasses,
  And blown as a tree through and through
With the winds of the keen mountain-passes, 10
  And tender as sun-smitten dew;
Sharp-tongued as the winter that shakes
The wastes of your limitless lakes,
  Wide-eyed as the sea-line's blue.

O strong-winged soul with prophetic 15
  Lips hot with the bloodbeats of song,
With tremor of heartstrings magnetic,
  With thoughts as thunders in throng,
With consonant ardors of chords
That pierce men's souls as with swords 20
  And hale them hearing along,

Make us too music, to be with us
  As a word from a world's heart warm,
To sail the dark as a sea with us,
  Full-sailed, outsinging the storm, 25
A song to put fire in our ears
Whose burning shall burn up tears,
  Whose sign bid battle reform;

A note in the ranks of a clarion,
  A word in the wind of cheer, 30
To consume as with lightning the carrion
  That makes time foul for us here;
In the air that our dead things[2] infest
A blast of the breath of the west,
  Till east way as west way is clear. 35

Out of the sun beyond sunset,
  From the evening whence morning shall be,
With the rollers in measureless onset,
  With the van of the storming sea,
With the world-wide wind, with the breath 40
That breaks ships driven upon death,
  With the passion of all things free,

With the sea-steeds footless and frantic,
  White myriads for death to bestride

---

7 Swinburne here adapts the Germanic myth that foretold the "twilight" and fall of the gods as a prelude to the emergence of a regenerated world.

1 Europe, which is here as much in question as England, was in the early and middle years of the century in the throes of casting off the despotism of its ecclesiastical and political rulers.
2 Contemporary heads of church and state and what they stood for.

In the charge of the ruining Atlantic
  Where deaths by regiments ride,
With clouds and clamors of waters,
  With a long note shriller than slaughter's
    On the furrowless fields world-wide,

With terror, with ardor and wonder,
  With the soul of the season that wakes
When the weight of a whole year's thunder
  In the tidestream of autumn breaks,
Let the flight of the wide-winged word
Come over, come in and be heard,   55
    Take form and fire for our sakes.

For a continent bloodless with travail
  Here toils and brawls as it can,
And the web of it who shall unravel
  Of all that peer on the plan;   60
Would fain grow men, but they grow not,
And fain be free, but they know not
    One name for freedom and man.

One name, not twain for division;
  One thing, not twain, from the birth;   65
Spirit and substance and vision,
  Worth more than worship is worth;
Unbeheld, unadored, undivined,
The cause, the center, the mind,
    The secret and sense of the earth.   70

Here as a weakling in irons,
  Here as a weanling in bands,
As a prey that the stake-net[3] environs,
  Our life that we looked for stands;
And the man-child naked and dear,   75
Democracy, turns on us here
    Eyes trembling with tremulous hands.

It sees not what season shall bring to it
  Sweet fruit of its bitter desire;
Few voices it hears yet sing to it,   80
  Few pulses of hearts reaspire;
Foresees not time, nor forehears
The noises of imminent years,
    Earthquake, and thunder, and fire:

When crowned and weaponed and curbless   85
  It shall walk without helm or shield
The bare burnt furrows and herbless
  Of war's last flame-stricken field,

45
Till godlike, equal with time,
  It stand in the sun sublime,   90
    In the godhead of man revealed.

Round your people and over them
  Light like raiment is drawn,
Close as a garment to cover them
  Wrought not of mail nor of lawn;[4]   95
Here, with hope hardly to wear,
Naked nations and bare
    Swim, sink, strike out for the dawn.

Chains are here, and a prison,
  Kings, and subjects, and shame;   100
If the God upon you be arisen,[5]
  How should our songs be the same?
How, in confusion of change,
How shall we sing, in a strange
    Land, songs praising his name?   105

God is buried and dead to us,
  Even the spirit of earth,
Freedom; so have they said to us,
  Some with mocking and mirth,
Some with heartbreak and tears;   110
And a God without eyes, without ears,
  Who shall sing of him, dead in the birth?[6]

The earth-god Freedom, the lonely
  Face lightening, the footprint unshod,
Not as one man crucified only,   115
  Nor scourged with but one life's rod;
The soul that is substance of nations,
Reincarnate with fresh generations:
    The great god Man, which is God.

But in weariest of years and obscurest   120
  Doth it live not at heart of all things,
The one God and one spirit, a purest
  Life, fed from unstanchable springs?
Within love, within hatred it is,
And its seed in the stripe[7] as the kiss,   125
    And in slaves is the germ, and in kings.

---

[3] Fishing net spread upon stakes as a kind of weir.

[4] These represent respectively the military and the ecclesiastical hierarchies: mail is armor and lawn is the material out of which bishops' sleeves are made.

[5] The god is identified below as Freedom or Man.

[6] They have told us that Freedom is dead and that in any event an abstraction, as opposed to a personal god, is no god at all.

[7] Blow of a lash.

Freedom we call it, for holier
  Name of the soul's there is none;
Surelier its labors, if slowlier,
  Than the meters of star or of sun;   130
Slowlier than life into breath,
Surelier than time into death,
  It moves till its labor be done.

Till the motion be done and the measure
  Circling through season and clime,   135
Slumber and sorrow and pleasure,
  Vision of virtue and crime;
Till consummate with conquering eyes,
A soul disembodied, it rise
  From the body transfigured of time.   140

Till it rise and remain and take station
  With the stars of the worlds that rejoice;
Till the voice of its heart's exultation
  Be as theirs an invariable voice;
By no discord of evil estranged,   145
By no pause, by no breach in it changed,
  By no clash in the chord of its choice.

It is one with the world's generations,
  With the spirit, the star, and the sod;
With the kingless and king-stricken nations,   150
  With the cross, and the chain, and the rod;
The most high, the most secret, most lonely,
The earth-soul Freedom, that only
  Lives, and that only is God.

Walter Horatio Pater
1839–1894

Pater was born in the East End of London in 1839. When he was five, his father, who was a physician, died, and perhaps some of his aloofness from the world of practical action and his delicate sense for distinctions of feeling may be traced to the feminine influence of the three women (mother, aunt, and grandmother) who brought him up. After school in Canterbury, where the Gothic beauty of the cathedral impressed him as deeply as it did Morris, he went to Oxford in 1858, and after graduation became a Fellow of Brasenose College, where he spent most of his life teaching and writing. His principal works are *Studies in the History of the Renaissance* (1873), a collection of critical essays mainly on Italian painters of that period, and a philosophical biography of an imaginary Roman, *Marius the Epicurean* (1885). He died at Oxford in 1894.

Arnold and Pater are the two major critics of the Victorian period, but the contrast between them is more striking, and more significant historically, than any similarity. Where Arnold has the characteristic longing of the mid-Victorians for certitude, and their characteristic faith in the discovery of truth and the resolution of practical problems, Pater by contrast is far closer to the twentieth century in his radical skepticism. The study of history made him conscious of the vast and bewildering variety of conflicting beliefs which men had held and abandoned in the past. Were their present beliefs likely to be more stable or true? Indeed, are not all institutions and all philosophies, secular or religious, simply manifestations of the particular state of civilization in any given time and place? And if so, then everything is "right" and "true" relative to its environment; nothing is Right and True absolutely. The philosopher, therefore, can hardly expect to arrive at final answers or to formulate positive creeds. He must be content "with suspension of judgment, at the end of the intellectual journey, to the very last asking: *Que scais-je?* Who knows?" Nothing could be more alien to the hopes and ideals of Arnold and the other Victorians of the middle century, or more fatal to the whole concept of the artist as prophet.

What did Pater advocate instead? What was *his* philosophy of life? and of art? The answer to the first is latent in his skepticism. If thought is impotent, the alternative is feeling. Not to reason but to burn always with a hard, gemlike flame, to respond ecstatically to every manifestation of beauty, is success in life. This conclusion was reinforced for Pater by his acceptance of the mechanistic universe which the new science was describing, where all things, material and human, were determined by a vast network of cause and effect. In such a world purposeful action was a delusion. All that man could do was to live in and for the impressions of the moment, to be as alert and sensitive as possible to the "forms of nature and human nature," in life and in art, which give the finest quality of sensuous pleasure. Not that Pater rules out "ideas," but an idea has become for him not something to believe and live by, but something to taste, some new or strange notion to add to his store of experience, or else a new angle of vision which will enable him to see and respond to what otherwise he would not have noticed. In short, what Pater offered his generation was fundamentally not a new criticism but a new philosophy, the philosophy of aestheticism. He was the architect, you might say, who built the Ivory Tower in which Morris was a visitor, and in which the aesthetes of the nineties, Wilde and Symons and the young Yeats, made their home. "As Pater offered instead of moral earnestness life lived as 'a pure gem-like flame' all accepted him for master" (Yeats). And in doing so, he offered a refuge from the physical ugliness and intellectual confusion of modern life.

Given this philosophy of aesthetic enjoyment, we can predict the attraction of the Renaissance for Pater and for his contemporaries. As a matter of fact, *Studies in the History of the Renaissance* (1873) was a pioneer work in England, followed presently by J. A. Symonds's *The Renaissance in Italy* (1875–86) and Vernon Lee's *Euphorion, Essays in the Renaissance* (1884). Strange as it now seems, there was no article on the period in the *Encyclopaedia Britannica* until the ninth edition of 1885, where the author (Symonds) explained that it was only during the previous twenty-five years that the importance of the Renaissance had been recognized—that is to say, in the very years when the new aesthetic attitude was displacing the moral and religious attitude of the mid-Victorians. The passage from Ruskin to Pater marks the transition. For by Pater's time the Renaissance is no longer viewed as a "bad" period of sensual luxury and pagan thought, as it had been by Ruskin (see p. 643), but as a "good" period of revolt against the narrow bounds of Christian asceticism, a freeing of the heart and imagination to enjoy once more the beauty of man and nature. The obvious analogy with the aesthetic revolt against the bounds of mid-Victorianism is the inciting cause of the Renaissance studies and the Renaissance enthusiasm of the period from 1860 to 1914. After the First World War, the next reaction (against aestheticism itself) and the rise of modern metaphysical poetry shifted literary sympathy to the seventeenth century.

Pater's poetic theory is a natural deduction from his philosophy. If the goal of life is the fullest enjoyment of lovely or curious sensations, the purpose of art is not profit (one is tempted to say, not prophet), but pleasure; and the artist's role is to record the most striking impressions, in their novelty or beauty, that his sensitive nature has experienced. In theory this did not rule out a defined content, psychological or even ideological; but the reaction against the Victorian poetry of ideas could very well lead—as it sometimes did in Morris and Swinburne and the early Yeats—to a "pure" poetry of mood and atmosphere, created out of image and rhythm. The critical rationale of this development is found in Pater's essay on "The School of Giorgione." There he suggests that "the highest and most complete form of poetry" is the lyric, where the very perfection depends, in part, "on a certain suppression or vagueness of mere subject," and argues that all art should strive "to be independent of the mere intelligence, to become a matter of pure perception, to get rid of its responsibilities to subject or material." This is the doctrine of Art for Art's Sake at its extreme, as we find it maintained by the artists of the eighties and nineties. Yeats was speaking for the poets of that period when he said that the revolt against Victorianism meant the revolt against introducing into poetry "curiosities about politics, about science, about religion . . . with moral purpose and educational fervour," and the determination, by reaction, to "purify poetry of all that is not poetry" by writing lyrical poems where music and color would suggest an "almost bodiless emotion." But Pater could also recognize, especially in later essays, the importance of character, action, even ideas in literature.

Pater's defense of claiming that all the arts should "aspire towards the condition of music" is that, their form and matter being so completely fused, they cannot be separated even by the critical intellect. But to demand that kind of fusion from poetry and painting is to sacrifice their special potentialities, which are different from those of music but no less expressive. In a top-notch poem or painting, form and matter *are* welded together, only not so tightly that analysis may not be able to disengage them. But this is inevitable, and entirely justified by the character of the mediums. But however faulty the argument, Pater's general insistence on the organic character of art was completely valid and very much needed. For the tendency of Victorian criticism was to focus too exclusively either on the content (the moral or religious ideas of a poet-prophet) or on the form (the technique of the painter, the artistry of the poet). "The legitimate contention," he claimed, was "not one age or school of literary art against another, but of all successive schools alike, against the stupidity which is dead to substance, and the vulgarity which is dead to form." The critic's first concern, therefore, must be with the essential quality of a work of art, with the particular kind and shade of experience it communicates by means of all its elements working together. Pater demands that we see a poem or picture as an organic whole to which we respond with a unified sensibility, with what he calls "imaginative reason." Furthermore, he wanted the object to be seen as it would have been by a contemporary: "Every intellectual product must be judged from the point of view of the age and the people in which it was produced." Though Pater's own criticism is inferior to Arnold's, his *conception* of criticism now seems more valid—and more modern. Here are the basic assumptions of the "new criticism," together with a principle which "new critics" have tended to disregard, that a poem should be read in its historical context.

TEXTS: *The Works of Walter Pater* have been published in ten volumes (1910). There is an unreliable biography by Thomas Wright (2 vols., 1907) and a short life by A. C. Benson (1906). Helen H. Young's *The Writings of Walter Pater. A Reflection of British Philosophical Opinion from 1860 to 1890* (1933) is a useful study. The *Letters* have been edited by Lawrence Evans (1970). Perhaps the best short criticisms are in Graham Hough, *The Last Romantics* (1949); in Geoffrey Tillotson, *Criticism and the Nineteenth Century* (1951), chapters 3–5; and in Ian Fletcher's pamphlet *Walter Pater* (1959).

from The Renaissance. Studies in Art and Poetry

PREFACE

Many attempts have been made by writers on art and poetry to define beauty in the abstract, to express it in the most general terms, to find some universal formula for it. The value of these attempts has most often been in the suggestive and penetrating things said by the way. Such discussions help us very little to enjoy what has been well done in art or poetry, to discriminate between what is more and what is less excellent in them, or to use words like beauty, excellence, art, poetry, with a more precise meaning than they would otherwise have. Beauty, like all other qualities presented to human experience, is relative; and the definition of it becomes unmeaning and useless in proportion to its abstractness. To define beauty, not in the most abstract but in the most concrete terms possible, to find not its universal formula, but the formula which expresses most adequately this or that special manifestation of it, is the aim of the true student of aesthetics.

"To see the object as in itself it really is," has been justly said to be the aim of all true criticism whatever;[1] and in aesthetic criticism the first step towards seeing one's object as it really is, is to know one's own impression as it really is, to discriminate it, to realise it distinctly. The objects with which aesthetic criticism deals —music, poetry, artistic and accomplished forms of human life—are indeed receptacles of so many powers or forces: they possess, like the products of nature, so many virtues or qualities. What is this song or picture, this engaging personality presented in life or in a book, to *me*? What effect does it really produce on me? Does it give me pleasure? and if so, what sort or degree of pleasure? How is my nature modified by its presence, and under its influence? The answers to these questions are the original facts with which the aesthetic critic has to do; and, as in the study of light, of morals, of number, one must realise such primary data for one's self, or not at all. And he who experiences these impressions strongly, and drives directly at the discrimination and analysis of them, has no need to trouble himself with the abstract question what beauty is in itself, or what its exact relation to truth or experience—metaphysical questions, as unprofitable as metaphysical questions elsewhere. He may pass them all by as being, answerable or not, of no interest to him.

The aesthetic critic, then, regards all the objects with which he has to do, all works of art, and the fairer forms of nature and human life, as powers or forces producing pleasurable sensations, each of a more or less peculiar or unique kind. This influence he feels, and wishes to explain, by analysing and reducing it to its elements. To him, the picture, the landscape, the engaging personality in life or in a book, *La Gioconda*, the hills of Carrara, Pico of Mirandola,[2] are valuable for their virtues, as we say, in speaking of a herb, a wine, a gem; for the property each has of affecting one with a special, a unique, impression of pleasure. Our education becomes complete in proportion as our susceptibility to these impressions increases in depth and variety. And the function of the aesthetic critic is to distinguish, to analyse, and separate from its adjuncts, the virtue by which a picture, a landscape, a fair personality in life or in a book, produces this special impression of beauty or pleasure, to indicate what the source of that

---

[1] By Arnold in first paragraph of "The Function of Criticism."

[2] The picture is the *Mona Lisa* by Leonardo da Vinci, the landscape a hilly section of Italy, and the personality an Italian humanist of the fifteenth century.

impression is, and under what conditions it is experienced. His end is reached when he has disengaged that virtue, and noted it, as a chemist notes some natural element, for himself and others; and the rule for those who would reach this end is stated with great exactness in the words of a recent critic of Sainte-Beuve:—*De se borner à connaître de près les belles choses, et à s'en nourrir en exquis amateurs, en humanistes accomplis.*[3]

What is important, then, is not that the critic should possess a correct abstract definition of beauty for the intellect, but a certain kind of temperament, the power of being deeply moved by the presence of beautiful objects. He will remember always that beauty exists in many forms. To him all periods, types, schools of taste, are in themselves equal. In all ages there have been some excellent workmen, and some excellent work done. The question he asks is always:—In whom did the stir, the genius, the sentiment of the period find itself? where was the receptacle of its refinement, its elevation, its taste? "The ages are all equal," says William Blake, "but genius is always above its age."

Often it will require great nicety to disengage this virtue from the commoner elements with which it may be found in combination. Few artists, not Goethe or Byron even, work quite cleanly, casting off all *débris,* and leaving us only what the heat of their imagination has wholly fused and transformed. Take, for instance, the writings of Wordsworth. The heat of his genius, entering into the substance of his work, has crystallised a part, but only a part, of it; and in that great mass of verse there is much which might well be forgotten. But scattered up and down it, sometimes fusing and transforming entire compositions, like the Stanzas on *Resolution and Independence,* or the *Ode on the Recollections of Childhood,* sometimes, as if at random, depositing a fine crystal here or there, in a matter it does not wholly search through and transmute, we trace the action of his unique, incommunicable faculty, that strange, mystical sense of a life in natural things, and of man's life as a part of nature, drawing strength and colour and character from local influences, from

the hills and streams, and from natural sights and sounds. Well! that is the *virtue,* the active principle in Wordsworth's poetry; and then the function of the critic of Wordsworth is to follow up that active principle, to disengage it, to mark the degree in which it penetrates his verse.

The subjects of the following studies are taken from the history of the *Renaissance,* and touch what I think the chief points in that complex, many-sided movement. I have explained in the first of them what I understand by the word, giving it a much wider scope than was intended by those who originally used it to denote that revival of classical antiquity in the fifteenth century which was only one of many results of a general excitement and enlightening of the human mind, but of which the great aim and achievements of what, as Christian art, is often falsely opposed to the Renaissance, were another result. This outbreak of the human spirit may be traced far into the middle age itself, with its motives already clearly pronounced, the care for physical beauty, the worship of the body, the breaking down of those limits which the religious system of the middle age imposed on the heart and the imagination. I have taken as an example of this movement, this earlier Renaissance within the middle age itself, and as an expression of its qualities, two little compositions in early French;[4] not because they constitute the best possible expression of them, but because they help the unity of my series, inasmuch as the Renaissance ends also in France, in French poetry, in a phase of which the writings of Joachim du Bellay[5] are in many ways the most perfect illustration. The Renaissance, in truth, put forth in France an aftermath, a wonderful later growth, the products of which have to the full that subtle and delicate sweetness which belongs to a refined and comely decadence, just as its earliest phases have the freshness which belongs to all periods of growth in art, the charm of *ascêsis,*[6] of the austere and serious girding of the loins in youth.

But it is in Italy, in the fifteenth century, that the interest of the Renaissance mainly lies,—in that solemn fifteenth century which can

---

[3] "To limit ourselves to knowing beautiful things at first hand, and to nourish ourselves by them like sensitive amateurs and accomplished humanists."

[4] *Amis and Amile* and *Aucassin and Nicolette.*
[5] French poet and critic of the sixteenth century, the subject of one of Pater's essays.
[6] Defined elsewhere by Pater as "self-restraint, a skilful economy of means."

hardly be studied too much, not merely for its positive results in the things of the intellect and the imagination, its concrete works of art, its special and prominent personalities, with their profound aesthetic charm, but for its general spirit and character, for the ethical qualities of which it is a consummate type.

The various forms of intellectual activity which together make up the culture of an age, move for the most part from different starting-points, and by unconnected roads. As products of the same generation they partake indeed of a common character, and unconsciously illustrate each other; but of the producers themselves, each group is solitary, gaining what advantage or disadvantage there may be in intellectual isolation. Art and poetry, philosophy and the religious life, and that other life of refined pleasure and action in the conspicuous places of the world, are each of them confined to its own circle of ideas, and those who prosecute either of them are generally little curious of the thoughts of others. There come, however, from time to time, eras of more favourable conditions, in which the thoughts of men draw nearer together than is their wont, and the many interests of the intellectual world combine in one complete type of general culture. The fifteenth century in Italy is one of these happier eras, and what is sometimes said of the age of Pericles is true of that of Lorenzo:[7]—it is an age productive in personalities, many-sided, centralised, complete. Here, artists and philosophers and those whom the action of the world has elevated and made keen, do not live in isolation, but breathe a common air, and catch light and heat from each other's thoughts. There is a spirit of general elevation and enlightenment in which all alike communicate. The unity of this spirit gives unity to all the various products of the Renaissance; and it is to this intimate alliance with mind, this participation in the best thoughts which that age produced, that the art of Italy in the fifteenth century owes much of its grave dignity and influence.

I have added an essay on Winckelmann,[8] as not incongruous with the studies which precede it, because Winckelmann, coming in the eighteenth century, really belongs in spirit to an earlier age. By his enthusiasm for the things of the intellect and the imagination for their own sake, by his Hellenism, his life-long struggle to attain to the Greek spirit, he is in sympathy with the humanists of a previous century. He is the last fruit of the Renaissance, and explains in a striking way its motive and tendencies.

THE SCHOOL OF GIORGIONE[9]

It is the mistake of much popular criticism to regard poetry, music, and painting—all the various products of art—as but translations into different languages of one and the same fixed quantity of imaginative thought, supplemented by certain technical qualities of color, in painting—of sound, in music—of rhythmical words, in poetry. In this way, the sensuous element in art, and with it almost everything in art that is essentially artistic, is made a matter of indifference; and a clear apprehension of the opposite principle—that the sensuous material of each art brings with it a special phase or quality of beauty, untranslatable into the forms of any other, an order of impressions distinct in kind—is the beginning of all true aesthetic criticism. For, as art addresses not pure sense, still less the pure intellect, but the "imaginative reason"[10] through the senses, there are differences of kind in aesthetic beauty, corresponding to the differences in kind of the gifts of sense themselves. Each art, therefore, having its own peculiar and incommunicable sensuous charm, has its own special mode of reaching the imagination, its own special responsibilities to its material. One of the functions of aesthetic criticism is to define these limitations; to estimate the degree in which a given work of art fulfils its responsibilities to its special material; to note in a picture that true pictorial charm, which is neither a mere poetical thought nor sentiment, on the one hand, nor a mere result of communicable technical skill in colour or design, on the other; to define in a poem that true poetical quality, which is neither descriptive nor meditative merely, but comes of an inventive handling of rhythmical language

---

7 Pericles, the Athenian statesman of the fifth century B.C., and Lorenzo de' Medici, prince of Florence and patron of Renaissance art.

8 Eighteenth-century historian of classical art.

9 Italian painter of the Renaissance.

10 What would now be called the unified sensibility, or the total feeling-thinking man responding directly to any object, in life or in art. In the next sentence Pater uses the term "imagination" for the same thing.

—the element of song in the singing; to note in music the musical charm—that essential music, which presents no words, no matter of sentiment or thought, separable from the special form in which it is conveyed to us.

To such a philosophy of the variations of the beautiful, Lessing's analysis of the spheres of sculpture and poetry, in the *Laocoön,* was a very important contribution.[11] But a true appreciation of these things is possible only in the light of a whole system of such art-casuistries.[12] And it is in the criticism of painting that this truth most needs enforcing, for it is in popular judgments on pictures that that false generalisation of all art into forms of poetry is most prevalent. To suppose that all is mere technical acquirement in delineation or touch, working through and addressing itself to the intelligence, on the one side, or a merely poetical, or what may be called literary interest, addressed also to the pure intelligence, on the other;—this is the way of most spectators, and of many critics, who have never caught sight, all the time, of that true pictorial quality which lies between (unique pledge of the possession of the pictorial gift) the inventive or creative handling of pure line and colour, which, as almost always in Dutch painting, as often also in the works of Titian or Veronese, is quite independent of anything definitely poetical in the subject it accompanies. It is the *drawing*—the design projected from that peculiar pictorial temperament or constitution, in which, while it may possibly be ignorant of true anatomical proportions, all things whatever, all poetry, every idea however abstract or obscure, floats up as a visible scene or image: it is the *colouring*—that weaving as of just perceptible gold threads of light through the dress, the flesh, the atmosphere, in Titian's *Lace-girl*—the staining of the whole fabric of the thing with a new, delightful physical quality. This *drawing,* then —the arabesque traced in the air by Tintoret's flying figures, by Titian's forest branches; this colouring—the magic conditions of light and hue in the atmosphere of Titian's *Lace-girl,* or Rubens's *Descent from the Cross:*[13]—these essential pictorial qualities must first of all delight the sense, delight it as directly and sensuously as a fragment of Venetian glass; and through this delight only be the medium of whatever poetry or science may lie beyond them, in the intention of the composer. In its primary aspect, a great picture has no more definite message for us than an accidental play of sunlight and shadow for a moment, on the wall or floor: is itself, in truth, a space of such fallen light, caught as the colours are caught in an Eastern carpet, but refined upon, and dealt with more subtly and exquisitely than by nature itself. And this primary and essential condition fulfilled, we may trace the coming of poetry into painting, by fine gradations upwards; from Japanese fan-painting, for instance, where we get, first, only abstract colour; then, just a little interfused sense of the poetry of flowers; then, sometimes, perfect flower-painting; and so, onwards, until in Titian we have, as his poetry in the *Ariadne,* so actually a touch of true childlike humour in the diminutive, quaint figure with its silk gown, which ascends the temple stairs, in his picture of the *Presentation of the Virgin,* at Venice.

But although each art has thus its own specific order of impressions, and an untranslatable charm, while a just apprehension of the ultimate differences of the arts is the beginning of aesthetic criticism; yet it is noticeable that, in its special mode of handling its given material, each art may be observed to pass into the condition of some other art, by what German critics term an *Anders-streben*—a partial alienation from its own limitations, by which the arts are able, not indeed to supply the place of each other, but reciprocally to lend each other new forces.

Thus some of the most delightful music seems to be always approaching to figure, to pictorial definition. Architecture, again, though it has its own laws—laws esoteric enough, as the true architect knows only too well—yet sometimes aims at fulfilling the conditions of a picture, as in the *Arena* chapel;[14] or of sculpture, as in the flawless unity of Giotto's tower at Florence; and often finds a true poetry, as in those strangely twisted staircases of the *châteaux* of

---

[11] Lessing was a German critic and dramatist of the eighteenth century.

[12] Casuistry is the application of general moral principles to particular cases of conscience or conduct.

[13] Titian, Veronese, and Tintoretto were Italian painters

---

of the Renaissance; Rubens was a Flemish painter of the seventeenth century.

[14] In Padua, Italy.

the country of the Loire,[15] as if it were intended that among their odd turnings the actors in a wild life might pass each other unseen: there being a poetry also of memory and of the mere effect of time, by which it often profits greatly. Thus, again, sculpture aspires out of the hard limitation of pure form towards colour, or its equivalent; poetry also, in many ways, finding guidance from the other arts, the analogy between a Greek tragedy and a work of Greek sculpture, between a sonnet and a relief, of French poetry generally with the art of engraving, being more than mere figures of speech; and all the arts in common aspiring towards the principle of music; music being the typical, or ideally consummate art, the object of the great *Anders-streben* of all art, of all that is artistic, or partakes of artistic qualities.

All art constantly aspires towards the condition of music. For while in all other works of art it is possible to distinguish the matter from the form, and the understanding can always make this distinction, yet it is the constant effort of art to obliterate it. That the mere matter of a poem, for instance—its subject, its given incidents or situation; that the mere matter of a picture—the actual circumstances of an event, the actual topography of a landscape—should be nothing without the form, the spirit, of the handling; that this form, this mode of handling, should become an end in itself, should penetrate every part of the matter:—this is what all art constantly strives after, and achieves in different degrees.

This abstract language becomes clear enough, if we think of actual examples. In an actual landscape we see a long white road, lost suddenly on the hill-verge. That is the matter of one of the etchings of M. Legros:[16] only, in this etching, it is informed by an indwelling solemnity of expression, seen upon it or half-seen, within the limits of an exceptional moment, or caught from his own mood perhaps, but which he maintains as the very essence of the thing, throughout his work. Sometimes a momentary tint of stormy light may invest a homely or too familiar scene with a character which might well have been drawn from the deep places of the imagination. Then we might say that this particular effect of light, this sudden inweaving of gold thread through the texture of the haystack, and the poplars, and the grass, gives the scene artistic qualities; that it is like a picture. And such tricks of circumstance are commonest in landscape which has little salient character of its own; because, in such scenery, all the material details are so easily absorbed by that informing expression of passing light, and elevated, throughout their whole extent, to a new and delightful effect by it. And hence the superiority, for most conditions of the picturesque, of a river-side in France to a Swiss valley, because, on the French river-side, mere topography, the simple material, counts for so little, and, all being so pure, untouched, and tranquil in itself, mere light and shade have such easy work in modulating it to one dominant tone. The Venetian landscape, on the other hand, has in its material conditions much which is hard, or harshly definite; but the masters of the Venetian school have shown themselves little burdened by them. Of its Alpine background they retain certain abstracted elements only, of cool colour and tranquillising line; and they use its actual details, the brown windy turrets, the straw-coloured fields, the forest arabesques, but as the notes of a music which duly accompanies the presence of their men and women, presenting us with the spirit or essence only of a certain sort of landscape—a country of the pure reason or half-imaginative memory.

Poetry, again, works with words addressed in the first instance to the mere intelligence; and it deals, most often, with a definite subject or situation. Sometimes it may find a noble and quite legitimate function in the expression of moral or political aspiration, as often in the poetry of Victor Hugo.[17] In such instances it is easy enough for the understanding to distinguish between the matter and the form, however much the matter, the subject, the element which is addressed to the mere intelligence, has been penetrated by the informing, artistic spirit. But the ideal types of poetry are those in which this distinction is reduced to its *minimum*; so that lyrical poetry, precisely because in it we are least able to detach the matter from the form, without a deduction of something from that matter itself,

---

[15] The valley of the Loire river in France.
[16] Alphonse Legros, a French artist of the nineteenth century.

[17] French novelist and poet (1802–1885) who was a passionate liberal in politics.

is, at least artistically, the highest and most complete form of poetry. And the very perfection of such poetry often seems to depend, in part, on a certain suppression or vagueness of mere subject, so that the meaning reaches us through ways not distinctly traceable by the understanding, as in some of the most imaginative compositions of William Blake, and often in Shakspere's songs, as pre-eminently in that song of Mariana's page in *Measure for Measure,* in which the kindling force and poetry of the whole play seems to pass for a moment into an actual strain of music.

And this principle holds good of all things that partake in any degree of artistic qualities, of the furniture of our houses, and of dress, for instance, of life itself, of gesture and speech, and the details of daily intercourse; these also, for the wise, being susceptible of a suavity and charm, caught from the way in which they are done, which gives them a worth in themselves; wherein, indeed, lies what is valuable and justly attractive, in what is called the fashion of a time, which elevates the trivialities of speech, and manner, and dress, into "ends in themselves," and gives them a mysterious grace and attractiveness in the doing of them.

Art, then, is thus always striving to be independent of the mere intelligence, to become a matter of pure perception, to get rid of its responsibilities to its subject or material; the ideal examples of poetry and painting being those in which the constituent elements of the composition are so welded together, that the material or subject no longer strikes the intellect only; nor the form, the eye or the ear only; but form and matter, in their union or identity, present one single effect to the "imaginative reason," that complex faculty for which every thought and feeling is twin-born with its sensible analogue or symbol.

It is the art of music which most completely realises this artistic ideal, this perfect identification of form and matter. In its ideal, consummate moments, the end is not distinct from the means, the form from the matter, the subject from the expression; they inhere in and completely saturate each other; and to it, therefore, to the condition of its perfect moments, all the arts may be supposed constantly to tend and aspire. Music, then, and not poetry, as is so often supposed, is the true type or measure of perfected

art. Therefore, although each art has its incommunicable element, its untranslatable order of impressions, its unique mode of reaching the "imaginative reason," yet the arts may be represented as continually struggling after the law or principle of music, to a condition which music alone completely realises; and one of the chief functions of aesthetic criticism, dealing with the products of art, new or old, is to estimate the degree in which each of those products approaches, in this sense, to musical law.

By no school of painters have the necessary limitations of the art of painting been so unerringly though instinctively apprehended, and the essence of what is pictorial in a picture so justly conceived, as by the school of Venice; and the train of thought suggested in what has been now said is, perhaps, a not unfitting introduction to a few pages about Giorgione, who, though much has been taken by recent criticism from what was reputed to be his work, yet, more entirely than any other painter, sums up, in what we know of himself and his art, the spirit of the Venetian school.

The beginnings of Venetian painting link themselves to the last, stiff, half-barbaric splendours of Byzantine decoration, and are but the introduction into the crust of marble and gold on the walls of the *Duomo* of Murano,[18] or of Saint Mark's,[19] of a little more of human expression. And throughout the course of its later development, always subordinate to architectural effect, the work of the Venetian school never escaped from the influence of its beginnings. Unassisted, and therefore unperplexed, by naturalism, religious mysticism, philosophical theories, it had no Giotto, no Angelico, no Botticelli. Exempt from the stress of thought and sentiment, which taxed so severely the resources of the generations of Florentine artists, those earlier Venetian painters, down to Carpaccio and the Bellini, seem never for a moment to have been tempted even to lose sight of the scope of their art in its strictness, or to forget that painting must be before all things decorative, a thing for the eye, a space of colour on the wall, only more dexterously blent than the marking of its precious stone or the chance interchange of sun and shade

---

18 A cathedral on an island a mile north of Venice.
19 The famous cathedral in Venice.

upon it—this, to begin and end with—whatever higher matter of thought, or poetry, or religious reverie might play its part therein, between. At last, with final mastery of all the technical secrets of his art, and with somewhat more than "a spark of the divine fire" to his share, comes Giorgione. He is the inventor of *genre,* of those easily movable pictures which serve neither for uses of devotion, nor of allegorical or historic teaching —little groups of real men and women, amid congruous furniture or landscape—morsels of actual life, conversation or music or play, refined upon or idealised, till they come to seem like glimpses of life from afar. Those spaces of more cunningly blent colour, obediently filling their places, hitherto, in a mere architectural scheme, Giorgione detaches from the wall; he frames them by the hands of some skilful carver, so that people may move them readily and take with them where they go, like a poem in manuscript, or a musical instrument, to be used, at will, as a means of self-education, stimulus or solace, coming like an animated presence, into one's cabinet, to enrich the air as with some choice aroma, and, like persons, live with us, for a day or a lifetime. Of all art like this, art which has played so large a part in men's culture since that time, Giorgione is the initiator. Yet in him too that old Venetian clearness or justice, in the apprehension of the essential limitations of the pictorial art, is still undisturbed; and, while he interfuses his painted work with a high-strung sort of poetry, caught directly from a singularly rich and high-strung sort of life, yet in his selection of subject, or phase of subject, in the subordination of mere subject to pictorial design, to the main purpose of a picture, he is typical of that aspiration of all the arts towards music, which I have endeavoured to explain,—towards the perfect identification of matter and form.

Born so near to Titian, though a little before him,[20] that these two companion pupils of the aged Giovanni Bellini may almost be called contemporaries, Giorgione stands to Titian in something like the relationship of Sordello to Dante, in Mr. Browning's poem.[21] Titian, when he leaves Bellini, becomes, in turn, the pupil of Giorgione; he lives in constant labour more than sixty years after Giorgione is in his grave; and

with such fruit, that hardly one of the greater towns of Europe is without some fragment of it. But the slightly older man, with his so limited actual product (what remains to us of it seeming, when narrowly examined, to reduce itself to almost one picture, like Sordello's one fragment of lovely verse),[22] yet expresses, in elementary motive and principle, that spirit—itself the final acquisition of all the long endeavours of Venetian art—which Titian spreads over his whole life's activity.

And, as we might expect, something fabulous and illusive has always mingled itself in the brilliancy of Giorgione's fame. The exact relationship to him of many works—drawings, portraits, painted idylls—often fascinating enough, which in various collections went by his name, was from the first uncertain. Still, six or eight famous pictures at Dresden, Florence and the Louvre, were undoubtedly attributed to him, and in these, if anywhere, something of the splendour of the old Venetian humanity seemed to have been preserved. But of those six or eight famous pictures it is now known that only one is certainly from Giorgione's hand. The accomplished science of the subject has come at last, and, as in other instances, has not made the past more real for us, but assured us that we possess of it less than we seemed to possess. Much of the work on which Giorgione's immediate fame depended, work done for instantaneous effect, in all probability passed away almost within his own age, like the frescoes on the façade of the *fondaco dei Tedeschi*[23] at Venice, some crimson traces of which, however, still give a strange additional touch of splendour to the scene of the *Rialto.*[24] And then there is a barrier or borderland, a period about the middle of the sixteenth century, in passing through which the tradition miscarries, and the true outlines of Giorgione's work and person become obscured. It became fashionable for wealthy lovers of art, with no critical standard of authenticity, to collect so-called works of Giorgione, and a multitude of imitations came into circulation. And now, in the "new Vasari,"[25] the great traditional

---

20 Titian's dates were 1477–1576; Giorgione's, 1477?–1511.
21 *Sordello,* published in 1840.

22 Part of his most famous song, written in Provençal about 1237, is translated by Karl Vossler in his *Mediaeval Culture* (New York, 1929), p. 66.
23 Headquarters of the German merchants.
24 Bridge over the Grand Canal in Venice.
25 The "old" Vasari was the author of *Lives of the . . .*

reputation, woven with so profuse demand on men's admiration, has been scrutinised thread by thread; and what remains of the most vivid and stimulating of Venetian masters, a live flame, as it seemed, in those old shadowy times, has been reduced almost to a name by his most recent critics.

Yet enough remains to explain why the legend grew up, above the name, why the name attached itself, in many instances, to the bravest work of other men. The *Concert* in the *Pitti Palace*,[26] in which a monk, with cowl and tonsure, touches the keys of a harpsichord, while a clerk, placed behind him, grasps the handle of a viol, and a third, with cap and plume, seems to wait upon the true interval for beginning to sing, is undoubtedly Giorgione's. The outline of the lifted finger, the trace of the plume, the very threads of the fine linen, which fasten themselves on the memory, in the moment before they are lost altogether in that calm unearthly glow, the skill which has caught the waves of wandering sound, and fixed them for ever on the lips and hands—these are indeed the master's own; and the criticism which, while dismissing so much hitherto believed to be Giorgione's, has established the claims of this one picture, has left it among the most precious things in the world of art.

It is noticeable that the "distinction" of this *Concert,* its sustained evenness of perfection, alike in design, in execution, and in choice of personal type, becomes for the "new Vasari" the standard of Giorgione's genuine work. Finding here enough to explain his influence, and the true seal of mastery, its authors assign to Pellegrino da San Daniele[27] the *Holy Family* in the Louvre, for certain points in which it comes short of that standard, but which will hardly diminish the spectator's enjoyment of a singular charm of liquid air, with which the whole picture seems instinct, filling the eyes and lips, the very garments, of its sacred personages, with some windsearched brightness and energy; of which fine air the blue peak, clearly defined in the distance, is, as it were, the visible pledge. Similarly, another favourite picture in the Louvre, the subject of a sonnet by a poet[28] whose own painted work often comes to mind as one ponders over these precious things—the *Fête Champêtre,* is assigned to an imitator of Sebastian del Piombo;[29] and the *Tempest,* in the Academy at Venice (a slighter loss, perhaps, though not without its pleasant effect of clearing weather, towards the left, its one untouched morsel), to Paris Bordone,[30] or perhaps to "some advanced craftsman of the sixteenth century." From the gallery at Dresden, the *Knight embracing a Lady,* where the knight's broken gauntlets seem to mark some well-known pause in a story we would willingly hear the rest of, is conceded to "a Brescian hand," and *Jacob meeting Rachel* to a pupil of Palma;[31] and, whatever their charm, we are called on to give up the *Ordeal,* and the *Finding of Moses* with its jewel-like pools of water, perhaps to Bellini.

Nor has the criticism, which thus so freely diminishes the number of his authentic works, added anything important to the well-known outline of the life and personality of the man: only, it has fixed one or two dates, one or two circumstances, a little more exactly. Giorgione was born before the year 1477, and spent his childhood at Castelfranco, where the last crags of the Venetian Alps break down romantically, with something of parklike grace, to the plain. A natural child of the family of the Barbarelli by a peasant-girl of Vedelago, he finds his way early into the circle of notable persons—people of courtesy; and becomes initiated into those differences of personal type, manner, and even of dress, which are best understood there—that "distinction" of the *Concert* of the *Pitti* Palace. Not far from his home lives Catherine of Cornara, formerly Queen of Cyprus;[32] and, up in the towers which still remain, Tuzio Costanzo, the famous *condottiére*[33]—a picturesque remnant of medieval manners, amid a civilisation rapidly changing. Giorgione paints their portraits; and

---

Architects, Painters, and Sculptors (1550 and 1568). The "new" Vasari, as Pater explains in a footnote, is J. A. Crowe and G. B. Cavalcaselle, *History of Painting in North Italy* (1862 in French, 1871 in English).
26 The famous picture gallery in Florence.
27 Venetian painter of altar pieces, c. 1467–1547.

28 The sonnet entitled "For a Venetian Pastoral by Giorgione (in the Louvre)" was written by Dante Gabriel Rossetti.
29 Venetian painter, 1485–1547.
30 Another Venetian painter, 1500–1571.
31 Giacomo Palma, c.1480–1528, also a painter.
32 Life dates: 1454–1510.
33 Military captain or leader of mercenaries painted by Giorgione.

when Tuzio's son, Matteo, dies in early youth, adorns in his memory a chapel in the church of Castelfranco, painting on this occasion, perhaps, the altar-piece, foremost among his authentic works, still to be seen there, with the figure of the warrior-saint, Liberale, of which the original little study in oil, with the delicately gleaming, silver-gray armour, is one of the greater treasures of the National Gallery, and in which, as in some other knightly personages attributed to him, people have supposed the likeness of his own presumably gracious presence. Thither, at last, he is himself brought home from Venice, early dead, but celebrated. It happened, about his thirty-fourth year, that in one of those parties at which he entertained his friends with music, he met a certain lady of whom he became greatly enamoured, and "they rejoiced greatly," says Vasari, "the one and the other, in their loves." And two quite different legends concerning it agree in this, that it was through this lady he came by his death: Ridolfi[34] relating that, being robbed of her by one of his pupils, he died of grief at the double treason;—Vasari, that she being secretly stricken of the plague, and he making his visits to her as usual, he took the sickness from her mortally, along with her kisses, and so briefly departed.

But, although the number of Giorgione's extant works has been thus limited by recent criticism, all is not done when the real and the traditional elements in what concerns him have been discriminated; for, in what is connected with a great name, much that is not real is often very stimulating; and, for the æsthetic philosopher, over and above the real Giorgione and his authentic extant works, there remains the *Giorgionesque* also—an influence, a spirit or type in art, active in men so different as those to whom many of his supposed works are really assignable —a veritable school, which grew together out of all those fascinating works rightly or wrongly attributed to him; out of many copies from, or variations on him, by unknown or uncertain workmen, whose drawings and designs were, for various reasons, prized as his; out of the immediate impression he made upon his contemporaries, and with which he continued in men's minds; out of many traditions of subject and

treatment, which really descend from him to our own time, and by retracing which we fill out the original image; Giorgione thus becoming a sort of impersonation of Venice itself, its projected reflex or ideal, all that was intense or desirable in it thus crystallising about the memory of this wonderful young man.

And now, finally, let me illustrate some of the characteristics of this *School of Giorgione,* as we may call it, which, for most of us, notwithstanding all that negative criticism of the "new Vasari," will still identify itself with those famous pictures at Florence, Dresden and Paris; and in which a certain artistic ideal is defined for us— the conception of a peculiar aim and procedure in art, which we may understand as the *Giorgionesque,* wherever we find it, whether in Venetian work generally, or in work of our own time —and of which the *Concert,* that undoubted work of Giorgione in the *Pitti* Palace, is the typical instance, and a pledge authenticating the connexion of the school with the master.

I have spoken of a certain interpenetration of the matter or subject of a work of art with the form of it, a condition realised absolutely only in music, as the condition to which every form of art is perpetually aspiring. In the art of painting, the attainment of this ideal condition, this perfect interpenetration of the subject with colour and design, depends, of course, in great measure, on dexterous choice of that subject, or phase of subject; and such choice is one of the secrets of Giorgione's school. It is the school of *genre,* and employs itself mainly with "painted idylls," but, in the production of this pictorial poetry, exercises a wonderful tact in the selecting of such matter as lends itself most readily and entirely to pictorial form, to complete expression by drawing and colour. For although its productions are painted poems, they belong to a sort of poetry which tells itself without an articulated story. The master is pre-eminent for the resolution, the ease and quickness, with which he reproduces instantaneous motion—the lacing-on of armour, with the head bent back so stately—the fainting lady—the embrace, rapid as the kiss caught, with death itself, from dying lips—the momentary conjunction of mirrors and polished armour and still water, by which all the sides of a solid image are presented at once, solving that casuistical

[34] Carlo Ridolfi, born in 1594, mainly known as a biographer of painters.

question whether painting can present an object as completely as sculpture. The sudden act, the rapid transition of thought, the passing expression—this, he arrests with that vivacity which Vasari has attributed to him, *il fuoco Giorgionesco*,[35] as he terms it. Now it is part of the ideality of the highest sort of dramatic poetry, that it presents us with a kind of profoundly significant and animated instant, a mere gesture, a look, a smile, perhaps—some brief and wholly concrete moment—into which, however, all the motives, all the interests and effects of a long history, have condensed themselves, and which seem to absorb past and future in an intense consciousness of the present. Such ideal instants the school of Giorgione selects, with its admirable tact, from that feverish, tumultuously coloured life of the old citizens of Venice—exquisite pauses in time, in which, arrested thus, we seem to be spectators of all the fulness of existence, and which are like some consummate extract or quintessence of life.[36]

It is to the law or condition of music, as I said, that all art like this is really aspiring; and, in the school of Giorgione, the perfect moments of music itself, the making or hearing of music, song or its accompaniment, are themselves prominent as subjects. On that background of the silence of Venice, which the visitor there finds so impressive, the world of Italian music was then forming. In choice of subject, as in all besides, the *Concert* of the *Pitti* Palace is typical of all that Giorgione, himself an admirable musician, touched with his influence; and in sketch or finished picture, in various collections, we may follow it through many intricate variations—men fainting at music, music heard at the pool-side while people fish, or mingled with the sound of the pitcher in the well, or heard across running water, or among the flocks; the tuning of instruments—people with intent faces, as if listening, like those described by Plato in an ingenious passage, to detect the smallest interval of musical sound, the smallest undulation in the air, or feeling for music in thought on a stringless instrument, ear and finger refining themselves infinitely, in the appetite for sweet sound—a momentary touch of an instru-

ment in the twilight, as one passes through some unfamiliar room, in a chance company.

In such favourite incidents, then, of Giorgione's school, music or music-like intervals in our existence, life itself is conceived as a sort of listening—listening to music, to the reading of Bandello's novels, to the sound of water, to time as it flies. Often such moments are really our moments of play, and we are surprised at the unexpected blessedness of what may seem our least important part of time; not merely because play is in many instances that to which people really apply their own best powers, but also because at such times, the stress of our servile, everyday attentiveness being relaxed, the happier powers in things without us are permitted free passage, and have their way with us. And so, from music, the school of Giorgione passes often to the play which is like music; to those masques in which men avowedly do but play at real life, like children "dressing-up," disguised in the strange old Italian dresses, particoloured, or fantastic with embroidery and furs, of which the master was so curious a designer, and which, above all the spotless white linen at wrist and throat, he painted so dexterously.

And when people are happy in this thirsty land water will not be far off; and in the school of Giorgione, the presence of water—the well, or marble-rimmed pool, the drawing or pouring of water, as the woman pours it from a pitcher with her jewelled hand in the *Fête Champêtre*, listening, perhaps, to the cool sound as it falls, blent with the music of the pipes—is as characteristic, and almost as suggestive, as that of music itself. And the landscape feels, and is glad of it also—a landscape full of clearness, of the effects of water, of fresh rain newly passed through the air, and collected into the grassy channels; the air, too, in the school of Giorgione, seeming as vivid as the people who breathe it, and literally empyrean, all impurities being burnt out of it, and no taint, no floating particle of anything but its own proper elements allowed to subsist within it.

Its scenery is such as in England we call "park scenery," with some elusive refinement felt about the rustic buildings, the choice grass, the grouped trees, the undulations deftly economised for graceful effect. Only, in Italy all natural things are, as it were, woven through

---

[35] The "fire" of Giorgione.
[36] See the end of the "Conclusion" to the *Renaissance*.

and through with gold thread, even the cypress revealing it among the folds of its blackness. And it is with gold dust, or gold thread, that these Venetian painters seem to work, spinning its fine filaments, through the solemn human flesh, away into the white plastered walls of the thatched huts. The harsher details of the mountains recede to a harmonious distance, the one peak of rich blue above the horizon remaining but as the visible warrant of that due coolness which is all we need ask here of the Alps, with their dark rains and streams. Yet what real, airy space, as the eye passes from level to level, through the long-drawn valley in which Jacob embraces Rachel among the flocks! Nowhere is there a truer instance of that balance, that modulated unison of landscape and persons—of the human image and its accessories—already noticed as characteristic of the Venetian school, so that, in it, neither personage nor scenery is ever a mere pretext for the other.

Something like this seems to me to be the *vraie vérité*[37] about Giorgione, if I may adopt a serviceable expression, by which the French recognise those more liberal and durable impressions which, in respect of any really considerable person or subject, anything that has at all intricately occupied men's attention, lie beyond, and must supplement, the narrower range of the strictly ascertained facts about it. In this, Giorgione is but an illustration of a valuable general caution we may abide by in all criticism. As regards Giorgione himself, we have indeed to take note of all those negations and exceptions, by which, at first sight, a "new Vasari" seems merely to have confused our apprehension of a delightful object, to have explained away out of our inheritance from past time what seemed of high value there. Yet it is not with a full understanding even of those exceptions that one can leave off just at this point. Properly qualified, such exceptions are but a salt of genuineness in our knowledge; and beyond all those strictly ascertained facts, we must take note of that indirect influence by which one like Giorgione, for instance, enlarges his permanent efficacy and really makes himself felt in our culture. In a just impression of that, is the essential truth, the *vraie vérité*, concerning him.

37 Essential truth.

CONCLUSION

Λέγει που Ἡράκλειτος ὅτι πάντα χωρεῖ καὶ οὐδὲν μένει[38]

To regard all things and principles of things as inconstant modes or fashions has more and more become the tendency of modern thought. Let us begin with that which is without—our physical life. Fix upon it in one of its more exquisite intervals, the moment, for instance, of delicious recoil from the flood of water in summer heat. What is the whole physical life in that moment but a combination of natural elements to which science gives their names? But those elements, phosphorus and lime and delicate fibres, are present not in the human body alone: we detect them in places most remote from it. Our physical life is a perpetual motion of them—the passage of the blood, the waste and repairing of the lenses of the eye, the modification of the tissues of the brain under every ray of light and sound—processes which science reduces to simpler and more elementary forces. Like the elements of which we are composed, the action of these forces extends beyond us: it rusts iron and ripens corn. Far out on every side of us those elements are broadcast, driven in many currents; and birth and gesture and death and the springing of violets from the grave are but a few out of ten thousand resultant combinations. That clear, perpetual outline of face and limb is but an image of ours, under which we group them—a design in a web, the actual threads of which pass out beyond it. This at least of flame-like our life has, that it is but the concurrence, renewed from moment to moment, of forces parting sooner or later on their ways.

Or, if we begin with the inward world of thought and feeling, the whirlpool is still more rapid, the flame more eager and devouring. There it is no longer the gradual darkening of the eye, the gradual fading of colour from the wall—movements of the shore-side, where the water flows down indeed, though in apparent rest—but the race of the mid-stream, a drift of momentary acts of sight and passion and thought. At first sight experience seems to bury us under

38 "Heraclitus says, 'All things give way; nothing remaineth'" (Pater's translation of a remark by Socrates in Plato's *Cratylus*).

a flood of external objects, pressing upon us with a sharp and importunate reality, calling us out of ourselves in a thousand forms of action. But when reflexion begins to play upon those objects they are dissipated under its influence; the cohesive force seems suspended like some trick of magic; each object is loosed into a group of impressions—colour, odour, texture—in the mind of the observer. And if we continue to dwell in thought on this world, not of objects in the solidity with which language invests them, but of impressions, unstable, flickering, inconsistent, which burn and are extinguished with our consciousness of them, it contracts still further: the whole scope of observation is dwarfed into the narrow chamber of the individual mind. Experience, already reduced to a group of impressions, is ringed round for each one of us by that thick wall of personality through which no real voice has ever pierced on its way to us, or from us to that which we can only conjecture to be without. Every one of those impressions is the impression of the individual in his isolation, each mind keeping as a solitary prisoner its own dream of a world. Analysis goes a step farther still, and assures us that those impressions of the individual mind to which, for each one of us, experience dwindles down, are in perpetual flight; that each of them is limited by time, and that as time is infinitely divisible, each of them is infinitely divisible also; all that is actual in it being a single moment, gone while we try to apprehend it, of which it may ever be more truly said that it has ceased to be than that it is. To such a tremulous wisp constantly reforming itself on the stream, to a single sharp impression, with a sense in it, a relic more or less fleeting, of such moments gone by, what is real in our life fines itself down. It is with this movement, with the passage and dissolution of impressions, images, sensations, that analysis leaves off—that continual vanishing away, that strange, perpetual weaving and unweaving of ourselves.

Philosophiren, says Novalis, *ist dephlegmatisiren, vivificiren.*[39] The service of philosophy, of speculative culture, towards the human spirit, is to rouse, to startle it to a life of constant and eager observation. Every moment some form grows perfect in hand or face; some tone on the hills or the sea is choicer than the rest; some mood of passion or insight or intellectual excitement is irresistibly real and attractive to us,—for that moment only. Not the fruit of experience, but experience itself, is the end. A counted number of pulses only is given to us of a variegated, dramatic life. How may we see in them all that is to be seen in them by the finest senses? How shall we pass most swiftly from point to point, and be present always at the focus where the greatest number of vital forces unite in their purest energy?

To burn always with this hard, gemlike flame, to maintain this ecstasy, is success in life. In a sense it might even be said that our failure is to form habits: for, after all, habit is relative to a stereotyped world, and meantime it is only the roughness of the eye that makes any two persons, things, situations, seem alike. While all melts under our feet, we may well grasp at any exquisite passion, or any contribution to knowledge that seems by a lifted horizon to set the spirit free for a moment, or any stirring of the senses, strange dyes, strange colours, and curious odours, or work of the artist's hands, or the face of one's friend. Not to discriminate every moment some passionate attitude in those about us, and in the very brilliancy of their gifts some tragic dividing of forces on their ways, is, on this short day of frost and sun, to sleep before evening. With this sense of the splendour of our experience and of its awful brevity, gathering all we are into one desperate effort to see and touch, we shall hardly have time to make theories about the things we see and touch. What we have to do is to be for ever curiously testing new opinions and courting new impressions, never acquiescing in a facile orthodoxy of Comte, or of Hegel,[40] or of our own. Philosophical theories or ideas, as points of view, instruments of criticism, may help us to gather up what might otherwise pass unregarded by us. "Philosophy is the microscope of thought." The theory or idea or system which requires of us the sacrifice of any part of this experience, in consideration of some interest into which we cannot enter, or some abstract theory

---

[39] "To philosophize is to cast off inertia, to make oneself alive." Novalis was a German writer of the Romantic school.

[40] French and German philosophers who each erected a large philosophic system purporting to be all-inclusive and final.

we have not identified with ourselves, or of what is only conventional, has no real claim upon us.

One of the most beautiful passages of Rousseau is that in the sixth book of the *Confessions,* where he describes the awakening in him of the literary sense. An undefinable taint of death had clung always about him, and now in early manhood he believed himself smitten by mortal disease. He asked himself how he might make as much as possible of the interval that remained; and he was not biassed by anything in his previous life when he decided that it must be by intellectual excitement, which he found just then in the clear, fresh writings of Voltaire. Well! we are all *condamnés,* as Victor Hugo says: we are all under sentence of death but with a sort of indefinite reprieve—*les hommes sont tous condamnés à mort avec des sursis indéfinis:* we have

10

an interval, and then our place knows us no more. Some spend this interval in listlessness, some in high passions, the wisest, at least among "the children of this world," in art and song. For our one chance lies in expanding that interval, in getting as many pulsations as possible into the given time. Great passions may give us this quickened sense of life, ecstasy and sorrow of love, the various forms of enthusiastic activity, disinterested or otherwise, which come naturally to many of us. Only be sure it is passion—that it does yield you this fruit of a quickened, multiplied consciousness. Of such wisdom, the poetic passion, the desire of beauty, the love of art for its own sake, has most. For art comes to you proposing frankly to give nothing but the highest quality to your moments as they pass, and simply for those moments' sake.

Gerard Manley Hopkins

1844–1889

Hopkins was born near London in 1844, the son of highly educated parents who had active interests in politics, philosophy, and art, and who were moderate Anglicans in religion. Early in life the boy's temperament showed the marked influence of Romanticism: a sensitive and almost ecstatic love of beauty, especially in nature, and a beauty full of rich and sensuous color; a fascinated interest in whatever was "counter, original, spare, strange" (see "Pied Beauty"); and a passion for individuality (he spoke later of "my consciousness and feeling of myself, that taste of myself, . . . more distinctive than the smell of walnutleaf or camphor"). We could predict a romantic poet of nature with a marked strain of originality in perception and in form.

After attending boarding school at Highgate, Hopkins matriculated at Balliol College, Oxford, in 1863, and was plunged into the violent religious controversy of the time and the place. The rival parties were led by Benjamin Jowett, the Broad Church Liberal, and Dr. Pusey, the High Church Anglican who had joined Keble and Newman a generation earlier to support the Oxford Movement. As one could have anticipated, it was the latter that claimed Hopkins's allegiance, partly because of the aesthetic appeal of its ritual and architecture, but partly, one suspects, because its ascetic practices and its authoritarian principles offered his insistent ego exactly the discipline and control he felt it most needed. His

reading in 1864 of Newman's *Apologia pro Vita Sua,* explaining and defending the famous conversion to Rome, and his subsequent conversations with Newman himself at Birmingham, prepared the way for Hopkins's own conversion in 1866. Two years later he entered the Society of Jesus. He spent the rest of his short life serving his Order in various ways, most notably by missionary work in the slums of Liverpool and by teaching at Dublin, where he was Professor of Classics in the new Catholic university.

When Hopkins entered the Jesuit Order in 1868, he burned most of his early verse and "resolved to write no more, as not belonging to my profession, unless it were by the wish of my superiors." Seven years later when he was asked to write an ode in memory of five Franciscan nuns who had been drowned at sea, his "Wreck of the Deutschland" revealed an original poet of major quality—indeed, its style was so new and unconventional that the editors of *The Month,* a Jesuit periodical to which Hopkins sent his manuscript, "dared not print it." Since this was the first poem written in his highly personal manner (the early verse is largely derivative, from Keats and George Herbert), it seems likely that the rigidly disciplined life of his Order, which Hopkins welcomed, surely, as an imperative check to his own *self-*indulgence, produced an indirect reaction in his verse. When his romantic ego was brought to heel in his vocation, it asserted itself all the more strongly in his avocation. Moreover, when Bridges told him to imitate classical poetry, Hopkins answered that "the effect of studying masterpieces is to make me admire and do otherwise. So it must be on every original artist to some degree, on me to a marked degree. Perhaps then more reading would only *refine my singularity,* which is not what you want." But his religious life was marked by entire and willing submission to traditional authority.

The poems which he felt free to compose, after writing the "Deutschland," are few in number and short, a handful of sonnets and lyrics. He could not find it in his conscience to spend time on poetry, nor did the pressure of his clerical work leave him leisure or creative energy for much composition. None of his verse was published during his lifetime, but he sent the manuscripts to his friend Robert Bridges, so that "if anyone should like, they might be published after my death." But Bridges, concluding that the public would be as much offended as he was by Hopkins's lack of literary decorum, did not print the *Poems of Gerard Manley Hopkins* until 1918. Even then the edition of 750 copies took ten years to sell out. But when the next printing appeared in 1930, it was gone in five months, and Hopkins rose suddenly to the rank of major Victorian poet. Or rather, modern poet. He began to appear in anthologies of twentieth-century verse, to be discussed in studies of contemporary poetry. By 1934 he was being called the "forerunner of the postwar poets, the first 'modern' poet, and a most evident link between them and Donne."

But if this is true (in ways to be considered in a moment), it is also true that much of Hopkins's work seems far from modern. One of his most characteristic poems begins:

Earnest, earthless, equal, attuneable, vaulty, voluminous, . . . stupendous
Evening strains to be time's vast, womb-of-all, home-of-all, hearse-of-all night.
Her fond yellow hornlight wound to the west, her wild hollow hoarlight hung to the height
Waste; her earliest stars, earl-stars, stars principal, overbend us,
Fire-featuring heaven.

This is no more like Donne than it is like Eliot. If anything, it suggests the musical art of Swinburne with its pronounced play of assonance and rime. But fundamentally it is unlike anyone else, a thing all its own, curious and strange in both imagery and rhythm. The first and often unfavorable impression that Hopkins makes is of a poet straining for originality and succeeding only in being eccentric. But we must remember his answer to a friend who protested

against the singularity of his style, that it was the spontaneous expression of his poetical feeling.

This is largely, if not wholly, true. Hopkins by nature saw things in a highly individual way. He had a passion for what he called "inscape," for the special individualizing quality which distinguishes one particular object or person or emotion from all other similar objects, persons, or emotions; and at the same time, a passion for "instress," the special individual response which the inscape of that object, person, or emotion awakened in him. In both respects (illustrated in "Henry Purcell") this is a romantic passion for what is singular and unique—and therefore rightly and inevitably to be expressed in a highly original style. The proof of this is in the reading. What at first seems merely eccentric is discovered, on further study, to carry a strange but entirely accurate perception. One passes through the image to an "idea" one can imaginatively grasp. You must not, he told Bridges, dismiss novelty and boldness offhand as affectation; and again, if the meaning is dark on first reading, see if it does not presently explode.

But sometimes the explosion never occurs. That was certain to be the case, given Hopkins's desire to capture the special and ultimate quality of every experience. He knew that no ordinary word would do. He had to find a unique expression for a unique emotion. And sometimes he failed to match the two. The strange image or the strange rhythm is not the right one, or at any rate not one which the average reader can assimilate. Instead of passing through it to a valid perception, he is simply stopped. "It is the vice of distinctiveness to become queer. This vice I cannot have escaped." But the instances grow fewer on every reading; the sense of oddness disappears as one catches Hopkins's angle of vision and shares his intuition.

In a similar fashion we modify our first impression that his art is largely verbal. There is no doubt that Hopkins was much attracted to the sensuous diction and the musical harmonies of Tennyson and the Pre-Raphaelites. His letters praise the popular poets of the day for their "poetical impetus, and . . . richness of diction," and Swinburne in particular for the extraordinary music of his words and his mastery of "a poetical dialect so ornate and continuously beautiful." Just as Pater was saying that poetry should aspire "towards the condition of music" (see p. 931), Hopkins was writing in his *Notebooks,* "Poetry is speech framed for contemplation of the mind by the way of hearing, or speech framed to be heard for its own sake and interest over and above its interest of meaning." This tendency to make prosody a primary end instead of a functional part can be seen at the close of the octave of "Spring" and in the opening lines of "Spelt from Sibyl's Leaves," quoted above.

On the other hand, the letters criticize contemporary poetry not only for the use of archaic and Elizabethan diction but also for weakness "in thought and insight." And Swinburne is blamed for "a perpetual functioning of genius without truth, feeling, or any adequate matter to be at function on." The effect is extraordinary, "but words only are only words." The fact is that Hopkins's serious concern with religious experience, together with his personal suffering during the final years of his life, made a primarily verbal art simply impossible. The depth and intensity of his feeling brought all his technical skill to bear organically on its expression.

At its best, indeed, his style is not musical but dramatic. The diction, though it departs widely from current idiom, as Shakespeare's does, is a living diction, capable of great psychological precision, and without sacrifice of the evocative and sensuous effects of a lyrical vocabulary. His Sprung Rhythm (an accentual verse in which the foot varies from one to four syllables) was founded on common speech, as he himself explained by citing nursery rimes like *Díng, dóng, béll; Pússy's ín the wéll; Whó pút her ín? Líttle Jóhnny Thín.* But like that example, it retained the movement of song. What he wanted to achieve was a metric flexible enough to catch the shifting emotions of felt experience and yet rhythmical enough to retain an incantatory effect, or in his own words, he wanted to combine "markedness of rhythm—that is rhythm's self—and naturalness of expression." If the first two lines of "Spring and Fall" are lyrical and the next two dramatic, those that follow are precisely the fusion which Hopkins aimed at, in which the speaking voice is mounted, so to speak, on a singing base. In the same way his pronounced use of alliteration, assonance, and internal rime serves a dramatic purpose over and above its musical effect. In the closing couplet of "Spring and Fall," both the "b" and the "m" alliterations, as well as the rime, enforce the irony.

When Hopkins spoke of masterly execution as the artist's most essential quality, he defined it as "the begetting one's thought on paper, on verse," and went on to insist that "the life must be conveyed into the work and displayed there, not suggested as having been in the artist's mind." It is this power of dramatic realization, which is possible only in living speech, that makes his poetry superior to most Victorian verse and connects it with modern art. Indeed, his ability to do this in a medium that retains the sensuous and evocative element in Elizabethan and Romantic poetry is found in various contemporary poets, notably Yeats, Frost, and MacNeice. Furthermore, his verse has a density and compression of meaning that is far more modern than Victorian. The merit of a work, he once said, "may lie for one

thing in its terseness. It is like a mate which may be given, one way only, in three moves; otherwise, various ways, in many." Hopkins's three-move checkmates are achieved by multiple meaning (cf. note 1 to "God's Grandeur"); by ambiguity of reference, where a phrase is linked grammatically in one way to what precedes it, in another to what follows (cf. "leaves and blooms" in line 6 of "Spring," which are first verbs and then nouns); by the use of ellipsis to suggest the immediacy of actual speech, or to follow and reproduce the very movement of the mind in the act of thought, leaping from image to image, or in the act of perception seizing in a single unity the various facets of observation (a falcon drawn toward and etched against the dappled sky of the morning becomes a "dapple-dawn-drawn falcon"). All these techniques are characteristic of twentieth-century verse. Finally, apart from form, if Hopkins's focus on nature is dated, his concern "with inner division, friction, and psychological complexities in general" has spoken directly to our own time.

This concern is to be traced to his personal life. His last years were filled with intense, if intermittent, suffering. From about 1880, and with increasing frequency, the letters speak of "a wretched state of weakness and weariness," of "a deep fit of nervous prostration" in which "I did not know but I was dying," of "that coffin of weakness and dejection in which I live, without even the hope of change," of "fits of sadness" which, "though they do not affect my judgment, resemble madness." It is hardly surprising that when he caught typhoid fever in June 1889, he made no effort for his life, and died at the age of forty-five.

The poems, especially the so-called "terrible sonnets" written in the last four years, not only express this suffering in metaphors and rhythms that make its pain tangible (see especially the superb "No Worst, There Is None"); they also reveal its focal point, an agonizing sense of frustration. "In the life I lead now," he says, "which is one of a continually jaded and harassed mind, if in any leisure I try to do anything [in poetry] I make no way." Or he cries out, "If I could but get on, if I could but produce work I should not mind its being buried, silenced, going no further; but it kills me to be time's eunuch and never to beget." It must not be supposed that it was only the poet who was frustrated. So, to a lesser degree, was the Jesuit priest: "I cannot produce anything at all, not only the luxuries like poetry, but the duties almost of my position." If the sonnet "To R. B." refers to his art, the previous sonnet ("Thou Art Indeed Just, Lord") asks, "Why must disappointment *all* I endeavour end?" and closes with a passionate prayer for God to send his roots rain that he may "breed one work that wakes"—in this context, plainly a Christian work.

Frustration is the normal expression of neurosis, of an inner conflict that is unresolved. Here we are on dangerous ground, since no layman, at any rate, is competent to diagnose Hopkins's illness. One thing is certain. The conflict was not that of the natural man, with his imperious ego and his artistic drive, fighting hopelessly to be free of Catholic and Jesuit bondage. No one can read the letters and imagine for a moment that Hopkins was not a profoundly religious person and a devout Catholic. Indeed, however much he wanted to be himself and to be the poet he knew he was, he wanted far more deeply to be Christian. If his profession demanded time and energy that he might have given to poetry, if it stood between him and the fame his published work might have won him, if it asked him to submit his mind to orthodox beliefs and ecclesiastical control, he gladly made the sacrifice. But not—much as he wished to—whole-heartedly. "I have never wavered in my vocation," he said, "but I have not lived up to it." In a revealing letter to Dixon, he confessed to the reluctance he had shown in giving up hopes of poetic fame, to "the backward glances I have given with my hand upon the plough," to the "thoughts of vain-glory" which his artistic ambitions had quickened. There was no conflict of decision between religion and art, between the Christian and the Romantic, but there was a conflict of desires. And it was intensified, as the above passage implies, by a sense of guilt. He would gladly have lived all his life, he said, in a monastery and been "busied only with God. But in the midst of outward occupations . . . unhappily the will is entangled, worldly interests freshen, and wordly ambitions revive." This tension in one form or another, between the Christian-Jesuit and the natural man, either poet or individualist, underlies "The Windhover," where it is momentarily resolved; may well be central in "Spelt from Sibyl's Leaves" (see note 9); and is explicit in milder tones in "My Own Heart Let Me More Have Pity On." No doubt it is not the whole story behind his suffering, but it is plainly an important source of the frustration he felt so keenly and profoundly.

Finally, equally modern in its appeal, there is the subtle and sophisticated attitude toward his suffering which Hopkins adopts. On the one hand, he feels it to be terribly unjust. He who has given his life to God, who has sacrificed so much in His service (parents, wife and children, the career of an artist), is not only desperately unhappy, but thwarted, defeated, in all he endeavors to do. On the other hand, his suffering is rightly and wisely imposed upon him by a just God: it is punishment for his sins, or it is Christian purgation, cleansing him of evil. These attitudes are not held singly in alternation, but at one and the same time. In "Carrion Comfort" and "Thou Art Indeed Just, Lord," this ambivalence, which is as true of human nature on the secular as on the religious level, is rendered with surpassing skill.

Hopkins's poetry is too small in bulk, too narrow in range of observation, perhaps a trifle too strained and highly wrought, to justify calling him a major poet. But nowhere else in the Victorian period, and rarely anywhere else outside *King Lear,* can one find suffering so intensely felt and so poignantly expressed.

TEXTS: The fourth edition of the *Poems,* edited with notes by W. H. Gardner and N. H. MacKenzie (1967), is now the standard text. Hopkins's *Letters to Robert Bridges,* his *Correspondence* with R. W. Dixon, and the *Further Letters, . . . including his Correspondence with Coventry Patmore* (all edited by C. C. Abbott, the first two in 1935, the third in 1938, enlarged ed. 1956), are indispensable for understanding his general aesthetics and the meaning of particular poems. *A Hopkins Reader,* ed. John Pick (1953) is a good selection from the poetry and letters. Perhaps the most valuable critical books are: W. H. Gardner's *Gerard Manley Hopkins* (2 vols., 1944 and 1949) and Robert Boyle's *Metaphor in Hopkins* (1960).

Heaven—Haven

A Nun Takes the Veil
I have desired to go
　　Where springs not fail,
To fields where flies no sharp and sided hail
　　And a few lilies blow.

And I have asked to be
　　Where no storms come,
Where the green swell is in the havens dumb,
　　And out of the swing of the sea.

God's Grandeur

The world is charged with the grandeur of God.
　　It will flame out, like shining from shook foil;[1]
　　It gathers to a greatness, like the ooze of oil
Crushed.[2] Why do men then now not reck his
　　　　rod?

---

[1] "I mean," said Hopkins (*Letters to Bridges,* p. 169), "foil in its sense of leaf or tinsel. . . . Shaken goldfoil gives off broad glares like sheet lightning and also, . . . owing to its zigzag dints and creasings and network of small many-cornered facets, a sort of fork lightning too."
[2] Presumably like oil crushed out of seed.

Generations have trod, have trod, have trod;   5
   And all is seared with trade; bleared, smeared
      with toil;
   And wears man's smudge and shares man's
      smell: the soil
Is bare now, nor can foot feel, being shod.

And for all this, nature is never spent;
   There lives the dearest freshness deep down   10
      things;
And though the last lights off the black West
      went
   Oh, morning, at the brown brink eastward,
      springs—
Because the Holy Ghost over the bent
   World broods with warm breast and with ah!
      bright wings.

Spring

Nothing is so beautiful as Spring—
   When weeds, in wheels, shoot long and lovely
      and lush;
   Thrush's eggs look little low heavens, and
      thrush
Through the echoing timber does so rinse and
      wring
The ear, it strikes like lightning to hear him sing;   5
   The glassy peartree leaves and blooms, they
      brush
   The descending blue; that blue is all in a rush
With richness; the racing lambs too have fair
      their fling.

What is all this juice and all this joy?
   A strain of the earth's sweet being in the be-   10
      ginning
In Eden garden.—Have, get, before it cloy,

   Before it cloud,[1] Christ, lord,[2] and sour with
      sinning,
Innocent mind and Mayday in girl and boy,
   Most, O maid's child, thy choice and worthy
      the winning.[3]

[1] The antecedent of "it" is line 10.
[2] These two words are vocatives.
[3] Cf. Newman's sermon on "The Second Spring" (1857), which Hopkins must have known: "How beautiful is the human heart, when it puts forth its first leaves, and opens and rejoices in its spring-tide. Fair as may be the bodily form, fairer far, in its green foliage and bright blossoms,

The Windhover

To Christ our Lord

I caught this morning morning's minion, king-
   dom of daylight's dauphin, dapple-dawn-
   drawn Falcon, in his riding
   Of the rolling level underneath him steady
     air, and striding
High there, how he rung upon the rein of a
     wimpling wing[1]
In his ecstasy! then off, off forth on swing,   5
   As a skate's heel sweeps smooth on a bow-
     bend: the hurl and gliding
   Rebuffed the big wind. My heart in hiding
Stirred for a bird,—the achieve of, the mastery of
   the thing![2]

Brute beauty and valour and act, oh, air, pride,
   plume,[3] here
   Buckle! AND the fire that breaks from thee   10
     then, a billion
Times told lovelier, more dangerous, O my
   chevalier![4]

---

is natural virtue. It blooms in the young, like some rich flower, so delicate, so fragrant, and so dazzling. . . . And yet, as night follows upon day, as decrepitude follows upon health, so surely are failure, and overthrow, and annihilation, the issue of this natural virtue, if time only be allowed to it to run its course. . . . Let the course of life proceed, let the bright soul go through the fire and water of the world's temptations and seductions and corruptions and transformations; and, alas for the in-sufficiency of nature! Alas for its powerlessness to per-severe, its waywardness in disappointing its own promise!"

[1] In falconry "to ring" means to rise in the air spirally, but this image is combined with that of "ringing a horse," i.e., guiding him in a circle on a long rein. "Wimpling" is turning and twisting.
[2] Cf. Hopkins's letter, written from a Jesuit monastery (*Letters to Dixon*, pp. 75–76): "My mind is here more at peace than it has ever been and I would gladly live all my life, if it were so to be, in as great or a greater seclu-sion from the world and be busied only with God. But in the midst of outward occupations not only the mind is drawn away from God, . . . but unhappily the will too is entangled, worldly interests freshen, and worldly ambi-tions revive." The image of the falcon suggests the natural life in all its energy and beauty and freedom.
[3] These terms, in general, carry on the chivalric imagery in lines 1–2, which reappears in line 11; it is particularly appropriate to the heroic Christian life he goes on to describe. "Air" is used in the sense of "peculiar or char-acteristic appearance, mien, manner," and here suggests the knightly or princely air of the falcon. I take "pride" to mean "proud, chivalric scorn" of everything mean or even earthly.
[4] The "thee" is Christ, my chevalier, but only the Christ that is "realized" in the lives of men, in Hopkins's own

No wonder of it: shéer plód makes plough
    down sillion[5]
Shine, and blue-bleak embers, ah my dear,
  Fall, gall themselves, and gash gold-vermil-
    lion.[6]

Pied Beauty

Glory be to God for dappled things—
  For skies of couple-colour as a brinded[1] cow;
    For rose-moles all in stipple[2] upon trout
      that swim;
Fresh-firecoal chestnut-falls;[3] finches' wings;
  Landscape plotted and pieced—fold, fallow,   5
    and plough;
  And áll trádes, their gear and tackle and trim.

All things counter,[4] original, spare,[5] strange;

---

life. It therefore really means "one's self as he takes on, or myself as I take on, the heroic Christian character of Christ." (Cf. one of the sonnets—"As Kingfishers Catch Fire"—where the just man by the grace of God
  "Acts in God's eye what in God's eye he is—
  Christ. For Christ plays in ten thousand places,
  Lovely in limbs, and lovely in eyes not his
  To the Father through the features of men's faces.")
"Buckle" is an imperative (Hopkins is talking to himself and to us). Here in the Christian life, in the priestly vocation, let one, or/and let me, buckle these heroic qualities together, and then the Christlike life of spiritual conquest will be far lovelier, though more dangerous, than any natural life they could inform. Or, for another possible reading, here in this mortal life or in the heart (in hiding), let one, or/and let me, buckle (in the sense of fasten down) these natural energies (under the Christian-Catholic rule), and then in sublimated form they will burst out in a Christlike life far lovelier, though more dangerous. (The second reading is suggested by Gardner, who quotes *Macbeth:* "He cannot buckle his distempered cause Within the belt of rule.")
5 The ridge between the furrows.
6 Both metaphors illustrate and apply the thesis of lines 9–11. Though the Christian life seems to lack the "beauty and valour and act" of the natural life, it requires and reveals these qualities in far higher degree. The hard, plodding work of plowing (of the priest) makes the plowshare shine as it goes down the row turning up the sillion. When embers, blue-bleak on the outside, fall and break open (the death of martyrdom is implied), they show forth a magnificent brightness ("gold-vermillion" suggesting both the blood and the gold crown of the martyr).

1 Streaked (an early form of "brindled").
2 Method in painting of applying colors in dots.
3 Chestnuts without their husks.
4 Opposite to what is expected, or to the ordinary run of things.
5 Rare.

Whatever is fickle, freckled (who knows how?)
  With swift, slow; sweet, sour; adazzle, dim;
He fathers-forth whose beauty is past change: 1
    Praise him.

Henry Purcell[1]

The poet wishes well to the divine genius of Purcell and praises him that, whereas other musicians have given utterance to the moods of man's mind, he has, beyond that, uttered in notes the very make and species of man as created both in him and in all men generally.

Have fair fallen, O fair, fair have fallen,[2] so dear
To me, so arch-especial a spirit as heaves in
    Henry Purcell,
An age is now since passed, since parted; with the
    reversal
Of the outward sentence low lays him, listed to a
    heresy, here.[3]

Not mood in him nor meaning, proud fire or
    sacred fear,
Or love or pity or all that sweet notes not his
    might nursle:
It is the forgèd feature finds me; it is the re-
    hearsal
Of own, of abrúpt sélf there so thrusts on, so
    throngs the ear.

Let him oh! with his air of angels then lift me,
    lay me! only I'll
Have an eye to the sakes of him,[4] quaint moon-   1
    marks, to his pelted plumage under

---

1 Pronounced *Púr-cell.* An English composer, and a Protestant, who died in 1695.
2 Hopkins explained (*Letters to Bridges,* p. 171) that he meant, May fair fortune have befallen Henry Purcell.
3 *Letters to Bridges,* pp. 170–71: "May Purcell, O may he have died a good death and that soul which I love so much and which breathes and stirs so unmistakably in his works have parted from the body and passed away, centuries since though I frame the wish, in peace with God! so that the heavy condemnation under which he outwardly or nominally lay for being out of the true Church may in consequence of his good intentions have been reversed. 'Low lays him' is merely '[which] lays him low,' that is, strikes him heavily, weighs upon him. . . . 'Listed,' by the by, is 'enlisted.' "
4 The "sakes of him" is his "arch-especial" spirit, his "forgèd feature," his "own" or "abrupt self," which Hopkins will listen for, over and above responding to the musical meaning ("his air of angels").

Wings:[5] so some great stormfowl, whenever he
    has walked his while

The thunder-purple seabeach plumèd purple-of-
    thunder,
If a wuthering of his palmy snow-pinions scat-
    ter a colossal smile
Off him, but meaning motion fans fresh our wits
    with wonder.[6]

Felix Randal

Felix Randal the farrier, O is he dead then? my
    duty all ended,
Who have watched his mould of man, big-boned
    and hardy-handsome
Pining, pining, till time when reason rambled
    in it and some
Fatal four disorders, fleshed there, all contended?

Sickness broke him. Impatient he cursed at first,   5
    but mended
Being anointed and all; though a heavenlier
    heart began some
Months earlier, since I had our sweet reprieve
    and ransom
Tendered to him. Ah well, God rest him all road
    ever[1] he offended!

This seeing the sick endears them to us, us too it
    endears.
My tongue had taught thee comfort, touch had   10
    quenched thy tears,
Thy tears that touched my heart, child, Felix,
    poor Felix Randal;

How far from then forethought of, all thy more
    boisterous years,
When thou at the random[2] grim forge, powerful
    amidst peers,

Didst fettle[3] for the great grey drayhorse his
    bright and battering sandal!

Spring and Fall

To a young child

Márgarét, are you gríeving
Over Goldengrove unleaving?
Leáves, líke the things of man, you
With your fresh thoughts care for, can you?
Áh! ás the heart grows older   5
It will come to such sights colder
By and by, nor spare a sigh
Though worlds of wanwood leafmeal[1] lie;
And yet you wíll weep and know why.[2]
Now no matter, child, the name: 10
Sórrow's spríngs áre the same.
Nor mouth had, no nor mind, expressed
What heart heard of, ghost guessed:[3]
It ís the blight man was born for,
It is Margaret you mourn for.   15

In the Valley of the Elwy

I remember a house where all were good
    To me, God knows, deserving no such thing:
    Comforting smell breathed at very entering,
Fetched fresh, as I suppose, off some sweet wood.

That cordial air made those kind people a hood   5
    All over, as a bevy of eggs the mothering wing
    Will, or mild nights the new morsels of
        Spring:
Why, it seemed of course; seemed of right it
    should.

Lovely the woods, waters, meadows, combes,
    vales,
All the air things wear that build this world of   10
    Wales;
    Only the inmate does not correspond:

God, lover of souls, swaying considerate scales,

---

[5] His special individuality is like the special markings, shaped like a new moon, on the plumage of a stormfowl under his wings.
[6] Just as the bird, intending only flight, reveals his moon-marks (like a "colossal smile" because of their shape) by a wuthering (fluttering) of his wings as he prepares to take off, so Purcell, though aiming only to communicate "proud fire or sacred fear," reveals his own unique character and personality in his style.

[1] In whatever way.
[2] Built with stones of irregular shapes and sizes.

---

[3] Prepare. (Notes 1–3 are by W. H. Gardner.)

[1] A fusion of "piecemeal" and "leaf-mold." The latter meaning reinforces the "wan" of "wanwood."
[2] "Will" is the future tense.
[3] Guessed intuitively by the spirit or soul.

Complete thy creature dear O where it fails,
  Being mighty a master, being a father and
    fond.[1]

Spelt from Sibyl's Leaves[1]

Earnest, earthless, equal, attuneable,[2] | vaulty,
  voluminous, . . . stupendous
Evening strains to be tíme's vást, | womb-of-all,
  home-of-all, hearse-of-all night.
Her fond yellow hornlight[3] wound to the west, |
  her wild hollow hoarlight hung to the height
Waste; her earliest stars, earl-stars, | stárs prin-
  cipal, overbend us,
Fíre-féaturing heaven. For earth | her being has
  unbound, her dapple is at an end, as-
tray or aswarm, all throughther,[4] in throngs; |
  self ín self steepèd and páshed[5]—quíte
Disremembering, dísmémbering | áll now. Heart,
  you round[6] me right
With: Óur évening is over us; óur night | whélms,
  whélms, ánd will end us.
Only the beakleaved boughs dragonish | damask[7]
  the tool-smooth bleak light; black,
Ever so black on it. Óur tale, O óur oracle! | Lét
  life, wáned, ah lét life wind
Off hér once skéined stained véined variety |
  upon, áll on twó spools; párt, pen, páck
Now her áll in twó flocks, twó folds—black,
  white; | right, wrong; reckon but, reck but,
    mind
But thése two; wáre of a wórld where bút these |
  twó tell, each off the óther; of a rack
Where, selfwrung, selfstrung, sheathe-[8] and shel-
  terless, | thóughts agáinst thoughts ín groans
    grínd.[9]

5

10

---

1 Hopkins's note to Bridges (*Letters*, pp. 76–77): "The
frame of the sonnet is a rule of three sum *wrong*, thus:
As the sweet smell to those kind people so the Welsh
landscape is NOT to the Welsh; and then the author and
principle of all four terms is asked to bring the sum
right."

1 The Sibyl was the prophetess at Cumae, near Naples,
who wrote down her oracles on leaves (see the *Aeneid*,
Bk. VI).
2 Everywhere harmonious and alike (equal), in contrast
to daylight with its varied color effects (cf. line 5).
3 The light of the new moon.
4 A dialect word meaning "through-other."
5 Enveloped and dashed to pieces.
6 Whisper or talk privately to (obsolete meaning) as well
as turn round upon.   7 Mark in variegated patterns.
8 Probably an error for "sheath-."
9 Lines 10–14 can be read in either one of two ways, each

(Carrion Comfort[1])

Not, I'll not, carrion comfort, Despair, not feast
  on thee;
Not untwist—slack they may be—these last
  strands of man
In me ór, most weary, cry *I can no more*. I can;
Can something, hope, wish day come, not choose
  not to be.

But ah, but O thou terrible, why wouldst thou
  rude on me
Thy wring-world right foot rock? lay a lionlimb
  against me? scan
With darksome devouring eyes my bruisèd bones?
  and fan,
O in turns of tempest, me heaped there; me
  frantic to avoid thee and flee?

  Why? That my chaff might fly; my grain lie
    sheer and clear.[2]
Nay in all that toil, that coil,[3] since[4] (seems) I
  kissed the rod,
Hand rather, my heart lo! lapped strength, stole
  joy, would laugh, chéer.
Cheer whom though? the hero whose heaven-
  handling flung me, fóot tród
Me? or me that fought him? O which one? is it

1

---

of which issues in a radically different meaning for the
poem. (1) Hopkins's "heart" is his natural self with all
its love for the dapple and mixture of things, and therefore is warning him against any intellectual discipline
which insists on his judging everything in black and
white (which, so to speak, would call Henry Purcell a
heretic, a black sheep). Beware of such a world, it tells
him: it is a rack on which the self will be tortured, and
thoughts of submission must clash violently and painfully
against thoughts of revolt. Or (2), the heart is his conscience finding in the reduction of everything to white
and black the prophecy of the Judgment Day, and therefore warning him to beware of the world where all souls
are to be divided into two flocks, and the rack (of hell)
where the self will be tortured, and thoughts of God and
virtue will grind violently against thoughts of horror and
guilt. Against the first reading, one may say that nowhere
else does Hopkins express any revolt against his Church
or his Order; against the second, that the "heart" for
Hopkins never seems to mean the conscience but the
natural self (in the sonnet below, for example, "My Own
Heart Let Me More Have Pity On").

1 The title was added by Bridges.
2 This line at once gives another interpretation to "fan"
in line 7: The tempest that fanned him was winnowing
the chaff from the grain.   3 Tumult.
4 Causal, not temporal: it was (apparently) because I
kissed the rod, . . .

each one? That night, that year
Of now done darkness I wretch lay wrestling with
  (my God!) my God.[5]

No Worst, There Is None

No worst, there is none. Pitched past pitch of
  of grief,
More pangs will, schooled at forepangs, wilder
  wring.
Comforter, where, where is your comforting?
Mary, mother of us, where is your relief?
My cries heave, herds-long;[1] huddle in a main, a   5
  chief
woe, world-sorrow; on an age-old anvil wince
  and sing[2]—
Then lull, then leave off, Fury had shrieked "No
  ling-
ering! Let me be fell:[3] force I must be brief."[4]
O the mind, mind has mountains; cliffs of fall
Frightful, sheer, no-man-fathomed. Hold them   10
  cheap
May who ne'er hung there. Nor does long our
  small
Durance deal with that steep or deep. Here!
  creep,
Wretch, under a comfort serves in a whirlwind:
  all
Life death does end and each day dies with sleep.

I Wake and Feel the Fell of Dark

I wake and feel the fell of dark,[1] not day.
What hours, O what black hoürs we have spent
This night! what sighs you, heart, saw; ways you
  went!
And more must, in yet longer light's delay.

With witness I speak this. But where I say   5

Hours I mean years, mean life. And my lament
Is cries countless, cries like dead[2] letters sent
To dearest him that lives alas! away.

I am gall, I am heartburn. God's most deep de-
  cree
Bitter[3] would have me taste: my taste was me;   10
Bones built in me, flesh filled, blood brimmed
  the curse.
Selfyeast of spirit a dull dough sours.[4] I see
The lost are like this, and their scourge to be
As I am mine, their sweating selves; but worse.[5]

My Own Heart Let Me More Have Pity On

My own heart let me more have pity on; let
Me live to my sad self hereafter kind,
Charitable; not live this tormented mind
With this tormented mind tormenting yet.[1]

I cast for comfort I can no more get   5
By groping round my comfortless, than blind
Eyes in their dark can day or thirst can find
Thirst's all-in-all in all a world of wet.[2]

Soul, self;[3] come, poor Jackself,[4] I do advise
You, jaded, let be; call off thoughts awhile   10
Elsewhere; leave comfort root-room; let joy size

At God knows when to God knows what,[5] whose
  smile

---

[2] Because undelivered.
[3] Both an adjective modifying "decree" and the object
of "taste." The bitter decree is that he taste the bitter.
[4] Cf. Hopkins's *Notebooks* (p. 309), where he speaks of
"my self-being, my consciousness and feeling of myself,
that taste of myself, of *I* and *me* above and in all things."
This spirit self, which should be a leaven to the bodily
self described in the previous line, only makes the latter
more bitter.
[5] Their fate is worse than his (at the moment); they are
in hell.

[1] That is, not living tormenting an already tormented
mind.
[2] "I can no more find comfort in my comfortless self than
blind eyes can find light in their dark selves or than thirst
can find relief in its yearning self"—Robert Boyle, *Metaphor in Hopkins*, p. 147.
[3] Think of the soul as simply the everyday self, Hopkins
is saying, and forget the tormented striving for a "gracious" soul.
[4] Hopkins's everyday, hard-working self. (Gardner's note.)
[5] Let joy grow in size, be released and expand, whenever
it will to whatever proportions it will.

---

[5] The parenthesis must be spoken in a horrified whisper.
(Gardner's note.)

[1] Like the successive cries of a herd (of frightened sheep).
Then they become one tremendous cry of the whole herd
huddled together in fear.
[2] On the anvil of human life, beaten by the hammer-
blows of Fury, I wince and sing out in cries of agony.
[3] Savage, brutal.
[4] Perforce I must be brief. Otherwise no man could survive at all (which explains the periodic lulls).

[1] The smothering coat of darkness. "Fell" is literally the
hairy hide of an animal.

's not wrung, see you;[6] unforeseen times rather
   —as skies
Betweenpie mountains[7]—lights a lovely mile.

Thou Art Indeed Just, Lord

*Justus quidem tu es, Domine, si disputem tecum:
verumtamen justa loquar ad te: Quare via impiorum
prosperatur? &c.*[1]

Thou art indeed just, Lord, if I contend
With thee; but, sir,[2] so what I plead is just.[3]
Why do sinners' ways prosper? and why must
Disappointment all I endeavour end?

Wert thou my enemy, O thou my friend,   5
How wouldst thou worse, I wonder, than thou
    dost
Defeat, thwart me? Oh, the sots and thralls of
    lust

---

[6] The smile of joy is not to be forced by an act of will,
but will break out spontaneously (provided comfort has
root-room) at unforeseen times and light a lovely mile of
life.

[7] As skies seen between dark mountains give a pied or
dappled light.

[1] The opening sentence of Jeremiah 12, but the "&c."
shows that Hopkins expected his reader to have the whole
chapter, called "The message on the broken covenant,"
in mind. The most important verses are: "Righteous art
thou, O Lord, when I plead with thee: yet let me talk
with thee of thy judgments: Wherefore doth the way
of the wicked prosper? wherefore are all they happy that
deal very treacherously? Thou has planted them, yea,
they have taken root: they grow, yea, they bring forth
fruit: thou art near in their mouth, and far from their
reins. But thou, O Lord, knowest me: thou hast seen me,
and tried mine heart toward thee. . . . I have forsaken
mine house, I have left mine heritage. . . . Many pastors
have destroyed my vineyard, they have trodden my portion under foot, they have made my pleasant portion a
desolate wilderness."

[2] The epithet "sir" is intended to catch the middle attitude which is defined in the poem. If the Lord is one's
friend, as he is, and yet treats one, or seems to, like an
enemy, the resulting emotional response will be neither
love nor hate, but a between feeling of respect, exactly
like that which one has toward a judge and expresses by
calling him "sir."

[3] So also what *I* plead is just.

Do in spare hours more thrive than I that spend,

Sir, life upon thy cause.[4] See, banks and brakes
Now, leavèd how thick! lacèd they are again   10
With fretty chervil, look, and fresh wind shakes
Them; birds build—but not I build; no, but
    strain,
Time's eunuch, and not breed one work that
    wakes.[5]
Mine, O thou lord of life, send my roots rain.

To R. B.[1]

The fine delight that fathers thought; the strong
Spur, live and lancing like the blowpipe flame,
Breathes once and, quenchèd faster than it came,
Leaves yet the mind a mother of immortal song.

Nine months she then, nay years, nine years she   5
    long
Within her wears, bears, cares and combs[2] the
    same:
The widow of an insight lost she lives, with aim
Now known and hand at work now never wrong.

Sweet fire the sire of muse, my soul needs this;
I want the one rapture of an inspiration.   10
O then if in my lagging lines you miss

The roll, the rise, the carol, the creation,
My winter world, that scarcely breathes that bliss
Now, yields you, with some sighs, our explana-
    tion.

---

[4] Cf. *Letters to Bridges*, p. 110, Where Hopkins is explaining his delay in answering a letter: "Time and spirits
were wanting; one is so fagged, so harried and gallied [i.e.,
galled] up and down. And the drunkards go on drinking,
the filthy, as the scripture says, are filthy still: human
nature is so inveterate."

[5] Cf. *Letters to Bridges*, p. 222: "It kills me to be time's
eunuch and never to beget."

[1] Robert Bridges.

[2] To unravel and arrange, and also probably (as Gardner
suggests) to "store, mature—as in a honeycomb."

Other Victorian Poets

Elizabeth Barrett Browning

1806–1861

The tremendous acclaim with which the poetry of Elizabeth Barrett Browning was received during her lifetime—greater than that accorded to her husband —was undoubtedly due to a deep and widely felt desire of her contemporaries for moral inspiration and guidance. She herself felt keenly that the poet should be a person apart, the mouthpiece of divine wisdom and truth. In her poem "The Dead Pan" she explicitly outlines the proper subjects of poetry and the mission of the poet:

> What is true and just and honest,
> What is lovely, what is pure . . .
> O brave poets . . .
> Look up Godward; speak the truth in
> Worthy song from earnest soul!

In "A Musical Instrument" she implicitly describes the poet as the reed in the service of divinity. In similar vein she speaks of Wordsworth, in the sonnet on his portrait by Haydon, as "poet-priest."

Her own talent, which was early apparent, was fostered by an unusually fine education in both classical and modern literatures, and was further developed during years of invalidism by wide reading. All of this, quite naturally, is reflected in her poetry, but less to be expected from one who was so isolated— at least before her marriage to Robert Browning in 1846—was her passionate interest in various humanitarian causes of the period, such as the amelioration of child labor and the abolition of slavery. When she had married and was living in Italy, she fervently championed Italian liberation from Austria and unity under an Italian ruler, conceiving of herself as an anointed spokesman for justice.

However, it is not by her humanitarian and political poems that Elizabeth Browning's reputation survives. They were too often marred by redundancy, a kind of patent overelaboration of ideas, and by a self-conscious didacticism which makes them seem to come more from the preacher than from the poet.

Elizabeth Barrett Browning (1806–1861). The story of her literary courtship and marriage to Robert Browning has perhaps somewhat obscured her individual achievement from the modern reader. In fact, during her lifetime, Elizabeth Barrett's poetry was probably more widely known and appreciated than her husband's. *National Portrait Gallery.*

Where she did excel was in the expression of personal experience, particularly in that series of sonnets where under the transparent fiction of a Portuguese troubadour she expressed her own feelings during the time of her courtship by Browning. Here where she was really addressing herself only to her lover—she had not originally intended the sonnets for publication—we find direct and moving expressions of her woman's love, analyzed with a detail and described with a freedom unusual for the age and untouched by any sense of poetic or moralistic mission. This is not to say that *Sonnets from the Portuguese* gives a realistic description of love; rather it is the characteristically idealized view of a period in which very gradually, and for the most part unconsciously, perfect love for another human being came to take the place of love for the Divine Being, who was becoming more and more remote.

TEXTS: Elizabeth Browning's poetry appears in her *Complete Works,* edited by C. Porter and H. A. Clark (6 vols., 1900). The best biography is by Gardner B. Taplin (1957). Her *Letters,* ed. F. G. Kenyon (2 vols., 1897), and *Elizabeth Barrett to Miss Mitford,* ed. Betty Miller (1954) throw valuable light on her mind and work. For critical comment see Douglas Bush, *Mythology and the Romantic Tradition* (1937), pp. 266–71.

A Musical Instrument

I

What was he doing, the great god Pan,
  Down in the reeds by the river?
Spreading ruin and scattering ban,
Splashing and paddling with hoofs of a goat,
And breaking the golden lilies afloat   5
  With the dragon-fly on the river.

II

He tore out a reed, the great god Pan
  From the deep cool bed of the river:
The limpid water turbidly ran,
And the broken lilies a-dying lay,   10
And the dragon-fly had fled away,
  Ere he brought it out of the river.

III

High on the shore sat the great god Pan
  While turbidly flowed the river;
And hacked and hewed as a great god can,
With his hard bleak steel at the patient reed,   15
Till there was not a sign of the leaf indeed
  To prove it fresh from the river.

IV

He cut it short, did the great god Pan,
  (How tall it stood in the river!)
Then drew the pith, like the heart of a man,   20

Steadily from the outside ring,
And notched the poor dry empty thing
  In holes, as he sat by the river.

V

"This is the way," laughed the great god Pan   25
  (Laughed while he sat by the river),
"The only way, since gods began
To make sweet music, they could succeed."
Then, dropping his mouth to a hole in the reed,
  He blew in power by the river.   30

VI

Sweet, sweet, sweet, O Pan!
  Piercing sweet by the river!
Blinding sweet, O great god Pan!
The sun on the hill forgot to die,
And the lilies revived, and the dragon-fly   35
  Came back to dream on the river.

VII

Yet half a beast is the great god Pan,
  To laugh as he sits by the river,
Making a poet out of a man:
The true gods sigh for the cost and pain,—   40
For the reed which grows nevermore again
  As a reed with the reeds in the river.

On a Portrait of Wordsworth by B. R. Haydon[1]

Wordsworth upon Helvellyn![2] Let the cloud
Ebb audibly along the mountain-wind
Then break against the rock, and show behind
The lowland valleys floating up to crowd
The sense with beauty. He with forehead bowed   5
And humble-lidded eyes, as one inclined
Before the sovran thought of his own mind,
And very meek with inspirations proud,
Takes here his rightful place as poet-priest
By the high altar, singing prayer and prayer   10
To the higher Heavens. A nobler vision free
Our Haydon's hand has flung out from the mist:
No portrait this, with Academic air!
This is the poet and his poetry.

---

[1] Benjamin Robert Haydon (1786–1846), English historical painter, a personal friend of Wordsworth.

[2] A peak in the English Lake Country, a frequent haunt of Wordsworth.

Grief

I tell you, hopeless grief is passionless;
That only men incredulous of despair,
Half-taught in anguish, through the midnight air
Beat upward to God's throne in loud access
Of shrieking and reproach. Full desertness, 5
In souls as countries, lieth silent-bare
Under the blanching, vertical eye-glare
Of the absolute Heavens. Deep-hearted man, ex-
    press
Grief for thy Dead in silence like to death—
Most like a monumental statue set 10
In everlasting watch and moveless woe
Till itself crumble to the dust beneath.
Touch it; the marble eyelids are not wet:
If it could weep, it could arise and go.

Sonnets from the Portuguese[1]

1847-1850

1

I thought once how Theocritus[2] had sung
Of the sweet years, the dear and wished-for years,
Who each one in a gracious hand appears
To bear a gift for mortals, old or young;
And, as I mused it in his antique tongue, 5
I saw, in gradual vision through my tears,
The sweet, sad years, the melancholy years,
Those of my own life, who by turns had flung
A shadow across me. Straightway I was 'ware,
So weeping, how a mystic Shape did move 10
Behind me, and drew me backward by the hair;
And a voice said in mastery, while I strove,—
"Guess now who holds thee?"—"Death," I said.
    But there,
The silver answer rang,—"Not Death, but Love."

3

Unlike are we, unlike, O princely Heart!
Unlike our uses and our destinies.
Our ministering two angels look surprise
On one another, as they strike athwart
Their wings in passing. Thou, bethink thee, art 5
A guest for queens to social pageantries,

With gages[3] from a hundred brighter eyes
Than tears even can make mine, to play thy part
Of chief musician. What hast *thou* to do
With looking from the lattice-lights at me, 10
A poor, tired, wandering singer, singing through
The dark, and leaning up a cypress tree?
The chrism[4] is on thine head,—on mine, the
    dew,—
And Death must dig the level where these agree.

4

Thou hast thy calling to some palace floor,
Most gracious singer of high poems! where
The dancers will break footing, from the care
Of watching up thy pregnant lips for more.
And dost thou lift this house's latch too poor 5
For hand of thine? and canst thou think and bear
To let thy music drop here unaware
In folds of golden fulness at my door?
Look up and see the casement broken in,
The bats and owlets builders in the roof! 10
My cricket chirps against thy mandolin.
Hush, call no echo up in further proof
Of desolation! there's a voice within
That weeps . . . as thou must sing . . . alone, aloof.

6

Go from me. Yet I feel that I shall stand
Henceforward in thy shadow. Nevermore
Alone upon the threshold of my door
Of individual life, I shall command
The uses of my soul, nor lift my hand 5
Serenely in the sunshine as before,
Without the sense of that which I forbore—
Thy touch upon the palm. The widest land
Doom takes to part us, leaves thy heart in mine
With pulses that beat double. What I do 10
And what I dream include thee, as the wine
Must taste of its own grapes. And when I sue
God for myself, He hears that name of thine,
And sees within my eyes the tears of two.

7

The face of all the world is changed, I think,
Since first I heard the footsteps of thy soul
Move still, oh, still, beside me, as they stole
Betwixt me and the dreadful outer brink
Of obvious death, where I, who thought to sink, 5
Was caught up into love, and taught the whole
Of life in a new rhythm. The cup of dole
God gave for baptism, I am fain to drink,

---

[1] Mrs. Browning was reluctant to publish these sonnets as being too intimate and autobiographical, but when she was persuaded to do so by her husband, she hoped to protect herself by the pretense that they were merely translations from some Portuguese originals.
[2] Greek writer of pastoral poetry in the third century B.C.

[3] Promises.   [4] Consecrated oil used in religious rites.

And praise its sweetness, Sweet, with thee anear.
The names of country, heaven, are changed away
For where thou art or shalt be, there or here;
And this . . . this lute and song . . . loved yester-
    day,
(The singing angels know) are only dear
Because thy name moves right in what they say.

14

If thou must love me, let it be for nought
Except for love's sake only. Do not say,
"I love her for her smile—her look—her way
Of speaking gently,—for a trick of thought
That falls in well with mine, and certes brought
A sense of pleasant ease on such a day"—
For these things in themselves, Belovèd, may
Be changed, or change for thee,—and love, so
    wrought,
May be unwrought so. Neither love me for
Thine own dear pity's wiping my cheeks dry,—
A creature might forget to weep, who bore
Thy comfort long, and lose thy love thereby!
But love me for love's sake, that evermore
Thou may'st love on, through love's eternity.

20

Belovèd, my Belovèd, when I think
That thou wast in the world a year ago,
What time I sat alone here in the snow
And saw no footprint, heard the silence sink
No moment at thy voice, but, link by link,
Went counting all my chains as if that so
They never could fall off at any blow
Struck by thy possible hand,—why, thus I drink
Of life's great cup of wonder! Wonderful,
Never to feel thee thrill the day or night
With personal act or speech,—nor ever cull
Some prescience of thee with the blossoms white
Thou sawest growing! Atheists are as dull,
Who cannot guess God's presence out of sight.

22

When our two souls stand up erect and strong,
Face to face, silent, drawing nigh and nigher,
Until the lengthening wings break into fire
At either curvèd point,—what bitter wrong
Can the earth do to us, that we should not long
Be here contented? Think. In mounting higher,
The angels would press on us and aspire
To drop some golden orb of perfect song
Into our deep, dear silence. Let us stay
Rather on earth, Belovèd,—where the unfit
Contrarious moods of men recoil away

And isolate pure spirits, and permit
A place to stand and love in for a day,
With darkness and the death-hour rounding it.

26

I lived with visions for my company,
Instead of men and women, years ago,
And found them gentle mates, nor thought to
    know
A sweeter music than they played to me.
But soon their trailing purple was not free
Of this world's dust, their lutes did silent grow,
And I myself grew faint and blind below
Their vanishing eyes. Then THOU didst come—
    to be,
Belovèd, what they seemed. Their shining fronts,
Their songs, their splendors (better, yet the same,
As river-water hallowed into fonts),
Met in thee, and from out thee overcame
My soul with satisfaction of all wants:
Because God's gifts put man's best dreams to
    shame.

35

If I leave all for thee, wilt thou exchange
And be all to me? Shall I never miss
Home-talk and blessing and the common kiss
That comes to each in turn, nor count it strange,
When I look up, to drop on a new range
Of walls and floors, another home than this?
Nay, wilt thou fill that place by me which is
Filled by dead eyes too tender to know change?
That's hardest. If to conquer love, has tried,
To conquer grief, tries more, as all things prove;
For grief indeed is love and grief beside.
Alas, I have grieved so I am hard to love.
Yet love me—wilt thou? Open thine heart wide,
And fold within the wet wings of thy dove.

43

How do I love thee? Let me count the ways.
I love thee to the depth and breadth and height
My soul can reach, when feeling out of sight
For the ends of Being and ideal Grace.
I love thee to the level of everyday's
Most quiet need, by sun and candle-light.
I love thee freely, as men strive for Right;
I love thee purely, as they turn from Praise.
I love thee with the passion put to use
In my old griefs, and with my childhood's faith.
I love thee with a love I seemed to lose
With my lost saints,—I love thee with the breath,
Smiles, tears, of all my life!—and, if God choose,
I shall but love thee better after death.

Edward FitzGerald

1809–1883

In 1859 appeared almost unnoticed *The Rubáiyát of Omar Khayyám,* rendered into English verse anonymously. By the turn of the century it had achieved a startling popularity. The rendering had been made by an unusually modest gentleman of adequate means and scholarly tastes, Edward FitzGerald, a friend from his days at Cambridge of Tennyson and Thackeray, who was primarily only indulging his own interest in Persian literature and his flair for verse translation. It was FitzGerald's goal so to paraphrase this series of random quatrains, originally composed about the time of the Norman Conquest, as to transmit the spirit of the Persian poet rather than his words, and in this process the poem became in a sense his own creation. But its epicurean and skeptical tone could probably only have been accepted by the general reader in 1859—and then not enthusiastically—as that of some long-departed Oriental poet. However, as the century advanced, the quatrains came increasingly to reflect the weariness of spirit and the expanding skepticism that followed the scientific revolution. As men came more and more to terms with the seemingly irrefutable facts of evolution and scientific materialism, the public found in the *Rubáiyát* what seemed the only wisdom left to it: we know not whence or whither, we are but dust, sentient, it is true, but hardly different from the grape and the rose. Why then trouble ourselves with seeking what we cannot find? Let us rather accept our ignorance and get what pleasure we can from our senses before we too pass. Brave words, but not even Horace or Omar, much less FitzGerald and his contemporaries, could escape the inevitable tinge of melancholy that rises from such a view, and the closing quatrains echo their sigh for a scheme of things nearer to man's deep desire for significance and value.

While it was almost certainly this correspondence to a mood of the time that primarily accounted for the tremendous popularity of the *Rubáiyát* at the turn of the century, the wealth of Oriental imagery and FitzGerald's haunting cadences then and now have appealed to the ears and imaginations of readers to whose thoughts and beliefs the message of Omar is indifferent or utterly hostile. For them it is a kind of magic carpet of gorgeous design and texture to waft them far away from the actual and its problems.

TEXTS: There is an elaborate edition of FitzGerald's work, both verse and prose, edited by George Benthan (7 vols., 1902–03). The four somewhat different versions of the *Rubáiyát* published in FitzGerald's lifetime have been printed together (1921). The volume on FitzGerald in the English Men of Letters series is by A. C. Benson (1905); a more recent biography is by A. McK. Terhune (1947). For a critical discussion of the translation of the *Rubáiyát,* consult A. Platt, "Edward FitzGerald," in *Nine Essays* (1927).

The Rubáiyát of Omar Khayyám of Naishápúr

I

Wake! For the Sun, who scattered into flight
The Stars before him from the Field of Night,
 Drives Night along with them from Heaven and strikes
The Sultán's Turret with a Shaft of Light.

II

Before the phantom of False morning[1] died,   5
Methought a Voice within the Tavern cried,
 "When all the Temple is prepared within,
Why nods the drowsy Worshiper outside?"

III

And, as the Cock crew, those who stood before
The Tavern shouted—"Open then the Door!   10
 You know how little while we have to stay,
And, once departed, may return no more."

IV

Now the New Year[2] reviving old Desires,
The thoughtful Soul to Solitude retires,
 Where the WHITE HAND OF MOSES on the   15
  Bough
Puts out, and Jesus from the Ground suspires.[3]

---

[1] "A transient Light on the Horizon about an hour before . . . the True Dawn; a well-known Phenomenon in the East." (FitzGerald)

[2] "Beginning with the Vernal Equinox, it must be remembered." (FitzGerald)

[3] The white blossoms emerging upon the branches in spring are likened to the hand of Moses when he withdrew it from his bosom (Exodus 4:6); and the flowers springing from the earth seem like an exhalation of the breath of Jesus.

V

Iram[4] indeed is gone with all his Rose,
And Jamshyd's[5] Seven-ringed Cup where no one
    knows;
    But still a Ruby kindles in the Vine,
And many a Garden by the Water blows.   20

VI

And David's[6] lips are locked; but in divine
High-piping Pehleví,[7] with "Wine! Wine! Wine!
    Red Wine!"—the Nightingale cries to the Rose
That sallow cheek of hers to incarnadine.

VII

Come, fill the Cup, and in the fire of Spring   25
Your Winter-garment of Repentance fling:
    The Bird of Time has but a little way
To flutter—and the Bird is on the Wing.

VIII

Whether at Naishápúr[8] or Babylon,
Whether the Cup with sweet or bitter run,   30
    The Wine of Life keeps oozing drop by drop,
The Leaves of Life keep falling one by one.

IX

Each morn a thousand Roses brings, you say;
Yes, but where leaves the Rose of Yesterday?
    And this first Summer month that brings the   35
        Rose
Shall take Jamshyd and Kaikobád[9] away.

X

Well, let it take them! What have we to do
With Kaikobád the Great, or Kaikhosrú?[10]
    Let Zál and Rustum[11] bluster as they will,
Or Hátim[12] call to Supper—heed not you.   40

XI

With me along the strip of Herbage strown
That just divides the desert from the sown,

---

[4] An ancient Persian garden, "now sunk somewhere in the Sands of Arabia." (FitzGerald)
[5] A legendary king of Persia. His cup "was typical of the 7 Heavens, 7 Planets, 7 Seas, etc." (FitzGerald) and had magic powers.
[6] Author of the Psalms.
[7] "The old Herioc *Sanskrit* of Persia." (FitzGerald)
[8] The home of Omar Khayyám.
[9] Founder of an ancient Persian dynasty.
[10] Early Persian hero.
[11] "The 'Hercules' of Persia, and Zál his Father." (Fitz-Gerald) See Matthew Arnold, *Sohrab and Rustum*, pp. 801–11.
[12] The typical figure of Oriental hospitality.

Where name of Slave and Sultán is forgot—
And Peace to Mahmúd[13] on his golden Throne!

XII

A Book of Verses underneath the Bough,   45
A Jug of Wine, a Loaf of Bread—and Thou
    Beside me singing in the Wilderness—
Oh, Wilderness were Paradise enow!

XIII

Some for the Glories of This World; and some
Sigh for the Prophet's[14] Paradise to come;   50
    Ah, take the Cash, and let the Credit go,
Nor heed the rumble of a distant Drum![15]

XIV

Look to the blowing Rose about us—"Lo,
Laughing," she says, "into the world I blow,
    At once the silken tassel of my Purse   55
Tear, and its Treasure[16] on the Garden throw."

XV

And those who husbanded the Golden Grain,[17]
And those who flung it to the winds like Rain,
    Alike to no such aureate Earth are turned
As, buried once, Men want dug up again.   60

XVI

The Worldly Hope men set their Hearts upon
Turns Ashes—or it prospers; and anon,
    Like Snow upon the Desert's dusty Face,
Lighting a little hour or two—is gone.

XVII

Think, in this battered Caravanserai[18]   65
Whose Portals are alternate Night and Day,
    How Sultán after Sultán with his Pomp
Abode his destined Hour, and went his way.

XVIII

They say the Lion and the Lizard keep
The Courts where Jamshyd gloried and drank   70
    deep:
    And Bahrám,[19] that great Hunter—the Wild
        Ass
Stamps o'er his Head, but cannot break his Sleep.

XIX

I sometimes think that never blows so red
The Rose as where some buried Caesar bled;
    That every Hyacinth the Garden wears   75

---

[13] The Sultan.

Dropped in her Lap from some once lovely
    Head.

XX

And this reviving Herb whose tender Green
Fledges the River-Lip on which we lean—
    Ah, lean upon it lightly! for who knows
From what once lovely Lip it springs unseen!   80

XXI

Ah, my Belovéd, fill the Cup that clears
TODAY of past Regrets and future Fears:
    Tomorrow!—Why, Tomorrow I may be
Myself with Yesterday's Seven thousand Years.

XXII

For some we loved, the loveliest and the best   85
That from his Vintage rolling Time hath pressed,
    Have drunk their Cup a Round or two before,
And one by one crept silently to rest.

XXIII

And we, that now make merry in the Room
They left, and Summer dresses in new bloom,   90
    Ourselves must we beneath the Couch of
        Earth
Descend—ourselves to make a Couch—for whom?

XXIV

Ah, make the most of what we yet may spend,
Before we too into the Dust descend;
    Dust into Dust, and under Dust to lie,   95
Sans[20] Wine, sans Song, sans Singer, and—sans
    End!

XXV

Alike for those who for TODAY prepare,
And those that after some TOMORROW stare,
    A Muezzín[21] from the Tower of Darkness cries,
"Fools, your Reward is neither Here nor There."   100

XXVI

Why, all the Saints and Sages who discussed
Of the Two Worlds so wisely—they are thrust

Like foolish Prophets forth; their Words to
    Scorn
Are scattered, and their Mouths are stopped with
    Dust.

XXVII

Myself when young did eagerly frequent   105
Doctor and Saint, and heard great argument
    About it and about; but evermore
Came out by the same door where in I went.

XXVIII

With them the seed of Wisdom did I sow,
And with mine own hand wrought to make it   110
    grow;
    And this was all the Harvest that I reaped—
"I came like Water, and like Wind I go."

XXIX

Into this Universe, and *Why* not knowing
Nor *Whence,* like Water willy-nilly flowing;
    And out of it, as Wind along the Waste,   115
I know not *Whither,* willy-nilly blowing.

XXX

What, without asking, hither hurried *Whence?*
And, without asking, *Whither* hurried hence!
    Oh, many a Cup of this forbidden Wine[22]
Must drown the memory of that insolence!   120

XXXI

Up from the Earth's Center through the Seventh
    Gate
I rose, and on the Throne of Saturn sate,[23]
    And many a Knot unraveled by the Road;
But not the Master-knot of Human Fate.

XXXII

There was the Door to which I found no Key;   125
There was the Veil through which I might not
    see;
    Some little talk awhile of ME and THEE[24]
There was—and then no more of THEE and ME.

---

14 Mohammed's.
15 "A Drum—beaten outside a Palace" (FitzGerald), signifying regal and worldly affairs.
16 "The Rose's Golden Center." (FitzGerald)
17 Money.
18 An Oriental inn, primarily for the use of caravans.
19 A Persian ruler, lost in a swamp while pursuing a wild ass.
20 Without.
21 One who calls the Mohammedans to prayer from a tower of the mosque.

22 The drinking of wine is forbidden to faithful Mohammedans.
23 The sphere of Saturn was the seventh of the concentric circles surrounding the earth in early concepts of the universe. Omar means that his studies had extended as far as man's knowledge of the universe.
24 "Some individual Existence or Personality distinct from the Whole." (FitzGerald)

XXXIII

Earth could not answer; nor the Seas that mourn
In flowing Purple, of their Lord forlorn;   130
   Nor rolling Heaven, with all his Signs revealed
And hidden by the sleeve of Night and Morn.

XXXIV

Then of the THEE IN ME[25] who works behind
The Veil, I lifted up my hands to find
   A lamp amid the Darkness; and I heard,   135
As from Without—"THE ME WITHIN THEE
   BLIND!"

XXXV

Then to the Lip of this poor earthen Urn
I leaned, the Secret of my Life to learn;
   And Lip to Lip it murmured—"While you
   live,
Drink!—for, once dead, you never shall return."   140

XXXVI

I think the Vessel, that with fugitive
Articulation answered, once did live,
   And drink;[26] and Ah! the passive Lip I kissed,
How many Kisses might it take—and give!

XXXVII

For I remember stopping by the way   145
To watch a Potter thumping his wet Clay;
   And with its all-obliterated Tongue
It murmured—"Gently, Brother, gently, pray!"

XXXVIII

And has not such a Story from of Old
Down Man's successive generations rolled   150
   Of such a clod of saturated Earth
Cast by the Maker into Human mold?[27]

XXXIX

And not a drop that from our Cups we throw
For Earth to drink of, but may steal below
   To quench the fire of Anguish in some Eye   155
There hidden—far beneath, and long ago.[28]

XL

As then the Tulip for her morning sup
Of Heavenly Vintage from the soil looks up,
   Do you devoutly do the like, till Heaven
To Earth invert you—like an empty Cup.   160

XLI

Perplexed no more with Human or Divine,
Tomorrow's tangle to the winds resign,
   And lose your fingers in the tresses of
The Cypress-slender Minister of Wine.[29]

XLII

And if the Wine you drink, the Lip you press,   165
End in what All begins and ends in—Yes;
   Think then you are TODAY what YESTERDAY
You were—TOMORROW you shall not be less.

XLIII

So when that Angel of the darker Drink
At last shall find you by the river-brink,   170
   And, offering his Cup, invite your Soul
Forth to your Lips to quaff—you shall not shrink.

XLIV

Why, if the Soul can fling the Dust aside,
And naked on the Air of Heaven ride,
   Were't not a Shame—were't not a Shame for   175
   him
In this clay carcass crippled to abide?

XLV

'Tis but a Tent where takes his one day's rest
A Sultán to the realm of Death addressed;
   The Sultán rises, and the dark Ferrásh[30]
Strikes, and prepares it for another Guest.   180

XLVI

And fear not lest Existence closing your
Account, and mine, should know the like no
   more;
   The Eternal Sákí from that Bowl has poured
Millions of Bubbles like us, and will pour.

XLVII

When You and I behind the Veil are past,   185
Oh, but the long, long while the World shall last,
   Which of our Coming and Departure heeds
As the Sea's self should heed a pebble-cast.

---

25 The universal spirit?
26 In a note FitzGerald refers to a Persian tale in which a thirsty traveler is told by a supernatural voice that the clay of which his bowl is made was once man.
27 As, indeed, in the Biblical story of creation.
28 The first two lines of this quatrain refer to a common Persian practice. "The precious Liquor is not lost, but sinks into the ground to refresh the dust of some poor Wine-worshipper foregone." (FitzGerald)

---

29 The maiden who passes the wine, later called Sákí.
30 A servant charged with setting up and "striking" or taking down the tents.

XLVIII

A Moment's Halt—a momentary taste
Of BEING from the Well amid the Waste—
    And Lo!—the phantom Caravan has reached
The NOTHING it set out from—Oh, make haste!

XLIX

Would you that spangle of Existence spend
About THE SECRET—quick about it, Friend!
    A Hair perhaps divides the False and True—
And upon what, prithee, may life depend?

L

A Hair perhaps divides the False and True;
Yes; and a single Alif[31] were the clue—
    Could you but find it—to the Treasure-house,
And peradventure to THE MASTER too;

LI

Whose secret Presence, through Creation's veins
Running Quicksilver-like eludes your pains;
    Taking all shapes from Máh to Máhi;[32] and
They change and perish all—but He remains;

LII

A moment guessed—then back behind the Fold
Immersed of Darkness round the Drama rolled
    Which, for the Pastime of Eternity,
He doth Himself contrive, enact, behold.

LIII

But if in vain, down on the stubborn floor
Of Earth, and up to Heaven's unopening Door,
    You gaze TODAY, while You are You—how then
TOMORROW, when You shall be You no more?

LIV

Waste not your Hour, nor in the vain pursuit
Of This and That endeavor and dispute;
    Better be jocund with the fruitful Grape
Than sadden after none, or bitter, Fruit.

LV

You know, my Friends, with what a brave
    Carouse
I made a Second Marriage in my house;
    Divorced old barren Reason from my Bed,
And took the Daughter of the Vine to Spouse.

LVI

For "Is" and "Is-NOT" though with Rule and Line
And "UP-AND-DOWN" by Logic I define,
    Of all that one should care to fathom, I
Was never deep in anything but—Wine.

LVII

Ah, but my Computations, People say,
Reduced the Year to better reckoning?[33]—Nay,
    'Twas only striking from the Calendar
Unborn Tomorrow, and dead Yesterday.

LVIII

And lately, by the Tavern Door agape,
Came shining through the Dusk an Angel Shape
    Bearing a Vessel on his Shoulder; and
He bid me taste of it; and 'twas—the Grape!

LIX

The Grape that can with Logic absolute
The Two-and-Seventy jarring Sects confute;
    The sovereign Alchemist that in a trice
Life's leaden metal into Gold transmute:

LX

The mighty Mahmúd, Allah-breathing Lord,
That all the misbelieving and black Horde
    Of Fears and Sorrows that infest the Soul
Scatters before him with his whirlwind Sword.[34]

LXI

Why, be this Juice the growth of God, who dare
Blaspheme the twisted tendril as a Snare?
    A Blessing, we should use it, should we not?
And if a Curse—why, then, Who set it there?

LXII

I must abjure the Balm of Life, I must,
Scared by some After-reckoning ta'en on trust,
    Or lured with Hope of some Diviner Drink,
To fill the Cup—when crumbled into Dust!

LXIII

Oh threats of Hell and Hopes of Paradise!
One thing at least is certain—*This* Life flies;
    One thing is certain and the rest is Lies;
The Flower that once has blown for ever dies.

---

31 A single stroke, the first letter of the Arabic alphabet.
32 "From Fish to Moon." (FitzGerald)

33 Omar was an astronomer and mathematician as well
as a poet and was instrumental in reforming the calendar.
34 "Alluding to Sultan Mahmúd's Conquest of India
and its dark people." (FitzGerald) It was carried out in
the name of Allah.

LXIV

Strange, is it not? that the myriads who
Before us passed the door of Darkness through,
    Not one returns to tell us of the Road,   255
Which to discover we must travel too.

LXV

The Revelations of Devout and Learned
Who rose before us, and as Prophets burned,
    Are all but Stories, which, awoke from Sleep
They told their comrades, and to Sleep returned.   260

LXVI

I sent my Soul through the Invisible,
Some letter of that After-life to spell;
    And by and by my Soul returned to me,
And answered, "I Myself am Heaven and Hell":

LXVII

Heaven but the Vision of fulfilled Desire,   265
And Hell the Shadow from a Soul on fire,
    Cast on the Darkness into which Ourselves,
So late emerged from, shall so soon expire.

LXVIII

We are no other than a moving row
Of Magic Shadow-shapes that come and go   270
    Round with the Sun-illumined Lantern held
In Midnight by the Master of the Show;

LXIX

But helpless Pieces of the Game He plays
Upon this Checker-board of Nights and Days;
    Hither and thither moves, and checks, and   275
        slays,
And one by one back in the Closet lays.

LXX

The Ball no question makes of Ayes and Noes,
But Here or There as strikes the Player goes;
    And He that tossed you down into the Field,
He knows about it all—HE knows—HE knows!   280

LXXI

The Moving Finger writes; and, having writ,
Moves on: nor all your Piety nor Wit
    Shall lure it back to cancel half a Line,
Nor all your Tears wash out a Word of it.

LXXII

And that inverted Bowl they call the Sky,   285

Whereunder crawling cooped we live and die,
    Lift not your hands to *It* for help—for It
As impotently moves as you or I.

LXXIII

With Earth's first Clay They did the Last Man
    knead,
And there of the Last Harvest sowed the Seed: 290
    And the first Morning of Creation wrote
What the Last Dawn of Reckoning shall read.

LXXIV

YESTERDAY *This* Day's Madness did prepare;
TOMORROW's Silence, Triumph, or Despair:
    Drink! for you know not whence you came,   295
        nor why;
Drink! for you know not why you go, nor where.

LXXV

I tell you this—When, started from the Goal,
Over the flaming shoulders of the Foal
    Of Heaven Parwín and Mushtarí they flung,[35]
In my predestined Plot of Dust and Soul   300

LXXVI

The Vine had struck a fiber; which about
If clings my Being—let the Dervish[36] flout;
    Of my Base metal may be filed a Key,
That shall unlock the Door he howls without.

LXXVII

And this I know: whether the one True Light   305
Kindle to Love, or Wrath-consume me quite,
    One Flash of It within the Tavern caught
Better than in the Temple lost outright.

LXXVIII

What! out of senseless Nothing to provoke
A conscious Something to resent the yoke   310
    Of unpermitted Pleasure, under pain
Of Everlasting Penalties, if broke!

LXXIX

What! from his helpless Creature be repaid
Pure Gold for what he lent him dross-allayed—
    Sue for a Debt he never did contract,   315
And cannot answer—Oh the sorry trade!

---

35 When over the equatorial constellation known as the
"Little Horse" they (the gods or supernatural forces; see
stanza LXXIII: "With Earth's first Clay They did the
Last Man knead") flung or placed the Pleiades and the
planet Jupiter.
36 A Mohammedan fanatic.

LXXX

Oh Thou, who didst with pitfall and with gin[37]
Beset the Road I was to wander in,
    Thou wilt not with Predestined Evil round
Enmesh, and then impute my Fall to Sin!　　320

LXXXI

O Thou, who Man of Baser Earth didst make,
And even with Paradise devise the Snake:
    For all the Sin wherewith the Face of Man
Is blackened—Man's forgiveness give—and take!

*   *   *   *   *   *

LXXXII

As under cover of departing Day　　325
Slunk hunger-stricken Ramazán[38] away,
    Once more within the Potter's house alone
I stood, surrounded by the Shapes of Clay.

LXXXIII

Shapes of all Sorts and Sizes, great and small,
That stood along the floor and by the wall;　　330
    And some loquacious Vessels were; and some
Listened perhaps, but never talked at all.

LXXXIV

Said one among them—"Surely not in vain
My substance of the common Earth was ta'en
    And to this Figure molded, to be broke,　　335
Or trampled back to shapeless Earth again."

LXXXV

Then said a Second—"Ne'er a peevish Boy
Would break the Bowl from which he drank in
    joy;
    And He that with his hand the Vessel made
Will surely not in after Wrath destroy."　　340

LXXXVI

After a momentary silence spake
Some Vessel of a more ungainly Make;
    "They sneer at me for leaning all awry:
What! did the Hand, then, of the Potter Shake?"

LXXXVII

Whereat someone of the loquacious Lot—　　345
I think a Súfi[39] pipkin—waxing hot—
    "All this of Pot and Potter—Tell me, then,
Who is the Potter, pray, and who the Pot?"

LXXXVIII

"Why," said another, "Some there are who tell
Of one who threatens he will toss to Hell　　350
    The luckless Pots he marred in making—Pish!
He's a Good Fellow, and 'twill all be well."

LXXXIX

"Well," murmured one, "Let whoso make or buy,
My Clay with long Oblivion is gone dry;
    But fill me with the old familiar Juice,　　355
Methinks I might recover by and by."

XC

So while the Vessels one by one were speaking,
The little Moon[40] looked in that all were seek-
    ing:
    And then they jogged each other, "Brother!
    Brother!
Now for the Porter's shoulder-knot[41] a-creaking!"　　360

*   *   *   *   *

XCI

Ah, with the Grape my fading Life provide,
And wash the Body whence the Life has died,
    And lay me, shrouded in the living Leaf,
By some not unfrequented Garden-side.

XCII

That even my buried Ashes such a snare　　365
Of Vintage shall fling up into the Air
    As not a True-believer passing by
But shall be overtaken unaware.

XCIII

Indeed the Idols I have loved so long
Have done my credit in this World much wrong:　　370
    Have drowned my Glory in a shallow Cup,
And sold my Reputation for a Song.

XCIV

Indeed, indeed, Repentance oft before
I swore—but was I sober when I swore?

---

37 Trap.
38 A month during which Mohammedans eat no food between sunrise and sunset.
39 A Persian mystic, or pantheist.

40 When the new moon appeared, it signaled the end of Ramazán.
41 The strap on which the jars were hung from the porter's shoulder.

And then and then came Spring, and Rose-in- 375
hand
My thread-bare Penitence apieces tore.

XCV

And much as Wine has played the Infidel,
And robbed me of my Robe of Honor—Well,
   I wonder often what the Vintners buy
One half so precious as the stuff they sell. 380

XCVI

Yet Ah, that Spring should vanish with the
   Rose!
That Youth's sweet-scented manuscript should
   close!
   The Nightingale that in the branches sang,
Ah whence, and whither flown again, who knows!

XCVII

Would but the Desert of the Fountain yield 385
One glimpse—if dimly, yet indeed, revealed,
   To which the fainting Traveler might spring,
As springs the trampled herbage of the field!

XCVIII

Would but some wingéd Angel ere too late
Arrest the yet unfolded Roll of Fate, 390

And make the stern Recorder otherwise
Enregister, or quite obliterate!

XCIX

Ah, Love! could you and I with Him conspire
To grasp this sorry Scheme of Things entire,
   Would not we shatter it to bits—and then 395
Remold it nearer to the Heart's Desire!

* * * * *

C

Yon rising Moon that looks for us again—
How oft hereafter will she wax and wane;
   How oft hereafter rising look for us
Through this same Garden—and for *one* in vain! 400

CI

And when like her, O Sákí, you shall pass
Among the Guests Star-scattered on the Grass,
   And in your joyous errand reach the spot
Where I made One—turn down an empty Glass!
                                        TAMÁN[42]

---

[42] It is ended.

George Meredith

1828–1909

In an age when men were torn by doubt and anxiety as to the meaning of life, Meredith seems to stand curiously aloof, one somehow removed from the hopes and fears of his contemporaries, who can record from a lofty and purely intellectual viewpoint his observations of his fellow man. These observations form the matter of his novels, which are primarily studies of character, as, indeed, their titles indicate: *The Ordeal of Richard Feverel* (1859), *The Adventures of Harry Richmond* (1871), *The Egoist* (1879), and *Diana of the Crossways* (1885), to name the best known.

   Even in his verse novel, *Modern Love,* where his own unhappy first marriage is reflected, Meredith remains the cool and detached observer of human character. This perceptive study of the dissolution of married love is presented in a loosely connected series of sixteen-line sonnets, each providing a glimpse of the tragic progress toward a final collapse. By deal-

ing so openly with the problem of marital adjustment, Meredith was probing an area Victorians evaded. It is interesting that the modern poet C. Day Lewis calls the poem "a revolutionary work because it adumbrated our present-day attitude toward the sexual relationship, our belief that marriage imposes obligations but does not confer rights."

   It is in his lyric poetry that Meredith comes to grips with the baffling questions posed by the conflict of the Christian tradition and scientific research, and yet here again his attitude seems relatively objective. His was essentially a naturalistic interpretation of the world and of man's role in it. For him the possibility of a personal God is ruled out in favor of nature itself, or Earth, as he prefers to call it. He believes only in the process of unalterable law, fulfilling itself in accord with the principles of evolution, without regard to individuals, but with some dimly perceived purpose of perfection for the human race. And it is characteristic of Meredith that this perfection is to be primarily that of the mind.

Fortunately for his poetry, abstract Earth and unalterable law had their concrete manifestations in sights and sounds and seasons, which Meredith never tired of watching carefully or of recording in pastorals and lyrics that capture both the general impressions and the sharp details of his natural surroundings. Where the philosophical implications do appear, they seem secondary to the delight in nature for its own sake. Even in such poems as "The Lark Ascending" and "Hard Weather," the passages of natural description, while obviously intended as springboards into the philosophical exposition, still convey a keen awareness and enjoyment of the phenomena of nature.

TEXTS: G. M. Trevelyan has edited the *Poetical Works* (1928), and has written the best critical book, *The Poetry and Philosophy of George Meredith* (1920). C. Day Lewis's introduction to his edition of *Modern Love* (1949) is illuminating. The best biography is Lionel Stevenson's *The Ordeal of George Meredith* (1953). The *Letters* have been edited by C. L. Cline in 3 vols. (1970).

from Modern Love

1

By this he knew she wept with waking eyes:
That, at his hand's light quiver by her head,
The strange low sobs that shook their common bed
Were called into her with a sharp surprise,
And strangled mute, like little gaping snakes, 5
Dreadfully venomous to him. She lay
Stone-still, and the long darkness flowed away
With muffled pulses. Then, as midnight makes
Her giant heart of Memory and Tears
Drink the pale drug of silence, and so beat 10
Sleep's heavy measure, they from head to feet
Were moveless, looking through their dead black years,
By vain regret scrawled over the blank wall.
Like sculptured effigies they might be seen
Upon their marriage-tomb, the sword between;[1] 15
Each wishing for the sword that severs all.

16

In our old shipwrecked days there was an hour,
When in the firelight steadily aglow,
Joined slackly, we beheld the red chasm grow
Among the clicking coals. Our library-bower
That eve was left to us: and hushed we sat 5
As lovers to whom Time is whispering.
From sudden-opened doors we heard them sing;
The nodding elders mixed good wine with chat.
Well knew we that Life's greatest treasure lay
With us, and of it was our talk. "Ah, yes! 10
Love dies!" I said: I never thought it less.
She yearned to me that sentence to unsay.
Then when the fire domed blackening, I found
Her cheek was salt against my kiss, and swift
Up the sharp scale of sobs her breast did lift:— 15
Now am I haunted by that taste! that sound!

17

At dinner, she is hostess, I am host.
Went the feast ever cheerfuller? She keeps
The Topic over intellectual deeps
In buoyancy afloat. They see no ghost.
With sparkling surface-eyes we ply the ball; 5
It is in truth a most contagious game:
HIDING THE SKELETON shall be its name.
Such play as this the devils might appal!
But here's the greater wonder; in that we,
Enamored of an acting naught can tire, 10
Each other, like true hypocrites, admire;
Warm-lighted looks, Love's ephemeridae,[2]
Shoot gayly o'er the dishes and the wine.
We waken envy of our happy lot.
Fast, sweet, and golden, shows the marriage-knot. 15
Dear guests, you now have seen Love's corpse-light[3] shine.

43

Mark where the pressing wing shoots javelin-like
Its skeleton shadow on the broad-backed wave!
Here is a fitting spot to dig Love's grave;
Here where the ponderous breakers plunge and strike,
And dart their hissing tongues high up the sand: 5
In hearing of the ocean, and in sight
Of those ribbed wind-streaks running into white.
If I the death of Love had deeply planned,
I never could have made it half so sure,
As by the unblest kisses which upbraid 10

---

[1] In medieval legend, the sword dividing lovers signified chastity or honor. Here its symbolizes spiritual separation.
[2] Short-lived creatures.
[3] A flame sometimes seen in cemeteries, viewed as a portent of death.

The full-waked sense; or failing that, degrade!
'Tis morning: but no morning can restore
What we have forfeited. I see no sin:
The wrong is mixed. In tragic life, God wot,
No villain need be! Passions spin the plot: 15
We are betrayed by what is false within.

47

We saw the swallows gathering in the sky,
And in the osier-isle we heard them noise.
We had not to look back on summer joys,
Or forward to a summer of bright dye:
But in the largeness of the evening earth   5
Our spirits grew as we went side by side.
The hour became her husband and my bride.
Love, that had robbed us so, thus blessed our
       dearth!
The pilgrims of the year waxed very loud
In multitudinous chatterings, as the flood   10
Full brown came from the West, and like pale
       blood
Expanded to the upper crimson cloud.
Love, that had robbed us of immortal things,
This little moment mercifully gave,
Where I have seen across the twilight wave   15
The swan sail with her young beneath her wings.

50

Thus piteously Love closed what he begat:
The union of this ever-diverse pair!
These two were rapid falcons in a snare,
Condemned to do the flitting of the bat.
Lovers beneath the singing sky of May,   5
They wandered once; clear as the dew on flowers:
But they fed not on the advancing hours:
Their hearts held cravings for the buried day.
Then each applied to each that fatal knife,
Deep questioning, which probes to endless dole.   10
Ah, what a dusty answer gets the soul
When hot for certainties in this our life!—
In tragic hints here see what evermore
Moves dark as yonder midnight ocean's force,
Thundering like ramping hosts of warrior horse,   15
To throw that faint thin line upon the shore!

Lucifer in Starlight

On a starred night Prince Lucifer[1] uprose.
Tired of his dark dominion swung the fiend

Above the rolling ball in cloud part screened,
Where sinners hugged their specter of repose.
Poor prey to his hot fit of pride were those.   5
And now upon his western wing he leaned,
Now his huge bulk o'er Afric's sands careened,
Now the black planet shadowed Arctic snows.
Soaring through wider zones that pricked his
       scars
With memory of the old revolt from Awe,   10
He reached a middle height, and at the stars,
Which are the brain of heaven, he looked, and
       sank.
Around the ancient track marched, rank on rank,
The army of unalterable law.

Hard Weather

Bursts from a rending East in flaws[1]
The young green leaflet's harrier, sworn
To strew the garden, strip the shaws,[2]
And show our Spring with banner torn.
Was ever such virago morn?   5
The wind has teeth, the wind has claws.
All the wind's wolves through woods are loose,
The wild wind's falconry aloft.
Shrill underfoot the grassblade shrews,[3]
At gallop, clumped, and down the croft   10
Bestrid by shadows, beaten, tossed;
It seems a scythe, it seems a rod.
The howl is up at the howl's accost;
The shivers greet and the shivers nod.
Is the land ship? we are rolled, we drive   15
Tritonly, cleaving hiss and hum;
Whirl with the dead, or mount or dive,
Or down in dregs, or on in scum.
And drums the distant, pipes the near,
And vale and hill are gray in gray,   20
As when the surge is crumbling sheer,
And sea-mews wing the haze of spray.
Clouds—are they bony witches?—swarms,
Darting swift on the robber's flight,
Hurry an infant sky in arms: 25
It peeps, it becks; 'tis day, 'tis night.
Black while over the loop of blue
The swathe is closed, like shroud on corse.
Lo, as if swift the Furies flew,
The Fates at heel at a cry to horse!   30

---

1 The angel who revolted against God and was exiled to
rule over hell.

1 Squalls.
2 The tops of potatoes or turnips.
3 Makes harsh noises.

Interpret me the savage whirr:
And is it Nature scourged, or she,
Her offspring's executioner,
Reducing land to barren sea?
But is there meaning in a day 35
When this fierce angel of the air,
Intent to throw, and haply slay,
Can for what breath of life we bear
Exact the wrestle? Call to mind
The many meanings glistening up 40
When Nature, to her nurslings kind,
Hands them the fruitage and the cup!
And seek we rich significance
Not otherwise than with those tides
Of pleasure on the sunned expanse, 45
Whose flow deludes, whose ebb derides?

Look in the face of men who fare
Lock-mouthed, a match in lungs and thews
For this fierce angel of the air,
To twist with him and take his bruise. 50
That is the face beloved of old
Of Earth, young mother of her brood:
Nor broken for us shows the mold
When muscle is in mind renewed:
Though farther from her nature rude, 55
Yet nearer to her spirit's hold:
And though of gentler mood serene,
Still forceful of her fountain-jet.
So shall her blows be shrewdly met,
Be luminously read the scene 60
Where Life is at her grindstone set,
That she may give us edging keen,
String us for battle, till as play
The common strokes of fortune shower.
Such meaning in a dagger-day 65
Our wits may clasp to wax in power.
Yea, feel us warmer at her breast,
By spin of blood in lusty drill,
Than when her honeyed hands caressed,
And Pleasure, sapping, seemed to fill. 70

Behold the life at ease; it drifts.
The sharpened life commands its course.
She[4] winnows, winnows roughly; sifts,
To dip her chosen in her source:
Contention is the vital force, 75
Whence pluck they brain, her prize of gifts,
Sky of the senses! on which height,
Not disconnected, yet released,
They see how spirit comes to light,
Through conquest of the inner beast, 80
Which Measure tames to movement sane,
In harmony with what is fair.
Never is Earth misread by brain:
That is the welling of her, there
The mirror: with one step beyond, 85
For likewise is it voice; and more,
Benignest kinship bids respond,
When wail the weak, and them restore
Whom days as fell as this may rive,
While Earth sits ebon in her gloom, 90
Us atomies of life alive
Unheeding, bent on life to come.
Her children of the laboring brain,
These are the champions of the race,
True parents, and the sole humane, 95
With understanding for their base.
Earth yields the milk, but all her mind
Is vowed to thresh for stouter stock.
Her passion for old giantkind,
That scaled the mount, uphurled the rock, 100
Devolves on them who read aright
Her meaning and devoutly serve;
Nor in her starlessness of night
Peruse her with the craven nerve:
But even as she from grass to corn, 105
To eagle high from grubbing mole,
Prove in strong brain her noblest born,
The station for the flight of soul.

---

4 Earth or nature.

Christina Georgina Rossetti

1830–1894

The daughter of an exiled Italian patriot and the sister of the gifted and exuberant Pre-Raphaelite painter and poet, Christina Rossetti seems, so far as we may judge from the expression she gave to her thoughts and feelings, to have lived somewhat remote from the political and artistic preoccupations which burned up so much of the energy of the rest of the household. Aside from a very occasional political utterance such as "To-day for me . . ." and a relatively few poems "Goblin Market" and "Paradise," her poetry is represented by a series of rather simple and restrained lyrics which, if not autobiographical, are certainly colored by her own personal history. Because of her restricted family circumstances and her own rather frail health, she had but a limited knowledge of the world to draw upon, and she used her gift mainly to express her major emotional experience. She was the victim of an inner conflict: on the one hand she responded eagerly to the beauties of nature and the warmth of human affection, and on the other she was almost tortured by a kind of religious asceticism, which called upon her to reject these earthly pleasures and dedicate herself completely to God. So strong was this spiritual compulsion that she refused two suitors, one of whom she loved deeply, on religious grounds; but such was the pain of this rejection of one whole side of her nature that although she seems to have convinced herself of the whole-heartedness of her surrender, the dominant theme of her poetry is the relief and resolution that death, and death alone, will be able to bring to her frustration.

> Life is not sweet. One day it will be sweet
> To shut our eyes and die

is her theme in "Life and Death," and the last poem she ever wrote tells of the peace that will come when she is sleeping at last.

Aside from the subject matter, the distinguishing characteristics of her work are the simple diction and the wonderfully natural musical cadences, which combine to produce an impression of sincerity and spontaneity. "I question," wrote her brother William Michael, "her having ever once deliberated with herself whether or not she would write something or other. . . . Instead of this, something impelled her feelings, or 'came into her head,' and her hand obeyed the dictation."

TEXTS: Christina Rossetti's *Poetical Works* were edited by her brother, W. M. Rossetti, together with a memoir (1904). Though too much permeated by a supposed love affair between Christina and William Bell Scott, Lona Packer's biography (1963) is the principal scholarly work. C. M. Bowra discusses her poetry in *The Romantic Imagination* (1949).

Song

When I am dead, my dearest,
  Sing no sad songs for me;
Plant thou no roses at my head,
  Nor shady cypress tree:
Be the green grass above me
  With showers and dewdrops wet;
And if thou wilt, remember,
  And if thou wilt, forget.

I shall not see the shadows,
  I shall not feel the rain;
I shall not hear the nightingale
  Sing on as if in pain:
And dreaming through the twilight
  That doth not rise nor set,
Haply I may remember,
  And haply may forget.

Up-Hill

Does the road wind up-hill all the way?
  Yes, to the very end.
Will the day's journey take the whole long day?
  From morn to night, my friend.

But is there for the night a resting-place?
  A roof for when the slow dark hours begin.
May not the darkness hide it from my face?
  You cannot miss that inn.

Shall I meet other wayfarers at night?
  Those who have gone before.
Then must I knock, or call when just in sight?
  They will not keep you standing at that door.

Shall I find comfort, travel-sore and weak?
  Of labor you shall find the sum.

Will there be beds for me and all who seek? 15
    Yea, beds for all who come.

A Better Resurrection

I have no wit, no words, no tears;
    My heart within me like a stone
Is numbed too much for hopes or fears.
    Look right, look left, I dwell alone; 5
I lift mine eyes, but dimmed with grief
    No everlasting hills I see;
My life is in the falling leaf:
    O Jesus, quicken me.

My life is like a faded leaf,
    My harvest dwindled to a husk: 10
Truly my life is void and brief
    And tedious in the barren dusk;
My life is like a frozen thing,
    No bud nor greenness can I see;
Yet rise it shall—the sap of Spring; 15
    O Jesus, rise in me.

My life is like a broken bowl,
    A broken bowl that cannot hold
One drop of water for my soul
    Or cordial in the searching cold; 20
Cast in the fire the perished thing;
    Melt and remold it, till it be
A royal cup for Him, my King:
    O Jesus, drink of me.

A Birthday

My heart is like a singing bird
    Whose nest is in a watered shoot:
My heart is like an apple-tree
    Whose boughs are bent with thickset fruit;
My heart is like a rainbow shell 5
    That paddles in a halcyon sea;
My heart is gladder than all these
    Because my love is come to me.

Raise me a dais of silk and down;
    Hang it with vair[1] and purple dyes; 10
Carve it in doves, and pomegranates,
    And peacocks with a hundred eyes;

Work it in gold and silver grapes, 15
    In leaves and silver fleurs-de-lys;
Because the birthday of my life 15
    Is come, my love is come to me.

An Echo from Willow-Wood[1]

O ye, all ye that walk in willow-wood.
D. G. ROSSETTI

Two gazed into a pool, he gazed and she,
    Not hand in hand, yet heart in heart, I think,
    Pale and reluctant on the water's brink,
As on the brink of parting which must be.
Each eyed the other's aspect, she and he, 5
    Each felt one hungering heart leap up and
        sink,
    Each tasted bitterness which both must drink,
There on the brink of life's dividing sea.
Lilies upon the surface, deep below
    Two wistful faces craving each for each, 10
    Resolute and reluctant without speech:—
A sudden ripple made the faces flow,
    One moment joined, to vanish out of reach:
    So those hearts joined, and ah were parted
        so.

A Fisher-Wife

The soonest mended, nothing said;
    And help may rise from east or west,
But my two hands are lumps of lead,
    My heart sits leaden in my breast.

O north wind, swoop not from the north, 5
    O south wind, linger in the south,
Oh come not raving raging forth,
    To bring my heart into my mouth;

For I've a husband out at sea,
    Afloat on feeble planks of wood; 10
He does not know what fear may be;
    I would have told him if I could.

I would have locked him in my arms,
    I would have hid him in my heart;

---

[1] A kind of squirrel fur.

[1] This poem is a "rewriting" of the first of four sonnets called "Willowwood" in Dante Gabriel Rossetti's *House of Life*: cf. p. 885, note 6. The epigraph is the opening line of the third sonnet in the group.

For oh the waves are fraught with harms, 15
    And he and I so far apart!

Endure Hardness

A cold wind stirs the blackthorn
    To burgeon and to blow,
Besprinkling half-green hedges
    With flakes and sprays of snow.

Thro' coldness and thro' keenness, 5
    Dear hearts, take comfort so:
Somewhere or other doubtless
    These make the blackthorn blow.

Life and Death

Life is not sweet. One day it will be sweet
    To shut our eyes and die;
Nor feel the wild flowers blow, nor birds dart by
    With flitting butterfly,
Nor grass grow long above our heads and feet, 5
Nor hear the happy lark that soars sky-high,
Nor sigh that spring is fleet and summer fleet,
    Nor mark the waxing wheat,
Nor know who sits in our accustomed seat.

Life is not good. One day it will be good 10
    To die, then live again;

To sleep meanwhile; so, not to feel the wane 15
    Of shrunk leaves dropping in the wood,
Nor hear the foamy lashing of the main,
Nor mark the blackened bean-fields, nor where 15
        stood
    Rich ranks of golden grain,
Only dead refuse stubble clothe the plain:
    Asleep from risk, asleep from pain.

Sleeping at Last

Sleeping at last, the trouble and tumult over,
    Sleeping at last, the struggle and horror past,
Cold and white, out of sight of friend and of
        lover,
    Sleeping at last.

No more a tired heart downcast or overcast, 5
No more pangs that wring or shifting fears that
        hover,
    Sleeping at last in a dreamless sleep locked
        fast.

Fast asleep. Singing birds in their leafy cover
    Cannot wake her, nor shake her the gusty
        blast.
Under the purple thyme and the purple clover 10
    Sleeping at last.

Francis Thompson
1859–1907

Thompson's expressed wish to be known primarily as the poet of the return to God sets the tone of the major part of his work. Although he was unfitted to enter the Roman Catholic Church as a priest—as indeed he was unfitted both physically and morally to cope with practical existence—his poetic life was almost wholly spent in the service of religion. His outstanding achievement, "The Hound of Heaven," in a sense a spiritual autobiography, reflects his lamentable moral condition, closely paralleled by his physical collapse, before he was able in some degree to redeem himself and devote his time and what strength he could salvage to his religious and mystical bent. (He was a drug addict in the last stages of tuberculosis, without roof, food, or friend, when he was rescued by the editor of a Catholic magazine and his poet-wife, Wilfrid and Alice Meynell.)

By his own admission his temperament and poetic gift were allied to the tradition of seventeenth-century metaphysical poetry, particularly to Crashaw and Cowley; his love of paradox, of imagery, of conceit, all these, as well as his awareness of a spiritual world so close as to be almost tangible, are the tokens of his kinship, and are all to be found in "The Hound of Heaven." He fell at times, though—probably under the uncritical influence of Shelley—into extravagances of diction and lavishness of imagery, thus weakening the force and integrity of a poem and vitiating the intensity of his mysticism. However, these are but limitations which in large measure he was able to transcend in "The Hound of Heaven," where the primary theme of unrelenting pursuit is built up by a series of images, first of tremendous speed and immense space, then, for an interlude, of imagined escape, only to reach a kind of awful breathlessness in those which describe his worthlessness and impotency. Here the imagery is functional, not ornamental. The effect is tremendously heightened by the rhythm of the poem: the feeling of imminent pursuit is echoed in the rushing movement of the early section, in which the insistent beat of feet moves swiftly and inexorably onward; then as the chase nears its end and the stricken soul cowers before its Creator, the rhythm slows and slows as it comes to the final image of the shadow of God's caressing hand.

TEXTS: Wilfrid Meynell edited Thompson's *Complete Poetical Works* (1913). M. A. Kelley has done a separate edition of "The Hound of Heaven" (1916). Two recent biographies, the first of which contains a good deal of useful criticism, are J. C. Reid's *Francis Thompson: Man and Poet* (1960) and Paul van Kuykendall Thompson's *Francis Thompson: A Critical Biography* (1961).

The Hound of Heaven

I fled Him, down the nights and down the days;
  I fled Him, down the arches of the years;
  I fled Him, down the labyrinthine ways
  Of my own mind; and in the mist of tears
I hid from Him, and under running laughter.   5
    Up vistaed hopes I sped;
    And shot, precipitated,
Adown Titanic[1] glooms of chasmèd fears,
  From those strong Feet that followed, followed
    after.
    But with unhurrying chase,
    And unperturbèd pace,   10
Deliberate speed, majestic instancy,[2]
    They beat—and a Voice beat
    More instant than the Feet—
  "All things betray thee, who betrayest Me."   15

    I pleaded, outlaw-wise,
By many a hearted casement, curtained red,
  Trellised with intertwining charities;[3]
(For, though I knew His Love Who followèd,
    Yet was I sore adread   20

Lest, having Him, I must have naught beside).
But, if one little casement parted wide,
  The gust of His approach would clash it to.
  Fear wist not to evade, as Love wist to pursue.
Across the margent[4] of the world I fled,   25
  And troubled the gold gateways of the stars,
  Smiting for shelter on their clangèd bars;
    Fretted to dulcet jars
And silvern chatter the pale ports o' the moon.[5]
I said to Dawn: Be sudden—to Eve: Be soon;   30
  With thy young skiey blossoms heap me over
    From this tremendous Lover—
Float thy vague veil about me, lest He see!
  I tempted all His servitors, but to find
My own betrayal in their constancy,   35
In faith to Him their fickleness to me,
  Their traitorous trueness, and their loyal deceit.
To all swift things for swiftness did I sue;
  Clung to the whistling mane of every wind.
    But whether they swept, smoothly fleet,   40
  The long savannahs of the blue;
    Or whether, Thunder-driven,
  They clanged his chariot 'thwart a heaven,
Plashy with flying lightnings round the spurn
    o' their feet:—[6]
  Fear wist not to evade as Love wist to pursue.   45
    Still with unhurrying chase,
    And unperturbèd pace,
  Deliberate speed, majestic instancy,
    Came on the following Feet,
    And a Voice above their beat—   50
  "Naught shelters thee, who wilt not shelter
    Me."

I sought no more that after which I strayed
    In face of man or maid;
But still within the little children's eyes
  Seems something, something that replies,   55
They at least are for me, surely for me!
I turned me to them very wistfully;
But just as their young eyes grew sudden fair
    With dawning answers there,
Their angel plucked them from me by the hair.   60
"Come then, ye other children, Nature's—share
With me" (said I) "your delicate fellowship;
    Let me greet you lip to lip,

---

[1] Immense (the Titans were giants).   [2] Insistency.
[3] The poet fled like a fleeing outlaw to human love, to the human heart, hoping to find sympathy and kindness.
[4] Margin, boundary.
[5] Agitated or shook the portals of the moon until they gave forth sweet sounds.
[6] The sky was sparkling with the lightning-like sparks struck out by their hooves.

Let me twine with you caresses,
    Wantoning   65
With our Lady-Mother's vagrant tresses,
    Banqueting
With her in her wind-walled palace,
Underneath her azured daïs,
Quaffing, as your taintless way is,   70
    From a chalice
Lucent-weeping[7] out of the dayspring."
So it was done:
I in their delicate fellowship was one—
Drew the bolt of Nature's secrecies.   75
    I knew all the swift importings[8]
    On the wilful face of skies;
    I knew how the clouds arise
    Spumèd[9] of the wild sea-snortings;
        All that's born or dies   80
Rose and drooped with; made them shapers
Of mine own moods, or wailful or divine;
    With them joyed and was bereaven.
    I was heavy with the even,
    When she lit her glimmering tapers   85
    Round the day's dead sanctities.
    I laughed in the morning's eyes.
I triumphed and I saddened with all weather,
    Heaven and I wept together,
And its sweet tears were salt with mortal mine;   90
Against the red throb of its sunset-heart
        I laid my own to beat,
        And share commingling heat;
But not by that, by that, was eased my human
    smart.
In vain my tears were wet on Heaven's gray   95
    cheek.
For ah! we know not what each other says,
    These things and I; in sound *I* speak—
Their sound is but their stir, they speak by
    silences.
Nature, poor stepdame, cannot slake my drouth;
    Let her, if she would owe[10] me,   100
Drop yon blue bosom-veil of sky, and show me
    The breasts o' her tenderness:
Never did any milk of hers once bless
    My thirsting mouth.
        Nigh and nigh draws the chase,   105
        With unperturbèd pace,
    Deliberate speed, majestic instancy,
        And past those noisèd Feet

    A Voice comes yet more fleet—
    "Lo! naught contents thee, who content'st   110
    not Me."

Naked I wait Thy love's uplifted stroke!
My harness piece by piece Thou hast hewn from
    me,
        And smitten me to my knee;
    I am defenseless utterly.
    I slept, methinks, and woke,   115
And, slowly gazing, find me stripped in sleep.
In the rash lustihead of my young powers,
    I shook the pillaring hours[11]
And pulled my life upon me; grimed with
    smears,
I stand amid the dust o' the moulded years—   120
My mangled youth lies dead beneath the heap.
My days have crackled and gone up in smoke,
Have puffed and burst as sun-starts[12] on a stream.
    Yea, faileth now even dream
The dreamer, and the lute the lutanist;   125
Even the linked fantasies,[13] in whose blossomy
    twist
I swung the earth[14] a trinket at my wrist,
Are yielding; cords of all too weak account
For earth with heavy griefs so overplussed.
    Ah! is Thy love indeed   130
A weed, albeit an amaranthine[15] weed,
Suffering no flowers except its own to mount?
    Ah! must—
    Designer infinite!—
Ah! must Thou char the wood ere Thou canst   135
    limn with it?
My freshness spent its wavering shower i' the
    dust;
And now my heart is as a broken fount,
Wherein tear-drippings stagnate, spilt down ever
    From the dank thoughts that shiver
Upon the sighful branches of my mind.   140
    Such is; what is to be?
The pulp so bitter, how shall taste the rind?
I dimly guess what Time in mists confounds;
Yet ever and anon a trumpet sounds
From the hid battlements of Eternity;   145
Those shaken mists a space unsettle, then
Round the half-glimpsèd turrets slowly wash
    again.

---

7 Dripping luminous drops.
8 Meanings.
9 Made from the spray that is cast up by the waves.
10 Own.

11 Like Samson when he pulled the temple down.
12 Bubbles.
13 Poetic imaginings.   14 My world, my life.
15 Immortal, from the name of a flower that was reputed
never to fade.

But not ere him who summoneth
I first have seen, enwound
With   glooming   robes   purpureal,   cypress-   150
crowned;[16]
His name I know, and what his trumpet saith.
Whether man's heart or life it be which yields
Thee harvest, must Thy harvest-fields
Be dunged with rotten death?[17]

Now of that long pursuit   155
Comes on at hand the bruit;[18]
That Voice is round me like a bursting sea:
"And is thy earth so marred,
Shattered in shard on shard?
Lo, all things fly thee, for thou fliest Me!   160
Strange, piteous, futile thing!
Wherefore should any set thee love apart?
Seeing none but I makes much of naught" (He
said),

"And human love needs human meriting:
How hast thou merited—   165
Of all man's clotted[19] clay the dingiest clot?
Alack, thou knowest not
How little worthy of any love thou art!
Whom wilt thou find to love ignoble thee,
Save Me, save only Me?   170
All which I took from thee I did but take,
Not for thy harms,
But just that thou might'st seek it in My arms.
All which thy child's mistake
Fancies as lost, I have stored for thee at home: 175
Rise, clasp My hand, and come!"

Halts by me that footfall:
Is my gloom, after all,
Shade of His hand, outstretched caressingly?
"Ah, fondest, blindest, weakest,   180
I am He Whom thou seekest!
Thou dravest love from thee, who dravest Me."

16 The cypress is associated with death and mourning.
17 Must man die spiritually as well as physically in order to nourish his salvation?
18 Noise, din.
19 Lumpish, without spark.

William Ernest Henley
1849–1903

Henley spent almost his entire life in a losing fight against tuberculosis, and much of his work reflects his reactions to the struggle. Primary among these is his preoccupation with death and suffering, which is lustily countered, and almost in the same breath, by his cry for life, life unflinching and lived to the full. The spirited defiance engendered by this battle, together with a strong sense of individuality, led him to revolt against the conventional attitudes and artistic forms of the mid-Victorians, giving him breadth of mind to appreciate in his critical essays the innovations made by others (he was among the first to recognize and admire Hardy, Swinburne, Meredith, and Conrad, among other writers, as well as Rodin and Whistler), and at the same time courage to experiment himself. He is the real founder of what came to be called "free verse," that is, verse free from any metrical pattern (and also, as a rule, from rime), so that shifting rhythms and changing lengths of line might fit more closely the successive emotional "units."

In content Henley's poetry is a curious mixture of new realism and old romanticism. "In Hospital," a series of poems written during a long stay in the Edinburgh Infirmary, is a sharp, graphic description of scenes and experiences in a big city hospital, acutely observed, and set down in the barest diction and in the most natural order of words. On the other hand, his passionate desire for dynamic life, extending sometimes into sheer worship of force, of the Strong Man, takes us back, in a poem like "Invictus," to Byron and the Byronic hero; while at the same time it links Henley with Kipling and British imperialism (besides explaining, incidentally, his blunt disgust with the aestheticism of the nineties). Equally romantic in a complementary way is the "I. M. Margaritae Sorori," where the longing to escape from the hard battle of life makes him imagine a lovely and painless death, and thus recalls a stanza in Keats's "Ode to a Nightingale" and another in Shelley's "Stanzas Written in Dejection, near Naples."

TEXTS: Henley's *Works* have been published in seven volumes (1908); the *Poems* appear in a separate volume (1912). The best general book is *William Ernest Henley: A Study in the "Counter-Decadence" of the Nineties,* by Jerome H. Buckley. Also see John Connell, *William Ernest Henley* (1949). Shorter essays are those by John Drinkwater, "William Ernest Henley," in *The Muse in Council* (1925) and Arthur Symons, "Modernity in Verse," in *Studies in Two Literatures* (1924).

from In Hospital

1

ENTER PATIENT

The morning mists still haunt the stony street;
The northern summer air is shrill and cold;
And lo, the Hospital, gray, quiet, old,
Where Life and Death like friendly chafferers
    meet.
Thro' the loud spaciousness and draughty gloom   5
A small, strange child—so agèd yet so young!—
Her little arm besplinted and beslung,
Precedes me gravely to the waiting-room.
I limp behind, my confidence all gone.
The gray-haired soldier-porter waves me on,   10
And on I crawl, and still my spirits fail:
A tragic meanness seems so to environ
These corridors and stairs of stone and iron,
Cold, naked, clean—half-workhouse and half-
    jail.

4

BEFORE

Behold me waiting—waiting for the knife.
A little while, and at a leap I storm
The thick, sweet mystery of chloroform,
The drunken dark, the little death-in-life.
The gods are good to me: I have no wife,   5
No innocent child, to think of as I near
The fateful minute; nothing all-too dear
Unmans me for my bout of passive strife.
Yet I am tremulous and a trifle sick,
And, face to face with chance, I shrink a little: 10
My hopes are strong, my will is something weak.
Here comes the basket?[1] Thank you. I am ready.
But, gentlemen my porters, life is brittle:
You carry Caesar and his fortunes—steady!

7

VIGIL

Lived on one's back,
In the long hours of repose,

---

[1] In which the patient is carried to the operating room.

Life is a practical nightmare—
Hideous asleep or awake.

Shoulders and loins   5
Ache — — — !
Ache, and the mattress,
Run into boulders and hummocks,
Glows like a kiln, while the bedclothes—
Tumbling, importunate, daft—   10
Ramble and roll, and the gas,
Screwed to its lowermost,
An inevitable atom of light,
Haunts, and a stertorous sleeper
Snores me to hate and despair.   15

All the old time
Surges malignant before me;
Old voices, old kisses, old songs
Blossom derisive about me;
While the new days   20
Pass me in endless procession:
A pageant of shadows
Silently, leeringly wending
On . . . and still on . . . still on!

Far in the stillness a cat   25
Languishes loudly. A cinder[2]
Falls, and the shadows
Lurch to the leap of the flame. The next man to
    me
Turns with a moan; and the snorer,
The drug like a rope at his throat,   30
Gasps, gurgles, snorts himself free, as the night-
    nurse,
Noiseless and strange,
Her bull's eye half-lanterned in apron[3]
(Whispering me, "Are ye no' sleepin' yet?"),
Passes, list-slippered[4] and peering,   35
Round . . . and is gone.

Sleep comes at last—
Sleep full of dreams and misgivings—
Broken with brutal and sordid
Voices and sounds that impose on me,   40
Ere I can wake to it,
The unnatural, intolerable day.

---

[2] The ward is heated by a coal fire.
[3] A protected candlestick, the equivalent of a flashlight.
[4] With felt-soled slippers.

28

DISCHARGED

Carry me out
Into the wind and the sunshine,
Into the beautiful world.

O, the wonder, the spell of the streets!
The stature and strength of the horses,
The rustle and echo of footfalls,
The flat roar and rattle of wheels!
A swift tram floats huge on us . . .
It's a dream?
The smell of the mud in my nostrils   10
Blows brave—like a breath of the sea!

As of old,
Ambulant, undulant drapery,
Vaguely and strangely provocative,
Flutters and beckons. O, yonder—   15
Is it?—the gleam of a stocking!
Sudden, a spire

Wedged in the mist! O, the houses,
The long lines of lofty, gray houses,
Cross-hatched⁵ with shadow and light!   20
These are the streets. . . .
Each is an avenue leading
Whither I will!

Free . . . !
Dizzy, hysterical, faint,
I sit, and the carriage rolls on with me
Into the wonderful world.

Invictus¹

Out of the night that covers me,
    Black as the Pit from pole to pole,
I thank whatever gods may be
    For my unconquerable soul.

In the fell clutch of circumstance
    I have not winced nor cried aloud.   5

Under the bludgeonings of chance
    My head is bloody, but unbowed.

Beyond this place of wrath and tears
    Looms but the Horror of the shade,   10
And yet the menace of the years
    Finds, and shall find, me unafraid.

It matters not how strait the gate,   5
    How charged with punishments the scroll,
I am the master of my fate;   15
    I am the captain of my soul.

I. M.
Margaritae Sorori¹
(1886)

A late lark twitters from the quiet skies;   15
And from the west,
Where the sun, his day's work ended,
Lingers as in content,
There falls on the old, gray city   5
An influence luminous and serene,
A shining peace.   20

The smoke ascends
In a rosy-and-golden haze. The spires
Shine, and are changed. In the valley   10
Shadows rise. The lark sings on. The sun,
Closing his benediction,   25
Sinks, and the darkening air
Thrills with a sense of the triumphing night—
Night with her train of stars   15
And her great gift of sleep.

So be my passing!
My task accomplished and the long day done,
My wages taken, and in my heart
Some late lark singing,   20
Let me be gathered to the quiet west,
The sundown splendid and serene,
Death.   5

Space and Dread and the Dark

Space and dread and the dark—
Over a livid stretch of sky

---

⁵ A technique of etching.

¹ Unconquered. The title in *The Works of W. E. Henley,*
7 vols. (1908) is "I.M. R.T. Hamilton Bruce (1846–1899)."
Since Henley died in 1903, and this title or no title
appeared in volumes during his lifetime, it looks as though
"Invictus" was the idea of some editor in the twentieth
century.

¹ To the Memory of Sister Margaret.

Cloud-monsters crawling, like a funeral train
Of huge, primeval presences
Stooping beneath the weight
Of some enormous, rudimentary grief;
While in the haunting loneliness
The far sea waits and wanders with a sound
As of the trailing skirts of Destiny,
Passing unseen
To some immitigable end
With her gray henchman, Death.

What larve,[1] what specter is this
Thrilling the wilderness to life
As with the bodily shape of Fear?
What but a desperate sense,
A strong foreboding of those dim
Interminable continents, forlorn
And many-silenced, in a dusk
Inviolable utterly, and dead

As the poor dead it huddles and swarms and
    styes[2]
5 In hugger-mugger[3] through eternity?

Life—life—let there be life!
Better a thousand times the roaring hours
When wave and wind,
10 Like the Arch-Murderer in flight
From the Avenger at his heel,
Storm through the desolate fastnesses
And wild waste places of the world!

Life—give me life until the end,
15 That at the very top of being,
The battle-spirit shouting in my blood,
Out of the reddest hell of the fight
I may be snatched and flung
Into the everlasting lull,
20 The immortal, incommunicable dream.

1 Ghost.

2 Herds into sties like pigs.   3 Disorder.

Rudyard Kipling

1865–1936

Kipling was born in India and returned to it for his first job as a young man; he was thus especially fitted to interpret the natives, the British soldiery, and Anglo-Indian officialdom. And this, as a member of the staff of a local newspaper in Lahore, is what he first set out to do in 1882, writing a series of short stories and poems that dealt rather acidly with the manners and foibles (or worse) of English military and official society, portrayed native loyalty and superstition with sympathy, and described the life of the common soldier in an understanding, if somewhat uproarious, tone. The young Kipling was not a profound thinker, but he was a keen observer, with great vitality and a talent for brisk narrative. He also had an ear for pronounced rhythm that enabled him to translate into verse the vigor of his subjects, especially in the form of ballad or chanty.

These swinging rhythms, of course, were one source of the tremendous popularity of *Departmental Ditties* and *Barrack-Room Ballads and Other Verses*. But the underlying theme, too, had its own definite appeal, for the last twenty years of the century were the heyday of imperial expansion: India and the soldiers and administrators who were forging this vast and mysterious territory into an English colony were subjects of great interest and pride at home.

It is a credit to Kipling's integrity as man and artist that, while swept along with the current of imperial enthusiasm (see the dedication to *Barrack-Room Ballads*), with its concomitant exaltation of "Strong Men" and central authority, he could yet point the finger of satire at least at the minor evils of the situation, such as the shabby treatment of Tommy Atkins by his fellow-countrymen and the mean or bullying attitude of the average Anglo-Indian to the natives; and that at the very apex of the imperial fever he dared to intone the warning of his "Recessional."

But around 1900 success translated Kipling from an obscure reporter, very much in touch with the natives and with the common soldier, into a person of distinction, the friend of generals and top administrators. He still worshipped "Strong Men," but it was now the strength of autocratic dictation from above based on unquestioning submission from below, with utter condemnation for anyone who opposed the will of England. He could no longer have written "The Ballad of East and West" or admitted the valor of Fuzzy-Wuzzy. However, the great days of imperialism were drawing to a close and the English themselves were beginning to question the validity of "the White Man's burden." Kipling was out of tune with the new generation. It was no doubt some sense of his isolation that led him to withdraw into a retired country existence and to turn in his poetry from the wide world of Empire to the rural English countryside.

TEXTS: The standard edition is *Rudyard Kipling's Verse: Inclusive Edition, 1885–1932* (1934). The best biography is by C. E. Carrington (1955). For critical commentary see the introduction by T. S. Eliot to *A Choice of Kipling's Verse* (1942); an essay by Edmund Wilson, "The Kipling that Nobody Read," in *The Wound and the Bow* (1941); *Kipling's Mind and Art: Selected Critical Essays,* ed. Andrew Rutherford (1964); and J. M. S. Tomkins's *The Art of Rudyard Kipling* (1959; reissue, 1965).

from *Barrack-Room Ballads*

Dedication

Beyond the path of the outmost sun through
    utter darkness hurled—
Farther than ever comet flared or vagrant star-
    dust swirled—
Live such as fought and sailed and ruled and
    loved and made our world.

They are purged of pride because they died;
    they know the worth of their bays;
They sit at wine with the Maidens Nine[1] and the   5
    Gods of the Elder Days—
It is their will to serve or be still as fitteth Our
    Father's praise.

'Tis theirs to sweep through the ringing deep
    where Azrael's[2] outposts are,
Or buffet a path through the Pit's red wrath
    when God goes out to war,
Or hang with the reckless Seraphim on the rein
    of a red-maned star.

They take their mirth in the joy of the Earth—   10
    they dare not grieve for her pain.
They know of toil and the end of toil; they
    know God's Law is plain;
So they whistle the Devil to make them sport
    who know that Sin is vain.

---

1 The Muses.
2 The angel in Jewish and Mohammedan mythology who severs body and soul at death.—The Pit (line 8) = hell.

And oft-times cometh our wise Lord God, master
    of every trade,
And tells them tales of His daily toil, of Edens
    newly made;
And they rise to their feet as He passes by, gentle-   15
    men unafraid.

To these who are cleansed of base Desire, Sorrow
    and Lust and Shame—
Gods for they knew the hearts of men, men for
    they stooped to Fame—
Borne on the breath that men call Death, my
    brother's spirit came.

He scarce had need to doff his pride or slough
    the dross of Earth—
E'en as he trod that day to God so walked he   20
    from his birth,
In simpleness and gentleness and honor and clean
    mirth.

So cup to lip in fellowship they gave him wel-
    come high
And made him place at the banquet board—the
    Strong Men ranged thereby,
Who had done his work and held his peace and
    had no fear to die.

Beyond the loom of the last lone star, through   25
    open darkness hurled,
Further than rebel comet dared or hiving star-
    swarm swirled,
Sits he with those that praise our God for that
    they served His world.

The Ballad of East and West

1889

*Oh, East is East, and West is West, and never the
    twain shall meet,*
*Till Earth and Sky stand presently at God's great
    Judgment Seat;*
*But there is neither East nor West, Border, nor
    Breed, nor Birth,*
*When two strong men stand face to face, though
    they come from the ends of the earth!*

Kamal is out with twenty men to raise the Border   5
    side,

And he has lifted the Colonel's mare that is the Colonel's pride.

He has lifted her out of the stable-door between the dawn and the day,

And turned the calkins[1] upon her feet, and ridden her far away.

Then up spoke the Colonel's son that led a troop of the Guides:

"Is there never a man of all my men can say where Kamal hides?"   10

Then up and spoke Mohammed Khan, the son of the Ressaldar,

"If ye know the track of the morning-mist, ye know where his pickets are.

At dusk he harries the Abazai—at dawn he is into Bonair,

But he must go by Fort Bukloh to his own place to fare,

So if ye gallop to Fort Bukloh as fast as a bird can fly,   15

By the favor of God ye may cut him off ere he win to the Tongue of Jagai.

But if he be passed the Tongue of Jagai, right swiftly turn ye then,

For the length and the breadth of that grisly plain is sown with Kamal's men.

There is rock to the left, and rock to the right, and low lean thorn between,

And ye may hear a breech-bolt snick where never a man is seen."   20

The Colonel's son has taken horse, and a raw rough dun was he,

With the mouth of a bell and the heart of Hell, and the head of the gallows-tree.

The Colonel's son to the Fort has won, they bid him stay to eat—

Who rides at the tail of a Border thief, he sits not long at his meat.

He's up and away from Fort Bukloh as fast as he can fly,   25

Till he was aware of his father's mare in the gut of the Tongue of Jagai,

Till he was aware of his father's mare with Kamal upon her back,

And when he could spy the white of her eye, he made the pistol crack.

He has fired once, he has fired twice, but the whistling ball went wide.

"Ye shoot like a soldier," Kamal said. "Show now if ye can ride!"   30

It's up and over the Tongue of Jagai, as blown dust-devils go,

The dun he fled like a stag of ten, but the mare like a barren doe.

The dun he leaned against the bit and slugged his head above,

But the red mare played with the snaffle-bars, as a maiden plays with a glove.

There was rock to the left and rock to the right, and low lean thorn between,   35

And thrice he heard a breech-bolt snick tho' never a man was seen.

They have ridden the low moon out of the sky, their hoofs drum up the dawn,

The dun he went like a wounded bull, but the mare like a new-roused fawn.

The dun he fell at a water-course—in a woeful heap fell he,

And Kamal has turned the red mare back, and pulled the rider free.   40

He has knocked the pistol out of his hand—small room was there to strive,

" 'Twas only by favor of mine," quoth he, "ye rode so long alive:

There was not a rock for twenty mile, there was not a clump of tree,

But covered a man of my own men with his rifle cocked on his knee.

If I had raised my bridle-hand, as I have held it low,   45

The little jackals that flee so fast were feasting all in a row.

If I had bowed my head on my breast, as I have held it high,

The kite that whistles above us now were gorged till she could not fly."

Lightly answered the Colonel's son: "Do good to bird and beast,

But count who come for the broken meats before thou makest a feast.   50

If there should follow a thousand swords to carry my bones away,

Belike the price of a jackal's meal were more than a thief could pay.

They will feed their horse on the standing crop, their men on the garnered grain,

The thatch of the byres will serve their fires when all the cattle are slain.

But if thou thinkest the price be fair,—thy brethren wait to sup,   55

---

[1] Reversed the horseshoes.

The hound is kin to the jackal-spawn,—howl,
dog, and call them up!
And if thou thinkest the price be high, in steer
and gear and stack,
Give me my father's mare again, and I'll fight my
own way back!"
Kamal has gripped him by the hand and set
him upon his feet.
"No talk shall be of dogs," said he, "when wolf 60
and gray wolf meet.
May I eat dirt if thou has hurt of me in deed or
breath;
What dam of lances brought thee forth to jest
at the dawn with Death?"
Lightly answered the Colonel's son: "I hold by
the blood of my clan:
Take up the mare for my father's gift—by God,
she has carried a man!"
The red mare ran to the Colonel's son, and 65
nuzzled against his breast;
"We be two strong men," said Kamal then, "but
she loveth the younger best.
So she shall go with a lifter's dower, my tur-
quoise-studded rein,
My 'broidered saddle and saddle-cloth, and silver
stirrups twain."
The Colonel's son a pistol drew, and held it
muzzle-end,
"Ye have taken the one from a foe," said he. 70
"Will ye take the mate from a friend?"
"A gift for a gift," said Kamal straight; "a limb
for the risk of a limb.
Thy father has sent his son to me, I'll send my
son to him!"
With that he whistled his only son, that dropped
from a mountain-crest—
He trod the ling[2] like a buck in spring, and he
looked like a lance in rest.
"Now here is thy master," Kamal said, "who 75
leads a troop of the Guides,
And thou must ride at his left side as shield on
shoulder rides.
Till Death or I cut loose the tie, at camp and
board and bed,
Thy life is his—thy fate it is to guard him with
thy head.
So, thou must eat the White Queen's meat, and
all her foes are thine,
And thou must harry thy father's hold for the 80
peace of the Border-line.

And thou must make a trooper tough and hack
thy way to power—
Belike they will raise thee to Ressaldar when I
am hanged in Peshawur!"

They have looked each other between the eyes,
and there they found no fault.
They have taken the Oath of the Brother-in-
Blood on leavened bread and salt:
They have taken the Oath of the Brother-in- 85
Blood on fire and fresh-cut sod,
On the hilt and the haft of the Khyber knife,
and the Wondrous Names of God.
The Colonel's son he rides the mare and Kamal's
boy the dun,
And two have come back to Fort Bukloh where
there went forth but one.
And when they drew to the Quarter-Guard, full
twenty swords flew clear—
There was not a man but carried his feud with 90
the blood of the mountaineer.
"Ha' done! Ha' done!" said the Colonel's son.
"Put up the steel at your sides!
Last night ye had struck at a Border thief—to-
night 'tis a man of the Guides!"

*Oh, East is East, and West is West, and never the
twain shall meet,*
*Till Earth and Sky stand presently at God's great
Judgment Seat;*
But there is neither East nor West, Border, nor 95
Breed, nor Birth,
*When two strong men stand face to face, though
they come from the ends of the earth.*

"Fuzzy-Wuzzy"[1]

(Sudan Expeditionary Force)

We've fought with many men acrost the seas,
An' some of 'em was brave an' some was not:
The Paythan an' the Zulu an' Burmese;
But the Fuzzy was the finest o' the lot.
We never got a ha'porth's change[2] of 'im: 5

---

2 Barren mountainside.

1 The natives of the Sudan were given this nickname by
the British soldiers because of their long, frizzy hair. In
1884 an English expeditionary force met defeat at their
hands.
2 A halfpenny's worth of change, i.e., even the slightest
advantage. This poem and the next express the sentiments
of the British private, and so are couched in the speech

'E squatted in the scrub an' 'ocked our 'orses,
'E cut our sentries up a Sua*kim,*
   An' 'e played the cat an' banjo with our forces.
      So 'ere's *to* you, Fuzzy-Wuzzy, at your 'ome
        in the Soudan;
      You're a pore benighted 'eathen but a   10
        first-class fightin' man;
      We gives you your certificate, an' if you
        want it signed
      We'll come an' 'ave a romp with you when-
        ever you're inclined.

We took our chanst among the Kyber 'ills,[3]
   The Boers knocked us silly at a mile,
The Burman give us Irriwaddy chills,
   An' a Zulu *impi* dished us up in style: 15
But all we ever got from such as they
   Was pop to what the Fuzzy made us swaller;
We 'eld our bloomin' own, the papers say,
   But man for man the Fuzzy knocked us 'oller.   20
      Then 'ere's *to* you, Fuzzy-Wuzzy, an' the
        missis and the kid;
      Our orders was to break you, an' of course
        we went an' did.
      We sloshed you with Martinis,[4] an' it
        wasn't 'ardly fair;
      But for all the odds agin' you, Fuzzy-Wuz,
        you broke the square.[5]

'E 'asn't got no papers of 'is own,   25
   'E 'asn't got no medals nor rewards,
So *we* must certify the skill 'e's shown,
   In usin' of 'is long two-'anded swords:
When 'e's 'oppin' in an' out among the bush
   With 'is coffin-'eaded shield an' shovel-spear,   30
An 'appy day with Fuzzy on the rush
   Will last an 'ealthy Tommy for a year.
      So 'ere's *to* you, Fuzzy-Wuzzy, an' your
        friends which are no more,
      If we 'adn't lost some messmates we would
        'elp you to deplore.
      But give an' take's the gospel, an' we'll call   35
        the bargain fair,
      For if you 'ave lost more than us, you crum-
        pled up the square!

'E rushes at the smoke when we let drive,
   An', before we know, 'e's 'ackin' at our 'ead;
'E's all 'ot sand an' ginger when alive,
   An' 'e's generally shammin' when 'e's dead.   40

'E's a daisy, 'e's a ducky, 'e's a lamb!
   'E's a injia-rubber idiot on the spree,
'E's the on'y thing that doesn't give a damn
   For a Regiment o' British Infantree!
      So 'ere's *to* you, Fuzzy-Wuzzy, with your   45
        'ome in the Soudan;
      You're a poor benighted 'eathen but a first-
        class fightin' man;
      An' 'ere's *to* you, Fuzzy-Wuzzy, with your
        'ayrick 'ead of 'air—
      You big black boundin' beggar—for you
        broke a British square!

Tommy[1]

I went into a public-'ouse[2] to get a pint o' beer,
The publican[3] 'e up an' sez, "We serve no red-
   coats here."
The girls be'ind the bar they laughed an' giggled
   fit to die,
I outs into the street again an' to myself sez I:
      O it's Tommy this, an' Tommy that,   5
        an' "Tommy, go away";
      But it's "Thank you, Mister Atkins,"
        when the band begins to play—
      The band begins to play, my boys, the
        band begins to play,
      O it's "Thank you, Mister Atkins," when
        the band begins to play.

I went into a theater as sober as could be,
They gave a drunk civilian room, but 'adn't   10
   none for me;
They sent me to the gallery or round the music-
   'alls,
But when it comes to fightin', Lord! they'll shove
   me in the stalls!
      For it's Tommy this, an' Tommy that,
        an' "Tommy, wait outside";
      But it's "Special train for Atkins" when
        the trooper's on the tide—

---

common to him, Cockney, the most pronounced feature
of which is the omission of initial h.—*Hocked* (line 6)
= cut the leg tendon.
[3] Lines 13–16 refer to British campaigns in India, South
Africa, Burma, and Southeast Africa respectively. An *impi*
was a Zulu regiment.
[4] A particular type of rifle.
[5] A famous defensive formation of the British.

---

[1] Tommy Atkins is the conventional nickname of the
British private.
[2] Tavern.   [3] Tavern keeper.

The troopship's on the tide, my boys,   15
    the troopship's on the tide,
O it's "Special train for Atkins" when
    the trooper's on the tide.

Yes, makin' mock o' uniforms that guard you
    while you sleep
Is cheaper than them uniforms, an' they're starva-
    tion cheap;
An' hustlin' drunken soldiers when they're goin'
    large a bit
Is five times better business than paradin' in full   20
    kit.
        Then it's Tommy this, an' Tommy that,
            an' "Tommy, 'ow's yer soul?"
        But it's "Thin red line of 'eroes" when
            the drums begin to roll—
        The drums begin to roll, my boys, the
            drums begin to roll,
        O it's "Thin red line of 'eroes" when the
            drums begin to roll.

We aren't no thin red 'eroes, nor we aren't no   25
    blackguards too,
But single men in barricks, most remarkable like
    you;
An' if sometimes our conduck isn't all your fancy
    paints,
Why, single men in barricks don't grow into
    plaster saints;
        While it's Tommy this, an' Tommy that,
            an' "Tommy, fall be'ind,"
        But it's "Please to walk in front, sir,"   30
            when there's trouble in the wind—
        There's trouble in the wind, my boys,
            there's trouble in the wind,
        O it's "Please to walk in front, sir," when
            there's trouble in the wind.

You talk o' better food for us, an' schools, an'
    fires, an' all:
We'll wait for extry rations if you treat us ra-
    tional.
Don't mess about the cook-room slops, but prove   35
    it to our face
The Widow's[4] Uniform is not the soldier-man's
    disgrace.
        For it's Tommy this, an' Tommy that,
            an' "Chuck him out, the brute!"

But it's "Savior of 'is country" when the
    guns begin to shoot;
An' it's Tommy this, an' Tommy that,
    an' anything you please;
An' Tommy ain't a bloomin' fool—you   40
    bet that Tommy sees!

from *Five Nations*

Recessional[1]

1897

God of our fathers, known of old,
    Lord of our far-flung battle-line,
Beneath whose awful Hand we hold
    Dominion over palm and pine—
Lord God of Hosts, be with us yet,   5
Lest we forget—lest we forget!

The tumult and the shouting dies;
    The Captains and the Kings depart:
Still stands Thine ancient sacrifice,
    An humble and a contrite heart.   10
Lord God of Hosts, be with us yet,
Lest we forget—lest we forget!

Far-called, our navies melt away;
    On dune and headland sinks the fire:
Lo, all our pomp of yesterday   15
    Is one with Nineveh and Tyre![2]
Judge of the Nations, spare us yet,
Lest we forget—lest we forget!

If, drunk with sight of power, we loose
    Wild tongues that have not Thee in awe,   20
Such boastings as the Gentiles[3] use,
    Or lesser breeds without the Law—
Lord God of Hosts, be with us yet,
Lest we forget—lest we forget!

For heathen heart that puts her trust   25
    In reeking tube and iron shard,[4]

---

4 The queen's. Victoria's husband had died in 1861.

1 Written as a closing hymn after the pomp and brilliance
of the celebration of Victoria's sixtieth anniversary as
queen.
2 Two important cities of ancient times whose glories
have long since departed.
3 Those who are not of the chosen race, i.e., not English.
4 Guns and shell fragments.

All valiant dust that builds on dust,
    And guarding, calls not Thee to guard,
For frantic boast and foolish word—
    Thy mercy on Thy people, Lord!

The White Man's Burden[1]

1899

Take up the White Man's burden—
    Send forth the best ye breed—
Go bind your sons to exile
    To serve your captives' need;
To wait in heavy harness,
    On fluttered folk and wild—
Your new-caught, sullen peoples,
    Half-devil and half-child.

Take up the White Man's burden—
    In patience to abide,   10
To veil the threat of terror
    And check the show of pride;
By open speech and simple,
    An hundred times made plain,
To seek another's profit,   15
    And work another's gain.

Take up the White Man's burden—
    The savage wars of peace—
Fill full the mouth of Famine
    And bid the sickness cease;   20
And when your goal is nearest
    The end for others sought,

Watch Sloth and heathen Folly
    Bring all your hope to nought.

Take up the White Man's burden—   30
    No tawdry rule of kings,
But toil of serf and sweeper—
    The tale of common things.
The ports ye shall not enter,
    The roads ye shall not tread,
Go make them with your living,
    And mark them with your dead.

Take up the White Man's burden—
    And reap his old reward:
The blame of those ye better,
    The hate of those ye guard—
The cry of hosts ye humor
    (Ah, slowly!) toward the light:—
"Why brought ye us from bondage,
    Our loved Egyptian night?"[2]

Take up the White Man's burden—
    Ye dare not stoop to less—
Nor call too loud on Freedom
    To cloak your weariness;
By all ye cry or whisper,
    By all ye leave or do,
The silent, sullen peoples
    Shall weigh your Gods and you.

Take up the White Man's burden—
    Have done with childish days—
The lightly proffered laurel,
    The easy, ungrudged praise.
Comes now, to search your manhood
    Through all the thankless years,
Cold, edged with dear-bought wisdom,
    The judgment of your peers!

---

[1] The poem was written to remind America of her responsibilities toward Cuba and the Philippines consequent upon her victory over Spain in 1898. It is, of course, founded upon the premise that the "White Man" was carrying out a divine and completely altruistic mission in conquering and ruling the native lands of those of darker skin.

[2] This was the reproach of the Israelites when Moses was leading them to the Promised Land (Exodus 16:3, 17:3).

The Modern Period

Nude Descending a Staircase, No. 2 *by Marcel Duchamp. Philadelphia Museum of Art, the Arensberg Collection.*

The Modern Period

The literature of a reader's own time offers rewards, varieties of interest, that are scarcely to be looked for in the literature of a past era, whatever its greatness. The writers of our own time live in our world, subject to the same social, intellectual, and spiritual forces, the same excitements and the same despair or disappointment that confront us every day; for that reason we read them with an eagerness that is somehow different from any sense with which we approach the literature of the past. To be sure, large areas of human experience are common to many places and many times, so that an epigram from *The Greek Anthology* or a Chinese poem of the eighth century may have the same poignance for us that it had for those who first heard it or read it. But in other areas there is change: the certainties of one generation become the uncertainties of the next; each age has its own absorbingly immediate problems; and it is only the contemporary writer who can speak to us with a complete clarity of focus about our own peculiar uncertainties and dilemmas. The surfaces of life are constantly changing, too—modes of behavior, all the material side of life, the exact ways we speak and the nature of the things we laugh at —and we take a natural pleasure in seeing our own ways of life reflected in literature. Contemporary literature is no less able than any other literature to interpret for us what is permanent in human life and the human situation, but in addition it does what no other literature can: to interpret the very aspects of the life of our own time that make it in some degree unique. We welcome the sense of familiarity that life wears for us when we encounter it in the literature of our own time.

Here, at the very outset of a presentation of some representative aspects of the literature of the Modern period, we encounter a problem, a problem that involves both dates and terminology. The Modern period, as a division of literary history that is quite clearly distinguishable from Victorian literature, is generally accepted as having begun to take shape in certain literary and cultural impulses of the 1870s and 1880s, impulses that are grouped by cultural historians under the headings of aestheticism, decadence, and symbolism. Though other tendencies and schools, notably realism and naturalism, have their important place in the formation of the Modern period, nevertheless much of what it most essentially stands for, in the work of many of its greatest individual representatives, is to be traced back to the attitudes toward the works of art or literature that are involved in the three tendencies first named. It is also generally agreed that the Modern period saw its time of most intense fulfillment in the years between 1910 and 1930: a time when British literature saw the publication of key works by Yeats, Eliot, Joyce, D. H. Lawrence, and Virginia Woolf, works that we continue to think of as centrally and typically "modern." Such a list could be expanded not only for British literature but also with the names of such modern writers from other literatures as Proust, Thomas Mann, Franz Kafka, Hemingway, Faulkner, and Gertrude Stein. And, finally, it may also be agreed that these writers continue to seem modern, even as the time comes when we realize that *The Waste Land* or *Ulysses*, *Remembrance of Things Past* or *To the Lighthouse*, is fifty years old or more. What to do, then, with the word *Modern*? And if we are going to apply that term to a period that may in some sense seem to have come to an end by 1945 or 1950, what word do we use for the literature produced *since* that time?

The word *Modern* does seem, at least for the present, to belong to the particular era of development in literature and the other arts that may be contained (always with reservations and qualifications) within the time-span 1910–1945. No era can have been more *conscious* than this one was of its modernity, of having made a sharp, clean break with the assumptions and practices of the past; and somehow the word seems to be permanently associated with certain poems, novels, paintings, or pieces of music from a particular time, even as that time recedes into the past: with such works as Stravinsky's "Le Sacre du Printemps" or Marcel Duchamp's "Nude Descending a Staircase" or—and they must be named again—*The Waste Land* or *Ulysses.* So, aside from the question of whether or not there does exist a discontinuity between works written before 1945 and works written later, and aside from the contradiction involved in using, to describe a period that is now past, a word which derives from the Latin adverb *modo,* "just now," the term *Modern period* seems still to belong to the opening decades of the twentieth century.

As to the question of what term to use for British literature as it has continued to flourish since 1945, posterity may well decide that it too is "Modern," that it represents merely a continuation or further development of the Modern period. For the time being, however, and for reasons that will be made apparent in the present introduction, as well as in the introduction to the selections from post-1950 writers with which this volume closes, it may be permissible, even if it is occasionally awkward, to use the term *Modern* for the phase in the development of twentieth-century literature that was complete by 1945 or 1950, and such terms as "contemporary" or "writing of the present day" to describe work published since 1945 or 1950.

We have mentioned some of the reasons why the literature of the Modern period seems more immediately attractive to us than the literature of earlier times: the feeling we have that it comes to us more directly than earlier literature, with no need of mediation between us and a remote past; and the feeling that in reading it we will be involved in issues, questions, life situations, and problems that have not yet been solved and that are not yet merely a matter of history.

And here it may be claimed that thus far, as we go forward into the 1970s, the reader of Yeats's poems or of Lawrence's or Joyce's novels is not at all beset by a sense that he is reading work belonging to the past, work whose measure has already been taken once and for all. On the contrary, today's reader still has a very lively sense of participating in the growth of our understanding of these works, which have by no means yet been fully and definitively understood.

Here it must be recognized that any special claims made for twentieth-century literature are likely to be countered by the charge that its practitioners have too often made a cult of obscurity, that, forgetting their obligations to the reader, they have produced works so difficult, so strange in form, so packed with recondite allusion that no reader can be expected to understand them. The rebellious plain reader is apt to declare that if modern poetry has no audience it is because it deserves none. What answer can the partisans of contemporary literature offer to such a complaint?

This first of all: that no educated reader who is willing to approach the modern poets with a view to discovering what they have tried to do in their poetry is likely to remain for long under the illusion that the best of them have willfully cultivated obscurity. It is true that many of them are difficult, especially for the reader who comes to their work expecting to find the same kind of poetry that the Victorians wrote. The poets who have done most to give the twentieth century a voice entirely its own have written from a range of erudition and with a studied concentration and subtlety of effect that have necessarily cut them off from the unhesitating, undiscriminating acceptance that the Victorians gave to the work of their major writers. What lies behind their way of writing will be analyzed in some detail in the following pages. But at the outset we may ask if there is any reason why a poet of cultivated interests, of subtle powers of response and expression, should lay aside his interests or blunt his powers when he writes. On the contrary: both writer and reader must operate at the pitch of their powers, for otherwise what is written and what is read will become relaxed, weak, and at least partially false. The French critic Pierre Mille, writing about the brilliant twentieth-century French novelist and playwright Jean Giraudoux, states a truth that should be taken with perfect literalness by the educated reader who approaches any reputedly "difficult" contemporary writer: "This author is filled with allusions not readily discernible to ignorance or to hasty reading. But no one is obliged to be ignorant or to read hastily."

If the question of the "difficulty" of contemporary literature, particularly of modern poetry, has been touched on, perhaps tactlessly, at the very beginning of this introductory essay, it is because the bugbear of unintelligibility has kept many readers away from poetry and fiction that, with good will, an open mind, and a certain amount of rudimentary instruction as to aims and methods, they will be able to read with pleasure and profit. Most modern poems, if they are read aright and for the right reasons, are scarcely more difficult to read than, say, Wordsworth's sonnet beginning "The World Is Too Much with Us." But a sloppy reader who takes from the Wordsworth sonnet only a vague statement of an ethical preconception which he believes he finds expressed in the first four lines (such a reader is apt to ignore the last six) may convince himself, quite wrongly, that he has enjoyed and possessed the poem to the full, where the same reader making the same undisciplined approach to a highly individual and closely worked poem by Eliot or Auden will know that he has had nothing. Actually, he will have had no less than in reading Wordsworth, but here he is made uncomfortably aware of his own inadequacy, and for that he is unable to forgive the modern poet. A large part of the difficulty of modern poetry arises because it does not lend itself to being read for the wrong reasons. What the right reasons are will be brought out most easily if we trace the development of poetry from the 1890s to the present.

THE PREPARATORY ROLE OF THE AESTHETIC MOVEMENT

The story of most that is specifically modern in twentieth-century British literature begins in the 1890s, in the brief flourishing of the Aesthetic Movement described in the introduction to the Victorian period. Whatever the intrinsic merit of the writers of the period, their work represented a righting of balances that the Victorians, in their very greatness and success, had upset.

"The forces which mould the thought of men change, or men's resistance to them slackens; with the change of men's thought comes a change of literature, alike in its inmost essence and in its outward form: after the world has starved its soul long enough in the contemplation and the rearrangement of material things, comes the turn of the soul. . . ." In this sentence from the introduction to *The Symbolist Movement in Literature* (1899), Arthur Symons was referring to the wider European movement of which the Aesthetic Movement was a part and, for England, a preparation. Undoubtedly the great Victorians had not really starved their souls in mere "contemplation and . . . rearrangement of material things," but they had tended more and more, as the century wore on, to make of their art a medium for communicating with a large public on matters of broad ethical, educational, or even practical import. It was only natural that their emphasis on social values, on the poet's role as prophet, on the search for and expression of general, permanent truths should be countered by an insistence on the poet's right to work within the limits of his most intensely individual experience, on the value of the momentary impression for its own sake and without regard to its significance in some ultimate ethical or philosophical scale.

The fundamental doctrine of the Aesthetic Movement had found expression as early as 1873 in Walter Pater's *Studies in the History of the Renaissance*. To read Pater is to be reminded of the origin of the word *aesthetic* in the Greek verb αἰσθάνομαι, "perceive, or, apprehend by the senses": the realm of the aesthetic is the realm of perception, embracing the whole stream of sensory experience. Moreover, for Pater and his followers in the nineties, that is *all* experience is, and "those impressions of the individual to which, for each one of us, experience dwindles down, are in perpetual flight"; what is real is each impression lasting but for the moment in which it is apprehended. Not the sum of our moments, not the pattern that prudence or faith or intellect urges us to impose upon them, but the moment itself, seized for its essential and unique quality: that alone is worthy of our passionate attention. The sentences of the original Conclusion to his book in which Pater expressed

Salome and John by Aubrey Beardsley, 1907. Symons described Beardsley's art as "abstract spiritual corruption revealed in beautiful form."

his central views are as moving today as when they were written, even while we recognize the inadequacy that lurks within them. It will be remembered that after describing the importance of discriminating the best that each of our few brief moments has to offer us, Pater goes on to rule out certain attitudes that had been characteristeric of the Victorian approach to life and to letters:

With this sense of the splendour of our experience and of its awful brevity, gathering all we are into one desperate effort to see and touch, we shall hardly have time to make theories about the things we see and touch. . . . The theory or idea or system which requires of us the sacrifice of any part of this experience, in consideration of some interest into which we cannot enter, or some abstract theory we have not identified with ourselves, or of what is only conventional, has no real claim upon us.

In Pater's view of man's life as "an interval," after which "our place knows us no more,"

the highest of human satisfactions are those derived from art—from an art chastened of preoccupation with questions external to it, "art for art's sake":

Some spend this interval in listlessness, some in high passions, the wisest . . . in art and song. For our one chance lies in expanding that interval, in getting as many pulsations as possible into the given time. Great passions may give us this quickened sense of life, ecstasy and sorrow of love, the various forms of enthusiastic activity, disinterested or otherwise, which come naturally to many of us. Only be sure it is passion—that it does yield you this fruit of a quickened, multiplied consciousness. Of such wisdom, the poetic passion, the desire of beauty, the love of art for its own sake, has most. For art comes to you professing frankly to give nothing but the highest quality to your moments as they pass, and simply for those moments' sake.

Pater's statement is touched throughout with bravery and splendor; it also foreshadows the tragedy of those who made of it their philosophy of life and art, the Aesthetic writers of the 1890s. But whatever else they did or failed to do, these writers cleared the air of a certain heaviness and prophetic solemnity that had characterized the Victorian writer's relationship to his public. They themselves had undergone the influence of the French Symbolists, but their role was not so much to become the representatives of Symbolism in British poetry as to prepare the way for more powerful poets who should do so. (One who fulfilled both roles was W. B. Yeats, who had begun his career as a writer of typical nineties poetry, but at his death in 1939 he had long been the most admired poet of the twentieth century.) At a time when the voices of the great Victorians had to all intents and purposes been stilled, the Aesthetic writers provided a medium of conductivity for the impulses of the French Symbolist movement, helping restore to British literature the European character that it had largely lost during the Victorian era. Of course, many poets—Hardy, Kipling, A. E. Housman—continued, during the nineties and later, to work in a tradition that, except for the usual classical influences, was entirely native. But for other writers there was henceforth to be the same direct contact with Continental influences that had proved fruitful and decisive at so many earlier periods.

THE MEANING OF SYMBOLISM AND THE IMPACT OF THE SYMBOLIST MOVEMENT

No term in contemporary criticism is used with greater frequency or with a more bewildering disregard for its appropriateness in any given instance than "symbolism." The new student of modern literature will be helped if at this point we distinguish three uses of the word. All three uses have something in common, but each has its own special area of meaning as well.

First, in its widest sense, symbolism describes a situation with which we are all familiar. Much of the thought and feeling of our daily lives goes on in terms of our reactions to easily recognized symbols: a flag, a cross, a lion on an armorial bearing, an elephant in a political cartoon. In such instances, the values are fixed and easily recognized; there is no difficulty in seeing past the symbol to what it represents. In all these cases, and in many more like them, a present object or verbal sign is assigned or acquires a value as representing something other than itself, something greater than itself, an abstraction, an ideal, a complex of events or entities—"an unseen reality," in Arthur Symons's phrase. And always the symbol offers the advantage of being easier to manipulate than the reality behind it would be.

Second, the term is used to describe a technique of expression that has been employed by writers widely separated in space and time who have not necessarily been adherents of a school whose program was consciously "symbolist." We constantly encounter symbolism, used in a way that is not entirely different from the way it was used by the professed Symbolists (to give them the distinguishing capital letter) of the mid-nineteenth century and after, in the work of writers who either lived before the Symbolist doctrine was articulated or who were not touched by it.

We miss a great deal in reading Shakespeare, for example, if we are unwilling to see that his plays are ultimately capable of being interpreted on a symbolic level. *Othello*, whatever else it may be, is on one level a symbolic representation of the struggle between the powers of Heaven and Hell for the possession of a human soul. Everything is done, in terms of diction, imagery, and dramatic situation, to establish Desdemona as the symbol of Heaven and salvation, and Iago as the symbol of Hell and damnation. Othello, deceived into taking appearance for reality, makes a diametrically wrong choice of allegiance and is destroyed. Symbolism is present in the details of the play, too, and the following passage provides a good example of what we mean when we speak in general of the use of symbols in poetry. Iago has landed in Cyprus after passing safely through a storm at sea, with Desdemona in his charge (Act II, scene i). Cassio says:

> He's had most favorable and happy speed.
> Tempests themselves, high seas, and howling winds,
> The gutter'd rocks, and congregated sands,—
> Traitors ensteep'd to clog the guiltless keel,
> As having sense of beauty, do omit
> Their mortal natures, letting go safely by
> The divine Desdemona.

Now, in the play as a whole the treachery of Iago is opposed to the divinity, the blessedness, of Desdemona. This passage offers a symbolic epitome of that arrangement of values, except that here the elements that symbolize treachery—ironically, in view of Desdemona's coming destruction through the machinations of Iago—forgo their characteristic deadly functions, allowing the element that symbolizes Desdemona and her innocence to go, for the time being, unscathed. The storm, the high seas, the rocks, the sands,

> Traitors ensteep'd to clog the guiltless keel,

are incidental, momentary *symbols* of the values for which Iago is himself a larger, permanent symbol. The "guiltless keel" is the symbol of innocence, of the "divine Desdemona" whom it carries. By the use of these particular symbols, Shakespeare is enabled to make, with ease and concentration, the ironic point that has been referred to.

There is no need to suppose that Shakespeare was conscious of using symbols in this passage, any more than we have to be *conscious* of taking in a symbolic import to receive its force as we read or hear the play. But consciously or unconsciously, the writer who uses symbolism will be found to have set up, in a passage or over a whole work, a set of objects or personages or signs whose relation to one another parallels the arrangement of another set of values that are themselves not explicitly mentioned or exhibited.

And the poet who uses symbols by necessity, rather than in order to follow a literary fashion, is using them because what he has to say cannot be said by any more straightforward way, or at least because it cannot be expressed in any other way without a loss of concentration, of power, or of suggestiveness. The reader may demonstrate this point by asking himself, after he has become familiar with Yeats's "Sailing to Byzantium," how much that poem gains in richness, in ease, and in concentration of effect and meaning by the use of the ancient city of Byzantium as a complex symbol.

In its third use, the use in which it would be well if the word were to be consistently capitalized, Symbolism designates a specific literary school, international in scope, which began to make itself heard about a hundred years ago, and which achieved its clearest articulation in France. When we thing of Symbolism, we think first of a series of French writers: Baudelaire (1821–1867), Gérard de Nerval (1808–1855), Villiers de l'Isle Adam (1838–1889), Stéphane Mallarmé (1842–1898), Paul Verlaine (1844–1896), Tristan Corbière (1845–1875), Arthur Rimbaud (1854–1891), and Jules Laforgue (1860–1887). There was actual personal contact between some of these writers and certain English writers and painters of the Aesthetic nineties. Yeats met Verlaine in Paris in 1895 or 1896, a few months before the latter's death. Arthur Symons, Whistler, Oscar Wilde, and George Moore attended Mallarmé's famous Tuesday evenings in the Rue de Rome. Such contacts were but symptoms, however, of a widespread receptivity to the ideas and formal influences of French Symbolism.

The doctrines underlying French Symbolism were described for British readers by Arthur Symons in an important book already referred to, *The Symbolist Movement in Literature*. After describing the more general uses of the terms *symbol* and *symbolism*, Symons quoted a sentence from *Sartor Resartus* in which, he says, Carlyle is "vindicating for the word its full value":

In the Symbol proper, what we can call a Symbol, there is ever, more or less distinctly and directly, some embodiment and revelation of the Infinite; the Infinite is made to blend itself with the Finite, to stand visible, and as it were, attainable there.

"It is in such a sense as this," Symons says, "that the word Symbolism has been used to describe a movement which, during the last generation, has profoundly influenced the course of French literature." In this sense, the word implies a specific philosophical view: the belief that the visible world reflects the invisible, that correspondences exist between the world of phenomena we know and a realm of the invisible lying behind it. The consequence of this principle is the belief that we can know the invisible through the visible, that by close, intuitive attention to the impulses received through the senses we can receive an inkling, at least, of impulses that derive from the Absolute. Moreover, correspondences exist not only between finite and infinite, between visible and invisible, but also between impulses received through one sense and those received through another.[1]

As a consequence of this mystic belief in the availability of the Infinite and in the ultimate unity of all impulses, the Symbolists could not be content merely to provide in their poetry accurate, recognizable copies of the visible world of natural appearances and social institutions. To do so would be to leave out all that was dazzling and eternal, all that was subtle and *true* in their vision. The hitherto inexpressible had somehow to be expressed, and it could only be done by the most subtle techniques of suggestion, by which each writer would attempt to render his own individual experience with the utmost fidelity. Symons urges his readers to remember Mallarmé's principle: that "to name is to destroy, to suggest is to create." Words must be used to suggest the poet's delicately apprehended sensation. They must be so selected and grouped that in their weight and rhythm and color, in their capacity to translate one sense impression into terms of another sense, they become symbols for the original perception. In this elaborate process there are obviously many points at which the poet and his reader will part company, and there is no poetry in English that for obscurity can rival what Symons calls the "frozen impenetrability" of Mallarmé's last sonnets.

---

[1] For an expression of both points of the doctrine, see Baudelaire's celebrated sonnet, "Correspondances," from *Les Fleurs du Mal* (1857).

The philosophical beliefs of the French Symbolists are not entirely easy to grasp, and they are far from easy to accept. Although their poetry seldom approximates the obscurity of Mallarmé's later verse, it sometimes betrays weaknesses—a bloodlessness, an exiguity, a preciousness, a remoteness—which are consequences of its very strengths. Yet these writers, both in their theory and in their practice, opened up to poetry domains of interest and power that lay at a wide remove from the areas habitually exploited by the Victorians in England. Few of the British writers who came under their spell went so far as to adopt their philosophic positions *in toto*, but for all who read them seriously and sympathetically the writing of poetry and the role of the poet were to be very different from what they had been in the fifty years between 1830 and 1880.

Symons insists that the artist's position is *outside* society, that

> the artist . . . has no more part in society than a monk in domestic life: he cannot be judged by its rules, he can be neither praised nor blamed for his acceptance or rejection of its conventions. Social rules are made by normal people for normal people, and the man of genius is fundamentally abnormal. It is the poet against society, society against the poet, a direct antagonism. . . .

An extreme position, to be sure, involving for the artist who adheres to it a terrible loneliness, a denial of many sources of life and strength, for all its affirmation of his freedom to pursue and express his own individual perception and experience. The writers of the present century who inherit from the French Symbolists by way of the Aesthetic nineties have brought back into the subject matter of poetry large areas of political, social, and ethical experience that the extreme Symbolists had cast out. But at the same time they have preserved the ideal of a poetry which shall be as true to the poet's most subtle intuitions as he can possibly make it, rejecting completely the idea that the poet must coarsen his perceptions in order to make them more readily available to as large a group of readers as possible.

Much of the obscurity of poets like Mallarmé or Rimbaud derives from their attempt to use words as the symbolic equivalents of experiences which had quite simply never occurred to other men. Few contemporary poets have gone as far in their search for an expression of the well-nigh inexpressible as did Mallarmé, few have produced poetry as genuinely obscure, even to the patient reader, as his. "But, apart from obscurity," Symons asks, at the end of his essay on Mallarmé, "which we may all be fortunate enough to escape, is it possible for a writer, at the present day, to be quite simple, with the old, objective simplicity, in either thought or expression?" This question, and the answer it implies, suggests the most profitable attitude to adopt when we approach for the first time the subtle, complex, and genuinely original poems and stories of our time:

> To be naïf, to be archaic, is not to be either natural or simple; I affirm that [it] is not natural to be what is called "natural" any longer. We have no longer the mental attitude of those to whom a story was but a story, and all stories good. . . . And, naturally, we can no longer write what we can no longer accept. Symbolism, implicit in all literature from the beginning, as it is implicit in the very words we use, comes to us now, at last quite conscious of itself, offering us the only escape from our many imprisonments. We find a new, an older, sense in the so worn out forms of things; the world, which we can no longer believe in as the satisfying material object it was to our grandparents, becomes transfigured with a new light; words, which long usage had darkened almost out of recognition, take fresh lustre. And it is on the lines of that spiritualising of the word, that perfecting of form in its capacity for allusion and suggestion, that confidence in the eternal correspondences between the visible and the invisible universe, which Mallarmé taught, and too intermittently practised, that literature must now move, if it is in any sense to move forward.

FROM THE 1890S TO THE NEW CENTURY: THE CAREER OF WILLIAM BUTLER YEATS

Symons dedicated *The Symbolist Movement in Literature* to Yeats as "the chief representative of that movement in our country." At that time Yeats was in his early thirties and had published two or three volumes of lyric poetry, including *Crossways* (1889) and *The Wind Among the*

Reeds (1899), as well as a long narrative poem, *The Wanderings of Oisin* (1889); but the literary career which was to be the most remarkable that the twentieth century has thus far seen had no more than begun. In any account of twentieth-century literature Yeats's life and work demand a separate treatment not only because of the intrinsic worth of the poetry itself, which is second to none in our time, but also because Yeats provides a link between the nineties and the developments of the new century. As a young man he had been closely associated with the figures whom we think of as typical of the nineties, sharing their views on art and the relation of art to life and their dissatisfaction with much that had been produced by the Victorians. But, unlike the majority of the poets and painters of the Aesthetic Movement, Yeats lived beyond the nineties and continued to develop until his death in 1939. Thus we are able to see in his later work what the immediate heirs of the nineties were to make of their heritage.

In his *Autobiography,* Yeats describes the forces and interests that shaped his life and art. We may read there of his childhood at Sligo, in Ireland, and of his schooling and youth in London, from which he returned to Ireland for a part of every year. We learn of the influence exerted on him by his father, the painter John Yeats, who at one time came under the influence of the Pre-Raphaelites (writing of the late eighties, Yeats says, "I was in all things pre-Raphaelite") and to whom the Victorian poetry of ideas was distasteful. He marks out the early stages in the development of his interest in the occult, in theosophy, in Buddhism; the decline of his interest in science; and his growing distrust of the vested interests of scientific thought and naturalistic art. But, above all, we see the great curve of his development from a poet wholly in key with the Aesthetic Movement to a poet wholly in key with the significant developments of the new century. He began by accepting the doctrine by which Pater and his followers had attempted to purify literature of its concern with externalities. He went on, with no slightest sacrifice of the power of subtle evocation that the nineties had found in Symbolism, to bring back into poetry the directness of focus, the hard clarity of point, the reference to the world of actual human concern that the nineties had banished.

From the beginning, Yeats rejected the kind of poetry that the Victorians wrote. "I saw," he said, in describing the meetings of the Rhymers' Club in the late eighties and early nineties, ". . . that Swinburne in one way, Browning in another, and Tennyson in a third, had filled their work with what I called 'impurities,' curiosities about politics, about science, about history, about religion; and that we must create once more the pure work." There was no place in poetry for abstractions, for observation simply for observation's sake, for "mere reality." "I wanted the strongest passions, passions that had nothing to do with observation, and metrical forms that seemed old enough to have been sung by men half-asleep or riding upon a journey."

On these principles, he wrote the poems in his first three or four volumes, poems which he later described as "all picture, all association, all mythology." "The Falling of the Leaves," from his 1889 volume *Crossways* (see the selections from Yeats), may be taken as typical of many of these early poems. It has great beauty, which it offers up to the reader immediately. The frequent alliteration, the easy sway of the rhythm, give an almost palpable embodiment to a mood. And in evoking, as it does, an encompassing sense of autumnal languor and resignation not only by the obvious means of an appropriate meter and the immediate presentation of autumnal imagery but also by the more occult images involving water (related here, as often in Yeats's early poetry, to the other archetypal motifs of age, twilight, autumn, and the west), the poem comes close to making its effect in a totally Symbolist way, constituting itself as a "symbol," an evocative equivalent for an emotional complex in an almost Mallarméan way. Yeats's early verse is superior to all but the best of the verse written by the other poets of the nineties, and it may be that we fail to do it justice because it is overshadowed by the poems in the later manner that he began to find as early as the first decade of the new century. The point is, however, that the passion and the beauty of the early poems exist in a vacuum; they are summoned up for their own sake. In Yeats's later poems they exist side by side with intellect, and are evoked out of contact with the full world of active men.

There were many influences responsible for the particular line of development that Yeats's poetry took, away from a disembodied, wistful passion to the stern, hard beauty, the passionate responsibility, the unified sensibility of the later poems, where intellect and passion feed one another. First of all, any such development would have been impossible without Yeats's great power of self-awareness and self-criticism. He saw, for instance, that a certain early habit of remorse "helped to spoil" his early poetry, "giving it an element of sentimentality through my refusal to permit it any share of an intellect which I considered impure." A passage in the first section of his *Autobiography* describes his concern for qualities that are notable in his later style:

When I had finished The Wanderings of Oisin, *dissatisfied with its yellow and dull green, with all that overcharged color inherited from the romantic movement, I deliberately reshaped my style, deliberately sought out an impression as of cold light and tumbling clouds. I cast off traditional metaphors and loosened my rhythm, and recognising that all the criticism of life known to me was alien and English, became as emotional as possible but with an emotion which I described to myself as cold.*

We are reminded by the language of this passage of "The Fisherman" (see selections from Yeats), from *The Wild Swans at Coole* (1919), which tells us much—when we compare it with an early poem like "The Falling of the Leaves"—of the development Yeats's style had undergone.

Not only awareness of the limitations which the nineties had placed upon the writer and artist, but also certain contacts with the world of actuality were responsible for Yeats's growth. These contacts were chiefly of two sorts, political and theatrical. Yeats owed both of them to his love of Ireland, his concern (however incompletely he might have been willing, at any given time, to identify himself with one Irish party or another) that Ireland should find herself as a nation and as a people. His *Autobiography* is full of political portraits—the Fenian leader John O'Leary, John Taylor, James Connolly, Padraic Pearce, Douglas Hyde—figures whom we encounter again, many of them, in the poems. Yeats was fond of quoting a statement of O'Leary's which has the same ring of grand simplicity that we find in many a line of his own poetry: "There are things that a man must not do to save a nation." Describing the meetings of

a Young Ireland Society with O'Leary as president, Yeats said: "From these debates, from O'Leary's conversation, and from the Irish books he lent or gave me has come all I have set my hand to since." Yeats deplored the split between Catholic and Protestant Ireland and was aware of the inadequacies of both. "I thought we might bring the halves together if we had a national literature that made Ireland beautiful in the memory, and yet had been freed from provincialism by an exacting criticism, an European pose." There were various ways of contributing to this end. Most important, both for an Irish literature and for his own poetry, was his work in establishing an Irish theatre. With the help of Lady Augusta Gregory he started around 1900 the Irish National Theatre Company, later to become the Abbey Theatre. The point has often been made that the discipline of writing plays for this group, imposing as it did the necessity for considering the demands and abilities of the actors and for aiming at bold, general effects that would not be lost on an audience, toughened the sinews of his style, helping to take his poetry out of the half-light of the Aesthetic Movement into the full light of day.

But for all the clarity and simplicity of line that these interests had brought into his poetry, Yeats was still a Symbolist with the Symbolist's distaste for the mere transcription of appearance for appearance's sake, and with the Symbolist's belief in a world of essences that is hinted at in the world of forms we know. Beside his remark about the importance of O'Leary's talk to his later work should be placed a passage about the influence of Arthur Symons:

My thoughts gained in richness and in clearness from his sympathy, nor shall I ever know how much my practice and my theory owe to the passages that he read me from Catullus and from Verlaine and Mallarmé. I had read Axel *[an elaborate prose work in dramatic form by Villiers de l'Isle Adam, first published in Paris in 1890] to myself or was still reading it, so slowly, and with so much difficulty, that certain passages had an exaggerated importance, while all remained so obscure that I could without much effort imagine that here at last was the Sacred Book I longed for.*

Beginning early, Yeats gradually built up—bit by bit from Irish folklore, from the visions of

William Butler Yeats (1865–1939). Yeats's ability to reshape his style to the changing demands of his aesthetic philosophy made him a unique transitional figure between the Symbolist and Modern poets. *The Granger Collection.*

second-sighted servants, from the occult traditions of Europe and the East, from the philosophy of Plato and of the neo-Platonists—a private system of mystic, symbolic correspondences. Sooner or later in one's acquaintance with Yeats one must tackle *A Vision,* the work in which these doctrines are systematically presented. There one will encounter his description of the Great Wheel, with its fixed and recurrent arrangement of human types in harmony with the phases of the moon (the characteristics of an age are determined by the place that age occupies on the Wheel: all that has come and gone will come again). There and in other places he has described his belief in the "anima mundi," the soul of the world "which has a memory independent of embodied individual memories, though they constantly enrich it with their images and their thoughts." There one also encounters implications, political and religious, that are a

consequence of his belief in this closed system: a determinism that makes nonsense of individual striving, and a belief in the desirability of a hierarchical order based on wealth and power. But it is only fair to add that with Yeats such elements remained at the level of implication and never issued in any program or course of action that would have involved a suppression of the human spirit or of human liberty.

Yeats's private symbols would be a serious obstacle to reading his poetry if that poetry depended on them more centrally than is actually the case. At times, it is true, he is a Symbolist in the exact sense of the word. At such times, when he is using the full panoply of his esoteric symbols, his poems reserve a part of their meaning for those who, having mastered his various doctrines, are able to give each symbol its proper place in the system. But two points need to be emphasized. In the first place, a given poem will often make its full effect upon us even when we accept in only a general sense statements in it that bear a different and more literal interpretation if they are referred to appropriate passages in *A Vision*. The opening of "The Second Coming," for example, involves Yeats's very definite conception of characteristics of the time he describes, a consequence and a sign of the place occupied by that time on the Great Wheel (see *A Vision* [London, 1927], pp. 210 ff.). Yet everything he says there has seemed a sufficiently accurate and powerful description of the state of the world at the end of the First World War to give the poem great force and meaning even without reference to *A Vision*. In the second place, the majority of Yeats's symbols are by no means esoteric. In "Sailing to Byzantium," for example, he is dealing with the conflicting claims of two approaches to human life: the one described in the many symbolic images of the first stanza; the other in the great symbol of Byzantium itself. All will recognize the direction of meaning that is common to the images in which he symbolizes the impermanence of the life of the flesh, the transitoriness of "that sensual music"; and it takes very little more trouble to find out enough about Byzantine civilization of the fifth and sixth centuries, with its characteristically abstract, fleshless art and its fondness for artifice, to see why Yeats chose Byzantium as the symbol for the renunciation of the flesh in favor of the intellect. Once the direction and the import of these symbols have been grasped, it is impossible not to see how much of its essential quality the poem owes to their use.

Some of Yeats's political and religious doctrines may repel us or fill us with dismay. But even when they do, we can accept the poetry as the full, clear expression of a state of mind and soul that, though not ours, was indubitably the poet's. It is one of the chief glories of Yeats's mature poetry that he made it the vehicle for the most complete expression of *all*, in mind and soul, that was relevant to the state of consciousness seeking expression in a particular poem. In his best poetry we encounter a marvelous blending of the firm control of art with complete freedom to say what is in his mind and to describe what he sees in the moment's outward circumstance. The poets of the nineties had sifted the subject matter of their poetry to exclude all that was not in their view strictly poetic. Yeats resembled other poets of the new century in seeing that *all* experience could provide subject matter for poetry, that to limit and exclude was to court a thin artificiality of tone and purpose. In "Among School Children," for example, the soaring appeal of the last stanza gains some of its power from the foundations laid for it in the opening stanzas, with their flat, unemphatic, deliberate—but never "unpoetic"—notation of all that Yeats saw in the schoolroom, described in his own voice.

For always it is Yeats's own voice, never a voice that we feel has been assumed with pose and strain for the purpose of poetic utterance. He describes in the *Autobiography* how he was led to formulate a poetic principle central to all that is best and most characteristic in his verse, from as early as *The Green Helmet* (1910) onward:

We should write out our own thoughts in as nearly as possible the language we thought them in, as though in a letter to an intimate friend. We should not disguise them in any way; for our lives give them force as the lives of people in plays give force to their words. Personal utterance, which had almost ceased in English literature, could be as fine an escape from rhetoric and abstraction as drama itself. . . . I tried from that on to write out of my emotions exactly as they came to me in life, not changing them to make them more beautiful. "If I can be sincere and make my language natural, and without becoming discursive, like a novelist, and so indiscreet and prosaic," I said to myself, "I shall, if good luck or bad luck make my life interesting, be a great poet; for it will be no longer a matter of literature at all."

This principle of "personal utterance," the belief that the poet should write out of his life, not hesitating to bring his life's actuality into the poem, goes far to help us understand the quality that so compels and moves us in poems like "Easter, 1916," "Coole and Ballylee, 1931," or "At Algeciras." It is a principle of integrity and truth which makes it a small matter that (for example) we accept only poetically and temporarily the doctrine of reincarnation, referred to in "Sailing to Byzantium," which Yeats himself may have accepted literally.

THE FIRST WORLD WAR AND ITS AFTERMATH. WILFRED OWEN AND T. E. HULME. IMAGISM

In Yeats we see how a man of great gifts made his own use of the doctrines and techniques of Symbolism. Those doctrines and techniques have touched, to one degree or another, the work of most of the twentieth-century writers whom we think of as writing for their own time rather than as being content to echo the late Victorians. In this respect, as in others, Yeats's development parallels the general development of poetry in the new century; yet he was in many ways (with the exception of his Irish interests and his place in the Irish Renaissance) an isolated figure, without attachment to the programs and schools that seem, at least in retrospect, to have determined the direction taken by literature in the past few decades.

There has been no time in the present century when British poets and novelists have not produced valuable and significant work. This is true even of the first decade of the century, a period which sometimes strikes the literary historian as a time of stagnation, when the comparative certainty of life in the Edwardian era produced a thickening of literary line and a dullness of spirit. Such generalizations are always dangerous, but they are not wholly meaningless if we take them not as objective descriptions of what writers were actually producing during the period, but rather as expressions of the attitude of the younger writers' viewing the techniques and interests of their elders as inadequate for their new purposes. Not every generation is a generation in revolt, of course, but the generation that came of age around the time of the First World War was as sharply in revolt against accepted literary conventions as any generation has ever been.

The shock of the war itself; the sense of monstrous futility that its suffering and destruction aroused; and, in the years following the war, the sense of bitter disillusionment as it became more and more obvious that the millions who had died in the war had died to no purpose —the difficult assimilation of these experiences was the major fact in the life of the European spirit from 1914 onward. It was as if mankind had suddenly seen how deep a pit it was capable of digging for itself, and how little it could trust

A Battery Shelled by Wyndham Lewis, 1919. Lewis's painting of mechanical men and the dehumanizing brutality which killed them parallels the disallusionment with human society of poets like Wilfred Owen who experienced these horrors at first hand. *Imperial War Museum, London.*

itself to follow the modes of idealism, of humanistic purpose, and of human charity that earlier generations had taken for granted. Henry James, the great American novelist who, living for the most part in Europe, had for decades devoted a sensitive power of observation and understanding to analyzing the subtlest motives of European civilization, expressed the general dismay in a letter dated August 5, 1914:

The plunge of civilization into this abyss of blood and darkness by the wanton feat of those two infamous autocrats is a thing that so gives away the whole long age during which we have supposed the world to be, with whatever abatement, gradually bettering, that to have to take it all now for what the treacherous years were all the while really making for and meaning is too tragic for any words.

Nor, unhappily, did it long remain possible to attach sole blame for civilization's betrayal to the German and Austrian emperors.

The brutality of the war years themselves and the hitherto unparalleled suffering of the men who fought and died in the trenches was nowhere expressed with greater poignancy, dignity, or clear, hard force than in the poems of Wilfred Owen. Owen, still in his twenties, was killed on November 4, 1918, at the Sambre Canal. A volume of his poems was first published in 1920 with an introduction by another distinguished war poet, Siegfried Sassoon. His complete poems, edited and with a memoir by Edmund Blunden, were published in 1931 and have been reprinted several times since, for Owen's verse has retained a strong hold on the imagination of succeeding generations, of poets as well as of readers of poetry. In some of his poems Owen used a new riming technique, off-rime or para-rime (some prefer the term *dissonance*), where the riming words are similar in their consonants but dissimilar in their vowels (see, for example, in "Strange Meeting," such rimes as *mystery-mastery, spoiled-spilled*), or in which rime is close but not exact. This device, which was particularly suitable for the wry pathos or bitterness of Owen's poems, also had the more general usefulness of allowing poets to retain the advantages of rime without the cramping disadvantages of the traditional English rime schemes. W. H. Auden and other poets of the generation

that began to publish around 1930 were to make considerable use of para-rime. But even more important than Owen's technique in winning the admiration and discipleship of the poets who came after him was the spirit of his poetry, the complete clarity and steadiness with which he fixed his regard on human suffering and human injustice. The few sentences with which he had thought to preface the volume of poems he was preparing at the time of his death have become famous. His book, he had warned, would not glorify conquest or salve the conscience of the English people by paying empty tribute to heroism. As to the heroes, "English poetry," he said, "is not yet fit to speak of them."

Above all I am not concerned with Poetry.
My subject is War and the pity of War.
The Poetry is in the pity.

Owen's conviction that the poet's success is to be judged by his faithfulness to his subject, by the truthfulness he attains, finds at least a partial parallel in some of the critical positions of T. E. Hulme, also killed in the war, notably in Hulme's belief that the time was ripe for a kind of poetry that would be "classical" rather than "romantic," according to his definition of those vexed terms. Owen and Hulme were both protesting against what they saw as a grave weakness in much of the poetry of their time: the poet's willingness, inherited from the Romantic Movement, to abandon himself to an excess of feeling without sufficient regard for the object or situation that occasioned it. This habit led to vagueness of the feeling itself and to a blunting of the instruments of expression. When Owen said that he was "not concerned with Poetry," he meant that he was too gravely concerned with suffering—of which he wanted to make the English people bitterly aware—ever to be content with mere self-satisfied phrase-making about it. The truths he had seen were not to be the subject matter of poems that would receive their value from the poet's treatment; rather, the poems were instruments for making the truth known. If it were faithfully rendered, the truth would give the poems their reason for being and their strength.

But such critical ideas were in the air, both during and after the war. An ideal of precision, of a controlling objectivity, of the greatest possible fidelity to the emotion or the appearance with which the poet was working: such an ideal figures in many of the critical programs of the time and has determined the direction taken by much of the most interesting poetry of the last few decades. In his autobiographical volume *The Innocent Eye,* Herbert Read says that around the time of the war "there was a general feeling that some new philosophy was necessary, much as it had been necessary when Wordsworth and Coleridge had published their *Lyrical Ballads* in 1798." He cites as the clearest summation of this feeling the six "common principles" stated in the preface to a collection of Imagist poetry (including poems by Richard Aldington, H. D., and D. H. Lawrence) published in 1915. Everything in these principles emphasizes the necessity for the poet of saying exactly what he himself sees or feels or thinks exactly as he himself sees or feels or thinks it, the necessity of finding his own rhythms, his own images, of being free from cramping conventions of experience or expression. Another statement of principles from the same period, recently reprinted (see "A Retrospect," in *Literary Essays of Ezra Pound,* 1954 and later reissues), insists on "direct treatment of the 'thing' whether subjective or objective."

Some of the work produced by poets who were too exclusively "imagist" (contenting themselves with fixing single images in two or three lines of verse) was so slight as to have retained no more than an antiquarian interest, just as much *vers libre,* or free verse, written with no more serious purpose than to celebrate a sense of escape from convention, is now wholly uninteresting and unreadable. But the principle of sharpness of image and the principle of correspondence of a poet's rhythms to his subject were of the greatest importance and usefulness in the hands of poets who had something to say and who were capable of adapting these principles to produce their own characteristic techniques.

BETWEEN THE TWO WARS: EZRA POUND AND T. S. ELIOT; D. H. LAWRENCE

We sometimes talk of literary schools and programs and tendencies as if they had an existence of their own, as if they had produced the works that we cite in discussing them. In truth, of course, the most cogent declarations of literary principle would be no sooner framed than forgotten if it were not for the poems or plays or novels that make the program worth talking about in the first place. The critical ideas that we have just glanced at began to be current around 1915 and are still interesting to us, and still operative, because of the writers who entertained them and who demonstrated them in works of great intrinsic value. To those who followed the little magazines that provided a vehicle for young writers of the new school— *The Egoist, The Little Review,* Harriet Monroe's *Poetry*—it may have been difficult to know which of the new movement's many adherents were its leaders. But in retrospect it is clear that—with the exception of D. H. Lawrence, who was a law unto himself—the chief figures, and certainly the most influential figures, were two Americans living in England, Ezra Pound and T. S. Eliot.

Ezra Pound, born in Idaho in 1885 and educated at the University of Pennsylvania and Hamilton College, first went to Europe in 1906, and lived abroad, except for brief visits to the United States, until 1945, at first in England and then chiefly in Italy. But, unlike T. S. Eliot, he retained his American citizenship, and for that reason he is not represented in the following pages.[2] His major work, on which a large part of his reputation may ultimately have to rest, is the *Cantos,* which appeared in various forms and various groupings, beginning in 1916, and finally numbered over a hundred. At the close of World War II, Pound was the subject of embittered and unhappy controversy in literary circles. In July 1943 he was indicted for treason by the United States government as a consequence of his alleged wartime broadcasts over Radio Roma. He was brought back to this country in 1945 but was never tried, and in 1960 he returned to Italy. An extensive literature has grown up concerning the controversial aspects of Pound's career before, during, and immediately following World War II. Besides *A Casebook for Ezra Pound* (ed. William Van O'Connor and Edward Stone, 1959), the reader seeking insight on these matters may well turn to the extremely interesting book *Discretions,* by Pound's daughter, Mary de

---

[2] Pound's version of the Anglo-Saxon poem, *The Seafarer,* is, however, included in Volume I.

Rachewiltz, published a few months before his death. Through all the controversy, one element remained constant: the loyal testimony of many prominent writers—among them T. S. Eliot, Edith Sitwell, Wyndham Lewis, and Ernest Hemingway—to their admiration of his work or to their recognition of his influence on theirs. Few names are more important in the literary history of the first half of the twentieth century.

In his early essays Pound constantly urged his readers to improve the *quality* of their attention to literature and to read valuable work that he thought was neglected or misunderstood: Provençal poetry, certain Scots and Elizabethan translations of the classics, French poetry of the nineteenth century and after. Some of these interests figured no less prominently in his poetry. Except for *A Lume Spento,* published in a limited edition in Venice, his first volume of poems, *Personae,* was published in London in 1909. These poems and those which followed were the focal point for many interests and influences.

Many of them are dramatic, in the manner of Browning's dramatic monologues (Browning was the one Victorian poet whom Pound and his associates were able to admire or follow), and often Pound chose a Provençal or Italian poet, or a figure encountered in his reading of Provençal or Italian poetry, to be the *persona* or "mask" through which he spoke. Or at other times, in the course of a poem in which he gave direct voice to his own feelings or thoughts, he would quote a phrase or a line or a brief passage from an earlier writer as a commentary, by contrast or by similarity, on the situation he was describing. The fifteenth-century French poet François Villon, for example, begins one of his poems with these lines—

En l'an trentiesme de mon aage
Que toutes mes hontes j'ay beues . . .

(*In the thirtieth year of my age*
When I have drunk down all my shame . . .),

Ford Madox Ford, James Joyce, Ezra Pound, and John Quinn in Paris, 1923. Pound's efforts to bring the influences of continental literatures to bear on modern English poetry bore fruit in the complex imagery and mythical dimensions of Eliot's *The Waste Land. The Granger Collection.*

—lines which Eliot was to use as the epigraph to "A Cooking Egg." The first section of a poem published in 1920, "E. P. Ode pour l'Élection de son Sépulcre," in which Pound is describing with ironic detachment the divergence between his poetic ideals and those of the time in which he writes, contains the following lines:

Unaffected by "the march of events,"
He passed from men's memory in l'an trentiesme
De son aage. . . .

Here the use of Villon's phrase has the effect of adding to Pound's sardonic account of his own situation a swift comparison with the situation of an earlier poet with whom Pound feels a genial kinship. It could not have been done so deftly, or perhaps so effectively, in any other way, nor is it too much to expect that a reader will recognize a phrase from one of Villon's better-known poems. Pound's poem contains a number of other examples of the same technique, not all so easy to recognize as this, and in fact throughout his poetry Pound makes the fullest use of his reading in several languages, drawing on it for subject matter, for characters, for points of view, and for citations of the sort illustrated. Admittedly such a habit raises a barrier between Pound and the general reader, but—in the early poems at any rate—the barrier is by no means insurmountable, and the poems themselves, in point of beauty and wit, are worth the trouble.

At the time of Pound's death in 1972, many obituary statements tried to sum up his varied and influential career as poet and critic and entrepreneur, to draw a balance between what had been valuable in it and what had been less so, but there is one point that should have been made more emphatically and more often than it was. In the early, crucial years of his career, Pound was motivated in everything that he did by a personally achieved vision of the great literary tradition of the Western world and, on the other hand, by a sense of the deplorable extent to which English writing, around the turn of the century, had lost sight of the standards set by that tradition. Looking back on the earlier time in an essay written in 1934, Pound said, "The common verse of Britain from 1890 to 1910 was a horrible agglomerate compost, not minted, most of it not even baked, all legato, a doughy mess of third-hand Keats, Wordsworth, heaven knows what, fourth-hand Elizabethan sonority blunted, half-melted, lumpy." It was Pound's own knowledge of what literature had been at many of the great times, from Homer onwards, that animated him to want a different, *better* poetry than he found being written in English around 1900 or 1910. He worked to improve the state of poetry, in accord with his own knowledge and vision, in everything he did: in his essays on Guido Cavalcanti and Arnaut Daniel, on Henry James or Jules Laforgue; in his own poems; and in the immediate help he could give to young writers like Eliot and Joyce who were only with difficulty able to get their own first works into print. All these activities harmonize, and all of them—as well as the technique of inserting quotations from foreign writers into his own poems—have the one aim of curing English writing of provincialism and staleness, and of bringing it once more into vital contact with what was best in Western literature wherever it could be found.

Pound would be an important figure in the literary history of the early twentieth century if for no other reason than that of his services to letters at a time when young writers were seeking both new forms and some kind of outlet for their work. T. S. Eliot has recorded his own indebtedness to Pound in an essay dated 1946 (see *An Examination of Ezra Pound*, ed. Peter Russell, New Directions, 1950), in which, besides describing Pound's general personal influence on him and his contemporaries in the London literary scene between 1915 and 1922, he mentions that it was through Pound's efforts that his first volume of verse, *Prufrock and Other Observations*, was published by the Egoist Press in 1917. He has also told how in Paris, in 1922, he gave Pound "the manuscript of a sprawling chaotic poem called *The Waste Land* which left his hands, reduced to about half its size, in the form in which it appears in print." That poem is dedicated to Pound with a phrase (*il miglior fabbro*, "the better workman") in which Dante pays tribute to the Provençal poet, Arnaut Daniel.

The modesty of the small, buff-paper-covered pamphlet in which *Prufrock and Other Observations* originally appeared gave scant indication of its importance as a literary event. Here, as in Pound's poetry, influences crossed and blended, but the result was something new to English poetry. "The Love Song of J. Alfred Prufrock" is, among other things, a dramatic monologue, just as "My Last Duchess" is a dramatic monologue. But the character revealed is unlike any character Browning would have been interested in, just as the tone and technique of the revelation are unlike the tones or techniques of nineteenth-century English verse (after all, Arthur Hugh Clough was something of an anomaly). Prufrock's diffidence, his heart-gnawing awareness of his own insufficiency, his sardonic self-scrutiny are poles apart from the major tonalities of, say, Tennyson's Ulysses or Browning's Ferrarese Duke. We are more likely to encounter people like Prufrock in the poems of Jules Laforgue, where we also encounter the disabused clarity of view, the intent to undercut the old romantic effects by some sharp incongruity in the way in which they are presented, that we find in "Prufrock." Prufrock's description of the evening sky, in the opening lines of the poem, is arresting because it compares the sky to something with which we would have thought it had no single quality in common. But we immediately perceive that to a certain gaze, to a certain mood, there is a resemblance between the evening sky and "a patient etherized upon a table"; the effect of the image is above all to communicate that mood, Prufrock's mood, to us.

There are similar sunsets in Laforgue; indeed, in Eliot's early poems the tone of many passages reminds one of Laforgue, and occasionally one encounters single lines that are virtually translations from the French poet. More important than this, the structure and the movement of the verse in poems like "Prufrock" or "Portrait of a Lady" reproduce the structure of poems in Laforgue's *Derniers Vers,* just as the brisk, polysyllabic quatrains of poems like "Sweeney Among the Nightingales" owe much to Laforgue's poems in the same form (see, for example, the "Complainte de l'Organiste de Notre Dame de Nice"). But all this does not mean that Eliot was producing pastiche. If we recognize in his early verse many echoes of notes first struck by Laforgue, there are others which are traceable to his interest in other poetry, particularly Elizabethan dramatic verse, but the final result is entirely his own. His indebtedness to the French Symbolists, to Laforgue's particular use of *vers libre,* is to be understood in exactly the same light as the indebtedness of the Elizabethan sonneteers to the forms and conventions of their Italian masters. In this as in other respects Eliot and Pound must be credited with having brought English poetry once more into life-giving contact with Continental forms and movements from which it had been cut off by the insularity—in matters of literary influence, at least—of the Victorians.

Such difficulties as the reader may experience at his first acquaintance with Eliot's poetry may be overcome if he will keep in mind certain features of that poetry. First of all, one who comes to Eliot straight from the poets of the late nineteenth century may need a period of adjustment before he can see that the "Preludes," for instance, are poetry at all. But with familiarity the strong, desperate rhythms of those poems will begin to make their effect, and the uncompromisingly realistic details will take on for him their wider character of symbols of the life of modern cities. He will see that out of such things as the smells of meals being cooked and the descent of dusk over a wintry city street Eliot has created a poetic experience far more poignant and far more *responsible* as an account of the forms of life we see all about us than any evocation of conventional, neo-Victorian beauties could be. The sense of strangeness, the sense of straining to catch the music in the voice, will soon give way to the recognition of a highly controlled, highly individual poetic tone—Eliot is a master of his craft—and, what is more, the reader will gradually discover in himself a grateful awareness that he is reading poetry written for his own day, out of its moods, its sights and sounds, its life.

At first the new reader may be disturbed by the structural principle of a poem like "Prufrock." In it and in his other poems Eliot presents a character or a situation by establishing certain points in an experience, but he does not necessarily make the connections between those points: the reader is left to do that for himself. The various episodes in an Eliot poem, as C. Day Lewis has pointed out, are arranged according to a principle of emotional sequence, rather than of intellectual sequence, one image or one episode taking on its full meaning when it is confronted, for comparison or contrast, with the one that precedes or follows: it is a highly flexible and expressive technique, resembling that of the film-cutter. Or a phrase or a sentence may be given a thematic value, to which it refers whenever it recurs, in the manner of a Wagnerian leitmotiv.

At first, too, the reader may want to know things about a character or a situation in an Eliot poem which Eliot has no interest in telling him. In reading "Sweeney among the Nightingales," for instance, it is possible to establish the locale and the cast of characters with some precision, but it is *not* possible to say quite definitely what happens to Sweeney. We see him as a victim of sordid machinations that are not specified beyond a certain point: F. O. Matthiessen says that Eliot "once remarked that all he consciously set out to create in 'Sweeney Among the Nightingales' was a sense of foreboding."

"Sweeney Among the Nightingales" illustrates one more feature of Eliot's technique that may occasion some difficulty to the unwary: the technique of allusion that we have already noted in talking about Pound. The Greek epigraph—Agamemnon's cry when, in Aeschylus' tragedy, he is murdered by his wife, Clytemnestra ("Alas, I have been struck a most deadly blow!")—is an integral part of the poem. Through its use Eliot reminds us of another instance of victimization by treachery, and we are meant to see Agamemnon's fate as both different from and similar to Sweeney's: different in that it was the doom of a hero and a king, struck down by his faithless queen, different in the aura and significance of great tragedy carried with it as opposed to the meanness of Sweeney's falling victim to a tavern intrigue; similar in that baseness and treachery, of one kind or another, are present in both episodes. The commentary on the poem's present action, which was begun by the epigraph, is concluded and rounded off by the reference to Agamemnon in the concluding lines of the poem. It is neither possible nor necessary to sum up in a phrase or two the total effect that is produced by this juxtaposition of Agamemnon's murder and Sweeney's meaner fate, but it will be seen that the interplay between the two sets of events and values is central to the poem's meaning and purpose. In *The Waste Land* the system of allusions is much more complex than in "Sweeney Among the Nightingales," but each particular allusion in that poem, as indeed in Eliot's poetry generally, will be found to depend on the technique we have noticed here.

The Waste Land is possibly the most celebrated poem of the twentieth century; it is certainly the most discussed. First published in 1922, it expressed the disillusionment, the sense of spiritual instability and inadequacy that the war had left behind it with devastating completeness, accuracy, and power. The essence of the various techniques that were employed in writing it is *concentration,* so that any commentary which aims at unfolding all it contains will be many times as long as the poem itself. It describes, in terms of symbolic characters and incidents, the spiritual aridity of our time. In his notes to the poem Eliot has pointed out that "not only the title, but the plan and a good deal of the incidental symbolism . . . were suggested by Miss Jessie L. Weston's book on the Grail Legend: *From Ritual to Romance. . . ."* In that book we find summarized the anthropological accounts of the myth by which, in various forms, primitive man accounted for the changing cycle of the year, particularly the return of the spring. The Waste Land is dry and sterile because the Fisher King, its ruler, is impotent; the life-giving waters will flow again when a Deliverer arrives who, after surviving a dangerous combat (in the Chapel Perilous of the medieval derivatives of the legend), will by sexual intercourse with the Woman restore the land to fertility. In Eliot's poem the Waste Land, its physical aridity powerfully suggested, becomes the symbol for the spiritually arid modern world of false values and misguided aims. All three characters of the legend appear many times, in many different guises: the Fisher King in lines 60–76, 173–214, 422–33, among other places; the Deliverer in the guise of the various men whose energies are devoted to pointless sexual or commercial activities; the Woman in the guise of all the women whose selfish, neurotic, or bewildered concerns and desires represent only a dead end. It is a world of fear, a world of dryness and emptiness, that Eliot describes; and by means of allusions to other literary works, he is able to set his world against an extraordinarily complex background of pertinent reminders of other worlds and ideals, sometimes for contrast, at other times for comparison. The way out is clear—it is made clear in "What the Thunder Said," as well as by implication throughout the poem—but that way is not taken and, as the poem ends, the Fisher King sits upon the shore,

> Fishing, with the arid plain behind me,

wondering what he can cling to in the general wreckage and failure.

Even in the early stages of one's acquaintance with *The Waste Land,* one is aware that new meanings are being expressed in new ways, that one has not read anything quite like it before. The opening lines, with their presentation of spring as cruelly disturbing, of winter as desirably negative and vegetative (these things viewed, of course, through the eyes of a generation whose emptiness causes it to see life as fear and death as a release from fear), make their compelling and characteristic impression long before we have begun to fit them into the total plan of the poem. It may be that much will escape us even after we have spent considerable time in studying the poem, in tracing out its allusions, and in analyzing the exact position, as part of the poem's total statement, to which the basic questions are carried in each of the poem's five sections. But any labor thus spent will reward us by increasing our admiration for the poem's beauty and force, for its great distinction of thought and style, and for the wealth of its tightly packed, detailed implications.

It seems evident, even in *The Waste Land* and *The Hollow Men* (1925), that Eliot's view of the plight of the Western world in the twentieth century carries with it by implication the idea that the way of salvation lies through a return to religious faith. By the time Eliot published *Ash-Wednesday* in 1930, he had himself joined the communion of the Church of England; and some of his later works dealt with explicitly religious themes, for example *The Rock* (1934), a pageant, and *Murder in the Cathedral* (1935). The latter is a verse play centering in the meaning, for the relations between Church and State, of the murder of Thomas à Becket in 1170. His best-known play, *The Cocktail Party,* which had long commercial runs in London and New York, is in its own way concerned once more with the problem which figures directly or indirectly in nearly all his work: the problem of helping our civilization to find a way out of the abyss. Nor was his later writing limited to the verse drama; *Four Quartets,* a long reflective poem with lyric episodes, whose four parts were first published collectively in 1943, reveals that his verse underwent a marked development since some of his earlier poems in the direction of an increased resonance and suppleness.

Eliot has been no less important a force in criticism than in poetry, and many of the particular directions taken by the instructed literary taste of our time have been owing to his lead, either as the author of numerous critical essays or as editor of the *Criterion* or as one of the directors of a firm of London publishers. The first impetus to a revival of active interest in the metaphysical poets of the seventeenth century was probably given by Professor H. J. C. Grierson of the University of Edinburgh shortly before the First World War, but Eliot's essays were greatly instrumental in furthering that interest. His criticism is essentially the criticism of an unusually acute reader—and a sensitive poet —who keeps his attention focused on the work before him, seeing it for what it is rather than for what it may always have been said to be, but always aware of its position in relation to other works, from several literatures, of the same order. A number of reasons may be cited for the high prestige that Eliot (who, at the beginning of his literary career looked, at least, like a poet of distinctly nonconformist tendency) had attained by the 1940s—in 1948 he was awarded the Nobel Prize and made a member of the Order of Merit—but one need seek no further justification than the poetic power and skill, the sharpness of mind, and the clear distinction of spirit that are visible in his work at all stages of its development.

If Eliot felt that the solution to the problems of the age lay in a return to established religion, D. H. Lawrence found his answer (or at least looked for it) in quite other places. He felt that the insufficiencies and grave errors of modern life were the consequence of too much civilization, of too great a preoccupation with the false values of an industrialized urban society, and of living too exclusively according to the dictates of the prudent, conscious mind. The way out lay in a return to the life of the instincts, to a recognition of the power and demands of the blood. Writing from Italy in 1913, Lawrence said, in a passage which finds echoes throughout his work:

My great religion is a belief in the blood, the flesh, as being wiser than the intellect. We can go wrong in our minds. But what our blood feels and believes and says, is always true. The intellect is only a bit and a bridle. What do I care about knowledge. All I want is to answer to my blood, direct, without fribbling intervention of mind, or moral, or what-not. I conceive a man's body as a kind of flame, like a candle flame, forever upright and yet flowing: and the intellect is just the light that is shed on to the things around—which is really mind—but with the mystery of the flame forever flowing, coming God knows how from out of practically nowhere, and being itself, whatever there is around it, that it lights up. We have got so ridiculously mindful, that we never know that we ourselves are anything—we think there are only the objects we shine upon. And there the poor flame goes on burning ignored, to produce this light. And instead of chasing the mystery in the fugitive, half-lighted things outside us, we ought to look at ourselves and say "My God, I am myself!" That is why I like to live in Italy. The people are so unconscious. They only feel and want: they don't know. We know too much. No, we only think we know such a lot. A flame isn't a flame because it lights up two, or twenty objects on a table. It's a flame because it is itself. And we have forgotten ourselves.

Lawrence's system of beliefs might seem, on the basis of such positions as are touched on in this passage, to be only a thoroughgoing and shallow antiintellectualism. But it is the positive side of the statement, the belief in the blood, that gave Lawrence's ideas their depth and weight, that cut the channels in which his art was to flow. His belief that the dark gods of the blood may not be denied, that they will have their revenge if we attempt to deny them, reminds us inevitably of the teachings of the Viennese psychiatrist, Sigmund Freud ("I never did read Freud," Lawrence wrote in 1913, "but I have heard about him since I was in Germany"), and may at the same time remind us of the degree to which twentieth-century literature has been colored and shaped by the development of the techniques of psychoanalysis and indeed by the diffusion of psychological knowledge generally. One of the master ideas of our time, an idea that has determined not only the content, the meaning, but also the very form of many important works in twentieth-century literature, has been the discovery that more is contained in a human mind than can be accounted for by exploring it at the level of consciously formulated thought. Lawrence believed that man should recognize and obey the dictates of the unconscious; other writers, without necessarily taking the same stand on this point, have believed that a character can be completely presented only by recording the content of his mind on all its levels, including the subconscious, and this belief has produced some striking technical developments, particularly in fiction and drama.

Alike because of health and inclination, Lawrence lived out of England for the greater part of his life, after his first visit to Germany and Italy in 1912. When he was in England he was often at odds with the authorities—some of his books were seized and banned, exhibitions of his paintings were closed—and he seemed to find something more nearly approaching contentment among other people than the English. "After us the Savage God," Yeats had said; Lawrence, for his part, sought out the savage god, the elements and forms of primitive belief, among the Indians of Mexico and New Mexico, among the natives in the Australian bush, and in the records of Etruscan civilization that he found in Italy. But he also wrote about England, the life he had known as a child and as a young man in the Nottinghamshire mining country, or as a teacher on the outskirts of London.

Lawrence is best known today as a novelist, the most serious recent criticism, beginning with F. R. Leavis's *D. H. Lawrence: Novelist* (1955), having established his novels as his central achievement. But fiction did not suffice as an outlet for all that he was eager to declare or to record or to describe. He wrote essays and pamphlets, more vehemently and impatiently as his life neared its end; he wrote absorbing travel books (see especially the brilliant account of a trip to Sardinia from Sicily, *Sea and Sardinia*); he wrote a few plays; and he was a painter from time to time. He was also a poet, possibly one of the three or four foremost poets of his generation, even though some of his early "rhyming poems" are flawed because of his impatience with the demands of traditional poetic form. In poems like "Snake," from *Birds, Beasts, and Flowers,* he is one of the few poets who made of free verse what its adherents claimed it could be: a vehicle that would make possible a truly effective fidelity in the transcription of an individual vision, a personal response to experience. "The essence of poetry with us," he wrote in a letter dated 1916, "in this age of stark and unlovely actualities is a stark directness, without a shadow of a lie, or a shadow of deflection anywhere. Everything can go, but this stark, bare rocky directness of statement, this along makes poetry, today." Others thought so, too, and such a statement places Lawrence against a background that includes Imagism and the critical ideas of Hulme, Herbert Read, and Ezra Pound.

The effort of recent critical attention to Lawrence has been to get away from the impassioned chatter about his personal life that filled the books written about him, soon after his death, by those whose lives had been involved with his. It is now attempting to work out a dependable reading of his fiction: to establish what he is saying in the sequence of his greatest novels, including *Sons and Lovers, The Rainbow,* and *Women in Love.* Lawrence's thought is not easy to grasp, and the various critics are by no means of one mind as to the ultimate meaning of each of his novels. For one thing, he is not merely a reporter of things seen, he is also a prophet, as E. M. Forster made plain as early as 1927 in *Aspects of the Novel;* and he is possibly also a mystic. But there is one certainty: Lawrence's vivid, subtle sensitivity to experience was matched by a power of evoking experience that makes his created world, whether in fiction or poetry or essay, still live with the life that pressed upon him in the real world. In real life he had a way of making any experience more stirring for the person who shared it with him. The testimony to this quality given by Dr. J. D. Chambers, who describes the young Lawrence as "certainly the most exciting person I had ever met," is typical. "I adored him for what he was," Dr. Chambers said. "High spirited, infectiously gay, galvanising every company, whether at work or at play, into new and more intense activity, making them bigger, better, cleverer than they were by nature, and imparting to them some of his own inexhaustible zest for life." Something of the sort happens to us now who see the things he saw through his writing, and by means that are so apparently simple as to defy analysis. Perhaps it was a gift of seeing into the very being of any life-phenomenon that caught his eye, seeing with an intensity of sympathy that enabled him to give back its essential quality in one or two telling details. This ability in Lawrence amounts to genius, and it is fully operative even in such a tiny image as this one that occurs in the description of preparations for Christmas at the Marsh, in *The Rainbow:* "In the cow-shed the boys were blacking their faces for a dress-rehearsal; the turkey hung dead, with opened, speckled wings, in the dairy. The time was come to make pies, in readiness." In the central image of this brief paragraph, the image of the turkey, we see something at work that is more important than any adherence to an Imagist program: we see the power to grasp experience with sympathetic inwardness and to render it with complete clarity. This power marks virtually every page that Lawrence wrote.

BETWEEN THE TWO WARS: FICTION

Any claims that one makes for the Modern period can be as fully vindicated when one scrutinizes its achievement in fiction as in poetry. Here, too, the inheritance from Symbolism is visible and effective, not merely in that many of the principal modern novelists use symbolism of one kind or another in their work but also in the more pervasive sense that the twentieth-century novelist is determined to give his work the form and the content called for by his artistic conscience rather than by the customary demands of a wide reading public. Modern fiction begins under the aegis of two lofty examples: the careers of Henry James and Joseph Conrad, one an American and the other a Pole but both eventually naturalized in England. Both devoted their lifetimes to the writing of fiction as subtle and as powerful as any that has been written anywhere, revealing the full extent to which the novel could be responsive to the highest demands that it is possible to make of art.

James and Conrad wrote a good deal about

the novel in both practical and theoretical terms, and what they wrote constitutes a body of aesthetic principles for fiction. No one has ever written more eloquently than James did in his essay on "The Art of Fiction" (1885) in defense of the idea that the novel should be seen not as mere idle entertainment but as an art form capable of dealing seriously with the whole range of man's most serious concerns, in a form worthy of the writer's best artistic skill and of the reader's fullest aesthetic sensitivity. To look at the novel as anything less than this, James said, is "to bring it down from its high, free character of an immense and exquisite correspondence with life." Such a belief in the novel's potentiality is implicit in all that James and Conrad wrote, and also—without its being at all a matter of direct influence—in the work of such writers of the next generation as Joyce, Lawrence, and Virginia Woolf.

The representation of novelists in such a book as this is only possible, of course, when a given novelist has written short stories that measure up to his work in the novel. "The Secret Sharer" is not a substitute for *Under Western Eyes* or *Nostromo*, but within its scope it is Conrad at his best. Joyce's "The Dead," besides being the most elaborate of the stories in *Dubliners,* may be seen as in quite important ways an introduction to *A Portrait of the Artist as a Young Man* and *Ulysses.* Virginia Woolf, however, whose short fictional sketches (contained in *Monday or Tuesday* and *A Haunted House*) do not measure up to her novels, is represented here by an essay, "Mr. Bennett and Mrs. Brown," which, despite a certain one-sidedness of emphasis, has been a key document in the history of modern fiction. She is also represented by a group of excerpts from her diary, allowing us an unusually clear idea of the intense and courageous devotion to her art which produced *Mrs. Dalloway* and *To the Lighthouse.*

The conviction common to the twentieth-century poets whom we have discussed (in most respects so different from one another) that the problems as well as the insights and knowledge of their time demanded new emphases, new techniques of expression, was shared by a number of writers of fiction among their contemporaries. In the years immediately following the First World War, the belief gained force that

novelists like John Galsworthy, H. G. Wells, and Arnold Bennett were too preoccupied with the external forces and appearances of the life that they described ever to capture and convey a sense of that life's true inwardness. It may be that when Mrs. Woolf wrote "Mr. Bennett and Mrs. Brown," she was so eager to state the claims of the psychological novelist that she did not do complete justice to the achievement of Galsworthy, Wells, and Bennett. There are now signs that the balance of judgment has swung so that they begin to be viewed more sympathetically than Mrs. Woolf viewed them. Meanwhile, however, the most interesting developments in twentieth-century fiction did indeed take the directions described and defended in that essay.

The Georgian novelist, as Mrs. Woolf described him, was seeking a precedent to support his belief that what went on in people's minds was more important than the physical and social circumstances in which they lived, but it is hard to believe that precedents were quite so far to seek as she seems to suggest. No novelist, before or since, has been more completely dedicated to tracing the life of the spirit than was Henry James, whose later novels—particularly *The Wings of the Dove* (1902), *The Ambassadors* (1903), and *The Golden Bowl* (1904)— might well seem to form the very portals of initiation for much that was to be most distinctive in twentieth-century fiction. Moreover, there was the example of the psychological cast given to fiction by Joseph Conrad. There was also the fictional practice of E. M. Forster, a friend and associate of Mrs. Woolf and himself a member of the loosely defined "Bloomsbury group" of which she seems, at least in retrospect, to have been the most prominent member. Forster's first novel, *Where Angels Fear to Tread,* was published in 1905. In that novel, as well as in his later ones, many of his approaches to technique were traditional, even old-fashioned; but they do put the emphasis on a careful attention to psychological values, for the exploration of which Forster developed his own individual and lively methods of handling symbol.

It is true, however, that Mrs. Woolf herself, particularly in *Mrs. Dalloway* (1925), *To the Lighthouse* (1927), and *The Waves* (1931), was more resolute and thorough than most other novelists in her insistence on taking up her stand in the minds of her characters. At her best she presents her characters through the mental and emotional reactions to crucial or typical sequences in their lives, with an unsurpassed clarity and elegance. Beginning with *Mrs. Dalloway*, it is as if the life of her novels were bathed in an entirely new medium of light and air. Her nervous prose, delicate yet tough and supple, gives to the threads of incident and plot—which, crossing and recrossing, weave a day or a few months or several years in the lives of her characters—a lyric beauty that nothing else in fiction could quite prepare us for. At the time of her tragic early death in 1941 she enjoyed a higher prestige, both as novelist and as critical essayist, than any other woman in British letters. Recently there has been increased interest in the women's-rights side of her writing: in the books *A Room of One's Own* and *Three Guineas,* she explored, long before the Women's Liberation Movement had been heard of, the injustices and disadvantages that women faced in modern society simply because they were women. But that is only one side of her writing; her reputation today, after a certain amount of fluctuation, seems to rest more solidly than ever on the originality, the artistry, and the integrity of vision that are clearly manifest in her best novels.

Nevertheless, hers is not the prime example to which we turn if we wish to estimate the full range or experiment that the modern psychological novel is capable of: for that we go to James Joyce. Joyce's early work—the volume of short stories called *Dubliners* (finally published, after many hazards, in 1914) and his first novel, *A Portrait of the Artist as a Young Man* (1916)—employs for the most part perfectly dependable techniques that Joyce might have found ready to his hand in French or Russian fiction (or in his acknowledged master, Ibsen). (It should be added that these techniques are employed with the utmost skill, sensitivity, and power, so that *Dubliners* may fairly claim to be one of the most perfect volumes of short stories in English.) But with *Ulysses* it is a different story.

Each of the stories in *Dubliners* presents an episode in the life of some one citizen of Dublin, usually an incident which reveals that character and the meaning of his life not only to us but also to himself; Joyce thought of the

The Joyce Memorial by Milton Hebald, Zürich. Hebald's sculpture was unveiled on June 16, 1966, the 62nd anniversary of Bloomsday, the date on which the action of *Ulysses* takes place. *A joint gift of Mr. Lee Nordness and the artist.*

stories as "epiphanies." One of the stories, possibly to be titled "Mr. Bloom's Day," was to have followed a middle-class Dublin Jew, Leopold Bloom, through a typical (but also completely specific) day in his life. But this subject outgrew even the novella form, and became the subject for Joyce's second novel, *Ulysses* (Paris, 1922), in which we accompany Mr. Bloom through as nearly as possible *all* the events in a single day—June 16, 1904, to be exact. Each main episode parallels an episode in the *Odyssey,* many of them having their own prose styles or techniques of presentation appropriate to the nature of the episode (for example, the chapter that parallels the Aeolus adventure in the *Odyssey*—the Cave of the Winds—takes place in and about a newspaper office and makes use of newspaper jargon, newspaper headlines, and extremely frequent references to wind of one kind or another to keep the parallel present to our minds). This book has demanded about as much critical analysis and explanation as *The Waste*

Land—and for the same reasons: Joyce is describing modern lives, but he felt impelled to base his description in a structure of parallel reference to an earlier work. (*The Odyssey* does something of the same work here as the legend of the Fisher King does in *The Waste Land*.) Again, like Eliot, Joyce has seen fit to pack his work with literary and historical allusions. Like *The Waste Land*, *Ulysses* rewards the reader who will make the effort to understand it with a rich and complex vision of the modern world.

Ulysses has been a crucial work in twentieth-century literary history for a number of reasons. In the first place, there was the perfect frankness with which Joyce detailed the actions and thoughts of his characters, involving him in the representation of biological functions and erotic imagery that novelists had hitherto been accustomed to suppress. In 1933 Judge John M. Woolsey of the United States District Court rendered a notable decision lifting the ban on *Ulysses,* thus, as has been said, "making an honest book of it." This decision, printed as a preface to the American edition of the book, has established a precedent by which other honest, serious books may be relieved of the undeserved stigma of dishonesty.

Then, for many people who have not looked at the book very closely, the mention of *Ulysses* automatically calls up the phrase "stream of consciousness," or another phrase, "interior monologue." While these terms are entirely relevant, they are applicable to the several parts of the book in different senses. The book is perhaps best known for its closing section, where for forty pages, consisting of eight sentences, each having no punctuation but the full stop at the end, we are stationed inside the mind of Molly Bloom as she gradually drifts off to sleep. Here Joyce is indeed attempting to render as accurately as possible a character's "stream of consciousness," the whole flow of the waking mental process, in all its apparent inconsequentiality, formlessness, and proliferation of detail. In the more standard episodes of the book, where the characters are not so isolated as Mrs. Bloom is in the closing episode, Joyce uses a method that is not essentially different, only more elliptical, from the method he had used in *A Portrait of the Artist as a Young Man.* Narration goes on from a point of view almost

unalterably fixed within the mind and perceptions of a single character, either Stephen Dedalus or Mr. Bloom. From that point of view we witness the character's actions, see anything that he sees in the world about him, and move back into his past life or outward into the projections of his imagination, as the principle of association dictates. The author himself never comes forward to explain or comment, and the reader must be alert to the operations of suggestion if he is to know exactly what is going on at any point during this most specific day. Nor is it enough, for ultimate interpretation of the *meaning* of *Ulysses,* to know what Stephen and Mr. Bloom do and say and think as they move about Dublin, for Joyce has entrusted a large part of his meaning to a structure, by no means obtrusive or obvious, of symbol and symbolic image. The principal characters are themselves symbolic, and it is by no means a matter of common agreement, among the writers of the many careful critical investigations of *Ulysses,* what is meant by the coming together, finally, of Stephen Dedalus, the conscience-ridden young intellectual, and Leopold Bloom, the genial, timid, courageous middle-aged ad-canvasser, whose mind is a repository for every half-understood scientific concept or popular superstition of his time. But if in many ways *Ulysses* is a unique book, and sometimes a bafflingly difficult one, with approaches to technique and meaning that criticism has not yet come to the end of, it is also a *novel.* Like other great novels, it can assuredly be read with the liveliest pleasure and interest by reason of the fullness, the resonance, and the penetration with which it presents its rendering of life. One of the more recent commentators, Michael Mason, ends a brief study of the book (*James Joyce: Ulysses,* London, 1972) by characterizing it as involving a "quite peculiarly Joycean mixture of freedom and discipline":

The freedom—the joyful, energetic bursting of such aesthetic constraints as the idea of an author's "style," and the calm but undeterred indifference to Grundyism—hardly needs stressing. The discipline has several aspects: the extraordinary trouble, quite self-enforced, taken over the expression; the patient, caring, humane detail of the characterisation; the serious investigation of some of the moral implications of Freud's kind of picture of the personality; the thoroughgoing commitment to the tradition of European realism. Ulysses is simultaneously one of the most responsible and one of the most emancipated novels in our literature. In combining these qualities it is unique.

Joyce's last novel, *Finnegans Wake* (1939), in which he used a kind of dream-language to explore and present the dream-consciousness, is even more prodigious than *Ulysses*. Here, too, as we try to find our path through its closely worked pattern of significance, we are constantly in the presence of the wit, the beauty, and the developing compassion that we have found in the earlier books. In some sense, perhaps a sense not yet fully understood, Joyce's four works of fiction form a whole, and no amount of commentary will help us more, when we approach the later books, than will a careful reading of *Dubliners* and *A Portrait of the Artist as a Young Man.*

For the most part the writers whose careers form the history of English literature between the two wars believed in the mind, retained a faith in the validity of its most subtle workings even in the face of evidence that man was using his intellect to destroy himself. Aldous Huxley, who seemed to those who read his early novels and stories to have taken all knowledge for his province, to be the very type of the twentieth-century intellectual, was at first the leading satirist of the period, a position that he later yielded to George Orwell and Evelyn Waugh. His view of the world and of modern man's problematical place in it was never tinged with easy optimism, but the surface gaiety and sparkle of the early work—particularly the novels *Crome Yellow* (1921), *Antic Hay* (1923), and *Point Counter Point* (1928)—gradually gave way to the bitter view of the future that he set down in *Ape and Essence* (1949). Later still, in the closing years of his life, his interest in the mind-expanding effects of such hallucinogenic drugs as peyotl brought him abreast of certain current social considerations; but it may well be that his permanent contribution to twentieth-century literature was made in the novels, stories, and essays that he wrote in the 1920s and 1930s.

Returning now to the period between the two wars, it may be possible to point to one or two of its achievements—achievements that must be seen as centrally characteristic of the Modern period, even if it is not possible to "summarize" it. In the first place, its major writers stand for a consistent devotion to the principles of subtlety and intensity in literature, as well as to a principle of complexity that is a result not of mere fondness for complicating simple meanings but of the writer's having complex things to say. As we have seen, certain poetic developments involved more effective literary contacts with Continental forms and ideas than British literature had seen for almost a century. It was a period during which the intellectual life of men of letters was active and vivid, fed by an interest in new ideas and in new concepts of the function of literature. These concepts involved new approaches to form, to technique; and all these interests were not infrequently stirred by eager controversy. (The period supported two exciting and distinguished reviews, among its other periodicals: *The Criterion,* edited by T. S. Eliot, published between 1922 and 1939; and *Scrutiny,* edited by F. R. Leavis, published from 1932 until 1953.) The belief prevailed, and is easily seen in the writings of those who represent their time most faithfully, that nothing should be taken for granted, that all principles, and all values, aesthetic and otherwise, should be subjected to searching and recurrent examination. Finally, in spite of the defeatism, in spite of the disillusionment that grew as the shock of the war gave way to the realization that the peace was doomed, these years produced work of the highest distinction and interest in all forms. In confirmation of this statement one might easily add a score or more of names to those already discussed: among them, certainly, Robert Graves, Edith Sitwell, Wyndham Lewis, Katherine Mansfield, Middleton Murry, Edmund Blunden, William Plomer, and Walter de la Mare.

W. H. AUDEN AND THE 1930s

In 1930 Faber and Faber in London published a volume of poems that seems, in retrospect at least, to have heralded the most interesting poetry of the thirties as clearly as *Prufrock and Other Observations* had heralded that of the twenties. This volume, W. H. Auden's *Poems,* was not its author's first appearance in print; in

1928 an earlier version of *Poems* had been hand-printed at Oxford by Stephen Spender, Auden's fellow poet, in an edition of about forty-five copies. Some of Auden's poems had also appeared in the annual collections of verse by Oxford undergraduates, *Oxford Poetry;* the volumes for 1926, 1927, and 1928 constitute a remarkable prediction of things to come in that they contain early poems not only by Auden but also by Stephen Spender, C. Day Lewis, Louis MacNeice, and Rex Warner.

The poems in Auden's 1930 volume were various in kind, but all were wholly new both in manner and matter. It is true, they owed much to Eliot's exploration of important areas of thought and feeling; they owed certain features of their technique to Wilfred Owen, others to G. M. Hopkins (whose poems, it will be remembered, were first published in 1918): which means merely that Auden built on the innovations and advances made by his immediate predecessors. But the total impression was of a new poetic voice whose tone and quality could not possibly have been predicted any more than it could henceforth be forgotten, an impression of an observed and created world whose problems and preoccupations differed widely from those of the immediate postwar world.

Just as it had taken readers some time to get used to the techniques of presentation and the subject matter of Eliot's early poems, so it took time to see beyond the apparent strangeness of poems like "This Lunar Beauty" or "Too Dear, Too Vague" (see selections from Auden) to the beauty which familiarity with them disclosed. In such poems as the two mentioned, with their arresting use of the short line, Auden cultivated a compression, a deliberate suppression of links and transitions, which some readers were at first baffled by. But although Auden produced poems and parts of poems which are rendered perfectly hermetic by their unexplained reference to private circumstances, private jokes, in general the way to "understand" his poetry lies in learning to see in it what is there and not to look for kinds of statement or explanation which we are accustomed to finding in other poetry but which Auden was not concerned with.

The way to "understand" a poem like "This Lunar Beauty," for example, is not to try to paraphrase it, to reduce what it is saying to other terms, to prose, but to take it in *completely,* as it stands, to "get it by heart," in every sense of the word. Some parts of it would be difficult to paraphrase, but is it not an easy matter to apprehend what in general it is saying, about the way moonlight seems to change life, to give it a different meaning from that of our daylight existence, to give us a glimpse of life and the world free from time or change as it appears to be under the influence of moonlight? "Too Dear, Too Vague," like other of Auden's poems, makes full use of what modern psychology, particularly as it involves psychoanalysis, has taught us about the human heart—do not lines like

> *For no is not love: no is no*

or

> *Love is not there*
> *Love has moved to another chair*

give in their measure a sharp new verbal apprehension of old truths?

Auden and his contemporaries came of age during the economic slump of the thirties, and economic, political, and social questions form one of their major subjects, besides giving the tone to much of their imagery. In Auden's early poems the general interest of his time in finding a solution to grave social problems is frequently reflected in charade-like imagery, in references to an imaginary war with imaginary sides and campaigns. Later, the recognition of the necessity for political action became explicit. The special number of *New Verse* (November, 1937) that was devoted to Auden contained brief statements about him and his work by a number of writers of his and the preceding generation, among them one in which Stephen Spender pointed out that at Oxford Auden had been interested not in politics but in "poetry, psychoanalysis and medicine," and that he "'arrived at' politics by way of psychology."

His early poems begin by being preoccupied with neurosis in individuals, but this gradually extends (at the time when he had left Oxford and gone to live in Berlin) to an interest in the epoch and capitalist society.

Like so many thinking people of the 1930s, these poets saw many places in the world where

W. H. Auden (1907–1973). This photo of the young Auden was taken about the time of the publication of his first volume of poetry in 1930. *Curtis Brown Ltd.*

Communism offered an alternative to suffocation from the forces of reaction. Spender, who described the need for decisive political alignment in *Forward from Liberalism* (1937) and who later described his generation's disillusionment with Communism (in an essay in *The God That Failed,* 1950), goes on to show in the statement from which we have just quoted how the alternatives looked in the early 1930s:

In post-war and pre-Hitler Berlin, one began by noticing symptoms of decadence, suffering and unemployment; one looked further and one saw beneath the decay of the liberal state, the virulent reaction of the Nazis and the struggle for a new life of the Communists. The one side stood for the suppression of the very objectivity which the poet required, perhaps also his life, certainly his intellectual standards; the other, however painful and disillusioning its birth pangs, promised finally a world in which one could see and tell the truth.

We must remember in reading the poetry of the thirties that hopes and beliefs were then green which have since withered past all recognition. The tone and direction of much of that poetry are determined by a conviction that the sardonic disillusionment of the twenties should be swept away by forceful, positive action—by political action.

After publication of his first volume, Auden's poetic range continued to expand and change. There were many notable volumes after 1930: *The Orators, an English Study* (1932), a combination of verse and prose as exciting and unforgettable as it was bewildering; *Look, Stranger* (1936; called *On This Island* in America), a collection of poems which to some readers represented the fulfillment of Auden's earlier promise, and which was in any case scarcely to be matched by any living poet for the perfect beauty, the wit, or the rich variety of its contents; *Another Time* (1940), with its remarkable poems about particular great men—Melville, Pascal, Voltaire, Yeats. A characteristic product of the 1930s were Auden's experiments in the verse drama, either alone (*The Dance of Death,* 1933) or in collaboration with the novelist Christopher Isherwood (*The Dog Beneath the Skin,* 1935, and *The Ascent of F-6,* 1936). Isherwood, whose stories and short novels about Berlin in the late twenties and early thirties offer a fascinating record of a tragic era, has presented in his semifictional autobiographical volume *Lions and Shadows* (1947) a lively and appealing description of the literary aspirations, the friendships and associations (with a young poet named "Hugh Weston," for example), that were to determine the tone and temper of the work of this new generation.

In work published during the 1940s, such as *For the Time Being* ("A Christmas Oratorio"), *The Sea and the Mirror* ("A Commentary on Shakespeare's *The Tempest*"), and *The Age of Anxiety* ("A Baroque Eclogue," whose meter is closely derived from Old English alliterative verse), Auden continued to experiment with form. Wherever, in these works, he uses prose, it is no less brilliant than the verse. In two of his books (*Journey to a War,* written in collaboration with Isherwood and describing their journey to China in 1938, and *New Year Letter,* a long philosophical poem published in 1941) sonnet sequences are included. Some critics feel that these sonnets (see selections from Auden), deriving in form and tone not from the English sonneteers but from Rainer Maria Rilke, the great German Symbolist poet who died in 1926, are the finest poetry Auden wrote. But he produced too much verse of the first order of excellence to make such questions easy to decide. One other point should be made: after the publication of those poems referred to here, Auden continued to publish volumes of new poems until his death in 1973. But both in our discussion and in the selection from his work printed in this volume, the aim is to represent the impact he made as a striking new talent in the first two decades of his career, at a time when he seemed to embody a renewal and a modification of the creative impulse that characteristically shaped the Modern period.

If Auden was the most commanding poetic figure of his generation, by reason of the variety, the scope, and the consistent interest of his achievement, there are a number of other poets who have a claim to be a part of the literary history of the thirties and forties. The publication of Stephen Spender's first volume of poems in 1933 was as pleasurable an event as Auden's first appearance had been, and Spender has continued to speak clearly and honestly for the conscience of his time, both in verse and in prose. Another salutary presence was that of Louis MacNeice, whose books include verse plays for theater and radio, translations of Aeschylus' *Agamemnon* and Goethe's *Faust,* books of travel and observation and of criticism, as well as the collections of shorter poems. Prominent in any detailed account of the thirties and forties would also be C. Day Lewis, William Empson, and George Barker, as well as a number of Welsh poets—Dylan Thomas, Vernon Watkins, and Alun Lewis—to name only those who come first to mind.

The present account of the development of modern British literature, then, brings the story up to a point shortly after the end of World War II, projecting it about as it looked at mid-century. At that point the student of modern literature had the sense of surveying a rich and varied continuum of literary events that, beginning with a new orientation toward received aesthetic and philosophical doctrines during the last two decades of the nineteenth century, continued unbroken up to 1939. The specific literary doctrines and programs, the particular works, and the strongly emergent literary per-

sonalities that constitute the literary history of those sixty years were certainly not all of one kind, and the period contains its own internal eddies of contradiction, revolt, or reaction. Yet it remains a coherent period, something that can be called—for the moment, anyway—Modern literature, by reason of the intense creative energy that characterized it, and by the equally intense belief, common to all the major figures who belong to it and who created it—figures as different in other ways as James, Conrad, Joyce, Lawrence, and Eliot—in the *seriousness* of literature, in the possibilities of making poetry and the novel do more things and different things than they had ever done before. This belief in literature as a uniquely valuable activity and the accompanying conviction that literary form should be mastered, exploited as knowingly and subtly as possible, go back in some of their elements to the similar faith of the Romantic Movement and in others to the principles and practice of Symbolism. Arthur Symons, introducing the French Symbolists to English readers in 1899, had affirmed that "to be naïf, to be archaic, is not to be either natural or simple; . . . it is not natural to be what is called 'natural' any longer," and in doing so he was synthesizing the inner discipline of a movement that, already strongly in being, would find its specific manifestations in such works as *The Wings of the Dove, Ulysses,* and *To the Lighthouse*, in Yeats's poems about Byzantium and in *The Waste Land,* in—for it has been an international movement—*Remembrance of Things Past, The Duino Elegies,* and *The Trial.*

To the question of what British literature has been like *since* 1950, what it has been doing, why it is necessary to make a separation between it and the literature whose development we have been surveying, we shall return in the introduction to the concluding section of this book. For the moment, there remains the question of the principles on which our selections from the literature of the Modern period are made. No attempt was made to include every writer who in some way distinguished himself during the years in question; instead, we aimed at directing attention to work that it is essential to know if we are to understand what the earlier twentieth century made of the British tradition. There are, of course, many writers not mentioned here whose books might well be seen as equal or parallel in importance to the books of those whom we included; the work of still others, while it is of great intrinsic interest and value, seems to be less strictly representative than that of the writers we have chosen of what was *specially,* even uniquely, characteristic of the period. Problems of bulk make it impracticable to include many plays, so that a writer who, while the first half of the century was in progress, seemed to have much to say about *all* its problems, George Bernard Shaw, is not represented.

It is hoped that the poems, critical documents, and stories that follow will enable the reader to form with some fullness an idea of the quality and direction of the writing which has been most nearly central to the literary development of the period. And here, as always, the anthologist's aim must be to stir an impulse that will send the reader back to the books from which the selections have been taken. For an acquaintance with the writers represented here will, we believe, put the reader in possession of a key to what has been best and most distinctive in British literature of the earlier twentieth century.

General References

Much has been written, and continues to be written, about individual writers and specific aspects of the Modern period, but there is no great range of books to choose from when one is seeking a treatment of the period as a whole. David Daiches's *The Present Age: After 1920* (1958), like the other volumes in the series of *Introductions to English Literature* (General Editor, Bonamy Dobrée), and like Edwin Muir's *The Present Age from 1914* (1940) which it replaces, offers conveniently classified lists of authors and works preceded by critical chapters surveying the general background and the achievement of the period in each of the forms. *The Modern Age* (Volume VII of *The Pelican Guide to English Literature*), edited by Boris Ford, contains chapters by various hands on the principal phases and writers of the period. The volume of the *Oxford History of English Literature* devoted to this period, *Eight Modern Writers,* by J.I.M. Stewart (1963), gives full and judicious treatment to each of the eight writers in question: Hardy, James, Shaw, Conrad, Kipling,

Yeats, Joyce, Lawrence, and provides a detailed bibliography for each. A very unusual kind of anthology, *The Modern Tradition: Backgrounds of Modern Literature,* edited by Richard Ellmann and Charles Feidelson, Jr. (1967), offers a monumentally wide reading of the theoretical, aesthetic, and philosophical backgrounds of the period.

Twentieth-Century Literature in Retrospect, edited by Reuben Brower (1971), while it disappoints some of the expectations raised by its title, does nevertheless collect critical essays, by various writers, on each of the twentieth-century figures "who have reached an almost canonical status," as well as a series of twentieth-century revaluations of writers of the past. *The Idea of the Modern in Literature and the Arts,* edited by Irving Howe (1967), contains essays and excerpts by many writers on a wide range of subjects related to the Modern movement.

Any serious study of the Modern period must be based on an understanding of the nineteenth-century background and beginnings of the period, particularly the late nineteenth-century movements that culminate in Symbolism. Edmund Wilson's *Axel's Castle: A Study in the Imaginative Literature of 1870–1930* (1931, and later reissues) was a pioneer work which has been by no means displaced. It consists of an introductory chapter on Symbolism followed by chapters on—among others—Yeats, Eliot, and Joyce. Similarly helpful are the introductory chapter and the chapter on Yeats in C. M. Bowra's *The Heritage of Symbolism* (1947). For Symbolism in general there is also *The Symbolist Movement: A Critical Appraisal,* by Anna Balakian (1967). The whole complex of cultural tendencies and events that comprise the Aesthetic Movement is engagingly and dependably chronicled in William Gaunt's *The Aesthetic Adventure* (1945, and later reissues). Critical anthologies that offer comprehensive readings in the several component movements are *The Religion of Beauty: Selections from the Aesthetes,* edited with introduction by Richard Aldington (1950); *Aesthetes and Decadents of the 1890's: An Anthology of British Poetry and Prose,* edited by Karl Beckson (1966); and *The Symbolist Poem: The Development of the English Tradition,* edited by Edward Engelberg (1967).

Enid Starkie's *From Gautier to Eliot* (1960), though not as solid as one would like it to be, does trace certain lines of crucial continental influence, and Frank Kermode's *Romantic Image* offers a philosophical consideration of the early modern period in the light of its nineteenth-century affinities and origins. Graham Hough's *The Last Romantics* (1949) includes chapters on Pater, *fin-de-siècle*, and Yeats. The same writer's *Image and Experience: Studies in a Literary Revolution* (1960) studies the wider impact on English poetry of Imagism, and also contains chapters on free verse and on the role of psychoanalysis in literary interpretation. John Bayley's *The Romantic Survival: A Study in Poetic Evolution* (1957), which relates the Modern period to its origins in Romanticism, concludes with chapters on Yeats, Auden, and Dylan Thomas.

Certain critical works may be seen as having themselves formed a part of the literary history of the period, even while they were helping the thirties and the forties to reach an articulate awareness of what the immediately preceding decades had stood for and accomplished. F. R. Leavis's *New Bearings in English Poetry: A Study of the Contemporary Situation* (1932, and later reissues, which include a final chapter, "Retrospect 1950") contains the kind of general discussion suggested by its title as well as chapters on Eliot, Pound, and Hopkins. Stephen Spender's *The Destructive Element: A Study of Modern Writers and Beliefs* (1935) was one of the first books to treat the Modern period from a perspective that saw its most important writers, including James and Conrad, Eliot and Yeats, as reacting to common problems in diverse ways which determined the content and tenor of their work. His later books, *The Creative Element: A Study of Vision, Despair, and Orthodoxy Among Some Modern Writers* (1953) and *The Struggle of the Modern* (1963), put the central manifestations and issues of modern literature into unusually clear-sighted, helpful, non-partisan perspective.

The poets who saw themselves as giving a new direction to the development of modern literature in the 1930s published a number of critical statements or manifestos which scrutinized the recent past in the light of their own aims and brought the history of modern poetry up to date in the then-present. C. Day Lewis's *A Hope for Poetry* (1934), after surveying the poetic practice of Owen, Hopkins, and Eliot, went on to describe the aims of the generation of poets to which he, Auden, Spender, and MacNeice belonged. Louis MacNeice's *Modern Poetry: A Personal Essay* (1938) is valuable not only for what it tells us of MacNeice's own development but also for its account of the demands and influences of which these poets were conscious at the beginning of their careers. Views of the function of poetry that were to some extent shared by all these writers are brought out in a short book by Stephen Spender, *Life and the Poet* (1942).

Dorothy Van Ghent's *The English Novel: Form and Function* (1953) includes excellent chapters on a number of the modern novelists. Other useful books treating one aspect or another of the period are: David Daiches, *The Novel and the Modern World* (1960); H. E. Bates, *The Modern Short Story: A Critical Survey* (1941); W. Y. Tindall, *Forces in Modern British Literature* (new edition, 1956); G. S. Fraser, *The Modern Writer and His World* (1953); and M. L. Rosenthal, *The Modern Poets: A Critical Introduction* (1960).

Oscar Wilde

1854–1900

Although one of Oscar Wilde's greatest works, *Salome*, is a tragedy, and although both his novelette *The Picture of Dorian Gray* and his best poem, "The Ballad of Reading Gaol," are of somber, melodramatic cast, his more habitual mode was comedy. An essential element of his genius was humor, just as a pleasant, even temperament was a consistent feature of his personality. But simply because much of what he said, whether in his writing or in his conversation, was said lightly, with elegance and wit, we must not make the mistake of dismissing him as a merely entertaining writer of no weight or consequence. Both in his writing and in his life he stood, as he said, "in symbolic relations to the art and culture of [his] age." His behavior—the striking dress, the carefully chosen scheme of decoration in his London house, the outrageously paradoxical turn he gave to his remarks—was calculated, no doubt, to gain attention, for throughout the years of his fame Wilde thoroughly enjoyed being in the limelight. But this very desire to attract attention was in a larger sense the embodiment of an idea: the idea common to the Decadence wherever it occurs at the end of the nineteenth century, whether in England or in France,[1] that the standardized behavior of the newspaper-reading, money-making bourgeois was intolerably limited, drab, hypocritical, and—above all—that it was utterly untouched by imagination. Wilde's brilliant critical dialogue, "The Decay of Lying," is a defense of the imagination and of the role of art as expanding the boundaries of men's vision, of teaching the race to see, to feel, to imagine: "the object of Art is not simple truth but complex beauty." One of the principles stated in this dialogue is a restatement, albeit in simpler terms, of principles encountered in the eloquent closing paragraphs of Shelley's *Defence of Poetry*: "All things exist as they are perceived," Shelley had said; and the idea is completed—with reference to the role of the poet in helping us to perceive—in much the same way as Wilde completes it when he says, "Things are because we see them, and what we see, and how we see it, depends on the Arts that have influenced us."

Wilde, as one of the centrally emblematic figures (another is the painter Whistler) of the nineties in England, brings together in his own person the principal ideas of two movements that, with the deeper and more momentous movement known as Symbolism, constitute the very foundation of the Modern period: the Decadence and the Aesthetic Movement. In Paris the Decadents who flourished in the 1880s protested in various ways against the rigidity and narrowness of bourgeois values, sometimes by a gutter-life that they tried to make as scandalous as possible; other times by a life of the most careful attentiveness to the whole range of aesthetic values. Wilde's *The Picture of Dorian Gray*, which owes a great deal, both in detail and in total conception, to *A Rebours*, portrays both modes of behavior. But another possible instrument of the Decadence, in its role of defying the false values it finds entrenched in the society around it, is humor, and Wilde more habitually chooses this instrument. Underneath the good-natured gibes of *The Importance of Being Earnest*—in the brilliant scene in which Lady Bracknell interrogates Jack Worthing, for instance—there is implicit a protest against the hypocrisy, the time-serving, and the sheer insensitivity, whether to feeling or to imagination, of "good" society.

In given instances, whether of a writer or of a fictional character, it is not always easy to distinguish between the Decadent and the Aesthete. Dorian Gray was both, and so perhaps was Wilde. In any event, the Aesthetic Movement, with its doctrine of "art for art's sake"—in England given its clearest statement by Pater—found its most flamboyant embodiment in the public career and in the writing of Oscar Wilde. Everything Wilde did or said, in the ten years before the collapse of his career in 1895, may be seen as a pushing to extreme consequences of the principles concerning the autonomy and unique importance of art that Pater had so quietly and compellingly enunciated in the Preface and Conclusion to the first edition (1873) of *The Renaissance*.

But although Wilde interests us greatly because of his role as representative of aesthetic and philosophic principles essential to the literature of the Modern period, he interests us no less because of the intrinsic value of his work. He achieved his highest stature as a comic dramatist, particularly for *The Importance of Being Earnest;* this play alone would assure him of a place in the history of British literature beside Congreve, Sheridan, Goldsmith, and Shaw. *Salome,* at least when it is deepened and strengthened by Richard Strauss's music, and with its theme of the abandonment of all prudence, all

---

[1] It occurs in its pure state, so to speak, in the life of Des Esseintes, the hero of J.-K. Huysmans's novel *A Rebours,* first published in 1884; English translations appear under such titles as *Against Nature* or *Against the Grain.*

Oscar Wilde (1854–1900) in 1882. Wilde is wearing the "aesthetic" dress he affected at the beginning of his public career. He later abandoned this style in favor of correctly elegant clothing in the current fashion. *The Granger Collection.*

reverence, all decency even, to a hopeless passion, is one of the most impressive works that the Decadence produced. Wilde was not a dependably good poet, but the stories, whether the long, rather melodramatic ones like "Lord Arthur Savile's Crime" or the beautifully poised, essentially melancholy modern fables like "The Selfish Giant" or "The Happy Prince," are works of great distinction, both for their lucidity of style and for their alertness of moral vision.

Oscar Wilde (his full name was Oscar Fingal O'Flahertie Wills Wilde) was born in Dublin on October 16, 1854. His father was Sir William Wilde, a famous eye-and-ear specialist, and his mother was a poetess of sorts who published her work under the pen name Speranza. Both Wilde's parents were the subject of much picturesque Dublin legend, some of it recounted in the early sections of Yeats's *Autobiography,* and both have been the subject of recent biographies. Wilde went to Trinity College, Dublin, as an exhibitioner, and from there went on a scholarship to Magdalen College, Oxford. At Oxford from

1874 to 1879, Wilde came under the spell not only of Pater but also of Ruskin, who had been Slade Professor of Fine Art since 1870, and who, as A.J. A. Symons reminds us in an article on "Wilde at Oxford" (*Horizon,* April and May, 1941), had expressed the hope that his young disciples in the Guild of St. George might "band themselves together, one day, and go out in a kind of Benedictine brotherhood to cultivate waste places and make life tolerable in our great cities for the children of the poor."

During the Oxford years, Wilde traveled in Italy and Greece, and won the Newdigate Prize with a poem entitled "Ravenna." He left Oxford with a first-class degree and went immediately to London, where his "aesthetic" dress and his carefully cultivated dandy pose were quickly immortalized in the character of Bunthorne in Gilbert and Sullivan's *Patience* (1881). In 1882 he undertook an American lecture tour, his subjects being "The New Hellenism" and the English Renaissance; the next year he lectured in England on "The House Beautiful." He was married in 1884 to Constance Lloyd, and Yeats has described in his *Autobiography* the beautifully decorated house, at 16 Tite St., Chelsea, in which Wilde lived with his wife and their two children. The years from 1887 to 1895 were the years of Wilde's greatest fame and productivity: in 1888 he published the collection of short tales called *The Happy Prince;* in 1890 the critical essays and dialogues in *Intentions,* the stories in *Lord Arthur Savile's Crime,* and *The Picture of Dorian Gray;* in 1891–92 he wrote *Salome* in French, the work then translated into English by Lord Alfred Douglas, the young man whose fatal acquaintance he had recently made; his comedies followed in quick succession—*Lady Windermere's Fan* in 1892, *A Woman of No Importance* in 1893, and both *An Ideal Husband* and *The Importance of Being Earnest* in 1895.

With only a little exaggeration, it is possible to see paradox as the mainspring of Wilde's life and art throughout his years of fame. It is probably his single most constant stylistic or rhetorical device. Sometimes his verbal paradoxes occur so frequently that they begin to seem mechanical; more often they are entirely delightful and expressive, and always they spring from the conviction voiced by someone in *The Picture of Dorian Gray:* "The way of paradoxes is the way of truth. To test reality we must see it on the tight-rope. When the Verities become acrobats we can judge them." After his disgrace, Wilde believed that he had discovered a deeper significance in paradox, or, to put it another way, that the deepest truths about human life were paradoxical. In *De Profundis,* the long letter of self-justification and self-exploration that he wrote in prison, Wilde said: "To be entirely free, and at the same time entirely dominated by law, is the eternal paradox of human life that we realize at every moment." This realization was linked to another, that "the secret of life is suffering. It is what is hidden behind everything. . . . Pain, unlike pleasure, wears no mask." This last sentence, by reminding us of a passage in *Dorian Gray,* may also remind us that during the years of success Wilde was obsessed by the dramatic paradox inherent in his own life: that while he was courted and admired by London society he was secretly involved, in whatever degree, in the world of homoerotic vice, and that if his involvement were to be uncovered his disgrace would be instantaneous. Dorian Gray's crime is heavier, but we see Wilde's own situation behind his as one evening, "exquisitely dressed and wearing a large button-hole of Parma violets," he is

ushered into Lady Narborough's drawing-room by bowing servants. His forehead was throbbing with maddened nerves, and he felt wildly excited, but his

manner as he bent over his hostess's hand was as easy and graceful as ever. Perhaps one never seems so much at one's ease as when one has to play a part. Certainly no one looking at Dorian Gray that night could have believed that he had passed through a tragedy as horrible as any tragedy of our age. Those finely-shaped fingers could never have clutched a knife for sin, nor those smiling lips have cried out on God and goodness. He himself could not help wondering at the calm of his demeanor, and for a moment he felt keenly the terrible pleasure of a double life.

For Wilde, the terrible pleasure of a double life was to end abruptly, and even if he had come out of prison in better health and more favorable circumstances than he did, it may be doubted whether he would have gone on writing, since the life-springs, the springs of paradox, had been broken.

In March 1895 Wilde had brought a suit for criminal libel against the Marquess of Queensbury, the father of his friend Lord Alfred Douglas: Queensberry had left at Wilde's club a card bearing the not entirely logical taunt, "To Oscar Wilde, posing as a sodomite." During the trial, Wilde was rigorously cross-examined, his case was thrown out, and he was himself arrested. Tried and convicted of offenses against Section 11 of the Criminal Law Amendment Act, 1885, which punishes "indecencies between grown-up men, in public or private," Wilde was sentenced on May 27 to two years hard labor. He was released from Reading Prison on May 19, 1897, and went immediately to France, living first at Berneval, on the coast, then in Paris. After visiting Italy in 1900, he died on November 30 of that year, in Paris, at the Hôtel d'Alsace. (He said, "If I were to survive into the twentieth century, it would be more than the English people could bear.") On his grave in Père Lachaise cemetery, Paris, the massive monument by Sir Jacob Epstein is inscribed with a stanza from "The Ballad of Reading Gaol":

> *Yet all is well; he has but passed*
> *To Life's appointed bourne:*
> *And alien tears will fill for him*
> *Pity's long-broken urn,*
> *For his mourners will be outcast men,*
> *And outcasts always mourn.*

The career ends somberly, and Wilde's last years were made bitter by poverty, illness, and the loneliness of exile. His work is not somber, however, at least not for the most part, but neither is it shallow. If his poses were sometimes vain and silly, they had their purpose and their meaning, and beneath them he was a good-natured, generous man—he was

Irish, after all—with a sharp eye for everything that is involved in being human. His wit is entirely healthy and constitutes a standard for clear-eyed, beneficent understanding, which we would do well to carry about with us always.

TEXTS: Wilde's works are available in a number of one-volume collections or selections: *The Works of Oscar Wilde,* edited by G. F. Maine (1948, new edition 1966); *Complete Works of Oscar Wilde,* with an introduction by Vyvyan Holland (1966); *The Portable Oscar Wilde,* selected and edited by Richard Aldington (1946); *Selected Writings of Oscar Wilde,* edited by Russell Fraser (1969); *Oscar Wilde: Selected Writings,* with an introduction by Richard Ellmann (1961). Ellmann has also edited *The Artist as Critic: Critical Writings of Oscar Wilde* (1969).

Wilde's *Letters,* superbly edited by Rupert Hart-Davis, were published in 1962. *Oscar Wilde: The Critical Heritage,* edited by Karl Beckson (1970), gathers reviews and critical articles from Wilde's own lifetime (including Pater's review of *The Picture of Dorian Gray*). The story of the Wilde trials is told by H. Montgomery Hyde in a volume of the Famous Trials series (1963).

To be recommended from the numerous biographies are: Frances Winwar, *Oscar Wilde and the Yellow Nineties* (1940); Edouard Roditi, *Oscar Wilde,* in the Makers of Modern Literature series (1947); Hesketh Pearson, *The Life of Oscar Wilde* (1954); and Philippe Jullian, *Oscar Wilde,* translated by Violet Wyndham (1969). *Oscar Wilde: A Pictorial Biography* (1960) was compiled by Wilde's son, Vyvyan Holland. Recent critical works include: *Oscar Wilde: A Critical Study,* by Arthur Ransome (1971); and *Eminent Domain: Yeats among Wilde, Joyce, Pound, Eliot, and Auden,* by Richard Ellmann (1967).

The Importance of Being Earnest

The persons of the play

JOHN WORTHING, J.P.	LADY BRACKNELL
ALGERNON MONCRIEFF	HON. GWENDOLEN
REV. CANON	FAIRFAX
CHASUBLE, D.D.	CECILY CARDEW
MERRIMAN, butler	MISS PRISM, governess
LANE, manservant	

ACT ONE

SCENE: *Morning-room in Algernon's flat in Half-Moon Street, London, W.* TIME: *The present.*

The room is luxuriously and artistically furnished. The sound of a piano is heard in the adjoining room.

LANE *is arranging afternoon tea on the table, and after the music has ceased,* ALGERNON *enters.*

ALGERNON. Did you hear what I was playing, Lane?

LANE. I didn't think it polite to listen, sir.

ALGERNON. I'm sorry for that, for your sake. I don't play accurately—any one can play accurately—but I play with wonderful expression. As far as the piano is concerned, sentiment is my forte. I keep science for Life.

LANE. Yes, sir.

ALGERNON. And, speaking of the science of Life, have you got the cucumber sandwiches cut for Lady Bracknell?

LANE. Yes, sir. (*Hands them on a salver.*)

ALGERNON (*inspects them, takes two, and sits down on the sofa*). Oh! . . . by the way, Lane, I see from your book that on Thursday night, when Lord Shoreman and Mr. Worthing were dining with me, eight bottles of champagne are entered as having been consumed.

LANE. Yes, sir; eight bottles and a pint.

ALGERNON. Why is it that at a bachelor's establishment the servants invariably drink the champagne? I ask merely for information.

LANE. I attribute it to the superior quality of the wine, sir. I have often observed that in married households the champagne is rarely of a first-rate brand.

ALGERNON. Good heavens! Is marriage so demoralising as that?

LANE. I believe it *is* a very pleasant state, sir. I have had very little experience of it myself up to the present. I have only been married once. That was in consequence of a misunderstanding between myself and a young person.

ALGERNON (*languidly*). I don't know that I am much interested in your family life, Lane.

LANE. No, sir; it is not a very interesting subject. I never think of it myself.

ALGERNON. Very natural, I am sure. That will do, Lane, thank you.

LANE. Thank you, sir.

LANE *goes out.*

ALGERNON. Lane's views on marriage seem somewhat lax. Really, if the lower orders don't set us a good example, what on earth is the use of them? They seem, as a class, to have absolutely no sense of moral responsibility.

Enter LANE

LANE. Mr. Ernest Worthing.

Enter JACK. LANE *goes out.*

ALGERNON. How are you, my dear Ernest? What brings you up to town?

JACK. Oh, pleasure, pleasure! What else should bring one anywhere? Eating as usual, I see, Algy!

ALGERNON (*stiffly*). I believe it is customary in good society to take some slight refreshment at five o'clock. Where have you been since last Thursday?

JACK (*smiling down on the sofa*). In the country.

ALGERNON. What on earth do you do there?

JACK (*pulling off his gloves*). When one is in town one amuses oneself. When one is in the country one amuses other people. It is excessively boring.

ALGERNON. And who are the people you amuse?

JACK (*airily*). Oh, neighbours, neighbours.

ALGERNON. Got nice neighbours in your part of Shropshire?

JACK. Perfectly horrid! Never speak to one of them.

ALGERNON. How immensely you must amuse them! (*Goes over and takes sandwich.*) By the way, Shropshire is your county, is it not?

JACK. Eh? Shropshire? Yes, of course. Hallo! Why all these cups? Why cucumber sandwiches? Why such reckless extravagance in one so young? Who is coming to tea?

ALGERNON. Oh! merely Aunt Augusta and Gwendolen.

JACK. How perfectly delightful!

ALGERNON. Yes, that is all very well; but I am afraid Aunt Augusta won't quite approve of your being here.

JACK. May I ask why?

ALGERNON. My dear fellow, the way you flirt with Gwendolen is perfectly disgraceful. It is almost as bad as the way Gwendolen flirts with you.

JACK. I am in love with Gwendolen. I have come up to town expressly to propose to her.

ALGERNON. I thought you had come up for pleasure? . . . I call that business.

JACK. How utterly unromantic you are!

ALGERNON. I really don't see anything romantic in proposing. It is very romantic to be in love. But there is nothing romantic about a definite proposal. Why, one may be accepted. One usually is, I believe. Then the excitement is all over. The very essence of romance is uncertainty. If ever I get married, I'll certainly try to forget the fact.

JACK. I have no doubt about that, dear Algy. The Divorce Court was specially invented for people whose memories are so curiously constituted.

ALGERNON. Oh! there is no use speculating on that subject. Divorces are made in Heaven—— (JACK *puts out his hand to take a sandwich.* ALGERNON *at once interferes.*) Please don't touch the cucumber sandwiches. They are ordered specially for Aunt Augusta. (*Takes one and eats it.*)

JACK. Well, you have been eating them all the time.

ALGERNON. That is quite a different matter. She is my aunt. (*Takes plate from below.*) Have some bread and butter. The bread and butter is for Gwendolen. Gwendolen is devoted to bread and butter.

JACK (*advancing to table and helping himself*). And very good bread and butter it is too.

ALGERNON. Well, my dear fellow, you need not eat as if you were going to eat it all. You behave as if you were married to her already. You are not married to her already, and I don't think you ever will be.

JACK. Why on earth do you say that?

ALGERNON. Well, in the first place girls never marry the men they flirt with. Girls don't think it right.

JACK. Oh, that is nonsense!

ALGERNON. It isn't. It is a great truth. It accounts for the extraordinary number of bachelors that one sees all over the place. In the second place, I don't give my consent.

JACK. Your consent!

ALGERNON. My dear fellow, Gwendolen is my first cousin. And before I allow you to marry her, you will have to clear up the whole question of Cecily. (*Rings bell.*)

JACK. Cecily! What on earth do you mean? What do you mean, Algy, by Cecily! I don't know any one of the name of Cecily.

Enter LANE

ALGERNON. Bring me that cigarette case Mr. Worthing left in the smoking-room the last time he dined here.

LANE. Yes, sir.

LANE *goes out.*

JACK. Do you mean to say you have had my cigarette case all this time? I wish to goodness you had let me know. I have been writing frantic letters to Scotland Yard about it. I was very nearly offering a large reward.

ALGERNON. Well, I wish you would offer one. I happen to be more than usually hard up.

JACK. There is no good offering a large reward now that the thing is found.

Enter LANE *with the cigarette case on a salver.*

ALGERNON *takes it at once.* LANE *goes out.*

ALGERNON. I think that is rather mean of you, Ernest, I must say. (*Opens case and examines it.*) However, it makes no matter, for, now that I look at the inscription inside, I find that the thing isn't yours after all.

JACK. Of course it's mine. (*Moving to him.*) You have seen me with it a hundred times, and you have no right whatsoever to read what is written inside. It is a very ungentlemanly thing to read a private cigarrette case.

ALGERNON. Oh! it is absurd to have a hard and fast rule about what one should read and what one shouldn't. More than half of modern culture depends on what one shouldn't read.

JACK. I am quite aware of the fact, and I don't propose to discuss modern culture. It isn't the sort of thing one should talk of in private. I simply want my cigarette case back.

ALGERNON. Yes; but this isn't your cigarette case. This cigarette case is a present from some one of the name of Cecily, and you said you didn't know any one of that name.

JACK. Well, if you want to know, Cecily happens to be my aunt.

ALGERNON. Your aunt!

JACK. Yes. Charming old lady she is, too. Lives at Tunbridge Wells. Just give it back to me, Algy.

ALGERNON (*retreating to back of sofa*). But why does she call herself little Cecily if she is your aunt and lives at Tunbridge Wells? (*Reading.*) "From little Cecily with her fondest love."

JACK (*moving to sofa and kneeling upon it*).

My dear fellow, what on earth is there in that? Some aunts are tall, some aunts are not tall. That is a matter that surely an aunt may be allowed to decide for herself. You seem to think that every aunt should be exactly like your aunt! That is absurd! For Heaven's sake give me back my cigarette case. (*Follows* ERNEST *round the room.*)

ALGERNON. Yes. But why does your aunt call you her uncle? "From little Cecily, with her fondest love to her dear Uncle Jack." There is no objection, I admit, to an aunt being a small aunt, but why an aunt, no matter what her size may be, should call her own nephew her uncle, I can't quite make out. Besides, your name isn't Jack at all; it is Ernest.

JACK. It isn't Ernest; it's Jack.

ALGERNON. You have always told me it was Ernest. I have introduced you to every one as Ernest. You answer to the name of Ernest. You look as if your name was Ernest. You are the most earnest-looking person I ever saw in my life. It is perfectly absurd your saying that your name isn't Ernest. It's on your cards. Here is one of them. (*Taking it from case.*) "Mr. Ernest Worthing, B.4, The Albany." I'll keep this as a proof that your name is Ernest if ever you attempt to deny it to me, or to Gwendolen, or to any one else. (*Puts the card in his pocket.*)

JACK. Well, my name is Ernest in town and Jack in the country, and the cigarette case was given to me in the country.

ALGERNON. Yes, but that does not account for the fact that your small Aunt Cecily, who lives at Tunbridge Wells, calls you her dear Uncle. Come, old boy, you had much better have the thing out at once.

JACK. My dear Algy, you talk exactly as if you were a dentist. It is very vulgar to talk like a dentist when one isn't a dentist. It produces a false impression.

ALGERNON. Well, that is exactly what dentists always do. Now, go on! Tell me the whole thing. I may mention that I have always suspected you of being a confirmed and secret Bunburyist; and I am quite sure of it now.

JACK. Bunburyist? What on earth do you mean by a Bunburyist?

ALGERNON. I'll reveal to you the meaning of that incomparable expression as soon as you are kind enough to inform me why you are Ernest in town and Jack in the country.

JACK. Well, produce my cigarette case first.

ALGERNON. Here it is. (*Hands cigarette case.*) Now produce your explanation, and pray make it improbable. (*Sits on sofa.*)

JACK. My dear fellow, there is nothing improbable about my explanation at all. In fact, it's perfectly ordinary. Old Mr. Thomas Cardew, who adopted me when I was a little boy, made me in his will guardian to his grand-daughter, Miss Cecily Cardew. Cecily, who addresses me as her uncle from motives of respect that you could not possibly appreciate, lives at my place in the country under the charge of her admirable governess, Miss Prism.

ALGERNON. Where is that place in the country, by the way?

JACK. That is nothing to you, dear boy. You are not going to be invited. . . . I may tell you candidly that the place is not in Shropshire.

ALGERNON. I suspected that, my dear fellow! I have Bunburyed all over Shropshire on two separate occasions. Now, go on. Why are you Ernest in town and Jack in the country?

JACK. My dear Algy, I don't know whether you will be able to understand my real motives. You are hardly serious enough. When one is placed in the position of guardian, one has to adopt a very high moral tone on all subjects. It's one's duty to do so. And as a high moral tone can hardly be said to conduce very much to either one's health or one's happiness, in order to get up to town I have always pretended to have a younger brother of the name of Ernest, who lives in the Albany, and gets into the most dreadful scrapes. That, my dear Algy, is the whole truth pure and simple.

ALGERNON. The truth is rarely pure and never simple. Modern life would be very tedious if it were either, and modern literature a complete impossibility!

JACK. That wouldn't be at all a bad thing.

ALGERNON. Literary criticism is not your forte, my dear fellow. Don't try it. You should leave that to people who haven't been at a University. They do it so well in the daily papers. What you really are is a Bunburyist. I was quite right in saying you were a Bunburyist. You are one of the most advanced Bunburyists I know.

JACK. What on earth do you mean?

ALGERNON. You have invented a very useful younger brother called Ernest, in order that you may be able to come up to town as often as you like. I have invented an invaluable permanent invalid called Bunbury, in order that I may be able to go down into the country whenever I choose. Bunbury is perfectly invaluable. If it wasn't for Bunbury's extraordinary bad health, for instance, I wouldn't be able to dine with you at Willis's to-night, for I have been really engaged to Aunt Augusta for more than a week.

JACK. I haven't asked you to dine with me anywhere to-night.

ALGERNON. I know. You are absolutely careless about sending out invitations. It is very foolish of you. Nothing annoys people so much as not receiving invitations.

JACK. You had much better dine with your Aunt Augusta.

ALGERNON. I haven't the smallest intention of doing anything of the kind. To begin with, I dined there on Monday, and once a week is quite enough to dine with one's own relations. In the second place, whenever I do dine there I am always treated as a member of the family, and sent down with either no woman at all, or two. In the third place, I know perfectly well whom she will place me next to, to-night. She will place me next Mary Farquhar, who always flirts with her own husband across the dinner-table. That is not very pleasant. Indeed, it is not even decent . . . and that sort of thing is enormously on the increase. The amount of women in London who flirt with their own husbands is perfectly scandalous. It looks so bad. It is simply washing one's clean linen in public. Besides, now that I know you to be a confirmed Bunburyist I naturally want to talk to you about Bunburying. I want to tell you the rules.

JACK. I'm not a Bunburyist at all. If Gwendolen accepts me, I am going to kill my brother, indeed I think I'll kill him in any case. Cecily is a little too much interested in him. It is rather a bore. So I am going to get rid of Ernest. And I strongly advise you to do the same with Mr. . . . with your invalid friend who has the absurd name.

ALGERNON. Nothing will induce me to part with Bunbury, and if you ever get married, which seems to me extremely problematic, you will be very glad to know Bunbury. A man who marries without knowing Bunbury has a very tedious time of it.

JACK. That is nonsense. If I marry a charming girl like Gwendolen, and she is the only girl I ever saw in my life that I would marry, I certainly don't want to know Bunbury.

ALGERNON. Then your wife will. You don't seem to realise, that in married life three is company and two is none.

JACK (*sententiously*). That, my dear young friend, is the theory that the corrupt French Drama has been propounding for the last fifty years.

ALGERNON. Yes; and that the happy English home has proved in half the time.

JACK. For heaven's sake, don't try to be cynical. It's perfectly easy to be cynical.

ALGERNON. My dear fellow, it isn't easy to be anything nowadays. There's such a lot of beastly competition about. (*The sound of an electric bell is heard.*) Ah! that must be Aunt Augusta. Only relatives, or creditors, ever ring in that Wagnerian manner. Now, if I get her out of the way for ten minutes, so that you can have an opportunity for proposing to Gwendolen, may I dine with you to-night at Willis's?

JACK. I suppose so, if you want to.

ALGERNON. Yes, but you must be serious about it. I hate people who are not serious about meals. It is so shallow of them.

Enter LANE

LANE. Lady Bracknell and Miss Fairfax.

ALGERNON *goes forward to meet them. Enter* LADY BRACKNELL *and* GWENDOLEN.

LADY BRACKNELL. Good-afternoon, dear Algernon, I hope you are behaving very well.

ALGERNON. I'm feeling very well, Aunt Augusta.

LADY BRACKNELL. That's not quite the same thing. In fact the two things rarely go together. (*Sees* JACK *and bows to him with icy coldness.*)

ALGERNON (*to* GWENDOLEN). Dear me, you are smart!

GWENDOLEN. I am always smart! Am I not, Mr. Worthing?

JACK. You're quite perfect, Miss Fairfax.

GWENDOLEN. Oh! I hope I am not that. It would leave no room for developments, and I intend to develop in many directions. (GWENDOLEN *and* JACK *sit down together in the corner.*)

LADY BRACKNELL. I'm sorry if we are a little late, Algernon, but I was obliged to call on dear Lady Harbury. I hadn't been there since her poor husband's death. I never saw a woman so altered; she looks quite twenty years younger. And now I'll have a cup of tea, and one of those nice cucumber sandwiches you promised me.

ALGERNON. Certainly, Aunt Augusta. (*Goes over to tea-table.*)

LADY BRACKNELL. Won't you come and sit here, Gwendolen?

GWENDOLEN. Thanks, mamma, I'm quite comfortable where I am.

ALGERNON (*picking up empty plate in horror*). Good heavens! Lane! Why are there no cucumber sandwiches? I ordered them specially.

LANE (*gravely*). There were no cucumbers in the market this morning, sir. I went down twice.

ALGERNON. No cucumbers!

LANE. No, sir. Not even for ready money.

ALGERNON. That will do, Lane, thank you.

LANE. Thank you, sir. (*Goes out.*)

ALGERNON. I am greatly distressed, Aunt Augusta, about there being no cucumbers, not even for ready money.

LADY BRACKNELL. It really makes no matter, Algernon. I had some crumpets with Lady Harbury, who seems to me to be living entirely for pleasure now.

ALGERNON. I hear her hair has turned quite gold from grief.

LADY BRACKNELL. It certainly has changed its colour. From what cause I, of course, cannot say. (ALGERNON *crosses and hands tea.*) Thank you. I've quite a treat for you to-night, Algernon. I am going to send you down with Mary Farquhar. She is such a nice woman, and so attentive to her husband. It's delightful to watch them.

ALGERNON. I am afraid, Aunt Augusta, I shall have to give up the pleasure of dining with you to-night after all.

LADY BRACKNELL (*frowning*). I hope not, Algernon. It would put my table completely out. Your uncle would have to dine upstairs. Fortunately he is accustomed to that.

ALGERNON. It is a great bore, and, I need hardly say, a terrible disappointment to me, but the fact is I have just had a telegram to say that my poor friend Bunbury is very ill again. (*Ex-*

changes glances with JACK.) They seem to think I should be with him.

LADY BRACKNELL. It is very strange. This Mr. Bunbury seems to suffer from curiously bad health.

ALGERNON. Yes; poor Bunbury is a dreadful invalid.

LADY BRACKNELL. Well, I must say, Algernon, that I think it is high time that Mr. Bunbury made up his mind whether he was going to live or to die. This shilly-shallying with the question is absurd. Nor do I in any way approve of the modern sympathy with invalids. I consider it morbid. Illness of any kind is hardly a thing to be encouraged in others. Health is the primary duty of life. I am always telling that to your poor uncle, but he never seems to take much notice . . . as far as any improvement in his ailment goes. I should be much obliged if you would ask Mr. Bunbury, from me, to be kind enough not to have a relapse on Saturday, for I rely on you to arrange my music for me. It is my last reception, and one wants something that will encourage conversation, particularly at the end of the season when every one has practically said whatever they had to say, which, in most cases, was probably not much.

ALGERNON. I'll speak to Bunbury, Aunt Augusta, if he is still conscious, and I think I can promise you he'll be all right by Saturday. Of course the music is a great difficulty. You see, if one plays good music, people don't listen, and if one plays bad music people don't talk. But I'll run over the programme I've drawn out, if you will kindly come into the next room for a moment.

LADY BRACKNELL. Thank you, Algernon. It is very thoughtful of you. (*Rising and following* ALGERNON.) I'm sure the programme will be delightful, after a few expurgations. French songs I cannot possibly allow. People always seem to think that they are improper, and either look shocked, which is vulgar, or laugh, which is worse. But German sounds a thoroughly respectable language, and indeed, I believe is so. Gwendolen, you will accompany me.

GWENDOLEN. Certainly, mamma.

LADY BRACKNELL *and* ALGERNON *go into the music-room;* GWENDOLEN *remains behind.*

JACK. Charming day it has been, Miss Fairfax.

GWENDOLEN. Pray don't talk to me about the weather, Mr. Worthing. Whenever people talk to me about the weather, I always feel quite certain that they mean something else. And that makes me so nervous.

JACK. I do mean something else.

GWENDOLEN. I thought so. In fact, I am never wrong.

JACK. And I would like to be allowed to take advantage of Lady Bracknell's temporary absence . . .

GWENDOLEN. I would certainly advise you to do so. Mamma has a way of coming back suddenly into a room that I have often had to speak to her about.

JACK (*nervously*). Miss Fairfax, ever since I met you I have admired you more than any girl . . . I have ever met since . . . I met you.

GWENDOLEN. Yes, I am quite well aware of the fact. And I often wish that in public, at any rate, you had been more demonstrative. For me you have always had an irresistible fascination. Even before I met you I was far from indifferent to you. (JACK *looks at her in amazement.*) We live, as I hope you know, Mr. Worthing, in an age of ideals. The fact is constantly mentioned in the more expensive monthly magazines, and has now reached the provincial pulpits, I am told; and my ideal has always been to love some one of the name of Ernest. There is something in that name that inspires absolute confidence. The moment Algernon first mentioned to me that he had a friend called Ernest, I knew I was destined to love you.

JACK. You really love me, Gwendolen?

GWENDOLEN. Passionately!

JACK. Darling! You don't know how happy you've made me.

GWENDOLEN. My own Ernest!

JACK. But you don't really mean to say that you couldn't love me if my name wasn't Ernest?

GWENDOLEN. But your name is Ernest.

JACK. Yes, I know it is. But supposing it was something else? Do you mean to say you couldn't love me then?

GWENDOLEN (*glibly*). Ah! that is clearly a metaphysical speculation, and like most metaphysical speculations has very little reference at all to the actual facts of real life, as we know them.

JACK. Personally, darling, to speak quite candidly, I don't much care about the name of

Ernest. . . . I don't think the name suits me at all.

GWENDOLEN. It suits you perfectly. It is a divine name. It has a music of its own. It produces vibrations.

JACK. Well, really, Gwendolen, I must say that I think there are lots of other much nicer names. I think Jack, for instance, a charming name.

GWENDOLEN. Jack? . . . No, there is very little music in the name Jack, if any at all, indeed. It does not thrill. It produces absolutely no vibrations. . . . I have known several Jacks, and they all, without exception, were more than usually plain. Besides, Jack is a notorious domesticity for John! And I pity any woman who is married to a man called John. She would probably never be allowed to know the entrancing pleasure of a single moment's solitude. The only really safe name is Ernest.

JACK. Gwendolen, I must get christened at once—I mean we must get married at once. There is no time to be lost.

GWENDOLEN. Married, Mr. Worthing?

JACK (astounded). Well . . . surely. You know that I love you, and you led me to believe, Miss Fairfax, that you were not absolutely indifferent to me.

GWENDOLEN. I adore you. But you haven't proposed to me yet. Nothing has been said at all about marriage. The subject has not even been touched on.

JACK. Well . . . may I propose to you now?

GWENDOLEN. I think it would be an admirable opportunity. And to spare you any possible disappointment, Mr. Worthing, I think it only fair to tell you quite frankly beforehand that I am fully determined to accept you.

JACK. Gwendolen!

GWENDOLEN. Yes, Mr. Worthing, what have you got to say to me?

JACK. You know what I have got to say to you.

GWENDOLEN. Yes, but you don't say it.

JACK. Gwendolen, will you marry me? (Goes on his knees.)

GWENDOLEN. Of course I will, darling. How long you have been about it! I am afraid you have had very little experience in how to propose.

JACK. My own one, I have never loved any one in the world but you.

GWENDOLEN. Yes, but men often propose for practice. I know my brother Gerald does. All my girl-friends tell me so. What wonderfully blue eyes you have, Ernest! They are quite, quite blue. I hope you will always look at me just like that, especially when there are other people present.

Enter LADY BRACKNELL.

LADY BRACKNELL. Mr. Worthing! Rise, sir, from this semi-recumbent posture. It is most indecorous.

GWENDOLEN. Mamma! (*He tries to rise; she restrains him.*) I must beg you to retire. This is no place for you. Besides, Mr. Worthing has not quite finished yet.

LADY BRACKNELL. Finished what, may I ask?

GWENDOLEN. I am engaged to Mr. Worthing, mamma. (*They rise together.*)

LADY BRACKNELL. Pardon me, you are not engaged to any one. When you do become engaged to some one, I, or your father, should his health permit him, will inform you of the fact. An engagement should come on a young girl as a surprise, pleasant or unpleasant, as the case may be. It is hardly a matter that she could be allowed to arrange for herself. . . . And now I have a few questions to put to you, Mr. Worthing. While I am making these inquiries, you, Gwendolen, will wait for me below in the carriage.

GWENDOLEN (*reproachfully*). Mamma!

LADY BRACKNELL. In the carriage, Gwendolen!

GWENDOLEN *goes to the door. She and* JACK *blow kisses to each other behind* LADY BRACKNELL'S *back.* LADY BRACKNELL *looks vaguely about as if she could not understand what the noise was. Finally turns round.*

Gwendolen, the carriage!

GWENDOLEN. Yes, mamma. (*Goes out, looking back at* JACK.)

LADY BRACKNELL (*sitting down*). You can take a seat, Mr. Worthing.

Looks in her pocket for note-book and pencil.

JACK. Thank you, Lady Bracknell, I prefer standing.

LADY BRACKNELL (*pencil and note-book in hand*). I feel bound to tell you that you are not down on my list of eligible young men, although I have the same list as the dear Duchess of Bolton has. We work together, in fact. However, I am quite ready to enter your name, should your answers be what a really affectionate mother requires. Do you smoke?

JACK. Well, yes, I must admit I smoke.

LADY BRACKNELL. I am glad to hear it. A man should always have an occupation of some kind. There are far too many idle men in London as it is. How old are you?

JACK. Twenty-nine.

LADY BRACKNELL. A very good age to be married at. I have always been of opinion that a man who desires to get married should know either everything or nothing. Which do you know?

JACK (*after some hesitation*). I know nothing, Lady Bracknell.

LADY BRACKNELL. I am pleased to hear it. I do not approve of anything that tampers with natural ignorance. Ignorance is like a delicate exotic fruit; touch it and the bloom is gone. The whole theory of modern education is radically unsound. Fortunately in England, at any rate, education produces no effect whatsoever. If it did, it would prove a serious danger to the upper classes, and probably lead to acts of violence in Grosvenor Square. What is your income?

JACK. Between seven and eight thousand a year.

LADY BRACKNELL (*makes a note in her book*). In land, or in investments?

JACK. In investments, chiefly.

LADY BRACKNELL. That is satisfactory. What between the duties expected of one during one's lifetime, and the duties enacted from one after one's death, land has ceased to be either a profit or a pleasure. It gives one position, and prevents one from keeping it up. That's all that can be said about land.

JACK. I have a country house with some land, of course, attached to it, about fifteen hundred acres, I believe; but I don't depend on that for my real income. In fact, as far as I can make out, the poachers are the only people who make anything out of it.

LADY BRACKNELL. A country house! How many bedrooms? Well, that point can be cleared up afterwards. You have a town house, I hope? A girl with a simple, unspoiled nature, like Gwendolen, could hardly be expected to reside in the country.

JACK. Well, I own a house in Belgrave Square, but it is let by the year to Lady Bloxham. Of course, I can get it back whenever I like, at six months' notice.

LADY BRACKNELL. Lady Bloxham? I don't know her.

JACK. Oh, she goes about very little. She is a lady considerably advanced in years.

LADY BRACKNELL. Ah, nowadays that is no guarantee of respectability of character. What number in Belgrave Square?

JACK. 149

LADY BRACKNELL (*shaking her head*). The unfashionable side. I thought there was something. However, that could easily be altered.

JACK. Do you mean the fashion, or the side?

LADY BRACKNELL (*sternly*). Both, if necessary, I presume. What are your politics?

JACK. Well, I am afraid I really have none. I am a Liberal Unionist.

LADY BRACKNELL. Oh, they count as Tories. They dine with us. Or come in the evening, at any rate. Now to minor matters. Are your parents living?

JACK. I have lost both my parents.

LADY BRACKNELL. Both? . . . That seems like carelessness. Who was your father? He was evidently a man of some wealth. Was he born in what the Radical papers call the purple of commerce, or did he rise from the ranks of the aristocracy?

JACK. I am afraid I really don't know. The fact is, Lady Bracknell, I said I had lost my parents. It would be nearer the truth to say that my parents seem to have lost me. . . . I don't actually know who I am by birth. I was . . . well, I was found.

LADY BRACKNELL. Found!

JACK. The late Mr. Thomas Cardew, an old gentleman of a very charitable and kindly disposition, found me, and gave me the name of Worthing, because he happened to have a first-class ticket for Worthing in his pocket at the time. Worthing is a place in Sussex. It is a seaside resort.

LADY BRACKNELL. Where did the charitable gentleman who had a first-class ticket for this seaside resort find you?

JACK (*gravely*). In a hand-bag.

LADY BRACKNELL. A hand-bag?

JACK (*very seriously*). Yes, Lady Bracknell. I was in a hand-bag—a somewhat large, black leather hand-bag, with handles to it—an ordinary hand-bag in fact.

LADY BRACKNELL. In what locality did this Mr. James, or Thomas, Cardew come across this ordinary hand-bag?

JACK. In the cloak-room at Victoria Station. It was given to him in mistake for his own.

LADY BRACKNELL. The cloak-room at Victoria Station?

JACK. Yes. The Brighton line.

LADY BRACKNELL. The line is immaterial. Mr. Worthing, I confess I feel somewhat bewildered by what you have just told me. To be born, or at any rate bred, in a hand-bag, whether it had handles or not, seems to me to display a contempt for the ordinary decencies of family life that reminds one of the worst excesses of the French Revolution. And I presume you know what that unfortunate movement led to? As for the particular locality in which the hand-bag was found, a cloak-room at a railway station might serve to conceal a social indiscretion—has probably, indeed, been used for that purpose before now—but it could hardly be regarded as an assured basis for a recognised position in good society.

JACK. May I ask you then what you would advise me to do? I need hardly say I would do anything in the world to ensure Gwendolen's happiness.

LADY BRACKNELL. I would strongly advise you, Mr. Worthing, to try and acquire some relations as soon as possible, and to make a definite effort to produce at any rate one parent, of either sex, before the season is quite over.

JACK. Well, I don't see how I could possibly manage to do that. I can produce the hand-bag at any moment. It is in my dressing-room at home. I really think that should satisfy you, Lady Bracknell.

LADY BRACKNELL. Me, sir! What has it to do with me? You can hardly imagine that I and Lord Bracknell would dream of allowing our only daughter—a girl brought up with the utmost care—to marry into a cloak-room, and form an alliance with a parcel. Good-morning, Mr. Worthing!

LADY BRACKNELL *sweeps out in majestic indignation.*

JACK. Good-morning! (ALGERNON, *from the other room, strikes up the Wedding March.*

JACK *looks perfectly furious, and goes to the door.*) For goodness' sake don't play that ghastly tune, Algy! How idiotic you are!

The music stops and ALGERNON *enters cheerily.*

ALGERNON. Didn't it go off all right, old boy? You don't mean to say Gwendolen refused you? I know it is a way she has. She is always refusing people. I think it is most ill-natured of her.

JACK. Oh, Gwendolen is as right as a trivet. As far as she is concerned, we are engaged. Her mother is perfectly unbearable. Never met such a Gorgon. . . . I don't really know what a Gorgon is like, but I am quite sure that Lady Bracknell is one. In any case, she is a monster, without being a myth, which is rather unfair. . . . I beg your pardon, Algy, I suppose I shouldn't talk about your own aunt in that way before you.

ALGERNON. My dear boy, I love hearing my relations abused. It is the only thing that makes me put up with them at all. Relations are simply a tedious pack of people, who haven't got the remotest knowledge of how to live, nor the smallest instinct about when to die.

JACK. Oh, that is nonsense!

ALGERNON. It isn't!

JACK. Well, I don't argue about the matter. You always want to argue about things.

ALGERNON. That is exactly what things were originally made for.

JACK. Upon my word, if I thought that, I'd shoot myself. . . . (*A pause.*) You don't think there is any chance of Gwendolen becoming like her mother in about a hundred and fifty years, do you, Algy?

ALGERNON. All women become like their mothers. That is their tragedy. No man does. That's his.

JACK. Is that clever?

ALGERNON. It is perfectly phrased! And quite as true as any observation in civilised life should be.

JACK. I am sick to death of cleverness. Everybody is clever nowadays. You can't go anywhere without meeting clever people. The thing has become an absolute public nuisance. I wish to goodness we had a few fools left.

ALGERNON. We have.

JACK. I should extremely like to meet them. What do they talk about?

ALGERNON. The fools? Oh! about the clever people of course.

JACK. What fools.

ALGERNON. By the way, did you tell Gwendolen the truth about your being Ernest in town, and Jack in the country?

JACK (*in a very patronising manner*). My dear fellow, the truth isn't quite the sort of thing one tells to a nice, sweet, refined girl. What extraordinary ideas you have about the way to behave to a woman!

ALGERNON. The only way to behave to a woman is to make love to her, if she is pretty, and to some one else, if she is plain.

JACK. Oh, that is nonsense.

ALGERNON. What about your brother? What about the profligate Ernest?

JACK. Oh, before the end of the week I shall have got rid of him. I'll say he died in Paris of apoplexy. Lots of people die of apoplexy, quite suddenly, don't they?

ALGERNON. Yes, but it's hereditary, my dear fellow. It's a sort of thing that runs in families. You had much better say a severe chill.

JACK. You are sure a severe chill isn't hereditary, or anything of that kind?

ALGERNON. Of course it isn't!

JACK. Very well, then. My poor brother Ernest is carried off suddenly, in Paris, by a severe chill. That gets rid of him.

ALGERNON. But I thought you said that . . . Miss Cardew was a little too much interested in your poor brother Ernest? Won't she feel his loss a good deal?

JACK. Oh, that is all right. Cecily is not a silly romantic girl, I am glad to say. She has got a capital appetite, goes for long walks, and pays no attention at all to her lessons.

ALGERNON. I would rather like to see Cecily.

JACK. I will take very good care you never do. She is excessively pretty, and she is only just eighteen.

ALGERNON. Have you told Gwendolen yet that you have an excessively pretty ward who is only just eighteen?

JACK. Oh! one doesn't blurt these things out to people. Cecily and Gwendolen are perfectly certain to be extremely great friends. I'll bet you anything you like that half an hour after they have met, they will be calling each other sister.

ALGERNON. Women only do that when they have called each other a lot of other things first. Now, my dear boy, if we want to get a good table

at Willis's, we really must go and dress. Do you know it is nearly seven?

JACK (*irritably*). Oh! it always is nearly seven.

ALGERNON. Well, I'm hungry.

JACK. I never knew you when you weren't. . . .

ALGERNON. What shall we do after dinner? Go to a theatre?

JACK. Oh, no! I loathe listening.

ALGERNON. Well, let us go to the Club?

JACK. Oh, no! I hate talking.

ALGERNON. Well, we might trot round to the Empire at ten?

JACK. Oh, no! I can't bear looking at things. It is so silly.

ALGERNON. Well, what shall we do?

JACK. Nothing!

ALGERNON. It is awfully hard work doing nothing. However, I don't mind hard work where there is no definite object of any kind.

Enter LANE

LANE. Miss Fairfax.

Enter GWENDOLEN. LANE *goes out.*

ALGERNON. Gwendolen, upon my word!

GWENDOLEN. Algy, kindly turn your back. I have something very particular to say to Mr. Worthing.

ALGERNON. Really, Gwendolen, I don't think I can allow this at all.

GWENDOLEN. Algy, you always adopt a strictly immoral attitude towards life. You are not quite old enough to do that. (ALGERNON *retires to the fireplace.*)

JACK. My own darling.

GWENDOLEN. Ernest, we may never be married. From the expression on mamma's face I fear we never shall. Few parents nowadays pay any regard to what their children say to them. The old-fashioned respect for the young is fast dying out. Whatever influence I ever had over mamma, I lost at the age of three. But although she may prevent us from becoming man and wife, and I may marry some one else, and marry often, nothing that she can possibly do can alter my eternal devotion to you.

JACK. Dear Gwendolen!

GWENDOLEN. The story of your romantic origin, as related to me by mamma, with unpleasing comments, has naturally stirred the deeper fibres of my nature. Your Christian name has an irresistible fascination. The simplicity of your character makes you exquisitely incomprehensible to me. Your town address at the Albany I have. What is your address in the country?

JACK. The Manor House, Woolton, Hertfordshire.

ALGERNON, *who has been carefully listening, smiles to himself, and writes the address on his shirt-cuff. Then picks up the Railway Guide.*

GWENDOLEN. There is a good postal service, I suppose? It may be necessary to do something desperate. That, of course, will require serious consideration. I will communicate with you daily.

JACK. My own one!

GWENDOLEN. How long do you remain in town?

JACK. Till Monday.

GWENDOLEN. Good! Algy, you may turn round now.

ALGERNON. Thanks, I've turned round already.

GWENDOLEN. You may also ring the bell.

JACK. You will let me see you to your carriage, my own darling?

GWENDOLEN. Certainly.

JACK (*To* LANE, *who now enters*). I will see Miss Fairfax out.

LANE. Yes, sir.

JACK *and* GWENDOLEN *go off.*

LANE *presents several letters on a salver to* ALGERNON. *It is to be surmised that they are bills, as* ALGERNON, *after looking at the envelopes, tears them up.*

ALGERNON. A glass of sherry, Lane.

LANE. Yes, sir.

ALGERNON. To-morrow, Lane, I'm going Bunburying.

LANE. Yes, sir.

ALGERNON. I shall probably not be back till Monday. You can put up my dress clothes, my smoking jacket, and all the Bunbury suits . . .

LANE. Yes, sir. (*Handing sherry.*)

ALGERNON. I hope to-morrow will be a fine day, Lane.

LANE. It never is, sir.

ALGERNON. Lane, you're a perfect pessimist.

LANE. I do my best to give satisfaction, sir.

Enter JACK. LANE *goes off.*

JACK. There's a sensible, intellectual girl! the only girl I ever cared for in my life. (ALGERNON *is laughing immoderately.*) What on earth are you so amused at?

ALGERNON. Oh, I'm a little anxious about poor Bunbury, that is all.

JACK. If you don't take care, your friend Bunbury will get you into a serious scrape some day.

ALGERNON. I love scrapes. They are the only things that are never serious.

JACK. Oh, that's nonsense, Algy. You never talk anything but nonsense.

ALGERNON. Nobody ever does.

JACK *looks indignantly at him and leaves the room.* ALGERNON *lights a cigarette, reads his shirt-cuff, and smiles.*

ACT TWO

SCENE: *Garden at the Manor House, Woolton. A flight of grey stone steps leads up to the house. The garden, an old-fashioned one, full of roses. Time of year, July. Basket chairs, and a table covered with books, are set under a large yew-tree.*

MISS PRISM *discovered seated at the table.* CECILY *is at the back watering flowers.*

MISS PRISM (*calling*). Cecily, Cecily! Surely such a utilitarian occupation as the watering of flowers is rather Moulton's duty than yours? Especially at a moment when intellectual pleasures await you. Your German grammar is on the table. Pray open it at page fifteen. We will repeat yesterday's lesson.

CECILY (*coming over very slowly*). But I don't like German. It isn't at all a becoming language. I know perfectly well that I look quite plain after my German lesson.

MISS PRISM. Child, you know how anxious your guardian is that you should improve yourself in every way. He laid particular stress on your German, as he was leaving for town yesterday. Indeed, he always lays stress on your German when he is leaving for town.

CECILY. Dear Uncle Jack is so very serious! Sometimes he is so serious that I think he cannot be quite well.

MISS PRISM (*drawing herself up*). Your guardian enjoys the best of health, and his gravity of demeanour is especially to be commended in one so comparatively young as he is. I know no one who has a higher sense of duty and responsibility.

CECILY. I suppose that is why he often looks a little bored when we three are together.

MISS PRISM. Cecily! I am surprised at you. Mr. Worthing has many troubles in his life. Idle merriment and triviality would be out of place in his conversation. You must remember his constant anxiety about that unfortunate young man his brother.

CECILY. I wish Uncle Jack would allow that unfortunate young man, his brother, to come down here sometimes. We might have a good influence over him, Miss Prism. I am sure you certainly would. You know German, and geology, and things of that kind influence a man very much.

CECILY *begins to write in her diary.*

MISS PRISM (*shaking her head*). I do not think that even I could produce any effect on a character that according to his own brother's admission is irretrievably weak and vacillating. Indeed I am not sure that I would desire to reclaim him. I am not in favour of this modern mania for turning bad people into good people at a moment's notice. As a man sows so let him reap. You must put away your diary, Cecily. I really don't see why you should keep a diary at all.

CECILY. I keep a diary in order to enter the wonderful secrets of my life. If I didn't write them down, I should probably forget all about them.

MISS PRISM. Memory, my dear Cecily, is the diary that we all carry about with us.

CECILY. Yes, but it usually chronicles the things that have never happened, and couldn't possibly have happened. I believe that Memory is responsible for nearly all the three-volume novels that Mudie sends us.

MISS PRISM. Do not speak slightingly of the three-volume novel, Cecily. I wrote one myself in earlier days.

CECILY. Did you really, Miss Prism? How wonderfully clever you are! I hope it did not end happily? I don't like novels that end happily. They depress me so much.

MISS PRISM. The good ended happily, and the bad unhappily. That is what Fiction means.

CECILY. I suppose so. But it seems very unfair. And was your novel ever published?

MISS PRISM. Alas! no. The manuscript unfortunately was abandoned. (CECILY *starts.*) I use the word in the sense of lost or mislaid. To your work, child, these speculations are profitless.

CECILY (*smiling*). But I see Dr. Chasuble coming up through the garden.

MISS PRISM (*rising and advancing*). Dr. Chasuble! This is indeed a pleasure.

Enter CANON CHASUBLE.

CHASUBLE. And how are we this morning? Miss Prism, you are, I trust, well?

CECILY. Miss Prism has just been complaining of a slight headache. I think it would do her so much good to have a short stroll with you in the Park, Dr. Chasuble.

MISS PRISM. Cecily, I have not mentioned anything about a headache.

CECILY. No, dear Miss Prism, I know that, but I felt instinctively that you had a headache. Indeed I was thinking about that, and not about my German lesson, when the Rector came in.

CHASUBLE. I hope, Cecily, you are not inattentive.

CECILY. Oh, I am afraid I am.

CHASUBLE. That is strange. Were I fortunate enough to be Miss Prism's pupil, I would hang upon her lips. (MISS PRISM *glares.*) I spoke metaphorically.—My metaphor was drawn from bees. Ahem! Mr. Worthing, I suppose, has not returned from town yet?

MISS PRISM. We do not expect him till Monday afternoon.

CHASUBLE. Ah yes, he usually likes to spend his Sunday in London. He is not one of those whose sole aim is enjoyment, as, by all accounts, that unfortunate young man his brother seems to be. But I must not disturb Egeria and her pupil any longer.

MISS PRISM. Egeria? My name is Lætitia, Doctor.

CHASUBLE (*bowing*). A classical allusion merely, drawn from the Pagan authors. I shall see you both no doubt at Evensong?

MISS PRISM. I think, dear Doctor, I will have a stroll with you. I find I have a headache after all, and a walk might do it good.

CHASUBLE. With pleasure, Miss Prism, with pleasure. We might go as far as the schools and back.

MISS PRISM. That would be delightful. Cecily, you will read your Political Economy in my absence. The chapter on the Fall of the Rupee you may omit. It is somewhat too sensational. Even these metallic problems have their melodramatic side.

Goes down the garden with DR. CHASUBLE.

CECILY (*picks up books and throws them back on table*). Horrid Political Economy! Horrid Geography! Horrid, horrid German!

Enter MERRIMAN *with a card on a salver.*

MERRIMAN. Mr. Ernest Worthing has just driven over from the station. He has brought his luggage with him.

CECILY (*takes the card and reads it*). "Mr. Ernest Worthing, B4, The Albany, W." Uncle Jack's brother! Did you tell him Mr. Worthing was in town?

MERRIMAN. Yes, Miss. He seemed very much disappointed. I mentioned that you and Miss Prism were in the garden. He said he was anxious to speak to you privately for a moment.

CECILY. Ask Mr. Ernest Worthing to come here. I suppose you had better talk to the housekeeper about a room for him.

MERRIMAN. Yes, Miss.

MERRIMAN *goes off.*

CECILY. I have never met any really wicked person before. I feel rather frightened. I am so afraid he will look just like every one else.

Enter ALGERNON, *very gay and debonair.* He does!

ALGERNON (*raising his hat*). You are my little cousin Cecily, I'm sure.

CECILY. You are under some strange mistake. I am not little. In fact, I believe I am more than usually tall for my age. (ALGERNON *is rather taken aback.*) But I am your cousin Cecily. You, I see from your card, are Uncle Jack's brother, my cousin Ernest, my wicked cousin Ernest.

ALGERNON. Oh! I am not really wicked at all, cousin Cecily. You mustn't think that I am wicked.

CECILY. If you are not, then you have certainly been deceiving us all in a very inexcusable manner. I hope you have not been leading a double life, pretending to be wicked and being really good all the time. That would be hypocrisy.

ALGERNON (*looks at her in amazement*). Oh! Of course I have been rather reckless.

CECILY. I am glad to hear it.

ALGERNON. In fact, now you mention the subject, I have been very bad in my own small way.

CECILY. I don't think you should be so proud of that, though I am sure it must have been very pleasant.

ALGERNON. It is much pleasanter being here with you.

CECILY. I can't understand how you are here at all. Uncle Jack won't be back till Monday afternoon.

ALGERNON. That is a great disappointment. I am obliged to go up by the first train on Monday morning. I have a business appointment that I am anxious . . . to miss!

CECILY. Couldn't you miss it anywhere but in London?

ALGERNON. No: the appointment is in London.

CECILY. Well, I know, of course, how important it is not to keep a business engagement, if one wants to retain any sense of the beauty of life, but still I think you had better wait till Uncle Jack arrives. I know he wants to speak to you about your emigrating.

ALGERNON. About my what?

CECILY. Your emigrating. He has gone up to buy your outfit.

ALGERNON. I certainly wouldn't let Jack buy my outfit. He has no taste in neckties at all.

CECILY. I don't think you will require neckties. Uncle Jack is sending you to Australia.

ALGERNON. Australia! I'd sooner die.

CECILY. Well, he said at dinner on Wednesday night, that you would have to choose between this world, the next world, and Australia.

ALGERNON. Oh, well! The accounts I have received of Australia and the next world are not particularly encouraging. This world is good enough for me, cousin Cecily.

CECILY. Yes, but are you good enough for it?

ALGERNON. I'm afraid I'm not that. That is why I want you to reform me. You might make that your mission, if you don't mind, cousin Cecily.

CECILY. I'm afraid I've no time, this afternoon.

ALGERNON. Well, would you mind my reforming myself this afternoon?

CECILY. It is rather Quixotic of you. But I think you should try.

ALGERNON. I will. I feel better already.

CECILY. You are looking a little worse.

ALGERNON. That is because I am hungry.

CECILY. How thoughtless of me. I should have remembered that when one is going to lead an entirely new life, one requires regular and wholesome meals. Won't you come in?

ALGERNON. Thank you. Might I have a button-hole first? I never have any appetite unless I have a buttonhole first.

CECILY. A Maréchal Niel? (*Picks up scissors.*)

ALGERNON. No, I'd sooner have a pink rose.

CECILY. Why? (*Cuts a flower.*)

ALGERNON. Because you are like a pink rose, cousin Cecily.

CECILY. I don't think it can be right for you to talk to me like that. Miss Prism never says such things to me.

ALGERNON. Then Miss Prism is a short-sighted old lady. (CECILY *puts the rose in his buttonhole.*) You are the prettiest girl I ever saw.

CECILY. Miss Prism says that all good looks are a snare.

ALGERNON. They are a snare that every sensible man would like to be caught in.

CECILY. Oh, I don't think I would care to catch a sensible man. I shouldn't know what to talk to him about.

They pass into the house. MISS PRISM *and* DR. CHASUBLE *return.*

MISS PRISM. You are too much alone, dear Dr. Chasuble. You should get married. A misanthrope I can understand—a womanthrope, never!

CHASUBLE. (*with a scholar's shudder*). Believe me, I do not deserve so neologistic a phrase. The precept as well as the practice of the Primitive Church was distinctly against matrimony.

MISS PRISM (*sententiously*). That is obviously the reason why the Primitive Church has not lasted up to the present day. And you do not seem to realise, dear Doctor, that by persistently remaining single, a man converts himself into a permanent public temptation. Men should be more careful; this very celibacy leads weaker vessels astray.

CHASUBLE. But is a man not equally attractive when married?

MISS PRISM. No married man is ever attractive except to his wife.

CHASUBLE. And often, I've been told, not even to her.

MISS PRISM. That depends on the intellectual sympathies of the woman. Maturity can always be depended on. Ripeness can be trusted. Young women are green. (DR. CHASUBLE *starts.*) I spoke horticulturally. My metaphor was drawn from fruit. But where is Cecily?

CHASUBLE. Perhaps she followed us to the schools.

Enter JACK *slowly from the back of the garden. He is dressed in the deepest mourning, with crepe hatband and black gloves.*

MISS PRISM. Mr. Worthing!

CHASUBLE. Mr. Worthing?

MISS PRISM. This is indeed a surprise. We did not look for you till Monday afternoon.

JACK (*shakes* MISS PRISM'S *hand in a tragic manner*). I have returned sooner than I expected. Dr. Chasuble, I hope you are well?

CHASUBLE. Dear Mr. Worthing, I trust this garb of woe does not betoken some terrible calamity?

JACK. My brother.

MISS PRISM. More shameful debts and extravagance?

CHASUBLE. Still leading his life of pleasure?

JACK (*shaking his head*). Dead!

CHASUBLE. Your brother Ernest dead?

JACK. Quite dead.

MISS PRISM. What a lesson for him! I trust he will profit by it.

CHASUBLE. Mr. Worthing, I offer you my sincere condolence. You have at least the consolation of knowing that you were always the most generous and forgiving of brothers.

JACK. Poor Ernest! He had many faults, but it is a sad, sad blow.

CHASUBLE. Very sad indeed. Were you with him at the end?

JACK. No. He died abroad; in Paris, in fact. I had a telegram last night from the manager of the Grand Hotel.

CHASUBLE. Was the cause of death mentioned?

JACK. A severe chill, it seems.

MISS PRISM. As a man sows, so shall he reap.

CHASUBLE (*raising his hand*). Charity, dear Miss Prism, charity! None of us are perfect. I myself am peculiarly susceptible to draughts. Will the interment take place here?

JACK. No. He seems to have expressed a desire to be buried in Paris.

CHASUBLE. In Paris! (*Shakes his head.*) I fear that hardly points to any very serious state of mind at the last. You would no doubt wish me to make some slight allusion to this tragic domestic affliction next Sunday. (JACK *presses his hand convulsively.*) My sermon on the meaning of the manna in the wilderness can be adapted to almost any occasion, joyful, or, as in the present case, distressing. (*All sigh.*) I have preached it at harvest celebrations, christenings, confirmations, on days of humiliation and festal days. The last time I delivered it was in the Cathedral, as a charity sermon on behalf of the Society for the Prevention of Discontent among the Upper Orders. The Bishop, who was present, was much struck by some of the analogies I drew.

JACK. Ah! that reminds me, you mentioned christenings, I think, Dr. Chasuble? I suppose you know how to christen all right? (DR. CHASUBLE *looks astounded.*) I mean, of course, you are continually christening, aren't you?

MISS PRISM. It is, I regret to say, one of the Rector's most constant duties in this parish. I have often spoken to the poorer classes on the subject. But they don't seem to know what thrift is.

CHASUBLE. But is there any particular infant in whom you are interested, Mr. Worthing? Your brother was, I believe, unmarried, was he not?

JACK. Oh yes.

MISS PRISM (*bitterly*). People who live entirely for pleasure usually are.

JACK. But it is not for any child, dear Doctor. I am very fond of children. No! the fact is, I would like to be christened myself, this afternoon, if you have nothing better to do.

CHASUBLE. But surely, Mr. Worthing, you have been christened already?

JACK. I don't remember anything about it.

CHASUBLE. But have you any grave doubts on the subject?

JACK. I certainly intend to have. Of course I don't know if the thing would bother you in any way, or if you think I am a little too old now.

CHASUBLE. Not at all. The sprinkling, and, indeed, the immersion of adults is a perfectly canonical practice.

JACK. Immersion!

CHASUBLE. You need have no apprehensions. Sprinkling is all that is necessary, or indeed I think advisable. Our weather is so changeable. At what hour would you wish the ceremony performed?

JACK. Oh, I might trot round about five if that would suit you.

CHASUBLE. Perfectly, perfectly! In fact, I have two similar ceremonies to perform at that time. A case of twins that occurred recently in one of the outlying cottages on your own estate. Poor Jenkins the carter, a most hard-working man.

JACK. Oh! I don't see much fun in being christened along with other babies. It would be childish. Would half-past five do?

CHASUBLE. Admirably! Admirably! (*Takes out watch.*) And now, dear Mr. Worthing, I will not intrude any longer into a house of sorrow. I would merely beg you not to be too much bowed down by grief. What seem to us bitter trials are often blessings in disguise.

MISS PRISM. This seems to me a blessing of an extremely obvious kind.

Enter CECILY *from the house.*

CECILY. Uncle Jack! Oh, I am pleased to see you back. But what horrid clothes you have got on! Do go and change them.

MISS PRISM. Cecily!

CHASUBLE. My child! my child!

CECILY *goes towards* JACK; *he kisses her brow in a melancholy manner.*

CECILY. What is the matter, Uncle Jack? Do look happy! You look as if you had toothache, and I have got such a surprise for you. Who do you think is in the dining-room? Your brother!

JACK. Who?

CECILY. Your brother Ernest. He arrived about half an hour ago.

JACK. What nonsense! I haven't got a brother.

CECILY. Oh, don't say that. However badly he may have behaved to you in the past he is still your brother. You couldn't be so heartless as to disown him. I'll tell him to come out. And you will shake hands with him, won't you, Uncle Jack? (*Runs back into the house.*)

CHASUBLE. These are very joyful tidings.

MISS PRISM. After we had all been resigned to his loss, his sudden return seems to me peculiarly distressing.

JACK. My brother is in the dining-room? I don't know what it all means. I think it is perfectly absurd.

Enter ALGERNON *and* CECILY *hand in hand. They come slowly up to* JACK.

JACK. Good heavens! (*Motions* ALGERNON *away.*)

ALGERNON. Brother John, I have come down from town to tell you that I am very sorry for all the trouble I have given you, and that I intend to lead a better life in the future. (JACK *glares at him and does not take his hand.*)

CECILY. Uncle Jack, you are not going to refuse your own brother's hand?

JACK. Nothing will induce me to take his hand. I think his coming down here disgraceful. He knows perfectly well why.

CECILY. Uncle Jack, do be nice. There is some good in every one. Ernest has just been telling me about his poor invalid friend Mr. Bunbury whom he goes to visit so often. And surely there must be much good in one who is kind to an invalid, and leaves the pleasures of London to sit by a bed of pain.

JACK. Oh! he has been talking about Bunbury, has he?

CECILY. Yes, he has told me all about poor Mr. Bunbury, and his terrible state of health.

JACK. Bunbury! Well, I won't have him talk to you about Bunbury or about anything else. It is enough to drive one perfectly frantic.

ALGERNON. Of course I admit that the faults were all on my side. But I must say that I think that Brother John's coldness to me is peculiarly painful. I expected a more enthusiastic welcome, especially considering it is the first time I have come here.

CECILY. Uncle Jack, if you don't shake hands with Ernest I will never forgive you.

JACK. Never forgive me?

CECILY. Never, never, never!

JACK. Well, this is the last time I shall ever do it. (*Shakes hands with* ALGERNON *and glares.*)

CHASUBLE. It's pleasant, is it not, to see so perfect a reconciliation? I think we might leave the two brothers together.

MISS PRISM. Cecily, you will come with us.

CECILY. Certainly, Miss Prism. My little task of reconciliation is over.

CHASUBLE. You have done a beautiful action to-day, dear child.

MISS PRISM. We must not be premature in our judgments.

CECILY. I feel very happy.

They all go off except JACK *and* ALGERNON.

JACK. You young scoundrel, Algy, you must get out of this place as soon as possible. I don't allow any Bunburying here.

Enter MERRIMAN.

MERRIMAN. I have put Mr. Ernest's things in the room next to yours, sir. I suppose that is all right?

JACK. What?

MERRIMAN. Mr. Ernest's luggage, sir. I have unpacked it and put it in the room next to your own.

JACK. His luggage?

MERRIMAN. Yes, sir, Three portmanteaus, a dressing case, two hat-boxes, and a large luncheon-basket.

ALGERNON. I am afraid I can't stay more than a week this time.

JACK. Merriman, order the dog-cart at once. Mr. Ernest has been suddenly called back to town.

MERRIMAN. Yes, sir. (*Goes back into the house.*)

ALGERNON. What a fearful liar you are, Jack. I have not been called back to town at all.

JACK. Yes, you have.

ALGERNON. I haven't heard any one call me.

JACK. Your duty as a gentleman calls you back.

ALGERNON. My duty as a gentleman has never interfered with my pleasures in the smallest degree.

JACK. I can quite understand that.

ALGERNON. Well, Cecily is a darling.

JACK. You are not to talk of Miss Cardew like that. I don't like it.

ALGERNON. Well, I don't like your clothes. You look perfectly ridiculous in them. Why on earth don't you go up and change? It is perfectly childish to be in deep mourning for a man who is actually staying for a whole week with you in your house as a guest. I call it grotesque.

JACK. You are certainly not staying with me for a whole week as a guest or anything else. You have got to leave . . . by the four-five train.

ALGERNON. I certainly won't leave you so long as you are in mourning. It would be most unfriendly. If I were in mourning you would stay with me, I suppose. I should think it very unkind if you didn't.

JACK. Well, will you go if I change my clothes?

ALGERNON. Yes, if you are not too long. I never saw anybody take so long to dress, and with such little result.

JACK. Well, at any rate, that is better than being always over-dressed as you are.

ALGERNON. If I am occasionally a little over-dressed, I make up for it by being always immensely over-educated.

JACK. Your vanity is ridiculous, your conduct an outrage, and your presence in my garden utterly absurd. However, you have got to catch the four-five, and I hope you will have a pleasant journey back to town. This Bunburying, as you call it, has not been a great success for you. (*Goes into the house.*)

ALGERNON. I think it has been a great success. I'm in love with Cecily, and that is everything.

Enter CECILY *at the back of the garden. She picks picks up the can and begins to water the flowers.*

But I must see her before I go, and make arrangements for another Bunbury. Ah, there she is.

CECILY. Oh, I merely came back to water the roses. I thought you were with Uncle Jack.

ALGERNON. He's gone to order the dog-cart for me.

CECILY. Oh, is he going to take you for a nice drive?

ALGERNON. He's going to send me away.

CECILY. Then have we got to part?

ALGERNON. I am afraid so. It is very painful parting.

CECILY. It is always painful to part from people whom one has known for a very brief space of time. The absence of old friends one can endure with equanimity. But even a momentary separation from any one to whom one has just been introduced is almost unbearable.

ALGERNON. Thank you.

Enter MERRIMAN.

MERRIMAN. The dog-cart is at the door, sir.

ALGERNON *looks appealing at* CECILY.

CECILY. It can wait, Merriman, for five minutes.

MERRIMAN. Yes, Miss.

Exit MERRIMAN.

ALGERNON. I hope, Cecily, I shall not offend you if I state quite frankly and openly that you seem to me to be in every way the visible personification of absolute perfection.

CECILY. I think your frankness does you great credit, Ernest. If you will allow me, I will copy your remarks into my diary. (*Goes over to table and begins writing in diary.*)

ALGERNON. Do you really keep a diary? I'd give anything to look at it. May I?

CECILY. Oh, no. (*Puts her hand over it.*) You see, it is simply a very young girl's record of her own thoughts and impressions, and consequently meant for publication. When it appears in volume form I hope you will order a copy. But pray, Ernest, don't stop. I delight in taking down from dictation. I have reached "absolute perfection." You can go on. I am quite ready for more.

ALGERNON (*somewhat taken aback*). Ahem! Ahem!

CECILY. Oh, don't cough, Ernest. When one is dictating one should speak fluently and not cough. Besides, I don't know how to spell a cough. (*Writes as* ALGERNON *speaks.*)

ALGERNON (*speaking very rapidly*). Cecily, ever since I first looked upon your wonderful and incomparable beauty, I have dared to love you wildly, passionately, devotedly, hopelessly.

CECILY. I don't think that you should tell me that you love me wildly, passionately, devotedly, hopelessly. Hopelessly doesn't seem to make much sense, does it?

ALGERNON. Cecily!

Enter MERRIMAN.

MERRIMAN. The dog-cart is waiting, sir.

ALGERNON. Tell it to come round next week, at the same hour.

MERRIMAN (*looks at* CECILY, *who makes no sign*). Yes, sir.

MERRIMAN *retires.*

CECILY. Uncle Jack would be very much annoyed if he knew you were staying on till next week, at the same hour.

ALGERNON. Oh, I don't care about Jack. I don't care for anybody in the whole world but you. I love you, Cecily. You will marry me, won't you?

CECILY. You silly boy! Of course. Why, we have been engaged for the last three months.

ALGERNON. For the last three months?

CECILY. Yes, it will be exactly three months on Thursday.

ALGERNON. But how did we become engaged?

CECILY. Well, ever since dear Uncle Jack first confessed to us that he had a younger brother who was very wicked and bad, you, of course, have formed the chief topic of conversation between myself and Miss Prism. And, of course, a man who is much talked about is always very attractive. One feels there must be something in him, after all. I dare say it was foolish of me, but I fell in love with you, Ernest.

ALGERNON. Darling. And when was the engagement actually settled?

CECILY. On the 14th of February last. Worn out by your entire ignorance of my existence, I determined to end the matter one way or the other, and after a long struggle with myself I accepted you under this dear old tree here. The next day I bought this little ring in your name, and this is the little bangle with the true lover's knot I promised you always to wear.

ALGERNON. Did I give you this? It's very pretty, isn't it?

CECILY. Yes, you've wonderfully good taste, Ernest. It's the excuse I've always given for your leading such a bad life. And this is the box in which I keep all your dear letters. (*Kneels at table, opens box, and produces letters tied up with blue ribbon.*)

ALGERNON. My letters! But, my own sweet Cecily, I have never written you any letters.

CECILY. You need hardly remind me of that, Ernest. I remember only too well that I was forced to write your letters for you. I wrote always three time a week, and sometimes oftener.

ALGERNON. Oh, do let me read them, Cecily?

CECILY. Oh, I couldn't possibly. They would make you far too conceited. (*Replaces box.*) The three you wrote me after I had broken off the engagement are so beautiful, and so badly spelled, that even now I can hardly read them without crying a little.

ALGERNON. But was our engagement ever broken off?

CECILY. Of course it was. On the 22nd of last March. You can see the entry if you like. (*Shows diary.*) "To-day I broke off my engagement with Ernest. I feel it is better to do so. The weather still continues charming."

ALGERNON. But why on earth did you break it off? What had I done? I had done nothing at all. Cecily, I am very much hurt indeed to hear you broke it off. Particularly when the weather was so charming.

CECILY. It would hardly have been a really serious engagement if it hadn't been broken off at least once. But I forgave you before the week was out.

ALGERNON (*crossing to her, and kneeling*). What a perfect angel you are, Cecily.

CECILY. You dear romantic boy. (*He kisses her, she puts her fingers through his hair.*) I hope your hair curls naturally, does it?

ALGERNON. Yes, darling, with a little help from others.

CECILY. I am so glad.

ALGERNON. You'll never break off our engagement again, Cecily?

CECILY. I don't think I could break it off now that I have actually met you. Besides, of course, there is the question of your name.

ALGERNON. Yes, of course. (*Nervously.*)

CECILY. You must not laugh at me, darling, but it had always been a girlish dream of mine to love some one whose name was Ernest.

ALGERNON *rises,* CECILY *also.*

There is something in that name that seems to inspire absolute confidence. I pity any poor married woman whose husband is not called Ernest.

ALGERNON. But, my dear child, do you mean to say you could not love me if I had some other name?

CECILY. But what name?

ALGERNON. Oh, any name you like—Algernon —for instance . . .

CECILY. But I don't like the name of Algernon.

ALGERNON. Well, my own dear, sweet, loving little darling, I really can't see why you should object to the name of Algernon. It is not at all a bad name. In fact, it is rather an aristocratic name. Half of the chaps who get into the Bankruptcy Court are called Algernon. But seriously, Cecily—(*moving to her*)—if my name was Algy, couldn't you love me?

CECILY (*rising*). I might respect you, Ernest, I might admire your character, but I fear that I should not be able to give you my undivided attention.

ALGERNON. Ahem! Cecily! (*Picking up hat.*) Your Rector here is, I suppose, thoroughly experienced in the practice of all the rites and ceremonials of the Church?

CECILY. Oh, yes. Dr. Chasuble is a most learned man. He has never written a single book, so you can imagine how much he knows.

ALGERNON. I must see him at once on a most important christening—I mean on most important business.

CECILY. Oh!

ALGERNON. I shan't be away more than half an hour.

CECILY. Considering that we have been engaged since February the 14th, and that I only met you to-day for the first time, I think it is rather hard that you should leave me for so long a period as half an hour. Couldn't you make it twenty minutes?

ALGERNON. I'll be back in no time. (*Kisses her and rushes down the garden.*)

CECILY. What an impetuous boy he is! I like his hair so much. I must enter his proposal in my diary.

Enter MERRIMAN.

MERRIMAN. A Miss Fairfax has just called to see Mr. Worthing. On very important business, Miss Fairfax states.

CECILY. Isn't Mr. Worthing in his library?

MERRIMAN. Mr. Worthing went over in the direction of the Rectory some time ago.

CECILY. Pray ask the lady to come out here; Mr. Worthing is sure to be back soon. And you can bring tea.

MERRIMAN. Yes, Miss. (*Goes out.*)

CECILY. Miss Fairfax! I suppose one of the many good elderly women who are associated with Uncle Jack in some of his philanthropic work in London. I don't quite like women who are interested in philanthropic work. I think it is so forward of them.

Enter MERRIMAN.

MERRIMAN. Miss Fairfax.

Enter GWENDOLEN. *Exit* MERRIMAN

CECILY (*advancing to meet her*). Pray let me introduce myself to you. My name is Cecily Cardew.

GWENDOLEN. Cecily Cardew? (*Moving to her and shaking hands.*) What a very sweet name! Something tells me that we are going to be great friends. I like you already more than I can say. My first impressions of people are never wrong.

CECILY. How nice of you to like me so much after we have known each other such a comparatively short time. Pray sit down.

GWENDOLEN (*still standing up*). I may call you Cecily, may I not?

CECILY. With pleasure!

GWENDOLEN. And you will always call me Gwendolen, won't you?

CECILY. If you wish.

GWENDOLEN. Then that is all quite settled, is it not?

CECILY. I hope so.

A pause. They both sit down together.

GWENDOLEN. Perhaps this might be a favourable opportunity for my mentioning who I am. My father is Lord Bracknell. You have never heard of papa, I suppose?

CECILY. I don't think so.

GWENDOLEN. Outside the family circle, papa, I am glad to say, is entirely unknown. I think that is quite as it should be. The home seems to me to be the proper sphere for the man. And certainly once a man begins to neglect his domestic duties he becomes painfully effeminate, does he not? And I don't like that. It makes men so very attractive. Cecily, mamma, whose views on education are remarkably strict, has brought me up to be extremely short-sighted; it is part of her system; so do you mind my looking at you through my glasses?

CECILY. Oh! not at all, Gwendolen. I am very fond of being looked at.

GWENDOLEN (*after examining* CECILY *carefully through a lorgnette*). You are here on a short visit, I suppose.

CECILY. Oh no! I live here.

GWENDOLEN (*severely*). Really? Your mother, no doubt, or some female relative of advanced years, resides here also?

CECILY. Oh no! I have no mother, nor, in fact, any relations.

GWENDOLEN. Indeed?

CECILY. My dear guardian, with the assistance of Miss Prism, has the arduous task of looking after me.

GWENDOLEN. Your guardian?

CECILY. Yes, I am Mr. Worthing's ward.

GWENDOLEN. Oh! It is strange he never mentioned to me that he had a ward. How secretive of him! He grows more interesting hourly. I am not sure, however, that the news inspires me with feelings of unmixed delight. (*Rising and going to her.*) I am very fond of you, Cecily; I have liked you ever since I met you! But I am bound to state that now that I know that you are Mr. Worthing's ward, I cannot help expressing a wish you were—well, just a little older than you seem to be—and not quite so very alluring in appearance. In fact, if I may speak candidly—

CECILY. Pray do! I think that whenever one has anything unpleasant to say, one should always be quite candid.

GWENDOLEN. Well, to speak with perfect candour, Cecily, I wish that you were fully forty-two, and more than unusually plain for your age. Ernest has a strong upright nature. He is the very soul of truth and honour. Disloyalty would be as impossible to him as deception. But even men of the noblest possible moral character are extremely susceptible to the influence of the physical charms of others. Modern, no less than Ancient History, supplies us with many most painful examples of what I refer to. If it were not so, indeed, History would be quite unreadable.

CECILY. I beg your pardon, Gwendolen, did you say Ernest?

GWENDOLEN. Yes.

CECILY. Oh, but it is not Mr. Ernest Worthing who is my guardian. It is his brother—his elder brother.

GWENDOLEN (*sitting down again*). Ernest never mentioned to me that he had a brother.

CECILY. I am sorry to say they have not been on good terms for a long time.

GWENDOLEN. Ah! that accounts for it. And now that I think of it I have never heard any man mention his brother. The subject seems distasteful to most men. Cecily, you have lifted a load from my mind. I was growing almost anxious. It would have been terrible if any cloud had come across a friendship like ours, would it not? Of course you are quite, quite sure that it is not Mr. Ernest Worthing who is your guardian?

CECILY. Quite sure. (*A pause.*) In fact, I am going to be his.

GWENDOLEN (*inquiringly*). I beg your pardon?

CECILY (*rather shy and confidingly*). Dearest Gwendolen, there is no reason why I should make a secret of it to you. Our little county newspaper is sure to chronicle the fact next week. Mr. Ernest Worthing and I are engaged to be married.

GWENDOLEN (*quite politely, rising*). My darling Cecily, I think there must be some slight error. Mr. Ernest Worthing is engaged to me. The announcement will appear in the *Morning Post* on Saturday at the latest.

CECILY (*very politely, rising*). I am afraid you must be under some misconception. Ernest proposed to me exactly ten minutes ago. (*Shows diary.*)

GWENDOLEN (*examines diary through her lorgnette carefully*). It is certainly very curious, for he asked me to be his wife yesterday afternoon at 5.30. If you would care to verify the incident, pray do so. (*Produces diary of her own.*) I never travel without my diary. One should always have something sensational to read in the train. I am so sorry, dear Cecily, if it is any disappointment to you, but I am afraid I have the prior claim.

CECILY. It would distress me more than I can tell you, dear Gwendolen, if it caused you any mental or physical anguish, but I feel bound to point out that since Ernest proposed to you he clearly has changed his mind.

GWENDOLEN (*meditatively*). If the poor fellow has been entrapped into any foolish promise I shall consider it my duty to rescue him at once, and with a firm hand.

CECILY (*thoughtfully and sadly*). Whatever unfortunate entanglement my dear boy may have got into, I will never reproach him with it after we are married.

GWENDOLEN. Do you allude to me, Miss Cardew, as an entanglement? You are presumptuous. On an occasion of this kind it becomes more than a moral duty to speak one's mind. It becomes a pleasure.

CECILY. Do you suggest, Miss Fairfax, that I entrapped Ernest into an engagement? How dare you? This is no time for wearing the shallow mask of manners. When I see a spade I call it a spade.

GWENDOLEN (*satirically*). I am glad to say that I have never seen a spade. It is obvious that our social spheres have been widely different.

Enter MERRIMAN, *followed by the footman. He*

carries a salver, table cloth, and plate stand. CECILY *is about to retort. The presence of the servants exercises a restraining influence, under which both girls chafe.*

MERRIMAN. Shall I lay tea here as usual, Miss?

CECILY (*sternly, in a calm voice*). Yes, as usual.

MERRIMAN *begins to clear table and lay cloth. A long pause.* CECILY *and* GWENDOLEN *glare at each other.*

GWENDOLEN. Are there many interesting walks in the vicinity, Miss Cardew?

CECILY. Oh! yes! a great many. From the top of one of the hills quite close one can see five counties.

GWENDOLEN. Five counties! I don't think I should like that; I hate crowds.

CECILY (*sweetly*). I suppose that is why you live in town?

GWENDOLEN *bites her lip, and beats her foot nervously with her parasol.*

GWENDOLEN (*looking round*). Quite a well-kept garden this is, Miss Cardew.

CECILY. So glad you like it, Miss Fairfax.

GWENDOLEN. I had no idea there were any flowers in the country.

CECILY. Oh, flowers are as common here, Miss Fairfax, as people are in London.

GWENDOLEN. Personally I cannot understand how anybody manages to exist in the country, if anybody who is anybody does. The country always bores me to death.

CECILY. Ah! This is what the newspapers call agricultural depression, is it not? I believe the aristocracy are suffering very much from it just at present. It is almost an epidemic amongst them, I have been told. May I offer you some tea, Miss Fairfax?

GWENDOLEN (*with elaborate politeness*). Thank you. (*Aside.*) Detestable girl! But I require tea!

CECILY (*sweetly*). Sugar?

GWENDOLEN (*superciliously*). No, thank you. Sugar is not fashionable any more.

CECILY *looks angrily at her, takes up the tongs and puts four lumps of sugar into the cup.*

CECILY (*severely*). Cake or bread and butter?

GWENDOLEN (*in a bored manner*). Bread and butter, please. Cake is rarely seen at the best houses nowadays.

CECILY (*cuts a very large slice of cake and puts it on the tray*). Hand that to Miss Fairfax.

MERRIMAN *does so, and goes out with footman.* GWENDOLEN *drinks the tea and makes a grimace. Puts down cup at once, reaches out her hand to the bread and butter, looks at it, and finds it is cake. Rises in indignation.*

GWENDOLEN. You have filled my tea with lumps of sugar, and though I asked most distinctly for bread and butter, you have given me cake. I am known for the gentleness of my disposition, and the extraordinary sweetness of my nature, but I warn you, Miss Cardew, you may go too far.

CECILY (*rising*). To save my poor, innocent, trusting boy from the machinations of any other girl there are no lengths to which I would not go.

GWENDOLEN. From the moment I saw you I distrusted you. I felt that you were false and deceitful. I am never deceived in such matters. My first impressions of people are invariably right.

CECILY. It seems to me, Miss Fairfax, that I am trespassing on your valuable time. No doubt you have many other calls of a similar character to make in the neighbourhood.

Enter JACK.

GWENDOLEN (*catching sight of him*). Ernest! My own Ernest!

JACK. Gwendolen! Darling! (*Offers to kiss her.*)

GWENDOLEN (*drawing back*). A moment! May I ask if you are engaged to be married to this young lady? (*Points to* CECILY.)

JACK (*laughing*). To dear little Cecily! Of course not! What could have put such an idea into your pretty little head?

GWENDOLEN. Thank you. You may! (*Offers her cheek.*)

CECILY (*very sweetly*). I knew there must be some misunderstanding, Miss Fairfax. The gentleman whose arm is at present round your waist is my guardian, Mr. John Worthing.

GWENDOLEN. I beg your pardon?

CECILY. This is Uncle Jack.

GWENDOLEN (*receding*). Jack! Oh!

Enter ALGERNON.

CECILY. Here is Ernest.

ALGERNON (*goes straight over to* CECILY *without noticing any one else*). My own love! (*Offers to kiss her.*)

CECILY (*drawing back*). A moment, Ernest!

May I ask you—are you engaged to be married to this young lady?

ALGERNON (*looking round*). To what young lady? Good heavens! Gwendolen!

CECILY. Yes! to good heavens, Gwendolen, I mean to Gwendolen.

ALGERNON (*laughing*). Of course not! What could have put such an idea into your pretty little head?

CECILY. Thank you. (*Presenting her cheek to be kissed.*) You may. (ALGERNON *kisses her.*)

GWENDOLEN. I felt there was some slight error, Miss Cardew. The gentleman who is now embracing you is my cousin, Mr. Algernon Moncrieff.

CECILY (*breaking away from* ALGERNON). Algernon Moncrieff! Oh!

The two girls move towards each other and put their arms round each other's waists as if for protection.

CECILY. Are you called Algernon?

ALGERNON. I cannot deny it.

CECILY. Oh!

GWENDOLEN. Is your name really John?

JACK (*standing rather proudly*). I could deny it if I liked. I could deny anything if I liked. But my name certainly is John. It has been John for years.

CECILY (*to* GWENDOLEN). A gross deception has been practised on both of us.

GWENDOLEN. My poor wounded Cecily!

CECILY. My sweet wronged Gwendolen!

GWENDOLEN (*slowly and seriously*). You will call me sister, will you not?

They embrace. JACK *and* ALGERNON *groan and walk up and down.*

CECILY (*rather brightly*). There is just one question I would like to be allowed to ask my guardian.

GWENDOLEN. An admirable idea! Mr. Worthing, there is just one question I would like to be permitted to put to you. Where is your brother Ernest? We are both engaged to be married to your brother Ernest, so it is a matter of some importance to us to know where your brother Ernest is at present.

JACK (*slowly and hesitatingly*). Gwendolen—Cecily—it is very painful for me to be forced to speak the truth. It is the first time in my life that I have ever been reduced to such a painful position, and I am really quite inexperienced in

doing anything of the kind. However, I will tell you quite frankly that I have no brother Ernest. I have no brother at all. I never had a brother in my life, and I certainly have not the smallest intention of ever having one in the future.

CECILY (*surprised*). No brother at all?

JACK (*cheerily*). None!

GWENDOLEN (*severely*). Had you never a brother of any kind?

JACK (*pleasantly*). Never. Not even of any kind.

GWENDOLEN. I am afraid it is quite clear, Cecily, that neither of us is engaged to be married to any one.

CECILY. It is not a very pleasant position for a young girl suddenly to find herself in. Is it?

GWENDOLEN. Let us go into the house. They will hardly venture to come after us there.

CECILY. No, men are so cowardly, aren't they?

They retire into the house with scornful looks.

JACK. This ghastly state of things is what you call Bunburying, I suppose?

ALGERNON. Yes, and a perfectly wonderful Bunbury it is. The most wonderful Bunbury I have ever had in my life.

JACK. Well, you've no right whatsoever to Bunbury here.

ALGERNON. That is absurd. One has a right to Bunbury anywhere one chooses. Every serious Bunburyist knows that.

JACK. Serious Bunburyist! Good heavens!

ALGERNON. Well, one must be serious about something, if one wants to have any amusement in life. I happen to be serious about Bunburying. What on earth you are serious about I haven't got the remotest idea. About everything, I should fancy. You have such an absolutely trivial nature.

JACK. Well, the only small satisfaction I have in the whole of this wretched business is that your friend Bunbury is quite exploded. You won't be able to run down to the country quite so often as you used to do, dear Algy. And a very good thing too.

ALGERNON. Your brother is a little off colour, isn't he, dear Jack? You won't be able to disappear to London quite so frequently as your wicked custom was. And not a bad thing either.

JACK. As for your conduct towards Miss Cardew, I must say that your taking in a sweet, simple, innocent girl like that is quite inexcusable. To say nothing of the fact that she is my ward.

ALGERNON. I can see no possible defence at all for your deceiving a brilliant, clever, thoroughly experienced young lady like Miss Fairfax. To say nothing of the fact that she is my cousin.

JACK. I wanted to be engaged to Gwendolen, that is all. I love her.

ALGERNON. Well, I simply wanted to be engaged to Cecily. I adore her.

JACK. There is certainly no chance of your marrying Miss Cardew.

ALGERNON. I don't think there is much likelihood, Jack, of you and Miss Fairfax being united.

JACK. Well, that is no business of yours.

ALGERNON. If it was my business, I wouldn't talk about it. (Begins to eat muffins.) It is very vulgar to talk about one's business. Only people like stockbrokers do that, and then merely at dinner parties.

JACK. How can you sit there, calmly eating muffins when we are in this horrible trouble, I can't make out. You seem to me to be perfectly heartless.

ALGERNON. Well, I can't eat muffins in an agitated manner. The butter would probably get on my cuffs. One should always eat muffins quite calmly. It is the only way to eat them.

JACK. I say it's perfectly heartless your eating muffins at all, under the circumstances.

ALGERNON. When I am in trouble, eating is the only thing that consoles me. Indeed, when I am in really great trouble, as any one who knows me intimately will tell you, I refuse everything except food and drink. At the present moment I am eating muffins because I am unhappy. Besides, I am particularly fond of muffins. (Rising.)

JACK (rising). Well, that is no reason why you should eat them all in that greedy way. (Takes muffins from ALGERNON.)

ALGERNON (offering tea-cake). I wish you would have tea-cake instead. I don't like tea-cake.

JACK. Good heavens! I suppose a man may eat his own muffins in his own garden.

ALGERNON. But you have just said it was perfectly heartless to eat muffins.

JACK. I said it was perfectly heartless of you, under the circumstances. That is a very different thing.

ALGERNON. That may be. But the muffins are the same. (He seizes the muffin-dish from JACK.)

JACK. Algy, I wish to goodness you would go.

ALGERNON. You can't possibly ask me to go without having some dinner. It's absurd. I never go without my dinner. No one ever does, except vegetarians and people like that. Besides, I have just made arrangements with Dr. Chasuble to be christened at a quarter to six under the name of Ernest.

JACK. My dear fellow, the sooner you give up that nonsense the better. I made arrangements this morning with Dr. Chasuble to be christened myself at 5.30, and naturally will take the name of Ernest. Gwendolen would wish it. We can't both be christened Ernest. It's absurd. Besides, I have a perfect right to be christened if I like. There is no evidence at all that I have ever been christened by anybody. I should think it extremely probable I never was, and so does Dr. Chasuble. It is entirely different in your case. You have been christened already.

ALGERNON. Yes, but I have not been christened for years.

JACK. Yes, but you have been christened. That is the important thing.

ALGERNON. Quite so. So I know my constitution can stand it. If you are not quite sure about your ever having been christened, I must say I think it rather dangerous your venturing on it now. It might make you very unwell. You can hardly have forgotten that some one very closely connected with you was very nearly carried off this week in Paris by a severe chill.

JACK. Yes, but you said yourself that a severe chill was not hereditary.

ALGERNON. It usen't to be, I know—but I dare say it is now. Science is always making wonderful improvements in things.

JACK (picking up the muffin-dish). Oh, that is nonsense; you are always talking nonsense.

ALGERNON. Jack, you are at the muffins again! I wish you wouldn't. There are only two left (Takes them.) I told you I was particularly fond of muffins.

JACK. But I hate tea-cake.

ALGERNON. Why on earth then do you allow tea-cake to be served up for your guests? What ideas you have of hospitality!

JACK. Algernon! I have already told you to go. I don't want you here. Why don't you go!

ALGERNON. I haven't quite finished my tea yet! and there is still one muffin left.

JACK *groans, and sinks into a chair.* ALGERNON *still continues eating.*

ACT THREE

SCENE: *Drawing-room at the Manor House, Woolton.* GWENDOLEN *and* CECILY *are at the window, looking out into the garden.*

GWENDOLEN. The fact that they did not follow us at once into the house, as any one else would have done, seems to me to show that they have some sense of shame left.

CECILY. They have been eating muffins. That looks like repentance.

GWENDOLEN (*after a pause*). They don't seem to notice us at all. Couldn't you cough?

CECILY. But I haven't got a cough.

GWENDOLEN. They're looking at us. What effrontery!

CECILY. They're approaching. That's very forward of them.

GWENDOLEN. Let us preserve a dignified silence.

CECILY. Certainly. It's the only thing to do now.

Enter JACK *followed by* ALGERNON. *They whistle some dreadful popular air from a British Opera.*

GWENDOLEN. This dignified silence seems to produce an unpleasant effect.

CECILY. A most distasteful one.

GWENDOLEN. But we will not be the first to speak.

CECILY. Certainly not.

GWENDOLEN. Mr. Worthing, I have something very particular to ask you. Much depends on your reply.

CECILY. Gwendolen, your common sense is invaluable. Mr. Moncrieff, kindly answer me the following question. Why did you pretend to be my guardian's brother?

ALGERNON. In order that I might have an opportunity of meeting you.

CECILY (*to* GWENDOLEN). That certainly seems a satisfactory explanation, does it not?

GWENDOLEN. Yes, dear, if you can believe him.

CECILY. I don't. But that does not affect the wonderful beauty of his answer.

GWENDOLEN. True. In matters of grave importance, style, not sincerity, is the vital thing.

Mr. Worthing, what explanation can you offer to me for pretending to have a brother? Was it in order that you might have an opportunity of coming up to town to see me as often as possible?

JACK. Can you doubt it, Miss Fairfax?

GWENDOLEN. I have the greatest doubts upon the subject. But I intend to crush them. This is not the moment for German scepticism. (*Moving to* CECILY.) Their explanations appear to be quite satisfactory, especially Mr. Worthing's. That seems to me to have the stamp of truth upon it.

CECILY. I am more than content with what Mr. Moncrieff said. His voice alone inspires one with absolute credulity.

GWENDOLEN. Then you think we should forgive them?

CECILY. Yes. I mean no.

GWENDOLEN. True! I had forgotten. There are principles at stake that one cannot surrender. Which of us should tell them? The task is not a pleasant one.

CECILY. Could we not both speak at the same time?

GWENDOLEN. An excellent idea! I always speak at the same time as other people. Will you take the time from me?

CECILY. Certainly.

GWENDOLEN *beats time with uplifted finger.*

GWENDOLEN *and* CECILY (*speaking together*). Your Christian names are still an insuperable barrier. That is all!

JACK *and* ALGERNON (*speaking together*). Our Christian names! Is that all? But we are going to be christened this afternoon.

GWENDOLEN (*to* JACK). For my sake you are prepared to do this terrible thing?

JACK. I am.

CECILY (*to* ALGERNON). To please me you are ready to face this fearful ordeal?

ALGERNON. I am!

GWENDOLEN. How absurd to talk of the equality of the sexes! Where questions of self-sacrifice are concerned, men are infinitely beyond us.

JACK. We are. (*Clasps hands with* ALGERNON.)

CECILY. They have moments of physical courage of which we women know absolutely nothing.

GWENDOLEN (*to* JACK). Darling.

ALGERNON (*to* CECILY). Darling!

They fall into each other's arms.

Enter MERRIMAN. *When he enters he coughs loudly, seeing the situation.*

MERRIMAN. Ahem! Ahem! Lady Bracknell!

JACK. Good heavens!

Enter LADY BRACKNELL. *The couples separate in alarm. Exit* MERRIMAN.

LADY BRACKNELL. Gwendolen! What does this mean?

GWENDOLEN. Merely that I am engaged to be married to Mr. Worthing, mamma.

LADY BRACKNELL. Come here. Sit down. Sit down immediately. Hesitation of any kind is a sign of mental decay in the young, of physical weakness in the old. (*Turns to* JACK.) Apprised, sir, of my daughter's sudden flight by her trusty maid, whose confidence I purchased by means of a small coin, I followed her at once by a luggage train. Her unhappy father is, I am glad to say, under the impression that she is attending a more than usually lengthy lecture by the University Extension Scheme on the Influence of a permanent income on Thought. I do not propose to undeceive him. Indeed I have never undeceived him on any question. I would consider it wrong. But, of course, you will clearly understand that all communication between yourself and my daughter must cease immediately from this moment. On this point, as indeed on all points, I am firm.

JACK. I am engaged to be married to Gwendolen, Lady Bracknell!

LADY BRACKNELL. You are nothing of the kind, sir. And now, as regards Algernon! . . . Algernon!

ALGERNON. Yes, Aunt Augusta.

LADY BRACKNELL. May I ask if it is in this house that your invalid friend Mr. Bunbury resides?

ALGERNON (*stammering*). Oh! No! Bunbury doesn't live here. Bunbury is somewhere else at present. In fact, Bunbury is dead.

LADY BRACKNELL. Dead! When did Mr. Bunbury die? His death must have been extremely sudden.

ALGERNON (*airily*). Oh! I killed Bunbury this afternoon. I mean poor Bunbury died this afternoon.

LADY BRACKNELL. What did he die of?

ALGERNON. Bunbury? Oh, he was quite exploded.

LADY BRACKNELL. Exploded! Was he the victim of a revolutionary outrage? I was not aware that Mr. Bunbury was interested in social legislation. If so, he is well punished for his morbidity.

ALGERNON. My dear Aunt Augusta, I mean he was found out! The doctors found out that Bunbury could not live, that is what I mean—so Bunbury died.

LADY BRACKNELL. He seems to have had great confidence in the opinion of his physicians. I am glad, however, that he made up his mind at the last to some definite course of action, and acted under proper medical advice. And now that we have finally got rid of this Mr. Bunbury, may I ask, Mr. Worthing, who is that young person whose hand my nephew Algernon is now holding in what seems to me a peculiarly unnecessary manner?

JACK. That lady is Miss Cecily Cardew, my ward.

LADY BRACKNELL *bows coldly to* CECILY.

ALGERNON. I am engaged to be married to Cecily, Aunt Augusta.

LADY BRACKNELL. I beg your pardon?

CECILY. Mr. Moncrieff and I are engaged to be married, Lady Bracknell.

LADY BRACKNELL (*with a shiver, crossing to the sofa and sitting down*). I do not know whether there is anything peculiarly exciting in the air of this particular part of Hertfordshire, but the number of engagements that go on seems to me considerably above the proper average that statistics have laid down for our guidance. I think some preliminary inquiry on my part would not be out of place. Mr. Worthing, is Miss Cardew at all connected with any of the larger railway stations in London? I merely desire information. Until yesterday I had no idea that there were any families or persons whose origin was a Terminus.

JACK *looks perfectly furious, but restrains himself.*

JACK (*in a clear, cold voice*). Miss Cardew is the grand-daughter of the late Mr. Thomas Cardew of 149 Belgrave Square, S.W.; Gervase Park, Dorking, Surrey; and the Sporran, Fifeshire, N.B.

LADY BRACKNELL. That sounds not unsatisfactory. Three addresses always inspire confidence, even in tradesmen. But what proof have I of their authenticity?

JACK. I have carefully preserved the Court Guides of the period. They are open to your inspection, Lady Bracknell.

LADY BRACKNELL (*grimly*). I have known strange errors in that publication.

JACK. Miss Cardew's family solicitors are Messrs. Markby, Markby and Markby.

LADY BRACKNELL. Markby, Markby and Markby? A firm of the very highest position in their profession. Indeed I am told that one of the Mr. Markby's is occasionally to be seen at dinner parties. So far I am satisfied.

JACK (*very irritably*). How extremely kind of you, Lady Bracknell! I have also in my possession, you will be pleased to hear, certificates of Miss Cardew's birth, baptism, whooping cough, registration, vaccination, confirmation, and the measles; both the German and the English variety.

LADY BRACKNELL. Ah! A life crowded with incident, I see; though perhaps somewhat too exciting for a young girl. I am not myself in favour of premature experiences. (*Rises, looks at her watch.*) Gwendolen! the time approaches for our departure. We have not a moment to lose. As a matter of form, Mr. Worthing, I had better ask you if Miss Cardew has any little fortune?

JACK. Oh! about a hundred and thirty thousand pounds in the Funds. That is all. Good-bye, Lady Bracknell. So pleased to have seen you.

LADY BRACKNELL (*sitting down again*). A moment, Mr. Worthing. A hundred and thirty thousand pounds! And in the Funds! Miss Cardew seems to me a most attractive young lady, now that I look at her. Few girls of the present day have any really solid qualities, any of the qualities that last, and improve with time. We live, I regret to say, in an age of surfaces. (*To* CECILY): Come over here, dear. (*CECILY goes across.*) Pretty child! your dress is sadly simple, and your hair seems almost as Nature might have left it. But we can soon alter all that. A thoroughly experienced French maid produces a really marvellous result in a very brief space of time. I remember recommending one to young Lady Lancing, and after three months her own husband did not know her.

JACK. And after six months nobody knew her.

LADY BRACKNELL (*glares at* JACK *for a few moments. Then bends, with a practised smile, to* CECILY). Kindly turn round, sweet child. (*CECILY turns completely round.*) No, the side view is what I want. (*CECILY presents her profile.*) Yes, quite as I expected. There are distinct social possibilities in your profile. The two weak points in our age are its want of principle and its want of profile. The chin a little higher, dear. Style largely depends on the way the chin is worn. They are worn very high, just at present. Algernon!

ALGERNON. Yes, Aunt Augusta!

LADY BRACKNELL. There are distinct social possibilities in Miss Cardew's profile.

ALGERNON. Cecily is the sweetest, dearest, prettiest girl in the whole world. And I don't care twopence about social possibilities.

LADY BRACKNELL. Never speak disrespectfully of Society, Algernon. Only people who can't get into it do that. (*To* CECILY): Dear child, of course you know that Algernon has nothing but his debts to depend upon. But I do not approve of mercenary marriages. When I married Lord Bracknell I had no fortune of any kind. But I never dreamed for a moment of allowing that to stand in my way. Well, I suppose I must give my consent.

ALGERNON. Thank you, Aunt Augusta.

LADY BRACKNELL. Cecily, you may kiss me!

CECILY (*kisses her*). Thank you, Lady Bracknell.

LADY BRACKNELL. You may also address me as Aunt Augusta for the future.

CECILY. Thank you, Aunt Augusta.

LADY BRACKNELL. The marriage, I think, had better take place quite soon.

ALGERNON. Thank you, Aunt Augusta.

CECILY. Thank you, Aunt Augusta.

LADY BRACKNELL. To speak frankly, I am not in favour of long engagements. They give people the opportunity of finding out each other's character before marriage, which I think is never advisable.

JACK. I beg your pardon for interrupting you, Lady Bracknell, but this engagement is quite out of the question. I am Miss Cardew's guardian, and she cannot marry without my consent until she comes of age. That consent I absolutely decline to give.

LADY BRACKNELL. Upon what grounds may I ask? Algernon is an extremely, I may almost say an ostentatiously, eligible young man. He has nothing, but he looks everything. What more can one desire?

JACK. It pains me very much to have to speak frankly to you, Lady Bracknell, about your nephew, but the fact is that I do not approve at all of his moral character. I suspect him of being untruthful.

ALGERNON and CECILY *look at him in indignant amazement.*

LADY BRACKNELL. Untruthful! My nephew Algernon? Impossible! He is an Oxonian.

JACK. I fear there can be no possible doubt about the matter. This afternoon during my temporary absence in London on an important question of romance, he obtained admission to my house by means of the false pretence of being my brother. Under an assumed name he drank, I've just been informed by my butler, an entire pint bottle of my Perrier-Jouet, Brut, '89; wine I was specially reserving for myself. Continuing his disgraceful deception, he succeeded in the course of the afternoon in alienating the affections of my only ward. He subsequently stayed to tea, and devoured every single muffin. And what makes his conduct all the more heartless is, that he was perfectly well aware from the first that I have no brother, that I never had a brother, and that I don't intend to have a brother, not even of any kind. I distinctly told him so myself yesterday afternoon.

LADY BRACKNELL. Ahem! Mr. Worthing, after careful consideration I have decided entirely to overlook my nephew's conduct to you.

JACK. That is very generous of you, Lady Bracknell. My own decision, however, is unalterable. I decline to give my consent.

LADY BRACKNELL (*to* CECILY). Come here, sweet child. (CECILY *goes over.*) How old are you, dear?

CECILY. Well, I am really only eighteen, but I always admit to twenty when I go to evening parties.

LADY BRACKNELL. You are perfectly right in making some slight alteration. Indeed, no woman should ever be quite accurate about her age. It looks so calculating. . . . (*In a meditative manner.*) Eighteen, but admitting to twenty at evening parties. Well, it will not be very long before you are of age and free from the restraints of tutelage. So I don't think your guardian's consent is, after all, a matter of any importance.

JACK. Pray excuse me, Lady Bracknell, for interrupting you again, but it is only fair to tell you that according to the terms of her grandfather's will Miss Cardew does not come legally of age till she is thirty-five.

LADY BRACKNELL. That does not seem to me to be a grave objection. Thirty-five is a very attractive age. London society is full of women of the very highest birth who have, of their own free choice, remained thirty-five for years. Lady Dumbleton is an instance in point. To my own knowledge she has been thirty-five ever since she arrived at the age of forty, which was many years ago now. I see no reason why our dear Cecily should not be even still more attractive at the age you mention than she is at present. There will be a large accumulation of property.

CECILY. Algy, could you wait for me till I was thirty-five?

ALGERNON. Of course I could, Cecily. You know I could.

CECILY. Yes, I felt it instinctively, but I couldn't wait all that time, I hate waiting even five minutes for anybody. It always makes me rather cross. I am not punctual myself, I know, but I do like punctuality in others, and waiting, even to be married, is quite out of the question.

ALGERNON. Then what is to be done, Cecily?

CECILY. I don't know, Mr. Moncrieff.

LADY BRACKNELL. My dear Mr. Worthing, as Miss Cecily states positively that she cannot wait till she is thirty-five—a remark which I am bound to say seems to me to show a somewhat impatient nature—I would beg of you to reconsider your decision.

JACK. But my dear Lady Bracknell, the matter is entirely in your own hands. The moment you consent to my marriage with Gwendolen, I will most gladly allow your nephew to form an alliance with my ward.

LADY BRACKNELL (*rising and drawing herself up*). You must be quite aware that what you propose is out of the question.

JACK. Then a passionate celibacy is all that any of us can look forward to.

LADY BRACKNELL. That is not the destiny I propose for Gwendolen. Algernon, of course, can choose for himself. (*Pulls out her watch.*) Come, dear—(GWENDOLEN *rises*)—we have already missed five, if not six, trains. To miss any more might expose us to comment on the platform.

Enter DR. CHASUBLE.

CHASUBLE. Everything is quite ready for the christenings.

LADY BRACKNELL. The christenings, sir! Is not that somewhat premature?

CHASUBLE (*looking rather puzzled, and pointing to* JACK *and* ALGERNON). Both these gentlemen have expressed a desire for immediate baptism.

LADY BRACKNELL. At their age? The idea is grotesque and irreligious! Algernon, I forbid you to be baptized. I will not hear of such excess. Lord Bracknell would be highly displeased if he learned that that was the way in which you wasted your time and money.

CHASUBLE. Am I to understand then that there are to be no christenings at all this afternoon?

JACK. I don't think that, as things are now, it would be of much practical value to either of us, Dr. Chasuble.

CHASUBLE. I am grieved to hear such sentiments from you, Mr. Worthing. They savour of the heretical views of the Anabaptists, views that I have completely refuted in four of my unpublished sermons. However, as your present mood seems to be one peculiarly secular, I will return to the church at once. Indeed, I have just been informed by the pew-opener that for the last hour and a half Miss Prism has been waiting for me in the vestry.

LADY BRACKNELL (*starting*). Miss Prism! Did I hear you mention a Miss Prism?

CHASUBLE. Yes, Lady Bracknell. I am on my way to join her.

LADY BRACKNELL. Pray allow me to detain you for a moment. This matter may prove to be one of vital importance to Lord Bracknell and myself. Is this Miss Prism a female of repellent aspect, remotely connected with education?

CHASUBLE (*somewhat indignantly*). She is the most cultivated of ladies, and the very picture of respectability.

LADY BRACKNELL. It is obviously the same person. May I ask what position she holds in your household?

CHASUBLE (*severely*). I am a celibate, madam.

JACK (*interposing*). Miss Prism, Lady Bracknell has been for the last three years Miss Cardew's esteemed governess and valued companion.

LADY BRACKNELL. In spite of what I hear of her, I must see her at once. Let her be sent for.

CHASUBLE (*looking off*). She approaches; she is nigh.

Enter MISS PRISM *hurriedly.*

MISS PRISM. I was told you expected me in the vestry, dear Canon. I have been waiting for you there for an hour and three-quarters. (*Catches sight of* LADY BRACKNELL, *who has fixed her with a stony glare.* MISS PRISM *grows pale and quails. She looks anxiously round as if desirous to escape.*)

LADY BRACKNELL (*in a severe, judicial voice*). Prism! (MISS PRISM *bows her head in shame.*) Come here, Prism! (MISS PRISM *approaches in a humble manner.*) Prism! Where is that baby? (*General consternation. The* CANON *starts back in horror.* ALGERNON *and* JACK *pretend to be anxious to shield* CECILY *and* GWENDOLEN *from hearing the details of a terrible public scandal.*) Twenty-eight years ago, Prism, you left Lord Bracknell's house, Number 104, Upper Grosvenor Street, in charge of a perambulator that contained a baby of the male sex. You never returned. A few weeks later, through the elaborate investigations of the Metropolitan police, the perambulator was discovered at midnight standing by itself in a remote corner of Bayswater. It contained the manuscript of a three-volume novel of more than usually revolting sentimentality. (MISS PRISM *starts in involuntary indignation.*) But the baby was not there. (*Every one looks at* MISS PRISM.) Prism! Where is that baby? (*A pause.*)

MISS PRISM. Lady Bracknell, I admit with shame that I do not know. I only wish I did. The plain facts of the case are these. On the morning of the day you mention, a day that is for ever branded on my memory, I prepared as usual to take the baby out in its perambulator. I had also with me a somewhat old, capacious handbag in which I had intended to place the manuscript of a work of fiction that I had written during my few unoccupied hours. In a moment of mental abstraction, for which I never can forgive myself, I deposited the manuscript in the basinette, and placed the baby in the hand-bag.

JACK (*who has been listening attentively*). But where did you deposit the hand-bag?

MISS PRISM. Do not ask me, Mr. Worthing.

JACK. Miss Prism, this is a matter of no small importance to me. I insist on knowing where you deposited the hand-bag that contained that infant.

MISS PRISM. I left it in the cloak-room of one of the larger railway stations in London.

JACK. What railway station?

MISS PRISM (*quite crushed*). Victoria. The Brighton line. (*Sinks into a chair.*)

JACK. I must retire to my room for a moment. Gwendolen, wait here for me.

GWENDOLEN. If you are not too long, I will wait here for you all my life.

Exit JACK *in great excitement.*

CHASUBLE. What do you think this means, Lady Bracknell?

LADY BRACKNELL. I dare not even suspect, Dr. Chasuble. I need hardly tell you that in families of high position strange coincidences are not supposed to occur. They are hardly considered the thing.

Noises heard overhead as if some one was throwing trunks about. Every one looks up.

CECILY. Uncle Jack seems strangely agitated.

CHASUBLE. Your guardian has a very emotional nature.

LADY BRACKNELL. This noise is extremely unpleasant. It sounds as if he was having an argument. I dislike arguments of any kind. They are always vulgar, and often convincing.

CHASUBLE (*looking up*). It has stopped now. (*The noise is redoubled.*)

LADY BRACKNELL. I wish he would arrive at some conclusion.

GWENDOLEN. This suspense is terrible. I hope it will last.

Enter JACK *with a hand-bag of black leather in his hand.*

JACK (*rushing over to* MISS PRISM). Is this the hand-bag, Miss Prism? Examine it carefully before you speak. The happiness of more than one life depends on your answer.

MISS PRISM (*calmly*). It seems to be mine. Yes, here is the injury it received through the upsetting of a Gower Street omnibus in younger and happier days. Here is the stain on the lining caused by the explosion of a temperance beverage, an incident that occurred at Leamington. And here, on the lock, are my initials. I had forgotten that in an extravagant mood I had had them placed there. The bag is undoubtedly mine. I am delighted to have it so unexpectedly restored to me. It has been a great inconvenience being without it all these years.

JACK (*in a pathetic voice*). Miss Prism, more is restored to you than this hand-bag. I was the baby you placed in it.

MISS PRISM (*amazed*). You?

JACK (*embracing her*). Yes . . . mother!

MISS PRISM (*recoiling in indignant astonishment*). Mr. Worthing, I am unmarried!

JACK. Unmarried! I do not deny that is a serious blow. But after all, who has the right to cast a stone against one who has suffered? Cannot repentance wipe out an act of folly? Why should there be one law for men, and another for women? Mother, I forgive you. (*Tries to embrace her again.*)

MISS PRISM (*still more indignant*). Mr. Worthing, there is some error. (*Pointing to* LADY BRACKNELL). There is the lady who can tell you who you really are.

JACK (*after a pause*). Lady Bracknell, I hate to seem inquisitive, but would you kindly inform me who I am?

LADY BRACKNELL. I am afraid that the news I have to give you will not altogether please you. You are the son of my poor sister, Mrs. Moncrieff, and consequently Algernon's elder brother.

JACK. Algy's elder brother! Then I have a brother after all. I knew I had a brother! I always said I had a brother! Cecily,—how could you have ever doubted that I had a brother! (*Seizes hold of* ALGERNON.) Dr. Chasuble, my unfortunate brother. Miss Prism, my unfortunate brother. Gwendolen, my unfortunate brother. Algy, you young scoundrel, you will have to treat me with more respect in the future. You have never behaved to me like a brother in all your life.

ALGERNON. Well, not till to-day, old boy, I admit. I did my best, however, though I was out of practice. (*Shakes hands.*)

GWENDOLEN (*to* JACK). My own! But what own are you? What is your Christian name, now that you have become some one else?

JACK. Good heavens! . . . I had quite forgotten that point. Your decision on the subject of my name is irrevocable, I suppose?

GWENDOLEN. I never change, except in my affections.

CECILY. What a noble nature you have, Gwendolen!

JACK. Then the question had better be cleared up at once. Aunt Augusta, a moment. At the time when Miss Prism left me in the hand-bag, had I been christened already?

LADY BRACKNELL. Every luxury that money could buy, including christening, had been lavished on you by your fond and doting parents.

JACK. Then I was christened! That is settled. Now, what name was I given? Let me know the worst.

LADY BRACKNELL. Being the eldest son you were naturally christened after your father.

JACK (*irritably*). Yes, but what was my father's Christian name?

LADY BRACKNELL (*meditatively*). I cannot at the present moment recall what the General's Christian name was. But I have no doubt he had one. He was eccentric, I admit. But only in later years. And that was the result of the Indian climate, and marriage, and indigestion, and other things of that kind.

JACK. Algy! Can't you recollect what our father's Christian name was?

ALGERNON. My dear boy, we were never even on speaking terms. He died before I was a year old.

JACK. His name would appear in tthe Army Lists of the period, I suppose, Aunt Augusta?

LADY BRACKNELL. The General was essentially a man of peace, except in his domestic life. But I have no doubt his name would appear in any military directory.

JACK. The Army Lists of the last forty years are here. These delightful records should have been my constant study. (*Rushes to bookcase and tears the books out.*) M. Generals . . . Mallam, Maxbohm, Magley, what ghastly names they have—Markby, Migsby, Mobbs, Moncrieff! Lieutenant 1840, Captain, Lieutenant-Colonel, Colonel, General 1869, Christian names, Ernest John. (*Puts book very quietly down and speaks quite calmly.*) I always told you, Gwendolen, my name was Ernest, didn't I? Well, it is Ernest after all. I mean it naturally is Ernest.

LADY BRACKNELL. Yes, I remember now that the General was called Ernest. I knew I had some particular reason for disliking the name.

GWENDOLEN. Ernest! My own Ernest! I felt from the first that you could have no other name!

JACK. Gwendolen, it is a terrible thing for a man to find out suddenly that all his life he has been speaking nothing but the truth. Can you forgive me?

GWENDOLEN. I can. For I feel that you are sure to change.

JACK. My own one!

CHASUBLE (*to* MISS PRISM). Lætitia! (*Embraces her.*)

MISS PRISM (*enthusiastically*). Frederick! At last!

ALGERNON. Cecily! (*Embraces her.*) At last!

JACK. Gwendolen! (*Embraces her.*) At last!

LADY BRACKNELL. My nephew, you seem to be displaying signs of triviality.

JACK. On the contrary, Aunt Augusta, I've now realised for the first time in my life the vital Importance of Being Earnest.

TABLEAU

CURTAIN

William Butler Yeats

1865–1939

Since Yeats's development as a poet forms such· an important chapter in twentieth-century literary history, that development and the events in his life that helped to determine it have been described with some fullness in the introduction to the Modern period. Here it may be added that Yeats was born at Sandymount, near Dublin, and was educated at schools in London and Dublin. The Yeats family moved to London in 1887, but Yeats was to move back and forth between England and Ireland throughout his life. "The Lake Isle of Innisfree," for instance, one of Yeats's best-known early poems, was inspired by a sudden fit of longing for the Irish countryside that overtook him in a crowded London street (*Autobiographies*, p. 134); he was in England when he heard the news of the Easter Rebellion that was the occasion of his magnificent tribute to the patriots, "Easter, 1916." But while it is sometimes easy (however mistaken it may be) to forget that Swift and Shaw were Irishmen, with Yeats we never for a moment do so.

Nor is this simply a matter of the external events of his life: of his work in founding an Irish National Theatre, for instance, or of his having been a Senator of the Irish Free State from 1922 to 1928. For like James Joyce he accepted Ireland, Irish life, Irish questions of conscience as the subject matter and guiding inspirational force of his art, without ever descending to a superficial picturesqueness or to the special pleading that provincialism must supply in its own behalf. If he eagerly accepted his Irish inheritance, the orientation he gave it in his writing was effectively European and cosmopolitan.

TEXTS: The publication of a variorum edition of the poems in 1957, edited by Peter Allt and Russell K. Alspach, makes easily possible the study of Yeats's revisions of his poems. *The Selected Poems of William Butler Yeats,* edited by M. L. Rosenthal, was published in the series of Macmillan Paperbacks in 1962 and has been reissued since. Yeats's plays, both in prose and verse, were published in a final collected edition in 1952. The volume of *Essays* (1924), which include three collections of Yeats's critical writings, *Ideas of Good and Evil* (1896–1903), *The Cutting of an Agate* (1903–15), and *Per Amica Silentia Lunae* (1916–17), was in 1961 incorporated in a volume entitled *Essays and Introductions.* A further collection of prose, *Explorations,* was published in 1962; Yeats's *Mythologies,* uniform with these two volumes, had been published in 1959. In 1970 was published the first of a projected series of volumes of *Uncollected Prose: The Autobiography of William Butler Yeats,* from which quotation is made in the introduction to the Modern period. It is the first book that should be consulted by the reader who wishes to supplement the reading of Yeats's poetry with a study of the forces and interests that lay behind it. (Under the title *Autobiographies,* and augmented by the inclusion of essays and addresses previously published in *Dramatis Personae,* the definitive edition of this work appeared in London in 1955, and has since been reprinted.) *The Letters on Poetry from W. B. Yeats to Dorothy Wellesley* (1940) are of great interest for the liveliness with which they present Yeats's views on poets and poetry, including his views of his contemporaries, during the period of remarkable creative activity of his last years (see also his introductory essay to *The Oxford Book of Modern Verse,* which he was engaged in editing at the time these letters were written). *The Letters of W. B. Yeats,* edited by Allan Wade (1955), offers a wide range of letters, to many correspondents and ranging from 1887 to 1939. *A Vision* was reissued in 1956, in an edition that incorporated the author's final revisions. Closer in the nature of its interest to Yeats's auto-

biographical writings than to the work of his critics and biographers is the volume of letters by Yeats's father, *J. B. Yeats: Letters to His Son W. B. Yeats and Others, 1869–1922* (1934).

To many of the earlier books about Yeats, all readers of his poetry are indebted. Some of the most important shorter pieces are collected in *The Permanence of Yeats: Selected Criticisms,* edited by James Hall and Martin Steinmann (1950, and later reissues). G. B. Saul, *Prolegomena to the Study of Yeats's Poems* (1957), offers the necessary factual information about each poem. Among the earlier books one would first want to recommend are: *The Poetry of W. B. Yeats,* by Louis MacNeice (1941); Richard Ellmann's two indispensable books, *Yeats, the Man and the Masks* (1948) and *The Identity of Yeats* (1954); *The Lonely Tower,* by T. R. Henn; *W. B. Yeats, Man and Poet,* by A. N. Jeffares (1949); and *A Reader's Guide to William Butler Yeats,* by John Unterecker (1959).

Of the numerous newer books, one can mention only a tithe. Among them would be a very useful short book by B. Rajan, *W. B. Yeats: A Critical Introduction* (1965); the essays by various hands in *In Excited Reverie: A Centenary Tribute to William Butler Yeats 1865–1939* (1965), edited by Jeffares and Cross; Giorgio Melchiori, *The Whole Mystery of Art: Pattern into Poetry in the Work of W. B. Yeats* (1960); Amy G. Stock, *W. B. Yeats: His Poetry and Thought* (1961); W. Y. Tindall, *W. B. Yeats* (1966); Edward Engelberg, *The Vast Design: Patterns in W. B. Yeats's Aesthetic* (1964); T. F. Parkinson, *W. B. Yeats, Self-Critic: A Study of His Early Verse* (1951) and *The Later Poetry* (1971); and Harold Bloom, *Yeats* (1970).

The Symbolism of Poetry[1]

"Symbolism, as seen in the writers of our day, would have no value if it were not seen also, under one disguise or another, in every great imaginative writer," writes Mr. Arthur Symons in *The Symbolist Movement in Literature,* a subtle book which I cannot praise as I would, because it has been dedicated to me; and he goes on to show how many profound writers have in the last few years sought for a philosophy of poetry in the doctrine of symbolism, and how even in countries where it is almost scandalous to seek for any philosophy of poetry, new writers are following them in their search. We do not

10

---

[1] The essay was written in 1900.

know what the writers of ancient times talked of among themselves, and one bull is all that remains of Shakespeare's talk, who was on the edge of modern times; and the journalist is convinced, it seems, that they talked of wine and women and politics, but never about their art, or never quite seriously about their art. He is certain that no one, who had a philosophy of his art or a theory of how he should write, has ever made a work of art, that people have no imagination who do not write without forethought and afterthought as he writes his own articles. He says this with enthusiasm, because he has heard it at so many comfortable dinner-tables, where some one had mentioned through carelessness, or foolish zeal, a book whose difficulty had offended indolence, or a man who had not forgotten that beauty is an accusation. Those formulas and generalisations, in which a hidden sergeant has drilled the ideas of journalists and through them the ideas of all but all the modern world, have created in their turn a forgetfulness like that of soldiers in battle, so that journalists and their readers have forgotten, among many like events, that Wagner spent seven years arranging and explaining his ideas before he began his most characteristic music; that opera, and with it modern music, arose from certain talks at the house of one Giovanni Bardi of Florence; and that the Pleiade laid the foundations of modern French literature with a pamphlet. Goethe has said, "a poet needs all philosophy, but he must keep it out of his work," though that is not always necessary; and almost certainly no great art, outside England, where journalists are more powerful and ideas less plentiful than elsewhere, has arisen without a great criticism, for its herald or its interpreter and protector, and it may be for this reason that great art, now that vulgarity has armed itself and multiplied itself, is perhaps dead in England.

All writers, all artists of any kind, in so far as they have had any philosophical or critical power, perhaps just in so far as they have been deliberate artists, at all, have had some philosophy, some criticism of their art; and it has often been this philosophy, or this criticism, that has evoked their most startling inspiration, calling into outer life some portion of the divine life, or of the buried reality, which could alone extinguish in the emotions what their philosophy or their criticism would extinguish in the intellect. They have sought for no new thing, it may be, but only to understand and to copy the pure inspiration of early times, but because the divine life wars upon our outer life, and must needs change its weapons and its movements as we change ours, inspiration has come to them in beautiful startling shapes. The scientific movement brought with it a literature, which was always tending to lose itself in externalities of all kinds, in opinion, in declamation, in picturesque writing, in word-painting, or in what Mr. Symons has called an attempt "to build in brick and mortar inside the covers of a book"; and now writers have begun to dwell upon the element of evocation, of suggestion, upon what we call the symbolism in great writers.

II

In "Symbolism in Painting," I tried to describe the element of symbolism that is in pictures and sculpture, and described a little the symbolism in poetry, but did not describe at all the continuous indefinable symbolism which is the substance of all style.

There are no lines with more melancholy beauty than these by Burns—

The white moon is setting behind the white wave,
And Time is setting with me, O!

and these lines are perfectly symbolical. Take from them the whiteness of the moon and of the wave, whose relation to the setting of Time is too subtle for the intellect, and you take from them their beauty. But, when all are together, moon and wave and whiteness and setting Time and the last melancholy cry, they evoke an emotion which cannot be evoked by any other arrangement of colours and sounds and forms. We may call this metaphorical writing, but it is better to call it symbolical writing, because metaphors are not profound enough to be moving, when they are not symbols, and when they are symbols they are the most perfect of all, because the most subtle, outside of pure sound, and through them one can the best find out what symbols are. If one begins the reverie with any beautiful lines that one can remember, one finds they are like those by Burns. Begin with this line by Blake—

> *The gay fishes on the wave when the moon*
> *sucks up the dew;*

or these lines by Nash—

> *Queens have died young and fair,*
> *Brightness falls from the air,*
> *Dust hath closed Helen's eye;*

or these lines by Shakespeare—

> *Timon hath made his everlasting mansion*
> *Upon the beached verge of the salt flood;*
> *Who once a day with his embossed froth*
> *The turbulent surge shall cover;*

or take some line that is quite simple, that gets its beauty from its place in a story, and see how it flickers with the light of the many symbols that have given the story its beauty, as a sword-blade may flicker with the light of burning towers.

All sounds, all colours, all forms, either because of their pre-ordained energies or because of long association, evoke indefinable and yet precise emotions, or, as I prefer to think, call down among us certain disembodied powers, whose footsteps over our hearts we call emotions; and when sound, and colour, and form are in a musical relation, a beautiful relation to one another, they become as it were one sound, one colour, one form, and evoke an emotion that is made out of their distinct evocations and yet is one emotion. The same relation exists between all portions of every work of art, whether it be an epic or a song, and the more perfect it is, and the more various and numerous the elements that have flowed into its perfection, the more powerful will be the emotion, the power, the god it calls among us. Because an emotion does not exist, or does not become perceptible and active among us, till it has found its expression, in colour or in sound or in form, or in all of these, and because no two modulations or arrangements of these evoke the same emotion, poets and painters and musicians, and in a less degree because their effects are momentary, day and night and cloud and shadow, are continually making and un-making mankind. It is indeed only those things which seem useless or very feeble that have any power, and all those things that seem useful or strong, armies, moving wheels, modes of architecture, modes of government, speculations of the reason, would have been a little different if some mind long ago

had not given itself to some emotion, as a woman gives herself to her lover, and shaped sounds or colours or forms, or all of these, into a musical relation, that their emotion might live in other minds. A little lyric evokes an emotion, and this emotion gathers others about it and melts into their being in the making of some great epic; and at last, needing an always less delicate body, or symbol, as it grows more powerful, it flows out, with all it has gathered, among the blind instincts of daily life, where it moves a power within powers, as one sees ring within ring in the stem of an old tree. This is maybe what Arthur O'Shaughnessy meant when he made his poets say they had built Nineveh with their sighing; and I am certainly never certain, when I hear of some war, or of some religious excitement or of some new manufacture, or of anything else that fills the ear of the world, that it has not all happened because of something that a boy piped in Thessaly. I remember once telling a seer to ask one among the gods who, as she believed, were standing about her in their symbolic bodies, what would come of a charming but seeming trivial labour of a friend, and the form answering, "the devastation of peoples and the overwhelming of cities." I doubt indeed if the crude circumstance of the world, which seems to create all our emotions, does more than reflect, as in multiplying mirrors, the emotions that have come to solitary men in moments of poetical contemplation; or that love itself would be more than an animal hunger but for the poet and his shadow the priest, for unless we believe that outer things are the reality, we must believe that the gross is the shadow of the subtle, that things are wise before they become foolish, and secret before they cry out in the market-place. Solitary men in moments of contemplation receive, as I think, the creative impulse from the lowest of the Nine Hierarchies, and so make and unmake mankind, and even the world itself, for does not "the eye altering alter all"?

> *Our towns are copied fragments from our breast;*
> *And all man's Babylons strive but to impart*
> *The grandeurs of his Babylonian heart.*

III

The purpose of rhythm, it has always seemed to me, is to prolong the moment of contemplation, the moment when we are both asleep and awake, which is the one moment of creation, by hushing us with an alluring monotony, while it holds us waking by variety, to keep us in that state of perhaps real trance, in which the mind liberated from the pressure of the will is unfolded in symbols. If certain sensitive persons listen persistently to the ticking of a watch, or gaze persistently on the monotonous flashing of a light, they fall into the hypnotic trance; and rhythm is but the ticking of a watch made softer, that one must needs listen, and various, that one may not be swept beyond memory or grow weary of listening; while the patterns of the artist are but the monotonous flash woven to take the eyes in a subtler enchantment. I have heard in meditation voices that were forgotten the moment they had spoken; and I have been swept, when in more profound meditation, beyond all memory but of those things that came from beyond the threshold of waking life. I was writing once at a very symbolical and abstract poem, when my pen fell on the ground; and as I stooped to pick it up, I remembered some phantastic adventure that yet did not seem phantastic, and then another like adventure, and when I asked myself when these things had happened, I found that I was remembering my dreams for many nights. I tried to remember what I had done the day before, and then what I had done that morning; but all my waking life had perished from me, and it was only after a struggle that I came to remember it again, and as I did so that more powerful and startling life perished in its turn. Had my pen not fallen on the ground and so made me turn from the images that I was weaving into verse, I would never have known that meditation had become trance, for I would have been like one who does not know that he is passing through a wood because his eyes are on the pathway. So I think that in the making and in the understanding of a work of art, and the more easily if it is full of patterns and symbols and music, we are lured to the threshold of sleep, and it may be far beyond it, without knowing that we have ever set our feet upon the steps of horn or of ivory.

IV

Besides emotional symbols, symbols that evoke emotions alone,—and in this sense all alluring or hateful things are symbols, although their relations with one another are too subtle to delight us fully, away from rhythm and pattern, —there are intellectual symbols, symbols that evoke ideas alone, or ideas mingled with emotions; and outside the very definite traditions of mysticism and the less definite criticism of certain modern poets, these alone are called symbols. Most things belong to one or another kind, according to the way we speak of them and the companions we give them, for symbols, associated with ideas that are more than fragments of the shadows thrown upon the intellect by the emotions they evoke, are the playthings of the allegorist or the pedant, and soon pass away. If I say "white" or "purple" in an ordinary line of poetry, they evoke emotions so exclusively that I cannot say why they move me; but if I bring them into the same sentence with such obvious intellectual symbols as a cross or a crown of thorns, I think of purity and sovereignty. Furthermore, innumerable meanings, which are held to "white" or to "purple" by bonds of subtle suggestion, and alike in the emotions and in the intellect, move visibly through my mind, and move invisibly beyond the threshold of sleep, casting lights and shadows of an indefinable wisdom on what had seemed before, it may be, but sterility and noisy violence. It is the intellect that decides where the reader shall ponder over the procession of the symbols, and if the symbols are merely emotional, he gazes from amid the accidents and destinies of the world; but if the symbols are intellectual too, he becomes himself a part of pure intellect, and he is himself mingled with the procession. If I watch a rushy pool in the moonlight, my emotion at its beauty is mixed with memories of the man that I have seen ploughing by its margin, or of the lovers I saw there a night ago; but if I look at the moon herself and remember any of her ancient names and meanings, I move among divine people, and things that have shaken off our mortality, the tower of ivory, the queen of waters, the shining stag among enchanted woods, the white hare sitting upon the hilltop, the fool of faery with his shining cup full of dreams, and it may be "make a friend of one of these images of wonder," and "meet the Lord in the air." So, too, if one is moved by Shakespeare, who is content with emotional symbols that he may come the nearer to our sympathy, one is mixed with the whole spectacle of the world; while if one is moved by Dante, or by the myth of Demeter, one is mixed into the shadow of God or of a goddess. So too one is furthest from symbols when one is busy doing this or that, but the soul moves among symbols and unfolds in symbols when trance, or madness, or deep meditation has withdrawn it from every impulse but its own. "I then saw," wrote Gérard de Nerval of his madness, "vaguely drifting into form, plastic images of antiquity, which outlined themselves, became definite, and seemed to represent symbols of which I only seized the idea with difficulty." In an earlier time he would have been of that multitude, whose souls austerity withdrew, even more perfectly than madness could withdraw his soul, from hope and memory, from desire and regret, that they might reveal those processions of symbols that men bow to before altars, and woo with incense and offerings. But being of our time, he has been like Maeterlinck, like Villiers de l'Isle Adam in *Axël,* like all who are preoccupied with intellectual symbols in our time, a foreshadower of the new sacred book, of which all the arts, as somebody has said, are begging to dream. How can the arts overcome the slow dying of men's hearts that we call the progress of the world, and lay their hands upon men's heart-strings again, without becoming the garment of religion as in old times?

V

If people were to accept the theory that poetry moves us because of its symbolism, what change should one look for in the manner of our poetry? A return to the way of our fathers, a casting out of descriptions of nature for the sake of nature, of the moral law for the sake of the moral law, a casting out of all anecdotes and of that brooding over scientific opinion that so often extinguished the central flame in Tennyson, and of that vehemence that would make us do or not do certain things; or, in other words, we should come to understand that the beryl stone was enchanted by our fathers that it might unfold the pictures in its heart, and not to mirror our own excited faces, or the boughs waving outside the window. With this change of substance, this return to imagination, this

understanding that the laws of art, which are the hidden laws of the world, can alone bind the imagination, would come a change of style, and we would cast out of serious poetry those energetic rhythms, as of a man running, which are the invention of the will with its eyes always on something to be done or undone; and we would seek out those wavering, meditative, organic rhythms, which are the embodiment of the imagination, that neither desires nor hates, because it has done with time, and only wishes to gaze upon some reality, some beauty; nor would it be any longer possible for anybody to deny the importance of form, in all its kinds, for although you can expound an opinion, or describe a thing when your words are not quite well chosen, you cannot give a body to something that moves beyond the senses, unless your words are as subtle, as complex, as full of mysterious life, as the body of a flower or of a woman. The form of sincere poetry, unlike the form of the popular poetry, may indeed be sometimes obscure, or ungrammatical as in some of the best of the Songs of Innocence and Experience, but it must have the perfections that escape analysis, the subtleties that have a new meaning every day, and it must have all this whether it be but a little song made out of a moment of dreamy indolence, or some great epic made out of the dreams of one poet and of a hundred generations whose hands were never weary of the sword.

The Falling of the Leaves[1]

Autumn is over the long leaves that love us,
And over the mice in the barley sheaves;
Yellow the leaves of the rowan above us,
And yellow the wet wild-strawberry leaves.

The hour of the waning of love has beset us,
And weary and worn are our sad souls now;
Let us part, ere the season of passion forget us,
With a kiss and a tear on thy drooping brow.

---

1 "The Falling of the Leaves" was printed in *Crossways* (1889).

The Man Who Dreamed of Faeryland[1]

He stood among a crowd at Dromahair;
His heart hung all upon a silken dress,
And he had known at last some tenderness,
Before earth took him to her stony care;
But when a man poured fish into a pile, 5
It seemed they raised their little silver heads,
And sang what gold morning or evening sheds
Upon a woven world-forgotten isle
Where people love beside the ravelled seas;
That Time can never mar a lover's vows 10
Under that woven changeless roof of boughs:
The singing shook him out of his new ease.

He wandered by the sands of Lissadell;
His mind ran all on money cares and fears,
And he had known at last some prudent years 15
Before they heaped his grave under the hill;
But while he passed before a plashy place,
A lug-worm with its grey and muddy mouth
Sang that somewhere to north or west or south
There dwelt a gay, exulting, gentle race 20
Under the golden or the silver skies;
That if a dancer stayed his hungry foot
It seemed the sun and moon were in the fruit:
And at that singing he was no more wise.

He mused beside the well of Scanavin, 25
He mused upon his mockers: without fail
His sudden vengeance were a country tale,
When earthy night had drunk his body in;
But one small knot-grass growing by the pool
Sang where—unnecessary cruel voice— 30
Old silence bids its chosen race rejoice,
Whatever ravelled waters rise and fall
Or stormy silver fret the gold of day,
And midnight there enfold them like a fleece
And lover there by lover be at peace.
The tale drove his fine angry mood away. 35

He slept under the hill of Lugnagall;
And might have known at last unhaunted sleep
Under that cold and vapour-turbaned steep,

Now that the earth had taken man and all: 40
Did not the worms that spired about his bones
Proclaim with that unwearied, reedy cry
That God has laid His fingers on the sky,
That from those fingers glittering summer runs
Upon the dancer by the dreamless wave. 45
Why should those lovers that no lovers miss
Dream, until God burn Nature with a kiss?
The man has found no comfort in the grave.

To Ireland in the Coming Times[1]

Know, that I would accounted be
True brother of a company
That sang, to sweeten Ireland's wrong,
Ballad and story, rann and song;
Nor be I any less of them, 5
Because the red-rose-bordered hem
Of her,[2] whose history began
Before God made the angelic clan,
Trails all about the written page.
When Time began to rant and rage 10
The measure of her flying feet
Made Ireland's heart begin to beat;
And Time bade all his candles flare
To light a measure here and there;
And may the thoughts of Ireland brood 15
Upon a measured quietude.

Nor may I less be counted one
With Davis, Mangan, Ferguson,
Because, to him who ponders well,
My rhymes more than their rhyming tell 20
Of things discovered in the deep,
Where only body's laid asleep.
For the elemental creatures go

---

1 From *The Rose* volume (1893). In Yeats's early system of symbolism, conjunction of gold and silver or of sun and moon (as for example in lines 6–7 or in line 21) connotes a state of blessedness, and this state can also be represented as "the dancing place." Thus the Faeryland that is dreamed of can be seen as attainment of the ideal, of perfection, so that the poem poses a conflict between the claims of the real and the ideal.

1 The concluding poem of *The Rose* volume. Like the opening poem, "To the Rose upon the Rood of Time," this poem is italicized to indicate a more directly personal mode of statement. The opening poem had invoked Yeats's complex early rose symbol, standing for a wide and shifting range of transcendental values—ideal beauty, ideal love, divinity—placed against the cross (rood) of actual earthly existence. In that poem, he at times wishes to dedicate himself to the Rose, at other times he holds back. In this poem, where he alludes to the idealizing habit of his Rose poems, he casts up his account as one who has also served Ireland, just as the Irish nationalist figures had done who are enumerated in line 18.
2 "Of her"—of woman: Yeats here alludes to a tradition, found in the Kabbala and elsewhere, that (as Ellmann puts it) "eternal womanhood is coeval with God."

About my table to and fro,
That hurry from unmeasured mind 25
To rant and rage in flood and wind;
Yet he who treads in measured ways
May surely barter gaze for gaze.
Man ever journeys on with them
After the red-rose-bordered hem. 30
Ah, faeries, dancing under the moon,
A Druid land, a Druid tune!

While still I may, I write for you
The love I lived, the dream I knew.
From our birthday, until we die, 35
Is but the winking of an eye;
And we, our singing and our love,
What measurer Time has lit above,
And all benighted things that go
About my table to and fro, 40
Are passing on to where may be,
In truth's consuming ecstasy,
No place for love and dream at all;
For God goes by with white footfall.
I cast my heart into my rhymes, 45
That you, in the dim coming times,
May know how my heart went with them
After the red-rose-bordered hem.

He Wishes for the Cloths of Heaven[1]

Had I the heavens' embroidered cloths,
Enwrought with golden and silver light,
The blue and the dim and the dark cloths
Of night and light and the half-light,
I would spread the cloths under your feet: 5
But, I, being poor, have only my dreams;
I have spread my dreams under your feet;
Tread softly because you tread on my dreams.

Adam's Curse[1]

We sat together at one summer's end,
That beautiful mild woman, your close friend,

And you and I, and talked of poetry.
I said, "A line will take us hours maybe;
Yet if it does not seem a moment's thought, 5
Our stitching and unstitching has been naught.
Better go down upon your marrow-bones
And scrub a kitchen pavement, or break stones
Like an old pauper, in all kinds of weather;
For to articulate sweet sounds together 10
Is to work harder than all these, and yet
Be thought an idler by the noisy set
Of bankers, schoolmasters, and clergymen
The martyrs call the world."

                              And thereupon
That beautiful mild woman for whose sake 15
There's many a one shall find out all heartache
On finding that her voice is sweet and low
Replied, "To be born woman is to know—
Although they do not talk of it at school—
That we must labour to be beautiful." 20

I said, "It's certain there is no fine thing
Since Adam's fall but needs much labouring.
There have been lovers who thought love should
     be
So much compounded of high courtesy
That they would sigh and quote with learned 25
     looks
Precedents out of beautiful old books;
Yet now it seems an idle trade enough."

We sat grown quiet at the name of love;
We saw the last embers of daylight die,
And in the trembling blue-green of the sky 30
A moon, worn as if it had been a shell
Washed by time's waters as they rose and fell
About the stars and broke in days and years.

I had a thought for no one's but your ears:
That you were beautiful, and that I strove 35
To love you in the old high way of love;
That it had all seemed happy, and yet we'd
     grown
As weary-hearted as that hollow moon.

The Cold Heaven[1]

Suddenly I saw the cold and rook-delighting
heaven

---

1 "He," as we know from the titles of a number of the other poems in *The Wind Among the Reeds* (1899), is to be taken as "the lover" or "the poet."

1 From *In the Seven Woods* (1904). For Adam's curse, see *Genesis* 3:17–19. Various commentators relate the incident described in the poem to Yeats's relationship with Maud Gonne, who is presumably the "you" of the poem, and to a remark she reported her sister as having made about how much work goes into being beautiful.

1 From *Responsibilities* (1914).

That seemed as though ice burned and was but
    the more ice,
And thereupon imagination and heart were
    driven
So wild that every casual thought of that and this
Vanished, and left but memories, that should be
    out of season
With the hot blood of youth, of love crossed
    long ago;
And I took all the blame out of all sense and
    reason,
Until I cried and trembled and rocked to and
    fro,
Riddled with light. Ah! when the ghost begins
    to quicken,
Confusion of the death-bed over, is it sent   10
Out naked on the roads, as the books say, and
    stricken
By the injustice of the skies for punishment?

The Wild Swans at Coole[1]

The trees are in their autumn beauty,
The woodland paths are dry,
Under the October twilight the water
Mirrors a still sky;
Upon the brimming water among the stones   5
Are nine-and-fifty swans.

The nineteenth autumn has come upon me
Since I first made my count;
I saw, before I had well finished,
All suddenly mount   10
And scatter wheeling in great broken rings
Upon their clamorous wings.

I have looked upon those brilliant creatures,
And now my heart is sore.
All's changed since I, hearing at twilight,   15
The first time on this shore,
The bell-beat of their wings above my head,
Trod with a lighter tread.

Unwearied still, lover by lover,
They paddle in the cold   20

Companionable streams or climb the air;
Their hearts have not grown old;
Passion or conquest, wander where they will,
Attend upon them still.

But now they drift on the still water,   25
Mysterious, beautiful;
Among what rushes will they build,
By what lake's edge or pool
Delight men's eyes when I awake some day
To find they have flown away?   30

An Irish Airman Foresees His Death[1]

I know that I shall meet my fate
Somewhere among the clouds above;
Those that I fight I do not hate,
Those that I guard I do not love;
My country is Kiltartan Cross,[2]   5
My countrymen Kiltartan's poor,
No likely end could bring them loss
Or leave them happier than before.
Nor law, nor duty bade me fight,
Nor public men, nor cheering crowds,   10
A lonely impulse of delight
Drove to this tumult in the clouds;
I balanced all, brought all to mind,
The years to come seemed waste of breath,
A waste of breath the years behind   15
In balance with this life, this death.

The Fisherman[1]

Although I can see him still,
The freckled man who goes

---

[1] Coole Park, the estate of Yeats's friend and patroness, Lady Augusta Gregory. Yeats had first visited there in 1897; the poem was written in October 1916. See also the note to "Coole Park and Ballylee, 1931," below.

[1] Yeats had in mind Major Robert Gregory, the son of Lady Augusta Gregory—

    ". . . my dear friend's dear son,
      Our Sidney and our perfect man, . . ."

as he calls him in the longer poem, "In Memory of Major Gregory," which precedes this one in *The Wild Swans at Coole* (1919). Lady Gregory's husband, Sir W. H. Gregory, had died in 1892; her only son, the *Dictionary of National Biography* tells us, "became a distinguished painter and was killed in action as an airman in Italy in January 1918."

[2] Kiltartan is a village near Coole Park, the Gregorys' estate, which is itself near Gort, County Galway, in the west of Ireland.

[1] Another poem from *The Wild Swans at Coole.* Connemara (line 4) is a district in County Galway.

To a grey place on a hill
In grey Connemara clothes
At dawn to cast his flies,　　　　　　　5
It's long since I began
To call up to the eyes
This wise and simple man.
All day I'd looked in the face
What I had hoped 'twould be　　　　　10
To write for my own race
And the reality;
The living men that I hate,
The dead man that I loved,
The craven man in his seat,　　　　　15
The insolent unreproved,
And no knave brought to book
Who has won a drunken cheer,
The witty man and his joke
Aimed at the commonest ear,　　　　20
The clever man who cries
The catch-cries of the clown,
The beating down of the wise
And great Art beaten down.

Maybe a twelvemonth since　　　　　25
Suddenly I began,
In scorn of this audience,
Imagining a man,
And his sun-freckled face,
And grey Connemara cloth,　　　　　30
Climbing up to a place
Where stone is dark under froth,
And the down-turn of his wrist
When the flies drop in the stream;
A man who does not exist,　　　　　35
A man who is but a dream;
And cried, "Before I am old
I shall have written him one
Poem maybe as cold
And passionate as the dawn."　　　　40

Easter, 1916[1]

I have met them at close of day
Coming with vivid faces

From counter or desk among grey
Eighteenth-century houses.
I have passed with a nod of the head　　　5
Or polite meaningless words,
Or have lingered awhile and said
Polite meaningless words,
And thought before I had done
Of a mocking tale or a gibe　　　　10
To please a companion
Around the fire at the club,
Being certain that they and I
But lived where motley is worn:
All changed, changed utterly:　　　　15
A terrible beauty is born.

That woman's days were spent
In ignorant good-will,
Her nights in argument
Until her voice grew shrill.　　　　20
What voice more sweet than hers
When, young and beautiful,
She rode to harriers?
This man had kept a school
And rode our wingèd horse;　　　　25
This other his helper and friend
Was coming into his force;
He might have won fame in the end,
So sensitive his nature seemed,
So daring and sweet his thought.　　30
This other man I had dreamed

---

insurgents proclaimed a republic; but by April 29, after the loss of three hundred lives, they had been forced to give in to the British. "The seven signatories of the republican proclamation, including Pearse and Connolly, and nine others were shot after court-martial between 3 and 12 May [see Yeats's poem "Sixteen Dead Men," which follows "Easter, 1916" in the *Collected Poems*], 75 were reprieved and over 2,000 held prisoners." (For a fuller account of the Easter Rebellion and its place in the history of the Irish Republic see the article by D. B. Quinn in *Chambers's Encyclopedia*, New Edition [1950], VII, 728, from which the above facts are taken.)

The remembered scene in the first section of the poem is, of course, Dublin. The woman and the men enumerated in the second section may be identified as follows: lines 17–23, the Countess Markiewicz; lines 24–25, Pádraic Pearse; lines 26–30, MacDonagh; lines 31 ff., Mac-Bride. In the third section Yeats establishes, as a symbol for the heart that is entirely dedicated to a high and harshly difficult political cause, the stone set in the midst of a stream, touched but unaffected by the accidental life and change of the stream—as the dedicated heart is unmoved by the other demands of its life.

This poem and the next are from *Michael Robartes and the Dancer* (1921).

---

1 A combination of Irish Nationalist groups had planned an insurrection for Easter Sunday, 1916. Despite attempts to postpone the uprising until a more favorable time (the ship that had been bringing arms from Germany had been intercepted on April 20), it began on Easter Monday in Dublin. Seizing key points in the city, the

A drunken, vainglorious lout.
He had done most bitter wrong
To some who are near my heart,
Yet I number him in the song;   35
He, too, has resigned his part
In the casual comedy;
He, too, has been changed in his turn,
Transformed utterly:
A terrible beauty is born.   40

Hearts with one purpose alone
Through summer and winter seem
Enchanted to a stone
To trouble the living stream.
The horse that comes from the road,   45
The rider, the birds that range
From cloud to tumbling cloud,
Minute by minute they change;
A shadow of cloud on the stream
Changes minute by minute;   50
A horse-hoof slides on the brim,
And a horse plashes within it;
The long-legged moor-hens dive,
And hens to moor-cocks call;
Minute by minute they live: 55
The stone's in the midst of all.

Too long a sacrifice
Can make a stone of the heart.
O when may it suffice?
That is Heaven's part, our part   60
To murmur name upon name,
As a mother names her child
When sleep at last has come
On limbs that had run wild.
What is it but nightfall?   65
No, no, not night but death;
Was it needless death after all?
For England may keep faith
For all that is done and said.
We know their dream; enough   70
To know they dreamed and are dead;
And what if excess of love
Bewildered them till they died?
I write it out in a verse—
MacDonagh and MacBride   75
And Connolly and Pearse
Now and in time to be,
Wherever green is worn,

Are changed, changed utterly:
A terrible beauty is born.   80

September 25, 1916

The Second Coming[1]

Turning and turning in the widening gyre
The falcon cannot hear the falconer;
Things fall apart; the centre cannot hold;
Mere anarchy is loosed upon the world,
The blood-dimmed tide is loosed, and every-   5
    where
The ceremony of innocence is drowned;
The best lack all conviction, while the worst
Are full of passionate intensity.
Surely some revelation is at hand;
Surely the Second Coming is at hand.   10
The Second Coming! Hardly are those words out
When a vast image out of *Spiritus Mundi*[2]
Troubles my sight: somewhere in sands of the
    desert
A shape with lion body and the head of a man,
A gaze blank and pitiless as the sun,   15
Is moving its slow thighs, while all about it
Reel shadows of the indignant desert birds.
The darkness drops again; but now I know
That twenty centuries of stony sleep
Were vexed to nightmare by a rocking cradle.   20
And what rough beast, its hour come round at
    last,
Slouches towards Bethlehem to be born?

---

[1] For a note on this poem, and a reference to the relevant pages in Yeats's *A Vision*, see p. 990. The scheme of the poem may be seen as follows: If the Second Coming were to occur in the present age, when evil is everywhere in power, it seems to the poet that it must take place under some such loathsome and terrible form as is described in the second part of the poem: not Christ, but some rough beast, an obscene and sphinxlike creature.

    For the meaning of "gyre" in the first line, see note 2 on the use of this term in the next poem, "Sailing to Byzantium."

[2] *Spiritus Mundi*, like *Anima Mundi*, was for Yeats "the general mind," the soul of the wide world dreaming on things to come, the collective consciousness (or subconscious) which the individual can touch and draw upon by giving free rein to his power of intuition: the *Anima Mundi* has remarkable image-making power—"if you suspend the critical faculty, . . . images pass rapidly before you." These images, moreover, are not merely fortuitous or fanciful but have prophetic relevance as well. For a full discussion of the concept and its place in the thought of Henry More, the Cambridge Platonist (1614–1687), see Yeats's essay "Anima Mundi" in *Per Amica Silentia Lunae* (reprinted in *Essays* by *W. B. Yeats,* 1924).

Sailing to Byzantium[1]

I

That is no country for old men. The young
In one another's arms, birds in the trees,
—Those dying generations—at their song,
The salmon-falls, the mackerel-crowded seas,
Fish, flesh, or fowl, commend all summer long   5
Whatever is begotten, born, and dies.
Caught in that sensual music all neglect
Monuments of unageing intellect.

II

An aged man is but a paltry thing,
A tattered coat upon a stick, unless   10
Soul clap its hands and sing, and louder sing
For every tatter in its mortal dress,
Nor is there singing school but studying
Monuments of its own magnificence;
And therefore I have sailed the seas and come   15
To the holy city of Byzantium.

III

O sages standing in God's holy fire
As in the gold mosaic of a wall,
Come from the holy fire, perne in a gyre,[2]

And be the singing-masters of my soul.   20
Consume my heart away; sick with desire
And fastened to a dying animal
It knows not what it is; and gather me
Into the artifice of eternity.

IV

Once out of nature I shall never take   25
My bodily form from any natural thing,
But such a form as Grecian goldsmiths make
Of hammered gold and gold enamelling
To keep a drowsy Emperor awake;
Or set upon a golden bough to sing   30
To lords and ladies of Byzantium
Of what is past, or passing, or to come.

Among School Children[1]

I

I walk through the long schoolroom questioning;
A kind old nun in a white hood replies;

---

1 A word has been said in the introduction to the Modern period about the arrangement of symbolic values in this poem. It should be noted that (in the first stanzas) the poet imagines himself as having already reached Byzantium, the ancient city which symbolizes for him the triumph of intellect and spirit over the life of the body; from this vantage point he looks back on the world he has left—"*that* is no country for old men." Then the situation changes slightly in stanza 3, where his plea to be gathered "into the artifice of eternity" is necessarily that of one who has not yet shaken off the "dying animal," the human body. In the fourth stanza he is frankly, completely, and calmly (after the fervor of stanza 3) in his own created being, in the world of nature, specifying a wish for future existences: never again to be a part of the natural world, to live in the flesh, but to exist only as spirit, symbolized by the goldsmith's artificial bird. In a note to stanza 4 Yeats says: "I have read somewhere that in the Emperor's palace at Byzantium was a tree made of gold and silver, and artificial birds that sang."—This poem and the next are from *The Tower* (1928).
2 Both "perne" and "gyre" have special meanings for Yeats, but here it is enough to see them as combining to describe a kind of motion—"to perne," to descend spiral-wise, but including the individual light dancing or revolving motion of the object or body as well as the spiraling. The gyre (whatever it symbolizes in other places in Yeats of the confusion of earthly existence) may be seen here as a descending whirlpool-like structure.

1 The first stanza describes the kind of school-visit which Yeats may have made when, in his sixties, he was a Senator of the Irish Free State. The sight of the children reminds him of a story told him in the past by a loved and beautiful woman of something that had happened to her as a child: a tale which, as it happened, had united them in sympathy. He tries then to see her as she had been when a child—did she look like one or the other of the children in the school-room there?—and succeeds all too well: it is as if she were suddenly before him as a living child. He then thinks of her (stanza 4) as she is now, aged as he is aged, but at the end of the stanza it is as if, for the moment of the school-visit, he had put an end to the somber reflections that have occurred to him there. But these reflections have started a train of thought, about the harshness of man's lot who must pass from youth to age, and about what values may eventually be seen as giving life its meaning. What young mother, he asks in stanza 5, if she could see her son grown old, would think his latter state worth the pains of birth or the care of setting him on his way? It would seem that he was being forced into a position where it would be necessary to affirm that only the soul has value, that the body must be spurned—but no: in the last three stanzas he dismisses the abstractions and the asceticism of the philosophers, invoking instead the images, the Presences that hold human feelings in thrall, whether the feelings of nuns or mothers. These images—images of the human body which claim human affection—have the power to break hearts, they doom to disappointment all who worship them, and yet they must be worshiped. Even to the man "with sixty winters on his head," who knows how life ends, the meaning of life lies in accepting it, in the faith in beauty and in the body which the last stanza affirms, as no poet has ever more eloquently affirmed it.

The children learn to cipher and to sing,
To study reading-books and history,
To cut and sew, be neat in everything 5
In the best modern way—the children's eyes
In momentary wonder stare upon
A sixty-year-old smiling public man.

II

I dream of a Ledaean body,[2] bent
Above a sinking fire, a tale that she 10
Told of a harsh reproof, or trivial event
That changed some childish day to tragedy—
Told, and it seemed that our two natures blent
Into a sphere from youthful sympathy,
Or else, to alter Plato's parable,[3] 15
Into the yolk and white of the one shell.

III

And thinking of that fit of grief or rage
I look upon one child or t' other there
And wonder if she stood so at that age—
For even daughters of the swan can share 20
Something of every paddler's heritage—
And had that colour upon cheek or hair,
And thereupon my heart is driven wild:
She stands before me as a living child.

IV

Her present image floats into the mind— 25
Did Quattrocento[4] finger fashion it
Hollow of cheek as though it drank the wind
And took a mess of shadows for its meat?
And I though never of Ledaean kind
Had pretty plumage once—enough of that, 30
Better to smile on all that smile, and show
There is a comfortable kind of old scarecrow.

V

What youthful mother, a shape upon her lap
Honey of generation had betrayed,[5]
And that must sleep, shriek, struggle to escape 35
As recollection or the drug decide,
Would think her son, did she but see that shape
With sixty or more winters on its head,
A compensation for the pang of his birth,
Or the uncertainty of his setting forth? 40

VI

Plato[6] thought nature but a spume that plays
Upon a ghostly paradigm of things;
Solider Aristotle played the taws
Upon the bottom of a king of kings;
World-famous golden-thighed Pythagoras 45
Fingered upon a fiddle-stick or strings
What a star sang and careless Muses heard:
Old clothes upon old sticks to scare a bird.

VII

Both nuns and mothers worship images,
But those the candles light are not as those 50
That animate a mother's reveries,
But keep a marble or a bronze repose.
And yet they too break hearts—O Presences
That passion, piety or affection knows,
And that all heavenly glory symbolise— 55
O self-born mockers of man's enterprise;

VIII

Labour is blossoming or dancing where
The body is not bruised to pleasure soul,

---

2 I.e., a body beautiful enough for a daughter of Leda, as Helen of Troy was. (In line 20 we are reminded that Helen was also the daughter of Zeus, who possessed Leda in the form of a swan.)

3 In the *Symposium,* where Aristophanes tells how Zeus had decided that it was necessary to split the double-formed primeval men. "He . . . cut men in two, like a sorb-apple which is halved for pickling, or as you might divide an egg with a hair." Consequently "each of us when separated is but the indenture of a man, having one side only like a flat fish, and he is always looking for his other half." (Jowett's translation)

4 The term used, from the Italian system of expressing dates, by art historians to describe the schools and style of fifteenth-century painting.

5 Yeats has explained in a note that the phrase "honey of generation" was taken from Porphyry's essay on "The Cave of the Nymphs"; but he adds, "[I] find no warrant in Porphyry for considering it the 'drug' that destroys the 'recollection' of prenatal freedom. . . ." In his essay on "Shelley's Poetry" (*Essays by W. B. Yeats,* especially p. 102) Yeats explains that for Porphyry, as for others of the ancients, "honey was the symbol . . . for 'pleasure arising from generation,'" the pleasure which had betrayed the infant on her lap from the prenatal world of nonexistence to the world of life.

6 In this stanza Plato and his predecessor Pythagoras (*fl.* 532 B.C.) serve to represent philosophical views that urge the freeing of the soul from the trammels of the flesh. The followers of Pythagoras, for instance, are said to have "had much in common with the Orphic communities which sought by rites and abstinences to purify the believer's soul and enable it to escape from the wheel of birth.'" "Solider Aristotle" (who for all his comparative solidity is dismissed with the other two in the last line of the stanza) was tutor to Alexander the Great, the "king of kings." *To play the taws* = to give a whipping.

Nor beauty born out of its own despair,
Nor blear-eyed wisdom out of midnight oil.   60
O chestnut tree, great rooted blossomer,
Are you the leaf, the blossom or the bole?
O body swayed to music, O brightening glance,
How can we know the dancer from the dance?

A Dialogue of Self and Soul[1]

I

My Soul. I summon to the winding ancient stair;
    Set all your mind upon the steep ascent,
    Upon the broken, crumbling battlement,
    Upon the breathless starlit air,
    Upon the star that marks the hidden pole;   5
    Fix every wandering thought upon
    That quarter where all thought is done:
    Who can distinguish darkness from the soul?

My Self. The consecrated blade upon my knees
    Is Sato's ancient blade, still as it was,   10
    Still razor-keen, still like a looking-glass
    Unspotted by the centuries;
    That flowering, silken, old embroidery, torn
    From some court-lady's dress and round
    The wooden scabbard bound and wound,   15
    Can, tattered, still protect, faded adorn.

My Soul. Why should the imagination of a man
    Long past his prime remember things that are
    Emblematical of love and war?
    Think of ancestral night that can,   20
    If but imagination scorn the earth
    And intellect its wandering
    To this and that and t'other thing,
    Deliver from the crime of death and birth.

My Self. Montashigi, third of his family, fash-   25
        ioned it
    Five hundred years ago, about it lie
    Flowers from I know not what embroidery—
    Heart's purple—and all these I set
    For emblems of the day against the tower
    Emblematical of the night,   30

---

[1] From *The Winding Stair* (1933). The sword, besides being a symbol, perhaps of life (its silken covering perhaps a symbol of beauty), was an actual sword given to Yeats by Sato, a Japanese friend.

And claim as by a soldier's right
A charter to commit the crime once more.

My Soul. Such fullness in that quarter overflows
    And falls into the basin of the mind
    That man is stricken deaf and dumb and   35
        blind,
    For intellect no longer knows
    Is from the *Ought,* or *Knower* from the
        Known—
    That is to say, ascends to Heaven;
    Only the dead can be forgiven;
    But when I think of that my tongue's a stone.   40

II

My Self. A living man is blind and drinks his
        drop.
    What matter if the ditches are impure?
    What matter if I live it all once more?
    Endure that toil of growing up;
    The ignominy of boyhood; the distress   45
    Of boyhood changing into man;
    The unfinished man and his pain
    Brought face to face with his own clumsiness;

    The finished man among his enemies?—
    How in the name of Heaven can he escape   50
    That defiling and disfigured shape
    The mirror of malicious eyes
    Casts upon his eyes until at last
    He thinks that shape must be his shape?
    And what's the good of an escape   55
    If honour find him in the wintry blast?

    I am content to live it all again
    And yet again, if it be life to pitch
    Into the frog-spawn of a blind man's ditch,
    A blind man battering blind men;   60
    Or into that most fecund ditch of all,
    The folly that man does
    Or must suffer, if he woos
    A proud woman not kindred of his soul.

    I am content to follow to its source   65
    Every event in action or in thought;
    Measure the lot; forgive myself the lot!
    When such as I cast out remorse
    So great a sweetness flows into the breast
    We must laugh and we must sing,   70
    We are blest by everything,
    Everything we look upon is blest.

Coole Park and Ballyee, 1931[1]

Under my window-ledge the waters race,
Otters below and moor-hens on the top,
Run for a mile undimmed in Heaven's face
Then darkening through "dark" Raftery's "cellar" drop,
Run underground, rise in a rocky place   5
In Coole demesne, and there to finish up
Spread to a lake and drop into a hole.
What's water but the generated soul?[2]

Upon the border of that lake's a wood
Now all dry sticks under a wintry sun,   10
And in a copse of beeches there I stood,
For Nature's pulled her tragic buskin on
And all the rant's a mirror of my mood:
At sudden thunder of the mounting swan
I turned about and looked where branches break   15
The glittering reaches of the flooded lake.

Another emblem there! That stormy white
But seems a concentration of the sky;
And, like the soul, it sails into the sight
And in the morning's gone, no man knows why;   20
And is so lovely that it sets to right
What knowledge or its lack had set awry,
So arrogantly pure, a child might think
It can be murdered with a spot of ink.

Sound of a stick upon the floor, a sound   25
From somebody that toils from chair to chair;

Beloved books that famous hands have bound,
Old marble heads, old pictures everywhere;
Great rooms where travelled men and children
        found
Content or joy; a last inheritor   30
Where none has reigned that lacked a name
        and fame
Or out of folly into folly came.

A spot whereon the founders lived and died
Seemed once more dear than life; ancestral trees,
Or gardens rich in memory glorified   35
Marriages, alliances and families,
And every bride's ambition satisfied.
Where fashion or mere fantasy decrees
Man shifts about—all that great glory spent—
Like some poor Arab tribesman and his tent.   40

We were the last romantics—chose for theme
Traditional sanctity and loveliness;
Whatever's written in what poets name
The book of the people; whatever most can bless
The mind of man or elevate a rhyme;   45
But all is changed, that high horse riderless,
Though mounted in that saddle Homer rode
Where the swan drifts upon a darkening flood.

At Algeciras[1]—A Meditation
upon Death

The heron-billed pale cattle-birds
That feed on some foul parasite
Of the Moroccan flocks and herds
Cross the narrow Straits to light
In the rich midnight of the garden trees   5
Till the dawn break upon those mingled seas.[2]

Often at evening when a boy
Would I carry to a friend—
Hoping more substantial joy
Did an older mind commend—   10
Not such as are in Newton's metaphor,
But actual shells of Rosses' level shore.[3]

---

1 Coole demesne, or Coole Park, is the Gregorys' estate
so often referred to in Yeats's poems. At the time the
poem describes, Lady Gregory (who died the next year,
1932) was living there old and alone, "a last inheritor"
(stanza 4). The geographical features mentioned in stanza
1 are described in "Dust Hath Closed Helen's Eye," one
of the chapters (dated 1900) of Yeats's *The Celtic Twilight*, where he speaks of a visit to "a little group of
houses, not many enough to be called a village, in the
barony of Kiltartan in County Galway, whose name,
Ballylee, is known through all the west of Ireland." He
mentions that Raftery, "a famous poet" of the early nineteenth century, in an Irish poem about Mary Hynes had
said "there is a strong cellar in Ballylee." Yeats's guide
had told him that the cellar was "the great hole where
the river sank under ground, and he brought me to a
deep pool, where an otter hurried away under a grey
boulder. . . ." Raftery was nearly blind, hence "dark
Raftery" (line 4). This poem and the next are from *The
Winding Stair and Other Poems* (1933); the last three
are from *Last Poems and Plays* (1940).
2 This idea, touched here only glancingly and incidentally,
Yeats derived from the philosophical writings of Henry
More, the seventeenth-century neo-Platonist.

---

1 A Spanish city a few miles west of Gibraltar.
2 In the Straits of Gibraltar, on which Algeciras faces, the
waters of the Atlantic and Mediterranean meet.
3 For Yeats's description of Rosses, see "Drumcliff and
Rosses " in *The Celtic Twilight*, where he calls it "a little
sea-dividing, sandy plain, covered with short grass, like a
green table-cloth, and lying in the foam mid-way between
the round cairn-headed Knocknarea and 'Ben Bulben,
famous for hawks. . . .'"

Greater glory in the sun,
An evening chill upon the air,
Bid imagination run   15
Much on the Great Questioner;
What He can question, what if questioned I
Can with a fitting confidence reply.

Byzantium[1]

The unpurged images of day recede;
The Emperor's drunken soldiery are abed;
Night resonance recedes, night-walkers' song
After great cathedral gong;
A starlit or a moonlit dome disdains   5
All that man is,
All mere complexities,
The fury and the mire of human veins.

Before me floats an image, man or shade,
Shade more than man, more image than a shade: 10
For Hades' bobbin bound in mummy-cloth
May unwind the winding path;
A mouth that has no moisture and no breath
Breathless mouths may summon;
I hail the superhuman;   15
I call it death-in-life and life-in-death.

Miracle, bird or golden handiwork,
More miracle than bird or handiwork,
Planted on the star-lit golden bough,
Can like the cocks of Hades crow,   20
Or, by the moon embittered, scorn aloud
In glory of changeless metal
Common bird or petal
And all complexities of mire or blood.

At midnight on the Emperor's pavement flit   25
Flames that no faggot feeds, nor steel has lit,
Nor storm disturbs, flames begotten of flame,
Where blood-begotten spirits come
And all complexities of fury leave,
Dying into a dance,   30
An agony of trance,
An agony of flame that cannot singe a sleeve.

Astraddle on the dolphin's mire and blood,
Spirit after spirit! The smithies break the flood.

The golden smithies of the Emperor!   35
Marbles of the dancing floor
Break bitter furies of complexity,
Those images that yet
Fresh images beget,
That dolphin-torn, that gong-tormented sea.   40

Crazy Jane and the Bishop[1]

Bring me to the blasted oak
That I, midnight upon the stroke,
(All find safety in the tomb.)
May call down curses on his head
Because of my dear Jack that's dead.   5
Coxcomb was the least he said:
The solid man and the coxcomb.

Nor was he Bishop when his ban
Banished Jack the Journeyman,
(All find safety in the tomb.)   10
Nor so much as parish priest,
Yet he, an old book in his fist,
Cried that we lived like beast and beast:
The solid man and the coxcomb.

The Bishop has a skin, God knows,   15
Wrinkled like the foot of a goose,
(All find safety in the tomb.)
Nor can he hide in holy black
The heron's hunch upon his back,
But a birch-tree stood my Jack: 20
The solid man and the coxcomb.

Jack had my virginity,
And bids me to the oak, for he
(All find safety in the tomb.)
Wanders out into the night   25
And there is shelter under it,
But should that other come, I spit:
The solid man and the coxcomb.

Lapis Lazuli[1]
(For Harry Clifton)

I have heard that hysterical women say
They are sick of the palette and fiddle-bow,

---

[1] From *The Winding Stair* (1933).

[1] The first of a series of poems whose protagonist is
Crazy Jane, from *Words for Music Perhaps.*

[1] This poem, and those that follow, are from *Last Poems*

Of poets that are always gay,
For everybody knows or else should know
That if nothing drastic is done
Aeroplane and Zeppelin will come out,
Pitch like King Billy bomb-balls in
Until the town lie beaten flat.

All perform their tragic play,
There struts Hamlet, there is Lear,
That's Ophelia, that Cordelia;
Yet they, should the last scene be there,
The great stage curtain about to drop,
If worthy their prominent part in the play,
Do not break up their lines to weep.

They know that Hamlet and Lear are gay;
Gaiety transfiguring all that dread.
All men have aimed at, found and lost;
Black out; Heaven blazing into the head:
Tragedy wrought to its uttermost.
Though Hamlet rambles and Lear rages,
And all the drop-scenes drop at once
Upon a hundred thousand stages,
It cannot grow by an inch or an ounce.

On their own feet they came, or on shipboard,
Camel-back, horse-back, ass-back, mule-back,
Old civilisations put to the sword.
Then they and their wisdom went to rack:
No handiwork of Callimachus,
Who handled marble as if it were bronze,

Made draperies that seemed to rise
When sea-wind swept the corner, stands;
His long lamp-chimney shaped like the stem
Of a slender palm, stood but a day;
All things fall and are built again,
And those that build them again are gay.

Two Chinamen, behind them a third,
Are carved in lapis lazuli,
Over them flies a long-legged bird,
A symbol of longevity;
The third, doubtless a serving-man,
Carries a musical instrument.

Every discoloration of the stone,
Every accidental crack or dent,
Seems a water-course or an avalanche,
Or lofty slope where it still snows
Though doubtless plum or cherry-branch
Sweetens the little half-way house
Those Chinamen climb towards, and I
Delight to imagine them seated there;
There, on the mountain and the sky,
On all the tragic scene they stare.
One asks for mournful melodies;
Accomplished fingers begin to play.
Their eyes mid many wrinkles, their eyes,
Their ancient, glittering eyes, are gay.

and Plays (1940). The *objet d'art* that provides the central image of the poem is a large square of lapis lazuli carved to represent the scene here described; it had been given to Yeats by the friend to whom the poem is dedicated.

In the poem Yeats raises the question of whether the tragic mood is unseemly (as hysterical women say) at a time when civilization seems about to topple. In answer he says that tragic art is not to be seen as sniveling, weak, and self-indulgent: its essence is a salutary gaiety that provides the race with the strength and courage it needs. Civilizations have always fallen, nor can they be preserved in their individual physical manifestations. What matters, and what must be preserved through the kind of wisdom that tragic art recognizes and safeguards, is the spirit that enables mankind to go on building its civilization perpetually anew, with joy. It does not matter that of particular works by Callimachus, the Greek sculptor of the fifth century B.C., only the fame has come down to us; it is more important to have his name and his example, that each succeeding sculptor should obey the same impulse, than it would be to have a few specific works by a specific artist of the past. In the concluding section of the poem Yeats makes a little parable of his meaning from what he sees (and from what he imagines as following from what he sees) on the lapis lazuli plaque.

An Acre of Grass

Picture and book remain,
An acre of green grass
For air and exercise,
Now strength of body goes;
Midnight, an old house
Where nothing stirs but a mouse.

My temptation is quiet.
Here at life's end
Neither loose imagination,
Nor the mill of the mind
Consuming its rag and bone,
Can make the truth known.

Grant me an old man's frenzy,
Myself must I remake
Till I am Timon and Lear
Or that William Blake

Who beat upon the wall
Till Truth obeyed his call;

A mind Michael Angelo knew
That can pierce the clouds,   20
Or inspired by frenzy
Shake the dead in their shrouds;
Forgotten else by mankind,
An old man's eagle mind.

Long-Legged Fly

That civilisation may not sink,
Its great battle lost,
Quiet the dog, tether the pony
To a distant post;
Our master Caesar is in the tent   5
Where the maps are spread,
His eyes fixed upon nothing,
A hand under his head.
Like a long-legged fly upon the stream
His mind moves upon silence.   10

That the topless towers be burnt
And men recall that face,[1]
Move most gently if move you must
In this lonely place.
She thinks, part woman, three parts a child,   15
That nobody looks; her feet
Practise a tinker shuffle
Picked up on a street.
Like a long-legged fly upon the stream
Her mind moves upon silence.   20

That girls at puberty may find
The first Adam in their thought,
Shut the door of the Pope's chapel,[2]
Keep those children out.
There on that scaffolding reclines   25
Michael Angelo.
With no more sound than the mice make
His hand moves to and fro.
Like a long-legged fly upon the stream
His mind moves upon silence.   30

---

[1] Of Helen of Troy.
[2] The Sistine Chapel at the Vatican in Rome, decorated by Michelangelo (and others); the Creation of Adam is depicted in one of the compartments on the ceiling.

John Kinsella's Lament
for Mrs. Mary Moore

A bloody and a sudden end,
    Gunshot or a noose,
For Death who takes what man would keep,
    Leaves what man would lose.
He might have had my sister,   5
    My cousins by the score,
But nothing satisfied the fool
    But my dear Mary Moore,
None other knows what pleasures man
    At table or in bed.   10
What shall I do for pretty girls
    Now my old bawd is dead?

Though stiff to strike a bargain,
    Like an old Jew man,
Her bargain struck we laughed and talked   15
    And emptied many a can;
And O! but she had stories,
    Though not for the priest's ear,
To keep the soul of man alive,
    Banish age and care,   20
And being old she put a skin
    On everything she said.
What shall I do for pretty girls
    Now my old bawd is dead?

The priests have got a book that says   25
    But for Adam's sin
Eden's Garden would be there
    And I there within.
No expectation fails there,
    No pleasing habit ends,   30
No man grows old, no girl grows cold,
    But friends walk by friends.
Who quarrels over halfpennies
    That plucks the trees for bread?
What shall I do for pretty girls   35
    Now my old bawd is dead?

The Circus Animals' Desertion[1]

I

I sought a theme and sought for it in vain,
I sought it daily for six weeks or so.

---

[1] Here Yeats harks back in old age to some of the mythological figures he had invoked in his earlier poems and

Maybe at last, being but a broken man,
I must be satisfied with my heart, although
Winter and summer till old age began
My circus animals were all on show,   5
Those stilted boys, that burnished chariot,
Lion and woman and the Lord knows what.

II

What can I but enumerate old themes?
First that sea-rider Oisin led by the nose   10
Through three enchanted islands, allegorical
    dreams,
Vain gaiety, vain battle, vain repose,
Themes of the embittered heart, or so it seems,
That might adorn old songs or courtly shows;
But what cared I that set him on to ride,   15
I, starved for the bosom of his faery bride?

And then a counter-truth filled out its play,
The Countess Cathleen was the name I gave it;
She, pity-crazed, had given her soul away,
But masterful Heaven had intervened to save it.   20
I thought my dear must her own soul destroy,
So did fanaticism and hate enslave it,
And this brought forth a dream and soon enough
This dream itself had all my thought and love.

And when the Fool and Blind Man stole the   25
    bread
Cuchulain fought the ungovernable sea;
Heart-mysteries there, and yet when all is said
It was the dream itself enchanted me:
Character isolated by a deed
To engross the present and dominate memory.   30
Players and painted stage took all my love,
And not those things that they were emblems of.

III

Those masterful images because complete
Grew in pure mind, but out of what began?

---

plays: Oisin (pronounced *Usheen*), the hero of his long
narrative poem *The Wanderings of Oisin* (1889), summarized in part II; the Countess Cathleen, heroine of the play
(1892) performed at the opening of the National Theater
in Dublin in 1899; and Cuchulain (pronounced *Cuhoolin*),
who appears in the poem "Cuchulain's Fight with the
Sea" (1892) and in the play *On Baile's Strand* (1904).
Characteristically for the poems of this last phase of his
art, Yeats rejects myth in favor of uncompromising acceptance of lived reality.

A mound of refuse or the sweepings of a street,   35
Old kettles, old bottles, and a broken can,
Old iron, old bones, old rags, that raving slut
Who keeps the till. Now that my ladder's gone,
I must lie down where all the ladders start,
In the foul rag-and-bone shop of the heart.   40

The Black Tower

Say that the men of the old black tower,
Though they but feed as the goatherd feeds,
Their money spent, their wine gone sour,
Lack nothing that a soldier needs,
That all are oath-bound men: 5
Those banners come not in.

There in the tomb stand the dead upright,
But winds come up from the shore:
They shake when the winds roar,
Old bones upon the mountain shake.   10

Those banners come to bribe or threaten,
Or whisper that a man's a fool
Who, when his own right king's forgotten,
Cares what king sets up his rule.
If he died long ago   15
Why do you dread us so?

There in the tomb drops the faint moonlight,
But wind comes up from the shore:
They shake when the winds roar,
Old bones upon the mountain shake.   20

The tower's old cook that must climb and clam-
    ber
Catching small birds in the dew of the morn
When we hale men lie stretched in slumber
Swears that he hears the king's great horn.
But he's a lying hound: 25
Stand we on guard oath-bound!

There in the tomb the dark grows blacker,
But wind comes up from the shore:
They shake when the winds roar,
Old bones upon the mountain shake.   30

January 21, 1939

Thomas Hardy

1840–1928

If we consider Hardy strictly as a novelist, it might be difficult to claim him for the Modern period, even though in his novels he is constantly subjecting the harsher, more repressive institutions and dogmas of his time to a current of critical inquiry that foreshadows the twentieth century, and even though his novels, like those of James and Conrad, have always stood rather as an inauguration of the fiction of the new century than as a conclusion to that of the old. When one considers him as a poet, however, the case is different, and here the matter of dates is significant.

Hardy had been writing poetry ever since he had been writing anything at all, from as early as the 1860s. But he began his literary career as a novelist, with the publication (anonymous) of *Desperate Remedies* (1871) and *Under the Greenwood Tree* (1872), and was to appear before the public as a writer of fiction for the next twenty-five years. Among the novels were *Far from the Madding Crowd* (1874), *The Return of the Native* (1878), *The Mayor of Casterbridge* (1886), *Tess of the D'Urbervilles* (1891), and *Jude the Obscure* (1895–96); the volumes of short stories include *Wessex Tales* (1888) and *Life's Little Ironies* (1894). With *Tess of the D'Urbervilles* and *Jude the Obscure*, Hardy encountered such severe difficulties from reactionary public opinion and official or semiofficial repression that he resolved to make an end to his career as a novelist, something which he had perhaps intended to do for some time, and to devote himself exclusively to his poetry. In a diary-entry dated October 17, 1896, and headed "Poetry," he says: "Perhaps I can express more fully in verse ideas and emotions which run counter to the inert crystallized opinion—hard as rock—which the vast body of men have vested interests in supporting. . . ."

His first collection of verse, *Wessex Poems and Other Verses*, was published in 1898, and other volumes appeared at intervals for the rest of his life. Their titles are characteristic and descriptive: *Poems of the Past and the Present* (1902), *Time's Laughingstocks and Other Verses* (1909), *Satires of Circumstance* (1914), *Moments of Vision and Miscellaneous Verses* (1917), *Late Lyrics and Earlier* (1922), *Human Shows and Far Fantasies* (1925), and the posthumously published *Winter Words* (1928). Two of these titles point to Hardy's habit, common to all the volumes, of publishing poems that he had had by him for some time alongside others that were new.

Still, it is not merely the fact that several of Hardy's individual volumes of poems were published during the decades that also saw the publication of the most epoch-making poems of the Modern period, but rather the specific qualities of the poetry itself that make Hardy a poet to be reckoned with in the history of Modern literature. It is significant that I. A. Richards, writing *Science and Poetry* in 1926, considered Hardy's poetry along with that of Yeats and Eliot when it was a question of determining the role of poetry in the modern world; and there is testimony from the poets who were beginning their careers around 1930 that Hardy was for them a distinct and forceful presence. Many readers owe their initiation into an awareness of the essential values of Hardy's poetry not to any written criticism but to having heard Dylan Thomas read a few of the poems, whether on his lecture tours or over the B.B.C. or on phonograph records.

On at least one occasion, Dylan Thomas prefaced his reading of Hardy's poems by saying that there were hundreds of them and that he loved them all. This is fully as appropriate an attitude as that of the critics who undertake to establish a canon of the dozen or so "best" poems. Certainly a reader will want to make discriminations: it is inevitable that, out of eight or nine hundred poems, some will seem weak or mechanical in conception or flaccid or unengaging in execution. A more debatable contention, but one that is defensible in that it helps us toward an appreciation of what it is that Hardy does *best,* is that his poems of individual instance, of individual tragic or frustrated circumstance, are to be preferred to his poems of direct cosmic statement. Sometimes, to be sure, one encounters both elements in a single poem, where they reinforce one another: when that is the case, it is apt to be Hardy's uncompromising attention to the exact circumstance, in all its shabbiness or awkwardness, that gives moving conviction to the total statement. The very phrasing is an effective working element of the poetic situation: phrases that do not slip off the tongue easily, so that we have to give every word its due weight and importance if we are to *say* the line at all. This is true also with Hardy's characteristic images, seldom conventionally beautiful or "poetic," so that if we are to accept them at all, we have to accept the vision they reflect of an awkward, harsh, uncompromising reality. In "The Darkling Thrush," with its bleak vision of the nineteenth century just ending, there are images of this kind, particularly that of the shabby, aged thrush, "frail, gaunt, and small,/In blast-beruffled plume," who has so little in common with the nightingales and skylarks we are accustomed to finding in the poetry of romantic vision.

Equally unaccommodating to accepted notions of euphony and grace are Hardy's diction and phrasing: in the very first stanza of "The Convergence of the Twain," for example, the description of the sunken liner in the phrase "stilly couches she," or the complex image in the second stanza of the ship's now-extinguished furnace-chambers. Hardy seemed to welcome awkwardness almost for its own sake, and this was one aspect of his practice that distanced his poetry unmistakably from the kind of late nineteenth-century poetry which continued to exploit Romantic and post-Romantic stereotypes of image, diction, and feeling long after the life had gone out of them.

The two-volume biography of Hardy by his second wife, Florence Emily Hardy (*The Early Life of Thomas Hardy,* 1928, and *The Later Years of Thomas Hardy,* 1930), which Hardy is now known to have had a larger part in writing than was formerly supposed, offers a wealth of authoritative statement as to his beliefs—never very complicated, whether in the realm of philosophical speculation or of poetic principle—and, even more suggestive when it is a question of understanding the poetry, as to the aspects of human experience that caught his attention and engaged his affections. He saw mankind as subject to "chance and change"—these are the first words of *Wessex Poems,* and they are the last words of the preface to his next volume, *Poems of the Past and the Present.* He saw the possibility of happiness for mankind as very slight indeed; and the contemplation of "the monotonous moils of strained, hard-run Humanity" brought out a strong vein of compassion, in which he included animals as well. Although he wanted to be called a "meliorist" rather than a pessimist, his view of the likely fate of mankind and the higher creatures is sufficiently bleak. " 'All is vanity,' saith the Preacher. But if all were only vanity, who would mind? Alas, it is too often worse than vanity; agony, darkness, death also." But in another place:

Thought of the determination to enjoy. We see it in all nature, from the leaf on the tree to the titled lady at the ball. . . . Like pent-up water it will find a chink of possibility somewhere. Even the most oppressed of men and animals find it, so that out of a thousand there is hardly one who has not a sun of some sort for his soul.

We learn in the biography of his lifelong fondness for the dance music played by the great bands at the public dance halls in his youth—Willis's Rooms, Cremorne, the Argyle—and just possibly it is more important to recognize in his poetry the presence of something like the strong, emotionally charged rhythms of such music than it is to see the poetry as just one more reflection of nineteenth-century religious doubt and agnostic disarray. This is the rhythm that animates a poem like "The Voice" —at least that poem makes rhythm do what it can to embody a strongly emotional sense of loss and longing.

We learn, too, in the biography about the sorts of juxtaposition of apparently disparate elements that caught his eye, forming, as he puts it in *Jude the Obscure,* "the basis of a beautiful crystallization." One such juxtaposition occurred when he and Mrs. Hardy were attending a First-Aid lecture:

A skeleton—the one used in these lectures—is hung up outside the window. We face it as we sit. Outside the band is playing, and the children are dancing. I can see their little figures through the window past the skeleton dangling in front.

The elements assembled here—death, life, and the dance or the music to underscore it emotionally— are similarly assembled in much of Hardy's poetry. "The Poet takes note of nothing," as he said in 1908, "that he cannot feel emotively."

Of course other features of Hardy's life, interests, and concerns are reflected in his poems. He was born near Dorchester—the Casterbridge of his novels —the principal town of the area of southwest England which Hardy called "Wessex," restoring the name of the ancient kingdom of the West Saxons. He was thoroughly versed in country life, country lore, and country music. Apprenticed to a Dorchester architect and church-restorer at the age of sixteen, he used to read Latin and Greek before going to work in the morning. In 1862 he went to London, "to pursue the art and science of architecture on more advanced lines," and worked for five or six years as an assistant architect. Returning to Dorchester in 1867, he was sent on a church-restoring mission to St. Juliot, Cornwall, where he met Lavinia Gifford, who was to become his first wife and who figures as the subject of many of his most intensely felt poems (for example, the series of poems written immediately after her death in 1912, which includes "The Voice," "The Going," and "After a Journey"). He had turned to writing as a relief from the monotony of his work as an architect, first writing poems ("Neutral Tones" is one of the early ones) and then, in 1867, making his first attempt to write a novel. But, as we have seen, when the long career as a novelist came to an end, Hardy was free to turn back to another career that had at first seemed merely impractical, that of being a poet. One aspect of his life as a poet should not be overlooked: the vast panoramic—even cinematic—verse-drama of the Napoleonic Era, *The Dynasts*, first published in three separate parts (1904–08) and then as a unit in 1910.

TEXTS: *The Collected Poems of Thomas Hardy* (1930 and subsequent reprintings) includes all of Hardy's verse except *The Dynasts*. (The American edition also omits *Winter Words*.) There are volumes of selections by G. M. Young (1940 and later reprintings) and John Crowe Ransom (1961). In the centenary year, 1940, *The Southern Review* devoted an expanded Summer issue to Hardy, printing essays on every aspect of his work, including essays on his poetry by W. H. Auden, R. P. Blackmur, Cleanth Brooks, F. R. Leavis, John Crowe Ransom, and Allen Tate; many of these essays have been reprinted in volumes by their respective authors. C. M. Bowra's *Inspiration and Poetry* (1947) includes an essay on "The Lyrical Poetry of Thomas Hardy," and there is another paper, with the same title, by C. Day Lewis in the *Proceedings of the British Academy*, Vol. XXXVII (1951). *Thomas Hardy: A Critical Biography*, by J. I. M. Stewart (1971), includes a chapter on the poetry. There is a volume on Hardy, by Irving Howe, in the Masters of World Literature series (1967). Books devoted entirely to Hardy as poet are: Kenneth Marsden, *The Poems of Thomas Hardy: A Critical Introduction* (1969); J. O. Bailey, *The Poetry of Thomas Hardy: A Handbook and Commentary* (1970); and Jean R. Brooks, *Thomas Hardy: The Poetic Structure* (1971). *Thomas Hardy: The Critical Heritage*, edited by R. G. Cox (1970), collects contemporary reviews and articles from 1871 to 1918.

Neutral Tones

We stood by a pond that winter day,
And the sun was white, as though chidden of
    God,
And a few leaves lay on the starving sod;
    —They had fallen from an ash, and were
      gray.

Your eyes on me were as eyes that rove   5
Over tedious riddles of years ago;
And some words played between us to and fro
    On which lost the more by our love.

The smile on your mouth was the deadest thing
Alive enough to have strength to die;   10
And a grin of bitterness swept thereby
    Like an ominous bird a-wing. . . .

Since then, keen lessons that love deceives,
And wrings with wrong, have shaped to me
Your face, and the God-curst sun, and a tree,   15
    And a pond edged with grayish leaves.

Thoughts of Phena

At News of Her Death

Not a line of her writing have I,
    Not a thread of her hair,
No mark of her late time as dame in her dwelling, whereby
    I may picture her there;
And in vain do I urge my unsight   5
    To conceive my lost prize
At her close, whom I knew when her dreams were upbrimming with light,
    And with laughter her eyes.

What scenes spread around her last days,
    Sad, shining, or dim?   10
Did her gifts and compassions enray and enarch
  her sweet ways
    With an aureate nimb?
    Or did life-light decline from her years,
    And mischances control
Her full day-star; unease, or regret, or forebodings, or fears   15
    Disennoble her soul?

Thus I do but the phantom retain
    Of the maiden of yore
As my relic; yet haply the best of her—fined in my brain
    It may be the more   20
That no line of her writing have I,
    Nor a thread of her hair,
No mark of her late time as dame in her dwelling, whereby
    I may picture her there.

"I Look into My Glass"

I look into my glass,
And view my wasting skin,

And say, "Would God it came to pass
My heart had shrunk as thin!"

For then, I, undistrest   5
By hearts grown cold to me,
Could lonely wait my endless rest
With equanimity.

But Time, to make me grieve,
Part steals, lets part abide;   10
And shakes this fragile frame at eve
With throbbings of noontide.

Drummer Hodge[1]

I

They throw in Drummer Hodge, to rest
    Uncoffined—just as found:
His landmark is a kopje-crest[2]
    That breaks the veldt[3] around;
And foreign constellations west   5
    Each night above his mound.

II

Young Hodge the Drummer never knew—
    Fresh from his Wessex home—
The meaning of the broad Karoo,[4]
    The Bush, the dusty loam,   10
And why uprose to nightly view
    Strange stars amid the gloam.

III

Yet portion of that unknown plain
    Will Hodge for ever be;
His homely Northern breast and brain   15
    Grow to some Southern tree,
And strange-eyed constellations reign
    His stars eternally.

A Broken Appointment

        You did not come,
And marching Time drew on, and wore me
    numb.—

Yet for loss of your dear presence there
Than that I thus found lacking in your make
That high compassion which can overbear   5
Reluctance for pure lovingkindness' sake
Grieved I, when, as the hope-hour stroked its
    sum,
        You did not come.

        You love not me,
And love alone can lend you loyalty;   10
—I know and knew it. But, unto the store
Of human deeds divine in all but name,
Was it not worth a little hour or more
To add yet this: Once you, a woman, came
To soothe a time-torn man; even though it be   15
        You love not me?

The Darkling Thrush

I leant upon a coppice gate
    When Frost was spectre-gray,
And Winter's dregs made desolate
    The weakening eye of day.
The tangled bine-stems scored the sky   5
    Like strings of broken lyres,
And all mankind that haunted nigh
    Had sought their household fires.

The land's sharp features seemed to be
    The Century's corpse outleant,   10
His crypt the cloudy canopy,
    The wind his death-lament.
The ancient pulse of germ and birth
    Was shrunken hard and dry,
And every spirit upon earth   15
    Seemed fervourless as I.

At once a voice arose among
    The bleak twigs overhead
In a full-hearted evensong
    Of joy illimited;   20
An aged thrush, frail, gaunt, and small,
    In blast-beruffled plume,
Had chosen thus to fling his soul
    Upon the growing gloom.

So little cause for carolings   25
    Of such ecstatic sound
Was written on terrestrial things
    Afar or nigh around,

That I could think there trembled through
   His happy good-night air   30
Some blessed Hope, whereof he knew
   And I was unaware.

A Church Romance

(Mellstock: circa 1835)

She turned in the high pew, until her sight
Swept the west gallery, and caught its row
Of music-men with viol, book, and bow
Against the sinking sad tower-window light.

She turned again; and in her pride's despite   5
One strenuous viol's inspirer seemed to throw
A message from his string to her below,
Which said: "I claim thee as my own forthright!"

Thus their hearts' bond began, in due time
   signed.
And long years thence, when Age had scared   10
   Romance,
At some old attitude of his or glance
That gallery-scene would break upon her mind,
With him as minstrel, ardent, young, and trim,
Bowing "New Sabbath" or "Mount Ephraim."

The Convergence of the Twain[1]

(Lines on the loss of the "Titanic")

I

    In a solitude of the sea
    Deep from human vanity,
And the Pride of Life that planned her, stilly
    couches she.

II

    Steel chambers, late the pyres
    Of her salamandrine fires,   5
Cold currents thrid, and turn to rhythmic tidal
    lyres.

III

    Over the mirrors meant
    To glass the opulent

---

[1] The White Star liner *Titanic* sank, with great loss of life, after collision with an iceberg on its maiden voyage from Southampton to New York on April 15, 1912.

The sea-worm crawls—grotesque, slimed, dumb,
    indifferent.

IV

    Jewels in joy designed   10
    To ravish the sensuous mind
Lie lightless, all their sparkles bleared and black
    and blind.

V

    Dim moon-eyed fishes near
    Gaze at the gilded gear
And query: "What does this vaingloriousness   15
    down here?". . .

VI

    Well: while was fashioning
    This creature of cleaving wing,
The Immanent Will that stirs and urges every-
    thing

VII

    Prepared a sinister mate
    For her—so gaily great—   20
A Shape of Ice, for the time far and dissociate.

VIII

    And as the smart ship grew
    In stature, grace, and hue,
In shadowy silent distance grew the Iceberg too.

IX

    Alien they seemed to be: 25
    No mortal eye could see
The intimate welding of their later history.

X

    Or sign that they were bent
    By paths coincident
On being anon twin halves of one august event,   30

XI

    Till the Spinner of the Years
    Said "Now!" And each one hears,
And consummation comes, and jars two hemi-
    spheres.

The Place on the Map

I

I look upon the map that hangs by me—
Its shires and towns and rivers lined in varnished

artistry—
    And I mark a jutting height
Coloured purple, with a margin of blue sea.

II

—'Twas a day of latter summer, hot and dry;   5
Ay, even the waves seemed drying as we walked
    on, she and I,
    By this spot where, calmly quite,
She unfolded what would happen by and by.

III

This hanging map depicts the coast and place,
And re-creates therewith our unforeboded trou-   10
    blous case
    All distinctly to my sight,
And her tension, and the aspect of her face.

IV

Weeks and weeks we had loved beneath that
    blazing blue,
Which had lost the art of raining, as her eyes to-
    day had too,
    While she told what, as by sleight,   15
Shot our firmament with rays of ruddy hue.

V

For the wonder and the wormwood of the
    whole
Was that what in realms of reason would have
    joyed our double soul
    Wore a torrid tragic light
Under order-keeping's rigorous control.   20

VI

So, the map revives her words, the spot, the
    time,
And the thing we found we had to face before
    the next year's prime;
    The charted coast stares bright,
And its episode comes back in pantomime.

The Going[1]

Why did you give no hint that night
That quickly after the morrow's dawn,

---

[1] This poem and the two that follow are from a series of poems written soon after the death of Hardy's first wife, and printed with the phrase *"Veteris vestigia flammae"* ("embers of an old fire") as epigraph, in which Hardy looked back with intense longing on the early years of a marriage that had later been an unhappy one.

And calmly, as if indifferent quite,
You would close your term here, up and be gone
    Where I could not follow   5
    With wing of swallow
To gain one glimpse of you ever anon!

    Never to bid good-bye,
    Or lip me the softest call,
Or utter a wish for a word, while I   10
Saw morning harden upon the wall,
    Unmoved, unknowing
    That your great going
Had place that moment, and altered all.

Why do you make me leave the house   15
And think for a breath it is you I see
At the end of the alley of bending boughs
Where so often at dusk you used to be;
    Till in darkening dankness
    The yawning blankness   20
Of the perspective sickens me!

    You were she who abode
    By those red-veined rocks far West,
You were the swan-necked one who rode
Along the beetling Beeny Crest,   25
    And, reining nigh me,
    Would muse and eye me,
While Life unrolled us its very best.

Why, then, latterly did we not speak,
Did we not think of those days long dead,   30
And ere your vanishing strive to seek
That time's renewal? We might have said,
    "In this bright spring weather
    We'll visit together
Those places that once we visited."   35

    Well, well! All's past amend,
    Unchangeable. It must go.
I seem but a dead man held on end
To sink down soon. . . . O you could not know
    That such swift fleeing   40
    No soul foreseeing—
Not even I—would undo me so!

The Voice

Woman much missed, how you call to me, call to
    me,
Saying that now you are not as you were

When you had changed from the one who was
    all to me,
But as at first, when our day was fair.

Can it be you that I hear? Let me view you, then,   5
Standing as when I drew near to the town
Where you would wait for me: yes, as I knew
    you then,
Even to the original air-blue gown!

Or is it only the breeze, in its listlessness
Travelling across the wet mead to me here,   10
You being ever dissolved to wan wistlessness.
Heard no more again far or near?

    Thus I; faltering forward,
    Leaves around me falling,
Wind oozing thin through the thorn from nor-   15
    ward,
    And the woman calling.

The waterfall, above which the mist-bow shone
    At the then fair hour in the then fair weather,   20
And the cave just under, with a voice still so
    hollow
    That it seems to call out to me from forty
    years ago,
      When you were all aglow,
And not the thin ghost that I now fraily follow!

Ignorant of what there is flitting here to see,   25
    The waked birds preen and the seals flop
    lazily,
Soon you will have, Dear, to vanish from me,
    For the stars close their shutters and the dawn
    whitens hazily.
Trust me, I mind not, though Life lours,
    The bringing me here; nay, bring me here   30
    again!
      I am just the same as when
Our days were a joy, and our paths through
    flowers.

After a Journey

Hereto I come to view a voiceless ghost;
    Whither, O whither will its whim now draw
    me?
Up the cliff, down, till I'm lonely, lost,
    And the unseen waters' ejaculations awe me.
Where you will next be there's no knowing,   5
    Facing round about me everywhere,
      With your nut-coloured hair,
And gray eyes, and rose-flush coming and going.

Yes: I have re-entered your olden haunts at last;
    Through the years, through the dead scenes I   10
    have tracked you;
What have you now found to say of our past—
    Scanned across the dark space wherein I have
    lacked you?
Summer gave us sweets, but autumn wrought
    division?
    Things were not lastly as firstly well
      With us twain, you tell?   15
But all's closed now, despite Time's derision.

I see what you are doing: you are leading me on
    To the spots we knew when we haunted here
    together,

The Blinded Bird

So zestfully canst thou sing?
And all this indignity,
With God's consent, on thee!
Blinded ere yet a-wing
By the red-hot needle thou.   5
I stand and wonder how
So zestfully thou canst sing!

Resenting not such wrong,
Thy grievous pain forgot,
Eternal dark thy lot,   10
Groping thy whole life long,
After that stab of fire;
Enjailed in pitiless wire;
Resenting not such wrong!

Who hath charity? This bird.   15
Who suffereth long and is kind,
Is not provoked, though blind
And alive ensepulchred?
Who hopeth, endureth all things?
Who thinketh no evil, but sings?   20
Who is divine? This bird.

The Children and Sir Nameless

Sir Nameless, once of Athelhall, declared:
"These wretched children romping in my park
Trample the herbage till the soil is bared,
And yap and yell from early morn till dark!
Go keep them harnessed to their set routines: 5
Thank God I've none to hasten my decay;
For green remembrance there are better means
Than offspring, who but wish their sires away."

Sir Nameless of that mansion said anon:
"To be perpetuate for my mightiness   10
Sculpture must image me when I am gone."
—He forthwith summoned carvers there express
To shape a figure stretching seven-odd feet
(For he was tall) in alabaster stone,
With shield, and crest, and casque, and sword   15
    complete:
When done a statelier work was never known.

Three hundred years hied; Church-restorers
    came,
And, no one of his lineage being traced,
They thought an effigy so large in frame
Best fitted for the floor. There it was placed,   20
Under the seats for schoolchildren. And they
Kicked out his name, and hobnailed off his nose;
And, as they yawn through sermon-time, they say,
"Who was this old stone man beneath our toes?"

No Buyers

A Street Scene

A load of brushes and baskets and cradles and
    chairs
Labours along the street in the rain:

With it a man, a woman, a pony with whitey-
    brown hairs.—
The man foots in front of the horse with a
    shambling sway
    At a slower tread than a funeral train,   5
While to a dirge-like tune he chants his wares,
Swinging a Turk's-head brush (in a drum-
    major's way
    When the bandsmen march and play).

A yard from the back of the man is the whitey-
    brown pony's nose:
He mirrors his master in every item of pace and   10
    pose:
    He stops when the man stops, without
        being told,
    And seems to be eased by a pause; too plainly
        he's old,
        Indeed, not strength enough shows
        To steer the disjointed waggon straight,
Which wriggles left and right in a rambling   15
    line,
Deflected thus by its own warp and weight,
And pushing the pony with it in each incline.

    The woman walks on the pavement verge,
        Parallel to the man:
She wears an apron white and wide in span,   20
And carries a like Turk's-head, but more in
    nursing-wise:
    Now and then she joins in his dirge,
    But as if her thoughts were on distant
        things.
    The rain clams her apron till it clings.—
So, step by step, they move with their   25
    merchandize,
    And nobody buys.

Joseph Conrad

1857-1924

The life of Joseph Conrad was only in its later decades the placid, regulated life of the man of letters.
In its earlier phases, until he was in his thirties, it
was as adventurous, as active as the lives of any of
his heroes; and, like their lives, it was lived in many
parts of the globe and as much on sea as on land. He
was born Teodor Josef Konrad Korzeniowski, in the

Polish Ukraine in 1857 (he took the name Joseph
Conrad when he was naturalized as a British subject
in 1886), shared his father's political exile in Russia,
went to sea at the age of sixteen (perhaps, it has been
suggested, to get as far away as possible from Central
Europe), first in French merchant vessels, then, beginning with his service on the *Mavis*, in the British

merchant marine. In this service he moved steadily up the ranks, taking his Master Mariner's papers in 1886.

During these early years he had seen at first hand the tyranny of Czarist Russia, he had perhaps participated in Carlist gun-running in Spain, he had known what it was to be improvident about money, and he had possibly attempted suicide. All this is recounted not for its interest as sensation but because of the resonance it gives to Conrad's later dedication to the intensely conservative traditions of the British merchant-navy and his avowed concern, in his writing, with what he called *"les valeurs idéales."* Jocelyn Baines, in his critical biography of Conrad, cites a passage from a letter, dated March 1, 1917, in which Conrad protests that the direction of his work had not always been well understood:

I have been called a writer of the sea, of the tropics, a descriptive writer, a romantic writer—and also a realist. But as a matter of fact all my concern has been with the "ideal" value of things, events and people. That and nothing else. The humorous, the pathetic, the passionate, the sentimental aspects came in of themselves—mais en vérité c'est les valeurs idéales des faits et gestes humains qui se sont imposés à mon activité artistique.

Not the events themselves, then, the stirring sea-adventures, the tropical backdrops, the vividly de-

Joseph Conrad (1857–1924). A pastel portrait by William Rothenstein. *National Portrait Gallery.*

tailed shipboard life; not the carefully constructed Central American silver republic of *Nostromo,* for its own sake, nor the vast Russian panorama of *Under Western Eyes* in which "an ordinary young man, with a healthy capacity for work and sane ambitions, . . . an average conscience" is caught between the forces of "senseless desperation provoked by senseless tyranny." And not the bomb outrage of *The Secret Agent,* the ugly, sterile activities of that novel's anarchists, for their interest as sheer exciting event. But all these things are arenas in which *"les valeurs idéales"* can be exhibited, tried, explored: in which we can learn what truly matters in human nature and human conduct. Or, as Lady Ottoline Morrell put it (the shrewd and perceptive woman who appears, somewhat traduced, as Hermione in D. H. Lawrence's *Women in Love*), "The sea, with its calm, its storms, to him was but a mirror of the restless motion of the souls of men."

In "The Secret Sharer," written in 1909, everything is perfectly handled (J.I.M. Stewart has called it the finest of all the short stories), and there are many sources of appeal. There is the evocation of the ship itself, as the young captain takes up his first command; the tautly managed series of small strategies as he tries to conceal the presence of the fugitive in his cabin; the sense we have from the very beginning that words and images have a meaning on more than a surface level. Then there is the even more pervasive sense that in the gradual blurring or merging of identities between the captain and the young man who swims up to his ship at this testing moment in the captain's career, will be found the important meaning, what the captain learns in the course of the story about himself, his powers, and his essential moral need. There is nothing cut and dried about this story; like most of Conrad's work it is "modern" in that it presents its meaning through a full range of symbol, symbolic image, and symbolic situation, with a resulting richness of ambiguity that makes it unwise to be dogmatic in laying down lines of interpretation.

TEXTS: Present-day readers owe a good deal to a number of critics who have called attention to what is centrally important in Conrad's work, as much as any to F. R. Leavis for the treatment of Conrad in *The Great Tradition* (1948), and to Morton Dauwen Zabel for his extensive work with Conrad, not only in *Craft and Character in Modern Fiction* (1957), but also in his reissue (1951) of *Under Western Eyes,* first published in 1911, and in his introductions to the several groupings of short stories in Doubleday's Anchor series. One of the principal effects of the best recent criticism of Conrad has been to give a central place in his achievement to three novels that are *not* about the sea: *Nostromo* (1904), *The Secret Agent* (1907), and *Under Western Eyes.* We understand the novels that *are* set at sea—*Lord Jim,* for example (1900), or *The Nigger of the Narcissus* (1897)—all the better for seeing them as involved in the same patient exploration of moral issues as the novels that present men as pitted not against the sea's inhuman forces but as standing up against other men, and against themselves in their own weakness and doubt, on dry land.

Among the critical works to be recommended are: O. Warner's booklet, *Joseph Conrad,* published as a supplement to *British Book News* in 1950, which contains a bibliography and lists the short stories separately; Albert J. Guerard's *Conrad the Novelist* (1957); J.I.M. Stewart's *Joseph Conrad* (1968), as well as the excellent chapter on Conrad in the same author's *Eight Modern Writers* (1963). *The Art of Joseph Conrad: A Critical Symposium,* edited by R. W. Stallman (1960), collects essays by various critics. The best biography, and one of the most useful of all the books on Conrad, is Jocelyn Baines's *Joseph Conrad: A Critical Biography.* Individual essays worth seeking out are: Henry James, "The New Novel," in *Notes on Novelists* (1914); Virginia Woolf, "Joseph Conrad," in *The Common Reader* (1925, and later reprints), and "Mr. Conrad: A Conversation," in *The Captain's Death Bed* (1950); and Ford Madox Ford, Chapter VIII in *Thus to Revisit* (1921, reprinted 1966). See also the appropriate chapters in Dorothy Van Ghent's *The English Novel: Form and Function* (1953) and in Graham Hough, *Image and Experience* (1960).

The Secret Sharer

I

On my right hand there were lines of fishing-stakes resembling a mysterious system of half-submerged bamboo fences, incomprehensible in its division of the domain of tropical fishes, and crazy of aspect as if abandoned forever by some nomad tribe of fishermen now gone to the other end of the ocean; for there was no sign of human habitation as far as the eye could reach. To the left a group of barren islets, suggesting ruins of stone walls, towers, and blockhouses, had its foundations set in a blue sea that itself looked solid, so still and stable did it lie below my feet; even the track of light from the westering sun shone smoothly, without that animated glitter which tells of an imperceptible ripple. And

when I turned my head to take a parting glance at the tug which had just left us anchored outside the bar, I saw the straight line of the flat shore joined to the stable sea, edge to edge, with a perfect and unmarked closeness, in one levelled floor half brown, half blue under the enormous dome of the sky. Corresponding in their insignificance to the islets of the sea, two small clumps of trees, one on each side of the only fault in the impeccable joint, marked the mouth of the river Meinam we had just left on the first preparatory stage of our homeward journey; and, far back on the inland level, a larger and loftier mass, the grove surrounding the great Paknam pagoda, was the only thing on which the eye could rest from the vain task of exploring the monotonous sweep of the horizon. Here and there gleams as of a few scattered pieces of silver marked the windings of the great river; and on the nearest of them, just within the bar, the tug steaming right into the land became lost to my sight, hull and funnel and masts, as though the impassive earth had swallowed her up without an effort, without a tremor. My eye followed the light cloud of her smoke, now here, now there, above the plain, according to the devious curves of the stream, but always fainter and farther away, till I lost it at last behind the mitre-shaped hill of the great pagoda. And then I was left alone with my ship, anchored at the head of the Gulf of Siam.

She floated at the starting-point of a long journey, very still in an immense stillness, the shadows of her spars flung far to the eastward by the setting sun. At that moment I was alone on her decks. There was not a sound in her—and around us nothing moved, nothing lived, not a canoe on the water, not a bird in the air, not a cloud in the sky. In this breathless pause at the threshold of a long passage we seemed to be measuring our fitness for a long and arduous enterprise, the appointed task of both our existences to be carried out, far from all human eyes, with only sky and sea for spectators and for judges.

There must have been some glare in the air to interfere with one's sight, because it was only just before the sun left us that my roaming eyes made out beyond the highest ridge of the principal islet of the group something which did away with the solemnity of perfect solitude. The tide of darkness flowed on swiftly; and with tropical suddenness a swarm of stars came out above the shadowy earth, while I lingered yet, my hand resting lightly on my ship's rail as if on the shoulder of a trusted friend. But, with all that multitude of celestial bodies staring down at one, the comfort of quiet communion with her was gone for good. And there were also disturbing sounds by this time—voices, footsteps forward; the steward flitted along the main-deck, a busily ministering spirit; a hand-bell tinkled urgently under the poop-deck. . . .

I found my two officers waiting for me near the supper table, in the lighted cuddy. We sat down at once, and as I helped the chief mate, I said:

"Are you aware that there is a ship anchored inside the islands? I saw her mastheads above the ridge as the sun went down."

He raised sharply his simple face, overcharged by a terrible growth of whisker, and emitted his usual ejaculations: "Bless my soul, sir! You don't say so!"

My second mate was a round-cheeked, silent young man, grave beyond his years, I thought; but as our eyes happened to meet I detected a slight quiver on his lips. I looked down at once. It was not my part to encourage sneering on board my ship. It must be said, too, that I knew very little of my officers. In consequence of certain events of no particular significance, except to myself, I had been appointed to the command only a fortnight before. Neither did I know much of the hands forward. All these people had been together for eighteen months or so, and my position was that of the only stranger on board. I mention this because it has some bearing on what is to follow. But what I felt most was my being a stranger to the ship; and if all the truth must be told, I was somewhat of a stranger to myself. The youngest man on board (barring the second mate), and untried as yet by a position of the fullest responsibility, I was willing to take the adequacy of the others for granted. They had simply to be equal to their tasks; but I wondered how far I should turn out faithful to that ideal conception of one's own personality every man sets up for himself secretly.

Meantime the chief mate, with an almost visible effect of collaboration on the part of his round eyes and frightful whiskers, was trying to evolve a theory of the anchored ship. His dominant trait was to take all things into earnest consideration. He was of a painstaking turn of mind. As he used to say, he "liked to account to himself" for practically everything that came in his way, down to a miserable scorpion he had found in his cabin a week before. The why and the wherefore of that scorpion—how it got on board and came to select his room rather than the pantry (which was a dark place and more what a scorpion would be partial to), and how on earth it managed to drown itself in the inkwell of his writing-desk—had exercised him infinitely. The ship within the islands was much more easily accounted for; and just as we were about to rise from table he made his pronouncement. She was, he doubted not, a ship from home lately arrived. Probably she drew too much water to cross the bar except at the top of spring tides. Therefore she went into that natural harbour to wait for a few days in preference to remaining in an open roadstead.

"That's so," confirmed the second mate, suddenly, in his slightly hoarse voice. "She draws over twenty feet. She's the Liverpool ship *Sephora* with a cargo of coal. Hundred and twenty-three days from Cardiff."

We looked at him in surprise.

"The tugboat skipper told me when he came on board for your letters, sir," explained the young man. "He expects to take her up the river the day after to-morrow."

After thus overwhelming us with the extent of his information he slipped out of the cabin. The mate observed regretfully that he "could not account for that young fellow's whims." What prevented him telling us all about it at once, he wanted to know.

I detained him as he was making a move. For the last two days the crew had had plenty of hard work, and the night before they had very little sleep. I felt painfully that I—a stranger—was doing something unusual when I directed him to let all hands turn in without setting an anchor-watch. I proposed to keep on deck myself till one o'clock or thereabouts. I would get the second mate to relieve me at that hour.

"He will turn out the cook and the steward at four," I concluded, "and then give you a call. Of course at the slightest sign of any sort of wind we'll have the hands up and make a start at once."

He concealed his astonishment. "Very well,

sir." Outside the cuddy he put his head in the second mate's door to inform him of my unheard-of caprice to take a five hours' anchor-watch on myself. I heard the other raise his voice incredulously—"What? The captain himself?" Then a few more murmurs, a door closed, then another. A few moments later I went on deck.

My strangeness, which had made me sleepless, had prompted that unconventional arrangement, as if I had expected in those solitary hours of the night to get on terms with the ship of which I knew nothing, manned by men of whom I knew very little more. Fast alongside a wharf, littered like any ship in port with a tangle of unrelated things, invaded by unrelated shore people, I had hardly seen her yet properly. Now, as she lay cleared for sea, the stretch of her main-deck seemed to me very fine under the stars. Very fine, very roomy for her size, and very inviting. I descended the poop and paced the waist, my mind picturing to myself the coming passage through the Malay Archipelago, down the Indian Ocean, and up the Atlantic. All its phases were familiar enough to me, every characteristic, all the alternatives which were likely to face me on the high seas—everything! . . . except the novel responsibility of command. But I took heart from the reasonable thought that the ship was like other ships, the men like other men, and that the sea was not likely to keep any special surprises expressly for my discomfiture.

Arrived at that comforting conclusion, I bethought myself of a cigar and went below to get it. All was still down there. Everybody at the after end of the ship was sleeping profoundly. I came out again on the quarter-deck, agreeably at ease in my sleeping-suit on that warm breathless night, barefooted, a glowing cigar in my teeth, and, going forward, I was met by the profound silence of the fore end of the ship. Only as I passed the door of the forecastle I heard a deep, quiet, trustful sigh of some sleeper inside. And suddenly I rejoiced in the great security of the sea as compared with the unrest of the land, in my choice of that untempted life presenting no disquieting problems, invested with an elementary moral beauty by the absolute straightforwardness of its appeal and by the singleness of its purpose.

The riding-light in the fore-rigging burned with a clear, untroubled, as if symbolic, flame,

confident and bright in the mysterious shades of the night. Passing on my way aft along the other side of the ship, I observed that the rope side-ladder, put over, no doubt, for the master of the tug when he came to fetch away our letters, had not been hauled in as it should have been. I became annoyed at this, for exactitude in small matters is the very soul of discipline. Then I reflected that I had myself peremptorily dismissed my officers from duty, and by my own act had prevented the anchor-watch being formally set and things properly attended to. I asked myself whether it was wise ever to interfere with the established routine of duties even from the kindest of motives. My action might have made me appear eccentric. Goodness only knew how that absurdly whiskered mate would "account" for my conduct, and what the whole ship thought of that informality of their new captain. I was vexed with myself.

Not from compunction certainly, but, as it were mechanically, I proceeded to get the ladder in myself. Now a side-ladder of that sort is a light affair and comes in easily, yet my vigorous tug, which should have brought it flying on board, merely recoiled upon my body in a totally unexpected jerk. What the devil! . . . I was so astounded by the immovableness of that ladder that I remained stock-still, trying to account for it to myself like that imbecile mate of mine. In the end, of course, I put my head over the rail.

The side of the ship made an opaque belt of shadow on the darkling glassy shimmer of the sea. But I saw at once something elongated and pale floating very close to the ladder. Before I could form a guess a faint flash of phosphorescent light, which seemed to issue suddenly from the naked body of a man, flickered in the sleeping water with the elusive, silent play of summer lightning in a night sky. With a gasp I saw revealed to my stare a pair of feet, the long legs, a broad livid back immersed right up to the neck in a greenish cadaverous glow. One hand, awash, clutched the bottom rung of the ladder. He was complete but for the head. A headless corpse! The cigar dropped out of my gaping mouth with a tiny plop and a short hiss quite audible in the absolute stillness of all things under heaven. At that I suppose he raised up his face, a dimly pale oval in the shadow of the ship's side. But even then I could only barely make out down there the shape of his black-haired head. However, it was enough for the horrid, frost-bound sensation which had gripped me about the chest to pass off. The moment of vain exclamations was past, too. I only climbed on the spare spar and leaned over the rail as far as I could, to bring my eyes nearer to that mystery floating alongside.

As he hung by the ladder, like a resting swimmer, the sea-lightning played about his limbs at every stir; and he appeared in it ghastly, silvery, fish-like. He remained as mute as a fish, too. He made no motion to get out of the water, either. It was inconceivable that he should not attempt to come on board, and strangely troubling to suspect that perhaps he did not want to. And my first words were prompted by just that troubled incertitude.

"What's the matter?" I asked in my ordinary tone, speaking down to the face upturned exactly under mine.

"Cramp," it answered, no louder. Then slightly anxious, "I say, no need to call any one."

"I was not going to," I said.

"Are you alone on deck?"

"Yes."

I had somehow the impression that he was on the point of letting go the ladder to swim away beyond my ken—mysterious as he came. But, for the moment, this being appearing as if he had risen from the bottom of the sea (it was certainly the nearest land to the ship) wanted only to know the time. I told him. And he, down there, tentatively:

"I suppose your captain's turned in?"

"I am sure he isn't," I said.

He seemed to struggle with himself, for I heard something like the low, bitter murmur of doubt. "What's the good?" His next words came out with a hesitating effort.

"Look here, my man. Could you call him out quietly?"

I thought the time had come to declare myself.

"*I* am the captain."

I heard a "By Jove!" whispered at the level of the water. The phosphorescence flashed in the swirl of the water all about his limbs, his other hand seized the ladder.

"My name's Leggatt."

The voice was calm and resolute. A good voice. The self-possession of that man had some-how induced a corresponding state in myself. It was very quietly that I remarked:

"You must be a good swimmer."

"Yes. I've been in the water practically since nine o'clock. The question for me now is whether I am to let go this ladder and go on swimming till I sink from exhaustion, or—to come on board here."

I felt this was no mere formula of desperate speech, but a real alternative in the view of a strong soul. I should have gathered from this that he was young; indeed, it is only the young who are ever confronted by such clear issues. But at the time it was pure intuition on my part. A mysterious communication was established already between us two—in the face of that silent, darkened tropical sea. I was young, too; young enough to make no comment. The man in the water began suddenly to climb up the ladder, and I hastened away from the rail to fetch some clothes.

Before entering the cabin I stood still, listening in the lobby at the foot of the stairs. A faint snore came through the closed door of the chief mate's room. The second mate's door was on the hook, but the darkness in there was absolutely soundless. He, too, was young and could sleep like a stone. Remained the steward, but he was not likely to wake up before he was called. I got a sleeping-suit out of my room and, coming back on deck, saw the naked man from the sea sitting on the main-hatch, glimmering white in the darkness, his elbows on his knees and his head in his hands. In a moment he had concealed his damp body in a sleeping-suit of the same grey-stripe pattern as the one I was wearing and followed me like my double on the poop. Together we moved right aft, barefooted, silent.

"What is it?" I asked in a deadened voice, taking the lighted lamp out of the binnacle, and raising it to his face.

"An ugly business."

He had rather regular features; a good mouth; light eyes under somewhat heavy, dark eyebrows; a smooth, square forehead; no growth on his cheeks; a small, brown moustache, and a well-shaped, round chin. His expression was concentrated, meditative, under the inspecting light of the lamp I held up to his face; such as a man thinking hard in solitude might wear. My sleeping-suit was just right for his size. A well-knit young fellow of twenty-five at most. He caught his lower lip with the edge of white, even teeth.

"Yes," I said, replacing the lamp in the binnacle. The warm, heavy tropical night closed upon his head again.

"There's a ship over there," he murmured.

"Yes, I know. The *Sephora*. Did you know of us?"

"Hadn't the slightest idea. I am the mate of her ——" He paused and corrected himself. "I should say I *was*."

"Aha! Something wrong?"

"Yes. Very wrong indeed. I've killed a man."

"What do you mean? Just now?"

"No, on the passage. Weeks ago. Thirty-nine south. When I say a man ——"

"Fit of temper," I suggested, confidently.

The shadowy, dark head, like mine, seemed to nod imperceptibly above the ghostly grey of my sleeping-suit. It was, in the night, as though I had been faced by my own reflection in the depths of a sombre and immense mirror.

"A pretty thing to have to own up to for a Conway boy," murmured my double, distinctly.

"You're a Conway boy?"

"I am," he said, as if startled. Then, slowly . . . "Perhaps you too ——"

It was so; but being a couple of years older I had left before he joined. After a quick interchange of dates a silence fell; and I thought suddenly of my absurd mate with his terrific whiskers and the "Bless my soul—you don't say so" type of intellect. My double gave me an inkling of his thoughts by saying:

"My father's a parson in Norfolk. Do you see me before a judge and jury on that charge? For myself I can't see the necessity. There are fellows that an angel from heaven——And I am not that. He was one of those creatures that are just simmering all the time with a silly sort of wickedness. Miserable devils that have no business to live at all. He wouldn't do his duty and wouldn't let anybody else do theirs. But what's the good of talking! You know well enough the sort of ill-conditioned snarling cur——"

He appealed to me as if our experiences had been as identical as our clothes. And I knew well enough the pestiferous danger of such a character where there are no means of legal repression. And I knew well enough also that my double there was no homicidal ruffian. I did not think of asking him for details, and he told me the story roughly in brusque, disconnected sentences. I needed no more. I saw it all going on as though I were myself inside that other sleeping-suit.

"It happened while we were setting a reefed foresail, at dusk. Reefed foresail! You understand the sort of weather. The only sail we had left to keep the ship running; so you may guess what it had been like for days. Anxious sort of job, that. He gave me some of his cursed insolence at the sheet. I tell you I was overdone with this terrific weather that seemed to have no end to it. Terrific, I tell you—and a deep ship. I believe the fellow himself was half crazed with funk. It was no time for gentlemanly reproof, so I turned round and felled him like an ox. He up and at me. We closed just as an awful sea made for the ship. All hands saw it coming and took to the rigging, but I had him by the throat, and went on shaking him like a rat, the men above us yelling, 'Look out! look out!' Then a crash as if the sky had fallen on my head. They say that for over ten minutes hardly anything was to be seen of the ship—just the three masts and a bit of the forecastle head and the poop all awash driving along in a smother of foam. It was a miracle that they found us, jammed together behind the forebits. It's clear that I meant business, because I was holding him by the throat still when they picked us up. He was black in the face. It was too much for them. It seems they rushed us aft together, gripped as we were, screaming 'Murder!' like a lot of lunatics, and broke into the cuddy. And the ship running for her life, touch and go all the time, any minute her last in a sea fit to turn your hair grey only a-looking at it. I understand that the skipper, too, started raving like the rest of them. The man had been deprived of sleep for more than a week, and to have this sprung on him at the height of a furious gale nearly drove him out of his mind. I wonder they didn't fling me overboard after getting the carcass of their precious ship-mate out of my fingers. They had rather a job to separate us, I've been told. A sufficiently fierce story to make an old judge and a respectable jury sit up a bit. The first thing I heard when I came to myself was the maddening howling of that endless gale, and on that the voice of the old man. He was hanging on to my bunk, staring into my face out of his sou'wester.

"'Mr. Leggatt, you have killed a man. You can act no longer as chief mate of this ship.'"

His care to subdue his voice made it sound monotonous. He rested a hand on the end of the skylight to steady himself with, and all that time did not stir a limb, so far as I could see. "Nice little tale for a quiet tea-party," he concluded in the same tone.

One of my hands, too, rested on the end of the skylight; neither did I stir a limb, so far as I knew. We stood less than a foot from each other. It occurred to me that if old "Bless my soul—you don't say so" were to put his head up the companion and catch sight of us, he would think he was seeing double, or imagine himself come upon a scene of weird witchcraft; the strange captain having a quiet confabulation by the wheel with his own grey ghost. I became very much concerned to prevent anything of the sort. I heard the other's soothing undertone.

"My father's a parson in Norfolk," it said. Evidently he had forgotten he had told me this important fact before. Truly a nice little tale.

"You had better slip down into my stateroom now," I said, moving off stealthily. My double followed my movements; our bare feet made no sound; I let him in, closed the door with care, and, after giving a call to the second mate, returned on deck for my relief.

"Not much sign of any wind yet," I remarked when he approached.

"No, sir. Not much," he assented, sleepily, in his hoarse voice, with just enough deference, no more, and barely suppressing a yawn.

"Well, that's all you have to look out for. You have got your orders."

"Yes, sir."

I paced a turn or two on the poop and saw him take up his position face forward with his elbow in the rat-lines of the mizzen-rigging before I went below. The mate's faint snoring was still going on peacefully. The cuddy lamp was burning over the table on which stood a vase with flowers, a polite attention from the ships' provision merchant—the last flowers we should see for the next three months at the very least. Two bunches of bananas hung from the beam symmetrically, one on each side of the rudder-casing. Everything was as before in the ship—except that two of her captain's sleeping-suits were simultaneously in use, one motionless in the cuddy, the other keeping very still in the captain's stateroom.

It must be explained here that my cabin had the form of the capital letter L the door being within the angle and opening into the short part of the letter. A couch was to the left, the bed-place to the right; my writing-desk and the chronometers' table faced the door. But any one opening it, unless he stepped right inside, had no view of what I call the long (or vertical) part of the letter. It contained some lockers surmounted by a bookcase; and a few clothes, a thick jacket or two, caps, oilskin coat, and such like, hung on hooks. There was at the bottom of that part a door opening into my bath-room, which could be entered also directly from the saloon. But that way was never used.

The mysterious arrival had discovered the advantage of this particular shape. Entering my room, lighted strongly by a big bulkhead lamp swung on gimbals above my writing-desk, I did not see him anywhere till he stepped out quietly from behind the coats hung in the recessed part.

"I heard somebody moving about, and went in there at once," he whispered.

I, too, spoke under my breath.

"Nobody is likely to come in here without knocking and getting permission."

He nodded. His face was thin and the sunburn faded, as though he had been ill. And no wonder. He had been, I heard presently, kept under arrest in his cabin for nearly seven weeks. But there was nothing sickly in his eyes or in his expression. He was not a bit like me, really; yet, as we stood leaning over my bed-place, whispering side by side, with our dark heads together and our backs to the door, anybody bold enough to open it stealthily would have been treated to the uncanny sight of a double captain busy talking in whispers with his other self.

"But all this doesn't tell me how you came to hang on to our side-ladder," I inquired, in the hardly audible murmurs we used, after he had told me something more of the proceedings on board the *Sephora* once the bad weather was over.

"When we sighted Java Head I had had time to think all those matters out several times over. I had six weeks of doing nothing else, and with only an hour or so every evening for a tramp on the quarter-deck."

He whispered, his arms folded on the side of my bed-place, staring through the open port. And I could imagine perfectly the manner of this thinking out—a stubborn if not a steadfast operation; something of which I should have been perfectly incapable.

"I reckoned it would be dark before we closed with the land," he continued, so low that I had to strain my hearing, near as we were to each other, shoulder touching shoulder almost. "So I asked to speak to the old man. He always seemed very sick when he came to see me—as if he could not look me in the face. You know, that foresail saved the ship. She was too deep to have run long under bare poles. And it was I that managed to set it for him. Anyway, he came. When I had him in my cabin—he stood by the door looking at me as if I had the halter around my neck already—I asked him right away to leave my cabin door unlocked at night while the ship was going through Sunda Straits. There would be the Java coast within two or three miles, off Angier Point. I wanted nothing more. I've had a prize for swimming my second year in the Conway."

"I can believe it," I breathed out.

"God only knows why they locked me in every night. To see some of their faces you'd have thought they were afraid I'd go about at night strangling people. Am I a murdering brute? Do I look it? By Jove! if I had been he wouldn't have trusted himself like that into my room. You'll say I might have chucked him aside and bolted out, there and then—it was dark already. Well, no. And for the same reason I wouldn't think of trying to smash the door. There would have been a rush to stop me at the noise, and I did not mean to get into a confounded scrimmage. Somebody else might have got killed—for I would not have broken out only to get chucked back, and I did not want any more of that work. He refused, looking more sick than ever. He was afraid of the men, and also of that old second mate of his who had been sailing with him for years—a grey-headed old humbug; and his steward, too, had been with him devil knows how long—seventeen years or more—a dogmatic sort of loafer who hated me like poison, just because I was the chief mate. No chief mate ever made

more than one voyage in the *Sephora*, you know. Those two old chaps ran the ship. Devil only knows what the skipper wasn't afraid of (all his nerve went to pieces altogether in that hellish spell of bad weather we had)—of what the law would do to him—of his wife, perhaps. Oh, yes! she's on board. Though I don't think she would have meddled. She would have been only too glad to have me out of the ship in any way. The 'brand of Cain' business, don't you see. That's all right. I was ready enough to go off wandering on the face of the earth—and that was price enough to pay for an Abel of that sort. Anyhow, he wouldn't listen to me. 'This thing must take its course. I represent the law here.' He was shaking like a leaf. 'So you won't?' 'No!' 'Then I hope you will be able to sleep on that,' I said, and turned my back on him. 'I wonder that *you* can,' cries he, and locks the door.

"Well, after that, I couldn't. Not very well. That was three weeks ago. We have had a slow passage through the Java Sea; drifted about Carimata for ten days. When we anchored here they thought, I suppose, it was all right. The nearest land (and that's five miles) is the ship's destination; the consul would soon set about catching me; and there would have been no object in bolting to these islets there. I don't suppose there's a drop of water on them. I don't know how it was, but to-night that steward, after bringing me my supper, went out to let me eat it, and left the door unlocked. And I ate it—all there was, too. After I had finished I strolled out on the quarter-deck. I don't know that I meant to do anything. A breath of fresh air was all I wanted, I believe. Then a sudden temptation came over me. I kicked off my slippers and was in the water before I had made up my mind fairly. Somebody heard the splash and they raised an awful hullabaloo. 'He's gone! Lower the boats! He's committed suicide! No, he's swimming.' Certainly I was swimming. It's not so easy for a swimmer like me to commit suicide by drowning. I landed on the nearest islet before the boat left the ship's side. I heard them pulling about in the dark, hailing, and so on, but after a bit they gave up. Everything quieted down and the anchorage became as still as death. I sat down on a stone and began to think. I felt certain they would start searching for me at daylight. There was no place to hide on those stony things—and if there had been, what would have been the good? But now I was clear of that ship, I was not going back. So after a while I took off all my clothes, tied them up in a bundle with a stone inside, and dropped them in the deep water on the outer side of that islet. That was suicide enough for me. Let them think what they liked, but I didn't mean to drown myself. I meant to swim till I sank—but that's not the same thing. I struck out for another of these little islands, and it was from that one that I first saw your riding-light. Something to swim for. I went on easily, and on the way I came upon a flat rock a foot or two above water. In the daytime, I dare say, you might make it out with a glass from your poop. I scrambled up on it and rested myself for a bit. Then I made another start. That last spell must have been over a mile."

His whisper was getting fainter and fainter, and all the time he stared straight out through the port-hole, in which there was not even a star to be seen. I had not interrupted him. There was something that made comment impossible in his narrative, or perhaps in himself; a sort of feeling, a quality, which I can't find a name for. And when he ceased, all I found was a futile whisper: "So you swam for our light?"

"Yes—straight for it. It was something to swim for. I couldn't see any stars low down because the coast was in the way, and I couldn't see the land, either. The water was like glass. One might have been swimming in a confounded thousand-feet deep cistern with no place for scrambling out anywhere; but what I didn't like was the notion of swimming round and round like a crazed bullock before I gave out; and as I didn't mean to go back . . . No. Do you see me being hauled back, stark naked, off one of these little islands by the scruff of the neck and fighting like a wild beast? Somebody would have got killed for certain, and I did not want any of that. So I went on. Then your ladder——"

"Why didn't you hail the ship?" I asked, a little louder.

He touched my shoulder lightly. Lazy footsteps came right over our heads and stopped. The second mate had crossed from the other side of the poop and might have been hanging over the rail, for all we knew.

"He couldn't hear us talking—could he?" My double breathed into my very ear, anxiously.

His anxiety was an answer, a sufficient answer, to the question I had put to him. An answer containing all the difficulty of that situation. I closed the port-hole quietly, to make sure. A louder word might have been overheard.

"Who's that?" he whispered then.

"My second mate. But I don't know much more of the fellow than you do.

And I told him a little about myself. I had been appointed to take charge while I least expected anything of the sort, not quite a fortnight ago. I didn't know either the ship or the people. Hadn't had the time in port to look about me or size anybody up. And as to the crew, all they knew was that I was appointed to take the ship home. For the rest, I was almost as much a stranger on board as himself, I said. And at the moment I felt it most acutely. I felt that it would take very little to make me a suspect person in the eyes of the ship's company.

He had turned about meantime; and we, the two strangers in the ship, faced each other in identical attitudes.

"Your ladder——" he murmured, after a silence. "Who'd have thought of finding a ladder hanging over at night in a ship anchored out here! I felt just then a very unpleasant faintness. After the life I've been leading for nine weeks, anybody would have got out of condition. I wasn't capable of swimming round as far as your rudder-chains. And, lo and behold! there was a ladder to get hold of. After I gripped it I said to myself, 'What's the good?' When I saw a man's head looking over I thought I would swim away presently and leave him shouting—in whatever language it was. I didn't mind being looked at. I—I liked it. And then you speaking to me so quietly—as if you had expected me—made me hold on a little longer. It had been a confounded lonely time—I don't mean while swimming. I was glad to talk a little to somebody that didn't belong to the *Sephora*. As to asking for the captain, that was a mere impulse. It could have been no use, with all the ship knowing about me and the other people pretty certain to be round here in the morning. I don't know—I wanted to be seen, to talk with somebody, before I went on. I don't know what I would have said. . . . 'Fine night, isn't it?' or something of the sort."

"Do you think they will be round here presently?" I asked with some incredulity.

"Quite likely," he said, faintly.

He looked extremely haggard all of a sudden. His head rolled on his shoulders.

"H'm. We shall see then. Meantime get into that bed," I whispered. "Want help? There."

It was a rather high bed-place with a set of drawers underneath. This amazing swimmer really needed the lift I gave him by seizing his leg. He tumbled in, rolled over on his back, and flung one arm across his eyes. And then, with his face nearly hidden, he must have looked exactly as I used to look in that bed. I gazed upon my other self for a while before drawing across carefully the two green serge curtains which ran on a brass rod. I thought for a moment of pinning them together for greater safety, but I sat down on the couch, and once there I felt unwilling to rise and hunt for a pin. I would do it in a moment. I was extremely tired, in a peculiarly intimate way, by the strain of stealthiness, by the effort of whispering and the general secrecy of this excitement. It was three o'clock by now and I had been on my feet since nine, but I was not sleepy; I could not have gone to sleep. I sat there, fagged out, looking at the curtains, trying to clear my mind of the confused sensation of being in two places at once, and greatly bothered by an exasperating knocking in my head. It was a relief to discover suddenly that it was not in my head at all, but on the outside of the door. Before I could collect myself the words "Come in" were out of my mouth, and the steward entered with a tray, bringing in my morning coffee. I had slept, after all, and I was so frightened that I shouted, "This way! I am here, steward," as though he had been miles away. He put down the tray on the table next the couch and only then said, very quietly, "I can see you are here, sir." I felt him give me a keen look, but I dared not meet his eyes just then. He must have wondered why I had drawn the curtains of my bed before going to sleep on the couch. He went out, hooking the door open as usual.

I heard the crew washing decks above me. I knew I would have been told at once if there had been any wind. Calm, I thought, and I was doubly vexed. Indeed, I felt dual more than ever. The steward reappeared suddenly in the doorway. I jumped up from the couch so quickly that he gave a start.

"What do you want here?"

"Close your port, sir—they are washing decks."

"It is closed," I said, reddening.

"Very well, sir." But he did not move from the doorway and returned my stare in an extraordinary, equivocal manner for a time. Then his eyes wavered, all his expression changed, and in a voice unusually gentle, almost coaxingly:

"May I come in to take the empty cup away, sir?"

"Of course!" I turned my back on him while he popped in and out. Then I unhooked and closed the door and even pushed the bolt. This sort of thing could not go on very long. The cabin was as hot as an oven, too. I took a peep at my double, and discovered that he had not moved, his arm was still over his eyes; but his chest heaved; his hair was wet; his chin glistened with perspiration. I reached over him and opened the port.

"I must show myself on deck," I reflected.

Of course, theoretically, I could do what I liked, with no one to say nay to me within the whole circle of the horizon; but to lock my cabin door and take the key away I did not dare. Directly I put my head out of the companion I saw the group of my two officers, the second mate barefooted, the chief mate in long india-rubber boots, near the break of the poop, and the steward half-way down the poop-ladder talking to them eagerly. He happened to catch sight of me and dived, the second ran down on the main-deck shouting some order or other, and the chief mate came to meet me, touching his cap.

There was a sort of curiosity in his eye that I did not like. I don't know whether the steward had told them that I was "queer" only, or downright drunk, but I know the man meant to have a good look at me. I watched him coming with a smile which, as he got into point-blank range, took effect and froze his very whiskers. I did not give him time to open his lips.

"Square the yards by lifts and braces before the hands go to breakfast."

It was the first particular order I had given on board that ship; and I stayed on deck to see it executed, too. I had felt the need of asserting myself without loss of time. That sneering young cub got taken down a peg or two on that occasion, and I also seized the opportunity of having a good look at the face of every foremast man as they filed past me to go to the after braces. At breakfast time, eating nothing myself, I presided with such frigid dignity that the two mates were only too glad to escape from the cabin as soon as decency permitted; and all the time the dual working of my mind distracted me almost to the point of insanity. I was constantly watching myself, my secret self, as dependent on my actions as my own personality, sleeping in that bed, behind that door which faced me as I sat at the head of the table. It was very much like being mad, only it was worse because one was aware of it.

I had to shake him for a solid minute, but when at last he opened his eyes it was in the full possession of his senses, with an inquiring look.

"All's well so far," I whispered. "Now you must vanish into the bath-room."

He did so, as noiseless as a ghost, and I then rang for the steward, and facing him boldly, directed him to tidy up my stateroom while I was having my bath—"and be quick about it." As my tone admitted of no excuses, he said, "Yes, sir," and ran off to fetch his dust-pan and brushes. I took a bath and did most of my dressing, splashing, and whistling softly for the steward's edification, while the secret sharer of my life stood drawn up bolt upright in that little space, his face looking very sunken in daylight, his eyelids lowered under the stern, dark line of his eyebrows drawn together by a slight frown.

When I left him there to go back to my room the steward was finishing dusting. I sent for the mate and engaged him in some insignificant conversation. It was, as it were, trifling with the terrific character of his whiskers; but my object was to give him an opportunity for a good look at my cabin. And then I could at last shut, with a clear conscience, the door of my stateroom and get my double back into the recessed part. There was nothing else for it. He had to sit still on a small folding stool, half smothered by the heavy coats hanging there. We listened to the steward going into the bath-room out of the saloon, filling the water-bottles there, scrubbing the bath, setting things to rights, whisk, bang, clatter—out again into the saloon—turn the key—click. Such was my scheme for keeping my second self invisible. Nothing better could be contrived under the circumstances. And there we sat; I at my

writing-desk ready to appear busy with some papers, he behind me, out of sight of the door. It would not have been prudent to talk in daytime; and I could not have stood the excitement of that queer sense of whispering to myself. Now and then, glancing over my shoulder, I saw him far back there, sitting rigidly on the low stool, his bare feet close together, his arms folded, his head hanging on his breast—and perfectly still. Anybody would have taken him for me.

I was fascinated by it myself. Every moment I had to glance over my shoulder. I was looking at him when a voice outside the door said:

"Beg pardon, sir."

"Well!" . . . I kept my eyes on him, and so, when the voice outside the door announced, "There's a ship's boat coming our way, sir," I saw him give a start—the first movement he had made for hours. But he did not raise his bowed head.

"All right. Get the ladder over."

I hesitated. Should I whisper something to him? But what? His immobility seemed to have been never disturbed. What could I tell him he did not know already? . . . Finally I went on deck.

II

The skipper of the *Sephora* had a thin red whisker all round his face, and the sort of complexion that goes with hair of that colour; also the particular, rather smeary shade of blue in the eyes. He was not exactly a showy figure; his shoulders were high, his stature but middling—one leg slightly more bandy than the other. He shook hands, looking vaguely around. A spiritless tenacity was his main characteristic, I judged. I behaved with a politeness which seemed to disconcert him. Perhaps he was shy. He mumbled to me as if he were ashamed of what he was saying; gave his name (it was something like Archbold—but at this distance of years I hardly am sure), his ship's name, and a few other particulars of that sort, in the manner of a criminal making a reluctant and doleful confession. He had had terrible weather on the passage out—terrible—terrible—wife aboard, too.

By this time we were seated in the cabin and the steward brought in a tray with a bottle and glasses. "Thanks! No." Never took liquor. Would have some water, though. He drank two tumblerfuls. Terrible thirsty work. Ever since daylight had been exploring the islands round his ship.

"What was that for—fun?" I asked, with an appearance of polite interest.

"No!" He sighed. "Painful duty."

As he persisted in his mumbling and I wanted my double to hear every word, I hit upon the notion of informing him that I regretted to say I was hard of hearing.

"Such a young man, too!" he nodded, keeping his smeary blue, unintelligent eyes fastened upon me. What was the cause of it—some disease? he inquired, without the least sympathy and as if he thought that, if so, I'd got no more than I deserved.

"Yes; disease," I admitted in a cheerful tone which seemed to shock him. But my point was gained, because he had to raise his voice to give me his tale. It is not worth while to record that version. It was just over two months since all this had happened, and he had thought so much about it that he seemed completely muddled as to its bearings, but still immensely impressed.

"What would you think of such a thing happening on board your own ship? I've had the *Sephora* for these fifteen years. I am a well-known shipmaster."

He was densely distressed—and perhaps I should have sympathised with him if I had been able to detach my mental vision from the unsuspected sharer of my cabin as though he were my second self. There he was on the other side of the bulkhead, four or five feet from us, no more, as we sat in the saloon. I looked politely at Captain Archbold (if that was his name), but it was the other I saw, in a grey sleeping-suit, seated on a low stool, his bare feet close together, his arms folded, and every word said between us falling into the ears of his dark head bowed on his chest.

"I have been at sea now, man and boy, for seven-and-thirty years, and I've never heard of such a thing happening in an English ship. And that it should be my ship. Wife on board, too."

I was hardly listening to him.

"Don't you think," I said, "that the heavy sea which, you told me, came aboard just then might have killed the man? I have seen the sheer weight of a sea kill a man very neatly, by simply breaking his neck."

"Good God!" he uttered, impressively, fixing his smeary blue eyes on me. "The sea! No man killed by the sea ever looked like that." He seemed positively scandalised at my suggestion. And as I gazed at him, certainly not prepared for anything original on his part, he advanced his head close to mine and thrust his tongue out at me so suddenly that I couldn't help starting back.

After scoring over my calmness in this graphic way he nodded wisely. If I had seen the sight, he assured me, I would never forget it as long as I lived. The weather was too bad to give the corpse a proper sea burial. So next day at dawn they took it up on the poop, covering its face with a bit of bunting; he read a short prayer, and then, just as it was, in its oilskins and long boots, they launched it amongst those mountainous seas that seemed ready every moment to swallow up the ship herself and the terrified lives on board of her.

"That reefed foresail saved you," I threw in.

"Under God—it did," he exclaimed fervently. "It was by a special mercy, I firmly believe, that it stood some of those hurricane squalls."

"It was the setting of that sail which——" I began.

"God's own hand in it," he interrupted me. "Nothing less could have done it. I don't mind telling you that I hardly dared give the order. It seemed impossible that we could touch anything without losing it, and then our last hope would have been gone."

The terror of that gale was on him yet. I let him go on for a bit, then said, casually—as if returning to a minor subject:

"You were very anxious to give up your mate to the shore people, I believe?"

He was. To the law. His obscure tenacity on that point had in it something incomprehensible and a little awful; something, as it were, mystical, quite apart from his anxiety that he should not be suspected of "countenancing any doings of that sort." Seven-and-thirty virtuous years at sea, of which over twenty of immaculate command, and the last fifteen in the *Sephora,* seemed to have laid him under some pitiless obligation.

"And you know," he went on, groping shamefacedly amongst his feelings, "I did not engage that young fellow. His people had some interest with my owners. I was in a way forced to take him on. He looked very smart, very gentlemanly, and all that. But do you know—I never liked him, somehow. I am a plain man. You see, he wasn't exactly the sort for the chief mate of a ship like the *Sephora*."

I had become so connected in thoughts and impressions with the secret sharer of my cabin that I felt as if I, personally, were being given to understand that I, too, was not the sort that would have done for the chief mate of a ship like the *Sephora*. I had no doubt of it in my mind.

"Not at all the style of man. You understand," he insisted, superfluously, looking hard at me.

I smiled urbanely. He seemed at a loss for a while.

"I suppose I must report a suicide."

"Beg pardon?"

"Sui-cide! That's what I'll have to write to my owners directly I get in."

"Unless you manage to recover him before to-morrow," I assented, dispassionately. . . . "I mean, alive."

He mumbled something which I really did not catch, and I turned my ear to him in a puzzled manner. He fairly bawled:

"The land—I say, the mainland is at least seven miles off my anchorage."

"About that."

My lack of excitement, of curiosity, of surprise, of any sort of pronounced interest, began to arouse his distrust. But except for the felicitous pretence of deafness I had not tried to pretend anything. I had felt utterly incapable of playing the part of ignorance properly, and therefore was afraid to try. It is also certain that he had brought some ready-made suspicions with him, and that he viewed my politeness as a strange and unnatural phenomenon. And yet how else could I have received him? Not heartily! That was impossible for psychological reasons, which I need not state here. My only object was to keep off his inquiries. Surlily? Yes, but surliness might have provoked a point-blank question. From its novelty to him and from its nature, punctilious courtesy was the manner best calculated to restrain the man. But there was the danger of his breaking through my defence bluntly. I could not, I think, have met him by a direct lie, also for psychological (not moral) reasons. If he had only known how afraid I was of his putting my feeling of identity with the other to the test! But, strangely enough—(I thought of it only afterward)—I believe that he was not a little disconcerted by the reverse side of that weird situation, by something in me that reminded him of the man he was seeking—suggested a mysterious similitude to the young fellow he had distrusted and disliked from the first.

However that might have been, the silence was not very prolonged. He took another oblique step.

"I reckon I had no more than a two-mile pull to your ship. Not a bit more."

"And quite enough, too, in this awful heat," I said.

Another pause full of mistrust followed. Neccessity, they say, is mother of invention, but fear, too, is not barren of ingenious suggestions. And I was afraid he would ask me point-blank for news of my other self.

"Nice little saloon, isn't it?" I remarked, as if noticing for the first time the way his eyes roamed from one closed door to the other. "And very well fitted out, too. Here, for instance," I continued, reaching over the back of my seat negligently and flinging the door open, "is my bath-room."

He made an eager movement, but hardly gave it a glance. I got up, shut the door of the bath-room, and invited him to have a look round, as if I were very proud of my accommodation. He had to rise and be shown round, but he went through the business without any raptures whatever.

"And now we'll have a look at my stateroom," I declared, in a voice as loud as I dared to make it, crossing the cabin to the starboard side with purposely heavy steps.

He followed me in and gazed around. My intelligent double had vanished. I played my part.

"Very convenient—isn't it?"

"Very nice. Very comf . . ." He didn't finish, and went out brusquely as if to escape from some unrighteous wiles of mine. But it was not to be. I had been too frightened not to feel vengeful; I felt I had him on the run, and I meant to keep him on the run. My polite insistence must have had something menacing in it, because he gave in suddenly. And I did not let him off a single item; mate's room, pantry, storerooms, the very sail-locker which was also under the poop—he had to look into them all. When at last I showed him out on the quarter-deck he drew a long, spiritless sigh, and mumbled dismally that he must really be going back to his ship now. I desired my mate, who had joined us, to see to the captain's boat.

The man of whiskers gave a blast on the whistle which he used to wear hanging round his neck, and yelled, *"Sephoras* away!" My double down there in my cabin must have heard, and certainly could not feel more relieved than I. Four fellows came running out from somewhere forward and went over the side, while my own men, appearing on deck too, lined the rail. I escorted my visitor to the gangway ceremoniously, and nearly overdid it. He was a tenacious beast. On the very ladder he lingered, and in that unique, guiltily conscientious manner of sticking to the point:

"I say . . . you . . . you don't think that——"

I covered his voice loudly:

"Certainly not. . . . I am delighted. Goodbye."

I had an idea of what he meant to say, and just saved myself by the privilege of defective hearing. He was too shaken generally to insist, but my mate, close witness of that parting, looked mystified and his face took on a thoughtful cast. As I did not want to appear as if I wished to avoid all communication with my officers, he had the opportunity to address me.

"Seems a very nice man. His boat's crew told our chaps a very extraordinary story, if what I am told by the steward is true. I suppose you had it from the captain, sir?"

"Yes. I had a story from the captain."

"A very horrible affair—isn't it, sir?"

"It is."

"Beats all these tales we hear about murders in Yankee ships."

"I don't think it beats them. I don't think it resembles them in the least."

"Bless my soul—you don't say so! But of course I've no acquaintance whatever with American ships, not I, so I couldn't go against your knowledge. It's horrible enough for me. . . . But the queerest part is that those fellows seemed to have some idea the man was hidden aboard here.

They had really. Did you ever hear of such a thing?"

"Preposterous—isn't it?"

We were walking to and fro athwart the quarterdeck. No one of the crew forward could be seen (the day was Sunday), and the mate pursued:

"There was some little dispute about it. Our chaps took offence. 'As if we would harbour a thing like that,' they said. 'Wouldn't you like to look for him in our coal-hole?' Quite a tiff. But they made it up in the end. I suppose he did drown himself. Don't you, sir?"

"I don't suppose anything."

"You have no doubt in the matter, sir?"

"None whatever."

I left him suddenly. I felt I was producing a bad impression, but with my double down there it was most trying to be on deck. And it was almost as trying to be below. Altogether a nerve-trying situation. But on the whole I felt less torn in two when I was with him. There was no one in the whole ship whom I dared take into my confidence. Since the hands had got to know his story, it would have been impossible to pass him off for any one else, and an accidental discovery was to be dreaded now more than ever. . . .

The steward being engaged in laying the table for dinner, we could talk only with our eyes when I first went down. Later in the afternoon we had a cautious try at whispering. The Sunday quietness of the ship was against us; the the stillness of air and water around her was against us; the elements, the men were against us—everything was against us in our secret partnership; time itself—for this could not go on forever. The very trust in Providence was, I suppose, denied to his guilt. Shall I confess that this thought cast me down very much? And as to the chapter of accidents which counts for so much in the book of success, I could only hope that it was closed. For what favourable accident could be expected?

"Did you hear everything?" were my first words as soon as we took up our position side by side, leaning over my bed-place.

He had. And the proof of it was his earnest whisper, "The man told you he hardly dared to give the order."

I understood the reference to be to that saving foresail.

"Yes. He was afraid of it being lost in the setting."

"I assure you he never gave the order. He may think he did, but he never gave it. He stood there with me on the break of the poop after the maintopsail blew away, and whimpered about our last hope—positively whimpered about it and nothing else—and the night coming on! To hear one's skipper go on like that in such weather was enough to drive any fellow out of his mind. It worked me up into a sort of desperation. I just took it into my own hands and went away from him, boiling, and—— But what's the use telling you? *You* know! . . . Do you think that if I had not been pretty fierce with them I should have got the men to do anything? Not it! The bo's'n perhaps? Perhaps! It wasn't a heavy sea—it was a sea gone mad! I suppose the end of the world will be something like that; and a man may have the heart to see it coming once and be done with it—but to have to face it day after day—— I don't blame anybody. I was precious little better than the rest. Only—I was an officer of that old coal-waggon, anyhow——"

"I quite understand," I conveyed that sincere assurance into his ear. He was out of breath with whispering; I could hear him pant slightly. It was all very simple. The same strung-up force which had given twenty-four men a chance, at least, for their lives, had, in a sort of recoil, crushed an unworthy mutinous existence.

But I had no leisure to weigh the merits of the matter—footsteps in the saloon, a heavy knock. "There's enough wind to get under way with, sir." Here was the call of a new claim upon my thoughts and even upon my feelings.

"Turn the hands up," I cried through the door. "I'll be on deck directly."

I was going out to make the acquaintance of my ship. Before I left the cabin our eyes met— the eyes of the only two strangers on board. I pointed to the recessed part where the little camp-stool awaited him and laid my finger on my lips. He made a gesture—somewhat vague— a little mysterious, accompanied by a faint smile, as if of regret.

This is not the place to enlarge upon the sensations of a man who feels for the first time a ship move under his feet to his own independent word. In my case they were not unalloyed. I was not wholly alone with my command; for there was that stranger in my cabin. Or rather, I was not completely and wholly with her. Part of me was absent. That mental feeling of being in two places at once affected me physically as if the mood of secrecy had penetrated my very soul. Before an hour had elapsed since the ship had begun to move, having occasion to ask the mate (he stood by my side) to take a compass bearing of the Pagoda, I caught myself reaching up to his ear in whispers. I say I caught myself, but enough had escaped to startle the man. I can't describe it otherwise than by saying that he shied. A grave, preoccupied manner, as though he were in possession of some perplexing intelligence, did not leave him henceforth. A little later I moved away from the rail to look at the compass with such a stealthy gait that the helmsman noticed it—and I could not help noticing the unusual roundness of his eyes. These are trifling instances, though it's to no commander's advantage to be suspected of ludicrous eccentricities. But I was also more seriously affected. There are to a seaman certain words, gestures, that should in given conditions come as naturally, as instinctively as the winking of a menaced eye. A certain order should spring on to his lips without thinking; a certain sign should get itself made, so to speak, without reflection. But all unconscious alertness had abandoned me. I had to make an effort of will to recall myself back (from the cabin) to the conditions of the moment. I felt that I was appearing an irresolute commander to those people who were watching me more or less critically.

And, besides, there were the scares. On the second day out, for instance, coming off the deck in the afternoon (I had straw slippers on my bare feet) I stopped at the open pantry door and spoke to the steward. He was doing something there with his back to me. At the sound of my voice he nearly jumped out of his skin, as the saying is, and incidentally broke a cup.

"What on earth's the matter with you?" I asked, astonished.

He was extremely confused. "Beg your pardon, sir. I made sure you were in your cabin."

"You see I wasn't."

"No, sir. I could have sworn I had heard you moving in there not a moment ago. It's most extraordinary . . . very sorry, sir."

I passed on with an inward shudder. I was

so identified with my secret double that I did not even mention the fact in those scanty, fearful whispers we exchanged. I suppose he had made some slight noise of some kind or other. It would have been miraculous if he hadn't at one time or another. And yet, haggard as he appeared, he looked always perfectly self-controlled, more than calm—almost invulnerable. On my suggestion he remained almost entirely in the bath-room, which, upon the whole, was the safest place. There could be really no shadow of an excuse for any one ever wanting to go in there, once the steward had done with it. It was a very tiny place. Sometimes he reclined on the floor, his legs bent, his head sustained on one elbow. At others I would find him on the camp-stool, sitting in his grey sleeping-suit and with his cropped dark hair like a patient, unmoved convict. At night I would smuggle him into my bed-place, and we would whisper together, with the regular footfalls of the officer of the watch passing and repassing over our heads. It was an infinitely miserable time. It was lucky that some tins of fine preserves were stowed in a locker in my stateroom; hard bread I could always get hold of; and so he lived on stewed chicken, paté de foie gras, asparagus, cooked oysters, sardines— on all sorts of abominable sham delicacies out of tins. My early morning coffee he always drank; and it was all I dared do for him in that respect.

Every day there was the horrible manœuvring to go through so that my room and then the bath-room should be done in the usual way. I came to hate the sight of the steward, to abhor the voice of that harmless man. I felt that it was he who would bring on the disaster of discovery. It hung like a sword over our heads.

The fourth day out, I think (we were then working down the east side of the Gulf of Siam, tack for tack, in light winds and smooth water)— the fourth day, I say, of this miserable juggling with the unavoidable, as we sat at our evening meal, that man, whose slightest movement I dreaded, after putting down the dishes ran up on deck busily. This could not be dangerous. Presently he came down again; and then it appeared that he had remembered a coat of mine which I had thrown over a rail to dry after having been wetted in a shower which had passed over the ship in the afternoon. Sitting stolidly at the head of the table I became terrified at the sight of the garment on his arm. Of course he made for my door. There was no time to lose.

"Steward," I thundered. My nerves were so shaken that I could not govern my voice and conceal my agitation. This was the sort of thing that made my terrifically whiskered mate tap his forehead with his forefinger. I had detected him using that gesture while talking on deck with a confidential air to the carpenter. It was too far to hear a word, but I had no doubt that this pantomime could only refer to the strange new captain.

"Yes, sir," the pale-faced steward turned resignedly to me. It was this maddening course of being shouted at, checked without rhyme or reason, arbitrarily chased out of my cabin, suddenly called into it, sent flying out of his pantry on incomprehensible errands, that accounted for the growing wretchedness of his expression.

"Where are you going with that coat?"

"To your room, sir."

"Is there another shower coming?"

"I'm sure I don't know, sir. Shall I go up again and see, sir?"

"No! never mind."

My object was attained, as of course my other self in there would have heard everything that passed. During this interlude my two officers never raised their eyes off their respective plates; but the lip of that confounded cub, the second mate, quivered visibly.

I expected the steward to hook my coat on and come out at once. He was very slow about it; but I dominated my nervousness sufficiently not to shout after him. Suddenly I became aware (it could be heard plainly enough) that the fellow for some reason or other was opening the door of the bath-room. It was the end. The place was literally not big enough to swing a cat in. My voice died in my throat and I went stony all over. I expected to hear a yell of surprise and terror, and made a movement, but had not the strength to get on my legs. Everything remained still. Had my second self taken the poor wretch by the throat? I don't know what I would have done next moment if I had not seen the steward come out of my room, close the door, and then stand quietly by the sideboard.

"Saved," I thought. "But, no! Lost! Gone! He was gone!"

I laid my knife and fork down and leaned

back in my chair. My head swam. After a while, when sufficiently recovered to speak in a steady voice, I instructed my mate to put the ship round at eight o'clock himself.

"I won't come on deck," I went on. "I think I'll turn in, and unless the wind shifts I don't want to be disturbed before midnight. I feel a bit seedy."

"You did look middling bad a little while ago," the chief mate remarked without showing any great concern.

They both went out, and I stared at the steward clearing the table. There was nothing to be read on that wretched man's face. But why did he avoid my eyes I asked myself. Then I thought I should like to hear the sound of his voice.

"Steward!"

"Sir!" Startled as usual.

"Where did you hang up the coat?"

"In the bath-room, sir." The usual anxious tone. "It's not quite dry yet, sir."

For some time longer I sat in the cuddy. Had my double vanished as he had come? But of his coming there was an explanation, whereas his disappearance would be inexplicable. . . . I went slowly into my dark room, shut the door, lighted the lamp, and for a time dared not turn round. When at last I did I saw him standing bolt-upright in the narrow recessed part. It would not be true to say I had a shock, but an irresistible doubt of his bodily existence flitted through my mind. Can it be, I asked myself, that he is not visible to other eyes than mine? It was like being haunted. Motionless, with a grave face, he raised his hands slightly at me in a gesture which meant clearly, "Heavens! what a narrow escape!" Narrow indeed. I think I had come creeping quietly as near insanity as any man who has not actually gone over the border. That gesture restrained me, so to speak.

The mate with the terrific whiskers was now putting the ship on the other tack. In the moment of profound silence which follows upon the hands going to their stations I heard on the poop his raised voice: "Hard alee!" and the distant shout of the order repeated on the maindeck. The sails, in that light breeze, made but a faint fluttering noise. It ceased. The ship was coming round slowly; I held my breath in the renewed stillness of expectation; one wouldn't

have thought that there was a single living soul on her decks. A sudden brisk shout, "Mainsail haul!" broke the spell, and in the noisy cries and rush overhead of the men running away with the main-brace we two, down in my cabin, came together in our usual position by the bedplace.

He did not wait for my question. "I heard him fumbling here and just managed to squat myself down in the bath," he whispered to me. "The fellow only opened the door and put his arm in to hang the coat up. All the same——"

"I never thought of that," I whispered back, even more appalled than before at the closeness of the shave, and marvelling at that something unyielding in his character which was carrying him through so finely. There was no agitation in his whisper. Whoever was being driven distracted, it was not he. He was sane. And the proof of his sanity was continued when he took up the whispering again.

"It would never do for me to come to life again."

It was something that a ghost might have said. But what he was alluding to was his old captain's reluctant admission of the theory of suicide. It would obviously serve his turn—if I had understood at all the view which seemed to govern the unalterable purpose of his action.

"You must maroon me as soon as ever you can get amongst these islands off the Cambodje shore," he went on.

"Maroon you! We are not living in a boy's adventure tale," I protested. His scornful whispering took me up.

"We aren't indeed! There's nothing of a boy's tale in this. But there's nothing else for it. I want no more. You don't suppose I am afraid of what can be done to me? Prison or gallows or whatever they may please. But you don't see me coming back to explain such things to an old fellow in a wig and twelve respectable tradesmen, do you? What can they know whether I am guilty or not—or of *what* I am guilty, either? That's my affair. What does the Bible say? 'Driven off the face of the earth.' Very well. I am off the face of the earth now. As I came at night so I shall go."

"Impossible!" I murmured. "You can't."

"Can't? . . . Not naked like a soul on the Day of Judgment. I shall freeze on to this sleeping-suit. The Last Day is not yet— and . . . you have understood thoroughly. Didn't you?''

I felt suddenly ashamed of myself. I may say truly that I understood—and my hesitation in letting that man swim away from my ship's side had been a mere sham sentiment, a sort of cowardice.

"It can't be done now till next night," I breathed out. "The ship is on the off-shore tack and the wind may fail us."

"As long as I know that you understand," he whispered. "But of course you do. It's a great satisfaction to have got somebody to understand. You seem to have been there on purpose." And in the same whisper, as if we two whenever we talked had to say things to each other which were not fit for the world to hear, he added, "It's very wonderful."

We remained side by side talking in our secret way—but sometimes silent or just exchanging a whispered word or two at long intervals. And as usual he stared through the port. A breath of wind came now and again into our faces. The ship might have been moored in dock, so gently and on an even keel she slipped through the water, that did not murmur even at our passage, shadowy and silent like a phantom sea.

At midnight I went on deck, and to my mate's great surprise put the ship round on the other tack. His terrible whiskers flitted round me in silent criticism. I certainly should not have done it if it had been only a question of getting out of that sleepy gulf as quickly as possible. I believe he told the second mate, who relieved him, that it was a great want of judgment. The other only yawned. That intolerable cub shuffled about so sleepily and lolled against the rails in such a slack, improper fashion that I came down on him sharply.

"Aren't you properly awake yet?"

"Yes, sir! I am awake."

"Well, then, be good enough to hold yourself as if you were. And keep a look-out. If there's any current we'll be closing with some islands before daylight."

The east side of the gulf is fringed with islands, some solitary, others in groups. On the blue background of the high coast they seem to float on silvery patches of calm water, arid and grey, or dark green and rounded like clumps of evergreen bushes, with the larger ones, a mile or two long, showing the outlines of ridges, ribs of grey rock under the dark mantle of matted leafage. Unknown to trade, to travel, almost to geography, the manner of life they harbour is an unsolved secret. There must be villages—settlements of fishermen at least—on the largest of them, and some communication with the world is probably kept up by native craft. But all that forenoon, as we headed for them, fanned along by the faintest of breezes, I saw no sign of man or canoe in the field of the telescope I kept on pointing at the scattered group.

At noon I gave no orders for a change of course, and the mate's whiskers became much concerned and seemed to be offering themselves unduly to my notice. At last I said:

"I am going to stand right in. Quite in— as far as I can take her."

The stare of extreme surprise imparted an air of ferocity also to his eyes, and he looked truly terrific for a moment.

"We're not doing well in the middle of the gulf," I continued, casually. "I am going to look for the land breezes to-night."

"Bless my soul! Do you mean, sir, in the dark amongst the lot of all them islands and reefs and shoals?"

"Well—if there are any regular land breezes at all on this coast one must get close inshore to find them, mustn't one?"

"Bless my soul!" he exclaimed again under his breath. All that afternoon he wore a dreamy, contemplative appearance which in him was a mark of perplexity. After dinner I went into my stateroom as if I meant to take some rest. There we two bent our dark heads over a half-unrolled chart lying on my bed.

"There," I said. "It's got to be Koh-ring. I've been looking at it ever since sunrise. It has got two hills and a low point. It must be inhabited. And on the coast opposite there is what looks like the mouth of a biggish river—with some town, no doubt, not far up. It's the best chance for you that I can see."

"Anything. Koh-ring let it be."

He looked thoughtfully at the chart as if surveying chances and distances from a lofty height—and following with his eyes his own figure wandering on the blank land of Cochin-China, and then passing off that piece of paper clean out of sight into uncharted regions. And it was as if the ship had two captains to plan her course for her. I had been so worried and restless running up and down that I had not had the patience to dress that day. I had remained in my sleeping-suit, with straw slippers and a soft floppy hat. The closeness of the heat in the gulf had been most oppressive, and the crew were used to see me wandering in that airy attire.

"She will clear the south point as she heads now," I whispered into his ear. "Goodness only knows when, though, but certainly after dark. I'll edge her in to half a mile, as far as I may be able to judge in the dark——"

"Be careful," he murmured, warningly— and I realised suddenly that all my future, the only future for which I was fit, would perhaps go irretrievably to pieces in any mishap to my first command.

I could not stop a moment longer in the room. I motioned him to get out of sight and made my way on the poop. That unplayful cub had the watch. I walked up and down for a while thinking things out, then beckoned him over.

"Send a couple of hands to open the two quarter-deck ports," I said, mildly.

He actually had the impudence, or else so forgot himself in his wonder at such an incomprehensible order, as to repeat:

"Open the quarter-deck ports! What for, sir?"

"The only reason you need concern yourself about is because I tell you to do so. Have them open wide and fastened properly."

He reddened and went off, but I believe made some jeering remark to the carpenter as to the sensible practice of ventilating a ship's quarter-deck. I know he popped into the mate's cabin to impart the fact to him because the whiskers came on deck, as it were by chance, and stole glances at me from below—for signs of lunacy or drunkenness, I suppose.

A little before supper, feeling more restless than ever, I rejoined, for a moment, my second self. And to find him sitting so quietly was surprising, like something against nature, inhuman. I developed my plan in a hurried whisper.

"I shall stand in as close as I dare and then put her round. I shall presently find means to smuggle you out of here into the sail-locker, which communicates with the lobby. But there is an opening, a sort of square for hauling the sails out, which gives straight on the quarter-deck and which is never closed in fine weather, so as to give air to the sails. When the ship's way is deadened in stays and all the hands are aft at the mainbraces you shall have a clear road to slip out and get overboard through the open quarter-deck port. I've had them both fastened up. Use a rope's end to lower yourself into the water so as to avoid a splash—you know. It could be heard and cause some beastly complication."

He kept silent for a while, then whispered, "I understand."

"I won't be there to see you go," I began with an effort. "The rest . . . I only hope I have understood, too."

"You have. From first to last"—and for the first time there seemed to be a faltering, something strained in his whisper. He caught hold of my arm, but the ringing of the supper bell made me start. He didn't, though; he only released his grip.

After supper I didn't come below again till well past eight o'clock. The faint, steady breeze was loaded with dew; and the wet, darkened sails held all there was of propelling power in it. The night, clear and starry, sparkled darkly, and the opaque, lightless patches shifting slowly against the low stars were the drifting islets. On the port bow there was a big one more distant and shadowily imposing by the great space of sky it eclipsed.

On opening the door I had a back view of my very own self looking at a chart. He had come out of the recess and was standing near the table.

"Quite dark enough," I whispered.

He stepped back and leaned against my bed with a level, quiet glance. I sat on the couch. We had nothing to say to each other. Over our heads the officer of the watch moved here and there. Then I heard him move quickly. I knew what that meant. He was making for the companion; and presently his voice was outside my door.

"We are drawing in pretty fast, sir. Land looks rather close."

"Very well," I answered. "I am coming on deck directly."

I waited till he was gone out of the cuddy, then rose. My double moved too. The time had come to exchange our last whispers, for neither of us was ever to hear each other's natural voice.

"Look here!" I opened a drawer and took

out three sovereigns. "Take this, anyhow. I've got six and I'd give the you the lot, only I must keep a little money to buy some fruit and vegetables for the crew from native boats as we go through Sunda Straits."

He shook his head.

"Take it," I urged him, whispering desperately. "No one can tell what——"

He smiled and slapped meaningly the only pocket of the sleeping-jacket. It was not safe, certainly. But I produced a large old silk handkerchief of mine, and tying the three pieces of gold in a corner, pressed it on him. He was touched, I suppose, because he took it at last and tied it quickly round his waist under the jacket, on his bare skin.

Our eyes met; several seconds elapsed, till, our glances still mingled, I extended my hand and turned the lamp out. Then I passed through the cuddy, leaving the door of my room wide open. . . . "Steward!"

He was still lingering in the pantry in the greatness of his zeal, giving a rub-up to a plated cruet stand the last thing before going to bed. Being careful not to wake up the mate, whose room was opposite, I spoke in an undertone.

He looked round anxiously. "Sir!"

"Can you get me a little hot water from the galley?"

"I am afraid, sir, the galley fire's been out for some time now."

"Go and see."

He fled up the stairs.

"Now," I whispered, loudly, into the saloon —too loudly, perhaps, but I was afraid I couldn't make a sound. He was by my side in an instant— the double captain slipped past the stairs— through the tiny dark passage . . . a sliding door. We were in the sail-locker, scrambling on our knees over the sails. A sudden thought struck me. I saw myself wandering barefooted, bareheaded, the sun beating on my dark poll. I snatched off my floppy hat and tried hurriedly in the dark to ram it on my other self. He dodged and fended off silently. I wonder what he thought had come to me before he understood and suddenly desisted. Our hands met gropingly, lingered united in a steady, motionless clasp for a second. . . . No word was breathed by either of us when they separated.

I was standing quietly by the pantry door when the steward returned.

"Sorry, sir. Kettle barely warm. Shall I light the spirit-lamp?"

"Never mind."

I came out on deck slowly. It was now a matter of conscience to shave the land as close as possible—for now he must go overboard whenever the ship was put in stays. Must! There could be no going back for him. After a moment I walked over to leeward and my heart flew into my mouth at the nearness of the land on the bow. Under any other circumstances I would not have held on a minute longer. The second mate had followed me anxiously.

I looked on till I felt I could command my voice.

"She will weather," I said then in a quiet tone.

"Are you going to try that, sir?" he stammered out incredulously.

I took no notice of him and raised my tone just enough to be heard by the helmsman.

"Keep her good full."

"Good full, sir."

The wind fanned my cheek, the sails slept, the world was silent. The strain of watching the dark loom of the land growing bigger and denser was too much for me. I had shut my eyes—because the ship must go closer. She must! The stillness was intolerable. Were we standing still?

When I opened my eyes the second view started my heart with a thump. The black southern hill of Koh-ring seemed to hang right over the ship like a towering fragment of the everlasting night. On that enormous mass of blackness there was not a gleam to be seen, not a sound to be heard. It was gliding irresistibly toward us and yet seemed already within reach of the hand. I saw the vague figures of the watch grouped in the waist, gazing in awed silence.

"Are you going on, sir," inquired an unsteady voice at my elbow.

I ignored it. I had to go on.

"Keep her full. Don't check her way. That won't do now," I said warningly.

"I can't see the sails very well," the helmsman answered me, in strange, quavering tones.

Was she close enough? Already she was, I won't say in the shadow of the land, but in the very blackness of it, already swallowed up as it were, gone too close to be recalled, gone from me altogether.

"Give the mate a call," I said to the young

man who stood at my elbow as still as death. "And turn all hands up."

My tone had a borrowed loudness reverberated from the height of the land. Several voices cried out together: "We are all on deck, sir."

Then stillness again, with the great shadow gliding closer, towering higher, without a light, without a sound. Such a hush had fallen on the ship that she might have been a bark of the dead floating in slowly under the very gate of Erebus.

"My God! Where are we?"

It was the mate moaning at my elbow. He was thunderstruck, and as it were deprived of the moral support of his whiskers. He clapped his hands and absolutely cried out, "Lost!"

"Be quiet," I said sternly.

He lowered his tone, but I saw the shadowy gesture of his despair. "What are we doing here?"

"Looking for the land wind."

He made as if to tear his hair, and addressed me recklessly.

"She will never get out. You have done it, sir. I knew it'd end in something like this. She will never weather, and you are too close now to stay. She'll drift ashore before she's round. O my God!"

I caught his arm as he was raising it to batter his poor devoted head, and shook it violently.

"She's ashore already," he wailed, trying to tear himself away.

"Is she? . . . Keep good full there!"

"Good full, sir," cried the helmsman in a frightened, thin, child-like voice.

I hadn't let go the mate's arm and went on shaking it. "Ready about, do you hear? You go forward"—shake—"and stop there"—shake—"and hold your noise"—shake—"and see these head-sheets properly overhauled"—shake, shake—shake.

And all the time I dared not look toward the land lest my heart should fail me. I released my grip at last and he ran forward as if fleeing for dear life.

I wondered what my double there in the sail-locker thought of this commotion. He was able to hear everything—and perhaps he was able to understand why, on my conscience, it had to be thus close—no less. My first order "Hard alee!" re-echoed ominously under the towering shadow of Koh-ring as if I had shouted in a mountain gorge. And then I watched the land intently. In that smooth water and light wind it was impossible to feel the ship coming-to. No! I could not feel her. And my second self was making now ready to slip out and lower himself overboard. Perhaps he was gone already . . . ?

The great black mass brooding over our very mast-heads began to pivot away from the ship's side silently. And now I forgot the secret stranger ready to depart, and remembered only that I was a total stranger to the ship. I did not know her. Would she do it? How was she to be handled?

I swung the mainyard and waited helplessly. She was perhaps stopped, and her very fate hung in the balance, with the black mass of Koh-ring like the gate of the everlasting night towering over her taffrail. What would she do now? Had she way on her yet? I stepped to the side swiftly, and on the shadowy water I could see nothing except a faint phosphorescent flash revealing the glassy smoothness of the sleeping surface. It was impossible to tell—and I had not learned yet the feel of my ship. Was she moving? What I needed was something easily seen, a piece of paper, which I could throw overboard and watch. I had nothing on me. To run down for it I didn't dare. There was no time. All at once my strained, yearning stare distinguished a white object floating within a yard of the ship's side. White on the black water. A phosphorescent flash passed under it. What was that thing? . . . I recognised my own floppy hat. It must have fallen off his head . . . and he didn't bother. Now I had what I wanted—the saving mark for my eyes. But I hardly thought of my other self, now gone from the ship, to be hidden forever from all friendly faces, to be a fugitive and a vagabond on the earth, with no brand of the curse on his sane forehead to stay a slaying hand . . . too proud to explain.

And I watched the hat—the expression of my sudden pity for his mere flesh. It had been meant to save his homeless head from the dangers of the sun. And now—behold—it was saving the ship, by serving me for a mark to help out the ignorance of my strangeness. Ha! It was drifting forward, warning me just in time that the ship had gathered sternway.

"Shift the helm," I said in a low voice to the seaman standing still like a statue.

The man's eyes glistened wildly in the binnacle light as he jumped round to the other side and spun round the wheel.

I walked to the break of the poop. On the overshadowed deck all hands stood by the forebraces waiting for my order. The stars ahead seemed to be gliding from right to left. And all was so still in the world that I heard the quiet remark "She's round," passed in a tone of intense relief between two seamen.

"Let go and haul."

The foreyards ran round with a great noise, amidst cheery cries. And now the frightful whiskers made themselves heard giving various orders. Already the ship was drawing ahead. And

I was alone with her. Nothing! no one in the world should stand now between us, throwing a shadow on the way of silent knowledge and mute affection, the perfect communion of a seaman with his first command.

Walking to the taffrail, I was in time to make out, on the very edge of a darkness thrown by a towering black mass like the very gateway of Erebus—yes, I was in time to catch an evanescent glimpse of my white hat left behind to mark the spot where the secret sharer of my cabin and of my thoughts, as though he were my second self, had lowered himself into the water to take his punishment: a free man, a proud swimmer striking out for a new destiny.

Thomas Stearns Eliot
1888–1965

T. S. Eliot's place in the development of twentieth-century British literature has been described in the introduction to the Modern period, but one or two biographical facts may be added here. He was born in St. Louis, Missouri, and was educated at Milton Academy and at Harvard, where he took his B.A. in three years and an M.A. in the fourth. He then spent a year in Paris studying French literature and philosophy at the Sorbonne. He returned to Harvard for further work in philosophy, and in 1914, unable because of the war to complete a projected stay in Germany on a traveling fellowship, went to Merton College, Oxford. His stay in England prolonged itself into permanent residence, with various jobs: school-teaching, working in a branch of Lloyd's Bank, acting as assistant editor of *The Egoist* from 1917 to 1919, working for the distinguished publishing firm of Faber and Faber, of which he later became a director. The story of these early years in England, and of the beginnings of his literary career, has been told in interesting and authoritative detail by his widow, Valerie Eliot, in her introduction to what is the most important recent Eliot publication: the facsimile edition (1971) of the original manuscript of *The Waste Land,* including the annotations of Ezra Pound.

Eliot acquired British citizenship in 1927. He made an extended visit to the United States in 1932–33, when he held the Charles Eliot Norton Professorship of Poetry at Harvard, in which capacity he delivered the lectures later published under the title *The Use of Poetry and the Use of Criticism.* During the same season he delivered the Page Bar-

bour Lectures at the University of Virginia, later published as *After Strange Gods: A Primer of Modern Heresy.*

T. S. Eliot (1888–1965) in 1939. *Photo by Gisele Freund for Photo Researchers, Inc.*

Eliot's statement in the preface to *For Lancelot Andrewes* (1928) that the "general point of view" of the essays in that volume might be described as "classicist in literature, royalist in politics, and anglo-catholic in religion" has a patness that has made for too frequent quotation. The statement does, however, bring out his conservatism, not the least of the many apparent paradoxes that one encounters in studying this poet whose work has at times, and in some respects, seemed so revolutionary. But the early poetry, which to its first readers seemed to discard accepted poetic practices completely and abruptly, is seen to imply, when we look at it more closely, a greater regard for tradition than Eliot's immediate predecessors or many of his contemporaries had shown. The individual's present experience must be presented and scrutinized with reference to comparable experiences from the history and from the literature of the past: the whole technique of literary allusion is there to implement this principle. Not only as poet but also as critic, much of Eliot's endeavor was guided by an instinct for seeing the present against the background of the past that produced it: the individual writer, for example, as working within a tradition, a line of development, which his work, if it is valid, will alter to one degree or another (see "Tradition and the Individual Talent").

TEXTS: Eliot's complete poems, with the exception of a small volume of *Poems Written in Early Youth* (1967), are contained in *Collected Poems, 1909–1962*. The five verse plays, *Murder in the Cathedral* (1935), *Family Reunion* (1939), *The Cocktail Party* (1950), *The Confidential Clerk* (1954), and *The Elder Statesman* (1959) are all included in *Collected Plays* (1962).

His earlier literary criticism, originally published in such celebrated volumes as *The Sacred Wood* (1920), *Homage to John Dryden* (1924), *For Lancelot Andrewes* (1928), *Dante* (1929), and *Essays Ancient and Modern* (1936), is contained in *Selected Essays* (new edition, 1950). *The Idea of a Christian Society* (1939) and *Notes Toward the Definition of Culture* (1948) are concerned less with literary matters than with the role of belief in the formation of a society and its culture. Eliot's later literary criticism is published in *On Poetry and Poets* (1957) and *To Criticize the Critic* (1965).

Of the many books about Eliot and his art, one of the earliest to give the beginning reader the help he needed was H. R. Williamson's *The Poetry of T. S. Eliot* (1933; reprinted 1972). F. O. Matthiessen's *The Achievement of T. S. Eliot* (1935; a new edition, 1958, includes a chapter by C. L. Barber on Eliot's later work) is detailed and authoritative. F. R. Leavis has been a consistently illuminating critic of Eliot, in

New Bearings in English Poetry (1932; reprinted 1950) as well as in essays contained in later volumes (see especially *The Common Pursuit*, 1952, and *Lectures in America*, 1969). Other books, of varied scope and specific intent, are: Northrop Frye, *T. S. Eliot* (1963, in Writers and Critics series); Helen Gardner, *The Art of T. S. Eliot* (1949); Elizabeth Drew, *T. S. Eliot: The Design of His Poetry* (1950); Herbert Howarth, *Notes on Some Figures Behind T. S. Eliot* (1965); Leonard Unger, *T. S. Eliot: Movements and Patterns* (1966); George Williamson, *A Reader's Guide to T. S. Eliot: A Poem by Poem Analysis* (1966); and Bernard Bergonzi, *T. S. Eliot* (1972).

The following volumes collect essays or other contributions by various individual writers: *T. S. Eliot: A Study of His Writings by Several Hands*, edited by B. Rajan (1947); *T. S. Eliot: A Selected Critique*, edited by Leonard Unger (1948); *T. S. Eliot: A Symposium for his Seventieth Birthday*, edited by Neville Braybrook (1958); *T. S. Eliot: A Collection of Critical Essays*, edited by Hugh Kenner (1962); *T. S. Eliot: The Man and His Work*, edited by Allen Tate (1967). Two important and helpful essays are the chapter on Eliot in Edmund Wilson's *Axel's Castle* (1931, and later reprintings), and the essay on *The Waste Land* in C. M. Bowra's *The Creative Experiment* (1949).

The Love Song of J. Alfred Prufrock

S'io credesse che mia risposta fosse
A persona che mai tornasse al mondo,
Questa fiamma staria senza piu scosse.
Ma perciocche giammai di questo fondo
Non torno vivo alcun, s'i'odo il vero,
Senza tema d'infamia ti rispondo.[1]

Let us go then, you and I,
When the evening is spread out against the sky
Like a patient etherised upon a table;
For the yellow smoke that slides along the street,
The muttering retreats
Of restless nights in one-night cheap hotels
And sawdust restaurants with oyster-shells:

5

---

[1] The epigraph, from Dante's *Inferno* (XXVII, 61–66), consists of the first six lines of the speech in which the spirit of Guido da Montefeltro (concealed, like the other spirits in this section of Hell, in the flame of its own sin) answers Dante's question as to his identity: "If I believed that my answer were given to anyone who would ever return to the world, this flame would stand without moving any more; but because no one ever returned alive from this depth, if what I hear is true, I answer you without fear of infamy."

Streets that follow like a tedious argument
Of insidious intent
To lead you to an overwhelming question . . .   10
Oh, do not ask, "What is it?"
Let us go and make our visit.

In the room the women come and go
Talking of Michelangelo.

The yellow fog that rubs its back upon the   15
    window-panes,
The yellow smoke that rubs its muzzle on the
    window-panes
Licked its tongue into the corners of the evening,
Lingered upon the pools that stand in drains,
Let fall upon its back the soot that falls from
    chimneys,
Slipped by the terrace, made a sudden leap,   20
And seeing that it was a soft October night,
Curled once about the house, and fell asleep.

And indeed there will be time
For the yellow smoke that slides along the street,
Rubbing its back upon the window-panes;   25
There will be time, there will be time
To prepare a face to meet the faces that you
    meet;
There will be time to murder and create,
And time for all the works and days[2] of hands
That lift and drop a question on your plate;   30
Time for you and time for me,
And time yet for a hundred indecisions,
And for a hundred visions and revisions,
Before the taking of a toast and tea.

In the room the women come and go   35
Talking of Michelangelo.

And indeed there will be time
To wonder, "Do I dare?" and, "Do I dare?"
Time to turn back and descend the stair,
With a bald spot in the middle of my hair—   40
[They will say: "How his hair is growing thin!"]
My morning coat, my collar mounting firmly to
    the chin,
My necktie rich and modest, but asserted by a
    simple pin—

[They will say: "But how his arms and legs are
    thin!"]
Do I dare   45
Disturb the universe?
In a minute there is time
For decisions and revisions which a minute will
    reverse.

For I have known them all already, known them
    all:—
Have known the evenings, mornings, afternoons,   50
I have measured out my life with coffee spoons;
I know the voices dying with a dying fall
Beneath the music from a farther room.
    So how should I presume?

And I have known the eyes already, known them   55
    all—
The eyes that fix you in a formulated phrase,
And when I am formulated, sprawling on a pin,
When I am pinned and wriggling on the wall,
Then how should I begin
To spit out all the butt-ends of my days and   60
    ways?
    And how should I presume?

And I have known the arms already, known
    them all—
Arms that are braceleted and white and bare
[But in the lamplight, downed with light brown
    hair!]
Is it perfume from a dress   65
That makes me so digress?
Arms that lie along a table, or wrap about a
    shawl.
    And should I then presume?
    And how should I begin?
                            · · ·

Shall I say, I have gone at dusk through narrow   70
    streets
And watched the smoke that rises from the pipes
Of lonely men in shirt-sleeves, leaning out of
    windows? . . .

I should have been a pair of ragged claws
Scuttling across the floors of silent seas.
                            · · ·

And the afternoon, the evening, sleeps so peace-   75
    fully!
Smoothed by long fingers,
Asleep . . . tired . . . or it malingers,

---

[2] A reference, made with ironic intent, to the *Works and Days* of Hesiod (eighth century B.C.), in which the Greek poet describes the simple productive labors of his people.

Stretched on the floor, here beside you and me.
Should I, after tea and cakes and ices,
Have the strength to force the moment to its 80
    crisis?
But though I have wept and fasted, wept and
    prayed,
Though I have seen my head [grown slightly
    bald] brought in upon a platter,[3]
I am no prophet—and here's no great matter;
I have seen the moment of my greatness flicker,
And I have seen the eternal Footman hold my 85
    coat, and snicker,
And in short, I was afraid.

And would it have been worth it, after all,
After the cups, the marmalade, the tea,
Among the porcelain, among some talk of you
    and me,
Would it have been worth while, 90
To have bitten off the matter with a smile,
To have squeezed the universe into a ball
To roll it toward some overwhelming question,
To say: "I am Lazarus, come from the dead,[4]
Come back to tell you all, I shall tell you all"— 95
If one, settling a pillow by her head,
    Should say: "That is not what I meant at all.
    That is not it, at all."

      .   .   .

And would it have been worth it, after all,
Would it have been worth while, 100
After the sunsets and the dooryards and the
    sprinkled streets,
After the novels, after the teacups, after the
    skirts that trail along the floor—
And this, and so much more?—
It is impossible to say just what I mean!
But as if a magic lantern threw the nerves in 105
    patterns on a screen:
Would it have been worth while
If one, settling a pillow or throwing off a shawl,
And turning toward the window, should say:
    "That is not it at all,
    That is not what I meant, at all." 110

      .   .   .

No! I am not Prince Hamlet, nor was meant to
    be;
Am an attendant lord, one that will do
To swell a progress, start a scene or two,

---

3 See the story of John the Baptist in Matthew 14.
4 For the resurrection of Lazarus, see John 11.

Advise the prince; no doubt, an easy tool,
Deferential, glad to be of use, 115
Politic, cautious, and meticulous;
Full of high sentence, but a bit obtuse;
At times, indeed, almost ridiculous—
Almost, at times, the Fool.

I grow old . . . I grow old . . . 120
I shall wear the bottoms of my trousers rolled.

Shall I part my hair behind? Do I dare to eat a
    peach?
I shall wear white flannel trousers, and walk
    upon the beach.
I have heard the mermaids singing, each to each.

I do not think that they will sing to me. 125

I have seen them riding seaward on the waves
Combing the white hair of the waves blown back
When the wind blows the water white and black.

We have lingered in the chambers of the sea
By sea-girls wreathed with seaweed red and 130
    brown
Till human voices wake us, and we drown.

Preludes

I

The winter evening settles down
With smell of steaks in passageways.
Six o'clock.
The burnt-out ends of smoky days.
And now a gusty shower wraps 5
The grimy scraps
Of withered leaves about your feet
And newspapers from vacant lots;
The showers beat
On broken blinds and chimney-pots, 10
And at the corner of the street
A lonely cab-horse steams and stamps.
And then the lighting of the lamps.

II

The morning comes to consciousness
Of faint stale smells of beer 15
From the sawdust-trampled street
With all its muddy feet that press

To early coffee-stands.
With the other masquerades
That time resumes,   20
One thinks of all the hands
That are raising dingy shades
In a thousand furnished rooms.

III

You tossed a blanket from the bed,
You lay upon your back, and waited;   25
You dozed, and watched the night revealing
The thousand sordid images
Of which your soul was constituted;
They flickered against the ceiling.
And when all the world came back   30
And the light crept up between the shutters
And you heard the sparrows in the gutters,
You had such a vision of the street
As the street hardly understands;
Sitting along the bed's edge, where   35
You curled the papers from your hair,
Or clasped the yellow soles of feet
In the palms of both soiled hands.

IV

His soul stretched tight across the skies
That fade behind a city block,   40
Or trampled by insistent feet
At four and five and six o'clock;
And short square fingers stuffing pipes,
And evening newspapers, and eyes
Assured of certain certainties,   45
The conscience of a blackened street
Impatient to assume the world.

I am moved by fancies that are curled
Around these images, and cling:
The notion of some infinitely gentle   50
Infinitely suffering thing.

Wipe your hand across your mouth, and laugh;
The worlds revolve like ancient women
Gathering fuel in vacant lots.

A Cooking Egg[1]

En l'an trentiesme de mon aage
Que toutes mes hontes j'ay beues . . .[2]

Pipit sate upright in her chair
    Some distance from where I was sitting;

Views of the Oxford Colleges
    Lay on the table, with the knitting.

Daguerreotypes and silhouettes,   5
    Her grandfather and great great aunts,
Supported on the mantelpiece
    An *Invitation to the Dance.*

                    . . .

I shall not want Honour in Heaven
    For I shall meet Sir Philip Sidney   10
And have talk with Coriolanus
    And other heroes of that kidney.

I shall not want Capital in Heaven
    For I shall meet Sir Alfred Mond.
We two shall lie together, lapt   15
    In a five per cent. Exchequer Bond.

I shall not want Society in Heaven,
    Lucretia Borgia shall be my Bride;
Her anecdotes will be more amusing
    Than Pipit's experience could provide.   20

I shall not want Pipit in Heaven:
    Madame Blavatsky will instruct me
In the Seven Sacred Trances;
    Piccarda de Donati will conduct me.
                    . . .

But where is the penny world I bought   25
    To eat with Pipit behind the screen?

1 Different readers may have different views as to just who the "I" is, and just who Pipit is: for two such individual readings, see Elizabeth Drew, *Discovering Poetry* (1933), pp. 112 ff., and F. O. Matthiessen, *The Achievement of T. S. Eliot*, pp. 130–31 (Oxford Bookshelf Edition). To the "I" of the poem—the "cooking egg" of its title—Sir Philip Sidney represents the Elizabethan ideal of the perfect nobleman, as Shakespeare's Coriolanus represents that of the towering, assured hero. Sir Alfred Mond, the British financier, represents great wealth, and Lucrezia Borgia (1480–1519), the brilliant and deadly Renaissance intrigante, stands for exciting, romantic, willful relationships with women. Yeats has described his meetings with Madame Blavatsky (1831–1891), the Russian theosophist, in various places: see especially his *Autobiography* (1938), p. 151.

Each of the figures evoked has been chosen for the extravagance with which it contrasts with the dull, limited actuality of the speaker's life. Kentish Town and Golder's Green are London workers' suburbs. In earlier editions of his *Poems*, Eliot included a note to the last line of the poem: "I.e. an endemic teashop, found in all parts of London. The initials signify: Aerated Bread Company, Limited."

2 The poem's epigraph, from Villon, is referred to, and translated, p. 995, in the introduction to the Modern period.

The red-eyed scavengers are creeping
  From Kentish Town and Golder's Green;

Where are the eagles and the trumpets?

  Buried beneath some snow-deep Alps.   30
Over buttered scones and crumpets
  Weeping, weeping multitudes
Droop in a hundred A.B.C.'s.

Sweeney Among the Nightingales[1]

ὦμοι πέπληγμαι καιρίαν πληγὴν ἔσω.

Apeneck Sweeney spreads his knees
Letting his arms hang down to laugh,
The zebra stripes along his jaw
Swelling to maculate giraffe.

The circles of the stormy moon   5
Slide westward toward the River Plate,[2]
Death and the Raven drift above
And Sweeney guards the hornèd gate.[3]

Gloomy Orion and the Dog
Are veiled; and hushed the shrunken seas;   10
The person in the Spanish cape
Tries to sit on Sweeney's knees

Slips and pulls the table cloth
Overturns a coffee-cup,
Reorganised upon the floor   15
She yawns and draws a stocking up;

The silent man in mocha brown
Sprawls at the window-sill and gapes;
The waiter brings in oranges
Bananas figs and hothouse grapes;   20

The silent vertebrate in brown
Contracts and concentrates, withdraws;

Rachel *née* Rabinovitch
Tears at the grapes with murderous paws;

She and the lady in the cape   25
Are suspect, thought to be in league;
Therefore the man with heavy eyes
Declines the gambit, shows fatigue,

Leaves the room and reappears
Outside the window, leaning in,   30
Branches of wistaria
Circumscribe a golden grin;

The host with someone indistinct
Converses at the door apart,
The nightingales are singing near   35
The Convent of the Sacred Heart,

And sang within the bloody wood
When Agamemnon cried aloud,
And let their liquid siftings fall
To stain the stiff dishonoured shroud.   40

The Waste Land[1]

*"Nam Sibyllam quidem Cumis ego ipse oculis meis
vidi in ampulla pendere, et cum illi pueri dicerent:*
Σίβυλλα τί θέλεις; *respondebat illa:* ἀποθανεῖν
θέλω."[2]

FOR EZRA POUND

il miglior fabbro

I. THE BURIAL OF THE DEAD

April is the cruellest month, breeding
Lilacs out of the dead land, mixing
Memory and desire, stirring
Dull roots with spring rain.
Winter kept us warm, covering   5
Earth in forgetful snow, feeding
A little life with dried tubers.

---

1 For a brief note of interpretation, and translation of the epigraph, see the discussion of Eliot in the introduction to the Modern period.
2 The River Plate (Río de la Plata) is the estuary of two South American rivers, between Paraguay and Argentina, which has led commentators to place the poem's otherwise unspecified scene in South America. Orion (line 9), in any event, is an equatorial constellation.
3 Through the gates of ivory, in Homer and in various succeeding mythologies, come the dreams that are pleasant but untrue; through the gates of horn, the dreams that are unpleasant but true.

1 It has occasionally been suggested (wrongly, this editor thinks) that in providing notes to *The Waste Land* (reprinted in this volume immediately following the poem) Eliot was in part guying the reader, and that in any event his notes are not very helpful. Now, a beginning reader who needs fundamental help with the poem needs *more* help than can be provided by interlacing Eliot's own notes with additional notes by the editor. For the reader who is in a position to follow the suggestions for approaching *The Waste Land* that have been made in the

Summer surprised us, coming over the Starn-
    bergersee[3]
With a shower of rain; we stopped in the colon-
    nade,
And went on in sunlight, into the Hofgarten,   10
And drank coffee, and talked for an hour.
Bin gar keine Russin, stamm' aus Litauen, echt
    deutsch.[4]
And when we were children, staying at the arch-
    duke's,
My cousin's, he took me out on a sled,
And I was frightened. He said, Marie,   15
Marie, hold on tight. And down we went.
In the mountains, there you feel free.
I read, much of the night, and go south in the
    winter.

What are the roots that clutch, what branches
    grow
Out of this stony rubbish? Son of man,   20
You cannot say, or guess, for you know only
A heap of broken images, where the sun beats,

And the dead tree gives no shelter, the cricket no
    relief,
And the dry stone no sound of water. Only
There is shadow under this red rock,   25
(Come in under the shadow of this red rock),
And I will show you something different from
    either
Your shadow at morning striding behind you
Or your shadow at evening rising to meet you;
I will show you fear in a handful of dust.   30
       Frisch weht der Wind
       Der Heimat zu.
       Mein irisch Kind,
       Wo weilest du?[5]
"You gave me hyacinths first a year ago;   35
"They called me the hyacinth girl."
—Yet when we came back, late, from the Hya-
    cinth garden,
Your arms full, and your hair wet, I could not
Speak, and my eyes failed, I was neither
Living nor dead, and I knew nothing,   40
Looking into the heart of light, the silence.
Oed' und leer das Meer.[6]

Madame Sosostris, famous clairvoyante,
Had a bad cold, nevertheless
Is known to be the wisest woman in Europe,   45
With a wicked pack of cards. Here, said she,
Is your card, the drowned Phoenician Sailor,
(Those are pearls that were his eyes. Look!)
Here is Belladonna, the Lady of the Rocks,
The lady of situations.   50
Here is the man with three staves, and here the
    Wheel,
And here is the one-eyed merchant, and this card,
Which is blank, is something he carries on his
    back,
Which I am forbidden to see. I do not find
The Hanged Man. Fear death by water.   55
I see crowds of people, walking round in a ring.
Thank you. If you see dear Mrs. Equitone,
Tell her I bring the horoscope myself:
One must be so careful these days.

Unreal City,[7]   60

---

introduction to the Modern period, Eliot's notes should be taken seriously and literally and will provide all the detailed help that is necessary once the right directions have been taken. The technique of allusion that is fundamental to the poem's structure depends on the reader's knowing not merely where each of the quoted passages comes from, as a simple fact, but something of the context of event, meaning, or tone which each allusion calls up: if a passage is not familiar to him, Eliot's notes will direct him, in most cases, to its source so that he can build up for himself a sense of the passage's context which will enable him to see what values the poet has hoped to summon up by citing it. The reader can easily see how the process works by examining the effect of juxtaposing a line (*Waste Land,* line 172) from Ophelia's speech in *Hamlet,* IV, v, with the banal good nights of the Cockneys in the pub. Nor is there any need to postpone "reading" the poem while one undertakes an elaborate course of reading the works to which allusion is made. Each reader should try to take in as much of the background of reference as he can profitably absorb, and avoid the pedantry which can so insidiously substitute itself for the genuine poetic pleasure which the work can give an early stage of one's acquaintance with it. The editor is above all anxious not to give the impression that the "key" to an understanding and appreciation of the poem lies in such notes on particular points as are appended here. The chief aim has been to provide help where the reader may not know the language in which the citation is made.

2 The epigraph is taken from the *Satyricon* of Petronius, the Roman satirist of the first century A.D.: " For indeed I myself, with my own eyes, have seen the Cumaean Sibyl hanging in a bottle, and when those boys would say to her, 'Sibyl, what do you want?' she would reply, 'I want to die.' "

3 A lake near Munich. The Hofgarten (line 10) is a formal garden in the center of Munich.

4 "I am no Russian, come from Lithuania, a real German."

5 (See Eliot's note.) The sailor's song from Wagner's *Tristan und Isolde:* "Fresh blows the wind/ towards the homeland./ My Irish child,/ where are you lingering?"

6 (See Eliot's note.) "Waste and empty the sea." (I.e., the ship bringing Isolde back to Tristan is nowhere in sight.)

7 (See Eliot's note.) The lines which Eliot cites from Baudelaire as providing the background of the phrase

Under the brown fog of a winter dawn,
A crowd flowed over London Bridge, so many,
I had not thought death had undone so many.[8]
Sighs, short and infrequent, were exhaled,[9]
And each man fixed his eyes before his feet. 65
Flowed up the hill and down King William
    Street,
To where Saint Mary Woolnoth kept the hours
With a dead sound on the final stroke of nine.
There I saw one I knew, and stopped him, cry-
    ing: "Stetson!
"You who were with me in the ships at Mylae! 70
"That corpse you planted last year in your gar-
    den,
"Has it begun to sprout? Will it bloom this year?
"Or has the sudden frost disturbed its bed?
"Oh keep the Dog far hence, that's friend to
    men,[10]
"Or with his nails he'll dig it up again! 75
"You! hypocrite lecteur!—mon semblable,—mon
    frère!"[11]

II. A GAME OF CHESS

The Chair she sat in, like a burnished throne,
Glowed on the marble, where the glass
Held up by standards wrought with fruited vines
From which a golden Cupidon peeped out 80
(Another hid his eyes behind his wing)
Doubled the flames of sevenbranched candelabra
Reflecting light upon the table as
The glitter of her jewels rose to meet it,
From satin cases poured in rich profusion; 85
In vials of ivory and coloured glass
Unstoppered, lurked her strange synthetic per-
    fumes,
Unguent, powdered, or liquid—troubled, con-
    fused

And drowned the sense in odours; stirred by the
    air
That freshened from the window, these ascended 9
In fattening the prolonged candle-flames,
Flung their smoke into the laquearia,[12]
Stirring the pattern on the coffered ceiling.
Huge sea-wood fed with copper
Burned green and orange, framed by the col- 9
    oured stone,
In which sad light a carvèd dolphin swam.
Above the antique mantel was displayed
As though a window gave upon the sylvan scene
The change of Philomel, by the barbarous king
So rudely forced; yet there the nightingale 10
Filled all the desert with inviolable voice
And still she cried, and still the world pursues,
"Jug Jug" to dirty ears.
And other withered stumps of time
Were told upon the walls; staring forms 10
Leaned out, leaning, hushing the room enclosed.
Footsteps shuffled on the stair.
Under the firelight, under the brush, her hair
Spread out in fiery points
Glowed into words, then would be savagely still. 110

"My nerves are bad to-night. Yes, bad. Stay with
    me.
"Speak to me. Why do you never speak. Speak.
"What are you thinking of? What thinking?
    What?
"I never know what you are thinking. Think."

I think we are in rats' alley 11
Where the dead men lost their bones.

"What is that noise?"
               The wind under the door.
"What is that noise now? What is the wind do-
    ing?"
               Nothing again nothing. 12
                   "Do
"You know nothing? Do you see nothing? Do
    you remember
"Nothing?"

              I remember
Those are pearls that were his eyes. 12

"Unreal City" are the opening lines of "Les Sept Vieil-
lards" (The Seven Old Men) in *Les Fleurs du Mal* (1857):
"Swarming city, city full of dreams,/ Where in broad
daylight the specter accosts the passer-by!"
[8] (See Eliot's note.) ". . . Such a long train/ of people,
that I would never have believed/ that death had undone
so many."
[9] (See Eliot's note.) "Here, as far as we could hear,/ there
was no weeping, but such sighs/ as made the eternal air
tremble."
[10] See Eliot's note 407.
[11] The last line of Baudelaire's verse Preface to *Les Fleurs
du Mal*. In this Preface Baudelaire has invoked *Ennui*, the
spirit of boredom: "His eye charged with an involuntary
tear, he dreams of scaffolds as he smokes his hookah. You
know him, reader, this monster of delicate tastes,—hypocrite reader,—my counterpart,—my brother!"

---

[12] The lines Eliot quotes from the *Aeneid* in his note may
be translated as follows: "Glowing lamps hang from the
gold-paneled ceiling, and the torches conquer the darkness
with their flames."

"Are you alive, or not? Is there nothing in your
    head?"
                                  But
O O O O that Shakespeherian Rag—
It's so elegant
So intelligent   130
"What shall I do now? What shall I do?
"I shall rush out as I am, and walk the street
"With my hair down, so. What shall we do
    tomorrow?
"What shall we ever do?"
                        The hot water at ten.   135
And if it rains, a closed car at four.
And we shall play a game of chess,
Pressing lidless eyes and waiting for a knock
    upon the door.

When Lil's husband got demobbed,[13] I said—
I didn't mince my words, I said to her myself,   140
HURRY UP PLEASE IT'S TIME[14]
Now Albert's coming back, make yourself a bit
    smart.
He'll want to know what you done with that
    money he gave you
To get yourself some teeth. He did, I was there.
You have them all out, Lil, and get a nice set,   145
He said, I swear, I can't bear to look at you.
And no more can't I, I said, and think of poor
    Albert,
He's been in the army four years, he wants a good
    time,
And if you don't give it him, there's others will,
    I said.
Oh is there, she said. Something o' that, I said.   150
Then I'll know who to thank, she said, and give
    me a straight look.
HURRY UP PLEASE IT'S TIME
If you don't like it you can get on with it, I said.
Others can pick and choose if you can't.
But if Albert makes off, it won't be for lack of   155
    telling.
You ought to be ashamed, I said, to look so an-
    tique.
(And her only thirty-one.)
I can't help it, she said, pulling a long face,
It's them pills I took, to bring it off, she said.

(She's had five already, and nearly died of young   160
    George.)
The chemist[15] said it would be all right, but I've
    never been the same.
You *are* a proper fool, I said.
Well, if Albert won't leave you alone, there it is,
    I said,
What you get married for if you don't want chil-
    dren?
HURRY UP PLEASE IT'S TIME   165
Well, that Sunday Albert was home, they had a
    hot gammon,
And they asked me in to dinner, to get the beauty
    of it hot—
HURRY UP PLEASE IT'S TIME
HURRY UP PLEASE IT'S TIME
Goonight Bill. Goonight Lou. Goonight May.   170
    Goonight.
Ta ta. Goonight. Goonight.
Good night, ladies, good night, sweet ladies, good
    night, good night.

III. THE FIRE SERMON

The river's tent is broken: the last fingers of leaf
Clutch and sink into the wet bank. The wind
Crosses the brown land, unheard. The nymphs   175
    are departed.
Sweet Thames, run softly, till I end my song.
The river bears no empty bottles, sandwich
    papers,
Silk handkerchiefs, cardboard boxes, cigarette
    ends
Or other testimony of summer nights. The
    nymphs are departed.
And their friends, the loitering heirs of city   180
    directors;
Departed, have left no addresses.
By the waters of Leman I sat down and
    wept . . .[16]
Sweet Thames, run softly till I end my song,
Sweet Thames, run softly, for I speak not loud or
    long.
But at my back in a cold blast I hear   185
The rattle of the bones, and chuckle spread from
    ear to ear.
A rat crept softly through the vegetation
Dragging its slimy belly on the bank
While I was fishing in the dull canal

---

13 Demobilized.
14 The reiterated "Hurry up please it's time" is typical of
the injunctions by which London barkeepers remind their
customers that it is closing time. Here, of course, it is
used for symbolic effect, as well as—in its literal sense—
to set the scene.

15 The British equivalent of our *druggist* or *pharmacist*.
16 Cf. Psalm 137.

On a winter evening round behind the gashouse 190
Musing upon the king my brother's wreck
And on the king my father's death before him.
White bodies naked on the low damp ground
And bones cast in a little low dry garret,
Rattled by the rat's foot only, year to year. 195
But at my back from time to time I hear
The sound of horns and motors, which shall
    bring
Sweeney to Mrs. Porter in the spring.
O the moon shone bright on Mrs. Porter
And on her daughter 200
They wash their feet in soda water
*Et O ces voix d'enfants, chantant dans la
    coupole!*[17]

Twit twit twit
Jug jug jug jug jug jug
So rudely forc'd. 205
Tereu

Unreal City[18]
Under the brown fog of a winter noon
Mr. Eugenides, the Smyrna merchant
Unshaven, with a pocket full of currants 210
C.i.f. London: documents at sight,
Asked me in demotic French
To luncheon at the Cannon Street Hotel
Followed by a weekend at the Metropole.

At the violet hour, when the eyes and back 215
Turn upward from the desk, when the human
    engine waits
Like a taxi throbbing waiting,
I Tiresias, though blind, throbbing between two
    lives,[19]

Old man with wrinkled female breasts, can see
At the violet hour, the evening hour that strives 220
Homeward, and brings the sailor home from
    sea,[20]
The typist home at teatime, clears her breakfast,
    lights
Her stove, and lays out food in tins.
Out of the window perilously spread
Her drying combinations touched by the sun's 225
    last rays,
On the divan are piled (at night her bed)
Stockings, slippers, camisoles, and stays.
I Tiresias, old man with wrinkled dugs
Perceived the scene, and foretold the rest—
I too awaited the expected guest. 230
He, the young man carbuncular, arrives,
A small house agent's clerk, with one bold stare,
One of the low on whom assurance sits
As a silk hat on a Bradford millionaire.
The time is now propitious, as he guesses, 235
The meal is ended, she is bored and tired,
Endeavours to engage her in caresses
Which still are unreproved, if undesired.
Flushed and decided, he assaults at once;
Exploring hands encounter no defence; 240
His vanity requires no response,

---

[17] The concluding line of Verlaine's sonnet "Parsifal": "And oh those children's voices singing in the choir loft!"
[18] Cf. lines 60–61, above.
[19] The passage from Ovid (*Metamorphoses*, III, 322 ff.) which Eliot quotes in his note on this line reads as follows in Golding's translation (1567):
They say that Jove, disposed to mirth as he and Juno sat
A-drinking nectar after meat in sport and pleasant rate,
Did fall a-jesting with his wife, and said: "A greater pleasure
In Venus' games ye women have than men beyond all measure."
She answered, no. To try the truth, they both of them agree
The wise Tiresias in this case indifferent judge to be,
Who both the man's and woman's joys by trial understood,
For finding once two mighty snakes engend'ring in a wood,

He struck them overthwart the backs, by means whereof behold
(As strange a thing to be of truth as ever yet was told)
He being made a woman straight, seven winters lived so.
The eighth he finding them again did say unto them tho:
"And if to strike ye have such power as for to turn their shape
That are the givers of the stripe, before you hence escape,
One stripe now shall I lend you more." He struck them as before
And straight returned his former shape in which he first was born.
Tiresias therefore being ta'en to judge this jesting strife,
Gave sentence on the side of Jove; the which the queen his wife
Did take a great deal more to heart than needed, and in spite
To wreak her teen upon her judge, bereft him of his sight;
But Jove (for to the gods it is unlawful to undo
The things which other of the gods by any means have do)
Did give him sight in things to come for loss of sight of eye,
And so his grievous punishment with honour did supply.
[20] The poem of Sappho in question in Eliot's note to this line is No. 120 in E. Diehl, *Anthologia Lyrica* (1922). It may be translated as follows:
  Hesperus, all things you bring, as many as light-bringing morning has scattered abroad.
  You bring the sheep,
  You bring the goat, you bring the child to its mother.
But see also R. L. Stevenson's "Requiem," line 7.

And makes a welcome of indifference.
(And I Tiresias have foresuffered all
Enacted on this same divan or bed;
I who have sat by Thebes below the wall   245
And walked among the lowest of the dead.)
Bestows one final patronising kiss,
And gropes his way, finding the stairs unlit . . .

She turns and looks a moment in the glass,
Hardly aware of her departed lover;   250
Her brain allows one half-formed thought to
    pass:
"Well now that's done: and I'm glad it's over."
When lovely woman stoops to folly and
Paces about her room again, alone,
She smoothes her hair with automatic hand,   255
And puts a record on the gramophone.

"This music crept by me upon the waters"
And along the Strand, up Queen Victoria Street.
O City city, I can sometimes hear
Beside a public bar in Lower Thames Street,   260
The pleasant whining of a mandoline
And a clatter and a chatter from within
Where fishmen lounge at noon: where the walls
Of Magnus Martyr hold
Inexplicable splendour of Ionian white and gold.   265

    The river sweats
    Oil and tar
    The barges drift
    With the turning tide
    Red sails   270
    Wide
    To leeward, swing on the heavy spar.
    The barges wash
    Drifting logs
    Down Greenwich reach   275
    Past the Isle of Dogs.
        Weialala leia
        Wallala leialala

    Elizabeth and Leicester
    Beating oars   280
    The stern was formed
    A gilded shell
    Red and gold
    The brisk swell
    Rippled both shores   285
    Southwest wind
    Carried down stream
    The peal of bells

    White towers
        Weialala leia   290
        Wallala leialala

"Trams and dusty trees.
Highbury bore me. Richmond and Kew[21]
Undid me. By Richmond I raised my knees
Supine on the floor of a narrow canoe."   295

"My feet are at Moorgate, and my heart
Under my feet. After the event
He wept. He promised 'a new start.'
I made no comment. What should I resent?"

"On Margate Sands.   300
I can connect
Nothing with nothing.
The broken fingernails of dirty hands.
My people humble people who expect
Nothing."   305
        la la

To Carthage then I came

Burning burning burning burning
O Lord Thou pluckest me out
O Lord Thou pluckest   310

burning

IV. DEATH BY WATER

Phlebas the Phoenician, a fortnight dead,
Forgot the cry of gulls, and the deep sea swell
And the profit and loss.
              A current under sea   315
Picked his bones in whispers. As he rose and fell
He passed the stages of his age and youth
Entering the whirlpool.
              Gentile or Jew
O you who turn the wheel and look to windward,   320
Consider Phlebas, who was once handsome and
    tall as you.

---

21 The verses from the *Purgatorio* which Eliot quotes in
his note to this line are from the moving speech of La
Pia, who says to Dante: "Pray, when you have returned to
the world and are rested from your long journey, . . .
remember me, who am La Pia; Siena made me, the
Maremma unmade me" (referring to the manner of her
death, possibly from being intentionally shut up by her
husband in the fever-ridden marshes around Siena known
as the Maremma).

V. WHAT THE THUNDER SAID

After the torchlight red on sweaty faces
After the frosty silence in the gardens
After the agony in stony places
The shouting and the crying   325
Prison and palace and reverberation
Of thunder of spring over distant mountains
He who was living is now dead
We who were living are now dying
With a little patience   330

Here is no water but only rock
Rock and no water and the sandy road
The road winding above among the mountains
Which are mountains of rock without water
If there were water we should stop and drink   335
Amongst the rock one cannot stop or think
Sweat is dry and feet are in the sand
If there were only water amongst the rock
Dead mountain mouth of carious teeth that can-
    not spit
Here one can neither stand nor lie nor sit   340
There is not even silence in the mountains
But dry sterile thunder without rain
There is not even solitude in the mountains
But red sullen faces sneer and snarl
From doors of mudcracked houses
                         If there were water   345

    And no rock
    If there were rock
    And also water
    And water
    A spring   350
    A pool among the rock
    If there were the sound of water only
    Not the cicada
    And dry grass singing
    But sound of water over a rock   355
    Where the hermit-thrush sings in the pine trees
    Drip drop drip drop drop drop drop
    But there is no water

Who is the third who walks always beside you?
When I count, there are only you and I together   360
But when I look ahead up the white road
There is always another one walking beside you
Gliding wrapt in a brown mantle, hooded
I do not know whether a man or a woman
—But who is that on the other side of you?   365

What is that sound high in the air[22]
Murmur of maternal lamentation
Who are those hooded hordes swarming
Over endless plains, stumbling in cracked earth
Ringed by the flat horizon only   370
What is the city over the mountains
Cracks and reforms and bursts in the violet air
Falling towers
Jerusalem Athens Alexandria
Vienna London   375
Unreal

A woman drew her long black hair out tight
And fiddled whisper music on those strings
And bats with baby faces in the violet light
Whistled, and beat their wings   380
And crawled head downward down a blackened
    wall
And upside down in air were towers
Tolling reminiscent bells, that kept the hours
And voices singing out of empty cisterns and ex-
    hausted wells.

In this decayed hole among the mountains   385
In the faint moonlight, the grass is singing
Over the tumbled graves, about the chapel
There is the empty chapel, only the wind's home.
It has no windows, and the door swings,
Dry bones can harm no one.   390
Only a cock stood on the rooftree
Co co rico co co rico
In a flash of lightning. Then a damp gust
Bringing rain

Ganga was sunken, and the limp leaves   395
Waited for rain, while the black clouds
Gathered far distant, over Himavant.
The jungle crouched, humped in silence.
Then spoke the thunder
DA   400
Datta: what have we given?
My friend, blood shaking my heart
The awful daring of a moment's surrender

---

22 The passage from Hermann Hesse's *Blick ins Chaos* (A
Glance into Chaos) which Eliot quotes in his note to this
passage may be translated as follows: "Already half of
Europe, already at least half of Eastern Europe is on the
road to Chaos, drives drunkenly in holy madness along
the abyss and sings the while, sings drunkenly a hymn
as Dimitri Karamazov sang. The bourgeois laughs, insulted, over these songs, but the saint and prophet hear
them with tears."

Which an age of prudence can never retract

By this, and this only, we have existed   405

Which is not to be found in our obituaries

Or in memories draped by the beneficent spider

Or under seals broken by the lean solicitor

In our empty rooms

DA   410

Dayadhvam: I have heard the key[23]

Turn in the door once and turn once only

We think of the key, each in his prison

Thinking of the key, each confirms a prison

Only at nightfall, aethereal rumours   415

Revive for a moment a broken Coriolanus[24]

DA

Damyata: The boat responded

Gaily, to the hand expert with sail and oar

The sea was calm, your heart would have re-   420

    sponded

Gaily, when invited, beating obedient

To controlling hands

                I sat upon the shore

Fishing, with the arid plain behind me

Shall I at least set my lands in order?   425

London Bridge is falling down falling down fall-

    ing down

Poi s'ascose nel foco che gli affina[25]

Quando fiam uti chelidon—O swallow swallow[26]

Le Prince d'Aquitaine à la tour abolie[27]

These fragments I have shored against my ruins   430

Why then Ile fit you. Hieronymo's mad againe.

Datta. Dayadhvam. Damyata.

    Shantih   shantih   shantih

Itylus is to think of Philomela the line has the effect of reminding us yet again of a theme that has been touched on many times in the poem. (See Eliot's note to line 99, and see also the nightingale's song, lines 203–06.)

27 Gérard de Nerval's sonnet *El Desdichado,* from which this line is taken, describes one who thinks of himself as in all senses "disinherited":

    Je suis le ténébreux,—le veuf,—l'inconsolé,

    Le prince d'Aquitaine à la tour abolie:

    Ma seule étoile est morte,—et mon luth constellé

    Porte le *Soleil noir* de la *Mélancholie.* . . .

"I am the shadowy one,—the widower,—the unconsoled,/ The prince of Aquitania in the disused tower:/ My only star is dead,—and my starred lute/ Carries as its sign the black sun of Melancholy. . . ."

NOTES ON THE WASTE LAND

Not only the title, but the plan and a good deal of the incidental symbolism of the poem were suggested by Miss Jessie L. Weston's book on the Grail legend: *From Ritual to Romance* (Cambridge). Indeed, so deeply am I indebted, Miss Weston's book will elucidate the difficulties of the poem much better than my notes can do; and I recommend it (apart from the great interest of the book itself) to any who think such elucidation of the poem worth the trouble. To another work of anthropology I am indebted in general, one which has influenced our generation profoundly; I mean *The Golden Bough;* I have used especially the two volumes *Adonis, Attis, Osiris.* Anyone who is acquainted with these works will immediately recognise in the poem certain references to vegetation ceremonies.

I. The Burial of the Dead

Line 20. Cf. Ezekiel II, i.

23. Cf. Ecclesiastes XII, v.

31. V. Tristan und Isolde, I, verses 5–8.

42. Id. III, verse 24.

46. I am not familiar with the exact constitution of the Tarot pack of cards, from which I have obviously departed to suit my own convenience. The Hanged Man, a member of the traditional pack, fits my purpose in two ways: because he is associated in my mind with the Hanged God of Frazer, and because I associate him with the hooded figure in the passage of the disciples to Emmaus in Part V. The Phoenician Sailor and the Merchant appear later; also the "crowds of people," and Death by Water is executed in Part IV. The Man with Three Staves (an authentic member of the Tarot pack) I associate, quite arbitrarily, with the Fisher King himself.

60. Cf. Baudelaire:

"Fourmillante cité, cité pleine de rêves,

"Où le spectre en plein jour raccroche le passant."

63. Cf. Inferno III, 55–57:

                "si lunga tratta

      di gente, ch'io non avrei mai creduto

      che morte tanta n'avesse disfatta."

64. Cf. Inferno IV, 25–27:

---

23 In his note to this line Eliot quotes a brief passage from the section of the *Inferno* in which Count Ugolino of Pisa recounts his imprisonment with his little sons in the Hunger Tower (Canto XXXII, lines 124–39, and Canto XXXIII, lines 1–90): "and I heard them below locking the entrance to the horrible tower."

24 The hero of Shakespeare's tragedy, the symbol of the great man and hero who seeks, with tragic outcome, to be utterly self-sufficient.

25 In his note to this line Eliot quotes part of the speech of the late twelfth-century poet Arnaut Daniel, whom Dante encounters among the lustful in Purgatory: " 'I am Arnaut, who weep and go singing. In thought I see my past folly, and with joy I see the day I hope for before me. And so I pray you, by that Virtue which guides you to the top of the stair, be reminded in time of my grief.' Then he disappeared in the fire that refines them." Each of the fragments quoted in this last group of eleven lines has its purpose in representing one or another of the themes of the whole poem: this line brings in again the theme of pointless sexual lust which has loomed so large in the poem's picture of the values of a sick world, and to that theme it adds the idea of a solution through repentance and purgation.

26 The first half of the line is from the conclusion of the *Pervigilium Veneris,* a Latin poem of some ninety lines, dating possibly from the late Empire, in praise of the power of Venus: "When shall I do as the swallow [i.e. sing] and cease to be silent?" The second half of the line is from Swinburne's "Itylus," and since to think of

"Quivi, secondo che per ascoltare,
"non avea pianto, ma' che di sospiri,
"che l'aura eterna facevan tremare."
68. A phenomenon which I have often noticed.
74. Cf. the Dirge in Webster's *White Devil*.
76. V. Baudelaire, Preface to *Fleurs du Mal*.

II. A Game of Chess

77. Cf. *Antony and Cleopatra*, II, ii, l. 190.
92. Laquearia. V. *Aeneid*, I, 726:
dependent lychni laquearibus aureis incensi, et
noctem flammis funalia vincunt.
98. Sylvan scene. V. Milton, *Paradise Lost*, IV, 140.
99. V. Ovid, *Metamorphoses*, VI, Philomela.
100. Cf. Part III, l. 204.
115. Cf. Part III, l. 195.
118. Cf. Webster: Is the wind in that door still?"
126. Cf. Part I, l. 37, 48.
138. Cf. the game of chess in Middleton's *Women beware Women*.

III. The Fire Sermon

176. V. Spenser, *Prothalamion*.
192. Cf. *The Tempest*, I, ii.
196. Cf. Marvell, *To His Coy Mistress*.
197. Cf. Day, *Parliament of Bees*:
"When of the sudden, listening, you shall hear,
"A noise of horns and hunting, which shall bring
"Actaeon to Diana in the spring,
"Where all shall see her naked skin . . ."
199. I do not know the origin of the ballad from which these lines are taken: it was reported to me from Sydney, Australia.
202. V. Verlaine, *Parsifal*.
210. The currants were quoted at a price "carriage and insurance free to London"; and the Bill of Lading etc. were to be handed to the buyer upon payment of the sight draft.
218. Tiresias, although a mere spectator and not indeed a "character," is yet the most important personage in the poem, uniting all the rest. Just as the one-eyed merchant, seller of currants, melts into the Phoenician Sailor, and the latter is not wholly distinct from Ferdinand Prince of Naples, so all the women are one woman, and the two sexes meet in Tiresias. What Tiresias *sees*, in fact, is the substance of the poem. The whole passage from Ovid is of great anthropological interest:
'. . . Cum Iunone iocos et maior vestra profecto est
Quam, quae contingit maribus,' dixisse, 'voluptas.'
Illa negat; placuit quae sit sententia docti
Quaerere Tiresiae: venus huic erat utraque nota.
Nam duo magnorum viridi coeuntia silva
Corpora serpentum baculi violaverat ictu
Deque viro factus, mirabile, femina septem
Egerat autumnos; octavo rursus eosdem
Vidit et 'est vestrae si tanta potentia plagae,'
Dixit 'ut auctoris sortem in contraria mutet,
Nunc quoque vos feriam!' percussis anguibus isdem
Forma prior rediit genetivaque venit imago.
Arbiter hic igitur sumptus de lite iocosa
Dicta Iovis firmat; gravius Saturnia iusto
Nec pro materia fertur doluisse suique
Iudicis aeterna damnavit lumina nocte,
At pater omnipotens (neque enim licet inrita cuiquam
Facta dei fecisse deo) pro lumine adempto
Scire futura dedit poenamque levavit honore.

221. This may not appear as exact as Sappho's lines, but I had in mind the "longshore" or "dory" fisherman, who returns at nightfall.
253. V. Goldsmith, the song in *The Vicar of Wakefield*.
257. V. *The Tempest*, as above.
264. The interior of St. Magnus Martyr is to my mind one of the finest among Wren's interiors. See *The Proposed Demolition of Nineteen City Churches*: (P. S. King & Son, Ltd.).
266. The Song of the (three) Thames-daughters begins here. From line 292 to 306 inclusive they speak in turn. V. *Götterdämmerung*, III, i: the Rhine-daughters.
279. V. Froude, *Elizabeth*, Vol. I, ch. iv, letter of De Quadra to Philip of Spain:
"In the afternoon we were in a barge, watching the games on the river. (The queen) was alone with Lord Robert and myself on the poop, when they began to talk nonsense, and went so far that Lord Robert at last said, as I was on the spot there was no reason why they should not be married if the queen pleased."
293. Cf. *Purgatorio*, V, 133:
"Ricorditi di me, che son la Pia;
"Siena mi fe', disfecemi Maremma."
307. V. St. Augustine's *Confessions*: "to Carthage then I came, where a cauldron of unholy loves sang all about mine ears."
308. The complete text of the Buddha's Fire Sermon (which corresponds in importance to the Sermon on the Mount) from which these words are taken, will be found translated in the late Henry Clarke Warren's *Buddhism in Translation* (Harvard Oriental Series). Mr. Warren was one of the great pioneers of Buddhist studies in the Occident.
309. From St. Augustine's *Confessions* again. The collocation of these two representatives of eastern and western asceticism, as the culmination of this part of the poem, is not an accident.

V. What the Thunder Said

In the first part of Part V three themes are employed: the journey to Emmaus, the approach to the Chapel Perilous (see Miss Weston's book) and the present decay of eastern Europe.
357. This is *Turdus aonalaschkae pallasii*, the hermit-thrush which I have heard in Quebec County. Chapman says (*Handbook of Birds of Eastern North America*) "it is most at home in secluded woodland and thickety retreats. . . . Its notes are not remarkable for variety or volume, but in purity and sweetness of tone and exquisite modulation they are unequalled." Its "water-dripping song" is justly celebrated.
360. The following lines were stimulated by the account of one of the Antarctic expeditions (I forget which, but I think one of Shackleton's): it was related that the party of explorers, at the extremity of their strength, had the constant delusion that there was *one more member* than could actually be counted.
366–76. Cf. Hermann Hesse, *Blick ins Chaos*: "Schon ist halb Europa, schon ist zumindest der halbe Osten Europas auf dem Wege zum Chaos, fährt betrunken im heiligem Wahn am Abgrund entlang und singt dazu, singt betrunken und hymnisch wie Dmitri Karamasoff sang. Ueber diese Lieder lacht der Bürger beleidigt, der Heilige und Seher hört sie mit Tränen."
401. "Datta, dayadhvam, damyata" (Give, sympathise, control). The fable of the meaning of the Thunder is found in the *Brihadaranyaka—Upanishad*, 5, 1. A transla-

tion is found in Deussen's *Sechzig Upanishads des Veda*, p. 489.

407. Cf. Webster, *The White Devil*, V, vi:

> ". . . they'll remarry
> Ere the worm pierce your winding-sheet, ere the spider
> Make a thin curtain for your epitaphs."

411. Cf. *Inferno*, XXXIII, 46:

> "ed io sentii chiavar l'uscio di sotto
> all' orribile torre:"

Also F. H. Bradley, *Appearance and Reality*, p. 346. "My external sensations are no less private to myself than are my thoughts or my feelings. In either case my experience falls within my own circle, a circle closed on the outside; and, with all its elements alike, every sphere is opaque to the others which surround it. . . . In brief, regarded as an existence which appears in a soul, the whole world for each is peculiar and private to that soul."

424. V. Weston: *From Ritual to Romance;* chapter on the Fisher King.

427. V. *Purgatorio*, XXVI, 148.

> " 'Ara vos prec per aquella valor
> 'que vos guida al som de l'escalina,
> 'sovegna vos a temps de ma dolor.'
> Poi s'ascose nel foco che gli affina."

428. V. *Pervigilium Veneris*. Cf. Philomela in Parts II and III.

429. V. Gerard de Nerval, Sonnet *El Desdichado*.

431. V. Kyd's *Spanish Tragedy*.

433. Shantih. Repeated as here, a formal ending to an Upanishad. "The Peace which passeth understanding" is our equivalent to this word.

The Hollow Men

Mistah Kurtz—he dead

A penny for the Old Guy[1]

I

We are the hollow men
We are the stuffed men
Leaning together

---

[1] The first of the poem's two epigraphs comes from Joseph Conrad's *Heart of Darkness;* perhaps here it may be taken as evoking the unspeakable horror and degradation of Kurtz's last days. Kurtz, the agent of a European company exploiting the resources and manpower of the African ivory district, had determined to stamp out savage beliefs and customs, but eventually he succumbs to their power— a power of darkness as opposed to the power of light that had been his inheritance as a European—and allows himself to be worshiped by the natives.

The second epigraph is typical of the phrases employed by English children on Guy Fawkes day, November 5, phrases that license them to solicit pennies from all comers. Such phrases, and the bonfires in which "the guy" is burnt in effigy, are all that remain of the conspiracy (and the religious zeal behind it, even though the conspiracy was traitorous) in which Guy Fawkes (1570–1606), a Roman Catholic, unsuccessfully attempted to blow up the Houses of Parliament.

Headpiece filled with straw. Alas!
Our dried voices, when   5
We whisper together
Are quiet and meaningless
As wind in dry grass
Or rats' feet over broken glass
In our dry cellar   10

Shape without form, shade without colour,
Paralysed force, gesture without motion;

Those who have crossed
With direct eyes, to death's other Kingdom
Remember us—if at all—not as lost   15
Violent souls, but only
As the hollow men
The stuffed men.

II

Eyes I dare not meet in dreams
In death's dream kingdom   20
These do not appear:
There, the eyes are
Sunlight on a broken column
There, is a tree swinging
And voices are   25
In the wind's singing
More distant and more solemn
Than a fading star.

Let me be no nearer
In death's dream kingdom   30
Let me also wear
Such deliberate disguises
Rat's coat, crowskin, crossed staves
In a field
Behaving as the wind behaves   35
No nearer—

Not that final meeting
In the twilight kingdom

III

This is the dead land
This is cactus land   40
Here the stone images
Are raised, here they receive
The supplication of a dead man's hand
Under the twinkle of a fading star.

Is it like this   45
In death's other kingdom

Waking alone
At the hour when we are
Trembling with tenderness
Lips that would kiss   50
Form prayers to broken stone.

IV

The eyes are not here
There are no eyes here
In this valley of dying stars
In this hollow valley   55
This broken jaw of our lost kingdoms

In this last of meeting places
We grope together
And avoid speech
Gathered on this beach of the tumid river   60

Sightless, unless
The eyes reappear
As the perpetual star
Multifoliate rose
Of death's twilight kingdom   65
The hope only
Of empty men.

V

Here we go round the prickly pear
Prickly pear prickly pear
Here we go round the prickly pear   70
At five o'clock in the morning.

Between the idea
And the reality
Between the motion
And the act   75
Falls the Shadow
        For Thine is the Kingdom

Between the conception
And the creation
Between the emotion   80
And the response
Falls the Shadow
        Life is very long

Between the desire
And the spasm   85
Between the potency
And the existence
Between the essence

And the descent
Falls the Shadow   90
        For Thine is the Kingdom

For Thine is
Life is
For Thine is the

This is the way the world ends   95
This is the way the world ends
This is the way the world ends
Not with a bang but a whimper.

from *Four Quartets*

Burnt Norton[1]

τοῦ λόγου δ'ἐόντος ξυνοῦ ζώουσιν οἱ πολλοὶ
ὡς ἰδίαν ἔχοντες φρόνησιν.

        I. p. 77. Fr. 2.

ὁδὸς ἄνω κάτω μία καὶ ὠντή.

        I. p. 89. Fr. 60.

   Diels: *Die Fragmente der Vorsokratiker*
(Herakleitos).

I

Time present and time past
Are both perhaps present in time future,
And time future contained in time past.
If all time is eternally present
All time is unredeemable.   5
What might have been is an abstraction
Remaining a perpetual possibility
Only in a world of speculation.
What might have been and what has been
Point to one end, which is always present.   10
Footfalls echo in the memory
Down the passage which we did not take
Towards the door we never opened
Into the rose-garden. My words echo
Thus, in your mind.

1 "Burnt Norton" was first published in 1936, when it
was included in Eliot's *Collected Poems, 1909–1935*. It
was published separately in 1941, and then—with "East
Coker," "The Dry Salvages," and "Little Gidding"—in
Four Quartets in 1943.
   The epigraphs may be translated as follows: "Although the Word is common to all, the majority live
as if they had intelligence peculiarity their own." "The
journey up and down is one and the same."

But to what purpose
Disturbing the dust on a bowl of rose-leaves
I do not know.
Other echoes
Inhabit the garden. Shall we follow?
Quick, said the bird, find them, find them, 20
Round the corner. Through the first gate,
Into our first world, shall we follow
The deception of the thrush? Into our first
world.
There they were, dignified, invisible,
Moving without pressure, over the dead leaves,
In the autumn heat, through the vibrant air, 25
And the bird called, in response to
The unheard music hidden in the shrubbery,
And the unseen eyebeam crossed, for the roses
Had the look of flowers that are looked at.
There they were as our guests, accepted and ac- 30
cepting.
So we moved, and they, in a formal pattern,
Along the empty alley, into the box circle,
To look down into the drained pool.
Dry the pool, dry concrete, brown edged,
And the pool was filled with water out of sun- 35
light,
And the lotos rose, quietly, quietly,
The surface glittered out of heart of light,
And they were behind us, reflected in the pool.
Then a cloud passed, and the pool was empty.
Go, said the bird, for the leaves were full of chil- 40
dren,
Hidden excitedly, containing laughter.
Go, go, go, said the bird: human kind
Cannot bear very much reality.
Time past and time future
What might have been and what has been 45
Point to one end, which is always present.

II

Garlic and sapphires in the mud
Clot the bedded axle-tree.
The trilling wire in the blood
Sings below inveterate scars 50
And reconciles forgotten wars.
The dance along the artery
The circulation of the lymph
Are figured in the drift of stars
Ascend to summer in the tree 55
We move above the moving tree
In light upon the figured leaf
And hear upon the sodden floor

Below, the boarhound and the boar 15
Pursue their pattern as before 60
But reconciled among the stars.

At the still point of the turning world. Neither
flesh nor fleshless;
Neither from nor towards; at the still point,
there the dance is,
But neither arrest nor movement. And do not
call it fixity,
Where past and future are gathered. Neither 65
movement from nor towards,
Neither ascent nor decline. Except for the point,
the still point,
There would be no dance, and there is only the
dance.
I can only say, *there* we have been: but I cannot
say where.
And I cannot say, how long, for that is to place
it in time.

The inner freedom from the practical desire, 70
The release from action and suffering, release
from the inner
And the outer compulsion, yet surrounded
By a grace of sense, a white light still and mov-
ing,
Erhebung[2] without motion, concentration
Without elimination, both a new world 75
And the old made explicit, understood
In the completion of its partial ecstasy,
The resolution of its partial horror.
Yet the enchainment of past and future
Woven in the weakness of the changing body, 80
Protects mankind from heaven and damnation
Which flesh cannot endure.
Time past and time future
Allow but a little consciousness.
To be conscious is not to be in time
But only in time can the moment in the rose- 85
garden,
The moment in the arbour where the rain beat,
The moment in the draughty church at smoke-
fall
Be remembered; involved with past and future.
Only through time time is conquered.

III

Here is a place of disaffection 90
Time before and time after

---

2 Elevation; uplift.

In a dim light: neither daylight
Investing form with lucid stillness
Turning shadow into transient beauty
With slow rotation suggesting permanence   95
Nor darkness to purify the soul
Emptying the sensual with deprivation
Cleansing affection from the temporal.
Neither plenitude nor vacancy. Only a flicker
Over the strained time-ridden faces   100
Distracted from distraction by distraction
Filled with fancies and empty of meaning
Tumid apathy with no concentration
Men and bits of paper, whirled by the cold wind
That blows before and after time,   105
Wind in and out of unwholesome lungs
Time before and time after.
Eructation of unhealthy souls
Into the faded air, the torpid
Driven on the wind that sweeps the gloomy hills 110
    of London,
Hampstead and Clerkenwell, Campden and Put-
    ney,
Highgate, Primrose and Ludgate. Not here
Not here the darkness, in this twittering world.

Descend lower, descend only
Into the world of perpetual solitude,   115
World not world, but that which is not world,
Internal darkness, deprivation
And destitution of all property,
Desiccation of the world of sense,
Evacuation of the world of fancy,   120
Inoperancy of the world of spirit;
This is the one way, and the other
Is the same, not in movement
But abstention from movement; while the world
    moves
In appetency, on its metalled ways   125
Of time past and time future.

IV

Time and the bell have buried the day,
The black cloud carries the sun away.
Will the sunflower turn to us, will the clematis
Stray down, bend to us; tendril and spray   130
Clutch and cling?
Chill
Fingers of yew be curled
Down on us? After the kingfisher's wing
Has answered light to light, and is silent, the 135
    light is still
At the still point of the turning world.

V

Words move, music moves
Only in time; but that which is only living
Can only die. Words, after speech, reach
Into the silence. Only by the form, the pattern, 140
Can words or music reach
The stillness, as a Chinese jar still
Moves perpetually in its stillness.
Not the stillness of the violin, while the note
    lasts,
Not that only, but the co-existence,   145
Or say that the end precedes the beginning,
And the end and the beginning were always
    there
Before the beginning and after the end.
And all is always now. Words strain,
Crack and sometimes break, under the burden,   150
Under the tension, slip, slide, perish,
Decay with imprecision, will not stay in place,
Will not stay still. Shrieking voices
Scolding, mocking, or merely chattering,
Always assail them. The Word in the desert   155
Is most attacked by voices of temptation,
The crying shadow in the funeral dance,
The loud lament of the disconsolate chimera.

The detail of the pattern is movement,
As in the figure of the ten stairs.   160
Desire itself is movement
Not in itself desirable;
Love is itself unmoving,
Only the cause and end of movement,
Timeless, and undesiring   165
Except in the aspect of time
Caught in the form of limitation
Between un-being and being.
Sudden in a shaft of sunlight
Even while the dust moves   170
There rises the hidden laughter
Of children in the foliage
Quick now, here, now, always—
Ridiculous the waste sad time
Stretching before and after.   175

Tradition and the Individual Talent

In English writing we seldom speak of tradition, though we occasionally apply its name in deploring its absence. We cannot refer to "the tradition" or to "a tradition"; at most, we employ the adjective in saying that the poetry of So-and-so is "traditional" or even "too traditional." Seldom, perhaps, does the word appear except in a phrase of censure. If otherwise, it is vaguely approbative, with the implication, as to the work approved, of some pleasing archaeological reconstruction. You can hardly make the word agreeable to English ears without this comfortable reference to the reassuring science of archaeology.

Certainly the word is not likely to appear in our appreciations of living or dead writers. Every nation, every race, has not only its own creative, but its own critical turn of mind; and is even more oblivious of the shortcomings and limitations of its critical habits than of those of its creative genius. We know, or think we know, from the enormous mass of critical writing that has appeared in the French language the critical method or habit of the French; we only conclude (we are such unconscious people) that the French are "more critical" than we, and sometimes even plume ourselves a little with the fact, as if the French were the less spontaneous. Perhaps they are; but we might remind ourselves that criticism is as inevitable as breathing, and that we should be none the worse for articulating what passes in our minds when we read a book and feel an emotion about it, for criticizing our own minds in their work of criticism. One of the facts that might come to light in this process is our tendency to insist, when we praise a poet, upon those aspects of his work in which he least resembles any one else. In these aspects or parts of his work we pretend to find what is individual, what is the peculiar essence of the man. We dwell with satisfaction upon the poet's difference from his predecessors, especially his immediate predecessors; we endeavour to find something that can be isolated in order to be enjoyed. Whereas if we approach a poet without this prejudice we shall often find that not only the best, but the most individual parts of his work may be those in which the dead poets, his ancestors, assert their immortality most vigorously. And I do not mean the impressionable period of adolescence, but the period of full maturity.

Yet if the only form of tradition, of handing down, consisted in following the ways of the immediate generation before us in a blind or timid adherence to its successes, "tradition" should positively be discouraged. We have seen many such simple currents soon lost in the sand; and novelty is better than repetition. Tradition is a matter of much wider significance. It cannot be inherited, and if you want it you must obtain it by great labour. It involves, in the first place, the historical sense, which we may call nearly indispensable to any one who would continue to be a poet beyond his twenty-fifth year; and the historical sense involves a perception, not only of the pastness of the past, but of its presence; the historical sense compels a man to write not merely with his own generation in his bones, but with a feeling that the whole of the literature of Europe from Homer and within it the whole of the literature of his own country has a simultaneous existence and composes a simultaneous order. This historical sense, which is a sense of the timeless as well as of the temporal and of the timeless and of the temporal together, is what makes a writer traditional. And it is at the same time what makes a writer most acutely conscious of his place in time, of his own contemporaneity.

No poet, no artist of any art, has his complete meaning alone. His significance, his appreciation is the appreciation of his relation to the dead poets and artists. You cannot value him alone; you must set him, for contrast and comparison, among the dead. I mean this as a principle of aesthetic, not merely historical, criticism. The necessity that he shall conform, that he shall cohere, is not onesided; what happens when a new work of art is created is something that happens simultaneously to all the works of art which preceded it. The existing monuments form an ideal order among themselves, which is modified by the introduction of the new (the really new) work of art among them. The existing order is complete before the new work arrives; for order to persist after the supervention of novelty, the *whole* existing order must be, if ever so slightly, altered; and so the relations, proportions, values of each work of art toward the whole are readjusted; and this is conformity between the old and the new. Whoever has approved this idea of order, of the form of European, of English literature will not find it preposterous that the past should be altered by the present as much as the present is directed by the past. And the poet who is aware of this will be aware of great difficulties and responsibilities.

In a peculiar sense he will be aware also that he must inevitably be judged by the standards of the past. I say judged, not amputated, by them; not judged to be as good as, or worse or better than, the dead; and certainly not judged by the canons of dead critics. It is a judgment, a comparison, in which two things are measured by each other. To conform merely would be for the new work not really to conform at all; it would not be new, and would therefore not be a work of art. And we do not quite say that the new is more valuable because it fits in; but its fitting in is a test of its value—a test, it is true, which can only be slowly and cautiously applied, for we are none of us infallible judges of conformity. We say: it appears to conform, and is perhaps individual, or it appears individual, and may conform; but we are hardly likely to find that it is one and not the other.

To proceed to a more intelligible exposition of the relation of the poet to the past: he can neither take the past as a lump, an indiscriminate bolus, nor can he form himself wholly on one or two private admirations, nor can he form himself wholly upon one preferred period. The first course is inadmissible, the second is an important experience of youth, and the third is a pleasant and highly desirable supplement. The poet must be very conscious of the main current, which does not at all flow invariably through the most distinguished reputations. He must be quite aware of the obvious fact that art never improves, but that the material of art is never quite the same. He must be aware that the mind of Europe—the mind of his own country—a mind which he learns in time to be much more important than his own private mind—is a mind which changes, and that this change is a development which abandons nothing *en route,* which does not superannuate either Shakespeare, or Homer, or the rock drawing of the Magdalenian draughtsmen. That this development, refinement perhaps, complication certainly, is not, from the point of view of the artist, any improvement. Perhaps not even an improvement from the point of view of the psychologist or not to the extent which we imagine; perhaps only in the end based upon a complication in economics and machinery. But the difference between the present and the past is that the conscious present is an awareness of the past in a way and to an extent which the past's awareness of itself cannot show.

Some one said: "The dead writers are remote from us because we *know* so much more than they did." Precisely, and they are that which we know.

I am alive to a usual objection to what is clearly part of my programme for the *métier* of poetry. The objection is that the doctrine requires a ridiculous amount of erudition (pedantry), a claim which can be rejected by appeal to the lives of poets in any pantheon. It will even be affirmed that much learning deadens or perverts poetic sensibility. While, however, we persist in believing that a poet ought to know as much as will not encroach upon his necessary receptivity and necessary laziness, it is not desirable to confine knowledge to whatever can be put into a useful shape for examinations, drawing-rooms, or the still more pretentious modes of publicity. Some can absorb knowledge, the more tardy must sweat for it. Shakespeare acquired more essential history from Plutarch than most men could from the whole British Museum. What is to be insisted upon is that the poet must develop or procure the consciousness of the past and that he should continue to develop this consciousness throughout his career.

What happens is a continual surrender of himself as he is at the moment to something which is more valuable. The progress of an artist is a continual self-sacrifice, a continual extinction of personality.

There remains to define this process of depersonalization and its relation to the sense of tradition. It is in this depersonalization that art may be said to approach the condition of science. I, therefore, invite you to consider, as a suggestive analogy, the action which takes place when a bit of finely filiated platinum is introduced into a chamber containing oxygen and sulphur dioxide.

II

Honest criticism and sensitive appreciation are directed not upon the poet but upon the poetry. If we attend to the confused cries of the newspaper critics and the *susurrus*[1] of popular repetition that follows, we shall hear the names of poets in great numbers; if we seek not Blue-book knowledge but the enjoyment of poetry, and ask for a poem, we shall seldom find it. I have tried

---

[1] Whispering, buzzing, muttering (Latin).

to point out the importance of the relation of the poem to other poems by other authors, and suggested the conception of poetry as a living whole of all the poetry that has ever been written. The other aspect of this Impersonal theory of poetry is the relation of the poem to its author. And I hinted, by an analogy, that the mind of the mature poet differs from that of the immature one not precisely in any valuation of "personality," not being necessarily more interesting, or having "more to say," but rather by being a more finely perfected medium in which special, or very varied, feelings are at liberty to enter into new combinations.

The analogy was that of the catalyst. When the two gases previously mentioned are mixed in the presence of a filament of platinum, they form sulphurous acid. This combination takes place only if the platinum is present; nevertheless the newly formed acid contains no trace of platinum, and the platinum itself is apparently unaffected; has remained inert, neutral, and unchanged. The mind of the poet is the shred of platinum. It may partly or exclusively operate upon the experience of the man himself; but, the more perfect the artist, the more completely separate in him will be the man who suffers and the mind which creates; the more perfectly will the mind digest and transmute the passions which are its material.

The experience, you will notice, the elements which enter the presence of the transforming catalyst, are of two kinds: emotions and feelings. The effect of a work of art upon the person who enjoys it is an experience different in kind from any experience not of art. It may be formed out of one emotion, or may be a combination of several; and various feelings, inhering for the writer in particular words or phrases or images, may be added to compose the final result. Or great poetry may be made without the direct use of any emotion whatever: composed out of feelings solely. Canto XV of the *Inferno* (Brunetto Latini) is a working up of the emotion evident in the situation; but the effect, though single as that of any work of art, is obtained by considerable complexity of detail. The last quatrain gives an image, a feeling attaching to an image, which "came," which did not develop simply out of what precedes, but which was probably in suspension in the poet's mind until the proper combination arrived for it to add itself to. The poet's mind is in fact a receptacle for seizing and storing up numberless feelings, phrases, images, which remain there until all the particles which can unite to form a new compound are present together.

If you compare several representative passages of the greatest poetry you see how great is the variety of types of combination, and also how completely any semi-ethical criterion of "sublimity" misses the mark. For it is not the "greatness," the intensity, of the emotions, the components, but the intensity of the artistic process, the pressure, so to speak, under which the fusion takes place, that counts. The episode of Paolo and Francesca[2] employs a definite emotion, but the intensity of the poetry is something quite different from whatever intensity in the supposed experience it may give the impression of. It is no more intense, furthermore, than Canto XXVI, the voyage of Ulysses, which has not the direct dependence upon an emotion. Great variety is possible in the process of transmutation of emotion: the murder of Agamemnon, or the agony of Othello, gives an artistic effect apparently closer to a possible original than the scenes from Dante. In the *Agamemnon,* the artistic emotion approximates to the emotion of an actual spectator; in *Othello* to the emotion of the protagonist himself. But the difference between art and the event is always absolute; the combination which is the murder of Agamemnon is probably as complex as that which is the voyage of Ulysses. In either case there has been a fusion of elements. The ode of Keats contains a number of feelings which have nothing particular to do with the nightingale, but which the nightingale, partly, perhaps, because of its attractive name, and partly because of its reputation, served to bring together.

The point of view which I am struggling to attack is perhaps related to the metaphysical theory of the substantial unity of the soul: for my meaning is, that the poet has, not a "personality" to express, but a particular medium, which is only a medium and not a personality, in which impressions and experiences combine in peculiar and unexpected ways. Impressions and experiences which are important for the

---

2 In Dante's *Inferno,* Canto V.

man may take no place in the poetry, and those which become important in the poetry may play quite a negligible part in the man, the personality.

I will quote a passage[3] which is unfamiliar enough to be regarded with fresh attention in the light—or darkness—of these observations:

> And now methinks I could e'en childe myself
> For doating on her beauty, though her death
> Shall be revenged after no common action.   10
> Does the silkworm expend her yellow labours
> For thee? For thee does she undo herself?
> Are lordships sold to maintain ladyships
> For the poor benefit of a bewildering minute?
> Why does yon fellow falsify highways,
> And put his life between the judge's lips,
> To refine such a thing—keeps horse and men
> To beat their valours for her? . . .

In this passage (as is evident if it is taken in its context) there is a combination of positive and negative emotions: an intensely strong attraction toward beauty and an equally intense fascination by the ugliness which is contrasted with it and which destroys it. This balance of contrasted emotion is in the dramatic situation to which the speech is pertinent, but that situation alone is inadequate to it. This is, so to speak, the structural emotion, provided by the drama. But the whole effect, the dominant tone, is due to the fact that a number of floating feelings, having an affinity to this emotion by no means superficially evident, have combined with it to give us a new art emotion.

It is not in his personal emotions, the emotions provoked by particular events in his life, that the poet is in any way remarkable or interesting. His particular emotions may be simple, or crude, or flat. The emotion in his poetry will be a very complex thing, but not with the complexity of the emotions of people who have very complex or unusual emotions in life. One error, in fact, of eccentricity in poetry is to seek for new human emotions to express; and in this search for novelty in the wrong place it discovers the perverse. The business of the poet is not to find new emotions, but to use the ordinary ones and, in working them up into poetry, to express feelings which are not in actual emotions at all.

And emotions which he has never experienced will serve his turn as well as those familiar to him. Consequently, we must believe that "emotion recollected in tranquillity" is an inexact formula. For it is neither emotion, nor recollection, nor, without distortion of meaning, tranquillity. It is a concentration, and a new thing resulting from the concentration, of a very great number of experiences which to the practical and active person would not seem to be experiences at all; it is a concentration which does not happen consciously or of deliberation. These experiences are not "recollected," and they finally unite in an atmosphere which is "tranquil" only in that it is a passive attending upon the event. Of course this is not quite the whole story. There is a great deal, in the writing of poetry, which must be conscious and deliberate. In fact, the bad poet is usually unconscious where he ought to be conscious, and conscious where he ought to be unconscious. Both errors tend to make him "personal." Poetry is not a turning loose of emotion, but an escape from emotion; it is not the expression of personality, but an escape from personality. But, of course, only those who have personality and emotions know what it means to want to escape from these things.

III

ὁ δὲ νοῦς ἴσως θειότερόν τι καὶ ἀπαθές ἐστιν[4]

This essay proposes to halt at the frontier of metaphysics or mysticism, and confine itself to such practical conclusions as can be applied by the responsible person interested in poetry. To divert interest from the poet to the poetry is a laudable aim: for it would conduce to a juster estimation of actual poetry, good and bad. There are many people who appreciate the expression of sincere emotion in verse, and there is a smaller number of people who can appreciate technical excellence. But very few know when there is an expression of *significant* emotion, emotion which has its life in the poem and not in the history of the poet. The emotion of art is impersonal. And the poet cannot reach this impersonality without surrendering himself wholly to the work to be done. And he is not likely to know what is to

---

[3] From *The Revenger's Tragedy* (1607), by the Jacobean playwright Cyril Tourneur.

[4] Aristotle, *De Anima*, 408b, 29: ". . . The mind is at once something more divine and impassible."

be done unless he lives in what is not merely the present, but the present moment of the past, unless he is conscious, not of what is dead, but of what is already living.

The Metaphysical Poets

By collecting these poems[1] from the work of a generation more often named than read, and more often read than profitably studied, Professor Grierson has rendered a service of some importance. Certainly the reader will meet with many poems already preserved in other anthologies, at the same time that he discovers poems such as those of Aurelian Townshend or Lord Herbert of Cherbury here included. But the function of such an anthology as this is neither that of Professor Saintsbury's admirable edition of Caroline poets nor that of the *Oxford Book of English Verse*. Mr. Grierson's book is in itself a piece of criticism and a provocation of criticism; and we think that he was right in including so many poems of Donne, elsewhere (though not in many editions) accessible, as documents in the case of "metaphysical poetry." The phrase has long done duty as a term of abuse or as the label of a quaint and pleasant taste. The question is to what extent the so-called metaphysicals formed a school (in our own time we should say a "movement"), and how far this so-called school or movement is a digression from the main current.

Not only is it extremely difficult to define metaphysical poetry, but difficult to decide what poets practise it and in which of their verses. The poetry of Donne (to whom Marvell and Bishop King are sometimes nearer than any of the other authors) is late Elizabethan, its feeling often very close to that of Chapman. The "courtly" poetry is derivative from Jonson, who borrowed liberally from the Latin; it expires in the next century with the sentiment and witticism of Prior. There is finally the devotional verse of Herbert, Vaughan, and Crashaw (echoed long after by Christina Rossetti and Francis Thomp-

son); Crashaw, sometimes more profound and less sectarian than the others, has a quality which returns through the Elizabethan period to the early Italians. It is difficult to find any precise use of metaphor, simile, or other conceit, which is common to all the poets and at the same time important enough as an element of style to isolate these poets as a group. Donne, and often Cowley, employ a device which is sometimes considered characteristically "metaphysical"; the elaboration (contrasted with the condensation) of a figure of speech to the farthest stage to which ingenuity can carry it. Thus Cowley develops the commonplace comparison of the world to a chessboard through long stanzas (*To Destiny*), and Donne, with more grace, in *A Valediction*, the comparison of two lovers to a pair of compasses. But elsewhere we find, instead of the mere explication of the content of a comparison, a development by rapid association of thought which requires considerable agility on the part of the reader.

> On a round ball
> A workman that hath copies by, can lay
> An Europe, Afrique, and an Asia,
> And quickly make that, which was nothing, All,
> So doth each teare,
> Which thee doth weare,
> A globe, yea, world by that impression grow,
> Till thy tears mixt with mine do overflow
> This world, by waters sent from thee, my
> heaven dissolvèd so.[2]

Here we find at least two connexions which are not implicit in the first figure, but are forced upon it by the poet: from the geographer's globe to the tear, and the tear to the deluge. On the other hand, some of Donne's most successful and characteristic effects are secured by brief words and sudden contrasts:

> A bracelet of bright hair about the bone,[3]

where the most powerful effect is produced by the sudden contrast of associations of "bright hair" and of "bone." This telescoping of images and multiplied associations is characteristic of the phrase of some of the dramatists of the period which Donne knew: not to mention

---

[1] *Metaphysical Lyrics and Poems of the Seventeenth Century: Donne to Butler.* Selected and edited, with an Essay, by Herbert J. C. Grierson (Oxford: Clarendon Press. London: Milford). (Eliot's note)

[2] Donne, "A Valediction: Of Weeping," lines 10–18.
[3] "The Relic," line 6 (See Vol. I).

Shakespeare, it is frequent in Middleton, Webster, and Tourneur, and is one of the sources of the vitality of their language.

Johnson, who employed the term "metaphysical poets," apparently having Donne, Cleveland, and Cowley chiefly in mind, remarks of them that "the most heterogeneous ideas are yoked by violence together."[4] The force of this impeachment lies in the failure of the conjunction, the fact that often the ideas are yoked but not united; and if we are to judge of styles of poetry by their abuse, enough examples may be found in Cleveland to justify Johnson's condemnation. But a degree of heterogeneity of material compelled into unity by the operation of the poet's mind is omnipresent in poetry. We need not select for illustration such a line as:

Notre âme est un trois-mâts cherchant son Icarie;[5]

we may find it in some of the best lines of Johnson himself (*The Vanity of Human Wishes*):

His fate was destined to a barren strand,
A petty fortress, and a dubious hand;
He left a name at which the world grew pale,
To point a moral, or adorn a tale.[6]

where the effect is due to a contrast of ideas, different in degree but the same in principle, as that which Johnson mildly reprehended. And in one of the finest poems of the age (a poem which could not have been written in any other age), the *Exequy* of Bishop King, the extended comparison is used with perfect success: the idea and the simile become one, in the passage in which the Bishop illustrates his impatience to see his dead wife, under the figure of a journey:

Stay for me there; I will not faile
To meet thee in that hollow Vale.
And think not much of my delay;
I am already on the way,
And follow thee with all the speed
Desire can make, or sorrows breed.
Each minute is a short degree,
And ev'ry houre a step towards thee.
At night when I betake to rest,

Next morn I rise nearer my West
Of life, almost by eight houres sail,
Than when sleep breath'd his drowsy gale....
But heark! My Pulse, like a soft Drum
Beats my approach, tells Thee *I* come;
And slow howere my marches be,
I shall at last sit down by Thee.

(In the last few lines there is that effect of terror which is several times attained by one of Bishop King's admirers, Edgar Poe.) Again, we may justly take these quatrains from Lord Herbert's Ode, stanzas which would, we think, be immediately pronounced to be of the metaphysical school:

So when from hence we shall be gone,
*   And be no more, nor you, nor I,*
*   As one another's mystery,*
Each shall be both, yet both but one.

This said, in her up-lifted face,
*   Her eyes, which did that beauty crown,*
*   Were like two starrs, that having faln down,*
Look up again to find their place:

While such a moveless silent peace
*   Did seize on their becalmèd sense,*
*   One would have thought some influence*
Their ravished spirits did possess.

There is nothing in these lines (with the possible exception of the stars, a simile not at once grasped, but lovely and justified) which fits Johnson's general observations on the metaphysical poets in his essay on Cowley. A good deal resides in the richness of association which is at the same time borrowed from and given to the word "becalmed"; but the meaning is clear, the language simple and elegant. It is to be observed that the language of these poets is as a rule simple and pure; in the verse of George Herbert this simplicity is carried as far as it can go—a simplicity emulated without success by numerous modern poets. The *structure* of the sentences, on the other hand, is sometimes far from simple, but this is not a vice; it is a fidelity to thought and feeling. The effect, at its best, is far less artificial than that of an ode by Gray. And as this fidelity induces variety of thought and feeling, so it induces variety of music. We doubt whether, in the eighteenth century, could be found two poems in nominally the same

---

[4] See the life of Cowley, in Johnson's *Lives of the Poets*.
[5] From Baudelaire's "Le Voyage" (in *Les Fleurs du Mal*): "Our soul is a three-master in quest of its Icaria."
[6] Lines 219 ff. (see Vol. I).

metre, so dissimilar as Marvell's *Coy Mistress* and Crashaw's *Saint Teresa*; the one producing an effect of great speed by the use of short syllables, and the other an ecclesiastical solemnity by the use of long ones:

> Love, thou art absolute sole lord
> Of life and death.

If so shrewd and sensitive (though so limited) a critic as Johnson failed to define metaphysical poetry by its faults, it is worth while to inquire whether we may not have more success by adopting the opposite method: by assuming that the poets of the seventeenth century (up to the Revolution) were the direct and normal development of the precedent age; and, without prejudicing their case by the adjective "metaphysical," consider whether their virtue was not something permanently valuable, which subsequently disappeared, but ought not to have disappeared. Johnson has hit, perhaps by accident, on one of their peculiarities, when he observes that "their attempts were always analytic"; he would not agree that, after the dissociation, they put the material together again in a new unity.

It is certain that the dramatic verse of the later Elizabethan and early Jacobean poets expresses a degree of development of sensibility which is not found in any of the prose, good as it often is. If we except Marlowe, a man of prodigious intelligence, these dramatists were directly or indirectly (it is at least a tenable theory) affected by Montaigne. Even if we except also Jonson and Chapman, these two were notably erudite, and were notably men who incorporated their erudition into their sensibility: their mode of feeling was directly and freshly altered by their reading and thought. In Chapman especially there is a direct sensuous apprehension of thought, or a recreation of thought into feeling, which is exactly what we find in Donne:

> in this one thing, all the discipline
> Of manners and of manhood is contained;
> A man to join himself with th' Universe
> In his main sway, and make in all things fit
> One with that All, and go on, round as it;
> Not plucking from the whole his wretched part,
> And into straits, or into nought revert,
> Wishing the complete Universe might be

> Subject to such a rag of it as he;
> But to consider great Necessity.[7]

We compare this with some modern passage:

> No, when the fight begins within himself,
> A man's worth something. God stoops o'er his head,
> Satan looks up between his feet—both tug—
> He's left, himself, i' the middle; the soul wakes
> And grows. Prolong that battle through his life![8]

It is perhaps somewhat less fair, though very tempting (as both poets are concerned with the perpetuation of love by offspring), to compare with the stanzas already quoted from Lord Herbert's Ode the following from Tennyson:

> One walked between his wife and child,
> With measured footfall firm and mild,
> And now and then he gravely smiled.
>   The prudent partner of his blood
> Leaned on him, faithful, gentle, good,
> Wearing the rose of womanhood.
> And in their double love secure,
> The little maiden walked demure,
> Pacing with downward eyelids pure.
>   These three made unity so sweet,
> My frozen heart began to beat,
> Remembering its ancient heat.[9]

The difference is not a simple difference of degree between poets. It is something which had happened to the mind of England between the time of Donne or Lord Herbert of Cherbury and the time of Tennyson and Browning; it is the difference between the intellectual poet and the reflective poet. Tennyson and Browning are poets, and they think; but they do not feel their thought as immediately as the odour of a rose. A thought to Donne was an experience; it modified his sensibility. When a poet's mind is perfectly equipped for its work, it is constantly amalgamating disparate experience; the ordinary man's experience is chaotic, irregular, fragmentary. The latter falls in love, or reads Spinoza, and these two experiences have nothing to do with each other, or with the noise of the typewriter or the smell of cooking; in the mind of

---

7 George Chapman, *The Revenge of Bussy d'Ambois*, IV, i, 139 ff.
8 Browning, "Bishop Blougram's Apology," ll. 693–97.
9 "The Two Voices," lines 412 ff.

the poet these experiences are always forming new wholes.

We may express the difference by the following theory: The poets of the seventeenth century, the successors of the dramatists of the sixteenth, possessed a mechanism of sensibility which could devour any kind of experience. They are simple, artificial, difficult, or fantastic, as their predecessors were; no less nor more than Dante, Guido Cavalcanti, Guinizelli, or Cino. In the seventeenth century a dissociation of sensibility set in, from which we have never recovered; and this dissociation, as is natural, was aggravated by the influence of the two most powerful poets of the century, Milton and Dryden. Each of these men performed certain poetic functions so magnificently well that the magnitude of the effect concealed the absence of others. The language went on and in some respects improved; the best verse of Collins, Gray, Johnson, and even Goldsmith satisfies some of our fastidious demands better than that of Donne or Marvell or King. But while the language became more refined, the feeling became more crude. The feeling, the sensibility, expressed in the *Country Churchyard* (to say nothing of Tennyson and Browning) is cruder than that in the *Coy Mistress.*

The second effect of the influence of Milton and Dryden followed from the first, and was therefore slow in manifestation. The sentimental age began early in the eighteenth century, and continued. The poets revolted against the ratiocinative, the descriptive; they thought and felt by fits, unbalanced; they reflected. In one or two passages of Shelley's *Triumph of Life,* in the second *Hyperion,* there are traces of a struggle toward unification of sensibility. But Keats and Shelley died, and Tennyson and Browning ruminated.

After this brief exposition of a theory—too brief, perhaps, to carry conviction—we may ask, what would have been the fate of the "metaphysical" had the current of poetry descended in a direct line from them, as it descended in a direct line to them? They would not, certainly, be classified as metaphysical. The possible interests of a poet are unlimited; the more intelligent he is the better; the more intelligent he is the more likely that he will have interests: our only condition is that he turn them into poetry, and not merely meditate on them poetically. A philosophical theory which has entered into poetry is established, for its truth or falsity in one sense ceases to matter, and its truth in another sense is proved. The poets in question have, like other poets, various faults. But they were, at best, engaged in the task of trying to find the verbal equivalent for states of mind and feeling. And this means both that they are more mature, and that they wear better, than later poets of certainly not less literary ability.

It is not a permanent necessity that poets should be interested in philosophy, or in any other subject. We can only say that it appears likely that poets in our civilization, as it exists at present, must be *difficult.* Our civilization comprehends great variety and complexity, and this variety and complexity, playing upon a refined sensibility, must produce various and complex results. The poet must become more and more comprehensive, more allusive, more indirect, in order to force, to dislocate if necessary, language into his meaning. (A brilliant and extreme statement of this view, with which it is not requisite to associate oneself, is that of M. Jean Epstein, *La Poésie d'aujourd'hui.*) Hence we get something which looks very much like the conceit—we get, in fact, a method curiously similar to that of the "metaphysical poets," similar also in its use of obscure words and of simple phrasing.

> *O géraniums diaphanes, guerroyeurs sortilèges,*
> *Sacrilèges monomanes!*
> *Emballages, dévergondages, douches! O pressoirs*
> *Des vendanges des grands soirs!*
> *Layettes aux abois,*
> *Thyrses au fond des bois!*
> *Transfusions, représailles,*
> *Relevailles, compresses et l'éternelle potion,*
> *Angélus! n'en pouvoir plus*
> *De débâcles nuptiales! de débâcles nuptiales!*[10]

The same poet could write also simply:

> *Elle est bien loin, elle pleure,*
> *Le grand vent se lamente aussi . . .*[11]

---

[10] From Jules Laforgue, *Derniers Vers,* X, lines 1–10. Translation of these lines can only do them a grave injustice.

[11] From Laforgue, *Derniers Vers,* XI, "Sur une Défunte," lines 57 f.: "She is far away, she weeps,/ The high wind too laments. . . ."

Jules Laforgue, and Tristan Corbière in many of his poems, are nearer to the "school of Donne" than any modern English poet. But poets more classical than they have the same essential quality of transmuting ideas into sensations, of transforming an observation into a state of mind.

> Pour l'enfant, amoureux de cartes et d'estampes,
> L'univers est égal à son vaste appétit.
> Ah, que le monde est grand à la clarté des lampes!
> Aux yeux du souvenir que le monde est petit![12]

In French literature the great master of the seventeenth century—Racine—and the great master of the nineteenth—Baudelaire—are in some ways more like each other than they are like any one else. The greatest two masters of diction are also the greatest two psychologists, the most curious explorers of the soul. It is interesting to speculate whether it is not a misfortune that two of the greatest masters of diction in our language, Milton and Dryden, triumph with a dazzling disregard of the soul. If we continued to produce Miltons and Drydens it might not so much matter, but as things are it is a pity that English poetry has remained so incomplete. Those who object to the "artificiality" of Milton or Dryden sometimes tell us to "look into our hearts and write." But that is not looking deep enough; Racine or Donne looked into a good deal more than the heart. One must look into the cerebral cortex, the nervous system, and the digestive tracts.

May we not conclude, then, that Donne, Crashaw, Vaughan, Herbert and Lord Herbert, Marvell, King, Cowley at his best, are in the direct current of English poetry, and that their faults should be reprimanded by this standard rather than coddled by antiquarian affection? They have been enough praised in terms which are implicit limitations because they are "metaphysical" or "witty," "quaint" or "obscure," though at their best they have not these attributes more than other serious poets. On the other hand, we must not reject the criticism of Johnson (a dangerous person to disagree with) without having mastered it, without having as-

similated the Johnsonian canons of taste. In reading the celebrated passage in his essay on Cowley we must remember that by wit he clearly means something more serious than we usually mean today; in his criticism of their versification we must remember in what a narrow discipline he was trained, but also how well trained; we must remember that Johnson tortures chiefly the chief offenders, Cowley and Cleveland. It would be a fruitful work, and one requiring a substantial book, to break up the classification of Johnson (for there has been none since) and exhibit these poets in all their difference of kind and of degree, from the massive music of Donne to the faint, pleasing tinkle of Aurelian Townshend—whose *Dialogue between a Pilgrim and Time* is one of the few regrettable omissions from the excellent anthology of Professor Grierson.

The Frontiers of Criticism[1]

The thesis of this paper is that there are limits, exceeding which in one direction literary criticism ceases to be literary, and exceeding which in another it ceases to be criticism.

In 1923 I wrote an article entitled *The Function of Criticism*. I must have thought well of this essay ten years later, as I included it in my *Selected Essays*, where it is still to be found. On re-reading this essay recently, I was rather bewildered, wondering what all the fuss had been about—though I was glad to find nothing positively to contradict my present opinions. For, leaving aside a wrangle with Mr. Middleton Murry about "the inner voice"—a dispute in which I recognize the old *aporia* of Authority *v.* Individual Judgment—I found it impossible to recall to mind the background of my outburst. I had made a number of statements with assurance and considerable warmth; and it would seem that I must have had in mind one or more well-established critics senior to myself whose writings did not satisfy my requirements of what literary criticism should be. But I cannot recall a single book or essay, or the name of a single critic, as representative of the kind of impression-

---

12 The opening lines of Baudelaire's "Le Voyage": "For the child in love with maps and prints,/ The universe is on a scale with his vast appetite./ Ah, how big the world is in the light of the study-lamp!/ To the eyes of memory, how small!"

1 The Gideon Seymour Lecture delivered at the University of Minnesota in 1956 and published by the University.

istic criticism which aroused my ire thirty-three years ago.

The only point in mentioning this essay now, is to call attention to the extent to which what I wrote on this subject in 1923 is "dated." Richards's *Principles of Literary Criticism* was published in 1925. A great deal has happened in literary criticism since this influential book came out; and my paper was written two years earlier. Criticism has developed and branched out in several directions. The term "The New Criticism" is often employed by people without realizing what a variety it comprehends; but its currency does, I think, recognize the fact that the more distinguished critics of to-day, however widely they differ from each other, all differ in some significant way from the critics of a previous generation.

Many years ago I pointed out that every generation must provide its own literary criticism; for, as I said, "each generation brings to the contemplation of art its own categories of appreciation, makes its own demands upon art, and has its own uses for art." When I made this statement I am sure that I had in mind a good deal more than the changes of taste and fashion: I had in mind at least the fact that each generation, looking at masterpieces of the past in a different perspective, is affected in its attitude by a greater number of influences than those which bore upon the generation previous. But I doubt whether I had in mind the fact that an important work of literary criticism can alter and expand the content of the term "literary criticism" itself. Some years ago I drew attention to the steady change in meaning of the word *education* from the sixteenth century to the present day, a change which had taken place owing to the fact that education not only comprised more and more subjects, but was being supplied for or imposed upon more and more of the population. If we could follow the evolution of the term *literary criticism* in the same way, we would find something similar happening. Compare a critical masterpiece like Johnson's *Lives of the Poets* with the next great critical work to follow it, Coleridge's *Biographia Literaria*. It is not merely that Johnson represents a literary tradition to the end of which he himself belongs, while Coleridge is defending the merits and criticizing the weaknesses of a new style. The difference more pertinent to what I have been saying, is due to the scope and variety of the interests which Coleridge brought to bear on his discussion of poetry. He established the relevance of philosophy, aesthetics and psychology; and once Coleridge had introduced these disciplines into literary criticism, future critics could ignore them only at their own risk. To appreciate Johnson an effort of historical imagination is needed; a modern critic can find much in common with Coleridge. The criticism of to-day, indeed, may be said to be in direct descent from Coleridge, who would, I am sure, were he alive now, take the same interest in the social sciences and in the study of language and semantics, that he took in the sciences available to him.

The consideration of literature in the light of one or more of these studies, is one of the two main causes of the transformation of literary criticism in our time. The other cause has not been so fully recognized. The increasing attention given to the study of English and American literature in our universities and indeed in our schools, has led to a situation in which many critics are teachers, and many teachers are critics. I am far from deploring this situation: most of the really interesting criticism to-day is the work of men of letters who have found their way into universities, and of scholars whose critical activity has been first exercised in the classroom. And nowadays, when serious literary journalism is an inadequate, as well as precarious means of support for all but a very few, this is as it must be. Only, it means that the critic to-day may have a somewhat different contact with the world, and be writing for a somewhat different audience from that of his predecessors. I have the impression that serious criticism now is being written for a different, a more limited though not necessarily a smaller public than was that of the nineteenth century.

I was struck not long ago by an observation of Mr. Aldous Huxley in a preface to the English translation of *The Supreme Wisdom*, a book by a French psychiatrist, Dr. Hubert Benoit, on the psychology of Zen Buddhism. Mr. Huxley's observation responded to the impression which I had myself received from that remarkable book when I read it in French. Huxley is comparing Western psychiatry with the discipline of the East as found in Tau and Zen:

"The aim of Western psychiatry (he says) is

to help the troubled individual to adjust himself to the society of less troubled individuals—individuals who are observed to be well adjusted to one another and the local institutions, but about whose adjustment to the fundamental Order of Things no enquiry is made. . . . But there is another kind of normality—a normality of perfect functioning. . . . Even a man who is perfectly adjusted to a deranged society can prepare himself, if he so desires, to become adjusted to the Nature of Things."

The applicability of this to my present matter is not immediately obvious. But just as Western psychiatry, from a Zen Buddhist point of view, is confused or mistaken as to what healing is for, and its attitude needs really to be reversed, so I wonder whether the weakness of modern criticism is not an uncertainty as to what criticism is for? As to what benefit it is to bring, and to whom? Its very richness and variety have perhaps obscured its ultimate purpose. Every critic may have his eye on a definite goal, may be engaged on a task which needs no justification, and yet criticism itself may be lost as to its aims. If so, this is not surprising: for is it not now a commonplace, that the sciences and even the humanities have reached a point in development at which there is so much to know about any specialty, that no student has the time to know much about anything else? And the search for a curriculum which shall combine specialized study with some general education has surely been one of the problems most discussed in our universities.

We cannot, of course, go back to the universe of Aristotle or of St. Thomas Aquinas; and we cannot go back to the state of literary criticism before Coleridge. But perhaps we can do something to save ourselves from being overwhelmed by our own critical activity, by continually asking such a question as: when is criticism not literary criticism but something else?

I have been somewhat bewildered to find, from time to time, that I am regarded as one of the ancestors of modern criticism, if too old to be a modern critic myself. Thus in a book which I read recently by an author who is certainly a modern critic, I find a reference to "The New Criticism," by which, he says, "I mean not only the American critics, but the whole critical movement that derives from T. S. Eliot." I don't understand why the author should isolate me so

sharply from the American critics; but on the other hand I fail to see any critical movement which can be said to derive from myself, though I hope that as an editor I gave the New Criticism, or some of it, encouragement and an exercise ground in *The Criterion*. However, I think that I should, to justify this apparent modesty, indicate what I consider my own contribution to literary criticism to have been, and what are its limitations. The best of my *literary* criticism—apart from a few notorious phrases which have had a truly embarrassing success in the world—consists of essays on poets and poetic dramatists who had influenced me. It is a by-product of my private poetry-workshop; or a prolongation of the thinking that went into the formation of my own verse. In retrospect, I see that I wrote best about poets whose work had influenced my own, and with whose poetry I had become thoroughly familiar, long before I desired to write about them, or had found the occasion to do so. My criticism has this in common with that of Ezra Pound, that its merits and its limitations can be fully appreciated only when it is considered in relation to the poetry I have written myself. In Pound's criticism there is a more didactic motive: the reader he had in mind, I think, was primarily the young poet whose style was still unformed. But it is the love of certain poets who had influenced him, and (as I said of myself) a prolongation of his thinking about his own work, that inspires an early book which remains one of the best of Pound's literary essays, *The Spirit of Romance*.

This kind of criticism of poetry by a poet, or what I have called workshop criticism, has one obvious limitation. What has no relation to the poet's own work, or what is antipathetic to him, is outside of his competence. Another limitation of workshop criticism is that the critic's judgment may be unsound outside of his own art. My valuations of poets have remained pretty constant throughout my life; in particular, my opinions about a number of living poets have remained unchanged. It is, however, not only for this reason, that what I have in mind, in talking as I am to-day about criticism, is the criticism of poetry. Poetry, as a matter of fact, is what most critics in the past have had in mind when generalizing about literature. The criticism of prose fiction is of comparatively recent institution, and I am not qualified to discuss it; but it seems to me to require a somewhat different set of weights and measures from poetry. It might, indeed, provide an interesting subject for some critic of criticism—one who was neither poet nor novelist—to consider the differences between the ways in which the critic must approach the various *genres* of literature, and between the kinds of equipment needed. But poetry is the most convenient object of criticism to have in mind, when talking about criticism, simply for the reason that its formal qualities lend themselves most readily to generalization. In poetry, it might seem that style is everything. That is far from being true; but the illusion that in poetry we come nearer to a purely aesthetic experience makes poetry the most convenient *genre* of literature to keep in mind when we are discussing literary criticism itself.

A good deal of contemporary criticism, originating at that point at which criticism merges into scholarship, and at which scholarship merges into criticism, may be characterized as the criticism of explanation by origins. To make clear what I mean I shall mention two books which have had, in this connection, a rather bad influence. I do not mean that they are bad books. On the contrary: they are both books with which everyone should be acquainted. The first is John Livingston Lowes's *The Road to Xanadu*—a book which I recommend to every student of poetry who has not yet read it. The other is James Joyce's *Finnegans Wake*—a book which I recommend every student of poetry to read—at least some pages of. Livingston Lowes was a fine scholar, a good teacher, a lovable man and a man to whom I for one have private reasons to feel very grateful. James Joyce was a man of genius, a personal friend, and my citation here of *Finnegans Wake* is neither in praise nor dispraise of a book which is certainly in the category of works that can be called *monumental*. But the only obvious common characteristic of *The Road to Xanadu* and *Finnegans Wake* is that we may say of each: one book like this is enough.

For those who have never read *The Road to Xanadu*, I will explain that it is a fascinating piece of detection. Lowes ferreted out all the books which Coleridge had read (and Coleridge was an omnivorous and insatiable reader) and from which he had borrowed images or phrases to be found in *Kubla Khan* and *The Ancient Mariner*. The books that Coleridge read are many of them obscure and forgotten books—he read, for instance, every book of travels upon which he could lay his hands. And Lowes showed, once and for all, that poetic originality is largely an original way of assembling the most disparate and unlikely material to make a new whole. The demonstration is quite convincing, as evidence of how material is digested and transformed by the poetic genius. No one, after reading this book, could suppose that he understood *The Ancient Mariner* any better; nor was it in the least Dr. Lowes's intention to make the *poem* more intelligible as poetry. He was engaged on an investigation of process, an investigation which was, strictly speaking, beyond the frontier of literary criticism. How such material as those scraps of Coleridge's reading became transmuted into great poetry remains as much of a mystery as ever. Yet a number of hopeful scholars have seized upon the Lowes method as offering a clue to the understanding of any poem by any poet who gives evidence of having read anything. "I wonder," a gentleman from Indiana wrote to me a year or more ago, "I wonder—it is possible that I am mad, of course" (this was his interjection, not mine; of course he was not in the least mad, merely slightly touched in one corner of his head from having read *The Road to Xanadu*) "whether 'the dead cats of civilization,' 'rotten hippo' and Mr. Kurtz have some tenuous connection with 'that corpse you planted last year in your garden'?" This sounds like raving, unless you recognize the allusions: it is merely an earnest seeker trying to establish some connection between *The Waste Land* and Joseph Conrad's *Heart of Darkness*.

Now while Dr. Lowes has fired such practitioners of hermeneutics with emulative zeal, *Finnegans Wake* has provided them with a model of what they would like all literary works to be. I must hasten to explain that I am not deriding or denigrating the labours of those exegetists who have set themselves to unravel all the threads and follow all the clues in that book. If *Finnegans Wake* is to be understood at all—and we cannot judge it without such labour—that kind of detection must be pursued; and Messrs. Campbell and Robinson (to mention the authors of one such piece of work) have done an admirable job. My grievance if any is against

James Joyce, the author of that monstrous masterpiece, for writing a book such that large stretches of it are, without elaborate explanation, merely beautiful nonsense (very beautiful indeed when recited by an Irish voice as lovely as that of the author—would that he had recorded more of it!). Perhaps Joyce did not realize how obscure his book is. Whatever the final judgment (and I am not going to attempt a judgment) of the place of *Finnegans Wake* may be, I do not think that most poetry (for it is a kind of vast prose poem) is written in that way or requires that sort of dissection for its enjoyment and understanding. But I suspect that the enigmas provided by *Finnegans Wake* have given support to the error, prevalent nowadays, of mistaking explanation for understanding. After the production of my play *The Cocktail Party,* my mail was swollen for months with letters offering surprising solutions of what the writers believed to be the riddle of the play's meaning. And it was evident that the writers did not resent the puzzle they thought I had set them—they liked it. Indeed, though they were unconscious of the fact, they invented the puzzle for the pleasure of discovering the solution.

Here I must admit that I am, on one conspicuous occasion, not guiltless of having led critics into temptation. The notes to *The Waste Land!* I had at first intended only to put down all the references for my quotations, with a view to spiking the guns of critics of my earlier poems who had accused me of plagiarism. Then, when it came to print *The Waste Land* as a little book —for the poem on its first appearance in *The Dial* and in *The Criterion* had no notes whatever—it was discovered that the poem was inconveniently short, so I set to work to expand the notes, in order to provide a few more pages of printed matter, with the result that they became the remarkable exposition of bogus scholarship that is still on view to-day. I have sometimes thought of getting rid of these notes; but now they can never be unstuck. They have had almost greater popularity than the poem itself— anyone who bought my book of poems, and found that the notes to *The Waste Land* were not in it, would demand his money back. But I don't think that these notes did any harm to other poets: certainly I cannot think of any good contemporary poet who has abused this same

practice. (As for Miss Marianne Moore, *her* notes to poems are always pertinent, curious, conclusive, delightful and give no encouragement whatever to the researcher of origins.) No, it is not because of my bad example to other poets that I am penitent: it is because my notes stimulated the wrong kind of interest among the seekers of sources. It was just, no doubt, that I should pay my tribute to the work of Miss Jessie Weston; but I regret having sent so many enquirers off on a wild goose chase after Tarot cards and the Holy Grail.

While I was pondering this question of the attempt to understand a poem by explaining its origins, I came across a quotation from C. G. Jung which struck me as having some relevance. The passage was quoted by Fr. Victor White, O.P. in his book *God and the Unconscious.* Fr. White quotes it in the course of exposing a radical difference between the method of Freud and the method of Jung.

"It is a generally recognised truth (says Jung) that physical events can be looked at in two ways, that is from the mechanistic and from the energic standpoint. The mechanistic view is purely causal: from this standpoint an event is conceived as the result of a cause. . . . The energic viewpoint on the other hand is in essence final; the event is traced from effect to cause on the assumption that energy forms the essential basis of changes in phenomena. . . ."

The quotation is from the first essay in the volume *Contributions to Analytical Psychology.* I add another sentence, not quoted by Fr. White, which opens the next paragraph: "both viewpoints are indispensable for the comprehension of physical phenomena."

I take this simply as a suggestive analogy. One can explain a poem by investigating what it is made of and the causes that brought it about; and explanation may be a necessary preparation for understanding. But to understand a poem it is also necessary, and I should say in most instances still more necessary, that we should endeavour to grasp what the poetry is aiming to be; one might say—though it is long since I have employed such terms with any assurance—endeavouring to grasp its entelechy.

Perhaps the form of criticism in which the danger of excessive reliance upon causal explanation is greatest is the critical biography, especially when the biographer supplements his knowledge of external facts with psychological conjectures about inner experience. I do not suggest that the personality and the private life of a dead poet constitute sacred ground on which the psychologist must not tread. The scientist must be at liberty to study such material as his curiosity leads him to investigate—so long as the victim is dead and the laws of libel cannot be invoked to stop him. Nor is there any reason why biographies of poets should not be written. Furthermore, the biographer of an author should possess some critical ability; he should be a man of taste and judgment, appreciative of the work of the man whose biography he undertakes. And on the other hand any critic seriously concerned with a man's work should be expected to know something about the man's life. But a critical biography of a writer is a delicate task in itself; and the critic or the biographer who, without being a trained and practising psychologist, brings to bear on his subject such analytical skill as he has acquired by reading books written by psychologists, may confuse the issues still further.

The question of how far information about the poet helps us to understand the poetry is not so simple as one might think. Each reader must answer it for himself, and must answer it not generally but in particular instances, for it may be more important in the case of one poet and less important in the case of another. For the enjoyment of poetry can be a complex experience in which several forms of satisfaction are mingled; and they may be mingled in different proportions for different readers. I will give an illustration. It is generally agreed that the greatest part of Wordsworth's best poetry was written within a brief span of years—brief in itself, and brief in proportion to the whole span of Wordsworth's life. Various students of Wordsworth have propounded explanations to account for the mediocrity of his later output. Some years ago, Sir Herbert Read wrote a book on Wordsworth—an interesting book, though I think that his best appreciation of Wordsworth is found in a later essay in a volume entitled *A Coat of Many Colours*—in which he explained the rise and fall of Wordsworth's genius by the effects upon him of his affair with Annette Vallon, about which information had at that time come to light. More recently still, Mr. F. W. Bateson has written a book about Wordsworth which is also of considerable interest (his chapter on "The Two Voices" does help to understand Wordsworth's style). In this book he maintains that Annette doesn't figure nearly so importantly as Sir Herbert Read had thought, and that the real secret was that Wordsworth fell in love with his sister Dorothy; that this explains, in particular, the Lucy poems, and explains why, after Wordsworth's marriage, his inspiration dried up. Well, he may be right: his argument is very plausible. But the real question, which every reader of Wordsworth must answer for himself, is: does it matter? does this account help me to understand the Lucy poems any better than I did before? For myself, I can only say that a knowledge of the springs which released a poem is not necessarily a help towards understanding the poem: too much information about the origins of the poem may even break my contact with it. I feel no need for any light upon the Lucy poems beyond the radiance shed by the poems themselves.

I am not maintaining that there is *no* context in which such information or conjecture as that of Sir Herbert Read and Mr. Bateson may be relevant. It is relevant if we want to understand Wordsworth; but it is not directly relevant to our understanding of his poetry. Or rather, it is not relevant to our understanding of *the poetry as poetry*. I am even prepared to suggest that there is, in all great poetry, something which must remain unaccountable however complete might be our knowledge of the poet, and that that is what matters most. When the poem has been made, something new has happened, something that cannot be wholly explained by *anything that went before*. That, I believe, is what we mean by "creation."

The explanation of poetry by examination of its sources is not the method of all contemporary criticism by any means; but it is a method which responds to the desire of a good many readers that poetry should be explained to them in terms of something else: the chief part of the letters I receive from persons unknown to me, concerning my own poems, consists of requests for a kind of explanation that I cannot possibly give. There are other tendencies such as that represented by Professor Richards's investigation of the problem of how the appreciation of poetry can be taught, or by the verbal subtleties of his distinguished pupil, Professor Empson. And I have recently noticed a development, which I suspect has its origin in the classroom methods of Professor Richards, which is, in its way, a healthy reaction against the diversion of attention from the poetry to the poet. It is found in a book published not long ago, entitled *Interpretations:* a series of essays by twelve of the younger English critics, each analysing one poem of his own choice. The method is to take a well-known poem—each of the poems analysed in this book is a good one of its kind—without reference to the author or to his other work, analyse it stanza by stanza and line by line, and extract, squeeze, tease, press every drop of meaning out of it that one can. It might be called the lemon-squeezer school of criticism. As the poems range from the sixteenth century to the present day, as they differ a good deal from one another—the book begins with "The Phoenix and the Turtle" and ends with "Prufrock" and Yeats's "Among School Children," and as each critic has his own procedure, the result is interesting and a little confusing—and, it must be admitted, to study twelve poems each analysed so painstakingly is a very tiring way of passing the time. I imagine that some of the poets (they are all dead except myself) would be surprised at learning what their poems mean: I had one or two minor surprises myself, as on learning that the fog, mentioned early in "Prufrock," had somehow got into the drawing-room. But the analysis of "Prufrock" was not an attempt to find origins, either in literature or in the darker recesses of my private life; it was an attempt to find out what the poem really meant—whether that was what I had meant it to mean or not. And for that I was grateful. There were several essays which struck me as good. But as every method has its own limitations and dangers, it is only reasonable to mention what seem to me the limitations and dangers of this one, dangers against which, if it were practised for what I suspect should be its chief use, that is, as an exercise for pupils, it would be the business of the teacher to warn his class.

The first danger is that of assuming that there must be just one interpretation of the poem as a whole, that must be right. There will be details of explanation, especially with poems written in another age than our own, matters of

fact, historical allusions, the meaning of a certain word at a certain date, which can be established, and the teacher can see that his pupils get these right. But as for the meaning of the poem as a whole, it is not exhausted by any explanation, for the meaning is what the poem means to different sensitive readers. The second danger—a danger into which I do not think any of the critics in the volume I have mentioned has fallen, but a danger to which the reader is exposed— is that of assuming that the interpretation of a poem, if valid, is necessarily an account of what the author consciously or unconsciously was trying to do. For the tendency is so general, to believe that we understand a poem when we have identified its origins and traced the process to which the poet submitted his materials, that we may easily believe the converse—that any explanation of the poem is also an account of how it was written. The analysis of "Prufrock" to which I have referred interested *me* because it helped *me* to see the poem through the eyes of an intelligent, sensitive and diligent reader. That is not at all to say that *he* saw the poem through my eyes, or that his account has anything to do with the experiences that led up to my writing it, or with anything I experienced in the process of writing it. And my third comment is, that I should, as a test, like to see the method applied to some new poem, some very good poem, and one that was previously unknown to me: because I should like to find out whether, after perusing the analysis, I should be able to enjoy the poem. For nearly all the poems in the volume were poems that I had known and loved for many years; and after reading the analyses, I found I was slow to recover my previous feeling about the poems. It was as if someone had taken a machine to pieces and left me with the task of reassembling the parts. I suspect, in fact, that a good deal of the value of an interpretation is—that it should be my own interpretation. There are many things, perhaps, to know about this poem, or that, many facts about which scholars can instruct me which will help me to avoid definite *mis*understanding; but a valid interpretation, I believe, must be at the same time an interpretation of my own feelings when I read it.

It has been no part of my purpose to give a comprehensive view of all the types of literary criticism practised in our time. I wished first to call attention to the transformation of literary criticism which we may say began with Coleridge but which has proceeded with greater acceleration during the last twenty-five years. This acceleration I took to be prompted by the relevance of the social sciences to criticism, and by the teaching of literature (including *contemporary* literature) in colleges and universities. I do not deplore the transformation, for it seems to me to have been inevitable. In an age of uncertainty, an age in which men are bewildered by new sciences, an age in which so little can be taken for granted as common beliefs, assumptions and background of all readers, no explorable area can be forbidden ground. But, among all this variety, we may ask, what is there, if anything, that should be common to all literary criticism? Thirty years ago, I asserted that the essential function of literary criticism was "the elucidation of works of art and the correction of taste." That phrase may sound somewhat pompous to our ears in 1956. Perhaps I could put it more simply, and more acceptably to the present age, by saying to "promote the understanding and enjoyment of literature." I would add that there is implied here also the negative task of pointing out what should *not* be enjoyed. For the critic may on occasion be called upon to condemn the second-rate and expose the fraudulent: though that duty is secondary to the duty of discriminating praise of what is praiseworthy. And I must stress the point that I do not think of *enjoyment* and *understanding* as distinct activities—one emotional and the other intellectual. By *understanding* I do not mean *explanation* though explanation of what can be explained may often be a necessary preliminary to understanding. To offer a very simple instance; to learn the unfamiliar words, and the unfamiliar forms of words, is a necessary preliminary to the understanding of Chaucer; it is explanation: but one could master the vocabulary, spelling, grammar and syntax of Chaucer—indeed, to carry the instance a stage further, one could be very well informed about the age of Chaucer, its social habits, its beliefs, its learning and its ignorance—and yet not *understand the poetry. To* understand a poem comes to the same thing as to enjoy it for the right reasons. One might say that it means getting from the poem such enjoyment as it is capable of giving: to enjoy a poem under a

misunderstanding as to what it is, is to enjoy what is merely a projection of our own mind. So difficult a tool to handle, is language, that "to enjoy" and "to get enjoyment from" do not seem to mean quite the same thing: that to say that one "gets enjoyment from" poetry does not sound quite the same as to say that one "enjoys poetry." And indeed, the very meaning of "joy" varies with the object inspiring joy; different poems, even, yield different satisfactions. It is certain that we do not fully enjoy a poem unless we understand it; and on the other hand, it is equally true that we do not fully understand a poem unless we enjoy it. And that means, enjoying it to the right degree and in the right way, relative to other poems (it is in the relation of our enjoyment of a poem to our enjoyment of other poems that *taste* is shown). It should hardly be necessary to add that this implies that one *shouldn't* enjoy bad poems—unless their badness is of a sort that appeals to our sense of humour.

I have said that explanation may be a necessary preliminary to understanding. It seems to me, however, that I understand some poetry without explanation, for instance Shakespeare's

Full fathom five thy father lies

or Shelley's

Art thou pale for weariness
Of climbing heaven and gazing on the earth

for here, and in a great deal of poetry, I see nothing to be explained—nothing, that is, that would help me to understand it better and therefore enjoy it more. And sometimes explanation, as I have already hinted, can distract us altogether from *the poem as poetry,* instead of leading us in the direction of understanding. My best reason, perhaps, for believing that I am not deluded in thinking that I understand such poetry as the lyrics by Shakespeare and Shelley which I have just cited, is that these two poems give me as keen a thrill when I repeat them today as they did fifty years ago.

The difference, then, between the literary critic, and the critic who has passed beyond the frontier of literary criticism, is not that the literary critic is "purely" literary, or that he has no other interests. A critic who was interested in nothing but "literature" would have very little to say to us, for his literature would be a pure abstraction. Poets have other interests beside poetry—otherwise their poetry would be very empty: they are poets because their dominant interest has been in turning their experience and their thought (and to experience and to think means to have interests beyond poetry)—in turning their experience and their thinking into poetry. The critic accordingly is a *literary* critic if his primary interest, in writing criticism, is to help his readers to *understand and enjoy*. But he must have other interests, just as much as the poet himself; for the literary critic is not merely a technical expert, who has learned the rules to be observed by the writers he criticizes: the critic must be the whole man, a man with convictions and principles, and of knowledge and experience of life.

We can therefore ask, about any writing which is offered to us as literary criticism, is it aimed towards understanding and enjoyment? If it is not, it may still be a legitimate and useful activity; but it is to be judged as a contribution to psychology, or sociology, or logic, or pedagogy, or some other pursuit—and is to be judged by specialists, not by men of letters. We must not identify biography with criticism: biography is ordinarily useful in providing explanation which may open the way to further understanding; but it may also, in directing our attention on the poet, lead us away from the poetry. We must not confuse knowledge—factual information—about a poet's period, the conditions of the society in which he lived, the ideas current in his time implicit in his writings, the state of the language in his period—with understanding his poetry. Such knowledge, as I have said, may be a necessary preparation for understanding the poetry; furthermore, it has a value of its own, as history; but for the appreciation of the poetry, it can only lead us to the door: we must find our own way in. For the purpose of acquiring such knowledge, from the point of view taken throughout this paper, is not primarily that we

should be able to project ourselves into a remote period, that we should be able to think and feel, when reading the poetry, as a contemporary of the poet might have thought and felt, though such experience has its own value; it is rather to divest ourselves of the limitations of our own age, and the poet, whose work we are reading, of the limitations of *his* age, in order to get the direct experience, the immediate contact with his poetry. What matters most, let us say, in reading an ode of Sappho, is not that I should imagine myself to be an island Greek of twenty-five hundred years ago; what matters is the experience which is the same for all human beings of different centuries and languages capable of enjoying poetry, the spark which can leap across those 2,500 years. So the critic to whom I am most grateful is the one who can make me look at something I have never looked at before, or looked at only with eyes clouded by prejudice, set me face to face with it and then leave me alone with it. From that point, I must rely upon my own sensibility, intelligence, and capacity for wisdom.

If in literary criticism, we place all the emphasis upon *understanding*, we are in danger of slipping from understanding to mere explanation. We are in danger even of pursuing criticism as if it was a science, which it never can be. If, on the other hand, we over-emphasize *enjoyment,* we will tend to fall into the subjective and impressionistic, and our enjoyment will profit us no more than mere amusement and pastime. Thirty-three years ago, it seems to have been the latter type of criticism, the impressionistic, that had caused the annoyance I felt when I wrote on "the function of criticism." To-day it seems to me that we need to be more on guard against the purely explanatory. But I do not want to leave you with the impression that I wish to condemn the criticism of our time. These last thirty years have been, I think, a brilliant period in literary criticism in both Britain and America. It may even come to seem, in retrospect, too brilliant. Who knows?

Thomas Ernest Hulme

1883–1917

During his short lifetime Hulme's principal publications were two translations: Bergson's *Introduction to Metaphysics* (1913) and Sorel's *Reflections on Violence* (1916). (The five little poems,[1] afterwards so strangely celebrated, had first been published in *The New Age* in 1911; in 1915 they appeared again as an appendix to Ezra Pound's *Ripostes*.) Yet after his death, as a result of the posthumous publication of his notes and papers, arranged and edited by Herbert Read, under the title *Speculations* (1924), Hulme seems to have exerted a continuous and decisive influence on the development of English poetry and critical thought between the two wars. At the very least it may be said that his critical principles and beliefs, particularly those outlined in the chapter from *Speculations* here reprinted, affirmed and paralleled the critical principles and poetic practice of writers who, in the years following World War I, were to determine the directions taken by English poetry of their time. It may be that some of Hulme's statements are overstatements, that in the form in which we have them they are understandably oversimplified; nevertheless they have their vitality and their clarity, and they are extremely interesting.

Of Hulme's life there is little to tell. He was born in Staffordshire and educated at the High School, Newcastle-under-Lyme, and at St. John's College, Cambridge. After being sent down from Cambridge in 1904 (he was readmitted in 1912), he traveled, worked, and studied independently, living at one time or another in London, in Canada, and on the Continent. He joined the Army in 1914 and was commissioned in 1916; he was killed in September 1917.

TEXTS: A book-length study by Michael Roberts, *T. E. Hulme,* was published in 1938, and another, *The Life and Opinions of T. E. Hulme,* by Alun Richard Jones, in 1960. *Further Speculations,* edited by Sam Hughes, was published in 1955.

Romanticism and Classicism

I want to maintain that after a hundred years of romanticism, we are in for a classical revival, and that the particular weapon of this new classical spirit, when it works in verse, will be fancy. And in this I imply the superiority of fancy—not superior generally or absolutely, for that would be obvious nonsense, but superior in the sense that we use the word good in empirical ethics—good for something, superior for something. I shall have to prove then two things, first that a classical revival is coming, and, secondly, for its particular purposes, fancy will be superior to imagination.

So banal have the terms Imagination and Fancy become that we imagine they must have always been in the language. Their history as two differing terms in the vocabulary of criticism is comparatively short. Originally, of course, they both mean the same thing; they first began to be differentiated by the German writers on aesthetics in the eighteenth century.

I know that in using the words "classic" and "romantic" I am doing a dangerous thing. They represent five or six different kinds of antitheses, and while I may be using them in one sense you may be interpreting them in another. In this present connection I am using them in a perfectly precise and limited sense. I ought really to have coined a couple of new words, but I prefer to use the ones I have used, as I then conform to the practice of the group of polemical writers who make most use of them at the present day, and have almost succeeded in making them political catchwords. I mean Maurras, Lasserre and all the group connected with *L'Action Française.*

At the present time this is the particular group with which the distinction is most vital. Because it has become a party symbol. If you asked a man of a certain set whether he preferred the classics or the romantics, you could deduce from that what his politics were.

The best way of gliding into a proper definition of my terms would be to start with a set of people who are prepared to fight about it—for in them you will have no vagueness. (Other people take the infamous attitude of the person with catholic tastes who says he likes both.)

About a year ago, a man whose name I think was Fauchois gave a lecture at the Odéon on Racine, in the course of which he made some

---

[1] These poems, not included here, are described by Herbert Read as "good textbook examples of imagist techniques."

disparaging remarks about his dullness, lack of invention and the rest of it. This caused an immediate riot: fights took place all over the house; several people were arrested and imprisoned, and the rest of the series of lectures took place with hundreds of gendarmes and detectives scattered all over the place. These people interrupted because the classical ideal is a living thing to them and Racine is the great classic. That is what I call a real vital interest in literature. They regard romanticism as an awful disease from which France had just recovered.

The thing is complicated in their case by the fact that it was romanticism that made the revolution. They hate the revolution, so they hate romanticism.

I make no apology for dragging in politics here; romanticism both in England and France is associated with certain political views, and it is in taking a concrete example of the working out of a principle in action that you can get its best definition.

What was the positive principle behind all the other principles of '89? I am talking here of the revolution in as far as it was an idea; I leave out material causes—they only produce the forces. The barriers which could easily have resisted or guided these forces had been previously rotted away by ideas. This always seems to be the case in successful changes; the privileged class is beaten only when it has lost faith in itself, when it has itself been penetrated with the ideas which are working against it.

It was not the rights of man—that was a good solid practical war-cry. The thing which created enthusiasm, which made the revolution practically a new religion, was something more positive than that. People of all classes, people who stood to lose by it, were in a positive ferment about the idea of liberty. There must have been some idea which enabled them to think that something positive could come out of so essentially negative a thing. There was, and here I get my definition of romanticism. They had been taught by Rousseau that man was by nature good, that it was only bad laws and customs that had suppressed him. Remove all these and the infinite possibilities of man would have a chance. This is what made them think that something positive could come out of disorder, this is what created the religious enthusiasm. Here is the root

of all romanticism: that man, the individual, is an infinite reservoir of possibilities; and if you can so rearrange society by the destruction of oppressive order then these possibilities will have a chance and you will get Progress.

One can define the classical quite clearly as the exact opposite to this. Man is an extraordinarily fixed and limited animal whose nature is absolutely constant. It is only by tradition and organisation that anything decent can be got out of him.

This view was a little shaken at the time of Darwin. You remember his particular hypothesis, that new species came into existence by the cumulative effect of small variations—this seems to admit the possibility of future progress. But at the present day the contrary hypothesis makes headway in the shape of De Vries's mutation theory, that each new species comes into existence, not gradually by the accumulation of small steps, but suddenly in a jump, a kind of sport, and that once in existence it remains absolutely fixed. This enables me to keep the classical view with an appearance of scientific backing.

Put shortly, these are the two views, then. One, that man is intrinsically good, spoilt by circumstance; and the other that he is intrinsically limited, but disciplined by order and tradition to something fairly decent. To the one party man's nature is like a well, to the other like a bucket. The view which regards man as a well, a reservoir full of possibilities, I call the romantic; the one which regards him as a very finite and fixed creature, I call the classical.

One may note here that the Church has always taken the classical view since the defeat of the Pelagian heresy and the adoption of the sane classical dogma of original sin.

It would be a mistake to identify the classical view with that of materialism. On the contrary it is absolutely identical with the normal religious attitude. I should put it in this way: That part of the fixed nature of man is the belief in the Deity. This should be as fixed and true for every man as belief in the existence of matter and in the objective world. It is parallel to appetite, the instinct of sex, and all the other fixed qualities. Now at certain times, by the use of either force or rhetoric, these instincts have been suppressed—in Florence under Savonarola, in Geneva under Calvin, and here under the Roundheads. The inevitable result of such a process is that the repressed instinct bursts out in some abnormal direction. So with religion. By the perverted rhetoric of Rationalism, your natural instincts are suppressed and you are converted into an agnostic. Just as in the case of the other instincts, Nature has her revenge. The instincts that find their right and proper outlet in religion must come out in some other way. You don't believe in a God, so you begin to believe that man is a god. You don't believe in Heaven, so you begin to believe in a heaven on earth. In other words, you get romanticism. The concepts that are right and proper in their own sphere are spread over, and so mess up, falsify and blur the clear outlines of human experience. It is like pouring a pot of treacle over the dinner table. Romanticism then, and this is the best definition I can give of it, is spilt religion.

I must now shirk the difficulty of saying exactly what I mean by romantic and classical in verse. I can only say that it means the result of these two attitudes towards the cosmos, towards man, in so far as it gets reflected in verse. The romantic, because he thinks man infinite, must always be talking about the infinite; and as there is always the bitter contrast between what you think you ought to be able to do and what man actually can, it always tends, in its later stages at any rate, to be gloomy. I really can't go any further than to say it is the reflection of these two temperaments, and point out examples of the different spirits. On the one hand I would take such diverse people as Horace, most of the Elizabethans and the writers of the Augustan age, and on the other side Lamartine, Hugo, parts of Keats, Coleridge, Byron, Shelley and Swinburne.

I know quite well that when people think of classical and romantic in verse, the contrast at once comes into their mind between, say, Racine and Shakespeare. I don't mean this; the dividing line that I intend is here misplaced a little from the true middle. That Racine is on the extreme classical side I agree, but if you call Shakespeare romantic, you are using a different definition to the one I give. You are thinking of the difference between classic and romantic as being merely one between restraint and exuberance. I should say with Nietzsche that there are two kinds of classicism, the static and the dynamic. Shakespeare is the classic of motion.

What I mean by classical in verse, then, is this. That even in the most imaginative flights there is always a holding back, a reservation. The classical poet never forgets this finiteness, this limit of man. He remembers always that he is mixed up with earth. He may jump, but he always returns back; he never flies away into the circumambient gas.

You might say if you wished that the whole of the romantic attitude seems to crystallise in verse round metaphors of flight. Hugo is always flying, flying over abysses, flying up into the eternal gases. The word infinite in every other line.

In the classical attitude you never seem to swing right along to the infinite nothing. If you say an extravagant thing which does exceed the limits inside which you know man to be fastened, yet there is always conveyed in some way at the end an impression of yourself standing outside it, and not quite believing it, or consciously putting it forward as a flourish. You never go blindly into an atmosphere more than the truth, an atmosphere too rarefied for man to breathe for long. You are always faithful to the conception of a limit. It is a question of pitch; in romantic verse you move at a certain pitch of rhetoric which you know, man being what he is, to be a little high-falutin. The kind of thing you get in Hugo or Swinburne. In the coming classical reaction that will feel just wrong. For an example of the opposite thing, a verse written in the proper classical spirit, I can take the song from Cymbeline beginning with "Fear no more the heat of the sun." I am just using this as a parable. I don't quite mean what I say here. Take the last two lines:

> "*Golden lads and lasses must,*
> *Like chimney sweepers come to dust.*"

Now, no romantic would have ever written that. Indeed, so ingrained is romanticism, so objectionable is this to it, that people have asserted that these were not part of the original song.

Apart from the pun, the thing that I think quite classical is the word lad. Your modern romantic could never write that. He would have to write golden youth, and take up the thing at least a couple of notes in pitch.

I want now to give the reasons which make

me think that we are nearing the end of the romantic movement.

The first lies in the nature of any convention or tradition in art. A particular convention or attitude in art has a strict analogy to the phenomena of organic life. It grows old and decays. It has a definite period of life and must die. All the possible tunes get played on it and then it is exhausted; moreover its best period is its youngest. Take the case of the extraordinary efflorescence of verse in the Elizabethan period. All kinds of reasons have been given for this— the discovery of the new world and all the rest of it. There is a much simpler one. A new medium had been given them to play with— namely, blank verse. It was new and so it was easy to play new tunes on it.

The same law holds in other arts. All the masters of painting are born into the world at a time when the particular tradition from which they start is imperfect. The Florentine tradition was just short of full ripeness when Raphael came to Florence, the Bellinesque was still young when Titian was born in Venice. Landscape was still a toy or an appanage of figure-painting when Turner and Constable arose to reveal its independent power. When Turner and Constable had done with landscape they left little or nothing for their successors to do on the same lines. Each field of artistic activity is exhausted by the first great artist who gathers a full harvest from it.

This period of exhaustion seems to me to have been reached in romanticism. We shall not get any new efflorescence of verse until we get a new technique, a new convention, to turn ourselves loose in.

Objection might be taken to this. It might be said that a century as an organic unity doesn't exist, that I am being deluded by a wrong metaphor, that I am treating a collection of literary people as if they were an organism or state department. Whatever we may be in other things, an objector might urge, in literature in as far as we are anything at all—in as far as we are worth considering—we are individuals, we are persons, and as distinct persons we cannot be subordinated to any general treatment. At any period at any time, an individual poet may be a classic or a romantic just as he feels like it. You at any particular moment may think that you can stand outside a movement. You may think that as an individual you observe both the classic and the romantic spirit and decide from a purely detached point of view that one is superior to the other.

The answer to this is that no one, in a matter of judgment of beauty, can take a detached standpoint in this way. Just as physically you are not born that abstract entity, man, but the child of particular parents, so you are in matters of literary judgment. Your opinion is almost entirely of the literary history that came just before you, and you are governed by that whatever you may think. Take Spinoza's example of a stone falling to the ground. If it had a conscious mind it would, he said, think it was going to the ground because it wanted to. So you with your pretended free judgment about what is and what is not beautiful. The amount of freedom in man is much exaggerated. That we are free on certain rare occasions, both my religion and the views I get from metaphysics convince me. But many acts which we habitually label free are in reality automatic. It is quite possible for a man to write a book almost automatically. I have read several such products. Some observations were recorded more than twenty years ago by Robertson on reflex speech, and he found that in certain cases of dementia, where the people were quite unconscious so far as the exercise of reasoning went, that very intelligent answers were given to a succession of questions on politics and such matters. The meaning of these questions could not possibly have been understood. Language here acted after the manner of a reflex. So that certain extremely complex mechanisms, subtle enough to imitate beauty, can work by themselves—I certainly think that this is the case with judgments about beauty.

I can put the same thing in slightly different form. Here is a question of a conflict of two attitudes, as it might be of two techniques. The critic, while he has to admit that changes from one to the other occur, persists in regarding them as mere variations to a certain fixed normal, just as a pendulum might swing. I admit the analogy of the pendulum as far as movement, but I deny the further consequence of the analogy, the existence of the point of rest, the normal point.

When I say that I dislike the romantics, I dissociate two things: the part of them in which they resemble all the great poets, and the part in which they differ and which gives them their character as romantics. It is this minor element which constitutes the particular note of a century, and which, while it excites contemporaries, annoys the next generation. It was precisely that quality in Pope which pleased his friends, which we detest. Now, anyone just before the romantics who felt that, could have predicted that a change was coming. It seems to me that we stand just in the same position now. I think that there is an increasing proportion of people who simply can't stand Swinburne.

When I say that there will be another classical revival I don't necessarily anticipate a return to Pope. I say merely that now is the time for such a revival. Given people of the necessary capacity, it may be a vital thing; without them we may get a formalism something like Pope. When it does come we may not even recognise it as classical. Although it will be classical it will be different because it has passed through a romantic period. To take a parallel example: I remember being very surprised, after seeing the Post Impressionists, to find in Maurice Denis's account of the matter that they consider themselves classical in the sense that they were trying to impose the same order on the mere flux of new material provided by the impressionist movement, that existed in the more limited materials of the painting before.

There is something now to be cleared away before I get on with my argument, which is that while romanticism is dead in reality, yet the critical attitude appropriate to it still continues to exist. To make this a little clearer: For every kind of verse, there is a corresponding receptive attitude. In a romantic period we demand from verse certain qualities. In a classical period we demand others. At the present time I should say that this receptive attitude has outlasted the thing from which it was formed. But while the romantic tradition has run dry, yet the critical attitude of mind, which demands romantic qualities from verse, still survives. So that if good classical verse were to be written to-morrow very few people would be able to stand it.

I object even to the best of the romantics. I object still more to the receptive attitude. I object to the sloppiness which doesn't consider that a poem is a poem unless it is moaning or whining about something or other. I always think in this

connection of the last line of a poem of John Webster's which ends with a request I cordially endorse:

"End your moan and come away."

The thing has got so bad now that a poem which is all dry and hard, a properly classical poem, would not be considered poetry at all. How many people now can lay their hands on their hearts and say they like either Horace or Pope? They feel a kind of chill when they read them.

The dry hardness which you get in the classics is absolutely repugnant to them. Poetry that isn't damp isn't poetry at all. They cannot see that accurate description is a legitimate object of verse. Verse to them always means a bringing in of some of the emotions that are grouped round the word infinite.

The essence of poetry to most people is that it must lead them to a beyond of some kind. Verse strictly confined to the earthly and the definite (Keats is full of it) might seem to them to be excellent writing, excellent craftsmanship, but not poetry. So much has romanticism debauched us, that, without some form of vagueness, we deny the highest.

In the classic it is always the light of ordinary day, never the light that never was on land or sea. It is always perfectly human and never exaggerated: man is always man and never a god.

But the awful result of romanticism is that, accustomed to this strange light, you can never live without it. Its effect on you is that of a drug.

There is a general tendency to think that verse means little else than the expression of unsatisfied emotion. People say: "But how can you have verse without sentiment?" You see what it is: the prospect alarms them. A classical revival to them would mean the prospect of an arid desert and the death of poetry as they understand it, and could only come to fill the gap caused by that death. Exactly why this dry classical spirit should have a positive and legitimate necessity to express itself in poetry is utterly inconceivable to them. What this positive need is, I shall show later. It follows from the fact that there is another quality, not the emotion produced, which is at the root of excellence in verse. Before I get to this I am concerned with a negative thing, a theoretical point, a prejudice that stands in the way and is really at the bottom of this reluctance to understand classical verse.

It is an objection which ultimately I believe comes from a bad metaphysic of art. You are unable to admit the existence of beauty without the infinite being in some way or another dragged in.

I may quote for purposes of argument, as a typical example of this kind of attitude made vocal, the famous chapters in Ruskin's *Modern Painters*, Vol. II, on the imagination. I must say here, parenthetically, that I use this word without prejudice to the other discussion with which I shall end the paper. I only use the word here because it is Ruskin's word. All that I am concerned with just now is the attitude behind it, which I take to be the romantic.

"Imagination cannot but be serious; she sees too far, too darkly, too solemnly, too earnestly, ever to smile. There is something in the heart of everything, if we can reach it, that we shall not be inclined to laugh at.... Those who have so pierced and seen the melancholy deeps of things, are filled with intense passion and gentleness of sympathy." (Part III, Chap. III, § 9.)

"There is in every word set down by the imaginative mind an awful undercurrent of meaning, and evidence and shadow upon it of the deep places out of which it has come. It is often obscure, often half-told; for he who wrote it, in his clear seeing of the things beneath, may have been impatient of detailed interpretation; for if we choose to dwell upon it and trace it, it will lead us always securely back to that metropolis of the soul's dominion from which we may follow out all the ways and tracks to its farthest coasts." (Part III, Chap. III, § 5.)

Really in all these matters the act of judgment is an instinct, an absolutely unstateable thing akin to the art of the tea taster. But you must talk, and the only language you can use in this matter is that of analogy. I have no material clay to mould to the given shape; the only thing which one has for the purpose, and which acts as a substitute for it, a kind of mental clay, are certain metaphors modified into theories of aesthetic and rhetoric. A combination of these, while it cannot state the essentially unstateable intuition, can yet give you a sufficient analogy to enable you to see what it was and to recognise it on condition that you yourself have been in a similar state. Now these phrases of Ruskin's con-

vey quite clearly to me his taste in the matter.

I see quite clearly that he thinks the best verse must be serious. That is a natural attitude for a man in the romantic period. But he is not content with saying that he prefers this kind of verse. He wants to deduce his opinion like his master, Coleridge, from some fixed principle which can be found by metaphysic.

Here is the last refuge of this romantic attitude. It proves itself to be not an attitude but a deduction from a fixed principle of the cosmos.

One of the main reasons for the existence of philosophy is not that it enables you to find truth (it can never do that) but that it does provide you a refuge for definitions. The usual idea of the thing is that it provides you with a fixed basis from which you can deduce the things you want in aesthetics. The process is the exact contrary. You start in the confusion of the fighting line, you retire from that just a little to the rear to recover, to get your weapons right. Quite plainly, without metaphor this—it provides you with an elaborate and precise language in which you really can explain definitely what you mean, but what you want to say is decided by other things. The ultimate reality is the hurly-burly, the struggle; the metaphysic is an adjunct to clear-headedness in it.

To get back to Ruskin and his objection to all that is not serious. It seems to me that involved in this is a bad metaphysical aesthetic. You have the metaphysic which in defining beauty or the nature of art always drags in the infinite. Particularly in Germany, the land where theories of aesthetics were first created, the romantic aesthetes collated all beauty to an impression of the infinite involved in the identification of our being in absolute spirit. In the least element of beauty we have a total intuition of the whole world. Every artist is a kind of pantheist.

Now it is quite obvious to anyone who holds this kind of theory that any poetry which confines itself to the finite can never be of the highest kind. It seems a contradiction in terms to them. And as in metaphysics you get the last refuge of a prejudice, so it is now necessary for me to refute this.

Here follows a tedious piece of dialectic, but it is necessary for my purpose. I must avoid two pitfalls in discussing the idea of beauty. On the one hand there is the old classical view which is supposed to define it as lying in conformity to certain standard fixed forms; and on the other hand there is the romantic view which drags in the infinite. I have got to find a metaphysic between these two which will enable me to hold consistently that a neo-classic verse of the type I have indicated involves no contradiction in terms. It is essential to prove that beauty may be in small, dry things.

The great aim is accurate, precise and definite description. The first thing is to recognise how extraordinarily difficult this is. It is no mere matter of carefulness; you have to use language, and language is by its very nature a communal thing; that is, it expresses never the exact thing but a compromise—that which is common to you, me and everybody. But each man sees a little differently, and to get out clearly and exactly what he does see, he must have a terrific struggle with language, whether it be with words or the technique of other arts. Language has its own special nature, its own conventions and communal ideas. It is only by a concentrated effort of the mind that you can hold it fixed to your own purpose. I always think that the fundamental process at the back of all the arts might be represented by the following metaphor. You know what I call architect's curves—flat pieces of wood with all different kinds of curvature. By a suitable selection from these you can draw approximately any curve you like. The artist I take to be the man who simply can't bear the idea of that "approximately." He will get the exact curve of what he sees whether it be an object or an idea in the mind. I shall here have to change my metaphor a little to get the process in his mind. Suppose that instead of your curved pieces of wood you have a springy piece of steel of the same types of curvature as the wood. Now the state of tension or concentration of mind, if he is doing anything really good in this struggle against the ingrained habit of the technique, may be represented by a man employing all his fingers to bend the steel out of its own curve and into the exact curve which you want. Something different to what it would assume naturally.

There are then two things to distinguish, first the particular faculty of mind to see things as they really are, and apart from the conventional ways in which you have been trained to see them. This is itself rare enough in all con-

sciousness. Second, the concentrated state of mind, the grip over oneself which is necessary in the actual expression of what one sees. To prevent one falling into the conventional curves of ingrained technique, to hold on through infinite detail and trouble to the exact curve you want. Wherever you get this sincerity, you get the fundamental quality of good art without dragging in infinite or serious.

I can now get at that positive fundamental quality of verse which constitutes excellence, which has nothing to do with infinity, with mystery or with emotions.

This is the point I aim at, then, in my argument. I prophesy that a period of dry, hard, classical verse is coming. I have met the preliminary objection founded on the bad romantic aesthetic that in such verse, from which the infinite is excluded, you cannot have the essence of poetry at all.

After attempting to sketch out what this positive quality is, I can get on to the end of my paper in this way: That where you get this quality exhibited in the realm of the emotions you get imagination, and that where you get this quality exhibited in the contemplation of finite things you get fancy.

In prose as in algebra concrete things are embodied in signs or counters which are moved about according to rules, without being visualised at all in the process. There are in prose certain type situations and arrangements of words, which move as automatically into certain other arrangements as do functions in algebra. One only changes the X's and the Y's back into physical things at the end of the process. Poetry, in one aspect at any rate, may be considered as an effort to avoid this characteristic of prose. It is not a counter language, but a visual concrete one. It is a compromise for a language of intuition which would hand over sensations bodily. It always endeavours to arrest you, and to make you continuously see a physical thing, to prevent you gliding through an abstract process. It chooses fresh epithets and fresh metaphors, not so much because they are new, and we are tired of the old, but because the old cease to convey a physical thing and become abstract counters. A poet says a ship "coursed the seas" to get a physical image, instead of the counter word "sailed." Visual meanings can only be transferred by the new bowl of metaphor; prose is an old pot that lets them leak out. Images in verse are not mere decoration, but the very essence of an intuitive language. Verse is a pedestrian taking you over the ground, prose—a train which delivers you at a destination.

I can now get on to a discussion of two words often used in this connection, "fresh" and "unexpected." You praise a thing for being "fresh." I understand what you mean, but the word besides conveying the truth conveys a secondary something which is certainly false. When you say a poem or drawing is fresh, and so good, the impression is somehow conveyed that the essential element of goodness is freshness, that it is good because it is fresh. Now this is certainly wrong, there is nothing particularly desirable about freshness *per se*. Works of art aren't eggs. Rather the contrary. It is simply an unfortunate necessity due to the nature of language and technique that the only way the element which does constitute goodness, the only way in which its presence can be detected externally, is by freshness. Freshness convinces you, you feel at once that the artist was in an actual physical state. You feel that for a minute. Real communication is so very rare, for plain speech is unconvincing. It is in this rare fact of communication that you get the root of aesthetic pleasure.

I shall maintain that wherever you get an extraordinary interest in a thing, a great zest in its contemplation which carries on the contemplator to accurate description in the sense of the word accurate I have just analysed, there you have sufficient justification for poetry. It must be an intense zest which heightens a thing out of the level of prose. I am using contemplation here just in the same way that Plato used it, only applied to a different subject; it is a detached interest. "The object of aesthetic contemplation is something framed apart by itself and regarded without memory or expectation, simply as being itself, as end not means, as individual not universal."

To take a concrete example. I am taking an extreme case. If you are walking behind a woman in the street, you notice the curious way in which the skirt rebounds from her heels. If that peculiar kind of motion becomes of such interest to you that you will search about until you can get the exact epithet which hits it off, there you have a properly aesthetic emotion. But

it is the zest with which you look at the thing which decides you to make the effort. In this sense the feeling that was in Herrick's mind when he wrote "the tempestuous petticoat" was exactly the same as that which in bigger and vaguer matters makes the best romantic verse. It doesn't matter an atom that the emotion produced is not of dignified vagueness, but on the contrary amusing; the point is that exactly the same activity is at work as in the highest verse. That is the avoidance of conventional language in order to get the exact curve of the thing.

I have still to show that in the verse which is to come, fancy will be the necessary weapon of the classical school. The positive quality I have talked about can be manifested in ballad verse by extreme directness and simplicity, such as you get in "On Fair Kirkconnel Lea." But the particular verse we are going to get will be cheerful, dry and sophisticated, and here the necessary weapon of the positive quality must be fancy.

Subject doesn't matter; the quality in it is the same as you get in the more romantic people.

It isn't the scale or kind of emotion produced that decides, but this one fact: Is there any real zest in it? Did the poet have an actually realised visual object before him in which he delighted? It doesn't matter if it were a lady's shoe or the starry heavens.

Fancy is not mere decoration added on to plain speech. Plain speech is essentially inaccurate. It is only by new metaphors, that is, by fancy, that it can be made precise.

When the analogy has not enough connection with the thing described to be quite parallel with it, where it overlays the thing it described and there is a certain excess, there you have the play of fancy—that I grant is inferior to imagination.

But where the analogy is every bit of it necessary for accurate description in the sense of the word accurate I have previously described, and your only objection to this kind of fancy is that it is not serious in the effect it produces, then I think the objection to be entirely invalid. If it is sincere in the accurate sense, when the whole of the analogy is necessary to get out the exact curve of the feeling or thing you want to express —there you seem to me to have the highest verse, even though the subject be trivial and the emotions of the infinite far away.

It is very difficult to use any terminology at all for this kind of thing. For whatever word you use is at once sentimentalised. Take Coleridge's word "vital." It is used loosely by all kinds of people who talk about art, to mean something vaguely and mysteriously significant. In fact, vital and mechanical is to them exactly the same antithesis as between good and bad.

Nothing of the kind; Coleridge uses it in a perfectly definite and what I call dry sense. It is just this: A mechanical complexity is the sum of its parts. Put them side by side and you get the whole. Now vital or organic is merely a convenient metaphor for a complexity of a different kind, that in which the parts cannot be said to be elements as each one is modified by the other's presence, and each one to a certain extent is the whole. The leg of a chair by itself is still a leg. My leg by itself wouldn't be.

Now the characteristic of the intellect is that it can only represent complexities of the mechanical kind. It can only make diagrams, and diagrams are essentially things whose parts are separate one from another. The intellect always analyses—when there is a synthesis it is baffled. That is why the artist's work seems mysterious. The intellect can't represent it. This is a necessary consequence of the particular nature of the intellect and the purposes for which it is formed. It doesn't mean that your synthesis is ineffable, simply that it can't be definitely stated.

Now this is all worked out in Bergson, the central feature of his whole philosophy. It is all based on the clear conception of these vital complexities which he calls "intensive" as opposed to the other kind which he calls "extensive," and the recognition of the fact that the intellect can only deal with the extensive multiplicity. To deal with the intensive you must use intuition.

Now, as I said before, Ruskin was perfectly aware of all this, but he had no such metaphysical background which would enable him to state definitely what he meant. The result is that he has to flounder about in a series of metaphors. A powerfully imaginative mind seizes and combines at the same instant all the important ideas of its poem or picture, and while it works with one of them, it is at the same instant working with and modifying all in their relation to it and never losing sight of their bearings on each other —as the motion of a snake's body goes through all parts at once and its volition acts at the same instant in coils which go contrary ways.

A romantic movement must have an end of the very nature of the thing. It may be deplored, but it can't be helped—wonder must cease to be wonder.

I guard myself here from all the consequences of the analogy, but it expresses at any rate the inevitableness of the process. A literature of wonder must have an end as inevitably as a strange land loses its strangeness when one lives in it. Think of the lost ecstasy of the Elizabethans. "Oh my America, my new found land," think of what it meant to them and of what it means to us. Wonder can only be the attitude of a man passing from one stage to another, it can never be a permanently fixed thing.

Sir Herbert Read

1893–1968

It is not easy to think of another writer in recent years who achieved such great distinction in both the criticism of art and the criticism of literature as Sir Herbert Read. He held important posts in the world of art—he was Assistant Keeper of the Victoria and Albert Museum from 1922 to 1931; he taught fine arts at the Universities of Edinburgh, Liverpool, and London; he was editor of the *Burlington Magazine* from 1933 to 1939; and he wrote a number of influential books about art, particularly modern art, and its place in the social structure: *The Meaning of Art* (1931), *Art Now* (1933), *Art and Industry* (1934), *Art and Society* (1936), *Education through Art* (1943), and *Art and Alienation: The Role of the Artist in Society* (1967). He was equally prolific as a literary critic, and here again he did work of the first order of usefulness not only in exhibiting the literature of the past in its potential relation to present-day needs, but also in teaching the present to look at the work of its own writers with sympathy and understanding. In books like *Reason and Romanticism* (1926 and later reissues), *Wordsworth* (1930, and later reissues), *Coleridge as Critic* (1949), *In Defence of Shelley* (1935), and especially in *The True Voice of Feeling: Studies* in *English Romantic Poetry* (1953), he did more than any other critic to assure a fair appraisal of the Romantic poets in a time that produced some formidable dissenting voices. His studies of literary form—*English Prose Style* (1928), *Phases of English Poetry* (1928), and *Form in Modern Poetry* (1932)—were all reprinted after their original publication. Some of Sir Herbert's longer essays—on Malory, Vauvenargues, Swift, Hawthorne, and Henry James—were brought together in *Collected Essays* (1938; revised edition, *Collected Essays in Literary Criticism,* 1951). *A Coat of Many Colors* (1945) consists of some seventy short essays on a very attractively wide range of subjects. Later collections of essays, on both literature and art, are: *The Tenth Muse: Essays in Criticism* (1957); *A Letter to a Young Painter* (1962); *Poetry and Experience* (1967); *The Cult of Sincerity* (1968).

The chapter from *The Innocent Eye* (1947) reprinted here has something to say about Read's early development as a poet, but it also has something to say (and this has been a primary reason for including it here) about his development as a reader, as a man in whose life literature was to hold an honored and happy place. One further word about *The Innocent Eye* (published in England as *Annals of Innocence and Experience* in 1940 and 1946, and later incorporated in the volume of Read's autobiographical writings called *The Contrary Experience: Autobiographies,* 1963): it is one of the best and most delightful essays in autobiography to have appeared during the Modern period and deserves to be read in its entirety. The opening section describes the author's childhood on a Yorkshire farm, and other chapters describe his experiences as an infantry officer in France and Belgium from 1915 to 1918; still others, like the chapter below, analyze his own spiritual and intellectual development, placing it against the background of the important cultural and aesthetic movements of his time.

Herbert Read: An Introduction to His Work by Various Hands, edited by Henry Treece, was published in 1969.

The Discovery of Poetry

It was not until my seventeenth year that I became conscious of the art of poetry. At school we read and even acted Shakespeare, and there were "recitations" which must have included some verse. But I never read a volume of poems for choice. It was only later, when I began to read for my matriculation, that I also began to listen more intently to the sound of what I was reading: words and phrases would now linger insistently in my mind. At the evening school I attended there was a teacher who had a genuine enthusiasm for his subject; he read aloud to us with feeling and expressiveness. He communicated his pleasure in poetry to at least one of his pupils. About the same time I made the acquaintance of one who was for many years to be my only confidant and my devoted patron. My brother, eighteen months younger than myself, had left school and found employment with a tailor in the city, who bore our family name—even the same Christian name as my brother—and childless himself, henceforth was to take a great interest in all of us. He belonged to a good Quaker family settled for many generations in the Isle of Axholme. Orphaned at an early age, he had been given into the care of two rich and cultured maiden aunts, who gave him a good education and destined him for a post in the British Museum. But at the age of sixteen or so he had suddenly revolted against the smug religious atmosphere in which he was being brought up, and he had run away. After various adventures he had been compelled to take whatever employment he could get, and this happened to be tailoring, a craft for which he had no liking, but which he was to follow for more than forty years with a quiet stoicism. He was a man of small proportions, gentle manners, and in physiognomy bore a close resemblance to the portraits of William Blake. He had two passions —the reading of poetry and the cultivation of flowers. His reading in every direction was wide, and it was in his house that I first made the acquaintance, not only of innumerable volumes of verse, but of the works of writers like Ibsen, Turgenev, Dostoevsky and Chekhov.

Hitherto my reading had been confined to what could be borrowed from the public library, and what I could buy out of an allowance of one shilling a week which I made to myself out of my meagre earnings as a bank-clerk. But now I not only had an enthusiast's library to draw from, but I rarely visited this friend without coming away with a gift of two or three volumes. It was probably to my advantage then that the blessings thus showered on me were indiscriminate. My friend praised with equal zest W. B. Yeats and Fiona Macleod, Browning and William Cullen Bryant, Francis Thompson and

Sir Edwin Arnold. If I failed to share his enthusiasm—as in the case of Emerson—he did not question or complain: he was convinced that I should one day see the light.

I cannot now be certain whether my own first poems preceded this fruitful friendship: I think they did. But I cannot forget the emotion with which my mentor learned for the first time that I was writing verses, and with what eagerness he received my efforts when I offered them for his criticism. His criticism was not very severe, though it did check my absurdities. But for the most part he encouraged me with his praise and was for a long time the only audience I had, but a sufficing one. It is to his memory that I have dedicated my collected poems.

It is difficult to recapture the first access of composition. It descended on me like a frenzy, and a day was not perfect unless it gave birth to a poem. Of one thing I am certain: the breath that first fanned my smouldering tinder was Tennyson's. I soon outgrew Tennyson, and for many years affected to despise him—it was a natural reaction, for we tend to turn on all our adolescent enthusiasms. Now that I have balanced my reactions, and can judge Tennyson with a detached mind, I find that I admire him for qualities which must have appealed, however unconsciously, to my awakening sensibility: for the ease and simplicity of his diction, for a broad if not a very profound intelligence, and for an exact rendering of a special landscape—the watery fens and long dim wolds which were not so remote from my own dales and moors. At times he seems to describe the actual scenes of my own childhood:

> The seven elms, the poplars four,
> That stand beside my father's door,
> . . . . . . the brook that loves
> To purl o'er matted cress and ribbed sand,
> Or dimple in the dark of rushy coves,
> Drawing into his narrow earthen urn,
> In every elbow and turn,
> The filter'd tribute of the rough woodland.[1]

There would be more to say in adequate appreciation of this poet—more to discover, perhaps, of poetic merit than we generally admit; and a very curious personality to analyse. But now I only seek to relate my own sensibility to his, and to explain why he in particular should have been

the reagent in the first poems precipitated from my mind. It would have been much more normal if my enthusiasm at this time had been for Shelley: but the very abstractness of Shelley's poetry kept him at a distance. Shelley, I would now say, demands a degree of intellectual development which I had not reached by the age of seventeen or eighteen. Tennyson had a more objective appeal and was therefore more open to my simple sensibility.

Even so, there were limits to my powers of absorption, and neither then, nor since, could I read the *Idylls of the King*. Romantic as I was, and am, this particular brand of archaism has always been repugnant to me. I hate every kind of literary fustian, every affectation of an earlier style, every exercise or experiment in an old measure. Such a whimsy attitude to the art of writing is impossible to anyone who believes in the immediacy of expression, in the automatism of inspiration, in the creative nature of even poetic evolution: and these are the doctrines of a true romanticism. The rest is dilettantism: not the vital function, but an academic diversion.

The compositions which came to me so easily in these adolescent days were destroyed long ago, and I have no very precise recollection of their nature. They were, I think, mostly short lyrics about flowers, birds, atmospheric moods; the more realistic of them may have attempted to catch something of the poetry of foggy, gas-lit streets, the glow of furnaces by night, the clatter of clogs on the stone pavements. There were no love poems, for my heart was not yet engaged.

It was then that the poetry of William Blake descended on me like an apocalypse. Tennyson had chimed in with my moods, and shown me felicity. Blake shook me to the depths of my awakening mind, scattered the world of my objective vision, and left me floundering in subjective fantasy. I did not, at that time, venture far into the Prophetic Books; but the Songs of Innocence and Experience, and the poems from the Rossetti and Pickering manuscripts, pierced me like gleaming steel, and their meaning was annealed to my mind. Their meaning?—I should rather say their mystery, for many of these poems were not easy to understand, and indeed I did not seek to understand

---

1 From the early "Ode to Memory," lines 56–63.

them. From the beginning I was content with the incantation of a poem, and I still maintain that this is the quality essential to poetry.

Blake kept his ascendancy in my mind for many years—indeed, though I have submitted to many influences and have been fired to more than one enthusiasm in the intervening years, there is no poet with whom to-day I would more readily identify the poetic essence. For me, Blake is absolute. Shakespeare is richer, Milton is more sonorous, Hopkins is more sensuous—one could make many more comparative statements; but Blake has no need of qualifying epithets: he is simply poetic, in imagination and in expression.

A discovery which I then made with some of the same emotional excitement that Blake had aroused was of a contemporary poet. There was published about this time a series of small yellow chapbooks, and in it appeared the first poems of Ralph Hodgson. The poems were in harmony with the archaic style of the production: they seemed to come from a world of gypsies and highwaymen, they were sometimes sentimental, and they had a simple insistent rhythm which haunted the mind:

> Eve with her basket, was
> Deep in the bells and grass,
> Wading in bells and grass
> Up to her knees,
> Picking a dish of sweet
> Berries and plums to eat,
> Down in the bells and grass
> Under the trees.

Ralph Hodgson is a genuine poet, and I think that in spite of his sentimentality and whimsicality he has a permanent place in our literature. But he was the worst, because the most superficial kind of influence. To be influenced by Shakespeare, Milton or Wordsworth cannot do a young poet any harm: at least, it is only a very poor creature who would be influenced by their idiosyncrasies without at the same time being profitably stirred by their profundities. There is nothing profound in the poetry of Ralph Hodgson, and I am far from implying that all poetry should be profound. But just as one would feel a little silly if one found oneself unconsciously imitating the antics or gestures of another man, and tend to blame the other man for having antics and gestures of an imitable

kind, so I feel inclined to criticize Hodgson's verse for its pretty jingle and infectious rhythm. These are qualities to be enjoyed by non-poetic people: the poet must go his own gait.

It is easy to retort that if a poet's genius is strong enough, his diction will be independent enough. But a poet has to undergo a process of birth and growth: he does not discover himself until he has rejected the alternative selves represented by the poetry already existing in the world. Here, perhaps, I am advancing a romantic doctrine. It is possible to conceive of poetry as an established form, and of the poet's duty as merely to add to the general fund. That is the classical conception of the poet. But my conception was, and still is, of poetry as a unique experience: the individual, with his particular moods, emotions, thoughts, trying to express himself integrally, in his own choice of words. It is true that he has to use words which are common to all his countrymen; but there is an infinite number of ways of selecting and combining these words, and from these infinite possibilities one exact, original correspondence of idea and expression must emerge, or the poem will be an affectation and a failure.

To discover what other influences were at work in this early phase of my poetic awakening, I should have to examine the verses themselves, and as I have already related, they no longer exist. But this acquisitive age actually continues until the end of my twentieth year, and for the later stage of it there is the evidence of a small "brochure" published by Elkin Mathews in 1915 and entitled *Songs of Chaos*. An epigraph from Nietzsche—"One must have chaos within one to give birth to a dancing star"—explains the title, but this sentence which I had printed on the title-page really belongs to a later phase of my development, and the poems in the modest little volume have none of the tremendous implications of such a motto. When, in January, 1915, I joined the Army, I was posted to a battalion stationed in Dorset. I had to travel via London and arrived in that city for the first time in my life. I carried, besides my military baggage, a large bundle of poems, and at King's Cross I told the taxi-driver to go to Waterloo via Cork Street. All I knew about Mr. Mathews was that he had been publishing the kind of poetry I was interested in: I had no introduction to him nor any means of obtaining one. However, he received me very kindly in the back of his shop and undertook to consider the publication of my poems if I would pay a reader's fee, which I willingly did. A few weeks later he sent me the reader's report, which was to the effect that though the poems were too slight and imitative to be published in bulk, a small selection that would pass might be made, and he indicated the ones he thought best. I was not so much dashed by his general criticism as angry at the selection he had made. I insisted on making my own selection, and Mr. Mathews published them at my expense—I do not remember what it cost me, but it was not exorbitant. Six months later twenty-two copies had been sold: but I had already regretted my rash and inexperienced venture, and at my request the remainder of the edition was pulped.

This abortive volume has been out of my mind for many years now, but I still possess a copy and I have unearthed it. It has the musty smell of forgotten books, but as I turn its pages I wonder if I have been too harsh with its simple conceits. I reprinted four of the poems in the 1926 edition of my *Collected Poems,* but in 1935 suppressed even these. The intensity with which I wrote some of these poems is still a vivid memory—it was not an intensity of emotion leading to expression, but an emotion generated by the act of creation. The intensity was due to the discovery that an image could be matched with exact words. The triviality of the image did not seem to matter. Even now, with all my literary and critical experience, I cannot be sure that it matters. I cannot be sure, for example, that a poem which now costs me a qualm to quote is not nevertheless a valid poem and therefore a good poem. It was called "A Little Girl":

> *I pluck a daisy here and there—*
> *O many a daisy do I take!*
> *And I string them together in a ring,*
> *But it's seldom the ring doesn't break.*
>
> *O daisies rosy, daisies white!*
> *If I could string them in a ring*
> *They'd make a bonny daisy chain—*
> *O why is a daisy a delicate thing?*

If, as a very childlike youth, I succeeded in evoking the simplicity of a child's outlook, even a child's insight, then the result is valid. It is only sentimental if as an adult I am trying to exploit childish things.

In looking through this booklet (it ran to no more than thirty-seven pages), the only other influence besides those of Blake and Hodgson which I can now discern is that of Yeats:

> *When Niordr arose from the burning deep*
> *And bade the waves no longer weep:—*
> *Niordr arose with a golden harp*
> *And touched the strings that never warp,*
> *Bidding the angry waves be still,*
> *And the Vanir gather to obey his will.*

Niordr and the Vanir are no longer my familiar spirits, but I am reminded that at this time, at the instigation of the friend to whom I already owed so much, I read many of the Northern myths and sagas, and played with the idea of writing a Viking epic. But other influences, and other ambitions, were to intervene.

At the beginning of the Michaelmas Term, in the year 1912, I enrolled myself as a student at the University of Leeds. I was still not very certain of my intentions: ostensibly I was to become a lawyer of some kind, but secretly (it was half a secret to myself) I was determined on a literary career. I already saw myself as a novelist, a dramatist, or perhaps a journalist—the future would decide which. I was conscious of the scrappiness of my general education, and therefore resolved to spend a year in a way which was not strictly utilitarian: I took the first year course for the B.A. degree. The following year I switched over to my proper studies, which I had decided were Law and Economics, and I was rash enough to attempt to take the two degrees (LL.B. and B.Sc. Econ.) simultaneously. I do not think the prescribed limits of these two curricula would have been too much for me; but I never for a day kept within these limits. I was an anomalous figure among my fellow-undergraduates, whose careers were already determined: they were going to be school-teachers, or clergymen, or practical scientists and technicians in the local industries. Not a single soul, so far as I ever discovered, was there for the disinterested purpose of acquiring a "liberal" education. It is true that I too had my purpose; but it was vague and self-selected, and not dependent on a grant or scholarship. I could pick and choose my subjects to suit my own idea of a career; and I did in fact choose my subjects with an abandon which ought undoubtedly to have been restrained. English and French literature, Latin, Logic, Roman Law, Jurisprudence, Common Law, Constitutional Law and History, Political Economy, Social Economics, European History, Geology—the mere list now makes me dizzy. The result was complete mental congestion and overwork. My days were filled with lectures and I read till the small hours every night. But this is not half the toll. I had at the same time been let loose in a library of seemingly infinite dimensions. I used to seat myself at a table in this library in every spare interval between the lectures. By a chance which was almost perverse, the seat to which my instinct first directed me, and which I continued to use whenever I found it free, was sheltered by a high bookcase which contained, like a mountain veined with shining gold, the very names with which my intellectual curiosity was now engaged—Dostoevsky, Ibsen and Nietzsche. I would open my *Gaius* or *Justinian,* Welton's *Logic* or Marshall's *Political Economy;* but soon my eyes would be caught by the tempting titles at my side, and one by one the volumes were drawn out and only the closing bell awakened me from my absorption. With Dostoevsky and Ibsen I was already partly acquainted, but Nietzsche was a new world, and since my discovery of Blake, the most cataclysmic. It was Nietzsche who first introduced me to philosophy—I read far more than I could understand in his pages, but I did not let my ignorance rest. From Nietzsche I passed to Schopenhauer, to Kant, Hegel, Hume, Pascal, Plato—in very much this indiscriminate order. It was as though I had tapped a central exchange of intellectual tendencies; from Nietzsche communications ran in every direction and for at least five years he, and none of my professors or friends, was my real teacher.

These years at the university were thus an orgy of acquisitiveness: what basis of disciplined education had been devised by the university authorities was completely swamped by my own proclivities. It must be remembered that these new universities have no such institution as the tutor—perhaps their greatest failing; and though I could have consulted the lecturers and professors, the very oddness of my position and the indeterminateness of my aims made this, however desirable, not strictly necessary. And this educational machine is so rigid in its workings that any action which is not strictly necessary is almost impossible. I remember that in my second year I did venture to send to the professor of English Literature, F. W. Moorman, two poetic dramas which I had written in North Riding dialect—I ventured to do this because he was a great enthusiast for the dialect, and perhaps the most inspiring teacher in the university. He was completely taken by surprise—though he had, some weeks earlier, been impressed by an essay I had written on Witchcraft and the Elizabethan Drama. It had never occurred to him that one of the hundred odd students who scribbled away taking notes as he lectured should attempt an original composition. He began to take a special interest in me and encouraged me to show him more of my efforts; but then came the war and before I could renew contact with this possible mentor, he had been accidentally drowned whilst bathing.

The experience of these years raises in its acutest form the whole question of disciplined education. Up to the age of fifteen my education had been perhaps more than usually disciplined, but from that age to the present day I have followed my own bent; the order has been of my own devising, and generally the order of my strongest inclinations. This is the kind of education which most authorities find reprehensible. "I hold very strongly," wrote Cardinal Newman in the best of all treatises on the subject, "that the first step in intellectual training is to impress upon a boy's mind the idea of science, method, order, principle, and system; of rule and exception, of richness and harmony. . . . Let him once gain this habit of method, of starting from fixed points, of making his ground good as he goes, of distinguishing what he knows from what he does not know, and I conceive he will be gradually initiated into the largest and truest philosophical views, and will feel nothing but impatience and disgust at the random theories and imposing sophistries and dashing paradoxes, which carry away half-formed and superficial intellects." These words, in which I recognize a large measure of truth, are a complete condemnation of the method of education which I pursued, and yet I am not entirely repentant. Admittedly

I had some good habits: what I read I tended to read thoroughly; I made notes and to the best of my unaided ability made the ground good as I went on my way. Nietzsche is not a starting-point that Newman would have approved—he would almost certainly have included his works among "the random theories and imposing sophistries and dashing paradoxes" which he scorns, and my intellect among the half-formed and superficial which are carried away by such theories and sophistries. Nevertheless, Nietzsche *was* a starting-point and all the circumstances considered, not one which I regret. He gave me vistas which were quite outside the range of formal education; he introduced me to the ferment of contemporary ideas. In his company I knew the excitement of an intellectual adventure, that highest exaltation which only comes when truth is conceived as a fleeting quarry in whose pursuit the whole mind must be engaged.

In my subsequent years I was often to come into contact with great men whose intellects had been formed in the gradual and disciplined manner indicated by Newman. Let me admit that I have always felt in their presence a sense of weakness; but it is the weakness of the runner who has returned from the chase and found the imperturbable god of reason still changeless in his niche. I had felt the earth spinning underneath my feet, and the clouds racing me in the sky; beauty had stirred like an animal in the covert and my senses had been assailed from a thousand directions. The flush on my features was a reflexion of the animation in my mind, where the images were as vivid as nature and as restless as the sea. If my ideal had been a static form, then I should have withered like a wreath at the feet of this impassive god; but my ideal was a labile green shoot, an emergent new world, a manifestation of the unknown in the desert of dead facts.

I have found that most people whose minds have responded to a formal university education are like monoliths. They are bodies at rest. They have acquired during their university years a choice armoury of information, and they assume that it will serve them for the rest of their lives. Many of them sell their classics to the secondhand bookseller before they "come down" from Oxford or Cambridge; or if they keep them, it is for the sake of sentimental associations. They are stored in a glazed bookcase behind the "chesterfield," with a college shield on the wall above and a tobacco-jar on the ledge. In a few years the once proud possessor of a first in Greats will have forgotten all but a few tags of his Greek and Latin, and will be reduced to defending a classical education for its supposed disciplinary virtues. He can boast of having "done" his Plato or his Aristotle, his Aeschylus or his Euripides; but these are names now, mingled with his sentimental recollections of professors and dons. They had not become a part of his life, a continuing influence and ever-present inspiration. They and the whole galaxy of classical poets and philosophers are dead and distant worlds.

There is another side to the argument. Some of these formally educated young men, on leaving the universities, have gone into the Civil Service or business, and have become very efficient administrators. Between their present efficiency and their education there is a very direct relation: not the relation of a vocational training to the vocation pursued (which is much more the ideal of the modern universities and technical colleges), but a relation sanctioned by the intangible virtues of "character"—in Newman's words, "the force, the steadiness, the comprehensiveness and the versatility of intellect, the command over our own powers, the instinctive just estimate of things as they pass before us, which sometimes indeed is a natural gift, but commonly is not gained without much effort and the exercise of years." These are the virtues which are needed in the upper ranks of any social hierarchy—these virtues rather than specialized knowledge or technical skill—and the Civil Service has quite rightly rejected the notion of a particularized training such as the Army, the Navy and the professions require. Its flexibility, its adaptability, its very humanity depend on this paradox in its recruitment.

The ideals of this kind of education are generally summed up in the word "character," though latterly the more equivocal word "leadership" has been used. But administration is not the only function of an educated man, nor is leadership a necessity in a community of free individuals. There is an alternative ideal of education, for which I have always attempted to reserve the word "personality." Character is the product of a disciplined education: discipline inculcates habits of mind as well as of body, and the result is a firm, dependable set of ideas and reactions upon which a definite type of society can be based. A character is not necessarily conservative: rather it is constructive, and in a time of stress or disintegration might well seem revolutionary. It is moral, though its morality is not necessarily conventional. It cultivates a "taste," but this taste is rational rather than aesthetic, retrospective and historical rather than experimental and contemporary.

A personality, on the other hand, is distinguished by immediacy and by what I would call lability, or the capacity to change without loss of integrity. Keats, who discerned the quality in himself, gave it the name of Negative Capability; and in Hamlet Shakespeare depicted the type in all its mutability.

Character is only attained by limitation. The senses, which would otherwise be open to the impact of every phenomenal event, must be canalized, protected by a hard cortex or shell, and only allowed to operate when they have been directed by the conscious will; and it can be argued that sensations and their attendant emotions are all the finer for being thus restricted. But the personality will have none of this arbitrary interference with the natural process of selectivity: the senses are open to every impression which falls upon them, and the mind surrenders to its environment. Admittedly, from a moral and social point of view, there is a danger that such a passive attitude will lead to instability and disintegration. But the values of the personality are neither moral nor social: they are religious or aesthetic. Here the word "religious," put in contrast to "moral," may cause some surprise; but I would be prepared to maintain that the essentially religious experience described by the great mystics of the East as well as the West, and now generally known in modern theology as the Kierkegaardian "instant," the Barthian "crisis" or "leap," is a surrender of the existential being only possible to a personality, a man of negative capability.

To question the values of the personality, therefore, is to question the values of mysticism and of art. The greatest mistake would be to suppose that a society can be based exclusively on one type of human being. Society needs for vitality, and for effective progress, the contrast

and opposition of types, more particularly of these two fundamental types which I have called characters and personalities. The tautness of the social fabric depends on their dialectical counterplay.

It would seem to follow from these considerations that there should be two systems of education, one for character and one for personality. That would obviously be impracticable, and the most we can hope for is an elasticity in the general system which would provide for both types of individual. The present system is directed almost exclusively to the creation of character, and at its best is very successful in this aim. The survival of personality in this system is a matter of chance: sometimes an understanding teacher will give his protection to a boy obviously not made for the mould; but more often the boy revolts and escapes from the system (as Shelley did), or by some chance is never submitted to it —is *privately* educated, as we say. My own case was still more exceptional: I entered the system as a casual and undirected unit, a misfit. I did not consciously reject the system: rather, it rejected me. I played the game, but I did not obey the rules. I did not conform to a regular routine, and before I could be punished for my dilettantism, the war had taken me to another and a more realistic school.

During the whole of this subsequent period I read avidly. Even in the most difficult circumstances—in the most desperate trench warfare— I was never without a book in my pocket. It was necessarily very unsystematic reading, but it included Henry James and Flaubert, Baudelaire and Rimbaud, Plato and Berkeley. But it is not really necessary to isolate this period: I would rather say that the process of self-education was uninterrupted by the war, the only difference being that before and after that event I was better equipped to find or refer to the books of which day by day I became conscious.

* * * * * *

I have not lost sight of the original purpose of this chapter, which was to relate my gradual discovery of the world of poetry. But a divagation has been necessary to show what part was played in the process by my education. I think I have shown that it was mainly negative. When I look back on this period of my life, and when I compare my experience with that of other people, my strongest feeling is one of relief. It is so easy to crush a nascent sensibility, or if not to crush it, then to deform it. The poetic sensibility is especially vulnerable, and especially in England. Socially the poet is despised: for the great majority of people he is merely a comic figure, the butt of *Punch* and the music-halls. Poetry as an art has become a secret and shame-faced activity: people are even shy of being seen reading poetry in a train, whereas the public declamation of poetry, as it was practised even in the nineteenth century, and as it is still practised in Russia, is quite unknown.[2] Attempts to reintroduce the art through the very suitable medium of broadcasting have so far been very disappointing.

If this social opposition to poetry is reinforced by what one might call a process of academic sterilization, it is very difficult to retain any trace of free sensibility. Actually the attempt to reduce an art to materia paedagogii is always fatal: poetry cannot be dissected unless it is first killed. I do not imply, however, that poetry—or art in general—should be excluded from the curriculum of our schools and universities. On the contrary, I think that the arts should play a greater part in education. But they should be treated as arts and not as "subjects," still less as sciences. This is not the place to enlarge on the question, but as a general indication of what I mean, I would say that it is necessary to make a clear separation of the historical and the technical aspects of each art. The history of literature or the history of painting (including, of course, the history of their technical development) would be distinct subjects, taught like the history of

any other aspect of social evolution. But the technique of literature, like the technique of painting, would be encouraged as a practical activity. Poetry and plays would be written, recited or produced, and the creative artist would be elevated above the academic scholar. It would, of course, revolutionize educational standards if marks were to be awarded, or even a degree granted, on the artistic merits of an original composition; but that, I contend, is the only way in which the arts can be brought into organic relation with a vital system of education.

Otherwise, it is better to let the aesthetic impulse develop unaided, as it did in my own case. Once I had become aware of this creative impulse in myself, I needed no encouragement to educate myself in the subject. I was filled with an insatiable curiosity which extended to all the poetry of the past, to the poetry of other languages, and to the poetry of my contemporaries. In a few years I had raced through all the poetry in my own language which I thought likely to appeal to me, and was then eager to discover the poetry of France, of Italy and of Germany. I doubt if I should ever have attempted to learn the languages of these countries but for the curiosity engendered by my poetic impulse. Latin poetry had been almost completely destroyed for me by the education I had received in this subject, but a measure of enjoyment was preserved in poets who by chance had never been "set," such as Catullus and Lucretius. But I must confess that Latin poetry in general has played an insignificant part in my poetic experience. I have excused myself by supposing a lack of sympathy, but this lack may have been due to a deficiency of knowledge. For Greek poetry, however, I have felt much sympathy on the basis of no knowledge at all. I have never had the time, nor perhaps the will, to teach myself Greek, and Greek poetry, in its essential nature, remains unknown to me. I say "in its essential nature" because it is only in translation that I have read the great classics of Greek poetry: and though this may have given me a certain insight into the Greek spirit, it is futile, as I know from my experience with foreign poetry in general, to pretend that my lips have even touched the rim of the hippocrene fountain. I console myself with the thought that I am still far from the age at which Cato first learned the language.

---

2 A few years ago I was one of a group of English poets invited to the Russian Embassy to meet three Russian poets (Lugovskoy, Selvinsky and one whose name I have forgotten). After tea and vodka, we adjourned to a drawing-room where our Russian colleagues recited in turn their own poems, magnificently. Though few, if any, of us knew the language, we were made to feel its music and its passion, and even the meaning penetrated by virtue of the poets' mime and rhetoric. When they had finished, they turned to us and asked us to recite some of our famous English poetry to them. We looked at each other in nervous embarrassment. After much shuffling and modest protestation, an elderly poet began to pipe out Shelley's "Ode to the West Wind" in a high monotonous voice; faltered and broke down. Someone else recited a little poem about a little bird. There were a few other irrelevancies and then we parted, feeling that we had betrayed, not only our country, but also the art for which our country is respected even when all our other qualities are despised. (Read's note)

In this account of my discovery of poetry I have so far not gone beyond Blake and Yeats. I have mentioned Ralph Hodgson, but his influence was short-lived and superficial. The next stage is represented by Donne and Browning among the poets of the past, and by a group of contemporary poets known as the Imagists. Together, these two influences may be said to have completed my poetic education. The years to follow held such surprises as Rimbaud and Apollinaire, Hölderlin and Rilke, but though such poets have deepened my conception of the content of poetry, they have not altered the attitude to the problems of technique which I formed under the influence of the Imagists.

Donne is an influence apart—not in any sense a technical influence, but rather an extension of sensibility, an education in emotional rectitude. The conceits which so disgusted Johnson appealed to me because they were an attempt to bridge the separate worlds of intellect and feeling, and I began to conceive of poetry as an intermediary between these conflicting forces. But it never occurred to me that poets of the twentieth century should use the language and diction of the seventeenth century—they might, with as good reason, dress in the costumes of that period. There was something even in this respect to learn from Donne: he did, after all, refuse to sacrifice his meaning to a conventional ideal of smoothness (which is not the same thing as felicity). Browning's technique I found entirely relevant. He too was occupied by this problem— the expression of intellectual concepts in the language of feeling—though his intelligence was historical and ethical rather than experimental and aesthetic, and his emotions were distorted by the moral conventions of his age. His technique, however, was free: a reaction against the Parnassian polish of Tennyson and Arnold, a return to the rugged exactitude of Donne. Until Hopkins was discovered (in 1918, though odd poems had appeared earlier) Browning was the only English poet of the immediate past who worked as anything like a ferment in the minds of the poets of the decade 1906–1915 (the decisive years in the formation of the modern poetic tradition in England). There was also Yeats, but he did not then appear as of the past: he was one of our contemporaries, himself subject to some of the same influences. But even

Yeats can to a great extent be discounted—his real influence came later, when his later poems grew realistic and political, and as such appealed to a still later generation. Even before the outbreak of the war, we distrusted Yeats's romanticism. Only the Irish could move freely in the Celtic twilight, though the Americans might assimilate it like any other foreign tradition, and it was the Americans among us, particularly Ezra Pound, who paid most respect to it. For the Anglo-Saxons it might be a fashionable craze, but as a poetic style it was racially foreign to us, only to be adopted as a mannerism and an affectation. The war finally killed it. An epigraph which appeared next to the title-page of the first edition of my war-poems, *Naked Warriors*, was intended as a parody of Yeats, and as a cynical expression of my own disillusionment:

War through my soul has driven
its jagged blades:
The riven
dream fades—
So you'd better grieve, heart, in the gathering night,
Grieve, heart, in the loud twilight.

What I wish to insist on is the importance of Browning in the pre-war years. It is only necessary to turn to the poems published by Ezra Pound—"il miglior fabbro" of us all—particularly the volumes *Personae* and *Exultations,* to see that influence predominant. Even when Pound is writing a poem with a Provençal or Romantic theme, it may be given the manner or diction of Browning. The same influence is not absent from the earlier poems of his friend T. S. Eliot.

Mr. Pound, I know, has many other gods— Fenollosa and Rémy de Gourmont, for example —and he is very jealous on their behalf. But I am not writing about critical influences, which were very various, but of direct mentors of the technique and diction of verse. The modification of Browning's influence came from France—from Rimbaud and Laforgue, and from the early verse of Duhamel, Jules Romains, Jean de Bosschère, André Spire and Apollinaire. There was also T. E. Hulme, but by now his five short poems have begun to assume rather too much prominence in the history of this period. They were certainly good textbook examples of imagist technique, but if Hulme had written fifty or a hundred poems as good, we should not have heard so much about them.

This explanation has been long enough, and I must pick up the residue of my own impressions. If Browning was the last of my historical discoveries, it will now be seen how he came to be fused in my imagination with the activities of a contemporary school which was at that time learning from Browning and applying his technique to the expression of a modern sensibility. I had now reached the vanguard of the art for which I had felt an affinity in my own being. Henceforth my discovery of poetry was to be directed by my passionate participation in its immediate destiny. Hitherto I had read for enjoyment and understanding: I was now to read as if I drew in the substance of life itself, creatively manifested in the minds of living poets.

From this experience, which lasted from the year 1913 to 1917, I quickly evolved what I would have called my philosophy of composition. There was a general feeling then that some new philosophy was necessary, much as it had been necessary when Wordsworth and Coleridge published their *Lyrical Ballads* in 1798, and several attempts to formulate one had been made by the young poets for whom I felt such a strong sympathy. The clearest statement of these years is the Preface to *Some Imagist Poets,* an anthology published in 1915 which included the work of Richard Aldington, H. D., F. S. Flint, and D. H. Lawrence. That preface still remains the locus classicus for the doctrines of the imagist school, and since it is not now generally available, I will quote the six "common principles"[3] which it set forth:

1. To use the language of common speech, but to employ always the *exact* word, not the nearly-exact, nor the merely decorative word.

2. To create new rhythms—as the expression of new moods—and not to copy old rhythms, which merely echo old moods. We do not insist upon "free-verse" as the only method of writing poetry. We fight for it as for a principle of liberty. We believe that the individuality of a poet may often be better expressed in free-verse than in conventional forms. In poetry, a new cadence means a new idea.

3. To allow absolute freedom in the choice of subject. It is not good art to write badly about aeroplanes and automobiles; nor is it necessarily bad art to write about the past. We believe passionately in the artistic value of modern life, but we wish to point out that there is nothing so uninspiring nor so old-fashioned as an aeroplane of the year 1911.

4. To present an image (hence the name: "Imagist"). We are not a school of painters, but we believe that poetry should render particulars exactly and not deal in vague generalities, however magnificent and sonorous. It is for this reason that we oppose the cosmic poet, who seems to us to shirk the real difficulties of his art.

5. To produce poetry that is hard and clear, never blurred nor indefinite.

6. Finally, most of us believe that concentration is of the very essence of poetry.

Three years later, in the third number of *Art and Letters,* I published my own "Definitions towards a Modern Theory of Poetry." I began with the following "axioms":

1. Form is determined by the emotion which requires expression.

Corollary: Form is not an unchanging mould into which any emotion can be poured.

2. The poem is an artistic whole demanding strict unity.

3. The criterion of the poem is the quality of the vision expressed, granted that the expression is adequate.

Corollary: Rhyme, metre, cadence, alliteration, are various decorative devices to be used as the vision demands, and are not formal quantities pre-ordained.

I was evidently reading Spinoza at the time, and the whole essay is written in a dry analytical style. Terms like "vision," "emotion," "value," "unity," and "form" are defined with the aid of a psychological jargon which I should now try to avoid; but the essay, differently worded, would still represent my views on the theory of poetry. What interests me now is to find myself criticizing my friends the Imagists. I admitted that they were the only modern school of poets which showed "any clarity of creative intention";

---

3 The best *defence* of these principles is F. S. Flint's Preface to *Otherworld,* a volume of "cadences" published in 1920 (Poetry Bookshop) and dedicated, I am proud to recall, to me. Flint had far more to do with the development of the Imagist school than has generally been acknowledged. (Read's note)

but I criticized them because "in their manifestoes they had renounced the decorative word, but their sea-violets and wild hyacinths tend to become as decorative as the beryls and jades of Oscar Wilde." I also accused them of lacking "that aesthetic selection which is the artist's most peculiar duty"—by which I meant, as far as I can now make out, that they thought any passing mood or emotion worthy of poetic expression— they did not apply an aesthetic (or did I mean intellectual?) judgment to the quality of the emotion itself. I concluded: "Modern England may be 'a nest of singing birds,' but it is well for us to realize that the poem is still rather a primitive affair, and to make it otherwise there is a call for stern artistic devotion. We must shrink from the exotic and the decadent, and from the sheltered garden of cultivated beauties. Beauty is a discipline, demanding all the intensity of a man's intelligence to present clear and undefiled the infinite quality in things. The artist's vision is the supreme value; the expression of it is the supreme difficulty."

This essay must have been written early in 1918, that is to say, before the end of the war, though I cannot remember where or in what circumstances I wrote it. I can look back with amusement on its earnest solemnity now, but I think it reflects something of the contradiction that was being forced on us by our daily experience. We were trying to maintain an abstract aesthetic ideal in the midst of terrorful and inhuman events. In my own case I am certain that this devotion to abstract notions and intellectual reveries saved me from a raw reaction to these events. But as the war went on, year after year, and there seemed no escape from its indignity except death, some compromise between dream and reality became necessary. The only worthy compromise, I even then dimly realized, was a synthesis—some higher reality in which the freedom of the mind and the necessity of experience became reconciled. If I had been older that solution might have been a philosophy; but I was not contemplative enough for that, nor wise enough. I therefore sought the solution in art: in a poetry which would represent my aesthetic ideals and yet at the same time deal with the experience that threatened to overwhelm me. The result was a series of war poems, some of which I afterwards destroyed, but most of which

I published in a small volume to which I gave the title *Naked Warriors*. (Incidentally, I am sure that I had not at that time seen Pollaiuolo's engraving which so perfectly illustrates the title and the epigraph which I put on the title-page: "And there were some that went into the battle naked and unarmed, fighting only with the fervour of their spirit, dying and getting many wounds.") It may seem that this was but a feeble response to such an immense event. In a later chapter I shall discuss my reactions to war in more detail, but on this level of aesthetic response, I would ask the reader to reflect on the millions who were engaged in that conflict and then to examine its poetic aftermath in any of the languages of the nations engaged. It is infinitesimal in quantity and almost negligible in poetic quality. Many years later, in his Introduction to the *Oxford Book of Modern Verse*, Yeats was to offer a reason for this strange disparity—"the same reason that made Arnold withdraw his 'Empedocles on Etna' from circulation; passive suffering is not a theme for poetry"; and for the same reason Yeats decided to exclude war poetry from his anthology. It was a judgment that was to arouse a good deal of resentment among the young poets of to-day, and I am not sure that I myself accept it—at least, not for the reason given. Another sentence in the same paragraph of Yeats's Introduction, though it is metaphorical, seems to me to be nearer the truth of the matter: "When man has withdrawn into the quicksilver at the back of the mirror no great event becomes luminous in his mind. . . ." In other words, the necessary element is the timelapse implicit in Wordsworth's phrase, "recollected in tranquillity," an element of "aesthetic distance." Even passive suffering can be a fit theme for poetry if it is seen objectively enough, against a wide background. The direct expression of suffering is an animal cry; poetry, too, is an animal cry, but of another kind. There is a difference which is the difference between the scream of a slaughtered pig and the song of a nightingale, and this is perhaps the difference between passive suffering and passive joy. But art begins—and I think this was Yeats's meaning— when the joy is purposive, an active sublimation even of suffering and tragedy.

In 1917 and 1918, in the intervals of leave from the Front, I gradually made the acquaintance of the poets whose work I admired—Flint, Aldington, Pound and Eliot—and met other writers with whom I was in sympathy, such as A. R. Orage and P. Wyndham Lewis. Influences which had been literary and indirect now became personal, and the cold communication of the page was exchanged for the intimate give-and-take of conversation. Some of these friendships were to endure without interruption to the present day, some became intermittent, some never developed at all. It is not my intention to discuss my personal relationships in this book, but I cannot avoid a reference to my friendship with Eliot, because it has certainly had a considerable effect on my intellectual development, perhaps just because we are so divergent in origin, education, character and ideals. He has called himself royalist, classicist, and anglo-catholic, whereas I (with qualifications similar to those he made) would call myself anarchist, romanticist and agnostic. A long and uninterrupted friendship has been possible because in spite of these divergences, we have always agreed about things which are perhaps finally more important: the sense of beauty in poetry, the quality of the expression of ideas, and the priority to be given to natural goodness even when the intelligence seems perverse. I think our friendship has a certain general significance, because too much importance, in history and criticism, is given to ideological similarities and not enough to human sympathies. Life, even in its intimate or arcane recesses, is still dialectical.

These friendships no doubt modified my poetic outlook, but I think I may say that by the end of the war I had discovered myself and my style—that is to say, I had made an equation between emotion and image, between feeling and expression. So long as I was true to this equation, I need not be afraid of influences or acquired mannerisms. Poetry was reduced to an instrument of precision. "Reduced" will imply, of course, a lack of bulk: from that time my output of verse was to be severely restricted. But what

I wrote I tended to keep: I no longer destroyed a large part of my writing. Criticism had become innate, composition an instinctive language; and though I am very far from claiming perfection or permanence for the poems I have retained, I do not think it will be necessary for a reader of the future to approach my work with squared shoulders: he can accept or reject me on the instant. By this statement I lay myself open to the charge that there is nothing in my poetry to detain the reader; but that, of course, is not what I mean. One of the essential characteristics of poetry is what Coleridge called "the power of reducing multitude into unity of effect." Whatever the nature of poetry, be it lyrical or dramatic, meditative or philosophical, this unity of effect should exist, and be immediately apparent. If that unity is achieved, the poem has that quality which is possessed by all true works of art—the quality of retaining our interest in spite of familiarity.

Here I will break off this account of my discovery of poetry—"break off" because it is an enterprise which still continues. I am not now likely to modify my own technique, and I have reached that becalmed stage of life, midway between youth and old age, in which the poetic impulse is often dormant. But I still retain the zest, the insatiable thirst for this pellucid essence of experience. All other sensuous experiences are as nothing to this perception of poetic beauty. A few years ago I took my son, then aged about eleven, to an open-air performance of A Midsummer Night's Dream. It was a brilliant sunny day, and everywhere, not least on the green and leafy stage, the atmosphere was gay. But time after time the impact of Shakespeare's words—the words themselves and not their meaning—would send a gush of tears to my eyes, and there was no darkness to hide my paradoxical visage from my neighbours. But they too were absorbed in the play—some in the antics, some in the atmosphere; some few in the cadence of the words that came winged with inexplicable sorrow through the summer air.

David Herbert Lawrence

1885–1930

D. H. Lawrence was born in the Midlands mining district of England, the son of a miner; the outward circumstances of his early life must fairly have resembled those of the miners' families depicted in his works—in *Sons and Lovers,* for instance, or in the story reprinted here, "Odour of Chrysanthemums." His first job was that of teacher; after taking his teaching certificate at Nottingham University College, he taught for a time at the Davidson Road School,

Croydon, in South London, but in this life he felt cramped and stifled. The publication of his early books made it clear that another vocation lay ahead of him, one that would allow him to live in the milder climates that were necessary to his always frail health. His first novel, *The White Peacock* (1911), was followed by others, with a certain regularity: *The Trespasser* (1912); *Sons and Lovers* (1913); *The Rainbow* (1915) (this one seized and banned in England, thus

Lawrence's Final Corrected Draft of "Bavarian Gentians." The manuscript is in The Humanities Research Center, University of Texas. *Used by permission of the Viking Press, Laurence Pollinger Ltd., and the Estate of Mrs. Frieda Lawrence Ravagli.*

cutting Lawrence off from the income he had hoped it would bring); *Women in Love* (1921); *Aaron's Rod* (1922); *Kangaroo* (1923); *St. Mawr* (1925); *The Plumed Serpent* (1926); and *Lady Chatterley's Lover* (1928). His short stories appeared in four principal collections: *The Prussian Officer* (1914), *England, My England* (1922), *The Woman Who Rode Away* (1928), and *The Lovely Lady* (1933).

After his first trip abroad, to Bavaria and Italy in 1912, he and his wife (he married Frieda, Baroness von Richthofen, in 1914) traveled widely—in Germany, Italy, Ceylon, Australia, the United States and Mexico, the south of France and Switzerland—living abroad, particularly in Italy, for long periods. Certain of the qualities that made him a great novelist and poet are responsible for the interest, vivacity, and power of his travel books: *Twilight in Italy* (1916), *Sea and Sardinia* (1921), *Mornings in Mexico* (1927), *Etruscan Places* (1933). *Psychoanalysis and the Unconscious* and its continuation, *Fantasia of the Unconscious* (1923, reprinted in one volume in 1960) are valuable as an explicit statement of some of the positions and beliefs that are worked out in the novels. *Studies in Classic American Literature* (1924 and later reprints), despite its conventional title, is a very lively and unconventional book, revealing a profound insight into the American writers he treats, among them Cooper, Melville, Hawthorne, and Whitman. *Phoenix: The Posthumous Papers of D. H. Lawrence* (1936), which includes the long *Study of Thomas Hardy*, gathers together a wide variety of nonfictional prose: critical papers and reviews, philosophical and psychological essays, sketches about people and places. A further and equally interesting collection of such pieces, *Phoenix II*, consists of uncollected, unpublished, and other prose works, edited by Warren Roberts and Harry T. Moore and was published in 1968.

There have been a number of collections of the poems, the best being the *Complete Poems*, edited by V. da Sola Pinto and Warren Roberts, first published in two volumes in 1964 and now available in a one-volume edition. The stories, including the impressive late novella, *The Man Who Died* (1931), were collected in a single volume in 1934, as *The Tales of D. H. Lawrence*. There is at present a three-volume paperback edition available in this country.

Lawrence died in the south of France, at Vence, Alpes Maritimes, on March 2, 1930. In a biographical note at the end of his edition of *The Letters of D. H. Lawrence* (1932), Aldous Huxley says: "No headstone is over his grave, save a phoenix (which was his own design), done in local stones by a peasant who loved him."

TEXTS: There has never been a shortage of books about Lawrence, but his earlier biographers were too often occupied, consciously or unconsciously, with the task of explaining their own respective relationships with him. More recently, however, critical and biographical studies have gained in clarity of perspective and in the essential seriousness with which they approach Lawrence as a serious writer. *D. H. Lawrence: A Composite Biography*, edited by Edward Nehls (3 vols., 1957–59), is both monumental and indispensable. The letters, originally edited, with a fine introductory essay by Aldous Huxley, still offer perhaps the most direct insight into Lawrence's life and temperament. A new edition, *The Collected Letters of D. H. Lawrence* (2 vols., 1962), which includes hitherto unpublished letters, is edited by Harry T. Moore, author of *The Intelligent Heart: The Story of D. H. Lawrence* (1954). Among the best critical studies—most of them directed primarily at analysis and criticism of the novels, because for recent criticism they constitute the heart of Lawrence's achievement—are the following: Mark Spilka, *The Love Ethic of D. H. Lawrence* (1955); F. R. Leavis, *D. H. Lawrence: Novelist* (1955); Mary Freeman, *D. H. Lawrence: A Basic Study of His Ideas* (1955); Graham Hough, *The Dark Sun: A Study of D. H. Lawrence* (1956); Eugene Goodheart, *The Utopian Vision of D. H. Lawrence* (1963); Julian Moynihan, *The Deed of Life: The Novels and Tales of D. H. Lawrence* (1963); and H. M. Daleskie, *The Forked Flame: A Study of D. H. Lawrence* (1965). *D. H. Lawrence: A Collection of Critical Essays*, edited by Mark Spilka (1963), presents excellent essays on many phases of Lawrence's work.

Return to Bestwood[1]

I came home to the Midlands for a few days, at the end of September. Not that there is any home, for my parents are dead. But there are my sisters, and the district one calls home; that mining district between Nottingham and Derby.

It always depresses me to come to my native district. Now I am turned forty, and have been more or less a wanderer for nearly twenty years, I feel more alien, perhaps, in my home place than anywhere else in the world. I can feel at ease in Canal Street, New Orleans, or in the Avenue Madero, in Mexico City, or in George Street, Sydney, in Trincomallee Street, Kandy, or in Rome or Paris or Munich or even London. But in Nottingham Road, Bestwood, I feel at once a devouring nostalgia and an infinite repulsion. Partly I want to get back to the place as it was when I was a boy, and I waited so long to be

---

1 From *Phoenix II: D. H. Lawrence,* collected and edited by Warren Roberts and Harry T. Moore (1968).

served in the Co-op. I remember our Co-op number, 1553A.L., better than the date of my birth—and when I came out hugging a string net of groceries. There was a little hedge across the road from the Co-op then, and I used to pick the green buds which we called bread-and-cheese. And there were no houses in Gabes Lane. And at the corner of Queen Street, Butcher Bob was huge and fat and taciturn.

Butcher Bob is long dead, and the place is all built up. I am never quite sure where I am, in Nottingham Rd. Walker Street is not very much changed though because the ash tree was cut down when I was sixteen, when I was ill. The houses are still only on one side the street, the fields on the other. And still one looks across at the amphitheatre of hills which I still find beautiful, though there are new patches of reddish houses, and a darkening of smoke. Crich is still on the sky line to the west, and the woods of Annesley to the north, and Coney Grey Farm still lies in front. And there is still a certain glamour about the country-side. Curiously enough, the more motor-cars and tram-cars and omnibuses there are rampaging down the roads, the more the country retreats into its own isolation, and becomes more mysteriously inaccessible.

When I was a boy, the whole population lived very much more *with* the country. Now, they rush and tear along the roads, and have joy-rides and outings, but they never seem to touch the reality of the country-side. There are many more people, for one thing: and all these new contrivances, for another.

The country seems, somehow, fogged over with people, and yet not really touched. It seems to lie back, away, unreached and asleep. The roads are hard and metalled and worn with everlasting rush. The very field-paths seem wider and more trodden and squalid. Wherever you go, there is the sordid sense of humanity.

And yet the fields and the woods in between the roads and paths sleep as in a heavy, weary dream, disconnected from the modern world.

This visit, this September, depresses me peculiarly. The weather is soft and mild, mildly sunny in that hazed, dazed, uncanny sunless sunniness which makes the Midlands peculiarly fearsome to me. I cannot, cannot accept as sunshine this thin luminous vaporousness which passes as a fine day in the place of my birth. Oh

Phœbus Apollo! Surely you have turned your face aside!

But the special depression this time is the great coal strike, still going on. In house after house, the families are now living on bread and margarine and potatoes. The colliers get up before dawn, and are away into the last recesses of the country-side, scouring the country for blackberries, as if there were a famine. But they will sell the blackberries at fourpence a pound, and so they'll be fourpence in pocket.

But when I was a boy, it was utterly *infra dig.* for a miner to be picking blackberries. He would never have demeaned himself to such an unmanly occupation. And as to walking home with a little basket—he would almost rather have committed murder. The children might do it, or the women, or even the half grown youths. But a married, manly collier!

But nowadays, their pride is in their pocket, and the pocket has a hole in it.

It is another world. There are policemen everywhere, great big strange policemen with faces like a leg of mutton. Where they come from, heaven only knows: Ireland or Scotland, presumably, for they are no Englishmen. And they exist, along the country-side, in thousands. The people call them "blue-bottles," and "meat-flies." And you can hear a woman call across the street to another: "Seen any blow-flies about?"—Then they turn to look at the alien policemen, and laugh shrilly.

And this in my native place! Truly, one no longer knows the palm of his own hand. When I was a boy, we had our own police sergeant, and two young constables. And the women would as leave have thought of calling Sergeant Mellor a "blue-bottle" as calling Queen Victoria one. The Sergeant was a quiet, patient man, who spent his life trying to keep people out of trouble. He was another sort of shepherd, and the miners and their children were a flock to him. The women had the utmost respect for him.

But the women seem to have changed most in this, that they have no respect for anything. There was a scene in the market-place yesterday, a Mrs Hufton and a Mrs Rowley being taken off to court to be tried for insulting and obstructing the police. The police had been escorting the black-legs from the mines, after a so-called day's work, and the women had made the usual row. They were two women from decent homes. In the past they would have died of shame, at having to go to court. But now, not at all.

They had a little gang of women with them in the market-place, waving red flags and laughing loudly and using occasional bad language. There was one, the decent wife of the post-man. I had known her and played with her as a girl. But she was waving her red flag, and cheering as the motor-bus rolled up.

The two culprits got up, hilariously, into the bus.

"Good luck, old girl! Let 'em have it! Give it the blue-bottles in the neck! Tell 'em what for! Three cheers for Bestwood! Strike while the iron's hot, girls!"

"So long! So long, girls! See you soon! Merry home coming, what, eh?"

"Have a good time, now! Have a good time! Stick a pin in their fat backsides, if you can't move 'em any other road. We s'll be thinking of you!"

"So long! So long! See you soon! Who says Walker!"

"E-eh! E-eh!"

The bus rolled heavily off, with the shouting women, amid the strange hoarse cheering of the women in the little market-place. The draughty little market-place where my mother shopped on Friday evenings, in her rusty little black bonnet, and where now a group of decent women waved little red flags and hoarsely cheered two women going to court!

O mamma mia!—as the Italians say. My dear mother, your little black bonnet would fly off your head in horrified astonishment, if you saw it now. You were so keen on progress: a decent working man, and a good wage! You paid my father's union pay for him, for so many years! You believed so firmly in the Co-op! You were at your Women's Guild when they brought you word your father, the old tyrannus, was dead! At the same time, you believed so absolutely in the ultimate benevolence of all the masters, of all the upper classes. One had to be grateful to them, after all!

Grateful! You can have your cake and eat it, while the cake lasts. When the cake comes to an end, you can hand on your indigestion. Oh my dear and virtuous mother, who believed in a Utopia of goodness, so that your own people were never quite good enough for you—not even the spoiled delicate boy, myself!—oh my dear and virtuous mother, behold the indigestion we have inherited, from the cake of perfect goodness you baked too often! Nothing was good enough! We must all rise into the upper classes! Upper! Upper! Upper!

Till at last the boots are all uppers, the sole is worn out, and we yell as we walk on stones.

My dear, dear mother, you were so tragic, because you had nothing to be tragic about! We, on the other side, having a moral and social indigestion that would raise the wind for a thousand explosive tragedies, let off a mild crepitus ventris and shout: Have a good time, old girl! Enjoy yourself, old lass!

Never-the-less, we have all of us "got on." The reward of goodness, in my mother's far-off days, less than twenty years ago, was that you should "get on." *Be good, and you'll get on in life.*

Myself, a snotty-nosed little collier's lad, I call myself at home when I sit in a heavy old Cinque-cento Italian villa, of which I rent only half, even then—surely I can be considered to have "got-on." When I wrote my first book, and it was going to be published—sixteen years ago—and my mother was dying, a fairly well-known editor wrote to my mother and said, of me: "By the time he is forty, he will be riding in his carriage."

To which my mother is supposed to have said, sighing, "Ay, if he lives to be forty!

Well, I am forty-one, so there's one in the eye for that sighing remark. I was always weak in health, but my life was strong. Why had they all made up their minds that I was to die? Perhaps they thought I was too good to live. Well, in that case they were had!

And when I was forty, I was not even in my own motor-car. But I did drive my own two horses in a light buggy (my own) on a little ranch (also my own, or my wife's, through me) away on the western slope of the Rocky Mountains. And sitting in my corduroy trousers and blue shirt, calling: "Get up Aaron! *Ambrose!*" then I thought of Justin Harrison's prophecy. Oh Oracle of Delphos! Oracle of Dodona! "Get up, Ambrose!" Bump! went the buggy over a rock, and the pine-needles slashed my face! See him driving his carriage, at forty!—driving it pretty badly too! Put the brake on!

So I suppose I've got on, snotty-nosed little

collier's lad, of whom most of the women said: "He's a *nice* little lad!" They don't say it now: if ever they say anything, which is doubtful. They've forgotten me entirely.

But my sister's "getting on" is much more concrete than mine. She is almost on the spot. Within six miles of that end dwelling in The Breach, which is the house I first remember—an end house of hideous rows of miners' dwellings, though I loved it, too—stands my sister's new house, "a lovely house!"—and her garden: "I wish mother could see my garden in June!"

And if my mother did see it, what then? It is wonderful the flowers that bloom in these Midlands, in June. A northern Persephone seems to steal out from the Plutonic, coal-mining depths and give a real hoot of blossoms. But if my mother *did* return from the dead, and see that garden in full bloom, and the glass doors open from the hall of the new house, what then? Would she then say: It is reached! Consummatum est!

When Jesus gave up the ghost, he cried: It is finished. Consummatum est! But was it? And if so, what? What was it that was consummate?

Likewise, before the war, in Germany I used to see advertised in the newspapers a moustache-lifter, which you tied on at night and it would make your mustache stay turned up, like the immortal moustache of Kaiser Wilhelm II, whose moustache alone is immortal. This moustache-lifter was called: Es ist erreicht! In other words: It is reached! Consummatum est!

Was it? Was it reached? With the moustache-lifter?

So the ghost of my mother, in my sister's garden. I see it each time I am there, bending over the violas, or looking up at the almond tree. Actually an almond tree! And I always ask, of the grey-haired, good little ghost: "Well what of it, my dear? What is the verdict?"

But she never answers, though I press her:

"Do look at the house, my dear! Do look at the tiled hall, and the rug from Mexico, and the brass from Venice, seen through the open doors, beyond the lilies and the carnations of the lawn beds! Do look! And do look at me, and see if I'm not a gentleman! Do say that I'm almost upper class!"

But the dear little ghost says never a word.

"Do say we've got on! Do say, we've ar-

rived. Do say, it is reached, es ist erreicht, consummatum est!"

But the little ghost turns aside, she knows I am teasing her. She gives me one look, which is a look I know, and which says: "I shan't tell you, so you can't laugh at me. You must find out for yourself." And she steals away, to her place, wherever it may be.—"In my father's house are many mansions. If it were not so, I would have told you."

The black-slate roofs beyond the wind-worn young trees at the end of the garden are the same thick layers of black roofs of blackened brick houses, as ever. There is the same smell of sulphur from the burning pit bank. Smuts fly on the white violas. There is a harsh sound of machinery. Persephone couldn't quite get out of hell, so she let Spring fall from her lap along the upper workings.

But no! There are no smuts, there is even no smell of the burning pit bank. They cut the bank, and the pits are not working. The strike has been going on for months. It is September, but there are lots of roses on the lawn beds.

"Where shall we go this afternoon! Shall we go to Hardwick?"

Let us go to Hardwick. I have not been for twenty years. Let us go to Hardwick:

Hardwick Hall
More window than wall.

Built in the days of good Queen Bess, by that other Bess, termagant and tartar, Countess of Shrewsbury.

Butterley, Alfreton, Tibshelf—what was once the Hardwick district is now the Notts-Derby coal area. The country is the same, but scarred and splashed all over with mines and mining settlements. Great houses loom from hill-brows, old villages are smotherd in rows of miners' dwellings, Bolsover Castle rises from the mass of the colliery village of Bolsover.—Böwser, we called it, when I was a boy.

Hardwick is shut. On the gates, near the old inn, where the atmosphere of the old world lingers perfect, is a notice: "This park is closed to the public and to all traffic until further notice. No admittance."

Of course! The strike! They are afraid of vandalism.

Where shall we go? Back into Derbyshire, or to Sherwood Forest.

Turn the car. We'll go on through Chesterfield. If I can't ride in my own carriage, I can still ride in my sister's motor-car.

It is a still September afternoon. By the ponds in the old park, we see colliers slowly loafing, fishing, poaching in spite of all notices.

And at every lane end there is a bunch of three or four policemen, "blue-bottles," big, big-faced, stranger policemen. Every field path, every stile seems to be guarded. There are great pits, coal mines, in the fields. And at the end of the paths coming out of the field from the colliery, along the high-road, the colliers are squatted on their heels, on the wayside grass, silent and watchful. Their faces are clean, white, and all the months of the strike have given them no colour and no tan. They are pit-bleached. They squat in silent remoteness, as if in the upper galleries of hell. And the policemen, alien, stand in a group near the stile. Each lot pretends not to be aware of the others.

It is past three. Down the path from the pit come straggling what my little nephew calls "the dirty ones." They are the men who have broken strike, and gone back to work. They are not many: their faces are black, they are in their pit-dirt. They linger till they have collected, a group of a dozen or so "dirty ones," near the stile, then they trail off down the road, the policemen, the alien "blue-bottles," escorting them. And the "clean ones," the colliers still on strike, squat by the wayside and watch without looking. They say nothing. They neither laugh nor stare. But here they are, a picket, and with their bleached faces they see without looking, and they register with the silence of doom, squatted down in rows by the road-side.

The "dirty ones" straggle off in the lurching, almost slinking walk of colliers, swinging their heavy feet and going as if the mine-roof were still over their heads. The big blue policemen follow at a little distance. No voice is raised: nobody seems aware of anybody else. But there is the silent, hellish registering in the consciousness of all three groups, clean ones, dirty ones and blue-bottles.

So it is now all the way into Chesterfield, whose crooked spire lies below. The men who have gone back to work—they seem few, indeed —are lurching and slinking in quiet groups, home down the high-road, the police at their heels. And the pickets, with bleached faces, squat and lean and stand, in silent groups, with a certain pale fatality, like Hell, upon them.

And I, who remember the homeward-trooping of the colliers when I was a boy, the ringing of the feet, the red mouths and the quick whites of the eyes, the swinging pit bottles, and the strange voices of men from the underworld calling back and forth, strong and, it seemed to me, gay with the queer, absolved gaiety of miners—I shiver, and feel I turn into a ghost myself. The colliers were noisy, lively, with strong underworld voices such as I have never heard in any other men, when I was a boy. And after all, it is not so long ago. I am only forty-one.

But after the war, the colliers went silent: after 1920. Till 1920 there was a strange power of life in them, something wild and urgent, that one could hear in their voices. They were always excited, in the afternoon, to come up above-ground: and excited, in the morning, at going down. And they called in the darkness with strong, strangely evocative voices. And at the little local foot-ball matches, on the damp, dusky Saturday afternoons of winter, great, full-throated cries came howling from the foot-ball field, in the zest and the wildness of life.

But now, the miners go by to the foot-ball match in silence like ghosts, and from the field comes a poor, ragged shouting. These are the men of my own generation, who went to the board school with me. And they are almost voiceless. They go to the welfare clubs, and drink with a sort of hopelessness.

I feel I hardly know any more the people I come from, the colliers of the Erewash Valley district. They are changed, and I suppose I am changed. I find it so much easier to live in Italy. And they have got a new kind of shallow consciousness, all newspaper and cinema, which I am not in touch with. At the same time, they have, I think, an underneath ache and heaviness very much like my own. It must be so, because when I see them, I feel it so strongly.

They are the only people who move me strongly, and with whom I feel myself connected in deeper destiny. It is they who are, in some peculiar way, "home" to me. I shrink away from them, and I have an acute nostalgia for them.

And now, this last time, I feel a doom over the country, and a shadow of despair over the hearts of the men, which leaves me no rest. Because the same doom is over me, wherever I go, and the same despair touches my heart.

Yet it is madness to despair, while we still have the course of destiny open to us.

One is driven back to search one's own soul, for a way out into a new destiny.

A few things I know, with inner knowledge.

I know that what I am struggling for is life, more life ahead, for myself and the men who will come after me: struggling against fixations and corruptions.

I know that the miners at home are men very much like me, and I am very much like them: ultimately, we want the same thing. I know they are, in the life sense of the word, good.

I know that there is ahead the mortal struggle for property.

I know that the ownership of property has become, now, a problem, a religious problem. But it is one we can solve.

I know I want to own a few things: my personal things. But I also know I want to own no more than those: I don't want to own a house, nor land, nor a motor-car, nor shares in anything. I don't want a fortune—not even an assured income.

At the same time, I don't want poverty and hardship. I know I need enough money to leave me free in my movements, and I want to be able to earn that money without humiliation.

I know that most decent people feel very much the same in this respect: and the indecent people must, in their indecency, be subordinated to the decent.

I know that we could, if we would, establish little by little a true democracy in England: we could nationalise the land and industries and means of transport, and make the whole thing work infinitely better than at present, *if we would*. It all depends on the spirit in which the thing is done.

I know we are on the brink of a class war.

I know we had all better hang ourselves at once, than enter on a struggle which shall be a fight for the ownership or non-ownership of property, pure and simple, and nothing beyond.

I know the ownership of property is a problem that may have to be fought out. But beyond the fight must lie a new hope, a new beginning.

I know our vision of life is all wrong. We must be prepared to have a new conception of what it means, *to live*. And everybody should try to help to build up this new conception, and everybody should be prepared to destroy, bit by bit, our old conception.

I know that man cannot live by his own will alone. With his soul, he must search for the sources of the power of life. It is life we want.

I know that where there is life, there is essential beauty. Genuine beauty, which fills the soul, is an indication of life, and genuine ugliness, which blasts the soul, is an indication of morbidity.—But prettiness is opposed to beauty.

I know that, first and foremost, we must be sensitive to life and to its movements. If there is power, it must be sensitive power.

I know that we must look after the quality of life, not the quantity. Hopeless life should be put to sleep, the idiots and the hopeless sick and the true criminal. And the birth-rate should be controlled.

I know we must take up the responsibility for the future, now. A great change is coming, and must come. What we need is some glimmer of a vision of a world that shall be, beyond the change. Otherwise we shall be in for a great débâcle.

What is alive, and open, and active, is good. All that makes for inertia, lifelessness, dreariness, is bad. This is the essence of morality.

What we should live for is life and the beauty of aliveness, imagination, awareness, and contact. To be perfectly alive is to be immortal.

I know these things, along with other things. And it is nothing very new to know these things. The only new thing would be to act on them.

And what is the good of saying these things, to men whose whole education consists in the fact that twice two are four?—which, being interpreted, means that twice tuppence is fourpence. All our education, the whole of it, is formed upon this little speck of dust.

Odour of Chrysanthemums

The small locomotive engine, Number 4, came clanking, stumbling down from Selston with seven full waggons. It appeared round the corner with loud threats of speed, but the colt that it startled from among the gorse, which still flickered indistinctly in the raw afternoon, outdistanced it at a canter. A woman, walking up the railway line to Underwood, drew back into the hedge, held her basket aside, and watched the footplate of the engine advancing. The trucks thumped heavily past, one by one, with slow inevitable movement, as she stood insignificantly trapped between the jolting black waggons and the hedge; then they curved away towards the coppice where the withered oak leaves dropped noiselessly, while the birds, pulling at the scarlet hips beside the track, made off into the dusk that had already crept into the spinney. In the open, the smoke from the engine sank and cleaved to the rough grass. The fields were dreary and forsaken, and in the marshy strip that led to the whimsey, a reedy pit-pond, the fowls had already abandoned their run among the alders, to roost in the tarred fowl-house. The pit-bank loomed up beyond the pond, flames like red sores licking its ashy sides, in the afternoon's stagnant light. Just beyond rose the tapering chimneys and the clumsy black headstocks of Brinsley Colliery. The two wheels were spinning fast up against the sky, and the winding-engine rapped out its little spasms. The miners were being turned up.

The engine whistled as it came into the wide bay of railway lines beside the colliery, where rows of trucks stood in harbour.

Miners, single, trailing and in groups, passed like shadows diverging home. At the edge of the ribbed level of sidings squat a low cottage, three steps down from the cinder track. A large bony vine clutched at the house, as if to claw down the tiled roof. Round the bricked yard grew a few wintry primroses. Beyond, the long garden sloped down to a bush-covered brook course. There were some twiggy apple trees, winter-crack trees, and ragged cabbages. Beside the path hung dishevelled pink chrysanthemums, like pink cloths hung on bushes. A woman came stooping out of the felt-covered fowl-house, halfway down the garden. She closed and padlocked the door, then drew herself erect, having brushed some bits from her white apron.

She was a tall woman of imperious mien, handsome, with definite black eyebrows. Her smooth black hair was parted exactly. For a few moments she stood steadily watching the miners as they passed along the railway: then she turned towards the brook course Her face was calm and set, her mouth was closed with disillusionment. After a moment she called:

"John!" There was no answer. She waited, and then said distinctly:

"Where are you?"

"Here!" replied a child's sulky voice from among the bushes. The woman looked piercingly through the dusk.

"Are you at that brook?" she asked sternly.

For answer the child showed himself before the raspberry-canes that rose like whips. He was a small, sturdy boy of five. He stood quite still, defiantly.

"Oh!" said the mother conciliated. "I thought you were down at that wet brook—and you remember what I told you—"

The boy did not move or answer.

"Come, come on in," she said more gently, "it's getting dark. There's your grandfather's engine coming down the line!"

The lad advanced slowly, with resentful, taciturn movement. He was dressed in trousers and waistcoat of cloth that was too thick and hard for the size of the garments. They were evidently cut down from a man's clothes.

As they went slowly towards the house he tore at the ragged wisps of chrysanthemums and dropped the petals in handfuls along the path.

"Don't do that—it does look nasty," said his mother. He refrained, and she, suddenly pitiful, broke off a twig with three or four wan flowers and held them against her face. When mother and son reached the yard her hand hesitated, and instead of laying the flower aside, she pushed it in her apron-band. The mother and son stood at the foot of the three steps looking across the bay of lines at the passing home of the miners. The trundle of the small train was imminent. Suddenly the engine loomed past the house and came to a stop opposite the gate.

The engine-driver, a short man with round grey beard, leaned out of the cab high above the woman.

"Have you got a cup of tea?" he said in a cheery, hearty fashion.

It was her father. She went in, saying she would mash. Directly, she returned.

"I didn't come to see you on Sunday," began the little grey-bearded man.

"I didn't expect you," said his daughter.

The engine-driver winced; then, reassuming his cheery, airy manner, he said:

"Oh, have you heard then? Well, and what do you think—?"

"I think it is soon enough," she replied.

At her brief censure the little man made an impatient gesture, and said coaxingly, yet with dangerous coldness:

"Well, what's a man to do? It's no sort of life for a man of my years, to sit at my own hearth like a stranger. And if I'm going to marry again it may as well be soon as late—what does it matter to anybody?"

The woman did not reply, but turned and went into the house. The man in the engine-cab stood assertive, till she returned with a cup of tea and a piece of bread and butter on a plate. She went up the steps and stood near the footplate of the hissing engine.

"You needn't 'a brought me bread and butter," said her father. "But a cup of tea"—he sipped appreciatively—"it's very nice." He sipped for a moment or two, then: "I hear as Walter's got another bout on," he said.

"When hasn't he?" said the woman bitterly.

"I heered tell of him in the 'Lord Nelson' braggin' as he was going to spend that b— afore he went: half a sovereign that was."

"When?" asked the woman.

"A' Sat'day night—I know that's true."

"Very likely," she laughed bitterly. "He gives me twenty-three shillings."

"Aye, it's a nice thing, when a man can do nothing with his money but make a beast of himself!" said the grey-whiskered man. The woman turned her head away. Her father swallowed the last of his tea and handed her the cup.

"Aye," he sighed, wiping his mouth. "It's a settler, it is—"

He put his hand on the lever. The little engine strained and groaned, and the train rumbled towards the crossing. The woman again looked across the metals. Darkness was settling over the spaces of the railway and trucks: the miners, in grey sombre groups, were still passing home. The winding-engine pulsed hurriedly, with brief pauses. Elizabeth Bates looked at the dreary flow of men, then she went indoors. Her husband did not come.

The kitchen was small and full of firelight; red coals piled glowing up the chimney mouth. All the life of the room seemed in the white, warm hearth and the steel fender reflecting the red fire. The cloth was laid for tea; cups glinted in the shadows. At the back, where the lowest stairs protruded into the room, the boy sat struggling with a knife and a piece of whitewood. He was almost hidden in the shadow. It was half-past four. They had but to await the father's coming to begin tea. As the mother watched her son's sullen little struggle with the wood, she saw herself in his silence and pertinacity; she saw the father in her child's indifference to all but himself. She seemed to be occupied by her husband. He had probably gone past his home, slunk past his own door, to drink before he came in, while his dinner spoiled and wasted in waiting. She glanced at the clock, then took the potatoes to strain them in the yard. The garden and fields beyond the brook were closed in uncertain darkness. When she rose with the saucepan, leaving the drain steaming into the night behind her, she saw the yellow lamps were lit along the high road that went up the hill away beyond the space of the railway lines and the field.

Then again she watched the men trooping home, fewer now and fewer.

Indoors the fire was sinking and the room was dark red. The woman put her saucepan on the hob, and set a batter pudding near the mouth of the oven. Then she stood unmoving. Directly, gratefully, came quick young steps to the door. Someone hung on the latch a moment, then a little girl entered and began pulling off her outdoor things, dragging a mass of curls, just ripening from gold to brown, over her eyes with her hat.

Her mother chid her for coming late from school, and said she would have to keep her at home the dark winter days.

"Why, mother, it's hardly a bit dark yet. The lamp's not lighted, and my father's not home."

"No, he isn't. But it's a quarter to five! Did you see anything of him?"

The child became serious. She looked at her mother with large, wistful blue eyes.

"No, mother, I've never seen him. Why?

Has he come up an' gone past, to Old Brinsley? He hasn't, mother, 'cos I never saw him."

"He'd watch that," said the mother bitterly, "he'd take care as you didn't see him. But you may depend upon it, he's seated in the 'Prince o' Wales.' He wouldn't be this late."

The girl looked at her mother piteously.

"Let's have our teas, mother, should we?" said she.

The mother called John to table. She opened the door once more and looked out across the darkness of the lines. All was deserted: she could not hear the winding-engines.

"Perhaps," she said to herself, "he's stopped to get some ripping done."

They sat down to tea. John, at the end of the table near the door, was almost lost in the darkness. Their faces were hidden from each other. The girl crouched against the fender slowly moving a thick piece of bread before the fire. The lad, his face a dusky mark on the shadow, sat watching her who was transfigured in the red glow.

"I do think it's beautiful to look in the fire," said the child.

"Do you?" said the mother. "Why?"

"It's so red, and full of little caves—and it feels so nice, and you can fair smell it."

"It'll want mending directly," replied her mother, "and then if your father comes he'll carry on and say there never is a fire when a man comes home sweating from the pit. A public-house is always warm enough."

There was silence till the boy said complainingly: "Make haste, our Annie."

"Well, I am doing! I can't make the fire do it no faster, can I?"

"She keeps wafflin' it about so's to make 'er slow," grumbled the boy.

"Don't have such an evil imagination, child," replied the mother.

Soon the room was busy in the darkness with the crisp sound of crunching. The mother ate very little. She drank her tea determinedly, and sat thinking. When she rose her anger was evident in the stern unbending of her head. She looked at the pudding in the fender, and broke out:

"It is a scandalous thing as a man can't even come home to his dinner! If it's crozzled up to a cinder I don't see why I should care. Past his very door he goes to get to a public-house, and here I sit with his dinner waiting for him—"

She went out. As she dropped piece after piece of coal on the red fire, the shadows fell on the walls, till the room was almost in total darkness.

"I canna see," grumbled the invisible John. In spite of herself, the mother laughed.

"You know the way to your mouth," she said. She set the dustpan outside the door. When she came again like a shadow on the hearth, the lad repeated, complaining sulkily:

"I canna see."

"Good gracious!" cried the mother irritably, "you're as bad as your father if it's a bit dusk!"

Nevertheless she took a paper spill from a sheaf on the mantelpiece and proceeded to light the lamp that hung from the ceiling in the middle of the room. As she reached up, her figure displayed itself just rounding with maternity.

"Oh, mother—!" exclaimed the girl.

"What?" said the woman, suspended in the act of putting the lamp glass over the flame. The copper reflector shone handsomely on her, as she stood with uplifted arm, turning to face her daughter.

"You've got a flower in your apron!" said the child, in a little rapture at this unusual event.

"Goodness me!" exclaimed the woman, relieved. "One would think the house was afire." She replaced the glass and waited a moment before turning up the wick. A pale shadow was seen floating vaguely on the floor.

"Let me smell!" said the child, still rapturously, coming forward and putting her face to her mother's waist.

"Go along, silly!" said the mother, turning up the lamp. The light revealed their suspense so that the woman felt it almost unbearable. Annie was still bending at her waist. Irritably, the mother took the flowers out from her apron-band.

"Oh, mother—don't take them out!" Annie cried, catching her hand and trying to replace the sprig.

"Such nonsense!" said the mother, turning away. The child put the pale chrysanthemums to her lips, murmuring:

"Don't they smell beautiful!"

Her mother gave a short laugh.

"No," she said, "not to me. It was chrysanthemums when I married him, and chrysanthemums when you were born, and the first time they ever brought him home drunk, he'd got brown chrysanthemums in his button-hole."

She looked at the children. Their eyes and their parted lips were wondering. The mother sat rocking in silence for some time. Then she looked at the clock.

"Twenty minutes to six!" In a tone of fine bitter carelessness she continued: "Eh, he'll not come now till they bring him. There he'll stick! But he needn't come rolling in here in his pit-dirt, for *I* won't wash him. He can lie on the floor—Eh, what a fool I've been, what a fool! And this is what I came here for, to this dirty hole, rats and all, for him to slink past his very door. Twice last week—he's begun now—"

She silenced herself, and rose to clear the table.

While for an hour or more the children played, subduedly intent, fertile of imagination, united in fear of the mother's wrath, and in dread of their father's home-coming, Mrs. Bates sat in her rocking-chair making a "singlet" of thick cream-coloured flannel, which gave a dull wounded sound as she tore off the grey edge. She worked at her sewing with energy, listening to the children, and her anger wearied itself, lay down to rest, opening its eyes from time to time and steadily watching, its ears raised to listen. Sometimes even her anger quailed and shrank, and the mother suspended her sewing, tracing the footsteps that thudded along the sleepers outside; she would lift her head sharply to bid the children "hush," but she recovered herself in time, and the footsteps went past the gate, and the children were not flung out of their play-world.

But at last Annie sighed, and gave in. She glanced at her waggon of slippers, and loathed the game. She turned plaintively to her mother.

"Mother!"—but she was inarticulate.

John crept out like a frog from under the sofa. His mother glanced up.

"Yes," she said, "just look at those shirt-sleeves!"

The boy held them out to survey them, saying nothing. Then somebody called in a hoarse voice away down the line, and suspense bristled in the room, till two people had gone by outside, talking.

"It's time for bed," said the mother.

"My father hasn't come," wailed Annie plaintively. But her mother was primed with courage.

"Never mind. They'll bring him when he does come—like a log." She meant there would be no scene. "And he may sleep on the floor till he wakes himself. I know he'll not go to work to-morrow after this!"

The children had their hands and faces wiped with a flannel. They were very quiet. When they had put on their nightdresses, they said their prayers, the boy mumbling. The mother looked down at them, at the brown silken bush of intertwining curls in the nape of the girl's neck, at the little black head of the lad, and her heart burst with anger at their father who caused all three such distress. The children hid their faces in her skirts for comfort.

When Mrs. Bates came down, the room was strangely empty, with a tension of expectancy. She took up her sewing and stitched for some time without raising her head. Meantime her anger was tinged with fear.

II

The clock struck eight and she rose suddenly, dropping her sewing on her chair. She went to the stairfoot door, opened it, listening. Then she went out, locking the door behind her.

Something scuffled in the yard, and she started, though she knew it was only the rats with which the place was overrun. The night was very dark. In the great bay of railway lines, bulked with trucks, there was no trace of light, only away back she could see a few yellow lamps at the pit-top, and the red smear of the burning pit-bank on the night. She hurried along the edge of the track, then, crossing the converging lines, came to the stile by the white gates, whence she emerged on the road. Then the fear which had led her shrank. People were walking up to New Brinsley; she saw the lights in the houses; twenty yards further on were the broad windows of the "Prince of Wales," very warm and bright, and the loud voices of men could be heard distinctly. What a fool she had been to imagine that anything had happened to him! He was merely drinking over there at the "Prince of Wales." She faltered. She had never yet been to fetch him, and she never would go. So she continued her walk towards the long straggling line of houses, standing blank on the highway. She entered a passage between the dwellings.

"Mr. Rigley?—Yes! Did you want him? No, he's not in at this minute."

The raw-boned woman leaned forward from her dark scullery and peered at the other, upon whom fell a dim light through the blind of the kitchen window.

"Is it Mrs. Bates?" she asked in a tone tinged with respect.

"Yes. I wondered if your Master was at home. Mine hasn't come yet."

"'Asn't 'e! Oh, Jack's been 'ome an' 'ad 'is dinner an' gone out. 'E's just gone for 'alf an hour afore bedtime. Did you call at the 'Prince of Wales'?"

"No—"

"No, you didn't like—! It's not very nice." The other woman was indulgent. There was an awkward pause. "Jack never said nothink about —about your Mester," she said.

"No!—I expect he's stuck in there!"

Elizabeth Bates said this bitterly, and with recklessness. She knew that the woman across the yard was standing at her door listening, but she did not care. As she turned:

"Stop a minute! I'll just go an' ask Jack if 'e knows anythink," said Mrs. Rigley.

"Oh, no—I wouldn't like to put—!"

"Yes, I will, if you'll just step inside an' see as th' childer doesn't come downstairs and set theirselves afire."

Elizabeth Bates, murmuring a remonstrance, stepped inside. The other woman apologized for the state of the room.

The kitchen needed apology. There were little frocks and trousers and childish undergarments on the squab and on the floor, and a litter of playthings everywhere. On the black American cloth of the table were pieces of bread and cake, crusts, slops, and a teapot with cold tea.

"Eh, ours is just as bad," said Elizabeth Bates, looking at the woman, not at the house. Mrs. Rigley put a shawl over her head and hurried out, saying:

"I shanna be a minute."

The other sat, noting with faint disapproval the general untidiness of the room. Then she fell to counting the shoes of various sizes scattered over the floor. There were twelve. She

sighed and said to herself, "No wonder!"—glancing at the litter. There came the scratching of two pairs of feet on the yard, and the Rigleys entered. Elizabeth Bates rose. Rigley was a big man, with very large bones. His head looked particularly bony. Across his temple was a blue scar, caused by a wound got in the pit, a wound in which the coal-dust remained blue like tattooing.

"'Asna'e come whoam yit?" asked the man, without any form of greeting, but with deference and sympathy. "I couldna say wheer he is—'e's non ower theer!"—he jerked his head to signify the "Prince of Wales."

"'E's 'appen gone up to th' 'Yew,'" said Mrs. Rigley.

There was another pause. Rigley had evidently something to get off his mind:

"Ah left 'im finishin' a stint," he began. "Loose-all 'ad bin gone about ten minutes when we com'n away, an' I shouted, 'Are ter comin', Walt?' an' 'e said, 'Go on, Ah shanna be but a 'ef a minnit,' so we com'n ter th' bottom, me an' Bowers, thinkin' as 'e wor just behint, an' 'ud come up i' th' next bantle—"

He stood perplexed, as if answering a charge of deserting his mate. Elizabeth Bates, now again certain of disaster, hastened to reassure him:

"I expect 'e's gone up to th' 'Yew Tree,' as you say. It's not the first time. I've fretted myself into a fever before now. He'll come home when they carry him."

"Ay, isn't it too bad!" deplored the other woman.

"I'll just step up to Dick's an' see if 'e *is* theer," offered the man, afraid of appearing alarmed, afraid of taking liberties.

"Oh, I wouldn't think of bothering you that far," said Elizabeth Bates, with emphasis, but he knew she was glad of his offer.

As they stumbled up the entry, Elizabeth Bates heard Rigley's wife run across the yard and open her neighbour's door. At this, suddenly all the blood in her body seemed to switch away from her heart.

"Mind!" warned Rigley. "Ah've said many a time as Ah'd fill up them ruts in this entry, sumb'dy 'll be breakin' their legs yit."

She recovered herself and walked quickly along with the miner.

"I don't like leaving the children in bed, and nobody in the house," she said.

"No, you dunna!" he replied courteously. They were soon at the gate of the cottage.

"Well, I shanna be many minnits. Dunna you be frettin' now, 'e'll be all right," said the butty.

"Thank you very much, Mr. Rigley," she replied.

"You're welcome!" he stammered, moving away. "I shanna be many minnits."

The house was quiet. Elizabeth Bates took off her hat and shawl, and rolled back the rug. When she had finished, she sat down. It was a few minutes past nine. She was startled by the rapid chuff of the winding-engine at the pit, and the sharp whirr of the brakes on the rope as it descended. Again she felt the painful sweep of her blood, and she put her hand to her side, saying aloud, "Good gracious!—it's only the nine o'clock deputy going down," rebuking herself.

She sat still, listening. Half an hour of this, and she was wearied out.

"What am I working myself up like this for?" she said pitiably to herself. "I s'll only be doing myself some damage."

She took out her sewing again.

At a quarter to ten there were footsteps. One person! She watched for the door to open. It was an elderly woman, in a black bonnet and a black woollen shawl—his mother. She was about sixty years old, pale, with blue eyes, and her face all wrinkled and lamentable. She shut the door and turned to her daughter-in-law peevishly.

"Eh, Lizzie, whatever shall we do, whatever shall we do!" she cried.

Elizabeth drew back a little, sharply.

"What is it, mother?" she said.

The elder woman seated herself on the sofa.

"I don't know, child, I can't tell you!"—she shook her head slowly. Elizabeth sat watching her, anxious and vexed.

"I don't know," replied the grandmother, sighing very deeply. "There's no end to my troubles, there isn't. The things I've gone through, I'm sure it's enough—!" She wept without wiping her eyes, the tears running.

"But, mother," interrupted Elizabeth, "what do you mean? What is it?"

The grandmother slowly wiped her eyes.

The fountains of her tears were stopped by Elizabeth's directness. She wiped her eyes slowly.

"Poor child! Eh, you poor thing!" she moaned. "I don't know what we're going to do, I don't—and you as you are—it's a thing, it is indeed!"

Elizabeth waited.

"Is he dead?" she asked, and at the words her heart swung violently, though she felt a slight flush of shame at the ultimate extravagance of the question. Her words sufficiently frightened the old lady, almost brought her to herself.

"Don't say so, Elizabeth! We'll hope it's not as bad as that; no, may the Lord spare us that, Elizabeth. Jack Rigley came just as I was sittin' down to a glass afore going to bed, an' 'e said, ' 'Appen you'll go down th' line, Mrs. Bates. Walt's had an accident. 'Appen you'll go an' sit wi' 'er till we can get him home.' I hadn't time to ask him a word afore he was gone. An' I put my bonnet on an' come straight down, Lizzie. I thought to myself, 'Eh, that poor blessed child, if anybody should come an' tell her of a sudden, there's no knowin' what'll 'appen to 'er.' You mustn't let it upset you, Lizzie—or you know what to expect. How long is it, six months—or is it five, Lizzie? Ay!"—the old woman shook her head—"time slips on, it slips on! Ay!"

Elizabeth's thoughts were busy elsewhere. If he was killed—would she be able to manage on the little pension and what she could earn?— she counted up rapidly. If he was hurt—they wouldn't take him to the hospital—how tiresome he would be to nurse!—but perhaps she'd be able to get him away from the drink and his hateful ways. She would—while he was ill. The tears offered to come to her eyes at the picture. But what sentimental luxury was this she was beginning? She turned to consider the children. At any rate she was absolutely necessary for them. They were her business.

"Ay!" repeated the old woman, "it seems but a week or two since he brought me his first wages. Ay—he was a good lad, Elizabeth, he was, in his way. I don't know why he got to be such a trouble, I don't. He was a happy lad at home, only full of spirits. But there's no mistake he's been a handful of trouble, he has! I hope the Lord'll spare him to mend his ways. I hope so, I hope so. You've had a sight o' trouble with him, Elizabeth, you have indeed. But he was a jolly enough lad wi' me, he was, I can assure you. I don't know how it is. . . ."

The old woman continued to muse aloud, a monotonous irritating sound, while Elizabeth thought concentratedly, startled once, when she heard the winding-engine chuff quickly, and the brakes skirr with a shriek. Then she heard the engine more slowly, and the brakes made no sound. The old woman did not notice. Elizabeth waited in suspense. The mother-in-law talked, with lapses into silence.

"But he wasn't your son, Lizzie, an' it makes a difference. Whatever he was, I remember him when he was little, an' I learned to understand him and to make allowances. You've got to make allowances for them—"

It was half-past ten, and the old woman was saying: "But it's trouble from beginning to end; you're never too old for trouble, never too old for that—" when the gate banged back, and there were heavy feet on the steps.

"I'll go, Lizzie, let me go," cried the old woman, rising. But Elizabeth was at the door. It was a man in pit-clothes.

"They're bringin' 'im Missis," he said. Elizabeth's heart halted a moment. Then it surged on again, almost suffocating her.

"Is he—is it bad?" she asked.

The man turned away, looking at the darkness:

"The doctor says 'e'd been dead hours. 'E saw 'im i' th' lamp-cabin."

The old woman, who stood just behind Elizabeth, dropped into a chair, and folded her hands, crying: "Oh, my boy, my boy!"

"Hush!" said Elizabeth, with a sharp twitch of a frown. "Be still, mother, don't waken th' children: I wouldn't have them down for anything!"

The old woman moaned softly, rocking herself. The man was drawing away. Elizabeth took a step forward.

"How was it?" she asked.

"Well, I couldn't say for sure," the man replied, very ill at ease. "'E wor finishin' a stint an' th' butties 'ad gone, an' a lot o' stuff come down atop 'n 'im."

"And crushed him?" cried the widow, with a shudder.

"No," said the man, "it fell at th' back of 'im. 'E wor under th' face, an' it niver touched 'im. It shut 'im in. It seems 'e wor smothered."

Elizabeth shrank back. She heard the old woman behind her cry:

"What?—what did 'e say it was?"

The man replied, more loudly: "'E wor smothered!"

Then the old woman wailed aloud, and this relieved Elizabeth.

"Oh, mother," she said, putting her hand on the old woman, "don't waken th' children, don't waken th' children."

She wept a little, unknowing, while the old mother rocked herself and moaned. Elizabeth remembered that they were bringing him home, and she must be ready. "They'll lay him in the parlour," she said to herself, standing a moment pale and perplexed.

Then she lighted a candle and went into the tiny room. The air was cold and damp, but she could not make a fire, there was no fireplace. She set down the candle and looked round. The candlelight glittered on the lustre-glasses, on the two vases that held some of the pink chrysanthemums, and on the dark mahogany. There was a cold, deathly smell of chrysanthemums in the room. Elizabeth stood looking at the flowers. She turned away, and calculated whether there would be room to lay him on the floor, between the couch and the chiffonier. She pushed the chairs aside. There would be room to lay him down and to step round him. Then she fetched the old red tablecloth, and another old cloth, spreading them down to save her bit of carpet. She shivered on leaving the parlour; so, from the dresser-drawer she took a clean shirt and put it at the fire to air. All the time her mother-in-law was rocking herself in the chair and moaning.

"You'll have to move from there, mother," said Elizabeth. "They'll be bringing him in. Come in the rocker."

The old mother rose mechanically, and seated herself by the fire, continuing to lament. Elizabeth went into the pantry for another candle, and there, in the little penthouse under the naked tiles, she heard them coming. She stood still in the pantry doorway, listening. She heard them pass the end of the house, and come awkwardly down the three steps, a jumble of shuffling footsteps and muttering voices. The old woman was silent. The men were in the yard.

Then Elizabeth heard Matthews, the manager of the pit, say: "You go in first, Jim. Mind!"

The door came open, and the two women

saw a collier backing into the room, holding one end of a stretcher, on which they could see the nailed pit-boots of the dead man. The two carriers halted, the man at the head stooping to the lintel of the door.

"Wheer will you have him?" asked the manager, a short, white-bearded man.

Elizabeth roused herself and came from the pantry carrying the unlighted candle.

"In the parlour," she said.

"In there, Jim!" pointed the manager, and the carriers backed round into the tiny room. The coat with which they had covered the body fell off as they awkwardly turned through the two doorways, and the women saw their man, naked to the waist, lying stripped for work. The old woman began to moan in a low voice of horror.

"Lay th' stretcher at th' side," snapped the manager, "an' put 'im on th' cloths. Mind now, mind! Look you now—!"

One of the men had knocked off a vase of chrysanthemums. He stared awkwardly, then they set down the stretcher. Elizabeth did not look at her husband. As soon as she could get in the room, she went and picked up the broken vase and the flowers.

"Wait a minute!" she said.

The three men waited in silence while she mopped up the water with a duster.

"Eh, what a job, what a job, to be sure!" the manager was saying, rubbing his brow with trouble and perplexity. "Never knew such a thing in my life, never! He'd no business to ha' been left. I never knew such a thing in my life! Fell over him clean as a whistle, an' shut him in. Not four foot of space, there wasn't—yet it scarce bruised him."

He looked down at the dead man, lying prone, half naked, all grimed with coal-dust.

" 'Sphyxiated,' the doctor said. It *is* the most terrible job I've ever known. Seems as if it was done o' purpose. Clean over him, an' shut 'im in, like a mouse-trap"—he made a sharp, descending gesture with his hand.

The colliers standing by jerked aside their heads in hopeless comment.

The horror of the thing bristled upon them all.

Then they heard the girl's voice upstairs calling shrilly: "Mother, mother—who is it? Mother, who is it?"

Elizabeth hurried to the foot of the stairs and opened the door:

"Go to sleep!" she commanded sharply. "What are you shouting about? Go to sleep at once—there's nothing—"

Then she began to mount the stairs. They could hear her on the boards, and on the plaster floor of the little bedroom. They could hear her distinctly:

"What's the matter now?—what's the matter with you, silly thing?"—her voice was much agitated, with an unreal gentleness.

"I thought it was some men come," said the plaintive voice of the child. "Has he come?"

"Yes, they've brought him. There's nothing to make a fuss about. Go to sleep now, like a good child."

They could hear her voice in the bedroom, they waited whilst she covered the children under the bedclothes.

"Is he drunk?" asked the girl, timidly, faintly.

"No! No—he's not! He—he's asleep."

"Is he asleep downstairs?"

"Yes—and don't make a noise."

There was silence for a moment, then the men heard the frightened child again:

"What's that noise?"

"It's nothing, I tell you, what are you bothering for?"

The noise was the grandmother moaning. She was oblivious of everything, sitting on her chair rocking and moaning. The manager put his hand on her arm and bade her "Sh—sh!!"

The old woman opened her eyes and looked at him. She was shocked by this interruption, and seemed to wonder.

"What time is it?"—the plaintive thin voice of the child, sinking back unhappily into sleep, asked this last question.

"Ten o'clock," answered the mother more softly. Then she must have bent down and kissed the children.

Matthews beckoned to the men to come away. They put on their caps and took up the stretcher. Stepping over the body, they tiptoed out of the house. None of them spoke till they were far from the wakeful children.

When Elizabeth came down she found her mother alone on the parlour floor, leaning over the dead man, the tears dropping on him.

"We must lay him out," the wife said. She

put on the kettle, then returning knelt at the feet, and began to unfasten the knotted leather laces. The room was clammy and dim with only one candle, so that she had to bend her face almost to the floor. At last she got off the heavy boots and put them away.

"You must help me now," she whispered to the old woman. Together they stripped the man.

When they arose, saw him lying in the naive dignity of death, the women stood arrested in fear and respect. For a few moments they remained still, looking down, the old mother whimpering. Elizabeth felt countermanded. She saw him, how utterly inviolable he lay in himself. She had nothing to do with him. She could not accept it. Stooping, she laid her hand on him, in claim. He was still warm, for the mine was hot where he had died. His mother had his face between her hands, and was murmuring incoherently. The old tears fell in succession as drops from wet leaves; the mother was not weeping, merely her tears flowed. Elizabeth embraced the body of her husband, with cheek and lips. She seemed to be listening, inquiring, trying to get some connection. But she could not. She was driven away. He was impregnable.

She rose, went into the kitchen, where she poured warm water into a bowl, brought soap and flannel and a soft towel.

"I must wash him," she said.

Then the old mother rose stiffly, and watched Elizabeth as she carefully washed his face, carefully brushing the big blond moustache from his mouth with the flannel. She was afraid with a bottomless fear, so she ministered to him. The old woman, jealous, said:

"Let me wipe him!"—and she kneeled on the other side drying slowly as Elizabeth washed, her big black bonnet sometimes brushing the dark head of her daughter-in-law. They worked thus in silence for a long time. They never forgot it was death, and the touch of the man's dead body gave them strange emotions, different in each of the women; a great dread possessed them both, the mother felt the lie was given to her womb, she was denied; the wife felt the utter isolation of the human soul, the child within her was a weight apart from her.

At last it was finished. He was a man of handsome body, and his face showed no traces of drink. He was blond, full-fleshed, with fine limbs. But he was dead.

"Bless him," whispered his mother, looking always at his face, and speaking out of sheer terror. "Dear lad—bless him!" She spoke in a faint, sibilant ecstasy of fear and mother love.

Elizabeth sank down again to the floor, and put her face against his neck, and trembled and shuddered. But she had to draw away again. He was dead, and her living flesh had no place against his. A great dread and weariness held her: she was so unavailing. Her life was gone like this.

"White as milk he is, clear as a twelve-month baby, bless him, the darling!" the old mother murmured to herself. "Not a mark on him, clear and clean and white, beautiful as ever a child was made," she murmured with pride. Elizabeth kept her face hidden.

"He went peaceful, Lizzie—peaceful as sleep. Isn't he beautiful, the lamb? Ay—he must ha' made his peace, Lizzie. 'Appen he made it all right, Lizzie, shut in there. He'd have time. He wouldn't look like this if he hadn't made his peace. The lamb, the dear lamb. Eh, but he had a hearty laugh. I loved to hear it. He had the heartiest laugh, Lizzie, as a lad—"

Elizabeth looked up. The man's mouth was fallen back, slightly open under the cover of the moustache. The eyes, half shut, did not show glazed in the obscurity. Life with its smoky burning gone from him, had left him apart and utterly alien to her. And she knew what a stranger he was to her. In her womb was ice of fear, because of this separate stranger with whom she had been living as one flesh. Was this what it all meant—utter, intact separateness, obscured by heat of living? In dread she turned her face away. The fact was too deadly. There had been nothing between them, and yet they had come together, exchanging their nakedness repeatedly. Each time he had taken her, they had been two isolated beings, far apart as now. He was no more responsible than she. The child was like ice in her womb. For as she looked at the dead man, her mind, cold and detached, said clearly: "Who am I? What have I been doing? I have been fighting a husband who did not exist. *He* existed all the time. What wrong have I done? What was that I have been living with? There lies the reality, this man." And her soul died in her for fear: she knew she had never seen him, he had never seen her, they had met in the dark and had fought in the dark, not knowing whom they met nor whom they fought. And now she saw, and turned silent in seeing. For she had been wrong. She had said he was something he was not; she had felt familiar with him. Whereas he was apart all the while, living as she never lived, feeling as she never felt.

In fear and shame she looked at his naked body, that she had known falsely. And he was the father of her children. Her soul was torn from her body and stood apart. She looked at his naked body and was ashamed, as if she had denied it. After all, it was itself. It seemed awful to her. She looked at his face, and she turned her own face to the wall. For his look was other than hers, his way was not her way. She had denied him what he was—she saw it now. She had refused him as himself. And this had been her life, and his life. She was grateful to death, which restored the truth. And she knew she was not dead.

And all the while her heart was bursting with grief and pity for him. What had he suffered? What stretch of horror for this helpless man! She was rigid with agony. She had not been able to help him. He had been cruelly injured, this naked man, this other being, and she could make no reparation. There were the children— but the children belonged to life. This dead man had nothing to do with them. He and she were only channels through which life had flowed to issue in the children. She was a mother—but how awful she knew it now to have been a wife. And he, dead now, how awful he must have felt it to be a husband. She felt that in the next world he would be a stranger to her. If they met there, in the beyond, they would only be ashamed of what had been before. The children had come, for some mysterious reason, out of both of them. But the children did not unite them. Now he was dead, she knew how eternally he was apart from her, how eternally he had nothing more to do with her. She saw this episode of her life closed. They had denied each other in life. Now he had withdrawn. An anguish came over her. It was finished then: it had become hopeless between them long before he died. Yet he had been her husband. But how little!

"Have you got his shirt, 'Lizabeth?"

Elizabeth turned without answering, though she strove to weep and behave as her mother-in-law expected. But she could not, she was silenced. She went into the kitchen and returned with the garment.

"It is aired," she said, grasping the cotton shirt here and there to try. She was almost ashamed to handle him; what right had she or any one to lay hands on him; but her touch was humble on his body. It was hard work to clothe him. He was so heavy and inert. A terrible dread gripped her all the while: that he could be so heavy and utterly inert, unresponsive, apart. The horror of the distance between them was almost too much for her—it was so infinite a gap she must look across.

At last he was finished. They covered him with a sheet and left him lying, with his face bound. And she fastened the door of the little parlour, lest the children should see what was lying there. Then, with peace sunk heavy on her heart, she went about making tidy the kitchen. She knew she submitted to life, which was her immediate master. But from death, her ultimate master, she winced with fear and shame.

Mercury[1]

It was Sunday, and very hot. The holiday-makers flocked to the hill of Mercury, to rise two thousand feet above the steamy haze of the valleys. For the summer had been very wet, and the sudden heat covered the land in hot steam.

Every time it made the ascent, the funicular was crowded. It hauled itself up the steep incline, that towards the top looked almost perpendicular, the steel thread of the rails in the gulf of pine-trees hanging like an iron rope against a wall. The women held their breath, and didn't look. Or they looked back towards the sinking levels of the river, steamed and dim, far-stretching over the frontier.

When you arrived at the top, there was nothing to do. The hill was a pine-covered cone; paths wound between the high tree-trunks, and

1 From *Phoenix: The Posthumous Papers of D. H. Lawrence,* edited and with an introduction by Edward D. McDonald (1936). Merkur is a mountain or hill to the east of Baden-Baden, Germany, and an excursion point for the region. On its summit was discovered a votive stone dedicated to the god Mercury.

you could walk round and see the glimpses of the world all round, all round: the dim, far river-plain, with a dull glint of the great stream, to westwards; southwards the black, forest-covered, agile-looking hills, with emerald-green clearings and a white house or two; east, the inner valley, with two villages, factory chimneys, pointed churches, and hills beyond; and north, the steep hills of forest, with reddish crags and reddish castle ruins. The hot sun burned overhead, and all was in steam.

Only on the very summit of the hill there was a tower, an outlook tower; a long restaurant with its beer-garden, all the little yellow tables standing their round disks under the horse-chestnut trees; then a bit of a rock-garden on the slope. But the great trees began again in wilderness a few yards off.

The Sunday crowd came up in waves from the funicular. In waves they ebbed through the beer-garden. But not many sat down to drink. Nobody was spending any money. Some paid to go up the outlook tower, to look down on a world of vapours and black, agile-crouching hills, and half-cooked towns. Then everybody dispersed along the paths, to sit among the trees in the cool air.

There was not a breath of wind. Lying and looking upwards at the shaggy, barbaric middle-world of the pine-trees, it was difficult to decide whether the pure high trunks supported the upper thicket of darkness, or whether they descended from it like great cords stretched downwards. Anyhow, in between the tree-top world and the earth-world went the wonderful clean cords of innumerable proud tree-trunks, clear as rain. And as you watched, you saw that the upper world was faintly moving, faintly, most faintly swaying, with a circular movement, though the lower trunks were utterly motionless and monolithic.

There was nothing to do. In all the world, there was nothing to do, and nothing to be done. Why have we all come to the top of the Merkur? There is nothing for us to do.

What matter? We have come a stride beyond the world. Let it steam and cook its half-baked reality below there. On the hill of Mercury we take no notice. Even we do not trouble to wander and pick the fat, blue, sourish bilberries. Just lie and see the rain-pure tree-trunks like chords of music between two worlds.

The hours pass by: people wander and disappear and reappear. All is hot and quiet. Humanity is rarely boisterous any more. You go for a drink: finches run among the few people at the tables: everybody glances at everybody, but with remoteness.

There is nothing to do but to return and lie down under the pine-trees. Nothing to do. But why do anything, anyhow? The desire to do anything has gone. The tree-trunks, living like rain, they are quite active enough.

At the foot of the obsolete tower there is an old tablet-stone with a very much battered Mercury, in relief. There is also an altar, or votive stone, both from the Roman times. The Romans are supposed to have worshipped Mercury on the summit. The battered god, with his round sun-head, looks very hollow-eyed and unimpressive in the purplish-red sandstone of the district. And no one any more will throw grains of offering in the hollow of the votive stone: also common, purplish-red sandstone, very local and un-Roman.

The Sunday people do not even look. Why should they? They keep passing on into the pine-trees. And many sit on the benches; many lie upon the long chairs. It is very hot, in the afternoon, and very still.

Till there seems a faint whistling in the tops of the pine-trees, and out of the universal semi-consciousness of the afternoon arouses a bristling uneasiness. The crowd is astir, looking at the sky. And sure enough, there is a great flat blackness reared up in the western sky, curled with white wisps and loose breast-feathers. It looks very sinister, as only the elements still can look. Under the sudden weird whistling of the upper pine-trees, there is a subdued babble and calling of frightened voices.

They want to get down; the crowd want to get down off the hill of Mercury, before the storm comes. At any price to get off the hill! They stream towards the funicular, while the sky blackens with incredible rapidity. And as the crowd presses down towards the little station, the first blaze of lightning opens out, followed immediately by a crash of thunder, and great darkness. In one strange movement, the crowd takes refuge in the deep veranda of the restaurant, pressing among the little tables in silence. There is no rain, and no definite wind, only a sudden coldness which makes the crowd press closer.

They press closer, in the darkness and the suspense. They have become curiously unified, the crowd, as if they had fused into one body. As the air sends a chill waft under the veranda the voices murmur plaintively, like birds under leaves, the bodies press closer together, seeking shelter in contact.

The gloom, dark as night, seems to continue a long time. Then suddenly the lightning dances white on the floor, dances and shakes upon the ground, up and down, and lights up the white striding of a man, lights him up only to the hips, white and naked and striding, with fire on his heels. He seems to be hurrying, this fiery man whose upper half is invisible, and at his naked heels white little flames seem to flutter. His flat, powerful thighs, his legs white as fire stride rapidly across the open, in front of the veranda, dragging little white flames at the ankles, with the movement. He is going somewhere, swiftly.

In the great bang of the thunder the apparition disappears. The earth moves, and the house jumps in complete darkness. A faint whimpering of terror comes from the crowd, as the cold air swirls in. But still, upon the darkness, there is no rain. There is no relief: a long wait.

Brilliant and blinding, the lightning falls again; a strange bruising thud comes from the forest, as all the little tables and the secret tree-trunks stand for one unnatural second exposed. Then the blow of the thunder, under which the house and the crowd reel as under an explosion. The storm is playing directly upon the Merkur. A belated sound of tearing branches comes out of the forest.

And again the white splash of the lightning on the ground: but nothing moves. And again the long, rattling, instantaneous volleying of the thunder, in the darkness. The crowd is panting with fear, as the lightning again strikes white, and something again seems to burst, in the forest, as the thunder crashes.

At last, into the motionlessness of the storm, in rushes the wind, with the fiery flying of bits of ice, and the sudden sea-like roaring of the pine-trees. The crowd winces and draws back, as the bits of ice hit in the face like fire. The roar of the trees is so great, it becomes like another silence. And through it is heard the crashing and splintering of timber, as the hurricane concentrates upon the hill.

Down comes the hail, in a roar that covers every other sound, threshing ponderously upon the ground and the roofs and the trees. And as the crowd surges irresistibly into the interior of the building, from the crushing of this ice-fall, still amid the sombre hoarseness sounds the tinkle and crackle of things breaking.

After an eternity of dread, it ends suddenly. Outside is a faint gleam of yellow light, over the snow and the endless debris of twigs and things broken. It is very cold, with the atmosphere of ice and deep winter. The forest looks wan, above the white earth, where the ice-balls lie in their myriads, six inches deep, littered with all the twigs and things they have broken.

"Yes! Yes!" say the men, taking sudden courage as the yellow light comes into the air. "Now we can go!"

The first brave ones emerge, picking up the big hailstones, pointing to the overthrown tables. Some, however, do not linger. They hurry to the funicular station, to see if the apparatus is still working.

The funicular station is on the north side of the hill. The men come back, saying there is no one there. The crowd begins to emerge upon the wet, crunching whiteness of the hail, spreading around in curiosity, waiting for the men who operate the funicular.

On the south side of the outlook tower two bodies lay in the cold but thawing hail. The dark-blue of the uniforms showed blackish. Both men were dead. But the lightning had completely removed the clothing from the legs of one man, so that he was naked from the hips down. There he lay, his face sideways on the snow, and two drops of blood running from his nose into his big, blond, military moustache. He lay there near the votive stone of the Mercury. His companion, a young man, lay face downwards, a few yards behind him.

The sun began to emerge. The crowd gazed in dread, afraid to touch the bodies of the men. Why had they, the dead funicular men, come round to this side of the hill, anyhow?

The funicular would not work. Something had happened to it in the storm. The crowd began to wind down the bare hill, on the sloppy ice. Everywhere the earth bristled with broken pine-boughs and twigs. But the bushes and the leafy trees were stripped absolutely bare, to a miracle. The lower earth was leafless and naked as in winter.

"Absolute winter!" murmured the crowd, as they hurried, frightened, down the steep, winding descent, extricating themselves from the fallen pine-branches.

Meanwhile the sun began to steam in great heat.

Reading a Letter

She sits on the recreation ground
    Under an oak whose yellow buds dot the pale
      blue sky.
The young grass twinkles in the wind, and the
    sound
    Of the wind in the knotted buds makes a
      canopy.

So sitting under the knotted canopy   5
    Of the wind, she is lifted and carried away as
      in a balloon.
Across the insensible void, till she stoops to see
    The sandy desert beneath her, the dreary pla-
      toon.

She knows the waste all dry beneath her, in one
    place
    Stirring with earth-coloured life, ever turning   10
      and stirring.
But never the motion has a human face
    Nor sound, only intermittent machinery whir-
      ring.

And so again, on the recreation ground
    She alights a stranger, wondering, unused to
      the scene;
Suffering at sight of the children playing around,   15
    Hurt at the chalk-coloured tulips, and the
      evening-green.

Song of a Man Who Has Come Through

Not I, not I, but the wind that blows through
    me!
A fine wind is blowing the new direction of
    Time.
If only I let it bear me, carry me, if only it carry
    me!
If only I am sensitive, subtle, oh, delicate, a
    winged gift!

If only, most lovely of all, I yield myself and am
    borrowed
By the fine, fine wind that takes its course
    through the chaos of the world
Like a fine, an exquisite chisel, a wedge-blade
    inserted;
If only I am keen and hard like the sheer tip of
    a wedge
Driven by invisible blows,
The rock will split, we shall come at the wonder,   10
    we shall find the Hesperides.

Oh, for the wonder that bubbles into my soul,
I would be a good fountain, a good well-head,
Would blur no whisper, spoil no expression.

What is the knocking?
What is the knocking at the door in the night?   15
It is somebody wants to do us harm.

No, no, it is the three strange angels.
Admit them, admit them.

Bat

At evening, sitting on this terrace,
When the sun from the west, beyond Pisa, be-
    yond the mountains of Carrara
Departs, and the world is taken by surprise . . .

When the tired flower of Florence is in gloom be-
    neath the glowing
Brown hills surrounding . . .   5

When under the arches of the Ponte Vecchio
A green light enters against stream, flush from
    the west,
Against the current of obscure Arno . . .

Look up, and you see things flying
Between the day and the night;   10
Swallows with spools of dark thread sewing the
    shadows together.

A circle swoop, and a quick parabola under the
    bridge arches
Where light pushes through;
A sudden turning upon itself of a thing in the
    air.
A dip to the water.   15

And you think:
"The swallows are flying so late!"

Swallows?

Dark air-life looping
Yet missing the pure loop . . .
A twitch, a twitter, an elastic shudder in flight
And serrated wings against the sky,
Like a glove, a black glove thrown up at the
    light,
And falling back.

Never swallows!   25
Bats!
The swallows are gone.

At a wavering instant the swallows give way to
    bats
By the Ponte Vecchio . . .
Changing guard.   30

Bats, and an uneasy creeping in one's scalp
As the bats swoop overhead!
Flying madly.

Pipistrello![1]   35
Black piper on an infinitesimal pipe.
Little lumps that fly in air and have voices in-
    definite, wildly vindictive;

Wings like bits of umbrella.

Bats!

Creatures that hang themselves up like an old
    rag, to sleep;
And disgustingly upside down.   40
Hanging upside down like rows of disgusting old
    rags
And grinning in their sleep.
Bats!

In China the bat is symbol of happiness.

Not for me!   45

Snake

A snake came to my water-trough
On a hot, hot day, and I in pyjamas for the heat,
To drink there.

---

1 The Italian word for bat ("little piper").

In the deep, strange-scented shade of the great
    dark carob-tree
I came down the steps with my pitcher   5
And must wait, must stand and wait, for there he
    was at the trough before me.

He reached down from a fissure in the earth-wall
    in the gloom
And trailed his yellow-brown slackness soft-
    bellied down, over the edge of the stone
    trough
And rested his throat upon the stone bottom,
And where the water had dripped from the tap,   10
    in a small clearness,
He sipped with his straight mouth,
Softly drank through his straight gums, into his
    slack long body,
Silently.

Someone was before me at my water-trough,
And I, like a second comer, waiting.   15

He lifted his head from his drinking, as cattle do,
And looked at me vaguely, as drinking cattle do,
And flickered his two-forked tongue from his lips,
    and mused a moment,
And stooped and drank a little more,
Being earth-brown, earth-golden from the burn-   20
    ing bowels of the earth
On the day of Sicilian July, with Etna smoking.

The voice of my education said to me
He must be killed,
For in Sicily the black, black snakes are innocent,
    the gold are venomous.

And voices in me said, If you were a man   25
You would take a stick and break him now, and
    finish him off.

But must I confess how I liked him,
How glad I was he had come like a guest in
    quiet, to drink at my water-trough
And depart peaceful, pacified, and thankless,
Into the burning bowels of this earth?   30

Was it cowardice, that I dared not kill him?
Was it perversity, that I longed to talk to him?
Was it humility, to feel so honoured?
I felt so honoured.

And yet those voices: 35
If you were not afraid, you would kill him!

And truly I was afraid, I was most afraid,
But even so, honoured still more
That he should seek my hospitality
From out the dark door of the secret earth.   40

He drank enough
And lifted his head, dreamily, as one who has
    drunken,
And flickered his tongue like a forked night on
    the air, so black,
Seeming to lick his lips,
And looked around like a god, unseeing, into   45
    the air,
And slowly turned his head,
And slowly, very slowly, as if thrice adream,
Proceeded to draw his slow length curving round
And climb again the broken bank of my wall-
    face.

And as he put his head into that dreadful hole,   50
And as he slowly drew up, snake-easing his
    shoulders, and entered farther,
A sort of horror, a sort of protest against his
    withdrawing into that horrid black hole,
Deliberately going into the blackness, and slowly
    drawing himself after,
Overcame me now his back was turned.

I looked round, I put down my pitcher,   55
I picked up a clumsy log
And threw it at the water-trough with a clatter.

I think it did not hit him,
But suddenly that part of him that was left be-
    hind convulsed in undignified haste,
Writhed like lightning, and was gone   60
Into the black hole, the earth-lipped fissure in
    the wall-front,
At which, in the intense still noon, I stared with
    fascination.

And immediately I regretted it.
I thought how paltry, how vulgar, what a mean
    act!
I despised myself and the voices of my accursed   65
    human education.

And I thought of the albatross,
And I wished he would come back, my snake.

For he seemed to me again like a king,
Like a king in exile, uncrowned in the under-
    world,
Now due to be crowned again.   70

And so, I missed my chance with one of the lords
Of life.
And I have something to expiate;
A pettiness.

                                    Taormina.

Bavarian Gentians

Not every man has gentians in his house
in Soft September, at slow, sad Michaelmas.

Bavarian gentians, big and dark, only dark
darkening the day-time, torch-like with the smok-
    ing blueness of Pluto's gloom,
ribbed and torch-like, with their blaze of darkness   5
    spread blue
down flattening into points, flattened under the
    sweep of white day
torch-flower of the blue-smoking darkness, Pluto's
    dark-blue daze,
black lamps from the halls of Dis,[1] burning dark
    blue,
giving off darkness, blue darkness, as Demeter's
    pale lamps give off light,
lead me then, lead the way.   10

Reach me a gentian, give me a torch!
let me guide myself with the blue, forked torch
    of this flower
down the darker and darker stairs, where blue is
    darkened on blueness
even where Persephone goes, just now, from the
    frosted September
to the sightless realm where darkness is awake   15
    upon the dark
and Persephone herself is but a voice
or a darkness invisible enfolded in the deeper
    dark
of the arms Plutonic, and pierced with the pas-
    sion of dense gloom,

---

[1] Another of the names for Pluto, ruler of the underworld, the world of the dead. He had abducted Persephone
(Roman Proserpina) from her mother, Demeter (Roman
Ceres), the goddess of vegetation and living nature, taking
her with him to rule over his kingdom. In symbolic
parallel to the changing seasons, she was allowed to return
for six months of each year to the world of the living.

among the splendour of torches of darkness,
 shedding darkness on the lost bride and her
 groom.

The Ship of Death[1]

I

Now it is autumn and the falling fruit
and the long journey towards oblivion.

The apples falling like great drops of dew
to bruise themselves an exit from themselves.

And it is time to go, to bid farewell   5
to one's own self, and find an exit
from the fallen self.

II

Have you built your ship of death, O have you?
O build your ship of death, for you will need it.

The grim frost is at hand, when the apples will   10
    fall
thick, almost thundrous, on the hardened earth.

And death is on the air like a smell of ashes!
Ah! can't you smell it?

And in the bruised body, the frightened soul
finds itself shrinking, wincing from the cold   15
that blows upon it through the orifices.

III

And can a man his own quietus make
with a bare bodkin?

With daggers, bodkins, bullets, man can make
a bruise or break of exit for his life;   20
but is that a quietus, O tell me, is it quietus?

Surely not so! for how could murder, even self-
    murder
ever a quietus make?

---

1 Lawrence found the image of the little ship of death
when he visited the Etruscan painted tombs in Central
Italy in the spring of 1927. In *Etruscan Places,* he describes
how, before the tombs were pillaged, each would contain
"the little bronze ship that should bear the [soul of the
dead] over to the other world."

IV

O let us talk of quiet that we know,
that we can know, the deep and lovely quiet   25
of a strong heart at peace!

How can we this, our own quietus, make?

V

Build then the ship of death, for you must take
the longest journey, to oblivion.

And die the death, the long and painful death   30
that lies between the old self and the new.

Already our bodies are fallen, bruised, badly
    bruised,
already our souls are oozing through the exit
of the cruel bruise.

Already the dark and endless ocean of the end   35
is washing in through the breaches of our wounds,
already the flood is upon us.

Oh build your ship of death, your little ark
and furnish it with food, with little cakes, and
    wine
for the dark flight down oblivion.   40

VI

Piecemeal the body dies, and the timid soul
has her footing washed away, as the dark flood
    rises.

We are dying, we are dying, we are all of us
    dying
and nothing will stay the death-flood rising
    within us
and soon it will rise on the world, on the outside   45
    world.

We are dying, we are dying, piecemeal our bodies
    are dying
and our strength leaves us,
and our soul cowers naked in the dark rain over
    the flood,
cowering in the last branches of the tree of our
    life.

VII

We are dying, we are dying, so all we can do   50
is now to be willing to die, and to build the ship

of death to carry the soul on the longest journey.

A little ship, with oars and food
and little dishes, and all accoutrements
fitting and ready for the departing soul.   55

Now launch the small ship, now as the body dies
and life departs, launch out, the fragile soul
in the fragile ship of courage, the ark of faith
with its store of food and little cooking pans
and changes of clothes,   60
upon the flood's black waste
upon the waters of the end
upon the sea of death, where still we sail
darkly, for we cannot steer, and have no port.

There is no port, there is nowhere to go   65
only the deepening blackness darkening still
blacker upon the soundless, ungurgling flood
darkness at one with darkness, up and down
and sideways utterly dark, so there is no direction
    any more.
and the little ship is there; yet she is gone.   70
She is not seen, for there is nothing to see her by.
She is gone! gone! and yet
somewhere she is there.
Nowhere!

VIII

And everything is gone, the body is gone   75
completely under, gone, entirely gone.
The upper darkness is heavy as the lower,
between them the little ship
is gone
she is gone.   80

It is the end, it is oblivion.

IX

And yet out of eternity, a thread
separates itself on the blackness,
a horizontal thread
that fumes a little with pallor upon the dark.   85

Is it illusion? or does the pallor fume
A little higher?
Ah wait, wait, for there's the dawn,
the cruel dawn of coming back to life
out of oblivion.   90

Wait, wait, the little ship
drifting, beneath the deathly ashy grey
of a flood-dawn.

Wait, wait! even so, a flush of yellow
and strangely, O chilled wan soul, a flush of rose.   95

A flush of rose, and the whole thing starts again.

X

The flood subsides, and the body, like a worn
    sea-shell
emerges strange and lovely.
And the little ship wings home, faltering and
    lapsing
on the pink flood,   100
and the frail soul steps out, into her house again
filling the heart with peace.

Swings the heart renewed with peace
even of oblivion.

Oh build your ship of death, oh build it!   105
for you will need it.
For the voyage of oblivion awaits you.

Virginia Woolf

1882–1941

Mrs. Woolf's contribution to the life of British letters was made both as a novelist and as a critic. Of her importance as a novelist a word has already been said in the introduction to the Modern period. Her first two books, *The Voyage Out* (1915) and *Night and Day* (1919), were comparatively conventional in form and spirit. With *Jacob's Room* (1922) there began the series of novels in which she developed her own impressionistic technique for communicating the inner life of her characters, the novels on which her reputation chiefly rests: *Mrs. Dalloway* (1925), *To the Lighthouse* (1927), *The Waves* (1931), *The Years* (1937), and *Between the Acts* (1941). In 1928 she published *Orlando*, a fantasy whose protagonist (no other term

Virginia Woolf As a Young Woman. *The Hogarth Press.*

is quite so convenient) lives from Elizabethan to modern times without aging but who changes from a young man to a young woman during the process.

As a critic she is best known for the two volumes of essays published during her lifetime, *The Common Reader* (1925) and *The Second Common Reader* (1932)—the two later reprinted in one volume, *The Common Reader*. In these essays a remarkably sure and delicate personal taste ranges over a wide variety of subjects—"The Russian Point of View," "The Strange Elizabethans," "How Should One Read a Book?," "How it Strikes a Contemporary," for example—though the larger number of them deal with fiction and fiction writers. The biographical skill that found expression in certain of these essays was later utilized in a full-length biography of the painter Roger Fry (1940). Her claims that women be given the same opportunities and be taken as seriously as men were stated in *A Room of One's Own* (1929) and *Three Guineas* (1938), and she frequently touches on this issue in the entries of her diary, selections from which, edited by her husband Leonard Woolf, were published as *A Writer's Diary* in 1953. *A Writer's Diary* affords an unusually compelling glimpse of Mrs. Woolf's mind and personality, and of the devotion and courage with which she carried

on her calling as a novelist, often in the face of the most discouraging conditions of mental health.

After her death four more collections of her critical essays were published: *The Death of a Moth* (1942), *The Moment* (1947), *The Captain's Death Bed* (1950), and *Granite and Rainbow* (1958). *Collected Essays* (1966) gathered all her essays into four volumes.

Virginia Woolf, who was the daughter of Sir Leslie Stephen, the late Victorian critic, married Leonard Woolf in 1912. In 1917 they started the Hogarth Press, working with a hand press in Hogarth House, Richmond. *Monday or Tuesday* (1921), a collection of short sketches by Mrs. Woolf, and *Kew Gardens*, a short fantasy, both illustrated with woodcuts by her sister, Vanessa Bell, are characteristic products of this interesting and important press in its early days. Her husband's autobiography, in five volumes (*Sowing*, 1960; *Growing*, 1961; *Beginning Again*, 1964; *Downhill All the Way*, 1967; and *The Journey Not the Arrival Matters*, 1970), is one of the best sources of information and insight into the life and career of Virginia Woolf.

CRITICAL STUDIES: It may be that the 1950s were a little cool in their attitude towards Mrs Woolf, but the 1960s and 1970s have more than made up for it. The authorized biography by her nephew, Quentin Bell (*Virginia Woolf: A Biography*, 1972) has been a best seller, but there are many other biographical and critical works that demand mention. Early studies include E. M. Forster's essay, *Virginia Woolf*, delivered as the Rede Lecture at Cambridge in 1942, as well as books by David Daiches (1942), Joan Bennett (1945), R. L. Chambers (1948), and Bernard Blackstone (1949). The first of the critical studies of her achievement as a novelist should perhaps be Jean Guiguet's book, *Virginia Woolf and Her Works*, translated by Jean Stewart (1965). Other recent studies include: *Virginia Woolf*, by Monique Nathan, translated by Herma Briffault (1961); *Virginia Woolf*, by Carl Woodring, in the Columbia Essays on Modern Writers series (1966); and *Feminism and Art: A Study of Virginia Woolf* (1968). *Virginia Woolf: A Collection of Critical Essays*, compiled by Claire Sprague, was published in 1971; also assembling material by various hands is *Recollections of Virginia Woolf*, edited by Joan Russell Noble (1972).

Mr. Bennett and Mrs. Brown

It seems to me possible, perhaps desirable, that I may be the only person in this room who has committed the folly of writing, trying to write, or failing to write, a novel. And when I asked myself, as your invitation to speak to you about modern fiction made me ask myself, what demon whispered in my ear and urged me to my doom, a little figure rose before me—the figure of a man, or of a woman, who said, "My name is Brown. Catch me if you can."

Most novelists have the same experience. Some Brown, Smith, or Jones comes before them and says in the most seductive and charming way in the world, "Come and catch me if you can." And so, led on by this will-o'-the-wisp, they flounder through volume after volume, spending the best years of their lives in the pursuit, and receiving for the most part very little cash in exchange. Few catch the phantom; most have to be content with a scrap of her dress or a wisp of her hair.

My belief that men and women write novels because they are lured on to create some character which has thus imposed itself upon them has the sanction of Mr. Arnold Bennett. In an article from which I will quote he says, "The foundation of good fiction is character-creating and nothing else. . . . Style counts; plot counts; originality of outlook counts. But none of these counts anything like so much as the convincingness of the characters. If the characters are real the novel will have a chance; if they are not, oblivion will be its portion. . . ." And he goes on to draw the conclusion that we have no young novelists of first-rate importance at the present moment, because they are unable to create characters that are real, true, and convincing.

These are the questions that I want with greater boldness than discretion to discuss tonight. I want to make out what we mean when we talk about "character" in fiction; to say something about the question of reality which Mr. Bennett raises; and to suggest some reasons why the younger novelists fail to create characters, if, as Mr. Bennett asserts, it is true that fail they do. This will lead me, I am well aware, to make some very sweeping and some very vague assertions. For the question is an extremely difficult one. Think how little we know about character—think how little we know about art. But, to make a clearance before I begin, I will suggest that we range Edwardians and Georgians into two camps; Mr. Wells, Mr. Bennett, and Mr. Galsworthy I will call the Edwardians; Mr. Forster, Mr. Lawrence, Mr. Strachey, Mr. Joyce, and Mr. Eliot I will call the Georgians. And if I speak in the first person, with intolerable egotism, I will ask you to excuse me. I do not want to attribute to the world at large the opinions of one solitary, ill-informed, and misguided individual.

My first assertion is one that I think you will grant—that every one in this room is a judge of character. Indeed it would be impossible to live for a year without disaster unless one practised character-reading and had some skill in the art. Our marriages, our friendships depend on it; our business largely depends on it; every day questions arise which can only be solved by its help. And now I will hazard a second assertion, which is more disputable perhaps, to the effect that in or about December, 1910, human character changed.

I am not saying that one went out, as one might into a garden, and there saw that a rose had flowered, or that a hen had laid an egg. The change was not sudden and definite like that. But a change there was, nevertheless; and, since one must be arbitrary, let us date it about the year 1910. The first signs of it are recorded in the books of Samuel Butler, in *The Way of All Flesh* in particular; the plays of Bernard Shaw continue to record it. In life one can see the change, if I may use a homely illustration, in the character of one's cook. The Victorian cook lived like a leviathan in the lower depths, formidable, silent, obscure, inscrutable; the Georgian cook is a creature of sunshine and fresh air; in and out of the drawing-room, now to borrow the *Daily Herald*, now to ask advice about a hat. Do you ask for more solemn instances of the power of the human race to change? Read the *Agamemnon*, and see whether, in process of time, your sympathies are not almost entirely with Clytemnestra. Or consider the married life of the Carlyles and bewail the waste, the futility, for him and for her, of the horrible domestic tradition which made it seemly for a woman of genius to spend her time chasing beetles, scouring saucepans, instead of writing books. All human relations have shifted—those between masters and servants, husbands and wives, parents and children. And when human relations change there is at the same time a change in religion, conduct, politics, and literature. Let us agree to place one of these changes about the year 1910.

I have said that people have to acquire a

good deal of skill in character-reading if they are to live a single year of life without disaster. But it is the art of the young. In middle age and in old age the art is practised mostly for its uses, and friendships and other adventures and experiments in the art of reading character are seldom made. But novelists differ from the rest of the world because they do not cease to be interested in character when they have learnt enough about it for practical purposes. They go a step further, they feel that there is something permanently interesting in character in itself. When all the practical business of life has been discharged, there is something about people which continues to seem to them of overwhelming importance, in spite of the fact that it has no bearing whatever upon their happiness, comfort, or income. The study of character becomes to them an absorbing pursuit; to impart character an obsession. And this I find it very difficult to explain: what novelists mean when they talk about character, what the impulse is that urges them so powerfully every now and then to embody their view in writing.

So, if you will allow me, instead of analysing and abstracting, I will tell you a simple story which, however pointless, has the merit of being true, of a journey from Richmond to Waterloo, in the hope that I may show you what I mean by character in itself; that you may realize the different aspects it can wear; and the hideous perils that beset you directly you try to describe it in words.

One night some weeks ago, then, I was late for the train and jumped into the first carriage I came to. As I sat down I had the strange and uncomfortable feeling that I was interrupting a conversation between two people who were already sitting there. Not that they were young or happy. Far from it. They were both elderly, the woman over sixty, the man well over forty. They were sitting opposite each other, and the man, who had been leaning over and talking emphatically to judge by his attitude and the flush on his face, sat back and became silent. I had disturbed him, and he was annoyed. The elderly lady, however, whom I will call Mrs. Brown, seemed rather relieved. She was one of those clean, threadbare old ladies whose extreme tidiness—everything buttoned, fastened, tied together, mended and brushed up—suggests more

extreme poverty than rags and dirt. There was something pinched about her—a look of suffering, of apprehension, and, in addition, she was extremely small. Her feet, in their clean little boots, scarcely touched the floor. I felt that she had nobody to support her; that she had to make up her mind for herself; that, having been deserted, or left a widow, years ago, she had led an anxious, harried life, bringing up an only son, perhaps, who, as likely as not, was by this time beginning to go to the bad. All this shot through my mind as I sat down, being uncomfortable, like most people, at travelling with fellow passengers unless I have somehow or other accounted for them. Then I looked at the man. He was no relation of Mrs. Brown's I felt sure; he was of a bigger, burlier, less refined type. He was a man of business I imagined, very likely a respectable corn-chandler from the North, dressed in good blue serge with a pocket-knife and a silk handkerchief, and a stout leather bag. Obviously, however, he had an unpleasant business to settle with Mrs. Brown; a secret, perhaps sinister business, which they did not intend to discuss in my presence.

"Yes, the Crofts have had very bad luck with their servants," Mr. Smith (as I will call him) said in a considering way, going back to some earlier topic, with a view to keeping up appearances.

"Ah, poor people," said Mrs. Brown, a trifle condescendingly. "My grandmother had a maid who came when she was fifteen and stayed till she was eighty" (this was said with a kind of hurt and aggressive pride to impress us both perhaps).

"One doesn't often come across that sort of thing nowadays," said Mr. Smith in conciliatory tones.

Then they were silent.

"It's odd they don't start a golf club there— I should have thought one of the young fellows would," said Mr. Smith, for the silence obviously made him uneasy.

Mrs. Brown hardly took the trouble to answer.

"What changes they're making in this part of the world," said Mr. Smith looking out of the window, and looking furtively at me as he did so.

It was plain, from Mrs. Brown's silence, from the uneasy affability with which Mr. Smith spoke, that he had some power over her which he was exerting disagreeably. It might have been her son's downfall, or some painful episode in her past life, or her daughter's. Perhaps she was going to London to sign some document to make over some property. Obviously against her will she was in Mr. Smith's hands. I was beginning to feel a great deal of pity for her, when she said, suddenly and inconsequently:

"Can you tell me if an oak-tree dies when the leaves have been eaten for two years in succession by caterpillars?"

She spoke quite brightly, and rather precisely, in a cultivated, inquisitive voice.

Mr. Smith was startled, but relieved to have a safe topic of conversation given him. He told her a great deal very quickly about plagues of insects. He told her that he had a brother who kept a fruit farm in Kent. He told her what fruit farmers do every year in Kent, and so on, and so on. While he talked a very odd thing happened. Mrs. Brown took out her little white handkerchief and began to dab her eyes. She was crying. But she went on listening quite composedly to what he was saying, and he went on talking, a little louder, a little angrily, as if he had seen her cry often before; as if it were a painful habit. At last it got on his nerves. He stopped abruptly, looked out of the window, then leant towards her as he had been doing when I got in, and said in a bullying, menacing way, as if he would not stand any more nonsense:

"So about that matter we were discussing. It'll be all right? George will be there on Tuesday?"

"We shan't be late," said Mrs. Brown, gathering herself together with superb dignity.

Mr. Smith said nothing. He got up, buttoned his coat, reached his bag down, and jumped out of the train before it had stopped at Clapham Junction. He had got what he wanted, but he was ashamed of himself; he was glad to get out of the old lady's sight.

Mrs. Brown and I were left alone together. She sat in her corner opposite, very clean, very small, rather queer, and suffering intensely. The impression she made was overwhelming. It came pouring out like a draught, like a smell of burning. What was it composed of—that overwhelming and peculiar impression? Myriads of irrelevant and incongruous ideas crowd into one's head on such occasions; one sees the person, one sees

Mrs. Brown, in the centre of all sorts of different scenes. I thought of her in a seaside house, among queer ornaments: sea-urchins, models of ships in glass cases. Her husband's medals were on the mantlepiece. She popped in and out of the room, perching on the edges of chairs, picking meals out of saucers, indulging in long, silent stares. The caterpillars and the oak-trees seemed to imply all that. And then, into this fantastic and secluded life, in broke Mr. Smith. I saw him blowing in, so to speak, on a windy day. He banged, he slammed. His dripping umbrella made a pool in the hall. They sat closeted together.

And then Mrs. Brown faced the dreadful revelation. She took her heroic decision. Early, before dawn, she packed her bag and carried it herself to the station. She would not let Smith touch it. She was wounded in her pride, unmoored from her anchorage; she came of gentlefolks who kept servants—but details could wait. The important thing was to realize her character, to steep oneself in her atmosphere. I had no time to explain why I felt it somewhat tragic, heroic, yet with a dash of the flighty, and fantastic, before the train stopped, and I watched her disappear, carrying her bag, into the vast blazing station. She looked very small, very tenacious; at once very frail and very heroic. And I have never seen her again, and I shall never know what became of her.

The story ends without any point to it. But I have not told you this anecdote to illustrate either my own ingenuity or the pleasure of travelling from Richmond to Waterloo. What I want you to see in it is this. Here is a character imposing itself upon another person. Here is Mrs. Brown making someone begin almost automatically to write a novel about her. I believe that all novels begin with an old lady in the corner opposite. I believe that all novels, that is to say, deal with character, and that it is to express character—not to preach doctrines, sing songs, or celebrate the glories of the British Empire, that the form of the novel, so clumsy, verbose, and undramatic, so rich, elastic, and alive, has been evolved. To express character, I have said; but you will at once reflect that the very widest interpretation can be put upon those words. For example, old Mrs. Brown's character will strike you very differently according to the age and country in which you happen to be born. It would be easy enough to write three different versions of that incident in the train, an English, a French, and a Russian. The English writer would make the old lady into a "character"; he would bring out her oddities and mannerisms; her buttons and wrinkles; her ribbons and warts. Her personality would dominate the book. A French writer would rub out all that; he would sacrifice the individual Mrs. Brown to give a more general view of human nature; to make a more abstract, proportioned, and harmonious whole. The Russian would pierce through the flesh; would reveal the soul—the soul alone, wandering out into the Waterloo Road, asking of life some tremendous question which would sound on and on in our ears after the book was finished. And then besides age and country there is the writer's temperament to be considered. You see one thing in character, and I another. You say it means this, and I that. And when it comes to writing, each makes a further selection on principles of his own. Thus Mrs. Brown can be treated in an infinite variety of ways, according to the age, country, and temperament of the writer.

But now I must recall what Mr. Arnold Bennett says. He says that it is only if the characters are real that the novel has any chance of surviving. Otherwise, die it must. But, I ask myself, what is reality? And who are the judges of reality? A character may be real to Mr. Bennett and quite unreal to me. For instance, in this article he says that Dr. Watson in *Sherlock Holmes* is real to him: to me Dr. Watson is a sack stuffed with straw, a dummy, a figure of fun. And so it is with character after character—in book after book. There is nothing that people differ about more than the reality of characters, especially in contemporary books. But if you take a larger view I think that Mr. Bennett is perfectly right. If, that is, you think of the novels which seem to you great novels—*War and Peace, Vanity Fair, Tristram Shandy, Madame Bovary, Pride and Prejudice, The Mayor of Casterbridge, Villette*—if you think of these books, you do at once think of some character who has seemed to you so real (I do not by that mean so lifelike) that it has the power to make you think not merely of it itself, but of all sorts of things through its eyes—of religion, of love, of war, of peace, of family life, of balls in country towns, of sunsets, moonrises, the immortality of the soul. There is hardly any subject of human experience that is left out of *War and Peace* it seems to me. And in all these novels all these great novelists have brought us to see whatever they wish us to see through some character. Otherwise, they would not be novelists; but poets, historians, or pamphleteers.

But now let us examine what Mr. Bennett went on to say—he said that there was no great novelist among the Georgian writers because they cannot create characters who are real, true, and convincing. And there I cannot agree. There are reasons, excuses, possibilities which I think put a different colour upon the case. It seems so to me at least, but I am well aware that this is a matter about which I am likely to be prejudiced, sanguine, and near-sighted. I will put my view before you in the hope that you will make it impartial, judicial, and broad-minded. Why, then, is it so hard for novelists at present to create characters which seem real, not only to Mr. Bennett, but to the world at large? Why, when October comes round, do the publishers always fail to supply us with a masterpiece?

Surely one reason is that the men and women who began writing novels in 1910 or thereabouts had this great difficulty to face—that there was no English novelist living from whom they could learn their business. Mr. Conrad is a Pole; which sets him apart, and makes him, however admirable, not very helpful. Mr. Hardy has written no novel since 1895. The most prominent and successful novelists in the year 1910 were, I suppose, Mr. Wells, Mr. Bennett, and Mr. Galsworthy. Now it seems to me that to go to these men and ask them to teach you how to write a novel—how to create characters that are real—is precisely like going to a bootmaker and asking him to teach you how to make a watch. Do not let me give you the impression that I do not admire and enjoy their books. They seem to me of great value, and indeed of great necessity. There are seasons when it is more important to have boots than to have watches. To drop metaphor, I think that after the creative activity of the Victorian age it was quite necessary, not only for literature but for life, that someone should write the books that Mr. Wells, Mr. Bennett, and Mr. Galsworthy have written. Yet what odd books they are! Sometimes I wonder if we are right to call them books at all. For they leave one with so strange a feeling of incompleteness and dissatisfaction. In order to complete them it seems necessary to do something—to join a society, or, more desperately, to write a cheque. That done, the restlessness is laid, the book finished; it can be put upon the shelf, and need never be read again. But with the work of other novelists it is different. *Tristram Shandy* or *Pride and Prejudice* is complete in itself; it is self-contained; it leaves one with no desire to do anything, except indeed to read the book again, and to understand it better. The difference perhaps is that both Sterne and Jane Austen were interested in things in themselves; in character in itself; in the book in itself. Therefore everything was inside the book, nothing outside. But the Edwardians were never interested in character in itself; or in the book in itself. They were interested in something outside. Their books, then, were incomplete as books, and required that the reader should finish them, actively and practically, for himself.

Perhaps we can make this clearer if we take the liberty of imagining a little party in the railway carriage—Mr. Wells, Mr. Galsworthy, Mr. Bennett are travelling to Waterloo with Mrs. Brown. Mrs. Brown, I have said, was poorly dressed and very small. She had an anxious harassed look. I doubt whether she was what you call an educated woman. Seizing upon all these symptoms of the unsatisfactory condition of our primary schools with a rapidity to which I can do no justice, Mr. Wells would instantly project upon the window-pane a vision of a better, breezier, jollier, happier, more adventurous and gallant world, where these musty railway carriages and fusty old women do not exist; where miraculous barges bring tropical fruit to Camberwell by eight o'clock in the morning; where there are public nurseries, fountains, and libraries, dining-rooms, drawing-rooms, and marriages; where every citizen is generous and candid, manly and magnificent, and rather like Mr. Wells himself. But nobody is in the least like Mrs. Brown. There are no Mrs. Browns in Utopia. Indeed I do not think that Mr. Wells, in his passion to make her what she ought to be, would waste a thought upon her as she is. And what would Mr. Galsworthy see? Can we doubt that the walls of Doulton's factory would take his fancy? There are women in that factory who make twenty-five dozen earthenware pots every day. There are mothers in the Mile End Road who depend upon the farthings which those women earn. But there are employers in Surrey who are even now smoking rich cigars while the nightingale sings. Burning with indignation, stuffed with information, arraigning civilization, Mr. Galsworthy would only see in Mrs. Brown a pot broken on the wheel and thrown into the corner.

Mr. Bennett, alone of the Edwardians, would keep his eyes in the carriage. He, indeed, would observe every detail with immense care. He would notice the advertisements; the pictures of Swanage and Portmouth; the way in which the cushion bulged between the buttons; how Mrs. Brown wore a brooch which had cost three-and-ten-three at Whitworth's bazaar; and had mended both gloves—indeed the thumb of the left-hand glove had been replaced. And he would observe, at length, how this was the non-stop train from Windsor which calls at Richmond for the convenience of middle-class residents, who can afford to go to the theatre but have not reached the social rank which can afford motor-cars, though it is true, there are occasions (he would tell us what) when they hire them from a company (he would tell us which). And so he would gradually sidle sedately towards Mrs. Brown, and would remark how she had been left a little copyhold, not freehold, property at Datchet, which, however, was mortgaged to Mr. Bungay the solicitor—but why should I presume to invent Mr. Bennett? Does not Mr. Bennett write novels himself? I will open the first book that chance puts in my way—*Hilda Lessways*. Let us see how he makes us feel that Hilda is real, true, and convincing, as a novelist should. She shut the door in a soft, controlled way, which showed the constraint of her relations with her mother. She was fond of reading *Maud;* she was endowed with the power to feel intensely. So far, so good; in his leisurely, surefooted way Mr. Bennett is trying in these first pages, where every touch is important, to show us the kind of girl she was.

But then he begins to describe, not Hilda Lessways, but the view from her bedroom window, the excuse being that Mr. Skellorn, the man who collects rents, is coming along that way. Mr. Bennett proceeds:

"The bailiwick of Turnhill lay behind her; and all the murky district of the Five Towns, of which Turnhill is the northern outpost, lay to the south. At the

foot of Chatterley Wood the canal wound in large curves on its way towards the undefiled plains of Cheshire and the sea. On the canal-side, exactly opposite to Hilda's window, was a flour-mill, that sometimes made nearly as much smoke as the kilns and the chimneys closing the prospect on either hand. From the flour-mill a bricked path, which separated a considerable row of new cottages from their appurtenant gardens, led straight into Lessways Street, in front of Mrs. Lessway's house. By this path Mr. Skellorn should have arrived, for he inhabited the farthest of the cottages."

One line of insight would have done more than all those lines of description; but let them pass as the necessary drudgery of the novelist. And now—where is Hilda? Alas. Hilda is still looking out of the window. Passionate and dissatisfied as she was, she was a girl with an eye for houses. She often compared this old Mr. Skellorn with the villas she saw from her bedroom window. Therefore the villas must be described. Mr. Bennett proceeds:

"The row was called Freehold Villas: a consciously proud name in a district where much of the land was copyhold and could only change owners subject to the payment of 'fines,' and to the feudal consent of a 'court' presided over by the agent of a lord of the manor. Most of the dwellings were owned by their occupiers, who, each an absolute monarch of the soil, niggled in his sooty garden of an evening amid the flutter of drying shirts and towels. Freehold Villas symbolized the final triumph of Victorian economics, the apotheosis of the prudent and industrious artisan. It corresponded with a Building Society Secretary's dream of paradise. And indeed it was a very real achievement. Nevertheless, Hilda's irrational contempt would not admit this."

Heaven be praised, we cry! at last we are coming to Hilda herself. But not so fast. Hilda may have been this, that, and the other; but Hilda not only looked at houses, and thought of houses; Hilda lived in a house. And what sort of a house did Hilda live in? Mr. Bennett proceeds:

"It was one of the two middle houses of a detached terrace of four houses built by her grandfather Lessways, the teapot manufacturer; it was the chief of the four, obviously the habitation of the proprietor of the terrace. One of the corner houses comprised a grocer's shop, and this house had been robbed of its just proportion of garden so that the seigneurial

garden-plot might be triflingly larger than the other. The terrace was not a terrace of cottages, but of houses rated at from twenty-six to thirty-six pounds a year; beyond the means of artisans and petty insurance agents and rent-collectors. And further, it was well-built, generously built; and its architecture, though debased, showed some faint traces of Georgian amenity. It was admittedly the best row of houses in that newly-settled quarter of the town. In coming to it out of Freehold Villas Mr. Skellorn obviously came to something superior, wider, more liberal. Suddenly Hilda heard her mother's voice. . . ."

But we cannot hear her mother's voice, or Hilda's voice; we can only hear Mr. Bennett's voice telling us facts about rents and freeholds and copyholds and fines. What can Mr. Bennett be about? I have formed my own opinion of what Mr. Bennett is about—he is trying to make us imagine for him; he is trying to hypnotize us into the belief that, because he has made a house, there must be a person living there. With all his powers of observation, which are marvellous, with all his sympathy and humanity, which are great, Mr. Bennett has never once looked at Mrs. Brown in her corner. There she sits in the corner of the carriage—that carriage which is travelling, not from Richmond to Waterloo, but from one age of English literature to the next, for Mrs. Brown is eternal, Mrs. Brown is human nature, Mrs. Brown changes only on the surface, it is the novelists who get in and out—there she sits and not one of the Edwardian writers has so much as looked at her. They have looked very powerfully, searchingly, and sympathetically out of the window; at factories, at Utopias, even at the decoration and upholstery of the carriage; but never at her, never at life, never at human nature. And so they have developed a technique of novel-writing which suits their purpose; they have made tools and established conventions which do their business. But those tools are not our tools, and that business is not our business. For us those conventions are ruin, those tools are death.

You may well complain of the vagueness of my language. What is a convention, a tool, you may ask, and what do you mean by saying that Mr. Bennett's and Mr. Wells's and Mr. Galsworthy's conventions are the wrong conventions for the Georgians? The question is difficult: I will attempt a short cut. A convention in writing is not much different from a convention in manners. Both in life and in literature it is necessary to have some means of bridging the gulf between the hostess and her unknown guest on the one hand, the writer and his unknown reader on the other. The hostess bethinks her of the weather, for generations of hostesses have established the fact that this is a subject of universal interest in which we all believe. She begins by saying that we are having a wretched May, and, having thus got into touch with her unknown guest, proceeds to matters of greater interest. So it is in literature. The writer must get into touch with his reader by putting before him something which he recognizes, which therefore stimulates his imagination, and makes him willing to co-operate in the far more difficult business of intimacy. And it is of the highest importance that this common meeting-place should be reached easily, almost instinctively, in the dark, with one's eyes shut. Here is Mr. Bennett making use of this common ground in the passage which I have quoted. The problem before him was to make us believe in the reality of Hilda Lessways. So he began, being an Edwardian, by describing accurately and minutely the sort of house Hilda lived in, and the sort of house she saw from the window. House property was the common ground from which the Edwardians found it easy to proceed to intimacy. Indirect as it seems to us, the convention worked admirably, and thousands of Hilda Lessways were launched upon the world by this means. For that age and generation, the convention was a good one.

But now, if you will allow me to pull my own anecdote to pieces, you will see how keenly I felt the lack of a convention, and how serious a matter it is when the tools of one generation are useless for the next. The incident had made a great impression on me. But how was I to transmit it to you? All I could do was to report as accurately as I could what was said, to describe in detail what was worn, to say, despairingly, that all sorts of scenes rushed into my mind, to proceed to tumble them out pell-mell, and to describe this vivid, this overmastering impression by likening it to a draught or a smell of burning. To tell you the truth, I was also strongly tempted to manufacture a three-volume novel about the old lady's son, and his adventures crossing the Atlantic, and her daughter, and how she kept a milliner's shop in Westminster, the past life of Smith himself, and his house at Sheffield, though such stories seem to me the most dreary, irrelevant, and humbugging affairs in the world.

But if I had done that I should have escaped the appalling effort of saying what I meant. And to have got at what I meant I should have had to go back and back and back; to experiment with one thing and another; to try this sentence and that, referring each word to my vision, matching it as exactly as possible, and knowing that somehow I had to find a common ground between us, a convention which would not seem to you too odd, unreal, and farfetched to believe in. I admit that I shirked that arduous undertaking. I let my Mrs. Brown slip through my fingers. I have told you nothing whatever about her. But that is partly the great Edwardians' fault. I asked them—they are my elders and betters—How shall I begin to describe this woman's character? And they said: "Begin by saying that her father kept a shop in Harrogate. Ascertain the rent. Ascertain the wages of shop assistants in the year 1878. Discover what her mother died of. Describe cancer. Describe calico. Describe—" But I cried: "Stop! Stop!" And I regret to say that I threw that ugly, that clumsy, that incongruous tool out of the window, for I knew that if I began describing the cancer and the calico, my Mrs. Brown, that vision to which I cling though I know no way of imparting it to you, would have been dulled and tarnished and vanished for ever.

That is what I mean by saying that the Edwardian tools are the wrong ones for us to use. They have laid an enormous stress upon the fabric of things. They have given us a house in the hope that we may be able to deduce the human beings who live there. To give them their due, they have made that house much better worth living in. But if you hold that novels are in the first place about people, and only in the second about the houses they live in, that is the wrong way to set about it. Therefore, you see, the Georgian writer had to begin by throwing away the method that was in use at the moment. He was left alone there facing Mrs. Brown without any method of conveying her to the reader. But that is inaccurate. A writer is never alone. There is always the public with him—if not on the same seat, at least in the compartment next door. Now the public is a strange travelling companion. In England it is a very suggestible and docile creature, which, once you get it to attend, will believe implicitly what it is told for a certain number of years. If you say to the public with sufficient conviction: "All women have tails, and all men humps," it will actually learn to see women with tails and men with humps, and will think it very revolutionary and probably improper if you say: "Nonsense. Monkeys have tails and camels humps. But men and women have brains, and they have hearts; they think and they feel,"—that will seem to it a bad joke, and an improper one into the bargain.

But to return. Here is the British public sitting by the writer's side and saying in its vast and unanimous way, "Old women have houses. They have fathers. They have incomes. They have servants. They have hot-water bottles. That is how we know that they are old women. Mr. Wells and Mr. Bennett and Mr. Galsworthy have always taught us that this is the way to recognize them. But now with your Mrs. Brown—how are we to believe in her? We do not even know whether her villa was called Albert or Balmoral; what she paid for her gloves; or whether her mother died of cancer or of consumption. How can she be alive? No; she is a mere figment of your imagination."

And old women of course ought to be made of freehold villas and copyhold estates, not of imagination.

The Georgian novelist, therefore, was in an awkward predicament. There was Mrs. Brown protesting that she was different, quite different, from what people made out, and luring the novelist to her rescue by the most fascinating if fleeting glimpse of her charms; there were the Edwardians handing out tools appropriate to house building and house breaking; and there was the British public asseverating that they must see the hot-water bottle first. Meanwhile the train was rushing to that station where we must all get out.

Such, I think, was the predicament in which the young Georgians found themselves about the year 1910. Many of them—I am thinking of Mr. Forster and Mr. Lawrence in particular—spoilt their early work because, instead of throwing away those tools, they tried to use them. They tried to compromise. They tried to combine their own direct sense of the oddity and signifi-

cance of some character with Mr. Galsworthy's knowledge of the Factory Acts, and Mr. Bennett's knowledge of the Five Towns. They tried it, but they had too keen, too overpowering a sense of Mrs. Brown and her peculiarities to go on trying it much longer. Something had to be done. At whatever cost of life, limb, and damage to valuable property Mrs. Brown must be rescued, expressed, and set in her high relations to the world before the train stopped and she disappeared for ever. And so the smashing and the crashing began. Thus it is that we hear all round us, in poems and novels and biographies, even in newspaper articles and essays, the sound of breaking and falling, crashing and destruction. It is the prevailing sound of the Georgian age—rather a melancholy one if you think what melodious days there have been in the past, if you think of Shakespeare and Milton and Keats or even of Jane Austen and Thackeray and Dickens; if you think of the language, and the heights to which it can soar when free, and see the same eagle captive, bald, and croaking.

In view of these facts—with these sounds in my ears and these fancies in my brain—I am not going to deny that Mr. Bennett has some reason when he complains that our Georgian writers are unable to make us believe that our characters are real. I am forced to agree that they do not pour out three immortal masterpieces with Victorian regularity every autumn. But, instead of being gloomy, I am sanguine. For this state of things is, I think, inevitable whenever from hoar old age or callow youth the convention ceases to be a means of communication between writer and reader, and becomes instead an obstacle and an impediment. At the present moment we are suffering, not from decay, but from having no code of manners which writers and readers accept as a prelude to the more exciting intercourse of friendship. The literary convention of the time is so artificial—you have to talk about the weather and nothing but the weather throughout the entire visit—that, naturally, the feeble are tempted to outrage, and the strong are led to destroy the very foundations and rules of literary society. Signs of this are everywhere apparent. Grammar is violated; syntax disintegrated; as a boy staying with an aunt for the week-end rolls in the geranium bed out of sheer desperation as the solemnities of the sabbath wear on. The more adult writers do not, of course, indulge in such wanton exhibitions of spleen. Their sincerity is desperate, and their courage tremendous; it is only that they do not know which to use, a fork or their fingers. Thus, if you read Mr. Joyce and Mr. Eliot you will be struck by the indecency of the one, and the obscurity of the other. Mr. Joyce's indecency in *Ulysses* seems to me the conscious and calculated indecency of a desperate man who feels that in order to breathe he must break the windows. At moments, when the window is broken, he is magnificent. But what a waste of energy! And, after all, how dull indecency is, when it is not the overflowing of a superabundant energy or savagery, but the determined and public-spirited act of a man who needs fresh air! Again, with the obscurity of Mr. Eliot. I think that Mr. Eliot has written some of the loveliest single lines in modern poetry. But how intolerant he is of the old usages and politenesses of society—respect for the weak, consideration for the dull! As I sun myself upon the intense and ravishing beauty of one of his lines, and reflect that I must make a dizzy and dangerous leap to the next, and so on from line to line, like an acrobat flying precariously from bar to bar, I cry out, I confess, for the old decorums, and envy the indolence of my ancestors who, instead of spinning madly through mid-air, dreamt quietly in the shade with a book. Again, in Mr. Strachey's books, *Eminent Victorians* and *Queen Victoria,* the effort and strain of writing against the grain and current of the times is visible too. It is much less visible, of course, for not only is he dealing with facts, which are stubborn things, but he has fabricated, chiefly from eighteenth-century material, a very discreet code of manners of his own, which allows him to sit at table with the highest in the land and to say a great many things under cover of that exquisite apparel which, had they gone naked, would have been chased by the men-servants from the room. Still, if you compare *Eminent Victorians* with some of Lord Macaulay's essays, though you will feel that Lord Macaulay is always wrong, and Mr. Strachey always right, you will also feel a body, a sweep, a richness in Lord Macaulay's essays which show that his age was behind him; all his strength went straight into his work; none was used for purposes of concealment or of conversion. But Mr. Strachey has had to open our eyes before he

made us see; he has had to search out and sew together a very artful manner of speech; and the effort, beautifully though it is concealed, has robbed his work of some of the force that should have gone into it, and limited his scope.

For these reasons, then, we must reconcile ourselves to a season of failures and fragments. We must reflect that where so much strength is spent on finding a way of telling the truth, the truth itself is bound to reach us in rather an exhausted and chaotic condition. Ulysses, Queen Victoria, Mr. Prufrock—to give Mrs. Brown some of the names she has made famous lately—is a little pale and dishevelled by the time her rescuers reach her. And it is the sound of their axes that we hear—a vigorous and stimulating sound in my ears—unless of course you wish to sleep, when, in the bounty of his concern, Providence has provided a host of writers anxious and able to satisfy your needs.

Thus I have tried, at tedious length, I fear, to answer some of the questions which I began by asking. I have given an account of some of the difficulties which in my view beset the Georgian writer in all his forms. I have sought to excuse him. May I end by venturing to remind you of the duties and responsibilities that are yours as partners in this business of writing books, as companions in the railway carriage, as fellow travellers with Mrs. Brown? For she is just as visible to you who remain silent as to us who tell stories about her. In the course of your daily life this past week you have had far stranger and more interesting experiences than the one I have tried to describe. You have overheard scraps of talk that filled you with amazement. You have gone to bed at night bewildered by the complexity of your feelings. In one day thousands of ideas have coursed through your brains; thousands of emotions have met, collided, and disappeared in astonishing disorder. Nevertheless, you allow the writers to palm off upon you a version of all this, an image of Mrs. Brown, which has no likeness to that surprising apparition whatsoever. In your modesty you seem to consider that writers are of different blood and bone from yourselves; that they know more of Mrs. Brown than you do. Never was there a more fatal mistake. It is this division between reader and writer, this humility on your part, these professional airs and graces on ours, that corrupt and emasculate the books which should be the healthy offspring of a close and equal alliance between us. Hence spring those sleek, smooth novels, those portentous and ridiculous biographies, that milk and watery criticism, those poems melodiously celebrating the innocence of roses and sheep which pass so plausibly for literature at the present time.

Your part is to insist that writers shall come down off their plinths and pedestals, and describe beautifully if possible, truthfully at any rate, our Mrs. Brown. You should insist that she is an old lady of unlimited capacity and infinite variety; capable of appearing in any place; wearing any dress; saying anything and doing heaven knows what. But the things she says and the things she does and her eyes and her nose and her speech and her silence have an overwhelming fascination, for she is, of course, the spirit we live by, life itself.

But do not expect just at present a complete and satisfactory presentment of her. Tolerate the spasmodic, the obscure, the fragmentary, the failure. Your help is invoked in a good cause. For I will make one final and surpassingly rash prediction—we are trembling on the verge of one of the great ages of English literature. But it can only be reached if we are determined never, never to desert Mrs. Brown.

from A Writer's Diary

Being Extracts from the Diary of Virginia Woolf*

Thursday, August 18th [1921]

Nothing to record; only an intolerable fit of the fidgets to write away. Here I am chained to my rock; forced to do nothing; doomed to let every worry, spite, irritation and obsession scratch and claw and come again. This is a day that I may not walk and must not work. Whatever book I read bubbles up in my mind as part of an article I want to write. No one in the whole of Sussex is so miserable as I am; or so conscious of an infinite capacity of enjoyment hoarded in me, could I use it. The sun streams (no, never streams; floods rather) down upon all the yellow fields and the long low barns; and what wouldn't I give to be coming through Firle woods, dirty and hot, with my nose turned home, every muscle tired and the brain laid up in sweet lavender, so sane and cool, and ripe for the morrow's task. How I should notice everything—the phrase for it coming the moment after and fitting like a glove; and then on the dusty road, as I ground my pedals, so my story would begin telling itself; and then the sum would be down; and home, and some bout of poetry after dinner, half read, half lived, as if the flesh were dissolved and through it the flowers burst red and white. There! I've written out half my irritation. I hear poor L. driving the lawn mower up and down, for a wife like I am should have a latch to her cage. She bites! And he spent all yesterday running round London for me. Still if one is Prometheus, if the rock is hard and the gadflies pungent, gratitude, affection, none of the nobler feelings have sway. And so this August is wasted.

Only the thought of people suffering more than I do at all consoles; and that is an aberration of egotism, I suppose. I will now make out a time table if I can get through these odious days.

Poor Mdlle. Lenglen,[1] finding herself beaten by Mrs. Mallory, flung down her racquet and burst into tears. Her vanity I suppose is colossal. I daresay she thought that to be Mdlle. Lenglen was the greatest thing in the world; invincible, like Napoleon. Armstrong, playing in the test match, took up his position against the gates and would not move, let the bowlers appoint themselves, the whole game became farcical because there was not time to play it out. But Ajax in the Greek play was of the same temper—which we all agree to call heroic in him. But then everything is forgiven to the Greeks. And I've not read a line of Greek since last year, this time, too. But I shall come back, if it's only in snobbery; I shall be reading Greek when I'm old; old as the woman at the cottage door, whose hair might be a wig in a play, it's so white, so thick. Seldom penetrated by love for mankind as I am, I sometimes feel sorry for the poor who don't read Shakespeare, and indeed have felt some generous democratic humbug at the Old Vic, when they played Othello and all the poor men and women and children had him there for themselves. Such

---

* Edited by Leonard Woolf, 1953.

1 Mlle. Suzanne Lenglen, international women's tennis champion in the 1920s.

splendour and such poverty. I am writing down the fidgets, so no matter if I write nonsense. Indeed, any interference with the normal proportions of things makes me uneasy. I know this room too well—this view too well—I am getting it all out of focus, because I can't walk through it.

Tuesday, June 19th [1923]

I took up this book[2] with a kind of idea that I might say something about my writing—which was prompted by glancing at what K. M.[3] said about her writing in *The Dove's Nest*. But I only glanced. She said a good deal about feeling things deeply: also about being pure, which I won't criticise, though of course I very well could. But now what do I feel about *my* writing?—this book, that is, *The Hours*,[4] if that's its name? One must write from deep feeling, said Dostoievsky. And do I? Or do I fabricate with words, loving them as I do? No, I think not. In this book I have almost too many ideas. I want to give life and death, sanity and insanity; I want to criticise the social system, and to show it at work, at its most intense. But here I may be posing. I heard from Ka[5] this morning that she doesn't like *In the Orchard*. At once I feel refreshed. I become anonymous, a person who writes for the love of it. She takes away the motive of praise, and lets me feel that without any praise I should be content to go on. This is what Duncan[6] said of his painting the other night. I feel as if I slipped off all my ball dresses and stood naked—which as I remember was a very pleasant thing to do. But to go on. Am I writing *The Hours* from deep emotion? Of course the mad part tries me so much, makes my mind squirt so badly that I can hardly face spending the next weeks at it. It's a question though of these characters. People, like Arnold Bennett, say I can't create, or didn't in *Jacob's Room*, characters that survive. My answer is—but I leave that to the *Nation:* it's only the old argument that character is dissipated into shreds now; the old post-Dostoievsky argument. I daresay it's true,

however, that I haven't that "reality" gift. I insubstantise, wilfully to some extent, distrusting reality—its cheapness. But to get further. Have I the power of conveying the true reality? Or do I write essays about myself? Answer these questions as I may, in the uncomplimentary sense, and still there remains this excitement. To get to the bones, now I'm writing fiction again I feel my force glow straight from me at its fullest. After a dose of criticism I feel that I'm writing sideways, using only an angle of my mind. This is justification; for free use of the faculties means happiness. I'm better company, more of a human being. Nevertheless, I think it most important in this book to go for the central things. Even though they don't submit, as they should, however, to beautification in language. No, I don't nail my crest to the Murrys, who work in my flesh after the manner of the jigger insect. It's annoying, indeed degrading, to have these bitternesses. Still, think of the eighteenth century. But then they were overt, not covert, as now.

I foresee, to return to *The Hours*, that this is going to be the devil of a struggle. The design is so queer and so masterful. I'm always having to wrench my substance to fit it. The design is certainly original and interests me hugely. I should like to write away and away at it, very quick and fierce. Needless to say, I can't. In three weeks from today, I shall be dried up.

Saturday, October 27th [1928]

A scandal, a scandal, to let so much time slip and I leaning on the Bridge watching it go. Only leaning has not been my pose; running up and down, irritably, excitedly, restlessly. And the stream viciously eddying. Why do I write these metaphors? Because I have written nothing for an age. *Orlando* has been published. I went to Burgundy with Vita.[7] It flashed by. How disconnected this is! My ambition is from this very moment, 8 minutes to 6, on Saturday evening, to attain complete concentration again. When I have written here, I am going to open Fanny Burney's diaries and work solidly at that article which poor Miss McKay cables about. I am going to read, to think. I gave up reading and thinking on 26th September when I went to France. I

---

2 I.e., the notebook in which she kept her diary.
3 Katherine Mansfield (1888–1923), the famous short-story writer, and wife of J. Middleton Murry, the critic.
4 Subsequently this title was altered to *Mrs. Dalloway* [Leonard Woolf's note].
5 Mrs. Arnold-Forster [L. W.'s note].
6 Duncan Grant, the painter.

7 Victoria Sackville-West (Mrs. Harold Nicolson), poet and novelist.

came back and we plunged into London and publishing. I am a little sick of *Orlando*. I think I am a little indifferent now what anyone thinks. Joy's life in the doing—I murder, as usual, a quotation; I mean it's the writing, not the being read, that excites me. And as I can't write while I'm being read, I am always a little hollow hearted; whipped up; but not so happy as in solitude. The reception, as they say, surpassed expectation. Sales beyond our record for the first week. I was floating rather lazily on praise, when Squire barked in the *Observer,* but even as I sat reading him on the Backs last Sunday in the showering red leaves and their illumination, I felt the rock of self esteem untouched in me. "This doesn't really hurt," I said to myself; even now; and sure enough, before evening I was calm, untouched. And now there's Hugh[8] in the *Morning Post* to spread the butter again, and Rebecca West—such a trumpet call of praise—that's her way—that I feel a little sheepish and silly. And now no more of that I hope.

Thank God, my long toil at the women's lecture is this moment ended. I am back from speaking at Girton,[9] in floods of rain. Starved but valiant young women—that's my impression. Intelligent, eager, poor; and destined to become schoolmistresses in shoals. I blandly told them to drink wine and have a room of their own. Why should all the splendour, all the luxury of life be lavished on the Julians and the Francises, and none on the Phares and the Thomases? There's Julian[10] not much relishing it, perhaps. I fancy sometimes the world changes. I think I see reason spreading. But I should have liked a closer and thicker knowledge of life. I should have liked to deal with real things sometimes. I get such a sense of tingling and vitality from an evening's talk like that; one's angularities and obscurities are smoothed and lit. How little one counts, I think: how little anyone counts; how fast and furious and masterly life is; and how all these thousands are swimming for dear life. I felt elderly and mature. And nobody respected me. They were very eager, egotistical, or rather not much impressed by age and repute. Very little

reverence or that sort of thing about. The corridors of Girton are like vaults in some horrid high church cathedral—on and on they go, cold and shiny, with a light burning. High Gothic rooms: acres of bright brown wood; here and there a photograph.

Wednesday, November 28th [1928]

Father's birthday. He would have been 96, 96, yes, today; and could have been 96, like other people one has known: but mercifully was not. His life would have entirely ended mine. What would have happened? No writing, no books;—inconceivable.

I used to think of him and mother daily; but writing the *Lighthouse* laid them in my mind. And now he comes back sometimes, but differently. (I believe this to be true—that I was obsessed by them both, unhealthily; and writing of them was a necessary act.) He comes back now more as a contemporary. I must read him some day. I wonder if I can feel again, I hear his voice, I know this by heart?

So the days pass and I ask myself sometimes whether one is not hypnotised, as a child by a silver globe, by life; and whether this is living. It's very quick, bright, exciting. But superficial perhaps. I should like to take the globe in my hands and feel it quietly, round, smooth, heavy, and so hold it, day after day. I will read Proust I think. I will go backwards and forwards.

As for my next book, I am going to hold myself from writing till I have it impending in me: grown heavy in my mind like a ripe pear; pendant, gravid, asking to be cut or it will fall. *The Moths*[11] still haunts me, coming, as they always do, unbidden, between tea and dinner, while L. plays the gramophone. I shape a page or two; and make myself stop. Indeed I am up against some difficulties. Fame to begin with. *Orlando* has done very well. Now I could go on writing like that—the tug and suck are at me to do it. People say this was so spontaneous, so natural. And I would like to keep those qualities if I could without losing the others. But those qualities were largely the result of ignoring the others. They came of writing exteriorly; and if I dig, must I not lose them? And what is my own position towards the inner and the outer? I think

---

8 Hugh Walpole, the novelist.
9 A college for women, founded at Hitchin in 1869, later moved to Cambridge.
10 Julian Bell, Virginia Woolf's nephew, son of Vanessa and Clive Bell, who was later killed in Spain.

11 Later entitled *The Waves*.

a kind of ease and dash are good;—yes: I think even externality is good; some combination of them ought to be possible. The idea has come to me that what I want now to do is to saturate every atom. I mean to eliminate all waste, deadness, superfluity: to give the moment whole; whatever it includes. Say that the moment is a combination of thought; sensation; the voice of the sea. Waste, deadness, come from the inclusion of things that don't belong to the moment; this appalling narrative business of the realist: getting on from lunch to dinner: it is false, unreal, merely conventional. Why admit anything to literature that is not poetry—by which I mean saturated? Is that not my grudge against novelists? that they select nothing? The poets succeeding by simplifying: practically everything is left out. I want to put practically everything in: yet to saturate. That is what I want to do in *The Moths*. It must include nonsense, fact, sordidity: but made transparent. I think I must read Ibsen and Shakespeare and Racine. And I will write something about them; for that is the best spur, my mind being what it is; then I read with fury and exactness; otherwise I skip and skip; I am a lazy reader. But no: I am surprised and a little disquieted by the remorseless severity of my mind: that it never stops reading and writing; makes me write on Geraldine Jewsbury,[12] on Hardy, on Women—is too professional, too little any longer a dreamy amateur.

Wednesday, May 9th [1934]

This, the 9th May, was our last day and fine. So we saw Warwickshire—but I've been reading the Monologue and note how oddly another style infects—at its best: thick green, thick leaves, stubby yellow stone houses and a fine sprinkling of Elizabethan cottages. All this led very harmoniously to Stratford on Avon; and all crabbers be damned—it is a fine, unselfconscious town, mixed, with eighteenth century and the rest all standing cheek by jowl. All the flowers were out in Shakespeare's garden. "That was where his study windows looked out when he wrote *The Tempest*," said the man. And perhaps it was true. Anyhow it was a great big house, looking straight at the large windows and the grey stone of the school chapel, and when the

clock struck, that was the sound Shakespeare heard. I cannot without more labour than my roadrunning mind can compass describe the queer impression of sunny impersonality. Yes, everything seemed to say, this was Shakespeare's, here he sat and walked; but you won't find me, not exactly in the flesh. He is serenely absent—present; both at once; radiating round one; yes; in the flowers, in the old hall, in the garden; but never to be pinned down. And we went to the church and there was the florrid foolish bust, but what I had not reckoned for was the worn simple slab, turned the wrong way, Kind Friend for Jesus' sake forbear—again he seemed to be all air and sun smiling serenely; and yet down there one foot from me lay the little bones that had spread over the world this vast illumination. Yes, and then we walked round the church and all is simple and a little worn; the river slipping past the stone wall, with a red breadth from some flowering tree, and the edge of the turf unspoilt, soft and green and muddy and two casual nonchalant swans. The church and the school and the house are all roomy spacious places, resonant, sunny today, and in and out [13]—yes, an impressive place; still living, and then the little bones lying there, which have created: to think of writing *The Tempest* looking out on that garden: what a rage and storm of thought to have gone over any mind; no doubt the solidity of the place was comfortable. No doubt he saw the cellars with serenity. And a few scented American girls and a good deal of parrot prattle from old gramophone discs at the birthplace, one taking up the story from the other. But isn't it odd, the caretaker at New Place agreed, that only one genuine signature of Shakespeare's is known; and all the rest, books, furniture, pictures etc. has completely vanished? Now I think Shakespeare was very happy in this, that there was no impediment of fame, but his genius flowed out of him and is still there, in Stratford. They were acting *As You Like It* I think in the theatre.

Duffers the biographers not to make more hum and melody out of New Place. I could, so I think. For the man told us that after the great grand-daughter's death there was a sale, and why shouldn't some of his things, he said, be lost,

12 See the essay "Geraldine and Jane," in *The Second Common Reader*.

13 Word illegible [L. W.'s note].

put away and come to light? Also, Queen H. Maria, Charles I's queen, stayed there at New Place with the grand-daughter(?) which shows how substantial it must have been. That he told us, and I had never heard. And he said Gaskell, the clergyman, had the original house, which stretched across the garden almost to the chapel, pulled down because people bothered him, asking to see Shakespeare's house. And there (between the window and the wall) was the room he died in. A mulberry reputes to be the scion of the tree that grew outside Shakespeare's window. Great cushions of blue, yellow, white flowers in the garden, which is open, so that the living go on walking and sitting there.

Saturday, April 3rd [1937]

Now I have to broadcast on 29th. It will go like this: can't be a craft of words. Am going to disregard the title and talk about words: why they won't let themselves be made a craft of. They tell the truth: they aren't useful. That there should be two languages: fiction and fact. Words are inhuman . . . won't make money—need privacy. Why. For their embraces, to continue the race. A dead word. The purists and the impurists. These are only impressions, not fixations. I respect words too. Associations of words. Felicity brings in absent thee. We can easily make new words. Squish squash: crick crack. But we can't use them in writing.

Tuesday, April 11th [1939]

I am reading Dickens; by way of a refresher. How he lives: not writes: both a virtue and a fault. Like seeing something emerge; without containing mind. Yet the accuracy and even sometimes the penetration—into Miss Squeers and Miss Price and the farmer for example—remarkable. I can't dip my critical mind, even if I try to. Then I'm reading Sévigné, professionally, for that quick amalgamation of books that I intend. In future, I'm to write quick, intense, short books, and never be tied down. This is the way to keep off the settling down and refrigeration of old age. And to float all preconceived theories. For more and more I doubt if enough is known to sketch even probable lines, all too emphatic and conventional. Maurice, the last of the Ll. Davies brothers, is dead; and Margaret

lives—lives too carefully of life, I used to feel Why drag on, always measuring and testing one's little bit of strength and setting it easy tasks so as to accumulate years? Also I'm reading Rochefoucauld. That's the real point of my little brown book—that it makes me read—with a pen —following the scent; and read the good books: not the slither of MSS and the stridency of the young chawking—the word expresses callow bills agape and chattering—for sympathy. Chaucer I take at need. So if I had any time—but perhaps next week will be more solitudinous—I should, if it weren't for the war—glide my way up and up into that exciting layer so rarely lived in: where my mind works so quick it seems asleep; like the aeroplane propellers. But I must retype the last Clifton passage; and so be quit for tomorrow and clear the decks for Cambridge. Rather good, I expect it is: condensed and moulded.

Friday, February 2nd [1940]

Only the fire sets me dreaming—of all the things I mean to write. The break in our lives from London to country is a far more complete one than any change of house. Yes, but I haven't got the hang of it altogether. The immense space suddenly becomes vacant: then illuminated. And London, in nips, is cramped and creased. Odd how often I think with what is love I suppose of the City: of the walk to the Tower: that is my England: I mean, if a bomb destroyed one of those little alleys with the brass bound curtains and the river smell and the old woman reading, I should feel—well, what the patriots feel.

Wednesday, January 15th [1941]

Parsimony may be the end of this book.[14] Also shame at my own verbosity, which comes over me when I see the 20 it is—books shuffled together in my room. Who am I ashamed of? Myself reading them. Then Joyce is dead: Joyce about a fortnight younger than I am. I remember Miss Weaver,[15] in wool gloves, bringing Ulysses in typescript to our teatable at Hogarth House.

---

14 I.e., the current notebook in which she was writing her diary.
15 Harriet Shaw Weaver, editor of The Egoist, to whom T. S. Eliot was later to dedicate his Selected Essays in gratitude for her service to the writers of his time.

Roger I think sent her. Would we devote our lives to printing it? The indecent pages looked so incongruous: she was spinsterly, buttoned up. And the pages reeled with indecency. I put it in the drawer of the inlaid cabinet. One day Katherine Mansfield came, and I had it out. She began to read, ridiculing: then suddenly said, But there's something in this: a scene that should figure I suppose in the history of literature. He was about the place, but I never saw him. Then I remember Tom[16] in Ottoline's[17] room at Garsington saying—it was published then—how could anyone write again after achieving the immense prodigy of the last chapter? He was, for the first time in my knowledge, rapt, enthusiastic. I bought the blue paper book, and read it here one summer I think with spasms of

wonder, of discovery, and then again with long lapses of intense boredom. This goes back to a pre-historic world. And now all the gents are furbishing up their opinions, and the books, I suppose, take their place in the long procession.

We were in London on Monday. I went to London Bridge. I looked at the river; very misty; some tufts of smoke, perhaps from burning houses. There was another fire on Saturday. Then I saw a cliff of wall, eaten out, at one corner; a great corner all smashed; a Bank; the Monument erect: tried to get a bus; but such a block I dismounted; and the second bus advised me to walk. A complete jam of traffic; for streets were being blown up. So by Tube to the Temple; and there wandered in the desolate ruins of my old squares: gashed; dismantled; the old red bricks all white powder, something like a builder's yard. Grey dirt and broken windows. Sightseers; all that completeness ravished and demolished.

---

[16] T. S. Eliot.
[17] Lady Ottoline Morrell; Garsington, her country house, is the Breadalby of D. H. Lawrence's *Women in Love*.

Edward Morgan Forster
1879–1970

Of E. M. Forster's five novels, four were published in the first decade of the century (*Where Angels Fear to Tread*, 1905; *The Longest Journey*, 1907; *A Room with a View*, 1908; *Howard's End*, 1910) and the fifth, *A Passage to India*, in 1927. A number of short stories that had first appeared in periodicals were collected in 1911 under the title of *The Celestial Omnibus;* and another such collection, *The Eternal Moment*, was published in 1928 (the stories in both volumes are at present obtainable in a single volume, *The Collected Tales of E. M. Forster*). Yet it would be a mistake to assume from glancing at these dates that one must approach E. M. Forster as an Edwardian, or perhaps even as a Georgian, for he has had a faculty for seeming to be exactly contemporary with the moment at which one reads him. Or one might put it this way: his works are shaped by a clear intelligence, by an ability to see through cant and sham and stuffiness, by a warmth of heart, and by a recognition of the difficulties inherent in the human situation, which must always strike us as pointing to the way out of the particular impasse in which at a given moment stupidity and hatred have succeeded in placing us. To follow the way out demands, of course, the same courage and bold faith that are demanded of

his characters by the crucial situations in which he places them; like some of them, we do not often find the courage, or even know that it is demanded, until too late.

Forster, who was born in 1879, was educated at Tonbridge and at King's College, Cambridge. At the time of the First World War he spent three years in Egypt, commemorated in *Alexandria: A History and a Guide* (1922) and in a collection of essays on Alexandrian history, *Pharos and Pharillon* (1923). He had traveled in India in 1912, and was there again in 1922. In 1927 he gave the Clark Lectures at Cambridge, published in the same year as *Aspects of the Novel*. Among his other books are a biography of Goldsworthy Lowes Dickinson (1934); two collections of critical essays, reviews, and shorter biographical sketches, *Abinger Harvest* (1936) and *Two Cheers for Democracy* (1951); an account of his experiences in India as a young man, *The Hill of Devi* (1953); and *Marianne Thornton: A Domestic Biography: 1797–1887* (1956).

Since Forster's death, two early works of fiction have been published: *Maurice: A Novel* (1971) and *The Life to Come and Other Stories* (1972). These books have their interest, as anything from Forster's pen inevitably has; and, dealing as they do with explicitly homerotic themes and situations, they cast a certain light on Forster's other novels, but they do not seem to come up to the already published work in quality.

CRITICAL STUDIES: There have been full-length studies of his work by Rose Macaulay (1938) and Lionel Trilling (1944; new and revised edition 1967), and Forster figures in J. K. Johnstone's study of *The Bloomsbury Group* (1954). There is a brief study, *E. M. Forster,* by Harry T. Moore, in the series of Columbia Essays on Modern Writers (1965), and a full-length study by Wilfred Stone, *The Cave and the Mountain* (1966). Collections of essays by various hands are: *Forster: A Collection of Critical Essays,* edited by Malcolm Bradbury (1966), and *Aspects of E. M. Forster: Essays and Recollections Written for His Ninetieth Birthday,* by John Arlott and Others (including Elizabeth and Benjamin Britten).

The Road from Colonus[1]

I

For no very intelligible reason, Mr. Lucas had hurried ahead of his party. He was perhaps reaching the age at which independence becomes valuable, because it is so soon to be lost. Tired of attention and consideration, he liked breaking away from the younger members, to ride by himself, and to dismount unassisted. Perhaps he also relished that more subtle pleasure of being kept waiting for lunch, and of telling the others on their arrival that it was of no consequence.

So, with childish impatience, he battered the animal's sides with his heels, and made the muleteer bang it with a thick stick and prick it with a sharp one, and jolted down the hillsides through clumps of flowering shrubs and stretches of anemones and asphodel, till he heard the sound of running water, and came in sight of the group of plane trees where they were to have their meal.

Even in England those trees would have been remarkable, so huge were they, so inter-

laced, so magnificently clothed in quivering green. And here in Greece they were unique, the one cool spot in that hard brilliant landscape, already scorched by the heat of an April sun. In their midst was hidden a tiny Khan or country inn, a frail mud building with a broad wooden balcony in which sat an old woman spinning, while a small brown pig, eating orange peel, stood beside her. On the wet earth below squatted two children, playing some primaeval game with their fingers; and their mother, none too clean either, was messing with some rice inside. As Mrs. Forman would have said, it was all very Greek, and the fastidious Mr. Lucas felt thankful that they were bringing their own food with them, and should eat it in the open air.

Still, he was glad to be there—the muleteer had helped him off—and glad that Mrs. Forman was not there to forestall his opinions—glad even that he should not see Ethel for quite half an hour. Ethel was his youngest daughter, still unmarried. She was unselfish and affectionate, and it was generally understood that she was to devote her life to her father, and be the comfort of his old age. Mrs. Forman always referred to her as Antigone, and Mr. Lucas tried to settle down to the role of Oedipus, which seemed the only one that public opinion allowed him.

He had this in common with Oedipus, that he was growing old. Even to himself it had become obvious. He had lost interest in other people's affairs, and seldom attended when they spoke to him. He was fond of talking himself but often forgot what he was going to say, and even when he succeeded, it seldom seemed worth the effort. His phrases and gestures had become stiff and set, his anecdotes, once so successful, fell flat, his silence was as meaningless as his speech. Yet he had led a healthy, active life, had worked steadily, made money, educated his children. There was nothing and no one to blame: he was simply growing old.

At the present moment, here he was in Greece, and one of the dreams of his life was realized. Forty years ago he had caught the fever of Hellenism, and all his life he had felt that could he but visit that land, he would not have lived in vain. But Athens had been dusty, Delphi wet, Thermopylae flat, and he had listened with amazement and cynicism to the rapturous exclamations of his companions. Greece was like

1 Colonus, which was the birthplace of Sophocles, "is a hill a mile north of Athens, where Oedipus [the protagonist of Sophocles's best-known tragedies, the *Oedipus Tyrannus* and the *Oedipus at Colonus*] found refuge and was buried" (*Oxford Classical Dictionary*). "In *Oedipus at Colonus* he is a wandering beggar, faithfully tended by Antigone," his daughter.

England: it was a man who was growing old, and it made no difference whether that man looked at the Thames or the Eurotas. It was his last hope of contradicting that logic of experience, and it was failing.

Yet Greece had done something for him, though he did not know it. It had made him discontented, and there are stirrings of life in discontent. He knew that he was not the victim of continual ill-luck. Something great was wrong, and he was pitted against no mediocre or accidental enemy. For the last month a strange desire had possessed him to die fighting.

"Greece is the land for young people," he said to himself as he stood under the plane trees, "but I will enter into it, I will possess it. Leaves shall be green again, water shall be sweet, the sky shall be blue. They were so forty years ago, and I will win them back. I do mind being old, and I will pretend no longer."

He took two steps forward, and immediately cold waters were gurgling over his ankle.

"Where does the water come from?" he asked himself. "I do not even know that." He remembered that all the hillsides were dry; yet here the road was suddenly covered with flowing streams.

He stopped still in amazement, saying: "Water out of a tree—out of a hollow tree? I never saw nor thought of that before."

For the enormous plane that leant towards the Khan was hollow—it had been burnt out for charcoal—and from its living trunk there gushed an impetuous spring, coating the bark with fern and moss, and flowing over the mule track to create fertile meadows beyond. The simple country folk had paid to beauty and mystery such tribute as they could, for in the rind of the tree a shrine was cut, holding a lamp and a little picture of the Virgin, inheritor of the Naiad's and Dryad's joint abode.

"I never saw anything so marvellous before," said Mr. Lucas. "I could even step inside the trunk and see where the water comes from."

For a moment he hesitated to violate the shrine. Then he remembered with a smile his own thought—"the place shall be mine; I will enter it and possess it"—and leapt almost aggressively on to a stone within.

The water pressed up steadily and noiselessly from the hollow roots and hidden crevices of the plane, forming a wonderful amber pool ere it spilt over the lip of bark on to the earth outside. Mr. Lucas tasted it and it was sweet, and when he looked up the black funnel of the trunk he saw sky which was blue, and some leaves which were green; and he remembered, without smiling, another of his thoughts.

Others had been before him—indeed he had a curious sense of companionship. Little votive offerings to the presiding Power were fastened on to the bark—tiny arms and legs and eyes in tin, grotesque models of the brain or the heart—all tokens of some recovery of strength or wisdom or love. There was no such thing as the solitude of nature, for the sorrows and joys of humanity had pressed even into the bosom of a tree. He spread out his arms and steadied himself against the soft charred wood, and then slowly leant back, till his body was resting on the trunk behind. His eyes closed, and he had the strange feeling of one who is moving, yet at peace—the feeling of the swimmer, who, after long struggling with chopping seas, finds that after all the tide will sweep him to his goal.

So he lay motionless, conscious only of the stream below his feet, and that all things were a stream, in which he was moving.

He was aroused at last by a shock—the shock of an arrival perhaps, for when he opened his eyes, something unimagined, indefinable, had passed over all things, and made them intelligible and good.

There was meaning in the stoop of the old woman over her work, and in the quick motions of the little pig, and in her diminishing globe of wool. A young man came singing over the streams on a mule, and there was beauty in his pose and sincerity in his greeting. The sun made no accidental patterns upon the spreading roots of the trees, and there was intention in the nodding clumps of asphodel, and in the music of the water. To Mr. Lucas, who, in a brief space of time, had discovered not only Greece, but England and all the world and life, there seemed nothing ludicrous in the desire to hang within the tree another votive offering—a little model of an entire man.

"Why, here's papa, playing at being Merlin."

All unnoticed they had arrived—Ethel, Mrs. Forman, Mr. Graham, and the English-speaking dragoman. Mr. Lucas peered out at them suspiciously. They had suddenly become unfamiliar, and all that they did seemed strained and coarse.

"Allow me to give you a hand," said Mr. Graham, a young man who was always polite to his elders.

Mr. Lucas felt annoyed. "Thank you, I can manage perfectly well by myself," he replied. His foot slipped as he stepped out of the tree, and went into the spring.

"Oh papa, my papa!" said Ethel, "what are you doing? Thank goodness I have got a change for you on the mule."

She tended him carefully, giving him clean socks and dry boots, and then sat him down on the rug beside the lunch basket, while she went with the others to explore the grove.

They came back in ecstasies, in which Mr. Lucas tried to join. But he found them intolerable. Their enthusiasm was superficial, commonplace, and spasmodic. They had no perception of the coherent beauty that was flowering around them. He tried at least to explain his feelings, and what he said was:

"I am altogether pleased with the appearance of this place. It impresses me very favourably. The trees are fine, remarkably fine for Greece, and there is something very poetic in the spring of clear running water. The people too seem kindly and civil. It is decidedly an attractive place."

Mrs. Forman upbraided him for his tepid praise.

"Oh, it is a place in a thousand!" she cried, "I could live and die here! I really would stop if I had not to be back at Athens! It reminds me of the Colonus of Sophocles."

"Well, *I* must stop," said Ethel. "I positively must."

"Yes, do! You and your father! Antigone and Oedipus. Of course you must stop at Colonus!"

Mr. Lucas was almost breathless with excitement. When he stood within the tree, he had believed that his happiness would be independent of locality. But these few minutes' conversation had undeceived him. He no longer trusted himself to journey through the world, for old thoughts, old wearinesses might be waiting to rejoin him as soon as he left the shade of the planes, and the music of the virgin water. To

sleep in the Khan with the gracious, kind-eyed country people, to watch the bats flit about within the globe of shade, and see the moon turn the golden patterns into silver—one such night would place him beyond relapse, and confirm him for ever in the kingdom he had regained. But all his lips could say was: "I should be willing to put in a night here."

"You mean a week, papa! It would be sacrilege to put in less."

"A week then, a week," said his lips, irritated at being corrected, while his heart was leaping with joy. All through lunch he spoke to them no more, but watched the place he should know so well, and the people who would so soon be his companions and friends. The inmates of the Khan only consisted of an old woman, a middle-aged woman, a young man and two children, and to none of them had he spoken, yet he loved them as he loved everything that moved or breathed or existed beneath the benedictory shade of the planes.

"*En route!*" said the shrill voice of Mrs. Forman, "Ethel! Mr. Graham! The best of things must end."

"To-night," thought Mr. Lucas, "they will light the little lamp by the shrine. And when we all sit together on the balcony, perhaps they will tell me which offerings they put up."

"I beg your pardon, Mr. Lucas," said Graham, "but they want to fold up the rug you are sitting on."

Mr. Lucas got up, saying to himself: "Ethel shall go to bed first, and then I will try to tell them about my offering too—for it is a thing I must do. I think they will understand if I am left with them alone."

Ethel touched him on the cheek. "Papa! I've called you three times. All the mules are here."

"Mules? What mules?"

"Our mules. We're all waiting. Oh, Mr. Graham, do help my father on."

"I don't know what you're talking about, Ethel."

"My dearest papa, we must start. You know we have to get to Olympia to-night."

Mr. Lucas in pompous, confident tones replied: "I always did wish, Ethel, that you had a better head for plans. You know perfectly well that we are putting in a week here. It is your own suggestion."

Ethel was startled into impoliteness. "What a perfectly ridiculous idea. You must have known I was joking. Of course I meant I wished we could."

"Ah! if we could only do what we wished!" sighed Mrs. Forman, already seated on her mule.

"Surely," Ethel continued in calmer tones, "you didn't think I meant it."

"Most certainly I did. I have made all my plans on the supposition that we are stopping here, and it will be extremely inconvenient, indeed, impossible for me to start."

He delivered this remark with an air of great conviction, and Mrs. Forman and Mr. Graham had to turn away to hide their smiles.

"I am sorry I spoke so carelessly; it was wrong of me. But, you know, we can't break up our party, and even one night here would make us miss the boat at Patras."

Mrs. Forman, in an aside, called Mr. Graham's attention to the excellent way in which Ethel managed her father.

"I don't mind about the Patras boat. You said that we should stop here, and we are stopping."

It seemed as if the inhabitants of the Khan had divined in some mysterious way that the altercation touched them. The old woman stopped her spinning, while the young man and the two children stood behind Mr. Lucas, as if supporting him.

Neither arguments nor entreaties moved him. He said little, but he was absolutely determined, because for the first time he saw his daily life aright. What need had he to return to England? Who would miss him? His friends were dead or cold. Ethel loved him in a way, but, as was right, she had other interests. His other children he seldom saw. He had only one other relative, his sister Julia, whom he both feared and hated. It was no effort to struggle. He would be a fool as well as a coward if he stirred from the place which brought him happiness and peace.

At last Ethel, to humour him, and not disinclined to air her modern Greek, went into the Khan with the astonished dragoman to look at the rooms. The woman inside received them with loud welcomes, and the young man, when no one was looking, began to lead Mr. Lucas' mule to the stable.

"Drop it, you brigand!" shouted Graham, who always declared that foreigners could understand English if they chose. He was right, for the man obeyed, and they all stood waiting for Ethel's return.

She emerged at last, with close-gathered skirts, followed by the dragoman bearing the little pig, which he had bought at a bargain.

"My dear papa, I will do all I can for you, but stop in that Khan—no."

"Are there—fleas?" asked Mrs. Forman.

Ethel intimated that "fleas" was not the word.

"Well, I am afraid that settles it," said Mrs. Forman, "I know how particular Mr. Lucas is."

"It does not settle it," said Mr. Lucas. "Ethel, you go on. I do not want you. I don't know why I ever consulted you. I shall stop here alone."

"That is absolute nonsense," said Ethel, losing her temper. "How can you be left alone at your age? How would you get your meals or your bath? All your letters are waiting for you at Patras. You'll miss the boat. That means missing the London operas, and upsetting all your engagements for the month. And as if you could travel by yourself!"

"They might knife you," was Mr. Graham's contribution.

The Greeks said nothing; but whenever Mr. Lucas looked their way, they beckoned him towards the Khan. The children would even have drawn him by the coat, and the old woman on the balcony stopped her almost completed spinning, and fixed him with mysterious appealing eyes. As he fought, the issue assumed gigantic proportions, and he believed that he was not merely stopping because he had regained youth or seen beauty or found happiness, but because in that place and with those people a supreme event was awaiting him which would transfigure the face of the world. The moment was so tremendous that he abandoned words and arguments as useless, and rested on the strength of his mighty unrevealed allies: silent men, murmuring water, and whispering trees. For the whole place called with one voice, articulate to him, and his garrulous opponents became every minute more meaningless and absurd. Soon they would be tired and go chattering away into the sun, leaving him to the cool grove and the moonlight and the destiny he foresaw.

Mrs. Forman and the dragoman had indeed already started, amid the piercing screams of the little pig, and the struggle might have gone on indefinitely if Ethel had not called in Mr. Graham.

"Can you help me?" she whispered. "He is absolutely unmanageable."

"I'm no good at arguing—but if I could help you in any other way—" and he looked down complacently at his well-made figure.

Ethel hesitated. Then she said: "Help me in any way you can. After all, it is for his good that we do it."

"Then have his mule led up behind him."

So when Mr. Lucas thought he had gained the day, he suddenly felt himself lifted off the ground, and sat sideways on the saddle, and at the same time the mule started off at a trot. He said nothing, for he had nothing to say, and even his face showed little emotion as he felt the shade pass and heard the sound of the water cease. Mr. Graham was running at his side, hat in hand, apologizing.

"I know I had no business to do it, and I do beg your pardon awfully. But I do hope that some day you too will feel that I was—damn!"

A stone had caught him in the middle of the back. It was thrown by the little boy, who was pursuing them along the mule track. He was followed by his sister, also throwing stones.

Ethel screamed to the dragoman, who was some way ahead with Mrs. Forman, but before he could rejoin them, another adversary appeared. It was the young Greek, who had cut them off in front, and now dashed down at Mr. Lucas' bridle. Fortunately Graham was an expert boxer, and it did not take him a moment to beat down the youth's feeble defence, and to send him sprawling with a bleeding mouth into the asphodel. By this time the dragoman had arrived, the children, alarmed at the fate of their brother, had desisted, and the rescue party, if such it is to be considered, retired in disorder to the trees.

"Little devils!" said Graham, laughing with triumph. "That's the modern Greek all over. Your father meant money if he stopped, and they consider we were taking it out of their pocket."

"Oh, they are terrible—simple savages! I

don't know how I shall ever thank you. You've saved my father."

"I only hope you didn't think me brutal."

"No," replied Ethel with a little sigh. "I admire strength."

Meanwhile the cavalcade reformed, and Mr. Lucas, who, as Mrs. Forman said, bore his disappointment wonderfully well, was put comfortably on to his mule. They hurried up the opposite hillside, fearful of another attack, and it was not until they had left the eventful place far behind that Ethel found an opportunity to speak to her father and ask his pardon for the way she had treated him.

"You seemed so different, dear father, and you quite frightened me. Now I feel that you are your old self again."

He did not answer, and she concluded that he was not unnaturally offended at her behaviour.

By one of those curious tricks of mountain scenery, the place they had left an hour before suddenly reappeared far below them. The Khan was hidden under the green dome, but in the open there still stood three figures, and through the pure air rose up a faint cry of defiance or farewell.

Mr. Lucas stopped irresolutely, and let the reins fall from his hand.

"Come, father dear," said Ethel gently.

He obeyed, and in another moment a spur of the hill hid the dangerous scene for ever.

II

It was breakfast time, but the gas was alight, owing to the fog. Mr. Lucas was in the middle of an account of a bad night he had spent. Ethel, who was to be married in a few weeks, had her arms on the table, listening.

"First the door bell rang, then you came back from the theatre. Then the dog started, and after the dog the cat. And at three in the morning a young hooligan passed by singing. Oh yes: then there was the water gurgling in the pipe above my head."

"I think that was only the bath water running away," said Ethel, looking rather worn.

"Well, there's nothing I dislike more than running water. It's perfectly impossible to sleep in the house. I shall give it up. I shall give notice next quarter. I shall tell the landlord plainly,

'The reason I am giving up the house is this: it is perfectly impossible to sleep in it.' If he says —says—well, what has he got to say?"

"Some more toast, father?"

"Thank you, my dear." He took it, and there was an interval of peace.

But he soon recommenced. "I'm not going to submit to the practising next door as tamely as they think. I wrote and told them so—didn't I?"

"Yes," said Ethel, who had taken care that the letter should not reach. "I have seen the governess, and she has promised to arrange it differently. And Aunt Julia hates noise. It will be sure to be all right."

Her aunt, being the only unattached member of the family, was coming to keep house for her father when she left him. The reference was not a happy one, and Mr. Lucas commenced a series of half articulate sighs, which was only stopped by the arrival of the post.

"Oh, what a parcel!" cried Ethel. "For me! What can it be! Greek stamps. This is most exciting!"

It proved to be some asphodel bulbs, sent by Mrs. Forman from Athens for planting in the conservatory.

"Doesn't it bring it all back! You remember the asphodels, father. And all wrapped up in Greek newspapers. I wonder if I can read them still. I used to be able to, you know."

She rattled on, hoping to conceal the laughter of the children next door—a favorite source of querulousness at breakfast time.

"Listen to me! 'A rural disaster.' Oh, I've hit on something sad. But never mind. 'Last Tuesday at Plataniste, in the province of Messenia, a shocking tragedy occurred. A large tree' —aren't I getting on well?—'blew down in the night and'—wait a minute—oh, dear! 'crushed to death the five occupants of the little Khan there, who had apparently been sitting in the balcony. The bodies of Maria Rhomaides, the aged proprietress, and of her daughter, aged forty-six, were easily recognizable, whereas that of her grandson'—oh, the rest is really too horrid; I wish I had never tried it, and what's more I feel to have heard the name Plataniste before. We didn't stop there, did we, in the spring?"

"We had lunch," said Mr. Lucas, with a faint expression of trouble on his vacant face.

"Perhaps it was where the dragoman bought the pig."

"Of course," said Ethel in a nervous voice. "Where the dragoman bought the little pig. How terrible!"

"Very terrible!" said her father, whose attention was wandering to the noisy children next door. Ethel suddenly started to her feet with genuine interest.

"Good gracious!" she exclaimed. "This is an old paper. It happened not lately but in April— the night of Tuesday the eighteenth—and we— we must have been there in the afternoon."

"So we were," said Mr. Lucas. She put her hand to her heart, scarcely able to speak.

"Father, dear father, I must say it: you wanted to stop there. All those people, those poor half savage people, tried to keep you, and they're dead. The whole place, it says, is in ruins, and even the stream has changed its course. Father, dear, if it had not been for me, and if Arthur had not helped me, you must have been killed."

Mr. Lucas waved his hand irritably. "It is not a bit of good speaking to the governess, I shall write to the landlord and say, 'The reason I am giving up the house is this: the dog barks, the children next door are intolerable, and I cannot stand the noise of running water.'"

Ethel did not check his babbling. She was aghast at the narrowness of the escape, and for a long time kept silence. At last she said: "Such a marvellous deliverance does make one believe in Providence."

Mr. Lucas, who was still composing his letter to the landlord, did not reply.

The Raison d'Etre of Criticism in the Arts

An Address Delivered at a Symposium on Music at Harvard University

Believing as I do that music is the deepest of the arts and deep beneath the arts, I venture to emphasise music in this brief survey of the raison d'être of criticism in the arts. I have no authority here. I am an amateur whose inadequacy will become all too obvious as he proceeds. Perhaps, though, you will remember in your charity that the word amateur implies love. I love music. Just to love it, or just to love anything or anybody is not enough. Love has to be clarified and controlled to give full value, and here is where criticism may help. But one has to start with love; one has, in the case of music, to want to hear the notes. If one has no initial desire to listen and no sympathy after listening, the notes will signify nothing, sound and fury, whatever their intellectual content.

The case *against* criticism is alarmingly strong, and much of my paper is bound to be a brief drawn up by the Devil's Advocate. I will postpone the evil day, and begin by indicating the case *for* criticism.

Most of us will agree that previous training is desirable before we approach the arts. We mistrust untrained appreciation, believing that it often defeats its own ends. Appreciation ought to be enough. But unless we learn by example and by failure and by comparison, appreciation will not bite. We shall tend to slip about on the surface of masterpieces, exclaiming with joy, but never penetrating. "Oh, I do like Bach," cries one appreciator, and the other cries, "Do you? I don't. I like Chopin." Exit in opposite directions chanting Bach and Chopin respectively, and hearing less the composers than their own voices. They resemble investors who proclaim the soundness of their financial assets. The Bach shares must not fall, the Chopin not fall further, or one would have been proved a fool on the aesthetic stock exchange. The objection to untrained appreciation is not its naïveté but its tendency to lead to the appreciation of no one but oneself. Against such fatuity the critical spirit is a valuable corrective.

Except at the actual moment of contact— and I shall have much to say on the subject of that difficult moment—it is desirable to know why we like a work, and to be able to defend our preferences by argument. Our judgment has been strengthened and if all goes well the contacts will be intensified and increased and become more valuable.

I add the provisio "if all goes well" because success lies on the knees of an unknown God. There is always the contrary danger; the danger that training may sterilise the sensitiveness that is being trained; that education may lead to knowledge instead of wisdom, and criticism to

nothing but criticism; that spontaneous enjoyment, like the Progress of Poesy in Matthew Arnold's poem, may be checked because too much care has been taken to direct it into the right channel. Still it is a risk to be faced, and if no care had been taken the stream might have vanished even sooner. We hope criticism will help. We have faith in it as a respectable human activity, as an item in the larger heritage which differentiates us from the beasts.

How best can this activity be employed? One must allow it to construct aesthetic theories, though to the irreverent eyes of some of us they appear as travelling laboratories, beds of Procrustes whereon Milton is too long and Keats too short. In an age which is respectful to theory— as for instance the seventeenth century was respectful to Aristotle's theory of the dramatic unities—a theory may be helpful and stimulating, particularly to the sense of form. French tragedy could culminate in Racine because certain leading strings had been so willingly accepted that they were scarcely felt. Corneille and Tasso were less happy. Corneille, having produced the *Cid,* wasted much time trying to justify its deviations from Aristotle's rules; and Tasso wasted even more, for he published his theory of Christian Epic Poetry before he wrote the *Gerusalemme Liberata* which was to illustrate it. His epic was attacked by the critics because it deviated from what Aristotle said and also from what Tasso thought he might have said. Tasso was upset, became involved in three volumes of controversy, tried to write a second epic which should not deviate, failed, and went mad. Except perhaps in Russia, where the deviations of Shostakovitch invite a parallel, a theory in the modern world has little power over the fine arts, for good or evil. We have no atmosphere where it can flourish, and the attempts of certain governments to generate such an atmosphere in bureaus are unlikely to succeed. The construction of aesthetic theories and their comparison are desirable cultural exercises: the theories themselves are unlikely to spread far or to hinder or help.

A more practical activity for criticism is the sensitive dissection of particular works of art. What did the artist hope to do? What means did he employ, subconscious or conscious? Did he succeed, and if his success was partial where did he fail? In such a dissection the tools should break as soon as they encounter any living tissue. The apparatus is nothing, the specimen all. Whether expert critics will agree with so extreme a statement is doubtful, but I do enjoy following particular examinations so far as an amateur can. It is delightful and profitable to enter into technicalities to the limit of one's poor ability, to continue as far as one can in the wake of an expert mind, to pursue an argument till it passes out of one's grasp. And to have, while this is going on, a particular work of art before one can be a great help. Besides learning about the work one increases one's powers. Criticism's central job seems to be education through precision.

A third activity, less important, remains to be listed, and since it lies more within my sphere than precision I will discuss it at greater length. Criticism can stimulate. Few of us are sufficiently awake to the beauty and wonder of the world, and when art intervenes to reveal them it sometimes acts in reverse, and lowers a veil instead of raising it. This deadening effect can often be dispersed by a well-chosen word. We can be awakened by a remark which need not be profound or even true, and can be sent scurrying after the beauties and wonders we were ignoring. Journalism and broadcasting have their big opportunity here. Unsuited for synthesis or analysis, they can send out the winged word that carries us off to examine the original.

There is in fact a type of criticism which has no interpretative value, yet it should not be condemned offhand. Much has been written about music, for instance, which has nothing to do with music and must make musicians smile. It usually describes the state into which the hearer was thrown as he sat on his chair at the concert and the visual images which occurred to him in that sedentary position. Here is an example, and a very lovely one, from Walt Whitman. Whitman has heard "one of Beethoven's master septets" performed at Philadelphia (there is only one Beethoven septet, but this the old boy did not know), and the rendering of it on a "small band of well-chosen and perfectly combined instruments" quite carried him away.

Dainty abandon, sometimes as of Nature laughing on a hillside in the sunshine; serious and firm monotonies, as of winds; a horn sounding through the tangle of the forest, and the dying echoes; soothing floating waves, but presently rising in surges, angrily lashing, muttering, heavy; piercing peals of laughter for interstices; now and then weird as Nature is herself in certain moods—but mainly spontaneous, easy, careless—often the sentiment of the postures of naked children playing or sleeping. It did me good even to see the violinists drawing their bows so masterly— every motion a study. I allowed myself, as I sometimes do, to wander out of myself. The conceit came to me of a copious grove of singing birds, and in their midst a simple harmonic duo, two human souls, steadily asserting their own pensiveness, joyousness.

Here is adorable literature, but what has it to do with Op. 20? A poet's imagination has been kindled. He has allowed himself to wander out of himself, but not into Beethoven's self, his presumable goal. He has evoked the visual images congenial to him, and though in the closing phrase there is a concert it is not the one he attended, for it took place in his garden of Eden.

Another example of such criticism is to be found in Proust. Proust is what Walt Whitman is not—sophisticated, soigné, rusé, maladif. But he too listens to a septet and reacts to it visually, he is carried off his seat into a region which has nothing to do with the concert. It is the septet of Vinteuil, whom we have hitherto known as the composer of a violin sonata. Vinteuil himself, an obscure and unhappy provincial organist, has scarcely appeared; but his sonata, and particularly a phrase in it, *la petite phrase,* has been an actor in the long-drawn inaction of the novel. Character after character has listened to it, and has felt hope, jealousy, despair, peace, according to the circumstances into which *la petite phrase* has entered. We do not know what it sounds like, but its arrival always means emotional heightening.

Towards the end of the novel, the hero goes to a musical reception in Paris where a new work is to be performed. He does not bother to look at the programme, being occupied by social trifles. It is a septet—the opening bars are sombre, glacial, as if dawn had not yet risen over the sea. He finds himself in an unknown world, where he understands nothing. Suddenly into this bewilderment there falls—*la petite phrase,* a reference to the sonata. He is listening to a posthumous work of Vinteuil, of whose existence he was unaware. Everything falls into shape. It is as if he has walked in an unknown region and come across the little gate which belongs to the garden of a friend. The septet expands its immensities, now comprehensible. The dawn rises crimson out of the sea, harsh midday rejoicings give way to more images, and the little phrase of the sonata, once virginal and shy, is august, quivering with colours, final, mature.

Now these visual wanderings are not entirely to my taste, nor perhaps to yours. Whitman's has its own naïve merit, but in the case of Proust, who is pretentious culturally, we feel uneasy. Shall we then say that they do not and cannot help us musically at all? I think this is too severe. The septets of Beethoven and of Vinteuil have come no nearer to us, but we have been excited, we have been disposed to listen to sounds, we have been challenged to test the descriptions and to decide whether we agree with them. This general sharpening of interest is desirable. It can be effected in various ways: by a legitimate critic like Donald Tovey, by a grand old boy at Philadelphia, or by a snobby Frenchman in the Faubourg St. Germain. Not all ways are equally good. Those who hear music will always interpret it best. But those who don't hear it after the first few notes have also their use. Their wanderings, their visual images, their dreams, help to sharpen us. They recall us to the importance of sounds, and, their inferior in other ways, we may perhaps manage to listen to the sounds longer than they did.

Examples of higher musical value are to be found in the early journalism of Bernard Shaw. Though Shaw is a man of letters, like Whitman and Proust, and readily runs after his own thoughts and pictorial images, he does manage to remember the music. He can interpret as well as stimulate. He can say for instance of Haydn: "Hayden would have been among the greatest had he been driven to that terrible eminence; but we are fortunate enough in having had at least one man of genius who was happy enough in the Valley of Humiliation to feel no compulsion to struggle on through the Valley of the Shadow of Death." What a sensitive and just reflection! How admirably it expresses that turning away from the tragic so often displayed by Haydn—for instance in the opening of the C Major Symphony, Op. 97: turning away not because he is afraid of tragedy, which would dis-

compose the listener, but because he prefers not to be tragic. This is an essential in Haydn, and, apprehending it, Shaw convinces us that he is inside music and could have criticised it more deeply, had his career and his inclinations allowed.

I like, in this connection, jokes about music, the irresponsible folly which sometimes kicks a door open as it flies. They too may incline us to listen to sounds. When the English humorist, Beachcomber, says "Wagner is the Puccini of music," he says rather more than he says. Besides guying a well-worn formula, he pierces Grand Opera itself, and reveals Brünnhilde and Butterfly transfixed on the same mischievous pin. I like, too, the remark of an uncle of mine, a huntin', fishin', shootin', sportin' sort of uncle, whose aversion to the arts was very genuine. "They tell me," he said one day thoughtfully, "they tell me music's like a gun; it hurts less when you let it off yourself." Besides getting in a well-directed gibe, and discomposing my aunt who adored Mendelssohn, he indicated very neatly the gulf between artist on the one hand and critic on the other. Those who are involved and those who appraise are never hurt in the same way. This is, as a matter of fact, going to be our chief problem here, and perhaps it will come the fresher because my uncle hit at it in his slapdash fashion before striding back to his dogs.

For now our trouble starts. We can readily agree that criticism has educational and cultural value; the artist helps to civilise the community, builds up standards, forms theories, stimulates, dissects, encourages the individual to enjoy the world into which he has been born; and on its destructive side criticism exposes fraud and pretentiousness and checks conceit. These are substantial achievements. But I would like if I could to establish its raison d'être on a higher basis than that of public utility. I would like to discover some spiritual parity between it and the objects it criticises, and this is going to be difficult. The difficulty has been variously expressed. One writer—Mr. F. L. Lucas—has called criticism a charming parasite; another—Chekhov—complains it is a gadfly which hinders the oxen from ploughing; a third—the eighteenth-century philosopher Lord Kames—compares it to an imp which distracts critics from their objective and incites them to criticise each other. My own trouble is not so much that it is a parasite, a gadfly, or an imp, but that there is a basic difference between the critical and creative states of mind, and to the consideration of that difference I would now invite your attention.

What about the creative state? In it a man is taken out of himself. He lets down as it were a bucket into his subconscious, and draws up something which is normally beyond his reach. He mixes this thing with his normal experiences, and out of the mixture he makes a work of art. It may be a good work of art or a bad one—we are not here examining the question of quality—but whether it is good or bad it will have been compounded in this unusual way, and he will wonder afterwards how he did it. Such seems to be the creative process. It may employ much technical ingenuity and worldly knowledge, it may profit by critical standards, but mixed up with it is this stuff from the bucket, this subconscious stuff, which is not procurable on demand. And when the process is over, when the picture or symphony or lyric or novel (or whatever it is) is complete, the artist, looking back on it, will wonder how on earth he did it. And indeed he did not do it on earth.

A perfect example of the creative process is to be found in Kubla Khan. Assisted by opium, Coleridge had his famous dream, and dipped deep into the subconscious. Waking up, he started to transcribe it, and was proceeding successfully when that person from Porlock unfortunately called on business.

> Weave a circle round him thrice
> And close your eyes with holy dread,
> For he on honeydew hath fed
> And drunk the milk of Paradise—

and in came the person from Porlock. Coleridge could not resume. His connection with the subconscious had snapped. He had created and did not know how he had done it. As Professor John Livingston Lowes has shown, many fragments of Coleridge's day-to-day reading are embedded in Kubla Khan, but the poem itself belongs to another world, which he was seldom to record.

The creative state of mind is akin to a dream. In Coleridge's case it was a dream. In other cases—Jane Austen's for instance—

the dream is remote or sedate. But even Jane Austen, looking back upon Emma, could have thought "Dear me, how came I to write that? It is not ill-contrived." There is always, even with the most realistic artist, the sense of withdrawal from his own creation, the sense of surprise.

The French writer, Paul Claudel, gives the best description known to me of the creative state. It occurs in La Ville. A poet is speaking. He has been asked whence his inspiration comes, and how is it that when he speaks everything becomes explicable although he explains nothing. He replies:

> I do not speak what I wish, but I conceive in sleep,
> And I cannot explain whence I draw my breath, for
> 　　it is my breath which is drawn out of me.
> I expand the emptiness within me, I open my mouth,
> 　　I breathe in the air, I breathe it out.
> I restore it in the form of an intelligible word,
> And having spoken I know what I have said.

There is a further idea in the passage, which my brief English paraphrase has not attempted to convey: the idea that if the breathing in is inspiration the breathing out is expiration, a prefiguring of death, when the life of a man will be drawn out of him by the unknown force for the last time. Creation and death are closely connected for Claudel. I'm confining myself, though, to his description of the creative act, and ask you to observe how precisely it describes what happened in Kubla Khan. There is conception in sleep, there is the connection between the subconscious and the conscious, which has to be effected before the work of art can be born, and there is the surprise of the creator at his own creation.

> Je restitue une parole intelligible,
> Et l'ayant dite, je sais ce que j'ai dit.

Which is exactly what happened to Coleridge. He knew what he had said, but as soon as inspiration was interrupted he could not say any more.

After this glance at the creative state, let us glance at the critical. The critical state has many merits, and employs some of the highest and subtlest faculties of man. But it is grotesquely remote from the state responsible for the works it affects to expound. It does not let down buckets into the subconscious. It does not conceive in sleep, or know what it has said after it has said it. Think before you speak is criticism's motto; speak before you think creation's. Nor is criticism disconcerted by people arriving from Porlock; in fact it sometimes comes from Porlock itself. While not excluding imagination and sympathy, it keeps them and all the faculties under control, and only employs them when they promise to be helpful.

Thus equipped, it advances on its object. It has two aims. The first and the more important is aesthetic. It considers the object in itself, as an entity, and tells us what it can about its life. The second aim is subsidiary: the relation of the object to the rest of the world. Problems of less relevance are considered, such as the conditions under which the work of art was composed, the influences which formed it (criticism adores influences), the influence it has exercised on subsequent works, the artist's life, the lives of the artist's father and mother, prenatal possibilities and so on, straying this way into psychology and that way into history. Much of the above is valuable, but what meanwhile has become of Monteverdi's Vespers, or the Great Mosque at Delhi, or the Frogs of Aristophanes, or any other work which you happen to have in mind? I throw these three objects at you because they happen to be in my own mind. I have been hearing the Vespers, seeing the Frogs, and thinking about the Delhi Mosque. If we wheel up an aesthetic theory—the best attainable, and there are some excellent ones—if we wheel it up and apply it with its measuring rods and pliers and forceps, its calipers and catheters, to Vespers, Mosque, and Frogs, we are visited at once by a sense of the grotesque. It doesn't work, two universes have not even collided, they have been juxtaposed. There is no spiritual parity. And if criticism strays from her central aesthetic quest to influences and psychological and historical considerations, something does happen then, contact is established. But no longer with a work of art.

A work of art is a curious object. Isn't it infectious? Unlike machinery, hasn't it the power of transforming the person who encounters it towards the condition of the person who created it? (I use the clumsy phrase "towards the condition" on purpose.) We—we the beholders or listeners or whatever we are—undergo a change analogous to creation. We are rapt into a region near to that where the artist worked, and like him when we return to earth we feel surprised. To claim we actually entered his state and became co-creators with him there is presumptuous. However much excited I am by Brahms' Fourth Symphony I cannot suppose I feel Brahms' excitement, and probably what he felt is not what I understand as excitement. But there has been an infection from Brahms through his music to myself. Something has passed. I have been transformed towards his condition, he has called me out of myself, he has thrown me into a subsidiary dream; and when the passacaglia is trodden out, and the transformation closed, I too feel surprise.

Unfortunately this infection, this sense of cooperation with a creator, which is the supremely important step in our pilgrimage through the fine arts, is the one step over which criticism cannot help. She can prepare us for it generally, and educate us to keep our senses open, but she has to withdraw when reality approaches, like Virgil from Dante on the summit of Purgatory. With the coming of love, we have to rely on Beatrice, whom we have loved all along, and if we have never loved Beatrice we are lost. We shall remain pottering about with theories and influences and psychological and historical considerations—supports useful in their time, but they must be left behind at the entry of Heaven. I would not suggest that our comprehension of the fine arts is or should be of a nature of a mystic union. But, as in mysticism, we enter an unusual state, and we can only enter it through love. Putting it more prosaically, we cannot understand music unless we desire to hear it. And so we return to the earth.

Let us reconsider that troublesome object, the work of art, and observe another way in which it is recalcitrant to criticism. I am thinking of its freshness. So far as it is authentic, it presents itself as eternally virgin. It expects always to be heard or read or seen for the first time, always to cause surprise. It does not expect to be studied, still less does it present itself as a crossword puzzle, only to be solved after much reexamination. If it does that, if it parades a mystifying element, it is, to that extent, not a work of art, not an immortal Muse but a Sphinx who dies as soon as her riddles are answered. The work of art assumes the existence of the perfect spectator, and is indifferent to the fact that no such person exists. It does not allow for our ignorance and it does not cater for our knowledge.

This eternal freshness in creation presents a difficulty to the critic, who when he hears or reads or sees a work a second time rightly profits by what he has heard or read or seen of it the first time, and studies and compares, remembers and analyses, and often has to reject his original impressions as trivial. He may thus in the end gain a just and true opinion of the work, but he ought to remain startled, and this is usually beyond him. Take Beethoven's Ninth Symphony, the one in A. Isn't it in A? The opening bars announce the key as explicitly as fifths can, leaving us only in doubt as to whether the movement will decide on the major or minor mode. In the fifteenth bar comes the terrifying surprise, the pounce into D minor, which tethers the music, however far it wanders, right down to the ineluctable close. Can one hope to feel that terror and surprise twice? Can one avoid hearing the opening bars as a preparation for the pounce— and thus miss the life of the pounce? Can we combine experience and innocence? I think we can. The willing suspension of experience is possible, it is possible to become like a child who says "Oh!" each time the ball bounces, although he has seen it bounce before and knows it must bounce.

It is possible but it is rare. The critic who is thoroughly versed in the score of the Ninth Symphony and can yet hear the opening bars as a trembling introduction in A to the unknown has reached the highest rank in his profession. Most of us are content to remain well-informed. It is so restful to be well-informed. We forget that Beethoven intended his Symphony to be heard always for the first time. We forget with still greater ease that Tchaikovsky intended the same for his Piano Concerto in B flat minor. Dubious for good reasons of that thumping affair, we sometimes scold it for being "stale"—a ridiculous accusation, for it too was created as an eternal virgin, it too should startle each time it galumphs down the waltz. No doubt the Concerto, and much music, has been too often performed, just as some pictures have been too often looked at.

Freshness of reception is exhausted more rapidly by a small or imperfect object than by a great one. Nevertheless the objects themselves are eternally new, it is the recipient who may wither. You remember how at the opening of Goethe's *Faust,* Mephistopheles, being stale himself, found the world stale, and reported it as such to the Almighty. The archangels took no notice of him and continued to sing of eternal freshness. The critic ought to combine Mephistopheles with the archangels, experience with innocence. He ought to know everything inside out, and yet be surprised. Virginia Woolf—who was both a creative artist and a critic—believed in reading a book twice. The first time she abandoned herself to the author unreservedly. The second time she treated him with severity and allowed him to get away with nothing he could not justify. After these two readings she felt qualified to discuss the book. Here is good rule of thumb advice. But it does not take us to the heart of our problem, which is superrational. For we ought really to read the book in two ways at once. (And we ought to look at a picture in two ways at once, and to listen to music similarly.) We ought to perform a miracle the nature of which was hinted at by the Almighty when he said he was always glad to receive Mephistopheles in Heaven and hear him chat.

I would speak tentatively in the presence of an expert audience, but it seems to me that we are most likely to perform that miracle in the case of music. Music, more than the other arts, postulates a double existence. It exists in time, and also exists outside time, instantaneously. With no philosophic training, I cannot put my belief clearly, but I can conceive myself hearing a piece as it goes by and also when it has finished. In the latter case I should hear it as an entity, as a piece of sound-architecture, not as a sound-sequence, not as something divisible into bars. Yet it would be organically connected with the concert-hall performance. Architecture and sequence would, in my apprehension, be more closely fused than the two separate readings of a book in Virginia Woolf's.

The claim of criticism to take us to the heart of the Arts must therefore be disallowed. Another claim has been made for it, a more precise one. It has been suggested that criticism can help an artist to improve his work. If that be true, a raison d'être is established at once. Criticism becomes an important figure, a hand-maid to beauty, holding out the sacred lamp in whose light creation proceeds, feeding the lamp with oil, trimming the wick when it flares or smokes. There must be many artists, musicians and others here, and it would be interesting to know whether criticism had helped them in their work, and if so how. Has she held up the lamp? No doubt she illuminates past mistakes or merits, that certainly is within her power, but has the better knowledge of them any practical value?

A remark of Mr. C. Day Lewis is interesting in this connection. It comes at the opening of *The Poetic Image*.

There is something formidable for the poet in the idea of criticism—something, dare I say it? almost unreal. He writes a poem, then he moves on to a new experience, the next poem: and when a critic comes along and tells him what is right or wrong about the first poem, he has a feeling of irrelevance.

Something almost unreal. That is a just remark. The poet is always developing and moving on, and when his creative state is broken into by comments on something he has just put behind him, he feels bewildered. His reaction is "What are you talking about? Must you?" Once again, and in its purest form, the division between the critical and creative states, the absence of spiritual parity, becomes manifest. In its purest form because poetry is an extreme form of art, and is a convenient field for experiment. My own art, the mixed art of fiction, is less suitable, yet I can truly say with Mr. Day Lewis that I have nearly always found criticism irrelevant. When I am praised, I am pleased; when I am blamed, I am displeased; when I am told I am elusive, I am surprised—but neither the pleasure nor the sorrow nor the astonishment makes any difference when next I enter the creative state. One can eliminate a particular defect perhaps; to substitute merit is the difficulty. I remember that in one of my earlier novels I was blamed for the number of sudden deaths in it, which were said to amount to forty-four per cent of the fictional population. I took heed, and arranged that characters in subsequent novels should die less frequently and give previous notice where possible by means of illness or some other acceptable

device. But I was not inspired to put anything vital in the place of the sudden deaths. The only remedy for a defect is inspiration, the subconscious stuff that comes up in the bucket. A piece of contemporary music, to my ear, has a good many sudden deaths in it; the phrases expire as rapidly as the characters in my novel, the chords cut each other's throats, the arpeggio has a heart attack, the fugue gets into a nose-dive. But these defects—if defects they be—are vital to the general conception. They are not to be remedied by substituting sweetness. And the musician would do well to ignore the critic even when he admits the justice of the particular criticism.

Only in two ways can criticism help the artist a little with his work. The first is general. He ought—if he keeps company at all—to keep good company. To be alone may be best—to be alone was that Fate reserved for Beethoven. But if he wishes to consort with ideas and standards and the works of his fellows—and he usually has to in the modern world—he must beware of the second-rate. It means a relaxation of fibre, a temptation to rest on his own superiority. I do not desire to use the words "superior" and "inferior" about human individuals; in an individual so many factors are present that one cannot grade him. But one can legitimately apply them to cultural standards, and the artist should be critical here, and alive in particular to the risks of the clique. The clique is a valuable social device, which only a fanatic would condemn; it can protect and encourage the artist. It is the artist's duty, if he wants to be in a clique, to choose a good one, and to take care it doesn't make him bumptious or sterile or silly. The lowering of critical standards in what one may call daily-studio life, their corruption by adulation or jealousy, may lead to inferior work. Good standards may lead to good work. That is all that there seems to be to say about this vague assistance, and maybe it was not worth saying.

The second way in which criticism can help the artist is more specific. It can help him over details, niggling details, minutiae of style. To refer to my own work again, I have certainly benefited by being advised not to use the word "but" so often. I have had a university education, you see, and it disposes one to overwork that particular conjunction. It is the strength of the academic mind to be fair and see both sides of a question. It is its weakness to be timid and to suffer from that fear-of-giving-oneself-away disease of which Samuel Butler speaks. Both its strength and its weakness incline it to the immoderate use of "but." A good many "buts" have occurred today, but not as many as if I had not been warned. The writer of the opposed type, the extrovert, the man who knows what he knows, and likes what he likes, and doesn't care who knows it—he should doubtless be subject to the opposite discipline; he should be criticised because he never uses "but"; he should be tempted to employ the qualifying clause. The man who has a legal mind should probably go easy on his "if's." Fiddling little matters. Yes, I know. The sort of trifling help which criticism can give the artist. She cannot help him in great matters.

With these random considerations my paper must close. The latter part of it has been overshadowed and perhaps obsessed by my consciousness of the gulf between the creative and critical states. Perhaps the gulf does not exist, perhaps it does not signify, perhaps I have been making a gulf out of a molehill. But in my view it does prevent the establishment of a first class raison d'être for criticism in the arts. The only activity which can establish such a raison d'être is love. However cautiously, with whatever reservations, after whatsoever purifications, we must come back to love. That alone raises us to the co-operation with the artist which is the sole reason for our aesthetic pilgrimage. That alone promises spiritual parity. My main conclusion on criticism has therefore to be unfavourable, nor have I succeeded in finding that it has given substantial help to the artists.

James Joyce

1882–1941

James Joyce was born on February 2, 1882, in the Dublin suburb of Rathgar. Like Stephen Dedalus, the hero of his closely autobiographical first novel, *A Portrait of the Artist as a Young Man* (1916), he had his first schooling at Clongowes Wood College, where he was sent at the age of six and where he remained until 1891. In 1893 he went to Belvedere College, Dublin, another Jesuit school (Herbert Gorman remarks—in the biography of Joyce from which come these facts about Joyce's early training—that he was to be educated by Jesuits until he was twenty), and in 1898 to University College, Dublin, where he studied for four years under the Faculty of Arts. *A Portrait of the Artist as a Young Man* gives a remarkably full and intensely wrought picture of Joyce's development up to the time he left Ireland for the first time in 1902, to go to Paris. "When the soul of a man is born in this country," Stephen Dedalus says, "there are nets flung at it to hold it back from flight. You talk to me of nationality, language, religion. I shall try to fly by those nets." Stephen's tutelary figure becomes an image of Daedalus fleeing from the Cretan labyrinth on the wings of his own artifice: "He seemed to hear the noise of dim waves and to see a winged form flying above the waves and slowly climbing the air. What did it mean? Was it a quaint device opening a page of some medieval book of prophecies and symbols, a hawklike man flying sunward above the sea, a prophecy of the end he had been born to serve and had been following through the mists of childhood and boyhood, a symbol of the artist forging anew in his workship out of the sluggish matter of the earth a new soaring impalpable imperishable being?" The novel ends as Stephen prepares to leave for Paris—"I go to encounter for the millionth time the reality of experience and to forge in the smithy of my soul the uncreated conscience of my race"; and its last sentence is a supplication to Daedalus—"Old father, old artificer, stand me now and ever in good stead."

The hand-to-mouth existence which Joyce led in Paris during the winter and spring of 1902–03 was brought to an end by a telegram—"Mother dying come home father"—received on Good Friday, 1903. He remained in Dublin until October 8, 1904, when he left it again, with his newly married wife, to take up a new life on the Continent. His life in Dublin during the interim is variously described, implied, or referred to in his second novel, *Ulysses* (Paris, 1922), whose entire action takes place in Dublin on June 16, 1904. With the exception of brief necessary visits to Ireland, the last of which ended in September 1912, the remaining years of Joyce's life were passed on the Continent: in Trieste; in Rome for a while; in Zurich, where he supported himself and his family by teaching languages; finally in Paris, where he was able to devote himself exclusively to writing. He died in 1941.

The commanding position that Joyce occupied in the world of letters between the two wars was first and foremost a result of the aims he realized, and the startling, varied techniques by which he realized them, in his two most ambitious novels, *Ulysses* and *Finnegans Wake* (1939). But these brilliant performances should not make us forget his earliest work of fiction, *Dubliners,* a collection of short stories ready for publication in 1905 which, because of unwarranted difficulties with censorship both in Dublin and in London, was not published until 1914. Each of these stories reveals the life of a citizen of Dublin, with the utmost economy and rightness of form: "My intention," Joyce said in a letter to Grant Richards, "was to write a chapter of the moral history of my country and I chose Dublin for the scene because that city seemed to me the centre of paralysis. . . . I have written it for the most part in a style of scrupulous meanness and with the conviction that he is a very bold man who dares to alter in the presentment, still more to deform, whatever he has seen and heard." The "scrupulous meanness," the precisely faithful rendering of Dublin life as he had seen and heard it, with no gratuitous false emphasis, produced a group of stories in which no word could be changed without damaging the taut fabric of the whole. Sometimes, as in the longest of the stories, "The Dead," reprinted here, an individual consciousness will soar in self-realization above the level inconscient mean, and then the prose soars with it, as at the end of "The Dead." The stories in *Dubliners* may be compared with the stories of Chekhov more appropriately than with those of any other writer, but in the end they are incomparable; there is a mood, experienced by the reader who has once come under the spell of their quiet power and precise beauty, when they seem, quite simply, to be the most perfect stories in English.

TEXTS: Of the wide array of critical and bio-

Grafton Street, Dublin, ca. 1904. All of Joyce's work, from *The Dubliners* to *Finnegans Wake,* is steeped in the stifling physical and spiritual atmosphere of the Dublin he had fled in 1904. *National Library of Ireland.*

graphical material concerning Joyce and his work that is now available, perhaps the most indispensable single book is Richard Ellmann's fine biography, *James Joyce* (1959). There is an edition of Joyce's *Letters,* in three volumes (the first volume edited by Stuart Gilbert, 1957; the second and third by Ellmann, 1966), and a volume of Joyce's *Critical Writings,* edited by Ellsworth Mason and Richard Ellmann (1959). *Stephen Hero,* the original, fuller version of *A Portrait of the Artist as a Young Man,* was published in 1944 (new, revised edition 1955). Among the helpful books which treat Joyce's career as a whole are: *Re Joyce,* by Anthony Burgess (1965); *Dublin's Joyce,* by Hugh Kenner (1956); *Joyce,* by S. L. Goldberg in the Writers and Critics series (1967); and, a pioneer book which is still to be consulted, *James Joyce: A Critical Introduction,* by Harry Levin (1941). Edward Brandabur's *A Scrupulous Meanness: A Study of Joyce's Early Work* was published in 1971. The greatest weight of recent critical effort seems to have been directed to the analysis and explanation of *Ulysses,* and here the following books may be recommended: Frank Budgen, *James Joyce and the Making of Ulysses* (1934, revised edition 1960); Stuart Gilbert, *James Joyce's Ulysses: A Study* (1952); R. M. Kain, *Fabulous Voyager: James Joyce's Ulysses* (1947; revised edition, 1959); S. L. Goldberg, *The Classical Temper: A Study of James Joyce's Ulysses* (1961); Stanley Sultan, *The Argument of Ulysses* (1964); Harry Blamires, *The Bloomsday Book: A Guide Through Joyce's Ulysses* (1966); Clive Hart, *James Joyce's Ulysses* (1968); and Richard Ellmann, *Ulysses on the Liffey* (1972).

The Dead

Lily, the caretaker's daughter, was literally run off her feet. Hardly had she brought one gentleman into the little pantry behind the office on the ground floor and helped him off with his overcoat than the wheezy hall-door bell clanged again and she had to scamper along the bare hallway to let in another guest. It was well for her she had not to attend to the ladies also. But Miss Kate and Miss Julia had thought of that and had converted the bathroom upstairs into a ladies' dressing-room. Miss Kate and Miss Julia were there, gossiping and laughing and fussing, walking after each other to the head of the stairs, peering down over the banisters and calling down to Lily to ask her who had come.

It was always a great affair, the Misses Morkan's annual dance. Everybody who knew them came to it, members of the family, old friends of the family, the members of Julia's choir, any of Kate's pupils that were grown up enough, and even some of Mary Jane's pupils too. Never once had it fallen flat. For years and years it had gone off in spendid style, as long as anyone could remember; ever since Kate and Julia, after the death of their brother Pat, had left the house in Stoney Batter and taken Mary Jane, their only niece, to live with them in the dark, gaunt house on Usher's Island, the upper part of which they had rented from Mr. Fulham, the corn-factor on the ground floor. That was a good thirty years ago if it was a day. Mary Jane, who was then a little girl in short clothes, was now the main prop of the household, for she had the organ in Haddington Road. She had been through the Academy and gave a pupils' concert every year in the upper room of the Antient Concert Rooms. Many of her pupils belonged to the better-class families on the Kingstown and Dalkey line. Old as they were, her aunts also did their share. Julia, though she was quite grey, was still the leading soprano in Adam and Eve's, and Kate, being too feeble to go about much, gave music lessons to beginners on the old square piano in the back room. Lily, the caretaker's daughter, did housemaid's work for them. Though their life was modest, they believed in eating well; the best of everything: diamond-bone sirloins, three-shilling tea and the best bottled stout. But Lily seldom made a mistake in the orders, so that she got on well with her three mistresses. They were fussy, that was all. But the only thing they would not stand was back answers.

Of course, they had good reason to be fussy on such a night. And then it was long after ten o'clock and yet there was no sign of Gabriel and his wife. Besides they were dreadfully afraid that Freddy Malins might turn up screwed. They would not wish for worlds that any of Mary Jane's pupils should see him under the influence; and when he was like that it was sometimes very hard to manage him. Freddy Malins always came late, but they wondered what could be keeping Gabriel: and that was what brought them every two minutes to the banisters to ask Lily had Gabriel or Freddy come.

"O, Mr. Conroy," said Lily to Gabriel when

she opened the door for him, "Miss Kate and Miss Julia thought you were never coming. Good-night, Mrs. Conroy."

"I'll engage they did," said Gabriel, "but they forget that my wife here takes three mortal hours to dress herself."

He stood on the mat, scraping the snow from his goloshes, while Lily led his wife to the foot of the stairs and called out:

"Miss Kate, here's Mrs. Conroy."

Kate and Julia came toddling down the dark stairs at once. Both of them kissed Gabriel's wife, said she must be perished alive, and asked was Gabriel with her.

"Here I am as right as the mail, Aunt Kate! Go on up. I'll follow," called out Gabriel from the dark.

He continued scraping his feet vigorously while the three women went upstairs, laughing, to the ladies' dressing-room. A light fringe of snow lay like a cape on the shoulders of his overcoat and like toecaps on the toes of his goloshes; and, as the buttons of his overcoat slipped with a squeaking noise through the snow-stiffened frieze, a cold, fragrant air from out-of-doors escaped from crevices and folds.

"Is it snowing again, Mr. Conroy?" asked Lily.

She had preceded him into the pantry to help him off with his overcoat. Gabriel smiled at the three syllables she had given his surname and glanced at her. She was a slim, growing girl, pale in complexion and with hay-coloured hair. The gas in the pantry made her look still paler. Gabriel had known her when she was a child and used to sit on the lowest step nursing a rag doll.

"Yes, Lily," he answered, "and I think we're in for a night of it."

He looked up at the pantry ceiling, which was shaking with the stamping and shuffling of feet on the floor above, listened for a moment to the piano and then glanced at the girl, who was folding his overcoat carefully at the end of a shelf.

"Tell me, Lily," he said in a friendly tone, "do you still go to school?"

"O no, sir," she answered. "I'm done schooling this year and more."

"O, then," said Gabriel gaily, "I suppose we'll be going to your wedding one of these fine days with your young man, eh?"

The girl glanced back at him over her shoulder and said with great bitterness:

"The men that is now is only all palaver and what they can get out of you."

Gabriel coloured, as if he felt he had made a mistake and, without looking at her, kicked off his goloshes and flicked actively with his muffler at his patent-leather shoes.

He was a stout, tallish young man. The high colour of his cheeks pushed upwards even to his forehead, where it scattered itself in a few formless patches of pale red; and on his hairless face there scintillated restlessly the polished lenses and the bright gilt rims of the glasses which screened his delicate and restless eyes. His glossy black hair was parted in the middle and brushed in a long curve behind his ears where it curled slightly beneath the groove left by his hat.

When he had flicked lustre into his shoes he stood up and pulled his waistcoat down more tightly on his plump body. Then he took a coin rapidly from his pocket.

"O Lily," he said, thrusting it into her hands, "it's Christmas-time, isn't it? Just . . . here's a little. . . ."

He walked rapidly towards the door.

"O no, sir!" cried the girl, following him. "Really, sir, I wouldn't take it."

"Christmas-time! Christmas-time!" said Gabriel, almost trotting to the stairs and waving his hand to her in deprecation.

The girl, seeing that he had gained the stairs, called out after him:

"Well, thank you, sir."

He waited outside the drawing-room door until the waltz should finish, listening to the skirts that swept against it and to the shuffling of feet. He was still discomposed by the girl's bitter and sudden retort. It had cast a gloom over him which he tried to dispel by arranging his cuffs and the bows of his tie. He then took from his waistcoat pocket a little paper and glanced at the headings he had made for his speech. He was undecided about the lines from Robert Browning, for he feared they would be above the heads of his hearers. Some quotation that they would recognise from Shakespeare or from the Melodies would be better. The indelicate clacking of the men's heels and the shuffling of their soles reminded him that their grade of culture differed from his. He would only make himself ridiculous by quoting poetry to them which they could not understand. They would think that he was airing his superior education. He would fail with them just as he had failed with the girl in the pantry. He had taken up a wrong tone. His whole speech was a mistake from first to last, an utter failure.

Just then his aunts and his wife came out of the ladies' dressing-room. His aunts were two small, plainly dressed old women. Aunt Julia was an inch or so the taller. Her hair, drawn low over the tops of her ears, was grey; and grey also, with darker shadows, was her large flaccid face. Though she was stout in build and stood erect, her slow eyes and parted lips gave her the appearance of a woman who did not know where she was or where she was going. Aunt Kate was more vivacious. Her face, healthier than her sister's, was all puckers and creases, like a shrivelled red apple, and her hair, braided in the same old-fashioned way, had not lost its ripe nut colour.

They both kissed Gabriel frankly. He was their favourite nephew, the son of their dead elder sister, Ellen, who had married T. J. Conroy of the Port and Docks.

"Gretta tells me you're not going to take a cab back to Monkstown tonight, Gabriel," said Aunt Kate.

"No," said Gabriel, turning to his wife, "we had quite enough of that last year, hadn't we? Don't you remember, Aunt Kate, what a cold Gretta got out of it? Cab windows rattling all the way, and the east wind blowing in after we passed Merrion. Very jolly it was. Gretta caught a dreadful cold."

Aunt Kate frowned severely and nodded her head at every word.

"Quite right, Gabriel, quite right," she said. "You can't be too careful."

"But as for Gretta here," said Gabriel, "she'd walk home in the snow if she were let."

Mrs. Conroy laughed.

"Don't mind him, Aunt Kate," she said. "He's really an awful bother, what with green shades for Tom's eyes at night and making him do the dumbbells, and forcing Eva to eat the stirabout. The poor child! And she simply hates the sight of it! . . . O, but you'll never guess what he makes me wear now!"

She broke out into a peal of laughter and

glanced at her husband, whose admiring and happy eyes had been wandering from her dress to her face and hair. The two aunts laughed heartily, too, for Gabriel's solicitude was a standing joke with them.

"Goloshes!" said Mrs. Conroy. "That's the latest. Whenever it's wet underfoot I must put on my goloshes. Tonight even, he wanted me to put them on, but I wouldn't. The next thing he'll buy me will be a diving suit."

Gabriel laughed nervously and patted his tie reassuringly, while Aunt Kate nearly doubled herself, so heartily did she enjoy the joke. The smile soon faded from Aunt Julia's face and her mirthless eyes were directed towards her nephew's face. After a pause she asked:

"And what are goloshes, Gabriel?"

"Goloshes, Julia!" exclaimed her sister. "Goodness me, don't you know what goloshes are? You wear them over your . . . over your boots, Gretta, isn't it?"

"Yes," said Mrs. Conroy. "Guttapercha things. We both have a pair now. Gabriel says everyone wears them on the continent."

"O, on the continent," murmured Aunt Julia, nodding her head slowly.

Gabriel knitted his brows and said, as if he were slightly angered:

"It's nothing very wonderful, but Gretta thinks it very funny because she says the word reminds her of Christy Minstrels."

"But tell me, Gabriel," said Aunt Kate, with brisk tact. "Of course, you've seen about the room. Gretta was saying . . ."

"O, the room is all right," replied Gabriel. "I've taken one in the Gresham."

"To be sure," said Aunt Kate, "by far the best thing to do. And the children, Gretta, you're not anxious about them?"

"O, for one night," said Mrs. Conroy. "Besides, Bessie will look after them."

"To be sure," said Aunt Kate again. "What a comfort it is to have a girl like that, one you can depend on! There's that Lily, I'm sure I don't know what has come over her lately. She's not the girl she was at all."

Gabriel was about to ask his aunt some questions on this point, but she broke off suddenly to gaze after her sister, who had wandered down the stairs and was craning her neck over the banisters.

"Now, I ask you," she said almost testily,

"where is Julia going? Julia! Julia! Where are you going?"

Julia, who had gone half way down one flight, came back and announced blandly:

"Here's Freddy."

At the same moment a clapping of hands and a final flourish of the pianist told that the waltz had ended. The drawing-room door was opened from within and some couples came out. Aunt Kate drew Gabriel aside hurriedly and whispered into his ear:

"Slip down, Gabriel, like a good fellow and see if he's all right, and don't let him up if he's screwed. I'm sure he's screwed. I'm sure he is."

Gabriel went to the stairs and listened over the banisters. He could hear two persons talking in the pantry. Then he recognised Freddy Malins' laugh. He went down the stairs noisily.

"It's such a relief," said Aunt Kate to Mrs. Conroy, "that Gabriel is here. I always feel easier in my mind when he's here. . . . Julia, there's Miss Daly and Miss Power will take some refreshment. Thanks for your beautiful waltz, Miss Daly. It made lovely time."

A tall wizen-faced man, with a stiff grizzled moustache and swarthy skin, who was passing with his partner, said:

"And may we have some refreshment, too, Miss Morkan?"

"Julia," said Aunt Kate summarily, "and here's Mr. Browne and Miss Furlong. Take them in, Julia, with Miss Daly and Miss Power."

"I'm the man for the ladies," said Mr. Browne, pursing his lips until his moustache bristled and smiling in all his wrinkles. "You know, Miss Morkan, the reason they are so fond of me is—"

He did not finish his sentence, but, seeing that Aunt Kate was out of earshot, at once led the three young ladies into the back room. The middle of the room was occupied by two square tables placed end to end, and on these Aunt Julia and the caretaker were straightening and smoothing a large cloth. On the sideboard were arrayed dishes and plates, and glasses and bundles of knives and forks and spoons. The top of the closed square piano served also as a sideboard for viands and sweets. At a smaller sideboard in one corner two young men were standing, drinking hop-bitters.

Mr. Browne led his charges thither and in-

vited them all, in jest, to some ladies' punch, hot, strong and sweet. As they said they never took anything strong, he opened three bottles of lemonade for them. Then he asked one of the young men to move aside, and, taking hold of the decanter, filled out for himself a goodly measure of whisky. The young men eyed him respectfully while he took a trial sip.

"God help me," he said, smiling, "it's the doctor's orders."

His wizened face broke into a broader smile, and the three young ladies laughed in musical echo to his pleasantry, swaying their bodies to and fro, with nervous jerks of their shoulders. The boldest said:

"O, now, Mr. Browne, I'm sure the doctor never ordered anything of the kind."

Mr. Browne took another sip of his whisky and said, with sidling mimicry:

"Well, you see, I'm like the famous Mrs. Cassidy, who is reported to have said: 'Now, Mary Grimes, if I don't take it, make me take it, for I feel I want it.' "

His hot face had leaned forward a little too confidentially and he had assumed a very low Dublin accent so that the young ladies, with one instinct, received his speech in silence. Miss Furlong, who was one of Mary Jane's pupils, asked Miss Daly what was the name of the pretty waltz she had played; and Mr. Browne, seeing that he was ignored, turned promptly to the two young men who were more appreciative.

A red-faced young woman, dressed in pansy, came into the room, excitedly clapping her hands and crying:

"Quadrilles! Quadrilles!"

Close on her heels came Aunt Kate, crying:

"Two gentlemen and three ladies, Mary Jane!"

"O, here's Mr. Bergin and Mr. Kerrigan," said Mary Jane. "Mr. Kerrigan, will you take Miss Power? Miss Furlong, may I get you a partner, Mr. Bergin. O, that'll just do now."

"Three ladies, Mary Jane," said Aunt Kate.

The two young gentlemen asked the ladies if they might have the pleasure, and Mary Jane turned to Miss Daly.

"O, Miss Daly, you're really awfully good, after playing for the last two dances, but really we're so short of ladies tonight."

"I don't mind in the least, Miss Morkan."

"But I've a nice partner for you, Mr. Bartell

D'Arcy, the tenor. I'll get him to sing later on. All Dublin is raving about him."

"Lovely voice, lovely voice!" said Aunt Kate.

As the piano had twice begun the prelude to the first figure Mary Jane led her recruits quickly from the room. They had hardly gone when Aunt Julia wandered slowly into the room, looking behind her at something.

"What is the matter, Julia?" asked Aunt Kate anxiously. "Who is it?"

Julia, who was carrying in a column of table-napkins, turned to her sister and said, simply, as if the question had surprised her:

"It's only Freddy, Kate, and Gabriel with him."

In fact right behind her Gabriel could be seen piloting Freddy Malins across the landing. The latter, a young man of about forty, was of Gabriel's size and build, with very round shoulders. His face was fleshy and pallid, touched with colour only at the thick hanging lobes of his ears and at the wide wings of his nose. He had coarse features, a blunt nose, a convex and receding brow, tumid and protruded lips. His heavy-lidded eyes and the disorder of his scanty hair made him look sleepy. He was laughing heartily in a high key at a story which he had been telling Gabriel on the stairs and at the same time rubbing the knuckles of his left fist backwards and forwards into his left eye.

"Good evening, Freddy," said Aunt Julia.

Freddy Malins bade the Misses Morkan good-evening in what seemed an offhand fashion by reason of the habitual catch in his voice and then, seeing that Mr. Browne was grinning at him from the sideboard, crossed the room on rather shaky legs and began to repeat in an undertone the story he had just told to Gabriel.

"He's not so bad, is he?" said Aunt Kate to Gabriel.

Gabriel's brows were dark but he raised them quickly and answered:

"O, no, hardly noticeable."

"Now, isn't he a terrible fellow!" she said. "And his poor mother made him take the pledge on New Year's Eve. But come on, Gabriel, into the drawing-room."

Before leaving the room with Gabriel she signalled to Mr. Browne by frowning and shaking her forefinger in warning to and fro. Mr. Browne nodded in answer and, when she had gone, said to Freddy Malins:

"Now, then, Teddy, I'm going to fill you out a good glass of lemonade just to buck you up."

Freddy Malins, who was nearing the climax of his story, waved the offer aside impatiently but Mr. Browne, having first called Freddy Malins' attention to a disarray in his dress, filled out and handed him a full glass of lemonade. Freddy Malins' left hand accepted the glass mechanically, his right hand being engaged in the mechanical readjustment of his dress. Mr. Browne, whose face was once more wrinkling with mirth, poured out for himself a glass of whisky while Freddy Malins exploded, before he had well reached the climax of his story, in a kink of high-pitched bronchitic laughter and, setting down his untasted and overflowing glass, began to rub the knuckles of his left fist backwards and forwards into his left eye, repeating words of his last phrase as well as his fit of laughter would allow him.

Gabriel could not listen while Mary Jane was playing her Academy piece, full of runs and difficult passages, to the hushed drawing-room. He liked music but the piece she was playing had no melody for him and he doubted whether it had any melody for the other listeners, though they had begged Mary Jane to play something. Four young men, who had come from the refreshment-room to stand in the doorway at the sound of the piano, had gone away quietly in couples after a few minutes. The only persons who seemed to follow the music were Mary Jane herself, her hands racing along the key-board or lifted from it at the pauses like those of a priestess in momentary imprecation, and Aunt Kate standing at her elbow to turn the page.

Gabriel's eyes, irritated by the floor, which glittered with beeswax under the heavy chandelier, wandered to the wall above the piano. A picture of the balcony scene in *Romeo and Juliet* hung there and beside it was a picture of the two murdered princes in the Tower which Aunt Julia had worked in red, blue and brown wools when she was a girl. Probably in the school they had gone to as girls that kind of work had been taught for one year. His mother had worked for him as a birthday present a waistcoat of purple tabinet, with little foxes' heads upon it, lined with brown satin and having round mulberry buttons. It was strange that his mother had had no musical talent though Aunt Kate used to call her the brains carrier of the Morkan family. Both she and Julia had always seemed a little proud of their serious and matronly sister. Her photograph stood before the pierglass. She held an open book on her knees and was pointing out something in it to Constantine who, dressed in a man-o'-war suit, lay at her feet. It was she who had chosen the names of her sons for she was very sensible of the dignity of family life. Thanks to her, Constantine was now senior curate in Balbriggan and, thanks to her, Gabriel himself had taken his degree in the Royal University. A shadow passed over his face as he remembered her sullen opposition to his marriage. Some slighting phrases she had used still rankled in his memory; she had once spoken of Gretta as being country cute and that was not true of Gretta at all. It was Gretta who had nursed her during all her last long illness in their house at Monkstown.

He knew that Mary Jane must be near the end of her piece for she was playing again the opening melody with runs of scales after every bar and while he waited for the end the resentment died down in his heart. The piece ended with a trill of octaves in the treble and a final deep octave in the bass. Great applause greeted Mary Jane as, blushing and rolling up her music nervously, she escaped from the room. The most vigorous clapping came from the four young men in the doorway who had gone away to the refreshment-room at the beginning of the piece but had come back when the piano had stopped.

Lancers were arranged. Gabriel found himself partnered with Miss Ivors. She was a frank-mannered talkative young lady, with a freckled face and prominent brown eyes. She did not wear a low-cut bodice and the large brooch which was fixed in the front of her collar bore on it an Irish device and motto.

When they had taken their places she said abruptly:

"I have a crow to pluck with you."

"With me?" said Gabriel.

She nodded her head gravely.

"What is it?" asked Gabriel, smiling at her solemn manner.

"Who is G. C.?" answered Miss Ivors, turning her eyes upon him.

Gabriel coloured and was about to knit his brows, as if he did not understand, when she said bluntly:

"O, innocent Amy! I have found out that you write for *The Daily Express*. Now, aren't you ashamed of yourself?"

"Why should I be ashamed of myself?" asked Gabriel, blinking his eyes and trying to smile.

"Well, I'm ashamed of you," said Miss Ivors frankly, "To say you'd write for a paper like that. I didn't think you were a West Briton."

A look of perplexity appeared on Gabriel's face. It was true that he wrote a literary column every Wednesday in *The Daily Express,* for which he was paid fifteen shillings. But that did not make him a West Briton surely. The books he received for review were almost more welcome than the paltry cheque. He loved to feel the covers and turn over the pages of newly printed books. Nearly every day when his teaching in the college was ended he used to wander down the quays to the second-hand booksellers, to Hickey's on Bachelor's Walk, to Webb's or Massey's on Aston's Quay, or to O'Clohissey's in the by-street. He did not know how to meet her charge. He wanted to say that literature was above politics. But they were friends of many years' standing and their careers had been parallel, first at the University and then as teachers: he could not risk a grandiose phrase with her. He continued blinking his eyes and trying to smile and murmured lamely that he saw nothing political in writing reviews of books.

When their turn to cross had come he was still perplexed and inattentive. Miss Ivors promptly took his hand in a warm grasp and said in a soft friendly tone:

"Of course, I was only joking. Come, we cross now."

When they were together again she spoke of the University question and Gabriel felt more at ease. A friend of hers had shown her his review of Browning's poems. That was how she had found out the secret: but she liked the review immensely. Then she said suddenly:

"O, Mr. Conroy, will you come for an excursion to the Aran Isles this summer? We're going to stay there a whole month. It will be splendid out in the Atlantic. You ought to come. Mr. Clancy is coming, and Mr. Kilkelly and Kathleen Kearney. It would be splendid for Gretta too if she'd come. She's from Connacht, isn't she?"

"Her people are," said Gabriel shortly.

"But you will come, won't you?" said Miss Ivors, laying her warm hand eagerly on his arm.

"The fact is," said Gabriel, "I have just arranged to go—"

"Go where?" asked Miss Ivors.

"Well, you know, every year I go for a cycling tour with some fellows and so—"

"But where?" asked Miss Ivors.

"Well, we usually go to France or Belgium or perhaps Germany," said Gabriel awkwardly.

"And why do you go to France and Belgium," said Miss Ivors, "instead of visiting your own land?"

"Well," said Gabriel, "it's partly to keep in touch with the languages and partly for a change."

"And haven't you your own language to keep in touch with—Irish?" asked Miss Ivors.

"Well," said Gabriel, "if it comes to that, you know, Irish is not my language."

Their neighbours had turned to listen to the cross-examination. Gabriel glanced right and left nervously and tried to keep his good humour under the ordeal which was making a blush invade his forehead.

"And haven't you your own land to visit," continued Miss Ivors, "that you know nothing of, your own people, and your own country?"

"O, to tell you the truth," retorted Gabriel suddenly, "I'm sick of my own country, sick of it!"

"Why?" asked Miss Ivors.

Gabriel did not answer for his retort had heated him.

"Why?" repeated Miss Ivors.

They had to go visiting together and, as he had not answered her, Miss Ivors said warmly:

"Of course, you've no answer."

Gabriel tried to cover his agitation by taking part in the dance with great energy. He avoided her eyes for he had seen a sour expression on her face. But when they met in the long chain he was surprised to feel his hand firmly pressed. She looked at him from under her brows for a moment quizzically until he smiled. Then, just as the chain was about to start again, she stood on tiptoe and whispered into his ear:

"West Briton!"

When the lancers were over Gabriel went away to a remote corner of the room where Freddy Malins' mother was sitting. She was a stout feeble old woman with white hair. Her voice had a catch in it like her son's and she stuttered slightly. She had been told that Freddy had come and that he was nearly all right. Gabriel asked her whether she had had a good crossing. She lived with her married daughter in Glasgow and came to Dublin on a visit once a year. She answered placidly that she had had a beautiful crossing and that the captain had been most attentive to her. She spoke also of the beautiful house her daughter kept in Glasgow, and of all the friends they had there. While her tongue rambled on Gabriel tried to banish from his mind all memory of the unpleasant incident with Miss Ivors. Of course the girl or woman, or whatever she was, was an enthusiast but there was a time for all things. Perhaps he ought not to have answered her like that. But she had no right to call him a West Briton before people, even in joke. She had tried to make him ridiculous before people, heckling him and staring at him with her rabbit's eyes.

He saw his wife making her way towards him through the waltzing couples. When she reached him she said into his ear:

"Gabriel, Aunt Kate wants to know won't you carve the goose as usual. Miss Daly will carve the ham and I'll do the pudding."

"All right," said Gabriel.

"She's sending in the younger ones first as soon as this waltz is over so that we'll have the table to ourselves."

"Were you dancing?" asked Gabriel.

"Of course I was. Didn't you see me? What row had you with Molly Ivors?"

"No row. Why? Did she say so?"

"Something like that. I'm trying to get that Mr. D'Arcy to sing. He's full of conceit, I think."

"There was no row," said Gabriel moodily, "only she wanted me to go for a trip to the west of Ireland and I said I wouldn't."

His wife clasped her hands excitedly and gave a little jump.

"O, do go, Gabriel," she cried. "I'd love to see Galway again."

"You can go if you like," said Gabriel coldly.

She looked at him for a moment, then turned to Mrs. Malins and said:

"There's a nice husband for you, Mrs. Malins."

While she was threading her way back across the room Mrs. Malins, without adverting to the interruption, went on to tell Gabriel what beautiful places there were in Scotland and beautiful scenery. Her son-in-law brought them every year to the lakes and they used to go fishing. Her son-in-law was a splendid fisher. One day he caught a beautiful big fish and the man in the hotel cooked it for their dinner.

Gabriel hardly heard what she said. Now that supper was coming near he began to think again about his speech and about the quotation. When he saw Freddy Malins coming across the room to visit his mother Gabriel left the chair free for him and retired into the embrasure of the window. The room had already cleared and from the back room came the clatter of plates and knives. Those who still remained in the drawing-room seemed tired of dancing and were conversing quietly in little groups. Gabriel's warm trembling fingers tapped the cold pane of the window. How cool it must be outside! How pleasant it would be to walk out alone, first along by the river and then through the park! The snow would be lying on the branches of the trees and forming a bright cap on the top of the Wellington Monument. How much more pleasant it would be there than at the supper-table!

He ran over the headings of his speech: Irish hospitality, sad memories, the Three Graces, Paris, the quotation from Browning. He repeated to himself a phrase he had written in his review: "One feels that one is listening to a thought-tormented music." Miss Ivors had praised the review. Was she sincere? Had she really any life of her own behind all her propagandism? There had never been any ill-feeling between them until that night. It unnerved him to think that she would be at the supper-table, looking up at him while he spoke with her critical quizzing eyes. Perhaps she would not be sorry to see him fail in his speech. An idea came into his mind and gave him courage. He would say, alluding to Aunt Kate and Aunt Julia: "Ladies and Gentlemen, the generation which is now on the wane among us may have had its faults but for my part I think it had certain qualities of hospitality, of humour, of humanity, which the new and very serious and hypereducated generation that is growing up around us seems to me to lack." Very good: that was one for Miss Ivors. What did he care that his aunts were only two ignorant old women?

A murmur in the room attracted his attention. Mr. Browne was advancing from the door, gallantly escorting Aunt Julia, who leaned upon his arm, smiling and hanging her head. An irregular musketry of applause escorted her also as far as the piano and then, as Mary Jane seated herself on the stool, and Aunt Julia, no longer smiling, half turned so as to pitch her voice fairly into the room, gradually ceased. Gabriel recognised the prelude. It was that of an old song of Aunt Julia's—*Arrayed for the Bridal*. Her voice, strong and clear in tone, attacked with great spirit the runs which embellish the air and though she sang very rapidly she did not miss even the smallest of the grace notes. To follow the voice, without looking at the singer's face, was to feel and share the excitement of swift and secure flight. Gabriel applauded loudly with all the others at the close of the song and loud applause was borne in from the invisible supper-table. It sounded so genuine that a little colour struggled into Aunt Julia's face as she bent to replace in the music-stand the old leather-bound song-book that had her initials on the cover. Freddy Malins, who had listened with his head perched sideways to hear her better, was still applauding when everyone else had ceased and talking animatedly to his mother who nodded her head gravely and slowly in acquiescence. At last, when he could clap no more, he stood up suddenly and hurried across the room to Aunt Julia whose hand he seized and held in both his hands, shaking it when words failed him or the catch in his voice proved too much for him.

"I was just telling my mother," he said, "I never heard you sing so well, never. No, I never heard your voice so good as it is tonight. Now! Would you believe that now? That's the truth. Upon my word and honour that's the truth. I never heard your voice sound so fresh and so . . . so clear and fresh, never!"

Aunt Julia smiled broadly and murmured something about compliments as she released her hand from his grasp. Mr. Browne extended his open hand towards her and said to those who were near him in the manner of a showman introducing a prodigy to an audience:

"Miss Julia Morkan, my latest discovery!"

He was laughing very heartily at this himself when Freddy Malins turned to him and said:

"Well, Browne, if you're serious you might make a worse discovery. All I can say is I never heard her sing half so well as long as I am coming here. And that's the honest truth."

"Neither did I," said Mr. Browne. "I think her voice has greatly improved."

Aunt Julia shrugged her shoulders and said with meek pride:

"Thirty years ago I hadn't a bad voice as voices go."

"I often told Julia," said Aunt Kate emphatically, "that she was simply thrown away in that choir. But she never would be said by me."

She turned as if to appeal to the good sense of the others against a refractory child while Aunt Julia gazed in front of her, a vague smile of reminiscence playing on her face.

"No," continued Aunt Kate, "she wouldn't be said or led by anyone, slaving there in that choir night and day, night and day. Six o'clock on Christmas morning! And all for what?"

"Well, isn't it for the honour of God, Aunt Kate?" asked Mary Jane, twisting round on the piano-stool and smiling.

Aunt Kate turned fiercely on her niece and said:

"I know all about the honour of God, Mary Jane, but I think it's not at all honourable for the pope to turn out the women out of the choirs that have slaved there all their lives and put little whippersnappers of boys over their heads. I suppose it is for the good of the Church if the pope does it. But it's not just, Mary Jane, and it's not right."

She had worked herself into a passion and would have continued in defence of her sister for it was a sore subject with her but Mary Jane, seeing that all the dancers had come back, intervened pacifically:

"Now, Aunt Kate, you're giving scandal to Mr. Browne who is of the other persuasion."

Aunt Kate turned to Mr. Browne, who was grinning at this allusion to his religion, and said hastily:

"O, I don't question the pope's being right. I'm only a stupid old woman and I wouldn't presume to do such a thing. But there's such a thing as common everyday politeness and gratitude. And if I were in Julia's place I'd tell that Father Healey straight up to his face . . ."

"And besides, Aunt Kate," said Mary Jane, "we really are all hungry and when we are hungry we are all very quarrelsome."

"And when we are thirsty we are also quarrelsome," added Mr. Browne.

"So that we had better go to supper," said Mary Jane, "and finish the discussion afterwards."

On the landing outside the drawing-room Gabriel found his wife and Mary Jane trying to persuade Miss Ivors to stay for supper. But Miss Ivors, who had put on her hat and was buttoning her cloak, would not stay. She did not feel in the least hungry and she had already overstayed her time.

"But only for ten minutes, Molly," said Mrs. Conroy. "That won't delay you."

"To take a pick itself," said Mary Jane, "after all your dancing."

"I really couldn't," said Miss Ivors.

"I am afraid you didn't enjoy yourself at all," said Mary Jane hopelessly.

"Ever so much, I assure you," said Miss Ivors, "but you really must let me run off now."

"But how can you get home?" asked Mrs. Conroy.

"O, it's only two steps up the quay."

Gabriel hesitated a moment and said:

"If you will allow me, Miss Ivors, I'll see you home if you are really obliged to go."

But Miss Ivors broke away from them.

"I won't hear of it," she cried. "For goodness' sake go in to your suppers and don't mind me. I'm quite well able to take care of myself."

"Well, you're the comical girl, Molly," said Mrs. Conroy frankly.

"*Beannacht libh*," cried Miss Ivors, with a laugh, as she ran down the staircase.

Mary Jane gazed after her, a moody puzzled expression on her face, while Mrs. Conroy leaned over the banisters to listen for the hall-door. Gabriel asked himself was he the cause of her abrupt departure. But she did not seem to be in ill humour: she had gone away laughing. He stared blankly down the staircase.

At the moment Aunt Kate came toddling out of the supper-room, almost wringing her hands in despair.

"Where is Gabriel?" she cried. "Where on earth is Gabriel? There's everyone waiting in there, stage to let, and nobody to carve the goose!"

"Here I am, Aunt Kate!" cried Gabriel, with sudden animation, "ready to carve a flock of geese, if necessary."

A fat brown goose lay at one end of the table and at the other end, on a bed of creased paper strewn with sprigs of parsley, lay a great ham, stripped of its outer skin and peppered over with crust crumbs, a neat paper frill round its shin and beside this was a round of spiced beef. Between these rival ends ran parallel lines of side-dishes: two little minsters of jelly, red and yellow; a shallow dish full of blocks of blanc-mange and red jam, a large green leaf-shaped dish with a stalk-shaped handle, on which lay bunches of purple raisins and peeled almonds, a companion dish on which lay a solid rectangle of Smyrna figs, a dish of custard topped with grated nutmeg, a small bowl full of chocolates and sweets wrapped in gold and silver papers and a glass vase in which stood some tall celery stalks. In the centre of the table there stood, as sentries to a fruit-stand which upheld a pyramid of oranges and American apples, two squat old-fashioned decanters of cut glass, one containing port and the other dark sherry. On the closed square piano a pudding in a huge yellow dish lay in waiting and behind it were three squads of bottles of stout and ale and minerals, drawn up according to the colours of their uniforms, the first two black, with brown and red labels, the third and smallest squad white, with transverse green sashes.

Gabriel took his seat boldly at the head of the table and, having looked to the edge of the carver, plunged his fork firmly into the goose. He felt quite at ease now for he was an expert carver and liked nothing better than to find himself at the head of a well-laden table.

"Miss Furlong, what shall I send you?" he asked. "A wing or a slice of the breast?"

"Just a small slice of the breast."

"Miss Higgins, what for you?"

"O, anything at all, Mr. Conroy."

While Gabriel and Miss Daly exchanged plates of goose and plates of ham and spiced beef Lily went from guest to guest with a dish of hot floury potatoes wrapped in a white napkin. This was Mary Jane's idea and she had also suggested apple sauce for the goose but Aunt Kate had said that plain roast goose without any apple sauce had always been good enough for her and she hoped she might never eat worse. Mary Jane waited on her pupils and saw that they got the best slices and Aunt Kate and Aunt Julia opened and carried across from the piano bottles of stout and ale for the gentlemen and bottles of minerals for the ladies. There was a great deal of confusion and laughter and noise, the noise of orders and counter-orders, of knives and forks, of corks and glass-stoppers. Gabriel began to carve second helpings as soon as he had finished the first round without serving himself. Everyone protested loudly so that he compromised by taking a long draught of stout for he had found the carving hot work. Mary Jane settled down quietly to her supper but Aunt Kate and Aunt Julia were still toddling round the table, walking on each other's heels, getting in each other's way and giving each other unheeded orders. Mr. Browne begged of them to sit down and eat their suppers and so did Gabriel but they said there was time enough, so that, at last, Freddy Malins stood up and, capturing Aunt Kate, plumped her down on her chair amid general laughter.

When everyone had been well served Gabriel said, smiling:

"Now, if anyone wants a little more of what vulgar people call stuffing let him or her speak."

A chorus of voices invited him to begin his own supper and Lily came forward with three potatoes which she had reserved for him.

"Very well," said Gabriel amiably, as he took another preparatory draught, "kindly forget my existence, ladies and gentlemen, for a few minutes."

He set to his supper and took no part in the conversation with which the table covered Lily's removal of the plates. The subject of talk was the opera company which was then at the Theatre Royal. Mr. Bartell D'Arcy, the tenor, a dark-complexioned young man with a smart moustache, praised very highly the leading contralto of the company but Miss Furlong thought she had a rather vulgar style of production. Freddy Malins said there was a Negro chieftain

singing in the second part of the Gaiety pantomime who had one of the finest tenor voices he
had ever heard.

"Have you heard him?" he asked Mr.
Bartell D'Arcy across the table.

"No," answered Mr. Bartell D'Arcy carelessly.

"Because," Freddy Malins explained, "now
I'd be curious to hear your opinion of him. I
think he has a grand voice."

"It takes Teddy to find out the really good
things," said Mr. Browne familiarly to the table.

"And why couldn't he have a voice too?"
asked Freddy Malins sharply. "Is it because he's
only a black?"

Nobody answered this question and Mary
Jane led the table back to the legitimate opera.
One of her pupils had given her a pass for
Mignon. Of course it was very fine, she said, but
it made her think of poor Georgina Burns. Mr.
Browne could go back farther still, to the old
Italian companies that used to come to Dublin—
Tietjens, Ilma de Murzka, Campanini, the great
Trebelli, Giuglini, Ravelli, Aramburo. Those
were the days, he said, when there was something like singing to be heard in Dublin. He told
too of how the top gallery of the old Royal used
to be packed night after night, of how one night
an Italian tenor had sung five encores to *Let me
like a Soldier fall,* introducing a high C every
time, and of how the gallery boys would sometimes in their enthusiasm unyoke the horses from
the carriage of some great *prima donna* and pull
her themselves through the streets to her hotel.
Why did they never play the grand old operas
now, he asked, *Dinorah, Lucrezia Borgia?* Because they could not get the voices to sing them:
that was why.

"O, well," said Mr. Bartell D'Arcy, "I presume there are as good singers today as there
were then."

"Where are they?" asked Mr. Browne defiantly.

"In London, Paris, Milan," said Mr. Bartell
D'Arcy warmly. "I suppose Caruso, for example,
is quite as good, if not better than any of the men
you have mentioned."

"Maybe so," said Mr. Browne. "But I may
tell you I doubt it strongly."

"O, I'd give anything to hear Caruso sing,"
said Mary Jane.

"For me," said Aunt Kate, who had been
picking a bone, "there was only one tenor. To
please me, I mean. But I suppose none of you
ever heard of him."

"Who was he, Miss Morkan?" asked Mr.
Bartell D'Arcy politely.

"His name," said Aunt Kate, "was Parkinson. I heard him when he was in his prime and
I think he had then the purest tenor voice that
was ever put into a man's throat."

"Strange," said Mr. Bartell D'Arcy. "I never
even heard of him."

"Yes, yes, Miss Morkan is right," said Mr.
Browne. "I remember hearing of old Parkinson
but he's too far back for me."

"A beautiful, pure, sweet, mellow English
tenor," said Aunt Kate with enthusiasm.

Gabriel having finished, the huge pudding
was transferred to the table. The clatter of forks
and spoons began again. Gabriel's wife served
out spoonfuls of the pudding and passed the
plates down the table. Midway down they were
held up by Mary Jane, who replenished them
with raspberry or orange jelly or with blanc-
mange and jam. The pudding was of Aunt Julia's
making and she received praises for it from all
quarters. She herself said that it was not quite
brown enough.

"Well, I hope, Miss Morkan," said Mr.
Browne, "that I'm brown enough for you because, you know, I'm all brown."

All the gentlemen, except Gabriel, ate
some of the pudding out of compliment to Aunt
Julia. As Gabriel never ate sweets the celery had
been left for him. Freddy Malins also took a
stalk of celery and ate it with his pudding. He
had been told that celery was a capital thing for
the blood and he was just then under doctor's
care. Mrs. Malins, who had been silent all
through the supper, said that her son was going
down to Mount Melleray in a week or so. The
table then spoke of Mount Melleray, how bracing
the air was down there, how hospitable the
monks were and how they never asked for a
penny-piece from their guests.

"And do you mean to say," asked Mr.
Browne incredulously, "that a chap can go down
there and put up there as if it were a hotel and
live on the fat of the land and then come away
without paying anything?"

"O, most people give some donation to the monastery when they leave," said Mary Jane.

"I wish we had an institution like that in our Church," said Mr. Browne candidly.

He was astonished to hear that the monks never spoke, got up at two in the morning and slept in their coffins. He asked what they did it for.

"That's the rule of the order," said Aunt Kate firmly.

"Yes, but why?" asked Mr. Browne.

Aunt Kate repeated that it was the rule, that was all. Mr. Browne still seemed not to understand. Freddy Malins explained to him, as best he could, that the monks were trying to make up for the sins committed by all the sinners in the outside world. The explanation was not very clear for Mr. Browne grinned and said:

"I like that idea very much but wouldn't a comfortable spring bed do them as well as a coffin?"

"The coffin," said Mary Jane, "is to remind them of their last end."

As the subject had grown lugubrious it was buried in a silence of the table during which Mrs. Malins could be heard saying to her neighbour in an indistinct undertone:

"They are very good men, the monks, very pious men."

The raisins and almonds and figs and apples and oranges and chocolates and sweets were now passed about the table and Aunt Julia invited all the guests to have either port or sherry. At first Mr. Bartell D'Arcy refused to take either but one of his neighbours nudged him and whispered something to him upon which he allowed his glass to be filled. Gradually as the last glasses were being filled the conversation ceased. A pause followed, broken only by the noise of the wine and by unsettlings of chairs. The Misses Morkan, all three, looked down at the tablecloth. Someone coughed once or twice and then a few gentlemen patted the table gently as a signal for silence. The silence came and Gabriel pushed back his chair and stood up.

The patting at once grew louder in encouragement and then ceased altogether. Gabriel leaned his ten trembling fingers on the tablecloth and smiled nervously at the company. Meeting a row of upturned faces he raised his eyes to the chandelier. The piano was playing a waltz tune and he could hear the skirts sweeping against the drawing-room door. People, perhaps, were standing in the snow on the quay outside, gazing up at the lighted windows and listening to the waltz music. The air was pure there. In the distance lay the park where the trees were weighted with snow. The Wellington Monument wore a gleaming cap of snow that flashed westward over the white field of Fifteen Acres.

He began:

"Ladies and Gentlemen,

"It has fallen to my lot this evening, as in years past, to perform a very pleasing task but a task for which I am afraid my poor powers as a speaker are all too inadequate."

"No, no!" said Mr. Browne.

"But, however that may be, I can only ask you tonight to take the will for the deed and to lend me your attention for a few moments while I endeavour to express to you in words what my feelings are on this occasion.

"Ladies and Gentlemen, it is not the first time that we have gathered together under this hospitable roof, around this hospitable board. It is not the first time that we have been the recipients—or perhaps, I had better say, the victims—of the hospitality of certain good ladies."

He made a circle in the air with his arm and paused. Everyone laughed or smiled at Aunt Kate and Aunt Julia and Mary Jane who all turned crimson with pleasure. Gabriel went on more boldly:

"I feel more strongly with every recurring year that our country has no tradition which does it so much honour and which it should guard so jealously as that of its hospitality. It is a tradition that is unique as far as my experience goes (and I have visited not a few places abroad) among the modern nations. Some would say, perhaps, that with us it is rather a failing than anything to be boasted of. But granted even that, it is, to my mind, a princely failing, and one that I trust will long be cultivated among us. Of one thing, at least, I am sure. As long as this one roof shelters the good ladies aforesaid—and I wish from my heart it may do so for many and many a long year to come—the tradition of genuine warm-hearted courteous Irish hospitality, which our forefathers have handed down to us and which we in turn must hand down to our descendants, is still alive among us."

A hearty murmur of assent ran round the table. It shot through Gabriel's mind that Miss Ivors was not there and that she had gone away discourteously: and he said with confidence in himself:

"Ladies and Gentlemen,

"A new generation is growing up in our midst, a generation actuated by new ideas and new principles. It is serious and enthusiastic for these new ideas and its enthusiasm, even when it is misdirected, is, I believe, in the main sincere. But we are living in a sceptical and, if I may use the phrase, a thought-tormented age: and sometimes I fear that this new generation, educated or hypereducated at it is, will lack those qualities of humanity, of hospitality, of kindly humour which belonged to an older day. Listening tonight to the names of all those great singers of the past it seemed to me, I must confess, that we were living in a less spacious age. Those days might, without exaggeration, be called spacious days: and if they are gone beyond recall let us hope, at least, that in gatherings such as this we shall still speak of them with pride and affection, still cherish in our hearts the memory of those dead and gone great ones whose fame the world will not willingly let die."

"Hear, hear!" said Mr. Browne loudly.

"But yet," continued Gabriel, his voice falling into a softer inflection, "there are always in gatherings such as this sadder thoughts that will recur to our minds: thoughts of the past, of youth, of changes, of absent faces that we miss here tonight. Our path through life is strewn with many such sad memories: and were we to brood upon them always we could not find the heart to go on bravely with our work among the living. We have all of us living duties and living affections which claim, and rightly claim, our strenuous endeavours.

"Therefore, I will not linger on the past. I will not let any gloomy moralising intrude upon us here tonight. Here we are gathered together for a brief moment from the bustle and rush of our everyday routine. We are met here as friends, in the spirit of good-fellowship, as colleagues, also to a certain extent, in the true spirit of *camaraderie*, and as the guests of—what shall I call them?—the Three Graces of the Dublin musical world."

The table burst into applause and laughter at this allusion. Aunt Julia vainly asked each of her neighbours in turn to tell her what Gabriel had said.

"He says we are the Three Graces, Aunt Julia," said Mary Jane.

Aunt Julia did not understand but she looked up, smiling at Gabriel, who continued in the same vein:

"Ladies and Gentlemen,

"I will not attempt to play tonight the part that Paris played on another occasion. I will not attempt to choose between them. The task would be an invidious one and one beyond my poor powers. For when I view them in turn, whether it be our chief hostess herself, whose good heart, whose too good heart, has become a byword with all who know her, or her sister, who seems to be gifted with perennial youth and whose singing must have been a surprise and a revelation to us all tonight, or, last but not least, when I consider our youngest hostess, talented, cheerful, hard-working and the best of nieces, I confess, Ladies and Gentlemen, that I do not know to which of them I should award the prize."

Gabriel glanced down at his aunts and, seeing the large smile on Aunt Julia's face and the tears which had risen to Aunt Kate's eyes, hastened to his close. He raised his glass of port gallantly, while every member of the company fingered a glass expectantly, and said loudly:

"Let us toast them all three together. Let us drink to their health, wealth, long life, happiness and prosperity and may they long continue to hold the proud and self-won position which they hold in their profession and the position of honour and affection which they hold in our hearts."

All the guests stood up, glass in hand, and turning towards the three seated ladies, sang in unison, with Mr. Browne as leader:

> *For they are jolly gay fellows,*
> *For they are jolly gay fellows,*
> *For they are jolly gay fellows,*
> *Which nobody can deny.*

Aunt Kate was making frank use of her handkerchief and even Aunt Julia seemed moved. Freddy Malins beat time with his pudding-fork and the singers turned towards one another, as if in melodious conference, while they sang with emphasis:

> *Unless he tells a lie,*
> *Unless he tells a lie,*

Then, turning once more towards their hostesses, they sang:

> *For they are jolly gay fellows,*
> *For they are jolly gay fellows,*
> *For they are jolly gay fellows,*
> *Which nobody can deny.*

The acclamation which followed was taken up beyond the door of the supper-room by many of the other guests and renewed time after time, Freddy Malins acting as officer with his fork on high.

The piercing morning air came into the hall where they were standing so that Aunt Kate said:

"Close the door, somebody. Mrs. Malins will get her death of cold."

"Browne is out there, Aunt Kate," said Mary Jane.

"Browne is everywhere," said Aunt Kate, lowering her voice. Mary Jane laughed at her tone.

"Really," she said archly, "he is very attentive."

"He has been laid on here like the gas," said Aunt Kate in the same tone, "all during the Christmas."

She laughed herself this time good-humouredly and then added quickly:

"But tell him to come in, Mary Jane, and close the door. I hope to goodness he didn't hear me."

At that moment the hall-door was opened and Mr. Browne came in from the doorstep, laughing as if his heart would break. He was dressed in a long green overcoat with mock astrakhan cuffs and collar and wore on his head an oval fur cap. He pointed down the snow-covered quay from where the sound of shrill prolonged whistling was borne in.

"Teddy will have all the cabs in Dublin out," he said.

Gabriel advanced from the little pantry behind the office, struggling into his overcoat and, looking round the hall, said:

"Gretta not down yet?"

"She's getting on her things, Gabriel," said Aunt Kate.

"Who's playing up there?" asked Gabriel.

"Nobody. They're all gone."

"O no, Aunt Kate," said Mary Jane. "Bartell D'Arcy and Miss O'Callaghan aren't gone yet."

"Someone is fooling at the piano anyhow," said Gabriel.

Mary Jane glanced at Gabriel and Mr. Browne and said with a shiver:

"It makes me feel cold to look at you two gentlemen muffled up like that. I wouldn't like to face your journey home at this hour."

"I'd like nothing better this minute," said Mr. Browne stoutly, "than a rattling fine walk in the country or a fast drive with a good spanking goer between the shafts."

"We used to have a very good horse and trap at home," said Aunt Julia sadly.

"The never-to-be-forgotten Johnny," said Mary Jane, laughing.

Aunt Kate and Gabriel laughed too.

"Why, what was wonderful about Johnny?" asked Mr. Browne.

"The late lamented Patrick Morkan, our grandfather, that is," explained Gabriel, "commonly known in his later years as the old gentleman, was a glue-boiler."

"O, now, Gabriel," said Aunt Kate, laughing, "he had a starch mill."

"Well, glue or starch," said Gabriel, "the old gentleman had a horse by the name of Johnny. And Johnny used to work in the old gentleman's mill, walking round and round in order to drive the mill. That was all very well; but now comes the tragic part about Johnny. One fine day the old gentleman thought he'd like to drive out with the quality to a military review in the park."

"The Lord have mercy on his soul," said Aunt Kate compassionately.

"Amen," said Gabriel. "So the old gentleman, as I said, harnessed Johnny and put on his very best tall hat and his very best collar and drove out in grand style from his ancestral mansion somewhere near Back Lane, I think."

Everyone laughed, even Mrs. Malins, at Gabriel's manner and Aunt Kate said:

"O, now, Gabriel, he didn't live in Back Lane, really. Only the mill was there."

"Out from the mansion of his forefathers," continued Gabriel, "he drove with Johnny. And everything went on beautifully until Johnny came in sight of King Billy's statue: and whether he fell in love with the horse King Billy sits on or whether he thought he was back again in the mill, anyhow he began to walk round the statue."

Gabriel paced in a circle round the hall in his goloshes amid the laughter of the others.

"Round and round he went," said Gabriel, "and the old gentleman, who was a very pompous old gentleman, was highly indignant. 'Go on, sir! What do you mean, sir? Johnny! Johnny! Most extraordinary conduct! Can't understand the horse!'"

The peal of laughter which followed Gabriel's imitation of the incident was interrupted by a resounding knock at the hall door. Mary Jane ran to open it and let in Freddy Malins. Freddy Malins, with his hat well back on his head and his shoulders humped with cold, was puffing and steaming after his exertions.

"I could only get one cab," he said.

"O, we'll find another along the quay," said Gabriel.

"Yes," said Aunt Kate. "Better not keep Mrs. Malins standing in the draught."

Mrs. Malins was helped down the front steps by her son and Mr. Browne and, after many manoeuvres, hoisted into the cab. Freddy Malins clambered in after her and spent a long time settling her on the seat, Mr. Browne helping him with advice. At last she was settled comfortably and Freddy Malins invited Mr. Browne into the cab. There was a good deal of confused talk, and then Mr. Browne got into the cab. The cabman settled his rug over his knees, and bent down for the address. The confusion grew greater and the cabman was directed differently by Freddy Malins and Mr. Browne, each of whom had his head out through a window of the cab. The difficulty was to know where to drop Mr. Browne along the route, and Aunt Kate, Aunt Julia and Mary Jane helped the discussion from the doorstep with cross-directions and contradictions and abundance of laughter. As for Freddy Malins he was speechless with laughter. He popped his head in and out of the window every moment to the great danger of his hat, and told his mother how the discussion was progressing, till at last Mr. Browne shouted to the bewildered cabman above the din of everybody's laughter:

"Do you know Trinity College?"

"Yes, sir," said the cabman.

"Well, drive bang up against Trinity College gates," said Mr. Browne, "and then we'll tell you where to go. You understand now?"

"Yes, sir," said the cabman.

"Make like a bird for Trinity College."

"Right, sir," said the cabman.

The horse was whipped up and the cab rattled off along the quay amid a chorus of laughter and adieus.

Gabriel had not gone to the door with the others. He was in a dark part of the hall gazing up the staircase. A woman was standing near the top of the first flight, in the shadow also. He could not see her face but he could see the terra-cotta and salmon-pink panels of her skirt which the shadow made appear black and white. It was his wife. She was leaning on the banisters, listening to something. Gabriel was surprised at her stillness and strained his ear to listen also. But he could hear little save the noise of laughter and dispute on the front steps, a few chords struck on the piano and a few notes of a man's voice singing.

He stood still in the gloom of the hall, trying to catch the air that the voice was singing and gazing up at his wife. There was grace and mystery in her attitude as if she were a symbol of something. He asked himself what is a woman standing on the stairs in the shadow, listening to distant music, a symbol of. If he were a painter he would paint her in that attitude. Her blue felt hat would show off the bronze of her hair against the darkness and the dark panels of her skirt would show off the light ones. *Distant Music* he would call the picture if he were a painter.

The hall-door was closed; and Aunt Kate, Aunt Julia and Mary Jane came down the hall, still laughing.

"Well, isn't Freddy terrible?" said Mary Jane. "He's really terrible."

Gabriel said nothing but pointed up the stairs towards where his wife was standing. Now that the hall-door was closed the voice and the piano could be heard more clearly. Gabriel held up his hand for them to be silent. The song seemed to be in the old Irish tonality and the singer seemed uncertain both of his words and of his voice. The voice, made plaintive by distance and by the singer's hoarseness, faintly illuminated the cadence of the air with words expressing grief:

> *O, the rain falls on my heavy locks*
> *And the dew wets my skin,*
> *My babe lies cold . . .*

"O," exclaimed Mary Jane. "It's Bartell D'Arcy singing and he wouldn't sing all the night. O, I'll get him to sing a song before he goes."

"O, do, Mary Jane," said Aunt Kate.

Mary Jane brushed past the others and ran to the staircase, but before she reached it the singing stopped and the piano was closed abruptly.

"O, what a pity!" she cried. "Is he coming down, Gretta?"

Gabriel heard his wife answer yes and saw her come down towards them. A few steps behind her were Mr. Bartell D'Arcy and Miss O'Callaghan.

"O, Mr. D'Arcy," cried Mary Jane, "it's downright mean of you to break off like that when we were all in raptures listening to you."

"I have been at him all the evening," said Miss O'Callaghan, "and Mrs. Conroy, too, and he told us he had a dreadful cold and couldn't sing."

"O, Mr. D'Arcy," said Aunt Kate, "now that was a great fib to tell."

"Can't you see that I'm as hoarse as a crow?" said Mr. D'Arcy roughly.

He went into the pantry hastily and put on his overcoat. The others, taken aback by his rude speech, could find nothing to say. Aunt Kate wrinkled her brows and made signs to the others to drop the subject. Mr. D'Arcy stood swathing his neck carefully and frowning.

"It's the weather," said Aunt Julia, after a pause.

"Yes, everybody has colds," said Aunt Kate readily, "everybody."

"They say," said Mary Jane, "we haven't had snow like it for thirty years; and I read this morning in the newspapers that the snow is general all over Ireland."

"I love the look of snow," said Aunt Julia sadly.

"So do I," said Miss O'Callaghan. "I think

Christmas is never really Christmas unless we have the snow on the ground."

"But poor Mr. D'Arcy doesn't like the snow," said Aunt Kate, smiling.

Mr. D'Arcy came from the pantry, fully swathed and buttoned, and in a repentant tone told them the history of his cold. Everyone gave him advice and said it was a great pity and urged him to be very careful of his throat in the night air. Gabriel watched his wife, who did not join in the conversation. She was standing right under the dusty fanlight and the flame of the gas lit up the rich bronze of her hair, which he had seen her drying at the fire a few days before. She was in the same attitude and seemed unaware of the talk about her. At last she turned towards them and Gabriel saw that there was colour on her cheeks and that her eyes were shining. A sudden tide of joy went leaping out of his heart.

"Mr. D'Arcy," she said, "what is the name of that song you were singing?"

"It's called *The Lass of Aughrim*," said Mr. D'Arcy, "but I couldn't remember it properly. Why? Do you know it?"

"*The Lass of Aughrim*," she repeated. "I couldn't think of the name."

"It's a very nice air," said Mary Jane. "I'm sorry you were not in voice tonight."

"Now, Mary Jane," said Aunt Kate, "don't annoy Mr. D'Arcy. I won't have him annoyed."

Seeing that all were ready to start she shepherded them to the door, where good-night was said:

"Well, good-night, Aunt Kate, and thanks for the pleasant evening."

"Good-night, Gabriel. Good-night, Gretta!"

"Good-night, Aunt Kate, and thanks ever so much. Good-night, Aunt Julia."

"O, good-night, Gretta, I didn't see you."

"Good-night, Mr. D'Arcy. Good-night, Miss O'Callaghan."

"Good-night, Miss Morkan."

"Good-night, again."

"Good-night, all. Safe home."

"Good-night. Good-night."

The morning was still dark. A dull, yellow light brooded over the houses and the river; and the sky seemed to be descending. It was slushy underfoot; and only streaks and patches of snow lay on the roofs, on the parapets of the quay and on the area railings. The lamps were still burning redly in the murky air and, across the river, the palace of the Four Courts stood out menacingly against the heavy sky.

She was walking on before him with Mr. Bartell D'Arcy, her shoes in a brown parcel tucked under one arm and her hands holding her skirt up from the slush. She had no longer any grace of attitude, but Gabriel's eyes were still bright with happiness. The blood went bounding along his veins; and the thoughts went rioting through his brain, proud, joyful, tender, valorous.

She was walking on before him so lightly and so erect that he longed to run after her noiselessly, catch her by the shoulders and say something foolish and affectionate into her ear. She seemed to him so frail that he longed to defend her against something and then to be alone with her. Moments of their secret life together burst like stars upon his memory. A heliotrope envelope was lying beside his breakfast cup and he was caressing it with his hand. Birds were twittering in the ivy and the sunny web of the curtain was shimmering along the floor: he could not eat for happiness. They were standing on the crowded platform and he was placing a ticket inside the warm palm of her glove. He was standing with her in the cold, looking in through a grated window at a man making bottles in a roaring furnace. It was very cold. Her face, fragrant in the cold air, was quite close to his; and suddenly he called out to the man at the furnace:

"Is the fire hot, sir?"

But the man could not hear with the noise of the furnace. It was just as well. He might have answered rudely.

A wave of yet more tender joy escaped from his heart and went coursing in warm flood along his arteries. Like the tender fire of stars moments of their life together, that no one knew of or would ever know of, broke upon and illumined his memory. He longed to recall to her those moments, to make her forget the years of their dull existence together and remember only their moments of ecstasy. For the years, he felt, had not quenched his soul or hers. Their children, his writing, her household cares had not quenched all their souls' tender fire. In one letter that he had written to her then he had said: "Why is it that words like these seem to me so dull and cold? Is it because there is no word tender enough to be your name?"

Like distant music these words that he had written years before were borne towards him from the past. He longed to be alone with her. When the others had gone away, when he and she were in the room in the hotel, then they would be alone together. He would call her softly:

"Gretta!"

Perhaps she would not hear at once: she would be undressing. Then something in his voice would strike her. She would turn and look at him . . .

At the corner of Winetavern Street they met a cab. He was glad of its rattling noise as it saved him from conversation. She was looking out of the window and seemed tired. The others spoke only a few words, pointing out some building or street. The horse galloped along wearily under the murky morning sky, dragging his old rattling box after his heels, and Gabriel was again in a cab with her, galloping to catch the boat, galloping to their honeymoon.

As the cab drove across O'Connell Bridge Miss O'Callaghan said:

"They say you never cross O'Connell Bridge without seeing a white horse."

"I see a white man this time," said Gabriel.

"Where?" asked Mr. Bartell D'Arcy.

Gabriel pointed to the statue, on which lay patches of snow. Then he nodded familiarly to it and waved his hand.

"Good-night, Dan," he said gaily.

When the cab drew up before the hotel, Gabriel jumped out and, in spite of Mr. Bartell D'Arcy's protest, paid the driver. He gave the man a shilling over his fare. The man saluted and said:

"A prosperous New Year to you, sir."

"The same to you," said Gabriel cordially.

She leaned for a moment on his arm in getting out of the cab and while standing at the curbstone, bidding the others good-night. She leaned lightly on his arm, as lightly as when she had danced with him a few hours before. He had felt proud and happy then, happy that she was his, proud of her grace and wifely carriage. But now, after the kindling again of so many memories, the first touch of her body, musical and strange and perfumed, sent through him a keen pang of lust. Under cover of her silence he pressed her arm closely to his side; and, as they stood at the hotel door, he felt that they had escaped from their lives and duties, escaped from home and friends and run away together with wild and radiant hearts to a new adventure.

An old man was dozing in a great hooded chair in the hall. He lit a candle in the office and went before them to the stairs. They followed him in silence, their feet falling in soft thuds on the thickly carpeted stairs. She mounted the stairs behind the porter, her head bowed in the ascent, her frail shoulders curved as with a burden, her skirt girt tightly about her. He could have flung his arms about her hips and held her still, for his arms were trembling with desire to seize her and only the stress of his nails against the palms of his hands held the wild impulse of his body in check. The porter halted on the stairs to settle his guttering candle. They halted, too, on the steps below him. In the silence Gabriel could hear the falling of the molten wax into the tray and the thumping of his own heart against his ribs.

The porter led them along a corridor and opened a door. Then he set his unstable candle down on a toilet-table and asked at what hour they were to be called in the morning.

"Eight," said Gabriel.

The porter pointed to the tap of the electric-light and began a muttered apology, but Gabriel cut him short.

"We don't want any light. We have light enough from the street. And I say," he added, pointing to the candle, "you might remove that handsome article, like a good man."

The porter took up his candle again, but slowly, for he was surprised by such a novel idea. Then he mumbled good-night and went out. Gabriel shot the lock to.

A ghastly light from the street lamp lay in a long shaft from one window to the door. Gabriel threw his overcoat and hat on a couch and crossed the room towards the window. He looked down into the street in order that his emotion might calm a little. Then he turned and leaned against a chest of drawers with his back to the light. She had taken off her hat and cloak and was standing before a large swinging mirror, unhooking her waist. Gabriel paused for a few moments, watching her, and then said:

"Gretta!"

She turned away from the mirror slowly and walked along the shaft of light towards him. Her face looked so serious and weary that the words would not pass Gabriel's lips. No, it was not the moment yet.

"You look tired," he said.

"I am a little," she answered.

"You don't feel ill or weak?"

"No, tired: that's all."

She went on to the window and stood there, looking out. Gabriel waited again and then, fearing that diffidence was about to conquer him, he said abruptly:

"By the way, Gretta!"

"What is it?"

"You know that poor fellow Malins?" he said quickly.

"Yes. What about him?"

"Well, poor fellow, he's a decent sort of chap, after all," continued Gabriel in a false voice. "He gave me back that sovereign I lent him, and I didn't expect it, really. It's a pity he wouldn't keep away from that Browne, because he's not a bad fellow, really."

He was trembling now with annoyance. Why did she seem so abstracted? He did not know how he could begin. Was she annoyed, too, about something? If she would only turn to him or come to him of her own accord! To take her as she was would be brutal. No, he must see some ardour in her eyes first. He longed to be master of her strange mood.

"When did you lend him the pound?" she asked, after a pause.

Gabriel strove to restrain himself from breaking out into brutal language about the sottish Malins and his pound. He longed to cry to her from his soul, to crush her body against his, to overmaster her. But he said:

"O, at Christmas, when he opened that little Christmas-card shop in Henry Street."

He was in such a fever of rage and desire that he did not hear her come from the window. She stood before him for an instant, looking at him strangely. Then, suddenly raising herself on tiptoe and resting her hands lightly on his shoulders, she kissed him.

"You are a very generous person, Gabriel," she said.

Gabriel, trembling with delight at her sudden kiss and at the quaintness of her phrase, put his hands on her hair and began smoothing it back, scarcely touching it with his fingers. The washing had made it fine and brilliant. His heart was brimming over with happiness. Just when he was wishing for it she had come to him of her own accord. Perhaps her thoughts had been running with his. Perhaps she had felt the impetuous desire that was in him, and then the yielding mood had come upon her. Now that she had fallen to him so easily, he wondered why he had been so diffident.

He stood, holding her head between his hands. Then, slipping one arm swiftly about her body and drawing her towards him, he said softly:

"Gretta, dear, what are you thinking about?"

She did not answer nor yield wholly to his arm. He said again, softly:

"Tell me what it is, Gretta. I think I know what is the matter. Do I know?"

She did not answer at once. Then she said in an outburst of tears:

"O, I am thinking about that song, *The Lass of Aughrim*."

She broke loose from him and ran to the bed and, throwing her arms across the bed-rail, hid her face. Gabriel stood stock-still for a moment in astonistment and then followed her. As he passed in the way of the cheval-glass he caught sight of himself in full length, his broad, well-filled shirtfront, the face whose expression always puzzled him when he saw it in a mirror, and his glimmering gilt-rimmed eye-glasses. He halted a few paces from her and said:

"What about the song? Why does that make you cry?"

She raised her head from her arms and dried her eyes with the back of her hand like a child. A kinder note than he had intended went into his voice.

"Why, Gretta?" he asked.

"I am thinking about a person long ago who used to sing that song."

"And who was the person long ago?" asked Gabriel, smiling.

"It was a person I used to know in Galway when I was living with my grandmother," she said.

The smile passed away from Gabriel's face. A dull anger began to gather again at the back of his mind and the dull fires of his lust began to glow angrily in his veins.

"Someone you were in love with?" he asked ironically.

"It was a young boy I used to know," she answered, "named Michael Furey. He used to sing that song, *The Lass of Aughrim*. He was very delicate."

Gabriel was silent. He did not wish her to think that he was interested in this delicate boy.

"I can see him so plainly," she said, after a moment. "Such eyes as he had: big, dark eyes! And such an expression in them—an expression!"

"O, then, you are in love with him?" said Gabriel.

"I used to go out walking with him," she said, "when I was in Galway."

A thought flew across Gabriel's mind.

"Perhaps that was why you wanted to go to Galway with that Ivors girl?" he said coldly.

She looked at him and asked in surprise:

"What for?"

Her eyes made Gabriel feel awkward. He shrugged his shoulders and said:

"How do I know? To see him, perhaps."

She looked away from him along the shaft of light towards the window in silence.

"He is dead," she said at length. "He died when he was only seventeen. Isn't it a terrible thing to die so young as that?"

"What was he?" asked Gabriel, still ironically.

"He was in the gasworks," she said.

Gabriel felt humiliated by the failure of his irony and by the evocation of this figure from the dead, a boy in the gasworks. While he had been full of memories of their secret life together, full of tenderness and joy and desire, she had been comparing him in her mind with another. A shameful consciousness of his own person assailed him. He saw himself as a ludicrous figure, acting as a pennyboy for his aunts, a nervous, well-meaning sentimentalist, orating to vulgarians and idealising his own clownish lusts, the pitiable fatuous fellow he had caught a glimpse of in the mirror. Instinctively he turned his back more to the light lest she might see the shame that burned upon his forehead.

He tried to keep up his tone of cold interrogation, but his voice when he spoke was humble and indifferent.

"I suppose you were in love with this Michael Furey, Gretta," he said.

"I was great with him at that time," she said.

Her voice was veiled and sad. Gabriel, feeling now how vain it would be to try to lead her whither he had purposed, caressed one of her hands and said, also sadly:

"And what did he die of so young, Gretta? Consumption, was it?"

"I think he died for me," she answered.

A vague terror seized Gabriel at this answer, as if, at that hour when he had hoped to triumph, some impalpable and vindictive being was coming against him, gathering forces against him in its vague world. But he shook himself free of it with an effort of reason and continued to caress her hand. He did not question her again, for he felt that she would tell him of herself. Her hand was warm and moist: it did not respond to his touch, but he continued to caress it just as he had caressed her first letter to him that spring morning.

"It was in the winter," she said, "about the beginning of the winter when I was going to leave my grandmother's and come up here to the convent. And he was ill at the time in his lodgings in Galway and wouldn't be let out, and his people in Oughterard were written to. He was in decline, they said, or something like that. I never knew rightly."

She paused for a moment and sighed.

"Poor fellow," she said. "He was very fond of me and he was such a gentle boy. We used to go out together, walking, you know, Gabriel, like the way they do in the country. He was going to study singing only for his health. He had a very good voice, poor Michael Furey."

"Well; and then?" asked Gabriel.

"And then when it came to the time for me to leave Galaway and come up to the convent he was much worse and I wouldn't be let see him so I wrote him a letter saying I was going up to Dublin and would be back in the summer, and hoping he would be better then."

She paused for a moment to get her voice under control, and then went on:

"Then the night before I left, I was in my grandmother's house in Nuns' Island, packing up, and I heard gravel thrown up against the window. The window was so wet I couldn't see, so I ran downstairs as I was and slipped out the back into the garden and there was the poor fellow at the end of the garden, shivering."

"And did you not tell him to go back?" asked Gabriel.

"I implored of him to go home at once and told him he would get his death in the rain. But he said he did not want to live. I can see his eyes as well as well! He was standing at the end of the wall where there was a tree."

"And did he go home?" asked Gabriel.

"Yes, he went home. And when I was only a week in the convent he died and he was buried in Oughterard, where his people came from. O, the day I heard that, that he was dead!"

She stopped, choking with sobs, and, overcome by emotion, flung herself face downward on the bed, sobbing in the quilt. Gabriel held her hand for a moment longer, irresolutely, and then, shy of intruding on her grief, let it fall gently and walked quietly to the window.

She was fast asleep.

Gabriel, leaning on his elbow, looked for a few moments unresentfully on her tangled hair and half-open mouth, listening to her deep-drawn breath. So she had had that romance in her life: a man had died for her sake. It hardly pained him now to think how poor a part he, her husband, had played in her life. He watched her while she slept, as though he and she had never lived together as man and wife. His curious eyes rested long upon her face and on her hair: and, as he thought of what she must have been then, in that time of her first girlish beauty, a strange, friendly pity for her entered his soul. He did not like to say even to himself that her face was no longer beautiful, but he knew that it was no longer the face for which Michael Furey had braved death.

Perhaps she had not told him all the story. His eyes moved to the chair over which she had thrown some of her clothes. A petticoat string dangled to the floor. One boot stood upright, its limp upper fallen down: the fellow of it lay upon its side. He wondered at his riot of emotions of an hour before. From what had it proceeded? From his aunt's supper, from his own foolish speech, from the wine and dancing, the merry-making when saying good-night in the hall, the pleasure of the walk along the river in the snow.

Poor Aunt Julia! She, too, would soon be a shade with the shade of Patrick Morkan and his horse. He had caught that haggard look upon her face for a moment when she was singing *Arrayed for the Bridal*. Soon, perhaps, he would be sitting in that same drawing-room, dressed in black, his silk hat on his knees. The blinds would be drawn down and Aunt Kate would be sitting beside him, crying and blowing her nose and telling him how Julia had died. He would cast about in his mind for some words that might console her, and would find only lame and useless ones. Yes, yes: that would happen very soon.

The air of the room chilled his shoulders. He stretched himself cautiously along under the sheets and lay down beside his wife. One by one, they were all becoming shades. Better pass boldly into that other world, in the full glory of some passion, than fade and wither dismally with age. He thought of how she who lay beside him had locked in her heart for so many years that image of her lover's eyes when he had told her that he did not wish to live.

Generous tears filled Gabriel's eyes. He had never felt like that himself towards any woman, but he knew that such a feeling must be love. The tears gathered more thickly in his eyes and in the partial darkness he imagined he saw the form of a young man standing under a dripping tree. Other forms were near. His soul had approached that region where dwell the vast hosts of the dead. He was conscious of, but could not apprehend, their wayward and flickering existence. His own identity was fading out into a grey impalpable world: the solid world itself, which these dead had one time reared and lived in, was dissolving and dwindling.

A few light taps upon the pane made him turn to the window. It had begun to snow again. He watched sleepily the flakes, silver and dark, falling obliquely against the lamplight. The time had come for him to set out on his journey westward. Yes, the newspapers were right: snow was general all over Ireland. It was falling on every part of the dark central plain, on the treeless hills, falling softly upon the Bog of Allen and, farther westward, softly falling into the dark mutinous Shannon waves. It was falling, too, upon every part of the lonely churchyard on the hill where Michael Furey lay buried. It lay thickly drifted on the crooked crosses and headstones, on the spears of the little gate, on the barren thorns. His soul swooned slowly as he heard the snow falling faintly through the universe and faintly falling, like the descent of their last end, upon all the living and the dead.

Edward Thomas
1878–1917

Philip Edward Thomas, of Welsh descent, was born in the Lambeth district of London. He was educated at St. Paul's School and at Oxford. He wrote books on nature (*The Woodland Life*, 1897) and books of familiar essays, as well as literary criticism, including studies of Swinburne (1912) and Pater (1913). The life of literary journalism had begun to be something of a burden by the time he gave it up in 1915 to enlist in the Artists' Rifles, from which he was later transferred to the Royal Garrison Artillery. He went to France in 1917, and was killed at Arras, in Flanders, on April 9 of that year. In a sense, he is one of the poets of World War I, but the war itself figures only in the background of his poetry or obliquely. Edward Garnett, in the article on Thomas in the *Dictionary of National Biography* which has supplied these facts, says that a few months before his enlistment, and inspired by the example of his friend Robert Frost, who was then living in England, he "bent all his energies to writing verse." But it may have worked the other way too, and there is at least a similarity between the work of the two poets, even if not an influence one way or the other. One of Frost's poems is entitled "To E.T.," and commemorates the friendship with Thomas, at the same time that it regrets the failure to "call you to your face/First soldier, and then poet, and then both,/ Who died a soldier-poet of your race."

The body of Edward Thomas's poetry is not large, the poems are never overemphatic in statement, and they can easily be overlooked if we study early twentieth-century literature too exclusively in terms of its main movements and its most striking declarations of innovative principle. But Thomas's was a first-rate poetic gift which it would be a pity to over-look. When we have learned to listen for what is distinctive in his style of utterance and in his approach to experience (Dylan Thomas's recording of "The Owl" can be a great help in initiating our understanding), the value of his poetry will go on increasing and deepening for us the longer we know it.

TEXTS: *The Collected Poems of Edward Thomas*, with a foreword by Walter de la Mare, was first published in 1920, and later reissued with additional poems. A volume of *The Prose of Edward Thomas*, selected by Roland Gant, was published in 1948. There is a booklet on Thomas, by Vernon Scannell, in the series of pamphlets published as supplements to *British Book News* (1963), and a full-length critical biography, *Edward Thomas*, by William Cooke (1970).

The Sign-Post

The dim sea glints chill. The white sun is shy,
And the skeleton weeds and the never-dry,
Rough, long grasses keep white with frost
At the hilltop by the finger-post;
The smoke of the traveller's-joy is puffed   5
Over hawthorn berry and hazel tuft.
I read the sign. Which way shall I go?
A voice says: You would not have doubted so
At twenty. Another voice gentle with scorn
Says: At twenty you wished you had never been   10
    born.

One hazel lost a leaf of gold
From a tuft at the tip, when the first voice told
The other he wished to know what 'twould be
To be sixty by this same post. "You shall see,"
He laughed—and I had to join his laughter—   15
"You shall see; but either before or after,
Whatever happens, it must befall,
A mouthful of earth to remedy all
Regrets and wishes shall freely be given;
And if there be a flaw in that heaven   20
'Twill be freedom to wish, and your wish may be
To be here or anywhere talking to me,
No matter what the weather, on earth,
At any age between death and birth,—
To see what day or night can be,   25
The sun and the frost, the land and the sea,
Summer, Autumn, Winter, Spring,—

With a poor man of any sort, down to a king,
Standing upright out in the air
Wondering where he shall journey, O where?"   30

The Owl

Downhill I came, hungry, and yet not starved;
Cold, yet had heat within me that was proof
Against the North wind; tired, yet so that rest
Had seemed the sweetest thing under a roof.

Then at the inn I had food, fire, and rest,   5
Knowing how hungry, cold, and tired was I.
All of the night was quite barred out except
An owl's cry, a most melancholy cry

Shaken out long and clear upon the hill,
No merry note, nor cause of merriment,   10
But one telling me plain what I escaped
And others could not, that night, as in I went.

And salted was my food, and my repose,
Salted and sobered, too, by the bird's voice
Speaking for all who lay under the stars,   15
Soldiers and poor, unable to rejoice.

Melancholy

The rain and wind, the rain and wind, raved
    endlessly.
On me the Summer storm, and fever, and melan-
    choly
Wrought magic, so that if I feared the solitude
Far more I feared all company: too sharp, too
    rude,
Had been the wisest or the dearest human voice.   5
What I desired I knew not, but whate'er my
    choice
Vain it must be, I knew. Yet naught did my des-
    pair
But sweeten the strange sweetness, while through
    the wild air
All day long I heard a distant cuckoo calling
And, soft as dulcimers, sounds of near water fall- 10
    ing,
And, softer, and remote as if in history,
Rumours of what had touched my friends, my
    foes, or me.

Haymaking

After night's thunder far away had rolled
The fiery day had a kernel sweet of cold,
And in the perfect blue the clouds uncurled,
Like the first gods before they made the world
And misery, swimming the stormless sea   5
In beauty and in divine gaiety.
The smooth white empty road was lightly strewn
With leaves—the holly's Autumn falls in June—
And fir cones standing up stiff in the heat.
The mill-foot water tumbled white and lit   10
With tossing crystals, happier than any crowd
Of children pouring out of school aloud.
And in the little thickets where a sleeper
For ever might lie lost, the nettle creeper
And garden-warbler sang unceasingly;   15
While over them shrill shrieked in his fierce glee
The swift with wings and tail as sharp and narrow
       row
As if the bow had flown off with the arrow.
Only the scent of woodbine and hay new mown
Travelled the road. In the field sloping down,   20
Park-like, to where its willows showed the brook,
Haymakers rested. The tosser lay forsook
Out in the sun; and the long waggon stood
Without its team: it seemed it never would
Move from the shadow of that single yew.   25
The team, as still, until their task was due,
Beside the labourers enjoyed the shade
That three squat oaks mid-field together made
Upon a circle of grass and weed uncut,
And on the hollow, once a chalk pit, but   30
Now brimmed with nut and elder-flower so clean.
The men leaned on their rakes, about to begin,
But still. And all were silent. All was old,
This morning time, with a great age untold,
Older than Clare and Cobbett, Morland and   35
       Crome,
Than, at the field's far edge, the farmer's home,
A white house crouched at the foot of a great
       tree.
Under the heavens that know not what years be
The men, the beasts, the trees, the implements
Uttered even what they will in times far hence— 40
All of us gone out of the reach of change—
Immortal in a picture of an old grange.

Birds' Nests

The summer nests uncovered by autumn wind,
Some torn, others dislodged, all dark,
Everyone sees them: low or high in tree,
Or hedge, or single bush, they hang like a mark.

Since there's no need of eyes to see them with   5
I cannot help a little shame
That I missed most, even at eye's level, till
The leaves blew off and made the seeing no
       game.

'Tis a light pang. I like to see the nests
Still in their places, now first known,   10
At home and by far roads. Boys knew them not,
Whatever jays and squirrels may have done.

And most I like the winter nests deep-hid
That leaves and berries fell into:
Once a dormouse dined there on hazel-nuts,   15
And grass and goose-grass seeds found soil and
       grew.

The Gallows

There was a weasel lived in the sun
With all his family,
Till a keeper shot him with his gun
And hung him up on a tree,
Where he swings in the wind and rain,   5
In the sun and in the snow,
Without pleasure, without pain,
On the dead oak tree bough.

There was a crow who was no sleeper,
But a thief and a murderer   10
Till a very late hour; and this keeper
Made him one of the things that were,
To hang and flap in rain and wind,
In the sun and in the snow.
There are no more sins to be sinned   15
On the dead oak tree bough.

There was a magpie, too,
Had a long tongue and a long tail;
He could both talk and do—
But what did that avail?   20
He, too, flaps in the wind and rain
Alongside weasel and crow,
Without pleasure, without pain,
On the dead oak tree bough.

And many other beasts   25
And birds, skin, bone, and feather,

Have been taken from their feasts
And hung up there together,
To swing and have endless leisure
In the sun and in the snow,   30
Without pain, without pleasure,
On the dead oak tree bough.

March

Now I know that Spring will come again,
Perhaps to-morrow: however late I've patience
After this night following on such a day.

While still my temples ached from the cold burn-
    ing
Of hail and wind, and still the primroses   5
Torn by the hail were covered up in it,
The sun filled earth and heaven with a great
    light
And a tenderness, almost warmth, where the hail
    dripped,
As if the mighty sun wept tears of joy.
But 'twas too late for warmth. The sunset piled   10
Mountains on mountains of snow and ice in the
    west:
Somewhere among their folds the wind was lost,
And yet 'twas cold, and though I knew that
    Spring
Would come again, I knew it had not come,
That it was lost too in those mountains chill.   15

What did the thrushes know? Rain, snow, sleet,
    hail,
Had kept them quiet as the primroses.
They had but an hour to sing. On boughs they
    sang,
On gates, on ground; they sang while they
    changed perches
And while they fought, if they remembered to   20
    fight:
So earnest were they to pack into that hour
Their unwilling hoard of song before the moon
Grew brighter than the clouds. Then 'twas no
    time
For singing merely. So they could keep off silence
And night, they cared not what they sang or   25
    screamed;
Whether 'twas hoarse or sweet or fierce or soft;
And to me all was sweet: they could do no wrong.
Something they knew—I also, while they sang
And after. Not till night had half its stars

And never a cloud, was I aware of silence   30
Stained with all that hour's songs, a silence
Saying that Spring returns, perhaps to-morrow.

The Word

There are so many things I have forgot,
That once were much to me, or that were not,
All lost, as is a childless woman's child
And its child's children, in the undefiled
Abyss of what will never be again.   5
I have forgot, too, names of the mighty men
That fought and lost or won in the old wars,
Of kings and fiends and gods, and most of the
    stars.
Some things I have forgot that I forget.
But lesser things there are, remembered yet,   10
Than all the others. One name that I have not—
Though 'tis an empty thingless name—forgot
Never can die because Spring after Spring
Some thrushes learn to say it as they sing.
There is always one at midday saying it clear   15
And tart—the name, only the name I hear.
While perhaps I am thinking of the elder scent
That is like food; or while I am content
With the wild rose scent that is like memory,
This name suddenly is cried out to me   20
From somewhere in the bushes by a bird
Over and over again, a pure thrush word.

Aspens

All day and night, save winter, every weather,
Above the inn, the smithy, and the shop,
The aspens at the cross-roads talk together
Of rain, until their last leaves fall from the top.

Out of the blacksmith's cavern comes the ringing   5
Of hammer, shoe, and anvil; out of the inn
The clink, the hum, the roar, the random sing-
    ing—
The sounds that for these fifty years have been.

The whisper of the aspens is not drowned,
And over lightless pane and footless road,   10
Empty as sky, with every other sound
Not ceasing, calls their ghosts from their abode,

A silent smithy, a silent inn, nor fails
In the bare moonlight or the thick-furred gloom,

In tempest or the night of nightingales,
To turn the cross-roads to a ghostly room.

And it would be the same were no house near.
Over all sorts of weather, men, and times,
Aspens must shake their leaves and men may
    hear
But need not listen, more than to my rhymes.

Whatever wind blows, while they and I have
    leaves
We cannot other than an aspen be
That ceaselessly, unreasonably grieves,
Or so men think who like a different tree.

The Gypsy

A fortnight before Christmas Gypsies were every-
    where:
Vans were drawn up on wastes, women trailed to
    the fair.
"My gentleman," said one, "you've got a lucky
    face."
"And you've a luckier," I thought, "if such a
    grace
And impudence in rags are lucky." "Give a penny
For the poor baby's sake." "Indeed I have not any
Unless you can give change for a sovereign, my
    dear."
"Then just half a pipeful of tobacco can you
    spare?"
I gave it. With that much victory she laughed
    content.

I should have given more, but off and away she
    went
With her baby and her pink sham flowers to
    rejoin
The rest before I could translate to its proper
    coin
Gratitude for her grace. And I paid nothing then,
As I pay nothing now with the dipping of my
    pen
For her brother's music when he drummed the
    tambourine
And stamped his feet, which made the workmen
    passing grin,
While his mouth-organ changed to a rascally
    Bacchanal dance
"Over the hills and far away." This and his
    glance
Outlasted all the fair, farmer, and auctioneer,
Cheap-jack, balloon-man, drover with crooked
    stick, and steer,
Pig, turkey, goose, and duck, Christmas corpses
    to be.
Not even the kneeling ox had eyes like the
    Romany.
That night he peopled for me the hollow wooded
    land,
More dark and wild than stormiest heavens, that
    I searched and scanned
Like a ghost new-arrived. The gradations of the
    dark
Were like an underworld of death, but for the
    spark
In the Gypsy boy's black eyes as he played and
    stamped his tune,
"Over the hills and far away," and a crescent
    moon.

Wilfred Owen

1893–1918

An account has been given, in the introduction to the Modern period, of Wilfred Owen's life and his place in the literary history of his time. An (unsigned) review, in the *Times Literary Supplement* for September 29, 1972, of Jon Silkin's book about the poets of World War I, *Out of Battle* (1972), makes a point about just what that place was—one that has not always been realized. It was not realized by Yeats, for instance, when he excluded Owen from *The Oxford Book of Modern Verse*. Speaking of the poems that came, as Owen's did, out of the direct experience of trench warfare, the reviewer says:

It is clear that by the middle of the war a radical poetic transformation had occurred, new subjects and new attitudes became possible, and what Isaac

Rosenberg called "trench poems" began to appear. It became possible to write realistically about death, not simply as a sentimental possibility, but as a statistical probability, and as a part of the environment. . . . This transformation is more radical than anything that had happened in poetry for a century or more; it made The Waste Land, *and thus all postwar poetry, possible.*

TEXTS: The definitive edition of Owen's poems is *The Collected Poems of Wilfred Owen,* edited by C. Day Lewis (1963). *Wilfred Owen: Collected Letters,* edited by Harold Owen and John Bell, was published in 1967. Also by Harold Owen is the three-volume *Journey from Obscurity: Memoirs of the Owen Family* (1963–65). There is a critical study of Owen, in Twayne's English Authors Series, by Gertrude M. White (1969), and another by D.S.R. Welland, *Wilfred Owen: A Critical Study* (1960). For books about the poets of World War I in general, see the book by Jon Silkin, *Out of Battle,* referred to above, which includes an extremely interesting bibliography of books concerned with the literature of both World Wars; and also *Heroes' Twilight,* by Bernard Bergonzi (1965).

Strange Meeting

It seemed that out of battle I escaped
Down some profound dull tunnel, long since scooped
Through granites which titanic wars had groined.
Yet also there encumbered sleepers groaned,
Too fast in thought or death to be bestirred.   5
Then, as I probed them, one sprang up, and stared
With piteous recognition in fixed eyes,
Lifting distressful hands as if to bless.
And by his smile, I knew that sullen hall,
By his dead smile I knew we stood in Hell.   10
With a thousand pains that vision's face was grained;
Yet no blood reached there from the upper ground,
And no guns thumped, or down the flues made moan.
"Strange friend," I said, "here is no cause to mourn."
"None," said the other, "save the undone years,   15
The hopelessness. Whatever hope is yours,
Was my life also; I went hunting wild

After the wildest beauty in the world,
Which lies not calm in eyes, or braided hair,
But mocks the steady running of the hour,   20
And if it grieves, grieves richlier than here.
For by my glee might many men have laughed,
And of my weeping something had been left,
Which must die now. I mean the truth untold,
The pity of war, the pity war distilled.   25
Now men will go content with what we spoiled.
Or, discontent, boil bloody, and be spilled.
They will be swift with swiftness of the tigress,
None will break ranks, though nations trek from progress.
Courage was mine, and I had mystery,   30
Wisdom was mine, and I had mastery;
To miss the march of this retreating world
Into vain citadels that are not walled.
Then, when much blood had clogged their chariot-wheels
I would go up and wash them from sweet wells,   35
Even with truths that lie too deep for taint.
I would have poured my spirit without stint
But not through wounds; not on the cess of war.
Foreheads of men have bled where no wounds were.
I am the enemy you killed, my friend.   40
I knew you in this dark; for so you frowned
Yesterday through me as you jabbed and killed.
I parried; but my hands were loath and cold.
Let me sleep now. . . ."

Miners

There was a whispering in my hearth,
    A sigh of the coal,
Grown wistful of a former earth
    It might recall.

I listened for a tale of leaves   5
    And smothered ferns;
Frond-forests; and the low, sly lives
    Before the fawns.

My fire might show steam-phantoms simmer
    From Time's old cauldron,   10
Before the birds made nests in summer,
    Or men had children.

But the coals were murmuring of their mine,
    And moans down there

Of boys that slept wry sleep, and men
    Writhing for air.

And I saw white bones in the cinder-shard,
    Bones without number;
For many hearts with coal are charred
    And few remember.

I thought of some who worked dark pits
    Of war, and died
Digging the rock where Death reputes
    Peace lies indeed.

Comforted years will sit soft-chaired
    In rooms of amber;
The years will stretch their hands, well-cheered
    By our lives' ember.

The centuries will burn rich loads
    With which we groaned,
Whose warmth shall lull their dreaming lids
    While songs are crooned.
But they will not dream of us poor lads
    Lost in the ground.

Anthem for Doomed Youth

What passing-bells for these who die as cattle?
    Only the monstrous anger of the guns.
    Only the stuttering rifles' rapid rattle

15 Can patter out their hasty orisons.
No mockeries for them from prayers or bells,
    Nor any voice of mourning save the choirs,—
The shrill, demented choirs of wailing shells;
    And bugles calling for them from sad shires.

20 What candles may be held to speed them all?
    Not in the hands of boys, but in their eyes
Shall shine the holy glimmers of good-byes.
    The pallor of girls' brows shall be their pall;
Their flowers the tenderness of silent minds,
And each slow dusk a drawing-down of blinds.

Futility

Move him into the sun—
Gently its touch awoke him once,
At home, whispering of fields unsown.
Always it woke him, even in France,
Until this morning and this snow.
If anything might rouse him now
The kind old sun will know.

Think how it wakes the seeds,—
Woke, once, the clays of a cold star.
Are limbs, so dear-achieved, are sides,
Full-nerved—still warm—too hard to stir?
Was it for this the clay grew tall?
—O what made fatuous sunbeams toil
To break earth's sleep at all?

Alfred Edward Housman
1859–1936

A. E. Housman led the austere life of a classics scholar, having been Professor of Latin at University College, London from 1892 until, in 1911, he went to Cambridge as Professor of Latin and Fellow of Trinity College; he remained at Cambridge for the rest of his life. Although he may have seen his editions of Manilius, Juvenal, and Lucan as the main work of his life, he also published two small volumes of verse for which he will be known and remembered by *more* people, at any rate. *A Shropshire Lad* appeared in 1896 and *Last Poems* twenty-six years later (1922). In 1936 a further volume, *More Poems,* was published posthumously under the care of Laurence Housman,

the poet's brother; and in 1939 *The Collected Poems* gathered together the contents of these three volumes plus a number of poems that had not appeared in them. Housman's Leslie Stephen Lecture, *The Name and Nature of Poetry,* delivered at Cambridge on May 9, 1933, says much that is memorable and individual about the poetic situation, as well as much that is interesting about Housman's own habits of composition.

    Housman the poet was not an innovator in the sense of producing changes in form and technique that contemporaries and successors can make use of: no subsequent poet can write "like Housman" with-

A. E. Housman (1859–1936). A drawing by Francis Dodd, 1936. *The Katherine Young Archive for Art and History.*

out being frankly imitative. To say this, however, is not to detract from the intrinsic value of his own verse: using conventional forms, coloring them by his classical training and his own highly individual moral temper, he produced a collection of poems that at their frequent best are both flawless and deeply moving.

TEXTS: After his death a number of memoirs appeared, including *A Buried Life: Personal Recollections of A. E. Housman,* by Percy Withers (1940); *A. E. Housman, a Sketch,* by A. S. F. Gow (1936); and *A. E. H.: Some Poems, Some Letters and a Personal Memoir by His Brother,* by Laurence Housman (1937). A later biographical study is *A. E. Housman: A Divided Life,* by George L. Watson (1957). Edmund Wilson's *The Triple Thinkers* (1938) contains a critical essay, and in 1959 Cleanth Brooks devoted a lecture to Housman at the Library of Congress. *The Name and Nature of Poetry,* mentioned above, is available in *Selected Prose of A. E. Housman,* edited by John Carter (1961). Essays on Housman by various hands are gathered together in *A. E. Housman: A Collection of Critical Essays,* edited by Christopher Ricks (1968). There is a volume of letters, *The Letters of A. E. Housman,* edited by Henry Maas (1971).

From Far, from Eve and Morning[1]

From far, from eve and morning
   And yon twelve-winded sky,
The stuff of life to knit me
   Blew hither: here am I

Now—for a breath I tarry   5
   Nor yet disperse apart—
Take my hand quick and tell me,
   What have you in your heart.

Speak now, and I will answer;
   How shall I help you, say;   10
Ere to the wind's twelve quarters
   I take my endless way.

Far in a Western Brookland

Far in a western brookland
   That bred me long ago
The poplars stand and tremble
   By pools I used to know.

There, in the windless night-time,   5
   The wanderer, marvelling why,
Halts on the bridge to hearken
   How soft the poplars sigh.

He hears: no more remembered
   In fields where I was known,   10
Here I lie down in London
   And turn to rest alone.

There, by the starlit fences,
   The wanderer halts and hears
My soul that lingers sighing   15
   About the glimmering weirs.

I Promise Nothing: Friends Will Part

I promise nothing: friends will part;
   All things may end, for all began;

---

[1] The first two poems were included in *A Shropshire Lad,* the last three in *More Poems.*

And truth and singleness of heart
　　Are mortal even as is man.

But this unlucky love should last　　　　　5
　　When answered passions thin to air;
Eternal fate so deep has cast
　　Its sure foundation of despair.

Diffugere Nives

Horace. Odes IV. 7.

The snows are fled away, leaves on the shaws
　　And grasses in the mead renew their birth,
The river to the river-bed withdraws,
　　And altered is the fashion of the earth.

The Nymphs and Graces three put off their fear　　5
　　And unapparelled in the woodland play.
The swift hour and the brief prime of the year
　　Say to the soul, *Thou wast not born for aye.*

Thaw follows frost; hard on the heel of spring
　　Treads summer sure to die, for hard on hers　　10
Comes autumn with his apples scattering;
　　Then back to wintertide, when nothing stirs.

But oh, whate'er the sky-led seasons mar,
　　Moon upon moon rebuilds it with her beams;
Come *we* where Tullus and where Ancus[1] are　　15
　　And good Aeneas,[2] we are dust and dreams.

[1] Legendary kings of Rome.
[2] Aeneas, a member of one of the branches of the Trojan royal house, was the son of Anchises and Aphrodite; in some legends, and of course in Vergil's *Aeneid*, he is the founder of the Roman State, from having founded a Trojan colony in Latium after his escape at the fall of Troy.

Torquatus,[3] if the gods in heaven shall add
　　The morrow to the day, what tongue has told?
Feast then thy heart, for what the heart has had
　　The fingers of no heir will ever hold.　　20

When thou descendest once the shades among,
　　The stern assize and equal judgment o'er,
Not thy long lineage nor thy golden tongue,
　　No, nor thy righteousness, shall friend thee
　　　　more.

Night holds Hippolytus the pure of stain,　　25
　　Diana steads him nothing, he must stay;
And Theseus leaves Pirithous in the chain[4]
　　The love of comrades cannot take away.

Crossing Alone the Nighted Ferry

Crossing alone the nighted ferry
　　With the one coin for fee,[1]
Whom, on the wharf of Lethe waiting,
　　Count you to find? Not me.

The brisk fond lackey to fetch and carry,
　　The true, sick-hearted slave,
Expect him not in the just city
　　And free land of the grave.

[3] A friend of Horace.
[4] Theseus, son of Aegeus, legendary king of Athens, was the hero of a series of adventures (slaying the Minotaur, etc.). Pirithous, king of the Lapiths, was his faithful friend. Hippolytus (line 25) was Theseus' son: see, for his story, the tragedy by Euripides (produced 429 B.C.), or *Phèdre,* by the French dramatist Racine, produced in 1677.

[1] In Greek mythology the shades of the dead were ferried across the rivers of the underworld by the aged boatman, Charon, who received a single coin, an obolus, for his charge: this coin was put in the mouths of the dead.

Robert Graves

1895–

Robert Graves has written interesting and distinguished books in an astonishing variety of forms, but it has become increasingly clear that his poetry is his central achievement. He was born in London in 1895, went to Charterhouse, and then, after serving with the British army in France during World War

I, returned to St. John's College, Oxford. Some of his first poems dealt with his experiences as a soldier, and the war experience also figured in his autobiography, *Goodbye to All That* (1929, revised edition 1957), one of the first and most celebrated of the books in which those who came of age during or after the war took stock of the world they found they had inherited. Besides a number of novels, of which the two novels of historical reconstruction, *I, Claudius* and *Claudius the God* (both 1934), are the best known, Graves has written short stories, essays, books about language, about mythology, and about twentieth-century life socially considered: with Alan Hodges, he wrote *The Long Week-End: A Social History of Great Britain, 1918–1939* (1940, second edition 1963), an extremely useful book for the lively insight it affords into the background of the Modern period.

Next in interest to his poetry, and equally marked by a total independence of any allegiance to schools or prescribed literary tendency, is his literary criticism, particularly of poetry. Still of interest today, when it can be found, is the pamphlet published by Leonard and Virginia Woolf at the Hogarth Press in 1925, *Contemporary Techniques of Poetry*, a survey of contemporary poetic modes made when the subject was not nearly so much canvassed as it is now. *The Common Asphodel: Collected Essays on Poetry, 1922–1949* (1949, reprinted 1970) includes the book-length treatment of "Modernist Poetry," which he wrote with Laura Riding and published in 1926. *The Crowning Privilege: Collected Essays on Poetry* (1956) takes its title from the first of the six Clark Lectures that Graves delivered at Trinity College, Cambridge, in 1954–55; the sixth lecture, "These Be Your Gods, O Israel!" takes a very sharp look indeed at the current idolatry of "the five living idols —namely, Yeats, Pound, Eliot, Auden, and Dylan Thomas." Graves was Professor of Poetry at Oxford from 1961 to 1966. His *Collected Poems* are frequently brought up to date, the most recent edition being that of 1965–66; since that time there have been two more small volumes of new *Poems* (1968 and 1970).

CRITICAL STUDIES: Among the critical works devoted to him, and in some cases to his poetry particularly, are: *Robert Graves*, by Martin Seymour-Smith (1965), in the series of pamphlets published as supplements to *British Book News*; *Robert Graves*, by George Stade (1967), one of the Columbia Essays on Modern Writing; *Swifter Than Reason: The Poetry and Criticism of Robert Graves*, by Douglas Day (1963); *Robert Graves*, by J. M. Cohen (1965); and *The Poetry of Robert Graves*, by Michael Kirkham (1969).

Lost Love

His eyes are quickened so with grief,
He can watch a grass or leaf
Every instant grow; he can
Clearly through a flint wall see,
Or watch the startled spirit flee   5
From the throat of a dead man.
    Across two counties he can hear
And catch your words before you speak.
The woodlouse or the maggot's weak
Clamour rings in his sad ear,   10
And noise so slight it would surpass
Credence—drinking sound of grass,
Worm talk, clashing jaws of moth
Chumbling holes in cloth;
The groan of ants who undertake   15
Gigantic loads for honour's sake
(Their sinews creak, their breath comes thin);
Whir of spiders when they spin,
And minute whispering, mumbling, sighs
Of idle grubs and flies.   20
    This man is quickened so with grief,
He wanders god-like or like thief
Inside and out, below, above,
Without relief seeking lost love.

Warning to Children

Children, if you dare to think
Of the greatness, rareness, muchness,
Fewness of this precious only
Endless world in which you say
You live, you think of things like this: 5
Blocks of slate enclosing dappled
Red and green, enclosing tawny
Yellow nets, enclosing white
And black acres of dominoes,
Where a neat brown paper parcel   10
Tempts you to untie the string.
In the parcel a small island,
On the island a large tree,
On the tree a husky fruit.
Strip the husk and pare the rind off: 15
In the kernel you will see
Blocks of slate enclosed by dappled
Red and green, enclosed by tawny
Yellow nets, enclosed by white
And black acres of dominoes,   20
Where the same brown paper parcel—
Children, leave the string alone!
For who dares undo the parcel
Finds himself at once inside it,
On the island, in the fruit,   25
Blocks of slate about his head,

Finds himself enclosed by dappled
Green and red, enclosed by yellow
Tawny nets, enclosed by black
And white acres of dominoes,   30
With the same brown paper parcel
Still unopened on his knee.
And, if he then should dare to think
Of the fewness, muchness, rareness,
Greatness of this endless only   35
Precious world in which he says
He lives—he then unties the string.

The Cool Web

Children are dumb to say how hot the day is,
How hot the scent is of the summer rose,
How dreadful the black wastes of evening sky,
How dreadful the tall soldiers drumming by.

But we have speech, to chill the angry day,   5
And speech, to dull the rose's cruel scent.
We spell away the overhanging night,
We spell away the soldiers and the fright.

There's a cool web of language winds us in,
Retreat from too much joy or too much fear: 10
We grow sea-green at last and coldly die
In brininess and volubility.

But if we let our tongues lose self-possession,
Throwing off language and its watery clasp
Before our death, instead of when death comes,   15
Facing the wide glare of the children's day,
Facing the rose, the dark sky and the drums,
We shall go mad no doubt and die that way.

The Castle

Walls, mounds, enclosing corrugations
Of darkness, moonlight on dry grass.
Walking this courtyard, sleepless, in fever;
Planning to use—but by definition
There's no way out, no way out—   5
Rope-ladders, baulks of timber, pulleys,
A rocket whizzing over the walls and moat—
Machines easy to improvise.
                              No escape,
No such thing; to dream of new dimensions,   10

Cheating checkmate by painting the king's robe
So that he slides like a queen;
Or to cry, "Nightmare, nightmare!"
Like a corpse in the cholera-pit
Under a load of corpses;
Or to run the head against these blind walls,
Enter the dungeon, torment the eyes
With apparitions chained two and two,
And go frantic with fear—
To die and wake up sweating by moonlight   20
In the same courtyard, sleepless as before.

The Devil's Advice to Story-Tellers

Lest men suspect your tale to be untrue,
Keep probability—some say—in view.
But my advice to story-tellers is:
Weigh out no gross of probabilities,
Nor yet make diligent transcriptions of   5
Known instances of virtue, crime or love.
To forge a picture that will pass for true,
Do conscientiously what liars do—
Born liars, not the lesser sort that raid
The mouths of others for their stock-in-trade: 10
Assemble, first, all casual bits and scraps
That may shake down into a world perhaps;
People this world, by chance created so,
With random persons whom you do not know—
The teashop sort, or travellers in a train   15
Seen once, guessed idly at, not seen again;
Let the erratic course they steer surprise
Their own and your own and your readers' eyes;
Sigh then, or frown, but leave (as in despair)
Motive and end and moral in the air;   20
Nice contradiction between fact and fact
Will make the whole read human and exact.

The Cloak

Into exile with only a few shirts,
Some gold coin and the necessary papers.
But winds are contrary: the Channel packet
Time after time returns the sea-sick peer
To Sandwich, Deal or Rye. He does not land,   5
But keeps his cabin; so at last we find him
In humble lodgings maybe at Dieppe,
His shirts unpacked, his night-cap on a peg,

Passing the day at cards and swordsmanship
Or merry passages with chambermaids,
By night at his old work. And all is well—
The country wine wholesome although so sharp,
And French his second tongue; a faithful valet
Brushes his hat and brings him newspapers.
This nobleman is at home anywhere, 15
His castle being, the valet says, his title.
The cares of an estate would incommode
Such tasks as now his Lordship has in hand.
His Lordship, says the valet, contemplates
A profitable absence of some years. 20
Has he no friend at Court to intercede?
He wants none: exile's but another name
For an old habit of non-residence
In all but the recesses of his cloak.
It was this angered a great personage. 25

End of Play

We have reached the end of pastime, for always,
Ourselves and everyone, though few confess it
Or see the sky other than, as of old,
A foolish smiling Mary-mantle blue;

Though life may still seem to dawdle golden 5
In some June landscape among giant flowers,
The grass to shine as cruelly green as ever,
Faith to descend in a chariot from the sky—

May seem only: a mirror and an echo
Mediate henceforth with vision and sound. 10
The cry of faith, no longer mettlesome,
Sounds as a blind man's pitiful plea of "blind."

We have at last ceased idling, which to regret
Were as shallow as to ask our milk-teeth back;
As many forthwith do, and on their knees 15
Call lugubriously upon chaste Christ.

We tell no lies now, at last cannot be
The rogues we were—so evilly linked in sense
With what we scrutinized that lion or tiger
Could leap from every copse, strike and devour 20
us.

No more shall love in hypocritic pomp
Conduct its innocents through a dance of shame,

From timid touching of gloved fingers 10
To frantic laceration of naked breasts.

Yet love survives, the word carved on a sill 25
Under antique dread of the headsman's axe;
It is the echoing mind, as in the mirror
We stare on our dazed trunks at the block kneel-
ing.

The Villagers and Death

The Rector's pallid neighbour at The Firs,
Death, did not flurry the parishioners.
Yet from a weight of superstitious fears
Each tried to lengthen his own term of years.
He was congratulated who combined 5
Toughness of flesh and weakness of the mind
In consequential rosiness of face.
This dull and not ill-mannered populace
Pulled off their caps to Death, as they slouched
by,
But rumoured him both atheist and spy. 10
All vowed to outlast him (though none ever did)
And hear the earth drum on his coffin-lid.
Their groans and whispers down the village
street
Soon soured his nature, which was never sweet.

To Juan at the Winter Solstice

There is one story and one story only
That will prove worth your telling,
Whether as learned bard or gifted child;
To it all lines or lesser gauds belong
That startle with their shining 5
Such common stories as they stray into.

Is it of trees you tell, their months and virtues,
Or strange beasts that beset you,
Of birds that croak at you the Triple will?
Or of the Zodiac and how slow it turns 10
Below the Boreal Crown,
Prison of all true kings that ever reigned?

Water to water, ark again to ark,
From woman back to woman:
So each new victim treads unfalteringly 15
The never altered circuit of his fate,

Bringing twelve peers as witness
Both to his starry rise and starry fall.

Or is it of the Virgin's silver beauty,
All fish below the thighs?
She in her left hand bears a leafy quince;
When with her right she crooks a finger, smiling,
How may the King hold back?
Royally then he barters life for love.

Or of the undying snake from chaos hatched,
Whose coils contain the ocean,
Into whose chops with naked sword he springs,
Then in black water, tangled by the reeds,
Battles three days and nights,
To be spewed up beside her scalloped shore?

Much snow is falling, winds roar hollowly,
The owl hoots from the elder,
Fear in your heart cries to the loving-cup:
Sorrow to sorrow as the sparks fly upward.
The log groans and confesses:
There is one story and one story only.

Dwell on her graciousness, dwell on her smiling,
Do not forget what flowers
The great boar trampled down in ivy time.
Her brow was creamy as the crested wave,
Her sea-grey eyes were wild
But nothing promised that is not performed.

The Frog and the Golden Ball

She let her golden ball fall down the well
    And begged a cold frog to retrieve it;
For which she kissed his ugly, gaping mouth—
    Indeed, he could scarce believe it.

And seeing him transformed to his princely
    shape,
    Who had been by hags enchanted,
She knew she could never love another man
    Nor by any fate be daunted.

But what would her royal father and mother say?
    They had promised her in marriage
To a cousin whose wide kingdom marched with
    theirs,
    Who rode in a jewelled carriage.

"Our plight, dear heart, would appear past hu-
    man hope
    To all except you and me: to all
Who have never swum as a frog in a dark well
    Or have lost a golden ball."

"What then shall we do now?" she asked her
    lover.
    He kissed her again, and said:
"Is magic of love less powerful at your Court
    Than at this green well-head?"

Edwin Muir
1887–1959

Born in Deerness on the Orkney mainland May 15, 1887, Edwin Muir grew up on small farms, first on the Orkney island of Wyre, and then near Kirkwall on the mainland. As a young man, after the death of his parents and two of his brothers, he worked as a clerk in Glasgow and Greenock. After his marriage to Wilhelmina (Willa) Johnstone, he moved to London, where he was assistant to the editor of *New Age*, A. R. Orage. At a still later stage of his life, from 1921 to 1924, he lived on the Continent, especially in Prague but also in Germany, Italy, and Austria. Although he had written verses while he was living in Glasgow, he began during these years to write the poems that were eventually to establish him as one of the most considerable poets of the

first half of the century. (He and his wife are also well known as the translators of Kafka, as well as of many other writers in German.) He wrote a great deal of criticism, much of it in the form of reviews, but also a number of books, including *The Present Age* (1940), already cited in the introduction to the Modern period, and *The State of Poetry* (1962), which contains the Charles Eliot Norton lectures delivered at Harvard in 1955–56. Some of his more substantial essays are collected in *Latitudes* (1924), *Transition* (1926), and *Essays on Literature and Society* (1949). Though he belongs to no particular school of criticism, he is always a critic to be reckoned with, by reason of his clear insight and firm independence of moral temper.

His poetry cannot be assimilated to any of the specific tendencies that have been most talked about in general historical accounts of the development of the Modern period, and it was only in the 1950s that it began to be at all widely realized that he was a poet of the very finest distinction. In his poems personal experience is transfigured into something like myth by the sheering off of any limiting specificity of detail: at other times, myths from the past, particularly Greek, are given a kind of modern actuality and applicability. In his *Autobiography* (1954), and in his wife's book, *Belonging: A Memoir*, perhaps the only secondary books one needs, many of the incidents from Muir's life are recounted that later came to figure in individual poems: for example, the ascent of Mt. Etna, in Sicily, which was the occasion for the observations embodied in "The Desolations." Even more revealing is the account of the dream about his brothers, who had died young, which is described in one of his most compelling poems, "The Brothers."

TEXTS: *Collected Poems, 1921–1958,* including poems not previously collected, was published in 1960. There is a full-length study, *Edwin Muir: Man and Poet* (1966), by P. H. Butler, and another, *The Poetry of Edwin Muir,* by Elizabeth Huberman (1971). The pamphlet on Muir, in the British Council series, is by J. C. Hall (1956). Helen Gardner's *Edwin Muir,* the W. D. Thomas Memorial Lecture, 1960, was published in pamphlet form in 1961.

Childhood

Long time he lay upon the sunny hill,
  To his father's house below securely bound.
Far off the silent, changing sound was still,
  With the black islands lying thick around.

He saw each separate height, each vaguer hue,   5
  Where the massed islands rolled in mist away,
And though all ran together in his view
  He knew that unseen straits between them lay.

Often he wondered what new shores were there.
  In thought he saw the still light on the sand,   10
The shallow water clear in tranquil air,
  And walked through it in joy from strand to
    strand.

Over the sound a ship so slow would pass
  That in the black hill's gloom it seemed to lie.
The evening sound was smooth like sunken glass,   15

And time seemed finished ere the ship passed
  by.

Grey tiny rocks slept round him where he lay,
  Moveless as they, more still as evening came,
The grasses threw straight shadows far away,
  And from the house his mother called his   20
    name.

The Bird

Adventurous bird walking upon the air,
Like a schoolboy running and loitering, leaping
  and springing,
Pensively pausing, suddenly changing your mind
To turn at ease on the heel of a wing-tip. Where
In all the crystalline world was there to find   5
For your so delicate walking and airy winging
A floor so perfect, so firm and so fair,
And where a ceiling and walls so sweetly ring-
  ing,
Whenever you sing, to your clear singing?

The wide-winged soul itself can ask no more   10
Than such a pure, resilient and endless floor
For its strong-pinioned plunging and soaring
  and upward and upward springing.

The Return of the Greeks

The veteran Greeks came home
Sleepwandering from the war.
We saw the galleys come
Blundering over the bar.
Each soldier with his scar   5
In rags and tatters came home.

Reading the wall of Troy
Ten years without a change
Was such intense employ
(Just out of the arrows' range),   10
All the world was strange
After ten years of Troy.

Their eyes knew every stone
In the huge heartbreaking wall
Year after year grown   15
Till there was nothing at all

But an alley steep and small,
Tramped earth and towering stone.

Now even the hills seemed low
In the boundless sea and land,
Weakened by distance so.
How could they understand
Space empty on every hand
And the hillocks squat and low?

And when they arrived at last
They found a childish scene
Embosomed in the past,
And the war lying between—
A child's preoccupied scene
When they came home at last.

But everything trite and strange,
The peace, the parcelled ground,
The vinerows—never a change!
The past and the present bound
In one oblivious round
Past thinking trite and strange.

But for their grey-haired wives
And their sons grown shy and tall
They would have given their lives
To raise the battered wall
Again, if this was all
In spite of their sons and wives.

Penelope in her tower
Looked down upon the show
And saw within an hour
Each man to his wife go,
Hesitant, sure and slow:
She, alone in her tower.

Dejection

I do not want to be
Here, there or anywhere;
My melancholy
Folds me beyond the reach of care
5 As in a valley
Whence long ago I tried to sally,
But dreamt and left my dream upon the air.

And now in lunar pleasure
I watch the undreaming folk of rock and stone

Lie side by side alone
Enjoying their enormous leisure,
That shall continue till the day
When rock and stone are put away;
20 And feel no more than they the sun that burns
On this unmoving scenery,
Nor count nor care to count the dull returns
Of day and month and year and century
Crowding within the crowding urns.

25 For every eloquent voice dies in this air
Wafted from anywhere to anywhere
And never counted by the careful clock,
That cannot strike the hour
Of power that will dissolve this power
30 Until the rock rise up and split the rock.

Song

Sunset ends the day,
35 The years shift their place,
Under the sun's sway
Times from times fall;
Mind fighting mind
The secret cords unwind
No power can replace:
40 Love gathers all.

The living and the dead
Centuries separate,
Man from himself is led
Through mazes past recall,
45 Distraction can disguise
The wastrel and the wise
Till neither knows his state:
Love gathers all.

Father at odds with son
Breeds ageless enmity,
Friendships undone
Build up a topless wall;
Achilles and Hector slain
Fight, fight and fight again
In measureless memory:
5 Love gathers all.

The quarrel from the start,
Long past and never past,
The war of mind and heart,
The great war and the small

That tumbles the hovel down
And topples town on town
Come to one place at last:
Love gathers all.

The Animals

They do not live in the world,
Are not in time and space.
From birth to death hurled
No word do they have, not one
To plant a foot upon,   5
Were never in any place.

For with names the world was called
Out of the empty air,
With names was built and walled,
Line and circle and square,   10
Dust and emerald;
Snatched from deceiving death
By the articulate breath.

But these have never trod
Twice the familiar track,   15
Never never turned back
Into the memoried day.
All is new and near
In the unchanging Here
Of the fifth great day of God,   20
That shall remain the same,
Never shall pass away.

On the sixth day we came.

The Island

Your arms will clasp the gathered grain
For your good time, and wield the flail
In merry fire and summer hail.
There stand the golden hills of corn
Which all the heroic clans have borne,   5
And bear the herdsmen of the plain,
The horseman in the mountain pass,
The archaic goat with silver horn,
Man, dog and flock and fruitful hearth.
Harvests of men to men give birth.   10
These the ancestral faces bred
And show as through a golden glass

Dances and temples of the dead.
Here speak through the transmuted tongue   30
The full grape bursting in the press,   15
The barley seething in the vat,
Which earth and man as one confess,
Babbling of what both would be at
In garrulous story and drunken song.
Though come a different destiny,   20
Though fall a universal wrong
More stern than simple savagery,
Men are made of what is made,
The meat, the drink, the life, the corn,
Laid up by them, in them reborn.   25
And self-begotten cycles close
About our way; indigenous art
And simple spells make unafraid
The haunted labyrinths of the heart,
And with our wild succession braid   30
The resurrection of the rose.

Sicily

The Desolations

The desolations are not the sorrows' kin.
Sorrow is gentle and sings her sons to rest.
The desolations have no word nor music,
Only an endless inarticulate cry
Inaudible to the poetry-pampered ear.   5
The desolations tell
Nothing for ever, the interminable
Civil war of earth and water and fire.
These have to do with our making.
                    What guards us here   10
Among the established and familiar things?
The leaf, the apple and the rounded earth
Where even imagination is an O,
And only endless harvest is gathered there,
Nothing but that. Yet sometimes absently   15
We pause and murmur "We came crying hither,"
Remembering, and set up a little stage
For our indigenous formal tragedy
Where we are all the actors.
                    The wild earth   20
Pours its hot entrails on the slopes of Aetna,
Blasting whatever's made. Yet in a while
Black house-rows like a pleasant street in Hell
Rise from the frozen slag, and safe within
The lava rooms Sicilian families   25
Follow their ancient ways; the vine-rows yield

Seven times a year, fed on earth's dearest dust.
And all forget the admonition of fire.
There, if you listen, you may hear them say,
"Love is at home, earth's joys lie all around us,   30
The vine-stock and the rose are guarded well.
The roof-tree holds, and friends come in the
    evening."
What saves us from the raging desolations
And tells us we shall walk through peace to
    peace?

The Brothers

Last night I watched my brothers play,
The gentle and the reckless one,
In a field two yards away.
For half a century they were gone
Beyond the other side of care   5
To be among the peaceful dead.
Even in a dream how could I dare
Interrogate that happiness
So wildly spent yet never less?
For still they raced about the green   10
And were like two revolving suns;

A brightness poured from head to head,
So strong I could not see their eyes
Or look into their paradise.
What were they doing, the happy ones?   15
Yet where I was they once had been.

I thought, How could I be so dull,
Twenty thousand days ago,
Not to see they were beautiful?
I asked them, Were you really so   20
As you are now, that other day?
And the dream was soon away.

For then we played for victory
And not to make each other glad.
A darkness covered every head,   25
Frowns twisted the original face,
And through that mask we could not see
The beauty and the buried grace.

I have observed in foolish awe
The dateless mid-days of the law   30
And seen indifferent justice done
By everyone on everyone.
And in a vision I have seen
My brothers playing on the green.

Wystan Hugh Auden

1907–1973

When W. H. Auden's second collection of poems, *On This Island,* appeared in this country in 1937, it was reviewed in the *New York Herald Tribune Books* section by the young American poet Frederick Prokosch with an enthusiasm that must have struck many readers who had been following Auden's development as echoing their own excitement and pleasure. Auden's earlier books had been interesting, but *On This Island* displayed a variety of accomplishment and degrees of beauty and skill which the earlier volumes had not reached, or had not reached quite so often: all promises had been fulfilled, and Auden emerged, as Prokosch put it, "as a poet of spectacular and exciting powers." And while different readers may have different preferences among the books Auden published after that time (for an account of his several volumes see the introduction to the Modern period), all will agree that he continued to exercise those powers in ways that are both varied and highly

engaging: to such an extent, indeed, that he seems quite clearly to be the leading poet of his generation.

Auden was born in York in 1907, the son of a doctor. He offers a certain amount of biographical information in the verse "Letter to Lord Byron" in the travel book on which he collaborated with Louis MacNeice, *Letters from Iceland* (1941). There, or in other places (Isherwood's *Lions and Shadows,* for instance), we learn of his early scientific leanings, of the Icelandic strain in his family background, and of his interest in Icelandic saga and folklore. He was educated at St. Edmund's School and Gresham's School, Holt, and went as an exhibitioner to Christ Church, Oxford. After leaving Oxford he was a schoolmaster for a time, and later taught at various institutions in the United States. In 1935 he wrote a short verse commentary ("This is the night mail crossing the border") for the British Post Office film *Night Mail.* In 1936 he went to Spain in support of his sympathies for the republican side in the civil war; his role there is described in Stephen Spender's candid autobiography, *World Within World* (1951), which is also valuable for its picture of Auden as Spender knew him at Oxford. He left England in 1939 to take up permanent residence in America, lived both here and in Europe until 1972 when he returned to England to live. He was Professor of Poetry at Oxford for the usual five-year term, delivering his inaugural lecture, "Making, Knowing, and Judging," on June 11, 1956.

TEXTS: Auden's poetry is currently available in a variety of forms. The first one-volume *Collected Poetry of W. H. Auden* (1945) arranged the poems alphabetically by first lines rather than chronologically. *Collected Shorter Poems: 1927–1957* and *Collected Longer Poems* (1969) offer an alternative format, and there is a *Selected Poetry* (1970), the poems chosen by the author. His later single-volumes include: *Homage to Clio* (1960); *About the House* (1967); *City Without Walls, and Other Poems* (1969); and *Epistle to a Godson, and Other Poems* (1972). There is a collection of his criticism, *The Dyer's Hand, and Other Essays* (1962), and a commonplace book, *A Certain World* (1970).

Among the books devoted to Auden's poetry are: Francis Scarfe, *Auden and After: The Liberation of Poetry, 1930–1941* (1942); Richard Hoggart, *Auden: An Introductory Essay* (1951); J. W. Beach, *The Making of the Auden Canon* (1957); Monroe Spears, *The Poetry of W. H. Auden* (1963); J. G. Blair, *The Poetic Art of W. H. Auden* (1965); Justin Replogle, *Auden's Poetry* (1969); and *The Case of the Helmeted Airman*, by François Duchêne (1972).

This Lunar Beauty

This lunar beauty
Has no history,
Is complete and early;
If beauty later
Bear any feature,   5
It had a lover
And is another.

This like a dream
Keeps other time,
And daytime is   10
The loss of this;
For time is inches
And the heart's changes,
Where ghost has haunted,

Lost and wanted.   15

But this was never
A ghost's endeavour
Nor, finished this,
Was ghost at ease;
And till it pass   20
Love shall not near
The sweetness here,
Nor sorrow take
His endless look.

Too Dear, Too Vague

Love by ambition
Of definition
Suffers partition
And cannot go
From yes to no,   5
For no is not love; no is no,
The shutting of a door,
The tightening jaw,
A wilful sorrow;
And saying yes   10
Turns love into success,
Views from the rail
Of land and happiness;
Assured of all,
The sofas creak,   15
And were this all, love were
But cheek to cheek
And dear to dear.

Voices explain
Love's pleasure and love's pain,   20
Still tap the knee
And cannot disagree,
Hushed for aggression
Of full confession,
Likeness to likeness   25
Of each old weakness;
Love is not there
Love has moved to another chair.
Aware already
Of what stands next   30
And is not vexed,
And is not giddy,
Leaves the North in place
With a good grace,

And would not gather
Another to another,
Designs his own unhappiness
Foretells his own death and is faithless.

A Summer Night

(To Geoffrey Hoyland)

Out on the lawn I lie in bed,
Vega conspicuous overhead
    In the windless nights of June,
As congregated leaves complete
Their day's activity; my feet   5
    Point to the rising moon.

Lucky, this point in time and space
Is chosen as my working-place,
    Where the sexy airs of summer,
The bathing hours and the bare arms,   10
The leisured drives through a land of farms
    Are good to a newcomer.

Equal with colleagues in a ring
I sit on each calm evening
    Enchanted as the flowers   15
The opening light draws out of hiding
With all its gradual dove-like pleading,
    Its logic and its powers

That later we, though parted then,
May still recall these evenings when   20
    Fear gave his watch no look;
The lion griefs loped from the shade
And on our knees their muzzles laid,
    And Death put down his book.

Now north and south and east and west   25
Those I love lie down to rest;
    The moon looks on them all,
The healers and the brilliant talkers
The eccentrics and the silent walkers,
    The dumpy and the tall.   30

She climbs the European sky,
Churches and power-station lie
    Alike among earth's fixtures:
Into the galleries she peers
And blankly as a butcher stares   35
    Upon the marvellous pictures

To gravity attentive, she   35
Can notice nothing here, though we
    Whom hunger does not move,
From gardens where we feel secure   4
Look up and with a sigh endure
    The tyrannies of love:

And, gentle, do not care to know,
Where Poland draws her eastern bow,
    What violence is done,   4
Nor ask what doubtful act allows
Our freedom in this English house,
    Our picnics in the sun.

Soon, soon, through dykes of our content
The crumpling flood will force a rent   5
    And, taller than a tree,
Hold sudden death before our eyes
Whose river dreams long hid the size
    And vigours of the sea.

But when the waters make retreat   5
And through the black mud first the wheat
    In shy green stalks appears,
When stranded monsters gasping lie,
And sounds of riveting terrify
    Their whorled unsubtle ears,   6

May these delights we dread to lose,
This privacy, need no excuse
    But to that strength belong,
As through a child's rash happy cries
The drowned parental voices rise   6
    In unlamenting song.

After discharges of alarm
All unpredicted let them calm
    The pulse of nervous nations,
Forgive the murderer in his glass,   7
Tough in their patience to surpass
    The tigress her swift motions.

In Memory of W. B. Yeats

(D. Jan. 1939)

He disappeared in the dead of winter:
The brooks were frozen, the airports almost deserted,
And snow disfigured the public statues;

The mercury sank in the mouth of the dying day.
What instruments we have agree   5
The day of his death was a dark cold day.

Far from his illness
The wolves ran on through the evergreen forests,
The peasant river was untempted by the fash-
    ionable quays;
By mourning tongues   10
The death of the poet was kept from his poems.

But for him it was his last afternoon as himself,
An afternoon of nurses and rumours;
The provinces of his body revolted,
The squares of his mind were empty,   15
Silence invaded the suburbs,
The current of his feeling failed: he became his
    admirers.

Now he is scattered among a hundred cities
And wholly given over to unfamiliar affections:
To find his happiness in another kind of wood   20
And be punished under a foreign code of con-
    science.
The words of a dead man
Are modified in the guts of the living.

But in the importance and noise of tomorrow
When the brokers are roaring like beasts on the   25
    floor of the Bourse,
And the poor have the sufferings to which they
    are fairly accustomed,
And each in the cell of himself is almost con-
    vinced of his freedom,
A few thousand will think of this day
As one thinks of a day when one did something
    slightly unusual.
What instruments we have agree   30
The day of his death was a dark cold day.

2

You were silly like us: your gift survived it all;
The parish of rich women, physical decay,
Yourself. Mad Ireland hurt you into poetry.
Now Ireland has her madness and her weather   35
    still,
For poetry makes nothing happen: it survives
In the valley of its making where executives
Would never want to tamper, flows on south
From ranches of isolation and the busy griefs,

Raw towns that we believe and die in; it survives,   40
A way of happening, a mouth.

3

Earth, receive an honoured guest;
William Yeats is laid to rest.
Let the Irish vessel lie
Emptied of its poetry.   45

In the nightmare of the dark
All the dogs of Europe bark,
And the living nations wait,
Each sequestered in its hate;

Intellectual disgrace   50
Stares from every human face,
And the seas of pity lie
Locked and frozen in each eye.

Follow, poet, follow right
To the bottom of the night,   55
With your unconstraining voice
Still persuade us to rejoice;

With the farming of a verse
Make a vineyard of the curse,
Sing of human unsuccess   60
In a rapture of distress;

In the deserts of the heart
Let the healing fountain start,
In the prison of his days
Teach the free man how to praise.   65

Our Bias

The hour-glass whispers to the lion's roar,
The clock-towers tell the gardens day and night,
How many errors Time has patience for,
How strong they are in being always right.

Yet Time, however loud its chimes or deep,   5
However fast its falling torrent flows,
Has never put one lion off his leap
Nor shaken the assurance of a rose.

For they, it seems, care only for success:

While we choose words according to their sound 10
And judge a problem by its awkwardness;

And Time with us was always popular.
When have we not preferred some going round
To going straight to where we are?

from Sonnets from China[1]

XII

Here war is harmless like a monument:
A telephone is talking to a man;
Flags on a map declare that troops were sent;
A boy brings milk in bowls. There is a plan

For living men in terror of their lives, 5
Who thirst at nine who were to thirst at noon,
And can be lost and are, who miss their wives,
And, unlike an idea, can die too soon.

Yet ideas can be true, although men die:
For we have seen a myriad faces 10
Ecstatic from one lie:

And maps can really point to places
Where life is evil now:
Nanking. Dachau.[2]

XIII

Far from a cultural centre he was used:
Abandoned by his general and his lice,
Under a padded quilt he turned to ice
And vanished. He will never be perused

When this campaign is tidied into books: 5
No vital knowledge perished in that skull;

His jokes were stale; like wartime, he was dull;
His name is lost for ever like his looks.

Though runeless, to instructions from headquar-
ters
He added meaning like a comma when 10
He joined the dust of China, that our daughters

Might keep their upright carriage, not again
Be shamed before the dogs, that, where are
waters,
Mountains and houses, may be also men.

XIV

They are and suffer; that is all they do:
A bandage hides the place where each is living,
His knowledge of the world restricted to
A treatment metal instruments are giving.

They lie apart like epochs from each other 5
(Truth in their sense is how much they can bear;
It is not talk like ours but groans they smother),
From us remote as plants: we stand elsewhere.

For who when healthy can become a foot?
Even a scratch we can't recall when cured, 10
But are boisterous in a moment and believe

Reality is never injured, cannot
Imagine isolation: joy can be shared,
And anger, and the idea of love.

XIX

When all our apparatus of report
Confirms the triumph of our enemies,
Our frontier crossed, our forces in retreat,
Violence pandemic like a new disease,

And Wrong a charmer everywhere invited, 5
When Generosity gets nothing done,
Let us remember those who looked deserted:
To-night in China let me think of one[3]

---

[1] The sonnets in this sequence originally appeared in *Journey to a War,* the book in which Auden and Isherwood recorded what they saw in China during their trip there in 1938. The Sino-Japanese War, one of the earliest outcroppings of the general fascist aggression which was later to bring on World War II, had broken out in July 1937. (Earlier hostilities beginning with the Japanese invasion of Manchuria in September 1931 had come to a temporary end with the Tangku truce in May 1933.)
[2] Gilbert Ernest Hubbard, in his article on Chinese History in Chambers's *Encyclopedia* (1950), points out that by the end of 1937 the Japanese were in Nanking, so that the Chinese government had had to move to Hankow, and adds: "The troops at Nanking sullied Japan's reputation by committing the grossest excesses against the civilian population and disarmed soldiery, of whom some 40,000 were massacred." Dachau was the site of one of the German concentration camps.

---

[3] Writing in the days when the meaning of fascism and fascist aggression was becoming more and more painfully apparent, Auden thinks of one who stood in his life and art for everything that totalitarianism would suppress: the great German symbolist poet Rilke (d. 1926). On February 11, 1922, Rilke wrote to a friend from the Château de Muzot sur Sierre, Valais, Switzerland, "At this moment . . . I lay my pen aside behind the last completed Elegy, the tenth. . . . This is what I have been struggling for. Through everything. Miracle. Grace.—All

Who for ten years of drought and silence waited,
Until in Muzot all his being spoke,   10
And everything was given once for all.

Awed, grateful, tired, content to die, completed,
He went out in the winter night to stroke
That tower as one pets an animal.

As I Walked Out One Evening

As I walked out one evening,
  Walking down Bristol Street,
The crowds upon the pavement
  Were fields of harvest wheat.

And down by the brimming river   5
  I heard a lover sing
Under an arch of the railway:
  "Love has no ending.

"I'll love you, dear, I'll love you
  Till China and Africa meet,
And the river jumps over the mountain   10
  And the salmon sing in the street.

"I'll love you till the ocean
  Is folded and hung up to dry,
And the seven stars go squawking   15
  Like geese about the sky.

"The years shall run like rabbits,
  For in my arms I hold
The Flower of the Ages,
  And the first love of the world."   20

But all the clocks in the city
  Began to whirr and chime:
"O let not Time deceive you,
  You cannot conquer Time.

"In the burrows of the Nightmare   25
  Where Justice naked is,
Time watches from the shadow
  And coughs when you would kiss.

"In headaches and in worry
  Vaguely life leaks away,   30
And Time will have his fancy
  Tomorrow or today.

"Into many a green valley
  Drifts the appalling snow;
Time breaks the threaded dances   35
  And the diver's brilliant bow.

"O plunge your hands in water,
  Plunge them in up to the wrist;
Stare, stare in the basin
  And wonder what you've missed.   40

"The glacier knocks in the cupboard,
  The desert sighs in the bed,
And the crack in the tea-cup opens
  A lane to the land of the dead.

"Where the beggars raffle the banknotes   45
  And the Giant is enchanting to Jack,
And the Lily-white Boy is a Roarer,
  And Jill goes down on her back.

"O look, look in the mirror,
  O look in your distress;   50
Life remains a blessing
  Although you cannot bless.

"O stand, stand at the window
  As the tears scald and start;
You shall love your crooked neighbor   55
  With your crooked heart."

It was late, late in the evening,
  The lovers they were gone;
The clocks had ceased their chiming,
  And the deep river ran on.   60

Casino

Only their hands are living, to the wheel at-
    tracted,
are moved, as deer trek desperately towards a
    creek
  through the dust and scrub of a desert, or
    gently,
    as sunflowers turn to the light,

---

in a few days. . . ." And later in the same letter, "I have
gone out and stroked my little Muzot for having guarded
all this for me and at last granted it to me, stroked it
like a great shaggy beast." (*Selected Letters of Rainer
Maria Rilke: 1902–1926*, trans. by R. F. C. Hull, 1947.)

and, as night takes up the cries of feverish chil-
    dren,
the cravings of lions in dens, the loves of dons,
    gathers them all and remains the night, the
        Great room is full of their prayers.

To a last feast of isolation self-invited,
they flock, and in a rite of disbelief are joined;
    from numbers all their stars are recreated,
        the enchanted, the worldly, the sad.

Without, calm rivers flow among the wholly
    living
quite near their trysts, and mountains part them,
    and birds,
        deep in the greens and moistures of summer,
        sing towards their work.

But here no nymph comes naked to the youngest
    shepherd,
the fountain is deserted, the laurel will not grow;
    the labyrinth is safe but endless, and broken
        is Ariadne's thread,

as deeper in these hands is grooved their fortune:
    lucky
were few, and it is possible that none was loved,
    and what was god-like in this generation
        was never to be born.

The Unknown Citizen

(TO JS/07/M/378 This Marble Monument
Is Erected by the State)

He was found by the Bureau of Statistics to be
One against whom there was no official com-
    plaint,
And all the reports on his conduct agree
That, in the modern sense of an old-fashioned
word, he was a saint,
For in everything he did he served the Greater
    Community.
Except for the War till the day he retired
He worked in a factory and never got fired,
But satisfied his employers, Fudge Motors Inc.
Yet he wasn't a scab or odd in his views,
For his Union reports that he paid his dues,
(Our report on his Union shows it was sound)
And our Social Psychology workers found
That he was popular with his mates and liked a
    drink.
The Press are convinced that he bought a paper
    every day
And that his reactions to advertisements were
    normal in every way.
Policies taken out in his name prove that he was
    fully insured,
And his Health-card shows he was once in hospi-
    tal but left it cured.
Both Producers Research and High-Grade Living
    declare
He was fully sensible to the advantages of the
    Instalment Plan
And had everything necessary to the Modern
    Man,
A phonograph, a radio, a car and a frigidaire.
Our researchers into Public Opinion are content
That he held the proper opinions for the time of
    year;
When there was peace, he was for peace; when
    there was war, he went.
He was married and added five children to the
    population,
Which our Eugenist says was the right number
    for a parent of his generation,
And our teachers report that he never interfered
    with their education.
Was he free? Was he happy? The question is
    absurd:
Had anything been wrong, we should certainly
    have heard.

Louis MacNeice

1907–1963

Louis MacNeice was born in Belfast, Ireland, in 1907. He was educated at Marlborough and at Merton College, Oxford. From 1930 to 1936 he was Lecturer in Classics at the University of Birmingham, and from 1936 to 1940 Lecturer in Greek at Bedford College for Women. He was associated with the British Broadcasting Corporation as feature-writer and producer; *Christopher Columbus* (1944), a play for radio, and *The Dark Tower* (1946), a collection of radio scripts, reflect this latter interest. His first volume of poems, *Blind Fireworks,* was published in 1929; his second volume, *Poems* (1935), attracted attention from those who were reading Auden and Spender and established his reputation as a lyric and reflective poet of individuality and distinction. His volumes of shorter poems include *The Earth Compels* (1938), *Plant and Phantom* (1941), *Springboard* (1944), *Holes in the Sky* (1948), *Visitations* (1957), and *Solstices* (1961). *Collected Poems: 1925–1948* was published in 1949, and *Eighty-five Poems,* the author's own selection from his work, in 1959. *Autumn Journal* (1939) is a long reflective poem, in twenty-four sections, written between August and December 1938, "a record of the author's intellectual and emotional experience during that time"; it was followed by *Autumn Sequel* in 1954. His translations and critical writing have been mentioned in the introduction to the Modern period. With Auden he made a trip to Iceland, which is recorded, in prose and verse, in their jointly written *Letters from Iceland* (1937). To Volume II of John Lehmann's *Orpheus: A Symposium of the Arts* (1949), he contributed an article called *Experiences with Images,* which offers some clear and helpful insights into his poetic method.

TEXTS: The definitive edition of his poems, *The Collected Poems of Louis MacNeice,* edited by E. R. Dodds, was published in 1966.

Sunday Morning

Down the road someone is practising scales,
The notes like little fishes vanish with a wink of
    tails,
Man's heart expands to tinker with his car
For this is Sunday morning, Fate's great bazaar,
Regard these means as ends, concentrate on this   5
    Now,

And you may grow to music or drive beyond
    Hindhead anyhow,
Take corners on two wheels until you go so fast
That you can clutch a fringe or two of the windy
    past,
That you can abstract this day and make it to
    the week of time
A small eternity, a sonnet self-contained in   10
    rhyme.

But listen, up the road, something gulps, the
    church spire
Opens its eight bells out, skulls' mouths which
    will not tire
To tell how there is no music or movement
    which secures
Escape from the weekday time. Which deadens
    and endures.

Plain Speaking

In the beginning and in the end the only decent
Definition is tautology: man is man,
Woman woman, and tree tree, and world world,
Slippery, self-contained; catch as catch can.

Which when caught between the beginning and   5
    end
Turn other than themselves, their entities un-
    furled,
Flapping and overlapping—a tree becomes
A talking tower, and a woman becomes world.

Catch them in nets, but either the thread is thin
Or the mesh too big or, thirdly, the fish die   10
And man from false communion dwindles back
Into a mere man under a mere sky.

But dream was dream and love was love and what
Happened happened—even if the judge said
It should have been otherwise—and glitter glit-   15
    ters
And I am I although the dead are dead.

The Sunlight on the Garden

The sunlight on the garden
Hardens and grows cold,
We cannot cage the minute
Within its nets of gold,
When all is told   5
We cannot beg for pardon.

Our freedom as free lances
Advances towards its end;
The earth compels, upon it
Sonnets and birds descend;   10
And soon, my friend,
We shall have no time for dances.

The sky was good for flying
Defying the church bells
And every evil iron   15
Siren and what it tells:
The earth compels,
We are dying, Egypt, dying

And not expecting pardon,
Hardened in heart anew,   20
But glad to have sat under
Thunder and rain with you,
And grateful too
For sunlight on the garden.

London Rain

The rain of London pimples
The ebony street with white
And the neon-lamps of London
Stain the canals of night
And the park becomes a jungle   5
In the alchemy of night.

My wishes turn to violent
Horses black as coal—
The randy mares of fancy,
The stallions of the soul—   10
Eager to take the fences
That fence about my soul.

Across the countless chimneys
The horses ride and across
The country to the channel   15
Where warning beacons toss,

To a place where God and No-God
Play at pitch and toss.

Whichever wins I am happy
For God will give me bliss   20
But No-God will absolve me
From all I do amiss
And I need not suffer conscience
If the world was made amiss.

Under God we can reckon   25
On pardon when we fall
But if we are under No-God
Nothing will matter at all,
Adultery and murder
Will count for nothing at all.   30

So reinforced by logic
As having nothing to lose
My lust goes riding horseback
To ravish where I choose,
To burgle all the turrets   35
Of beauty as I choose.

But now the rain gives over
Its dance upon the town
Logic and lust together
Come dimly tumbling down,   40
And neither God nor No-God
Is either up or down.

The argument was wilful,
The alternatives untrue,
We need no metaphysics   45
To sanction what we do
Or to muffle us in comfort
From what we did not do.

Whether the living river
Began in bog or lake,   50
The world is what was given,
The world is what we make.
And we only can discover
Life in the life we make.

So let the water sizzle   55
Upon the gleaming slates,
There will be sunshine after
When the rain abates
And rain returning duly
When the sun abates.   60

My wishes now come homeward,
Their gallopings in vain,
Logic and lust are quiet
And again it starts to rain;
Falling asleep I listen   65
To the falling London rain.

Explorations

The whale butting through scarps of moving
    marble,
The tapeworm probing the intestinal darkness,
The swallows drawn collectively to their magnet,
    These are our prototypes and yet,
Though we may envy them still, they are merely   5
    patterns
    To wonder at—and forget.

For the ocean-carver, cumbrous but unencum-
    bered,
Who tired of land looked for his freedom and
    frolic in water,
Though he succeeded, has failed; it is only in-
    stinct
    That plots his graph and he,
Though appearing to us a free and a happy   10
    monster, is merely
    An appanage of the sea.

And the colourless blind worm, triumphantly
    self-degraded,
Who serves as an image to men of the worst
    adjustment—
Oxymoron of parasitical glory—   15
    Cannot even be cursed,
Lacking the only pride of his way of life, not
    knowing
    That he has chosen the worst.

So even that legion of birds who appear so gladly
Purposeful, with air in their bones, enfranchised 20
Citizens of the sky and never at odds with
    The season or out of line,
Can be no model to us; their imputed purpose
    Is a foregone design—

And ours is not. For we are unique, a conscious   25
Hoping and therefore despairing creature, the
    final
Anomaly of the world, we can learn no method
    From whales or birds or worms;

Our end is our own to be won by our own en-
    deavour
    And held on our own terms.   30

Hiatus[1]

The years that did not count—Civilians in the
    towns
Remained at the same age as in Nineteen-Thirty-
    Nine,
Saying last year, meaning the last of peace;
Yet eyes began to pucker, mouth to crease,
The hiatus was too packed with fears and frowns,   5
The would-be absent heart came forth a magnetic
    mine.

As if the weekly food queue were to stretch,
Absorb all future Europe. Or as if
The sleepers in the Tube had come from Goya's
    Spain
Or Thucydides' Corcyra[2]—a long way to fetch   10
People to prove that civilization is vain,
Wrapped in old quilts; no wonder they wake stiff.

Yes, we wake stiff and older; especially when
The schoolboys of the Thirties reappear,
Fledged in the void, undubitably men,   15
Having kept vigil on the Unholy Mount
And found some dark and tentative things made
    clear,
Some clear made dark, in the years that did not
    count.

The National Gallery[1]

The kings who slept in the caves are awake and
    out,
The pictures are back in the Gallery; Old Masters
    twirl their cadenzas, whisper and shout,

---

1 From *Holes in the Sky*, copyright, 1948, by Louis Mac-
Neice. Reprinted by permission of Random House, Inc.
2 The great Spanish painter Francisco Goya y Lucientes
(1746–1828) recorded his bitter impressions of the Napoleonic armies' invasion of Spain in a series of etchings
called "The Disasters of War," disasters and disruptions
of human lives of which the poet is reminded by the
sight of the London subway stations filled with sleepers
seeking refuge from bombing attacks during the Battle
of Britain. He is also reminded of the varying fortunes
of the island of Corcyra (modern Corfu) during the Pelo-
ponnesian War (431–404 B.C.), described by Thucydides
in his *History* of that war (I, 24–55; III, 70–85; IV, 46–48).

1 The poem takes as its occasion the return to the National Gallery, at Trafalgar Square, London, of the works
of art that had been stored in caves for safekeeping during
World War II.

Hundreds of windows are open again on a vital
but changeless world—a day-dream free from
doubt.

Here are the angels playing their lutes at the
Birth—
Clay become porcelain; the pattern, the light, the   5
ecstasy which make sense of the earth;
Here is Gethsemane scooped like a glacier, here is
Calvary calmly assured of its own worth.

Here are the gold haloes, opaque as coins,
The pink temple of icing-sugar, the blandly scalloped rock which joins
Primitive heaven and earth; here is our Past wiping the smuts from his eyes, girding his loins.

Here saint may be gorgeous, hedonist austere,   10
The soul's nativity drawn of the earth and
earthy, our brother the Ass being near,
The petty compartments of life thrown wind-
wide open, our lop-sided instincts and customs atoned for here.

Here only too have the senses unending joy:
Draperies slip but slip no further and expectation cannot cloy;
The great Venetian buttocks, the great Dutch   15
bosoms, remain in their time—their prime—
beyond alloy.

And the Painter's little daughter, far-off-eyed,
Still stretches for the cabbage white,[2] her sister
dawdling at her side;
That she grew up to be mad does not concern
us, the idyl and the innocent poise abide.

Aye; the kings are back from their caves in the
Welsh hills,
Refreshed by darkness, armed with colour,   20
sleight-of-hand and imponderables,
Armed with Uccello's lances, with beer-mugs,
dragons' tongues, peacocks' eyes, bangles and
spangles and flounces and frills;

Armed with the full mystique of the commonplace,
The lusts of the eye, the gullet, the loins, the
memory—grace after living and grace
Before some plain-clothes death grabs at the ar-

_____
[2] A kind of small yellow butterfly.

tist's jemmy, leaves us yet one more half-
solved case.

For the quickness of the heart deceives the eye,   25
Reshuffling the themes: a Still Life lives while
portrayed flesh and feature die
Into fugues and subterfuges of being as enveloping and as aloof as a frosty midnight sky.

So fling wide the windows, this window and that,
let the air
Blowing from times unconfined to Then, from
places further and fuller than There,
Purge our particular time-bound unliving lives,   30
rekindle a pentecost in Trafalgar Square.

Time for a Smoke

Sitting once more outside the British Museum,
Behind me seekers for truth perusing a bottom-
less well,
I wonder on which floor in the building opposite
When I was a small boy and it a hotel
I stayed and, waiting for the gates to open,   5
Ran upstairs, trying to beat the lift;

Which was neither good manners, they said, nor
good for the heart.
I turn to my left and Queen Victoria's gift,
An Easter Island idol, looks back through me
And I turn to my right and an Easter Island idol   10
Looks back, over my head. We remain apart
While behind us a million books wait to be
opened;

Still, I have time for a smoke. Striking a match,
My mind knows less about it than my hand
To which this town means merely rough and   15
smooth,
Means moving handrails, knobs, revolving glass,
Or the swing doors behind me which just now
It thrust to let its appended torso pass

From the room where buckets knock on the rim
of the well;
But the child come down in the lift which he   20
failed to beat
Prefers to linger here with pigeons and sparrows
For whom neither truth nor falsehood, heaven
nor hell,
Holds any purport, who have no regrets,
No ideals and no history—only wings.

Dylan Thomas

1914–1953

At the time of his death it was clear that Dylan Thomas had not had time to fulfill the promise manifest in the relatively small body of his poetry, prose sketches, and fiction, or possibly even to find the poetic style and form toward which he had been working. Interest in his appealing and tragic life story has been fostered by such books as *Letters to Vernon Watkins* (ed. Vernon Watkins, 1957)—they are often very lively and amusing letters—or *Dylan Thomas in America: An Intimate Journal,* by J. M. Brinnin (1957). But interest also continues in Thomas as a poet, perhaps the last poet, when considered from the point of view of later developments, to write in an unmistakably individual idiom—an idiom so personal as sometimes to become hermetic—in the way that we have come to think of as typical of the Modern period but a good deal less typical of the decades that have followed 1950.

TEXTS: His principal volumes of poems had been *18 Poems* (1934), *25 Poems* (1936), and *Deaths and Entrances* (1946); *Collected Poems* was published in 1952, but Daniel Jones's recent edition (1971) adds more than a hundred poems to the *Collected Poems 1934–52*. Thomas recorded many of his poems, as well as *Under Milk Wood: A Play for Voices.* The fiction includes *A Portrait of the Artist as a Young Dog* (1940), stories of Welsh life as seen through the sharp, frank eyes of boyhood, and one of the most original and vivid books produced by the writers of the 1930s; there is another novel-like book, *Adventures in the Skin Trade* (published in 1955). The texts of some of his very delightful broadcast talks, some about personal experience, some about poetry and poets, were collected under the title of one of them, *Quite Early One Morning* (1954). A selection of Thomas's work with an introduction by John L. Sweeney is offered in *Selected Writings of Dylan Thomas* (1947). Recent publications include: *Dylan Thomas: Early Prose Writings,* edited by Walford Davies, and *Dylan Thomas: New Critical Essays,* also edited by Walford Davies (1972). Among the critical studies are Elder Olsen's *The Poetry of Dylan Thomas* (1954) and Ralph Maud's *Poet in the Making* (1972).

Dylan Thomas (1914–1953). Drawing by Michael Ayrton. *Courtesy of the National Portrait Gallery and the Artist.*

Quite Early One Morning

Quite early one morning in the winter in Wales, by the sea that was lying down still and green as grass after a night of tar-black howling and rolling. I went out of the house, where I had come to stay for a cold unseasonable holiday, to see if it was raining still, if the outhouse had been blown away, potatoes, shears, rat-killer, shrimp-nets, and tins of rusty nails aloft on the wind, and if all the cliffs were left. It had been such a ferocious night that someone in the smoky shipped-pictured bar had said he could feel his tombstone shaking even though he was not dead, or at least was moving; but the morning shone as clear and calm as one always imagines to-morrow will shine. 10

The sun lit the sea town, not as a whole —from topmost down—reproving zinc-roofed chapel to empty but for rats and whispers grey warehouse on the harbour, but in separate bright pieces. There, the quay shouldering out, nobody on it now but the gulls and the capstans like small men in tubular trousers. Here, the roof of 20 the police-station, black as a helmet, dry as a summons, sober as Sunday. There, the splashed church, with a cloud in the shape of a bell poised above it, ready to drift and ring. Here the chimneys of the pink-washed pub, the pub that was waiting for Saturday night as an over-jolly girl waits for sailors.

The town was not yet awake. The milkman lay still lost in the clangour and music of his Welsh-spoken dreams, the wish-fulfilled tenor voices more powerful than Caruso's, sweeter than Ben Davies's, thrilling past Cloth Hall and Manchester House up to the frosty hills. The town was not yet awake. Babies in upper bedrooms of salt-white houses dangling over water, or of bow-windowed villas squatting prim in neatly treed but unsteady hill streets, worried the light with their half in sleep cries. Miscellaneous retired sea captains emerged for a second from deeper waves than ever tossed their boats, then drowned again, going down down into a perhaps Mediterranean-blue cabin of sleep, rocked to the sea-beat of their ears. Landladies, shawled and bloused and aproned with sleep in the curtained, bombasined black of their once spare rooms, remember their loves, their bills, their visitors—dead, decamped, or buried in English deserts till the trumpet of next expensive August roused them again to the world of holiday rain, dismal cliff and sand seen through the weeping windows of front parlours, tasselled table-cloths, stuffed pheasants, ferns in pots, fading photographs of the bearded and censorious dead, autograph albums with a lock of limp and colourless beribboned hair lolling out between the thick black boards.

The town was not yet awake. Birds sang in eaves, bushes, trees, on telegraph wires, rails, fences, spars, and wet masts, not for love or joy, but to keep other birds away. The landlords in feathers disputed the right of even the flying light to descend and perch.

The town was not yet awake, and I walked through the streets like a stranger come out of the sea, shrugging off weed and wave and darkness with each step, or like an inquisitive shadow, determined to miss nothing—not the preliminary tremor in the throat of the dawn-saying cock or the first whirring nudge of arranged time in the belly of the alarm clock on the trinketed chest of drawers under the knitted text and the done-by-hand water-colours of Porthcawl or Trinidad.

I walked past the small sea-spying windows, behind whose trim curtains lay mild-mannered men and women not yet awake and, for all I could know, terrible and violent in their dreams. In the head of Miss Hughes, "The Cosy," clashed the cymbals of an eastern court. Eunuchs struck gongs the size of Bethesda Chapel. Sultans with voices fiercer than visiting preachers demanded a most un-Welsh dance. Everywhere there glowed and rayed the colours of the small, slate-grey woman's dreams, purple, magenta, ruby, sapphire, emerald, vermilion, honey. But I could not believe it. She knitted in her tidy sleep-world a beige woollen shroud with "thou shalt not" on the bosom.

I could not imagine Cadwallader Davies the grocer in his near-to-waking dream, riding on horse-back, two-gunned and Cody-bold, through the cactus prairies. He added, he subtracted, he receipted, he filed a prodigious account with a candle dipped in dried egg.

What big seas of dreams ran in the Captain's sleep? Over what blue-whaled waves did he sail through a rainbow hail of flying fishes to the music of Circe's swinish island? Do not let him be dreaming of dividends and bottled beer and onions.

Someone was snoring in one house. I counted ten savage and indignant grunts and groans like those of a pig in a model and mudless farm which ended with a window rattler, a wash-basin shaker, a trembler of tooth glasses, a waker of dormice. It thundered with me to the chapel railings, then brassily vanished.

The chapel stood grim and grey, telling the day there was to be no nonsense. The chapel was not asleep, it never cat-napped nor nodded nor closed its long cold eye. I left it telling the morning off and the sea-gull hung rebuked above it.

And climbing down again and up out of the town I heard the cocks crow from hidden farmyards, from old roosts above waves where fabulous sea-birds might sit and cry: "Neptune!" And a far-away clock struck from another church in another village in another universe, though the wind blew the time away. And I walked in the timeless morning past a row of white cottages almost expecting that an ancient man with a great beard and an hour-glass and a scythe under his night-dressed arm might lean from the window and ask me the time. I would have told him:

"Arise old counter of the heart beats of albatrosses, and wake the cavernous sleepers of the town to a dazzling new morning." I would have told him: "You unbelievable Father of Eva and Dai Adam, come out, old chicken, and stir up the winter morning with your spoon of a scythe." I would have told him—I would have scampered like a scalded ghost over the cliffs and down to the bilingual sea.

Who lived in these cottages? I was a stranger to the sea town, fresh or stale from the city where I worked for my bread and butter wishing it were laver-bread and country salty butter yolk-yellow. Fisherman certainly; no painters but of boats; no man-dressed women with shooting-sticks and sketch-books and voices like macaws to paint the reluctant heads of critical and sturdy natives who posed by the pint against the chapel-dark sea which would be made more blue than the bay of Naples—though shallower.

I walked on to the cliff path again, the town behind and below waking up now so very slowly; I stopped and turned and looked. Smoke from one chimney—the cobbler's I thought, but from that distance it may have been the chimney of the retired male nurse who had come to live in Wales after many years successful wrestling with the mad rich of southern England. He was not liked. He measured you for a strait jacket carefully with his eye; he saw you bounce from rubber walls like a sorbo ball. No behaviour surprised him. Many people of the town found it hard to resist leering at him suddenly around the corner, or convulsively dancing, or pointing with laughter and devilish good humour at invisible dog fights merely to prove to him that they were normal.

Smoke from another chimney now. They were burning their last night's dreams. Up from a chimney came a long-haired wraith like an old politician. Someone had been dreaming of the Liberal party. But no, the smoky figure wove, attentuated into a refined and precise grey comma. Someone had been dreaming of reading Charles Morgan. Oh! the town was waking now and I heard distinctly insistent over the slow-speaking sea the voices of the town blown up to me. And some of the voices said:

I am Miss May Hughes "The Cosy," a lonely lady,
Waiting in her house by the nasty sea,

Waiting for her husband and pretty baby
To come home at last from wherever they may be.

I am Captain Tiny Evans, my ship was the Kidwelly, 5
And Mrs. Tiny Evans has been dead for many a year.
"Poor Captain Tiny all alone," the neighbours whisper,
But I like it all alone and I hated her.

Clara Tawe Jenkins, "Madam" they call me,
An old contralto with her dressing-gown on, 10
And I sit at the window and I sing to the sea,
For the sea does not notice that my voice has gone.

Parchedig Thomas Evans making morning tea,
Very weak tea, too, you mustn't waste a leaf.
Every morning making tea in my house by the sea, 15
I am troubled by one thing only, and that, belief.

Open the curtains, light the fire, what are servants for?
I am Mrs. Ogmore Pritchard and I want another snooze.
Dust the china, feed the canary, sweep the drawing-room floor;
And before you let the sun in, mind he wipes his shoes. 20

I am only Mr. Griffiths, very short-sighted, B.A., Aber.
As soon as I finish my egg I must shuffle off to school.
O patron saint of teachers, teach me to keep order,
And forget those words on the blackboard—"Griffiths Bat is a fool."

Do you hear that whistling?—It's me, I am Phoebe, 25
The maid at the King's Head, and I am whistling like a bird.
Some spilt a tin of pepper in the tea.
There's twenty for breakfast and I'm not going to say a word.

Thus some of the voices of a cliff-perched town at the far end of Wales moved out of sleep and darkness into the new-born, ancient, and ageless morning, moved and were lost.

The Hand That Signed the Paper Felled a City

The hand that signed the paper felled a city;
Five sovereign fingers taxed the breath,
Doubled the globe of dead and halved a country;
These five kings did a king to death.

The mighty hand leads to a sloping shoulder, 5
The finger joints are cramped with chalk;
A goose's quill has put an end to murder
That put an end to talk.

The hand that signed the treaty bred a fever,
And famine grew, and locusts came; 10
Great is the hand that holds dominion over
Man by a scribbled name.

The five kings count the dead but do not soften
The crusted wound nor pat the brow;
A hand rules pity as a hand rules heaven; 15
Hands have no tears to flow.

Light Breaks Where No Sun Shines

Light breaks where no sun shines;
Where no sea runs, the waters of the heart
Push in their tides;
And, broken ghosts with glow-worms in their
heads,
The things of light 5
File through the flesh where no flesh decks the
bones.

A candle in the thighs
Warms youth and seed and burns the seeds of
age;
Where no seed stirs,
The fruit of man unwrinkles in the stars, 10
Bright as a fig;
Where no wax is, the candle shows its hairs.

Dawn breaks behind the eyes;
From poles of skull and toe the windy blood
Slides like a sea;
Nor fenced, nor staked, the gushers of the sky 15
Spout to the rod
Divining in a smile the oil of tears.

Night in the sockets rounds,
Like some pitch moon, the limit of the globes;
Day lights the bone; 20
Where no cold is, the skinning gales unpin
The winter's robes;
The film of spring is hanging from the lids.

Light breaks on secret lots, 25

On tips of thought where thoughts smell in the
rain;
When logics die,
The secret of the soil grows through the eye,
And blood jumps in the sun;
Above the waste allotments the dawn halts. 30

After the Funeral

(In Memory of Ann Jones)

After the funeral, mule praises, brays,
Windshake of sailshaped ears, muffle-toed tap
Tap happily on one peg in the thick
Grave's foot, blinds down the lids, the teeth in
black,
The spittled eyes, the salt ponds in the sleeves,
Morning smack of the spade that wakes up sleep,
Shakes a desolate boy who slits his throat
In the dark of the coffin and sheds dry leaves,
That breaks one bone to light with a judgment
clout,
After the feast of tear-stuffed time and thistles 10
In a room with a stuffed fox and a stale fern,
I stand, for this memorial's sake, alone
In the snivelling hours with dead, humped Ann
Whose hooded, fountain heart once fell in pud-
dles
Round the parched worlds of Wales and drowned 15
each sun
(Though this for her is a monstrous image blindly
Magnified out of praise; her death was a still
drop;
She would not have me sinking in the holy
Flood of her heart's fame; she would lie dumb
and deep
And need no druid of her broken body). 20
But I, Ann's bard on a raised hearth, call all
The seas to service that her wood-tongued virtue
Babble like a bellbuoy over the hymning heads,
Bow down the walls of the ferned and foxy woods
That her love sing and swing through a brown 25
chapel,
Bless her bent spirit with four, crossing birds.
Her flesh was meek as milk, but this skyward
statue
With the wild breast and blessed and giant skull
Is carved from her in a room with a wet window
In a fiercely mourning house in a crooked year. 30
I know her scrubbed and sour humble hands

Lie with religion in their cramp, her threadbare
Whisper in a damp word, her wits drilled hollow,
Her fist of a face died clenched on a round pain;
And sculptured Ann is seventy years of stone.   35
These cloud-sopped, marble hands, this monu-
    mental
Argument of the hewn voice, gesture and psalm,
Storm me forever over her grave until
The stuffed lung of the fox twitch and cry Love
And the strutting fern lay seeds on the black sill.   40

The Hunchback in the Park

The hunchback in the park
A solitary mister
Propped between trees and water
From the opening of the garden lock
That lets the trees and water enter   5
Until the Sunday sombre bell at dark

Eating bread from a newspaper
Drinking water from the chained cup
That the children filled with gravel
In the fountain basin where I sailed my ship   10
Slept at night in a dog kennel
But nobody chained him up.

Like the park birds he came early
Like the water he sat down
And Mister they called Hey mister   15
The truant boys from the town
Running when he had heard them clearly
On out of sound

Past lake and rockery
Laughing when he shook his paper   20
Hunchbacked in mockery
Through the loud zoo of the willow groves
Dodging the park keeper
With his stick that picked up leaves.

And the old dog sleeper   25
Alone between nurses and swans
While the boys among willows
Made the tigers jump out of their eyes
To roar on the rockery stones
And the groves were blue with sailors   30

Made all day until bell time
A woman figure without fault

Straight as a young elm
Straight and tall from his crooked bones
That she might stand in the night   35
After the locks and chains

All night in the unmade park
After the railings and shrubberies
The birds the grass the trees the lake
And the wild boys innocent as strawberries   40
Had followed the hunchback
To his kennel in the dark.

Poem in October

It was my thirtieth year to heaven
Woke to my hearing from harbor and neighbor
    wood
And the mussel pooled and the heron
    Priested shore
The morning beckon   5
With water praying and call of seagull and rook
And the knock of sailing boats on the net webbed
    wall
Myself to set foot
That second
In the still sleeping town and set forth.   10

My birthday began with the water-
Birds and the birds of the winged trees flying my
    name
Above the farms and the white horses
And I rose
In rainy autumn   15
And walked abroad in a shower of all my days.
High tide and the heron dived when I took the
    road
Over the border
And the gates
Of the town closed as the town awoke.   20

A springful of larks in a rolling
Cloud and the roadside bushes brimming with
    whistling
Blackbirds and the sun of October
Summery
On the hill's shoulder,   25
Here were fond climates and sweet singers sud-
    denly
Come in the morning where I wandered and
    listened

To the rain wringing
    Wind blow cold
In the wood faraway under me.   30

Pale rain over the dwindling harbor
And over the sea wet church the size of a snail
    With its horns through mist and the castle
        Brown as owls
    But all the gardens   35
Of spring and summer were blooming in the tall
tales
Beyond the border and under the lark full cloud.
    There could I marvel
        My birthday
Away but the weather turned around.   40

It turned away from the blithe country
And down the other air and the blue altered sky
    Streamed again a wonder of summer
        With apples
    Pears and red currants   45
And I saw in the turning so clearly a child's
Forgotten mornings when he walked with his
mother.
    Through the parables
        Of sun light
And the legends of the green chapels   50

And the twice told fields of infancy
That his tears burned my cheeks and his heart
moved in mine.
    These were the woods the river and sea
        Where a boy
    In the listening   55
Summertime of the dead whispered the truth of
his joy
To the trees and the stones and the fish in the
tide.
    And the mystery
        Sang alive
Still in the water and singingbirds.   60

And there could I marvel my birthday
Away but the weather turned around. And the
true
    Joy of the long dead child sang burning
        In the sun.
    It was my thirtieth   65
Year to heaven stood there then in the summer
noon

Though the town below lay leaved with October
blood.
    O may my heart's truth
        Still be sung
On this high hill in a year's turning.   70

A Refusal to Mourn the Death, by Fire, of a Child in London

Never until the mankind making
Bird beast and flower
Fathering and all humbling darkness
Tells with silence the last light breaking
And the still hour   5
Is come of the sea tumbling in harness

And I must enter again the round
Zion of the water bead
And the synagogue of the ear of corn
Shall I let pray the shadow of a sound   10
Or sow my salt seed
In the least valley of sackcloth to mourn

The majesty and burning of the child's death.
I shall not murder
The mankind of her going with a grave truth   15
Nor blaspheme down the stations of the breath
With any further
Elegy of innocence and youth.

Deep with the first dead lies London's daughter,
Robed in the long friends,   20
The grains beyond age, the dark veins of her
    mother,
Secret by the unmourning water
Of the riding Thames.
After the first death, there is no other.

Fern Hill

Now as I was young and easy under the apple
    boughs
About the lilting house and happy as the grass
    was green,
    The night above the dingle starry,
        Time let me hail and climb
    Golden in the heydays of his eyes,   5

And honoured among wagons I was prince of
   the apple towns
And once below a time I lordly had the trees
   and leaves
     Trail with daisies and barley
   Down the rivers of the windfall light.

And as I was green and carefree, famous among   10
   the barns
About the happy yard and singing as the farm
   was home,
   In the sun that is young once only,
     Time let me play and be
   Golden in the mercy of his means,
And green and golden I was huntsman and herds-   15
   man, the calves
Sang to my horn, the foxes on the hills barked
   clear and cold,
   And the sabbath rang slowly
   In the pebbles of the holy streams.

All the sun long it was running, it was lovely,
   the hay-
Fields high as the house, the tunes from the   20
   chimneys, it was air
   And playing, lovely and watery
     And fire green as grass.
   And nightly under the simple stars
As I rode to sleep the owls were bearing the farm
   away,
All the moon long I heard, blessed among stables,   25
   the night-jars
   Flying with the ricks, and the horses
     Flashing into the dark.

And then to awake, and the farm, like a wanderer
   white
With the dew, come back, the cock on his shoul-
   der: it was all
   Shining, it was Adam and maiden,   30
     The sky gathered again
   And the sun grew round that very day.
So it must have been after the birth of the simple
   light
In the first, spinning place, the spellbound horses
   walking warm
   Out of the whinnying green stable   35
   On to the fields of praise.

And honoured among foxes and pheasants by the
   gay house

Under the new made clouds and happy as the
   heart was long,
   In the sun born over and over,
     I ran my heedless ways,   40
   My wishes raced through the house-high hay
And nothing I cared, at my sky blue trades, that
   time allows
In all his tuneful turning so few and such morn-
   ing songs
   Before the children green and golden
     Follow him out of grace,   45

Nothing I cared, in the lamb white days, that
   time would take me
Up to the swallow thronged loft by the shadow of
   my hand,
   In the moon that is always rising,
     Nor that riding to sleep
   I should hear him fly with the high fields   50
And wake to the farm forever fled from the child-
   less land.
Oh as I was young and easy in the mercy of his
   means,
     Time held me green and dying
    Though I sang in my chains like the sea.

In My Craft or Sullen Art

In my craft or sullen art
Exercised in the still night
When only the moon rages
And the lovers lie abed
With all their griefs in their arms,   5
I labour by singing light
Not for ambition or bread
Or the strut and trade of charms
On the ivory stages
But for the common wages   10
Of their most secret heart.

Not for the proud man apart
From the raging moon I write
On these spindrift pages
Nor for the towering dead   15
With their nightingales and psalms
But for the lovers, their arms
Round the griefs of the ages,
Who pay no praise or wages
Nor heed my craft or art.   20

Do Not Go Gentle into That Good Night

Do not go gentle into that good night,
Old age should burn and rave at close of day;
Rage, rage against the dying of the light.

Though wise men at their end know dark is right,
Because their words had forked no lightning they   5
Do not go gentle into that good night.
Good men, the last wave by, crying how bright
Their frail deeds might have danced in a green
    bay,
Rage, rage against the dying of the light.

Wild men who caught and sang the sun in flight,   10
And learn, too late, they grieved it on its way,
Do not go gentle into that good night.

Grave men, near death, who see with blinding
    sight
Blind eyes could blaze like meteors and be gay,
Rage, rage against the dying of the light.

And you, my father, there on the sad height,
Curse, bless, me now with your fierce tears, I
    pray.
Do not go gentle into that good night.
Rage, rage against the dying of the light.

The 1950s and After

Courtesy of Southern Methodist University Sustentation.

The 1950s and After

The aim of the concluding section of this anthology is to offer a selection from the work of writers whose careers are still actively in progress and thus to give an idea of the continuity of British literature into the present, of what its salient qualities have been since the end of World War II. The assumption was made, at the end of the introduction to the Modern period, that that period, considered as a segment of literary history beginning in the 1870s or 1880s, had run its course by about 1945 or 1950. The Modern period, having had its origins in the activities of the Aesthetic Movement, and receiving much of its characteristic stamp from the doctrines and practical literary consequences of the Symbolist Movement, was seen as having had its era of most signal achievement in the years from 1910 to 1940. Its principal figures were Yeats, Eliot, and Pound, D. H. Lawrence, James Joyce, and Virginia Woolf; while there are a score of other names to be cited if one were attempting to describe all the valid, interesting, and distinguished writing of the period, these are the names that absolutely must be accounted for in any literary history of the period. However these writers differ from one another in other respects, their work shares certain characteristics: it is notably complex, subtle, and sometimes—at least on first approach—seems arcane or hermetic. It is innovative, adventurous, highly individual, and it owes all these qualities to a fundamental conviction about the importance, even the sacred importance, of the work of art. Not the importance to a wide audience, or for immediate social purpose, but to the very *idea* of art and its ultimate importance in human life, so that the writer must make every effort to realize *his* ideal of what his work must be and, in doing so, come as close as possible to realizing the never-quite-to-

be-fathomed potential that art can have if it can find its right form. "Art for art's sake" is too often thought of as having trivialized art: what it did was to take art and literature out of the service of the immediate contingent tasks and interests that society would like to impose upon them, doing so in order that art might realize more essential, more grandiose aims than those. "To create once more the pure work . . .": Yeats's words might well serve as the motto for the Modern period, for what is most central to the theoretical assumptions and the creative impulse that determined it—and this is true even with writers like Lawrence or Joyce, part of whose effort was indeed directed toward altering the forms of life in their own time.

In order "to create once more the pure work," the first necessary step, as we have seen, was to eliminate impurities—the elements of philosophical discursiveness, or the habit of attention to matters of immediate practical or ethical concern, which Yeats found in the work of Tennyson and Browning, even of Swinburne. Virginia Woolf, too, a little later, insists on the necessity of removing from literature—and from the novel, this time, where they had seemed most at home—all the concerns of social realism, the recording of factual detail, the concern with the whole material side of living, as she found these things in the novels of Bennett, Wells, and Galsworthy, in order to present the essence of character with greater purity and intensity. There is nothing casual or relaxed about such aims, and in fact the principal works of Modern literature involve both writer and reader in a certain degree of tension, of ambitious and discriminating attentiveness to just what is being done at every moment in a work, even to *how* it is being done.

If at this point we say that such aims were relaxed after a while, that they no longer seem to be so centrally operative in the work of the British writers who have succeeded the writers of the Modern period, that is not meant as a value judgment, but simply to point out what seems to be a recognizable difference between the way that things were done in the first half of the twentieth century and the way that they more often tend to be done since.

It is not so easy to see the literature of the 1950s, 1960s, and 1970s in perspective as it is with the literature of the earlier decades, and it may not even be desirable to try. Perhaps the best one can do is to respect the concluding sentence of John Wain's essay on "The Conflict of Forms in Contemporary English Literature" (included in a volume of essays collected in 1963 under the title *Essays on Literature and Ideas*): "Certainly I myself believe that contemporary English writing, despite the harm done to it by its parasites, can fairly be called abundant, inventive, original and interesting." Such words will be entirely acceptable to anyone who, perhaps without worrying too much about imposing patterns of tendency or school or critical intention, has been reading the novels, poems, and plays that English writers have produced since 1950.

A few generalizations can be attempted, but they are not meant to be tendentious. Some of the concerns that the writers of the Modern period tried to eliminate from literature seem to have come back in: it is important not to forget Virginia Woolf's essay "Mr. Bennett and Mrs. Brown," if only *because* much of the most interesting writing of the years following World War II seems to have brought back into the novel the very elements that she was anxious to reject. Social concerns, social satire, dissatisfaction with the impact of institutions on individual lives, and a very lively, documented awareness of the way that Englishmen are living at the particular time in history, are all present in a small array of novels that appeared at about the same moment in the early 1950s, and that are still among the books one must look at first for an understanding of the direction English writing has been taking: John Wain's *Hurry on Down* (1953; published in the United States as *Born in Captivity* in 1954); Kingsley Amis's *Lucky Jim* (1953); John Braine's *Room at the Top* (1957); Alan Sil-

litoe's *Saturday Night and Sunday Morning* (1958) and *The Loneliness of the Long Distance Runner* (1959); and John Osborne's play, *Look Back in Anger* (1957). John Wain has protested vigorously against the shibboleth that was used to group some of these writers together, in the criticism and critical chatter of these years and later, the phrase "Angry Young Men." He has patiently explained the journalistic maneuvers responsible for a term that he believes to have been inaccurate and inappropriate; and anyone who plans to go on using the phrase should first read the essay on contemporary English literature that we have just cited; also Wain's "Reply to a Letter from Joe" in the same volume.

Without wishing to pigeonhole these novels as having limited aims of social protest or description of contemporary social modes, we nevertheless feel that they bring back into English fiction an objectivity, a casualness of approach, a willingness to be entertaining, even an interest in plot (how diffident E. M. Forster had been about plot in *Aspects of the Novel*!). A precedent for such interests and procedures can be found in the somewhat earlier work of George Orwell (1903–1950). Orwell is most widely known today for his short political satire, *Animal Farm* (1946), and for the novel of sociopolitical prediction, *Nineteen Eighty-Four* (1949), but throughout the 1930s he had been writing novels, books of observation or reportage, and critical essays that were in a quite different tone and insisted on quite different values and centers of interest, both social and literary, from anything we were accustomed to find in the generally more characteristic writers of the Modern period. Two of his novels, *Keep the Aspidistra Flying* (1936) and *Coming up for Air* (1939), firmly and unmistakably established the possibility of writing thoroughly absorbing novels about some of the very matters, such as the danger of political oppression, the ways in which men can be enslaved even in societies that claim to be free, that the great Modern writers had been inclined to turn away from or to be involved with only at a remove, indirectly. In everything he wrote—his book about his experiences as a dish-washer in Paris and as a tramp in England (*Down and Out in Paris and London*, 1933), his book about the Spanish people (*Homage to Catalonia*, 1938), or his essays on certain aspects of the literature of the Modern period itself—he was moved by an instinct to keep a sharp eye on the effect of politics on life, on the way, for instance, that a corrupt political tendency will vitiate language and literature. He is a serious, disciplined writer, with very high standards for prose, but he is also a casual writer, an entertaining one. In defiance of a dictum made by Arthur Symons at the end of his little book on Symbolism—"I affirm that it is not natural to be what is called 'natural' any longer"—Orwell wrote always with the most successful and attractive naturalness. (The opening sentence of *Coming up for Air* is: "The idea really came to me the day I got my new false teeth.") And whether the new novelists were consciously following Orwell's example or not, they may permissibly be seen as continuing a tradition that he had affirmed. It may be noted in passing that much of the writing that had come out of World War II—direct description of firsthand experience during the war, whether by civilians or by members of the armed services —had the effect of keeping prose casual, supple, and informal; nor was the war itself much of a respecter of ivory towers.

George Orwell was interested in the popular arts as being symptomatic of values and assumptions that may be implicit in a society without the society's being clearly aware of them. He was also interested in the ways, often insidious, in which writing or art that seems to propose nothing but entertainment can involve and proselytize attitudes and modes of conduct that may ultimately prove sinister. He wrote seriously about subjects that literary criticism had not taken seriously before: the weekly story-papers for boys ("Boys' Weeklies"), the comic postcards of Donald McGill, or James Hadley Chase's novel of violence, *No Orchids for Miss Blandish*. The volume which collects some of these essays— *Dickens, Dali and Others* (1946), subtitled "Studies in Popular Culture"—also contains an essay "In Defence of P. G. Wodehouse." Kingsley Amis's interest in certain other manifestations of popular culture, for example, his study of Ian Fleming's James Bond novels (*The James Bond Dossier,* 1965), or his survey of science fiction (*New Maps of Hell,* 1960), is indicative that in this respect, too, Orwell's example continues to be followed.

Other writers who began their careers in the years immediately after World War II, while they might at first have seemed to be turning away from the intense care for form and for the uniquely personal vision of the writers of the Modern period, in the direction of a certain relaxation of effort, a willingness to write quite directly about the real world and its immediate concerns or foibles—and often to do these things very entertainingly—soon demonstrated that the inheritance from the Modern period was not to be denied or neglected. It was often, in fact, to be very fully exploited. Angus Wilson, one of the most consistently distinguished fiction writers of the postwar period, first published a volume of very amusing, but often bitter, satiric stories called *The Wrong Set* (1949), to be followed by another collection, *Such Darling Dodos* (1950). But as the 1950s went on, he began to publish novels—*Hemlock and After* (1952) and *Anglo-Saxon Attitudes* (1956) were the first of a long series—in which he showed that a skilful post-Modern novelist was free to be casual and offhand in his satiric or comic treatment of contemporary human types and situations at the same time that he could invoke and exploit the earlier novelists' legacy of a demanding subtlety of analysis and give full attention to the serious moral and philosophical dilemmas of a time that has been conscious of living under the shadow of a crisis of faith. Iris Murdoch, an equally distinguished novelist and one who likewise began her career in the 1950s, at first rather dazzled her readers by the apparent raciness, exciting narrative, and complex plotting of novels like *The Flight from the Enchanter* (1956) and *The Sandcastle* (1957); but it soon became evident that in these novels, as well as in her later ones, she was by no means concerned merely to provide sensation, but was also deeply engaged in the often fully symbolic presentation of events and crises of human conduct that posed the most serious moral problems of the time, indeed of the century. If we have claimed that the postwar writers approached considerations of form in a more relaxed way than, say, Virginia Woolf had done, some degree of correction has to be made by a reader, who will often find that the contemporary novelist always has available to him the possibility of a return to the high degree of conscious artistic concern that the Modern novelists, from James and Conrad on, had seen as being both the novelist's right and his duty. A reader of Doris Lessing's *The Golden Notebook* (1962), for instance, is in the presence of quite as articulate a concern with the problems that a writer faces in his attempt to capture truth, reality, as he would find in André Gide's *The Counterfeiters* (*Les Faux-Monnayeurs*, 1925), that archetype of the earlier twentieth-century novelist's self-consciousness in the face of his task. (But Mrs. Lessing's work is also characterized, as is evidenced by any of her splendid short stories, by a power of evoking the real world in a most convincing and moving way.)

Perhaps it may be said, again without any wish to make an invidious statement, that since the 1950s there have been a great many British novelists whose work has been of much more than average or merely passing interest, without there having been any two or three figures who have seemed to attain—or even to aspire to—the monumentality of James or Conrad, of Lawrence or Joyce. It may be that there are such figures—perhaps even among those we have mentioned here—but that we are still too close to recognize the ultimate pattern or scope of their work. Another possibility is that the period has tended to shun monumentality, though a number of novelists seem to be aiming at it by the very fact of conceiving of certain of their novels as forming sequences: there is Lawrence Durrell's *Alexandria Quartet,* completed during the 1950s, for instance, as well as sequences by Lord Snow (C. P. Snow), Doris Lessing, Anthony Burgess, and Anthony Powell. This theory seems to receive support when we turn from the novelists to the poets. It was of the very essence of Yeats's career as a poet that he was constantly shaping the total structure that his work would eventually constitute, shaping not only the form and style of particular poems but also the ideology which underlay them and the personal character —his own character—of which they were a sign, or for which they were an instrument of discovery. Again, of course, contemporary poets may be doing the same thing, without our being able to recognize the fact, just as the scope of Yeats's achievement was not at all generally recognized until the publication of the 1933 *Collected Poems.* Yet in general the poets of the 1940s and after come to us more casually than did Yeats or Eliot or Pound. They seem to wish to write in-

dividual poems that treat quite immediately of specific experiences, poems that can be approached by a reader without his needing preliminary initiation into a system of thought or belief that is assumed in the poems. Certainly there have been models available in the work of the best of the 1930s poets, Auden, Spender, MacNeice (and for that matter, in the work of poets who belong to no particular decade, like Graves and Edwin Muir). These poets of the thirties did write poems that offered to take the reader very directly and candidly into a self-sustaining account of a specific personal experience, short poems, on the whole, each complete in itself, each capable of being read by and for itself. This is the pattern—despite the presence of poem-sequences here and there, or occasionally of a long poem—that we encounter in the separate volumes by the poets we read today: Thom Gunn, Ted Hughes, Dannie Abse, Donald Davie, Charles Tomlinson, Elizabeth Jennings, and really a great many others. "Personal utterance," which Yeats had recognized as a necessary principle of poetic strength, had a somewhat different meaning for him than it was to have for Auden and the other poets of recent decades. Yeats had written about himself and his own immediate life-concerns and circumstances, but he brought such matters into the aura of a spirit that somehow distanced them; they became a part of the impressiveness that was involved in the very fact of *each* poem's being a facet of a total lofty statement. When Auden begins an early poem by saying, "Now from my window-sill I watch the night," and goes on to fill in the circumstances of the boys' school in which he is teaching, with a very casual, unexplained specificity, something has happened to the principle of personal utterance; it has moved a bit farther on in the direction of a more easy-going, discursive tone. And such a tone is very widely diffused in the work of the most recent generation of British poets.

After the Modern period's tendency to attach maximum importance to the concept of art, and to produce individual works that should match that idea in their weight, complexity, and scope, it is only natural that later writers should be moved to minimize the idea, to produce work that, while never failing to be serious and carefully wrought, should look as little portentous and imposing as possible. Today *more* poetry seems to be being written than ever before—this is true for the United States as well as for Britain—moreover the work of the many contemporary poets whose work one encounters either in their individual volumes or in a great range of periodicals maintains a standard of quality, of distinction and seriousness, that is astonishing when one considers how widely diffused it is. Perhaps this is to be seen as the most dependable generalization one can make about the writing of the post-Modern decades: that while the great, somewhat isolated individual figure may be absent, his absence is compensated for by the presence of *more* writers whose work consistently measures up to very firm standards of strictness and subtlety than one could have been sure of finding in the Modern period.

Needless to say, these standards and qualities are themselves a part of the inheritance from the Modern period. Nobody had to say, in the years after World War II, what Pound and Herbert Read and their associates had had to say around the time of World War I, that "poetry should be at least as well written as prose"—post-Modern poetry has been very well written indeed. Another inheritance from the Modern period is open for exploitation at any time: the clause in the post-Symbolist writer's charter that allows him to do what he feels he must do, even if the result is baffling to his reader or his audience. Some of the playwrights, particularly, have put audiences of the 1950s and 1960s up against the situation that was common during the Modern period, of not knowing quite how to respond to the work before them. One thinks of *Waiting for Godot,* the play with which Samuel Beckett—again the year is 1953—gained the wide attention to his bleakly reductive view of man's situation that his earlier novels (*Molloy,* 1951; *Malone Dies,* 1951; *L'Innommable—The Unnamable—,* 1953) had not won. A little later came the somewhat similarly challenging plays of Harold Pinter (*The Birthday Party,* 1959; *The Caretaker,* 1960; *A Night Out,* 1961; and *The Homecoming,* 1965), who belongs more rightfully than Beckett (who had been Joyce's younger associate) to the generation which came of age in the fifties and sixties.

We live today, literarily speaking, in a highly self-conscious time. Writers are aware not only of coming at the end of a *long* tradition of literary achievement, but also of following directly on a period whose great writers are still a part of our consciousness, who cannot be simply rejected or reacted against. The reading public is as hard to be sure of as ever, but critics are totally aware of everything that is being written, or that has been written; and, of course, the question of what literature can do for us, in the present disarray of society and its values, is often raised, and not always in a very hopeful or friendly way. But for the reader or student of contemporary literature the situation is a straightforward one. Now, as much as at any time in the long history of British literature, each year sees the publication of novels, short stories, poems, books of reporting or analysis of contemporary experience, essays in literary criticism, that have the clearest possible claim on our attention, because they are about—to use the title of John Wain's novel—"Living in the Present." The following pages offer samples of the work of at least a few of these writers, in the belief that familiarity with the names represented here will lead the reader outward to familiarity with the much greater number of contemporary writers whom these may serve to represent.

General References

More concerted critical attention has been given to the work of the novelists of the post-World War II period than to that of the poets. James Gindin's *Postwar British Fiction: New Accents and Attitudes* (1962) treats (among others) Amis, Durrell, William Golding, Thomas Hinde, Doris Lessing, Iris Murdoch, Alan Sillitoe, C. P. Snow, John Wain, and Angus Wilson. An even wider range of individual figures is accounted for in Frederick R. Karl's *The Contemporary English Novel* (1962), since here the emphasis is not so squarely on the most recent generation. Later studies include Bernard Bergonzi's *The Situation of the Novel* (1969) and David Lodge's *The Novelist at the Crossroads, and Other Essays on Fiction and Criticism* (1971). *Continuance and Change: The Contemporary British Novel Sequence,* by Robert K. Morris (1972), deals specifically with novelists who have conceived of several of their novels as forming a sequence.

For sorting out the poetry of the period, M. L. Rosenthal's *The New Poets*: *American and British Poetry since World War II* (1967) is indispensable. See also "The State of Poetry: A Symposium" in the Tenth Anniversary Issue of *The Review* (Spring-Summer, 1972). Certain anthologies are also among the useful means of developing an acquaintance with the many individual writers who have achieved one degree of prominence or another, among them Robert Conquest's *New Lines*: *An Anthology* (1956), and its successor, *New Lines II* (1963); Edward Lucie-Smith's *A Group Anthology* (1963), and the same editor's *British Poetry Since 1945* (Penguin, 1970); A. Alvarez's *The New Poetry* (Penguin, 1962); and *Children of Albion*: *Poetry of the Underground in Britain*, edited by Michael Horovitz (1969). The Penguin Modern Poets series (three poets to a volume) is also helpful, but not all the volumes are available in the United States. *Writing in England Today*: *The Last Fifteen Years*, edited by Karl Miller (1968), offers often very brief selections from a large number of writers of both prose and verse, including excerpts from novels and plays, and constitutes an attractive sampling of the whole field.

George Orwell

1903–1950

"George Orwell" was the pseudonym assumed, close to the beginning of his career as a writer, by Eric Arthur Blair, who had been born in Bengal, the son of an official of the Bengal Civil Service, who was educated at Eton, and who on leaving Eton in 1921, instead of going on to one of the universities, went to Burma to serve in the Imperial Police. After five years in Burma he returned to Europe, and for the next few years followed a variety of occupations that enabled him to live, sometimes on the barest subsistence level, but also to penetrate the workings of the society of his time without committing himself to it, and, presumably, to generate the resolve and to amass the experience which would contribute to his being—what he eventually and completely was— a writer. Soon after his return to Europe, for instance, he worked as a dishwasher in Paris hotels and lived the precarious but instructive existence of a tramp in England: these are the experiences which he described in *Down and Out in Paris and London* (1933) and in such an essay as "How the Poor Die," describing his time as a charity patient in a Paris hospital in 1929. He also worked for a time as a schoolmaster and as an assistant in a bookshop; he was writing his first novels; and later in the 1930s he fought in the Spanish Civil War as a militiaman. We are apt to think of Orwell first as a novelist, no doubt because he gained his widest fame as the author of *Animal Farm* (1946)—though this is more strictly a political fable or allegory than a novel—and of *Nineteen Eighty-Four* (1949), but a large part of his work consists of essays, about literature or about socialism or about the interactions of literature and society, and of book-length treatments of the life of his time, always considered from the point of view of the necessity of socialism.

To return for a moment to the question of his pseudonym. The authors of *The Unknown Orwell* (1972), Peter Stansky and William Abrahams, point out that at the end of his life, during which he had to all intents and purposes *become* "George Orwell," he returned by his own wish to being Eric Blair. They cite the inscription on his tombstone in the village churchyard of Sutton Courtenay ("Here Lies/ Eric Arthur Blair/ Born June 25th 1903/ Died January 21st 1950"), and go on to say that this inscription "was specified by Orwell himself, in the first part of the final sentence of his last will. The will was drawn up on January 18, 1950, three days before his death, in University College Hospital, London, where he had been a patient since the preceding September. Having chosen his epitaph, he went on to conclude the sentence with a request that no memorial service be held for him and no biography be written; and then he signed his name, Eric Blair." All this has been stated here because it suggests the complexity of personality and of literary intention that lies behind the life and work of a writer whom we are perhaps too ready to consider as an exponent of simple, direct objectivity. Stansky and Abrahams, at a later point in their book, point out another instance of the distinction between Blair and Orwell that may manifest itself at any time and that must always be kept in mind in assessing Orwell's writing. They compare the impression of his childhood which is given in the autobiographical essay "Such, Such Were the Joys" with the idea of that childhood which they have established from other sources, including his early letters; and they conclude that, valuable as the essay may be as Orwell's "interpretation of Eric Blair's childhood, . . . it is less satisfactory as a biographical account. Written with admirable directness, these straightforward sentences create effortlessly an air of candour and intelligence, and lead one to believe that one is being told everything. In fact, Orwell has written a highly selective and purposive work of art, an 'indictment' of the cruelty inflicted on children in the name of boarding-school education, and whatever will lessen the force of the argument has been omitted." The phrasing here, singling out the impression a reader receives from Orwell's writing, of directness, straightforwardness of style, candor and intelligence, will commend itself to the reader of any part of his work, not just of the essay in question. But the upshot of the matter, which is also the upshot of the whole distinction between Blair and Orwell, is that Orwell *was* a writer, and artist, who can mistakenly be seen as offering an unmediated account of actual biographical experience, and who must instead be seen as using a highly developed literary skill—including a style of the utmost lucidity and simplicity—to produce works of art that are "highly selective and purposive," and that are none the less works of art for being so.

All this is poignantly dramatized by Orwell's reassumption on his deathbed of his own civil identity: the life of the artist, for which he had needed the distancing of the pseudonym, is over. In "Why I Write" Orwell makes his purpose as a writer perfectly clear. Enumerating what seemed to him the various motives for writing ("Sheer Egoism"; "Aesthetic Enthusiasm"; "Historical Impulse," i.e., to "find out true facts and store them up for the use of posterity"; and "Political purpose. . . . Desire to push the world in a certain direction, to alter other people's idea of the kind of society that they should strive after."), he declares that although by nature he was a person in whom the first three motives would outweigh the fourth, he was forced by the times in which he lived to become "a sort of pamphleteer." He goes on to describe the various phases of his early life, such as we have mentioned above, including "poverty and a sense of failure," and the increasingly strong impact upon him, during the 1930s, of political events—"Hitler, the Spanish civil war, etc.," until "the Spanish war and other events in 1936–37 turned the scale and thereafter I knew where I stood. Every line of serious work that I have written since 1936 has been written, directly or indirectly, *against* totalitarianism and *for* democratic Socialism, as I understand it." Fair enough: but it does *not* mean that the writing was devoid of artistry, or even of artistic indirection or selectivity. Nor should we forget his account, in the same essay, of a habit that began in his school days,

going on at the same time that he was writing the usual things demanded by school occasions and that continued for fifteen years: "a literary exercise of quite a different kind: this was the making up of a continuous 'story' about myself, a sort of diary existing only in the mind. . . . This habit continued till I was about twenty-five, right through my non-literary years."

George Orwell, who published his first book in 1933 and who died in 1950, is placed in this book at the beginning of the section that carries the story of British literature on after 1950 because his books deal explicitly and directly with social issues and conditions in a way that makes him the forerunner of the writers of the fifties rather than with the more subjectively oriented writers of the Modern period as we have defined it. Only it should be emphasized—as the whole question of the pseudonym and the purposefully adopted identity may show—that the reportorial simplicity and directness of his work are to be taken not as naïve and unavoidable. They were elements of a style and approach that were themselves consciously chosen, after what may have been a period of painful gestation of George Orwell's entire literary character, as being best fitted to what he saw as the necessary aim of a writer whose conscience forbade him to turn his back on the social evils and the sinister historical direction of his time.

TEXTS: Orwell is best known, as we have said, and on a widely international scale, for his two novels of political satire: the anti-Stalinist *Animal Farm* (1946, but completed by 1944, a year in which it was difficult to find a publisher for it in England) and *Nineteen Eighty-Four* (1949); but his other novels are fully as interesting and ought not to be overlooked: *Burmese Days* (1934), *A Clergyman's Daughter* (1935), *Keep the Aspidistra Flying* (1936), and *Coming up for Air* (1939). The last two, especially, might be seen as the prototype for many of the novels of relaxed social observation—including the two novels that usually *are* seen as inaugurating the trend, Amis's *Lucky Jim* and John Wain's *Hurry on Down* (both 1953)—that have been such a prominent feature of the literature of the 1950s and after. The books of direct nonfictional analysis or historical report begin with Orwell's first book, *Down and Out in Paris and London* (1933), the category including *The Road to Wigan Pier* (1937), *Homage to Catalonia* (1938), and *The Lion and the Unicorn* (1941).

Orwell's essays appeared in two collections during his lifetime, *Inside the Whale* (1940) and *Critical Essays* (London, 1946; published in New York, in the same year, under the title *Dickens, Dali and Others*). Further collections published after his death were *Shooting an Elephant* (1950), *Such, Such Were the Joys* (1953), *England Your England* (1953), and *Collected Essays* (1961). In 1968 appeared the indispensable *Collected Essays, Journalism and Letters of George Orwell,* in four volumes, edited by Sonia Orwell and Ian Angus. Critical interest in Orwell, far from dying down after his death, has increased in intensity, so that it is possible to list here only a tithe of the many books about him and his work that are now available. The recent biographical study by Stansky and Abrahams has been cited above. For reminiscences and impressions of Orwell by those who knew him, see Cyril Connolly, *Enemies of Promise* (1939); Anthony Powell, "George Orwell: A Memoir," in *The Atlantic Monthly,* October 1967; Julian Symons, "Orwell: A Reminiscence," *London Magazine,* September 1963; and Rayner Heppenstall, *Four Absentees* (1960). Among the critical works to be consulted first are: Christopher Hollis, *A Study of George Orwell: The Man and His Works* (1956); Sir Richard Rees, *George Orwell: Fugitive from the Camp of Victory* (1961); George Woodcock, *The Crystal Spirit: A Study of George Orwell* (1966); and Richard Voorhees, *The Paradox of George Orwell* (1961). The pamphlet-length general introduction to Orwell, in the "Writers and Their Work" series published for the British Council and the National Book League, is by Tom Hopkinson (1953). *The World of George Orwell,* illustrated with many photographs, is edited by Miriam Gross (1971).

Politics and the English Language

Most people who bother with the matter at all would admit that the English language is in a bad way, but it is generally assumed that we cannot by conscious action do anything about it. Our civilization is decadent and our language —so the argument runs—must inevitably share in the general collapse. It follows that any struggle against the abuse of language is a sentimental archaism, like preferring candles to electric light or hansom cabs to aeroplanes. Underneath this lies the half-conscious belief that language is a natural growth and not an instrument which we shape for our own purposes.

Now, it is clear that the decline of a language must ultimately have political and economic causes: it is not due simply to the bad influence of this or that individual writer. But an effect can become a cause, reinforcing the original cause and producing the same effect in an intensified form, and so on indefinitely. A man may take to drink because he feels himself to be a failure, and then fail all the more completely because he drinks. It is rather the same thing that is happening to the English language. It becomes ugly and inaccurate because our thoughts are foolish, but the slovenliness of our language makes it easier for us to have foolish thoughts. The point is that the process is reversible. Modern English, especially written English, is full of bad habits which spread by imitation and which can be avoided if one is willing to take the necessary trouble. If one gets rid of these habits one can think more clearly, and to think clearly is a necessary first step towards political regeneration: so that the fight against bad English is not frivolous and is not the exclusive concern of professional writers. I will come back to this presently, and I hope that by that time the meaning of what I have said here will have become clearer. Meanwhile, here are five specimens of the English language as it is now habitually written.

These five passages have not been picked out because they are especially bad—I could have quoted far worse if I had chosen—but because they illustrate various of the mental vices from which we now suffer. They are a little below the average, but are fairly representative samples. I number them so that I can refer back to them when necessary:

"(*1*) *I am not, indeed, sure whether it is not true to say that the Milton who once seemed not unlike a seventeenth-century Shelley had not become, out of an experience ever more bitter in each year, more alien* [sic] *to the founder of that Jesuit sect which nothing could induce him to tolerate.*"

Professor Harold Laski
(*Essay in* Freedom of Expression)

"(*2*) *Above all, we cannot play ducks and drakes with a native battery of idioms which prescribes such egregious collocations of vocables as the* Basic *put up with* for *tolerate* or *put at a loss* for *bewilder.*"

Professor Lancelot Hogben (Interglossa)

"(*3*) *On the one side we have the free personality: by definition it is not neurotic, for it has neither conflict nor dream. Its desires, such as they are, are transparent, for they are just what institu-*

tional approval keeps in the forefront of consciousness; another institutional pattern would alter their number and intensity; there is little in them that is natural, irreducible, or culturally dangerous. But on the other side, the social bond itself is nothing but the mutual reflection of these self-secure integrities. Recall the definition of love. Is not this the very picture of a small academic? Where is there a place in this hall of mirrors for either personality or fraternity?"

Essay on Psychology in Politics *(New York)*

"*(4) All the 'best people' from the gentlemen's clubs, and all the frantic fascist captains, united in common hatred of Socialism and bestial horror of the rising tide of the mass revolutionary movement, have turned to acts of provocation, to foul incendiarism, to medieval legends of poisoned wells, to legalize their own destruction of proletarian organizations, and rouse the agitated petty-bourgeoisie to chauvinistic fervour on behalf of the fight against the revolutionary way out of the crisis.*"

Communist pamphlet

"*(5) If a new spirit is to be infused into this old country, there is one thorny and contentious reform which must be tackled, and that is the humanization and galvanization of the B.B.C. Timidity here will bespeak canker and atrophy of the soul. The heart of Britain may be sound and of strong beat, for instance, but the British lion's roar at present is like that of Bottom in Shakespeare's* Midsummer Night's Dream—*as gentle as any sucking dove. A virile new Britain cannot continue indefinitely to be traduced in the eyes or rather ears, of the world by the effete languors of Langham Place, brazenly masquerading as 'standard English'. When the Voice of Britain is heard at nine o'clock, better far and infinitely less ludicrous to hear aitches honestly dropped than the present priggish, inflated, inhibited, school-ma'amish arch braying of blameless bashful mewing maidens!*"

Letter in Tribune

Each of these passages has faults of its own, but, quite apart from avoidable ugliness, two qualities are common to all of them. The first is staleness of imagery: the other is lack of precision. The writer either has a meaning and cannot express it, or he inadvertently says something else, or he is almost indifferent as to whether his words mean anything or not. This mixture of vagueness and sheer incompetence is the most marked characteristic of modern English prose, and especially of any kind of political writing. As soon as certain topics are raised, the concrete melts into the abstract and no one seems able to think of turns of speech that are not hackneyed: prose consists less and less of *words* chosen for the sake of their meaning, and more and more of *phrases* tacked together like the sections of a prefabricated hen-house. I list below, with notes and examples, various of the tricks by means of which the work of prose-construction is habitually dodged:

Dying Metaphors. A newly invented metaphor assists thought by evoking a visual image, while on the other hand a metaphor which is technically "dead" (e.g. *iron resolution*) has in effect reverted to being an ordinary word and can generally be used without loss of vividness. But in between these two classes there is a huge dump of worn-out metaphors which have lost all evocative power and are merely used because they save people the trouble of inventing phrases for themselves. Examples are: *Ring the changes on, take up the cudgels for, toe the line, ride roughshod over, stand shoulder to shoulder with, play into the hands of, no axe to grind, grist to the mill, fishing in troubled waters, on the order of the day, Achilles' heel, swan song, hotbed.* Many of these are used without knowledge of their meaning (what is a "rift," for instance?), and incompatible metaphors are frequently mixed, a sure sign that the writer is not interested in what he is saying. Some metaphors now current have been twisted out of their original meaning without those who use them even being aware of the fact. For example, *toe the line* is sometimes written *tow the line.* Another example is *the hammer and the anvil,* now always used with the implication that the anvil gets the worst of it. In real life it is always the anvil that breaks the hammer, never the other way about: a writer who stopped to think what he was saying would be aware of this, and would avoid perverting the original phrase.

Operators or *Verbal False Limbs.* These save the trouble of picking out appropriate verbs and nouns, and at the same time pad each sentence with extra syllables which give it an appearance of symmetry. Characteristic phrases are: *render inoperative, militate against, make contact with, be subjected to, give rise to, give grounds for, have the effect of, play a leading part (role) in, make itself felt, take effect, exhibit a tendency to, serve the purpose of, etc., etc.* The keynote is the elimination of simple verbs. Instead of being a single word, such as *break, stop, spoil, mend, kill,* a verb becomes a *phrase,* made up of a noun or adjective tacked on to some general-purposes verb such as *prove, serve, form, play, render.* In addition, the passive voice is wherever possible used in preference to the active, and noun constructions are used instead of gerunds (*by examination of* instead of *by examining*). The range of verbs is further cut down by means of the *-ize* and *de-* formations, and the banal statements are given an appearance of profundity by means of the *not un-* formation. Simple conjunctions and prepositions are replaced by such phrases as *with respect to, having regard to, the fact that, by dint of, in view of, in the interests of, on the hypothesis that;* and the ends of sentences are saved from anticlimax by such resounding commonplaces as *greatly to be desired, cannot be left out of account, a development to be expected in the near future, deserving of serious consideration, brought to a satisfactory conclusion,* and so on and so forth.

Pretentious Diction. Words like *phenomenon, element, individual* (as noun), *objective, categorical, effective, virtual, basic, primary, promote, constitute, exhibit, exploit, utilize, eliminate, liquidate,* are used to dress up simple statements and give an air of scientific impartiality to biased judgments. Adjectives like *epoch-making, epic, historic, unforgettable, triumphant, age-old, inevitable, inexorable, veritable,* are used to dignify the sordid processes of international politics, while writing that aims at glorifying war usually takes on an archaic colour, its characteristic words being: *realm, throne, chariot, mailed fist, trident, sword, shield, buckler, banner, jackboot, clarion.* Foreign words and expressions such as *cul de sac, ancien régime, deus ex machina, mutatis mutandis, status quo, gleichschaltung, weltanschauung,* are used to give an air of culture and elegance. Except for the useful abbreviations *i.e., e.g.,* and *etc.,* there is no real need for any of the hundreds of foreign phrases now current in English. Bad writers, and especially scientific, political and sociological writers, are nearly always haunted by the notion that Latin or

Greek words are grander than Saxon ones, and unnecessary words like *expedite, ameliorate, predict, extraneous, deracinated, clandestine, subaqueous* and hundreds of others constantly gain ground from their Anglo-Saxon opposite numbers.[1] The jargon peculiar to Marxist writing (*hyena, hangman, cannibal, petty bourgeois, these gentry, lacquey, flunkey, mad dog, White Guard,* etc.) consists largely of words and phrases translated from Russian, German or French; but the normal way of coining a new word is to use a Latin or Greek root with the appropriate affix and, where necessary, the *-ize* formation. It is often easier to make up words of this kind (*deregionalize, impermissible, extramarital, non-fragmentatory* and so forth) than to think up the English words that will cover one's meaning. The result, in general, is an increase in slovenliness and vagueness.

Meaningless Words. In certain kinds of writing, particularly in art criticism and literary criticism, it is normal to come across long passages which are almost completely lacking in meaning.[2] Words like *romantic, plastic, values, human, dead, sentimental, natural, vitality,* as used in art criticism, are strictly meaningless, in the sense that they not only do not point to any discoverable object, but are hardly ever expected to do so by the reader. When one critic writes, "The outstanding feature of Mr. X's work is its living quality," while another writes, "The immediately striking thing about Mr. X's work is its peculiar deadness," the reader accepts this as a simple difference of opinion. If words like *black* and *white* were involved, instead of the jargon words *dead* and *living,* he would see at once that

---

1 An interesting illustration of this is the way in which the English flower names which were in use till very recently are being ousted by Greek ones, *snapdragon* becoming *antirrhinum, forget-me-not* becoming *myosotis,* etc. It is hard to see any practical reason for this change of fashion: it is probably due to an instinctive turning-away from the more homely word and a vague feeling that the Greek word is scientific. (This footnote and the following are Orwell's.)

2 Example: "Comfort's catholicity of perception and image, strangely Whitmanesque in range, almost the exact opposite in aesthetic compulsion, continues to evoke that trembling atmospheric accumulative hinting at a cruel, an inexorably serene timelessness . . . Wrey Gardiner scores by aiming at simple bull's-eyes with precision. Only they are not so simple, and through this contented sadness runs more than the surface bitter-sweet of resignation." (*Poetry Quarterly.*)

language was being used in an improper way. Many political words are similarly abused. The word *Fascism* has now no meaning except in so far as it signifies "something not desirable." The words *democracy, socialism, freedom, patriotic, realistic, justice,* have each of them several different meanings which cannot be reconciled with one another. In the case of a word like *democracy,* not only is there no agreed definition, but the attempt to make one is resisted from all sides. It is almost universally felt that when we call a country democratic we are praising it: consequently the defenders of every kind of régime claim that it is a democracy, and fear that they might have to stop using the word if it were tied down to any one meaning. Words of this kind are often used in a consciously dishonest way. That is, the person who uses them has his own private definition, but allows his hearer to think he means something quite different. Statements like *Marshal Pétain was a true patriot, The Soviet Press is the freest in the world, The Catholic Church is opposed to persecution,* are almost always made with intent to deceive. Other words used in variable meanings, in most cases more or less dishonestly, are: *class, totalitarian, science, progressive, reactionary, bourgeois, equality.*

Now that I have made this catalogue of swindles and perversions, let me give another example of the kind of writing that they lead to. This time it must of its nature be an imaginary one. I am going to translate a passage of good English into modern English of the worst sort. Here is a well-known verse from *Ecclesiastes:*

"I returned and saw under the sun, that the race is not to the swift, nor the battle to the strong, neither yet bread to the wise, nor yet riches to men of understanding, nor yet favour to men of skill; but time and chance happeneth to them all."

Here it is in modern English:

"Objective consideration of contemporary phenomena compels the conclusion that success or failure in competitive activities exhibits no tendency to be commensurate with innate capacity, but that a considerable element of the unpredictable must invariably be taken into account."

This is a parody, but not a very gross one. Exhibit (3), above, for instance, contains several patches of the same kind of English. It will be seen that I have not made a full translation. The beginning and ending of the sentence follow the orginal meaning fairly closely, but in the middle the concrete illustrations—race, battle, bread—dissolve into the vague phrase "success or failure in competitive activities." This had to be so, because no modern writer of the kind I am discussing—no one capable of using phrases like "objective consideration of contemporary phenomena"—would ever tabulate his thoughts in that precise and detailed way. The whole tendency of modern prose is away from concreteness. Now analyse these two sentences a little more closely. The first contains forty-nine words but only sixty syllables, and all its words are those of everyday life. The second contains thirty-eight words of ninety syllables: eighteen of its words are from Latin roots, and one from Greek. The first sentence contains six vivid images, and only one phrase ("time and chance") that could be called vague. The second contains not a single fresh, arresting phrase, and in spite of its ninety syllables it gives only a shortened version of the meaning contained in the first. Yet without a doubt it is the second kind of sentence that is gaining ground in modern English. I do not want to exaggerate. This kind of writing is not yet universal, and outcrops of simplicity will occur here and there in the worst-written page. Still, if you or I were told to write a few lines on the uncertainty of human fortunes, we should probably come much nearer to my imaginary sentence than to the one from *Ecclesiastes.*

As I have tried to show, modern writing at its worst does not consist in picking out words for the sake of their meaning and inventing images in order to make the meaning clearer. It consists in gumming together long strips of words which have already been set in order by someone else, and making the results presentable by sheer humbug. The attraction of this way of writing is that it is easy. It is easier—even quicker, once you have the habit—to say *In my opinion it is a not unjustifiable assumption that* than to say *I think.* If you use ready-made phrases, you not only don't have to hunt about for words; you also don't have to bother with the rhythms of your sentences, since these phrases are generally so arranged as to be more or less euphonious. When you are composing in a hurry

—when you are dictating to a stenographer, for instance, or making a public speech—it is natural to fall into a pretentious, Latinized style. Tags like *a consideration which we should do well to bear in mind* or *a conclusion to which all of us would readily assent* will save many a sentence from coming down with a bump. By using stale metaphors, similes and idioms, you save much mental effort, at the cost of leaving your meaning vague, not only for your reader but for yourself. This is the significance of mixed metaphors. The sole aim of a metaphor is to call up a visual image. When these images clash—as in *The Fascist octopus has sung its swan song, the jackboot is thrown into the melting pot*—it can be taken as certain that the writer is not seeing a mental image of the objects he is naming; in other words he is not really thinking. Look again at the examples I gave at the beginning of this essay. Professor Laski (1) uses five negatives in fifty-three words. One of these is superfluous, making nonsense of the whole passage, and in addition there is the slip *alien* for akin, making further nonsense, and several avoidable pieces of clumsiness which increase the general vagueness. Professor Hogben (2) plays ducks and drakes with a battery which is able to write prescriptions, and, while disapproving of the everyday phrase *put up with,* is unwilling to look *egregious* up in the dictionary and see what it means. (3), if one takes an uncharitable attitude towards it, is simply meaningless: probably one could work out its intended meaning by reading the whole of the article in which it occurs. In (4), the writer knows more or less what he wants to say, but an accumulation of stale phrases chokes him like tea leaves blocking a sink. In (5), words and meaning have almost parted company. People who write in this manner usually have a general emotional meaning—they dislike one thing and want to express solidarity with another—but they are not interested in the detail of what they are saying. A scrupulous writer, in every sentence that he writes, will ask himself at least four questions, thus: What am I trying to say? What words will express it? What image or idiom will make it clearer? Is this image fresh enough to have an effect? And he will probably ask himself two more: Could I put it more shortly? Have I said anything that is avoidably ugly? But you are not obliged to go to all this trouble. You can shirk it by simply throwing your mind open and letting the ready-made phrases come crowding in. They will construct your sentences for you—even think your thoughts for you, to a certain extent—and at need they will perform the important service of partially concealing your meaning even from yourself. It is at this point that the special connection between politics and the debasement of language becomes clear.

In our time it is broadly true that political writing is bad writing. Where it is not true, it will generally be found that the writer is some kind of rebel, expressing his private opinions and not a "party line." Orthodoxy, of whatever colour, seems to demand a lifeless, imitative style. The political dialects to be found in pamphlets, leading articles, manifestos, White Papers and the speeches of under-secretaries do, of course, vary from party to party, but they are all alike in that one almost never finds in them a fresh, vivid, home-made turn of speech. When one watches some tired hack on the platform mechanically repeating the familiar phrases—*bestial atrocities, iron heel, bloodstained tyranny, free peoples of the world, stand shoulder to shoulder*—one often has a curious feeling that one is not watching a live human being but some kind of dummy: a feeling which suddenly becomes stronger at moments when the light catches the speaker's spectacles and turns them into blank discs which seem to have no eyes behind them. And this is not altogether fanciful. A speaker who uses that kind of phraseology has gone some distance towards turning himself into a machine. The appropriate noises are coming out of his larynx, but his brain is not involved as it would be if he were choosing his words for himself. If the speech he is making is one that he is accustomed to make over and over again, he may be almost unconscious of what he is saying, as one is when one utters the responses in church. And this reduced state of consciousness, if not indispensable, is at any rate favourable to political conformity.

In our time, political speech and writing are largely the defence of the indefensible. Things like the continuance of British rule in India, the Russian purges and deportations, the dropping of the atom bombs on Japan, can indeed be defended, but only by arguments which are too brutal for most people to face, and which do not square with the professed aims of political parties. Thus political language has to consist largely of euphemism, question-begging and sheer cloudy vagueness. Defenceless villages are bombarded from the air, the inhabitants driven out into the countryside, the cattle machine-gunned, the huts set on fire with incendiary bullets: this is called *pacification*. Millions of peasants are robbed of their farms and sent trudging along the roads with no more than they can carry: this is called *transfer of population* or *rectification of frontiers*. People are imprisoned for years without trial, or shot in the back of the neck or sent to die of scurvy in Arctic lumber camps: this is called *elimination of unreliable elements*. Such phraseology is needed if one wants to name things without calling up mental pictures of them. Consider for instance some comfortable English professor defending Russian totalitarianism. He cannot say outright, "I believe in killing off your opponents when you can get good results by doing so." Probably, therefore, he will say something like this:

"While freely conceding that the Soviet régime exhibits certain features which the humanitarian may be inclined to deplore, we must, I think, agree that a certain curtailment of the right to political opposition is an unavoidable concomitant of transitional periods, and that the rigours which the Russian people have been called upon to undergo have been amply justified in the sphere of concrete achievement."

The inflated style is itself a kind of euphemism. A mass of Latin words falls upon the facts like soft snow, blurring the outlines and covering up all the details. The great enemy of clear language is insincerity. When there is a gap between one's real and one's declared aims, one turns as it were instinctively to long words and exhausted idioms, like a cuttlefish squirting out ink. In our age there is no such thing as "keeping out of politics." All issues are political issues, and politics itself is a mass of lies, evasions, folly, hatred and schizophrenia. When the general atmosphere is bad, language must suffer. I should expect to find—this is a guess which I have not sufficient knowledge to verify—that the German, Russian and Italian languages have all deteriorated in the last ten or fifteen years, as a result of dictatorship.

But if thought corrupts language, language can also corrupt thought. A bad usage can spread by tradition and imitation, even among people who should and do know better. The debased language that I have been discussing is in some ways very convenient. Phrases like *a not unjustifiable assumption, leaves much to be desired, would serve no good purpose, a consideration which we should do well to bear in mind,* are a continuous temptation, a packet of aspirins always at one's elbow. Look back through this essay, and for certain you will find that I have again and again committed the very faults I am protesting against. By this morning's post I have received a pamphlet dealing with conditions in Germany. The author tells me that he "felt impelled" to write it. I open it at random, and here is almost the first sentence that I see: "(The Allies) have an opportunity not only of achieving a radical transformation of Germany's social and political structure in such a way as to avoid a nationalistic reaction in Germany itself, but at the same time of laying the foundations of a co-operative and unified Europe." You see, he "feels impelled" to write—feels, presumably, that he has something new to say—and yet his words, like cavalry horses answering the bugle, group themselves automatically into the familiar dreary pattern. This invasion of one's mind by ready-made phrases (*lay the foundations, achieve a radical transformation*) can only be prevented if one is constantly on guard against them, and every such phrase anaesthetizes a portion of one's brain.

I said earlier that the decadence of our language is probably curable. Those who deny this would argue, if they produced an argument at all, that language merely reflects existing social conditions, and that we cannot influence its development by any direct tinkering with words and constructions. So far as the general tone or spirit of a language goes, this may be true, but it is not true in detail. Silly words and expressions have often disappeared, not through any evolutionary process but owing to the conscious action of a minority. Two recent examples were *explore every avenue* and *leave no stone unturned,* which were killed by the jeers of a few journalists. There is a long list of flyblown metaphors which could similarly be got rid of if enough people would interest themselves in the job; and it should also be possible to laugh the *not un-* formation out of existence,[3] to reduce the amount of Latin and Greek in the average sen-

[3] One can cure oneself of the *not un-* formation by memorizing this sentence: *A not unblack dog was chasing a not unsmall rabbit across a not ungreen field.* [Orwell's note.]

tence, to drive out foreign phrases and strayed scientific words, and, in general, to make pretentiousness unfashionable. But all these are minor points. The defence of the English language implies more than this, and perhaps it is best to start by saying what it does *not* imply.

To begin with it has nothing to do with archaism, with the salvaging of obsolete words and turns of speech, or with the setting up of a "standard English" which must never be departed from. On the contrary, it is especially concerned with the scrapping of every word or idiom which has outworn its usefulness. It has nothing to do with correct grammar and syntax, which are of no importance so long as one makes one's meaning clear, or with the avoidance of Americanisms, or with having what is called a "good prose style." On the other hand it is not concerned with fake simplicity and the attempt to make written English colloquial. Nor does it even imply in every case preferring the Saxon word to the Latin one, though it does imply using the fewest and shortest words that will cover one's meaning. What is above all needed is to let the meaning choose the word, and not the other way about. In prose, the worst thing one can do with words is to surrender to them. When you think of a concrete object, you think wordlessly, and then, if you want to describe the thing you have been visualizing you probably hunt about till you find the exact words that seem to fit it. When you think of something abstract you are more inclined to use words from the start, and unless you make a conscious effort to prevent it, the existing dialect will come rushing in and do the job for you, at the expense of blurring or even changing your meaning. Probably it is better to put off using words as long as possible and get one's meaning as clear as one can through pictures or sensations. Afterwards one can choose —not simply *accept*—the phrases that will best cover the meaning, and then switch round and decide what impression one's words are likely to make on another person. This last effort of the mind cuts out all stale or mixed images, all prefabricated phrases, needless repetitions, and humbug and vagueness generally. But one can often be in doubt about the effect of a word or a phrase, and one needs rules that one can rely on when instinct fails. I think the following rules will cover most cases:

(i) Never use a metaphor, simile or other figure of speech which you are used to seeing in print.

(ii) Never use a long word where a short one will do.

(iii) If it is possible to cut a word out, always cut it out.

(iv) Never use the passive where you can use the active.

(v) Never use a foreign phrase, a scientific word or a jargon word if you can think of an everyday English equivalent.

(vi) Break any of these rules sooner than say anything outright barbarous.

These rules sound elementary, and so they are, but they demand a deep change of attitude in anyone who has grown used to writing in the style now fashionable. One could keep all of them and still write bad English, but one could not write the kind of stuff that I quoted in those five specimens at the beginning of this article.

I have not here been considering the literary use of language, but merely language as an instrument for expressing and not for concealing or preventing thought. Stuart Chase and others have come near to claiming that all abstract words are meaningless, and have used this as a pretext for advocating a kind of political quietism. Since you don't know what Fascism is, how can you struggle against Fascism? One need not swallow such absurdities as this, but one ought to recognize that the present political chaos is connected with the decay of language, and that one can probably bring about some improvement by starting at the verbal end. If you simplify your English, you are freed from the worst follies of orthodoxy. You cannot speak any of the necessary dialects, and when you make a stupid remark its stupidity will be obvious, even to yourself. Political language—and with variations this is true of all political parties, from Conservatives to Anarchists—is designed to make lies sound truthful and murder respectable, and to give an appearance of solidity to pure wind. One cannot change this all in a moment, but one can at least change one's own habits, and from time to time one can even, if one jeers loudly enough, send some worn-out and useless phrase—some *jackboot, Achilles' heel, hotbed, melting pot, acid test, veritable inferno* or other lump of verbal refuse—into the dustbin where it belongs.

Kingsley Amis

1922–

Kingsley Amis was born in Clapham, a district of London, and educated at St. John's College, Oxford. He has taught English at University College, Swansea, at Cambridge, and has been a visiting professor at various American colleges.

Amis, although he is best known as a novelist, has written poetry and critical essays as well. His poems have so far appeared in three collections: *A Case of Samples: Poems 1946–56* (1957), *A Look Round the Estate: Poems 1957–67* (1967), and *The Evans Country* (1967). Some of the critical essays he has contributed to journals and reviews are published under the title *What Became of Jane Austen? and Other Questions* (1970). His interest in the late Ian Fleming's James Bond has produced not only *The James Bond Dossier,* but also a further James Bond adventure, *Colonel Sun,* published under the pseudonym David Markham. There is a volume of short stories, *My Enemy's Enemy* (1962), from which the following selection is taken. Since *Lucky Jim* (1953), his first novel, which immediately drew the attention of readers and critics to Amis, he has published a number of other novels, including *That Uncertain Feeling* (1956), *I Like It Here* (1958), *Take a Girl Like You* (1960), *The Egyptologists* (with Robert Conquest, 1965), *The Anti-Death League* (1966), *I Want It Now* (1968), and *Girl, 20* (1971).

Interesting Things

Gloria Davies crossed the road towards the Odeon on legs that weaved a little, as if she was tipsy or rickety. She wasn't either really; it was just the high-heeled shoes, worn for the first time specially for today. The new hoop earrings swayed from her lobes, hitting her rhythmically on the jaws as she walked. No. They were wrong. They had looked fine in her bedroom mirror, but they were wrong, somehow. She whipped them off and stuffed them into her handbag. Perhaps there'd be a chance to try them again later, when it was the evening. They might easily make all the difference then.

She stopped thinking about the earrings when she found she couldn't see Mr. Huws-Evans anywhere in the crowd of people waiting for their friends on the steps of the Odeon. She knew at once then that he hadn't really meant it. After all, what could an Inspector of Taxes (Assessment Section) see in an eighteen-year-old comptometer operator? How stuck-up she'd been, congratulating herself on being the first girl in the office Mr. Huws-Evans had ever asked out. Just then a tall man who'd been standing close by took off his beige mackintosh hat with a drill-like movement, keeping his elbow close to his chest. It was Mr. Huws-Evans.

"Hallo, Gloria," he said. He watched her for a bit, a smile showing round the curly stem of the pipe he was biting. Then he added: "Didn't you recognise me, Gloria?"

"Sorry, Mr. Huws-Evans, I sort of just didn't see you." The hat and the pipe had put her off completely, and she was further confused by being called Gloria twice already.

He nodded, accepting her apology and explanation. He put his hat on again with a ducking gesture, then removed his pipe. "Shall we go in? Don't want to miss the News."

While Mr. Huws-Evans bought two two-and-fourpennies Gloria noticed he was carrying a string bag full of packets of potato crisps. She wondered why he was doing that.

It was very dark inside the cinema itself, and Mr. Huws-Evans had to click his fingers for a long time, and tremendously loudly, before an usherette came. The Odeon was often full on a Saturday when the football team was playing away, and Gloria and Mr. Huws-Evans couldn't help pushing past a lot of people to get to their seats. A good deal of loud sighing, crackling of sweet-packets and uncoiling of embraces marked their progress. At last they were settled in full view of the screen, on which the Duke of Edinburgh was playing polo. Mr. Huws-Evans asked Gloria loudly whether she could see all right, and when she whispered that she could he offered her a chocolate. "They're rather good," he said.

Almost nothing happened while the films were shown. The main feature was on first. As soon as Gloria could tell that it was old-fashioned she was afraid she wouldn't enjoy it. Nobody did anything in it, they just talked. Some of the talking made Mr. Huws-Evans laugh for a long time at a time, and once or twice he nudged Gloria.

When he did this she laughed too, because it was up to her to be polite and not spoil his pleasure. The film ended with a lot of fuss about a Gladstone bag and people falling into each other's arms in a daft, put-on way.

Gloria kept wondering if Mr. Huws-Evans was going to put his arm around her. She'd never yet gone to the pictures in male company without at least this happening, and usually quite a lot more being tried on, but somehow Mr. Huws-Evans didn't seem the man for any of that. He was older than her usual escorts, to start with, and to go on with there was something about that mackintosh hat and that string bag which made it hard to think of him putting his arm round anyone, except perhaps his mother. Once she caught sight of his hand dangling over the arm of the seat towards her, and she moved her own hand carefully so that he could take hold of it easily if he wanted to, but he didn't. He leaned rather closer to her to light her cigarettes than he strictly needed to, and that was all.

After a pair of tin gates had been shown opening in a slow and dignified way, there was about half an hour of advertisements while everybody whistled the tunes that were playing. The cereals and the detergents came up, then a fairly long and thorough episode about razor-blades. During it Mr. Huws-Evans suddenly said: "It's a damned scandal, that business."

"What's that, then?"

"Well, all this business about the modern shave. All these damned gadgets and things. It's just a way of trying to get you to use a new blade every day, that's all."

"Oh, I get you. You mean because the——"

"Mind you, with the kind of blade some of these firms turn out you've got to use a new blade. I grant them that." He laughed briefly. "If you don't want to skin yourself getting the beard off, that is. And of course they don't give a damn how much they spend on publicity. It's all off tax. Doesn't really cost them a bean."

Gloria was going to say "How's that, then?" but Mr. Huws-Evans's manner, that of one with a comprehensive explanation on instant call, warned her not to. She said instead: "No, of course it doesn't."

He looked at her with mingled scepticism and wistfulness, and ended the conversation by saying violently: "Some of these firms."

While the lights went down again, Gloria thought about this brief exchange. It was just the kind of talk older men went in for, the sort of thing her father discussed with his butties when they called to take him down to the pub, things to do with the Government and pensions and jobs and the Russians, things that fellows who went dancing never mentioned. She saw, on the other hand, that that kind of talk wasn't only tied up in some way with getting old, it also had to do with having money and a car, with speaking properly and with being important. So a girl would show herself up for a lump with no conversation and bad manners if she gave away to an older man the fact that uninteresting things didn't interest her. Next time Mr. Huws-Evans got on to them she must do better.

The second film promised to be full of interesting things. There were some lovely dresses, the star looked just like another star Gloria had often wished she looked like, and there was a scene in a kind of flash night-club with dim lights, men in tail coats and a modern band. The star was wearing a terrific evening dress with sequins and had a white fur round her shoulders. A man with a smashing profile sitting at the bar turned and saw her. Her eyes met his for a long moment. Gloria swallowed and leant forward in her seat.

Mr. Huws-Evans nudged Gloria and said: "Don't think much of this, do you? What about some tea?"

"Oh, we haven't got to go yet, have we?"

"Well, we don't want to sit all through this, do we?"

Gloria recollected herself. "No, right you are, then."

They moved effortfully back along the row, taking longer this time because some of the embraces were slower in uncoiling. In the foyer, Gloria said: "Well, thank you very much, Mr. Huws-Evans, I enjoyed the film ever so much," but he wasn't listening; he was looking wildly about as if he'd just found himself in a ladies' cloakroom, and beginning to say: "The crisps. I've left them inside."

"Never mind, don't you worry, it won't take a minute fetching them. I don't mind waiting at all."

He stared out at her from under the mackintosh hat, which he'd pulled down for some reason so that it hid his eyebrows. "I shan't be able to remember the seat. You come too, Gloria. Please."

After a lot more finger-clicking inside they found the row. In the beam of the usherette's torch Gloria saw that their seats were already occupied. Even more slowly than before, Mr. Huws-Evans began shuffling sidelong away from her; there was some disturbance. Gloria, waiting in the aisle, turned and looked at the screen. The man with the profile was dancing with the star now and all the other people had gone back to their tables and were watching them. Gloria watched them too, and had forgotten where she was when a moderate uproar slowly broke out and slowly moved towards her. It was Mr. Huws-Evans with the crisps, which were rustling and crunching like mad. Men's voices were denouncing him, some of them loudly and one of the loud ones using words Gloria didn't like, in fact one word was the word she called "that word." Her cheeks went hot. Mr. Huws-Evans was saying things like "Very sorry, old boy" and "Hurts me as much as it hurts you," and every so often he laughed cheerily. Everywhere people were calling "Ssshh." Gloria couldn't think of anything to do to help.

A long time later they were outside again. It was clear at once that the rain had stopped holding off hours ago. Mr. Huws-Evans took her arm and said they'd better run for it, and that was what they did. They ran a long way for it, and fast too, so that the high heels were doing some terrible slipping and skidding. Opposite Woolworth's Gloria nearly did the splits, but Mr. Huws-Evans prevented that, and was just as effective when she started a kind of sliding football tackle towards a lady in bifocal glasses carrying a little boy. That was just outside Bevan & Bevan's, and Gloria didn't mind it much because she'd guessed by now that they were going to Dalessio's, a fairly flash Italian restaurant frequented by the car-owning classes—unless, of course, they were making for Cwmbwrla or Portardulais on foot.

There was a queue in Dalessio's and Gloria panted out the news that she was going to the cloakroom, where there was another, but shorter, queue. While she waited her turn she felt her hair, which must have been looking dreadful, and wondered about her face, to which she'd applied some of the new liquid make-up everyone was talking about. She was glad to find, in due

time, that she hadn't been looking too bad. Touching up with the liquid stuff didn't quite provide the amazing matt finish the advertisements described, in fact she wondered if she didn't look a bit like one of the waxworks she'd seen that time in Cardiff, but there was no time to re-do it and it must surely wear off a little after a bit. She gazed longingly at the earrings in her bag, and at the new mascara kit, but these must certainly wait. Taking a last peep at herself, she reflected gratefully, as her father had often exhorted her to do, that she was very lucky to be quite pretty and have all that naturally curly naturally blonde hair.

Mr. Huws-Evans had a table for two when she joined him. He took the bag of crisps off her chair and laid them reverently at his side. Gloria thought he seemed very attached to them. What did he want them for, and so many of them too? It was a puzzle. Perhaps he guessed her curiosity, because he said: "They're for the party. They said I was to get them."

"Oh, I see. Who'll be there? At the party? You did tell me when you asked me, but I'm afraid I've forgotten."

"Not many people you'll know, I'm afraid. There'll be Mr. Pugh, of course, from Allowances, and his wife, and Miss Harry from Repayments, and my brother—you've met him, haven't you?— and my dentist and his, er, and his friend, and two or three of my brother's friends. About a dozen altogether."

"It sounds lovely," Gloria said. A little tremor of excitement ran through her; then she remembered about poise. She arranged herself at the table like one of the models who showed off jewellery on TV, and purposely took a long while deciding what to have when the waitress came, though she'd known ever since passing Bevan & Bevan's that she was going to have mixed grill, with French fried potatoes. She was soon so lost in thoughts of the party and in enjoying eating that it was like a voice in a dream when Mr. Huws-Evans said:

"Of course, the real difficulties come when we have to decide whether something's income or capital."

Gloria looked up, trying not to seem startled. "Oh yes."

"For instance," Mr. Huws-Evans went on, drawing a long fishbone from his mouth, "take the case of a man who buys a house, lives in it for a bit and then sells it. Any profit he might make wouldn't be assessable. It's capital, not income."

"So he wouldn't have to pay tax on it, is that right?"

"Now for goodness' sake don't go and get that mixed up with the tax on the property itself, the Schedule A tax."

"Oh yes, I've heard of that. There were some figures I——"

"That still has to be paid." He leaned forward in an emphatic way. "Unless the man is exempt, of course."

"Oh yes."

"Now it'd be much easier, as you can imagine, to catch him on the sale of several houses. But even then we'd need to show that there was a trade. If the chap simply buys them as investments, just to get the rents, well then you couldn't catch him if he sold out later at a profit. There'd be no trade, you see."

"No." Gloria swallowed a mushroom-stalk whole. "No trade."

"That's right." He nodded and seemed pleased, then changed his tone to nonchalant indulgence. "Mind you, even the profit on an isolated transaction could be an income profit. There was the case of three chaps who bought some South African brandy, had it shipped over here and blended with French brandy, and sold it at a profit. But the Court still said there was a trade. They'd set up a selling organisation."

"Ah, I get it."

"You'll be perfectly all right just so long as you remember that income tax is a tax on income."

Gloria felt a little dashed when Mr. Huws-Evans found nothing to add to his last maxim. She hadn't spoken up enough and shown she was taking an interest. He couldn't just go on talking, with nobody helping to make it a proper conversation. And yet—what could she have said? It was so hard to think of things.

Mr. Huws-Evans launched off again soon and she cheered up. He questioned her about herself and her parents and friends and what she did in the evenings. He watched her with his big brown eyes and tended to raise his eyebrows slowly when she got near the end of each bit she said. Then, before asking his next question,

he'd let his eyes go vacant, and drop his jaw without opening his mouth at all, and nod slightly, as if each reply of hers was tying up, rather disturbingly, with some fantastic theory about her he'd originally made up for fun: that she was a Communist spy, say, or a goblin in human form. During all this he dismantled, cleaned, reassembled, filled and lit his pipe, finally tamping down the tobacco with his thumb and burning himself slightly.

At last it was time to go. In the street Gloria said: "Well, thank you very much, Mr. Huws-Evans, I enjoyed the food ever so much," but he wasn't listening; he was rubbing his chin hard with some of his fingers, and beginning to say: "Shave. Got to have a shave before the party. That blade this morning."

They boarded a bus and went a long way on it. Mr. Huws-Evans explained, quoting figures, that a taxi wasn't worth while and that he personally was damned if he was going to lay out all that cash on a car simply to make a splash and impress a few snobs. He paid the conductor with coins from a leather purse that did up with two poppers. This purse, Gloria thought, was somehow rather like the mackintosh hat and the string bag with the crisps. After doing up the purse and putting it safely away Mr. Huws-Evans said that his digs, where the shave was going to happen, were quite near Mr. Pugh's house, which was where the party was going to happen. He added that this would give them just nice time.

They got off the bus and walked for a few minutes. The rain had stopped and the sun was out. Gloria cheered up again, and didn't notice at first when Mr. Huws-Evans suddenly stopped in the middle of the pavement. He was looking about in rather the same way as he'd done in the foyer of the Odeon. He said: "Funny. I could have sworn."

"What's the matter, then?"

"Can't seem to remember the right house. Ridiculous of me, isn't it? Just can't seem to remember at all."

"Not your digs it isn't, where you can't remember, is it?"

"Well yes, my digs. This is it. No, there's no TV aerial."

"Never mind, what's the number?"

"That's the silly part. I don't know the number."

"Oh, but you must. How ever do you manage with letters and things? Come on, you must know. Try and think, now."

"No good. I've never known it."

"What?"

"Well, you see, the landlady's got one of those stamp things to stamp the address at the top of the notepaper and I always use that. And then when I get a letter I just see it's for me and that's all I bother about, see?" He said most of this over his shoulder in the intervals of trying to see through some lace curtains. Then he shook his head and walked on, only to bend forward slightly with hands on knees, like a swimmer waiting for the starting-pistol, and stare at a photograph of a terrier which someone had arranged, thoughtfully turned outward, on a windowsill. "The number's got a three in it, I do know that," he said then. "At least I think so."

"How do you manage as a rule?"

"I know the house, you see."

Mr. Huws-Evans now entered a front garden and put his eye to a gap in the curtains. Quite soon a man in shirtsleeves holding a newspaper twitched the curtain aside and stood looking at him. He was a big man with hair growing up round the base of his neck, and you could guess that he worked at some job where strength was important. Mr. Huws-Evans came out of the garden, latching its gate behind him. "I don't think that's the one," he said.

"Come on, why not just knock somewhere and ask?"

"Can't do that. They'd think I was barmy."

Eventually Mr. Huws-Evans recognised his house by its bright red door. "Eighty-seven," he murmured, studying the number as he went in. "I must remember that."

Gloria sat in the sitting-room, which had more books in it than she'd ever seen in a private house before, and looked at the book Mr. Huws-Evans had dropped into her lap before going up to have his shave. It was called *Income Taxes in the Commonwealth,* and he'd said it would probably interest her.

She found it didn't do that and had gone to see if there were any interesting books in the bookcase when the door opened and an old lady looked in. She and Gloria stared at each other for about half a minute, and Gloria's cheeks felt hot again. The old lady's top lip had vertical furrows and there was something distrustful about her. She gave a few grunts with a puff of breath at the beginning of each one, and went out. Gloria didn't like to touch the bookcase now and told herself that the party would make everything worth while.

When Mr. Huws-Evans came back he had a big red patch on his neck. "These razor-blade firms," he said bitterly, but made no objection when Gloria asked if she could go and wash her hands. He even came to the foot of the stairs to show her the right door.

The liquid make-up looked fine, the mascara went on like distemper on a wall and the earrings were just right now. She only hoped her white blouse and rust cocktail-length skirt, the only clothes she had that were at all evening, were evening enough. When she came out the old lady was there, about thirty inches away. This time she gave more puffing grunts than before and started giving them sooner. She was still giving them when Gloria went downstairs. But then Mr. Huws-Evans, as soon as he saw her, jumped up and said: "You look absolutely stunning, Gloria," so that part was worth while.

After they'd left, what Gloria had been half-expecting all along happened, though not in the way she'd half-expected. It now appeared that they were much too early, and Mr. Huws-Evans took her into a park for a sit-down. Before long he said: "You know, Gloria, it means a lot to me, you coming out with me today."

This was hard to answer, so she just nodded.

"I think you're the prettiest girl I've ever been out with."

"Well, thank you very much, Mr. Huws-Evans."

"Won't you call me Waldo? I wish you would."

"Oh no, I don't think I could, really."

"Why not?"

"I . . . I don't think I know you well enough."

He stared at her with the large brown eyes she'd often admired in the office, but which she now thought looked soft. Sadly, he said: "If only you knew what I feel about you, Gloria, and how much you mean to me. Funny, isn't it? I couldn't have guessed what you were going to do to me, make me feel, I mean, when I first saw you." He lurched suddenly towards her, but drew back at the last minute. "If only you could feel for me just a tiny bit of what I feel for you, you've no idea what it would mean to me."

An approach of this kind was new to Gloria and it flustered her. If, instead of all this daft talk, Mr. Huws-Evans had tried to kiss her, she'd probably have let him, even in this park place; she could have handled that. But all he'd done was make her feel foolish and awkward. Abruptly, she stood up. "I think we ought to be going."

"Oh, not yet. Please. Please don't be offended."

"I'm not offended, honest."

He got up too and stood in front of her. "I'd give anything in the world to think that you didn't think too hardly of me. I feel such a worm."

"Now you're not to talk so silly."

When it was much too late, Mr. Huws-Evans did try to kiss her, saying as he did so: "Oh, my darling."

Gloria side-stepped him. "I'm not your darling," she said decisively.

After that neither spoke until they arrived at the house where the party was. Mr. Huws-Evans's daft talk, Gloria thought, was to be expected from the owner of that mackintosh hat—which he still wore.

When Mr. Huws-Evans's brother caught sight of her their eyes met for a long moment. It was because of him—she'd seen him once or twice when he called in at the office—that she'd accepted Mr. Huws-Evans's invitation. Originally she'd intended just to look at him across the room while she let Mr. Huws-Evans talk to her, but after what had happened she left Mr. Huws-Evans to unpack his crisps and put them in bowls while the brother (it was funny to think that he was Mr. Huws-Evans too, in a way) took her across the room, sat her on a sofa and started talking about interesting things.

Angus Wilson

1913–

Born at Bexhill, Wilson spent part of his childhood in South Africa. He was educated at Westminster School, London, and at Oxford. Between 1942 and 1946 he worked in the Foreign Office, and later in the British Museum, where he was Deputy Superintendent of the Reading Room. He retired in 1955 to devote himself entirely to his writing.

Angus Wilson's novels are: *Hemlock and After* (1952); *Anglo-Saxon Attitudes* (1956); *The Middle Age of Mrs. Eliot* (1958); *The Old Men at the Zoo* (1961); *Late Call* (1964); and *No Laughing Matter* (1967). A third volume of short stories, besides the two mentioned in the introduction, *A Bit off the Map*, was published in 1957; and stories from all three volumes are grouped in *Dance of Death: Twenty-Five Stories* (1969). *The Wild Garden; or, Speaking of Writing* (1963) is a brief autobiographical account in which Wilson talks about the relation of his books to his own life and describes the themes he had in mind in specific novels and stories. He has also written a study of Zola, *Emile Zola: An Introductory Study of His Novels* (1952). There is a brief treatment of Wilson, by K. W. Grandsden, in the "Writers and Their Work" series (1969) and another comparatively brief treatment by J. L. Halio in the "Writers and Critics" series (1964).

What Do Hippos Eat?

She seemed such a little bit of a thing as she peered through the railings at the huge, cumbrous bison, her neat boyish head of short-cut, tight red curls such a contrast to the matted chocolate wool that lay in patches around the beast's long, mournful features. "Ginger for pluck" Maurice always called her, and indeed her well-knit little figure and firm stance were redolent of determination and cheek, and cried out her virtues as a real good pal, her Dead End Kid appeal that went through to the heart.

"My! My!" she said to the bison, "someone forgot to bring his comb." She was such a round-eyed urchin that one felt almost surprised when she did not put out her tongue.

Maurice smiled paternally and fingered his little grey first world war moustache. "How would you like to have a couple of rounds in the ring with that?" he asked laughing.

"Oh! I'd take it on all right," she said, and gave him one of her funny straight looks. She had only two roles with men—tomboy and good scout

—even they were very alike, except that the good scout was full of deep, silent understanding and could hold her drink.

Maurice guffawed, "My God! I believe you would. Size means nothing to you." His admiration was perfectly genuine, for under his ostentatious virility he was a physically timorous man with a taste for the brutal. As he looked appraisingly at her slender shoulders and tight little breasts, he felt wonderfully protective and sentimental. All the same it irked him that he wasn't getting on faster with his scheme. It was true, he reflected, that he hadn't paid a sausage out in rent for the last two months and she'd cashed two stumers for him without batting an eyelid when they came back "R.D."; but now that he'd turned fifty-five he wanted a more secure berth than that. The truth was that Maurice had experienced some unpleasant bouts of giddiness in the mornings recently, and his heart—he called it "the old ticker" even to himself—often missed a beat when he climbed upstairs. Under such circumstances, a partnership in the boarding house—it was his name for legalized use of her capital—would just suit him, with a liberal supply of pocket money for the "dogs." Earls Court wasn't exactly the neighbourhood he would have chosen, indeed, when he remembered his brief residence in Clarges Street, now seen in retrospect as lasting for years, he felt ashamed that he should have sunk so low, but he had known too much of Camden Town and the York Road, Waterloo, in the interval not to count his blessings while they lasted. He was, in fact, worn out with schemes and lies and phoney deals, he slept badly and his nerves were giving way. Temporary setbacks made him act, as now, precipitately.

"It's grand to see you enjoying yourself, Greta," he said. "You ought to be having lots of fun whilst you're still young. It's a damned shame the way you have to work. You had a hard enough life as a kid, God knows, and now this blasted house hanging round your neck. It's too much even for your heavyweight shoulders," and he laughed.

Greta stuck out her chin, "I had my fun all right," she said. "You don't have to be rich to enjoy life as a kid."

"Oh, I know," Maurice replied, with a smile as though she had been referring to hopscotch in the back alley. "You can take it on the chin all right, I'll say that for you. But all the same," he continued with a sigh, "I'd give my right hand to have known you when I still had a bit of money. *I'd* have put an end to all these worries."

Greta had decided not to notice Maurice's remarks for a few moments, so she turned to watch a scarlet ibis wading in the pool behind them.

"Aren't you a lucky bird not to be a hat?" she asked. She had her special brand of humour —the gang at the local called it "Greta's dopey jokes." Then. "You're my only money worry, Maurice Legge," she said, her Manchester accent more emphasized than usual, "and what are you going to do about *that*?"

Self-pity and suppressed anger brought beads of sweat to his temples and he mopped them with the silk handkerchief which he kept in his cuff—an old ex-officer habit, he was always careful to explain. Two pictures flashed before him in quick succession. First, the young ex-subaltern, a possible for the Harlequins; handsome, easy-going; a man to whom stockbrokers offered £2,000 a year jobs on his social contacts alone. Then the other picture—still a handsome man, old and tired now, but unmistakably a gentleman for all the doubtful shifts into which life had forced him—he bent before the cheap snubs and insults of a common little creature, whom the ex-subaltern would not have noticed in a crowd. He could almost hear the commentator say, "Look upon this picture and on *this*," and his eyes filled with tears. This cinematographic representation of life had grown on him in middle age. It was not a surprising phenomenon, since his days were passed in a highly coloured histrionic blur. He would move from Prince's to the Cri, from the Cri to the Troc, from the Troc to Odennino's, trying with a closely-knit web of circumstantial narrative to pull off complicated deals or, at the very least, to cadge a drink from some toughly sentimental whisky-soaking Colonial or American. In the intervals of this "work," he went to the "pictures" or sat before the gasfire of his bed-sitting room working out large betting schemes which he had not the capital to realize, or reading cheap thrillers. Past, present and future, truth and lies, all moved before him in short, vivid, dramatic scenes that merged into a background mist of anxiety, imagined grandeur and sticky sentiment. But behind

it all was a certain hard core of determination to
survive. It was this that made him swallow
Greta's snub and turn to the buffaloes.

"Nice mild-looking fellows, you would say
about those, wouldn't you?" he asked. Greta
looked at their large, brown calf's eyes and their
shapely horns, and nodded.

"How wrong you'd be," said Maurice. "I
shall never forget once up country from Nairobi
going through a village after buffalo had stam-
peded. Not a pleasant sight at all. Harry Brand
was with me and I've never seen a chap turn so
green. 'So help me, God, Maurice,' he said, 'I
shall have to call it a day and turn back.' Funny
thing, really, because he was a beefy sort of cove.
But you remember him, anyhow."

Greta shook her head. "Oh yes you do, darling," said Maurice, "great red-faced fellow we
met one evening outside the Plaza." Greta looked
puzzled but denied it. "I'm sure you did,"
Maurice went on. Then he added thoughtfully,
"But wait a minute though, perhaps you're right.
Yes, you are. I was with Dolly." And, glad to
have checked this point, he returned to Kenya
with renewed ardour.

Greta listened to his stories with rapt attention. However her business acumen and natural
hardness might protect her against his wilder
financial schemes, her pride and delight in his
recounted exploits were for once in her life quite
unselfconsciously childlike. His attraction as a
gentleman was enhanced for her by the cosmopolitan background which every day of their
intimacy revealed a little more. She felt, more
justly than she realized, that it was an authentica-
tion of all that the films had hinted to her. The
digressions, irrelevant ramifications and long-
winded checks of memory in which Maurice indulged might have been expected to bore his
listeners, but strangely enough they were exactly
the features which finally convinced the sceptical,
banishing suspicions of glibness and lending realism to art. To Greta they were the supreme pleasure, for they seemed somehow to involve her
own participation in these exciting adventures.
After all she had, it seemed, only just missed
meeting Harry Brand outside the Plaza. For
Maurice himself they formed a reassurance which
his self-confidence badly needed. He had told so
many stories for so many years, truth and fiction
were so inextricably mixed, that to check a new

falsehood by a poorly remembered old one made
him feel that in some way truth must be involved
somewhere.

As they walked into the Lion House Maurice felt his confidence returning. He was ready
for any audience. And there, gazing at the
Siberian tiger, an audience awaited him—an elderly solicitor and his wife, a working-class
woman with two small children. Maurice began
to talk to Greta in a voice pitched loudly enough
for the others to hear.

"Siberian tiger, eh?" he said. "A present
from our not such dear friends the Russians. He's
a beautiful creature, though. Never had any experience with them myself, but I should think
they might be very ugly customers. Don't you
agree, sir?" he asked the solicitor, who replied
embarrassedly, "Yes, yes, I should imagine so."

"No," said Maurice loudly and self-depre-
catingly. "I've only run across this chap's Indian
cousin who's altogether smaller fry. Most of this
stuff about man-eaters, you know, is a lot of nonsense. No tiger turns to human flesh until he's
too old to hold his own in the jungle."

"Do you hear that, Billy?" said the woman
to her son.

"Oh, yes," Maurice continued, "all these
round-ups of tigers for important people, makes
you laugh if you know about it, half the poor
blighters can hardly stand up with old age. So if
anyone asks you to a tiger shoot, laddy," he said
to the boy, "you can be sure of bringing your
mother back a nice new rug."

"There you are, Billy," said the woman,
"you hear what the gentleman says," and everyone laughed.

Greta felt so proud of Maurice. He looked
so handsome, despite all his wrinkles and
pouches, and the line of his arm appeared so
strong and manly as he gripped the rail in front
of him, that she longed to take his hand in hers
and to stroke it. He had told her so often, however, that physical caresses in public were "just
not done," and she was able now to check herself
in time. Greta was both anxious and quick to
learn as she climbed up the economic ladder, and
she felt it was one of the great advantages of
her relations with Maurice that he could teach
her so much. She no longer said "serviette" or
dropped her shoes off under restaurant tables.
She never went out now without gloves—Mau-

rice's ideas of polite behaviour belonged rather to his early years—but she also no longer blew into them when she took them off. She could hardly guess that he had mixed little with respectable people of any class for over fifteen years, and thus she was able to retain many of her humorous phrases—"he's a smell on the landing to me" was a favourite—without qualms, for Maurice greeted them with a smile. She was jealous sometimes of his larking with waitresses, but he told her not to be suburban, and in any case she felt ready to forgive anything as she watched him finger the knot of his old school tie whilst he studied the menu, and heard him refer to her as "Madam" when he finally gave the order.

As the keeper passed the tiger cage with a bucket of dung Maurice asked him which the biggest lion was now and how many pounds of meat the black leopard consumed in a day. He was one of the older keepers and received Maurice's officer-to-batman manner in a more friendly spirit than was often the case these days. Soon the whole party was being taken behind the scenes to watch a puma cross one of the little bridges to its outdoor cage. Greta felt quite queenly when she saw the respectful manner in which the keeper received Maurice's tip, and she attempted a new charming bow and smile as the party broke up. She even approved Maurice's giving sixpence to the two little children, though in general she did not care to spend her money too lavishly.

Maurice looked ten years younger as they walked away from the Lion House. He had always been interested in wild animals, felt a mastery over them that he lacked with men, and these boyish sensations combined with a genuine aesthetic feeling for their shape and colour were now re-awakened. It was so seldom that he experienced any pleasure divorced from his own schemes and anxieties these days, and his body expanded and revelled in the carefree mood. He stroked the soft nose of the caribou as it pushed through the bars in quest of food. It was not, therefore, surprising that he felt little pleasure in Greta's urchin impudence when she gave the animal the raspberry. But he was too happy to comment on her vulgarity. For her, wild animals were an alarming and remote tribe, that once secured behind bars or in travelling circuses, could be treated as comic turns.

But Greta's thoughts were not, in any case, on the beasts, they were very much upon Maurice. She had seldom felt him so desirable, and it worried her to see the creases of his suit—so overcleaned and repaired—shine in the sunlight. She knew the pitiable state of his few underclothes and threadbare second suit as they reposed in the chest of drawers in a litter of important-looking papers, solicitors' letters, unpaid bills and pawntickets—knew only too well, for in the first weeks of his failure to pay his rent she searched in vain for any saleable articles. Though she could not allow him to handle her money since he was obviously so foolish about business, he *was* her man and she wanted him to look nice. She made up her mind to buy him a whole new outfit. She had done very well out of letting her rooms in the last few years and could afford to spend a little and still leave the good margin in the bank which represented respectability to her. Greta's realism had begun at sixteen as a waitress, Maurice's had never really got going: it was hardly an even match. In her greater sense of reality she was far clearer about what she did and did not want. She wanted a man, and the fact that he was twenty years older did not trouble her, for she liked experience. Nevertheless she did not want to tie herself to someone who might play fast and loose with her savings, nor even perhaps would she want that man at all when he had passed sixty. However if he was not to have her money he should certainly have a suit.

Greta's friendly thoughts, her increased desire for him, communicated themselves to Maurice and, added to his own happy mood, made him walk on air. Tips passed lavishly as they fed the sealions from the rocks—Greta screamed and jumped like a little girl as the shapely, blubbery creatures flopped about her—gave honey to the brown bear—Maurice smiled in his old way as she cried "Who's got a bear behind?"—how devil-may-care he was with a carefully selected snake coiled round his arm! The monkeys rather damped their ardour, for they were both united in their prudish disapproval of certain antics. But an incident in front of the spider monkeys' cage finally broke up their happy mood. They were laughing delightedly as the monkeys snatched the bread they offered and swung away with feet, hands and tails alike, when a young

couple approached the cage. In general Greta
did not care for freaks and there was certainly
something a bit cranky about the young woman's
long, shapeless grey frock and the young man's
corduroys and knapsack. They were, in fact,
R.A.D.A. students at play. But their studied seriousness and carefully beautiful voices impressed
Greta.

"Their movements *are* rather heavenly,"
said the girl. "Almost a ghostlike flitting."

"It's immensely interesting that they should
have developed prehensile tails," said the boy,
and seeing Greta watching him, he smiled the
new shy smile he was developing to play Oswald
in "Ghosts." Greta was completely conquered
and smiled back. Maurice began to talk loudly,
but Greta frowned impatiently, for the boy was
speaking again.

"You see they're really gibbons, at least I
think so," and he smiled shyly again, "and yet
they've developed prehensile tails as well as arms
and legs for swinging. It's a complete vindication
of Lamarck really."

"You do find the oddest things interesting,
darling," said the girl. Greta felt so angry with
her.

"You can always learn something if you
keep your ears open," she said and smiled again
at the boy.

"Come along," said Maurice impatiently.
"We don't want to watch these damned monkeys
all day," but Greta waited a few minutes before
following.

They stood surveying the hideous flat features of the lion-faced baboon in angry silence.
"Why the hell you want to encourage that
damned unwashed long-haired young swine,"
said Maurice, "I can't imagine."

"Because," replied Greta—she snapped like
a turtle when she was annoyed—"I'm willing to
learn from others occasionally."

"And you've got a hell of a lot to learn."

"I fully appreciate the lessons," Greta cried,
"and I hope you appreciate what I pay for them."

Maurice's eyes narrowed with rage. "What
exactly do you mean by that?"

"Two months' rent. That's what I mean by
that, Maurice Legge." He raised his fist as though
to hit her, and she ran from him, calling, "You
keep away from me." An elderly woman turned
to stare at them.

"I'll leave your bloody house to-night," he
shouted. "You'll get your cheque to-morrow
morning."

"Yes," said Greta, "and it'll come back R.D.
by the end of the week."

"You little so-and-so," Maurice cried; it was
one of his favourite phrases. He was trembling
with rage, but behind his anger he could see all
his hopes crumbling. He felt completely at the
end of his tether; a night on the streets at his
age might finish him off. With a tremendous effort he controlled his temper.

"Don't let's be greater fools than God made
us," he said.

Greta watched his collapse with genuine
pity, she felt more than ever determined to look
after him. But first, like all men, he must be
taught a lesson, a lesson for spoilt children. From
the pages of her favourite woman's journal she
recalled the advice, "He will accept you at the
price you put on yourself, so don't make yourself
cheap"—it was not exactly the situation the edi-
tress had in mind, but it seemed to apply.

"No thank you, Maurice. I've had enough.
We're friends if you like, but friends apart," she
felt very pleased with the phrase. Sturdy, jaunty,
independent, she walked away from him, past the
pelicans and the ravens, towards the tunnel.
Maurice stood sullenly for a few minutes, then
he ran after her. He saw her at the far end of the
tunnel and shouted "Greta! Greta!" until his
ears were filled with the echoes. His heart was
pounding heavily and his legs felt like lead. He
noticed the flood level mark and wished he were
under the waters. Greta stood and waited for
him.

"I'm sorry, kiddie," he said, "I can't say
more."

"That's all right," she replied, the perfect
good scout. "Well say no more about it."

They went slowly back through the tunnel
to the tearoom.

The "set" tea with watercress *ad lib* was
like a children's picnic, as they laughed and
teased away the memory of the angry outburst.
Greta was determined to bring back Maurice's
pleasure. She felt sure of her mastery now and
was anxious to erase all trace of the events that
had revealed it. She stuffed herself almost sick
with bread and butter and buns, because he so
delighted to tease her about her "kid's appetite."

"Greedy guts," he said smiling, as she took a second helping of watercress. He was quite sentimental now, as he thought of where he would be without her generosity; she might not be a lady but she certainly had a heart of gold. Ever sanguine and tenacious, he began to consider new ways of putting his little scheme to her.

"Shall we have a dekko at the elephants and then make for home?" he asked.

As they passed through the tunnel once more, Greta thought how alike all men are, just children really, and she purred as she thought how well she understood him. When they approached the pool where the orange-teethed coypus sat on the rocks, cleaning their whiskers, she began to sing, "He's my guy. Heaven knows why I love him, but he's my guy."

"There's your famous musquash coats," said Maurice, pointing at the huge rats, with their wet, coarse bristles.

"I *should* believe you," Greta cried. They were both delighted when he convinced her—he because she was such a funny ignorant little rascal, she because it really was surprising what he knew. "Well I'll never have a musquash coat," she cried, "not from creatures with teeth like that."

They watched the otter as it swam in crazy circles round its pool, trying ceaselessly to dig a way through the concrete sides down to the open sea. "The way it keeps scrabbling," said Greta, "I should think it wanted to get out." They both had to laugh at its antics.

When they reached the Elephant House Maurice asked the keeper if they could go to the back of the hippopotamus pool. He was quite a young Cockney who didn't respond to Maurice's manner at all.

"It's not usual," he said. "There's nothing to see, you know, that you can't see from here."

"All the same," replied Maurice, "I'd like to take the lady round the back."

"O.K. Colonel," the boy said, winking across at Greta, "but it's not the place I'd choose to take my girl friend."

It was, indeed, most unattractive on closer inspection. The hot steam from the muddy water smelt abominably and the sides of the pool were slippery with slime. Every now and again the huge black forms would roll over, displacing ripples of brown foam-flecked water, and malevolent eyes on the end of stalks would appear above the surface for a moment. Maurice offered the keeper half-a-crown.

"That's all right," he said. "You keep your money. I get paid, you know." It was most difficult to walk on the slimy surface and Maurice, who was exhausted from the afternoon's events, slipped and would have fallen had not the boy caught his arm. As he recovered his balance, he noticed Greta returning the keeper's amused smile. A moment later, a hippopotamus surfaced, blowing sprays of water from its great pink nostrils. Maurice's suit was flecked with mud.

"Sorry about that," said the keeper.

But Greta begged him not to worry. "It's a terrible old thing, anyway. I'm going to get him a new one to-morrow," she explained.

Maurice felt his throat fill with rage, anger that almost blinded him. He put his hands on her hips and in a moment he would have pushed her into the thick vaporous water; then he suddenly realized that he had no idea what would happen. Hippos, he felt sure, were not carnivorous, but in their anger at the disturbance they might destroy her, and that would be the end of both of them, he reflected with bitter satisfaction. On the other hand, they might just turn away from the floating Greta in disgust, in which case he would simply have mucked up all his schemes. He withdrew his hands in despair. Once again he had to control his fury.

Greta was most surprised when she felt his hands on her waist. How funny men were, she reflected, just when you thought you understood them, they did something unexpected like that. Maurice, who was always lecturing her for showing her affection in public! She was really rather touched by the gesture. All the same, she decided, it would be wiser not to notice it then. So turning her wide-eyed gaze up at him, "What *do* hippos eat, darling?" she asked, in her childlike way.

Doris Lessing

1919–

Mrs. Lessing, who was born in Kermanshah, Iran, was educated in Southern Rhodesia, and lived in Rhodesia from 1924 until 1959, when she settled in London. She has published several volumes of short stories, including (with some repetitions from one volume to another) *This Was the Old Chief's Country* (1952), *A Man and Two Women: Stories* (1963), and *The Temptation of Jack Orkney, and Other Stories* (1972). Her first novel, *The Grass Is Singing*, was published in 1950. Among those that followed it, besides the novels in the Children of Violence series which began with *Martha Quest* in 1952, are *Retreat to Innocence* (1956), *The Golden Notebook* (1962), *Briefing for a Descent into Hell* (1971) and *The Summer Before Dark* (1973). Her books about her own experiences of the world around her are as interesting as her novels: *Going Home* (1957) describes a return visit to Southern Rhodesia after having lived in England for several years, and *In Pursuit of the English: A Documentary* (1960) tries to capture London as it looks through the eyes of its many strangers.

A Sunrise on the Veld

Every night that winter he said aloud into the dark of the pillow: Half-past four! Half-past four! till he felt his brain had gripped the words and held them fast. Then he fell asleep at once, as if a shutter had fallen; and lay with his face turned to the clock so that he could see it first thing when he woke.

It was half-past four to the minute, every morning. Triumphantly pressing down the alarm-knob of the clock, which the dark half of his mind had outwitted, remaining vigilant all night and counting the hours as he lay relaxed in sleep, he huddled down for a last warm moment under the clothes, playing with the idea of lying abed for this once only. But he played with it for the fun of knowing that it was a weakness he could defeat without effort; just as he set the alarm each night for the delight of the moment when he woke and stretched his limbs, feeling the muscles tighten, and thought: Even my brain—even that! I can control every part of myself.

Luxury of warm rested body, with the arms and legs and fingers waiting like soldiers for a word of command! Joy of knowing that the precious hours were given to sleep voluntarily!— for he had once stayed awake three nights running, to prove that he could, and then worked all day, refusing even to admit that he was tired; and now sleep seemed to him a servant to be commanded and refused.

The boy stretched his frame full-length, touching the wall at his head with his hands, and the bedfoot with his toes; then he sprung out, like a fish leaping from water. And it was cold, cold.

He always dressed rapidly, so as to try and conserve his night-warmth till the sun rose two hours later; but by the time he had on his clothes his hands were numbed and he could scarcely hold his shoes. These he could not put on for fear of waking his parents, who never came to know how early he rose.

As soon as he stepped over the lintel, the flesh of his soles contracted on the chilled earth, and his legs began to ache with cold. It was night: the stars were glittering, the trees standing black and still. He looked for signs of day, for the greying of the edge of a stone, or a lightening in the sky where the sun would rise, but there was nothing yet. Alert as an animal he crept past the dangerous window, standing poised with his hand on the sill for one proudly fastidious moment, looking in at the stuffy blackness of the room where his parents lay.

Feeling for the grass-edge of the path with his toes, he reached inside another window further along the wall, where his gun had been set in readiness the night before. The steel was icy, and numbed fingers slipped along it, so that he had to hold it in the crook of his arm for safety. Then he tiptoed to the room where the dogs slept, and was fearful that they might have been tempted to go before him; but they were waiting, their haunches crouched in reluctance at the cold, but ears and swinging tails greeting the gun ecstatically. His warning undertone kept them secret and silent till the house was a hundred yards back: then they bolted off into the bush, yelping excitedly. The boy imagined his parents turning in their beds and muttering: Those dogs again! before they were dragged back in sleep; and he smiled scornfully. He always looked back over his shoulder at the house before he passed a wall of trees that shut it from sight. It looked so low and small, crouching there under a tall and brilliant sky. Then he turned his back on it, and on the frowsting sleepers, and forgot them.

He would have to hurry. Before the light grew strong he must be four miles away; and already a tint of green stood in the hollow of a leaf, and the air smelled of morning and the stars were dimming.

He slung the shoes over his shoulder, veld skoen that were crinkled and hard with the dews of a hundred mornings. They would be necessary when the ground became too hot to bear. Now he felt the chilled dust push up between his toes, and he let the muscles of his feet spread and settle into the shapes of the earth; and he thought: I could walk a hundred miles on feet like these! I could walk all day, and never tire!

He was walking swiftly through the dark tunnel of foliage that in daytime was a road. The dogs were invisibly ranging the lower travelways of the bush, and he heard them panting. Sometimes he felt a cold muzzle on his leg before they were off again, scouting for a trail to follow. They were not trained, but free-running companions of the hunt, who often tired of the long stalk before the final shots, and went off on their own pleasure. Soon he could see them, small and wild-looking in a wild strange light, now that the bush stood trembling on the verge of colour, waiting for the sun to paint earth and grass afresh.

The grass stood to his shoulders; and the trees were showering a faint silvery rain. He was soaked; his whole body was clenched in a steady shiver.

Once he bent to the road that was newly scored with animal trails, and regretfully straightened, reminding himself that the pleasure of tracking must wait till another day.

He began to run along the edge of a field, noting jerkily how it was filmed over with fresh spiderweb, so that the long reaches of great black clods seemed netted in glistening grey. He was using the steady lope he had learned by watching the natives, the run that is a dropping of the weight of the body from one foot to the next in a slow balancing movement that never tires, nor shortens the breath; and he felt the blood pulsing down his legs and along his arms, and the exultation and pride of body mounted in him till he was shutting his teeth hard against a violent desire to shout his triumph.

Soon he had left the cultivated part of the farm. Behind him the bush was low and black. In front was a long vlei, acres of long pale grass that sent back a hollowing gleam of light to a satiny sky. Near him thick swathes of grass were bent with the weight of water, and diamond drops sparkled on each frond.

The first bird woke at his feet and at once a flock of them sprang into the air calling shrilly that day had come; and suddenly, behind him, the bush woke into song, and he could hear the guinea-fowl calling far ahead of him. That meant they would now be sailing down from their trees into thick grass, and it was for them he had come: he was too late. But he did not mind. He forgot he had come to shoot. He set his legs wide, and balanced from foot to foot, and swung his gun up and down in both hands horizontally, in a kind of improvised exercise, and let his head sink back till it was pillowed in his neck muscles, and watched how above him small rosy clouds floated in a lake of gold.

Suddenly it all rose in him: it was unbearable. He leapt up into the air, shouting and yelling wild, unrecognizable noises. Then he began to run, not carefully, as he had before, but madly, like a wild thing. He was clean crazy, yelling mad with the joy of living and a superfluity of youth. He rushed down the vlei under a tumult of crimson and gold, while all the birds of the world sang about him. He ran in great leaping strides, and shouted as he ran, feeling his body rise into the crisp rushing air and fall back surely on to sure feet; and thought briefly, not believing that such a thing could happen to him, that he could break his ankle any moment, in this thick tangled grass. He cleared bushes like a duiker, leaped over rocks; and finally came to a dead stop at a place where the ground fell abruptly away below him to the river. It had been a two-mile-long dash through waist-high growth, and he was breathing hoarsely and could no longer sing. But he poised on a rock and looked down at stretches of water that gleamed through stooping trees, and thought suddenly, I am fifteen! Fifteen! The words came new to him; so that he kept repeating them wonderingly, with swelling excitement; and he felt the years of his life with his hands, as if he were counting marbles, each one hard and separate and compact, each one a wonderful shining thing. That was what he was: fifteen years of this rich soil, and this slow-moving water, and air that smelt like a challenge whether it was warm and sultry at noon, or as brisk as cold water, like it was now.

There was nothing he couldn't do, nothing! A vision came to him, as he stood there, like when a child hears the word "eternity" and tries to understand it, and time takes possession of the mind. He felt his life ahead of him as a great and wonderful thing, something that was his; and he said aloud, with the blood rising to his head: all the great men of the world have been as I am now, and there is nothing I can't become, nothing I can't do; there is no country in the world I cannot make part of myself, if I choose. I contain the world. I can make of it what I want. If I choose, I can change everything that is going to happen: it depends on me, and what I decide now.

The urgency, and the truth and the courage of what his voice was saying exulted him so that he began to sing again, at the top of his voice, and the sound went echoing down the river gorge. He stopped for the echo, and sang again: stopped and shouted. That was what he was!—he sang, if he chose; and the world had to answer him.

And for minutes he stood there, shouting and singing and waiting for the lovely eddying sound of the echo; so that his own new strong thoughts came back and washed round his head, as if someone were answering him and encouraging him; till the gorge was full of soft voices clashing back and forth from rock to rock over the river. And then it seemed as if there was a new voice. He listened, puzzled, for it was not his own. Soon he was leaning forward, all his nerves alert, quite still: somewhere close to him there was a noise that was no joyful bird, nor tinkle of falling water, nor ponderous movement of cattle.

There it was again. In the deep morning hush that held his future and his past, was a sound of pain, and repeated over and over: it was a kind of shortened scream, as if someone, something, had no breath to scream. He came to

himself, looked about him, and called for the dogs. They did not appear: they had gone off on their own business, and he was alone. Now he was clean sober, all the madness gone. His heart beating fast, because of that frightened screaming, he stepped carefully off the rock and went towards a belt of trees. He was moving cautiously, for not so long ago he had seen a leopard in just this spot.

At the edge of the trees he stopped and peered, holding his gun ready; he advanced, looking steadily about him, his eyes narrowed. Then, all at once, in the middle of a step, he faltered, and his face was puzzled. He shook his head impatiently, as if he doubted his own sight.

There, between two trees, against a background of gaunt black rocks, was a figure from a dream, a strange beast that was horned and drunken-legged, but like something he had never even imagined. It seemed to be ragged. It looked like a small buck that had black ragged tufts of fur standing up irregularly all over it, with patches of raw flesh beneath . . . but the patches of rawness were disappearing under moving black and came again elsewhere; and all the time the creature screamed, in small gasping screams, and leaped drunkenly from side to side, as if it were blind.

Then the boy understood: it *was* a buck. He ran closer, and again stood still, stopped by a new fear. Around him the grass was whispering and alive. He looked wildly about, and then down. The ground was black with ants, great energetic ants that took no notice of him, but hurried and scurried towards the fighting shape, like glistening black water flowing through the grass.

And, as he drew in his breath and pity and terror seized him, the beast fell and the screaming stopped. Now he could hear nothing but one bird singing, and the sound of the rustling, whispering ants.

He peered over at the writhing blackness that jerked convulsively with the jerking nerves. It grew quieter. There were small twitches from the mass that still looked vaguely like the shape of a small animal.

It came into his mind that he should shoot it and end its pain; and he raised the gun. Then he lowered it again. The buck could no longer feel; its fighting was a mechanical protest of the nerves. But it was not that which made him put down the gun. It was a swelling feeling of rage and misery and protest that expressed itself in the thought: if I had not come it would have died like this: so why should I interfere? All over the bush things like this happen; they happen all the time; this is how life goes on, by living things dying in anguish. He gripped the gun between his knees and felt in his own limbs the myriad swarming pain of the twitching animal that could no longer feel, and set his teeth, and said over and over again under his breath: I can't stop it. I can't stop it. There is nothing I can do.

He was glad that the buck was unconscious and had gone past suffering so that he did not have to make a decision to kill it even when he was feeling with his whole body: this is what happens, this is how things work.

It was right—that was what he was feeling. *It was right and nothing could alter it.*

The knowledge of fatality, of what has to be, had gripped him and for the first time in his life; and he was left unable to make any movement of brain or body, except to say: "Yes, yes. That is what living is." It had entered his flesh and his bones and grown in to the furthest corners of his brain and would never leave him. And at that moment he could not have performed the smallest action of mercy, knowing as he did, having lived on it all his life, the vast unalterable, cruel veld, where at any moment one might stumble over a skull or crush the skeleton of some small creature.

Suffering, sick, and angry, but also grimly satisfied with his new stoicism, he stood there leaning on his rifle, and watched the seething black mound grow smaller. At his feet, now, were ants trickling back with pink fragments in their mouths, and there was a fresh acid smell in his nostrils. He sternly controlled the uselessly convulsing muscles of his empty stomach, and reminded himself: the ants must eat too! At the same time he found that the tears were streaming down his face, and his clothes were soaked with the sweat of that other creature's pain.

The shape had grown small. Now it looked like nothing recognizable. He did not know how long it was before he saw the blackness thin, and bits of white showed through, shining in the sun—yes, there was the sun, just up, glowing over the rocks. Why, the whole thing could not have taken longer than a few minutes.

He began to swear, as if the shortness of the time was in itself unbearable, using the words he had heard his father say. He strode forward, crushing ants with each step, and brushing them off his clothes, till he stood above the skeleton, which lay sprawled under a small bush. It was clean-picked. It might have been lying there years, save that on the white bone were pink fragments of gristle. About the bones ants were ebbing away, their pincers full of meat.

The boy looked at them, big black ugly insects. A few were standing and gazing up at him with small glittering eyes.

"Go away!" he said to the ants, very coldly. "I am not for you—not just yet, at any rate. Go away." And he fancied that the ants turned and went away.

He bent over the bones and touched the sockets in the skull; that was where the eyes were, he thought incredulously, remembering the liquid dark eyes of a buck. And then he bent the slim foreleg bone, swinging it horizontally in his palm.

That morning, perhaps an hour ago, this small creature had been stepping proud and free through the bush, feeling the chill on its hide even as he himself had done, exhilarated by it. Proudly stepping the earth, tossing its horns, frisking a pretty white tail, it had sniffed the cold morning air. Walking like kings and conquerors it had moved through this free-held bush, where each blade of grass grew for it alone, and where the river ran pure sparkling water for its slaking.

And then—what had happened? Such a swift surefooted thing could surely not be trapped by a swarm of ants?

The boy bent curiously to the skeleton. Then he saw that the back leg lay uppermost and strained out in the tension of death, was snapped midway in the thigh, so that broken bones jutted over each other uselessly. So that was it! Limping into the ant-masses it could not escape, once it had sensed the danger. Yes, but how had the leg been broken? Had it fallen, perhaps? Impossible, a buck was too light and graceful. Had some jealous rival horned it?

What could possibly have happened? Perhaps some Africans had thrown stones at it, as they do, trying to kill it for meat, and had broken its leg. Yes, that must be it.

Even as he imagined the crowd of running,

shouting natives, and the flying stones, and the leaping buck, another picture came into his mind. He saw himself, on any one of these bright ringing mornings, drunk with excitement, taking a snap shot at some half-seen buck. He saw himself with the gun lowered, wondering whether he had missed or not; and thinking at last that it was late, and he wanted his breakfast, and it was not worth while to track miles after an animal that would very likely get away from him in any case.

For a moment he would not face it. He was a small boy again, kicking sulkily at the skeleton, hanging his head, refusing to accept the responsibility.

Then he straightened up, and looked down at the bones with an odd expression of dismay, all the anger gone out of him. His mind went quite empty: all around him he could see trickles of ants disappearing into the grass. The whispering noise was faint and dry, like the rustling of a cast snakeskin.

At last he picked up his gun and walked homewards. He was telling himself half defiantly that he wanted his breakfast. He was telling himself that it was getting very hot, much too hot to be out roaming the bush.

Really, he was tired. He walked heavily, not looking where he put his feet. When he came within sight of his home he stopped, knitting his brows. There was something he had to think out. The death of that small animal was a thing that concerned him, and he was by no means finished with it. It lay at the back of his mind uncomfortably.

Soon, the very next morning, he would get clear of everybody and go to the bush and think about it.

Philip Larkin

1922–

Philip Larkin was one of the first of the new generation of poets to impress his voice and poetic personality—very quietly, to be sure, but also distinctively and unmistakably—in the years immediately following World War II. Except for *The North Ship* (a book of poems that first appeared in 1945 and was republished, unaltered, in 1966, even though Larkin recognizes the derivative quality of many of the poems), his first books were novels. Both are comparatively light without therefore being slight: *Jill* (1946) and *A Girl in Winter* (1947). His best work, however, seems to be the two volumes of poems for which he is chiefly known, *The Less Deceived* (1955) and *The Whitsun Weddings* (1964).

Larkin was born in Coventry and educated at Coventry and St. John's College, Oxford. Since 1955 he has been Librarian at the University of Hull.

Next, Please

Always too eager for the future, we
Pick up bad habits of expectancy.
Something is always approaching; every day
Till then we say,

Watching from a bluff the tiny, clear,   5
Sparkling armada of promises draw near.
How slow they are! And how much time they
          waste,
Refusing to make haste!

Yet still they leave us holding wretched stalks
Of disappointment, for, though nothing balks   10
Each big approach, leaning with brasswork
          prinked,
Each rope distinct,

Flagged, and the figurehead with golden tits
Arching our way, it never anchors; it's
No sooner present than it turns to past.   15
Right to the last

We think each one will heave to and unload
All good into our lives, all we are owed
For waiting so devoutly and so long.
But we are wrong: 20

Only one ship is seeking us, a black-
Sailed unfamiliar, towing at her back

A huge and birdless silence. In her wake
No waters breed or break.

Church Going

Once I am sure there's nothing going on
I step inside, letting the door thud shut.
Another church: matting, seats, and stone,
And little books; sprawlings of flowers, cut
For Sunday, brownish now; some brass and stuff   5
Up at the holy end; the small neat organ;
And a tense, musty, unignorable silence,
Brewed God knows how long. Hatless, I take off
My cycle-clips in awkward reverence,

Move forward, run my hand around the font.   10
From where I stand, the roof looks almost new—
Cleaned, or restored? Someone would know: I
     don't.
Mounting the lectern, I peruse a few
Hectoring large-scale verses, and pronounce
"Here endeth" much more loudly than I'd meant.   15
The echoes snigger briefly. Back at the door
I sign the book, donate an Irish sixpence,
Reflect the place was not worth stopping for.

Yet stop I did: in fact I often do,
And always end much at a loss like this,   20
Wondering what to look for; wondering, too,
When churches fall completely out of use
What we shall turn them into, if we shall keep
A few cathedrals chronically on show,
Their parchment, plate and pyx in locked cases,   25
And let the rest rent-free to rain and sheep.
Shall we avoid them as unlucky places?

Or, after dark, will dubious women come
To make their children touch a particular stone;
Pick simples for a cancer; or on some   30
Advised night see walking a dead one?
Power of some sort or other will go on
In games, in riddles, seemingly at random;
But superstition, like belief, must die,
And what remains when disbelief has gone?   35
Grass, weedy pavement, brambles, buttress, sky,

A shape less recognisable each week,
A purpose more obscure. I wonder who
Will be the last, the very last, to seek
This place for what it was; one of the crew   40

That tap and jot and know what rood-lofts were?
Some ruin-bibber, randy for antique,
Or Christmas-addict, counting on a whiff
Of gown-and-bands and organ-pipes and myrrh?
Or will he be my representative,   45

Bored, uninformed, knowing the ghostly silt
Dispersed, yet tending to this cross of ground
Through suburb scrub because it held unspilt
So long and equably what since is found
Only in separation—marriage, and birth,   50
And death, and thoughts of these—for whom was
     built
This special shell? For, though I've no idea
What this accoutred frowsty barn is worth,
It pleases me to stand in silence here;

A serious house on serious earth it is,   55
In whose blent air all our compulsions meet,
Are recognised, and robed as destinies.
And that much never can be obsolete,
Since someone will forever be surprising
A hunger in himself to be more serious,   60
And gravitating with it to this ground,
Which, he once heard, was proper to grow wise
     in,
If only that so many dead lie round.

Myxomatosis

Caught in the centre of a soundless field
While hot inexplicable hours go by
What trap is this? Where were its teeth con-
     cealed?
You seem to ask.
               I make a sharp reply,   5
Then clean my stick. I'm glad I can't explain
Just in what jaws you were to suppurate:
You may have thought things would come right
     again
If you could only keep quite still and wait.

At Grass

The eye can hardly pick them out
From the cold shade they shelter in,
Till wind distresses tail and mane;
Then one crops grass, and moves about

—The other seeming to look on— 5
And stands anonymous again.

Yet fifteen years ago, perhaps
Two dozen distances sufficed
To fable them: faint afternoons
Of Cups and Stakes and Handicaps, 10
Whereby their names were artificed
To inlay faded, classic Junes—

Silks at the start: against the sky
Numbers and parasols: outside,
Squadrons of empty cars, and heat, 15
And littered grass: then the long cry
Hanging unhushed till it subside
To stop-press columns on the street.

Do memories plague their ears like flies?
They shake their heads. Dusk brims the shadows. 20
Summer by summer all stole away,
The starting-gates, the crowds and cries—
All but the unmolesting meadows.
Almanacked, their names live; they

Have slipped their names, and stand at ease, 25
Or gallop for what must be joy,
And not a fieldglass sees them home,
Or curious stop-watch prophesies:
Only the groom, and the groom's boy,
With bridles in the evening come. 30

Ambulances

Closed like confessionals, they thread
Loud noons of cities, giving back
None of the glances they absorb.
Light glossy grey, arms on a plaque,
They come and rest at any kerb: 5
All streets in time are visited.

Then children strewn on steps or road,
Or women coming from the shops
Past smells of different dinners, see
A wild white face that overtops 10
Red stretcher-blankets momently
As it is carried in and stowed,

And sense the solving emptiness
That lies just under all we do,
And for a second get it whole, 15

So permanent and blank and true. 5
The fastened doors recede. *Poor soul,*
They whisper at their own distress;

For borne away in deadened air
May go the sudden shut of loss 20
Round something nearly at an end,
And what cohered in it across
The years, the unique random blend
Of families and fashions, there

At last begin to loosen. Far 25
From the exchange of love to lie
Unreachable inside a room
The traffic parts to let go by
Brings closer what is left to come,
And dulls to distance all we are. 30

An Arundel Tomb

Side by side, their faces blurred,
The earl and countess lie in stone,
Their proper habits vaguely shown
As jointed armour, stiffened pleat,
And that faint hint of the absurd— 5
The little dogs under their feet.

Such plainness of the pre-baroque
Hardly involves the eye, until
It meets his left-hand gauntlet, still
Clasped empty in the other; and 10
One sees, with a sharp tender shock,
His hand withdrawn, holding her hand.

They would not think to lie so long.
Such faithfulness in effigy
Was just a detail friends would see: 15
A sculptor's sweet commissioned grace
Thrown off in helping to prolong
The Latin names around the base.

They would not guess how early in
Their supine stationary voyage 20
The air would change to soundless damage,
Turn the old tenantry away;
How soon succeeding eyes begin
To look, not read. Rigidly they

Persisted, linked, through lengths and breadths 25
Of time. Snow fell, undated. Light

Each summer thronged the glass. A bright
Litter of birdcalls strewed the same
Bone-riddled ground. And up the paths
The endless altered people came,   30

Washing at their identity.
Now, helpless in the hollow of
An unarmorial age, a trough
Of smoke in slow suspended skeins

Above their scrap of history,   35
Only an attitude remains:

Time has transfigured them into
Untruth. The stone fidelity
They hardly meant has come to be
Their final blazon, and to prove   40
Our almost-instinct almost true:
What will survive of us is love.

Thom Gunn

1929–

Since Thom Gunn (the full name is Thomson William Gunn) now lives in California and writes poems with a markedly American background—the scene is often San Francisco—it should perhaps be mentioned that he did grow up in England and was educated at University College School, London, and at Trinity College, Cambridge. His individual volumes of poems are: *Fighting Terms* (1954, with a revised edition 1962); *The Sense of Movement* (1957); *My Sad Captains* (1961); *Touch* (1967); *Positives: Verses by Thom Gunn; Photographs by Ander Gunn* (1967); and *Moly* (1971). *Poems, 1950–1966: A Selection* (1969) was published in paperback in England.

Market at Turk

At the street corner, hunched up,
he gestates action, prepared
for some unique combat in
boots, jeans, and a curious cap
whose very peak, jammed forward,   5
indicates resolution.

It is military, almost,
how he buckles himself in,
with bootstraps and Marine belt,
reminders of the will, lest   10
even with that hard discipline
the hardness should not be felt.

He waits, whom no door snatches
to unbuckling in the close
commotion of bar or bed,   15
he presides in apartness,

not yet knowing his purpose
fully, and fingers the blade.

Puss in Boots to the Giant

In fine simplicity
I cry On either side
Far as the eye can see
These fields as green as wide
Are my master's property.   5

The cattle browze their fill,
All day the tall boys sweat
With the bags in the mill,
And after sun set
Jack has his Jill.   10

And then upon the grass
How lasting and how clean
Without token alas
They banish the lean
Highway beggars that pass.   15

It is not selfishness
But when they enjoy
Two triumphs in one place
Every girl and boy
Like the defeated less.   20

So praise the pitiless, hot
In each other's arms.
Gigglers, gossips, do not
Come near. You, Itching Palms,
We condemn to Thought.   25

In fine simplicity
I cry On either side
Far as the eye can see
These fields as green as wide
Are my master's property.   30

Black Jackets

    In the silence that prolongs the span
Rawly of music when the record ends,
    The red-haired boy who drove a van
In weekday overalls but, like his friends,

    Wore cycle boots and jacket here   5
To suit the Sunday hangout he was in,
    Heard, as he stretched back from his beer,
Leather creak softly round his neck and chin.

    Before him, on a coal-black sleeve
Remote exertion had lined, scratched, and burned   10
    Insignia that could not revive
The heroic fall or climb where they were earned.

    On the other drinkers bent together,
Concocting selves for their impervious kit,
    He saw it as no more than leather   15
Which, taut across the shoulders grown to it,

    Sent through the dimness of a bar
As sudden and anonymous hints of light
    As those that shipping give, that are
Now flickers in the Bay, now lost in night.   20

    He stretched out like a cat, and rolled
The bitterish taste of beer upon his tongue,
    And listened to a joke being told:
The present was the things he stayed among.

    If it was only loss he wore,   25
He wore it to assert, with fierce devotion,
    Complicity and nothing more.
He recollected his initiation,

    And one especially of the rites.
For on his shoulders they had put tattoos: 30
    The group's name on the left, The Knights,
And on the right the slogan Born To Lose.

The Value of Gold

The hairs turn gold upon my thigh,
And I am gold beneath the sun,
Losing pale features that the cold
Pinched, pointed, for an instant I
Turn blind to features, being one   5
With all that has, like me, turned gold.

I finish up the can of beer,
And lay my head on the cropped grass:
Now bordering flag, geranium,
And mint-bush tower above me here,   10
Which colour into colour pass
Toward the last state they shall become.

Of insect size, I walk below
The red, green, greenish-black, and black,
And speculate. Can this quiet growth   15
Comprise at once the still-to-grow
And a full form without a lack?
And, if so, can I too be both?

I darken where perpetual
Action withdraws me from the sun.   20
Then from one high precocious stalk
A flower—its fulness reached—lets fall
Features, great petals, one by one
Shrivelling to gold across my walk.

Considering the Snail

The snail pushes through a green
night, for the grass is heavy
with water and meets over
the bright path he makes, where rain
has darkened the earth's dark. He   5
moves in a wood of desire,

pale antlers barely stirring
as he hunts. I cannot tell
what power is at work, drenched there
with purpose, knowing nothing.   10
What is a snail's fury? All
I think is that if later

I parted the blades above
the tunnel and saw the thin
trail of broken white across   15

litter, I would never have
imagined the slow passion
to that deliberate progress.

Taylor Street

The small porch of imitation
marble is never sunny, but
outside the front door he
sits on his kitchen chair facing
the street. In the bent yellowish   5
face, from under the brim
of a floppy brown hat,
his small eyes watch what
he is not living. But he
lives what he can: 10
watches without a smile, with
a certain strain, the warmth
of his big crumpled
body anxiously cupped
by himself in himself, as   15
he leans over himself not
over the cold railing, unmoving but carefully getting
a little strength from the sight of the
passers-by. He has it   20
all planned: he will live
here morning by morning.

Memoirs of the World

It has turned cold. I have been gathering wood,
Numb-fingered, hardly feeling what I touched,
Turning crisp leaves to pick up where I could
The damp sticks from beneath them. I have
      crouched
Piling them up to dry, all afternoon,   5
And have heard all afternoon, over and over,
Two falling notes—a sweet disconsolate tune,
As if the bird called, from its twiggy cover,
            Nót now, nót now, nót now.

I dislodge sticks for kindling, one by one,   10
From brambles. Struck by shade, I stand and see
Half-blinding me, the cold red setting sun
Through the meshed branches of a leafless tree.
It calls old sunsets to my mind, one most

Which coloured, similarly, the white grey, black-   15
      ened
Iron and slabbed concrete of a sentry post
With its cold orange. Let me live, one second,
            Nót now, nót now, nót now.

Most poignant and most weakening, that recall.
Although I lived from day to day, too, there.   20
Yet the comparison makes me sensible
Of the diminishing warmth and light, which
      were,
Or seem to have been, diminished less than now.
The bird stops. Hardening in the single present,
I know, hearing wind rattle in a bough,   25
I have always harked thus after an incessant
            Nót now, nót now, nót now.

From the Wave

It mounts at sea, a concave wall
      Down-ribbed with shine,
And pushes forward, building tall
      Its steep incline.

Then from their hiding rise to sight   5
      Black shapes on boards
Bearing before the fringe of white
      It mottles towards.

Their pale feet curl, they poise their weight
      With a learn'd skill.   10
It is the wave they imitate
      Keeps them so still.

The marbling bodies have become
      Half wave, half men,
Grafted it seems by feet of foam   15
      Some seconds, then,

Late as they can, they slice the face
      In timed procession:
Balance is triumph in this place,
      Triumph possession.   20

The mindless heave of which they rode
      A fluid shelf
Breaks as they leave it, falls and, slowed,
      Loses itself.

Clear, the sheathed bodies slick as seals   25
      Loosen and tingle;

And by the board the bare foot feels
   The suck of shingle.

They paddle in the shallows still;
   Two splash each other;
Then all swim out to wait until   30
   The right waves gather.

Street Song

I am too young to grow a beard
But yes man it was me you heard
In dirty denim and dark glasses.
I look through everyone who passes
But ask him clear, I do not plead,   5
Keys lids acid and speed.

My grass is not oregano.
Some of it grew in Mexico.
You cannot guess the weed I hold,
Clara Green, Acapulco Gold,   10
Panama Red, you name it man,
Best on the street since I began.

My methedrine, my double-sun,
Will give you two lives in your one,
Five days of power before you crash.   15
At which time use these lumps of hash
—They burn so sweet, they smoke so smooth,
They make you sharper while they soothe.

Now here, the best I've got to show,
Made by a righteous cat I know.   20
Pure acid—it will scrape your brain,
And make it something else again.
Call it heaven, call it hell,
Join me and see the world I sell.

Join me, and I will take you there,   25
Your head will cut out from your hair

Into whichever self you choose.
With Midday Mick man you can't lose,
I'll get you anything you need.
Keys lids acid and speed.   30

The Discovery of the Pacific

They lean against the cooling car, backs pressed
Upon the dusts of a brown continent,
And watch the sun, now Westward of their West,
Fall to the ocean. Where it led they went.

Kansas to California. Day by day   5
They travelled emptier of the things they knew.
They improvised new habits on the way,
But lost the occasions, and then lost them too.

One night, no-one and nowhere, she had woken
To resin-smell and to the firs' slight sound,   10
And through their sleeping-bag had felt the
   broken
Tight-knotted surfaces of the naked ground.

Only his lean quiet body cupping hers
Kept her from it, the extreme chill. By degrees
She fell asleep. Around them in the firs   15
The wind probed, tiding through forked estu-
   aries.

And now their skin is caked with road, the grime
Merely reflecting sunlight as it fails.
They leave their clothes among the rocks they
   climb,
Blunt leaves of iceplant nuzzle at their soles.   20

Now they stand chin-deep in the sway of ocean,
Firm West, two stringy bodies face to face,
And come, together, in the water's motion,
The full caught pause of their embrace.

Ted Hughes

1930–

Ted Hughes's first volume of poems was *The Hawk in the Rain* (1957), followed by *Lupercal* (1960), *Wodwo* (1967), and *Crow: from the Life and Songs of the Crow* (1971). A small volume of *Selected Poems, by Thom Gunn and Ted Hughes*, was published in 1969.

Griefs for Dead Soldiers

I

Mightiest, like some universal cataclysm,
Will be the unveiling of their cenotaph:
The crowds will stand struck, like the painting
    of a terror
Where the approaching planet, a half-day off,
Hangs huge above the thin skulls of the silenced   5
    birds;
Each move, each sound, a fresh-cut epitaph—
Monstrousness of the moment making the air
    stone.

Though thinly, the bugle will then cry,
The dead drum tap, and the feet of the columns
And the sergeant major's voice blown about by   10
    the wind
Make these dead magnificent, their souls
Scrolled and supporting the sky, and the national
    sorrow,
Over the crowds that know of no other wound,
Permanent stupendous victory.

II

Secretest, tiniest, there, where the widow watches   15
    on the table
The telegram opening of its own accord
Inescapably and more terribly than any bomb
That dives to the cellar and lifts the house. The
    bared
Words shear the hawsers of love that now lash
Back in darkness, blinding and severing. To a   20
    world
Lonely as her skull and little as her heart

The doors and windows open like great gates to
    a hell.

Still she will carry cups from table to sink.
She cannot build her sorrow into a monument
And walk away from it. Closer than thinking   25
The dead man hangs around her neck, but never
Close enough to be touched, or thanked, even,
For being all that remains in a world smashed.

III

Truest, and only just, here, where since
The battle passed the grass has sprung up   30
Surprisingly in the valleyful of dead men.
Under the blue sky heavy crow and black fly
    move.
Flowers bloom prettily to the edge of the mass
    grave
Where spades hack, and the diggers grunt and
    sweat.
Among the flowers the dead wait like brides   35

To surrender their limbs; thud of another body
    flung
Down, the jolted shape of a face, earth into the
    mouth—
Moment that could annihilate a watcher!
Cursing the sun that makes their work long
Or the black lively flies that bite their wrists,   40
The burial party works with a craftsman calm.
Weighing their grief by the ounce, and burying
    it.

Wind

This house has been far out at sea all night,
The woods crashing through darkness, the boom-
    ing hills,
Winds stampeding the fields under the window
Floundering black astride and blinding wet

Till day rose; then under an orange sky   5
The hills had new places, and wind wielded
Blade-light, luminous black and emerald,
Flexing like the lens of a mad eye.

At noon I scaled along the house-side as far as
The coal-house door. I dared once to look up—   10

Through the brunt wind that dented the balls of
    my eyes
The tent of the hills drummed and strained its
    guyrope,

The fields quivering, the skyline a grimace,
At any second to bang and vanish with a flap:
The wind flung a magpie away and a black-   15
Back gull bent like an iron bar slowly. The house

Rang like some fine green goblet in the note
That any second would shatter it. Now deep
In chairs, in front of the great fire, we grip
Our hearts and cannot entertain book, thought,   20

Or each other. We watch the fire blazing,
And feel the roots of the house move, but sit on,
Seeing the window tremble to come in,
Hearing the stones cry out under the horizons.

Roarers in a Ring

Snow fell as for Wenceslas.
    The moor foamed like a white
Running sea. A starved fox
    Stared at the inn light.

In the red gridded glare of peat,   5
    Faces sweating like hams,
Farmers roared their Christmas Eve
    Out of the low beams.

Good company kept a laugh in the air
    As if they tossed a ball   10
To top the skip of a devil that
    Struck at it with his tail,

Or struck at the man who held it long.
    They so tossed laughter up
You would have thought that if they did not   15
    Laugh, they must weep.

Therefore the ale went round and round.
    Their mouths flung wide
The cataract of a laugh, lest
    Silence drink blood.   20

And their eyes were screwed so tight,
    While their grand bellies shook—

O their flesh would drop to dust
    At the first sober look.

The air was new as a razor,
    The moor looked like the moon,
When they all went roaring homewards
    An hour before dawn.

Those living images of their deaths
    Better than with skill
Blindly and rowdily balanced
    Gently took their fall

While the world under their footsoles
    Went whirling still
Gay and forever, in the bottomless black
    Silence through which it fell.

The Casualty

Farmers in the fields, housewives behind steamed
    windows,
Watch the burning aircraft across the blue sky
    float,
As if a firefly and a spider fought,
Far above the trees, between the washing hung
    out.
They wait with interest for the evening news.

But already, in a brambled ditch, suddenly-
    smashed
Stems twitch. In the stubble a pheasant
Is craning every way in astonishment.
The hare that hops up, quizzical, hesitant,
Flattens ears and tears madly away and the wren
    warns.

Some, who saw fall, smoke beckons. They jostle
    above,
They peer down a sunbeam as if they expected
    there
A snake in the gloom of the brambles or a rare
    flower,—
See the grave of dead leaves heave suddenly, hear
It was a man fell out of the air alive,

Hear now his groans and senses groping. They
    rip
The slum of weeds, leaves, barbed coils; they
    raise

A body that as the breeze touches it glows,
Branding their hands on his bones. Now that he has
No spine, against heaped sheaves they prop him up,   20

Arrange his limbs in order, open his eye,
Then stand, helpless as ghosts. In a scene
Melting in the August noon, the burned man
Bulks closer greater flesh and blood than their own,
As suddenly the heart's beat shakes his body and the eye   25

Widens childishly. Sympathies
Fasten to the blood like flies. Here's no heart's more
Open or large than a fist clenched, and in there
Holding close complacency its most dear
Unscratchable diamond. The tears of their eyes   30

Too tender to let break, start to the edge
Of such horror close as mourners can,
Greedy to share all that is undergone,
Grimace, gasp, gesture of death. Till they look down
On the handkerchief at which his eye stares up.   35

The Thought-Fox

I imagine this midnight moment's forest:
Something else is alive
Beside the clock's loneliness
And this blank page where my fingers move.

Through the window I see no star: 5
Something more near
Though deeper within darkness
Is entering the loneliness:

Cold, delicately as the dark snow,
A fox's nose touches twig, leaf;   10
Two eyes serve a movement, that now
And again now, and now, and now

Sets neat prints into the snow
Between trees, and warily a lame
Shadow lags by stump and in hollow   15
Of a body that is bold to come

Across clearings, an eye,
A widening deepening greenness,
Brilliantly, concentratedly,
Coming about its own business   20

Till, with a sudden sharp hot stink of fox
It enters the dark hole of the head.
The window is starless still; the clock ticks,
The page is printed.

Her Husband

Comes home dull with coal-dust deliberately
To grime the sink and foul towels and let her
Learn with scrubbing brush and scrubbing board
The stubborn character of money.

And let her learn through what kind of dust   5
He has earned his thirst and the right to quench it
And what sweat he has exchanged for his money
And the blood-weight of money. He'll humble her

With new light on her obligations.
The fried, woody chips, kept warm two hours in the oven,   10
Are only part of her answer.
Hearing the rest, he slams them to the fire back

And is away round the house-end singing
"Come back to Sorrento" in a voice
Of resounding corrugated iron.   15
Her back has bunched into a hump as an insult.

For they will have their rights.
Their jurors are to be assembled
From the little crumbs of soot. Their brief
Goes straight up to heaven and nothing more is   20
heard of it.

Fern

Here is the fern's frond, unfurling a gesture,
Like a conductor whose music will now be pause
And the one note of silence
To which the whole earth dances gravely.

The mouse's ear unfurls its trust, 5
The spider takes up her bequest,
And the retina
Reins the creation with a bridle of water.

And, among them, the fern
Dances gravely, like the plume 10
Of a warrior returning, under the low hills,

Into his own kingdom.

The Rescue

That's what we live on: thinking of their rescue
And fitting our future to it. You have to see it:
First, the dry smudge above the sea-line,
Then the slow growth of a shipful of strangers
Into this existence. White bows, the white bow-
    wave 5
Cleaving the nightmare, slicing it open,
Letting in reality. Then all the sailors white
As maggots waving at the rail. Then their shout-
    ing—
Faintly at first, as you can think
The crowd coming with Christ sounded 10
To Lazarus in his cave.
Then the ship's horn giving blast after blast out
Announcing the end of the island. Then the row-
    boat.
I fancy I saw it happen. The five were standing
In the shallows with the deathly sea 15
Lipping their knees and the rattle of oar-locks
Shaking the sand out of their brain-cells,
The flash of wet oars slashing their eyes back
    alive—
All the time the long white liner anchoring the
    world
Just out there, crowded and watching. 20
Then there came a moment in the eternity of
    this island
When the rowboat's bows bit into the beach
And the lovely greetings and chatter scattered—
This is wrong.
            The five never moved.
They just stood sucked empty 25
As grasses by this island's silence. And the crew
Helped them into the boat not speaking
Knowing the sound of a voice from the world
Might grab too cheery-clumsy

Into their powdery nerves. Then they rowed off 30
Toward the shining ship with carefully
Hushed oars dipping and squeaking. And the five
    sat all the time
Like mummies with their bandages lifted off—
While the ship's dazzling side brimmed up the 35
    sky
And leaned over, pouring faces.

Pibroch

The sea cries with its meaningless voice
Treating alike its dead and its living,
Probably bored with the appearance of heaven
After so many millions of nights without sleep,
Without purpose, without self-deception. 5

Stone likewise. A pebble is imprisoned
Like nothing in the Universe.
Created for black sleep. Or growing
Conscious of the sun's red spot occasionally,
Then dreaming it is the foetus of God. 10

Over the stone rushes the wind
Able to mingle with nothing,
Like the hearing of the blind stone itself.
Or turns, as if the stone's mind came feeling
A fantasy of directions. 15

Drinking the sea and eating the rock
A tree struggles to make leaves—
An old woman fallen from space
Unprepared for these conditions.
She hangs on, because her mind's gone com- 20
    pletely.

Minute after minute, aeon after aeon,
Nothing lets up or develops.
And this is neither a bad variant nor a tryout.
This is where the staring angels go through.
This is where all the stars bow down. 25

Gnat-Psalm

The Gnat is of more ancient lineage than man.
                        Proverb.

When the gnats dance at evening
Scribbling on the air, sparring sparely,

Scrambling their crazy lexicon,
Shuffling their dumb Cabala,
Under leaf shadow   5

Leaves only leaves
Between them and the broad thrusts of the sun
Leaves muffling the dusty stabs of the late sun
From their frail eyes and crepuscular tempera-
    ments

Dancing   10
Dancing
Writing on the air, rubbing out everything they
    write
Jerking their letters into knots, into tangles
Everybody everybody else's yoyo

Immense magnets fighting around a centre   15

Not writing and not fighting but singing
That the cycles of this Universe are no matter
That they are not afraid of the sun
That the one sun is too near
It blasts their song, which is of all the suns   20
That they are their own sun
Their own brimming over
At large in the nothing
Their wings blurring the blaze
Singing   25
Singing

That they are the nails
In the dancing hands and feet of the gnat-god
That they hear the wind suffering
Through the grass   30
And the evening hill suffering
And the towns, camped by their graveyards,
Saddening into an utter darkness

The wind bowing with long cat-gut cries
And highways and airways   35

Dancing in the wind
The wind's dance, the death-dance,
Plunging into marshes and undergrowth
And cities like cowdroppings huddling to dust

But not the gnats, their agility   40
Has outleaped that threshold
And hangs them a little above the claws of the
    grass
Dancing
Dancing
In the glove shadows of the sycamore   45

A dance never to be altered
A dance giving their bodies to be burned

And their mummy faces will never be used

Their little bearded faces
Weaving and bobbing on the nothing   50
Shaken in the ear, shaken, shaken
And their feet dangling like the feet of victims

O little Hasids
Ridden to death by your own bodies
Riding your bodies to death   55
You are the angels of the only heaven!

And God is an Almighty Gnat!
You are the greatest of all the galaxies!
My hands fly in the air, they are follies
My tongue hangs up in the leaves   60
My thoughts have crept into crannies

Your dancing

Your dancing

Rolls my staring skull slowly away into outer
    space.

Stevie Smith

1902–1972

Stevie Smith was the name under which Florence Margaret Smith wrote some of the most brilliantly inimitable novels and poems that have been produced in England for quite some time. In both poetry and fiction, her highly personal, apparently careless and self-indulgent style can be mistakenly seen as not very serious, and she has, in fact, not always been taken seriously by critics surveying the writing of the past few decades. Yet she had a unique talent, and her verse is not merely comic verse or light verse, despite the frequent wry, throwaway tone or the sardonic little line drawings with which she decorated her books. Her verse often jests; but, just when we feel that it is all amounting to nothing much more than a kind of sardonic fun, it is apt to become suddenly harsh, bitterly censorious of foolishness or cant, and fully aware of suffering—sometimes aware of the kind of suffering that is no easier to bear by reason of being ridiculous. The way to her values is through a responsiveness to her particular tone of poetic voice. While this came through immediately to anyone who heard her read her verse, over the BBC for instance, it may be harder to develop it for oneself off the printed page.

TEXTS: Her novels are: *Novel on Yellow Paper* (1936, reissued in 1969); *Over the Frontier* (1938); and *The Holiday* (1949). There are several books of poems, including *A Good Time Was Had by All* (1937); *Mother, What Is Man?* (1942); *Harold's Leap* (1950); *Not Waving but Drowning* (1957); *The Best Beast* (1969); and *Scorpion* (1972). *Selected Poems* was published in 1962, and an interview with Stevie Smith is recorded in *Ivy and Stevie: Ivy Compton-Burnett and Stevie Smith: Conversations and Reflections,* by Kay Dick (1971).

Mr. Over

Mr. Over is dead
He died fighting and true
And on his tombstone they wrote
Over to You.

And who pray is this You   5
To whom Mr. Over is gone?
Oh if we only knew that
We should not do wrong.

But who is this beautiful You
We all of us long for so much   10
Is he not our friend and our brother
Our father and such?

Yes he is this and much more
This is but a portion
A sea-drop in a bucket   15
Taken from the ocean

So the voices spake
Softly above my head
And a voice in my heart cried: Follow
Where he has led   20

And a devil's voice cried: Happy
Happy the dead.

Deeply Morbid

Deeply morbid deeply morbid was the girl who
    typed the letters
Always out of office hours running with her social
    betters
But when daylight and the darkness of the office
    closed about her
Not for this ah not for this her office colleagues
    came to doubt her
It was that look within her eye   5
Why did it always seem to say goodbye?

Joan her name was and at lunchtime
Solitary solitary
She would go and watch the pictures
In the National Gallery   10
All alone all alone
This time with no friend beside her
She would go and watch the pictures
All alone.

Will she leave her office colleagues   15
Will she leave her evening pleasures
Toil within a friendly bureau
Running later in her leisure?

All alone all alone
Before the pictures she seems turned to stone.   20

Close upon the Turner pictures
Closer than a thought may go
Hangs her eye and all the colours
Leap into a special glow
All for her, all alone   25
All for her, all for Joan.

First the canvas where the ocean
Like a mighty animal
With a really wicked motion
Leaps for sailors' funeral   30

Holds her panting. Oh the creature
Oh the wicked virile thing
With its skin of fleck and shadow
Stretching tightening over him.
Wild yet captured wild yet captured   35
By the painter, Joan is quite enraptured.

Now she edges from the canvas
To another loved more dearly
Where the awful light of purest
Sunshine falls across the spray,   40
There the burning coasts of fancy
Open to her pleasure lay.
All alone, all alone
Come away, come away
All alone.   45

Lady Mary, Lady Kitty
The Honourable Featherstonehaugh
Polly Tommy from the office
Which of these shall hold her now?
Come away, come away   50
All alone.

The spray reached out and sucked her in
It was a hardly noticed thing
That Joan was there and is not now
(Oh go and tell young Featherstonehaugh)   55
Gone away, gone away
All alone.

She stood up straight
The sun fell down
There was no more of London Town   60
She went upon the painted shore
And there she walks for ever more

Happy quite
Beaming bright
In a happy happy light   65
All alone.

They say she was a morbid girl, no doubt of it
And what befell her clearly grew out of it
But I say she's a lucky one
To walk for ever in that sun   70
And as I bless sweet Turner's name
I wish that I could do the same.

Not Waving but Drowning

Nobody heard him, the dead man,
But still he lay moaning:
I was much further out than you thought
And not waving but drowning.

Poor chap, he always loved larking   5
And now he's dead
It must have been too cold for him his heart gave
          way,
They said.

Oh, no no no, it was too cold always
(Still the dead one lay moaning)   10
I was much too far out all my life
And not waving but drowning.

Dido's Farewell to Aeneas

(from Virgil)

I have lived and followed my fate without flinch-
          ing, followed it gladly
And now, not wholly unknown, I come to the
          end.
I built this famous city, I saw the walls rise,
As for my abominable brother, I don't think I've
          been too lenient.
Was I happy? Yes, at a price, I might have been   5
          happier
If our Dardanian Sailor had condescended to put
          in elsewhere.
Now she fell silent, turning her face to the pillow,
Then getting up quickly, the dagger in her hand,
I die unavenged, she cried, but I die as I choose,

Come Death, you know you must come when   10
    you're called
Although you're a god. And this way, and this
    way, I call you.

I Remember

It was my bridal night I remember,
An old man of seventy-three
I lay with my young bride in my arms,
A girl with t.b.
It was wartime, and overhead   5
The Germans were making a particularly heavy
    raid on Hampstead.
Harry, do they ever collide?
I do not think it has ever happened,
Oh my bride, my bride.

But Murderous

A mother slew her unborn babe
In a day of recent date
Because she did not wish him to be born in a
    world
Of murder and war and hate
"Oh why should I bear a babe from my womb   5
To be broke in pieces by the hydrogen bomb?"

I say this woman deserves little pity
That she was a fool and a murderess
Is a child's destiny to be contained by a mind
That signals only a lady in distress?   10

And why should human infancy be so superior
As to be too good to be born in this world?
Did she think it was an angel or a baa-lamb
That lay in her belly furled?

Oh the child is the young of its species   15
Alike with that noble, vile, curious and fierce
How foolish this poor mother to suppose
Her act told us aught that was not murderous

(As, item, That the arrogance of a half-baked
    mind
Breeds murder; makes us all unkind.)   20

Dear Little Sirmio

Catullus Recollected

Dear little Sirmio
Of all capes and islands
Wherever Neptune rides the coastal waters and
    the open sea
You really are the nicest.

How glad I am to see you again, how fondly I
    look at you.

No sooner had I left Bithynia—and what was
    the name of the other place?
And was safely at sea
I thought only of seeing you.

Really is anything nicer
After working hard and being thoroughly wor-   10
    ried
Than to leave it all behind and set out for home
Dear old home and one's own comfortable bed?

Even if one wears oneself out paying for them.

The Celts

I think of the Celts as rather a whining lady
Who was beautiful once but is not so much now
She is not very loving, but there is one thing she
    loves
It is her grievance which she hugs and takes out
    walking.

The Celtic lady likes fighting very much for
    freedom
But when she has got it she is a proper tyrant
Nobody likes her much when she is governing.

The Celtic lady is not very widely popular
But the English love her oh they love her very
    much
Especially when the Celtic lady is Irish they love   10
    her
Which is odd as she hates them then more than
    anyone else,
When she's Welsh the English stupidly associate
    her chiefly

With national hats, eisteddfods and Old Age
    Pensions.
(They don't think of her at all when she is Scotch,
    it is rather a problem.)

Oh the Celtic lady when she's Irish is the one 15
    for me
Oh she is so witty and wild, my word witty,
And flashing and spiteful this Celtic lady we love
All the same she is not so beautiful as she was.

John Wain

1925–

John Wain has continued to publish novels regularly
since the first one, *Hurry on Down* (1953), which impressed a wide range of readers, not only in England
but also abroad, as offering a clear indication of what
some, at least, of the new writing was to be like.
Some of his other novels are *Living in the Present*
(1955), *The Contenders* (1958), *Strike the Father Dead*
(1962), *The Smaller Sky* (1967), and *A Winter in the
Hills* (1971). Wain himself has said that his best
writing is to be found in his poetry; among the
volumes of his poems are: *A Word Carved on a Sill*
(1956), *Weep Before God* (1961), and *Hidden Life,
and Other Poems* (1962). His criticism is always worth
reading for its clarity, its independent sensitivity to
values that lie a little outside current fashion (as in
the attention he gives, in his essay on G. M. Hopkins
to an early Hopkins poem like "The Alchemist in the
City"), its willingness to cut Gordian knots, and its
refusal to be pretentious. His essays have so far appeared in two volumes, *Preliminary Essays* (1957) and
Essays on Literature and Ideas (1963), and there have
been three collections of short stories.

    Born at Stoke-on-Trent, educated at Newcastle-
under-Lyme and at St. John's College, Oxford, Wain
has taught English at the University of Reading, as
well as in France and the United States. There is a
very interesting volume of autobiography, *Sprightly
Running: Part of an Autobiography* (1962).

The New Puritanism, The New
Academicism, The New, The New . . .

It is well-known that the Puritan mentality is
hostile to art. And I count it among the misfortunes of my life that, having at last attained
maturity as an imaginative writer, I should have
found myself living in an increasingly Puritan
society.

    The description will seem surprising only to
those who, by a pardonable etymological confusion, associate Puritanism with "purity" in its
specifically sexual sense of chastity. Obviously no
one could look at our society and say that chastity
was near the top in any dominant scale of values.
Puritanism, however, need not involve an insistence on chastity. Many of our most Puritan
types, at the present moment, are fierce in their
demand for as much unchastity as possible, on
their own and everyone else's part. No, Puritanism, as historically understood, signifies the all-
or-nothing attitude, the horror of compromise,
the impulse to simplify. To the Puritan, only
one thing is needful. We may classify Puritans
according to the particular thing that they specify
as needful, but they are all equally Puritans.

    In our time, naturally enough, the domi-
nant type of Puritanism has been the revolutionary. A certain kind of political action, tending
always towards the ruthless and the extreme, has
been held up as the one thing needful. The year
1968 saw the rise to pre-eminence of the student
with the Afro-Asian coiffure who would take his
place at a university seminar on Kant's *Critique
of Pure Reason* or Shakespeare's *Antony and
Cleopatra,* and before the professor could get the
discussion moving, come in with the flat demand,
"Tell me first—what has this to do with the
revolution?" (Or perhaps I should have shown
more respect by giving it a capital letter: "the
Revolution.") Such students are Puritans because
they believe not only that one issue can over-ride
all others—which will, inevitably, happen from
time to time—but that it *ought* to do so, that this
is a moral imperative.

    One tries to be sympathetic; if only because
mere indignation, mere uncomprehending opposition, is an empty emotion. Puritanism has,
in its time, moved mountains. What one fears is
that when the mountains have been moved, we

are left with a featureless plain that is easily covered over with concrete. The Puritanism that worked within the societies of northern Europe in the sixteenth and seventeenth centuries was motivated by a wish to have done with the Middle Ages and in particular with the multiplicity of religious observances, and the consequent proliferation of religious attitudes, that characterized the Age of Faith. This Puritanism acted as a valuable catalyst on the literary culture of the West inasmuch as it provoked the Renaissance "Defences of Poetry," which were not, of course, defences of verse-writing but of imaginative writing itself. The conflict sharpened until we find Oliver Cromwell ordering his soldiers to smash the stained glass windows in English churches and knock the heads off statues. Much good art was lost. We, the inheritors, are the poorer for his action. Yet the Puritanism he represented was no merely negative thing. It contributed, and we have what it contributed. The art that Cromwell ordered to be destroyed was associated in the Puritan mind with idolatry, with a plurality of vision that menaced the single eye of Protestant worship; and, politically, with a governing class that was soft on Popery. The Puritan of the 1640's was intent on replacing these things with a marvellously bracing theocentric vision of the universe. He attacked art in the name of something greater: of course the Puritan always does this, but Cromwell's vision of what religion and society might be, his dedication to a City of Man that really might achieve a certain very direct relationship with a City of God, was at any rate something important. In the name of what greater thing do our modern Puritans attack art? For they, make no mistake, would knock the heads off statues if they could. Indeed, the determined effort to substitute Anti-Art for Art, the sustained attempt to interest us in Campbell's soup tins and heaps of gravel tossed on to the studio floor, *is* a way of knocking the heads off statues and throwing acid on paintings, just as the "sound poem" is an attack on the notion of a poetic language which can compass a wide range of human emotions.

The criteria of the modern Puritan are social. He postulates no City of God overarching his City of Man. He wants, or claims to want, social justice, a world dedicated to the interests of the majority, an end to the plight of the poor.

These, by themselves, are noble aims. One's misgivings begin when one contemplates the people who voice these aims. Some of them, indeed are all that they claim to be. These, the ones who truly mean what they say and are prepared to make sacrifices, usually meddle very little with art. Their lives are filled with a blazing, acrid vision that leaves them in no need of the colour and rhythm and movement that art would offer; while towards the inevitable complication of art, arising from the fact that art mirrors the complication of life, they would feel, if they came face to face with it, only a virtuous horror.

It is the Puritan who does meddle with art, who does try to police it, to forbid it, to channel it into a purpose that suits his emotional needs, who must—to be blunt—be rejected out of hand as a nuisance, a fractious child interfering with grown-up people. He is a simplifier, and art can have no truck with simplification. It cannot simply preach Liberation or Revolution, inasmuch as these are two-dimensional things, belonging to the world of imperatives, and art is rich with the multi-dimensional richness of life. It has a memory, and Revolution has no memory. It includes negatives and counterstresses, and Liberation cannot afford these. It glows with colour, and Puritanism is black and white like a newspaper headline.

The Puritan attempt to simplify art, so as to muzzle and direct it and also to avoid its challenge, is usually carried out by failed artists who have adopted the Puritan ethos as a cover for their failure. At the level of art-chatter, therefore, Puritanism joins hands with that other arch-simplifier, sensationalism.

Pseudo-art takes many forms. In our time, the pseudo-artist is generally both a Puritan and a sensation-monger. To be sensational is to attract attention, and it is the duty of the Puritan, the man with a simplifying mission, to attract attention if he can. Hence the cult of the extreme statement. It is as if our age had grown deaf to any language except that of the superlative. Slender talents, competing with one another in staking out the ultimate boundaries of whatever they are trying to express, occupy the forefront of attention. The pornography of sexuality, which has always been with us, is now challenged by the pornography of violence, the pornography of disgust, and the pornography of despair. (It is not at all my purpose, in this essay, to attack individuals, but I should like to take this opportunity of going on record with the opinion that Samuel Beckett, whom I have never met and against whom I feel no personal animus whatsoever, is a writer with a very minor talent and that the present inflation of his reputation will come to seem, in retrospect, one of those interesting collective lapses of taste like the Victorian admiration for Martin Tupper.)

The rise of pornography, of course, has other explanations. It is connected with the Puritan insistence on explicitness. To the Puritan, it is a deadly sin to sweep anything under the carpet. Imagination is suspect because imagination so often works best on what is under the carpet or behind a veil of one kind or another. There must be no carpets, no veils! The Puritan fiercely disapproves, and perhaps rightly, of the merely suggestive; of the kind of play or novel, for instance that won a large public by encouraging people to think about sex, without making any explicit sexual statement. And, since it is now considered a moral weakness to shy away from sex and say nothing about it, the Puritan is left with only one alternative: the totally explicit which sometimes passes for "permissiveness," though there is nothing permissive about it: it is authoritarian, exhortatory, a categorical imperative. Do this, or be damned! Sit in your theatre seat and watch a couple on stage actually having intercourse—because to avert your eyes, or walk out, merely on the grounds that such acts have no proper audience except the people concerned in them, is to reject the explicit statment: and Puritanism lives by the explicit statement, and will accept nothing else. And if it is compulsory to accept copulation on stage, it is necessarily just as compulsory to swallow a book like *Last Exit to Brooklyn* without gagging—even, if one is a determined enough Puritan, to get up in court and testify that it is Literature.

That last thought, of course, brings us into contact with another wing of the present onslaught on imaginative writing. It brings us to the academic, since one of the functions that academic teachers of literature have agreed to take over is that of helping the legal system to decide what is, or is not, an offence against public decency. I suppose the historic date here is the *affaire Lady Chatterley* in 1960 or there-

abouts. It was that hearing which first alerted the legal and political mind to the fact that the scholarly-critical mind was, on the whole, in favour of the removal of restraints. Academic here joins with Puritan in the insistence on explicitness and the sin of sweeping anything under the carpet. If it is wrong that a fiercely moral Puritan like D. H. Lawrence should be muzzled, then it quickly becomes wrong that *anyone* should be muzzled.

What I personally miss, in the to-and-fro of this argument, is any concern for the nature of art, the way in which art gets its effects. The assumption all along is that anything that can't be said in so many words can't be said at all. Yet Shakespeare in *Antony and Cleopatra* managed to convey the full range of sexual passion without using a single word that we should recognize as indecent. Sexually, it is probably the most highly charged work in English literature, yet it contains actually less bawdy, less indecency for indecency's sake, than almost any other Shakespearean play. Shakespeare is a great enough artist to work by suggestion. He harnesses the reader's sexual imagination instead of pouring out the untreated contents of his own. In this, he is merely being true to the fundamentals of his art. All art works by suggestion as much as by explicitness, and suggestion is a means of working on the recipient's mind which resembles judo: throw him by his own weight! The modern liberated writer, splattering the page with every four-letter word in the language, actually chills the reader's imagination, producing a sense of weariness and surfeit not only with his own efforts but, what is much more serious, with the natural impulses he is trying to exploit. So that one hears time and time again the complaint from ordinary intelligent readers that this or that sex-obsessed book is "enough to put me off sex." This is the result of that denial of imagination which allows the reader no participatory role.

This denial, in turn, comes from the Puritan belief that the imagination is hostile because unbiddable. That belief is very dominant in the world nowadays. All totalitarian régimes hold it as a matter of course (the imagination feeds on freedom, therefore it deserves to starve). But it is also widespread in those societies whose governmental systems disclaim any such total wish to process the individual. (I had almost written "democracies," but that word must now be deemed obsolete; the technological world has screened out individual freedom and with it the political ideal of interpreting the will of Demos, on any large scale. There can be democracy within the village cricket club, but not at national level —a fact which by itself constitutes the major argument for decentralization.) This distrust of the imagination is a predictable result of the immense speeding-up of the means of communication which has resulted in our present state of perpetual wooziness, that "information overload" of which we have learnt to speak blandly. When everything that happens everywhere in the world is instantaneously reported, not only does any one separate event become meaningless, we quickly arrive at a state in which *all* events are meaningless, and since that way lies nothing but insanity and disintegration, we strive vainly to subject this torrent of events to a simultaneous, production-line process of interpretation. Naturally this interpretation cannot be pursued rigorously, since there is a long queue of other subjects waiting to be processed; hence the mania for interviewing (a form of exposure which does not really expose anything, the subject of the interview being always a puppet with strings pulled by the hard-faced professional who is working him over) and for the panel discussion (another means of appearing to put a topic into perspective while actually involving it in a hall-of-mirrors of conflicting perspectives, a perfect recipe for the intellectual slapstick which television has taught us to accept instead of thought). In this state of grogginess, a non-stop mainlining on the potent mix peddled by the media in all countries, there is no place for the imagination, if only because the imagination works in depth and at leisure, and the effect of our collective media trip is to seal off the depths of our minds and to deny us any slackening of pace.

This situation is not irremediable. One of the features I like and admire about young people at the present time, those below twenty-five in particular, is their complete and casual rejection of the electronic-and-plastic world their parents rushed forward so eagerly, between 1945 and 55, to embrace. And, since many of these young people are to be found in the universities, that alone makes the universities so much the more healthy and pleasant to the spirit. As regards their elders, however, the hard-line professional academics, I feel less certain of grounds for optimism. It is disconcerting, for one thing, to note how, with no apparent inner conflict, academics as a whole have accepted the opportunity to "reach a wider audience" (i.e. travesty their intellectual tradition with maximum publicity and profitableness) by means of the television panel industry. For another, and this particularly concerns those whose stamping-ground is what used to be called "the humanities," I am disturbed by the symptoms of what I discern as a new academicism, as crippling as anything in the old: refusal to join in the complex, wide-ranging and subtly tinged interchange between present and past.

Let me explain. I belong to the generation of men of letters formed in the era of T. S. Eliot, and I still accept Eliot as an important authority in matters that concern me professionally. One of Eliot's main preoccupations, as we all know, was the dialogue between past and present. His first really influential utterance, the essay "Tradition and the Individual Talent" (1919), was to the effect that, while it has long been understood that the past influences the present, it is also true that the present influences the past. If a new artist arises whose work modifies our way of looking at his particular art, we then apply that modified vision to the masterpieces of our tradition, and we may have to do some adjusting of reputations. The backward look alters the object. This view, needless to say, was very unpopular with academics, who live on received judgments and dislike having to make changes, and who also derive income from text-books which they do not wish to see outdated. But Eliot, blandly immovable, persisted in it. He never budged from the position, stated in "Tradition and the Individual Talent," that the historical sense is "nearly indispensable to anyone who would continue to be a poet beyond his twenty-fifth year"; nor from his view that the useful critic is the man who is aware of the reach of the past, and who uses this awareness to illuminate the problems of the present.

It has happened to me many times, in the last five or six years, to meet people employed in university literary studies, both research and teaching, who have taken up a quite contrary line.

To these people, the present age is so totally new, so totally unlike any former age in human history, that nothing from the past can be carried over. Certain figures who constantly recur in my conversation as measuring-points, people as diverse as Shakespeare and Samuel Johnson and Ovid and Chekhov and Marvell, were waved aside as belonging to that sealed-off, unreachable "past." Listening to these opinions, I have been haunted by a sense of having heard them, or something not quite unlike them, in my youth; I have murmured inwardly,

For [she] is like to something I remember
A great while since, a long, long time ago.

And now it comes back to me. When I was a young student, the older professors were very firmly of the opinion that there could be no fruitful dialogue between past and present. They wanted the contemporary artist to be the docile servant of his great predecessors. In poetry, for instance, they liked best the kind of gentle, well-smoothed lyrical verse that derived primarily from Tennyson; and if such verse was not quite as important as Tennyson's, who was troubled by that? Innovation, in any of the arts, earned their fierce hostility. The arts were complete; great painters, great composers, great writers, had lived and had shown the way. Where was the sense in trying to meddle with things that were settled and done with?

Not all senior academics took this line; but it can fairly be called the characteristic attitude among them. And when I hear the trendy young academic of today dismiss the past as unreachable, I realize that I am in the presence of a new academicism as hidebound as the old. Obviously, the claim that present-day life is unrecognizably different from anything that went before is so much self-important twaddle. The emotional infrastructure of human life is apt to show small but interesting differences from one epoch to another; it was not quite the same in sixteenth-century Europe as in classical antiquity, to say nothing of the racial differences between Africa, the East and the West; but to cut it off with a chopper, to say that since certain technological disorientations the entire nature of the human animal has altered—this is merely another symptom of "information overload" and the failure of imagination.

After all this, what?

I am trying to resist the temptation to turn this essay into a jeremiad, because a jeremiad is a self-indulgently enjoyable thing to write and I am not, at the moment, writing to enjoy myself but to get certain matters into a clearer perspective. In any case, a jeremiad would be foolish. This is a good period of literature; it is the age of Neruda and Paz and Günter Grass and Moravia and Golding and Iris Murdoch and Larkin and R. S. Thomas and Leonardo Sciascia and dozens more whose names do not come to me at this moment, including that marvellous Latin American writer whose name escapes me who wrote *A Hundred Years of Solitude;* and though Pasternak is dead, Borges and Montale and Ezra Pound are still alive. Yes, and Isaac Bashevis Singer! And even North American literature, dominated as it is at the moment by the showmen and the brass-lunged shouters, will be heard to speak again when the deafening parade has gone by. Its voice will come from directions we have neglected, from the absolutely professional craftsmanship of a novelist like Alfred Hayes or the quiet, unstressed meaningfulness of a poet like David Wagoner. No, mere pessimism about "the state of things," the writer's habitual snivel, would be out of place. What we need, those of us who enjoy the art of literature, whether as readers or writers, and wish to see it continue, is a sense of the importance of what is at stake and a quiet determination to face down the opposition. If imaginative writing goes, what remains? If language is never to be used for anything but information and analysis, if poetry, from being a repository of emotions and associations that would otherwise remain undefined and unfelt, becomes a play-area for delinquent children, how is a civilization possible?

The modern Puritanism of fact would imprison us in a straitjacket of statement. And when poets retreat into the kindergarten and begin to turn out babble and doodle under such various earnest names as "sound poetry" and "concrete poetry," they are showing a flaccid willingness to cede the central territory they should be defending. Unreverberative factual statement on the one hand, play-patterns on the other, and in between only the crude slogans of the propagandists—is this what we want?

One thing that language can do better than any other form of communication is to liberate the individual by setting his imagination to work. If twenty people read the sentence, "Autumn had come to the woods, and a thin white mist hung between the wet tree-trunks," twenty separate imaginative pictures will be formed. They will relate to a central core provided by the author, but they will be individual. And so on. In a novel, each reader imagines the physical appearance of the characters, hears the timbre of their voices, pictures to himself the physical setting of the action. In the cinema, by contrast, we all see what the camera puts in front of us. Only one imagination is at work—the director's. I used to quote with approval Cocteau's definition of a film as "a dream that can be dreamed by many people at the same time." I still think this is a good definition of film, but I no longer look on it with complacency: it seems to me, now, a dangerous thing for a crowd of people to dream their dreams in unison. Dangerous, because it ministers to that collective hypnosis in which a people, having long since lost touch with reality, is led to embrace ever more evil delusions. What, after all, was Fascism but a dream dreamed by a lot of people at the same time?—and those sleep-walkers proved expensive to wake up.

At this point, the modern academic steps in again, to remind me that my values are based on an obsolete regard for the individual. In an age of collectivism, here am I, quaintly, still making the unargued assumption that it is better for human beings to think and feel as individuals than as a Mass. Haven't I realized (asks the modern academic, with a tolerant shake of his Arnoldian side-whiskers) that individualism was merely an episode in the history of human attitudes, that in any case it was never world-wide, being confined to the West and only there among relatively privileged people?—and that it arose from a purely fortuitous association between *laissez-faire* economics, small-scale means of production, and Christianity with its stress on the value of the individual soul? All of which have just about had their day?

I do, of course, realize all these things. But, while the factors that produced Western individualism may all be in decline, the individualism itself, having been called into being, may well outlast its causes. (It wouldn't be the first example of such a turn of events.) And the mere fact that the spirit of individualism, the assump-

tion that the unique personality in each of us is valuable because of its uniqueness and not in spite of it, has found beautiful and memorable expression in literature, will surely act as a continuing force. One sees the concern for the individual in the process of coming into the European consciousness with Chaucer and Villon—to pin-point two names merely representative—and, by the time we reach the epoch of Shakespeare, the individual has moved into the centre of the stage. All Shakespeare's plays, particularly the major tragedies on which his reputation mainly rests, are concerned with the clash between large-scale personalities, aflame with the incandescence of their uniqueness, and the vast impersonal universe to which, somehow or other, they must temper themselves. Indeed, Shakespeare's main service to the world may well have been that his plays dramatized, and so brought into full consciousness, the nature of the human conflict as it was to be during the centuries of individualism. If this is so, the lives of the gigantic individuals who act out Western history from the Renaissance to our own time were made possible by Shakespeare and the other writers who were nourished by him. Because large-scale individual characters had been imagined and portrayed and set talking and moving on a lighted stage, they were free to exist in "real" life. And this, after all, is no more than the *cliché* that life imitates art; as one feels that Wilde and Pater were to a large extent creations of a movement in literature that began when they were children.

Western art, and particularly the art of literature, focused, defined, and in general gave a tremendous push to, the notion of the individual. And the cultural muddle of the present time is due, very largely, to the antagonism between the kind of art which keeps alive the spirit of individualism, drawing strength from it and channeling back strength in return, and the new collectivized art or anti-art which screens out the individual. And here we circle back to revolutionary Puritanism, because Asiatic peasants are too poor to know or care about individualism, and the Asiatic peasant is the kind of man we must all strive to resemble, because he is exploited and poor and holy and a Mass, and there is one thing needful. Or so the Puritans tell us, howling in the echo-chamber of a technological society.

We may be sure of one thing: the pushing and shoving will go on. The novel is an individual form, the film is not. Poetry which uses the full resources of its tradition is an individual form, though less so than the novel because the poetic use of language is always to some extent tribal; concrete-and-gimmick poetry is anti-individual because its means are too simplified to express the complexity of the individual nature; it is a means of togetherness. Narrative is individual because we all have our own way of telling a story; plotless, static mood-writing is anti-individual because it induces hypnosis, and the "trip" is a shared experience if it is to be an experience at all.

The most easily available trip, if only because it costs nothing, does not involve the services of a pusher, and does not come into collision with the law, is of course the trip into one's own inner failures and miseries. To let down a bucket into the well of despair that we can all locate inside ourselves is not only easy and even, in its release from tension, rather pleasant; it is also a reliable claptrap. George Orwell, in the essay "Inside the Whale," took a bearing on the self-indulgent hopelessness of so much of the minor literature of the 1920s: "Everyone with a safe £500 a year turned highbrow and began training himself in *taedium vitae*. It was an age of eagles and crumpets, facile despairs, backyard Hamlets, cheap return tickets to the end of the night. In some of the minor characteristic novels of the period, books like *Told by an Idiot,* the despair-of-life reaches a Turkish-bath atmosphere of self-pity."

Orwell, at any rate, can be cleared of the suspicion of being a hearty beer-swilling optimist refusing to face facts. It is he who remarked, almost as a parenthesis that needed no proof and no emphasis, "A man who gives a good account of himself is probably lying, since any life when viewed from the inside is simply a series of defeats" ("Benefit of Clergy"). His own intimate knowledge of suffering and foreboding, the chaos at the heart of the individual experience, is as profound as Samuel Johnson's. Yet he does not, for that reason, issue the prescriptive criterion that has once again become fashionable in recent years: exhibit that chaos, in all its seething dis-

order and to the exclusion of everything else, if you want to be taken seriously!

People who lack the talent to produce art, yet want to get into the act in some way, nearly always try to legislate for it. There is always a lot of coaching from the touch-line, in the literary weeklies and such-like; all that changes is the nature of the advice, delivered loudly and with the threat of total failure and isolation at the back of it. Thirty years ago the writer was threatened with excommunication if he failed to show social responsibility and contemporary sensibility, which in effect meant writing about hydro-electric schemes from the correct class-angle. Today the shouting goes on but the orders have changed. The up-to-date critic now maintains that, since human life is cruel and ugly, therefore art must be cruel and ugly. A classic *non sequitur*. And also a prescription which would have narrowed the field of art intolerably ever since its first inception; human life has always, over vast areas and for vast numbers of people, been cruel and ugly, so that if these critics had existed from the beginning and had been able to impose their views, humanity would never have had any but cold, squalid, narrow, despairing art, in which case the human race would probably have died out by this time.

However, this school of critics has certainly imposed its views at present, as witness Ted Hughes's *Crow*, the most praised poem of the last five or six years. *Crow*, with its relentless probing of the depths of horror and violence, reads very much like a poem written expressly to appeal to the reigning critical *cénacle*; obviously Mr. Hughes is too serious and too sincere a poet to write for this kind of motive, which makes the poem even more of a depressing example; it can only be that the incessant demand for horrors has got under his skin and produced this rash. Bad criticism is a joke, until it begins to spoil good artists, and then it becomes a crime.

Back in 1964—but how freshly it comes to mind to-day!—the indispensable *Critical Quarterly* carried an interesting article by C. B. Cox and A. R. Jones, "After the Tranquilized Fifties." In it, the authors took approving note of the "concern with violence and neurotic breakdown" which was beginning to be evident at that time in the work of writers as diverse as Robert Lowell, Sylvia Plath and James Baldwin. In the course of a lucid and skillful discussion of these tendencies—the exploration of intimate personal experience, the owning-up to anarchic impulses, the "assumption that in a deranged world, a deranged response is the only possible reaction of the sensitive mind"—the authors note with apparent approval, or at any rate a total absence of expressed disapproval, such attitudes as that which they attribute to James Baldwin:

To Baldwin, therefore, to live, to perceive reality, is to submit oneself to suffering and chaos. Breakdown, neurosis, even suicide, are a proper reaction to the human condition, for otherwise we are escaping from the truth.

What Professors Cox and Jones here state calmly and dispassionately can easily become fuel for the superheated demand for more violence, more sickness, more perversity, with which we are now bombarded by the hopheads of the literary underworld. As I said, their article appeared in 1964. I must take some opportunity of asking these distinguished critics, for I know and respect both of them, whether, after the passing of nearly a decade, they are still quite so happy about it all. Certainly, in those days, they appeared very sure that wisdom lay in this descent into violence and perversity, rather than in the attempt at distancing and poise which they discerned in the English writing of the ("tranquilized") 'fifties:

Many of the new writers of the 1950s had been young men during the last war. Their writing appears to stem from a denial of the horror of such facts as Dachau, Belsen and Hiroshima, a refusal to be contaminated by the chaos in which their youth had been involved. They withdrew from politics and fighting, and tried to celebrate the inviolate quality of their personal emotions in lucid, disciplined verse. Philip Larkin's recently published The Whitsun Weddings *includes some of the best poems written in this mode, combining lucidity and compression of meaning with orthodox metres and rhyme. Larkin often makes the point that for him withdrawal from life is necessary for the preservation of the self, though in poems such as "Dockery and Son," "Self's the Man" and "Send No Money" he explores with subtlety his own doubts and the heavy price he has had to pay. In the novel, Kingsley Amis and John Wain tried to return to the fictional modes of H. G. Wells and Arnold Bennett, to show the problems of man in society in a conven-*

tional manner, but in their fictions they withdraw from serious problems into farce. Both of them touch on problems of mental sufferings such as suicide in Wain's *Living in the Present* or fear of death in Amis's *Take a Girl Like You*, but find it difficult to make an extensive study of such problems. Their humour comes from a deliberate refusal to be involved, a sense that life is so chaotic and irrational that farce is the only possible medium for its expression.*

This is certainly a pertinent criticism; personally I would accept the implied limiting judgment on my very early work (the only book of mine actually mentioned here was published in 1955, since when I have consistently striven to deepen as well as broaden my area of attention). What worries me is the apparently bland acceptance that what we need in place of this "deliberate refusal to be involved" (if that's what it is) is a plunge into sickness and hysteria. Are Professors Cox and Jones, in view of the flood-gates that have opened in the years since they wrote their article, still as happy about the love affair with disintegration and death?

The irrationality which overwhelms man comes, not from without but from within; the individual will, the urge towards order and stability, is in direct conflict with the anarchic depths of the individual subconsciousness. To know thyself, once the ideal of reason, is now a call to anarchy. Moreover, writers co-operating in their perversity with these forces, through drugs or homosexuality or what have you, ally themselves with the forces of irrationality in the belief that reality, happiness and truth lie in such an alliance. Nonetheless they all appear to assume that self-knowledge must bring man into conflict not only with his society and its mores but, more importantly, in conflict with his conscious self. Self-expression is no longer expression of the conscious but of the subconscious self. Thus in the war between the conscious and the subconscious mind the forces are heavily committed on the side of irrationality, violence, hatred and perversity.

The trouble is that this sacred quartet of qualities—"irrationality, violence, hatred and perversity"—can be faked as easily as any other qualities: much more easily, indeed, than wit or irony or compassion. The overwrought, hysterical tone which seems to be mandatory in present-day writing must be one of the easiest tones to reproduce mechanically; eighteenth-century poetic diction, by contrast, must have been at least as difficult as playing some game like whist. And *Crow*, in the end, won't prove as helpful a model as *The Dunciad*—which also has its climax of barely controlled terror, its vision of the cold, dark waters which lie under the thin ice of reason and tolerance.

There is an unmistakeable panic, a powerful unfocussed dread, behind Pope's vision of "the sable throne" of "Night primeval, and of Chaos old." The Puritan with his all-or-nothing logic may assert that to express this panic in beautifully poised couplets and honed language is to be paradoxical. Yes. By such paradoxes, art lives.

Iris Murdoch

1919–

Iris Murdoch was born in Dublin and educated in London, Bristol, and at Somerville College, Oxford. Since 1948 she has been a Fellow and Tutor in philosophy at St. Anne's College, Oxford.

Her first book was not a novel but a short book on the French Existentialist novelist and philosopher Jean-Paul Sartre, published in 1953; more recently she has published another book on a philosophical subject, *The Sovereignty of Good* (1970). Since the first novel, *Under the Net* (1954), there have been more than a dozen others, including *The Flight from the Enchanter* (1956), *The Sandcastle* (1957), *The Bell* (1958), *A Severed Head* (1961), *The Italian Girl* (1964), *The Nice and the Good* (1968), and *An Accidental Man* (1971). There is an essay on her and her work, by Rubin Rabinovitz, in the series of Columbia Essays on Modern Writers (1968), and a book by Peter Wolfe, *The Disciplined Heart: Iris Murdoch and Her Novels* (1966).

Salvation by Words

51st Address on the Evangeline Wilbour Blashfield Foundation Ceremonial of the American Academy of Arts and Letters and the National Institute of Arts and Letters, May, 17, 1972

We are told that art is now under attack. Of course it has often been under attack. Tyrants always fear art because tyrants want to mystify while art tends to clarify. The good artist is a vehicle of truth, he formulates ideas which would otherwise remain vague and focuses attention upon facts which can then no longer be ignored. The tyrant persecutes the artist by silencing him or by attempting to degrade or buy him. This

has always been so. However it may be admitted that in this age art seems to have rather more enemies than usual. The tyrants of course are still here, and we know what they do. But now science, philosophy, and forces arising within art itself threaten this traditional activity: an activity which we are so used to, which we take so much for granted, and which is perhaps more frail and unstable than it might seem.

10 The Romantics felt instinctively that science was an enemy of art, and of course in certain simple and obvious ways they were right. A technological society, quite automatically and without any malign intent, upsets the artist by taking over and transforming the idea of craft, and by endlessly reproducing objects which are not art objects but sometimes resemble them. Technology steals the artist's public by inventing sub-artistic forms of entertainment and by offer-
20 ing a great counter-interest and a rival way of grasping the world.

Of course science affects the artist not only in his public relations but in his soul. What is called "anti-art" is not a novel phenomenon. The latest art has often seemed like an anti-art and been so regarded by its friends as well as its enemies. At regular intervals in history the artist has tended to be a revolutionary or at least an instrument of change in so far as he has tended
30 to be a sensitive and independent thinker with a job which is a little outside established society. And in this century we have already seen the completed history of a movement, surrealism, which fought art by art on behalf of revolution. The surrealist movement, of course, ended by dividing into two, some of its members returning

into art via anti-art, and others abandoning art for politics. The motives of surrealism are not unlike the motives of our contemporary anti-art revolutionaries. The artist has a particular way of making his own a very general revulsion against a materialistic reproductive industrial society, he is particularly well equipped to attack and caricature this society, and he may elect to do so by deliberately deforming his own art and turning it into a mockery and a provocation.

A motive for change in art has always been the artist's own sense of truth. Artists constantly react against their tradition, finding it pompous and starchy and out of touch. Today's reaction seems only more extreme than before, in that many young artists, especially in the visual arts, seem to want to reject the whole of the European tradition and to challenge the very idea of the work of art, that well known and well loved idol of so many past generations. The work of art and the artist as its creator have lost some of their old grandeur and dignity. Writers and painters are not so much revered now as they were, say, in the nineteenth century. And there is a deep crisis of confidence in the very idea of art as the making of completed statements. I think that technological entertainment sub-art affects the artist here by showing him how what is utterly ephemeral can have an immensely attractive technical perfection and can be, because it is so unpretentious, curiously honest. European art, the great art upon which we were once brought up, is certainly very grand stuff by comparison, claiming serious attention, professing to purvey universal truths, offering big complicated completed statements about the world. Many people today, especially young people, instinctively mistrust this claim to completeness. They want to challenge the completeness of the art object itself as a way of challenging the authority of the statement it appears to be making. Traditional art is seen as far too grand, and is *then* seen as a half truth.

There is also, and has been, only now it is stronger than ever, a decent and comprehensible kind of utilitarian reaction against art. Philistines of course we have always with us, but I am thinking here not of Mr. Gradgring, but of sincere people who feel that in a world reeling with misery it is frivolous to enjoy art, which is after all a kind of play. There is a familiar puritanical

and protestant ancestry to this thinking, which expresses itself in the philosophy of Jeremy Bentham, who refused to allow poetry a dignity which was higher than that of push-pin. Today technology further disturbs the artist and his client not only by actually threatening the world, but by making its wretchedness apparent upon the television screen. And the desire to attack art, to neglect it or to harness it or to transform it out of recognition, is a natural and in a way respectable reaction to this display. Western moral philosophy, which has of late been moving quietly from existentialist behaviourism to sociological utilitarianism has in fact thereby exhibited in philosophical form two of the possible hostile reactions to art. Existentialism, the last fling of liberal Romanticism in philosophy, by putting a value upon sincerity and immediacy, suggests a criticism of old solemn art as being in *mauvaise foi*. The "happening" is a proper child of existentialism. In fact Romanticism has always held the seeds of anti-art in its cult of sincere feeling. Rousseau: the beginning of the end. While sociological utilitarianism, with a bent which is scientific rather than humanist, represents a certain deliberate and even high-minded philistinism.

I have mentioned several, sometimes overlapping, anti-art forces: dictators, scientists, technologists, revolutionaries, anti-art artists, existentialists, utilitarians. I cannot here discuss these multifarious foes. I want simply to do two things: to diagnose what I think is a fundamental *malaise* which afflicts us (in the west) about art; and to make a resultant recommendation. To help the diagnosis I want to draw in two great and notorious, and in many ways sympathetic, critics of art: Plato and Freud. Freud says that "before the problem of the creative artist psychoanalysis must lay down its arms." However, Freud does not lay down his arms. He tells us that art is essentially the fantasy life of the artist stimulating the fantasy life of the artist's client. The work of art lies in between acting as a sort of concealed bribe. The formal and "innocent" aesthetic charm of the art work leads the client, as it has already led the artist, on toward an end-pleasure of quite another sort, a sexual satisfaction in a licensed play of fantasy, which provides the work with a spurious air of completion. Art then consoles, but does so by secret and unacknowledged means; the unity and the dignity of the work of art are in a sense sham.

Freud is actually too loyal and traditional a European to make his attack upon art in any savage style. He interlards his criticism with compliments, though the criticism is none the less devastating. No such polite respect for a large established institution hampered Plato when he decided to exclude artists from his ideal state. Plato outlaws the artist for reasons which are remarkably Freudian. He regards art as the base addressing the base, created by and for and about the lowest part of the soul. Art studies the unstable and the various, what we might call the neurotic, which it can easily and amusingly depict. Goodness, which is steady and unified and "uninteresting," art cannot understand or represent. (Plato is thinking mainly of writers of course.) Art moreover makes us "relax our guard" (Plato's phrase) and indulge vicariously in adventures of emotion which we would not tolerate as part of our "real life" activity. Art is a false consolation, celebrating the mediocre and the mean and excusing self-indulgent emotion.

This powerful attack, which occurs at the end of the *Republic,* may be effectively read in conjunction with a remarkable passage in the *Phaedrus* (275) in which Plato criticises writing. I mean the use of a visual symbolism to express words, then of course still a comparative novelty. Plato says that written statements can only properly be reminders of genuinely understood communications which occur *viva voce* face to face. A written statement, like a picture, is only itself and cannot answer back. It is portable and can be moved from one place to another and so is able to be degraded and misunderstood by ill-wishing and mediocre minds. The written word should always be thought of as ancillary to real direct communication, by which it must be constantly refreshed, and not as an end in itself. Literature then, verbal art, would of course be open to this criticism too if it were written down. Thus Plato anticipates not only Freud (whose therapy depends, incidentally, upon the spoken, not written, word), but existentialist aesthetics and Marshall McLuhan as well.

I think these two great critics have suggested an unease about art which perhaps especially afflicts us now. Of course it can be said at once that what Freud and Plato have to say applies with a prime obviousness to bad art: the lowest part of the soul amusing the lowest part of the soul. But what is interesting about it is that it has its application to good art too. Many people, including many artists, feel now that art affects a false dignity and purveys a false consolation, and that the work of art is a false unity. Much visual art exhibits a consciousness of this false unity by an attack upon unity as such. Pictures fall out of frames, objects are made too large or too senselessly complex to be grasped by a unified vision. The printed word too is thought of as somehow essentially insincere, and hence a preference for immediate experience, participation, happenings, which cannot lie.

It may in fact be, in this age of frightful self-consciousness, wise and healthy to admit that art is a sort of conjuring trick and that the work of art is a sort of pseudo-object. Of course works of art are not, though they are linked more or less closely to, "material objects." The work of art however appears as a *sui generis* "object" in so far as it appears as a quasi-sensuous self-contained unity. W. H. Auden describes a poem as a "contraption," but adds that there is a guy inside it. This felicitous image suggests something a good deal less formally complete than many advocates of art would like to think that works of art manage to be. Of course the arts differ among themselves, and certain arts, perhaps music, can attain a degree of formal completeness which is impossible in literature; and I mainly have literature in mind here, though what I say does, I believe, apply *mutatis mutandis* to all the arts. Of course no poem, no play and *a fortiori* no novel, can be as clarified and as non-accidental and complete as it seems, and as it aims at seeming, to us when we are absorbed in it, or when we vaguely brood upon it when not studying it. How small in compass a Shakespeare play often looks when we return to the text from a more vague enjoyment of our general sense of it as an object.

There is certainly a conjuring trick. But our discovery of the trick need not discredit the trickster. We in the west have always been perhaps too fascinated by the idea of the work of art, that grand safe authoritative benign resplendent transcendent entity. And now we express uneasiness about art by means of criticism of the art object, and feel that if the object is attacked art is attacked. I myself very much believe in the importance of the work of art as an attempted formal unity and completed statement. There is no substitute for the discipline of this sort of attempt to tell truth succinctly and clearly. This particular effort is uniquely world-revealing. I do not think that the traditional production of works of art is ending or should end. But art is not discredited if we realise that it is based on and partly consists of ordinary human jumble, incoherence, accident, sex. (Sex, though it produces great thought-forms, is fundamentally jumble: not even roulette so much as mish-mash.) Great art, especially literature, but the other arts too *mutatis mutandis,* carries a built-in self-critical recognition of its incompleteness. It accepts and celebrates jumble, and the bafflement of the mind by the world. The incomplete pseudo-object, the work of art, is a lucid commentary upon itself. Andrey Sinyavsky has defined art as telling truth by the absurd and leading up to simplicity. These words are important. Art makes a place for precision in the midst of chaos by inventing a language in which contingent details can be lovingly noticed and obvious truths stated with simple authority. The incompleteness of the pseudo-object need not affect the lucidity of the mode of talk which it bodies forth, in fact the two aspects of the matter ideally support each other. In this sense all good art is its own intimate critic, celebrating in simple and truthful utterance the broken nature of its formal complexity. All good tragedy is anti-tragedy. *King Lear*. Lear wants to enact the false tragic, the solemn, the complete. Shakespeare forces him to enact the true tragic, the absurd, the incomplete.

Great art then, by introducing a chaste self-critical precision into its *mimesis*, its representation of the world by would-be complete, yet incomplete, forms, inspires truthfulness and humility. (So Plato, though partly right, was partly wrong.) Great art is able to display and discuss the central area of our reality, our actual consciousness, in a more exact way than science or even philosophy can. And I want to speak finally about one of the main tools of this exploration: words. If we wish to exhibit to ourselves the unpretentious unbogus piercing lucidity of which art is capable we may think of certain pictures, certain music. (Bach, Piero.) Or we may think

of a use of words by Homer or Shakespeare. It is perhaps pointless to argue about which is the highest art, whatever that may mean, but there is no doubt which art is the most practically important for our survival and our salvation, and that is literature. Words constitute the ultimate texture and stuff of our moral being, since they are the most refined and delicate and detailed, as well as the most universally used and understood, of the symbolisms whereby we express ourselves into existence. We became spiritual animals when we became verbal animals. The *fundamental* distinctions can only be made in words. Words are spirit. Of course eloquence is no guarantee of goodness, and an inarticulate man can be virtuous. But the quality of a civilisation depends upon its ability to discern and reveal truth, and this depends upon the scope and purity of its language.

Any dictator attempts to degrade the language because this is a way to mystify. And many of the quasi-automatic operations of capitalist industrial society tend also toward mystification and the blunting of verbal precision. Some misguided people even attack the printed word and hence words themselves in the name of sincerity and genuine feeling. But we have to realise that, in our world, the quality of words is the quality of printed words. Of course Plato is right that words are best understood, are most precise and profound, when used in particular face to face contexts. The printed word has inevitable ambiguities. And doubtless there are some things, such as Zen Buddhism or the philosophy of Wittgenstein, which can only be communicated at all by *viva voce* discussion. But since we do not live in a city-state we have to use print, and though this is a danger it can also be an inspiration and a challenge. We must not be tempted to leave lucidity and exactness to the scientist. Whenever we write we ought to write as well as we can, in order to meet the dangers of which Plato spoke, and in order to defend our language and render subtle and clear that stuff which is the deepest texture of our spirit. When George Jackson deplored time wasted upon Latin which could have been used for maths or science he was wrong from his own point of view. Of course the exactness of science has an importance which is not likely to be underestimated. But the study of a language or a literature or any study which will increase and refine our ability to *be* through words is part of a battle for civilisation and justice and freedom, for clarity and truth, against vile fake-scientific jargon and spiritless slipshod journalese and tyrannical mystification. There are not two cultures. There is only one culture and words are its basis; words are where we live as human beings and as moral and spiritual agents. This is obvious, but needs now constantly to be repeated.

As I said earlier, I do not think that the art object as would-be complete statement either will or should perish. It is important to try to make such statements because they challenge our ability to discern and express truth and often constitute the only form in which certain truths can be expressed at all. And I think that the work of art, as a pseudo-thing, is profoundly suited to the nature of beings who inhabit a thingy planet and are themselves pseudo-things. I believe that, as in the past, art will take over anti-art and make it its own. This is an anti-metaphysical age in our part of the world. The rejection of art is in many ways an aspect of a general rejection of metaphysics, in philosophy, in religion, and in the popular beliefs which are compounded out of these. This stripping down of the scene certainly produces shock. But it has also perhaps made possible a kind of healing agnosticism, a natural mysticism, a new humility which favors clarity and plain speech and the expression of obvious and unpretentious truths: truths which are often unconnected and unhallowed by system, reflections of the somewhat random creatures that we are. Both art and philosophy constantly recreate themselves by returning to the deep and obvious and ordinary things of human existence and making there a place for cool speech and wit and serious unforced reflection. Long may this central area remain to us, the homeland of freedom and of art. The great artist, like the great saint, calms us by a kind of unassuming simple lucidity, he speaks with the voice that we hear in Homer and in Shakespeare and in the Gospels. This is the human language of which, whenever we write, as artists or as word-users of any other kind, we should endeavour to be worthy.

An ABC of Prosody

by Karl Shapiro

Prosody, or versification, is the science of poetical forms, of the way in which syllables and words are combined so that they become verse as distinguished from prose. There is no need to approach this technical side of poetry with fear if we keep in mind a few general truths about it. One of these is that prosody appears after the poetry has been written. It is not a set of rules which a poet follows; it is a partial account of how a poet writes, a description of verse as we find it. Another point to keep in mind is that prosody can be called a "science" only in the broadest sense of the term: no one has ever set down a complete body of rules for the right analysis of verse. Indeed, poets themselves often disagree about the scansion, or measuring, of a line of verse, as we find exemplified by those poets who have written directly about prosody—Coleridge, Poe, Hopkins, Lanier, Bridges, Patmore, to name only a few. And finally we should remember that one may know little about prosody and yet may develop a mature and sensitive knowledge of poetry. A knowledge of prosody will be helpful in our analysis of the patterns of sounds which we find in poetry, but at the best it is an imperfect implement, and we may develop our awareness of the melody of poetry quite apart from it.

Beyond question, the most valuable approach to prosody is the memorizing of good poems in one's own language. In committing to memory a fine passage of English verse, one becomes aware of prosody in several ways at once. He fixes in his mind a specific metrical pattern—for every poem has its own metrical character—which will be helpful in learning to judge other poems with discrimination. Second, he fixes in his mind a definite sound-structure, which will apply to no other poem, but which will be retained as a model of the music of English.

Thirdly, when he recites the poem he will grasp and understand the union of meter, sound, and sense which makes poetry. If he but knows the pronunciation of English words, the meter will speak itself to his ear. And if he but knows the sense of the words, the larger rhythms of phrase and stanza will speak to his mind and his feelings.

A complete prosody would include all the elements of sound that enter into the making of poetry. It would embrace not only the basic rhythmical pattern, or meter, of the line, but also rime schemes, the melody of vowel and consonant sounds, rhythmic phrasing, even tempo, volume, and pitch, and the relation of all these elements to meaning. Prosody has too often been considered in the narrow sense of meter; it is much more. Yet the study of meter alone is a good approach to the wider range of effects if we bear in mind that it is only one characteristic of verse. For meter is probably the most significant as well as the most obvious formal characteristic, and the harmony of poetry can be traced largely to it.

We have said that meter is the basic rhythmical pattern of verse—what might be called the ground rhythm, as distinguished from larger and vaguer rhythms of phrase and period. Rhythm, of course, is found also in prose. It is found wherever sounds are broken into more or less regular intervals of time. It is in the familiar words of the Lord's Prayer: "Thy Kingdom come, Thy will be done, on earth, as it is in heaven." But the rhythm of prose is not regular; it is occasional. The metrical pattern of verse is continuous and highly regular. What is the nature of this rhythm of verse and what different kinds of rhythm do the English poets use? The answers to these questions, which follow, form a brief introduction to the study of meters.

THE METRICAL SYSTEM OF ENGLISH

The rhythm of English verse is governed by two main factors. One of these is stress, or accent. The other is time, or what was called *quantity* in classical Greek and Latin versification. Some writers have claimed that English verse is based on time durations alone—that its basis is temporal variations—and they have attempted to scan our poetry by using a system of time measurement similar to musical notation. Others have disregarded the time element completely and

have merely marked the accents of the line. Take what is the commonest type of verse in English poetry, the ten-syllable line:

Ti-tum ti-tum ti-tum ti-tum ti-tum.

The accentualist, reading the line with alternating light and heavy accents, would represent it thus:

Tĭ-túm tĭ-túm tĭ-túm tĭ-túm tĭ-túm.

The quantitivist, reading it with alternating short and long syllables, would represent it thus:

Tĭ-tumm tĭ-tumm tĭ-tumm tĭ-tumm tĭ-tumm.

Neither system is truly satisfactory. By reading aloud any actual line of poetry, one can see that the melody of the line is in fact based on both accentual and temporal variations. Some syllables are more heavily accented than others. And it may be further observed that heavy accent and prolongation of sound usually occur in the same syllable. A syllable or word on which an accent falls is likely to be more prolonged in pronunciation than the same syllable or word if it does not receive an accent. Either system of notation is an approximation, not a full description of the facts. We use below the notation of the accentualist (x ′) in order to avoid unnecessary complication in the marking of lines.

In the preceding paragraph we represented a typical line of poetry by alternate unstressed and stressed syllables. The reading of a real line of poetry will show us that there is almost never a completely regular alternation of this sort. Such an alternation (ti-tum ti-tum ti-tum ti-tum ti-tum) is, as it were, an imaginary pattern against which the line plays, but which is seldom reproduced exactly. For example, in a typical line from *Hamlet* the imaginary pattern or "ideal" meter would be

Ŏh, thăt thĭs tóo, tŏo sólĭd flésh wŏuld mélt.

But actually no one would wrench the words thus. We make the ideal metrical pattern yield to normal speech habits, distributing the accents approximately as follows:

Óh, thăt thĭs tóo, tŏo sólĭd flésh wŏuld mélt.

The stress we give to produce this variation from the ideal comes from the accent given to a word in normal speech. It is obvious that no two readers will render a given line identically. Verse, like music, must be "interpreted." Anyone who can read English prose should be able to give a reasonably satisfactory rendering of an English poem. To analyze one's rendering, to identify the meter of the poem, is what is meant by *scanning* a poem.

We have seen that meter is a rhythm, more or less regular but not completely so, produced by combinations of accented and unaccented syllables. Considering again the line from *Hamlet,* we notice the following combinations:

> (1) *Óh, thàt*
> (2) *thìs tóo*
> (3) *tòo sól-*
> (4) *ìd flésh*
> (5) *wòuld mélt*

Or, as commonly written:

Óh, thàt| thìs tóo| tòo sól|ìd flésh| wòuld mélt.|

The units into which we thus divide a line in scanning it are technically known as *feet.* Names have been given to the kinds of feet shown here (and to others), and the kinds of line are identified by the nature and number of the feet they contain. A one-foot line is called monometer; lines of two, three, four, five, six, seven, and eight feet are called respectively dimeter, trimeter, tetrameter, pentameter, hexameter, heptameter, and octameter.

The Iambic Foot

By far the commonest English foot is the one we have represented by x ′ above—the one occurring in the second, fourth, and fifth feet of the line from *Hamlet.* It has two syllables, the first lightly stressed, the second heavily stressed. On the analogy of the Greek iambus, which was composed of two syllables, the first half as long in time as the second, we call this English foot the iambus or the iambic foot.

English iambic is most successful in lines of five and four feet. Below four it has a certain lyrical value but cannot be used for sustained passages. The six-foot iambic, called the alexandrine, is used sparingly because of its tendency to break in two; it occurs most frequently in combination with lines of other length, as in the Spenserian stanza, where it follows eight five-foot lines. It is the five-foot iambic line that has proved the real backbone of English poetry. Its pre-eminence is due to its immense adaptability and internal fluidity. There is no kind of poetry, from the lightest to the most heroic, that cannot find expression in this meter. Dramatic, narrative, elegiac, epic, and didactic poets have all used it with great success. It is the meter of the sonnet as well.

The English developed this line from one of the very old French meters. It existed in English long before Chaucer, but Chaucer was the first great English poet to recognize its power and flexibility. From his time to ours the essential nature of this line has remained unaltered and has proved adaptable to the linguistic and ideational changes of five and a half centuries.

The Trochaic Foot

If we examine a collection of Shakespeare's lyrics, we will notice a remarkable fact, namely, that many of them are written not in the iambic foot of the plays themselves but in a foot that is the reverse of the iambus—a foot in which the accented syllable precedes the unaccented one (′ x). This foot is called a trochee or a trochaic foot. Trochaic meter, or *falling meter,* as it is sometimes called in contrast to the *rising meter* of the iambus, is hardly ever successful in the five-foot line, and it has never competed with the iambic as a vehicle for the larger verse forms. On the other hand, it is the meter chosen for such poems as "Who is Sylvia?"; "Where the bee sucks, there suck I"; "Tell me where is fancy bred"; "Take, O take those lips away." It is, in short, the meter of songs. We know that many nursery rimes are in falling meters:

Jáck ànd| Jíll wènt| úp the| híll|

or

Bóbby| Sháftoe's| góne tò| séa.|

(The last unaccented syllable of a trochaic line is frequently omitted.) In music, measures begin with the accent in the initial place, and a great deal of English lyric verse, especially that intended for singing, is therefore quite naturally trochaic. Blake's *Songs of Innocence* are frequently in falling meters, and the "sprung rhythm" of Gerard Manley Hopkins is an elaboration of this "musical" structure for the purposes of spoken poetry.

The Spondaic Foot

The spondaic foot or spondee consists of two accented syllables (′ ′). This foot is not used in English verse as a basic meter; it occurs, as we see it in the third foot of our line from *Hamlet*, as an occasional substitute for some other type of foot.

The Anapestic Foot and the Dactylic Foot

The anapest (x x ′) and the dactyl (′ x x) are relatively infrequent in English poetry as basic meters. There are illustrious examples throughout the literature of poems in these trisyllabic meters, and we note an increase in them in the Victorian period and the twentieth century, but on the whole such poems are exhibition pieces and feats of metrical skill. The chief importance of trisyllabic feet is as substitute feet in iambic or trochaic verse.

Substitution

We have already seen that the usual verse line does not reproduce exactly the regular structure of the "ideal" line. An iambic line, for example, is only predominantly iambic; one or more of its feet may be trochaic or anapestic or spondaic. Consider

We two| alone| will sing| like birds| in the cage,|

or

Come then| and take| the last| warmth of| my lips,|

or

Lady,| by yon|der bless|ed moon| I swear,
That tips| with sil|ver all| these fruit-|tree tops.|

Substitutions such as these play one of the largest parts in producing variety and metrical beauty in verse. In scanning a poem, recognition

of the basic foot is necessary for the identification of the meter. Recognition of substitutions for this foot lead the beginner to an understanding of much of the subtlety of English verse. The following examples of typical English meters are fairly regular in movement, but the student will profit by analyzing the variations and considering their effect.

Iambic Hexameter

So dark are earthly things compared to things divine.
SPENSER, Faery Queen

Like pageantry of mist on an autumnal stream.
SHELLEY, Adonais

Iambic Pentameter

Alas, 'tis true I have gone here and there
And made myself a motley to the view,
Gored mine own thoughts, sold cheap what is most
    dear,
Made old offences of affections new.
SHAKESPEARE, Sonnet 110

Iambic Tetrameter

I sometimes hold it half a sin
To put in words the grief I feel;
For words, like Nature, half reveal
And half conceal the Soul within.
TENNYSON, In Memoriam

Iambic Trimeter

Grow old along with me;
The best is yet to be.
BROWNING, Rabbi Ben Ezra

Trochaic Octameter

Hope the best, but hold the Present fatal daughter of
    the Past,
Shape your heart to front the hour, but dream not
    that the hour will last.
TENNYSON, Locksley Hall Sixty Years After

Trochaic Pentameter

Weary of myself and sick of asking
What I am and what I ought to be,
At this vessel's prow I stand, which bears me
Forwards, forwards, o'er the starlit sea.
ARNOLD, Self-Dependence

Trochaic Tetrameter

Queen and huntress, chaste and fair,
Now the sun is laid to sleep,
Seated in thy silver chair,
State in wonted manner keep.
Hesperus entreats thy light,
Goddess excellently bright.

JONSON, Hymn to Diana

Anapestic Hexameter

In the darkness of time, in the deeps of the years, in
the changes of things,
Ye shall sleep as a slain man sleeps, and the world
shall forget you for kings.

SWINBURNE, Hymn to Proserpine

Anapestic Pentameter

"I have gone the whole round of creation: I saw and
I spoke:
I, a work of God's hand for that purpose, received
in my brain
And pronounced on the rest of his handwork—re-
turned him again
His creation's approval or censure: I spoke as I saw."

BROWNING, Saul

Anapestic Tetrameter

Not a word to each other; we kept the great pace
Neck by neck, stride by stride, never changing our
pace.

BROWNING, How They Brought the Good News

Dactylic Hexameter

Hope evermore and believe, O man, for e'en as thy
thought
So are the things that thou seest; e'en as thy hope and
belief.

CLOUGH, Hope Evermore and Believe

Dactylic Pentameter

What will it please you, my darling, hereafter to be?
Fame upon land will you look for, or glory by sea?
Gallant your life will be always, and all of it free.

SWINBURNE, A Child's Future

Dactylic Trimeter

Yes! I believe that there lived
Others like thee in the past,
Not like the men of the crowd
Who all round me today

Blunder or cringe, and make life
Hideous, and arid, and vile.

ARNOLD, Rugby Chapel

RIME, BLANK VERSE, AND THE MUSIC OF ENGLISH

Two words are said to rime when they are alike in their stressed vowel and all that follows it and unlike in the sound or sounds preceding the stressed vowel. *Day-May* and *ride-hide* are monosyllabic or so-called masculine rimes. When an entire unstressed syllable follows the stressed syllable, the rime is called double or feminine, as is *riding-hiding*. When two unstressed syllables follow the stressed syllable, the rime is called triple, as in *tenderly-slenderly*.

Particularly in recent poetry, two types of partial rime have been utilized by poets as occasional or regular substitutes for complete rime in a poem. In *assonance* two words have the same accented vowel but different consonants before and after the vowel, as in *gold-rode*. Assonance was characteristic of much early Romance poetry—it occurs, for example, in the early French *Song of Roland*—but it has not achieved much prominence in English. *Dissonance* (also called half-rime, para-rime, and off-rime) is the reverse of assonance in that the accented vowel in the pair is changed while the surrounding consonants remain the same, as in *leaves-lives, scooped-escaped*. The masters of this radical device are Yeats and Wilfred Owen, the World War poet. Yeats used it tentatively, and in reality developed the use of *imperfect rime,* that is, pairs of words which are spelled for riming but which are pronounced differently (for example, *love-move*). Owen was the first to employ dissonance systematically and in place of the conventional complete rime. The introduction of this half-riming scale has enriched English riming a thousandfold.

At its best, rime is not simply poetic ornament, enriching the musical texture, but a structural factor. It is a time-beater for the poem and it gives to the stanza an inner pattern of temporal design. Because of its conspicuousness among the sound effects of verse, its importance may be overestimated by some readers. It must be remembered that much of the greatest English verse has dispensed with rime. True, unrimed lyrics are rare in English, though notable exceptions may be mentioned, such as Campion's "Rose-cheeked

Laura," Collins's "Ode to Evening," and some of Tennyson's lyrics. But *blank verse*—that is, un-rimed iambic pentameter—has been one of the mainstays of longer English poems, especially of our verse drama and our epics. Blank verse, however, implies much more than the mere absence of rime. It is a form that implies size, together with the great variety of internal rhythmical and musical device and the great range of dramatic feeling that are appropriate to size.

We have been speaking of rime used at the ends of lines. End-rime, however, is only one (though the most conspicuous) type of sound-echo in poetry. Assonance and dissonance occur within lines as well as at their end. Another device involving repetition of sound is *alliteration* (sometimes described as initial rime), once a structural element of English poetry, as we have seen in *Beowulf, Piers Plowman,* and *Sir Gawain and the Green Knight,* but now employed sporadically, not only to provide a second pattern of prosody but also to emphasize phrasing.

How poor are they that have not patience!
Thou know'st we work by wit and not by witchcraft.

Shadwell alone of all my sons is he
Who stands confirmed in full stupidity.

Beyond such definable devices, patterns of similar or related vowel and consonant sounds appear in infinite variety to help create the music of English verse. The ear picks up, for example, the repetitions of *l* and of *m* and *n,* as well as the pattern of related vowels, in the following passage:

The long day wanes; the slow moon climbs; the deep
Moans round with many voices,

and finds the music of the lines exquisitely adapted to their sense. It is impossible here to do more than suggest the variety of means by which such marriage of sound and meaning has been achieved; the student will find his ear becoming more delicately attuned to them the more he reads of English poetry.

FORM IN THE SHORT POEM

It has been overwhelmingly the practice of the poet who works in the "short poem" to devise or borrow a pattern which results in a group of stanzas. What is a stanza? It is essentially a kind of larger rhythm, larger than foot and larger than line or verse, which forms a suitable period. It becomes a stanza by virtue of its repetition within a single poem. It corresponds in some ways to a paragraph in prose; but it has more internal regularity and, as between stanzas, more external similarity. The word *stanza* originally meant a room; thus the stanza is a spatial conception, the area where a significant section of a poem takes place.

Ordinarily a poem in stanzas employs the same stanza throughout, though there are poems in which the stanzas are not all alike, and even poems in which all the stanzas are different. A stanza may have as its recurrent feature only a set number of unrimed lines of equal length. Most unrimed stanzaic poems, however, use a pattern of lines of varying length; for example, the stanza of Collins's "Ode to Evening" has two iambic pentameter lines followed by two iambic trimeter lines. By far the majority of English stanzas employ a pattern of end-rime, either with or without a pattern of different line-lengths.

The simplest type of rimed stanza is the couplet, which appears in a variety of meters, most notably in iambic pentameter. Occasionally used is a three-line stanza, with all lines riming; so is another three-line stanza, the Italian *terza rima,* with interlinking rime (*aba bcb cdc ded,* etc.). Four-line stanzas, or quatrains, appear in a great variety of forms. One of these is the "ballad stanza," which rimes *abcb,* the first and third lines iambic tetrameter, the second and fourth iambic trimeter. Quatrains riming *abab* occur in a variety of meters. Mention should also be made of the *In Memoriam* stanza, an iambic tetrameter quatrain riming *abba.*

Of longer stanzas there is room here to name only three particularly important ones: *rime royal,* which is composed of seven iambic pentameter lines riming *ababbcc;* the *Spenserian stanza,* which has eight iambic pentameter lines and an alexandrine, riming *ababbcbcc;* and *ottava rima,* used notably by Byron in *Don Juan* and other poems, which consists of eight iambic pentameter lines riming *abababcc.*

In the Romance languages there are many elaborate poetic structures which are carried intact from poem to poem. For example, the *triolet* consists of eight lines riming *abaaabab*, with the first line repeated entire as the fourth and seventh lines and the second repeated as the eighth. Versifying of this kind is relatively foreign to English poetry except in its early stages, and our prosodists usually refer to such forms as "artificial." One "set" form, however, has been of the utmost importance in English poetry since its importation from Italy in the sixteenth century. This is the *sonnet*, a fourteen-line iambic pentameter poem with rime in one or another of several established schemes. The sonnet has proved peculiarly adaptable to many serious poetic occasions.

MODERN VERSE

The English prosody we have described up to this point is characterized, in comparison with much recent verse, by its regularity of metrical pattern. It is, as we have seen, by no means rigid in its regularity; it is an extraordinarily subtle medium in which repetition and variation of feet give almost unlimited opportunity of wedding ever-varying thought to form. In the twentieth century, however, has appeared a development of prosody, only suggested in earlier poetry, which has remarkably extended the boundaries of English verse forms. Modern verse, with little regularity of rhythm—or, at least, with a regularity hard to describe—offers the obstacle of newness to the reader whose ear is not yet accustomed to it, and to anyone who expects that all poetry must be measurable entirely by the counting of syllables.

The new movement in versification was largely of American origin, although it occurred simultaneously in England. It began, of course, in practice and not in theory; the new poetry appeared before it began to be explained. And the new poetry was never purely and simply a question of verse and meters; at the root of the change lay a new conception of imagery in poetry, a new conception of poetic diction, and a whole re-examination of earlier notions of what poetry is. The metrical change, while certainly not a minor innovation, was not the fundamental cause of the reaction.

What the new poets—Free Versers and Imagists—advocated was a line based on the natural flow of the contemporary language, not on syllable counting. The rhythmic phrasing therefore was not measured by the foot but, more broadly, by cadence, or the *fall of the voice*. Cadences usually include more syllables than traditional feet, and, in fact, there is usually no point in attempting to scan them in the ordinary sense. They are marked for the most part by the grammatical or rhetorical pauses of normal speech. Take three lines from T. S. Eliot's *The Waste Land*:

> He who was living is now dead
> We who were living are now dying
> With a little patience.

These lines do not conform to any traditional pattern of metrics; they are the cadences of ordinary everyday modern speech. The first two lines can be divided into phrasal groups by observing a pause after the word "living" and another at the end of the line. The third line is a phrase in itself.

If we know, as Ezra Pound put it, that free verse proceeds by the sequence of the musical phrase, we know that the foot scansion does not apply to poetry composed in this style. And if we know, as T. S. Eliot suggested, that free verse does not imply complete metrical license, we are aware that limitations exist in this form too. The following illustration will show the problem of finding a "typical" meter for a free verse poem.

SALUTATION

> O| generation| of the thoroughly| smug|
>   and thoroughly| uncomfortable,|
> I have seen| fishermen| picnicking| in the sun,|
> I have seen them| with untidy| families,|
> I have seen| their smiles| full of teeth|
>   and heard| ungainly| laughter.|
> And I| am happier| than you are,|
> And they| were happier| than I am;|
> And the fish| swim| in the lake|
>   and do not| even| own clothing.|

The cadences are read as they are marked off above—at least by the present reader. It is obvious that the feet named earlier have little utility in describing the rhythmical movement here. A reader beginning the poem might identify the first line as iambic pentameter, but he need not go much farther before discovering that that is not the metrical principle of the poem. He will discover recognizable feet, but he will find them combined with other rhythms to which he can give no name. He must give up any attempt at exact syllabic reading and try to savor the rhythms of the cadences. He may be puzzled and at first repelled by the unorthodoxy of the lines, but wider reading will train his ear and eventually enable him to distinguish good free verse from bad.

Following the liberation of English verse in the early twentieth century, poets began in earnest to experiment with meters, some reviving forms as old as the Anglo-Saxon, and others drawing more and more freely on prose rhythms for their verse effects. The result has been to produce two parallel tendencies in present-day poetry. One is the free verse line, which offers infinite metrical possibilities; the other is a new formalism, the revival of stanzaic and metrical forms for the sake of those forms. It appears that the two tendencies are not at variance, for poets today recognize that old meters may be used in new ways, and that new meters do not always signify new poetry.

Index of Authors and Titles

Index of First Lines of Poems

A Literary Map of
The British Isles

ATLANTIC

OCEAN

NORTH SEA

SHETLAND ISLANDS

ORKNEY
ISLANDS

Deerness
Muir

OUTER HEBRIDES

□ Battles

+ Religious significance

Byron
Aberdeen •

Dundee •

Lower Largo
Defoe

Boswell

Ruskin
Perth •

Dumfermline

Edinburgh
Scott

• Glasgow

Hawthornden

Inverness
Macbeth
□ Culloden

Aberdour Castle

Iona +

Berwick upon Tweed

Lindisfarne Island